# Children's Needs III:

## Development, Prevention, and Intervention

---

*Edited by*

George G. Bear

Kathleen M. Minke

National Association of School Psychologists

**From the NASP Publications Board Operations Manual**

The content of this document reflects the ideas and positions of the authors. The responsibility lies solely with the authors and does not necessarily reflect the position or ideas of the National Association of School Psychologists.

Published by the National Association of School Psychologists



Copies may be ordered from:
NASP Publications
4340 East West Highway, Suite 402
Bethesda, MD 20814
(301) 657-0270
(301) 657-0275, fax
e-mail: *publications@naspweb.org*
*www.nasponline.org*

ISBN 0-932955-79-7 and 978-0932955-79-1

Printed in the United States of America

First Printing, February 2006

10 9 8 7 6 5 4 3 2 1

# Contents

# Preface

Since the previous edition of this book was published in 1997, children's needs have not become less grave. Increasing numbers of children live in poverty, especially children of color and children in single-parent families (see chapter 62). Around 12 children per 1,000 experienced abuse or neglect in 2002 (see chapters 60 and 61). Although children are safer in school than in many of their communities, still around one quarter of students report being the victim of a crime at school (DeVoe et al., 2004) and about 4,500 children under age 18 are arrested each day (Federal Bureau of Investigation [FBI], n.d.). Academically, children continue to struggle, with 37% of fourth graders and 26% of eighth graders reading below a basic reading level for their grade (Donahue, Daane, & Jin, 2005).

There are some encouraging statistics. For example, the number of infants infected with HIV through their mothers has decreased dramatically in recent years, and aggressive treatment has greatly increased the survival rates of these children (see chapter 65). From 1995 to 2004 the number of juveniles arrested for violent crimes decreased 31% (FBI, n.d.). Similarly, the rate of teenage pregnancy is falling, as is the use of illicit drugs among adolescents (see chapters 53 and 76). Nevertheless, rates of HIV infection, criminal offenses, teen pregnancy, and alcohol, tobacco, and drug use remain unacceptably high.

It is clear that children need our help more than ever. School-based practitioners, including school psychologists, social workers, counselors, nurses, teachers, and administrators, are called upon to be knowledgeable about a wide range of academic, mental health, and physical health issues in order to support children's success in schools. Furthermore, with recent analyses indicating that as many as one in three children will have one or more psychiatric disorders by age 16 (Costello, Mustillo, Erkanli, Keeler, & Angold, 2003), it is plain that prevention efforts are critical.

This book is designed to provide an authoritative resource to assist school-based practitioners in developing effective prevention and intervention activities. In keeping with the emphasis on promoting evidence-based practice in school psychology (Kratochwill & Shernoff, 2004), authors were asked to focus their chapters on recent research and to present, wherever possible, prevention and intervention strategies that have adequate research support. Readers should recognize that not all areas addressed in the book, at present, have specific strategies supported by enough research to qualify as "evidence based." Therefore, readers enacting strategies described in this edition are called upon to evaluate the activities for effectiveness in their particular context (see Stoiber & Kratochwill, 2002).

The book is divided into four major sections: (1) children's social and emotional needs, (2) children's academic needs, (3) children's family-related needs, and (4) children's health-related needs. As in the last edition, chapters follow the same general format. Each chapter addresses relevant background information on the topic, including any developmental issues, and then reviews problems and implications related to the topic. These first two sections of each chapter are critical for the problem analysis phase of a systematic problem-solving process. Each chapter concludes with alternative actions to address the topic, with an emphasis on school-based strategies. Where appropriate, prevention strategies are discussed explicitly and separately from intervention activities.

Chapter authors are recognized experts in their fields, and over 30 chapters have lead authors who are new to this edition. The book contains over 20 new chapters, which address issues that have become more important in schools over the past 10 years. For example, we have included chapters on psychiatric disorders that are on the rise (e.g., bipolar disorders, high-functioning autism/Asperger's syndrome, self-mutilation), social–emotional issues that may affect academic performance in light of high-stakes testing (e.g., perfectionism, test and performance anxiety), and social context issues that are of current relevance (e.g., poverty, family mobility). Because we believe that school-based practitioners must become more active in prevention, there is a particular emphasis on building effective and supportive classroom and school environments; thus, we have included new chapters on peer-assisted learning, character education, school discipline, school engagement, social–emotional learning, and relationships among children, teachers, and parents.

In choosing chapters to delete from this volume, we focused on decreasing the overlap between *Children's Needs* and other NASP publications. Chapters that were retained from the previous edition have been completely updated and reflect state-of-the-art knowledge in addressing challenges related to classroom practices, psychophysiological concerns, and family-based issues. Thus, this volume provides distinct, yet critical, information that school-based practitioners can use every day in their efforts to support the healthy development of children.

## REFERENCES

Costello, E. J., Mustillo, S., Erkanli, A., Keeler, G., & Angold, A. (2003). Prevalence and development of psychiatric disorders in childhood and adolescence. *Archives of General Psychiatry, 60,* 837–844.

DeVoe, J. F., Peter, K., Kaufman, P., Miller, A., Noonan, M., Snyder, T. D., & Baum, K. (2004). *Indicators of school crime and safety, 2004* (NCES Publication No. 2005–002/NCJ 205290). U.S. Departments of Education and Justice. Washington, DC: U.S. Government Printing Office.

Donahue, P. L., Daane, M. C., & Jin, Y. (2005). *The nation's report card: Reading* (NCES Publication No. 2005–453). U.S. Department of Education. Washington, DC: U.S. Government Printing Office.

Federal Bureau of Investigation (n.d.). *Crime in the United States, 2004.* Retrieved October 20, 2005, from http://www.fbi.gov/ucr/cius_04/

Kratochwill, T. R., & Shernoff, E. S. (2004). Evidence-based practice: Promoting evidence-based interventions in school psychology. *School Psychology Review, 33,* 34–48.

Stoiber, K. C., & Kratochwill, T. R. (2002). *Outcomes: Planning, monitoring, evaluating.* San Antonio, TX: The Psychological Corporation.

# Acknowledgments

A volume of this size cannot be completed without the skills and efforts of many individuals. We would like to thank first the authors who took such care in the development and revision of their chapters. These revisions were made possible by the many reviewers, both practitioners and researchers, who volunteered their time to offer careful, detailed feedback on the chapter drafts. Our reviewers included:

Leigh Armistead
Rhonda Armistead
Eileen Baker
Tom Barry
Susan Bartels
Ron Benner
Jessica Blom-Hoffman
John Boyle
Stephen Brock
Andrea Canter
Elaine Clark
Sylvia Cohen
Christian Connell
Richard Cowen
Elliot Davis
Tom Delaney
John Desrochers
Beth Doll
Oliver Edwards
Laura Eisenman
Lori Fernald
Michael Furlong
Richard Gilman
Joelene Goodover
Betsy Grier
Robyn Hess
Jan Hughes
Deborah Johnson
Joan Kelly
Jennifer Kitson
Emily Klein
Maureen Manning
Kara McGoey
Nancy Metzler Peterson
Daniel Miller
Michael Minor
Gale Morrison
Leslie Munson
Stacy Overstreet
Ronald Palomares
LeAdelle Phelps
Kathy Pluymert
Tom Power
Fred Provenzano
Joseph Prus
Yvonne Rafferty
Stephanie Rahill
Ron Reeve
Melissa Reeves
Robert Rhodes
Ken Rice
Abby Royston
Gail Rys
Cindi Schulmeyer
Robbie Sharp
Diane Smallwood
William Strein
Vicki Tepper
Rosemary Virtuso
Nancy Waldron
Steven Welsh
Peter Whelley
David Wodrich
Lisa York
Joseph Zins

We owe particular gratitude to our research assistant, Julie Watkins, who tracked all of the drafts, reviews, and tiny details, all while maintaining her good humor (and GPA!) as a school psychology graduate student. Thanks also to Kathy Kelly who provided expert and detailed copy editing. We are grateful to the NASP Publications department, including Denise Ferrenz, Director of Publications, and Nancy Metzler Peterson, chair of the NASP Publications Board, for their guidance and support of the project. Special thanks goes to Linda Morgan, NASP's Director of Production, for her incredibly careful attention to each chapter and every phase of the book's development. She was a pleasure to work with and never once yelled at us, even when we deserved it.

Finally, we thank all of the school-based practitioners who work tirelessly every day to help children reach their best possible futures. We hope you find this volume helpful in your efforts.

GGB
KMM

# 1

# Social and Emotional Learning

**Joseph E. Zins**

*University of Cincinnati, Cincinnati, OH*

**Maurice J. Elias**

*Rutgers University, New Brunswick, NJ*

## BACKGROUND AND DEVELOPMENT

High-stakes tests. Substance abuse. Suicide. Academic standards. Delinquency. Media and technology. Teacher retention. Interpersonal violence. Dropouts. Changes in families. The list of issues facing today's educators and students is daunting. But genuinely effective schools—those that prepare students not only to pass tests at school but also to pass the tests of life—are finding that social–emotional competence and academic achievement are interwoven and that integrated, coordinated instruction in both areas maximizes students' potential to succeed in school and throughout their lives. Schools are now seen as "an important if not central arena for health promotion [and] primary prevention . . . in addition to the education of students" (Roeser, Eccles, & Samoroff, 2000, p. 467). These findings are not surprising, as shown in the work of Wang, Haertel, and Walberg (1997). They examined 28 categories of influences on learning, which they based on reviews of 179 handbook chapters, 91 research syntheses, and surveys of 61 national experts. Wang et al. found that 8 of the 11 most influential categories involved social and emotional factors (e.g., student–teacher social interactions, classroom climate, and peer group). Further, according to the National Center for Education Statistics (2002), among the major reasons cited for dropping out of school several involve social and emotional factors: not getting along with teachers or peers (35.0% and 20.1%, respectively), feeling left out (23.2%), and not feeling safe (12.1%). Thus, it is understandable that Wang et al. concluded that "direct intervention in the psychological determinants of learning promises the most effective avenues of reform" (p. 210), which supports providing social and emotional learning in schools.

### Social and Emotional Learning Defined

In simple terms, social and emotional learning (SEL) is the capacity to recognize and manage emotions, solve problems effectively, and establish positive relationships with others, competencies that clearly are essential for all students. Thus, SEL targets a combination of behaviors, cognitions, and emotions. As described by the Collaborative for Academic, Social, and Emotional Learning (CASEL), SEL is the process of acquiring and effectively applying the knowledge, attitudes, and skills necessary to recognize and manage emotions; developing caring and concern for others; making responsible decisions; establishing positive relationships; and handling challenging situations capably. Similar to the way students learn academic skills, they learn, practice, and apply SEL skills by engaging in positive activities in and out of the classroom. Initial skills that they have learned become enhanced, nuanced, and better integrated over time to address the increasingly complex situations children face in terms of academics, social relationships, citizenship, and health (Elias et al., 1997; Collaborative for Academic, Social, and Emotional Learning [CASEL], 2003).

SEL largely evolved from research on prevention and resilience (see Consortium on the School-Based Promotion of Social Competence, 1994), and interest in SEL sparked in the mid-1990s with the publication of Goleman's *Emotional Intelligence* (1995) and Gardner's *Multiple Intelligences* (1993). A high level of interest continues today, with research showing an increasing number of positive outcomes of SEL, and states and school districts adopting requirements for teaching SEL. Indeed, growing numbers of educators and parents recognize the relationships between academic and social–emotional learning, particularly within the context of schools' systems of support.

## Systems of Support

Instruction in SEL is provided in the context of caring, safe, well-managed, and participatory classroom, school, and other learning environments. These learned skills are then reinforced in the school, home, and community. All children might benefit from social–emotional instruction, including those who are at risk, those beginning to engage in negative behaviors, and those already displaying significant problems. The focus of most SEL programs is universal prevention and promotion—that is, preventing behavior problems by promoting social and emotional competence—rather than direct intervention. Smaller numbers of students may require moderate to intensive treatment that focuses on social–emotional competence, but SEL programming is intended to enhance the growth of all children, to help them develop healthy behaviors, and to prevent their engaging in maladaptive and unhealthy behaviors.

Such efforts should be viewed within the context of systems of support that provide a comprehensive continuum of services based on student needs. The continuum involves three system levels that support the academic and social–emotional development of all students. A diagram illustrating these relationships is shown in Figure 1, which closely parallels the conceptual framework of Adelman and Taylor (2000). The different sizes of the circles represent numbers of children served by each system, the overlapping signifies the interrelationships among the three systems, and the bottom box indicates that school–family–community partnerships are the foundation for promoting the development of all students. Additionally, the costs associated with providing the necessary support at each level are spread out across many students at the prevention and promotion level, which results in a relatively small cost per student; however, the costs rise as the intensity of the support increases. Hence, the cost per student is much higher for early intervention and treatment, particularly for the latter.

As a system of support, SEL is a unifying concept for organizing, coordinating, and integrating school-based

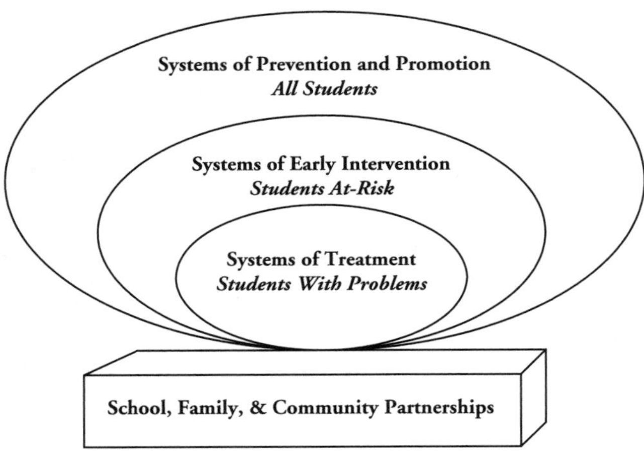


**Figure 1.** *Integrated and coordinated systems to support the development of all children.*

prevention and promotion programs that minimizes fragmentation and reduces marginalization of these efforts. The most effective, sustained approaches involve students, parents, educators, and community members as partners in planning, implementing, and evaluating SEL efforts. Systematic social and emotional education begins in preschool, continues through high school, is intentionally linked to academics, and is an integral component of the school curriculum (Elias et al., 1997; CASEL, 2003).

# PROBLEMS AND IMPLICATIONS

In today's society, children face countless situations that can have a negative effect on their social–emotional and academic development and ultimately on their happiness in life. For example, the United States arguably is more deeply divided and confused today than it has been since the civil rights and Vietnam War eras, as we grapple with issues such as preemptive war, civil liberties, and personal freedoms versus national security, abortion, the definition of marriage, affirmative action, and immigration. Inequities between the richest and poorest households continue to widen and are the widest since these data were first recorded in the 1960s (Wollman et al., 2003). In the past, menaces to world peace were well-known; now they may be anonymous, fanatical terrorists who don't discriminate between soldiers and civilians, who hide within the general populace, and who might be the person sitting next to you on a plane or walking by you at the mall, which can lead to a generalized sense of insecurity and fear.

Fifty years ago social institutions and political leaders were highly respected and influential. Children did not pick up the morning paper to learn about sexual abuse by religious leaders or the lurid details of the president's marital indiscretions. The evening television news was not filled with stories of business executives and cultural icons being sent to prison because of their unethical, illegal behavior that betrayed and harmed the future of thousands of their employees and investors; allegations of their sexual relationships with young children; and charges of rape and murder.

Previous generations of parents did not have to be Internet savvy. "Dangerous strangers" supposedly lurked around the corner or on the other side of town, but they didn't exist in children's bedrooms or the family room via Internet chat rooms and easily accessible pornographic websites. Video games such as Grand Theft Auto had not been invented, and the media weren't as notorious about delivering messages that encourage unhealthy behaviors. In the past, children's sporting events weren't scheduled every day of the week and from morning to late evening on weekends, thereby putting tremendous pressures on families and their values. Today many role models are tarnished, unethical behavior is commonplace, and new opportunities to develop and engage in negative behaviors abound. More than ever, students are faced with uncertainty in their daily lives and in their futures, and many feel a sense of insecurity, disenfranchisement, disillusionment, and even fear. For all of these reasons, SEL is perhaps more important than ever as an essential component of school reform (Zins, Walberg, & Weissberg, 2004).

## ACTIONS FOR PREVENTION AND PROMOTION

### Why Students Should Be Taught SEL

Developing social–emotional competence is a key to success in school and in life. We know that emotions affect how and what we learn, that caring relationships provide the foundation for lasting learning, and that important SEL skills and knowledge can be taught. Research shows that SEL has positive effects on academic performance, benefits physical health, improves citizenship, is demanded by employers, is essential for lifelong success, and reduces the risk of maladjustment, failed relationships, interpersonal violence, substance abuse, and unhappiness (Elias et al., 1997; Zins, Weissberg et al., 2004).

Many of today's prevention and promotion initiatives are fragmented, which does not contribute to their collective effectiveness. Schools nationally implement a median of 14 practices (among them, metal detectors, advisory periods, recreational activities, architectural features of the school, school change management practices, and informational posters and brochures) to prevent problem behavior and promote safe environments (Gottfredson & Gottfredson, 2001), so it is easy to understand why such efforts may not be coordinated. The result is lost opportunities to reinforce skills across programs and activities, as well as competition for resources. However, SEL can serve as the organizing framework for a broad array of prevention and promotion efforts (Elias et al., 1997).

### Key Components of Effective SEL

Five key competencies are taught, practiced, and reinforced through SEL programming (CASEL, 2003):

- *Self-awareness*—Identification and recognition of one's own emotions, recognition of strengths in self and others, sense of self-efficacy, and self-confidence.
- *Social awareness*—Empathy, respect for others, and perspective taking.
- *Responsible decision making*—Evaluation and reflection, and personal and ethical responsibility.
- *Self-management*—Impulse control, stress management, persistence, goal setting, and motivation.
- *Relationship skills*—Cooperation, help seeking and providing, and communication.

As noted earlier, these competencies are taught most effectively within caring, supportive, and well-managed learning environments. Development of autonomy, self-discipline, and ethics is more likely in environments in which mutual respect, cooperation, caring, and decision making are the norm (Bear, 2005). Such contexts are structured in ways that encourage students to explore and try new learning activities, provide them with easily accessible opportunities to address their personal needs and problems, and support them in establishing positive relationships with peers and adults. As a result, students feel safe and secure and are not fearful of making mistakes. Ultimately, a reciprocal relationship exists between SEL skills and school climate. A positive school environment promotes SEL, and SEL facilitates a supportive climate. Because social, emotional, and academic growth are interdependent, the result is synergistic progress in all of these areas.

A comprehensive list of 37 guidelines for developing SEL can be found in *Promoting Social and*

**Table 1** *Outline of Effective Social and Emotional Learning Instruction*

- Based on theory and research and carefully planned
- Interactively teaches SEL skills for applications to daily life
- Builds connections to school through caring, engaging classroom and school practices
- Promotes developmentally and culturally appropriate instruction
- Leads to coordinated, integrated, and unified programming linked to academic outcomes
- Enhances school performance by addressing emotional and social dimensions of learning by engaging and interactive methods
- Involves school–family–community partnerships
- Establishes organizational supports and policies that foster success
- Provides high-quality staff development and support
- Addresses key implementation and sustainability factors, including continuous improvement, outcomes evaluation, and dissemination factors

*Note.* Based on *Promoting Social and Emotional Learning: Guidelines for Educators*, by M. J. Elias et al., 1997, Alexandria, VA: Association for Supervision and Curriculum Development; and *Safe and Sound: An Educational Leader's Guide to Evidence-Based Social and Emotional Learning (SEL) Programs,* by the Collaborative for Academic, Social, and Emotional Learning, 2003, Chicago: Author.

*Emotional Learning: Guidelines for Educators* (Elias et al., 1997). These guidelines, which are summarized in 10 major points in Table 1, describe in detail what effective SEL instruction entails. For example, it must be systematic, provided over multiple years, integrated with the academic curriculum, and supported by school–family–community partnerships and a caring supportive environment. In addition, nine useful guidelines specific to school climate, which were developed by the Ohio Department of Education, are presented in Table 2.

SEL programming should be approached from a risk and resilience perspective. In other words, children may acquire risk processes, such as school failure, involvement with antisocial peers, or family poverty, that make it more likely that they will develop problem behaviors. The more risk processes they have, the higher their relative risk, although having risk processes does not guarantee that a student will develop problems, and many of them do not. On the other hand, protective mechanisms or development of competencies—such as bonding to school, learning to consider the perspectives of others, or possessing adequate social decision-making skills—keep children from harm's way or buffer them from the negative effects, and thus lead to more successful adaptation. These positive, health-promoting processes may be found within the child and at the family and community levels.

**Table 2** *Ohio Guidelines for School Climate*

*Guideline 1.* Operational principles for local schools that are grounded in best practices for academic achievement and are espoused by the community will produce effective systems.

*Guideline 2.* School–community partnerships enable the provision of comprehensive services for students and staff.

*Guideline 3.* Regular, thorough assessment and evaluation result in continuous improvement.

*Guideline 4.* High-quality staff development and administrative support lead to effective program implementation.

*Guideline 5.* Addressing real and perceived threats to safety and security enables students to focus on learning and teachers to focus on instruction.

*Guideline 6.* A student's sense of belonging in the classroom encourages classroom participation, positive interactions, and good study habits.

*Guideline 7.* Engagement of parents and families in school–home learning partnerships maximizes the potential for effective instruction and student learning.

*Guideline 8.* Youth engagement in forming school policy and procedures integrates an essential perspective into proposed solutions.

*Guideline 9.* High-quality food service supports improvements in academic performance and behavior.

*Note.* From *Ohio Guidelines for School Climate*, by the Ohio Department of Education, 2004, Columbus, OH: Center for Students, Families, and Community.

## Evidence-Based SEL

***Research support.*** The past two to three decades have seen great progress in educational researchers' and practitioners' knowledge of how to prevent social–emotional and other problems, and in how to promote competence and health-enhancing behaviors. A growing number of programs, strategies, and techniques are available for promoting healthy development and preventing negative outcomes, and a stronger empirical base has emerged in the SEL field (Greenberg et al., 2003). Thus, a number of evidence-based SEL curricula and programs are available that lead to outcomes such as the prevention of substance abuse and interpersonal violence and to the promotion of mental health, positive youth development, and academic achievement (e.g., Catalano,

Berglund, Ryan, Lonczak, & Hawkins, 2002; Durlak & Wells, 1997; Gottfredson & Wilson, 2003; Tobler et al., 2000; Zins, Weissberg et al., 2004). Many of the positive outcomes found to be associated with SEL interventions are summarized in Table 3.

Although many research and practice issues still need to be addressed, the empirical investigations behind current SEL evaluation efforts include better study designs, use of manualized and readily replicable interventions, more analyses of longitudinal data leading to a better understanding of the operation of risk and protective processes, and improvements in knowledge of pathways and stages associated with development of maladaptive behaviors (Greenberg, 2004; Mrazek & Haggerty, 1994). Consequently, the quality of the research support for school-based preventive interventions is substantially stronger (i.e., more than 60 randomized controlled trials) than four other areas of educational research (e.g., math education and staff development) examined by the U.S. Department of Education's Institute for Education Sciences (Whitehurst, 2003). A number of organizations have identified, reviewed, and rated evidence-based programs (see Table 4), and a National Registry of Effective Programs and Practices (NREPP; see *http://modelprograms.samhsa.gov*) has been established that includes the category of general substance abuse and treatment programs.

***Costs.*** Evidence shows that effective SEL programs can provide a good return for their costs; that is, the value of their benefits exceeds their costs (Aos, Lieb, Mayfield, Miller, & Pennucci, 2004). For instance, providing the Seattle Social Development Program (Hawkins, Smith, & Catalano, 2004) costs $4,590 per student served annually, but its benefits were $14,426, or $3.14 per dollar spent per student. Likewise, the Child Development Project (now known as Caring School Community; Schaps, Battistich, & Solomon, 2004) has benefits of $28.42 for each dollar spent, and Life Skills Training (Botvin, 1998, 2002) has $25.61 in benefits. Examples of demonstrated benefits include improved educational outcomes (e.g., test scores, graduation rates), reduced crime, lowered substance abuse, and decreased teen suicide attempts. However, such programs do not result in positive benefits across the board, as some generate more costs than benefits. For example, Drug Abuse Resistance Education (D.A.R.E.) costs $99 per student served but resulted in no benefit according to the criteria used (Aos et al., 2004). As with other areas of education, SEL programs must be examined carefully before being adopted.

**Table 3** *Examples of SEL Outcomes Related to Success in School and Life*

*Attitudes*

- Higher sense of self-efficacy
- Better sense of community (bonding) and view of school as caring
- Stronger commitment to democratic values
- More positive attitudes toward school and learning
- Improved ethical attitudes and values
- Higher academic motivation and educational aspirations
- Greater trust and respect for teachers
- Improved coping with school stressors
- Increased understanding of consequences of behavior

*Behaviors*

- More prosocial behavior
- Fewer absences and suspensions; maintained or improved attendance
- More likely to work out own way of learning
- Reductions in aggression, disruptions, and interpersonal violence
- Fewer hostile negotiations, lower rate of conduct problems, better conflict resolution skills
- More classroom participation and higher engagement
- Greater effort to achieve, more frequent reading outside of school
- Better transitions
- Less drug, tobacco, and alcohol use and delinquent behavior
- Decreases in sexually transmitted diseases, HIV/AIDS, suicide
- More involvement in positive activities (e.g., sports)

*Performance*

- Improved math, language arts, and social studies skills
- Increases in achievement over time (elementary to middle school)
- Higher achievement test scores and no decreases in scores
- More progress in phonological awareness
- Improved learning-to-learn skill
- Better problem solving and planning
- Improved nonverbal reasoning

*Note.* Reprinted from "Facilitating Success in School and in Life Through Social and Emotional Learning," by J. E. Zins, M. J. Elias, and M. T. Greenberg, 2003, *Perspectives in Education, 21*(4), pp. 59–60. Copyright 2003 by *Perspectives in Education*. Reprinted with permission. See also Consortium on the School-Based Promotion of Social Competence (1994); Elias et al., (1997); Fredericks (2003); U.S. Department of Health and Human Services (2002); and Wilson, Gottfredson, & Najaka (2001).

**Table 4** *Examples of Effective Social and Emotional Learning Programs*

| | Ratings Organization | | | | |
|---|---|---|---|---|---|
| **Program** | **Center for Substance Abuse Prevention** | **Collaborative for Academic, Social, and Emotional Learning** | **National Institute on Drug Abuse** | **Office of Juvenile Justice and Delinquency Prevention** | **U.S. Department of Education** |
| Al's Pals: Kids Making Healthy Choices | Model | | | | Promising |
| Caring School Community | | Select | Effective | | Promising |
| I Can Problem Solve | Promising | Select | | Promising | Promising |
| Life Skills Training | Model | | Effective | Blueprints Model | Exemplary |
| Lions-Quest Skills | Model | Select | | | Promising |
| Michigan Model for Comprehensive School Health Education | | Select | | | Promising |
| Olweus Bullying Prevention | Model | | | Blueprints Model | |
| Promoting Alternative Thinking Strategies | Effective | Select | | Blueprints Model | Promising |
| Project Achieve | Model | Select | | | |
| Project Northland | Model | | | Promising | Exemplary |
| Second Step: A Violence Prevention Curriculum | Model | Select | | | Exemplary |
| Resolving Conflicts Creatively Program | | Select | | | |
| Social Problem Solving/ Social Decision Making | Promising | Select | | | Promising |

*Note.* These ratings are subject to change as programs are revised and reassessed.

***Use.*** Evidence-based practices are not used as widely and effectively as they could be (Biglan, Mrazek, Carnine, & Flay, 2003), and we do not know enough about how to influence teachers, educational leaders, and schools to adopt and maintain such practices (Glasgow, Vogt, & Boles, 1999). As discussed later, the manner in which social–emotional instruction is delivered is also important (e.g., with fidelity to how it was planned), and we need to learn more about what reinforces the adoption of, adherence to, and sustainability of these interventions (Elias, Zins, Graczyk, & Weissberg, 2003). Significant "person power" issues also exist; far fewer personnel have been trained in SEL approaches than are needed for widespread dissemination. Although some progress is being made in making SEL part of the preparation of professionals such as school psychologists, counselors, and educators, efforts in these directions must be more extensive if they are to touch the many children who need them (Zins, 2001).

## The Implementation Process

This section contains a brief overview of key implementation issues. The following are examples of activities for school psychologists and other support staff members who wish to be involved in implementation efforts (these are discussed in more detail in Elias et al., 2003):

- *Conduct school and community risk and needs assessments for program planning.* Determine the need and readiness for social–emotional programming. Identify specific issues that could be addressed and examine what already is in place.
- *Consult with school personnel.* Assist in exploring, adopting, implementing, and continuing SEL programming. Support educational leaders who are involved in implementing and integrating SEL into the school culture and organizational routines.
- *Be a champion for SEL.* Be a leader and promote the case for SEL instruction. Help create a safe, caring learning environment at school, in the home, and in extracurricular activities.
- *Promote organizational support.* Help develop policies and practices that will enhance SEL so that adequate support and resources are devoted to these efforts. Encourage the adoption of SEL in district curriculum standards.
- *Act as a liaison to coordinate and integrate school–family–community SEL efforts.* Work with parents and community members to ensure continuity and coordination of prevention messages and services, and to avoid redundancy and conflicts over resources.
- *Help ensure maintenance and sustainability.* Examine the integrity with which SEL programs are adopted and monitor the adaptations that occur to promote high quality. Ensure that support and resources will continue to be devoted to these efforts.
- *Engage in program monitoring and evaluation services.* Assess the extent and quality of SEL program implementation using identified benchmarks, and evaluate formatively and summatively whether goals are attained.

Before examining more specific implementation issues, we must express two caveats. First, the field is a long way from systematically preparing school-based professionals to engage in the activities that make up SEL programs. Even with qualified personnel, the process of implementation takes time. It is common for adoption and institutionalization to take 3 to 5 years, so expectations about outcomes must be tempered based on that reality (Elias et al., 1997; Lippitt, Langseth, & Mossop, 1985).

***Readiness and sanction.*** To begin, how does a school know if it is ready to devote more efforts and resources to SEL? And if it is ready to adopt specific programming? The school will have many considerations, but among the first is to understand its organizational motivations and the need for change, as well as the outcomes it hopes to achieve. A first step is to perform an organizational analysis, involving interviews, observations, questionnaires, rating scales, examination of permanent products and records, and so forth, that targets staff members, students, parents, and community members. The data collected will help the participants understand issues such as organizational climate and health, communication processes, boundaries, roles, leadership styles, and external influences. Of particular importance at this early stage is an understanding of current related efforts and how new programming might help to better meet identified needs by either supplementing or replacing what is being done (Lippitt et al., 1985; Zins & Illback, 1993).

Once participants determine the school's readiness, they should identify program goals and reach consensus about which goals to address. In addition, sanction for implementation must be gained at the administrative, staff, and parent–community levels. Having champions of the cause within the organization is important, but beyond those individuals the position taken by educational leaders such as principals is critical to ensuring sufficient support for role changes, ongoing staff development and coaching, scheduling, program monitoring and evaluation, and resource allocation. Ongoing staff development and coaching, for instance, are likely to lead to high-quality programming, fidelity, and sustainability.

***Programming.*** Among the challenges at this point is to select appropriate evidence-based programming from the myriad of potential approaches. Fortunately, several program reviews are available that include ratings of effectiveness. Examples of overall ratings of several selected programs are shown in Table 4. These reviews help promote standards for quality SEL programming and enable educators to compare and select appropriate programs, based on the match between local needs and program effectiveness, goals, intervention techniques, strengths and limitations, costs, and so forth.

An excellent resource for ratings is *Safe and Sound: An Educational Leader's Guide to Evidence-Based Social and Emotional Learning (SEL) Programs* (CASEL, 2003). The guide contains reviews and comparisons of 80 programs across 17 variables of interest, including the five key SEL skills listed earlier. To be included in the review, programming had to be school based and pertain to general education; consist of multiyear, sequenced instruction or an organizational structure to promote lessons beyond the first year; be systematic and comprehensive; have at least eight lessons in one program year; and be nationally available. The programs were rated on outcome effectiveness; how well the five key SEL skills are addressed; the availability of student assessment measures; if it includes support for school-wide, family, and community involvement; and whether professional development is offered. Of this group, 21 were identified as *select* because they met CASEL standards for high-quality SEL instruction, ongoing professional development support, and evidence of effectiveness based on well-designed evaluations. Within the programs that included methods to promote the integration of SEL with academic curricula and teaching practices, an impressive 83% produced academic gains.

The core, active elements of the intervention (i.e., specifically what will be implemented; what are negotiable versus non-negotiable aspects of program integrity; how can differences compared with current practices, systems, and values be resolved) must be well understood by those seeking to adopt a program. Visiting a site to see the program operating, or talking with current users, usually provides insights that cannot be obtained elsewhere. Furthermore, all programs have limitations; schools must be wary of programs that are oversold by overzealous champions who build unwarranted expectations for them. Rather, by being aware of the strengths and limits of programs, and being able to predict many roadblocks and sources of resistance, schools often can learn to manage and address these problems (e.g., resistance, fear of failure, changing roles, scaling-up too rapidly, more ecological intrusion that results in unanticipated challenges) so that implementation may proceed more smoothly.

***Ownership.*** Programs have associated values that must be supported by and compatible with relevant school policies, practices, and goals if they are to succeed. Buy-in from constituencies at different organizational levels, including parents and the community, must be ascertained and their commitment established. School leadership and high-status individuals need to be involved early in the implementation process, and ultimately, ownership needs to be created among all constituencies.

Roles and functions of stakeholders may be altered, but SEL program planners should recognize that the same job can be done in different ways. For instance, school psychologists do not have to spend the majority of their time conducting psychoeducational assessments and developing individual interventions. Instead, they may focus more energy on systems change by implementing SEL programs, which may decrease the press for direct services (Zins, 2001). Parents too can be true partners in deciding how SEL programming is delivered to their children, rather than being uninvolved or passive recipients.

Another implementation challenge is dealing with competing agendas. Elements of the organization may have different priorities, but consensus must be achieved to avoid battles over resources and direction of efforts, because such competition increases fragmentation and marginalization. The organization should review potential areas of conflict and fragmentation, such as for resources, roles of staff, boundaries, time allocation, priorities, and overlap (Novick, Kress, & Elias, 2002). Likewise, when the staff overspecializes or focuses too much on one area, such as Positive Behavioral Interventions and Supports or conflict resolution, rather than being broad based, too much energy may inadvertently be devoted to providing services rather than empowering individuals within the school.

***Application.*** Numerous opportunities exist for the application of SEL concepts, such as the following (see Zins, Weissberg et al., 2004):

- Adopt specific SEL curricula (e.g., Second Step program).
- Infuse SEL activities into regular academic curricula (e.g., literacy, history).

- Develop supportive, caring learning environments (e.g., improve school climate).
- Alter instructional processes (e.g., cooperative learning).
- Reinforce SEL skills as part of the informal curriculum (e.g., lunch, playground).
- Promote school–family–community partnerships.
- Engage students actively and experientially in the learning process (e.g., service learning).
- Reflect SEL in behavior management and discipline practices and policies.
- Integrate SEL methods into extracurricular activities (e.g., sports).

One of the more common concerns about adopting SEL programming is how it will fit into an already packed school day. As seen in the list above, the options require a range of adaptations, from relatively minor to more substantial changes in the school ecology. Introducing a specific SEL curriculum may be difficult in some schools, but using SEL principles to guide school discipline and behavior management practices may be less intrusive to organizational routines and resources. The goal is to infuse SEL into ongoing activities and program delivery systems in schools and communities to make the intervention sustainable. Likewise, organizational processes and structures must be established to ensure high-quality implementation and to promote sustainability (Greenberg, 2004). Without such safeguards, programs can easily drift from what was planned and intended, and core program elements inadvertently may be omitted because of time concerns. Such deviations from the program may affect outcomes. Often, the core, active elements of the intervention are not clear, so practitioners, researchers, and program developers must work together to identify them. Fortunately, many schools have successfully navigated these dilemmas and can serve as models for organizations embarking on this work (Elias, Arnold, & Hussey, 2002; Elias et al., 1997; Lantieri, 2002).

The issue of adaptation versus fidelity must be addressed, as there is evidence that it is related to program outcomes. Fidelity to program procedures has been found to lead to better outcomes; conversely, poor fidelity results in decreased effectiveness (Elliott & Mihalic, 2004). For example, Botvin, Baker, Dusenbury, Botvin, and Diaz (1995) found that the strongest outcomes with Life Skills Training (Botvin, 1998, 2002) occurred with students who received a more complete version of the intervention. Because implementing a program will almost always involve making adaptations, even with highly structured, manualized interventions, one way to view this issue is to examine the quality and nature of the changes. Support staff members and classroom teachers should work together to anticipate and plan for modifications while they work to ensure that core program elements are maintained. Some adaptations are beneficial in terms of improving outcomes and facilitating ownership (and thus durability), whereas others harm program integrity. Furthermore, programs need to be tailored culturally to ethnic and racial minority children to maximize the programs' effectiveness (Botvin, 2004). In other words, the better the cultural fit is, the more likely that buy-in and perceptions of the program's relevance will occur.

Finally, systems to support SEL must be integrated across levels of prevention/promotion and treatment services (e.g., universal to indicated prevention and treatment (Adelman & Taylor, 2000), across student developmental levels, and across school, family, and community systems, as shown in Figure 1. The fragmentation and marginalization that characterize the educational and mental health systems today largely result from a lack of coordination and integration (Illback, Cobb, & Joseph, 1997); however, the systemwide adoption of SEL can reduce fragmentation and be a unifying conceptual scheme (Elias et al., 1997, 2003).

## Standards and Accountability

More attention should be devoted to state department of education instructional standards that include teaching SEL to further institutionalize and sustain such efforts. For example, in 2003 Illinois passed the Children's Mental Health Act (Public Act 93-0495) in which social and emotional development are defined as integral to schools' mission and essential to students' academic readiness and school success. The act is intended to ensure that schools incorporate the following:

- Regard social and emotional development as integral to their mission and a critical component of student academic readiness and school success.
- Take concrete steps to address their students' social and emotional development.
- Have the flexibility to include social and emotional learning in their school improvement plans.
- Develop a policy for incorporating social and emotional development into the district's educational program, including assessing social and emotional skills.

- Develop a policy for responding to children with social, emotional, or mental health problems that affect learning.

Social and emotional development standards are now included as part of the Illinois Learning Standards, which means that children's social–emotional development must be addressed in the curriculum. Consequently, all students in the state receive such instruction. One result of the Illinois legislation is that it has made paramount the need to measure social–emotional skills because every district must have a policy for incorporating social–emotional development into the district's educational program. That policy includes not only teaching and assessing SEL for all students, but also responding to children who have social, emotional, or mental health problems that affect their learning. Likewise, it requires schools to be accountable for conducting valid and reliable assessments of social–emotional, academic, and health-related outcomes, as well as of school climate, based on input obtained from multiple constituencies (e.g., students, parents, teachers, and community members).

Thus, SEL assessment is one area in need of further development and may be of special interest to many school psychologists. For purposes of accountability and acceptability, we need to determine that SEL has value-added outcomes for student learning, and we need to be able to assess the quality of the SEL instruction that occurs in the classroom. While some school psychologists are involved in developing measures, others could examine indicators of competence, health, and the like, to see how well they align with SEL constructs. There is no reason to delay making SEL part of standard assessment processes using the best measures available.

## SUMMARY

Students today must be prepared not only to pass tests at school but also to pass the tests of life. Social–emotional competence and academic achievement are highly related, and effective schools are focusing efforts on integrated, coordinated instruction in both areas to maximize students' potential to succeed in school and throughout their lives. A growing body of research demonstrates that evidence-based SEL interventions are associated with academic achievement, health, and citizenship, so a major challenge for schools is how to make SEL a core element of the curriculum and how to implement relevant programming with fidelity and in ways that are sustainable. Tremendous opportunities exist for school psychologists to assist schools in these endeavors, and additional training opportunities must be made available to prepare them for such roles.

## RECOMMENDED RESOURCES

### Books and Other Printed Material

Elias, M. J., Zins, J. E., Weissberg, R. P., Frey, K. S., Greenberg, M. T., Haynes, N. M., Kessler, R., Schwab-Stone, M. E., & Shriver, T. P. (1997). *Promoting social and emotional learning: Guidelines for educators.* Alexandria, VA: Association for Supervision and Curriculum Development.

The authors define the field of social and emotional learning. They draw upon the most recent scientific studies, the best theories, site visits carried out around the country, and their own extensive experiences to describe effective approaches to SEL. The discussion is framed by 39 concise guidelines for promoting SEL.

Greenberg, M. T., Weissberg, R. P., O'Brien, M. U., Zins, J. E., Fredericks, L., Resnik, H., & Elias, M. J. (2003). Enhancing school-based prevention and youth development through coordinated social and emotional learning. *American Psychologist, 58,* 466–474.

In this article the authors make the case for the widespread implementation of beneficial prevention programming. They advocate for research-based, comprehensive school reform models that improve social, health, and academic outcomes; school policies that demand accountability for fostering children's overall development; professional development related to helping educators implement programs effectively; and ongoing monitoring and evaluation to guide school improvement.

Zins, J. E., Weissberg, R. P., Wang, M. C., & Walberg, H. J. (Eds.). (2004). *Building academic success on social and emotional learning: What does the research say?* New York: Teachers College Press.

This comprehensive book contains a concise review of the field of social and emotional learning (SEL), with a specific examination of its effects on academic achievement and school success. Relevant outcomes from a number of the best SEL programs nationally are reviewed, leading the editors to conclude that "there is a growing body of scientifically based research supporting the strong impact that enhanced social and emotional behaviors can have on success in school and ultimately in life" (p. 19).

## Websites

*http://www.casel.org*

The Collaborative for Academic, Social, and Emotional Learning (CASEL) is a major national organization whose mission is to enhance children's success in school and in life by promoting coordinated, evidence-based social, emotional, and academic learning as an essential part of education from preschool through high school. CASEL's three primary goals are to advance the science of SEL; expand coordinated, evidence-based practice; and build a sustainable and collaborative organization to accomplish its mission.

*http://www.csee.net*

The Center for Social and Emotional Education (CSEE) is an educational and professional development organization dedicated to supporting effective social–emotional learning, teaching, and leadership in K–12 schools. It integrates research and best practices in education, including risk prevention, health promotion, mental health, effective citizenry, character education, and social–emotional learning, to promote students' ability to learn and develop in healthy ways.

*http://www.samhsa.gov*

The mission of the Substance Abuse and Mental Health Services Administration (SAMHSA), U.S. Department of Health and Human Services, is to build resilience and facilitate recovery for people with or at risk for substance abuse problems and mental illness. Its vision is a life in the community for everyone, and it supports a variety of school-based prevention efforts.

*http://smhp.psych.ucla.edu*

The mission of the UCLA School Mental Health Project (SMHP) is to improve outcomes for young people by enhancing the field of mental health in schools. It connects mental health and psychosocial concerns with school reform and improvement by integrating health and related concerns into a broad perspective that includes addressing barriers to learning and promoting healthy development.

# REFERENCES


Adelman, H., & Taylor, L. (2000). Moving prevention from the fringes into the fabric of school improvement. *Journal of Educational and Psychological Consultation, 11,* 7–26.

Aos, S., Lieb, R., Mayfield, J., Miller, M., & Pennucci, A. (2004). *Benefits and costs of prevention and early intervention programs for youth.* Olympia: Washington State Institute for Public Policy.

Bear, G. G. (with Cavalier, A., & Manning, M.). (2005). *Developing self-discipline and preventing and correcting misbehavior.* Boston: Allyn and Bacon.

Biglan, A., Mrazek, P., Carnine, D. W., & Flay, B. R. (2003). The integration of research and practice in the prevention of youth problem behaviors. *American Psychologist, 58,* 433–440.

Botvin, G. J. (2004). Advancing prevention science and practice: Challenges, critical issues, and future directions. *Prevention Science, 5,* 69–72.

Botvin, G. J. (1998). Preventing adolescent drug abuse through Life Skills Training: Theory, methods, and effectiveness. In J. Crane (Ed.), *Social programs that work* (pp. 225–257). New York: Russell Sage Foundation.

Botvin, G. J. (2002). *Life skills training.* White Plains, NY: Princeton Health Press.

Botvin, G. J., Baker, E., Dusenbury, L., Botvin, E. M., & Diaz, T. (1995). Long-term follow-up results of a randomized drug abuse prevention trial in a white middle-class population. *Journal of the American Medical Association, 273,* 1106–1112.

Catalano, R. F., Berglund, M. L., Ryan, J. A. M., Lonczak, H. S., & Hawkins, J. D. (2002). Positive youth development in the United States: Research findings on evaluations of positive youth development programs. *Prevention & Treatment, 5,* Article 15. Retrieved September 8, 2003, from http://journals.apa.org/prevention/volume5/pre0050015a.html

Collaborative for Academic, Social, and Emotional Learning. (2003). *Safe and sound: An educational leader's guide to evidence-based social and emotional learning (SEL) programs.* Chicago: Author.

Consortium on the School-Based Promotion of Social Competence. (1994). The promotion of social competence: Theory, research, practice, and policy. In R. J. Haggerty, L. Sherrod, N. Garmezy, & M. Rutter (Eds.), *Stress, risk, resilience in children and adolescents: Processes, mechanisms, and interaction* (pp. 268–316). New York: Cambridge University Press.

Durlak, J. A., & Wells, A. M. (1997). Primary prevention mental health programs for children and adolescents: A meta-analytic review. *American Journal of Community Psychology, 25,* 115–152.

Elias, M. J., Arnold, H., & Hussey, C. (Eds.). (2002). *Leadership practices for caring and successful schools.* Thousand Oaks, CA: Corwin.

Elias, M. J., Zins, J. E., Graczyk, P. A., & Weissberg, R. P. (2003). Implementation, sustainability, and scaling up of social–emotional and academic innovations in public schools. *School Psychology Review, 32,* 303–319.

Elias, M. J., Zins, J. E., Weissberg, R. P., Frey, K. S., Greenberg, M. T., Haynes, N. M., Kessler, R., Schwab-Stone, M. E., & Shriver, T. P. (1997). *Promoting social and emotional learning: Guidelines for educators.* Alexandria, VA: Association for Supervision and Curriculum Development.

Elliott, D. S., & Mihalic, S. (2004). Issues in disseminating and replicating effective prevention programs. *Prevention Science, 5,* 47–53.

Fredericks, L. (2003). *Social and emotional learning, service-learning, and educational leadership.* Chicago: Collaborative for Academic, Social, and Emotional Learning.

Gardner, H. (1993). *Multiple intelligences: The theory in practice.* New York: Basic.

Glasgow, R. E., Vogt, T. M., & Boles, S. M. (1999). Evaluating the public health impact of health promotion interventions: The RE-AIM framework. *American Journal of Public Health, 89,* 1322–1327.

Goleman, D. (1995). *Emotional intelligence.* New York: Bantam.

Gottfredson, D. C., & Wilson, D. B. (2003). Characteristics of effective school-based substance abuse prevention. *Prevention Science, 4,* 27–38.

Gottfredson, G. D., & Gottfredson, D. C. (2001). What schools do to prevent problem behaviors and promote safe environments. *Journal of Educational and Psychological Consultation, 12,* 313–344.

Greenberg, M. T. (2004). Current and future challenges in school-based prevention. *Prevention Science, 5,* 5–13.

Greenberg, M. T., Weissberg, R. P., O'Brien, M. U., Zins, J. E., Fredericks, L., Resnik, H., & Elias, M. J. (2003). Enhancing school-based prevention and youth development through coordinated social and emotional learning. *American Psychologist, 58,* 466–474.

Hawkins, J. D., Smith, B. H., & Catalano, R. F. (2004). Social development and social and emotional learning. In J. E. Zins, R. P. Weissberg, M. C. Wang, & H. J. Walberg (Eds.), *Building academic success on social and emotional learning: What does the research say?* (pp. 135–150). New York: Teachers College Press.

Illback, R. J., Cobb, C. T., & Joseph, H. M., Jr. (Eds.). (1997). *Integrated services for children and families.* Washington, DC: American Psychological Association.

Lantieri, L. (Ed.). (2002). *Schools with spirit: Nurturing the inner lives of children and teachers.* Boston: Beacon.

Lippitt, G. L., Langseth, P., & Mossop, J. (1985). *Implementing organizational change: A practical guide to managing change efforts.* San Francisco: Jossey-Bass.

Mrazek, P. J., & Haggerty, R. J. (Eds.). (1994). *Reducing risks for mental disorders: Frontiers for preventive intervention research.* Washington, DC: National Academy Press.

National Center for Education Statistics. (2002). *Dropout rates in the United States 2000.* Washington, DC: U.S. Department of Education, Offices of Educational Research and Improvement.

Novick, B., Kress, J. S., & Elias, M. J. (2002). *Building learning communities with character: How to integrate academic, social, and emotional learning.* Alexandria, VA: Association for Supervision and Curriculum Development.

Ohio Department of Education. (2004). *Ohio guidelines for school climate.* Columbus, OH: Center for Students, Families, and Community.

Roeser, R. W., Eccles, J. S., & Samoroff, A. J. (2000). School as a context of early adolescents' academic and social–emotional development: A summary of research findings. *The Elementary School Journal, 100,* 443–471.

Schaps, E., Battistich, V., & Solomon, D. (2004). Community in school as key to student growth: Findings from the Child Development Project. In J. E. Zins, R. P. Weissberg, M. C. Wang, & H. J. Walberg (Eds.), *Building academic success on social and emotional learning: What does the research say?* (pp. 189–205). New York: Teachers College Press.

Tobler, N. S., Roona, M. R., Ochshorn, P., Marshall, D. G., Streke, A. V., & Stackpole, K. M. (2000). School-based adolescent drug prevention programs: 1998 meta-analysis. *Journal of Primary Prevention, 20,* 275–337.

U.S. Department of Health and Human Services, Substance Abuse and Mental Services Administration. (2002). SAMHSA model programs: Model prevention programs supporting academic achievement. Retrieved January 23, 2003, from http://modelprograms.samsha.gov

Wang, M. C., Haertel, G. D., & Walberg, H. J. (1997). Toward a knowledge base for school learning. *Review of Educational Research, 63,* 249–294.

Whitehurst, G. R. (2003, October). *Evidence-based safe and drug-free schools programs.* Keynote address at Office of Safe and Drug-Free Schools National Conference, Washington, DC.

Wilson, D. B., Gottfredson, D. C., & Najaka, S. S. (2001). School-based prevention of problem behaviors: A meta-analysis. *Journal of Quantitative Criminology, 17,* 247–272.

Wollman, N., Yoder, B. L., Brumbaugh-Smith, J. P., Gross, H., Leiter, B. E., Fry-Miller, A. L., & McCourt, E. H. (2003). *Poverty gaps in the U.S. between the races, age groups, and genders decreased steadily since 1995—but still a ways to go.* Available from Manchester College website: http://www.manchester.edu/links/violenceindex/NewsReleases/PovertyGapsInUS.pdf

Zins, J. E. (2001). Examining opportunities and challenges for school-based prevention and promotion: Social and emotional learning as an exemplar. *The Journal of Primary Prevention, 21*(4), 441–446.

Zins, J. E., & Illback, R. J. (1993). Implementing consultation in child services systems. In J. E. Zins, T. R. Kratochwill, & S. N. Elliott (Eds.), *Handbook of consultation services for children* (pp. 204–226). San Francisco: Jossey-Bass.

Zins, J. E., Elias, M. J., & Greenberg, M.T. (2003). Facilitating success in school and in life through social and emotional learning. *Perspectives in Education, 21,* 59–60.

Zins, J. E., Walberg, H. J., & Weissberg, R. P. (2004). Getting to the heart of school reform: Social and emotional learning for school success. *NASP Communiqué, 33*(3), 35.

Zins, J. E., Weissberg, R. P., Wang, M. C., & Walberg, H. J. (Eds.). (2004). *Building academic success on social and emotional learning: What does the research say?* New York: Teachers College Press.

# 2

# Character Education

**Marvin W. Berkowitz**
*University of Missouri–St. Louis*

**Merle Schwartz**
*Character Education Partnership, Washington, DC*

## BACKGROUND AND DEVELOPMENT

### Character Education Defined

Character education is a widely misunderstood discipline. Some think it is a recent phenomenon, when in fact it probably dates back, at least in the Western world, to the classical Greeks over 2,000 years ago. Some think it is a religious phenomenon (particularly a conservative Christian one), when in fact it is a widely accepted secular phenomenon that is taught in public schools. Some think it is a usurpation of uniquely family roles, when in fact it is grounded in human development, the civic mission of schools (especially in a democratic society), and universal ethical principles such as justice and caring.

Essentially, character education consists of practices and strategies schools use to help students not only become smart but also become good. The Character Education Partnership (CEP), a national organization of educational and professional associations (including the National Association of School Psychologists and the National Education Association), defines it as the way in which schools help students "understand, care about, and act upon core ethical values" (Character Education Partnership, 2004, p. 1).

Consistent with this definition, NASP's position paper on character education (NASP, 2003) states the following:

> [Character education] enhances the development of students' value systems which embrace not only social norms, but also cultural diversity—the students' understanding of why it is important to hold such values as fairness, caring, or responsibility, and their desire to live by them and act on them. When these programs are intentional in this way, they become a part of character education. Character education confirms the belief that ethical, social, and emotional development of young people is as important as their academic achievement. (p. 1)

Character education is a multifaceted approach that is best accomplished through comprehensive school reform (Berkowitz & Bier, 2005). As noted in CEP's *Eleven Principles Sourcebook* (Beland & Tolman, 2003), character education includes a clear values mission, focuses on child development, relies on intrinsic motivation, includes a range of stakeholders (such as students, teachers, administrators, and parents), is incorporated into the academic curriculum, and offers community service opportunities. Character education ultimately focuses on building a caring school and classroom community, in particular on relationship building, a pedagogy that incorporates issues of values and ethics, a clear values-based mission, and a developmental approach to discipline and behavior management that is intentionally aligned with the school's explicit values.

Of course, all of this depends on the developmental level of the students and on what is meant by character. Character is the complex "set of psychological characteristics that affect that person's ability and inclination to function morally" (Berkowitz, 2002, p. 48). It consists of seven types of psychological characteristics: moral values, moral action, moral emotion, moral reasoning, moral personality, moral identity, and foundational characteristics.

**Table 1** *The Stages of Moral Reasoning*

| Stage | Moral Issue | Nature of Moral Reasoning |
|---|---|---|
| *Stage 0*<br>*Egocentric Reasoning* | WHAT'S RIGHT:<br>REASON TO BE GOOD: | I should get my own way.<br>To get rewards and avoid punishment. |
| *Stage 1*<br>*Unquestioning Obedience* | WHAT'S RIGHT:<br>REASON TO BE GOOD: | I should do what I'm told.<br>To stay out of trouble. |
| *Stage 2*<br>*What's-In-It-For-Me Fairness* | WHAT'S RIGHT:<br>REASON TO BE GOOD: | I should look out for myself but be fair to those who are fair to me.<br>Self-interest: What's in it for me? |
| *Stage 3*<br>*Interpersonal Conformity* | WHAT'S RIGHT:<br>REASON TO BE GOOD: | I should be a nice person and live up to the expectations of people I know and care about.<br>So others will think well of me (social approval) and so I can think well of myself (self-esteem). |
| *Stage 4*<br>*Responsibility to "The System"* | WHAT'S RIGHT:<br>REASON TO BE GOOD: | I should fulfill my responsibilities to the social or value system I feel part of.<br>To keep the system from falling apart and to maintain self-respect as somebody who meets my obligations. |
| *Stage 5*<br>*Principled Conscience* | WHAT'S RIGHT:<br>REASON TO BE GOOD: | I should show the greatest possible respect for the rights and dignity of every individual person and should support a system that protects human rights.<br>The obligation of conscience to act in accordance with the principle of respect for all human beings. |

*Note.* Adapted from *The Eleven Principles Sourcebook: How to Achieve Quality Character Education in K–12 Schools*, by K. Beland (Series Ed.), 2003, Washington, DC: Character Education Partnership. Copyright 2003 by the Character Education Partnership. Adapted with permission.

## Three Aspects of Character

The Character Education Partnership defines character as a three-part concept: understanding, caring about, and acting upon core ethical values. A useful mnemonic for the three parts is *head, heart, and hand.* In other words, in the CEP definition (which comes from leaders in the field such as Thomas Lickona and Kevin Ryan) character includes a cognitive component, an affective component, and a behavioral component. Thus, to become a person of character, a student (or any person) needs to develop all three aspects.

The cognitive aspect of character (the head) is best understood as having two sides: knowledge and reasoning. Students need to know what is right and wrong (knowledge) and be able to figure it out themselves (reasoning). The latter is especially true when facing novel, ambiguous, or contradictory circumstances, because students cannot be taught the correct response to all possible moral situations. Instead, they often need to figure out responses to moral circumstances on their own. Schools therefore need to teach (didactically and in other ways) knowledge relevant to ethical issues and to implement pedagogical practices that promote the development of relevant reasoning structures, such as moral reasoning, perspective taking, and interpersonal understanding. In other words, schools need to promote critical thinking about sociomoral phenomena.

Kohlberg (1984) developed stages of moral reasoning that may serve as a developmental guide for understanding and stimulating higher order thinking about moral issues, as seen in Table 1 (Beland, 2003). Although there is controversy over some aspects of this model of moral reasoning (e.g., whether it applies across cultures and genders, whether it is related to affect and behavior), extensive research suggests that is very helpful for understanding how students make meaning of the moral world. Theorists and researchers like Kohlberg readily acknowledge that the *head* of character is only part of the picture; a cognitive focus alone is insufficient for understanding moral functioning.

The second aspect, the affective component of character (the heart), requires a different approach than the cognitive aspect of character development does. It entails emotions and motivation. It has to do with valuing goodness; with caring about right and wrong; and with committing to core values such as respect, responsibility, fairness, and caring. As suggested above, one cannot really separate the heart from the head. It is the fostering of empathy and related moral emotions (e.g., sympathy, compassion, guilt, and shame) that ignites the heart—and, in order to foster such emotions, one needs the cognitive skills to recognize another's feelings and perspectives as well as to understand the related moral issues.

Teaching the heart is something for which educators tend not to be well trained. It can be more slippery and difficult for many educators. If the development of character, however, is reliant on developing both the head and the heart, it becomes vital that the adults in schools address this. Therefore, it is at the center of what character-based school reform and effective implementation need to be and do. Key to teaching the heart is the development of empathy and emotions that lead to other-focused responses (Hoffman, 2000).

The third aspect, the behavioral element of character (the hand), has recently become a broader and richer concept. One way to conceptualize the hand of character is by thinking about a helping hand (*hands*, really). This aspect of character is the *doing* aspect, and in character education, there are two forms of doing that become part of the curriculum—moral action and skills of social–emotional behavior.

Moral action starts with opportunities, which Tolman described as follows (2003):

> When teachers take their students to a local nursing home and schools organize canned food drives, they are creating opportunities for moral action. Schools also provide such opportunities when they help students resolve their own conflicts, when they set up student-led honor committees, or when they encourage student clubs to take on school problems. These activities go by many names: service learning, cooperative learning, conflict resolution, class meetings, peer mediation, student leadership, peer tutoring, youth-adult partnerships, and community service, among many others. (p. 5)

By reflecting on experiences that involve moral action, students strengthen the cognitive and emotional aspects of character. Studies have shown that students involved in a variety of opportunities for civic engagement while in high school are more likely to continue being civically engaged up to three decades later (Davidson & Youniss 1991; Youniss, McLellan, & Yates, 1997). As students develop, they can become increasingly involved in the creation of such opportunities, increasingly reflective about the experiences, and increasingly abstract in understanding the social and moral meaning of them.

The second form of hand, or *doing*, comes from learning and practicing behavioral skills that help the student act with good character. Teaching behavior skills not only helps students develop individual character, it also lays the foundation of primary prevention. Therefore, many schools have begun to focus on building students' social and emotional skills (see chapter 1, "Social and Emotional Learning"). These skills are driven by the theory and research that support what many developmental guidance curricula have been trying to do for a while, typically as mental health "carve-out" or stand-alone add-on curricula.

The notion of developmental discipline has also contributed to this revolution by highlighting the need to build classroom management and discipline around two concepts: (a) the critical importance of teacher–student relations and school climate and (b) a shifting of the goal of classroom management and discipline from the immediate reduction of the undesirable behavior to the long-term positive development of the child, including the development of their cognitive, affective, and behavioral competencies (Bear, 2005; Watson, 2003).

Regardless of which definition of character one adopts, character should clearly be understood to be (a) psychological, (b) multifaceted, and (c) developmental. Thus, the obvious conclusion would be that character education needs to focus on the multifaceted psychological development of students and therefore needs to rely on a range of diverse educational strategies. Not as clear, but equally important, is the importance of adult behavior in schools. A crucial aspect of providing character education is to promote the development of responsible, respectful adult behaviors, relationships, and communities in schools. Adults need to "walk the talk" if they expect students to follow that path, to borrow from the title of Theodore and Nancy Faust Sizer's (1999) book, *The Students Are Watching.*

## PROBLEMS AND IMPLICATIONS

In his book, *Character Matters* (2004), Lickona makes a compelling case about the state of our nation's character.

The following are the critical statistics for the 30-year period from the 1960s to the early 1990s:

- Violent crime increased by 500%.
- Teen suicide tripled.
- The divorce rate more than doubled.
- About 40% of children go to sleep in homes where their fathers do not live.
- Births to unmarried mothers increased more than 400%.
- More than one in five children now live in poverty.
- The average teen now spends less than two hours each week reading and more than 20 hours each week watching television.

Lickona goes on to give a "2002 Report Card on American Youth Ethics":

- Three out of four students admitted to cheating on an exam in school during the past year.
- Nearly 4 in 10 students said they had stolen something from a store during the past year.
- Nearly 4 in 10 said they "would lie to get a good job."
- More than a third of college students told a 1999 *U.S. News & World Report* survey that they would steal from an employer (only 6% of those over 45 said they would do so) (p. 13).

The implication from these dismal statistics is that students are not developing the competencies and motives necessary to provide our democracy with responsible and caring citizens who work toward the common good. To develop the necessary civic character in students, some states are taking action. Fifteen states specifically *mandate* character education, another 14 *encourage* character education through legislation, and 10 or more *support* character education, often through a State Board of Education resolution or rule, through specific programs or partnerships, or even through language in state standards that does not invoke character education but refers to specific positive behaviors.

## ALTERNATIVE ACTIONS: DEVELOPMENT AND IMPLEMENTATION OF CHARACTER EDUCATION PROGRAMS

More than half of the 2003 National Schools of Character (NSOC) award winners (a CEP contest based on CEP's *Eleven Principles of Effective Character Education* [Lickona, Schaps, & Lewis, 2003], outlined in the *CEP Quality Standards* [CEP, 2002]) began their character education initiatives in response to an existing problem such as poor academic achievement, financial crisis, lack of civility, or safety issues. When these "turnaround" schools examined the causes of their problems, they concluded that they needed to emphasize character development and to make it a major part of their transformation. Using the *Eleven Principles* as a guide, the schools were able to examine what they were strong in and what areas of concern needed a coordinated effort as part of their plan to implement character education.

## ORGANIZATION OF AN EFFECTIVE CHARACTER EDUCATION PROGRAM USING THE 11 PRINCIPLES

Although effective character education follows no single script, some important principles should be considered when designing and evaluating an effective program. These inclusive principles, which are discussed in *Eleven Principles of Effective Character Education* (Lickona et al., 2003), serve as a conceptual framework for planning and sustaining an effective program that will provide methods for both prevention and intervention. Using these broad parameters for character education as a foundation, this section offers more concrete guidance on effective character education methods.

### Principle 1: Effective Character Education Promotes Core Ethical Values as the Basis of Good Character

Schools should have a clear character education mission. Ideally, they should collaboratively develop a touchstone or some other representation of what they consider to be the end goal of character education; that is, they should define what good character entails. In the process of defining the mission, or stating the school's core ethical values, the school will agree on what kind of school it hopes to be by answering questions such as the following: *What kind of school do we want to be? What will our behavior look like if we reach our goal? What kind of people are we?*

Schools that create their own core ethical values go through a process of gathering the community members or stakeholders, developing a list of possible core ethical values

**Table 2** *Sample of Scope and Sequence of Behavior Skill Sets*

Elementary School

*Care and respect:* actively listening, making conversation, including others, comforting others, interrupting politely.

*Responsibility:* dealing with distractions, asking for help, admitting wrongs and mistakes, apologizing and making amends, setting goals.

*Honesty:* resisting the temptation to lie and steal.

*Fairness:* sharing, trading, taking turns, negotiating a fair solution.

*Trustworthiness:* keeping a promise.

Middle School and High School

*Care and respect:* communicating feelings, active listening, including others.

*Responsibility:* dealing with peer pressure, resisting labeling and stereotyping, standing up for the rights of self and others, taking responsibility for your actions, setting goals.

*Honesty:* resisting the temptation to cheat.

*Fairness:* negotiating a fair solution.

*Trustworthiness:* keeping a promise, avoiding gossip, keeping a confidence.

*Note.* From *The Eleven Principles Sourcebook: How to Achieve Quality Character Education in K–12 Schools,* by K. Beland (Series Ed.), 2003, Washington, DC: Character Education Partnership. Copyright 2003 by the Character Education Partnership. Adapted with permission.

or statements, evaluating the list, agreeing on a set of values or statements, and defining the values (Beland & Tolman, 2003). Whether the school chooses a program with core values that are already established or creates the consensus using a process, everyone in the school needs to understand and agree on the meaning of and means of enacting these statements. In other words, the guiding principles and values need to be both behaviorally anchored and communally generated or reviewed and accepted.

## Principle 2: Effective Character Education Defines Character Comprehensively to Include Thinking, Feeling, and Behavior

In defining character to include the head (cognitive), the heart (affective), and the hand (behavioral, or doing), as discussed earlier, behavioral definitions allow school and community members to describe what abstract concepts—such as *respect, care, fairness,* and *responsibility*—look like when exhibited by a student or an adult. For some schools, this definition process brings ethnic groups together, as sharing their differences becomes a way of finding common ground.

When school professionals know how character has been comprehensively defined, it becomes easier for them to plan how to teach the concepts and develop the students' skills and motives needed to function as persons of character. It also becomes easier for educators to assess the presence or absence of these skills. Social–emotional skills need to be taught directly, as does much of character knowledge. Schools need to commit to teaching peer conflict resolution skills, anger management competencies, emotional literacy, and so forth. To develop character, students need to achieve certain intrapersonal and interpersonal competencies. Table 2 demonstrates how one district went about planning for social and emotional learning by first broadly defining the competencies that were to be taught by developmental age.

Of course, skill training in isolation is not likely to result in a pervasive demonstration of good character throughout the school. For these lessons to be of value, they must be omnipresent in the structures and practices and people of the school.

## Principle 3: Effective Character Education Uses a Comprehensive, Intentional, Proactive, and Evidence-Based Approach to Character Development

Lickona et al. (2003) describe this principle in the following way:

> Schools committed to character development look at themselves through a moral lens to assess how virtually everything that goes on in school affects the character of students. A *comprehensive* approach uses all aspects of schooling as opportunities for character development. This includes what is sometimes called the *hidden curriculum*; the *academic curriculum*; and *extracurricular programs* . . . Finally, rather than simply waiting for opportunities to arise, with an *intentional* and *proactive* approach, the school staff takes deliberate steps for developing character, drawing wherever possible on practices shown by research to be effective. (p. 2)

Of all the principles to consider, this one underpins what the school really is *doing* to infuse character development throughout the campus. It answers the question *Who should be involved?* (Answer: *Everyone.*) It also emphasizes the important role of adult behavior and modeling. Teachers, by how they treat children, are critical to the development of student character. For that reason, teachers (and all other adults in schools) need to examine what are often their own unreflective patterns of interacting with students. How does the teacher respond to a student who asks a question that shows a severe lack of understanding or lack of attention? How does the teacher respond to students in emotional crisis, especially when the teacher is busy or annoyed, or feels the student is overreacting?

Students learn character in the hidden curriculum by watching how other people treat each other in the student's presence. How does the teacher or administrator speak to the student's uncooperative parents (with the child present) in a frustrating conference? How does the teacher talk to the custodian who finally attends to a long-standing classroom problem after repeated requests? How do teachers interact with each other in the parking lot on Friday afternoon? All educators are, after all, role models whether they want to be or not, whether they try to be or not. One elementary school teacher once commented that "if you want to know what kind of teacher you are, watch your students playing school." High school teachers have indicated that the same process occurs as students try to act like their teacher when making class presentations. An early childhood educator said that when she wants to check on how she is doing as a teacher she simply asks one of her four-year-olds to lead a lesson.

Educators need to reflect on how they treat each other and the students and how committed they are to promoting learning (for themselves and their students). They need to model among themselves, as well as with their students, the kind of people they want students to become. Students are watching, and they will see the hypocrisy if it is there; educators cannot expect students to be and become something they themselves are unwilling or unable to be. Punishing students for late assignments must be done only if teachers are willing to accept consequences when they return assignments late or show up to faculty meetings late. Educators can demand respect from students only if they treat students with respect.

Thomas Lickona, one of leaders in the field of character education, wrote for parents that "it's not only important to practice what you preach, but it's also important to preach what you practice" (1985, p. 136). This applies equally well to educators. We not only send these messages directly, but we often convey them indirectly as well. One boy came home from middle school and asked his father, "Why do all of my teachers think it is okay to cheat?" When asked why he thought that, he replied, "Because students cheat on homework all the time and teachers know it and don't do anything. Besides, one of my teachers caught a kid cheating on a test and said, 'At least it shows he wants to do well.' " These are powerful examples of how teachers explicitly and implicitly say what matters to them.

Being intentional about character education means providing opportunities for students to experience character and issues related to character. That includes giving them the opportunity to negotiate and resolve their own interpersonal challenges. It includes sharing authority with them in the governance of their classrooms and schools. It also includes providing opportunities for them to be of service to others. Students tend to perceive themselves as having little autonomy and voice in schools, and they are right. Schools tend to be very hierarchical, and students are at the bottom of the food chain. A large part of character education involves reforming governance structures and systems of power in classrooms and schools. Rather than telling students what to do, educators should start by asking them what ought to be done.

## Principle 4: Effective Character Education Develops Caring Relationships in the School Community

Research shows that when schools do not meet students' need for safety, caring, and significance, students are more likely to feel alienated and engage in at-risk behaviors (Resnick, Bearman et al. 1997). Character education requires a different kind of teaching staff. Ideally, educators in a character education school are committed to the school's core ethical values, deeply care about children, reflect on and consistently strive to model what they want their students to become, and are willing to share power and voice with students. Furthermore, school staff members (and this includes teachers, administrators, school counselors and psychologists, paraprofessionals, and support staff) must strive to become a caring community of learning professionals themselves.

"The experience of being connected, supported, valued, helpful, and influential in the daily life of the classroom and school" (Schaps, 2002) creates a sense of community in school. Contemporary leaders in the field, such as John Gardner (1991), Nel Noddings (1992), and

Tom Sergiovanni (1994), have emphasized the importance of community building in schools, especially in relation to developing caring relationships and promoting student engagement in learning. Findings of research-based programs with a focus on community have shown increases in students' and staff members' sense of community in school. They have also shown other significant student outcomes, such as increased prosocial behaviors, decreased aggressive and at-risk behaviors, and improved academic achievement (Schwartz, 2004).

Effective character education schools frequently create structures that build relationships (Berkowitz & Bier, 2005). Peer interactive methods are one means. Cross-age practices, such as classroom buddying, peer mentoring, multi-age classes and homerooms, are another. Such relationships should not just be among students, however. Elementary classrooms can adopt nonclassroom adults such as art teachers, counselors, custodians, and cafeteria workers. Staff can adopt at-risk students and create special supportive relationships with them. Teachers can mentor each other or create small friendship groups among themselves.

## Principle 5: Effective Character Education Provides Students With Opportunities for Moral Action

In the ethical as in the intellectual domain, students are constructive learners; they learn best by doing. To develop good character, they need many and varied opportunities to apply values such as compassion, responsibility, and fairness in everyday interactions and discussions as well as through community service. By grappling with real-life challenges—how to divide the labor in a cooperative learning group, how to reach consensus in a class meeting, how to reduce fights on the playground, how to carry out a service learning project—and reflecting on these experiences, students develop practical understanding of the requirements of cooperating with others and giving of oneself. Through repeated experiences that cause them to consider their moral beliefs, students develop and practice the skills and behavioral habits that make up the action side of character (Lickona et al., 2003).

Students need to be given the opportunity to consider, challenge, debate, collaboratively explore, and contrast perspectives on moral issues. Class meetings provide one format for these types of discussion and student interaction, but academic class discussions can provide more open interaction as well. Students not only learn the academic content better through such methods, they also develop character competencies through the interactive experiences.

Service learning is one technique that combines academic learning with moral action. For example, if the curriculum in a literature, health, or social studies class leads to a discussion of poverty and hunger, students may use their academic time to research these issues, discuss moral implications, and talk about experiences from their own lives or communities to connect with their learning. Given the opportunity to research how prevalent hunger might be within their own community, students not only practice their academic skills but also engage in a course of action that leads to a relevant service project. Because the elements of reflection, such as discussion, journal writing, and exhibitions, are included in the study, students experience how *service* is connected to *learning*.

Schools need to increase the expectation of and opportunities for students to engage in meaningful service to others, whether within the school or outside of it, whether connected to the academic curriculum (as in service learning) or not. Community service, service learning, and peer tutoring are examples. Table 3 illustrates areas to consider in matching moral action experiences to child development.

## Principle 6: Effective Character Education Includes a Meaningful and Challenging Academic Curriculum That Respects All Learners and Helps Them to Succeed

Character development results from caring yet demanding relationships in which adults have the students' best interests at heart (including their long-term development) while expecting high levels of both academic performance and general behavior. These high levels of expectation, however, need to be both realistic and supported. The child must be reasonably capable of meeting the expectations. Educators need to put supports in place that will help students make headway toward meeting the high expectations of their schools. This scaffolding entails understanding the unique needs of all the children and providing the appropriate level and type of support for them, monitoring their progress, and dismantling the scaffold appropriately and systematically.

A meaningful curriculum includes active teaching and learning methods such as cooperative learning, problem-solving approaches, and experience-based projects. These approaches increase students' autonomy by appealing to their interests, providing them with opportunities to think creatively and test their ideas, and fostering a sense of "voice and choice"—having a say in decisions and plans that affect them (Lickona et al., 2003).

Schools need to build character content into their curricula, identify and use the character content already in their curricula, and commit to teaching about character. Lessons on honesty in short stories, courage in social studies lessons, responsibility in the health curriculum or science, and so forth are prime opportunities for character education. When teachers help students find the links between core ethical values and the characters, historical figures, and issues they are studying, they infuse character education into the curriculum and avoid the perception that character education is "something extra."

## Principle 7: Effective Character Education Strives to Develop Students' Intrinsic Motivation

How educators respond evaluatively to children and their behavior will either contribute to building their ideas about and commitment to being a person of character or inhibit their internalizing the values and experiences that would help them become a person of good character. Responses include both affirming responses, such as praise, and critiquing responses, such as reprimand. One aspect of this is whether educators respond at all. For instance, many educators fail to give many affirming responses. Some educators have begun to institutionalize affirmations through "caught in the act of doing good" programs such as character slips and character assemblies. Others have instituted positive office referrals, in which students are sent to the principal's office for praise for a noteworthy act. Some teachers make positive phone calls or write notes to parents to let them know of the praiseworthy acts of their children. The undergirding principle here is to be sure to acknowledge the character-related successes of students.

Educators are debating, however, about whether the acknowledgments should be material (reward) or social (affirmation) and whether individuals or groups (that is, classes or the entire school) should be the focus or recipients of the acknowledgments. The first question revolves around the intrinsic versus extrinsic nature of consequences and motives. On one side is the argument that extrinsic rewards are highly salient and students respond to them. On the other side, however, is the argument that students do not internalize the extrinsically rewarded behavior or value and learn instead to do whatever gets them good things. One elementary school, for example, discovered that after a year in which service activities increased when the school rewarded students' acts of service, the students had not internalized the value of service and instead were only willing to engage in service activities if there was a material reward attached. The debate about having an individual versus a social focus of affirmations can be shown in the example in which an elementary school principal terminated the long-running tradition of monthly character assemblies in her new school because only a few children were affirmed for showing good character each month. She claimed that she did not want to send the message that only a few children deserved recognition for acting with character, when every day in her school hundreds of children actually did so. Some educators prefer to acknowledge the entire class or school for having had a good day or week rather than singling out individual students and actions.

Another critical aspect of evaluative responses to students involves discipline and classroom management. Much of the traditional approach to behavior management is reactive; that is, the teacher responds to the student or students after they have engaged in some undesirable behavior. Of course, this is an inevitable phenomenon in school (and life, for that matter). However, much of what educators do for behavior management is proactive and preemptive, and it is in these approaches that character education has its greatest potential for contributing to behavior management—by *preventing* misbehavior. Clearly, character education is intended to foster positive psychological strengths in students, including prosocial values, social and emotional competencies, and an affective attachment to the class and school. By promoting the development of character in students, schools are, by definition, reducing misbehavior. For example, a recent review of outcome studies of 33 character education programs showed that quality character education reduces violence and aggression, substance use, premature sexual behavior, school misbehavior, and general misbehavior (Berkowitz & Bier, 2005).

Behavior management, however, is inevitably reactive at times. Character education suggests that responses to misbehavior should be crafted with a long-term developmental focus, rather than a short-term organizational focus (Berkowitz & Begun 2003). In other words, the purpose of behavior management should be the long-term prosocial development of the child and not the immediate cessation of the disruptive event (unless, of course, the event is clearly dangerous or even potentially

**Table 3** *A Growing Reach: Moral Action and Development*

| Developmental Domain | Developmental Issue | Early Elementary >>> Late Elementary | | >>> Middle School >>> High School |
|---|---|---|---|---|
| *Cognitive* | *Patterns in Development* | Concrete thinking, learning through play and action. | → | Abstract, self-reflective thinking skills more developed; ability to understand multiple viewpoints. |
| | *Implications for Action* | Focus on local actions and tangible work while also drawing on student imagination. Provide a clear step-by-step plan. | → | Provide opportunities to take on complex, long-term projects involving design, inquiry, and global and controversial issues with growing independence. |
| *Social* | *Patterns in Development* | Growing abilities to work with others, have close friends, identify with others. Students like trying on adult roles. | → | Peer friendships central; exploration of different social groups. Students are interested in adult world. Social connectedness is vital to overall success. |
| | *Implications for Action* | Have students build one-on-one relationships with elders, "big brothers and sisters"; learn to work in cooperative groups; and help peers. | → | Provide opportunities to try out adult roles, meet new people and role models, and work closely with diverse peers, all in a safe setting. |
| *Physical* | *Patterns in Development* | Regular physical activity critical; coordination increasing with age. | → | Identity issues, self-awareness with physical maturity. New health issues (e.g., sexuality, substances) emerge. |
| | *Implications for Action* | Incorporate physical work and play into action opportunities. Stretch students to do tasks that involve fine motor abilities (art, construction). | → | Continue to incorporate physical work. Address issues of self-image, sexuality, substance abuse. |
| *Identity* | *Patterns in Development* | Identity based largely on action, behavior. | → | Identity based largely on beliefs, internal features; students increasingly focused on defining self. |
| | *Implications for Action* | Provide opportunities for learning from modeling and practicing good behavior. | → | Encourage actions that involve self-expression, communication skills, finding voice. |
| *Moral and Ethical* | *Patterns in Development* | Ethics based largely on self-interest, and later on social norms, though able to experience empathy at an early age. | → | Ethics increasingly based on concern for others and rules, and later on concern for social welfare and justice. |
| | *Implications for Action* | Provide actions that involve clear rules and that stretch students to take on other people's perspectives. | → | Introduce actions involving larger social issues and competing values. Actions should stretch students to use values as the basis for decision making. |

*Note.* From "Providing Opportunities for Moral Action," by Joel Tolman. In K. Beland (Series Ed.), *The Eleven Principles Sourcebook: How to Achieve Quality Character Education in K–12 Schools*, 2003, Washington, DC: Character Education Partnership. Copyright 2003 by the Character Education Partnership. Reprinted with permission.

dangerous). When a child is punished in a demeaning or unfair way to stop a behavior that a teacher finds undesirable, for instance by public humiliation in the classroom, it is likely that child will act out later. The punishment may ultimately result in an overall increase in misbehavior, just not at the offending moment and perhaps not even in the teacher's line of sight. School counselors, school psychologists, and administrators understand this delayed effect as a dynamic in which teachers with poor and often harsh behavior management styles breed playground, bus, and cafeteria misbehavior, in effect increasing the case loads of the counselors and psychologists.

Teachers need to align their classroom management styles with the philosophy of the school and with the goal of promoting the positive long-term development of students. Developmental discipline, fair and relevant consequences, positive teacher–student relations, and peer-mediated discipline are examples of such strategies (Bear, 2005; Watson, 2003).

## Principle 8: Effective Character Education Engages the School Staff as a Learning and Moral Community

The commitment and expertise of administrators and the school's investment in professional development for all adults who work and volunteer in the school are pivotal for the effective implementation of character education. Most of the character education initiative hinges on the capacity of staff members to implement it, and success is fairly unlikely without schools' and educators' priority commitment to developing the professional skills and knowledge involved in character education. In addition to setting aside in-service days, schools should have a character education staff committee that will take the lead in planning learning groups, organizing assessments, and ensuring that time is set aside for teachers, students, parents, and administrators to reflect on and talk about how things are going and what changes are needed.

As part of a learning community, staff members need to identify areas of need. If in studying character education they learn that class meetings, for example, are a good way to develop skills that lead to character development, then the staff might form a small committee dedicated to reviewing resources and presenting their findings. The same thing is true for skill areas that include teaching strategies (for example, Socratic discussions), conflict resolution and peer mediation, service learning, assessment, and curriculum integration. When staff members model how they learn, students observe that learning and cooperative endeavors are lifelong activities.

## Principle 9: Effective Character Education Fosters Shared Moral Leadership and Long-Range Support of the Character Education Initiative

One of the hallmarks of caring school communities is that they truly are communities, with shared commitments to other members of the community and to the institution and its mission. Governance is shared, and members have respect for all voices in the community and for external stakeholders. This idea of community suggests rethinking the governance structure of the school, its decision-making practices, and the relationships among its members. Reform models such as Professional Learning Communities (DuFour & Eaker, 1998) and Ethical Professional Learning Communities (Lickona & Davidson, 2005) provide examples of how the adult organization in a school can be radically transformed. Such models are perfectly aligned with what needs to happen to share moral leadership (Sergiovanni 1994).

Administrative leaders, including principals and superintendents, need to deeply understand what character is, how it develops, and how schools must change to promote it. These leaders are critical to the saliency of and emphasis on character education in a school, but they also are critical to its long-term viability. Although no educational reform is "principal proof" (an antagonistic leader can easily undermine a reform effort or the culture of the school), it is possible to institutionalize policies and practices that will maximize the likelihood of a character education initiative surviving significant turnover of staff and students. Such policies and practices include hiring faculty who fit the school's vision; providing effective orientation for new students, staff members, and families; and sharing responsibility for implementing, assessing, and improving the initiative.

Depending on their developmental levels, students may take leadership roles in planning for character education activities as well as helping new peers understand what the school community has committed to.

## Principle 10: Effective Character Education Engages Families and Community Members as Partners in the Character-Building Effort

One of the most common laments of schools attempting to effectively promote character development in students is that it is futile because parents and the broader community either are apathetic or even counterproductive to these efforts. Students are more likely to learn and to develop if parents are productively involved in their education. Schools of character routinely find ways to attract such involvement by creating opportunities for families and the community to be involved, by motivating family and community members to want to be involved, and by authentically valuing such involvement and empowering families and community members to share ownership of the character education initiative (and of the school in general).

Building a successful character education program requires participation from all the stakeholders—school leaders, school staff (both teaching and nonteaching), students, parents, and community members. The school's character education committee should have more than a few active parent representatives, and it should do more than simply inform parents of character education activities and goals. Parents and others should be actively involved in planning, implementing, and supporting character education.

### Principle 11: Effective Character Education Endorses the Evaluation of the School's Character Education Program and Its Supporting School Community

The growing body of empirical research on the effectiveness of character education (Berkowitz & Bier, 2005) has shown that some character education is quite effective and some is not. Schools need to understand that not all attempts at promoting character education are likely to be successful and that what works elsewhere may not work in their unique setting. Therefore it is important for schools to evaluate whether they are actually implementing character education (not all good intentions lead to productive results) and, if they are, whether it is having a positive effect.

Posey, Davidson, and Korpi (2003) offer excellent guidance on how to decide on, plan, and implement the various forms of evaluation for character education in schools. It is beyond the scope of this chapter to review what they suggest. Instead, we offer a few major points. First, plan well in advance so that meaningful baseline data are collected. Second, feed data back to the school to improve practice (Marshall & Caldwell 2002). Third, be sure to use evaluative methods that have an evidence base; i.e., for which there is a scientifically justifiable body of evidence supporting the effectiveness of the methods selected (Berkowitz & Bier, 2005).

## SUMMARY

Character education is the intentional efforts a school takes to promote students' understanding of, capacity to critically reason about, motivation for, and ability to act in accordance with ethical values and principles. Character education is ultimately a matter of school reform. Therefore it requires committed leadership and takes multiple years to accomplish. In truth, character education is a journey that is ongoing. Leadership changes, children graduate, and teachers retire or relocate. Each year brings a new opportunity for the school to recommit to the development of good character in all members of a school community. Without the active support of school and district leadership, and without the patience and commitment of school teachers and administrators to stay the course, character education is much less likely to be effectively implemented. The stakes for character education are high—our nation depends on it. In reflecting on character education, Peter Yarrow argues in Berkowitz (2005) that "though it may sound calamitous to some, and for others these words will resonate as a wake-up call, I believe that such work might be decisive in determining, not only the future well-being of our world, but … the survival of everything we value in our society and of society itself" (pp. xiv and xxi).

## RECOMMENDED RESOURCES

### Books and Other Printed Material

Beland, K. (Series Ed.) (2003). *The eleven principles sourcebook: How to achieve quality character education in K–12 schools.* Washington, DC: Character Education Partnership.

The *Sourcebook* binder provides a guidebook for each of the *Eleven Principles of Effective Character Education*, complete with research and examples of application by National Schools of Character.

Collaborative for Academic, Social, and Emotional Learning. (2003). *Safe and sound: An educational leader's guide to evidence-based social and emotional learning (SEL) programs.* Chicago: Author.

This is a very useful resource and guide to K–12 programs used throughout the nation that are designed to develop character and social and emotional learning.

Lickona, T. (1991). *Educating for character: How schools can teach respect and responsibility.* New York: Bantam Books.

This foundational text gives the basics for why character education is important and how it can work in schools.

Lickona, T. (2004). *Character matters: How to help our children develop good judgment, integrity, and other essential virtues.* New York: Simon & Schuster.

*Character Matters* offers more than 100 practical strategies that parents and schools have used to help young people build strong personal character as the foundation for a purposeful, productive, and fulfilling life.

Ryan, K., & Bohlin, K. (1999). *Building character in our schools.* San Francisco: Jossey-Bass.

This book outlines the principles and strategies of effective character education and explains what schools must do to teach students the habits and dispositions that lead to responsible adulthood.

Watson, M. (2003). *Learning to trust: Transforming difficult elementary classrooms through developmental discipline.* San Francisco: Jossey-Bass.

The book uses a case study to illustrate how developmental discipline can be critical to helping difficult students learn to trust, which is part of the foundation for character development.

## Websites

*http://www.bu.edu/education/caec*

The Center for the Advancement of Ethics and Character (CAEC) offers insights and practical approaches to the exploration of virtue, ethics, and curricular integration by providing both the theory and practice of character education.

*http://www.character.org*

The Character Education Partnership (CEP) is a national, nonprofit resource center that provides advocacy and leadership for quality character education initiatives.

*http://www.casel.org*

The goals of the Collaborative for Academic, Social, and Emotional Learning (CASEL) are to advance the science of SEL (social and emotional learning), translate scientific knowledge into effective school practice, and disseminate sound SEL strategies.

## REFERENCES

Bear, G. G. (with Cavalier, A., & Manning, M.). (2005). *Developing self-discipline and preventing and correcting misbehavior.* Boston: Allyn and Bacon.

Beland, K. (2003). Understanding character development. In K. Beland (Series Ed.), *The Eleven principles sourcebook: How to achieve quality character education in K–12 schools.* Washington, DC: Character Education Partnership.

Beland, K., & Tolman, J. (2003). Creating a foundation. In K. Beland (Series Ed.), *Eleven principles sourcebook: How to achieve quality character education in K–12 schools.* Washington, DC: Character Education Partnership.

Berkowitz, M. W. (2002). The science of character education. In W. Damon (Ed.), *Bringing in a new era in character education* (pp. 43–63). Stanford, CA: Hoover Institution.

Berkowitz, M. W. (2005). *Parenting for good.* Chapel Hill, NC: Character Development Group.

Berkowitz, M. W., & Begun, A. L. (2003). Designing prevention programs: The developmental perspective. In Z. Sloboda & W. J. Bukoski (Eds.), *Handbook of drug abuse prevention: Theory, science, and practice* (pp. 327–348). Hingham, MA: Kluwer Academic Publishers.

Berkowitz, M. W., & Bier, M. C. (2005). *What works in character education: A research-driven guide for educators.* Washington, DC: Character Education Partnership.

Character Education Partnership (2002). *CEP's quality standards.* Washington, DC: Author.

Character Education Partnership (2004). *Character education: Questions and answers.* Washington, DC: Author.

Davidson, P., & Youniss, J. (1991). Which comes first, morality or identity? In W. Kurtines & J. L. Gewirtz (Eds.), *Handbook of moral development and behavior* (pp. 105–121). Hillsdale, NJ: Erlbaum.

DuFour, R., & Eaker, R. (1998). *Professional learning communities at work: Best practices for enhancing student achievement.* Alexandria, VA: Association for Supervision and Curriculum Development.

Gardner, J. W. (1991). *Building community.* Washington, DC: Independent Sector.

Hoffman, M. L. (2000). *Empathy and moral development: Implications for caring and justice.* Cambridge, UK: Cambridge University Press.

Kohlberg, L. (1984). *Essays on moral development: The psychology of moral development.* New York: Harper and Row.

Lickona, T. (1985). *Parents as moral educators. Moral education: Theory and application.* Hillsdale, NJ: Erlbaum.

Lickona, T. (2004). *Character matters: How to help our children develop good judgment, integrity, and other essential virtues.* New York: Touchstone.

Lickona, T., & Davidson, M. (2005). *Smart and good high schools: Developing excellence and ethics for success in school, work, and beyond.* Cortland, NY: Center for the 4th and 5th Rs.

Lickona, T., Schaps, E., & Lewis, C. (2003). *Eleven principles of effective character education.* Washington, DC: Character Education Partnership.

Marshall, J., & Caldwell, S. (2002). *Evaluation resource guide.* St. Louis, MO: CharacterPlus.

National Association of School Psychologists. (2003). *Position statement on character education.* Bethesda, MD: Author.

Noddings, N. (1992). *The challenge to care in schools.* New York: Teachers College Press.

Posey, J., Davidson, M., & Korpi, M. (2003). Evaluation toolkit. In K. Beland (Series Ed.), *The eleven principles sourcebook: How to achieve quality character education in K–12 schools.* Washington, DC: Character Education Partnership.

Resnick, M. D., Bearman, P. S., Blum, R. W., Bauman, K. E., Harris, K. M., Jones, J., et al. (1997). Protecting adolescents from harm: Findings from the national longitudinal study on adolescent health. *Journal of the American Medical Association, 278,* 823–832.

Schaps, E. (2002, October). Revealing the hidden curriculum: The new ABC's for success. Paper presented at the Character Education Partnership Ninth National Forum, Atlanta.

Schwartz, M. (2004, March). Character education: Constructing the big picture through FBA. *NASP Communiqué* (p. 12, 14). Bethesda, MD.

Sergiovanni, T. J. (1994). *Building community in schools.* San Francisco: Jossey-Bass.

Sizer, T. R., & Sizer, N. F. (1999). *The students are watching: Schools and the moral contract.* Boston: Beacon Press.

Tolman, J. (2003). Providing opportunities for moral action. In K. Beland (Series Ed.), *Eleven principles sourcebook: How to achieve quality character education in K–12 schools.* Washington, DC: Character Education Partnership.

Watson, M. (2003). *Learning to trust.* San Francisco: Jossey-Bass.

Youniss, J., McLellan, J. A., & Yates, M. (1997). What we know about engendering civic identity. *The American Behavioral Scientist, 40,* 620–631.

# 3

# Developing Self-Discipline

**George G. Bear**
**Julie M. Watkins**
*University of Delaware*

## BACKGROUND AND DEVELOPMENT

### Self-Discipline Defined

Although the term *self-discipline* often is used in the context of a number of nonacademic and academic behaviors, such as exercising, dieting, practicing a sport or music, managing one's finances, and studying, in this chapter it is used specifically in the context of *school discipline*. As such, self-discipline refers to socially and morally responsible behavior (i.e., behavior concerning others and distinguishing right from wrong) that is self-regulated. It entails inhibiting socially and morally inappropriate behavior and exhibiting prosocial behavior, and doing so under one's own volition. It also entails assuming responsibility for one's decisional choices and actions (both good and bad).

Self-discipline requires much more than simply knowing right from wrong (e.g., being able to cite the school's five rules and their consequences) and obeying rules in order to avoid punishment or receive external rewards. In addition to knowing rules, avoiding punishment, and seeking rewards, individuals who have self-discipline employ a variety of more complex social, cognitive, and emotional mechanisms that mediate, support, enhance, or augment the influence of environmental factors (Bandura, 1989, 2001; Dodge & Pettit, 2003). It is through these mechanisms that children come to perceive themselves as the cause, source, or agent of their own behavior and strive to act accordingly even when they know that adults are not watching.

Thus, self-discipline connotes the critical notion of *internalization*—the idea that children internalize the values, standards, beliefs, and attitudes of their parents, teachers, peers, and others in society, and in the process of doing so, they actively transform these values and endorse them as their *own*. Internalization has repeatedly been shown to be related to what Kochanska (2002) refers to as *committed* compliance and what Brophy (1996) refers to as *willing* compliance, in which children accept the directives and rules of their parents and teachers, and do so without requiring external rewards or punishment. The motivation to comply comes from the inside and is associated with a sense of pride and autonomy (Kochanska). This is in contrast to *situational* compliance (Kochanska) or *grudging* compliance (Brophy) that comes from the outside and is contingent upon parent or teacher control.

In school, internalization, as observed in self-discipline, is perhaps most evident when students assume responsibility for their own actions and follow school rules in the absence of adult supervision, external rewards, sanctions, and the likelihood of punishment. Self-discipline often is used interchangeably with the terms autonomy, responsibility, self-regulation, and self-control. We prefer the team *self-discipline*, however, because it highlights the need for schools to view the development of *self*-discipline as a primary component of their school discipline plans, policies, and practices. Self-discipline is widely recognized as a critical aspect of character (see chapter 2, "Character Education"), emotional intelligence (Mayer & Salovey, 1997), and social and emotional learning (see chapter 1, "Social and Emotional Learning"). Although many programs that address each of these areas also address the importance of developing self-discipline, they tend to emphasize much more than self-discipline per se (i.e., multiple elements of character and emotional and social development).

### The Importance of Self-Discipline

The educational aim of helping students develop self-discipline is not new. Since the outset of education in the

United States, it has been a primary aim, if not *the* primary aim, of education (Bear, 2005; Wentzel, 1991). This still holds true today, although perhaps to a lesser extent, at least as viewed by the general public. A recent Gallup poll presented members of the general public with seven reasons public schools were created and asked them to rate each one as to its importance today. The highest rated reason was "to prepare students to be responsible citizens" (Rose & Gallup, 2000). On a 10-point scale, with 10 being of highest importance, that reason received a mean score of 9.0. However, when asked to rate the public schools' effectiveness in achieving that aim, with 10 being highly effective, the mean score was 6.1.

For obvious reasons, developing self-discipline is important to educators as well as to society in general. Both desire students or citizens who act in a socially responsible manner and require minimal external regulation. There are three additional reasons that developing self-discipline should be a primary aim of education (Bear, Manning, & Izard, 2003). First, it promotes positive relations with others and a positive school climate. As one might suspect, research shows that students prefer, and are less likely to socially reject, peers who demonstrate self-discipline, as reflected in prosocial and responsible behavior and the lack of aggression and antisocial behavior (Rubin, Bukowski, & Parker, 1998). Likewise, teachers prefer students who demonstrate self-discipline and prosocial behavior rather than antisocial behavior (Birch & Ladd, 1998). These students tend to receive more social support, both from teachers (Hughes, Cavel, & Willson, 2001) and from peers (Wentzel, 1991), and they experience a sense of belonging to the school community (Osterman, 2000). Such support and acceptance is an important characteristic of a positive school climate, which is seen in the greater empathy among students, caring about others, increased conflict resolution skills, and reduced delinquency (Battistich, Schaps, Watson, Solomon, & Lewis, 2000). It should be noted, however, that the relationship between student behavior and teacher or school factors is bidirectional. Whereas self-discipline fosters positive relations with others and an overall positive school climate, the opposite also is true: A positive and supportive school climate, including caring and support from teachers and peers, promotes self-discipline.

A second reason self-discipline is important to schools is that it fosters academic achievement. Research shows that academic achievement and self-discipline are positively and reciprocally related (Berkowitz & Bier, 2005; Collaborative for Academic, Social, and Emotional Learning [CASEL], 2003; Malecki & Elliott, 2002). Both share many of the same social, cognitive, and emotional skills and processes, including problem-solving skills, the motivation to please others, the ability to inhibit impulsive behavior, and the desire to achieve or act in a manner that is consistent with one's internalized standards, goals, and self-concept.

A third reason self-discipline is important is that it promotes self-worth and emotional well-being. One of the most important determinants of children's feelings of overall self-worth, or self-esteem, is their perception of behavioral or moral conduct (Harter, 1999; see chapter 26, "Self-Concept and Self-Esteem"). Children tend to judge their specific behavior as good or bad based on whether their behavior is consistent with the moral standards they have developed. They tend to view their overall self-worth the same way. That is, because nearly all children view positive behavioral conduct as important to their self-worth, they find it quite difficult to view themselves favorably when they view their behavior as wrong or inconsistent with their own moral standards. However, children can protect their self-worth in spite of poor behavior when they have low moral standards or when they apply various strategies of moral disengagement (as discussed later in the chapter). Not only is a positive self-concept important in its own right; it also is important because it fosters general emotional well-being and helps motivate further good behavior (Harter, 1999; Kochanska, 2002).

## Influence of Developmental Factors

Self-discipline develops with age and reflects a gradual shift in expectations and socialization practices of parents and other adults. Over the course of the child's development, the emphasis of socialization shifts from directly teaching young children social skills and socially appropriate behavior to inculcating in older children and adolescents self-discipline or responsibility for their own decisions and behaviors (Grusec & Goodnow, 1994). The success of socialization is determined largely by a wide range of family and parenting factors and teacher and school factors (e.g., see chapters 5, 7, and 8, "Student-Teacher Relationships," "School Disciplinary Systems," and "School Completion"). However, successful socialization also is determined by the development of a variety of social, cognitive, emotional processes and skills, as discussed below. Many of these processes and skills underlie both moral behavior and antisocial behavior, influencing both an individual's behavior and the

**Table 1** *Social Cognitive Abilities and Emotions Related to Self-Discipline That Develop During the School-Age Years*

- Growth of self-awareness and self-understanding, enabling children to view themselves as objects of evaluation by others and to attribute responsibility for their behavior to themselves as causal agents. Such growth also is related to development of the moral emotions of empathy, pride, guilt, and shame.

- Increased social perspective taking and social referencing, as seen in increased awareness, sensitivity, and understanding of the intentions, emotions, and needs of others, and their relation to one's own behavior.

- Increased use of social comparisons in evaluating the behavior of self and others and a related desire to conform to social expectations of others (e.g., parents, teachers, peers, close friends).

- Development of sociomoral reasoning. Students shift from a preconventional hedonistic perspective limited primarily to seeking rewards and avoiding punishment to a conventional perspective based more on concern about others: issues of fairness, trust, and mutual relationships; maintaining one's reputation and the social order; and principles of justice and caring. With respect to school discipline, and particularly rule-following behavior, this shift can be seen in the following:
    - Decreased belief that rules are to be followed because punishment is inevitable.
    - Decreased unilateral respect for authority and rules.
    - Increased mutual respect for rules and obligations and the understanding that rules are alterable.
    - Increased understanding that just rules are rules that are fair to everyone: A rule is not fair simply because it is dictated by an authority.
    - Increased understanding that rules foster cooperation and are needed to coordinate and maintain social order.

- Increased sophistication of competence in the social information processing skills, including encoding hostile and nonhostile cues; interpreting hostile intent; generating more behavioral responses; endorsing aggressive responses less; and improving enactment skills (see chapter 9, "Anger and Aggression").

- Increased cognitive abilities related to attending, storing, retrieving, and understanding information, including standards and rules of conduct, and applying such standards and rules to different situations.

- Growth in executive functioning applied to self-regulation of behavior, as seen in increased ability to delay gratification, monitor one's own behavior, suppress impulsive urges and prohibited acts, and act prosocially in the absence of adult supervision or external control.

- Development of feelings of empathy; pride in moral behavior; and anxiety, guilt, remorse, and shame over wrongdoing. These emotions become less overgeneralized and increasingly linked to attributions of responsibility, controllability, and intentionality.

- Increased understanding of the dynamics of the feelings and behaviors of others and of feelings as not just specific to immediate situations but as lasting and pervasive.

environment in an ongoing and reciprocal fashion (Bandura, 1997).

It is beyond the scope of this chapter to review each of the many social, cognitive, and emotional processes and skills related to self-discipline and to prosocial and antisocial behavior (see Coie & Dodge, 1998; Dodge & Pettit, 2003; and Eisenberg, Fabes, & Spinrad, in press, for reviews). A brief list of critical social, cognitive, and emotional processes and skills related to self-discipline is presented in Table 1. Not only do these processes and skills develop within the social context of relationships with parents, peers, and close friends, they also develop within the context of student-teacher relationships, which includes teaching and classroom or school discipline. Clearly, what happens in schools significantly affects the development of self-discipline.

## PROBLEMS AND IMPLICATIONS: LINKING SOCIAL COGNITION AND EMOTION TO SELF-DISCIPLINE

At one time or another all kids misbehave. They talk or get out of their seats without permission, fail to complete class work or homework assignments, tease others, and so forth. Fortunately, most do so infrequently and are responsive to common techniques of prevention and mild correction of misbehavior, and they rarely, if ever, engage in moral transgressions that harm others, such as acts of violence and delinquency. Moreover, they tend to learn from their mistakes, including from the *use* of discipline by adults to correct misbehavior. They learn to recognize and understand the effect of their behavior on others, respect moral authority, and appreciate the value of self-discipline. Unfortunately, a small percentage frequently fail to exhibit self-discipline or to behave responsibly. They are resistant to common interventions and require constant monitoring, supervision, and multiple interventions, including those that emphasize external control.

In this section, social, cognitive, and emotional processes that contribute to misbehavior are reviewed, with a focus on those processes that often account for a lack of self-discipline or resistance to intervention. It should be noted, however, that these processes are much stronger predictors of differences between extreme groups of students, such as aggressive versus nonaggressive students and delinquent versus nondelinquent students, than of individual acts of misbehavior in given situations. Nevertheless, many of the factors not only help explain group differences but also explain why individuals, including normal children, exhibit common, as well as more deviant and harmful, acts of misbehavior.

Bear et al. (2003) offer a useful social, cognitive, and emotional framework consisting of four components for viewing why students fail to act in a socially responsible manner (either in a given situation or over time). Although they focus on social, cognitive, and emotional processes, it is clear that these responses operate reciprocally with multiple biological and environmental factors. Consistent with Dodge's (Crick & Dodge, 1994) model of social information processing, Bear et al.'s framework also recognizes that (a) processes and skills within each component influence those within other components, both through feed-forward and feedback loops, (b) processes and skills within any one component may occur simultaneously with processes within another component, (c) not all components are necessarily involved in a given behavior, and (d) a combination of processes and skills is a much greater predictor of behavior than any one process or skill. The four components, which are based on an earlier model of moral reasoning and behavior developed by Rest (1983), are described in the next section.

### Component 1: Perceiving the Need to Exhibit Prosocial Behavior or Inhibit Antisocial Behavior

Knowledge of what is right and wrong is a necessary and important aspect of self-discipline. However, it certainly is not sufficient. Very few students are unaware that their misbehavior violates a rule or is otherwise undesirable. Beginning in the early 20th century with the classic research studies of Hartshorne and May (1928), researchers have shown that moral knowledge (e.g., being able to cite the Boy Scouts or Girl Scouts code of behavior, Biblical scripture, school rules, or lessons learned in a Drug Abuse Resistance Education, or DARE, program) is not a good predictor of moral behavior. Research shows that a host of other abilities and skills influence a student's awareness of the need to exhibit prosocial behavior and inhibit misbehavior. Central among these is the ability to read social cues (e.g., recognize and understand differences in facial expressions, assume the perspectives of others, and recognize that situational context often determines the appropriateness of a given behavior) and the ability to foresee and anticipate the consequences of decisions and actions (or lack thereof) on both self and others.

Highlighting the importance of this component, a large body of research shows that aggressive children are overly likely to interpret hostile intentions in others, especially in ambiguous situations, and to ignore mitigating circumstances (see Orobio de Castro, Veerman, Koops, Bosch, & Monshouwer, 2002, for review). Aspects of temperament, especially impulsivity, also come into play (this is also true within the other three components). For example, failing to interpret social cues accurately and before deciding on a response is a common characteristic both of children with Attention Deficit/Hyperactivity Disorder (ADHD) and of angry children (see chapter 9, "Anger and Aggression"). With respect to prosocial behavior, research shows that acts of caring and helping are associated with greater empathy and sensitivity to the perspectives and needs of others (see chapter 24, "Prosocial Behavior").

## Component 2: Determining What One Ought to Do—Thinking About Consequences Rather Than Responding Automatically

Many social situations call for little processing of information. That is, relevant information is automatically retrieved from well-established cognitive scripts (or schemas) that are stored in memory and reinforced often (Huesmann, 1988). These scripts are grounded in personal beliefs, attitudes, and experiences, in values that guide behavior without the need for much reflection. Similar to scripts in a film, cognitive scripts are repeated over time. They can support either prosocial and responsible behavior (e.g., "Listen to your teacher," "Respect adults," or "Be nice to others") or antisocial and irresponsible behavior (e.g., "Don't let others push you around" or "Look out for yourself").

Although both responsible and irresponsible behaviors in the classroom often occur without much social-cognitive processing, on many occasions students must stop and reflect upon what they *ought* to do. In making a decision, they may retrieve one or more alternative responses from memory or generate a novel response, depending on what is called for in a given situation. Each alternative response is then evaluated, with moral reasoning and moral emotions playing critical roles (i.e., reasoning and emotions that focus on matters of justice, fairness, empathy, and caring). That is, in deciding what they ought to do, students think about issues such as the consequences of their behavior on self and others, friendship, reputation, fairness, justice, and the rights and welfare of others. Their decisions are influenced not only by moral reasoning per se but also by moral emotions that are interrelated with moral reasoning, particularly empathy, pride, guilt, and shame (Eisenberg et al., in press; Hoffman, 2000).

Research shows that antisocial children tend to generate alternative solutions that are inferior in both quantity and quality (i.e., more atypical, maladaptive, and aggressive) and to view these solutions as being good ones (see Coie & Dodge, 1998, and Dodge & Pettit, 2003, for reviews of this literature). Research also shows that certain types of moral reasoning tend to be associated with disruptive and aggressive behavior in the classroom (Manning & Bear, 2002), as well as with a variety of delinquent behaviors in the community (e.g., violence, theft, and substance abuse; Kuther, 2000; Palmer & Hollin, 2001). In particular, these behaviors consistently have been shown to be associated with moral reasoning that is hedonistic or self-centered in perspective, focusing on the personal consequences of behavior instead of its effect on others.

Of significant practical importance, research indicates that students who are *most likely* to violate school rules are the same ones who are most likely to say that the best reason they should not violate rules is because they *might* get caught and punished (Manning & Bear, 2002). This is consistent with the disciplinary practices of most schools. Because these students focus on whether or not they might get caught, if the school were to remove the risk of being caught, students would have no reason *not* to misbehave (e.g., "No one's watching now"). Similarly, research shows that delinquent adolescents often believe that they will not get caught and view both legal and social consequences (to self and others) less negatively than do nondelinquents (Guerra, 1989). In addition to having less fear of actually getting caught, delinquents see few reasons for not stealing, lying, and harming others. Bullies have a similar pattern of hedonistic moral reasoning. They think more about whether or not they will get caught than about the effect of their behavior on others (Menesini et al., 2003). Although this form of moral reasoning (or lack thereof) characterizes many students who are disruptive and aggressive, it is much less common among those who act more prosocially and inhibit antisocial behavior. The moral reasoning of more prosocially oriented students tends to be based less on external motivators of behavior than on concerns about the needs and welfare of others, which are grounded in empathy, caring, and anticipation of feelings of guilt.

## Component 3: Deciding to Act (or Not to Act) in Accordance With One's Sociomoral Reasoning

It is not uncommon for students to interpret social cues correctly and voice moral reasoning that is not hedonistic and self-centered but to then fail to demonstrate socially responsible behavior. Just as moral knowledge is not sufficient for self-discipline, neither is moral reasoning. A wide range of environmental factors and additional social, cognitive, and emotional processes interact to mediate the relation between moral reasoning and behavior. All too frequently, one or a combination of these factors and processes leads students to decide to act in ways that are inconsistent with their moral knowledge and reasoning. In the classroom, peers and student-teacher relations are perhaps the most widely recognized environmental factors. However, the influence of these factors is largely mediated by an individual student's personal values and social goals. For example, whereas some students may choose to act out against "mean" teachers, others do not.

Unfortunately, in a given situation, certain values and goals commonly associated with responsible behavior in the classroom (e.g., desire to please teachers as well as parents) often compete with values and goals that support irresponsible behavior (e.g., getting what one wants, attention). For example, research shows that among aggressive children, the self-centered goal of getting what one wants tends to preempt goals of not harming others and of maintaining friendships (Erdley & Asher, 1996). When others are perceived as blocking that self-centered goal, aggression is viewed as justified. In contrast, the behavior of children who are more prosocial tends to be motivated by the values and goals of social acceptance, respect of others, and a sense of integrity (Covington, 2000).

Although the values and goals of antisocial students are more self-centered than those of other students, it is clear that antisocial students are not the only ones who look out for themselves. Nearly everyone has a self-serving bias (Nisan, 1991). This is seen in instances of good intentions being undermined by contingencies of the moment, especially the presence or absence of immediate rewards and punishments. In addition to a self-serving bias, modeling by others and perceived social norms often have a profound influence on moral decision making and behavior. For example, perceived social norms about what people do, as well as what they should do, predict aggressive behavior (Guerra, Nucci, & Huesmann, 1994). The strong influence of group norms and modeling in harmful behavior can be seen in the recent national controversy over the use of steroids in baseball.

Research also demonstrates the strong influences of student-teacher relations and classroom management on self-discipline and antisocial behavior, including a student's decision about whether to act in accordance with his or her moral reasoning (Bear, 2005). Research shows that students are much better behaved in classrooms in which they view teachers and rules as fair and teachers as caring (Arum, 2003).

Irrespective of the above factors, it is not uncommon, and is normal and healthy, for students to understand mature moral reasons for helping and not harming others but to nevertheless question school rules. Research on children's differentiation of the moral and social conventional domains helps explain why this often occurs (Nucci, 2001). Such research shows that students tend to perceive behaviors that typically lead to disciplinary actions as falling into one of three domains: moral (i.e., behaviors that harm others), social-conventional (i.e., arbitrary rules for purposes of maintaining social conventions, such as "Do your homework"), and personal (i.e., behaviors based on personal preference and choice, such as choice of clothing, friends, music, and smoking). School rules apply to behavior in all three domains, but it is rules pertaining to behaviors in the social-conventional and personal domains that students are most likely to question and disobey (Nucci). However, not all students distinguish moral, social-conventional, and personal domains as clearly as do others, which helps explain many disciplinary problems. In particular, antisocial students tend to fail to distinguish between the three domains, perceiving most moral, social-conventional, and personal behaviors similarly—as matters of personal choice that should not be governed by others (Blair, Monson, & Frederickson, 2001; Guerra, Nucci, & Huesmann, 1994). To them, cheating, stealing, and fighting have no more moral basis than wearing certain clothing or listening to different styles of music.

## Component 4: Acting in Accordance With One's Moral Convictions and Intentions

The above processes often account for why students decide that they ought to behave in a socially responsible manner but decide against doing so. Researchers have recently focused on three social, cognitive, and emotional processes, or mechanisms, that often explain why individuals act consistently, or inconsistently, with their moral intentions: (a) moral emotions that motivate behavior, (b) perceptions of self-efficacy, and (c) attributions and judgments of responsibility.

Hoffman's theory of moral development and its supporting research (see Hoffman, 2000; Eisenberg et al., in press) highlight the importance of *moral emotions*, particularly empathy, sympathy, and guilt. Whether or not individuals can assume and share the perspective of others (empathy) and care or feel sorry about others (sympathy) often motivates individuals to act consistently with their intentions. Guilt serves a similar purpose, motivating individuals to assist others in need or to refrain from moral transgressions because they anticipate feelings of guilt for failing to act responsibly or for harming others. The absence of guilt and empathy, which often is reflected in low moral reasoning, has been shown to be associated with low behavioral inhibition; individuals are insensitive to cues of danger and punishment and to the effect of their behavior on others, and they are oversensitive to potential rewards (Frick et al., 2003; Pardini, Lochman, & Frick, 2003). In turn, this absence of guilt and empathy is recognized as a major pathway to serious conduct problems that have an early onset. (The more common pathway, however, is that of high emotional reactivity and poorly regulated behavior associated with dysfunctional parenting practices and low intelligence [Wooton, Frick, Shelton, & Silverthorn, 1997]).

*Perceived self-efficacy* refers to believing that one has the ability to achieve what he or she intends to do (Bandura, 1997). High perceptions of self-efficacy motivate individuals to engage or persist in prosocial acts and refrain from immoral acts. For example, extremely altruistic individuals, or moral exemplars, tend to hold strong beliefs that they can successfully help others (Colby & Damon, 1999), whereas antisocial individuals tend to hold feelings of low self-efficacy with respect to their ability to act prosocially (Goldstein, Harootunian, & Conoley, 1994). Yet high perceptions of self-efficacy also can motivate an individual to engage in antisocial behavior, as seen in aggressive students, including bullies, who believe that their aggressive behavior will be successful in achieving their self-serving goals (Arsenio & Lemerise, 2001).

*Attributions and judgments of responsibility* refer to an individual's perception of the cause of his or her behavior (e.g., "Why did this happen?" or "Am I responsible?"; Weiner, 2001). Perceptions of controllability and intentionality are of particular importance in attributing responsibility to oneself: Individuals seldom accept full responsibility for their actions when they are viewed as being uncontrollable (e.g., "I couldn't help it" or "I have ADHD") or unintentional ("That's not what I meant to do" or "It was an accident"). Bandura (1991, 2001) argues that individuals often use *mechanisms of disengagement*, or cognitive distortions, to avoid attributing responsibility to themselves and that such mechanisms are a main reason for a lack of consistency between the individual's moral reasoning and behavior. Mechanisms of *moral disengagement* are seen when students deny responsibility for their actions (and are reflected in the lack of self-discipline). By denying responsibility, they not only avoid punishment but also protect themselves from self-punitive affect and thinking that lowers self-esteem.

Bandura (1991, 2001) argues that moral disengagement explains not only the behavior of delinquents and criminals but also why *good* people sometimes commit reprehensible acts. Bandura's mechanisms of moral disengagement that are most relevant to violations of classroom and school rules are (a) moral or social justification, (b) euphemisms and convoluted language, (c) exonerative or advantageous comparison, (d) displacement and diffusion of responsibility, and (e) blame shifting.

***Moral or social justification.*** Self-condemnation for a rule-violating action is avoided by justifying to oneself (and hopefully to others) that "It was the 'right' thing to do." Common examples are "But I meant well," "I didn't mean for that to happen," and "If I hadn't done that, something worse would have happened."

***Euphemisms and convoluted language.*** Individuals use labels of "convoluted and sanitizing verbiage" (Bandura, 1991, p. 67) to convince others, and themselves, that their irresponsible behavior is benign. Common examples are "I was just kidding," "It was just clowning around," "I was just joking," and "It was just horseplay."

***Exonerative or advantageous comparison.*** In the eyes of the offender, and compared with the greater violations of others, a violation of rules is insignificant and certainly not deserving of punishment. Common examples include "But others were worse," "But did you see what they did?" and "Others weren't punished when they did it."

***Displacement and diffusion of responsibility.*** By placing the responsibility on someone else, individuals minimize not only internal self-prohibiting reactions but also personal concern about the consequences of their irresponsible behavior on others. Common examples are "But he forced me to do it," "He told me to do it," "If she had locked her locker I wouldn't have stolen it," and "No one said I couldn't do it."

***Blame shifting.*** Displacement of responsibility can often take the form of blaming the victim (e.g., "He shouldn't have said that" and "She started it.").

These mechanisms of moral disengagement, or cognitive distortions, are typically used, and often in combination with one another, when irresponsible behavior has obvious negative consequences to oneself or to others (Bandura, 1991, 2001). They may either be kept internal or be verbalized as excuses and denial of responsibility, depending largely on whether the situation involves a potential need to escape punishment. Although mechanisms of moral disengagement are a common characteristic of antisocial children and adolescents, they also are used at one time or another by nearly everyone (Bandura, Caprara, Barbaranelli, & Regalia, 2001).

## ALTERNATIVE ACTIONS FOR DEVELOPING SELF-DISCIPLINE

Guided by research and theory consistent with the four components of moral behavior presented above, educators are encouraged to help students develop self-discipline by embracing the following four goals:

1. Develop sensitivity to social and moral problems.
2. Develop social perspective-taking, empathy, and moral reasoning.
3. Develop decision making that is responsive to the needs of others and to a sense of responsibility (rather than to peer pressure and self-serving interests).
4. Develop self-confidence and the social skills needed to carry out behaviors consistent with personal intentions and decisions.

Adopting these goals is a clear alternative to the common strategy of attempting to develop students' self-discipline by focusing exclusively on the external use of rewards, rules, and punishment for displaying obedience or rule-following behavior. To be sure, rewards, rules, and punishment (but particularly punishment that is noncorporal, fair, reasonable, and used only in combination with reinforcement of replacement behaviors) *are* appropriate in developing self-discipline. Likewise, they are critical techniques for correcting and preventing misbehavior (Bear, 2005). However, we emphasize that although the goals of developing self-discipline, correcting misbehavior, and preventing misbehavior are interrelated (and share many of the same techniques), schools cannot achieve the long-term goal of developing self-discipline by focusing exclusively on the prevention and correction of misbehavior. For example, a teacher may be quite effective in classroom management and the use of behavioral techniques but fail to foster self-discipline. Students do not learn self-discipline when teachers emphasize external control and fail to equip students with social and emotional competencies that guide behavior when external supervision, rewards, and punishment are not present or clear.

Below are six critical strategies for helping to achieve the four goals:

### Strategy 1: Recognize the Critical Importance of Student-Teacher Relationships and School Climate in Developing Self-Discipline

Ample research demonstrates the importance of positive teacher-student relationships (see chapter 5, "Student-Teacher Relationships"). It is a critical element of both effective classroom management and the development of self-discipline. Students who perceive teachers as being caring and respectful and providing emotional support are less likely to misbehave in the classroom. Positive outcomes include less opposition to teachers and greater on-task behavior (Bru, Stephens, & Torsheim, 2002), less cheating (Murdock, Hale, & Weber, 2001), less antisocial behavior toward peers (Bru, Murberg, & Stephens, 2001), fewer discipline problems in the classroom (Murdock, 1999), and greater motivation to act responsibly and prosocially (Wentzel, 1996). Students also are more likely to feel comfortable and supported in this type of environment, especially when the teacher shows interest in the student's life (see chapter 5). When students and teachers have positive relationships, teachers have greater opportunities to influence how students think and behave. Certainly, students emulate the behaviors of those with whom they share an attachment.

Positive student-teacher relationships not only help develop self-discipline but also help create and maintain a positive school climate that prevents behavior problems and is conducive to learning and safety. The learning experience is much more enjoyable for all when the students and teacher share positive feelings for one another and are working toward a common goal. In working toward positive student-teacher relationships, the focus should be on the *relational unit* that consists of the student *and* the teacher, because both bring different characteristics to the relationship (Pianta, Hamre, & Stuhlman 2003). Of course, although student-teacher relationships should be a primary focus with respect to school discipline, the critical roles of families and communities also should receive ample attention in promoting a positive school climate (see chapter 6, "Parent-Teacher Relationships").

## Strategy 2: Provide Multiple Models of Social and Moral Problem Solving, Moral and Regulated Emotions, and Responsible Behavior

Modeling is a powerful way to teach students how to think, feel, and act appropriately. Educators can use different methods to model social and moral problem-solving skills; the regulation of "negative" emotions of anger, contempt, hatred, and frustration; habits of socially and morally responsible behavior; a sense of pride in one's good behavior; and even the "moral emotions" of guilt and empathy. The advantages of modeling are that it (a) informs students of appropriate ways of thinking and acting, (b) motivates students to engage in the observed behaviors, (c) promotes values and standards underlying the observed behavior, and (d) often triggers emotional reactions that lead to prosocial behavior (e.g., empathy, sorrow, and pride) (Bandura, 1986).

Teachers and support staff should routinely use various forms of modeling (e.g., self, peers, video, or literature) to target processes and skills associated with the four goals above, while explaining to students how and why they (and others) think, feel, and act in certain ways. Parents should be encouraged to do the same at home. Likewise, teachers should be encouraged to capitalize on *real-life* situations in which students themselves exhibit such processes and skills, providing reinforcement and highlighting the processes and skills to peers. When processes and skills are modeled, emphasis should be placed on their importance, including positive outcomes to self and others. Moreover, opportunities should be provided for the practice and reinforcement of the processes and skills modeled.

## Strategy 3: Implement Curriculum Activities That Directly Teach Social, Emotional, and Behavioral Competencies

As mentioned previously, self-discipline does not necessarily develop on its own. It is critical that social and moral problem solving, along with related emotional competencies, be taught in a planned, deliberate, and systematic fashion using modeling and a combination of additional direct and indirect methods of instruction. This teaching approach may entail the use of a packaged curriculum or the infusion of lessons throughout the curriculum. Several useful resources exist for choosing among the multiple curriculum packages that target many of the processes and skills shown in Table 1 (see chapter 1, "Social and Emotional Learning," for additional important skills). Among empirically validated programs, *Second Step: A Violence Prevention Curriculum* (Committee for Children, 2003) contains units that specifically focus not only on social problem solving but also on impulse control and the critical element of empathy. For example, using discussion, direct teaching, and role-playing, the program teaches students to follow five steps for handling interpersonal problems using the social and moral problem-solving skills that they have learned: (1) What is the problem? (2) What are some solutions? (3) For each solution ask: Is it safe? How might people feel? Is it fair? Will it work? (4) Choose a solution and use it. (5) Determine if it is working and, if not, what to do next? Step 3 emphasizes issues of fairness and the effect of the student's behavior on others, including aspects of moral reasoning and empathy that are often lacking in other social skills training programs.

Instead of, or in addition to, using a curriculum program, a teacher may decide to infuse social and moral problem-solving skills and related emotions into the general curriculum. This method is more advantageous because it is less expensive, is more realistic, and does not involve an "add-on" to the curriculum. Thus, teachers are likely to be less resistant to adopting and implementing the instruction. The general curriculum, especially language arts and social studies, has a rich source of content that provides teachers with many opportunities to teach skills related to social, moral, and emotional competence. Teachers can infuse in the general curriculum the same methods that are used in packaged programs, such as verbal instruction, discussion, modeling, role-playing, and reinforcement, while covering similar content.

## Strategy 4. Provide Opportunities for Students to Practice Social and Moral Problem Solving, Moral and Regulated Emotions, and Responsible Behavior

Self-discipline is more likely to develop when students are given a variety of opportunities to apply and practice the skills they have observed and been taught. The following recommendations suggest ways of providing such opportunities (Bear, 2005):

- Provide guidance and support when students encounter situations of interpersonal conflict, as in the following examples:

- Prompt students to use social and moral problem-solving skills. Help students work through problems and possible solutions by providing guiding questions (scaffolding), through which they come to apply problem-solving skills with little or no teacher intervention.
- Prompt students to think about how others might feel in a given situation and remind them to use positive emotions and to assume responsibility for their own behavior. Focus more on establishing a sense of pride in good behavior, instead of simply earning external rewards and avoiding punishment.
- Encourage students to explain how they feel by starting with *I* and an emotion instead of *you*. By using *I*, the student is less likely to put the other person on the defensive and may prevent a conflict from occurring.
- Teach and encourage students to regulate emotions that are likely to lead to negative outcomes when unregulated, such as frustration and anger. (See chapter 9, "Anger and Aggression.")

- Provide peer-assisted and cooperative learning opportunities, sports and extracurricular activities, and service learning opportunities to help students learn and practice social and moral problem solving. (See chapters 48, 37, and 24, respectively.)
- Use class meetings to help students learn and practice the above skills by discussing and addressing social and moral problems students see in the classroom, school, and community. The meetings can be used to help students identify and share their feelings and to learn how to predict and understand the feelings of others. Class meetings are likely to be successful when (a) the topics are developmentally appropriate, (b) the teacher's role is that of a facilitator, not lecturer, (c) the meeting is held in a nonthreatening environment, (d) students have the skills necessary to participate in the discussion, and (e) all students are included in the discussion.

## Strategy 5. Use Disciplinary Encounters to Help Develop Self-Discipline

Corrective techniques, including the judicious use of punishment, are often necessary and appropriate when students violate school rules. Research clearly shows, however, that when punishment, such as response cost or time-out, is used it is much more effective when combined with techniques for teaching and reinforcing replacement behaviors. Likewise, research clearly shows that among the best predictors of the technique's effectiveness is the perception among students that the discipline is fair (Arum, 2003). With respect to developing self-discipline, a particular focus during disciplinary encounters should be on using *induction*, which is a disciplinary technique that fosters internalization and responsibility for one's behavior. Induction focuses on the effect of one's behavior on others, as opposed to the consequences to oneself, and emphasizes empathy, values, and sociomoral reasoning. Where appropriate, this includes a healthy dose of inducing empathy-based guilt (e.g., "How do you think your teasing makes Marty feel?") and emphasizing a sense of pride about good behavior (e.g., "I'm sure you feel good about your improved behavior"). Anticipated guilt and pride are two emotions most linked to responsible behavioral choices in the classroom, regardless of the presence of social sanctions (Ford, Wentzel, Wood, Stevens, & Sisfield, 1989).

Inducing empathy-based guilt and pride is much more effective in developing self-discipline and social conformity than the common techniques of correcting misbehavior by inducing fear or shame (Izard, 1991). Of course, the induction of guilt must be used selectively, cautiously, infrequently, and always in combination with strategies and techniques for teaching and developing behaviors that should be associated with feelings of pride. In addition to induction, techniques listed in Table 2 should help promote the development of self-discipline during disciplinary encounters. These techniques should also simultaneously increase the effectiveness of more specific corrective techniques that might be appropriate for teaching and increasing replacement behaviors and for reducing inappropriate behavior.

## Strategy 6. Help Students Cope With Stress and Situations in Which They Have Little Control

The above strategies may be of little help to students in difficult situations in which they (and their teachers) have very little control (e.g., ongoing peer rejection or chronic bullying both in and out of school). In these cases it may be more beneficial to teach the students strategies to help cope with the situation. Although coping strategies are not a solution to the problem, they can help the student learn how to *feel differently by thinking differently* about the situation. Two fairly simple

**Table 2** *Recommendations for Helping to Develop Self-Discipline During Disciplinary Encounters*

- Recognize that minor misbehavior is developmentally normal for children and adolescents. Hold high behavior expectations but understand that such expectations will not always be met. Don't expect perfect behavior.
- Be patient. Understand that behaviors rarely improve immediately and that the development of self-discipline takes a long time.
- Recognize that thoughts, emotions, and behaviors are interrelated. When correcting misbehavior, consider how thoughts and emotions influence and are influenced by one's behavior.
- Closely examine environmental factors that might have contributed to the misbehavior. Reflect on how the curriculum, your teaching, and other classroom (and school) factors might be adapted to improve the student's behavior.
- Be sensitive to cultural and racial differences. Respect the feelings, thoughts, and dignity of *all* students.
- Do not argue: speak calmly, firmly, and respectfully.
- Focus on how the behavior is to improve.
- Use the occasion as an opportunity to develop social and moral problem-solving skills and emotional competencies (e.g., ask the student to identify the problem, its consequences, and personal goals; consider feelings and thoughts of others; think of alternatives; try a plan and evaluate it).
- Reinforce effort and achievement, not obedience.
- Include the student in developing intervention plans. Allow for student input and negotiation when appropriate.
- Recognize the multiple limitations to the use of punishment and the student's right to due process when certain types of punishment are used (e.g., suspension).
- Before correcting misbehavior, make sure that the student is actually responsible for the misbehavior, especially when correction entails the use of punitive techniques. Students are entitled to the right to due process.
- Make sure that students understand what they did wrong, why it was wrong, and what they should have done differently.
- Intervene early, before the misbehavior escalates.
- Do not model aggression, either verbally or nonverbally. If you're very angry or upset, wait until you calm down, or have someone else deal with the misbehavior.
- Be fair. Consequences should be consistent with the severity of the misbehavior.
- Be consistent. The same consequences should be used when the same behavior is exhibited under the same circumstances.

*(Continued)*

**Table 2** *Continued*

- Make sure your expectations and standards for improvement are clear, reasonable, and realistic.

- Convey a sense of optimism and trust that the student's behavior will improve and meet your expectations.

- Use the least amount of external control necessary to bring about a change in behavior.

- Work to establish and maintain a positive teacher-student relationship. If the relationship is harmed as a result of the use of correction, work to restore it by demonstrating warmth, caring, and support.

- Support a positive self-concept:
  - Focus on the behavior, not the person.
  - Respect the student's need to feel a sense of belonging. Thus, avoid public humiliation. If the misbehavior requires more than a mild verbal correction, make every attempt to handle the correction privately.
  - Respect the student's need for autonomy. Give choices, when appropriate.
  - Emphasize that you are trying to *help* the student.
  - When feasible, point out the student's strengths and progress.
  - View the correction of misbehavior as similar to the correction of an academic problem: The problem presents an opportunity for the student to learn and practice important skills.

- Use induction. Your message should do the following:
  - Arouse empathy and perspective-taking but not anger.
  - Focus on the effect of the behavior on others.
  - Emphasize the values and moral reasoning that underlie the inhibition of inappropriate behavior and the exhibition of prosocial behavior.
  - Emphasize responsibility for one's own actions.
  - Involve parents, especially when correction needs to be repeated. Establish a support system to help the students improve their behavior.
  - Don't hesitate to seek assistance and support from others, including fellow teachers, administrators, school psychologists, and counselors.

- In general, be authoritative, not authoritarian!

*Note.* From *Developing Self-Discipline and Preventing and Correcting Misbehavior* (pp. 228–229), by G. Bear, 2005, Boston: Allyn & Bacon. Copyright 2005 by Allyn and Bacon. Adapted with permission.

techniques that teachers can teach their students are *cognitive restructuring* (e.g., a student reframes the situation in a way that allows him or her to find something positive about the situation or some meaning in it) and *distraction* (e.g., actively taking one's mind off of a situation by "distracting" oneself with something more pleasurable).

## SUMMARY

Self-discipline refers to socially and morally responsible behavior that is a result of internalizing prosocial values. Self-discipline is important because it (a) promotes positive relations with others, (b) fosters academic achievement, and (c) promotes self-worth and emotional well-being. Whereas the systematic use of rewards and punishment is certainly critical in the development of self-discipline, it is not sufficient. Far too often, children and adolescents find little motivation or reason to exhibit socially and morally responsible behavior in the absence of concrete rewards or the fear of getting caught and being punished. Schools that focus entirely on the use of external rewards and punishment for rule-following behaviors in their disciplinary policies, procedures, and practices run the great risk of fostering, rather than preventing, future behavior problems. That is, they encourage a self-centered, hedonistic perspective that has consistently been linked to increased behavior problems. Although the use of rewards and punishment should clearly be a part of school discipline, these methods should always be combined with additional strategies and techniques, such as those presented in this chapter, for developing self-discipline.

## RECOMMENDED RESOURCES

### Books and Other Printed Material

Bear, G. G. (with M. Manning & A. Cavalier). (2005). *Developing self-discipline and preventing and correcting misbehavior.* Boston: Allyn & Bacon.

Consistent with the focus of this chapter, this book argues that developing students' self-discipline should be the primary goal of classroom and school discipline. Numerous practical techniques guided by theory and research are given for preventing and correcting misbehavior and for addressing serious and chronic behavior problems.

Lickona, T. (2004). *Character matters: How to help our children develop good judgment, integrity, and other essential virtues.* New York: Touchstone.

Written for the general public, this book is extremely valuable to educators interested in developing students' character and self-discipline. In addition to building a strong case for the need for character education, the book presents multiple practical strategies and techniques for schools.

Watson, M. (2003). *Learning to trust: Transforming difficult elementary classrooms through developmental discipline.* San Francisco: Jossey-Bass.

Using her experience as an educator and researcher with the Child Development Project (see website below), Marilyn Watson emphasizes the critical importance of student-teacher relationships and a caring and trusting school climate. She also presents excellent advice on using "developmental discipline" to foster students' self-discipline.

### Websites

*http://www.cortland.edu/www/c4n5rs*

The website for the Center for the 4th and 5th Rs offers useful information, a newsletter, and resources on character education and promoting self-discipline.

*http://www.character.org*

The Character Education Partnership is a non-partisan coalition dedicated to developing moral character and civic virtue. Their website offers useful resources for character education.

*http://www.casel.org*

The website for the Collaborative for Academic, Social, and Emotional Learning (CASEL) provides a very informative electronic newsletter, links to related sites and new resources, and reports on research and effective practices for developing self-discipline and other social and emotional competencies.

*http://www.devstu.org*

This is the website for the Developmental Studies Center, the Child Development Project, and the Caring School Community, which are dedicated to promoting children's academic, ethical, and social development. Supported by ample research conducted by these projects, the site provides resources and curriculum materials on child development and education and for promoting self-discipline.

## REFERENCES

Arsenio, W. F., & Lemerise, E. A. (2001). Varieties of childhood bullying: Values, emotion processes, and social competence. *Social Development, 10,* 59–73.

Arum, R. (2003). *Judging school discipline: The crisis of moral authority* Cambridge, MA: Cambridge University Press.

Bandura, A. (1986). *Social foundations of thought and action: A social cognitive theory.* Upper Saddle River, NJ: Prentice-Hall.

Bandura, A. (1989). Self-regulation of motivation and action through internal standards and goal systems. In L. A. Pervin (Ed.), *Goal concepts in personality and social psychology* (pp. 19–85). Hillsdale, NJ: Erlbaum.

Bandura, A. (1991). Social cognitive theory of moral thought and action. In W. M. Kurtines & J. L. Gewirtz (Eds.), *Handbook of moral behavior and development* (pp. 45–103). Hillsdale, NJ: Erlbaum.

Bandura, A. (1997). *Self-efficacy: The exercise of control.* New York: Freeman.

Bandura, A. (2001). *Social cognitive theory: An agentic perspective. Annual review of psychology* (Vol. *52,* pp. 1–26). Palo Alto, CA: Annual Reviews.

Bandura, A., Caprara, G. V., Barbaranelli, C., & Regalia, C. (2001). Sociocognitive self-regulatory mechanisms governing transgressive behavior. *Journal of Personality and Social Psychology, 80,* 125–135.

Battistich, V., Schaps, E., Watson, M., Solomon, D., & Lewis, C. (2000). Effects of the Child Development Project on students' drug use and other problem behaviors. *Journal of Primary Prevention, 21,* 75–99.

Bear, G. G. (with Cavalier, A., & Manning, M.) (2005). *Developing self-discipline and preventing and correcting misbehavior.* Boston: Allyn & Bacon.

Bear, G. G., Manning, M., & Izard, D. (2003). Responsible behavior: The importance of social cognition and emotion. *School Psychology Quarterly, 18,* 140–157.

Berkowitz, M. W., & Bier, M. C. (2005). *What works?* Washington, DC: Character Education Partnership.

Birch, S. H., & Ladd, G. W. (1998). Children's interpersonal behaviors and the teacher–child relationship. *Developmental Psychology, 34,* 934–946.

Blair, R. J. R., Monson, J., & Frederickson, N. (2001). Moral reasoning and conduct problems in children with emotional and behavioural difficulties. *Personality and Individual Differences, 31,* 799–811.

Brophy, J. E. (1996). *Teaching problem students.* New York: Guilford Press.

Bru, E., Murberg, T. A., & Stephens, P. (2001). Social support, negative life events and pupil misbehavior among young Norwegian adolescents. *Journal of Adolescence, 24,* 715–727.

Bru, E., Stephens, P., & Torsheim, T. (2002). Students' perceptions of class management and reports of their own misbehavior. *Journal of School Psychology, 40,* 287–307.

Coie, J. D., & Dodge, K. A. (1998). Aggression and antisocial behavior. In W. Damon (Series Ed.) & N. Eisenberg (Vol. Ed.) *Handbook of child psychology, Vol. 3. Social, emotional, and personality development* (5th ed., pp. 779–862). New York: Wiley.

Colby, A., & Damon, W. (1999). The development of extraordinary moral commitment. In M. Killen & D. Hart (Eds.), *Morality in everyday life: Developmental perspectives* (pp. 342–370). New York: Cambridge University Press.

Collaborative for Academic, Social, and Emotional Learning. (2003). *Safe and sound: An educational leader's guide to evidence-based social and emotional learning (SEL) programs.* Retrieved July 8, 2003, from http://www.CASEL.org

Committee for Children. (2003). *Second Step: A violence prevention curriculum (Preschool-kindergarten teacher's guide).* Seattle, WA: Author.

Crick, N. R., & Dodge, K. A. (1994). A review and reformulation of social information-processing mechanisms in children's social adjustment. *Psychological Bulletin, 115,* 74–101.

Covington, M. V. (2000). Goal theory, motivation, and school achievement: An integrative review. *Annual Review of Psychology, 51,* 171–200.

Dodge, A. K., & Pettit, G. S. (2003). A biopsychosocial model of the development of chronic conduct problems in adolescence. *Developmental Psychology, 39,* 349–371.

Eisenberg, N., Fabes, R. A., & Spinrad, T. L. Prosocial development. In W. Damon & R. M. Lerner (Series Eds.) & N. Eisenberg (Vol. Ed.), *Handbook of child psychology: Vol. 3. Social, emotional, and personality development* (6th ed). New York: Wiley. (in press).

Erdley, C. A., & Asher, S. R. (1996). Children's social goals and self-efficacy perceptions as influences on their responses to ambiguous provocation. *Child Development, 67,* 1329–1344.

Ford, M. E., Wentzel, K. R., Wood, D., Stevens, E., & Sisfield, G. A. (1989). Processes associated with integrative social competence: Emotional contextual influences on adolescent social responsibility. *Journal of Adolescent Research, 4,* 405–425.

Frick, P. J., Cornell, A. H., Bodin, S. D., Dane, H. E., Barry, C. T., & Loney, B. R. (2003). Callous-unemotional traits and conduct problems in the prediction of conduct problem severity, aggression, and self-report of delinquency. *Journal of Abnormal Child Psychology, 31,* 457–470.

Goldstein, A. P., Harootunian, B., & Conoley, J. C. (1994). *Student aggression: Prevention, management, and replacement training.* New York: Guildford Press.

Grusec, J. E., & Goodnow, J. J. (1994). Impact of parental discipline methods on the child's internalization of values: A reconceptualization of current points of view. *Developmental Psychology, 30,* 4–19.

Guerra, N. G. (1989). Consequential thinking and self-reported delinquency in high-school youth. *Criminal Justice and Behavior, 16,* 440–454.

Guerra, N. G., Nucci, L., & Huesmann, L. R. (1994). Moral cognition and childhood aggression. In L. R. Huesmann (Ed.), *Aggressive behavior: Current perspectives* (pp. 13–33). New York: Plenum Press.

Harter, S. (1999). *The construction of the self: A developmental perspective.* New York: Guilford Press.

Hartshorne, H., & May, M. A. (1928). *Studies in the nature of character: Vol. I: Studies in deceit.* New York: Macmillan.

Hoffman, M. L. (2000). *Empathy and moral development: Implications for caring and justice.* Cambridge, UK: Cambridge University Press.

Huesmann, L. R. (1988). An information processing model for the development of aggression. *Aggressive Behavior, 14,* 13–24.

Hughes, J. N., Cavell, T. A., & Willson, V. (2001). Further support for the developmental significance of the quality of the teacher-student relationship. *Journal of School Psychology, 39,* 289–301.

Izard, C. E. (1991). *The psychology of emotions.* New York: Plenum Press.

Kochanska, G. (2002). Committed compliance, moral self, and internalization: A mediational model. *Developmental Psychology, 38,* 339–351.

Kuther, T. L. (2000). Moral reasoning, perceived competence, and adolescent engagement in risky activity. *Journal of Adolescence, 23,* 599–604.

Malecki, C. K., & Elliott, S. (2002). Children's social behaviors as predictors of academic achievement: A longitudinal analysis. *School Psychology Quarterly, 17,* 1–23.

Manning, M. A., & Bear, G. G. (2002). Are children's concerns about punishment related to their aggression? *Journal of School Psychology, 40,* 523–539.

Mayer, J. D., & Salovey, P. (1997). What is emotional intelligence? In P. Salovey & D. Sluyter (Eds.), *Emotional development and emotional intelligence: Implications for educators* (pp. 3–31). New York: Basic Books.

Menesini, E., Sanchez, V., Fonzi, A., Ortega, R., Costabile, A., & Lo Feudo, G. (2003). Moral emotions and bullying: A cross-national comparison of differences between bullies, victims and outsiders. *Aggressive Behavior, 29,* 515–530.

Murdock, T. B. (1999). The social context of risk: Predictors of alienation in middle school. *Journal of Educational Psychology, 91,* 62–75.

Murdock, T. B., Hale, N. M., & Weber, M. J. (2001). Predictors of cheating among early adolescents: Academic and social motivations. *Contemporary Educational Psychology, 26,* 96–115.

Nisan, M. (1991). The moral balance model: Theory and research extending our understanding. In W. M. Kurtines & J. L. Gewirtz (Eds.), *Handbook of moral behavior and development, Vol. 3. Application* (pp. 213–249). Hillsdale, NJ: Erlbaum.

Nucci, L. P. (2001). *Education in the moral domain.* New York: Cambridge University Press.

Orobio de Castro, B., Veerman, J. W., Koops, W., Bosch, J., & Monshouwer, J. J. (2002). Hostile attribution of intent and aggressive behavior: A meta-analysis. *Child Development, 73,* 916–934.

Osterman, K. F. (2000). Students' need for belonging in the school community. *Review of Educational Research, 70,* 323–367.

Palmer, E. J., & Hollin, C. R. (2001). Sociomoral reasoning, perceptions of parenting, and self-reported delinquency in adolescents. *Applied Cognitive Psychology, 15,* 85–100.

Pardini, D. A., Lochman, J. E., & Frick, P. J. (2003). Callous/unemotional traits and social–cognitive processes in adjudicated youths. *Journal of the American Academy of Child & Adolescent Psychiatry, 42,* 364–371.

Pianta, R. C, Hamre, B., & Stuhlman, M. (2003). Relationships between teachers and children. In W. Reynolds & G. Miller (Eds.), *Comprehensive Handbook of Psychology (Vol. 7) Educational Psychology* (pp. 199–234).

Rest, J. R. (1983). Morality. In P. H. Musen (Series Ed.) & J. H. Flavell & E. M. Markman (Vol. Eds.), *Handbook of child psychology: Vol. 3. Cognitive development* (4th ed., pp 556–629). New York: Wiley.

Rose, L. C., & Gallup, A. M. (2000). The 32nd annual Phi Delta Kappa/Gallup poll of the public's attitudes toward the public schools. *Phi Delta Kappan, 82,* 41–66.

Rubin, K. H., Bukowski, W., & Parker, J. G. (1998). Peer interactions, relationships, and groups. In W. Damon (Series Ed.) & N. Eisenberg (Vol. Ed.), *Handbook of child psychology: Vol. 3. Social, emotional, and personality development* (5th ed., pp. 619–700). New York: Wiley.

Weiner, B. (2001). Responsibility for social transgressions: An attributional analysis. In B. F. Malle, L. J. Moses, & D. A. Baldwin (Eds.), *Intentions and intentionality: Foundations of social cognition* (pp. 331–344). Cambridge, MA: MIT Press.

Wentzel, K. R. (1991). Social competence at school: Relation between social responsibility and academic achievement. *Review of Educational Research, 61,* 1–24.

Wentzel, K. R. (1996). Social and academic motivation in middle school: Concurrent and long-term relations to academic effort. *Journal of Early Adolescence, 16,* 390–406.

Wooton, J. M., Frick, P. J., Shelton, K. K., & Silverthorn, P. (1997). Ineffective parenting and childhood conduct problems: The moderating role of callous-unemotional traits. *Journal of Consulting and Clinical Psychology, 65,* 301–308.

# 4

# School Engagement

**Stacy L. O'Farrell**
*Fairfield-Suisun Unified School District, CA*

**Gale M. Morrison**
**Michael J. Furlong**
*University of California, Santa Barbara*

"Johnny's just not motivated." "Susie just doesn't care." "Sam is turned off by school." "These kids are really alienated from their peers."

These are comments frequently heard from teachers and parents describing students who, for some reason, seem out of touch with school and the goals of schooling. Listening carefully to the wording of these comments suggests that there is a *continuum of connectedness* to school, which ranges from not being motivated by the academic aspects of school to being totally turned off by the content of the curriculum. There are also the affective connections to school. For example, students who are disengaged have a diminished sense of feeling they are a part of school. As a result, they do not fully participate in the school environment. At its most extreme, disengaged students feel alienated from the academic and social contexts of school. Clearly, those who are concerned about a student's connection to school must consider the multiple dimensions of that connection.

School engagement has recently received increased attention as a topic of interest to researchers and educators because of its association with negative student outcomes such as delinquency (Hawkins, Guo, Hill, Battin-Pearson, & Abbott, 2001; O'Donnell, Hawkins, & Abbott, 1995), school dropout (Rumberger & Larson, 1998), poor academic achievement (Abbott et al., 1998; Anderman & Anderman, 1999; Connell, Spencer, & Aber, 1994), and substance use (Hawkins et al., 2001; O'Donnell, Hawkins, & Abbott, 1995). Students who are not psychologically and behaviorally engaged in school are more likely to experience negative outcomes, such as those mentioned above, than students who have high levels of school engagement. A recent international study investigating school engagement in high school students indicates that as many as one in four students could be classified as experiencing low levels of school engagement (Willms, 2003). Because school engagement facilitates student social and academic development, these alarming statistics suggest that school engagement is an issue worthy of attention both in the schools and in the research community.

The purpose of this chapter is to examine the concept of school engagement as a construct that exemplifies the multidimensional nature of a student's connections to school. After thoroughly examining the many terms used to express the concept of *engagement*, emphasis will be placed on the role of school contexts in enhancing or detracting from a student's engagement in school. Problems that seem to be motivation based are often thought to originate primarily within the child, rather than emanating from the interaction of the child with his or her environment. For educators to be maximally effective in their efforts to improve student engagement in school, thereby increasing the chances for student success, they must know about the influences of the multiple, modifiable contexts that positively or negatively influence student engagement.

## BACKGROUND AND DEVELOPMENT

School engagement has been represented in the research and practice literature by many terms, including school connectedness, membership, bonding, belonging, engagement, and affiliation (Jimerson, Campos, & Greif, 2003; Osterman, 2000). The study of school engagement originated within the school dropout literature in the work of Jeremy Finn. Finn (1989) found that school engagement, which consists of identification and participation, was an important factor associated with school completion. Finn describes identification as an "internal state with two components, *belonging* and *valuing*" (p. 127, emphasis added). In contrast, participation is a behavioral component of school engagement (e.g., homework completion, involvement in extracurricular activities, and class participation). Since Finn's seminal work, school engagement has received increasing attention in the school dropout literature and elsewhere, including the motivation and resilience literatures (Goodenow, 1993; Mouton, Hawkins, McPherson, & Copley, 1996).

A second perspective that is often cited in studies utilizing school engagement as a measured construct is the self-systems processes model, which posits that individuals are motivated to participate in activities that serve their needs for autonomy, competence, and relatedness (Pierson & Connell, 1992). When these needs are met, individuals become engaged within the institution. This motivational process has been applied to explain student engagement in school.

In summary, the school engagement construct has roots in literature that examines schooling and adjustment outcomes, such as dropping out or engaging in delinquent acts, and in the examination of the processes involved in a student's performance at school. These distinct research traditions have led to some of the variations in definition and measurement described below.

## Definition and Measurement of Engagement

Despite the apparent simplicity of the idea of school engagement, there has been some divergence among researchers in the terms used to describe this broad phenomenon. Several terms overlap with school engagement, with regard to both definition and measurement. Two of the most common are *school bonding* and *school belonging*. Hirschi (1969) introduced the concept of *school bonds* in his theory of social control, which was developed to describe the factors associated with youth engagement in delinquent acts. According to Hirschi's theory, youths who harbor positive feelings, or bonds, to social institutions such as school are less likely to commit delinquent acts and are more likely to succeed in school. Hawkins and his colleagues tested Hirschi's theory of social control in their own research, adapted it based on their findings, and created what they call the social development model (Hawkins & Lishner, 1987; O'Donnell, Hawkins, & Abbott, 1995). The social development model expands upon Hirschi's theory of social control by hypothesizing that bonding to social institutions such as schools is determined by the amount of opportunity for involvement, the skills applied in participation, and the reinforcements provided for behavior. *School belonging* is defined as "the extent to which students feel personally accepted, respected, included, and supported by others in the school environment" (Goodenow, 1993, p. 80). It is often cited synonymously with school bonding and is used in studies of resilience, academic achievement, and general school adjustment.

The use of multiple terms that appear to describe similar, if not identical constructs has made the synthesis and interpretation of the literature difficult. Translating results from empirical studies into practical interventions for use in the schools becomes tricky when the existing research has used a variety of measurement tools and definitions. Thus, as the result of extensive literature reviews, several researchers have tried to consider the overlapping school engagement terms, positing the existence of one multidimensional construct (Fredericks, Blumenfeld, & Paris, 2004; Furlong et al., 2003; O'Farrell & Morrison, 2003).

The literature suggests that the broad phenomenon of school engagement consists of at least three related components: behavioral, emotional, and cognitive engagement (Fredericks et al., 2004; Furlong et al., 2003). Sinclair, Christenson, Lehr, and Anderson (2003) add academic engagement to these three components. In a factor analysis that examined measures of school bonding and related constructs, O'Farrell and Morrison empirically identified five dimensions within the greater construct: peer and general school relations; school support, competency, and participation; adult acceptance and general belonging; academic orientation; and personal and family educational expectations. Currently, there is agreement that school engagement and its associated terms are important within the context of positive school adjustment; however, researchers and practitioners are still pursuing definitional and measurement precision. Nonetheless, we can state confidently that school engagement has multiple dimensions and is formed within multiple contexts.

### Developmental Considerations

Some of the variation in constructs used in this body of research may be the result of differing age-group foci. It is important for educators to understand how school engagement issues may present themselves differently at the various school levels (elementary, junior high school, and high school). Studies investigating differences between school belonging and related constructs across developmental stages suggest that it may differ qualitatively across the elementary and junior high school years (Morrison, Cosden, O'Farrell, & Campos, 2003; O'Farrell, Fisher, & Redding, 2004). In these studies, school belonging is correlated with different variables within the two periods. Specifically, school belonging is associated with factors from multiple contexts in elementary school (e.g., home, classroom, peer, and individual). In contrast, during the junior high school years, only individual and peer contexts remain significantly related with levels of school belonging (O'Farrell et al., 2004). This pattern suggests that age is important when considering an intervention strategy. Recent research suggests that during the elementary years, students, on average, experience high levels of belonging to school (O'Farrell, 2004). Given this average high level of belonging, those students who experience low levels of belonging during the elementary years appear at risk. Monitoring and catching these students before they fall into a negative trajectory becomes even more important. In comparison, once students enter secondary school, an approach that considers the significant role that peers play in an individual student's sense of belonging will enhance interventions and support programs.

## PROBLEMS AND IMPLICATIONS

As shown in the current literature base and its origins, knowledge is limited regarding the "normal" development of school engagement across time. Rather, research has focused on low levels of school engagement and the association of that condition with various negative developmental outcomes. Understanding the characteristics of disengaged students, who often have low levels of school engagement, can help educators identify these students and develop prevention and intervention plans. In addition to these individual student factors, peer, classroom, school, and family contexts are associated with low levels of school engagement. These factors can be considered with regard to context, from an interactive ecological perspective (e.g., Bronfenbrenner, 1986). Table 1 presents a summary of contextual considerations and actions to enhance student engagement.

### Individual Student Variables

Multiple studies have shown that self-efficacy is associated with school engagement (Caraway, Tucker, Reinke, & Hall, 2003; Gutman & Midgley, 2000). That relationship has held for both high school (Caraway et al.) and elementary students (Gutman & Midgley). Students who harbor a higher sense of self-efficacy and are more oriented toward process goals than task completion tend to be more engaged in school. In addition, studies show that students with a higher sense of academic competence tend to feel a greater sense of belonging in school (O'Farrell et al., 2004). That is, students who feel that they have the academic skills necessary to succeed are more engaged in school. This is true both in upper elementary and junior high school. In addition, students who have a high expectancy for school success and who value schoolwork tend to do better academically and are more engaged in school than their counterparts (Goodenow, 1993).

Academic achievement has been found to be associated with both emotional and behavioral school engagement and related constructs (Connell et al., 1994; Gutman & Midgley, 2000; Hawkins et al., 2001). Interestingly, whereas emotional engagement appears to be related only to short-term outcomes, behavioral engagement continues to have an effect on academic outcomes over time. This suggests, for example, that students who are more closely bonded with their teacher and peers one year will immediately perform better academically, but persistent behavioral engagement is associated with longer-term, stable academic attainment. The relationship between school belonging and grade point average during the transition from elementary to junior high school appears to work similarly. For example, Gutman and Midgley (2000) studied the transition between elementary and junior high school with regard to grade point average, school belonging, and various psychological variables. Their findings suggest that the emotional or belonging dimension of school engagement is situation-specific and emerges from the quality of the student's classroom, peer, and school contexts each year. Therefore, it is possible that the quality and level of a student's affective connection to school may change from year to year and students who persist in their behavioral engagement show the most stable academic outcomes.

**Table 1** *School Engagement: Contextual Considerations and Actions*

| Level | Considerations | Actions |
|---|---|---|
| *Individual* | Student's age. | Implement developmentally appropriate interventions. |
| | Level of self-efficacy and academic self-concept. If self-efficacy is low, is it an appropriate evaluation of skill level? | Consult with teacher to consider student academic skill level and possible modifications in the classroom (e.g., additional instructional time or modified assignments). |
| | Does the student value school? What are his or her expectations with regard to school? | Investigate student educational goals and attitudes toward school. Does the student see the relevance of school? Consider familial and peer influences. |
| | Does the student have a disability? | Consider the educational environment of the student (e.g., resource program) and the potential barriers to school engagement. Also consider possible peer effects (e.g., victimization and teasing). |
| | Is the student involved in extracurricular activities or school-related activities that emphasize personal strengths? | Explore alternate avenues of involvement in school if academics are not a strength (e.g., drama, music, art, or sports). |
| *Peer* | What are the academic aspirations of the student's peer group? | Consider implementing a study skills group or involving the student in an existing group that holds high academic aspirations. |
| | Does the student have peer support for academics? | Would involvement in a homework club be beneficial? |
| | Is the students' peer group generally resistant to school norms? | Consider group intervention or involving the group in a school-sponsored activity in which they may feel success. This opportunity could lead to greater acceptance of school norms. |
| | Is the student experiencing victimization from peers? | Consider a targeted or school-wide bullying prevention program. |
| | Does the student have strong peer affiliations? | Consider the benefits of involvement in a school activity that emphasizes student strengths and provides opportunities for peer interaction. |

*(Continued)*

**Table 1** *Continued*

| Level | Considerations | Actions |
|---|---|---|
| *Classroom* | What is the classroom goal orientation (i.e., ability focused or task focused)? | Consult with the teacher to develop task- and goal-oriented activities and strategies. Try to minimize competition among peers and emphasize personal goal achievement. |
| | How does the teacher encourage students? How does the teacher communicate high expectations for success? | Observe the classroom environment and provide specific suggestions or modeling for the teacher. |
| | What opportunities are available for cooperative learning? | Observe the classroom environment and provide specific suggestions or modeling for the teacher. |
| | What types of classroom management strategies are implemented? Are they proactive or reactive? | Observe the classroom environment and provide specific suggestions or modeling for the teacher. |
| *School* | How is the school disciplinary policy communicated and reinforced? | Examine reinforcement opportunities for positive behavior. Communicate appropriate behaviors in addition to providing consequences for inappropriate behaviors. |
| | How are expectations for student success communicated at the school-wide level? | Consider suggesting a weekly or daily address to the student body that emphasizes student success (both behavioral and academic). |
| | Are students involved in decision making at the school-wide level? | Examine opportunities for input on decision making and the relevance of these opportunities, as perceived by students. |
| | What are the opportunities for parent–school communication? | Work with teachers and administrators to improve parent–school communication (i.e., reinforce the importance of relaying positive messages regarding student behavior and achievement). |
| | How are school-wide data used with regard to programming (e.g., academic, behavioral, and attendance)? | Consider developing a climate and student monitoring system so that school-wide data can be used to increase student engagement. |

*(Continued)*

**Table 1** *Continued*

| Level | Considerations | Actions |
|---|---|---|
| *Family* | What are the educational expectations for the child? How do parents communicate high expectations? | Explore the educational expectations for the child through conversations with parents, either individually or at parent nights. Provide explicit examples for parents about how they can communicate and model high expectations. |
| | How are parents involved in their children's education? | Provide multiple opportunities for involvement, such as parent volunteering and classroom visits. |
| | Do parents want or need additional education regarding parenting or development? | Provide parenting classes after conducting a needs assessment to determine what type of education is wanted and relevant. |
| | Are community resources accessible to parents? | Provide connections between families and community resources. |

*Note.* From Morrison, G. M. (2005). *Turning Points.* Unpublished manuscript, University of California, Santa Barbara.

Research indicates that students with disabilities experience lower levels of school bonding than their peers. For example, in one study (Fulk, Brigham, & Lohman, 1998), junior high students with learning disabilities reported feeling more alienated than did students with emotional or behavioral disorders or average achievement. In another study that investigated school bonding among fifth- and sixth-graders with and without disabilities, students with disabilities tended to have lower levels of school bonding than students without disabilities (Murray & Greenberg, 2001). Finally, in a comparison of at-risk, learning-disabled, speech-impaired, and not-at-risk elementary students (Robertson, Harding, & Morrison, 1998), students receiving speech services reported low school bonding and poorer self-concept than the other groups. Thus, it appears that disability status may affect bonds with school across the elementary and junior high years. As such, students with disabilities are at greater risk of low levels of school engagement than their non-disabled counterparts, perhaps reflecting their marginalized involvement in the broader educational academic mission of schools.

Thus, at the individual level, both psychological and status variables may contribute to low levels of school engagement. Many of the psychological variables can potentially be influenced through environmental interventions. For example, receiving an academic intervention may increase a student's sense of academic self-concept, whereas a student's disability status is not as easily affected. Considering engagement contexts is of utmost importance when evaluating possible avenues for intervention. When it comes to addressing the needs of disengaged (those with few bonds to school) and disengaging (those in the process of psychologically and socially withdrawing from school) students, schools have tended to take the approach that the problem is in the individual rather than a reciprocal interactive process involving contexts within the school environment. This process is discussed in a later section.

## Peer Variables

Peers clearly play a significant role in students' sense of belonging at school. For example, in a study of seventh-graders, peer academic constructs (including academic aspirations and support) and resistance to school norms were found to be related to student alienation. Illustrating the influence of social isolation on school engagement, a new body of research is emerging that suggests that adolescents who experience attraction to same-sex peers also experience lower levels of school belonging (Galliher, Rostosky, & Hughes, 2004; Rostosky, Owens, Zimmerman, & Riggle, 2003). Alienation may be worsened by a peer or school culture that includes victimization of sexual minority youth. Indeed, victimization has been found to have a strong link to low levels of school belonging, with students who perceive themselves as victimized tending to report lower levels of belonging at school (Morrison & O'Farrell, 2004; O'Farrell et al., 2004). That issue is worthy of additional attention in the schools, as students who experience victimization may be loath to report bullying behavior to school personnel for fear of additional harassment. The same stream of research points to the importance of schools creating welcoming contexts that help all students feel bonded and providing niches that nurture and support.

## Classroom Variables

It is difficult to imagine how students could be meaningfully engaged in school without feeling that they are part of their classroom. In one study (Anderman & Anderman, 1999), school belonging was examined across the transition from elementary to junior high school as it related to classroom goal orientation. Anderman and Anderman conceived of goal orientation as being toward either task completion or ability level, which emphasizes competition in the classroom. School belonging was found to relate to classroom goal orientations—significant and positive associations were found with task goal orientation, whereas negative associations were found with ability goal orientations. School belonging related positively to task-completion and goal orientation and negatively to ability goal orientation. This finding implies that students' sense of belonging at school is systematically tied to the goal orientation of the teacher. Students who have teachers who structure their classrooms to emphasize ability have a lower sense of belonging to school than students whose teachers use a task-completion approach.

Research shows that teacher variables such as disapproval and criticism, encouragement, and long-term expectations are associated with alienation (with alienation being defined as disengagement from school tasks and involvement in discipline problems). Discipline problems tend to be positively associated with teachers' disapproval and criticism and negatively related to teachers' encouragement, teachers' long-term expectations, and student engagement. For example, in a study by Murdock (1999), student engagement was positively related to teachers' long-term expectations and negatively related to teachers' disapproval and criticism. Teachers' expectations and peer aspirations were associated with engagement. After controlling for previous achievement, only the motivational variables (teachers' expectations) predicted behavioral engagement. These findings suggest that student perception of teachers' affective variables (expectations, approval, and encouragement) bear significantly on behavioral engagement (as it was measured in this study). Murdock's measure did not tap an affective element of engagement, so these relationships are unknown.

In another study of teacher variables in elementary schools, Skinner and Belmont (1993) found that a significant predictor of students' behavioral engagement was their perception of teacher structure, whereas a significant predictor of students' emotional engagement was perception of teacher involvement. The multidimensionality of school engagement is revealed in that study. This point is important for educators to recognize because it implies that students may have high levels of behavioral engagement, for example, but diminished emotional engagement.

## School Variables

School climate has been shown to be associated with the strength of students' school engagement. In one study, school bonding was positively associated with school climate and school adjustment and negatively associated with problem behavior (Simons-Morton, Crump, Haynie, & Saylor, 1999). In a similar study, school characteristics were investigated as they relate to school engagement in high school students (Willms, 2003). Schools with a strong disciplinary climate, good student–teacher relations, and high expectations for student success tended to have a higher percentage of students with high levels of student engagement.

Evidence shows a significant link between student engagement and school climate, in particular the extent to which students experience their school as a caring community (Battistich & Hom, 1997; Battistich, Schaps, & Wilson, 2004). Specifically, an environment that emphasizes interpersonal relationships among students and teachers and allows students to participate in decision-making opportunities tends to achieve higher levels of student engagement than one that does not. Students in such environments tend to enjoy school more and are involved in less problem behavior than their counterparts. When students attend elementary schools that highlight their role as a caring community, the positive effects continue beyond elementary and into junior high school (Battistich, Schaps, & Wilson).

Additional studies that have focused on school-wide variables suggest that students are more likely to be engaged at schools that are effective and have a clear school mission, high expectations for students' learning and behavior, instructional leadership, a safe and orderly environment, opportunities and time to learn, frequent monitoring of and feedback on student performance, and positive home–school relationships (Block, Everson, & Guskey, 1995; Reynolds, Teddlie, Creemers, Scheerens, & Townsend, 2000).

### Family Variables

Hirschi's (1969) original research looking at student bonds to school indicated that familial bonds preceded social bonds with peers and institutions such as school. Since his seminal work, research has confirmed this relationship, suggesting that poor familial bonds correlate with lower levels of school engagement and related constructs (Dornbusch, Erickson, Laird, & Wong, 2001; O'Donnell, Hawkins, & Abbott, 1995; O'Donnell, Hawkins, Catalano, Abbott, & Day, 1995). For example, parental behavior and presence in the home seem to affect school engagement in high school (Johnson, Crosnoe, & Elder, 2001). Furthermore, students from intact homes, with parents who have higher levels of educational attainment and who hold high educational expectations, tend to be more engaged than students without these characteristics. The level of parent involvement in education relates to school engagement. For example, youth who show disaffected patterns of behavior and emotion in school (low levels of school engagement) experience less support from their families than those who report higher levels of engagement (Connell et al., 1994). Students with high levels of family involvement and school factors (i.e., school belonging and perceived teacher support) have higher grade point averages than do their classmates who have high levels of only one or none of these variables (Gutman & Midgley, 2000).

Interventions that include families have been shown to positively affect student bonding to school. Family-based interventions implemented to prevent substance use have resulted in increased levels of school engagement in both pre-kindergarten and early elementary school students (Kaminski, Stormshack, Good, & Goodman, 2002; Kumpfer, Alvarado, Tait, & Turner, 2002). In junior high school, results have been mixed. For example, a family-based intervention program increased parental investment and decreased behavior problems in the students with the intervention but did not affect school bonding or academic achievement (Pantin et al., 2003). These findings emphasize the importance of developmental considerations, suggesting that at the junior high level interventions directed toward parents may not be the most effective method of increasing school engagement. Together, the results indicate that family factors may, indeed, be another important context of influence with regard to school engagement.

## SCHOOL ENGAGEMENT INTERVENTIONS

The following sections describe specific actions educators can take in preventing or intervening with regard to school engagement at the individual, group, classroom, or school-wide level. The discussion is framed using Furlong, Morrison, and colleagues' three-tiered model of school violence prevention (Furlong & Morrison, 2000; Furlong, Morrison, & Pavelski, 2000). The model is intended to reaffirm, reconnect, and reconstruct student bonds to school, depending on their level of disengagement and need. The model is based on Hawkins' social development model (Hawkins & Lishner, 1987), which emphasizes the importance of providing opportunities for students to contribute to their school environment, to gain the skills necessary for such involvement, and to experience reinforcement for using these skills. We categorize programs from the literature as *reaffirming*, *reconnecting*, or *reconstructing* ties to school based on their scope. In general, school-wide programs have been categorized as preventing or reaffirming ties to school. These programs do not target students specifically based on their apparent level of school engagement. Programs that do target specific students have been categorized as interventions, which occur at either the reconnecting or the reconstructing level of need.

### Reaffirmation: Alternative Actions for Prevention

In general, most students appear to feel a sense of belonging at their school (O'Farrell, 2004; Willms, 2003). However, up to 25% of students have reported low levels of school engagement (Willms), which has been demonstrated as a predictor of negative outcomes such as school dropout and delinquency, as described previously. An important role for all educators, and specifically school psychologists, is to monitor the students' level of school engagement at their schools and to establish methods of prevention to maintain their healthy bonds to school. Risks that may affect such bonds include victimization by peers, failure to meet academic or social expectations, frustrated attempts to join in school activities (e.g., sports or drama), or parent attitudes toward school or academic performance.

For some students, school engagement can be described as tenuous, with potential risk of disconnection from school. Therefore, creating methods of *reaffirming* ties to school as a way of preventing low levels of school engagement may be beneficial. Two empirically tested programs for preventing eventual negative outcomes and strengthening bonds to school are the Child Development Project and the Seattle Social Development Project.

The Child Development Project (CDP; Battistich, Schaps, Watson, Solomon, & Lewis, 2000) aims to increase the sense of community within elementary schools. The four major principles of the CDP are (a) build stable, warm, and supportive relationships; (b) attend to the social and ethical dimensions of learning; (c) teach to the active mind; and (d) honor intrinsic motivation. The program is applied at the classroom, school-wide, and familial levels. Within the classroom, these principles are infused into every classroom activity, primarily through cooperative learning. Recently, a follow-up study was conducted on students from 6 of the 12 elementary schools involved in the original program implementation study to investigate their adjustment to junior high school (Battistich et al., 2004). The authors found that the level of implementation was an important factor in the overall results of the program. For the high implementation group, almost 65% of all indicators showed marked improvement favoring the students involved in the project. School-related attitudes (i.e., sense of school as a community, educational aspirations, trust in and respect for teachers, and liking for school) and academic performance were especially strong for students involved in the intervention. The results suggest, as will be seen throughout this discussion, that prevention efforts geared toward multiple contexts with a high level of implementation fidelity tend to be the most successful in strengthening and maintaining high levels of school engagement.

The Seattle Social Development Project (SSDP; Abbott et al., 1998; Hawkins et al., 2001; O'Donnell et al., 1995) is similar to the CDP in that it is a multicomponent, school-wide intervention that is implemented in elementary schools. The program is designed to promote school bonding and positive youth development while preventing negative outcomes such as school failure, drug use, and delinquency. The SSDP includes three strands of intervention—modified teaching practices, social skills training for students, and developmentally adjusted parent training. The teachers are trained in three instructional components—proactive classroom management, interactive teaching, and cooperative learning. These strategies are infused throughout the school day. The child intervention (cognitive and social skills training) is implemented in grades one through six. The parent intervention, a voluntary component, is offered for each grade level in the form of parent workshops. Topics include child behavior management, academic support, and antisocial behavior prevention.

The SSDP has been evaluated with regard to the prevention of school failure, drug use, and delinquency (O'Donnell et al., 1995) and to the promotion of school bonding (Abbott et al., 1998; Hawkins et al., 2001) and academic achievement (Abbott et al.). These studies indicate that with high levels of fidelity to implementation and with full intervention (all components of the intervention design), school bonding can be affected well into high school (Hawkins et al., 2001). Specifically, students who received the full intervention (classroom, child, and parent levels in grades one through six) were significantly more bonded to school in junior high and high school than students in the control group or in the group receiving intervention only in grades five and six. More immediate effects include increased academic achievement (Abbott et al.) and school commitment and class participation (O'Donnell et al.). These results reinforce the idea that adherence to intervention design is essential in implementing a program such as the SSDP. In addition, it appears that multicomponent interventions seem to have more long-term impacts than programs based only on portions of the intervention.

In summary, prevention efforts found in the literature consisted primarily of programs that contain multiple components and target the classroom, individual, and home contexts. For example, the school populations targeted in the SSDP were considered to be at risk because they were from an urban, low-income environment. Thus, the intervention targeted the home environment through parent training in addition to the school environment through teacher and student training. To be successful, prevention programs designed at the school level should consider the specific needs of the population with regard to the multiple contexts of influence.

## Reconnection: Alternative Actions for Intervention

As previously mentioned, the *reaffirm, reconnect, and reconstruct* model is based on a three-tiered concept representing students' differing levels of need. This section describes interventions that may be appropriate for students requiring a reconnection to school. These students may show signs of disengagement in their attendance and grade patterns, such as grades that have declined compared with previous grading periods or school years, or they may seem suddenly unmotivated. School personnel must reach out to connect with students for whom bonds with school have been damaged (Furlong et al., 2000).

One such targeted intervention was implemented in four urban high schools in an effort to prevent drug abuse and school dropout (Eggert, Thompson, Herting, Nicholas, & Dicker, 1994). The intervention, which was implemented in the format of a personal growth class, was offered as a one-semester elective for students who were considered at risk for drug use or dropping out of school. The teachers, who volunteered to teach the personal growth class, received intensive training and had biweekly meetings with the trainers throughout the semester. The class consisted of three primary components: (a) it provided a social network support, such as group support, friendship development, and teacher–student and peer group relationships; (b) teachers and other students modeled support behaviors in the class setting; and (c) it taught students specific skills such as self-esteem enhancement, decision making, personal control, and interpersonal communication. These skills were presented to the class and practiced as part of class discussion. That is, they were introduced in response to the students rather than to a predetermined curriculum.

Evaluation of the personal growth class (see Eggert et al., 1994) revealed that the intervention had a significant impact on a number of variables. Compared with student controls, participants had a significant increase in their grade point average, self-esteem, and school bonding and a decrease in drug use and, for girls, bonding with deviant peers. The design of the intervention reflected the developmental level of the students in need. Because peer relationships appear to become more important aspects of school bonding and engagement as students enter adolescence, the personal growth class intervention capitalizes on the power of peer relationships and uses them as a mechanism for increasing students' engagement in school. That approach appears promising for students at the high school and possibly junior high school levels.

## Reconstruction: Intervention Efforts From the Literature

The third tier of intervention efforts aim to reach the most disconnected students—those who require the reconstruction of their bonds to school. These students may have patterns of involvement in school disciplinary events and may engage in delinquent activities in their communities. Students who require this level of intervention are likely to have teachers who are already frustrated with them, who feel exasperated and unsure of how to handle the students' behavior. Often, these students lack the academic skills to gain the recognition they need that would foster their future engagement (Furlong et al., 2000). Therefore, school personnel must be creative in finding ways to connect with these students and to provide opportunities for positive involvement.

The Check & Connect program is designed to increase school engagement and prevent school dropout (Sinclair, Christenson, Evelo, & Hurley, 1998; Sinclair et al., 2003; also see chapter 8, "School Completion"). The program is described as a highly targeted, schoolwide model designed to identify students who appear to be at risk for low levels of school engagement and to intervene. Check & Connect is outcome driven, making use of the data that are regularly collected by school personnel, such as attendance, grades, and disciplinary events. Within the program, two key school personnel are primarily involved with surveying the data and intervening. The first is the monitor, who serves as a mentor or advocate. This person extends services to the student and his or her family as the need arises and is hired by the school for that purpose only. The second person, the coordinator, is typically part of the school staff, such as a school psychologist, who directs the day-to-day workings of the intervention. The coordinator provides supervision and continued staff development for the monitors at the school or in the district.

The core elements of the Check & Connect intervention model include (a) relationship building; (b) a persistent source of academic motivation (through the monitor and the family); (c) routine monitoring of alterable indicators (e.g., attendance, school performance, and behavior); (d) individualized and timely intervention; (e) tracking of students and families who move from school to school within a district, and help with problem-solving; and (f) affiliation with the school (student access to school-sponsored activities and events). These components, plus other considerations for effective interventions, can be found in chapter 8, "School Completion."

Evaluation of early implementation of the Check & Connect program suggested that students who receive continued intervention are more likely to be engaged in school than students in the control group (Sinclair et al., 1998). The students in the program attended school more regularly than students in the control group. Furthermore, special education teachers tended to perceive the program's students as more academically competent than control students, and general education teachers rated treatment students as having less behavioral difficulty than nontreatment students. The evaluation of Check & Connect focused primarily on behavioral engagement; however, an evaluation of affective engagement (identification with school) found no differences between treatment and control students (Sinclair et al., 1998).

## SUMMARY

This chapter presented school engagement as it represents students' multidimensional connections to school, including affective, behavioral, and cognitive dimensions. Terms related to school engagement were defined and described—*school bonding, school attachment, school connectedness*, and *school belonging*—to give a perspective on the various contexts that may affect a child's connections to the school. Variables were considered that may affect student connections to school, including the individual, peer, classroom, school, and family. Finally, programs were reviewed that involve both prevention and intervention to provide educators with tools to aid in creating stronger ties between students and the school.

## RECOMMENDED RESOURCES

### Books and Other Printed Material

Jimerson, S. R. (Ed.). (2003). Special topic section: School engagement, youth development, and school success. *California School Psychologist, 8,* 3–140.

Volume 8 of the *California School Psychologist* contains numerous articles covering multiple perspectives of school engagement. The reader will gain an understanding of the multiple facets of this important topic, from the theoretical to the empirical. Available at www.education.ucsb.edu/school-psychology

National Academies. (2004). *Engaging schools: Fostering high school students' motivation to learn.* A report by the Committee on Increasing High School Students' Engagement and Motivation to Learn. Washington, DC: National Academies Press. Available at http://www.nap.edu

This book provides a thorough description of school engagement and ways in which school personnel can intervene for students who are at risk of disengaging from school. The book focuses on interventions for students at the high school level.

Finn, J. D. (1989). Withdrawing from school. *Review of Educational Research, 59,* 117–142.

This is one of the early seminal works that synthesizes information about school engagement.

Osterman, K. F. (2000). Students' need for belonging in the school community. *Review of Educational Research, 70,* 323–367.

This review takes a social–cognitive perspective to examine what is known about how schools can build a stronger sense of community and how that supports students' sense of acceptance and belonging in the school.

### Websites

*http://www.childtrends.org/what_works/clarkwww/civic/table_engage.asp*

The website "Child Trends: What Works—Civic Engagement Programs" organizes information related to schools' civic engagement programs that implement service learning programs in classrooms and the school. The website documents associated benefits of service learning on school engagement and bonding and provides information about promising evidence-based programs.

*http://www.truancyprevention.org*

The National Center for School Engagement's website provides information on promising programs, detailed annotated bibliographies, and access to a program evaluation service to support attendance, attachment, and achievement.

*http://www.bocyf.org/Increasing_High_School_Students_Engagement.html*

The website of the National Academy of Sciences' Board on Children, Youth, and Families provides a link to the expert committee report *Engaging Schools:*

*Fostering High School Students' Motivation to Learn.* The report gives the conclusions of the BOCYF Committee on Increasing High School Students' Engagement and Motivation to Learn.

*http://www.allaboutkids.umn.edu*

The website for the Division of General Pediatrics and Adolescent Health, University of Minnesota has information taken from the National Study of Adolescent Health, which includes updates about the protective influence of school connectedness.

## REFERENCES

Abbott, R. D., O'Donnell, J., Hawkins, J. D., Hill, K. G., Kosterman, R., & Catalano, R. F. (1998). Changing teaching practices to promote achievement and bonding to school. *American Journal of Orthopsychiatry, 68,* 542–552.

Anderman, L. H., & Anderman, E. M. (1999). Social predictors of changes in students' achievement goal orientations. *Contemporary Educational Psychology, 25,* 21–37.

Battistich, B., & Hom, A. (1997). The relationship between students' sense of their school as a community and their involvement in problem behaviors. *American Journal of Public Health, 87,* 1997–2001.

Battistich, V., Schaps, E., Watson, M., Solomon, D., & Lewis, C. (2000). Effects of the Child Development Project on students' drug use and other problem behaviors. *Journal of Primary Prevention, 21,* 75–99.

Battistich, V., Schaps, E., & Wilson, N. (2004). Effects of an elementary school intervention on students' "connectedness" to school and social adjustment during middle school. *Journal of Primary Prevention, 24,* 243–262.

Block, J., Everson, S., & Guskey, T. (1995). *School improvement programs: A handbook for educational leaders.* New York: Scholastic. (ERIC Number: ED381856).

Bronfenbrenner, U. (1986). Ecology of the family as a context for human development: Research perspectives. *Developmental Psychology, 22,* 723–742.

Caraway, K., Tucker, C. M., Reinke, W. M., & Hall, C. (2003). Self-efficacy, goal orientation, and fear of failure as predictors of school engagement in high school students. *Psychology in the Schools, 40,* 417–427.

Connell, J. P., Spencer, M. B., & Aber, J. L. (1994). Educational risk and resilience in African-American youth: Context, self, action, and outcomes in school. *Child Development, 65,* 493–506.

Dornbusch, S. M., Erickson, K. G., Laird, J., & Wong, C. A. (2001). The relation of family and school attachment to adolescent deviance in diverse groups and communities. *Journal of Adolescent Research, 16,* 396–422.

Eggert, L. L., Thompson, E. A., Herting, J. R., Nicholas, L. J., & Dicker, B. G. (1994). Preventing adolescent drug abuse and high school dropout through an intensive school-based social network development program. *American Journal of Health Promotion, 8,* 202–215.

Finn, J. D. (1989). Withdrawing from school. *Review of Educational Research, 59,* 117–142.

Fredericks, J. A., Blumenfeld, P. C., & Paris, A. H. (2004). School engagement: Potential of the concept, state of the evidence. *Review of Educational Research, 74,* 59–109.

Fulk, B. M., Brigham, F. J., & Lohman, D. A. (1998). Motivation and self-regulation: A comparison of students with learning disabilities and behavior problems. *Remedial and Special Education, 19,* 300–309.

Furlong, M. J., & Morrison, G. M. (2000). The SCHOOL in school violence. *Journal of Emotional and Behavioral Disorders, 8,* 71–82.

Furlong, M. J., Morrison, G. M., & Pavelski, R. (2000). Trends in school psychology for the 21st century: Influences of school violence on professional change. *Psychology in the Schools, 37,* 81–90.

Furlong, M. J., Whipple, A. D., St. Jean, G., Simental, J., Soliz, A., & Panthuna, S. (2003). Multiple contexts of school engagement: Moving toward a unifying framework for educational research and practice. *California School Psychologist, 8,* 99–114.

Galliher, R. V., Rostosky, S. S., & Hughes, H. K. (2004). School belonging, self-esteem, and depressive symptoms in adolescents: An examination of sex, sexual attraction status, and urbanicity. *Journal of Youth and Adolescence, 33,* 235–245.

Goodenow, C. (1993). The psychological sense of school membership among adolescents: Scale development and educational correlates. *Psychology in the Schools, 30,* 79–90.

Gutman, L. M., & Midgley, C. (2000). The role of protective factors in supporting the academic achievement of poor African American students during the middle school transition. *Journal of Youth and Adolescence, 29,* 223–248.

Hawkins, D. J., Guo, J., Hill, K. G., Battin-Pearson, S., & Abbott, R. D. (2001). Long-term effects of the Seattle Social Development Intervention on school bonding trajectories. *Applied Developmental Science, 5,* 225–236.

Hawkins, D. J., & Lishner, D. (1987). Etiology and prevention of antisocial behavior in children and adolescents. In D. H. Crowell & I. M. Evans (Eds.), *Childhood aggression and violence: Sources of influence, prevention, and control* (pp. 263–282). New York: Plenum Press.

Hirschi, T. (1969). *Causes of delinquency.* Berkeley, CA: University of California Press.

Jimerson, S., Campos, E., & Greif, J. (2003). Towards an understanding of definitions and measures of school engagement and related terms. *California School Psychologist, 8,* 7–28.

Johnson, M. K., Crosnoe, R., & Elder, G. H. (2001). Students' attachment and academic engagement: The role of race and ethnicity. *Sociology of Education, 74,* 318–340.

Kaminski, R. A., Stormshack, E. A., Good, R. H., & Goodman, M. R. (2002). Prevention of substance abuse with rural Head Start children and families: Results of Project STAR. *Psychology of Addictive Behaviors, 16*(4S), 11–26.

Kumpfer, K. L., Alvarado, R., Tait, C., & Turner, C. (2002). Effectiveness of school-based family and children's skills training for substance abuse prevention among 6- to 8-year-old rural children. *Psychology of Addictive Behaviors, 16*(4S), 65–71.

Morrison, G. M., Cosden, M. A., O'Farrell, S. L., & Campos, E. (2003). If all students belong at school, why don't they believe it? Factors related to perceptions of school belonging for Latino students. *California School Psychologist, 8,* 87–98.

Morrison, G. M., & O'Farrell, S. L. (2004). *Victimization and problem behavior: Influence of social contextual factors.* Poster session presented at the annual meeting of the American Psychological Association, Honolulu, HI.

Mouton, S. G., Hawkins, J., McPherson, R. H., & Copley, J. (1996). School attachment: Perspectives of low-attached high school students. *Educational Psychology, 16,* 297–304.

Murdock, T. (1999). The social context of risk: Status and motivational predictors of alienation in middle school. *Journal of Educational Psychology, 91,* 62–75.

Murray, C., & Greenberg, M. T. (2001). Relationships with teachers and bonds with school: Social emotional adjustment correlates for children with and without disabilities. *Psychology in the Schools, 38,* 25–41.

O'Donnell, J., Hawkins, D. J., & Abbott, R. D. (1995). Predicting serious delinquency and substance use among aggressive boys. *Journal of Consulting and Clinical Psychology, 63,* 529–537.

O'Donnell, J., Hawkins, D. J., Catalano, R. F., Abbott, R. D., & Day, L. E. (1995). Preventing school failure, drug use, and delinquency among low-income children: Long-term intervention in elementary schools. *American Journal of Orthopsychiatry, 65,* 87–100.

O'Farrell, S. L. (2004). *Exploring school belonging trajectories in upper elementary students using latent variable growth curve modeling.* Unpublished doctoral dissertation, University of California: Santa Barbara.

O'Farrell, S. L., Fisher, E., & Redding, M. (2004). *School belonging in Latino communities: An investigation of trajectories in behaviorally at-risk students.* Poster session presented at the 10th biennial meeting of the Society for Research on Adolescence, Baltimore, MD.

O'Farrell, S. L., & Morrison, G. M. (2003). A factor analysis exploring school bonding and related constructs among upper elementary aged students. *California School Psychologist, 8,* 53–72.

Osterman, K. F. (2000). Students' need for belonging in the school community. *Review of Educational Research, 70,* 323–367.

Pantin, H., Coatsworth, J. D., Feaster, D. J., Newman, F. L., Briones, E., Proado, et al. (2003). *Familias unidas*: The efficacy of an intervention to promote parental investment in Hispanic immigrant families. *Prevention Science, 4,* 189–201.

Pierson, L. H., & Connell, J. P. (1992). Effect of grade retention on self-system processes, school engagement, and academic performance. *Journal of Educational Psychology, 84,* 300–307.

Reynolds, D., Teddlie, C., Creemers, B., Scheerens, J., & Townsend, T. (2000). An introduction to school effectiveness research. In C. Teddlie & D. Reynolds (Eds.), *The international handbook of school effectiveness research* (pp. 3–25). New York: Falmer Press.

Robertson, L. M., Harding, M. S., & Morrison, G. M. (1998). A comparison of risk and resilience indicators among Latino/a students: Differences between students identified as at-risk, learning disabled, speech impaired, and not at-risk. *Education and Treatment of Children, 21,* 333–353.

Rostosky, S. S., Owens, G. P., Zimmerman, R. S., & Riggle, E. D. B. (2003). Associations among sexual attraction status, school belonging, and alcohol and marijuana use in rural high school students. *Journal of Adolescence, 26,* 741–751.

Rumberger, R. W., & Larson, K. A. (1998). Student mobility and the increased risk of high school dropout. *American Journal of Education, 107,* 1–35.

Simons-Morton, B. G., Crump, A. D., Haynie, D. L., & Saylor, K. E. (1999). Student-school bonding and adolescent problem behavior. *Health Education Research, 14,* 99–107.

Sinclair, M. F., Christenson, S. L., Evelo, D. L., & Hurley, C. M. (1998). Dropout prevention for youth with disabilities: Efficacy of a sustained school engagement procedure. *Exceptional Children, 65,* 7–21.

Sinclair, M. F., Christenson, S. L., Lehr, C. A., & Anderson, A. R. (2003). Facilitating student engagement: Lessons learned from Check & Connect longitudinal studies. *California School Psychologist, 8,* 29–42.

Skinner, E. A., & Belmont, M. J. (1993). Motivation in the classroom: Reciprocal effects of teacher behavior and student engagement across the school year. *Journal of Educational Psychology, 85,* 571–581.

Willms, J. D. (2003). *Student engagement at school: A sense of belonging and participation—Results from PISA 2000.* Paris, France: Organization for Economic Cooperation and Development, Program for International Student Assessment.

# 5

# Student–Teacher Relationships

**Bridget K. Hamre**
**Robert C. Pianta**
*University of Virginia*

## BACKGROUND AND DEVELOPMENT

### The Importance of Student–Teacher Relationships

A sizable literature provides evidence that strong and supportive relationships between teachers and students are fundamental to the healthy development of all students in schools (e.g., see Birch & Ladd, 1998; Hamre & Pianta, 2001; Pianta, 1999). Positive student–teacher relationships serve as a resource for students at risk of school failure, whereas conflict or disconnection between students and adults may compound that risk (Ladd & Burgess, 2001). Although the nature of these relationships changes as students mature, the need for connection between students and adults in the school setting remains strong from preschool to 12th grade (Crosnoe, Johnson, & Elder, 2004). Furthermore, even as schools place increasing attention on accountability and standardized testing, the social quality of student–teacher relationships contributes to both academic and social–emotional development (e.g., Gregory & Weinstein, 2004; Hamre & Pianta, 2001). As such, student–teacher relationships provide a unique entry point for educators and others working to improve the social and learning environments of schools and classrooms. These relationships may be a direct focus of intervention or may be viewed as one important feature of successful implementation of many of the other interventions described in this volume.

As children enter formal school settings, either in preschool or kindergarten, relationships with teachers provide the foundation for successful adaptation to the social and academic environment. From the first day of school, young children must rely on teachers to provide them with the understanding and support that will allow them to get the most out of their daily interactions in the classroom. Children who form close relationships with teachers enjoy school more and get along better with peers. Positive relationships with teachers can also serve as a secure base for young children; they are better able to play and work on their own because they know that if things get difficult or if they are upset, they can count on their teacher to recognize and respond to these problems.

Relationships with teachers may be particularly important for children who display early academic or behavior problems. In one study examining children at academic risk, a group of children were designated as at risk for referral for special education or retention on the basis of low kindergarten screening scores. Those who ultimately did get retained or referred between kindergarten and second grade were compared with those who, despite being high risk, were promoted or not referred (Pianta, Steinberg, & Rollins, 1995). The children who, despite predictions of retention or referral, were ultimately promoted or not referred had far more positive relationships with their teachers than their high-risk peers who were retained or referred. Similarly, highly aggressive third- and fourth-graders who are able to form supportive relationships with teachers are more likely than other aggressive students to be well liked by peers (Hughes, Cavell, & Willson, 2001). Positive relationships with teachers may even help those behaviorally at-risk students learn more adaptive behavior, as evidenced in one recent study among a group of aggressive African American and Hispanic students in which supportive student–teacher relationships were associated with declines in aggressive behavior between second and third grade (Meehan, Hughes, & Cavell, 2003).

The need for positive relationships with teachers does not diminish as children mature. Support in teacher–student relationships may be particularly salient at transition points, such as the transition from elementary to middle school (Wentzel, 1998). Middle school

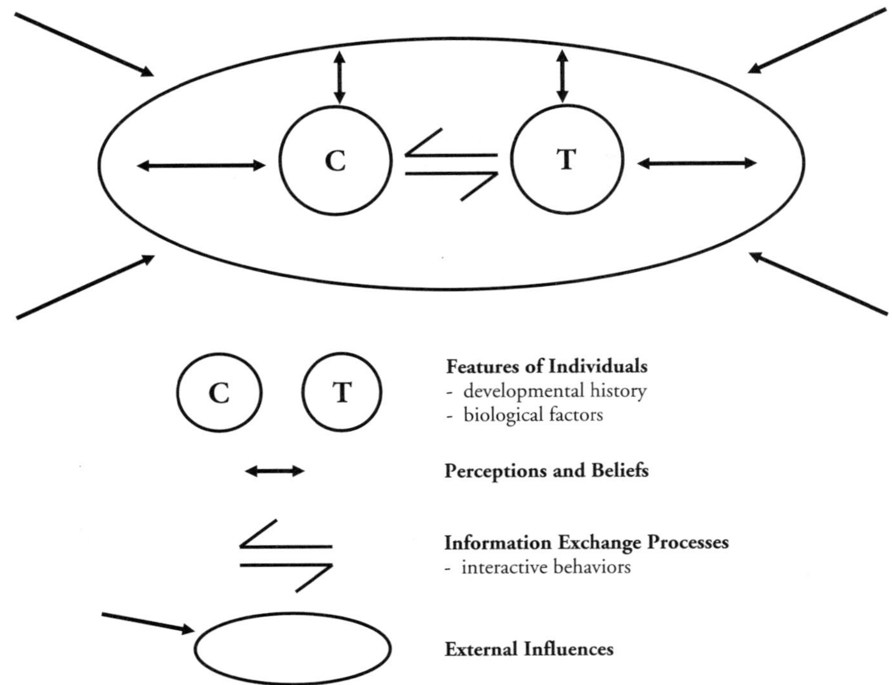


**Figure 1.** *A Conceptual Model of Teacher–Child Relationships*

teachers who convey emotional warmth and acceptance as well as make themselves available regularly for personal communication with students foster the positive relational processes characteristic of support. These supportive relationships help maintain students' interests in academic and social pursuits, which in turn lead to better grades and more positive peer relationships. Although teachers are not the only source of support for middle school students, the support students receive from their parents, peers, and teachers seemed to have additive, thus fairly independent, effects. Thus, teacher support among this age group may be particularly salient for students who have low levels of parent support (Harter, 1996).

Although students have less time with teachers during high school, there is strong evidence that relationships with adults in these settings are among the most important predictors of success. Data from the National Longitudinal Study of Adolescent Health indicate that high school students reporting greater connectedness to teachers display lower rates of emotional distress, suicidal ideation, suicidal behavior, violence, substance abuse, and early sexual activity (Resnick et al., 1997). Connection with teachers was a better predictor of many outcomes than was students' sense of family connectedness. As with young students, the benefits of positive relationships with adults are not limited to social and emotional outcomes. Although both parental and teacher support are important in predicting students' achievement, a recent study indicated that student-perceived teacher connection was the factor most closely associated with growth in achievement from 8th to 12th grade (Gregory & Weinstein, 2004).

## A Conceptual Model of Student–Teacher Relationships

Developmental systems theory (e.g., Lerner, 1998) informs the core conceptual model for student–teacher relationships. Using this theory, the development of the person-in-context is depicted as a function of dynamic processes embedded in multilevel interactions between a person and his or her contexts over time. Consistent with developmental systems theory, the conceptual model of teacher–child relationships presented by Pianta (1999) is reproduced as Figure 1. As discussed below, the primary components of relationships between teachers and students include (a) features of the individuals and their representation of the relationship, (b) processes by which information is exchanged between the relational partners, and (c) external influences of the systems in which the relationship is embedded.

***Individuals: Demographic, psychological, and developmental factors.*** At the most basic level, relationships incorporate features of individuals. They include biological facts such as gender; biological processes such as temperament, genetics, and responsiveness to stressors; developed features such as personality, self-esteem, or social skills; as well as the perceptions each individual holds of their relational partner and the relationship itself. Below teacher and student characteristics that contribute to the development of their relationships with one another are discussed.

Teacher demographic factors show a fairly inconsistent association with quality of the teacher–student relationship. Teacher experience and education have shown little relation to teachers' or students' reports about the qualities of their relationships (Stuhlman & Pianta, 2001; Wentzel, 2003). In contrast, teachers' beliefs and perceptions about students and about their own roles are much more salient to the formation of supportive relationships in the classroom. Brophy (1985) suggested that teachers view themselves primarily as instructors or socializers and that their perceptions in relation to these two roles affect the way they interact with students. Instructors tend to respond more negatively to students who are underachievers, unmotivated, or disruptive during learning tasks, whereas teachers who are socializers tend to act more negatively toward students they view as hostile, aggressive, or interpersonally disconnected. Teachers' self-efficacy beliefs may also affect the nature of the relationship they develop with students. Teachers who believe that they have an influence on students tend to interact in ways that enhance student investment and achievement (Midgley, Feldlaufer, & Eccles, 1989). Furthermore, when teachers hold high generalized expectations for student achievement, students tend to achieve more, experience a greater sense of self-esteem and competence as learners, and resist involvement in problem behaviors during both childhood and adolescence (e.g., Roeser, Eccles, & Sameroff, 1998); thus, these expectations are quite salient to student–teacher relationships.

Teachers' mental health may also play a role in relational experiences, as evidenced by two recent studies. Among a group of child care providers and preschool teachers, caregivers reporting more depressive symptoms were less sensitive and more likely to engage in negative interactions with young students (Hamre & Pianta, 2004), likely resulting in less positive relationships. Teachers experiencing a recent loss or depression in their personal lives were also more likely to respond in a dependent fashion to students' needs and have difficulty establishing emotional or behavioral boundaries for students (Zeller & Pianta, 2004). These teachers report their relationships with students as being a source of emotional support and comfort. Little is known about the consequences of this type of emotional investment on the part of teachers, but an extensive body of research on parenting suggests that a lack of boundaries can be harmful to children's social development.

Just as teachers bring features of themselves into the classroom, students begin to make impressions on a teacher from the moment they enter a classroom, impressions that are important in the formation of the relationships that develop over the course of the school year. Some characteristics, such as gender, are both static and readily apparent to teachers, whereas others are more psychological or behavioral in nature.

Students' relationships with teachers change from elementary to junior high school. Relationships between teachers and students become less personal, more formal, more evaluative, and more competitive (Harter, 1996; Lynch & Cicchetti, 1997). These changes can lead to more negative self-evaluations and attitudes toward learning because the impersonal and evaluative nature of the relational context in junior high does not match well with the students' relational needs (Roeser & Galloway, 2002). This disparity applies particularly to students who have lower levels of intrinsic motivation, in that teacher–student relationships (typically viewed as potential resources) can actually exacerbate risk if they either are not positive or do not match the developmental needs of the student (Harter, 1996).

Across grade levels, girls tend to form closer and less conflictual relationships with their teachers than do boys (e.g., Bracken & Craine, 1994; Ryan, Stiller, & Lynch, 1994). Unfortunately the disproportionately female teaching workforce in elementary and middle schools makes it difficult to determine whether this consistent finding is a reflection of gender bias. Findings from the adolescent literature suggest that relational closeness may be higher for gender-matched dyads (Drevets, Benton, & Bradley, 1996), but absent a major shift in staffing of elementary and middle schools, the consequence remains the same: Boys are at greater risk of relational difficulties in schools.

Other student characteristics that may be linked to the relationships students develop with teachers include their own social and academic competencies and problems. In particular, disruptive behavior (observed, self-reported, and teacher-reported) is consistently associated with formation of less supportive and more conflictual relationships (Hamre & Pianta, 2001; Ladd, Birch, & Buhs, 1999; Murray & Greenberg, 2000). According to Ladd et al., this connection between behavior and relationships may be the result, in part, of the relational style of the student (moving toward, away, or against), as discussed later in this chapter.

***Information exchange processes: Feedback loops between student and teacher.*** As with any system, the components of the student–teacher relationship interact in reciprocal exchanges, or loops, in which feedback is provided across components, allowing information to be calibrated and integrated in the feedback loops. In one way, dyadic relationships can be characterized by these feedback processes. This view of interaction as *carrying information* is somewhat broader than that of interaction as *reinforcing* or not. This perspective makes explicit the link between interaction and the participants' interpretation of the information embedded in the interaction, which is consistent with the focus on relational units of analysis. Furthermore, the qualities of information or how it is exchanged (tone of voice, posture and proximity, timing of behavior, or contingency or reciprocity of behavior) may be even more important than what is actually said or done.

Research on student–teacher interactions as they relate to student motivation provides some insight into associations between these interactions and the quality of student–teacher relationships. For example, a study of upper elementary teachers found that students had positive perceptions of the teacher when teachers were more involved with students within the social environment (Skinner & Belmont, 1993). A reciprocal association was found between teacher and student behavior: Teacher involvement fostered students' classroom engagement, and that engagement, in turn, led teachers to become more involved. This study and others suggest that students who are able to form strong relationships with teachers are at an advantage that may grow exponentially as the year progresses.

***External influences.*** Teachers and students do not interact in isolation; they are a part of a larger school community that may support or constrain the development of positive relationships. It is difficult to disentangle the extent to which student–teacher relationships and school climate influence one another, and the extent to which the balance of influence shifts as students grow older and their experiences become more widely distributed within a school. Nonetheless, there is ample evidence that school climate and the quality of student–teacher relationships share a reciprocal association (e.g., Crosnoe et al., 2004).

One interesting line of research in this area has highlighted the increasing mismatch between students' continuing need for emotional support and schools' increasing departmentalization and impersonal climate as students move from elementary to middle school (e.g., Roeser et al., 1998). Teacher–student interactions that lead students to feel supported by their teachers, and smaller communities of teachers and students, are important in enhancing young adolescents' motivation and emotional well-being. Unfortunately, in most middle schools, students spend very little time each day with any one teacher, thus limiting their ability to form close connections. Furthermore, many middle schools approach students' social and instructional needs from a perspective in which management is the goal. The ensuing control-oriented organization and techniques often backfire, creating less motivation and increasing student disengagement and hostility. These school-level effects on student–teacher relations have important implications for school-wide intervention, as discussed in the next section.

In sum, in student–teacher relationships, both parties bring an assortment of goals, feelings, needs, and behavioral styles that will ultimately affect the quality of the relationship they form and, in turn, influence the value of their experiences with one another in the classroom. These relationships may be further enhanced or constrained by external factors such as the climate and physical features of schools and classrooms.

## PROBLEMS AND IMPLICATIONS

Over the past 10 years, research on student–teacher relationships has focused on the ways in which these relationships may affect students' peer relations, parent–child relationships, academic competence, and social and emotional adjustment (for review see Pianta, Hamre, & Stuhlman, 2003). In the previous section some of the ways in which relationships between students and teachers can promote more positive outcomes were considered. In contrast, students who have difficulty forming supportive relationships with teachers are at greater risk of school failure. Poor relationships may be conceptualized as producing concurrent risk, with conflict between a student and teacher that leads to problems in the classroom during that school year, or chronic risk, with students developing a pattern of negative relationships with teachers over time. Unfortunately, most of the research on poor student–teacher relationships as a source of risk has focused on elementary school students. Research on student–teacher relationships with older students has generally focused on the supportive context of relationships (e.g., Harter, 1996; Wentzel, 1998).

At least for younger children, relational stressors, such as student–teacher conflict, may be more powerful predictors of school adjustment than relational supports (Ladd et al., 1999). For example, in a study of kindergartners (Birch & Ladd, 1998; Ladd et al., 1999), children with greater conflict with teachers displayed lower levels of classroom participation and achievement. For some children, these early relational problems develop into more long-standing, chronic risks. Children develop a generalized interpersonal style (moving toward, moving against, or moving away) that characterizes their interactions with peers and with teachers. That relational style, which crosses socioeconomic levels, is related in predictable ways to the quality of relationships children form with teachers and peers in the classroom during early elementary school (Birch & Ladd, 1998). Those children who display *moving against* behaviors in kindergarten, such as verbal and physical aggression toward teachers and peers, are more likely to form negative relationships with teachers in first and second grade (Ladd & Burgess, 1999). Also, chronic student–teacher conflict is associated with increased problems of attention and behavior and decreased cooperation, participation, and positive attitude toward school from kindergarten to first grade (Ladd & Burgess, 2001). Chronic student–teacher conflict is a particularly strong predictor of poor outcomes for aggressive children.

These findings suggest that early relational difficulties are important indicators of problems throughout students' school careers. Indeed, a study by Hamre and Pianta (2001) demonstrated that conflict in the student–teacher relationship reported by kindergarten teachers predicted achievement test scores, disciplinary infractions, and school suspensions through eighth grade. Conflict was a better predictor of sustained academic and disciplinary problems than were teacher ratings of students' behavior problems. That suggests that students' relational capacities may be more salient than behavior problems to students' ability to adjust to the classroom environment and thus a better indicator of future school difficulties.

Although we know something about how the nature of student–teacher relationships may change as students mature (Harter, 1996), we know almost nothing about the implications of the developmental changes on the function of student–teacher relationships within the school environment. For example, young children rely extensively on teachers to structure their daily experiences, regulate their emotions and behavior, and facilitate connections with peers. Consequently, student–teacher relationships are likely to have a somewhat diffuse influence on many aspects of young children's classroom experiences. As children get older and their ability to form relationships with teachers becomes more circumscribed, however, the function of these relationships may move toward providing links to resources outside of classroom.

To better understand these potential developmental shifts, researchers need to perform longitudinal studies that specifically examine changes in the nature and function of student–teacher relationships and to perform more studies on the consequences of negative relationships among older students and teachers.

## ALTERNATIVE ACTIONS FOR PREVENTION

In considering applications of knowledge about student–teacher relationships across the many levels of organization and processes in schools, researchers approach the task with a bias toward deploying resources (or techniques) before problems emerge, with the distinct goal of enhancing wellness and strengthening developmental competencies (Cowen, 2000). It is in that context that improved relationships between teachers and students are either (a) a focus of intervention efforts or (b) a by-product of other efforts directed at students, teachers, classrooms, or schools. Using Eccles's and Roeser's (1999) model of school processes and structure, researchers can discuss an assortment of educational and psychological applications that improve student–teacher relationships, either directly or indirectly, as a consequence of other improvements in the network of systems in which the relationship is embedded. Eccles's and Roeser's model of the context of schooling (Eccles & Roeser, 1999) is a helpful organizing framework because of its focus on understanding the multiple layers of school organization and processes. Below, applications are discussed related to (a) organizational ethos of the school, its structure, and its resources; (b) classroom ethos and structure and the characteristics of the teacher; and (c) social interactions between teachers and students.

**Table 1** *School-Wide Steps Supporting Positive Student–Teacher Relationships*

| Goal | Steps |
|---|---|
| *Increase the amount of time that students and teachers spend together.* | Organize nonacademic extracurricular activities for students and teachers to participate in together.<br>Have students and teachers eat lunch together in small, consistent groups at least a few times a week.<br>Have homeroom teachers act as advisers for students. Decrease the number of transitions and "pullouts" (e.g., art, P.E., library) during the school day.<br>Have parents and paraprofessionals in classrooms to facilitate more small-group and individual time between teachers and students. |
| *Expand the network of adults who are available to students.* | Create opportunities for nonclassroom staff, such as specialists, office staff, janitors, and others, to engage with students in fun, after-school activities. |
| *Model caring relationships from the top down.* | Involve administrators in teachers' planning and activities.<br>Teachers who feel that administrators are genuinely interested and supportive of their work are likely to impart this same interest and support to their students.<br>Have teams of teachers and administrators meet regularly to discuss problems and successes with individual students. |
| *Develop disciplinary policies that carry high expectations for students while fostering caring relationships.* | Use mediation strategies as alternatives to punitive discipline.<br>Have teachers, parents, and administrators form collaborative teams to work together on comprehensive plans for students with chronic behavioral difficulties.<br>Develop school-wide systems that reward positive behavior, rather than just punish misbehavior. |

## Influence of School-Level Approaches on Student–Teacher Relationships

In a comprehensive review of whole-school restructuring projects and their consequences for student mental health, Felner, Favazza, Shim, & Brand (2001) concluded that often there is a "mismatch between the conditions and practices students encounter in grades K–12 and the developmental needs, readiness, and capacities of students" (p. 179). One of these needs is to form functional, effective, supportive relationships with peers and with adults in the school setting. The structure or organization of a school community greatly affects the way students and teachers feel about the time they spend at school. An emotionally and socially positive school climate contributes to the development of students' self-confidence, teachers' belief that they can be effective in their jobs, and an atmosphere of cordiality in student–teacher relationships. Results from several large studies that examined mechanisms for creating such "caring communities" suggest that schools would benefit from emphasizing the importance of building and maintaining supportive, caring relationships between teachers and students (Battistich, Solomon, Watson, & Schaps, 1997).

The ability of middle and high school students to form supportive relationships with teachers is often constrained by the structure of the school day. They have short periods of time with up to six or seven different teachers over the course of the day. Changes to that structure can foster relationships by increasing the amount of time that teachers and students spend together. In Felner et al.'s (2001) approach to that challenge (which is widely used in large schools), teams of 60 to 100 students have classes together and have consistent homeroom advisers and counselors. Time is allotted for all teachers to meet and discuss students, to integrate curriculum, and to increase coherence and the support available to students. Such school restructuring efforts reduce complexity for students and build a sense of continuity and community, critically, increasing and stabilizing contact between students and a teacher or teachers. Schools report 40–50% declines in school dropout, maintenance of achievement levels, and fewer student- and teacher-reported behavioral or emotional problems. Not surprisingly, teachers also report higher job satisfaction and less burnout. Table 1 presents some other practical steps that schools can take to create a more caring community.

One underlying goal of many of these strategies is to encourage staff members to learn more about students' lives outside the classroom so that they can connect with students on a more personal level. These efforts communicate to students that adults are genuinely interested in them as individuals and that they care about what is going on in their students' lives.

## Classroom Practices and Student–Teacher Relationships

Although the school-level preventions described above often contain classroom-level efforts, other prevention programs have focused exclusively on improving the classroom climate and the quality of interaction between students and teachers.

***Teaching teachers and students about social and emotional development.*** Explicit teaching of social and emotional skills and behavioral regulation fosters relational development by providing students with opportunities to talk about difficult feelings and situations in a safe and supportive environment. Social–emotional curriculums, such as PATHS (Promoting Alternative Thinking Strategies), as described in Greenberg, Kusche, Cook, & Quamma (1995), are designed to help students identify and label feelings and social interactions, reflect on these feelings and interactions, and generate solutions and alternatives for interpretation and behavior, and allow them to test such alternatives. Social–emotional programs are effective in altering the quality of the classroom climate and relationships within the classroom (Conduct Problems Prevention Research Group, 1999) by providing students with a larger emotional vocabulary, a more advanced ability to connect basic emotions to personal experiences, a more advanced understanding of emotional cues, and more confidence that they can manage their feelings (Greenberg et al., 1995). All of these factors are essential building blocks to the development of positive student–teacher relationships.

Student–teacher relationships, and the student–teacher interactions that promote them, may also be the specific target of intervention in professional development efforts involving teachers. Teachers can learn specific strategies and techniques that will help them form more supportive relationships with all students in their classroom. A few such strategies are discussed below.

***Engaging in frequent social conversation with students.*** Talking with students about their lives outside of school is one way teachers can show an interest in and appreciation for students. Teachers may ask students questions about how things are going in other classes, in their after-school activities, or at home. It is important for teachers to show genuine interest in students' responses by spending time listening, asking follow-up questions, and remembering key information (such as the name of a sports team, or the class that the student is having a hard time in) to ask about later. Such conversations are often made more comfortable by having them during fun activities such as playing a board game or shooting baskets with a student during recess. Young students, in particular, often initiate conversations with teachers at inopportune times, such as during the middle of a lesson. Teachers can easily convey interest without sacrificing productivity by saying something such as, "I'm really interested in hearing more about that. Let's talk about it some more after we are done with this."

***Being available to students who are having a hard time.*** Adults in schools can provide an important resource for students who are having difficulties, but often the school day is too busy for teachers to make themselves available to the students in that way. By letting students know that they are available 15 or 30 minutes before or after school, even if it is just a few days a week, teachers can provide an important opening for students who need to talk with an adult.

***Displaying regard for students' perspectives and ideas.*** Teachers can work on establishing more positive relationships even during academic times of the school day. One way to do that is by actively seeking and facilitating opportunities for students to share their views and thoughts on academic subjects. Teachers who try to make curriculum meaningful to students, by incorporating aspects of their and the students' real lives and going with the flow of students' ideas during discussions, also indicate a greater regard for their students.

***Using behavior management strategies that clearly communicate expectations and caring.*** The way teachers choose to deal with misbehavior is key to developing supportive relationships in the classroom. From a relational perspective (Pianta, 1999), well-designed behavior management systems (a) provide clear limits and tolerances that help regulate students' behavior, (b) reinforce the idea that teachers will respond in expected (and fair) ways, (c) create opportunities to give students positive feedback about their behavior, and (d) are implemented in a way that communicates care and respect of students. A relational perspective of behavior management, as distinguished from a strict behavior modification framework, applies the notion that teachers can reduce behavior problems most effectively by spending more time with students. That is in contrast to some behavioral models, which suggest that students' misbehavior may be reinforced by attention from teachers.

These behavior management approaches are the centerpiece of an Internet-based tool that is currently being evaluated in a randomized field trial in prekindergarten classrooms (Pianta, Kinzie, Justice, Pullen, Fan, & Lloyd, 2003). The Internet resource MyTeachingPartner (*http://www.MyTeachingPartner.net*) offers teachers a two-level mechanism of professional development content and support. Using this resource, teachers can access hundreds of video examples of classroom interactions with students, along with detailed text descriptions of aspects of interaction that promote, among other things, more positive relationships. The resource provides a second layer of support to teachers who are in situations requiring intervention by giving them ongoing and individualized feedback on interactions in their own classrooms. Teachers can send in videotapes of their classrooms on a regular two-week cycle. The MyTeachingPartner consultant edits the tapes and gives feedback, then makes the edited tape with feedback available on the teacher's private webpage. After the teacher has reviewed the edited tape and comments, the teacher and the consultant then meet face-to-face for conversation that takes place over the Internet. This two-week cycle repeats continuously over the course of the academic year. In theory, this consulting process, because it is based on actual observations of the teachers' own classroom interactions, will provide them with a resource for professional development as well as lead to higher quality student–teacher interactions. This method of delivery needs further study but offers an innovative option for providing highly individualized feedback to teachers on a large scale.

## ALTERNATIVE ACTIONS FOR INTERVENTION

The prevention efforts described above focus largely on enhancing the promotive and protective relational resources available to students at the school and classroom level. However, even the best teachers struggle at times to form positive relationships with certain students. These strained relationships begin to interfere with the learning environment, draining energy from teachers and leading to more frequent and serious disruptions in the classroom. Thus, even a single negative student–teacher relationship can affect many students in the classroom.

The most important components of a relationally based intervention with students who are having difficulties in the classroom include (a) conducting a thorough assessment, (b) creating time to spend with the student in which the focus is on building more positive interactions, and (c) finding ways to support the student throughout the day by creating and communicating consistent relational themes.

### Relational Assessment

Although it is beyond the scope of this chapter to describe in detail some options for assessing relationships between teachers and students (see Pianta, Hamre, & Stuhlman, 2003), we present here a few key points that will help teachers, psychologists, or others to create the most effective and responsive interventions for students with relational difficulties. When describing the quality of relationships, one must approach the task from multiple points of view using multiple assessments of relational components. Relationships can be described from the inside and from the outside, with data on both the student's and the teacher's perceptions, behaviors, and beliefs. Using any one source of information about relationships almost always results in an indirect and incomplete assessment; therefore, talking with the teacher and student and conducting observations in the classroom provide important and unique information for designing an intervention. Looking for and assessing potential resources in the student–teacher relationship are also important. Being able to identify times in which things go relatively well for the student and teacher may provide information about positive aspects of the teacher–student relationship or context that the teacher can draw on in more challenging times.

## Creation of Relational Capital

A number of interventions are designed specifically to create more positive interactions between teachers and the students with whom they have the most conflict. These interventions include Primetime (Hughes, Cavell, & Jackson, 1999); Teacher–Child Interaction Therapy (McIntosh, Rizza, & Bliss, 2000); and Students, Teachers and Relationship Support (STARS; Pianta & Hamre, 2001). Although the interventions are relatively new and need more research to demonstrate efficacy, each has a strong theoretical base and derives from well-validated student–teacher interventions.

Common to all of these interventions is a focus on helping teachers and students develop new and more supportive ways of interacting with one another throughout the school day. Banking Time, the technique used in STARS to improve student–teacher interactions (Pianta, 1999; Pianta & Hamre, 2001), uses brief, regular play and interaction sessions in which the teacher plays the role of follower and listener. Its name is derived from the idea that relationships can be a resource that teachers and students rely on during their day-to-day interactions. When interactions are positive, the relationship provides support or "capital" that can be drawn on in stressful circumstances.

In Banking Time sessions, the teacher's behavior is highly constrained in order to produce changes in interaction style and in beliefs. The emphasis in Banking Time sessions is on the student's choice of activities, the regular occurrence of sessions (not contingent on the student's good behavior), neutral verbalizations from the teacher (not focused on the student's performance), and relational messages that convey safety, support for exploration, or predictability, to help the student and teacher define their relationship. When implementing Banking Time with a target student (typically a student with whom the teacher reports high levels of relational conflict), teachers report changes in communication with the student (the student more readily shares personal information) and less relational conflict. They also feel more effective in their interactions with the student and report knowing the student better than before.

The Banking Time technique acts on nearly every component of a relationship between a student and an adult; thus, it is a powerful source of pressure on the relationship system. By constraining the adult's behavior, a variant of the typical interaction is created that is reportedly viewed as different, novel, and better by most student and adult participants. The student is freed to display behaviors (and competencies) that are not typically seen in routine interactions between teacher and student. The student often explores interacting at a higher level and shows interest in the teacher and the teacher's attention. In turn, the teacher may reexamine or change his or her perceptions. Thus, new pathways or dimensions of feedback and communication between teacher and student become possible.

The STARS approach also involves a set of other procedures that act on teachers' perceptions about students. The procedures include videotaping interactions with students in the classroom for review with the consultant, reflecting on relationships with students through directed interviews, and analyzing classroom instruction and disciplinary practices. In combination with Banking Time sessions, the techniques offer a comprehensive approach to interventions in student–teacher relationships.

## Creation and Communication of Relational Themes

Teachers have opportunities throughout the school day to help change the nature and quality of their relationships with the most difficult students. One way they can do this is to identify specific themes or messages that may need to be communicated to the student and then to seek opportunities to reinforce these themes throughout the school day. Relational themes that will help reinforce the work being done during one-on-one sessions include messages such as "You are important," "Adults can be helpers," and "I am consistent." Table 2 lists some possible relational themes, along with examples of ways teachers can reinforce these throughout the school day (Pianta & Hamre, 2001).

# SUMMARY

Throughout this chapter it was argued that students' relationships with teachers are fundamental to their success in school, and as such, these relationships should be explicitly targeted in school-based prevention and intervention efforts. Student–teacher relationships develop over the course of the school year through a complex intersection of student and teacher beliefs, attitudes, behaviors, and interactions with one another. Forming strong and supportive relationships with teachers allows students to feel safer and more secure in the school setting, feel more competent, make more positive

**Table 2** *Relational Themes and Ways to Communicate Them in the Classroom*

| Relational Themes | Ways to Communicate Relational Themes in the Classroom |
|---|---|
| *I am interested in you.* | Take a few minutes out of class preparation time to watch the child during P.E., her forte. |
| *I accept you.* | When the teacher or adult brings the student to you for starting a fight on the playground for the second time in a day, make an effort to communicate your frustration with compassion and calmness. |
| *Adults can be helpers.* | During an activity that you know is hard for the student, make a point of telling him before he begins that if he is having trouble you are available to support him. |
| *I am consistent.* | Tell the student that you are always around for the last 5 minutes of lunch if he needs to talk. Make sure you are there. |
| *I am safe.* | When he comes to you in tears because other children are teasing him, you listen, provide support, and take appropriate action to prevent a recurrence. |
| *You have competencies.* | Praise the student the first time she is able to sit through circle time without being asked to keep her hands to herself. |
| *I will be here even when things get tough.* | Make a point of listening to his side even when he is to blame for starting a fight with a classmate. |
| *I can read your signals and will respond to them.* | Notice when the student comes in more quietly than usual from recess and take a moment to ask how she's doing. |

connections with peers, and make greater academic gains. In contrast, conflict with teachers may place students on a trajectory of school failure in which they are unable to connect to academic and social resources offered within classrooms and schools.

The theoretical and empirical study of student–teacher relationships has led to the development of programs designed to promote students' school success by improving student–teacher relationships. Research is accumulating to support the efficacy of these efforts, but more empirical evidence is needed on aspects of these programs, such as the following: (a) the relative power of the student–teacher relationship to alter developmental trajectories in relation to the influence of the parents or peers; (b) the most effective ways to go to scale with intervention efforts targeting the student-teacher relationship; (c) how best to identify students and teachers in need of relationship support and thus target interventions; and (d) how to sustain these efforts over time and to effectively integrate them into the myriad programs for which schools are responsible. Answering these questions will refine our understanding of how teachers' relationships with students may further positive social development and academic growth and, ultimately, help make schools and classrooms more responsive to the diverse needs of today's students.

## RECOMMENDED RESOURCES

### Books and Other Printed Material

Eccles, J. S., & Gootman, J. A. (Eds.). (2002). *Community programs to promote youth development.* Washington, DC: National Academy Press.

This book discusses the features of community programs that can contribute to successful transition from adolescence to adulthood. It offers insight into ways adolescents' relationships with teachers and other adults may facilitate that transition.

Pianta, R. C, Hamre, B., & Stuhlman, M. (2003). Relationships between teachers and children. In W. Reynolds & G. Miller (Eds.), *Comprehensive handbook of psychology: Vol. 7. Educational psychology* (pp. 199–234). Hoboken, NJ: Wiley & Sons, Inc.

This chapter provides a comprehensive review of the literature on teachers' relationships with children. It summarizes historic trends in the research on child–teacher relationships and advances theoretical and applied efforts by organizing the available work that has been done across diverse areas.

Pianta, R. C. (1999). *Enhancing relationships between children and teachers.* Washington, DC: American Psychological Association.

This book aims to provide school psychologists, child psychologists, and other mental health professionals who work with children with the theoretical and technical basis for designing interventions that enhance relationships between children and teachers. The author draws on research in social development and relationship-systems theory to describe the role of child–adult relationships in the development of social and academic competencies and the potential of child–teacher relationships to promote healthy development.

### Websites

*http://www.casel.org*

This is the website for the Collaborative for Academic, Social, and Emotional Learning (CASEL). CASEL was founded in 1994 and works to establish social and emotional learning as an essential part of education, from preschool through high school. The website offers extensive resources for educators, school psychologists, and others, including reviews on the effectiveness prevention efforts in the field of social and emotional learning.

*http://www.myteachingpartner.org*

The MyTeachingPartner (MTP) website provides preschool teachers with web-based support and consultancy on effective teaching practice, with a focus on helping them develop students' language, literacy, and social relationships. An evaluation on the effectiveness of MTP is currently under way with over 230 preschool teachers throughout Virginia.

*http://www.smhp.psych.ucla.edu*

The School Mental Health Project (SMHP) was created in 1986 to pursue theory, research, practice, and training related to addressing mental health and psychosocial concerns through school-based interventions. To these ends, SMHP works closely with school districts, local and state agencies, special initiatives, organizations, and colleagues across the country.

## REFERENCES


Battistich, V., Solomon, D., Watson, M., & Schaps, E. (1997). Caring school communities. *Educational Psychologist, 32,* 137–151.

Birch, S. H., & Ladd, G. W. (1998). Children's interpersonal behaviors and the teacher–child relationship. *Developmental Psychology, 34,* 934–946.

Bracken, B. A., & Craine, R. M. (1994). Children's and adolescents' interpersonal relations: Do age, race, and gender define normalcy? *Journal of Psychoeducational Assessment, 12,* 14–32.

Brophy, J. (1985). Teachers' expectations, motives, and goals for working with problem students. In C. Ames & R. Ames (Eds.), *Research on motivation in education: Vol. 2. The classroom milieu* (pp. 175–213). New York: Academic Press.

Conduct Problems Prevention Research Group. (1999). Initial impact of the fast track prevention trial for conduct problems: II. Classroom effects. *Journal of Consulting and Clinical Psychology, 67,* 648–657.

Cowen, E. L. (2000). Psychological wellness: Some hopes for the future. In D. Cicchetti & J. Rappaport (Eds.), *The promotion of wellness in children and adolescents* (pp. 477–503). Washington, DC: Child Welfare League of America.

Crosnoe, R., Johnson, M. K., & Elder, G. H. (2004). Intergenerational bonding in school: The behavioral and contextual correlates of student–teacher relationships. *Sociology of Education, 77,* 60–81.

Drevets, R. K., Benton, S. L., & Bradley, F. O. (1996). Students' perceptions of parents' and teachers' qualities of interpersonal relations. *Journal of Youth and Adolescents, 25,* 787–802.

Eccles, J., & Roeser, R. (1999). School and community influences on human development. In M. H. Bornstein & M. E. Lamb (Eds.), *Developmental psychology: An advanced textbook* (4th ed., pp. 503–554). Mahwah, NJ: Erlbaum.

Felner, R., Favazza, A., Shim, M., & Brand, S. (2001). Whole school improvement and restructuring as prevention and promotion: Lessons from project STEP and the project on high performance learning communities. *Journal of School Psychology, 39,* 177–202.

Greenberg, M., Kusche, C., Cook, E., & Quamma, J. (1995). Promoting emotional competence in school-aged children: The effects of the PATHS curriculum. *Development and Psycholopathology, 7,* 117–136.

Gregory, A., & Weinstein, R. S. (2004). Connection and regulation at home and in school: Predicting growth in achievement for adolescents. *Journal of Adolescent Research, 19,* 405–427.

Hamre, B., & Pianta, R. (2001). Early teacher–child relationships and the trajectory of children's school outcomes through eighth grade. *Child Development, 72,* 625–638.

Hamre, B. K., & Pianta, R. C. (2004). Self-reported depression in nonfamilial caregivers: Prevalence and associations with caregiver behavior in child-care settings. *Early Childhood Research Quarterly, 19,* 297–318.

Harter, S. (1996). Teacher and classmate influences on scholastic motivation, self-esteem, and level of voice in adolescents. In J. Juvonen & K. Wentzel (Eds.), *Social motiva-tion: Understanding children's school adjustment.* New York: Cambridge University Press.

Hughes, J. N., Cavell, T. A., & Jackson, T. (1999). Influence of the teacher–student relationship on childhood conduct problems: A prospective study. *Journal of Clinical Child Psychology, 28,* 173–184.

Hughes, J. N., Cavell, T. A., & Willson, V. (2001). Further support for the developmental significance of the quality of the teacher–student relationship. *Journal of School Psychology, 39,* 289–302.

Ladd, G. W., & Burgess, K. B. (1999). Charting the relationship trajectories of aggressive, withdrawn, and aggressive/withdrawn children during early grade school. *Child Development, 70,* 910–929.

Ladd, G. W., & Burgess, K. B. (2001). Do relational risks and protective factors moderate the linkages between childhood aggression and early psychological and school adjustment? *Child Development, 72,* 1579–1601.

Ladd, G. W., Birch, S. H., & Buhs, E. S. (1999). Children's social and scholastic lives in kindergarten: Related spheres of influence? *Child Development, 70,* 1373–1400.

Lerner, R. M. (1998). Theories of human development: Contemporary perspectives. In W. Damon (Series Ed.) & R. M. Lerner (Ed.), *Handbook of child psychology: Vol. XX (5th Ed.): Theoretical Models of Human Development* (5th ed., pp. 1–24). New York: John Wiley & Sons, Inc.

Lynch, M., & Cicchetti, D. (1997). Children's relationships with adults and peers: An examination of elementary and junior high school students. *Journal of School Psychology, 35,* 81–100.

McIntosh, D. E., Rizza, M. G., & Bliss, L. (2000). Imple-menting empirically supported interventions: Teacher–child interaction therapy. *Psychology in the Schools, 37,* 453–462.

Meehan, B. T., Hughes, J. N., & Cavell, T. A. (2003). Teacher–student relationships as compensatory resources for aggressive children. *Child Development, 74,* 1145–1157.

Midgley, C., Feldlaufer, H., & Eccles, J. S. (1989). Student/teacher relations and attitudes toward mathematics before and after the transition to junior high school. *Child Development, 60,* 981–992.

Murray, C., & Greenberg, M. T. (2000). Children's relationships with teachers and bonds with schools: An investigation of patterns and correlates in middle childhood. *Psychology in the Schools, 38,* 425–446.

Pianta, R. C. (1999). *Enhancing relationships between children and teachers.* Washington, DC: American Psychological Association.

Pianta, R. C., & Hamre, B. (2001). *Students, teachers, and relationship support [STARS]: User's guide.* Lutz, FL: Psychological Assessment Resources, Inc.

Pianta, R. C., Hamre, B., & Stuhlman, M. (2003). Relationships between teachers and children. In W. Reynolds & G. Miller (Eds.), *Comprehensive handbook of psychology: Vol. 7. Educational psychology* (199–234). Hoboken NJ: Wiley & Sons.

Pianta, R., Kinzie, M., Justice, L., Pullen, P., Fan, X., & Lloyd, J. (2003). *Web training: Pre-K teachers, literacy, and relationships. Effectiveness of Early Childhood Program, Curricula, and Interventions.* Washington, DC: National Institute of Child Health and Human Development.

Pianta, R. C., Steinberg, M. S., & Rollins, K. B. (1995). The first two years of school: Teacher–child relationships and deflections in children's classroom adjustment. *Development and Psychopathology, 7,* 295–312.

Resnick, M. D., Bearman, P. S., Blum, R. W., Bauman, K., Harris, K. M., Jones, J., Tabor, J., Beuhring, T., Sieving, R. E., Shew, M., Ireland, M., Behringer, L. H., & Udry, J. R. (1997). Protecting adolescents from harm: Findings from the National Longitudinal Study of Adolescent Health. *Journal of the American Medical Association, 278,* 823–832.

Roeser, R., Eccles, J., & Sameroff, A. (1998). Academic and emotional functioning in early adolescence: Longitudinal relations, patterns, and prediction by experience in middle school. *Development and Psychopathology, 10,* 321–352.

Roeser, R. W., & Galloway, M. K. (2002). Studying motivation to learn during early adolescence: A holistic perspective. In F. Pajares & T. Urban (Eds.), *Academic motivation of adolescents* (pp. 331–372). Greenwich, CT: LAP Information Age Publishing.

Ryan, R. M., Stiller, J. D., & Lynch, J. H. (1994). Representations of relationships to teachers, parents, and friends as predictors of academic motivation and self-esteem. *Journal of Early Adolescence, 14,* 226–249.

Skinner, E. A., & Belmont, M. J. (1993). Motivation in the classroom: Reciprocal effects of teacher behavior and student engagement across the school year. *Journal of Educational Psychology, 85,* 571–581.

Stuhlman, M. W., & Pianta, R. C. (2001). Teachers' narratives about their relationships with children: Associations with behavior in classrooms. *School Psychology Review, 31,* 148–163.

Wentzel, K. (1998). Social relationships and motivation in middle school: The role of parents, teachers, and peers. *Journal of Educational Psychology, 90*(2), 202–209.

Wentzel, K. (2003). School adjustment. In W. Reynolds & G. Miller (Eds.), *Handbook of psychology: Volume 7 Educational psychology* (pp. 235–258). Hoboken, NJ: John Wiley & Sons, Inc.

Zeller, J. J., & Pianta, R. C. (2004). *Teachers' childhood attachments and teacher–student relationships.* Unpublished manuscript, University of Virginia, Charlottesville.

# 6

# Parent–Teacher Relationships

**Kathleen M. Minke**

*University of Delaware*

*"The fact of the matter is, parents and teachers just haven't known how to get along together. Because of this, we haven't been able to use the resources and good will of children, of teachers, of administrators, of parents and other citizens in developing . . . a community-centered education."*

Lane, 1948, p. 155

Over a half-century after the publication of this passage, not much has changed in helping parents and teachers "get along together." However, the need for them to do so has probably never been greater. The demand for schools to involve parents in education continues to grow, with federal regulations specifying roles for parents in planning and implementing educational programming. At the same time, increasing cultural and language diversity in U.S. schools makes it exceedingly challenging for parents and teachers to communicate and understand one another.[1]

Schools have responded by implementing an array of parent involvement (PI) initiatives, and it is generally accepted that such initiatives yield positive benefits for students, parents, and schools. However, the supporting literature has many methodological weaknesses (see Mattingly, Prislin, McKenzie, Rodriguez, & Kayzar, 2002, for a review), making it difficult to know which efforts are truly successful and what the essential variables are for creating success. This chapter briefly reviews some of the issues surrounding PI activities and posits that constructive interpersonal relationships between parents and educators are a key element in successfully marshaling family and school assets to support children's academic achievement. Although evidence-based practices in this area are still underdeveloped, the chapter also presents promising school-based strategies to create and maintain productive working relationships between parents and educators.

## BACKGROUND AND DEVELOPMENT

### The Pros and Cons of Parent Involvement

Mandated parent involvement in education has long been part of federal special education and compensatory education regulations. More recently, under the No Child Left Behind Act of 2001 (NCLB), local school districts are required to develop a parent involvement policy that not only supports effective PI activities for individual children, but also increases schools' capacity to involve parents, increases parents' capacity to participate, involves parents in the development and implementation of school review and improvement efforts, and coordinates PI activities among other programs receiving federal funds, such as Head Start (U.S. Department of Education, 2004). These ambitious goals are supported by research indicating that when parents are involved in their children's education, students show a variety of positive outcomes, including higher grades, better school attendance, greater likelihood of promotion, and higher rates of enrollment in post-secondary programs. These outcomes have been demonstrated in families from diverse cultural backgrounds, income levels, and education levels (see Henderson & Mapp, 2002, for a review). Despite the largely correlational nature of the research base (Mattingly et al., 2002), mandated PI initiatives appear to be based on the causal assumption that increasing PI improves student achievement.

[1] In this chapter, *parent* refers to any adult in a primary caregiving role. The term *teacher* is used to emphasize that relationships occur among individuals; however, all school-based personnel, not just teachers, have important roles in developing relationships with families.

There is some evidence to support that assumption. For example, students participating in Title I services whose parents were more involved (e.g., attended parent workshops) made greater gains in math and reading than students whose parents participated less (Shaver & Walls, 1998). Among low-income, urban preschool students, PI activities, especially those conducted at home such as reading to the child and asking the child about school, predicted several positive end-of-year outcomes, including better attention, persistence and receptive vocabulary (Fantuzzo, McWayne, Perry, & Childs, 2004). Furthermore, a recent meta-analysis showed an effect size of approximately 0.30 (Fan & Chen, 2001), suggesting a moderate relationship between parent involvement and subsequent student achievement. It is important to note that parents' aspirations and expectations for their children appeared to have a stronger relationship to achievement than specific parent behaviors such as supervision (see also Hong & Ho, 2005).

Such findings lead to the question of whether schools have the means to influence parents' involvement choices. Again, evidence shows that they do. For example, at the secondary school level, parents who perceived more frequent contacts from the school with respect to volunteering, helping at home, and planning post–secondary school options also reported greater involvement with education (e.g., more conversations with their teenagers about school activities, coursework, and post–high school plans and more frequent attendance at school-based workshops and activities). These relationships were observed even after controlling for socioeconomic status, ethnicity, family structure, and prior achievement (Simon, 2004). Similarly, parents who perceived greater teacher outreach—through teachers' valuing parent contributions, providing information about their children's strengths and needs, and offering suggestions on ways to help—were more involved at home and at school (Patrikakou & Weissberg, 2000). In sum, the literature generally supports the notion that increasing parent involvement is possible and that increased PI should be beneficial to students.

However, when schools reach out to families, not all families respond as anticipated. Often described as "hard to reach," these families may be labeled as uncaring and may be blamed for their children's lack of success. A downward spiral can begin wherein the teacher views the child as having parents who do not value education, leading to lowered expectations for the child's competence and future success (Hauser-Cram, Sirin, & Stipek, 2003). Low expectations of the child's ability lead to less outreach by the teacher, and parents respond with less trust in the school (Stone, 2003), presumably reinforcing the teacher's view of value differences with the family. This pattern is particularly unfortunate in that parents who are viewed as uninvolved by school personnel often see themselves as highly involved in their children's education (Lawson, 2003). The way they express that involvement, for example, by getting their children to school each day and by keeping them off the street and safe after school, often goes unrecognized (see also Huss-Keeler, 1997). Lawson describes these parents as taking a broad, "community-centric" view of what it means to be involved, whereas educators typically take a narrow, "school-centric" view in which the primary indicators of PI are being present at the school and responding to teacher requests. School-centric approaches, however, fail to account for important differences among families—in social resources, occupational flexibility, prior negative school experiences, and beliefs about what is appropriate in interactions with school personnel (e.g., Lareau & Shumar, 1996). In particular, families from cultural and linguistic minorities and families who are living in challenging socioeconomic contexts are likely to have difficulty meeting schools' expectations for involvement (e.g., Coll et al., 2002; Grolnick, Benjet, Kurowski, & Apostoleris, 1997).

## Family–School Collaboration and the Significance of Relationships

In contrast to traditional PI activities, family–school collaborative efforts have the potential to ameliorate some of the difficulties described in the previous section. Collaborative approaches are based in systems theory. From a systems perspective, the family and school contexts have overlapping influences on the child, and may support or impede optimal developmental outcomes. Furthermore, a relationship always exists between families and schools, regardless of whether this connection is acknowledged and even if school personnel never meet a particular parent (Pianta & Walsh, 1996). Through collaboration, parents and educators increase their understanding of one another's expectations for the child and for the relationship, which is expected to be beneficial to the child's success.

Collaboration requires educators and families to develop shared goals, bidirectional communication, and joint problem-solving methods. There is greater emphasis on understanding and accommodating families' diverse views, needs, and desires with respect to the families' interactions with the school. Rather than focusing solely on what educators need from parents (as is often the case in traditional PI approaches), attention is also given to finding out what families need from educators. From this perspective, educators, families, and students are seen as having complementary areas of expertise that can support student achievement. In short, collaboration relies on the development of productive interpersonal relationships, through which the expertise of all parties can be tapped (see Christenson & Sheridan, 2001, and Minke, 2000, for a more detailed discussion of family–school collaboration).

Collaborative strategies are complex and do not lend themselves to easy evaluation. Still, programs based in collaborative principles have been shown to have positive effects on a variety of outcomes, including school safety (Smith et al., 2004), adolescent behavior problems (Coatsworth, Pantin, & Szapocznik, 2002), and student achievement as part of school reform efforts (e.g., Noblit, Malloy, & Malloy, 2001).

If it is true that productive working relationships among the individuals involved are critical in collaboration, then the elements of such relationships must be defined. Although the literature uses a variety of terms, collaborative relationships are typically described as involving honesty; perceived integrity, competence, and commitment by both sides; respectfulness; and inclusiveness in decision making (e.g., Blue-Banning, Summers, Frankland, Nelson, & Beegle, 2004; Friesen, Koren, & Koroloff, 1992). As noted by Sarason (1995), "The assets of parents cannot be perceived and realized by educators unless the relationship between the two parties bears the stamp of respect and trust. And when those features are absent you have the situation where people talk, if they talk at all, past and not with each other" (p. 50).

Indeed, productive working relationships in the family–school context can be more succinctly described as trusting relationships (the following discussion of relational trust draws primarily from Adams & Christenson, 2000, and Bryk & Schneider, 2002). Relationships between parents and teachers are characterized by mutual dependence for achieving highly valued outcomes, especially children's academic success, in an environment of unequal power. Each party has expectations for the roles and responsibilities of the other in the relationship. When those expectations are similar and when both parties perceive that the other is fulfilling his or her obligations, trust grows within the relationship. Several dimensions are critical: (a) respect, demonstrated through listening and taking the other's perspective into account when planning future actions; (b) competence, or the fulfillment of one's role obligations; (c) personal regard, demonstrated through efforts to decrease the other's sense of vulnerability in the relationship; and (d) integrity or commitment to acting in the best interests of the others involved in the relationship. When any one of these elements is perceived as deficient, trust is harmed.

The development of trust depends on repeated interactions that allow each party to make judgments about the other's intentions with respect to the relationship. Although the quality of interactions, rather than the quantity, is a better predictor of trust (Adams & Christenson, 2000), when opportunities to interact are limited, each party continues to seek evidence that the other is trustworthy and the relationship remains stuck at a superficial level. Furthermore, under circumstances of limited interaction, positive behaviors may be overlooked and negative behaviors may be given undue weight, further undermining the development of trust (Bryk & Schneider, 2002). Thus, even when the elements of a trusting relationship are available, limited interaction time may harm the process.

In circumstances in which trusting relationships develop between parents and teachers, this trust becomes a resource for future interactions. For example, when problems arise, participants in a trusting relationship are much more likely to give the other the benefit of the doubt, making disagreements easier to resolve. Significantly, trust as a resource extends beyond particular problem-solving experiences. For example, even after accounting for demographic characteristics, including race, gender, ethnicity, and prior achievement, trust among parents, teachers, and students has been shown to predict academic achievement (e.g., Goddard, Tschannen-Moran, & Hoy, 2001).

It is important to remember that trusting relationships at all levels of family–school interaction are by themselves insufficient for supporting positive outcomes for students; they serve as a starting point for collaboration, not the end goal. Comprehensive, well-planned school improvement initiatives that are adapted to local needs are critical. However, the presence of relationships characterized by mutual respect, trust, and commitment to student success make it more likely that such collaborations will prosper (Bryk & Schneider, 2002).

## PROBLEMS AND IMPLICATIONS

Given the emphasis on increased parent involvement through family–school collaboration, and the recognition that trusting relationships are a critical component of collaborative efforts, why are such relationships so often missing in schools? Although reasons have been summarized in a variety of ways (see Christenson, 2003), three broad influences are cited here.

## Risks Inherent in Relationships

Relationships, in general, are not emotionally neutral. Parent–teacher relationships, in particular, have a strong emotional valence in that both parties are highly invested in the outcomes of the relationship with respect to student success. Unlike other emotionally charged relationships, however, parents and teachers do not have a choice about entering the relationship, because students typically are assigned to teachers by administrators with limited, if any, input from parents or the teachers themselves. Furthermore, their behavior in the relationship is embedded within a complex array of expectations, prior experiences, and interaction rules that may or may not be explicit and shared by both sides. In other words, it is a confusing and sometimes frightening terrain for both.

Parents often enter the relationship with little understanding of how schools work. They may have only their own, sometimes negative, experiences to draw on. They often report feeling intimidated by teachers and worry that they may somehow make things worse for their children if they speak up (e.g., Hanafin & Lynch, 2002). Teachers, too, report feelings of discomfort when interacting with parents. They worry that they will not communicate their concerns clearly and that their professional judgments will be unfairly challenged (e.g., Minke & Anderson, 2003). These concerns and anxieties make it easy for miscommunications and misunderstandings to develop, leading to conflict. Indeed, asking teachers to develop more personal relationships with parents has been described as requiring them to "move towards the danger" of emotional involvements they feel ill-equipped to manage (Maurer, 1996, cited in Hargreaves, 2001, p. 1076).

## Cultural and Language Differences

Families from cultural minorities and those living in difficult circumstances often find it challenging to meet school expectations for involvement, in part because these parents define involvement differently than teachers do. Misunderstandings grounded in these differing expectations can lead to poor relationships between parents and teachers. For example, Chinese parents' high expectations for their children and demands for perfection were seen as unduly harsh by British teachers. The parents and teachers also used different words to describe students, with teachers preferring to stress positives and parents requesting information about weaknesses. These differences in perspective and vocabulary kept parents and teachers from identifying shared goals for student improvement (Ran, 2001). Similarly, Pakistani families expressed confusion about the informal environment of British schools and did not think it appropriate for them to come to the school. Teachers tended to see these parents as uninterested in their children's education and therefore did not invest a lot of effort into forging relationships with the families (Huss-Keeler, 1997). Misunderstandings such as these occur in U.S. schools as well (see, for example, the review by Kalyanpur, Harry, & Skrtic, 2000).

When families are from groups that have experienced discrimination by the majority culture, they may approach teachers with less trust and greater worry that their children will not be treated fairly. These parents' efforts to express their concerns are sometimes interpreted by teachers as unhelpful and hostile (Lareau & Horvat, 1999). Teachers may respond by approaching interactions as an opportunity to convince parents what is best for the child, rather than as an opportunity to understand parents' perceptions (Valle & Aponte, 2002). These interactions can lead to avoidance and placating rather than genuine dialogue, problem solving, and relationship development.

## Organization and Operation of Schools

Schools typically are not organized in ways that are conducive to developing relationships. Time allotment, skills training, and specific policies may present obstacles to parents' and teachers' efforts to work collaboratively.

***Time.*** Relationships will not develop unless the parties have time and opportunities to interact. Time is a scarce commodity in schools, and lack of time is frequently cited as a primary barrier for both parents and teachers (U.S. Department of Education, 1998). The current emphasis on testing and accountability is likely to further drain time from relationship-development activities. Policies that limit time allotted to parent–teacher conferences or that fail to compensate teachers for their efforts beyond the contracted school day may also inhibit relationship development. Nevertheless, when a crisis arises with a particular student, in many cases large allotments of time become available as teachers, administrators, and parents try to repair situations that might have been prevented (Swap, 1993).

***Training.*** Relationships do not develop automatically. Especially in circumstances in which perspectives are very diverse, educators need well-developed communication skills to successfully elicit parents' views and clearly articulate their own views without shutting down the exchange. Because conflict is more likely when diverse views are expressed, educators must be able to use disagreements constructively and to solve problems effectively. The absence of these skills can lead to what Walker (1998) called "meetings without communication." However, teachers report that they receive limited training in communication skills, either at the preservice or inservice level (U.S. Department of Education, 1998). Furthermore, they report dissatisfaction with the training they do receive (e.g., Young & Hite, 1994).

***School policies and structures.*** For most students and their families, the relationship with a teacher lasts a single academic year. Furthermore, with departmentalization at the middle and high school levels, students may need to interact with many teachers, further subdividing time for relationship development. Teachers facing a six-period day with 30 students in each class have a monumental task simply getting to know their students, let alone their students' families. Very large schools may be administratively convenient, but their students find it more difficult to develop a sense of belonging and connection to the school (see chapter 5, "Student–Teacher Relationships"). Although the literature on student–teacher relationships tends to exclude discussion of families, it is reasonable to assume that school structures that limit relationship development between teachers and students have a similar effect on relationships between teachers and parents.

## ALTERNATIVE ACTIONS FOR PREVENTION AND INTERVENTION

Although some of these challenges are difficult to overcome, particularly those grounded in district-wide policies, actions can be taken at the school level to influence the quality of parent–teacher relationships. Consistent with the premise that trusting relationships are at the core of any successful PI or family–school collaboration initiative, the focus in this section is on strategies and activities specific to promoting the development of these relationships, rather than on particular PI programs. Also, given evidence that school outreach practices are a key element in effective PI (e.g., Patrikakou & Weissberg, 2000), this section emphasizes ways in which educators can promote the development of relationships, rather than ways that parents can approach educators. The strategies discussed should be considered promising for the most part because they have not yet undergone rigorous evaluation (see Shepard & Carlson, 2003). Indeed, although much is known about *what* constructive family–school relationships look like, much less is known about *how* these relationships can be developed and nurtured (Christenson & Sheridan, 2001).

### Planning for Action

The literature on organizational change makes clear that top-down initiatives, those that are imposed without the participation and support of the people who have to make the process work, are likely to fail, as are bottom-up initiatives undertaken without sufficient infrastructure support (e.g., Fullan, 2003). Because PI initiatives may grow from federal, state, and local mandates, rather than from locally identified needs, the risk is high that educators asked to implement them will perceive the initiatives negatively. Similarly, if a group of teachers and families at the local level attempt to implement change without administrative support, they may meet resistance, frustration, and defeat. Thus, efforts to improve family–school relationships must begin with a careful planning process that includes engaging in self-assessment; developing a commitment to family–school relationships among educators, administrators, and families; and creating a sustainable plan for implementing and evaluating whatever activities are initiated. Several resources in the literature may be useful to educators beginning the planning process.

Constantino (2003) describes a five-step process for engaging families (see Table 1). The process begins with a critical first step, helping participants understand why family engagement is important and how it may be useful to students, families, and educators. The process also emphasizes needs assessment and consensus building. Christenson and Sheridan (2001) are even more explicit regarding the need to take a comprehensive approach to planning. Their "four A's" (see Table 2) provide a

**Table 1** *Five-Step Model for Implementing Family Engagement Initiatives*

| Steps in Process | Overview |
|---|---|
| Awareness | • Help participants understand how the initiative will be helpful to students, families, and educators. |
| Self-Assessment | • Involve administrators, teachers, parents, and students in the evaluation.<br>• Assess the extent to which the school is welcoming to families and the ways in which outreach to families is conducted. |
| Conceptualization and Development | • Work with all stakeholders in developing shared understanding of the goals of family engagement and the roles of all involved. |
| Implementation | • Prioritize among generated ideas by examining current assets and needs.<br>• Develop policies, procedures, and practices to support changes over time. |
| Evaluating and Sustaining | • Gather and analyze data to evaluate and modify initiatives. |

*Note.* Content adapted from *Engaging All Families: Creating a Positive School Culture by Putting Research Into Practice*, by S. M. Constantino, 2003, Lanham, MD: Scarecrow Education.

blueprint that encompasses all phases of implementing a successful relationship-building process. They recommend addressing the general approach, attitudes, and atmosphere of the school context before any specific actions are contemplated. They also provide a detailed review of the literature that communicates why family–school relationships matter and the theoretical and empirical bases for supporting these relationships, giving particular attention to the ecosystemic approach (see also Vickers & Minke, 1997). Finally, they offer an inventory for needs assessment and action planning that schools may find useful. The important point is that process variables, such as attitudes toward families and beliefs about the causes of problems, are at least as important in family–school relationship building as the nature of particular practices and activities. Thus, these variables require careful attention and explicit exploration prior to embarking on relationship-building initiatives.

## Communication Skills

Trusting, productive relationships between parents and teachers cannot occur in the absence of effective communication. However, teachers receive limited preparation in this area. School-based mental health service providers, given their background in counseling and consultation, have the training and expertise to provide inservice workshops to help teachers develop communication skills. Unfortunately, although the literature contains many communication tips for teachers, well-developed and tested curricula are not easily available, and few, if any, outcome studies have been done. This situation leaves school professionals to draw on their own creativity in developing such training. Nevertheless, an examination of the communication and counseling literature (e.g., Fujishin, 2000; Ivey & Ivey, 2003) suggests a number of specific skills that should be included.

***Intrapersonal communication.*** Intrapersonal communication refers to the internal dialogue or self-talk that occurs during interactions (Ehrlich, 2000). This process allows individuals to interpret the communications of others and consider a range of possible responses. It is a form of self-reflection that influences future interactions. However, internal dialogue can interfere with communication when it is excessively negative or self-focused. That is, people cannot listen effectively when they focus primarily on how they are being received by the other person, on making a good impression, or on judging the other's intent.

A helpful exercise is to explore the kind of self-talk that is typical in parent–teacher interactions. This could be done through discussion groups or through brief sentence completions or other questionnaires (e.g., What are you likely to say to yourself when a parent drops by your classroom unexpectedly? When a parent misses an appointment? When a parent sends a gift?). Discussions of such issues should reveal some of the teachers' assumptions and interpretations of parents' behavior, which can then be explored for accuracy using an ecosystemic theoretical lens. It might also lead to the introduction of cognitive restructuring and other self-talk strategies for those teachers who find interactions with parents particularly anxiety provoking.

***Attending to nonverbal communication.*** In any communication, words form only a small part of the total information that is exchanged. Moreover, when individuals perceive a contradiction between verbal and

**Table 2** *Processes for Developing Family–School Relationships*

| Component | Definition | Sample Key Concepts to Include in Planning, Training, and Interventions |
|---|---|---|
| Approach | The framework for interaction with families | • Families are essential in supporting children's learning.<br>• Students are at the center of the family–school relationship.<br>• Interactions between families and educators are best understood through an ecological–systemic lens. |
| Attitudes | The values and perceptions held about family–school relationships | • Educators approach families with a positive attitude and a focus on strengths.<br>• Relationships are characterized by mutual respect, willingness to listen, and attention to the views of all.<br>• Educators support a nonblaming, no-fault problem-solving stance in interactions with families. |
| Atmosphere | The climate in schools for families and educators | • The school is characterized by a welcoming, respectful, inclusive, positive, and supportive climate.<br>• Family input is actively sought in making decisions.<br>• There are opportunities for parents and educators to learn from each other. |
| Actions | Strategies for building shared responsibility | • Trust building and relationship building are considered when planning family–school interactions.<br>• Attention is given to shared roles and responsibilities.<br>• Joint problem-solving across home and school settings is emphasized. |

*Note.* Content adapted from *Schools and Families: Creating Essential Connections for Learning*, by S. L. Christenson and S. M. Sheridan, 2001, New York: Guilford Press.

nonverbal elements in a message, they are more likely to put credence in their interpretation of the nonverbal message (e.g., Erhlich, 2000). Because nonverbal cues are ambiguous and vary across cultures, they are easily misinterpreted.

Training should include increasing educators' awareness of the nonverbal cues they send and the interpretations they make of others' cues. During role-playing or video demonstrations of parent–teacher interactions, participants should be invited to explore the possible meaning of variations in body posture, eye contact, use of touch, and so forth. It is important to avoid cultural stereotypes. For example, although low levels of eye contact may be more common in some cultural groups, there is great variation within groups, and assumptions should never be made about the meaning of a particular behavior. Instead, judicious use of listening and responding skills (discussed below) will enhance the chances of both parties developing a clear understanding of each other's intent. For example, if a teacher notices that a parent is looking down and is very quiet during a conference, rather than ignore the behavior or make an unverified interpretation of its meaning, the teacher could say, "I notice that I'm doing most of the talking and wonder if you are getting a chance to say everything you want." This comment might invite more participation from the parent or an explanation that the parent prefers to listen to the teacher.

***Active listening and empathic responding.*** Social listening primarily involves attending to what another is saying and engaging in reasonable turn-taking. The natural responses of relating the speaker's message to one's own experience or offering advice are usually considered appropriate in social exchanges. However, in active listening the listener's goal is to be sure the speaker's intent

**Table 3** *Guidelines for Active Listening and Empathic Responding*

- Stay quiet and focused on the other. Ask yourself, "What is the main thing this person needs me to understand?"
- Avoid making judgments or offering advice. Avoid interrupting.
- Offer a brief paraphrase of your understanding of the message. Attend to both content and affect, if appropriate.
- Try to reflect just the core message; don't list everything the other just said.
- Keep your interpretation flexible and tentative.
- Keep your response short.
- Eliminate *why* questions because they tend to make the other defensive.
- Limit the use of "I" so that the response focuses on the other, not you.
- Invite the person to continue talking.
- If the other rejects your response, try again.

is understood correctly and to communicate that understanding back to the speaker (see Table 3). It seems simple, but the technique actually requires a great deal of skill and practice.

Active listening and empathic responding are not the only skills used in relationship-building or problem-solving exchanges. Eventually the conversation will include participants' sharing ideas about ways to approach particular problems, but only after they are clearly "on the same page." The example in Table 4 illustrates the value of using empathic responding to develop shared understanding prior to problem solving. In this common scenario, a parent directly elicits advice from the teacher. The most likely teacher response would be to begin to solve the problem of homework issues. And, indeed, if the parent's central concern is homework, little harm is done if an empathic response is not given. However, if homework is not the central issue (as in the second possible parent response) and the teacher goes immediately to problem solving, both teacher and parent are likely to become frustrated with the conversation and the relationship may be harmed.

***Delivering clear messages.*** It is important for educators to feel confident in their ability to deliver information clearly and effectively. Teachers sometimes worry that in their efforts to be tactful, they may not adequately convey the degree of concern they feel about a particular

**Table 4** *Use of Empathic Responding Before Problem Solving*

*Parent*: My son is driving me crazy. At 10 years old you would think he could be responsible for himself at least a little bit! He can't accomplish a single thing unless I'm standing right there, nagging him all the way through. Homework is a nightmare! I feel like I'm the one with homework, and we struggle for at least 2 hours before it is done. This can't go on. He's not learning and I'm out of patience! How can I help him?

*Teacher (responding empathically):* It sounds as if you're very frustrated that he can't be more independent in completing his jobs and worried that what you're doing now isn't helping either one of you. Is that close?

*The parent might respond as follows:* Yes, that's it exactly. I could handle everything else if I got him on the right track with homework. (This will lead to more exploration of homework and ways the parent is already trying to solve the problem.)

*But what if the parent responded instead:* Yes, that's it exactly. I've been feeling so helpless and overwhelmed since Johnny's father has been in the hospital for these past 2 months. (This will lead to an entirely different discussion.)

problem (Minke & Anderson, 2003). However, teachers also must frame their messages in ways that parents can understand them. Table 5 offers suggestions for constructing clear messages.

***Other communication skills.*** Space does not permit a thorough review of all skills that could be included in communications training for teachers, but trainers should consider reframing, summarizing, searching for strengths,

**Table 5** *Constructing Clear Messages*

- Use a warm tone and open body posture.
- Use specific, behavioral language rather than labels or jargon (e.g., "Anthony talks to others during quiet work times nearly every day" versus "Anthony gets in other people's business and shows signs of ADHD").
- State only one or two issues at a time; avoid laundry lists of problems.
- Be brief and give the other a chance to respond.
- Convey willingness to listen to other points of view (e.g., "Is this something you have noticed also?") and optimism that the problem can be solved.

**Table 6** *Creating Relationship Development Opportunities*

| Area | Questions to Ask | Possible Changes |
|---|---|---|
| The Physical Plant | • How welcoming does the school appear?<br>• Are visitors a priority? | • Post welcome signs and mission statement in several languages.<br>• Arrange the main office in an inviting way.<br>• Greet all visitors promptly and courteously.<br>• Maintain a comfortable space for routine interactions between parents and teachers. |
| Written Communications | • Are forms and policies written in a jargon-free, readable way?<br>• How do families of limited English proficiency gain access to this information?<br>• Do documents encourage two-way communication between parents and school?<br>• Do notes home from teachers convey respect and willingness to work together? | • Review all documents for reading level.<br>• Translate documents into languages used by families.<br>• Provide access to information through oral means.<br>• Request feedback from families regarding user-friendliness of documents.<br>• Use "good news" notes.<br>• Use face-to-face communication whenever possible when problems need to be discussed. |
| School Improvement Teams | • Are parents active members of the teams?<br>• How is family input sought on school discipline, curriculum, and so forth? | • Have at least two members of all decision-making teams who are parents.<br>• Regularly collect and analyze school climate data with input from families. |
| Conferences and Problem-Solving Meetings | • How can conferences and meetings be made more relevant to family concerns?<br>• How can we ease barriers to participation? | • Develop teachers' skills in alternative conferencing methods (e.g., family–school conferences, student–led conferences).<br>• Conduct some conferences in community settings.<br>• Use conjoint behavioral consultation or family–school problem-solving meetings. |

*Note.* From *Family–School Collaboration and Positive Behavior Support: Applications at the School-wide Level*, by K. M. Minke, 2004, Newark, DE: University of Delaware, Center for Disabilities Studies; and Delaware Department of Education. Also see Christenson and Sheridan (2001) for information on conjoint behavioral consultation and family–school problem-solving meetings.

blocking blame, using questions effectively, and using immediacy comments (see Christenson & Sheridan, 2001; Minke, 2000). Counseling skills textbooks (e.g., Ivey & Ivey, 2003) can be valuable in developing specific activities to teach these skills; examples should be created that are specific to parent–teacher interactions. Trainers should emphasize application of the skills to cross-cultural and conflict situations. For example, activities might be developed to demonstrate the use of empathic responding to help an angry parent calm down prior to problem solving or the use of immediacy comments to explore the meaning of observed nonverbal cues.

## Creating Relationship-Building Opportunities

Once educators have a well-developed repertoire of communication skills, they can search for outlets where those skills can be used. Most schools have a variety of activities already in place that include families, such as Back-to-School Night, regularly scheduled conferences, performances, and athletic events. Teachers can adapt those encounters to focus more clearly on developing relationships with parents and sharing responsibility for student success (see Christenson & Sheridan, 2001, for review). For example, rather than a single Back-to-School Night, schools might choose to hold several similar events in community-based centers, such as the neighborhood library, to allow more parents to attend. In addition, teachers could broadly examine their current practices (see Table 6) and seek ways to modify those practices—not to require teachers to do more but to inspire them to do differently those activities that are already part of their routines.

The traditional parent–teacher conference is one such activity that has received some empirical attention, and several alternative models have been identified in the literature. Because conferences are already a typical part of parent–teacher interactions, but often do not fulfill their potential for effective communication (e.g., Swap, 1993), they provide fertile ground for modification. Student-led conferences (e.g., Bailey & Guskey, 2001) and family–school conferences (Minke & Anderson, 2003) are alternative approaches that give students a central role in their conferences. These methods emphasize preconference preparation by students, parents, and teachers, along with increasing students' sense of responsibility for their own learning. Student-led conferences typically involve students presenting their accomplishments to their parents through portfolios. Multiple conferences usually occur at the same time, and the teacher serves as the facilitator in the process. These conferences have been shown to increase parent participation dramatically, with 95% to 100% participation reported in some cases, creating opportunities for parent–teacher relationship development.

Family–school conferences are similar to traditional parent–teacher conferences in that teachers have individual meetings with each family. However, unlike traditional conferences, meetings are structured to give all participants, including the student, the opportunity to discuss the student's learning and behavioral strengths and needs. Family–school conferences, compared with traditional parent–teacher conferences, have more dyadic exchanges (dialogues, rather than teacher monologues), and parents and teachers report a better understanding of each other and the student. Although more outcome research is needed, these kinds of adjustments in traditional practices show promise in promoting effective parent–teacher relationships.

### A Brief Look at Intervention

Intervention, with respect to parent–teacher relationships, is needed when a relationship is low in trust, high in negative emotion, and high in conflict. There may be unwillingness to continue the relationship on both sides. Given that parent–teacher relationships are typically short term, lasting only one school year, and given that conflict in schools is often avoided (e.g., Swap, 1993), it is perhaps unsurprising to find little in the research literature that specifically addresses relationship repair between parents and teachers. However, even if empirically supported interventions were to be developed in this area, the primary approach should be prevention.

As discussed above, having trusting relationships in place increases the likelihood that parents and teachers will give each other the benefit of the doubt if a problem arises with the child's behavior or school work; highly negative interactions are less likely to occur and effective problem solving is more likely. In situations in which a trusting relationship has not been established, the communication skills described earlier should be used to defuse emotion on both sides before problem solving is attempted. Furthermore, even when processes are in place for developing relationships between parents and teachers, there will still be some who are unsuccessful in working together. The conflict resolution literature (e.g., Deutsch & Coleman, 2000) may be helpful for developing interventions in those cases and for planning relationship repair strategies.

## SUMMARY

Parent involvement in education is widely believed to be important in student achievement. However, many school-based initiatives to promote parent involvement yield frustration on both sides, in part because of the individuals' different definitions of what it means to be involved. Collaborative approaches attempt to circumvent some of the problems associated with traditional parent involvement activities by emphasizing the need to learn from families, develop shared goals, and engage in joint problem solving. Productive, trusting parent–teacher relationships are a critical component of family–school collaboration initiatives. However, developing these relationships can be difficult because they involve emotional risk, cross-cultural differences, and school structures that allow little time for parents and teacher to work together. Educators can make progress in this area through well-planned strategies that build on examination of current practices, development of communication skills, and adjustment of current activities to enhance the probability that trusting relationships develop.

## RECOMMENDED RESOURCES

### Books and Other Printed Material

Christenson, S. L., & Sheridan, S. M. (2001). *Schools and families: Creating essential connections for learning.* New York: Guilford Press.

This book is an excellent resource for school teams considering plans of action for improving family–school relationships. It presents a strong rationale for engaging in such activities and offers many resources for planning and implementation.

Constantino, S. M. (2003). *Engaging all families: Creating a positive school culture by putting research into practice.* Lanham, MD: Scarecrow Education.

This book offers a brief but comprehensive guide to approaching family–school relationship development. It includes an interesting section on the benefits and difficulties posed by increasing access to communication technologies.

Swap, S. M. (1993). *Developing home school partnerships: From concepts to practice.* New York: Teachers College Press.

This classic text offers a good overview of barriers to family–school collaboration and means to address them.

### Website

*http://www.ncpie.org*

The website of the National Coalition for Parent Involvement in Education offers resources for parents, teachers, and administrators interested in developing effective family–school partnerships.

## REFERENCES

Adams, K. S., & Christenson, S. L. (2000). Trust and the family–school relationship: Examination of parent–teacher differences in elementary and secondary grades. *Journal of School Psychology, 38,* 477–497.

Bailey, J. M., & Guskey, T. R. (2001). *Implementing student-led conferences.* Thousand Oaks, CA: Sage.

Blue-Banning, M., Summers, J. A., Frankland, H. C., Nelson, L. L., & Beegle, G. (2004). Dimensions of family and professional partnerships: Constructive guidelines for collaboration. *Exceptional Children, 70*(2), 167–184.

Bryk, A. S., & Schneider, B. (2002). *Trust in schools: A core resource for improvement.* New York: Russell Sage Foundation.

Christenson, S. L. (2003). The family–school partnership: An opportunity to promote the learning competence of all children. *School Psychology Quarterly, 18,* 454–482.

Christenson, S. L., & Sheridan, S. M. (2001). *Schools and families: Creating essential connections for learning.* New York: Guilford Press.

Coatsworth, J. D., Pantin, H., & Szapocznik, J. (2002). Familia unidas: A family-centered ecodevelopmental intervention to reduce risk for problem behavior among Hispanic adolescents. *Clinical Child and Family Psychology Review, 5*(2), 113–132.

Coll, C. G., Akiba, D., Palacios, N., Bailey, B., Silver, R., DiMartino, L., & Chin, C. (2002). Parental involvement in children's education: Lessons from three immigrant groups. *Parenting: Science and Practice, 2,* 300–324.

Constantino, S. M. (2003). *Engaging all families: Creating a positive school culture by putting research into practice.* Lanham, MD: Scarecrow Education.

Deutsch, M., & Coleman, P. T. (Eds.). (2000). *The handbook of conflict resolution: Theory and practice.* San Francisco: Jossey-Bass.

Ehrlich, L. G. (2000). *Fatal words and friendly faces: Interpersonal communication in the twenty-first century.* Lanham, MD: University Press.

Fan, X., & Chen, M. (2001). Parental involvement and students' academic achievement: A meta-analysis. *Educational Psychology Review, 13,* 1–22.

Fantuzzo, J., McWayne, C., Perry, M. A., & Childs, S. (2004). Multiple dimensions of family involvement and their relations to behavioral and learning competencies for urban, low income children. *School Psychology Review, 33,* 467–480.

Friesen, B. J., Koren, P. E., & Koroloff, N. M. (1992). How parents view professional behaviors: A cross-professional analysis. *Journal of Child and Family Studies, 1,* 209–231.

Fujishin, R. (2000). *Creating communication: Exploring and expanding your fundamental communication skills.* San Francisco: Acada Press.

Fullan, M. (2003). *Change forces with a vengeance.* New York: Routledge Falmer.

Goddard, R. D., Tschannen-Moran, M., & Hoy, W. K. (2001). A multilevel examination of the distribution and effects of teacher trust in students and parents in urban elementary schools. *Elementary School Journal, 102,* 3–17.

Grolnick, W. S., Benjet, C., Kurowski, C. O., & Apostoleris, N. H. (1997). Predictors of parent involvement in children's schooling. *Journal of Educational Psychology, 89,* 538–548.

Hanafin, J., & Lynch, A. (2002). Peripheral voices: Parental involvement, social class, and educational disadvantage. *British Journal of Sociology of Education, 23,* 35–49.

Hargreaves, A. (2001). Emotional geographies of teaching. *Teachers College Record, 103,* 1056–1080.

Hauser-Cram, P., Sirin, S. R., & Stipek, D. (2003). When teachers' and parents' values differ: Teachers' ratings of academic competence in children from low-income families. *Journal of Educational Psychology, 95,* 813–820.

Henderson, A. T., & Mapp, K. L. (2002). *A new wave of evidence. The impact of school, family and community connections on student achievement.* Southwest Educational Development Laboratory. Retrieved February 22, 2005, from http://www.sedl.org/connections/resources/evidence.pdf

Hong, S., & Ho, H. (2005). Direct and indirect longitudinal effects on parental involvement on student achievement: Second-order latent growth modeling across ethnic groups. *Journal of Educational Psychology, 97,* 32–42.

Huss-Keeler, R. L. (1997). Teacher perception of ethnic and linguistic minority parental involvement and its relationship to children's language and literacy learning: A case study. *Teaching and Teacher Education, 13,* 171–182.

Ivey, A. E., & Ivey, M. B. (2003). *Intentional interviewing and counseling: Facilitating client development in a multicultural society.* Pacific Grove, CA: Thomson Brooks/Cole.

Kalyanpur, M., Harry, B., & Skrtic, T. (2000). Equity and advocacy expectations of culturally diverse families' participation in special education. *International Journal of Disability, Development and Education, 47,* 119–136.

Lane, B. B. (1948). *Your part in your child's education: An activity program for parents.* New York: Dutton.

Lareau, A., & Horvat, E. M. (1999). Moments of social inclusion and exclusion: Race, class, and cultural capital in family–school relationships. *Sociology of Education, 72* (January), 37–53.

Lareau, A., & Shumar, W. (1996). The problem of individualism in family-school policies. *Sociology of Education, 69* (Extra Issue), 24–39.

Lawson, M. A. (2003). School-family relations in context: Parent and teacher perceptions of parent involvement. *Urban Education, 38,* 77–133.

Mattingly, D. J., Prislin, R., McKenzie, T. L., Rodriguez, J. L., & Kayzar, B. (2002). Evaluating evaluations: The case of parent involvement programs. *Review of Educational Research, 72,* 549–576.

Maurer, R. (1996). *Beyond the wall of resistance.* Austin, TX: Bard Books.

Minke, K. M. (2000). Preventing school problems and promoting school success through family–school–community collaboration. In K. M. Minke & G. G. Bear (Eds.), *Preventing school problems—promoting school success: Strategies and programs that work* (pp. 337–420). Bethesda, MD: National Association of School Psychologists.

Minke, K. M. (2004). *Family–school collaboration and positive behavior support: Applications at the school-wide level.* Newark, DE: University of Delaware,

Center for Disabilities Studies; and Delaware Department of Education.

Minke, K. M., & Anderson, K. J. (2003). Restructuring routine parent–teacher conferences: The family–school conference model. *Elementary School Journal, 104,* 49–69.

Noblit, G. W., Malloy, W. W., & Malloy, C. E. (2001). *The kids got smarter: Case studies of successful Comer schools.* Creskill, NJ: Hampton Press.

Patrikakou, E. N., & Weissberg, R. P. (2000). Parents' perceptions of teacher outreach and parent involvement in children's education. *Journal of Prevention and Intervention in the Community, 20,* 103–119.

Pianta, R., & Walsh, D. B. (1996). *High-risk children in schools: Constructing sustaining relationships.* New York: Routledge.

Ran, A. (2001). Travelling on parallel tracks: Chinese parents and English teachers. *Educational Research, 43,* 311–328.

Sarason, S. B. (1995). *Parental involvement and the political principle.* San Francisco: Jossey-Bass.

Shaver, A. V., & Walls, R. T. (1998). Effect of Title I parent involvement on student reading and mathematics achievement. *Journal of Research and Development in Education, 31*(2), 90–97.

Shepard, J., & Carlson, J. S. (2003). An empirical evaluation of school-based prevention programs that involve parents. *Psychology in the Schools, 40,* 641–656.

Simon, B. S. (2004). High school outreach and family involvement. *Social Psychology of Education, 7,* 185–209.

Smith, E. P., Gorman-Smith, D., Quinn, W. H., Rabiner, D. L., Tolan, P. H., & Winn, D. M. (2004). Community-based multiple family groups to prevent and reduce violent and aggressive behavior: The GREAT families program. *American Journal of Preventive Medicine, 26*(Suppl. 1), 39–47.

Stone, S. (2003). The transition to high school: Teacher perspectives in a large, urban, predominantly minority school system. *Journal of Ethnic & Cultural Diversity in Social Work, 12,* 47–67.

Swap, S. M. (1993). *Developing home school partnerships: From concepts to practice.* New York: Teachers College Press.

U.S. Department of Education. (2004). *Parental involvement. Title 1, Part A: Non-regulatory guidance.* Retrieved February 22, 2005, from http://www.ed.gov/programs/titleiparta/parentinvguid.doc

U.S. Department of Education, National Center for Education Statistics. (1998). *Parent involvement in children's education: Efforts by public elementary schools (NCES 98–032).* Washington, DC: Author.

Valle, J. W., & Aponte, E. (2002). IDEA and collaboration: A Bakhtinian perspective on parent and professional discourse. *Journal of Learning Disabilities, 35,* 471–481.

Vickers, H. S., & Minke, K. M. (1997). Family systems and the family–school connection. In G. G. Bear, K. M. Minke, & A. Thomas (Eds.), *Children's needs II: Development, problems, and alternatives* (pp. 547–558). Bethesda, MD: National Association of School Psychologists.

Walker, B. M. (1998). Meetings without communication: A study of parents' evenings in secondary schools. *British Educational Research Journal, 24,* 163–178.

Young, J. R., & Hite, S. J. (1994). The status of teacher preservice preparation for parent involvement: A national study. *Education, 115,* 153–160.

# 7

# School Disciplinary Systems: Alternatives to Suspension and Expulsion

**Russell Skiba**
**M. Karega Rausch**
*Center for Evaluation and Education Policy, Indiana University*

Without question, schools need sound disciplinary systems to maintain school safety and promote student learning. In the face of multiple-victim homicides in the late 1990s, schools have been increasingly motivated to address issues of disruption and violence. The fear created by such incidents also has generated support for more punitive methods of school discipline, often under the broad rhetoric of *zero tolerance.* The shift toward punitive and exclusionary discipline has substantially increased the number of students suspended or expelled from school (Wald & Losen, 2003).

Thus, schools face what appears to be a profound dilemma. To fulfill their responsibility to promote safety, many schools and school districts have turned to procedures that remove some children from the opportunity to learn. Under federal education legislation, schools are under a mandate to use "only practices that are evidence-based, so only the best ideas with proven results are introduced into the classroom" (No Child Left Behind Act Fact Sheet, 2001). The purpose of this chapter is to examine what is known about the use of school exclusion as a disciplinary strategy. Are zero tolerance, suspension, and expulsion effective methods for promoting safe and effective school climates? Are there effective alternatives that can keep schools safe without removing students from the opportunity to learn?

## BACKGROUND AND DEVELOPMENT

### Purposes of School Discipline

Although in the public mind school discipline has become increasingly associated with the use of punishment and school exclusion (Skiba & Peterson, 1999), in fact a number of important instructional and organizational purposes underlie any school's disciplinary system:

- *To ensure the safety of students and teachers.* The increased awareness that deadly violence brought to this nation has drawn attention to the acute need to guarantee the safety of students and teachers.
- *To create a climate conducive to learning.* Effective disciplinary systems should improve academic outcomes by increasing the amount and quality of time teachers can spend teaching rather than responding to behavioral disruptions.
- *To teach students skills needed for successful interaction in school and society.* Children will always require socialization, instruction, and correction to shape fundamentally egocentric behavior into interpersonal skills that make children capable of interacting successfully with others in school and beyond.
- *To reduce rates of future misbehavior.* Behavioral psychology (Skinnner, 1953) suggests that those

disciplinary interventions that are effective will lead to reduced rates of inappropriate or disruptive behavior in the school setting.

Among the most dominant disciplinary approaches in the past 15 years has been the philosophy of *zero tolerance.* Zero tolerance is based on the philosophy of *deterrence*, that is, the belief that increasing the severity of punishment for both minor and major misbehavior will send a message that disruptive behavior will not be tolerated. Before we examine whether the disciplinary practices favored by this approach have been effective in meeting the primary purposes of school discipline, we review the background and definition of zero tolerance.

## Zero Tolerance: Background and Definition

Zero tolerance first received national attention as the title of a program developed in 1986 by U.S. Attorney Peter Nuñez to impound seagoing vessels carrying any amount of drugs. U.S. Attorney General Edwin Meese highlighted the program as a national model in 1988 and ordered U.S. Customs officials to seize the vehicles and property of anyone crossing the border with even trace amounts of drugs, and to charge those individuals in federal court. Beginning in 1989, school districts in California, New York, and Kentucky picked up on the term *zero tolerance* and mandated expulsion for drugs, fighting, and gang-related activity. By 1993, zero tolerance policies had been adopted across the country, and often were broadened to include not only drugs and weapons but also smoking and school disruption. This tide swept zero tolerance into national policy when the Clinton administration signed the Gun-Free Schools Act into law. The law mandates a 1-year expulsion for possession of a firearm, referral of students who violate the law to the criminal or juvenile justice system, and the provision that state law must authorize local administrators to conduct a case-by-case review of all such expulsions.

State legislatures and local school districts have broadened the mandate of zero tolerance beyond the federal mandates of weapons, to drugs and alcohol, fighting, threats, or swearing. Many school boards continue to toughen their disciplinary policies; some have begun to experiment with permanent expulsion from the system for some offenses. Others have begun to apply school suspensions, expulsions, or transfers to behaviors that occur outside of school (Ayers, Dohrn, & Ayers, 2001; Michigan Public Policy Initiative, 2003; Potts, Njie, Detch, & Walton, 2003).

As a philosophy more than an intervention, zero tolerance is difficult to define. The National Center on Education Statistics (NCES) report, *Violence and Discipline Problems in America's Public Schools: 1996–1997* (Heaviside, Rowand, Williams, & Farris, 1998) defined zero tolerance as a policy that mandates predetermined consequences or punishments for specified offenses. Yet the NCES definition of zero tolerance may be unnecessarily broad. One would expect that few school disciplinary policies exist that do not mandate some predetermined consequences for specific behaviors. A more limited definition of zero tolerance is as a disciplinary policy that is "intended primarily as a method of sending a message that certain behaviors will not be tolerated, by punishing all offenses severely, no matter how minor" (Skiba & Peterson, 1999, p. 373).

## Frequency of Use of Suspension and Expulsion

At the national level, it has been estimated that the number of suspensions and expulsions nationwide has doubled since the 1970s (U.S. Department of Education, 2000; Wald & Losen, 2003). Both state and local district reports suggest increases in out-of-school suspension rates at the local level (Raffaele Mendez & Knoff, 2003; Rausch & Skiba, 2004). Studies of school discipline (Bowditch, 1993; Skiba, Peterson, & Williams, 1997) have consistently found that suspension is among the most widely used disciplinary techniques—perhaps the most frequently used disciplinary tool—but studies also found that rates of usage vary widely. For example, reports of rates of suspension at the high school level have ranged from below 9.3% of enrolled students (Kaeser, 1979) to 92% (Thornton & Trent, 1988). Out-of-school suspension rates appear to be the highest in urban schools, compared with schools in suburban, town, or rural locales (Massachusetts Advocacy Center, 1986; Wu, Pink, Crain, & Moles, 1982). Suspension rates appear to be the lowest in elementary school; they increase and peak during middle school, then drop slightly from middle school to high school (Raffaele Mendez & Knoff, 2003; Rausch & Skiba, 2004). School expulsion, though less widely studied, appears to be used relatively infrequently relative to other disciplinary techniques (Heaviside et al., 1998).

## PROBLEMS AND IMPLICATIONS

Out-of-school suspension and expulsion are, by their very nature, interventions that pose some risk to educational opportunity. One of the most important findings of educational psychology of the past 30 years is the central importance of academic engagement to learning (Greenwood, Horton, & Utley, 2002). Thus, suspension and expulsion, which remove students from the opportunity to learn, must be viewed as potentially risky interventions.

Questions about suspension and expulsion as disciplinary tools are essentially issues of costs and benefits. Does the removal of troublesome students from school through suspension and expulsion provide sufficient benefits in terms of safety and improved learning climate to offset the risks to the suspended students' educational opportunity and school bonding that are inherent in disciplinary removal? In the following sections we address that question by reviewing the literature on the efficacy of out-of-school suspension and expulsion.

### Efficacy of Disciplinary Removal

How effective is school disciplinary removal in preserving safe school climates that are conducive to learning, in teaching students the behaviors they need to succeed in school, or in deterring students from disruptive behavior? To address that question, we examine research findings on the efficacy of out-of-school suspension and expulsion pertaining to treatment integrity, nondiscriminatory application, and educational outcomes.

***Measuring treatment integrity.*** Treatment integrity, the extent to which an intervention is implemented as planned, has been increasingly viewed as a key factor in judging the effectiveness of behavioral interventions (Lane, Bocian, MacMillan, & Gresham, 2004). Unless an intervention is implemented with some degree of consistency, any changes in school climate or student behavior cannot be attributed to that intervention. For traditional disciplinary interventions, one might expect two indicators of treatment integrity. First, because removal from the opportunity to learn is in most cases the most extreme form of punishment a school could administer, one measure of treatment fidelity would be whether out-of-school suspension and expulsion are reserved for those offenses for which they are intended—the most serious offenses. Second, because disciplinary techniques are intended as methods of behavior change, one would expect that variations in the use of suspension and expulsion would be based largely upon variations in student behavior, not upon idiosyncratic characteristics of schools or school staff. Both of these aspects of the treatment integrity of disciplinary removal are reviewed below.

***Are suspension and expulsion reserved for most serious offenses?*** Looking across studies of school discipline, it is clear that school suspension tends not to be reserved for serious or dangerous behaviors. Fighting or physical aggression among students is consistently found to be among the most common reasons for suspension (Skiba et al., 1997; Stone, 1993). The majority of offenses for which students are suspended, however, appear to be nonviolent, less-disruptive offenses (Children's Defense Fund, 1975; Raffaele Mendez & Knoff, 2003). Rausch and Skiba (2004) reported that 5% of all out-of-school suspensions in one Midwestern state were in categories such as weapons or drugs that are typically considered more serious or dangerous; the remaining 95% of suspensions fell into two categories: *disruptive behavior* and *other*. These data are consistent with Stone's (1993) conclusions from a national survey of 35 school districts representing over a million students: "It appears clear that on reviewing the data to determine if the crime fits the punishment, the answer is no" (p. 367).

One might expect that expulsion, because it is used less frequently, would be reserved for more serious infractions. In one of the few reported studies of school expulsion in American education, Morrison and D'Incau (1997) found that student offenses resulting in expulsion tended to be offenses of moderate to high severity. The authors also reported, however, that the majority of offenses in the sample they investigated were committed by students who would not generally be considered dangerous to the school environment. Some researchers have also suggested that zero tolerance and the increased involvement of law enforcement in schools has led to the criminalization of some relatively minor misbehavior (Wald & Losen, 2003).

***Are suspension and expulsion primarily a response to student misbehavior?*** There can be little doubt that certain students are at a much higher risk for office referral and school suspension and thus account for a disproportionate share of disciplinary effort (Tobin, Sugai, & Colvin, 1996; Wu et al., 1982). Yet the data also indicate that certain classrooms and schools appear to be responsible for a disproportionate share of disciplinary referrals. Skiba et al. (1997) reported that at one middle school they studied, 25% of classroom teachers were responsible for 66% of all referrals to the office. In a national study to identify predictors of school suspension, Wu et al. (1982) found that student behavior and attitude did make a significant contribution to the probability of suspension in that model. However, their analyses also showed that a number of school characteristics contributed significantly to the probability of a student's being suspended, including overall school suspension rate, teacher attitudes, administrative centralization, school governance, perceptions of achievement, socioeconomic disadvantage, and racial status. In fact, school and demographic characteristics made a more significant contribution to predicting school suspension than did student behavior and attitude, leading Wu et al. to the following conclusion:

> One could argue from this finding that if students are interested in reducing their chances of being suspended, they will be better off by transferring to a school with a lower suspension rate than by improving their attitudes or reducing their misbehavior. (pp. 255–256)

Rates of out-of-school suspension and expulsion also appear to be determined by attitudes of school principals. Principals who were interviewed regarding their disciplinary practices for the national report *Opportunities Suspended* (Advancement Project/Civil Rights Project, 2000) used school suspension in direct proportion to their support for the policy of zero tolerance. Skiba et al. (2003) surveyed 325 principals regarding their attitudes toward zero tolerance, suspension and expulsion, and violence prevention strategies and found a correlation between the attitudes of school principals and school disciplinary outcomes. That is, they found that rates of out-of-school suspension were lower, and the use of preventive measures more frequent, at schools whose principals believed that suspension and expulsion were unnecessary in a positive school climate.

Given the range of school and teacher characteristics that contribute to rates of suspension and expulsion, it is not surprising that district-level research has found the use of disciplinary removal to be extremely inconsistent from school to school (Massachusetts Advocacy Center, 1986). Ultimately, then, one must assume that the treatment integrity of out-of-school suspension and expulsion as a disciplinary intervention is low.

## Nondiscriminatory Practice

Both special education regulations and federal education policy prohibit discrimination in the application or outcomes of intervention. Yet almost 30 years of research has documented racial and socioeconomic disparities in the use of out-of-school suspension and expulsion.

***Disproportionality due to socioeconomic status.*** Studies of school suspension have consistently documented disproportionality due to socioeconomic status. Research has found that students from economically disadvantaged backgrounds are at greater risk of school suspension (Wu et al., 1982). In a qualitative study of student reactions to school discipline, both high- and low-income adolescents reported that students from lower socioeconomic status were likely to commit more frequent and more serious disciplinary infractions than higher income groups (Brantlinger, 1991). Both groups, however, also believed that their school discriminated systematically by social class and agreed that how, and even whether, a student is punished for a given infraction depends on student reputation, achievement, and socioeconomic status.

***Disproportionality due to minority status.*** National, state-, district-, and school-level data for the past 30 years shows that African American students have been suspended at rates two to three times that of other students. They are similarly overrepresented in office referrals, corporal punishment, and school expulsion (Children's Defense Fund, 1975; Raffaele Mendez & Knoff, 2003; Skiba, Michael, Nardo, & Peterson, 2002; Wu et al., 1982). Disciplinary overrepresentation of Latino students has been reported in some studies (Raffaele Mendez & Knoff, 2003; Rausch & Skiba, 2004), but the finding is not universal across locations or studies.

Racial disparities in discipline cannot be fully accounted for by the lower economic status of minority students. Although low socioeconomic status has been consistently found to be a risk factor for school suspension, minority overrepresentation in school punishment remains significant even after statistically controlling for socioeconomic status (Skiba et al., 2002; Wu et al., 1982).

Furthermore, no studies show that African American students have higher rates of misbehavior that would result in disproportionate rates of discipline. African American students have been punished for less severe rule violations than white students (Shaw & Braden, 1990) or have been punished more severely than others who committed the same offense (McFadden & Marsh, 1992). In a study devoted specifically to African American disproportionality in school discipline, Skiba et al. (2002) tested alternate hypotheses for racial disparities in an urban school setting. They found that white students were referred to the office significantly more frequently for offenses that can be objectively documented, such as smoking, vandalism, leaving without permission, and obscene language. In contrast, African American students were referred more often for disrespect, excessive noise, threats, and loitering. Such results suggest a clear pattern of increased subjectivity for African American office referrals. In short, far from showing that African American students act out more than other students, the available evidence suggests that African American students may be subject to office referrals for less serious or more subjective reasons.

***Factors associated with disciplinary disparities.*** Some evidence suggests that the disproportionate representation of African American students originates at the classroom level. Skiba et al. (2002) found that racial disparities in the rate of out-of-school suspension in a large urban district could be almost entirely accounted for by the fact that African American students were twice as likely as white students to be referred to the office by classroom teachers. In an ethnographic observational study, Vavrus and Cole (2002) found that many office referrals leading to school suspension in urban classrooms were not the result of serious classroom disruptions. Rather, the authors concluded:

> Suspensions are the result of a complex sequence of events that together form a disciplinary moment, a moment when one disruptive act among many is singled out for action by the teacher. This singling-out process, we contend, disproportionately affects students whose race and gender distance them from their teachers, and this subtle, often unconscious process may be one of the reasons why students of color often experience suspension in the absence of violent behavior. (p. 109)

Together, these results are consistent with suggestions that cultural discontinuities may create interactional patterns that increase the likelihood that African American students, especially African American male adolescents, will be removed from class. Townsend (2000) suggested that many teachers, especially those of European American origin, may be unfamiliar or uncomfortable with the more active and boisterous style of interaction that characterizes African American males. Teachers prone to accepting stereotypes of adolescent African American males as threatening or dangerous may thus be more likely to react more quickly to relatively minor threats to authority that might be ignored for other ethnic or racial groups.

In summary, it is hard to argue that disciplinary removal is not discriminatory. Rather, students of color, particularly African American students, and students from disadvantaged backgrounds are at increased risk of being removed from school through suspension or expulsion. These disparities cannot be explained simply by socioeconomic status or the behavior of the students themselves. The evidence suggests that these disparities are, at least in part, a product of cultural discontinuity or insufficient training in culturally responsive classroom management practices. Together with findings that racial disproportionality in suspension increases in schools that use suspension more frequently (Massachusetts Advocacy Center, 1986), these data make a case that the use, and especially the overuse, of disciplinary removal carries with it an inherent risk of racial disparity.

## Outcomes of Disciplinary Removal

Any frequently used behavioral intervention must consider outcomes to justify their use. Federal educational legislation has increasingly mandated that schools use only evidence-based educational interventions. Disciplinary removal could be judged an effective educational or behavioral intervention if it led to improvements in either individual rates of disruptive or violent behavior or overall school safety or school climate. Data on the outcomes of exclusionary disciplinary approaches are reviewed below.

***Do zero tolerance suspensions and expulsions improve student behavior?*** Behavioral psychology defines an effective punisher as one that reduces the future probability of responding (Skinner, 1953). Yet descriptive studies of out-of-school suspension have consistently shown a high rate of repeat offending (Bowditch, 1993; Massachusetts Advocacy Center, 1986). Furthermore, out-of-school suspension in late elementary school has been found to be among the strongest predictors of out-of-school suspension in middle school (Raffaele Mendez, 2003), prompting some researchers to conclude that, for some students, "suspension functions as a reinforcer ... rather than as a punisher" (Tobin, Sugai, & Colvin, 1996, p. 91).

In the long term, school suspension has been found to be a moderate to strong predictor of dropout, retention, and late graduation. Research on at-risk students in the 1980s found a moderate and stable correlation between out-of-school suspension and high school dropout (Ekstrom, Goertz, Pollack, & Rock, 1986). Raffaele Mendez (2003) also reported that the number of out-of-school suspensions a student received as a sixth-grader correlated negatively with the probability that the student would graduate with his or her cohort of students 6 years later as a 12th-grade student. Interestingly, this relationship was stronger for African American students than for White students.

Unfortunately, there is evidence that the relationship between school suspension and school dropout may not be entirely accidental. Ethnographic field studies of school discipline, which included interviewing administrators and observing the school discipline process, have noted that disciplinarians in troubled urban schools often view their role in large measure as dealing with persistent troublemakers who challenge the institution's authority (Bowditch, 1993). In such a context, suspension may be used as a push-out tool to encourage low-achieving students and those viewed as troublemakers to leave school before graduation.

***Do suspension and expulsion improve school climate?*** Rather than making a contribution to school safety, the increased use of suspension and expulsion seems to be associated with student and teacher perceptions of a less effective and less inviting school climate. Schools with higher rates of suspension have been reported to have higher student–teacher ratios and a lower level of academic quality (Hellman & Beaton, 1986). Wu et al. (1982) found that attending a school with less satisfactory school governance was a significant predictor of a student's being suspended at least once in her or his school career.

Because an important purpose of school discipline is to maintain a school climate that is conducive to learning, a positive correlation could be expected between effective school discipline and a school's average academic achievement. However, emerging data suggest a negative relationship between the use of school suspension and expulsion and academic achievement. Skiba et al. (2003) reported that states with higher rates of out-of-school suspension had lower average scores on the National Assessment of Educational Progress (NAEP), and Raffaele Mendez, Knoff, and Ferron (2002) found that student achievement in writing was negatively associated with out-of-school suspensions for middle and high school students.

The simple relationship between achievement and discipline could of course result from a number of factors. For example, schools in more disadvantaged areas might have a higher percentage of difficult students who are suspended and also exhibit lower achievement. To test this hypothesis, Skiba and Rausch (2004) conducted a multivariate analysis testing the relationship of school discipline and academic achievement, controlling for a number of demographic variables, including the school's percentage of students accepting free and reduced lunch (poverty), enrollment of African American students, and school type (elementary or secondary). Results indicated that higher school rates of out-of-school suspension were associated with lower passing rates on the state accountability test, regardless of the demographic or the economic or racial makeup of the school.

## Summary: The Failure of Zero Tolerance as a Disciplinary Paradigm

Schools must use all effective methods at their disposal to prevent violence and to ensure a school climate that is maximally conducive to learning. Schools have a right and responsibility to minimize disruptions that can threaten the integrity of the learning environment. In the wake of frightening violence in some U.S. schools in the 1990s, there can be little doubt about the depth of the consensus around these propositions.

Among the key words in that understanding, however, is the term *effective*. In the climate of fear generated by real and perceived threats to the safety of schools, many schools and school districts adopted a get-tough deterrent philosophy of zero tolerance as an intuitive method for addressing perceived threats to school safety. It makes logical sense that strict levels of enforcement for both major and minor incidents will be effective in sending a message to students that disruption will not be tolerated. It makes sense that removing troublemakers will be effective in improving and strengthening the school climate for those students who remain. Yet as data on zero tolerance, out-of-school suspension, and expulsion have emerged, they have overwhelmingly failed to support these commonsense notions that lie at the heart of the zero tolerance philosophy. Suspension and expulsion appear to be used too inconsistently to guarantee treatment integrity. Over 30 years of consistent data on African American overrepresentation in suspension and expulsion indicate that disciplinary school exclusion may carry inherent risks for creating or exacerbating racial and socioeconomic disadvantage. No evidence as yet shows that zero tolerance contributes to school safety or improves student behavior; rather, increased levels of out-of-school suspension and expulsion are related to less adequate school climates, lower levels of achievement at the school level, a higher probability of future student misbehavior, and eventually lower levels of school completion. These data indicate that the actual benefits of removing a child from school for disciplinary reasons are in no way sufficient to counterbalance other concerns created by those interventions in terms of loss of educational opportunity and threats to school bonding.

Expecting that schools will simply cease suspending and expelling disruptive students is of course unrealistic. In the absence of any other effective strategy, removing the tool many administrators believe is their only or best option might simply increase school disruption and chaos. Thus, it becomes extremely important to examine the available alternatives to suspension and expulsion and the potential for the effective implementation of those alternatives in schools.

## ALTERNATIVE ACTIONS FOR PREVENTION

Given the mandate of No Child Left Behind to use only effective strategies, one would assume that over time pressure will increase on schools to develop more effective disciplinary approaches that can maintain safe school climates with a lower risk to student learning. To what extent do such alternatives exist? How widely are they implemented? How can schools begin to move away from ineffective and punitive discipline toward more evidence-based procedures?

### Evidence-Based Alternatives to Suspension and Expulsion

Effective alternatives for reducing the threat of youth violence have been identified nationally. In the past 10 years, the U.S. government has convened or sponsored a number of research efforts and panels on school-based prevention of youth violence, including a report to Congress on youth violence (Sherman et al., 1997), the Department of Education/Juvenile Justice response to school shootings (see Dwyer, Osher, & Warger, 1998), and the report of the U.S. Surgeon General on violence prevention (Elliott, Hatot, Sirovatka, & Potter, 2001). Those panels have in general relied on relatively rigorous methodological criteria in the selection of effective and promising programs. Their findings have been remarkably consistent, with each other and with scholarly reviews (e.g., Gagnon & Leone, 2001), in outlining an emerging conceptual model and in identifying programs that appear to be most effective within that model.

In 1993, the American Psychological Association (APA) released its report *Violence and Youth: Psychology's Response* (APA, 1993), which addressed what was then widely perceived as an epidemic of youth violence. That report framed youth violence prevention efforts in terms of a three-tiered primary prevention model. Since the publication of that report, a large number of researchers, policy makers, and professional organizations have articulated similar prevention models that can be applied to mental health (Mrazek & Haggerty, 1994), youth violence in general (Elliott et al., 2001; Tolan & Guerra, 1994), or school violence in particular (Walker et al., 1996). The model became the centerpiece for efforts by the U.S. Department of Education to provide guidance to America's schools concerning the prevention of violence (Dwyer, et al., 1998).

Figure 1 represents the three levels of a primary prevention model. As applied in school settings, the framework acts as a useful schematic for organizing violence prevention and school disciplinary interventions. The model represents the following three levels: First, to promote a safe and responsive climate for all students, schools implement *primary* or *universal prevention* efforts, such as the following, school-wide: conflict resolution (Bodine & Crawford, 1998), bullying prevention (see chapter 10), social and emotional learning (see chapter 1), teaching to instill self-discipline (see chapter 3) and improved classroom management (Gottfredson et al., 2000).

At the *secondary or selected prevention* level, schools implement early screening or identification efforts for children who may be at risk for violence (Walker & Shinn, 2002) and programs such as anger management (see chapter 9) or mentoring that can reconnect students with schools and other institutions.

Third, despite schools' best efforts, some form of disruption, aggression, or perhaps violence will likely occur that requires an appropriate response. *Tertiary* or *indicated prevention* interventions, such as multisystemic

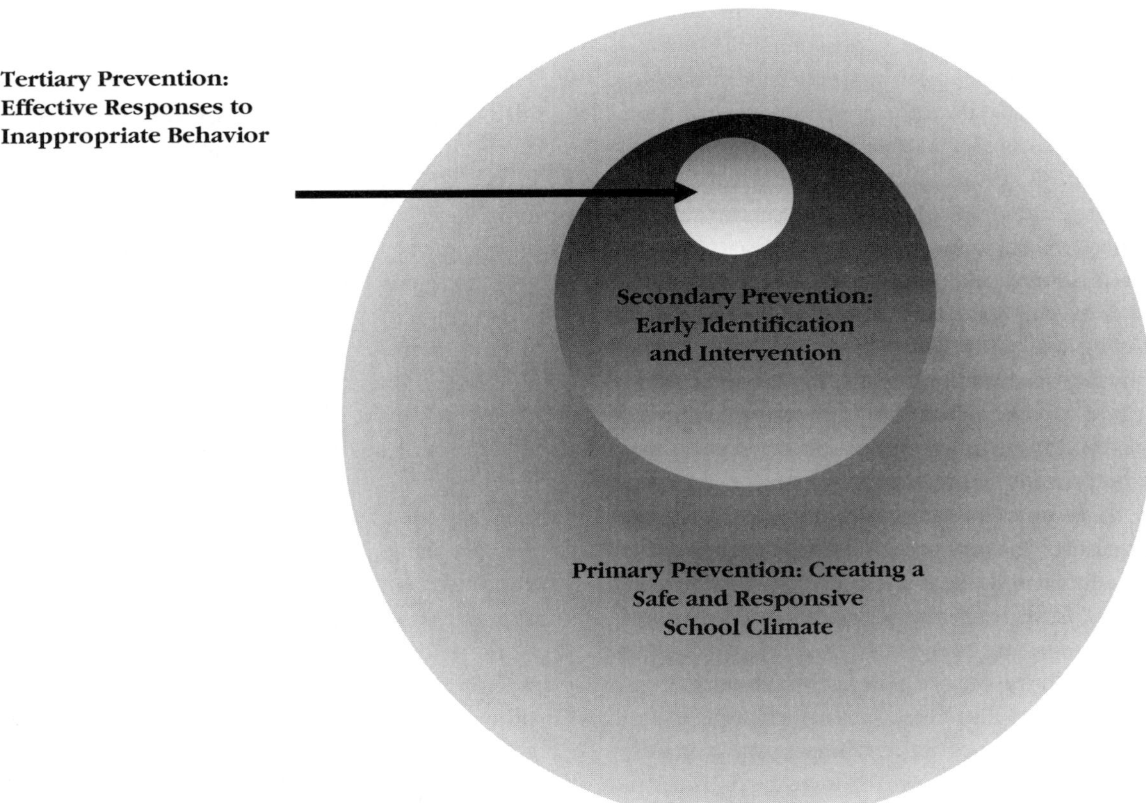


*Note.* From "Beyond guns, drugs, and gangs: The structure of student perceptions of school safety," by R. Skiba, A. B. Simmons, R. Peterson, J. McKelvey, S. Forde, and S. Gallini. In M. Furlong, G. Morrison, R. Skiba, and D. Cornell (Eds.), *Issues in School Violence Research*, p. 154, Binghamton, NY: Hawthorn. Copyright 2004 by The Hawthorn Press. Adapted with permission.

**Figure 1.** *The Safe and Responsive Schools Model of school violence prevention. Primary prevention approaches to create a safe and positive school climate are applied universally to address issues of day-to-day disruption and school climate. Secondary prevention strategies of early identification and early intervention are applied to a smaller proportion of the school population that may be at risk for violence or disruption. Effective response strategies and intervention are in place for those students who are already engaging in disruptive behavior.*

therapy, are targeted at those students who have already engaged in violence and disruption. Such efforts are characterized by a planned and coordinated response that seeks to minimize the future damage of aggression to the child and others (Bear, Webster-Stratton, Furlong, & Rhee, 2000; Walker & Shinn, 2002).

Increasingly, policy pressures from federal (e.g., No Child Left Behind) and state government have emphasized student outcomes in the areas of academic achievement, attendance, and dropout. This reality has forced schools to reorganize their practices to produce positive changes in those performance indicators. The increased academic focus necessitated by accountability planning may increase schools' resistance to considering programs that are not viewed as directly relating to mandated outcomes, such as programs that focus on interpersonal competence. However, the emerging research base that documents the relationship between a positive school climate and academic outcomes suggests that, by minimizing disruption and improving student engagement, preventive and social–emotional interventions represent a key element in attaining strong academic outcomes (Brophy, 1988; Greenberg et al., 2003; Zins, Weissberg, Wang, & Walberg, 2004). Thus, the perception that improving academic outcomes and improving social–emotional outcomes are somehow contradictory is probably in error. Rather, the data suggest that prevention-based programs that focus on social–emotional learning are an important component in achieving the improved academic outcomes mandated by federal and state accountability requirements.

### Implementation of Preventive Alternatives

The existence of an extensive and relatively consistent database on school-based intervention for the prevention of violence does not guarantee that schools will implement those strategies. G. Gottfredson et al. (2000) surveyed a nationally representative sample of school principals and teachers regarding the implementation of prevention programs at their school. More than 50% of the principals reported a prevention activity in most of the 20 prevention categories surveyed. However, teachers reported that implementation of prevention activities was typically at a level that would be considered unacceptable for guaranteeing efficacy. In addition, the most widely used prevention practices were not necessarily those identified in evidence-based literature but instead tended to be less widely researched procedures with respect to their effect on student behavior.

Nor has is been demonstrated that schools can implement prevention programs with a high degree of treatment integrity. Gottfredson, Gottfredson, and Skroban (1998) attempted to implement a multicomponent violence prevention strategy, using only evidence-based strategies, in a single middle school. Despite the school's personnel having levels of training well in excess of typical school research, Gottfredson et al. (1998) reported that few of the components of the program were received by more than 60% of the students, and that the intensity of the interventions was lower than expected.

The problem of implementing evidence-based violence prevention programs in school settings may be the result of an overfocus in the field on the notion of internal validity and experimental control. Schoenwald and Hoagwood (2001) argue that the majority of evidence-based practices have been developed under "test tube conditions" that fail to mirror the realities of school settings. Generally, the programs most often identified as effective or promising in violence prevention research have been implemented by highly trained professionals, researchers, or graduate assistants and often have been accompanied by a large influx of grant support. Such rigorous experimental conditions are critical to demonstrate internal validity and to enable judgments that the treatments, and not nuisance variables, are responsible for observed effects. Yet such conditions do not guarantee that evidence-based procedures will be feasible in real-world settings, which typically lack highly trained researchers, graduate assistants, and large amounts of discretionary funds.

## ALTERNATIVE ACTIONS FOR INTERVENTION

### Restructuring of School Disciplinary Methods: Two Alternatives

Extensive study with fairly rigorous experimental criteria has identified a number of effective nonexclusionary, evidence-based alternatives capable of reducing the threat of school violence and of maintaining an instructional climate conducive to learning. However, the existence of effective evidence-based alternatives unfortunately has not guaranteed widespread implementation of those alternatives in school settings. The most critical challenge facing alternative approaches to school discipline, therefore, is to find effective methods of implementing research-based practices in school discipline and school violence prevention.

A number of strategies have been designed to improve implementation of such alternatives. Those strategies typically are characterized by attention to the process by which schools implement effective alternatives that are tailored to local needs. Two of those efforts, Positive Behavior Interventions and Supports and Safe and Responsive Schools, are highlighted below.

***Positive Behavioral Interventions and Supports.*** Origi-nally developed to address the persistently challenging behavior of students with disabilities, the Positive Behavior Interventions and Supports (PBIS) model focuses on providing schools, especially classroom teachers, with comprehensive, positive, and locally generated systems of proactive resources (Sugai et al., 2000). One key assumption of PBIS is that human behavior is learned. Thus, PBIS seeks to teach students appropriate behaviors that promote academic and social engagement by intentionally altering environmental contexts, including the behaviors of teachers and administrators, that may contribute to student misbehavior. The system creates and fosters support systems at the school-wide level (i.e., all students and all staff), in specific school settings (e.g., hallways, transition periods), at the classroom level (e.g., improved classroom management practices), and at the individual student level (e.g., functional behavior assessment). It also assumes that behavior occurs in a unique social and cultural context, and any proposed changes must be socially and culturally responsive.

PBIS is structured to be responsive to local needs, allowing schools to address local issues. A school PBIS plan is typically created and implemented by a team of local educators, community members, and parents. That team is charged with reviewing their school's discipline and other relevant data to identify areas of concern and the contextual variables hypothesized to be contributing to the concerns, and generate positive interventions to change those relationships. The team also implements selected interventions, tracks the effects of the interventions, and modifies the program as needed.

A growing body of evidence suggests that PBIS can be effective as an alternative to disciplinary removal (Rosenberg & Jackman, 2003; Scott & Barrett, 2004; Sugai et al., 2000). Reductions in office referrals for misbehavior, suspensions, expulsions, teacher attrition, and turnover have been noted, as well as increases in positive school climates and results from state-mandated assessments (Rosenberg & Jackman, 2003). Results also suggest that well-designed PBIS systems produce significant decreases in time spent on discipline by classroom teachers, students, and administrative staff, freeing up time to focus on instruction and a more productive educational environment. For example, as a result of reductions in office disciplinary referrals and suspensions, one urban elementary school's comprehensive PBIS implementation resulted in a total 2-year gain of 31.4 days of administrator time and 158.9 additional school days for students (Scott & Barrett, 2004). After taking into consideration the expenditures on PBIS training and implementation and converting administrator and student time into monetary values, this particular school realized a net savings of almost $7,000 in the first year of implementation and close to $10,000 in the second implementation year, compared with baseline levels.

***Safe and Responsive Schools.*** The Safe and Responsive Schools (SRS) project (Skiba, Peterson, Miller, Ritter, & Simmons, in press) has sought to enable schools and school districts to develop a broader perspective on school safety, stressing comprehensive planning, prevention, and parent and community involvement. The goal of the project has been to increase the knowledge base of teachers and administrators concerning what works in discipline and violence prevention, and to develop a comprehensive model of systems change in school discipline. Working from a three-tiered primary prevention model, the SRS project has worked with rural, suburban, and urban schools in two states to assist them in developing school safety plans.

Skiba et al. (in press) describe the implementation of the SRS model in two states (Indiana and Nebraska) over 3 years. To proceed strategically toward a school safety plan that would address key school issues, participating schools engaged in a year of structured school planning that consisted of four phases.

1. *Team Formation.* Participating schools developed a team, including general and special educators, school psychologists, administrators, parents, and students, which met biweekly to carry out the planning activities.
2. *Needs Assessment.* SRS teams engaged in two needs assessment activities that helped the team identify their most significant school safety problems and the resources available at their school to address those problems.
3. *Best Practices Review.* Once the SRS team had identified their school's areas of greatest need in terms of safety and violence prevention, they reviewed fact sheets and Internet-based materials that might address the safety needs of the school. Team discussion considered (a) the key components of the strategy, (b) the general evidence available to determine the effectiveness of that strategy, and (c) the extent to which that intervention appeared to fit the needs and resources of their own school.
4. *Strategic Planning.* Finally, guided by a series of strategic planning worksheets, each school team considered both their needs assessment data and available best-evidence strategies to design a Safe and Responsive Schools plan.

Evaluation data after 1 year of the SRS plans' implementation are highly encouraging. Table 1 shows that among the first four participating secondary schools in the state of Indiana, out-of-school suspensions for the entire school showed a decline of 40% to 60%. Gains also extended to students with disabilities. One middle school showed a drop from 39 suspensions for students with disabilities in 1999–2000 to no suspensions in 2000–2001.

The process was exemplified by the experience of one participating school: Owen Valley High School in rural Spencer, Indiana. During the planning year, the SRS team identified one of the school's major problems as being the large number of disciplinary referrals to the office, especially for minor misbehavior. To respond to that issue, the school developed an innovative new

**Table 1** *Total Number of Suspensions for Participating SRS Schools: 1999–2000 and 2000–2001 School Years*[a]

| School | 1999–2000 Total Suspensions | 2000–2001 Total Suspensions |
|---|---|---|
| Spencer Owen | | |
| Owen Valley High School | 397 | 171 |
| Owen Valley Middle School | 1293 | 687 |
| Richland Bean Blossom | | |
| Edgewood High School | 205 | 179 |
| Edgewood Junior High School | 577 | 42 |

[a]Data were taken from the Suspension Report submitted by all Indiana schools each year to the Indiana Department of Education.

program called the *intervention room*. Before making an office referral, any teacher can refer a student exhibiting a behavioral problem to the intervention room, which is staffed by both a general and a special education teacher. Students referred to the intervention room for behavioral issues meet with the intervention room teachers, who process the incident with the student, attempt to help the student take responsibility for his or her behavior, and assist the student in returning to the classroom with a plan for avoiding future problems. SRS team members at Owen Valley High School attribute many of the changes in their disciplinary data to the implementation of the intervention room. Finally, these improvements reflect the relationship between positive discipline and academic excellence. In the 2001–2002 school year, Owen Valley High School was one of six schools in the nation that won the prestigious New American High School award from the U.S. Department of Education in recognition of its reform efforts and increased academic excellence.

## Recommendations for Practitioners

Recommendations for modifying or moving away from a zero tolerance model have begun to emerge. School psychologists who wish to move their school toward best-practices school discipline and violence prevention programs might consider advocating for the following recommendations.

- *Reserve zero tolerance disciplinary removals for only the most serious and severe of disruptive behaviors, and define those behaviors explicitly.* The need to protect against the most serious infractions should be balanced with the lack of efficacy data supporting the use of zero tolerance for less serious offenses. A best-evidence approach would suggest restricting zero tolerance to only the most serious of infractions, such as possession of firearms on school property.
- *Replace one-size-fits-all disciplinary strategies with graduated systems of discipline, wherein consequences are geared to the seriousness of the infraction.* In response to community concerns about punishments that do not fit the crime under zero tolerance, many school districts are implementing graduated systems of discipline, reserving severe punishment for only the most serious, safety-threatening offenses. Less serious offenses, such as classroom disruption, attendance-related behaviors, or even minor fights among students are met with less severe consequences that might range from in-school suspension to parent contact, reprimands, community service, or counseling.
- *Define all infractions, whether major or minor, carefully.* Garibaldi, Blanchard, and Brooks (1996) argued that inadequate reporting of disciplinary information allows individual bias to creep in, which can lead to disproportional discipline. Carefully drawn definitions of all behaviors subject to the school disciplinary code protect students from inequitable consequences and protect school officials from charges of unfair and arbitrary application of school policy.
- *Expand the array of options available to schools for dealing with disruptive or violent behavior.* One must assume that school boards or administrators implementing zero tolerance policies are not doing so because they take pleasure in removing children from school. Rather, many school disciplinarians may simply be unaware of more effective alternatives. School psychologists can play a critical role in the

development of more effective disciplinary systems by becoming aware of best practices for effective preventive alternatives and by disseminating that information to administrators and teachers.

- *Implement preventive measures that can improve school climate and reconnect alienated students.* Osher, Sandler, and Nelson (2001) noted that many of the most effective programs in the nation for dealing with student disruption are characterized by high levels of student support and community. Solutions to the zero tolerance dilemma might also seek to shift the focus from relying on punishment strategies of questionable efficacy, to using research-supported strategies such as conflict resolution and bullying prevention to improve the sense of school community and belonging.
- *Improve collaboration and communication among schools, parents, juvenile justice professionals, and mental health workers to develop an array of alternatives for challenging youth.* The behaviors of the most challenging of youth can seriously disrupt school environments, and the problems faced by those youth and their families often exceed the abilities of any one agency to address them. Collaborative approaches such as "wraparound" (Eber, Sugai, Smith, & Scott, 2002) are promising as ways of providing additional resources to schools to address the most serious and challenging behaviors.
- *Evaluate all school discipline or school violence prevention strategies to ensure that all disciplinary interventions, programs, or strategies are truly affecting student behavior and school safety.* Accountability of instruction has become a national priority. There is no reason why behavioral or disciplinary procedures should be held to a lower standard of accountability. The implementation of any procedure addressing student behavior or school violence—whether it be zero tolerance, conflict resolution, school security, or classroom management—must be accompanied by an evaluation adequate to determine whether that procedure has indeed made a positive contribution to improving school safety or student behavior. Without such data, time and resources could be wasted on strategies that sound appealing but, in fact, do little to decrease a school's chances of disruption or violence.

Using data from reform efforts such as PBIS and Safe and Responsive Schools, Table 2 presents a four-step process as a guide for school psychologists and other school leaders who seek to restructure their school's or district's disciplinary practices. Previous efforts have shown that a school- or district-wide commitment to exploring alternatives is a critical first step in school reform. Thus, school psychologists can work with school administrators to ensure that initial efforts are led by a team of respected professionals with the mandate to consider alternatives and with the authority to have their recommendations accepted. Once the planning team is in place, a structured needs assessment process enables the team to identify both the key local disciplinary concerns and the resources currently in place or needed for addressing those concerns. With that information, the team explores the availability of evidence-based programs that can address the most important concerns raised by the needs assessment. Finally, in the strategic planning phase, the team begins to implement the new program or programs to meet identified needs and evaluate the outcomes of that effort.

**Table 2** *A Four-Step Process for Disciplinary Reform: Putting the Safe and Responsive Schools Process Into Action*

1. *Making a commitment*

   Develop school-based teams composed of respected representatives of key school and community constituencies, and ensure that the time and accomplishments of that team are valued and recognized.

2. *Looking at local data*

   Review available data (questionnaires, surveys, team discussion, and disciplinary data) to (a) identify the greatest local needs or concerns with respect to violence, disruption, school discipline, and school climate; and (b) identify the school's strengths and resources in school violence prevention.

3. *Finding and examining resources*

   Review evidence-based practices for addressing violence and disruption at all three levels of prevention to identify promising practices and assess how those practices could be adopted within local resource constraints.

4. *Using strategic planning to create change*

   Use data from all previous phases to develop a comprehensive plan that addresses local violence and disciplinary prevention needs.

## SUMMARY

Clear and effective school discipline systems are critical in maintaining safe school environments conducive to learning. Yet the evidence has failed to support disciplinary exclusion as an intervention capable of ensuring such a climate. Viewed as behavioral interventions, out-of-school suspension and expulsion appear to lack treatment integrity, to show consistent evidence of racial and socioeconomic disparities, and to be associated with negative outcomes in terms of school climate, student behavior, student achievement, and school dropout. Fortunately, effective alternatives are emerging, many with strong empirical support. Problems of implementation clearly remain to be solved, although school reform strategies such as *Positive Behavior Interventions and Supports* and *Safe and Responsive Schools* appear to hold promise as methods for reforming school discipline systems. The challenge ahead for research and practice will be to identify ways to increase the implementation of effective disciplinary systems that maintain school safety without removing students from the opportunity to learn.

## RECOMMENDED RESOURCES

### Books and Other Printed Material

Ayers, W., Dohrn, B., & Ayers, R. (Eds.). *Zero tolerance: Resisting the drive for punishment in our schools* (pp. 176–187). New York: New Press.

This collection of articles addresses the issue of zero tolerance interventions that are designed with a non-technical audience in mind.

Casella, R. (2001). *At zero tolerance: Punishment, prevention, and school violence.* New York: Peter Lang.

This book thoughtfully considers the forces that maintain zero tolerance policies and the consequences of those policies.

Skiba, R. J., & Noam, G. G. (Eds.). *New directions for youth development. No. 92: Zero tolerance: Can suspension and expulsion keep schools safe?* (pp. 17–43). San Francisco: Jossey-Bass.

This collection of six reviews consider the data on zero tolerance, suspension and expulsion, and the alternatives to those procedures.

### Websites

*http://www.colorado.edu/cspv/blueprints/*

Blueprints for Violence Prevention, the website of the Center for the Study and Prevention of Violence, presents findings of its evidence-based evaluations identifying effective violence prevention programs.

*http://www.pavnet.org*

The Partnerships Against Violence Network is a virtual library of information about violence and youth at risk with data from seven federal agencies. Professionals can communicate and share resources using the network.

*http://www.surgeongeneral.gov/library/youthviolence/*

Youth Violence: A Report of the Surgeon General was a collaboration of three federal agencies (the Centers for Disease Control and Prevention (CDC), the National Institutes of Health (NIH), and the Substance Abuse and Mental Health Services Administration (SAMHSA) to describe the status of knowledge about youth violence prevention, and especially to identify effective and promising practices for addressing youth violence.

*http://www.unl.edu/srs/* or *http://www.indiana.edu/safeschl*

The Safe and Responsive Schools Project at University of Nebraska–Lincoln and Indiana University is a framework that enables schools to engage in a strategic planning process to restructure school discipline and school safety planning.

*http://www.tolerance.org/teach/index.jsp*

Tolerance.org is a web project of the Southern Poverty Law Center that helps educators and others teach tolerance.

*http://ceep.indiana.edu/ChildrenLeftBehind*

Children Left Behind is the website of a project analyzing one state's disciplinary data in order to create a meaningful dialogue among policymakers, educators, and community members about suspension, expulsion, and their alternatives.

## REFERENCES

Advancement Project/Civil Rights Project. (2000, February). *Opportunities suspended: The devastating consequences of zero tolerance and school discipline.* Cambridge, MA: Author.

American Psychological Association. (1993). *Violence and youth: Psychology's response.* Washington, DC: Author.

Ayers, W., Dohrn, B., & Ayers, R. (Eds.). (2001). *Zero tolerance: Resisting the drive for punishment in our schools* (pp. 176–187). New York: New Press.

Bear, G. C., Webster-Stratton, C., Furlong, M. J., & Rhee, S. (2000). Preventing aggression and violence. In K. M. Minke & G. G. Bear (Eds.), *Preventing school problems, promoting school success: Strategies and programs that work* (pp. 1–70). Bethesda, MD: National Association of School Psychologists.

Bodine, R. J., & Crawford, D. K. (1998). *The handbook of conflict resolution education: A guide to building quality programs in schools.* San Francisco: Jossey-Bass.

Bowditch, C. (1993). Getting rid of troublemakers: High school disciplinary procedures and the production of dropouts. *Social Problems, 40,* 493–507.

Brantlinger, E. (1991). Social class distinctions in adolescents' reports of problems and punishment in school. *Behavioral Disorders, 17,* 36–46.

Brophy, J. (1988). Research linking teacher behavior to student achievement: Potential implications for instruction of chapter 1 students. *Educational Psychologist, 23,* 235–286.

Children's Defense Fund. (1975). *School suspensions: Are they helping children?* Cambridge, MA: Washington Research Project.

Dwyer, K., Osher, D., & Warger, C. (1998). *Early warning, timely response: A guide to safe schools.* Washington, DC: U.S. Department of Education.

Eber, L., Sugai, G., Smith, C. R., & Scott, T. M. (2002). Wraparound and positive behavioral interventions and supports in the schools. *Journal of Emotional and Behavioral Disorders, 10,* 171–181.

Ekstrom, R. B., Goertz, J. M., Pollack, D. A., & Rock, D. A. (1986). Who drops out of high school and why? Findings from a national study. In G. Natriello (Ed.), *School dropouts: Patterns and policies.* New York: Teachers College Press.

Elliott, D., Hatot, N. J., Sirovatka, P., & Potter, B. B. (2001). *Youth violence: A report of the Surgeon General.* Washington, DC: U.S. Department of Health and Human Services.

Gagnon, J. C., & Leone, P. E. (2001). Alternative strategies for youth violence prevention. In R. J. Skiba & G. G. Noam (Eds.), *New directions for youth development. No. 92: Zero tolerance: Can suspension and expulsion keep school safe?* (pp. 101–125). San Francisco: Jossey-Bass.

Garibaldi, A., Blanchard, L., & Brooks, S. (1996). Conflict resolution training, teacher effectiveness and student suspension: The impact of a health and safety initiative in the New Orleans public schools. *Journal of Negro Education, 65,* 408–413.

Gottfredson, D. C., Gottfredson, G. D., & Skroban, S. (1998). Can prevention work where it is needed most? *Evaluation Review, 22,* 315–339.

Gottfredson, G. D., Gottfredson, D. C., Czeh, E. R., Cantor, D., Crosse, S., & Hantman, I. (2000). *The national study of delinquency prevention in schools.* Ellicott City, MD: Gottfredson Associates.

Greenberg, M. T., Weissberg, R. P., O'Brien, M. U., Zins, J. E., Fredericks, L., Resnik, H., & Elias, M. J. (2003). Enhancing school-based prevention and youth development through coordinated social, emotional, and academic learning. *American Psychologist, 58,* 466–474.

Greenwood, C. R., Horton, B. T., & Utley, C. A. (2002). Academic engagement: Current perspectives on research and practice. *School Psychology Review, 31,* 328–349.

Heaviside, S., Rowand, C., Williams, C., & Farris, E. (1998). Violence and discipline problems in U.S. public schools: 1996–97. (NCES 98-030). Washington, DC: U.S. Department of Education, National Center for Education Statistics.

Hellman, D. A., & Beaton, S. (1986). The pattern of violence in urban public schools: The influence of school and community. *Journal of Research in Crime and Delinquency, 23,* 102–127.

Kaeser, S. C. (1979). Suspensions in school discipline. *Education and Urban Society, 11,* 465–484.

Lane, K. L., Bocian, K. M., MacMillan, D. L., Gresham, F. M. (2004). Treatment integrity: An essential—but often forgotten—component of school-based interventions. *Preventing School Failure, 48,* 36–44.

Massachusetts Advocacy Center. (1986). *The way out: Student exclusion practices in Boston middle schools.* Boston, MA: Author.

McFadden, A. C., & Marsh, G. E. (1992). A study of race and gender bias in the punishment of school children. *Education and Treatment of Children, 15,* 140–147.

Michigan Public Policy Initiative. (2003). Zero tolerance policies and their impact on Michigan students [Online]. Retrieved July 28, 2004, from http://www.mnaonline.org/pdf/spotlight%202002_12.pdf

Morrison, G. M., & D'Incau, B. (1997). The web of zero tolerance: Characteristics of students who are recommended for expulsion from school. *Education and Treatment of Children, 20,* 316–336.

Mrazek, P. J., & Haggerty, R. J. (Eds.). (1994). *Reducing risks for mental disorders: Frontiers for preventive intervention research.* Washington, DC: National Academy Press.

No Child Left Behind Act Fact Sheet. (2001). The facts about investing in what works [Online]. Retrieved July 21, 2004, from http://www.ed.gov/nclb/methods/whatworks/what_works.pdf

Osher, D. M., Sandler, S., & Nelson, C. L. (2001). The best approach to safety is to fix schools and support children and staff. In R. J. Skiba & G. G. Noam (Eds.), *New directions for youth development. No. 92: Zero tolerance: Can suspension and expulsion keep school safe?* (pp. 127–154). San Francisco: Jossey-Bass.

Potts, K., Njie, B., Detch, E. R., & Walton, J. (2003). *Zero tolerance in Tennessee schools: An update.* Nashville: Office of Education Accountability, State of Tennessee. (ERIC Document Reproduction Service No. ED481971).

Raffaele Mendez, L. M. (2003). Predictors of suspension and negative school outcomes: A longitudinal investigation. In J. Wald & D. J. Losen (Eds.), *New directions for youth development. No. 99: Deconstructing the school-to-prison pipeline* (pp. 17–34). San Francisco: Jossey-Bass.

Raffaele Mendez, L. M., & Knoff, H. M. (2003). Who gets suspended from school and why: A demographic analysis of schools and disciplinary infractions in a large school district. *Education and Treatment of Children, 26,* 30–51.

Raffaele Mendez, L. M., Knoff, H. M., & Ferron, J. F. (2002). School demographic variables and out-of-school suspension rates: A quantitative and qualitative analysis of a large, ethnically diverse school district. *Psychology in the Schools, 39,* 259–277.

Rausch, M. K., & Skiba, R. J. (2004). Unplanned outcomes: Suspensions and expulsions in Indiana. Bloomington, IN: Center for Evaluation and Education Policy [Online]. Retrieved July 21, 2004, from http://ceep.indiana.edu/ChildrenLeftBehind

Rosenberg, M. S., & Jackman, L. A. (2003). Development, implementation, and sustainability of comprehensive school-wide behavior management systems. *Intervention in School and Clinic, 39,* 10–21.

Schoenwald, S. K., & Hoagwood, K. (2001). Effectiveness, transportability, and dissemination of intervention: What matters when? *Psychiatric Services, 52,* 1190–1197.

Scott, T. M., & Barrett, S. B. (2004). Using staff and student time engaged in disciplinary procedures to evaluate the impact of school-wide PBS. *Journal of Positive Behavior Interventions, 6,* 21–27.

Shaw, S. R., & Braden, J. P. (1990). Race and gender bias in the administration of corporal punishment. *School Psychology Review, 19,* 378–383.

Sherman, L. W., Gottfredson, D. C., MacKenzie, D. L., Eck, J., Reuter, P., & Bushway, S. D. (Eds.). (1997). *Preventing crime: What works, what doesn't, what's promising. A report to the United States Congress* (NCJ 171676). Washington, DC: U.S. Department of Justice, Office of Justice Programs.

Skiba, R. J., Michael, R. S., Nardo, A. C., & Peterson, R. (2002). The color of discipline: Sources of racial and gender disproportionality in school punishment. *Urban Review, 34,* 317–342.

Skiba, R. J., & Peterson, R. L. (1999). The dark side of zero tolerance: Can punishment lead to safe schools? *Phi Delta Kappan, 80,* 372–376, 381–382.

Skiba, R. J., Peterson, R., Miller, C., Ritter, S., & Simmons, A. (in press). The safe and responsive schools project: A school reform model for implementing best practices in violence prevention. In S. Jimerson & M. Furlong (Eds.), *Handbook of school violence and school safety: From research to practice.* Mahwah, NJ: Lawrence Erlbaum Associates.

Skiba, R. J., Peterson, R. L., & Williams, T. (1997). Office referrals and suspension: Disciplinary intervention in middle schools. *Education and Treatment of Children, 20,* 295–315.

Skiba, R. J., & Rausch, M. K. (2004). *The relationship between achievement, discipline, and race: An analysis of factors predicting ISTEP scores.* Bloomington, IN: Center for Evaluation and Education Policy [Online]. Retrieved July 21, 2004, from http://ceep.indiana.edu/ChildrenLeftBehind

Skiba, R. J., Simmons, A. B., Peterson, R. L., McKelvey, J., Forde, S., & Gallini, S. (2004). Beyond guns, drugs, and gangs: The structure of student perceptions of school safety. In M. Furlong, G. Morrison, R. Skiba, and D. Cornell (Eds.), *Issues in school violence research.* Binghamton, NY: Hawthorn.

Skiba, R. J., Simmons, A. B., Staudinger, L. P., Rausch, M. K., Dow, G., & Feggins, L. R. (2003). *Consistent removal: Contributions of school discipline to the school-prison pipeline.* Paper presented at the Harvard Civil Rights Conference School-to-Prison Pipeline Conference, Cambridge, MA.

Skinner, B. F. (1953). *Science and human behavior.* New York: Free Press.

Stone, D. H. (1993). Crime & punishment in public schools: An empirical study of disciplinary proceedings. *Journal of Trial Advocacy, 17,* 351–398.

Sugai, G., Horner, R. H., Dunlap, G., Hieneman, M., Lewis, T. J., Nelson, C. M., et al. (2000). Applying positive behavior support and functional behavioral assessment in schools. *Journal of Positive Behavior Interventions, 2,* 131–143.

Thornton, C. H., & Trent, W. (1988). School desegregation and suspension in East Baton Rouge Parish: A preliminary report. *Journal of Negro Education, 57,* 482–501.

Tobin, T., Sugai, G., & Colvin, G. (1996). Patterns in middle school discipline records. *Journal of Emotional and Behavioral Disorders, 4,* 82–94.

Tolan, P. H., & Guerra, N. (1994). *What works in reducing adolescent violence: An empirical review of the field.* Boulder, CO: Center for the study and prevention of violence, Institute for Behavioral Sciences, University of Colorado, Boulder.

Townsend, B. (2000). Disproportionate discipline of African American children and youth: Culturally responsive strategies for reducing school suspension and expulsions. *Exceptional Children, 66,* 381–391.

U.S. Department of Education. (2000). The 2000–2001 elementary and secondary school survey: National and state projections. Washington, DC: U.S. Government Printing Office [Online]. Retrieved July 26, 2004, from http://205.207.175.84/ocr2000r/wdsdata.html

Vavrus, F., & Cole, K. (2002). "I didn't do nothin": The discursive construction of school suspension. *Urban Review, 34,* 87–111.

Wald, J., & Losen, D. J. (2003). Defining and redirecting a school-to-prison pipeline. In J. Wald & D. J. Losen (Eds.), *New directions for youth development. No. 99: Deconstructing the school-to-prison pipeline* (pp. 9–15). San Francisco: Jossey-Bass.

Walker, H. M., Horner, R. H., Sugai, G., Bullis, M., Sprague, J. R., Bricker, D., & Kaufman, M. J. (1996). Integrated approaches to preventing antisocial behavior patterns among school-age children and youth. *Journal of Emotional and Behavioral Disorders, 4*(4), 194–209.

Walker, H. M., & Shinn, M. R. (2002). Structuring school-based interventions to achieve integrated primary, secondary, and tertiary prevention goals for safe and effective schools. In M. R. Shinn, H. M. Walker, & G. Stoner (Eds.), *Interventions for academic and behavior problems. II: Preventive and remedial approaches* (pp. 1–26). Bethesda, MD: National Association of School Psychologists.

Wu, S. C., Pink, W. T., Crain, R. L., & Moles, O. (1982). Student suspension: A critical reappraisal. *Urban Review, 14,* 245–303.

Zins, J. E., Weissberg, R. P., Wang, M. C., & Walberg, H. J. (Eds.). (2004). *Building academic success on social and emotional learning: What does the research say?* New York: Teachers College Press.

# 8

# School Completion

**Amy Reschly**

*University of South Carolina*

**Sandra L. Christenson**

*University of Minnesota*

High school completion is increasingly important in American society. Although school completion has been a significant national issue for the past two decades, at no time in our nation's history have dropout and school completion garnered so much attention and concern or have the stakes been so high. As our nation has become increasingly technological, the importance of postsecondary education has increased. At the same time, job opportunities and wages for high school dropouts are diminishing. Furthermore, the consequences of not completing high school, personally and for society, are well documented and severe.

With the recent passage of the No Child Left Behind Act, completion and dropout have become a high-stakes issue for schools and districts as well. Under that legislation, schools and districts are held accountable for the completion rates of *all* students, including those who have traditionally not fared well in the U.S. educational system, including students who receive special education services, students of color, students who are English Language Learners, and students living in poverty. The focus on promoting successful school completion is more relevant and imperative today than ever before.

## BACKGROUND AND DEVELOPMENT

### Interpreting Dropout Statistics

Headlines and stories about dropout rates appear frequently in newspapers, both locally and nationally. However, a note of caution regarding the interpretation of dropout statistics is warranted. First, there are different types of dropout statistics. For example, the National Center for Education Statistics (NCES) reports event, status, and cohort dropout rates (Kaufman, Alt, & Chapman, 2001). *Event* rates reflect the proportion of students within a certain age range who drop out of school each year. *Status* rates are cumulative and provide a measure of dropout among all youth within a given age range. *Cohort* rates follow a group of students over time (Kaufman, Alt, & Chapman, 2001). In addition, several issues are related to the estimation of dropout rates, such as the following (Wolman, Bruininks, & Thurlow, 1989):

- Length of time a student is absent from school before he or she is classified as a dropout.
- Inclusion or exclusion of students in special education.
- Inclusion of all students in the district, regardless of program, or only those enrolled in traditional high schools.
- Inclusion of students who drop out during the summer months.
- Age of students classified as dropouts.
- Grade levels included in the report.
- Student mobility to other districts and states.

Recent statistics indicate that dropout continues to be a significant problem in the United States. According to the status dropout rate, 11% of 16- to 24-year-olds were out of school without a high school credential in 2001. Although the status dropout rate declined for young adults in that age range between the early 1970s and 2001, it remained quite stable between 1992 and 2001 (U.S. Department of Education, 2003).

Some groups of students are at particularly high risk for dropping out: those who are from low socioeconomic status (SES) backgrounds, students who are Hispanic, African American, or Native-American, and students with disabilities (Christenson, Sinclair, Lehr, & Hurley, 2000; Rumberger, 1995). In terms of SES and regional differences, 12.7% of students in the lowest 20% of the income distribution dropped out of school in 1998, compared with 3.8% of students from middle income families and 2.7% of students with families in the top 20% of the income distribution. Young adults living in the Northeast and Midwest have higher completion rates (88%) than those in the South (83.4%) and the West (80.4%; Kaufman, Kwon, Klein, & Chapman, 1999). Finally, students with disabilities complete school at a rate far below their general education peers. For example, in the 1998–1999 school year, the most recent year for which data are available, only 57.4% of students with disabilities graduated from high school with a standard diploma (U.S. Department of Education, 2001), compared to approximately 75% of the general population of students. This status completion rate of 75% is based on receipt of a standard diploma. Another 10% of students in the total population complete high school by an alternative method (Kaufman et al., 1999).

## Research on Dropout

Research on dropout has generally been descriptive. The literature currently addresses predictors of dropout, but much less information is available on the development of effective prevention and intervention strategies (Christenson, Sinclair, Lehr, & Godber, 2001). One useful distinction in the classification of dropout predictors is that of amenability to intervention (alterable vs. unalterable). Unalterable predictors of dropout are variables such as race or ethnicity, SES, or having a sibling or parent that dropped out of school. Alterable predictors of dropout are those that may be useful in prevention and intervention efforts. Those variables may be classified according to level (students, families, and schools) and by whether the predictor is a protective or risk factor for dropout. Although not an exhaustive list, several examples of alterable predictors associated with dropout may be found in Table 1. It is important to note, however, that as with all important developmental outcomes, dropout is best understood as an interaction, over time, between individuals and the systems in which they are embedded (home, schools, peers, and community). As such, it is impossible to characterize any single predictor of a complex outcome as an *internal child* or an *external (family, school, or peers)* predictor.

**Table 1** *Alterable Variables Associated With School Dropout*

| | **Protective** | **Risk** |
|---|---|---|
| Students | • Complete homework<br>• Come to class prepared<br>• High locus of control<br>• Good self-concept<br>• Expectations for school completion | • High rate of absences<br>• Behavior problems<br>• Poor academic performance<br>• Grade retention<br>• Working |
| Families | • Academic support (e.g., help with homework) and motivational support (e.g., high expectations, talk to children about school) for learning<br>• Parental monitoring | • Low educational expectations<br>• Mobility<br>• Permissive parenting styles |
| Schools | • Orderly school environments<br>• Committed, caring teachers<br>• Fair discipline policies | • Weak adult authority<br>• Large school size (>1,000 students)<br>• High pupil–teacher ratios<br>• Few caring relationships between staff and students<br>• Poor or uninteresting curricula<br>• Low expectations and high rates of truancy |

*Note.* The contents of this table were drawn from the following sources: Bryk & Thum, 1989; Ekstrom, Goertz, Pollack, & Rock, 1986; Hess & D'Amato, 1996; Rumberger, 1995; Wehlage & Rutter, 1986.

Another distinction that may be useful when considering predictors of dropout is what Jordan, McPartland, and Lara (1999) describe as "push/pull effects." *Push effects* (e.g., suspending students or assigning failing grades for excessive absences) describe situations or experiences in which students are unable to cope with policies and practices within the school environment. These school-based practices exacerbate rather than ameliorate failure and dropout. The widespread adoption of zero tolerance policies for managing students' behavior, which result in suspension or expulsion, is both a vivid and a troubling example of a practice that pushes students out of school. In addition to such policies' ineffectiveness in deterring misbehavior, they also are applied capriciously, result in lost opportunities to learn, and are associated with students dropping out and not graduating on time. Often, these disciplinary actions are used to rid schools of the most difficult students (see chapter 7, "School Disciplinary Systems: Alternatives to Suspension and Expulsion"). *Pull effects*, on the other hand, refer to external factors or pressures that undermine the emphasis on schooling for the student (e.g., pregnancy, employment, or family demands). Using data from the National Educational Longitudinal Study of 1988, Jordan et al. (1999) found that push factors were most important for predicting a student's decision to drop out. Approximately half of the 25,000 students in the 1,000 schools in the study reported not liking or failing school, whereas only 7% indicated they needed to help support their families, and 17% indicated they had to get a job. School-related factors were the most frequently cited reasons for dropping out, regardless of gender or ethnicity.

At the student level, evidence clearly shows that students who drop out often experience difficulties with academics (DeBettencourt, Zigmond, & Thornton, 1989; Ekstrom, Goertz, Pollack, & Rock, 1986; Kortering, Horing, & Klockars, 1992; Zigmond & Thornton, 1985). However, studies of dropouts and the literature on peer and student–teacher relationships reveal the importance of the personal side of schooling. There is considerable evidence that students' feelings of belonging and their relationships with teachers and peers are associated with important educational processes (e.g., work completion, attitudes, and participation) and outcomes (e.g., achievement, dropout; Christenson & Anderson, 2002). It has been argued that relationships with teachers and peers set a path toward school completion or dropout (Marcus & Sanders-Reio, 2001). Studies of students who dropped out have found that dropouts frequently reported not getting along with teachers or peers, feeling as though they did not belong at school, having friends that dropped out (Berktold, Geis, & Kaufman, 1998), and finding the teachers uncaring and school boring (Tidwell, 1988).

School-level differences are another important consideration in understanding and predicting dropout and completion. It is no surprise that dropout rates vary by school. Although some of the school-level variation can be attributed to the characteristics of students who attend the school, the composition of the student body, school resources, and policies also influence dropout rates. For example, after accounting for student characteristics, Rumberger and Thomas (2000) found that high-SES schools had a lower adjusted dropout rate than average-SES schools, and average SES schools had lower adjusted dropout rates than low-SES schools. Similar results were reported for students' perceptions of teacher quality, student–teacher ratios, and teacher salaries and for school-wide attendance. In general, policies supporting grade retention and suspension are associated with higher school-level dropout rates, whereas schools with fair discipline policies, opportunities for participation, high attendance by students and staff, and caring and devoted teachers are associated with lower dropout rates (see Table 1). Rumberger and Thomas (2000) argued that schools affect dropout and mobility in two ways: *directly*, through explicit policies and decisions that cause students to involuntarily withdraw from school, and *indirectly*, with the implementation of policies and practices designed to promote the effectiveness of schools but that instead contribute to voluntary student turnover by negatively affecting conditions that keep students engaged.

## Development

The word *dropout* implies an event, or something short term; however, there is evidence that dropout and completion are best conceptualized as a process that occurs over many years. Early childhood experiences have been related to school adjustment and to dropout or completion years later (e.g., Jimerson, Egeland, Sroufe, & Carlson, 2000). Others have delineated developmental pathways to dropout that involve early school difficulties, childhood exposure to drug use, and cumulative family stress at a young age (Garnier, Stein, & Jacobs, 1997). Furthermore, it is possible to predict from early elementary school which students will later drop out (e.g., Alexander, Entwisle, & Horsey, 1997; Barrington & Hendricks, 1989; Ensminger & Slusarcick, 1992). For example, after accounting for demographic variables, Alexander et al. (1997) found that students' engagement behaviors (attendance and behavior) and attachment to school in the first grade predicted dropout years later.

Arguably, the most influential theory, or model, for understanding the dropout process is the Participation-Identification Model proposed by Finn (1989). In that theory, the process of dropout is described in terms of engagement. Engagement consists of students' behavior

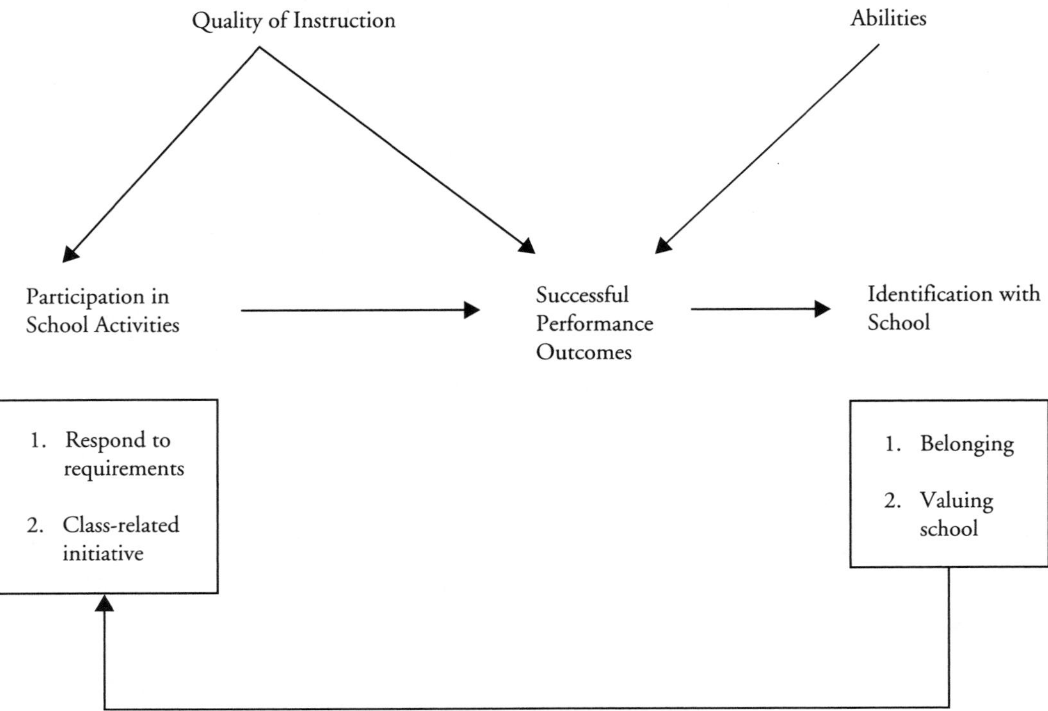


*Note.* From "Withdrawing from School," by J. D. Finn, 1989, *Review of Educational Research, 59,* p. 130. Copyright 1989 by the American Educational Research Association. Reprinted with permission.

**Figure 1.** *Finn's Participation-Identification Model of School Engagement.*

(involvement with classroom and school activities) and identification with school. Finn delineated levels of participation in the school environment. In its most basic form, participating in the school environment involves attending school, being prepared to work, and responding to the teacher's directions and questions. Other levels represent students' initiative to be involved in the classroom and school, participation in social and extracurricular activities, and involvement in decision making. The theory is developmental in that it reflects how participation in the school environment changes as students progress through school, with greater opportunities to become involved in the nonacademic aspects of the school environment.

Figure 1 provides a graphic representation of Finn's theory. Student participation in school activities is directly related to successful school performance, which in turn promotes identification with school. In the next step of the model, students' identification with school affects their ongoing participation. Most children arrive at school with a set of skills and the behaviors and attitudes needed for successful participation in the school environment. Although they encounter difficulties along the way, the cycle of participation and identification continues. These students are on the path toward school completion.

Other students, however, do not enter school with the behaviors and skills necessary for success. Over time, the cycle of participation and identification breaks down. These students are less likely than their peers to demonstrate increased and varied forms of participation in the school environment, such as initiative-taking in the classroom or participating in extracurricular activities, and are likely to develop increased feelings of alienation as they progress through school. According to this model, if not addressed, these students may exhibit the most extreme form of disengagement—dropping out of school (Finn, 1989).

# PROBLEMS AND IMPLICATIONS

## Consequences of Dropout

For both students and society, a host of negative consequences are associated with not completing high school. Students who do not complete high school are more likely to live in poverty, be dependent on welfare and other government assistance programs, have health problems, engage in criminal behavior and be incarcerated, and experience unemployment or underemployment (Christenson et al., 2000; Rumberger, 1995). Census data from 2002 indicate a difference in annual salary of dropouts and high school graduates of $6,700 ($22,500 vs. $29,200), while other estimates show even more disparate incomes (e.g., $15,334 vs. $29,294; Lehr, Clapper, & Thurlow, in press). In addition, the difference in wages between dropouts and graduates has become greater over time. In 1967, a male dropout earned 76% of what someone with a diploma earned, whereas by 1992 this had decreased to 58% (Grubb, 1997). Quite simply, the outlook for high school dropouts is bleak.

For society, the costs of government assistance programs for employment, housing, and medical care are staggering. It is estimated that each year of dropouts costs the United States $200 billion during their lifetimes in lost earnings and taxes (Catterall, 1985). Furthermore, school completion is increasingly considered an indicator of school effectiveness and is one of the criteria in the No Child Left Behind Act.

## Prevention and Intervention: Critical Concepts in School Completion

Although dropout has been a prominent issue for a number of years, most attention has been paid to preventing a negative outcome, dropping out, rather than promoting a positive one, completing school. Preventing school dropout, in and of itself, is not a sufficient goal (Christenson et al., 2001). Instead, society's focus must shift to promoting school completion with competence in academic and social domains.

An important step in promoting school completion is to understand the current research base on prevention and intervention strategies. Recently, independent reviews of the literature were conducted by Prevatt and Kelly (2003) and Lehr, Hansen, Sinclair, and Christenson (2003). They found that relatively few intervention studies have been published in peer-reviewed journals, and much of the published research in that area is of poor methodological quality. For example, in the Prevatt and Kelly (2003) literature review, only 30 of 259 articles published between 1982 and 2002 on the topic of dropout and school completion were dropout intervention studies, and only 18 of those included dropout as a dependent variable. Both reviews found that most interventions were implemented at the secondary level and included more than one type of intervention strategy (e.g., academic, personal and affective, psychosocial skills, family outreach, school structure, and work related). Prevatt and Kelly (2003) noted that, whereas interventions were often research based, few were grounded in theory. They also noted that most articles failed to provide information on the relative importance of various intervention components and that few interventions had been replicated or provided enough information in the article for others to replicate. Furthermore, Lehr et al. (2003) found that the focus of most interventions was on change within students, rather than on important contextual influences, such as peers, families, and schools, and few interventions were systematically implemented with students who have disabilities. Although Lehr et al. (2003) concluded that educational researchers currently lack the research foundation about dropout prevention and intervention from which to make definitive statements regarding policy and practice, some research has indicated that comprehensive, long-term interventions do yield positive results for students (e.g., Sinclair, Christenson, & Thurlow, 2005; Christenson & Thurlow, 2004).

The most important concept in understanding the development of dropout and its implications for prevention and intervention is the concept of student engagement. Finn's (1989) Participation-Identification Model describes dropout and completion in terms of students' engagement—participation in the classroom and in school environments and feelings of identification with school. Dropout can therefore be viewed as a process of disengagement that occurs over many years. That model is supported by the findings of investigations related to student engagement (e.g., Finn & Cox, 1992; Finn & Rock, 1997) and of past research on dropout and school completion.

McPartland (1994) proposed a conceptual framework to examine the causes and alleviation of dropout and to serve as a basis for dropout prevention programs. The framework is based on research regarding students at risk for poor outcomes, including dropout, and effective schools, and has garnered some empirical support for its four essential components of dropout prevention programs. The framework adopts the student's perspective and categorizes sources of motivation to stay in school by the type of organizational environment (formal and informal) and the nature of organizational problems (internal and external). The following are fundamental tenets of the framework:

- Students need to experience success at school.
- A positive interpersonal climate is a crucial part of students' school experiences.

- Coursework should be relevant to students' lives and future goals.
- Students need help with serious personal problems in order to be successful as learners.

Recently, we have proposed a taxonomy of student engagement. This taxonomy is based on experiences with the dropout prevention program Check & Connect (Sinclair, Christenson, Evelo, & Hurley, 1998), and links the conceptual work of McPartland (1994) in the area of dropout intervention with the work of Finn (1989) on student engagement and dropout.

*Academic* engagement is the amount of time students spend on task. There is a strong association between the amount of time a student spends on task and his or her achievement; however, engagement is a broader, multidimensional construct that includes *behavioral* (e.g., attendance, participation, and preparation for class and school), *cognitive* (self-regulation and perceived relevance of education to the future), and *psychological/interpersonal* engagement (i.e., relationships with teachers and peers and a sense of belonging). Academic and behavioral engagement are observable indicators, whereas cognitive and psychological engagement are internal indicators of students' engagement, requiring a higher level of inference (Sinclair, Christenson, Lehr, & Anderson, 2003). These types of engagement provide a useful heuristic for understanding students' experiences and performance in school and may be helpful in designing interventions to address these important components. Finally, a useful distinction in this conceptualization of student engagement can be made between *indicators* and *facilitators* of student engagement. Indicators refer to students' connections to school and learning (e.g., behavior, attendance, or homework completion), whereas facilitators refer to contextual influences (peers, families, and schools) that promote student engagement (Sinclair et al., 2003).

## ALTERNATIVE ACTIONS FOR PREVENTION

The next two sections describe prevention and intervention activities to address dropout. Although these sections are separate for the purposes of this chapter, there is considerable overlap in prevention and intervention activities designed to promote school completion. To prevent dropout, one must look beyond the individual student to the different systems, or contexts, of students' lives. Early childhood education is one avenue for promoting later student success. Students enter kindergarten with a wide range of skills and experiences. Many students who are at risk for dropping out have not had exposure to preacademic skills and experiences that facilitate success at school entry (e.g., rich verbal environment; trips to the zoo, museums, or libraries; knowledge of the alphabet and letter sounds; numeral concepts; and group social interactions). Quality preschool education is one means of promoting success for students at risk for school failure and later dropout. For example, students who participated in the Perry Preschool Project, a high-quality preschool program, were more likely than controls to graduate from high school, attend postsecondary institutions, have employment, and own homes (see *http://www.highscope.org*). Once in school, frequently monitoring students' academic progress and behavior and providing early and effective interventions when students are experiencing difficulties will also help promote completion. Problem-solving methodology (e.g., see Tilly, 2002) may be a particularly useful means of approaching students' academic and behavioral difficulties.

Although descriptive, predictors of dropout and completion found in the literature make logical connections to prevention efforts. Families that provide academic support (e.g., helping with homework, volunteering at school) and motivational support (e.g., setting high expectations for children, and talking to children about school) for learning[1], and that monitor children's activities are more likely to have children who complete school. At the school level, providing opportunities for meaningful participation, including decision-making, and success in the school environment; promoting fair disciplinary policies that are applied to *all* students; creating school environments that are warm and caring (e.g., having small teacher–student ratios, providing access to teachers and additional help, and promoting positive peer relationships); and having high expectations for students and staff will help keep students engaged with school and learning. In addition, across studies grade retention is the most robust predictor of dropout. This evidence remains even after retained students are matched to those who were promoted on demographic characteristics and achievement variables (Jimerson, 2001). Ensuring that schools and districts do not implement retention policies is an important facet of prevention efforts. The case for early and continued intervention for students experiencing academic and behavioral

[1]The distinction between academic and motivational support for learning comes from Bempechat (1998).

difficulties cannot be emphasized enough. By addressing students' difficulties before problems become severe, schools may have the solution to the long-standing debate on retention versus social promotion.

Transitions are another aspect of schooling that warrant particular care and attention. Students are often "lost" as they transition from elementary to middle school and from middle school to high school. Typically, when students move to the next level, they begin in an entirely new environment with more students (sometimes with thousands more students than in the previous school) and fewer opportunities to connect with teachers and staff. Helping students adjust to new environments (e.g., what to expect and school routines and rules), providing opportunities to be involved, and ensuring that students are aware that teachers and other staff, such as school psychologists and counselors, are receptive and available to students may help students navigate these transitions.

One of the most important activities for those interested in promoting school completion is to first systematically monitor students for signs of disengagement: behavioral, academic, and psychological indicators of withdrawal from school, including poor attendance, academic difficulties, behavior problems, low participation in class and extracurricular activities, difficulty with or isolation from peers, failure to achieve criterion levels of performance on mandated state achievement tests, and insufficient credits earned toward graduation. Next, school personnel should follow up with students who demonstrate signs of withdrawal (Anderson, Christenson, & Lehr, 2004). Following up may entail any number of activities, depending on the students' needs. What is important is that signs of disengagement are caught early and students are not lost from schools.

## ALTERNATIVE ACTIONS FOR INTERVENTION

There is no one "right" intervention that will work for every student, all the time. The strategies and interventions that are chosen will vary as a function of student needs and context. Schools and districts, like students, have different strengths, difficulties, and access to resources. Furthermore, many interventions that are commonly used in schools, though easy to implement, have little effect on student outcomes, including attendance, grades, and dropout rates (Dynarski & Gleason, 2002). However, there is promising evidence for the positive effects of long-term, systematic, personalized interventions (Christenson & Thurlow, 2004). An example of one intervention, Check & Connect, is presented in Table 2. In addition, it is important to intervene early, before problems become so severe that interventions are less likely to be effective.

There is some agreement regarding the essential components of dropout prevention programs. These components include the following (Anderson et al., 2004):

- Provide students with opportunities to experience academic success.
- Offer coursework that is relevant to students' lives and goals.
- Give students individual assistance.
- Foster a positive, interpersonal climate.
- Make sure resources are available to help students with their personal problems.
- Intervene early when addressing academic and behavior problems.

Interventions must address student engagement in a comprehensive way. Programs that address a single indicator of engagement, such as behavior or attendance, are unlikely to stem the trajectory of school withdrawal and later dropout. As is evident in the above list of intervention components, effective interventions must address students' academic, behavioral, cognitive, and psychological engagement with school. Furthermore, attention must also be paid to the context of students' lives. Families, peers, and schools are important facilitators of student engagement.

## SUMMARY

School completion is increasingly important in American society. Outcomes for dropouts are poor, and the costs to society are staggering. The current literature base on school dropout is largely descriptive. Demographic characteristics of students who drop out tend to be Native American, Hispanic, or African American, live in single-parent homes, come from low-SES families, or have disabilities. Other predictors of dropout may be organized according to student, family, or school-level variables. Protective factors for dropout include homework completion, parental monitoring, parental expectations for school completion, interesting curricula, and caring school environments; risk factors include attendance or behavior problems, high mobility, and large, impersonal schools.

Dropout is increasingly viewed as a process of withdrawal from school over many years. The construct of student engagement is used to describe this process of withdrawal and is the foundation of prevention and

**Table 2** *Intervention Program Example: Check & Connect*

Principal Developers: Sandra Christenson, Mary Sinclair, Martha Thurlow, and David Evelo, University of Minnesota

Background:

- Designed to promote student engagement and school completion through relationship building, problem solving, and persistence.
- Based on resilience literature and the theoretical and empirical work on student engagement and school completion.

Intervention Staff:

- A *monitor/mentor* who works individually with students and collaboratively with families, school staff, and community personnel regarding students' educational success. Monitors are asked to make 2-year commitments to the program.

Components:

- *Relationship building*: mutual trust and open communication, nurtured through a long-term commitment that is focused on student's educational success.
- *Problem solving*: designed to promote the acquisition of skills to resolve conflict constructively and to look for solutions rather than a source of blame.
- *Persistence Plus*: refers to a persistent source of academic motivation, a continuity of familiarity with the youth and family, and a consistency in the message that "education is important for your future."
- *Routine monitoring of alterable indicators*: systematic checks of warning signs of withdrawal (attendance, academic performance, behavior) that are readily available to school personnel and that can be altered through intervention.
- *Timely and individualized interventions*: support that is tailored to individual student needs, based on level of engagement with school, associated influences of home and school, and the leveraging of local resources.

Empirical Results:

- *Pilot Study 1992–1995*: students with learning and emotional/behavior disorders, grades 7–9 (Sinclair, Christenson, Evelo, & Hurley, 1998). Treatment students more likely than controls to be enrolled in school at the end of 9th grade and to graduate within 5 years (68% vs. 29%).
- *School Success Truancy Intervention 1996–2002*: students with and without disabilities, ages 11–17 (Sinclair & Kaibel, 2002). Reduction in the percentage of students absent more than 15% of the time (45% at time of referral to 32% after 2 years of Check & Connect) and an increase in the percentage of students present more than 95% of the time (from 11% at referral to 34% after 2 years).
- *Persistence Plus 1996–2001*: Persistence Plus 1996–2001: students with emotional and behavioral disorders, grades 9–12 (Sinclair, Christenson, & Thurlow, 2005). Check & Connect students were significantly less likely than controls to drop out of school (39% vs. 43%).
- *Elementary Truancy Prevention Pilot 1997–2001*: elementary students and their families (Lehr, Sinclair, & Christenson, 2004). After 2 years, the percentage of students present 95% of the time increased from 17% to 40% while the percentage of students arriving on time increased from 42% to 86%.
- Also used as a service delivery model for students with aggressive behavior (Early Risers Check & Connect) and combined with early literacy screening and interventions for kindergartners and first-graders (Project ELSE; O'Shaughnessy et al., 2004).

*Note.* Information drawn from Check & Connect website. Retrieved August 10, 2004 from *http://ici.umn.edu/checkandconnect/*.

intervention efforts. Engagement is multidimensional, involving academic, behavioral, cognitive, and psychological components. Although definitive statements regarding intervention programs cannot be made at this time, evidence is promising for interventions that are personalized, systematic, and long term.

The answer to preventing early school departure, or promoting school completion, is not easy. There is no magic bullet to remedy the dropout problem. Furthermore, intensive interventions require time, resources, and sustained effort. Though federal initiatives promote, or even require, the use of evidence-based practices, the knowledge base in the area of dropout prevention and intervention is in the earliest stages. *Sound research is needed to guide practice in schools* (Christenson & Thurlow, 2004). Despite these challenges, this is also an exciting time of change and opportunity in our nation's schools. Interventions that comprehensively address students' engagement (academic, cognitive, behavioral, and psychological) and facilitators of student engagement (families, peers, and schools) have the potential to change students' lives and ensure that all students complete high school with the academic and social skills necessary for success in our society.

# RECOMMENDED RESOURCES

## Books and Other Printed Material

Christenson, S. L., & Thurlow, M. L. (2004). School dropouts: Prevention considerations, interventions, and challenges. *Current Directions in Psychological Science, 13,* 36–39.

This recent article reviews the state of the evidence for dropout prevention and intervention and the particular challenges arising from the NCLB legislation.

Contemporary Psychological Perspectives on School Completion [Special issue]. *School Psychology Quarterly, 16,* 351–484.

This special issue of *School Psychology Quarterly* is devoted to the topic of dropout and completion. Articles review past research on dropout and describe predictors of dropout at the individual and school levels and the state of intervention research.

Dynarski, M., & Gleason, P. (2002). How can we help? What we have learned from recent federal dropout prevention evaluations. *Journal of Education for Students Placed At-Risk, 7,* 43–69.

This publication summarizes implementation and impact findings from more than 20 federally funded dropout prevention programs for secondary students. The findings suggest that alternative schools for students in grades 6–8, GED programs for students in high school, and personalizing education show promise for reducing or preventing dropout.

## Websites

*http://www.dropoutprevention.org*

This website is for the National Dropout Prevention Center/Network, based at Clemson University. The Center is a research and resource network for policy makers, practitioners, and researchers.

*http://www.nces.ed.gov*

The website is for the National Center for Education Statistics in the U.S. Department of Education. The most recent dropout and completion statistics are available here, as are research reports related to dropout and school completion.

*http://www.ici.umn.edu/checkandconnect/*

This is the website for the Check & Connect intervention program developed at the University of Minnesota.

# REFERENCES

Alexander, K. L., Entwisle, D. R., & Horsey, C. S. (1997). From first grade forward: Early foundations of high school dropouts. *Sociology of Education, 70,* 87–107.

Anderson, A. R., Christenson, S. L., & Lehr, C. A. (2004). *Promoting student engagement to enhance school completion: Information and strategies for educators. Helping children at home and at school.* Bethesda, MD: National Association of School Psychologists.

Barrington, B. L., & Hendricks, B. (1989). Differentiating characteristics of high school graduates, dropouts, and nongraduates. *Journal of Educational Research, 82*(6), 309–319.

Bempechat, J. (1998). *Against the odds: How "at-risk" students EXCEED expectations.* San Francisco: Jossey-Bass.

Berktold, J., Geis, G., & Kaufman, P. (1998). *Subsequent educational attainment of high school dropouts.* Washington, DC: U.S. Department of Education, National Center for Education Statistics.

Bryk, A. S., & Thum, Y. M. (1989). The effects of high school organization on dropping out: An exploratory investigation. *American Educational Research Journal, 26,* 353–383.

Catterall, J. S. (1985). On the social costs of dropping out of schools. (Report No. 86-SEPT-3).Stanford, CA: Stanford University, Center for Educational Research.

Christenson, S. L., & Anderson, A. R. (2002). Commentary: The centrality of the learning context for students' academic enabler skills. *School Psychology Review, 31,* 378–393.

Christenson, S. L., Sinclair, M. F., Lehr, C. A., & Godber, Y. G. (2001). Promoting successful school completion: Critical conceptual and methodological guidelines. *School Psychology Quarterly, 16,* 468–484.

Christenson, S. L., Sinclair, M. F., Lehr, C., & Hurley, C. (2000). Promoting successful school completion. In Kathleen M. Minke & George G. Bear (Eds.), *Preventing school problems—Promoting school success: Strategies and programs that work.* Bethesda, MD: National Association of School Psychologists.

Christenson, S. L., & Thurlow, M. L. (2004). School dropouts: Prevention considerations, interventions, and challenges. *Current Directions in Psychological Science, 13,* 36–39.

DeBettencourt, L. U., Zigmond, N., & Thornton, H. (1989). Follow-up of postsecondary-age rural learning disabled graduates and dropouts. *Exceptional Children, 56,* 40–49.

Dynarski, M., & Gleason, P. (2002). How can we help? What we have learned from recent federal dropout prevention evaluations. *Journal of Education for Students Placed At-Risk, 7,* 43–69.

Ekstrom, R. B., Goertz, M. E., Pollack, J. M., & Rock, D. A. (1986). Who drops out of high school and why? Findings from a national study. *Teachers College Record, 87,* 356–373.

Ensminger, M. E., & Slusarcick, A. L. (1992). Paths to high school graduation or dropout: A longitudinal study of a first-grade cohort. *Sociology of Education, 65,* 95–113.

Finn, J. D. (1989). Withdrawing from school. *Review of Educational Research, 59,* 117–142.

Finn, J. D., & Cox, D. (1992). Participation and withdrawal among fourth-grade pupils. *American Educational Research Journal, 29,* 141–162.

Finn, J. D., & Rock, D. A. (1997). Academic success among students at-risk for school failure. *Journal of Applied Psychology, 82,* 221–234.

Garnier, P., Stein, J. A., & Jacobs, J. K. (1997). The process of dropping out of high school: A 19-year perspective. *American Educational Research Journal, 34,* 395–419.

Grubb, W. N. (1997). The returns of education in the sub-baccalaureate labor market 1984–1990. *Economics of Education Review, 16,* 231–245.

Hess, R. S., & D'Amato, R. C. (1996). High school completion among Mexican-American children: Individual and family background variables. *School Psychology Quarterly, 11,* 353–368.

Jimerson, S. (2001). Meta-analysis of grade retention research: Implications for practice in the 21st century. *School Psychology Review, 30,* 420–437.

Jimerson, S., Egeland, B., Sroufe, L. A., & Carlson, E. (2000). A prospective longitudinal study of high school dropouts: Examining multiple predictors across development. *Journal of School Psychology, 38,* 525–549.

Jordan, W. J., McPartland, J. M., & Lara, J. (1999). Rethinking the causes of high school dropout. *The Prevention Researcher, 6,* 1–4.

Kaufman, P., Alt, M. N., & Chapman, C. D. (2001). *Dropout rates in the United States: 2000.* Washington, DC: U.S. Department of Education, National Center for Education Statistics.

Kaufman, P., Kwon, J. Y, Klein, S., & Chapman, C. D. (1999). *Dropout rates in the United States: 1998.* [Online]. Retrieved August 23, 2005 from http://nces.ed.gov

Kortering, L., Horing, N., & Klockars, A. (1992). The identification of high school dropouts as learning disabled: Evaluating the utility of discriminant analysis function. *Exceptional Children, 58,* 422–435.

Lehr, C. A., Clapper, A. T., & Thurlow, M. (in press). *Graduation for all: A practical guide to decreasing school dropout.* Thousand Oaks, CA: Corwin Press.

Lehr, C. A., Hansen, A., Sinclair, M. F., & Christenson, S. L. (2003). An integrative review of data-based interventions: Moving beyond dropout towards school completion. *School Psychology Review, 32,* 342–364.

Lehr, C. A., Sinclair, M. F., & Christenson, S. L. (2004). Addressing student engagement and truancy prevention during the elementary years: A replication study of the Check & Connect model. *Journal of Education for Students Placed At-Risk, 9,* 279–301.

Marcus, R. G., & Sanders-Reio, J. (2001). The influence of attachment on school completion. *School Psychology Quarterly, 16,* 427–444.

McPartland, J. M. (1994). Dropout prevention in theory and practice. In R. J. Rossi (Ed.), *Schools and students at risk: Context and framework for positive change* (pp. 255–276). New York: Teachers College Press.

O'Shaughnessy, T. E., Draper, K., Christenson, S. L., Militch, A., Waldbart, A., & Gabriel, S. (2004). Preventive intervention for kindergarten children at risk for school failure: Efficacy of a sustained early literacy-school engagement procedure.

Prevatt, F., & Kelly, F. D. (2003). Dropping out of school: A review of intervention programs. *Journal of School Psychology, 41,* 377–395.

Rumberger, R. W. (1995). Dropping out of middle school: A multilevel analysis of students and schools. *American Educational Research Journal, 32,* 583–625.

Rumberger, R. W., & Thomas, S. L. (2000). The distribution of dropout and turnover rates among urban and suburban high schools. *Sociology of Education, 73,* 39–67.

Sinclair, M. F., Christenson, S. L., Evelo, D., & Hurley, C. (1998). Dropout prevention for high-risk youth with disabilities: Efficacy of a sustained school engagement procedure. *Exceptional Children, 65,* 7–21.

Sinclair, M. F., Christenson, S. L., Lehr, C. A., & Anderson, A. R. (2003). Facilitating student engagement: Lessons learned from Check & Connect longitudinal studies. *California School Psychologist, 8,* 29–42.

Sinclair, M. F., Christenson, S. L., & Thurlow, M. L. (2005). Promoting school completion of urban secondary youth with emotional or behavioral disabilities. *Exceptional Children, 71,* 465–482.

Sinclair, M., & Kaibel, C. (2002, October). *Dakota county: Secondary check & connect program. Final summary report.* University of Minnesota, College of Education and Human Development, Institute on Community Integration.

Tidwell, R. (1988). Dropouts speak out: Qualitative data on early school departures. *Adolescence, 23,* 939–954.

Tilly, W. D. (2002). Best practices in school psychology as a problem-solving enterprise. In A. Thomas & J. Grimes (Eds.), *Best practices in school psychology IV* (pp. 21–36). Bethesda, MD: National Association of School Psychologists.

U.S. Department of Education. (2001). *Twenty-third annual report to Congress on the implementation of the Individuals with Disabilities Education Act.* Washington, DC: Author.

U.S. Department of Education, National Center for Education Statistics. (2003). *The Condition of Education 2003* (NCES Publication No. 2003–067). Washington, DC: Author.

Wehlage, G. G., & Rutter, R. A. (1986). Dropping out: How much do schools contribute to the problem? *Teachers College Record, 87,* 374–392.

Wolman, C., Bruininks, R., & Thurlow, M. L. (1989). Dropouts and dropout programs: Implications for special education. *Remedial and Special Education, 10,* 6–20.

Zigmond, N., & Thornton, H. (1985). Follow-up of postsecondary age learning disabled graduates and drop-outs. *Learning Disabilities Research, 1,* 50–55.

# 9

# Anger and Aggression

**John E. Lochman**
**Nicole R. Powell**
**Nancy Clanton**
**Heather K. McElroy**

*University of Alabama*

Anger and aggression in children and adolescents are increasingly important topics to today's educators and school psychologists. School professionals are confronted not only with the direct effects of anger and aggression, such as threats of violence and fighting among students, but also with the indirect effects that appear in the form of learning difficulties and social adjustment problems. This chapter aims to take a comprehensive look at the problems associated with anger and aggression in today's youth and at some of the current methods and interventions designed to address those problems.

## BACKGROUND AND DEVELOPMENT

Anger is defined as a person's response to a threat or the perception of a threat against an individual or group (Lazarus, 1991). The types of threats that tend to trigger an anger response are broad in scope and include both physical threats and psychological threats, or threats to a person's pride or dignity. Anger can also evolve from empathic concern or perceptions of injustice and is related to cognitive factors such as hostility (Spielberger et al., 1985) and cynicism (Martin, Watson, & Wan, 2000). Anger can be adaptive by energizing an individual and heightening cognitive awareness to take action against a threat or perceived threat (Goleman, 1995). Anger is an emotion that is often difficult to control because of the intense physiological reactions involved in the fight or flight response that triggers anger. The fight response is a response triggered naturally by the body to protect itself against the instigating situation (Lazarus, 1991). Intense, uncontrolled feelings of anger are often associated with externalizing behavior problems, particularly aggression.

Aggression is generally defined as a behavioral act that results in harming or hurting others. However, there are numerous types of aggression, depending on the intentions of the aggressor and the situation that stimulated the aggressive response. Because aggressive behavior, and thus the treatment of aggression, varies greatly according to the intentions and conditions surrounding the aggression, aggression is typically categorized according to type. Aggression is commonly viewed as being either proactive or reactive; overt or covert; or physical, verbal, or relational (e.g., Werner & Crick, 2004). Because proactive and reactive types of aggression have been the focus of recent research and offer both an explanation and description of aggression, they receive primary emphasis here.

Children engaging in *proactive aggression* typically use aggression to meet a goal. For example, if the child wants to have an object that belongs to another child, the proactively aggressive child will simply use aggression to take the object from the other child. Proactively aggressive children also use aggression to obtain social goals (Dodge, 1991). When the aggressive behavior yields the desired reward, the child is more likely to engage in proactive aggression the next time he or she intends to meet a goal. Conversely, *reactively aggressive* children do not seek to meet goals through their aggressive behavior. Instead, those children react negatively to perceived or actual threats and are easily irritated and provoked.

There is increasing evidence that reactive and proactive types of aggression exist independently and relate differently to different expressions of anger. Reactive aggression, which is characterized by hot-blooded anger and is more emotionally driven, is likely to occur with visible displays of anger, whereas proactive aggression, which is more calculated and cold-blooded, does not appear to relate to the expression of anger in the same manner (Hubbard et al., 2002).

Reactive and proactive aggression appear to differ in social outcomes. In terms of peer relations, reactive aggression is associated with peer rejection and peer victimization, whereas proactive aggression is not (Dodge, Lochman, Harnish, Bates, & Pettit, 1997). In contrast, proactive aggression is related to leadership skills and a sense of humor (Dodge & Coie, 1987). The social–cognitive correlates of reactive and proactive aggression also appear to differ. Children who demonstrate reactive aggression tend to incorrectly believe that others have acted hostilely toward them, but proactively aggressive children do not display this bias (Hubbard, Dodge, Cillessen, Coie, & Schwartz, 2001). In addition, proactive aggression, but not reactive aggression, is related to expectations of positive outcomes for aggressive acts (Smithmyer, Hubbard, & Simons, 2000). Children who engage in proactively aggressive acts tend to expect that their goals (e.g., dominance or revenge) will be reached through their aggression.

### Developmental Aspects

Anger is a developmentally appropriate and normal reaction to threatening stimuli. Anger motivates the individual for action and protects and preserves the individual and the individual's needs. The anger response and its frequency, the types of aggression exhibited, and the situations that elicit an anger or aggressive response change as children progress through developmental stages from preschool through adolescence and into adulthood.

During infancy, expressions of anger are difficult to differentiate; however, as children age, their facial expressions and vocalizations differentiate more clearly such emotions as fear, sadness, and anger. As children age, they are more likely and capable of directing their negative feelings toward the source of the emotion (Stenberg & Campos, 1990). However, this tends to be counterbalanced as parents and other socializing agents respond more negatively to expressions of anger. Social information–processing skills also improve with age. For example, older children are more likely to accurately consider the context of the incident and are more capable of correctly identifying the underlying intentions of another person's behavior (Crick & Dodge, 1994).

The types of incidents that elicit aggression in children also appear to change developmentally. Younger children are more likely to act aggressively toward someone or something that blocks their means to some goal. However, older children are more likely to use aggression to react to threats to their self-esteem. As children age, their reactions to insults, putdowns, and other threats to their self-concept become more important triggers of aggressive behavior.

Because boys are typically reported as being more aggressive than girls, a significant amount of research on aggression focuses specifically on males. However, females certainly experience anger and commit acts of aggression. Research has begun to emerge that specifically examines female aggression, particularly relational aggression. *Relational aggression* harms others not through the use of physical violence, but instead through acts that damage peer relationships or threaten to do so. Although relational aggression is the predominant type of aggression among females, it should be noted that the rate of physical aggression among girls has been increasing at a higher rate than among boys (U.S. Department of Justice, 2000).

## PROBLEMS AND IMPLICATIONS

Angry and aggressive behaviors are expected among young children, and the occurrence of such behaviors provides important opportunities for socialization and the development of self-control. Temper tantrums, for example, are common in preschool-age children, occurring two to three times per week in typically developing 18-month-old children (Ounsted & Simons, 1978). However, severe and frequent tantrums that persist into the preschool and school-age years are cause for concern, demonstrating the importance of developmental context in labeling problem behaviors. In addition to developmental appropriateness, practitioners should also consider social context when attempting to understand or evaluate anger and aggressive behavior. That is, displays of anger or aggression may be common and accepted in certain situations but not in others. For example, aggressive acts during roughhousing among friends are likely to be well tolerated, whereas similar behaviors may provoke a physical fight outside of a positive social relationship.

Although some problems with anger and aggression are expected during childhood, the distinction between typical and atypical behaviors is a matter of degree. Increases in the severity and frequency of aggressive behavior lead to disruptions in the child's functioning and, in extreme cases, may cause harm to others. Aggression that is serious enough to meet the criteria for Conduct Disorder is estimated to occur in 6% to 16% of males under age 18, and in 2% to 9% of females in that age range (American Psychiatric Association, 1994). A diagnosis of Conduct Disorder is often one part of a developmental trajectory that starts with aggression during early childhood and continues into adolescence and adulthood in the form of antisocial behavior (Schaeffer, Petras, Ialongo, Poduska, & Kellam, 2003). Early aggression has been related to a host of social problems in adolescence and adulthood, including substance abuse, unconventionality, and low achievement (Brook & Newcomb, 1995).

Children who demonstrate problems with anger and aggression are at increased risk for a number of negative outcomes. Aggression is related to mental health problems in children, including externalizing disorders such as Oppositional Defiant Disorder and Conduct Disorder, as well as internalizing problems with depression and anxiety (American Psychiatric Association, 1994). Aggressive behavior compromises children's social relationships, causing children to be rejected by their peers at a high rate (e.g., Dodge, 1983). About half of all rejected children are identified as aggressive (Cillessen, Van IJzendoorn, Van Lieshout, & Hartup, 1992). Problems with anger and aggression are also likely to disrupt children's educational experiences. Aggressive children demonstrate higher levels of academic problems, are more likely to be retained, and are also more likely to prematurely drop out of school (Risi, Gerhardstein, & Kistner, 2003).

## FACTORS THAT CONTRIBUTE TO PROBLEMS WITH ANGER AND AGGRESSION

Problems with anger and aggression are influenced by a multitude of factors and can be conceptualized within a contextual social–cognitive model (Lochman & Wells, 2002a). Thus, the next sections examine the roles of emotional, physiological, social–cognitive, and contextual factors in the development and maintenance of anger and aggression.

### Emotional Factors

Individual differences in temperament and emotional arousability play a role in the expression of angry and aggressive behaviors, according to studies (Russell, Hart, Robinson, & Olsen, 2003). A more specific link between angry emotional arousal and aggression has also been documented (Arsenio, Cooperman, & Lover, 2000). However, other research has not substantiated the relationship between anger and aggression. For example, Hubbard (2001) found no differences in the expression of anger between aggressive and nonaggressive children. She suggested that the lack of a significant relationship may have resulted from the study's focus on the proactive rather than the reactive type of aggression.

An understanding of the physiological processes involved can elucidate the relationship between angry arousal and aggression and helps to distinguish proactive and reactive aggression. Perception of threat or endangerment activates two physiological processes, which lead to different types of anger. In the first, the thalamus signals the amygdala, which triggers an increase in cardiovascular activity and an energy rush. This can result in an immediate rage response. The amygdala's effects on the adrenocortical branch of the nervous system also lead to longer lasting effects in the form of a general background state of action readiness that can last for hours or days. In this state of arousal, intense anger outbursts may be brought on by seemingly minor irritations and frustrations. Therefore, once initiated, the anger process tends to be maintained and exacerbated and can be difficult to break. This process is consistent with the reactive form of aggression, which is characterized by impulsivity and lashing out.

In the second pathway, the thalamus signals the neocortex, which processes the threatening information and attributes causes and motivations to the event, then develops possible responses to it. In this second case, the anger response is likely to be deliberate and controlled, as in proactive aggression.

### Social–Cognitive Factors

Anger and aggression often are conceptualized within a social–cognitive framework (Crick & Dodge, 1994; Dodge, Laird, Lochman, Zelli, & Conduct Problems Prevention Research Group, 2002). This model of social information processing entails six steps: (a) encoding social cues, (b) interpreting the cues, (c) identifying social goals, (d) generating possible solutions to the problem event, (e) evaluating the solutions, and (f) enacting the behavior of the chosen response. As shown later, understanding how aggressive children's social–cognitive processing differs from that of nonaggressive children has led to the development of interventions and programs that seek to decrease aggressive behavior by correcting deficits in social–cognitive processes.

As a group, aggressive children have been shown to have deficits at each of the six steps, although individual aggressive children are likely to have deficits at only certain steps (Orobio de Castro, Veerman, Koops, Bosch, & Monshouwer, 2002). In the first step of processing, *encoding*, aggressive children recall fewer relevant cues about a situation, use fewer cues in interpreting an event, show a preference for hostile rather than neutral cues when attending to and recalling an event, and demonstrate a pronounced recency effect for cues in a sequence (Crick & Dodge, 1994).

In the second step, *interpreting cues*, aggressive children tend to excessively infer that others' actions are malevolent, a cognitive distortion known as the hostile attribution bias. The hostile attribution bias has been shown in aggressive children across a number of studies involving both boys and girls, and in both live and hypothetical situations. Many aggressive children also have distortions in their interpretations of their own behaviors. While they tend to overinterpret hostility in others' actions, they tend to underestimate their own aggressive behavior (Lochman & Dodge, 1998). The cognitive errors made in this step of processing may cause aggressive children to react strongly in situations that are generally perceived as neutral or only mildly irritating, and to feel justified in assigning blame to another person for their own aggressive responses.

In the third step of processing, *identifying social goals*, aggressive children tend to assign higher value to goals of retaliation and dominance and to value social affiliation goals less. For example, compared with prosocial and withdrawn children, aggressive children tend to give higher ratings to goals of revenge, self-protection, and appearance of strength, while they give lower ratings to prosocial affiliation goals and constructive problem solving (Erdley & Asher, 1996).

In the fourth step of processing, *generating possible solutions*, aggressive children display deficits in the quality of solutions they generate for problem situations. For example, they are less likely to offer verbal assertion or compromise solutions and are more likely to offer direct action solutions, help-seeking or adult-intervention solutions, and more physically aggressive responses (see Larson & Lochman, 2002). The fifth step of processing, *evaluating solutions*, involves identifying the potential consequences of the possible solutions to a problem and evaluating each solution in terms of the desired outcome. For aggressive children, this step is influenced by their perceptions and beliefs about aggressive behavior in that they tend to view aggression as less negative (Deluty, 1983) and more positive (Crick & Werner, 1998) than do nonaggressive children.

The final processing step, *enacting the behavior of the chosen response*, appears to be a problem for aggressive children who have been found to have difficulties in carrying out positive and prosocial behaviors (Dodge, Pettit, McClaskey, & Brown, 1986). For example, aggressive children may know that verbal assertion can be a useful strategy in resolving conflicts with peers, but they may fail to state their wants in a confident manner and may neglect important nuances such as tone and body language, causing peers to reject their attempts at verbal assertion.

It is important to note that social information processing at each of these steps interacts with emotional and physiological factors in at least three ways. First, children's perceptions that another person is behaving with hostile intentions toward them can contribute to increased arousal and anger. Second, angry mood states that are due to prior conflicts can lead a child to misperceive causes of problems in subsequent interactions with other individuals. As children become more physiologically aroused in response to provocations, they have accompanying increases in their hostile attributions of others' intentions (Williams, Lochman, Phillips, & Barry, 2003). Third, schemas, or cognitive-emotional beliefs, are also responsible for the experience of anger and influence how information is processed. Once children develop a schema—learned expectations about a particular situation—that their peers are hostile, then subsequent interactions with peers will trigger that schema and taint the current information processing. As the schema is invoked, those children anticipate being treated unfairly; angry feelings and physiological arousal can be triggered and they may respond with aggressive behavior (Lochman, Dunn, & Wagner, 1997).

## Contextual Factors

Just as social, cognitive, emotional, and physiological factors interact in an ongoing and reciprocal fashion, so too do each of these factors interact with contextual factors. External influences on anger and aggression in children include family, peers, and neighborhood factors. Within the family, parenting practices, child abuse, and exposure to domestic violence have all been related to aggression in children. Patterson's (1982) family coercion model outlines how parent–child interactions can unwittingly reinforce and maintain problem behaviors, including aggression, in children. In the model, parental requests are met with resistance from the child, which leads to an escalating pattern of parental demands and child noncompliance. The cycle eventually ends with the parent becoming frustrated and backing down from his or her request, which reinforces the child's negative behavior and sets the stage for similar reactions from the child in response to future parental instructions. From such interactions, the child may learn that coercive behavior is an effective means to achieve their own goals.

Children who are subjected to abusive behaviors, either through direct victimization or as a witness to domestic violence, are also at increased risk for angry, aggressive behaviors. For example, in a recent study of children who had witnessed physical violence in their homes or had been physically abused, Johnson and colleagues (2002) found that child victimization was a significant predictor of child aggression and that witnessing violence significantly predicted aggression and anger in children.

Peer relationships are another important influence (see chapter 25, "Peer Relationships"). Research examining aggressive children's peer relationships has consistently found that aggressive children tend to associate with other aggressive children (Poulin & Boivin, 2000). That tendency increases the probability that their aggressive behaviors will be maintained or will escalate as a result of modeling effects and reinforcement of deviant behaviors (e.g., Dishion, Andrews, & Crosby, 1995).

The school environment also has been shown to affect children's aggression (see chapters 3 and 7, "Developing Self-Discipline" and "School Disciplinary Systems"). Barth, Dunlap, Dane, Lochman, and Wells (2004) found that the aggressiveness of children's classmates directly affected children's own rates of aggressive behaviors. Teachers' management of the classroom has also been related to the prevalence of students' aggression toward classmates (Roland & Galloway, 2002).

Exposure to neighborhood violence also has been shown to increase children's aggressive behaviors. For example, Guerra, Huesmann, & Spindler (2003), in a study of a large sample of children living in urban neighborhoods, indicated that exposure to violence resulted in an increase in aggressive behavior and in social cognitions supporting aggression.

Exposure to various types of violent media, including movies, television, video games, and music, is associated with increased aggression in children and youth (see Anderson et al., 2003, for a review). Studies have shown immediate effects as well as effects over time, with exposure to violent media in childhood predicting aggressive behavior in young adults. Exposure to violent media affects aggression in a number of ways, including physical aggression, verbal aggression, aggressive emotions, and aggressive cognitions.

## ALTERNATIVE ACTIONS FOR PREVENTION

Researchers and government agencies have identified several universal programs that specifically address the prevention of aggression and associated anger and substance abuse problems (see Mrazek & Haggerty, 1994, for a review). The universal prevention programs outlined in this section include those that incorporate rigorous research methodologies and evaluations, such as randomized, controlled design or quasi-experimental design. Because many of the programs target different age groups, they are discussed and categorized according to the predominant developmental age group targeted: elementary or middle school and adolescent.

### Elementary School Universal Preventive Interventions

***Second Step program.*** The primary goal of the Second Step program is to prevent impulsive and aggressive behavior by teaching social competence and thus increasing prosocial behavior. Second Step targets the skill areas of anger management, empathy, and impulse control. Exercises that encourage generalization are built into each session (Grossman et al., 1997). Outcome research for the elementary school program has indicated increased knowledge and improved skills in anger management, impulse control, empathy, social problem solving, and conflict resolution. Comparisons of intervention versus control schools indicated that the schools did not significantly differ on parent and teacher ratings of child behavior. However, behavioral observations did show a decrease in physical aggression immediately following the universal intervention and at a 6-month follow-up. In addition, increases in prosocial behavior were noted through behavioral observations (Grossman et al., 1997).

Smaller scale studies that compared one intervention school and one control school found significant increases in teacher-rated social competence and decreases in teacher-rated antisocial behavior at the intervention school (Taub, 2001).

***Child Development Project (CDP).*** The CDP's main objective is to increase children's respect and responsibility within the auspice of creating a caring school community (Lewis, Watson, & Schaps, 2003). Some of the components include cooperative learning in which students are encouraged to work together (not compete), nonpunitive discipline, reading activities, cross-grade "buddies" activities in which older and younger students work in pairs to complete activities, parental activities for home use, and community-building activities that involve all of the students, parents, teachers, and staff working together within a school (Berryhill & Prinz, 2003; Lewis et al., 2003). Overall, the results indicate that students in schools that had a high fidelity of curriculum implementation had increases in personal, social, and ethical values and attitudes compared with control schools and schools that did not implement the curriculum with a high degree of fidelity (Solomon, Battistich, Watson, Schaps, & Lewis, 2000). Three- and 4-year follow-ups of schools with a high degree of program fidelity had reductions in many measures of substance use and delinquency compared with control schools (Berryhill & Prinz, 2003; Solomon et al., 2000).

***Good Behavior Game.*** The Good Behavior Game was created by Barrish, Saunders, and Wolf (1969). The prevention focuses on increasing children's acceptance of authority and rules within the school classroom. The Good Behavior Game is a type of behavioral technique that is taught to children instead of a standard curriculum-based prevention (Barrish et al., 1969; Embry, 2002). Children in the classroom are divided into teams and a scoreboard keeps track of which teams have accrued the fewest "fouls" (i.e., a rule that is broken). Rewards are given to the team with the fewest fouls, and smaller rewards are given to teams that earned a number of fouls below an established threshold (Embry, 2002). In several studies comparing the effects of the game and another intervention designed to increase family and school communication and partnership, the Good Behavior Game yielded the strongest results for the reduction of aggressive behavior, poor achievement, and shy behaviors (e.g., Embry, 2002).

***Linking the Interests of Families & Teachers (LIFT).*** LIFT targets students and parents within an elementary school. Parents receive behavior management training, and are encouraged to initiate more communication with teachers with the use of a phone and answering machine installed in each intervention classroom (Reid & Eddy, 2002). Child participants are taught social and problem-solving skills and receive a recess behavior management program that uses an adaptation of the Good Behavior Game (Reid & Eddy, 2002). A review of the long-term effects of LIFT indicated that the frequency of police arrest and alcohol use during the middle school years was less likely for participants receiving the preventive intervention in elementary school than for participants in the control condition. However, differences were not found between the two groups in terms of the frequency and onset of using other substances such as tobacco or marijuana (Eddy, Reid, Stoolmiller, & Fetrow, 2003; Reid & Eddy, 2002).

***Seattle Social Development Project (SSDP).*** The SSDP is a universal prevention designed to reduce aggression by creating a positive school environment. The prevention has been used predominantly for public elementary schools serving high-crime areas of Seattle, Washington. The SSDP includes training for teachers to increase the use of nonpunitive classroom behavior management such as positive reinforcement, and more recent versions of the intervention have also included parent training and child problem solving and social skills training (Berryhill & Prinz, 2003; Hawkins, Catalano, Kosterman, Abbott, & Hill, 1999). Longitudinal research conducted with the SSDP found significant prevention or reductions of alcohol use (Hawkins et al., 1999), reductions in delinquency, a lower frequency of sexual intercourse and number of sexual partners, and decreased reports of becoming pregnant or causing pregnancy (Hawkins et al., 1999). In addition, students receiving the prevention reported more positive feelings and commitment to school compared with control groups, improved academic achievement, and less student-reported school misbehavior (Hawkins et al., 1999).

***Promoting Alternative THinking Strategies (PATHS).*** Greenberg, Domitrovich, and Bumbarger developed the PATHS universal preventive intervention, which teaches children three steps for calming down: stop, take a deep breath, and identify the problem and your feelings (Kusche & Greenberg, 1994). Parent and teacher components are also included to enhance the skills child participants learn (Greenberg et al., 2001). Overall, results at 1- and 2-year follow-ups have indicated that children receiving the PATHS intervention were better at understanding emotions, were better at problem solving, and reported decreases in conduct problems and impulsivity compared with children in a control group (Greenberg et al., 2001).

***Fast Track Program.*** The Fast Track program is a multisite intervention with a universal prevention program that uses a PATHS component (Kusche & Greenberg, 1994) and addresses child, family, school, and community levels in one intervention (Conduct Problems Prevention Research Group, 1992, 1999). For elementary school children, the intervention emphasizes understanding and communicating emotions, learning self-control, and learning problem solving (Conduct Problems Prevention Research Group, 1992). Intervention starts in first grade and continues through tenth grade. The outcome effects of Fast Track indicate significant effects on peer ratings of aggression, disruptive behavior, and classroom atmosphere. In addition, at the end of first grade, moderate positive social effects were reported on children's social, emotional, and academic skills (Conduct Problems Prevention Research Group, 1999). Many of those effects have been maintained in assessments at the end of third grade (Conduct Problems Prevention Research Group, 2002) and up to the end of elementary school, through fourth and fifth grades (Conduct Problems Prevention Research Group, 2004).

***Bullying Prevention Program.*** The Bullying Prevention Program was a nationwide universal preventive intervention conducted in Norway. The program's objectives include reducing the acceptance of bullying among children and school staff and improving school supervision and deterrence of bullying. The program instills awareness through booklets, suggestions for preventing bullying, initiation of classroom meetings, and videos (Berryhill & Prinz, 2003). Results from the 42 elementary and middle schools in Norway showed at least a 50% decrease in bullying and decreased reports of delinquency, including vandalism, fighting, intoxication, theft, and truancy. The results indicated even greater positive effects at a 2-year follow-up than at the 1-year follow-up (Greenberg et al., 2001).

## Middle School/Adolescent Universal Preventive Interventions

***Responding in Peaceful & Positive Ways (RIPP).*** RIPP interventionists teach middle school adolescents problem-solving steps, better communication skills, and achievement techniques to promote nonviolence. Teens are encouraged to internalize these skills through repetition and mental rehearsal of problem-solving steps, experiential learning, and didactic teaching (Farrell, Meyer, & White, 2001). Results show that teens in the RIPP intervention had decreased incidence of school punishment for engaging in violent acts, including fewer suspensions, compared with teens in control groups. As for gender differences, boys maintained fewer suspensions compared with the control group 1 year later, whereas girls' suspensions compared with controls were not significantly different after 1 year. Adolescents in the RIPP program also indicated that they used peer mediation more frequently than controls did. Overall, students who had the highest rates of disruptive behaviors prior to receiving the prevention achieved the greatest benefit from RIPP (Farrell, Meyer, Sullivan, & Kung, 2003; Farrell et al., 2001).

***Positive Youth Development (PYD).*** PYD is a universal preventive intervention created to increase adolescents' personal and social competence. Sessions specifically cover topics such as stress management, self-esteem, problem solving, substance use and health information, assertiveness, and social networks (Caplan, Weissberg, Grober, & Sivo, 1992). Studies comparing PYD with control groups found that teens receiving the intervention improved in terms of ability to positively solve conflicts, impulse control, and popularity according to teacher ratings. Teens in the PYD groups also reported increases in the use of problem solving and decreases in the intent to use substances and alcohol (Caplan et al., 1992; Greenberg et al., 2003).

***The School Transitional Environment Project (STEP).*** STEP targets adolescents' adaptation skills during transitional stages, such as the transition from elementary to middle school and the transition from middle school to high school. One of the main components of STEP is reorganizing the school social system, including creating smaller class sizes and maintaining a consistent set of peers. STEP also restructures the homeroom teacher's role by encouraging the teacher to be the main communicator between parents and the school and by increasing overall teacher support (Felner et al.,

2001). Long-term follow-up of middle school and high school students receiving STEP indicates a 50% reduction in dropout rates and significant increases in school achievement and attendance (Felner et al., 1993). In particular, when fidelity to treatment methods are high, STEP has been found to incite a "whole school" change in which social–emotional, behavioral, and academic difficulties; developmental competency; and adaptation are all significantly improved compared with control groups (Felner et al., 1993; Felner et al., 2001).

## ALTERNATIVE ACTIONS FOR INTERVENTION

Several intervention or prevention programs have been developed to help reduce anger problems and aggressive behavior in children (see Table 1). These programs have been presented in school settings as indicated prevention programs for high risk aggressive children (Mrazek & Haggerty, 1994) or as treatment programs for children with diagnosable disruptive disorders. As can be noted in Table 1, common elements in these effective programs include teaching skills to manage the affective arousal associated with anger, instruction on social problem solving skills, and development of social skills. Some programs have multiple components and include both parent and child interventions. The various intervention programs will be reviewed in turn.

### The Anger Coping and Coping Power Programs

The Anger Coping Program is a structured 18-session group intervention for aggressive children that has been refined over a period of 20 years. The program evolved from an earlier 12-session Anger Control Program. The Anger Coping Program has been used in school settings for prevention and early intervention purposes and in specialty programs for children with oppositional defiant disorder and conduct disorder in outpatient mental health clinics. Sessions typically last 45 to 60 minutes in school-based groups. Sessions are moderately structured, with specific goals, objectives, and planned exercises for each session. The model was designed for use with elementary school and middle school children and has been used primarily with children in the fourth to sixth grades. The groups typically have four to six children.

A detailed session-by-session outline of the Anger Coping Program can be found in Larson and Lochman (2002). The goals for the program's group sessions include introduction and establishment of the group rules and reinforcement systems, goal setting, anger management training, perspective-taking, awareness of physiological arousal and anger, and social problem solving. The two overarching goals for this cognitive–behavioral program are, first, to help children find ways to cope with the intense surge of physiological arousal and anger they experience immediately after a provocation or frustration, and, second, to help children retrieve from memory an array of possible strategies to resolve the problem or conflict they are experiencing.

The program's anger management training teaches children to recognize the triggers that lead to their high arousal reactions in difficult interpersonal situations. The training then assists them in using several coping techniques to manage the arousal and to avoid an impulsive, rage-filled response. The coping techniques include distraction, relaxation, and self-talk. In the social problem-solving sessions, children brainstorm multiple possible solutions to social problems and then evaluate the long-term and short-term consequences of each solution. Role-playing and videotaping are used to reinforce the problem-solving process.

Outcome research indicates that program participants displayed less disruptive-aggressive behavior, more time on-task in the classroom, lower levels of parent-rated aggression, higher self-esteem or perceived social competence, and a trend toward a reduction in teacher-rated aggression. These findings were noted using pre–post assessments as well as comparisons between program participants and control groups. Examination of the longer-term preventive effects of the program indicated that gains and preventive effects were maintained but has also found that some other behavioral gains were not maintained (Lochman, 1992). Compared with untreated controls and nonaggressive boys, program participants had higher levels of self-esteem; lower rates of irrelevant solutions to problems on a problem-solving measure; and lower rates of alcohol, marijuana, and other drug use at a follow-up period 3 years after the intervention. On the follow-up measures, the program participants were functioning in a range comparable to the nonaggressive boys, indicating a prevention effect for substance use and a relative normalization of self-esteem and social problem-solving skills.

The Coping Power Program (Lochman & Wells, 2002a) is a lengthier, multicomponent version of the

**Table 1** *Alternate Actions for Intervention*

| Program | Age Range | Program Length | Components | Skill Areas | Program Effects Relative to Control Group | Effects at Follow-Up |
|---|---|---|---|---|---|---|
| Anger Coping (Lochman, 1992) | Children in fourth to sixth grade | 18 sessions | Child only | Goal setting; anger management; perspective-taking; awareness of physiological arousal and anger; social problem solving | Decreased disruptive–aggressive behavior; more time on-task in the classroom; lower levels of parent-rated aggression; higher self-esteem or perceived self-competence; reduction in teacher-rated aggression (trend) | Higher levels of self-esteem; lower rates of irrelevant solutions to problems on a problem-solving measure; lower rates of substance use |
| Coping Power (Lochman & Wells, 2002a) | Children in fourth to sixth grade | 33 child sessions and 16 parent sessions over 15–18 months | Parent and child | Emotional awareness; relaxation training; social skills enhancement; positive social and personal goals; dealing with peer pressure | Improvements in children's social information processing and locus of control; improvements in parenting practices | Significant reductions in risk for self-reported delinquency, parent-reported substance use, and teacher-reported behavior problems |
| The Art of Self-Control (Feindler & Ecton, 1986) | 13- to 17-year-old adolescents | 12 sessions | Child only | Relaxation; self-instruction; coping statements; assertiveness; self-monitoring of anger and conflictual situations; problem solving | Reductions in aggressive and disruptive behavior; improvements in problem-solving abilities, social skills, cognitive reflectivity, and adult-rated impulsivity and self-control | Not available |
| Dinosaur School (Webster-Stratton & Hammond, 1997) | 4- to 7-year-old children | 6 months | Parent and child | Social skills; empathy; perspective-taking, conflict resolution; dealing with loneliness, stress, and anger | Reduction in conduct problems reported in the home; increases in social problem-solving skills | Parent ratings of behavioral problems in the normal rather than the clinically significant range (75% of children) |

*(Continued)*

**Table 1** *Continued*

| Program | Age Range | Program Length | Components | Skill Areas | Program Effects Relative to Control Group | Effects at Follow-Up |
|---|---|---|---|---|---|---|
| Montreal Delinquency Prevention Program (Tremblay, Masse, Pagani, & Vitaro, 1996) | Early elementary school age | 2 years | Parent and child | Social skills and self-control training | Decreased risk of serious school adjustment problems; less delinquent behavior | Decreased gang involvement, lower levels of delinquency and substance use during adolescence |
| Problem-Solving Skills Training (Kazdin, Esveldt-Dawson, French, & Unis, 1987) | Elementary school age | 20–25 child sessions; 16 parent sessions | Parent and child | Prosocial problem-solving skills | Reductions in externalizing and internalizing problems; increased social activities and school adjustment; improvements in social and behavioral functioning at school | Reductions in disruptive behavior and increases in prosocial activities at home and school |

Anger Coping Program and is designed to enhance outcome effects and provide better maintenance of gains over time. The Coping Power Program added sessions to the basic Anger Coping framework to create a child component (for a total of 33 group sessions) that addresses additional substantive areas such as emotional awareness, relaxation training, social skills enhancement, positive social and personal goals, and techniques for dealing with peer pressure. The program also has a parent component that is designed to be integrated with the child component and to cover the same 15- to 18-month period. The program's 16 parent group sessions address parents' use of social reinforcement and positive attention, establishment of clear house rules, behavioral expectations and monitoring procedures, use of a range of appropriate and effective discipline strategies, family communication, positive connection to school, and stress management capability. Parents are informed of the skills their children are working on in their sessions, and parents are encouraged to facilitate and reinforce their children's use of the new skills.

Outcome analyses in randomized, controlled intervention studies indicate that the Coping Power intervention had broad effects at post-intervention on boys' social information processing and locus of control and on parents' parenting practices (Lochman & Wells, 2002a). In analyses of the 1-year follow-up effects of the program, Coping Power produced significant reductions in risks for self-reported delinquency, parent-reported substance use, and teacher-reported behavioral problems, especially for boys who received both the child and parent components (Lochman & Wells, 2004). A second effectiveness study explored whether the Coping Power Program effects could be augmented by delivering the program along with a classroom-based intervention involving teacher training. Outcome analyses with 245 aggressive children indicate that Coping Power produced significant postintervention effects on children's social competence and aggressive behavior (Lochman & Wells, 2002b). That study replicated the 1-year follow-up results from the prior study: Coping Power children had reduced levels of delinquency, substance use, and aggressive behaviors in the school setting (Lochman & Wells, 2003).

## The Art of Self-Control

This cognitive–behavioral adolescent control program for groups and individuals is described in a session-by-session format in Feindler and Ecton (1986). The group program consists of 12 sessions lasting from 45 to 90 minutes once weekly in outpatient settings and twice weekly in residential treatment settings. The groups typically consist of 8 to 12 members, and the leaders may come from a variety of settings (e.g., child care workers, counselors, nurses, probation officers, psychiatrists, psychologists, social workers, teachers, or even involved parents). This program to teach the art of self-control provides training in relaxation, self-instruction, the use of coping statements, assertiveness, self-monitoring of anger and conflictual situations, and problem solving. It uses stress inoculation training (SIT) based on Meichenbaum and Goodman's (1971) and Novaco's (1975) intervention program. SIT particularly emphasizes the cognitive components of anger and encourages adolescents to moderate, regulate, and prevent out-of-control anger and to use problem-solving skills in response to conflictual situations. In this program, the SIT approach involves an educational–cognitive preparation phase, a skill acquisition phase (consisting of a cognitive component and a behavioral skills training component), and a skill application phase. In the first phase, participants are taught to recognize their personal anger patterns (including cognitive, physiological, and behavioral components) and their situational antecedents, or triggers, that lead to their out-of-control anger. Leaders then encourage adolescents to use these cues to "chill out" and to substitute cognitive–behavioral anger control techniques.

In the skill acquisition phase, participants are taught cognitive–behavioral techniques to use in anger-provoking situations. Feindler and Ecton (1986) use the mnemonic "C-A-L-M-D-O-W-N" to indicate the different cognitive and behavioral skills to be learned: (a) *C*ue for anger provocation, (b) *A*lter views of anger provocation, (c) *L*et adolescents use self-instructions to help with anger control, (d) *M*oderate physiological anger arousal by providing skills in relaxation, (e) *D*irect adolescents to communicate anger verbally and nonverbally by providing them with training in assertiveness, (f) *O*rganize the manner in which anger-related problems are solved by teaching problem-solving skills, (g) *W*ork through the proper timing sequences and conditions that will enhance the effectiveness of the skills learned (using modeling and behavioral rehearsal formats), and (h) *N*egotiate a contract to use the skills learned (to promote generalization to other settings).

In the skill application phase, participants are taught to use the skills in the acquisition phase by exposing them to graduated anger-provoking situations through role-playing and real-life situations. Videotapes and written homework are used to assist with this process. The three phases of this program occur simultaneously, rather than successively as they are described here.

As summarized in Feindler and Ecton (1986), outcome research for this program indicated reductions in aggressive and disruptive behavior and improvements in problem-solving abilities, social skills, cognitive reflectivity, and adult-rated impulsivity and self-control. The improvements were noted from pre–post comparisons as well as when comparisons were made between program participants and a control group. The populations examined consisted of adolescents who had experienced fairly extreme or chronic histories of aggression (e.g., adolescents at an in-school junior high school program for youth suspended multiple times and delinquent youth and for adolescents at an inpatient psychiatric facility).

This self-control training program also has been adapted for use primarily with incarcerated adolescents. This adaptation, called Anger Control Training, is part of a larger program (i.e., Aggression Replacement Training) aimed to help reduce adolescent aggression. A detailed description of this program (in a session-by-session format) can be found in Goldstein and Glick (1994).

## Dinosaur School—Child Training

This program was initially developed as part of a larger preventive intervention designed to examine the relative and additive effectiveness of parent training and child training for 4- to 7-year-olds with early-onset conduct problems (Webster-Stratton & Hammond, 1997). The child component, which was referred to as Dinosaur School, addresses issues that young children with conduct problems frequently face: social skills problems, an inability to emotionally empathize or engage in perspective-taking, effective conflict resolution, and feelings of loneliness, stress, and anger. The parenting component consisted of videotaped programs on parenting and interpersonal skills that have proved to be effective in reducing noncompliant behaviors (Webster-Stratton, 1990). Analysis of treatment groups revealed that the child training led to a significant reduction in conduct problems reported in the home and increases in social problem-solving skills in comparison to controls. Moreover, at 1-year follow-up nearly two-thirds of children in the child treatment group had parent ratings of behavioral problems in the normal rather than clinically significant range. Although the combination of child and parent training proved superior to each of the component pieces, this finding indicates that cognitive–behavioral treatments directed at young children can be effective in reducing disruptive behavior problems and could potentially be used when parents are unwilling or unable to participate in treatment.

## The Montreal Delinquency Prevention Program

This intervention took place over 2 years and consisted of a parent-training component based on the strategy developed by the Oregon Social Learning Center (Patterson, 1982) and a child component consisting of social skills and self-control trainings that took place in the second and third grades (Tremblay, Masse, Pagani, & Vitaro, 1996). Investigations have revealed that by age 12, boys who received the intervention were less likely than untreated boys to have serious adjustment problems in school (Tremblay et al., 1992) or to have antisocial friends (Vitaro & Tremblay, 1994), and they reported fewer instances of trespassing and stealing (McCord, Tremblay, Vitaro, & Desmarais-Gervais, 1994). Moreover, during adolescence individuals who received the treatment were less likely to be involved in gangs (Tremblay et al., 1996) and reported lower levels of delinquency and substance use (Tremblay, Kurtz, Masse, Vitaro, & Pihl, 1995) than the untreated controls. Since many of those treatment effects emerged at age 12 and remained stable up until the age of 15, the results of this preventive intervention provide substantial evidence that early cognitive–behavioral interventions during the elementary school years can produce effects that last throughout adolescence. It should be noted that these effects are for the parent and child training combined, making it difficult to interpret the unique effect that the child-centered cognitive–behavioral component had on treatment gains.

## Problem-Solving Skills Training

Problem-solving skills training (PSST) is probably one of the most extensively researched cognitive–behavioral treatments for antisocial behavior in childhood. The program itself focuses on teaching and reinforcing prosocial problem-solving skills among children with disruptive behavior disorders to promote their ability to effectively manage potentially volatile interpersonal situations. Research examining PSST has indicated that it is superior to nondirective relationship therapy and control conditions in reducing global measures of externalizing and internalizing problems, including aggression, and increasing social activities and overall school adjustment among psychiatric inpatient children (Kazdin, Esveldt-Dawson, French, & Unis, 1987). A subsequent study also revealed that the addition of an in vivo practice component to PSST can help improve children's social and behavioral functioning at school. However, that effect was found only at post-treatment, not at 1-year follow-up. Despite this finding, both the original and the modified training were more effective in reducing disruptive behaviors and increasing prosocial activities both at home and at school in comparison to nondirective behavior therapy, and those effects remained at 1-year follow-up (Kazdin, Bass, Siegel, & Thomas, 1989). Another study indicated that PSST could be better than parent management training at increasing children's social competence at school and reducing self-reports of aggression and delinquency, although a combination of both treatments seems to be optimal (Kazdin, Siegel, & Bass, 1992). This accumulation of evidence not only suggests that PSST is an effective and long-lasting treatment for antisocial behavior in children, it also indicates that cognitive–behavioral treatments for disruptive behavior disorders may be superior to other forms of treatment.

## SUMMARY

Anger and aggression are normal experiences in childhood, but when taken to excess they can lead to significant impairment in a child's functioning. Problems with anger and aggression have been associated with an array of factors, including emotional arousability, social information processing, and contextual influences. Understanding how these different factors may precipitate and maintain problems with anger and aggression has led to the development of prevention and intervention programs. Prevention programs are particularly promising in that they can be distributed widely and have the potential to prevent a broad range of problems and symptoms. Prevention programs are available for delivery at both the elementary and middle school level, and this chapter presents summaries on several empirically tested programs at each level. Intervention programs for children who display high-risk aggressive behaviors or who have diagnosable disruptive disorders are also reviewed in this chapter. The target groups of the programs vary, from very young children displaying early-onset conduct problems to adolescents who are incarcerated or hospitalized in an inpatient psychiatric facility. Topics addressed in these programs include anger management training, social skills development, and instruction in social problem solving. Each program's curriculum covers one or more of these areas. In addition, several programs contain a parenting component. The programs reviewed are supported by outcome research, some of which indicates reductions in disruptive behavior problems that are maintained a year or more after treatment has ended.

## AUTHOR NOTE

The preparation of this chapter has been supported by grants from the Centers for Disease Control and Prevention (R49/CCR418569), the Center for Substance Abuse Prevention (KD1 SP08633; UR6 5907956), the National Institute on Drug Abuse (R01 DA08453; R01 DA16135), and the U.S. Department of Justice (2000; CKWX0091). Correspondence about this paper can be directed to John E. Lochman, PhD, Department of Psychology, Box 870348, The University of Alabama, Tuscaloosa, AL 35487–0348.

## RECOMMENDED RESOURCES

### Books

Larson, J., & Lochman, J. E. (2002). *Helping schoolchildren cope with anger: A cognitive behavioral intervention.* New York: Guilford Press.

This volume is designed to be a practical resource for school-based professionals, including counselors, psychologists, social workers, and special education consultants, in their work with aggressive children. The authors provide a full manual of the empirically validated Anger Coping Program, along with up-to-date information on childhood aggression, the principles underlying the program, and supporting evidence of the program's effectiveness.

Kazdin, A. E., & Weisz, J. R. (2003). *Evidence-based psychotherapies for children and adolescents.* New York: Guilford Press.

In this book, leading experts review current interventions for a range of childhood problems, including conduct problems, ADHD, autism, and severe emotional disturbance. Chapters provide detailed descriptions of therapeutic interventions, highlighting evidence for treatment effects and presenting strengths and weaknesses of the various programs.

Lochman, J. E., Wells, K. C., & Murray, M. The Coping Power Program: Preventive intervention at the middle school transition. In P. Tolan, J. Szapocznik, & S. Sambrano (Eds.), *Preventing substance abuse: 3 to 14.* Washington, DC: American Psychological Association (in press). This article provides detailed information on the Coping Power Program, including an explanation of the model on which the program is based and session-by-session descriptions of the parent and child interventions. A case example is provided that highlights relevant implementation issues. The authors also review research findings that lend support for the program's efficacy and effectiveness.

Reinecke, M., & Clark, D. (2003). *Cognitive therapy across the lifespan: Evidence and practice.* Cambridge, England: Cambridge University Press.

This volume presents a critical review of cognitive and cognitive–behavioral approaches in the conceptualization and treatment of clinical problems. Several chapters focus specifically on childhood problems, including disruptive behavior, anxiety, depression, and ADHD. The theoretical models underlying therapeutic interventions are presented, along with research on relevant treatment outcomes, which allows readers to make informed decisions in selecting a course of treatment.

## Websites

*http://www.actagainstviolence.org*

ACT—Adults and Children Together Against Violence—is designed to prevent violence in young children 0 to 8 years of age by providing information and training to the individuals involved in their care. This website includes information on early violence prevention and child development, as well as user-friendly handouts on topics such as anger management in children and ways to minimize classroom behavior problems. The website also provides articles in Spanish.

*http://www.excellence-earlychildhood.ca*

The website of the Centre of Excellence for Early Childhood Development provides information on the social and emotional development of young children 0 to 5 years of age. The site includes an encyclopedia of information on various topics related to child development, including aggression, prevention of maltreatment, and peer relations.

*http://www.clinicalchildpsychology.org*

Included in the website of the Society of Clinical Child and Adolescent Psychology (Division 53 of the American Psychological Association) is an evidence-based treatment site that covers conduct and oppositional problems, anxiety disorders, depression and dysthymia, and ADHD. For each disorder, the website presents descriptions of various treatment options that have been rated as well established or probably efficacious. In addition, the site provides a helpful list of high-quality references for each of the disorders covered.

## REFERENCES

American Psychiatric Association. (1994). *Diagnostic and statistical manual of mental disorders* (4th ed.). Washington, DC: Author.

Anderson, C. A., Berkowitz, L., Donnerstein, E., Huesmann, L. R., Johnson, J. D., Linz, D., Malamuth, N. M., & Wartella, E. (2003). The influence of media violence on youth. *Psychological Science in the Public Interest, 4,* 81–110.

Arsenio, W. F., Cooperman, S., & Lover, A. (2000). Affective predictors of preschoolers' aggression and peer acceptance: Direct and indirect effects. *Developmental Psychology, 36,* 438–448.

Barrish, H. H., Saunders, M., & Wolf, M. M. (1969). Good behavior game: Effects of individual contingencies for group consequences on disruptive behavior in a classroom. *Journal of Applied Behavior Analysis, 2,* 119–124.

Barth, J. M., Dunlap, S. T., Dane, H., Lochman, J. E., & Wells, K. C. (2004). Classroom environment influences on aggression, peer relations, and academic focus. *Journal of School Psychology, 42,* 115–133.

Berryhill, J. C., & Prinz, R. J. (2003). Environmental interventions to enhance student adjustment: Implications for prevention. *Prevention Science, 4,* 65–87.

Brook, J. S., & Newcomb, M. D. (1995). Childhood aggression and unconventionality: Impact on later academic achievement, drug use, and workforce involvement. *Journal of Genetic Psychology, 156,* 393–410.

Caplan, M., Weissberg, R. P., Grober, J. S., & Sivo, P. J. (1992). Social competence promotion with inner-city and suburban young adolescents: Effects on social adjustment and alcohol use. *Journal of Consulting and Clinical Psychology, 60,* 56–63.

Cillessen, A. H., Van IJzendoorn, H. W., Van Lieshout, C. F., & Hartup, W. W. (1992). Heterogeneity among peer-rejected boys: Subtypes and stabilities. *Child Development, 63,* 893–905.

Conduct Problems Prevention Research Group. (1992). A developmental and clinical model for the prevention of conduct disorder: The FAST Track Program. *Development & Psychopathology, 4,* 509–527.

Conduct Problems Prevention Research Group. (1999). Initial impact of the fast track prevention trial for conduct problems: II. Classroom effects. *Journal of Consulting and Clinical Psychology, 67,* 648–657.

Conduct Problems Prevention Research Group. (2002). Predictor variables associated with positive Fast Track outcomes at the end of third grade. *Journal of Abnormal Child Psychology, 30,* 37–52.

Conduct Problems Prevention Research Group. (2004). The effects of the Fast Track program on serious problem outcomes at the end of elementary school. *Journal of Clinical Child and Adolescent Psychology, 33,* 650–661.

Crick, N. R., & Dodge, K. A. (1994). A review and reformulation of social information-processing mechanisms in children's social adjustment. *Psychological Bulletin, 115,* 74–101.

Crick, N. R., & Werner, N. E. (1998). Response decision processes in relational and overt aggression. *Child Development, 69,* 1630–1639.

Deluty, R. H. (1983). Children's evaluations of aggressive, assertive, and submissive responses. *Journal of Clinical Child Psychology, 12,* 124–129.

Dishion, T. J., Andrews, D. W., & Crosby, L. (1995). Antisocial boys and their friends in early adolescence: Relationship characteristics, quality, and interactional process. *Child Development, 66,* 139–151.

Dodge, K. A. (1983). Behavioral antecedents of peer social status. *Child Development, 54,* 1386–1399.

Dodge, K. A. (1991). The structure and function of reactive and proactive aggression. In D. J. Pepler & K. H. Rubin (Eds.), *Development and treatment of childhood aggression* (pp. 201–218). Hillsdale, NJ: Lawrence Erlbaum Associates, Inc.

Dodge, K. A., & Coie, J. D. (1987). Social-information-processing factors in reactive and proactive aggression in children's peer groups. *Journal of Personality & Social Psychology, 53,* 1146–1158.

Dodge, K. A., Laird, R., Lochman, J. E., Zelli, A., & Conduct Problems Prevention Research Group. (2002). Multidimensional latent-construct analysis of children's social information processing patterns: Correlations with aggressive behavior problems. *Psychological Assessment, 14,* 60–73.

Dodge, K. A., Lochman, J. E., Harnish, J. D., Bates, J. E., & Pettit, G. S. (1997). Reactive and proactive aggression in school children and psychiatrically impaired chronically assaultive youth. *Journal of Abnormal Psychology, 106,* 37–51.

Dodge, K. A., Pettit, G. S., McClaskey, C. L., & Brown, M. M. (1986). Social competence in children. *Monographs of the Society for Research in Child Development, 51,* 1–85.

Eddy, J. M., Reid, J. B., Stoolmiller, M., & Fetrow, R. A. (2003). Outcomes during middle school for an elementary school-based preventive intervention for conduct problems: Follow-up results from a randomized trial. *Behavior Therapy, 34,* 535–552.

Embry, D. D. (2002). The Good Behavior Game: A best practice candidate as a universal behavioral vaccine. *Clinical Child & Family Psychology Review, 5,* 273–297.

Erdley, C. A., & Asher, S. R. (1996). Children's social goals and self-efficacy perceptions as influences on their responses to ambiguous provocation. *Child Development, 67,* 1329–1344.

Farrell, A. D., Meyer, A. L., Sullivan, T. N., & Kung, E. M. (2003). Evaluation of the responding in peaceful and positive ways (RIPP) seventh grade violence prevention curriculum. *Journal of Child & Family Studies, 12,* 101–120.

Farrell, A. D., Meyer, A. L., & White, K. S. (2001). Evaluation of Responding in Peaceful and Positive Ways (RIPP): A school-based prevention program for reducing violence among urban adolescents. *Journal of Clinical Child Psychology, 30,* 451–463.

Feindler, E. L., & Ecton, R. B. (1986). *Adolescent anger control: Cognitive-behavior techniques.* New York: Pergamon Books.

Felner, R. D., Brand, S., Adan, A. M., Mulhall, P. F., Flowers, N., Sartain, B., & DuBois, D. L. (1993). Restructuring the ecology of the school as an approach to prevention during school transitions: Longitudinal follow-ups and extensions of the School Transitional Environment Project (STEP). *Prevention in Human Services, 10,* 103–136.

Felner, R. D., Favazza, A., Shim, M., Brand, S., Gu, K., & Noonan, N. (2001). Whole school improvement and restructuring as prevention and promotion: Lessons from STEP and the Project on High Performance Learning Communities. *Journal of School Psychology, 39,* 177–202.

Goldstein, A. P., & Glick, B. (1994). Aggression replacement training: Curriculum and evaluation. *Simulation & Gaming, 25,* 9–26.

Goleman, D. (1995). *Emotional intelligence.* New York: Bantam Books.

Greenberg, M. T., Domitrovich, C., & Bumbarger, B. (2001). The prevention of mental disorders in school-aged children: Current state of the field. *Prevention & Treatment, 4 Article 1.* Retrieved January 14, 2005, from http://journals.apa.org/prevention/volume4/pre0040001a.html

Greenberg, M. T., Weissberg, R. P., O'Brien, M. U., Zins, J. E., Fredericks, L., Resnik, H., & Elias, M. J. (2003). Enhancing school-based prevention and youth development through coordinated social, emotional, and academic learning. *American Psychologist, 58,* 466–474.

Grossman, D. C., Neckerman, H. J., Koespell, T. D., Liu, P. Y., Asher, K. N., Beland, K., Frey, K., & Rivera, F. P. (1997). Effectiveness of a violence prevention curriculum among children in elementary school. *Journal of the American Medical Association, 277,* 1605–1611.

Guerra, N. G., Huesmann, L. R., & Spindler, A. (2003). Community violence exposure, social cognition, and aggression among urban elementary school children. *Child Development, 74,* 1561–1576.

Hawkins, J. D., Catalano, R. F., Kosterman, R., Abbott, R. D., & Hill, K. G. (1999). Preventing adolescent health-risk behaviors by strengthening protection during childhood. *Archives of Pediatrics and Adolescent Medicine, 153,* 226–234.

Hubbard, J. A. (2001). Emotion expression processes in children's peer interaction: The role of peer rejection, aggression, and gender. *Child Development, 72,* 1426–1438.

Hubbard, J. A., Dodge, K. A., Cillessen, A. H. N., Coie, J. D., & Schwartz, D. (2001). The dyadic nature of social information processing in boys' reactive and proactive aggression. *Journal of Personality & Social Psychology, 80,* 268–280.

Hubbard, J. A., Smithmyer, C. M., Ramsden, S. R., Parker, E. H., Flanagan, K. D., Dearing, K. F., Relyea, N., & Simons, R. F. (2002). Observational, physiological, and self-report measures of children's anger: Relations to reactive versus proactive aggression. *Child Development, 73,* 1101–1118.

Johnson, R. M., Kotch, J. B., Catellier, D. J., Winsor, J. R., Dufort, V., Hunter, W., & Amaya-Jackson, L. (2002). Adverse behavioral and emotional outcomes from child abuse and witnessed violence. *Child Maltreatment: Journal of the American Professional Society on the Abuse of Children, 7,* 179–186.

Kazdin, A. E., Bass, D., Siegel, T., & Thomas, C. (1989). Cognitive-behavioral therapy and relationship therapy in the treatment of children referred for antisocial behavior. *Journal of Consulting and Clinical Psychology, 57,* 522–535.

Kazdin, A. E., Esveldt-Dawson, K., French, N. H., & Unis, A. S. (1987). Problem-solving skills training and relationship therapy in the treatment of antisocial child behavior. *Journal of Consulting and Clinical Psychology, 55,* 76–85.

Kazdin, A. E., Siegel, T. C., & Bass, D. (1992). Cognitive problem-solving skills training and parent management training in the treatment of antisocial behavior in children. *Journal of Consulting and Clinical Psychology, 60,* 733–747.

Kusche, C., & Greenberg, M. (1994). *The PATHS curriculum: Promoting alternative thinking strategies.* Seattle, WA: Developmental Research and Programs.

Larson, J., & Lochman, J. E. (2002). *Helping schoolchildren cope with anger: A cognitive behavioral intervention.* New York: Guilford Press.

Lazarus, R. S. (1991). Progress on a cognitive-motivational-relational theory of emotion. *American Psychologist, 46,* 819–834.

Lewis, C., Watson, M., & Schaps, E. (2003). Building community in school: The Child Development Project. In M. J. Elias & H. Arnold (Eds.), *EQ + IQ = best leadership practices for caring and successful schools* (pp. 100–108). Thousand Oaks, CA: Corwin Press.

Lochman, J. E. (1992). Cognitive behavioral intervention with aggressive boys: Three-year follow-up and preventive effects. *Journal of Consulting and Clinical Psychology, 60,* 426–432.

Lochman, J. E., & Dodge, K. A. (1998). Distorted perceptions in dyadic interactions of aggressive and nonaggressive boys: Effects of prior expectations, context, and boys' age. *Development & Psychopathology, 10,* 495–512.

Lochman, J. E., Dunn, S. E., & Wagner, E. E. (1997). Anger. In G. G. Bear, K. M. Minke, & A. Thomas (Eds.), *Children's Needs II: Development, problems, and alternatives* (pp. 149–160). Bethesda, MD: National Association of School Psychologists.

Lochman, J. E., & Wells, K. C. (2002a). Contextual social–cognitive mediators and child outcome: A test of the theoretical model in the Coping Power Program. *Development & Psychopathology, 14,* 945–967.

Lochman, J. E., & Wells, K. C. (2002b). The Coping Power Program at the middle-school transition: Universal and indicated prevention effects. *Psychology of Addictive Behaviors, 16,* S40–S54.

Lochman, J. E., & Wells, K. C. (2003). Effectiveness of the Coping Power Program and of classroom intervention with aggressive children: Outcomes at a 1-year follow-up. *Behavior Therapy, 34,* 493–515.

Lochman, J. E., & Wells, K. C. (2004). The Coping Power Program for preadolescent aggressive boys and their parents: Outcome effects at the one-year follow-up. *Journal of Consulting and Clinical Psychology 72,* 571–578.

Martin, R., Watson, D., & Wan, C. K. (2000). A three-factor model of trait anger: Dimensions of affect, behavior, and cognition. *Journal of Personality, 68,* 869–897.

McCord, J., Tremblay, R. E., Vitaro, F., & Desmarais-Gervais, L. (1994). Boys' disruptive behaviour, school adjustment, and delinquency: The Montreal prevention experiment. *International Journal of Behavioral Development, 17,* 739–752.

Meichenbaum, D. H., & Goodman, J. (1971). Training impulsive children to talk to themselves: A means of developing self-control. *Journal of Abnormal Psychology, 77,* 115–126.

Mrazek, P. J., & Haggerty, R. J. (1994). *Reducing risks for mental disorders: Frontiers for preventive intervention research* (pp. 215–315). Washington, DC: National Academy Press.

Novaco, R. W. (1975). *Anger control: The development and evaluation of an experimental treatment.* Oxford, England: Lexington.

Orobio de Castro, B., Veerman, J. W., Koops, W., Bosch, J. D., & Monshouwer, H. J. (2002). Hostile attribution of intent and aggressive behavior: A meta-analysis. *Child Development, 73,* 916–934.

Ounsted, M. K., & Simons, C. D. (1978). The first-born child: Toddlers' problems. *Developmental Medicine & Child Neurology, 20,* 710–719.

Patterson, G. R. (1982). *Coercive family process.* Eugene, OR: Castalia.

Poulin, F., & Boivin, M. (2000). The role of proactive and reactive aggression in the formation and development of boys' friendships. *Developmental Psychology, 36,* 233–240.

Reid, J. B., & Eddy, J. M. (2002). Preventive efforts during the elementary school years: The Linking the Interests of Families and Teachers Project. In J. B. Reid & G. R. Patterson (Eds.), *Antisocial behavior in children and adolescents: A developmental analysis and model for intervention* (pp. 219–233). Washington, DC: American Psychological Association.

Risi, S., Gerhardstein, R., & Kistner, J. (2003). Children's classroom peer relationships and subsequent educational outcomes. *Journal of Clinical Child & Adolescent Psychology, 32,* 351–361.

Roland, E., & Galloway, D. (2002). Classroom influences on bullying. *Educational Research, 44,* 299–312.

Russell, A., Hart, C. H., Robinson, C. C., & Olsen, S. F. (2003). Children's sociable and aggressive behavior with peers: A comparison of the U.S. and Australia, and contributions of temperament and parenting styles. *International Journal of Behavioral Development, 27,* 74–86.

Schaeffer, C. M., Petras, H., Ialongo, N., Poduska, J., & Kellam, S. (2003). Modeling growth in boys' aggressive behavior across elementary school: Links to later criminal involvement, conduct disorder, and antisocial personality disorder. *Developmental Psychology, 39,* 1020–1035.

Smithmyer, C. M., Hubbard, J. A., & Simons, R. F. (2000). Proactive and reactive aggression in delinquent adolescents: Relations to aggression outcome expectancies. *Journal of Clinical Child Psychology, 29,* 86–93.

Solomon, D., Battistich, V., Watson, M., Schaps, E., & Lewis, C. (2000). A six-district study of educational change: Direct and mediated effects of the child development project. *Social Psychology of Education, 4,* 3–51.

Spielberger, C. D., Johnson, E. H., Russell, S. F., Crane, R. J., Jacobs, G. A., & Worden, T. J. (1985). The experience and expression of anger: Construction and validation of an anger expression scale. In M. A. Chesney & R. H. Rosenman (Eds.), *Anger and hostility in cardiovascular and behavioral disorders* (pp. 5–30). New York: Hemisphere/ McGraw-Hill.

Stenberg, C. R., & Campos, J. J. (1990). The development of anger expressions in infancy. In N. L Stein, B. Leventhal, & T. Trabasso (Eds.), *Psychological and biological approaches to emotion* (pp. 247–282). Hillsdale, NJ: Lawrence Erlbaum Associates.

Taub, J. (2001). Evaluation of the Second Step Violence Prevention Program at a rural elementary school. *School Psychology Review, 31,* 186–200.

Tremblay, R. E., Kurtz, L., Masse, L. C., Vitaro, F., & Pihl, R. O. (1995). A bimodal preventive intervention for disruptive kindergarten boys: Its impact through mid-adolescence. *Journal of Consulting and Clinical Psychology, 63,* 560–568.

Tremblay, R. E., Masse, L. C., Pagani, L., & Vitaro, F. (1996). From childhood physical aggression to adolescent maladjustment: The Montreal prevention experiment. In R. D. Peters & R. J. McMahon (Eds.), *Preventing childhood disorders, substance abuse, and delinquency* (pp. 268–298). Thousand Oaks, CA: Sage.

Tremblay, R. E., Vitaro, F., Bertrand, L., LeBlanc, M., Beauchesne, H., Boileau, H., & David, L. (1992). Parent and child training to prevent early onset of delinquency: The Montreal longitudinal-experimental study. In J. McCord & R. E. Tremblay (Eds.), *Preventing antisocial behavior: Interventions from birth through adolescence* (pp. 117–138). New York: Guilford Press.

U.S. Department of Justice, Federal Bureau of Investigation. (2000, April). Age-specific arrest rates and race-specific arrest rates for selected offenses. 1965–1988. Washington, DC: U.S. Government Printing Office.

Vitaro, F., & Tremblay, R. E. (1994). Impact of a prevention program on aggressive children's friendships and social adjustment. *Journal of Abnormal Child Psychology, 22,* 457–475.

Webster-Stratton, C. (1990). Enhancing the effectiveness of self-administered videotape parent training for families with conduct-problem children. *Journal of Abnormal Child Psychology, 18,* 479–492.

Webster-Stratton, C., & Hammond, M. (1997). Treating children with early-onset conduct problems: A comparison of child and parent training interventions. *Journal of Consulting and Clinical Psychology, 65,* 93–109.

Werner, N. E., & Crick, N. R. (2004). Maladaptive peer relationships and the development of relational and physical aggression during middle childhood. *Social Development, 13,* 495–514.

Williams, S. C., Lochman, J. E., Phillips, N. C., & Barry, T. D. (2003). Aggressive and nonaggressive boys' physiological and cognitive processes in response to peer provocations. *Journal of Clinical Child & Adolescent Psychology, 32,* 568–576.

# 10

# Bullying

**George M. Batsche**
**Larry J. Porter**
*University of South Florida*

## BACKGROUND AND DEVELOPMENT

Bullying among students has become a topic of increasing concern in countries throughout the world. In the United States a significant catalyst of this concern was the school shootings at Columbine and the reported relationship between bullying and school shootings (Vossekuil, Fein, Reddy, Borum, & Modzeleski, 2002). Since 2001, more than 15 states have passed laws pertaining to bullying in schools, with such laws often mandating prevention and intervention programs (Limber & Small, 2003).

The results of prevalence studies of bullying provide inconsistent data based on the age of students studied, the country in which the research was conducted, and the definition of bullying used in the study. In a survey of 15,686 students in grades 6 through 10 in the United States (Nansel et al., 2001), almost 30% of the students reported being involved in bullying either moderately (sometimes) or frequently (once or more each week), either as a bully (13.0%), a victim (10.6%), or both (bully/victim, 6.3%). In another study of 5,171 students in grades 5 through 9 in Norway (Solberg & Olweus, 2003), 6.5% of all students reported bullying others, 10.1% reported being bullied, and 1.6% reported both bullying and being bullied. In both studies, significantly more boys reported being involved in bullying (as a bully, victim, or bully/victim) than did girls. It is clear from both studies, however, that the problem of bullying is prevalent in schools both in the United States and abroad.

### Bullying Defined

Bullying in school is defined by the presence of four key factors: (a) the *harming* of a person directly through physical or verbal means or indirectly through harming interpersonal relationships or reputations; (b) the presence of an *unfair advantage* over the victim because the bully is physically stronger, because the bully has more social power, or because the bullying is perpetrated by a group against an individual (age difference alone is insufficient); (c) the occurrence *at school* or on the way to or from school; and (d) the *repetition* of the act (Hazler, Miller, Carney, & Green, 2001; Olweus, Limber, & Mihalic, 1999). The U.S. Department of Education (1998) defined bullying as "intentional, repeated hurtful acts, words or other behavior, such as name-calling, threatening and/or shunning committed by one or more children against another. The victim does not intentionally provoke these negative acts, and for such acts to be defined as bullying, an imbalance in real or perceived power must exist between the bully and the victim. Bullying may be physical, verbal, emotional, or sexual in nature" (p. 1).

How often must bullying occur for an individual to be considered a bully or a victim of bullying? In a study designed to improve the accuracy of the prevalence estimation of school bullying, Solberg and Olweus (2003) concluded that a frequency of two or three times a month is a functional lower-bound cutoff point to use for the identification of bullies and victims. This is an important statistic for two reasons. First, school systems must have criteria for the identification of bullying that are clear and have sufficient inter-rater agreement in order to develop and enforce policies and to identify students or situations in need of interventions. School districts and school buildings can use the presence or absence of the four factors above in combination with the frequency cutoff in order to ensure consistent identification of bullies and their victims. Second, the negative effects of bullying on a victim is related to the frequency and intensity of those aversive events. Clearly, victims of repeated, frequent bullying are at greatest risk for negative social, emotional, and school performance outcomes.

*Bullies* are individuals (or a group) that bully others and are not bullied themselves while *victims* are bullied but do not bully others. In one sense these definitions represent the *pure* bullies and victims. However, some children and youth bully others and are victimized. These individuals are known as *bully/victims*. In the Nansel et al. study (2001), 6.3% of the sample reported being both a bully and a target of bullying. *Bystanders* are those who witness bullying. Although bullying and victimization can be private, interpersonal events, many such events occur in public settings in schools. Therefore, it is very likely that the greatest numbers of students involved in the bully process are, in fact, bystanders. This group is generally ignored both in the research and in the implementation of prevention and intervention programs (Harris & Petrie, 2003). Finally, a group of students exists who are not involved in any way in the bully–victim process. Those students are often referred to as controls or uninvolved students.

## Forms of Bullying

The behavioral repertoire of bullies can be characterized as direct and indirect bullying or aggression. *Direct* bullying usually occurs through verbal or physical aggression, or both, with direct verbal aggression being the most common form of bullying (Batsche, 1997; Hunter & Boyle, 2002; Nansel et al., 2001). Males are more likely to use direct forms of bullying. Two types of direct bullying or aggression have been identified: proactive (object oriented, person directed) and reactive (in response to anger and frustration). *Proactive* aggression is goal directed and can be associated with high levels of social competence and peer status (Coie & Dodge, 1998). *Reactive* aggression often is associated with individuals who have low levels of social competence and does not necessarily correlate with high peer status. Reactive aggression can be viewed as an ineffective form of aggression that is not likely to move an individual to a higher position of dominance in the peer group (Prinstein & Cillessen, 2003).

The use of social exclusion, gossip, malicious rumors, and the like are behaviors associated with *indirect* or *relational* bullying (Crick & Grotpeter, 1995; Woods & Wolke, 2004). Traditionally, relational bullying has been associated with females and, in general, with nonphysical means of harming someone (Crick & Grotpeter, 1995). However, it is now clear that relational aggression is also common among males (Espelage & Swearer, 2003). Recent research has expanded our understanding of the concepts of relational bullying and aggression and how they are related to gender bias, social competence, and popularity. For example, research by Xie, Swift, Cairns, and Cairns (2002) suggests that two types of relational aggression exist: relational and reputational. *Relational* aggression is defined as using a personal relationship to harm someone. *Reputational* aggression is defined as an attempt to harm someone's social reputation. The results of this research concluded that relational aggression is used to maintain the conflict or to retaliate or escalate the conflict, whereas reputational aggression is used during the initiation of some type of conflict.

Rodkin, Farmer, Pearl, and Van Acker (2000) suggest that some bullying behaviors are demonstrated by socially competent, high-status children and youth (whom they refer to as "popular-toughs"). These students are motivated to use aggression to garner resources and to control status within a group. They require a social network within which to operate and are very popular but not necessarily liked. Xie's (Xie et al., 2002) work has helped our understanding of how these popular-toughs use bullying to attain status—primarily by using aggression to bring down someone's reputation. The target of reputational aggression has to be someone *with* a reputation or status. As such, this form of bullying may occur between students of high (or at least equal) status—students who do not fit the traditional definition of bullies and victims (e.g., weak or socially incompetent).

## Factors That Contribute to Bullying

The development and application of effective interventions, both to reduce the levels of bullying and victimization and to increase the levels of prosocial behaviors, require an understanding of the factors that contribute to the bullying process. A rubric is needed to organize all of the information on bullying to address the behaviors efficiently using a problem-solving process. One such rubric is the Referral-Question Consultation (RQC) process (Batsche & Ulman, 1984), which organizes hypotheses for school-based problem solving into six factors: student, peers, home and family, classroom and school environment, curriculum, and teachers or school-based adults. Examples of hypotheses drawn from empirical research for each factor are presented in Table 1. In addition, this approach reinforces a problem-solving process that supports a social–ecological perspective

**Table 1** *Examples of Hypotheses for Each Factor in the RQC Problem-Solving Process*

| Factors | Hypotheses |
|---|---|
| Child | The bully falsely attributes a victim's actions as hostile.<br>The bully does not possess adequate social skills to appropriately deal with anger and frustration.<br>The bully believes that the positive personal outcomes of bullying justify the actions.<br>The bully is using reputational aggression to establish status within a group or to limit a threat from a similar out-group student. |
| Peer | The bully or victim in question is rejected by the peer group.<br>The peer group plays no role (other than rejection) in helping to explain the bully process.<br>*Bully assistants* serve to reinforce the role of the bully in the bully's absence or to manipulate low-level threats.<br>Bystanders reinforce bullying yet are not involved directly in the group. They reinforce bullying because the process does not offer any threat to them, they are perceived as a nonthreat by the bully, and they view the bully as cool or popular.<br>Bystanders do nothing to intervene with the bully or victim because they do not know what to do or are afraid of becoming involved.<br>Bystanders aid the victim, particularly when they are empathetic toward the victim, offer no threat to the bully, and are not at risk for retaliation from the bully or bully's supporters. |
| Family | The household has low levels of parental supervision.<br>There is physical violence in the household.<br>One or both parents or guardians model or reinforce bully behavior. |
| Classroom and School Environment | No school or classroom rules are in place to discourage bullying and being a bystander.<br>There are low levels of administrator and teacher supervision in the school outside of the classroom.<br>The school has no bully prevention or awareness programs. |
| Curriculum | The curriculum is not inclusive of all students.<br>The curriculum is too difficult.<br>The curriculum is not relevant to the students.<br>Progress within the curriculum is competitive between students.<br>Few resources exist for students who are not successful with the curriculum. |
| Teacher, School, and Adult Factors | Teachers do not know how to identify bullying when it is occurring.<br>Teachers do not possess the skills to intervene with the bully, victim, or bystanders when the incident occurs.<br>School staff believe that bullying is a natural part of student behavior.<br>Staff believe that bullying is limited to overt physical and verbal aggression.<br>Staff are unaware of covert forms of bullying. |

(Espelage & Swearer, 2004). This rubric provides a valuable "blueprint" with which to complete the problem analysis step of the problem-solving process for bullying. A review of the existing literature results in a wealth of information to explain how each of the hypothesis areas potentially contributes to the development of bullying behavior.

***Student-based factors.*** Research has identified a range of deficits and deficiencies in the social cognitive processes of children who exhibit frequent acts of aggression, including bullying. For example, Dodge's (Crick & Dodge, 1994) model of social information processing shows how aggressive children attribute hostile intentions to others; possess fewer prosocial solutions to provocations than same-age peers; label levels of arousal as anger rather than fear, anxiety, or other appropriate emotions; underestimate their own level of aggressiveness; are deficient in short-term memory, impulse control, and concentration; lack empathy for victims; and view aggression positively (see chapter 9, "Anger and Aggression," and 3, "Developing Self-Discipline"). The social information processing model may apply best when trying to explain reactive aggression or proactive aggression that seems to occur outside the context of a social network.

Another model for viewing the thoughts and emotions of children that have been shown to be associated with aggression and bullying is the theory of mind model (Salmivalli, Lagerspetz, Bjorkqvist, Osterman, & Kaukiainen, 1996), which focuses on the ability to attribute mental states to oneself and to others. This is perhaps best applied to bully behavior that is more indirect or that serves to modify an individual's status within the social network. The conclusions of Xie et al. (2002) regarding reputational aggression would lead one to assume that bullies have the ability to evaluate the social status of their victim, the victim's tolerance of the bullying, and the peer group's acceptance of the bully's new status following successful aggression (direct or relational). As such, behaviors such as lying and spreading rumors about the victim and making continued threats toward a victim would indicate the presence of relational aggression for the purpose of maintaining the status in the peer group and above the victim. Therefore, assessment of the outcome served by the bullying (improved status) and the topography of the bullying (reputational, relational, direct, or indirect) could serve to confirm or reject the hypothesis.

Consistent with both models—social information processing and theory of mind—is the role that moral emotions play in bullying. Menesini et al. (2003) concluded that bullies demonstrate a pattern of egocentric reasoning. Menesini et al. demonstrated that bullies believe that their motives and the goals of their actions help them to justify their negative and harmful behavior. This research found that 30% of the bullies in the study had some type of awareness of the negative effects of their behavior on victims. However, what the bullies feared most was the potential consequences of the bully behavior on themselves (e.g., punishment). The combination of egocentric responsibility and disengagement from the effects of bullying helps to explain how bullies can affirm their understanding of the negative effects on others yet, at the same time, seem not to care. Arsenio and Lemerise (2001) concluded that although some bullies (especially those with proactive aggression) have well-developed skills in understanding the intentions of others (theory of mind), they use these skills not for prosocial acts but to attain their own goals at the expense of others (victims).

***Peer factors.*** Peers are involved, at some level, in 85% of bullying episodes (Atlas & Pepler, 1998). Salmivalli et al. (1996) identified four participant roles in the bullying process other than the bully and the victim. They are reinforcer of the bully, assistant of the bully, defender of the victim, and outsider. Some bullies have few friends and very limited interaction with social groups. Others belong to small fringe groups made up of individuals such as themselves (unpopular bullies). However, more recent research (e.g., Prinstein & Cillessen, 2003) has identified bullies who are popular, are socially engaged at complex levels, and operate within an ecology where they skillfully manipulate their environment. These bullies require other players, confederates if you will, to carry out catalytic, reinforcing, and supportive roles—both for bullies and victims. Salmivalli et al. concluded that bullies rely on their network of reinforcers, assistants, and scapegoats to establish influence within the peer culture. Peer groups tend to be similar on a number of behavioral and demographic characteristics, and groups to which bullies belong are similarly consistent. Clearly, peer influence plays an important role in bullying: Students who affiliate with bullies engage in more bullying. This is generally true for both males and females.

The findings of Ojala and Nesdale (2004) are similar to those of Salmivalli et al. (1996). When Ojala and Nesdale applied social identity theory to bullying, they found that in- and out-group differences were important. Bullying an out-group member was not justified by the group when the out-group member offered no threat to the in-group. Furthermore, when the out-group member shared similarities with the in-group, then bullying was not viewed as less acceptable. Behavioral similarities and level of perceived threat seemed to predict an episode of bullying. However, other studies show that aggressive children do not limit their affiliation to other aggressive children alone. A study conducted by Farmer et al. (2002) investigated the degree to which children within groups are aggressive, and how the aggressive and nonaggressive students were viewed by other members of the group. The investigators found that two-thirds of aggressive boys and half of aggressive girls affiliated in groups whose members were mostly nonaggressive. Aggressive children nominated peers who were aggressive as "cool," and nominated nonaggressive children as cool as well, but only if they were in a nonaggressive peer group (offering no threat to the aggressive group). Interestingly, some aggressive boys were disproportionately nominated by nonaggressive girls as cool.

Given the above studies, it can be concluded that many bullies belong to established social groups of students who share similar characteristics. However, unlike previous understandings of bully groups, these are not deviant groups; rather, they are groups that enjoy a broad base of social support both from similar students within the group and from nonaggressive (dissimilar) students outside the group. These socially networked bullies (and supporters) use both reputational aggression and relational aggression to establish and maintain their status in the group. However, because they do not offer a threat to other peers who do not threaten them, these bullies can maintain a level of popularity within and across groups.

***Family factors.*** The following family factors have been shown to be associated with bullying: low levels of supervision and the presence of physical violence; inconsistent, harsh discipline (a form of bullying in itself); parents who value aggression as a way to achieve goals (Espelage & Swearer, 2003); and bullying by siblings (Duncan, 1999). In addition, some evidence exists to support the idea that overcontrolling mothers and parents who are significantly involved in their child's school (Nansel et al., 2001) are associated with an increased risk for victimization. Nansel et al. suggest that greater parent involvement might limit the development of independence in their children. This lowered level of independence may make the children more vulnerable to being bullied.

***Classroom and school environment factors.*** Two particular domains of hypotheses are included in these factors: classroom and school climate. The presence of classroom rules that prohibit bullying and discourage bystanding and the use in the classroom of cooperative learning and other activities (Doll, Song, & Siemers, 2004) that facilitate the development of friendships are consistent with lower rates of bullying. Pellegrini and Long (2002) found that being popular and having a number of friends serve as a buffer against victimization. Bullies are less likely to aggress toward a popular student or those with a number of friends who could retaliate against the bully. Bullies are interested in maintaining status (Xie et al., 2002) and are less likely to risk losing it by attacking students with a social support group. Close or frequent proximity to one another is likely to occur in classroom settings in which peer inclusion strategies are encouraged and supported. Bullies are more likely to victimize students who are isolated physically or socially. Therefore, the level of teacher supervision available is related to levels of bullying. This is particularly true in classrooms and school buildings where the architecture prevents or inhibits visual scans. Strong levels of peer and social inclusion are also related to lower levels of bullying (Doll et al., 2004). The use of strategies to teach autonomy, self-control, and problem-solving skills reduces the possibility of bullying. These skills are particularly important since a significant amount of bullying occurs when adults are not present. The use of self-monitoring, self-evaluation, and self-reinforcement are examples of strategies that increase behavioral self-control.

School climate factors include policies and practices that influence all of the educators, students, and families in a school setting. Some school climate factors that are related to bullying, and can be used in the problem-solving process, include the following:

- Schools in which there are high levels of student–student and student–teacher conflict report more conduct problems.
- Schools that have administration and staff actively involved in supervision outside of the classroom report few incidents of bullying and other aggressive behaviors.
- Schools that openly communicate expectations for prosocial behavior, involve students in school-wide campaigns for prosocial behavior, and have peer mediation programs report fewer incidents of bullying.
- Schools that have high expectations for students and provide support for those expectations report fewer conduct problems.
- Schools that promote and have high levels of parent involvement report fewer incidents of harassment and aggressive behaviors.

- Schools that use high rates of exclusion consequences, such as suspension (in and out of school), expulsion, referrals to the office, report a greater number of student–student conflicts.
- Schools that include curricula that provide training in and reinforcement for prosocial behaviors report fewer student–student conflicts.
- Schools that promote collaborative, rather than competitive, learning are viewed as more harmonious by the students. Schools labeled as harmonious report fewer student–student conflicts and are evaluated as positive environments by students.

***Curriculum factors.*** The way in which students are expected to engage the curriculum, the difficulty level, and the relevance of the curriculum all contribute to classroom climate. Curriculum that requires the inclusion of all students, provides for collaborative work (source of social support), and focuses on student progress facilitates a climate of involvement and success. In a collaborative environment, fewer students become isolated (and thus are vulnerable as victims) or angry and retaliative (and become bullies). Students who are forced to engage in curriculum that is above their instructional level experience frustration and stress. Repeated exposure to this type of experience makes the student vulnerable, either as a victim or a bully. Students who do not find the curriculum relevant, whether based on interest, experience, or culture, engage the curriculum at lower levels than students who find the curriculum to be relevant. The lower levels of engagement are associated with lower levels of academic performance and further disengagement. Students who cannot attain status through academic achievement will seek status through other means, such as reputational aggression.

***Teacher or school-based adult factors.*** Teachers and other adults in the school setting are critical players in bully prevention and intervention. However, to be successful in addressing bullying, the adults in a building must know what bullying is and have the skills to address it when it occurs. Teachers view physical threat as more severe than verbal or emotional abuse and often rate physical conflict as bullying when it is not and rate verbal or emotional behaviors as not bullying when in fact they are (Hazler et al., 2001). In addition, teachers tend to report lower rates of bullying in a given setting than do students (Stockdale, Hangaduambo, Duys, Larson, & Sarvela, 2002). They also report less confidence in their ability to intervene with bullying than with other school-related behaviors. Questions that must be answered and addressed when engaging in problem solving to develop a bully prevention or intervention program include the following:

- Do teachers and other adults have a clear understanding of the definition of bullying so they know it when they see it?
- Do adults possess the skills to intervene with the bully, victim, and bystanders when an incident occurs?
- Is there adequate adult supervision in areas of the school building other than classrooms (e.g., lunchroom, halls, and bathrooms)?
- Are students treated with respect by adults in the building?

## PROBLEMS AND IMPLICATIONS

A number of problems are associated with being a bully, a victim, a bully/victim, or a bystander. Nansel et al. (2001) conducted a comprehensive study of bullying in grades 6 through 10 in the United States and demonstrated the degree to which bullying is a serious problem that affects school-age children and youth. Overall, students who were bullies, victims, or bully/victims had poorer psychosocial adjustment than noninvolved students. In Nansel et al.'s study of adolescents, being a bully was positively related to poor school adjustment, lower academic achievements, alcohol consumption, fighting, and smoking. At the same time, bullies reported that it was easier to make friends. This is consistent with the recent research (Xie et al., 2002) identifying popular bullies who are part of viable social networks. Being a victim was related to difficulty making friends, poorer relationships with classmates, and increased loneliness. Being a victim was associated with a less frequent use of alcohol. Bully/victims had the poorest adjustment across social–emotional dimensions and problem behaviors. Being a bully/victim was associated with poorer academic achievement, smoking, fighting, and alcohol use. A permissive parental attitude toward drinking and poor relationships with classmates were also associated with being a bully/victim.

Although few studies have been conducted on the long-term effects of bullying, all verify that the effects of bullying last into adulthood. Olweus (1994) reported that 60% of former bullies had at least one conviction and 35%–40% had three or more convictions. In addition, Olweus reported that victims reported higher levels of depression and poorer self-esteem at age 23.

The impact on bystanders of witnessing bullying is significant. Bystanders experience a wide range of emotions, including anger, fear, guilt, and sadness (Harris & Petrie, 2003; Hazler, 1996). Bystanders typically do not help the victim because they do not know strategies to prevent bullying, feel that it is none of their business, or are afraid of retaliation by the bully (Hazler). Bystanders report that they lose their confidence in their ability to intervene, lose self-respect, and become desensitized to the bullying over time. In addition, male bystanders report that they become less sympathetic to the victim over time (Harris & Petrie).

It is clear that bullying also has a detrimental effect on school climate. The loss of trust that school is a safe place, the emergence of fear (and avoidance), and the general reduction in the quality of the environment for both students and adults all affect perceptions of climate. The negative effect of bullying on school climate is exacerbated when the school does not respond to bullying in a systematic, visible way. Schools that do not address bullying in a systematic way tend to have lower levels of supervision outside the classroom, fewer rules and prevention programs for bully behavior, and an environment where communication about prosocial behavior is sparse. In that climate, students conclude that bullying and aggression are sanctioned. The belief that bullying is sanctioned (and therefore that there is little that can be done about it) is particularly devastating to victims, by deepening their already negative affect (Dill, Vernberg, Fonagy, Twemlow, & Gamm, 2004).

The negative effects of bullying are perhaps greatest on students who are victimized repeatedly. Repeated victimization produces increased anger and depression, low self-esteem, social withdrawal, and a perception of loss of control (Hunter & Boyle, 2002). The process of repeated victimization can occur for a number of reasons, including lack of supervision and adult inattention to the bullying. A more insidious (and less visible) cyclical process can develop with students who have less assertive behaviors. Some bullies target vulnerable victims, those who are less assertive, shy, withdrawn, or socially isolated. Students who possess these characteristics tend to have fewer friends, are less integral to the social network, remain on the fringe of the group, and have fewer allies if bullied. Moreover, when bullied, students with these characteristics also tend to invite further and more intense victimization (Hodges & Perry, 1999). The increased victimization predicts an increase in adjustment problems. Hunter and Boyle found that a student's perception of control over bullying was related to the length of time that the bullying occurred. Perceptions of greater control over the situation occurred earlier, rather than later, in the bullying process. Hunter and Boyle concluded that "a failure to intervene early may lead to victims developing appraisals which discourage proactive behaviour, leading to an increase in the likelihood of extended victimization." (p. 331). Girls (but not boys) felt less in control with frequent, compared with infrequent, bullying. Interestingly, perceived control was not related to the type of bullying (direct or indirect) or to the age difference between the bully and the victim.

The problems associated with bullying and the implications of not preventing and intervening are clearly severe. The short-term effects on all parties involved in the bullying process put children and youth at risk for some type of adaptational failure. The long-term effects on levels of criminal behavior and emotional maladjustment appear to serve as a mandate for early prevention and intervention programs in schools.

## ALTERNATIVE ACTIONS FOR PREVENTION

### Universal Interventions

Bullying is all about school climate. The climate of a school either sustains bully behavior or limits its possibilities. Some level of bullying, however, is likely to occur in any environment, regardless of the level of prevention and intervention efforts. Our need for dominance, status, and affiliation all support behaviors that, at one time or another, are bully-like. In addition, feelings of anger, isolation, rejection, and ineptness are fertile ground for reactive aggression. However, the presence of prevention programs limits the growth and maturity of the social network and culture that support bullying and aggression.

A comprehensive approach to bully prevention and intervention should take a scaffolding approach, with broad-based, school-wide policies and prevention programs that, at their core, support and empower classroom-level activities, leading to more intense interventions based on the response to lower-level ones. Consistent with the model of school-wide positive behavioral supports, universal prevention efforts should constitute the core program, which should affect 80% to 90% of the students. Strategic and intensive interventions should focus on the remaining 10% to 20%

of the student population that do not respond to the prevention efforts.

The primary effect of core prevention programs will be on mild levels of bullying and victimization. Long-term bully/victim problems are resistant to prevention-only efforts (Sharp, Thompson, & Arora, 2000). Olweus's & Limber's (1999) Bully Prevention Program offers a wide range of prevention strategies, including staff education, school conference days, staff discussion groups, and supervision, along with rule development, student and parent meetings, and direct work with bullies and victims. The program has a component to facilitate the development of individual intervention plans. In addition, the program has assessment protocols to evaluate levels of need and the pervasiveness of the problem. A number of the program's essential components define a comprehensive bully prevention effort. The components must address problem assessment, staff education and involvement, policy development, school climate issues, specific skills to be taught to students and staff, supervision, and a program evaluation strategy. The following sections briefly address each component.

## Problem Assessment

In a research study designed to predict teacher and school implementation of the Olweus Bullying Prevention Program, Kallestad and Olweus (2003) found that teachers' perceptions of the degree of bullying in their classrooms predicted their use of classroom intervention strategies. A number of surveys and peer nomination practices exist to collect school-wide data on the nature and extent of the bullying problem in a school. In addition, the frequency of suspension, expulsion, office discipline referral associated with bullying can be assessed.

Olweus's and Limber's (1999) Bullying Prevention Program is one source of data collection tools, and the appendices of *Bullying* (Harris & Petrie, 2003) contain surveys. The data collected in these surveys can be used to establish student and staff perceptions of the levels of bullying, sources of bullying, and its impact. This information can be communicated to staff implementing the prevention program to establish an understanding of the need for a prevention program. In addition, the data can be used for formative and summative assessment. The steps in Table 2 can be used to complete the problem identification phase of the problem-solving process. Data collected from these steps will establish levels of baseline data prior to implementing the prevention program.

**Table 2** *Problem Identification*

| Step | Activity |
|---|---|
| 1 | Define bullying using the U.S. Department of Education definition, including the four key factors: harmful, repeated, unfair advantage, and setting. |
| 2 | Ensure that the definition includes both direct (e.g., physical, verbal) and indirect (relational, reputational) forms of bullying. |
| 3 | Communicate the definition and criteria to staff and students. |
| 4 | Administer a student and staff survey to identify perceptions of both the *levels* and *types* of bullying and to identify student and staff perceptions of social supports to prevent and intervene with bully behavior. |
| 5 | Collect data on office discipline referrals, suspensions, and expulsions related to bullying behavior. |

## Staff Education and Involvement

Ensuring that the school staff has basic knowledge about the bullying process is important. This is particularly true given the results of the Hazler et al. (2001) study in which teachers consistently misidentified exemplars and nonexemplars of bullying. Kallestad and Olweus (2003) found that the degree to which teachers implemented classroom interventions was most strongly predicted by a staff efficacy measure, or perceived staff importance (the degree to which staff saw themselves as important agents of change). Teachers and other staff first must know that a problem exists, and second, must have enough knowledge about the prevention program and its components to believe that they have the skills to carry out the program successfully.

## Policy Development

Schools and districts must develop policies to support the prevention and intervention program, to support the development of school-wide rules, and to provide consistency in the implementation of responses to bullying. In particular, the school's code of conduct should be modified to ensure that fighting and bullying are differentiated. Harris and Petrie (2003) provide examples of policy statements that can be used as blueprints by schools and districts.

## School Climate

A number of factors must be present to ensure that the school climate provides enough "oxygen" to support prosocial behavior and limit bullying. Students are most likely to communicate with school staff regarding bullying when they believe that the staff are responsive to bullying behaviors, when bullying problems are addressed early in their development, when few (if any) students are victimized repeatedly, and when the school has open discussion and programs regarding elimination of bully behavior. Open communication between teachers contributes to a climate in which teachers are more willing to implement prevention activities (Kallestad & Olweus, 2003). The presence of concrete indicators, such as school assemblies, signs, surveys, rules and policies, and parent involvement, all contribute to students and staff perceiving that the school climate does not harbor and nurture bullies. The presence of teachers who are emotionally responsive and empathetic toward victims not only contributes to a positive school climate but also is a predictor of the degree to which teachers will implement prevention programs (Kallestad & Olweus, 2003).

## Prevention Skills

Staff can draw on a number of skills to reduce the probability of bullying behavior, including the following:

- Develop firm but realistic behavioral and academic expectations for all students.
- Develop a few clear rules regarding interpersonal behavior.
- Provide consistent, close supervision of students. This is particularly important in school settings outside the classroom.
- Treat students with respect and value their contributions. Expect the same from them.
- Provide frequent opportunities for students with behavioral and academic problems to respond in class and to receive positive feedback for their behavior. These students actually need more opportunities to participate in class than students who do not demonstrate these problems.
- Ensure that all students are included in activities, have classmates with whom to affiliate, and are not isolated and rejected.
- Conduct classroom discussions to ensure that students gain knowledge about bullying, the impact of bullying, and the roles of bullies, victims, and bystanders.
- Select collaborative rather than competitive activities in the classroom.
- Resolve conflict between students with a stepwise problem-solving process such as Skillstreaming (Goldstein, McGinnis, Sprafkin, Gershaw, & Klein, 1997).
- Engage in school-wide campaigns, with activities, signs, assemblies, and other student-led activities that promote prosocial behavior and discourage bullying.
- Ensure that students can communicate information about bullying through both open, direct methods and anonymous methods.
- Involve parents in the prevention program through parent education, involvement in school-wide assemblies about bullying, school celebrations, and home–school communication strategies (e.g., home–school notes).

## Supervision

Adequate supervision, in the classroom and in noninstructional settings (e.g., halls, lunchroom, and school grounds), is essential for an effective prevention program. Supervision provides students with the message that the environment is safe and that the school staff members are there to support the program. Adequate supervision is the best defense against repeated victimization, and it communicates to victims that someone other than the bully is in control. Victims are more likely to be receptive to interventions if they believe that they have some control over the situation. Schools can identify areas in need of supervision by plotting the location of bullying and other aggressive events on a school map. Over a period of just a couple of months, the hot spots in need of supervision will become obvious. Administrators can deploy additional supervision to those areas, make them known to school staff for additional vigilance, or create off-limits areas to enhance safety.

## Program Evaluation

The primary purpose of a program evaluation component is to provide students and staff with data to demonstrate the effectiveness of the program. Data can enhance teacher efficacy (related to level of program implementation), provide students with evidence that their efforts are working and that they do have control to overcome the bullying, and provide district-level decision makers with evidence to continue program support. Most bullying prevention programs use a repeated-measures format to collect data by readministering the assessment tools used in the problem identification step (Olweus, Limber & Mihalic, 1999; Harris & Petrie, 2003). In addition, the collection of suspension, expulsion, and office discipline referrals for bully behavior provides data on frequency and per capita data in addition to student and staff perceptions of program effectiveness. Comparing pre- and postprogram results is one method to assess student and staff response to the program and will provide some evidence of program effectiveness. The use of a *comparison school* (one with similar demographics and problem levels) to collect similar data will provide additional support for program effectiveness. This is particularly powerful when the comparison school is slated to participate in the prevention program in the future. Data aggregated across multiple settings at different times provide more rigorous program evaluations.

## ALTERNATIVE ACTIONS FOR INTERVENTION

The most effective intervention programs for bullying and school violence focus on a change in the school climate and expectations for student behavior (Limber, 2004). Mulvey and Cauffman (2001) found that schools that used strategies that focus on improving the school environment appear to have more success than schools that use specific curricular strategies. Many of the packaged curriculum programs for bullying prevention and intervention do not have empirical evidence to support their use. In addition, some of the interventions with face validity may, in fact, exacerbate the problem. For example, Limber (2004) warns that the use of conflict resolution and mediation strategies may be inappropriate. The use of these approaches assumes that a relatively even power relationship exists between the two parties involved. This is not the case with bullying. Bullying is always inappropriate and there is nothing to "mediate." The message should be clear—don't do it.

Staff education is important: Teachers and administrators must have the skills to differentiate bullying from other forms of aggression to avoid empowering the bully with inappropriate interventions. The use of some group and individual therapy approaches also may exacerbate the problem (Limber, 2004). The group process itself may foster an increase in bullying if group members are allowed to reinforce each other's behavior and strengthen their social network as a result of the group meetings. The content of some group therapy programs may be problematic. Although there is a general belief that bullies have low self-esteem, the work of Olweus (1994), Xie et al. (2002), and others suggest that is not the case. Therefore, it is possible that participation in groups designed to enhance self-esteem could increase the confidence of bullies and make matters worse.

The research support for differentiated intervention programs is increasing rapidly. Practitioners who work with bullies should ensure that they adhere to evidence-based practices and put the majority of their efforts into school-wide programs designed to improve school climate. A number of school-wide programs exist that can be adapted by practitioners for school-based use. Examples of such programs include the Olweus Bullying Prevention Program (Olweus et al., 1999) and the Bully Busters Program (Horne, Bartolomucci, & Newman-Carlson, 2003). A number of other interventions exist that have empirical support but must be used appropriately.

### Mentoring

Mentoring meets three critical needs of bullies, victims, and bully/victims. First, mentoring provides the opportunity to experience positive role models with the behavior appropriate to the role (e.g., bully or victim). Second, it sends a message to the student that someone in the school is there every day with a caring, nurturing attitude and provides a person with whom the bully or victim can develop trust and communication (social support). Third, it meets a supervision need to ensure the safety of all parties involved. Every bully, victim, or bully/victim who is identified in a school should have a mentor. Research to date has not evaluated the effects of mentoring on bully behavior. However, strategies such as increased supervision, social modeling, school and parent involvement, and a protective environment all reduce bully behavior (Northwest Regional Laboratory, 2001). Mentors can be used to ensure that these strategies are implemented in the school setting.

### Social Skills Training

Social skills training programs should only be used with students who have skill deficits that are important to ensuring success in the school or community setting. Social skills programs are less effective for students who possess the skills but demonstrate performance deficits. Many of the existing curricula for social skills training curricula, such as

Skillstreaming, share a similar training format (skill steps, modeling, role-playing, prompting, and reinforcement), and current research on the effectiveness of social skills training supports its use with skill or acquisition deficits (Gresham, Cook, Crews, & Kern, 2004). The appropriate application of social skills training with the bullying process would be to enhance particular skills of victims (assertiveness and group affiliation) and bully/victims when behavioral deficits are related to victimization. Some research also supports the effectiveness of social skills training with delinquent populations and with the development of social interaction skills (Mathur, Kavale, Quinn, Forness, & Rutherford, 1998). One advantage of social skills training is that teachers and other staff members can learn the behavioral prompts quickly and easily, making it easy to transfer training from the group to the classroom and providing teachers and other staff with additional skills to manage student behavior.

## Anger Control Training

Anger control training (see chapter 9, "Anger and Aggression") would have its most logical application with bullies who engaged in direct, reactive bullying. Often these students have anger control problems and are reinforced for their anger by eliminating sources of stress or feeling powerful. These students are the least socially competent of the bully types, are more rejected, and have low status in the group. Their inappropriate use of anger continues the cycle of rejection and isolation, which in turn increases the need to feel some level of power and validation. The use of anger control training, combined with opportunities for prosocial training, reinforcement, and affiliation with a peer group, would be an appropriate intervention. Anger control training with bullies who are the popular-tough types would not be appropriate. These students use bullying to enhance their status (reputational aggression), are socially networked, enjoy some level of popularity, and would most likely use the anger control group experience to enhance their status even further.

## Empathy and Perspective-Taking Training

The use of these interventions should be reserved for situations in which the practitioner has evidence (e.g., functional behavior assessment) that the lack of empathy and perspective-taking is central to the problem (bully or bystander) and does not exacerbate the problem. If the bullying involves a student who inappropriately attributes hostile intent to others or is related to the underestimation of the effects of bullying on others, then these curricula might have some utility. The practitioner should be careful to ensure that the group process itself does not foster additional bully behavior.

## Expulsion and Exclusion

Intervention involving expulsion and exclusion certainly has face validity for applications to bullying. In fact, they may be the most logical and desired interventions from the viewpoint of individuals who do not fully understand how bullying develops. Expulsion or other types of exclusion are certainly appropriate when no other interventions are working, when the bully continues to victimize repeatedly, and when the presence of the bully threatens the health and safety of students. Sometimes educators have no other choice. However, these interventions should be used only as a time-out until a comprehensive plan can be developed for the student. The primary problem with expulsion is that it removes the immediate problem from the school building but not from the lives of other bullies and victims. The results of the Nansel et al. (2001) study demonstrated the problems associated with bullying (e.g., alcohol use and fighting). Schools offer the best opportunity for positive role models and supervision during the daytime. Exclusion from school removes the opportunity both for intervention and supervision.

# SUMMARY

Bullying is the most pervasive form of interpersonal violence and victimization that occurs during childhood and adolescence. School settings, by virtue of their organization and purpose, are ideal places for bullying to occur. Given what is now known about bullying, schools have no choice but to develop and implement prevention and intervention programs. In fact, many states have a legal mandate to do so. Educators and researchers now understand the degree to which bullying constitutes a social–ecological problem and is not simply a bully and victim situation. Bullying occurs under many circumstances and for many reasons. It involves different types of bullies, victims, and bully/victims and affects the noninvolved (bystanders) in many ways. The number of studies of bullying has increased dramatically and is providing more up-to-date guidance on how to prevent and intervene with bullying; however, schools have much to learn about managing the problem.

Bullying is not going to go away. It is part of the human condition, and just because schools are now interested in it does not mean that a problem for the ages will soon be solved. Far from it. Perhaps the best approach to bullying is to understand it well enough to manage it effectively. Expecting to eradicate it is unreasonable. Managing it is reasonable if it is viewed on a continuum of awareness–prevention–intervention. A significant percentage of bullying can be managed with core interventions (awareness and prevention), more still can be managed with strategic interventions (mentoring and social skills training), and a smaller percentage can be managed with intensive interventions (school and community, law enforcement, or alternative education). The goal of every school district should be to have such a management plan that is implemented effectively and evaluated continuously.

## RECOMMENDED RESOURCES

### Books and Other Printed Material

Espelage, D. L., & Swearer, S. M. (2004). *Bullying in American schools: A social–ecological perspective on prevention and intervention* London: Erlbaum.

Provides practitioners with information about individual, peer, and classroom characteristics related to bullying. In addition, school climate, family factors, innovative school partnerships, and effective prevention and intervention programs are presented.

Harris, S., & Petrie, G. F. (2003). *Bullying.* Lanham, MD: Scarecrow Press.

Provides a straightforward, practical approach to understanding bullying at the elementary, middle, and high school levels. Particular attention is paid to the role of bystanders. Prevention and intervention programs are reviewed. The appendices contain school-wide bully assessment instruments and examples of text that can be used to develop district policies regarding bullying.

Limber, S. P. (2004). Implementation of the Olweus Bullying Prevention Program in American schools: Lessons learned from the field. In D. L. Espelage & S. Swearer (Eds.), *Bullying in American schools: A social–ecological perspective of prevention and intervention* (pp. 37–61). Hillsdale, NJ: Erlbaum.

Information presented in this chapter will assist the practitioner in selecting interventions that are appropriate for bullying behaviors. The author cautions practitioners to avoid selecting interventions that might have face validity (e.g., conflict resolution) but might be inappropriate for bullies.

### Websites

*http://www.stopbullyingnow.hrsa.gov*

The U.S. Department of Health and Human Services, the Health Resources and Services Administration, and the Maternal and Child Health Bureau created this website.

*http://www.interventioncentral.org*

Intervention Central offers free tools and resources to help school staff and parents promote positive classroom behaviors and foster effective learning for all children and youth. The site was created by Jim Wright, a school psychologist from Syracuse, NY.

*http://www.sofie.org/SOFIEfiles/faculty/FacultyResources.htm*

This Schools Online for Interactive Education (SOFIE) web page is devoted to a comprehensive listing of Internet sites related to bullying. The target audience for this site consists of teachers, administrators, and students.

## REFERENCES

Arsenio, F. W., & Lemerise, E. A. (2001). Varieties of childhood bullying: Emotional processes and social competence. *Social Development, 1,* 59–73.

Atlas, R. S., & Pepler, D. J. (1998). Observations of bullying in the classroom. *Journal of Educational Research, 92,* 86–99.

Batsche, G. M. (1997). Bullying. *Children's needs II: Development, problems and alternatives.* Bethesda, MD: National Association of School Psychologists.

Batsche, G. M., & Ulman, J. (1984). *Referral-oriented, consultative approach to assessment/decision-making* Washington, DC: National Association of School Psychologists.

Coie, J. D., & Dodge, K. A. (1998). Aggression and antisocial behavior. In W. Damon (Series Ed.) & N. Eisenberg (Vol. Ed.), *Handbook of child psychology,*

*Vol. 3. Social, emotional, and personality development* (5th ed., pp. 779–862). New York: Wiley.

Crick, N. R., & Dodge, K. A. (1994). A review and reformulation of social information-processing mechanisms in children's social adjustment. *Psychological Bulletin, 115,* 74–101.

Crick, N. R., & Grotpeter, J. K. (1995). Relational aggression, gender, and social–psychological adjustment. *Child Development, 66,* 710–722.

Dill, E. J., Vernberg, E. M., Fonagy, P., Twemlow, S. W., & Gamm, B. K. (2004). Negative affect in victimized children: The roles of social withdrawal, peer rejection, and attitudes toward bullying. *Journal of Abnormal Child Psychology, 32,* 159–173.

Dodge, K. A., & Coie, J. D. (1987). Social-information-processing factors in reactive and proactive aggression in children's peer groups. *Journal of Personality and Social Psychology, 53,* 1146–1158.

Doll, B., Song, S., & Siemers, E. (2004). Classroom ecologies that support or discourage bullying. In D. L. Espelage & S. Swearer (Eds.), *Bullying in American schools: A social–ecological perspective of prevention and intervention* (pp. 37–61). Hillsdale, NJ: Erlbaum.

Duncan, R. D. (1999). Maltreatment by parents and peers. The relationship between child abuse, bully victimization, and psychological distress. *Child Maltreatment, 4,* 45–55.

Espelage, D. L., & Swearer, S. M. (2003). Research on school bullying and victimization: What have we learned and where do we go from here? *School Psychology Review, 32,* 365–383.

Espelage, D. L., & Swearer, S. M. (2004). *Bullying in American schools.* London: Lawrence Erlbaum Associates.

Farmer, T. W., Leung, M-C., Pearl, R., Rodkin, P. C., Cadwallader, T. W., & Van Acker, R. (2002). Deviant or diverse peer groups? The peer affiliations of aggressive elementary students. *Journal of Educational Psychology, 94,* 611–620.

Goldstein, A. P., McGinnis, E., Sprafkin, R. P., Gershaw, N. J., & Klein, P. (1997). *Skillstreaming the adolescent: New strategies and perspectives for teaching prosocial skills.* Champaign, IL: Research Press.

Gresham, F. M., Cook, C. R., Crews, S. G., & Kern, L. (2004). Social skills training for children and youth with emotional and behavioral disorders: Validity considerations and future directions. *Behavioral Disorders, 30,* 32–46.

Harris, S., & Petrie, G. F. (2003). *Bullying.* Lanham, MD: Scarecrow Press.

Hazler, R. (1996). *Breaking the cycle of violence: Interventions for bullies and victims.* Bristol, PA: Accelerated Development.

Hazler, R. J., Miller, D. L., Carney, J. V., & Green, S. (2001). Adult recognition of school bullying situations. *Educational Research, 43,* 133–146.

Hodges, E. V. E., & Perry, D. G. (1999). Personal and interpersonal antecedents and consequences of victimization by peers. *Journal of Personality and Social Psychology, 76,* 677–685.

Horne, A. M., Bartolomucci, C. L., & Newman-Carlson, D. (2003). *Bully Busters: A teacher's manual for helping bullies, victims, and bystanders (Grades K-5).* Champaign, IL: Research Press.

Hunter, S. C., & Boyle, J. M. E. (2002). Perceptions of control in the victims of school bullying: The importance of early intervention. *Educational Research, 44,* 323–336.

Kallestad, J. H., & Olweus, D. (2003). Predicting teachers' and schools' implementation of the Olweus Bullying Prevention Program: A multilevel study. *Prevention & Treatment, 6,* Article 21. Retrieved August 20, 2005, from http://journals.apa.org/prevention/volume6/

Limber, S. P. (2004). Implementation of the Olweus Bullying Prevention program in American schools: Lessons learned from the field. In D. L. Espelage & S. Swearer (Eds.), *Bullying in American schools: A social–ecological perspective of prevention and intervention* (pp. 37–61). Hillsdale, NJ: Erlbaum.

Limber, S. P., & Small, M. A. (2003). State laws and policies to address bullying in schools. *School Psychology Review, 32,* 445–455.

Mathur, S. R., Kavale, K. A., Quinn, M. M., Forness, S. R., & Rutherford, R. B. (1998). Social skills interventions with students with emotional and behavioral problems: A quantitative synthesis of single-subject research. *Behavioral Disorders, 21,* 193–201.

Menesini, E., Sanchez, V., Fonzi, A., Ortega, R., Costabile, A., & Lo Feudo, G. (2003). Moral emotions and bullying: A cross-national comparison of differences between bullies, victims and outsiders. *Aggressive Behavior, 29,* 515–530.

Mulvey, E. P., & Cauffman, E. (2001). The inherent limits of predicting school violence. *American Psychologist, 56,* 797–802.

Nansel, T. R., Overpeck, M., Pills, R. S., Ruan, W. J., Simons-Morton, B., & Scheidt, P. (2001). Bullying behaviors among US youth. *Journal of the American Medical Association, 285,* 2094–2100.

Northwest Regional Laboratory. (2001, December). *Schoolwide prevention of bullying.* Retrieved December 1, 2004, from http://www.nwrel.org/request/dec01/schoolwide

Ojala, K., & Nesdale, D. (2004). Bullying and social identity. The effects of group norms and distinctiveness threat on attitudes towards bullying. *British Journal of Developmental Psychology, 22,* 19–35.

Olweus, D. (1994). Bullying at school: Long-term outcomes for the victims and an effective school-based intervention program. In L. R. Huesmann (Ed.), *Aggressive behavior: Current perspectives* (pp. 97–130). New York: Plenum Press.

Olweus, D., & Limber, S. (1999). *Blueprints for violence prevention: Bullying Prevention Program.* Institute of Behavioral Science, University of Colorado, Boulder.

Olweus, D., Limber, S., & Mihalic, S. F. (1999). *Blueprints for violence prevention, book nine: Bullying Prevention Program.* Boulder, CO: Center for the Study and Prevention of Violence.

Pellegrini, A. D., & Long, J. (2002). A longitudinal study of bullying, dominance, and victimization during the transition from primary to secondary school. *British Journal of Developmental Psychology, 20,* 259–280.

Prinstein, M. J., & Cillessen, A. H. N. (2003). Forms and functions of adolescent peer aggression associated with high levels of peer status. *Merrill-Palmer Quarterly, 49,* 310–342.

Rodkin, P. C., Farmer, T. W., Pearl, R., & Van Acker, R. (2000). Heterogeneity of popular boys: Antisocial and prosocial configurations. *Developmental Psychology, 36,* 14–24.

Salmivalli, C., Lagerspetz, K., Bjorkqvist, K., Osterman, K., & Kaukiainen, A. (1996). Bullying as a group process: Participant roles and their relationship to social status within the group. *Aggressive Behavior, 22,* 1–15.

Sharp, S., Thompson, D., & Arora, T. (2000). How long before it hurts? An investigation into long-term bullying. *School Psychology International, 21,* 37–46.

Solberg, M. E., & Olweus, D. (2003). Prevalence estimation of school bullying with the Olweus bully/victim questionnaire. *Aggressive Behavior, 29,* 239–268.

Stockdale, M. S., Hangaduambo, S., Duys, D., Larson, K., & Sarvela, P. D. (2002). Rural elementary students', parents', and teachers' perceptions of bullying. *American Journal of Health Behavior, 26,* 266–277.

U.S. Department of Education. (1998). *Preventing bullying: A manual for schools and communities.* Washington, DC: Author.

Vossekuil, B., Fein, R. A., Reddy, M., Borum, R., & Modzeleski, W. (2002). *The final report and findings of the Safe School Initiative: Implications for the prevention of school attacks in the United States.* Washington, DC: U.S. Secret Service and U.S. Department of Education.

Woods, S., & Wolke, D. (2004). Direct and relational bullying among primary school children and academic achievement. *Journal of School Psychology, 42,* 135–155.

Xie, J., Swift, D. J., Cairns, B. D., & Cairns, R. B. (2002). Aggressive behaviors in social interaction and developmental adaptation. A narrative analysis of interpersonal conflicts during early adolescence. *Social Development, 11,* 205–224.

# 11
# Temper Tantrums

**Merilee McCurdy**
**Gina M. Kunz**
**Susan M. Sheridan**
*University of Nebraska–Lincoln*

## BACKGROUND AND DEVELOPMENT

When children are not given what they need or want, they sometimes engage in behaviors that are undesirable and emotionally painful to the adults in their environment (Clark, 1996). Collectively, displays of these types of behaviors often are referred to as temper tantrums, which are defined as a "fit of bad temper" (*Webster's New Collegiate Dictionary*, 2003). Although there is often consensus among observers as to when a temper tantrum is occurring, there is no such consensus regarding the discrete set of behaviors or characteristics a tantrum comprises (Sheridan & Russman, 1997). One explanation for this lack of a definite description is that several different behaviors and combinations of behaviors constitute temper tantrums. Behaviors associated with temper tantrums include crying, screaming, yelling verbal insults, kicking, flailing arms and legs, throwing objects, head banging, and biting. Among professionals, however, the consensus appears to be that temper tantrums (a) contain verbal or physical aggressive behaviors, (b) are extreme and spontaneous reactions not justified by the situation, (c) involve at least one adult and one child, and (d) are likely to occur in a public setting (Bath, 1994; Douglas, 1989; Schaefer & Millman, 1981).

In this chapter, temper tantrums are defined as overt displays of unpleasant behaviors that are extreme and severe in nature and are disproportionate to the situation. The conceptual framework for temper tantrums in this chapter considers a tantrum to be a learned response that, through a series of repetitions, results in desired outcomes for the child (Sheridan & Russman, 1997). Interventions discussed in this chapter focus on behavioral techniques designed to eliminate a child's temper tantrums and increase appropriate behaviors while still meeting the child's needs and suitable desires. Although temper tantrums can continue through early and late childhood and into adolescence, that review is beyond the scope of this chapter. This chapter focuses exclusively on temper tantrums exhibited by young children and children with disabilities.

### Prevalence of Temper Tantrums

Although temper tantrums have long been identified as among the most common childhood behavior problems (Christophersen & Mortweet, 2001; McMahon & Forehand, 2003; Potegal, Kosorok, & Davidson, 2003; Wandling, 1939), prevalence rates differ depending on the definitions used, the population examined, and the chronological age and developmental levels of children identified (Sheridan & Russman, 1997). In general, studies have shown that for children ages 1 through 5 years, approximately 5%–7% of the general, non-clinic-referred population have temper tantrums that last 15 minutes or longer three or more times a week (Needleman, Stevenson, & Zuckerman, 1991). Prevalence rates are much higher among outpatient-clinic-referred populations of children in the same age range (i.e., about 75%; Bhatia et al., 1990), and temper tantrums are among the most common reasons for referral in outpatient clinic settings (Sobel, Roberts, Rayfield, Barbard, & Rapoff, 2001). Generally speaking, the prevalence, frequency, and duration of temper tantrums decrease with age; however, temper tantrums in early childhood have been associated with higher rates of externalizing behavior problems in middle childhood and adolescence (Campbell, 1995; Douglas, 1989; Stoolmiller, 2001).

### Developmental Aspects of Temper Tantrums

Temper tantrums are found in children from infancy through adolescence and into the adult years. Depending upon the developmental stage of the child, tantrums may be characterized as normal behavior or be associated with more severe behavior problems. Although temper tantrums are considered to be a part of the normal development of children between the ages of 3 and 5 years, infants also can express tantrum-like behaviors. In the course of normal development, infants express their needs by smiling, crying, gurgling, and grabbing at interesting objects. When their basic needs are compromised (e.g., warmth, food, and drink) or when they experience pain, illness, or fatigue, infants are likely to express their rage with screaming and flailing limbs (Bath, 1994). These behaviors typically are attended to immediately and readily by parents and caregivers, both to appease the infant and to calm the adult.

Professionals and parents seem to agree that temper tantrums are a rite of passage into the toddler years and are rarely considered a serious emotional disturbance during this time (Schaefer & Millman, 1981). Toddlers are actively striving for competence and autonomy by achieving developmental milestones such as walking and talking. However, the child's newfound freedom means that household rules and consequences need to be established and enforced to ensure safety and maintain control of the child. Attempts at exploration by the toddler are often met with adult intervention. Lacking the ability to understand why their efforts have been thwarted by the adult, combined with natural physical and verbal inabilities, toddlers may become frustrated and will often respond with a temper tantrum. It is theorized that between the ages of 18 months and 3 years, children begin asserting themselves and developing a sense of autonomy (Erikson, 1950) and may begin to test limits as they expand their boundaries and attempt to exert more control over their environment. In this context, tantrums are not considered abnormal behavior. However, they become a sign of abnormality when they are used frequently and over a prolonged period of time (Schaefer, Millman, Sichel, & Zwilling, 1986), especially into the middle childhood years.

As toddlers advance into the early childhood years, the occurrence of tantrums significantly decreases. Prevalence researchers found that only 21% of children between the ages of 6 and 8 had temper tantrums, a marked reduction from children in their toddler years (Bhatia et al., 1990). The reduction in tantrums is associated with a longer time between tantrums, lower tantrum intensity, decreased post-tantrum pouting, and decreased tantrum duration. Finally, as the age of the child increases parents and caregivers often find that they can discuss problems with the child and avert the tantrum behaviors altogether.

Temper tantrums can continue into later childhood, adolescence, and even adulthood; however, these anger outbursts may begin to appear differently. For example, adolescents may express their anger or disappointment by becoming withdrawn or becoming violent. Adolescent anger or aggression may be caused by emotional factors, social–cognitive factors, or contextual factors, or by a combination of these. Readers interested in the cognitive and emotional determinants of anger in older children are directed to see chapter 9, "Anger and Aggression," in this volume.

## PROBLEMS AND IMPLICATIONS

### Problems Associated With Temper Tantrums

Disruptive behaviors, including tantrums, are among the most common concerns reported by parents of typically developing children (McMahon & Forehand, 2003). From a clinical perspective, it is important to distinguish between children who present with isolated incidents of temper tantrums and those whose tantrums are accompanied by other severe behaviors. This knowledge will affect both diagnostic and therapeutic decisions. In situations in which tantrums persist or escalate beyond expected levels, additional childhood problems may be indicated. For example, children with separation anxiety disorder are at risk for severe temper tantrums, especially if they are forced to separate from their parents or to leave their homes or other familiar areas (Ingersoll & Goldstein, 1995). In addition, "loss of temper" is an essential feature of oppositional defiant disorder (ODD) as defined by the *Diagnostic and Statistical Manual of Mental Disorders, Fourth Edition, Text Revision* (DSM-IV-TR; American Psychiatric Association, 2000). Children with ODD also exhibit behaviors such as arguing with adults, failing to comply, annoying others, blaming others, and demonstrating anger, resentment, and vindictiveness.

Temper tantrums can also be accompanied by myriad other behavior problems not necessarily associated with a DSM-IV-TR diagnosis (Bath, 1994; Douglas, 1989;

Needleman et al., 1991). In a study on tantrum prevalence and etiology, Bhatia et al. (1990) reported that the following problems were exhibited at a higher rate among children who exhibited tantrums compared with control children: thumb sucking, head banging, sleep disturbances, mutism, school avoidance, underachievement, speech and eating problems, and delinquent behavior.

Needleman et al. (1991) investigated the psychosocial correlates of temper tantrums in a study of 502 mothers and found that 6.8% of the mothers identified severe tantrums in their child, with 52% also identifying other behavior problems. Factors associated with increased reporting of temper tantrums included maternal depression and stress, low maternal education, use of corporal punishment, low social class, child care provided predominately by the mother, and poor child health. Gender of the child, maternal employment, low social support, and single parenthood were not associated with tantrums.

## Problem Analysis of Temper Tantrums

Tantrums occur within the context of environmental conditions, and as such, serve a function (Repp & Karsh, 1994). Events and situations in a child's environment can increase the likelihood of a child exhibiting tantrum behavior. A child's poor communication abilities and ineffective interpersonal interactions are additional factors that contribute to the occurrence of tantrums (Durand, 1993; Needleman et al., 1991). Therefore, the pressing question should not be, "What *causes* temper tantrums?" but, "What is the *function* of the temper tantrum?"

Tantrums may serve a communication function for children with language impairments (Durand, 1993). Children with communication disorders, mental retardation, or a pervasive developmental disorder may develop a pattern of severe temper tantrums (Durand; Gross, 1994). For example, children with severe disabilities may exhibit temper tantrums as a means to communicate needs, wishes, or messages. Attempts to communicate using aggressive tantrum behaviors are often reinforced by others who respond to the child, even if the child is using inappropriate communication gestures. Therefore, tantrums become a learned or adaptive response. Once these behaviors have been reinforced and communication has occurred, children are likely to continue to use inappropriate methods (i.e., tantrums) to communicate their needs in future interactions.

Interpersonal factors are also known to contribute to the behavioral outbursts of a tantrum-prone child. Patterson, Reid, Jones, and Conger (1975) explained dysfunctional interactions between children and their parents in terms of a *coercive cycle*. Specifically, the coercion hypothesis states that unclear boundaries and limits on a child's behavior may lead to a power struggle between a parent and child. In some situations, a child's behavior may escalate to a violent or severe tantrum until the parent accommodates the child's wishes. In other situations, the parent may continue engaging in the negative interaction by yelling or screaming until the child discontinues the inappropriate behaviors. In each situation, a cycle of anger and aggression often develops, with the parent and child becoming increasingly more negative toward each other. This recurrent interactional pattern models aggression for the child and reinforces the behavior when it results in a desired outcome (Patterson, Reid, Jones, & Conger, 1975).

Typically, children engage in tantrum behavior for two reasons: they get what they want (i.e., positive reinforcement) or they avoid or escape negative stimuli (i.e., negative reinforcement). Imagine the checkout line in a grocery store. A child may engage in a tantrum because he wants a candy bar or pack of gum and his parent refuses to buy it. If that parent gives in to the child and buys the item, the child is placated and calms down. In this common situation, each person's behavior has been reinforced. The child has received positive reinforcement by receiving the grocery store item. In addition, the parent has been negatively reinforced because he or she has escaped the negative stimuli (i.e., embarrassment of a child having a tantrum). Because the behaviors of the parent and the child have been reinforced, they are likely to be repeated in the future.

Although the termination of tantrums may be negatively reinforcing for parents, tantrums may also serve a negative reinforcement function for children. Children may engage in temper tantrums to escape or avoid adult commands (Carr, Taylor, & Robinson, 1991; Shriver, 1998). Consider this sequence of events: (a) an adult presents a command to a child, (b) the child refuses to comply and begins to have a tantrum, (c) the parent repeats the command with increased intensity, (d) the child increases the intensity of the tantrum, and (e) the parent becomes frustrated and withdraws the request. In this situation, the child's tantrum has been negatively reinforced by avoiding an aversive stimulus (i.e., parental command). With repetitions of these occurrences (i.e., the coercive cycle), children move more rapidly through this cycle, with mild inappropriate behaviors always preceding more severe behaviors (Harding, Wacker, Berg, Barretto, Winborn, & Gardner, 2001).

Knowing the function of the tantrum is instrumental for developing interventions to eliminate the tantrum (Vollmer, Northup, Ringdahl, LeBlanc, & Chauvin, 1996). A functional behavior assessment can be conducted to determine the function of the behavior (O'Neill, Horner, Albin, Storey, & Sprague, 1990). The assessment identifies the antecedents and consequences of a tantrum as well as the situational events or conditions that coincide with the occurrence of the tantrum. Once this information has been identified, effective prevention and intervention techniques can be implemented to modify the relevant antecedents and consequences in the child's environment.

## ALTERNATIVE ACTIONS FOR PREVENTION

The most efficient way to manage a tantrum is by implementing prevention procedures that modify the child's environment and reduce the probability of future tantrums. Prevention techniques such as antecedent control and functional communication training can be used to reduce the frequency, duration, and strength of temper tantrums. The use of antecedent manipulation procedures will result in a modified, enriched environment that promotes positive child behaviors. Functional communication training teaches children appropriate techniques for obtaining what they desire; therefore, reducing their reliance on a tantrum to access preferred outcomes.

### Environmental Modifications

The primary environmental modification required to prevent tantrums involves changing the current child–adult interactions so that positive child behaviors are reinforced and the relationship is strengthened. *Time-in* (Christophersen & Mortweet, 2001) and *differential attention* (Mallot & Trojan Suarez, 2004) are two reinforcement procedures that contribute to the creation of a preventive environment. The basic rationale for providing reinforcement as a prevention technique posits that attention provided in sufficient quantities for displays of appropriate behaviors (e.g., compliance, self-calming, absence of inappropriate behaviors) decreases the motivation for children to seek adult attention by engaging in inappropriate behaviors or tantrums. Time-in procedures are based on the delivery of brief intervals of positive attention contingent upon the absence of inappropriate behaviors (Christophersen & Mortweet, 2001). Attention can include a pat on the back or a thumbs-up accompanied by verbal praise (e.g., "Thank you for sharing your toy with your brother."). The main goal of any time-in procedure is to create an enriched environment where a child receives positive adult attention as a result of appropriate behavior.

The frequency of time-in needed to effectively increase appropriate behaviors differs for each child. For example, very young children may initially require 20 seconds of time-in every 5 to 10 minutes. Once behavior change is observed, the frequency of parental attention can decrease until the nonreinforcement interval extends to 15 or 20 minutes. The child's behavior should be the guide for determining the frequency of time-in, with the goal being to increase appropriate behavior and decrease inappropriate behavior.

Differential attention or differential reinforcement is another effective strategy for preventing tantrums. Differential reinforcement of alternative behaviors (DRA; Vollmer & Iwata, 1992) and differential reinforcement of other behaviors (DRO; Poling & Ryan, 1982) involve providing desirable events and outcomes (e.g., attention, tangible objects, or escape from a demand) contingent on the occurrence of alternative, nontantrum behaviors or the absence of inappropriate tantrum behavior (i.e., other behaviors). In developing DRA programs, adults must be careful to identify appropriate behaviors that are exhibited in place of tantrum behaviors. For example, instead of screaming and crying after being told to put her toys away, a child complies and begins to clean up. Compliance is the alternative behavior to having a tantrum, and the adult using DRA immediately praises the child's compliant behavior. In contrast to DRA, DRO programs generally do not identify specific alternative behaviors with which to replace tantrum behaviors. Rather, reinforcement is delivered at specific times or in specific intervals if tantrums have not been exhibited. With regard to the previous example, a parent using DRO would reinforce the child after a predetermined period of time without tantrums. This period of time could be placed on a fixed (e.g., every 30 minutes) or variable (e.g., interval length varies but remains between 20 minutes and 40 minutes) reinforcement system.

### Functional Communication Training

In some cases, children may engage in problem behaviors, including temper tantrums, as a means of communicating with others. This is especially true for children with severe language or cognitive impairments. Functional communication training (FCT) can allow those children to convey their needs, desires, or frustrations using socially appropriate alternatives to tantrums (Durand & Merges, 2001). FCT assumes children will engage in behaviors that result in preferred consequences, such as attention or escape from difficult tasks. Therefore, it teaches children a new response that will allow them to achieve the desired consequence in an efficient, appropriate manner. If a child is engaging in tantrums to escape a difficult academic task, FCT would teach him or her to ask for help or to ask to take a break, each of which are appropriate responses to challenging activities. Similarly, FCT could be used to teach a child to use language to solicit attention (e.g. "Look at what I'm doing"), rather than engaging in a tantrum.

Durand (1993) provided functional communication training to children with severe language and cognitive disabilities who exhibited temper tantrums and other challenging behaviors. The children were taught to appropriately request objects and activities previously obtained by displaying tantrum behaviors. Assistive communication devices were used to augment their communication. Following a functional analysis of their problem behaviors, they were taught to use their devices to request the object or activities (e.g., social attention, breaks from work) that were maintaining their tantrums. Multiple baseline data collected across students showed decreases in negative behavior in all children following the onset of communication training.

Response match and response mastery are two important concepts to consider when using FCT to prevent tantrum behaviors (Durand & Merges, 2001). *Response match* refers to the relationship or match between the consequence of the new communicative response and the function of the tantrums. In other words, if tantrums permit the child to gain access to preferred tangibles, then the new communication statement must also result in acquired tangibles. In addition, the new response must result in the desired outcome (i.e., *response mastery*). A reduction in tantrums will not occur if use of the new response produces an undesired effect or no effect at all. Therefore, if a child is taught to ask for help when frustrated, then he or she should receive help each time it is requested.

By modifying a child's environment and using functional communication training, tantrums can be prevented or greatly reduced. However, tantrums are normal occurrences in a child's development, and the adult response to an ongoing tantrum when it is occurring is extremely important. The following section discusses intervention strategies that should be implemented when a child is exhibiting a tantrum.

## ALTERNATIVE ACTIONS FOR INTERVENTION

Managing the child's behavior during a tantrum is extremely difficult, and any reactions by adults may result in an increase in the severity or duration of the tantrum. In addition, the adult response may positively or negatively reinforce future tantrum behavior. Therefore, extinction procedures are the recommended response to active, ongoing tantrums.

*Extinction* involves the removal of reinforcement for previously reinforced behaviors (Martin & Pear, 2003). If tantrums have been positively reinforced in the past by attention or access to tangibles, extinction procedures will remove this reinforcement and reduce the tantrum behaviors. For example, a child may engage in tantrum behavior when her mother refuses to give her candy before bedtime. If the child's tantrums result in her eventually receiving the candy, she will engage in this behavior in the future. However, if the parent ignores the tantrum and does not provide the child with the candy, the child will likely stop the tantrum because it does not result in the desired item. In this situation, the application of extinction procedures (i.e., ignoring) resulted in a decrease in tantrums.

The most common extinction procedures are ignoring and time-out from reinforcement. Endo, Sloane, Hawkes, McLoughlin, and Jenson (1991) taught parents to use both types of extinction procedures to reduce the frequency of home-based temper tantrums. In Phase 1 of the program, parents were given specific instructions on ignoring a tantrum by leaving the room and not returning for five minutes or until the child stopped the tantrum. If another tantrum occurred, they repeated the procedure and responded to any verbalization of the child with "I don't have to listen to that." Whenever Phase 1 was ineffective, parents were taught to use a five-minute time–out procedure by placing the child in a room. At the end of the program, 6 of the 10 children showed improvement from baseline to treatment. When measuring outcomes based on the final phase of treatment (i.e., time out), all but one child showed improvement. Furthermore, all parents reported satisfaction with the extinction-based program.

Extinction procedures can also be very effective as a response to bedtime tantrums (i.e., excessive crying; Durand, Mindell, Mapstone, & Gernert Dott, 1998; Kuhn & Weidinger, 2000). They include several variations, such as unmodified extinction and graduated extinction. Unmodified extinction procedures require parents to put their child to bed and to ignore any crying that occurs prior to sleep onset or during night awakenings. Because unmodified extinction procedures are often difficult for parents and were found to be unacceptable to many, modified extinction procedures, such as graduated extinction, were developed and have been found to rapidly decrease bedtime crying. *Graduated extinction*, also called graduated systematic ignoring, requires parents to gradually reduce the amount of attention they provide for nighttime crying. Parents are allowed to check on their child, then they either gradually extend response times (wait longer each night before responding) or respond immediately but gradually decrease the amount of time spent with the crying child (Kuhn & Weidinger, 2000).

Whether extinction procedures are used to reduce daytime tantrums or nighttime crying, three main cautions exist. First, it is difficult to control all sources of reinforcement that occur when a child has a tantrum. For example, one of the child's parents may decide to ignore the child who is having a tantrum for candy, but the other parent may give in, thus reinforcing the tantrum behavior. In addition, other students and peers may provide attention in response to tantrum behaviors at school and reinforce their occurrence. Second, it is often difficult to consistently ignore tantrum behaviors. Petty (1976) reported two cases in which extinction was used in combination with contingent reinforcement to decrease tantrums. Because of the stress caused by ignoring tantrums, parents participated in additional training in desensitization and relaxation techniques, which increased their compliance with the extinction procedures. Finally, extinction procedures often result in extinction bursts (Lerman & Iwata, 1995), which are initial and temporary increases in the targeted behavior (e.g., tantrums), or result in extinction-induced aggression (i.e., an increase in aggressive behaviors). Therefore, a child's tantrums may increase in frequency, duration, or intensity, or aggressive behaviors may occur immediately following initiation of extinction procedures. In some cases, extinction bursts and extinction-induced aggression have been found in up to 40% of children (Lerman, Iwata, & Wallace, 1999). If an extinction burst or aggressive behaviors do appear, it is typically for a brief time. However, the intensity of the negative behaviors may be difficult for parents and teachers to manage, and continuation of extinction should be recommended only if strategies to manage these side effects are developed (e.g., positive reinforcement and differential reinforcement procedures).

# SUMMARY

Temper tantrums are developmentally expected behaviors exhibited by most children between 1 and 4 years of age. However, tantrums are also among the most common referral concern found in outpatient clinic settings. As tantrums increase in frequency, duration, or severity, the child's behavior may become extremely disruptive to parents, teachers, and peers.

The focus of this chapter has been to describe temper tantrums in young children and children with disabilities and to review developmental expectations. The chapter explored factors that contribute to the occurrence of temper tantrums, such as environmental influences and behavior–maintaining variables, and the role of prevention as an early intervention technique. That technique emphasizes the role of parent–child interactions in increasing or decreasing tantrum behavior and possible maintaining variables (i.e., positive and negative reinforcement). Techniques such as environmental modifications, differential reinforcement, and functional communication training have been demonstrated empirically to prevent the occurrence of tantrum behaviors. In addition, several interventions are successful in the treatment of temper tantrums. These techniques, including various types of extinction, have been shown to be effective in reducing the occurrence and severity of tantrums. In many cases, a combination of prevention and intervention strategies is recommended.

# RECOMMENDED RESOURCES

## Books and Other Printed Material

Barkley, R. A. (1997). *Defiant children: A clinician's manual for assessment and parent training.* New York: Guilford Press.

The primary goal of this parent training manual is to provide clinicians with guidelines for teaching parents methods to decrease their child's inappropriate behavior while increasing their child's positive behaviors. In this second edition, the modifications have been made to incorporate recommendations specific to children's Attention Deficit Hyperactivity Disorder, oppositional defiant disorder, and conduct disorder. In addition, the manual provides the clinician with helpful resources, such as behavior rating forms, progress monitoring tools, and parent handouts.

McMahon, R. L., & Forehand, R. J. (2003). *Helping the noncompliant child* (2nd ed.). New York: Guilford Press.

This newest version of the popular text incorporates the research gains made in the parent training literature over the past 20 years. Similar to its predecessor, this book is a training manual that provides concrete, research-based steps to reduce negative child behaviors. Although written for use in an outpatient clinic setting, the principles and components described are useful in all settings, including schools. This book exemplifies the scientist–practitioner approach by incorporating the authors' research into their clinical practice.

Shriver, M. D. (1998). Teaching parenting skills. In T. S. Watson & F. M. Gresham (Eds.), *Handbook of child behavior therapy* (pp. 165–182). New York: Plenum Press.

This article provides a general framework for teaching parents skills to modify child behavior. Parent training procedures are described by following the steps of a problem-solving model, specifically problem identification, problem analysis, plan implementation, and plan evaluation.

### Websites

*http://www.pcit.org*

This website describes Parent Child Interaction Therapy (PCIT), which was developed and researched by Dr. Sheila Eyberg and her research teams at the University of Florida. PCIT is a parent training program that emphasizes changing negative parent and child interactions. Included on the website are downloadable manuscripts evaluating the efficacy of PCIT from 1976 to the present. In addition, group and individual treatment manuals are available, along with slide presentations about the main PCIT components.

*http://www.parenting-ed.org*

The Center for Effective Parenting's website is a collaborative project of the University of Arkansas for Medical Services, Arkansas Children's Hospital, and the Jones Center for Families and serves as a source of information on effective parenting. The Parent Handouts link is potentially useful for professionals as readily available handouts and for parents who are interested in learning more about children's development and behavior management. Two handouts, "Time-in" and "Time-out," are most directly relevant to information provided in this chapter.

## REFERENCES

American Psychiatric Association. (2000). *Diagnostic and statistical manual of mental disorders* (4th ed., text revision). Washington, DC: Author.

Bath, H. I. (1994). Temper tantrums in group care. *Child and Youth Care Forum, 23,* 5–27.

Bhatia, M. S., Dhar, N. K., Singhal, P. K., Nigam, V. R., Milik, S. C., & Mullick, D. N. (1990). Temper tantrums: Prevalence and etiology in a non-referral outpatient setting. *Clinical Pediatrics, 29,* 311–315.

Campbell, S. B. (1995). Behavior problems in preschool children: A review of recent research. *Journal of Child Psychology and Psychiatry and Allied Disciplines, 36,* 113–149.

Carr, E. G., Taylor, J. C., & Robinson, S. (1991). The effects of severe behavior problems in children on the teaching behavior of adults. *Journal of Applied Behavior Analysis, 24,* 523–535.

Christophersen, E. R., & Mortweet, S. L. (2001). *Treatments that work with children: Empirically supported strategies for managing childhood problems.* Washington, DC: American Psychological Association.

Clark, L. (1996). *SOS help for parents.* Bowling Green, KY: Parents Press.

Douglas, J. (1989). *Behavior problems in young children: Assessment and management.* New York: Tavistock/ Routledge.

Durand, V. M. (1993). Functional communication training using assistive devices: Effects on challenging behavior and affect. *Augmentative and Alternative Communication, 9,* 168–176.

Durand, V. M., & Merges, E. (2001). Functional communication training: A contemporary behavior analytic intervention for problem behaviors. *Focus on Autism & Other Developmental Disabilities, 16,* 110–119.

Durand, V. M., Mindell, J. A., Mapstone, E., & Gernert Dott, P. (1998). Sleep problems. In T. S. Watson &

F. M. Gresham (Eds.) *Handbook of child behavior therapy: Issues in clinical child psychology* (pp. 203–219). New York: Plenum Press.

Endo, G. T., Sloane, H. N., Hawkes, T. W., McLoughlin, C., & Jenson, W. R. (1991). Reducing child tantrums through self-instructional parent training materials. *School Psychology International, 12,* 95–109.

Erikson, E. H. (1950). *Childhood and society.* New York: Norton.

Gross, E. R. (1994). Nonaversive olfactory conditioning to control aggressive behaviors of a blind, hearing impaired, and noncommunicating child. *Journal of Developmental and Physical Disabilities, 9,* 77–82.

Harding, J. W., Wacker, D. P., Berg, W. K., Barretto, A., Winborn, L., & Gardner, A. (2001). Analysis of response class hierarchies with attention-maintained problem behaviors. *Journal of Applied Behavior Analysis, 34,* 61–64.

Ingersoll, B. D., & Goldstein, S. (1995). *Lonely, sad, and angry: A parent's guide to depression in children and adolescents.* New York: Doubleday.

Kuhn, B. R., & Weidinger, D. (2000). Intervention for infant and toddler sleep disturbance: A review. *Child and Family Behavior Therapy, 22,* 33–50.

Lerman, D. C., & Iwata, B. A. (1995). Prevalence of the extinction burst and its attenuation during treatment. *Journal of Applied Behavior Analysis, 28,* 93–94.

Lerman, D. C., Iwata, B. A., & Wallace, M. D. (1999). Side effects of extinction: Prevalence of bursting and aggression during the treatment of self-injurious behavior. *Journal of Applied Behavior Analysis, 32,* 1–8.

Mallot, R. W., & Trojan Suarez, E. A. (2004). *Principles of behavior.* Upper Saddle River, NJ: Pearson Education, Inc.

Martin, G., & Pear, J. (2003). *Behavior modification: What it is and how to do it.* New Jersey: Prentice Hall.

McMahon, R. J., & Forehand, R. L. (2003). *Helping the noncompliant child: Family-based treatment for oppositional behavior* (2nd ed.). New York: Guilford Press.

Needleman, R., Stevenson, J., & Zuckerman, B. (1991). Psychosocial correlates of severe temper tantrums. *Journal of Developmental & Behavioral Pediatrics, 12,* 77–83.

O'Neill, R. E., Horner, R. H., Albin, R. W., Storey, K., & Sprague, J. R. (1990). *Functional analysis: A practical assessment guide.* Pacific Grove, CA: Brooks/Cole.

Patterson, G. R., Reid, J. G., Jones, R. R., & Conger, R. E. (1975). *A social learning approach to family interaction.* Eugene, OR: Castalia Press.

Petty, G. L. (1976). Desensitization of parents to tantrum behavior. *The American Journal of Clinical Hypnosis, 19,* 95–97.

Poling, A., & Ryan, C. (1982). Differential reinforcement of other behavior schedules: Therapeutic applications. *Behavior Modification, 6,* 3–21.

Potegal, M., Kosorok, M. R., & Davidson, R. J. (2003). Temper tantrums in young children: 1. Behavioral composition. *Journal of Developmental & Behavioral Pediatrics, 24,* 140–147.

Repp, A. C., & Karsh, K. G. (1994). Hypothesis-based interventions for tantrum behaviors of persons with developmental disabilities in school settings. *Journal of Applied Behavior Analysis, 27,* 21–31.

Schaefer, C. E., & Millman, H. L. (1981). *How to help children with common problems.* New York: Van Nostrand Reinhold.

Schaefer, C. E., Millman, H. L., Sichel, S. M., & Zwilling, J. R. (1986). *Advances in therapies for children.* San Francisco: Jossey-Bass.

Sheridan, S. M., & Russman, S. (1997). Temper tantrums. In G. Bear, K. Minke, & A. Thomas (Eds.), *Children's needs II: Development, problems and alternatives* (pp. 161–169). Bethesda, MD: National Association of School Psychologists.

Shriver, M. D. (1998). Teaching parenting skills. In T. S. Watson & F. M. Gresham (Eds.), *Handbook of child behavior therapy* (pp. 165–182). New York: Plenum Press.

Sobel, A. B., Roberts, M. C., Rayfield, A. D., Barbard, M. U., & Rapoff, M. A. (2001). Evaluating outpatient pediatric psychology services in a primary care setting. *Journal of Pediatric Psychology, 26,* 395–405.

Stoolmiller, M. (2001). Synergistic interaction of child manageability problems and parent-discipline tactics in predicting future growth in externalizing behavior for boys. *Developmental Psychology, 37,* 814–825.

Vollmer, T. R., & Iwata, B. A. (1992). Differential reinforcement as treatment for behavior disorders: Procedural and functional variations. *Research in Developmental Disabilities, 13,* 393–417.

Vollmer, T. R., Northup, J., Ringdahl, J. E., LeBlanc, L. A., & Chauvin, T. M. (1996). Functional analysis of severe tantrums displayed by children with language delays: An outclinic assessment. *Behavior Modification, 20,* 97–115.

Wandling, A. R. (1939). *Ten behavior problems common with pre-school children.* Oxford, England: House of Field.

*Webster's new collegiate dictionary (11th ed.).* (2003). Springfield, MA: G & C Merriam Company.

# 12

# Lying

**Jan N. Hughes**
**Crystal Renee' Hill**
*Texas A&M University*

## BACKGROUND AND DEVELOPMENT

In its broadest sense, a lie refers to a nonaccidental false statement. However, not all forms of lying serve the same function or have the same developmental and psychological significance. Antisocial lying, the focus of this chapter, is defined as a deliberate attempt to deceive another person in order to avoid blame, obtain a reward, avoid an obligation, or inflict harm. Thus, antisocial lying serves hedonistic or malicious motivations. Antisocial lying also is often associated with other behaviors that violate societal norms or rules and may be either a precursor to or a manifestation of conduct disorder (Loeber, Kennan, Lahey, Green, & Thomas, 1993). Examples of antisocial lies include the following: (a) A girl accidentally breaks a vase; her mother asks how the vase broke, and the girl replies, "I don't know." (b) A boy falsely tells his mother that he has finished his homework in order to watch television. (c) A girl tells a classmate that another classmate is spreading unkind rumors about her, in hopes of starting a fight between the two classmates; however, the accusation is false.

Excluded from consideration are lies motivated by the desire to protect oneself from threats to one's sense of security and self-worth. For example, an 8-year-old girl whose neglectful mother abandoned her to the care of an aunt tells classmates that her mother is on a business trip and is going to bring her lots of presents when she returns, or a 10-year-old peer-rejected boy says that he is one of the most popular children in his class. Also excluded from consideration in this chapter are prosocial falsehoods, or white lies. Prosocial falsehoods are motivated by positive social motives, such as avoiding hurting another's feelings, entertaining another, and helping another. Finally, false statements that reflect one's beliefs are also excluded from our definition of lying.

### Prevalence

Prevalence of lying refers to the percentage of individuals in the population who lie, and research shows that lying is a common behavior. In a study on developmental changes in conceptions of lying, Peterson, Peterson, and Seeto (1983) found that adults and children 11 years of age and older admitted to lying at least some of the time (although the type of lie was not ascertained). Because everyone lies at some time, the frequency and nature of the lying, and the severity of the consequences of lying, are important considerations in defining lying as a problem behavior. In her review of seven studies on the prevalence of lying in normal children ages 4 to 16 years, Stouthamer-Loeber (1986) reported an overall prevalence rate of 19.4% for parent reports and 14.4% for teacher reports of occasional lying (defined as a verbal statement intended to deceive). The prevalence rate for frequent or chronic lying was 3%, as reported by parents and teachers, and rates for retrospective self-reports of chronic lying were much higher (15%–23%). Because these prevalence data are based on raters' definitions of "*often*," "*sometimes*," and "*rarely*," the criteria or exact frequencies that determine these ratings cannot be ascertained.

In one of the few longitudinal studies of lying, Gervais, Tremblay, Desmarais-Gervais, and Vitaro (2000) reported on the prevalence, stability, and developmental significance of occasional and frequent lying over a 3-year period in a community sample of children who were in kindergarten at the beginning of the study. For both boys and girls, a similar percentage of mothers (58% and 59%, respectively) reported occasional lying. A higher percentage of mothers of boys than of girls reported frequent lying (9% versus 4%). Teachers reported somewhat lower prevalence rates, generally, and reported higher rates for boys than girls for both occasional and frequent lying (23% versus 16% for occasional lying, and 4% versus 1.5% for frequent lying). These authors did not define occasional and frequent lying. Compared with the gender differences found in the Gervais et al. study, other studies have reported no gender differences (Tiet, Wasserman, Loeber, McReynolds, & Miller, 2001). In general, findings on gender differences tend to be mixed, with inconsistent results probably due to differences in samples, definitions of lying, and the person reporting on the lying.

The frequency of lying at any given age may be less important, in terms of risk for future behavioral problems, than the consistency of lying across settings and time. Gervais et al. (2000) reported that 4.9% of boys and 2.2% of girls were identified as persistent liars, which were defined as those rated by both teachers and parents as either occasional or frequent liars for 3 consecutive years. Furthermore, being rated as a consistent liar (i.e., rated at one point in time by both teachers and parents as an occasional or frequent liar) at age 7, but not at age 6, was associated with being rated as a consistent liar the following year. This finding suggests that beginning at age 7, children who lie across settings are likely to persist in lying. Although both consistent liars and persistent liars of either gender were rated as having more disruptive behavior problems than children who lied in no setting or only one setting, persistent liars had the highest rates of disruptive behaviors.

### Developmental Considerations

Research on lying conducted by developmental psychologists has a long tradition in psychology (Bandura, 1986; Piaget, 1932). Much of this research has focused either on children's conceptualization of a lie (Berthoud-Papandropoulou & Kilcher, 2003; Taylor, Lussier, & Maring, 2003) or on children's moral evaluation of lying (Johnson, 1997). Research on children's conceptualization of a lie examined lying from the perspective of children's cognitive reasoning and mindfulness. Beginning around age 3, children appear to be able to distinguish between a false statement (i.e., misinformed) and a lie (i.e., deliberate distortion of secret knowledge; Johnson, 1997; Berthoud-Papandropoulou & Kilcher, 2003). Children as young as 3 lie to conceal a misdeed (Newton, Reddy, & Bull, 2000); which also is the most common reason for lying across ages (Stouthamer-Loeber, 1986).

Research on children's moral evaluation of lying reveals a developmental progression in children's moral reasoning. In a study of preschoolers, second graders, and fifth graders, Bussey (1992) charted changes in children's moral reasoning about lying. Children as young as 4 years of age weighed a child's intent in evaluating a false statement as good or bad. If a child intended to tell the truth but was operating under a false belief, preschool children evaluated the false statement as less "naughty." Preschool children's judgments of the naughtiness of lying were also influenced by whether a lie was punished or not, with punished lies being evaluated more negatively. By kindergarten, however, punishment did not weigh into the evaluative judgments and indicated feelings of pride associated with truth telling. With increasing maturity, greater reliance on internal satisfaction for truth telling and less reliance on punishment are consistent with a general shift in childhood's behavioral regulation from external control to self-regulation. "If socialization is successful, there is a transfer from external forms of control to more internal controls, that is, there is less reliance on external factors such as punishment" (Bussey, 1992, p. 136).

As children age, their conscious motivations for lying may also change; consequently, their moral evaluations of lying change. In a cross-sectional study of high school and college students, Jensen, Arnett, Feldman, and Cauffman (2004) found that lying to adults about such behaviors as alcohol and drug use, friends, dating, money, and sex was normative among high school students but declined in college students. Boys were more likely than girls to lie about issues pertaining to money and alcohol or drugs. When adolescents are seeking greater autonomy, they justify lying to their parents on the basis of asserting their right to make decisions regarding "personal" issues. As adolescents reach college age and their parents grant greater autonomy, lying both decreases and is judged as less acceptable.

## PROBLEMS AND IMPLICATIONS

Given the common occurrence of lying, knowing when lying is indicative of a problem is important. Whereas lying has been studied in association with several childhood problems, including poor interpersonal relationships, conduct disorders, and disturbed parent–child relationships, lying as a whole has been understudied. Stouthamer-Loeber (1986) found an average prevalence rate of lying among clinical populations of 49%, or 2.5

times that of normal samples. In addition, a lower-than-normal rate for lying was indicated in children with a diagnosis of neurotic problems, and a higher-than-normal rate was indicated in children with a diagnosis of conduct problems. Thus, viewing lying as part of a constellation of behaviors is more useful than viewing lying as an isolated behavior problem.

### Lying and Interpersonal Relationships

Trust is an essential characteristic of friendship, especially in later childhood and adolescence. Thus, the child who lies will have difficulty being accepted by peers and developing close friendships. In turn, satisfactory peer relationships are very important to a child's behavioral adjustment and learning. It is well established that children who are rejected by their peers are poorer achievers in school and are more likely to experience a wide range of adjustment difficulties in later adolescence (for review see Bierman, 2004). Lying also undermines family trust and cohesion. Because a supportive and close relationship with their parents is a resource that protects children from multiple risks, children who frequently lie to their parents may erode this important social support.

### Lying and Conduct Problems

According to the *Diagnostic and Statistical Manual of Mental Disorders, Fourth Edition* (American Psychiatric Association, 1994), lying is one of the criteria for a diagnosis of conduct disorder. The child or adolescent with a conduct disorder violates societal norms of conduct by persistently engaging in behaviors that violate the basic rights of others, societal norms, or rules. A diagnosis of conduct disorder requires that the individual manifest at least 3 of 15 criteria in the past 12 months, with at least 1 of the criteria present in the past 6 months. These 15 criteria are grouped into four categories of antisocial behavior: aggression to people and animals, destruction of property, deceitfulness or theft, and serious violation of rules. The criterion "often lies to obtain goods or favors or to avoid obligations" is one of three criteria within the "deceitfulness or theft" grouping.

Although lying is a behavior that is listed as a symptom of conduct disorder, it forms an exception to the established pattern of other conduct disorder symptoms. Specifically, unlike other conduct disorder symptoms, lying is common in young children, often declines in frequency with age, and is equally associated with oppositional defiant disorder and conduct disorder diagnoses. In contrast, other conduct disorder symptoms are pathologic at any age and are more common in conduct-disordered children (Loeber et al., 1993).

When lying is included as an item on behavior rating scales, it is invariably included in a delinquent, conduct problem, or antisocial scale (Achenbach & Edelbrock, 1991). Loeber and Schmaling (1985) subjected data from 28 factor and cluster analytic studies on child psychopathology to a multidimensional scaling analysis in order to empirically determine the dimensions of antisocial behavior. The analysis yielded one dimension with two poles: overt or confrontational behaviors and covert or concealing behaviors. Lying falls on the covert side and is related to behaviors such as theft, truancy, and drug use. This distinction between overt and covert antisocial behavior has been replicated by other researchers (Achenbach, 1993) and is found in preschoolers (Willoughby, Kupersmidt, & Bryant, 2001) as well as in children ages 4–18 (Tolan, Gorman-Smith, & Loeber, 2000). When covert and overt behaviors are considered together, both contribute uniquely to a general measure of conduct problems, hyperactivity, and peer and adult conflict for preschool boys and girls (Willoughby et al., 2001). As the child enters into adolescence, covert behaviors contribute to a general measure of conduct problems, hyperactivity, and peer and adult conflict as well (Tolan et al., 2000).

## ALTERNATIVE ACTIONS FOR PREVENTION

Lying occurs in an interpersonal context and often has moral overtures. Thus, interventions that improve the quality (i.e., closeness and trust) of parent–child and teacher–student relationships and interventions that increase children's empathy and moral reasoning would be expected to deter lying. For example, a considerable body of research has documented relationships between parenting strategies and children's internalization of prosocial values (see Grusec, 1997). Specifically, parenting characterized by warmth and acceptance and moderate control (i.e., discipline and monitoring) is associated with higher levels of moral behavior and moral reasoning. Maccoby and Martin (1983) developed the concept of *receptive compliance* to refer to a generalized willingness to cooperate with (i.e., to share) a parent's goals. Children who enjoy a secure (close and warm) relationship with their parents and whose parents do not rely extensively on power-assertive strategies are likely to evince receptive compliance. Receptive compliance is distinguished from situational compliance, which Maccoby and Martin see as stemming from external pressure. Receptive compliance reduces conflicts and the motivation to deceive others. Parenting classes that focus on acceptance skills, communication skills, strategies for promoting child independence, and strategies for making one's values explicit would be expected to increase receptive compliance and prevent lying.

Teachers also can prevent lying by creating close and open relationships with students and by making their values explicit (see chapter 5, "Student–Teacher Relationships"). School-wide interventions that focus on enhancing students' social and emotional competencies and on creating school climates in which students feel a sense of belonging would also be expected to reduce the prevalence of lying (see chapters 1, "Social and Emotional Learning," 2, "Character Education," 3, "Developing Self-Discipline," and 24, "Prosocial Behavior").

# ALTERNATIVE ACTIONS FOR INTERVENTION

## Linking of Assessment to Intervention

When lying is part of a pattern of antisocial, rule-violating behavior, it requires a broad-based approach to assessment and to intervention. A broad-based approach is required because conduct disorders are the result of multiple and interactive causes. Also, single-focused interventions have been found to be ineffective in altering the negative developmental trajectory of children exhibiting high levels of physical and covert aggression. Among the factors contributing to conduct disorders are home and parenting factors (e.g., harsh and inconsistent parenting, low parental monitoring, low maternal warmth and acceptance, marital discord, and parent criminality); school factors (e.g., school failure and school norms); community factors (e.g., high levels of neighborhood violence, few recreational facilities, poverty, and media violence); child factors (e.g., temperament and intelligence), and peer group factors (e.g., association with antisocial peers; Hughes & Cavell, 1995). All of these factors should be considered when lying is the reason for referring a child for psychological services.

When a teacher or parent asks for help regarding a child's lying, it is important to conduct an assessment of the lying behavior as well as an assessment of the child's overall functioning. The assessment of the lying behavior establishes the parameters of the lying, its frequency, and associated antecedents and consequences. The assessment of the child's overall functioning determines whether the child's lying is best understood as a precursor, consequence, or manifestation of conduct disorder, peer rejection, a disturbed parent–child relationship, or other problem. Alternatively, a child's false statements may reflect the psychological defense of denial or a child's inability to discriminate between reality and fantasy, rather than intent to deceive others.

The following are among the questions to be addressed for children referred for lying:

- What behaviors does the referring adult classify as lying?
- What is the content and context of the child's lying?
- How frequently does the child lie?
- Is lying a recent or a long-standing problem?

In an interview with the referring adult, the adult would be asked for specific examples of the referred child's lying behavior. By analyzing the context of the child's lies and environmental antecedents and consequences, one can formulate hypotheses about the child's motivations. The following questions also might be asked:

- Is the child avoiding punishment?
- Is the child attempting to harm another or to gain some advantage?

Antisocial motives, as reflected in the latter two questions, would indicate antisocial lying. On the other hand, the child's lies may reflect a psychological defense against potentially threatening information or an attempt to gain acceptance of the peer group.

Obtaining an accurate count of lying is very hard to do. Lying is difficult to observe; a child may be a skilled liar and may only get caught occasionally. Nevertheless, an estimate of the frequency of lying helps determine the seriousness of the problem and serves as an important baseline against which to evaluate improvement following the intervention. The referring adult should be asked to maintain a written record of the child's lying for a period of 7 to 14 days. The definition of lying arrived at in the interview serves as the operational definition. If possible, both the child's parents and teachers should record instances of lying in order to determine the specifics of the behavior. Because the adults may not be able to judge, with complete confidence, whether an assertion made by the child is true or false, they record all assertions they have just reason to believe are false. When possible, the adults should attempt to determine the veracity of the child's suspected lie. For example, a teacher could contact the parent to check out the child's assertion that he was unable to complete his homework due to a family emergency. When lying is part of covering up for stealing, intervention should focus on stealing.

Conducting a functional assessment of the lying may be helpful for determining the situations associated with lying and the consequences that follow lying. For each reported or suspected lie, the observer records the following information: the actual content of the suspected lie, antecedent events, and consequent events. Antecedent events refer to all the characteristics of the situation just before the lie occurred and the person to whom the lie was directed. Consequent events are simply whatever happened just after the lie occurred. Examples of antecedent events include bragging by another child, criticism of the target child, or an unstructured play situation. Examples of consequent events include someone calling the target child a liar; the child avoiding punishment; or another child being unjustly blamed. A notepad with three columns can be used for the record keeping. In the center column, the observer writes the child's suspected false assertion, then the antecedents and consequences are recorded in the left and right columns, respectively. The results of the functional assessment may be used to identify motivations as well as unintended rewards for lying.

Another goal is to determine if lying is part of other childhood problems, such as peer rejection, conduct problems, or a disturbed parent–child relationship. Behavioral rating scales and checklists are useful in assessing a child's overall behavioral problems and social competencies. By taking a broad view of the child's behavioral problems as well as the child's strengths, the lying can be put into perspective. When lying is part of a pattern of antisocial behavior, the assessment and the intervention should target the broader class of conduct problems rather than only the lying. When the lying is part of peer rejection, an assessment of the child's social competencies is appropriate, using behavioral observations, teacher ratings, or peer ratings.

## Co-Occurrence With Antisocial Behavior

When lying is part of a pattern of antisocial behavior, the assessment should include an assessment of the multiple factors associated with the development of conduct problems in children. These factors include biological, family, parenting, peer, academic, school, and community factors (Hughes & Cavell, 1995). Among family factors to assess are the parents' effectiveness as disciplinarians, their reliance on overly punitive forms of discipline, the extent to which they provide emotional acceptance to their child, their level of involvement and monitoring, and the level of family stress. Some families view lying and other antisocial behavior as justified because of perceived mistreatment by society and a sense of alienation from mainstream society. In this case, lying to "outsiders" may constitute part of a deviant lifestyle that may be valued by the child's extended family. Similarly, the level of peer and community support for antisocial behavior and attitudes should be assessed. If the child associates with antisocial peers, it is likely that rule-breaking behavior receives peer support. The level of violence in the school and community should also be considered.

## Co-Occurrence With Social–Cognitive and Moral Reasoning Deficits

Lying may reflect deficiencies in social and moral reasoning. Aggressive and rejected children, compared with nondeviant peers, exhibit poor perspective-taking ability, underattention to relevant social cues, selective attention to hostile cues, a tendency to infer hostile intent to others in ambiguous situations, a reliance on ineffective and aggressive solutions to interpersonal conflict, belief that aggression results in positive consequences for the aggressor, and a lack of empathy for the victim of aggression (see chapters 9, "Anger and Aggression," and 3, "Developing Self-Discipline"). These social-information processes can be assessed through semistructured, vignette-based interviewing procedures (Heidgerken, Hughes, & Cavell, in press). In the interviews, the child is presented with a situation involving some provocation and is asked a series of questions that elicit his or her attributions, likely behavioral responses, and beliefs about the effectiveness of both antisocial and socially competent responses. A child's reasoning about lying should also be assessed. The child may believe that lying is justified when one's needs have been thwarted by another or when the person lied to is an "outsider" versus a member of the child's social network. A child may be unaware or unperturbed by the effect of lying on another person or may expect that "everyone lies, so it is okay."

## Selection of an Intervention Approach

There is no intervention specifically for lying that meets consensual standards for evidence of efficacy.

Intervention research specifically on lying is limited because lying both is hard to assess and is likely to co-occur with other problems that are assessed at a more general level rather than a symptom level. Thus, interventions for lying often target either the presumed underlying cause (e.g., overcontrolling parents, peer rejection, or antisocial syndrome). The following sections first review interventions that target lying as a discrete behavior, followed by a discussion of interventions that address the broader dimensions and correlates of lying.

## Lying as a Target of Behavioral Intervention Programs

In applied behavior analysis, specific target behaviors are first identified and then modified using principles of learning. The concept of target behaviors in behavior therapy has been criticized on the grounds that it encourages a simplistic, static, and monosymptomatic view of client difficulties (Hughes, 2000). The target behavior metaphor has particular problems when applied to a complaint of lying. Lying is the *deceleration* target behavior (the behavior to be eliminated or decreased), and telling the truth is the incompatible *acceleration* behavior. According to applied behavior analysis, the problem behavior is either ignored or punished, and the incompatible behavior is rewarded. Yet rewarding telling the truth is problematic. A child could easily obtain rewards by making truthful assertions while continuing unabated lying. But punishing lying behavior also poses problems. Punishing each lie a child tells may succeed only in making the child a more skillful liar. Also, "getting at the truth" places parents and teachers in the role of grand inquisitor and provides the child with attention that may inadvertently reinforce the lying behavior.

Whereas a strict contingency-management approach to lying may be unproductive, it is important to alter contingencies of reinforcement for lying and telling the truth so that the rewards for lying are lessened, and the rewards for telling the truth are increased. For example, when the child lies to avoid punishment and is detected in the lie, the punishment that would have been administered for the original behavior should stand, and a punishment for lying should be added. When a child admits to a wrongdoing on his or her own, the punishment for the wrongdoing should be less than it would be if the child had not admitted guilt. Results of a naturalistic study of parents of children ages 2 to 4 years of age (Wilson, Smith, & Ross, 2003) suggest that lying is frequently positively reinforced by parents. These researchers found that parents rarely directly address their children's lie. They were most likely to ignore the lie, address the transgression that prompted the lie, or believe the lie. Only 3% of the time did parents directly address the lie (i.e., by saying that lying is wrong). As a result, children whose parents did not confront the lie were more likely to lie 2 years later.

## Lying as Part of Parent–Child and Student–Teacher Relationships

Sometimes lying occurs in the context of a parent–child relationship characterized by high parental expectations and contingent approval. In this case, the child's lying may occur only at home and may result from the child's desire to avoid perceived parental displeasure or rejection. When this dynamic is present, the recommended intervention is one that addresses the quality of the emotional bond between the parent and the child. Specifically, the parents need to more clearly communicate acceptance of the child and distinguish between approving of the child's behaviors and approving of the child. When the child is given more security, affection, and positive attention, the need for lying may disappear.

Parents and teachers should also look for opportunities to make explicit their values regarding lying and truth telling. Cavell (2000) suggests that parental acceptance skills and clarity regarding the parents' own moral values are essential to helping children internalize such prosocial values as truth telling. In an experimental study, Huffman, Warren, and Larson (1999) found that children's lying was decreased when children were reminded to tell the truth. This reminder apparently activated the children's moral inhibitions against lying. This strategy also is likely to help in the classroom, especially when combined with an emphasis on the importance of trust and relationships with others.

Lying may also occur within a parent–child relationship characterized by overcontrolling and intrusive parenting (Jensen et al., 2004; for review see Barber, 2002). This is especially likely in adolescence, when the youth is striving for greater autonomy and resents parental intrusion into issues such as selection of friends and sexual behavior, which the youth views as within his or her realm of decision making (Jensen et al., 2004). When this is the case, family therapy can help by focusing on communication skills and on the reciprocal responsibilities of parents to gradually grant their children more freedoms and autonomy and of youth to be responsible with new freedoms.

## Lying as Part of Peer Rejection

Interventions for peer rejection focus on rejected children's social–cognitive deficits and distortions. Bierman (2004) describes in detail the implications of three guiding principles for the design of effective social competence coaching programs for rejected children: (a) Interventions focus on skill domains of effective social interaction rather than specific discrete behaviors; (b) they include components that target associated deficits rejected children may have, such as poor emotion regulation, poor impulse control, and poor social problem-solving skills; and (c) they incorporate components designed to enhance the generalization and maintenance of social skills and improved peer relations. Whereas social competence interventions have not been evaluated specifically with respect to lying, they have been found to produce moderate effect sizes in measures of children's social competencies (see Bierman, 2004).

## Lying as Part of a Cluster of Antisocial Behaviors

When lying is part of a constellation of other disruptive or delinquent behaviors, single-focused interventions are unlikely to be effective (Kazdin, 2003). A consensus holds that early intervention in the development of conduct disorders, before a relative "window of opportunity" closes, is most likely to be effective in altering the negative developmental trajectory. Furthermore, interventions will need to be broad based, addressing at least two of the multiple systems that influence the development and maintenance of antisocial behavior. The most extensively researched interventions for childhood antisocial behaviors are parent-training approaches and skills-training approaches.

***Parent-training approaches.*** The efficacy of parent training with parents of children with conduct disorders is supported by research spanning three decades (Kazdin, 2003). Patterson et al. were pioneers in developing and evaluating parent-training programs (Patterson, Chamberlain, & Reid, 1982). Their approach to parent training was based on social learning principles, especially on altering parent-delivered contingencies for antisocial and prosocial behaviors. Other researchers have modified this approach and contributed to the systematic evaluation of parent-training approaches with parents of conduct-disordered children. These research programs have greatly increased the knowledge of who responds to parent training, mechanisms responsible for improved child functioning, and the effect of modifications in treatment procedures on client outcomes.

In recent years, training in parental management skills has been combined with training in positive parent–child interactional skills, especially nondirective play skills (Eyberg, Boggs, & Algina, 1995). The emphasis on parental acceptance and positive parenting skills is based on findings that a combination of parental warmth and appropriate behavioral controls result in best child outcomes and that parents of conduct-disordered children are overly controlling and provide lower levels of acceptance (Cavell, 2000). Thus, current programs represent a merger of behavioral management and relationship enhancement approaches (Eyberg et al., 1995).

Both individual and group formats of parent training have been found to be effective, and therapist or leader manuals are available for both formats (Barkley, 1987; Eyberg et al., 1995; Webster-Stratton, 1987). Despite variations, all programs in this genre include instruction, modeling, and rehearsal of targeted parenting skills, homework assignments to promote generalization of skills to home settings, and discussion of homework assignments to identify obstacles and modifications needed in strategies.

Despite the overall effectiveness of parent training, 30% to 40% of treated parents report that children's problems remain in the clinical range after treatment, and 25% to 50% of teachers report that children's externalizing problems are within the clinical range (Webster-Stratton, 1990). Parents least likely to respond positively to parent training are those experiencing significant stress. Mothers who are socially isolated, with few sources of social support outside the family; socioeconomically disadvantaged families; children whose problems are more severe; and parents who evince psychopathology are less likely to benefit from parent training (Webster-Stratton, 1985). These same characteristics predict attrition from parent training (Kazdin, 1990). Multiple demands interfere with parents' commitment to learning and practicing skills they are taught. With such parents, attention to family stress and parents' personal issues and worries may be a necessary adjunct to parent training.

Parent training is less successful with adolescents (Henggeler & Borduin, 1990). Whereas parenting factors loom as the most significant influence on the development of aggression and conduct problems in the preschool years, other systems become increasingly important after children enter school. By adolescence, the peer group is the preeminent influence on conduct disorders. Adolescents need multisystemic approaches that recognize the influence of additional systems, such as the peer group and school.

Only one parent intervention study specifically targeted lying. Venning, Blampied, and France (2003) found that the Triple-P program (Sanders, Markie-Dadds, Tully, & Bor, 2000), when modified to include a specific focus on lying, reduced the frequency of lying. Because the Triple-P program is a comprehensive parent training program, one cannot isolate the effect of the treatment component that focuses on lying from effects of the broader program.

***Skill-training approaches.*** Children experiencing disruptive behavior problems are likely to have poor self-regulatory skills, social skills, and problem-solving skills and are likely to demonstrate social–cognitive deficits and distortions. Interventions designed to remedy antisocial children's social–cognitive deficits and distortions have produced positive but limited effects (Kazdin, 2003). In an effort to boost the strength and duration of treatment benefits, researchers have developed and tested multicomponent interventions that address the multiple factors that contribute to the development of antisocial behavior.

***Comprehensive approaches.*** The Fast Track intervention program (Conduct Problems Prevention Research Group, 1999, 2002) exemplifies a comprehensive approach to preventing and treating early antisocial problems. Fast Track combines selective interventions for aggressive, high-risk children with a universal intervention that targets school-wide normative beliefs in and use of social competencies and alternatives to aggression. Results indicate that Fast Track's combination of selective and universal interventions implemented over multiple years led to significant, albeit modest, benefits in disruptive children's social and behavioral functioning.

## Example of Integrating Assessment Information and Intervention

Heather, a 12-year-old girl, was referred by her parents for lying. Example lies included saying she did not phone the emergency 911 number after calling it three times, spilling honey and then blaming it on her sister, and telling her parents she made a B on a spelling test so that she could stay up late to watch a TV program. A meeting was held with the parents, teacher, and school psychologist to determine whether Heather also lied at school, as well as to assess Heather's overall school functioning. The school psychologist also interviewed Heather.

The teacher reported that Heather had made up some highly unlikely excuses for not turning in her homework. It was also discovered during the parent and teacher meeting that Heather had told lies that the teacher had not detected. Although her parents did not allow her to wear makeup to school, Heather wore a great deal of it at school, especially eye makeup. When the teacher asked her what her mother thought about her wearing so much makeup, Heather had responded that her mother did not mind. She was putting the makeup on when she got to school and washing it off before going home. Heather also had signed her mother's name to a note excusing her from dressing out for physical education class.

Heather's teachers and parents agreed to record instances of Heather's lying for 2 weeks, and they agreed to communicate with each other two or three times a week to verify information that Heather had given one of them. The teacher detected five lies, four involving untrue reasons for not doing homework and one involving reasons for being tardy to class. The parents recorded 10 lies at home, all of which involved avoiding blame or getting out of some obligation. Additionally, Heather had been found with a cassette recorder she said she borrowed from a friend, when she actually had stolen it from the library.

Heather hangs out with a small group of girls who tend to be troublemakers at school. She is a C student, but her aptitude test scores indicate that she is underachieving. On the teacher version of the Child Behavior Checklist (Achenbach & Edelbrock, 1991), her teacher endorsed a large number of items reflecting the externalizing syndrome, particularly within the aggression scale (argues, disobeys at school, lies and cheats, and is stubborn).

Heather's parents are overly critical of her and tend to rely primarily on punitive discipline techniques. Relatively minor behavior infractions result in significant punishment, including spanking and being grounded for several weeks. On the parent version of the Child Behavior Checklist, Heather obtained elevated scores on the aggression and delinquency scales. Heather is one of four siblings, and high levels of family conflict characterize her home environment.

Heather was talkative and outgoing in the interview. She is socially oriented but her friendships have been characterized by high levels of conflict and, therefore, are of short duration. She finds school boring but reports enjoying PE classes and expressed an interest in joining a community soccer team (but she said her parents had indicated she would have to earn that privilege through good grades). In discussing various problems, Heather demonstrated little awareness of her contribution and reported being misunderstood and picked on by others.

On the basis of this assessment, the school psychologist hypothesized that Heather's lying was part of a pattern of child defiance against parental authority and of covert aggression. Thus, Heather exhibited characteristics of both the covert and authority conflict pathways to delinquency. The recommended intervention included parent training that incorporates both control skills and acceptance of the child, such as the Parent and Child Series (Webster-Stratton, 1990), involvement in peer group activities with prosocial peers, ongoing monitoring of her behavior, and continued consultation with the parent, teacher, and school psychologist. Specifically, Heather's parents agreed to enroll her in soccer, a sport in which she could excel and that would increase her time spent with prosocial peers. Heather was assigned a college student mentor who provided an additional source of acceptance and a positive role model.

## SUMMARY

Lying is associated with several childhood problems, and an assessment of the child's overall adjustment and relationships with parents, teachers, and peers is necessary in order to focus intervention efforts on the constellation of problems of which lying is a part. Lying may signify difficulty in peer relationships, conduct disorder, a disturbed parent–child relationship, or an inability to acknowledge information that is potentially threatening to the child's self-system. Effective interventions also need to address the broader constellation of problems rather than focusing exclusively on lying as an isolated, discrete behavior.

## RECOMMENDED RESOURCES

Bussey, K. (1992). Lying and truthfulness: Children's definitions, standards, and evaluative reactions. *Child Development, 63,* 129–137.

In this cross-sectional study, the authors investigate preschool, second-grade, and fifth-grade children's definitions of lying and their moral reasoning about lying. The authors found developmental changes in children's understanding of lying, evaluative reactions to lying, and moral standards related to lying. For example, as children mature, they rely more on internal standards and reactions and less on external aspects of the lying in evaluating lying. Older children report feeling proud when they tell the truth. The authors provide some implications of their findings for encouraging children to be truthful.

Cavell, T. A. (2000). *Working with parents of aggressive children: A practitioner's guide.* Washington, DC: American Psychological Association.

This book presents Responsive Parent Therapy, which blends several principles and practices that are derived from social-learning-based parent management, relationship enhancement, and structural family therapies. It provides practical advice for practitioners using current empirical knowledge.

Eisenstadt, T. H., Eyberg, S., McNeil, C. B., Newcomb, K., & Funderburk, B. (1993). Parent-child interaction therapy with behavior problem children: Relative effectiveness of two stages and overall outcome. *Journal of Clinical Child Psychology, 22,* 42–51.

This empirical article describes Parent–Child Interaction Therapy (PCIT) and reports evidence of its efficacy. PCIT is especially helpful in reducing child behavioral problems with younger children (ages 3–7). PCIT emphasizes teaching parents child-relationship skills, such as play skills, as well as strategies for managing behavior problems.

Forgatch, M., & Patterson, G. (1989). *Parents and adolescents living together: Part 2. Family problem solving.* Eugene, OR: Castalia.

Patterson, G. R., & Forgatch, M. S. (1987). *Parents and adolescents living together: Part I. The basics.* Eugene, OR: Castalia.

These two volumes provide parents sage advice about how to establish healthy, mutually respectful relationships with their adolescents. The books stress the importance of the quality of the relationship with the adolescent as well as strategies for preventing and responding to behavioral problems, including lying.

Stouthamer-Loeber, M. (1986). Lying as a problem behavior in children: A review. *Clinical Psychology Review, 6,* 267–289.

This article presents a review of empirical studies on lying by children. It provides data on prevalence of lying in normal and clinical samples of children and on adults' perceptions of the seriousness of lying. Longitudinal and cross-sectional studies are reviewed that demonstrate an association between lying and conduct problems and delinquency. The article provides a few suggestions for treatment. For example, they suggest increasing parental monitoring and supervision and punishing the lie and the misbehavior that prompted the lie separately.

## REFERENCES


Achenbach, T. M. (1993). Taxonomy and comorbidity of conduct problems: Evidence from empirically based approaches. *Development and Psychopathology, 5,* 51–64.

Achenbach, T. M., & Edelbrock, C. (1991). *Manual for the Child Behavior Checklist and revised child behavior profile* (2nd ed.). Burlington, VT: University of Vermont, Department of Psychiatry.

American Psychiatric Association. (1994). *Diagnostic and statistical manual of mental disorders* (4th ed.). Washington, DC: Author.

Bandura, A. (1986). *Social foundations of thought and action: A social cognitive theory.* Englewood Cliffs, NJ: Prentice-Hall.

Barber, B. K. (2002). Reintroducing parental psychological control. In B. K. Barber (Ed.), *Intrusive parenting: How psychological control affects children and adolescents* (pp. 3–13). Washington, DC: American Psychological Association.

Barkley, R. A. (1987). *Defiant children: A clinician's manual for parent training.* New York: Guilford Press.

Berthoud-Papandropoulou, I., & Kilcher, H. (2003). Is a false belief statement a lie or a truthful statement? Judgments and explanations of children aged 3 to 8. *Developmental Science, 6,* 173–177.

Bierman, K. L. (2004). *Peer rejection: Developmental processes and intervention strategies.* New York: Guilford Press.

Bussey, K. (1992). Lying and truthfulness: Children's definitions, standards, and evaluative reactions. *Child Development, 63,* 129–137.

Cavell, T. A. (2000). *Working with parents of aggressive children: A practitioner's guide.* Washington, DC: American Psychological Association.

Conduct Problems Prevention Research Group. (1999). Initial impact of the Fast Track prevention trial for conduct problems: I. The high-risk sample. *Journal of Consulting and Clinical Psychology, 67,* 631–647.

Conduct Problems Prevention Research Group. (2002). Evaluation of the first 3 years of the Fast Track prevention trial with children at high risk for adolescent conduct problems. *Journal of Abnormal Child Psychology, 30,* 19–35.

Eyberg, S. M., Boggs, S. R., & Algina, J. (1995). Parent-child interaction therapy: A psychosocial model for the treatment of young children with conduct problem behavior and their families. *Psychopharmacology Bulletin, 31,* 83–91.

Gervais, J., Tremblay, R. E., Desmarais-Gervais, L., & Vitaro, F. (2000). Children's persistent lying, gender differences, and disruptive behaviors: A longitudinal perspective. *International Journal of Behavioral Development, 24,* 213–221.

Grusec, J. E. (1997). A history of research on parenting strategies and children's internalization of values. In J. E. Grusec & L. Kuczynski (Eds.), *Parenting and children's internalization of values* (pp. 3–22). New York: Wiley.

Heidgerken, A., Hughes, J. N., & Cavell, T. A. (in press). Direct and indirect effects of parenting and children's goals on child aggression. *Journal of Clinical Child and Adolescent Psychology.*

Henggeler, S. W., & Borduin, C. M. (1990). *Family therapy and beyond: A multisystemic approach to treating the behavior problems of children and adolescents.* Pacific Grove, CA: Brooks/Cole.

Huffman, M. L., Warren, A. R., & Larson, S. M. (1999). Discussing truth and lies in interviews with children: Whether, why, and how? *Applied Developmental Science, 3,* 6–15.

Hughes, J. N. (2000). Reconsideration of the role of theory in psychosocial intervention. *Journal of School Psychology, 38,* 389–401.

Hughes, J. N., & Cavell, T. A. (1995). Enhancing competence in aggressive children. In G. Cartledge &

J. F. Milburn (Eds.), *Teaching social skills to children: Innovative approaches* (3rd ed., pp. 199–236). New York: Pergamon Press.

Jensen, L. A., Arnett, J. J., Feldman, S. S., & Cauffman, E. (2004). The right to do wrong: Lying to parents among adolescents and emerging adults. *Journal of Youth and Adolescence, 33,* 101–112.

Johnson, E. A. (1997). Children's understanding of epistemic conduct in self-deception and other false belief stories. *Child Development, 68,* 1117–1132.

Kazdin, A. E. (1990). Premature termination from treatment among children referred for antisocial behavior. *Journal of Child Psychology and Psychiatry, 31,* 415–425.

Kazdin, A. E. (2003). Problem-solving skills training and parent management training for conduct disorder. In A. E. Kazdin (Ed.), *Evidence-based psychotherapies for children and adolescents* (pp. 241–262). New York: Guilford Press.

Loeber, R., Keenan, K., Lahey, B. B., Green, S. M., & Thomas, C. (1993). Evidence for developmentally based diagnoses of oppositional defiant disorder and conduct disorder. *Journal of Abnormal Child Psychology, 21,* 377–410.

Loeber, R., & Schmaling, K. B. (1985). Empirical evidence of overt and covert patterns of antisocial conduct problems: A meta-analysis. *Journal of Abnormal Child Psychology, 13,* 337–352.

Maccoby, E. E., & Martin, J. A. (1983). Socialization in the context of the family: Parent-child interaction. In P. H. Mussen (Ed.), *Handbook of child psychology* (4th ed., pp. 1–102). New York: Wiley.

Newton, P., Reddy, V., & Bull, R. (2000). Children's everyday deception and performance on false-belief tasks. *British Journal of Developmental Psychology, 18,* 297–317.

Patterson, G. R., Chamberlain, P., & Reid, J. B. (1982). A comparative evaluation of a parent-training program. *Behavior Therapy, 13,* 638–650.

Peterson, C. C., Peterson, J. L., & Seeto, D. (1983). Developmental changes in the ideas about lying. *Child Development, 54,* 1529–1535.

Piaget, J. (1932). *Le jugement moral chez l'enfant.* Paris: Alcan.

Sanders, M. R., Markie-Dadds, C., Tully, L. A., & Bor, W. (2000). The Triple-P Positive Parenting Program: A comparison of enhanced, standard and self-directed behavioral family intervention for parents of children with early onset conduct problems. *Journal of Consulting and Clinical Psychology, 68,* 624–640.

Stouthamer-Loeber, M. (1986). Lying as a problem behavior in children: A review. *Clinical Psychology Review, 6,* 267–289.

Taylor, M., Lussier, G. L., & Maring, B. L. (2003). The distinction between lying and pretending. *Journal of Cognition and Development, 4,* 299–323.

Tiet, Q. Q., Wasserman, G. A., Loeber, R., McReynolds, L. S., & Miller, L. S. (2001). Developmental and sex differences in types of conduct problems. *Journal of Child and Family Studies, 10*(2), 181–197.

Tolan, P. H., Gorman-Smith, D., & Loeber, R. (2000). Developmental timing of onsets of disruptive behaviors and later delinquency of inner-city youth. *Journal of Child and Family Studies, 9,* 203–220.

Venning, H. B., Blampied, N. M., & France, K. G. (2003). Effectiveness of a standard parenting-skills program in reducing stealing and lying in two boys. *Child and Family Behavior Therapy, 25,* 31–44.

Webster-Stratton, C. (1985). Predictors of treatment outcome in parent training for conduct disordered children. *Behavior Therapy, 16,* 223–242.

Webster-Stratton, C. (1987). *The parents and children series.* Eugene, OR: Castalia.

Webster-Stratton, C. (1990). Long-term follow-up of families with young conduct problem children: From preschool to grade school. *Journal of Consulting and Clinical Psychology, 19,* 144–149.

Willoughby, M., Kupersmidt, J., & Bryant, D. (2001). Overt and covert dimensions of antisocial behavior in early childhood. *Journal of Abnormal Child Psychology, 29,* 177–187.

Wilson, A. E., Smith, M. D., & Ross, H. S. (2003). The nature and effects of young children's lies. *Social Development, 12,* 21–45.

# 13

# Stealing

**Gloria E. Miller**
**Elizabeth Zimprich**
*University of Denver*

## BACKGROUND AND DEVELOPMENT

### Definitions of Stealing

Youth stealing often defies a clear definition because it is discussed in various ways depending on the age of the child, the worth of the stolen items, or whether it is accompanied by other antisocial acts. Stealing acts are commonly observed in young children as they explore the boundaries of normative social behavior. In fact, engagement in minor stealing can be considered a typical means of learning social norms by trial and error. When referring to younger children who take objects of lesser value, the term stealing is often used, whereas theft typically refers to similar behavior in older youth or to taking objects of greater value (Weger, 1987).

Another important distinction is made between nonconfrontational or covert stealing and confrontational or overt antisocial behavior. The latter typically includes instances in which theft incurs physical or personal harm. The covert versus overt distinction is important for official adjudication and also because treatment implications differ for each type. Formal definitions used in the U.S. Federal Bureau of Investigation's (FBI's) *Uniform Crime Reports* (2002) program to track national-level incidents of juvenile crime differentiate between burglary, robbery, and motor vehicle theft. Burglary involves breaking and entering to remove objects or things of value and involves no direct harm to others. Motor vehicle theft also typically involves no infliction of harm. Robbery, however, pertains to instances of theft in which a victim has incurred or been threatened with bodily harm.

For the purposes of this review, stealing is broadly defined as a covert, nonconfrontational antisocial behavior. It focuses on theft that does not typically inflict harm on the victim because that type has a high rate of occurrence and profound negative effect in school settings. Nonconfrontational stealing pertains to instances in which a child is in possession of something that does not explicitly belong to him or her. It can involve items of any value, including money or personal property, it can involve fraud (e.g., use of a stolen phone card), and it can be identified on the basis of direct observation or through the report or suspicion of others.

Developmental researchers have acknowledged that nonconfrontational stealing incidents are common manifestations of social development as children learn societal and cultural norms and rule-based behavior (Eisenberg, 1982). Increased social awareness of personal property precedes an understanding that there are restrictions about taking another person's possessions. Such social norm restrictions may be less obvious in environments where communal sharing is accepted or necessary. Minor stealing is more probable when differences in personal property boundaries exist across home or school settings. Over time, increases in empathy and interpersonal perspective-taking advance a child's moral reasoning and the social skills that lessen the likelihood of stealing. However, continued patterns of excessive stealing after a child enters formal schooling is cause for concern and often is a leading cause of clinical referrals.

### Incidence and Prevalence of Stealing

Normative studies about problem behaviors in the general population indicate that 4% to 6% of parental and adult concerns regarding problem behaviors are about youth stealing (Miller, 1997) Information about the prevalence of youth stealing also can be found by reviewing school and community crime incident reports of stolen property or adjudication and arrest records. Formal school records documenting stealing appear to have steadily declined since the early 1990s, but in 2001 more than 1.2 million acts of stealing were reported on school grounds across the nation (DeVoe et al., 2003). Inspections of official school reports also indicate that theft of personal property on school grounds is more common in 9th through 12th grade and more common for males than for females, or 46% versus 31%, respectively (Kingery, Coggeshall, & Alford, 1998).

Documentation systems to record youth crime, especially less obvious, covert antisocial behaviors such as theft or drug use, inherently under-represent the scope of the problem. Other approaches that assess the extent of youth stealing include unobtrusive observations of deliberately placed items, third-party reports, and self-reports. The latter approach gives the most accurate indication of the extent or acceptance of delinquent behavior in a general population (Kingery et al., 1998). The reliability and validity of self-reported surveys have been enhanced through strategic use of effective formats, wording, and administration procedures that guarantee anonymity (Miller & Moncher, 1988). Self-report instruments also are useful for assessing attitudes, contextual issues, and reasons that children and youth engage in delinquent acts (Moncher & Miller, 1999).

General student surveys about how they are affected by others' stealing indicate that between 25% and 46% of youth (depending on the age and gender of the respondent) have been victims of stealing during school or while traveling to and from school (Kingery, Coggeshall, & Alford, 1998). In nationally representative surveys in which students are asked to report on their own levels of stealing, up to 10% of middle and high school students reported personal participation in at least one act of nonconfrontational stealing on school grounds (Gottfredson et al., 2002).

A slightly higher level of self-reported involvement in theft behavior was found in a survey of 186 nondelinquent youth ages 10 to 15 who were attending a summer camp program. In that study, 45% of the youth indicated occasional engagement and 7% indicated frequent engagement in school or community stealing (i.e., defined as more than eight times during the past school year). Involvement was higher for males than females and for older rather than younger respondents (Moncher & Miller, 1999). Finally, comparable incidence rates of nonconfrontational stealing have been observed across urban, suburban, and rural youth on self-reports and victimization surveys (Chandler, Chapman, Rand, & Taylor, 1998).

These results support earlier national school safety studies that point to nonconfrontational theft as the most pervasive crime occurring in elementary and secondary schools. Significant numbers of children and adolescents report that they encounter or engage in nonconfrontational stealing on a regular basis while in school or while traveling to or from school (National Institute of Education, 1977). Over the past 20 years, nationally representative self-report studies have led to remarkably similar and relatively stable conclusions about youth criminal behavior in general and about youth stealing in particular (Loeber & Farrington, 2001). This type of offense now accounts for the largest portion of youth crime occurring in and out of school settings. Like other anonymously reported delinquent activities, self-reported incidents of stealing and theft typically increase during later elementary and middle school and then subsequently decrease in high school. Moreover, predictable patterns of this behavior can be observed in children as young as age 6 (Loeber & Farrington, 2001).

## Prevalence of Stealing as a Criminal Offense

Another means of assessing the prevalence of stealing, albeit imprecise, is to review data on youth crime. Youth criminal offenses, including stealing, are included in yearly FBI Uniform Crime Reports, but these statistics do not reflect incidents by offenders below age 13. Currently, no nationally adopted standards legally define child delinquency. In fact, each state derives its own definition and minimum age of criminal responsibility, which can vary from age 6 to age 10.

A national panel recently used a combination of databases to ascertain levels of antisocial and criminal behavior in children below age 13 (Loeber & Farrington, 2001). The panel concluded that although serious youth crime offenses decreased over the past two decades, incidents of less serious crimes, including minor theft and vandalism, increased markedly during the same period. Also, even though serious youth crime rose only slightly (about 6%), there was a substantial rise in the number of juvenile arrests and documented court cases (up 33%). This suggests an increased tendency to adjudicate juveniles even if they only engaged in minor criminal acts such as stealing (Loeber & Farrington, 1998).

Several conclusions can be drawn from information derived from various crime reports and studies. First, although males still predominate in all areas of antisocial offenses, females now make up about a quarter of the total juvenile arrests up to age 18. Second, although reports of stealing and other criminal offenses are higher for some minority youth, researchers caution that racial differences must be qualified by contextual mediators that include higher than average exposure to poverty and crime-ridden neighborhoods (Loeber & Farrington, 2001). Third, it is clear that most children and adolescents who steal will not have an adjudicated criminal theft record. The lack of a criminal record, however, should not be the sole determinant of intervention. Children or adolescents who have exhibited persistent patterns of nonconfrontational stealing alone or in combination with other disruptive behaviors for at least 6 months are in dire need of further remediation to avoid important detrimental outcomes.

## PROBLEMS AND IMPLICATIONS

### Negative Impacts of Stealing

A persistent pattern of stealing or other disruptive antisocial behavior over a 6-month duration, especially if noted before age 12, is a potential stepping stone on the pathway to more serious chronic or violent offenses (Loeber & Farrington, 2001). Engagement in such behavior also has far-reaching negative personal consequences in the form of increased mental health impairment and lower overall educational attainment. A more immediate personal hazard connected to problematic stealing is the development of an antisocial reputation, which mediates peer rejection and social isolation (Patterson, Capaldi, & Bank, 1991). A negative peer reputation bias has been linked to subsequent disengagement from adults and peers and an increased likelihood of association with an antisocial adolescent group over time for both males (Elliot & Menard, 1996) and females (Talbot & Thiede, 1999).

The most worrisome, consistent finding is the strong predictive association between early patterns of disruptive antisocial behavior (especially when theft is involved) and an increased trajectory of more serious delinquency (Loeber, 1990; Taylor et al., 2001). Criminal offending later in life is now viewed as part of a broader deviant developmental configuration that usually begins with less acute patterns of antisocial behavior, including stealing (Loeber & Farrington, 1998). Disheartening personal outcomes are even more probable when persistent stealing behavior is serious enough to warrant a referral to juvenile court. Youth adjudicated before age 13 are substantially more likely to become chronic juvenile offenders than youth whose initial court contact occurs at a later age.

Indirect negative economic and social impacts are associated with high levels of stealing in school and community settings. Important adverse consequences have been reported for victims and others who witness or know people affected by theft. Self-reported victimization or fear of theft while at or when traveling to and from school are related to lower student perceptions of personal and property safety and to greater school avoidance (i.e., feigned illness or truancy). Such worries about school or neighborhood safety have been linked to a limited sense of community and to lower levels of achievement and individual student success (Chandler, Chapman, Rand, & Taylor, 1998). Clearly, significant direct and secondary personal and societal costs are associated with youth stealing and its dire long-term prognosis for individual and community well-being.

### Risk and Contributory Factors

Consistent individual, peer, and family factors have been found to appreciably affect the promotion or desistance of stealing and other antisocial behaviors within the delinquency and resiliency literature (Miller, Brehm, & Whitehouse, 1998). Prevention and intervention efforts are best designed to mitigate involvement in more serious criminal behavior when guided by the strength of such risk and resiliency relationships as well as by the ease and cost associated with changing a particular variable (Stouthamer-Loeber, Loeber, Wei, Farrington, & Wikstrom, 2002).

Escalating involvement in antisocial behavior has been linked to individual emotional and social development and to moral reasoning. Children as young as 4 years of age possess a working knowledge of the needs of others and are able to demonstrate empathetic behavior (Eisenberg, 1982). Family social conditions that provide strong prosocial adult models lead to the development of these significant skills, the absence of which are strongly linked to stealing and other antisocial behavior later in life (Taylor et al., 2001). Sociomoral reasoning that affects judgments of right and wrong, fairness, and reward and punishment can influence decision making about stealing and have been associated with aggressive behavior in the classroom and with delinquent behaviors, including theft, in the community (Greening, 1997). Sociomoral knowledge structures and prosocial cognitive scripts can contribute to prosocial judgments and affect a student's decision to engage in antisocial behavior (see chapter 3, "Developing Self-Discipline"). Theft behavior also has been connected to negative self-feelings and attitudes toward delinquency, school, and authority, which can lead to rationalizations that stealing is a means of gaining power or revenge or reflects defiance against the conventional world (Moncher & Miller, 1999; Taylor et al., 2001). Such personal attitudes and motivations become increasingly influential in early adolescence (Zhang, Loeber, & Stouthamer-Loeber, 1997).

Peer and family contextual variables have been implicated in prevalent theories regarding the onset of delinquency in general and of stealing in particular (Hawkins, 1996). Many youth succumb to external pressures and are socialized into deviant conduct through involvement with delinquent peers (Keltikangas-Jarvinen & Lindeman, 1997). In one study, young adolescent males in particular were more likely to self-report attitudes that indicated greater peer acceptance of theft behaviors whereas females in the same study indicated less peer acceptance and also indicated that family values and the fear of punishment would likely deter a female peer from stealing (Moncher & Miller, 1999). Researchers have long attributed delinquent behavior to inadequate social bonding with adults in family and school (Wilson, 1993) and to less than adequate school engagement or academic progress (Hinshaw, 1992a). Displays of antisocial behavior, such as stealing, are highly related to peer rejection and academic failure (Wentzel, 1994). Many of these identified risk and contributory factors have been linked to the larger issue of limited relationships between students and adults in schools (Baker, Terry, Bridger, & Winsor, 1997).

The interrelationship between peer and family influences was critically examined in a prospective study in which three waves of adolescents and their best friends were surveyed repeatedly over several years (Aseltine, 1995). Results from this and other studies strongly suggest that peer influences are a primary source of youth delinquency, but that key adults also have important socialization influences and play a critical role in the formation of deviant friendships. Supportive adult relationships can help shield youth from deviancy, even though a highly deviant peer group can affect an adolescent's adoption of deviant or antisocial attitudes and behaviors. Some important family variables, however, such as coercive parent–child interaction, punitive parenting, parental disengagement, and less than adequate parental monitoring have consistently been found to escalate involvement in antisocial behavior in general and theft in particular (Hawkins, 1996). Thus, the evidence is strong that peer and adult factors play a complex, interactive role in the prevention and treatment of youth delinquency, especially in regard to covert deviant behavior like stealing (Keltikangas-Jarvinen & Lindeman, 1997; Moncher & Miller, 1999).

### Diagnostic Decisions Regarding Stealing

According to the American Psychiatric Association (1994), nonconfrontational stealing is one of several diagnostic criteria for conduct disorder. Although acts of stealing alone certainly do not indicate the need for such a diagnosis, instances of such behavior documented across settings over a 6-month period clearly must be considered when assessing a student's mental health and social–emotional development. Stealing behavior alone also cannot qualify a student for services under the Individuals with Disabilities Education Act (IDEA). Behaviors, including delinquent acts such as stealing, are considered socially maladjusted under IDEA, but these behaviors per se do not meet the conditions necessary to qualify under the domain of emotionally disturbed. Although the law does not completely exclude students who are socially maladjusted, it does require that emotional or behavioral problems be a certain degree and interfere substantially with a student's educational progress. This distinction is important for practitioners working with students who demonstrate antisocial behavior, particularly when discussing intervention options, individualized education plans, and behavior plans.

## ALTERNATIVE ACTIONS FOR PREVENTION

Rarely does a student exhibit significant antisocial behavior, including stealing, as an isolated concern mitigated by a single risk or resiliency factor (Tremblay & Drabman, 1997). This point is extremely important when considering prevention efforts within school and community settings. A comprehensive prevention approach is best designed from a broad understanding of the risk and resiliency factors affecting individuals, peers, and community members. Such a comprehensive understanding has led to dual-focused school-based prevention geared toward the promotion of healthy, prosocial attitudes, skills, and behaviors and the reduction of general antisocial behavior. This shift in thinking has dramatically influenced the way educators approach prevention programs to reduce stealing and other antisocial behavior in children and adolescents. This section is based on a review of empirically driven prevention strategies that reflect this dual focus.

Current school-based prevention programs are commonly classified as (a) universal approaches delivered to an entire school population, (b) selective approaches that focus on subsets of the school population deemed at risk or on factors predictive of antisocial behavior, and (c) indicated approaches that target individual students already demonstrating developmental precursors to antisocial behaviors (Kellam, Prinz, & Sheley, 2000). The remainder of this section discusses examples of universal and selective prevention efforts in relation to individual, peer, and family factors. Indicated or targeted approaches that closely resemble intervention efforts are addressed in a subsequent section.

## Universal Approaches to Prevention of Stealing

School-based universal prevention programs generally attempt to create a physical and emotional school climate in which all students and staff feel safe, appreciated, and respected. School-wide reductions in antisocial behavior have been observed after well-designed, empirically supported affective and character curricula are introduced that reinforce empathy, interpersonal problem solving, and conflict resolution (Stetson, Hurley, & Miller, 2003; also see chapter 2, "Character Education"). These outcomes, however, are mitigated by high fidelity in implementation as well as by general acceptance of all critical constituents (i.e., administrators, staff, students, and parents). Successful universal prevention programs also have been designed to foster supportive, high-quality interpersonal relationships between teachers and students and between peer groups, leading to successful reductions in school crime and improved academic engagement (Wentzel, 1998). Other effective universal school prevention programs have sought to improve the overall school climate by building caring communities where positive social relationships are fostered between students, teachers, parents, peer groups, and even wider local, national, and global neighborhoods. Finally, reduced levels of reported and perceived delinquency have been linked to universal prevention programs that strengthen bonds between teachers and parents through school–family–community partnerships (see chapter 6, "Parent–Teacher Relationships"). The effectiveness of such programs may lie in their ability to moderate, counteract, or override peer influence, especially in regard to covert antisocial behavior such as stealing and drug use (Elliot & Menard, 1996).

School-based prevention also has included educational efforts to improve social–emotional and moral reasoning skills throughout the school day. Judy and Nelson (2000) found that adolescents who reported higher levels of theft or burglary had significantly lower scores on a standard morality test, leading them to conclude that educators should encourage discussions and applications of moral reasoning in the school environment. Indeed, studies have consistently linked hedonistic, self-centered moral reasoning to a variety of antisocial and harmful behaviors, and a number of techniques and programs have been shown to be effective in targeting moral reasoning (see chapters 1–3, "Social and Emotional Learning," "Character Education," and "Developing Self-Discipline"). Included among these techniques are open Socratic class dialogues and problem-solving discussions concerning moral decisions and behavior that focus on the perspectives and feelings of others (Bear, 2005). Students who routinely engage in such discussions are more likely to provide advanced explanations for why stealing is wrong. Their arguments go beyond self-serving reasons such as "it leads to punishment and peer rejection," to stress the harm it brings to people and society because of a damaged sense of communal trust and well-being. School-based efforts to involve students in rule making, governance, and decisions for resolving peer conflicts also have led to significant increases in prosocial behavior and sociomoral reasoning and have reduced antisocial behavior (Lickona, 2004). Finally, educational programs that are accompanied by school citizenship or community-service opportunities also are effective universal approaches to preventing delinquency (Keltikangas-Jarvinen & Lindeman, 1997).

## Selected Approaches to Prevention of Stealing

Youth delinquency, violence, and conduct problems are socially embedded (Kellam et al., 2000), thus societal risk factors associated with some students place them at an elevated risk for developing stealing tendencies or other delinquent behaviors. For these students, selective prevention efforts may be needed to augment universal prevention efforts already in place. Selective prevention efforts typically emphasize means to thwart environmental, behavioral, and social precursors of antisocial behavior.

Theft and other school crime have been reduced through selective environmental prevention measures. These efforts have included increased surveillance, screening, or placement of technological safeguards such as video cameras in high crime areas. Other relatively straightforward environmental engineering efforts include selective changes in the physical layout of a school by setting up obstacles or systems for decreasing access to certain areas. Theft also can be deterred through improved lighting and increased adult monitoring in high crime areas. Finally, simple public displays that chart changing levels of targeted problem behaviors have reduced theft and other antisocial behaviors in school settings (Miller & Prinz, 1991).

Selective school prevention approaches have emphasized the creation of system-wide prosocial normative expectations, rule-making systems that outline consequences for documented infringements, and consistent positive behavioral supports. The success of such approaches is enhanced when they are collaboratively developed, widely publicized, and perceived as fair and reliably applied. The input of staff, students, parents, and community members must be sought to create successful school-wide expectations and effective positive behavior supports related to stealing or other problem behaviors (see chapter 7, "School Disciplinary Systems").

Other selective school prevention efforts have sought to build strong interpersonal social bonds for students affected by negative environmental conditions. Indeed, youth crime is higher in neighborhoods characterized by high poverty, dropout, unemployment, and gang activity, and much delinquent behavior occurs in the presence of or as a result of social pressure from delinquent peers (Judy & Nelson, 2000). Students who can identify one or more adult figures in their school, community, or home setting with whom they have a supportive, prosocial relationship are better able to cope with adversity and are less likely to engage in antisocial behavior (Miller, Brehm, & Whitehouse, 1998). Such findings have led to selective mentorship projects in which students from high-risk neighborhoods or who associate with known delinquents are paired with a long-term school or community adult who can model and engage the student in alternative prosocial activities. One example of a national mentorship program that strives to accomplish these goals is Big Brothers, Big Sisters of America (BBBSA). Grossman and Tierney (1998) found that, in contrast with youth who did not have a mentor, those who participated in BBBSA reported lower levels of substance use, more positive parent and peer relationships, increased school attendance, and higher grades. Aseltine (1995) suggests that well-designed mentorship programs help mitigate antisocial attitudes and norms and decrease the amount of time spent with delinquent peers, which in turn lessen the likelihood that a student will succumb to antisocial peer pressure.

A strong relationship has been consistently observed between delinquency and school failure (Hinshaw, 1992b). Lower rates of delinquent behavior, including stealing, are reported in schools where high academic aspirations are stressed and personal versus comparative achievement is recognized (Kasen, Cohen, & Brook, 1998). These findings support the need for prevention programs that build effective school environments where academic as well as social skills are underscored and individual accomplishments and school–community engagement are promoted. Selective prevention that involves individual remediation is especially important for students demonstrating early indications of academic and/or behavioral trouble (Hinshaw, 1992a, b). Edmondson and White (1998) describe a combined academic tutorial and counseling program for at-risk middle school students that they found to be successful in promoting students' self-esteem and academic achievement and reducing antisocial school and community behavior. In the future, other recently identified "academic enablers" across the domains of motivation, engagement, communication, and interpersonal skills also may prove to be fruitful targets in school prevention efforts to reduce acceptance of and involvement in stealing and other antisocial behaviors (DiPerna, Volpe, & Elliott, 2001).

## ALTERNATIVE ACTIONS FOR INTERVENTION

Clear actions to take with children or adolescents who steal often stymie the most sophisticated educational and mental health professionals. In contrast to the many interventions designed to reduce overt antisocial behaviors in children and adolescents, relatively few interventions have been designed solely to reduce problematic covert behaviors such as stealing. Most likely, this lack of interventions is because stealing, by its nature, is hard to detect and because, by the time a child is referred for stealing, he or she has developed a constellation of other conduct and academic problems.

Reviews of empirically valid stealing interventions across community, school, and home settings published before 1996 can be found in several previous articles and chapters (e.g., Miller, 1997; Miller & Prinz, 1991). This review focuses on several additional studies published since those reviews and summarizes eight key empirically supported intervention components reflected in the subsequent literature.

## 1. Develop a Consensus Definition of Stealing

A successful intervention for stealing must begin with the development of an overly inclusive definition of the target behavior. An *overly inclusive definition* of stealing includes any actual or suspected incidents in which the child (a) is in possession of any unfamiliar or unspecified item, (b) has purchased or bestowed unaccounted-for gifts, or (c) has engaged in any secretive or other actions that might lead an adult to suspect theft. This overly inclusive definition may result in false positive identification where a theft is recorded even when the behavior did not occur. However, it is critically important that all adults who live and work with the child reach a consensus about identifying stealing acts in an overly inclusive way that rests with a presumption of guilt. The rationale for such an assumption is that the burden of proof about instances of stealing is transferred to the child. To demonstrate progress (i.e., a reduction of stealing) the child must engage in behaviors that allow adults to clearly judge that stealing did not occur. Any questionable possessions, purchases, or actions must be viewed by all adults as potential instances of theft. In this way, adults are less likely to engage in extended discussions, arguments, or ill-advised searches that can provide a form of social attention, unintentionally reinforce stealing, or result in social or legal disapproval.

Developing and maintaining such an overly inclusive definition seems counterintuitive and overly stigmatizing to many parents and professionals. However, with covert behaviors such as stealing, a presumption of guilt is necessary to ensure that all instances of theft are identified. This step is essential to effectively decrease this negative behavior (Tremblay & Drabman, 1997). It also is possible to maintain a definition that assumes a "presumption of guilt" while simultaneously avoiding or overcoming negative biases using techniques that are discussed later.

## 2. Develop Effective Means to Monitor Stealing

After adults collaborate on a consensus definition of stealing, they must agree on a means to consistently monitor this behavior. However, it is critically important that all instances of theft be detected, because any undetected theft results in an immediate emotional and tangible reward. Without a reliable means to identify all stealing incidents across settings, an intermittent reinforcement schedule is created that in essence prolongs or strengthens continued stealing. Thus, all adults in a child's major life environments must approve and fully understand the rationale behind the system developed to detect stealing.

An effective monitoring strategy typically begins with a full accounting of all of the child's personal items both at school and at home. This leads to a comprehensive "ownership list" that is collaboratively developed and accepted by the child and all participating adults. This documented list of possessions then serves as a baseline against which to judge subsequent suspected or actual stealing acts. A practical daily routine is set up so that participating adults can easily and unobtrusively monitor or check for items in a child's locker, desk, backpack, or room. Items found during these inspections are compared with the itemized list. The expectation is that the child would only be in possession of designated items on his or her ownership list.

## 3. Maximize Environmental Deterrents

Successful interventions for stealing depend on comprehensive behavioral interviews with the child and adults to identify important antecedents that can contribute to a child's stealing and to understand the purpose and function of stealing from the child's perspective. This information should then be incorporated into the design of a variety of environmental deterrents. Effective deterrent strategies to prevent occurrences of stealing and other covert antisocial behavior are most effective when they are individualized to the particular needs of each child. Prior deterrent strategies have included restricted access and increased monitoring of a student's activities. In schools and homes, this may involve designating certain locations as off-limits or altering a student's seating, daily routine, free time, or after-school schedule to allow for increased levels of supervision. The student is then able to earn back unrestricted access and privileges once reductions in actual or suspected stealing are observed over a designated period of time.

## 4. Administer Immediate Consequences

Differential reinforcement strategies have a long history of success in reducing theft behavior. In a *differential reinforcement of other* behavioral plan (DRO), positive reinforcement is provided when the student has not exhibited or been suspected of stealing for a prearranged length of time. In a *differential reinforcement of alternative* behavioral plan (DRA), positive reinforcement is administered when a specified alternative behavior incompatible with stealing is observed. Restitution and overcorrection procedures, in which a child is asked to reimburse or compensate a victim affected by the theft, also are frequent components of successful comprehensive behavioral interventions to reduce stealing (Miller & Prinz, 1991).

After reviewing the existing intervention literature on childhood stealing, Tremblay and Drabman (1997) developed a multicomponent behavioral intervention for children and adolescents that combined differential reinforcement, restitution, and overcorrection procedures. Their approach involves several steps. Once a stealing event is identified, the child is asked to apologize to the victim and to return the stolen object. In addition, two additional overcorrection steps are included. First, the child is required to pay the victim (or to perform chores or tasks sufficient to substitute for financial restitution). Second, the child is required to relinquish one of his or her own possessions of approximately equal value (and similar in function) to the stolen item. During this second step, the child is expected to play an active role in the selection and presentation of the forfeited possession. Although the independent contributions of these two overcorrection steps cannot be ascertained from this study, such additional role reversal requirements likely increase effectiveness because the child experiences restitutional empathy.

## 5. Promote Alternative Prosocial Skills

A strong consensus of professionals holds that successful stealing interventions should emphasize social responsibility and prosocial alternatives in addition to strategies to reduce stealing. Students who engage in theft and other delinquent behaviors also exhibit less effective interpersonal decision making and conflict resolution (Greening, 1997). These findings have led to interventions that emphasize instruction in and practice of such skills to overcome specific cognitive attribution biases that reduce a student's ability to generate alternative prosocial solutions. Leeman, Gibbs, and Fuller (1993) reported significant reductions in incarcerated adolescents' self-reported delinquency, including theft, and improvements in means-end thinking (i.e., the ability to generate alternative prosocial behaviors instead of stealing during hypothetical problem-solving situations) following a dual-focused, multicomponent group treatment. Antisocial youth, including those who engage in impulsive stealing, have demonstrated reductions in overt and covert conduct problems following structured, self-control, and cognitive–behavioral treatments (Kendall, 1993). Reductions in antisocial behavior also are found following interventions designed to enhance and support academic skills (Hinshaw, 1992b). Decisions about which prosocial skills and strategies to target may need to vary depending upon evidence of early-onset versus later-onset stealing or upon evidence of overt aggressive behavior in addition to stealing. Interventions for younger students who also have concomitant behavioral or social concerns must encompass a multisystemic emphasis that includes individual, classroom, and family components (Loeber, 1990). For youth who evidence stealing or increased involvement in antisocial behavior during adolescence, heightened peer group intervention or mentorship efforts also may be required.

## 6. Overcome Biases and Social Rejection

Children who steal are particularly at risk of developing a negative antisocial reputation that can contribute to peer rejection and social isolation (see chapter 25, "Peer Relationships"). Reputational biases are especially critical when designing interventions for older children, since peers commonly hold onto negative biases even though a student has stopped stealing (Waas & Homer, 1990). Thus, successful interventions for stealing must combat the effects of a negative reputation but also must strive to improve a child's social status among peers. In general, this has been accomplished by getting teachers and support personnel to work together to structure opportunities in which children are not only monitored for instances of theft but also are provided opportunities to assist in situations that help to disconfirm negative reputation expectancies (White, Sherman, & Jones, 1996). This might occur when a target student is routinely placed in situations that require high levels of responsibility and honesty (i.e., taking the class lunch money to the office). Students who steal also could be strategically grouped with other youth to participate in beneficial academic, school, and community projects that involve cooperative and mutually reinforcing activities (see chapter 24, "Prosocial Behavior"). Following the successful completion of such tasks, teachers and other adults are asked to highlight the salience of these efforts through public recognition. Intervention efforts would also heighten adult feedback about any prosocial actions observed in the target child. Such increased positive recognition of acceptable behavior would optimally occur throughout the day through a combination of individual and peer group strategies.

Taking such explicit steps to fight peer biases and rejection may seem contrary to the presumption-of-guilt stance that teachers, parents, and school practitioners must take when working with children who steal, but both can exist simultaneously. Teachers, parents, and students recognize the uniqueness of different children. Often all they need is a reminder about the importance of individualized learning programs that build on strengths and compensate for weaknesses. From this perspective, stealing interventions can be reframed as efforts to improve an individual child's understanding of property rights. Reframing the target of the intervention in this way can help peers and adults view children who steal through a more positive learning framework. Reframing the target of the intervention also can reduce concerns about labeling or stigmatizing and can overcome reputation biases that contribute to peer or adult rejection. Thus, when designing treatments to reduce serious problem behavior in children and adolescents, the most successful outcomes will be obtained from interventions that focus both on changing an individual's behavior and changing the attitudes and perceptions of others.

## 7. Foster Home–School Collaboration

Home–school partnerships built on trust and effective communication play a major role in any successful intervention to curb a student's stealing (see chapter 6, "Parent–Teacher Relationships"). Collaborative efforts are essential to establish a consensus definition of stealing. The establishment of an inclusive definition of theft is highly dependent on teachers and family members who are willing to adopt a nonjudgmental stance and to commit to a high level of vigilance so that stealing does not go unnoticed (Miller & Prinz, 1991). Teachers and parents must feel comfortable reporting on their suspicions rather than waiting until they have documented proof of theft behavior, since rarely is it possible to catch someone in the act of stealing.

Parents and teachers often need affirmation that long-standing patterns of antisocial behavior can have a significant negative effect on a student's well-being and self-esteem and that elimination of such behaviors is most successful when the problem is identified early and when solutions are implemented across settings (Kellam et al., 2000). Once adults overcome their hesitancy to report stealing, collaborative problem solving sessions with all concerned adults can be conducted to develop effective prevention and intervention efforts. Such interventions clearly will be most effective when all adults involved can evaluate a wide range of contributing factors, including individual characteristics, behavioral standards and expectations, ownership rules, strategies for monitoring learning and behavior, interpersonal relationships, and exposure to prosocial models. From this vantage point, consistent interventions can then be developed and more easily implemented across settings. Successful home–school interventions are those in which adults can consistently use a wide array of agreed-upon strategies that are adapted into daily classroom and home routines.

## 8. Work Directly With Families

Family-focused interventions that target improved parent–child communication, discipline, interpersonal relationships, and increased supervision have been highly successful in curbing stealing. Family-based interventions that combine social learning and behavioral strategies to reduce negative or coercive family communication patterns, foster positive child management, and promote supportive adult–child interactions lead to significant reductions in deviant child and adolescent behavior (Farrington & Welsh, 1999). Families whose children have significant conduct problems often benefit from discussions and implementation of strategies to enhance personal coping as well as child management or supervision strategies (Miller & Prinz, 1990). Parents of adolescents may need additional education on effective communication and monitoring skills to help curtail detrimental friendships, since exposure to deviant activities in close friends and association with an antisocial peer group have a strong influence on initial and continued delinquency (Aseltine, 1995).

# SUMMARY

Consistent nonconfrontational stealing, especially when it occurs across settings or as part of a constellation of disruptive conduct, is a critical keystone behavior that can predict a trajectory toward more serious delinquency.

The prevention and treatment of youth stealing are of grave importance to promoting long-term well-being in individuals and communities. Schools represent one of the most critical environments for successful intervention. School-based prevention and intervention, in combination with community programs, are highly cost effective because of their clear long-term and economic benefits (Welsh, 2001).

A limited number of empirical investigations have been conducted on prevention and interventions designed specifically for stealing; however, recommendations that are effective in reducing overt, aggressive behaviors are relevant for treating covert antisocial behavior. Clearly, interdisciplinary, multi-environmental, collaborative solutions derived from various theoretical perspectives and approaches are required to effect the most change and to reduce negative long-term outcomes. Effective school-based efforts require collaborative problem solving to develop clear identification strategies that can be consistently employed across the school day and within home and community settings. Prevention and intervention strategies to reduce stealing have targeted individuals, peer groups, teachers, and families. Efforts have included methods to improve sociomoral reasoning, academic, and prosocial skills; to enhance peer and adult relationships; and to change negative perceptions and reputational biases. There is a strong recognition among professionals that proactive peer, classroom, and school-wide programs are as important as physical safeguards and deterrents. Effective school, home, and community collaboration can include combinations of curriculum activities, community mentorships, and service learning projects along with focused child treatment, peer group interventions, and family-based services.

# RECOMMENDED RESOURCES

## Books and Other Printed Material

Algozzine, B., & Kay, P. (Eds.). (2002). *Preventing problem behaviors: A handbook of successful prevention strategies.* Thousand Oaks, CA: Sage Publications.

This text provides practitioners with information and resources regarding the prevention of antisocial behaviors, including stealing at the universal, selected, and indicated levels. Social skills instruction, school-wide discipline, parent–teacher and community partnerships, and conflict resolution are a few of the prevention methods discussed. Implementation suggestions as well as form templates are also provided.

Loeber, R., & Farrington, D. P. (Eds.). (2001). *Child delinquents: Developmental, intervention, and service needs.* Thousand Oaks, CA: Sage Publications.

Though broad in scope, this book provides readers with a thorough explanation of the epidemiology, development, risk factors, and interventions associated with child delinquency. In addition, the issue of child delinquency, including behaviors such as stealing, is discussed in relation to societal issues such as mental health, the juvenile justice system, and child welfare. Practitioners can gain a more complete understanding of the context in which child delinquency occurs, as well as general intervention strategies.

Miller, G. E., & Prinz, R. J. (1989). Designing interventions for stealing. In G. Stoner, M. R. Shinn, & H. M. Walker (Eds.), *Interventions for achievement and behavior problems* (pp. 593–617). Silver Spring, MD: National Association of School Psychologists.

This chapter reviews the development and nature of juvenile stealing behavior and discusses the difficulties associated with its definition and assessment. Specific suggestions are provided regarding ways in which school professionals and family members can approach prevention and intervention techniques.

## Websites

*http://www.hamfish.org*

The Hamilton Fish Institute is a branch of George Washington University that is committed to decreasing violence in and around schools. From this website, practitioners are able to gain national and state-level data of violence trends, including theft. A thorough review of measures of school violence are available for added reference, and access to foundation grant applications for school and community violence prevention efforts are provided.

*http://ojjdp.ncjrs.org*

This website for the U.S. Office of Juvenile Justice and Delinquency Prevention provides readers with the most recent government information related to juvenile violence and prevention, including stealing. Reports of government programs, grant applications, and congressional rulings are easily accessible. Additionally, the website houses a library of journals, bulletins, fact sheets, reports, summaries, and videotapes on matters of juvenile delinquency and violence at home, in schools, and in the broader community.

## REFERENCES


American Psychiatric Association. (1994). *Diagnostic and statistical manual of mental disorders* (4th ed.). Washington, DC: Author.

Aseltine, R. H. (1995). A reconsideration of parental and peer influences on adolescent deviance. *Journal of Health and Social Behavior, 36,* 103–122.

Baker, J. A., Terry, T., Bridger, R., & Winsor, A. (1997). Schools as caring communities: A relational approach to school reform. *School Psychology Review, 26,* 586–602.

Bear, G. G. (2005). *Developing self-discipline and preventing and correcting misbehavior.* Boston: Allyn & Bacon.

Chandler, K. A., Chapman, C. D., Rand, M. R., & Taylor, B. M. (1998). *Students' reports of school crime: 1989 and 1995.* Washington, DC: U.S. Departments of Education and Justice. (NCES 98241/ NCJ-169607).

DeVoe, J. F., Peter, K., Kaufman, P., Ruddy, S. A., Miller, A. K., Planty, M., et al. (2003). *Indicators of school crime and safety* (NCJ No. 201257). Washington, DC: U.S. Department of Education and U.S. Department of Justice.

DiPerna, J. C., Volpe, R. J., & Elliott, S. N. (2001). A model of academic enablers and elementary reading/ language arts achievement. *School Psychology Review, 31,* 298–312.

Edmondson, J. H., & White, J. (1998). A tutorial and counseling program: Helping students at risk of dropping out of school. *Professional School Counseling, 1,* 43–47.

Eisenberg, N. (1982). *The development of prosocial reasoning.* New York: Academic Press.

Elliot, D. S., & Menard, S. (1996). Delinquent friends and delinquent behavior: Temporal and developmental patterns. In J. D. Hawkins (Ed.), *Delinquency and crime: Current theories* (pp. 28–67). New York: Cambridge University Press.

Farrington, D. P., & Welsh, B. C. (1999). Delinquency prevention using family-based interventions. *Children and Society, 13,* 287–303.

Gottfredson, G., Cantor, D., Gottfredson, D., Czeh, E., Crosse, S., & Hantman, D. (2002). *National study of delinquency prevention in schools, final report.* (Grant No. 96-MU-MU-0008). Ellicott City, MD: Gottfredson Associates, Inc.

Greening, L. (1997). Adolescent stealers' and nonstealers' social problem-solving skills. *Adolescence, 32,* 51–55.

Grossman, J. P., & Tierney, J. P. (1998). Does mentoring work? An impact study of the Big Brothers/Big Sisters program. *Evaluation Review, 22,* 403–426.

Hawkins, J. D. (1996). *Delinquency and crime: Current theories.* New York: Cambridge University Press.

Hinshaw, S. P. (1992a). Academic underachievement, attention deficits, and aggression: Comorbidity and implications for intervention. *Journal of Consulting and Clinical Psychology, 60,* 893–903.

Hinshaw, S. P. (1992b). Externalizing behavior problems and academic underachievement in childhood and adolescence: Causal relationships and underlying mechanisms. *Psychological Bulletin, 111,* 127–155.

Judy, B., & Nelson, E. S. (2000). Relationship between parents, peers, morality, and theft in an adolescent sample. *High School Journal, 83*(3), 31–42.

Kasen, S., Cohen, P., & Brook, J. S. (1998). Adolescent school experiences and dropout, adolescent pregnancy, and young adult deviant behavior. *Journal of Adolescent Research, 13,* 49–72.

Kellam, S., Prinz, R., & Sheley, J. (2000). *Preventing school violence* (NCJ No. 180972). Washington, DC: U.S. Department of Justice.

Keltikangas-Jarvinen, L., & Lindeman, M. (1997). Evaluation of theft, lying and fighting in adolescence. *Journal of Youth and Adolescence, 26,* 467–483.

Kendall, P. C. (1993). Cognitive-behavioral therapies with youth: Guiding theory, current status, and emerging developments. *Journal of Consulting and Clinical Psychology, 61,* 235–247.

Kingery, P. M., Coggeshall, M. B., & Alford, A. A. (1998). Violence at school: Recent evidence from four national surveys. *Psychology in the Schools, 35,* 247–258.

Leeman, L. W., Gibbs, J. C., & Fuller, D. (1993). Evaluation of a multi-component group treatment program for juvenile delinquents. *Aggressive Behavior, 19,* 281–292.

Lickona, T. (2004). *Character matters: How to help our children develop good judgment, integrity, and other essential virtues.* New York: Touchstone.

Loeber, R. (1990). Development and risk factors of juvenile antisocial behavior and delinquency. *Clinical Psychology Review, 10,* 1–41.

Loeber, R., & Farrington, D. P. (1998). *Serious and violent offenders: Risk factors and successful offenders.* Thousand Oaks, CA: Sage Publications.

Loeber, R., & Farrington, D. P. (Eds.). (2001). *Child delinquents: Developmental, intervention, and service needs.* Thousand Oaks, CA: Sage Publications.

Miller, G. E. (1997). Stealing. In G. G. Bear, K. M. Minke, & A. Thomas (Eds.), *Children's needs II: Development, problems, and alternatives* (pp. 193–202). Bethesda, MD: National Association of School Psychologists.

Miller, G. E., Brehm, K., & Whitehouse, S. (1998). Reconceptualizing school-based prevention for antisocial behavior within a resiliency framework. *School Psychology Review, 27,* 364–379.

Miller, G. E, & Moncher, F. J. (1988). Critical issues in the assessment of childhood stealing behavior. In R. J. Prinz (Ed.), *Advances in behavioral assessment of children and families* (Vol. 4, pp. 73–96). Greenwich, CT: JAI Press.

Miller, G. E., & Prinz, R. J. (1990). Enhancement of social learning family interventions for childhood conduct disorder. *Psychological Bulletin, 108,* 29–307.

Miller, G. E., & Prinz, R. J. (1991). Designing interventions for stealing. In G. Stoner, M. R. Shinn, & H. M. Walker (Eds.), *Interventions for achievement and behavior problems* (pp. 593–617). Silver Spring, MD: National Association of School Psychologists.

Moncher, F. J., & Miller, G. E. (1999). Nondelinquent youth's stealing behavior and their perceptions of parents, school, and peers. *Adolescence, 34,* 577–591.

National Institute of Education, U.S. Dept. of Health, Education, and Welfare. (1977). *Violent schools–Safe schools. The safe school study report to Congress* (Vol. 1). Washington, DC: U.S. Government Printing Office.

Patterson, G. R., Capaldi, D. M., & Bank, L. (1991). An early starter model for predicting delinquency. In D. J. Pepler & K. H. Rubin (Eds.), *The development and treatment of childhood aggression* (pp. 139–168). Hillside, NJ: Erlbaum.

Stetson, E. A., Hurley, A. M., & Miller, G. E. (2003). Can universal affective education programs be used to promote empathy in elementary aged children? A review of five curriculum. *Journal of Research in Character Education, 1,* 129–147.

Stouthamer-Loeber, M., Loeber, R., Wei, E., Farrington, D. P., & Wikstrom, P. (2002). Risk and promotive effects in the explanation of persistent serious delinquency in boys. *Journal of Consulting and Clinical Psychology, 70,* 111–123.

Talbot, E., & Thiede, K. (1999). Pathways to antisocial behavior among adolescent girls. *Journal of Emotional and Behavioral Disorders, 7,* 31–40.

Taylor, E., Kelly, J., Valescu, S., Reynolds, G., Sherman, J., & German, V. (2001). Is stealing a gateway crime? *Community Mental Health Journal, 37*(4), 347–358.

Tremblay, G. C., & Drabman, R. S. (1997). An intervention for childhood stealing. *Child and Family Behavior Therapy, 19,* 33–40.

U.S. Federal Bureau of Investigation. (2002). *Uniform crime reports: Crime in the United States.* Washington, DC: U.S. Government Printing Office.

Waas, G. A., & Homer, S. A. (1990). Situational attributions and dispositional inferences: The development of peer reputation. *Merrill-Palmer Quarterly, 36,* 239–260.

Weger, R. M. (1987). Children and stealing. In A. Thomas & J. Grimes (Eds.), *Children's needs and psychological perspectives* (pp. 571–578). Washington, DC: National Association of School Psychologists.

Welsh, B. C. (2001). Economic costs and benefits of early developmental prevention. In R. Loeber & D. P. Farrington (Eds.), *Child delinquents: Developmental, intervention, and service needs* (pp. 339–355). Thousand Oaks, CA: Sage Publications.

Wentzel, K. R. (1994). Relations of social goal pursuit to social acceptance, classroom behavior, and perceived social support. *Journal of Educational Psychology, 86,* 173–182.

Wentzel, K. R. (1998). Social relationships and motivation in middle school: The role of parents, teachers, and peers. *Journal of Educational Psychology, 90,* 202–209.

White, K. J., Sherman, M. D., & Jones, K. (1996). Children's perceptions of behavior problem peers: Effects of teacher feedback and peer-reputed status. *Journal of School Psychology, 34,* 53–72.

Wilson, J. Q. (1993). *The moral sense.* New York: The Free Press.

Zhang, Q., Loeber, R., & Stouthamer-Loeber, M. (1997). Developmental trends of delinquent attitudes and behaviors: Replications and synthesis across domains, time, and samples. *Journal of Quantitative Criminology, 13,* 181–215.

# 14

# Cheating

**F. Clark Power**
**Ann Marie R. Power**
*University of Notre Dame*

## BACKGROUND AND DEVELOPMENT

Cheating is a very general term for deceptive behavior that gives students an unfair grade on a particular task. Cheating may thus involve a variety of behaviors, including plagiarism and copying another student's homework or answers on a test. Whether a student is thought to be cheating depends on directly stated and implied rules for collaboration and research. These rules may change abruptly from one grade level to another. For example, in the third grade children may be permitted to copy a research report directly from an encyclopedia. In the seventh grade such copying may be seen as plagiarism, yet paraphrasing from an encyclopedia without proper citation may be permitted.

The seriousness of cheating is often difficult to gauge because the cheater's intentions and the negative consequences of the action are difficult to apprehend. For example, suppose Billy was unable to prepare for his seventh-grade math test because his parents got into a terrible fight the night before. If his teacher does not grade on a curve, then Billy's cheating seems to hurt no one but himself. Billy may even rationalize that cheating is simply a way of coping with an unfortunate situation. Calabrese and Cochran (1990) note that the seriousness of cheating seems to depend on whether one student is helping another, for example, by letting him or her copy an assignment (passive cheating) or whether the student is behaving dishonestly to improve his or her grade, for example, by using crib notes on an exam (active cheating).

Cheating in school has always been a significant problem, but it has become decidedly worse in recent years. In 1969, for example, 33.8% of high school students confessed to using a cheat sheet on a test; in 1989, more than double that number (67.8%) confessed to such use (Schab, 1991). In a nationwide survey of students in public and private high schools, 74% admitted to at least one form of serious cheating in the past year, and more than half acknowledged that they had plagiarized off the Internet (Stricherz, 2001). On a survey of ethics among American high school students, 62% reported that they had cheated on a test in the past year, and 83% admitted to copying another student's homework at least once during the past year (Josephson Institute of Ethics, 2004). Finally, in a survey of undergraduate students in upper-level courses, 70% to 80% responded positively to having cheated during high school, with no significant differences found between male and female respondents, and 40% to 60% reported that they had cheated during their college years (Davis & Ludvigson, 1995).

Although the high incidence of cheating evokes cries of outrage from adult leaders, few students seem concerned. An overwhelming majority of students (78%) report that they are not at all offended by cheating, and more students approve of cheating than disapprove (Johnston, Bachman, & O'Malley, 1990). Some educators and social scientists believe that the pervasiveness of student cheating signals the moral decay of the nation's youth; others, however, attribute cheating to broader problems in the culture and organization of schools and society. Cheating in school is, after all, not a new problem. Over 70 years ago, Willard Waller (1932) reported widespread use of "cribbing" on examinations: "Certainly, a large percentage of any student body cribs occasionally, and another group cribs habitually" (p. 360). The purpose of this chapter is to discuss why students cheat; what the rising incidence of cheating means for those who work in schools; and how teachers, administrators, school psychologists, and counselors can effectively address this problem.

## Why Students Cheat—Character or Social Context?

In the popular media, cheating is typically seen as a defect of character or as a lack of virtue. This view led Hartshorne and May (1928–1930) to conduct their well-known Studies in the Nature of Character. Hartshorne and May found very little consistency in cheating behavior across a number of situations in which students were tempted to cheat. They discovered that in spite of what students say about honesty, they will cheat when the rewards are high and the risks are low. The Hartshorne and May studies debunked the then-popular notions of character and virtue by showing that situational factors, such as the probability of detection, were far more powerful in predicting behavior than internal factors such as the virtue of honesty.

Since the Hartshorne and May studies, social learning theorists have elaborated how situational factors regulate moral behavior. Their research shows that anticipated sanctions, whether in the form of concrete rewards and punishments or of social approval and disapproval greatly influence behavior (e.g., Anderson, 1989). Anticipated sanctions help explain why children may espouse the virtue of honesty but not always practice it. Adults want to hear that children esteem the virtues, but they also want children to get good grades. Adults, moreover, do not practice what they preach. When conflicts occur between preaching and practice, research on modeling shows that practice takes precedence over preaching (Bandura, 1986).

The rise of cheating over the past 30 years may in part be the result of a lack of positive role models, leading to a growing cynicism about adult society. In 1969, 49.1% of high school students agreed that people in the United States were honest; in 1989, 23.8% agreed (Schab, 1991). In the Josephson Institute's 2004 survey, 84% of the high school respondents agreed that most of the adults in their lives consistently set a good example of ethics and character, but 59% also agreed that in the real world, successful people do what they have to do to win, even if others consider it cheating. The majority of students think that adults in almost all professions (the exceptions are judges and medical doctors) are dishonest sometimes. Whether or not adolescents' perceptions are correct, they no doubt influence how seriously students regard their own and their peers' cheating. If students believe that everyone cheats some of the time, it is easy to excuse cheating as a human foible or even as a necessity. Moreover, it is easy to dismiss moral admonitions about cheating as hypocritical.

The rise of cheating may also be explained as a reaction to ever-constricting opportunities for social advancement (Michaels & Miethe, 1989). In this sense, cheating is the by-product of a highly competitive society that values winning at any cost (Kohn, 1992). Examples abound of athletes, business executives, building contractors, and adults from all walks of life who cheat to gain a competitive edge. Competition is fruitful insofar as individuals are willing to abide by the rules that regulate any particular activity. Unfortunately, the heat of competition often seems to lead individuals to focus selfishly on their own goals, making it easier to cheat and to disregard others' welfare (Staub, 1978). The negative effects of competition may well be magnified by a meritocratic system that richly compensates the winners and provides little or nothing to the losers. The recognition given to virtue pales in comparison with that given to material success.

Many students report feeling considerable pressure to cheat, and they cite "fear of failure" and "parental insistence on grades" among the top three reasons for cheating (Schab, 1991). Students who feel a high demand for success and low self-efficacy are especially likely to resort to cheating (Finn & Frone, 2004; Murdock, Hale, & Weber, 2001). The pressure to cheat appears to vary depending on students' motivational goal orientation and the goal orientation of the classroom climate (Anderman, Griesinger, & Westerfield, 1998; Anderman & Midgley, 2004; Murdock et al., 2001). Students who are performance oriented focus on how they compare with others and seek to project an image of being intelligent. Compared with mastery- or task-oriented students, who are concerned about learning for its own sake, performance-oriented students attribute more personal importance to grades and may be tempted to cheat as a means of protecting their sense of self-esteem. Classroom climates that accentuate the importance of grades appear to exert considerable influence on the achievement orientations that students adopt and the adaptive or maladaptive strategies they use to succeed (Anderman et al., 1994; Anderman & Midgley, 2004; Murdock et al., 2001).

Although psychologists now recognize that situational factors have a major influence on cheating, they are coming to a renewed appreciation for the role of character in moral behavior. Reanalyses of the Hartshorne and May data indicate that there is greater behavior consistency across situations than had originally been noticed (Burton, 1963). Moreover, Kohlberg's (1984) research bridged the gap between words and deeds by showing that stages of moral reasoning are related to moral action. More recently, cognitive developmentalists have begun to identify personality factors that influence moral agency (Blasi, 1995; Colby & Damon, 1992; Power & Khmelkov, 1997). Adolescents, for example, may be more likely to resist the temptation to cheat if their self-concept or sense of identity is rooted in moral values. On the other hand, those most inclined to cheat and to accept cheating appear to be lacking in self-control (Cochran, Wood, Sellars, Wilkerson, & Chamlin, 1998; Jensen, Arnett, Feldman, & Cauffman, 2002).

## Developmental Perspective

Most studies of cheating, whether focused on the individual or the social context, fail to examine the problem from a developmental perspective. Cheating is all too often regarded as the violation of a socially approved standard for behavior. Yet, it is clear that cheating has different meanings for students as they mature. Young children, for example, may violate rules unknowingly. Older children may think of cheating as wrong only if it would hurt the teacher's feelings. The escalating severity of sanctions for cheating from elementary school through college suggests that as children develop, the social significance of their cheating grows, as does their moral responsibility for honest behavior. Likewise, the development of children's standards of moral behavior become more cognitively complex and internalized as children grow older (Bandura, 1991, 1997). Initially, parents give children simple prohibitions backed by concrete rewards and punishments. Later, parents and other authorities teach children more abstract rules and rely on more subtle expressions of social approval and disapproval. Ultimately, parents and teachers attempt to help children regulate their own behavior according to agreed-upon standards of conduct.

Jean Piaget (1932/1965) offered a penetrating developmental analysis of cheating that is particularly sensitive to the social context. He described cheating as a "defensive reaction" brought on by an unnecessarily individualistic educational system (p. 287). In Piaget's view, children are logically disposed to learn cooperatively and, in particular, to emulate successful students. The social structure of schools forces students either to comply with the teacher or to resist. In either case, cheating is likely to result.

Compliance encourages the weaker students to cheat in order to keep up with their peers; resistance takes the form of organized cheating, or at the very least a strictly enforced code of silence. Given the significant role that authority plays in maintaining the competitive system, Piaget was not surprised to find that children regarded cheating primarily as the violation of teachers' rules and expectations. Piaget and his colleagues asked children between the ages of 6 and 12 to respond to the question: "Why must you not copy from your friend's book?" They coded the children's answers into one of the following categories: (a) authority, because copying violates an adult prohibition, (b) equality, because copying hurts another student, and (c) utility, because cheating is useless, you learn nothing. They found that the appeal to authority was made by 100% of children between the ages 6 and 7 but that reason dropped to 15% at age 12. On the other hand, the appeal to equality was not made by children until age 10 (26%) and rose to 62% by the ages 11 and 12. The appeal to utility was relatively uncommon; it did not appear until age 10 (5%) and rose to only 25% by age 12.

Piaget's results indicate that children's reasons for not cheating develop with age, beginning with authority and ending with equality. His results less clearly support his view of cheating as the by-product of a competitive and adult-dominated social structure. Although young children view cheating as disobedience rather than dishonesty, the majority of older children see cheating as unfairness or hurting others. Few children, moreover, state that cheating is justifiable "solidarity" in response to a harsh social order, although Piaget suggests that many more may have thought it. Piaget cites the following example from an 11-year-old as an expression of this kind of solidarity: "For those who can't learn they ought to be allowed to have a little look, but for those who can learn it isn't fair . . . He ought not have copied. But if he was not clever it was more or less all right for him to do it" (p. 289). This answer indicates a genuine moral conflict. On the one hand, cheating is clearly seen as wrong ("one ought not to cheat"); on the other hand, a child's inability to learn entitles that child to extra help. This example suggests that children's understanding of the problem of cheating should not be isolated from their understanding of larger issues of justice in the process of classroom instruction.

Kohlberg's moral stage theory provides the most sensitive approach to the reasoning that informs children's and adolescents' notions of honesty and rationalizations for cheating. Studies conducted on the relationship between Kohlberg's stages of moral judgment and cheating indicate that the higher a student's stage of moral judgment, the less likely that the student will cheat (e.g., Blasi, 1980; Kohlberg, 1984). Kohlberg (1970) first explained this relationship in terms of the Socratic principle that reasoning leads directly to action. Later, however, Kohlberg (1984), in his moral action studies, offered a more nuanced interpretation, not only of the cheating studies but of other moral judgment. Kohlberg pointed out that an individual's moral stage does not lead to different conclusions about whether cheating is right or wrong; most subjects at all stages acknowledge that cheating is wrong. On the other hand, moral stage does correlate with the likelihood that a student will refuse to cheat in a tempting situation (Kohlberg, 1984). This latter fact led Kohlberg to conclude that moral stage may influence one's sense of responsibility to act on the judgment that cheating is wrong by supporting or rejecting "excuses" to cheat. Kohlberg's earlier and later positions are not mutually exclusive. At higher stages, individuals will be more motivated to act because they have a better understanding of the value of honesty and because their higher reasoning makes it more difficult to rationalize cheating than at the lower stages.

Research on moral development suggests that elementary and high school students think of cheating very differently. Cheating in the elementary grades seems largely synonymous with disobedience. Students are likely to see little intrinsic value in making sure that individuals do their own work, because they equate learning with completing assignments or acquiring information. Cheating at the junior high school and high school levels takes on more significance as students move to a stage 3 morality, which is based on meeting expectations of good behavior and upholding trust (see chapter 2, "Character Education," for a table of the stages of moral reasoning). Students also come to appreciate differences in achievement and how these differences are reflected in grading.

## Cheating Within the Context of the School—Social Psychological Theories of Deviance

Many social psychologists regard cheating as a form of deviance insofar as cheating entails the violation of an agreed-upon expectation for behavior. Michaels and Miethe (1989), for example, maintain that cheating is explicable by an integrated model of deviance that is drawn from deterrence, rational choice, social bond, and social learning theories.

*Deterrence theory* stipulates that undesirable behavior can be curtailed by a high risk of detection and swift and severe sanctions. The high incidence of cheating may in part be due to the perception that cheating is easy to get away with and that those who get caught are not severely punished. Teachers and administrators endorse deterrence theory insofar as they typically respond to cheating and other discipline problems with greater surveillance and harsher punishments. *Rational choice theory* unmasks the simplicity of deterrence theory by proposing that anticipated rewards, as well as punishments, enter into the calculated choice to engage in deviant behavior (Piliavin, Gartner, Thornton, & Matsueda, 1986). Schools mimic the wider society by ignoring the virtuous (except with token citizenship awards) and rewarding top athletes and scholars. Therefore, students may decide to cheat in order to gain the rewards most readily proffered by schools. One serious shortcoming of rational choice theory, however, is that it focuses on the decision maker without considering the social context in which choices are made. *Social bond theory* postulates that deviant behavior occurs as a result of loosened ties to society (Hirschi, 1969). Michaels and Miethe (1989) note, however, that strong social ties may predict cheating if those ties are to peers who cheat.

All of the above theories may be related to *social learning theory.* Of particular relevance is differential association-reinforcement theory, which builds on social bond theory by postulating that deviant behavior is fostered through relationships with those who engage in such behaviors. Thus, students who socialize with others who cheat will find reinforcement in the form of social approval for their cheating and social disapproval when they refuse to cooperate in cheating or in covering it up.

## Cheating as Normative Behavior

Michaels and Miethe (1989) concluded that all four of the above social psychological theories of deviance predicted self-reported cheating (in a sample of college students at a large university with an honor code). In reaching this conclusion, however, they criticize the premise that cheating is a form of deviance. Because the majority of students in their sample perceived cheating as an acceptable way of attaining good grades and the benefits that go with them, they suggest that cheating, from a statistical point of view, is a normative behavior (Michaels & Miethe, 1989, p. 882). However, the term *normative* is misleading, because although the majority of students may engage in and accept cheating, they also see cheating as wrong (e.g., Jensen et al., 2002). Norms can be defined from a descriptive, behavioral perspective as being how most subjects *do* act and from a prescriptive, evaluative perspective as being how most subjects believe they *should* act. The fact that students may tolerate and sometimes encourage the violation of rules against cheating does not mean that students think that cheating ought to be practiced as a moral ideal (Power, Higgins, & Kohlberg, 1989). Many students recognize that cheating is wrong but see cheating as a way of life.

Unfortunately, in many schools the honesty norm (considered from a prescriptive, evaluative perspective) has not taken hold or become institutionalized as a group norm (Power et al., 1989). That is, students may have personal objections to cheating but do not see cheating as violating a shared expectation for behavior. In such schools, peer pressure to share answers and to cover up cheating constitutes a counternorm to honesty insofar as students experience a need to conform, in the sense of fitting in with others in the group. Yet this expectation to go along with the crowd does not have the obligatory force of an expectation based on values and on reason. Thus cheating may be a quasi-norm from a descriptive point of view and a form of deviance from a prescriptive point of view.

## Cheating and Student Alienation

In addition to cheating being viewed from the perspective of normative or deviant behavior, it also can be viewed as a manifestation of student alienation (Finn & Frone, 2004). Students who dislike school and feel that their teachers are unfair are more likely to cheat than peers who have more positive perceptions of the school and teachers. Students are less likely to conform to classroom and school norms if they do not experience a meaningful connection to a classroom and school community.

## Cheating as Viewed by Students

Surprisingly little attention has been given to understanding how students regard cheating (Jensen et al., 2002). Most students of all ages think that cheating is wrong, but few stress that cheating is unfair to or harms others. For example, a survey of high school students found that 73.5% agreed with the statement, "Cheating only hurts the cheater" (Schab, 1991). Likewise, in a study of middle school students (seventh and eighth grade), Eisenberg (2004) found that less than half the students perceived cheating as a moral issue (an issue involving fairness or the welfare of another). Those students who perceived cheating as a moral issue were far more disapproving of cheating than those who saw it as a conventional issue (an issue of an arbitrary social norm, such as raising your hand before speaking in class; e.g., Nucci, 2001). Why did so many students perceive cheating as a conventional rather than a moral issue? Perhaps these students reasoned at the second stage of morality, which is focused on concrete self-interest. It may also be the case that students were capable of a higher stage of reasoning but were influenced by the school culture to view the rules about cheating in a conventional way.

Perhaps the fact that cheating rules are imposed from above leads students to focus primarily on the risks and consequences of getting caught rather than on the intrinsic immorality of cheating. Students may, of course, realize that cheating is unfair in the abstract but in the context of school regard such unfairness as trivial. As Nisan (1985) agrees, individuals allow themselves and others to deviate to a degree from the moral ideal insofar as the deviations are seen as excusable. These deviations are permitted presumably because they are due to strong temptations or because they are relatively unimportant in the context of competing considerations. In Nisan's view, individuals define a level of "limited acceptable morality" in which they may knowingly violate moral norms without believing that they are immoral persons or that they have done something really wrong. Students may regard cheating as limited acceptable morality (or immorality) insofar as they acknowledge that cheating is wrong but excuse cheating as necessary in certain situations (Schab, 1991).

Perhaps the acceptance of cheating among so many students can best be understood within the context of a school structure that is meritocratic and authoritarian. Students are required to earn status in schools through their performance on daily assignments, periodic tests, and papers. Teachers assign grades by comparing students with each other, although the teachers may not distribute student grades strictly along a bell curve. Though children also learn to compete in other contexts, such as by playing games with their friends or in more structured athletic programs, classrooms are the main locus of competition in childhood.

The assignment of students to classes and tracks based on their level of ability and the emphasis given to grades and academic awards are predicated on the assumption that students will work independently and achieve according to their abilities and effort. According to Dreeben (1968), students need to internalize the norms of independence and achievement in order to be prepared for adult society. Teachers play a major role in helping students become independent workers by regulating when they can work with one another and when they must work alone. Teachers must sometimes intervene in children's relationships with their parents and friends in order to foster children's independence. This intervention may sometimes appear to be artificial because parents and friends are naturally inclined to offer help. This intervention may also appear to be arbitrary because the teacher decides which tasks are to be done independently for the sake of evaluation and which are to be done cooperatively for the sake of instruction. Yet even when teachers attempt to clarify their expectations, the line between cooperation and collusion remains fuzzy. This fuzziness is due to the fact that helping behavior that is ordinarily thought of as praiseworthy can be construed as cheating in certain teacher-defined situations.

## PROBLEMS AND IMPLICATIONS

The research evidence indicates that cheating should be approached as a problem at both the individual and classroom and school levels. Thus, it is reviewed below as a problem at each of those two levels.

### Individual Level

Because of the prevalence of cheating at the junior high and high school level, interpretations of the seriousness of particular instances of cheating should be made with caution. Generally, cheating behavior can be attributed to situational factors and most efficiently remedied through interventions at the level of the classroom group. Cheating may, however, be a manifestation of a character problem. The *Diagnostic and Statistical Manual of Mental Disorders, Fourth Edition* (American Psychiatric Association, 1994) does not specifically include cheating as a criterion of a conduct disorder, although the manual does include the related behaviors of deceitfulness and theft. Cheating is, of course, a form of deceit and may in certain instances be seen as a form of theft (e.g., in cases of plagiarism, copying another's exam answers, or fraudulently obtaining a test). Achenbach and Edelbrock (1981) include cheating with lying as a single item on the Child Behavior Checklist. They find that approximately 50% to 85% of children referred for professional treatment are reported to lie or cheat, whereas only 15% to 20% of children in a normal sample are. In the more recent and comprehensive Achenbach–Conners–Quay Questionnaire (ACQ), cheating and lying are distinguished, and both are found to contribute to a delinquency factor (Kazdin, 1995). A delinquent pattern typically includes not only lying and cheating but also such behaviors as theft, running away, setting fires, and truancy (Achenbach, 1993). Another way of classifying cheating is to see it along with lying and stealing as a part of a covert (as opposed to an overt) polarity of antisocial behavior (Loeber, Lahey, & Thomas, 1991).

The chapters on lying and stealing (chapters 12 and 13 in this volume) provide a good summary of the research on conduct disorders and the issues relevant to the clusters of behaviors labeled as delinquent or covert. These chapters note that particular attention must be paid to early manifestations of antisocial behavior because the onset of conduct disorders typically occurs in early childhood. Conduct disorders may also be accompanied by other disorders such as the Attention Deficit Hyperactivity Disorder and the oppositional defiant disorder (Kazdin, 1995). Thus, cheating may, in certain instances, be a response to difficulties in paying attention during class and preparing for an examination or a way of opposing teachers' authority. Clearly, assessing the significance of any particular act of cheating or a pattern of cheating requires that the context in which cheating occurs and the motivation for the cheating be ascertained.

Several personality factors have been shown to be correlated with cheating, such as low self-esteem, fear of failure, and difficulty with authority figures (Bushway & Nash, 1977; Evans & Craig, 1990; Murphy, 1993). Cheating has also been related to pressures at home, part-time work, and absences from school (Evans & Craig, 1990). Recent studies also link cheating to the perception of teachers as incompetent (Murdock, Miller, & Kohlhardt, 2004).

### Classroom and School Level

Differences between the ways in which teachers and students think about cheating can lead to problems. While teachers may see cheating as a matter of character and honesty, students may see it as a coping strategy, a cause for peer solidarity, or a game of fooling the teacher. Students and teachers define cheating differently because of the different cultural contexts in which they reside. Within the students' culture, letting others copy their answers and keeping silent about cheating violations are well-established counternorms. Teachers, on the other hand, belong to an adult culture that opposes cheating and encourages vigilance, particularly in the school setting. Teachers often behave as though students will cheat if they have an opportunity to do so. Students recognize that their teachers do not trust them and are trying to catch them cheating. Both teachers and students thus find themselves engaged in a cat-and-mouse dynamic that severely limits possible ways teachers can address the cheating problem. The dynamic also leads students to conclude that schools are ill-equipped to teach honesty.

Only 5.4% of high school students agree that schools are an effective source of guidance for learning about honesty (Schab, 1991). Why are schools so ineffective? Part of the problem may well be structural; schools, as noted in the background section of this chapter, are meritocracies. Rewards, such as track placement, access to special classes, recognition in awards ceremonies, scholarships, and admission into selective prep schools and universities, depend on getting high grades. Failure to achieve high grades can lead to such negative sanctions as teacher and parent disapproval, disadvantageous track and course placement, and diminished employment opportunities. Students may find that the teachers' pleas for honesty ring hollow in a highly competitive environment in which so much emphasis is placed on grades. Many students seem to feel that teachers simply do not understand the pressures of getting good grades, and many teachers are appalled at their students' dismissal of cheating as a serious moral problem.

Students and teachers appear to live in different cultures, cultures that reflect not simply a generational gap but differences in values. If those differences are to be overcome, teachers and administrators must address the authority structure of the school, which inhibits moral communication and restricts students' sense of responsibility. Teachers and administrators have almost absolute responsibility for making and enforcing school rules. This allocation of responsibility might be justifiable if students were ignorant of what is right and wrong and so immature that they need almost complete external regulation. Yet there is no evidence that students are so ignorant and irresponsible that they can have no meaningful role in the disciplinary process.

In fact, this allocation of responsibility alienates students and thus undermines the effectiveness of disciplinary policies. Is it surprising to find that students care little about violations of school rules, such as the cheating rule, when they have no investment in those rules? Or is it surprising to find that students band together to protect themselves from teachers and administrators who do not seek their opinion or seem to care about the effects of school rules on the students? An authoritarian structure of schools drives students and teachers apart and fosters mutual ignorance and suspicion. Furthermore, an authoritarian structure aimed at control rather than moral education deprives students of an opportunity to learn responsibility.

## ALTERNATIVE ACTIONS FOR PREVENTION

Because cheating is so pervasive and typically rooted within the student peer culture, successful interventions would be advised to include the following five strategies:

### 1. Frame Cheating as a Moral Problem

Although most students acknowledge that cheating is wrong, they do not have a clear understanding of why. Moreover, many students typically excuse cheating as a way of coping with pressures at home and school to get good grades. Students tend to think that cheating hurts no one but the teacher, possibly, who lays down the rules about cheating and is responsible for trying to prevent it. The first step in preventing cheating must be to develop a shared understanding among students that cheating is unfair to other students and violates the trust that is essential to an academic community. Teachers who complain that students who cheat are only hurting themselves send the wrong message by treating cheating as a pragmatic concern for the individual student. What makes cheating morally wrong is not that it short-circuits genuine learning (which it does); what makes cheating wrong is that it is unjust. In the terminology of domain theory, teachers need to treat cheating as a moral, rather than as a personal or conventional, concern (Nucci, 2001). Teachers should help students value honesty for its own sake (moral domain) and not simply as a means to develop academically (personal domain) or as an act of obedience or conformity (conventional domain).

Teachers can most effectively promote a common understanding about the moral nature of cheating by discussing cheating with their students. Teachers should resist the temptation to give students a lecture on honesty or to ask closed questions, such as, "Don't you all see that cheating is wrong?" The moral discussion approach presupposes that students develop their moral judgment by thoughtfully engaging moral problems. A good discussion stimulates cognitive conflict, challenging students to rethink why they hold certain values and behave as they do.

Moral discussion over the course of a semester has been shown to promote significant moral stage development (Higgins, 1980). Although resistance to cheating is positively correlated with stage development, moral discussion interventions alone have limited effectiveness in changing student behavior (Blatt & Kohlberg, 1975). This lack of effectiveness is probably because moral discussions produce only a modest amount of change and because the hypothetical moral dilemmas used in these discussions do not address cheating directly. Moral discussion can be used more profitably in the context of making real decisions about classroom cheating.

## 2. Develop a Sense of Community in the Classroom and School

Cheating is unlikely to occur in a classroom community characterized by trust and caring (see Battistich & Hom, 1997; Battistich, Schaps, Watson, Solomon, & Lewis, 2000; also see chapter 24, "Prosocial Behavior"). Deterrence tactics, such as strict test supervision, alternate test forms, and greater spacing between desks, may curtail cheating behavior but fail to address the mentality that gives rise to cheating in the first place. Moreover, such tactics are based on the presupposition that students will cheat if they have the opportunity to do so. Many students do, in fact, construe teachers' lack of vigilance as an invitation to cheat, because students have become accustomed to their teachers' mistrust. On the other hand, students typically respond favorably to teachers who cultivate a trusting and supportive relationship with their students (Murdock et al., 2001; Pianta, Stuhlman, & Hamre, 2002; also see chapter 5, "Student–Teacher Relationships"). Many students excuse cheating because they feel that teachers make unrealistic and inflexible demands. This problem is exacerbated when students feel that their teachers are not teaching them well and are not approachable for extra help.

In a classroom community students and teachers work together to foster each other's learning and to attend to each other's needs, both personal and academic. In a genuine community, all students feel a sense of belonging and identify with school as a whole. Teachers cultivate this sense of community by finding ways in which all students can experience success in the classroom, by caring for each student and encouraging students to care for each other, and by sharing responsibility for building community with the students.

## 3. Develop Clear Rules and Policies That Address Cheating

Establishing clear rules and policies about cheating is simply good common sense. However, teachers and administrators should not establish rules and policies in a vacuum, that is, without the participation of students. Students need to understand the reasoning behind the rules prohibiting cheating. If the rule is to be effective, students should see it as following from what it means to be a good member of their classroom community. In other words, observing the rules about cheating ought to be seen as part of what it means to be a good citizen of the classroom and school. Explicit rules about cheating are also necessary simply because students are often confused about what constitutes cheating. Some teachers allow students to prepare by looking at old exams. Other teachers forbid that practice. Sometimes students are expected to collaborate on assignments; other times students are forbidden to collaborate.

Although the Internet is a valuable research tool, it has also made plagiarism quick and easy. One way to detect Internet plagiarism is through the use of Internet-based programs such as Turnitin.com. If the school makes use of such detection aides, the students should be advised of this. More importantly, however, students should be helped to understand the importance of proper citation and the conventions for doing so.

## 4. Establish a Student-Supported Honor Code or Honesty Contract

Rules that address cheating in the context of a community ideally should take the form of an honor code or honesty contract. Generally the greatest obstacle to implementing an honor code is student reluctance to "snitch" on another student and faculty reluctance to trust students to follow the rules about honesty without monitoring. Students' concern about reporting another student can be partly alleviated by using a system in which students provide information to an honesty committee consisting of students and teachers, rather than turn in a fellow student to an adult authority. Schools that have enjoyed success with honor codes have active student-led honor code committees. These committees may receive adult input as long as students play a major role. Students' concerns about reporting can also be lessened by granting the honor code committee some flexibility in determining the severity of punishment. Students are understandably reluctant to report other students if the penalties are likely to be severe. Severe penalties are also likely to inhibit students from admitting to cheating.

Much of the spirit of an honor code can be preserved through a negotiated student–teacher contract. Such a contract is best implemented within an intentional classroom community that applies certain features of the "just community" approach to moral education described by Power et al. (1989). The just community approach involves students and teachers in a democratic process of making and enforcing disciplinary rules and policies. The key to this process is to have teachers share responsibility with all students, not only those elected to a student council or appointed to an honor board. Teachers' unilateral use of prevention tactics sends students the message that cheating is the teacher's problem. A contractual approach lets students know that the cheating problem belongs to everyone, especially the students. The purpose of negotiating a contract is to break the barrier between the student and teacher cultures in order to build a common norm opposed to cheating.

Negotiating such a contract requires time and effort. In the just community approach, problems such as cheating are discussed in regularly scheduled community meetings. Teachers who wish to use a contractual approach to cheating need to set aside time for discussing why students should not cheat. Research on moral discussion indicates that teachers are effective only when they facilitate student participation (Colby, Kohlberg, Fenton, Speicher-Dubin, & Lieberman, 1977). However, this approach requires that teachers give up their role as sole authority and encourage students to think about how cheating affects other students and why cheating is wrong.

Teachers who use the contractual approach should be willing to discuss and modify their testing and grading practices. Teachers will have an easier time persuading students to not cheat to be fair to their fellow students if their students perceive that they are making a sincere effort to make their tests fair. Moreover, teachers will have an easier time building a climate of trust if students feel that they can openly raise issues concerning, for example, when a test is being given, the amount of material that is to be tested, and whether special help may be required.

### 5. Foster a Mastery Climate

A growing body of research suggests that cheating will decline if the teacher strikes a better balance between competition and cooperation in the classroom. The academic and social benefits of peer-assisted learning and cooperative learning strategies are well documented, and approaches are readily available (see chapter 48, "Peer-Assisted Learning Strategies"). As Thorkildsen (1989) has found, students of all ages believe that they should help other students in the learning process. She also reports that, unfortunately, few teachers take advantage of approaches that involve peers in learning. Using peer-assisted approaches demonstrates that teachers sincerely support students' natural desire to help one another. Once teachers have legitimized cooperation, they are in a better position to explain why, in certain cases, individual assignments and tests are necessary.

A related way to curtail cheating is to establish a "mastery climate" (Anderson, 1989) in which students pursue self-referenced achievement goals. Such a climate fosters each student's sense of competence and emphasizes the importance of learning for its own sake. Teachers focus on academic development, not testing and grading. Students endeavor to improve and learn, rather than to avoid failure or the appearance of failure. Teachers, moreover, encourage students to increase their understanding and to put forth their best efforts (e.g., Ames, 1992; Turner & Patrick, 2004).

## ALTERNATIVE ACTIONS FOR INTERVENTION

### Assessment of Cheating Problems

Although instances of cheating can generally be approached at the level of the classroom community, individual students who are flagrant cheaters may require special attention. Assessment of a cheating problem should proceed cautiously with an awareness that many students simply do not perceive cheating as a serious moral issue. School professionals must first determine the forms of cheating that the child has engaged in, their severity, their frequency, and their history. Certain forms of cheating, such as plagiarism, may result from teachers' failures to explain their expectations effectively or to students' inattention to those explanations. Because cheating is such a widespread phenomenon, and because teachers do not always have an accurate view of the cheating situation in the classroom (Evans & Craig, 1990), school professionals who are dealing with a referred child may need to ask some of the child's classmates about the extent of cheating in their classrooms.

For a child's cheating to be understood in the context of the classroom, it is necessary to determine the extent to which the problem may be influenced by peer pressure, test anxiety, learning or study problems, low self-esteem, hostility toward a particular teacher (or toward authority figures in general), the child's concern about meeting parents' and teachers' high expectations, stressful family or peer relations, or a fear of humiliation. Cheating is often symptomatic of problems related to learning and social adjustment. Given that children with conduct disorders generally manifest a cluster of behavior problems, ratings scales or checklists may be a helpful way of ascertaining whether cheating is a symptom of a more pervasive antisocial problem. Finally, the child's moral reasoning about cheating should be evaluated. This can be done by asking the child who has been referred for cheating to discuss whether different kinds of cheating are wrong and why.

## Individual Interventions

The therapeutic approaches discussed in the chapters on lying and stealing (chapters 12 and 13) are all applicable to the cheating problem. Parental training approaches are most relevant when cheating is symptomatic of a character disorder or when cheating is a response to parental pressure to succeed. Skills training approaches are helpful in addressing children's difficulties in coping with their schoolwork and with problems of peer acceptance. Behavioral approaches are difficult to apply to cheating because the rewards for cheating are so great in contrast to the risks of being caught. Moreover, students caught cheating are likely to excuse their cheating by saying "everyone is doing it" and they simply had the misfortune of being caught.

Because cheating is so prevalent and widely accepted, interventions with students who cheat will be far more effective in classrooms that have successfully employed the prevention strategies described above. In such cases, students are more likely to feel that by cheating they have let down their fellow students as well as their teachers. Moreover, they will feel motivated to stop cheating if they see their actions as important to membership in a community that they value.

Interventions with students who cheat should help those students understand why cheating is wrong and is prohibited. The five prevention strategies presented in the previous section (Alternative Actions for Prevention) can be adapted for use in the process of disciplining and counseling students who have cheated. For example, students caught cheating could be brought before a committee in which peer discussion of cheating as a moral and community problem would take place. In such a committee, both the teacher and student members should personalize cheating as a violation of a shared expectation of trust. The purpose of such a meeting is not to browbeat the student accused of cheating but to communicate that members of the community take cheating seriously. Members of the committee should balance an expression of disapproval for cheating with an expression of concern for the individual who has cheated. Often in such meetings, students will suggest ways in which students who cheat might become better integrated into the classroom and school community.

Students suspected of cheating should be encouraged to admit to it. All too often the harsh penalties adopted to express strong disapproval of cheating or to deter cheating discourage students from confessing dishonesty. A goal of teachers and the school professionals should be to design the disciplinary process so that students believe it is in their best interest to admit to cheating, if rightfully accused. Of course, if students are wrongfully accused, procedures need to be in place that students believe will give them a fair opportunity to defend themselves.

Many students who cheat do so out of a sense of desperation and inadequacy. Interventions with such students should not stop with moral education but should address the problems that interfere with classroom success. Those problems are typically complex and may range from learning disabilities to maladaptive social behavior.

# SUMMARY

Cheating in school is a growing problem brought about by factors in society and the school as well as in the individual student. Although teachers regard cheating as an antisocial behavior, many children accept cheating as part of coping with the demands of school. Because of its pervasiveness, cheating must be addressed at the level of the classroom, approaches that elicit the cooperation of the teacher and the students. In individual cases, cheating may be symptomatic of a character disorder, of attentional and learning disabilities, and of difficulties in peer and parental relationships. Interventions at the individual level should take into account the extent to which cheating is part of a broader problem or complex of problems.

# RECOMMENDED RESOURCES

## Books and Other Printed Material

Cizek, G. J. (2004). *Detecting and preventing classroom cheating: Promoting integrity in assessment.* Thousand Oaks, CA: Corwin Press.

This is a teacher-friendly resource for understanding and responding to classroom cheating.

Power, F. C., Higgins, A., & Kohlberg, L. (1989). *Lawrence Kohlberg's approach to moral education.* New York: Columbia University Press.

In this book, the authors provide an overview of Kohlberg's theory of moral development and the just community approach to moral education. They discuss how the problem of cheating was resolved through a democratic process of rulemaking.

## Websites

*http://www.academicintegrity.org*

This is the official website of the Center for Academic Integrity (CAI), which is affiliated with the Kenan Institute for Ethics at Duke University in Durham, North Carolina. The website has two tiers. A public tier contains information about the center and its activities. A members-only tier features information about projects and research and an e-mail discussion list for members to exchange ideas and information.

*http://www.charactercounts.org*

This is the website for Character Counts, a broad coalition of schools, communities, and nonpartisan organizations committed to promoting "the six pillars of character: trustworthiness, respect, responsibility, fairness, caring, and citizenship." This website provides free and easy access to a plethora of information, including teaching tools, research, projects, and discussions.

# REFERENCES


Achenbach, T. M. (1993). Taxonomy and comorbidity of conduct problems: Evidence from empirically based approaches. *Development and Psychopathology, 5,* 51–64.

Achenbach, T. M., & Edelbrock, C. (1981). Behavioral problems and competencies reported by parents of normal and disturbed children aged 4 through 16. *Monographs of the Society for Research in Child Development, 46,* 1–82.

American Psychiatric Association. (1994). *Diagnostic and statistical manual of mental disorders* (4th ed.). Washington, DC: Author.

Ames, C. (1992). Classrooms: Goals, structures, and student motivation. *Journal of Educational Psychology, 84,* 261–271.

Anderman, E., Griesinger, T., & Westerfield, G. (1998). Motivation and cheating during early adolescence. *Journal of Educational Psychology, 80,* 84–93.

Anderman, E., & Midgley, C. (2004). Changes in self-reported academic cheating across the transition from middle school to high school. *Contemporary Educational Psychology, 29,* 499–517.

Anderson, L. M. (1989). Classroom instruction. In M. C. Reynolds (Ed.), *Knowledge base for the beginning teacher* (pp. 101–115). Oxford: Pergamon Press.

Bandura, A. (1986). *Social foundations of thought and action: A social cognitive theory.* Englewood Cliffs, NJ: Prentice Hall.

Bandura, A. (1991). Social cognitive theory of moral thought and action. In W. M. Kurtines and J. L. Gewirtz (Eds.), *Handbook of moral behavior and development: Volume 1. Theory.* Hillsdale, NJ: Lawrence Erlbaum Associates.

Bandura, A. (1997). *Self-efficacy: The exercise of control.* New York: W. H. Freeman.

Battistich, V., & Hom, A. (1997). The relationship between students' sense of their school as a community and their involvement in problem behaviors. *American Journal of Public Health, 87,* 1997–2001.

Battistich, V., Schaps, E., Watson, M., Solomon, D., & Lewis, C. (2000). Effects of the Child Development Project on students' drug use and other problem behaviors. *Journal of Primary Prevention, 21,* 75–99.

Blasi, A. (1980). Bridging moral cognition and moral action: A critical review of the literature. *Psychological Bulletin, 88,* 1–45.

Blasi, A. (1995). Moral understanding and the moral personality: The process of moral integration. In

W. M. Kurtines & J. L. Gewirtz (Eds.), *Moral development: An introduction* (pp. 229–253). Boston: Allyn & Bacon.

Blatt, M., & Kohlberg, L. (1975). The effects of classroom moral discussion upon children's moral judgement. *Journal of Moral Education, 4,* 129–161.

Burton, R. V. (1963). Generality of honesty reconsidered. *Psychological Review, 70,* 481–499.

Bushway, A., & Nash, W. R. (1977). School cheating behavior. *Review of Educational Research, 47,* 623–632.

Calabrese, R. L., & Cochran, J. T. (1990). The relationship of alienation to cheating among a sample of American adolescents. *Journal of Research and Development in Education, 23,* 65–72.

Cochran, J. K., Wood, P. B., Sellars, C. S., Wilkerson, W., & Chamlin, M. B. (1998). Academic dishonesty and low social control: An empirical test of a general theory of crime. *Deviant Behavior: An Interdisciplinary Journal, 19,* 227–255.

Colby, A., & Damon, W. (1992). *Some do care: Contemporary lives of moral commitment.* New York: The Free Press.

Colby, A., Kohlberg, L., Fenton, T., Speicher-Dubin, B., & Lieberman, M. (1977). Secondary school moral discussion programmes led by social studies teachers. *Journal of Moral Education, 6,* 90–111.

Davis, S. F., & Ludvigson, H. W. (1995). Additional data on academic dishonesty and a proposal for remediation. *Teaching of Psychology, 22,* 119–121.

Dreeben, R. (1968). *On what is learned in school.* Reading, MA: Addison-Wesley.

Eisenberg, J. (2004). To cheat or not to cheat: Effects of moral perspective and situational variables on students' attitudes. *Journal of Moral Education, 33,* 163–178.

Evans, E. D., & Craig, D. (1990). Teachers and student perceptions of academic cheating in middle and senior high schools. *Journal of Educational Research, 84* (September/October), 44–52.

Finn, K. V., & Frone, M. R. (2004). Academic performance and cheating: Moderating role of school identification and self-efficacy. *Journal of Educational Research, 97,* 115–122.

Hartshorne, H., & May, M. A. (1928–1930). *Studies in the nature of character: Vol. 1. Studies in deceit.* New York: Macmillan.

Higgins, A. (1980). Research and measurement issues in moral education interventions. In R. Mosher (Ed.), *Moral education: A first generation of research and development* (pp. 92–107). New York: Praeger.

Hirschi, T. (1969). *Causes of delinquency.* Berkeley: University of California Press.

Jensen, L. A., Arnett, J. A., Feldman, S. S., & Cauffman, E. (2002). Everybody does it: Academic dishonesty among high school and college students. *Contemporary Educational Psychology, 27,* 209–229.

Johnston, L., Bachman, J., & O'Malley, P. (1990). (1990). *Monitoring the future: A continuing study of the lifestyles and values of youth.* [1989 computer file]. Conducted by University of Michigan, Survey Research Center. ICPSR Ed. Ann Arbor, MI: Inter-University Consortium for Political and Social Research, Producer and Distributor.

Josephson Institute of Ethics. (2004). *Report card on ethics of American youth.* Retrieved February 2, 2005, from http://josephsoninstitute.org/Survey2004

Kazdin, A. E. (1995). *Conduct disorders in childhood and adolescence* (2nd ed.). Thousand Oaks, CA: Sage Publications.

Kohlberg, L. (1970). Education for justice: A modern statement of the Platonic view. In N. Sizer & T. Sizer (Eds.), *Moral education: Five lectures.* Cambridge, MA: Harvard University Press.

Kohlberg, L. (1984). *Essays on moral development: Vol. 2. The psychology of moral development.* San Francisco: Harper and Row.

Kohn, A. (1992). *No contest: The case against competition.* Boston: Houghton Mifflin.

Loeber, R., Lahey, B. B., & Thomas, C. (1991). Diagnostic conundrum of oppositional defiant disorder and conduct disorder. *Journal of Abnormal Psychology, 100,* 379–390.

Michaels, J. W., & Miethe, T. D. (1989). Applying theories of deviance to academic cheating. *Social Science Quarterly, 70,* 870–885.

Murdock, T. B., Hale, N. M., & Weber, M. J. (2001). Predictors of cheating among early adolescents: Academic and social motivators. *Contemporary Educational Psychology, 26,* 96–115.

Murdock, T. B., Miller, A., & Kohlhardt, J. (2004). Effects of classroom context variables on high school students' judgments of the acceptability and likelihood of cheating. *Journal of Education Psychology, 96,* 765–777.

Murphy, J. P. (1993). The nature of cheating. In J. J. Cohen and M. C. Fish (Eds.), The nature of cheating. *The handbook of school-based interventions: Resolving student problems and promoting healthy educational environments* (pp. 18–20). San Francisco: Jossey-Bass.

Nisan, M. (1985). Limited morality: A concept and its educational implications. In M. Berkowitz and F. Oser (Eds.), *Moral education: Theory and application* (pp. 403–420). Hillsdale, NJ: Lawrence Erlbaum Associates.

Nucci, L. P. (2001). *Education in the moral domain.* Cambridge, UK: Cambridge University Press.

Piaget, J. (1932/1965). *The moral judgment of the child.* Glencoe, IL: Free Press.

Pianta, R. C., Stuhlman, M. W., & Hamre, B. K. (2002). How schools can do it better: Fostering stronger connections between students and teachers. *New Directions for Youth Development, 93* (Spring), 91–107.

Piliavin, I., Gartner, R. I., Thornton, C., & Matsueda, R. L. (1986). Crime, deterrence, and rational choice. *American Sociological Review, 51,* 101–119.

Power, F. C., Higgins, A., & Kohlberg, L. (1989). *Lawrence Kohlberg's approach to moral education.* New York: Columbia University Press.

Power, F. C., & Khmelkov, V. T. (1997). The development of the moral self: Implications for moral education. *International Journal of Educational Psychology, 27,* 539–551.

Schab, F. (1991). Schooling without learning: Thirty years of cheating in high school. *Adolescence, 26,* 839–847.

Staub, E. (1978). *Positive social behavior and morality: Vol. 1. Social and personality differences.* New York: Academic Press.

Stricherz, M. (2001). Many teachers ignore cheating, survey finds. *Education Week, 20*(34), 3.

Thorkildsen, T. (1989). Justice and the classroom: The student's view. *Child Development, 60,* 323–334.

Turner, J., & Patrick, H. (2004). Motivational influences of student participation in classroom learning activities. *Teachers College Record, 106,* 1759–1785.

Waller, W. (1932). *The sociology of teaching.* New York: John Wiley & Sons.

# 15

# Depressive Disorders

**Dawn H. S. Reinemann**

*Cardinal Stritch University*

**Kevin D. Stark**
**Johanna Molnar**
**Jane Simpson**

*University of Texas at Austin*

Depressive disorders are increasingly being viewed as potentially chronic, recurrent conditions that often have their origin in youth. When left unidentified and untreated, depression in children and adolescents can lead to long-term adverse outcomes and life-threatening behaviors. Depression negatively affects children's functioning at school, with peers, and at home. It is important for school professionals to recognize the magnitude and clinical importance of this disorder and to become educated regarding the identification, assessment, and treatment of depression in youth (Reynolds, 1990). School psychologists and other school-based mental health service providers can offer education regarding depression to teachers and other school staff so that these personnel can assist in the identification process. School practitioners can directly assess at-risk youngsters, refer those who are experiencing a depressive disorder for treatment, and coordinate school-based intervention efforts with other treatments. In addition, they can develop and implement classroom-based depression prevention programs.

Even though schools have many individuals who are concerned about children's social–emotional and educational development, depressed children and adolescents are typically underdiagnosed. Reasons for this oversight include the fact that depressed children rarely act out and often present with somatic complaints that may confound accurate diagnosis. Furthermore, school psychologists spend a majority of their time evaluating and treating children referred for special education services. However, when depression is discussed, it is usually in regard to regular education students, and the possibility that depressive disorders can co-occur with intellectual deficits and learning disabilities is overlooked (Stark, 1990).

To qualify for psychological and related services in the schools, a child must demonstrate an academic need, which usually presents as poor classroom performance. The symptoms of depression—including anhedonia, negative self-evaluations, difficulty concentrating, indecisiveness, fatigue, and psychomotor disturbances—may lead to decreased academic performance. These symptoms can affect the child's motivation as well as cognitive processing. A depressed child is also likely to engage in negative self-evaluations, which can be detrimental to his or her performance, motivation, and confidence regarding academic achievement (Stark, 1990).

Many school professionals have not had extensive training regarding the ways depression manifests itself during childhood, which may also contribute to underidentification. This problem is serious, because although 1 in 10 youngsters suffer from mental illness serious enough to cause functional impairment, estimates indicate that fewer than 1 in 5 receives any form of treatment (U.S. Public Health Service, 2001). However, with education and training, school practitioners can effectively treat psychological disorders such as depression within the educational setting. It is hoped that this chapter will alert school personnel to the growing problem of childhood depression and that it will promote greater involvement of school practitioners in the identification and treatment of depressed youth.

## BACKGROUND AND DEVELOPMENT

### Definitions

Although depression can be defined as a symptom, syndrome, or disorder, it is most accurately viewed as a *disorder* or a constellation of behaviors and emotions that co-occur for a minimum duration. The *Diagnostic and Statistical Manual of Mental Disorders, Fourth Edition, Text Revision* (DSM-IV-TR; American Psychiatric Association, 2000) recognizes three major diagnostic categories of unipolar depressive disorders: major depressive disorder (MDD), dysthymic disorder (DD), and depressive disorder not otherwise specified (DDNOS). The primary difference between these disorders is the number, severity, and duration of depressive symptoms. All three categories of depressive disorders are associated with significant impairment in current functioning.

The diagnostic criteria for MDD stipulate that five or more symptoms must be present over a 2-week period, including one symptom of either depressed mood, loss of interest or pleasure (anhedonia), or irritability. In addition to the mood disturbance, the syndrome also includes at least four of the following symptoms: (a) changes in weight or failure to make necessary weight gains, (b) sleep disturbance, (c) psychomotor agitation or retardation, (d) fatigue or loss of energy, (e) excessive feelings of worthlessness or guilt, (f) lack of concentration and decision-making ability, (g) suicidal ideation or attempts or plans of suicide (American Psychiatric Association, 2000).

Dysthymic disorder is characterized by a chronic mood disturbance of either dysphoria or anger and at least two other depressive symptoms. These symptoms must be present for a minimum of 1 year without more than two symptom-free months. Children who exhibit depressive symptoms but do not meet the diagnostic criteria for either MDD or DD may receive a diagnosis of DDNOS.

School-age youth can experience all three depressive disorders; however, the manner in which depressive symptoms cluster may vary as a function of development. For example, prepubertal children commonly display depressed appearance, somatic complaints, and social withdrawal, whereas psychomotor retardation, hypersomnia, and delusions are more commonly displayed in adolescence and adulthood (American Psychiatric Association, 2000).

### Prevalence

A relatively large percentage of youth are experiencing a depressive disorder at any given time, and prevalence rates increase with age. Prevalence of depressive disorders in prepubertal children ranges from approximately 1% to 3% for lifetime episodes (Stark, 1990). Prevalence rates dramatically increase around the time of puberty. For example, the National Comorbidity Study (NCS) examined a nationally represented community sample, which included adolescents ages 15–18, and found a lifetime prevalence rate for MDD of 14% (Kessler & Walters, 1998). Moreover, a 10-year longitudinal study found that between the ages of 11 and 15, lifetime prevalence rates of depression increased from 1% to 5.6%, and by age 18, rates increased to approximately 21% (Hankin et al., 1998). Thus, youth appear to be particularly susceptible to the emergence of MDD during the adolescent period.

Fewer studies have examined the prevalence rates of DD. However, it is important to understand the prevalence of DD because it is a serious, long-lasting disturbance that places the youngster at risk for a variety of psychosocial disturbances and the later development of MDD. The Third National Health and Nutrition Examination Survey (NHANES III) indicated that 4.7% of 17- to 19-year-olds had a lifetime history of DD (Jonas, Brody, Roper, & Narrow, 2003).

The gender ratio of depressive disorders during the elementary school years is about equal. However, beginning with the middle school years and extending through high school, the ratio of females to males who are experiencing a depressive disorder progressively increases until adulthood, at which time a 2:1 ratio is evident (Stark, 1990). Gender differences in depression appear to emerge between ages 13 and 15 (Hankin et al., 1998).

### Ethnic, Cultural, and Socioeconomic Differences

The literature on ethnicity and depression suggests that some racial groups experience more severe depression, experience different symptoms, and are less likely to receive help from a mental health professional. Minority students have been found to report higher rates of depression (e.g., Rushton, Forcier, & Schectman, 2003). There may be an increased risk for depression among various subgroups including children from families of lower socioeconomic status (Reinherz, Giaconia, Lefkowitz, Pakiz, & Frost, 1993) and gay, lesbian, and bisexual youth (Anhalt & Morris, 1998). Also, the way that different ethnic groups respond to self-report measures of depressive symptoms may differ. Assessing minority children's, adolescents', and parents' beliefs about depression appears important, such as the meaning that symptoms of depression hold for them and how they are experiencing their symptoms emotionally, physically, and cognitively.

### Comorbidity

Substantial comorbidity exists among youth who evidence depression. For example, it has been estimated that 43% of adolescents with MDD have a lifetime comorbid psychiatric disorder, with anxiety disorders being the most common (Lewinsohn, Rohde, & Seeley, 1998). Depressed youth also often experience comorbid disruptive behavior disorders and substance abuse (Lewinsohn et al.). Youth with comorbid disorders appear to have more negative outcomes and poorer prognoses than those who experience a single disorder (Lewinsohn et al.). In particular, a diagnosis of comorbid depression plus conduct disorder or comorbid depression plus substance abuse increases the risk of suicide in youth. Comorbidity also predicts the use of treatment, with those who have more than one disorder more likely to receive services (Lewinsohn et al.).

### Course and Prognosis

Episodes of MDD and DD during childhood remit naturally. However, children who have experienced an episode of depression are likely to develop a subsequent episode while still in their teens, suggesting that for many youth, depression represents a recurrent, and in some instances chronic, disorder. Furthermore, youth depression is considered a serious risk factor for adult depression (Lewinsohn, Rohde, Klein, & Seeley, 1999). Youngsters who suffer from depressive disorders have impaired social, emotional, behavioral, and academic functioning. Adolescent depression also predicts adverse outcomes in adulthood, including early marriage, marital dissatisfaction, impaired occupational functioning, reduced physical well-being, and potential suicide (e.g., Lewinsohn, Rohde, Seeley, Klein, & Gotlib, 2003). Therefore, primary prevention and early intervention efforts in educational settings become important means by which school professionals can affect the course of depression during children's formative years and throughout their lives.

## PROBLEMS AND IMPLICATIONS

Disturbances in multiple areas of functioning appear to lead to the development and maintenance of a depressive disorder, and different patterns of disturbances may be evident in different children. Thus, the historically dominant unidimensional models of depressive disorders probably present inadequate explanations of the etiology of depression (Stark, 1990). Although major etiological determinants will be reviewed separately for convenience, a more accurate view considers a multidimensional and integrated model that recognizes the reciprocal influence of cognitive, behavioral, interpersonal, and biochemical factors.

### Cognitive Variables

The major cognitive models (e.g., Abramson, Metalsky, & Alloy, 1989; Beck, 1967) are diathesis-stress models in which cognitive variables are assumed to interact with stressful life events to produce depression. In Beck's model, exposure to stressful, negative life events activates maladaptive schemata, which filter and guide the processing of information in a negatively distorted manner. As a result, individuals engage in biased information processing that leads them to hold negative views of the self, world, and future (the negative cognitive triad). The self-schema plays a crucial role in depression and contains cognitive content that is unrealistically negative and characterized by a sense of loss, unlovability, and inadequacy. When activated, the schema leads individuals to seek out and incorporate environmental stimuli that confirm their negative self-view and ignore or distort contradictory evidence. Thus, schema-driven, biased information processing leads to reinforcement of the negative self-schema and cognitive triad, producing and maintaining depression through a feedback loop (Beck, 1967). Beck proposed that such maladaptive schemata develop early in life in response to stress related to real or perceived loss.

According to the learned helplessness/hopelessness model, individuals who evidence a pessimistic (depressogenic) attributional style are vulnerable to developing hopelessness and subsequent depressive symptoms when exposed to negative life events (Abramson et al., 1989). First, individuals are likely to develop hopelessness and subsequent depression when they attribute important negative life events to stable (over time) and global (affecting many areas of life) causes. Second, if individuals believe that adverse consequences of the event are important, are not likely to change, or may lead to other negative consequences, they will be prone to experience hopeless depression. Third, Abramson et al. stressed the importance of the effect the negative life event has on individuals' beliefs about the self, such as worth, abilities, and personality. However, if negative life events do not occur, or if positive events take place, the depressogenic attributional style will not become activated and depression will not develop.

Research has examined the applicability of Beck's (1967) and Abramson et al.'s (1989) cognitive theories of depression to youth. Studies have confirmed an association between each component of the negative cognitive triad and the severity of depressive symptoms in children and have differentiated youngsters with depressive disorders from those with anxiety disorders or no disturbance (e.g., Kaslow, Stark, Printz, Livingston, & Tsai, 1992). Recently, longitudinal research has shown that a negative view of the self and, to a lesser extent, of the future, interacted with stress in the form of exposure to community violence, to predict change in middle school students' depressive symptoms over a 1-year period (Reinemann, Eckert, Brodigan, & Ellison, 2004). Prospective investigations also have found that older children and adolescents who evidence depressogenic attributional styles are more likely to develop subsequent depressive symptoms after experiencing negative life events than those who do not evidence this predisposition (e.g., Robinson, Garber, & Hilsman, 1995). However, for younger children, stressful life events appear to have both a direct and an indirect effect on depressive symptoms through cognitive disturbances. Thus, it appears that cognitive models of depression need to be modified when applied to younger students, as stressful events during this developmental period may in fact lead to the development of the disturbances in cognition (Cole & Turner, 1993). However, the adult models that stipulate that stress and cognition interact to predict depression appear applicable from later childhood into adulthood.

## Behavioral and Interpersonal Variables

Behavioral and interpersonal theories have recently been expanded to explain another possible pathway to the development of depression. According to Joiner, Coyne, and Blalock (1999), "interpersonal experience, especially involving significant others (e.g., parents), affects mood outcomes by laying down a negative and stable view of the interpersonal world" (p. 13). Thus, new theories are integrating cognitive and interpersonal components into their explanation of the etiology of depression.

Interpersonal risk factors for depression include relationship problems and social skills deficits (Joiner, 2002). Depressed youths experience disturbances in interpersonal relationships. They are less popular, less liked, and more likely to be rejected by their peers (e.g., Rudolph & Clark, 2001). Furthermore, the degree of impairment appears to be related to the duration of the depressive episode.

Interpersonal dependency also may serve as a risk factor for depression. When exposed to stress, individuals are likely to seek reassurance. In individuals at risk for depression, information processing biases will affect this reassurance-seeking process. Maladaptive, negative schema lead to increased detection of social stressors and more negative interpretation of these stressors, which in turn lead to greater reassurance seeking. These schemata may also produce ineffective reassurance-seeking behaviors, more negative and ambiguous perceptions of interpersonal feedback, and ultimately depression. Research has shown that excessive reassurance seeking in depressed youth seems to play a role in eliciting negative reactions from peers (Joiner, Metalsky, Katz, & Beach, 1999).

In addition, excessive need for and concern about interpersonal attachment is believed to lead to behaviors that contribute to and maintain depression (Joiner, 2002). Perceived negative parental messages about the self, world, and future, as well as punitive parent–child interchanges, contribute to a negative affective home atmosphere and an insecure parent–child attachment. Within this type of home experience, the child may develop an internal working model of relationships that is dysfunctional and yields a negative core self-schema. When the child is exposed to stressors, this schema guides information processing and subsequent behavior in ways that elicit rejection and isolation, further solidifying the negative self-view and producing and maintaining depression (Stark, Laurent, Livingston, Boswell, & Swearer, 1999).

## Family Variables

***Genetic basis.*** Evidence supports a link between genetic vulnerability and depressive disorders during childhood. Twin studies show higher concordance rates for depressive disorders among monozygotic twins relative to dizygotic twins (see Garber & Horowitz, 2002, for a review). According to Eaves et al. (1997), genes appear to account for between 30% and 50% of the variance in childhood depression. Nonshared environmental factors also appear to play a role in the etiology of depression in youth

(Eaves et al.). However, the roles of genetic and environmental factors are quite complex and likely vary by age and informant (Garber & Horowitz).

***Psychosocial factors.*** Evidence indicates that many depressed youngsters come from disturbed families. Specifically, families of depressed youth are characterized by greater conflict, chaos, abuse and neglect, and harsh parenting. These families also show communication difficulties, less cohesion, and structural disturbances. The tone of the mother–child relationship, and to a somewhat lesser extent the father–child relationship, is characterized as cold, hostile, tense, and at times rejecting. It is likely that a bidirectional relationship exists in which children's depressive symptoms or dysfunctional behavior elicits negative responses from parents, leading to further problematic child behaviors and increased symptomatology (Stark et al., 1999). However, prospective investigations regarding the contributions of the family environment to childhood depression are needed to test such hypotheses (Garber & Horowitz, 2002).

## Psychophysiology and Depression

Psychophysiological variables that have been implicated in the development of depressive disorders in adults and youth include neurotransmitter systems, neuroendocrine dysfunction, biological rhythms, and neuroanatomical abnormalities. The model of depression involving the monoamine neurotransmitter system implicates norepinephrine, serotonin, and dopamine in the expression of depressive symptoms. The central premise is that a decrease in norepinephrine, serotonin, and dopamine produces depression, and an increase in these neurotransmitters alleviates depressive symptoms. Prolonged exposure to stress in genetically vulnerable individuals is believed to affect vital areas of the brain, ultimately leading to the reduction in levels of these monoamines and subsequent symptoms of depression (Thase, Jindal, & Howland, 2002).

The monoamine neurotransmitters and neuroendocrine systems are closely linked. Serotonin and norepinephrine are found in the limbic system, which influences the regulation of eating, sleeping, and emotion. Two endocrine systems, the hypothalamic–pituitary–thyroid (HPT) axis and the hypothalamic–pituitary–adrenal (HPA) axis, are closely linked to depression (Plotsky, Owens, & Nemeroff, 1998). Neuroendocrine dysfunction and the role of both the HPA axis and the HPT axis in depression have been examined in adults and children (Thase et al., 2002). However, findings for youth have been inconsistent. Further investigation is needed to determine the extent to which HPA axis dysfunction is a stable vulnerability marker for depression in children (Garber & Horowitz, 2002). In addition, mild hypothyroidism is seen in some patients with clinical depression, and thyroid hormone replacement decreases depressive symptoms. This relationship between hypothyroidism and depression suggests that the HPT axis is implicated in depressive disorders. However, similar responses to thyroid hormone replacement have not been found in prepubertal depressed children (Burke & Puig-Antich, 1990), suggesting that this response may be mediated by age.

Abnormalities in growth hormone (GH) have been linked to depression. GH release during sleep in depressed prepubertal children has been found to be significantly greater than in controls; however, this pattern has not been found in depressed adolescents (Burke & Puig-Antich, 1990). Thus, age and puberty appear to interact in the control of GH release. Recent investigations comparing depressed youth to their nondepressed counterparts have shown that they secrete less GH in response to pharmacological challenges designed to stimulate the GH system with continued blunted responses following remission of the depressive episode (Dahl et al., 2000). These studies imply that GH system dysregulation may be a marker for depression (Garber & Horowitz, 2002).

Biological rhythms that involve circadian and ultradian rhythms may provide another possible explanation for the biological basis of depression and focus on the mutual influences of the sleep–wake cycle, neuroendocrine activity, and body temperature that follow the daily light–dark cycle. Disruptions in these processes are potential links to the expression of depressive symptoms. Depressed children have demonstrated some sleep abnormalities, including prolonged sleep latencies, reduced REM latencies, and inefficient sleep. However, other studies have failed to find differences in depressed and nondepressed children's electroencephalogram (EEG) sleep patterns (see Garber & Horowitz, 2002, for a review). Results of studies conducted with adolescents are similar to studies with adults and suggest that sleep disturbances associated with depression become more evident with age (Garber & Horowitz).

Finally, several EEG studies of adolescents and adults have reported brain asymmetries in those with depression, including higher right frontal brain activity and lower left frontal brain activity (Davidson, Pizzagalli, &

Nitschke, 2002). According to Davidson et al., left frontal brain regions are more active during positive experiences of emotion, whereas the right frontal regions are more active during negative emotional experiences. Thus, asymmetries in brain activation, in which left hypoactivation occurs, appear to lead to reduced ability to experience positive affect and an increased responsivity to negative stimuli, the hallmark characteristic of those who are depressed. Investigations of infants and toddlers of depressed mothers reveal similar left front hypoactivation, implying that brain activation abnormalities may be genetically transmitted, acquired prenatally, or acquired during early stressful mother–child interactions (Dawson, 1994).

## ALTERNATIVE ACTIONS FOR PREVENTION

Because of the chronicity, severity, long-term adverse effects, and high recurrence rate of depressive disorders, interventions to prevent initial onset or relapse are needed. Results of investigations designed to evaluate prevention programs for depressed youths yield mixed, although generally encouraging, results. Jaycox, Reivich, Gillham, and Seligman (1994) reported that a 12-session prevention program that emphasized training in cognitive and social problem solving reduced the severity of depressive symptoms and behavior problems in the classroom immediately following completion of the program and prevented symptoms from recurring for 6 months. Subsequent research on the program was conducted with groups of middle school students who were identified as being at risk for developing depressive disorders because of the chronic stress of poverty. According to the study, the program significantly reduced depressive symptoms among participants of Latino and Chinese descent but not among African American participants (Muñoz, Penilla, & Urizar, 2002). These results raise important questions about the need for, and potential benefits of, developing culturally sensitive interventions.

Another group of researchers has developed and evaluated a series of manualized cognitive–behavioral programs for the prevention and treatment of depressive disorders in youth, titled Coping with Stress (CWS) and Coping with Depression (CWD), respectively (Clarke et al., 1995; Clarke, Rohde, Lewinsohn, Hops, & Seeley, 1999). Components focus on experiential learning and skills training, with attention to increasing pleasant activities, improving social interaction, and coping with maladaptive thoughts. These programs have been administered in school settings, and the materials can be downloaded at no cost for use by mental health professionals (see Recommended Resources). In an evaluation, adolescents who reported subclinical levels of depressive symptoms, which placed them at risk for developing a depressive disorder, completed the 15-session CWS group prevention program (Clarke et al.). When compared with a "usual care" control condition, the prevention program significantly reduced the number of adolescents who developed diagnosable depressive disorders over a 12-month period. However, because a number of adolescents in the study still developed depressive disorders, additional research is needed in order to identify the variables that predict those who are resilient versus those who subsequently experience depression.

## ALTERNATIVE ACTIONS FOR INTERVENTION

### Pharmacological Interventions

Although antidepressants have been prescribed to depressed youth for many years, until recently little research had been done to support their effectiveness with this population. However, antidepressant medications have demonstrated efficacy for the treatment of depressive disorders in youth.

***Selective serotonin reuptake inhibitors (SSRIs).*** SSRIs increase the amount of serotonin signaling between neurons by preventing reuptake of serotonin. The SSRIs include fluoxetine, sertraline, paroxetine, fluvoxamine, citalopram, and escitalopram (see Table 1). Fluoxetine has the longest record for safety. Thus far, no irreversible damage has been reported from SSRI use in children and adolescents. Fluoxetine was the first antidepressant to receive empirical support with depressed youth and currently has the most empirical support for its efficacy.

Preliminary results of the most ambitious and methodologically rigorous study of the treatment of depression in adolescents are beginning to appear in the literature (March). The Treatment for Adolescents With Depression Study (TADS) evaluated the relative efficacy of fluoxetine, cognitive–behavioral therapy (CBT), a combination of fluoxetine and CBT, and a placebo. Results based on the first 100 participants indicate that 71% of participants receiving fluoxetine and CBT

**Table 1** *Generic and Brand Names of Current Antidepressant Medications*

| Generic Name | Brand Name |
|---|---|
| SSRIs | |
| Citalopram | Celexa |
| Escitalopram | Lexapro |
| Fluoxetine | Prozac |
| Fluvoxamine | Luvox |
| Paroxetine | Paxil |
| Sertraline | Zoloft |
| Atypical Antidepressants | |
| Bupropion | Wellbutrin |
| Mirtazepine | Remeron |
| Nefazodone | Serzone |
| Venlafaxine | Effexor |

no longer reported a diagnosable depressive disorder. In comparison, 61% of those taking fluoxetine alone, 43% of those receiving CBT alone, and 35% of those receiving a placebo were no longer depressed at post-treatment assessment (March).

A number of additional SSRIs have demonstrated efficacy in less ambitious studies. Sertraline (Wagner, Ambrosini, & Ryan, 2003) and citalopram (Wagner et al., 2001) have demonstrated efficacy with depressed youths, and escitalopram is currently being studied for use in pediatric depression in a multisite, controlled trial (Wagner et al., 2003).

Though the SSRIs have demonstrated efficacy for depressed adolescents, their use with this age group remains controversial. Currently, fluoxetine is the only medication approved by the U.S. Food and Drug Administration (FDA) for children and adolescents, yet it is common for psychiatrists and primary care physicians to prescribe other SSRIs. Controversy emerged following a 2003 report by the British Medicines and Healthcare Products Regulatory Agency (MHRA), which concluded that most of the SSRIs do not show benefits that exceed their risks of suicidal ideation and thus should not be prescribed to youth. In response to the MHRA report, the FDA (FDA, 2004) reanalyzed the results of existing drug studies. Results of the reanalysis indicated that youths who took antidepressants were 78% more likely to exhibit suicidal behaviors relative to children who took a placebo. The FDA recommended that paroxetine not be used to treat depression in youth under age 18 and that caution be used when administering other antidepressants to children and adolescents. In addition, parents should be warned of possible suicidality concerns, especially early in treatment. Results of TADS have implications for this debate. Participants in general from all four experimental conditions reported less suicidal ideation with treatment, although five of the medication-only participants attempted suicide compared to only one of the participants in the other conditions that included CBT. The decrease in suicidal ideation in all active treatment groups suggests that the therapies, including fluoxetine, were protective. The FDA has not yet responded to the results of TADS.

***Alternate antidepressants.*** A number of antidepressants also have been developed that affect other neurotransmitters (see Table 1). None of these medications have been approved by the FDA for treatment of depressed youths, although bupropion-SR has demonstrated efficacy with depressed youth (Daviss et al., 2001). Although nefazodone has also demonstrated efficacy in a clinical trial of 28 depressed children and adolescents (Findling et al., 2000), the FDA required that a "black box" warning be added to the product information as a result of nefazodone's association with liver abnormalities, liver failure, and death. Other antidepressants have not demonstrated efficacy with depressed youth. Thus, additional research into the effectiveness of psychopharmacological treatments is necessary.

## Psychosocial Interventions

This is a very exciting time in the study of the treatment of depression in children and adolescents. After decades of surprisingly little research, large-scale, methodologically rigorous, multisite, multiyear investigations are underway. The majority of evaluations of psychosocial treatments to date have evaluated CBT. In reviews of the existing literature, CBT has been classified as possibly efficacious for depressed children and probably efficacious for depressed adolescents (Kaslow & Thompson, 1998) according to the criteria for empirically supported treatments (Chambless & Hollon, 1998). However, given the preliminary results of TADS, the combination of CBT and medication may prove more efficacious than CBT alone. The following sections briefly examine a few of the promising treatments for depressed adolescents and children.

***Psychosocial treatment with adolescents.*** One of the interventions that has received empirical support is Clarke et al.'s (1999) Coping with Depression Course (CWDC). The CWDC is a cognitive–behavioral intervention that is delivered to large groups of adolescents. The program consists of 16 two-hour meetings delivered over 8 weeks. Participants are educated about the nature of depression and are provided with a cognitive–behavioral rationale for treatment. During subsequent meetings, participants are taught a variety of behavioral and cognitive skills. Self-monitoring is used to help the participants become more aware of their moods and the strategies that they use to try to improve mood, including pleasant events scheduling. Participants are taught to identify and change negative thoughts. In addition to these core cognitive–behavioral treatment components, CWDC teaches participants social skills, skills for improving communication and decreasing conflict, and skills for reducing anxiety. The skills are taught through didactic presentations, coaching, rehearsal, and feedback and are applied through structured homework assignments. Evaluations of the CWDC have shown that recovery rates for depressed adolescents in the program were greater than for those in a wait-list control group, and improvements were maintained over two years (Clarke et al., 1995; Clarke et al., 1999).

Another form of psychosocial treatment for depressed adolescents is Interpersonal Therapy for Adolescents (IPT-A; e.g., Mufson & Fairbanks, 1996). The primary therapeutic goals of IPT-A are to decrease depressive symptoms and to improve interpersonal functioning. To accomplish these goals, the youngster and therapist identify one or two problem areas from among the following: grief, interpersonal role disputes, role transitions, interpersonal deficits, and single-parent families.

Treatment is divided into three phases of four sessions each. During the initial phase, problem areas are identified, a rationale for treatment is provided, a formal therapeutic contract is written and signed, and the adolescent's role in therapy is defined. Some psychological education about the nature and effects of depression is provided to the youngster and parents. The therapist works with the youngster and parents together to ensure that the child is socially engaged in the family, in school, and with friends. Parents are asked to encourage their child to engage in as many normal activities as possible.

During the middle phase of treatment, the nature of each previously identified problem is clarified, effective strategies for attacking the problems are identified, and relevant plans are developed and implemented. When developing plans, an overarching goal is to improve interpersonal functioning. Youngsters are taught to monitor the experience of depressive symptoms and their emotional experiences.

The primary objectives of the final phase are to prepare the youngster for the program's termination and to establish a sense of personal competence for dealing with future problems. The youngster's feelings about termination are discussed and feelings of competence are engendered.

A pilot study of IPT-A conducted with 14 depressed adolescents (Mufson & Fairbanks, 1996) provided initial support for the treatment; at 1-year follow-up, only one adolescent met criteria for an affective disorder. A controlled trial with 48 depressed adolescents (Mufson, Moreau, Weissman, & Garfinkel, 1999) demonstrated that participants who received IPT-A experienced a greater decrease in depressive symptoms, were more likely to meet recovery criteria, and experienced greater improvement in social functioning and social problem solving than participants in the control group.

CBT and IPT-A share numerous treatment components that may account for their efficacy (Stark et al., 1999). An artful cognitive–behavioral therapist is likely to apply treatment strategies to interpersonal difficulties when those are the source of distress for a youngster, reducing the distinction between the two interventions. The primary difference between the implementation of the two treatments is that CBT includes cognitive restructuring and IPT-A does not. However, changing interactions between children and parents is a powerful way to change children's thinking about relationships as well as their self-perceptions of lovability.

***Psychosocial treatment with children.*** Currently, Stark is starting the third year of a large-scale investigation of the efficacy of CBT with and without parent training for the treatment of girls between the ages of 9 and 13 who are depressed. The intervention is gender specific and developmentally sensitive, and it is being conducted within the schools. The CBT condition consists of 20 group sessions and two individual meetings completed over 11 weeks. A treatment manual has been developed to ensure consistency in the implementation of the treatment (Stark et al., 2005). The girls participate in education about the nature of depression and set personal goals for treatment. Goals are tied to the acquisition of coping, problem-solving, and cognitive-restructuring skills. In addition, the girls participate in activities that are designed to enhance their sense of self. Skills are learned through in-session activities and applied through therapeutic homework. The delivery format is more intense in frequency of meetings and duration of treatment relative to interventions used in other investigations with depressed children. Parent training consists of eight meetings completed over the same 11 weeks. Parents learn positive behavior management strategies, problem-solving skills, empathic listening, communication skills, conflict management skills, and methods for helping their daughters to think more positively. The girls are present during half of the meetings so that the parents can practice the skills that they are learning. Preliminary results with the first 62 participants are very promising and suggest that more children improve through treatment than from the normal passage of time.

Trials of CBT with children and younger adolescents have shown generally positive results in comparisons with no treatment (Butler, Miezitis, Friedman, & Cole, 1980; Weisz, Thurber, Sweeney, Proffitt, & LeGagnoux, 1997), attention placebo (Butler et al.), and traditional school counseling groups (Stark, 1990). However, when CBT is compared with other types of treatments, several studies have found no differences in children's outcomes. It is important to note that most of these studies compared CBT and a similar type of treatment and determined that both were effective in reducing symptoms (e.g., Liddle & Spence, 1990).

## SUMMARY

Prevalence rates of depressive disorders in youth dramatically increase during adolescence. Depression adversely affects youngsters' functioning and may lead to long-term impairment. School psychologists and other school-based mental health service providers can assist in the identification, assessment, and treatment of depression within the school setting. Knowledge about variables that contribute to the onset and maintenance of depressive disorders will aid professionals in the development of appropriate interventions. According to cognitive theories of depression, youngsters experiencing a depressive disorder hold negative views of the self, world, and future, and they have a pessimistic (depressogenic) attributional style for explaining the causes of life events. Such depressive cognitive styles likely are formed through early caregiver attachments and learning experiences within the family. Depressed children and adolescents also experience social skills deficits, leading to interpersonal rejection. As in adults, genetic and biochemical factors also appear to play a role in the development and maintenance of depressive disorders in youth. Prevention programs designed to reduce the incidence of depressive disorders in the general population or in those at risk have shown preliminary promise and can be implemented in small group or classroom settings. Pharmacological interventions are often implemented with depressed youngsters, and ongoing evaluation of the efficacy of their use is crucial. Recent research indicates that a combination of medication and cognitive–behavioral therapy may be the most effective treatment for childhood depression.

## RECOMMENDED RESOURCES

### Books and Other Printed Material

Gotlib, I. H., & Hammen, C. L. (Eds.). (2002). *Handbook of depression.* New York: Guilford Press.

This book provides the reader with a comprehensive review of the current state of depression research, with writings by some of the most prominent experts on the topic. Major sections of the book focus on (a) the descriptive aspects of depression, such as prevalence rates, course, and outcome; (b) vulnerability, risk, and etiological models of depression; (c) prevention and treatment; and (d) depression in specific populations. Specific chapters provide in-depth coverage of depression and its treatment in children and adolescents.

Stark, K. D. (1990). *The treatment of depression during childhood: A school-based program.* New York: Guilford Press.

This book provides background information about the nature of depressive disorders during childhood from the perspective of a psychologist working in the schools. It includes discussion of symptoms, diagnosis, special education classification, prevalence, natural course, and comorbid conditions associated with depression during the elementary school years. A school-based identification and assessment model are described as well as an empirically based treatment program for depressed youth.

Stark, K. D., Laurent, J., Livingston, R., Boswell, J., & Swearer, S. (1999). Implications of research for the treatment of depressive disorders during childhood. *Applied & Preventive Psychology, 8,* 79–102.

This article provides an overview of depressive disorders in childhood, with an emphasis on implications of research on treatment. It includes an integrated model of depressive disorders in youth that encompasses biological, interpersonal and family, and cognitive factors. It includes a major section on alternative forms of treatment for depressed youth, including pharmacotherapy, interpersonal therapy, and Stark's cognitive-behavioral treatment program.

## Websites

*http://www.nimh.nih.gov/healthinformation/depressionmenu.cfm*

This website of the National Institute of Mental Health provides comprehensive general information about depression. It provides basic information on symptomatology and treatment options. It also includes research updates and information regarding depression resources and publications.

*http://www.dbsalliance.org*

This website of the Depression and Bipolar Support Alliance provides general information about depression and bipolar disorders. It includes resources to locate treatment professionals and information on support groups and chapters throughout the country.

*http://www.kpchr.org/public/acwd/acwd.html*

This website makes available free downloads of Clarke et al.'s (1995) Coping With Depression Course. Mental health professionals may download group treatment or group prevention programs, as well as individual treatment and parent intervention manuals.

*https://trialweb.dcri.duke.edu/tads*

This website provides an overview of the Treatment for Adolescents with Depression Study (TADS), including information on its organization and participating locations. It also provides answers to commonly asked questions about the study.

## REFERENCES

Abramson, L. Y., Metalsky, G. I., & Alloy, L. B. (1989). Hopelessness depression: A theory-based subtype of depression. *Psychological Review, 96,* 358–372.

American Psychiatric Association. (2000). *Diagnostic and statistical manual of mental disorders* (4th ed., text revision). Washington, DC: Author.

Anhalt, K., & Morris, T. L. (1998). Developmental and adjustment issues of gay, lesbian, and bisexual adolescents: A review of the empirical literature. *Clinical Child and Family Psychology Review, 1,* 215–230.

Beck, A. T. (1967). *Depression: Clinical, experimental and theoretical aspects.* New York: Harper & Row.

Burke, P., & Puig-Antich, J. (1990). Psychobiology of childhood depression. In M. Lewis & S. M. Miller (Eds.), *Handbook of developmental psychopathology* (pp. 327–339). New York: Plenum Press.

Butler, L., Miezitis, S., Friedman, R., & Cole, E. (1980). The effect of two school-based intervention programs on depressive symptoms in preadolescents. *American Educational Research Journal, 17,* 111–119.

Chambless, D. L., & Hollon, S. D. (1998). Defining empirically supported therapies. *Journal of Consulting and Clinical Psychology, 66,* 7–18.

Clarke, G. N., Hawkins, W., Murphy, M., Sheeber, L. B., Lewinsohn, P. M., & Seeley, J. R. (1995). Targeted prevention of unipolar depressive disorder in an at-risk sample of high school adolescents: A randomized trial of a group cognitive intervention. *Journal of the American Academy of Child and Adolescent Psychiatry, 34,* 312–321.

Clarke, G. N., Rohde, P., Lewinsohn, P. M., Hops, H., & Seeley, J. R. (1999). Cognitive-behavioral treatment of adolescent depression: Efficacy of acute group treatment and booster sessions. *Journal of the American Academy of Child and Adolescent Psychiatry, 38,* 272–279.

Cole, D., & Turner, J., Jr. (1993). Models of cognitive mediation and moderation in child depression. *Journal of Abnormal Psychology, 102,* 271–281.

Dahl, R. E., Birmaher, B., Williamson, L. D., Perel, J., Kaufman, J., Brent, D. A., et al. (2000). Low growth hormone response to growth hormone-releasing hormone in child depression. *Biological Psychiatry, 48,* 981–988.

Davidson, R. J., Pizzagalli, D., & Nitschke, J. B. (2002). The representation and regulation of emotion in depression: Perspectives from affective neuroscience. In I. H. Gotlib & C. L. Hammen (Eds.), *Handbook of depression* (pp. 219–244). New York: Guilford Press.

Daviss, W. B, Bentivoglio, P., Racusin, R., Brown, K., Bostic, J., & Wiley, L. (2001). Bupropion sustained release in adolescents with comorbid attention-deficit/hyperactivity and depression. *Journal of the American Academy of Child and Adolescent Psychiatry, 40,* 307–314.

Dawson, G. (1994). Development of emotional expression and emotion regulation in infancy: Contributions of the frontal lobe. In G. Dawson & K. W. Fischer (Eds.), *Human behavior and the developing brain* (pp. 346–379). New York: Guilford Press.

Eaves, L. J., Silberg, J. L., Meyer, J. M., Maes, H. H., Simonoff, E., Pickles, A., et al. (1997). Genetics and developmental psychopathology: 2. The main effects of genes and environment on behavioral problems in the Virginia Twin Study of Adolescent Behavioral Development. *Journal of Child Psychology and Psychiatry, 38,* 965–980.

Federal Drug Administration (2004). *FDA updates its review of antidepressant drugs in children: Agency details plans to present data to advisory committees in September and seek advice on appropriate regulatory actions.* Retrieved August 28, 2004, from http://www.fda.gov/bbs/topics/ANSWERS/2004/ANS01306.html

Findling, R. L., Preskorn, S. H., Marcus, R. N., Magnus, R. D., D'Amico, F., Marathe, P., et al. (2000). Nefazodone pharmacokinetics in depressed children and adolescents. *Journal of the American Academy of Child and Adolescent Psychiatry, 39,* 1008–1016.

Garber, J., & Horowitz, J. L. (2002). Depression in children. In I. H. Gotlib & C. L. Hammen (Eds.), *Handbook of depression* (pp. 510–540). New York: Guilford Press.

Hankin, B. L., Abramson, L. Y., Moffitt, T. E., Silva, P. A., McGee, R., & Angell, K. E. (1998). Development of depression from preadolescence to young adulthood: Emerging gender differences in a 10-year longitudinal study. *Journal of Abnormal Psychology, 107,* 128–140.

Jaycox, L. H., Reivich, K. J., Gillham, J., & Seligman, M. E. P. (1994). Prevention of depressive symptoms in school children. *Behavior Research and Therapy, 32,* 801–816.

Joiner, T. E. (2002). Depression in its interpersonal context. In I. H. Gotlib & C. L. Hammen (Eds.), *Handbook of depression* (pp. 295–313). New York: Guilford Press.

Joiner, T. E., Coyne, J. C., & Blalock, J. (1999). On the interpersonal nature of depression: Overview and synthesis. In T. E. Joiner & J. C. Coyne (Eds.), *Advances in interpersonal approaches: The interactional nature of depression* (pp. 3–19). Washington, DC: American Psychological Association.

Joiner, T. E., Metalsky, G. I., Katz, J., & Beach, S. R. H. (1999). Depression and excessive reassurance-seeking. *Psychological Inquiry, 10,* 269–278.

Jonas, B. S., Brody, D., Roper, M., & Narrow, W. E. (2003). Prevalence of mood disorders in a national sample of young American adults. *Social Psychiatry and Psychiatric Epidemiology, 38,* 618–624.

Kaslow, N. J., Stark, K. D., Printz, B., Livingston, R., & Tsai, Y. (1992). Cognitive Triad Inventory for Children: Development and relationship to depression and anxiety. *Journal of Clinical Child Psychology, 21,* 339–347.

Kaslow, N. J., & Thompson, M. P. (1998). Applying the criteria for empirically supported treatments to studies of psychosocial interventions for child and adolescent depression. *Journal of Clinical Child Psychology, 27,* 146–155.

Kessler, R. C., & Walters, E. E. (1998). Epidemiology of DSM-III-R major depression and minor depression among adolescents and young adults in the National Comorbidity Survey. *Depression and Anxiety, 7,* 3–14.

Lewinsohn, P. M., Rohde, P., Klein, D. M., & Seeley, J. R. (1999). Natural course of adolescent major depressive disorder: I. Continuity into young adulthood. *Journal of the American Academy of Child and Adolescent Psychiatry, 38,* 56–63.

Lewinsohn, P. M., Rohde, P., & Seeley, J. R. (1998). Major depressive disorder in older adolescents: Prevalence, risk factors, and clinical implications. *Clinical Psychology Review, 18,* 765–794.

Lewinsohn, P. M., Rohde, P., Seeley, J. R, Klein, D. N., & Gotlib, I. H. (2003). Psychosocial functioning of young adults who have experienced and recovered from major depressive disorder during adolescence. *Journal of Abnormal Psychology, 112,* 353–363.

Liddle, B., & Spence, S. H. (1990). Cognitive behaviour therapy with depressed primary school children: A cautionary note. *Behavioural Psychotherapy, 18,* 85–102.

March, J. (2004). The Treatment for Adolescents with Depression Study (TADS): Short-term effectiveness and safety outcomes. *Journal of the American Medical Association, 292,* 807–820.

Mufson, L., & Fairbanks, J. (1996). Interpersonal psychotherapy for depressed adolescents: A one-year naturalistic follow-up study. *Journal of the American Academy of Child and Adolescent Psychiatry, 35*(9), 1145–1155.

Mufson, L., Moreau, D., Weissman, M. M., & Garfinkel, R. (1999). Efficacy of interpersonal psychotherapy for depressed adolescents. *Archives of General Psychiatry, 56,* 573–579.

Muñoz, R. F., Penilla, C., & Urizar, G. (2002). Expanding depression prevention research with children of diverse cultures. *Prevention & Treatment 5,* Article 13. Retrieved August 16, 2004, from http://journals.apa.org/prevention/volume5/pre0050013c.html

Plotsky, P. M., Owens, M. J., & Nemeroff, C. B. (1998). Psychoneuroendocrinology of depression: Hypothalamic-pituitary-adrenal axis. *The Psychiatric Clinics of North America, 21,* 293–307.

Reinemann, D. H., Eckert, L., Brodigan, M., & Ellison, P. A. (2004). *Stress and cognitive triad interact to predict depressive symptoms 1 year later in urban children.* Manuscript in preparation, University of Wisconsin-Milwaukee.

Reinherz, H. Z., Giaconia, R. M., Lefkowitz, E. S., Pakiz, B., & Frost, A. K. (1993). Prevalence of psychiatric disorders in a community population of older adolescents. *Journal of the American Academy of Child and Adolescent Psychiatry, 32,* 369–377.

Reynolds, W. M. (1990). Depression in children and adolescents: Nature, diagnosis, assessment, and treatment. *School Psychology Review, 19,* 158–174.

Robinson, N. S., Garber, J., & Hilsman, R. (1995). Cognitions and stress: Direct and moderating effects of depressive versus externalizing symptoms during the junior high school transition. *Journal of Abnormal Psychology, 104,* 453–463.

Rudolph, K. D., & Clark, A. G. (2001). Conceptions of relationships in children with depressive and aggressive symptoms: Social-cognitive distortion or reality? *Journal of Abnormal Child Psychology, 29,* 41–56.

Rushton, J. L., Forcier, M., & Schectman, R. M. (2003). Epidemiology of depressive symptoms in the national longitudinal study of adolescent health. *Journal of the American Academy of Child and Adolescent Psychiatry, 41,* 199–205.

Stark, K. D. (1990). *The treatment of depression during childhood: A school-based program.* New York: Guilford Press.

Stark, K. D., Laurent, J., Livingston, R., Boswell, J., & Swearer, S. (1999). Implications of research for the treatment of depressive disorders during childhood. *Applied & Preventive Psychology, 8,* 79–102.

Stark, K. D., Schnoebelen, S., Simpson, J., Hargrave, J., Glenn, R., & Molnar, J. (2005). *Treating depressed children: Therapist manual for "ACTION."* Ardmore, PA: Workbook Publishing.

Thase, M. E., Jindal, R., & Howland, R. H. (2002). Biological aspects of depression. In I. H. Gotlib & C. L. Hammen (Eds.), *Handbook of depression* (pp. 192–218). New York: Guilford Press.

U.S. Public Health Service. (2001). *Report of the surgeon general's conference on children's mental health: A national action agenda.* Washington, DC: U.S. Department of Health and Human Services.

Wagner, K. D., Ambrosini, P., & Ryan, M. (2003). Efficacy of sertraline in the treatment of children and adolescents with major depressive disorder: Two randomized controlled trials. *Journal of the American Medical Association, 290,* 1033–1041.

Wagner, K. D., Robb, A. S., Findling, R., et al. (2001, December). *Citalopram is effective in the treatment of major depressive disorder in children and adolescents: Results of a placebo-controlled trial.* Poster presented at the 40th meeting of the American College of Neuropsychopharmacology, Waikoloa, HI.

Weisz, J. R., Thurber, C. A., Sweeney, L., Proffitt, V. D., & LeGagnoux, G. L. (1997). Brief treatment of mild-to-moderate child depression using primary and secondary control enhancement training. *Journal of Consulting and Clinical Psychology, 65,* 703–707.

# 16

# Bipolar Disorders

**Nicholas Lofthouse**
**Mary A. Fristad**
*Ohio State University*

## BACKGROUND AND DEVELOPMENT

Over the past decade, bipolar disorder in children has received increasing attention from the scientific community, media, and general public (see review by Lofthouse & Fristad, 2004). Although interest has grown, continued research is essential, as bipolar disorder in children often devastates family life, school functioning, and peer relationships. If left untreated, it may have a prolonged, highly relapsing course; be less responsive to treatment; and lead to legal difficulties, multiple hospitalizations, and increased rates of substance abuse and suicide (Findling, Kowatch, & Post, 2003; Geller et al., 2003). Despite the detrimental effects of bipolar disorder, few studies have examined the specific effects it has on academic performance, school behavior and peer functioning, clinical–educational implications, or treatment options. This chapter describes the presentation of bipolar disorder in children, its development, specific problems in the school environment, and interventions.

### Definition of Key Concepts and Terms

Various terms have been used to describe bipolar disorder in children, including pediatric, juvenile, early-onset, childhood, and prepubescent bipolar disorder. However, the singular term *bipolar disorder* is misleading, as there appear to be a group of disorders (bipolar I [BP-I], bipolar II [BP-II], cyclothymia, and bipolar not otherwise specified [BP-NOS]). A more fitting reference frequently used in the adult literature is *bipolar spectrum disorders* (Akiskal, 1983). Furthermore, because of differences between adult-onset and childhood- or adolescent-onset bipolar spectrum disorders (see discussion below), the term *early-onset bipolar spectrum disorder* (EOBPSD) is used when describing bipolar disorders that occur in persons younger than 18.

Although no epidemiological studies currently exist for children, Lewinsohn, Klein, and Klein's (1995) community school survey of 14- to 18-year-olds found lifetime prevalence rates for BP-I to be about 0.12% and for BP-II and cyclothymia to be about 1%. They reported an additional 5.7% with subthreshold symptoms, multiple comorbidities, and associated psychosocial impairment, which may constitute a group of adolescents with BP-NOS. By comparison, the cross-national lifetime prevalence for adults with bipolar spectrum disorders ranges from 3% to 6% (Weissman et al., 1996). A retrospective survey of 500 National Depressive and Manic-Depressive Association group members self-identified with "bipolar illness" found that nearly one-third (31%) recalled a variety of depressive and manic symptoms during childhood. An additional 28% reported onset during adolescence. Thus, over half of adults in this survey reported that their symptoms began prior to adulthood (Lish, Dime-Meenan, Whybrow, Price, & Hirschfeld, 1994).

According to the *Diagnostic and Statistical Manual of Mental Disorders, Fourth Edition* (DSM-IV; American Psychiatric Association, 1994), the four types of bipolar disorder can be distinguished on the basis of the frequency and severity of manic and depressive symptoms. An episode of mania involves a 1-week period or more (no duration, if hospitalized) of persistently and excessively elevated mood (i.e., inappropriately happy) or irritable mood (i.e., temper tantrums and rages out of proportion to events) that causes an observable change in functioning. A less severe and durable episode of mania, called hypomania, is characterized by a mood alteration of at least 4 days but without any noticeable functional impairment. For both mania and hypomania, altered mood is accompanied by three or more (four, if mood is irritable and not elated) other symptoms. These symptoms include inflated self-esteem or grandiosity; decreased need for sleep; rapid, loud, or uninterruptible speech; racing thoughts; increased distractibility; increased goal-directed activity or psychomotor agitation; and excessive involvement in pleasurable or dangerous activities.

A major depressive episode involves a sad, empty, or irritable mood or a loss of interest and pleasure in previously enjoyable activities that lasts most of the day, nearly every day, for a 2-week period or longer. The depressed mood and/or loss of interest or pleasure is accompanied by three or four additional symptoms (for a total of five symptoms). These symptoms include insomnia or hypersomnia, significant weight loss or gain, fatigue, psychomotor agitation or retardation, difficulty concentrating, feelings of worthlessness or excessive guilt, and recurrent thoughts of death or suicide.

With regard to the four DSM-IV types of EOBPSD, BP-I is characterized by at least one manic episode, with or without a major depressive episode. The diagnosis of BP-I can be further specified by noting the nature (manic, hypomanic, depressed, or mixed) of the current and previous mood episodes. BP-II is typified by the occurrence of one or more major depressive episodes and one or more hypomanic episodes, without any history of a manic or mixed episode. Cyclothymic disorder is not as severe as either BP-I or BP-II, but the condition is more chronic, lasting for 1 year or more in children and adolescents. In contrast, BP-NOS is a disorder with bipolar features that does not meet the criteria for BP-I, BP-II, or cyclothymic disorder.

Accurate diagnosis of children with EOBPSD requires that bipolar symptoms be differentiated from normal behaviors of childhood. For example, children may become elated, giddy, and silly several days before a trip to Disneyland. However, if this mood change is extreme (e.g., described by parents as "out of the blue" or "way too high") in reaction to ongoing events, it may be diagnostically significant. Similarly, children often engage in imaginative play in which they assume many roles, such as teacher, fireman, or superhero. This is typical in the context of play; however, this behavior becomes problematic when the child continues to assume such roles outside the context of play. For example, instead of pretending to instruct an imaginary classroom full of students, a child with EOBPSD may stand up in class and begin teaching her classmates because she believes she has more knowledge than the teacher.

EOBPSDs are some of the most difficult childhood disorders to assess, diagnose, and classify. Not only must clinicians differentiate clinically significant grandiosity and elation from normal temperamental differences in childhood, such as recklessness and bragging, they need to identify and discriminate EOBPSD symptoms from symptoms of other psychological and behavioral disorders, such as Attention Deficit Hyperactivity Disorder (ADHD), oppositional defiant disorder (ODD), and conduct disorder (CD); learning disabilities and various anxiety, psychotic, and pervasive developmental disorders; medical disorders; substance abuse; and poor child-rearing (Kowatch et al., 2005). In addition, clinicians must identify the presence of manic symptoms in terms of a significant change from baseline, even if that baseline is already disrupted by another condition such as ADHD. In that case, the overlapping manic symptoms of distractibility, psychomotor agitation, involvement in dangerous activities, and pressure to keep talking must increase, along with a change in mood, above and beyond the baseline ADHD symptoms of inattention, hyperactivity, and impulsivity.

Another problem with accurately diagnosing EOBPSD is that manic symptoms in children may not be clearly episodic. However, the child still must show evidence of waxing and waning mood symptoms that frequently arise unexpectedly and are often unrelated to environmental events. During the altered (expansive, euphoric, or irritable) mood state, additional manic symptoms (e.g., grandiosity, racing thoughts, and decreased need for sleep) also must be present. Additional areas to assess include a thorough family, developmental, medical, social, and school history to understand symptom manifestation in the larger context of the child's life. Finally, a life chart should be developed to clearly demarcate onset, duration, severity, impairment, and offset of mood symptoms during the child's life to further distinguish the variety of EOBPSD subtype (BP-I, BP-II, cyclothymia, or BP-NOS). For a more detailed review of key issues and methods related to the assessment of EOBPSD, see Quinn and Fristad (2004).

## Developmental Aspects of EOBPSD

Although the etiology of EOBPSD is not known, substantial evidence in the adult literature and more recent research with children and adolescents suggest a biological basis involving genetics, various neurochemicals, and certain affected brain regions (see review by Findling et al., 2003). Because EOBPSD appears to have biological origins that affect brain functioning, and as it is not intentional or caused by bad parenting, it can be considered a no-fault brain disorder. The initial manifestation of EOBPSD can be activated, and its developmental course exacerbated, by certain environmental factors, such as family, teacher, or peer conflict; academic stress; and disruption in the sleep–wake cycle (see review by Lofthouse & Fristad, 2004). Therefore, EOBPSD is best conceptualized as a biopsychosocial disorder and, as such, requires biopsychosocial interventions.

Regarding the onset of EOBPSD, Quinn, Lofthouse, Fristad, and Dingus (2004) found that parents reported their 8- to 11-year-old children's manic and depressive symptoms starting at 8.8 and 8.6 years, respectively. In an interesting finding, the ages of onset reported by their children were younger: at ages 8.3 and 7.8 for symptoms of mania and depression, respectively. Currently, no studies exist charting the early development of EOBPSD from infancy to early childhood. However, the clinical history of children with EOBPSD, from toddler years or even infancy, often includes reports of intense colic that evolves into ongoing extreme irritability, "terrible two's" that morph into "terrifying three's," and beyond. Many such children have preexisting problems with ADHD, ODD, CD, anxiety, and depression long before they are actually diagnosed with EOBPSD (McClellan, Werry, & Ham, 1993; Werry, McClellan, & Chard, 1991). It is important to note, however, that most children with colic and difficulties at ages 2 and 3 do not develop EOBPSD.

Retrospective research on 8- to 11-year-old children with EOBPSD (Kljun, Lofthouse, Fristad, & Dingus, 2004) suggests that the majority (77%) of parents recalled their children experienced past behavior problems in school and had previous special education services (80%). More than half of the parents reported their children continue to have current behavior problem at school (55%) and receive special education services (64%). The only longitudinal study to date of children with EOBPSD (Geller, Tillman, Craney, & Bolhofner, 2004) followed a sample of 86 7- to 16-year-olds diagnosed with BP-I for 4 years. Although most of these youth were in treatment of some kind, at 6 months most participants (86%) still met criteria for mania. Rates of recovery (defined as 8 consecutive weeks without any DSM-IV diagnoses of mania or hypomania) and of relapse (defined as 2 consecutive weeks with DSM-IV diagnoses of mania or hypomania) were reported at 6-month, 2-year, and 4-year follow-up. Although many youth with EOBPSD recovered over time, the mean time for recovery became longer between the 2- and 4-year assessments. After recovery, they relapsed at an increasingly higher rate over time, but the mean time to relapse after recovery also lengthened. For instance, at 6 months after baseline, recovery rates were low (14%), but they rose quite dramatically 1, 2, and 4 years later (37%, 65%, and 87%, respectively). Relapse rates after recovery followed a similar pattern, starting low at 6 months (16.7%), then increasing at 1, 2, and 4 years' follow-up (38%, 55%, and 64%, respectively). Furthermore, polarity switches, from mania and hypomania to MDD and minor depression, occurred on average 1.1 times every year.

Geller et al. (2004) also found low maternal–child warmth predicted relapse at the 2- and 4-year follow-up interviews, similar to research in the adult literature on the deleterious effect of high "expressed emotion" (which, in this case, refers to an intrusive, critical, or overinvolved style of interacting within a family) on the course of bipolar disorder in adults. Although the Geller study requires replication, no other characteristics of baseline symptoms that were assessed (e.g., MDD, ODD or CD, psychosis, mixed mania, continuous cycling, or global functioning) predicted relapse. However, the presence of psychosis at baseline did predict longer manic and hypomanic episodes.

Very little research has examined how EOBPSD may manifest differently with age. In comparison to adults, who are more likely to present with discrete cycles of mania and depression, children with EOBPSD may exhibit both manic and depressive symptoms at the same time or within the same day (Kowatch et al., 2005). Mood shifts in children are characterized by mixed states (i.e., simultaneous manic and depressive symptoms) and by rapid cycling (i.e., four or more mood episodes per year) and short duration (e.g., several hours, several times daily for several days in a row). Whereas mood states in adults with bipolar disorder are often expressed as euphoric or sad, manic and depressive moods in children often manifest as intense irritability. For children, this atypical presentation of symptoms often fails to meet the diagnostic criteria associated with BP-I, BP-II, or cyclothymia. Therefore, many children with EOBPSD are given the catchall diagnosis BP-NOS.

With respect to prognosis, as previously described, EOBPSD may include a prolonged and highly relapsing course; significant impairments in home, school, and peer functioning; legal difficulties; multiple hospitalizations; and increased rates of substance abuse and suicide. In short, children with EOBPSD have a chronic brain disorder that is biopsychosocial in nature and, at this current time, cannot be cured or grown out of. However, children and their families can buffer themselves against further impairment by learning to manage dysfunctional mood, related comorbid symptoms, and environmental stressors. Means to do so are described later in this chapter. The more families can minimize symptoms and stressors, the closer children can come to experiencing normal developmental functioning.

## PROBLEMS AND IMPLICATIONS

### Problems Caused by the Core Manic and Depressive Symptoms

Mood symptoms wax and wane and may or may not be related to environmental triggers. They represent a significant change from the child's typical functioning. A child with EOBPSD can experience extremely intense emotions of sadness, tearfulness, rage, or elation and mixed states of simultaneously occurring manic and depressive symptoms.

Manic and depressive symptoms may express themselves in a variety of ways in the school environment (see Tables 1 and 2, respectively). Manic or depressive symptoms also can escalate and become potentially harmful to the child (e.g., engaging in suicidal behaviors or dangerous activities) or others (e.g., hitting the teacher or fellow pupils, destroying property, or making sexually inappropriate advances to classmates). Furthermore, severe mania or depression may lead to psychotic symptoms such as paranoia (e.g., a child truly believes someone is spying on him), delusions (e.g., a child believes a war in another country was his fault), and auditory or visual hallucinations (e.g., a child hears voices telling her to do bad things or sees skeletons playing basketball). Psychotic symptoms in the presence of manic or depressive symptoms do not mean the child has schizophrenia or a related psychotic disorder. Typically, these psychotic symptoms disappear when mood symptoms improve.

### Stressors Associated With EOBPSD

In addition to the impairment of school functioning caused by core manic and depressive symptoms, children with EOBPSD may have additional problems in school as a result of a combination of various stressors. One of these stressors is comorbidity. Children and adolescents diagnosed with EOBPSD typically have a large number of co-occurring conditions, including ADHD (57%–98%), ODD or CD (41%–76%), and various anxiety disorders (13%–78%; see review by Lofhouse & Fristad, 2004). Substance abuse is less commonly an issue for children with EOBPSD, but Findling et al. (2003) suggested 50% to 70% of diagnosed adolescents will use and occasionally abuse various substances. School professionals need to be aware of the signs of substance abuse in youth with EOBPSD, as it can trigger further episodes of mania or be used to self-medicate symptoms in place of more safe and effective pharmacology.

Although children with EOBPSD have a high rate of ADHD, there are significant differences between these two disorders. Geller, Zimmerman, et al. (2000) compared a group of children and adolescents diagnosed with EOBPSD, with or without ADHD, to a group with ADHD alone. They found five DSM-IV mania-specific symptoms provided the best discrimination between the EOBPSD/ADHD and ADHD-only groups: Elated mood (89% and 14%, respectively), grandiosity (86% and 5%, respectively), flight of ideas/racing thoughts (71% and 10%, respectively), decreased need for sleep (40% and 6%, respectively), and hypersexuality (43% and 6%, respectively).

The presence of multiple disorders in adolescents with EOBPSD has also been associated with greater psychosocial impairment (Lewinsohn et al., 1995). Among children diagnosed with both ADHD and CD, those who also had manic episodes showed far greater impairment (Biederman et al., 1997). Of those children with mania, ADHD, and CD, 38% were retained in school, 86% needed extra help, and 71% were in a special education class. In contrast, only 18% of children with ADHD and CD, without mania, were retained, 35% needed extra help, and 3% were in a special education class.

Comorbid conditions might act as stressors, triggering future episodes of mania or depression (e.g., an increase in separation anxiety disorder symptoms and poor-quality sleep related to moving to a new middle school could prompt a manic episode). Additionally, these co-occurring conditions often warrant clinical attention in their own right because of their debilitating effects on academic, behavioral, and peer dysfunction. Therefore, as a result of the prevalence and impairments associated with comorbidity, the evaluation, accurate identification, and effective treatment of comorbid conditions in children and adolescents with EOBPSD are essential.

In addition, other factors that may contribute to the above problems include teacher, parent, and sibling

**Table 1** *Manic Symptoms and Their Expression in the School Environment*

| Symptom and Definition | Example |
|---|---|
| **Euphoria:** Elevated (too happy, silly, giddy) and expansive (about everything) mood, "out of the blue" or as an inappropriate reaction to external events for an extended period of time. | A child laughs hysterically for 30 minutes after a mildly funny comment by a peer and despite other students staring at him. |
| **Irritability:** Energized, angry, raging, or intensely irritable mood, "out of the blue" or as an inappropriate reaction to external events for an extended period of time. | In reaction to meeting a substitute teacher, a child flies into a violent 20-minute rage. |
| **Inflated Self-Esteem or Grandiosity:** Believing, talking, or acting as if he is considerably better at something or has special powers or abilities despite clear evidence to the contrary. | A child believes and tells others she is able to fly from the top of the school building. |
| **Decreased Need for Sleep:** Unable to fall or stay asleep or waking up too early because of increased energy, leading to a significant reduction in sleep yet feeling well rested. | Despite only sleeping 3 hours the night before, a child is still energized throughout the day. |
| **Increased Speech:** Dramatically amplified volume, uninterruptible rate, or pressure to keep talking. | A child suddenly begins to talk extremely loudly, more rapidly, and cannot be interrupted by the teacher. |
| **Flight of Ideas or Racing Thoughts:** Report or observation (via speech/writing) of speeded-up, tangential, or circumstantial thoughts. | A teacher cannot follow a child's rambling speech that is out of character for the child (i.e., not related to any cognitive or language impairment the child might have). |
| **Distractibility:** Increased inattentiveness beyond child's baseline attentional capacity. | A child is distracted by sounds in the hallway, which would typically not bother her. |
| **Increase in Goal-Directed Activity or Psychomotor Agitation:** Hyper-focused on making friends, engaging in multiple school projects or hobbies or in sexual encounters, or a striking increase in and duration of energy. | A child starts to rearrange the school library or clean everyone's desks, or plans to build an elaborate fort in the playground, but never finishes any of these projects. |
| **Excessive Involvement in Pleasurable or Dangerous Activities:** Sudden unrestrained participation in an action that is likely to lead to painful or very negative consequences. | A previously mild-mannered child may write dirty notes to other children in class or attempt to jump out of a moving school bus. |

stress; sleep disruptions; and time spent out of school related to an escalation of symptoms, treatment, and school-mandated suspensions or expulsions. As resources only recently have become available to educate and train teachers about EOBPSD and how to manage it in the classroom (see Recommended Resources), it is likely that teachers and other school professionals feel doubly frustrated, as they are dealing with significant and acute problems, often while lacking knowledge and training in how to handle these situations.

Two potential sources of stress that occur within the home—the effects of which may extend to the school

**Table 2** *Depressive Symptoms and Their Expression in the School Environment*

| Symptom and Definition | Example |
|---|---|
| **Depressed Mood:** Feels or looks sad or irritable (low energy) for an extended period of time. | A child appears down or flat or is cranky or grouchy in class and on the playground. |
| **Markedly Diminished Interest or Pleasures in All Activities:** Complains of feeling bored or finding nothing fun anymore. | A child reports feeling empty or bored and shows no interest in previously enjoyable school or peer activities. |
| **Significant Weight Lost/Gain or Appetite Increase/ Decrease:** Weight change of >5% in 1 month or significant change in appetite. | A child looks much thinner and drawn or a great deal heavier, or has no appetite or an excessive appetite at lunchtime. |
| **Insomnia or Hypersomnia:** Difficulty falling asleep, staying asleep, waking up too early or sleeping longer and still feeling tired. | A child looks worn out, is often groggy or tardy, or reports sleeping through alarm despite getting 12 hours of sleep. |
| **Psychomotor Agitation/Retardation:** Looks restless or slowed down. | A child is extremely fidgety or can't stay seated. His speech or movement is sluggish or he avoids physical activities. |
| **Fatigue or Loss of Energy:** Complains of feeling tired all the time. | Child looks or complains of constantly feeling tired even with adequate sleep. |
| **Low Self-Esteem, Feelings of Worthlessness or Excessive Guilt:** Thinking and saying more negative than positive things about self or feeling extremely bad about things one has done or not done. | A child frequently tells herself or others "I'm no good, I hate myself, no one likes me, I can't do anything." She feels bad about and dwells on accidentally bumping into someone in the corridor or having not said hello to a friend. |
| **Diminished Ability to Think or Concentrate, or Indecisiveness:** Increased inattentiveness, beyond child's baseline attentional capacity; difficulty stringing thoughts together or making choices. | A child can't seem to focus in class, complete work, or choose unstructured class activities. |
| **Hopelessness:** Negative thoughts or statements about the future. | A child frequently thinks or says "nothing will change or will ever be good for me." |
| **Recurrent Thoughts of Death or Suicidality:** Obsession with morbid thoughts or events, or suicidal ideation, planning, or attempts to kill self. | A child talks or draws pictures about death, war casualties, natural disasters, or famine. He reports wanting to be dead, not wanting to live anymore, wishing he'd never been born; he draws pictures of someone shooting or stabbing him, writes a suicide note, gives possessions away or tries to kill self. |

environment—are child–sibling and child–parent conflict. Being the sibling or a parent of a child with EOBPSD is associated with a high level of stress (e.g., coping with unpredictable and severe outbursts, which often draw support away from other family members), physical demands (e.g., dealing with extreme and extended bouts of aggression, high energy, insomnia, and dangerous behaviors), and financial pressures (e.g., multiple and long-term treatments and time off work), some of which may intensify intrafamily conflicts. Given these multiple sources of stress, interventions designed to reduce sibling and parent stress should contribute to improved outcomes for the child at home that might carry over to improved school functioning.

Although a reduced need for sleep has been identified as a cardinal symptom of EOBPSD, very little research has explored sleep difficulties in this population, and no research we are aware of has examined sleep problems in children with EOBPSD that are associated with their depressive or comorbid psychopathology. However, preliminary results from an ongoing study of 104 8- to 11-year-olds with EOBPSD suggest that 94% of children with EOBPSD have sleep problems associated with either their manic, depressive, or comorbid psychopathology (Lofthouse, Fristad, Splaingard, & Kelleher, 2004). Presumably, sleep disruptions in children with EOBPSD will deleteriously affect academic, behavioral, and social functioning at school.

Taking the necessary time out of school for escalating and debilitating symptoms or for inpatient or outpatient treatment can further set back the already delayed child with EOBPSD in terms of developing the essential skills to function academically, behaviorally, and socially. Similarly, school-enforced suspensions and expulsions, often used for disciplining behaviors that may well be beyond the control of the mood-disordered child, not only can disrupt the learning and socialization process but also can lead to failing grades and increased dropout rates. Contemplating the transition back to school also can be a potent stressor for a child with EOBPSD. Furthermore, parents, children, and teachers often report the child with EOBPSD has great difficulty with simple classroom transitions.

## Educational Implications of EOBPSD

Although research is limited on academic functioning of children with EOBPSD, studies reported that 24% of children with EOBPSD repeated a grade, 13% had learning disabilities, 43% had special education placements, 58% received tutoring (Biederman, Faraone, Chu, & Wozniak, 1999), and 30% and 42% had math and reading disabilities, respectively (Wozniak, et al., 1995). Compared with children with MDD or dysthymic disorder, children with EOBPSD evidence a trend toward more placements in special education classrooms (Fristad, Goldberg-Arnold, & Gavazzi, 2002).

As discussed earlier, in the retrospective study of 8- to 11-year-old children with EOBPSD, the majority of parents reported past and current special education services (Kljun et al., 2004). A related study that used similar participants reported that most parents (79%) and teachers (72%) and many children (46%) reported current difficulties with academics at school (Griffith, Lofthouse, Fristad, & Dingus, 2004).

Adolescents with EOBPSD also experience significant impairments in academic functioning. Quackenbush, Kutcher, Robertson, Boulos, and Chaban (1996) examined 44 adolescents with EOBPSD and found that prior to onset of their illness, 71% had good-to-excellent work effort, 58% were identified as having specific academic strengths, and 83% were taking college preparatory classes. After the onset of the disorder, however, teachers reported adolescents' work effort had diminished drastically; 67% had significant difficulties in math, and only 38% of the 37 students who were of age had graduated from high school.

Others have reported that children and adolescents with EOBPSD score higher on verbal measures of IQ than on visual–spatial measures of IQ (Shear, DelBello, Rosenberg, & Strakowski, 2002). This discrepancy may contribute to the difficulties children with EOBPSD often have with math achievement and decoding of nonverbal social cues, both of which require good visual–spatial abilities. Children with EOBPSD also have functional deficits on measures of attentional set-shifting and visual–spatial memory (Dickstein et al., 2004), whereas adolescents with EOBPSD have demonstrated impairment on tasks requiring executive functioning, such as systematic problem-solving and self-monitoring behavior (Shear et al.). Retrospective data on adolescents with EOBPSD also reveal developmental histories with significantly more language and motor delays than adolescents with unipolar depression (Sigurdsson, Fombonne, Sayal, & Checkley, 1999).

## Social Implications of EOBPSD

Very little research exists on the social problems of children and adolescents with EOBPSD in the school environment. However, difficulties with social skills and having few or no friends have been reported (Geller, Bolhofner, et al., 2000), and these children may show higher levels of aggression than their peers (Geller, Warner, Williams, & Zimmerman, 1998). For 8- to 11-year-olds with EOBPSD, the majority of parents and children report difficulties with peers; over half of the children report having no friends, and over half of the parents report their child does not have a best friend (Kljun et al., 2004). Similarly, teachers report 8- to 11-year-olds with EOBPSD have moderate to severe difficulties with antisocial behavior, social competence, withdrawn behavior, interpersonal skills, and self-management skills (Griffith et al., 2004).

### Problems and Implications—Summary

Despite the scarcity of studies, research suggests children and adolescents with EOBPSD have numerous, severe, and durable problems with manic and depressive symptoms with serious developmental, educational, and social implications. The high level of comorbidity associated with EOBPSD; teacher, parent, and sibling stress; sleep disruptions; and time spent out of school may all contribute to these problems.

## ALTERNATIVE ACTIONS FOR PREVENTION AND INTERVENTION

Although studies on the offspring of adults with bipolar disorders are in progress (see Chang & Steiner, 2003), currently no evidence-based prevention programs, strategies, or techniques exist for promoting healthy development and preventing negative outcomes in predisposed children. However, many of the strategies and techniques described below may be helpful for preventing continued impairment in children diagnosed with EOBPSD. Given the chronic nature of EOBPSD, efforts should be made to increase resiliency and recovery using a combination of effective pharmacological, psychosocial, and school interventions.

### Pharmacological Treatments

Pharmacological intervention is the foundation of effective treatment for EOBPSD. Research and clinical practice indicate that most children require multiple medications to alleviate symptoms of mania, depression, and co-occurring conditions. Although medications have not been adequately studied in children with EOBPSD, clinical practice indicates their potential utility. Because most school professionals will be informed about the brand rather than chemical names of medications children take, the following section notes brand names only.

Mood stabilizers (e.g., Depakote, Lithium, Gabitril, Lamictal, Tegretol, Trileptal, and Topamax) are considered the first line of pharmacological intervention. Antipsychotic medications (e.g., Abilify, Clozaril, Geodon, Risperdal, Seroquel, and Zyprexa) may help reduce aggressive or psychotic symptoms, and antihypertensive medications (e.g., Clonidine and Tenex) are sometimes used to improve the sleep–wake cycle. After a child's mood has been stabilized with a mood stabilizer, low-dose adjunctive antidepressant medications (e.g., Celexa, Lexapro, Luvox, Prozac, Remeron, Serzone, Wellbutrin, and Zoloft) may reduce depressive and anxiety symptoms, and adjunctive psychostimulants (e.g., Adderal, Concerta, Dexedrine, Focalin, Metadate, and Ritalin) and norepinephrine reuptake inhibitors (e.g., Strattera) may reduce ADHD symptoms of inattention, impulsivity, and hyperactivity. However, both antidepressants and psychostimulants pose a risk of activating manic symptoms, so they must be carefully monitored. Furthermore, school professionals should be aware of the major side effects students' medications may have in the school environment (e.g., chronic thirst, increased urination, and drowsiness) and should know how to help their students cope with them (e.g., more frequent bathroom breaks or changes in school schedule). For a more detailed review of the findings and issues in pharmacotherapy of EOBPSD, see Findling et al. (2003).

Finally, although dietary interventions such as Omega-3 fatty acids and high-intensity vitamin–mineral complexes have been tried in children, their efficacy is still being tested, and only case series data are available (Kaplan, Crawford, Gardner, & Farrelly, 2002). As evidence for efficacy in some of the medicines being used for EOBPSD is currently stronger, families are encouraged to begin treatment with those agents first.

### Psychological Treatments

Whereas pharmacological interventions are viewed as the foundation for effective treatment for EOBPSD, psychological interventions can be seen as the real-world building blocks of resiliency and recovery. Psychological interventions might include some combination of family therapy, individual therapy, parental guidance, group therapy, school-based intervention, home-based treatment, respite, out-of-home placement, or web-based support.

As recently as 1999, no evidence-based guidelines existed for psychosocial interventions with children who have EOBPSD (Fristad et al., 2002). Since then, three groups have developed interventions for children (Fristad, Gavazzi, & Mackinaw-Koons, 2003), children and adolescents (Pavuluri, Graczyk et al., 2004), and adolescents (Miklowitz et al., 2004). To date, only the multifamily psychoeducational groups (MFPG) and individual–family psychoeducation (IFP) developed by Fristad et al. (2003) have been tested in randomized clinical trials. MFPG and IFP teach parents and children about mood disorders, symptoms, and co-occurring disorders; pharmacological, mental health, and school- and community-focused interventions; and coping and self-preservation skills. Interventions are time limited, with the expectation that ongoing work of a similar nature will be required to maintain treatment gains over time for this chronic illness. Participation is expected to increase parents' and children's knowledge of EOBPSD and its treatment and to expand their repertoire of individual and family coping skills, which it is hoped will lead to more effective and efficient use of existing and future treatments. For a more detailed description of the MFPG's session contents and clinical tools, see Fristad and Goldberg-Arnold (2003) and Goldberg-Arnold and Fristad (2003).

Originally, MFPG consisted of a 6-week, 75-minute group treatment. It has since expanded to an 8-week, 90-minute format. MFPG has separate parent and child groups with combined check-in and check-out sessions at the beginning and end of each group. In the first study, families were randomized into immediate treatment or a 6-month wait-list prior to receiving treatment. All families continued to receive treatment as usual, which included medication management, as MFPG is an adjunctive intervention. Results from 35 participating 8- to 11-year-old children and their 47 participating parents indicate parents' knowledge about childhood mood disorders increased; parent–child relationships, as rated by parents, improved; children's ratings of perceived social support from parents increased (Fristad et al., 2002); and parents' consumer skills (i.e., their ability to obtain appropriate services) improved (Goldberg-Arnold, Fristad, & Gavazzi, 1999). A full-scale, randomized study ($N$ = 165) of the expanded 8-week, 90-minute format is now under way to further establish efficacy of the MFPG program.

In an uncontrolled pilot study of 34 participating 5- to 17-year-olds with EOBPSD, Pavuluri, Graczyk, Henry et al. (2004) assessed the impact of their child- and family-focused cognitive–behavioral therapy program (CFF-CBT or "Rainbow Program"). After all children were initially prescribed medication according to a specific algorithm (Pavuluri, Henry et al., 2004), CFF-CBT was delivered through 12 individual parent-and-child sessions. Parent-and-child treatment components included psychoeducation regarding the neuropsychiatric basis of bipolar disorder and the importance of routines; and skill building to improve affect regulation and anger control, increase positive self-statements, restructure negative thinking for living in the now, promote a balanced lifestyle (for parents), increase interpersonal and situational problem-solving, and develop support systems. Additionally, the child's school received a work folder of the individual sessions, and the school staff had a teleconference with the treatment therapist. Participants showed reductions in symptoms of ADHD, aggression, mania, psychosis, depression, and sleep disturbance; increases in global functioning; and high levels of treatment adherence and satisfaction (Pavuluri, Graczyk et al.).

Finally, Miklowitz et al. (2004) tested an adolescent version of Functional Family Therapy for Adolescents (FFT-A) combined with mood-stabilizing medications in an open trial of twenty 13- to 17-year-olds with BP-I. Treatment components, delivered by a standardized manual, included psychoeducation, family problem-solving, communication, crisis management, and the rehearsal of coping strategies for future relapses. Adolescents who received a combination of FFT-A and mood stabilizers experienced improvements in depressive, mania, and behavioral symptoms 1 year later. Although psychosocial treatment for families of children and adolescents with EOBPSD is a relatively new area, these new studies offer some hopeful and exciting future possibilities.

## School-Based Treatments

Unfortunately no research-supported, school-based interventions currently exist for EOBPSD. However, a number of potentially beneficial clinical and educational recommendations for school difficulties are available from several sources:

- The website of the Child and Adolescent Bipolar Foundation (CABF), at *http://www.bpkids.org*.

- The Juvenile Bipolar Research Foundation (JBRF) at *http:// www.jbrf.org.*
- The Josselyn Center's *Understanding and Educating Children and Adolescents with Bipolar Disorder: A Guide for Educators* (Anderson, Kubisak, Field, & Vogelstein, (2003).
- Fristad and Goldberg-Arnold's 2004 book, *Raising a Moody Child: How to Cope with Depression and Bipolar Disorder.*

The seven fundamental recommendations that appear below are adapted from these four sources.

1. *Build, maintain, and educate the school-based team.* It is critical for the child, family, and school personnel to work together. Working in isolation or at cross-purposes with other team members can be highly ineffective, frustrating, and potentially devastating. The first step involves thinking broadly about who might be included on an education team. Qualified persons could be anyone in the school environment (e.g., secretary or custodian) or child's life (e.g., Cub Scout leader or rabbi) who can provide consistent and effective support in assisting the child to cope with and recover from symptoms and related impairments. Second, successful maintenance of an education team rests on communication among its members and the setting and monitoring of observable goals. Third, it is important for the education team to have a firm foundation of knowledge about EOBPSD to be able to identify, understand, and flexibly work with the kinds of educational challenges EOBPSDs present.
2. *Prioritize individualized education plan (IEP) goals.* The Josselyn Center's *Guide for Educators* presents a hierarchy of basic priorities for educating children with EOBPSD. These include attendance, emotional stability and physical safety, knowledge acquisition, relationship building, and work production.
3. *Provide a predictable, positive, and flexible classroom environment.* Although predictability in the classroom environment is no doubt good for all students, it appears to be exponentially more important for children with EOBPSD, perhaps because of their unpredictable mood cycles. School professionals can increase predictability by providing organized classrooms, daily routines that are structured and consistent, and clear expectations coupled with a positive discipline strategy.

   Negative consequences, such as ignoring attention-getting behaviors, giving time-outs, removing privileges, assigning remedial work, and using suspension and expulsion, are often used to reduce unwanted behaviors. However, if the behavior (e.g., a euphoric or irritable mood) is not one the child has the cognitive, emotional, or behavioral skills to control, negative consequences may not only be ineffective in reducing that behavior, they could actually increase it.

   As symptoms of EOBPSD wax and wane within the developing child, maintaining flexibility is critical. It may be necessary to modify expectations regarding the amount, content of, and time allowed for activities, assignments, and tests, based on the child's fluctuations in mood, attention, energy, and motivation.
4. *Be aware of and manage medication side effects.* Children with EOBPSD are frequently prescribed multiple medications. It is important for school professionals to be kept up-to-date with the child's medications and any related side effects (e.g., increased thirst and urination, drowsiness, or sluggishness). Common classroom interventions include unlimited access to fluids and the restroom, and rescheduling of the most challenging activities to times when side effects are less pronounced (e.g., after lunch).
5. *Develop social skills.* Many children with EOBPSD have social–emotional skills deficits. They may misinterpret jokes, act shy, be bossy or bully, or become a victim of bullying. Providing support from the guidance counselor, psychologist, or social worker; allowing the child to participate in a social skills group; and increasing playground supervision to avert bullying can all help the child with EOBPSD function better at school.
6. *Be prepared for episodes of intense emotion.* Because a child with EOPBSD may experience dramatic, unexpected, and intense shifts of mood and emotion during the school day, a functional behavior assessment can help identify triggers that may precede losses of control and can guide the development of a behavior plan to help the child and school professional prevent or cope with stressors and frustrations. For instance, if episodes are triggered by boredom, school professionals can provide enrichment activities; if episodes are due to hunger or low blood sugar, the child should eat mid-morning and afternoon snacks; or if episodes occur during particularly difficult activities, temporarily reducing demands to a level the child can manage will reduce stressors. An important intervention for

children with EOBPSD is to have available the use of a safe or private place the child can visit to regain control (e.g., guidance office or resource room) and to establish a secret signal for the child and teacher to covertly communicate the need to take a brief time-out during class.

Preparation for episodes of intense emotion also may include the development of a crisis management plan that involves crisis prevention strategies. This crisis management plan should include the following:

- Explicit instructions to manage unsafe behaviors (i.e., who does what, when, and where).
- Details regarding the location, supervision of, and expectations surrounding safe and private places (e.g., designating the guidance counselor's office as a safe place and making sure the child gets there and returns to the classroom as soon as possible after calming down).
- The development and practice of a specific communication system to implement procedures quickly (e.g., a child could give a "T" hand signal to communicate the need to go to his or her safe place).
- Alternative backup plans (e.g., walking around the gym with an adult if time in the safe place didn't work).
- Recovery procedure for all involved following the crisis (e.g., destress and debrief as a class, with the child included, in order not to ostracize the child).

Following hospitalization or after an upsurge in symptoms that precludes success in negotiating an entire school day, it is critical that the education team prepare for the child's transition back to school to prevent further disruption. The team might arrange for temporary homebound instruction, followed by a gradual transition back to school, if needed, or the team might arrange for partial days at school.

7. *Consider alternatives to regular classrooms.* If symptoms escalate and become potentially harmful to the child and others in the regular classroom, the education team may need to consider the temporary or even permanent support of more restrictive educational environments. These may include (in order of least to most restrictive) regular classroom with a one-to-one aide, special education teacher or resource room support, self-contained classroom, home schooling, therapeutic day school, hospital day treatment program, residential treatment center, or therapeutic boarding school. The website for the National Association of Therapeutic Schools and Programs (*http://www.natsap.org*) can be helpful in locating programs suited to a child's particular needs. Though no research to date has evaluated these alternatives to standard educational placements, it can be assumed their effectiveness will be enhanced if their staff have accurate and up-to-date knowledge of EOBPSD and its manifestations in school settings.

## SUMMARY

Early-onset bipolar spectrum disorders (EOBPSD) are severe, highly comorbid, chronic, cyclical, and frequently relapsing biopsychosocial mood disorders of childhood and adolescence. The core symptoms of manic and depressive symptoms can be further exacerbated by the secondary problems of comorbidity; teacher, parent, and sibling stress; sleep disruptions; and time spent out of school. Interacting in a dynamic, caustic, debilitating cycle, this constellation of problems can lead to a further escalation of core symptoms, secondary problems, and devastating effects on developmental, home, school, and peer functioning.

Although EOBPSD cannot currently be cured or grown out of, children, their families, and school professionals can help to increase resiliency and recovery by the combined use of effective medications, psychoeducation, and psychosocial and school interventions designed to manage dysfunctional mood, related comorbid symptoms, and environmental stressors. Despite the recent development and testing of family-based psychosocial treatments for EOBPSD, no empirically supported school-based programs currently exist. One of the main challenges facing researchers of treatment outcomes is how to scientifically examine school interventions for a group of disorders that are relatively infrequent.

Despite the lack of research on school interventions, a number of potentially beneficial clinical and educational recommendations are available. Seven fundamental recommendations were described in this chapter. In conclusion, although EOBPSD is often chronic, variable, and damaging to family life, school functioning, and peer relationships, it is important not to lose hope. Several effective treatment tools currently exist, and with the increasing professional and public interest EOBPSD has received in recent years, additional treatments are likely to become available in the future.

# RECOMMENDED RESOURCES

## Books and Other Printed Material

Anderson, M., Kubisak-Boyd, J., Field, R., & Vogelstein, S. (2003). *Understanding and educating children and adolescents with bipolar disorder: A guide for educators.* Northfield, IL: The Josselyn Center.

This manual for educators provides ideas and principles to guide the assessment and intervention of children and adolescents with EOBPSD in educational settings.

Fristad, M., & Arnold, J. G. (2004). *Raising a moody child: How to cope with depression and bipolar disorder.* New York: Guilford Press.

This book for parents offers direct, easy-to-follow information and recommendations for families with children who suffer from mood disorders. Incorporating real-life examples, practical suggestions, and answers to frequently asked questions, this book covers important issues, including knowing when a child needs help, how parents can get a good evaluation, medical and psychological treatment options, crisis management, coping tools for the whole family, and how parents can help their child cope in school.

## Websites

*http://www.bpkids.org*

The Child & Adolescent Bipolar Foundation is a parent-led, not-for-profit, Internet-based organization of families raising children diagnosed with EOBPSD. The Resources—Printed Materials section of the website includes a brochure for educators called "Educating the Child with Bipolar Disorder." The Learning Center page has information on educational issues of pediatric bipolar disorder. In its bookstore, the CABF also sells an interactive CD for school personnel, "What is Pediatric Bipolar Disorder? A Resource for Educators."

*http://www.jbrf.org*

The Juvenile Bipolar Research Foundation (JBRF) is a web-based charitable organization of parents, clinicians, and researchers dedicated to the support of research on EOBPSD. The Discussion Forums section of the website provides information on the educational issues of students with bipolar disorder. Also in this section, the JBRF sells a DVD of a Janice Papolos presentation, "Educating and Nurturing the Bipolar Child."

# REFERENCES


Akiskal, H. S. (1983). The bipolar spectrum: new concepts in classification and diagnosis. In L. Grinspoon (Ed.), *Psychiatry update: The American Psychiatric Association annual review, Vol. 2* (pp. 271–292). Washington, DC: American Psychiatric Press.

American Psychiatric Association. (1994). *Diagnostic and statistical manual of mental disorders* (4th ed.). Washington, DC: Author.

Biederman, J., Faraone, S. V., Chu, M. P., & Wozniak, J. (1999). Further evidence of a bidirectional overlap between juvenile mania and conduct disorder in children. *Journal of the American Academy of Child and Adolescent Psychiatry, 38,* 468–476.

Biederman, J., Faraone, S. V., Hatch, M., Mennin, D., Taylor, A., & George, P. (1997). Conduct disorder with and without mania in a referred sample of ADHD children. *Journal of Affective Disorders, 44,* 177–188.

Chang, K., & Steiner, H. (2003). Offspring studies in child and early adolescent bipolar disorder. In B. Geller & M. P. DelBello (Eds.), *Bipolar disorder in childhood and early adolescence* (pp. 107–129). New York: Guilford Press.

Dickstein, D. P., Treland, J. E., Snow, J., McClure, E. B., Mehta, M. S., Towbin, K. E., et al. (2004). Neuro-psychological performance in pediatric bipolar disorder. *Biological Psychiatry, 55,* 32–39.

Findling, R. L., Kowatch, R. A., & Post, R. M. (2003). *Pediatric bipolar disorder.* London: Dunitz.

Fristad, M. A., Gavazzi, S. M., & Mackinaw-Koons, B. (2003). Family psychoeducation: An adjunctive intervention for children with bipolar disorder. *Biological Psychiatry, 53,* 1000–1008.

Fristad, M. A., & Goldberg-Arnold, J. S. (2003). Family interventions for early-onset bipolar disorder. In B. Geller & M. P. DelBello (Eds.), *Bipolar disorder in childhood and early adolescence* (pp. 295–313). New York: Guilford Press.

Fristad, M. A., Goldberg-Arnold, J. S., & Gavazzi, S. M. (2002). Multifamily psychoeducation groups (MFPG) for families of children with bipolar disorder. *Bipolar Disorder, 4,* 254–262.

Geller, B., Bolhofner, K., Craney, J. L., Williams, M., DelBello, M. P., & Gundersen, K. (2000). Psychosocial functioning in a prepubertal and early adolescent bipolar disorder phenotype. *Journal of the American Academy of Child and Adolescent Psychiatry, 39,* 1543–1548.

Geller, B., Craney, J. L., Bolhofner, K., DelBello, M. P., Axelson, D., & Luby, J. (2003). Phenomenology and longitudinal course of children with a prepubertal and early adolescent bipolar disorder phenotype. In B. Geller & M. P. DelBello (Eds.), *Bipolar disorder in childhood and early adolescence* (pp. 25–50). New York: Guilford Press.

Geller, B., Tillman, R., Craney, J. L., & Bolhofner, K. (2004). Four-year prospective outcome and natural history of mania in children with a prepubertal and early adolescent bipolar disorder phenotype. *Archives of General Psychiatry, 61,* 459–467.

Geller, B., Warner, K., Williams, M., & Zimmerman, B. (1998). Prepubertal and young adolescent bipolarity versus ADHD: Assessment and validity using the WASH-UKSADS, CBCL, and TRF. *Journal of Affective Disorders, 51,* 93–100.

Geller, B., Zimerman, B., Williams, M., Bolhofner, K., Craney, J. L., & Delbello, M. P. (2000). Diagnostic characteristics of 93 cases of prepubertal and early adolescent bipolar disorder phenotype by gender, puberty and comorbid attention deficit hyperactivity disorder. *Journal of Child and Adolescent Psychopharmacology, 10,* 157–164.

Goldberg-Arnold, J. S., & Fristad, M. A. (2003). Psychotherapy for children with bipolar disorder. In B. Geller & M. P. DelBello (Eds.), *Bipolar disorder in childhood and early adolescence* (pp. 272–294). New York: Guilford Press.

Goldberg-Arnold, J. S., Fristad, M. A., & Gavazzi, S. M. (1999). Family psychoeducation: Giving caregivers what they want and need. *Family Relations: Interdisciplinary Journal of Applied Family Studies, 48,* 411–417.

Griffith, A., Lofthouse, N., Fristad, M. A., & Dingus, C. (2004, October). *The school behavior and academic performance peer functioning of children with early-onset bipolar spectrum disorders.* Poster session presented at the Kansas Conference on Clinical Child and Adolescent Psychology, Lawrence, KS.

Kaplan, B. J., Crawford, S. G., Gardner, B., & Farrelly, G. (2002). Treatment of mood lability and explosive rage with mineral and vitamins: Two case studies in children. *Journal of Child and Adolescent Psychopharmacology, 12,* 205–219.

Kljun, J., Lofthouse, N., Fristad, M. A., & Dingus, C. (2004, October). *The effects of early-onset bipolar spectrum disorders on past and current school and peer functioning.* Poster session presented at the Kansas Conference on Clinical Child and Adolescent Psychology, Lawrence, KS.

Kowatch, R. A., Fristad, M. A., Birmaher, B., Wagner, K. D., Findling, R., & Hellander, M. (2005). Treatment guidelines for children and adolescents with bipolar disorder: Child Psychiatric Workgroup on Bipolar Disorder. *Journal of the American Academy of Child and Adolescent Psychiatry, 44,* 213–235.

Lewinsohn, P. M., Klein, J. R., & Klein, D. N. (1995). Bipolar disorder in a community sample of older adolescents: Prevalence, phenomenology, comorbidity and course. *Journal of the American Academy of Child and Adolescent Psychiatry, 34,* 454–463.

Lish, J. D., Dime-Meenan, S., Whybrow, P. C., Price, R. A., & Hirschfeld, R. M. (1994). The National Depressive and Manic-Depressive Association (NDMDA) survey of bipolar members. *Journal of Affective Disorders, 31,* 281–294.

Lofthouse, N., & Fristad, M. A. (2004). Psychosocial interventions for children with early-onset bipolar spectrum disorders. *Clinical Child and Family Psychology Review, 7*(2), 71–88.

Lofthouse, N., Fristad, M. A., Splaingard, M., & Kelleher, K. (2004, October). *Sleep problems associated with early-onset bipolar spectrum disorder.* Poster session presented at the Kansas Conference on Clinical Child and Adolescent Psychology, Lawrence, KS.

McClellan, J. M., Werry, J. S., & Ham, M. (1993). A follow-up study of early onset-psychosis: Comparison between outcome diagnoses of schizophrenia, mood disorders and personality disorders. *Journal of Autism and Developmental Disorders, 23,* 243–262.

Miklowitz, D. J., George, E. L., Axelson, D. A., Kim, E. Y., Birmaher, B., Schneck, C., et al. (2004). Family-focused treatment for adolescents with bipolar disorder. *Journal of Affective Disorders, 82*(11), S113–S128.

Pavuluri, M. N., Graczyk, P. A., Henry, D. B., Carbray, J. A., Heidenreich, J., & Miklowitz, D. J. (2004). Child and family focused cognitive-behavioral therapy for pediatric bipolar disorder: Development and preliminary results. *Journal of the American Academy of Child and Adolescent Psychiatry, 43,* 528–537.

Pavuluri, M. N., Henry, D. B., Devineni, B., Carbray, J. A., Naylor, M. W., & Janicak, P. G. (2004). A pharmacotherapy algorithm for stabilization and maintenance of pediatric bipolar disorder. *Journal of the American Academy of Child and Adolescent Psychiatry, 43,* 859–867.

Quackenbush, D., Kutcher, S., Robertson, H., Boulos, C., & Chaban, P. (1996). Premorbid and postmorbid school functioning in bipolar adolescents: Descriptive and suggested academic interventions. *Canadian Journal of Psychiatry, 41,* 16–22.

Quinn, C. A., & Fristad, M. A. (2004). Defining and identifying early-onset bipolar spectrum disorders. *Current Psychiatric Reports, 6,* 101–107.

Quinn, C. A., Lofthouse, N., Fristad, M. A., & Dingus, C. (2004). *Comorbidity and early onset mood spectrum disorders in childhood: Profiles, gender associations, developmental onset, and psychosocial functioning.* Poster session presented at the Association for the Advancement of Behavior Therapy (AABT), New Orleans, LA.

Shear, P. K., DelBello, M. P., Rosenberg, H. L., & Strakowski, S. M. (2002). Parental reports of executive dysfunction in adolescents with bipolar disorder. *Child Neuropsychology, 8,* 285–295.

Sigurdsson, E., Fombonne, E., Sayal, K., & Checkley, S. (1999). Neurodevelopmental antecedents of early-onset bipolar affective disorder. *British Journal of Psychiatry,* 121–127.

Weissman, M. M., Blanc, R. C., Canino, G. J., Faravelli, C., Greenwald, S., & Hwu, H. (1996). Cross-national epidemiology of major depression and bipolar disorder. *Journal of the American Medical Association, 276,* 293–299.

Werry, J. S., McClellan, J. M., & Chard, L. (1991). Childhood and adolescent schizophrenic, bipolar and schizoaffective disorders: A clinical and outcome study. *Journal of the American Academy of Child and Adolescent Psychiatry, 30,* 457–465.

Wozniak, J., Biederman, J., Kiely, K., Ablon, J. S., Faraone, S. V., & Mundy, E. (1995). Mania-like symptoms suggestive of childhood-onset bipolar disorder in clinically referred children. *Journal of the American Academy of Child and Adolescent Psychiatry, 34,* 867–876.

# 17

# Suicidal Ideation and Behaviors

**Stephen E. Brock**

*California State University, Sacramento*

**Jonathan Sandoval**

*University of California, Davis*

**Shelley Hart**

*California State University, Sacramento*

In 2001 more than 30,000 Americans died by suicide (Anderson & Smith, 2003), and within each of the age groups from 10 to 64 years, suicide ranks within the top 10 leading causes of death. Other forms of non-lethal suicidal behaviors are even more common. In 2002 it was estimated that 132,353 individuals were hospitalized following suicide attempts (Centers for Disease Control and Prevention [CDC], 2004). However, encouraging statistics show that youth suicide rates are currently at their lowest point in 20 years and have been declining since 1992 (Lubell, Swahn, Crosby, & Kegler, 2004). Since 1991, the percentage of students who seriously considered suicide also declined (Grunbaum et al., 2004).

Still, the U.S. statistics for youth are alarming. Despite the recent decline in youth suicide rates, they are still more than three times higher than what they were in 1950 (Prager, 2003). In the United States, suicide currently ranks as the third leading cause of death in the 10- to 24-year-old age group (Centers for Disease Control, 2005). Given these statistics, it is critical that providers of school psychological services understand this phenomenon and be informed about suicide prevention and intervention.

## BACKGROUND AND DEVELOPMENT

Although suicidal ideation and the decision to engage in suicidal behavior is idiosyncratic, consisting of both cumulative exposure to multiple risk factors and the relative lack of protective factors, it is possible to evaluate the prevalence of suicidal behaviors by groups—age, gender, ethnicity, sexual orientation, and access to firearms—and to consider the unique risks associated with each group.

### Age

Suicide rates increase as a function of age. Suicide is rare among children under 5 years. On the other hand, older adults have the most suicide deaths of any group (Anderson & Smith, 2003). The converse is true of the rate of suicide attempts, which is highest among adolescents and young adults and lowest among the elderly (Hjelmeland et al., 2002).

### Gender

Females of all races are more likely to report having had suicidal ideation and are almost twice as likely to attempt suicide (CDC, 2002). However, males of all races are almost five times as likely as females to die by suicide. Males are also significantly more likely than females to attempt suicide impulsively (Simon et al., 2001), whereas females are more likely to tell someone about suicidal thoughts and plans (O'Donnell, O'Donnell, Wardlaw, & Stueve, 2004).

### Ethnicity

Among Native American and Asian American youth age 25 and under, suicide ranks second among causes of death. Despite a recent decline, the suicide rate among adolescent

Native American males continues to be the highest of any group, whereas Caucasian males still have the highest absolute number of suicide deaths, accounting for approximately 70% of suicides. Among adolescent females, the Asian and Pacific Islander group has the highest suicide rate (Anderson & Smith, 2003).

### Sexual Orientation

Gay and lesbian youth have been reported to be at increased risk for suicidal behavior when compared to the general population. Studies have suggested a two- to fourfold increased risk for this group (O'Donnell et al., 2004).

### Access to Firearms

The availability of firearms is associated with increased suicidal ideation (Bearman & Moody, 2004), and the presence of a gun in the home is associated with a five times greater risk of suicide (Kellermann et al., 1992). Firearms have consistently ranked first among methods of suicide, accounting for nearly three of five youth suicides (American Association of Suicidology, 2003).

## PROBLEMS AND IMPLICATIONS

It is rare for an individual to suddenly and unexpectedly commit suicide. Rather, suicide is typically the result of a relative lack of resiliency factors and an accumulation of risk. In addition, a suicidal person typically displays warning signs that predict their behavior. Table 1 summarizes these resiliency factors, risk factors, and warning signs. The absence of resiliency factors and the presence of risk factors do not perfectly predict suicidal ideation and behaviors. However, these variables do signal the need to increase vigilance for suicide warning signs.

### Resiliency Factors

The presence of resiliency factors appears to mitigate the potential of risk factors to generate suicidal ideation and behaviors (CDC, 2004). Perhaps the most powerful resiliency factors exist within interpersonal systems, including family (e.g., feeling supported by, and having an open line of communication with, family members; O'Donnell et al., 2004) and peers (e.g., supportive and dense social networks; Rutter & Soucar, 2002). To the extent these systems are present and functional, they may protect individuals from suicide. To the extent they are absent or dysfunctional, they may result in an increased vulnerability to suicidal ideation and behaviors.

### Risk Factors

In addition to a lack of resiliency factors, the following risk factors may also signal the need to increase vigilance for suicide warning signs.

***Prior suicide attempts.*** A previous suicide attempt is one of the most significant predictors of future suicidal behavior. In one study, at a 3-month follow-up of adolescents who had attempted suicide, 12% had made another attempt (Spirito, Valeri, Boergers, & Donaldson, 2003). A long-term follow-up of first-time suicide attempters with depression found that 38% had died by suicide within 5 years and 8% had made at least one additional attempt after more than 10 years (Brådvik, 2003). In assessing this risk factor, it is important to make a distinction between suicidal and other self-injurious behaviors. For example, what is commonly referred to as cutting behavior is not necessarily suicidal (see chapter 72, "Self-Mutilation"). For a prior behavior to be considered a suicide attempt, the individual must have had conscious thoughts of ending his or her own life.

***History of psychopathology.*** Over 90% of people who engage in suicidal behaviors have a psychiatric disorder (Seeley, Rohde, Lewinsohn, & Clarke, 2002). Mood disorders, specifically depression, are the most common diagnoses, followed by substance abuse, disruptive behavior, and anxiety disorders (Bearman & Moody, 2004; Seeley et al.; Simon et al., 2001). It is estimated that the risk of suicide among individuals with major depression is 20 times greater than that of the general population (American Association of Suicidology, 2004), and a greater intent to die has been reported among individuals who are more significantly depressed (Haw, Hawton, Houston, & Townsend, 2003). Individuals diagnosed with depression in childhood, with chronic and frequent depressive episodes, and with more depressive symptoms have been shown to be more likely to make multiple suicide attempts (Spirito et al., 2003). Although typically associated with depression, the symptom of hopelessness appears to be valuable as a stand-alone predictor of suicidal ideation and behaviors (Spirito et al.).

Psychopharmacological treatments for depression have also been suggested to be a risk factor for suicidal

**Table 1** *Resiliency Factors, Risk Factors, and Warning Signs*

| ***Resiliency Factors*** | |
|---|---|
| Family support and cohesion | General life satisfaction |
| Good family communication | Ties to neighborhood and community |
| Parent involvement and engagement | High self-esteem |
| Peer support and close social networks | Easy access to mental health resources |
| School connectedness | Restricted access to lethal means (guns) |
| Cultural or religious beliefs that discourage suicide | Feeling that one has a purpose in life |
| Adaptive coping and problem-solving skills | Effective medical and mental health care |
| Good conflict-resolution skills | |
| ***Risk Factors*** | |
| Previous suicide attempt(s) | Mental disorder (particularly depression) |
| Alcohol/substance abuse | Comorbid disorders |
| Family history of suicide | Hopelessness/helplessness |
| Impulsive or aggressive behavior | Self-injurious behavior (e.g., cutting) |
| Sexual and/or physical abuse | Easy access to lethal suicide methods |
| Impulsive or aggressive tendencies | Physical illness |
| Isolation | Significant others who have died by suicide |
| Barriers to access to mental health treatment | Relational, social, work, or financial loss |
| Cultural or religious beliefs that allow suicide | Local epidemics of suicide |
| Unwillingness to seek mental health assistance | |
| ***Warning Signs*** | |
| Displaying overt suicidal statements and/or behaviors | Increased use/abuse of alcohol and/or drugs |
| Giving indirect clues of suicidal thoughts and plans | Making abrupt changes in appearance |
| Putting personal affairs in order | Altering patterns of sleeping or eating |
| Giving away prized possessions | Demonstrating inability to concentrate or think rationally |
| Talking about suicide and death | Acting happy suddenly and unexpectedly |
| Talking about having no reason to live | Showing improvement in mood after a period of depression |
| Withdrawing from family and friends | Running away from home |
| Losing interest in once pleasurable activities | |
| Showing drastic changes in behavior or mood | |

*Sources.* ASA (2004), Capuzzi (2002), and *The Surgeon General's Call to Action to Prevent Suicide.* Washington, DC: Author. U.S. Public Health Service (1999)

ideation and behaviors. Antidepressants such as Paxil and Prozac have been reported to increase suicide risk, especially during the first few days and weeks of treatment (Jick, Kaye, & Jick, 2004). Thus, students with depression who have recently been prescribed an antidepressant should be closely monitored for the emergence of suicidality (U.S. Food and Drug Administration, 2004).

***Biology.*** Twin studies have suggested a link between genetic factors and youth suicide attempts, with the combination of genetic and environmental factors accounting for 33% to 73% of the variance in the risk for suicidal behavior (Glowinski et al., 2001). Other biological risk factors may exist within the central nervous system. For example, low levels of serotonin metabolite in the cerebrospinal fluid have been indicated as a significant correlate of current and future suicidal behavior (Goldsmith, Pellmar, Kleinman, & Bunney, 2002).

***Family.*** Dysfunctional family environments have been studied frequently in suicide research. Low levels of parental support and involvement (Bearman & Moody, 2004), a parental history of mental disorders such as substance abuse (King et al., 2001), and both physical and sexual abuse (Glowinski et al., 2001) have been significantly associated with suicidal ideation and behaviors.

***Situations.*** The situations that lead to suicidality include stressors that consume available resources and produce an overwhelming sense of loss. For example, among adolescents, a relationship breakup or a rejection resulting in questions about an individual's sexual orientation may generate such feelings of loss and hopelessness (Moscicki, 1995). Although these events may appear to be the precipitating factor that triggers a suicide, in most cases these events typically have built upon a series of other circumstances and risk factors (Ramsay, Tanney, Lang, & Kinzel, 2004). Nevertheless, research has suggested some specific situations that increase risk for suicidal ideation and behaviors. These include (a) exposure to the suicidal behavior of a family member or friend, (b) social isolation and lack of connection to school, and (c) the presence of a firearm in the home (Bearman & Moody, 2004).

### Warning Signs of Suicidal Ideation and Behaviors

Whereas risk factors suggest the need to be vigilant for signs of suicidal ideation and behaviors, warning signs imply their presence. Warning signs are the ways in which an individual communicates distress and signals the possibility of suicidal ideation. Even individuals who engage in impulsive suicide attempts typically give some indication of their plans (Simon et al., 2001). Especially when combined with risk factors, warning signs require direct inquiry about the presence of suicidal ideation (i.e., asking the question: "Are you thinking about suicide?") and may indicate the need for immediate suicide intervention. Table 1 provides a list of both direct and indirect suicide warning signs.

## ALTERNATIVE ACTIONS FOR PREVENTION

Suicidal ideation and behaviors have a tremendous effect on learning. Within a typical high school classroom of 30 students, it is likely that three students have made a suicide attempt within the past year (CDC, 2004). These students are psychologically unavailable for academic instruction and their behavior may be negatively affecting other non-suicidal students in the class (Brock, Lazarus, & Jimerson, 2002). Furthermore, districts have been found liable by the courts when they failed to provide suicide prevention programs and adequate supervision of suicidal students (Lieberman & Davis, 2002). Thus, well-developed plans are needed for suicide prevention, intervention, and postvention (i.e., the response to a completed suicide).

### Suicide Prevention and Awareness Curricula

Curriculum programs typically target the entire student body. In general, these programs strive to raise the overall responsiveness within the at-risk student's environment. In doing so, they recognize that peers are an important part of an adolescent's life, and it is more likely that a youth will share concerns with a peer rather than an adult. Goals of curriculum programs include increasing awareness of the problem, providing knowledge about the behaviors associated with suicide, and describing the resources available to help.

These programs have not always been viewed as effective. Concerns have included the observation that very few adolescents attending these programs commit suicide (Shaffer, Garland, Gould, Fisher, & Trautman, 1988) and that most students already hold accurate views of suicide (Shaffer, Garland, & Whittle, 1987). It has been argued, therefore, that prevention resources should be allocated to programs for at-risk youngsters, instead of targeting the entire student body.

A second concern is the tendency of these programs to normalize suicidal behavior. Garland, Shaffer, and Whittle (1989) reported that many curriculum programs employ a *stress model* of suicide (i.e., suicide as a response to stress or pressures that could happen to anyone) rather than a *mental illness model* (i.e., suicide as a consequence of mental illness). This view is contrary to the fact that suicide is typically associated with emotional disturbance and may increase the tendency to view suicidal behavior as a mainstream solution to problems.

A final concern regarding student body programs is their effect on suicidal students. Garland et al. (1989) suggest that students who had made suicide attempts and had attended a suicide prevention program did not appear to respond aş favorably to these programs as did nonattempters. When compared with suicide attempters who did not attend a suicide prevention program, suicide attempters who were program participants were less likely to reveal suicidal intentions, less likely to believe that a mental health professional could help them, and more likely to view suicide as a reasonable solution.

Recently developed programs have responded to these potential shortcomings and have been shown to be promising. Specifically, the Signs of Suicide (SOS) program is an approach that incorporates a curriculum component with a brief screening for depression and other suicide risk factors. The goal is to make automatic the "action steps" taken when confronting suicide (i.e., Acknowledge, Care, and Tell, or ACT). The SOS program subscribes to a mental illness model. Making use of a randomized control group model, a recent study demonstrated that the SOS program significantly lowered self-reported suicide attempts over a 3-month period. In addition, relative to the control group, evaluation data suggested that SOS program participants had greater knowledge and more adaptive attitudes about depression and suicide (see Recommended Resources; Aseltine & DeMartino, 2004).

In addition, programs that promote resiliency factors are often reported to be helpful in the prevention of suicidal behaviors (Edwards & Holden, 2001). These may include programs that enhance problem-solving, decision-making, and coping skills. Examples of such programs include *I Can Problem Solve* (Aberson & Shure, 2002) and social skills training (Elliott, McKevitt, & DiPerna, 2002). Because of developmental issues and the fact that suicide is rare among children, elementary schools' suicide prevention efforts should focus more exclusively on these types of prevention programs (Capuzzi, 2002).

### School Gatekeeper Training

Education of school staff members is frequently identified as an essential component of any prevention program (Helsel, 2001). Teachers are the school professionals who spend the most time with at-risk students. It is thus crucial for them to be able to identify and bring these individuals to the attention of school psychologists and counselors. A good practice for school districts is to provide staff with periodic training sessions, using suicide intervention scenarios and role-playing to apply the knowledge and to practice skills. The *Technical Assistance Sampler on School Interventions to Prevent Youth Suicide* (Center for Mental Health in Schools at UCLA, 2003) provides a wealth of information on suicide prevention, intervention, and postvention and identifies specific gatekeeper training programs available throughout the country.

### Suicide Risk Screening

It is possible to efficiently and briefly (in less than 15 minutes) screen an individual for suicide risk (Gutierrez, Osman, & Kopper, 2000). An example of such a screening tool is the *Suicidal Ideation Questionnaire* (Reynolds, 1988). These screenings rarely yield false negatives but will frequently yield false positives. Thus, a second-stage evaluation of all positive results is required. Limitations of school-wide screening include the fact that suicidal ideation waxes and wanes over time and circumstances. Thus, multiple screenings may be necessary to capture all potentially at-risk students. An additional limitation is the acceptability of large-scale suicide risk screenings. Survey results suggest that school psychologists rate school-wide screenings as unacceptable (relative to curriculum programs and gatekeeper training) primarily due to their intrusiveness. However, the authors of this study also speculated that these screenings may be viewed as relatively unacceptable due to the time and effort they require (Eckert, Miller, DuPaul, & Riley-Tillman, 2003). Given these difficulties, school-wide screening may be most practical and acceptable when there is concern regarding suicide contagion.

### Restriction of Access to Lethal Means

Although an area of controversy, restrictive gun control laws are associated with lower suicide rates (Carrington & Moyer, 1994). In particular, study findings have suggested that these regulations would be helpful in reducing the rate of suicide in the 15- to 24-year-old age group (Sloan, Rivara, Reay, Ferris, & Kellermann, 1990).

## ALTERNATIVE ACTIONS FOR INTERVENTION

Despite the best of prevention efforts, suicidal ideation and behaviors will continue to occur. Thus, schools must

**Table 2** *General Suicide Intervention Procedures for School Staff*

1. *Stay with the student.* A suicidal student should never be left alone. A staff member should maintain constant visual contact with the student until help is obtained. This is true regardless of whether the student has made a direct or indirect threat. Until a suicide risk assessment is conducted, every student who appears to have suicidal ideation should be viewed as being at risk for a suicidal behavior.

2. *Do not allow the student to leave the school.* A student who has threatened suicide should not be allowed to leave school until the appropriate personnel (ideally a school psychologist or counselor) have conducted a risk assessment and until adequate supervision has been ensured. If a student does attempt to leave, staff members should ask the student to stay but should not do anything that puts themselves, or other students or staff members, in danger. If the student will not stay when requested, the police should be called.

3. *Do not promise confidentiality.* All staff members have a legal and ethical responsibility *not* to honor confidentiality when a student is threatening harm to self or others. No matter how much a student implores, a suicide plan must not be kept secret. It is better to have the student angry and alive than dead because a confidence was maintained.

4. *Determine if the student will relinquish the means.* If the student has the means to attempt suicide readily accessible, staff members should request that the student relinquish the means. They should not force the student or put themselves or others in danger. If a student refuses to voluntarily relinquish the means of a threatened suicide, then the police should be called.

5. *Take the student to a prearranged room.* As soon as possible, the student should be taken to a prearranged, nonthreatening room away from other students. There should be a phone in the room and another adult close by.

6. *Notify the designated reporter.* Schools should have a designated reporter (this would likely be a school psychologist or counselor) who will receive and immediately act upon all reports of suicide threats. It is important that this person is accessible and able to quickly respond to the suicide threat. The actions of the designated reporter are reviewed in Table 3.

7. *Notify the principal.* The principal should be made aware of any suicidal ideation or behavior. Given the high stakes and the principal's responsibilities for the school, it is essential that the principal be aware that a student is being assessed for suicide risk.

8. *Inform the youth of actions taken.* Before leaving a potentially suicidal student with the designated reporter, it is important to let the student know that help has been called and to describe what will happen next. The student should be told that his or her parents or guardians will need to be contacted. If the student is resistant to this idea, that information should be relayed to the designated reporter. If it is suspected that a student's resistance to parental contact is a consequence of abuse, a referral to child protective services must be made. Though staff members cannot promise that parents will not be informed of the suicidal threats, it would be appropriate to let a suicidal student know his or her concerns have been heard and are understood.

develop procedures for responding to the presence of a suicide threat and the occurrence of a suicidal behavior.

## Suicide Intervention

Goals of suicide intervention include ensuring student safety, assessing and responding to suicide risk, determining needed services, and ensuring appropriate care. Both general staff procedures and specific risk assessment and referral procedures need to be developed. An example of general staff procedures is provided in Table 2. These procedures should be followed whenever a staff member suspects a student is at risk for a suicidal behavior and identify how such a student will be brought to the attention of a "designated reporter" (Davis & Sandoval, 1991). A designated reporter is typically a school psychologist or counselor who has been trained to conduct suicide risk assessment and who is competent to make referral decisions. A model risk assessment and referral procedure is provided in Table 3.

## Suicide Postvention

It has been estimated that the number of individuals in the United States who have had close relationships with suicide victims (suicide survivors) is over 4 million, and

**Table 3** *Risk Assessment and Referral Procedures*

1. Discuss the reasons for referral with the referring staff member and begin to establish rapport with the student suspected to be suicidal.

2. Conduct an assessment to determine the student's risk of engaging in a suicidal behavior. The risk assessment should include the following:
   a. Identify suicidal ideation.
      i. Once the student has been engaged (through a demonstration of empathy, respect, and warmth), identify suicidal intent through direct questioning (e.g., "Sometimes when people have had your experiences and feelings they have thoughts of suicide. Is this something that you're thinking about?").
      ii. If thoughts of suicide are not present, a suicide intervention is not needed, but support and assistance with the student's referring concerns will likely be required.
      iii. If thoughts of suicide are present, continue to assess the student's risk of acting upon such ideation.
   b. Assess suicide risk in the following areas.
      i. *Current suicide plan.* Directly inquire about the presence of a plan (e.g., "Do you have a plan for how you might act on your thoughts of suicide?"). The greater the planning, the greater the risk. Other specific questions to ask include (a) "How might you do it?" (b) "How soon are you planning on suicide?" and (c) "How prepared are you to commit suicide?" (access to means of attempt).
      ii. *Pain.* Directly inquire about the degree to which the individual is desperate (e.g., "Does your physical or emotional pain feel unbearable?"). The more unbearable the pain, the greater the risk.
      iii. *Resources.* Directly inquire about the individual's perceptions of being alone (e.g., "Do you have any resources or reasons for living?"). The more "alone," the greater the risk.
      iv. *Prior suicidal behavior.* Directly inquire about the individual's history of suicidal behavior (e.g., "Have you or anyone close to you ever attempted suicide before?"). The more frequent the prior suicidal behavior the greater the risk.
      v. *History of mental illness.* Directly inquire about the individual's mental health history (e.g., "Have you ever had mental health care?"). Depression, schizophrenia, alcohol and substance abuse, trauma, and borderline personality disorders are particular concerns.

3. Consult with fellow staff members regarding risk assessment results. A school-based suicide risk assessment should never be done alone.

4. Consult with community mental health professionals. These are typically the individuals to whom the suicidal student would be referred.

5. Use risk assessment information and consultation guidance to develop an action plan. Action plan options are as follows:
   a. *Extreme Risk.* If the student has the means of his or her threatened suicide at hand and refuses to relinquish it, follow these procedures:
      i. Call the police.
      ii. Calm the student by talking and reassuring until the police arrive.
      iii. Continue to request that the student relinquish the means of the threatened suicide and try to prevent the student from harming himself or herself. When doing so, make certain that such requests do not place anyone else in danger.
      iv. Call the parents and inform them of the actions taken.
   b. *Crisis Intervention Referral.* If the student's risk of harming himself or herself is judged to be moderate to high (i.e., there is a probability of the student acting on suicidal thoughts, but the threat is not immediate), then follow these procedures.
      i. Determine if the student's distress is the result of parent or caregiver abuse, neglect, or exploitation. If so, contact child protective services instead of a parent or caregiver.
      ii. Meet with the student's parents (or child protective services).
      iii. Make appropriate referrals.
      iv. Determine what to do if the parents are unable or unwilling to assist with the suicidal crisis (e.g., call the police).

*(Continued)*

**Table 3** *Continued*

c. *Low Risk.* If the student's risk of harming himself or herself is judged to be low (i.e., although the student has thoughts of suicide, the risk assessment suggests a very low probability of engaging in a suicidal behavior), then follow these procedures.
   i. Determine if the student's distress is the result of parent or caregiver abuse, neglect, or exploitation. If so, contact child protective service instead of a parent or caregiver.
   ii. Meet with the student's parents (or child protective services).
   iii. Make appropriate referrals.

6. When making referrals, protect the privacy of the student and family.

7. Follow up with the hospital or clinic to ensure that the student is receiving the appropriate care.

*Note.* Source of risk assessment variables: R. F. Ramsay, B. L. Tanney, W. A. Lang, & T. Kinzel. (2004). *Suicide Intervention Handbook* (10th ed.). Calgary, AB: LivingWorks.

that number is growing by 180,000 per year (Jobes, Luoma, Hustead, & Mann, 2000). When taking into account those who have had relationships with individuals exhibiting other suicidal behaviors, estimates of the number of people affected by suicidality become staggering. These facts point to the need for schools to be prepared to respond to the aftermath of suicidal behavior. This response is referred to as *suicide postvention.*

Postvention assists in the identification of individuals who are having difficulty coping with a suicide and facilitates adaptive coping. Following a suicide, it is not unusual for some students and staff members to enter into a crisis state. In addition to the emotions felt after other types of loss, this state may consist of a set of unique emotional reactions, such as guilt, anger, shame, and isolation associated with the stigma attached to suicide (Brock, 2002). An additional postvention concern is the possibility of contagion. Although such imitative behavior accounts for only an estimated 1% to 3% of all adolescent suicides (Moscicki, 1995), the potential to imitate suicidal behavior appears to be a unique issue for adolescents (Askland, Sonnenfeld, & Crosby, 2003). Jobes et al. (2000) describe suicide postvention's guiding principles. They emphasize the importance of not dramatizing or glorifying the suicide. They also point out that doing nothing can be as dangerous as doing too much and that students cannot be helped until school staff are helped.

To effectively provide suicide postvention, schools should form a suicide postvention (or crisis intervention) team that will follow a specific protocol. The following describes the essential elements of the postvention protocol developed by Brock (2002). Ideally, different staff members would be working on several of these tasks simultaneously.

***Verify that a death has occurred.*** The legal classification of a death as a suicide is complex and is usually made by medical examiners; therefore, it is essential to avoid labeling any death a suicide, even what may seem to be an obvious suicide, until an official determination is made.

***Mobilize the crisis intervention team.*** Successful suicide postvention requires a team effort, with specific postvention response roles carried out by specific individuals. Each element of this postvention protocol should be addressed as part of a team effort.

***Assess the suicide's impact on the school and estimate the level of postvention response.*** As soon as the death is verified and the facts are known, the school should assess the effects of the loss on the student body. A suicide's impact is assessed by estimating the number of students affected by the death. Proximity is an important way of assessing such impact, including physical and emotional proximity to the current suicide, and temporal proximity to prior instances of suicidal behavior. Variables to consider when estimating the number of students affected by a suicide are given in Table 4. To the extent these variables are present, the suicide's impact will be greater.

***Notify other involved school personnel.*** The crisis team should next contact other school personnel who will likely be affected by the death or will participate in the response. Assessment of impact on these individuals

**Table 4** *Variables to Consider When Assessing the Impact of a Suicide on a School*

| Risk Factor | Examples |
|---|---|
| Facilitated the suicide | 1. Were involved in a suicide pact.<br>2. Helped write the suicide note.<br>3. Provided the means of the suicide.<br>4. Knew about and did not try to stop the suicide. |
| Failed to recognize the suicidal intent | 1. Observed events that were later learned to be signs of the impending suicide.<br>2. Did not take a suicide threat seriously.<br>3. Had been too busy to talk to a person who committed suicide and had asked for help. |
| Believe they may have caused the suicide | 1. Feel guilty about things said or done to the victim before the suicide.<br>2. Recently punished or threatened to punish the person who committed suicide for some misdeed. |
| Had a relationship or identify with the person who committed suicide | 1. Were mentioned in the suicide note.<br>2. Were relatives, best friends, or self-appointed therapists of the person who committed suicide.<br>3. Identify with the situation of the person who committed suicide.<br>4. Have life circumstances that parallel those of the suicide victim. |
| Have a history of prior suicidal behavior | 1. Have previously attempted or threatened suicide.<br>2. Have family members, acquaintances, or role models who have died by suicide. |
| Have a history of psychopathology | 1. Have poor baseline mental health.<br>2. Have substance abuse problems.<br>3. Have a history of impulsive or violent behavior directed either toward self or others. |
| Show symptoms of helplessness, hopelessness, or both | 1. Are feeling desperate and now consider suicide a viable alternative.<br>2. Feel powerless to change distressing life circumstances.<br>3. Are depressed. |
| Have suffered significant life stressors or losses | 1. Had family members or acquaintances that have died by accident or homicide.<br>2. Had someone they were close to die violently.<br>3. Had recently broken up with a girlfriend or boyfriend.<br>4. Have been disrupted by changes in residence, schools, or parental figures. |

*Note.* Adapted from "The School Psychologist's Role in Suicide Prevention." By J. Sandoval, & S. E. Brock, (1996), *School Psychology Quarterly, 11*, 169–185. Used by permission of publisher.

or school sites, and estimated response needs, should be considered when evaluating whom to contact.

***Contact the family of the suicide victim.*** The goals of this contact include expression of the school's sympathy and, if needed, offers of postvention assistance. The family may be helpful in identifying others who may need crisis intervention (e.g., the victim's close friends).

***Determine what information to share about the death.*** An announcement regarding the death should be made as soon as possible. Delay fuels rumors that can be damaging and difficult to dispel. Because not all of the facts may be immediately available, several communications may be needed (e.g., before and after the death is certified as a suicide). Students could be provided the basic facts about the death, but excessive details should be avoided. Postvention should avoid glorifying or sensationalizing the death while at the same time providing a timely flow of accurate information.

***Determine how to share information about the death.*** Options for sharing information with students include written bulletins, letters, phone calls, classroom presentations and discussions, and individual conferences. Regardless of the method all students should receive the information at the same time. A communication to the parents must also be prepared.

Working with the media is an important postvention task. To minimize the risk of suicide contagion, the CDC (2004) provides recommendations for the media when reporting suicide deaths. Specifically, they recommend that the media (a) downplay the death, such as by not placing the word suicide in the headline, not including a picture of the individual, and placing the article on an inside page, if it's necessary to report it at all; (b) not romanticize the death; (c) discourage opportunities for students to identify with the individual and not illuminate the pathological aspects of the suicide act; and (d) provide resources for individuals who may be at risk.

***Identify students significantly affected by the suicide and initiate referral procedures.*** During the crisis intervention team's assessment of the impact of the death on the school, high-risk individuals will be identified. Physical and emotional proximity to the current suicide and temporal proximity to prior suicides are the primary concerns when identifying students who may need crisis intervention.

***Conduct a faculty planning session.*** In addition to the initial staff meeting, the school should hold other meetings to provide the staff with updated information regarding the death. At these meetings, teachers should be informed that they are a vital component of the postvention response. Guidance should be offered regarding the potential need to suspend normal instruction for the postvention. However, at the same time it should be remembered that keeping to as normal a schedule as possible is reassuring to many. During this staff meeting, teachers should also be given permission to feel uncomfortable about discussing the suicide with their students. Such feelings may result in some staff members not being able to provide students with needed support and guidance, and the school should provide alternative opportunities for helping students cope.

***Initiate crisis intervention services.*** Planned interventions should be implemented (e.g., classroom activities, group sessions, individual sessions, parent meetings, or staff meetings) and referrals made to outside agencies. Typical intervention tasks include (a) facilitating the expression and acceptance of emotions over the loss through both verbal and nonverbal communications while ensuring that students do not identify with the person who committed suicide, (b) refraining from romanticizing or glorifying the person's behavior or circumstances, and (c) discouraging dwelling on real or imagined guilt. To prevent students' identification with the suicide, crisis counselors should point out how the survivors are different from the person who committed suicide and discuss how suicide was a poor choice (e.g., how feelings and situations can change quickly, what the individual will miss out on in life). Postvention providers can prevent the glorification of the act by not making the suicide seem exciting or the person who committed suicide admirable.

***Conduct daily planning sessions.*** Planning sessions should be held to evaluate the progress of the postvention as well as to make plans for the following day. These sessions also provide ongoing debriefing opportunities for the crisis team.

***Memorialize.*** After a crisis event, many people feel the need to express their grief, say goodbye, and do something as a memorial. Working together on a memorial can help survivors focus their grief, fears, and anger constructively. However, when choosing memorials following a suicide, postvention providers should take

**Table 5** *Memorial Activities Following a Suicide: A List of "Dos" and "Don'ts"*

| *DO* | *DON'T* |
|---|---|
| *Do* something to prevent other suicides from happening. | *Don't* make special arrangements to send all students from school to funerals. |
| *Do* develop living memorials (e.g., student assistance programs that help other students cope with feelings and problems). | *Don't* have memorial or funeral services at school. |
| *Do* allow any student, with parental permission, to attend the funeral. | *Don't* stop classes for a funeral. |
| *Do* encourage affected students, with parental permission, to attend the funeral. | *Don't* put up plaques in memory of the suicide victim. |
| *Do* mention to families and ministers the need to distance the person who committed suicide from survivors to avoid glorifying the suicide act. | *Don't* dedicate yearbooks, songs, or sporting events to the person who committed suicide.<br>*Don't* fly the flag at half-staff.<br>*Don't* have a moment of silence in all-school assemblies.<br>*Don't* have mass assemblies focusing on the suicide victim. |

*Note.* Adapted from "The School Psychologist's Role in Suicide Prevention." By J. Sandoval, & S. E. Brock, (1996), *School Psychology Quarterly, 11,* 169–185. Used by permission of publisher.

particular care to not romanticize the suicide. Table 5 provides a list of dos and don'ts regarding memorial activities following a suicide.

***Evaluate the postvention response.*** This is an opportunity to help interveners cope with the crisis. The goals are to review and evaluate the postvention response, as well as to provide an opportunity for crisis interveners to receive support and to continue to deal with their own emotions and reactions.

One final point should be made. If there is no chance of students becoming aware of a death that is a suicide, it is not necessary to report the situation to them or to provide crisis intervention services. Suicide is only contagious if other people know about it. If knowledge of suicidal behavior can be kept out of a school building, it is probably best to do so. However, the worst-case scenario is for students to know of a suicide and to have the school pretend that it did not occur.

## SUMMARY

Suicide is a reality in U.S. public schools. Prevalence data suggest that one suicide within a 5-year period and somewhere around 170 suicidal acts occur each year in a typical high school (Davis & Sandoval, 1991). Many of these incidents will not come directly to the school's attention. Suicidal behavior is a problem that diligent school psychologists, in partnership with other school personnel and community-based professionals, can do something about. This chapter has presented strategies for prevention, intervention, and postvention in the hope that readers will be stimulated to seek further education on this topic and be better prepared for suicidal crises. To that end, the following resources are recommended.

## RECOMMENDED RESOURCES

### Books and Other Printed Material

Hawton, K., & van Heeringen, K. (Eds.). (2002). *The international handbook of suicide and attempted suicide.* New York: Wiley.

This is a comprehensive and authoritative compilation of the incidence of suicide and attempted suicide, risk factors, and prevention and intervention for suicide behaviors..

Maris, R. W., Berman, A. L., & Silverman, M. M. (2000). *The comprehensive textbook of suicidology.* New York: Guilford Press.

The foundations of suicidology are covered, along with theory, research, and clinical applications.

## Websites

*http://www.save.org*

Suicide Awareness/Voices of Education (SAVE) offers information on prevention, postvention, coping, and depression, as well as links to other websites. It is a good starting point.

*http://www.suicidology.org*

American Association of Suicidology is an informative website by the organization that publishes the journal *Suicide and Life-Threatening Behaviors.* Many articles and fact sheets are available for download, and the site has many links to other organizations.

*http://www.nopcas.com*

National Organization for People of Color Against Suicide (NOPCAS) is an organization whose goal is to bring awareness to minority communities. The website offers articles and links.

*http://www.mentalhealthscreening.org/sos_highschool*

This website provides access to the SOS Signs of Suicide® Program. SOS is a nationally recognized, easily implemented, cost-effective ($200) program of suicide prevention for secondary school students.

# REFERENCES

Aberson, B., & Shure, M. (2002). Problem-solving training as a form of crisis prevention. In S. E. Brock, P. J. Lazarus, & S. R. Jimerson (Eds.), *Best practices in school crisis prevention and intervention* (pp. 109–130). Bethesda, MD: National Association of School Psychologists.

American Association of Suicidology. (2003). *Youth suicide fact sheet.* Retrieved June 2, 2004, from http://www.suicidology.org

American Association of Suicidology. (2004). *Some facts about suicide and depression.* Retrieved June 2, 2004, from http://www.suicidology.org

Anderson, R. N., & Smith, B. L. (2003). Deaths: Leading causes for 2001. *National Vital Statistics Report, 52*(9), 1–47.

Aseltine, R. H., & DeMartino, R. (2004). An outcome evaluation of the SOS suicide prevention. *American Journal of Public Health, 94,* 446–451. Retrieved August 2, 2005, from http://www.mentalhealthscreening.org/downloads/sites/docs/sos/AJPHarticle.pdf

Askland, K. D., Sonnenfeld, N., & Crosby, A. (2003). A public health response to a cluster of suicidal behaviors: Clinical psychiatry, prevention and community health. *Journal of Psychiatric Practice, 9,* 219–227.

Bearman, P. S., & Moody, J. (2004). Suicide and friendships among American adolescents. *American Journal of Public Health, 94,* 89–95.

Brådvik, L. (2003). Suicide after suicide attempt in severe depression: A long-term follow-up. *Suicide and Life-Threatening Behavior, 33,* 381–388.

Brock, S. E. (2002). School suicide postvention. In S. E. Brock, P. J. Lazarus, & S. R. Jimerson (Eds.), *Best practices in school crisis prevention and intervention* (pp. 211–223). Bethesda, MD: National Association of School Psychologists.

Brock, S. E., Lazarus, P. J., & Jimerson, S. R. (Eds.). (2002). *Best practices in school crisis prevention and intervention* Bethesda, MD: National Association of School Psychologists.

Capuzzi, D. (2002). Legal and ethical challenges in counseling suicidal students. *Professional School Counseling, 6,* 36–46.

Carrington, P. J., & Moyer, S. (1994). Gun control and suicide in Ontario. *American Journal of Psychiatry, 154,* 606–608.

Center for Mental Health in Schools at UCLA. (2003). *A technical assistance sampler on school interventions to prevent youth suicide.* Los Angeles, CA: Author.

Centers for Disease Control and Prevention. (2002, June). Surveillance summaries. *Morbidity and Mortality Weekly Report, 51,* (No. SS-4).

Centers for Disease Control and Prevention. (2004). *Web-based injury statistics query and reporting system (WISQARS).* Retrieved June 21, 2004, from http://www.cdc.gov/ncipc/wisqars

Centers for Disease Control and Prevention. (2005). *WISQARS leading causes of death reports, 1999–2002,* Retrieved August 3, 2005, from http://webappa.cdc.gov/sasweb/ncipc/leadcaus10.html

Davis, J. M., & Sandoval, J. (1991). *Suicidal youth: School-based intervention and prevention.* San Francisco: Jossey-Bass.

Eckert, T. L., Miller, D. N., DuPaul, G. J., & Riley-Tillman, T. C. (2003). Adolescent suicide prevention: School psychologists' acceptability of school-based programs. *School Psychology Review, 32,* 57–76.

Edwards, M. J., & Holden, R. R. (2001). Coping, meaning in life, and suicidal manifestations: Examining gender differences. *Journal of Clinical Psychology, 59,* 1133–1150.

Elliott, S. N., McKevitt, B. C., & DiPerna, J. C. (2002). Promoting social skills and development of socially supportive learning environments. In S. E. Brock, P. J. Lazarus, & S. R. Jimerson (Eds.), *Best practices in school crisis prevention and intervention* (pp. 151–170). Bethesda, MD: National Association of School Psychologists.

Garland, A. F., Shaffer, D., & Whittle, B. (1989). A national survey of school-based adolescent suicide prevention programs. *Journal of the American Academy of Child and Adolescent Psychiatry, 28,* 931–934.

Glowinski, A. L., Bucholz, K. K., Nelson, E. C., Fu, Q., Madden, P. A., Reich, W., & Heath, A. C. (2001). Suicide attempts in an adolescent female twin sample. *Journal of the American Academy of Child and Adolescent Psychiatry, 40,* 1300–1308.

Goldsmith, S. K., Pellmar, T. C., Kleinman, A. M., & Bunney, W. E. (Eds.). (2002). *Reducing suicide: A national imperative.* Washington, DC: National Academies Press.

Grunbaum, J. A., Kann, L., Kinchen, S., Ross, J., Hawkins, J., Lowry, R., et al. (2004, May). Youth risk behavior surveillance—United States, 2003. *Morbidity and Mortality Weekly Report, 53* (No. SS-02), 1–96. Retrieved July 20, 2004, from http://www.cdc.gov/mmwr/preview/mmwrhtml/ss5302a1.htm

Gutierrez, P. M., Osman, A., & Kopper, B. A. (2000). Suicide risk assessment in a college student population. *Journal of Counseling Psychology, 47,* 403–413.

Haw, C., Hawton, K., Houston, K., & Townsend, E. (2003). Correlates of relative lethality and suicidal intent among deliberate self-harm patients. *Suicide and Life-Threatening Behavior, 33,* 353–364.

Helsel, D. C. (2001). Tracking the suicidal student. *The Clearing House, 75*(2), 92–95.

Hjelmeland, H., Hawton, K., Nordvik, H., Bille-Brahe, U., De Leo, D., Fekete, S., et al. (2002). Why people engage in parasuicide: A cross-cultural study of intentions. *Suicide and Life-Threatening Behavior, 32,* 380–393.

Jick, H., Kaye, J. A., & Jick, S. S. (2004). Antidepressants and the risk of suicidal behaviors. *Journal of the American Medical Association, 292,* 338–343.

Jobes, D. A., Luoma, J. B., Hustead, L. A., & Mann, R. E. (2000). In the wake of suicide: Survivorship and postvention. In R. W. Maris, A. L. Berman, & M. M. Silverman (Eds.), *Comprehensive textbook of suicidology* (pp. 536–561). New York: Guilford Press.

Kellermann, A. L., Rivara, F. P., Somes, G., Reay, D. T., Francisco, J., Banton, J. G., et al. (1992). Suicide in the home in relation to gun ownership. *The New England Journal of Medicine, 327,* 467–472.

King, K. A., Schwab-Stone, M., Flisher, A. J., Greenwald, S., Kramer, R. A., Goodman, S. H, et al. (2001). Psychosocial and risk behavior correlates of youth suicide attempts and suicidal ideation. *Journal of the American Academy of Child and Adolescent Psychiatry, 40,* 837–846.

Lubell, K. M., Swahn, M. H., Crosby, A. E., & Kegler, S. R. (2004). Methods of suicide among persons aged 10–19 years—United States, 1992–2001. *Morbidity and Mortality Weekly Report, 53,* 471–473. Retrieved July 20, 2004, from http://www.cdc.gov/mmwr/PDF/wk/mm5322.pdf

Maris, R. W., Berman, A. L., & Silverman, M. M. (2000). *The comprehensive textbook of suicidology.* New York: Guilford Press.

Moscicki, E. K. (1995). Epidemiology of suicidal behavior. *Suicide and Life-Threatening Behavior, 25,* 22–35.

O'Donnell, L., O'Donnell, C., Wardlaw, D. M., & Stueve, A. (2004). Risk and resiliency factors influencing suicidality among urban African American and Latino youth. *American Journal of Community Psychology, 33,* 37–49.

Prager, K. (2003). *Health, United States, 2003: With chart book on trends in the health of Americans.* Hyattsville, MD: U.S. Department of Health and Human Services, Centers for Disease Control and Prevention, National Center for Health Statistics.

Ramsay, R. F., Tanney, B. L., Lang, W. A., & Kinzel, T. (2004). *Suicide intervention handbook* (10th ed.). Calgary, AB: LivingWorks.

Reynolds, W. M. (1988). *Suicidal ideation questionnaire: Professional manual.* Odessa, FL: Psychological Assessment Resources.

Rutter, P. A., & Soucar, E. (2002). Youth suicide risk and sexual orientation. *Adolescence, 37,* 289–299.

Sandoval, J., & Brock, S. E. (1996). The school psychologist's role in suicide prevention. *School Psychology Quarterly, 11,* 169–185.

Seeley, J. R., Rohde, P., Lewinsohn, P. M., & Clarke, G. N. (2002). Depression in youth: Epidemiology, identification, and intervention. In M. R. Shinn, G. M. Walker, & G. Stoner (Eds.), *Interventions for academic and behavior problems. II: Preventive and remedial approaches* (pp. 885–911). Bethesda, MD: National Association of School Psychologists.

Shaffer, D., Garland, A. F., Gould, M., Fisher, P., & Trautman, P. (1988). Preventing teenage suicide: A critical review. *Journal of the American Academy of Child and Adolescent Psychiatry, 27,* 675–687.

Shaffer, D., Garland, A., & Whittle, B. (1987). *An evaluation of three youth suicide prevention programs in New Jersey.* Unpublished report, Division of Child Psychiatry, New York State Psychiatric Institute, Columbia University, NY.

Simon, T. R., Swann, A. C., Powell, K. E., Potter, L. B., Kresnow, M., & O'Carroll, P. W. (2001). Characteristics of impulsive suicide attempts and attempters. *Suicide and Life-Threatening Behavior, 32*(Suppl), 49–59.

Sloan, J. H., Rivara, F. P., Reay, D. T., Ferris, J. A., & Kellermann, A. L. (1990). Firearm regulations and rates of suicide: A comparison of two metropolitan areas. *New England Journal of Medicine, 322,* 369–373.

Spirito, A., Valeri, S., Boergers, J., & Donaldson, D. (2003). Predictors of continued suicidal behavior in adolescents following a suicide attempt. *Journal of Clinical Child and Adolescent Psychology, 32,* 284–289.

U.S. Food and Drug Administration. (2004, March 22). *FDA public health advisory. Subject: Worsening depression and suicidality in patients being treated with antidepressant medications.* Retrieved July 25, 2004, from http://www.fda.gov/cder/drug/antidepressants/AntidepressanstPHA.htm

U.S. Public Health Service. (1999). *The surgeon general's call to action to prevent suicide.* Washington, DC: Author.

# 18

# Grief

**Gary W. Mauk**

*Scotland County Schools, Laurinburg, NC*

**Jim D. Sharpnack**

*The Guidance Center, Leavenworth, KS*

*"Well, everyone can master a grief but he that has it."*

– William Shakespeare, *Much Ado About Nothing,* Act III, Scene 2

## BACKGROUND AND DEVELOPMENT

### Loss: The Core of Grief

Loss is universal and resides at the core of grief; someone or something we love and value is gone, and we grieve (react to) the loss. From birth until death, as long as we continue to form attachments to and love other people—as long as we ascribe personal value to particular persons, pets, places, experiences, and objects—we assume the risk of the pain of grief when these cherished things are lost. In addition to losing a loved one through death, children and adolescents potentially experience sundry perceived minor and major losses and associated grieving from a variety of causes, such as losing a favorite toy to the ravages of time; experiencing parental separation, divorce, or imprisonment; moving to a new residence; changing schools; having a friend move away; being bullied; being rejected by peers; breaking up with a romantic partner; or not being chosen for a team or other group.

Despite the fact that children and adolescents can grieve many types of losses, loss is most severe when it involves the death of a person who was an integral part of the survivor's life. The losses from such deaths fall into four major classes: (a) relationship losses (e.g., loss of intimacy, emotional support, companionship, validation, instrumental support, a sense of being needed); (b) lifestyle losses (e.g., loss of social and school- or work-related activities, status or position in a peer group, and financial and material resources); (c) loss of biography (e.g., loss of personal history, shared memories, vision of and plans for the future); and (d) loss of the self or identity (e.g., loss of personal aspects of the survivor—such as positive feedback and specific roles and identities—that were interdependent with the relationship with the deceased) (Mullan, Skaff, & Pearlin, 2003).

### Grief, Mourning, and Bereavement

The various terms used to describe youths' reactions to loss are differentiated as follows. *Grief* is the normal, dynamic, unique, and multidimensional set of feelings, thoughts, and related reactions of an individual following a personally significant loss. Because grieving is a personally unique and highly variable dynamic process, grief responses among children and adolescents vary. Factors affecting grief responses include manner of death, nature and significance of the relationship to the deceased, age and related developmental tasks, gender, physical and mental status, social–emotional development and personality, prior loss experiences, death-specific religious beliefs, adequacy of personal coping resources, and availability of helpful social support. *Mourning,* which has both personal and interpersonal components and is embedded in an individual's religious and cultural tradition, is the way the bereaved individual personally manages and overtly expresses grief after the death of a loved one. Mourning includes formalized rituals such as memorial services, funerals, wakes, specific modes of dress, or other comforting behavior. *Bereavement* refers to an individual's complete reaction to the loss and encompasses both the unique grief experience and its expression through the work of mourning.

## Prevailing Theories and Models of Bereavement

The work of Kato and Mann (1999) explicates four major theories of bereavement: (a) psychoanalytic theories that stem from the work of Sigmund Freud and focus on the bereaved individual's withdrawal of libido from the deceased (the lost object) and reinvestment of the libido in a new object (e.g., a new friend); (b) stage or phase theories that view the bereaved individual's grief response as progressing through a systematic pattern of stages or phases that the individual may skip or revisit (e.g., Kübler-Ross's stages of grief—denial, anger, bargaining, depression, and acceptance [1969]); (c) stress theories that consider bereavement a major life stressor that requires significant life adjustments and may directly and indirectly affect a bereaved individual's mental and physical health; and (d) social support theories that view bereavement as a loss of a critical member of a family group or friend network that has both direct and indirect effects on the survivor's physical and mental well-being and functioning.

Although dominant 20th-century models of grieving have held that the function of grief and mourning is to cut bonds with the deceased, thereby freeing the survivor to reinvest in new relationships in the present, an emerging consensus among bereavement scholars is that the understanding of the grief process needs to be expanded. Recent discussions of loss and grief have revolved around (a) individual patterns of loss and grief (e.g., the changing intensity of grief experience over time) and (b) whether bereaved individuals should psychologically let go of or maintain a bond with the deceased (e.g., Klass, Silverman, & Nickman, 1996). Once a child or adolescent has accepted the death of a friend or loved one as reality, such continued attachments and bonds can serve as resources for continued healthy functioning in the present. Rather than being a representation of bereaved youths' denial of death, continuation of attachments allows them to talk honestly and openly about the deceased with others who knew them. By actively reflecting on their personal stories of loss, grief, and bereavement, youth can make sense of what has happened. They can experience suffering and sorrow as part of the memory of the deceased, and also experience comfort, warmth, connection, and celebration by holding on to mementos and memories of experiences with the deceased (e.g., Davis & Nolen-Hoeksema, 2001). Because deceased individuals can live on in the memories and everyday lives of the children and adolescents left behind to grieve their loss, they can continue to influence survivors' thoughts and actions. Thus, it is important to acknowledge the significance of the bereaved youth's self-appraised meaning of the loss and the adaptive coping of the continued attachment and ongoing relationship with the deceased.

## Common Misconceptions, Facts, and Developmental Aspects of Grief

All children and adolescents grieve various losses, especially the death of a loved one. Understanding and working with youths who are grieving a loss usually entail navigating a sea of misconceptions, some of which are presented in Table 1.

As children grow up and experience life, their understanding of death evolves, along with their cognitive and social–emotional development. Children's grief experiences will be affected by their understanding of each of five components of the death concept: (a) universality (i.e., all living things die); (b) irreversibility (i.e., once something dies, it does not become alive again); (c) nonfunctionality (i.e., when a living thing dies, it ceases to be able to engage in life-related behaviors such as communicating, thinking, eating, or moving); (d) causality (i.e., understanding and attributing realistic internal and external causes of death); and (e) noncorporeal continuation (i.e., the idea that some type of personal continuation occurs after the physical body has died; e.g., Speece & Brent, 1996).

Clear developmental differences exist between children and adolescents in their experience, understanding, and expression of grief (Adams et al., 1999). Table 2 contains a developmental matrix of death-related concepts, potential "acting-out" reactions that are considered normal, and indicators of possible problems. It is important to remember that a youth's cognitive developmental age (i.e., the ability to understand what has happened) rather than chronological age is the primary influence on his or her concept and perception of death.

Bereaved youth must undertake several tasks as they work toward active resolution of a loss, including the following: (a) overcoming denial and accepting the reality of the loss; (b) experiencing and processing the pain of grief incident to losing a loved one; (c) adjusting to an environment in which the deceased is missing by accepting and acquiring requisite postloss concepts, roles, and skills; and (d) finding realistic cognitive and emotional ways to think about the deceased and to move on with life and form new relationships (Worden, 2002).

**Table 1** *Misconceptions and Facts About Youths and Grief*

| Misconceptions | Facts |
|---|---|
| The child does not understand what has happened. He/she is too young. | Even very young children know when those around them are upset. Most children understand more than adults realize. |
| Going to the funeral would just upset him/her. | Not including the child in family rituals could be even more upsetting. It helps the child to see how adults grieve. |
| I must protect him/her from loss and pain. | All children experience losses and need help in learning ways to deal/cope with them. |
| Children do not feel grief the same as adults. | Every person grieves in his/her own way, depending on circumstances, developmental level, and life experiences. This is usual and healthy. |
| When the child has grieved once, it should be over. | As they develop, children must re-grieve losses in light of new understanding and abilities. |
| I will not say or do the right thing; I must be in control to talk with him/her. | There are no right answers, only honest ones. Saying "something" acknowledges the child's grief and dispels fears and misunderstandings. |
| He/she will not want to talk about it. | Let that be the child's choice, not yours. Often, that is all they *do* want to talk about. |
| I might upset him/her. | He/she is already upset—that is a natural part of grieving. |
| He/she needs to keep busy. | Routine activities are important, but new activities can be confusing. The child's grief may be deferred or perceived as being discounted by *not* thinking about it. |
| Getting rid of reminders helps; encourage only good memories. | This suggests it is wrong to think about the person who died or to have bad memories. |
| I will not mention it unless he/she does. | This suggests it is wrong to mention the person who died, that there is something bad about them or their death, and that you do not care. |
| Once he/she has been angry or has felt guilty, that should be the end of it. | Grief is a process, not steps. Thus, the same feelings will surface repeatedly, as each aspect of the loss is realized. |
| It is morbid to want to touch or talk about the body. | This is normal for children. It is a good way to say "goodbye," and make the death real. |
| I should use terms like "has passed away" or "is in eternal sleep." | These terms are misleading, and will likely confuse and frighten the child. "Dead" is better. |

*(Continued)*

**Table 1** *Continued*

| Misconceptions | Facts |
|---|---|
| If he/she is not expressing grief, then he/she is not grieving. | The child may not know how to express feelings or know if he/she has permission to grieve. The child may repress his/her grief to avoid upsetting others. When ready, the child will express his or her grief in personally necessary and meaningful ways, sometimes other than talking (e.g., play, artwork, music, writing, etc.). |
| I should tell him/her all the facts regarding the death immediately. | The child may not be able to understand or be able to handle the intensity of the situation. If allowed, the child will set the pace of disclosure. |

*Note.* The material in this table was adapted and used with written permission from Wendy Wainwright, Manager of Counseling and Spiritual Care, Victoria Hospice Society, Victoria, British Columbia, Canada.

Among the variables mediating youths' process of loss resolution are the nature of the losses they have experienced; the psychological, social, and economic resources available to manage their grief in the wake of loss; and the ability to reconstitute their life (Mullan et al., 2003). In particular, grieving adolescents may need frequent reassurance that certain behaviors are part of normal mourning or grief work and will dissipate in time (e.g., anger, anhedonia, difficulty concentrating, feelings of helplessness, and reduced energy). Also, although adolescents experience loss at a deep emotional level, they might expend a great deal of energy cloaking their feelings, presenting an outwardly brave and dispassionate public face while actively denying or postponing dealing with the pain of loss that begs for validation and healing support from caring peers and adults.

The Greek physician, Hippocrates, observed: "Healing is a matter of time, but it is sometimes also a matter of opportunity." Although the passage of quantitative chronological time (*Chronos*) is an essential element in youth's bereavement processes, and though developmental aspects and grief reactions have commonalities, bereaved youths come to terms with the reality of their unique losses in their own qualitative psychological time (*Kairos*) by seizing healing opportunities and experiencing personal growth. Young people who are grieving need four interrelated empowering essentials from adults: routine, love, honesty, and security (Rathkey, 2004). During times of confusion and uncertainty, routine provides children with familiar experiences to depend on, allowing them to engage in activities that they understand and expect. Unconditional love, demonstrated through adults' words and actions, is a powerful tool for the insecurity caused by grief. Because a once-broken trust is difficult to repair, adults should practice judicious honesty when sharing aspects of a death and grief-related feelings, honesty that is informed and guided by the grieving child's age and needs. The foregoing three essentials all contribute to the bereaved child's sense of security. Children experience a security that mitigates their fears, allows them to move through sadness with strengthened self-esteem and self-efficacy, and empowers them to challenge their vulnerabilities, accept loss, heal, and confidently grow.

## Gender-Related Differences

Although the understanding of death and the internal experience of grief may not differ substantially by gender, the facility and willingness of males and females to express that grief, the social acceptability of and opportunities for such expression, and the ways in which they prefer to express their grief appear to be another story. In combination with the generally death-denying, grieving-impatient, mourning-avoiding, and support-deficient nature of our society, gender conditioning may foster unhealthy restraint in expressing grief. In particular, adolescent boys may have a difficult time grieving, especially when they have been inculcated with the belief that only girls are supposed to display emotion when they experience a loss.

Eschewing gender-related terms and stereotypes regarding grief responses but still acknowledging distinct patterns of grieving or strategies of adapting to loss, Martin and Doka (2000, p. 5) have proffered the notion of "instrumental" and "intuitive" grievers. Instrumental grievers "tend to have a tempered affect to a loss," describe their grief "in physical or cognitive terms," and "are more likely to cognitively process or immerse themselves in activity." Conversely, intuitive grievers "are more

**Table 2** *Developmental Matrix of Death-Related Concepts, Potential "Acting Out" Reactions Considered Normal, and Indicators of Possible Problems*

| Age Groups | Concepts of Death | Potential "Acting Out" Reactions | Indicators of Possible Problems |
|---|---|---|---|
| **Under age 2** | Little understanding of death; Sense of separation, loss, abandonment. | Increased crying, fussiness, clinginess; Change in eating/ toileting/sleeping habits; Regression to earlier developmental tasks/ behaviors. | Exacerbation of any extant behavioral or emotional difficulties; Continual developmental regression; Persistent, detachment, indifference, and/or lack of trust. |
| **Ages 2–6** | Death is seen as reversible/ temporary; Displays magical thinking (i.e., if you wish it, it can happen– such as, you can "wish" someone dead; the deceased person will return). | Confusion; Sadness; Guilt; Aggression; Regression to earlier developmental tasks/behaviors; Nightmares; Bladder/bowel problems; Noncompliance. | Exacerbation of any extant behavioral or emotional difficulties; Inability to engage in usual activities; Significant interference with developmental tasks/ progress; Persistent unhappiness; Sleep problems; Continual developmental regression. |
| **Ages 6–9** | Gradual comprehension that death is final; Retains some magical thinking; Develops interest in death etiologies; Personifies death (e.g., a "monster" took the deceased person away). | Anger; Guilt/self-blame; Compulsive care-giving; Phobias; Possessiveness; Aggression; Regression to earlier developmental tasks/behaviors; Difficulty putting grief feelings into words; Difficulty concentrating; Psychosomatic symptoms (headaches, stomachaches); Identification with/ acting out being like the deceased. | Exacerbation of any extant behavioral or emotional difficulties; Inability to engage in usual activities; Significant interference with developmental tasks/progress; Excessive guilt and/or compulsiveness; Persistent belief deceased is still alive. |
| **Ages 9–12** | Cognitive awareness of death and its finality; Curiosity about the biological details and associated psychosocial processes and spiritual aspects of death; Difficulty conceiving own death. | Anger; Guilt/self-blame; Defiance; Phobias; Possessiveness; Aggression; Psychosomatic symptoms. | Exacerbation of any extant behavioral or emotional difficulties; Inability to engage in usual activities; Significant interference with developmental tasks/progress; Feelings of self-punishment; Physical symptoms of deceased. |
| **Adolescence** | Death is irreversible, universal, and inevitable; Abstract and philosophical reasoning–Understand that all people and self must die, but believe death is in the distant future. | Anger; Denial; Avoidance of discussion of the death; Defiance; Risk taking; Increased sexual activity; Substance abuse; Aggression; Possessiveness; Psychosomatic symptoms. | Exacerbation of any extant behavioral or emotional difficulties; Inability to engage in usual activities; Significant interference with developmental tasks/progress; Persistent anger; Suicidal ideation; Increase in harmful coping and impulsive-compulsive behaviors; Social withdrawal and isolation. |

*Note.* Adapted from "Grieving children: Are we meeting the challenge?" by Busch, T., and Kimble C. S. (2001). *Pediatric Nursing, 27*(4), 415. Reprinted with permission of the publisher, Jannetti Publications, Inc., East Holly Avenue – Box 56, Pitman, NJ 08071-0056; Phone (856) 256-2300; FAX (856) 589-7463. For a sample copy of the journal, please contact the publisher.

likely to experience their grief as waves of affect" and frequently "need to express their feelings and seek the support of others." Although many boys might be instrumental grievers and many girls might be intuitive grievers, gender only influences grieving patterns, it does not determine them (Doka, 1999).

## Cultural and Religious or Spiritual Considerations

Although grief responses might be more similar than different across cultures, it is important to acknowledge and respect the ways individuals from diverse cultures and religious or spiritual backgrounds deal with reactions to death and grieving. In particular, death-specific religious beliefs can be central to a bereaved youth's coping and adjustment process. Prior knowledge and sensitive inquiry regarding students' traditions and beliefs can provide school practitioners with valuable information to help them plan and implement appropriate support services following a death (Jimerson & Huff, 2002). Culture-specific information should be sought regarding acceptable coping, grieving, and mourning behaviors; language and communication issues; religious and funeral practices; coping styles and social support resources; time orientation; definitions of wellness and illness; and attitudes toward counseling.

## Vulnerability and Resilience: Risk and Protective Factors in Bereavement

Growing up consists of a dynamic interplay of potential vulnerabilities for psychological and behavioral difficulties (risks) and resources and opportunities for thriving and empowerment (protections). Although the accumulation of risk factors increases a youth's probability of developing mental health or behavioral problems from a significant loss, a fair balance between risk and protective factors might moderate the effects of the risk factors and help the youth to progress developmentally in the midst of adversity. In general, youths reportedly are at highest risk for loss-related adjustment difficulties in the first year after the loss, with 10% to 15% of bereaved youth considered at risk for problems such as depression (Goodman, 2001).

Several bereavement-specific risk factors contribute to healthy or unhealthy grieving outcomes for children and adolescents (Stroebe & Schut, 2001). First, the circumstances surrounding the death of a significant other (e.g., whether the death was sudden, expected, violent, or traumatic) affect the construction of the grief experience and the course of bereavement of a child or adolescent. Second, specific characteristics of the bereaved individual (e.g., age, gender, personality, and religiosity) will affect the process. High self-esteem and self-efficacy and strong personal adaptability and resilience (e.g., an ability to go with the flow, tolerance of affect, and self-soothing ability), low sensitivity to loss and anxiety, a secure rather than avoidant attachment style, an internal versus external locus of control, and strong religious beliefs can serve as protective or moderating factors for bereaved youths. Also, gender differences regarding perceived or actual social constraints on coping with or expressing grief might affect grief responses and help-seeking behavior. Finally, the interpersonal context of the loss (e.g., social support and the nature of the relationship) is important. The quality and number of psychologically accessible and socially supportive relationships, both inside and outside the family, can play a major role in a young person's postloss adjustment by strengthening his or her ability to experience and healthily manage distress. Also, the nature of the bereaved youth's relationship with the deceased (i.e., whether the relationship was ambivalent, conflicted, or socially sanctioned) and the functional role of the deceased person in the youth's construction of self might influence the course of bereavement.

# PROBLEMS AND IMPLICATIONS

## Healthy and Maladaptive Grieving and Bereavement

Grief can have a substantial effect on students' educational performance and behavior. School professionals may observe increased feelings of anxiety and stress; impaired memory or ability to concentrate; expressions of fear of the future and the possibility of other losses; physical or emotional fatigue; somatic complaints (which may be psychosomatic in origin) resulting in increased visits to the school nurse; poor academic performance; acting-out or punishment-seeking behavior instigated by feelings of anger or guilt related to the deceased; increased absenteeism; and emotional numbing (Stevenson, 2002).

There are no magic approaches to alleviating the pain of loss, and no right or best ways for bereaved youths to grieve healthily. When compared with the grief of an adult, a child's grief may appear more sporadic and short-lived. However, because children have more limited oral language and verbal communication skills for expression of feelings, their grief actually might be of a longer duration. Because adult-level intensity and pace of grief may interfere with normal developmental progress (i.e., the business of growing up), bereaved youths tend to grieve intermittently. They grieve for a while, resume their normal activities of living and maturing, and return to grieve again (e.g., Oltjenbruns, 2001). Also, as they progress through developmental tasks and transitional phases, children and adolescents likely reexperience grief in new ways during transition periods and significant life events (Jimerson & Huff, 2002). In addition, particular youths' prolonged pattern of grieving and apparent lack of readjustment to life without the deceased may be unrelated or only tangentially associated with the loss. Their behaviors may stem from conflicts or ambivalences that preceded the loss or from unidentified current psychosocial difficulties (Attig, 1995).

Although some bereaved children and adolescents may present with symptoms associated with a major depressive episode (e.g., feelings of sadness, insomnia, poor appetite, and loss of weight), grieving behavior (bereavement) is nosologically considered a normal reaction to the death of a loved one, not a clinical syndrome (American Psychiatric Association, 2000). However, if a surviving youth exhibits guilt unrelated to the death, thoughts of self-demise, morbid preoccupation with lack of self-worth, conspicuous psychomotor retardation, prolonged and noticeable functional impairment, or hallucinatory experiences unrelated to or not involving the deceased individual, a complicated grief reaction might be present. *Complicated grief* is defined as an abnormal or unhealthy grief reaction or mourning process that overwhelms the grieving individual, results in maladaptive behaviors, and impedes progress toward a healthy outcome (Zeitlin, 2001). Risk factors include a previous history of psychiatric disorder; an ambivalent or overly close or intense relationship with the deceased; a history of multiple, recent losses; loss of a parent or significant individual during childhood; lack of social support; and death by AIDS, suicide, homicide, or other unexpected cause that may cause the grief to be disenfranchised.

*Disenfranchised* grief refers to situations in which the grief of a child or adolescent is not openly recognized or socially sanctioned or validated (e.g., the survivor's relationship with the deceased is not recognized, the griever is excluded from discussions and rituals, or the mode of grieving is considered inappropriate; Doka, 2002). In addition to those deaths that involve social stigma, loss-related events that might often involve disenfranchised grief include a friend moving away, the death of a friend or peer, divorce, adoption, placement in foster care, incarceration of one or both parents, death of a pet, moving to a new residence, or losses involving very young children or children or adolescents with disabilities. Also, children might experience self-disenfranchisement (a) by failing to acknowledge or by forgoing their own feelings and expressions of grief when they desire to protect parents or siblings, (b) out of fear of emotional flooding, and (c) because they have memories of receiving disappointing responses from adults with respect to sad feelings (Crenshaw, 2002). Thus, informed awareness of the youth's baseline mental health and knowledge about the current situation are critical, if adults are to understand individual reactions to loss and to gauge the validity of presumptions regarding excessive grieving and the need for further assessment and intervention.

## "Who Died?"—Types of Deaths in the Lives of Children and Adolescents

The following sections provide a brief overview of a few types of deaths children and adolescents experience during their development, as well as special aspects and associated personal contextual factors that may facilitate or complicate the grieving process.

***Death of a parent.*** About one in seven children experience the death of a parent before age 10 (Batts, 2004). Although the death of a parent during childhood is a critical life event that can permanently influence a child's future, the grieving needs of children who experience parental death and the long-term psychological and psychosocial effects of such a loss have often been ignored (Schuurman, 2003). Consequently, many children, especially those who have conflicted, abusive, or neglectful relationships with parents, carry unresolved feelings regarding the parent's death into adulthood. Those feelings can negatively influence self-esteem, coping skills, and relationships (Schuurman & Lindholm, 2002). Four major variables mediate the effect of a parent's death on a child: (a) the distinctive characteristics of the child (i.e., age and developmental level; personality and coping style; loss history; social, cultural, and religious background); (b) the personal–social significance and strength and quality of the relationship with the parent; (c) the particular circumstances of the death (e.g., sudden or anticipated, natural or traumatic, and time of year); and (d) the types and availability of custodial, social, and emotional support (Hatter, 1996).

***Death of a sibling.*** The death of a sibling can have special significance in the life of surviving children. To protect them from additional distress, well-meaning adults might create an unhealthy atmosphere of silence in which surviving siblings' feelings, reactions, and grieving needs incident to the loss are neglected and invalidated. Also, parents who are involved in their own process of adjusting to their child's death might at times be psychologically inaccessible to assist surviving siblings with grieving. Parents should be helped to understand that children may need to grieve in unique ways following the death of a sibling and have the right to know about and share in family grief. Given opportunities within safe environments, many children are able and willing to discuss issues surrounding death (Dowden, 1995).

***Death of a friend or peer.*** Peers left behind in the wake of a friend's death are frequently indirect victims and forgotten or invisible mourners who may experience survivor guilt and disenfranchised grief. Bereavement as a result of a friend's death might lead to losses of other friends who are not grieving or who find the bereaved individual's grief both uncomfortable and tedious (Balk, 1998). Also, because youths' friends play crucial roles in helping them accomplish various psychosocial tasks (e.g., achieving individuation or consolidating a personal identity), the death of a friend may delay or jeopardize successful completion of those developmental tasks (Oltjenbruns, 1996). Thus, adults need to recognize the developmentally important nature of the intertwined roles that friends play in each other's lives, roles that are lost when one of them dies.

***Death of a pet.*** Although the first death a child experiences is often the death of an animal companion, the developmental significance of the death of a pet, and the incident grieving, are rarely acknowledged. Some of the factors that could affect a child's reactions to pet loss include the child's level of cognitive and emotional maturity; the role played by the pet in the child's life; the child's loss history, concurrent life events, and coping ability; the circumstances of the pet's death, including whether the child played any role in the death; and the quality and availability of parental and other support (Butler & Lagoni, 1996). Adults should provide honest and clear information to children and adolescents about what happened to their pet and support them socially and emotionally after the death.

## Secondary Losses: Grief Ripples in the Pool of Life

Secondary losses are psychosocial sequelae that are not directly related to a person's death but instead result from the initial consequences of the death, or they occur concomitantly with the person's process of dying or during the child's or adolescent's bereavement (Mahon, 1999). Among the cascade of secondary losses that can complicate the grieving process, and that often go unacknowledged in their effects on the child or adolescent, are factors such as loss of income, loss of future together, loss of special relationship, change in household routines, family disintegration, moving or having to live with relatives, and witnessing of parental grief or increased parental stress.

## A Special Case: Traumatic Death

Approximately 5 million children annually experience some form of traumatic experience (i.e., physical or sexual abuse, domestic violence, natural disasters, vehicular accidents, community violence, and so forth) that increases their risk for a multitude of social, neuropsychiatric, and physical health problems (Perry, 2002). When a death is traumatic, children and adolescents must deal with the interacting symptoms of trauma and grief. If the traumatic nature of the death is not attended to first, the youth's normal grief resolution may be impeded by the concomitant intrusion of thoughts about the deceased and thoughts and memories about the calamitous circumstances incident to the death (e.g., Regehr & Sussman, 2004). In cases of traumatic death, school personnel should be alert to signs of difficulty in adjustment, including being preoccupied with how the loved one died; reliving or reenacting the traumatic death through artwork or play; demonstrating signs of emotional or behavioral distress when reminded of the loss; attempting to avoid physical reminders of the traumatic death (e.g., activities, people, or placed related to the death); withdrawing from important aspects of their environment and previously enjoyed activities; showing signs of emotional constriction; being excessively jumpy or easily startled; and demonstrating signs of losing their sense of purposes and meaning in life (Goodman et al., 2004).

## ALTERNATIVE ACTIONS FOR PREVENTION

Because many children and adolescents cope well with and adjust to the death of a loved one (or other loss experience) without any clinically significant psychological difficulties, formal therapeutic interventions might not be necessary. Many times, assisting a student who is grieving a loss is as simple as being there to listen. Of course, some bereaved youths might need and benefit from vigilant monitoring and professional intervention and support, such as children and adolescents with extant mental health concerns, youth involved with traumatic deaths, and currently healthy young people who are emotionally or environmentally vulnerable (e.g., those who experienced the death of a parent or those who typically receive little or no emotional support from adults in their lives).

When young people experience a significant loss or the death of a loved one, it can negatively affect their overall wellness and behavior and can interfere with the learning process. Some children and adolescents who are considered difficult (i.e., exhibiting various academic, behavioral, and emotional problems) may really be covertly grieving various personal losses that they have incurred but have been unable to process and resolve (Le Count, 2000). Thus, just as schools ascertain and implement appropriate interventions, accommodations, or modifications for students experiencing specific learning difficulties, schools should plan for and provide appropriate support for students experiencing behavior and emotional problems as a result of loss and grief and bereavement processes, because such difficulties can be barriers to their learning and healthy psychosocial development.

### School-Based Death Education Programs

Rather than waiting for a death to occur and then providing death education in the midst of a grief-filled atmosphere, school personnel might consider providing planned learning experiences to examine the concepts of loss and death when students' grief potential is low. Such experiences can help youths acquire an understanding of personal patterns of loss experiences, identify loss-related feelings, and learn to seek or provide support (e.g., Metzgar & Zick, 1996). Integrated school-based death education programs for students should involve three major aspects: (a) cultural education (e.g., acknowledging that death is a reality and part of our culture); (b) suicide and violence prevention, intervention, and postvention (e.g., training in prosocial, anger management, and conflict-resolution skills presented as alternatives to violent behavior); and (c) media education to help young people deal with the presence and potentially negative effects of violent death in entertainment media (e.g., present actual crime data and discuss natural dying, with appropriate correction of distorted images that glorify or trivialize death) (Wass, 2004). Death education programs in school communities could entail (a) preparing for loss experiences by developing and implementing courses for students, educators, and parents and developing clear lines of communication and crisis preparation plans; (b) intervening by implementing comprehensive response plans for deaths and similar crises; and (c) following up by considering, developing, and implementing appropriate rituals and commemoration activities for students, educators, and parents, and offering judicious longer-term (postvention) support for relevant members of the school community (Adams et al., 1999).

### Loss-Related Interviewing and Monitoring

When a student has experienced a death-related loss, performing a loss inventory (Goldman, 2000a) or structured interview involving the student's parent or guardian may be helpful in providing support and determining whether intervention is desirable. Topics should include the manner of death, the student's connection to or involvement with the deceased, and the student's current resources and stressors. Although no gold standard exists with respect to assessment of grieving, some promising approaches and useful instruments are available for assessing loss and grief. In the Tripartite Assessment of the Bereaved Child (Webb, 2002), the assessment considers individual factors (e.g., age, cognitive level, previous coping and adjustment and experience with death or loss, and medical history); death-related factors (e.g., type and circumstances of death, relationship to the deceased, contact with the deceased, and grief reactions); and family, social, religious, and cultural factors (e.g., grief reactions of nuclear and extended family members, recognition of bereavement by the school, grief reactions of peers, religious affiliation, and cultural practices). School psychologists might also find the following instruments useful in planning and implementing prevention and intervention efforts: the *Assessment of Grief,* for children and adolescents who have experienced

**Table 3** *Actions by School Personnel That Can Facilitate Healthy Grieving and Adjustment of Students in the Aftermath of a Death of a Member of the School Community*

- Acknowledge the death in a timely manner and engage in honest communication of known facts (e.g., cause, time, and place of death; funeral plans), keeping in mind students' death-related cognitive and affective developmental limitations.
- Dispel rumors and provide truthful responses to students' questions.
- Encourage and permit expression of feelings in various ways (i.e., verbally, through art or writing activities) and non-judgmentally affirm the validity and variety of possible grief reactions.
- Discuss common grief responses and serve as a role model for appropriate grieving, suitably sharing personal feelings.
- When appropriate, allow participation in the funeral or memorial service, and suitable remembrance activities.
- Recognize and practice some flexibility in academic workload for a few days following the death, while maintaining routine as much as possible.
- Provide reassurance and inform students about available school-based assistance.

*Note.* The material in this table was adapted from Goldman (2000b), Klicker (2000), Miller (2000), and Wolfelt (1996). See References for complete citations.

death-related losses and the *Assessment of Loss/Transition* for youths who have experienced a loss other than death (e.g., illness, divorce, or moving; Aldrich, 2001).

### Proactive Postloss Actions by School Personnel

Visible, proactive school-based support activities provided in the aftermath of a death can promote an accepting atmosphere for students who might typically eschew, yet potentially benefit from, some level of care (e.g., students who have experienced prior but unrelated losses and disenfranchised grievers). Gleaned from the work of several professionals who have discussed appropriate school-based responses to loss (Goldman, 2000b; Klicker, 2000, Miller, 2000; Wolfelt, 1996), Table 3 outlines actions by school personnel that can facilitate healthy grieving and adjustment of students in the aftermath of the death of a member of the school community. In addition, in cases of traumatic grief school professionals should be aware of the need to coordinate services and make mental health referrals when necessary and to provide extra support to the child and family (Goodman et al., 2004).

### Rituals and Bereavement

Although providing constructive helping and social–emotional support (e.g., psychological and physical accessibility to the bereaved to listen and love and to be sympathetic) to youths who have experienced a loss can significantly mediate a pathway between grief and recovery, often parents, other family members, and friends who may be potential support providers are caught up in their own grief or psychosocial difficulties incident to the loss; thus, they are physically or psychologically inaccessible to the bereaved youth. Families sometimes question whether bereaved youths should attend and participate in funerals and other commemorative rituals. It may be helpful to share with families that such participation, when not coerced, can (a) provide children with opportunities to ask questions and express their feelings, (b) provide social modeling of adult grief reactions and coping behaviors that can help legitimate and guide children in their own bereavement, and (c) enable them to experience social support and enfranchisement that can increase their sense of control and help them not feel so isolated, helpless, and confused in their grief experience (e.g., Adams et al., 1999; Doka, 2002).

## ALTERNATIVE ACTIONS FOR INTERVENTION

As discussed in the background to this chapter, many children and adolescents are psychologically resilient and able to deal effectively with the experience of a significant loss. In fact, it has been proffered that routine therapeutic intervention of any kind is not justified for bereaved individuals (Raphael, Minkov, & Dobson, 2001). Indeed, few controlled studies of preventive interventions for bereaved youths have been published and some reviewers have judged the available research findings to be equivocal with respect to "the optimal combination of format, technique, and content" (Ayers & Sandler, 2003, p. 219). However, research in this area is difficult because of the myriad factors that influence bereavement intervention efficacy and mediate healthy outcomes (e.g., nature of the death; age, gender, and pre-loss mental and physical health of participants; available social-emotional support and resources). Furthermore, bereavement intervention research is often characterized by weak methodologies that make it difficult to draw meaningful conclusions and may obscure positive effects (Jordan & Neimeyer, 2003). Therefore, reports of the ineffectiveness of bereavement intervention should be viewed cautiously through the filter of both clinical experience and common sense.

In fact, some reviews of bereavement interventions have noted positive effects. Sharpnack (2000) conducted a meta-analysis of the research literature pertaining to the efficacy of group bereavement interventions for youths and adults. He located six bereavement intervention studies involving children's groups in which the mean age of the bereaved was 10.9 years. All of the studies used some form of psychotherapy, and the majority addressed deaths of parents and family members. The mean effect size for the six studies was .50, and for those studies for which an effect size could be computed, children in the experimental group appeared to benefit from the interventions relative to their control group counterparts. In another meta-analysis of randomized, controlled studies that provided individual, family, or group interventions to persons who were bereaved by the death of a loved one, Neimeyer (2000) found an overall positive but small intervention effect. The positive effect was stronger, however, for individuals receiving counseling for more complicated grief (e.g., grief incident to violent death). Although formal intervention or professionally facilitated grief management may not be routinely appropriate for all bereaved youths, school professionals should be clinically prudent by following apposite guidelines for good practice and offer or provide appropriate and timely support to loss-affected children and adolescents (Melvin & Lukeman, 2000).

## Intervention Options for Bereaved Youths

Although grief is a natural process, the course of grief may not always come naturally, and it may be beneficial to assist bereaved youths with integrating the loss into their lives. Because students differ in their comfort levels for and preferred modes of expressing grief after a death, it is important to have a variety of opportunities and activities available (Poland & Poland, 2004). Also, because children and adolescents experience social–emotional difficulties beyond the first year of bereavement (e.g., development-related transitions and anniversary reactions), grief support should remain available for a long time.

***Counseling.*** Although not all children and adolescents will need formal counseling after they experience a death, some might benefit from therapeutic assistance to facilitate mourning by giving them opportunities to express their feelings and ask questions about death. Certain elements appear to be important in grief counseling with bereaved youths, including giving the student time for the following:

- Relating the detailed story of the loss, including who and what were involved, when and how it happened, how they felt about how they were informed of the loss, and what part, if any, they played in family rituals associated with the loss.
- Remembering the lost person, place, or thing, including discussing positive and negative qualities; important times, experiences, and events; and times when they most miss the lost person, place, or thing.
- Expressing all kinds of feelings in all their intensities.
- Offering renewal and looking toward the future, which entails considering the bereaved youth's coping skills, identifying support resources, anticipating particularly difficult times (i.e., anniversaries and holidays), and reestablishing hope (McGlauflin, 1992).

When a few or several youths have experienced a common loss (e.g., a parent, sibling, or pet), forming a therapeutic bereavement group might be beneficial. Although research on the efficacy of youth bereavement groups is limited, group counseling activities and support groups can provide a normalizing and safe environment of commonality and universality in which bereaved youths can talk about their loss, express feelings, acquire and practice coping skills, and experience personal validation and social support. Finally, because play is the nonverbal language and expressive work of children, one through which they can both learn and grieve, some bereaved youths may benefit from play therapy techniques (e.g., puppets, drawing, and painting) that allow them to express their grief-related emotions in symbolic ways, at their own level of understanding and pace in a safe environment (Webb, 2000).

***Creative arts and visual media.*** Developmentally appropriate creative arts–based activities can provide opportunities for bereaved youths to express their thoughts and feelings about a death. Bereaved youths who engage in creative arts–based activities might be more likely to explore and communicate their feelings and less likely to internalize or act out their emotions in unhealthy and destructive ways (Le Count, 2000). Because drawing is a natural exploratory and expressive activity, it can be an ideal vehicle for bereaved youths to explore and communicate loss-related thoughts and feelings. Also, because death and grief are part of the story lines of many films, giving individuals or groups of bereaved youths opportunities to view such films in the presence of adult support might open areas for therapeutic discussion (e.g., Sedney, 1999).

***Literature and music.*** Literature-based interventions (bibliotherapy) assist bereaved youths through the use of books, providing them with opportunities to identify with and draw comfort and strength from characters who have experienced similar losses. Books can address particular circumstances and needs, and perhaps normalize the intensity and vicissitudes of grief (Thornton, 2001). Music therapy is another medium through which bereaved youths might explore and express their grief in nonconfrontational and creative ways. Music-based interventions (e.g., listening to personally meaningful recorded music, composing song lyrics, playing improvisational music on a chosen instrument) can help youths by validating their personal experiences of grief; letting them compare their experiences and strategies for coping with stressful, confusing, and conflicting emotions; and supporting and nurturing their potential for healing (e.g., Skewes & Erdonmez-Grocke, 2000).

***Written expression.*** Some children and adolescents may not feel comfortable talking about or sharing their grief-related feelings either individually with a helping professional or in a group setting. In such cases, creative writing activities, such as journaling, writing poetry or essays, or writing letters, can be useful clinical tools. Writing allows the student to express his or her emotions without the direct evaluation of another person; it does not need a real recipient to be present; and it may help the student structure and find meaning in thoughts and feelings (e.g., Pennebaker, Zech, & Rimé, 2001). For example, students who understand the finality and irreversibility of death could write a letter to the deceased to express something they wanted to say to the deceased person, such as caring statements, requests for forgiveness for something done or not done, said or not said before the death (Riely, 2003). These can then be placed in a journal or memory box or be disposed of in a symbolic way.

The grieving process has been compared metaphorically to a journey. For the bereaved individual it is a unique, meandering, uncharted journey of crawling, walking, and running over hills and through valleys, from the often lonely and isolated sorrow of loss toward the hope of personal peace, endeavoring to derive meaning from misfortune, struggling to move forward yet sometimes glancing over a shoulder at the past, and occasionally wandering back over previously traversed, memory-laden territory that one longs to visit or that unexpectedly beckons.

School professionals who are given and seize opportunities to provide caring counsel to bereaved children and adolescents on their grief journeys often enter a realm in which they not only can support, guide, and offer hope to youths, they also can learn something about themselves and the ecumenical human experience of loss and its seemingly paradoxical potential for personal growth.

## SUMMARY

All children and adolescents experience losses of various types, losses that they grieve in sundry ways and whose attendant pain they bring with them into their homes, schools, and neighborhoods. When the loss is death-related, the youth's unique relationship with the deceased and the circumstances of the loss or the death affect grieving. Youths' individual and interpersonal risk and protective factors, and their gender-based grieving expectancies, can affect postloss mourning and social–emotional adjustment. Prior knowledge and sensitive inquiry regarding cultural and developmental issues can be valuable in planning and providing appropriate support. School professionals can implement educational activities to examine the concepts of loss and death, they can interview youths who have experienced losses and monitor those who might be at greater risk for bereavement complications, and they can engage in proactive postloss actions to help students cope with personal losses. Although grief is a natural process resulting from a loss experience, the course of a youth's grief may not always proceed readily and healthily. In such cases, referral for outside mental health assessment and treatment may be needed.

## RECOMMENDED RESOURCES

### Books and Other Printed Material

Goldman, L. (2000). *Life and loss: A guide to help grieving children* (2nd ed.). Philadelphia: Accelerated Development.

The author creates a framework for working with grieving children in the contexts of contemporary society. The book contains extensive resources sections that include community and national resources and lists of books, videos, manuals, guides, curricula, CD-ROMS, and websites.

Webb, N. (2002). *Helping bereaved children: A handbook for practitioners* (2nd ed.). New York: Guilford Press.

This edited book provides in-depth case examples and explicates an array of therapeutic approaches and interventions for youth who have experienced loss through natural and violent or traumatic deaths of loved ones.

Wolfelt, A. D. (1996). *Healing the bereaved child: Grief gardening, growth through grief and other touchstones for caregivers.* Fort Collins, CO: Companion Press.

Using a holistic model of the normal, natural, and necessary process of grief, the author delineates guidelines for caregivers and discusses topics such as what makes each child's grief unique; how a grieving child thinks, feels, and mourns; how the bereaved child heals; foundations of counseling and counseling techniques with bereaved children; and how to help grieving children at school. The following books published by Dr. Wolfelt in 2001 are also recommended and available from Companion Press: *Healing Your Grieving Heart for Kids: 100 Practical Ideas; Healing Your Grieving Heart for Teens: 100 Practical Ideas;* and *Healing a Child's Grieving Heart: 100 Practical Ideas for Families, Friends and Caregivers.*

### Websites

*http://www.dougy.org*

Founded in 1982, the Dougy Center for Grieving Children and Families is a nonprofit organization that is totally privately supported and does not charge a fee for services. Although the Dougy Center's primary mission is to provide support and services to bereaved children, adolescents, and families in the Portland, Oregon, region, it also provides local, national, and international support and training to individuals and organizations seeking to assist children in grief.

*http://www.centerforloss.com*

Founded more than two decades ago by Dr. Alan D. Wolfelt, the Center for Loss and Life Transition (CLLT) in Fort Collins, Colorado, is a private organization dedicated to furthering understanding of and compassion for the complex set of emotions called grief. The website contains a Mourner's Corner that contains links to both free text resources and CLLT publications on general grief issues and other topics for both mourners and caregivers.

*http://www.americanhospice.org*

As a public service to people who wish to help a grieving child or adolescent (as well as a grieving friend, family member, colleague, employee, or client), this American Hospice Foundation website offers free access to several PDF articles and to GriefZone, a compendium of constructive ideas and resources for educators to help students deal with grief and loss.

## REFERENCES


Adams, D. W., Corr, C. A., Davies, B., Deveau, E., de Veber, L. L., Martinson, I. M., et al. (1999). Children, adolescents, and death: Myths, realities, and challenges—A statement from the Work Group on Palliative Care of the International Work Group on Death, Dying, and Bereavement. *Death Studies, 23,* 443–463.

Aldrich, L. M. (2001). *Facilitating grief, loss, and trauma support groups: A guidebook for mental health professionals dealing with grief, loss, and trauma issues among children and adolescents.* Cherry Hill, NJ: M & K Publishing.

American Psychiatric Association. (2000). *Diagnostic and statistical manual of mental disorders* (4th ed., text revision). Washington, DC: Author.

Attig, T. W. (1995). Respecting bereaved children and adolescents. In D. W. Adams & E. J. Deveau (Eds.), *Beyond the innocence of childhood. Vol. 3: Helping children and adolescents cope with death and bereavement* (pp. 43–60). Amityville, NY: Baywood Publishing.

Ayers, T. S., & Sandler, I. N. (2003). Bereavement, childhood. In T. P. Gullotta & M. Bloom (Eds.), *Encyclopedia of primary prevention and health promotion* (pp. 213–220). New York: Kluwer Academic/ Plenum Publishing.

Balk, D. E. (1998). Looking at adolescent grief: The need for proper spectacles. *Grief Matters: The Australian Journal of Grief and Bereavement, 1*(3), 3–5.

Batts, J. (2004). Death and grief in the family: Providing support at school. In A. S. Canter, L. Z. Paige, M. D. Roth, I. Romero, & S. A. Carroll (Eds.), *Helping children at home and school. II: Handouts for families and educators* (pp. S9-13–15). Bethesda, MD: National Association of School Psychologists.

Busch, T., & Kimble, C. S. (2001). Grieving children: Are we meeting the challenge? *Pediatric Nursing, 27*(4), 414–418.

Butler, C. L., & Lagoni, L. S. (1996). Children and pet loss. In C. A. Corr & D. M. Corr (Ed.), *Handbook of childhood death and bereavement* (pp. 179–200). New York: Springer.

Crenshaw, D. A. (2002). The disenfranchised grief of children. In K. J. Doka (Ed.), *Disenfranchised grief: New directions, challenges, and strategies for practice* (pp. 293–306). Champaign, IL: Research Press.

Davis, C. G., & Nolen-Hoeksema, S. (2001). Loss and meaning: How do people make sense of loss? *American Behavioral Scientist, 44,* 726–741.

Doka, K. J. (1999). A primer on loss and grief. In J. D. Davidson & K. J. Doka (Eds.), *Living with grief: At work, at school, at worship* (pp. 5–12). Washington, DC: Hospice Foundation of America.

Doka, K. (2002). Introduction. In K. J. Doka (Ed.), *Disenfranchised grief: New directions, challenges, and strategies for practice* (pp. 5–22). Champaign, IL: Research Press.

Dowden, S. (1995). Young children's experiences of sibling death. *Journal of Pediatric Nursing, 10*(1), 72–79.

Goldman, L. (2000a). *Life and loss: A guide to help grieving children* (2nd ed.). Philadelphia: Accelerated Development.

Goldman, L. (2000b). *Helping the grieving child in school.* Bloomington, IN: Phi Delta Kappa Educational Foundation.

Goodman, R. F. (2001). *Children and grief: What they know, how they feel, how to help.* New York: New York University Child Study Center. Retrieved January 3, 2005, from http://www.aboutourkids.org/aboutour/articles/grief.html

Goodman, R. F., Cohen, J., Epstein, C., Kliethermes, M., Layne, C., Macy, R., & Ward-Wimmer, D. (2004). *Childhood traumatic grief educational materials.* Los Angeles, CA, and Durham, NC: National Child Traumatic Stress Network, Child Traumatic Grief Task Force. Retrieved January 3, 2005, from http://www.nctsnet.org/nctsn_assets/pdfs/reports/childhood_traumatic_grief.pdf

Hatter, B. S. (1996). Children and the death of a parent or grandparent. In C. A. Corr & D. M. Corr (Eds.), *Handbook of childhood death and bereavement* (pp. 131–148). New York: Springer Publishing.

Jimerson, S. R., & Huff, L. C. (2002). Responding to a sudden, unexpected death at school: Chance favors the prepared professional. In S. E. Brock, P. J. Lazarus, & S. R. Jimerson (Eds.), *Best practices in school crisis prevention and intervention* (pp. 449–485). Bethesda, MD: National Association of School Psychologists.

Jordan, J. R., & Neimeyer, R. A. (2003). Does grief counseling work? *Death Studies, 27,* 765–786.

Kato, P. M., & Mann, T. (1999). A synthesis of psychological interventions for the bereaved. *Clinical Psychology Review, 19,* 275–296.

Klass, D., Silverman, P. R., & Nickman, S. L. (Eds.). (1996). *Continuing bonds: New understandings of grief.* Washington, DC: Taylor and Francis.

Klicker, R. L. (2000). *A student dies, a school mourns: Dealing with death and loss in the school community.* New York: Brunner-Routledge.

Kübler-Ross, E. (1969). *On death and dying.* New York: Macmillan.

Le Count, D. (2000). Working with "difficult" children from the inside out: Loss and bereavement and how the creative arts can help. *Pastoral Care in Education, 18*(2), 17–27.

Mahon, M. A. (1999). Secondary losses in bereaved children when both parents have died: A case study. *Omega: Journal of Death and Dying, 39,* 297–314.

Martin, T. L., & Doka, K. J. (2000). *Men don't cry . . . Women do: Transcending gender stereotypes of grief.* Philadelphia: Brunner/Mazel.

McGlauflin, H. (1992). How children grieve: Implications for counseling. In G. R. Walz & J. C. Bleuer (Eds.), *Developing support groups for students: Helping students cope with crises* (pp. 11–20). Ann

Arbor, MI: ERIC Counseling and Personnel Services Clearinghouse.

Melvin, D., & Lukeman, D. (2000). Bereavement: A framework for those working with children. *Clinical Child Psychology and Psychiatry, 5,* 521–539.

Metzgar, M. M., & Zick, B. C. (1996). Building the foundation: Preparation before a trauma. In C. A. Corr & D. M. Corr (Eds.), *Handbook of childhood death and bereavement* (pp. 245–264). New York: Springer Publishing.

Miller, S. D. (2000). *Mourning and dancing for schools: A grief and recovery sourcebook for students, teachers and parents.* Deerfield Beach, FL: Health Communications, Inc.

Mullan, J. T., Skaff, M. M., & Pearlin, L. I. (2003). The bereavement process: Loss, grief, and resolution. In I. Corless, B. B. Germino, & M. A. Pittman (Eds.), *Dying, death, and bereavement* (2nd ed., pp. 225–246). New York: Springer Publishing.

Neimeyer, R. A. (2000). Searching for the meaning of meaning: Grief therapy and the process of reconstruction. *Death Studies, 24,* 541–558.

Oltjenbruns, K. A. (1996). Death of a friend during adolescence: Issues and impacts. In C. A. Corr & D. E. Balk (Eds.), *Handbook of adolescent death and bereavement* (pp. 196–215). New York: Springer Publishing.

Oltjenbruns, K. A. (2001). Developmental context of childhood: Grief and regrief phenomena. In M. S. Stroebe, R. O. Hansson, W. Stroebe, & H. Schut (Eds.), *Handbook of bereavement research: Consequences, coping, and care* (pp. 169–197). Washington, DC: American Psychological Association.

Pennebaker, J. W., Zech, E., & Rimé, B. (2001). Disclosing and sharing emotion: Psychological, social, and health consequences. In M. S. Stroebe, R. O. Hansson, W. Stroebe, & H. Schut (Eds.), *Handbook of bereavement research: Consequences, coping, and care* (pp. 517–534). Washington, DC: American Psychological Association.

Perry, B. D. (2002). *Helping traumatized children: A brief overview for caregivers.* Houston, TX: Child Trauma Academy.

Poland, S., & Poland, D. (2004). Death at school: Tips for school administrators and support personnel. In A. S. Canter, L. Z. Paige, M. D. Roth, I. Romero, & S. A. Carroll (Eds.), *Helping children at home and school. II: Handouts for families and educators* (pp. S9-25–28). Bethesda, MD: National Association of School Psychologists.

Raphael, B., Minkov, C., & Dobson, M. (2001). Psychotherapeutic and pharmacological intervention for bereaved persons. In M. S. Stroebe, R. O. Hansson, W. Stroebe, & H. Schut (Eds.), *Handbook of bereavement research: Consequences, coping, and care* (pp. 587–612). Washington, DC: American Psychological Association.

Rathkey, J. W. (2004). *What children need when they grieve: The four essentials—Routine, love, honesty, and security.* New York: Three Rivers Press.

Regehr, C., & Sussman, T. (2004). Intersections between grief and trauma: Toward an empirically based model for treating traumatic grief. *Brief Treatment and Crisis Intervention, 4,* 289–309.

Riely, M. (2003). Facilitating children's grief. *The Journal of School Nursing, 19*(4), 212–218.

Schuurman, D. (2003). *Never the same: Coming to terms with the death of a parent.* New York: St. Martin's Press.

Schuurman, D., & Lindholm, A. B. (2002). Teens and grief. *The Prevention Researcher, 9*(2), 1, 3–5.

Sedney, M. A. (1999). Children's grief narratives in popular films. *Omega: Journal of Death and Dying, 39,* 315–324.

Sharpnack, J. D. (2000). The efficacy of group bereavement interventions: An integrative review of the research literature. *Dissertation Abstracts International, 61*(12): 671B. (UMI No. 9999114).

Skewes, K., & Erdonmez-Grocke, D. (2000). What does group music therapy offer to bereaved young people: A rounded approach to the grieving adolescent. *Grief Matters: The Australian Journal of Grief and Bereavement, 3*(3), 54–61.

Speece, M. W., & Brent, S. B. (1996). The development of children's understanding of death. In C. A. Corr & D. M. Corr (Eds.), *Handbook of childhood death and bereavement* (pp. 29–50). New York: Springer Publishing.

Stevenson, R. G. (2002). Sudden death in schools. In N. B. Webb (Ed.), *Helping bereaved children: A handbook for practitioners* (2nd ed., pp. 194–213). New York: Guilford Press.

Stroebe, W., & Schut, H. (2001). Risk factors in bereavement outcome: A methodological and empirical review. In M. S. Stroebe, R. O. Hansson, W. Stroebe, & H. Schut (Eds.), *Handbook of bereavement research: Consequences, coping, and care* (pp. 349–371). Washington, DC: American Psychological Association.

Thornton, C. M. (2001). Using children's literature to help the grieving child. *Physical Disabilities: Education and Related Services, 19*(2), 5–20.

Wass, H. (2004). A perspective on the current state of death education. *Death Studies, 28,* 289–304.

Webb, N. B. (2000). Using play therapy to help bereaved children. In K. J. Doka (Ed.), *Children, adolescents, and loss: Living with grief* (pp. 139–152). Washington, DC: Hospice Foundation of America.

Webb, N. B. (2002). Assessment of the bereaved child. In N. B. Webb (Ed.), *Helping bereaved children: A handbook for practitioners* (2nd ed., pp. 19–42). New York: Guilford Press.

Wolfelt, A. D. (1996). *Healing the bereaved child: Grief gardening, growth through grief and other touchstones for caregivers.* Fort Collins, CO: Companion Press.

Worden, J. W. (2002). *Grief counseling and grief therapy: A handbook for the mental health practitioner* (3rd ed.). New York: Springer Publishing.

Zeitlin, S. V. (2001). Grief and bereavement. *Primary Care: Clinics in Office Practice, 28,* 415–425.

# 19

# Stress

**Robyn S. Hess**
*University of Northern Colorado*

**Ellis P. Copeland**
*Chicago School of Professional Psychology*

The healthy development and well-being of children and adolescents can be compromised by too many stressful life events. These stressors can vary in both intensity and duration and occur in the form of acute traumatic events, chronic strain and adversity, and accumulated stressful life events and daily hassles (Haggerty, Sherrod, Garmezy, & Rutter, 1994). A strong belief among researchers is that stressors are part of the etiology of child and adolescent psychopathology. More than 1,500 empirical studies on the relationship between stressors and psychological symptoms among youth have been conducted over the past 15 years (Grant, Compas, Thurm, McMahon, & Gipson, 2004). Understanding the role of stressful life events in children and adolescents represents a significant step toward reducing exposure to stressors and enhancing the adaptive capability of youth to manage these events (Compas, 1995).

## BACKGROUND AND DEVELOPMENT

### Definitions of Stress

Despite the recognized role of stressors in child development and psychopathology, research on stress in childhood has been slow in comparison to similar research with adults (Grant et al., 2003). Part of the difficulty in studying stress is related to the lack of consistent definition and related instrumentation in measuring stress and stressful life events. Historically, there have been two prevailing definitions of stress. The first focuses on the environmental circumstances or conditions that threaten, challenge, exceed, or harm the psychological or biological capacities of the individual (Cohen, Kessler, & Gordon, 1995). A second approach, and one that is most widely accepted, is the transactional model put forth by Lazarus and Folkman (1984), which views stress as a relationship between environmental events or conditions and the individual's cognitive appraisals of the degree and type of challenge, threat, harm, or loss.

Recently, this second definition has been called into question because of subsequent research suggesting that cognitive appraisals may not always be present (e.g., stress during infancy) or are not as significant for young children (Turner & Cole, 1994). Furthermore, as theoretical statistical models have become more sophisticated, there is a growing understanding of the role of mediating and moderating processes that influence the relationship between stressors and psychopathology across development (Cicchetti & Cohen, 1995). That is, mediators (e.g., biological, psychological, and social processes) can help explain the relationship between stressors and a particular outcome (e.g., psychopathology), and moderators (e.g., child and environmental characteristics) are thought to influence this relationship. Although the individual's cognitive appraisal of a stressful event is understood to be an important aspect of stress, it may be considered a mediating or moderating process rather than a fundamental component in the definition of stress. Consistent with this new perspective, Grant et al. (2003, p. 449) suggest a broad definition of stress that "refers not only to the environmental stressors themselves but also to the range of processes set into motion by exposure to environmental stressors." In other words, stress is a biological and psychological response to the demands made upon individuals by their environment, perceptions, and relationships.

People's bodies are affected by stress (and distress) in ways that are often beyond their control. The three stages in the physical response are alarm, resistance, and exhaustion (Selye, 1978). In the first stage, *alarm*, the body goes into alert, with an increase in heart rate and breathing as the individual considers a course of action (analogous to the fight or flight response). *Resistance* follows alarm when the body attempts to slow down and return to normal, or homeostasis. Back in the fight or flight days (when a person either ran or fought back successfully), people's bodies naturally made this change. Today, stress is typically more continuous. The body attempts to adapt, but if the event continues or if the individual is unable to adapt to the situation, *exhaustion* may follow. Exhaustion may mean aches and pains to the adult, but often manifests as behavioral changes in the child. However, the body does not need to get to the exhaustion phase for physical and psychological problems to occur.

Stressful life events vary in duration, severity, and type of occurrence. For example, cumulative life experiences and daily hassles can include normal, developmental experiences (e.g., transition to kindergarten or high school) and nonnormative events (e.g., death of a family member) and chronic stressors (e.g., excessive crowding or noise in a low-income neighborhood). The experience of stress appears to be complex and depends on the psychological resources and contextual factors that interact with one another (Thoits, 1995). Unfortunately, practitioners can do little to decrease the number of stressors experienced by children and adolescents. Instead, efforts are best directed at enhancing the individual's coping capacity and mobilizing supportive resources in the environment to mediate the circumstances of the experience. To accomplish those goals, it is necessary for practitioners to understand the typical stressors and responses experienced by children and adolescents across different ages.

## Developmental Aspects of Stress

The source of stress, an individual's vulnerability and resiliency, and available supports to deal with stressors vary with developmental stage. The negative effects of stress are experienced very early in life through both direct and indirect channels. For example, poverty negatively affects parenting behaviors, which in turn predict increased risks of problem behaviors among children and adolescents (Grant et al., 2003). Initially, infants learn how to organize and regulate stress systems through their interactions with a primary caregiver. As a result, stress during infancy and early childhood is commonly viewed as a reciprocal activity between the infant and the environment. The quality of the attachment relationship is associated with the caregiver's ability to act as a buffer between the infant and a stressor in the environment. For example, infants who are both insecurely attached and temperamentally prone to approach new situations with caution are particularly at risk for elevated stress reactivity (Nachmias, Gunnar, Mangelsdorf, Parritz, & Buss, 1996). At these early stages, the sources of stress generally are related to meeting developmental milestones, addressing separation issues, and encountering family problems. Children who experienced more family stressors in the preschool years are more aggressive and anxious and less socially competent in kindergarten than their peers who were exposed to less family stress in those same years (Schmidt, Demulder, & Denham, 2002).

As children enter their school years, the major sources of stress expand to include school, peers, and neighborhood variables. In an impressive series of studies, Yamamoto and colleagues (e.g., Yamamoto, 2001) surveyed nearly 4,000 children, from preschool to ninth grade, from six different countries to determine the types of events that children found to be most stressful. The results were surprisingly consistent across gender and grade level and were grouped into two broad categories. The first cluster of stressors related to the child's sense of security and was expressed by such items as loss of a parent, going blind, parental fighting, and getting lost. The second cluster of stressful events appeared to be related to a child's sense of dignity and honor. Events such as "being kept in the same grade next year" and "telling the truth but no one believing me" were especially upsetting to children. Other items in this cluster included anything that might be considered embarrassing or shameful, such as being sent to the principal's office, wetting one's pants in class, or being laughed at in class. These findings reflect the more advanced cognitive abilities of middle childhood and the greater sense of inquiry and exploration of the world. This curiosity and risk taking brings about the desire for mastery of tasks and also the accompanying chance of failure, which can become a source of stress to children. At this stage, parents continue to play an important role as they help children to understand the world and gain a sense of control over stressful situations (e.g., Wyman, Cowen, Work, & Parker, 1991).

As children get older, normal events such as puberty, advancement to middle school, and peer relations can become stressors. Entry into adolescence represents a crucial time in the development of the individual, with accompanying rapid cognitive, social, emotional, and physical changes (Copeland & Hess, 1995). This period represents a particularly vulnerable time for youth; individuals who encounter multiple simultaneous stressful life changes are more likely to experience emotional and behavioral disturbances (e.g., Grant et al., 2003). Support from significant adults and feelings of worth appear to be the important foundation for effective coping at this developmental stage (Dubois et al., 2002).

As adolescents progress toward adulthood, yet another transition occurs, from dependence on the family to an increased reliance on one's friends and one's self. Researchers have proposed that successful transition into adolescence occurs when the individual has found a balance among achieving greater involvement with friends, handling significant roles and responsibilities within the family, and succeeding in the challenging demands of the school environment (Lerner et al., 1996). For older adolescents, the biological changes that affected them in early adolescence have largely subsided, and cognitive growth is nearly complete. As adolescents progress through subsequent developmental stages, they develop increasing capacities for abstract thought and self-reflection, allowing them to internalize sources of support to build self-system resources (e.g., self-esteem; Harter, 1999). These changes allow adolescents to exert greater control over their perceptions of stress and to regulate their subsequent actions, allowing for a broader range of coping strategies, especially those directed toward problem solving.

## PROBLEMS AND IMPLICATIONS

As the preceding discussion pointed out, all children and adolescents experience stress. However, even when high levels of stress are present in an individual's life, resources and supports can act as buffers to reduce the resulting distress caused by these events. Examples of such buffers might include coping styles, cognitive attributions, and family processes (Grant et al., 2003). For example, a positive relationship with primary caregivers, a stable family environment, and consistent family discipline practices are predictive of positive adjustment in highly stressed children (Wyman et al., 1991).

A growing body of literature supports the notion that certain preexisting characteristics increase or decrease the likelihood that stressors will result in psychopathology. Variables such as age, gender, genetic vulnerabilities, or environmental influences (e.g., parenting or peer groups) are considered to be significant in predicting how children react when stressed. For example, boys and girls tend to differ in their behavioral response to stressors, with boys showing more externalizing and girls exhibiting more internalizing symptoms (Grant et al., 2003). Thus, these variables (whether protective or risk factors) include sources that are internal to the child (e.g., biological and cognitive factors) as well as those that are environmental (e.g., parents, peers, school, and community).

### Biological and Cognitive Factors

Children possess both biological and cognitive factors that influence or moderate their responses to stressful life events. For example, those with lower thresholds for novel events and external stimuli are more prone to alarm and will likely find a wider variety of events to be stressful. This pattern of response can begin very early in the child's development, when stressful experiences are not successfully regulated by the caregiver and the infant is not yet able to self-regulate (Gunnar, 2000). It has been hypothesized, based on animal studies, that these unregulated stressful experiences may negatively influence brain structures as well as the reactivity of the hypothalamic–pituitary–adrenal (HPA) axis (Gunnar). The HPA axis is part of the human stress-response system, and when it operates at heightened levels it produces cortisol. These physiological changes are associated with behavioral and physiological responses to threats.

Adverse early life experiences may program the HPA system to be over- or underactive, which in turn interferes with healthy emotional and physical development. Although no causal information is available, cortisol levels are higher in children with internalizing behaviors, and children with lower levels of cortisol tend to be more outgoing and more engaged in school (Smider et al., 2002). Higher activity of the HPA axis may reflect an underlying biobehavioral tendency to withdraw when faced with normative social challenges. This line of research is quite new and largely based on animal models, but it does provide an interesting hypothesis as to why some children are overly stressed in novel social situations and others are not. Additional research is also needed to determine whether sociocontextual interventions have an effect on cortisol levels, allowing practitioners to raise children's thresholds to effectively manage stress.

Pubertal transition may be another biologically based factor that contributes to stress. For example, girls who experience early physical maturation are significantly more at risk for developing depression than those who develop at a more typical rate (Ge, Conger, & Elder, 1996). It is thought that when children mature too early, their adaptive and coping skills have not had time to develop and strengthen before the child is exposed to the higher levels of stress that accompany this transition. Recent research suggests that there may be important differences between males' and females' pubertal transition and its relationship to stress. Although both boys and girls experience heightened levels of stress associated with puberty, they tend to be affected by this transition in different ways. For girls, the research showed that the distress of early maturation seemed to have a more lasting effect on emotional functioning (Ge et al., 2003).

Another aspect of the individual's response to stress is the perception or cognitive appraisal of the stressful event. Children who tend to interpret stress events positively may be more likely to adapt effectively after the event (Jackson & Warren, 2000). It has been suggested that children's assessment of an event may be related to their perceptions of themselves as effective problem solvers, and in turn this appraisal affects their choice of coping actions (Fallin, Wallinga, & Coleman, 2001). For example, individuals with high self-esteem or a high feeling of control will choose active coping strategies focused on problems, whereas individuals with low self-esteem will adopt passive-avoidant coping styles focused on emotions (Thoits, 1995). Positive appraisal of stressful events and one's coping ability may act as a protective factor for children, especially those who do not have many protective factors (Jackson & Warren). Thus, the individual appears to bring certain biological and cognitive factors to the stress context, although some of these (e.g., reactivity of the HPA axis) may be indirectly related to family influences.

## Family Factors

Caregivers play an important role in helping buffer the negative effects of stress on children. Conversely, certain aspects of family functioning can also place a child at greater risk for distress when he or she is faced with stressful environmental stimuli. For example, mothers' expression of negative dominant emotion (e.g., anger or hostility) has been shown to be negatively related to children's constructive coping (Valiente, Fabes, Eisenberg, & Spinrad, 2004). Even when high levels of stress are present, children whose parents expressed higher levels of positive emotions (e.g., praising or demonstrating gratitude or admiration) were better able to demonstrate constructive coping than were those with less expressive parents. Unexpectedly, this same finding held true for families where mothers had high levels of expressed negative submissive emotion (e.g., crying or expressing sorrow). In low-stress situations, children who had parents with low levels of positive expression used high levels of constructive coping, but they were less able to do so in high-stress situations. These complex interactions suggest the importance of considering parental expressivity and incorporating it into educational activities and parenting support and training programs.

A common belief is that as children move toward adolescence their source of support changes from parents to peers; however, for most youth, parents remain a critical source of support. Among young adolescents, social support received from family members was associated with reduced levels of prospective psychological distress and conduct problems (DuBois, Felner, Meares, & Krier, 1994). A supportive family environment may help children develop positive coping responses to family stress, which reduces the chances of developing maladaptive behavior (Jackson, Sifers, Warren, & Velasquez, 2003). Although family relationships may have the greatest impact on children's reactions to stress, when that support is missing, young adolescents often begin to turn to peers for support (Dornbusch, Laird, & Crosnoe, 1999).

## Peer Relationships

Although positive peer support is commonly believed to help adolescents manage stressful life events, research has generally not supported this relationship (e.g., DuBois et al., 1994). Instead, it appears that social support plays an indirect role in an adolescent's adjustment to stress (DuBois et al.). That is, social support from peers (and adults) appears to help develop an individual's self-esteem, leading to better levels of adjustment. Furthermore, it is important that the sources of social support are balanced between peer- and adult-orientations. Young adolescents who rely more heavily on peer-oriented sources of support tend to have higher levels of negative adjustment in the form of externalizing behaviors (DuBois et al., 2002).

Conversely, peer rejection can be one of the most stressful experiences faced by a young person and has been correlated with poor adjustment (Zakriski, Jacobs, & Coie, 1996). Rejected children who are able to change this status are more likely to demonstrate a combination of behavioral (e.g., awareness) and self-system (e.g., self-efficacy and autonomy) variables related to coping than those who are not able to change their rejection status.

Social skills programs offered within the school can help young people change their social behaviors and can reinforce their efforts when natural peer rewards are not readily available (Zakriski et al.).

### Community and Environmental Factors

A number of environmental factors beyond family and friends affect the level of stress experienced by youth. One of the clearest findings is that children living in poverty are at greater risk for socioemotional difficulties than children from middle-class backgrounds (e.g., McLoyd, 1998). Furthermore, urban children in impoverished settings experience more stressful events than their middle-class, urban peers (e.g., Attar, Guerra, & Tolan, 1994). This finding holds true for rural poor children as well (Evans & English, 2002). That is, rural White children who live in impoverished settings experienced more stressors, had greater psychological distress, more difficulty with self-regulation, and higher levels of blood pressure and stress hormones than children who live in middle-class settings. This study also presented preliminary support for the hypothesis that cumulative negative life stressors account for part of the negative correlation between poverty and socioemotional development.

Just as gender affects an individual's perception of and reaction to stressful life events, so too does culture play an important role. Minority youth often experience additional stress related to chronic stressors, such as cultural conflicts, negative stereotypes, and socioeconomic disadvantage (Phinney, Lochner, & Murphy, 1990). For example, nearly half of a population of Puerto Rican children reported incidents of perceived discrimination (Szalacha et al., 2003). Perceived discrimination among adolescents is related to depression and stress and to some dimensions of self-esteem. It is impossible from this study to determine causation, but basing conclusions on the previous work of others and these most recent findings, Szalacha et al. proposed that perceived discrimination works in a reciprocal feedback loop. That is, some characteristics of a child (e.g., higher depression and anxiety and lower intergroup competence) put that individual at greater risk for perceiving discrimination (Phinney, Madden, & Santos, 1998; Szalacha et al.). In turn, these children may then experience more discrimination from peers because of their vulnerability, which then leads to further depression and anxiety. Unfortunately, this type of reciprocal loop is evident in many aspects of the relationship between stress and adaptive functioning.

High levels of stress and insufficient buffers can lead to long-term difficulties in children and adolescents. In some instances, the child's reactivity to stress begins quite early and may contribute to difficulty in effectively meeting developmental, educational, and social expectations. Children who experience frequent stressors are generally less available for new learning, which can negatively affect their academic achievement and educational decisions in adolescence (Garnier, Stein, & Jacobs, 1997). Problems such as weak academic performance, pregnancy, and poor relationships with peers and teachers may reflect an inability to cope successfully with more serious underlying problems created by chronic stressful living conditions (Kaplan, Damphousse, & Kaplan, 1994).

Researchers continue to puzzle over the best strategies for helping youth with stress-related problems to become more resilient. In a study examining stress and support variables across several contexts, DuBois et al. (1994) found that although adolescents who experience multiple conditions of socioeconomic disadvantage were more vulnerable to the effects of stressors, support from school personnel contributed to subsequent positive school performance. These data support the idea that school personnel can play an important role in ameliorating some of the risks associated with chronic stressors in the lives of adolescents. Still, many questions remain about the relationship between the specific strategies that students use to cope with stressful life events and educational outcomes.

## ALTERNATIVE ACTIONS FOR PREVENTION

Because all children experience stress, two dominant goals of school practitioners are to help youth build protective assets and competencies and to develop coping strategies that reduce or manage stress. From this perspective, universal prevention programs that alter educational practices for every student may be the best approach for enhancing students' ability to cope with life stressors and daily hassles. Because so many stressors are related to the school environment, lessons about stress and coping are appropriate for inclusion in the general curriculum (Fallin et al., 2001). Additionally, schools can provide supportive environmental structures and adult–child interactions that allow children the autonomy to solve their own problems and learn a wider variety of coping strategies (Hardy, Power, & Jaedicke, 1993).

One of the key components of a preventive school-based approach is ensuring that the school environment is safe. School climates that are organized and strong, have clear leadership and high academic and behavioral standards, have a belief and expectation that all children can learn, and involve families and communities in positive ways are more supportive to children (Epstein, 1990). Furthermore, instructional approaches that encourage cooperation and interaction with peers, particularly when combined with effective classroom management strategies, result in more positive attitudes toward school, more interest and engagement in learning activities, and fewer suspensions and expulsions, particularly among lower achieving students (Abbott et al., 1998).

To build positive coping behaviors in schools, excellent models for developing assets and competencies in children can now be found in the psychological and educational literature. Three noteworthy organizations that promote diverse yet interrelated competencies in youth and communities, on a school- or district-wide basis, are the Character Education Program network, the Search Institute, and the Collaborative for Academic, Social, and Emotional Learning (CASEL; see Recommended Resources). The mission of these organizations is to promote learning communities that advocate the development of problem-solving and decision-making skills, emotional regulation, interpersonal and relationship skills, and self-awareness of youth. Such competencies enable children to better confront stress and ameliorate its potentially harmful effects (see also chapter 1, "Social and Emotional Learning").

A variety of methods can be implemented by the teacher in the classroom to model effective stress management and encourage children to use appropriate coping strategies (Copeland, 2004). One of the most important components is having an adult act as a positive role model. Another example includes creating expectations for children that are realistic and clearly explained. When a child makes a poor decision, the best approach is to listen without being critical. The child can then be involved as a helper and be encouraged to make responsible decisions. The teacher can encourage children to express feelings by creating opportunities for them to talk and share problems that they are experiencing. One example is through the morning meeting format, in which a teacher meets with the class to check in and provide a format for discussing classroom problems or issues (Charney, 1992). Through morning meetings, children can be taught self-respect as well as respect for others. In addition to these more focused activities, children can be taught strategies for releasing stress through physical activity and humor.

Although data are limited on prevention programs that specifically increase coping skills, some programs have been shown to effectively increase skills associated with positive coping, such as problem-solving and cause-and-effect reasoning. For example, I Can Problem Solve (ICPS), a prevention program designed for children ages 4 through 12, is designed to enhance children's thinking skills and in turn, prevent high-risk behaviors (Shure, 1992). This program has a structured format that includes formal lessons as well as suggestions for incorporating the ICPS principles across the curriculum. The lessons take about 20 minutes, and the content is grouped into two major categories: pre-problem-solving skills and problem-solving skills. One of the central components of the program is problem-solving dialogue, in which the teacher guides the child in applying ICSP concepts to solve a real-life problem. Additionally, skills are taught through the use of games, stories, puppets, and role-playing. Results from large-scale, longitudinal studies suggest that this program is effective for helping children improve their prosocial behaviors, and these differences were sustained at the 3-year follow-up (Reddy et al., 2004). Furthermore, various programs are available that positively affect behavioral outcomes by decreasing aggression and behavioral problems while helping students increase their prosocial behavior and resolve problems and conflicts nonviolently (Rones & Hoagwood, 2000).

Another key component in building an effective prevention network involves home–school–community partnerships. Effective partnerships are established by fostering good communication between home and school and by providing multiple opportunities for parental involvement in children's learning activities (Abbot et al., 1998). In the broadest sense, schools can play an important role by providing access to low-cost, quality preschool education and before- and after-school care that monitors children's activities and supports homework completion (Smith, Boutte, Zigler, & Finn-Stevenson, 2004). These types of universal approaches may decrease overall stress on families as well as provide community resources. Additionally, schools can help educate parents about the importance of their role in mediating stress in their children's lives by offering parent training opportunities and newsletters that incorporate knowledge and strategies around parental expressivity and parental support.

## ALTERNATIVE ACTIONS FOR INTERVENTION

For students who are known to be at high levels of risk because of multiple stressors and lack of sufficient supports, secondary and tertiary interventions directed at stress management and effective coping are most appropriate. Fundamental to coping is the ability to evaluate an issue, select from a variety of possible coping options, and implement one or more strategies that effectively resolve the problem. Coping strategies can be either *primary* (i.e., a stressful condition or event that an individual has the opportunity to change) or *secondary* (i.e., stressful conditions that cannot be changed and to which the individual must adapt; Hardy et al., 1993). Coping skills work best when children can differentiate between these two types of conditions and can then select an appropriate strategy. As children mature, they are better able to differentiate between conditions they can influence and those they cannot; they begin to demonstrate more secondary coping strategies as they approach adolescence (Hardy et al.). Coping strategies can also be viewed as *functional* or *dysfunctional*. Functional coping refers to active efforts to manage a problem or think of a solution; dysfunctional coping focuses on denying or avoiding a problem instead attempting to regulate the emotions (Seiffge-Krenke, 1995). Coping styles that tend to avoid or ignore the stressor are associated with higher levels of depression and anxiety (e.g., Seiffge-Krenke & Klessinger, 2000).

Given this framework, programs directed toward more effective coping would focus on both managing stress and restructuring cognitions to help children appraise events as accurately as possible and reassure themselves that they can cope. Additional efforts might be directed at helping students understand and use a broader array of effective coping strategies. Practitioners should use theoretically driven and statistically supported models to understand the stress response and to develop and evaluate intervention approaches for children in stressful situations (Sandler, Wolchik, MacKinnon, Ayers, & Roosa, 1997). The Coping With Stress program (Clarke et al., 1995), an early-intervention program that incorporates these components, was designed to prevent depression in high-risk adolescents by helping them develop adaptive coping skills. Developed in 1990 by Clarke, Lewinsohn, and Hops (cited in Clarke et al.), Coping With Stress is a manualized program that incorporates cartoons, group activities, and role-playing to teach adolescents techniques such as cognitive restructuring to reorganize their negative or irrational thoughts. The program consists of 15 group sessions of 45 minutes each and is conducted by group leaders who are trained as school psychologists or counselors. A randomized, controlled trial of the Coping With Stress course found that although there were no differences between experimental and control groups at the end of the program, a follow-up assessment after 12 months demonstrated a significantly lower incidence of major depressive disorder or dysthymia in the treatment group versus the control group.

To date, many studies related to development of stress management and coping skills have focused on narrow programs delivered within school or clinic settings. Nevertheless, these findings provide a starting point for enhancing the resiliency of children, families, and communities. Unfortunately, the fragmentation among home, school, and community environments can present a considerable barrier to schools' providing effective interventions (Smith et al., 2004). Furthermore, in situations in which children are experiencing chronic stressors related to socioeconomic disadvantage and parental conflict, school personnel cannot be realistically expected to decrease these stressors. In such instances, the practitioner can work with the child to identify alterable stressors related to the overarching concerns. For example, the child may have difficulty completing homework at night because of overcrowding and disruptions due to fighting, which, in turn, leads to stress about going to school and interacting with the classroom teacher. In this case, the school practitioner might work with the child to problem-solve, using active coping strategies for completing homework at school or after school in a quieter setting and using secondary coping strategies, such as cognitive restructuring and stress relief, to cope with the larger stressors.

As can be seen in the example provided above, child-focused programs that teach skills to deal with stressful situations must include key social network members such as parents, teachers, and school practitioners. This feature is important across developmental stages because adolescents who perceive that a teacher both cares and has high expectations for them are less susceptible to negative peer influences (Dornbusch et al., 1999). Perceived teacher support appears to be a protective factor that contributes to students' feeling competent and understood, especially when other sources of support are lacking (Bowen, Richman, Brewster, & Bowen, 1998; see also chapter 5, "Student–Teacher Relationships").

This chapter covered strategies for helping children with common environmental stressors related to home, peers, school, and community. The important issue of traumatic stress was not addressed. Although traumatic events are not common, many people experience at least one or more traumatic events in their lifetimes. There are many actions that schools can take to reduce the subsequent stress experienced by children and adolescents who have been witnesses to these events (e.g., Brock, Sandoval, & Lewis, 2001). Additionally, group counseling interventions have been suggested by Williams (2004) as a strategy for helping students who have experienced traumatic events. These groups provide an opportunity for youth to share their feelings, reactions, and responses. The group might also serve a psychoeducational function by teaching participants about symptoms of post-traumatic stress.

## SUMMARY

The experience of stress is universal, yet its impact is so complex and variable that it is impossible to predict how it will affect any one child or adolescent. However, new advances in the field of stress research are beginning to provide a picture of how children begin to cope with stress and the mediating processes and moderating factors along the way that buffer or intensify the stress experienced by the individual. The types of stressors and the corresponding mediating processes are related to the developmental age of the child, with different processes taking on more importance at certain stages. For the youngest children, caregiver attachment and parental expressivity appear to be critical in helping manage the effects of stress. As the child grows, parental support continues to exert the greatest influence, and this support (along with that of peers) sets the foundation for a child's self-esteem and ability to realistically appraise both stressful events and coping resources. As the child grows into adolescence, school personnel, in addition to parents, begin to emerge as a source of support, especially when other resources are lacking.

The prevalence of research that demonstrates the negative effect of multiple stressors on child development and mental health outcomes demands the attention of school practitioners. Because of the long-term nature of some stressors, there are many points at which school personnel can intervene. At the primary prevention level, programs can be directed at creating safe school environments, teaching children about stress and coping, and enhancing supportive relationships between students and teachers. For more vulnerable youth, personnel can implement targeted interventions using psychoeducational and cognitive behavioral approaches and ensuring access to adult resources within the school setting. Although it is recognized that many youth suffer extreme stressors that are beyond parents' and adults' capacity to change, efforts can focus on helping children and adolescents enhance their own resources and resilience to the daily stressors of life.

## RECOMMENDED RESOURCES

### Books and Other Printed Material

Maton, K. I., Schellenbach, C. J., Leadbeater, B. J., & Solarz, A. L. (2004). *Investing in children, youth, families, and communities.* Washington, DC: American Psychological Association.

This text looks at a comprehensive array of negative issues and examines how to address them with strength-based, contextual approaches. It provides an exciting alternative view on how to address the problems faced by children and families.

Wolchik, S. A., & Sandler, I. N. (1997). *Handbook of children's coping: Linking theory and interventions.* New York: Plenum Press.

The editors provide a general framework for understanding stress and coping responses in children, with each subsequent chapter addressing a specific stressor and effective interventions for helping children cope.

### Websites

Three noteworthy organizations that promote leadership, knowledge, and resources for character education for youth and communities, school or district wide, are the Character Education Partnership (*http://www.character.org*), the Search Institute (*http://www.search-institute.org*), and the Collaborative for Academic, Social, and Emotional Learning (CASEL—*http://www.casel.org*). These websites contain multiple resources for planning, implementing, and evaluating interventions for youth.

## REFERENCES

Abbott, R. D., O'Donnell, J., Hawkins, J. D., Hill, K. G., Kosterman, R., & Catalano, R. F. (1998). Changing teaching practices to promote achievement and bonding to school. *American Journal of Orthopsychiatry, 68,* 542–552.

Attar, B. K., Guerra, N. G., & Tolan, P. H. (1994). Neighborhood disadvantage, stressful life events, and adjustment in urban elementary-school children. *Journal of Clinical Child Psychology, 23,* 391–400.

Bowen, G. L., Richman, J. M., Brewster, A., & Bowen, N. (1998). Sense of school coherence, perceptions of danger at school, and teacher support among youth at risk for school failure. *Child and Adolescent Social Work Journal, 15,* 273–286.

Brock, S. E., Sandoval, J., & Lewis, S. (2001). *Preparing for crises in the schools: A manual for building school crisis response teams* (2nd ed.). New York: Wiley.

Charney, R. S. (1992). *Teaching children to care: Management in the responsive classroom.* Greenfield, MA: Northeast Foundation for Children.

Cicchetti, D., & Cohen, D. (1995). Perspectives on developmental psychopathology. In D. Cicchetti & D. Cohen (Eds.), *Developmental psychopathology: Vol. 1. Theory and methods* (pp. 3–20). New York: Wiley.

Clarke, G. N., Hawkins, W., Murphy, M., Sheeber, L. B., Lewinsohn, P. M., & Seeley, J. R. (1995). Targeted prevention of unipolar depressive disorder in an at-risk sample of high school adolescents: A randomized trial of a group cognitive intervention. *Journal of the American Academy of Child and Adolescent Psychiatry, 34,* 312–321.

Cohen, S., Kessler, R. C., & Gordon, L. U. (1995). *Measuring stress: A guide for health and social scientists.* New York: Oxford University Press.

Compas, B. E. (1995). Promoting successful coping during adolescence. In M. Rutter (Ed.), *Psychosocial disturbances in young people: Challenges for prevention* (pp. 247–273). New York: Cambridge University Press.

Copeland, E. P. (2004). Stress in children: Strategies for parents and educators. In A. S. Canter, L. Z. Paige, M. D. Roth, I. Romero, & S. Carroll (Eds.), *Helping children at home and school II: Handouts for families and educators* (pp. 123–125). Bethesda, MD: National Association of School Psychologists.

Copeland, E. P., & Hess, R. S. (1995). Differences in young adolescents' coping strategies based on gender and ethnicity. *Journal of Early Adolescence, 15,* 203–219.

Dornbusch, S. M., Laird, J., & Crosnoe, R. (1999). Parental and school resources that assist adolescents in coping with negative peer influences. In E. Frydenberg (Ed.), *Learning to cope: Developing as a person in complex societies* (pp. 277–298). New York: Oxford University Press.

DuBois, D. L., Burk-Braxton, C., Swenson, L. P., Tevendale, H. D., Lockerd, E. M., & Moran, B. L. (2002). Getting by with a little help from self and others: Self-esteem and social support as resources during early adolescence. *Developmental Psychology, 38,* 822–839.

DuBois, D. L., Felner, R. D., Meares, H., & Krier, M. (1994). Prospective investigation of the effects of socioeconomic disadvantage, life stress, and social support on early adolescent adjustment. *Journal of Abnormal Psychology, 103,* 511–522.

Epstein, J. L. (1990). School and family connections: Theory, research, and implications for integrating sociologies of education and family. In D. G. Unger & M. B. Sussman (Eds.), *Families in community settings: Interdisciplinary perspectives* (pp. 99–126). New York: Haworth.

Evans, G. W., & English, K. (2002). The environment of poverty: Multiple stressor exposure, psychophysiological stress, and socioemotional adjustment. *Child Development, 73,* 1238–1248.

Fallin, K., Wallinga, C., & Coleman, M. (2001). Helping children cope with stress in the classroom setting. *Childhood Education, 78,* 17–29.

Garnier, H. E., Stein, J. A., & Jacobs, J. K. (1997). The process of dropping out of high school: A 19-year perspective. *American Educational Research Journal, 34,* 395–419.

Ge, X., Conger, R. D., & Elder, G. H., Jr. (1996). Coming of age too early: Pubertal influences on girls' vulnerability to psychological distress. *Child Development, 67,* 3386–3400.

Ge, X., Kim, I. J., Brody, G. H., Conger, R. D., Simons, R. L., Gibbons, F. X., & Cutrona, C. E. (2003). It's about timing and change: Pubertal transition effects on symptoms of major depression among African

American youths. *Developmental Psychology, 39,* 430–439.

Grant, K. E., Compas, B. E., Stuhlmacher, A. F., Thurm, A. E., McMahon, S. D., & Halpert, J. A. (2003). Stressors and child and adolescent psychopathology: Moving from markers to mechanisms of risk. *Psychological Bulletin, 129,* 447–466.

Grant, K. E., Compas, B. E., Thurm, A. E., McMahon, S. D., & Gipson, P. Y. (2004). Stressors and child and adolescent psychopathology: Measurement issues and prospective effects. *Journal of Clinical Child and Adolescent Psychology, 33,* 412–415.

Gunnar, M. R. (2000). Early adversity and the development of stress reactivity and regulation. In C. A. Nelson (Ed.), *The effects of early adversity on neurobehavioral development.* The Minnesota Symposia on Child Psychology (Vol. 31, pp. 163–200). Mahwah, NJ: Erlbaum.

Haggerty, R. J., Sherrod, L. R., Garmezy, N., & Rutter, M. (Eds.). (1994). *Stress, risk, and resilience in children and adolescents: Processes, mechanisms, and interventions.* New York: Cambridge University Press.

Hardy, D., Power, T., & Jaedicke, S. (1993). Examining the relation of parenting to children's coping with everyday stress. *Child Development, 64,* 1829–1841.

Harter, S. (1999). *The construction of self: A developmental perspective.* New York: Guilford Press.

Jackson, Y., Sifers, S. K., Warren, J. S., & Velasquez, D. (2003). Family protective factors and behavioral outcome: The role of appraisal in family life events. *Journal of Emotional Behavioral Disorders, 11,* 103–111.

Jackson, Y., & Warren, J. (2000). Appraisal, social support, and life events: Predicting outcome behavior in school-age children. *Child Development, 71,* 1441–1453.

Kaplan, D. S., Damphousse, K. R., & Kaplan, H. B. (1994). Mental health implications of not graduating from high school. *Journal of Experimental Education, 62,* 105–123.

Lazarus, R. S., & Folkman, S. (1984). *Stress, appraisal and coping.* New York: Springer.

Lerner, R. M., Lerner, J. V., von Eye, A., Ostrom, C. W., Nitz, K., Talwar-Suni, R., & Tubman, J. G. (1996). Continuity and discontinuity across the transition of early adolescence: A developmental contextual perspective. In J. A. Graber, J. Brooks-Gunn, & A. C. Petersen (Eds.), *Transitions through adolescence: Interpersonal domains and context* (pp. 3–22). Mahwah, NJ: Erlbaum.

McLoyd, V. C. (1998). Socioeconomic disadvantage and child development. *American Psychologist, 53,* 185–204.

Nachmias, M., Gunnar, M., Mangelsdorf, S., Parritz, R. H., & Buss, K. (1996). Behavioral inhibition and stress reactivity: The moderating role of attachment security. *Child Development, 67,* 508–522.

Phinney, J. S., Lochner, B. T., & Murphy, R. (1990). Ethnic identity development and psychological adjustment in adolescence. In A. R. Stiffman & L. E. Davis (Eds.), *Ethnic issues in adolescent mental health* (pp. 53–72). Newbury Park, CA: Sage.

Phinney, J. S., Madden, T., & Santos, L. J. (1998). Psychological variables as predictors of perceived ethnic discrimination among minority and immigrant adolescents. *Journal of Applied Social Psychology, 28,* 937–953.

Reddy, L. A., Atamoff, T., Spring, C., Hauch, Y., Braunstein, D., & Kranzler, R. (2004). Psychosocial group prevention and intervention programs for children and adolescents. *Child and Adolescent Psychiatric Clinics in North America, 13,* 363–380.

Rones, M., & Hoagwood, K. (2000). School-based mental health services: A research review. *Clinical Child and Family Psychology Review, 3,* 223–241.

Sandler, I. N., Wolchik, S. A., MacKinnon, D., Ayers, T. S., & Roosa, M. W. (1997). Developing linkages between theory and intervention in stress and coping processes. In S. A. Wolchik & I. N. Sandler (Eds.), *Handbook of children's coping: Linking theory and intervention* (pp. 3–40). New York: Plenum Press.

Schmidt, M. E., Demulder, E. K., & Denham, S. A. (2002). Kindergarten social-emotional competence: Developmental predictors and psychosocial implications. *Early Child Development and Care, 172,* 451–462.

Seiffge-Krenke, I. (1995). *Stress, coping and relationships in adolescence.* Mahwah, NJ: Erlbaum.

Seiffge-Krenke, I., & Klessinger, N. (2000). Long-term effects of avoidant coping on adolescents' depressive symptoms. *Journal of Youth and Adolescence, 29,* 617–630.

Selye, H. (1978). *The stress of life* (Rev. ed.). New York: McGraw-Hill.

Shure, M. B. (1992). *I can problem solve.* Champaign, IL: Research Press.

Smider, N. A., Essex, M. J., Kalin, N. H., Buss, K. A., Klein, M. H., Davidson, R. J., & Goldsmith, H. H. (2002). Salivary cortisol as a predictor of socioemotional adjustment during kindergarten: A prospective study. *Child Development, 73,* 75–92.

Smith, E. P., Boutte, G. S., Zigler, E., & Finn-Stevenson, M. (2004). Opportunities for schools to promote resilience in children and youth. In K. I. Maton, C. J. Schellenbach, B. J. Leadbeater, & A. L. Solarz (Eds.), *Investing in children, youth, families, and communities: Strength-based research and policy* (pp. 213–231). Washington, DC: American Psychological Association.

Szalacha, L. A., Erkut, S., García Coll, C., Alarcón, O., Fields, J. P., & Ceder, I. (2003). Discrimination and Puerto Rican children's and adolescents' mental health. *Cultural Diversity and Ethnic Minority Psychology, 9,* 141–155.

Thoits, P. A. (1995). Stress, coping, and social support processes: Where are we? What next? [Special issue]. *Journal of Health and Social Behavior,* 53–79.

Turner, J. E., Jr., & Cole, D. A. (1994). Developmental differences in cognitive diatheses for child depression. *Journal of Abnormal Child Psychology, 22,* 15–32.

Valiente, C., Fabes, R. A., Eisenberg, N., & Spinrad, T. L. (2004). The relations of parental expressivity and support to children's coping with daily stress. *Journal of Family Psychology, 18,* 97–106.

Williams, M. B. (2004). How schools respond to traumatic events. In N. B. Webb (Ed.), *Mass trauma and violence: Helping families and children cope* (pp. 120–141). New York: Guilford Press.

Wyman, P. A., Cowen, E. L., Work, W. C., & Parker, G. R. (1991). Developmental and family milieu correlates of resilience in urban children who have experienced major life stress. *American Journal of Community Psychology, 19,* 405–426.

Yamamoto, K. (2001). Stress: The view from the inside. In B. H. Stanford, & K. Yamamoto (Eds.), *Children and stress: Understanding and helping* (pp. 19–31). Olney, MD: Association for Childhood Education International.

Zakriski, A., Jacobs, M., & Coie, J. (1996). Coping with childhood peer rejection. In S. A. Wolchik & I. N. Sandler (Eds.), *Handbook of children's coping: Linking theory and intervention* (pp. 423–451). New York: Plenum Press.

# 20

# Fears and Anxiety Disorders

**Sylvia Z. Ramirez**
*University of Texas–Pan American*

**Kelly Ann Feeney-Kettler**
*University of Wisconsin–Madison*

**Leila Flores-Torres**
*University of Texas–Pan American*

**Thomas R. Kratochwill**
*University of Wisconsin–Madison*

**Richard J. Morris**
*University of Arizona*

## BACKGROUND AND DEVELOPMENT

Fears and anxiety are a normal part of child development and are adaptive in particular situations, such as in alerting children to potential dangers. When excessive, however, they can be debilitating and seriously affect children's current and long-term psychological functioning (Warren & Sroufe, 2004). This chapter provides a brief review of definitional and diagnostic issues related to children's fears, phobias, and anxiety disorders, as well as factors related to the development of these disorders. This background is followed by an overview of prevention and intervention strategies that mental health professionals have used successfully with children and adolescents.

### Definitional and Diagnostic Issues

The professional literature contains no clear consensus on the definitions and criteria of the multiple terms associated with fears and anxiety disorders (the discussion of these issues in this chapter is drawn primarily from Albano, Causey, & Carter, 2001; Dadds, James, Barrett, & Verhulst, 2004; Ginsburg & Walkup, 2004; and Warren & Sroufe, 2004). The terms *fear*, *phobia*, *anxiety*, and other related concepts (e.g., stress, panic, worry, avoidance reactions, and refusal behavior) often overlap and are used interchangeably. Fears are emotions that occur in response to threat, and mild fears are a part of normal development. Phobias are special forms of fear that "are associated with severe distress, usually lead to avoidance of the fear-provoking object or situation, do not remit with reassurance or information, and result in significant impairment in the daily functioning of children and their families" (Ginsburg & Walkup, p. 176). Traditionally, anxiety has been viewed as involving more diffuse reactions to nonspecific stimuli. In contrast to a fear's immediate alarm reaction, anxiety is characterized by negative affect that includes feelings of uneasiness, tension, apprehension, and worry that a negative event or situation will occur in the future.

The clinical manifestations of fears, phobias, and anxieties have been conceptualized in terms of three response systems or channels: cognitive, motor, and physiological. The cognitive channel is a subjective system of self-reported cognitions, feelings, and emotions associated with the fear (e.g., reporting the feeling of being afraid). In the motor channel, a child may act by confronting or avoiding the feared stimulus. The physiological channel involves an alarm reaction (i.e., the fight-or-flight response) to a perceived threat. Autonomic arousal reactions include elevated blood pressure, heart and respiration rate, and galvanic skin response. Additionally, the physiological channel can include sleep disturbance, impaired concentration, and the experience of tension.

Several approaches are used to diagnose anxiety disorders, including categorical, dimensional, and functional analysis models. Categorical diagnostic systems, particularly the *Diagnostic and Statistical Manual of Mental Disorders, Fourth Edition, Text Revision* (DSM-IV-TR; American Psychiatric Association, 2000), are widely used despite problems with the systems, such as questionable reliability and validity of the diagnostic categories. Categorical systems treat anxiety disorders as discrete entities. The model assumes that all anxiety disorders share similar features but differ with respect to the specific focus of the fear. In DSM-IV-TR, separation anxiety disorder and selective mutism are the only anxiety disorders that are specific to children and adolescents. The remaining anxiety disorders are described under adult disorders but may be applied to youth. Table 1 outlines the characteristics of some of the more common (DSM-IV-TR) anxiety disorders in youth.

The dimensional and functional models are diagnostic approaches that can be viewed as complementary to the DSM-IV-TR and other categorical systems. For example, the dimensional model is based on rating scales (e.g., the *Child Behavior Checklist*; see Dadds et al., 2004) and the assumption that anxiety disorders are a quantitative (rather than qualitative) deviation from normality. All individuals vary on a number of anxiety symptom dimensions that are derived from multivariate statistical procedures. Dimensional systems are recommended for research and clinical screening purposes, but they are also useful in conjunction with categorical systems for child diagnosis and treatment. For example, dimensional systems have cutoff scores that can aid in assessing levels of impairment.

The functional system of diagnosis is based on behavioral analytic theory. Rather than classifying on the basis of simple presence or absence of a behavior, the functional system classifies on the basis of the functional characteristics of behavior. For example, using the *School Refusal Assessment Scale* as a model, a child's behavior can be classified as being the result of one of several motivating conditions: attention-seeking behavior, avoidance of anxiety-provoking stimuli, escape from unpleasant social or evaluative situations, or positive tangible reinforcement. As a result, a primary advantage of the functional analysis model is that the analysis is highly relevant to treatment.

Regardless of the diagnostic system used, multiple methods should be used in assessing the nature and degree of impairment. Available assessment methods parallel the three channel components of fear and anxiety: behavioral assessment (e.g., naturalistic observation of behavior), physiological monitoring (e.g., galvanic skin response), and self- and other reports as illustrated in Table 2 (for a review of fear and anxiety assessment, see Greco & Morris, 2004). Specific assessment procedures include rating scales, diagnostic interviews, and broad-band measures of child and adolescent behavior that assess dimensions of anxiety. Additionally, behavioral and naturalistic observation is a particularly important part of the assessment of fears and anxiety disorders in children because it can provide information that may not be available when using other assessment methods.

## Development of Anxiety Disorders

***Risk and protective factors.*** Risk factors are variables that increase the likelihood that a particular disorder will occur, whereas protective factors are variables that reduce the likelihood of a particular disorder's occurrence. Whether a child will actually develop an anxiety disorder is not typically the result of any one risk or protective factor alone. Rather, anxiety disorders result from the interaction between protective factors, risk factors, and characteristics of the child and his or her environment (Donovan & Spence, 2000). Knowledge about anxiety disorder risk and protective factors can help educators identify those students most in need of prevention services (see Table 3).

Risk and protective factors and the development of anxiety disorders can be understood by examining theoretical perspectives with the most empirical support: biological–genetic and behavioral, including cognitive–behavioral theories (for a more complete discussion of the theoretical perspectives and findings described in this section, see Silverman & Kurtines, 2001; Manassis, Hudson, Webb, & Albano, 2004; and Sweeney & Pine, 2004).

***Biological and genetic theories.*** In biological and genetic theories, children are viewed as having a biological predisposition for developing anxiety disorders. A familial aggregation for the anxiety disorders has been revealed in

**Table 1** *Characteristics of Common DSM-IV-TR Anxiety Disorders in Youth*

| Disorder | Essential Features | Typical Age of Onset | Age Most Characteristic |
|---|---|---|---|
| Agoraphobia | Anxiety about being in places or situations from which escape might be difficult (or embarrassing) or in which help may not be available in the event of a panic attack or panic-like symptoms (e.g., fear of having a sudden attack of dizziness or a sudden attack of diarrhea). | Late adolescence | Late adolescence |
| Generalized Anxiety Disorder[a] | Excessive anxiety and worry (apprehensive expectation), occurring more days than not for a period of at least 6 months, about a number of events or activities (e.g., school performance). | Childhood | Adolescence |
| Obsessive–Compulsive Disorder | Recurrent obsessions or compulsions that are severe enough to be time-consuming (i.e., they take more than 1 hour a day) or cause marked distress or significant impairment. | Late childhood | Adolescence or early adulthood |
| Panic Attack | Discrete period of intense fear or discomfort in the absence of real danger that is accompanied by at least 4 of 13 somatic or cognitive symptoms (e.g., trembling, sweating, chest pain, and dizziness). | Adolescence or adulthood (can be childhood) | Adolescence or adulthood |
| Panic Disorder | Presence of recurrent, unexpected panic attacks followed by at least 1 month of persistent concern about having another panic attack, worry about the possible implications or consequences of the panic attacks, or a significant behavioral change related to the attacks. | Middle adolescence or early adulthood | Late-middle adolescence or young adulthood |
| Selective Mutism | Persistent failure to speak in specific social situations (e.g., school, with playmates) where speaking is expected, despite speaking in other situations. | Childhood | Childhood |
| Separation Anxiety Disorder | Excessive anxiety concerning separation from the home or from those to whom the person is attached. | Childhood | Childhood |
| Social Phobia | Marked and persistent fear of social or performance situations in which embarrassment can occur. | Middle adolescence | Adolescence |

*(Continued)*

**Table 1** *Continued*

| Disorder | Essential Features | Typical Age of Onset | Age Most Characteristic |
|---|---|---|---|
| Specific Phobia | Marked and persistent fear of clearly discernible, circumscribed objects or situations. | Childhood | Dependent on the phobia |

*Note.* Information regarding typical age of onset and age most characteristic is from "Fear and Anxiety in Children," by A. M. Albano, D. Causey, and B. D. Carter, 2001, in C. E. Walker and M. C. Roberts (Eds.), *Handbook of Clinical Child Psychology* (pp. 291–316), New York: Wiley; "Diagnostic Issues," by M. R. Dadds, R. C. James, P. M. Barrett, and F. C. Verhulst, 2004, in T. H. Ollendick and J. S. March (Eds.), *Phobic and Anxiety Disorders in Children and Adolescents: A Clinician's Guide to Effective Psychosocial and Pharmacological Interventions* (pp. 3–33), New York: Oxford University Press; "Developmental Variations in the Prevalence and Manifestation of Anxiety Disorders," by D. D. Weiss and C. Last, 2001, in M. W. Vasey and M. R. Dadds (Eds.), *The Developmental Psychopathology of Anxiety* (pp. 27–42), New York: Oxford University Press; and *Diagnostic and Statistical Manual of Mental Disorders, Fourth Edition, Text Revision* (DSM-IV-TR), by the American Psychiatric Association, 2000, Washington, DC: Author. Essential features are from DSM-IV-TR (pp. 121, 125, 430, 432, 433, 443, 450, 456, and 472). Copyright 2000 by the American Psychiatric Association. Reprinted with permission from the author.

[a]This category includes overanxious disorder of childhood, since the core criteria of GAD (DSM-IV-TR) and OAD (DSM-III-R) are similar.

studies that have examined parents of children with anxiety disorders and children of adults with anxiety disorders. Genetic influences account for about one-third of the variance in anxiety in most studies, although there appears to be less heritability for girls than boys. In particular, child temperament (e.g., behavioral inhibition) has received a great deal of attention as a neurobiological precursor. But since approximately 70% of children with behavioral inhibition do not develop anxiety disorders, more research is needed in this area (Silverman & Kurtines, 2001).

Anxiety sensitivity is another genetic influence that is implicated in anxiety disorders, in particular panic disorder. Children with anxiety sensitivity are more sensitive to their own physiological responses to stress and, as such, experience symptoms of anxiety as more threatening than those children without anxiety sensitivity. Cognitions also play a role in anxiety sensitivity because when children believe that harmful or aversive effects are linked to the experience of anxiety, their symptoms of anxiety further increase their perceived levels of stress.

***Behavior theories.*** Various behavioral theoretical perspectives have been advanced to conceptualize the development of fears and anxiety disorders, including classical and operant conditioning, social learning, and cognitive–behavioral theories. For example, from a classical conditioning perspective, anxiety problems result when a neutral stimulus, such as a dog, is paired with an aversive stimulus, such as a loud noise. The neutral stimulus becomes a conditioned stimulus and the aversive stimulus becomes an unconditioned stimulus. In the example, dogs become associated with loud noises, and the conditioned response is avoidance of dogs. Operant conditioning involves one additional component: a consequence following the conditioned response that results in the increased likelihood of the conditioned response occurring in the future. The parent of a child who becomes visibly upset in the presence of a dog may try to keep dogs away from the child, increasing the likelihood of the child's future avoidance of dogs. Similarly, a child screaming in the presence of a dog reinforces parent protective behavior, which indicates to the child that he or she should avoid dogs in the future. In another scenario, parents who punish or criticize a child for screaming in the presence of a dog, or for avoiding a dog, also may inadvertently promote avoidance of dogs. The punishment in response to the avoidance behavior indirectly intensifies the avoidance of dogs with the ultimate goal of avoiding criticism.

Social learning theory and cognitive–behavioral theories also describe pathways to the development of anxiety disorders. In social learning theory, children may learn to fear a situation through modeling or vicarious learning. If a child sees a parent or peer scream and run away every time a dog comes near, the child may emulate the parent's or peer's response to dogs and learn to believe that dogs are to be feared. In addition, the child may learn that he or she is unable to cope with fearful experiences, except through avoidance. Avoidance of anxious situations can result in the inability to develop mastery experiences, creating low self-efficacy and future avoidance of situations perceived to be threatening. With regard to cognitive–behavioral theory, some children have a propensity for appraising or expecting otherwise neutral stimuli to be threatening. These appraisals are often biased, distorted, and maladaptive, and reflect negative perceptions of the environment and the self. Consistent distorted self- and environmental

**Table 2** *Common Methods to Assess Fears and Anxiety in Children and Adolescents*

| Self-Reports | Behavior Rating Scales | Diagnostic Interviews | Other |
|---|---|---|---|
| Anxiety Sensitivity Index for Children (ASIC) | Behavior Assessment System for Children, Second Edition | Anxiety Disorders Interview Schedule for DSM-IV, Child Version (ADIS-IV-C) | Physiological measures |
| Fear Survey Schedule for Children, Revised (FSSC-R) | Child Behavior Checklist | Schedule for Affective Disorders and Schizophrenia for School-Age Children (K-SADS) | Behavioral observations |
| Multidimensional Anxiety Scale for Children (MASC) | | | |
| Revised Children's Manifest Anxiety Scale (RCMAS) | | | |
| School Refusal Assessment Scale | | | |
| Screen for Child Anxiety–Related Emotional Disorders (SCARED) | | | |
| Social Phobia and Anxiety Inventory for Children (SPAIC) | | | |
| Spence Children's Anxiety Scale (SCAS) | | | |
| State Trait Anxiety Inventory for Children (STAIC) | | | |

*Note.* Citations and reviews of these and other measures are from "Assessment," by L. A. Greco and T. L. Morris, 2004, in T. L. Morris and J. S. March (Eds.), *Anxiety Disorders in Children and Adolescents* (2nd ed., pp. 98–121), New York: Guilford; and from "Diagnostic Issues," by M. R. Dadds, R. C. James, P. M. Barrett, and F. C. Verhulst, 2004, in T. H. Ollendick and J. S. March (Eds.), *Phobic and Anxiety Disorders in Children and Adolescents: A Clinician's Guide to Effective Psychosocial and Pharmacological Interventions* (pp. 3–33), New York: Oxford University Press.

appraisals can result in fear-based responses. For example, if children expect or appraise dogs to be threatening, they will respond with fear. Their fearful responses can be reinforced and perpetuated as discussed in the paragraph above. Information processing and causal attribution theories also explore the relationship between the role of children's cognitions and anxiety (e.g., selective attention, thought patterns, judgment, and memory).

## Normative Fears

Research on fears and anxiety is plagued with methodological problems that make comparisons across studies difficult. These problems include the (a) lack of specificity of exclusionary criteria, (b) varying definitions of fear and anxiety, (c) type of behavior measurement (e.g., checklist versus direct observation), (d) type of informant (e.g., child, parent, or teacher), and (e) differences in the populations studied (e.g., race or ethnicity). Nonetheless, it is widely accepted that fears are a normal part of development, with children having an average of about 14 fears. Most children have fears that are mild, transient, and age specific, with girls tending to report more fears and greater fear intensity than boys. A young child's fears, for example, are of imaginary figures such as monsters, and older children and adolescents are more likely to fear anticipatory, abstract, and global stimuli. Why children of varying ages develop different fears can be explained

**Table 3** *Example Protective and Risk Factors in the Development of Fears and Anxiety Disorders*

**Protective Factors**
- Problem-focused coping style
  - Relaxation
  - Rational thinking and interpretations
- Observation of coping behaviors
- Social support

**Risk Factors**
- Emotion-focused coping style
- Child temperament
  - Behavioral inhibition
- Genetic predisposition
  - Anxiety sensitivity
- Gender
  - Female
- Attachment style
  - Insecure (Anxious, Resistant)
- Parental variables
  - Psychopathology, especially anxiety disorders
  - Overprotective behavior
  - Overcontrolling behavior
  - Inconsistent or restrictive parenting
  - Low levels of affection
  - Modeling of fearful behavior
- Peer relationships
  - Social withdrawal
  - Level of competence
- Stressful, negative, and traumatic life events
  - Disasters
  - Deaths
  - School transitions
  - Major accidents
  - Health problems

*Note.* From "Primary Prevention of Anxiety Disorders," by J. L. Hudson, E. Flannery-Schroeder, and P. C. Kendall, 2004, in J. A. Dozois and K. S. Dobson (Eds.), *The Prevention of Anxiety and Depression: Theory, Research, and Practice* (pp. 101–130), Washington, DC: American Psychological Association; and "Prevention Strategies," by S. H. Spence, 2001, in M. W. Vasey and M. R. Dadds (Eds.), *The Developmental Psychopathology of Anxiety* (pp. 325–351), New York: Oxford University Press.

by cognitive and environmental changes. For example, because of children's increased cognitive ability to differentiate reality from fantasy in the early school years, fears of imaginary creatures tend to give way to fears of physical harm. Also, fears change depending on experiential and environmental factors (e.g., adolescents tend to have more sexual fears than children). Ginsburg and Walkup (2004) and Warren and Sroufe (2004) provide a detailed discussion of these and other normative issues and the types of fears and anxieties associated with different ages in children and adolescents.

### Prevalence of Anxiety Disorders

Anxiety disorders are among the most common mental health problems experienced by school-age children (Ollendick & March, 2004). The prevalence rate for any anxiety disorder is from about 6% to 18%, with the most frequent disorders being overanxious/generalized anxiety disorder, separation anxiety disorder, and specific phobia (Silverman & Kurtines, 2001). These prevalence values may even be an underestimate, as they do not include the cases of children who remain unidentified and untreated. With the exception of separation anxiety disorder, however, most anxiety disorders tend to increase with age. Additionally, there is no clear gender pattern for most anxiety disorders in youth. Although relatively few studies have been done of the prevalence differences by race/ethnicity and religion, some differences have been reported (e.g., that Muslim children have fewer fears than Christian children, and African American children have more fears and higher fear intensity than White American children; see Manassis et al., 2004).

## PROBLEMS AND IMPLICATIONS

Anxiety disorders that remain untreated may persist, leading to impairments in emotional, social, and academic development, as well as future mental health problems (Ferdinand, Barrett, & Dadds, 2004). Greenberg et al. (1999) estimated that $42 billion per year ($1,542 per anxious individual each year) is spent in the United States on medical treatment for anxiety disorders, not including the cost of mental health treatment or emotional suffering by children and their families. Some evidence also exists regarding other consequences of having an anxiety disorder, such as comorbidity with other disorders (Dadds et al., 2004; Ginsburg & Walkup, 2004). For example, 60% of children with specific phobias have been reported to have other types of psychiatric disorders. Of children with specific phobia and another disorder, 50%–75% have a related anxiety disorder, most frequently separation anxiety disorder (Ginsburg & Walkup). In clinic samples, the rates of comorbid anxiety and other internalizing disorders (especially depression) are 24%–70%, and the comorbid rates with externalizing disorders are 8%–61% (see, e.g., Dadds et al.).

Fears and anxiety reactions can become clinical concerns when the reactions (a) are out of proportion to the situation's demands or threat, (b) occur with increased frequency and cannot be reasoned away through reassurance or information, (c) seem to be focused on innocuous stimuli that are not likely to cause harm, (d) appear to be spontaneous and out of the child's voluntary control, and (e) lead to avoidance of or escape from the situation (Albano et al., 2001). Unfortunately, children's fears and anxieties are not often identified by teachers or parents because children with internalizing problems do not usually disrupt classroom functioning. The longer children suffer with an unidentified anxiety problem, the more adverse the effects anxiety can have on children's development (e.g., low self-esteem, social rejection, avoidance of social activities, or academic failure), which are typically difficult to reverse (e.g., Spence, 2001). In addition, there is evidence that anxiety disorders may contribute to the development of other psychopathology, such as depression and substance abuse disorders (e.g., Hudson, Flannery-Schroeder, & Kendall, 2004).

## ALTERNATIVE ACTIONS FOR PREVENTION

High prevalence rates, coupled with the economic and emotional consequences of anxiety disorders, have resulted in a focus on preventing the development of anxiety disorders in children and adolescents. A three-tiered model of prevention (universal, selective, and indicated) is described below.

### Universal Prevention

Universal prevention, formerly referred to as primary prevention, includes programs applied to all students, no matter what their risk for a particular disorder (National Institute of Mental Health [NIMH], 2001). Universal prevention may be especially important in the prevention of anxiety disorders, since children with anxiety problems are often unidentified and untreated (Hudson et al., 2004).

Few universal prevention programs for anxiety disorders have been published. One is the FRIENDS program (Barrett, et al., 2000), which consists of a 12-week, family-based cognitive–behavioral intervention that teaches children to cope with daily experiences. The FRIENDS acronym stands for the steps in the program: F—Feeling worried; R—Relax and feel good; I—Inner thoughts; E—Explore plans; N—Nice work so reward yourself; D—Don't forget to practice; and S—Stay calm, you know how to cope now (Barrett et al.). Although applied as a universal prevention program, FRIENDS is similar to cognitive–behavioral and evidence-based programs for the treatment of anxiety disorders, such as the Coping Cat Program (Kendall, 1992, 2000). Children who participated in the FRIENDS program reported a decrease in self-reported symptoms of anxiety (Barrett et al.).

Another example of a universal prevention program is the Ready ... Set ... RELAX program (Allen & Klein, 1996). This program helps children manage stress by developing coping skills through the use of self-talk, music, progressive muscle relaxation, and imagination techniques (Tomb & Hunter, 2004). The program consists of 66 scripts that teach children coping skills using the acronym RELAX: R—Releasing tension; E—Enjoying life; L—Learning; A—Appreciating others; and X—Expanding your knowledge. Scripts can be selected and implemented based on individual needs. One of the program's strengths is that it can be administered by teachers, parents, or medical and mental health professionals. Students participating in Ready ... Set ... RELAX reported decreased anxiety and depression and increased self-esteem (Allen & Klein). The program can also be applied at the selective and indicated prevention intervention levels.

### Selective Prevention

Selective prevention, formerly referred to as secondary prevention, includes programs that are applied to students who have a greater-than-average risk for a particular disorder (NIMH, 2001). Children are particularly vulnerable to anxiety during periods of school transition (Donovan & Spence, 2000). The School Transitional Environment Project (STEP; Felner et al., 2001) is a program designed to help students decrease the stress associated with transitioning from elementary to middle school or from middle to high school. STEP changes the school environment by organizing students into groups for main academic classes and homeroom. The result is a community of teachers and students that yields social support and connection between the students, the rest of the school, and the outside community (Tomb & Hunter, 2004). Students participating in STEP reported improved academic achievement and improved adjustment to their new school settings (Greenberg, Domitrovich, & Bumbarger, 2001).

***Indicated Prevention.*** Indicated prevention, formerly referred to as tertiary prevention, includes programs that are applied to students who are at high risk for, have predispositions for, or have beginning symptoms of a particular disorder (NIMH, 2001). An example of an indicated prevention program is the Queensland Early Intervention and Prevention of Anxiety Project (QEIPAP; Dadds, Spence, Holland, Barrett, & Laurens, 1997; Dadds et al., 1999). Students with mild to moderate anxiety symptoms received a cognitive–behavioral child–parent intervention, named the Coping Koala, that was adapted from the Coping Cat Program (described in the cognitive–behavioral section below). The Coping Koala is analogous to the Coping Cat, except that it is conducted over 10 weeks rather than 12 weeks. Children learn to manage symptoms of anxiety during weekly 1- to 2-hour sessions, through the use of the FEAR acronym: F—Feel good through relaxation; E—Expect positive outcomes by using adaptive self-talk; A—Actions to take before and when exposed to threatening stimuli; R—Rewards for coping efforts (Dadds et al., 1997). Two of the 10 sessions are to provide parents with psychoeducation about anxiety disorders. Following participation in Coping Koala, only 16% of children were diagnosed with an anxiety disorder, compared to 54% of children who did not receive the intervention (Dadds et al., 1997). Two years later, 20% of the children who participated in Coping Koala had an anxiety disorder, compared to 39% of the children who did not receive the intervention (Dadds et al., 1999). The QEIPAP is viewed as a model program that can be used in a group format for students with low-anxiety symptoms (Tomb & Hunter, 2004).

## ALTERNATIVE ACTIONS FOR INTERVENTIONS

Intervention should be considered when children's fears or anxieties begin to interfere with their academic or social functioning. The focus of such interventions has moved to evidence-based treatment techniques and programs, including behavioral, cognitive–behavioral, and psychopharmacological interventions, as well as a combination of treatments (see, e.g., Ollendick & March, 2004; Silverman & Kurtines, 2001). Although other treatments (e.g., play and family therapies) are commonly used, their efficacy has not been sufficiently evaluated and demonstrated.

### Behavioral Interventions

Contemporary treatments often integrate different strategies to effectively manage fears, phobias, and other anxiety disorders in children and adolescents. Systematic desensitization, modeling, contingency management, and relaxation training are among the most effective behavioral therapies (Society of Clinical Child and Adolescent Psychology, 2004).

***Systematic desensitization.*** Systematic desensitization (also referred to as graduated exposure) has been used effectively for a variety of anxiety disorders and conditions, including separation anxiety disorder, specific phobias, and test anxiety. The intervention procedures are sequential and consist of gradually exposing a child to a feared stimulus, from the least to the most anxiety-provoking stimulus (fear hierarchy). To reduce fear using counterconditioning procedures, exposure is provided through imaginary or genuine experience, while concurrently inducing an incompatible response, such as relaxation. The relaxation component usually involves progressive muscle relaxation exercises (tensing and relaxing different muscle groups) combined with deep, slow breathing (Weisz, Hawley, & Doss, 2004). A variation of systematic desensitization uses positive imagery, games, or fun activities instead of the relaxation component.

***Contingency management.*** Contingency management procedures focus on modifying fears and related anxieties by manipulating the consequences associated with the performance of anxious behaviors (Albano et al., 2001). The procedures related to contingency management are shaping, reinforced practice, extinction, and contingency contracting (Morris & Kratochwill, 1998). The effectiveness of contingency management procedures depends on the construction and implementation of a contract between the parent, a teacher or therapist, and the child. In the contract, a list of rewards is devised and administered to the child upon the completion of a desired target behavior or upon the completion of successive behaviors leading toward a target behavior (Ginsburg & Walkup, 2004).

***Modeling.*** Modeling provides an opportunity for a child to perform behaviors that have not been performed or were inhibited in the feared anxiety-producing situation. This treatment is based on an observational learning approach in which the child observes a model interacting successfully with the feared situation (Morris & Kratochwill, 1998). There are two main types of modeling: live (or participant) modeling and symbolic (or filmed) modeling. Compared with symbolic modeling, live modeling has more empirical support in alleviating fears and phobias in children (see Ginsburg & Walkup, 2004).

## Cognitive-Behavioral Therapy

Cognitive–behavioral therapy (CBT) can be divided into three subcategories: self-instruction, rational–emotive therapy, and self-control (Morris & Kratochwill, 1998). Self-instructional interventions involve reflective problem-solving whereby a child uses self-talk to effectively handle anxiety-producing situations. Rational–emotive therapy focuses on replacing irrational thoughts that underlie the particular problem with rational beliefs (Weisz et al., 2004). Self-control strategies are designed to modify thoughts, perceptions, images, and beliefs by manipulating and restructuring maladaptive thoughts. Because it is based on the premise that maladaptive cognitions produce maladaptive behaviors, self-control allows for cognitive changes that, in turn, produce behavior changes (Albano et al., 2001). A child's negativistic self-talk increases and perpetuates his or her anxiety in the presence of anxiety-provoking stimuli. By changing the self-talk to be more positive, the child should experience less anxiety when exposed to an anxiety-provoking stimulus, such as entering a social situation (Dadds & Barrett, 2001).

Cognitive–behavioral therapy for childhood anxiety disorders consists of five major components (Albano & Kendall, 2002):

- Psychoeducation, which teaches the cognitive–behavioral conceptualization of anxiety and its treatment (Ginsburg & Schlossberg, 2002) and provides corrective information about feared stimuli and anxiety.
- Somatic management skills training, which targets autonomic arousal and related physiological responses.
- Cognitive restructuring, which must be developmentally appropriate and is focused on identifying maladaptive thoughts and teaching realistic thinking that focuses on coping.
- Exposure methods, which involve graduated, systematic, and controlled exposure to feared situations and stimuli.
- Relapse prevention plans, which focus on consolidating and generalizing treatment gains over time.

Most evidence-based interventions available for the treatment of fears and anxiety in children and adolescents involve these five components of cognitive-behavioral therapy.

The Coping Cat Program is one of the most effective interventions in the treatment of fears and related anxieties in children. The program also includes an adolescent version: the CAT project. The Coping Cat Program has demonstrated efficacy for a variety of ages and anxiety-based conditions and has proved to be adaptable to group formats as well as to diverse cultures (Albano & Kendall, 2002; Kendall, 1992, 2000).

The Coping Cat Program consists of 14 to 18 sixty-minute sessions. The first six to eight sessions focus on teaching new skills to the child; the second eight sessions give the child the opportunity to practice the skills learned both in-vivo and within sessions. The Coping Cat protocol consists of six main principles: (a) recognize anxious feelings and somatic reactions to anxiety, (b) identify cognitions in anxiety-provoking situations, (c) develop a plan to cope with anxiety-provoking situations, (d) practice the coping plan using behavioral exposure techniques, (e) evaluate performance, and (f) learn self-reinforcement techniques. To help reinforce and generalize the skills the child has learned, each session includes specific homework tasks along with specific techniques to enhance relapse prevention. In addition, parental involvement in the child's treatment occurs at several levels, including parent sessions during the course of treatment and inclusion in exposure exercises with the child. Parents play an important role, as they engage as collaborators and consultants in the child's treatment process.

## Selected Approaches to Cognitive–Behavioral Treatment

***Group cognitive–behavioral treatment.*** Although individual CBT interventions have been the focus of most research on treatment of child and adolescent anxiety disorders, some research has also focused on group-oriented treatments. Findings suggest that group treatment may be as effective as individual cognitive–behavioral therapy. Additionally, group treatment may be the treatment of choice for some youth with anxiety disorders (Flannery-Schroeder & Kendall, 2000). The group format provides the therapist with the opportunity to use peers for social support, social interactions, corrective instruction, modeling, and feedback. Group treatment also allows for leadership and exposure to different interpersonal contexts, objects, or situations. A further advantage of group CBT is that it may reduce the feelings of stigma and isolation in those children and adolescents experiencing social anxiety. Finally, group treatments incorporate the key treatment strategies of individual cognitive–behavioral therapy, have approximately the same number of sessions, and are believed to be more cost-effective than individual approaches.

Researchers have compared the efficacy of individual and group-based cognitive–behavioral treatments for youth anxiety disorders. In one study, Flannery-Schroeder and Kendall (2000) evaluated three treatment conditions (group cognitive–behavioral therapy, individual cognitive–behavioral therapy, and a wait-list control condition) using a sample of 37 children 8 to 14 years of age with anxiety disorders. The individual and group CBT conditions were based on the Coping Cat Program. At the end of the 18-week treatment cycle, more children in the two treatment groups than in the wait-list group no longer met diagnostic criteria for their primary anxiety disorder. The percentages of children who no longer met their primary anxiety disorder criteria were 73% for individual therapy, 50% for group therapy, and 8% for wait-list control. The treatment groups were superior to the wait-list control on other dependent measures (including self- and other reports), but there were few differences in outcomes between the two treatment groups.

***Family-based treatment.*** Another variation of CBT is family-based treatment. Cognitive–behavioral family-based treatment involves teaching parents specific strategies to reduce anxiety in their children. The treatment incorporates several therapeutic strategies, including psychoeducation, contingency management, cognitive restructuring, reduction of parental anxiety, improvement of the parent–child relationship, and relapse prevention (Ginsburg & Schlossberg, 2002). Involvement of the family in CBT treatments for children's phobic and anxiety disorders can enhance the efficacy of these treatments, since therapy is extended to the home environment. As a result, children experience consistency across environments as they use their CBT strategies to overcome fears and anxiety. In some cases, clinicians recommend adjunctive treatment for the parents, especially if the child's symptoms are believed to be present as a response to the parent's psychopathology (Albano et al., 2001; Albano & Kendall, 2002).

Several studies have included sessions with parents as a component of anxiety treatment programs. For example, Barrett, Dadds, and Rapee (1996) compared individual cognitive–behavioral therapy with CBT plus a family anxiety management component (CBT-FAM) in a sample of 79 children ages 7 to 14 years. Both treatments used the Coping Koala program, while the CBT-FAM program added a family component. CBT-FAM involved teaching parents to (a) reward their child's coping behaviors and to extinguish anxious behaviors; (b) use similar CBT strategies to manage their own anxiety; and (c) build better family communication and problem-solving skills. Upon completion of the program, 84% of the children treated with CBT-FAM no longer met DSM-III-R diagnostic criteria for anxiety disorders, compared with 57% of children treated with CBT alone. At follow-up, children who received CBT-FAM continued to show superior outcomes compared with children who received CBT alone, based on clinician ratings of overall functioning, avoidant and anxious behaviors, and parent and child skills in coping with difficult situations (84% vs. 71% at 6 months, and 96% vs. 70% at 12 months).

## Combined Interventions

Some clinicians and researchers believe that the combination of CBT and medication is the initial treatment of choice for most children and adolescents with a diagnosable anxiety disorder (March, 2002). Certain guidelines are recommended when considering whether to include a psychopharmacological intervention in the child's treatment (see Albano et al., 2001). Clinicians are urged to consider the following:

1. Judge whether the symptomatology presented produces significant distress and interference in the child's or adolescent's functioning.
2. Reflect on the probability that pharmacotherapy will help reduce symptoms.
3. Judge whether the symptoms are severe enough to require the child or adolescent to be exposed to the risks of taking a specific psychiatric medication.
4. Consider whether the parents have requested a psychopharmacological intervention.
5. Consider whether the child or adolescent has tried CBT or other treatment and whether it was not found to be effective.

6. Evaluate the presence of a comorbid disorder that suggests a more aggressive treatment component.
7. Consider whether the child or adolescent has suicidal tendencies.
8. Observe patterns of relapse and how frequent and severe they are in spite of previous CBT attempts.

Further research is needed to evaluate the effectiveness of combined pharmacotherapy and CBT in treating anxious and phobic children and to determine which approach—psychiatric medications or CBT—should be used first with youth. Moreover, additional research is needed to determine the safety and efficacy of long-term medication treatment, and the optimal duration of such treatment, to avoid prolonging it more than necessary (Walkup, Labellarte, & Ginsburg, 2002).

## SUMMARY

This chapter presented an overview of definitions, prevalence, diagnosis, assessment, risk factors, theories, and interventions associated with fears, phobias, and related anxiety disorders in children and adolescents. The primary focus was on the descriptions of evidence-based prevention and intervention approaches for youths. Anxiety disorders are quite common and may be diagnosed through categorical, dimensional, and functional analysis approaches. Behavioral (especially cognitive–behavioral) and genetic theories have received the most support with respect to etiology in recent years. In the treatment of fears, phobias, and related anxiety disorders, the most efficacious interventions appear to be behavioral, cognitive–behavioral, psychopharmacological, and a combination of treatments.

Until recently, the majority of previous research on anxiety disorders has focused less on prevention than on treatment (Donovan & Spence, 2000). Researchers are beginning to identify anxiety disorder prevention programs at each level in the three-tiered model of prevention. Anxiety prevention research, however, remains in its infancy. Much more work needs to be done before youth can be immunized against this highly prevalent, persistent, and costly mental health issue.

## RECOMMENDED RESOURCES

### Books and Other Printed Material

Dozois, D. J. A., & Dobson, K. S. (Ed.). (2004). *The prevention of anxiety and depression: Theory, research, and practice.* Washington, DC: American Psychological Association.

This text provides up-to-date information on the prevention of both anxiety and depression. Of particular interest are the chapters on each of the three tiers (primary, secondary, and tertiary) of a comprehensive prevention model for anxiety disorders. Current theories on risk and protective factors for anxiety disorders, research advances, and existing prevention programs are explored.

Morris, T. L., & March, J. S. (Eds.). (2004). *Anxiety disorders in children and adolescents* (2nd ed.). New York: Guilford Press.

This text provides current information on the etiology, assessment, diagnosis, prevention, and treatment (pharmacotherapy, cognitive–behavioral therapy, and combined treatments) of anxiety disorders in children and adolescents. Of particular interest are the seven chapters dedicated to specific anxiety disorders (e.g., obsessive–compulsive disorder and selective mutism).

Ollendick, T. H., & March, J. S. (Eds.). (2004). *Phobic and anxiety disorders in children and adolescents: A clinician's guide to effective psychosocial and pharmacological interventions.* New York: Oxford University Press.

This text presents a broad range of topics that address etiological, developmental, and diagnostic issues related to anxiety disorders in youth. Of particular interest are the separate chapters on the assessment and treatment of specific anxiety disorders in youth, including psychosocial and pharmacological interventions.

### Websites

*http://www.effectivechildtherapy.com*

This website of the Society of Clinical Child and Adolescent Psychology (Division 53, American Psychological Association) provides current information about child and adolescent mental health practice and evidence-based treatment of various psychological disorders, including anxiety disorders. The site includes case examples and recommended readings.

*http://smhp.psych.ucla.edu*

This website, sponsored by the Center for Mental Health in Schools, University of California, Los Angeles, offers information, materials, and technical support (e.g., with consultation cadres of professionals) about mental health issues in schools. Of particular interest is their introductory packet, which is available online: "An Introductory Packet on Fears, Phobias, and Related Problems: Intervention and Resources for School-Aged Youth."

## REFERENCES

Albano, A. M., Causey, D., & Carter, B. D. (2001). Fear and anxiety in children. In C. E. Walker & M. C. Roberts (Eds.), *Handbook of clinical child psychology* (pp. 291–316). New York: John Wiley & Sons.

Albano, A. M., & Kendall, P. C. (2002). Cognitive behavioural therapy for children and adolescents with anxiety disorders: Clinical research advances. *International Review of Psychiatry, 14,* 129–134.

Allen, J. S., & Klein, R. J. (1996). *Ready ... Set ... R.E.L.A.X.: A research-based program of relaxation, learning and self-esteem for children.* Watertown, WI: Inner Coaching.

American Psychiatric Association. (2000). *Diagnostic and statistical manual of mental disorders* (4th ed., text revision). Washington, DC: Author.

Barrett, P. M., Dadds, M. R., & Rapee, R. M. (1996). Family treatment of childhood anxiety: A controlled trial. *Journal of Consulting and Clinical Psychology, 64,* 333–342.

Barrett, P. M., Lowry-Webster, H., & Turner, C. (2000). *Friends program for children: Group leaders manual.* Brisbane: Australian Academic Press.

Dadds, M. R., & Barrett, P. M. (2001). Practitioner review: Psychological management of anxiety disorders in childhood. *Journal of Child Psychology and Psychiatry, 42,* 999–1011.

Dadds, M. R., Holland, D. E., Laurens, K. R., Mullins, M., Barrett, P. M., & Spence, S. H. (1999). Early intervention and prevention of anxiety disorders in children: Results at 2-year follow up. *Journal of Consulting and Clinical Psychology, 67,* 145–150.

Dadds, M. R., James, R. C., Barrett, P. M., & Verhulst, F. C. (2004). Diagnostic issues. In T. H. Ollendick & J. S. March (Eds.), *Phobic and anxiety disorders in children and adolescents: A clinician's guide to effective psychosocial and pharmacological interventions* (pp. 3–33). New York: Oxford University Press.

Dadds, M. R., Spence, S. H., Holland, D. E., Barrett, P. M., & Laurens, K. R. (1997). Prevention and early intervention for anxiety disorders: A controlled trial. *Journal of Consulting Psychology, 65,* 627–635.

Donovan, C. L., & Spence, S. H. (2000). Prevention of childhood anxiety disorders. *Clinical Psychology Review, 20,* 509–531.

Felner, R. D., Favazza, A., Shim, M., Brand, S., Gu, K., & Noonan, N. (2001). Whole school improvement and restructuring as prevention and promotion: Lessons from STEP and the Project on High Performance Learning Communities. *Journal of School Psychology, 39,* 177–202.

Ferdinand, R. F., Barrett, P. M., & Dadds, M. R. (2004). Anxiety and depression in childhood: Prevention and intervention. In T. Ollendick & J. S. March (Eds.), *Phobic and anxiety disorders in children and adolescents: A clinician's guide to effective psychosocial and pharmacological interventions* (pp. 459–475). New York: Oxford University Press.

Flannery-Schroeder, E. C., & Kendall, P. C. (2000). Group and individual cognitive-behavioral treatments for youth with anxiety disorders: A randomized clinical trial. *Cognitive Therapy and Research, 24,* 251–278.

Ginsburg, G. S., & Schlossberg, M. C. (2002). Family-based treatment of childhood anxiety disorders. *International Review of Psychiatry, 14,* 143–154.

Ginsburg, G. S., & Walkup, J. T. (2004). Specific phobia. In T. H. Ollendick & J. S. March (Eds.), *Phobic and anxiety disorders in children and adolescents: A clinician's guide to effective psychosocial and pharmacological interventions* (pp. 175–197). New York: Oxford University Press.

Greco, L. A., & Morris, T. L. (2004). Assessment. In T. L. Morris & J. S. March (Eds.), *Anxiety disorders in children and adolescents* (2nd ed., pp. 98–121). New York: Guilford Press.

Greenberg, M. T., Domitrovich, C., & Bumbarger, B. (2001). The prevention of mental disorders in school-aged children: Current state of the field. *Prevention and Treatment, 4,* 1–63.

Greenberg, P. E., Sisitsky, T., Kessler, R. C., Finkelstein, S. N., Berndt, E. R., Davidson, J. R. T., et al. (1999). The economic burden of anxiety disorders in the 1990s. *Journal of Clinical Psychiatry, 60,* 427–435.

Hudson, J. L., Flannery-Schroeder, E., & Kendall, P. C. (2004). Primary prevention of anxiety disorders. In J. A. Dozois & K. S. Dobson (Eds.), *The prevention of anxiety and depression: Theory, research, and practice* (pp. 101–130). Washington, DC: American Psychological Association.

Kendall, P. C. (1992, 2000). *Coping Cat Program for Anxious Youth.* Ardmore, PA: Workbook Publishing, Inc.

Manassis, K., Hudson, J. L., Webb, A., & Albano, A. M. (2004). Beyond behavioral inhibition: Etiological factors in childhood anxiety. *Cognitive and Behavioral Practice, 11,* 3–12.

March, J. S. (2002). Combining medication and psychosocial treatments: An evidence-based medicine approach. *International Review of Psychiatry, 14,* 155–163.

Morris, R. J., & Kratochwill, T. R. (1998). Childhood fears and phobias. In R. J. Morris & T. R. Kratochwill (Eds.), *The practice of child therapy* (3rd ed., pp. 91–131). Boston: Allyn & Bacon.

National Institute of Mental Health. (2001). National Advisory Mental Health Council Workgroup on Mental Disorders Prevention Research. Priorities for prevention research at NIMH. *Prevention & Treatment, 4,* Article 17. Retrieved May 1, 2004, from http://journals.apa.org/prevention/volume4/pre0040017a.html

Ollendick, T. H., & March, J. S. (Eds.) (2004). *Phobic and anxiety disorders in children and adolescents: A clinician's guide to effective psychosocial and pharmacological interventions.* New York: Oxford University Press.

Silverman, W. K., & Kurtines, W. M. (2001). Anxiety disorders. In J. N. Hughes, A. M. La Greca, & J. C. Conoley (Eds.), *Handbook of psychological services for children and adolescents* (pp. 225–244). New York: Oxford University Press.

Society of Clinical Child and Adolescent Psychology. (2004). *Evidence-based treatment for children and adolescents.* Washington, DC: American Psychological Association. Retrieved July 10, 2004, from http://www.effectivechildtherapy.com/

Spence, S. H. (2001). Prevention strategies. In M. W. Vasey & M. R. Dadds (Eds.), *The developmental psychopathology of anxiety* (pp. 325–351). New York: Oxford University Press.

Sweeney, M., & Pine, D. (2004). Etiology of fear and anxiety. In T. Ollendick & J. S. March (Eds.), *Phobic and anxiety disorders in children and adolescents: A clinician's guide to effective psychosocial and pharmacological interventions* (pp. 34–60). New York: Oxford University Press.

Tomb, M., & Hunter, L. (2004). Prevention of anxiety in children and adolescents in a school setting: The role of school-based practitioners. *Children & Schools, 26*(2), 87–101.

Walkup, J. T., Labellarte, M. J., & Ginsburg, G. S. (2002). The pharmacological treatment of childhood anxiety disorders. *International Review of Psychiatry, 14,* 135–142.

Warren, S. L., & Sroufe, L. A. (2004). Developmental issues. In T. Ollendick & J. S. March (Eds.), *Phobic and anxiety disorders in children and adolescents: A clinician's guide to effective psychosocial and pharmacological interventions* (pp. 92–115). New York: Oxford University Press.

Weiss, D. D., & Last, C. (2001). Developmental variations in the prevalence and manifestation of anxiety disorders. In M. W. Vasey & M. R. Dadds (Eds.), *The developmental psychopathology of anxiety* (pp. 27–42). New York: Oxford University Press.

Weisz, J. R., Hawley, K. M., & Doss, A. J. (2004). Empirically tested psychotherapies for youth internalizing and externalizing problems and disorders. *Child & Adolescent Psychiatric Clinics of North America, 13,* 729–815.

# 21

# Performance and Test Anxiety

**Thomas J. Huberty**
**Amy C. Dick**
*Indiana University*

## BACKGROUND AND DEVELOPMENT

Anxiety is a common experience for everyone and can be viewed both positively and negatively. It is most often viewed negatively, however, because it is associated with behaviors that interfere with cognitive, social, personal, and academic functioning. Indeed, anxiety, at its extremes, can interfere significantly with task performance and the ability to do well on tests and other evaluative procedures. In the school setting, where performance and evaluation occur frequently, anxiety can have significant effects on academic achievement and social functioning. This chapter discusses the nature of performance and evaluation anxiety and offers some suggestions for school-based professionals and parents to address both anxiety and its consequences for academic success.

For purposes of this chapter, *performance anxiety* refers to behaviors that are affected by anxiety. *Evaluation anxiety*, commonly called test anxiety, refers to anxiety demonstrated when a child or adolescent is being evaluated formally or informally. In some cases, children can demonstrate both types of anxiety, such as when giving a speech in class that is also being evaluated for a grade. Definitions of performance anxiety and test anxiety typically incorporate behaviors seen under evaluative conditions that also may be seen in other anxiety disorders. A working definition of performance and test anxiety for this chapter is excessive degrees of fear, worry, and apprehension about outcomes associated with performance and evaluative procedures. Performance and test anxiety are on a continuum of degrees of severity and are not merely present or absent.

Although almost all students experience test anxiety at some time, a subset of students experience high levels over many situations. Incidence figures are difficult to determine, because the types and severity of performance and test anxiety depend on the conditions under which tasks are to be performed. In one study, 52% of African American and 38% of White elementary school students met cutoff criteria for test anxiety (Beidel, Turner, & Trager, 1994). A conservative estimate is that at least 20% of elementary school students suffer from some form of test anxiety (Goonan, 2003). In general, girls tend to report test anxiety more often than boys, but the differences may reflect boys' reluctance to admit to anxiety. Sociocultural factors also may play a role, because adults may be more likely to accept reports of anxiety from girls than from boys. Also, boys' anxiety and fears tend to dissipate faster than girls'. Few gender differences are noted up to about 10 or 11 years of age, but during adolescence, girls tend to report higher levels of anxiety than do boys, including test anxiety.

The central component of anxiety is *worry*, which is defined as "an anticipatory cognitive process involving repetitive thoughts related to possible threatening outcomes and their potential consequences" (Vasey, Crnic, & Carter, 1994, p. 530). In performance and evaluation anxiety, worry is demonstrated by the child being overly concerned about failure, about being embarrassed, or about disappointing self or others. The specific conditions for a child to experience worry and anxiety are unknown, but Vasey et al. suggest that the ability to anticipate even one threatening situation may cause anxious reactions. Children with performance and test anxiety worry excessively about failure and anticipate negative outcomes of their efforts.

### Characteristics of Anxiety

In general, anxiety can be shown in three ways: cognitive, behavioral, and physiological responses. Not all signs will be seen in all children experiencing performance or test anxiety nor will they be seen to the same degree. The primary characteristics of anxiety are detailed in Table 1 (see also chapter 20, "Fears and Anxiety Disorders").

Early conceptualizations of test anxiety offered a rather simplistic explanation by describing it merely as failure to retrieve information during an assessment period. More recently, emphasis has turned to information-processing orientations that posit two classifications: (a) cognitive interference during assessment, and (b) general deficits in cognitive processing skills that impair test preparation and test performance (Cassady, 2004).

Of particular relevance to performance and test anxiety are two types of cognitive dysfunctions: *cognitive distortions* and *cognitive deficiencies.* Children who have cognitive distortions misconstrue or misperceive social and environmental events and may "catastrophize" situations. Although the distortions may have some rational basis, they are out of proportion to reality or to likely possibilities, such as fear that failing a single math test will prevent being accepted to a university. Cognitive deficiencies may be seen in the classroom in the form of impairment or absence of processing skills, and the child may become immobilized because he or she is unable to select an option or to act on a choice. During examinations and performances, children may "go blank," engage in negative self-talk (e.g., "I'm stupid" or "I can't do this"), feel overwhelmed, become distracted, or have difficulty organizing their thoughts (e.g., McDonald, 2001).

**Table 1** *Characteristics of Anxiety*

| Cognitive | Behavioral | Physiological |
|---|---|---|
| • Concentration problems<br>• Memory problems<br>• Attention problems<br>• Oversensitivity<br>• Problem-solving difficulties<br>• Worry<br>• Cognitive dysfunctions<br>  ○ Distortions<br>  ○ Deficiencies<br>• Attributional style problems | • Motor restlessness<br>• Fidgeting<br>• Task avoidance<br>• Rapid speech<br>• Erratic behavior<br>• Irritability<br>• Withdrawal<br>• Perfectionism<br>• Lack of participation<br>• Failure to complete tasks<br>• Seeking easy tasks | • Tics<br>• Recurrent, localized pain<br>• Rapid heart rate<br>• Flushing of the skin<br>• Perspiration<br>• Headaches<br>• Muscle tension<br>• Sleeping problems<br>• Nausea<br>• Vomiting<br>• Enuresis |

## Development of Anxiety

Because anxiety is a common emotion and is demonstrated in various forms across the age span, it is often difficult to determine what is typical and what is problematic. In certain situations, a moderate amount of anxiety is normal and alerts people to threats and the need for action. Too little anxiety may be associated with lack of motivation and lower performance, whereas excessive anxiety impairs concentration and the ability to act, also leading to decreased functioning. Thus, a moderate amount of anxiety about an upcoming performance or test may motivate a student to prepare, rehearse, and develop strategies to increase chances of success.

## Trait Anxiety and State Anxiety

Charles Spielberger is credited with developing the concepts of trait anxiety and state anxiety. *Trait anxiety* is characterized by relatively high levels of anxiety over a long period of time and a range of situations. Children with high trait anxiety often are tense and apprehensive in a variety of circumstances, to the extent that social, educational, or personal performance is impaired. *State anxiety* refers to anxiety that is shown in specific situations, such as public speaking or test taking (Spielberger, 1967). People who show state anxiety do not necessarily have high trait anxiety; however, children who have high trait anxiety tend to view more situations as potentially threatening, increasing the likelihood of developing state anxiety. Trait anxiety has been described as being the best predictor of test anxiety (Hodge, McCormick, & Elliott, 1997). A high level of trait anxiety acts as a predisposing condition that is exacerbated when a child is asked to perform a task or is being evaluated. Therefore, a child who has high trait anxiety is more likely to become increasingly apprehensive and worried when asked to perform a task, such as giving a speech. When both types of anxiety are present, interventions to help reduce trait anxiety may be needed, as well as strategies to cope with specific (state) anxiety-producing situations.

# PROBLEMS AND IMPLICATIONS

These patterns have implications for children in social and schooling processes. For example, children high in trait anxiety are more likely to select more avoidant solutions to situations they perceive as threatening than nonanxious children (Barrett, Rapee, Dadds, & Ryan, 1996; Chorpita, Albano, & Barlow, 1996). Children with high trait anxiety are also more likely to select maladaptive solutions to threatening situations (Bell-Dolan, 1995), are much more likely than their nonanxious peers to interpret neutral or ambiguous situations as potentially threatening (e.g., Hadwin, Frist, French, & Richards, 1997), and have a bias toward excessive attention to threat cues (Kindt, Brosschot, & Everaerd, 1997).

Highly anxious children also may demonstrate deficits in their performance in daily work and in evaluative situations. Anxiety interferes with encoding, organization, retrieval, and storage of information, and these effects are greater under external evaluative conditions. The effects of anxiety in these conditions are mediated, however, by the testing conditions and individual differences. For example, some students may report having an "anxiety block"—they knew the information when they entered the testing room but forgot it. Anxiety blocks are reported most often when anxiety is high and the test items are easy (Covington & Omelich, 1987).

A child's history of educational success and failure is a determining factor in the development of performance anxiety. Students who repeatedly fail in evaluative situations begin to doubt their ability and feel ashamed and humiliated and become anxious in the future (e.g., Prins & Hanewald, 1997). Furthermore, students who have had few successful experiences tend to develop maladaptive coping strategies, including negative self-talk, a characteristic of students with test anxiety. Most often, the content of students' negative self-talk is ruminations about beliefs of inability to complete tasks, fears of failure, or other undesirable outcomes. These thoughts distract the student from concentrating on developing solutions to problems, making it difficult to perform optimally. Lack of ability to function well socially may also contribute to difficulties in the classroom, such as not being able to participate well in group projects and assignments.

Sarason, Lighthall, Davidson, Waite, and Ruebush (1960) conducted the seminal study on performance and test anxiety in children. They gave high-anxiety and low-anxiety students two tasks that required analytic problem-solving skills under timed (pressured) and untimed (unpressured) conditions. The high-anxiety students made fewer errors in the untimed condition, whereas the low-anxiety students performed better in the timed condition. Consequently, highly anxious children may be motivated to perform if there is little pressure. Subsequent research has found that highly anxious children show debilitating self-evaluative thoughts that interfere with task completion, they tend to have attention problems, and they are off-task more often than nonanxious children (e.g., Kindt et al., 1997). Off-task thoughts tend to be characterized as being negatively self-evaluative, irrelevant, self-deprecatory, and interfering with performance.

## Test Anxiety During School Years

The experience of test anxiety varies in intensity across school years. In general, it increases during the elementary school years, declines slightly, and then returns in intensity at about age 11. Although the reasons for this pattern are unclear, it is likely that parent and teacher expectations play a role. Schools inherently are places where students are evaluated continuously, both formally and informally. As children go through school, they learn how to evaluate feedback from parents, teachers, and peers, which can result in the formation of attitudes and perceptions about their ability (see also chapter 26, "Self-Concept and Self-Esteem"). Consequently, determining if anxiety causes performance problems or if performance problems cause anxiety becomes difficult. As grading standards change and more emphasis is put on test performance, test anxiety may increase.

There is some concern that anxiety in schools is increasing with the increased use of standardized assessment and the associated pressures of high-stakes graduation examinations. Although research on the association between high-stakes testing and anxiety is not substantial, it seems likely that the importance attached to these tests may contribute to difficulties for anxiety-prone students (McDonald, 2001). With the enactment of the No Child Left Behind legislation, which requires ongoing, standardized assessment of academic progress, opportunities for the development of test anxiety will increase.

Anxious children may be prone to difficulties in taking tests, making oral presentations, and participating in class. Moreover, because they tend to have social problems, they may not be selected to participate in social and academic tasks, be seen as leaders, or be perceived as academically competent by teachers or peers. Over time, these factors can accumulate, causing a repeated pattern of underachievement and low performance. Therefore, intervention and prevention for anxious children in the school setting must consider both academic and social performance at the individual, classroom, and group levels. Treating just the anxious behaviors shown by a child may be only a part of intervention and not help prevent long-term consequences.

## Parents' Role in Performance Anxiety

Anxiety may develop when parents with unrealistically high expectations react critically to their child's performance. Consequently, the child becomes sensitive to adult reactions and is motivated to avoid future criticism and failure. Relatively few studies have tested this hypothesis, but research on childhood anxiety disorders suggests that children whose parents are critical and overprotective are at a higher risk for developing an anxiety disorder (Spence, 2001). Parents of anxious children tend to have lower expectations of their children's abilities, leading to overprotection, which helps to maintain childhood anxiety (Cobham, Dadds, & Spence, 1998). Discrepancies between parents' and adolescents' perceptions of the family environment and adolescents' trait and test anxieties have been found to be significantly related (Peleg & Klingman, 2002). This finding suggests that, when parents and adolescents have different views about the quality and cohesiveness of their families, adolescents are more likely to show generalized anxiety, leading to an increased likelihood that social and academic functioning will be negatively affected.

Other aspects of the parent–child relationship are associated with the emergence of performance or evaluation anxiety. The parents of highly anxious children provide less support and do not offer constructive feedback to children engaged in a task. In addition, these parents may withhold reinforcement following completion of a task. Conversely, parents of children with low test anxiety provide support by helping their children find problem-solving strategies (Cobham et al., 1998). By providing a moderate amount of cognitive structure in problem-solving situations, parents can help the child acquire strategies that can be used during evaluative situations. Thus, parents must strike a balance between encouraging independent thinking and providing feedback and support.

# ALTERNATIVE ACTIONS FOR PREVENTION

Prevention of test and performance anxiety in children has not received as much attention from the research community as has the area of intervention. Therefore, practitioners do not have a significant amount of group data examining the effectiveness of preventive techniques. Nevertheless, school psychologists, educators, and parents can design activities that may have beneficial preventive effects for children. These activities should include reducing risk factors for the development of performance and test anxiety and enhancing protective factors (Spence, 2001). Prevention of performance and test anxiety requires working with teachers, parents, and children, often simultaneously.

## Educating Teachers

Because performance anxiety may become more debilitating across school years, it is imperative that students receive early intervention. As the primary administrators of tests in schools, teachers should be knowledgeable about how to recognize and identify the test anxiety indicators. Because anxious children often withdraw to cope with anxiety, they may appear unmotivated by teachers, and their difficulties may go unrecognized. The list of characteristics provided in Table 1 may help teachers identify anxiety. Frequently, younger children who are anxious often are absent on the day of a test or presentation, or they may become ill or cry. Some students with anxiety in evaluative situations may report being easily distracted during testing and having difficulty organizing or recalling relevant information (e.g., their mind goes blank). Somatic complaints such as stomachaches or excessive sweating before or during tests also may be signs of test or performance anxiety. Educating teachers to notice these patterns may help to identify students with these anxieties and develop plans to assist them.

One benefit of experiencing academic success is the development of effective coping strategies. The types of coping strategies children use when faced with a stressful situation are significantly related to their psychological adjustment, including the appearance of debilitating anxiety. Lower levels of anxiety are associated with the use of problem-focused coping strategies, whereas avoidant or emotion-focused coping methods that are not effective in reducing the distress of a situation are more likely to be used by anxious students (Spence, 2001). Therefore, prevention methods should aim to teach students skills and strategies for coping with the stress of evaluation. Relaxation techniques, positive self-talk, and rational interpretation of events are strategies that can increase a child's ability to cope with stress and reduce anticipatory anxiety about pending tasks. These strategies, which also can be used as intervention techniques, are described in more detail later in this chapter.

***Grading practices.*** Several aspects of the school environment are associated with the development of anxiety and should be targeted by prevention efforts. For instance, the practice of assigning grades can be a significant factor in the development of anxiety because it inherently compares students. It is not uncommon for students and parents to be overly concerned about grades because students' grades affect future educational opportunities (see chapter 46, "Grades and Grading Practices"). However, educators can reduce the negative effects of assigning letter grades by developing alternative methods of grading. Working in collaboration with elementary school teachers, Hill and Wigfield (1984) developed a grading method that replaced letter grades with teacher reports of student achievement, effort, and strengths and weaknesses, using individual comments for each student. This alternative grading method also allowed teachers to include suggestions for improvement that were motivating for students.

At the junior high school level, teachers assigned grades for effort in addition to traditional achievement or ability grades. With such a grading method, teachers also have the option of including comments that relate to students' personal and social development. Overall, this type of grading emphasizes intraindividual comparison rather than group comparison and is assumed to aid in the prevention of evaluative anxiety. Although it may be necessary to report letter grades, schools can provide additional forms of performance feedback that may help reduce anxiety.

***Testing procedures.*** In conjunction with changing grading procedures, assessment methods may also be modified to reduce the likelihood of anxiety among students. Most teachers would agree that the primary purpose of testing is to determine if a student has mastered material. However, this purpose can be fulfilled by assessment methods other than traditional objective tests. McDaniel (1998) provides suggestions for alternative assessment procedures, such as developing a Jeopardy-type game. By adding an element of enjoyment and presenting tests in a different format, the expectation of performance evaluation may be less threatening and less stressful for students in the classroom.

When traditional tests are used, teachers can help to alleviate test anxiety by relaxing time constraints and modifying instructions. Previous research has established that high-anxiety students perform more poorly than low-anxiety students when time pressures are introduced (e.g., Sarason et al., 1960). Furthermore, when time constraints are eliminated, the performance of highly anxious students improves. One possible reason for this finding is that highly anxious students become so preoccupied with their physiological arousal or maladaptive thoughts that they progress slowly through a test (Zeidner, 1998). On the other hand, some students with test anxiety may work very quickly at the expense of accuracy when time limits are established. By relaxing time pressures, a major source of stress for students is eliminated, and they are more likely to work at an intermediate rate, which positively influences accuracy. In situations such as standardized testing, in which time constraints cannot be removed, teachers should instruct students how to work at an intermediate rate.

Testing instructions are another parameter that can have a significant effect on the anxiety levels of test-anxious students. Instructions that stress the evaluative nature of a task by using words such as *intelligence* or *achievement* appear to negatively affect the performance of highly text-anxious students (Sarason, 1973), although this finding has not been consistent across studies. Rather than introducing tasks as measures of students' ability, teachers can modify instructions to deemphasize evaluation. They also can tell students that some problems will be difficult and that the students are expected to try their best, not to answer every question correctly.

***Skills training.*** For some students, a lack of study skills or test-taking skills may contribute to the development of test anxiety. Likewise, students who have not received instruction in public speaking may feel incompetent and anxious before giving a speech. As part of the curriculum, teachers may institute study skills programs designed to teach students time management skills and strategies for studying. Students may also find it valuable to learn test-taking strategies for different test formats. For example, on multiple-choice tests, when two or more options are similar and essentially mean the same thing, they are probably wrong. In addition, administering practice tests as part of the skills training will help students become familiar with test formats and testing situations. For the treatment of public speaking anxiety, skills training sessions may include learning how to outline and organize ideas, conducting thorough research, and making practice speeches (Allen, Hunter, & Donohue, 1989).

### Working With Parents

Parents can influence children by providing feedback that supports good coping strategies. School practitioners could help prevent students' debilitating anxiety by teaching parents supportive skills, such as how to recognize signs of performance anxiety, how to help their child develop good study skills, how to help their child rehearse and practice public performances such as speeches, and how to give their child feedback about successes. As part of recognizing signs of anxiety, parents should be alert to children's difficulty adhering to sleeping, eating, and exercise routines before a test. Similarly, parents should be aware of the child who, as a way of coping with anxiety, avoids studying or preparing for a test, or the child who reports having trouble concentrating, which can lead to an inefficient use of study time. Parents also may need to know how to avoid negatively evaluating their child or applying pressure that might increase anxiety. This point may be especially important, because parental expectations can be major contributors to persistent patterns of childhood anxiety (e.g., McDonald, 2001). School practitioners also should communicate to parents the importance of ensuring that their child is well prepared physically, emotionally, and academically for evaluative situations. Along those lines, parents should encourage their child to maintain proper sleeping and eating habits prior to a test.

In sum, teaching parents how they may be contributing to the problem and helping them develop alternative expectations and behaviors may be valuable preventive efforts. This kind of information for parents can be communicated through workshops. For example, an outline for a brief workshop might include helping parents to recognize trait and test anxiety, to see how their expectations can inadvertently increase test anxiety, to emphasize effort over outcomes, and to prepare their child for a test by rehearsing and practicing using role-playing.

## ALTERNATIVE ACTIONS FOR INTERVENTION

The ability to effectively manage anxiety is an issue of central importance for highly anxious students because significant consequences, such as grade retention, are attached to poor test performance. This section discusses interventions designed for delivery in individual and small group formats. Available methods include behavioral, cognitive, cognitive–behavioral, and skill-deficit approaches, plus hypnosis and biofeedback, among many others. Interventions that combine both individual and group therapy appear to be most effective, followed by interventions administered in a group format (Ergene, 2003). Although individual therapy can be effective in reducing performance or test anxiety, interventions provided solely on an individual basis appear to produce the smallest effects.

### Behavioral Techniques

Behavioral interventions are designed to address the affective aspect of test anxiety, commonly termed *emotionality*. Emotionality refers to the physiological and autonomic reactions one experiences in response to an evaluative situation (McDonald, 2001). Highly anxious students may report excessive sweating, nausea, or stomachaches, or increased heart rate. The goal of behavioral interventions, such as relaxation training and systematic desensitization, is to teach students how to manage their physiological arousal so that it does not become a focus of attention and interfere with performance.

Relaxation techniques, such as deep breathing exercises and progressive muscle relaxation, are frequently used as performance or test anxiety interventions. Deep breathing exercises lower arousal by releasing tension with a series of deep, controlled breaths. These breathing exercises are also designed to produce mental relaxation in addition to reducing physiological arousal. Deep breathing exercises can be combined with progressive muscle relaxation, which entails systematically tensing and relaxing different muscle groups throughout the body one at a time. Typically, the client is instructed to begin by tensing and relaxing the major muscle groups in the upper body and then progresses to focus on the muscle groups in the lower body. This technique teaches clients how to induce a state of relaxation to replace the tension that often accompanies anxiety.

For younger children, relaxation techniques can be given names that facilitate recall of the steps. For example, Cheek, Bradley, Reynolds, and Coy (2002) developed the "Stop, Drop, and Roll" method for highly test-anxious students. Students who become anxious are instructed to stop taking the test, drop their heads forward, and roll them around while taking deep breaths (for additional suggestions on conducting relaxation training and for sample relaxation scripts, see Austin & Partridge, 1995; Collins, 1999; and Sapp, 1999).

Systematic desensitization, one of the most popular and effective interventions for the treatment of test or performance anxiety, expands on relaxation training. After students receive instruction in relaxation procedures, the next step is to identify situations that frequently evoke anxiety. The situations are then ranked, beginning with the items that produce the least amount of anxiety to those that are highly anxiety-provoking (see Table 2 for a sample hierarchy.) Because individuals respond differently to situations, anxiety hierarchies will differ among students. If treatment is being provided in a group format, it is possible to construct a group hierarchy by including all the items from the individually constructed hierarchies.

The final step of systematic desensitization involves guiding students through the hierarchy of anxiety-provoking situations. Students use relaxation techniques to remain calm while imagining scenes in the hierarchy. Once they master remaining calm during an imagined scene, they proceed to the next item in the hierarchy. Because anxiety is incompatible with the feeling of relaxation, the goal of systematic desensitization is to help students learn to replace the anxiety reaction with relaxation. Ultimately, students will be able to associate the items on the hierarchy with feeling calm and composed.

For younger children, the Stop, Drop, and Roll method can also be incorporated as part of systematic desensitization. As students proceed through the anxiety hierarchy, they yell "Fire!" when they begin to feel anxious and then practice the relaxation method of rolling the head and taking deep breaths (Cheek et al., 2002).

To improve the efficacy of behavioral interventions, the school practitioner should give students ample opportunity to practice the skills in therapy before using the procedures outside of treatment. Doing homework assignments to practice the skills in nonthreatening situations can help students become proficient with the techniques and can promote generalization to situations outside of the therapy setting (Suinn & Deffenbacher, 1988). It may also be beneficial for students to initially apply the techniques in moderately stressful situations, such as taking a quiz or speaking in front of a small group, and then advance to more anxiety-provoking situations. Finally, students should be cautioned that these behavioral techniques are not intended to eliminate anxiety completely, because a moderate level of anxiety is adaptive, but they are meant to help students control their anxiety so that it does not interfere with performance.

**Table 2** *Example Anxiety Hierarchies*

Test Anxiety Hierarchy

1. Teacher reminds you of an upcoming test.
2. The night before the exam, you still feel unprepared despite studying for several days.
3. Twenty minutes before the test, you overhear other students quizzing each other and you do not know all the answers to their questions.
4. While taking the test, you come across some questions on material that you did not study.
5. Most of the other students have finished the test and you are still working.
6. You only have 10 minutes left and you have an entire essay left to write.
7. You receive a grade lower than what you had hoped for.

Speech Anxiety Hierarchy

1. Teacher announces that you are required to give a 15-minute oral presentation as part of a project.
2. You are next in line to give your presentation.
3. Several students who are listening to your presentation appear bored and uninterested.
4. In the midst of the presentation, you realize your note cards are out of order.
5. You stutter and stumble over your words and your hands are shaking uncontrollably.
6. You are nearing the end of your presentation and you rush through the presesentation so that you have not filled up the entire 15 minutes.
7. A peer asks you a question about your topic that you cannot answer.

## Cognitive–Behavioral Techniques

Whereas behavioral techniques are intended to address the emotionality aspect of anxiety, cognitive methods focus primarily on the worry component of anxiety. *Worry* refers to the cognitive concerns about one's performance (e.g., Zeidner, 1998). More specifically, students may have concerns about the consequences of failure and how their performance compares with the performance of others. They often do not feel confident about their abilities.

Cognitive–behavioral interventions are constructed to address the worry component while also incorporating behavioral techniques. In cognitive–behavioral therapy, relaxation training approaches such as those previously described are frequently combined with cognitive approaches designed to recognize and dispute irrational thought patterns and alter negative attributional patterns. Consequently, cognitive–behavioral approaches can be effective for reducing both emotionality and worry in students. Among the cognitive techniques available to the therapist are "decatastrophizing," reattribution of faulty beliefs, and positive self-statements.

Decatastrophizing is a cognitive–behavioral technique that may be used to decrease the student's tendency to overestimate the importance of a task or the importance of doing well on the task. Students who catastrophize may envision failing a course or not getting accepted to a college because of a single test score. Decatastrophizing involves asking the student what the most likely outcome would be, based on all the facts (Friedberg & McClure, 2002). For instance, the therapist might ask the client, "What evidence do you have that you will fail if you don't get an A on this test?" By asking the student questions that challenge their irrational beliefs, the therapist can help students acquire a new set of rational thoughts such as "Even if I don't earn an A on this test, I've done well on my other work and that will help my grade."

Performance-anxious individuals tend to possess internal and stable attributional styles; that is, they attribute failure to lack of ability and success to luck (Zeidner, 1998). An internal, stable, and global attributional style is associated with a negative view of one's abilities and the expectation of failure, which may lead to elevated levels of anxiety. Reattribution is a method that encourages students to find alternate explanations for lack of success. In the case of a student who fails a test and attributes the failure to a lack of ability, the therapist may ask a question such as "What is another way of explaining your grade other than your conclusion that you are stupid?" The same technique can also be used so that students begin to attribute their success to their efforts, rather than to external factors such as the ease of the test.

Often, students who experience test or public speaking anxiety exhibit the irrational belief that one must be perfect in order to be considered a successful or worthy person. This belief may be expressed by thoughts such as "I am a terrible speaker because my presentation didn't go exactly as planned," or "I'm stupid if I receive a grade lower than an A." Negative and irrational statements such as these represent a cognitive style that becomes habitual and automatic for students with evaluation anxiety. Cognitive–behavioral approaches seek to eradicate negative thoughts and replace them with more positive self-statements. Self-affirmations, such as "I am well-prepared for this speech, so even if I make a mistake, I will be able to recover," or "Even though that test was difficult, I was able to remain calm and stay focused," can help students cope with anxiety before, during, and after an evaluative situation.

The following example shows how a therapist might address a student's anxiety about an upcoming test in class.

*Child:* I have a science test in 2 days and I'm so scared about it that I can't sleep at night.

*Therapist:* What scares you about taking the science test?

*Child:* I'm scared that if I don't get close to a 100 on my test, my teacher will think I'm stupid.

*Therapist:* So you're worried that your teacher will think you are smart only if you get a high score on your test. What convinces you that if you don't get close to a 100 on your test that your teacher will think you're stupid?

*Child:* Well, smart people always get really high grades. I've gotten really good grades so far but I'm scared that if I don't do well on this test, then all my good grades won't mean a thing anymore.

*Therapist:* Okay. I'm wondering if there are other traits that you think make someone a smart student.

*Child:* Yeah, sure there are.

*Therapist:* Let's make a list of all the things you think make someone smart. Earning high grades on tests is the first thing we can put on the list. What else might make someone smart?

*Child:* Getting good grades on other assignments. Doing your homework. Answering questions in class.

*Therapist:* Anything else you would like to add to the list?

*Child:* Maybe trying your best. I think that's all.

*Therapist:* Okay, now let's make a pie using all the traits you have listed. Do you know what a pie chart looks like?

*Child:* Yeah.

*Therapist:* We are going to make a pie chart so that each trait you mentioned gets a piece of the pie. We'll have to decide how big a pie piece each trait gets. A bigger piece of pie means that a trait contributes a lot to whether someone is smart. A smaller piece means that a trait isn't as important as some others we've listed. Do you understand?

*Child:* Yeah.

*Therapist:* Okay, then how about you start to divide the pie into its pieces. (Child draws the pie.) Now let's talk about your pie. It looks like getting high grades on tests is your biggest piece of the pie.

*Child:* Yeah, it is, but getting good grades on other assignments is a big piece too.

*Therapist:* Yes, it is. As you look at the pie, what would be left if we took the "grades on tests" piece out of the pie?

*Child:* There would be about three quarters of the pie left.

*Therapist:* What does that tell you about how much test grades contribute to being a smart person?

*Child:* Well, test grades are important, but there are other things that contribute a lot too.
*Therapist:* So the test grades aren't the majority of the pie, and when we take out that piece, we still have three quarters of the pie. How does that make you feel about your upcoming test?
*Child:* I guess I shouldn't be so scared because if I do all the other things on the pie, my teacher will still think I'm smart.
*Therapist:* Remember we've talked about making positive self-statements. What is an example of something you could tell yourself to remind you of your new conclusion?
*Child:* Well, I could say, "Even if this test doesn't go as well as I would like, I can still be smart, since test grades aren't the only thing that makes someone smart."

In this example, the therapist was successful in helping to change the child's belief about being considered stupid based on his score on one test, a thought that is irrational and contributes to his test anxiety. By encouraging the student to consider all the characteristics that make someone smart, and by assigning a piece of the pie to each trait, the therapist helped the student to decatastrophize the possible consequences of not performing at an extremely high level on the test. The student also adopted a more rational view of the importance of tests. Finally, the therapist asked the student to think of a positive self-statement that can help the student manage his anxiety if it becomes excessive (for more details on using cognitive–behavioral techniques, see Friedberg & McClure, 2002).

Cognitive–behavioral treatments can be combined with the skills training noted earlier to reduce anxiety and improve performance (Ergene, 2003). Furthermore, meta-analytic research indicates that the most effective treatments are those that combine skills training approaches with behavior or cognitive approaches (Allen et al., 1989; Ergene, 2003; Sapp, 1999). Multimodal treatment approaches are more comprehensive because they focus on both the worry and emotionality components of anxiety, in addition to remediating any deficits in study skills or test-taking.

## SUMMARY

Intervention and prevention of anxiety and performance problems in children and youth requires a multifaceted approach, including having a thorough understanding of the typical and atypical developmental aspects of anxiety. School professionals must be prepared to work with the child, teachers, and parents to develop individual and group interventions and prevention. Working with the child who has performance anxiety often involves addressing a variety of contributing factors, which may require using many approaches simultaneously. At a minimum, knowledge of behavioral and cognitive–behavioral techniques is necessary, as well as knowledge of classroom-based consultation, environmental interventions, and social skills training. Because some children may have high trait anxiety when they enter school, it may not be possible to prevent its occurrence, but it is possible to reduce its negative effects. The overall goal of intervention and prevention should not be to eliminate anxiety, which is unrealistic. Rather, emphasis should be placed on helping the child and others in collaborative efforts to manage performance and test anxiety.

## RECOMMENDED RESOURCES

### Books and Other Printed Material

Casbaro, J. (2003). *Test anxiety and what you can do about it.* Port Chester, NY: National Professional Resources.

This book is helpful for people who want to learn how to manage test anxiety or how to help others assist children, such as teachers or interventionists.

Methia, D. (2004). *Help your child overcome test anxiety and achieve higher test scores.* College Station, TX: Virtualbookworm.com publishing.

This book is directed at parents. It gives information about test anxiety and suggestions on how parents can help their children.

### Websites

*http://www.kidshealth.org*

This website addresses a variety of topics concerning children's health, including test anxiety. It also discusses other topics that are related to doing well on tests, such as getting enough sleep and having adequate nutrition.

*http://www.webmd.com*

This site discusses many health-related concerns of children, including anxiety and how anxiety can affect personal and social functioning.

## REFERENCES


Allen, M., Hunter, J., & Donohue, W. A. (1989). Meta-analysis of self-report data on the effectiveness of public speaking anxiety treatment techniques. *Communication Education, 38,* 54–76.

Austin, J. S., & Partridge, E. (1995). Prevent school failure: Treat test anxiety. *Preventing School Failure, 40,* 10–13.

Barrett, P. M., Rapee, R. M., Dadds, M. R., & Ryan, S. (1996). Family enhancement of cognitive style in anxious and aggressive children: Threat bias and the FEAR effect. *Journal of Abnormal Child Psychology, 24,* 187–203.

Beidel, D. C., Turner, S. M., & Trager, K. N. (1994). Test anxiety and childhood anxiety disorders in African American and White school children. *Journal of Anxiety Disorders, 8,* 169–179.

Bell-Dolan, D. J. (1995). Social cue interpretation in anxious children. *Journal of Clinical Child Psychology, 24,* 1–10.

Cassady, J. (2004). The influence of cognitive test anxiety across the learning–testing cycle. *Learning and Instruction, 14,* 569–592.

Cheek, J. R., Bradley, L. J., Reynolds, J., & Coy, D. (2002). An intervention for helping elementary students reduce test anxiety. *Professional School Counseling, 6,* 162–164.

Chorpita, B. F., Albano, A. M., & Barlow, D. H. (1996). Cognitive processing in children: Relationship to anxiety and family influences. *Journal of Clinical Child Psychology, 25,* 170–176.

Cobham, V. E., Dadds, M. R., & Spence, S. H. (1998). The role of parental anxiety in the treatment of childhood anxiety: A controlled trial. *Journal of Consulting and Clinical Psychology, 66,* 893–905.

Collins, L. (1999). *Effective strategies for dealing with test anxiety: Teacher to teacher series.* East Lansing, MI: National Center for Research on Teacher Learning. (ERIC Document Reproduction Service No. ED426214).

Covington, M. V., & Omelich, C. L. (1987). "I knew it cold before the exam": A test of the anxiety-blockage hypothesis. *Journal of Educational Psychology, 79,* 393–400.

Ergene, T. (2003). Effective interventions on test anxiety reduction: A meta-analysis. *School Psychology International, 24,* 313–328.

Friedberg, R. D., & McClure, J. M. (2002). *Clinical practice of cognitive therapy with children and adolescents.* New York: Guilford Press.

Goonan, B. (2003). *Overcoming test anxiety: Giving students the chance to show what they know* East Lansing, MI: National Center for Research on Teacher Learning. (ERIC Document Reproduction Service No. ED480053).

Hadwin, J., Frist, S., French, C. C., & Richards, A. (1997). Cognitive processing and trait anxiety in typically developing children: Evidence for an interpretation bias. *Journal of Abnormal Psychology, 106,* 486–490.

Hill, K. T., & Wigfield, A. (1984). Test anxiety: A major educational problem and what can be done about it. *Elementary School Journal, 85,* 105–126.

Hodge, G. M., McCormick, J., & Elliott, R. (1997). Examination-induced distress in a public examination at the completion of secondary schooling. *British Journal of Educational Psychology, 67,* 185–197.

Kindt, M., Brosschot, J. S., & Everaerd, W. (1997). Cognitive processing bias of children in a real life stress situation and a neutral situation. *Journal of Experimental Child Psychology, 64,* 79–97.

McDaniel, L. C. (1998). *T.E.S.T.S. (Taking Every Student to Success): Another way to assess.* East Lansing, MI: National Center for Research on Teacher Learning. (ERIC Reproduction Document Service No. ED422988).

McDonald, A. S. (2001). The prevalence and effects of test anxiety in school children. *Educational Psychology, 21,* 89–101.

Peleg, O., & Klingman, A. (2002). Family environment, discrepancies between perceived actual and desirable environment and children's test and trait anxiety. *British Journal of Guidance and Counseling, 30,* 451–466.

Prins, P. J. M., & Hanewald, G. J. F. P. (1997). Self-statements of test-anxious children: Thought-listing and questionnaire approaches. *Journal of Consulting and Clinical Psychology, 65,* 440–447.

Sapp, M. (1999). *Test anxiety: Applied research, assessment, and treatment interventions* (2nd ed.). Lanham, MD: University Press of America.

Sarason, I. G. (1973). Test anxiety and social influence. *Journal of Personality, 41,* 261–271.

Sarason, S. B., Lighthall, F. F., Davidson, K. S., Waite, R. R., & Ruebush, B. K. (1960). *Anxiety in elementary school children.* New York: Wiley.

Spence, S. H. (2001). Prevention strategies. In M. W. Vasey & M. R. Dadds (Eds.), *The developmental psychopathology of anxiety* (pp. 325–351). New York: Oxford Press.

Spielberger, C. (1967). *State-trait anxiety inventory for children manual.* Palo Alto, CA: Consulting Psychologists Press.

Suinn, R. M., & Deffenbacher, J. L. (1988). Anxiety management training. *The Counseling Psychologist, 16,* 31–49.

Vasey, M. W., Crnic, K. A., & Carter, W. G. (1994). Worry in childhood: A developmental perspective. *Cognitive Therapy and Research, 18,* 529–549.

Zeidner, M. (1998). *Test anxiety: The state of the art.* New York: Plenum.

# 22

# Selective Mutism

**Thomas J. Kehle**
**Melissa A. Bray**
*University of Connecticut*

**Lea A. Theodore**
*Queens College*

## BACKGROUND AND DEVELOPMENT

Children exhibiting selective mutism do not speak in specific settings where speech is expected, such as in school, although they freely converse in other settings. The condition is severe enough to impede academic and social functioning and is not due solely to a lack of knowledge of the spoken language or to embarrassment as result of a communication disorder. According to the *Diagnostic and Statistical Manual of Mental Disorders, Fourth Edition, Text Revision* (DSM-IV-TR), selective mutism tends to be associated with several features, including excessive shyness, social isolation, withdrawal, negativism, compulsive traits, temper tantrums, fear of social embarrassment, anxiety, and controlling oppositional behavior (American Psychiatric Association, 2000). It is a rare disorder, with a less than 0.7% prevalence rate (Bergman, Piacentini, & McCracken, 2002). Also, in contrast to DSM-IV-TR estimates, it appears to be substantially more prevalent in females than males, with a ratio that may be greater than 2:1 (Bergman, Holloway, & Piacentini, 1999).

Selective mutism is usually diagnosed about the time the child enters school; however, the age of onset is most likely considerably earlier, perhaps around 2.5 years (Drewes & Akin-Little, 2002). Selective mutism typically lasts for several years (Ford, Sladeczek, Carson, & Kratochwill, 1998), but it may persist throughout the child's entire educational career and even into adulthood. For example, in a 12-year longitudinal study from initial diagnosis of selective mutism, only 39% of participants had a complete remission (Remschmidt, Poller, Herpertz-Dahlman, Hennighausen, & Gutenbrunner, 2001). However, even those in remission described themselves as being relatively less independent, confident, mature, and physically healthy than those who made up the reference group. The best predictor variable of poor outcome was whether or not selective mutism was present in an immediate family member at the time of the child's diagnosis.

Some researchers suggest that the disorder might be an extreme form of social anxiety (Black & Uhde, 1995). However, it is not clear whether this is true. When comparing children with selective mutism to children with social phobia who are not selectively mute, children with selective mutism tend to score higher on indices of delinquency, suggesting the existence of a broader clinical syndrome (Yeganeh, Beidel, Turner, Pina, & Silverman, 2003). Furthermore, not all children with selective mutism exhibit social anxiety. Quite the contrary, some of these children can also be socially popular and excellent nonverbal communicators (Segal, 2003).

Numerous theoretical formulations regarding the etiology and treatment of selective mutism have been described. Commonly, these explanations are based on either psychodynamic or behavioral theories, but the definitive cause of selective mutism remains obscured. It is now generally accepted that there is a genetic predisposition for the disorder (Black & Uhde, 1995). However, it is not necessarily, as previously assumed, the result of abuse, neglect, or trauma (Shipon-Blum, 2002).

A poor prognostic indicator is the presence of mental illness in an immediate family member (Sluckin, Foreman, & Herbert, 1991) or more generally, the presence of family psychopathology (Spasaro & Schaefer, 1999). Components of a psychopathological family environment associated with selective mutism included social isolation, disharmony, an absent or emotionally distant father, and an overprotective, depressed mother who established and maintained a highly enmeshed relationship with her child (Shvarztman, Hornshtein, Klein, & Yechezkel, 1990). This symbiotic relationship between the mother and child was often the most prominent component of the family. The mother was commonly described as "lonely, depressed, and distant, even hostile, in her relationship with the father" (Spasaro & Schaefer, p. 4), in addition to being passive and having difficulty verbally expressing her needs.

In contrast, etiology based on behavioral theory suggests that selective mutism is a learned pattern of behavior that is shaped and maintained by the consequences of being selectively mute. If selective mutism is learned and maintained by its consequences, then operant conditioning techniques should be successful in treating the disorder.

From this perspective, the first step in the design of an intervention is a functional analysis of variables that maintain a child's selective mutism. However, reliable and valid determination of the behavioral function is difficult, which may be why interventions based on functional behavior assessments have been found to be no more effective than interventions that did not use functional behavior assessments (Gresham et al., 2004; Schill, Kratochwill, & Gardner, 1996). The child's discriminative decisions to be mute are idiosyncratic and complex, making the determination of the functional relationship between the child's environment and his or her selective mutism very difficult to detect. For example, one of the children treated by Kehle and his colleagues included a second grader who, in addition to being completely mute in school, also refused to have verbal interaction with any of her father's male relatives but spoke to her mother's male relatives (Kehle, Madaus, Baratta, & Bray, 1998).

## PROBLEMS AND IMPLICATIONS

Historically, this condition has been shown to be particularly intractable and highly resistant to intervention (Standart & Le Couteur, 2003). Teachers and parents allowing or reinforcing the child's nonverbal responding may maintain and even strengthen the resistance to intervention. Teacher requests are often ignored or avoided. In either situation, requests for compliance are often suspended, resulting in the mutism being negatively reinforced. Additionally, the child's mutism may be reinforced by classmates, who often assume a protective role and interpret the child's needs to the teacher.

Therefore, the assumption among researchers is that the longer the condition persists, the more resistant it is to intervention (Ford et. al., 1998). However, this assumption is at times violated, in that some children who are selectively mute spontaneously recover. For example, Lysne (1999) stated that "intervention at an early age, shortly after mutism has commenced, can be effective" (p. 88). This is particularly true if the condition has not been of a prolonged duration. However, if the condition has been present for years, self-recovery or recovery due to treatment are rare (Lysne). For those individuals the prognosis is poor.

For example, the first author of this chapter was unsuccessful in addressing selective mutism in a 38-year-old woman who was originally selectively mute within the school setting. She did not converse at all from kindergarten through her senior year in high school. After graduation, she became even more selective in the settings where she would speak. By age 38, she would only converse with her mother in the kitchen while making the evening meal. She had no verbal communication with any other human. Although this was an exceptionally severe case, and certainly is not typical, it nevertheless illustrates that the condition, if left untreated, appears to progressively worsen. The refusal to speak in school or in other social settings is unquestionably delimiting, particularly with respect to friendship formation and in academic or occupational pursuits.

As in the case of many children with internalizing disorders, early detection is crucial. However, because of the rarity of the disorder, teachers may not be familiar with the diagnostic indicators. When a teacher notices a child who does not verbally respond, the following criteria should be used to guide the decision to refer the child for intervention:

- If the child's failure to speak lasts at least 1 month, excluding the first month of the school year.
- If the child consistently fails to speak in expected situations but parental reports indicate expected or normal speech in the home setting.
- If the child's lack of speech will be detrimental to his or her academic and social functioning, and is not the result of a lack of knowledge of spoken language or a communication disorder.

As noted above, some of the following associated features may be present, including excessive shyness, fear of social embarrassment, social isolation, withdrawal, clinging, compulsive traits, negativism, temper tantrums, intentional enuresis, vomiting, physical rigidity, and, quite commonly, controlling oppositional behavior (American Psychiatric Association, 2000). In one study, controlling oppositional behavior was noted in 90% of children diagnosed with selective mutism (Krohn, Weckstein, & Wright, 1992). Furthermore, a high rate (59%) of maternal–child enmeshment was apparent (Krohn et al.). It is reasonable to assume that the associated feature of controlling oppositional behavior is perhaps related to the overenmeshed style of maternal–child interaction. When this constellation of symptoms is apparent, treatment strategies should be planned and implemented as soon as possible.

## ALTERNATIVE ACTIONS FOR PREVENTION

The design and implementation of preventive actions are difficult because selective mutism has no known definitive cause. Without a known cause, preventive procedures are without empirical justification. However, early detection and treatment are important because the disorder tends to become more resistant to intervention the longer the child remains selectively mute (Kehle, Hintze, & DuPaul, 1997).

Because of the rarity of the disorder, school personnel usually lack experience with selectively mute children and may unknowingly negatively reinforce the child's behavior. Preschool and kindergarten screening procedures should incorporate an assessment of the possible presence of selective mutism using the criteria presented in the background section. This assessment would require observation of the child in the home and school, plus acquisition of teacher and parent data regarding the child's verbal behavior in varied settings. Because many of these children will select not to talk in the presence of strangers, the assessment may also require the parent to videotape the child's typical verbal behavior at home.

## ALTERNATIVE ACTIONS FOR INTERVENTION

Because selective mutism is typically manifested around the time the child starts school, school psychologists will likely direct the design of the intervention and treatment coordination efforts. Interventions will ideally include cooperation between the family and school personnel. Establishing and maintaining an effective therapeutic relationship with the family, particularly the mother, to alter the maternal–child relationship can be a challenging task. The high frequency of the child's troublesome controlling oppositional behavior will most likely require any family-based intervention to focus on the maternal–child interaction. Although it has been suggested that treatment for selective mutism involving the family could occur within the home setting, the school setting, because it is the primary environment where the selective mutism is most prevalent, is the preferred treatment environment.

Implementing an intervention within the school involves the coordination of school personnel, family, and administrative policies and, depending on the type of intervention employed, classmates' parental approval and scheduling of equipment and space needs. Because selective mutism is rare and highly resistant to intervention, school personnel typically have not had previous experience with these children. Following an initial meeting of a placement and planning team, the student may be placed for a proportion of the school day in a self-contained class for children with emotional disturbance (Kehle, Madaus, Baratta, & Bray, 1998). However, such placements may not be appropriate.

Special education teachers of students with emotional disturbances most commonly use interventions designed to reduce problematic externalizing behaviors, but these methods may not be suitable for a child who exhibits considerable problematic internalizing behaviors. Also, teachers with a relative lack of experience treating children with selective mutism may unknowingly employ strategies that could negatively reinforce the child's resistance to intervention. Basically, failed attempts to eliminate the selective mutism may result in the child increasing his or her ability to resist future attempts at intervention.

Psychotherapeutic approaches are relatively ineffective in treating children with selective mutism (Spasaro & Schaefer, 1999). Treatment gains are most often realized with behaviorally based interventions that include stimulus fading and generalization (Drewes & Akin-Little, 2002). The most common of these behaviorally based strategies include contingency management, stimulus fading, shaping, escape-avoidance techniques, self-modeling, and combined treatment strategies. These treatments each have been empirically validated for the treatment of selective mutism (Ford et al., 1998; Spasaro & Schaefer).

## Contingency Management

Contingency management, which involves both reinforcing the child's verbal behavior and ignoring the child's nonverbal attempts to communicate, results in greater treatment effectiveness than either of these approaches alone (Piersal & Kratochwill, 1981).

## Stimulus Fading

Stimulus fading involves the transfer of stimulus control by reducing the strength of, or fading, the stimulus that typically causes the child's selective mutism. The procedure involves providing stimuli that reliably result in the child speaking in situations where he or she typically does not speak, most notably school-related settings (Kratochwill, 1981). For example, the procedure could involve having the child play a board game in the classroom after school with a few people (mother or siblings) with whom the child feels comfortable speaking. A few classmates are then introduced one at a time and invited to participate in the game. After the first classmate has been successfully integrated into the game, another classmate is introduced, thus fading the stimuli for mutism. This procedure can then be repeated in a semiprivate corner of the classroom during regularly scheduled classes. Eventually, other classmates and the teacher would be invited to enter the game, until the child's selective mutism is attenuated.

## Shaping

Shaping involves the systematic reinforcement of successive approximations toward normal speech. Kehle et al. (1998) used a shaping technique as a component of an augmented self-modeling intervention. They showed a 9-year-old girl with selective mutism an edited videotape of herself. As the child viewed the videotape, she was to say "stop" whenever she saw herself verbally responding to the teacher's questions. The videotape was paused and the child was allowed to select one of several inexpensive wrapped presents that were placed on a table directly in front of her. Subsequently, to get another one of the gifts, the child was required to increase her speech production by saying "stop the tape," and then "please stop the tape, Tom." Eventually, after receiving the gift, the child was required to describe the object (stickers, clothing for one of her dolls, pencils, etc.) to the therapist. This procedure continued until the child exhibited relatively normal speech within the therapeutic setting.

## Escape-Avoidance Techniques

Escape-avoidance procedures involve situations where the child can avoid an unpleasant event contingent upon talking. In an escape-avoidance technique referred to as *response initiation* (Krohn, Weckstein, & Wright, 1992), the child remains alone with the therapist until he or she verbally asks to leave the session. Most children do in fact choose to escape the session by talking or whispering within an hour or so (Drewes & Akin-Little, 2002). However, escape-avoidance procedures should not be used with a young child or as the initial treatment of choice because it can result in considerable stress. Furthermore, a supportive and trustful relationship between the therapist and child is requisite for its effective use. Also, considerable caution is recommended with this technique, because if it fails the child may be negatively reinforced for not speaking (Lysne, 1999).

## Self-Modeling

Self-modeling involves the child's repeated and spaced viewings of edited videotapes depicting the child performing exemplary behaviors (Dowrick & Dove, 1980). The procedure has been used effectively to address various problematic disorders, including behavior disorders (Kehle, Clark, Jenson, & Wampold, 1986), depression (Kahn, Kehle, Jenson, & Clark, 1990), and selective mutism (Kehle, Owen, & Cressy, 1990; Kehle et al., 1998). It is perhaps the most efficacious treatment strategy designed to address selective mutism, but it is the least used (Edwards & Prouxl, 1997).

Dowrick and Hood (1978), in the first published study to use self-modeling to treat selective mutism, described a procedure in which they filmed two selectively mute children talking normally in their home settings. Dowrick and Hood subsequently edited the films by inserting scenes of typical classroom activities so that the children appeared to be talking normally in their respective classrooms. The children were shown the edited films on eight different occasions, after which their classroom verbal interactions became normal. A 6-month follow-up indicated maintenance of relatively normal speech.

Kehle et al. (1990) effectively employed a self-modeling intervention with a 6-year-old male with selective mutism. The child had not uttered a word in school since he was 3 years old and attending preschool. However, in other settings he was not at all selectively mute. The procedure involved videotaping the classroom teacher asking the children approximately 10 questions that were written by the psychologist. The teacher asked each classmate a question, then asked the child with selective mutism, and finally asked another classmate. As expected, the child with selective mutism did not respond to any of the questions. On the same day, but after the school day, the child's mother was asked to come to the child's classroom and was instructed to ask the child the same questions (e.g., "What is your favorite flavor of ice cream?" "Who is your best friend?" etc.). No one else was present in the classroom. The video camera was set up on the tripod. A black piece of electrician's tape was placed over the videotaping indicator to lessen the child's reaction to being videotaped. With some prodding, the child eventually verbally responded to his mother's questions. The child's mother confirmed that the quality of the child's speech production was indistinguishable from that evidenced in the home.

The videotape was edited to portray the child with selective mutism supposedly responding with exemplary expected speech to the teacher's questions during what appeared to be a typical teacher-directed question-and-answer session. The 5-minute edited intervention videotape was then viewed in a setting that included only the child, the psychologist, and the social worker on two different occasions over a period of a week. On the second day of intervention, the child abruptly began to converse in a normal tone of voice with the experimenters, his teachers, and other school children. The treatment gains were maintained after 9 months. Most interestingly, the child could not remember why he chose not to talk for over 3 years. He stated, "I don't remember not talking."

## Pharmacological Treatment

Fluoxetine (Prozac) was used in a double-blind, placebo-controlled study of 16 children diagnosed with selective mutism (Black & Uhde, 1994). In comparison with the placebo group, the children treated with fluoxetine (0.6 milligrams per kilogram of weight) showed significantly greater improvement on indices of mutism, anxiety, and social functioning. However, the children remained symptomatic. In an open trial study, fluoxetine was administered to 21 children with selective mutism over a period of 9 weeks. Sixteen of the 21 children evidenced substantial improvement. However, 19% of the children experienced the side effect of behavioral disinhibition. Ten percent experienced sleep problems, jitteriness, and headaches, and 5% were irritable and agitated as a result of the fluoxetine treatment (Dummitt, Kleine, Tancer, Asche, & Martin, 1996). More recently, these pharmacological treatments and combined behavioral and pharmacological approaches have been used (Kehle et al., 1998). However, pharmacological treatment should not be recommended until other psychologically based treatments have been shown to be ineffective (Kehle et al.).

## Combined Treatment Strategies

Kehle et al. (1998) employed an augmented self-modeling intervention designed for a child who was selectively mute and had intentional diurnal enuresis. Intentional diurnal enuresis is rare but has been reported as an associated behavior of selective mutism (Barlow, Strother, & Landreth, 1986).

Jane was 9 years old at the time of treatment. At age 4, beginning from the first day she attended preschool, she remained totally mute and appeared severely depressed and frightened, with her head lowered and fists clenched. She typically would stand in the doorway of the classroom and remain there motionless until a staff member helped her remove and hang up her coat. Throughout the half-day preschool program, Jane walked using tiny, hardly measurable steps and her breathing was labored. Jane remained completely mute, having no verbal interaction with the staff or other children. Probably because of Jane's ability to wait until she got home to go to the bathroom, the teachers were not aware that she did not use the school's bathroom facilities.

Outside of school, Jane communicated easily, appeared happy, and engaged in many play activities with the neighborhood children. Jane's behavior in kindergarten was the same as that in preschool. She remained totally mute, refused to engage in any classroom activities, appeared depressed, and refused to use, or even go into, the school's bathroom facilities. As in preschool, Jane waited until she returned home to urinate. However, when she started the first grade and had to attend school on a full-day schedule, she chose to urinate in her clothing rather than use the school's bathroom. Accommodations were made to allow Jane to go to the nurse's office to change into a fresh diaper and a dry set of clothing. Even with these problematic and socially isolating behaviors, Jane evidenced considerable academic competencies. Nevertheless, she was placed in a self-contained classroom for children with emotional disturbance shortly after starting the first grade. She was the only girl in a class of seven students. Jane's special education teacher described her as "a very scared and nervous" young girl. She typically entered the classroom slowly and stood motionless near the coat rack.

Jane's behavior outside of school was normal, with two exceptions: (a) She refused to discuss any of her school experiences with her parents, and (b) she demanded that her mother come into the bathroom and place her hands over her (Jane's) ears during bowel movements.

A self-modeling intervention was designed that also incorporated the spacing effect, mystery motivators, controlled self-reinforcement, peer expectations, and stimulus fading. An edited self-modeling intervention videotape was constructed in a similar fashion as that described in the Kehle et al. (1990) study. The 7-minute-long self-modeling videotape depicted Jane supposedly responding to the special education teacher's questions. In reality, Jane was answering questions asked by her father. Jane viewed the self-modeling videotape on five different occasions over a period of 4 weeks to ensure a spacing effect. The spacing effect refers to the finding that for a given amount of study time, spaced presentations of the material (i.e., Jane's exemplary verbal behavior) will yield more pronounced learning than a single massed presentation.

Immediately before the self-modeling intervention began, a manila envelope was prominently placed on the bulletin board in the front of the class. A big question mark and the name "Jane" were written on the envelope. It was explained to Jane and the other children that the envelope contained a mystery motivator—a picture of a gift for Jane that was comparable to a birthday present. She could have the envelope and receive the gift that afternoon when she returned home if she asked her teacher for the mystery motivator in a tone of voice audible to the other children. Mystery motivators were designed to increase the anticipation and value of a reinforcer (Rhode, Jenson, & Reavis, 1993). The decision of what to include as Jane's mystery motivator was determined by her parents.

During Jane's viewings of the intervention videotape, she was instructed to pause the tape (using a remote control) whenever she saw herself verbally responding to the teacher's questions. At each pausing of the tape, Jane was allowed to select from several inexpensive gift-wrapped reinforcers (i.e., controlled self-reinforcement). In addition, and with Jane's permission, the edited self-modeling videotape was shown to her classmates to increase peer expectation for Jane to speak.

The intervention also used stimulus fading by inviting Jane's grandmother and brother to play Monopoly with her in the special education classroom after school. Jane conversed normally during the game. One by one, three of Jane's classmates, who had volunteered to stay after school to be involved in the intervention, were introduced into the room to play the game. Eventually, all three had been introduced and integrated into the Monopoly game.

Subsequent to the stimulus fading technique, Jane's selective mutism was completely eliminated to the point that her speech was indistinguishable from the other children's. A day after beginning to speak within the school setting, the intentional enuresis was eliminated by having another girl in general education escort Jane into the school's bathroom. After Jane's mutism was eliminated, she was interviewed to ascertain what components of the augmented self-modeling intervention she thought helped her overcome her selective mutism and enuresis. She was also asked if she knew why she had decided not to talk or use the bathroom. About the intervention, she stated she liked watching herself on the edited videotapes and also liked the mystery motivator. She said she did not know why she was selectively mute.

Nine months after this initial interview, Jane was asked to respond to the same series of follow-up questions. Again, Jane stated that she liked the mystery motivator, referring to it as "cool." In addition, she restated that she liked the self-modeling tapes. However, in response to the questions about why she chose not to talk and why she did not use the school's bathroom, Jane said she was just shy and that she did not know, respectively.

One year after the intervention, Jane's academic and social functioning had substantially improved. On the basis of her teacher's report, Jane not only was an academically superior student; she also enjoyed considerable popularity among her general education classmates. Jane also indicated to the second-grade teacher that she would like to help other children who were suffering from selective mutism.

In another case study, Kehle et al. (1998) used an augmented self-modeling intervention that eventually incorporated the use of fluoxetine with a 9-year-old girl. In addition to being completely mute throughout her schooling, Elaine exhibited intentional vomiting. For the past 4 years, since kindergarten, Elaine's school placement was in a self-contained special education classroom.

Elaine's vomiting usually occurred as a consequence of the teacher's request for compliance. The vomiting was preceded by a slight cough. The vomiting episodes occurred approximately twice per week. The classroom teacher indicated that Elaine exhibited immaturity, poor concentration, stubbornness, depression, and sulking behaviors. Additionally, she appeared nervous and fearful. She also tended to fidget and had stiff, awkward, and clumsy motor responses. Academically, Elaine was reported to be an underachiever who often failed to carry out assigned tasks.

Intervention tapes were constructed in the same manner as described in Kehle et al. (1990). Elaine viewed the initial 7-minute self-modeling intervention videotape on eight occasions over a 5-week period. In addition, mystery motivators were used for both Elaine and her classmates. Elaine was told that she would receive her mystery motivator if she asked for it in an audible tone of voice. A classmate would receive a mystery motivator if he or she could get Elaine to say the name of her cat. Using a class mystery motivator and showing the class Elaine's intervention videotape were intended to increase peer expectations for Elaine's speaking.

After five viewings of the edited intervention videotape, a stimulus-fading technique was implemented. A family member came to school and engaged Elaine in conversation in a room by themselves. These conversations with a family member faded her discrimination between speaking outside and inside the school. Gradually, several school personnel and peers became involved in these conservations.

However, Elaine's speech production within the school was not consistent with the quality and volume of speech in the home setting. At best, Elaine's school verbal behavior could be described as restricted. Consequently, a pharmacological component was added that consisted of administering 10 mg of fluoxetine for 4 weeks. The dosage was increased to 20 mg, at which point Elaine's speaking became indistinguishable from her general education classmates; she initiated conversations, volunteered to ask and answer teacher questions, and spontaneously conversed with her peer group. The fluoxetine was gradually withdrawn over a period of 7 weeks. Treatment effects were maintained at a 6-month follow-up.

### Alternative Explanation for Treatment Effects

The augmented self-modeling allowed two important aspects of novel learning to occur simultaneously. First, the technique takes advantage of the notion that behavior precedes feelings and beliefs (Skinner, 1964). The self-modeling videotape depicts the child exhibiting exemplary verbal behavior, and consequently the child's fear and anxiety associated with speaking are attenuated and come into concert with the exemplary behaviors he or she sees on the videotape. Subsequently, the child's efficacious belief that she can successfully speak, and the eventual speaking behavior, become circuitous, each influencing the other (Kehle, Bray, Margiano, Theodore, & Zhou, 2002). However, Kehle and his colleagues (1998) noted that in interviews following the self-modeling intervention, children who were successfully treated often responded to the question of why they did not speak by stating they did not remember being selectively mute. Consequently, the second component of the self-modeling intervention could be the complementary effect of fading the child 's memory of being selectively mute.

Kehle et al. noted that the research paradigms that use self-modeling are very similar to studies on the alteration of children's memories. The process of altering or changing memories of actual events has been well documented by several investigators (e.g., Loftus, 1997; Schacter, 1995). Loftus noted that it was relatively easy to "create complex and elaborate false memories in the minds of research subjects, and the subjects are confident that these false memories are real" (p. 61). Loftus simply asked her research subjects to induce mental images of events that had never occurred, which altered their memories. Having children repeatedly view edited videotapes of themselves successfully engaging in expected speech within the classroom setting may have created false memories that they had previously replicated the visually depicted behavior and could do so subsequently (Kehle et al., 2002).

Visual information is substantially more powerful than verbal information in changing memories. Furthermore, if the memory is changed using visual techniques, it is quite difficult to alter, even when verbal arguments are presented that are designed to discredit the newly acquired false memories (Braum & Loftus, 1998). Individuals exposed to visual misinformation "really believe in the veracity and strength of the newly created memories and they report visually re-experiencing the misinformation" (p. 577).

## SUMMARY

The causes of selective mutism remain unknown; however, it does appear that the condition is influenced by genetic predisposition. The etiology for the disorder typically involves behavioral or psychodynamically based explanations. There is considerable empirical support for treatments based on behavior theory and little or no support for psychodynamic treatments. The interventions summarized above have generally produced positive change in short periods of time. However, the magnitude of effects varies. The efficacy of behavior-based treatments is most commonly explained as being the result of the child relearning to speak in formerly problematic settings. However, with respect to self-modeling, another tenable explanation for treatment efficacy was presented as being based on memory alteration.

## RECOMMENDED RESOURCES

### Books and Other Printed Material

Kehle, T. J., Madaus, M. M. R., Baratta, V. S., & Bray, M. A. (1998). Augmented self modeling as a treatment for children with selective mutism. *Journal of School Psychology, 36,* 377–399.

This paper includes three case studies that employed variations of combined treatment strategies to successfully treat children with selective mutism.

Spasaro, S. A., & Schaefer, C. E. (Eds.). (1999). *Refusal to speak: Treatment of selective mutism in children.* Northvale, NJ: Jason Aronson, Inc.

The 17-chapter edited book provides a comprehensive and eclectic overview of the assessment and treatment of children with selective mutism. It addresses treatments based on behavioral, psychodynamic, group, and family therapies. It also includes chapters on the effectiveness of psychopharmacologic and multimodal treatments.

### Website

*http://www.selectivemutism.org*

The Selective Mutism Group—Childhood Anxiety Network is the largest and most comprehensive association dedicated to helping individuals learn about the causes, diagnosis, and treatment of selective mutism.

## REFERENCES

American Psychiatric Association. (2000). *Diagnostic and statistical manual of mental disorders* (4th ed., text revision). Washington, DC: Author.

Barlow, K., Strother, J., & Landreth, G. (1986). Sibling group play therapy: An alternative with the electively mute child. *The School Counselor, 34,* 44–50.

Bergman, R. L., Holloway, J., & Piacentini, J. (1999, March). *Selective mutism questionnaire: Preliminary findings.* Paper presented at the 19th National Conference of the Anxiety Disorders Association of America, San Diego, CA.

Bergman, R. L., Piacentini, J., & McCracken, J. T. (2002). Prevalence and description of selective mutism in a school-based sample. *Journal of the American Academy of Child and Adolescent Psychiatry, 41,* 938–946.

Black, B., & Uhde, T. W. (1994). Treatment of elective mutism with fluoxetine: A double-blind, placebo-controlled study. *Journal of the American Academy of Child and Adolescent Psychiatry, 33,* 1000–1006.

Black, B., & Uhde, T. W. (1995). Psychiatric characteristics of children with selective mutism: A pilot study. *Journal of the American Academy of Child and Adolescent Psychiatry, 34,* 847–856.

Braum, K. A., & Loftus, E. F. (1998). Advertising's misinformation effect. *Applied Cognitive Psychology, 12,* 569–591.

Dowrick, P. W., & Dove, C. (1980). The use of self-modeling to improve the swimming performance of spina bifida children. *Journal of Applied Behavior Analysis, 13,* 51–56.

Dowrick, P. W., & Hood, M. (1978). Transfer of talking behavior across settings using faked films. In E. L. Glynn & S. S. McNaughton (Eds.), *Proceedings of the New Zealand Conference for Research in Applied Behavior Analysis.* Auckland, New Zealand: University of Auckland Press.

Drewes, K. M., & Akin-Little, A. (2002, Spring). Children with selective mutism: Seen but not heard. *The School Psychologist, 56,* 37 ff.

Dummitt, E. S., Kleine, R. G., Tancer, N. K., Asche, B., & Martin, J. (1996). Fluoxetine treatment of children with selective mutism: An open trial. *Journal of the American Academy of Child and Adolescent Psychiatry, 35,* 615–621.

Edwards, T. M., & Prouxl, G. A. (1997, July). The use of edited videos for the treatment of selective mutism. *Institute for Applied Behavior Analysis—Positive Practices, 2,* 3–7.

Ford, M. A., Sladeczek, I. E., Carson, J., & Kratochwill, T. R. (1998). Selective mutism: Phenomenological characteristics. *School Psychology Quarterly, 13,* 192–227.

Gresham, F. M., McIntyre, L. L., Olson-Tinker, H., Dolstra, L., McLaughlin, V., & Van, M. (2004). Relevance of functional behavioral assessment research for school-based interventions and positive behavioral support. *Research in Developmental Disabilities, 25,* 19–37.

Kahn, J., Kehle, T. J., Jenson, W. R., & Clark, E. (1990). Comparison of cognitive-behavioral, relaxation, and self-modeling interventions for depression among middle-school students. *School Psychology Review, 19,* 196–211.

Kehle, T. J., Bray, M. A., Margiano, S., Theodore, L. A., & Zhou, Z. (2002). Self-modeling as an effective intervention for students with serious emotional disturbance: Are we modifying children's memories? *Psychology in the Schools, 39,* 203–207.

Kehle, T. J., Clark, E., Jenson, W. R., & Wampold, B. E. (1986). Effectiveness of self-observation with behavior disordered elementary school children. *School Psychology Review, 15,* 289–295.

Kehle, T. J., Hintze, J., & DuPaul, G. J. (1997). Selective mutism. In G. Bear, K. Minke, & A. Thomas (Eds.), *Children's needs II.* Washington, DC: National Association of School Psychologists.

Kehle, T. J., Madaus, M. M. R., Baratta, V. S., & Bray, M. A. (1998). Augmented self-modeling as a treatment for children with selective mutism. *Journal of School Psychology, 36,* 377–399.

Kehle, T. J., Owen, S. V., & Cressy, E. T. (1990). The use of self-modeling as an intervention in school psychology: A case study of an elective mute. *School Psychology Review, 19,* 115–121.

Kratochwill, T. R. (1981). *Selective mutism: Implications for research and treatment.* Hillsdale, NJ: Erlbaum.

Krohn, D. D., Weckstein, S. M., & Wright, H. L. (1992). A study of the effectiveness of a specific treatment for elective mutism. *Journal of the American Academy of Child and Adolescent Psychiatry, 31,* 711–718.

Loftus, E. F. (1997). Memories for a past that never was. *Current Directions in Psychological Science, 6,* 60–65.

Lysne, A. (1999). Elective mutism: Special treatment of a special case. In S. Spasaro & C. Schaefer (Eds.), *Refusal to speak: Treatment of selective mutism in children* (pp. 83–90). Northvale, NJ: Jason Aronson, Inc.

Piersal, W. C., & Kratochwill, T. R. (1981). A teacher-implemented contingency management package to assess and treat selective mutism. *Behavioral Assessment, 3,* 371–382.

Remschmidt, H., Poller, M., Herpertz-Dahlman, B., Hennighausen, K., & Gutenbrunner, C. (2001). A follow-up study of 45 patients with elective mutism. *European Archives of Psychology & Clinical Neuroscience, 251,* 284–296.

Rhode, G., Jenson, W. R., & Reavis, H. K. (1993). *The tough kid book: Practical classroom management strategies.* Longmont, CO: Sopris West, Inc.

Schacter, D. L. (1995). *Memory distortion: How minds, brains, and societies reconstruct the past.* Cambridge, MA: Harvard University Press.

Schill, M. T., Kratochwill, T. R., & Gardner, W. I. (1996). An assessment protocol for selective mutism: Analogue assessment using parents as facilitators. *Journal of School Psychology, 34,* 1–26.

Segal, N. L. (2003). "Two" quiet: Monozygotic female twins with selective mutism. *Clinical Child Psychology and Psychiatry, 8,* 473–488.

Shipon-Blum, E. (2002, February). "When the words just won't come out"—Understanding selective mutism. [Insert]. *NASP Communiqué, 30.*

Shvarztman, P., Hornshtein, I., Klein, E., & Yechezkel, A. (1990). Elective mutism in family practice. *Journal of Family Practice, 31,* 319–320.

Skinner, B. F. (1964). Behaviorism as a philosophy of psychology. In T. W. Wann (Ed.), *Behaviorism and phenomenology.* Chicago: University of Chicago Press.

Sluckin, A., Foreman, N., & Herbert, M. (1991). Behavioural treatment programs and selectivity of speaking at follow-up in a sample of 25 selective mutes. *Psychologist, 26,* 132–137.

Spasaro, S. A., & Schaefer, C. E. (1999). An introduction to selective mutism. In S. A. Spasaro & C. E. Schaefer (Eds.), *Refusal to speak: Treatment of selective mutism in children* (pp. 1–15). Northvale, NJ: Jason Aronson, Inc.

Standart, S., & Le Couteur, A. (2003). The quiet child: A literature review of selective mutism. *Child and Adolescent Mental Health, 8,* 154–160.

Yeganeh, R., Beidel, D. C., Turner, S. M., Pina, A. A., & Silverman, W. K. (2003). Clinical distinctions between selective mutism and social phobia: An investigation of childhood psychopathology. *Journal of the American Academy of Child and Adolescent Psychiatry, 49,* 1069–1075.

# 23

# Perfectionism

**Rich Gilman**

*University of Kentucky*

**Jeffrey S. Ashby**

*Georgia State University*

Academic success requires that students develop strategies oriented toward goal attainment (Schunk & Zimmerman, 1997). Such strategies include setting specific goals (or standards), holding positive beliefs toward achieving those standards, and modifying behaviors and cognitions upon realizing that the preestablished standards will not likely be achieved (Schunk, 1994). In general, youth who maintain healthy goal pursuits through the establishment of realistic standards also tend to perform better in school-related activities.

For some youth, the standards greatly exceed those established by the majority of same-age peers. These youth are identified under the general label of *perfectionists*. The term *perfectionist* has a long history in the lay, medical, and psychological literature, with most of the writings largely based on case histories and anecdotal reports. Within this literature, parents and teachers report that perfectionistic children and adolescents are relatively easy to recognize, as they are more likely to (a) forgo recess to complete assignments, (b) be very disappointed that they did not get the perfect grade, or (c) engage in compulsive behaviors such as continually rewriting assignments but stating that the final product is never good enough (Kottman & Ashby, 2000). Other observed characteristics of perfectionists include excessive indecisiveness, underachievement, and severe procrastination (Adderholdt-Elliott, 1987). The majority of research on perfectionism, which is influenced by these anecdotal reports, has thus focused on maladaptive outcomes that range from mild aggravations (e.g., expressed discouragement whenever standards are not achieved) to more severe problems, including depression and suicide attempts (see Flett & Hewitt, 2002). These findings have led some authors to conclude that the "insidious nature of perfectionism" (Pacht, 1984, p. 387) inevitably leads to potentially harmful psychological problems that are difficult to treat.

Nevertheless, as empirical research begins to replace anecdotal literature, perfectionism can be differentiated into adaptive and maladaptive aspects, with negative outcomes being the product of the latter (Enns & Cox, 2002). Although research investigating perfectionism in youth remains in its embryonic stage, enough findings have been published to warrant a synthesis of the literature. Thus, one focus of this chapter is to review research related to perfectionism among school-age students. It also describes strategies designed to prevent maladaptive forms of perfectionism from manifesting among youth. The final section focuses on specific interventions that mental health professionals and school personnel can use to help perfectionistic youth achieve their maximum potential.

## BACKGROUND AND DEVELOPMENT

### Definition of Perfectionism

One of the most problematic issues in perfectionism has been defining the nature and scope of the construct (Enns & Cox, 2002). For example, early anecdotal claims and theoretical discourse from eminent authors such as Sigmund Freud, Anna Freud, Karen Horney, and Albert Ellis all suggested that individuals who established exceedingly high personal standards inevitably experienced psychological distress. Words most encapsulating of this school of thought can be found in Pacht (1984), who conceptualized perfectionists as caught in a

"God/scum phenomenon ... [where] despite their striving they find it impossible to be perfect, and, as a result, spend a lot of their time wallowing on the low end of the continuum" (p. 387).

In contrast, other authors such as Alfred Adler and Abraham Maslow viewed the setting of high standards as an essential element of the human condition. For example, Adler contended that striving for high standards is normal and innate and constitutes a major component of healthy psychological functioning. It is only when strivings for success are born out of fear of criticism or failure, or when perfection is felt to be necessary to enhance self-esteem or gain admiration, that such standards become problematic.

Hamachek's (1978) seminal paper was the first to integrate these disparate views by proposing that perfectionism consists of two separate but related subtypes: normal (or adaptive) and neurotic (maladaptive). Adaptive perfectionists set high standards but gain a sense of pleasure from pursuing them. Although their standards are high, adaptive perfectionists are flexible enough that if their standards are not met they still feel satisfied with their performance. Thus, adaptive perfectionists are motivated by a desire to maximize their capabilities. Conversely, maladaptive perfectionists emphasize high standards in every situation and have an extremely inflexible range of acceptable performance. Furthermore, they are more concerned about elements of their performance that are considered "wrong" than about elements that are considered to be "correct" (Rice & Preusser, 2002). In this regard, maladaptive perfectionists are driven by a fear of failure and are never really satisfied with themselves or their efforts.

## Assessment of Perfectionism in Youth

Largely influenced by Hamachek's (1978) conceptualization, the current assessment of perfectionism in youth is based on a multidimensional model that encompasses both personal and social components. The most widely researched perfectionism measures are two separate scales that share the title of the Multidimensional Perfectionism Scale (MPS), and the Almost Perfect Scale-Revised (APS-R). Both forms of the MPS were developed independently by Hewitt and Flett (1991) and Frost, Marten, Lahart, and Rosenblate (1990); and the APS-R was developed by Slaney, Rice, Mobley, Trippi, and Ashby (2001).

In all the scales, perfectionism is conceived of as containing specific core dimensions, which include self-oriented perfectionism (setting high standards for oneself), other-oriented perfectionism (setting high standards for others), and socially prescribed perfectionism (having high standards set by others; see Enns & Cox, 2002). Each scale is designed to assess one or more of these dimensions. All scales were first conducted with adult samples and have been extended to school-age students. Nevertheless, youth-focused studies have supported the use of these instruments to assess multidimensional perfectionism along these core dimensions.

## Development of Perfectionism

Various authors (Burns, 1980; Driscoll, 1982; Flett, Hewitt, Oliver, & Macdonald, 2002) contend that perfectionism has its roots in childhood development, particularly with respect to parent–child interactions. That is, children receive strong messages as to what constitutes acceptance if they grow up in households in which their parents maintain an authoritarian parenting style, base their own self-esteem on the successes of their child, and are perfectionists themselves. In this regard, parents reinforce their child's excellence in academic and social endeavors and react adversely to instances of failure. In time, the child begins to believe that the way to gain and maintain identity within the family is to accept parental criticism, which leads to a continued quest to perform flawlessly. Retrospective studies conducted among college students have found some evidence to support these beliefs. For example, one study among college females found that harsh authoritarian discipline among parents with high expectations of their children was related to maladaptive perfectionism but not to adaptive perfectionism (Kawamura, Frost, & Harmatz, 2002). Other studies (e.g., Frost, Lahart, & Rosenblate, 1991; Vieth & Trull, 1999) reported that the relationship between maternal perfectionism and perfectionism in daughters was significant, whereas the relationship between paternal perfectionism and daughter perfectionism was not. Psychological distress experienced by perfectionistic daughters was significantly related to mother's (but not father's) perfectionism.

Collectively, these findings suggest that perfectionistic parents display characteristics that increase the probability that their child will become a perfectionist and that manifestations of the construct are transmitted along same-sex lines. However, given that few published studies have examined this topic, and given the fact that most studies are based on cross-sectional designs using retrospective reports, additional research incorporating a longitudinal methodology is necessary to test the veracity of these findings.

In addition to parent factors, environmental pressures (from peers, teachers, and society in general) may also emphasize the need to be perfect among many youth. For example, federal and state legislative mandates (e.g., No Child Left Behind) have placed pressure for success on school districts. Although the prospect of evaluation is a ubiquitous experience for students, these experiences may have particular ramifications among youth with exceedingly high standards.

Furthermore, the overall sense of competitiveness that is currently stressed in America indicates a shift toward perfectionistic thinking, particularly among cultures that emphasize high conformity to parental and societal expectations (Flett et al., 2002). For example, studies among college students have found that Caucasian respondents reported higher concern over mistakes and levels of parental criticism than African American respondents (Nilsson, Paul, Lupini, & Tatem, 1999). Asian Americans reported significantly higher concerns about making mistakes and doubts about their actions than the other two groups (Chang, 1998). Similar differences have been noted among youth. For example, African American male and female high school students reported greater levels of self-oriented and other-oriented perfectionism than their Caucasian peers, possibly because of a perceived need to overcompensate for their status in the broader society (van Hanswijk de Jonge & Waller, 2003).

Other studies have examined multidimensional perfectionism across international samples. For both American and Croatian youth, adaptive perfectionists reported higher global and self-satisfaction than maladaptive perfectionists and nonperfectionists (Gilman, Ashby, Sverko, Florell, & Varjas, 2005). Nevertheless, American adaptive perfectionists reported higher satisfaction with friends and family than the other groups, and the mean scores were invariant across groups for the Croatian sample. These findings indicate that the construct can differ as a result of unique cultural characteristics. Finally, it has also been noted that cultures that emphasize the quest for physical perfection (typically observed among Caucasian, middle-class females) also report higher incidences of perfectionism than cultures that have traditionally placed less emphasis on physical perfection (Smolak & Striegel-Moore, 2001). Nevertheless, as the message to obtain the perfect figure and face becomes omnipresent, increasing rates of perfectionism have been noted among women and school-age students in these less physically self-conscious cultures.

Researchers have suggested that characteristics such as temperament, attachment style, and personality also contribute significantly to the development of perfectionism (Flett et al., 2002). For example, high levels of emotionality, which would include fearfulness combined with high levels of task persistence, could be predispositions that lead a child to be highly sensitive to parental feedback (Flett, Hewitt, Endler, & Tassone, 1995). This increased sensitivity may lead to increased risk of developing perfectionism. However, few empirical studies have been conducted among youth samples to test this hypothesis.

A recent transactional model (Flett et al., 2002) represents a preliminary attempt to explain how child characteristics, parenting style, and environmental pressures share a reciprocal relationship in the development and maintenance of perfectionism. In brief, the child's internal characteristics, combined with a family environment that emphasizes high achievement, along with various environmental pressures, result in situations in which youth compare their own and others' expectations of success to their actual performance. With increasing age come many forms of rejection from various sources. In response to this perceived failure, some youth view the rejection as a threat to their self-esteem and self-worthiness. These youth, who are considered to be maladaptive perfectionists, constantly strive to prove their worthiness at all costs (Halgin & Leahy, 1989). Conversely, adaptive perfectionists make similar comparisons between internalized messages and actual performance but do not view their perceived failures as a threat to their self-worth.

Although there is some research to support this model, more information is needed if researchers are to understand how perfectionism develops among youth, particularly with respect to how parental factors may mediate the difference between youth becoming adaptive perfectionists and youth becoming maladaptive perfectionists. For example, although perfectionism is significantly related to parents' perfectionistic goals and standards, other factors may contribute to perfectionism subtype, such as the importance placed on these standards by the parents, the types of goals set (i.e., learning versus performance goals), and how these standards are applied across various life domains. Furthermore, the role of stress and coping management strategies may also play a mediating role between parenting style and perfectionistic subtype.

## PROBLEMS AND IMPLICATIONS

### Gifted Youth

Most of the studies of multidimensional perfectionism among youth have thus far focused on gifted samples, with the works by Parker and colleagues (e.g., Parker, 1997, 2002; Ablard & Parker, 1997; Parker & Stumpf, 1998) contributing the majority of findings. An implicit assumption is that most if not all gifted youth have perfectionistic tendencies. Furthermore, in considering the relationship between maladaptive perfectionism and poor adjustment, it is assumed that gifted children are likely to have been predisposed to various types of psychological and psychosocial stressors. Finally, gifted children are considered more likely to be maladaptive perfectionists because of parental demands for high achievement. Extant findings have refuted some commonly accepted notions. For example, the relationship between perfectionism and giftedness appears equivocal at best, with some studies reporting higher frequency of perfectionism among gifted youth and others reporting negligible differences in perfectionistic tendencies between gifted and nongifted peers (see Parker, 2002). One explanation for these mixed results may be the method used to assess perfectionism; earlier studies focused solely on the negative dimension, whereas more recent studies have measured both positive and negative dimensions.

Moreover, the relationship between giftedness and maladaptive perfectionism has not been entirely supported. If anything, gifted perfectionistic adolescents are more likely to be identified as adaptive rather than maladaptive perfectionists. In one of the few longitudinal studies to date, Parker (1997) found that gifted youth identified as adaptive perfectionists in year 1 remained in this category 4 years later. Also, more maladaptive perfectionists transitioned to the adaptive perfectionist category across the 4-year period, rather than transitioning to the nonperfectionist category. This result suggests that although holding high standards is relatively stable over time, cognitive strategies may change to more positively and flexibly adapt to these standards.

Finally, although some studies suggest that parents of gifted youth have higher achievement expectations than parents of nongifted youth (Siegle & Schuler, 2000), the size of parental influence on the initial development of perfectionism is small (accounting for less than 4% of the variance in children's self-reports). Thus, other factors, such as peer influences, are likely contributors to developing perfectionistic tendencies in this population. Most parents of gifted children report an orientation that facilitates adaptive perfectionism rather than maladaptive perfectionism. These findings collectively reveal that perfectionistic strivings among most gifted students, if they occur, are likely to result in adaptive outcomes rather than personal or academic maladjustment. Nevertheless, maladaptive perfectionism can and does occur among gifted youth (see chapter 34, "Giftedness").

### Nongifted Youth

Studies using nongifted samples have been rare, although measures of multidimensional perfectionism consistently support the distinction between adaptive and maladaptive subtypes. Perhaps the greatest difference is the manner in which each subtype manages high standards and sensitivity to mistakes. For example, among a general sample of elementary school students identified as perfectionists, maladaptive perfectionists were more hypersensitive about making mistakes and had greater difficulty accepting when their work was less than perfect (Rice & Preusser, 2002). Furthermore, these students expressed a strong need for approval from others and were highly compulsive in avoiding mistakes. This compulsion may lead many perfectionists to avoid tasks that contain a high likelihood of failure (see Adderholdt-Elliott, 1987). This avoidance may be manifested in behaviors that include refusing to participate in class discussions (for fear of giving an incorrect answer), and chronic delays in completing school assignments. Adaptive perfectionists, on the other hand, set just as high personal standards as their maladaptive counterparts but were more flexible in their willingness to make and accept mistakes. Moreover, although adaptive perfectionists reported compulsivity that was as high as that of maladaptive perfectionists, this compulsivity tended to be related to meeting personal goals rather than to avoiding making mistakes.

Other studies (Gilman & Ashby, 2003a, b; Kottman & Ashby, 2000) have reported different psychological and psychoeducational outcomes related to perfectionistic subtype. Among middle school students, adaptive perfectionists report significantly more positive school experiences, higher grade-point averages, and lower psychological distress than maladaptive perfectionists. Furthermore, adaptive perfectionists report more positive coping skills (particularly academic confidence) than maladaptive perfectionists. Moreover, although both perfectionistic groups tend to maintain high standards for others (such as expecting teachers, peers, and school administrators to value structure and organization), adaptive perfectionists are more cognitively flexible than maladaptive perfectionists in adapting to situations in which their standards for others are not met.

Although there are negative outcomes inherent to maladaptive perfectionism, maintaining high standards appears to yield benefits that are not found among youth identified as nonperfectionists (i.e., those holding comparatively lower standards). For example, a series of studies (e.g., Gilman & Ashby, 2003a, b; Gilman et al., 2005) found that both maladaptive and adaptive perfectionists reported significantly higher self-satisfaction than nonperfectionists. Furthermore, although maladaptive perfectionists reported significantly lower grade-point averages and fewer positive school experiences in comparison with adaptive perfectionists, their reports were significantly higher than nonperfectionists. Thus, holding high standards, even among individuals who report significant amounts of distress when their standards are not always attained, appears to yield some benefits in comparison to youth who do not establish such high standards. Nevertheless, when one considers that adaptive perfectionists consistently report significantly higher positive outcomes than maladaptive perfectionists, the inflexible standards held by maladaptive perfectionists likely limit optimal achievement, or at least achievement levels that are on par with their adaptive peers.

## ALTERNATIVE ACTIONS FOR PREVENTION

The traditional view that establishing high standards is synonymous with maladaptive outcomes no longer appears to be supported. Rather, the greatest difficulty for some perfectionistic youth appears to be the inflexibility experienced in dealing with the inevitable instances in which high standards are not attained. One should not strive to "prevent" youth from establishing high standards, because such standards have conceptually and empirically been shown to positively influence mental health and may play a role in a variety of positive psychosocial and psychoeducational outcomes (Slaney et al., 2001). Indeed, striving to maximize one's potential is fundamental to the human condition, and attempts to compromise this striving can present psychological, educational, and vocational difficulties. Therefore, this section focuses on strategies to prevent the development of maladaptive perfectionism among youth.

The foremost approach for mental health and education professionals is to dispel the myth that perfectionism is a unidimensional construct that inevitably leads to a variety of psychological, interpersonal, and psychoeducational difficulties. Workshops, inservices, and parent forums can provide a more balanced perspective of the multidimensional nature of perfectionism and can help dispel notions that maintaining high standards leads to impairment. It is important to stress to key adult figures that maintaining high standards can be adaptive, provided that such standards are not taken to the extreme and that students do not experience strong internal discord when their standards are not met. Likewise, such forums can help parents and school personnel better understand the subtle messages that are inherent in pursuing high achievement goals.

As children proceed through school, expectations from teachers and parents to produce flawless work may increase as students are prepared for life beyond graduation. Such pressures may serve as motivators for nonperfectionists but may hinder many students with exceedingly high expectations for success. It is one message to strive for success to the best of one's ability; it is another to strive for success at all costs. For many maladaptive perfectionistic youth, the latter becomes the accepted and internalized message. The message that should be heard by these youth is not "success at all costs"; rather, it should be "success within limits." This message must also be conveyed to parents who place exceedingly high standards on their children, because evidence shows a strong relationship between parenting style (particularly an authoritarian style) and maladaptive perfectionism (Flett et al., 2002). Thus, information disseminated through parent forums, school newsletters, and workshops is important in teaching parents to be aware of the messages they send through their style of child rearing.

Case reports that emphasize the destructive nature of perfectionism (Blatt, 1995; Pacht, 1984) are based on perfectionism that is inner-directed, with little evidence of social interest. As noted by prominent theorists (Adler, 1956), perfectionism in this form will likely lead to psychological distress, because striving for success is believed to be a necessary requisite to feelings of self-worth.

Although research directly investigating this relationship has not been conducted among youth, findings obtained among adults demonstrate a relationship between perfectionism and social interest. If such findings can be extended to youth, many maladaptive perfectionists may be setting standards to achieve individualistic needs, without benefit to the larger good.

Schools and communities have recently focused on developing programs in which students can participate in a variety of structured activities that are designed to allow students to not only enhance skills and achieve personal goals but also work with others to achieve a common goal. Structured extracurricular activities (e.g., fine arts, athletics, and school government) have been shown to influence a variety of psychological and psychoeducational outcomes (see Gilman, Meyers, & Perez, 2004, for a review). In the case of maladaptive perfectionists, participation in such activities may help them focus on outer-directed goals, which may foster more realistic striving toward goals and an understanding of how high standards may benefit a number of individuals.

## ALTERNATIVE ACTIONS FOR INTERVENTION

Prior to intervening, clinicians would be well served by discriminating between children who are more adaptive in their perfectionism and those who are maladaptive. Although the three perfectionism measures described earlier have primarily been used for research purposes, information obtained from these measures can help clinicians distinguish adaptive perfectionists from their maladaptive counterparts. Interviews with teachers, parents, and other adult figures provide useful information, and behavioral observations are strongly recommended. Behaviors of adaptive perfectionists often appear designed to meet high standards, but these children generally are able to exercise moderation and a willingness to learn from mistakes. In contrast, maladaptive perfectionists are governed by their own extremely high standards, coupled with strong dissatisfaction and discouragement and elevated levels of anxiety. They may be paralyzed by their mistakes and have a tendency to develop negative attributions about themselves and their abilities. These children may be distraught or even angry in response to what they perceive to be criticism, perseverating on anything they view as negative feedback.

Although no published outcome studies for the treatment of perfectionism in children and adolescents are available, a number of conceptual articles provide guidance to the clinician. For instance, Kottman and Ashby (2000) highlight several potential interventions for maladaptive perfectionists from different psychotherapeutic orientations. One important caveat in the discussion of personal counseling for maladaptive perfectionists is the finding of Blatt (1995) that maladaptive perfectionism interferes significantly with therapeutic response to a variety of short-term interventions for depression. This finding is consistent with research (e.g., Slaney & Ashby, 1996) suggesting that perfectionists are ambivalent at best and resistant at worst to change. Pacht (1984) notes that for the maladaptive perfectionist, "being perfect is the magic formula for success" (p. 387), and as a result, the perfectionist is extremely reluctant to give it up. Adding to the difficulty of treating maladaptive perfectionists is their fear of appearing inadequate or being "found out" as imperfect in some way (Burns, 1980). As a result, it may be particularly problematic to develop a counseling relationship with these youth, given their reticence to share inner thoughts and feelings. Clinicians might profit from efforts to share the responsibility and power in the counseling relationship. Kottman (2003) notes that these efforts are likely to help reticent youth engage in a therapeutic alliance. She suggests initially asking child clients about their understanding of why they are being seen in counseling, what happens in counseling, and their understanding of the presenting problem. These initial impressions can assist the clinician in developing the emotional bond and sense of shared goals and tasks necessary to the therapeutic alliance.

The majority of references to the dynamics of maladaptive perfectionism focus on cognitions and beliefs. Consistent with the early theoretical work of Burns (e.g., 1980), Kottman and Ashby (2000) noted that maladaptive perfectionists are prone to "all or nothing" thinking. Burns (1980) illustrates this dichotomous thinking pattern with the example of a straight A student who receives a B on an assignment and concludes "Now I am a total failure" (p. 38). Maladaptive perfectionists experience a number of cognitive distortions, including chronic, negative self-statements ("Why would anyone want to be my friend?"), negative interpretations of the reactions of others (interpreting silence as extreme rejection), and dichotomous or overgeneralized patterns of thinking (events are either wonderful or they are horrible) (Ashby, Kottman, & Martin, 2004).

A number of traditional cognitive interventions could be used to target the structure of distorted thoughts and irrational beliefs that underlie a youth's maladaptive perfectionism. Clinicians can help clients identify the distortions in their thoughts and teach them to evaluate their thoughts for logic and reasonableness (Burns, 1980). For instance, to highlight the unreasonableness of dichotomous thinking, clinicians can use an exercise in which clients investigate whether the world can be meaningfully evaluated using all-or-nothing categories. Afterwards, clients can learn to catch themselves thinking in a dichotomous manner ("I got an A– on the exam, so I'm a complete failure") and exchange a more reasonable evaluation ("I got an A– on the exam. I'm disappointed but it's not the end of the world, just a little less than what I had aimed for").

Similarly, using a Rational Emotive Behavioral Therapy (REBT) technique (Ellis & Bernard, 1986), clinicians can help youth identify the irrational beliefs underlying their maladaptive perfectionistic behavior ("I must be perfect in everything I do or I am unlovable"). Using REBT, the clinician would refute this belief by pointing out evidence in the youth's life that is inconsistent with the belief (e.g., positive regard from parents or others even when the youth's performance is not perfect).

Kottman and Ashby (2000) suggest a number of similar interventions for younger children, which specifically target maladaptively perfectionistic cognitions, including the use of metaphoric stories. Using this strategy, the clinician might tell a younger child stories about animals or other characters who did their best, did not achieve their perfectionistic goals, but were able to resolve the situation with a realistic belief about their performance and relative self-worth. Another technique targeting cognitive distortions for smaller children is mutual storytelling (Kottman, 2003). Using this method, the clinician and client use puppets to act out scenes where one puppet (acted out by the clinician) does not meet its perfectionistic standard and the other puppet (acted out by the client) helps it deal with the disappointment in a rational manner. The authors note that part of the power of the technique is that the child co-constructs the plot of the puppet show by responding rationally to the irrational beliefs of the puppet who does not meet its perfectionistic standards. A similar technique that might be used with older students is to have clients role-play scenarios in which they set standards for themselves in a variety of areas (e.g., academics, athletics, music, social). After this initial role-playing, the youth brainstorms adaptive ways to handle not meeting these hypothetical standards and then role-plays what they would say to themselves in the situation.

Clinicians may also want to explore with maladaptively perfectionistic youth how the desire to be perfect relates to parental expectations and values. This strategy may work well in play form with younger children and in discussion form with older students. With the latter group, the clinician can discuss the youth's perspective of family pressures or desires for perfectionism. As a follow-up these youth can talk with their parents and teachers to see how their perceptions match the statements of the adults (Adderholdt-Elliot, 1987). With younger children, the clinician can use a puppet to "interview" them about family interactions and expectations while the child assumes a variety of roles (e.g., themselves, their parents, their teachers).

A number of behavioral interventions may also effectively target maladaptive perfectionism. For instance, Antony and Swinson (1998) suggest having youth chart and evaluate their perfectionistic thoughts and behaviors. Clinicians might ask older youth to keep track of times when their perfectionism is working and times when it is self-defeating. In this manner, students can see which thought patterns are related to negative behaviors and feelings and which ones to positive. Using their observation, youth can work with clinicians to devise strategies to increase the incidence of positive perfectionistic patterns and decrease the negative patterns.

Hamachek (1978) identified several goals to work toward with clients who are trying to reduce their "neurotic" perfectionism. These goals included helping clients to be task selective—helping them choose one or two areas in which to apply their perfectionistic standards and related energy. Helping clients give themselves permission to be perfectionistic in one or two areas will, according to Hamachek, likely free them up to be less perfectionistic in other areas, and thus less hard on themselves. Another of Hamachek's goals was to help clients set reasonable goals for themselves by taking stock of strengths and weaknesses and setting goals accordingly. Hamachek's final goal for reducing neurotic perfectionism was to help clients choose at least one activity they would do without criticizing themselves. By avoiding perfectionistic standards, and related self-criticism and degradation, clients practice nonperfect behavior without the requisite damage to self-esteem. This exception to their perfectionistic rules provides additional evidence to help them counter their cognitive distortions about their performance in all areas.

Although most of the literature addressing the treatment of maladaptive perfectionism is focused on individual interventions, most of the techniques and approaches suggested could also be used in group counseling settings. Barrow and Moore (1983) suggested several group strategies to help clients discriminate self-worth from performance and to develop cognitive coping processes to moderate and control cognitive distortions and irrational beliefs. Groups also offer a unique opportunity for youth with different levels of adaptive and maladaptive perfectionism to model successful behaviors and learn from the successes and failures of others (Kottman & Ashby, 2000). Clinicians may want to include students who exhibit behaviors more consistent with adaptive perfectionism in groups treating maladaptive perfectionism. These students can act as models for positive striving without self-critical and destructive beliefs and behaviors.

Regardless of the treatment modality used, treatment of maladaptive perfectionistic clients typically shares several goals. These include helping youth (a) recognize self-defeating themes in their social and intrapersonal lives and begin to shift these cognitions, (b) learn to moderate their reaction to perceived criticism from others, (c) restructure their distorted cognitions, (d) develop greater flexibility and expand their choices of cognitive strategies, (e) readjust their attitudes toward and behavior related to orderliness and control, (f) learn strategies to recognize and cope with anxiety, and (g) accept greater responsibility for themselves by developing greater tolerance for taking risks and making mistakes.

## SUMMARY

Although previous conceptualizations and research focused on perfectionism as a unidimensional construct, more contemporary research finds that perfectionism consists of two specific subtypes: adaptive and maladaptive. Contrary to previous claims, perfectionism is not wholly synonymous with distress and can result in a number of positive outcomes as long as flexibility is maintained in concordance with high standards. Perfectionism becomes maladaptive when the established high standards are highly inflexible. In maladaptive perfectionism, goal pursuits are no longer considered to be healthy, and optimal psychological, interpersonal, and psychoeducational functioning may be compromised.

This chapter provided a number of suggestions for the prevention and treatment of maladaptive perfectionism. Through workshops, inservices, and teacher and parent consultation, key figures in a youth's life could better understand the complex nature of perfectionism and how messages for success may unwittingly hinder some perfectionist youth from achieving optimal psychological and academic functioning. Furthermore, because maladaptive perfectionism may result from high standards that are predominantly inner-directed, participation in structured extracurricular activities may help youth understand that goal-related standards can be beneficial to others as well. Finally, treatment of maladaptive perfectionism is not designed to lower preestablished standards but to help the maladaptive perfectionistic youth become more flexible in adapting to instances in which their performance will not meet their expectations.

## RECOMMENDED RESOURCES

Flett, G. L., & Hewitt, P. L. (2002). *Perfectionism: Theory, research, and treatment.* Washington, DC: American Psychological Association.

This edited book provides a comprehensive review of the most recent findings in perfectionism. Although the book largely focuses on perfectionism in adults, chapters focusing on perfectionism among gifted youth and on family characteristics are included. The book also includes an excellent discussion of theories and suggestions for future research.

Parker, W. D. (1997). An empirical typology of perfectionism in academically talented children. *American Education Research Journal, 34,* 545–562.

This paper is an excellent study of the subtypes found among a sample of over 800 gifted sixth graders. Cluster analysis identified that the majority of the sample were identified as healthy (adaptive) perfectionists, followed by nonperfectionists and dysfunctional (maladaptive) perfectionists, respectively. The paper addresses and dispels some myths surrounding perfectionism and gifted youth.

The following papers each provide a theoretical rationale and empirical validation for the construction of their respective multidimensional perfectionism scales. Although all three scales were first validated with adult samples, each scale has been administered and validated with school-age populations.

Frost, R. O., Marten, P., Lahart, C., & Rosenblate, R. (1990). The dimensions of perfectionism. *Cognitive therapy and research, 14,* 449–468.

Hewitt, P. L., & Flett, G. L. (1991). Perfectionism in the self and social contexts: Conceptualization, assessment, and association with psychopathology. *Journal of Personality and Social Psychology, 60,* 456–470.

Slaney, R. B., Rice, K. G., Mobley, M., Trippi, J., & Ashby, J. S. (2001). The Almost Perfect Scale-Revised. *Measurement and Evaluation in Counseling and Development, 34,* 130–145.

# REFERENCES


Ablard, K. E., & Parker, W. D. (1997). Parents' achievement goals and perfectionism in their academically talented children. *Journal of Youth and Adolescence, 26,* 651–667.

Adderholdt-Elliott, M. (1987). *Perfectionism: What's bad about being too good?* Minneapolis, MN: Free Spirit.

Adler, A. (1956). The neurotic disposition. In H. L. Ansbacher & R. R. Ansbacher (Eds.), *The individual psychology of Alfred Adler* (pp. 239–262). New York: Harper.

Antony, M., & Swinson, R. (1998). *When perfect isn't good enough: Strategies for coping with perfectionism.* Oakland, CA: New Harbinger.

Ashby, J. S., Kottman, T., & Martin, J. (2004). Play therapy with young perfectionists. *International Journal of Play Therapy, 13,* 34–55.

Barrow, J. C., & Moore, C. A. (1983). Group interventions with perfectionist thinking. *Personnel and Guidance Journal, 61,* 612–615.

Blatt, S. J. (1995). The destructiveness of perfectionism: Implications for the treatment of depression. *American Psychologist, 50,* 1003–1020.

Burns, D. (1980, November). The perfectionist's script for self-defeat. *Psychology Today,* 34–52.

Chang, E. C. (1998). Cultural differences, perfectionism, and suicidal risk in a college population: Does social problem solving still matter? *Cognitive Therapy and Research, 22,* 237–254.

Ellis, A., & Bernard, M. E. (1986). What is rational-emotive therapy (RET)? In R. M. Grieger & A. Ellis (Eds.), *Handbook of rational-emotive therapy, Vol. 2.* (pp. 3–30). New York: Springer.

Enns, M. W., & Cox, B. J. (2002). The nature and assessment of perfectionism: A critical analysis. In G. L. Flett & P. L. Hewitt (Eds.), *Perfectionism: Theory, research, and treatment* (pp. 33–62). Washington, DC: American Psychological Association.

Flett, G. L., & Hewitt, P. L. (2002). *Perfectionism: Theory, research, and treatment.* Washington, DC: American Psychological Association.

Flett, G. L., Hewitt, P. L., Endler, N. S., & Tassone, C. (1995). Perfectionism and components of state and trait anxiety. *Current Psychology, 13,* 326–350.

Flett, G. L., Hewitt, P. L., Oliver, J. M., & Macdonald, S. (2002). Perfectionism in children and their parents: A developmental analysis. In G. L. Flett & P. L. Hewitt (Eds.), *Perfectionism: Theory, research, and treatment* (pp. 89–132). Washington, DC: American Psychological Association.

Frost, R. O., Lahart, C. M., & Rosenblate, R. (1991). The development of perfectionism: A study of daughters and their parents. *Cognitive Therapy and Research, 15,* 469–489.

Frost, R. O., Marten, P., Lahart, C. M., & Rosenblate, R. (1990). The dimensions of perfectionism. *Cognitive Therapy and Research, 14,* 449–468.

Gilman, R., & Ashby, J. S. (2003a). Multidimensional perfectionism in a sample of middle school students: An exploratory investigation. *Psychology in the Schools, 40,* 677–689.

Gilman, R., & Ashby, J. S. (2003b). A first study of perfectionism and multidimensional life satisfaction among adolescents. *Journal of Early Adolescence, 23,* 218–235.

Gilman, R., Ashby, J. S., Sverko, D., Florell, D., & Varjas, K. (2005). The relationship between perfectionism and multidimensional life satisfaction among Croatian and American youth. *Personality and Individual Differences, 39,* 155–166.

Gilman, R., Meyers, J. J., & Perez, L. (2004). Structured extracurricular activities among adolescents: Findings and implications for school psychologists. *Psychology in the Schools, 41,* 31–42.

Halgin, R. P., & Leahy, P. M. (1989). Understanding and treating perfectionistic college students. *Journal of Counseling and Development, 68,* 222–225.

Hamachek, D. E. (1978). Psychodynamics of normal and neurotic perfectionism. *Psychology, 15,* 27–33.

Hewitt, P. L., & Flett, G. L. (1991). Perfectionism in the self and social contexts: Conceptualization, assessment, and association with psychopathology. *Journal of Personality and Social Psychology, 60,* 456–470.

Kawamura, K. Y., Frost, R. O., & Harmatz, M. G. (2002). The relationship of perceived parenting styles to perfectionism. *Personality and Individual Differences, 32,* 317–327.

Kottman, T. (2003). *Partners in play: An Adlerian approach to play therapy* (2nd ed.). Alexandria, VA: American Counseling Association.

Kottman, T., & Ashby, J. S. (2000). Perfectionistic children and adolescents: Implications for school counselors. *Professional School Counseling, 3,* 182–188.

Nilsson, J. E., Paul, B. D., Lupini, L. N., & Tatem, B. (1999). Cultural differences in perfectionism: A comparison of African-American and White college students. *Journal of College Student Development, 40,* 141–150.

Pacht, A. R. (1984). Reflections on perfection. *American Psychologist, 39,* 386–390.

Parker, W. D. (1997). An empirical typology of perfectionism in academically talented children. *American Education Research Journal, 34,* 545–562.

Parker, W. D. (2002). Perfectionism and adjustment in gifted children. In G. L. Flett & P. L. Hewitt (Eds.), *Perfectionism: Theory, research, and treatment* (pp. 133–148). Washington, DC: American Psychological Association.

Parker, W. D., & Stumpf, H. (1998). A validation of the five-factor model of personality in academically talented youth across observers and instruments. *Personality and Individual Differences, 25,* 1005–1025.

Rice, K. G., & Preusser, K. J. (2002). The Adaptive/Maladaptive Perfectionism Scale. *Measurement and Evaluation in Counseling and Development, 34,* 210–222.

Schunk, D. H. (1994). *Self-regulation of learning and performance: Issues and educational applications.* Hillsdale, NJ: Erlbaum.

Schunk, D. H., & Zimmerman, B. J. (1997). Social origins of self-regulatory competence. *Educational Psychologist, 32,* 195–208.

Siegle, D., & Schuler, P. A. (2000). Perfectionism differences in gifted middle school students. *Roeper Review, 23,* 39–44.

Slaney, R. B., & Ashby, J. S. (1996). Perfectionists: Study of a criterion group. *Journal of Counseling and Development, 74,* 393–398.

Slaney, R. B., Rice, K. G., Mobley, M., Trippi, J., & Ashby, J. S. (2001). The Almost Perfect Scale-Revised. *Measurement and Evaluation in Counseling and Development, 34,* 130–145.

Smolak, L., & Striegel-Moore, R. H. (2001). Challenging the myth of the golden girl: Ethnicity and eating disorders. In L. Smolak & R. H. Striegel-Moore (Eds.), *Eating disorders: Innovative directions in research and practice* (pp. 111–132). Washington, DC: American Psychological Association.

van Hanswijk de Jonge, L., & Waller, G. (2003). Perfectionism levels in African-American and Caucasian adolescents. *Personality and Individual Differences, 34,* 1447–1451.

Vieth, A. Z., & Trull, T. J. (1999). Family patterns of perfectionism: An examination of college students and their parents. *Journal of Personality Assessment, 72,* 49–67.

# 24
# Prosocial Behavior

**Nancy Eisenberg**
*Arizona State University*

When preschooler Sally deftly grabs a puzzle from Eric's hand, Eric immediately breaks into tears. Classmate Randy, observing this exchange, pats Eric on the back and offers to share the toy helicopter with which he has been playing.

The focus of this chapter is not on Sally or Eric but on Randy—or more correctly, on Randy's prosocial response to a classmate. This interest in Randy's behavior is different from the focus in much of this volume. The target behavior is not problematic; that is, it does not occur more often than is desirable and it usually does not occur under the wrong circumstances. Nor is the absence of prosociality normally considered a deficit that deserves the same attention as the many other social and academic deficits that come to the attention of educators and school psychologists. For example, concern for a child who is exceptionally socially reticent or who has failed to master basic reading skills is typically greater than concern for a child who bypasses opportunities to be helpful to others. Nonetheless, there is reason to assert the value—both to the individual and to society—of fostering children's tendencies for caring, sharing, and helping. Thus, this chapter focuses primarily on identifying effective means of promoting prosocial behavior, not on interventions for the lack of such behavior.

## BACKGROUND AND DEVELOPMENT

In the psychological literature, *prosocial behavior* often is defined as voluntary behavior that is intended to benefit another and that includes helping, donating, sharing, and comforting. Prosocial behavior that is intrinsically motivated is said to be altruistic. Thus, *altruism* refers to assisting others when one's acts are internally motivated by concern for others or by internalized values, goals, and self-rewards (Eisenberg & Fabes, 1998). Altruistic acts generally are viewed as reflecting moral rather than egoistic motivation. However, behaviors helpful to others may also reflect mere compliance with the demands of the situation or fear of punishment, the desire for reward, or some other nonmoral factor.

Observers usually cannot differentiate between altruistically motivated actions and those motivated by less noble concerns. As children develop, altruistic motives and behaviors may evolve from their nonaltruistic prosocial actions. Thus, understanding factors that influence the broader domain of prosocial behavior is valuable.

Prosocial behavior, including altruism, is frequently motivated by empathy-related emotional reactions. *Empathy* is commonly defined in developmental psychology as an affective response that stems from the apprehension of another's emotional state or condition and is identical or very similar to what the other person is feeling or would be expected to feel. Thus, if Randy is saddened by Eric's crying, or from what he infers from the crying about Eric's emotional state, he is experiencing empathy (Eisenberg & Fabes, 1998). If Eric recovers and cheerfully plays with the new toy and Randy feels happy as a consequence of Eric's shift in emotion, this would also be an empathic response.

It is important to differentiate empathy from related emotional responses, especially sympathy and personal distress. *Sympathy*, an affective response that frequently stems from empathy, consists of feelings of concern for a distressed or needy other. Thus, if Randy feels concern regarding Eric's well-being (rather than empathic sadness alone), he is experiencing sympathy. However, personal distress may also result when one vicariously experiences another's emotional state or condition. *Personal distress* involves a self-focused, aversive emotional reaction such as discomfort, anxiety, or self-oriented distress. Accordingly, if Randy's affective response to Eric's crying is a feeling of negative emotional arousal or discomfort, a reaction that might also motivate him to act or to escape from Eric, then Randy is feeling personal distress.

Empathy-related emotional reactions have been strongly implicated in prosocial development and action (see Hoffman, 2000). However, sympathy and personal distress are believed to be associated with different motivations and to relate differently to prosocial behavior. Specifically, sympathy is viewed as associated with other-oriented motives and, consequently, with other-oriented, altruistic helping behavior. In contrast, personal distress is believed to evoke the egoistic motivation of alleviating one's own distress. For example, if Randy responds to Eric's crying with personal distress, he would be expected to engage in prosocial behavior only if that is the easiest way to stop Eric's crying. If personal distress motivates Randy's action, and if he can easily escape contact with Eric's crying, he would be expected to leave the situation rather than help.

In general, the empirical research is consistent with the notion that helping is more likely to be associated with sympathy than with personal distress when it is easy for the distressed person to escape contact with the person needing assistance. In a series of studies, Eisenberg, Fabes and their colleagues (see Eisenberg & Fabes, 1998) examined the relationships of self-report, facial, and physiological (e.g., heart rate and skin conductance) markers of sympathy and personal distress to prosocial behavior in situations in which escape was relatively easy. When children were shown a variety of empathy-inducing videotapes, those who exhibited facial or physiological markers of sympathy tended to be relatively prosocial if given an opportunity to assist someone in the film or a group of people similar to those in the film (e.g., hospitalized children). In contrast, children (especially boys) who exhibited evidence of personal distress tended to be less prosocial (see Eisenberg & Fabes, 1998). Because of the conceptual and empirical links between empathy-related reactions and prosocial behavior, understanding the factors that promote sympathy will provide information relevant to fostering prosocial behavior.

For a long time most philosophers, psychologists, and others believed infants, toddlers, and young children to be quite self-interested and amoral. This view was exemplified by Sigmund Freud's theory in which infants were born possessing only the id, the structure of personality concerned with innate, instinctual, irrational impulses and self-gratification. In most of Freud's writings, the superego, or conscience, was said to develop only after children were 4 to 6 years of age. Jean Piaget also promulgated the belief that children are unable to understand others' perspectives until they are 6 or 7 years of age. If children are unaware of another's perspective, they are unlikely to assist. It is now clear from empirical work, however, that children develop a rudimentary understanding of others' perspectives in the first few years of life. Furthermore, children engage in other-oriented, prosocial behavior at an early age, although the nature of prosocial responding does seem to change somewhat during the first few years of life.

## The Development of Prosocial Tendencies

Much of the research on the early development of prosocial behavior concerns infants' and toddlers' reactions to the distress of others. Six-month-old infants infrequently respond with distress to the distress of a peer, although they often display interest in peers' discomfort (Hay, Nash, & Pedersen, 1981). Hoffman (2000) argued that infants in the first year of life do not clearly differentiate between self and other and, therefore, are unsure who is experiencing any distress they witness. By 10 to 14 months of age, infants often become agitated and disturbed when they view others in distress (e.g., Radke-Yarrow & Zahn-Waxler, 1984). It is not entirely clear in these situations whether children are genuinely concerned about the other person or whether the other person's distress merely upsets the infant. However, children of this age often seek comfort for themselves as a reaction to viewing another's distress, which supports the latter explanation. Becoming distressed as a response to the distress of others decreases in relative frequency during the second year of life.

Between 12 and 18 months, children sometimes try to interact in a positive manner with others in distress, for example, they pat someone who is upset. Randy's sharing of a toy in response to Eric's whimpering is typical of comforting behaviors that emerge and become more common during this period. Hoffman (2000) argued that although the 1- to 2-year-old appears to experience empathy and sometimes is prosocial, the child experiences "egocentric empathy." Thus, although some children have become fully aware of the difference between the self and another as physical entities and recognize who is experiencing distress, they do not yet fully distinguish between the other person's inner states and their own. Thus, a young child is prone to assist in ways appropriate for oneself but perhaps not for the other person. For example, a girl may give a distressed adult her own beloved doll or bring her own mother to comfort a crying peer, even if the other child's mother is present.

Although increasing in frequency during the second year of life, prosocial behavior, including attempts to help others in distress, is far from commonplace during this period. Children 18 to 36 months of age often ignore or watch their siblings' or peers' distress. In one study of 16- to 33-month-olds, a peer responded to another's distress within a play episode only 22% of the time, and children were three times as likely to respond to the distress of a friend than to that of a peer who was not a friend (Howes & Farver, 1987).

These findings notwithstanding, children's prosocial interventions do increase in frequency in the first few years of life (Eisenberg & Fabes, 1998). Moreover, it appears that 3-year-olds can respond to others' distress more appropriately and competently than can 18-month-olds (Radke-Yarrow & Zahn-Waxler, 1984). These changes are perhaps due to increases in children's ability, as they age, to take another's perspective or to understand how other people think and feel. Conversely, Zahn-Waxler, Schiro, Robinson, Emde, and Schmitz (2001), in a study of toddlers' empathy-related responses (at 14, 20, 24, and 36 months of age) to an experimenter and the toddler's mother feigning injuries found that nonempathic responses, such as self-oriented distress reactions, seemed to decrease in the second and third year of life. In addition, toddlers' indifference toward another's distress declined between 14 and 20 months of age but then increased between 24 and 36 months of age.

Because preschool children are better able to understand the perspective of others than younger children are, they are more motivated and better able to pinpoint the source of another's distress and to help in ways that are sensitive to the other's needs (Hoffman, 2000). Nonetheless, comforting others who are showing distress, particularly peers, is still a relatively infrequent act, especially in the preschool classroom (see Eisenberg & Fabes, 1998). Across the preschool years, however, preschoolers are increasingly likely to respond to others' distress with empathy and prosocial behaviors (Eisenberg & Fabes, 1998).

Not only do young children sometimes intervene when another is distressed, they also share with and help others in a variety of ways. Young children's sharing of objects may not be motivated primarily by concern for others; rather, the exchange of objects appears to be an effective way for young children to sustain positive interactions with other people. In the preschool years and beyond, sharing increases more consistently with age (Eisenberg & Fabes, 1998).

In general, prosocial behaviors (e.g., sharing, instrumental helping, and comforting) increase across the school years into adolescence (Eisenberg & Fabes, 1998). In addition, children of school age typically spend more time with their peers than do younger children, and they begin to develop intimate friendships. With increasing age children are more likely to view emotional support as an important component of friendship and thus to provide more support (Youniss, 1980). Older children are also more likely than younger children to take the perspective of the distressed person when attempting to help or comfort them. Hence, the quality of their assistance often is superior to that of younger children (see Bar-Tal, 1982; Eisenberg & Fabes, 1998).

Across the elementary school years, prosocial behavior becomes increasingly stable. For example, Tremblay, Nagin, Zoccolillo, and Vitaro (2002) found that children who entered kindergarten with specific levels of helpfulness finished primary school at very similar levels. In addition, spontaneously offered sharing in preschool predicts children's prosocial behaviors in later elementary school and in adolescence (Eisenberg et al., 1999).

Prosocial tendencies appear to increase from childhood into adolescence, although there is limited evidence of an increase in prosocial responding across adolescence, that is, from age 12 to 17 or 18 (Eisenberg & Fabes, 1998). One exception may be instances of helping victims of aggression (Lindeman, Harakka, & Keltikangas-Jarvinen, 1997). Hoffman (2000) hypothesized that the ability to sympathize with the distress of abstract others (i.e., those who are not in the immediate situation) and with the chronic distress of others develops in late childhood or early adolescence. Hoffman suggested that this age-related change is based on the child's newfound ability to view others as having personal identities and life experiences beyond the immediate situation. If Hoffman is correct, adolescents, in comparison to younger children, would be expected to be more sympathetic (and therefore more prosocial) toward members of disadvantaged groups and other individuals whose distress is chronic or not immediately observable.

In adolescence, volunteering becomes a common mode of prosocial behavior. In general, researchers have found that volunteering is associated with increases in adolescents' self-esteem and self-acceptance, moral development, and belief that they have a personal responsibility to help. Volunteering also demonstrates their concern for social issues and intended future service (Eisenberg, Fabes, & Spinrad, in press; Metz, McLellan, & Youniss, 2003).

### Age-Related Changes in Motives and Reasoning About Prosocial Behavior

Older and younger children also seem to differ somewhat in their motivations for engaging in prosocial behaviors. For example, older children are more likely to help or donate in situations in which they are not promised a reward or pressured to help (see Bar-Tal, 1982; Eisenberg, 1986). Moreover, there are developmental trends in the reasons children give for their prosocial actions. Even preschoolers may occasionally give simple, other-oriented, and pragmatic reasons for their peer-directed prosocial actions, but with increasing age, children are more inclined to cite reasons that reflect perspective taking and empathy or sympathy (Bar-Tal, 1982; Eisenberg, 1986). Moreover, there is evidence that children who express more mature motives for their prosocial actions engage in more prosocial behavior (see Eisenberg, 1986; Eisenberg & Fabes, 1998). Similar age-related trends have been noted in studies of children's moral reasoning, most of which involved interviews of children regarding hypothetical moral dilemmas (Eisenberg, 1986). Respondents were asked what a story's protagonist, faced with a dilemma, should do and why. The responses of young children tended to emphasize hedonistic reasoning (i.e., reasoning related to self-gain) or needs-oriented (primitive empathic) prosocial reasoning. Needs-oriented reasoning involves mere recognition of the other person's needs or condition. For example, Randy might explain that he helped "because Eric was crying," with no further elaboration. In general, self-oriented, hedonistic reasons for prosocial behavior appear to decrease with age. In elementary school, children's moral reasoning begins to reflect concern with approval and enhanced interpersonal relationships, as well as with the desire to behave in stereotypically good ways. However, the use of such reasoning appears to decrease somewhat in high school.

Beginning in late elementary school or thereafter, children begin to express reasoning that reflects abstract principles, internalized affective reactions (e.g., guilt or positive affect about the consequences for others of behaving a certain way or of living up to internalized principles), and self-reflective sympathy and perspective taking. However, individuals of all ages sometimes verbalize immature modes of reasoning, and developmental trends do not always involve linear progressions (see Eisenberg, 1986; Eisenberg & Fabes, 1998). Nonetheless, in general, children, as they age, tend to become less self-oriented in the preschool and elementary school years and more other-oriented and concerned with abstract value-related reasons for prosocial behavior.

## PROBLEMS AND IMPLICATIONS

Most of the research pertaining to developing children's prosocial behavior falls into two categories: promoting the behavior through multiple techniques and preventing deficits in this area, although the absence of prosocial behavior generally is not considered a serious problem. Nonetheless, knowledge of prosocial development is important to understanding children's success at school. Children who are prosocial may be somewhat less likely to develop difficulties in peer relationships. Prosocial, sympathetic children tend to be popular (i.e., well liked by peers, albeit not necessarily viewed as high status), to have friends, to be socially competent, and to not be bullies or aggressive (Eisenberg & Fabes, 1998; Warden & Mackinnon, 2003). Additionally, boys with poor prosocial skills have been found to be at risk of being bullied (Johnson et al., 2002). Grade point average also has been linked to prosocial behavior, even across time (Caprara, Barbaranelli, Pastorelli, Bandura, & Zimbardo, 2000).

Although cause-and-effect relationships between prosocial tendencies and variables such as social competence, adjustment, and grade point average are based primarily on correlational data, the initial findings indicate that these dimensions of children's functioning are interrelated. Causation probably goes both directions; for example, children who are prosocial are likely to be well liked, and having positive peer relationships provides opportunities to further develop sympathy and prosocial skills.

Although schools are generally considered to be primarily a resource for academic development, children receive indirect (and in some cases direct) classroom instruction on aspects of morality, such as prosocial behavior and its value in society. Prosocial behavior is regarded by most people in our society as desirable, at least in the abstract, and such norms and values are embedded in instructional materials and practices. Promotion of prosocial behavior and reasoning would also be expected to have a positive effect on the quality of classroom interaction. Thus, many teachers may wish to promote prosocial behavior as a way of optimizing the learning environment.

## ALTERNATIVE ACTIONS FOR PROMOTION OF PROSOCIAL BEHAVIOR

Although biological factors may play a role in the development of empathy and prosocial behavior (see Eisenberg & Fabes, 1998; Zahn-Waxler et al., 2001), children's prosocial behavior is clearly also related to some types of socialization experiences. Eight general types of socialization experiences are discussed in this section: disciplinary practices, parents' and teachers' warmth, modeling, nondisciplinary verbalizations, positive reinforcement, assignment to prosocial activities, emphasis on prosocial values, and emotion-related practices. More specific techniques that parents and teachers can use to enhance prosocial development are listed in Table 1.

Some of the relevant data on socialization are correlational, but other research involves experimental designs from which inferences about causality can be made with some confidence. Moreover, patterns of findings from laboratory and naturalistic studies generally converge, which increases professional confidence in this body of knowledge concerning parental practices. Unfortunately, relatively little of this research pertains directly to teachers' promotion of children's prosocial tendencies.

### Socialization Practices Related to Prosocial Behavior

***Disciplinary practices.*** Parental discipline that involves inductive discipline (i.e., reasoning), rather than assertion of power, appears to be associated with prosocial behavior, particularly for middle-class children in Western cultures. Reasoning that points out the consequences of the child's behavior on others has been linked to children's prosocial behavior. However, inductions seem to be most effective for children who have a history of exposure to inductive discipline (Hoffman, 1963; also see Dlugokinski & Firestone, 1974). Inductions also appear to be most effective when combined with a democratic parenting style, including support and demands for mature behavior (see Eisenberg & Fabes, 1998; Hoffman, 2000).

**Table 1** *Summary of Recommended Practices and Related Factors Associated With Prosocial Development*

- Use authoritative discipline, including inductive discipline and low levels of power assertion.
- Provide prosocial modeling.
- Use preachings and other verbalizations that encourage the child to empathize.
- Use dispositional praise for prosocial behavior.
- Provide practice in prosocial behavior.
- Encourage constructive regulation of negative emotion.
- Encourage and value prosocial values.
- Express positive emotion rather than conflict at home.
- Participate in cooperative activities.
- Develop supportive relationships in classrooms, including teacher expression of affection and approval.
- Encourage emotional perspective taking through discussion of naturally occurring events at school.
- Allow student participation in classroom governance and rule setting.
- Create a caring, cohesive school community.

*Note.* Listed practices and related factors are discussed in text.

Hoffman (2000) reasoned that inductions are likely to promote moral development for a number of reasons, including the following:

- They induce an optimal level of arousal for learning; that is, they elicit the child's attention but are unlikely to produce high levels of arousal that are disruptive to learning.
- Inductions are unlikely to be viewed by the child as arbitrary and therefore are not apt to cause resistance.
- Inductions focus children's attention on the consequences of their behavior for others, thereby capitalizing on children's capacity to empathize and experience guilt.

Hoffman further argued that over time, inductive messages are experienced as internalized messages, that is, deriving from within the child, because the child plays an active role in processing the information embedded in the induction. This information is integrated with information contained in other inductions and becomes disassociated from the particular disciplinary event. Furthermore, the focus when socializers use inductions is on the child's action and its consequences rather than on the parent as the disciplinary agent. Consequently, over time children are likely to remember the causal link between their actions and consequences for others rather than the external pressure or the specific disciplinary context.

In contrast to inductive discipline, power-assertive discipline involves physical punishment, deprivation of privileges, or the threat of these punishments. In general, power assertion has been found to be either unrelated or negatively related to children's prosocial behavior (physical abuse has been negatively related; Eisenberg & Fabes, 1998). According to Hoffman (2000), children often may attribute prosocial behavior resulting from power assertion techniques to external motives such as fear of detection or punishment. Furthermore, power assertion may focus children's attention on punishment rather than on the consequences of their behavior and it likely results in a level of arousal detrimental to learning.

Of course, discipline involving power assertion, such as physical punishment or threats, can cause immediate compliance with the adults demands for prosocial behavior if the adult monitors the child's behavior. However, there is little evidence that physical punishment, particularly when used as a primary mode of discipline, fosters the development of internalized prosocial behavior (see Eisenberg & Fabes, 1998).

***Parents' and teachers' warmth.*** The relationship between children's prosocial behavior and the variables of parental or teachers' warmth and support is a complex one. Adult warmth by itself is not consistently related to prosocial behavior (see Eisenberg & Fabes, 1998), although sympathetic parents tend to have children who are prone to sympathy rather than to personal distress (particularly if they are of the same gender as the parent; Eisenberg et al., 1992). Moreover, there is evidence, albeit limited, that children with secure attachments at a young age are more sympathetic and prosocial as preschoolers (Eisenberg & Fabes, 1998).

In general, however, a positive parent–child relationship is associated with children's prosocial tendencies (Eisenberg & Fabes, 1998). Similarly, warm, supportive interactions with teachers have been associated with preschool children's modeling of teachers' prosocial actions (Yarrow, Scott, & Waxler, 1973) and with sympathetic, prosocial reactions to distress (Kienbaum, Volland, & Ulich, 2001). Howes, Matheson, and Hamilton (1994) found that children classified as securely attached to their current and first preschool teachers were rated as more considerate and empathic with unfamiliar peers than children who were classified as having an insecure relationship (especially ambivalent) with their teachers. Thus, a supportive relationship between young children and their teachers may be important for prosocial development.

It is likely that adults' warmth and support provide a context within which other positive socialization practices are optimally effective, such as using democratic discipline (involving both warmth and control, combined with inductions) and providing suggestions, information, and positive comments. In contrast, adults' warmth combined with a highly permissive socialization style may result in low levels of prosocial behavior.

***Modeling.*** One of the most consistent findings in the prosocial literature is that children emulate prosocial and selfish behavior that they observe, whether it is enacted by unknown adults or by parents (see Eisenberg & Fabes, 1998). This finding has occurred regularly in laboratory studies that manipulate children's exposure to models as well as in correlational studies of families. Nurturant models, including teachers, who have ongoing relationships with children may be particularly effective. For example, preschoolers who viewed lifelike prosocial behaviors enacted by adults with whom they had nurturant interactions over a period of time in the classroom (acting like teachers) were likely to exhibit prosocial behavior later (Yarrow et al., 1973; also see chapter 5, "Student–Teacher Relationships"). Although powerful and competent models are imitated more than other models, children may also imitate the prosocial actions of their peers (Owens & Ascione, 1991). Moreover, adolescents who volunteer are relatively likely to have friends who feel it is important to do well in school and to be involved in community and volunteer work (Zaff, Moore, Papillo, & Williams, 2003).

***Nondisciplinary verbalizations.*** In general, children are more likely to share with or donate to others if they hear an adult say that he or she is going to help. In addition, children tend to engage in more prosocial behavior if they are exposed to pronouncements from adults such as teachers (usually called *preachings* in the literature) that are other oriented (e.g., point out the effects of assisting another) and that focus on the positive effects of prosocial action on others' emotional states (e.g., "They would be so happy and excited if they could buy food and toys."). Typically, preachings whose content is normative, that is, they indicate that it is good or right to give, are less effective than preachings that emphasize the effects of prosocial behavior on others. Preachings also may be most effective when children feel that they have a choice about whether to provide assistance (see Eisenberg & Fabes, 1998).

***Positive reinforcement.*** Concrete rewards and social reinforcement, such as praise, often increase the rate or frequency of children's prosocial behavior in the immediate context. However, concrete rewards do not seem to enhance prosocial tendencies outside the context in which the reward is given (Eisenberg & Fabes, 1998).

The effects of praise seem to vary with the type of praise and the age of the recipient. Praise that attributes a child's positive behavior to dispositional kindness seems to be more effective than praise that simply labels the act as positive (e.g., Grusec & Redler, 1980). In this context, *dispositional kindness* refers to motives that stem from the child's stable traits or dispositions (e.g., "I guess you're the kind of person who likes to help others whenever you can. You are a very nice and helpful person."). Social reinforcement for prosocial actions, with or without a dispositional attribution, appears to be positively related to the occurrence of prosocial behavior in the immediate context among elementary school children. However, in Grusec and Redler's study, praise without a dispositional attribution was not associated with the generalization of prosocial behavior to a new situation for 5- or 8-year-olds. In contrast, 10-year-olds exposed to either dispositional praise or nondispositional praise evidenced generalization to a different prosocial behavior (one that had not been reinforced; Grusec & Redler, 1980). Grusec and Redler hypothesized that older children may interpret reinforcement for a specific action (i.e., nondispositional praise) as having implications for a variety of situations, whereas younger children do not view praise for a given act as having broader relevance.

***Assignment of prosocial activities.*** Children who are persuaded to engage in prosocial behavior (either in the home or elsewhere) without feeling forced to do so seem to be relatively more prosocial in other contexts. In addition, the assignment of chores that have positive consequences for others has been linked to prosocial proclivities in children. Thus, practice in assisting others or learning by doing seems to foster prosocial tendencies, at least in some circumstances (Eisenberg & Fabes, 1998).

Participation in organized youth activities and nonvoluntary service required by school programs also has been linked to prosocial behavior, especially subsequent volunteerism or intentions to volunteer (Metz & Youniss, 2003). For example, Youniss and Metz (2004) found that required school-based service was related to increased volunteerism and intentions to volunteer for students who were less inclined to participate (and had little effect for those students who quickly completed their requirement and went on to participate in voluntary activities).

***Parental emphasis on prosocial values.*** As might be expected, parents who hold and try to teach prosocial values to their children tend to have children who are relatively kind and helpful (Eisenberg & Fabes, 1998). One of the more dramatic pieces of evidence for this assertion comes from a study of people who have exhibited unusual tendencies toward altruism, such as rescuers in Nazi Europe. These individuals assisted potential victims of concentration camps, often at the risk of losing their own lives. Many rescuers recalled learning values of caring from parents or from another person influential in their development. Rescuers also reported that their parents felt that ethical values were universal, that is, were to be extended to all human beings. However, rescuers did not differ from nonrescuers in reported exposure to nonprosocial values such as honesty or equity, only to prosocially relevant values (Oliner & Oliner, 1988).

***Emotion-related practices.*** Frequency and valence of emotion expressed in the family seem to play a role in children's prosocial behavior, albeit in a complex manner. In regard to positive emotion, relationships of these factors to prosocial behavior, when obtained, generally are positive. Conversely, children exposed to high levels of negative emotion in the home tend to be prone to personal distress rather than sympathy and tend to exhibit relatively low levels of prosocial behavior outside the home (although they may try to help parents or siblings during parental conflicts; see Eisenberg & Fabes, 1998; Eisenberg et al., 1992).

Parental practices that help children cope with their own negative emotions appear to foster sympathy and prosocial behavior rather than egoistic personal distress. This may occur because children who fail to adequately cope with their emotions tend to become overly aroused and, consequently, when confronted with another's distress experience a self-focused aversive response (i.e., personal distress) rather than sympathy. For example, investigators have found that parental emphasis on controlling one's own self-focused negative emotion (e.g., sadness or anxiety) is related to levels of personal distress among boys who are confronted with an empathy-inducing stimulus. In contrast, parental focus on instrumentally dealing with the cause of the negative emotion has been associated with boys' sympathy. Parents' willingness to discuss emotion with their children is related to children's empathy and prosocial behavior; however, such discussions likely foster sympathy and prosocial behavior primarily when the parents explain emotions and do not allow their children to become overaroused emotionally (see Eisenberg & Fabes, 1998).

## Promotion of Prosocial Behavior in Schools: The Child Development Project

Given the potential impact of educational institutions, it is surprising that the knowledge base regarding the effects of the school experience on children's prosocial behavior is not extensive. One finding from this limited body of research literature is that a relationship exists between quality of out-of-home care in the early years (e.g., preschool or day care) and children's prosocial development. Although differences between children in home care and those in group care may be small, the quality of the caregiving situation likely moderates the degree and type of influence preschools have on children's prosocial behavior and attitudes. For example, the quality of the day care or preschool environment has been associated with children's empathy and social competence (Vandell, Henderson, & Wilson, 1988) and considerateness (Phillips, McCartney, & Scarr, 1987). Another finding from descriptive studies is that naturally occurring prosocial behaviors are not very frequent in the classroom and that teachers, although presumed to value prosocial behaviors, usually do not actively reward instances of such behaviors (see Eisenberg & Fabes, 1998).

Among the best-known school-based programs designed to promote prosocial behavior is the Child Development Project (conducted primarily in the 1980s; see Battistich, Watson, Solomon, Schaps, & Solomon, 1991; Solomon, Watson, Delucchi, Schaps, & Battistich, 1988). This longitudinal program, which was first implemented in three schools and across five consecutive years of enrollment (kindergarten through fourth grade), included some school-wide elements and parental involvement, but the primary component of the prevention program focused on teacher education. Teachers were trained in procedures for creating classrooms conducive to the development of prosocial behavior and reasoning, then were assisted in implementing these procedures. Treatment integrity was monitored on an ongoing basis. Teachers learned techniques for expressing affection and approval, for interacting informally with children through games and other activities, and for discussing personal opinions and experiences. Moreover, teachers were trained to use a child-centered, developmental approach to classroom management that emphasized inductive discipline. For example, in the scenario discussed earlier, when Sally took the toy from Eric the teacher might have directed Sally's attention to Eric's affective response and to how Sally might have felt if the situation had been reversed.

The project also emphasized student participation in rule setting and self-control and on student commitment to agreed-upon rules and shared values. In another important program element, students participated in cooperative, interdependent activities in which they worked together toward common goals and learned to negotiate, state their positions, and compromise. Other aspects of the program that played less prominent roles included promoting social understanding, highlighting prosocial values, and providing helping activities (Battistich et al., 1991). The project attached considerable importance to discussing the classroom's naturally occurring events. A generous act or a classroom conflict often became a springboard for a discussion of the need to consider others' perspectives, needs, and feelings.

Researchers found that students in the project classrooms, compared with control classes, obtained higher ratings for spontaneous prosocial behavior across all five grades (although the difference was marginally significant during first grade and nonsignificant during fourth grade). These patterns were maintained when both teachers' general competence and students' participation in cooperative activities were controlled, suggesting that program effects on children's prosocial behavior were not simply the result of differences in teacher-initiated cooperative interactions or in more efficiently organized and managed classrooms.

This pattern of findings was replicated in a second cohort that consisted of kindergarten and first-grade classrooms. Moreover, there was evidence that supportive and friendly behavior at school increased, particularly in the first cohort (Solomon et al., 1988). Children enrolled in the project (but not children in the control group) evidenced the highest ratings for prosocial behavior and harmony in kindergarten. Thus, it appears that the effect of this program was greatest when it was first introduced. The degree to which program effects generalized beyond the immediate classroom environment was unclear (Battistich et al., 1991). Participation in the program did not affect children's academic performance or their observed negative interpersonal behavior.

The Child Development Project findings are particularly impressive because teachers in the first cohort had only 1 year of experience in implementing program components. Giving teachers additional time to refine their technique and fully integrate the program components into the routine of the classroom might be expected to result in even stronger effects. However, one caveat of the findings is that the program was initially implemented in schools that consisted of mostly white, middle-to-upper-class students who were, for the most part, academically and socially competent.

Solomon, Battistich, and Watson (1993) also examined the Child Development Project's effects on children's prosocial moral reasoning and conflict resolution skills. All students in one group participated in the program from kindergarten until at least fourth grade, with some taking part through sixth grade. Monitoring of effects continued through eighth grade. In kindergarten, comparison students earned higher prosocial moral reasoning scores than did program children, but the program group subsequently obtained higher scores. Program students also received higher scores on conflict resolution (indicating consideration of others' needs and a reliance on the use of compromise and sharing) than did comparison students at each grade level, and program students scored significantly higher at fourth- and eighth-grade levels.

These results provide some evidence that the program can have prolonged effects. It should be noted that the outcomes of the program were greater when data were aggregated across years; findings were not consistently significant within years. Moreover, because of the relatively small sample size in the later grades and the high attrition rate, any conclusions must be viewed cautiously.

More recently, the Child Development Project was implemented in six school districts over a 3-year period, with two additional schools in each district serving as a control group (Battistich, Schaps, Watson, Solomon, & Lewis, 2000; Solomon, Battistich, Watson, Schaps, & Lewis, 2000). This sample included schools that varied considerably in socioeconomic status and proportion of minority students. For those schools that made significant progress in implementing the program, students showed positive gains in personal, social, and ethical values, attitudes, and motives, and showed a reduction of substance abuse and other problem behaviors.

The concept of the school as community has become central to these researchers' understanding of the efficacy of their program. In general, prosocial behavior and reasoning appear to be fostered in schools and classrooms in which a sense of a caring community exists. The caring school community is one in which members support and care about one another; participate in and influence group decisions; share values, goals, and norms; and feel a sense of belonging (Battistich, Solomon, Kim, Watson, & Schaps, 1995).

Some school-based attempts to promote prosocial tendencies have extended the scope of the intervention to include animals as beneficiaries. For example, Ascione (1992) examined the effects of a humane education program involving first through fifth graders who engaged in about 40 hours of activities across the school year. Younger children showed relatively little immediate effect on humane attitudes, but an effect was noted a year later (Ascione & Weber, 1993). In an immediate posttest analysis, humane attitudes were enhanced for fourth graders; in a 1-year follow-up, humane attitudes were enhanced among fourth and fifth graders. The most notable finding, perhaps, was that human-directed empathy also increased for both fourth and fifth graders on both the initial test and the 1-year follow-up.

## ALTERNATIVE ACTIONS FOR INTERVENTIONS

Studies of interventions for specific children lacking prosocial behavior are few and usually involve very few subjects. Typically they were designed to promote preschoolers' prosocial behavior through a variety of techniques, such as modeling and reinforcement. Moreover, most formal attempts to intervene with children low in prosocial behavior in schools have involved relatively weak, short-term interventions. Evaluation of programs also has been difficult in some cases because control groups have been exposed to some aspects of the intervention. Treatment integrity has suffered in some instances when teachers have improvised rather than adhered to the planned curriculum. Thus, relatively little is known about enhancing prosocial tendencies in children who are especially deficient in these behaviors (see Eisenberg & Fabes, 1998, for some relevant references).

## SUMMARY

Although prosocial development in children is likely partly the result of factors other than socialization, it appears that adults can foster prosocial tendencies by using a variety of socialization practices. These practices are listed in Table 1. Although many people and factors clearly play a role in the development of prosocial actions, motives, and reasoning, schools, teachers, and parents can also play a role in enhancing prosocial development.

A constellation of practices, beliefs, and characteristics, combined with the emotional atmosphere of a child's home, seems to have an effect on the child's prosocial development. Parents are most likely to rear prosocial children if they are supportive; use inductive discipline; provide opportunities for prosocial activity; model, value, and preach other-oriented behavior; uphold high standards for their children; and encourage the development of sympathy and perspective taking. Moreover, practices that help children manage their own negative emotions, along with an emotionally positive home environment, seem to be related to the development of prosocial and sympathetic responding.

Prevention studies have shown that teachers likely can use the same practices to promote prosocial tendencies, although research with teachers is quite limited. It is likely that the child's characteristics, such as temperament, compliance, and other aspects of personality, interact with parents' and teachers' characteristics and beliefs in determining the quality of the adult–child relationship and adults' socialization efforts. To date, however, researchers studying correlates of prosocial responding have given relatively little consideration to the role of the child's characteristics in the socialization process (see Eisenberg & Fabes, 1998). Furthermore, most of the research has involved middle-class children and mothers or unknown experimenters, so the generalizability of the work to other populations and to real-life socializers besides mothers is not known. Fortunately, however, the results of research conducted in schools generally are consistent with findings from studies of socialization effects in the family.

Prosocial behavior and reasoning are doubtlessly valued by most educators although not frequently reinforced in typical classrooms. Quality early schooling and supportive relationships between children and their teachers have been associated with the development of prosocial behavior. Moreover, school-based programs designed to enhance prosocial values, behaviors, and attitudes in children can be effective in enhancing children's prosocial proclivities with respect to both humans and animals. Prosociality can be enhanced in classrooms in which teachers communicate well and share governance with students, use inductive discipline, focus on feelings, and structure cooperative learning activities. These conditions are associated with the perception of the school as a caring community.

## RECOMMENDED RESOURCES

Eisenberg, N. (1992). *The caring child.* Cambridge, MA: Harvard University Press.

Written for a general audience, this book is part of the Harvard University Press series on the developing child. It provides an account of the motives underlying prosocial behavior and the evolution of these motives. Biological bases, cultural influences, and socialization are discussed, as is the role played by situational factors.

Eisenberg, N., & Fabes, R. A. (1998). Prosocial development. In W. Damon (Series Ed.) & N. Eisenberg (Vol. Ed.), *Handbook of child psychology: Vol. 3. Social and personality development* (5th ed.). New York: Wiley.

This chapter presents perhaps the most extensive and up-to-date summary of major research findings and theory regarding prosocial behavior and reasoning. The reference list includes mostly studies in this area published in English prior to 1996. A version of the chapter in the sixth edition of the handbook is scheduled for publication in 2006 or 2007.

Both of the following references describe the Child Development Project and present results following several years of the project's implementation. These papers explain program methodology and present effects on classroom behavior for two cohorts of students.

Battistich, V., Watson, M., Solomon, D., Schaps, E., & Solomon, J. (1991). The Child Development Project: A comprehensive program for the development of prosocial character. In W. M. Kurtines & J. L. Gerwirtz (Eds.), *Handbook of moral behavior and development: Vol. 3. Application* (pp. 1–34). New York: Erlbaum.

Solomon, D., Battistich, V., Watson, M., Schaps, E., & Lewis, C. (2000). A six-district study of educational changes: Direct and mediated effects of the Child Development Project. *Social Psychology of Education, 4,* 3–51.

## REFERENCES

Ascione, F. R. (1992). Enhancing children's attitudes about the humane treatment of animals: Generalization to human-directed empathy. *Antrozoos, 5,* 176–191.

Ascione, F. R., & Weber, C. V. (1993, March). *Children's attitudes about the humane treatment of animals and empathy: One-year follow-up of a school-based intervention.* Paper presented at the biennial meeting of the Society for Research in Child Development, New Orleans, LA.

Bar-Tal, D. (1982). Sequential development of helping behavior: A cognitive-learning approach. *Developmental Review, 2,* 101–124.

Battistich, V., Schaps, E., Watson, M., Solomon, D., & Lewis, C. (2000). Effects of the Child Development Project on students' drug use and other problem behaviors. *The Journal of Primary Prevention, 21,* 75–99.

Battistich, V., Solomon, D., Kim, D-I., Watson, M., & Schaps, E. (1995). Schools as communities, poverty levels of student populations, and students' attitudes, motives, and performance: A multilevel analysis. *American Educational Research Journal, 32,* 627–658.

Battistich, V., Watson, M., Solomon, D., Schaps, E., & Solomon, J. (1991). The Child Development Project: A comprehensive program for the development of prosocial character. In W. M. Kurtines & J. L. Gerwirtz (Eds.), *Handbook of moral behavior and development: Vol. 3. Application* (pp. 1–34). New York: Erlbaum.

Caprara, G. V., Barbaranelli, C., Pastorelli, C., Bandura, A., & Zimbardo, P. G. (2000). Prosocial foundations of children's academic achievement. *Psychological Science, 11,* 302–306.

Dlugokinski, E. L., & Firestone, I. J. (1974). Other centeredness and susceptibility to charitable appeals: Effects of perceived discipline. *Developmental Psychology, 10,* 21–28.

Eisenberg, N. (1986). *Altruistic emotion, cognition, and behavior.* Hillsdale, NJ: Erlbaum.

Eisenberg, N., & Fabes, R. A. (1998). Prosocial development. In W. Damon (Series Ed.) & N. Eisenberg (Vol. Ed.), *Handbook of child psychology: Vol. 3. Social, emotional, and personality development* (5th ed., pp. 701–778). New York: Wiley.

Eisenberg, N., Fabes, R. A., Carlo, G., Troyer, D., Speer, A. L., Karbon, M., & Switzer, G. (1992). The relations of maternal practices and characteristics to children's vicarious emotional responsiveness. *Child Development, 63,* 583–602.

Eisenberg, N., Fabes, R. A., & Spinrad, T. L. (in press). Prosocial development. In W. Damon & R. M. Lerner (Series Eds.) & N. Eisenberg (Vol. Ed.), *Handbook of child psychology: Vol. 3. Social, emotional, and personality development* (6th ed.). New York: Wiley.

Eisenberg, N., Guthrie, I. K., Murphy, B. C., Shepard, S. A., Cumberland, A., & Carlo, G. (1999). Consistency and development of prosocial dispositions: A longitudinal study. *Child Development, 70,* 1360–1372.

Grusec, J. E., & Redler, E. (1980). Attribution, reinforcement, and altruism: A developmental analysis. *Developmental Psychology, 16,* 525–534.

Hay, D. F., Nash, A., & Pedersen, J. (1981). Responses of six-month-olds to the distress of their peers. *Child Development, 52,* 1071–1075.

Hoffman, M. L. (1963). Parent discipline and the child's consideration for others. *Child Development, 34,* 573–588.

Hoffman, M. L. (2000). *Empathy and moral development: Implications for caring and justice.* New York: Cambridge University Press.

Howes, C., & Farver, J. (1987). Toddlers' responses to the distress of their peers. *Journal of Applied Developmental Psychology, 8,* 441–452.

Howes, C., Matheson, C. C., & Hamilton, C. E. (1994). Maternal, teacher, and child care history correlates of children's relationships with peers. *Child Development, 65,* 264–273.

Johnson, H. R., Thompson, M. J. J., Wilkinson, S., Walsh, L., Balding, J., & Wright, V. (2002). Vulnerability to bullying: Teacher-reported conduct and emotional problems, hyperactivity, peer relationship difficulties, and prosocial behaviour in primary school children. *Educational Psychology, 22,* 553–556.

Kienbaum, J., Volland, C., & Ulich, D. (2001). Sympathy in the context of mother-child and teacher-child relationships. *International Journal of Behavioral Development, 25,* 302–309.

Lindeman, M., Harakka, T., & Keltikangas-Jarvinen, L. (1997). Age and gender differences in adolescents' reactions to conflict situations: Aggression, prosociality, and withdrawal. *Journal of Youth and Adolescence, 26,* 339–351.

Metz, E., McLellan, J., & Youniss, J. (2003). Types of voluntary service and adolescents' civic development. *Journal of Adolescent Research, 18,* 188–203.

Metz, E., & Youniss, J. (2003). PSOnline (http://www.apsanet.org), April, 281–286.

Oliner, S. P., & Oliner, P. M. (1988). *The altruistic personality: Rescuers of Jews in Nazi Europe.* New York: Free Press.

Owens, C. R., & Ascione, F. R. (1991). Effects of the model's age, perceived similarity, and familiarity on children's donating. *Journal of Genetic Psychology, 152,* 341–357.

Phillips, D., McCartney, K., & Scarr, S. (1987). Child-care quality and children's social development. *Developmental Psychology, 23,* 537–543.

Radke-Yarrow, M., & Zahn-Waxler, C. (1984). Roots, motives, and patterns in children's prosocial behavior. In E. Staub, D. Bar-Tal, J. Karylowski, & J. Reykowski (Eds.), *Development and maintenance of prosocial behavior: International perspectives on positive behavior* (pp. 81–99). New York: Plenum Press.

Solomon, D., Battistich, V., & Watson, M. (1993, March). *A longitudinal investigation of the effects of a school intervention program on children's social development.* Paper presented at the biennial meeting of the Society for Research in Child Development, New Orleans, LA.

Solomon, D., Battistich, V., Watson, M., Schaps, E., & Lewis, C. (2000). A six-district study of educational changes: Direct and mediated effects of the Child Development Project. *Social Psychology of Education, 4,* 3–51.

Solomon, D., Watson, M. S., Delucchi, K. L., Schaps, E., & Battistich, V. (1988). Enhancing children's prosocial behavior in the classroom. *American Educational Research Journal, 25,* 527–554.

Vandell, D. L., Henderson, V. K., & Wilson, K. S. (1988). A longitudinal study of children with daycare experiences of varying quality. *Child Development, 59,* 1286–1292.

Warden, D., & Mackinnon, S. (2003). Prosocial bullies, bullies, and victims: An investigation of their sociometric status, empathy, and social problem-solving strategies. *British Journal of Developmental Psychology, 21,* 367–385.

Yarrow, M. R., Scott, P. M., & Waxler, C. Z. (1973). Learning concerning for others. *Developmental Psychology, 8,* 240–260.

Youniss, J. (1980). *Parents and peers in social development: A Sullivan-Piaget perspective.* Chicago: University of Chicago Press.

Youniss, J., & Metz, E. (2004). Longitudinal gains in civic development through school-based required service. Manuscript submitted for editorial review. Catholic University, Washington, DC.

Zaff, J. F., Moore, K. A., Papillo, A. R., & Williams, S. (2003). Implications of extracurricular activity participation during adolescence on positive outcomes. *Journal of Adolescent Research, 18,* 599–630.

Zahn-Waxler, C., Schiro, K., Robinson, J. L., Emde, R. N., & Schmitz, S. (2001). Empathy and prosocial patterns in young MZ and DZ twins: Development and genetic and environmental influences. In R. N. Emde & J. K. Hewitt (Eds.), *Infancy to early childhood* (pp. 141–162). New York: Oxford University Press.

# 25

# Peer Relationships

**Gregory A. Waas**

*Northern Illinois University*

## BACKGROUND AND DEVELOPMENT

Since the earliest research on sociometry, in the 1930s, the importance of children's peer relationships has been well established. A cursory review of this scholarship reveals a burgeoning professional literature exploring a wide array of topics that involve the development of peer relationships and the effect such relationships have on children's social, emotional, and cognitive development. However, given the large number of important influences in a child's life, including parents, teachers, siblings, and even mass media, it is appropriate to ask: Why this focus on children's peer relationships?

Discussing the developmental significance of children's friendships, Willard Hartup (1992) provided a compelling theoretical argument for such emphasis. According to Hartup, children's friendships are important for four reasons. First, at the most basic level, they provide a *social context* in which various key social skills are acquired and elaborated. It is during such social interactions that children experiment with and refine a wide array of social skills related to communication, cooperation, conflict resolution, emotion regulation, and group entry. Friendships also serve as a critical *information source* to children. Through observation of how peers navigate their social worlds, children learn how others cope, both successfully and unsuccessfully, with such issues as social problems, upsetting emotions, and friendship building. Moreover, through such observations children gain greater understanding of how their own skills and characteristics compare with others.

Hartup (1992) also proposed that friendships serve as both *emotional and cognitive resources* for children. When confronted with a social problem or negative social experience, a child's peer group provides emotional support, such as sympathy and companionship, to help ameliorate the upsetting consequences of these events. Peers also may provide more direct, instrumental support as well, such as offering direct suggestions and other forms of problem-solving assistance. Finally, early friendship relationships may serve as *forerunners* of future social relationships. Hartup argued that many of the skills that are learned during early peer relationships (e.g., the ability to listen, share feelings, negotiate conflict, and understand the perspectives of others) are central features of adult intimate relationships, and failure to attain mastery of these skills places a child at risk for both concurrent and future difficulties with peer relationships.

The importance of children establishing and maintaining positive peer relationships is appreciated by both scientists and practitioners and has generated extensive research on numerous topics relating to the development, characteristics, and consequences of the peer relationships that children form. Although a comprehensive review of this literature is beyond the scope of this chapter (see Kupersmidt & Dodge, 2004; Gifford-Smith & Brownell, 2003, for more extensive reviews), two aspects of children's peer relationships are examined more closely: dyadic friendships and peer group status. Finally, this chapter examines those children who have difficulty establishing positive peer relationships and discusses alternative intervention approaches. Throughout this review, the emphasis is on children's peer relationships during the elementary school years.

### Friendships

In the research literature on children's friendships, a variety of definitions have been used to identify friendship pairs, and the specific definition used may have implications for the characteristics and consequences of friendship relationships (e.g., Newcomb & Bagwell, 1995).

The use of peer nominations has been the most common method of identifying children's friendships. *Mutual* or *reciprocal* friendships involve both members of a friendship dyad nominating the other member as a "best" or "close" friend, whereas *unilateral* friendships are defined as only one member of the dyad identifying the other as a best friend. Both of these friendship types can be differentiated from acquaintances, strangers, and disliked peers.

A number of methodological limitations are associated with such nomination procedures (Gifford-Smith & Brownell, 2003). First, children may use idiosyncratic definitions of *friend* (e.g., nominating a peer with whom they would *like* to be friends). Second, nomination procedures require children to dichotomize friendship (i.e., friend vs. nonfriend) when, in fact, friendships may more accurately be described on a continuum (e.g., casual to intense). And third, the nomination procedures provide no information about the quality of the friendship relationship being identified. Other approaches to the identification of children's friendships include direct observations of children's peer interactions (e.g., proximity, frequency, stability, or affective quality), as well as parent and teacher nominations.

In a meta-analytic review of research on children's friendships, Newcomb and Bagwell (1995) reported a number of important characteristics that differentiate friend and nonfriend relationships. For example, reciprocal friends shared a greater sense of equality, closeness, and loyalty; engaged in higher levels of cooperation and positive affect; and were more productive in completing tasks than were mere acquaintances. Although friends were found to be just as likely to experience disagreements and other forms of conflict as acquaintances, they were more likely to achieve successful resolution when conflicts did arise.

Close friendships have been shown to influence children's and adolescents' attitudes, behavior, and adjustment, with a tendency for friends to share similar characteristics and interests (Berndt & Murphy, 2002). The precise nature of friendship influences, however, is less well understood and is complicated by measurement and methodological issues. For example, Berndt and Murphy noted that both positive and negative influences of friends are likely to depend on the characteristics of the friend and on the quality of the friendship relationship. Moreover, the strength and direction of these influences may vary for different attitudes and behaviors. For example, one mechanism by which friends may influence each other is through the process of magnification (Berndt & Murphy, 2002). According to this hypothesis, children may tend to select friends with whom they already share attitudes, interests, and other characteristics. Within such relationships, friends tend to influence each other toward greater similarity through a system of reinforcement, modeling, information giving, and persuasion.

Our understanding of children's friendships is complicated further by the fact that the characteristics and functions of friendship change with age. The friendships of preschool children, for example, are most typically marked by positive and coordinated play between dyads and among small groups. During the elementary years, friendships among children are increasingly based on shared personal qualities and activities. As children move into adolescence, friendships involve greater intimacy and personal commitment (Parker & Gottman, 1989). Gender differences in the characteristics of childhood friendships have also been noted (Underwood, 2004). Girls are more likely to emphasize dyadic friendships, whereas boys form relationships both in dyads and with the larger peer group. Girls' reciprocal friendships tend to be characterized by higher levels of intimacy, self-disclosure, validation, help-giving, and successful conflict resolution than boys' friendships. Boys, however, tend to engage in greater levels of mutual participation in activities (Underwood, 2004). These developmental and gender differences underscore the complexity of research on children's friendships. Gifford-Smith and Brownell (2003) highlight many of these complexities and note that researchers' understanding of friendship types, functions, and characteristics remains quite limited. It will be important for future research to continue the examination of this important social relationship in children's development.

## Peer Group Status

Whereas children's friendships involve the close relationship between two individuals or among a small group of children, a child's peer group or social status refers to perceptions of the child by his or her entire peer group. An enormous body of research has accumulated regarding the behavioral, cognitive, emotional, and social factors related to children's peer group status. Researchers have also documented the developmental outcomes associated with peer group status and possible early life experiences that may contribute to such status in later life. Although a comprehensive review of these topics is beyond the scope of this chapter (see Gifford-Smith & Brownell,

2003, and Kupersmidt & Dodge, 2004, for a more extensive discussion), a brief review of identification procedures is provided, followed by a discussion of commonly identified subgroups of children and a review of intervention approaches for children who experience negative peer relationships.

Several methods are available for assessing a child's social behavior, including self, teacher, parent, and peer ratings and a variety of analogue and direct observation techniques (Bierman, 2004). However, to estimate a child's peer group status, the most common approach involves the completion of a sociometric measure. The two most frequently used sociometric procedures for identifying children's social status are peer ratings and peer nominations. For peer ratings, each child in a class or grade rates how much he or she likes to be friends with or play or work with every other same-sex peer. Such a unidimensional rating procedure provides an index of general social acceptance among a child's peers. Peer nominations involve children identifying a specified number of children (e.g., two to three peers, depending on group size) they most like to work or play with and the same number of children they least like. Using this approach results in a frequency index of the child's positive and negative peer relationships. Children's scores on sociometric measures often are standardized within classroom or grade level and gender.

One of the advantages of using the nomination type of sociometric measure is the ease with which four extreme subgroups of children can be identified. Popular children are those individuals receiving a high number of positive nominations (e.g., 1 standard deviation above the group mean; above chance level) and a low number of negative nominations (e.g., 1 standard deviation below the mean; below chance level). Conversely, rejected children are those who receive many negative nominations from peers and few positive nominations. Controversial children are defined as those students who are frequently nominated both as best and least liked, and neglected children are those individuals who receive very few nominations on either dimension. Researchers have also used this method to examine children's level of social preference (i.e., positive nominations minus negative nominations) and overall social impact (i.e., positive nominations plus negative nominations).

Rating procedures have the advantage of involving all peers in rating each child in the classroom group, thus increasing the reliability of derived scores and providing more detailed information about a child's general level of social acceptance (e.g., Gifford-Smith & Brownell, 2003). Moreover, some teachers and parents prefer the rating approach because it avoids having children make negative nominations of classmates. Although this approach does not lend itself as easily to the identification of extreme groupings, researchers have suggested strategies for accomplishing such classification (Bierman, 2004).

Extensive research has been conducted that uses each of these sociometric procedures and, although important differences exist, they have been shown to produce reasonably consistent findings (e.g., Gifford-Smith & Brownell, 2003). Teachers, also, can be a useful source of information about children's social status. Comparison studies of teacher and student perceptions indicate that, when peer evaluations are not available, teacher ratings or nominations may provide a viable alternative for estimating a child's peer group status. For example, French and Waas (1985) reported that, although teachers' ratings resulted in a significant number of both false negative and false positive identifications of rejected students when compared with peer nominations, teachers were generally successful in identifying those children experiencing the most severe peer rejection.

Using such sociometric procedures, researchers have long been able to identify popular children, as well as those who are well liked, prosocial toward peers, outgoing, and socially skilled. More recent research, however, has begun to distinguish between popularity as it relates to social preference (e.g., positive nominations) and popularity as a function of social visibility. Children in this latter group, who are *perceived* as popular by peers, may be characterized by a very different behavioral profile than children with high levels of social preference. For example, some research indicates that children who have high visibility scores only may be characterized by higher levels of arrogance, dominance, and physical and relational aggression (e.g., Parkhurst & Hopmeyer, 1998). Neglected children are typically defined as those individuals with low social impact. Although often viewed by peers as somewhat withdrawn, these children have been shown to be similar to their average-status peers in behavioral characteristics and do not appear to be at increased risk for negative adjustment outcomes (e.g., Gifford-Smith & Brownell, 2003). Controversial children exhibit the opposite sociometric profile from neglected students and receive high social impact scores. In some respects, these individuals resemble the popular sociometric group in that they are often quite active socially and are frequently viewed as leaders by peers.

However, these children may also be viewed as aggressive, arrogant, and snobbish.

Peer-rejected children exhibit a sociometric profile that is the reverse of popular children in that they tend to receive few positive nominations and are likely to be nominated frequently by peers as least liked. On peer ratings, rejected children are those children who receive the lowest average rating scores in the class. These procedures typically identify 13% to 16% of children as peer rejected. However, although the use of rating and nomination sociometric procedures provides important screening information about a child's general level of peer acceptance, such procedures provide very little information about the specific behaviors and characteristics of a child that are causal contributors to his or her peer difficulties. Peer rejection, therefore, can be viewed as an important indicator variable alerting the teacher, school psychologist, social worker, or others to a child's possible adjustment difficulties and triggering more intensive investigation into the nature of those difficulties.

# PROBLEMS AND IMPLICATIONS

## Friendship

Only relatively recently have researchers focused on the characteristics of children's friendships and the role that such relationships play in their social, emotional, and behavioral adjustment. Hartup (1996) suggested that understanding the effects of such relationships on a child's or adolescent's development required that three aspects of friendship be considered: whether the child has friends, the quality of the friendship, and the identity and characteristics of the friend or friends. A growing body of research indicates that each of these factors plus the interaction of these factors play an important role in children's adjustment. Parker and Asher (1993), for example, reported that over 77% of third- through fifth-grade children had at least one reciprocal friendship, and the absence of a friend was associated with higher levels of self-reported loneliness. Vandell and Hembree (1994) reported that reciprocal friendship status was related to third-grade children's self-concept, academic adjustment, and teacher-reported social–emotional adjustment.

In addition to the presence of a friendship, the quality of the friendship also appears to be an important factor in predicting loneliness. Parker and Asher (1993) found that children with higher quality friendships were less lonely than children with low quality friendships. They speculated that the presence of a positive, reciprocated friendship may provide children with important emotional and social support that serve as buffers against the experience of loneliness. Moreover, the link between the absence of reciprocal friendships and loneliness was found to be robust even after controlling for children's overall peer social status.

Berndt and Murphy (2002) have suggested that friend identity and friendship quality may interact to affect children's behavior and adjustment. In an interesting demonstration of this interaction, Bagwell and Coie (2004) reported that when fourth- and fifth-grade boys were given the opportunity to engage in rule-breaking behavior during a contrived game situation, aggressive boys and their friends were more likely to entice one another to engage in rule breaking than did nonaggressive dyads. These findings suggest that among aggressive children, friendships can be a source of reinforcement for increased deviant behavior. As part of the longitudinal Oregon Youth Study, Dishion, Poulin, and Burraston (2001) videotaped interactions between antisocial adolescent boys and documented what they referred to as "deviancy training" between friends. Deviancy training involved positive affective reactions to statements about rule breaking. Moreover, Dishion et al. reported that deviancy training scores were associated with substance abuse, delinquency, and violent behavior in adolescence.

## Peer Rejection

In comparison to the growing but still relatively small body of research examining the characteristics and effects of children's friendships, a very large body of evidence has accumulated about the difficulties confronted by children experiencing peer rejection. At the most basic level, peer-rejected children are most often identified by their ineffectiveness in dealing with peers. Rejected children often exhibit a wide variety of socially inappropriate behavior that militates against their inclusion in peer activities and the development of positive friendships. For example, when attempting to join an ongoing group activity, such as a game, peer-rejected children tend to use high-risk and unsuccessful strategies such as attention-seeking and disruptive behaviors (e.g., Putallaz & Wasserman, 1989). These behaviors often lead to disruption of the group activity, negative responses by peers, and further ostracism of the rejected child. In contrast to the use of such unsuccessful strategies, peer-accepted children tend to engage in a variety of socially appropriate strategies to gain entry. They are likely to use group-oriented statements and engage in behaviors that are consistent with the group activity. They are also sensitive to the importance of timing when making requests for group entry so as not to interrupt the ongoing flow of the activity. This is just one example of how rejected children may be ineffective in their social interactive strategies: The rejected child's maladaptive behavior may reflect an array of deficits that involve behavioral, social–cognitive, and emotional factors.

By far the most frequently cited characteristic of peer-rejected children is aggression (see chapter 9, "Anger and Aggression") and other externalizing characteristics such as explosiveness, impulsivity, immaturity, attention seeking, hyperactivity, and disruptiveness (e.g., Newcomb, Bukowski, & Pattee, 1993). It is estimated that 40% to 50% of the rejected group exhibit an externalizing–aggressive behavior pattern. However, rejected children are also often viewed by peers as being oversensitive, sad, and socially isolated. Indeed, peer-rejected children often report greater loneliness and higher levels of stress than others (Crick & Ladd, 1993).

Given these behavioral difficulties, it is not surprising that the friendships that peer-rejected children develop tend to be marked by lower quality than the friendships of other children. They are less likely to have reciprocal friendships, and the friendships they do have tend to be marked by less successful conflict resolution and lower levels of validation, caring, and help giving (Parker & Asher, 1993). Rejected children's perceptions of their friendships are often inconsistent with their friends' perceptions of the relationship. Brendgen, Little, and Krappmann (2000) reported that rejected children's friends viewed the quality of their friendship less positively than did the rejected children themselves. Moreover, the tendency of peer-rejected children to form friendships with other children who also exhibit peer-relationship difficulties may increase the likelihood that they will negatively influence each other and perpetuate the pattern of maladaptive behavior that led to social ostracism in the first place (Bagwell, 2004).

In addition to behavioral problems, peer-rejected children tend to have difficulties in the social–cognitive domain as well. When evaluating social situations, they tend to underuse relevant interpersonal information, and they are more likely to attribute hostile intent to others during interpersonal encounters (e.g., Dozier, 1988). They also view aggressive behavior in a more favorable light as a strategy to use during conflict, and they are more interested in the instrumental outcomes of social interactions than relational outcomes. For example, whereas most children view the goals of a game as winning and having fun, rejected children are more likely to focus exclusively on winning, regardless of the negative impact this may have on their relationship with playmates. These children also tend to be more emotionally reactive than others. They are more quickly aroused to intense anger and have more difficulty controlling their anger once aroused. These difficulties are likely related to both their lack of understanding of emotions and their inability to regulate their emotional experiences (Hubbard & Dearing, 2004).

Given the multitude of social, behavioral, emotional, and cognitive difficulties confronted by peer-rejected children, it is not surprising that they exhibit more negative long-term outcomes than nonrejected children. Indeed, peer-rejected children are more likely to experience difficulties later in life, such as poor academic performance (e.g., later grade retention, absenteeism, truancy, and lower success in later grades), increased risk of psychopathology during adolescence and adulthood, higher levels of delinquency and criminality, and depression (e.g., McDougall, Hymel, Vailancourt, & Mercer, 2001).

The specific links between peer rejection during childhood and adjustment difficulties later in life remain unclear. It is likely, however, that peer rejection serves as both an indicator of concurrent deficits and a possible contributor to an individual's future difficulties. Albee (1984) has argued that the experience of poor peer relationships during childhood contributes to future difficulties in four important ways: (a) difficult peer relationships act as an ongoing stressor, (b) socially ostracized children have fewer social resources with which to deal with life stressors, (c) such children are less likely to develop adequate social competence, and (d) the chronic experience of negative peer relations will likely lead to lower self-esteem. It will be important for future research to more clearly delineate the specific mechanisms by which peer rejection predicts future adjustment problems.

## Subgroups of Peer-Rejected Children and Gender Differences

Of course, not every peer-rejected child exhibits each of the characteristics noted above. Emerging research suggests that subgroups likely exist within the rejected population, and gender differences may as well.

Rejected-aggressive children, who exhibit inappropriate aggressive, coercive, and other externalizing behaviors, likely constitute the largest subgroup of the peer-rejected population. However, rejected-nonaggressive children, who often exhibit excessive social withdrawal and anxiety, have also emerged as an important subgroup of peer-rejected children (Bierman, 2004). Other characteristics, as well, such as low achievement, disabilities, and Attention Deficit Hyperactivity Disorder, may also form subgroups of peer-rejected children.

To date, the majority of studies examining peer rejection have focused on boys, but among those studies that included peer-rejected girls, many of the same characteristics have been found across genders. Nevertheless, emerging research including girls has documented some gender differences in the characteristics of peer-rejected children and in the types of behaviors likely to result in peer rejection (Underwood, 2004). For example, a large body of recent research suggests that, although girls are less likely than boys to engage in physical and verbal aggression, they may be more likely to engage in various forms of relational aggression, such as gossip and social exclusion. Gender differences may also exist in the way in which the peer group evaluates the behaviors of a child. For example, the use of gender nonnormative behaviors, such as physical aggression among girls, may place children at increased risk for rejection (e.g., Underwood, 2004). Clearly, additional research is needed that more clearly delineates subgroup and gender differences among the peer-rejected population.

## Role of the Peer Group

A growing body of converging evidence indicates that peer rejection, in addition to involving the individual characteristics of the rejected child, also involves the way that others think about and evaluate the rejected child. Bierman (2004), for example, reviewed research documenting the prevalence of negative stereotypes, distorted perceptions, and negative reputational bias directed at peer-rejected children. Such biased perceptions may reflect what Baldwin (1992) referred to as negative relational schemas. According to Baldwin, relational schemas are cognitive representations of social relationships that are developed through repeated interpersonal experiences. These schemas include representations of the self and other, and behavioral scripts for expected patterns of interactions. Individuals use these relational schemas to form working models of their interpersonal relationships, which serve as cognitive maps to help them navigate their social world.

Once such negative relational schemas and reputational bias are established about a rejected child, they may have a self-fulfilling effect on future interactions involving the child and are resistant to change. For example, Dodge (1980) reported that a child's reputation (aggressive vs. nonaggressive) was an important factor in determining how classmates evaluated his or her social behaviors, and that the use of reputation in making evaluations about a peer tended to increase with age. Consistent with these findings, Coie and Kupersmidt (1983) reported results from a study in which small groups of children previously unknown to each other were formed and observed during free-play sessions. The play groups consisted of four fourth-grade boys representing popular, average, neglected, and rejected sociometric groups. Coie and Kupersmidt noted that after six half-hour sessions, the rejected children had reestablished their negative sociometric status. Interestingly, however, group members rated socially rejected peers as more aggressive than others in the group when, in fact, the rejected peers had engaged in no more aggressive exchanges than their playmates. Moreover, although peer-rejected children did exhibit higher rates of inappropriate solitary behavior, this pattern tended to emerge only after their rejected status had been established within the playgroup.

These studies are suggestive of a negative cycle in which peer rejection increases deviant behavior on the part of the child, which in turn contributes to further rejection by the child's peers. This negative cycle results in both the rejected child and his or her peers developing rigid beliefs (i.e., negative relational schemas) about how the other child behaves, and these beliefs in turn affect how each child interacts with the other. For example, a child who maintains a relational schema that a rejected peer is aggressive and socially incompetent will likely seek confirmation of these negative beliefs and will tend to behave in a manner that is consistent with these beliefs (e.g., ostracism and social rejection).

Examination of the extensive literature on children who experience severe difficulties with peer relationships reveals peer rejection to be a multifaceted process involving the rejected child's social, emotional, behavioral, and cognitive skills as well as the response of the child's peer group. Coie (1990) has argued that, whereas the individual child's skill deficits may be primarily responsible for the *acquisition* of peer-rejected status, the perceptions and behaviors of the peer group play a primary role in the *maintenance* of rejected status. Both facets of the peer rejection process, however, are important targets to be addressed if prevention and intervention efforts are to be effective.

## ALTERNATIVE ACTIONS FOR PREVENTION

Classroom- and school-based programs designed to *prevent* the development of peer relationship difficulties among students emphasize many of the same actions as interventions for students having problems with peer relationships. Prevention programs have focused on developing students' social competence, teaching social problem solving, decreasing aggressive and disruptive behaviors, peer-pairing, fostering cooperative learning, and building and maintaining a positive school climate or sense of community (see McGrath, 1999, and the following chapters in this volume: 2, "Character Education"; 3, "Developing Self-Discipline"; 7, "School Disciplinary Systems"; 8, "School Completion"; 9, "Anger and Aggression"; 10, "Bullying"; and 24, "Prosocial Behavior").

As with direct interventions, effective prevention is a multifaceted, complicated process. Coie et al. (1993) identified five fundamental principles that should guide prevention efforts, and these same principles can be used in the evaluation of such programs:

- Prevention programs should identify and target critical causal processes most related to outcomes.
- Prevention programs should seek to address risk factors early in the developmental trajectory before they stabilize as predictors of dysfunction.
- Programs should target children at greatest risk for dysfunction.
- Prevention programs should target each domain identified in the risk model, using multicomponent programs.
- Developmental research should be used in the construction of prevention programs.

Given the complexity involved in the development of effective prevention efforts, it is not surprising that relatively few such programs have been developed and validated for children at risk for peer rejection. One program that shows considerable promise, however, is the Fast Track project (Conduct Problems Prevention Research Group, 2004). The elementary school phase of Fast Track (a middle and high school phase is also available) is a comprehensive and intensive program that addresses six areas of risk and protective factors based on developmental–psychopathology theory and research. These areas of focus include parenting, children's social problem-solving and emotional coping skills, peer relations, classroom atmosphere and curriculum, academic achievement, and home–school relations.

Of particular relevance for school-based programs, the elementary school phase of Fast Track includes an adaptation of the Promoting Alternative Thinking Strategies program (PATHS; Kusche & Greenberg, 1993). This classroom-based component involves a curriculum taught by teachers two to three times per week and targets skills deemed important to school functioning and to the development of positive peer relationships. These target skills include decision making, goal setting, character development, coping techniques for dealing with peer pressure, and problem solving. Teachers also receive individualized consultation support regarding behavioral management issues. In addition to the classroom-based intervention, parents participate in parent training groups and at-risk students participate in social skill training groups. Fast Track also provides peer pairing, academic tutoring, and home visits.

Although evaluation studies of Fast Track are ongoing, after 3 years of prevention services, children in Fast Track groups exhibited improved levels of social–cognitive skills, reduced levels of aggressive behaviors, reduced need for special education services, higher levels of positive peer interactions, and improved sociometric scores (Bierman, 2004). Both the Fast Track and PATHS programs have been identified as demonstrating strong promise of effectiveness by Blueprints for Violence Prevention (n.d.) of the Center for the Study and Prevention of Violence. This research is needed to continue evaluation efforts and to identify the most critical components of both Fast Track and PATHS.

A second type of prevention program relevant to peer relations involves antibullying efforts. Although a review of these programs is outside the purview of this chapter, the problem has received extensive attention in recent years, and effective bullying prevention programs have been put in place (see chapter 10, "Bullying"). Those programs facilitate positive peer relations by curtailing aggressive behaviors (thus ameliorating the negative effects of aggression on both the bully and victim) and by creating a more positive social milieu in which positive peer relationships can flourish and social ostracism is diminished. Successful antibullying programs typically involve intervening at multiple levels within the school and working with multiple stakeholders and participants (Olweus, 1994). These interventions include close examination of environmental factors that allow peer harassment to occur, including faculty and staff supervision and responsiveness. They also incorporate interventions directed at children who engage in bullying activities, children who experience victimization, and interventions designed to change general attitudes about bullying and social norms. Such programs not only decrease the prevalence of bullying and peer harassment within a school, they also promote a more tolerant and positive social atmosphere in which positive peer relationships are facilitated.

## ALTERNATIVE ACTIONS FOR INTERVENTION

Given the complexity of children's friendships and the peer rejection phenomenon, it is not surprising that intervention efforts have achieved only limited and inconsistent success. Most intervention approaches directed at children who experience peer relationship difficulties have traditionally targeted inadequate social skills identified as responsible for the child's social adjustment problems. Unfortunately, an exclusive focus on a child's skill deficits often fails to improve the sociometric status of the child. As a result, researchers and clinicians have increasingly recognized the importance of accounting for the multiple behavioral, cognitive, emotional, and social factors involved in peer relationship difficulties when intervening with these children (Bierman, 2004; Kupersmidt & Dodge, 2004).

Given this emerging, more complicated picture of peer relationships, interventions have begun to (a) target a wide array of social competence domains, including social, cognitive, and emotional skills that are relevant to the development of positive peer relationships; (b) structure interactions within the peer group to change negative reputation and facilitate positive friendships; and (c) use multifaceted approaches designed to address a wide array of needs experienced by these children. This more comprehensive approach to intervention necessarily involves more than traditional individual or group counseling with the at-risk child. It also involves extensive consultation with teachers and parents, and it may necessitate work at the classroom, school, family, and community levels as well.

### Promoting Social Competence

The development of effective social skills has long been recognized as critical to children achieving and sustaining positive peer relationships. Some of the most common skills targeted in treatment intervention studies with peer-rejected children include social participation (e.g., joining and attending to peers), communication and cooperation (e.g., sharing, turn-taking, conversation, and empathic responding), and techniques for dealing with conflict (e.g., teasing, aggression, and negotiation). Because not all children will exhibit deficits in each of these domains, it is important that a close match exists between the social skill taught and the specific needs of the child.

A large body of literature indicates that social skills can be taught most effectively through a social learning approach. In summary, this approach involves developing children's understanding of skill concepts, promoting skill performance, and fostering skill maintenance (e.g., Elliott & Gresham, 1991). Although such work can be done in both individual and group settings, small groups provide a powerful context within which social skills can be developed and practiced (Waas & Graczyk, 1998). The first step in the skill-building process is introducing the concept of a particular skill and increasing children's motivation for learning the skill. Because peer-rejected children often have a poor understanding of the causal connection between inappropriate behavior (e.g., aggression) and the negative consequences associated with peer rejection (e.g., loneliness), it is important to point out explicitly the benefits of learning better social skills. Both the group leader and other children in the group can play an important role in increasing participants' motivation for learning a given skill. All members of the group can participate in identifying the benefits of learning a particular social skill, and peers within the group often can serve as a "reality check" for each other's perception of the consequences of a behavior.

Whereas group discussion provides therapy participants with language-based information about the targeted skill, participant modeling provides visual information on how to perform the skill. In modeling procedures a child learns the target skill by watching others perform the component behaviors under a variety of conditions. A major advantage of social skill modeling is that observers are shown how behaviors are integrated and sequenced to result in successful performance.

A group format provides the opportunity for children to observe a variety of models, which promotes generalization of the trained skills and provides a wide sampling of behavioral solutions for group members to evaluate. For example, the therapist may initially model the target skill, providing group members with performance criteria toward which to strive. Group members then may take turns attempting to implement the skill. Throughout this process, children's understanding of the skill being taught is developed further by having group members enact both positive and negative exemplars of the skill.

The central component of social competence training focuses on skill performance through guided rehearsal, feedback, reinforcement, and practice. Guided rehearsal is a structured form of role-playing in which a particular skill (e.g., entering an ongoing activity) is rehearsed under supervision. The goal of guided rehearsal is to help children replace maladaptive responses with more appropriate ones through repeated practice. Supervision typically involves coaching children on the specific behaviors required to perform the skill successfully, as well as highlighting the relevant social cues occurring in a particular interaction. Such supervised practice is particularly helpful to many peer-rejected children, who have difficulty using social cues and social feedback effectively.

Feedback is a natural extension of the role-playing process that involves the constructive analysis of the actor's performance of the skill. Under the guidance of the group leader, other children can also provide important verbal feedback about a group member's use of a particular skill. Both group members and the role-players might be asked to answer questions such as What did the actor want to happen? What did they try? Did it work? What might they do differently next time? Additional questions might ask how each participant in the role-played situation might feel and probable short-term and long-term consequences.

Providing group members the opportunity to practice newly learned skills under less structured and less closely supervised conditions is an important part of training for generalization and maintenance. The group setting provides an ideal opportunity for such practice to occur through such activities as independent role-play practice, therapeutic games, structured activities, and free play. For example, Bierman and Furman (1984) conducted a social skills intervention with low-peer-accepted fifth- and sixth-grade students who also exhibited poor conversation skills. Children were coached in self-expression (e.g., sharing information about self and feelings), questioning (e.g., asking others about themselves and feelings), and leadership bids (e.g., giving advice or invitations). Children were also given opportunities to practice the skills through role-playing and a structured activity in which children made videotapes of group members engaged in the target skills. Participants who engaged in such skill training and practice increased their conversation skills and peer interactions.

Although social skill learning–based procedures have been widely used with children who experience peer relationship difficulties, such procedures have typically resulted in only moderate treatment effect (e.g., Beelmann, Pfingsten, & Losel, 1994). Moreover, there has been an increased recognition that the heterogeneity of the peer-rejected group is an important factor in predicting response to intervention (Bierman, 2004). For example, some research has suggested that children exhibiting shyness and withdrawal may be more responsive than aggressive children to traditional social skills training procedures (e.g., Schneider, 1992). As a result, researchers and clinicians have increasingly included treatment components designed to reduce impulsive, coercive, and aggressive behaviors in addition to increasing the use of prosocial behaviors by these children. Bierman, Miller, and Stabb (1987), for example, reported that when traditional coaching procedures were combined with a response-cost procedure designed to reduce negative behaviors, rejected-aggressive first- to third-grade boys achieved sustained improvements in peer interactions and significantly fewer "least liked" sociometric nominations. In addition to including such contingency management strategies to reduce negative behaviors, researchers and clinicians have also become interested in the use of a variety of social–cognitive peer-based interventions in their work with socially rejected children.

## Promoting Social–Cognitive Skills

Whereas behavioral skill training is used primarily to build specific social skills thought to be important to peer acceptance and the development of friendships, cognitive–behavioral procedures have been widely used to decrease impulsive responding, facilitate a more reflective approach to thinking about a given problem, and increase the child's self-monitoring, emotional regulation, and self-reinforcement.

One cognitive intervention commonly used with children is self-instructional training. This procedure targets a number of problem-solving skills that often are difficult for peer-rejected children, including generating multiple alternative solutions, examining consequences, and remaining focused on the problem task. Self-instructional training involves the group members and therapist working together to generate a series of questions or self-reminders the children can use to help work through the problem-solving process and be more reflective in their responses (e.g., Kendall & Braswell, 1993). Questions such as What is the problem? What are all the ways to solve it? What might happen? Which one should I choose? typically are developed, rehearsed, and used by the child in various practice situations. Self-instructional training is a common component of intervention directed at a wide variety of adjustment difficulties including impulsivity, ADHD, conduct disorder, anxiety, and depression (e.g., Kendall & Braswell, 1993; Kendall et al., 1992). Among the many programs that focus on the development of social problem-solving skills, the programs I Can Problem Solve (Shure, 1997) and Improving Social Awareness/Social Problem Solving (Elias & Tobias, 1992) have demonstrated evidence for improving children's social–cognitive abilities and adjustment (e.g., Frauenknecht & Black, 2004; Greenberg, Domitrovich, & Bumbarger, 2001).

A second target for intervention is coping and self-control in uncomfortable situations. Coping self-statements are designed to help children control their level of emotional arousal and decrease impulsive responding when they are upset. This procedure involves the therapist and children working together to identify especially problematic situations (e.g., being denied participation in a playground game) and then collaboratively developing self-statements that peer-rejected children can use to help them maintain self-control. As with social skills training, the use of coping statements is developed through modeling, coaching, and practice (see Bernard & Joyce, 1984, for review). Other types of arousal-reducing procedures, such as progressive relaxation, often are used in conjunction with coping self-statements. As with self-instructional training, coping self-statements have been used frequently in interventions directed at such problems as anger arousal (Feindler & Guttman, 1994), impulsive responding (Kendall & Braswell, 1993), and depression and anxiety (Stark, Raffaelle, & Reysa, 1994).

A third common target of social–cognitive procedures is the child's self-monitoring of emotional arousal, awareness of situations that lead to overreaction, and the regulation of affect. The approach often uses procedures to expand children's emotional vocabulary and help them understand the differences in intensity of emotional experience. For example, children might use an "emotional thermometer" to help differentiate levels of intensity, or they may be asked to participate in role-playing or to observe others as they cope with target emotions. The use of "hassle logs" and charts to identify the antecedents, behaviors, and consequences associated with emotion-arousing events are also often used with children experiencing difficulties with emotion regulation. Such procedures have been used successfully with children exhibiting both externalizing difficulties such as aggression and impulsivity (e.g., Feindler & Guttman, 1994) and internalizing difficulties such as depression and anxiety (e.g., Stark et al., 1994). Attributional retraining has also been used successfully with reactive–aggressive children who exhibit biased attributions of hostility toward others (Hudley et al., 1998).

Social–cognitive interventions tend to be most effective when combined with other social competence and behavioral interventions. Lochman, Coie, Underwood, and Terry (1993), for example, provided rejected-aggressive fourth-grade boys with training in social problem solving (e.g., identifying problem situations and goals, considering alternative solutions and consequences, inhibiting impulsive responding), social skills (e.g., cooperation, communication, negotiation, group entry, acceptance of rejection), and coping with angry feelings (e.g., use of self-statements). They reported that after 34 half-hour sessions involving both individual and group sessions, rejected-aggressive boys were more socially accepted by peers and were viewed as less aggressive by both teachers and peers than the control group. Moreover, these gains were maintained at 1-year follow-up.

## Changing Negative Reputation

An emerging focus of intervention with children experiencing peer rejection involves the use of the peer group itself to target negative relational schemas that both rejected children and their peers may develop. Such negative perceptions are likely developed by the rejected child as a result of the high frequency of conflictive interactions in which he or she has been engaged. Other children, as well, tend to develop negative relational schemas of the rejected child based on their direct experience with the child or observations and general reputation of the rejected child. Such schemas are likely to result in an increasingly negative reputation of such children, leading peers to direct additional rejecting behaviors toward them. As a result, both researchers and clinicians have become interested in interventions that target the negative cycle of rejection that often exists with these children (Bierman, 2004).

Price and Dodge (1989) suggested that direct reputation change will be most likely to occur if the peer group observes a rejected child performing highly salient behaviors that disconfirm the reputation. For example, a rejected child who has the reputation for argumentative behavior might be included in activities that require high levels of cooperation and sharing among peers. Such an intervention would be salient to peers and would be most likely to modify the child's reputation for hostility. Price and Dodge noted that the rejected child must be allowed to perform these disconfirming activities many times in order for peers to accept the behaviors as part of the rejected child's repertoire.

The literature on stereotypes also offers possible intervention strategies for changing a child's reputation among his or her peers. In discussing the modification of negative stereotypes, Cook (1985) identified four conditions that promote positive attitude change among group members. Applied to the domain of children's peer relations, these conditions include the following: (a) All members of the group should enjoy equal status, and the norms of the group should promote a sense of equality among members; (b) the attributes of the rejected children in the group must disconfirm prevailing stereotypes; (c) cooperation among group members in the achievement of joint goals should be encouraged; and (d) rejected children should be allowed to communicate personal information about themselves so they are perceived as unique individuals and not as stereotypes.

There are a number of different approaches that one might take in attempting to accomplish the objective of changing the negative relational schemas that children have developed about a rejected child. Regardless of the particular activity used, the focus of the intervention should be to increase positive interactions between the rejected child and his or her peers. One method of accomplishing this objective is to combine traditional social skills training with group participation in a positive, cooperative task.

A cooperative task involves children working together to achieve a common goal that demands interdependence and prosocial behaviors among group members. Bierman and Furman (1984), for example, had children work together in small groups of three to make films of students involved in friendly interactions. While the children were engaged in this activity, the therapist monitored their interactions, provided reinforcing comments, gave feedback to group members, and made suggestions on the social skills they were being taught. In using this activity, Bierman and Furman ensured that the social skills being taught in the group would be practiced actively. Moreover, the structured nature of the activity, combined with the close monitoring by the therapist, ensured that the rejected children were involved in multiple disconfirming behaviors (i.e., positive and cooperative interactions). Bierman and Furman reported that only those children who participated in both the social skills coaching and the peer involvement activities exhibited lasting improvements in peer partner acceptance ratings as well as improved social skills and peer interaction rates.

Other researchers have used various types of games to accomplish this dual goal of social skills practice and involvement in cooperative tasks. More important than the particular activity chosen, however, is the way that the therapist structures the activity. First, it is important that participants be given the opportunity to practice newly learned skills. To that end, the therapist may need to give the student explicit cues for using the skill, make suggestions and give feedback on the child's performance of the skill, and reinforce the child's skill enactment. Additionally, the therapist must structure the activities so that the target skills are practiced to mastery. Finally, activities should be monitored so that potential conflict among group members is minimized.

The use of such peer group interventions is not without risks. Dishion, McCord, and Poulin (1999), for example, reviewed several interventions in which peer group involvement appeared to have an iatrogenic effect on antisocial adolescents' long-term adjustment. They suggested that participants' close association with other antisocial youth as part of these interventions may have exposed them to "deviancy training" in which their participation in antisocial behavior was actively reinforced through laughter, social attention, and interest in such activities. Dishion et al. (1999) noted that such iatrogenic effects may be less likely with younger than with older participants and that the use of mixed groups in which at-risk youth are paired with prosocial youth may minimize this effect. Clearly, additional research is needed to explicate the role of the peer group in both the rejection process and intervention outcomes.

Most efforts to intervene with children who exhibit peer relationship difficulties have focused on the skills commonly thought to be important to enhancing peer acceptance. However, relatively little research has been devoted to interventions specifically designed to promote the development of high-quality, prosocial friendships among at-risk children. Given that peer acceptance and friendship are distinct dimensions of children's peer relationships, treatments that emphasize the development of positive friendships are warranted. Asher, Parker, and Walker (1996) proposed that a number of social skills required for forming and maintaining successful friendships are worthy of future investigation. These skills include recognizing that friendships involve a spirit of equality and reciprocity; using self-disclosure to promote intimacy; being willing to express concern, admiration, and affection; providing support when friends are in need; being consistently available; and having the ability to manage and resolve conflicts. As in interventions directed at general peer acceptance, such friendship qualities can be taught within a social learning framework and the active involvement of peers would be an important part of such efforts (Asher et al., 1996).

### Designing Consultative and Multifaceted Interventions

Given the complexity of peer relationship difficulties, researchers and clinicians are increasingly examining the use of more comprehensive interventions that address behavioral, emotional, social, family, and academic needs (Bierman, 2004). At the classroom and school levels, the use of consultative interventions with teachers and staff is an important extension of direct intervention services (Waas & Graczyk, 1998). Consultation with teachers might involve collaboratively designing strategies to promote generalization of social skills training to the classroom and playground settings. These might include the teacher monitoring a child's use of social skills, cuing the child in the use of targeted skills, and providing feedback and reinforcement to the child following his or her use of social skills.

Teachers can also facilitate the peer-mediated modification of a rejected child's negative reputation among classmates. A variety of peer-mediated interventions have shown promise in this regard. At the simplest level, the teacher might strategically control the membership of classroom work groups to promote positive interactions between the rejected child and his or her peers. More formal cooperative group techniques that involve students working together toward a common goal can be used to promote positive social interactions (Nastasi & Clements, 1991). A variety of peer-pairing techniques also have been used, both to promote a child's use of target social skills and to foster friendship development (Odom & Strain, 1984). For example, peer proximity interventions involve placing socially popular and unpopular children together during activities. Peers can also be taught to prompt and reinforce a child's use of a targeted behavior.

Achieving long-term sociometric change with children experiencing peer rejection is difficult, as documented in numerous studies; therefore, the use of consultative strategies and multifaceted programs may be critical to successful intervention. Bierman (2004) noted that there is a need for research on the most effective mechanisms, strategies, and content for different kinds of problems. Moreover, although such issues as friendship quality, social networks, victimization, and negative reputational bias have all been identified in recent research as important components of children's peer relations, very little systematic research has been conducted demonstrating how these can best be addressed in the context of both direct and indirect interventions. However, some of the most comprehensive efforts to address children's and adolescents' multifaceted peer relationships have been through primary and secondary prevention programs.

## SUMMARY

Establishing and maintaining positive peer relationships is an important part of a child's healthy social, emotional, and cognitive development. Research has demonstrated that children who fail to successfully accomplish this important developmental task are at increased risk for a wide variety of concurrent and future difficulties. Therefore, it is important for child professionals such as school psychologists, teachers, and social workers to identify and respond to these children. Although such children can be identified relatively easily through the use of sociometric and other procedures, successful intervention with these children has proved more difficult.

Researchers and clinicians recognize the importance of using multifaceted approaches when intervening with children who fail to establish positive peer relationships. Such interventions often involve working directly with the child across multiple domains, including social competence, social problem solving, emotional regulation, and positive interactions with peers, as well as holding consultative interventions with the child's teachers and families. Numerous prevention programs (e.g., social problem solving, friendship building, and anti- bullying) have been developed and adopt many of the same goals as direct interventions for children experiencing peer relationship difficulties. However, very few of these programs have explicitly targeted the prevention of peer rejection. Nevertheless, programs that emphasize a combination of training children in social skills, addressing environmental factors, and promoting positive social norms appear to hold the most promise for the prevention of social difficulties and the building of positive peer relationships.

# RECOMMENDED RESOURCES

## Books and Other Printed Material

Bierman, K. L. (2004). *Peer rejection.* New York: Guilford Press.

This volume, written by a leading scholar in the field, provides a comprehensive review of both theory and research on children who experience severe peer relationship difficulties. It also provides extensive discussion of school- and clinic-based interventions for this at-risk population.

Kupersmidt, J. B., & Dodge, K. A. (Eds.). (2004). *Children's peer relations: From development to intervention.* Washington, DC: American Psychological Association.

This edited volume addresses a wide array of critical topics in the peer relations literature while effectively integrating theory and extensive research. In addition to covering peer rejection, it also covers issues such as dyadic relationships, cliques, and family influences and examines intervention and prevention approaches.

Slee, P. T., & Rigby, K. (Eds.). (1999). *Children's peer relations.* New York: Routledge.

An international group of researchers review research and intervention strategies regarding children's peer relations. Topics covered include peer status, gender and ethnicity, disability, illness, and loneliness.

## Websites

*http://www.colorado.edu/cspv/blueprints*

The Blueprints for Violence Prevention project provides an extensive matrix and overview of program effectiveness. The project documents how various federal and private agencies have rated the effectiveness of prevention programs designed to reduce problem behaviors such as delinquency, aggression, substance abuse, and school behavioral problems.

*http://www.sp-ebi.org*

The Taskforce on Evidence-Based Interventions in School Psychology provides extensive information on the criteria for evaluating intervention programs. As this site develops, it will provide links to other evidence-based initiatives.

*http://www.w-w-c.org*

The What Works Clearinghouse (WWC), established in 2002 by the U.S. Department of Education's Institute of Education Sciences, gathers and reports on studies of the effectiveness of a wide array of educational interventions.

# REFERENCES

Albee, G. W. (1984). Prologue: A model for classifying prevention programs. In J. M. Joffe, G. W. Albee, & L. D. Kelly (Eds.), *Readings in primary prevention of psychopathology: Basic concepts* (pp. 228–245). Hanover, NH: University Press of New England.

Asher, S., Parker, J., & Walker, D. (1996). Distinguishing friendships from acceptance: Implications for intervention and assessment. In W. Bukowski, A. Newcomb, & W. Hartup (Eds.), *The company they keep: Friendships in childhood and adolescence* (pp. 336–405). Cambridge, UK: Cambridge University Press.

Bagwell, C. L. (2004). Friendships, peer networks, and antisocial behavior. In J. B. Kupersmidt & K. A. Dodge (Eds.), *Children's peer relations* (pp. 37–57). Washington, DC: American Psychological Association.

Bagwell, C. L., & Coie, J. D. (2004). The best friendships of aggressive boys: Relationship quality, conflict management, and rule-breaking behavior. *Journal of Experimental Child Psychology, 88,* 5–24.

Baldwin, M. W. (1992). Relational schemas and the processing of social information. *Psychological Bulletin, 112,* 461–484.

Beelmann, A., Pfingsten, U., & Losel, F. (1994). Effects of training social competence in children: A meta-analysis of recent evaluation studies. *Journal of Clinical Child Psychology, 23,* 260–271.

Bernard, M. E., & Joyce, M. R. (1984). *Rational-emotive therapy with children and adolescents.* New York: Wiley.

Berndt, T. J., & Murphy, L. M. (2002). Influences of friends and friendships: Myths, truths, and research recommendations. In R. V. Kail (Ed.), *Advances in child development and behavior* (Vol. 30, pp. 275–310). New York: Academic Press.

Bierman, K. L. (2004). *Peer rejection.* New York: Guilford Press.

Bierman, K. L., & Furman, W. (1984). The effects of social skills training and peer involvement on the social adjustment of preadolescents. *Child Development, 55,* 151–162.

Bierman, K. L., Miller, C. L., & Stabb, S. D. (1987). Improving the social behavior and peer acceptance of rejected boys: Effects of social skill training with instructions and prohibitions. *Journal of Consulting and Clinical Psychology, 55,* 194–200.

Blueprints for Violence Prevention. (n.d.). Matrix of programs as identified by various federal and private agencies. Retrieved November 15, 2004, from http://www.colorado.edu/cspv/blueprints/matrix/overview.html

Brendgen, M., Little, T. D., & Krappmann, L. (2000). Rejected children and their friends: A shared evaluation of friendship quality? *Merrill-Palmer Quarterly, 46,* 45–70.

Coie, J. D. (1990). Toward a theory of peer rejection. In S. R. Asher & J. D. Coie (Eds.), *Peer rejection in childhood* (pp. 365–401). New York: Cambridge University Press.

Coie, J. D., & Kupersmidt, J. B. (1983). A behavioral analysis of emerging social status in boys' groups. *Child Development, 54,* 1400–1416.

Coie, J. D., Watt, N. F., West, S. G., Hawkins, J. D., Asarnow, J. R., Markman, H. J., et al. (1993). The science of prevention: A conceptual framework and some directions for a national research program. *American Psychologist, 48,* 1013–1022.

Conduct Problems Prevention Research Group. (2004). The Fast Track experiment: Translating the developmental model into a prevention design. In J. B. Kupersmidt & K. A. Dodge (Eds.), *Children's peer relations* (pp. 181–208). Washington, DC: American Psychological Association.

Cook, S. W. (1985). Experimenting of social issues: The case of school desegregation. *American Psychologist, 40,* 452–460.

Crick, N. R., & Ladd, G. W. (1993). Children's perceptions of their peer experiences: Attributions, loneliness, social anxiety, and social avoidance. *Developmental Psychology, 29,* 244–254.

Dishion, T. J., McCord, J., & Poulin, F. (1999). When interventions harm: Peer groups and problem behavior. *American Psychologist, 54,* 755–764.

Dishion, T. J., Poulin, F., & Burraston, B. (2001). Peer-group dynamics associated with iatrogenic effects in group interventions with high-risk young adolescents. In D. W. Nangle & C. A. Erdley (Vol. Eds.), *The role of friendship in psychological adjustment: No. 91. New directions for child and adolescent development* (pp. 79–92). San Francisco, CA: Jossey-Bass.

Dodge, K. A. (1980). Social cognition and children's aggressive behavior. *Child Development, 51,* 162–170.

Dozier, M. (1988). Rejected children's processing of interpersonal information. *Journal of Abnormal Child Psychology, 16,* 141–149.

Elias, M., & Tobias, S. (1992). *Building social problem-solving skills.* San Francisco: Jossey-Bass.

Elliott, S. N., & Gresham, F. M. (1991). *Social skills intervention guide.* Circle Pines, MN: American Guidance Service.

Feindler, E. L., & Guttman, J. (1994). Cognitive-behavioral anger control training. In C. W. LeCroy (Ed.), *Handbook of child and adolescent treatment manuals* (pp. 170–199). New York: Lexington Books.

Frauenknecht, M., & Black, D. R. (2004). Problem-solving training for children and adolescents. In E. C. Chang, T. J. D'Zurilla, & L. J. Sanna (Eds.), *Social problem solving* (pp. 153–170). Washington, DC: American Psychological Association.

French, D. C., & Waas, G. A. (1985). Teachers' ability to identify peer-rejected children: A comparison of sociometrics and teacher ratings. *Journal of School Psychology, 23,* 347–353.

Gifford-Smith, M. E., & Brownell, C. A. (2003). Childhood peer relationships: Social acceptance, friendships, and peer networks. *Journal of School Psychology, 41,* 235–284.

Greenberg, M. T., Domitrovich, C., & Bumbarger, B. (2001). The prevention of mental disorders in school-aged children: Current state of the field. *Prevention and Treatment, 4,* 1–57.

Hartup, W. W. (1992). Friendships and their developmental significance. In H. McGurk (Ed.), *Childhood social development* (pp. 175–205). Hillsdale, NJ: Erlbaum.

Hartup, W. W. (1996). The company they keep: Friendships and their developmental significance. *Child Development, 67,* 1–13.

Hubbard, J. A., & Dearing, K. F. (2004). Children's understanding and regulation of emotion in the context of their peer relations. In J. B. Kupersmidt & K. A. Dodge, *Children's peer relations* (pp. 81–99). Washington, DC: American Psychological Association.

Hudley, C., Britsch, B., Wakefield, W. D., Smith, T., Demorat, M., & Cho, S. J. (1998). An attribution retraining program to reduce aggression in elementary school students. *Psychology in the Schools, 35,* 271–282.

Kendall, P. C., & Braswell, L. (1993). *Cognitive-behavioral therapy for impulsive children* (2nd ed.). New York: Guilford Press.

Kendall, P. C., Chansky, T. E., Kane, M. T., Kim, R. S., Kortlander, E., Ronan, K. R., Sessa, F. M., & Siqueland, L. (1992). *Anxiety disorders in youth.* Boston: Allyn & Bacon.

Kupersmidt, J. B., & Dodge, K. A. (Eds.). (2004). *Children's peer relations.* Washington, DC: American Psychological Association.

Kusche, C. A., & Greenberg, M. T. (1993). *The PATHS curriculum.* Seattle, WA: EXCEL.

Lochman, J. E., Coie, J. D., Underwood, M. K., & Terry, R. (1993). Effectiveness of a social relations intervention program for aggressive and nonaggressive, rejected children. *Journal of Consulting and Clinical Psychology, 61,* 1053–1058.

McDougall, P., Hymel, S., Vailancourt, T., & Mercer, L. (2001). The consequences of childhood peer rejection. In M. R. Leary (Ed.), *Interpersonal rejection* (pp. 219–247). Oxford, England: Oxford University Press.

McGrath, H. (1999). An overview of prevention and treatment programmes for developing positive peer relations. In P. T. Slee & K. Rigby (Eds.), *Children's peer relations* (pp. 229–241). New York: Routledge.

Nastasi, B. K., & Clements, D. H. (1991). Research on cooperative learning: Implications for practice. *School Psychology Review, 20,* 110–131.

Newcomb, A. F., & Bagwell, C. L. (1995). Children's friendship relations: A meta-analytic review. *Psychological Bulletin, 117,* 306–347.

Newcomb, A. F., Bukowski, W. M., & Pattee, L. (1993). Children's peer relations: A meta-analytic review of popular, rejected, neglected, controversial, and average sociometric status. *Psychological Bulletin, 113,* 99–128.

Odom, S. L., & Strain, P. S. (1984). Peer-mediated approaches to promoting children's social interaction: A review. *American Journal of Orthopsychiatry, 54,* 544–557.

Olweus, D. (1994). *Bullying at school: What we know and what we can do.* New York: Blackwell.

Parker, J. G., & Asher, S. R. (1993). Friendship and friendship quality in middle childhood: Links with peer group acceptance and feelings of loneliness and social dissatisfaction. *Developmental Psychology, 29,* 611–621.

Parker, J., & Gottman, J. (1989). Social and emotional development in a relational context: Friendship interaction from early childhood to adolescence. In T. Berndt & G. Ladd (Eds.), *Peer relationships in child development* (pp. 95–131). New York: Wiley.

Parkhurst, J. T., & Hopmeyer, A. (1998). Sociometric popularity and peer-perceived popularity: Two distinct dimensions of peer status. *Journal of Early Adolescence, 18,* 125–144.

Price, J. M., & Dodge, K. A. (1989). Peers' contributions to children's social maladjustment. In T. J. Berndt & G. W. Ladd (Eds.), *Peer relationships in child development* (pp. 341–370). New York: Wiley.

Putallaz, M., & Wasserman, A. (1989). Children's naturalistic entry behavior and sociometric status: A developmental perspective. *Developmental Psychology, 25,* 297–305.

Schneider, B. H. (1992). Didactic methods for enhancing children's peer relations: A quantitative review. *Clinical Psychology Review, 12,* 363–382.

Shure, M. (1997). Interpersonal cognitive problem solving: Primary prevention of early high-risk behaviors in the preschool and primary years. In G. Albee & T. Gullotta (Eds.), *Primary prevention works* (pp. 167–188). Thousand Oaks, CA: Sage Publications.

Underwood, M. K. (2004). Gender and peer relations: Are the two gender cultures really that different? In J. B. Kupersmidt & K. A. Dodge (Eds.), *Children's peer relations* (pp. 21–36). Washington, DC: American Psychological Association.

Vandell, D., & Hembree, S. (1994). Social status and friendship: Independent contributors to children's social and academic adjustment. *Merrill-Palmer Quarterly, 38,* 382–400.

Waas, G. A., & Graczyk, P. A. (1998). Group interventions for the peer-rejected child. In K. C. Stoiber & T. R. Kratochwill (Eds.), *Handbook of group intervention for children and families* (pp. 141–158). Needham Heights, MA: Allyn & Bacon.

# 26

# Self-Concept and Self-Esteem

**Maureen A. Manning**
*Anne Arundel County Public Schools*

**George G. Bear**
**Kathleen M. Minke**
*University of Delaware*

## BACKGROUND AND DEVELOPMENT

Inside the teacher's lounge, at individualized education plan (IEP) meetings, and elsewhere around the school building, educators can often be heard expressing concerns about students' self-esteem. In supermarket checkout lines, around the dinner table, and even during legislative assemblies, the self-esteem of students can be a lively topic as well. The term *self-esteem* has become a "household word" (Baumeister, Campbell, Krueger, & Vohs, 2003, p. 1), and "there is perhaps no aspect of students' psychosocial functioning that evokes stronger reactions from parents and educators" (Elbaum & Vaughn, 2003, p. 107). Low self-esteem has come to be viewed as the cause of all evil and high self-esteem as the cause of all good. In fact, as stated by the California Task Force to Promote Self-Esteem and Personal and Social Responsibility (1990), "the lack of self-esteem is central to most personal and social ills plaguing our state and nation" (p. 4). In contrast, the presence of self-esteem is portrayed as a "social vaccine, something that empowers us to live responsibly and that inoculates us against the lures of crime, violence, substance abuse, teen pregnancy, child abuse, chronic welfare dependency, and educational failure" (California Task Force, 1990, p. 4).

As a result of these beliefs, a number of educational and governmental initiatives have been undertaken to prevent low self-esteem and foster high self-esteem among students. Because of the positive relationship that is assumed to exist between self-esteem and academic achievement, many self-esteem programs have been implemented in the hopes of raising students' achievement. Furthermore, decisions about programming and placement in special education are sometimes made based on the assumptions that children with disabilities, especially children with learning disabilities (LD), have low self-esteem. For example, it is often assumed that classification labels result in lowered self-esteem and that children with LD will have higher self-esteem when placed in general education classrooms than when placed in special education environments (Bear, Minke, Griffin, & Deemer, 1997). Unfortunately, these "truths" are often taken to be self-evident, and beliefs are maintained (and important decisions made) despite empirical evidence to the contrary. Before a review of this research is presented, a few fundamental misconceptions about self-esteem are addressed.

### Distinction Between Self-Concept and Self-Esteem

Although the terms *self-esteem* and *self-concept* are often used interchangeably, many theorists argue that they are separate but related constructs (e.g., Harter, 1999; Marsh & Hattie, 1996). Self-esteem refers to an individual's overall evaluation of him- or herself, including feelings of general happiness and satisfaction. Self-esteem therefore involves global feelings of self-worth and self-acceptance. In contrast, self-concept refers to more than simply self-esteem. In addition to self-esteem, it refers to an individual's perceptions of competence or adequacy in specific domains, including academic (e.g., reading, writing, or math) and nonacademic (e.g., social, behavioral, or athletic) areas. The specific domains proposed by two prominent theorists and researchers in the field are displayed in Table 1. Both

**Table 1** *Comparison of Domains Assessed in Several Theoretically and Empirically Derived Multidimensional Measures of Self-Concept*

| Harter's Measures | | |
|---|---|---|
| *Pictorial Scale of Perceived Competence and Social Acceptance*[a] (Preschool–Grade 2) | *Self-Perception Profile for Children* (SPP-C)[b] (Grades 3–8) | *Self-Perception Profile for Adolescents* (SPP-A)[c] (Grades 9–12) |
| | Global self-worth | Global self-worth |
| Cognitive competence | Scholastic competence | Scholastic competence |
| Peer acceptance | Social acceptance | Social acceptance |
| Physical competence | Athletic competence | Athletic competence |
| Maternal acceptance | Behavioral conduct | Behavioral conduct |
| | Physical appearance | Physical appearance |
| | | Job competence |
| | | Close friendship |
| | | Romantic appeal |
| **Marsh's Measures** | | |
| *Self-Description Questionnaire for Preschoolers* (SDQP)[d] (Ages 4–5) | *Self-Description Questionnaire I* (SDQ-I)[e] (Grades 2–6) | *Self-Description Questionnaire II* (SDQ-II)[f] (Grades 7–10) |
| | General self | General self |
| Verbal | Reading | Verbal |
| Math | Mathematics | Math |
| | General school | General school |
| Physical | Physical abilities | Physical abilities |
| Appearance | Physical appearance | Physical appearance |
| Parents | Parent relations | Parent relations |
| Peers | Peer relations | Same-sex relations |
| | | Opposite-sex relations |
| | | Emotional stability |
| | | Honesty/trustworthiness |

[a]From "The Pictorial Scale of Perceived Competence and Social Acceptance for Young Children," by S. Harter & R. Pike, 1984, *Child Development, 55,* pp. 1969–1982.
[b]From *The Self-Perception Profile for Children*, by S. Harter, 1985, unpublished manual, University of Denver, CO.
[c]From *The Self-Perception Profile for Adolescents*, by S. Harter, 1988, unpublished manual, University of Denver, CO.
[d]From "How Do Preschool Children Feel About Themselves? Unraveling Measurement and Multidimensional Self-Concept Structure," by H. W. Marsh, L. A. Ellis, and R. G. Craven, 2002, *Developmental Psychology, 38,* pp. 376–393.
[e]From *Self-Description Questionnaire—I,* by H. W. Marsh, 1988, San Antonio, TX: Psychological Corporation.
[f]From *Self-Description Questionnaire—II,* by H. W. Marsh, 1990, San Antonio, TX: Psychological Corporation.

Harter (1999) and Marsh (1989; Marsh & Hattie, 1996) have developed self-concept instruments for different age groups, with the number of domains assessed on each scale increasing with age. Both sets of scales have received substantial theoretical, empirical, and psychometric support (Bear, Minke, & Manning, 2002).

## Multidimensional and Hierarchical Nature of Self-Concept

Consistent with the view of self-concept as an individual's perceptions of competence or adequacy in specific areas, as well as overall self-esteem, many theorists argue that self-concept is best represented by a *profile* of self-perceptions across specific domains, not by one aggregate score (e.g., Harter, 1999; Marsh & Hattie, 1996). As such, self-concept represents a multidimensional rather than unidimensional construct. According to this view, self-esteem is a distinct dimension of self-concept that is best measured by asking students a separate set of questions about their general happiness and satisfaction with themselves (Harter, 1999). On the Harter scales, the subscale that best represents self-esteem is known as "global self-worth," whereas on the Marsh scales it is known as "general self."

Another scale that has received substantial theoretical, empirical, and psychometric support is the Multidimensional Self-Concept Scale for Children (MSCS; Bracken, 1992). The MSCS targets students in grades 5 through 12 and consists of the following domains: affect, academic, social, physical, competence, and family. The affect, physical, and competence subscales do not appear to measure the same constructs as similarly named domains on other scales (Bear et al., 1997). However, the affect score rather than the total score better represents global feelings of satisfaction with oneself (Bear et al., 2002).

In addition to sharing a view of self-concept as multidimensional, theorists also tend to agree that self-concept is hierarchical. There is much debate, however, about the specific organization of this hierarchy. For example, although both Harter (1999) and Marsh (Marsh & Hattie, 1996) envision global self-concept (or self-esteem) at the apex of the hierarchy, they propose different organizational structures. According to Marsh, there are two separate levels below global self-concept; one consists of broad domains and the other consists of more specific subdomains. The nonacademic domain includes the subdomains of physical abilities and peer relations, and the academic domain includes the subdomains of reading and math. In contrast, Harter proposes several domains (e.g., scholastic competence, social acceptance, and behavioral conduct) that are similar to Marsh's subdomains but fall directly below global self-concept in the hierarchy (i.e., there is no intermediate level as there is in Marsh's model). Because researchers have failed to replicate a clearly defined hierarchical structure across age groups, the specific hierarchical nature of self-concept remains unclear. Furthermore, as noted by Harter (1999), the hierarchy may vary across individuals.

## Development of Self-Concept

Children as young as 4 or 5 perceive differences in their competence across various domains (Marsh, Ellis, & Craven, 2002). As shown in Table 1, the domains recognized by young children include relations with peers and parents, physical competence, and cognitive competence. According to Marsh et al., young students also make judgments about their physical appearance. Neither of the scales that Marsh or Harter developed for young children measure global self-worth, as students do not develop an understanding of this construct until middle childhood (Harter, 1999). As children become older, they not only develop a sense of their own worth as a person, they also recognize a greater number of specific areas in which they may demonstrate competence or incompetence. The increased number of domains students recognize with age has been supported by factor analyses on the different scales that have been developed for different age groups (Harter, 1999). On Harter's scales, the number of specific domains increases from four for children in preschool and early elementary school, to five for children in grades 3 through 8, to eight for students in grades 9 through 12. Similarly, the number of subdomains on Marsh's scales increases from six for preschoolers, to eight for students in grades 2 through 6, to 10 for students in grades 7 through 10.

Young children between the ages of 4 and 7 display positively biased self-perceptions. During this period of development, children often overestimate their social and behavioral functioning and view themselves as competent at everything. These biased self-perceptions do not represent intentional distortions of reality (Harter, 1999). Rather, young children lack the cognitive maturity to critically evaluate their abilities. As a result of this cognitively unsophisticated "all or none" thinking (Harter, 1999, p. 42), they believe that they cannot possess attributes of opposing valence (i.e., they cannot be good at one thing and bad at another); therefore, they tend to view themselves as either all good or all bad (typically the former). Furthermore, young children lack the cognitive maturity to determine whether their self-perceptions are realistic. For example, they cannot differentiate between their ideal and real selves and between their actual and desired competence (Harter, 1999).

Several other factors also help explain young children's overly positive self-perceptions (e.g., Harter, 1999; Nicholls, 1978; Stipek & Tannatt, 1984). Instead of considering the difficulty level of tasks performed, young children tend to evaluate their ability based on the amount of effort expended. Furthermore, they lack the ability to integrate information from multiple sources (e.g., parents, teachers, and peers), they ignore evidence of low competence, and they engage in few social comparisons (i.e., they do not evaluate their own competence by considering the performance of their peers). Despite their failure to engage in social comparisons, young children do engage in temporal comparisons, in which they compare their present performance to their previous performance. However, the growth students make in their skills over time contributes to the perpetuation of overly positive perceptions. Overall, given that inflated self-perceptions among young children are not only widespread but also developmentally appropriate, Harter (1999) recommends that they be viewed as "normative distortions" (p. 319) rather than as signs of pathology.

With development, children's self-perceptions become not only more negative but also increasingly accurate, as children recognize that they can be good at some things and bad at others (or "smart" in some situations and "dumb" in others; Harter, 1999). The decline of "all or none" thinking, coupled with an increase in social comparisons, helps children become better judges of their functioning. Another factor contributing to the decline of positive self-perceptions involves students' ability to adopt the perspectives of others and thereby better understand how others view their skills (Harter, 1999). In addition, they can better distinguish between their efforts and their abilities and between their real and ideal selves (Harter, 1999). As a result, children's self-evaluations become increasingly consistent with external indicators, including evaluations by teachers and evaluations based on objective criteria such as grades (Wigfield et al., 1997). A likely reason is that evaluations and competition become more important as students advance through school (Wigfield & Eccles, 2002).

Self-perceptions decline not only as children move into middle childhood (grades 2 through 6) but also as they move into early adolescence (grades 7 through 9; Harter, 1999). The latter decline often coincides with the transition to junior high school and the onset of puberty. As students move from junior to senior high school (grades 10 and 11), however, their self-esteem gradually grows. Increasing freedom allows students greater opportunities to participate in activities in which they are competent (e.g., sports and music), whereas increased perspective-taking abilities enable them to gain more support from others by behaving in more socially acceptable ways. Overall, these fluctuations in self-esteem across stages of development are present in both boys and girls and are reasonably consistent across different dimensions of self-concept (Harter, 1999).

In sum, declines in self-esteem that many children experience during elementary and middle school should not necessarily be cause for concern, as they can largely be explained by the extremely positive self-perceptions children display during the first few years of school. Furthermore, a tendency to overestimate one's abilities remains apparent not only in adolescence (Harter, 1999) but also in adulthood, when it is characteristic of individuals with high self-esteem (Baumeister et al., 2003). Despite their normative nature (and often adaptive function), overly positive self-perceptions may be problematic when they persist despite objective evidence to the contrary and when they contribute to the individual's denial of negative affect and behaviors, to external attributions of blame, and to a resistance to change.

## Gender Differences

A popular belief in American culture is that males have higher self-esteem than females (Kling, Hyde, Showers, & Buswell, 1999). In a recent meta-analysis, Kling et al. found support for a difference in self-esteem favoring males. However, the difference is rather small (effect size = .21), not nearly the magnitude that is often assumed. Gender differences in more specific domains of self-concept tend to be consistent with stereotypes of gender roles. For example, boys tend to have higher self-perceptions on scales for math, science, problem solving, athletic competence, physical appearance, and emotional stability, whereas girls tend to have higher self-perceptions on scales for reading, behavioral conduct, honesty–trustworthiness, and religion–spirituality (Harter, 1999; Marsh, 1989). These gender differences emerge in elementary school and remain stable from preadolescence to adulthood (Jacobs, Lanza, Osgood, Eccles, & Wigfield, 2002). As was true with self-esteem, however, these differences tend to be quite small, suggesting that the self-perceptions of boys and girls are quite similar.

# PROBLEMS AND IMPLICATIONS

## Myths and Misunderstandings

Many myths and misunderstandings about self-concept as a construct persist despite empirical evidence to the contrary. Many individuals believe that low self-esteem causes negative outcomes and that high self-esteem facilitates positive outcomes (Baumeister et al., 2003). Popular belief, clinical impressions, and anecdotal evidence have contributed to these assumptions, and studies that contradicted these beliefs typically have been neglected or dismissed because of methodological limitations and the lack of supporting data (Salmivalli, 2001). However, as noted by Baumeister et al. (2003) upon completing a comprehensive review of the research literature on self-esteem, "the excuse of inadequate data is beginning to wear thin" (p. 2), with a wealth of research indicating that "self-esteem per se is not the social panacea that many people once hoped it was" (p. 38).

***Self-concept and academic achievement.*** The relationship between self-concept and academic achievement has been studied more than any other relationship. Results indicate that self-esteem is often positively correlated with academic performance (Baumeister et al., 2003). These correlations, however, are typically low (e.g., low to mid .20s; Marsh, 1993). Consistent with the multidimensional nature of self-concept, correlations are higher when achievement in specific academic domains is correlated with self-perceptions of competence in those domains (e.g., correlations are higher when students' academic achievement is correlated with academic self-concept rather than global self-concept). Despite the small positive relationship between the two variables, self-esteem does not appear to influence academic achievement. Instead, high self-esteem appears to function more frequently as a consequence rather than a cause of high academic achievement. However, this relationship is also weak. Nevertheless, although high self-esteem does not seem to cause students to perform well in school, it may motivate them to persist longer in the face of failure (Baumeister et al., 2003).

As mentioned earlier, students with LD are often assumed to have lower self-esteem than their nondisabled peers, given the academic, social, and behavioral deficits that they often experience. Supporting the results of an earlier meta-analysis by Chapman (1988), a recent meta-analysis by Bear et al. (2002) confirmed that children with LD perceive their academic ability less favorably than children without LD. In contrast to Chapman's findings, however, Bear et al. found that students with LD do not seem to think less of themselves overall than their non-LD peers. Students with LD appear to perceive their academic deficits accurately, but such accurate appraisals do not prevent them from feeling fairly good about themselves. These results call into question the practice of providing interventions to improve self-concept among students with LD solely on the basis of their disability.

***Self-concept and aggression.*** Another popular assumption, based on clinical impressions rather than on theory or research, is that aggressive students suffer from low self-esteem and subsequently use aggressive behavior as a means of enhancing their self-esteem. Research has increasingly contradicted this assumption by showing that many aggressive students express adequate, if not inflated, self-perceptions (Baumeister et al., 2003). For example, a positive relationship has been demonstrated between children's tendencies to idealize and inflate their competence and their engagement in aggressive behavior (Hughes, Cavell, & Grossman, 1997). Similarly, more positively biased self-perceptions of social acceptance have been associated with more peer nominations of overt and relational aggression (David & Kistner, 2000). And, in a study of aggressive and nonaggressive rejected children (Verschueren & Marcoen, 2002), only the nonaggressive rejected children had significantly lower self-perceptions of global self-worth, scholastic competence, and physical appearance compared with children of average and popular social status. Thus, high self-esteem appears to have a "dark side" (David & Kistner, 2000, p. 327) and may function as a risk rather than protective factor among aggressive children.

In their comprehensive review of the literature on self-esteem, Baumeister et al. (2003) concluded that high self-esteem is associated with both the presence and the absence of aggression. In the most rigorous study included in their review (Salmivalli, Kaukiainen, Kaistaniemi, & Lagerspetz, 1999), high self-esteem predicted two contradictory behaviors: being a bully and defending a victim against a bully. The contradiction between these behaviors was explained by differences in the type of self-esteem exhibited by each group of students. Those who exhibited high levels of *genuine* self-esteem (i.e., recognizing one's strengths and weaknesses and accepting oneself in spite of the weaknesses) were more likely to defend victims of bullying. In contrast, those who exhibited high levels of *defensive* self-esteem (i.e., thinking highly of oneself and refusing to accept criticism) were more likely to approve of, engage in, and encourage bullying. Because high self-esteem can serve both prosocial and antisocial functions, the construct should not be studied on a unidimensional continuum from "low" to "high"; instead, distinctions should be made between qualitatively different types of self-esteem (Salmivalli, 2001).

***Self-esteem, depression, and risky health-related behaviors.*** In addition to academic achievement and aggression, Baumeister et al. (2003) examined the relationship of self-esteem to depression and risky health-related behaviors. They noted that although low self-esteem is often considered a defining characteristic of depression (American Psychiatric Association, 1994), the evidence for such a relationship is weak. However, Baumeister et al. showed a strong positive relationship between self-esteem and happiness, although the causal direction of this relationship has yet to be established.

Baumeister et al. (2003) found that few studies have investigated the relationship of self-esteem to risky health-related behaviors such as using illegal substances (e.g., alcohol, cigarettes, and drugs) and engaging in early sexual activity. The relationship between self-esteem and the use of alcohol and other drugs has little support. The same appears to be true for smoking, although there is some evidence to suggest that low self-esteem may be a weak risk factor in girls. As for early sexual activity, prospective studies suggest that the effect appears to be the opposite of what would be expected. That is, instead of low self-esteem leading to early sexual activity (i.e., as a means of enhancing one's self-esteem), it appears as though high self-esteem may actually precipitate premature sexual activity among girls. This unexpected finding may be related to the tendency of individuals with high self-esteem to be less inhibited, more willing to disregard risks, and more popular than individuals with low self-esteem, which may make young girls more prone to engage in early sexual activity. Another health issue that appears related to self-esteem is that of bulimia. Evidence from concurrent and prospective studies suggests that low self-esteem may be both a cause and consequence of bulimia. The relationship of low self-esteem to this particular eating disorder appears especially strong in the presence of other factors, such as body dissatisfaction and perfectionism.

In general, the results of Baumeister et al.'s (2003) review suggest that self-esteem is "not a major predictor or cause of almost anything" (p. 37). Among girls, some evidence suggests that low self-esteem may be a risk factor for smoking or bulimia, whereas high self-esteem may be a risk factor for early sexual activity, but more research in these areas is necessary before definitive conclusions are drawn. At this time, there appears to be little theoretical or empirical support for educators, school counselors, and school psychologists to focus on improving self-esteem in hopes of preventing or remediating children's academic or interpersonal problems. However, given its direct relation to feelings of happiness, positive self-esteem should be an important goal of education in its own right.

## Measurement Problems

The self-concept literature is complicated by various measurement problems, some of which contribute to the contradictory findings and misunderstandings noted above. One major problem is that the development of many instruments has not been guided by theory. Several popular instruments are based on an outdated, unidimensional model of self-concept. For example, the Piers-Harris Children's Self Concept Scale (Piers, 1969) measures general, or total, self-concept by aggregating students' responses to 80 items across a variety of areas that were neither theoretically nor empirically derived (Bear et al., 2002). Furthermore, many self-concept instruments have inadequate technical qualities, particularly with respect to representative norms, including the Piers-Harris (Piers, 1969), the Coopersmith Self-Esteem Inventories (Coopersmith, 1981), the various Harter scales (Harter, 1985, 1988; Harter & Pike, 1984), and the Self-Description Questionnaire (SDQ; Marsh, 1988, 1990; Marsh et al., 2002). Self-concept instruments are also subject to the same limitations that plague all self-reports in that results may be distorted by socially desirable responding, and thus they may measure how people want to present themselves to others rather than how people truly view themselves (Salmivalli, 2001).

The measurement of self-esteem is further complicated by the heterogeneity of the construct itself. One factor contributing to heterogeneity is the fact that self-concept scales tend to include both affect-related *self-evaluations* (e.g., "I am pleased with my reading") and non-affect-related *self-descriptions* of competence (e.g., "I receive good grades in reading"). Although these different item types correlate highly and positively, they have been found to load on separate factors (e.g., Marsh & Ayotte, 2003; Pietsch, Walker, & Chapman, 2003). Thus, combining them into a single subscale score may obscure important differences among children and among children's responses to interventions. For example, an intervention might improve self-descriptions of competence but not of affect, or vice versa. Furthermore, although many instruments combine perceptions of intellectual ability and academic competence on a single scale (MSCS, Harter scales, Piers-Harris), students with LD appear to differentiate between intellectual and academic abilities (Bear & Minke, 1996), perhaps because a defining characteristic of LD for a long time has been the discrepancy between the two. Finally, correlations between math and verbal self-concepts are often negligible (Marsh, 1986), suggesting that perceptions of these different skills should not be combined into a general academic subscale (as on the Self-Perception Profile for Children and MSCS). As noted by Bear et al. (2002), the many difficulties associated with the measurement of self-concept have contributed to the myths and inconsistent findings in the field.

## ALTERNATIVE ACTIONS FOR PREVENTION

Although self-concept itself does not appear to have a causal role in developmental outcomes, it remains an important construct, given its relationship with general happiness. However, focusing simply on helping students "feel better" about themselves is clearly insufficient; rather, prevention and intervention activities should focus on the primary antecedents of self-worth, defined by Harter (1999) as (a) perceived success in areas where students desire success and (b) approval from significant others. Therefore, preventing low self-esteem involves developing children's skills in domains they deem important and promoting positive relationships with others, particularly parents and peers. These two factors are highly related, especially when students value and feel competent in domains that are important to significant others. Parents tend to value scholastic competence and behavioral conduct, whereas peers tend to value physical appearance, social competence, and athletic competence. Furthermore, there appears to be a relationship between students' perceptions of competence in valued domains and their perceptions of support from others. Thus, increasing students' skills in areas valued by others may help increase students' perceptions of support from others and thereby help protect their feelings of self-worth. However, despite the positive relationship between these factors, excesses in one area cannot compensate for deficits in the other. Both factors are important, and the effects are additive rather than compensatory (Harter, 1999).

### Promoting Competence in Domains of Importance

Although students may not always be or feel competent in areas that are valued by parents and peers, they may not necessarily experience distress. Self-esteem may be protected in such cases if students feel competent in areas that they themselves value (e.g., feeling satisfied with their musical or artistic abilities) and if they can discount the importance of the domains others value but in which they struggle (e.g., discounting the importance of their athletic ability or physical appearance). A critical difference between students with high and low self-worth, therefore, is the ability of students with high self-worth to discount the importance of domains in which they feel incompetent (Harter, 1999). This pattern has been demonstrated among three different groups of students: those with average achievement, those with learning disabilities, and those with behavioral disorders. However, some researchers have failed to replicate these results and thus the value of importance ratings remains controversial. For example, Marsh and Hattie (1996) argue that importance ratings add little to the prediction of self-worth because few students discount the importance of various domains.

Of the domains studied, individuals' physical appearance has the strongest relationship to their self-worth, whereas their athletic competence has the weakest relationship (Harter, 1999). The high importance placed on physical appearance is evident across ages (i.e., children, adolescents, and adults), countries (e.g., Ireland, Greece, and Japan), and exceptionalities (i.e., including gifted, learning disabled, and behaviorally disordered populations). As is true with students' perceptions of competence in other domains, how attractive they perceive themselves to be affects their self-esteem more than how attractive they actually are. Given the tendency for children and adolescents to base their perceptions of attractiveness on media figures, parents and educators may need to help them understand that it is unrealistic and unhealthy to adopt such lofty standards (Harter, 1999).

### Enhancing Support From Significant Others

Among the different types of support that significant others may provide, approval or acceptance is the most predictive of self-worth, instrumental support is the least predictive, and emotional support falls between the two (Harter, 1999). The presence of nurturance and approval causes children to view themselves favorably, whereas the absence of nurturance, encouragement, and approval, or the presence of frequent rejection or punishment, causes children to view themselves negatively.

Although support can be provided by a number of different individuals, support from parents and peers seems particularly important. When children are young, parental approval is more predictive of self-worth than approval from others. Contrary to popular assumption, although the influence of peers increases over the course of development, the influence of parents does not decline (Harter, 1999). As was true with perceptions of competence, perceived, not actual, support predicts students' feelings of self-worth. Thus, school professionals may help prevent feelings of low self-worth by working not only with parents and peers to increase the actual support they provide to students, but also with students to increase their awareness of the support that is provided (Harter, 1999).

Surprisingly little research has investigated the effects of teacher support on student self-esteem. However, positive teacher–student relationships have been linked to decreased dropout, risk taking, and aggression, as well as increased academic and social competence (see chapter 6, "Parent–Teacher Relationships"). Furthermore, much of the research on parenting styles may apply to teachers as well. For example, adolescents raised by authoritative parents display significantly higher academic and social self-concepts than peers raised by authoritarian or neglectful parents (Lamborn, Mounts, Steinberg, & Dornbusch, 1991). It is likely that similar results might be obtained when teachers adopt authoritative teaching styles. Characteristics of such a style include providing unconditional acceptance, warmth, affection, and encouragement; involving children in decision making; setting clear limits on students' behavior; and consistently applying fair and reasonable consequences for misbehavior (see chapter 3, "Developing Self-Discipline"). Additional strategies teachers can use to prevent or reduce low self-worth are presented in Table 2 (see also Bear, 2005).

## ALTERNATIVE ACTIONS FOR INTERVENTION

Over the years, myriad strategies have been implemented to raise children's self-esteem, including simply telling them they are wonderful and implementing lessons and activities from the hundreds of books and curriculum packages on self-esteem. Instead of being based on theoretical or empirical support about the multidimensional nature of self-concept and the variety of factors that affect it, these strategies have been based on a unidimensional understanding of self-esteem and a simple one-size-fits-all approach. It should come as little surprise, then, that the results "do not provide a ringing endorsement" (Baumeister et al., 2003, p. 20) for the effectiveness of self-esteem interventions.

Effective intervention begins with a comprehensive problem-solving analysis of the multiple cognitive, affective, behavioral, and environmental factors that influence self-concept and with identification of the specific causes of low self-worth in each child. Carefully selecting an appropriate instrument and completing a clinical interview are critical steps in beginning the intervention process. Table 3 gives sample questions, and the information that should be gleaned from the interview is discussed below (see Bear et al., 1997, for a more extended discussion).

A detailed problem-solving analysis should lead to hypotheses that suggest whether intervention is necessary. Low levels of self-esteem may not necessitate intervention if they are restricted to a specific domain and represent a fairly accurate appraisal of a student's competence in that domain. If intervention is warranted, the next step is to determine whether it would be most efficaciously directed toward the child, the classroom, or the family, or toward a combination of these. Typically, all three should be the focus of intervention, with an emphasis on the home and school environments (Swann, 1996).

### Interventions Directed Toward the Child

One reason for the failure of self-concept interventions relates to their failure to address the specific causes of low self-worth in each individual child. Such causes may include lack of skills, lack of support, or lack of accurate perceptions about the skills students display or support they receive.

***Building skills.*** If children lack skills in areas they view as important, interventions that seek to build their skills in those areas may be appropriate. For example, students

**Table 2** *Educators' Techniques for Fostering Self-Esteem*

- Demonstrate social support by showing personal interest in each individual.
  - Discover each student's strengths, interests, favorite sports, hobbies, television shows, family background, and so on and refer to this information during daily discourse with the individual student and the class.
    - Such information can be gathered by distributing a simple survey (e.g., What are your favorite hobbies? What do you enjoy doing the most?), by asking students to write about what they are most proud of or what they do best, by personally interviewing each student, or by having students interview one another and report their results to the class.
    - Students can also be asked to develop an autobiography in which they profile their backgrounds, achievements, hobbies, and future goals.
  - Demonstrate sincere concern and strong support for students during times of need and hardship. Encourage students to do the same with their peers. One way to discover when students need emotional support is by requiring a journal in which students may (but are not required to) express emotional needs.

---

- Consistently demonstrate respect, acceptance, and care for all students, regardless of their backgrounds or past or present behavior.
  - When addressing misbehavior, the message should be that although the student's misbehavior is unacceptable, the student is always acceptable and worthwhile. Avoid attacks on the student's character and instead focus remarks on the student's behavior (e.g., instead of "you're irresponsible," say "what you did was irresponsible").
  - Draw a distinction between students' feelings and their behaviors. Teach students that all feelings are okay but all behaviors are not okay. For example, emphasize that it is okay for them to feel angry, but it is not okay for them to express their anger in a way that could hurt themselves or others. One way that students can often express their feelings without hurting anyone is simply by telling someone how they feel.
  - Display a positive and optimistic attitude. Even when working with students with the most challenging behavior problems, demonstrate confidence that their behavior will improve. Research shows that effective classroom managers view every day as a new day, and do not hold the past behaviors of students against them (Brophy, 1996).
  - View mistakes of behavior as learning experiences, not failures. Use these mistakes as opportunities to teach students more responsible behavior.
  - Exhibit "random acts of kindness" and encourage students to do the same.

---

- Avoid social comparisons (e.g., posting of grades). Encourage students to compare their performance (including behavior) to personal goals or previous performance rather than to their peers' (e.g., instead of saying, "Why don't you act like others in the class?" you should say, "Your behavior is much better than last week when you show that you can ignore others when they bother you").

---

- Avoid public humiliation. When possible, handle discipline problems privately, not publicly.

---

- Garner social support from others, especially parents and peers, to help bolster positive emotions and behavior. A 2-minute phone call to tell parents that their child could use some emotional support after experiencing an unexpected failure is likely to be time well spent.

---

- To help protect feelings of autonomy and, thus, self-esteem, apply only as much external regulation as necessary to bring about compliance (referred to as the "principle of minimal sufficiency"; Lepper, 1983). Educators should use just enough external pressure to bring about compliance without making students feel that they are being coerced. When external pressure is not obvious, students tend to believe that they perform a requisite behavior for reasons that are intrinsically motivated and, thus, are more likely to engage in that behavior in the future (Hoffman, 2000).

---

*Note.* From *Developing Self-Discipline and Preventing and Correcting Misbehavior* (pp. 180–181), by G. G. Bear (with A. R. Cavalier and M. A. Manning), 2005, Boston: Allyn & Bacon. Copyright 2005 by Allyn & Bacon. Reprinted with permission.

**Table 3** *Clinical Interview Sample Questions*

| Goal | Sample Questions |
|---|---|
| Elicit and examine self-perceptions and self-evaluations across a variety of domains. | How would you describe yourself? How might others describe you? |
| | How do you feel about yourself? What are you most proud of? |
| | What do you do very well? What things are difficult for you? What are some things you would like to do much better? |
| Assess importance attached to domains, especially areas of concern. | On a scale from 1 to 10, how important do you think it is to be good at ________________? |
| Explore individual item responses that are strongly negative or that differ from other items in the domain. | I noticed that you disagreed with the item, "My parents understand me." Tell me more about that. |
| Examine individual items for inconsistencies in responses to descriptions of competence and feelings about competence. | You said that you get good grades in reading but that you're not pleased with your reading. Tell me about that. |
| Determine frames of reference (social and ipsative comparisons). | When I asked you about how well you're doing in ____________, how did you decide how well (or poorly) you're doing? Were you thinking about kids who are your own age? Older? In other classes? Were you thinking of how you do in other areas? |
| | How about if you compare how well you're doing in ____________ (weak area) with ______________ (other group or other area)? |
| Evaluate perceptions of social support. | When you're having problems, whom can you turn to for help? How about others (e.g., parents, teachers, peers, close friends, relatives, and neighbors)? |

who express low academic self-concept, experience decoding difficulties, and view reading ability as vital to their self-worth may benefit from interventions designed to build their word attack skills. Similarly, students who display poor athletic ability but aspire to be successful in that area may benefit from learning and practicing specific sports techniques. According to Harter, however, an individual "does not have to be a superstar in the decathlon of life" in order to develop adequate or high self-esteem (1999, p. 316). In other words, students do not need to experience success in every possible domain. Rather, they simply need to have a few domains in which they both value and experience success. An important distinction of that success, as perceived by the student, is that it not be based on comparisons to others or on unrealistic goals and criteria. For example, students with reading difficulties should be encouraged to focus on their progress in learning specific skills rather than on their performance in relation to others.

***Building support.*** Students may benefit from learning skills that not only help them increase their competence in personally important areas (e.g., academic or athletic competence) but also help them gain more support from others. Because academic competence and behavioral conduct are highly valued by parents, interventions that promote greater success in these domains should lead to higher levels of support. Some students may also benefit from learning specific social skills that help them elicit support from others (e.g., learning how to ask for help or how to join a game). Furthermore, students who lack particular attributes that are valued by peers, such as physical appearance and athletic ability, may benefit from interventions that address these areas as well (Harter, 1999). In some cases, however, it may be more effective for students to reevaluate the importance they attach to particular sources of support. For example, students may need to discount the importance of the support they lack from particular sources (e.g., the "popular" crowd at school) and focus on the support that is forthcoming from other sources (e.g., one's own group of friends). In other cases, compensatory support may need to be provided by alternative sources.

***Changing perceptions.*** Sometimes students may not lack skills or support but rather may lack accurate perceptions of the skills they have or the support that is provided. In such cases, students may benefit from therapeutic techniques designed to help them see that they are more competent (or supported) than they believe. Some students may need to learn to adopt more realistic standards for themselves or to evaluate their performance in relation to their previous performance rather than to the performance of others. Others may benefit from techniques that help them internalize the positive opinions of others and make internal attributions for their successes (Harter, 1999).

Research supports the effectiveness of cognitive–behavioral techniques in modifying children's self-perceptions For example, Craven, Marsh, and Debus (1991) describe an attribution-retraining intervention in which students received internally focused feedback that emphasized their strengths in a particular academic subject and modeled an internal attribution for success (e.g., "Look at how well you add and subtract. You must feel good about your ability in math"). Improvements in academic self-concept and overall self-worth were evident, but only when the intervention was delivered by researchers rather than classroom teachers. These results suggest the importance of providing interventions by properly trained individuals (Hattie, 1992).

***Planning interventions for students with LD.*** The popular assumption that students with LD experience low self-concepts has resulted in their involvement in a number of different types of interventions. As reviewed by Elbaum and Vaughn (2001), these interventions have included counseling (e.g., cognitive–behavioral therapy and relaxation techniques), academic interventions (e.g., peer tutoring and cooperative learning), physical interventions (e.g., physical recreation and fitness programs), sensory–perceptual interventions (e.g., sensory integration and perceptual–motor therapy), and mediated interventions (in which parents and teachers have been trained to change the way they interact with students). In findings consistent with the multidimensional nature of self-concept, Elbaum and Vaughn (2001, 2003) determined that the effectiveness of the interventions varied according to specific self-concept domain and to grade level. Counseling and mediated interventions were the only techniques that influenced overall self-worth, mediated interventions were the only ones that affected social self-concept, and physical interventions were the only ones that influenced physical self-perceptions. Both academic and counseling interventions had a significant effect on academic self-concept, although counseling was effective only with older students. Academic interventions were the only effective interventions for students in elementary school, whereas counseling was the only effective intervention for middle and high school students. Overall, middle school students benefited more from interventions than did elementary or high school students, and interventions had more of an effect on students' academic self-concept than on other dimensions of self-concept. The latter results are consistent with Hattie (1992), which suggests that academic self-perceptions may be most amenable to change.

Further analysis of these studies by Elbaum and Vaughn (2003) indicated that only those students who experienced low self-concept benefited significantly from the interventions. These results call into question the practice of implementing self-concept interventions among students with LD solely on the basis of the students' disability category. Similar results might be expected for interventions aimed at students with behavior problems, especially because they often experience inflated, rather than deflated, self-esteem (e.g., David & Kistner, 2000). Consequently, some researchers suggest that the effectiveness of such interventions may be indicated by a decrease, rather than an increase, in self-concept (e.g., Hughes et al., 1997). In sum, these findings suggest that deficits in self-concept should be assessed, not assumed, prior to intervention and that a one-size-fits-all approach should be avoided.

## Classroom Interventions

***Special education placement.*** Two different perspectives have influenced beliefs about the relationship between self-concept and educational placement (Elbaum, 2002). One perspective has emphasized the processes of labeling and segregation, whereas the other has emphasized the process of social comparison.

According to the first perspective, students who are segregated from nondisabled peers develop low perceptions of self-worth because they believe that they are treated differently from their peers and viewed as inferior; placing students in inclusive settings is believed to ameliorate the problem. According to the second perspective, students' self-perceptions differ depending on the frame of reference they use when judging their own competence. When taught in general education classes, students with disabilities compare themselves to their nondisabled peers, which makes their deficits more apparent and results in negative self-perceptions. In contrast, when students are educated in segregated settings, where their interactions are limited to students who also have disabilities, their deficits may not be as apparent and their self-worth not as likely to suffer. Thus, segregated settings should be protective of children's self-worth.

Recent meta-analyses have put these assumptions to the test by comparing the self- concepts of students with LD across different settings. Bear et al. (2002) and Elbaum (2002) found no differences in self-concept among students with learning disabilities who received different degrees of special education support within regular education schools. Results suggest that students taught in inclusive settings do not seem to have higher self-perceptions because of the lessened stigma, nor do they seem to be harmed as a result of more readily available social comparisons with higher-achieving peers. Therefore, special educators should avoid making placement recommendations based on the presumed effects of settings on self-perceptions.

***Teacher practices.*** Although individual interventions may produce short-term gains in self-esteem, significant long-term benefits may not occur if the classroom environment does not support students' academic endeavors, sustain their achievement, and promote their feelings of acceptance (Elbaum & Vaughn, 2003). Practices such as peer tutoring and cooperative learning, when implemented in general education classrooms, can promote positive self-concepts by increasing students' academic skills and perceptions of social support (Elbaum & Vaughn, 2001). As noted in Table 4, teachers can help prevent or reduce feelings of low self-esteem by reducing the salience of social comparison cues in the classroom and by encouraging students to rely on other standards for self-evaluation, such as personal improvement and effort. Teachers should also be aware of the power of positive feedback in maintaining children's positive self-perceptions. For example, positive feedback from teachers

**Table 4** *Methods to Reduce the Availability of Social Comparison Cues and Limit Negative Social Comparison Effects*

| Area of Practice | Method to Reduce Social Comparisons |
|---|---|
| Grading and evaluation | Make grades private not public (e.g., do not post grades or "best work"). |
| | Allow students to improve grades by redoing work. |
| | Avoid grading that allows only a few students to achieve high grades (e.g., use of normal curve). |
| Grouping | Avoid use of ability groups for instruction. |
| | Make group membership flexible; allow for movement from one group to another. |
| Tasks | Provide individualized tasks at which all children can be successful. |
| | Reduce emphasis on competition against other students; emphasize improvement over the child's own prior performance. |
| | Use cooperative learning strategies that allow all children to participate successfully. |

has been shown to be related to students' self-satisfaction with regard to reading, which in turn is related to self-perception of academic competence (Bear, Minke, Griffin, & Deemer, 1998). However, the effects of positive feedback are difficult to measure because they are complex and embedded in the child's interpretation of factors, such as task difficulty and the overall quality of the relationship with the teacher. Likewise, the relationship between students' self-perceptions and motivation and teachers' feedback and judgments is cyclical (Meltzer et al., 2004).

Teachers can also help increase students' feelings of self-worth by fostering supportive relationships among students. Friendships serve as an important protective factor, buffering children against the negative effects of peer rejection (Bear, Juvonen, & McInerney, 1993) and bullying (Hodges, Malone, & Perry, 1997). However, across age groups, support from classmates is more strongly related to self-worth than is support from close friends (Harter, 1999). Perhaps the most effective way for teachers to foster feelings of acceptance among students is by creating a sense of community within the classroom. Through programs such as the Child Development Project (Solomon, Battistich, Watson, Schaps, & Lewis, 2000), teachers can create a sense of community by emphasizing prosocial values and using developmental discipline, cooperative learning activities, helping activities, and activities that promote social understanding (see also chapter 3, "Developing Self-Discipline"). Students' perceptions of their classroom as a community in which they care about each other, and are cared about, are positively related to their academic self-concept, global self-worth, and social competence (Battistich, Solomon, Kim, Watson, & Schaps, 1995). The relationship between sense of community and academic self-concept is particularly pronounced among high-poverty schools (Battistich et al.), suggesting that feelings of belonging at school may serve a powerful protection against negative outcomes, particularly for students who are at high risk.

### Interventions Directed Toward Families

Because parents' perceptions of their children powerfully influence the views students develop about themselves, parents are an important component of any self-esteem intervention. Parents may need assistance in understanding students' strengths and weaknesses, particularly if students display limited competence in areas valued by parents but greater competence in areas overlooked by parents. In cases in which students' abilities are limited, parents may need support in developing more realistic expectations for their children.

Another avenue for intervention involves improving the interactions between parents and children (Harter, 1999). Techniques based on attachment theory, such as Parent–Child Interaction Therapy (PCIT), have been effective in increasing students' self-esteem (Eisenstadt, Eyberg, McNeil, Newcomb, & Funderburk, 1993). However, these results have been based on students with behavior problems; therefore, it is questionable whether increased self-esteem is desirable. Nevertheless, given the relationship between parental discipline style and children's self-esteem (see Chapter 3, "Developing Self-Discipline"), school professionals may be able to not only prevent but also reduce low self-esteem in many students by helping parents adopt more authoritative discipline practices. Finally, self-esteem is consistently lower among children in families characterized by abuse or alcoholism (Feiring & Taska, 1996), perhaps because parents are not emotionally available to their children and therefore may not provide them the support they need. These families should be assisted in accessing resources that enable them to cope more effectively with such challenges.

## SUMMARY

Self-concept is one of the most widely discussed but least understood constructs in the fields of psychology and education. Current theory and research support the multidimensionality of self-concept, which is best represented by a profile of perceptions across specific domains of competence (e.g., academic and social) rather than by a single score. The construct of *global self-concept* represents one's overall feelings toward oneself, or what is traditionally known as self-esteem. Many myths and misunderstandings about self-esteem persist. For example, the idea that self-esteem is lower among children with learning disabilities or aggressive behavior problems has little empirical support. Increasingly, research suggests that aggressive children often display an inflated sense of self-worth. There is also little support for the notion that inclusion will increase students' self-concept or that segregated settings will decrease it.

Children's sense of self-worth is based on their sense of accomplishment in domains they value and on their feelings of support from peers and adults. Positive relationships and success lead to self-worth, which is associated with feelings of happiness. Many attempts to ameliorate low self-esteem have failed for one of two reasons: because they have been based on the mistaken assumption that all students in a particular group lack self-esteem, or because they fail to identify the factors that contribute to a particular student's low self-esteem. Effective prevention and intervention reflect a general understanding of the antecedents of self-concept, which include feelings of competence in highly valued areas and perceptions of support from significant others, with interventions tailored to meet the unique needs of each child.

## RECOMMENDED RESOURCES

### Books and Other Printed Material

Baumeister, R. F., Campbell, J. D., Krueger, J. I., & Vohs, K. D. (2003). Does high self-esteem cause better performance, interpersonal success, happiness, or healthier lifestyles? *Psychological Science in the Public Interest, 4,* 1–44.

This article provides a comprehensive review of research on self-esteem, including the relationship of self-esteem to school performance, job and task performance, interpersonal relations, aggression, violence, delinquency, antisocial behavior, happiness, coping, depression, smoking, alcohol and other drugs, sexual activity, and eating disorders.

Crocker, J., & Park, L. E. (2004). The costly pursuit of self-esteem. *Psychological Bulletin, 130,* 392–414.

This is one of several articles in a special issue devoted to the topic of self-esteem and the controversy surrounding its benefits.

Harter, S. (1999). *The construction of the self.* New York: Guilford Press.

This book provides a comprehensive review of Harter's extensive research on self-concept and discusses practical implications for educators.

## Websites

*http://self.uws.edu.au*

This is the website for the SELF (Self-Esteem Enhancement and Learning Facilitation) Research Centre in Australia, directed by Herbert Marsh. The website contains information regarding recent research conducted by the center as well as information on purchase of self-concept instruments. It is most useful to those conducting research in self-concept.

*http://www.devstu.org/cdp/*

This website describes the comprehensive Child Development Project, which combines a focus on developing children's reading skills with developing their sense of community and belonging in school. Links are provided to materials for creating a Caring School Community.

## REFERENCES

American Psychiatric Association. (1994). *Diagnostic and statistical manual for mental disorders* (4th ed.). Washington, DC: Author.

Battistich, V., Solomon, D., Kim, D., Watson, M., & Schaps, E. (1995). Schools as communities, poverty levels of student populations, and students' attitudes, motives, and performance: A multilevel analysis. *American Educational Research Journal, 32,* 627–658.

Baumeister, R. F., Campbell, J. D., Krueger, J. I., & Vohs, K. D. (2003). Does high self-esteem cause better performance, interpersonal success, happiness, or healthier lifestyles? *Psychological Science in the Public Interest, 4,* 1–44.

Bear, G. G. (with Cavalier, A., & Manning, M. A.). (2005). *Developing self-discipline and preventing and correcting misbehavior.* Boston: Allyn & Bacon.

Bear, G. G., Juvonen, J., & McInerney, F. (1993). Self-perceptions and peer relations of boys with and boys without learning disabilities in an integrated setting: A longitudinal study. *Learning Disability Quarterly, 16,* 127–136.

Bear, G. G., & Minke, K. M. (1996). Positive bias in the maintenance of self-worth among children with LD. *Learning Disability Quarterly, 19,* 23–31.

Bear, G. G., Minke, K. M., Griffin, S. M., & Deemer, S. A. (1997). Self-concept. In G. G. Bear & K. M. Minke (Eds.), *Children's needs II: Development, problems, and alternatives* (pp. 257–269). Washington, DC: National Association of School Psychologists.

Bear, G. G., Minke, K. M., Griffin, S. M., & Deemer, S. A. (1998). Achievement-related perceptions of children with learning disabilities and normal achievement: Group and developmental differences. *Journal of Learning Disabilities, 31,* 91–104.

Bear, G. G., Minke, K. M., & Manning, M. A. (2002). The self-concepts of students with learning disabilities: A meta-analysis. *School Psychology Review, 31,* 405–427.

Bracken, B. (1992). *Examiner's manual for the Multidimensional Self-Concept Scale.* Austin, TX: Pro-Ed.

Bracken, B. (1996). Clinical applications of a context-dependent, multidimensional model of self-concept. In B. A. Bracken (Ed.), *Handbook of self-concept: Developmental, social, and clinical considerations* (pp. 463–504). New York: Wiley.

Brophy, J. E. (1996). *Teaching problem students.* New York: Guilford Press.

California Task Force to Promote Self-Esteem and Personal and Social Responsibility. (1990). *Toward a state of esteem: The final report of the California Task Force to Promote Self-Esteem and Personal and Social Responsibility.* Sacramento, CA: Author.

Chapman, J. W. (1988). Learning disabled self-concepts. *Review of Educational Research, 58,* 347–371.

Coopersmith, S. (1981). *Coopersmith Self-Esteem Inventories.* Palo Alto, CA: Consulting Psychologists.

Craven, R. G., Marsh, H. W., & Debus, R. L. (1991). Effects of internally focused feedback and attributional feedback on the enhancement of academic self-concept. *Journal of Educational Psychology, 83,* 17–26.

David, C. F., & Kistner, J. A. (2000). Do positive self-perceptions have a "dark side"? Examination of the link between perceptual bias and aggression. *Journal of Abnormal Child Psychology, 28,* 327–337.

Eisenstadt, T. H., Eyberg, S., McNeil, C. B., Newcomb, K., & Funderburk, B. (1993). Parent-child interaction therapy with behavior problem children: Relative effectiveness of two stages and overall treatment outcome. *Journal of Clinical Child Psychology, 22,* 42–51.

Elbaum, B. (2002). The self-concept of students with learning disabilities: A meta-analysis of comparisons across different placements. *Learning Disabilities Research and Practice, 17,* 216–226.

Elbaum, B., & Vaughn, S. (2001). School-based interventions to enhance the self-concept of students with learning disabilities: A meta-analysis. *Elementary School Journal, 101,* 303–329.

Elbaum, B., & Vaughn, S. (2003). For which students with learning disabilities are self-concept interventions effective? *Journal of Learning Disabilities, 36,* 101–108.

Feiring, C., & Taska, L. S. (1996). Family self-concept: Ideas on its meaning. In B. Bracken (Ed.), *Handbook of self-concept* (pp. 317–373). New York: Wiley.

Harter, S. (1985). *The Self-Perception Profile for Children.* Un-published manual, University of Denver, Denver, CO.

Harter, S. (1988). *The Self-Perception Profile for Adolescents.* Unpublished manual, University of Denver, Denver, CO.

Harter, S. (1999). *The construction of the self: A developmental perspective.* New York: Guilford Press.

Harter, S., & Pike, R. (1984). The pictorial scale of Perceived Competence and Social Acceptance for Young Children. *Child Development, 55,* 1969–1982.

Hattie, J. (1992). *Self-concept.* Hillsdale, NJ: Erlbaum.

Hodges, E. V. E., Malone, M. J., Jr., & Perry, D. G. (1997). Individual risk and social risk as interacting determinants of victimization in the peer group. *Developmental Psychology, 35,* 94–101.

Hoffman, M. L. (2000). *Empathy and moral development: Implications for caring and justice.* Cambridge, UK: Cambridge University Press.

Hughes, J. N., Cavell, T. A., & Grossman, P. B. (1997). A positive view of self: Risk or protection for aggressive children? *Development and Psychopathology, 9,* 75–94.

Jacobs, J. E., Lanza, S., Osgood, D. W., Eccles, J. S., & Wigfield, A. (2002). Changes in children's self-competence and values: Gender and domain differences across grades one through twelve. *Child Development, 73,* pp. 509–527.

Kling, K. C., Hyde, J. S., Showers, C. J., & Buswell, B. N. (1999). Gender differences in self-esteem: A meta-analysis. *Psychological Bulletin, 125,* 470–500.

Lamborn, S. D., Mounts, N. S., Steinberg, L., & Dornbusch, S. M. (1991). Patterns of competence and adjustment among adolescents from authoritative, authoritarian, indulgent, and neglectful families. *Child Development, 62,* 1049–1065.

Lepper, M. (1983). Social-control processes and the internalization of social values: An attributional perspective. In E. T. Higgins, D. Ruble, & W. Hartup (Eds.), *Social cognition and social development: A social-cultural perspective.* (pp. 294–330). New York: Cambridge University Press.

Marsh, H. W. (1986). Verbal and math self-concepts: An internal/external frame of reference model. *American Educational Research Journal, 23,* 129–149.

Marsh, H. W. (1988). *Self-Description Questionnaire—I.* San Antonio, TX: Psychological Corporation.

Marsh, H. W. (1989). Age and sex effects in multiple dimensions of self-concept: Preadolescence to early adulthood. *Journal of Educational Psychology, 81,* 417–430.

Marsh, H. W. (1990). *Self-Description Questionnaire—II.* San Antonio, TX: Psychological Corporation.

Marsh, H. W. (1993). Academic self-concept: Theory, measurement, and research. In J. Suls (Ed.), *Psychological perspectives on the self.* (Vol. 4, pp. 59–98). Hillsdale, NJ: Erlbaum.

Marsh, H. W., & Ayotte, V. (2003). Do multiple dimensions of self-concept become more differentiated with age? The differential distinctiveness hypothesis. *Journal of Educational Psychology, 95,* 687–706.

Marsh, H. W., Ellis, L. A., & Craven, R. G. (2002). How do preschool children feel about themselves? Unraveling measurement and multidimensional self concept structure. *Developmental Psychology, 38,* 376–393.

Marsh, H. W., & Hattie, J. (1996). Theoretical perspectives on the structure of self-concept. In B. A. Bracken (Ed.), *Handbook of self-concept: Developmental, social, and clinical considerations.* (pp. 38–90). Oxford, UK: Wiley.

Meltzer, L., Reddy, R., Pollica, L. S., Roditi, B., Sayer, J., & Theokas, C. (2004). Positive and negative self-perceptions: Is there a cyclical relationship between teachers' and students' perceptions of effort, strategy use, and academic performance? *Learning Disabilities Research and Practice, 19,* 33–44.

Nicholls, J. G. (1978). The development of the concept of effort and ability, perceptions of academic attainment, and the understanding that difficult tasks require more ability. *Child Development, 49,* 800–814.

Piers, E. V. (1969). *Manual for the Piers-Harris Self-Concept Scale.* Nashville, TN: Counselor Recordings and Tests.

Pietsch, J., Walker, R., & Chapman, E. (2003). The relationship among self-concept, self-efficacy, and performance in mathematics during secondary school. *Journal of Educational Psychology, 95,* 589–603.

Salmivalli, C. (2001). Feeling good about oneself, being bad to others? Remarks on self-esteem, hostility, and aggressive behavior. *Aggression and Violent Behavior, 6,* 375–393.

Salmivalli, C., Kaukiainen, A., Kaistaniemi, L., & Lagerspetz, K. M. J. (1999). Self-evaluated self-esteem, peer-evaluated self-esteem, and defensive egotism as predictors of adolescents' participation in bullying situations. *Personality and Social Psychology Bulletin, 25,* 1268–1278.

Solomon, D., Battistich, V., Watson, M., Schaps, E., & Lewis, C. (2000). A six-district study of educational change: Direct and mediated effects of the child development project. *Social Psychology of Education, 4,* 3–51.

Stipek, D., & Tannatt, L. (1984). Children's judgements of their own and their peers' academic competence. *Journal of Educational Psychology, 76,* 75–84.

Swann, W. B., Jr. (1996). *Self-traps.* New York: Freeman.

Verschueren, K., & Marcoen, A. (2002). Perceptions of self and relationship with parents in aggressive and nonaggressive rejected children. *Journal of School Psychology, 40,* 501–522.

Wigfield, A., & Eccles, J. S. (2002). The development of competence beliefs, expectancies for success, and achievement values from childhood through adolescence. In A. Wigfield & J. S. Eccles (Eds.), *Development of achievement motivation* (pp. 91–120). San Diego, CA: Academic Press.

Wigfield, A., Eccles, J. S., Yoon, K. S., Harold, R. D., Arbreton, A., Freedman-Doan, K., & Blumenfeld, P. C. (1997). Change in children's competence beliefs and subjective task values across the elementary school years: A three-year study. *Journal of Educational Psychology, 89,* 451–569.

# 27

# Life Satisfaction

**E. Scott Huebner**
*University of South Carolina*

**Shannon M. Suldo**
*University of South Florida*

**Rich Gilman**
*University of Kentucky*

## BACKGROUND AND DEVELOPMENT

### Importance of Life Satisfaction

A central mission of mental health professionals and educators is to promote the psychological well-being of *all* students. Nevertheless, past and present approaches toward achieving this goal have largely focused on studies of factors that contribute to psychological distress and maladaptive outcomes, with the inference that such studies should directly inform understanding of the development of optimal mental health. Recent empirical evidence calls this inference into question. For example, Greenspoon and Saklofske (2001) identified a subgroup of elementary school children that reported low psychological distress but also low subjective well-being. Given that psychological assessment practices have focused on the identification of psychopathological symptoms, such students would appear psychologically "healthy" even though well-being reports would indicate otherwise. These findings suggest that the absence of psychopathological symptoms is not necessarily concordant with optimal mental health and are consistent with researchers who contend that the study of psychological well-being is an important endeavor in its own right.

In addition to mental health professionals' interest in this topic, other groups recognize the distinction between well-being and absence of disease. For example, the foremost goal of most parents is *not* to create environments or instill characteristics that are simply meant to prevent psychopathology from occurring; rather, their goal is to instill and promote characteristics that contribute to healthy development and a productive life. Such characteristics are also believed to serve as protective barriers against the development of psychological difficulties. Among school professionals, an important goal of psychoeducational interventions is to enhance the quality of life among youth. To be sure, ethical considerations necessitate that any intervention for students (e.g., placement in remedial or special education programs, behavioral modification strategies) should at the very least *not* result in decreased quality of life. In keeping with this goal, measurement of positive psychological well-being factors, such as life satisfaction, should contribute information that informs multiple groups regarding the impact of care and services provided to children.

Interpretation of the term *well-being* has been inconsistent in the human sciences. Until recently, research has focused on external, objective indicators such as family income level, recreational opportunities, and per capita expenditures on schooling. However, such objective indicators have consistently yielded low correlations with individuals' subjective evaluations of their life circumstances, suggesting that objective and subjective indicators provide unique information relevant to persons' well-being. Furthermore, given that objective indicators account for only a small portion of the variance in subjective well-being reports, the study of subjective well-being has been emphasized by some researchers. As Csikszentmihalyi (1990) noted, "subjective experience is not just one dimension of life, it *is* life itself" (p. 192).

Subjective well-being is theoretically composed of three components: life satisfaction, positive affect, and negative affect (Diener, Suh, Lucas, & Smith, 1999). Given that the affect domains represent one's frequency of experienced moods and emotions (e.g., joy, pride, guilt, and sadness), which change relatively rapidly within an individual, life satisfaction is considered to be the more stable component of subjective well-being and, therefore, the indicator most amenable for inclusion in comprehensive studies of youths' perceptions of their life circumstances. *Life satisfaction* is defined as a cognitive appraisal of life based on self-selected standards (Diener et al., 1999). At its most fundamental level, *general* life satisfaction refers to one's satisfaction with life as a whole. In addition, satisfaction judgments can be made for specific life domains that contribute to general life satisfaction. Most authors investigating multidimensional models of child and adolescent life satisfaction agree on several central domains, such as satisfaction with family, school, and friends, which should be included in formations of general life satisfaction. Research tends to support a hierarchical model, with general life satisfaction viewed as a superordinate factor along with multiple, lower-order specific life domains (Huebner, Laughlin, Ash, & Gilman, 1998).

Over the past decade, a number of life satisfaction scales appropriate for children and youth have been constructed on the basis of unidimensional (i.e., general) or multidimensional models. Most measures have been self-reports and have been primarily used to illustrate similarities and differences between life satisfaction and related psychological constructs, such as self-concept. Global self-concept generally refers to a summary evaluation of one's self-worth (i.e., appraisal of one's behavior or characteristics). In contrast, life satisfaction is conceptualized as a more comprehensive construct, which may include but is not limited to judgments related to the self. Life satisfaction evaluations reflect both inner-directed (e.g., self) and outer-directed evaluations of other life domains, such as family life or living environment. Research has supported the distinction between the two constructs through factor analytic procedures and the demonstration of differential correlates (e.g., Huebner, Gilman, & Laughlin, 1999).

Although conceptually distinguishable from various measures of psychopathology, life satisfaction has been found to be negatively related to depression, anxiety, health and risk behaviors such as alcohol or illicit drug use, and aggressive behavior (see Gilman & Huebner, 2003, for a review). Perhaps more important, with regard to the utility of the construct, seminal research with adult subjects indicates life satisfaction is not merely an outcome of negative life experiences or personal characteristics; it can influence adaptive outcomes. For example, low life satisfaction has been shown to precede the onset of depression in adulthood (Lewinsohn, Redner, & Seeley, 1991). Low life satisfaction has also been found to predict suicidal behavior, physical health, and compliance with treatment protocols (see Frisch, 1999, for a review).

Recent studies with youth have demonstrated that life satisfaction is not just a desirable outcome but also serves important functions in adolescent mental health. For instance, life satisfaction is one pathway through which perceived social relationships influence adolescents' own behavior. Specifically, adolescent life satisfaction serves as a mediator, that is, a cognitive link through which adolescents' perceptions of their parents' parenting behaviors influence their own levels of psychopathological behavior (Suldo & Huebner, 2004b). Similarly, it is a path through which stressful life experiences influence internalizing behavior (McKnight, Huebner, & Suldo, 2002). The level of initial life satisfaction has been successful in determining which youth are likely to develop later aggressive and delinquent behavior in the face of stressful life experiences (Suldo & Huebner, 2004a). Specifically, Suldo and Huebner found that among adolescents with high life satisfaction, frequency of stressful life experiences did not predict later increases in externalizing behavior; however, subsequent externalizing behavior increased linearly as a function of stressful life events experienced 1 year earlier in the sample of students with low life satisfaction. Thus, life satisfaction appears to function as a protective factor against the development of aggressive and delinquent behaviors. Taken together, these findings demonstrate that the promotion of high life satisfaction is more than simply a hedonistic pursuit. Rather, life satisfaction operates as a key psychological strength, facilitating adaptive development in children and youth.

Research also reveals that life satisfaction judgments contain both state- and trait-like characteristics. Life satisfaction reports have been shown to change in response to stressful life experiences such as homelessness or change in living status (Bearsley & Cummins, 1999; Gilman & Handwerk, 2001). These changes suggest sensitivity to differences between one's current circumstances and previous life circumstances. Nevertheless, life satisfaction reports also demonstrate substantial test–retest reliability (Huebner, Funk, & Gilman, 2000). Furthermore, most youth, regardless of life circumstance, report positive general life satisfaction and satisfaction with specific domains (Huebner, Drane, & Valois, 2000). Incorporating Lazarus's (1991) theory of coping, a positive satisfaction "set point," partially based on dispositional characteristics, may serve as a baseline against which ongoing cognitive appraisals, affective states, and environmental circumstances are compared. Most acute life experiences exert modest, short-term influences on life satisfaction at best. However, when negative events or circumstances overwhelm the coping resources of the individual, significant fluctuations in life satisfaction can be observed, signaling the need for new coping responses to manage the threats. In this manner, a positive set point supports sociability, creativity, environmental exploration, and other important approach tendencies that facilitate human survival (Diener & Diener, 1996). In short, a positive life-satisfaction set point, coupled with sensitivity to important environmental challenges, appears adaptive.

## Factors Related to Life Satisfaction

It has only been within the past 15 years that researchers have set out to discover what determines life satisfaction during normal childhood development. The initial research has primarily involved identifying variables that are correlated with life satisfaction at one point in time. For comprehensive reviews of literature pertinent to life satisfaction in youth, the reader is referred to Huebner, Suldo, Smith, and McKnight (2004) and Gilman and Huebner (2003). The following sections contain summaries of major findings pertinent to the study of life satisfaction during childhood and adolescence.

## Age, Gender, Race, and Socioeconomic Status

With respect to age, most studies find that children and adolescents, in general, report life satisfaction above the neutral range. For example, in a sample of 5,544 American students, 73% reported positive life satisfaction; specifically, life satisfaction ratings were within the "mostly satisfied" to "delighted" range (Huebner, Drane, & Valois, 2000). Global life satisfaction reports tend to decline slightly from childhood to adolescence, a finding confirmed in samples of youth from America (Suldo & Huebner, 2004b), Israel (Ullman & Tatar, 2001), China (Chang, McBride-Chang, Stewart, & Au, 2003), and the United Kingdom (Marks, Shah, & Westall, 2004).

Whereas age differences in life satisfaction have been identified, differences in gender, race, and socioeconomic status have not been found; however, studies have been limited to African American and Caucasian youth.

## Intrapersonal Factors

Several personality, cognitive, and psychopathology factors explain a substantial amount of variance in life satisfaction. Specifically, elevated life satisfaction during youth co-occurs with high levels of extroversion and perceived social self-efficacy (Fogle, Huebner, & Laughlin, 2002), as well as with increased social interest (i.e., desire for prosocial behavior; Gilman, 2001), self-esteem (Dew & Huebner, 1994), perfectionism (Gilman & Ashby, 2003), adaptive attributional style (Rigby & Huebner, 2004), and an internal locus of control (Ash & Huebner, 2001). Life satisfaction has an inverse relationship with neuroticism and psychopathology, including depression, anxiety, aggression, and conduct disorder (Huebner, Funk, & Gilman, 2000; Valois, Zullig, Huebner, & Drane, 2001). Indeed, diminished life satisfaction has been found among children diagnosed with emotional disabilities compared with children with learning disorders or those without any diagnosed handicap (Huebner & Alderman, 1993).

## School-Related Factors

Although schooling is a primary activity during youth, adolescents' global life satisfaction is unrelated to objective indicators of academic achievement, such as risk for school failure (Huebner & Alderman, 1993) or even special education placement due to cognitive or learning disabilities (Brantley, Huebner, & Nagle, 2002; McCullough & Huebner, 2003). Moreover, students with above-average intellectual abilities (i.e., labeled as gifted) and their nongifted classmates report comparable levels of life satisfaction (Ash & Huebner, 1998). Of note, recent cross-cultural surveys of students in environments with a particularly high emphasis on academic achievement have discovered diminished life satisfaction in students; specifically, in the United Kingdom life satisfaction was lowest among students attending the school with elite test scores (Marks, Shah, & Westall, 2004), and among elementary school students in China (where test scores in the primary years solely determine placement in an esteemed secondary school), achievement test scores were significantly correlated with life satisfaction (Chang et al., 2003). Although research on life satisfaction in normal childhood development downplays the influence of objective school grades, students' global life satisfaction is correlated with their *perceptions* of both their academic competence (Leung, McBride-Chang, & Lai, 2004; Suldo, 2004) and the quality of their school experiences (i.e., school satisfaction; Huebner, Drane, & Valois, 2000). Taken together, children's attitudes toward their school and feelings regarding their personal ability to achieve in such an environment are generally more strongly related to their life satisfaction than to objective indicators of achievement.

Some school factors may not relate to life satisfaction because school is mandated, and therefore is largely beyond adolescents' control (similar to demographic variables). In contrast, children's life satisfaction is associated with involvement in activities in which they *choose* to participate, including meaningful instrumental behaviors and extracurricular activities (Gilman, 2001; Maton, 1990). Specifically, the frequency with which adolescents engage in meaningful instrumental activity, such as actively contributing to the goals of a group or helping someone in need, is positively associated with global life satisfaction, whereas satisfaction with school is related to the number of structured extracurricular activities in which an adolescent participates.

Positive relationships with peers are common among children and adolescents with high life satisfaction (Dew & Huebner, 1994; Man, 2001). Moreover, life satisfaction partly explains both the quality of later peer relations (Huebner, Funk, & Gilman, 2000) and how peer stressors and peer resources influence adolescents' social behavior. Recent research that attempted to identify crucial aspects of the peer relationship found peer trust (i.e., loyalty, mutual caring, and commitment) to be the dimension of peer attachment most predictive of life satisfaction among children and early adolescents (Nickerson & Nagle, 2004). Additionally, perceived social self-competence (but not teacher-reported social competence) not only is correlated with life satisfaction but also is one cognitive mechanism by which extroversion influences life satisfaction (Fogle, Huebner, & Laughlin, 2002).

Life satisfaction is also related to teacher-reported behavior in school (Huebner & Alderman, 1993). Students who are more satisfied with their lives are less likely to engage in maladaptive behavior, including both externalizing and internalizing problem behavior.

## Home-Related Factors

***Environmental stressors.*** Consistent with Cowen's (1994) assertion that psychological health requires "exposure to settings that favor wellness outcomes" (p. 158), global life satisfaction in youth is related to the quality of children's surroundings, including location and diversity of neighborhoods, family environment, and stressful life experiences. For instance, children with high life satisfaction are more likely to reside in residential areas (vs. inner-city commercial or industrial areas) and neighborhoods with a relatively homogeneous ethnic composition (Homel & Burns, 1989; Sam, 1998). The latter finding is particularly salient among immigrant youth (Neto, 2001), whose life satisfaction increases as a function of length of residence in the new country (Liebkind & Jasinskaja-Lahti, 2000).

Family environment factors pertinent to adolescent life satisfaction include parents' marital status and involvement of caregivers. Although simple divorced or remarried family status is related to diminished well-being (Demo & Acock, 1996), more complex indicators of family discord, namely lack of paternal involvement and children's perceptions of a poor relationship between their parents, appear to exert more profound negative effects on life satisfaction (Grossman & Rowat, 1995; Flouri & Buchanan, 2002). Among teenage girls, multi-generational caregiving is associated with higher life satisfaction (Zimmerman, Salem, & Maton, 1995).

Similar to chronic daily stressors such as poor quality neighborhoods and unhappy home environments, the frequency of positive or negative *acute* life events is negatively related to life satisfaction during youth (Ash & Huebner, 2001). In one study, adolescents' recent experiences of major life events such as changing schools, parental divorce, and change in family income predicted their level of life satisfaction beyond that already predicted by their relevant personality traits (McKnight, Huebner, & Suldo, 2002). In addition to the direct effects of negative life events on life satisfaction, they also have indirect effects through their influence on children's locus-of-control attributions (Ash & Huebner, 2001). For example, frequent negative life events are associated with an increasingly external locus of control, which in turn is predictive of lower life satisfaction. Clearly, there are multiple paths by which acute stressful events affect adolescents' life satisfaction; nevertheless, research has indicated that *positive* daily events (e.g., hobbies or frequent opportunities to help others) predict life satisfaction better than the accumulation of major or daily life *stressors* (McCullough, Huebner, & Laughlin, 2000). Taken together, research on strains associated with an adolescent's environment, culture, and other stressful major experiences suggests that adolescent life satisfaction is likely to be at least temporarily influenced by acute and chronic life circumstances.

***Parent–child relations.*** Parent–child relationship variables are among the strongest correlates of life satisfaction during youth. For example, frequency and magnitude of parent–adolescent disagreements are inversely related to life satisfaction in adolescents from European American and Vietnamese American cultures (Phinney & Ong, 2002) as well as in Chinese youth (Shek, 1997). Although conflict between parents and their children is relatively ordinary during adolescence, research has pinpointed specific parenting behaviors that contribute to children's positive life satisfaction. First and foremost, parental social support and warmth is strongly associated with life satisfaction at every developmental stage of youth (Suldo & Huebner, 2004b); the magnitude of the relationship even persists during stressful adolescent life experiences such as teenage pregnancy (Stevenson, Maton, & Teti, 1999), high school dropout (Zimmerman, Salem, & Maton, 1995), and immigration (Liebkind & Jasinskaja-Lahti, 2000). Parental support and warmth is one aspect of a multidimensional style of parenting labeled authoritative, which is commonly found to relate to desirable child outcomes (Steinberg, Lamborn, Dornbusch, & Darling, 1992). Studies that include adolescent life satisfaction as a criterion variable have indicated positive relationships between life satisfaction and other components of authoritative parenting, namely strictness-supervision and promotion of adolescents' psychological autonomy (Suldo & Huebner, 2004b), as well as general use of authoritative parenting techniques during family decision-making (Petito & Cummins, 2000).

## PROBLEMS AND IMPLICATIONS

Research reviewed in the last section delineated several risk factors for diminished life satisfaction. Indeed, the survey of 5,544 American students referenced in the previous section indicated that 11% of respondents possessed overall life satisfaction far below the neutral point. Specifically, the average rating of their satisfaction with multiple domains of life was at or between "mostly dissatisfied" and "terrible" (Huebner et al., 2000). Such subgroups of children are in need of intervention to increase their life satisfaction in order to foster feelings of happiness in their life, but also to prevent later pathological outcomes.

Clearly, the sheer number of children who experience risk factors for low life satisfaction and the small but important number who report diminished life satisfaction are central problems with regard to life satisfaction in youth. However, an even larger problem involves the lack of attention paid to the construct itself. For example, life satisfaction as an indicator of optimal development is rarely included in either case studies or large-scale research studies of children's well-being. Data provided in the former paragraph are a notable exception and demonstrate the necessity of monitoring all children's life satisfaction. Unfortunately, many school professionals and researchers continue to shy away from strengths-based assessments in favor of assessing indicators of pathology.

This emphasis on pathology ignores research that attests to the importance of life satisfaction and related positive psychology constructs in comprehensive, balanced assessments of children and their environments. The main implication of life satisfaction studies is that psychologists will likely benefit from additional efforts in measuring, monitoring, and promoting positive aspects of child and youth well-being. Examples of strengths-based assessments of children in a school context can be found in Epstein et al. (2003).

## ALTERNATIVE ACTIONS FOR PREVENTION AND INTERVENTION

More than a decade ago, Phillips (1993) recommended that "the allocation of energies and resources in our schools must go increasingly to building wellness and lifetime competence rather than just struggling to contain the school failures of children and adolescents... The challenge is to identify factors or conditions that advance optimal development" (p. 14). This perspective is similar to Pollard and Rosenberg's (2003) thesis that efforts to dramatically improve the lives of children require a strengths-based approach "which focuses on cultivating children's strengths, assets, positive relationships, morals, and capacities that give them the resources they need to grow successfully across the life course" (p. 15).

These recommendations continue to be timely, both with respect to the school and nonschool environments of children and youth. On the basis of the research reviewed in the previous section, findings clearly indicate that life satisfaction is a crucial psychological strength that relates to healthy adaptation in youth. Thus, efforts to enhance life satisfaction in youth are warranted. However, research related to the development, implementation, and evaluation of programs to enhance the life satisfaction of children and youth has been scant, although some efforts are under way. The development of prevention and intervention programs for individuals and groups necessitates the development of a priori models to serve as a guide for clarifying the determinants and consequences of changes in life satisfaction. Some researchers distinguish between the goal of a program (e.g., increased life satisfaction) and the target of interventions, arguing that interventions should be directed at the goal's determinants. Consistent with this distinction, the extant research points toward a number of environmental, personal, and activity determinants, or pathways, that should inform the development of effective life-satisfaction promotion and intervention programs. Specifically, these pathways include supportive relationships, cognitive attribution training, positive life experiences, and involvement in meaningful activities.

## Promote Supportive Relationships

Studies of life satisfaction of children and youth demonstrate that supportive interpersonal relationships, including both family and peers, are crucial throughout childhood and adolescence. Moreover, parents who provide emotional and social support can foster healthy life satisfaction in their children during the challenging adolescent years, even when this stage is compounded by problems, such as pregnancy, high school dropout, and acculturation issues. Thus, despite the increasing importance of autonomy among adolescents, programs designed to enhance life satisfaction likely necessitate the inclusion of strong family components. Examples include the programs for family-centered positive psychology (Sheridan, Warnes, Cowan, Schemm, & Clarke, 2004) and the Building Family Strengths program (Thomason, Brown, & Thames, 2001). The latter program focuses on the identification of family strengths within a developmental framework. The potential contribution of age effects is illustrated in studies that have explicitly compared the magnitude of relationships between life satisfaction and its correlates across stages of childhood development. For instance, Suldo and Huebner's (2004b) research revealed changes in the relative importance of the dimensions of authoritative parenting across the adolescent years. With regard to peer relationships, research with Chinese youth indicated social self-concept was critical to life satisfaction among adolescents but not elementary school children (Chang et al., 2003). Thus, it is critical to consider developmental differences in the design of programs aimed at enhancing life satisfaction.

However, the provision of emotional support appears critical to high life satisfaction across developmental stages. Thus, parents of children who fail to experience them as emotionally supportive may benefit from traditional therapeutic procedures (e.g., family counseling, parenting skills training) to assess family dynamics and develop recommendations for more supportive parental behavior. One such family-strengthening intervention is Family Check-Up, which is noted for its emphasis on supporting parenting strengths and providing motivation to change maladaptive parenting (Dishion & Kavanagh, 2003). This assessment-based intervention is particularly amenable for implementation in the schools because of its brevity (specifically, its three-session design). In cases in which family interventions are unsuccessful, efforts to increase the provision of nonparental sources of support may be necessary to compensate for the lack of appropriate parental support. Resilient children who overcome significant adversity often turn to teachers and other adults for support. Mentoring programs, such as Big Brothers and Big Sisters, have been developed to provide such nonparental support.

High-quality peer relationships assume increasing importance across development (see chapter 25, "Peer Relationships"). Thus, programs that aid in the development of social competence and provide opportunities for constructive interactions with peers will also be critical ingredients of interventions for enhancing life satisfaction. Numerous social skills training programs have been developed and empirically validated. Similarly, numerous structured extracurricular activities affect child and adolescent well-being in positive ways (Gilman, Meyers, & Perez, 2004). For example, children benefit from participating in interpersonal activities such as sports, although the degree of positive outcome may be influenced by the quality of coaching, the peers involved, and the cultural meaning of the particular activity within the school and community (Larson & Verma, 1999; also see chapter 37, "Sports and Physical Activities").

For children who are experiencing low-quality peer relationships, efforts should be undertaken to differentiate the particular determinants of peer problems. If the child lacks appropriate social skills, then approaches that include social skills training would likely be the first line of intervention. Studies with adults suggest that prosocial behaviors, such as acts of kindness and expressions of gratitude, may be particularly instrumental in developing greater long-term life satisfaction (Abbe, Tkach, & Lyubormirsky, 2003). In some cases, however, it may be most appropriate to consider removing a child from an unsupportive peer group environment and relocating him or her to a potentially more supportive environment (e.g., a new school or new classroom). Given that adolescents with low life satisfaction are more likely to be victimized, special attention should be paid to this latter option if organizational and individual changes have not been successfully implemented to reduce bullying behavior.

## Promote Adaptive Attribution Styles

Attribution styles, which determine what forces individuals hold responsible for their successes and failures, are important to improving life satisfaction. Students who frequently make maladaptive attributions should be encouraged to use more adaptive explanatory styles for good events. For example, they might be reinforced for assuming responsibility for a positive interpersonal outcome (e.g., making a new friend) by attributing the outcome to an internal, stable, and global cause, such as their social skill. Similarly, they might be encouraged to avoid maladaptive attributions, such as attributing failure to an internal, stable, and global cause (e.g., "I'm just stupid.").

Formal attribution retraining programs may be helpful for students in general. One successful approach is that of Gillham, Reivich, Jaycox, and Seligman (1995), which teaches children to make constructive attributions using cognitive–behavioral techniques. Research by Rigby and Huebner (2005) underscores the need to focus attention on increasing adaptive attributions for positive events as much as on decreasing maladaptive attributions for negative events. In this manner, attribution retraining efforts are applicable to all students, not just to at-risk students.

## Promote Positive Self-Perceptions

Self-esteem and self-concept judgments are strongly related to overall life satisfaction in children and youth in the United States. Thus, efforts targeted toward sustainable changes in self-esteem or critical aspects of self-concept may increase life satisfaction (see chapter 26, "Self-Concept and Self-Esteem"). Much has been written about self-concept interventions, and a number of reviews of the literature are available. Additionally, Frisch's clinical work (1999) with adult patients in therapy points toward potential intervention targets for changing adolescents' self-perceptions. Frisch's comprehensive Quality of Life Therapy (QOLT) approach involves consideration of changes in a person's life circumstances, attitudes, goals and standards, and priorities to enhance life satisfaction. This collaborative approach, which could likely be modified for use with adolescents, would offer an integrative framework for altering maladaptive self-perceptions that negatively affect life satisfaction (see Frisch, 1999, for an example of a comprehensive case study illustrating the application of QOLT).

## Promote Involvement in Meaningful Activities

Research by Csikszentmihalyi (1990) and others has underscored the importance of encouraging adolescent participation in a variety of structured, meaningful activities (e.g., sports, arts, social clubs, or service activities). His research demonstrates the importance of engaging in activities that are challenging, intrinsically motivating, and voluntary, in contrast to mindless leisure activities. This body of research also underscores the importance of differentiating behavior and activities related to longer-term goals from those related to ongoing experience, suggesting that particular activities may be more essential to sustainable, long-term well-being. Gilman et al. (2004) provide an overview of the role of school psychologists in facilitating and evaluating student participation in such activities. Their discussion underscores the need to provide *all* students with access to extracurricular activities, not just those who do well academically. Thus, the students who are most at risk for school failure are not denied access to opportunities that are likely to enhance their potential to succeed in school and to develop positive relationships with peers and nonfamilial adults.

Work experiences may also provide the opportunity for adolescents to participate in meaningful activities that enhance life satisfaction. When work experiences do not consume too much time, they may be helpful to the extent that they provide opportunities to learn new skills and earn positive feedback from adults (Greenberger & Steinberg, 1986). However, negative outcomes are associated with jobs that involve long hours, repetitive work, and little involvement with positive adult role models. Again, educators and support staff (e.g., school psychologists or counselors) can help students plan, monitor, and evaluate their work experience to optimize their chances of increasing student life satisfaction.

In conclusion, given the positive intrapersonal, interpersonal, and school-related outcomes associated with high life satisfaction, it seems that *all* children and youth can benefit from efforts to increase their life satisfaction. Efforts to increase adolescents' life satisfaction and other aspects of their psychological well-being should be more cost-effective than simply treating those adolescents who display psychopathological or at-risk behaviors. Nevertheless, interventions to promote positive life satisfaction should consider cultural and gender differences and be tailored to specific national cultural groups. For example, Park and Huebner's (2005) research suggests that the global life satisfaction of students in Korea is much more strongly related to school satisfaction than for their American counterparts. Furthermore, although gender differences have not been found in mean levels of general life satisfaction, the possibility remains for differences in the determinants of overall life satisfaction or satisfaction with specific domains. Gender differences appear to moderate the relationships between life satisfaction and a variety of risk behaviors (e.g., eating behaviors, physical activity, and sexual behavior) in adolescence (Valois et al., 2001).

## SUMMARY

Research has progressed slowly but surely since the summary provided in the previous edition of *Children's Needs*. Most children and adolescents are satisfied with their lives. However, a noteworthy minority of children are very dissatisfied. Individual differences in the global life satisfaction reports of children and adolescents are associated with a variety of intrapersonal, interpersonal, and activity variables, suggesting that life satisfaction is determined by a complex interplay of environmental and personal factors. Low life satisfaction is associated with important adverse outcomes, including those related to mental health, physical health, and school. Although early research focused on life satisfaction as an outcome variable, current research is exploring the functional role of life satisfaction, that is, its role in mediating and moderating the relationship between adolescents' experiences and their adaptive and maladaptive behaviors. Most important, recent research has demonstrated that life satisfaction functions as a true psychological strength. Life satisfaction is not simply a by-product of positive life experiences; it actively fosters resilience.

Although much additional research is needed, the developing body of research points to several likely critical components of programs to promote wellness. The components include attention to interpersonal relationships, cognitive attributions, self-perceptions, and structured activities. The research concludes that life satisfaction is a key psychological construct in the positive psychology movement and a meaningful indicator and determinant of child and youth well-being.

## RECOMMENDED RESOURCES

### Books and Other Printed Material

Diener, E., Suh, E. M., Lucas, R. E., & Smith, H. (1999). Subjective well-being research: Three decades of progress. *Psychological Bulletin, 125,* 276–302.

The authors provide an outstanding synthesis of life satisfaction research among adults. The article also includes an excellent discussion of theories and needed future research.

Frisch, M. B. (1999). Quality of life assessment/intervention and the Quality of Life Inventory (QOLI). In M. R. Maruish (Ed.), *The use of psychological testing for treatment planning and outcome assessment* (2nd ed., pp. 1227–1331). Hillsdale, NJ: Erlbaum.

This chapter provides a thorough discussion of the application of life satisfaction research to clinical practices with adults. It also contains a case study illustrating the use of life satisfaction measures in treatment planning and evaluation.

Gilman, R., & Huebner, E. S. (2000). Review of life satisfaction measures for adolescents. *Behaviour Change, 3,* 178–195.

This article contains additional information about life satisfaction assessment instruments appropriate for adolescents. Furthermore, several well-validated assessment tools are available at Scott Huebner's website at the University of South Carolina: *http://www.cla.sc.edu/PSYC/facdocs/huebner.html*

Seligman, M. E. P. (2002). *Authentic happiness.* New York: Free Press.

This author distinguishes between the pleasant life, the good life, and the meaningful life. He provides an intriguing discussion of the need to identify and promote human strengths in an effort to obtain authentic happiness in various life domains, including work, love, and child rearing.

In addition, two special issues below provide information regarding life satisfaction and other positive psychology constructs as they pertain to children and practitioners in schools.

Chafouleas, S. M., & Bray, M. A. (2004, January). Positive psychology and wellness in children [Special issue]. *Psychology in the Schools, 41.*

Huebner, E. S., & Gilman, R. (2003). *School Psychology Quarterly, 18*(Summer).

## Websites

*http://www.cob.vt.edu/market/isqols*

This is the official website for the International Society for Quality-of-Life Studies, a professional society devoted to the study of quality of life. The website provides information about conferences, newsletters, and publications pertaining to quality of life, such as *Social Indicators Research and Journal of Happiness Studies.*

*http://www.eur.nl/fsw/research/happiness*

The World Database of Happiness, directed by Ruut Veenhoven, is a continuing register of research findings on subjective enjoyment of life. Empirical findings on life satisfaction are summarized in abstracts and categorized by subject for easy retrieval.

## REFERENCES


Abbe, A., Tkach, C., & Lyubormirsky, S. (2003). The art of living by dispositionally happy people. *Journal of Happiness Studies, 4,* 385–404.

Ash, C., & Huebner, E. S. (1998). Life satisfaction reports of gifted middle school students. *School Psychology Quarterly, 13,* 310–321.

Ash, C., & Huebner, E. S. (2001). Environmental events and life satisfaction reports of adolescents: A test of cognitive mediation. *School Psychology International, 22,* 320–336.

Bearsley, C., & Cummins, R. A. (1999). No place called home: Life quality and purpose of homeless youths. *Journal of Social Distress and the Homeless, 8,* 207–236.

Brantley, A., Huebner, E. S., & Nagle, R. J. (2002). Multidimensional life satisfaction reports of adolescents with mild mental disabilities. *Mental Retardation, 40,* 321–329.

Chang, L., McBride-Chang, C., Stewart, S. M., & Au, E. (2003). Life satisfaction, self-concept, and family relations in Chinese adolescents and children. *International Journal of Behavioral Development, 27,* 182–189.

Cowen, E. L. (1994). The enhancement of psychological wellness: Challenges and opportunities. *American Journal of Community Psychology, 22,* 149–179.

Csikszentmihalyi, M. (1990). *Flow: The psychology of optimal experience.* New York: Harper & Row.

Demo, D. H., & Acock, A. C. (1996). Family structure, family process, and adolescent well-being. *Journal of Research on Adolescence, 6,* 457–488.

Dew, T., & Huebner, E. S. (1994). Adolescents' perceived quality of life: An exploratory investigation. *Journal of School Psychology, 33,* 185–199.

Diener, E., & Diener, C. (1996). Most people are happy. *Psychological Science, 7,* 181–185.

Diener, E., Suh, E. M., Lucas, R. E., & Smith, H. L. (1999). Subjective well-being: Three decades of progress. *Psychological Bulletin, 125,* 276–302.

Dishion, T. J., & Kavanagh, K. (2003). *Intervening in adolescent problem behavior: A family-centered approach.* New York: Gilford Press.

Epstein, M. H., Harniss, M. K., Robbins, V., Wheeler, L., Cyrulik, S., Kriz, M., & Nelson, J. R. (2003). Strengths-based approaches to assessment in schools. In M. D. Weist, S. W. Evans, & N. A. Lever (Eds.), *Handbook of school mental health: Advancing practice and research* (pp. 285–299). New York: Kluwer Academic Publishers.

Flouri, E., & Buchanan, A. (2002). Life satisfaction in teenage boys: The moderating role of father involvement and bullying. *Aggressive Behavior, 28,* 126–133.

Fogle, L., Huebner, E. S., & Laughlin, J. E. (2002). The relationship between temperament and life satisfaction in early adolescence: Cognitive and behavioral mediation models. *Journal of Happiness Studies, 3,* 373–392.

Frisch, M. B. (1999). Quality of life assessment/intervention and the Quality of Life Inventory (QOLI). In M. R. Maruish (Ed.), *The use of psychological assessment for treatment planning and outcome assessment* (2nd ed.; pp. 1227–1331). Hillsdale, NJ: Erlbaum.

Gillham, J. E., Reivich, K. J., Jaycox, L. H., & Seligman, M. E. P. (1995). Prevention of depression symptoms in schoolchildren: Two year follow-up. *Psychological Science 6,* 343–351.

Gilman, R. (2001). The relationship between life satisfaction, social interest, and frequency of extracurricular activities among adolescent students. *Journal of Youth and Adolescence, 30,* 749–767.

Gilman, R., & Ashby, J. S. (2003). A first study of perfectionism and multidimensional life satisfaction among adolescents. *Journal of Early Adolescence, 23,* 218–235.

Gilman, R., & Handwerk, M. L. (2001). Changes in life satisfaction as a function of stay in residential setting. *Residential Treatment for Children and Youth, 18,* 47–65.

Gilman, R., & Huebner, E. S. (2003). A review of life satisfaction research with children and adolescents. *School Psychology Quarterly, 18,* 192–205.

Gilman, R., Meyers, J., & Perez, L. (2004). Structured extracurricular activities among adolescents: Findings and implications for school psychologists. *Psychology in the Schools, 41,* 31–42.

Greenberger, E., & Steinberg, L. (1986). *When teenagers work: The psychological and social costs of adolescent employment.* New York: Basic Books.

Greenspoon, P. J., & Saklofske, D. (2001). Toward an integration of subjective well-being and psychopathology. *Social Indicators Research, 54,* 81–108.

Grossman, M., & Rowat, K. M. (1995). Parental relationships, coping strategies, received support and well-being in adolescents of separated or divorced and married parents. *Research in Nursing & Health, 18,* 249–261.

Homel, R., & Burns, A. (1989). Environmental quality and the wellbeing of children. *Social Indicators Research, 21,* 133–158.

Huebner, E. S., & Alderman, G. L. (1993). Convergent and discriminant validation of a children's life satisfaction scale: Its relationship to self- and teacher-reported psychological problems and school functioning. *Social Indicators Research, 30,* 71–82.

Huebner, E. S., Drane, W., & Valois, R. F. (2000). Levels and demographic correlates of adolescent life satisfaction reports. *School Psychology International, 21,* 187–198.

Huebner, E. S., Funk, B. A., & Gilman, R. (2000). Cross-sectional and longitudinal psychosocial correlates of adolescent life satisfaction reports. *Canadian Journal of School Psychology, 16,* 53–64.

Huebner, E. S., Gilman, R., & Laughlin, J. E. (1999). A multimethod investigation of the multidimensionality of children's well-being reports: Discriminant validity of life satisfaction and self-esteem. *Social Indicators Research, 46,* 1–22.

Huebner, E. S., Laughlin, J. E., Ash, C., & Gilman, R. (1998). Further validation of the Multidimensional Students' Life Satisfaction Scale. *Journal of Psychoeducational Assessment, 15,* 118–134.

Huebner, E. S., Suldo, S. M., Smith, L. C., & McKnight, C. G. (2004). Life satisfaction in children and youth: Empirical foundations and implications for school psychologists. *Psychology in the Schools, 41,* 81–93.

Larson, R. W., & Verma, S. (1999). How children and adolescents spend their time across the world: Work, play, and developmental opportunities. *Psychological Bulletin, 125,* 701–736.

Lazarus, R. (1991). *Emotion and adaptation.* New York: Oxford University Press.

Leung, C. Y., McBride-Chang, C., & Lai, B. P. (2004). Relations among maternal parenting style, academic competence, and life satisfaction in Chinese early adolescents. *Journal of Early Adolescence, 24,* 113–143.

Lewinsohn, P., Redner, J., & Seeley, J. (1991). The relationship between life satisfaction and psychosocial variables: New perspectives. In F. Strack, M. Argyle, & N. Schwartz (Eds.), *Subjective well-being* (pp. 193–212). New York: Plenum Press.

Liebkind, K., & Jasinskaja-Lahti, I. (2000). Acculturation and psychological well-being among immigrant adolescents in Finland: A comparative study of adolescents from different cultural backgrounds. *Journal of Adolescent Research, 15,* 446–469.

Marks, N., Shah, H., & Westall, A. (2004). *The power and potential of well-being indicators: Measuring young people's well-being in Nottingham.* London: New Economics Foundation. (Available from http://www.neweconomics.org)

Maton, K. I. (1990). Meaningful involvement in instrumental activity and well-being: Studies of older adolescents and at-risk urban teen-agers. *American Journal of Community Psychology, 18,* 297–320.

McCullough, G., & Huebner, E. S. (2003). Life satisfaction reports of adolescents with learning disabilities and normally achieving adolescents. *Journal of Psychoeducational Assessment, 21,* 311–324.

McCullough, G., Huebner, E. S., & Laughlin, J. E. (2000). Life events, self-concept, and adolescents' positive subjective well-being. *Psychology in the Schools, 37,* 281–290.

McKnight, C. G., Huebner, E. S., & Suldo, S. M. (2002). Relationships among stressful life events, temperament, problem behavior, and global life satisfaction in adolescents. *Psychology in the Schools, 39,* 677–687.

Neto, F. (2001). Satisfaction with life among adolescents from immigrant families in Portugal. *Journal of Youth and Adolescence, 30,* 53–67.

Nickerson, A. B., & Nagle, R. J. (2004). The influence of parent and peer attachments on life satisfaction in middle childhood and early adolescence. *Social Indicators Research, 66,* 35–60.

Park, N., & Huebner, E. S. (2005). A cross-cultural study of the levels and correlates of life satisfaction among children and adolescents. *Journal of Cross-Cultural Research, 36,* 444–456.

Petito, F., & Cummins, R. A. (2000). Quality of life in adolescence: The role of perceived control, parenting style and social support. *Behaviour Change, 17,* 196–207.

Phillips, B. N. (1993). *Educational and psychological perspectives on stress in students, teachers, and parents.* Brandon, VT: Clinical Psychology Publishing Company.

Phinney, J. S., & Ong, A. D. (2002). Adolescent-parent disagreements and life satisfaction in families from Vietnamese- and European-American backgrounds. *International Journal of Behavioral Development, 26,* 556–561.

Pollard, E. L., & Rosenberg, M. L. (2003). The strengths-based approach to child well-being: Let's begin with the end in mind. In M. C. Bornstein, L. Davidson, C. L. M. Keyes, & K. A. Moore (Eds.), *Well-being: Positive development across the life course* (pp. 13–21). Mahwah, NJ: Erlbaum.

Rigby, B., & Huebner, E. S. (2005). Do causal attributions mediate the relationship between personality and life satisfaction in adolescence? *Psychology in the Schools, 41,* 91–100.

Sam, D. L. (1998). Predicting life satisfaction among adolescents from immigrant families in Norway. *Ethnicity & Health, 3,* 5–18.

Shek, D. T. L. (1997). The relation of parent-adolescent conflict to adolescent psychological well-being, school adjustment, and problem behavior. *Social Behavior and Personality, 25,* 277–290.

Sheridan, S. M., Warnes, E. D., Cowan, R., Schemm, A. V., & Clarke, B. L. (2004). Family-centered positive psychology: Focusing on strengths to build student success. *Psychology in the Schools, 41,* 7–18.

Steinberg, L., Lamborn, S. D., Dornbusch, S. M., & Darling, N. (1992). Impact of parenting practices on adolescent achievement: Authoritative parenting, school involvement, and encouragement to succeed. *Child Development, 63,* 1266–1281.

Stevenson, W., Maton, K. I., & Teti, D. M. (1999). Social support, relationship quality, and well-being among pregnant adolescents. *Journal of Adolescence, 22,* 109–121.

Suldo, S. M. (2004). *A longitudinal study identifying variables that describe youth with very high or low life satisfaction, and variables that predict and co-occur with changes in adolescents' life satisfaction.* Unpublished doctoral dissertation, University of South Carolina, Columbia, SC.

Suldo, S. M., & Huebner, E. S. (2004a). Does life satisfaction moderate the effects of stressful life events on psychopathological behavior during adolescence? *School Psychology Quarterly, 19,* 93–105.

Suldo, S. M., & Huebner, E. S. (2004b). The role of life satisfaction in the relationship between authoritative parenting dimensions and adolescent problem behavior. *Social Indicators Research, 66,* 165–195.

Thomason, D. J., Brown, B., & Thames, B. J. (2001, November). Building family strengths for children, youth and families at risk. Paper presented at the meeting of the International Society for Quality-of-Life Studies, Washington, DC.

Ullman, C., & Tatar, M. (2001). Psychological adjustment among Israeli adolescent immigrants: A report on life satisfaction, self-concept, and self-esteem. *Journal of Youth and Adolescence, 30,* 449–463.

Valois, R. F., Zullig, K. J., Huebner, E. S., & Drane, J. W. (2001). Relationship between life satisfaction and violent behaviors among adolescents. *American Journal of Health Behavior, 25,* 353–366.

Zimmerman, M. A., Salem, D. A., & Maton, K. I. (1995). Family structure and psychosocial correlates among urban African-American adolescent males. *Child Development, 66,* 1598–1613.

# 28

# Religion and Spirituality

**Renee Staton**
**Harriet Cobb**
*James Madison University*

## BACKGROUND AND DEVELOPMENT

### Religion and Spirituality

What distinguishes spirituality from religion? This question has confounded both researchers and practitioners. Although sometimes used interchangeably, the two terms are not synonymous. Spilka, Hood, Hunsberger, and Gorsuch (2003) suggest that *spirituality* involves a quest to find meaning in life and understand one's place in the universe. Spirituality is personal and does not necessarily fit into an "organizational framework" (Spilka et al., p. 10). A spiritual person would emphasize values, perhaps as guiding principles, without necessarily believing in a deity. *Religiousness*, on the other hand, may be manifested by membership in a church or congregation and participation in religious services, as well as through a person's beliefs, values, and experiences. Both religion and spirituality are concerned with seeking meaning in life and constructing an understanding of the relationship between humankind and the universe. "Religiousness is a subset of spirituality, which means that religiousness invariably involves spirituality, but that there may be nonreligious spirituality as well" (Spilka et al., p. 11). Miller (2003) echoes this idea, suggesting that religion is an organized endeavor rooted in societal and communal traditions, whereas spirituality is a personally defined relationship with others and the universe. This view of spirituality, therefore, includes secular humanists, atheists, and agnostics. This chapter distinguishes between spirituality and religion based on the above descriptions.

Any discussion of spirituality and religion has the potential to affect readers because of the sensitive nature of the topic. It is crucial to acknowledge the wide range of beliefs and practices that exist. At the same time, a professional, that is, objective, stance toward the topic is essential.

Psychology's view of religion has an intriguing history, beginning with William James and G. Stanley Hall, who advocated the legitimacy of religion as a subject of study. Freud later held that religion is primarily a form of neurosis, and, later still, behaviorists emphasized studying only behavior that could be observed and measured: Religion and spirituality, in their view, were not appropriate topics for research. During the past 20 years, however, researchers and practitioners have demonstrated renewed interest in studying religion and spirituality, as components of cultural diversity, and how they relate to mental and physical health. Although research has been limited on the topic (Hill & Pargament, 2003), religiousness and spirituality clearly have the potential to significantly influence children's development, both positively and negatively (D'Andrea & Daniels, 2001). Moreover, educators—including school psychologists—can expect to confront challenging religious and spiritual issues when working with children.

This chapter presents an overview of the few studies of children and religion or spirituality, then discusses the implications of those studies for educators. The topic is approached from a practice perspective that acknowledges that spirituality and religion can have a significant effect on an individual's worldview and relationships, and that beliefs can change over a lifetime. The position taken in this chapter—that educators should not promote any particular religious belief system—is shared by professional organizations in school psychology (National Association of School Psychologists, n.d.) and education (National Education Association, 2002).

### Religion in the United States

Documenting the state of religions, faith, and spiritual practices in the United States is a difficult task. The U.S.

Census Bureau is prohibited from surveying residents about their religious affiliations—a prohibition that reveals the problematic relationship between church and state in this country (Public Law 94-521). The Statistical Abstract of the United States (U.S. Census Bureau, 2001) offers some information, as does the American Religious Identification Survey (Kosmin, Mayer, & Keysar, 2001). However, these sources cannot adequately portray the range and depth of various beliefs and practices. Professing a religious preference, for instance, is different from actually observing religious practices and attending services.

Moreover, whereas Eck (2002) states that the United States is now the most religious nation in the world, others assert that it is becoming an increasingly secular nation (Kosmin et al., 2001). In fact, according to the 2001 Religious Identification Survey (Kosmin et al., 2001), the number of adults in the United States who report that they are not religious has grown from 8% in 1990 to more than 13% in 2001. However, more than half (62%) belong to religious organizations, and 60% say they believe that religion is a very important part of their lives (*Harvard Mental Health Letter*, 2001). According to Kosmin et al., the majority of people in the United States identify their religious preference as Christian (76.5%), with Roman Catholic the largest subgroup (24.5%) and Baptist the second largest (16.3%). More than 13% reported having no religious preference. Jews represent about 1.3% of the population, Muslims and Buddhists about 0.5%, and Hindus about 0.4%. (Note: 5.4% of respondents refused to answer this question.) Within religions, of course, there are distinctions between conservative and liberal denominations or different branches.

With regard to ethnicity, Latinos constitute 29% of the Catholics in the United States and 20% of the evangelical and born-again Christians. African Americans make up 37% of the Jehovah's Witnesses and 29% of the Baptists. Asians constitute 61% of the Buddhists, and 34% of the Muslim and Islamic group, and more than 90% of the religiously Jewish population is white (Kosmin et al., 2001).

These figures will likely change over time. The ethnic composition of various religions in the United States, for instance, has been significantly affected by immigration patterns. Since 1965, when the Immigration Act led to changes in government policy, the number of immigrants entering the country has increased. However, unlike previous immigrants, those arriving today are less likely to strive for assimilation into mainstream U.S. culture and instead are more likely to retain the beliefs and practices of their native religions. Between 1990 and 2001, for instance, the proportion of Asian immigrants to the United States who were Christian dropped from 63% to 43%, while the percentage who followed religions such as Buddhism, Hinduism, and Islam increased from 15% to 28% (Kosmin et al., 2001). Especially in gateway cities, immigrants are able to create or join networks of immigrants from their own cultures. They are also better able to stay in contact with people in their native countries (Eck, 2002). This shift also means that Christians, Jews, and others who have never lived outside the United States and have encountered little, if any, religious diversity are now being exposed to a greater variety of religions. In addition, until recently immigration primarily affected larger cities. Now, however, the effects can be felt even in rural areas. These changes suggest that today's American children and youth may well experience religion and spirituality differently from earlier generations.

## Stages of Religious Development in Children

Research in this area, while limited, has provided general templates that describe how faith develops, within age cohorts, in children. Fowler (1981) provides a framework for conceptualizing children's evolving religious and faith beliefs and posits that religious faith evolves in stages similar to Piaget's theory of cognitive development and Erickson's theory of psychosocial development. As with Piaget and Erickson, Fowler believes that development may stop at any stage as a result of cognitive or experiential limitations. Fowler's concept of faith, however, refers to a generic human experience that includes—but is not identical to—religion. It addresses deeply held values of primary importance such as power, family, sexuality, and religion.

The stages of faith begin with *primal faith* (infancy), in which basic trust emerges within the context of early attachments. The second stage is *intuitive/projective faith* (early childhood), during which the child merges his fantasy world with the real world. Spiritual images may invoke terror, guilt, awe, or benevolent care. A child may conclude that illness or death is a punishment from God or see such events in similarly concrete terms. During this stage the child becomes aware of mortality, what is considered sacred, and what is prohibited.

The third stage, *mythical/literal faith* (middle childhood), corresponds with Piaget's stage of concrete operations: Children can discriminate between fantasy and reality and comprehend others' perspectives. They can conceive of a higher being as caring and just—but also, in some cases, controlling and able to reward good behavior and punish transgressions. They view the concepts of God, prayer, and religion in a literal, concrete fashion, believing with confidence. Religion can provide an immediate answer to questions about the purpose of life and death and an explanation for pain and suffering.

The fourth stage, *synthetic/conventional faith* (early adolescence), is associated with Piaget's formal operations and Erickson's identity formation. At this point, early adolescents are capable of more abstract thinking and realize that perceptions are somewhat personal. They see that belief systems exist that are different from their own and their families'. They begin to think more about past experiences and may integrate other belief systems into their own structures for making meaning and sense of life. Some may wish for a more personal relationship with God.

Fowler's descriptions include development beyond childhood. In the fifth stage, *individuative/reflective faith*, adolescents and young adults reflect critically on their belief and value systems, as well as those of others, and sometimes move from reliance on external authorities to their own philosophy and ideas about the meaning of life.

During the sixth and seventh stages of middle and older adulthood, *conjunctive faith* and *universalizing faith*, adults may move beyond earlier belief-system boundaries and integrate "truths" from multiple perspectives. Additionally (although Fowler believes this is less common), individuals may feel oneness with the "power of being" (or God), as well as a commitment to justice and compassion. Those who have reached this final stage contribute to the well-being of others by offering some form of sanctuary and opposing inhumane treatment.

Fowler's stage theory has been criticized for a lack of empirical research that confirms its accuracy. However, Elkind's (1964) early studies supported the theory of a general move from the concrete to the abstract in children's religious concepts. Similarly, Tamminen (1994) described the religious experiences of Finnish late adolescents as also involving questions of personal identity and the meaning of life. Moreover, in prayer development, children move from prayer that asks God to change life events to prayer that is seen more as communication with God. This is not to suggest that their environment does not influence children's responses to religion and spirituality; stage theories alone are insufficient to explain the process of faith exploration and development. For instance, Spilka et al. (2003) confirm the important role parents play in the development of concepts of God as either loving or authoritarian. Even so, Fowler's theory remains a bellwether in the field and offers a framework for how children process questions of religion and spirituality.

## Research on Children's Religion and Behavior

Although most studies of religion primarily involve White, middle-class subjects, there are a few notable exceptions. In his classic qualitative study, *The Spiritual Life of Children*, Robert Coles (1990) interviewed children in several different countries who were Christian, Islamic, or Jewish, or who subscribed to secular belief systems. He found some universality across different cultural and religious backgrounds, in that young children have similar spiritual questions, and their quest for understanding and harmony with the universe is expressed through words, gestures, songs, and drawings. He came to perceive children as "pilgrims" who are aware that life is a finite journey and are as eager as adults to make sense of the universe and their place in it.

In a cross-cultural study of 5- to 7-year-olds of Muslim, Hindu, or Christian backgrounds, Nazar and Kouzekanani (2003) asked children questions such as, "Do you know God?" and "Where do people go when they die?" Although the authors noted some differences (e.g., fewer Muslim children thought that good people go to heaven), they also found similarities. The majority of children in all three groups, for instance, stated that they know God and that God can see them. The authors concluded that children follow the path of their culture, but common to all three religions is an awareness of goodness and truth: Children share similar goals of comforting people, appreciating the beauty of the world, and expressing awe and humility toward the unknown.

Sharing faith beliefs with others, attending religious services, and participating in spiritual and religious practices can offer children a valuable sense of community and belonging. Poland and McCormick (1999) state that one factor that promotes mental health in children is the consistent presence in the child's life of a caring adult who is not a family member. Rabbis, pastors, Sunday school teachers, and other spiritual mentors can fill this role. Furthermore, religion can contribute to a stable family life by encouraging strong marital bonds and prosocial behavior, which encourage favorable outcomes for children. Its effects on parenting, however, can be either positive or negative. When it stimulates nurturance, family togetherness, and effective behavior management, obviously, religion can be an enormous support for parents.

The relationship between early childhood attachments and religion is somewhat complex. Some findings suggest that avoidant parent–child attachments predict higher levels of adult religiousness. Adults with nonreligious mothers and secure attachments tend to report lower levels of religiousness, according to Kirkpatrick and Shaver (1990). Granqvist and Hageskull (1999) found that individuals with anxious–ambivalent attachments are more likely to have religious conversion experiences at some point in their lives. Kirkpatrick (1998), however, found that university students with positive feelings about themselves and others also had positive images of God. In general, parents are the strongest influence on religiousness in their children and adolescents, although their influence decreases during young adulthood. Most strongly religious adults come from strongly religious homes, and, conversely, most nonreligious adults are reared in homes in which religion is absent or not strongly emphasized. Altemeyer and Hunsberger (1997) found that after abandoning their beliefs, previously religious college students initially experience a great deal of fear and guilt. In retrospect, however, they feel that leaving their religion had more advantages than disadvantages. They were also more tolerant and nonauthoritarian than their highly religious peers in the study.

Most studies that specifically address the relationship between religion and morality report a weak but negative correlation between religion, nonmarital sexual behavior, and the use of alcohol, tobacco, and drugs, and to a lesser degree, delinquency and some criminal acts (Benson, Donahue, & Erickson, 1989; Gorsuch, 1995). On the other hand, faith is not related strongly to honesty, altruism, or tolerance of diversity (Spilka et al., 2003). Instead, prosocial behavior is primarily influenced by the values, moral reasoning, emotions, and behaviors of one's parents and family, irrespective of religion.

## PROBLEMS AND IMPLICATIONS

Certain faith-related perspectives can create challenges for educators. Since the 1960s, for instance, Supreme Court rulings have led to a ban on certain forms of religious expression in public schools, such as prayer. Many parents, in response, have called for a return to Judeo-Christian tenets of education (Seigler, 2003). Dissatisfaction with a more secular education is expressed in a number of ways, all of which may influence educators' daily practices. Censorship for religious reasons, for example, can be an issue for public schools. In *Counts v. Cedarville School District* (2003), the U.S. District Court ruled that school administrators violated students' rights by requiring parental permission for students to check out Harry Potter books from the school library. The case was filed by a parent and her pastor who charged that the books included witchcraft and the occult. The court's ruling stated that school administrators may not restrict access to books based solely on their dislike of the book's contents. Even so, attempts to remove or restrict materials remain relatively common in U.S. schools (American Library Association, n.d.).

Similarly, some parents may use religious beliefs to limit their children's participation in educational experiences. The Hatch Amendment to the General Education Provisions Act (1974) states that parents and guardians have the right to inspect all instructional materials and to refuse psychological examination, testing, or treatment for their children. Although this amendment empowers parents to be well informed, some have used it to restrict—at times severely—their children's experiences in schools. The organization Family Friendly Libraries, for example, provides templates of model letters parents can use to invoke the Hatch Amendment to exempt their children from activities that include values clarification; use of moral dilemmas; discussion of religious or moral standards; open-ended discussions of situations that involve moral issues; self-evaluation, curricula, books, or reading materials that pertain to religious beliefs (including elements of witchcraft); and evolution.

Evolution is an especially inflammatory topic in schools. Despite the notoriety of the Scopes Monkey Trial of 1925, which concluded that science—not religion—is the domain of public schools, challenges to the teaching of evolution have continued. Benen (1998) provides the following sequence of events. In 1966 the U.S. Supreme Court ruled that an Arkansas law preventing the teaching of evolution was unconstitutional, and in 1987 it ruled that a Louisiana statute that required the teaching of creationism as well as evolution violated the separation of church and state. Even so, since 1996 at least six state legislatures have considered promoting creationism—or even banning the teaching of evolution altogether. In 1997, professors from several state universities in Arizona testified before the state school board that students who graduate from public schools without an understanding of evolutionary biology are educationally disadvantaged compared to other college-bound students. Nevertheless, some school boards continue to challenge the teaching of evolution and to demand that it be presented as theory and not fact.

Schools in the United States reflect the controversy in society at large over religious or spiritual expression and secularism. For instance, although the Supreme Court has upheld rulings that separate church and state, the constitutionality of the phrase "under God" in the Pledge of Allegiance remains in dispute. Although not every educator will experience the potential legal ramifications of religion and spirituality in schools, situations may arise that require educators to be knowledgeable about students' needs as well as their rights. For example, Christianity in general promotes caring and compassion, but the tendency of any majority belief system can be to overlook different philosophies and traditions. At a minimum, children who are religious minorities in the United States may face ignorance and stereotypes; at worst, they may be subjected to ostracism or harassment.

Moreover, some faiths, such as certain evangelical and fundamentalist Christian groups in the United States, interpret the Bible literally and teach that people will be judged harshly and can never be good enough to please God (Thurston, 2000). In addition to their potentially negative effects on a child's sense of self-esteem (Siegel, Choldin, & Orost, 1995), such views are at odds with accepted beliefs in the field of psychology about the development of positive self-worth and mastery. A "Spare the rod and spoil the child" philosophy, for example, can be used to validate excessively harsh discipline and result in guilt, shame, or difficulty in individuating (Mahoney, Pargament, Tarakeshwar, & Swank, 2001). Similarly, the rigid views of some paternalistic religions, including certain Islamic, Jewish, and Christian sects, are likely to have a significant negative effect on females struggling with identity development (Siegel et al., 1995), at least in the United States.

School professionals may also encounter challenges when working with children who are distressed or confused by their beliefs. For example, adolescents who are exploring their sexual identity or emerging as gay, lesbian, or bisexual may struggle to reconcile their view of themselves as being worthy with religious doctrines that label homosexuality as a sin or abomination. In such instances, school mental health professionals must be able to build rapport while acknowledging the conflict.

## ALTERNATIVE ACTIONS FOR PREVENTION

The achievement of cultural competence can serve as the organizing framework for working with religious and spiritual diversity. If school personnel are expected to be multiculturally competent, they also should be expected to understand that religion and spirituality can be major components of diversity. The school professional's knowledge of a child's religious or spiritual orientation leads to deeper understanding and empathy. In particular, understanding the religious or spiritual beliefs of children and their families is essential in developing effective relationships with children and working effectively with families and caregivers. An understanding of religious and spiritual differences can also help to avoid or minimize discomfort when sensitive issues are raised. For example, wishing a Jewish child a Merry Christmas or Happy Easter is a clear sign that the well-wisher does not understand the child's experience. Complimenting an Amish child on her appearance is usually inappropriate because of the religion's attitude toward personal pride and vanity, and expecting a child who is a Jehovah's Witness to have a birthday party is inconsistent with his faith's practices regarding celebrations.

Educators should also appreciate that the child who does *not* participate in Weekly Religious Education (a program in some communities that offers Christian Biblical instruction during the school day but off school grounds) may be ostracized by peers and stigmatized by teachers. Understanding local political issues that involve religion and diversity is also vital to effective relationships with students, school personnel, families, and the community. School professionals must therefore be prepared to address religious intolerance in children and, perhaps, in school personnel as well.

The following recommendations extend this theme of cultural competency and sensitivity.

1. Explore and understand your own spiritual and religious beliefs, and be aware of how those beliefs place you in either the majority or minority in the United States. This exploration means coming to terms with prejudice or stereotypes that can arise when interacting with children and families who have differing perspectives and results in an awareness that is essential for school professionals who respond to divergent beliefs and practices.

2. Encourage staff to recognize each child's unique experience of religion and spirituality. As D'Andrea and Daniels (2001) point out, although school professionals cannot always accurately measure the influence of religion and spirituality, they should understand that faith beliefs can have a profound effect on children. Many families, for instance, rely on religious and spiritual

teachings to help children deal with loss and grief. Understanding religiousness and spirituality as a potential strength—or as a potential source of emotional conflict—is a key consideration in working with children.

3. Encourage school staff members to be familiar with the beliefs, customs, and practices of both majority and minority religious and spiritual groups represented in their school. Reading about religious and spiritual groups and observing faith practices, when appropriate, can be informative. In addition, although some religious groups are reluctant to talk with nonmembers, speaking with members—and former members—is another resource. These contacts may also serve as resources for consultation and referral.

4. Stay abreast of current state and federal laws and school district policies. Because the separation between church and state can be elusive, educators are advised to understand student and parental rights as stated in documents such as the Hatch Amendment and to be sensitive to the viewpoints represented in challenges to school curriculum. Because interpretations of the First Amendment vary—and challenges such as the evolution–creationism debate remain unresolved—educators should be aware of the potential for violation of students' rights by schools and of the sometimes contradictory messages sent by courts.

Haynes and Thomas (2002) provide information for educators sensitive to separation of church and state. Their guidelines include the following:

- Educate school personnel about their rights and limitations when teaching about religion.
- Provide resources on different religions and religious holidays that are educationally appropriate.
- Learn about religious groups represented in the school district.

In addition, Haynes and Thomas suggest that before planning displays or activities that involve religious holidays, educators should ask and answer the following:

- How will this event help students reach their academic goals?
- Could this activity make anyone feel like an outsider?
- Will this activity promote or inhibit religion?
- Will the display or party help students to better understand history and culture?

5. Work to positively influence school climate and foster an environment of tolerance and respect. Religious minorities may be discriminated against in a manner similar to cultural and ethnic minorities. To combat this, educators must use advocacy and consultation skills. Ortiz and Flanagan (2002) provide guidelines for working with children and families from diverse cultures that apply to religious differences as well.

6. Teachers and families may seek assistance regarding issues that can arise in the classroom, such as "Why doesn't Rachel celebrate Christmas?" or "What is Kwanzaa?" Providing accurate information and helping teachers handle religious and spiritual diversity in a sensitive manner are part of the school professional's role as consultant.

## ALTERNATIVE ACTIONS FOR INTERVENTION

To ensure that children's emotional needs are met in a therapeutic manner, while maintaining respect for their religious and spiritual beliefs, counselors and school psychologists are encouraged to consider the following recommendations for intervention.

1. Listen closely for any references the child or family makes to their belief system and respond openly and sensitively. This is especially important when assessing potential emotional disturbance in a child or when making recommendations for social–emotional interventions. The child psychiatric literature has some helpful information about assessing a child's spirituality or religion in the context of providing care. For instance, McEnvoy's (2003) mnemonic, "B-E-L-I-E-F," stands for understanding the family's *belief* system, their values and *ethics*, their practices and rituals *lifestyle*, the extent of the family's *involvement* in a religious community (including participation in religious *education*), and any thoughts about the child's *future* that may be affected by religious beliefs.

2. In developing a positive relationship with the family, explore how the family understands and explains emotional problems and serious mental disorders, including their own child's distress. Children who believe that pain and suffering can be healed or made meaningful through religious or spiritual beliefs and practices, for instance, may be better able to tolerate illness and loss. On the other hand, if they believe that such events are inflicted as punishment, their ability to withstand negative life events may be limited. Religious or spiritual coping skills such as praying or meditating, going to

confession, or seeking comfort from a higher power or God can produce positive mental health (Mabe & Josephson, 2004). Religion can also help children and families cope with illness, death, and other types of suffering (Spilka, Zwartjes, & Zwartjes, 1991). As another example, some religious groups also encourage moderation or abstention from alcohol, which can serve as a protective factor for adolescents exposed to alcohol or drugs.

3. If religion plays a major role, family members are likely to mention this during an initial interview. If it does play a major role, determine who the family believes is qualified to provide interventions for the child (Barnes, Ploinikoff, Fox, & Pendleton, 2000). That is, does the family favor religious leaders exclusively, or may school personnel and community mental health providers play a role as well? The answer will determine whether school staff members will need to work with other healers in the community—or at least respect their interventions and guidance—in coordinating the child's care.

Note that this type of collaboration can be complex when the family's belief system has the potential for inadequate or inappropriate care of children. Specific cultural beliefs that obstruct access to medical care, for instance, may require an educator's intervention. Nevertheless, learning about this aspect of the family allows the educator to understand the child's beliefs and assumptions about what is happening.

4. In some situations, a counselor or school psychologist may believe that a child could benefit by thinking critically about a problem. To be effective, professionals must first assess the child's religiousness and spirituality. This demands training and supervised practice beyond basic counseling techniques; in particular, it requires that the professional be aware of his or her own beliefs. In addition, the school professional must understand that encouraging individuals to come to their own conclusions can have discomfiting consequences. An adolescent, for example, may begin to experience distress while considering options that conflict with religious teachings. The school professional must be sensitive to the student's dilemma; in such situations, the warmth and caring that are essential to a good school professional–student relationship are especially important.

5. Consultation with parents about child rearing may also be affected by religious and spiritual beliefs. Maintaining an approachable and compassionate stance is the most effective way to establish a therapeutic alliance with the parents and to encourage positive outcomes for the child. School professionals can use their counseling skills to help children and family enlist the support that many religious or spiritual communities offer.

The following case illustrates the need for school professionals to be comfortable with religious and spiritual issues that can arise in counseling with children. Anna, a 9-year-old girl, was referred to the school psychologist for assessment and counseling following a serious car accident in which she suffered broken bones and internal injuries and in which her older brother had severe head trauma. His recovery was a slow, frightening, and expensive process. While the family struggled to find meaning in the crisis, Anna became phobic about riding in cars. Her counseling included cognitive behavioral techniques such as systematic desensitization and relaxation. But because her family was deeply religious, the counselor was able to incorporate the child's prayers into the process. Eventually, Anna was able to ride in cars without anxiety. The family also received emotional support and assistance from their church, as well as special educational services from the school. This situation illustrates the positive integration of a child's spiritual and emotional issues with a psychoeducational approach to intervention.

## SUMMARY

Children's religious or spiritual beliefs are important elements of personal identity. It is crucial, therefore, for school professionals to be aware of the potential impact of religiousness and spirituality when working with children. Educators must be self-aware and assess their own beliefs, as well as learn about belief systems different from their own. A commitment to respecting the origins and importance of others' beliefs is essential.

One of the difficulties inherent in any discussion of religion/spirituality and schools is the controversial nature of the issues raised. Public schools, although secular in the United States, are nevertheless influenced by the belief systems of administrators, teachers, and families. Religion as a concept commands respect because it is an important underpinning of so many cultures. On the other hand, the science and practice of psychology is dedicated to the investigation and exploration of what promotes healthy development and functioning in individuals and systems. Effective school professionals are expected to balance these sometimes competing concerns.

Each child is unique and demands objective, professional assessment. A commitment to the well-being of children, groups, and organizations is the foundation of sound practice. Therefore, in addition to learning about a diversity of beliefs, from secular humanism to religious fundamentalism, school professionals must acknowledge religiousness and spirituality as critical points of conceptualization in their work with children.

# RECOMMENDED RESOURCES

## Books and Other Printed Material

Coles, R. (1998). *The moral intelligence of children.* New York: Plume.

Through case histories and interviews, Coles provides a view of how children make sense of the world. The implications for parenting and preventive interventions regarding moral development are compelling.

Farrington, K. (1998). *The history of religion.* New York: Barnes & Noble.

This illustrated book provides a description of the major world religions and includes types of worship, gods, leading figures, beliefs, and practices.

Haynes, C., & Thomas, O. (2002). *Finding common ground: A guide to religious liberty in public schools.* Arlington, VA: First Amendment Center.

This book includes broad guidelines for effectively managing religious activities and issues in schools. The guide has been endorsed by a number of faith-based groups as well as by organizations such as the National Education Association.

Wood, D., & Chee, C. K. (2001). *Old turtle.* New York: Scholastic.

This children's book presents the concept of God as a metaphor and promotes the idea of tolerance and acceptance.

## Websites

*http://www.tolerance.org*

This website, sponsored by the Southern Poverty Law Center, includes resources and information for educators regarding religious tolerance as well as multiculturalism and education.

*http://www.youthandreligion.org*

This is a useful website for school professionals who want to follow research on religion and children and adolescents. It is the website of the National Study of Youth and Religion, which is based at the University of North Carolina at Chapel Hill. The website features abstracts for a variety of studies on such topics as Internet use by religious versus nonreligious teenagers, religious habits and movie-viewing habits, and time spent talking about religious and spiritual matters by Jewish families.

# REFERENCES

Altemeyer, B., & Hunsberger, B. (1997). *Amazing conversions: Why some turn to faith and others abandon religion.* Amherst, NY: Prometheus Books.

American Library Association. (n.d.). *Challenged and banned books.* Retrieved August 28, 2005, from http://www.ala.org/ala/oif/bannedbooksweek/challengedbanned/challengedbanned.htm

Barnes, L. P., Ploinikoff, G. A., Fox, K., & Pendleton, S. (2000). Spirituality, religion, and pediatrics: Intersecting worlds of healing. *Pediatrics, 104,* 899–908.

Benen, S. (1998). Evolving debate. *Church and state, 51,* 13–16.

Benson, P. L., Donahue, M. J., & Erickson, J. A. (1989). Adolescence and religion: A review of the literature from 1970 to 1986. *Research in the Social Scientific Study of Religion, 1,* 153–181.

Coles, R. (1990). *The spiritual life of children.* Boston: Houghton Mifflin.

*Counts v. Cedarville School District,* 295 F. Supp.2d 996 (W.D. Ark. 2003).

D'Andrea, M., & Daniels, J. (2001). RESPECTFUL counseling: An integrative multidimensional model for counselors. In D. B. Pope-Davis & H. L. K. Coleman (Eds.), *The intersection of race, class, and gender in multicultural counseling* (pp. 417–466). Thousand Oaks, CA: Sage Publications.

Eck, D. L. (2002). *A new religious America: How a "Christian country" has become the world's most religiously diverse nation.* San Francisco: Harper.

Elkind, D. (1964). Piaget's semi-clinical interview and the study of spontaneous religion. In B. Spilka, R. W. Hood, B. Hunsberger, & R. Gorsuch (Eds.), *The* psychology of religion: An empirical approach (1st ed.; 78). New York: Guilford Press.

Fowler, J. (1981). *Stages of faith: The psychology of human development and the quest for meaning.* San Francisco: Harper & Row.

Gorsuch, R. L. (1995). Religious aspects of substance abuse and recovery. *Journal of Social Issues, 51,* 65–83.

Granqvist, P., & Hageskull, B. (1999). Religiousness and perceived childhood attachment: Profiling socialized correspondence and emotional compensation. *Journal for the Scientific Study of Religion, 38,* 254–273.

Hatch Amendment to the General Education Provisions Act, 20 U.S.C. § 1232h (1974).

Haynes, C., & Thomas, O. (2002). *Finding common ground: A guide to religious liberty in public schools.* Arlington, VA: First Amendment Center.

Hill, P. C., & Pargament, K. I. (2003). Advances in the conceptualization and measurement of religion and spirituality. *American Psychologist, 58,* 64–74.

Kirkpatrick, L. A. (1998). God as a substitute attachment figure: A longitudinal study of adult attachment style and religious change in college students. *Personality and Social Psychology Bulletin, 24,* 961–973.

Kirkpatrick, L. A., & Shaver, P. R. (1990). Attachment theory and religion: Childhood attachments, religious beliefs, and conversion. *Journal for the Scientific Study of Religion, 29,* 315–334.

Kosmin, B. A., Mayer, E., & Keysar, A. (2001). *American Religious Identification Survey 2001.* New York: Graduate Center for the City University of New York.

Mabe, P. A., & Josephson, A. M. (2004). Child and adolescent psychopathology: Spiritual and religious perspectives. *Child Adolescent Psychiatric Clinics in North America, 13,* 111–125.

Mahoney, A., Pargament, K. I., Tarakeshwar, N., & Swank, A. B. (2001). Religion in the home in the 1980s and 1990s: A meta-analytic review and conceptual analysis of links between religion, marriage, and parenting. *Journal of Family Psychology, 15,* 559–596.

McEnvoy, M. (2003). Culture and spirituality as an integrated concept in pediatric care. *The American Journal of Child Nursing, 28,* 39–43.

Miller, G. (2003). *Incorporating spirituality in counseling and psychotherapy.* Hoboken, NJ: Wiley.

National Association of School Psychologists. (n.d.). *The provision of culturally competent services in the school setting.* Retrieved September 8, 2004, from http://www.nasponline.org

National Education Association. (2002, November). *Navigating religion in the classroom.* Retrieved May 4, 2005, from http://www.nea.org/neatoday/0211/cover.html

Nazar, F., & Kouzekanani, K. (2003). A cross-cultural study of children's perceptions of selected religious concepts. *Alberta Journal of Education Research, 49,* 155–162.

Ortiz, S. O., & Flanagan, D. P. (2002). Best practices in working with culturally diverse children and families. In A. Thomas & J. Grimes (Eds.), *Best practices in school psychology IV* (pp. 337–351). Bethesda, MD: National Association of School Psychologists.

Poland, S., & McCormick, (1999). *Coping with crisis: Lessons learned.* Longmont, CO: Sopris West.

Religion and mortality: New data. (2001, June). *Harvard Mental Health Letter, 17,* 7–8.

Seigler, T. J. (2003). Understanding original intent and stare decisis: Two methods of interpreting the establishment clause. *Educational Administration Quarterly, 39,* 208–237.

Siegel, R. J., Choldin, S., & Orost, J. H. (1995). Impact of three patriarchal religions on women. In J. C. Chrisler & A. H. Hemstreet (Eds.), *Variations on a theme: Diversity and the psychology of women* (pp. 107–144). Albany: State University of New York Press.

Spilka, B., Hood, R. W., Hunsberger, B., & Gorsuch, R. (2003). *The psychology of religion: An empirical approach* (3rd ed.). New York: Guilford Press.

Spilka, B., Zwartjes, W. J., & Zwartjes, B. M. (1991). The role of religion in coping with childhood cancer. In B. Spilka, R. W. Hood, B. Hunsberger, &

R. Gorsuch (Eds.), *The psychology of religion: An empirical approach* (2nd ed.; p. 503). New York: Guilford Press.

Tamminen, K. (1994). Religious experiences in childhood and adolescence: A viewpoint of religious development between the ages of 7 and 20. *International Journal for the Psychology of Religion, 4,* 61–85.

Thurston, N. (2000). Psychotherapy with evangelical and fundamentalist Protestants. In P. S. Richards & A. E. Bergin (Eds.), *Handbook of psychotherapy and religious diversity* (pp. 131–153). Washington, DC: American Psychological Association.

U.S. Census Bureau. (2001). *Statistical abstract of the U.S.* Retrieved September 9, 2004, from http://www.census.gov/statab/www/

# 29

# Attachment

**Kristyn Zajac**
**Roger Kobak**
*University of Delaware*

## BACKGROUND AND DEVELOPMENT

### Developmental Changes in Attachment

Attachment theory provides a guide to understanding how children's primary relationships develop and how these relationships influence children's capacities to cope with stress and manage academic and social challenges. During infancy, children form relationships with their caregivers and develop expectations of how their caregivers will respond to their needs. Over time, these expectations organize their strategies for maintaining and using relationships at times of threat or challenge. According to Bowlby (1969/1982), these expectations and strategies organize internal working models of both self and others and continually interact with the quality of care available to children. Children who experience sensitive and responsive care will form a secure attachment bond, whereas those who are not confident in the availability of the caregiver will form an insecure bond. Thus, while children's expectations are carried forward and influence the way they interact with other caregivers, the quality of care available to children in family and school environments continues to have an important impact on their coping and adaptation. Attachment-related aspects of children's personalities, including their ability to rely on adults at times of stress and challenge, continue to evolve throughout childhood and adolescence.

By charting how children's important relationships influence their ability to manage stress and challenge in the classroom, an attachment framework can provide educators, school psychologists, and other school personnel insight into problematic and disruptive classroom behavior. Much of this behavior results from children's negative views of themselves and others and from subsequent problems in coping with stress and challenge. However, attachment-related aspects of children's personalities and behaviors continue to be influenced by the quality of current caregiving relationships. As an alternative caregiver, a teacher has the opportunity to understand problematic behaviors and form supportive relationships with children with attachment-related problems and thus may serve an important role in enhancing children's confidence and capacity to manage stress in the classroom. Though children who are managing successfully often require less attention from teachers, they can also be influenced in positive and negative ways by the overall school environment. Attachment theory provides a general model for relationship development that can enhance teachers' understanding of children's emotional needs and how best to respond to them.

According to Bowlby's theory (1969/1982), attachment is a behavioral system that becomes active when children perceive cues of danger or challenge. When activated, the attachment system motivates behavior oriented toward seeking comfort and support from a primary caregiver. The attachment system is frequently activated during infancy and, under most conditions, results in the formation of an attachment bond between infants and their primary caregivers, typically during the first 18 months of life. From an evolutionary point of view, this attachment bond serves a protective function insofar as children who form such relationships increase their chances of survival and growth. Thus, children who seek proximity to their caregivers at times of distress or challenge and who engage in behaviors that elicit care and protection have an advantage over children who fail to form such a relationship.

Children's emotions play a central role in maintaining the attachment bond. Children typically experience a sense of safety and enjoyment when they achieve contact with their caregiver and become fearful and upset when access to the caregiver is threatened. Emotions also function as signals to the caregiver, with attachment behaviors such as crying and clinging serving to alert caregivers of children's need for care and contact. Through repeated interactions with their caregiver, children develop expectations about how the caregiver will respond to their needs and use these expectations to develop strategies to regulate attachment behaviors and the attachment relationship. As children mature through the toddler and early childhood periods, these expectations and patterns of attachment behavior provide children with a stable way of interacting with their caregivers and maintaining the attachment bond.

Internal expectations for caregiver availability and response also provide children with an initial sense of self-efficacy and a coping strategy for managing distress. When children have experienced available and responsive care, they usually develop confident expectations that a caregiver is trustworthy and will respond if needed. Inasmuch as children learn about the trustworthiness of others from their attachment relationships, they also form expectations about themselves as worthy and confident in the face of challenging situations. Depending on their experiences with caregivers, children grow to see themselves as more or less worthy of care and effective in obtaining the care that they need.

The expectations that children first develop in the attachment relationship gradually become internalized as working models. These working models are thought to guide children's expectations in future relationships with other adults, as well as with peers, and lead to the development of strategies for seeking the support of others (Cicchetti, Toth, & Lynch, 1995). In this way, children form basic beliefs about relationships through parent–child interactions and carry these forward to other relationships.

During the toddler and early childhood periods, children begin to explore the world and use the attachment relationship as a secure base to maintain their confidence when faced with challenges. By early childhood, the attachment relationship undergoes a major developmental change and is transformed into a goal-corrected partnership (Bowlby, 1969/1982). As children gain language and cognitive abilities to plan and regulate arousal and feeling, they become capable of forming cooperative relationships. This requires a change in caregiver response, with an increase in the use of verbal guidance and limit setting with children. Caregivers may support children's self-regulation by structuring challenges to an optimal level, gauging their level of frustration, and responding with support and guidance, which fosters the development of self-confidence. By the time children enter kindergarten, most have developed basic self-management skills that help them modulate arousal levels and balance challenge with the continued need for adult support.

In addition to developing increased capacity for self-regulation, children gradually reduce the amount of time they spend in close physical proximity to the primary caregiver. This ability to function in situations in which the caregiver is not physically accessible creates the need for children to learn to derive support from alternative caregivers. Alternative caregivers, such as day care providers, relatives, or preschool teachers, may respond to children in ways that reassure them of support or in ways that create or maintain negative expectations. The many challenges associated with entering school often result in teachers serving as temporary or ad hoc attachment figures who provide children with emotional support in distressing or challenging situations.

Elementary school is a period in which the development of competence is a primary contributor to successful adaptation. Competence includes success in academics, peer relationships, and good conduct. As a result, the teacher–student relationship may support children not only in academics but also in domains involving peers and self-regulation. Supportive teacher–student relationships can help children effectively manage their emotional experiences (Pianta, 1999). By late elementary school, children may increasingly turn to peers as sources of support and use teachers as attachment figures only in situations involving more extreme distress. Middle school and high school include the development of a more differentiated view of self that fosters later adult decisions about work and family. Here again, teacher involvement can play an important role in supporting adolescents in developing a sense of competence. Although the quality of the parent–child relationship continues to influence children's developmental trajectories, relationships with others become increasingly important. Throughout the school years, teachers and peers may serve as ad hoc attachment figures who can either provide support or undermine children's confidence in their abilities to face academic and social challenges.

## Individual Differences in Children's Expectations for Self and Others

A great deal of attachment research derives from Ainsworth et al.'s Strange Situation laboratory procedure, which is used with children between 12 and 18 months of age (Ainsworth, Blehar, Waters, & Wall, 1978). Ainsworth et al. observed three distinct patterns of infant behavior during this 20-minute procedure: a secure, an anxious–avoidant, and an anxious–resistant pattern. Children classified as secure engaged in behaviors that reflected an enjoyment of the relationship and positive expectations that the caregiver would be available and responsive. In contrast, children classified as avoidant tended to reject the caregiver's attempts at reassurance and physical comfort when distressed, whereas resistant children tended to be passive and were not easily soothed by the caregiver.

The secure and anxious patterns of attachment have been linked to the quality of care provided over the course of infancy (Ainsworth et al., 1978; Belsky, 1999). In middle-class samples, about 30%–40% of infants have anxious attachments, presumably because they have experienced insensitive care during the first year of life. These infants develop strategies for maintaining their relationship with a caregiver from whom they have come to expect a lack of responsive care. The anxious–avoidant infants are thought to have developed expectations for rejection and a corresponding strategy of minimizing expressions of attachment feeling and behaviors. They are likely to inhibit these attachment signals and divert their attention from feelings of distress. The strategy is adaptive for these infants because it prevents the caregiver from pushing them away, allowing them to maintain some proximity. Anxious–resistant infants who receive inconsistent or chaotic care are likely to adopt a maximizing strategy in which they closely monitor the attachment figure and exaggerate feelings of distress and attachment signals. This strategy increases the likelihood that they will receive the attention they need from an inconsistently available caregiver.

The expectations of self and others and attachment strategies that emerge during infancy are not rigid or deterministic and may change with development. Changes can occur in caregivers and the quality of care they provide to the child. As a result, children's expectations can be modified. Relationships and interactions outside the family may provide children with novel experiences that alter expectations for self and others. Longitudinal studies of attachment demonstrate substantial instability in attachment security from infancy through childhood (Scharfe, 2003). Whereas attachment security is dependent on the quality of care available to the child, the caregiver's behavior is subject to the stresses and supports that occur in the larger context of the family. Different aspects of family are constantly in flux, and the changes that directly influence the life of the caregiver are likely to have the greatest effect on the child (Pianta, Egeland, & Sroufe, 1990).

Yet despite the possibility of changes in the caregiving environment and in children's internal expectancies for self and others, data from the Parent–Child Project at the University of Minnesota suggest that as children transition into preschool and later elementary school classrooms, those who were secure during infancy have a marked advantage over those who were anxiously attached (Sroufe, Egeland, Carlson, & Collins, 2005). In preschool, children with secure histories are more independent in the classroom and spend more time interacting with peers than they do interacting with teachers or by themselves. Secure children generally have more flexibility and socially appropriate emotional expression, allowing them to adapt to the varying situations presented in the classroom (Cassidy, 1994). They have more self-confidence and they tend to seek out and receive the support they need, presumably because of their internal representations of themselves as worthy of care (Jacobsen & Hofmann, 1997). When faced with difficult tasks, children manifest this self-confidence in their persistence and enthusiasm in problem solving and, as a result, are less likely than their anxious counterparts to become frustrated and give up when they do not succeed with a task on the first try (Sroufe et al., 2005). In general, children with secure histories have better relationships with their teachers and are rated by their teachers as more competent and ready to learn (Pianta, 1999). In addition, secure children also tend to be popular with peers, show very little negative emotion, and are generally empathetic toward other children (Kerns, 1996). These skills help them to initiate and maintain close friendships. Jacobsen and Hofmann (1997) found that secure attachment representations continue to predict favorable outcomes in late childhood and adolescence, including higher levels of attention and participation in the classroom and higher grades.

The available and responsive care that contributes to children's attachment security provides a model for how teachers can develop an emotionally supportive relationship with students in the classroom. Although the types of challenges that children face gradually change over the course of elementary and secondary school, the teacher–child relationship may play an important compensatory role for children with insecure parent–child attachments.

## PROBLEMS AND IMPLICATIONS

Children's adaptation to the school environment is a product of multiple factors. On one hand, children enter school with a relationship history and expectations for self and others. On the other hand, children's adjustment continues to be influenced by the current environment and the quality of relationships with parents, peers, and teachers (Sroufe, 2002). Bowlby used the concept of developmental pathways to describe the dynamic transaction between children's personalities and the caregiving environment and to conceptualize how this transaction influences children's adjustment over time. For example, adjustment in first grade is understood to be the product of children's internal models of self and others that were shaped by their relationship history, by their experiences with peers, and by ad hoc attachment figures from infancy through preschool. Although children's internal expectations and the quality of the caregiving environment often remain stable, the current caregiving environment may alter children's expectations in both negative and positive ways.

A number of studies have shown that internal models influence behavior in the classroom. Overall, research has shown that children with histories of anxious attachment tend to show a more disordered pattern of classroom behavior than do children with secure histories. However, the types of disordered behavior may be distinctively different depending on the type of insecurity. For example, anxious–avoidant children are likely to be emotionally isolated, show aggression toward their peers, and be involved in antisocial behaviors (Rosenstein & Horowitz, 1996). Their behaviors toward teachers are often uncooperative or defiant and they tend to lie or blame others when they misbehave. In addition, some anxious–avoidant children show strong dependency needs but are conflicted in the way they display these needs (Sroufe et al., 2005). They may make desperate efforts to maintain contact with the teacher during group activities or when the school day is over, but they deliberately avoid the teacher when hurt or upset. In contrast, children with anxious–resistant attachment histories tend to demand a lot of attention from teachers, rushing to them immediately if upset or anxious (Sroufe, Carlson, Levy, & Egeland, 1999). They appear immature because of their low tolerance for stress, lack of independence, and low capacity for self-management. Anxious—resistant children are often socially isolated (Jacobsen & Hofmann, 1997), either in the form of neglect or bullying by their classmates. Although they are more oriented toward peers than avoidant children, they tend to hover on the outskirts of a group of children and struggle with one-on-one interactions (Rubin, Bukowski, & Parker, 1998).

Studies of children at high risk for psychopathology have identified more extreme problems in attachment relationship, usually stemming from early abuse or neglect. Using the Strange Situation procedure, Main and Solomon (1990) discovered an atypical pattern characterized by momentary disorganized or disoriented behavior. They hypothesized that these infants had parents who displayed frightening or frightened behavior in the presence of the child and, as a result, were conflicted between viewing their caregiver as a source of safety or as a source of alarm.

Children classified as disorganized or disoriented during infancy show the most serious behavioral problems throughout childhood and adolescence (Carlson, 1998). Theoretically, these children lack a consistent way of dealing with stress, presumably because they are unable to approach a frightening caregiver when they are frightened themselves (Main & Hesse, 1990). Disorganized attachment is a risk factor for the later development of psychopathology, especially dissociative symptoms (Carlson, 1998). These children also show higher levels of deviant hostile behavior toward their peers and display both aggressive behaviors and social withdrawal in preschool and elementary school (Lyons-Ruth, Alpern, & Repacholi, 1993).

Children diagnosed with reactive attachment disorder have even more severe attachment difficulties. These children are characterized by "markedly disturbed and developmentally inappropriate social relatedness in most contexts" (American Psychiatric Association, 2000) and may display either an inhibited pattern characterized by withdrawal or avoidance of physical contact with others along with self-stimulating behaviors, or a disinhibited pattern characterized by indiscriminate affection toward strangers and developmentally inappropriate childishness. This diagnosis also requires the experience of pathogenic care and may be linked to the experiences of neglect, abuse, and repeated change in caregiver that prevents the development of an attachment relationship. These children may display symptoms of anxiety, aggression, conduct problems, and academic problems (Haugaard & Hazen, 2004). Overall, the development of a warm and stable relationship with any responsive adult, including teachers and school personnel, has been found to be beneficial (Hanson & Spratt, 2000).

## ALTERNATIVE ACTIONS FOR PREVENTION

Although the relationship histories and expectations that children bring to the classroom influence their school adjustment, the quality of the school environment may either alter or reinforce children's negative expectations for self and others. By considering the aspects of caregiving that support confident and secure expectations, school professionals can systematically develop a classroom environment that prevents many of the problems associated with children's histories of anxious attachment. During the early years in elementary school, children are likely to turn to their teacher as a source of security and a secure base for academic and social challenges. The sensitive and responsive care that contributes to attachment security in the parent–child relationship can be a guide for how teachers can develop an emotionally supportive relationship with students (Pianta, 1999). An emotionally supportive teacher–student relationship can serve as a compensatory factor when children come from homes that lack parental support (Cicchetti & Lynch, 1993). Children's ability to trust and depend on their teacher for emotional support has been found to be directly related to their ability to manage stress in the classroom, particularly stress that stems from interactions with peers (Little & Kobak, 2003).

Prevention can occur during different developmental periods. On one hand, findings of attachment research conducted on the infant and preschool periods indicate that preventive interventions should occur relatively early in children's lives. Once children begin school, teachers inherit children's histories of relationships and are not in a position to prevent insecure or disorganized attachment from becoming a problem for a student. Because problems of attachment begin to take shape during the infant, toddler, and preschool years, the best programs for preventing later adjustment problems target the caregiver–child relationship. They are not actual prevention programs as much as they are early interventions. Interventions with mother–infant dyads have focused on improving the attachment relationship by teaching caregivers how to respond appropriately to the needs of infants and young children (van den Boom, 1995). They target not only caregivers' behavior but also caregivers' understanding of the children's behavior. This includes education about infants' expressions of positive and negative emotion, as well as reinforcement of healthy interaction in place of intrusive or detached involvement with the infant. Caregivers are taught how to perceive and correctly interpret their infants' signals and how to implement an appropriate and effective response. These interventions have had some success at improving attachment security and, as a result, improving children's social skills later in childhood.

Attachment interventions have also been extended to preschool children and their parents. Preschool parent psychotherapy (PPP) is an approach to intervening with parent–child dyads that is based on the concepts of attachment theory (Toth, Maughan, Manly, Spagnola, & Cicchetti, 2002). PPP has been used with children 4 years of age. The program is based on the idea that caregivers' own childhood experiences are unconsciously affecting the way they perceive and respond to their children. A therapist works with caregivers to raise their awareness of this connection. Because many caregivers who maltreat their children have histories of negative childhood relationships, one of the therapist's goals is to develop a positive supportive relationship with caregivers by providing them with respect, empathy, and unconditional positive regard. By targeting the caregivers' internal representations of self and others, this program increases caregivers' involvement with and attention to their children. Because children's internal working models are open to change during the preschool years, these methods can have a substantial impact on later adjustment. Research has shown substantial decreases in negative self-representations and increases in both positive self-representations and positive expectations of the mother–child relationship among children who have received the PPP intervention.

Intervention techniques have also been developed for use by teachers in early elementary school classrooms. The Play and Language to Succeed (PALS) program is designed to foster secure teacher–student relationships through play therapy in the classroom (Chaloner, 2001). It has been used by teachers with high-risk children in classrooms from pre-K through second grade and includes training and continued support from a school psychologist. PALS focuses on the three key elements of bonding, boundaries, and language to teach social skills to at-risk children and to build positive teacher–student relationships. Teachers are trained to understand children's feelings, needs, and beliefs by observing play behavior in the classroom. Play activities are used to foster warm and caring relationships with individual children. Boundaries are set using consistent and appropriate rules to structure playtime, and the process of establishing boundaries is used to model social skills. Teachers attend to the use of language to teach children how to label emotions and to identify behavioral manifestations of feelings with their peers. These skills are taught during free-play periods in the classroom and structured so the teacher is available to roam from one child to another. The teacher interacts one-on-one with children for brief periods of time, observing and commenting on play behavior, helping children to label themes during play, and responding proactively to behavior problems. PALS is designed to reduce behavior problems by helping children understand their behaviors through language and play and by fostering a positive teacher–child relationship. A small study has provided some preliminary support for the efficacy of the PALS program in reducing teacher-rated social-emotional problems and aggression among high-risk children (Chaloner, 2001).

Teachers' knowledge and understanding of children's developmental histories may also aid understanding of disruptive or inappropriate classroom behavior. By elementary school, sensitive caregiving requires both acceptance of children's need for support and the capacity to contain children's inappropriate behavior (Cavell, 2000). Acceptance can be fostered by teachers' contact and involvement with children's families.

## ALTERNATIVE ACTIONS FOR INTERVENTION

School-based interventions often focus on changing children's caregiving environments after they have developed disruptive or problematic behaviors. Managing the behavioral problems of anxious or disorganized children begins with understanding the core expectations of self and others and the strategies that children have developed to manage feelings of frustration and anxiety. From an attachment perspective, effective interventions that target the caregiving environment should include both teachers and parents. If children are currently experiencing caregiver instability, violence, or threats to the availability of their parents, it is doubtful that any level of intervention in the school will be successful without also addressing the stressors that these children are facing in the home. In addition, caregivers who are not getting their own relationship needs met may be less able to attend to the attachment needs of their children (Kobak & Mandelbaum, 2003). This is especially true of caregivers who are under high stress and lack the social support to help them cope.

A number of school-based interventions encourage parent involvement. The Chicago Parent–Child Center (CPC) program is a multifaceted, school-based early intervention program that relies heavily on parental involvement to promote both academic and social skills (Reynolds & Robertson, 2003). The CPC provides services from preschool through third grade. In addition to providing enriched classroom environments, the program requires parents to participate in educational activities both at school and in the home. The parent component of the intervention aims to improve the quality of parent–child interactions, provide social support for the parents, and improve children's school competence. Parents are encouraged to increase their participation in all aspects of the children's schooling, including attending special classroom activities and receiving home visits from school–community representatives. In addition, children receive intensive instruction in basic learning skills. Reynolds and Robertson (2003) have used the CPC intervention with a large sample of low-income, minority children, and the program has demonstrated effectiveness in improving school achievement and the quality of the parent–child relationship through the adolescent years. Children's participation in the CPC program was also related to decreased incidences of later child abuse and neglect.

Interventions that are designed to improve the quality of care available to children must take into account the overall context of parenting. Stress in the lives of parents increases the number of negative interactions with their children and can promote the development of aggression and antisocial behavior problems (Patterson, 1988). Interventions that include stress management for parents can have positive effects on their parenting practices and decrease deviant behavior in their children. Stress management interventions focus on the development of problem-solving skills that can be used to cope with the parenting stress of everyday life. It is useful for therapists to help parents to identify the stress in their lives and to use resources available to solve or at least cope with the problems. Including a parenting stress component in intervention has been shown to improve child treatment outcomes and reduce child deviance (Kazdin & Whitley, 2003).

In addition to their emphasis on parental involvement, school-based attachment interventions should focus on fostering positive relationships between teachers and children. The teacher–student relationship plays an important role in children's adaptation in school, both socially and academically (see chapter 5, "Student–Teacher Relationships"). Positive, supportive teacher–child relationships lead to children's greater classroom participation, higher achievement, and greater overall satisfaction with school. Teacher–child relationships that are characterized by conflict predict lower school achievement and aversion to school (Birch & Ladd, 1998).

However, it is also true that this relationship is heavily influenced by the interpersonal patterns of behavior that children bring to school. Attachment theory suggests that intervention with teacher–student relationships should help teachers to identify and understand the attachment styles of students and to recognize them as a reflection of their relationship history.

Children with insecure attachment histories may have some more general difficulties in the classroom functioning. These difficulties are likely to be most evident when children with insecure histories are faced with stressful situations. Children's negative expectations for self and others often lead to behaviors that shape teachers' perceptions and result in responses that tend to confirm the children's expectations. For instance, teachers may perceive children with avoidant histories as more aggressive and withdrawn and, as a result, find themselves using more discipline and less support with these children. The teachers' responses in turn confirm these children's expectations of rejection and potential conflict with caregivers.

Alternatively, teachers may perceive children with resistant histories as dependent and impulsive, and disorganized children as unpredictable and highly reactive. Because each child brings his or her own relational style to the classroom, teachers often form differential expectations that shape the way they react to the child. A teacher's beliefs about some students may lead to differential treatment and an inconsistent classroom environment. Differential expectations of behavior tend to become a self-fulfilling prophecy, mainly because the teacher's responses to anxiously attached children allow those students' maladaptive internal working models to remain intact. In that type of situation, the teacher's behavior is more likely to be shaped by the children's expectations and behaviors, thus confirming and perpetuating the children's negative expectations (Sroufe & Fleeson, 1988).

As teachers learn to monitor their own behavior and respond firmly but empathetically to disruptive behavior, they can make positive adjustments in the overall emotional climate of the classroom. Frustration and anger on the part of the teacher will only serve to reinforce children's attitudes about themselves and what they can expect from others. In order to be a secure base for children, teachers must be sensitive to their emotional needs. They must learn to tolerate the immaturity and dependence of anxious–resistant children while building these children's confidence in their ability to function independently. Anxious–avoidant children may be hesitant to approach teachers for help, so teachers must reassure them that they are available and will comfort them when upset. Finally, disorganized children, often the most difficult to handle in the classroom (Lyons-Ruth et al., 1993), must be treated with the consistency and care that they are missing in their parent–child relationship. Teachers should be aware that they might need outside help dealing with a disorganized child who may be severely disruptive to the classroom.

Although improving teacher–child relationships can lead to long-term improvement in classroom behavior, it is not a quick fix for a difficult child. Many problem behaviors that children display can be conceptualized as attempts to elicit attention and caregiving behavior from adults. However, these problems often stem from insufficient parental attention and monitoring. Although effective intervention should acknowledge and respond to children's attachment needs, a behavioral approach can help to address the disruption that causes distress in the classroom. School psychologists and educators may use a behavior modification program along with an attachment-based strategy to address current behavioral classroom disruptions while providing possibilities for long-term change (Speltz, 1990). This type of intervention is likely to be most effective when the parents are also involved, especially with at-risk children who may be experiencing abuse or neglect at home.

Management of aggressive behavior represents a major impediment to the development of a secure teacher–student relationship. Researchers have begun to combine both attachment and social learning theory in the understanding of aggressive children and the formulation of treatment approaches (Greenberg, Speltz, & DeKlyen, 1993). Interventions informed by social learning theory traditionally include parent training and education of children about the use of problem-solving skills. Because attachment security is thought to interact with environmental factors in determining levels of aggression, interventions that address children's internal working models and foster a sense of security are likely to enhance the effectiveness of skills–based techniques.

Although social learning approaches have established efficacy, interventions such as the PrimeTime treatment model (Cavell, 2000) have attempted to improve the quality of aggressive children's relationships with adults before attempting skills training. The theoretical underpinnings of this approach are that aggressive children have negative views of self and others, which may make it difficult for them to learn prosocial skills. The PrimeTime treatment involves 16 months of consultation with parents and teachers that emphasizes emotional acceptance of aggressive children's behavior and provides emotional support that acknowledges the difficulties of managing these aggressive children. Parents are also educated on behavioral control and family structure. In addition, target children receive 46 group sessions of problem-solving skills training that emphasizes empathy and understanding of social skills. Preliminary studies of the efficacy of this intervention showed significant decreases in teacher- and parent-rated aggression, but these improvements were also seen in the control group in which standard mentoring was used with the target children (Cavell & Hughes, 2000). The data also suggest that grouping aggressive children for treatment may have exacerbated aggression as a result of co-occurring peer deviancy training (Dishion & Andrews, 1995). Research using an updated PrimeTime protocol that includes prosocial peers in the skills groups is currently under way.

Many other school-based interventions are relevant to concepts of attachment theory. Providing children with a stable adult–child relationship may be the most important aspect of these interventions by having a positive effect on their internal working models of self and others. It is important to keep in mind that interventions with children are most useful when they address issues both at school and in the home. It is unrealistic to expect children's behavior to change dramatically in the school if the home environment remains conflicted and stressful.

Overall, attachment theory provides a broad background for conceptualizing processes that influence children's adaptation in the classroom. For teachers, it provides a way to understand both the problems students may develop in academic and social functioning and the importance of the teacher–student relationship in compensating children for problems begun in earlier relationships. This perspective provides an integrative framework for thinking of the kinds of parenting, classroom, and peer interventions that would be helpful for these children. The overall focus of the interventions is to increase the children's confidence in themselves and in the responsiveness of significant adults and peers.

## SUMMARY

Attachment theory has many implications for understanding children's behavior in the classroom. During infancy, children develop expectations of how the caregiver will respond to their needs through repeated interaction. Over time, this pattern of interaction provides children with a strategy for maintaining the relationship with the caregiver. These expectations and strategies are carried forward and influence the way children interact with other adults and, later, with peers throughout childhood and adolescence. These internal models of self and others exert a strong influence on children's adjustment; however, children remain open to new experiences with parents, teachers, and peers. School professionals can use the knowledge gained from attachment research to develop strategies for establishing a school environment that supports children's confidence in self and others.

In the classroom, children with secure attachment histories can appear markedly different from those with anxious patterns of attachment. Secure children are more competent in peer relationships, function more independently in the classroom, and are more resilient in the face of challenge. Their insecure counterparts tend to be more withdrawn, anxious, and dependent, or are more aggressive and engage in deviant behaviors. In addition, children's internal working models are likely to affect the relationships that they form with teachers. Attachment theory can provide a framework for the teacher to understand the children's behaviors in the classroom and adjust accordingly how they interact with children.

Programs for prevention of behavior problems stemming from anxious attachment histories often focus on the parent–child relationship during the preschool years. However, many school-based programs for intervention are relevant to attachment theory. The overall focus of such interventions is to increase the children's confident beliefs in their own capabilities and in the responsiveness of significant adults and peers. This chapter discussed several such interventions.

## RECOMMENDED RESOURCES

### Books and Other Printed Material

Brisch, K. H. (1999). *Treating attachment disorders: From theory to therapy.* New York: Guilford Press.

This book contains both theoretical and practical guidance for practitioners working with a range of psychological, behavioral, and psychosomatic problems. The author draws on principles of attachment theory to inform treatment of children and families.

Cavell, T. A. (2000). *Working with parents of aggressive children: A practitioner's guide.* Washington, DC: American Psychological Association.

This book integrates current research on child and adolescent aggression and a relationship enhancement model of treatment. It provides practitioners with a school-based intervention to help parents of children with behavior problems.

Sroufe, L. A., Egeland, B., Carlson, E. A., & Collins, W. A. (2005). *The development of the person: The Minnesota study of risk and adaptation from birth to adulthood.* New York: Guilford Press.

This book is a comprehensive review of the findings of the Minnesota study, defining both maladaptive and positive development from early childhood through adulthood. The theory presented here highlights the importance of early experiences, family and peer relationships throughout childhood and adolescence, and contextual factors in shaping individual outcomes.

## Websites

*http://www.psychology.sunysb.edu/attachment/*

This is the website for the State University of New York at Stony Brook Attachment Lab. In addition to providing a rich source of information regarding the history of findings in the attachment field, it is a valuable resource for current research and interventions.

*http://www.education.umn.edu/icd/parent-child/default.html*

This is the website for the University of Minnesota's Minnesota Longitudinal Study of Parents and Children. In addition to giving an overview of the project, this site lists publications in the field of attachment and education.

## REFERENCES

Ainsworth, M., Blehar, M., Waters, E., & Wall, S. (1978). *Patterns of attachment.* Hillsdale, NJ: Erlbaum.

American Psychiatric Association. (2000). *Diagnostic and statistical manual of mental disorders* (4th ed., Text rev.). Washington, DC: Author.

Belsky, J. (1999). Modern evolutionary theory and patterns of attachment. In J. Cassidy & P. R. Shaver (Eds.), *Handbook of attachment: Theory, research, and clinical applications* (pp. 141–161). New York: Guilford Press.

Birch, S. H., & Ladd, G. W. (1998). Children's interpersonal behaviors and the teacher-child relationship. *Developmental Psychology, 34,* 934–946.

Bowlby, J. (1969/1982). *Attachment and loss: Vol. 1. Attachment.* New York: Basic Books.

Carlson, E. A. (1998). A prospective longitudinal study of attachment disorganization/disorientation. *Child Development, 69,* 1107–1128.

Cassidy, J. (1994). Emotion regulation: Influence of attachment relationships. In N. A. Fox (Ed.), *The development of emotional regulation: Biological and behavioral considerations. Monographs of the Society for Research in Child Development, 59,* 228–249.

Cavell, T. A. (2000). *Working with parents of aggressive children: A practitioner's guide.* Washington, DC: American Psychological Association.

Cavell, T. A., & Hughes, J. N. (2000). Secondary prevention as context for assessing change processes in aggressive children. *Journal of School Psychology, 38,* 199–235.

Chaloner, W. B. (2001). Counselors coaching teachers to use play in classrooms: The Play and Language to Succeed (PALS) early, school-based intervention for behaviorally at-risk children. In A. A. Drewes, L. J. Carey, & C. E. Schaefer (Eds.), *School-based play therapy* (pp. 368–390). New York: Wiley.

Cicchetti, D., & Lynch, M. (1993). Toward an ecological/transactional model of community violence and child maltreatment: Consequences for children's development. *Psychiatry: Interpersonal and Biological Processes, 56,* 96–118.

Cicchetti, D., Toth, S. L., & Lynch, M. (1995). Bowlby's dream comes full circle: The application of attachment theory to risk and psychopathology. In T. H. Ollendick & R. J. Prinze (Eds.), *Advances in clinical and child psychology* (pp. 1–75). New York: Plenum Press.

Dishion, T. J., & Andrews, D. W. (1995). Preventing escalation in problem behaviors with high-risk young adolescents: Immediate and 1-year outcomes. *Journal of Consulting and Clinical Psychology, 63,* 538–548.

Greenberg, M. T., Speltz, M. L., & DeKlyen, M. (1993). The role of attachment in the early development of disruptive behavior problems. *Development and Psychopathology, 5,* 191–214.

Hanson, R. F., & Spratt, E. G. (2000). Reactive attachment disorder: What we know about the disorder and implications for treatment. *Child Maltreatment, 5,* 137–145.

Haugaard, J. J., & Hazen, C. (2004). Recognizing and treating uncommon behavioral and emotional disorders in children and adolescents who may have been severely maltreated: Reactive attachment disorder. *Child Maltreatment, 9,* 154–160.

Jacobsen, T., & Hofmann, V. (1997). Children's attachment representations: Longitudinal relations to school behavior and academic competency in middle childhood and adolescence. *Developmental Psychology, 33,* 703–710.

Kazdin, A. E., & Whitley, M. K. (2003). Treatment of parental stress to enhance therapeutic change among children referred for aggressive and antisocial behavior. *Journal of Counseling and Clinical Psychology, 71,* 504–515.

Kerns, K. (1996). Individual differences in friendship quality: Links to child-mother attachment. In W. Bukowski, A. Newcomb, & W. Hartup (Eds.), *The company they keep: Friendship in childhood and adolescence* (pp. 137–157). New York: Cambridge University Press.

Kobak, R., & Mandelbaum, T. (2003). Caring for the caregiver: An attachment approach to assessment and treatment of child problems. In S. Johnson & V. Whiffen (Eds.), *Attachment processes in couple and family therapy* (pp. 144–164). New York: Guilford Press.

Little, M., & Kobak, R. (2003). Emotional security with teachers' and children's stress reactivity: A comparison of special-education and regular-education classrooms. *Journal of Clinical Child and Adolescent Psychology, 32,* 127–138.

Lyons-Ruth, K., Alpern, L., & Repacholi, B. (1993). Disorganized infant attachment classification and maternal psychosocial problems as predictors of hostile-aggressive behavior in the preschool classroom. *Child Development, 64,* 572–585.

Main, M., & Hesse, E. (1990). Parents' unresolved traumatic experiences are related to infant disorganized attachment status: Is frightened and/or frightening behavior the linking mechanism? In M. T. Greenberg, D. Cicchetti, & E. M. Cummings (Eds.), *Attachment in the preschool years: Theory, research, and intervention* (pp. 161–182). Chicago: University of Chicago Press.

Main, M., & Solomon, J. (1990). Procedures for identifying infants as disorganized/disoriented during the Ainsworth Strange Situation. In M. T. Greenberg, D. Cicchetti, & E. M. Cummings (Eds.), *Attachment in the preschool years: Theory, research, and intervention* (pp. 121–160). Chicago: University of Chicago Press.

Patterson, G. R. (1988). Stress: A change agent for family process. In N. Garmezy & M. Rutter (Eds.), *Stress, coping, and development in children* (pp. 235–264). Baltimore: Johns Hopkins University Press.

Pianta, R. C. (1999). *Enhancing relationships between children and teachers.* Washington, DC: American Psychological Association.

Pianta, R. C., Egeland, B., & Sroufe, L. A. (1990). Maternal stress and children's development: Prediction of school outcomes and identification of protective factors. In J. E. Rolf & A. S. Masten (Eds.), *Risk and protective factors in the development of psychopathology* (pp. 213–235). New York: Cambridge University Press.

Reynolds, A. J., & Robertson, D. L. (2003). School-based early intervention and later child maltreatment in the Chicago Longitudinal Study. *Child Development, 74,* 2–26.

Rosenstein, D. S., & Horowitz, H. A. (1996). Adolescent attachment and psychopathology. *Journal of Consulting and Clinical Psychology, 64,* 244–253.

Rubin, K. H., Bukowski, W., & Parker, J. G. (1998). Peer interactions, relationships, and groups. In W. Damon (Series Ed.) & R. M. Lerner (Vol. Ed.), *Handbook of child psychology: Vol. 1. Theoretical models of human development* (5th ed., pp. 619–700). New York: Wiley.

Scharfe, E. (2003). Stability and change of attachment representations from cradle to grave. In S. M. Johnson & V. E. Whiffen (Eds.), *Attachment processes in couple and family therapy* (pp. 64–84). New York: Guilford Press.

Speltz, M. L. (1990). The treatment of preschool conduct problems. In M. T. Greenberg, D. Cicchetti, & E. M. Cummings (Eds.), *Attachment in the preschool years: Theory, research, and intervention* (pp. 399–426). Chicago: University of Chicago Press.

Sroufe, L. A. (2002). From infant attachment to promotion of adolescent autonomy: Prospective, longitudinal data on the role of parents in development. In J. Borkowski, S. Ramey, & M. Bristol-Power (Eds.), *Parenting and the child's world* (pp. 187–202). Mahwah, NJ: Erlbaum.

Sroufe, L. A., Carlson, E. A., Levy, A. K., & Egeland, B. (1999). Implications of attachment theory for developmental psychopathology. *Development and Psychopathology, 11,* 1–13.

Sroufe, L. A., Egeland, B., Carlson, E. A., & Collins, W. A. (2005). *The development of the person: The Minnesota study of risk and adaptation from birth to adulthood.* New York: Guilford Press.

Sroufe, L. A., & Fleeson, J. (1988). The coherence of family relationships. In R. A. Hinde & J. Stevenson-Hinde (Eds.), *Relationships within families: Mutual influences* (pp. 27–47). Oxford, UK: Oxford University Press.

Toth, S. L., Maughan, A., Manly, J. T., Spagnola, M., & Cicchetti, D. (2002). The relative efficacy of two interventions in altering maltreated preschool children's representational models: Implications for attachment theory. *Development and Psychopathology, 14,* 877–908.

van den Boom, D. C. (1995). Do first-year intervention effects endure? Follow-up during toddlerhood of a sample of Dutch irritable infants. *Child Development, 66,* 1798–1816.

# 30

# Temperament

**Hedwig Teglasi**

*University of Maryland*

## BACKGROUND

Temperament refers to biologically-based dimensions of individuality that influence developmental outcomes by shaping how persons engage with their surroundings (Rothbart & Bates, 1998; Rothbart, Ahadi, & Evans, 2000). Although temperamental predispositions are heritable, early appearing, and relatively stable across types of situations, their expression is influenced by maturation, experience, and environment. All children are born with a set of temperamental attributes, each distributed along the normal continuum and each exerting its influence on learning and development in the context of other traits and situational factors. In light of their association with emotional development, social competence, and general adjustment, various temperamental predispositions are regarded as risk factors or as protective factors. Prevention and early intervention strategies are built on an understanding of how temperamental predispositions affect the growth of children's coping and self-regulatory mechanisms needed to meet increasingly complex social and academic demands.

Although specific temperamental dimensions that have been identified vary somewhat across theories and research studies, four are common across all models (Buss & Plomin, 1984; Derryberry & Rothbart, 1988; and Thomas & Chess, 1977) and are well documented, particularly with respect to their heritability, early appearance, stability into adulthood, and relationship to adjustment. The dimensions of temperament are activity, emotionality, approach–avoidance/sociability, and attention/distractibility.

### Dimensions of Temperament

***Activity.*** Activity level refers to the tempo and vigor of motoric movement (Buss & Plomin, 1984). High and low activity levels are associated, respectively, with preferences for activities that are exciting or low key (Rothbart & Ahadi, 1994; Tarter, Moss, & Vanyukov, 1995). High levels of activity have been linked with increased risk for externalizing behavior problems (Moss, Blackson, Martin, & Tarter, 1992). Concomitant features of high activity level, such as restlessness and irritability, may predispose individuals to interpersonal and academic difficulties (Tarter, 1988). At the high end of this dimension are children with boundless energy, high tempo, and impatience to start a task before hearing all of the instructions. At the low end are those who are slow to respond in class or to start their assignments or appear lethargic or unmotivated. Items on questionnaires that refer to activities that are not appropriate to the context (e.g., being out of seat in class) assess not only the amount or energy of motor movement but also problems with its regulation.

***Emotionality.*** Emotions, central to all conceptions of temperament, are studied in relation to prevailing valence (positive or negative), intensity (degree of arousal), and ease of arousal of emotional states (threshold). Positive and negative emotions are largely independent of each other, are associated with different biological systems, and are evoked by different external variables (Clark & Watson, 1988). *Negative reactivity* is defined as sensitivity to stimuli that evoke negative affect, whereas *positive reactivity* is defined as sensitivity to stimuli that evoke positive affect. Negative emotions encompass general distress, anger and frustration, sadness, and fear; positive emotions include happiness, interest, and pride. Risk factors for internalizing and externalizing disorders, respectively, include pre-existing tendencies toward high negative reactivity (low threshold for physiological arousal) in novel or ambiguous situations (e.g., anxiety disorders; Kagan & Snidman, 1999) or unusually low reactivity (e.g., conduct disorders; Cooper, Wood, Orcutt, & Albino, 2003).

***Approach–Avoidance/Sociability.*** Inclinations to approach or avoid certain situations tend to correlate respectively with positive and negative emotions evoked in those situations (Clark, Watson, & Mineka, 1994; Rothbart & Mauro, 1990) and serve to maintain the preferred level of physiological or emotional arousal, thereby moderating reactivity (Losoya, Eisenberg, & Fabes, 1998). Approach–avoidance has been studied in relation to aspects of situations (e.g., whether they are novel, risky, intense, social or nonsocial, or rewarding or nonrewarding) that are salient for emotional reactivity. Children with high negative reactivity usually approach new situations with caution or may fearfully avoid such situations, whereas those low in negative reactivity tend to seek novelty or risk to attain a desired emotional state (Zuckerman, 1983, 1994). *Sociability* involves positive emotional reactions to other people and preference to seek the company of others regardless of their familiarity (Buss & Plomin, 1984; Cheek & Buss, 1981).

***Attention/Distractibility.*** Individual differences in the regulation of attention have been variously referred to as attention span, persistence, distractibility, or task orientation (Martin, 1989). *Inhibitory control,* defined as the capacity to plan ahead and to inhibit prepotent responses to engage in alternative behaviors, is related to two aspects of attention: selective focus and flexibility in shifting the focus (Rothbart, Ahadi, Hershey, & Fisher, 2001). Both of these aspects support social and emotional adjustment (Rothbart & Ahadi, 1994), possibly through their links to effortful self-regulation and to the development of executive functions such as planning and organization (Posner & Rothbart, 1998).

## Temperament and Personality

Tendencies that are intrinsic to the child are considered within the temperament rubric whereas tendencies that are outgrowths of the synthesis of experiences are subsumed within the personality construct. Rather than dichotomizing between them, it may be fruitful to view temperament dispositions as building blocks that contribute to the development of personality. By shaping how a person engages with his or her surroundings, temperament dispositions influence what is learned from experience. Hence, the relationship between temperament and personality is that of the parts to the whole. Such a part-to-whole association is consistent with the difficulties in empirically distinguishing between temperament and personality (Rothbart et al., 2000). Criteria for considering traits as temperament apply equally well when considering personality traits. Further confounding distinctions is the role of self-regulation, a term that is used in both fields.

***Overlapping criteria for identifying traits as temperament and as personality.*** Criteria for designating traits under the temperament rubric, such as early appearance, stability over time, cross-situational consistency, heritability, and biological bases, are also applicable to traits classified under the rubric of personality. Heritability estimates for temperament traits rarely exceed 50%, and although this level is substantial, the rest of the story is told by other influences, including environment (see Plomin, 1994). The other side of the coin is that perceptions of the "environment" show genetic influences. Children's perceptions of parents' behaviors toward them have a substantial genetic component. Plomin concludes that "correlations between environmental measures and developmental outcomes cannot be assumed to be environmental in origin" (p. 184). When more than one child is studied in a family, differences between siblings are striking and differences in outcomes are associated with non-shared perceptions of the "same" environment (Dunn, Stocker, & Plomin, 1990). Temperament and personality are characterized by similar heritability estimates, and concepts such as values, interests, and attitudes may be influenced by biological factors (Eaves, Eysenck, & Martin, 1989).

Researchers have argued that temperament should not be restricted to early appearing traits, even if the genetic basis is kept, because genes come into play at different times over the course of development as features of the nervous system mature. Also, heritability for most traits has been said to increase with age, at least up to middle childhood (see Rutter, 1994). As for personality, some traits seem to meet criteria of early appearance and stability into adulthood, including novelty seeking or sensation seeking (e.g., Hur & Bouchard, 1997) and empathy (Eisenberg et al., 1999).

Documenting cross-situational consistency has been elusive for both personality and temperament traits (e.g., Goldsmith & Campos, 1990). However, when situations are considered in terms of salience for temperament dimensions, consistency improves to the point that there is adequate prediction of behavior within well-defined classes of situations (Eliasz, 1990). Accordingly, shyness entails negative reactivity to situations that are novel, ambiguous, interpersonal, or have evaluative components. Yet, even within particular classes of situations, the expectation of generality in behavior is complicated by (a) effortful control over the expression of temperament, which may vary across contexts such as school or home, (b) temporary effect of inner states (e.g., fatigue or upset) on self-regulation, and (c) reciprocal influences within temperament dimensions and between temperament and personality. Thus, the expression of high empathy in a particular situation depends on appraisal of the costs of action or inaction (Batson & Oleson, 1991) and on the capacity to regulate emotional responses because, in a given context, those who become emotionally overwhelmed by the plight of another (personal distress) are less likely to act altruistically (Eisenberg & Okun, 1996). Thus, the expression of empathy as a personality trait depends on appraisal of the situation and on emotional self-regulation.

***Role of self-regulation in temperament and personality.*** The various temperamental dimensions are subsumed under two overarching constructs: reactivity and self-regulation (Rothbart & Derryberry, 1981). *Reactivity*, or the ease of arousal of behavioral or emotional systems, includes the dimensions of activity and emotionality, whereas *self-regulation*, which comprises the processes that moderate reactive tendencies, includes attentional control and approach or avoidance of stimuli that evoke reactivity. The temperament dimension of *adaptability*, proposed to differentiate between a persons' initial tendencies to withdraw from novel or unexpected stimuli and the ease of eventually getting used to them (introduced by Thomas & Chess, 1977) and later called Flexibility [Windle & Lerner, 1986]), appears relevant to self-regulation. Adaptable (or flexible) children easily handle changes in routine as well as other unexpected events or transitions (e.g., a new learning task, new school year, or class trip). A quick return of initial reactivity to baseline arousal (the temperament dimension of *falling reactivity*; Rothbart et al., 2001) would facilitate the process of acclimating to changes. Unlike the four dimensions of temperament discussed previously, adaptability does not emerge clearly in factor analytic studies (McClowry, Hegvik, & Teglasi, 1993), probably because the process of adapting to novel circumstances involves complex combinations of reactive tendencies and self-regulatory resources.

Within the temperament field, two distinct types of self-regulation have been distinguished, one type requiring deliberate effort and the other type comprising automatic reactions. The term *effortful control* refers to self-regulation that involves inhibiting a dominant response to perform a less dominant one (Posner & Rothbart, 1998; Ruff & Rothbart, 1996). Self-regulation that is automatic or reactive would be exemplified by avoidance of uncomfortable situations (e.g., stress or novelty) or behavioral inhibition (rigid constraint) in the face of emotional provocation.

*Effortful self-regulation* entails deliberate strategies for coping with the emotions or with the situations that evoke negative reactivity and may include plans for approaching other situations to accomplish goals. However, the use of willful effort to resist the expression of temperamental tendencies requires the capacity to sustain attention and to shift focus as needed to inhibit or activate behavior for deliberate purposes (Derryberry & Rothbart, 1997). The conceptual boundary between temperament and personality is blurred by the definition of effortful control offered by Rothbart et al. (2001) as the deliberate choice to replace a prepotent response tendency with an alternative that is more suited to the situation or to the pursuit of goals. Indeed, a central function of the personality is to act as an executive to balance multiple considerations, including the manner in which temperament is expressed (Karoly, 1993).

The contrast between effortful and reactive aspects of temperamental self-regulation has important parallels in the field of personality. Limitations in the human capacity to engage in sustained effortful self-regulation have been documented in temperament and personality. The effort expended to override temperamental inclinations, such as high negative emotional reactivity or distractibility, draws resources from other endeavors (i.e., academic or social activities) and may take its toll in stress (Strelau, 1995). Likewise, the difficulty of sustaining effortful self-regulation (Muraven, Tice, & Baumeister, 1998) has been highlighted in the field of personality. The importance of automaticity of perceptions and cognitions in daily functioning has been demonstrated (Bargh & Ferguson, 2000). In the educational enterprise, automatic access to knowledge structures that have been solidified through previous strategic processing of information is valued because it frees resources to focus effort on higher order learning (Borkowski, Carr, & Pressely, 1987).

In both the academic and social realms, current problem solving is expected to be informed by knowledge structures or schemas, consolidated through the synthesis of past learning opportunities, whether direct

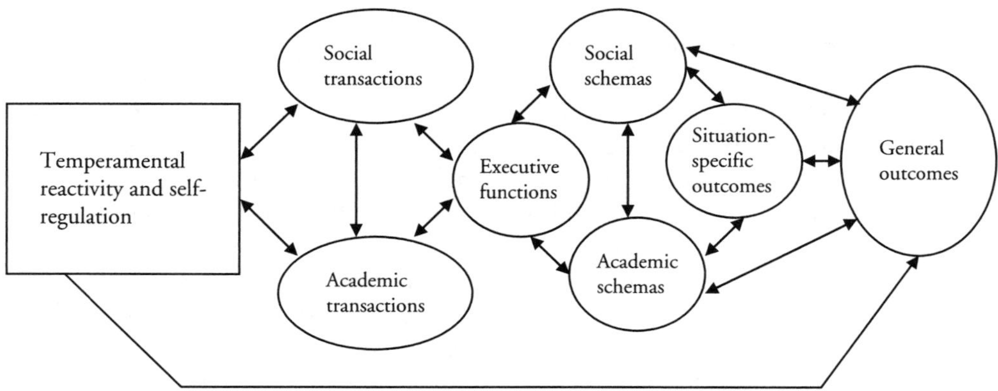


*Note.* From "Temperament and Learning Disability," by H. Teglasi, A. Cohn, and N. Meshbesher, 2004, *Learning Disability Quarterly, 27*, p. 13. Copyright 2004 by Council for Learning Disabilities. Reprinted with permission.

**Figure 1.** *Temperamentally Influenced Transactions and Outcomes.*

instruction or ongoing experiences. In social situations, activation of relevant schemas enables individuals to act spontaneously, without agonizing about the meaning of each situation or the appropriateness of each potential response. The science of early intervention and prevention relies on an understanding of how temperamental reactivity and self-regulation contribute to the development of effortful and automatic resources for self-regulation to enable the executive functions of the personality. Conversely, it would be important to understand how personality processes contribute to the regulation of temperamental reactivity.

## IMPLICATIONS FOR DEVELOPMENT

Individual differences in temperament influence development and contribute to the growth of personality (Rothbart et al., 2000). As depicted in Figure 1, temperamental reactivity and self-regulation set the patterns of reactions to stimuli and thereby influence the continuous process of learning from social and academic experiences. Responses to any situation, including learning tasks or interpersonal encounters, are understood in terms of adaptive implications for an individual's temperamental dispositions and the meaning of the situation in a specific culture (Kerr, 2001; Triandis, 1994). Thus, preferences to seek certain types of situations (e.g., novel or familiar, ambiguous or structured) are rooted in temperament, but the particular situations chosen are socially influenced (Oetting, Donnermeyer, Trimble, & Beauvais, 1998). Likewise, the tendency to worry may be a manifestation of temperament, but exactly what the person worries about is specific to culture, context, gender, and age. Thus, what the individual takes out of day-to-day experiences in various situations is shaped by the combination of temperamental dispositions and environmental factors. In turn, the individual's moment-to-moment experiences are consolidated into memory structures or schemas that comprise the rules for anticipating and coping with future situations. The schemas themselves become resources that inform and organize subsequent experiences and confer protection or risk for continued development (Lohr, Teglasi, & French, 2004).

Temperamental assets promote the growth of schemas, which give rise to a wide range of competencies that enhance subsequent development; conversely, adverse temperamental dispositions detract from the cumulative acquisition of such competencies. For instance, attentional control (persistence and duration of orienting) and positive affectivity (smiling or laughter) at 13 months predict language production and comprehension at 20 months (Dixon & Smith, 2000). At later ages, these temperament dimensions predict good self-control (Wills, 2002). In light of findings that behavioral regulation may be mediated by language (Denckla, 1996, 1998), it appears that temperament may be a building block of both. Moreover, positive emotion, particularly interest, facilitates attention and sustained intellectual pursuits (Renninger, Hidi, & Krapp, 1992). Temperament-based resources, to organize information from the surroundings and to plan behaviors accordingly, noted as *executive functions* in Figure 1, are vital to ongoing processes in the development and use of schemas. Together, the developing schemas and executive functions increase the individual's capacity to adapt to age-appropriate demands of specific contexts or to pursue autonomous goals. In effect, the situation-specific outcomes and more general developmental trajectories are influenced jointly by the manner in which the individual coordinates the processes of registering and interpreting new information (current experience) with knowledge structures or schemas (what is known on the basis of past experience).

Risk-promoting temperamental reactivity, particularly in concert with difficulties in working memory and self-regulation of attention, may disrupt the consolidation of higher order schemas or competencies needed to keep pace with social and academic demands that increase with advancing age (Zeidner, Matthews, Roberts, & MacCann, 2003). Among elementary school children, negative emotionality is associated with less organized, less complex, and less accurate cognitive self-regulatory schemas (Bassan-Diamond, Teglasi, & Schmitt, 1995), and in turn, limitations in schema development are associated with maladjustment (Lohr et al., 2004).

Social competence, an important developmental outcome, is associated with individual differences in both temperament (emotional reactivity and self-regulation) and social cognitions (e.g., Denham, et al., 2003). Regulation of emotions, a prerequisite of social competence, is a complex process that includes monitoring, evaluating, and modifying the expression of emotions to attune its timing and intensity to the context and to the accomplishment of intentions (Thompson, 1994). Typically, the systematic organization of social cognitions increases resources for emotional self-regulation by allowing past learning to influence appraisal of current situations in ways that increase the nuances of emotional experiences and expression. However, the synthesis of past experiences and growth of social cognitions are shaped by temperamental individuality in the attentional, cognitive, emotional, and behavioral processes.

Emotions play a central role in the development of children's social cognitions (Lemerise & Arsenio, 2000). Schemas encapsulate the ebb and flow of emotions in relation to ongoing life events as well as the connections of actions (or inactions) with outcomes (short or long term) in various contexts. The coordination of information from the inner (emotions and intentions) and outer worlds (events, actions, and outcomes) is represented in schemas that set the rules for how the various strands of life experiences "go together." The schemas, including the manner in which emotions are woven into the fabric of ongoing events, comprise data sets for understanding emotions in future encounters and may be used to reflect on prior emotional experiences.

In sum, temperamental dispositions associated with resilience (defined as the ability to maintain functioning in adverse conditions; Smith & Prior, 1995), including dimensions of task persistence and regulation of emotional reactivity, exert their influences on development not only by their affecting moment-by-moment encounters but also by their contributing to the incremental acquisition of schemas and social cognitions. Resilience is furthered by the growth of competencies and coping resources that continue to play a protective role in development. In contrast, temperamental vulnerability is compounded if adverse temperament dispositions disrupt the incremental consolidation of social cognitions and schemas needed to adapt or to pursue autonomous goals. To fully utilize knowledge about temperament, researchers need to generate new constructs to integrate what is known about temperament into models of development and intervention. Kagan (2001) suggested that new constructs are needed to solve three problems: (a) find theoretically useful ways to conceptualize childhood histories, (b) delineate the temperamental attributes that bias developmental profiles, and (c) determine how social factors maintain or alter previously acquired profiles.

## PROBLEMS AND IMPLICATIONS

Children's temperamental dispositions are often included in popular models of risk or resilience (e.g., Mash & Barkley, 2003). Predictive relationships between temperament and adjustment, both academic and social–emotional, have led to the view that certain temperamental attributes increase risk (vulnerability) or confer protection (resilience) in the face of adversity. The relationships between temperament and outcomes, though well documented, are considered probabilistic, not deterministic. In line with the developmental principles of equifinality and multifinality, different constellations of temperament characteristics may result in the same outcome, and the same constellation may result in different outcomes (Cicchetti & Rogosch, 1996). Vulnerability due to temperament is not static because it is modified by the growth of coping resources (Tarter, Mezzich, Hsieh, & Parks, 1995).

Generally, having a greater number of risk factors reduces the likelihood of acquiring higher order coping resources such as social competence (Diener & Kim, 2004) and increases the probability of adjustment problems (Siefer, 1995). The prediction of adverse outcomes often involves configurations of temperamental attributes because attributes work together, and each modifies the expression of the others. Negative emotionality and high activity level are two common risk factors during early childhood (see Rothbart & Bates, 1998). However, regulation of attention moderates problems with behavioral self-control and buffers individuals against the adverse impact of temperament dimensions such as high negative emotional reactivity (Belsky, Friedman, & Hsieh, 2001). The detrimental influence of high activity level on academic and social adjustment is more evident when combined with other temperament attributes such as low attention span (Nelson, Martin, Hodge, Havill, & Kamphaus, 1999). When well regulated, however, higher activity may be adaptive (Campbell, Eaton, & McKeen, 2002).

Decisions about when and how to intervene require understanding (a) developmental processes engendered by the configuration of risk and protective characteristics within the child; (b) patterns of interactions with the external world, as well as anticipated future patterns; and (c) growth of schemas and information-processing strategies (social and academic) that comprise higher order coping resources.

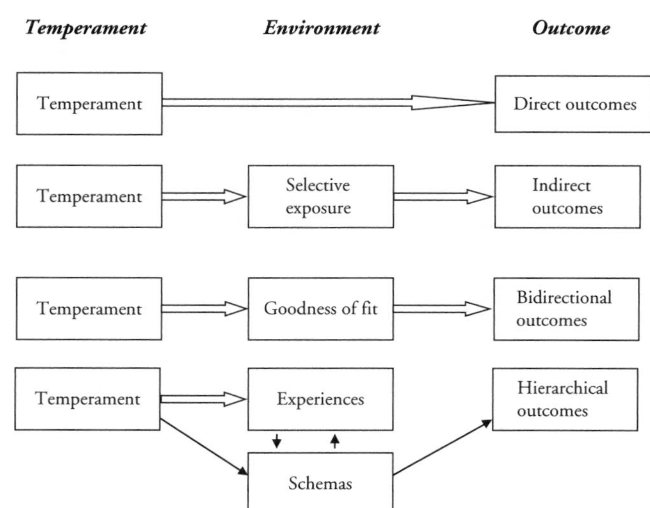


*Note.* From "Temperament and Learning Disability," by H. Teglasi, A. Cohn, and N. Meshbesher, 2004, *Learning Disability Quarterly, 27*, p. 14. Copyright 2004 by Council for Learning Disabilities. Reprinted with permission.

**Figure 2.** *Multiple Pathways Between Temperament and Outcomes.*

## ALTERNATIVE ACTIONS FOR PREVENTION OR INTERVENTION

Selecting the point of entry for prevention or intervention requires an understanding of the mechanisms linking temperament and the presenting problems. As shown in Figure 2, temperament influences outcomes in ways that may be described as direct, indirect, bidirectional, or hierarchical (see Teglasi & Epstein, 1998).

### Direct Outcomes

A wide range of variability in the expression of temperamental individuality is considered normal. However, at the extremes, the expression of temperament directly signals problems in adjustment that may be characterized by one or more of the four D's:

- *Disorganization* of the developmental and learning processes of the individual.
- *Disturbance* of the well-being of others.
- *Dysfunction* in relationships with families, peers, or teachers.
- *Distress* engendered by intense negative emotions or stress.

Even when temperamental dispositions such as extremely high negative reactivity are not behaviorally expressed, the stress or distressing emotions engendered are maladaptive and confer risk for negative outcomes (Strelau, 1995), including school phobia, test anxiety, social withdrawal, somatic complaints, or depressive episodes (Sears & Milburn, 1990). Moreover, the ability to mask the expression of emotions that are not socially acceptable does not ensure adjustment if the individual is internally disorganized (Cicchetti, Ackerman, & Izard, 1995).

The chronic arousal of intense emotions in the classroom setting or during social encounters impedes learning and social functioning, as the child may be too overwhelmed (overstimulated) or preoccupied with thoughts to focus on the tasks at hand or to organize the myriad social cues.

Responses of parents or other caregivers to the child's distressing or happy emotions may have a profound influence on how the child learns to regulate emotions. When mothers of infants classified as highly irritable at birth were trained to respond sensitively to their child's emotional displays, their children were more sociable, expressed less negative affect, and seemed more self-regulated at nine months of age than children of mothers who did not receive the training (van den Boom & Hoeksma, 1994). In general, preventive interventions at home or in the classroom aim to achieve two outcomes. First, to minimize the likelihood of a child's becoming overwhelmed by intense negative reactivity, interventions foster feelings of comfort or safety in threatening situations by countering the child's perception of the situation as upsetting or risky (i.e., the classroom or a visit to the dentist). Second, to minimize disturbance of others, interventions provide appropriate structures and alternative ways to express temperament (release pent-up energy by having well-timed breaks).

Should the child be overtaken by intense negative emotions (frustration, anger, and anxiety) or exhibit disorganized behaviors, interventions should do the following:

- Remove the stressor, help the child calm down, and normalize feelings.
- Manage behaviors in ways that help the child organize future responses to the situation and are sensitive to the self-regulatory functions of the child's behavior.
- Avoid fostering maladaptive cycles, such as giving time-out to a child who feels relieved to escape the situation.

## Indirect Outcomes

Cumulative influences of temperament on how the individual engages with the environment shape adjustment indirectly by affecting what is learned from experiences. Temperamentally rooted tendencies toward selective attention or inattention and selective approach or avoidance of certain types of information, situations, or activities limit the child's range of exposure to life experiences. For instance, an attentional bias to center on signals of embarrassment or potential rejection may explain individual differences in more complex cognitions that include maladaptive causal attributions in situations that evoke negative responses (Teglasi & Hoffman, 1982). Mastery of academic subjects is also influenced by temperamental variations in tendencies to persist on tasks, to resist distraction, and to engage in active, effortful processing of information in various domains. With the passage of time, biased attention, superficial or minimal processing of information, or the tendency to rush through homework limit the type and depth of knowledge acquired.

The focus of prevention is to avert the negative effect on development caused by temperamental tendencies that limit or bias exposure to experiences a child needs to acquire age-appropriate competencies for academic or social adjustment. Effective strategies would achieve the following:

- Maximize positive experiences by encouraging activities or interactions that bring out the best in the child, including the pursuit of hobbies or interests, and by fostering meaningful interpersonal bonds.
- Reduce the perceived risks of approaching activities or situations that are age-appropriate by helping the child gain insight about the nature of the situation as well as the feelings it evokes.
- Increase self-regulatory resources to resist the pull of temperamental avoidance or distractibility by helping the child to anticipate, plan, and cope with temperamental reactivity.
- Consider the difficulty of undertaking activities that go against the temperamental grain and balancing the demands of those activities with the child's resources and need for external supports.

## Bidirectional Outcomes

The concept of *goodness of fit* captures the two-way influences between the child and the environment as contributors to developmental outcomes (Lerner & Lerner, 1983). A poor fit occurs when a child's temperamental proclivities are at odds with the learning or behavioral demands of settings considered important for development or when temperamentally rooted behaviors evoke negative responses from others. Configurations of temperamental dispositions that foster poor fit have been referred to as "difficult" because they promote negative interactions between the child and the milieu. The concept of children's difficultness is general across cultures, but the attributes that are problematic may be specific to cultures (De Vries, 1987).

The behaviors of children with "difficult" temperaments, particularly negative emotional reactivity, high activity, or low task orientation (low persistence and high distractibility), may elicit responses from others that further disorganize behavior and disrupt higher order thinking. Children with difficult dispositions often receive negative messages from others, including peers (Walker, Berthelsen, & Irving, 2001), become embroiled in repeated hassles within their families (Teglasi & MacMahon, 1990), and are rated by their teachers as less teachable (Bender, 1986; Keogh, 1983). In contrast, children with positive temperamental characteristics elicit more favorable responses from peers and adults

(Rutter, 1987; Thomas & Chess, 1977). To improve goodness of fit, educators should become aware of how their own temperaments influence their responses to students' individuality (Richardson & Shupe, 2003). Teacher ratings of their relationships with students predict children's subsequent academic and social development (Hamre & Pianta, 2001; Ladd & Burgess, 2001), but bidirectional influences need further investigation. Programs exist to help parents or other caregivers and teachers learn to respond in ways that recognize and reframe the temperamental roots of problematic behaviors (McClowry, 2003).

Strategies to improve goodness of fit in the classroom are grounded in awareness of the wide range of variability in students' responses to routine classroom events, such as being called on, being corrected, taking tests, or being introduced to new activities or people. Highly reactive students may apprehensively ruminate about the potential public embarrassment of a mistake or the possibility of freezing on a test, whereas their less reactive peers may thrive on change, stimulation, or competition. Preventive interventions may pre-empt problems in various contexts by anticipating and averting a poor fit. After a history of poor fit, interventions to improve fit must consider the accumulated negative effect of prior interactions.

The following classroom-wide strategies can be adapted for enhancing goodness of fit (see Keogh, 2003):

- Provide structure that supports children who have extreme difficulties with self-regulation of learning, performance, behavior, or emotional reactivity. For some students, it is necessary to provide cues, prompts, explicit instruction, or feedback to draw attention or to help individuals shift from one aspect of a task or social situation to another.
- Individualize incentives for learning and performance according to what draws interest and maintains persistence (external rewards, emotional engagement, or growing sense of mastery).
- Vary the challenges and supports to optimize the match between requirements and individuals' resources to meet the demands for self-regulation of emotion or attention, application of prior knowledge, effortful persistence, self-direction, planning, or organization.
- Foster the sense of emotional safety in the classroom by considering the world of peer relationships, because children differ in their involvement in negative peer exchanges. The same environment is unlikely to be an equally good fit with every child, but it is important for children to feel that their teachers and other caregivers are sensitive to their individuality.

## Hierarchical Outcomes

At any point in time and in any given context, all of the developing resources within the child, including temperament, motivation, and prior knowledge, are called into play to meet demands or pursue goals. As described earlier, temperament contributes to the development of increasingly complex self-regulatory and adaptive resources that emerge hierarchically. Thus, peer acceptance, considered to be a protective factor in development, hinges on social competence (Eisenberg et al., 1999; Prior, Sanson, Smart, & Oberklaid, 2000), and social competence is predicated on self-regulation of emotion and attention (Denham et al, 2003; Diener & Kim, 2004). For children whose temperaments have impeded the growth of social–emotional competencies, a variety of interventions are available, including training in social skills, problem solving, or emotion management.

Despite the popularity of social compentency interventions, their effect sizes have been modest (for a review, see Kavale & Mostert, 2004), possibly because the programs do not address the various mechanisms that disrupted the child's acquisition of specific skills in relation to specific contexts. In keeping with the hierarchical view of development, the sequencing of skills warrants careful consideration. Some children need to start with gaining a basic understanding of emotions, such as recognizing, labeling, and appropriately expressing emotions, whereas others are ready to undertake the critical evaluation of problem situations or simply need the confidence to deal with the perceived problem. Structured group interventions that use narrative to increase social–emotional awareness and problem solving (STORIES; Rahill & Teglasi, 2003; Teglasi & Rothman, 2001) may be adapted to the needs of the participants through the selection of the books and through discussions or activities that acknowledge individuality. The story structure connects the various strands of experience, including the external circumstance, emotions and intentions, actions and outcomes, which may be viewed in the moment and in the long term. Systematic review of these connections promotes understanding emotions and social problem-solving (e.g., labeling feelings of various characters in the pictures prior to reading the text; identifying the emotions of the characters using cues in the story; identifying characters' goals and intentions and their influences on actions; and connecting events, emotions, actions, and outcomes).

The assessment of temperament adds important information beyond what is obtained in a typical psychoeducational battery by providing a broader range of attributes to be considered when making determinations about school readiness (Pianta & Walsh, 1996) or interventions (Keogh, 2003). Accurate assessment of temperament at an early age may make it possible to identify children at risk for social–emotional or academic difficulties and to monitor their developing schemas and self-regulatory resources. Interventions with older children may require that maladaptive social cognitions be repaired without invalidating the reality of children's day-to-day emotional experiences associated with their temperamental styles. As development proceeds, responses to the environment are expected to become increasingly self-regulated and filtered through the lens of prior learning (schemas), rather than directly evoked by impinging stimuli or immediate incentives. Therefore, the understanding of children's needs would be further enhanced by assessing schemas that constitute these filtering mechanisms (Teglasi, 1998, 2001) and by understanding the processes that contribute to their development.

## SUMMARY

Children's adverse temperamental dispositions entail greater challenges in their acquisition of the increasingly more complex social or academic competencies expected with development, whereas resilience-promoting dispositions facilitate their cumulative consolidation. Intervention strategies that are informed by temperament are grounded in four assumptions. First, the aim is not to change basic dispositions but to work with them to minimize potential adverse effects of temperamental tendencies and to maximize the development of higher order protective resources. Framing the child's behaviors in temperament terms expands options, enabling the intervention to avert the vicious cycles fueled by misunderstandings of the behavior's functions and to promote long-term self-regulatory competencies that moderate the expression of temperament.

Second, temperament is understood as a configuration of dimensions that interact with one another and with variables that do not fall under the temperament rubric. Adjustment, in a particular context, is a function of all of the child's inner attributes, including temperament and the accumulated knowledge structures that come together as the "team" to meet the demands of the environment or to pursue goals.

Third, interventions are based on an understanding of the multiple ways in which temperament places individuals at risk for problems in adjustment: direct, indirect, bidirectional, and hierarchical.

Fourth, interventions are aimed at the "big picture" of the developmental trajectory, keeping in mind the adaptive requirements of past, present, and future contexts. Goodness of fit between child and context may vary from one age to another, and environmental adjustments to improve the fit should be mindful of the child's long-term developmental needs.

## RECOMMENDED RESOURCES

Keogh, B. K. (2003). *Temperament in the classroom: Understanding individual differences.* Baltimore: Brookes Publishing.

This book explains the temperamental roots of many problems that children experience in educational settings and offers practical applications geared to educators and school psychologists.

McClowry, S. G. (2003). *Your child's unique temperament: Insights and strategies for responsive parenting.* Champaign, IL: Research Press.

This book, based on research conducted by the author, provides parents with insights and strategies to handle behavioral difficulties in ways that are responsive to the child's temperamental individuality.

## REFERENCES


Bargh, J. A., & Ferguson, M. L. (2000). Beyond behaviorism: On the automaticity of higher mental processes. *Psychological Bulletin, 126,* 925–945.

Bassan-Diamond, L., Teglasi, H., & Schmitt, P. (1995). Temperament and a story telling measure of self-regulation. *Journal of Research in Personality, 29,* 109–120.

Batson, C. D., & Oleson, K. C. (1991). Current status of the empathy-altruism hypothesis. In M. Clark

(Ed.), *Prosocial behavior* (pp. 62–85). Newbury Park, CA: Sage Publications.

Belsky, J., Friedman, S. L., & Hsieh, K. (2001). Testing a core emotion-regulation prediction: Does early attentional persistence moderate the effect of infant negative emotionality on later development? *Child Development, 72,* 123–133.

Bender, W. N. (1986). Teachability and personality of learning disabled children: Prediction of teachers' perceptions from personality variables. *Learning Disabilities Research, 2,* 4–9.

Borkowski, J., Carr, M., & Pressely, M. (1987). "Spontaneous" strategy use: Perspectives from metacognitive theory. *Intelligence, 11,* 61–75.

Buss, A., & Plomin, R. (1984). *Temperament: Early developing personality traits.* Hillsdale, NJ: Erlbaum.

Campbell, D. W., Eaton, W. O., & McKeen, N. A. (2002). Motor activity level and behavioral control in young children. *International Journal of Behavioral Development, 26,* 289–296.

Cheek, J. M., & Buss, A. H. (1981). Shyness and sociability. *Journal of Personality and Social Psychology, 41,* 330–339.

Cicchetti, D., Ackerman, B. P., & Izard, C. E. (1995). Emotions and emotion regulation in developmental psychopathology. *Development and Psychopathology, 7,* 1–10.

Cicchetti, D., & Rogosch, F. A. (1996). Equifinality and multifinality in developmental psychopathology. *Development and Psychopathology, 8,* 597–600.

Clark, L. A., & Watson, D. (1988). Mood and the mundane: Relations between daily life events and self-reported mood. *Journal of Personality and Social Psychology, 54,* 296–308.

Clark, L. A., Watson, D., & Mineka, S. (1994). Temperament, personality, mood and anxiety disorders. *Journal of Abnormal Psychology, 103,* 103–116.

Cooper, M. L., Wood, P. K., Orcutt, H. K., & Albino, A. (2003). Personality and the predisposition to engage in risky or problem behaviors during adolescence. *Journal of Personality and Social Psychology, 84,* 390–410.

Denckla, M. B. (1996). Biological correlates of learning and attention: What is relevant to learning disability and attention-deficit hyperactivity disorder? *Journal of Developmental and Behavioral Pediatrics, 17,* 114–119.

Denham, S. A., Blair, K. A., DeMulder, E., Levitas, J., Sawyer, K. S., Auerbach-Major, S. T., & Queenan, P. (2003). Preschoolers' emotional competence: Pathway to mental health? *Child Development, 74,* 238–256.

Derryberry, D., & Rothbart, M. K. (1988). Affected, arousal, and attention as components of temperament. *Journal of Personality and Social Psychology, 55,* 958–966.

Derryberry, D., & Rothbart, M. K. (1997). Reactive and effortful processes in the organization of temperament. *Development and Psychopathology, 9,* 633–652.

De Vries, M. W. (1987). Cry babies, culture, and catastrophe: Infant temperament among the Masai. In N. Schiper-Hughes (Ed.), *Child survival* (pp. 165–185). Dordrecht, Netherlands: Reidel Publishing.

Diener, M. L., & Kim, D. Y. (2004). Maternal and child predictors of preschool children's social competence. *Journal of Applied Developmental Psychology, 25,* 3–24.

Dixon, W. E., & Smith, P. H. (2000). Links between early temperament and language acquisition. *Merrill-Palmer Quarterly, 46,* 417–440.

Dunn, J., Stocker, C., & Plomin, R. (1990). Assessing the relationship between young siblings. *Journal of Child Psychology and Psychiatry, 31,* 983–991.

Eaves, L. J., Eysenck, H. J., & Martin, N. G. (1989). *Social attitudes: A model of cultural inheritance.* London: Academic Press.

Eisenberg, N., Guthrie, I. K., Murphy, B. C., Shepard, S. A., Cumberland, A., & Carlo, G. (1999). Consistency and development of prosocial dispositions: A longitudinal study. *Child Development, 70,* 1360–1372.

Eisenberg, N., & Okun, M. A. (1996). The relations of dispositional regulation and emotionality to elders' empathy-related responding and affect while volunteering. *Journal of Personality, 64,* 157–183.

Eliasz, A. (1990). Broadening the concept of temperament: From disposition to hypothetical construct. *European Journal of Personality, 4,* 287–302.

Goldsmith, H. H., & Campos, J. J. (1990). The structure of temporal fear and pleasure in infants: A psychometric perspective. *Child Development, 61,* 1944–1964.

Hamre, B. K., & Pianta, R. C. (2001). Early teacher-child relationships and the trajectory of children's school outcomes through eighth grade. *Child Development, 72,* 625–638.

Hur, Y., & Bouchard, T. J. (1997). The genetic correlation between impulsivity and sensation-seeking traits. *Behavior Genetics, 27,* 455–463.

Kagan, J. (2001). The need for new constructs. *Psychological Inquiry, 12,* 84–87.

Kagan, J., & Snidman, N. (1999). Early childhood predictors of adult anxiety disorders. *Biological Psychiatry, 46,* 1536–1541.

Kavale, K. A., & Mostert, M. P. (2004). Social skills interventions for individuals with learning disabilities. *Learning Disability Quarterly, 25,* 3–24.

Keogh, B. K. (1983). Individual differences in temperament: A contribution to the personal, social, and educational competence of learning disabled children. In J. D. McKinney & L. Feagens (Eds.), *Current topics in learning disabilities* (pp. 34–35). Norwood, NJ: Ablex.

Keogh, B. K. (2003). *Temperament in the classroom: Understanding individual differences.* Baltimore: Paul H. Brookes.

Kerr, M. (2001). Culture as a context for temperament: Suggestions from the life courses of shy Swedes and Americans. In T. D. Wachs & G. A. Kohnstamm (Eds.), *Temperament in context* (pp. 139–152). Mahwah, NJ: Erlbaum.

Ladd, G. W., & Burgess, K. B. (2001). Do relational risks and protective factors moderate the linkages between childhood aggression and early psychological and school adjustment? *Child Development, 72,* 1579–1601.

Lemerise, E. A., & Arsenio, W. F. (2000). An integrated model of emotion processes and cognition in social information processing. *Child Development, 71,* 107–118.

Lerner, J. V., & Lerner, R. M. (1983). Temperament and adaptation across life: Theoretical and empirical issues. In P. B. Baltes & O. G. Brim, Jr. (Eds.), *Life-span development and behavior* (pp. 197–231). New York: Academic Press.

Lohr, L., Teglasi, H., & French, M. (2004). Schemas and temperament as risk factors for emotional disability. *Personality and Individual Differences, 36,* 1637–1654.

Losoya, S., Eisenberg, N., & Fabes, R. A. (1998). Developmental issues in the study of coping. *International Journal of Behavioral Development, 22,* 287–313.

Martin, R. P. (1989). Activity level, distractibility, and persistence: Critical characteristics in early schooling. In G. A. Kohnstamm, J. E. Bates, & M. K. Rothbart (Eds.), *Temperament in childhood* (pp. 451–461). New York: Wiley.

Mash, E. J., & Barkley, R. A. (2003). *Child psychopathology* (2nd ed.). New York: Guilford Press.

McClowry, S. G. (2003). *Your child's unique temperament: Insights and strategies for responsive parenting.* Champaign, IL: Research Press.

McClowry, S., Hegvik, R., & Teglasi, H. (1993). An examination of the construct validity of the Middle Childhood Temperament Questionnaire. *Merrill-Palmer Quarterly, 39,* 279–293.

McCrae, R. R., & Costa, P. T. (1997). Personality trait structure as a human universal. *American Psychologist, 52,* 509–516.

Moss, H. B., Blackson, T. C., Martin, C. S., & Tarter, R. E. (1992). Heightened motor activity level in male offspring of substance abusing fathers. *Biological Psychiatry, 32,* 1135–1147.

Muraven, M., Tice, D. M., & Baumeister, R. F. (1998). Self-control as limited resource: Regulatory depletion patterns. *Journal of Personality and Social Psychology, 74,* 774–789.

Nelson, B., Martin, R. P., Hodge, S., Havill, V., & Kamphaus, R. W. (1999). Modeling the prediction of elementary school adjustment from preschool temperament. *Personality and Individual Differences, 26,* 687–700.

Oetting, E. R., Donnermeyer, J. R., Trimble, J., & Beauvais, F. (1998). Primary socialization theory: Culture, ethnicity, and cultural identification: The links between culture and substance use. *Substance Use and Misuse, 33,* 2075–2107.

Pianta, R. C., & Walsh, D. J. (1996). *High-risk children in schools.* New York: Routledge.

Plomin, R. (1994). *Genetics and experience: The interplay between nature and nurture.* Thousand Oaks, CA: Sage Publications.

Posner, M. I., & Rothbart, M. K. (1998). Attention, self regulation and consciousness. *Philosophical Transactions of the Royal Society of London, 353,* 1915–1927.

Prior, M., Sanson, A., Smart, D., & Oberklaid, F. (2000). *Pathways from infancy to adolescence—Australian Temperament Project 1983–2000.* Melbourne, Australia: Australian Institute of Family Studies.

Rahill, S. A., & Teglasi, H. (2003). Process and outcomes of story-based and skill-based social competency programs for children with emotional disabilities. *Journal of School Psychology, 41,* 413–429.

Renninger, K., Hidi, S., & Krapp, A. (1992). *The role of interest in learning and development.* Hillsdale, NJ: Erlbaum.

Richardson, B. G., & Shupe, M. J. (2003). The importance of teacher self-awareness in working with students with emotional and behavioral disorders. *Teaching Exceptional Children, 36,* 8–13.

Rothbart, M. K., & Ahadi, S. (1994). Temperament and the development of personality. *Journal of Abnormal Psychology, 103,* 55–66.

Rothbart, M. K., Ahadi, S. A., & Evans, D. E. (2000). Temperament and personality: Origins and outcomes. *Journal of Personality and Social Psychology, 78,* 122–135.

Rothbart, M. K., Ahadi, S. A., Hershey, K., & Fisher, P. (2001). Investigation of temperament at three to seven years: The Children's Behavior Questionnaire. *Child Development, 72,* 1394–1408.

Rothbart, M., & Bates, J. (1998). Temperament. In W. Damon (Series Ed.) and N. Eisenberg (Vol. Ed.), *Handbook of child development: Vol. 3. Social, emotional, and personality development* (pp. 105–176). New York: Wiley.

Rothbart, M., & Derryberry, D. (1981). Development of individual differences in temperament. In M. Lamb & A. Brown (Eds.), *Advances in developmental psychology* (Vol. 1; pp. 37–86). Hillsdale, NJ: Erlbaum.

Rothbart, M. K., & Mauro, J. A. (1990). Temperament, behavioral inhibition, and shyness in childhood. In H. Leitenberg (Ed.), *Handbook of social and evaluation anxiety* (pp. 139–160). New York: Plenum Press.

Ruff, H. A., & Rothbart, M. K. (1996). *Attention in early development: Themes and variations.* New York: Oxford University Press.

Rutter, M. (1987). Temperament, personality and personality disorder. *British Journal of Psychiatry, 150,* 443–458.

Rutter, M. (1994). Concepts of causation, tests of causal mechanisms, and implications for intervention. In A. C. Petersen & J. T. Mortimer (Eds.), *Youth unemployment and society* (pp. 147–171). Cambridge, UK: Cambridge University Press.

Sears, S. J., & Milburn, J. (1990). School-age stress. In L. E. Arnold (Ed.), *Childhood stress* (pp. 224–246). New York: Wiley.

Siefer, R. (1995). Perils and pitfalls of high risk research. *Developmental Psychology, 31,* 420–424.

Smith, J., & Prior, M. (1995). Temperament and stress resilience in school-age children: A within families study. *Journal of the American Academy of Child and Adolescent Psychiatry, 34,* 168–179.

Strelau, J. (1995). Temperament risk factor: The contribution of temperament to the consequences of the state of stress. In S. E. Hobfoll & M. W. de Vries (Eds.), *Extreme stress and communities: Impact and intervention* (pp. 63–81). The Netherlands: Kluwer Academic Publishers.

Tarter, R. E. (1988). Are there inherited behavioral traits that predispose to substance abuse? *Journal of Consulting and Clinical Psychology, 56,* 189–196.

Tarter, R., Mezzich, A., Hsieh, Y.-C., & Parks, M. (1995). Cognitive capacities in female adolescent substance abusers: Association with severity of drug abuse. *Drug and Alcohol Dependence, 39,* 15–21.

Tarter, R. E., Moss, H. B., & Vanyukov, M. M. (1995). Behavior genetic perspective of alcoholism etiology. In H. Begleiter & B. Kissin (Eds.), *The genetics of alcoholism* (pp. 294–326). New York: Oxford University Press.

Teglasi, H. (1998). Assessment of schema and problem-solving strategies with projective techniques. In M. Hersen & A. Bellack (Series Eds.) & C. Reynolds (Vol. Ed.), *Comprehensive clinical psychology: Vol. 4. Assessment* (pp. 459–499).

Teglasi, H. (2001). *Essentials of TAT and other storytelling instruments assessment.* New York: Wiley.

Teglasi, H., Cohn, A., & Meshbesher, N. (2004). Temperament and learning disability. *Learning Disability Quarterly, 27,* 9–20.

Teglasi, H., & Epstein, S. (1998). Temperament and personality theory: The perspective of cognitive-experiential self-theory. *School Psychology Review, 27,* 534–548.

Teglasi, H., & Hoffman, M. A. (1982). Causal attributions of shy subjects. *Journal of Research in Personality, 16,* 376–385.

Teglasi, H., & MacMahon, B. (1990). Temperament and common problem behaviors of children. *Journal of Applied Developmental Psychology, 11,* 331–349.

Teglasi, H., & Rothman, L. (2001). STORIES: A classroom-based program to reduce aggressive behavior. *Journal of School Psychology, 39,* 71–94.

Thomas, A., & Chess, S. (1977). *Temperament and development.* New York: Brunner/Mazel.

Triandis, H. C. (1994). *Culture and social behavior.* New York: McGraw-Hill.

van den Boom, D. C., & Hoeksma, J. B. (1994). The effect of infant irritability on mother-infant interaction: A growth curve analysis. *Developmental Psychology, 30,* 581–590.

Walker, S., Berthelsen, D., & Irving, K. (2001). Temperament and peer acceptance in early childhood: Sex and social status differences. *Child Study Journal, 31,* 177–192.

Windle, M., & Lerner, R. (1986). Reassessing the dimensions of temperament individuality across the life span: The revised Dimensions of Temperament Survey (DOTS-R). *Journal of Adolescent Research, 1,* 213–230.

Zeidner, M., Matthews, G., Roberts, R. D., & MacCann, C. (2003). Development of emotional intelligence: Toward a multi-level investment model. *Human Development, 46,* 69–97.

Zuckerman, M. (1983). *Biological bases of sensation seeking, impulsivity, and anxiety.* Hillsdale, NJ: Erlbaum.

Zuckerman, M. (1994). *Behavioral expressions and biosocial bases of sensation-seeking.* New York: Cambridge University Press.

# 31

# Sexual Interest and Expression

**Deborah Tharinger**
**Alison Wilkinson**
*University of Texas at Austin*

**Jon Lasser**
*Texas State University–San Marcos*

## BACKGROUND AND DEVELOPMENT

Understanding the development and meaning of children's sexual interest and expression is of utmost importance for educators and mental health professionals. These individuals need a certain amount of expertise and a comfort level that allows them to navigate this complex and sensitive area. They must work within a cultural and political context and are influenced and often constricted by public policy. They must balance these concerns with the best interests of the children and families with whom they work. Trained professionals in the schools are in a unique position to provide sexuality education, encourage understanding of normal or typical sexuality development, prevent common challenges through improved communication, detect problem and abnormal behaviors, and promote needed intervention. However, they must consider the diverse values and views of individual families as well as of the community and surrounding society, including legal parameters.

Much attention is devoted to sexuality today by parents, educators, religious leaders, lawmakers, politicians, and students. The public increasingly is concerned with public health problems, such as sexually transmitted diseases and teenage pregnancy as well as the psychological consequences of sexual activity of young teenagers and preteens. Risky sexual behaviors and their consequences can hamper the normal developmental tasks of adolescence and lead to psychological distress and an impairment in the ability to form healthy relationships (Beausang, 2000). An abstinence-only focus currently dominants the landscape of sex or sexuality education, although most experts agree that this approach alone is not satisfactory. Society continues to focus attention predominantly on the sexuality of adolescents, although research has shown that sexual development begins at conception and continues throughout life (Masters, Johnson, & Kolodny, 1995) and that sexual development in infancy and childhood can influence sexual health in adolescence and adulthood (Bancroft, 2003). Thus, sexuality development in infancy and childhood remains cloaked in denial, even in the 21st century.

Literature on child sexuality has largely been based on theoretical assumptions and data from small clinical case studies and anecdotal evidence (Larsson, 2001). Systematic research studies are largely nonexistent. Although Freud first published psychological writings on infant and childhood sexuality in 1905, the barriers that hamper the empirical study of children's sexuality remain pervasive and powerful. Parents, school officials, and community agencies are often of the mindset that involving children in studies of sexuality will trigger unhealthy sexual curiosity and experimentation. Institutional review boards (IRBs) strongly scrutinize and frequently reject research on such "socially sensitive" issues (O'Sullivan, 2003). Funding for research on childhood sexuality in this country is often denied or undermined. Much of the current research on childhood sexuality originates from other countries, such as England, Finland, Greece, or Sweden.

Thus, a science of the complex development of sexuality, including a description of the phenomena and an understanding of mediating and moderating variables, is lacking. In addition, research to track the effects of sexuality education is rare, and the outcome variables are often defined more by ideology than by science. The research that has been supported in the past two decades has focused on understanding the impact of sexual abuse on children, as well as children and youth who are sexual offenders. Several studies have found a link between "sexualized" behavior in children and children's having been the victims of sexual abuse (Cosentino, Meyer-Mahlenburg, Alpert, Weinberg, & Gaines, 1995; Friedrich et al., 1992; Kendall-Tackett, Williams, & Finkelhor, 1993).

These research efforts have produced a beginning body of knowledge that aids the practitioner in identifying when observed feelings, thoughts, and behaviors of children may indicate that sexual abuse has occurred and when responses of safety and treatment are needed. However, efforts to help prevent sexual abuse by educating children about inappropriate touch and imbalance of power have resulted in the development of programs and curricula that work from an inadequate understanding. Teaching children about sexual abuse without also providing them with the means for understanding healthy sexual development and expression can be extremely confusing and detrimental to children, because their first formal instruction regarding sexuality may be in the context of learning about sexual abuse.

Unfortunately, many children are left to seek out information about sexuality on their own because of the prevalence of adult denial, ignorance, confusion, and inability to communicate effectively or comfortably about sexuality. Peers, siblings, older children, and the media often fill this gap by providing information that can misinform and even frighten or shame. Children talk about the peer or school network as an underground source of information, but what they learn is likely to be misinformation or at the wrong level for them. Furthermore, the presence of sexual themes and images in today's popular culture continues to expand and such images are targeted to an increasingly younger audience. In the 1999–2000 television season, more than two-thirds of the programs contained some sort of sexual content (Brown, 2002). Children's access to Internet sites that address sexual material is increasingly a concern. Adult awareness and supervision are needed to help children make sense of often overwhelming and contradictory information.

Although parents and teachers can provide this supervision, trained school psychologists and other professionals in the schools can help by providing consultation, facilitating prevention efforts, and providing or referring for interventions in problem areas at the individual, family, and system levels. For educators and mental health professionals to fill these roles, they need to have a comprehensive understanding of the development of children's sexual interest and expression across the lifespan, sensitivity to relevant community and familial values, and openness to the topic of children's sexuality.

Although sexuality development is a major and complex domain of development and interfaces with the other more researched developmental domains—such as social, cognitive, emotional, physical, and moral—the topic is not well represented in courses on child development, teacher education programs, or professional psychology training programs. Also, most teachers and support staff have little education, training, or experience in this area, perhaps because of the long-held attitude that sexual matters are not part of the school curriculum and because few graduate training programs exist to provide the knowledge and experiential base. Although school psychologists interview and consult with parents and teachers about children's physical, intellectual, educational, social, and emotional development, they typically do not inquire about children's sexual development. In addition, school psychologists are rarely asked questions about children's sexuality, although almost all parents, teachers, and children have questions or concerns in this area. Before communication can begin, children's sexuality must be considered a domain of human life that can be discussed with both adults and children, not a difficult and embarrassing topic to be avoided.

Thus, school psychologists and other health and mental health professionals in the schools must endorse sexuality as a legitimate topic of discussion and intervention and be approachable and knowledgeable. They should be open and comfortable with the topic, which requires obtaining knowledge and examining and clarifying personal attitudes about sexuality. In addition, they must constantly examine the effects of changing sexual mores within the broader social context. Once professionals give permission to talk about sexuality by modeling comfort with the subject, parents, teachers, and children will raise questions. Most adults' questions pertain to behavior within the normal range, that is, questions about children who are manifesting basically normal behavior that adults regard as questionable, wrong, abnormal, or inappropriate for a given setting. For most of these situations, parents and educators can be helped by education, reassurance, and possibly brief counseling, interventions that help them respond to children in a manner that does not create a problem or exacerbate a minor problem.

Most children's questions focus on the normality of thoughts, feelings, and behaviors, and can be addressed by similar psychoeducational and counseling interventions. However, other questions asked may suggest a serious problem, as exemplified by sexual behavior that is extremely developmentally inappropriate and precocious, obsessive and compulsive, beyond control when under stress, or coercive and aggressive. Often, but not always, these behaviors are related to having been sexually abused or exploited. These concerns require thorough assessment and intervention for the child and family and typically involve referral to outside mental health agencies.

This chapter seeks to help educators, school psychologists, and other mental health specialists prepare to competently negotiate the complex area of children's developing sexual interest and expression, both healthy and unhealthy. Although reading background information such as that contained and recommended in this chapter is necessary, it is not sufficient. To support children's healthy sexual development, educators and mental health specialists in schools should use an approach that is open and honest, acknowledges the complex nature of sexuality, and is respectful.

This chapter addresses children's sexual interest and expression from birth to late childhood. *Sexual interest* in this chapter is defined as children's curiosity and concern about the many aspects of sexuality: physical, biological, cognitive, emotional, social, moral, and behavioral. *Sexual expression* is defined as children's behavioral manifestation of sexual interest. The chapter first outlines the development of sexual interest and expression from infancy to late childhood. That is followed by a discussion of problems ranging from commonly occurring challenges to serious problems in need of extensive intervention. Finally, the implications of these challenges and problems for the child, family, and school are explored, with an eye toward prevention and intervention activities and actions.

## Sexual Development

Children are sexual beings—they are developing physically, biologically, cognitively, emotionally, socially, morally, and behaviorally in relation to their sexuality. Sexual development is a natural, necessary, and complex process that begins at conception and continues throughout the life cycle (Chilman, 1983; Masters, Johnson, & Kolodny, 1995; Petty, 1995). During the prenatal period, sexual development is controlled mainly by biological factors. However, from the moment of birth, a child's sexual development is profoundly influenced by psychosocial factors, primarily parents and extended family, schooling, peers, and media, all interacting with the child's biological heritage. This process of being acculturated about sexuality cannot be prevented; it happens in one way or another. However, it can be weighted toward the healthy or the unhealthy.

The goal is to develop individuals who are sexually adjusted, who at every stage of their life are confident, competent, and responsible in their sexuality. Viewing sexual interest and expression as a function of development is useful for understanding the ranges of behavior included in the concept of normality. In addition, knowing what is normal is essential to not perceiving all childhood sexual interest and behavior as abnormal and thus determining what is in fact abnormal. A description of the normal developmental progressions of children's sexual interest can be organized into the stages of infancy, early childhood, middle childhood, and late childhood.

***Sexual development in infancy.*** Children's sexual development begins at birth. The capacity for physical arousal is present from the very beginning of life. Male babies can have erections and female babies can exhibit vaginal lubrication (DeLamater & Friedrich, 2002). Behaviors can be seen even in very young infants that resemble orgasm (Martinson, 1991). Young babies will touch and feel all of their body parts, including their genitals. This touching is an important first step in the development of identity, as infants learn the difference between their bodies and the world around them. They will also learn that touching their genitals can feel good. As this connection becomes more solidified, infants will engage in more purposeful acts. They may touch their genitals in a rhythmic fashion not unlike adult masturbation (DeLamater & Friedrich, 2002), or they may rub themselves against objects such as dolls or pillows, and they may even experience orgasm (Crooks & Baur, 1999). Many parents and caregivers may ignore these behaviors or not recognize them as sexual in nature, and infants will typically continue to engage in them unless they experience some sort of punishment or reprimand.

At this early stage of life, the infant is being cared for and learning to form caring relationships. The attachment bond with the primary caregivers is facilitated by experiences that can be considered sensual in nature. These interactions, including touching and cuddling, are essential in forming the bond between parent and child and will also influence the way the child will approach future relationships (Lively & Lively, 1991). Many of the activities involved in caregiving of a young child, such as breast feeding, diapering, and bathing, involve touching primary and secondary sex organs. For a very young child, the pleasurable sensations associated with these acts, as well as those associated with more purposeful touching of the genitals, are not necessarily different from other enjoyable sensations (Crooks & Baur, 1999). These behaviors occur before the memory system is fully formed and thus cannot usually be clearly recalled in adulthood. However, even this early in development, preferences for different types of stimulation may be established that will persist throughout life (DeLamater & Friedrich, 2002).

***Sexual development in early childhood (ages 3 to 6).*** As development continues through the preschool and early elementary school years, sexuality continues to emerge and intersect with other spheres of development. One important change that occurs in these years is the acquisition of language. Vocabulary blossoms during this time, and children may be eager to learn labels for body parts, feelings, and acts related to sex and reproduction. Toilet training, which typically occurs in early childhood, is a time in which young children may either learn a sense of pride and ownership over their bodies or they may learn that their genitals are "dirty" and shameful. Additionally, gender identity starts to form in the early childhood years. The child begins to have a sense of being a boy or being a girl, as well as develops a first understanding of the differences between the sexes. At the same time, society begins to impress upon the child some of the norms and expectations of his or her gender (DeLamater & Friedrich, 2002). These lessons are often reflected in the themes of young children's play, such as "house" or "mommies and daddies."

Sexual expression during these years may typically include nudity. Being without clothing in front of others, even in public, is common up to age 3 or 4 (Jensen, 1979), at which time negative reactions from others generally encourage the youngster to cover up. The pride that young children feel in displaying their genitals is a part of overall pride in their bodies and themselves.

Children's fascination with their bodies extends to masturbation (Lasser & Foster, 2004). By this time, children have clearly learned that touching themselves in this way feels good. They may fondle themselves as a way to be soothed or entertained. Parents' reactions to these behaviors can greatly influence the development of the child's sexuality as a whole. Parents are often conflicted about how to approach this situation, fearing that expressing acceptance may lead to excessive masturbation. However, even children at this age are beginning to be capable of understanding the difference between public and private behaviors, and most children are unlikely to engage in very frequent self-pleasuring (Crooks & Baur, 1999). Adults can treat children in a respectful manner by not reacting negatively to these behaviors while at the same time teaching children appropriate boundaries. Punishment and shame should be avoided. Parents who are uncomfortable talking to their children about masturbation may choose to ignore the behavior, whereas others may gently suggest that the child go to a private space such as a bedroom. Parents who are more comfortable discussing sexuality might use observations of genital touching as "teachable moments" to talk about their children's sexual interests (Lasser & Foster).

During the period of early childhood, children are continuing to experience and learn about relationships. Parents can be role models, demonstrating a loving and physically affectionate bond. Children also learn about closeness and intimacy directly, through hugs, kisses, and other loving contact. In preschool and elementary school, children have their first experiences with peers. These interactions with parents, friends, and other significant people can form the groundwork for relationships later in life. Some success in early relationships is needed if the child is to grow and develop a healthy sexuality as an adult.

***Sexual development in middle childhood (ages 7 to 9).*** As children progress through the elementary school years, many of the experiences and tasks that were relevant during early childhood continue to be relevant and are expanded. Cognitive and reasoning abilities blossom during this time, and consequently these children may become more curious about sexuality. They will continue to try to understand their own bodies, and they are curious about reproduction. It is important but sometimes difficult to provide children with information that is honest yet developmentally appropriate (Lasser, 2004). Our society in particular has difficulty with this task. Cross-cultural studies have shown that children in the United States are not as knowledgeable about sexual matters as children in other Western countries (e.g., Goldman & Goldman, 1982).

School personnel, however, are not always free to inform children as they wish. It is often readily apparent which children have received correct and appropriate information about sexuality at home and which children have not. School personnel must pay careful attention to the context in which the child lives and they must sometimes deal with the effects of an environment that is not conducive to healthy sexual development. At the same time they must respect the wishes of parents who may be uncomfortable with or have negative attitudes toward children's sexuality (Lively & Lively, 1991).

Although the home environment and relationships with caregivers continue to have a major influence on development, peer relationships are very important at this stage of life. Children continue to be open to interactions with the opposite sex; however, peer groups tend to be gender segregated. In these same-sex groups it is common to see children talking negatively about the opposite sex (Sandnabba, Santtila, Wannas, & Krook, 2003). Other discussions and play of a sexual nature are quite typical in these peer groups. Because of the separation of the genders at this age, sexual expression generally occurs with members of the same sex (DeLamater & Friedrich, 2002). These experiences are commonplace and are not always indicative of an enduring sexual orientation (Crooks & Baur, 1999).

Although exact percentages vary, research has shown that the majority of both boys and girls engage in some sort of sex play (Crooks & Baur, 1999). Behaviors may include kissing, touching, or imitating intercourse or other sexual and reproductive acts. For girls of this age, sexual expression is typically characterized by the exploration and imitation of social behavior and relationships. For boys, interest in showing and viewing genitals is common (Sandnabba et al., 2003). Although most girls discover masturbation on their own, most boys learn about it through friends (Crooks & Baur, 1999).

Children at this age are quite aware of the difference between "clean" and "dirty" jokes and will commonly use adult slang and obscene words. Unfortunately, these can sometimes reinforce negative attitudes toward sexuality, especially the idea that sex is something bad. The joke is often passed around that our message to kids is that "sex is dirty and awful—save it for someone you love." Children at this age have generally become aware that sex play should be done in private, and many will go to great lengths to ensure secrecy. Most adults who are asked to recall childhood sexual experiences can generally recall things that took place after the age of 4. They tend to report that their sexual behaviors took place with siblings or peers and without adults' knowledge (Ryan, 2000). However, if adults are aware of these activities and do not squelch this behavior or react in a way that induces guilt or shame, children will be more likely to develop healthy and positive attitudes toward sex (Lively & Lively, 1991). As long as sexual play involves children of roughly the same age and size, all of whom are participating voluntarily, it is not harmful and in fact has positive implications for later relationships.

***Sexuality in late childhood (ages 10 to 12).*** The physical changes associated with the onset of puberty constitute a major factor in the development of sexuality in the latter part of childhood. Levels of sex hormones begin to rise, triggering the beginnings of sexual attraction and sexual fantasies, as well as more visible bodily changes. This stage of sexual maturation and rapid growth occurs over a span of several years, roughly between the ages of 9 and 18. As the individual goes through the transition from childhood to adolescence, physical changes are accompanied by increased awareness of and interest in sexual thoughts, feelings, and expressions.

Puberty is characterized by an increase in size of the primary and secondary sex organs, appearance of pubic hair, gains in weight and height, and the development of reproductive capacity. The timing and sequence of physical changes vary (Berger, 2001). The mean age for the onset of breast development is 9.5 for African American girls, 9.8 for Mexican American girls, and 10.3 for Caucasian girls (Wu, Mendola, & Buck, 2002). The onset of the capacity for ejaculation in boys is typically between the ages of 8 and 15 (Martinson, 1991). These body changes can spark a renewed curiosity in the preadolescent. Some children are excited about these changes and await them eagerly, and some children become self-conscious as their bodies begin to change (Crooks & Baur, 1999). Those children for whom the onset of puberty is either early or late compared with their peers may be especially prone to feeling embarrassed. Early development for boys is often associated with positive self-esteem in later years, whereas early development for girls can be a negative experience. Early onset of menstruation for girls is also associated with early initiation of intercourse (Meschke & Silbereisen, 1997).

During the later years of childhood, peer relationships become even more central. These children are beginning the process of forming an identity separate from the family, and therefore they seek to form close friendships. Peer groups continue to be predominantly same-sex, and older children begin to develop crushes and are interested in romantic relationships. Group dates and boy–girl parties are common for children of this age

(DeLamater & Friedrich, 2002). These first experiences are important in helping the youngster learn to navigate dating relationships in adolescence and adulthood. As children begin experimenting with dating relationships, they may also begin experimenting with physical intimacy. For girls, the mean age of first having a boyfriend is 10.9 and the mean age of a first romantic kiss is 11.9 (Kornreich, Hearn, Rodriguez, & O'Sullivan, 2003). The older child's early forays into the world of romantic relationships can be an exciting but confusing and complicated time, and the child may greatly benefit from respectful and sensitive input from adults (Martinson, 1991). It is important to include the development of children whose trajectory includes same-sex or homosexual attraction. Evidence indicates that the average age of awareness of same-sex attraction is age 10, although some children are aware as young as age 5 (see chapter 32, "Gay, Lesbian, and Bisexual Youth").

## PROBLEMS AND IMPLICATIONS

The problems associated with children's sexual interest and expression can be divided into two categories, often referred to as normal sexual behavior that causes distress to others, and abnormal sexual behavior. *Normal* sexual behavior refers to sexual behavior that is a result of a natural human biological and psychological developmental process (Larsson, 2001) but is seen as a problem because of cultural values and standards. *Abnormal* sexual behavior typically is used to describe behavior that indicates something has happened to disrupt or change expected sexual behavior or the natural developmental process, but the behavior may also be influenced by cultural values (Larsson, 2001).

The first category of normal involves typically seen challenges that are not necessarily cause for major concern and potentially can be prevented. These types of challenges are generally related to problems in the child's environment. Problems may involve parents' negative modeling of sexuality and relationships; denial, ignorance, or negative reactions toward developmentally appropriate sexual interest and expression; failure to provide appropriate information or open communication to children; or parents' and educators' difficulty in understanding and supporting children who are questioning their sexual orientation. It is likely that professionals working in the schools will be faced with these types of challenges quite often and can likely offer supportive prevention or intervention activities.

The second category of abnormal problems is worthy of more serious concern with regard to the child's safety and well-being, as well as the safety and well-being of others. These types of problems may include severe symptoms, including sexual thoughts, feelings, and behaviors that are extremely developmentally inappropriate and precocious, obsessive and compulsive, beyond control when under stress, or coercive and aggressive. These symptoms may indicate that a child has been sexually abused or exploited or is at risk for becoming a perpetrator of sexual abuse. A good resource for further information is the website of the National Center on Sexual Behavior of Youth *(http://www.ncsby.org)*. Although these serious problems are usually treated outside of the school, they may be identified at school and will need immediate crisis response and referral from the school psychologist, counselor, or social worker as well as coordination with the child's needs at school.

### Promoting the Development of Normal Sexual Behavior

Development of sexuality begins at birth and therefore can be negatively affected starting in the infancy period. Because a major task in infancy is to form a secure attachment, most of the problems that have implications for healthy sexuality have to do with attachment (see chapter 29, "Attachment"). Infants who do not form a successful bond will likely be hindered in their ability to form trusting relationships, including romantic relationships, in their later lives (Lively & Lively, 1991). One of the key ways in which the secure bond is established is through touching. Just as sensual touching helps the infant to feel loved as well as reinforces the principle that touching feels good, a lack of touching or unkind touching may cause the infant to feel unloved and thus unable to build a foundation for pleasurable physical intimacy (Crooks & Baur, 1999).

The quality of interactions between caregiver and infant clearly has implications for the child's development, but the quality of interactions between caregivers can be cause for concern as well. Parents are the first role models for adult relationships. Infants lack the cognitive ability to understand adult conflicts, which makes them especially vulnerable to the negative effects of these conflicts. If infants are constantly exposed to fighting between the most important people in their life, they may form a concept of the world as a place where everyone fights. Adults' retrospective reports of learning about sexuality indicate that when loving relationships between adults were present in the home, they noticed it, and when these relationships were not present, they missed them (Beausang, 2000).

Many of the challenges in the development of sexuality of young children are related to adult denial, ignorance, and reactions to what can be considered normal sexual development. In American society, most adults do not react positively to young children's genital stimulation, whether it occurs alone or with peers. Parents especially tend to ignore or disapprove of this behavior. In one study asking adults to recall their childhood sexual experiences, 47% of those who "got caught" engaging in sex play were punished (Ryan, 2000). However, these negative reactions rarely result in the elimination of these behaviors and are more likely to result in increased guilt and anxiety (Crooks & Baur, 1999). Similarly, negative reactions to nudity can lead to feelings of shame about the body, and the child may grow to have difficulties in situations where nudity is necessary, such as gym class or summer camp (Lively & Lively, 1991). For both masturbation and nudity, adults must strike the tricky balance of teaching children the difference between public and private behaviors while not expressing disapproval of the child's developmentally appropriate activities (Lasser & Foster, 2004).

Children are naturally curious about many things related to sexuality; however, many adults are uncomfortable with children's questions. In fact, many adults assume that the typically developing child has no interest or knowledge of sex (Bancroft, 2003). Some adults deal with this discomfort by providing inaccurate information, such as giving the genitals cute names and passing on myths such as the stork when referring to reproduction, or by simply shutting down communication. Because children often discuss sexual matters with their peers, a child who has been given misinformation will likely soon become confused. Also, a child who has been armed with incorrect information will have to learn the correct information later in life, and this process of relearning can have a negative effect on sexuality (Lively & Lively, 1991). When adults demonstrate a shocked or disapproving emotional response to children's questions, children may become confused as to what they have done to provoke this response. These types of reactions will discourage children from asking more questions, and they will be left to seek out information about sex from unreliable sources.

By the time children reach middle childhood, they will have developed an understanding that things related to sexuality are culturally sensitive. Children who have received no information or wrong information may be discouraged from asking parents and other responsible adults about sexual matters. At the same time, children of this age are increasingly exposed to the media and are also seeking out more peer interactions, so sources of misinformation become more abundant. Between children and parents, a conspiracy of silence can be formed: children have learned not to ask questions, and because children do not ask, parents do not teach (Beausang, 2000).

In the later years of childhood, the peer group is incredibly important, and therefore the influence of peers is quite strong. If children have not already been prepared with a healthy sense of sexuality, they will be even more vulnerable to misinformation about sex and peer pressure. Adults should be prepared to monitor children's peer groups, especially if the groups are mixed in age and include teenagers. Children will typically begin to experiment with dating in these years, and adult guidance will be needed to ensure that the peer interactions remain positive. Even preadolescents can be fertile (Wu et al., 2002), and many lack the reasoning ability to understand the potential consequences of sexual activities, such as pregnancies or sexually transmitted diseases.

As adolescence approaches, children who have not been provided with accurate information will not be prepared for the changes of puberty. Children who have not been informed about menstruation or nocturnal emission may be traumatized when it happens to them. Even if children have developed healthy attitudes toward their bodies prior to puberty, if others react negatively to the natural development of the body during puberty, children can develop a sense of shame. Adults must actively encourage an open attitude toward sexuality, and they should not wait for children's questions before teaching appropriate lessons. This open attitude is important, considering that one risk factor for early sexual intercourse is having parents who do not communicate with their children about sex (Beausang, 2000).

## Identifying the Development of Abnormal Sexual Behavior

Although children can exhibit a wide range of sexual behaviors throughout the course of development, some behaviors can be considered unusual enough to merit attention, and some merit serious attention. Some types of expression are so rarely seen in children that if they are observed, they are most likely indicative of a larger problem, often that the child is being or has been sexually abused or has perpetrated abuse against others.

Problematic sexual interest and expression may include sexual thoughts, feelings, and behaviors that are extremely developmentally inappropriate and precocious; obsessive and compulsive sexual thoughts and behaviors; feelings, fantasies, and behavior that are very difficult to control when under stress; or communication and behavior that are aggressive and coercive.

Caregivers may observe a child of any age who is masturbating more than might be expected or desired. Although there are no specific statistics regarding how often young children self-stimulate and some subjective judgment is required, most young children do not stop other activities to masturbate and do not masturbate continuously (Ryan, 2000). Overzealous masturbation is occasionally a sign that the child is being distressed by something and is then engaging in the behavior as a method of self-soothing. It is also possible that the child may have some cognitive or neurological impairment, or there may be some sort of physical problem with the genitals that is causing the child pain or irritation (Lively & Lively, 1991).

Children rarely engage in behaviors that can be considered invasive. Acts such as inserting fingers or objects into one's vagina or anus or the vagina or anus of another child, engaging in oral–genital contact, or demanding that others take part in specific sexual activities with the child are very uncommon in the general population (Sandnabba et al., 2003), but they are more common among children who have been the victims of abuse. Additionally, the simulation of intercourse while wearing clothes is not entirely unusual, but when this behavior occurs without clothing it is more worthy of concern (Ryan, 2000). Although these behaviors are not conclusively indicative of abuse, they warrant adult attention to identify their source.

In general, children under the age of 12 do not frequently act in a way that can be considered seductive, either in behavior or speech. These behaviors are even more rarely directed toward adults (Sandnabba, et al., 2003). However, it may occasionally be difficult to differentiate seductive behavior in sex play from that in fantasy play. The more similar these behaviors are to adult behaviors, the more concerning they are. In general, sexual knowledge and behaviors that can be considered precocious in light of what might be expected at a certain age and culture are cause for further investigation (Ryan, 2000).

Sometimes, the cause for concern is not necessarily the behavior itself but rather the quality of the interaction. Any behaviors that include elements of coercion or force merit the concerns of an adult. Retrospective reports of adolescent and preadolescent perpetrators of sexual abuse toward younger children reveal that they sometimes practice their abusive behaviors beforehand (Ryan, 2000). Interactions between children that involve some sort of coercion (e.g., teasing, bribery, or force) may be traumatic for children even if the act is not technically sexual abuse. In the case of any of these types of behaviors, a responsible adult is needed to investigate and intervene.

## ALTERNATIVE ACTIONS FOR PREVENTION

Prevention efforts, specifically primary prevention efforts, are likely to be effective in decreasing the occurrence of what has been referred to in this chapter as "typically occurring problems," problems that often involve the misunderstanding or rejection of normal sexual interest and expression. As discussed earlier, typical problems may entail parents' negative modeling of sexuality and relationships; parents' and educators' denial, ignorance, or negative reactions toward developmentally appropriate sexual interest and expression; parents' and educators' failure to provide appropriate information or open communication to children; and difficulty of parents and educators in understanding and supporting children who are questioning their sexual orientation. Prevention efforts aimed at these concerns need to target parents, educators, and the children themselves, as well as interpersonal communication, particularly with children and their parents, but also with children and their educators. Because of the factors discussed throughout this chapter, there is a paucity of research evaluation studies on prevention activities.

The key to prevention is education—education of children and education of adults (parents and educators). This sounds so easy, but it is quite difficult. The Sexuality Information and Education Council of the United States reported that almost 90% of parents want their children to have sexuality education, 23 states require sexuality education and 13 others encourage its teaching, and more than 90 national organizations believe that all children and youth should receive sexuality education. Yet only 5% of children in America receive it (SIECUS, 2004). The controversy appears to be driven by extremely mixed views in this country as to how to educate children and adolescents about sexual intercourse. Concerns regarding the health consequences of adolescent sexual behavior have fueled the controversy over sexuality education. Whereas some maintain that educational efforts ought to teach abstinence only, others advocate for curricula that also include basic, accurate information about the risks of participating in, and the methods of avoiding, unprotected intercourse, and that inform youth about contraception.

Since 1996, when the U.S. Congress established a program that funded abstinence-only programs, programs that are based on a comprehensive orientation to sexuality education have struggled to find support and funding. A review of this literature and extensive examination of the controversy surrounding initiation of sex is beyond the scope of this chapter (see Halstead & Reiss, 2003; Irvine, 2003; Mayo, 2004; Ridini, 1998). However, it is important to note that the focus on prevention of sexual intercourse has served to equate sexuality education with sex. One of the results has been continuation of the denial that children are sexual beings and need support and education. Thus, the current controversy surrounding abstinence-only programs has strengthened the cloak of silence about children and sexuality, inhibiting educational efforts.

Despite this cultural and political atmosphere of denial, efforts have persisted at laying the groundwork for comprehensive sexuality education in this country. SIECUS has published the third edition of *Developing Guidelines for Comprehensive Sexuality Education* (Sexuality Information and Education Council of the United States [SIECUS], 2004), which has been formally supported by the National Association of School Psychologists, the American Psychological Association, and the National Education Association Health Information Network.

The Guidelines reflect attitudes, values, and insights; relationships and interpersonal skills; and responsibility. Six of the key concepts they address include human development, relationships, personal skills, sexual behavior, sexual health, and society and culture. The Guidelines are directed at teachers, parents, researchers, peer programs, schools, community agencies, and churches and synagogues. They are designed to provide a framework to help local communities design new curricula or evaluate existing programs. They can serve as an important catalyst for community discussion about how sexuality education can be addressed, specifically in local schools. The Guidelines are not a curriculum per se, but are best viewed as a starting point. The local community and school must determine the lesson plans that are appropriate for them. The Guidelines include four developmental levels: ages 5 to 8, 9 to 12, 13 to 15, and 16 to 18. In addition to the guidelines offered by SIECUS, faith communities' sexuality education curricula that span preschool through high school are available for consideration through the website of the Religious Institute on Sexual Morality, Justice, and Health.

Beyond their work through the school curriculum, school personnel need be prepared to work with parents and communities in the area of childhood sexuality and communication. Basic information can be provided to large groups, small groups, and parents, either directly or through recommendations for reading and for other information about resources in the community. Two books, *Sex and Sensibility: The Thinking Parent's Guide to Talking Sense About Sex* (Roffman, 2001) and *Everything You Never Wanted Your Kids to Know About Sex (but Were Afraid They'd Ask)* (Richardson & Schulster, 2003) are excellent resources for parents. Both books are recent and are comprehensive in their approach, span the ages from birth to 18, and suggest many other helpful resources. School psychologists and other support staff may also find that individual consultations with teachers and parents serve a useful function. The goal with teachers is to promote ways school personnel can respond more appropriately and effectively to children's normal sexual interest and behavior and to assist them in differentiating between normal and deviant sexual behaviors.

Caregivers and school professionals must recognize that children with disabilities also require sexuality education and that many have the same needs, desires, rights, and responsibilities as the nondisabled child. To teach sexuality education to children with disabilities, professionals need a positive attitude toward the children and knowledge of the particular medical and psychosocial implications of their disabilities. An excellent source is provided by the National Information Center for Children and Youth with Disabilities (NICHCY), titled *Sexuality Education for Children and Youth with Disabilities* (NICHCY, 1992). Children with disabilities may also be more vulnerable to sexual abuse than their nondisabled peers. Therefore, sexuality education efforts directed at the disabled population should promote awareness of the potential when working with children and their caregivers.

## ALTERNATIVE ACTIONS FOR INTERVENTION

Intervention (or secondary or tertiary prevention) activities typically fall under the purview of the school psychologist, counselor, social worker, or nurse. Activities involve providing services to children who have been identified as or are at high risk of exhibiting difficulties in sexual development. Children who would fit this description may be exhibiting normal behaviors that are not understood or acceptable by their parents or teachers, or they may be exhibiting abnormal behaviors, as described earlier.

As a general rule, interventions designed to address normal behaviors focus on providing a forum to discuss the reaction to the behavior and on proposing a plan to resolve the disagreements or misunderstandings. The plan will likely involve providing information, examining values and attitudes, and enhancing communication. The guiding principle of such plans is that children and adults are well served by accurate information, endorsement of the normality of children's sexual feelings and desires and their right to be sexual, and an opportunity to learn culturally acceptable sociosexual skills. With informed consent from parents, it may be beneficial for support staff to work directly with children at risk, individually or in groups, to provide them with age-appropriate information about sexuality and the means to feel comfortable in communicating about their sexuality.

Some children may be at risk and in need of intervention because they are questioning their sexual orientation and are receiving negative and even abusive reactions from their parents, educators, and peers. These children may need the psychological protection of a counseling or therapy relationship from which they can explore these interests and determine their meaning. This support may be available in some school communities or may involve a referral to a community agency. Education about the normality of homosexual and bisexual feelings and behavior in childhood can relieve fears and distress and perhaps end the crisis. Children who determine that their sexual orientation is exclusively or primarily toward members of the same sex need continued support to integrate this information into their identity and relationships in the world. In this case, parents also need support, perhaps through outside counseling and community support groups, to cope with what they will perceive as a loss and rejection and to reach the stage of acceptance. Family therapy also can be effective. In addition, school support staff can aid teachers by providing consultation to allow them to work on their own emotional reactions to homosexuality and bisexuality and to assist them with other students' reactions.

Children who are exhibiting abnormal sexual behavior likely are in need of extensive intervention, usually out of the scope of services provided within schools. These types of problems may include severe symptoms that involve sexual thoughts, feelings, and behaviors that are (a) extremely developmentally inappropriate and precocious, (b) obsessive and compulsive, (c) beyond control when under stress, or (d) coercive and aggressive.

Developmentally inappropriate and precocious sexual behaviors include engaging in extensive sexual behaviors with other children, including sodomy, oral copulation, and vaginal and anal intercourse (Berliner & Rawlings, 1991). Sexual behaviors at the coercive or aggressive end of this continuum are the most serious and may be associated with other forms of antisocial behavior. Aggressive sexual behavior may involve physical force to obtain submission and to prevent reporting. Coercive sexual behavior does not use force; however, serious threats to gain compliance are used. These symptoms often indicate that a child is being or has been sexually abused or exploited or is at risk for becoming a perpetrator of sexual abuse. Sexual abuse has serious initial and long-term behavioral and psychological consequences that often continue if untreated and also may endanger others. On the basis of clinical reports, a common belief is that children who demonstrate extreme or inappropriate sexual behaviors have almost always been sexually abused or sexually overstimulated (Johnson, 1990). Useful identification and intervention resources are offered by Bonner, Walker, and Berliner (1999); Gray, Pithers, Busconi, and Houchens (1999); and Silovsky and Niec (2002).

## SUMMARY

Although most people associate sexuality solely with adolescence and adulthood, infants and children are developing sexual beings, and they express natural interest and curiosity about their sexuality. Many adults, including parents and educators, find it difficult to accept and to allow expression of childhood sexuality, to communicate with children about sexuality, and to provide a supportive and developmentally appropriate environment for children. As a result, many children may associate the negative feelings of shame, guilt, embarrassment, fear, and helplessness with sexuality.

To help prepare educators, school psychologists, and other mental health professionals, this chapter discussed the controversies that ensue in this area and presented the normal developmental progressions of children's sexual interest from infancy through late childhood. Problem areas were described and were differentiated as "normal" behaviors that others are having negative reactions to and "abnormal" behaviors, often a consequence of sexual abuse. School psychologists and other mental health professionals in schools are in a key position, through prevention activities, to recognize children as sexual persons, to educate adults and children about sexual development, and to promote honest, accurate, and open communication about sexuality among parents, educators, and children. They also can evaluate concerns about children's sexual interest and expression and recommend and provide appropriate interventions. The goal is to support and promote practices that allow children to feel confident, competent, accepting, and responsible about their sexuality. To be effective, school professionals must be knowledgeable, comfortable, approachable, and willing to enter a controversial area.

## RECOMMENDED RESOURCES

### Books and Other Printed Material

Irvine, J. M. (2003). *Talk about sex: The battles over sex education in the United States.* Berkeley: University of California Press.

This book offers a comprehensive history of the culture wars over sex education and examines the politics of sexual speech in the United States. The author argues that the New Right draws on the tenacious power of sexual shame and fear to galvanize opposition to sex education.

Richardson, J., & Schulster, M. A. (2003). *Everything you NEVER wanted your kids to know about SEX (but were afraid they'd ask).* New York: Three Rivers Press.

This book provides a one-of-a-kind survival guide that is designed to help parents successfully navigate every stage of their child's sexual development. The authors, Harvard-trained physicians, combine their expertise with interview data and an analysis of the scientific research to offer parents a roadmap.

Roffman, D. M. (2001). *The thinking parent's guide to talking sense about sex.* Cambridge, MA: Perseus.

The author, an experienced sexuality educator, provides much well-founded wisdom to parents to help them understand and respond wisely and compassionately to their children's sexual development. The book would also be useful to teachers.

### Websites

*http://www.ncsby.org*

The website for the National Center on Sexual Behavior of Youth offers technical assistance for the management of children with sexual behavior problems.

*http://www.nichcy.org*

The National Information Center for Children and Youth with Disabilities, funded by the Office of Special Education Programs of the U.S. Department of Education, offers information pertaining to providing sexuality education to children with disabilities.

*http://www.religiousinstitute.org/curricula*

The website for the Religious Institute on Sexual Morality, Justice, and Health provides sexuality education curricula for faith communities.

*http://www.siecus.org*

The website for the Sexuality Information and Education Council of the United States provides information on sexuality education and curriculum guidelines.

## REFERENCES

Bancroft, J. (2003). Introduction. In J. Bancroft (Ed.), *Sexual development in childhood* (pp. xi–xiv). Bloomington: Indiana University Press.

Beausang, C. C. (2000). Personal stories of growing up sexually. *Issues in Comprehensive Pediatric Nursing, 23,* 175–192.

Berger, K. S. (2001). *The developing person through the lifespan.* New York: Worth Publishers.

Berliner, L., & Rawlings, L. (1991). *A treatment manual: Children with sexual behavior problems.* Unpublished manuscript.

Bonner, B. L., Walker, C. E., & Berliner, L. (1999). *Children with sexual behavior problems: Assessment and treatment* (Final Report, Grant No90-A-1469). Washington, DC: U.S. Department of Health and Human Services, Administration of Children, Youth, and Families. Retrieved from http://www.calib.com/nccanch/pubs/otherpubs/childassessment/index.cfm

Brown, J. D. (2002). Mass media influences on sexuality. *Journal of Sex Research, 39,* 42–45.

Chilman, C. S. (1983). The development of adolescent sexuality. *Journal of Research and Development in Education, 16,* 16–26.

Cosentino, C. E., Meyer-Mahlenburg, H., Alpert, J., Weinberg, S., & Gaines, R. (1995). Sexual behavior problems and psychopathology symptoms in sexually abused girls. *Journal of American Academy of Child and Adolescent Psychiatry, 34,* 1033–1042.

Crooks, R., & Baur, K. (1999). *Our sexuality.* Pacific Grove, CA: Brooks/Cole.

DeLamater, J., & Friedrich, W. N. (2002). Human sexual development. *Journal of Sex Research, 39,* 10–15.

Friedrich, W. N., Grambsch, P., Damn, L., Hewitt, S., Koverola, C., Lang, R., et al. (1992). Child sexual behavior inventory: Normative and clinical comparisons. *Psychological Assessment, 4,* 303–311.

Goldman, R., & Goldman, J. (1982). Children's sexual thinking: A comparative study of children aged 5–15 years in Australia, North America, Britain, and Sweden. London: Routledge & Kegan Paul.

Gray, A. S., Pithers, W. D., Busconi, A., & Houchens, P. (1999). Developmental and etiological characteristics of children with sexual behavior problems: Treatment implications. *Child Abuse and Neglect, 23,* 601–621.

Halstead, J. M., & Reiss, M. J. (2003). *Values in sex education: From principles to practice.* London: Routledge Falmer.

Irvine, J. M. (2003). *Talk about sex: The battles over sex education in the United States.* Berkeley: University of California Press.

Jensen, G. D. (1979). Childhood sexuality. In R. G. Green (Ed.), *Human sexuality: A health practitioner's text* (2nd ed.). Baltimore: Williams & Wilkins.

Johnson, T. C. (1990). Children who act out sexually. In J. McNamara & B. H. McNamara (Eds.), *Adoption and the sexually abused child.* Portland, ME: University of Southern Maine Human Services Development Institute.

Kendall-Tackett, K. E., Williams, L., & Finkelhor, D. (1993). The impact of sexual abuse on children: A review and synthesis of recent empirical studies. *Psychological Bulletin, 113,* 164–180.

Kornreich, J. L., Hearn, K. D., Rodriguez, G., & O'Sullivan, L. F. (2003). Sibling influence, gender roles, and the sexual socialization of urban early adolescent girls. *Journal of Sex Research, 40,* 101–121.

Larsson, I. (2001). *Child sexuality and sexual behaviour.* Stockholm, Sweden. Swedish National Board of Health and Welfare (Socialstyrelsen).

Lasser, J. (2004). Sexuality education. In A. Canter, L. Paige, M. Roth, I. Romero, & S. Carroll (Eds.), *Helping children at home and school II: Handouts for families and educators.* Bethesda, MD: National Association of School Psychologists.

Lasser, J., & Foster, I. (2004). Masturbation and genital touching. In A. Canter, L. Paige, M. Roth, I. Romero, & S. Carroll (Eds.), *Helping children at home and school II: Handouts for families and educators.* Bethesda, MD: National Association of School Psychologists.

Lively, V., & Lively, E. (1991). *Sexual development of young children.* Albany, NY: Delmar.

Martinson, F. M. (1991). Normal sexual development in infancy and childhood. In G. D. Ryan & S. L. Lane (Eds.), *Juvenile sexual offending: Causes, consequences, and correction* (pp. 57–82). Lexington, KY: Lexington Books.

Masters, W. H., Johnson, V. E., & Kolodny, R. C. (1995). *Human sexuality.* London: Harper Collins.

Mayo, C. (2004). *Disputing the subject of sex: Sexuality and public school controversies.* Lanham, MD: Rowman and Littlefield.

Meschke, L. L., & Silbereisen, R. K. (1997). The influence of puberty, family processes, and leisure activities on the timing of first sexual experience. *Journal of Adolescence, 20,* 403–418.

National Information Center for Children and Youth with Disabilities (1992). *Sexuality education for children and youth with disabilities.* Author. Retrieved September 15, 2005, from http://www.nichcy.org

O'Sullivan, L. (2003). Methodological issues associated with studies of child sexual behavior. In J. Bancroft (Ed.), *Sexual development in childhood* (pp. xi–xiv). Bloomington: Indiana University Press.

Petty, D. L. (1995). Sex education toward the prevention of sexual problems. In G. A. Rekers (Ed.), *Handbook of child and adolescent sexual problems* (pp. 1–54). Lexington, KY: Lexington Books.

Richardson, J., & Schulster, M. A. (2003). *Everything you NEVER wanted your kids to know about SEX (but were afraid they'd ask).* New York: Three Rivers Press.

Ridini, S. P. (1998). *Health and sexuality education in schools: The process of social change.* Westport, CT: Bergin & Garvey.

Roffman, D. M. (2001). *Sex and sensibility: The thinking parent's guide to talking sense about sex.* Cambridge, MA: Perseus.

Ryan, G. (2000). Childhood sexuality: A decade of study. Part I—Research and curriculum development. *Child Abuse and Neglect, 24,* 33–48.

Sandnabba, N. K., Santtila, P., Wannas, M., & Krook, K. (2003). Age and gender specific sexual behaviors in children. *Child Abuse and Neglect, 27,* 579–605.

Sexuality Information and Education Council of the United States (SIECUS). (2004). *Developing guidelines for comprehensive sexuality education.* Retrieved September 15, 2005, from http://www.siecus.org/

Silovsky, J. F., & Niec, L. (2002). Characteristics of young children with sexual behavior problems: A pilot study. *Child Maltreatment, 7,* 187–197.

Wu, T., Mendola, P., & Buck, G. M. (2002). Ethnic differences in the presence of secondary sex characteristics and menarche among U.S. girls: The third national health and nutrition examination survey, 1988–1994. *Pediatrics, 110,* 752–758.

# 32

# Gay, Lesbian, and Bisexual Youth

**Jon Lasser**

*Texas State University–San Marcos*

**Deborah Tharinger**
**Allison Cloth**

*University of Texas at Austin*

## BACKGROUND AND DEVELOPMENT

All adolescents, including gay, lesbian, and bisexual (GLB) youth, experience universal developmental tasks involving identity, independence, connectedness, achievement, and sexuality. The unique experiences of GLB youth, shaped largely by often uncaring if not hostile social environments, place this population at an increased risk for negative developmental outcomes such as school failure, substance abuse, depression, and suicide. Educators, including school psychologists, need to be aware of the experiences of GLB youth, potential risk factors affecting their development, and actions that can be taken to foster and promote positive outcomes.

As an often invisible population, GLB youth have proved challenging to study. Researchers have struggled with numerous barriers that are unique to this population. For example, many GLB youth have not disclosed their orientation to their parents and consequently cannot bring an informed consent form home for a signature. Those GLB youth who have not disclosed to anyone are de facto unavailable to researchers. Other GLB youth who fear stigma and victimization likely refrain from participating in research, yielding samples that are less representative than researchers would like them to be. That being said, estimates of the prevalence of adolescent homosexuality and bisexuality vary greatly. It has been estimated that of the approximately 45 million school-age children in the United States, over 1 million of those students are gay, lesbian, or bisexual (Reis & Saewyc, 1999). When one considers the siblings, parents, and friends of GLB youth, the number of lives touched increases significantly.

This chapter focuses on the development of GLB youth and operates on the assumption that gender, race, ethnicity, religiosity, culture, and socioeconomic status; individual qualities such as resilience and coping abilities; as well as family, peer, and school support play an important role in shaping the experiences of GLB youth, though little research has been done in this area. Disproportionate emphasis only on the child's or adolescent's sexual orientation may blind parents and service providers to other salient factors of development (e.g., cognitive and social development). Therefore, researchers, parents, and educators working with GLB youth are encouraged to consider how other relevant variables could potentially affect the GLB experience.

### Homophobia and Heterosexism

Discussions of GLB development also need to consider the impact of homophobia and heterosexism, as many theoretical models of homosexual development implicate these as the factors that make the development of GLB youth unique (Patterson, 1995). *Homophobia* is a term used to describe the set of negative attitudes about homosexuality and is therefore better understood as a prejudice rather than as a phobia or irrational fear as the name implies (Haaga, 1991). *Heterosexism* refers to the assumption that everyone is heterosexual or that heterosexuality is inherently superior to homosexuality (Francoeur, 1991). Teens who may be questioning their sexual orientation or are mistakenly perceived to be gay, lesbian, or bisexual may also be affected by the very same challenges as homosexual youth if they are targeted and stigmatized as homosexual youth are (D'Augelli & Dark, 1995; Schneider & Tremble, 1985). Furthermore, sanctioned prejudice and discrimination regarding any group of individuals perpetuate the vulnerability of all persons. Thus, whereas lesbian, gay, and bisexual youth are clearly the focus of this chapter, it is acknowledged that the effect of homophobia and heterosexism extends beyond GLB individuals.

## Homosexual and Bisexual Identity and Development

Sexual orientation has often been described as a dichotomous trait (Diamond, 2003), in spite of Kinsey's (1948/1953) now classic continuum that included thoughts, feelings, and behaviors ranging from exclusive heterosexuality to exclusive homosexuality. Today's youth may be less likely to make a clear gay versus straight distinction. In a recent national survey, the number of adolescents reporting bisexuality exceeded the number reporting homosexuality (Russell, Sief, & Truoung, 2001). As contemporary youth increasingly self-identify as "queer or questioning" or "bicurious," they are saying that the traditional gay versus straight model does not work for them (Diamond, 2003). When working with GLB youth, educators need to be aware that some students may experience same-sex attractions without self-identifying as GLB. More recently, attention has also been given to transsexual and transgendered individuals (Chen-Hayes, 2001). Because the experiences of transsexual and transgendered individuals appear to be quite distinct from the GLB population, the length of this chapter does not allow their inclusion. However, educators are encouraged to inform themselves of the unique hurdles of youth that are struggling with their sense of biological and gender correctness.

Historically, efforts to understand the development of homosexual and bisexual orientations have revolved around stage models (Cass, 1979; Troiden, 1989). These models, which have received some empirical support, posit that GLB individuals proceed through an ordered set of stages, from earliest awareness of homosexuality to fully integrated self-identification. These stage models serve an important function in that they provide a foundation for the study of GLB lives and development. Acknowledging that the stage models are useful both historically and as foundational theories, interested readers are referred to sources that discuss those models (e.g., Patterson, 1995), as more current approaches to understanding GLB development are presented here.

More recently, greater attention has been called to the complexities and diversity of GLB lives and the variations from fixed stages, with a new focus on developmental trajectories and "contextual factors, including gender, bisexual orientation, age, living circumstances, parental attitudes, and time since coming out" (Floyd & Stein, 2002, p. 173). This new focus considers whether GLB males and females follow similar or distinct pathways, differences between those who self-identify as children and those who self-identify as adults, and the stability of orientation over time. Whereas bisexuals have traditionally been categorized with gays and lesbians, their unique experiences have increasingly received greater attention.

The etiology of sexual orientation is unknown, and a wide range of often conflicting theories exist regarding the cause of sexual orientation (Patterson, 1995). Biological explanations have attempted to attribute sexual orientation to hormones (Meyer-Bahlburg et al., 1995), genetic factors (Bailey & Pillard, 1991), and brain structure (LeVay, 1993), whereas other theorists have focused on environmental and social constructivist perspectives (Kitzinger & Wilson, 1995). Critics of biological explanations argue that sexual orientation, like many other traits, results from a combination of both biological and psychosocial influences, and that efforts to identify a single cause of sexual orientation are overly simplistic given the complexity of human sexual behavior (Parker & DeCecco, 1995). Given the high level of uncertainty regarding the determinants of sexual orientation, this chapter emphasizes the development interactions of homosexual identities and sociocultural environments rather than the etiology of sexual orientation.

GLB development appears to have multiple developmental trajectories. Floyd and Stein (2002) collected data on the milestone events (self-awareness, sexual experiences, and disclosure to parents and others) of 72 gay, lesbian, and bisexual youths. Five clusters emerged, suggesting considerable variability in development. Although the overall mean age of first awareness of same-sex attraction was 10.39 years, the range was 3–18 years. The participants in the first three clusters generally met milestones early relative to the other two clusters. The participants in the last two clusters had, relative to the first three clusters, later ages of first awareness (11.76 years and 12.60 years, respectively). Floyd and Stein's discussion of the results validate the movement from linear stage models to multiple pathways. "The cluster groups were not merely at different stages of a single developmental course, but rather, their patterns represented clearly distinct developmental paths" (Floyd & Stein, p. 185).

## Visibility of GLB Youth

Much attention has been given to the "coming out" milestone, as it represents a transition from an internal awareness and acceptance to a more public identity. Coming out is generally regarded as a verbal disclosure of one's orientation. With such disclosures come the risks of rejection, victimization, stigma, and harassment. The way in which GLB youth make decisions about their disclosures has been an important area of study. Conceptualized as an ongoing process rather than a discrete event, coming out is considered to be an important phenomenon of the GLB experience.

When homophobia and heterosexism are pervasive, many GLB individuals selectively disclose their sexual orientation to avoid the costs associated with increased visibility. *Visibility management* refers to an ongoing process by which individuals employ multiple strategies to actively regulate the degree to which they disclose or reveal invisible traits or characteristics to others (Lasser & Tharinger, 2003; Lasser, 2005). Depending on a GLB adolescent's individual circumstances (e.g., perceived parental support, school climate with respect to GLB orientations, religious views on sexual orientation, and cultural values), an adolescent may find that more restrictive visibility management strategies (i.e., minimal disclosure) are more adaptive than less restrictive strategies. Visibility management for GLB youth appears to be central to the process of negotiating their social worlds.

Qualitative interview data from Lasser and Tharinger (2003) provide clear examples of how GLB youth think about and practice visibility management as they navigate school environments. Derek, age 17, said, "I don't see why [sexual orientation is] anyone's business at school. I mean, high school can be a really tough time, for a lot of kids. And I don't think someone's sexual preference is anyone's business but theirs. That's just me personally. I don't think it's healthy to keep it bottled in for your whole life, but I think that people you want to tell you should tell." Denise, an 18-year-old lesbian, noted that whereas it may be helpful to pass as straight, there are costs: "It's hard because you know that it's not you." Similarly, Rebecca, an 18-year-old bisexual student, reported that "the way being in the closet affects school is that you're on such guard and stuff and you're not really who you are." As these examples suggest, visibility management plays a significant role in the social development of GLB youth.

## Friends and Family: The Social Worlds of GLB Youth

Researchers are just beginning to develop a better understanding of GLB adolescent lives in terms of peer relationships, friendships, and leisure activities. Leisure activities (e.g., reading, sports, or artistic expression) contribute to the identity development of GLB youth, but more restrictive visibility management tends to mitigate the development of social identities (Kivel & Kleiber, 2000). One study found that, compared with heterosexual adolescents, GLB youth report that they have known their friends for less time and live farther from their friends (Schneider & Witherspoon, 2000). Given the potential for peer rejection and social isolation, further attention needs to be focused on the peer relationships of GLB youth.

Familial factors that may affect parental responses to disclosure, and the subsequent impact of such responses, are beginning to be investigated. Consider that the GLB adolescent is usually raised by one or more heterosexual parents or caregivers and is therefore unlikely to be supported the way, for example, an Asian American child could be supported by a parent who experienced similar discrimination (Harrison, 2003). Whereas most parents eventually accept the sexual orientation of their sons and daughters, many are unprepared for their adolescent's disclosure and detach emotionally at a time in which their child needs even greater connectedness (Saltzburg, 2004).

## Family Support and Personal Attributes as Protective Factors

The impact of rejection from family, peers, and other significant individuals on GLB youth has also been explored in the developmental context of attachment theory (Tharinger & Wells, 2000). Attachment theory posits that secure, foundational attachment relationships with primary caregivers build resiliency throughout the lifespan, and that connectedness to family and school are central to healthy outcomes (see chapter 29, "Attachment"). When GLB youth disclose their orientation and are shunned, isolated, rejected, and sometimes physically attacked by parents and peers, the experience may be that the "previously securely attached adolescents have the 'attachment rug' pulled our from under them" (Tharinger & Wells, p. 164). This disruption may place GLB youth at greater risk for depression, substance abuse, and other risk factors, thereby complicating their transition to adulthood.

The literature on resiliency has provided evidence that specific intrapersonal qualities and interpersonal processes are beneficial in protecting from stable negative outcomes those youth who are undergoing stressful life experiences. Intrapersonal attributes, such as average to above average cognitive capacities (Masten et al., 1999); perseverance and optimism (Floyd, 1996); hope and faith (Worrell & Hale, 2001); self-esteem (Harter, 1999); internal locus of control (Luthar, 1991); curiosity and compassion (Wolin & Wolin, 1996); and agreeableness, openness to new experiences, emotional regulation, and extroversion (Davey, Eaker, & Walters, 2003), all have been shown to be important characteristics in protecting youth from negative, aversive experiences and in increasing their capacity for successful adaptation.

Specific interpersonal processes also have been shown repeatedly to be critical protective factors. These include positive parenting practices (Masten et al., 1999); a supportive home, connection with competent adult role models, and community affiliation (Luthar, Cicchetti, & Becker, 2000); and positive school climate (Worrell & Hale, 2001). It is not surprising that being a member of a "rejected" peer group has been shown by Ellenbogen and Chamberland (1997) to be associated with negative developmental outcomes. When reflecting on their difficult childhoods, resilient youth have been found to mention the specific influences of family members, coaches, teachers, and counselors who were important in their successful developmental trajectories (Floyd, 1996).

Being resilient is not seen as a quality that one either has or does not have, but a dynamic process that can change across development (Luthar et al., 2000; Masten & Coatsworth, 1998). Youth are seen as constantly interacting with their environment in meaningful transactions, the outcomes of which are internalized and serve as building blocks for future experiences (Rhee, Furlong, Turner, & Harari, 2001). Over time, youth learn how to negotiate risks and use intrapersonal qualities and interpersonal relationships to enhance positive developmental outcomes. Furthermore, it is not a single risk or protective factor that determines a child's competence; rather, it is the transactions among these risk and protective factors that lead to resilient or nonresilient outcomes (Werner, 1989). It has also been suggested that parents might experience a process similar to the Kubler-Ross (1969) stages of grief, in which the family reacts to the disclosure of homosexuality or bisexuality with denial, anger, bargaining, depression, and acceptance (Harrison, 2003). Parents tend to react most unfavorably when they believe that their child has chosen to be homosexual or bisexual (Armesto, 2001).

## PROBLEMS AND IMPLICATIONS

### Mental Health and Suicide

In comparison to heterosexual youth, GLB youth have increased rates of mental health disorders (anxiety and depression) and suicidal tendencies (DeAngelis, 2002), high-risk behaviors (Blake et al., 2001), substance abuse (Garofalo, Wolf, Kessel, Palfrey, & DuRant, 1998), school failure and dropout (Elia, 1993; Savin-Williams, 1994), and homelessness. It is important to note that although the high suicide rate of GLB youth has been well publicized, findings in this area are mixed. Much research has stated that GLB youth's suicide rate has been in the range of two to three times that of their non-GLB peers (Garofalo, Wolf, Wissow, Woods, & Goodman, 1999; Munoz-Plaza, Quinn, & Rounds, 2002). However, a study by Savin-Williams (2001) found that GLB youth were two times more likely to report false suicide attempts than their heterosexual peers and had approximately the same number of actual attempts. Although the distinction between attempts and false reports is clearly significant, the underlying need to address the risk of suicide in the GLB youth remains paramount.

### Victimization of GLB Youth

GLB youth also have been found to be more likely to experience peer rejection, harassment, and isolation (Kosciw & Cullen, 2001; Marinoble, 1998); victimization and discrimination (McFarland, 2001; Roffman, 2000); and family rejection and communication problems (Saltzburg, 2004). Verbal discrimination has been reported by 83% of GLB students (Kosciw & Cullen, 2001); 68% of GLB youth reported feeling unsafe in their school environment because of their sexual orientation (Kosciw & Cullen, 2001); 21% of GLB youth reported being victimized in school; and 11% reported being physically assaulted because of their sexual orientation (D'Augelli, Pilkington, & Hershberger, 2002). Garofalo et al. (1998) found that 33% of GLB youth had been threatened with a weapon in school versus 7% of their straight peers. Similarly, 38% of GLB students reported having been involved in physical fights versus 14% of their peers, with as many as three times as many GLB youth requiring medical treatment for their injuries. It was also reported that 25% of GLB students indicated they had missed a day of school in the previous 30 days as a result of fear versus 5% of their non-GLB peers.

Research of broader cultural influences show that many GLB youth are also members of oppressed ethnic minority groups, some of which hold extremely negative views toward GLB individuals. Similarly, many religious affiliations in which GLB youth may have been raised have extremely negative associations with homosexuality (Weiler, 2003), making the GLB youth's relationship with religion challenging at best.

Thus, the interpersonal relationships that have been proposed and widely supported to buffer risk and promote resiliency in youth are systematically weakened in current society when it comes to GLB youth. The support of family, peers, school, culture, and religion often is missing or spotty, resulting in GLB youth being expected to rely more fully on their intrapersonal qualities to buffer themselves. However, this strategy is usually inadequate, as many of these youth have poor coping capacity and skills (Munoz-Plaza et al., 2002), especially when confronting their challenges feeling so alone. Therefore, it is not surprising to see consistent associations in the research between lack of intrapersonal and interpersonal protection and negative developmental outcomes for GLB youth.

### Risk-Taking Behavior

Social rejection and isolation experienced by GLB youth have been found to contribute to risk-taking behaviors such as substance abuse (Rosario, Hunter, & Gwadz, 1997) and unsafe sex (Blake et al., 2001). Whereas typical reasons for adolescent substance use and abuse are present for GLB youth (i.e., peer pressure, individuation, novelty, increased pleasure, and decreased stress), the additional experiences of isolation, rejection, lack of social support, and stressful life events serve to increase GLB youth's rate of risk-taking behaviors and substance use and abuse. Furthermore, it has been reported that up to one in four GLB youth drop out of school, likely because of social rejection, harassment, and victimization at school (Savin-Williams, 1994). Finally, researchers estimate that between 25% and 40% of homeless youth are GLB, some of whom report being kicked out of their homes because their sexual orientation is totally unacceptable to their families (Marinoble, 1998; Van Wormer & McKinney, 2003).

The task of trying to negotiate (with oneself and with one's immediate communities—family, peers, and school) same-sex sexual and romantic attraction in a society that assumes heterosexism and primarily condemns homosexuality is made all the more challenging by the interaction of (a) overwhelmed personal resources, (b) the pervasive lack of interpersonal protective factors, and (c) the pervasive presence of rejecting interpersonal factors. This combination predisposes many GLB youth to negative developmental outcomes, including increased rates of mental health disorders and suicidal tendencies, high-risk behaviors, substance abuse, school failure and dropout, and homelessness. This combination fortunately also provides a clear template for prevention and intervention activities and actions.

## ALTERNATIVE ACTIONS FOR PREVENTION

The template referred to above for prevention and intervention includes targeting of interpersonal processes and relationships by promoting positive parenting practices, connection with competent adult role models, positive community affiliation, and positive school climate. It also includes promoting intrapersonal processes by helping to cultivate individual perseverance and optimism, hope and faith, self-esteem, internal locus of control, curiosity and compassion, agreeableness, openness to new experiences, emotional regulation, and extroversion in the youth themselves. Although all these suggestions are needed to prevent negative outcomes for GLB youth, the focus in this section is on school-based efforts, with a recognition that broader action will be needed to affect positive parenting, expand connection with competent role models, and promote positive community affiliations. Thus, the major actions for prevention that are proposed in this section involve making schools healthy and supportive environments for *all* students, explicitly including GLB youth. This approach will require inclusive school policies (e.g., antidiscrimination policies that specify GLB youth), integration of GLB issues into the curriculum (e.g., health education, history, and literature), staff development, and accessible resource information and support services (Marinoble, 1998). This section enumerates the concerns that need to be assessed, addressed, and changed in order to beneficially serve GLB youth in schools.

## Providing School-Based Supports

Although the focus of prevention efforts may be clear, implementation can be complex and difficult, primarily because of heterosexism and homophobia, but also because of society's and the schools' hesitancy to address the topic of sexuality (Hollander, 2000). For example, Roffman (2000) found that 85% of prospective teachers do not want to include discussions about homosexuality in their classrooms.

Within the school environment, educators and other professionals are advised to initiate a climate assessment of being a GLB student in their school. Internal assessments should include levels of GLB acceptance, ways schools currently address GLB students, incidences of discrimination, and staff understanding of GLB student needs. From that information personnel can tailor school and community education, counseling, and support services. Assessments can also establish a knowledge base for service needs in the school or community (Travers & Paoletti, 1999) for future evaluation of directed efforts in this area.

Issues that need to be openly addressed in schools include discrimination; the philosophy, culture, and values of the school; and the self-esteem (community belonging) and safety (harassment and violence policies) of all students. In addressing these items, schools should address the need to make all events, such as proms and dances, and clubs open to GLB participation. These types of events should not be presumed heterosexual (Marinoble, 1998). School, community, or national news stories regarding GLB issues, interests, and events need to be covered by school newspapers (Marinoble, 1998). If there is interest, a teacher or school psychologist should sponsor GLB clubs, Gay–Straight Alliances (GSAs), or GLB speakers for the school.

## Staff Training

Teacher and staff training can be an effective form of prevention. Teacher and school staff development needs to focus on their knowledge and understanding of GLB issues and explore their views and biases about GLB orientation. Training also needs to instruct staff on homosexuality and youth (Lipkin, 2001), emphasize that religion is separate from school, and educate about the particular needs and issues of concern to GLB youth (such as depression, coming out, discrimination and harassment, dropping out, safe sex, healthy relationships, and substance abuse; Association of Gay, Lesbian, and Bisexual Issues in Counseling, 2004). Finally, training should empower staff to embrace school as a positive and inclusive community committed to all students. Schools can use the opportunity of training to challenge traditional definitions of gender, identity, sexuality, and psychopathology as well as make strides to depathologize homosexuality and encourage compassion (Marinoble, 1998).

These trainings need to include reinvigorating a school commitment to the safety of all children in school and including in school safety regulations specific language protecting GLB students from harm (Marinoble, 1998). Appointing a GLB point person for staff and students and making this resource person's role known by the whole school community may be effective. Staff would be instructed that there is zero tolerance for overhearing or seeing harassment of GLB students and not intervening. The training and GLB point person would encourage and guide the staff in how to be more receptive and accepting of student differences. Positive relationships with teachers have been found to be mitigating factors in school adjustment and school trouble (Russell, Sief, & Truoung, 2001).

## Curricular and Legal Concerns

General school curricula need to be inclusive of diversity and homosexuality. Sexual education, substance abuse education, and health education all need to include gay-sensitive and gay-informative elements. Health curricula need to be inclusive of the diversity of sexual development. In a study exploring the benefits of gay-sensitive HIV instruction in schools (Blake et al., 2001), general findings included that GLB youth reported more substance abuse, high-risk sexual behaviors, suicidal thoughts or attempts, and personal safety issues than their heterosexual peers. GLB youth from schools with gay-sensitive HIV instruction reported fewer sexual partners, less recent sex, and less substance abuse before sex than those without gay-sensitive instruction.

Many models for school support of GLB students exist and generally include the philosophy of acceptance—that is, the inclusion, equality, and belonging of all students. Hollander (2000) emphasized also not labeling students, as many adolescents may be questioning their sexual identity.

Tolerance and protection are actually mandated, and schools must protect the safety of GLB students. Under Title IX of the Federal Education Amendments of 1972, schools are being held financially and procedurally accountable for upholding these basic civil rights laws, which protect all students from harm, invasion of privacy, and intimidation (Callahan, 2000). Many court rulings require changes directly to school policies, as well as financial compensation. Teachers, students, and school personnel should be aware of their school's zero tolerance policy for homophobic or heterosexist slurs, jokes, harassment, and violence. Those who overlook these offenses should meet serious consequences (Marinoble, 1998).

### Visibility and a Vehicle for Support

The simplest and most powerful ways to support GLB youth in schools are to increase their positive visibility and prevent hostile environments that are rejecting and isolating them, increase their safety, and reduce their instigation to use substances and take other risks (Shifrin & Solis, 1992). Recommendations for change include investigating incidents, educating the offenders, educating staff, supporting and providing services to targets, and educating the whole school together (staff and students; Callahan, 2000). Schools may choose to use teachers who have come out as role models (McFarland, 2001), and actively hire GLB teachers (Van Wormer & McKinney, 2003). By dealing with GLB issues openly, schools can make incidences of hate unacceptable to the community. In keeping with a democratic society and the values of equality and civil rights, all members of a school community should feel safe and be protected. School culture must promote healthy development and respect for individuals as well as affirm diversity in the curriculum and elsewhere (e.g. by putting up posters of famous GLB contributors to society). Inclusive schools are positive and supportive environments for GLB youth. Like any minority, GLB students should experience exposure to role models (expert speakers), accurate accessible GLB information, and creative works in the library (by GLB authors or inclusive of GLB issues) (McFarland, 2001). This openness will give GLB youth the feeling that it is safe to come to school, belong, get an education, and be able to access services and materials.

## ALTERNATIVE ACTIONS FOR INTERVENTION

### Counseling Services

Counseling services to GLB youth need to be available in the schools to foster healthy development, build resiliency and coping skills, and address the consequences of social stigma and victimization. Those working directly with GLB youth are advised to examine their own thoughts, feelings, and attitudes regarding sexual orientation in an effort to avoid judgment of GLB youth (Tharinger & Wells, 2000). Additionally, while maintaining the confidentiality of all children, those working with GLB youth must be aware of nonheterosexual students' concerns and heightened sensitivity regarding the disclosure of their orientation to others (Harrison, 2003; Lasser & Tharinger, 2003).

Counseling and general support can be delivered individually or in groups (Muller & Hartman, 1998). Some schools have established confidentiality policies for counseling GLB youth without parental consent when coming out to families would place youth at risk. In such situations, advocates from within the school will have sought informed assent (Weiler, 2003). Whenever appropriate, school counselors and psychologists should provide family and parent counseling or should refer the family for such services outside of the school (Saltzburg, 2004). What follows are considerations for possible counseling scenarios for GLB youth.

***I think I might be gay.*** Some questioning youth may refer themselves for counseling to explore the possibility of a homosexual or bisexual identity (Hollander, 2000). Counselors should not be quick to make any assumptions about the student's sexual orientation. Rather, those counseling youth who present as questioning should offer their acceptance and focus on the student's needs, which may or may not include transition from questioning to homosexual, bisexual, or heterosexual identity status. A developmental–ecosystemic approach (Lasser & Gottlieb, 2004) applied to the questioning student would take into account adolescent social and identity development, cultural and environmental factors, and systemic variables in conceptualizing the referral. An initial interview may indicate that the student holds misconceptions about sexual orientation (e.g., confusing gender-atypical behavior with homosexuality), so the counselor could first correct such misunderstandings with factual information (Shidlo & Schroeder, 2002).

The counselor should not rush or push the student to make a decision with respect to selecting an orientation, but rather should provide the student with space to explore his or her thoughts and feelings, with the ultimate goal of reducing any distress the student might feel over the questioning status. Conversely, students should not be advised that their same-sex attractions are "just a passing phase," as their presenting feelings may develop into an enduring sexual orientation.

***I'm gay/lesbian/bisexual. Is there something wrong with me?*** Many GLB youth have internalized societal stereotypes about sexual orientation. They have heard the word *fag* used as a derogatory term in the school yard, seen homosexual characters victimized in the media and in their communities, and heard countless jokes that denigrate gays, lesbians, and bisexuals. Therefore, it is not surprising that many GLB youth wonder whether there is something wrong with them. School counselors and psychologists have an ethical obligation to communicate acceptance of the GLB student and send a clear message that there is nothing wrong with homosexual and bisexual orientations. Initially, the primary counseling goal should be to foster self-acceptance (Cooley, 1998). Psychoeducational approaches that provide GLB youth with basic, accurate information about sexual orientation may also be helpful in communicating that GLB orientations are normative.

***I feel so isolated.*** Many GLB students feel isolated from family members and peers. To address this isolation, school counselors and psychologists can link GLB students to counseling support groups with other GLB students (Muller & Hartman, 1998) or GSAs, which function less like counseling groups and more like student clubs or organizations (Russell, 2002). There are many benefits to linking GLB youth to support groups and GSAs, including peer support, role models, and shared experiences. Referrals to such groups should be made cautiously, given the concerns that many GLB youth have about disclosure to others (Harrison, 2003). Using the construct of visibility management, school counselors and psychologists could engage GLB youth in a cost–benefit analysis with respect to disclosure to others in the context of joining a support group or GSA (Lasser & Tharinger, 2003). Potential risks of joining (e.g., possible breaches of confidentiality) could be weighed against possible gains (e.g., social support and connectedness).

***What about my parents?*** Many GLB youth have concerns about disclosure of their sexual orientation to parents and other family members, knowing that they risk verbal abuse, physical abuse, and abandonment (Tharinger & Wells, 2000). Those working with GLB youth should discuss the potential costs and benefits of disclosure to parents. Parental adjustment to disclosure may take time, and not all parents are accepting. Discussing the student's disclosure to his or her parents in the context of an overall visibility management strategy may prove helpful (Lasser & Tharinger, 2003).

When working with parents, school counselors and psychologists are encouraged to empathize with those who are having difficulty accepting their child's orientation and to provide accurate information about GLB lives (see Recommended Resources at the end of this chapter). Many parents also express feelings of shame and guilt (Armesto, 2001). To facilitate greater acceptance, school counselors and psychologists should help parents understand that their child's orientation is not the product of parenting style or behavior.

## SUMMARY

GLB youth share many characteristics with their heterosexual peers, yet their unique developmental and social experiences warrant attention. Raised in a homophobic and heterosexist culture, GLB youth face discrimination and abuses in their schools, homes, and communities. The resiliency and positive developmental outcomes of GLB youth are often seriously compromised because of overwhelmed personal resources, pervasive lack of interpersonal protective factors, and pervasive presence of rejecting interpersonal factors. This combination predisposes many GLB youth to negative developmental outcomes, including increased rates of mental health disorders and suicidal tendencies, high-risk behaviors, substance abuse, school failure and dropout, and homelessness. Fortunately, this awareness also provides a clear template for prevention and intervention activities and actions for schools. That template includes promoting supportive attitudes and behaviors, promoting safe and secure educational environments, and working with GLB youth and their families to facilitate positive outcomes.

## RECOMMENDED RESOURCES

### Books and Other Printed Material

Griffen, C. W., Wirth, M. J., & Wirth, A. G. (1997). *Beyond acceptance: Parents of lesbians and gays talk about their experiences.* New York: St. Martin's Press.

*Beyond Acceptance* provides parents of gay, lesbian, and bisexual youth with helpful information and guidance for the coming out process. As the title suggests, the book focuses on strengthening the family following disclosure.

Lipkin, A. (1999). *Understanding homosexuality, changing schools.* Boulder, CO: Westview Press.

Arthur Lipkin has written what many regard as an essential text for those working to improve school climates for gay, lesbian, and bisexual youth. Geared toward educators, *Understanding Homosexuality* builds a strong case for supporting GLB youth in education, as well as practical strategies for accomplishing this goal.

## Websites

*http://www.Project10.org*

Project 10 is a school-based program that serves GLB students in Los Angeles, California. The Project 10 website provides useful information for parents, teachers, and youth.

*http://www.hmi.org*

The Hetrick-Martin Institute provides a wealth of resources for GLB youth. The institute founded the Harvey Milk High School in New York.

*http://www.glsen.org*

The Gay, Lesbian and Straight Education Network (GLSEN) was formed to make schools safe for GLB youth. Their website contains details about forming gay–straight alliances as school clubs.

## REFERENCES

Armesto, J. C. (2001). Attributions and emotional reactions to the identity disclosure ("coming out") of a homosexual child. *Family Process, 40,* 145–163.

Association of Gay, Lesbian, and Bisexual Issues in Counseling (AGLBIC). *Competencies for counseling gay, lesbian, bisexual and transgender (GBLT) clients.* Retrieved August 24, 2005, from http://www.aglbic.org/resources/competencies/html

Bailey, J. M. & Pillard, R. C. (1991). A genetic study of male sexual orientation. *Archives of General Psychiatry, 48,* 1089–1096.

Blake, S. M., Ledsky, R., Lehman, T., Goodenow, C., Sawyer, R., & Hack, T. (2001). Preventing sexual risk behaviors among gay, lesbian and bisexual adolescents: The benefits of gay-sensitive HIV instruction in schools. *American Journal of Public Health, 91,* 940–946.

Callahan, C. (2000). Schools that have not protected and worked with gay and lesbian students have been sanctioned by the courts. *Education, 121,* 313–327.

Cass, V. C. (1979). Homosexual identity formation: A theoretical model. *Journal of Homosexuality, 4,* 219–235.

Chen-Hayes, S. F. (2001). Counseling and advocacy with transgendered and gender-variant persons in schools and families. *Journal of Humanistic Counseling, Education, and Development, 40,* 34–46.

Cooley, J. J. (1998). Gay and lesbian adolescents: Presenting problems and the counselor's role. *Professional School Counseling, 1,* 30–39.

D'Augelli, A. R., & Dark, L. J. (1995). Vulnerable populations: Lesbian, gay, and bisexual youth. In L. D. Eron, J. Gentry, & P. Schlegel (Eds.), *Reason to hope: A psychosocial perspective on violence and youth* (pp. 177–196). Washington, DC: American Psychological Association.

D'Augelli, A. R., Pilkington, N. W., & Hershberger, S. L. (2002). Incidence and mental health impact of sexual orientation victimization of lesbian, gay and bisexual youths in high school. *School Psychology Quarterly, 17,* 148–167.

Davey, M., Eaker, D. G., & Walters, L. H. (2003). Resilient processes in adolescents: Personality profiles, self worth, and coping. *Journal of Adolescent Research, 18,* 347–362.

DeAngelis, T. (2002). New data on lesbian, gay and bisexual mental health. *Monitor on Psychology, 33,* 1–5.

Diamond, L. M. (2003). New paradigms for research on heterosexual and sexual minority development. *Journal of Clinical Child and Adolescent Psychology, 32,* 490–498.

Elia, J. P. (1993). Homophobia in the high school: A problem in need of resolution. *High School Journal, 77,* 177–185.

Ellenbogen, S., & Chamberland, C. (1997). The peer relations of dropouts: A comparative study of at-risk youths. *Journal of Adolescence, 20,* 355–367.

Floyd, C. (1996). Achieving despite the odds: A study of resilience among a group of African American high school seniors. *Journal of Negro Education, 65,* 181–189.

Floyd, F. J., & Stein, T. S. (2002). Sexual orientation identity formation among gay, lesbian, and bisexual youths: Multiple patterns of milestone experiences. *Journal of Research on Adolescence, 12,* 167–191.

Francoeur, R. T. (1991). *Becoming a sexual person.* New York: Macmillan.

Garofalo, R., Wolf, R. C., Kessel, S., Palfrey, J., & DuRant, R. H. (1998). The association between health risk behaviors and sexual orientation among a school-based sample of adolescents. *Pediatrics, 101,* 895–902.

Garofalo, R., Wolf, R. C., Wissow, L. S., Woods, E. R., & Goodman, E. (1999). Sexual orientation and risk of suicide attempts among a representative sample of youth. *Archives of Pediatric and Adolescent Medicine, 153,* 487–493.

Haaga, J. (1991). "Homophobia?" *Journal of Social Behavior and Personality, 6,* 171–174.

Harrison, T. W. (2003). Adolescent homosexuality and concerns regarding disclosure. *Journal of School Health, 73,* 107–113.

Harter, S. (1999). *The construction of the self.* New York: Guilford Press.

Hollander, G. (2000). Questioning youths: Challenges to working with youths forming identities. *School Psychology Review, 29,* 173–180.

Kinsey, A. C., Pomeroy, W. B., & Martin, C. E. (1948). *Sexual behavior in the human male.* Philadelphia: W. B. Saunders.

Kinsey, A. C., Pomeroy, W. B., Martin, C. E., & Gebhard, P. H. (1953). *Sexual behavior in the human female.* Philadelphia: W. B. Saunders.

Kitzinger, C., & Wilson, S. (1995). Transitions from heterosexuality to lesbianism: The discursive production of lesbian identities. *Developmental Psychology, 31,* 95–104.

Kivel, B. D., & Kleiber, D. A. (2000). Leisure in the identity formation of lesbian/gay youth: Personal, but not social. *Leisure Sciences, 22,* 215–232.

Kosciw, J. G., & Cullen, M. K. (2001). *The school-related experiences of our nation's lesbian, gay, bisexual and transgender youth: The GLSEN 2001 National School Climate Survey.* New York: GLSEN. Retrieved September 21, 2004, from http://www.glsen.org/cgi-bin/iowa/all/library/record/1413.html

Kubler-Ross, E. (1969). *On death and dying.* London: Collier-MacMillan LTD.

Lasser, J. (2005). Visibility management and the school psychologist. *School Psychology International. 26,* 44–54.

Lasser, J. S., & Gottlieb, M. C. (2004). Treating patients distressed regarding their sexual orientation: Clinical and ethical alternatives. *Professional Psychology: Research and Practice, 35,* 194–200.

Lasser, J., & Tharinger, D. (2003). Visibility management in school and beyond: A qualitative study of gay, lesbian, bisexual youth. *Journal of Adolescence, 26,* 233–244.

LeVay, S. (1993). *The sexual brain.* Cambridge, MA: MIT Press.

Lipkin, A. (2001). Teacher education must include homosexuality. *Community Youth Development Journal, 2.* Retrieved September 12, 2004, from http://www.cydjournal.org/2001Summer/contents.html

Luthar, S. S. (1991). Vulnerability and resilience: A study of high risk adolescents. *Child Development, 62,* 600–616.

Luthar, S. S., Cicchetti, D., & Becker, B. (2000). The construct of resilience: A critical evaluation and guidelines for future work. *Child Development, 71*(3), 543–562.

Marinoble, R. (1998). Homosexuality: A blind spot in the school mirror. *Professional School Counseling, 1,* 4–7.

Masten, A. S., & Coatsworth, J. D. (1998). The development of competence in favorable and unfavorable environments: Lessons from research on unsuccessful children. *American Psychologist, 52,* 205–220.

Masten, A. S., Hubbard, J. J., Gest, S. D., Tellegen, A., Garmezy, N., & Ramirez, M. (1999). Competence in the context of adversity: Pathways to resilience and maladaptation from childhood to late adolescence. *Development and Psychopathology, 11,* 143–169.

McFarland, W. P. (2001). The legal duty to protect gay and lesbian students from violence in school. *Professional School Counseling, 4,* 171–180.

Meyer-Bahlburg, H. F. L., Ehrhardt, A. A., Rosen, L. R., Gruen, R. S., Veridiano, N. P., Vann, F. H., & Neuwalder, H. F. (1995). Prenatal estrogens and the development of homosexual orientation. *Developmental Psychology, 31,* 12–21.

Muller, L. E., & Hartman, J. (1998). Group counseling for sexual minority youth. *Professional School Counseling, 3,* 58–82.

Munoz-Plaza, C., Quinn, S. C., & Rounds, K. (2002). Lesbian, gay, bisexual and transgender students: Perceived social support in the high school environment. *High School Journal, 85,* 52–64.

Parker, A. P., & DeCecco, J. P. (1995). Sexual expression: A global perspective. *Journal of Homosexuality, 28,* 427–430.

Patterson, C. J. (1995). Sexual orientation and human development: An overview. *Developmental Psychology, 31,* 3–11.

Reis, B., & Saewyc, E. (1999). *Eighty-three thousand youth: Selected findings of eight population-based studies as they pertain to anti-gay harassment and the safety and well-being of sexual minority students.* Seattle: Safe Schools Coalition of Washington.

Rhee, S., Furlong, M. J., Turner, J. A., & Harari, I. (2001). Integrating strength-based perspectives in psychoeducational evaluations. *California School Psychologist, 6,* 5–17.

Roffman, D. M. (2000). A model for helping schools address policy options regarding gay and lesbian youth. *Journal of Sex Education and Therapy, 25,* 130–137.

Rosario, M., Hunter, J., & Gwadz, M. (1997). Exploration of substance use among lesbian, gay and bisexual youth: Prevalence and correlates. *Journal of Adolescent Research, 12,* 454–476.

Russell, S. T. (2002). Queer in America: Citizenship for sexual minority youth. *Applied Developmental Science, 6,* 258–263.

Russell, S. T., Franz, B. T., & Driscoll, A. K. (2001). Same-sex romantic attraction and experiences of violence in adolescence. *American Journal of Public Health, 91,* 903–906.

Russell, S. T., Sief, H., & Truoung, N. L. (2001). School outcomes of sexual minority youth in the United States: Evidence from a national study. *Journal of Adolescence, 24,* 111–127.

Saltzburg, S. (2004). Learning that an adolescent child is gay or lesbian: The parent experience. *Social Work, 49,* 109–119.

Savin-Williams, R. C. (1994). Verbal and physical abuse as stressors in the lives of lesbian, gay male and bisexual youths: Associations with school problems, running away, substance abuse, prostitution, and suicide. *Journal of Consulting and Clinical Psychology, 62,* 261–269.

Savin-Williams, R. C. (2001). Suicide attempts among sexual-minority youth: Population and measurement issues. *Journal of Consulting and Clinical Psychology, 69,* 983–991.

Schneider, M. S., & Tremble, B. (1985). Gay or straight? Working with the confused adolescent. *Journal of Social Work and Human Sexuality, 4,* 71–82.

Schneider, M. S., & Witherspoon, J. J. (2000). Friendship patterns among lesbian and gay youth: An exploratory study. *Canadian Journal of Human Sexuality, 9,* 239–246.

Shidlo, A., & Schroeder, M. (2002). Changing sexual orientation: A consumer's report. *Professional Psychology: Research and Practice, 33,* 249–259.

Shifrin, F., & Solis, M. (1992). Chemical dependency in gay and lesbian youth. *Journal of Chemical Dependency Treatment, 5,* 67–76.

Tharinger, D., & Wells, G. (2000). An attachment perspective on the developmental challenges of gay and lesbian adolescents: The need for continuity of care giving from family and schools. *School Psychology Review, 29,* 158–172.

Travers, R., & Paoletti, D. (1999). The lesbian, gay and bisexual youth program: A model for communities seeking to improve quality of life for gay, lesbian and bisexual youth. *Canadian Journal of Human Sexuality, 8,* 293–304.

Troiden, R. R. (1989). The formation of homosexual identities. *Journal of Homosexuality, 17,* 43–73.

Van Wormer, K., & McKinney, R. (2003). What schools can do to help gay/lesbian/bisexual youth: A harm reduction approach. *Adolescence 38,* 409–421.

Weiler, E. M. (2003). Making schools safe for sexual minority students. *Principal Leadership Magazine, 4,* 10–16.

Werner, E. E. (1989). Vulnerability and resiliency: A longitudinal perspective. In M. Barmbring, F. Loesel, & H. Skowronek (Eds.), *Children at risk: Assessment, longitudinal research, and intervention* (pp. 173–185). New York: deGruyter.

Wolin, S., & Wolin, S. J. (1996). The challenge model: Working with strengths in children of substance-abusing parents. *Child & Adolescent Psychiatry Clinics of North America, 5,* 243–256.

Worrell, F. C., & Hale, R. L. (2001). Relationship of hope in the future and perceived school climate to school completion. *School Psychology Quarterly, 16*(4), 370–388.

# 33

# Achievement Motivation

**Anastasia S. Morrone**

*Indiana University–Purdue University Indianapolis*

**Paul R. Pintrich**[†]

*University of Michigan*

The quality that often differentiates children of similar abilities is motivation, which explains why one student might receive all A's, whereas another is referred for special services because of poor achievement. Indeed, with the exception of specific reading problems and behavior problems, lack of motivation is perhaps the most common reason why many children are identified by teachers and parents as needing help. Achievement motivation concerns certain types of goals, particularly mastery and performance goals (Ames, 1992; Dweck & Leggett, 1988; Grant & Dweck, 2003; Pintrich, 2000). In the classroom, these goals are often reflected in the types of questions students ask themselves when faced with a challenging academic assignment, such as: "What will I learn from the assignment?" "What is the best way to approach the assignment?" "Will I get a high grade on this assignment?" "Will I do better than other students in my classes?" "Will this be too difficult for me?" and "Will others think I am stupid if I can't do the assignment?"

## BACKGROUND AND DEVELOPMENT

Two theories of achievement motivation—attribution theory and achievement goal theory—are most prevalent in the literature. Attribution theory provides a theoretical foundation for achievement goal theory. Achievement goal theory helps to explain children's learning and performance on academic tasks in school settings, and it has been one of the most active areas of motivation research in the past decade (Pintrich & Schunk, 2002).

### Attribution Theory

There are two related attribution theories of motivation: *interpersonal* and *intrapersonal*. The interpersonal attribution theory includes beliefs about who is responsible for the outcome and the emotions that are expressed, given how responsibility has been assigned. The metaphor guiding the interpersonal theory is that of the person as a *judge* rather than as a scientist (Weiner, 2000). The intrapersonal theory, which is described in this chapter, emphasizes causal attributions for success and failure outcomes. As Weiner (2000) noted, the approach to intrapersonal motivation is "guided by the metaphor that people are scientists, trying to understand themselves and their environment and then acting on the basis of this knowledge" (p. 2).

Both the intrapersonal and interpersonal theories begin at the point that a person experiences an outcome that is unexpected, negative, or important. Reaching this point causes the person to retrospectively search for possible reasons why the outcome might have occurred. For example, if a student expected to earn a B on an assignment but instead earned a D, the student is likely to search for an explanation of why the grade is much lower than expected. The student would go through a similar process if a higher-than-expected grade had been earned.

[†]Paul R. Pintrich died suddenly on July 12, 2003, at the age of 50. This was a devastating loss not only to the field of motivation research, but also to those of us whose lives he touched through our professional relationships with him. Because Paul was a co-author on this chapter in 1997 and his voice is very much a part of this chapter, I have retained him as an author on this revision.

The perceived causes of success and failure in achievement settings can be located along three causal dimensions: locus of causality (internal vs. external), stability (stable vs. unstable), and controllability (controllable vs. uncontrollable). *Locus of causality* refers to whether the cause of the outcome is attributed to something within the person (internal) or outside the person (external). Aptitude, temporary and long-term effort, skills and knowledge, and mood are internal attributions because they describe characteristics of the person, whereas perceived teacher bias, help from others, objective task difficulty, and chance are considered external because they are outside of the person. *Stability* refers to whether the cause of the outcome is attributed to something that will not change (stable) or something that is variable and can change (unstable). Therefore, long-term effort, aptitude, perceived teacher bias, and objective task difficulty are considered stable causes, whereas temporary effort, skills and knowledge, mood, help from others, and chance are considered to be unstable. The third causal dimension, *controllability*, reflects whether the cause is something over which students perceive themselves to have control. Long-term and temporary effort, perceived teacher bias, and help from others are considered controllable causes; aptitude, mood, objective task difficulty, and chance are considered uncontrollable causes.

Generally when students attribute an outcome to their aptitude, they consider information such as how successful they have been in the past with similar tasks as well as the objective difficulty of the task. In a failure situation, a student making an aptitude attribution might reason, "Even though this was a hard test, I never do well in math. I'm just not good at math." If the task is perceived to be based on skill, and if other variables such as objective task difficulty are held constant, then the cause is usually attributed to temporary effort. In the same failure situation, another student making an effort attribution might reason, "I have always been good at math, and this test was not that difficult. So I must not have studied hard enough."

It is clear that these two explanations for failure will result in different future behavior. The reason for these two different outcomes is that the stability of a cause, rather than its locus, determines expectancy for future success (Weiner, 2000). For example, the student who attributed failure to low aptitude is likely to have low expectancy for future success because aptitude is considered an internal, stable cause. This student is likely to conclude, "I will never do well in math, no matter how hard I study." But the student who attributed the cause of failure to insufficient effort is likely to have high expectancy for future success because temporary effort is an internal, unstable cause. This student is likely to conclude, "I just need to study harder next time. I know I can do better if I work harder."

The controllability dimension further highlights the importance of attributing past failures to insufficient effort. Not only is temporary effort an unstable cause, it also is something over which students have full control. If students believe that working harder will produce success, they are likely to persist longer at the task and achieve at higher levels than if they attribute their failures to aptitude, which is an uncontrollable cause.

Although attribution theory has made important contributions to the study of achievement motivation, the theory primarily emphasizes reactions to events after they have occurred, rather than how beliefs and cognitions might influence the way students approach new academic tasks. In other words, attribution theory provides an explanation of the way students retrospectively attribute the cause of achievement outcomes but is less clear about how students' anticipatory beliefs and cognitions influence the way they approach academic tasks. Achievement goal theory focuses on these anticipatory beliefs and cognitions.

## Achievement Goal Theory

Ames (1992) defined an achievement goal orientation as an "integrated pattern of beliefs, attributions, and affect that produces the intentions of behavior (Weiner, 1986) and that is represented by different ways of approaching, engaging in, and responding to achievement-type activities" (p. 261). This quote by Ames underscores the way in which achievement goal theory has attempted to integrate and elaborate on the motivational processes proposed by previous theories of achievement motivation. Goal orientations reflect the reasons *why* students pursue achievement-related tasks, not just the outcome they hope to achieve (Urdan, 1997). As Pintrich and Schunk (2002) suggested, goal orientation "includes not just the purposes or reasons for achievement, but reflects a type of standard by which individuals judge their performance and success or failure in reaching that goal" (p. 214).

***Mastery versus performance goals.*** Achievement goal theory has typically emphasized two different types

**Table 1** *Two-Dimensional Framework for Revised Goal Theory*

| | Approach Tendency | Avoidance Tendency |
|---|---|---|
| Mastery orientation | Primary focus is on learning or mastering the task; students monitor their progress based on self-set standards. | Primary focus is on avoiding misunderstanding or *not* mastering the task; students use the standard of not performing the task incorrectly when evaluating their performance. |
| Performance orientation | Primary focus is on performing better than others on the task; students use normative standards when evaluating their performance. | Primary focus is on avoiding poor performance on the task; students use normative standards to evaluate their performance. |

Adapted from *Motivation in Education: Theory, Research, and Applications* (2nd ed., p. 219), P. R. Pintrich and D. H. Schunk, 2002, Englewood Cliffs, NJ: Merrill/Prentice Hall.

of goals: *mastery* (learning), or task-focused goals, and *performance*, or ego-focused goals (Anderman & Maehr, 1994; Grant & Dweck, 2003). Research on the role of mastery goals in motivation suggests that when students have mastery goals, their primary focus is on learning or mastering something new. Because they value learning for its own sake, they tend to choose more challenging assignments and work harder in school. These students also tend to use more effective learning strategies while studying (Middleton & Midgley, 1997; Pintrich, 2000; Wolters, Yu, & Pintrich, 1996).

Conversely, earlier research suggested that when students have performance goals they tend to focus on the external reward or consequence associated with their learning, such as getting a good grade or avoiding a bad grade. It was argued that students with performance goals often approach academic tasks by first determining how difficult the task is and whether they believe they will be successful. It was further hypothesized that because the focus is on the outcome, students spend less time deciding on the best learning strategies to use, which often results in the use of less effective strategies (Ames & Archer, 1988; Elliott & Dweck, 1988; Pintrich, 2000).

Recent advances in achievement motivation research suggest that the distinction between mastery and performance goals is incomplete because it does not acknowledge earlier contributions to the field of motivation, namely, approach and avoidance tendencies that are related to achievement motivation. Recent conceptualizations of achievement goal theory integrate contemporary views of mastery and performance goals with classic approach and avoidance distinctions. Elliot and McGregor (2001) and Pintrich (2000) have each proposed a two-dimensional framework that includes an approach and avoidance tendency for mastery and performance goals. The columns in Table 1 reflect the approach and avoidance tendencies associated with both mastery and performance goals.

With respect to performance goals, recent research suggests that there are important differences in cognitive outcomes for students who approach a task with the goal to outperform their peers (performance approach goal) versus students who approach a task with the goal to avoid looking less capable than their peers (performance avoidance goal; Middleton & Midgley, 1997). Specifically, students with performance approach goals may employ very effective strategies to help them achieve their goals, and these strategies may lead them to become more involved in a given task than students with performance avoidance goals. Students with performance avoidance goals are likely to avoid setting challenging goals, which in turn could lead to less involvement in the task (Harackiewicz, Barron, & Elliot, 1998; Pintrich, 2000). With respect to revised goal theory, correlational and experimental research findings have consistently demonstrated that "where mastery, approach performance, and avoidance performance goals are compared, maladaptive patterns of intrinsic motivation and actual performance occur only in the avoidance performance groups" (Pintrich, 2000, p. 544).

As noted earlier in this section, some aspects of revised goal theory have not yet been fully investigated. The most noteworthy of these are mastery avoidance goals. As Pintrich and Schunk (2002) noted, a mastery avoidance goal appears counterintuitive because the definition of mastery implies an approach tendency. Yet there are students who want to avoid doing something wrong, not because they are worried about how they will compare with their peers but because they have high standards for themselves and worry that they may not be able to live up to those standards. For example, if a student has the mastery avoidance goal of not getting the wrong answers on her long-division problems, but her teacher is really only interested in her process for solving the problems, it could be frustrating for the student because her goal conflicts with that of her teacher. Although there is some empirical support for mastery avoidance goals, more research is needed to better understand the nature of these goals and their implications in the classroom (Elliot & McGregor, 2001).

The differences in behavior between students with performance goals and mastery goals are similar to the behavioral differences between individuals who are ego involved and those who are task involved (Nicholls, 1989). The term *ego involvement* refers to situations in which students seek to demonstrate their own ability as compared to the ability of a normative reference group. *Task involvement*, on the other hand, refers to situations in which the focus is on improving mastery at a task rather than on demonstrating ability relative to others. The difficulty that arises with ego involvement is that individuals must determine whether they can master a task and to what extent this implies higher ability than others. If the amount of effort required to master the task is too high, this implies low ability. Ego involvement is seen more frequently in competitive situations, whereas task involvement is more often present in noncompetitive situations (Nicholls, 1989).

Mastery and performance goals are also conceptually similar to the distinctions between intrinsic and extrinsic motivation (Ryan & Deci, 2000; Harter, 1999). *Intrinsic* motivation refers to engaging in activities for their own sake, such as out of curiosity or interest, without the need for an accompanying external reward (Harter, 1999; Ryan & Deci, 2000). Conversely, *extrinsic* motivation refers to engaging in activities in order to acquire some type of reward, such as good grades or positive attention from teachers and parents. An intrinsic-motivation orientation characterizes students who tend to seek challenges and opportunities for independent mastery. In contrast, an extrinsic-motivation orientation characterizes students who tend to avoid challenges and opportunities for independent mastery.

***Entity and incremental theories of intelligence.*** What are the reasons behind the selection of one goal over another? Two researchers have taken different approaches in their explanation of why students have mastery goals or performance goals. Dweck and Leggett (1988) suggested that students may select achievement goals based on their own implicit theories of intelligence. The two implicit theories of intelligence that students differentially subscribe to, according to Dweck and Leggett, are the entity and incremental theories of intelligence.

Students with an entity theory of intelligence believe that intelligence is a fixed, global trait. In the context of attribution theory, the primary emphasis is on the internal, stable factor of ability, that is, aptitude (Weiner, 1986). Thus, students with an entity view see effort as being inversely related to ability (Dweck & Leggett, 1988) such that if they have to work hard to succeed, they must not be very smart. Because this view of intelligence focuses on ability, students who subscribe to it are likely to be mastery oriented in their approach to academic tasks only when they believe they are already good at something. The mastery-oriented pattern of behavior involves seeking challenging tasks, showing positive affect, and demonstrating high persistence (performance approach goal). If students believe they are not very good at something, a very different behavioral pattern is likely to emerge (performance avoidance goal). In this case, they are likely to exhibit helplessness, which is characterized by challenge avoidance, negative affect, and low persistence, especially in the face of difficulty. The entity view of intelligence favors performance goals because these goals either reinforce students' ability (they get good grades) or protect students' ability from being evaluated negatively (they withdraw from the task).

Conversely, students with an incremental theory of intelligence believe that their intelligence increases as they acquire new skills and knowledge. The primary emphasis of this view of intelligence is on the unstable, internal factor of effort, that is, temporary effort (Weiner, 1986). These students see a positive relationship between effort and ability, such that the harder they work, the smarter they will become. This view of intelligence favors learning or mastery approach goals in which students seek challenging tasks from which they will be able to learn. These students also understand that making mistakes is part of learning. It is important to note that these students are also aware of their present ability in a particular area, just as students with an entity view of intelligence are, but the former students place less importance on demonstrating that they are smart. Instead, they use what they know about their ability as a guide in determining the strategies that would best help them achieve their goals. At this time, it is unclear how mastery avoidance goals are related to children's theories of intelligence, and research is needed to clarify this distinction.

## Developmental Differences

An interesting question that emerges concerns the relationship between effort and ability and the ways in which the perceived relationship changes as children develop. Young children see effort and ability as positively related to one another (Nicholls, 1990), but gradually they become more concerned with how their ability compares with other children's. This developmental trend begins around age 9 and continues until approximately eighth grade, at which time students have developed "adult-like" (entity theory of intelligence) views concerning the relationship between effort and ability (Nicholls, 1990).

Similarly, with respect to children's ability to differentiate ability and task difficulty, Nicholls suggested that children move through three levels: egocentric (age 3–5), objective (age 5–6), and normative (age 7). In the egocentric level, young children equate task difficulty with how difficult the task is for them to perform and do not take into consideration how difficult the task may be for other children. For example, a child who is struggling to solve a challenging puzzle would be likely to state that "puzzles are really hard," even if other children are more successful in solving the same puzzle. In the objective level, children are beginning to understand that some tasks are objectively more difficult than other tasks, but if a child experiences a failure, he or she is still likely to equate task difficulty with low ability. For example, a child who consistently fails to identify the adverbs in a set of sentences would be likely to conclude that the task is difficult *for him or her* to perform, which may lead the child to the conclusion that he or she is not smart enough to do well in school (low ability attribution). Finally, in the normative level, children understand that task difficulty is based on how difficult the task is for most children. Children at this level are able to differentiate between task difficulty and ability, such that failure on a very difficult task is not equated with low ability.

Similarly, there are age-related changes in children's intrinsic motivation. Harter (1999) found that preferences for challenge, curiosity and interest, and independent mastery all declined beginning at the third-grade level and continuing through ninth grade, whereas independent judgment and the ability of children to evaluate their own performance increased with age. As Stipek (2002) noted, students "apparently tend to become less motivated to engage in academic activities for their own pleasure, but become better able to judge the quality of their performance" (p. 135). The reasons for these declines in motivation are not clear, but as is discussed in the next section, the classroom context can positively influence students' motivation for learning.

## The Role of the Classroom Context

An important question that still remains concerns how the classroom might influence the types of goals students adopt. This question has been addressed in research on how classroom context contributes to students' achievement goals. The results from both laboratory and classroom studies suggest that it is possible to manipulate achievement goals (Ames & Archer, 1988; Elliott & Dweck, 1988; Graham & Golan, 1991). However, most of these earlier studies did not differentiate between performance approach goals and performance avoidance goals, which makes the findings more difficult to interpret in light of the revisions to the theory.

Research suggests that competitive and individualistic goal structures result in the patterns of achievement cognitions commonly associated with performance-oriented and mastery-oriented students, respectively. For example, in a study by Ames (1984), the goal structure was experimentally manipulated through the instructions given to the children. Children in the competitive structure were paired with another child and told that the goal was to try to be the winner by solving more puzzles than their partner. In the individualistic structure, children worked alone and were encouraged to try to solve as many puzzles as possible and to improve their performance on the second set of puzzles. The results indicated that children in the individualistic structure selected more effort-attribution statements and self-instruction statements than children in the competitive structure. In contrast, children in the competitive structure selected more ability-attribution statements and fewer self-instruction statements. The findings are consistent with the attributional emphasis of children who have mastery and performance goals. In a similar study, Elliott and Dweck (1988) found that children more frequently selected a mastery (learning) task when the importance of acquiring new knowledge was emphasized, but selected a performance task more often when evaluation of their skill was emphasized. When mastery goals were highlighted, the children selected more challenging tasks and were more mastery oriented in their approach, regardless of their perceived ability. When performance goals were highlighted, children were more likely to show a helpless pattern of behavior, especially in the face of difficulty.

Studies conducted in actual classrooms rather than the laboratory suggest that highlighting mastery goals in the classroom promotes increased motivation for learning. Ames and Archer (1988) found that students who perceived mastery goals to be emphasized in their classrooms reported using more effective learning strategies, selected more challenging tasks, and had more positive attitudes toward the class. Conversely, students who perceived performance goals to be emphasized had more negative attitudes toward the class as well as lower perceived ability. Similarly, Patrick, Anderman, Ryan, Edelin, and Midgley (2001) examined teacher statements and practices in four classrooms with different goal structures (high mastery—low performance, high mastery—high performance, low mastery—low performance, and low mastery—high performance). The findings from this study indicate that teachers in mastery-focused classrooms stress the importance of active learning and emphasize student involvement, effort, and interaction to a greater extent than performance-focused classrooms. Teachers in performance-focused classrooms, on the other hand, tend to emphasize grades and normative assessment of student learning to a greater extent than low performance-focused teachers.

Two studies in which goal orientation was manipulated illustrate how the social context influences information processing. Graham and Golan (1991) examined the influence of task-involving versus ego-involving instructions on children's level of cognitive processing. (Recall that task involvement is conceptually similar to having mastery goals, whereas ego involvement is similar to having performance goals.) The children who received the task-involving instructions were told that people often make mistakes when they first learn how to solve puzzles but that they usually get better at solving them over time. These children were also encouraged to see the activity as a challenge and to have fun trying to master it. Conversely, the children who received ego-involving instructions were told that the experimenter had a good idea, based on their performance, of how good they were at solving puzzles compared with other children their age. The results indicate that when a task requires deeper levels of processing, ego-involved children are likely to show poorer recall than task-involved children.

In a related study, Bryson (1993) manipulated goal value using an adapted procedure from Elliott and Dweck (1988). The children in this study were placed in three groups based on their actual school achievement: high achieving, low achieving, and low achieving with "persistent learning difficulties" (Bryson, 1993, p. 302). The results suggest that when mastery goals are highlighted, children's verbalizations tend to show more evidence of deep-processing cognitive strategies rather than surface-level cognitive strategies, regardless of achievement group.

## PROBLEMS AND IMPLICATIONS

Many teachers are frustrated in their attempts to motivate their students. They often express their frustration by saying, "My students seem so unmotivated. No matter what I do, it doesn't seem to make any difference in their motivation." As discussed in chapter 4 of this volume, "School Engagement," low student motivation is often considered to be a problem that comes from "within the child" rather than the result of the interaction of that child in his or her environment. The authors point to the need for educators to understand the influence of the classroom and school context on student engagement.

It is not surprising that tasks students see as repetitive and boring tend to lower intrinsic motivation. A consistent finding in motivation research has been that students are the most motivated when they are given moderately challenging tasks (Ames, 1992; Lepper & Hodell, 1989). But many teachers say that it is difficult to provide challenging tasks to all students because their students have very different levels of ability. This often causes teachers to tailor their assignments so that all students can complete them. The difficulty that arises from this approach is that the assignments are often seen as unchallenging by many students. Even students who are generally motivated are less likely to feel motivated when the tasks are too easy. It is when students are not challenged that behavior problems also tend to surface, which often causes teachers to rely more on rewards and punishments to maintain control in the classroom. These rewards and punishments, although effective in maintaining control, often work to lower intrinsic motivation. The result is that students engage in academic tasks only to earn some external reward or to avoid some type of punishment.

Another aspect of academic tasks that often lowers intrinsic motivation is a task's lack of relevancy to the students, also described as the utility value of the task. A task's utility value is the extent to which the task is seen as instrumental in helping students reach some long-term goal (Wigfield & Eccles, 2000). When academic tasks have low utility value for a student, the student is likely to say, "I will never need to know this. Why should I learn it?"

Although many academic tasks seem uninteresting to students, it is often difficult for teachers to know how to make the material interesting. Impressing upon students that they will need this information in the future often increases the utility value associated with the task, but it does not guarantee that the task will be more interesting. Classroom practices that emphasize social comparison, especially as it relates to students' ability, also frequently reduce the focus on mastery goals. For example, posting the top scorers or a grade distribution encourages social comparisons of ability. This shifts the focus from mastery to performance goals, because how much students are learning becomes less important than how well they are doing compared with other students. Whereas many teachers believe that a little "healthy competition" is helpful to students, there is evidence that these practices can be devastating to the child who consistently finds himself or herself at the bottom of the distribution (Covington, 1998). Students who constantly receive feedback that they have low ability come to believe that no matter how hard they try it will not make a difference. This can result in the helpless behavior pattern described earlier in this chapter.

The way in which teachers attribute the causes of their students' successes and failures also affects students' self-perceptions of ability. Graham (1991) found that students make inferences about ability and effort based on how the teacher responds to their failures. When teachers react with pity toward students who fail, those students are likely to infer that the teacher believes they have low ability. However, when a teacher reacts with frustration or anger, students are likely to infer that the teacher is attributing the cause of failure to a lack of effort. These attributional inferences are important because ability (aptitude) is considered an internal, stable, uncontrollable cause, whereas effort (temporary exertion) is considered to be an internal, unstable, controllable cause.

Because these attributions are related to mastery and performance goals, students with mastery goals are more likely to emphasize the importance of effort, whereas students with performance goals are more likely to emphasize the importance of ability. The role that teachers play is very important, because if students come to believe that their success depends on how smart they are (ability attribution), they are more likely to adopt performance goals. However, students who come to believe that the key to academic success is effort (effort attribution) are more likely to adopt mastery goals.

With respect to authority in the classroom, there is evidence that practices perceived by students as controlling tend to lower intrinsic motivation, whereas practices that promote student autonomy tend to increase intrinsic motivation (Ames, 1992). Students see themselves as being the *origin* when they have some control over what happens to them in the classroom, but they see themselves as *pawns* when they are subjected to a great deal of control (Ryan & Deci, 2000). Although it is becoming clear that controlling strategies lower intrinsic motivation, recent research demonstrates that parents and teachers favor controlling classroom techniques to motivate children (Boggiano & Katz, 1991). One common use of a controlling strategy occurs when external rewards are used to control students' behavior, for example, when teachers say things such as, "If you complete your worksheets, you will be able to go to recess early." Many teachers (and parents) consider this technique to be effective because it seems that the students are working hard to complete the task. The problem with these kinds of controlling strategies is that they tend to promote increased interest in the reward and decreased interest in the academic task (Boggiano, 1998).

The reason interest in the task decreases is that engaging in the academic task becomes a means to an end. Thus, the students are doing their work not because they want to learn, but because it will lead to some external reward. Another problem is that rewards tend to increase motivation only as long as the possibility for additional rewards exists. When the rewards are not present, students often lack the motivation to engage in the task for its own sake. However, the detrimental effects of rewards are most pronounced when students are already intrinsically motivated. When students are not intrinsically motivated, rewards can have positive effects, especially when the rewards are used to convey information to the student (Pierce, Cameron, Banko, & So, 2003). For example, verbal praise generally increases intrinsic motivation, especially when it provides specific information to students about their performance.

## ALTERNATIVE ACTIONS FOR PREVENTION AND INTERVENTION

This section provides six basic recommendations for addressing the motivation problems discussed in this chapter. Following these recommendations, a useful framework, TARGET (Task, Authority, Recognition, Grouping, Evaluation, and Time), is presented for helping teachers apply the recommendations for motivating academic achievement.

## Basic Recommendations for Motivating Academic Achievement

***1. Provide challenging tasks for students with different ability levels.*** This can be accomplished by designing activities with a variety of difficulty levels. For example, an assignment might have some problems that are relatively easy, some that are moderately difficult, and some that are quite difficult. Using this assignment, a teacher might say to students, "Some of the problems at the end of this assignment are really hard, so don't worry if you can't solve them yet. You know how to do the problems at the beginning of the assignment, so practice on those first. Then just try some of the harder problems. You might just surprise yourself." The purpose of these kinds of assignments is to provide challenging problems to all students but also to make sure that students who are struggling do not feel bad if they are not immediately able to complete the more difficult problems.

***2. Emphasize the utility value of the learning.*** To increase the utility value of academic tasks, teachers should think about the ways in which the information might be relevant to their students' lives. This can be done by using problems that reflect real situations students might encounter rather than problems that have no apparent relevance. For example, asking students to calculate the area of a rectangle is likely to be viewed as less useful than asking students to measure the dimensions of their bedroom so that they can then calculate what it would cost to have new carpet installed.

Another way to increase utility value is to find out about the students' interests and goals and incorporate them into lessons. This approach is used in many classrooms where students are encouraged to write about topics that are interesting and relevant (Oldfather, 1993). After writing and editing, students often spend the time to illustrate their stories before they are "published," thus making their experiences in art class relevant to their interests as well. The approach differs from more traditional approaches in which all of the students read and write about the same topics. The advantage of this approach is that it increases the utility value of reading and writing for the students and also allows them to make choices, which increases intrinsic motivation.

***3. Use novel or unexpected tasks to promote interest.*** This can be difficult because it requires not only a strong grasp of the content but also creative thinking on the part of teachers about how to present the material in new and innovative ways. Despite the difficulty of the method, thinking about how to make something interesting to students is fundamentally important in increasing intrinsic motivation. Hidi (1990) described interesting information as something that is "novel or unusual, has characters or life themes with which readers can identify, and/or involves high activity or intensity level" (p. 557). Although it is difficult to make every academic task extremely interesting to all students, it is possible for teachers to present the material in ways that might interest their students. A classic example of the use of the unexpected is when a history teacher comes to class dressed as the person being discussed that day. The students do not expect this and therefore are intrigued by the novel approach. Of course, simply dressing and acting as a famous historical figure does not guarantee students' learning. The lesson must also be pedagogically sound such that the teacher conveys accurate and meaningful information about the historical figure.

Providing students with hands-on experiences or framing problems in interesting ways are two additional strategies likely to increase intrinsic motivation. For example, a particularly creative teacher in Delaware taught her students geometry during the World Cup Soccer tournament by illustrating how knowledge of angles helped soccer players score more goals.

***4. Minimize classroom practices that emphasize competition among students.*** Although many teachers believe that competition will help motivate students, the problem with competitive practices is that they highlight ability rather than effort. Consequently, students who have improved greatly, but who are still behind their classmates, fail to receive the encouragement necessary to keep trying because they continue to see themselves at the bottom of the distribution. Rather than emphasizing how students compare with one another, self-competition allows students to compete with themselves to see how much they have improved over their previous performance. This allows students to feel good about their academic gains, without the burden of being compared with other students. Self-competition is also much less likely to result in the pattern of learned helplessness discussed earlier in this chapter, because the students understand that their effort, rather than their ability relative to other students, has resulted in their academic gains.

Another way to minimize the emphasis on competition among students is through the use of cooperative learning techniques (see chapter 48, "Peer-Assisted Learning Strategies"). These techniques allow students of all ability levels to work together toward some common goal (Slavin, 1995). Cooperative learning also helps students focus more on the effort needed to accomplish the goal and less on their ability relative to other students in the class.

***5. Emphasize that failures are due to lack of effort or ineffective strategy use.*** Emphasizing that failures result from the student's lack of effort or from ineffective strategy use reinforces an incremental rather than an entity view of intelligence. The strategy attribution is especially important for students with learning disabilities because they are often working very hard and still having trouble in school (Borkowski, Carr, Rellinger, & Pressley, 1990). To continue to tell these students that they need to try even harder may cause them to give up and begin exhibiting the learned helplessness pattern of attributing failures to low ability. For these students, the importance of strategy use should be emphasized, because attributing a failure to ineffective strategy use allows them to remain optimistic that, with the right strategy, they can be successful in the future.

***6. Provide students with opportunities to participate in instructional decisions.*** To increase intrinsic motivation, teachers should provide students with opportunities to participate in instructional decisions. This does not mean that students should be given the ability to do as they please, but rather that they be part of the decision-making process. For example, many classrooms have class rules that the students are expected to follow. Instead of the teacher giving these rules to the students, which is often perceived by students as controlling, it is better if teachers can allow the students to help come up with these rules (and also the consequences of not following the rules). Not only do the students feel more autonomous, they are also more likely to follow the rules if they helped establish them in the first place.

## The TARGET Framework

The TARGET framework refers to tasks, authority, recognition, grouping, evaluation, and time. Ames (1992) extended the TARGET framework originally proposed by Epstein (1989) to schools and also integrated achievement goal theory (see also Maehr and Midgley, 1991). The framework provides a way to integrate the strategies presented in the previous section by helping teachers structure the classroom context in ways that promote mastery approach goals and minimize performance avoidance goals.

***Task.*** The most motivating learning tasks are meaningful for students, reflect the students' interests, and are moderately challenging for all students (Ames, 1992). As Brophy (2004) noted, rather than using tests, grades, or extrinsic rewards, teachers should design activities to maximize their intrinsic appeal and to help students appreciate the value of what they are learning. To ensure that academic tasks are challenging for all students, teachers also should help students set challenging goals for themselves and monitor their progress toward achieving their goals.

***Authority.*** To promote mastery approach goals in the classroom, teachers must share authority with students. Teachers give students the opportunity to participate in the decision making that takes place in the classroom, which in turn helps students develop responsibility and independence (Ames, 1992; Bear, 2005).

***Recognition.*** Teachers should recognize students for their individual academic progress by emphasizing how each student has improved over time, rather than compared with the performance of other students. In this way the accomplishments of *all* students are recognized, not just the high achieving students. Furthermore, most recognition of student progress should be done privately rather than by "public celebration of the accomplishments of the highest achievers" (Brophy, 2004, p. 105).

***Grouping.*** Grouping allows teachers to create learning communities that promote the social construction of knowledge. Group assignments should be varied and can be formed on the basis of friendships, common interests, and, when appropriate, by achievement level. The emphasis should be on cooperation rather than competition between groups (Brophy, 2004).

***Evaluation.*** Evaluation of student learning should focus on the student's individual improvement, with an emphasis on their progress and effort. Teachers should also encourage students to view making mistakes as an important part of learning, rather than as an indication of failure (Ames, 1992).

***Time.*** The use of flexible scheduling provides increased opportunities for students to engage in meaningful learning activities and to exercise their autonomy in making decisions about how best to spend their time engaged in these activities (Brophy, 2004). Motivation is increased when students are given additional time to complete their work, especially when the task is complex.

## SUMMARY

Teachers can look for ways to increase the intrinsic motivation of students by shifting the emphasis away from practices that involve competition among students. Although such practices are prevalent in schools today, they often cause students to see engaging in academic tasks as a means to end, rather than an end in itself. The TARGET framework provides an integrated approach to promoting mastery goals in the classroom. The framework includes emphasizing tasks and activities that increase students' interest and motivation for learning, sharing authority between teachers and students, recognizing students for their accomplishments, and providing meaningful evaluation of students' work. The use of rewards can also promote student motivation, especially when the rewards are used to reinforce appropriate academic and social behavior (Akin-Little, Eckert, Lovett, and Little, 2004). Though earlier research suggested detrimental effects from the use of rewards, recent research suggests that rewards may have a positive effect on motivation. Thus, integrating the appropriate use of rewards within the TARGET framework may provide optimal motivation for learning.

## RECOMMENDED RESOURCES

### Books and Other Printed Material

Ames, C. (1992). Classrooms: Goals, structures, and student motivation. *Journal of Educational Psychology, 84,* 261–271.

This seminal article provides a synthesis of the research on achievement motivation and also discusses how the classroom environment might influence students' goals. The framework discussed in this chapter is elaborated in more detail in this article, with an emphasis on instructional strategies that promote mastery goals in the classroom.

Brophy, J. (2004). *Motivating students to learn* (2nd ed.). Boston: McGraw-Hill.

This book does an excellent job of discussing the motivation of students. The second edition has been greatly expanded and includes an extensive review of the major theories of motivation, together with many practical classroom applications for motivating students.

Pintrich, P. R., & Schunk, D. H. (2002). *Motivation in education: Theory, research, and applications* (2nd ed.). Englewood Cliffs, NJ: Merrill/Prentice Hall.

The second edition of this textbook on motivation provides a comprehensive review of the major theories of motivation and also provides classroom applications of these theories. The book represents one of the most complete references on motivation in education.

Stipek, D. J. (2002). *Motivation to learn: Integrating theory and practice* (4th ed.). Needham, MA: Allyn & Bacon.

This textbook does an excellent job of making motivation theories understandable. The classroom applications of these theories are particularly helpful, especially for elementary school teachers.

### Websites

*http://www.apa.org/ed/lcp.html#Background*

This website from the American Psychological Association represents more than a century of research on teaching and learning. The 14 learner-centered psychological principles provide a framework for dialogue on current educational reform and school redesign efforts. The three principles that focus on motivation include motivational and emotional influences on learning, intrinsic motivation to learn, and the effects of motivation on effort.

*http://www.kidsource.com/kidsource/content2/Student_Motivatation.html*

KidSource OnLine is a website created by a group of parents who want to help parents and caregivers take greater responsibility for their children's health and education by providing up-to-date information and resources. Several links to student motivation within the website provide an excellent overview of students' motivation to learn.

## REFERENCES


Akin-Little, K. A., Eckert, T. L., Lovett, B. J., & Little, S. G. (2004). Extrinsic reinforcement in the classroom: Bribery or best practice. *School Psychology Review, 33*(3), 344–362.

Ames, C. (1984). Achievement attributions and self-instructions under competitive and individualistic goal structures. *Journal of Educational Psychology, 76,* 478–487.

Ames, C. (1992). Classrooms: Goals, structures, and student motivation. *Journal of Educational Psychology, 84,* 261–271.

Ames, C., & Archer, J. (1988). Achievement goals in the classroom: Students' learning strategies and motivation processes. *Journal of Educational Psychology, 80,* 260–267.

Anderman, E. M., & Maehr, M. L. (1994). Motivation and schooling in middle grades. *Review of Educational Research, 64,* 287–309.

Bear, G. G. (with Cavalier, A., & Manning, M. A.). (2005). *Developing self-discipline and preventing and correcting misbehavior.* Boston: Allyn & Bacon.

Boggiano, A. K. (1998). Maladaptive achievement patterns: A test of a diathesis-stress analysis of helplessness. *Journal of Personality and Social Psychology, 74,* 1681–1695.

Boggiano, A., & Katz, P. (1991). Maladaptive achievement patterns in students: The role of teachers' controlling strategies. *Journal of Social Issues, 47,* 35–51.

Borkowski, J. G., Carr, M., Rellinger, E., & Pressley, M. (1990). Self-regulated cognition: Interdependence of metacognition, attributions and self-esteem. In B. F. Jones & L. Idol (Eds.), *Dimensions of thinking and cognitive instruction* (pp. 54–92). Hillsdale, NJ: Erlbaum.

Brophy, J. (2004). *Motivating students to learn* (2nd ed.). Boston: McGraw-Hill.

Bryson, M. (1993). "School-based epistemologies"?: Exploring conceptions of how, what and why students know. *Learning Disability Quarterly, 16,* 299–315.

Cameron, J., & Pierce, W. D. (1994). Reinforcement, reward, and intrinsic motivation: A meta analysis. *Review of Educational Research, 64,* 363–423.

Covington, M. V. (1998). *The will to learn: A guide for motivating young people.* New York: Cambridge University Press.

Dweck, C. S., & Leggett, E. L. (1988). A social-cognitive approach to motivation and personality. *Psychological Review, 95,* 256–273.

Elliot, A. J., & McGregor, H. (2001). A 2 × 2 achievement goal framework. *Journal of Personality and Social Psychology, 80,* 501–519.

Elliott, E. S., & Dweck, C. S. (1988). Goals: An approach to motivation and achievement. *Journal of Personality and Social Psychology, 54,* 5–12.

Epstein, J. (1989). Family structure and student motivation: A developmental perspective. In C. Ames & R. Ames (Eds.), *Research on motivation in education* (Vol. 3, pp. 259–295). San Diego, CA: Academic Press.

Graham, S. (1991). A review of attribution theory in achievement contexts. *Educational Psychology Review, 3,* 5–39.

Graham, S., & Golan, S. (1991). Motivational influences on cognition: Task involvement, ego involvement, and depth of information processing. *Journal of Educational Psychology, 83,* 187–194.

Grant, H., & Dweck, C. S. (2003). Clarifying achievement goals and their impact. *Journal of Personality and Social Psychology, 85,* 541–553.

Harackiewicz, J. M., Barron, K. E., & Elliot, A. J. (1998). Rethinking achievement goals: When are they adaptive for college students and why? *Educational Psychologist, 33,* 1–21.

Harter, S. (1999). *The construction of the self: A developmental perspective.* New York: Guilford Press.

Hidi, S. (1990). Interest and its contribution as a mental resource for learning. *Review of Educational Research, 60,* 549–571.

Lepper, M. R., & Hodell, M. (1989). Intrinsic motivation in the classroom. In C. Ames & R. Ames (Eds.), *Research on motivation in education* (Vol. 3, pp. 73–105). San Diego, CA: Academic Press.

Maehr, M. L., & Midgley, C. (1991). Enhancing student motivation: A schoolwide approach. *Educational Psychologist, 26,* 399–427.

Middleton, M. J., & Midgley, C. (1997). Avoiding the demonstration of lack of ability: An underexplored aspect of goal theory. *Journal of Educational Psychology, 89,* 710–718.

Nicholls, J. G. (1989). *The competitive ethos and democratic education.* Cambridge, MA: Harvard University Press.

Nicholls, J. G. (1990). What is ability and why are we mindful of it? A developmental perspective. In R. Sternberg & J. Kolligan (Eds.), *Competence considered* (pp. 11–40). New Haven, CT: Yale University Press.

Oldfather, P. (1993). What students say about motivating experiences in a whole language classroom. *Reading Teacher, 46,* 672–681.

Patrick, H., Anderman, L. H., Ryan, A. M., Edelin, K. C., & Midgley, C. (2001). Teachers' communication of goal orientations in four fifth-grade classrooms. *Elementary School Journal, 102,* 35–58.

Pierce, W. D., Cameron, J., Banko, K. M., & So, S. (2003). Positive effects of rewards and performance standards on intrinsic motivation. *Psychological Record, 53,* 561–579.

Pintrich, P. R. (2000). Multiple goals, multiple pathways: The role of goal orientation in learning and achievement. *Journal of Educational Psychology, 92,* 544–555.

Pintrich, P. R., & Schunk, D. H. (2002). *Motivation in education: Theory, research, and applications* (2nd ed.). Englewood Cliffs, NJ: Merrill/Prentice Hall.

Ryan, R. M., & Deci, E. L. (2000). Intrinsic and extrinsic motivations: Classic definitions and new directions. *Contemporary Educational Psychology, 25,* 54–67.

Slavin, R. E. (1995). *Cooperative learning: Theory, research and practice* (2nd ed.). Boston: Allyn & Bacon.

Stipek, D. J. (2002). *Motivation to learn: Integrating theory and practice* (4th ed.). Needham, MA: Allyn & Bacon.

Urdan, T. (1997). Achievement goal theory: Past results, future directions. In M. L. Maehr & P. R. Pintrich (Eds.), *Advances in motivation and achievement* (Vol. 10, pp. 99–141). Greenwich, CT: JAI Press.

Weiner, B. (1986). *An attributional theory of achievement motivation and emotion.* New York: Springer-Verlag.

Weiner, B. (2000). Intrapersonal and interpersonal theories of motivation from an attributional perspective. *Educational Psychology Review, 12,* 1–14.

Wigfield, A., & Eccles, J. (2000). Expectancy-value theory of achievement motivation. *Contemporary Educational Psychology, 27,* 552–565.

Wolters, C., Yu, S., & Pintrich, P. R. (1996). The relation between goal orientation and students' motivational beliefs and self-regulated learning. *Learning and Individual Differences, 8,* 211–238.

# 34
# Giftedness

**Carolyn M. Callahan**
*University of Virginia*

## BACKGROUND AND DEVELOPMENT

The population of gifted children brings a unique set of characteristics and needs to schools. Gifted students are traditionally viewed as being able to succeed on their own. Hence, school personnel often do not recognize or respond to the traits that suggest that differentiated curricula and instructional strategies, programs, and support systems may be needed. These approaches are often necessary for maximizing potential and avoiding the problems that may surface if the family and schools do not recognize and provide for the differences gifted students manifest. Being a gifted child or adolescent is sometimes a double-edged sword. On the one hand, being gifted is obviously characterized by many learning characteristics that are deemed highly desirable. On the other hand, with those traits come a variety of potential inhibitors to achieving high potential. For example, the high expectations that others hold for the gifted child and adolescent may translate into stress or perfectionism. Or the traits of advanced vocabulary, knowledge, and language skills may result in isolation from peers who view the student as too different. Or boredom with the regular curriculum may result in acting out behavior or underachievement.

That little is done in America's classrooms to address the learning needs of the gifted student has been repeatedly documented. Many gifted and talented students receive little differentiation of curriculum and instruction and spend a great deal of time in school in activities geared toward teaching them what they already know, understand, and are able to do (Archambault et al., 1993; Moon, Callahan, Tomlinson, & Miller, 2002). Even in subject areas such as reading, where grouping has been a long-standing instructional practice, classroom teachers often fail to challenge talented readers (Reis et al., 2003). Common reasons for lack of attention to the needs of gifted students in schools include beliefs about the gifted students and educational values—"They will make it on their own." "Those who are already 'blessed' should not be provided with even more advantages and opportunities to excel." Also, teachers may lack the skill and knowledge of ways to effectively differentiate instruction. Finally, teachers are under increased pressure to "bring the bottom up," or raise test scores of the lowest achieving students (Moon, Brighton, & Callahan, 2003; Reis et al., 2003).

### Definitions of Key Concepts and Terms

***Giftedness.*** Definitions of giftedness offered in the literature are highly varied. Most states and school districts use the following definition, or a variation thereof, from the Javits Gifted and Talented Education Act (U.S. Department of Education, 1993). Although this federal act provides funding of programs for the gifted, the federal government does not mandate services for gifted students.

> Children and youth with outstanding talent perform or show the potential for performing at remarkably high levels of accomplishment when compared with others of their age, experience or environment.
>
> These children and youth exhibit high performance capability in intellectual, creative, and/or artistic areas, possess an unusual leadership capacity, or excel in specific academic fields. They require services or activities not ordinarily provided by the schools.
>
> Outstanding talents are present in children and youth from all cultural groups, across all economic strata, and in all areas of human endeavor. (p. 3)

Schools that adopt this definition may embrace the full spectrum of types of giftedness included in this definition or choose to identify and provide services for a very narrow range of giftedness (e.g., only intellectual ability, specified as students with high scores on intelligence tests or some combination of high scores on intelligence tests and language or mathematics achievement tests). Or a school district may elect to adopt a definition that includes students with talent in music and art, underachieving gifted students, or gifted students who also have a learning disability.

Several other definitions of giftedness have emerged from critical analyses of the federal definition. The most widely discussed and adopted alternative is the three-ring definition (Renzulli, 1978), which gained acceptance in conjunction with its relationship to a particular model for curricular modification, the Enrichment Triad Model (Renzulli, 1977). In this definition, giftedness is a confluence of the traits of above-average ability, task commitment, and creativity in a particular area of endeavor. Although above-average ability is considered a stable trait, the other two traits are tied to particular times and experiences in the students' lives, and accordingly, Renzulli calls for the identification of gifted behaviors rather than gifted persons.

Conceptions of intelligence offered by Sternberg (1988; Sternberg & Clinkenbeard, 1994) and Gardner (1983) have also been used as a basis for other definitions of giftedness. Sternberg has demonstrated that students whose curriculum is matched to exceptional ability in one of the three areas of intelligence in his theory (analytic, synthetic, or practical) demonstrate greater achievement than those whose curriculum is not matched. Gardner's multifaceted conception of intelligence has received extensive attention, but assessments and curricular interventions have not been validated. Each of these conceptions broadens the concept of giftedness to include more types of giftedness, and districts that adopt these definitions are more likely to serve more diverse populations of gifted students. However, even when programs are provided for a wide range of students, there are likely to be issues that surface for individual gifted students.

***Creativity as giftedness.*** Considerable attention has been given to creativity as one dimension of the federal definition of giftedness, as one of the areas of intelligence identified by Sternberg, and as one of the factors critical to the manifestation of giftedness as defined by Renzulli. Both the assessment of individual differences in creativity and the modifiability of creativity through instruction are part of an ongoing debate. The debate begins with the ways the literature has variously defined creativity as (a) part of the thinking process, (b) a personality variable, or (c) reflected by the ideas or creations of the individual. Accordingly, measurement of differences among school-age children and adults has resulted in the creation of measurement tools ranging from personality tests to evaluations of the processes and products of creative productivity.

***Talent.*** At times talent or academic talent is used as a synonym for giftedness. In the past decade a sense that the term *gifted* carries negative connotations has sometimes led educators to substitute the word academic talent. In other cases, the term talent is used to refer to students with exceptional abilities in nonacademic areas such as art, music, or drama. Tannenbaum (1985) has cautioned strongly against using the phrase "gifted and talented" or separating these two categories because of the danger that it will lead to differential values and favoritism toward some children over others.

***Prodigy.*** Prodigies are defined by researchers as children age 10 or younger who already are performing at an adult professional's level of skill in a cognitively complex area. Prodigies have been identified only in chess, music, creative writing, languages, and mathematics (Feldman, 1979, 1991). Their talents lie in areas in which other developmental factors or time and life experiences are not necessary for performance at the exceptional adult level. Although prodigies constitute only a very small segment of the total gifted population, the public image of giftedness is often associated with this extraordinary early performance—unfortunately resulting in dismissal of the needs of other gifted students.

***Highly gifted or genius.*** Stratification of the gifted population into categories such as highly gifted or genius stems from the use of the IQ score as a determinant of giftedness. The early studies by Hollingsworth (1942) and later writings of Gross (1993) on children whose IQ scores exceeded 140 were the basis of the use of this term. Though this group is characterized by extraordinary school performance, the danger of more severe social and emotional problems resulting from being even more different from peers than those identified as "*moderately gifted*" has also been noted.

## Developmental Aspects of Giftedness

Discussion of the primary developmental concerns associated with the development of prodigies should be separated from discussion of the development of the rest of the gifted population. Research (e.g., Feldman, 1991, 1994) indicates that the child prodigy does not generally differ from the general population of gifted students in overall IQ score. Moreover, the few prodigies that have been systematically studied have tended to perform at age-appropriate levels in logic, role taking, spatial reasoning, and moral judgment. The conclusion reached by Feldman based on his work and that of others is that prodigious performance is domain specific rather than a generalized endowment, and particular biological and psychological factors, environmental factors (family, societal, and cultural), and historical factors must all come together for prodigies to emerge developmentally (coincidence theory).

The very young age at which prodigious development occurs and patterns of instruction and behavior associated with development of the prodigious talent may lead to social and emotional issues for these children. The first is the isolation and consequent difficulty in developing peer relationships that result from the prodigy's intrinsic drive to master his or her domain of interest. Long hours of solitary practice or involvement with a very small group of similar prodigies may limit friendship opportunities and bonds. Very intense parental involvement in the development of the prodigy may result in a longer period of dependency and difficulties in becoming an independent adolescent and adult.

Prodigies make up only a very small proportion of students in the gifted population. The educational and developmental approach used for the general gifted population will depend on the definition of giftedness that is adopted and the subpopulations within the school that are considered. For example, students with very high general intellectual ability manifested across many domains and those with very advanced specific abilities (including those in the arts) can be viably identified at the preschool or kindergarten level because children at that age already exhibit patterns of extraordinary behaviors (not specifically taught facts and skills). Characteristics that are indicative of intellectual or academic giftedness are presented in Table 1. These characteristics may be exhibited across many areas of school performance or they may manifest themselves in only one area.

Although early identification is possible in some cases, developmental factors, including opportunity and maturity, clearly result in later manifestations of giftedness in other students. Furthermore, the manifestation of giftedness in populations of poor or minority students may be influenced by cultural and environmental influences that reduce exposure to experiences that enhance talent development. Hence, if students from at-risk populations—that is, some populations of minority students, students for whom English is a second language, and students at-risk because of conditions of poverty—are to develop the behaviors that characterize giftedness, they may need to be given specific opportunities in classrooms that parallel those that traditional students have in their homes or preschools. School staff may also need very specific examples of ways the behaviors that are characteristic of gifted students may be manifested in these at-risk students.

## Factors That Contribute to Normal Growth and Development

As with all students, the development of gifted students is a result of the interaction between innate abilities and the environment. Bloom (1985) and Csikszentmihalyi, Rathunde, and Whalen (1993) isolated family, school, and peer factors that enhance or inhibit both the intellectual and the affective development of gifted students. They found the following:

1. Potential talents were recognized early, cultivated, and nurtured. At home, in the early stages of talent development, the parents were child oriented and stressed doing one's best and achieving. They modeled a work ethic, and although children were expected to share household chores, they did not have to expend unreasonable time or energy in those chores. Family routines were structured to give students responsibilities and help them become self-disciplined.
2. Family support and challenge enhanced development of talent. Where family context was perceived as complex (both integrated and differentiated), talented teens spent more time on homework and were more goal directed.
3. Emphasis in the family was on excellence, hard work, and constructive use of time.
4. Talent development was easier for children who shared active and challenging pursuits with friends (e.g., hobbies or studying rather than just socializing or hanging out).
5. In early stages of talent development, teachers made initial learning pleasant and rewarding, with much playful activity and reinforcement for small gains. They were rarely critical, but they set standards, expected progress, and quickly rewarded steps toward reaching success. They set tasks to be accomplished that were just beyond the student's zone of proximal

**Table 1** *Characteristics of Intellectually or Academically Gifted Students*

- Displays early language development and uses language fluently and with unusual analogies, similes, and metaphors.
- Uses advanced vocabulary for age.
- Has a large knowledge base, excellent memory, and a large store of information.
- Exhibits superior analytic ability and advanced logical reasoning.
- Has keen observational skills.
- Learns rapidly and easily.
- Exercises superior problem-solving skills, thinks of many solutions to everyday problems, and is able to delay closure in problem solving.
- Manipulates symbol systems easily.
- Makes efficient use of strategies for learning.
- Applies knowledge, skills, and understanding to new situations; generalizes from specific to general principles easily.
- Thinks abstractly and understands complex ideas at an earlier age.
- Shows extraordinary insight.
- Exhibits great concentration and long attention span in areas of challenge and interest; becomes intensely involved in activities of his or her own choosing.
- Sees patterns and relationships easily.
- Has unusual curiosity and asks questions.
- Creates original solutions to problems.
- Thinks independently.
- Displays an advanced sense of justice and extraordinary idealism.
- Understands cause and effect, draws conclusions, and makes decisions from complex data.
- Has high energy.
- Thinks metacognitively (thinks about thinking).
- Is likely to be an early reader.

*Note.* Characteristics may be displayed across one or more disciplines or talent areas. The characteristics are synthesized from *Bringing Out the Giftedness in Your Child*, by R. Dunn, K. Dunn, and D. J. Treffinger, 1992, New York: Wiley; and *Education of the Gifted and Talented* (4th ed.), by G. A. Davis and S. B. Rimm, 1998, Needham Heights, MA: Allyn & Bacon.

development and helped students reach the goals and correct flaws in performance. Helping students grasp larger patterns and underlying processes in the subject area was paralleled by encouraging discovery of the "big ideas" of the discipline.

6. As talent developed, students required interactions with and instruction from teachers who were more expert. Teachers expected high levels of attainment, emphasized precision and excellence in the talent area, and helped students set short- and long-term goals.
7. In the later years of talent development, students needed master teachers who conveyed that the option of studying with them meant that the student would "go far" in the given field of study. They raised demands and expectations constantly. For students who were to become notable in their achievement, these teachers raised those expectations until it was clearly communicated that the student was expected to do what had never been done before (set Olympic records, solve heretofore unsolved math problems, etc.). Finally, these teachers conveyed that real learning was based on doing what experts in the field do.

## PROBLEMS AND IMPLICATIONS

Most often, academically or intellectually gifted students are viewed as ideal students because of the ease with which they master the curriculum. Most gifted students do succeed in school and experience few social or emotional problems or issues (Robinson, Reis, Neihart, & Moon, 2002). However, even traits that present themselves as positive in the profiles of many gifted students may translate into negative behaviors if parents and schools do not respond to the unique challenges their needs present. Whereas the resilience of gifted students is enhanced by their remarkable problem-solving ability, that resilience alone may be insufficient to result in both fulfillment of potential and normal development and adjustment. When social and emotional problems present themselves, they are frequently the result of family issues or the lack of appropriate curricular and school modifications. There is ample evidence that such modifications are often not in place in schools or are poorly implemented (Colangelo, Assouline, & Gross, 2004). Table 2 provides examples of ways in which gifted students' positive characteristics *may* present specific challenges to those students when the needs that emanate from those characteristics are not addressed.

### The Underachieving Gifted Student

Perhaps the greatest enigma to parents, teachers, counselors, and psychologists (and perhaps to the gifted student) is underachievement. The underachiever is defined and recognized in many ways, but all conceptions of underachievement include a discrepancy between some measure of potential and current performance (on achievement tests or in the classroom). Reis and McCoach (2002) categorized the factors identified as potential causes of underachievement as environmental or within the individual. Primary among environmental factors are unchallenging classroom learning tasks. Boredom with school and insufficient challenge often result in lack of interest and motivation. Pressure to be like everyone else, especially in early adolescence (and especially among females and minorities), is another common environmental factor and may lead to hiding one's abilities and achieving only at the level of peer expectations. Family dynamics also have received considerable attention in the literature, and researchers have associated underachievement with expectations that are too low or too high, overindulgence of the student, and unclear messages (Rimm, 1986). Factors within the individual include internalizing problems such as depression, anxiety, perfectionism, failure-avoidance, low self-esteem, and externalization problems such as rebelliousness, irritability, nonconformity, anger, or unrecognized learning deficits.

## The Perfectionist Gifted Child

In the study of perfectionism in gifted students, the distinction is often made between *normal*, or enabling perfectionistic behaviors, and *neurotic*, or disabling perfectionism (Bransky, Jenkins-Friedman, & Murphy, 1987; Hamachek, 1978). Some researchers conclude that gifted students as a group are perfectionistic, that on average they are more perfectionistic than average-ability peers, and that this behavior can be a positive force in their achievement. However, for other researchers, perfectionism is always a negative construct, and the exaggerated form of this behavior may lead to immobilization accompanied by depression, nagging self-doubt, shame, and self-deprecation (Hamachek, 1978). For gifted students, the experience of always having the right answer and always being the one from whom much is expected may result in an internalization of unrealistic self-expectations, intense self-scrutiny, and then self-doubt and self-criticism when those expectations cannot be met. As a result, students may internalize a need to present perfect products regardless of the task, the time, the resource parameters, or the expectations of others. At early ages this may manifest itself in the recopying and reediting of exemplary products, disappointment in final products even after maximum effort has been expended, refusal to submit products because of beliefs that the product fails to meet standards, and so forth. The development of these behaviors over time may lead to underachievement. That is, perfectionistic students decide (consciously or unconsciously) that it is better to fail by not trying, and thus not completing or submitting work, rather than to be judged as less than perfect (see chapter 23, "Perfectionism").

Many strategies have been suggested for addressing perfectionism, but empirical research on the effectiveness of these strategies is lacking. Key recommendations focus on the roles of teachers, parents, counselors, and psychologists in respecting healthy perfectionism and helping gifted students to understand that wanting to achieve at a high level is admirable, but that learning to set priorities, taking time to reflect on the value of learning from mistakes, relaxing, and pursuing one's passion with joy also are important. Helping students see setbacks as learning opportunities rather than failure, praising students for their efforts rather than for being smart, and encouraging them to focus on areas important to themselves are critical intervention steps (Schuler, 2002).

## The Socially Isolated Gifted Child

One potential issue for gifted students is becoming socially isolated. The subtleties of this issue are rooted in being "different" and either adjusting and coping appropriately or failing to find ways to establish suitable relationships. A critical factor to recognize before exploring this issue is that imposition of traditional notions of social isolation on gifted students may be artificial. First, one must explore whether the only satisfactory relationships for gifted students are age peers. In some cases, the advanced thinking, reasoning, and performance in the talent domain will place them in situations in which they may relate regularly in a very satisfactory way with older students or even adults who are similar to them. The many cases of radically accelerated students who develop such relationships and suffer no regrets for not having age peer relationships illustrate the satisfactory adjustment of these students. A second question may be whether gifted students are satisfied with a small group of close friends rather than a larger cadre of acquaintances.

However, when gifted students are unable to establish social relationships with either intellectual or age

**Table 2** *Characteristics of Gifted Children as They Relate to Issues and Difficulties These Children May Face*

| Differentiating Characteristics | Possible Issues or Problems |
|---|---|
| Extraordinary ability to absorb and retain information. | Bored in class, impatient with classmates, possibly resulting in socially isolating behavior. |
| Advanced understanding of complex concepts and ideas for age level; unusual capacity for processing information. | Unable to "suffer fools gladly," which is isolating socially; considered sassy or smart-alecky, resulting in poor interpersonal relationships. Bored with regular curriculum and repetition of already understood concepts, maybe resulting in unwillingness to engage in classroom tasks and assignments. |
| Unusually varied interests and curiosity and heightened capacity for seeing unusual and diverse relationships. | Tendency to take on too many projects at the same time, maybe leading to not completing tasks; inability to conform to routine tasks, maybe leading to disruptive classroom behavior. |
| High level of verbal behavior; high level of language development. | May dominate discussions; may be perceived as a showoff; may be perceived by teachers as negative and disruptive because of constant questioning; may use verbalization to rationalize inappropriate behavior or to avoid difficult thinking tasks or expressions of emotions. |
| Flexible thought processes. | Resistance to authority and to rules for completing tasks. |
| Extraordinary ability to see unusual and diverse relationships; rare ability to integrate ideas within and across disciplines. | May seem off the subject; may seek to pursue interests outside the classroom; may be perceived as weird or strange by others. |
| High expectations of self and others; evaluative approach toward self and others. | Frustration with self; neurotic perfectionism or immobilization due to fear of being unable to meet self-imposed standards; difficulty in maintaining relationships with others who do not meet expectations; possibly perceived as elitist. |
| Unusual capacity to process information; accelerated rate of information processing. | Frustration with inactivity or inability of others to keep up; dislike of drill and routine. |
| Ability to delay closure. | Resentment of externally imposed deadlines for product completion when still interested in further investigation of topic; may refuse to complete products. |
| Ability to generate original ideas and solutions. | Difficulty with tasks requiring conformity; may refuse to follow directions; may deal with rejection by becoming rebellious. |

*(Continued)*

**Table 2** *Continued*

| Differentiating Characteristics | Possible Issues or Problems |
|---|---|
| Advanced patterns of thought processing (thinking of alternatives, using abstract reasoning, sensing consequences, making generalizations, etc.). | Rejects or omits details in work; questions assumptions and generalizations of others, which can be considered disrespectful; may consider linear or detailed tasks boring. |
| Early ability to use and form conceptual frameworks. | Frustration with inability of others to understand or appreciate original solutions or insights; personally derived systems that may conflict with those taught in the curriculum. |
| Unusual intensity; persistent goal-directed behavior. | Perceived as stubborn and uncooperative. |
| Internal locus of control. | Rejects external validation; not willing to "work for grades"; chooses to live by personal values that may be viewed as rebellious or as a challenge to authority and tradition. |
| Unusual sensitivity to the expectations and feelings of others. | Unusually vulnerable to criticism of others; high level of need for success and recognition. |
| Keen sense of humor. | May use humor for critical attack on others in defense, resulting in damage to interpersonal relationships. |
| Heightened self-awareness, accompanied by feelings of being different. | Isolates self, resulting in being considered aloof; feeling rejected; perceives difference as a negative attribute resulting in low self-esteem; may result in deliberate masking of abilities, particularly in women and minorities. |
| Idealism, sense of justice, unusual depth and sensitivity, and advanced moral judgments. | May attempt unrealistic reform with resulting intense frustration; unusual vulnerability; may have problems focusing on realistic goals for life's work; intolerance of and lack of understanding from peer group, leading to rejection and possible isolation. |
| Discrepancy between physical and intellectual development. | Discomfort with physical activity; consequent inhibiting of physical development; limiting of experiences in otherwise pleasurable, constructive activity. |

*Note.* Adapted from *Growing Up Gifted* (6th ed., pp. 57–62), by B. Clark, 2002, Upper Saddle River, NJ: Merrill/Prentice Hall. Copyright 2002 by Merrill/Prentice Hall. Adapted with permission.

peers, then issues of loneliness and isolation may appear. Students' inability to adjust their behavior or unwillingness to adapt to peers, especially among early adolescents, has been shown to result from extreme reliance on process adjustment in the developmental process (Callahan et al., 2004). Research suggests that gifted students from families that have a family structure in which rules are erratically enforced, where the individual (usually the gifted child) dominates, and where the family system is modified to fit the gifted individual are most likely to experience social isolation. These students develop a strong sense of self, which is often reinforced by teachers who admire their independence of thinking, but they may be negatively affected as they become adolescents and begin turning to their peers for approval and support without having learned how to appropriately compromise, listen to the views of others, tolerate less gifted students, and respect others' points of view or circumstances. Sometimes, the opportunity to interact with like peers in special classes or to attend special programs will suffice for both finding a peer group and learning to understand alternative points of view. However, when a student's inability to relate to peers results in unhappiness, anxiety, or depression, then the student needs help developing appropriate social skills.

## Depression and Suicide

In a thorough review of the literature on gifted youth, Gust-Brey and Cross (1999) concluded that there is no empirical evidence that the rates of suicide or depression among the gifted are any greater or any lower than those of the general population. However, some researchers have questioned the conclusion that rates of suicide or depression do not differ between gifted and normal populations. For example, Neihart (2002) posits that many gifted students who experience serious emotional problems may not be referred or identified. According to Neihart, the data suggest that some gifted students are at risk for depression or suicide. While noting that high cognitive functioning, asynchronous development, perfectionism, and social isolation are suggested as possibly contributing to depression or suicide, Neihart points out that the relationships between these factors and depression and suicide are not clear. High cognitive functioning combined with intense sensitivity may make gifted children or adolescents aware of personal and global injustices over which they have little or no control. Asynchronous development that results in great academic, intellectual, or performance achievements but slower (average) physical or social development may lead to the frustration of not being able to succeed physically or socially at the level of intellectual peers. Perfectionism may create frustration when students feel unable to perform at levels that meet the expectations they set for themselves. Finally, as discussed above, social isolation, when associated with loneliness, may lead to depression. Neihart also notes that the role of protective factors is not given sufficient attention in the literature on gifted students. She enumerates several factors that may increase resilience and counter negative forces: high intelligence and problem-solving ability, advanced moral reasoning, androgyny, advanced social skills, and multiple interests.

## Specific Issues Faced by the Twice-Exceptional Gifted Child

***Gifted students with learning disabilities.*** The recognition of gifted students with learning disabilities (LD) is difficult because extraordinary intellectual ability and resultant problem-solving strategies may mask the disability, allowing the student to achieve at average levels (precluding referral). Moreover, the learning disability may camouflage the giftedness because teachers see only average performance. As a result, many gifted students with learning disabilities are not identified or provided services as either gifted students or as students with learning disabilities. The limited number of studies of gifted/LD students identify the serious problems faced by these students. Problems include unhealthy perfectionism, unrealistic expectations of self, intense frustration with difficult tasks that often produces a general lack of motivation and may result in underachievement, feelings of low self-esteem, and learned helplessness (Olenchak & Reis, 2002). College-age gifted/LD students reported having sought counseling for emotional problems, having negative school experiences, and having a sense that educators consider all students with learning disabilities to be below-average in ability (Reis, McGuire, & Neu, 2000; Reis, Neu, & McGuire, 1995).

***The gifted student with ADHD.*** Some authors have contended that giftedness is often misconstrued as Attention Deficit Hyperactivity Disorder (ADHD) and that the medical field has overdiagnosed ADHD among those who are really gifted or creative individuals (e.g., Baum, Olenchak, & Owen, 1998). By contrast, Kaufmann, Kalbfleisch, and Castellanos (2000) point out that "*no empirical data in the medical, educational, or psychological literature* [emphasis in original] substantiate this concern" (p. xiii).

The similarities between the sustained attention of a gifted child in a high-interest activity (described as *flow* by Csikszentmihalyi, 1990) and the hyperfocus of a student with ADHD have contributed to the confusion between the two categories of learner and have led some to dismiss the category of students who may be both ADHD and gifted. Recent work by Kaufmann et al. (2000) suggests that there may be gifted students with ADHD and that these students would be predisposed to manifest the state of intensely focused attention. When this state is applied appropriately to problem solving and becomes an aspect of task commitment, it takes on positive valence. However, when students are unable to shift from task to task, the trait can become a negative behavior (Moon, 2002).

Kaufmann et al. (2000) noted that ADHD is not characterized by an inability to sustain attention but by inability to appropriately regulate the application of attention to tasks that are not intrinsically rewarding or to those that require effort. They caution educators that the condition of ADHD can coexist with giftedness and can both inhibit and enhance the realization of potential. However, they note the importance of considering all aspects of a student's environment in diagnosing ADHD, using a multidisciplinary team to arrive at diagnosis, and being "cautious about 'quick fixes'" (p. 35) that claim to ameliorate the barriers that ADHD may place in the way of students achieving their potential.

The lack of research on the coexistence of ADHD and giftedness precludes specific recommendations for interventions beyond a creative and carefully monitored attempt to meld those already recommended for the two groups independently.

### Specific Issues Faced by the Gifted Female

The data on gifted females are quite limited, as are recent studies on the barriers faced by this population, and yet females continue to be underrepresented in the traditionally male domains of math, science, and technology. Schuler (2002) suggests that females are more likely to be identified as perfectionists, who are fixated on avoiding mistakes and who work to please others rather than themselves. Furthermore, there is evidence that gifted females' beliefs in their ability and their feelings of self-confidence are diminished during childhood and adolescence (Callahan, Cunningham, & Plucker, 1994).

### The At-Risk Gifted Student

There is little question that at-risk students (minority and poor) are underidentified and underserved by programs for the gifted (National Research Council, 2002). The difficulties in identifying gifted students in those populations has been well documented; however, research on programs that foster the development of talent and the specific issues surrounding psychosocial development is rare. Difficulties that are associated with gifted African American students include conflict between success and peer relationships, the lack of multicultural curriculum, the isolation of being in a separate gifted program, and lack of role models (Ford, 2002). Mentoring is one strategy that has shown promise for addressing these concerns. (See the section below on mentoring for one strategy which has shown promise for addressing these concerns.)

## ALTERNATIVE ACTIONS FOR EDUCATING THE GIFTED

Discussion of best practice for meeting the needs of gifted students has been complicated by unclear distinctions in the literature between curricular and instructional models and grouping arrangements, the entanglement of those two constructs in research designs, the multiple definitions of giftedness used in the research literature, and the lack of experimental research to document effects of different approaches. For example, the term *acceleration* has been used to signify early entrance to kindergarten, grade skipping, early entrance to college, or simply acceleration of the curriculum for one or a group of students to compress multiple years of study in a discipline into a shorter time frame. The concept of *enrichment* covers models ranging from just providing supplemental instruction in an area not related to the curriculum to curricular interventions that have specific guidelines for the selection of content and instructional strategies to supplement classroom learning. Furthermore, the ways in which curriculum is delivered through various administrative arrangements complicates the interpretation of effective practice.

### Ability Grouping

One administrative or programming arrangement recommended for enhancing the achievement of gifted students has been ability grouping (see chapter 44, "Ability Grouping"). Controversy surrounding the practice of grouping stems from confusion between the terms *ability grouping* and *tracking*. Ability grouping refers to the practice of using test scores or other indicators of student ability or achievement to assign students to classes or instructional groups within a class or across classrooms. The term tracking was once restricted to the practice of recommending to students that they elect a course of high school studies leading to a particular vocational goal. Tracking was considered to be a selection process left to the students. However, tracking has come to be applied to the practice of sorting students at an early age into high-, medium-, and low-level classes in which students remain through high school. As a rigid and immutable practice, tracking has received great criticism, which has been extended to the practice of ability grouping. The intention of ability grouping was not to create permanent configurations of students; however, when schools do not provide the opportunity for students to gain the knowledge and skills necessary to move between groups, or they do not use frequent assessment to reassign students appropriately, tracking may result. The wide range of alternative grouping models are described in the chapter on ability grouping (see chapter 44).

***Studies of grouping alternatives.*** Meta-analyses of the research on ability grouping have consistently concluded that significantly greater achievement results from between- or within-class grouping for high-achieving, high-ability students (Kulik, 1992; Kulik & Kulik, 1992; Lou et al., 1996). Kulik and Kulik found no negative effects on self-concept, and the meta-analysis by Lou et al. found that within-class grouping resulted in more positive attitudes toward the subject matter and higher general self-concept. Recent studies that looked specifically at the effects of grouping practices and curricular practices reaffirmed that when students who received a differentiated curriculum, in combination with cluster grouping and flexible grouping practices, the academic achievement of middle- and high-ability groups was significantly greater than compared with students without grouping or differentiated instruction (Gentry & Owen, 1999; Tieso, 2002). The self-esteem and self-efficacy of students at all achievement levels was not influenced by the grouping arrangements (Tieso). Rogers (1991) concluded that ability grouping for curriculum extension in pullout programs produces an academic effect size of .65, which is considered high.

Finally, a comparative study of the effects of special schools, separate classrooms, and pullout programs documented higher levels of achievement for students served in gifted programs than those not in gifted programs, with no one arrangement yielding consistently better results than the others (Delcourt, Loyd, Cornell, & Goldberg, 1994).

***Misapplication of cooperative learning strategies.*** Cooperative learning is considered by some to be a grouping arrangement, by others to be an instructional strategy (see chapter 48, "Peer-Assisted Learning Strategies"). The widespread acceptance of cooperative learning as a substitute for other program or curricular adaptations for gifted students, particularly at the middle school level, has been criticized by experts in gifted education based on the paucity of research evidence that specifically includes and carefully analyzes the effects on gifted learners. In some studies, for example, the top 25% of the class is considered the high-ability group; in others, high ability is defined as above the median on a teacher-made test. Furthermore, the outcome measures in most studies are basic skill measures. And in these studies outcomes of curricular and instructional practices appropriate for gifted students are not compared to cooperative learning; rather only traditional curricular and instructional practices are compared with cooperative learning, As a consequence, educators have made generalizations about the positive effects of cooperative learning on gifted learners, but those conclusions have not been documented and have been severely criticized by parents.

## Compacting

Compacting is the practice in which students are preassessed prior to the introduction of an instructional unit. Students are exempted from instruction in areas they have mastered and are required to participate in whole group or individualized instruction only in areas they have not mastered. Reis et al. (1993) documented that at the elementary level, gifted students who had 40% to 50% of their curriculum eliminated in this way had scores that were not significantly different from those of students who experienced all of the instructional activities. In several areas gifted students with compacted curriculum earned higher achievement scores than their classmates who did not have their curriculum compacted.

## Acceleration

Use of acceleration is based on the assumption that the gifted learner is a rapid learner, has already mastered advanced-level curriculum, and is ready to learn curriculum offered at a higher grade or school level. Models of acceleration do not demand change in the school curriculum; the learner is served by placement in a more advanced level of the existing curriculum within a school or by attendance at another school or in college. Typically, curricular goals and instructional strategies are not modified to accommodate gifted students. A recent review of the studies of acceleration identified 18 types of acceleration (Colangelo et al., 2004). Programs of radical acceleration allow students to skip one or more grade levels, enter kindergarten early, enter college early, and enroll in college and high school courses simultaneously. Two less dramatic forms of acceleration are telescoping (condensing two or more grade levels for content into 1 year) and course-by-course acceleration (e.g., going to the high school in 7th grade to take geometry or taking advanced placement courses). The theoretical rationale of the acceleration options is that the more advanced courses will provide a sufficient level of challenge.

Studies of acceleration conclude that the practice yields clear advantages in academic achievement (Colangelo et al., 2004). Arguments against acceleration have focused on fears regarding the social or emotional difficulties that may result. However, considerable follow-up research, based primarily on post hoc surveys, suggests that students are academically successful, with few if any indications of social or emotional problems, when (a) acceleration is implemented with students whose levels of achievement and maturity clearly suggest that this modification in their school program is warranted, (b) careful monitoring and support are available, and (c) the practice is flexible (Colangelo, Assouline, & Gross, 2004; Hunsaker & Callahan, 1991). Southern and Jones (1991) summed up the literature on acceleration succinctly by noting that although group results appear very positive, concentration on whether or not groups are helped or harmed masks the effects on individuals. Because the differing options present different challenges, not all acceleration options are equally appropriate for all gifted children.

## Enrichment Programs and Differentiated Curriculum

Enrichment options and differentiated curriculum are often offered as the alternative to acceleration. Study of enrichment and differentiated curriculum has been hampered by the lack of consistency in the specification of sampled gifted students' characteristics and lack of careful study of particular curriculum models. In addition, models vary in their degrees of implementation (e.g., time spent in enrichment programs often range from half an hour a week to a full day a week), and the studies lack valid and reliable instruments to measure the outcomes of instruction. Despite these limitations, meta-analyses of studies of grouping arrangements show significant and meaningful effects when the curriculum is adjusted to match student strengths (Kulik, 1992; Kulik & Kulik, 1997).

## Mentorships

Although controlled experimental studies of the effects of mentoring programs for the gifted do not exist, case study and qualitative studies suggest positive influences of mentoring relationships and programs and the processes through which different types of influence may occur. Gifted students involved in mentoring perceive mentoring relationships as beneficial in the further development of interests and motivation. They report learning about the lifestyles of professionals in specific careers as well as the specific roles, functions, activities, and goals of individuals who are accomplished in those careers, and they feel that mentors help them become socialized in the field and develop self-efficacy (Arnold, 1995; Pleiss & Feldhusen, 1995). Other identified benefits of mentoring programs include helping students take risks, developing talents, learning about advanced subject matter, developing the ability to work independently, using technical skills, finding out about career entrance requirements, seeing how professionals interact, learning to conduct research in the field, and making contacts and establishing networks (Callahan & Kyburg, 2005).

***Mentoring gifted females.*** Mentors have been identified as important in influencing gifted adolescent females' career choices and success, including supporting decisions of ethnically and socioeconomically diverse females in the choice of careers in science, mathematics, and engineering. Mentors also have helped them examine ways to integrate career and family (Kerr, 1994; Packard & Nguyen, 2003).

***Mentoring underachievers and twice-exceptional students.*** Case study analysis of underachieving gifted adolescent males suggests the following characteristics of mentoring relationships contribute positively to improved school behaviors and academic achievement: (a) social and emotional support, (b) advocacy that supplements the more direct instructor–student relationship, (c) help in identifying barriers to developing creative productivity, and (d) help in developing and testing strategies for overcoming those barriers (Hébert & Olenchak, 2000).

***Mentoring students from minority groups and low socioeconomic backgrounds.*** Gifted Latino students perceived mentors to be of great importance in helping them set and achieve academic goals, and those whose parents possessed less *cultural capital* (access to resources and information networks) identified mentors as critical in helping them gain access to information they would not have otherwise obtained (Arellano and Padilla, 1996). Early mentoring of at-risk students has been an influential factor in the development of talent in very young minority students and students from impoverished environments (Moon & Callahan, 2001; Wright & Borland, 1992).

***Mentoring prodigies.*** Bloom (1985) concluded that optimal cultivation of talent requires different mentors at different stages of development. The first or initial mentors of young, talented students should emphasize making the study interesting, playful, and engaging. In contrast, as students mature into middle childhood, mentors should provide instruction that stresses precision and accuracy, while at the same time providing the encouragement and support required to develop a commitment to the field. Finally, adolescents may need help in identifying and developing a personal style as well as targeted coaching to achieve peak performance.

### Reversal of Underachievement Through Curricular Interventions

Case study research has identified factors that appear to play a role in reversing underachievement among gifted students: engagement in challenging out-of-school activities, parental support, development of goals associated with grades, teachers, and self-development. Students most likely to develop achievement-oriented behaviors described themselves as having been stimulated in class and provided with opportunities to pursue topics of interest (Baum, Renzulli, & Hebert, 1995; Emerick, 1992).

### Methods of Addressing the Twice-Exceptional Student

Although experimental studies of particular interventions are lacking, studies of successful twice-exceptional students suggest that certain programs and strategies have led to productive outcomes. These include mentoring; provision of early services to gifted students with learning disabilities, including differentiating the curriculum in areas of strength and with appropriate supports (e.g., books on tape and readers for exams); counseling (both responsive to issues that are identified and proactive); and summer or after-school programs that provide compensatory strategies. Curriculum that was based on projects derived from individual interests and learning style reduced frustration and enhanced self-esteem among gifted/LD students (Baum, Owen, & Dixon, 1991).

## SUMMARY

Although many gifted students are provided adequate school opportunities and most do not develop social or emotional problems as they move through childhood and adolescence, it is a myth that gifted students will make it without positive and supportive interventions from school and family. Although gifted students may achieve in school, schools are failing these students, as well as society and schools themselves, when they do not provide gifted students the opportunities to achieve their full potential. The evidence indicates that schools are not responding fully to the educational and learning needs suggested by the defining characteristics of giftedness. Failure to respond to those needs creates an environment that is likely to foster frustration, underachievement, and social and emotional problems.

## RECOMMENDED RESOURCES

### Books and Other Written Material

Colangelo, N., Assouline, S., & Gross, M. U. M. (2004). *A nation deceived: How schools hold back America's brightest students. Volume 1.* Iowa City: The Connie Belin and Jacqueline N. Blade International Center for Gifted Education and Talent Development, University of Iowa.

A comprehensive review of acceleration that explains and categorizes the many forms that acceleration may take, this publication also presents inclusive summaries of the empirical studies of acceleration and the various academic, social, and emotional outcomes of acceleration

Neihart, M., Reis, S. M., Robinson, N. M., & Moon, S. M. (2002). *The social and emotional development of gifted children: What do we know?* Waco, TX: Prufrock.

This compendium includes reviews of the literature ranging from psychosocial issues such as perfectionism, depression, and underachievement among gifted students to issues faced by special populations of the gifted, including gifted females; African Americans; and gays, lesbians, and bisexuals. It also includes reviews of acceleration and recommended practices in counseling gifted students.

Robinson, N. M. (2002). *Assessing and advocating for gifted students: Perspectives for school and clinical psychologists* (Research Monograph 02166). Storrs, CT: The National Research Center on the Gifted and Talented, University of Connecticut.

Robinson provides a comprehensive plan for assessment, including guidelines for individual testing and the possibility of out-of-level testing. In addition, the paper explores issues surrounding testing of highly gifted, very young, the rare student who has been coached in correct test answers, underserved minorities, and ethnically isolated families.

## Websites

*http://www.gifted.uconn.edu/nrcgt.html*

The website for the National Research Center on the Gifted and Talented provides abstracts of the more than 75 publications and video resources on topics including identification, counseling, twice-exceptional students, underachievement, school programming options, specific social and emotional adjustment issues, and brochures for parents in Spanish. The website provides access to more than 20 online publications on topics such as school dropouts, as well as resources for parents and advice for economically disadvantaged and first-generation college attendees.

*http://www.nagc.org*

The website for the National Association for Gifted Children includes information on conferences and conventions, a specific division for those interested in counseling the gifted, public policy, legislative issues, summer programs for the gifted, publications on gifted education, and a toy list for parents.

# REFERENCES


Archambault, F. X., Westberg, K. L., Brown, S., Hallmark, B. W., Emmons, C., & Zhang, W. (1993). *Regular classroom practices with gifted students: Results of a national survey of classroom teachers* (Research Monograph 93102). Storrs, CT: National Research Center on the Gifted and Talented, University of Connecticut.

Arellano, A. R., & Padilla, A. M. (1996). Academic invulnerability among a select group of Latino university students. *Hispanic Journal of Behavioral Sciences, 18,* 485–508.

Arnold, K. D. (1995). *Lives of promise.* San Francisco: Jossey-Bass.

Baum, S. M., Olenchak, F. R., & Owen, S. V. (1998). Gifted students with attention deficits: Fact or fiction? *Gifted Child Quarterly, 42,* 96–104.

Baum, S. M., Owen, S. V., & Dixon, J. (1991). *To be gifted and learning disabled: From definitions to practical intervention strategies.* Mansfield Center, CT: Creative Learning Press.

Baum, S. M., Renzulli, J. S., & Hebert, T. P. (1995). Reversing underachievement: Creative productivity as a systemic intervention. *Gifted Child Quarterly, 39,* 224–235.

Bloom, B. S. (Ed.). (1985). *Developing talents in young people.* New York: Ballentine.

Bransky, P. S., Jenkins-Friedman, R., & Murphy, D. (1987). *Identifying gifted students at risk for disabling perfectionism: The role of the school psychologist.* Paper presented at the annual conference of the American Psychological Association, New York.

Callahan, C. M., Cunningham, C. M., & Plucker, J. A. (1994). Foundations for the future: The socio-emotional development of gifted, adolescent women. *Roeper Review, 17,* 99–105.

Callahan, C. M., & Kyburg, R. M. (2005). Talented and gifted youth. In D. L. Dubois & M. S. Karcher (Eds.), *Handbook of youth mentoring* (pp. 424–439). Thousand Oaks, CA: Sage.

Callahan, C. M., Sowa, C. J., May, K. M., Tomchin, E. M., Plucker, J. A., Cunningham, C. M., & Taylor, W. (2004). *The social and emotional development of gifted students* (Research Monograph 04188). Storrs, CT: National Research Center on the Gifted and Talented, University of Connecticut.

Clark, B. (1992). *Growing up gifted: Developing the potential of children at home and at school* (4th ed.). New York: Macmillan.

Clark, B. (2002). *Growing up gifted* (6th ed.). Upper Saddle River, NJ: Prentice Hall.

Colangelo, N., Assouline, S., & Gross, M. U. M. (2004). *A nation deceived: How schools hold back America's brightest students* (Vol. 1). Iowa City: The Connie Belin & Jacqueline N. Blade International Center for Gifted Education and Talent Development, University of Iowa.

Csikszentmihalyi, M. (1990). *Flow: The psychology of optimal experience.* New York: Harper & Row.

Csikszentmihalyi, M., Rathunde, K., & Whalen, S. (1993). *Talented teenagers: The roots of success and failure.* Cambridge, UK: Cambridge University Press.

Davis, G. A., & Rimm, S. B. (1998). *Education of the gifted and talented* (4th ed.). Needham Heights, MA: Allyn & Bacon.

Delcourt, M. A. B., Loyd, B. H., Cornell, D. G., & Goldberg, M. D. (1994). *Evaluation of the effects of programming arrangements on student outcomes* (Research Monograph 94108). Storrs, CT: National Research Center on the Gifted and Talented, University of Connecticut.

Dunn, R., Dunn, K., & Treffinger, D. J. (1992). *Bringing out the giftedness in your child.* New York: Wiley.

Emerick, L. J. (1992). Academic underachievement among the gifted: Students' perceptions of factors that reverse the pattern. *Gifted Child Quarterly, 36,* 140–146.

Feldman, D. H. (1979). The mysterious case of extreme giftedness. In A. H. Passow (Ed.), *The gifted and talented: Their education and development: The seventy-eighth yearbook of the National Society for the Study of Education* (pp. 335–351). Chicago: University of Chicago.

Feldman, D. H. (1991). *Nature's gambit: Child prodigies and the development of human potential.* New York: Teachers College Press.

Feldman, D. H. (1994). *Beyond universals in cognitive development* (2nd ed.). Norwood, NJ: Ablex.

Ford, D. Y. (2002). Racial identity among gifted African American students. In M. Neihart, S. M. Reis, N. M. Robinson, & S. M. Moon (Eds.), *The social and emotional development of gifted children: What do we know?* (pp. 155–163). Waco, TX: Prufrock.

Gardner, H. (1983). *Frames of mind.* New York: Basic Books.

Gentry, M., & Owen, S. V. (1999). An investigation of the effects of total school flexible cluster grouping on identification, achievement, and classroom practices. *Gifted Child Quarterly, 43,* 224–43.

Gross, M. U. M. (1993). *Exceptionally gifted children.* London: Routledge.

Gust-Brey, K., & Cross, T. L. (1999). An examination of the literature base on the suicidal behaviors of gifted children. *Roeper Review, 22,* 28–35.

Hamachek, D. E. (1978). Psychodynamics of normal and neurotic perfectionism. *Psychology, 15,* 27–33.

Hébert, T. P., & Olenchak, F. R. (2000). Mentors for gifted underachieving males: Developing potential and realizing promise. *Gifted Child Quarterly, 44,* 196–207.

Hollingsworth, L. M. (1942). *Children above 180 IQ Stanford-Binet: Origin and development.* Yonkers-on-Hudson, NY: World Books.

Hunsaker, S. L., & Callahan, C. M. (1991). Student assessment and evaluation. In W. T. Southern & E. D. Jones (Eds.), *The academic acceleration of gifted children* (pp. 207–222). New York: Teachers College.

Kaufmann, F., Kalbfleisch, M. L., & Castellanos, F. X. (2000). *Attention deficit disorders and gifted students: What do we really know?* (Research Monograph 00146). Storrs, CT: National Research Center on the Gifted and Talented, University of Connecticut.

Kerr, B. A. (1994). *Smart girls: A new psychology of girls, women and giftedness.* Scottsdale, AZ: Gifted Psychology Press.

Kulik, J. A. (1992). *An analysis of the research on ability grouping: Historical and contemporary perspectives* (Research Monograph 9204). Storrs, CT: National Research on the Gifted and Talented, University of Connecticut.

Kulik, J. A., & Kulik, C. C. (1992). Meta-analytic findings on grouping programs. *Gifted Child Quarterly, 36,* 73–77.

Kulik, J. A., & Kulik, C. C. (1997). Ability grouping. In N. Colangelo & G. Davis (Eds.), *Handbook of gifted education* (pp. 230–342). Needham Heights, MA: Allyn & Bacon.

Lou, Y., Abrami, P. C., Spence, J. C., Poulsen, C., Chambers, B., & d'Apollonia, S. (1996). Within-class grouping: A meta-analysis. *Review of Educational Research, 66,* 423–458.

Moon, S. M. (2002). Gifted children with attention-deficit/hyperactivity disorder. In M. Neihart, S. M. Reis, N. M. Robinson, & S. M. Moon (Eds.), *The social and emotional development of gifted children: What do we know?* (pp. 193–203). Waco, TX: Prufrock.

Moon, T. R., Brighton, C. M., & Callahan, C. M. (2003). State standardized testing program: Friend or foe of gifted education? The influences of state testing programs on elementary teachers and students. *Roeper Review, 25,* 49–60.

Moon, T. R., & Callahan, C. M. (2001). Impacts of a mentoring program intervention. *Journal for the Education of the Gifted, 24,* 305–321.

Moon, T. R., Callahan, C. M., Tomlinson, C. A., & Miller, E. M. (2002). *Middle school classrooms: Teachers' reported practices and student perceptions* (Research Monograph 02164b). Storrs, CT: National Research Center on the Gifted and Talented, University of Connecticut.

National Research Council. (2002). *Minority students in special and gifted education.* Washington, DC: National Academy Press.

Neihart, M. (2002). Gifted children and depression. In M. Neihart, S. M. Reis, N. M. Robinson, & S. M. Moon (Eds.), *The social and emotional development of gifted children: What do we know?* (pp. 93–101). Waco, TX: Prufrock.

Neihart, M., Reis, S. M., Robinson, N. M., & Moon, S. M. (2002). *The social and emotional development of gifted children: What do we know?* Waco, TX: Prufrock.

Olenchak, F. R., & Reis, S. M. (2002). Gifted students with learning disabilities. In M. Neihart, S. Reis, N. M. Robinson, & S. M. Moon (Eds.), *The social and emotional development of gifted children: What do we know?* (pp. 177–191). Waco, TX: Prufrock.

Packard, B. W., & Nguyen, D. (2003). Science career-related possible selves of adolescent girls: A longitudinal study. *Journal of Career Development, 29,* 251–263.

Pleiss, M. K., & Feldhusen, J. F. (1995). Mentors, role models, and heroes in the lives of gifted children. *Educational Psychologist, 30,* 159–169.

Reis, S. M., Gubbins, E. J., Briggs, C., Schreiber, F. J., Richards, S., Jacobs, J., et al. (2003). *Reading instruction for talented readers: Case studies documenting few opportunities for continuous progress* (Research Monograph 03184). Storrs, CT: National Research Center on the Gifted and Talented, University of Connecticut.

Reis, S. M., & McCoach, D. B. (2002). Underachievement in gifted students. In M. Neihart, S. M. Reis, N. M. Robinson, & S. M. Moon (Eds.), *The social and emotional development of gifted children: What do we know?* (pp. 81–91). Waco, TX: Prufrock.

Reis, S. M., McGuire, J. M., & Neu, T. W. (2000). Compensation strategies used by high ability students with learning disabilities who succeed in college. *Gifted Child Quarterly 44,* 123–144.

Reis, S. M., Neu, T. W., & McGuire, J. M. (1995). *Talents in two places: Case studies of high ability students with learning disabilities who have achieved* (Research Monograph 95113). Storrs, CT: National Research Center on the Gifted and Talented, University of Connecticut.

Reis, S. M, Westberg, K. L., Kulikowich, J., Caillard, F., Hebert, T., Plucker, J., et al. (1993). *Why not let high ability students start school in January? The curriculum compacting study* (Research Monograph 93106). Storrs, CT: National Research Center on the Gifted and Talented, University of Connecticut.

Renzulli, J. S. (1977). *The enrichment triad model: A guide for developing defensible programs for the gifted.* Mansfield Center, CT: Creative Learning Press.

Renzulli, J. S. (1978). What makes giftedness? Reexamining a definition. *Phi Delta Kappan, 60,* 180–184.

Rimm, S. B. (1986). Underachievement syndrome: Causes and cures. Watertown, WI: Apple. 180–184.

Robinson, N. M., Reis, S. M., Neihart, M., & Moon, S. M. (2002). *Social and emotional issues: what have we learned and what should we do now?* In M. Neihart, S. M. Reis, N. M. Robinson, & S. M. *The social and emotional development of gifted students: What do we know?* (pp. 267–288). Waco, TX: Prufrock.

Rogers, K. B. (1991). *The relationship of grouping practices to the education of the gifted and talented* (Research Monograph 9102). Storrs, CT: National Research

Center on the Gifted and Talented, University of Connecticut.

Schuler, P. (2002). Perfectionism in gifted children and adolescents. In M. Neihart, S. M. Reis, N. M. Robinson, & S. M. Moon (Eds.), *The social and emotional development of gifted children: What do we know?* (pp. 71–79). Waco, TX: Prufrock.

Southern, W. T., & Jones, E. D. (Eds.). (1991). *The academic acceleration of gifted children.* New York: Teachers College.

Sternberg, R. J. (1988). *The triarchic mind: A new theory of human intelligence.* New York: Viking.

Sternberg, R. J., & Clinkenbeard, P. R. (1994). The triarchic model applied to identifying, teaching, and assessing gifted children. *Roeper Review, 17,* 255–260.

Tannenbaum, A. J. (1985). The enrichment matrix model. In J. S. Renzulli (Ed.), *Systems and models for developing programs for the gifted and talented* (pp. 391–428). Mansfield Center, CT: Creative Learning Press.

Tieso, C. L. (2002). *The effects of grouping and curricular practices on intermediate students' math achievement* (Research Monograph 02154). Storrs, CT: National Research Center on the Gifted and Talented, University of Connecticut.

U.S. Department of Education (1993). *National excellence: A case for developing American's talent.* Washington, DC: U.S. Government Printing Office.

Wright, L., & Borland, J. H. (1992). A special friend: Adolescent mentors for young economically disadvantaged, potentially gifted students. *Roeper Review, 14,* 124–129.

# 35

# Study Skills

**Maribeth Gettinger**
**Carrie Ball**
*University of Wisconsin–Madison*

## BACKGROUND AND DEVELOPMENT

Knowing how to study is essential for successful academic performance. Effective study skills are associated with positive outcomes across multiple academic content areas and for diverse learners. Deficits in knowledge and ineffective use of study skills can pose substantial problems for students, including failure to accomplish classroom tasks or meet teachers' expectations. Capable learners at all grade levels may experience academic difficulty and personal frustration, not because they lack ability, but because they lack effective approaches for studying. Despite the importance of study skills for success in school, many teachers do not teach study skills directly in their classrooms, instead assuming that students will acquire these skills on their own. Although some students develop effective study skills through trial and error, many others, especially students who struggle in school, require direct instruction and repeated practice to become effective studiers.

### Importance of Study Skills

There are several compelling reasons for schools to focus on developing study skills among students. First, strong study skills play an important role in learning and achievement. According to Devine (1987), study skills are the tools associated with all components of the learning process, specifically acquiring, recording, organizing, synthesizing, remembering, and using information taught in school. The ability to use study skills maximizes students' chance of being successful on assignments and tests in school and enables them to take advantage of multiple learning opportunities.

Achievement in most academic skill areas is often associated with effective study skills (Waldron & McLeskey, 2000). Success in reading, for example, is linked to several study strategies. Specifically, good readers (a) assess the demands of reading tasks and activities, (b) plan their reading approach, (c) allocate their attention appropriately to concentrate on important ideas and skim less critical information, and (d) monitor their comprehension through review and self-questioning. Similarly, effective writers implement several study skills, including (a) setting writing goals; (b) outlining or organizing related ideas into categories before they write; and (c) editing, reviewing, or asking themselves questions about what they wrote. Finally, successful math students have a well-organized knowledge base that allows them to assess the demands of math problems and select appropriate problem-solving strategies and requisite computation facts.

Effective study skills also enhance students' sense of personal control and self-efficacy. Students with good study skills feel competent and confident as they learn; they are more likely to approach schoolwork with positive expectations and attitudes, which in turn contribute to achievement. Finally, study skills are basic life skills that apply to many activities outside of school. Study skills go beyond helping students achieve success in a classroom; they also help individuals function effectively in multiple contexts, such as academic, athletic, social, or vocational. The development of study skills contributes to an individual's overall growth as an independent and lifelong learner. Indeed, studying has been described as the "principal means of self-education throughout life" (Rohwer, 1984, p. 1).

### Study Skills, Tactics, and Strategies

A comprehensive definition of *study skills* derives from an understanding of what is meant by studying. Studying is defined on the basis of four key dimensions. First, studying is skillful. To be effective, individuals must select the best method to accomplish a learning task and apply the method appropriately. For students to reach this level of competence in studying, they need explicit instruction and practice with specific skills or techniques to help them acquire, organize, retain, and use information on their own. Second, studying is intentional. Studying requires not only the knowledge and application of skills, but also volition on the part of the individual learner. The act of studying is a deliberate, conscious, self-initiated effort by students. It depends as much on personal efficacy and motivational factors as it does on organizational or procedural skills. Many learners may attempt to study while watching television or sitting with friends and are easily distracted from the demanding task of studying. Learning, however, does not happen incidentally; it requires significant effort and concentration by students. Third, studying is typically an individually guided activity. Whereas classroom learning occurs within a social context through interaction and guidance from teachers or peers, studying often occurs in isolation, away from the classroom setting. Many of the social cues or learning scaffolds available to students in classrooms are not present during individual periods of study. Finally, studying involves a self-regulatory dimension. When individuals study, they must engage in a process of self-monitoring to ensure success. Evaluating whether they understand and remember material, keeping themselves on task, setting personal learning goals, and taking the initiative to answer their own questions are a few examples of self-regulatory behaviors in which learners engage when they study (Gettinger & Seibert, 2002).

Given these characteristics of the process of studying, what does it mean to have good study skills? Study skills encompass a wide range of coordinated cognitive skills and processes that allow students to learn more effectively and efficiently. A useful distinction relevant to defining study skills is often made between a study tactic and a study strategy. A *study tactic* is a specific technique or skill, such as note taking, outlining, summarizing, or self-questioning, that individuals use while studying. Study tactics are often defined in terms of observable behaviors and broken down into a series of concrete steps. Because specific techniques lend themselves to direct instruction and classroom evaluation, teachers who incorporate study skill instruction into their regular content teaching often choose to focus on study tactics. It is sometimes assumed that good studying is associated with using a particular tactic; however, there is no consistent evidence that any one tactic is more effective than another. Additionally, knowing how to follow a set of sequential steps does not necessarily lead students to think about or monitor their studying behaviors.

The effectiveness of study tactics can be improved by employing a study strategy. A *study strategy* goes beyond using specific tactics; it refers to a configuration of different tactics, deliberately selected by the learner for a designated purpose or learning situation. A key distinction between study tactics and study strategies lies in the metacognitive process involved in strategy selection and application. Study tactics become strategies when learners demonstrate knowledge of when, where, and how to apply them effectively. Implementing study strategies requires knowledge about how to make decisions concerning the use of study tactics and how to take responsibility for one's own learning.

Study skills encompass a variety of tactics that are used both flexibly and intentionally by students, depending on the requirements of different learning situations. Good studiers are good strategy users; they know how to use a variety of goal-specific tactics, to execute them in a planned sequence, and to monitor their use. Instead of applying a single study tactic, effective studiers are more likely to choose from and use a collection of tactics in purposeful ways. Research has shown that effective studying (measured on the basis of accuracy of text recall) is associated with using a diverse range of study tactics as well as being able to explain why a given tactic was chosen at a particular time, as opposed to using the same single study tactic on a consistent basis, irrespective of the type of task (Winne & Hadwon, 1997).

It appears, therefore, that students use different collections of study tactics, leading to various ways of learning the same material under the same conditions. No study skill is appropriate for all students or for all academic tasks, and a number of different tactics may be equally effective for learning and remembering the same information. In spite of this flexibility, however, students may not develop a sufficiently broad and effective repertoire of study skills without explicit training. In fact, some learners continue to use ineffective or inefficient tactics as primary methods of studying even when the methods they have chosen do not help them learn.

## Developmental Considerations

Whereas problems with study skills are evident among students of all ages, the importance of study skills increases as students get older. Study skill deficits may be manifested in elementary school children as problematic classroom behaviors, such as poor attention, low persistence, weak motivation, or low task engagement and completion (Henley, Ramsey, & Algozzine, 1996). Among middle and high school students, however, study skills are considered more cognitive than behavioral and tend to be associated with thinking and reading skills.

The majority of research on study skills has been conducted with students in middle or high school. Weak study skills are considered more frequent among adolescents and older students, largely because expectations for and use of independent textbook study increase substantially in middle and high school. As students mature and advance in school, they face special challenges and expectations beyond paying attention and learning academic skills. In high school, students are expected to handle multiple courses (which are not as well integrated as in an elementary curriculum), read dozens or even hundreds of pages each week, and be skillful and motivated as studiers. Organizational and time management skills become especially important components of effective studying for adolescents. For instance, good studiers at the high school level are usually proficient at managing their time and are aware of their own strengths and weaknesses when approaching novel learning tasks. These students typically organize their books, notes, and related materials in preparation for studying and have individualized routines for identifying and recording new information. They are also less likely to study with distractions such as music or television.

Secondary school students with inadequate study skills experience significant difficulty acquiring new information and understanding course material. They often feel overwhelmed with the amount of material they are expected to learn, yet they continue to employ inefficient and ineffective study tactics (Wood, Woloshyn, & Willoughby, 1995). For example, high school students with study skill deficits rely heavily on passive study strategies such as rote memorization and rereading. They have been shown to memorize details to the exclusion of main ideas and fail to establish goals or priorities when studying. When these students study, they do so in long, infrequent sessions. Not surprisingly, they find studying unpleasant because they associate it with frustration and failure. Older students with weak study skills usually experience negative academic and nonacademic outcomes. They may receive failing grades, drop classes, drop out of school, or experience limited success in the workplace.

In addition to deficits in cognitive, organizational, or thinking strategies, low-achieving high school students may not exhibit desirable study behaviors. For example, they often report that the purpose of studying is to remember material just long enough to take a test. Thus, a common test-preparation strategy is to study only the night before an exam. In addition, low-achieving high school students do not allocate sufficient time to study, and the time they do allocate is frequently interrupted by friends, daydreaming, music, or poor concentration. Finally, academically weak high school students fail to self-regulate their studying; they do not monitor their comprehension of material, nor do they realize when a particular study tactic is not effective for them.

## PROBLEMS AND IMPLICATIONS

### Academic Achievement

Weak study skills contribute to negative outcomes for students in general classroom learning as well as in specific content domains. Many students with academic difficulties are simply not aware of the strategies used by successful students when they study. Therefore, an assessment of study skills should be part of a comprehensive evaluation for children who experience academic problems.

Assessment of study skills should be guided by what is known about the nature of effective studying among high-versus low-achieving students. Much of the knowledge about study skills used by successful students has been obtained through *think-aloud* methods in which students express their thoughts and verbalize their strategies while engaged in studying. Think-aloud methods have allowed researchers to move beyond a narrow focus on observable behaviors and to explore the cognitive and metacognitive processes involved in studying. Rich descriptive information gained from think-aloud assessment, as well as from other methods of assessment (e.g., interviews, observations, and self-report checklists), has contributed to a profile of study behaviors that differentiate successful from unsuccessful students. This information has also led to the identification of strategies that low-achieving students may need to acquire to become more successful in school.

Pressley and Afflerbach (1995), for example, identified several study strategies that successful learners use to understand and remember new material. Common practices include (a) scanning a passage prior to reading,

**Table 1** *Study Approaches of High-Achieving Versus Low-Achieving Students*

| *High-Achieving Students* | *Low-Achieving Students* |
|---|---|
| • Choose from a repertoire of study tactics and select tactics in a purposeful manner, depending on the task content, structure, or expectations. | • Have a restricted range of tactics and use the same, often ineffective, study approach for all learning, regardless of the task content, structure, or expectations. |
| • Take an active role in studying, and justify the use of study tactics for a given learning task. | • Assume a passive role in learning and rely on others to tell them what and how to study. |
| • Allocate attention appropriately to focus on important information, jumping forward and backward to process information effectively. | • Are unaware they must extend effort beyond simply reading content to fully comprehend and retain information. |
| • Monitor their own studying, and look back and "fix up" inaccuracies in their comprehension or change their study approaches. | • Fail to monitor their own studying, and show little evidence of looking back or employing "fix up" strategies to remedy comprehension problems when they occur. |
| • Establish personal goals for their studying, integrate new strategies into their study routines, use study strategies, and evaluate the benefits of a variety of learning strategies. | • Do not establish goals for learning, are discouraged from using study strategies because they do not know how to apply them, and have difficulty integrating strategies as part of their study routines. |

(b) identifying and attending to important information (which often includes skipping ahead or rereading), (c) connecting and integrating main ideas included in the content to be learned, (d) activating and using prior knowledge, (e) changing study tactics when one becomes ineffective, and (f) monitoring comprehension accuracy and correcting problems or mistakes.

Compared with successful students, students who experience difficulty in school often have not developed the study skills necessary for success, or they demonstrate weak and ineffective use of study tactics. Students with academic difficulties often take a passive role in the learning process and rely on others (e.g., parents or teachers) to regulate their own studying. Several cognitive and behavioral characteristics reflect this passivity in learning. Specifically, low-achieving students do not monitor their understanding of content; they are often not aware of the purpose of studying and show little evidence of looking back or using "fix-up" strategies (looking back and fixing inaccuracies caused by their prior comprehension or changing their study approaches) to remedy comprehension problems.

Students who have difficulty learning new or complex information seem to be unaware that they must extend effort beyond simply reading the content to understand it. Children with learning disabilities, in particular, do not exhibit an executive level of thinking in which they plan, organize, and monitor their approaches to studying or completing work. Their studying tends to be haphazard and disorganized. An assessment of students with academic problems, based on both teacher and parent ratings and self-report, revealed challenges with personal organization as well, which is important for success in the general education classroom. Particular areas of difficulty related to organization may include keeping track of materials and assignments, following directions, completing class assignments, and completing homework assignments. Finally, unlike good studiers who use a variety of study tactics in a flexible, yet purposeful manner, low-achieving students use a restricted range of skills; they cannot explain why good study strategies are important for learning; and they tend to use the same, often ineffective study approach for all learning tasks, irrespective of task content, structure, or difficulty (Strichart, Mangrum, & Iannuzzi, 1998). A summary of these characteristics of studying among high- versus low-achieving students is presented in Table 1.

Not surprisingly, students with study skill deficits typically struggle in reading, writing, and math. Poor readers, for example, display an array of problems that reflect weak study skills. Unlike successful readers, they typically do not monitor their understanding of what they read, nor do they adjust their reading rate to match the demands of the reading task. They are often unaware of the purpose of reading and may show little evidence of study tactics such as skimming, looking back, or self-questioning. Similarly, poor writers engage in minimal, if any, planning prior to writing. They tend to focus on organizing individual words rather than main ideas or the overall structure, and they seldom review, edit, or revise their written products. Finally, students with low success in math do not organize

**Table 2** *Self-Analysis of Study Skills*

| Do I . . . | Almost Always | Sometimes | Very Seldom |
|---|---|---|---|
| Understand directions provided in class? | | | |
| Take notes that are helpful? | | | |
| Ask questions when I don't understand? | | | |
| Understand lectures and discussions? | | | |
| Keep up with assigned work? | | | |
| Feel disorganized most of the time? | | | |
| Participate in class discussions? | | | |
| Find it difficult to complete assignments? | | | |
| Feel well-prepared most of the time? | | | |
| Find vocabulary in reading too difficult? | | | |
| Have a regular place where I study? | | | |
| Have a regular time to study? | | | |
| Outline or summarize what I read? | | | |
| Keep a calendar of tests and assignments? | | | |
| Review class and reading notes regularly? | | | |
| Set study goals for myself? | | | |
| Follow a routine study method for tests? | | | |
| Concentrate when I study? | | | |
| Motivate and reward myself for studying? | | | |
| Know when I don't understand something? | | | |

information and fail to identify and select appropriate strategies to apply to a problem. In sum, weaknesses in academic performance among low-achieving students may be as much the result of the limited effectiveness and efficiency of the study skills they use as of their academic skill deficits.

## Explaining Study Skill Deficits

There are several explanations for weak study skills. In many cases, students simply have not learned good study strategies and do not have a repertoire of well-developed study skills. Students may have deficiencies in their existing study strategies. Although teachers expect students to acquire skills for effective studying and test-taking during their school experience, the development of good study strategies is seldom a focus of systematic classroom instruction (Zimmerman, 1998).

Another explanation for study skill deficits is that students cannot self-select appropriate study methods or self-regulate their use, despite having acquired a repertoire of effective study tactics. Few high school students know how to regulate their own study strategies because they have received ineffective instruction; teachers fail to explain when, where, how, and why to use a new strategy (Scanlon, Deshler, & Schumaker, 1996). Students may be able to recite the steps of a study procedure without knowing when to apply it, how to modify it for different tasks or content areas, or why it is even important to their own learning. Many students who exhibit poor study skills have received little direct instruction related to studying, thus underscoring the need to prepare teachers to incorporate study skills training into regular classroom activities. Teachers may neglect study skills instruction because they assume students have already mastered the skills necessary for studying, or they may not be familiar with methods to help students develop good study skills.

Finally, poor studying habits can be due to a lack of motivation. When confronted with competing goals or outside pressures, students may choose activities other than studying or completing schoolwork. Students who lack a good repertoire of study skills are especially prone to low motivation. Because they associate studying with negative emotions and outcomes, they show less initiative and are more easily distracted than students with good study skills. Instructional practices may also inadvertently contribute to low motivation (Adams & Hamm, 1994). For example, when teachers, parents, and administrators define learning objectives, students are not given the opportunity to set individual goals or become self-directed learners. As a result, students rely too heavily on the structure imposed by teachers and parents and do not initiate studying behaviors on their own.

### Evaluating Study Skills

One way to determine if students need to improve their study skills is to ask questions directly about their study habits and strategies or observe work samples and other evidence of study skills. Some instruments have been developed for evaluating study skills, such as the Learning and Study Strategies Inventory (Weinstein & Palmer, 1990). Harvey (2002) recommended that informative and comprehensive assessment of study skills include interviews with parents, teachers, and students. Interviews should focus on key components of study skills not addressed in most inventories or checklists, such as motivation or self-regulation. The Metacognitive Awareness of Reading Strategies Inventory (MARSI) was designed to evaluate students' metacognitive awareness and self-perceptions regarding their use of study strategies while reading and studying school-related materials (Mokhtari & Reichard, 2002).

Because students must be aware of and responsible for their own study patterns, they should complete checklists or questionnaires at different times during the school year (see example in Table 2). The objective of this type of self-analysis is to provide information about students' study skills and general classroom behavior so that students and teachers together can develop a specific plan for improving areas of weakness. To enhance their study skills, students must identify both effective and ineffective study behaviors and assume some responsibility for modifying their own strategies.

## ALTERNATIVE ACTIONS FOR PREVENTION

### Essential Features of Study Skills Instruction

The link between student achievement and study skills is well established and underscores the need to focus on study skills at all grade levels. In response to this need, comprehensive models have been developed and evaluated for implementing study strategy training in all classes. Because these instructional models are intended to provide study skills training to all students to promote academic success, they are viewed as prevention approaches. A focus on study skills within a prevention framework includes three essential elements. The first critical feature of study skills training is one that incorporates principles of effective teaching and learning, such as focusing on important information and providing corrective feedback (Harvey, 2002). Second, study skills training should be initiated early in the elementary grades so that skills are practiced and established before students enter middle or high school (Gleason, Archer, & Colvin, 2002). Finally, study skills training should be integrated with classroom instruction in basic skills or content domains, rather than provided as separate instruction. When teachers incorporate training in study strategies into their regular curriculum, they can be effective in preventing academic problems for many students in their classrooms. During the past 20 years, research has provided evidence supporting the effectiveness of study skills instruction that incorporates these elements. By receiving explicit training in study skills as early as third grade, students become more efficient, thoughtful, and independent as learners, and they perform better in school (Scheid, 1993). Even students who develop study skills on their own learn to study more effectively and efficiently through explicit instruction.

### Phases of Study Skills Instruction

Although commercial materials have been developed to serve as curriculum guides for classroom instruction in study skills, these tend to focus on the identification and teaching of discrete study tactics, such as outlining, note taking, time management, and organizational skills. In recent years, there has been a shift toward developing and evaluating strategy-based teaching models that emphasize the flexible use of interrelated study tactics. Controlled evaluations of two approaches, in particular, have documented positive effects of strategy training on the learning and achievement of all learners, especially low-achieving or at-risk students. These approaches are the Strategies Intervention Model, developed by Deshler and other researchers at the Kansas Institute for Research in Learning Disabilities and Center for Research on Learning (Deshler, Ellis, & Lenz, 1996), and the Good

Information Processing Approach, stemming from the work of Pressley and his colleagues (Pressley, Woloshyn, & Associates, 1995). Both approaches are based on a model of effective study-strategy instruction, which incorporates a sequence of standard instructional phases that proceed gradually from social modeling by the teacher to self-directed studying by students. The model is consistent with a social cognitive perspective of academic competence, which posits that academic performance develops initially from social sources (e.g., teachers and peers) and eventually shifts to internal sources (students themselves). Within a social cognitive perspective, three phases of study-strategy development map directly onto standard elements of effective instruction (Zimmerman & Kitsantas, 1997).

In the first phase, students initially acquire study strategies through social modeling, task structuring, and social praise. The first step in effective strategy instruction, therefore, begins with breaking the study strategy into basic steps, followed by giving explicit instruction and frequent modeling of strategy use by the teacher. Research highlights the importance of showing students, not just telling them, how to use a study skill. This type of modeling is termed *cognitive modeling* because the teacher demonstrates the use of a study strategy while thinking aloud to verbalize the rationale and reasoning behind its use. Students who understand the potential benefit of a study skill are more likely to apply the skill on their own in multiple situations.

For some learners, the first phase, cognitive modeling, is sufficient for them to apply the strategy effectively on their own. Most students, however, require actual performance of the strategy before it becomes incorporated into their study routine. Thus, the second phase of strategy development is imitation, whereby the learner applies the strategy in a way that approximates the teacher's performance. The primary role of the teacher during this step of instruction is to provide multiple opportunities for students to practice study skills and receive feedback and guidance through scaffolding. Scaffolding involves providing help to students on an as-needed basis, such that students continue to make progress in applying a strategy. As part of the scaffolding process, teacher guidance is gradually reduced over practice trials, and students assume increasing responsibility for using the strategy on their own. Strategy practice during this gradual shift in responsibility from the teacher to students occurs through a process called *cognitive coaching*. Through cognitive coaching, the teacher continues to provide coaching or assistance (e.g., cues, prompts, and guiding questions) to support students in the transition from teacher guidance to self-regulation.

In the third phase of study-strategy development, referred to as *self-regulation*, learners use the study skills independently. Whereas the source of learning and reinforcement for the first two phases of strategy acquisition is primarily social, the locus of control shifts to the individual student in this phase. During this phase, students' use of study strategies becomes internalized. In practice, opportunities are provided for students to use study skills while completing their daily assignments. Although teachers may provide minimal guidance, students are expected to initiate the use of a study strategy on their own and make adjustments or adapt the strategy to meet their individual needs. Students are prompted to look for authentic situations to apply the study skills they have learned. Success at this level of training may be limited if students believe they must adhere to a narrow, scripted use of a strategy in all study situations. Thus, study skills instruction must make clear to learners that strategies can and should be used flexibly. One particular tactic may not be appropriate for all students, and most often study skills must be tailored to individual students (Archambeault, 1992).

## Applications of Study Skills Instruction

In summary, effective study skills instruction for all learners incorporates three components: (a) simplification of the strategy so that the procedural steps are explicit, justified, and amenable to individualization; (b) frequent modeling or demonstration of the study strategy; and (c) guided instruction, practice, and feedback to help students move from teacher dependence to self-dependence in selecting and implementing study strategies.

Despite the documented benefits of study skills training, instructional challenges may limit the widespread application of the training in classrooms for all students. For strategy instruction to be implemented in classroom contexts as a preventive action, adaptations for group situations are necessary. For example, teachers may not choose to sacrifice coverage of curriculum content in order to teach study skills to their students, especially at the secondary school level. One way to address this concern is for teachers to teach study skills in conjunction with their curriculum, that is, to merge their teaching of content with the teaching of study strategies that aid students in learning the content. Specifically, teachers can

**Table 3** *Clusters of Study Skills to Target for Intervention*

| Strategy Cluster | Description | Purpose | Examples | Age |
|---|---|---|---|---|
| *Repetition-based* | Rehearse and repeat material to be learned | To remember small amounts of discrete information for a limited amount of time | Flashcards Spelling lists | Young children (K–2) Any age for basic facts |
| *Procedural* | Use personalized and consistent routines or steps to maximize the benefits of study time | To enhance time management, organization of materials, and structured studying | SQ3R | Elementary school (Grade 3 and above) |
| *Cognitive* | Think about, integrate, or connect new content with existing knowledge | To engage in appropriate thinking about content, and to connect new information to existing knowledge and personal experience | Graphic organizers Question generation Summarization | Elementary school (Grade 3 and above) |
| *Metacognitive* | Monitor and regulate the use of cognitive strategies | To adjust studying to task demands and expectations, and to use and monitor appropriate and effective strategies | Self-questioning | Middle school and above |
| *Peer assisted* | Model skills, strategies, and thought processes | To use peer modeling or cooperative learning to teach content and develop new skills | Tutoring Mentoring Cooperative learning | Any age with developmentally appropriate adjustment |

teach and prompt the application of strategies that are most effective for their academic content. There is some evidence that strategies are more readily learned if strategy training is embedded within content instruction. That is, students witness firsthand the immediate application and benefit of strategies for learning and remembering content, rather than learning study strategies in isolation (Lenz, Ellis, & Scanlon, 1996).

Additional principles are important to keep in mind when designing and implementing preventive study skills training for all students. First, students must recognize the need for varied approaches to studying, and they should not be expected to apply all study methods for every learning situation. Appropriate study strategies vary depending on the type of task, students' personal learning style and habits, and the teachers' expectations. For example, the most effective strategy for studying spelling words is likely to be different from an effective approach for studying for a history test. Furthermore, any single study tactic will likely require modification and personalization on the part of the students themselves. In developing an awareness of different strategies, students should be encouraged to explain the appropriateness of a particular strategy for different tasks.

Second, the key to effective study skills training is to help students guide their own thinking, organization, and use of study behaviors. One reason that students fail to use strategies they have been taught is that they are not able to integrate the new strategies into their personal study habits, and attempting to do so requires too much time (Rauch & Fillenworth, 1995). The most effective study-skill instruction does so by helping all students develop strategies that work for them. Students should be actively involved in developing their own personalized study strategies, instead of being taught a scripted set of steps. Including the students in developing their own strategies (e.g., cue words for a study step), establishing personal study goals, and evaluating their study plans enhances maintenance and generalization to other study situations. Sweidel (1996), for example, recommends the use of a study strategy portfolio in which students keep a portfolio of different study strategies they use and self-evaluate how well they were able to implement each study strategy and the strategy's overall effectiveness in terms of graded assignments or tests. Through this approach, students are encouraged to think about their study methods, self-evaluate their effectiveness, and modify these approaches as necessary for studying different academic content.

# ALTERNATIVE ACTIONS FOR INTERVENTION

## Conceptual Framework for Study Strategies

Not all students benefit from preventive study skill instruction in general education classrooms. For some students, it may be necessary to provide more intensive and explicit instruction in study strategies. Intervention is necessary when children have failed to develop or apply effective study skills through classroom instruction. Although different theoretical perspectives support the benefit of equipping students with study skills, the most applicable theory is information processing. In brief, an information-processing perspective assumes that information to be learned is manipulated by the student to enhance both acquisition and retention.

The level or depth of processing, or manipulation, is affected by the type of study strategy the learner uses. The more elaborate the strategy, the deeper the level of processing. Weinstein and Mayer (1985) offered a useful classification of study skills within this information-processing perspective. They grouped study skills on the basis of the degree of manipulation or level of processing required for the information to be learned. Within this framework, the four clusters of study skills are repetition based, procedural, cognitive, and metacognitive. Alternative intervention approaches for students at greatest risk for school failure focus on any or all of these four clusters of study skills, depending on students' strengths and needs. In contrast to classwide study skills instruction for prevention of learning problems, intervention for study skills is characterized as being more intense and explicitly focused on one or more specific types of study skills. Table 3 summarizes each cluster of skills and offers suggestions for the developmental appropriateness of each cluster.

***Repetition-based study strategies.*** The most basic study skills are based on repetition. Intervention at this level involves teaching students to repeat, reread, or rehearse information to be learned. Rehearsal strategies are easy to learn and use; they are useful interventions for students who experience difficulty remembering small amounts of information for the short term (e.g., studying 15 weekly spelling words) or when the content being studied is used frequently (e.g., multiplication facts). From an information-processing perspective, repetition-based study skills, although easy to acquire and apply, afford minimal processing of content. For many low-achieving students, repetition strategies must be augmented to promote deeper processing of information. For example, a variety of mnemonic devices, such as mental imagery, have been shown to enhance the effectiveness of repetition-based study skills, particularly for long-term retention and acquisition of complex information (Levin, 1993).

***Procedural study strategies.*** The second type of study skills that may be targeted for intervention are procedural. These study skills encompass the routines, behaviors, or habits that allow students to maximize the benefits of their available study time. Many students who require study skills intervention demonstrate lack of organization. Although they may have an awareness of organizational skills, they fail to use them consistently and effectively. Several competencies underlie the development of procedural study skills, including time management, materials organization, and development of schedules or consistent study routines. A common problem for students with deficits in procedural or organizational skills is the inability to structure their study time and, when necessary, to adapt their schedules to provide sufficient time for studying and work completion. Organizational routines and study procedures are most effective when they are personalized and when students construct their own goals for monthly, weekly, and daily study. Although the research has failed to document benefits for any single study routine over another, such as SQ3R (survey, question, read, respond, and review), what does contribute to positive outcomes is the consistency with which a study routine is implemented and the extent to which individual learners have adapted it to their own style.

***Cognitive study strategies.*** Cognitive study strategies make up the third type of study skills. The goal of cognitive strategies is to guide students to engage in appropriate thinking about the information they are studying. According to information-processing theory, the more knowledge students have about content, the more likely they are to think about, understand, and remember it. Therefore, studying can be improved when the material to be learned is meaningful to students and integrated or connected with their existing knowledge. In addition, when information is stored in a network of connected facts and concepts, called *schemata*, it is more easily learned and retained. Interventions involving cognitive study skills, therefore, are designed to help students (a) activate or assemble background knowledge prior to studying a topic, e.g., through discussion; (b) connect new information or concepts to what students already know or to their personal experiences; and (c) develop new schemata, when necessary, to integrate content to be learned.

Several evidence-based intervention tools are available that allow students to achieve these cognitive goals. Cognitive organizers, for example, are effective in activating students' knowledge about a topic, organizing information during studying, and establishing connections among key concepts. Cognitive organizers, also called cognitive or semantic maps, are visual or graphic representations of the interrelatedness of ideas. Typically, a map contains a hierarchical diagram or arrangement of concepts, ideas, and facts about the content to be studied (often written on individual cards), which enables students to manipulate information cards and describe the relationship between content ideas (Baumann & Bergeron, 1993). Two other evidence-based cognitive interventions—question generation and summarization—also help students activate and make connections with prior knowledge (Rosenshine, Meister, & Chapman, 1996; Malone & Mastropieri, 1992). These cognitive strategies are most effective when they are generative, i.e., when the learner's own words and experiences are used to construct novel connections and relationships among ideas. When learners use their own words to formulate questions or summarize content, connections between new material and existing knowledge are automatically constructed, because those words are associated with information that is already stored in the learner's memory.

***Metacognitive study strategies.*** The final cluster of study skills to target for intervention are metacognitive-based skills. The extent to which students apply study skills when the need arises depends largely on their metacognitive capabilities—their ability to assess the need for studying and to plan, implement, monitor, and evaluate their study approaches. Whereas cognitive-based study skills relate to how learners process information, metacognitive strategies relate to how students select, monitor, and use strategies.

Metacognition involves knowledge about and regulation of cognition, and students' use of these strategies results in the ability to evaluate, monitor, and make goals and plans for studying. Students with well-developed metacognitive skills are able to adjust their studying according to varying task demands; they know how to study effectively; they understand which study strategies to use; and they monitor their studying and allocate study time wisely. In contrast, students who require metacognitive skill interventions are often disorganized in their studying and have limited understanding about what to do or how to proceed with studying. Intervention can significantly improve students' metacognitive abilities.

In typical metacognitive skill training, students are given explicit instruction in self-questioning strategies. For example, students may be taught to ask themselves questions such as "Do I understand the material I am studying?" "Should I reread or revise my study strategy?" "What strategies are necessary for solving this problem?" (Zimmerman, Bonner & Kovach, 1996).

## Peer-Assisted Approaches

In recent years, there has been a growing awareness of the benefits of using peers to model cognitive study strategies. Peer-assisted approaches (see chapter 48, "Peer-Assisted Learning Strategies"), including tutoring, mentoring, and cooperative learning, have assumed a critical role in study skills interventions. For example, the work of Fuchs, Fuchs, Mathes, and Simmons (1997) has demonstrated the effectiveness of Peer Assisted Learning Strategies (PALS), a peer tutoring program involving partner reading, summarization, prediction, and other cognitive study strategies. Peer models who demonstrate strategies, verbalize their thought processes as they perform tasks, and provide guidance to other students contribute to better studying among low-achieving students than do teacher or adult models.

## Developmental Appropriateness of Study Strategies

Because all study strategies require varying levels of cognitive processing to be implemented effectively, it is important to consider the developmental appropriateness of strategies to be taught. Peer-assisted study strategies, for example, may be used with children of any age, although the setting and structure of such activities will change depending on the age of students and the content to be learned. Other clusters of study strategies, however, may be more or less effective with certain age groups. For very young children, repetition-based strategies are most useful, as they are the easiest to learn and require relatively little cognitive processing. They also have a logical connection to early skill instruction in that repetition plays a key role in developing automaticity with letter-sound correspondences and basic math facts.

As children enter Piaget's concrete operational stage, they learn to follow step-by-step instructions and gradually learn to organize information. Procedural study skills, which typically rely on sequences of steps to help organize information, are most useful for children at this developmental level. In addition, children in first through third grade may benefit from basic cognitive study strategies. Graphic organizers, in particular, create a visual, concrete representation of interconnected information, which helps elementary school age children grasp the abstract concept of cognitively organizing information. More complicated cognitive strategies such as question generation and summarization may be taught in the context of procedural skills (e.g., SQ3R). These strategies become more fully developed as children acquire a better understanding of their purpose and learn to individualize strategies for their own benefit. These procedural and cognitive clusters of study strategies become essential during middle and late elementary school, when children begin to use reading skills independently and are expected to study material on their own for quizzes and tests.

Metacognitive strategies require a high level of cognitive processing in addition to the capacity for abstract thought. Strategies that involve selecting, monitoring, and regulating the use of other study skills are probably most appropriate for students in middle and high school. Beginning in middle school, subject areas tend to be taught in relative isolation, and study strategies must be selected on the basis of their usefulness for learning specific information. Additionally, adjustments are often necessary to meet the expectations of multiple instructors. This shift in educational structure coincides with cognitive development, whereby students gain the ability to think abstractly and to understand their own cognitive processes. At this juncture, employing metacognitive strategies to monitor and regulate study habits becomes an important factor in students' academic performance.

In sum, students of any age who have good study skills demonstrate an understanding of task demands and an ability to implement flexible, effective strategies. In addition to knowing the steps associated with specific study tactics, study skills involve an understanding of when, how, and why to use them. Studying requires that students be able to direct their own learning and to determine what information is important and how it can be learned and retained. As children develop cognitively, they tend to create their own strategies for learning and studying based on previous successes and failures in school. Some students, however, fail to develop strategies independently. The result is ineffective studying, often leading to low success and low motivation in school.

# SUMMARY

Study skills are essential components in student success yet they are often neglected in education. Teachers often assume that study skills will be acquired without direct teaching and guided practice. More often than not, however, effective and efficient study skills are not mastered by all students. An understanding of the nature of studying and knowledge of evidence-based approaches that help students acquire and apply study skills are important tools for designing effective prevention and intervention programs. Many "how to study" programs and instruction are implemented independent of actual classroom activities.

Because study skills are applied differently within each content area, study skills instruction designed to prevent learning problems is most effective when it is integrated into the context of regular classroom instruction. Actions designed to prevent study skill deficits in students require teachers to implement an effective model of instruction that includes three components: (a) modeling study strategies, (b) giving guided practice and feedback in applying the strategy, and (c) providing authentic opportunities for independent practice in using the strategy. For some students, however, more intensive, individualized, and skill-based intervention is necessary. In particular, students need to learn strategies for remembering and organizing information and for monitoring their own study behaviors. Framed within an information-processing perspective, study skills interventions are aimed at equipping students with methods for more effective and more elaborate processing of information to be learned.

## RECOMMENDED RESOURCES

### Books and Other Printed Materials

Lenz, B. K., Ellis, E. S., & Scanlon, D. (1996). *Teaching learning strategies to adolescents and adults with learning disabilities.* Austin, TX: Pro-Ed.

This book focuses on how educators can design preventive instruction to teach and strengthen learning strategies among all learners, especially students with learning disabilities. The authors describe the principles and procedures associated with an evidence-based approach for strategy instruction, called the Strategies Intervention Model. A particular strength of this text is the inclusion of a section that presents information on collaboration among special educators, pupil services staff, and general education content-area teachers for incorporating study strategy training in content-area instruction.

Pressley, M., Woloshyn, V., & Associates. (1995). *Cognitive strategy instruction that really improves children's academic performance* (2nd ed.). Cambridge, MA: Brookline.

This book is part of a Cognitive Strategy Training Series published by Brookline that includes books focusing on specific aspects of effective studying (e.g., test-taking skills, strategies for learning mnemonically). The book provides a review of the research on approaches for teaching cognitive strategies that are appropriate for all learners and that can be incorporated into the content of regular classroom instruction. As such, it is a good resource for alternative actions in prevention of academic problems linked to ineffective study strategies. The chapter titled "Getting Started Teaching Strategies" is particularly useful in terms of offering suggestions for teachers to follow, both for training and for supporting strategy use among students.

Strichart, S. S., Mangrum, C. T., & Iannuzzi, P. (1998). *Teaching study skills and strategies to students with learning disabilities, attention deficit disorders, or special needs* (2nd ed.). Boston: Allyn & Bacon.

This book is an excellent resource that includes activities and guidelines for teaching specific study methods to at-risk learners in Grades 4 through 12. Each chapter focuses on one type of study approach (e.g., Strategies for Remembering Information) and contains learning objectives and practice activities to promote both acquisition and application of study methods. Because the activities are designed to provide explicit instruction in repetition-based, procedural (e.g., Using Time and Space), and cognitive (Solving Math Word Problems) study skills, the focus is on alternative actions for intervention. The aim is to enable teachers or special educators to provide study skill to students with academic needs to enable them to be more successful and independent learners.

### Websites

*http://www.appliedscholastics.org*

This website for Applied Scholastics International, a nonprofit organization, provides training, materials, and support for teachers to help their students learn how to learn and to achieve academic goals.

*http://www.score-ed.com*

This is the website for SCORE (Success in the CORE for Everyone), which works with schools to establish academic supports, including study skills and staff development related to study skills training.

*http://www.teachersandfamilies.com/open/parent/homework1.cfm*

The Parenting Perspectives website provides a study skills guide for parents. The site, which was developed by the National Association of School Psychologists, includes suggestions for teaching children organizational skills and for helping them understand the value of homework. It may be helpful for education professionals interested in forming home–school collaborations.

*http://www.how-to-study.com/index.html*

The website of How-to-Study.com provides concise tips for sharpening skills in reading, writing, mathematics, note taking, and even listening. This is a good resource for older students who enjoy using the Internet or for teachers who want to help students sharpen a particular skill.

*http://www.studygs.net*

This website, Study Guides and Strategies, provides a very comprehensive set of links to maximize the benefits of studying, tutoring, doing research, and working collaboratively. Although most useful for teachers of late elementary or secondary students, the website contains an extensive amount of material and is well worth a visit.

## REFERENCES


Adams, D., & Hamm, M. (1994). *New designs for teaching and learning: Promoting active learning in tomorrow's schools.* San Francisco: Jossey-Bass.

Archambeault, B. (1992). Personalizing study skills in secondary students. *Journal of Reading, 35,* 468–472.

Baumann, J. F., & Bergeron, B. S. (1993). Story map instruction using children's literature. *Journal of Reading Behavior, 25,* 407–437.

Deshler, D. D., Ellis, E. S., & Lenz, B. K. (1996). *Teaching adolescents with learning disabilities: Strategies and methods.* Denver, CO: Love Publishing.

Devine, T. G. (1987). *Teaching and study skills: A guide for teachers.* Boston: Allyn & Bacon.

Fuchs, D., Fuchs, L. S., Mathes, P. G., & Simmons, D. C. (1997). Peer-assisted learning strategies: Making classrooms more responsive to diversity. *American Educational Research Journal, 34,* 174–206.

Gettinger, M., & Seibert, J. K. (2002). Contributions of study skill to academic competence. *School Psychology Review, 31,* 350–365.

Gleason, M. M., Archer, A. L., & Colvin, G. (2002). Interventions for improving study skill. In M. R. Shinn, H. M. Walker, & G. Stoner (Eds.), *Interventions for academic and behavior problems II: Preventive and remedial approaches* (pp. 651–680). Bethesda, MD: National Association of School Psychologists.

Harvey, V. (2002). Best practices in teaching study skills. In A. Thomas & J. Grimes (Eds.), *Best practices in school psychology IV* (pp. 831–849). Bethesda, MD: National Association of School Psychologists.

Henley, M., Ramsey, R. S., & Algozzine, R. F. (1996). *Characteristics and strategies for teaching students with mild disabilities* (2nd ed.). Boston: Allyn & Bacon.

Lenz, B. K., Ellis, E. S., & Scanlon, D. (1996). *Teaching learning strategies to adolescents and adults with learning disabilities.* Austin, TX: Pro-Ed.

Levin, J. R. (1993). Mnemonic strategies and classroom learning: A twenty-year report card. *Elementary School Journal, 94,* 235–244.

Malone, L. D., & Mastropieri, M. A. (1992). Reading comprehension instruction: Summarization and self-monitoring training for students with learning disabilities. *Exceptional Children, 58,* 270–279.

Mokhtari, K., & Reichard, C. A. (2002). Assessing students' metacognitive awareness of reading strategies. *Journal of Educational Psychology, 94,* 249–259.

Pressley, M., & Afflerbach, P. (1995). *Verbal reports of reading: The nature of constructively responsive reading.* Hillsdale NJ: Erlbaum.

Pressley, M., Woloshyn, V., & Associates. (1995). *Cognitive strategy instruction that really improves children's academic performance* (2nd ed.). Cambridge, MA: Brookline.

Rauch, M., & Fillenworth, C. (1995). Motivating students to use newly learned study strategies. *Journal of Reading, 38,* 567–578.

Rohwer, W. D. (1984). An invitation to an educational psychology of studying. *Educational Psychologist, 9,* 1–14.

Rosenshine, B., Meister, J., & Chapman, S. (1996). Teaching students to generate questions: A review of the intervention studies. *Review of Educational Research, 66,* 181–221.

Scanlon, D. J., Deshler, D. D., & Schumaker, J. B. (1996). Can a strategy be taught and learned in secondary inclusive classrooms? *Learning Disabilities Research and Practice, 7,* 142–146.

Scheid, K. (1993). *Helping students become strategic learners: Guidelines for teaching.* Cambridge, MA: Brookline.

Strichart, S. S., Mangrum, C. T., & Iannuzzi, P. (1998). *Teaching study skills to students with learning disabilities, attention deficit disorders, or special needs* (2nd ed.). Boston: Allyn & Bacon.

Sweidel, G. B. (1996). Study strategy portfolio: A project to enhance study skills and time management. *Teaching of Psychology, 23,* 246–258.

Waldron, N. L., & McLeskey, J. (2000). Preventing academic failure. In K. M. Minke & G. G. Bear (Eds.), *Preventing school problems-Promoting school success: Strategies and programs that work* (pp. 171–209). Bethesda, MD: National Association of School Psychologists.

Weinstein, C. E., & Mayer, R. F. (1985). The teaching of learning strategies. In M. C. Wittrock (Ed.), *Handbook of research on teaching* (3rd ed., pp. 315–329). New York: Macmillan.

Weinstein, C. E., & Palmer, D. R. (1990). *Learning and Study Strategies Inventory-High school version.* Clearwater, FL: H&H Publishing.

Winne, P. H., & Hadwon, A. F. (1997). Studying as self-regulated learning. In D. J. Hacker, J. Dunlosky, & A. C. Graesser (Eds.), *Metacognition in educational theory and practice* (pp. 234–256). Hillsdale, NJ: Erlbaum.

Wood, E., Woloshyn, V. E., & Willoughby, T. (Eds.). (1995). *Cognitive strategy instruction for middle and high school.* Cambridge, MA: Brookline.

Zimmerman, B. J. (1998). Academic studying and the development of personal skill: A self-regulatory perspective. *Educational Psychologist, 33,* 73–86.

Zimmerman, B. J., Bonner, S., & Kovach, R. (1996). *Developing self-regulated learners: Beyond achievement to self-efficacy.* Washington, DC: American Psychological Association.

Zimmerman, B. J., & Kitsantas, A. (1997). Developmental phases in self-regulation: Shifting from process to outcome goals. *Journal of Educational Psychology, 89,* 29–36.

# 36

# Strategic Learning

**Mary Ann Rafoth**

*Indiana University of Pennsylvania*

## BACKGROUND AND DEVELOPMENT

Jean Piaget (1964) said that the goals of education are simply to prepare students to do things that have never been done before; to educate people who can invent, discover, and create; and to develop students who can think logically and reason. In other words, educators need to help students learn strategically and solve problems effectively. Successful students differ from unsuccessful students in the degree to which they are able to attach meaning to new information, select appropriate strategies to aid in retention, and match the way in which information is encoded to the performance demands of the criterion task. The teaching of learning strategies helps students with special needs experience successful inclusion in the regular classroom and promotes academic achievement and independent learning skills among *all* students.

A *learning strategy* is a voluntary activity that children use to learn or remember information. Strategies may be domain specific, such as applying a specific strategy to solve a particular kind of math problem, or higher order, such as using a strategy to sequence or coordinate other strategies (Bruning, Schraw, & Ronning, 1995). Table 1 describes common types of learning strategies. Students with effective learning strategies (behaviors that are directed at improving the processing of new information to aid learning) become independent learners by acting as a teacher to themselves. They recognize when they are experiencing difficulty or successfully retaining information, and they adapt their strategies accordingly.

### Developmental Aspects of Strategic Learning and Metacognition

Developmental aspects of independent learning must be considered when developing a strategic learning curriculum. In the classroom, teachers check students' comprehension and memory using questions, activities, and evaluations. Students do this for themselves when they learn what learning strategies to successfully employ. Because younger children have less developed executive processing skills to set expectations, focus, direct, and maintain direction; choose appropriate strategies; and monitor their learning, teachers typically play a more directive role in overseeing and guaranteeing these events in the primary grades. As children mature and curriculum demands for independent learning escalate, teachers place an increasing amount of responsibility on the learner.

This progression follows nicely the developmental sequence of learning strategies and metacognition (our knowledge and awareness of our cognitive processes), which emerge during the upper elementary grades and throughout middle and high school. Teachers assume that young children lack learning strategies and metacognitive skills and that their learning needs to be directed to a large extent. Likewise, as students progress in school many teachers assume that students are aware of appropriate strategies when studying and are capable of monitoring their own learning to a greater degree. However, while some students may spontaneously develop strong metacognitive skills, many do not.

The onset of metacognitve maturity (coinciding with acquisition of concrete thinking and, later, formal thinking in a Piagetian framework) explains increases in use of strategies and the improved memories of older children and adolescents. Actual short-term memory capacity reaches its potential (about seven meaningful units of information) by the time children are of school age. Flavell (1970) wrote that metacognition consists of three major factors: person, task, and strategy. Everything one knows about oneself and others as processors and retainers of information make up *person* factors. For instance, knowing that older children

**Table 1** *Types of Learning Strategies*

| Types of Strategies | Definition | Examples |
|---|---|---|
| 1. *Rehearsal* | Reviewing verbally or in writing; includes rereading or "looking over" something multiple times. | Writing spelling words five times.<br>Reading a text chapter over and over. |
| 2. *Elaboration* | Inserting or increasing meaning to enhance ease of memory. | Acronyms.<br>Acrostics.<br>Visualizations.<br>Rhymes, songs, and raps. |
| 3. *Organizational* | Enhancing meaningfulness and memory by grouping information. | Note-taking.<br>Concept webs.<br>Graphic organizers.<br>Assignment books. |
| 4. *Comprehension monitoring* | Enhancing understanding by predicting, reflecting, paraphrasing, self-testing, and reviewing. | SQ4R (survey, question, read, reflect, recite, review) technique. |
| 5. *Affective* | Enhancing motivation and/or decreasing performance anxiety. | Strategic learning.<br>Relaxation exercises.<br>Goal setting. |
| 6. *Problem solving* | Improving ability to solve problems by application of specific steps or techniques. | Visualization.<br>Personalization (changing a problem to increase personal relevancy).<br>Algorithms.<br>Heuristic approaches. |

are likely to remember more information on a memory task than younger children is person knowledge. Similarly, self-awareness about tasks that are difficult for an individual is representative of person knowledge. As students become aware of their own learning, this information is incorporated into their knowledge of metacognition and makes it possible for them to increase the efficiency and accuracy of their learning. *Task* factors involve information about how a particular task can best be handled and how successful one is likely to be at it. A student devoting more study time to difficult material is an example of a task factor. Knowledge about potentially employable strategies and their effectiveness characterize *strategy* factors. A student writing down a homework assignment to help remember the assignment is also an example of strategy knowledge. Children between 4 and 12 years of age become progressively more aware of person, task, and strategy variables as metacognitive awareness increases.

As with strategy use, distinct age-related changes in metacognitive knowledge have been reported in the literature, with older children demonstrating a better understanding of memory. Older children are also more aware that items they fail to recall on a test are more in need of further study than items they recalled successfully. By the end of elementary school, children know that memory skills vary from person to person and from situation to situation, that they do not have equally good memories in all situations, and their knowledge of various memory strategies has increased dramatically from what it was in kindergarten (Bruning et al., 1995). Metamemory, however, is not completely developed by the end of childhood. Many adolescents and college students have little knowledge about some important memory strategies (Schneider & Pressley, 1989). It is not unusual for college students to know little about elaborative or organizational study strategies or to have difficulty identifying what is important when studying from a text and to fail to effectively monitor learning (Schraw, 1994). However, students who believe that they control the learning process through the use of effective strategic techniques are more likely to be successful students than those who believe success is due to chance or luck (Margolis & McCabe, 2003; McCombs & Marzano, 1990; Palmer & Goetz, 1988).

The development of organizational study strategies parallels the development of rehearsal strategies, although rehearsal strategies develop earlier. Common strategies for organization include concept webbing, which is used with young children as well as high school students (Hyerle, 1995), outlining, and note-taking methods. Time management strategies include keeping assignment books, using calendars to plan study activity, and organizing study time around task difficulty and importance (Rafoth, 1999). Elaboration strategies involve creating connections that add meaning to the material to be remembered or understood. As a strategy for remembering, elaboration works because it requires children to create connections that have special meaning to them. The first elaboration strategies that children use, however, are often ineffective because their elaborations are not memorable. In fact, research has found that younger children remember more when elaborations are suggested by the experimenter than when children produce their own (Pressley, Borkowski, & Schneider, 1987). In contrast, the performance of adolescents and adults is better when they produce their own elaborations. Adolescents are more likely than older elementary school children to report that they use elaboration while studying. Ideally, note taking is a form of elaboration on what is learned as well as a written memory aid. Note-taking styles should develop as the student matures, with individuals developing a system that best matches their individual preference.

One of the last study strategies to develop during childhood involves activity aimed at determining if one can safely stop studying. Self-testing is one way to decide if study activity can be terminated, and this can be accomplished in several ways. Students who do not self-test are unlikely to engage in strong test-taking strategies. Students often make errors because they fail to read all distracters or to refer back to test questions (Scruggs, White, & Bennion, 1986). In general, older children are better than younger children at using retrieval strategies. From the ages of 4 to 12, children become more efficient and sophisticated in their use of retrieval strategies when they are having difficulty recalling information.

For similar reasons, young children are very poor at monitoring their own comprehension. That is, they are often unaware that they do not understand something. Children often do not monitor comprehension problems while reading (Mayer, 1992). Good readers monitor their comprehension while reading and adjust their reading strategies once miscomprehension is detected. Adjusting reading strategies in response to detected comprehension failures is a late-developing skill. Strategies used to lessen anxiety (e.g., relaxation training) or to self-motivate (e.g., goal setting, self-reinforcement, or self-management) are also increasingly important as children mature.

### Gender Differences

Research indicates that elementary school girls may be more competent than boys of the same age in their use of study and learning strategies (Pressley, Levin, Ghatala, & Ahmad, 1987). Waters (1981) suggested that this developmental lag for males is maintained from elementary school to college, at least in the use of organizational strategies. Cox and Waters (1986) demonstrated that consistent gender differences favoring girls occur across ages in the processing of verbal materials and in the use of organizational study strategies. Boys are also more likely than girls to be oblivious to their past failures as they make predictions about future performance (Parsons & Ruble, 1977). After failure, girls make lower predictions about performance. If children are oblivious to previous failures, it is unlikely that they will improve or adjust their study techniques accordingly. The available evidence indicates that strategies for learning develop at a faster pace in girls than in boys. What causes this acceleration is unclear. It may be related to physical–cognitive maturation, to school achievement, or to other related factors. Because few studies of memory and learning have systematically looked for possible gender differences, those studies that do report gender differences should be interpreted cautiously at present.

## PROBLEMS AND IMPLICATIONS

Students who do not leave school with a strong sense of how they learn and what strategies they may employ successfully to learn and remember are at a distinct disadvantage in postsecondary settings and will not be able to learn independently as adults. Much research has demonstrated that students with memory and study skill deficits present as immature learners. For example, research involving children with learning problems—including those with mild to moderate retardation and those with learning disabilities—has shown their memory to be similar to that of the younger, "normal" learner. In addition, children with reading disabilities have been found to lack study strategies appropriate for their age and intellectual level. Similarly, children with learning disabilities (LD) are less aware of how to effectively organize and study prose, spend less time studying, and are less likely than average readers to use an organization strategy on a memory task (Wong & Wilson, 1984). These students also have more difficulty generalizing strategies beyond the immediate task (Ryan, Ledger, Short, & Weed, 1982). Results similar to those reported for children with LD have been reported for children with mental retardation (Brown & Barclay, 1976). Moreover, all students who leave high school without a sense of personal study style and the ability to learn independently are not likely to reach their potential in postsecondary settings or vocationally later in life.

## ALTERNATIVE ACTIONS FOR PREVENTION AND INTERVENTION

### Development of Study Style

Knowledge of appropriate learning strategies and the ability to choose them appropriately and to judge their effectiveness may well differentiate successful from unsuccessful students more so than ability (Morris, 1990; Swanson, 1990). For this reason, it is essential that schools directly teach independent learning skills. Schmeck (1988) and Rafoth (1999) argue that the best way to aid students is to make the student's learning style more versatile by teaching strategies that allow for greater adaptation. Encouraging the development of deeper, more elaborative cognitive styles (in which students use strategies to enhance meaningfulness and accept personal responsibility for learning outcomes) enhances student learning (Schmeck, 1988). Accomplishing these goals is a challenge, but it can be pursued using a cohesive strategic learning program to strengthen the overall curriculum and support students with a variety of needs.

### Instructional Strategies

A recommended approach to teaching strategic learning skills is to embed related instructional strategies into content areas. To develop an embedded approach, schools should do the following:

- Develop a list of strategic learning objectives.
- Identify learning strategies to be gained by students.
- Identify instructional strategies and activities useful in teaching strategies across content areas.
- Identify evaluation methods (performance activities and portfolio samples).

An instructional consultation process is helpful in implementing a strategic learning curriculum. Table 2 describes a consultative process that outlines how to integrate learning strategy and study skills instruction into classroom and school-wide consultation based on the steps identified by Rosenfield (2002). Successfully creating a curriculum that uses embedded learning strategies involves engaging faculty in the process at an entry stage to establish the role of the teacher and support personnel in solving instructional problems. The second stage, *identification and analysis*, involves (a) identifying and analyzing the problem by isolating the teacher's or curricular objectives for a student or students, including examining for inclusion of strategic learning skills; (b) identifying prerequisite knowledge and skills, including those necessary for the acquisition or development of strategic learning skills; (c) assessing the students' level of acquisition; (d) identifying the strategies used to modify instruction or materials, including learning strategy instruction; and (e) assessing the quality of the students' use of strategies. The second stage flows logically into the third, or *intervention*, stage, in which the intervention is designed. Integral to successful strategic learning interventions is the establishment of feedback loops to both students and teachers regarding the efficacy of learning strategies and their impact on student achievement and learning. Finally, as in all successful consultations, the intervention must include a way to assess the extent to which students have met strategic learning goals (see Table 2).

### The Role of Strategic Learning in Basic and Advanced Skill Attainment

To learn independently, students must have a minimum level of competency in the basics of reading, writing, and mathematics. Adopting a mastery approach in these core

**Table 2** *Integrating Strategic Learning Instruction Into Classroom or School District–Wide Consultation*

1. Entry and contracting
   - Establish the role of the teacher and support personnel in solving instructional problems.
   - Establish importance of strategic learning.
   - Review the information processing model and the importance of interactive learning.
   - Reinforce the problem-solving model for solving instructional problems.
2. Problem identification and analysis
   - Identify the teacher's objectives for the student (e.g., whether any learning strategies are included in the objectives).
   - Identify the prerequisite skills (e.g., whether any learning strategies are required).
   - Identify if the student has the skills that are required.
   - Identify strategies that have been tried for modifying instruction or instructional materials.
   - Conduct observations, including observation of students' study and strategic learning skills; also assess what the teacher has suggested to students regarding the acquisition of such skills.
   - Conduct a curriculum-based assessment that includes (a) instructional level (include developmental level), (b) task analysis (ask what learning strategies are needed to accomplish the task), and (c) process and error analysis (ask whether strategies are ineffective for the task).
3. Intervention
   - Provide the classroom teacher and student with feedback regarding the efficacy of strategy instruction.
   - Realize that there are no pat answers (some trial and error will be involved in instruction in strategic learning skills).
4. Termination
   - Include progress made toward strategic learning goals and outcomes and what future development should be expected.

areas (students must achieve a mastery level of at least 80% accuracy on all identified objectives) helps ensure that all students are reaching competency in important skill areas. This, of course, is the main rationale behind the No Child Left Behind Act. In order to accomplish this in the classroom, teachers need to design instruction so that a portion of class time in these skill areas allows students to work at their own pace and on materials matched to their individual instructional levels. Moreover, to meet the demands of the act students must be taught to be strategic learners who routinely apply strategies to aid comprehension and solve problems.

Direct instruction in strategic study skills, such as taking notes, reading for factual information and independent comprehension, and in general, absorbing skills seen as necessary for success in high school and college, must occur in middle school. One approach is to help students form effective elaborative connections by providing them with questions to consider when reading or listening. Without such prompts, it is doubtful that children will create their own elaborations, and even when elaborations are created, it is unlikely that they will be memorable ones. Instruction on using time wisely, avoiding errors, guessing, using deductive reasoning, and preventing carelessness can significantly increase student test performance (Sarason, 1980). Length of training is related to success, as is developmental level.

To address the need to provide students with direct instruction in strategic study, schools must adopt and embed strategic learning skill objectives across the curriculum and evaluate students to determine successful acquisition. To help accomplish this, the whole faculty should adopt a series of strategic learning and organizational objectives. A variety of instructional strategies can be used to teach a specific set of learning strategies and study skills that support objectives embedded across content areas (see chapter 35, "Study Skills"). Performance checklists and portfolios are helpful techniques for assessing acquisition of learning strategies and study skills. For example, students should be responsible for developing study plans for several exams that can be included in their portfolios. Students can complete brief performance checklists to document their application of strategies to the required problem solving.

The emphasis on strategic learning enables students with special needs to gain skills that will help them succeed in the regular classroom and gives *all* students exposure to study skills they will need in competitive classroom environments in the future. Moreover, the likelihood that *all* students will become independent learners is greatly enhanced. Table 3 presents a method for helping students acquire strategic learning skills by teaching them how to take and use notes in mathematics.

Strategic learning skills are also essential to students who are given opportunities for acceleration in content areas. Acceleration in the curriculum (allowing students to move through the regular curriculum at a quicker pace and increase exposure to more content than usual) has been found to be an effective means of increasing

**Table 3** *Teaching Strategic Learning: Advice to Students on Using Their Notes to Prepare for a Math Test*

1. Identify the type or types of problems that will be on the test. If you are not sure, ask the teacher.
2. Find the selection in your notes that covers each type of problem. You should have written a heading at the beginning of each day's notes.
3. Read through your notes and rework the examples step by step. Highlight or underline main headings and important information. Put a star next to or a box around examples. Add extra notes of explanation where needed.
4. If there is something you don't understand in your notes, find the section in your textbook and read it over. If you still don't understand something, check with a classmate or your teacher.
5. Once you think you understand the examples in your notes, make up new practice problems and see if you can solve them, following the same procedures as in the examples in your notebook.
6. If possible, exchange practice problems with a classmate. Check to make sure you both come out with the same answers.
7. If you are permitted to use your notebook during a test, follow these same procedures during the test, using the test questions instead of new practice problems. Of course, omit Step 6—do not check answers with a classmate—but do check your own work on a test.

achievement among able learners (see chapter 34, "Giftedness"). Good study habits, including strategic learning skills and the ability to learn independently, are essential to successful acceleration. Many students with strong motivation, good study habits, and above-average ability levels reach their highest potential through acceleration. When acceleration is limited to students who meet state qualifications for giftedness, however, this option is closed to many. Intentional instruction of learning strategies, coupled with enrichment experiences built into the curriculum horizontally, increases the likelihood that all students will become both lifelong and independent learners. Strategic learning skills are essential for the advanced as well as the at-risk learner.

## Specific Strategies for Learning Problems

When services are brought to the regular classroom more frequently, resource staff can work with more students and assist the classroom teacher in improving overall instruction using the methods outlined above. Studies have shown that it is possible to instruct underachieving students in self-testing and other strategies (Leal, Crays, & Moely, 1985; Weinstein, Ridley, Dahl, & Weber, 1989). The following are examples of successful strategy instruction with special populations, particularly students with learning disabilities:

- When students have difficulty with acquisition of rote information, such as the times tables, embedding the information into a meaningful context, such as a game, rap, or rhyme, is helpful for drill and practice (Leal & Rafoth, 1991; Fulk, 1994; Rafoth, 1999).
- When students cannot organize ideas, use visual maps and webs (Hyerle, 1995; Rafoth, Leal, & DeFabo, 1993).
- When students have difficulty with comprehension and recall of new concepts, teach elaboration strategies (Weinstein et al., 1989; Colson & Mehring, 1990).
- When students are not motivated to self-regulate learning, teach them to self-evaluate in relation to a study task and to connect the task to a future goal (McCombs & Marzano, 1990; Duchardt, Deshler & Shumaker, 1995).
- When students have difficulty with problem solving, teach heuristic approaches within specific domain contexts (Bransford, Sherwood, Vye, & Riesser 1986).
- For students with high test anxiety, teach relaxation exercises and test-taking strategies (Sarason, 1980).
- For students with poor note-taking skills, teach strategies for paraphrasing lecture information, using abbreviations and symbols, and note-review strategies (Hughes & Suritsky, 1991; McAndrew, 1983).
- For students with poor written language, provide structure through strategies for planning, production, and revision, such as the WRITER and COPS models or the PLEASE strategy (see Welch, 1992).
- For students with poor reading comprehension, teach strategies for enhancing comprehension, such as the SQ4R and POSSE strategies, across disciplines. Increasing student awareness and ability to analyze text structures can also improve comprehension (see Englert & Mariage, 1991; Simmons, Kameenui, & Darch, 1988; Wilheim, 2001).

- For students with difficulty in recalling new vocabulary or essential detail, use mnemonic instruction (see Scruggs & Mastropieri, 1989).
- For students who have difficulty self-monitoring and predicting achievement accurately, teach them to self-test and predict their success by monitoring their performance (Reid & Harris, 1989; Mushinski & Mastropieri, 1990).

## Modification of Instruction to Enhance Strategic Learning

In general, learning strategies are perhaps best assessed by directly observing and interviewing a student. Teachers should also encourage students to consider which strategies work best for them, to predict their grades on tests, and to practice self-testing to increase their ability to know when they have mastered the task. At this juncture, students may begin to learn to tailor their learning strategies to match their individual learning needs. For example, students may choose the problem-solving strategy that works best for them, including algorithmic solutions, personalization strategies, and visualization strategies. Students who are person-oriented, field-dependent learners may prefer personalization strategies in which they substitute their name or friends' names and interests for details in problems to make them more concrete and solvable. Students who prefer spatial and visual learning may prefer to visualize solutions by drawing pictures. Students, once exposed and reinforced with a variety of learning strategies, may choose those strategies that complement their own learning so that a personal study approach emerges (Rafoth, et al., 1993).

Table 4 presents a Learning Strategies Checklist that can be used to help teachers analyze their instruction to adapt to a variety of instructional strategies and to include learning strategies instruction. In high school many of the skills described earlier for use in middle school will need to be reinforced. The most important task during these years is to develop as strategic learners and to improve skills such as taking notes, taking tests, and improving comprehension. Secondary school teachers must consider how to reinforce the development of effective note-taking. For example, not only should they present information in an organized fashion, cite frequent examples, and indicate key relationships to foster selective perception, semantic encoding, and retention, they also should encourage students to do the same. This can be accomplished by making specific suggestions about how to record information in notes, providing a skeletal outline, and using a note-taking system as an advanced organizer. Teachers might also cue students to regularly generate their own examples to test their understanding of new concepts. Again, initially teachers will have to check examples and provide feedback to the learner about their accuracy. Likewise, requiring students to frequently paraphrase information they have read or heard in the form of oral and written responses aids in comprehension (Aaron & Joshi, 1992). It is critical that students are directly taught that this strategy will aid in comprehension and will help them monitor their learning (Paris & Jacobs, 1984; Paris, Cross, & Lipson, 1984).

Although systems for improving comprehension, such as the SQ4R technique and reciprocal teaching (Palinscar & Brown, 1984), are helpful in training students, frequent embedded practice is necessary for skill acquisition and generalization. Through consistent and coordinated instruction, schools can embed strategic learning skill objectives into the curriculum and take a more active and direct role in shaping independent learning.

# SUMMARY

A major difference between mature and immature learners is the spontaneous use of efficient learning strategies. That is, in learning and study situations successful learners employ a variety of acquisition and retrieval strategies that less mature learners do not. Schools have not intentionally taught students to acquire strategic learning skills and thus develop the capability for independent learning.

Less effective learners include not only young children but also students with average ability that are underachieving, that is, those who have been identified as having learning disabilities, cognitive deficiencies, or other developmental disabilities in school. Study after study has shown that younger and less proficient students are less strategic in their learning efforts. They generally know fewer strategies and have little awareness of when and how to use the strategies that they do know. Students become more active in initiating strategy use in a variety of settings as they become older. Older students also know more about the workings of memory. Improvements in performance occur when children are taught to use more effective strategies.

However, strategies should not be taught by discussion alone. Children require intensive training and

**Table 4** *Learning Strategies Checklist for Teachers*

1. First, analyze the lesson by putting a checkmark in each category and underlining the types of activities included in the lesson. Mark any learning strategies that are included as well.
2. Second, consider what instructional strategies are not used and what activities might be added to the lesson. Put a plus sign in the categories that could be added and circle the activities that might be included, or write in your own suggestions.

***Instructional Strategies Style Categories***

_____ *Visual* (students have something to look at)
Example activities: viewing a model or real object or animal; viewing an overhead, chart, or concept web; watching a video; reviewing a handout; readings; ________________ ________________

_____ *Auditory* (students have something to listen to)
Example activities: oral preview, summary, or review; audiotapes; actual sounds from the environment; ________________ ________________

_____ *Kinesthetic* (students learn by doing some activity)
Example activities: *conduct an experiment,* work through an exercise, make a model, ________________

_____ *Part-to-whole cognitive style* (students move from part to whole in the thinking process)
Example activities: put facts together to construct a concept web, assemble pieces into a model, discover information gradually to solve a problem, complete a puzzle, ________________

_____ *Whole-to-part cognitive style* (students move from whole to part analysis in the thinking process)
Example activities: break out parts of a task, make an outline from a reading, take a model apart, dissections, identify components of a process, ________________

_____ *Field dependent* (students interact with the environment and social context)
Example activities: large or small group discussion, think-pair-share, cooperative learning, buddy exercises, teacher-student dialogues, ________________

_____ *Field independent* (students work on their own to complete a project or analyze data)
Example activities: independent field or seat work, ________________

***What Learning Strategies Are Embedded in the Lesson?***

_____ *Elaboration strategies* (visual imagery, acrostics, acronyms, etc.)

_____ *Organizational strategies* (note-taking aids such as skeletal outlines, information chunking, cluster cards, concept webs, etc.)

_____ *Comprehension strategies* (SQ4R, problem-solving cues, strategies for following directions, etc.)

_____ *Monitoring strategies* (check sheets, etc.)

_____ *Problem-solving strategies* (personalization, visualization, algorithm identification cues, etc.)

_____ *Affective strategies* (goal setting, relaxation, reinforcement, etc.)

practice in the use of any one study strategy as well as feedback about why and when they should employ the strategy. In addition, students should be encouraged to evaluate strategies. What choices work best for them? Which strategies meet their individual needs? As students move through school, helping them to develop a personally effective approach to learning and studying should be a priority. The development of a strategic learning curriculum that includes embedded strategy instruction in all classes is essential for the creation of independent learning skills in all students.

# RECOMMENDED RESOURCES

## Books and Other Printed Material

Bransford, J. D., Brown, A. L., & Cocking, R. R. (1999). *How people learn: Brain, mind, experience, and school.* Washington, DC: National Academy Press.

This book is both comprehensive and readable in its approach to explaining the learning process and what facilitates learning. Part II of the book, Learners and

Learning, speaks most directly to how strategic learning occurs and the relationship between the mind and brain. The book presents an excellent overview and discussion of research on memory, developmental acquisition of strategies, the voyage from novice to expert, and learning and transfer.

Campbell, L. (2003). *Mindful learning: 101 proven strategies for student and teacher success.* Thousand Oaks, CA: Corwin Press.

This book includes 101 instructional and learning strategies that reflect current learning theory and research. The strategies are well presented and easily understood and are integrated into classroom practice. The author reviews cognitive style and individual differences in learning and provides concrete teaching and learning strategies to help instructors teach more effectively and build strategic learning in students.

Rafoth, M. A. (1999). *Inspiring independent learning.* Washington, DC: National Education Association Professional Library.

This book provides practical examples of embedded learning and study strategies. Chapter 1 provides an overview of the teacher's role in developing strategic learning behavior in students from a developmental perspective that speaks to classroom teachers, curriculum directors, school administrators, and support professionals working to help every student succeed in the regular classroom. Chapters 2 through 4 include many examples of strategies that facilitate student learning and increase the likelihood that they will learn independently in the future. The final two chapters deal with assessing strategy use and metacognition and related interventions, including peer tutoring. A peer tutoring program and manual, study skills interview, and metacognitive interview are included. The book's text is available free online from the NEA's Professional Library website.

## Websites

*http://www.newhorizons.org*

At this website you will find information on researched and widely implemented methods of helping students learn more successfully. The information includes a description of how the teaching and learning strategies work, where they have been applied, and where to find further information.

*http://www.ku-crl.org*

This site presents the University of Kansas's Center for Research on Learning's learning strategies curriculum. Topic areas include strategies for reading, studying, and remembering information; writing; improving assignment and test performance; interacting effectively with others; motivation; and math.

*http://www.ldonline.org*

The LD Online site focuses on articles that discuss helping students with learning disabilities become more efficient and effective learners by teaching them how to learn. The goal is to equip students with a repertoire of strategies for learning.

# REFERENCES

Aaron, P. G., & Joshi, R. M. (1992). *Reading problems: Consultation and remediation.* New York: Guilford Press.

Bransford, J., Sherwood, R., Vye, N., Rieser, J. (1986). Teaching thinking and problem solving. *American Psychologist, 41,* 1078–1089.

Brown, A. L., & Barclay, C. R. (1976). The effects of training specific mnemonics on the metamnemonic efficiency of retarded children. *Child Development, 47,* 71–80.

Bruning, R., Schraw, G., & Ronning, R. (1995). *Cognitive psychology and instruction.* Englewood Cliffs, NJ: Prentice Hall.

Colson, S., & Mehring, T. (1990). Facilitating memory in students with learning disabilities. *LD Forum, 16,* 75–79.

Cox, D., & Waters, H. S. (1986). Sex differences in the use of organization strategies: A developmental analysis. *Journal of Experimental Child Psychology, 41,* 18–37.

Duchardt, B. A., Deshler, D., & Shumaker, J. B. (1995). A strategic intervention for enabling students with learning disabilities to identify and change their ineffective beliefs. *Learning Disability Quarterly, 18,* 186–201.

Englert, C., & Mariage, T. (1991). Making students partners in the comprehension process: Organizing the reading POSSE. *Learning Disability Quarterly 14,* 123–140.

Flavell, J. H. (1970). Developmental studies of mediated memory. In H. W. Reese & L. P. Lipsitt (Eds.), *Advances in child development* (pp. 181–211). New York: Academic Press.

Fulk, B. M. (1994). Mnemonic keyword strategy training for students with learning disabilities. *Learning Disabilities Research, 9,* 179–185.

Hughes, C. A., & Suritsky, K. A. (1994). Note-taking skills of university students with and without learning disabilities. *Journal of Learning Disabilities, 27,* 20–25.

Hyerle, D. (1995). Thinking maps: Seeing is understanding. *Educational Leadership, 53,* 85–88.

Leal, L., Crays, N., & Moely, B. E. (1985). Training children to use a self-monitoring study strategy in preparation for recall: Maintenance and generalization effects. *Child Development, 56,* 643–653.

Leal, L., & Rafoth, M. (1991). Memory strategy development: What teachers do makes a difference. *Intervention in School and Clinic, 26,* 234–237.

Margolis, H., & McCabe, P. (2003). Self-efficacy: A key to improving the motivation of struggling learners. *Preventing School Failure, 47,* 162–170.

Mayer, R. E. (1992). *Thinking, problem-solving, and cognition* (2nd ed.). New York: Freeman.

McAndrew, D. A. (1983). Underlining and note-taking: Some suggestions from research. *Journal of Reading, 27,* 103–108.

McCombs, B., & Marzano, R. (1990). Putting the self in self-regulated learning: The self as agent in integrated will and skill. *Educational Psychologist, 25,* 51–69.

Morris, C. C. (1990). Retrieval processes underlying confidence in comprehension judgements. *Journal of Experimental Psychology: Learning, Memory, and Cognition, 16,* 223–232.

Mushinski, B. M., & Mastropieri, M. A. (1990). Training positive attitudes. *Intervention in School and Clinic, 26,* 79–83.

Palinscar, A., & Brown, A. (1984). Reciprocal teaching of comprehension fostering strategies and comprehension monitoring strategies. *Cognition and Instruction, 1,* 117–175.

Palmer, D. J., & Goetz, E. (1988). Selection and use of study strategies: The role of the studier's beliefs about self and strategies. In C. E. Weinstein, C. E. Goetz, & P. Alexander (Eds.), *Learning and study strategies* (pp. 41–57). San Diego, CA: Academic Press.

Paris, S., Cross, D., & Lipson, M. (1984). Informal strategies for learning: A program to improve children's reading awareness and comprehension. *Journal of Educational Psychology, 76,* 1239–1252.

Paris, S., & Jacobs, J. (1984). The benefit of informed instruction for children's reading and comprehension. *Child Development, 55,* 2083–2093.

Parsons, J., & Ruble, D. (1977). The development of achievement-related expectancies. *Child Development, 48,* 1075–1079.

Piaget, J. (1964). Development and learning. In R. E. Ripple & V. N. Rockcastle (Eds.), *Readings in learning and human abilities: Educational Psychology* (pp. 208–256). Oxford England: Harper & Row.

Pressley, M., Borkowski, J., & Schneider, W. (1987). Cognitive strategies: Good strategy users coordinate metacognition and knowledge. In R. Vasta & G. Whitehurst (Eds.), *Annals of child development* (Vol. 5, pp. 89–129). Greenwich, CT: JAI.

Pressley, M., Levin, J., Ghatala, E., & Ahmad, M. (1987). Test monitoring in young grade school children. *Journal of Experimental Child Psychology, 43,* 96–111.

Rafoth, M. A. (1999). Inspiring independent learning. Washington DC: NEA Professional Library.

Rafoth, M. A., Leal, L., & DeFabo, L. (1993). *Strategies for learning and remembering: Study skills across the curriculum.* Washington, DC: NEA Professional Library.

Reid, R., & Harris, K. (1989). Self-monitoring of performance. *LD Forum, 15,* 39–42.

Rosenfield, S. (2002). Instructional consultation. In A. Thomas & J. Grimes (Eds.), *Best practices in school psychology IV* (pp. 608–623). Bethesda, MD: National Association of School Psychologists.

Ryan, E., Ledger, G., Short, E., & Weed, K. (1982). Promoting the use of active comprehension strategies by poor readers. *Topics in Learning Disabilities, 2,* 53–60.

Sarason, I. (1980). *Test anxiety: Theory, research, and applications.* Hillsdale, NJ: Erlbaum.

Schmeck, R. (1988). Individual differences and learning strategies. In C. E. Weinstein, E. Goetz, & P. Alexander (Eds.), *Learning and study strategies* (pp. 171–188). San Diego, CA: Academic Press.

Schneider, W., & Pressley, M. (1989). *Memory development between 2 and 20.* New York: Springer-Verlag.

Schraw, G. (1994). The effect of metacognitive knowledge on local and global monitoring. *Contemporary Educational Psychology, 19,* 143–154.

Scruggs, T., & Mastropieri, M. (1989). Mnemonic instruction of LD students: A field-based evaluation. *Learning Disability Quarterly, 12,* 119–125.

Scruggs, T., White, K., & Bennion, K. (1986). Teaching test-taking skills to elementary-grade students: A meta-analysis. *Elementary School Journal, 87,* 69–82.

Simmons, D. C., Kameenui, E. J., & Darch, C. (1988). The effect of textual proximity on fourth- and fifth-grade L.D. students' metacognitive awareness and strategic comprehension behavior. *Learning Disability Quarterly, 11,* 380–395.

Swanson, H. L. (1990). Influence of metacognitive knowledge and aptitude on problem-solving. *Journal of Educational Psychology, 82,* 306–314.

Waters, H. S. (1981). Organizational strategies in memory for prose: A developmental analysis. *Journal of Experimental Child Psychology, 32,* 223–246.

Weinstein, C. E., Ridley, D., Dahl, T., & Weber, E. (1989). Helping students develop strategies for effective learning. *Educational Leadership, 46,* 17–19.

Welch, M. (1992). The PLEASE strategy: A metacognitive learning strategy for improving the paragraph writing of students with mild learning disabilities. *Learning Disability Quarterly, 15,* 119–128.

Wilheim, J. D. (2001). *Improving comprehension with think-aloud strategies.* New York: Scholastic.

Wong, B. Y. L., & Wilson, M. (1984). Investigating awareness of and teaching passage organization in learning disabled children. *Journal of Learning Disabilities, 17,* 477–482.

# 37

# Sports and Physical Activities

**Ronald E. Reeve***
**Maureen R. Weiss***
*University of Virginia*

## BACKGROUND AND DEVELOPMENT

Sport participation is a ubiquitous phenomenon among children and adolescents in American society. An estimated 30 million youth between the ages of 5 and 18 years engage in community-based or agency-sponsored sports (e.g., Little League, U.S. Olympic Development programs, YMCA, Boys' and Girls' Clubs), ranging from individual sports such as swimming and gymnastics to team sports such as baseball and basketball (Weiss & Hayashi, 1996). Another 7 million adolescents compete in organized school sports, the most popular among boys being football, basketball, track and field, baseball, and soccer. Among girls, the highest participation rates occur in basketball, track and field, volleyball, fast-pitch softball, and soccer (National Federation of State High School Associations, 2003).

Girls and boys participate in sport for a multitude of reasons, most notably to learn and improve skills, to be with and make friends, to feel part of a group, and to have fun (Weiss & Williams, 2004). When caring and competent adults supervise youth activities, children experience positive feelings that translate to a desire to continue participation and opportunities to reap the benefits afforded by involvement in such activities.

A substantial knowledge base in youth sport psychology documents the potential benefits of athletic participation. Some of these benefits include self-esteem, social relationships, intrinsic motivation, self-regulation skills, and character development (Weiss, 1993; Weiss & Smith, 2002). Studies based in the school setting have demonstrated positive long-term effects of sport participation on academic achievement, development of peer networks, and formation of self-identity (Barber, Eccles, & Stone, 2001; Eccles & Barber, 1999; Marsh & Kleitman, 2003). Moreover, consistent participation in structured extracurricular activities has been associated with lower dropout rates, lower aggression and other antisocial behaviors, and higher educational status (including greater likelihood of college attendance) among adolescents (Mahoney, 2000; Mahoney, Cairns, & Farmer, 2003). In sum, youth involvement in sport and physical activity affords many physical, social, and mental health outcomes.

It is important to note, however, that improvements in self-perceptions, motivation, and interpersonal competence, among other personal characteristics, are not automatic consequences of sport involvement. A growing literature on risk prevention and resiliency demonstrates that effective youth development programs are those that emphasize personal skill development (e.g., self-regulation, social responsibility), include positive adult leadership styles and behaviors, and are characterized by a climate focused on learning and mastery (Catalano, Berglund, Ryan, Lonczak, & Hawkins, 2002; Petitpas, Cornelius, Van Raalte, & Jones, 2005). Educators and parents are responsible for ensuring that youth glean positive experiences from their activity participation.

In this chapter we review what we know and what we can do to maximize children's skill and health outcomes through sport participation. First, we review research on potential positive outcomes of sport participation—self-perceptions, social relationships, intrinsic motivation, and character development. Next, we review potential negative aspects inherent in competitive sport and implications for psychosocial development. Finally, we synthesize the research to offer recommendations for parents

*Note: Authors are listed alphabetically. Each contributed equally to the chapter.

and psychologists to maximize positive effects and minimize negative effects of participating in organized sport.

## POSITIVE PSYCHOSOCIAL OUTCOMES OF SPORT PARTICIPATION

A number of social–psychological theories have been productive for understanding and explaining children's thoughts, beliefs, emotions, and behaviors in sport contexts (see Horn, 2004; Weiss & Ferrer-Caja, 2002; Weiss & Smith, 2002). Foremost are Harter's (1978, 1999) theories on competence motivation and global self-worth, Eccles et al.'s (1983) expectancy-value theory, Deci and Ryan's (1985) self-determination theory, achievement goal theories (Ames, 1992; Nicholls, 1989), and moral development theories (Bandura, 1986; Haan, 1977; Rest, 1984). These theories have guided research on youth sport psychology over the past 20 years, resulting in a wealth of knowledge about children's self-perceptions, social relationships, motivation, and character development. Several robust findings on these developmental outcomes suggest how educators, psychologists, and parents may structure situations and modify their behaviors to maximize children's positive experiences through sport involvement. We review research on each of these important topics in the following sections.

### Self-Perceptions

Self-perceptions refer to an individual's global and domain-specific self-evaluations. *Self-esteem* is an individual's global self-evaluation of worthiness and significance as a person, whereas *perceived competence* refers to one's beliefs or judgments about abilities in a particular domain (e.g., academics, sports) or subdomain (e.g., math, swimming) (Weiss & Ebbeck, 1996). When considering the child's self-perceptions in sports and physical activities, it is important to understand how perceptions of physical competence are developed and how these self-appraisals influence motivated behavior, such as choosing to continue a sport from year to year, persisting when learning difficult skills, and maintaining an intrinsic desire to improve skills.

Because perceived competence is a critical variable within most theories, a logical question is "How do children make judgments about how competent they are?" Sources of information include parent feedback, coach evaluation, peer comparison, peer evaluation, performance statistics, skill improvement, ease of learning skills, effort, goal attainment, and event outcome. Research shows age-related differences in the use of these sources (Horn, 2004). Children under 10 years of age report greater use of parent feedback and game outcome to judge physical competence than do older children. Older children (ages 10 to 15 years) use peer comparison and evaluation, as well as coach feedback, relatively more than younger children do. Older adolescents (ages 16 to 18 years) use self-referenced information (e.g., skill improvement, effort, goal achievement) more frequently in comparison to younger adolescents and also use a wider variety of information sources, including social comparison and evaluation.

Children and adolescents frequently use feedback by parents and coaches, and peer comparison and evaluation, as sources for judging how athletically skilled they are. If young participants interpret these and other sources of information positively, level of perceived competence (how high or low a child judges his or her ability) will be positively affected. In turn, belief that one is good at sports is associated with greater enjoyment and a "love of the game," as well as greater likelihood of continuing one's involvement and trying hard when the going gets tough. In sum, perceptions of competence are key to understanding the quality of children's experiences in sport and physical activity.

Consistent with Harter's (1999) model of global self-worth, perceptions of domain-specific competence, together with reflected appraisals and social comparison, are primary sources of self-esteem development (Horn, 2004; Weiss & Ebbeck, 1996). *Reflected appraisals* refer to verbal and nonverbal behaviors from significant adults and peers that convey approval or judgment of the child's mastery attempts and performances. When a coach rolls his eyes following a fielding error, the child is likely to interpret this as disapproval, whereas hand clapping by a parent following the same performance may be viewed as acceptance and encouragement to do better next time. *Social comparison* is the child's attempt to "measure up" or evaluate his or her skills and abilities relative to those of teammates or other peers.

Research demonstrates the predictive value of perceived competence and adult and peer influence on youths' self-esteem. Ebbeck and Stuart (1996) found that youth sport participants who reported higher physical competence and greater importance placed by parents and teammates on being successful in sport were also higher in self-esteem. Ebbeck and Weiss (1998) found that participants who had more positive beliefs about their physical competence reported greater positive affect toward sport, which in turn related to self-esteem. A. L. Smith (1999) found that youth who perceived greater peer acceptance and close friendship in physical activity reported higher physical self-worth, attraction toward physical activity, intrinsic motivation, and physical activity behavior (frequency, intensity, duration). Together, reflected appraisals by parents, coaches, and peers, and social comparison to peers are significant ways by which youth form judgments about their ability in sport (perceived competence) and worth as a person (self-esteem). These findings lead naturally to the next important developmental outcome of sport participation—social relationships with parents, coaches, and peers.

## Social Relationships: Parents, Coaches, and Peers

Social acceptance and affiliation motives are major reasons why youth initiate, continue, and sustain their participation in sport (Weiss & Williams, 2004). Examples include being with and making friends, gaining social recognition or approval from parents and coaches, and achieving social status among one's peer group. Children's perceptions of social acceptance and approval from significant adults and peers figure prominently in whether they view their sport experiences as positive or negative. Therefore, it should not be surprising that abundant research has explored children's relationships with parents, coaches, and peers, and how these relationships influence self-perceptions, emotional reactions, and motivated behavior.

***Parents.*** Parents influence their child's achievement-related attitudes and behaviors through role modeling, providing experiences, and interpreting experiences (Fredricks & Eccles, 2004). Role modeling refers to parents' exhibition of attitudes and behaviors concerning the value of being successful in a domain. Parents may do this by expressing positive affect following a workout or after coaching their child. Providing experiences refers to opportunities parents afford their child, such as buying sports equipment, transporting the child to practices and games, and paying for specialty camps and coaches. Interpreting experiences refers to parents' verbal and nonverbal communication about their child's participation behaviors. A parent's value judgment speaks loudly when he or she asks a daughter or son after a game, "What did you learn today?" as opposed to "Did you win?"

Several studies illustrate a strong link between parental beliefs, expectancies, and behaviors with children's psychosocial responses in sport (see Weiss, 2003; Weiss & Ferrer-Caja, 2002). First, parents who express positive competence beliefs and value toward being successful in sport for their child have children who report higher perceived competence, enjoyment, and motivation to participate. Second, parental feedback and interactions that are interpreted as social support and encouragement, and not as pressure, positively influence children's competence judgments and enjoyment of sport. Finally, parents who are positive role models (e.g., are physically active, play or coach sports, enjoy working out) have a positive effect on their child's enjoyment of and involvement in physical activity.

***Coaches.*** Coaches are also significant socializers of children's self-perceptions, emotional reactions, and achievement behaviors in sport (see Horn, 2002; Weiss & Ferrer-Caja, 2002). Coaches' feedback, leadership style, and structuring of the motivational climate influence a child's perceived competence and self-determination, which in turn affect their motivational orientation and motivated behavior (effort, persistence). Coaches' feedback and reinforcement can be characterized as informational or evaluative in nature; both are strongly related to young athletes' ability beliefs, enjoyment, satisfaction with their sport experience, and inclination to continue participation. Consistent findings show that coaches who engage in more frequent contingent and appropriate praise combined with instruction following successful attempts (i.e., specific to level of performance; given sincerely based on the athlete's potential), and who offer encouragement combined with corrective instruction following errors, are associated with athletes who report higher perceived competence, enjoyment, and motivation. By contrast, coaches who use a punitive style, characterized by criticism for mistakes or instruction provided in a negative manner ("How many times do I have to tell you to use two hands?"), are associated with athletes who report more negative psychosocial outcomes.

Coach leadership style is also linked with athletes' psychosocial responses in sport. Coaches who provide children with some autonomy or choice in activities help foster feelings of self-determination and enhance motivational attitudes and behaviors. By contrast, an autocratic or controlling coach may thwart a child's feeling of autonomy, ultimately affecting desire to engage in the activity. Finally, coaches color the practice and competition climate in which youngsters participate. A mastery climate is characterized by coach recognition and evaluation for self-referenced forms of success (i.e., improving skills, achieving goals), and is most conducive to positive achievement-related attitudes, emotions, and behaviors. By contrast, a performance climate that emphasizes norm-referenced forms of success, such as comparison to others' performances and winning, is conducive to high anxiety, low perceived competence, and decreased intrinsic motivation. Several studies show a positive relationship between coach-structured mastery climate and positive attitudes, beliefs about competency, and motivated behaviors among youth participants (see Weiss & Ferrer-Caja, 2002).

***Peers.*** Children's peer relationships in sport are important determinants of self-evaluations, affective reactions, and motivation to participate (see Weiss & Stuntz, 2004). Peer acceptance, or one's popularity and status within one's peer group, is positively associated with being good in sports and being a leader of activities. Moreover, greater peer acceptance is positively associated with positive emotional responses and greater motivation to participate in sport and physical activities. Close friendship refers to a mutual dyadic peer relationship, one that is characterized by similarity of interests, self-esteem enhancement, emotional support, and loyalty (Weiss, Smith, & Theeboom, 1996). Children who identify high friendship quality in sport and physical activity report more positive self-perceptions, greater attraction toward physical activity, and higher intrinsic motivation and commitment to sport (e.g., Smith, 1999; Weiss & Smith, 2002).

Sport is a context in which salient peer relationships may develop, and such relationships are key to children's positive sport experiences and psychosocial development. Thus parents, coaches, and psychologists should pay special attention to structuring physical activity environments so that positive peer relationships are fostered and youth may benefit from the social support (emotional, instrumental, companionship) that emanates from such relationships. Several recent studies that emphasize team-building and other activities to enhance group cohesion represent efforts to highlight the importance of peer relationships within sport and physical activity groups (Carron & Hausenblas, 1998).

## Motivation

Motivation refers to the *why* of behavior, such as why children participate in a sport year after year, why they may choose to discontinue a program, and why some try hard and persist at learning skills and others slack off or simply give up (Weiss & Williams, 2004). The early descriptive research on children's reasons for participation pointed to three key motives: (a) to develop or demonstrate physical competence (learn and improve skills, get physically fit), (b) to attain social acceptance and approval (make friends, be recognized by the coach), and (c) to enjoy experiences related to sport involvement (have fun, experience excitement). Key motivation theories incorporate perceptions of competence, social influence, and positive affect as key ingredients for understanding and explaining motivated behavior, and thus capture the major reasons for children's sport involvement.

Competence motivation refers to an individual's desire to develop or demonstrate ability in an achievement domain (e.g., academics, sport, social relationships). According to Harter (1978), a child's intrinsic desire to develop or display mastery leads her or him to attempt optimal skill challenges. Successful mastery will result in higher perceptions of competence and internal control, positive affective reactions, and intrinsic motivation to continue the activity (i.e., competence motivation is maintained or enhanced). Significant adults and peers are also important sources of competence motivation. For example, children whose parents encourage them to participate and respond positively to their efforts, regardless of outcome, will feel better about their competencies, enjoy their experiences, and want to continue their participation.

An expectancy-value approach to motivation (Eccles et al., 1983) focuses on expectations of success and subjective task values as determinants of participation choice, effort, and persistence. Success expectancies are similar to perceived competence, in that individuals' beliefs about their ability in a domain will strongly relate to participation behaviors. Subjective task values refer to how important, interesting, and useful an individual believes an achievement domain to be. Higher expectations of success and greater importance, interest, and utility placed on being successful in sports predict stronger motivation in the form of activity choice, effort, and persistence. A host of variables influence a child's development of expectancies and values, and consequently achievement motivation—notably socializers' (parents, teachers, coaches, peers) beliefs and behaviors.

In achievement goal theories, individuals' goal orientations or definitions of success are key to predicting achievement-related cognitions, emotions, and behaviors (Weiss & Williams, 2004; also see chapter 33, "Achievement Motivation"). A child is task-oriented if she defines success and competence as inherent in the task itself—mastery, learning, and effort. That is, success is defined in self-referenced terms such as improvement relative to past performance and individual task mastery. By contrast, a child is ego-oriented if he judges whether or not he is successful based on comparing performance relative to others. That is, success is defined in norm-referenced terms such as beating an opponent or winning a race. Individuals may be high in both goal orientations, low in both, or high in one and low in the other. The important point is that achievement goals (i.e., task, ego) are associated with beliefs about the causes of success, emotional responses, and motivation (Weiss & Williams, 2004). Individuals who are high in task orientation, regardless of level of ego orientation, report higher self-perceptions, enjoyment, and intrinsic motivation. They also view personal effort, rather than normative ability, as a major contributor to performance attempts and outcome, and they are less likely to view unsportsmanlike play as a legitimate means for achieving success. One key to fostering high task goal orientation in young participants is emphasizing a mastery motivational or psychological climate (Ames, 1992).

## Character Development

Character development is without doubt one of the most hotly debated topics regarding the benefits and costs of sport involvement. On the one hand, educators and parents have long attested that participation in sport can teach children values such as honesty, respect, cooperation, and fair play. On the other hand, sport critics implore that sport develops characters, not character, by lowering the bar for what behaviors are deemed acceptable during the course of play (see Weiss & Smith, 2002). The bottom line is that sport has the potential to build character or characters, depending on the quality of adult leadership and the types of experiences afforded children in the competitive environment.

Examples of both prosocial and antisocial behaviors in youth sport are associated with children's observational learning of adults' and teammates' behaviors, as well as with perceptions of significant others' approval of actions that may physically or psychologically harm others (Weiss & Smith, 2002). The research to date has focused on issues such as the social learning of sportsmanlike behaviors, moral reasoning and aggressive attitudes and behaviors, and interventions to promote character development in sport and physical activity contexts (Weiss & Smith, 2002). These strands of research are summarized in the following paragraphs.

According to social learning theory (Bandura, 1986), *moral development* is defined as prosocial behaviors that align with societal norms and conventions. Such behaviors are shaped through observational learning, reinforcement and punishment, and approval by significant others. Of course, antisocial behaviors may be learned through similar mechanisms. The social learning of sportsmanlike and unsportsmanlike behaviors is well documented in the youth sport psychology literature (Weiss & Smith, 2002). For example, youth hockey players report learning legal and illegal hits from watching hockey on television and performing illegal hits at least once during the season. Players also report that fathers, teammates, and coaches moderately or highly approve of body checking and fighting back, among other aggressive behaviors (Mugno & Feltz, 1985; Smith, 1974, 1975, 1978). These studies have been replicated and extended over the years to both male and female athletes, and to varying sports, age groups, and skill levels (see Weiss & Smith, 2002). Stuart and Ebbeck (1995) found a strong relationship between children's perceptions of significant others' approval of unsportsmanlike play and their moral judgment, reasoning, intentions, and behaviors. If parents, coaches, and teammates were viewed as disapproving of unfair play, this was associated with children's higher moral reasoning and lower likelihood of aggressive intentions and behaviors.

Structural developmental theories focus on moral reasoning processes underlying behavior (Weiss & Smith, 2002). These theories define moral development as concern for the physical and emotional welfare of self and others, and believe moral development is shaped through social interactions in response to moral dilemmas. Haan's (1977) emphasis on *dialogue and balance* exemplifies the processes of conflict and conflict resolution necessary to achieve moral equilibrium in dilemma situations. Rest's (1984) model of moral action specifies that moral judgment, reasoning, intention, and behavior are all crucial to understanding character. Rest's model has been applied successfully to the sport context, ranging from studies of what children define as moral dilemmas (Stuart, 2003), to studies of relationships between moral reasoning and aggressive tendencies (Bredemeier, Weiss, Shields, & Cooper, 1987), to intervention studies targeted at improving moral reasoning and prosocial behaviors (Gibbons, Ebbeck, & Weiss, 1995).

Several studies show links among moral reasoning, perceptions of legitimacy of aggression, and sport behaviors (Weiss & Smith, 2002). Children who reason at higher levels see injurious actions as less acceptable and are likely to engage in assertive, rather than aggressive, play. By contrast, children demonstrating lower moral reasoning perceive aggression as a legitimate means of maximizing chances of winning and are rated by coaches as more violent players. Several studies have assessed young athletes' moral reasoning in daily life and sport contexts and show that, by age 12, youth reason at lower levels in sport than for life contexts. Shields and Bredemeier (1995) coined this phenomenon "*game reasoning*"—meaning that sport is seen as a context separate from larger society, where certain behaviors are deemed acceptable, or even celebrated, in an effort to beat an opponent. Game reasoning is seen when professional athletes' violent actions are ignored or minimally punished, compared with similar actions in real life, in which individuals may be arrested and given jail time (e.g., high sticking in ice hockey, intentionally throwing "payback" pitches at a baseball player, blindside blocking in football).

The most encouraging research on moral development in sport contexts comes from intervention studies designed to promote prosocial and discourage antisocial behaviors among youth. The Fair Play for Kids program developed in Canada has been shown to be effective (Gibbons et al., 1995), as has the Social Responsibility Model (Hellison & Walsh, 2002). These and other interventions unequivocally show that when environments are structured to purposefully teach youth positive values and beliefs about sportsmanlike play, and positive role models are available to reinforce such behaviors, effects on character development are not only significantly different from control group participants, but the effect sizes are meaningful and enduring. The foundation of these programs—competent and caring adults and activities that are specifically designed to teach life skills—serves as an exemplar for developing after-school and extracurricular physical activity and sports programs that target positive youth development (Larson, 2000).

# PROBLEMS AND IMPLICATIONS

The millions of youngsters who participate in sport and physical activities each year experience many positive outcomes of youth sport participation. Unfortunately, sport participation also has numerous possible drawbacks. Several of these are summarized here.

## Competitive Stress and Burnout

When competition becomes excessive and extends over a long period of time, anxiety and loss of fun may result. Burnout and dropout may follow. When competitive stress is kept at low to moderate levels, children can learn to cope better with competition, a skill that they can carry into their adult lives (Gould, 1993). Sport competition thus might serve to inoculate participants against debilitating stress reactions in competitive situations later in life. Coaches should be aware of and sensitive to young athletes who experience high levels of stress in sport; they should deemphasize the importance of winning and engage in supportive, rather than punitive, behaviors concerning performance errors and losing (Gould, Wilson, Tuffey, & Lochbaum, 1993). Stress management techniques such as goal setting, relaxation training, and mental imagery can be taught in the context of youth sports (Weiss, 1991) and can transfer to nonsport settings (e.g., academics, work, social relationships).

About one-third of youth participants may drop out each year in any given sport (Weiss & Ferrer-Caja, 2002). Sometimes this occurs as a natural process of sampling activities, or "dropping in and out" of different sports, because other activities are seen as more appealing. However, dropping out may serve as a remedy to problems in the way sports are organized for children. Martens (1980) listed some reasons given by children for dropping out of sports. These included not getting to play, constant criticism of mistakes by coaches, not being successful, mismatching (e.g., child whose size and strength are markedly different from competitors), overorganization (e.g., lengthy practices, little fun in practices and games), and competitive stress, such as feelings of dread experienced prior to game time.

Research on stress experienced by young athletes has distinguished between state and trait anxiety. Children who are highly trait anxious have "... a predisposition to perceive certain environmental stimuli as threatening ... and to respond to these stimuli with varying levels of state anxiety" (Martens, 1977, p. 9). *State anxiety* is a negative feeling experienced at a given moment in a specific context. Consequently, children who are high in competitive trait anxiety are those who experience elevated feelings of anxiety in competitive sport settings, and specifically high levels of state anxiety in competitive sport situations. Adult leaders should try to identify youth who experience excessive levels of competitive stress, as these athletes could benefit from receiving supportive coaching and parenting as well as from learning stress management techniques (Gould, 1993; Smith, Smoll, & Barnett, 1995; Weiss, 1991).

Several situational factors are associated with experiencing higher levels of competitive anxiety and stress (Gould, 1993; Passer, 1988). These include (a) type of sport or activity, (b) amount of time prior to competition (i.e., the closer to game time the higher the anxiety), (c) game or event criticality (i.e., "the big game," game against a rival team), (d) situation criticality (i.e., bottom of the 9th inning, two outs, two on base, and one run behind), and (e) game or event outcome (winners report lower postgame anxiety than do losers). If the sport or activity type is conducive to high social evaluation by significant adults and peers, the potential for experiencing high anxiety increases. Simon and Martens (1979) demonstrated this phenomenon in a classic study. They compared state anxiety levels of children competing in several sports, taking an academic test, participating in physical education, playing in band, and performing in a music solo. Children playing in band solos reported the highest anxiety, followed by wrestling and gymnastics. The activities for which youth recorded the lowest anxiety levels were participating in physical education class and competing in football and ice hockey. One take-home message was that activities that carried the most potential for social evaluation—instrumental music solos and individual sports—were associated with the highest anxiety. Important adults and peers are in a position to observe, evaluate, and make judgment about one's competence in these activities. A second take-home message is that, overall, youth sport participants did not experience greater anxiety than youth in other activities—taking an academic test, playing music, and participating in physical education. Thus, unless children are to be protected from all evaluative situations, there is little evidence to suggest that sport participation places undue stress on children.

Several individual difference factors are also associated with higher levels of anxiety and stress (Gould, 1993; Passer, 1988). These are children who (a) are high in competitive trait anxiety, (b) worry about fear of failure and fear of negative social evaluation, (c) have low self-esteem or low performance expectancies, and (d) are high in ego and low in task goal orientation. Thus, the child who is likely to benefit most from good experiences in sport (i.e., low self-esteem, high trait-anxious) is most at-risk for manifesting high levels of anxiety and stress. Because these individual differences are highly influenced by the quality of parent–child interactions, quality of interactions with other adults and peers, and history of successes and failures, educators and psychologists occupy an important position in helping youth who experience competitive stress and may suffer from potential negative motivational and health outcomes (Passer, 1988).

## Age and Intensity of Sport Involvement

At what age is sport competition appropriate for children? Around the world, many children begin sport participation at a young age (as young as 3 or 4 years in some sports), although most children do not begin competition until later (De Knop, Engstrom, Skirstad, & Weiss, 1996; Weiss & Hayashi, 1996). Passer (1996) suggested three criteria for when children should begin competition in sports. First is motivational readiness, defined as children becoming attracted to and seeking out opportunities for social comparison in achievement situations such as sports. Second is cognitive readiness, which varies with the complexity of the sport involved. For team sports, children need to be able to organize and store information (such as the coach's instructions, plays to be used in the game, and opponent's tendencies) and be able to retrieve such information and use it at the appropriate time. A third criterion for determining a minimum age to begin sport competition is the possibility of physical or psychological harm.

Motivational readiness—the desire to compete—clearly is a social comparison process. The intent is to compare one's skills with those of peers. Very young children (younger than 6 or 7) do not care to make such comparisons for the purpose of evaluating their own ability, although they do observe others to learn how to do certain tasks or activities (Passer, 1996). The other two criteria, cognitive readiness and potential physical and psychological harm, depend on the particular sport, emphasis of a competitive program, skill and sensitivity of the adults in charge, and physical setting in which sport takes place. Applying all these criteria, Passer (1996) recommends that children do not start sport competition before the age of 7 or 8. However, joining an organized sport program that emphasizes skill development and learning is certainly appropriate for young children, as evidenced by the popularity and success of such programs as Mom and Me swimming, The Little Gym, and community leagues that emphasize learning the skills and strategies of the game, as well as those that create child-friendly environments for maximizing success and enjoyment (e.g., smaller equipment, smaller facilities, fewer players per side, more flexible rules).

One argument for starting some children in competitive sports at an early age is that potential elite athletes need to be selected and groomed for their sport. It is common in some countries to screen 4- to 5-year-old children and start them in intensive training programs, with the expectation that an Olympic gold medal may await someday. Research does not exist supporting a relationship between early identification of athletic potential and success as an elite athlete. Moreover, only a tiny percentage of individuals ever make it to more elite levels (professional leagues, Olympics). Thus, a more rational approach is to emphasize skill development and fun, rather than intensive training and competition, for youth during the early and middle childhood years (Passer, 1996).

### Coaches, Parents, and Spectators

Adults are essential for forming programs, organizing leagues, and scheduling practices and competitions. Some adults may adopt values, such as an overemphasis on winning, that contradict the overarching purposes of youth sport participation and may get in the way of healthier motives for athletic activity. Some adults may strive to live out their sports fantasies vicariously through their own children or others they coach. Parents may threaten to (or may actually) withhold love and affection to motivate their children to meet parents' goals for their children's performance (see Fredricks & Eccles, 2004).

Youth coaches also may be part of the problem, and many serve dual roles as parents and coaches of participants. Coaches sometimes model their own behavior after the most visible models available, such as college and professional coaches whose jobs are on the line with every call (and whose players are at elite skill levels and are much older). Or they coach as they themselves were coached. The bottom line is that there is considerable variability among youth coaches' knowledge of emotional, social, cognitive, and physical characteristics and needs of children at varying stages of development. The variability stems from the fact that some agencies and programs offer, or even require, a certain level of coach certification whereas others require nothing more than a ready volunteer. To remedy this problem, many school and nonschool programs require that coaches meet minimum criteria of knowledge and skills related to the specific sport in question *and* the developmental needs of the specific age groups and skill levels they coach (e.g., American Sport Education Program [ASEP], The First Tee, National Youth Sport Coaching Association [NYSCA]).

### Elitism

The most gifted children often get the bulk of playing time and occupy the central positions, such as baseball pitcher, football quarterback, and basketball point guard. Certainly baseball is not much fun for either team if a great pitcher strikes out everyone on the opposing team. Children may get stereotyped at an early age; heavier and slower children play catcher in baseball or on the line in football, never getting a chance to develop skills at other positions. Yet children's body types change dramatically over the childhood years, with especially dramatic changes occurring during early and middle adolescence. The chubby, slow 10-year-old may have a tailback or shortstop body at age 14, but if he was not afforded opportunities earlier on to develop skills necessary for playing tailback or shortstop, odds are good that the child will have given up on football or baseball some time before.

Prime examples of stereotyping youth are given by Michael Jordan and Orel Hershiser, who were skinny, scrawny adolescents and were cut by their coaches in their respective sports in high school. Fortunately, their resilience to stick with the sport resulted in eventually making their teams and becoming stars. Coaches make a serious error by trying to get maximum payoff in the present (i.e., winning) by playing children only in their current best positions, no matter what the child wants or needs, and with no eye to the child's future as an athlete or active participant in recreational activities in adulthood.

## RECOMMENDATIONS FOR PARENTS AND PROFESSIONALS

Common threads emerge for translating research to practical applications for parents and psychologists (Weiss & Williams, 2004). Several take-home messages are available to inform practitioners how to maximize children's self-perceptions, positive affect, motivation, social relationships, and character development.

***1. Provide optimal challenges.*** Ensuring realistic but difficult skill challenges in relation to the child's ability will maximize chances to achieve mastery, enhance perceived competence, experience enjoyment, and promote intrinsic or competence motivation (i.e., the desire to continue participating in the activity for the joy, pleasure, and mastery). Tasks or skills that are not developmentally appropriate are likely to invoke anxiety and decrease motivation to participate.

***2. Make sure sport experiences are fun.*** Positive experiences are strongly related to motivation to continue involvement. When children enjoy and take pleasure in their participation, they will be more likely to try hard and persist at skills, resulting in skill development and ensuing perceptions of competence.

***3. Create a mastery motivational climate.*** When adults define success as improving skills, trying hard, and mastering new skills, this creates a nonthreatening environment where children feel their efforts, regardless of outcome, are valued and recognized, and where errors are viewed as a natural part of the learning process. Such an environment is conducive to adopting a task goal orientation, positive self-beliefs about ability, intrinsic motivation, and sportsmanlike attitudes and behaviors.

***4. Maximize social support.*** Positive regard by parents, coaches, and peers is crucial for making an impact on children's perceived competence, self-esteem, affective responses, and motivated behaviors. In addition, parents' approval of desirable behaviors and disapproval of undesirable behaviors are key to children's moral development. As such, parents and coaches should strive to provide appropriate praise and constructive criticism following performances (e.g., don't give excessive praise for an easy task; couple criticism with instruction on how to improve). Parents and coaches should provide frequent and contingent skill-relevant feedback, because such feedback communicates positive competence beliefs and expectancies for success to children that, in turn, translate to greater effort and persistence. Parents and coaches could promote positive peer relationships and respect and empathy for others by organizing activities that require cooperation to achieve goals and by emphasizing group cohesiveness and mutual respect through team-building activities.

***5. Be a moral mentor.*** Children are our legacy—how will they reflect our values and behaviors on the field or in the gym? Damon (1988) coined the term *moral mentor* to suggest that children need to be exposed to exemplary individuals in the community who have distinguished themselves in fighting for social justices such as reducing discriminatory behaviors, eliminating physical and psychological abuse, and promoting behaviors that reflect "the right thing to do." Parents and coaches are significant mentors in children's lives—why not upgrade that status to moral mentor?

***6. Deemphasize winning.*** This message is especially critical at young ages, when children's self-concepts are forming. Adults' role in sports should be to teach the necessary skills, rules, and strategies of the sport in a safe and appropriate environment. Most leagues for young children (below age 11 or 12) should have a philosophy of and be oriented toward skill development. For younger children, league standings, playoffs, and all-star games should be downplayed or eliminated. The goals of skill development and fun should be paramount. Team sports at a recreational level could be realigned as necessary to equalize competition, even during the season. Equal playing time should be ensured for all children, and all should have the opportunity to play all positions.

***7. Require a coach education program.*** Clinics should be available in all leagues, at all levels, and for all coaches. Content should include injury prevention and care, effective teaching of skills and strategies, and, most importantly, the psychological needs of children in the age group involved. Several agencies, clubs, or school systems in many countries, including Canada, Australia, New Zealand, and the United States, require coaches to be certified (see De Knop et al., 1996; Weiss & Hayashi, 1996). Requiring a coach training program requires time and energy for those providing the training as well as for coaches. Most sports for preadolescent children rely on volunteer coaches, typically drawn from the ranks of parents. Fortunately, good models exist that have been successful in the United States and can be adapted to fit local needs (e.g., ASEP, The First Tee, NYSCA). In addition to receiving training, coaches should be evaluated by the sponsoring agency to ensure that positive behaviors predominate (e.g., playing children in different positions) and negative behaviors are minimized or absent (e.g., arguing with officials, yelling at players).

***8. Keep adult spectators at a distance.*** Parents and other spectators also can be a problem. Parents may yell inappropriately at their own and at other children, and they too often vocally dispute referees' calls. They also may interfere with the coaches' ability to coach during games. Some leagues have successfully required adults other than coaches to stay behind fences or in the stands, rather than allowing them to roam the sidelines. If such rules were implemented and made clear early on, most adults would understand and comply with the rules, and the experience for children would be improved substantially.

***9. Adapt special rules to increase action and the likelihood of success.*** Sports such as Little League baseball, which has been steadily losing participants, might experience a rebirth if hitters and fielders spent more time hitting and fielding than standing around and watching. At T-ball levels, the batting tee allows every batter to put the ball in play, and there is a defensive opportunity for every batter. Similarly, coaches or other players could pitch to their own hitters, a pitching machine could be used, or a different player could pitch each inning rather than having the one or two most precocious 12-year-olds do all the pitching. Similar rule modifications in other sports could improve the likelihood of greater participation and success as well. In basketball, using smaller balls and lowering the goal to 8 or 9 feet can improve dribbling, passing, and shooting mechanics. Forbidding teams from using a full-court press would help children who might not yet have developed the advanced skills necessary to evade several defenders while maintaining a dribble. In many sports (e.g., soccer, football), changing the court or field dimensions and limiting the number of players per side also are likely to aid skill development, enhance probability of success, and increase fun.

***10. Provide opportunities commensurate with age and skill level.*** Certainly the perspective that skill development and fun be emphasized makes good sense from a developmental standpoint for most sports for children under the age of 11 or 12. However, consistent with what is known about typical emotional and physical development of youth, older children are much better prepared to deal with the psychological and physical demands of highly competitive sports. Thus, advanced levels of sport competition should be available as an avenue for more skilled athletes beginning at age 12 or 13. At that point, programs catering to two or more ability levels are appropriate (e.g., select, travel, elite). Those who choose to compete at a higher level, with more emphasis on skilled performance, have opportunities to do so while those who wish to continue to play primarily for the joy of the activity also will be able to participate.

***11. Help parents decide if their child should participate in sports.*** Parents face this question often, and school psychologists can help parents answer the question by reviewing with them which issues must be considered. In general, all children should be given the opportunity to participate. Some cautions are in order, however. Parents and educators should use an "intelligent consumers" mindset and consider the following questions when investigating the sport under consideration:

- Is the sport, as offered in this specific locale, safe? For example, check out the condition of the facilities and ask questions about equipment. Is first-aid equipment, including ice, available at all practices and games? Is there an emergency plan in the event of injury to a child? Do the coaches have training in first-aid and CPR?
- Who are the coaches; how are they selected, trained, and evaluated; and what rules or principles guide their behavior? Is the emphasis of the sport on skill building and fun, or is it on winning? Do all players get to play? How are players selected and assigned?
- Does the child *want* to play, or is he or she being asked to play to meet other needs, such as helping parents relive lost (or never found) sports glory through the child, or to keep pace with neighbors' or friends' children?

## SUMMARY

Youth sports comprise an important part of most children's experiences in our society. When experiences are positive, results can include enhanced self-esteem, character, social relationships, and motivation to maintain an active and healthy lifestyle. To maximize such outcomes, and minimize anxiety and stress, parents and coaches are crucial in helping to shape positive attitudes and behaviors through feedback, expectancies, and the motivational climate surrounding sport participation. Based on theory and research, we provide several take-home messages for ensuring positive experiences and maximizing the potential for positive youth development through sport and physical activity participation.

# RECOMMENDED RESOURCES

## Books and Other Printed Material

Cahill, B. R., & Pearl, A. J. (Eds.). (1993). *Intensive participation in youth sports.* Champaign, IL: Human Kinetics.

This book covers a range of topics, from training and conditioning to societal issues in youth sport. It contains excellent sections on competitive stress and burnout, self-esteem, motivation, and social development.

Malina, R. M., & Clark, M. A. (Eds.). (2003). *Youth sports—Perspectives for a new century.* Monterey, CA: Coaches Choice.

This book contains articles from a conference held at the Youth Sports Institute at Michigan State University for practitioners and academics. Topics range from those on psychosocial issues (e.g., social influence, moral development) to issues on growth and physical maturation, physiological topics, and sports medicine.

Marriott, L., & Nilsson, P. (2005). *Sport parent for the future.* Phoenix: Vision54/Coaching for the Future, Inc. (available from *http://www.coachingforthefuture.com*).

This 40-page booklet features vivid examples and take-home messages from two of the most successful teaching golf professionals. They have drawn from their vast experiences of teaching youth, and their recommendations are consistent with youth sport research on the role of parents in their child's experiences.

Murphy, S. (1999). *The cheers and the tears: A healthy alternative to the dark side of youth sports today.* San Francisco: Jossey-Bass.

This is an outstanding book for parents and professionals, written in user-friendly form and translating concepts that stem from theory and research on children in sport.

Weiss, M. R. (2004). *Developmental sport and exercise psychology: A lifespan perspective.* Morgantown, WV: Fitness Information Technology.

This book covers topics such as parent influence, self-perceptions, emotional experiences, motivation, self-regulation, and moral development. Each chapter reviews theory and research and then translates these concepts into practical applications for professionals.

## Websites

*http://curry.edschool.virginia.edu/kinesiology/sprtpsy/*

This is the website of the University of Virginia Sport and Exercise Psychology program, directed by Maureen Weiss. The program focuses on youth sport issues such as self-perceptions, social relationships, motivation, character development, and observational learning. Publications, recent studies, and ongoing projects are featured.

*http://ed-web3.educ.msu.edu/ysi/*

This is the website of the Youth Sports Institute at Michigan State University, directed by Daniel Gould. The mission of the Institute is to provide educational materials and workshops to coaches and parents and to conduct research to advance the knowledge base in youth sport.

*http://www.footballfoundation.com/Center/center_about.php*

This is the website of the National Football Foundation Center for Youth Development Through Sport, located at Springfield College, Massachusetts, and directed by Albert Petitpas. This Center provides educational materials related to Play It Smart, a school-based mentoring program that targets kids from underserved communities for help with their personal and academic development.

# REFERENCES

Ames, C. A. (1992). Achievement goals, motivational climate, and motivational processes. In G. C. Roberts (Ed.), *Motivation in sport and exercise* (pp. 161–176). Champaign, IL: Human Kinetics.

Bandura, A. (1986). *Social foundations of thought and action: A social cognitive theory.* Englewood Cliffs, NJ: Prentice-Hall.

Barber, B. L., Eccles, J. S., & Stone, M. R. (2001). Whatever happened to the Jock, the Brain, and the Princess? Young adult pathways linked to adolescent activity involvement and social identity. *Journal of Adolescent Research, 16,* 429–455.

Bredemeier, B. J., Weiss, M. R., Shields, D. L., & Cooper, B. A. B. (1987). The relationship between children's legitimacy judgments and their moral reasoning, aggression tendencies, and sport involvement. *Sociology of Sport Journal, 4,* 48–60.

Carron, A. V., & Hausenblas, H. A. (1998). *Group dynamics in sport* (2nd ed.). Morgantown, WV: Fitness Information Technology.

Catalano, R. F., Berglund, L., Ryan, J. A. M., Lonczak, H. S., & Hawkins, D. (2002). *Positive youth development in the United States: Research findings on evaluations of positive youth development programs.* Retrieved August 1, 2004, from http://aspe.os.dhhs.gov/hsp/Posiitive YouthDev99/index.html

Damon, W. (1988). *The moral child.* New York: The Free Press.

Deci, E. L., & Ryan, R. M. (1985). *Intrinsic motivation and self-determination in human behavior.* New York: Plenum Press.

De Knop, P., Engstrom, L.-M., Skirstad, B., & Weiss, M. R. (1996). *Worldwide trends in youth sport.* Champaign, IL: Human Kinetics.

Ebbeck, V., & Stuart, M. E. (1996). Predictors of self-esteem with youth basketball players. *Pediatric Exercise Science, 8,* 368–378.

Ebbeck, V., & Weiss, M. R. (1998). Determinants of children's self-esteem: An examination of perceived competence and affect in sport. *Pediatric Exercise Science, 10,* 285–298.

Eccles, J. S., Adler, T. E., Futterman, R., Goff, S. B., Kaczala, C. M., Meece, J. L., & Midgley, C. (1983). Expectancies, values, and academic behaviors. In J. T. Spence (Ed.), *Achievement and achievement motivation* (pp. 75–146). San Francisco: W. H. Freeman.

Eccles, J. S., & Barber, B. L. (1999). Student council, volunteering, basketball, or marching band: What kind of extracurricular involvement matters? *Journal of Adolescent Research, 14,* 10–43.

Fredricks, J. A., & Eccles, J. S. (2004). Parental influences on youth involvement in sports. In M. R. Weiss (Ed.), *Developmental sport and exercise psychology: A lifespan perspective* (pp. 145–164). Morgantown, WV: Fitness Information Technology.

Gibbons, S. L., Ebbeck, V., & Weiss, M. R. (1995). Fair Play for Kids: Effects on the moral development of children in physical education. *Research Quarterly for Exercise and Sport, 66,* 247–255.

Gould, D. (1993). Intensive sport participation and the prepubescent athlete: Competitive stress and burnout. In B. R. Cahill & A. J. Pearl (Eds.), *Intensive participation in children's sports* (pp 19–38). Champaign, IL: Human Kinetics.

Gould, D., Wilson, C. J., Tuffey, S., & Lochbaum, M. (1993). Stress and the young athlete: The child's perspective. *Pediatric Exercise Science, 5,* 286–297.

Haan, N. (1977). *Coping and defending: Processes of self-environment organization.* New York: Academic Press.

Harter, S. (1978). Effectance motivation reconsidered. *Human Development, 21,* 34–64.

Harter, S. (1999). *The construction of the self: A developmental perspective.* New York: Guilford Press.

Hellison, D., & Walsh, D. (2002). Responsibility-based youth programs evaluation: Investigating the investigations. *Quest, 54,* 292–307.

Horn, T. S. (2002). Coaching effectiveness in the sport domain. In T. S. Horn (Ed.), *Advances in sport psychology* (2nd ed., pp. 309–354). Champaign, IL: Human Kinetics.

Horn, T. S. (2004). Developmental perspectives on self-perceptions in children and adolescents. In M. R. Weiss (Ed.), *Developmental sport and exercise psychology: A lifespan perspective* (pp. 101–143). Morgantown, WV: Fitness Information Technology.

Larson, R. (2000). Toward a psychology of positive youth development. *American Psychologist, 55,* 170–183.

Mahoney, J. L. (2000). School extracurricular activity participation as a moderator in the development of antisocial patterns. *Child Development, 71,* 502–516.

Mahoney, J. L., Cairns, B. D., & Farmer, T. W. (2003). Promoting interpersonal competence and educational success through extracurricular activity participation. *Journal of Educational Psychology, 95,* 409–418.

Marsh, H. W., & Kleitman, S. (2003). School athletic participation: Mostly gain with little pain. *Journal of Sport & Exercise Psychology, 25,* 205–228.

Martens, R. (1977). *Sports competition anxiety test.* Champaign, IL: Human Kinetics.

Martens, R. (1980). The uniqueness of the young athlete: Psychological considerations. *American Journal of Sports Medicine, 8,* 382–385.

Mugno, D. A., & Feltz, D. L. (1985). The social learning of unsportsmanlike play in youth football in the United States. *Canadian Journal of Applied Sport Sciences, 10,* 26–35.

National Federation of State High School Associations. (2003). *2002–2003 participation survey.* Retrieved August 1, 2004, from http://www.nfhs.org

Nicholls, J. G. (1989). *The competitive ethos and democratic education.* Cambridge, MA: Harvard University Press.

Passer, M. W. (1988). Determinants and consequences of children's competitive stress. In F. Smoll, R. A. Magill, & M. A. Ash (Eds.), *Children in sport* (2nd ed., pp. 203–227). Champaign, IL: Human Kinetics.

Passer, M. W. (1996). At what age are children ready to compete? Some psychological considerations. In F. L. Smoll & R. E. Smith (Eds.), *Children and youth sport: A biopsychosocial perspective* (pp. 125–141). Madison, WI: Brown & Benchmark.

Petitpas, A. J., Cornelius, A. E., Van Raalte, J. L., & Jones, T. (2005). A framework for planning youth sport programs that foster psychosocial development. *The Sport Psychologist, 19,* 63–80.

Rest, J. R. (1984). The major components of morality. In W. Kurtines & J. Gewirtz (Eds.), *Morality, moral behavior, and moral development* (pp. 24–40). New York: Wiley.

Shields, D. L. L., & Bredemeier, B. J. L. (1995). *Character development and physical activity.* Champaign, IL: Human Kinetics.

Simon, J. A., & Martens, R. (1979). Children's anxiety in sport and nonsport evaluative activities. *Journal of Sport Psychology, 1,* 160–169.

Smith, A. L. (1999). Perceptions of peer relationships and physical activity participation in early adolescence. *Journal of Sport & Exercise Psychology, 21,* 329–350.

Smith, M. D. (1974). Significant others' influence on the assaultive behavior of young hockey players. *International Review of Sport Sociology, 3–4,* 45–56.

Smith, M. D. (1975). The legitimation of violence: Hockey players' perceptions of their reference groups' sanctions for assault. *Canadian Review of Sociology and Anthropology, 12,* 72–80.

Smith, M. D. (1978). Social learning of violence in minor hockey. In F. L. Smoll & R. E. Smith (Eds.), *Psychological perspectives in youth sports* (pp. 91–106). Washington, DC: Hemisphere Publishing.

Smith, R. E., Smoll, F. L., & Barnett, N. P. (1995). Reduction of children's sport performance anxiety through social support and stress-reduction training for coaches. *Journal of Applied Developmental Psychology, 16,* 125–142.

Stuart, M. E. (2003). Moral issues in sport: The child's perspective. *Research Quarterly for Exercise and Sport, 74,* 445–454.

Stuart, M. E., & Ebbeck, V. (1995). The influence of perceived social approval on moral development in youth sport. *Pediatric Exercise Science, 7,* 270–280.

Weiss, M. R. (1991). Psychological skill development in children and adolescents. *The Sport Psychologist, 5,* 335–354.

Weiss, M. R. (1993). Psychological effects of intensive sport participation on children and youth: Self-esteem and motivation. In B. R. Cahill & A. J. Pearl (Eds.), *Intensive participation in children's sports* (pp. 39–69). Champaign, IL: Human Kinetics.

Weiss, M. R. (2003). Social influences on children's psychosocial development in youth sports. In R. M. Malina & M. A. Clark (Eds.), *Youth sports–Perspectives for a new century* (pp. 109–126). Monterey, CA: Coaches Choice.

Weiss, M. R., & Ebbeck, V. (1996). Self-esteem and perceptions of competence in youth sport: Theory, research, and enhancement strategies. In O. Bar-Or (Ed.), *Encyclopaedia of sports medicine: The child and adolescent athlete* (pp. 364–382). Oxford: Blackwell Science.

Weiss, M. R., & Ferrer-Caja, E. (2002). Motivational orientations and sport behavior. In T. S. Horn (Ed.), *Advances in sport psychology* (2nd ed., pp. 101–183). Champaign, IL: Human Kinetics.

Weiss, M. R., & Hayashi, C. T. (1996). The United States. In P. De Knop, L. M. Engstrom, B. Skirstad, & M. R. Weiss (Eds.), *Worldwide trends in child and youth sport* (pp. 43–57). Champaign, IL: Human Kinetics.

Weiss, M. R., & Smith, A. L. (2002). Moral development in sport and physical activity: Theory, research, and intervention. In T. S. Horn (Ed.), *Advances in sport psychology* (2nd ed., pp. 243–280). Champaign, IL: Human Kinetics.

Weiss, M. R., Smith, A. L., & Theeboom, M. (1996). "That's what friends are for": Children's and teenagers' perceptions of peer relationships in the sport domain. *Journal of Sport & Exercise Psychology, 18,* 347–379.

Weiss, M. R., & Stuntz, C. P. (2004). A little friendly competition: Peer relationships and psychosocial development in youth sport and physical activity contexts. In M. R. Weiss (Ed.), *Developmental sport and exercise psychology: A lifespan perspective* (pp. 165–196). Morgantown, WV: Fitness Information Technology.

Weiss, M. R., & Williams, L. (2004). The *why* of youth sport involvement: A developmental perspective on motivational processes. In M. R. Weiss (Ed.), *Developmental sport and exercise psychology: A lifespan perspective* (pp. 223–268). Morgantown, WV: Fitness Information Technology.

# 38

# Language Development

**Amanda C. Brandone**
**Sara J. Salkind**
**Roberta Michnick Golinkoff**
*University of Delaware*

**Kathy Hirsh-Pasek**
*Temple University*

## BACKGROUND AND DEVELOPMENT

What is language? Language has been hailed as the hallmark of humanity, the ability that separates humans from animals (Berko-Gleason, 1997). As humans in society, we use our language ability continuously to embrace ideas, share our feelings, comment on the world, and understand each other's minds. *Language* can be defined as an organized system of arbitrary signals and rule-governed structures that are used as a means for communication. Language occurs both receptively and expressively through reading, listening, writing, and speaking. In order to become fully functioning members of school and society, children must learn the elements, the rules, the structure, and the conventions of this system.

Our working definition of language encompasses five structural components: phonology, semantics, syntax, morphology, and pragmatics. *Phonology* refers to the sounds and the intonation patterns that are associated with spoken language. *Semantics* encompasses the words of a language and the meanings associated with those words. *Syntax* describes the grammatical rules of a language—how words combine into phrases and sentences. *Morphology* refers to the rules that govern the use of morphemes. Morphemes are the smallest units of meaning in a language, including the prefixes and suffixes that mark syntactic and semantic information, such as number (i.e., plurals), gender, and tense (i.e., past, present, or future). Finally, *pragmatics* is how we adjust our speech to our audience and use language toward the goal of communication.

To better address typical and atypical language development as well as strategies of prevention and intervention, the five structural components of language may be simplified into three essential aspects of communication: content, form, and use (Bloom & Lahey, 1978). *Content* refers to the semantics of language—the concepts and ideas that are encoded in words. *Form* is the way in which meaning is represented, including speech, sign language, and writing. In the context of spoken language, form encompasses phonology, morphology, and syntax. Finally, *use* refers to the function of language in context. Although each of these aspects of language can be identified separately, they are inherently interconnected elements in communication (Bloom & Lahey). Language problems may arise when there is a disruption within any one component of the model or in their integration. The following sections consider the typical development of each of these aspects of language.

### Language Content

Relations between words and their referents are arbitrary and symbolic. Words themselves do not lend the language learner any clues to the identity of what is being labeled. Thus, learning the meaning of words involves learning how one's own language community labels content in the world. This is not an easy task. Consider, for example, seeing a rabbit hopping by and hearing the word *rabbit*. How does one know whether the word applies to the whole rabbit or to its fur? To its twitching whiskers or to its hopping? Research suggests that even very young children are guided in this initial word-to-referent mapping by a default set of assumptions or predispositions (see Woodward & Markman, 1998, for a review of these principles). Hypotheses based on these assumptions are then supplemented by input and feedback from mature speakers, allowing children to test and revise their label-to-referent mappings in order to conform to those of their speech community (see Table 1 for developmental milestones of language content).

The semantic achievement of the production of the first word typically occurs around the child's first birthday; however, it may appear as early as 8 months or as late as 16 months without indicating serious concern. By this time, children have already been exposed to a great deal of language and possess a receptive vocabulary of about 50 words (Fenson et al., 1994). Once vocabulary learning begins, progress is slow and measured. However, by 18 months of age productive vocabularies typically expand to about 50 words. Great individual differences appear during this period. For example, although at 16 months the average number of words a baby can say is 40, the top 10% of 16-month-olds can say 180 words, and the bottom 10% can say fewer than 10, and in some cases none at all (Fenson et al., 1994). This variation among children is completely normal and should be expected.

During the toddler, preschool, and school years, children continue to acquire a varied lexicon. Semantic development expands from the concrete nouns of infancy to complex, abstract, and relational concepts, such as words for actions, emotions, and colors; and deictic terms, such as *I, you, this*, and *that*. Children also make connections among the words in their vocabulary, building a complex network of interrelated words and concepts. Semantic development does not end in childhood. Even into adulthood we continue to add new words to our lexicon (e.g., blog and latte), and fine-tune the content of our communication as we increase our knowledge and experiences (see Pan, 2001, for a review of semantic development).

## Language Form

For typically developing children, sensitivity to language *form* originates in the womb (see Golinkoff & Hirsh-Pasek, 1999, for a review). The growing fetus can hear a number of sounds generated both inside and outside of the mother's abdomen. As a result of these experiences, infants at birth are already familiar with some of the phonology of their language, including its intonational patterns and prosodic contours (see Table 2 for developmental milestones of language form). Young infants also enter the world able to discriminate between most of the sounds that are used in language, including those in languages to which they have never been exposed.

Soon after birth, infants begin to make noises of their own, beginning with vegetative sounds, cooing, and laughing (see Vihman, 1996). By about 4 months of age the nature of these noises changes as infants begin to manipulate their vocal apparatus in vocal play. Starting around 6 or 7 months of age, cooing develops into real, language-like sounds, called *babbling*. A significant language milestone, babbling consists of sequences of consonant–vowel syllables (e.g., "mamama"). Though babbling is itself meaningless, it is through babbling that infants are able to experiment with producing the sounds of their language. Infants' ability to hear their own vocalizations and those of the people around them takes on increased importance during this period, and babies who are deaf produce fewer well-formed syllables than their hearing counterparts (Oller & Eilers, 1988). The final stage of prelinguistic vocalization, the *jargon* stage, generally overlaps with the child's first true words. Beginning at around 9 to 12 months of age, jargon consists of strings of sounds and syllables produced with the rich variety of stress and intonation that mimic the sounds of adult speech. Although not all babies engage in jargon, its presence is an indicator that children have nearly mastered the sounds of their language; they have only to formulate those sounds into approximations of meaningful words (see Vihman, 1996, for a review of early phonological development).

The next crucial milestone in the development of language form occurs when the child discovers that rule-based combinations of words actually express more than the meaning of any of the individual words. For example, by 17 months children are able to discriminate between "Cookie Monster is tickling Big Bird" and "Big Bird is tickling Cookie Monster" (Hirsh-Pasek & Golinkoff, 1996). Comprehension of these rule-based combinations comes prior to production using these rules.

Children begin to combine words into two-word utterances (e.g., "car go" and "more juice") between 18 and 24 months. These early word combinations express meaningful relationships yet tend to be missing function words (*the, a*), auxiliary verbs (*am, is, has*), and the bound morphemes that mark plural (*s*), possessive (*-'s*), or tense (*-ing, -ed*). As children learn to combine words into longer sequences, they add the function words and bound morphemes that were absent from their first

**Table 1** *Milestones of Language Content*

| Typical Age | Content Milestones |
|---|---|
| 8–12 mos. | Understand 3–50 words.<br>First words are used for names of familiar people and objects; communicative games and routines; to talk about appearance, disappearance, recurrence. |
| 12–18 mos. | Average expressive vocabulary size: 50–100 words at 18 mos.<br>Semantic roles are expressed in one-word speech, including agent, action, object, location, possession, rejection, disappearance, nonexistence, denial.<br>Words are understood outside of routine games; still need contextual support for lexical comprehension. |
| 18–24 mos. | Average expressive vocabulary size: 200–300 words at 24 mos.<br>Prevalent relations expressed: agent–action, agent–object, action–object, action–location, entity–location, possessor–possession, demonstrative–entity, attribute–entity. |
| 24–30 mos. | Understanding and use of questions about objects (What?), people (Who?), and basic events (What is x doing? Where is x going?). |
| 30–36 mos. | Use and understand *Why?* questions.<br>Use and understand basic spatial terms (*in, on, under,* etc.). |
| 36–42 mos. | Use and understand semantic relationship between adjacent and conjoined sentences, including additive, temporal, causal, contrastive.<br>Understand basic color words.<br>Use and understand basic kinship terms. |
| 42–48 mos. | Use and understand "when" and "how" questions.<br>Understand words for basic shapes (circle, square, triangle).<br>Use and understand basic size vocabulary (big, small).<br>Use conjunctions *and* and *because* to conjoin sentences. |
| 48–60 mos. | Knowledge of letter names and sounds emerges.<br>Knowledge of numbers and counting emerges.<br>Use conjunctions *when, so, because,* and *if.* |
| 5–7 years | Reorganization of lexical knowledge from episodic to semantic networks occurs.<br>Average expressive vocabulary size: 5,000 words. |
| 7–9 years | School introduces new words not encountered in conversation.<br>Pronouns used anaphorically to refer to nouns previously named.<br>Word definitions include synonyms and categories.<br>Some words understood to have multiple meanings.<br>Capacity for production of figurative language increases. |

*(Continued)*

**Table 1** *Continued*

| Typical Age | Content Milestones |
|---|---|
| 9–12 years | Vocabulary in school texts is more abstract and specific than that in conversation.<br>Students are expected to acquire new information from written texts.<br>Can explain relationships between meanings of multiple-meaning words.<br>Begin using adverbial conjunctions.<br>Understand most common idioms. |
| 12–14 years | Abstract dictionary definitions given for words.<br>Can explain meaning of proverbs in context. |
| 15–18 years | Average vocabulary size of high school graduate: 10,000 words. |

*Note.* From *Language Disorders From Infants Through Adolescence: Assessment and Intervention*, by R. Paul, 2001, Philadelphia: Mosby. Copyright 2000 by Elsevier. Adapted with permission. Based on previous works of Chapman (2000), Miller (1981), Nippold (1998).

word combinations. Negative sentences and questions join the simple declarative sentences of early childhood. Finally, complex, multiclause sentences appear (see Tager-Flusberg, 2001, for a review of the development of syntax and morphology).

Although most grammatical structures are in place by the age of 5, children continue to acquire more complex forms and rules of grammar in the school setting. Here the focus of language development expands to incorporate written communication, including reading and writing. Learning to read and write requires the active analysis of certain aspects of language that were experienced only passively by the younger child. One example of this is *phonemic awareness*, or the understanding that letters map to sounds and that those sounds can be combined to make words. The ability to read and write dramatically transforms the language learner. Through these new language experiences, children gain *metalinguistic competence*, or the ability to conceptualize, reflect upon, and analyze language as an entity in and of itself (see Nippold, 1998, for a review of later language development).

## Language Use

Children learn to communicate long before they develop the form and content of language (see Table 3 for milestones of language use). Infants are born with a repertoire of affective behaviors that allow for the communication of basic needs, and as early as the first year of life they are able to further communicate their intention to others through a combination of eye gaze, vocalization, and gesture (e.g., Harding & Golinkoff, 1979). Although initially infants are unaware of the impact of these prelinguistic behaviors, the consistent and contingent responses of caregivers during early protoconversational exchanges highlight and teach the communicative nature of language (Sachs, 2001).

Through interaction with family, peers, teachers, and caregivers, children learn *communicative competence*, or how to use language appropriately and strategically in social situations (Hymes, 1967). Because we use language for so many purposes, many skills are involved in communicative competence (see Becker-Bryant, 2001). Children need to learn to ask questions, make requests, give orders, express agreement or disagreement, apologize, refuse, joke, praise, and tell stories. They must learn social routines (such as saying "Trick or treat" on Halloween), terms of politeness, and ways to address others. Children must also understand how to initiate, maintain, and conclude conversations, as well as take turns, provide and respond effectively to feedback, and stay on-topic. Crucially, they must learn to be sensitive to their audience and to the situations in which they are communicating. Sophistication in pragmatics continues to develop throughout childhood and into adulthood.

## Factors Contributing to Normal Growth and Development

The single most important factor contributing to the development of the content, use, and form of language is

**Table 2** *Milestones of Language Form*

| Typical Age | Form Milestones |
|---|---|
| 0–8 mos. | 0–2 mos.—vegetative sounds.<br>2–4 mos.—cooing, laughing.<br>4–6 mos.—vocal play. |
| 8–12 mos. | 6–10 mos.—canonical babbling (e.g., dadada), variegated babbling (e.g., digaba).<br>Jargon babble with intonational contours of language being learned. |
| 12–18 mos. | Production of first 50 words. |
| 18–24 mos. | Understand basic semantic roles and relations.<br>Two-word utterances and two-syllable words emerge.<br>Word order is consistent.<br>Utterances are "telegraphic," with few grammatical markers.<br>Speech is 50% intelligible; 70% of consonant sounds produced are correct. |
| 24–30 mos. | Grammatical morphemes appear.<br>Early emerging acquisition: *-ing*, *in*, *on*, plural *s*.<br>Use of *no*, *not*, *can't*, *don't* as negation between subject and verb.<br>Questions formed with rising intonation only.<br>Use of sentences with semi-auxiliaries: *gonna*, *wanna*, *gotta*, *hafta*.<br>Awareness of rhyme emerges. |
| 30–36 mos. | Present-tense auxiliaries appear.<br>*Be* verbs used inconsistently.<br>Overgeneralized past-tense forms appear.<br>Speech is 75% intelligible at 36 mos.<br>Ability to produce rhyme emerges. |
| 36–42 mos. | Emergence of embedded sentences.<br>First complex sentence forms appear.<br>Auxiliary verbs are placed correctly in questions and negatives.<br>Irregular past tense, articles (*a*, *the*), possessive *'s* acquired. |
| 42–48 mos. | Early emerging complex sentence types, including full prepositional clauses, *wh* clauses, simple infinitives.<br>Errors in production of *s*, *r*, *l*, *th* may persist. |
| 5–7 years | Use and understanding of passive sentences emerges.<br>Mastery of exceptions to basic grammar rules emerges.<br>Ability to segment words into phonemes emerges.<br>Understand concept of *word* separate from its referent. |

*(Continued)*

**Table 2** *Continued*

| Typical Age | Form Milestones |
|---|---|
| 7–9 years | Literate language syntax needed for academic participation develops.<br>A few errors in noun phrases ("much bricks") persist.<br>Articulation is mostly error-free; some difficulty with complex words may persist (e.g., aluminum).<br>Phonological knowledge is used in spelling. |
| 9–12 years | Syntax used in school texts is more complex than that used in oral language.<br>Use of word order variations increase in writing ("Near the pool I put a fence").<br>Metacognitive skills emerge. |
| 12–14 years | Use of perfect aspect (*have/had* +[verb]) increases.<br>Syntax used in writing is more complex than that used in speech.<br>Knowledge of stress rules (yellowjacket vs. yellow jacket) is acquired. |
| 15–18 years | Complexity in written language is greater than in spoken language.<br>Full adult range of syntactic constructions reached. |

*Note.* From *Language Disorders From Infants Through Adolescence: Assessment and Intervention,* by R. Paul, 2001, Philadelphia: Mosby. Copyright 2000 by Elsevier. Adapted with permission. Based on previous works of Chapman (2000), Miller (1981), and Nippold (1998).

*input.* To learn language, children must hear language and experience it being used in the context of communication. Accordingly, the most important factor contributing to the commencement of language development is infants' ability to hear. Research suggests that hearing problems, including those stemming from recurring ear infections in infancy and early childhood, may have long-term effects on language development ("Who has Hearing, Speech, and Language Problems?" 1995). However, hearing the sounds of language is not enough. Children must hear their world discussed and described to learn the intricacies of language. They must be invited to contribute to the conversation and allowed to experience language within a rich and stimulating linguistic environment.

Language is not taught explicitly; instead, it is learned through communication. Thus, the more opportunities children have to interact with other language users, the more linguistic input they have to analyze and learn from. Not surprisingly, research suggests that children exposed to larger amounts of adult input develop larger, richer vocabularies and more advanced syntactic skills than children exposed to more limited input (Huttenlocher, 1998). Parents and caregivers who encourage conversation, ask questions, and build on conversations that their children start, have children with more advanced language abilities (Hoff & Naigles, 2002).

Results from the National Institute of Child Health and Human Development (NICHD) Early Child Care Research Network (2000) likewise demonstrate that regardless of whether child care takes place at home, with family members, or in a formal child care setting, input is nevertheless crucial to language development. When teachers and caregivers talk to children, ask questions, and wait for answers, they create a more stimulating language environment. This environment results in children who know more letters, colors, and shapes at age 3 than children who are not addressed as frequently. Early language stimulation remains one of the best predictors of later vocabulary, reading, and mathematical skills.

## PROBLEMS AND IMPLICATIONS

For most children, the development of language proceeds without difficulty. By the age of 5, typically developing children have mastered the building blocks of the system and are left only to refine and integrate their skills in order to use language in an increasingly complex range of tasks. During the course of the development of language, there is a tremendous range of what can be considered normal. Many harmless problems inevitably occur (e.g., sound substitutions, such as "f" for "th" in *birthday*;

**Table 3** *Milestones of Language Use*

| Typical Age | Use Milestones |
|---|---|
| 0–8 mos. | Caregivers attribute intent to child's actions. |
| 8–12 mos. | Intent expressed with gestures and vocalizations: requesting objects and actions, refusing, commenting, playing communicative games.<br>Frequency of communicative acts: 2.5/min. of free play. |
| 12–18 mos. | Words replace preverbal means in expressing intent.<br>Frequency of communicative acts: 5/min. of free play. |
| 18–24 mos. | Word use increases as preverbal communication decreases.<br>New intents include requesting information, answering questions.<br>Frequency of communicative acts: 7.5/min. of free play. |
| 24–30 mos. | "Please" used for polite requests.<br>New intents include symbolic play, talk about absent objects, misrepresentation.<br>Narratives are characterized primarily by labels and descriptions. |
| 30–36 mos. | Some requests for clarification provided.<br>Use of language in play increases.<br>Narratives express theme but no plot. |
| 36–42 mos. | More flexibility in requesting, including permission directives (Can you … ?) and indirect requests (Would you … ?); direct requests decrease in frequency.<br>Narratives express theme and some temporal organization. |
| 42–48 mos. | New functions emerge, including reporting on past events, reasoning, predicting, expressing empathy, creating imaginary roles and props, and maintaining interactions. |
| 48–60 mos. | Ability to address specific requests for clarification increases.<br>Narratives express some plot but no high point or resolution. |
| 5–7 years | Narratives are true stories expressing central focus, high point, and resolution. |
| 7–9 years | Stories contain complete episodes with internal goals, motivations, and reactions of characters; some multi-episode stories appear.<br>Language is used to establish and maintain social status.<br>Increased perspective-taking allows for more successful persuasion.<br>Provide conversational repairs: defining terms, giving background information.<br>Begin to understand jokes and riddles based on sound similarities.<br>Can perform successfully in simple referential communication tasks. |

*(Continued)*

**Table 3** *Continued*

| Typical Age | Use Milestones |
|---|---|
| 9–12 years | Stories include complex, embedded, and interactive episodes.<br>Understand jokes and riddles based on lexical ambiguity. |
| 12–14 years | Expository texts are used in school writing.<br>Most information is presented in expository formats.<br>Understand jokes and riddles based on deep structure ambiguity. |
| 15–18 years | Language is used to maintain social bonds.<br>Persuasive and argumentative skills reach near-adult levels. |

*Note.* From *Language Disorders From Infants through Adolescence: Assessment and Intervention*, by R. Paul, 2001, Philadelphia: Mosby. Copyright 2000 by Elsevier. Adapted with permission. Based on previous works of Chapman (2000), Miller (1981), Nippold (1998).

over- or underextension of meaning, as when all animals are called *dog*; or overgeneralization of grammatical rules, as when children overapply "-ed" as a past-tense indicator, resulting in *goed* instead of *went*); nevertheless, more severe problems do arise.

## Classification of Language Problems

The literature often draws a distinction between delay and disorder when discussing language. The term *delay* refers to language that is similar to that which would be expected from a younger child, whereas *disorder* refers to language that is qualitatively different from what is typical. In practice, however, this distinction is often unclear. Recent studies of the prevalence of language delay give an incidence of between 3% and 15% (Lees & Urwin, 1997). Yet these studies fail to agree about where the distinction between delay and disorder should be drawn. In this chapter, the following definition of language disorder, from the American Speech-Language-Hearing Association (1993), is used:

> A language disorder is the impaired comprehension and/or use of a spoken, written, and/or other symbol system. The disorder may involve (1) the form of language (phonology, morphology, syntax), (2) the content of language (semantics), and/or (3) the function of language in communication (pragmatics) in any combination. (p. 41)

Under the Individuals with Disabilities Education Act of 1997 (IDEA) a language disorder is recognized as a primary disability under the categories of speech or language impairment, specific learning disabilities, and developmental delay. Language disorders are also widely recognized as characteristic of other disabilities, particularly hearing impairment, mental retardation, autism, traumatic brain injury, and certain types of emotional disturbance. Students with severe language impairments typically are identified at an early age and receive speech or language therapy. However, a larger number of students experience more subtle language problems that become manifest as the demands of school increase. Table 4 describes the difficulties associated with each language dimension.

Language skills underpin all human interaction and are therefore crucial to children's success in school and society. As a result, problems with language have pervasive effects on the ability to read, write, and interact with others. A great deal of evidence links spoken language problems to reading disabilities (e.g., Catts, Fey, Tomblin, & Zhang, 2002). Children with early language impairment have been found to be at significantly higher risk for reading disabilities later in life. Attention to children's development of vocabulary, grammar, narrative structure and content, and other aspects of spoken language functioning is thus crucial in the early identification of children at risk for reading disabilities. In a study of normally developing children, Walker, Greenwood, Hart, & Carta (1994) found that general language skills acquired prior to age 5 predicted both reading and academic achievement in later grades. Anywhere between 50% and 100% of children with preschool speech and language disorders experience persistent language problems and academic difficulties (see Lewis, Freebairn, & Taylor, 2000). Language skills grease the wheels of human social interaction. Thus, they are also related to children's acceptance into a group, the ease with which they form friendships, and their ability to interact appropriately with others.

## Risk Factors for Language Problems

The causes of language problems are developmental in nature. Although no specific etiology has been found, three major risk factors for language delay have been identified (Olswang, Rodriquez, & Timler, 1998). The first is prolonged periods of untreated otitis media, or inflammation of the middle ear. Moderate hearing loss associated with otitis media may interfere with children's ability to decode and practice language. Second is a family history of language and learning problems. Approximately half of families of children with language impairments have at least one other family member who has a language problem (Spitz, Tallal, Flax, & Benasich, 1997). The final risk factor for language delay is parental characteristics, including a directive rather than responsive interaction style, high parental concern about children's language, and low socioeconomic status. With respect to the impact of socioeconomic status on language development, a study by Hart and Risley (1995) found that in an average hour of interaction with children under 3 years of age, professional parents (as compared with their working-class and welfare counterparts) used more words of all kinds, more multiclause sentences, more past and future verb tenses, more declaratives, and more questions of all kinds. The average number of words children heard per hour in professional families was 2,150, as compared with 1,250 in working-class families, and a mere 620 were heard per hour in welfare families. Given the cumulative effects of this variation in linguistic input, it is no surprise that socioeconomic status is associated with language impairment and success in school.

In addition to these risk factors, Olswang and colleagues (1998) have identified a series of behaviors in children in the 18- to 36-month range that are predictors of the need for language intervention. These include the following:

- A smaller than average vocabulary, including few verbs, a lack of variety of verbs, and a predominance of general verbs (e.g., make, go, do).
- A language comprehension delay of 6 months or a comprehension deficit with a large comprehension-production gap.
- Phonological problems, including limited vocalizations and restricted babbling.
- Few spontaneous vocal imitations and reliance on direct modeling in imitation tasks.
- Little combinatorial or symbolic play.
- Few communicative or symbolic gestures (e.g., pointing, waving).
- Behavior problems.
- Few conversational initiations.
- Difficulty interacting with peers as compared with adults.

When a toddler with slow language development shows significant risk factors, intervention is warranted.

# ALTERNATIVE ACTIONS FOR PREVENTION

Though language impairment generally first becomes a serious challenge during the school years, the seeds of language problems are in place much earlier and relate to children's prior medical history and family life. Accordingly, early identification and intervention services for children thought to be at risk for language impairment remain the most promising methods of prevention. The role of school personnel, including school psychologists, in the prevention of language impairment is twofold. First, they should screen the hearing and language skills of all children upon entry into school, if not sooner. They also should assess the language skills of infants and preschoolers considered to be at risk for a language disorder based on results of screening or the presence of risk factors reviewed above. Older school-age students at risk for a language disorder also should be screened or monitored periodically for the need of services throughout their schooling (see Paul, 2001, for a review of screening and language assessment procedures). Early identification of hearing and language problems helps to ensure that children receive intervention to minimize the effects of delay on language development.

The second role of schools in the prevention of language impairments (as well as other impairments related to language) is the provision of preventive programs for children found during screening to be at risk for a language disorder. This finding would be indicated by low scores on screening measures, which are likely to reflect the risk factors discussed previously. Because language emerges from natural interactions that occur between children and their caregivers, early intervention programs

**Table 4** *Language Difficulties*

| Language Dimension | Difficulties |
|---|---|
| Use | Does not consider who the listener is, the familiarity of the listener, or the degree of formality of the situation or environment. |
| | Maintains poor eye contact, infringes on conversational partner's turn to speak, fails to maintain appropriate conversational distance. |
| | Does not consider perspective of listeners, including their ability to follow the speaker's train of thought, what and how much information to provide to them, and their verbal and nonverbal responses. |
| | Neglects polite terms and uses imperative statements inappropriately. |
| | Has difficulty with conversation initiation and topic maintenance. |
| Form | Has difficulty using possessives, past tense, prefixes, noun derivation (*-er*), adverb derivation (*-ly*), and *wh*-questions. |
| | Has difficulty learning rules for subject–verb agreement, reflexives, irregular past tense, irregular plural nouns, noun possessives, comparatives and superlatives, and auxiliary verbs. |
| | Has difficulty processing complex syntactic structures such as interrogatives and embedded, passive, and negative sentences. |
| | Has difficulty transforming sentences to create new sentences. |
| | Produces shorter, less elaborated sentences that lack syntactical complexity; relies on basic sentence structure. |
| | Ignores or omits word endings (plurals, verb tense, superlatives) and low-stress words (prepositions, conjunctions). |
| | Begins sentences with "um" or "uh," reflecting inability to order thoughts and words. |
| | Displays sound omissions or substitutions; demonstrates difficulty discriminating sounds. |
| Content | Displays restricted, literal, and concrete receptive and expressive word knowledge. |
| | Substitutes nonspecific words or phrases and indefinite terms for specific words when describing objects or events. |
| | Has difficulty using and understanding linguistic concepts (e.g., before/after, if/then, many, some, few), conjunctions, transition words, relational terms, and words with multiple meanings. |
| | Has difficulty understanding synonyms, antonyms, and verbal analogies and perceiving logical relationships among words. |
| | Has difficulty with figurative language, including idioms, proverbs, metaphors, similes, sarcasm, and jokes. |

*Note.* Compiled from material presented in *Speech, Language, and Hearing Disorders: A Guide for the Teacher* (3rd ed.), by B. J. Hall, H. J. Oyer, and W. H. Haas, 2001, Boston: Allyn & Bacon; *Speech and Language Difficulties in the Classroom* (2nd ed.), by D. Martin and C. Miller, 2003, London: David Fulton Publishers.

aim to enhance and supplement children's social and linguistic experiences by establishing natural, interactive, communication-based relationships between at-risk children and their environment, including the adults within that environment (Rossetti, 2001).

Early intervention often requires significant involvement by the caregiver, as caregivers must be taught how to respond to children in ways that will ultimately enhance and increase their language behaviors. One of the most successful and widely used models for effectively training caregivers as language facilitators is the Hanen Early Language Parent Program (Girolametto, Greenburg, & Manolson, 1986). The basic notion behind this program is that parents can be their children's language facilitators only if they are taught how. The Hanen approach thus instructs caregivers in becoming better communicative partners to help their children learn to communicate. Parents are taught to identify

**Table 5** *Specific Intervention Techniques*

| Technique | Explanation |
|---|---|
| Modeling | Adult models a word or function for the child to imitate after the child demonstrates an interest in an object or activity. A correct imitation of the model is followed by praise, verbal expansion, and immediate access to the desired object/activity. |
| Mand modeling | Adult uses a prompt (e.g., "Tell me what you want") or a request for response to a direct question (e.g., "What's this?") followed by corrective imitation or reinforcement and access to the desired object or activity. |
| Conversational recasting | Adult replies to child's utterances by maintaining the child's basic meaning but syntactically changing one or more of the sentence components and incorporating elements that are slightly above the child's current language level (e.g., Child: "Book fall." Adult: "Oh no! Did the book fall off the table?"). |
| Labeling | Adult attends to focus of child's attention and verbalizes the name of the item of focus. |
| Expansion | Adult repeats child's utterance with the addition of relevant grammatical and semantic details (e.g., Child: "Dog in house." Adult: "Yes! The dog is inside the house."). |
| Extension and expatiation | Adult responds contingently to the child's utterance by contributing something new and extending some aspect of meaning (e.g., Child: "Dog in house." Adult: "Yes. He went inside. He got too cold."). |
| Buildups and breakdowns | Adult expands and breaks down the child's utterance to draw attention to its grammatical components (e.g., Child: "I make a mess." Adult: "You did. You made a big mess. A big mess. You sure did make a mess. You made a mess, all right! Didn't you?"). |

*Note.* Adapted from material presented in *Language Intervention With Young Children*, by M. E. Fey, 1986, San Diego, CA: College-Hill Press.

children's attempts to communicate and to respond to them contingently using techniques that facilitate interaction and ultimately language growth (see Table 5). Results suggest that children of parents in the Hanen program were more responsive, initiated more conversational topics, used more verbal turns, and displayed a more diverse vocabulary than children in a matched control group. Implementing the teachings of the Hanen program with parents and other adults may be useful in enhancing the communication environment and thus the language abilities of children of all ages, but especially those in the preschool years. Home visitation programs targeting parents of children at risk have also been shown to have a small but significant impact on cognitive and socioemotional outcomes (Sweet & Appelbaum, 2004).

Federally funded community-based programs for low-income families with infants and toddlers, such as Head Start and Early Head Start, also function as effective tools in the prevention of language problems (U.S. Department of Health and Human Services Administration for Children and Families, 2002). Early Head Start programs were found to enhance children's cognitive and language development at both 2 and 3 years of age, leading to improvement in receptive vocabulary and the extent and complexity of children's spoken language. Through proactive, supportive, high-quality interaction, immersion in such early intervention programs is a small step toward equalizing the disparate early language experiences of children from different socioeconomic backgrounds.

Data suggest that, in general, early intervention programs have enduring effects on children's cognitive and social–emotional development into middle school (Nelson, Westhues, & McLeod, 2003). Investment in such programs can be considered an investment in the future, resulting in dramatic savings for both school districts and society. For example, cost-effectiveness analyses of the Perry Preschool program, an early intervention program for children with low IQs from low-income African American families, demonstrated monetary savings of more than $95,000 per participant by the age of 27 (Barnett, 1996). More specifically, 2 years of enrollment in the Perry Preschool program resulted in school cost savings of $5,500 per participant (Barnett, 1985). Although this program did not specifically target language development, these findings illustrate the remarkable generalized long-term effects of intervention before the age of 3. By implementing early intervention programs, schools can promote the language development of their students in a way that is both effective and cost-efficient.

## ALTERNATIVE ACTIONS FOR INTERVENTION

The general premise of the many methods of language intervention is to enhance the natural language development process by augmenting, highlighting, or modifying the linguistic input students receive. It is beyond the scope of this chapter to review the various approaches and techniques used by speech and language pathologists to remediate a language disorder. However, direct intervention from a speech and language pathologist should not be the only service provided to children with or at risk for language disorders. Intervention should include a strong collaborative problem-solving component in which team members, including the students' teacher(s), parents, speech and language pathologists, and school psychologists, work together in planning and delivering interventions for the classroom and home.

Given their familiarity with cognitive and behavioral theory, school psychologists can act as effective partners to the speech and language pathologist in the design and delivery of developmentally appropriate language intervention services (Telzrow, Fuller, Siegel, Lowe, & Lowe, 1989). The school psychologist can assist the speech and language pathologist in the development of appropriate goals for the student's behavior management, social interaction, and developmental play. They can also offer insight and support to speech and language pathologists regarding the psychological and adjustment aspects of the language intervention process. Because of the clear relationship between early language difficulties and future reading problems, school psychologists should ensure that students receive treatment that targets not only spoken language problems but also anticipated problems in reading. Together the school psychologist and the speech and language pathologist can develop a language intervention program that is both effective and appropriate for the individual student.

A critical component of intervention should be collaboration and consultation with the parents of children requiring language intervention. By incorporating parents and the natural home setting into the intervention process, the effects of intervention procedures taking place outside of the home may be maximized. If properly trained, parents can serve as powerful and effective agents of intervention, helping to improve parent–child communication in general, as well as advancing specific intervention goals (Fey, 1986). Parents can be instructed in the communication methods suggested by the Hanen Early Language Parent Program, as well as in joint book reading techniques (see Kirchner, 1991) and specific intervention practices such as modeling, mand modeling, conversational recasting, labeling, expansion and extension, and buildups and breakdowns (see Table 5 for descriptions of these techniques). If parents are equipped with knowledge of how to help children with language problems, language facilitation can occur not only at school, but also at home.

Finally, speech and language pathologists and school psychologists should collaborate with teachers in developing daily classroom lessons that foster language development. The classroom environment offers an ideal setting for intervention aimed at stimulating overall language development in a meaningful and naturalistic context. For those students already displaying language difficulties, classroom-based interventions can present language instruction that is rich, frequent, and relevant to students' daily experiences. By enriching the everyday language environment, classroom-based services can also potentially help children who have not been formally identified as having language impairment (Fey, 1986). Regrettably, children's classroom language experiences often fall short of stimulating. There is a fundamental disparity between *natural* language and *school* language. Unlike natural language that is authentic and relevant, school language is characterized by unnatural, disembodied, teacher-dominated talk that is "directed toward pedagogical ends and not toward communication with children" (Piper, 1998, p. 242).

Nonetheless, school language environments can be modified in ways that will ultimately enhance students' learning experiences. Suggestions derive roughly from a whole-language perspective or, "a child-centered, literature-based approach to language teaching that immerses students in real communication situations whenever possible" (Froese, 1990, p. 2). In contrast to that in the typical classroom, talk in whole-language classrooms is genuine and natural. Students participate daily in authentic tasks involving authentic language (e.g., predicting daily newspaper headlines based on recent events and writing or discussing the content of the accompanying articles). In this way, both reading and writing are incorporated as a means of learning, yet not at the expense of oral language. Whole-language classrooms also typically integrate subject areas so that language plays a central role across the curriculum. For example, lessons in science, math, language arts, social studies, art, and music all focus on a single, overarching theme, such as rivers or dinosaurs. As a result, genuine and meaningful learning across content areas is connected by a common language (Piper, 1998).

Mercer and Mercer (1998) also provide the following techniques that teachers can use to incorporate language intervention into normal classroom instruction (they also provide activities and specific strategies for increasing language comprehension and production in students with language problems):

1. Teach language in context through authentic and relevant communication.
2. Follow the sequence of normal language development (see Tables 1–3).
3. Vocalize thoughts and describe ongoing actions.
4. Use parallel talk to describe what others are doing.
5. Use modeling to provide practice on a specific language skill.
6. Use expansion to demonstrate how an idea can be expressed in a more complex manner (see Table 5).
7. Use elaboration to show how to provide more information (see Table 5).
8. Use everyday activities to provide skill practice within a context.
9. Recognize the relationship between comprehension and production.
10. Plan and teach the generalization of classroom lessons to natural communication.

Language forms the basis for success in the classroom. As a team, the school psychologist, speech and language pathologists, parents, and teachers can ensure that students receive language intervention that will enable them to be effective learners and communicators.

## SUMMARY

School success hinges on language knowledge, as language skills are the single best predictor of later school readiness, reading skills, and mathematics ability. Although language development continues throughout the lifespan, the formative years occur in infancy and preschool when, through interaction with others, children discover the meanings of words (language *content* or *semantics*), the way in which meaning is represented (language *form*, including *phonology*, *morphology*, and *syntax*), and the way in which language is used toward the purpose of communication (language *use* or *pragmatics*).

The ages at which children achieve language milestones vary greatly. Most children easily acquire the complexities of language; yet many children experience difficulty with language form, content, or use. Severe language impairments are typically identified at an early age. However, more subtle language problems often become manifest as the demands of school increase. Language impairment has no single cause. However, research indicates that frequent ear infections, a family history of language and learning problems, and low socioeconomic status are each associated with language impairment.

Language emerges from natural interactions that occur between children and their caregivers, and language input is a crucial factor in determining language ability. Accordingly, methods of prevention and intervention aim to create an optimally stimulating and responsive language environment for all children, particularly those at risk of language impairment. The enrichment and enhancement of children's language experiences, both in the classroom and at home, necessitate the partnership of school psychologists, speech and language pathologists, teachers, and parents. This collaborative commitment to language stimulation may have enduring effects on students' cognitive, social, and linguistic development.

## RECOMMENDED RESOURCES

### Books and Other Printed Material

Berko-Gleason, J. (2001). *The development of language.* New York: Pearson Education, Inc.

This text thoroughly explores the development of syntax, morphology, semantics, phonology, and pragmatics. It also examines individual differences in language development and covers atypical development. Written by a panel of experts and including the most recent research findings, this text is a masterful resource on the development of language.

Golinkoff, R. M., & Hirsh-Pasek, K. (1999). *How babies talk: The magic and mystery of language in the first three years of life.* New York: Dutton.

This book provides a light-hearted, yet comprehensive, research-based account of language development during the first 3 years of life. Outlining language milestones, ways to facilitate the language-learning process, and warning signs of potential problems, this book is a valuable resource for school psychologists, teachers, and parents alike.

Paul, R. (2001). *Language disorders from infancy through adolescence: Assessment and intervention.* Philadelphia, PA: Mosby.

Written by a speech and language pathologist, this book provides a clear and extremely comprehensive review of the full spectrum of topics in language disorders, including assessment, intervention, causation, and prevention. Paul also includes specific approaches for assessment and treatment of infants, toddlers, preschoolers, school-age children, and older adolescents with language or learning deficits. This book is an extremely useful resource for anyone involved in the intervention process.

## Websites

*http://www.asha.org/public/*

The public page of the website for the American Speech-Language-Hearing Association offers resources to help all audiences better understand communication and communication disorders. It also provides links to early intervention references and professional referral services for access to qualified care.

*http://www.bamford-lahey.org*

The Bamford-Lahey Children's Foundation is a foundation dedicated to conducting and supporting programs that will enhance the linguistic, cognitive, social, and emotional development of children. The Foundation's current focus is improving the language development of children with language difficulties. This website provides a thorough list of references on language disorders as well as information relevant to the goal of developing guidelines on evidence-based practices in child language disorders.

# REFERENCES

American Speech-Language-Hearing Association Ad Hoc Committee on Service Delivery in the Schools. (1993). Definitions of communication disorders and variations. *ASHA, 35* (Suppl. 10), 40–41.

Barnett, W. S. (1985). The Perry Preschool program and its long-term effects: A benefit-cost analysis. *High/Scope Early Childhood Policy Papers* (No. 2). Ypsilanti, MI: High/Scope Press.

Barnett, W. S. (1996). Lives in balance: Benefit-cost analysis of the Perry Preschool program through age 2. *Monographs of the High/Scope Educational Research Foundation, 11.* Ypsilanti, MI: High/Scope Press.

Becker-Bryant, J. (2001). Language in social contexts: Communicative competence. In J. Berko-Gleason (Ed.), *The development of language* (pp. 191–229). New York: Allyn & Bacon.

Berko-Gleason, J. (1997). *The development of language.* Boston: Allyn & Bacon.

Bloom, L., & Lahey, M. (1978). *Language development and language disorders.* New York: Wiley.

Catts, H. W., Fey, M. E., Tomblin, J. B., & Zhang, Z. (2002). A longitudinal investigation of reading outcomes in children with language impairments. *Journal of Speech, Language, and Hearing Research, 45,* 1142–1157.

Chapman, R. (2000). Children's language learning: An interactionist perspective. *Journal of Child Psychology and Psychiatry, 41,* 33–54.

Fenson, L., Dale, P. S., Reznick, J. S., Bates, E., Thal, E. J., & Stephen, J. (1994). Variability in early communicative development. *Monographs of the Society for Research in Child Development* (Serial No. 242).

Fey, M. E. (1986). *Language intervention with young children.* San Diego, CA: College-Hill Press.

Froese, V. (Ed.). (1990). *Whole-language practice and theory.* Scarborough, ON: Prentice Hall Canada, Inc.

Girolametto, L., Greenburg, J., & Manolson, A. (1986). Developing dialogue skills: The Hanen early language training program. *Seminars in Speech and Language, 4,* 367.

Golinkoff, R. M., & Hirsh-Pasek, K. (1999). *How babies talk: The magic and mystery of language in the first three years of life.* New York: Dutton.

Hall, B. J., Oyer, H. J., & Haas, W. H. (2001). *Speech, language, and hearing disorders: A guide for the teacher* (3rd ed.). Boston: Allyn & Bacon.

Harding, C. G., & Golinkoff, R. M. (1979). The origins of intentional vocalizations in prelinguistic infants. *lChild Development, 50,* 33–40.

Hart, B., & Risley, T. (1995). *Meaningful differences in the everyday experiences of young American children.* Baltimore, MD: Brookes.

Hirsh-Pasek, K., & Golinkoff, R. M. (Eds.). (1996). *The origins of grammar: Evidence from early language comprehension.* Cambridge, MA: MIT Press.

Hoff, E., & Naigles, L. (2002). How children use input to acquire a lexicon. *Child Development, 73,* 418–433.

Huttenlocher, J. (1998). Language input and language growth. *Preventive Medicine, 27*(2), 195–199.

Hymes, D. (1967). Models of the interaction of language and social setting. *Journal of Social Issues, 23*(2), 8–28.

Kirchner, D. (1991). Reciprocal book reading: A discourse-based intervention strategy for the child with atypical language development. In T. Gallagher (Ed.), *Pragmatics of language: Clinical practice issues* (pp. 307–332). San Diego, CA: Singular Publishing Group.

Lees, J., & Urwin, S. (1997). *Children with language disorders* (2nd ed.). San Diego, CA: Singular Publishing Group.

Lewis, B. A., Freebairn, L. A., & Taylor, H. G. (2000). Academic outcomes in children with histories of speech sound disorders. *Journal of Communication Disorders, 33,* 11–30.

Martin, D., & Miller, C. (2003). *Speech and language difficulties in the classroom* (2nd ed.). London: Fulton.

Mercer, C. D., & Mercer, A. R. (1998). *Teaching students with learning problems* (5th ed.). Upper Saddle River, NJ: Prentice Hall.

Miller, J. (1981). *Assessing language production in children.* Boston: Allyn & Bacon.

National Institute of Child Health and Human Development (NICHD) Early Child Care Research Network. (2000). The relation of child care to cognitive and language development. *Child Development, 71,* 960–980.

Nelson, G., Westhues, A., & McLeod, J. (2003, December 18). A meta-analysis of longitudinal research on preschool prevention programs for children. *Prevention and Treatment, 6,* Article 31. Retrieved October 18, 2004, from http://journals.apa.org/prevention/volume6/pre0060031a.html

Nippold, M. A. (1998). *Later language development.* Austin, TX: PRO-ED, Inc.

Oller, D. K., & Eilers, R. (1988). The role of audition in infant babbling. *Child Development, 59,* 441–449.

Olswang, L. B., Rodriguez, B., & Timler, G. (1998). Recommending intervention for toddlers with specific language learning difficulties: We may not have all the answers, but we know a lot. *American Journal of Speech-Language Pathology, 7,* 23–32.

Pan, B. A. (2001). Semantic development: Learning the meaning of words. In J. Berko-Gleason (Ed.), *The development of language* (pp. 112–147). New York: Allyn & Bacon.

Paul, R. (2001). *Language disorders from infants through adolescence: Assessment and intervention.* Philadelphia, PA: Mosby.

Piper, T. (1998). *Language and learning: The home and school years* (2nd ed.). Upper Saddle River, NJ: Prentice Hall.

Rossetti, L. M. (2001). *Communication intervention: Birth to three* (2nd ed.). Albany, NY: Thomson Learning.

Sachs, J. (2001). Communication development in infancy. In J. Berko-Gleason (Ed.), *The development of language* (pp. 39–61). New York: Allyn & Bacon.

Spitz, R. V., Tallal, P., Flax, J., & Benasich, A. A. (1997). Look who's talking: A prospective study of familial transmission of language impairments. *Journal of Speech and Hearing Research, 40,* 990–1001.

Sweet, M. A., & Appelbaum, M. I. (2004). Is home visiting an effective strategy? A meta-analytic review of home visiting programs for families with young children. *Child Development, 75,* 1435–1456.

Tager-Flusberg, H. (2001). Putting words together: Morphology and syntax in the preschool years. In J. Berko-Gleason (Ed.), *The development of language* (pp. 148–190). New York: Allyn & Bacon.

Telzrow, C. F., Fuller, A., Siegel, C., Lowe, A., & Lowe, B. (1989). Collaboration in the treatment of children's communication disorders: A five-year case study. *School Psychology Review, 18,* 463–474.

U.S. Department of Health and Human Services. Administration for Children and Families. (2002). *Making a difference in the lives of infants and toddlers and their families: The impacts of Early Head Start* (Under Contract DHHS-95-1936). Princeton, NJ: Mathematica Policy Research, Inc.

Vihman, M. M. (1996). *Phonological development: The origins of language in the child.* Oxford: Basil Blackwell.

Walker, D., Greenwood, C. R., Hart, B., & Carta, J. (1994). Prediction of school outcomes based on early language production and socioeconomic factors. *Child Development, 65,* 606–621.

Who has hearing, speech, and language problems? (1995). *ASHA, 37*(2), 38–39.

Woodward, A. L., & Markman, E. M. (1998). Early word learning. In W. Damon, D. Kuhn, & R. Siegler (Eds.), *Handbook of child psychology: Vol. 2: Cognition, perception and language* (pp. 371–420). New York: Wiley.

# 39

# Career Development

**Edward M. Levinson**

*Indiana University of Pennsylvania*

**Denise L. Ohler**

*Edinboro University of Pennsylvania*

## BACKGROUND AND DEVELOPMENT

Schools have done an inadequate job of preparing young people for work. Sixty percent of American adults believe high schools devote enough attention to preparing students for college, but *not* enough attention to helping students get jobs. Schools direct most of their resources toward preparing students for college. Yet only about 15% of incoming ninth graders go on to graduate from high school and then obtain a 4-year college degree within 6 years of their high school graduation (Morra, 1993). Moreover, only 34% of students who left high school in 2002 were reported to possess the skills and qualifications necessary to attend college (Greene & Winters, 2005). Recent data citing unemployment rates for students with disabilities underscore these concerns. Students' unemployment rate has hovered around 70% for the past 12 years (National Council on Disability, 2000). College graduates with disabilities experience higher unemployment rates and longer job searches than do college students without disabilities, and they are more likely to be employed outside their chosen field than are their peers without disabilities.

In light of the above, it should not be surprising that the National Standards for School Counseling Programs (Campbell & Dahir, 1997) identified career development as an essential component of effective school counseling programs, and recent legislation (e.g., the School-to-Work Opportunities Act and the Individuals with Disabilities Education Improvement Act 2004) assists schools in developing and implementing this important component. Changing demographics and cultural plurality have influenced the career development intervention process, as non-Whites, women, and immigrants have begun to dominate the workforce. Many of these individuals face tremendous barriers to achieving satisfying careers and are concentrated in low paying or low skill level jobs. Despite legislation to protect their rights, one half of persons with disabilities are "outside the work structure" (Isaacson & Brown, 1997; p. 313), and women and people of color continue to experience career-related difficulties.

*Career development* refers to the lifelong psychological, behavioral, and contextual influences shaping one's career over the life span. It is beyond the scope of this chapter to review the multiple theories of career development (at least 10 theories have been proposed and subjected to research), the various stages of career development, and the many career-related issues that confront individuals throughout the life span. The previous version of this chapter (Levinson & Brandt, 1997) focused on two of the most popular theories of career development: the theories of Holland (1992) and Super (1957). As such, these are not repeated here. Instead, this chapter focuses on two of the more recent, and popular, theories: social cognitive career theory (Lent, Brown, and Hackett, 1996) and Linda Gottfredson's theory of circumscription and compromise (Gottfredson, 1996). Following a brief review of these two theories, common perspectives on career development are presented that are based on a synthesis of the career development literature.

### Social Cognitive Career Theory

Social cognitive career theory (SCCT) (Lent et al., 1996) is based on the assumption that social and cognitive factors play an important role in career development and career decision making. SCCT draws heavily from

Krumboltz's (Mitchell & Krumboltz, 1996) learning theory of career counseling and from Bandura's (1986) social learning theory. Specifically, SCCT highlights *self-efficacy beliefs*, outcome expectations, and *personal goals*. Self-efficacy beliefs are defined as people's judgments of their capabilities to organize and execute courses of action required to attain designated types of performances. Self-efficacy beliefs provide answers to questions regarding whether one can perform specific tasks (e.g., Can I write business letters?). *Outcome expectations* refer to desired consequences of a specific course of action. *Personal goals* pertain to the effort required to engage in an activity.

The theory also emphasizes the interaction of environment, self-referent thought, and behavior, referred to as the triadic reciprocal interaction system. In this system four general factors are seen as influencing career decision making: genetic, environmental, instrumental and associative learning experiences, and task approach skills. These factors influence students' beliefs about themselves and about the world. In essence, person inputs (e.g., predisposition, gender, and race) interact with contextual factors (e.g., culture and family) and learning experiences to influence self-referent thoughts, including self-efficacy beliefs, outcome expectations, and personal goals. In turn, these thoughts shape behavior. Likewise, both of these dimensions are influenced by, and influence, environmental factors (e.g., job opportunities and access to training) and "planned happenstance." Planned happenstance is a conceptual framework used by counselors to encourage individuals to generate, recognize, and take advantage of chance events.

Several studies have demonstrated positive outcomes for SCCT-based interventions used with diverse client groups (Hackett & Byars, 1996). However, because SCCT is a relatively recent addition to the literature on career development, research addressing the theory is still in its infancy.

## Linda Gottfredson's Theory of Circumscription and Compromise

Gottfredson's (1996) theory offers a developmental, sociological perspective on career development that is focused on the types of compromises people make in formulating their occupational aspirations. *Circumscription* involves the process of eliminating unacceptable occupations based primarily on gender and social class. *Compromise* involves the process of modifying career choices as a response to limiting factors. Gottfredson proposes four stages of cognitive development:

***Stage 1. Orientation to size and power (ages 3–5).*** Children orient themselves to differences in size and power between themselves and adults.

***Stage 2. Orientation to sex roles (ages 6–8).*** Children develop their "tolerable sextype boundary." That is, they believe that certain jobs are only for boys, and others are only for girls.

***Stage 3. Orientation to social valuation (ages 9–13).*** Children and early adolescents develop a zone of occupations as acceptable based on social class and ability level. In other words, they rule out careers they consider to be beneath them; those that are above the upper limit of effort and risk they are willing to take.

***Stage 4. Orientation to internal, unique self (age 14 +).*** Adolescents, and adults, become more introspective and self-aware, establishing a self-identity or self-concept and related personal goals. Compromise occurs as preferred careers are eliminated as a result of external realities such as job opportunities.

Gottfredson (1996) highlights the importance of career education programs to promote systematic exploration of career choices. Research on the theory has not been extensive; however, her concepts describing boundaries and motivation related to choice and aspiration are noteworthy.

## Common Themes Among Theories of Career Development

Several common themes can be found among the various theories of career development, including the two briefly discussed above. First, career development is commonly viewed as a lifelong process that is influenced by an interaction of environmental and genetic factors. Second, it is characterized by progression through a series of hierarchical stages, each associated with certain developmental tasks or objectives. At each stage the career development process entails a series of ongoing, interrelated decisions that individuals must make. These decisions influence the career development of the individual, and the decision-making process itself is influenced by vocational and career experiences. Third, personality development and traits assume an important role in career development and choice. Because different people possess different traits, and because different traits are required for success in different occupations, certain types of people are best suited for certain types of occupations. Finally, feelings about oneself (self-concept and self-efficacy) influence career development and choice.

## PROBLEMS AND IMPLICATIONS

In general, the operationalization of career choice problems individuals face is dependent on the particular theoretical approach to which the counselor subscribes. For example, according to Gottfredson, career choice difficulties may occur because of a premature narrowing of viable occupational alternatives. In contrast, from a social cognitive career theory perspective, students who experience career choice difficulties may do so because they have faulty self-efficacy beliefs and outcome expectations.

Career problems are as individual as each student; however, career choice is recognized as a common problem in most theories and has received much attention in the career counseling literature. Among students, the problem of career choice is seen in the unnecessary restriction of their occupational options (Gottfredson, 1996). This often is reflected in the following: (a) the student is unable to name one or more career options, (b) the student's interests and abilities are inadequate for the chosen career, (c) the student is not satisfied with the alternatives, (d) the student has unnecessarily restricted alternatives, and (e) the student is unaware of career opportunities or unrealistic about obstacles for implementing their chosen occupation. In that these factors tend to focus on circumscription of career options as they relate to social class, gender, and intellectual assets, they place women, racial and ethnic minorities, and students with disabilities at especially high risk for problems in career development.

### Issues in the Career Development of Females

Two-thirds of the new entrants into the workforce between the late 1980s and 2000 were women (Niles & Harris-Bowlsbey, 2002). During this period, the total percentage of American women in the workforce increased from 51.5% to 61.1% (Niles & Harris-Bowlsbey, 2002). Results of a longitudinal study of adolescents suggest that during the first 7 years following high school, students' expectations regarding their occupations at age 30 are highly unstable, females are more inconsistent in their expectations than are men, and family events (such as marriage and children) have a greater impact on occupational expectations and attainment among women than men. Collectively, these findings suggest that family and career issues are more interdependent for females than for males (Ridfuss, Cooksey, & Sutterlin, 1999).

In support of both Gottfredson's stage development approach and social cognitive career theory, Helwig (2001) found that occupational aspirations form and develop among second- to sixth-grade students as their age advances, and they tend to be based on gender stereotypes that circumscribe career options for females at an early age. However, some evidence suggests that females tend to demonstrate higher levels of career maturity and career development knowledge, including knowledge about decision making and the world of work, than do men (Ohler, Levinson, & Damiani, 1998).

Factors associated with occupational and educational aspirations of school-age children and adolescents include continued gender differences, socioeconomic status, and parental expectations and supports, and the latter is especially true for students of color. Adolescents who showed aspiration–expectation discrepancies made anticipatory compromises by shifting toward more realistic and accessible occupations (Armstrong & Crombie, 2000) as described by Gottfredson's theory of compromise.

### Ethnic and Racial Issues

Certain ethnic and social groups of students are at high risk for dropping out of school, particularly African Americans and Hispanics with backgrounds of low socioeconomic status (see chapter 8, "School Completion"). Many of these students also face stereotyping, discrimination, and environmental barriers. A number of factors contribute to these career-related problems. Some are factors that schools can affect, such as the scarcity of successful role models with similar backgrounds, limited expectations and aspirations, lack of ethnic identity and related self-efficacy, and limited opportunities to explore a wide range of careers.

### Individuals With Disabilities

Unemployment rates among working-age individuals with disabilities have hovered around 70% for the past 12 years (National Council on Disability, 2000). As a consequence, 29% of workers with a disability live in poverty, compared with 10% of workers without a disability (National Organization on Disability, 2002). To some extent, unemployment and income limitations that characterize individuals with disabilities can be traced to elevated school dropout rates that also characterize this population. Individuals with disabilities are often subjected to low career expectations, which further limits their career development. For example, both parents and teachers of individuals with disabilities believe that counselors typically suggest fields other than science and engineering to students with disabilities (Alston & Hampton, 2000).

The Individuals with Disabilities Education Act of 1997 (IDEA) required schools to develop a plan designed to help students with disabilities make a successful transition from school to work and/or postsecondary education and community living. The act required that transition services be identified and included in the student's individual education plan by age 14. The Individuals with Disabilities Education Act of 2004 now requires that services designed to assist students in making a successful transition from school to postschool plans be included in the student's Individualized Education Plan (IEP) and in effect by the time the child is 16 years of age.

## ALTERNATIVE ACTIONS FOR PREVENTION

To prevent problems in the area of career development, schools must do a better job of planning, implementing, and evaluating K–12 career education programs. Programs should be based on career development theory, with clear career-related objectives at each grade level. Comprehensive transdisciplinary vocational and career assessment (Levinson, 1993) should be included and should be designed to identify the extent to which individual students are meeting career development objectives in a manner consistent with career development theory. Students identified as not meeting objectives can then be identified and provided with interventions to assist them in career development. Interventions can be provided at both the systems level and the individual student level.

Activities designed to further students' acquisition of career-related objectives should occur both as part of (for all students) and outside of (for students needing additional assistance) regular education. Schools must also target for career services those populations that are at high risk for career-related difficulties (women, minorities, and individuals with disabilities). Though high-risk students should be given special attention and consideration in the process, no evidence suggests that these students would benefit from any specialized or unique career intervention. That is, interventions that work effectively for the general population of students are likely to work effectively for high-risk students and vice versa. Finally, schools must provide transition services designed to assist students in making a successful transition from high school to post-school life as part of a comprehensive K–12 career education program.

Schools have done an inadequate job of planning and implementing programs designed to address students' career development needs. Many programs currently in operation have been hastily developed in response to federal or state mandates. Moreover, they have had as their primary focus accountability and compliance rather than the identification and accommodation of individual students' needs. For example, in response to the prior IDEA mandate that schools offer transition services to students with disabilities by age 14, many schools simply developed transition plans for students without any additional assessment or consideration of the individual students' needs and attached these plans to the student's IEP to document compliance. Too often the transition plans translate into services that differ little from those provided to students without disabilities. Hence, to truly prevent career-related problems, schools must do a better job of planning, implementing, and evaluating career development programs. Additionally, they must ensure that students receive a comprehensive, transdisciplinary vocational or career assessment so that career development needs are identified and individual interventions are designed to address individual needs.

### Planning, Implementation, and Evaluation of Career Development Programs

The first step in program development entails planning, which should begin with establishing a task force that adequately represents all school and community personnel likely to be involved in providing services. The task force first should conduct a needs assessment designed to identify school and community resources and services that can be utilized in the program and potential obstacles to successful provision of services. Next, a K–12 career development model should be designed that makes use of local resources. Formal interagency agreements between school and community agencies should be established that clearly identify (a) services to be provided, (b) the agencies that will provide these services,

(c) which students will be provided services, and (d) when the services will be provided. Funding requirements also should be identified, and sources of funding secured, if necessary.

In the implementation phase, a K–12 program coordinator should be identified who will oversee implementation of the program and, in conjunction with other involved personnel, will develop a procedures manual, purchase equipment and materials, and train and orient involved professionals. Next, the program should be pilot tested, revised, and fully implemented. In the final phase, after the program has been implemented for a predetermined period of time, the program should be evaluated and revised as necessary.

### Vocational and Career Assessment

Assessment should meet the following criteria. First, assessment results should be viewed, along with a student's self-knowledge and intentionality, past educational experience, and best predictions about work demands of the future. Second, results should be used less for predicting options and more for identifying new concepts of self, areas for growth, and new possibilities for exploration. Finally, with respect to prevention, the student should be involved as an equal participant—that is, the student should assist in guiding the process and should be involved in offering his or her own interpretation of assessment results and should be given an opportunity to add to or delete occupational options generated by the assessment (Niles & Harris-Bowlsbey, 2002). The role of assessment in the early stages of career development helps prevent career decision-making problems in that it increases a student's readiness for making career decisions.

Effective vocational and career assessment helps increase students' understanding of themselves. Many school systems have established vocational assessment programs, which are often dual-level programs and involve a variety of school and community-based (adult service agencies) personnel. Thus, the term *transdisciplinary* has been applied to describe this type of vocational and career assessment model (Levinson, 2004). Level 1 assessments typically include measures of mental ability, academic achievement, motor coordination, personality, vocational interests, vocational aptitudes, vocational adaptive behavior, and career maturity. These measures consist of paper-and-pencil tests, performance tests, interviews, and observations. Level 2 assessments may evaluate these same areas but typically emphasize vocational adaptive behavior, vocational interests, and vocational aptitudes. These measures tend to consist of more expensive and time-consuming techniques, such as work samples and real and simulated work experiences (see Levinson [2002a] for more information on both planning of programs and vocational and career assessment).

## ALTERNATIVE ACTIONS FOR INTERVENTION

In this section, two levels of intervention for career development are reviewed: systems-level interventions and individual-level interventions.

### Systems-Level Interventions

Systems-level interventions are designed to be part of a K–12 regular education program and be available to all students. Career education and school-to-work transition programs are examples of systems-level interventions.

***Career education.*** Career education is the systematic attempt to influence the career development of students through the use of various types of educational strategies, including providing occupational information, infusing career-related concepts into the academic curriculum, offering various worksite-based experiences, and offering career planning courses (Isaacson & Brown, 1997). Comprehensive career guidance programs that are an integral part of the school's educational program and that enhance student development should be provided to all students. Unfortunately, many school districts do not provide such systematic and coordinated programs, but instead offer them in a haphazard and piecemeal fashion.

Developing a systematic and coordinated career development program requires that school professionals understand the developmental tasks confronting students in grades K–12. Understanding the tasks that students deal with at all levels of schooling prepares school personnel to work collaboratively in program development and implementation. The specific career development competencies that have been identified as being appropriate for elementary school children are self-knowledge (e.g., importance of self-concept), educational and occupational exploration (e.g., awareness of the relationship between work and learning), and career planning (e.g., awareness of different occupations and

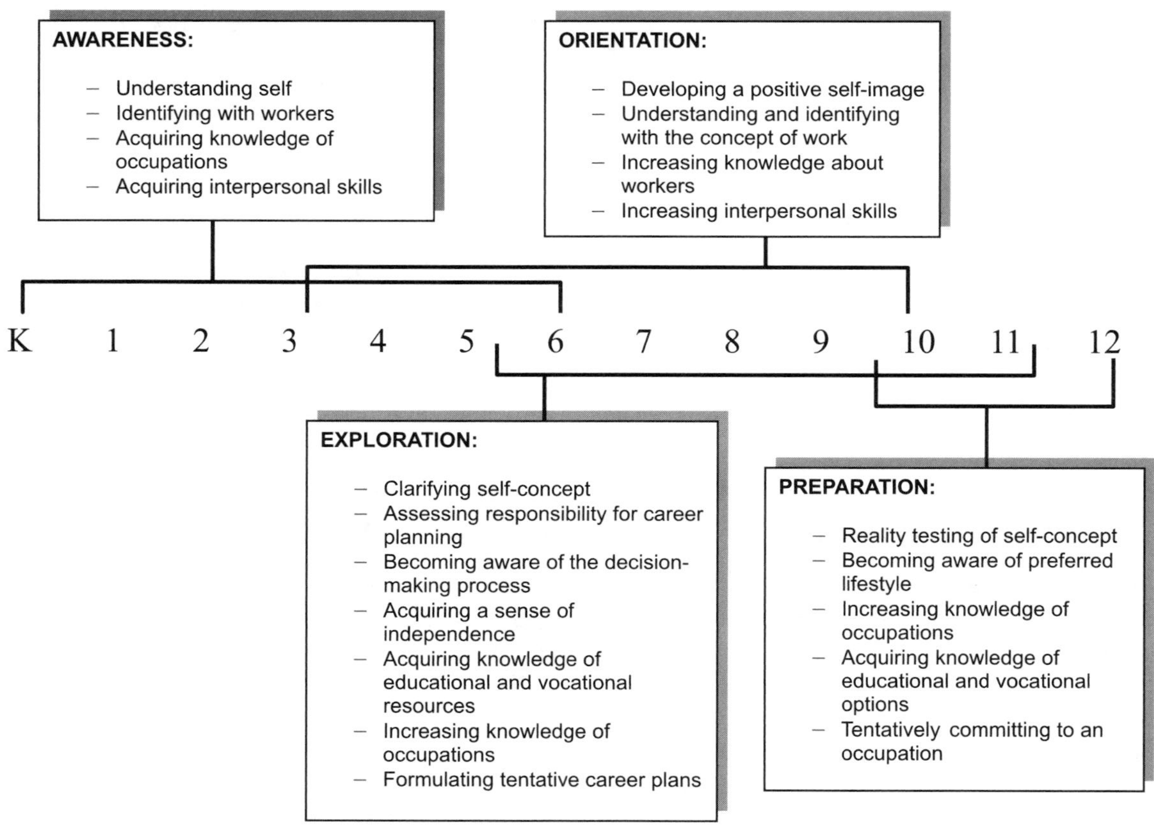


**Figure 1.** *Stages of career education*

changing gender roles) (National Occupational Information Coordinating Committee, 1992). Students who do not accomplish the career development tasks they encounter in elementary school are likely to be at risk for even more difficulty when they encounter career development tasks presented to them during secondary school (Super, 1957). As such, the programs offering career development or transition services are appropriate for all K–12 students, not just those in middle school or high school.

Career education programs operate in many schools and are designed to help students achieve the career competencies identified above: self-knowledge, educational and occupational exploration, and career planning. Such programs usually follow a model similar to that depicted in Figure 1 and are based on normal career development theory. The activities and experiences that make up career education programs usually include career assessment, career counseling, and the provision of educational and occupational information. These programs are usually integrated into the regular education curriculum and are implemented by a variety of school personnel. Life career planning should begin in elementary school through such strategies as school-wide career days, career education classes, and discussion of career development issues into the classroom. The planning of programs should involve the developmental implications involving gender, parental influence, socioeconomic status, school experiences, and self-efficacy.

A meta-analysis of studies of K–12 career development programs and career education interventions concluded that moderate, positive outcomes (i.e., improved levels of career maturity) were present across studies (Baker & Popowicz, 1983). Several interventions designed to enhance self-efficacy and career confidence have been demonstrated to be empirically effective. Examples include career education classes, group counseling sessions based on self-efficacy information, small group career exploration and planning sessions, and computerized assessment and individual career counseling (McWhirter, Rasheed, & Crothers, 2000). In fact, some authors have suggested that career education should form the basis for K–12 education and that all instruction should be linked to career development objectives to make instruction more relevant to students.

***School-to-work transition programs.*** Recent federal legislation (the School-to-Work Opportunities Act and the Individuals with Disabilities Education Act of 2004) have provided the impetus for the development of school-to-work transition programs. Unfortunately, many of these programs are designed to service only students with disabilities, focus solely on employment as a goal, and are not made available to students until age 14 or later. Our current knowledge of career development clearly suggests that transition services should incorporate a process rather than a single event or series of events. That is, rather than conceptualizing transition planning as a separate process that is initiated at age 14 (or age 16 as is now required by law), transition planning should be considered a natural part of the lifelong process of career development and career planning and be embedded within a K–12 career education program. The knowledge and skills individuals need in order to make a successful transition from school to work and to community living actually begin to develop at birth and continue throughout the life span. Hence, issues such as understanding oneself and getting along with others, which should be addressed as early as the elementary school years, will ultimately affect transition from school to work. Planning for students' successful transition actually begins in elementary school and continues throughout their educational career. Transition planning, therefore, should be understood to be an ongoing process that is inextricably linked to career development and begins the moment a student sets foot in school (Levinson, 2004).

Ongoing career development and transition programs are particularly important for students with disabilities and should ensure the following (Levinson, 2004):

- Planning for postschool adjustment that begins early in a student's educational career.
- Written, individualized plans that specify transition services that are part of each student's IEP.
- Attempts to integrate individuals with disabilities with individuals without disabilities.
- Educational curriculum that focuses on instruction of relevant and functional life skills.
- Instruction that takes place in the community.
- Curricula that include academic, vocational, and social skills instruction.
- Program planning based on a comprehensive, transdisciplinary vocational assessment.
- Transition programs that shift from the traditional practice of intervening on the individual level to focusing on the systemic level to promote change and to understand students' transition from school to work to life. Specifically, such programs should include work-based learning activities, adult world orientation, and support from adults, taking into account the diverse background of students.

## Individual-Level Interventions

As students progress though the career education activities afforded them in regular education and are subjected to an ongoing vocational and career assessment, professionals should identify those who are not profiting sufficiently from these activities or are not meeting career development objectives in a timely manner. For these students, individual career development activities, designed to supplement what occurs in a K–12 career education program, must be developed. Career development interventions, defined broadly, involve any activity that empowers students to cope effectively with career development tasks.

Generally, research has suggested that career interventions have positive effects, and no consistent body of literature suggests that any one intervention is more effective than any other (Savickas, 1989). More research is needed to determine which interventions seem to be most effective for whom and under what circumstances (Luzzo & MacGregor, 2001). All interventions should have the purpose of facilitating one or more of the following, each of which is critical to mature career decision making (National Occupational Information Coordinating Committee, 1992): increasing self-awareness, increasing educational and occupational awareness, improving decision-making skills, and facilitating job readiness and placement. In addition, Levinson (2002b) suggests that individual interventions should focus on providing accommodations needed for success, teaching advocacy skills, and offering activities designed to improve self-efficacy. Some specific activities, as described by Niles and Harris-Bowlsbey (2002) follow. These activities can be used to further some of the objectives noted previously.

### Sample Career Development Activities for Elementary School Students

***Self-knowledge.*** The objective of an activity, such as "What is a friend?," is to determine valued attributes in a friend. Students would either list individually or discuss in small groups the definitions of friendship and what personal attributes describe a friend.

***Educational and occupational exploration.*** For the activity ABC List of Occupations, students list as many occupations as they can think of alphabetically and what they require from a worker. Students then discuss energy required versus pay, which jobs earn the most money, and so forth. Students learn about the importance of knowing about jobs and job requirements and how personal preferences influence people's opinions about jobs.

***Career planning.*** Students list school subjects, such as math, science, and music, on the chalkboard. They then divide into small groups to list occupations that require the knowledge of that subject (e.g., math for accounting) in order to reinforce the connection between school and work.

### Sample Career Development Activities for Middle School and Junior High and High School Students

***Self-knowledge.*** Students record in a journal how they spend their out-of-school time over the course of 1 week. They then rate their enjoyment of each activity. By focusing on those activities they like most, students can clarify those that they should incorporate into their career plans.

***Educational and occupational exploration.*** Students interview workers who enjoy their jobs and are good at them in order to identify training requirements, working conditions, specific responsibilities, and so forth. Students then review their responses and share them with a group and respond to the following statement: This job would or would not (select one) be a good match for me because ... Additionally, the following activities can be useful to increase occupational awareness: structured site visits, shadowing, simulated site visits, simulated work samples, vocationally related classroom experiences, academic classroom experiences, and visits to work settings.

***Career planning.*** Students collect and document their course work, activities, career exploration, special awards, transition plan, goal statements, and contacts in an educational and career portfolio, which begins as early as middle school in preparation for continued education or work.

## SUMMARY

Many students are at risk for career-related difficulties. In particular, female students, minorities, and individuals with disabilities experience the highest risk of experiencing career-related problems. To prevent problems in the area of career development, schools must develop K–12 career education programs that, based on career development theory, establish clear career-related objectives at each grade level. Activities designed to aid students' acquisition of these objectives must be an established part of the regular education curriculum. Schools must target populations that are at high risk for career-related difficulties (women, minorities, and individuals with disabilities) and must incorporate a multilevel vocational and career assessment program to determine the extent to which students are mastering objectives in a timely manner. The program would then assist in planning individual or group interventions for students who were not mastering these objectives. Finally, schools must provide transition services designed to help students make a successful transition from high school to postschool life as part of a comprehensive K–12 career education program.

Perhaps most important, though, is that educators must provide the same level of emphasis, and the same level of commitment and resources, to planning and developing programs to meet the career development needs of the job-bound majority as they do the needs of the college-bound minority. In addition, schools need to focus on the development of programs that are truly oriented toward identifying and meeting student needs rather than meeting school needs for accountability and statutory compliance. Until this fundamental shift in educational priorities occurs, a dramatic shift in career development outcomes among students is unlikely, particularly those students who are at the greatest risk of experiencing career-related problems.

## RECOMMENDED RESOURCES

### Books and Other Printed Material

Levinson, E. M. (1993). *Transdisciplinary vocational assessment: Issues in school-based programs.* Brandon, VT: Clinical Psychology Publishing Co.

This book summarizes theories of career development, discusses assessment techniques that can be used to assess aspects of career development, and discusses the development and implementation of vocational assessment, career education, and school-to-work transition programs in the schools. Six models of school-based vocational assessment program are discussed, and sample forms are included.

Levinson, E. M. (2004). *Transition from school to postschool life for individuals with disabilities: Assessment from an educational and school psychological perspective.* Springfield, IL: Charles C. Thomas.

This book addresses the domains that should be included in a comprehensive assessment designed to assist in planning for a student's transition from school to postschool life. With chapters written by practicing school psychologists, this book attempts to blend theory and practice and reviews research issues and assessment methods in each of six transition domains. Separate chapters address issues associated with transition to work and transition to postsecondary education.

Niles, S. G., & Harris-Bowlsbey, J. (2002). *Career development interventions in the 21st century.* Upper Saddle River, NJ: Merrill/Prentice Hall.

This book used the National Career Development Association (NCDA) career development competencies to guide the identification of topics designed to merge theory and practice inclusively and to provide the requisite skills for career development interventions.

Pope, M., & Minor, C. W. (2000). *Experiential activities for teaching career counseling classes and for facilitating career groups.* Columbus, OH: National Career Development Association.

This book is a refreshing resource to generate interest and learning about career exploration and planning. It contains 70 suggested activities ranging from discussions to reflective research to role-plays.

## Websites

*http://www.careerkey.org/english/*

This website provides free assessments of career interests using the Career Key published by Lawrence Jones, PhD. The assessment is based on the Holland typology. Related resources are very useful.

# REFERENCES

Alston, R. J., & Hampton, J. L. (2000). Science and engineering as viable career choices for students with disabilities: A survey of parents and teachers. *Rehabilitation Counseling Bulletin, 43,* 158–164.

Armstrong, P. I., & Crombie, G. (2000). Compromises in adolescents' occupational aspirations and expectations from grades 8 to 10. *Journal of Vocational Behavior, 56,* 82–98.

Baker, S. B., & Popowicz, C. L. (1983). Meta-analysis as a strategy for evaluating effects of career education interventions. *Vocational Guidance Quarterly, 31,* 178–186.

Bandura, A. (1986). *Social foundations of thought and action: A social cognitive theory.* Englewood Cliffs, NJ: Prentice Hall.

Campbell, C. A., & Dahir, C. A. (1997). *The national standards for school counseling programs.* Alexandria, VA: American School Counselor Association.

Gottfredson, L. S. (1996). Gottfedson's theory of circumscription and compromise. In D. Brown, L. Brooks, & Assoc. (Eds.), *Career choice and development* (3rd ed., pp. 179–232). San Francisco: Jossey-Bass.

Greene, J. P., & Winters, M. A. (2005). *Public high school graduation and college-readiness rates: 1991–2002.* Retrieved March 18, 2005, from www.manhattan-institute.org/html/ewp_08.htm

Hackett, G., & Byars, A. (1996). Social cognitive theory and career development of African American women. *Career Development Quarterly, 44,* 322–340.

Helwig, A. A. (2001). A test of Gottfredson's theory using a ten-year longitudinal study. *Journal of Career Development, 27,* 77–95.

Holland, J. L. (1992). Making vocational choices: A theory of vocational personalities and work environments. (2nd ed.). Odessa, FL: Psychological Assessment Resources.

Isaacson, L. E., & Brown, D. (1997). *Career information, career counseling, and career development.* Boston: Allyn & Bacon.

Lent, R. W., Brown, S. D., & Hackett, G. (1996). Career development from a social cognitive perspective. In D. Brow, L. Brooks, & Assoc. (Eds.), *Career choice and development* (3rd ed., pp. 373–416). San Francisco: Jossey-Bass.

Levinson, E. M. (1993). *Transdisciplinary vocational assessment: Issues in school-based programs.* Brandon, VT: Clinical Psychology Publishing Co.

Levinson, E. M. (2002a). Best practices in school-based vocational assessment. In A. Thomas & J. Grimes (Eds.), *Best practices in school psychology IV* (pp. 1569–1584). Bethesda, MD: National Association of School Psychologists.

Levinson, E. M. (2002b). Career development interventions for young adults with disabilities. In S. Niles (Ed.), *Adult career development: Concepts, issues, and practices* (pp. 233–252). Tulsa, OK: National Career Development Association.

Levinson, E. M. (2004). Introduction to transition assessment. In E. M. Levinson (Ed.), *Transition from school to post-school life for individuals with disabilities: Assessment from an educational and school psychological perspective.* Springfield, IL: Charles C. Thomas.

Levinson, E. M., & Brandt, J. (1997). Career development. In G. Bear, K. Minke, & A. Thomas (Eds.), *Children's needs: Psychological perspectives II* (pp. 533–545). Bethesda, MD: National Association of School Psychologists.

Luzzo, D. A., & MacGregor, M. W. (2001). Practice and research in career counseling and development 2000. *Career Development Quarterly, 50,* 98–139.

McWhirter, E. H., Rasheed, S., & Crothers, M. (2000). The effects of high schoool career education on social-cognitive variables. *Journal of Counseling Psychology, 47,* 330–341.

Mitchell, L. K., & Krumboltz, J. D. (1996). Krumboltz's learning theory of career choice counseling. In D. Brown, L. Brooks, & Assoc. (Eds.), *Career choice and development* (3rd ed., pp. 233–276). San Francisco: Jossey-Bass.

Morra, L. G. (1993). *Transition from school to work: H.R. 2884 addresses components of comprehensive strategy* (GAO/HRD-93-32) (Testimony before the Committee on Education and Labor, U.S. House of Representatives). Washington, DC: General Accounting Office.

National Council on Disability. (2000). *National disability policy: A progress report, November 1, 1998–November 19, 1999.* Washington, DC: Author. (ERIC Document Reproduction Service No. ED442240).

National Occupational Information Coordinating Committee, U.S. Department of Labor (1992). *The national career development guidelines project.* Washington, DC: U.S. Department of Labor.

National Organization on Disability (2002). *Executive summary: 2000 N.O.D./Harris Survey of Americans with Disabilities.* Retrieved January 11, 2004, from http://www.nod.org/index.cfm?fuseaction=page.viewPage&pageID=1430&nodeID=1&FeatureID=861&redirected=1&CFID=656927&CFTOKEN=55331917

Niles, S. G., & Harris-Bowlsbey, J. (2002). *Career development interventions in the 21st century.* Upper Saddle River, NJ: Merrill/Prentice Hall.

Ohler, D. L., Levinson, E. M., & Damiani, V. B. (1998). Gender, disability and career maturity among college students. *Special Services in the Schools, 13*(1/2), 149–161.

Ridfuss, R. R., Cooksey, E. C., & Sutterlin, L. S. (1999). Young adult occupational achievement: Early expectation versus behavioral reality. *Work and Occupations, 26,* 220–263.

Savickas, M. L. (1989). Annual review: Practice and research in career counseling and development, 1988. *Career Development Quarterly, 38*(2), 100–134.

Super, D. (1957). *The psychology of careers.* New York: Harper & Row.

# 40

# Response to Intervention

**Frank M. Gresham**

*Louisiana State University Project REACH University of California–Riverside*

## BACKGROUND AND DEVELOPMENT

Applied psychologists historically have addressed children's academic and behavioral needs by receiving referrals, conducting comprehensive assessments, making classification recommendations, and providing suggestions for interventions. For school psychologists, this process typically begins with a referral from teachers and results in an eligibility recommendation for 1 of the 13 disability categories specified in the Individuals With Disabilities Education Act of 2004 (IDEA). For child clinical psychologists, this process typically begins with a referral from parents and results in a diagnosis using the *Diagnostic and Statistical Manual of Mental Disorders* (DSM-IV; American Psychiatric Association, 1994). In both of these cases, there is often very little relationship between the referral concern, the assessments conducted, and the interventions that are recommended. That is, typical assessments for diagnosis in DSM-IV and eligibility determination under IDEA lack treatment validity (Fuchs & Fuchs, 1998; Gresham, 2002a; Gresham & Gansle, 1992).

*Treatment validity* (sometimes called treatment or instructional utility) can be defined as the extent to which any assessment procedure contributes to beneficial outcomes for individuals (Cone, 1989; Hayes, Nelson, & Jarrett, 1987). A central feature of treatment validity is that there must be a clear and unambiguous relationship between the assessment data collected and the recommended intervention. Although the concept of treatment validity evolved from the behavioral assessment field, it shares several characteristics and concepts with the traditional psychometric literature.

First, treatment validity is based in part on the idea of incremental validity; that is, it requires that an assessment procedure improve prediction above and beyond existing assessment procedures (Sechrest, 1963). Second, treatment validity involves the notions of utility and cost–benefit analysis, which are common concepts in the personnel selection literature (Mischel, 1968; Wiggins, 1973). Third, treatment validity involves Messick's (1995) notion of the evidential basis for test interpretation and use, particularly as it relates to construct validity, relevance and utility, and social consequences of testing. Although an assessment procedure might have construct validity, it could have little, if any, relevance or utility for treatment planning (i.e., absence of treatment validity).

For any assessment procedure to have treatment validity, it must lead to identification of relevant areas of concern (academic or behavioral), inform treatment planning, and be helpful in evaluating treatment outcomes. Traditionally, assessment procedures in applied psychology have failed to demonstrate treatment validity because they do not inform instructional and behavioral intervention practices (Cronbach, 1975; Gresham, 2002a; Reschly & Ysseldyke, 2002). The concept of *response to intervention* depends largely on the treatment validity of measures used to determine adequate or inadequate treatment response. This chapter proposes that the field adopt the logic of response to intervention as a more beneficial means of addressing children's academic and behavioral needs.

### Response to Intervention Defined

The response to intervention (RTI) concept is based on an adequate or inadequate change in academic performance or behavior as a function of intervention (Gresham, 2002a). In an RTI approach, eligibility determinations of diagnostic decisions are based on how children respond to evidence-based interventions implemented with integrity. This approach is also used to select, change, or titrate interventions based on how the child responds to the intervention. RTI assumes that if a child shows an inadequate response to the best interventions available, then that child can and should be eligible for additional assistance, including, but not limited to, special education and related services. The goal of all interventions is to produce a *discrepancy* between the child's current performance and the child's expected level of performance. In fact, in a problem-solving model, a *problem* is defined as the discrepancy between current and expected levels of performance (Tilly, 2002). The larger this discrepancy, the larger the problem and the more resistant the problem will be to change.

RTI uses data-based decision making as a basis for modifying, titrating, or changing the nature of interventions. This logic is not unlike physicians changing the dosage level or type of drug based on a patient's unacceptable response to that drug. RTI gives school personnel the latitude to function within an intervention framework rather than a psychometric eligibility framework, as the latter often results in dubious intervention recommendations based on assessment procedures that have little or no treatment validity (Gresham, 2002a; Reschly & Tilly, 1999).

## Brief History of RTI

The origins of the RTI approach can be traced back to the National Research Council (NRC) investigation (Heller, Holtzman, & Messick, 1982) in which the validity of the special education classification system was evaluated using three criteria: (a) the quality of the general education program, (b) the value of the special education program in producing important outcomes for students, and (c) the accuracy and meaningfulness of the assessment process in the identification of a disability. The first two of the above criteria emphasize the quality of instruction, whereas the third criterion described in the NRC study involves judgments of the quality of instructional environments and the student's response to instruction delivered in those environments (Vaughn & Fuchs, 2003). The third criterion described in the NRC study is consistent with Messick's (1995) evidential and consequential bases for test use and interpretation.

Speece (2002) argued that IQ-achievement discrepancy approaches are problematic because of the unintended social consequences they produce. Two such unintended social consequences are the difficulty young children have in qualifying for services and the overrepresentation of males and minority children with the discrepancy approach. Additionally, the discrepancy approach does not inform instructional decisions that might be made to improve student outcomes (Gresham, 2002a; Reschly & Tilly, 1999). Heller et al. (1982) concluded that only when all three criteria are met could a special education classification be considered valid.

***Operationalizing of the NRC criteria.*** Fuchs and Fuchs (1997, 1998) operationalized the NRC criteria using curriculum-based measurement (CBM), which measures students' responsiveness or unresponsiveness to intervention delivered in a general education classroom. Earlier, Fuchs (1995) compared the RTI approach to the practice used in medicine (endocrinology) in which a child's growth over time is compared with that of same-age children. A child showing a large discrepancy between his or her height and that of a normative sample may be considered a candidate for certain types of medical treatment, such as growth hormone therapy. In education, a child showing a large discrepancy between the current level of academic performance and that of same-age peers in the same classroom might be considered a candidate for more intensive intervention. It should be emphasized that a low-performing child who shows a growth rate similar to that of peers in a low-performing classroom would not be considered a candidate for more intensive intervention because the child is deriving similar educational benefits, although low, from that classroom (Fuchs, 1995).

Fuchs and Fuchs (1998) argued for a reconceptualization of the process used to identify children with learning disabilities (LD), to base the process on the idea of treatment validity. This approach does not classify students as LD unless and until it has been demonstrated that they are not benefiting from the general education curriculum. The treatment validity approach repeatedly measures the student's progress in the general education curriculum using CBM rather than assessing students at one point in time using ability, achievement, and processing measures characteristic of traditional LD assessments. The dynamic and ongoing nature of assessment using CBM probes to assess growth (or lack thereof) characterizes the treatment validity approach to LD assessment. In this approach, special education is considered only if a student's performance shows a *dual discrepancy* (DD), in which performance *level* is below that of classroom peers and the student's learning rate (*growth*) is substantially below that of classroom peers.

The CBM-DD approach for identifying students as LD consists of three phases. Phase I requires the documentation of adequate classroom instruction and dual discrepancies (both level and growth). It involves the collection of periodic CBM assessments for all students in a general education classroom (three 1-minute CBM reading probes). During this phase, overall classroom performance is compared with the performance of other classrooms, with district norms, or with grade-level benchmarks. If classroom performance is adequate, then individual student data are evaluated based on the following criteria: (a) a difference of 1 standard deviation between a student's CBM median score and that of classmates and (b) a difference of 1 standard deviation between a student's CBM slope of improvement (growth) and that of classmates. Students who meet these criteria and who do not have accompanying exclusionary conditions (e.g., mental retardation, sensory disabilities, or autism) move to Phase II of the process.

Phase II of this process involves implementation of a prereferral intervention that focuses on remediating the student's dual discrepancy. CBM data are collected to judge the effectiveness of the intervention, with the provision that the teacher implements a minimum of two interventions over a 6-week period. If a student does not show adequate progress in terms of level and slope, the student enters Phase III of the process.

Phase III involves the design and implementation of an extended intervention plan. This phase represents a special-education diagnostic trial period in which the student's responsiveness to more intense instruction is measured. This phase lasts about 8 weeks, after which a team reconvenes and makes decisions about the student's placement. The team could decide that the intervention was successful in eliminating the dual discrepancy, and an individual education plan (IEP) would be developed and the plan continued. In contrast, the team could decide that the intervention was unsuccessful in eliminating the dual discrepancy and consider alternative decisions such as changing the nature and intensity of the intervention, collecting additional assessment information, considering a more restrictive placement, or changing to a school having additional resources that better address the student's needs.

To qualify a student as LD in the above model, a three-pronged test must be passed: (a) a dual discrepancy must exist between the student's performance level and growth (1 standard deviation for each), (b) the student's rate of learning is inadequate, even with adaptations made in the general education classroom, and (c) the provision of special education must result in improved growth (i.e., it results in educational benefit).

***Replication of the CBM-DD approach.*** Speece and Case (2001) provided further validity evidence for the CBM-DD model's use in identifying students as LD. Children were identified as being at risk for reading failure if their mean performance on CBM reading probes placed them in the lower quartile of their classrooms. A contrast group was identified that included five students from each classroom based on scores at the median (2 students) and the 30th, 75th, and 90th percentiles (1 student at each level). At-risk students were placed into one of three groups: CBM dual discrepancy (CBM-DD), regression-based IQ–reading achievement (IQ-DS), and low achievement (LA). Students in the CBM-DD group were given 10 CBM oral reading probes administered across the school year. Slopes (based on ordinary least squares regression for each child and classroom) were calculated, and each student's performance level was based on the mean of the last two data points. Children were placed in the CBM-DD group ($n$ = 47) if their slope across the year and level of performance at the end of the year was greater than 1 standard deviation below that of classmates. Students were placed in the IQ-DS group ($n$ = 17) if their IQ–reading achievement discrepancy was 1.5 or more standard errors of prediction (approximately a 20-point discrepancy). Children were placed in the LA group ($n$ = 28) if their total reading score was less than 90 (< 25th percentile).

Speece and Case showed that students in the CBM-DD group were more deficient on measures of phonological processing and were rated by teachers as having lower academic competence and social skills and more problem behaviors than students in the IQ-DS and LA groups. The CBM-DD and IQ-DS groups were not different on a standardized measure of reading achievement. These data offer further support for the CBM-DD model's ability to identify students as LD, specifically those with phonological deficits.

***The LD summit and IDEA reauthorization.*** The RTI approach received further attention as a viable alternative to IQ–achievement discrepancy from the LD Initiative. The initiative was sponsored by the Office of Special Education Programs (U.S. Department of Education) and culminated in the Learning Disabilities Summit, a national conference held in Washington, DC, in August 2001. Nine white papers were written and presented over a 2-day period. One paper (Gresham, 2002a) specifically addressed the literature on RTI, which was responded to by four highly respected professionals within the field of LD (Fuchs, 2002; Grimes, 2002;

Vaughn, 2002; Vellutino, 2002). Subsequent to the Learning Disabilities Summit, the President's Commission on Excellence in Special Education (2002) emphasized RTI as a viable alternative to IQ–achievement discrepancy in the identification of LD.

In December 2004 President Bush signed into law the reauthorization of IDEA. The law now reads as follows, with respect to specific learning disabilities:

> Specific learning disabilities: (A) General: Notwithstanding section 607 of this Act, or any other provision of law, when determining whether a child has a specific learning disability as defined by this Act, the LEA shall *not be required* to take into consideration whether a child has a severe discrepancy between achievement and intellectual ability in oral expression, listening comprehension, reading recognition ... (B) Additional Authority: In determining whether a child has a specific learning disability, a LEA *may use* a process which determines if a child *responds to a scientific, research based intervention* (Italics added).

The reauthorized version of IDEA does not require, nor does it eliminate, IQ–achievement discrepancy as a basis for identifying students as LD. It also allows, but does not require, school districts to use an RTI approach to identify LD.

# PROBLEMS AND IMPLICATIONS

## Advantages of RTI

There are four advantages of adopting an RTI approach in the identification of children's learning and behavioral problems: (a) early identification of learning and behavioral deficits leads to more effective interventions; (b) it conceptualizes learning and behavioral problems in terms of a risk rather than a deficit model, (c) it can lead to a reduction of identification biases, and (d) it focuses on student outcomes (Fletcher et al., 2002; Gresham, 2002; Vaughn & Fuchs, 2003). Each of these advantages is discussed in the following sections.

***Early identification of learning and behavior problems.*** Many fields have well-established practices of early identification of problems, which leads to more effective treatments. For example, in medicine, routine screening procedures such as mammograms to detect breast cancer and prostate-specific antigen tests to detect prostate cancer have been routine for years. Unfortunately, similar proactive, early identification practices are not universally used for identifying children with learning or behavioral problems (Walker, Ramsey, & Gresham, 2004).

Perhaps the most compelling reason for adopting an RTI approach is that it provides the opportunity to help struggling children immediately rather than wait until these children have a well-ingrained pattern of academic or behavioral difficulties. The current use of IQ–achievement discrepancy to identify children as LD has been termed a "wait to fail" approach because it requires that a student fail severely enough and long enough for the teacher to make a decision to refer. The developmental odds of being classified as LD increase dramatically from first to fourth grades. For example, between first and second grades the LD rate doubles, from second to third grades the rate doubles again, and between third and fourth grades the odds increase by a factor of 1.5 (U.S. Department of Education, 2002). Thus, between first and fourth grades, the odds of being labeled LD increase linearly by 450%. Discrepancy approaches penalize younger children because they are much more likely to demonstrate a discrepancy than older children (Fletcher et al., 1998).

In the area of children's emotional and behavioral difficulties, schools often wait until it is too late for effective interventions to address these children's difficulties. Bullis and Walker (1994) argued that it is ironic that teachers consistently rank children's severe behavioral difficulties as one of their highest service priorities, even though prevalence studies indicate that this school population continues to be underidentified (Walker, Nishioka, Zeller, Severson, & Feil, 2000). Kauffman (1999) has argued that schools often "prevent prevention" of behavior disorders of at-risk children through well-meaning efforts to protect them from such factors as labeling and stigmatization associated with the early identification process.

Professionals have known for years that children who have not learned to achieve their social goals other than through inappropriate or coercive behavioral strategies by around 8 years of age (end of third grade) will likely continue displaying some degree of antisocial behavior throughout their lives (Kazdin, 1987; Loeber & Farrington, 1998; Walker et al., 2004). It is also known that the longer such children go without access to effective intervention services, the more resistant their behavior problems will be to later intervention efforts (Gresham, 1991). In the absence of early intervention, these problem behaviors will likely escalate and morph into more serious and debilitating behavior patterns. Early identification of problem behaviors and subsequent intervention efforts using an RTI approach hold great promise for preventing serious problem behaviors as children get older.

***Risk versus deficit models of practice.*** The field of school psychology historically has operated under a deficit model in which either underlying cognitive and processing deficits or social–emotional deficits are identified, and instructional or behavioral strategies subsequently are recommended to remediate those identified deficits (Mann, 1979; Reschly & Tilly, 1999; Ysseldyke, 2001). In the field of LD, Vaughn and Fuchs (2003) noted that the field simply has not been successful in reliably identifying underlying processing deficits and linking that information to effective instructional strategies. Current LD assessment relies heavily on aptitude by treatment interaction (ATI) logic, in which instructional treatments are matched to aptitude strengths, presumably to produce better outcomes. After 20 years of disappointing research, Cronbach (1975) abandoned ATI logic as a basis for applied psychology and recommended a process akin to what is now called problem solving and short-run empiricism (see Reschly & Ysseldyke, 2002; Tilly, Reschly, & Grimes, 1999).

RTI operates under a risk model in which early identification of learning and behavioral difficulties is emphasized. Under this model, *all* students are screened for potential learning and behavioral difficulties early in their school careers (e.g., kindergarten to first grade). Those students identified as being at risk are given supplemental instruction or positive behavioral support that has been shown to be an effective practice through research (i.e., evidence-based practice) to remediate these learning and behavioral difficulties.

The most important concept in an RTI approach is the idea of matching the *intensity* of the intervention to the *severity* and *resistance* of the problem to intervention. This approach characterizes interventions that differ in terms of their nature, comprehensiveness, and intensity, as well as the degree of unresponsiveness of behavior to those interventions (Gresham, 1991, 2002a). The RTI approach also offers enhanced opportunities to integrate services between general and special education (Vaughn & Fuchs, 2003).

***Reduction of identification biases.*** Special education eligibility in the public schools almost always begins with a general education teacher's decision to refer a child for special education consideration. The decision to refer a child for an LD assessment is almost always based on academic difficulties, particularly in reading (Bocian, Beebe, MacMillan, & Gresham, 1999). In contrast, the decision to refer a child for an assessment as emotionally disturbed (ED) is almost always based on social behavioral difficulties, particularly for externalizing or undercontrolled behavior problems (Kauffman, 2000; Walker et al., 2004).

Two fundamental principles guide teacher referral: *relativity* and *tolerance.* Relativity deals with the child's level of academic or behavioral performance relative to the modal or expected performance of the class or the gap between the referred child's academic or behavioral performance and relative to other members of the class. Tolerance deals with the degree to which a child's academic or behavioral difficulties are tolerated by the teacher and meet that teacher's behavioral demands and expectations (see Walker, Irvin, Noell, & Singer, 1992). The extent to which a child's academic or behavioral difficulties exceed that teacher's tolerance level predicts the probability of referral to special education.

A teacher's decision to refer is influenced not only by academic difficulties and behavioral excesses but also by factors such as the child's gender, socioeconomic status, and group membership (MacMillan & Siperstein, 2002; Reschly, 2002). Donovan and Cross (2002) argued that an RTI approach to the referral process has the potential of reducing and perhaps eliminating the disproportionate overrepresentation of certain minority groups in special education that result from biases in the teacher referral process (e.g., overrepresentation of African American males in the ED category). Also, it is well established that there is a bias in overidentifying males and underidentifying females as LD by the current teacher referral process (Donovan & Cross, 2002; Shaywitz, Shaywitz, Fletcher, & Escobar, 1990). In addition, researchers have empirically demonstrated the power of iterative problem-solving efforts that are implemented as part of an RTI approach to reduce disproportionate identification by race and sex, as well as the RTI approach's superiority to other methods of identification, such as teacher referral (VanDerHeyden, Witt, & Naquin, 2003).

***Focus on student outcomes.*** RTI is based on the premise that measures and domains assessed should be determined by their relationships to child outcomes. Useful and appropriate measures and domains should have a documented relationship to positive child outcomes, not just to predictions of failure. Measures without such relationships do little for children and may cause harm because they deflect attention away from measures and domains that can be used to produce positive outcomes (Reschly & Tilly, 1999). RTI emphasizes direct measurement of achievement, behavior, and the instructional environment as the core foci of a comprehensive evaluation of children's academic and behavioral difficulties. RTI is concerned primarily with the assessment of measurable and changeable aspects of the instructional environment that are related to positive child outcomes. Assessment in an RTI approach concentrates on factors that are related to achievement or positive behavior and on interventions designed to improve rates and levels of skill development.

The RTI approach assumes, for example, that a significant proportion of children who are or might be identified as LD may be more accurately characterized as "instructional causalities" (Vaughn, Linan-Thompson, & Hickman, 2003). Clay (1987) argued that many children "learn to be learning disabled" because they are not exposed to early fundamental literacy skills in kindergarten and first grade (e.g., phoneme awareness, print concepts, and letter–sound correspondence). In addition, many of these children are exposed to marginally effective general education reading curricula and instruction that either have not been scientifically validated or have been implemented with poor integrity (National Reading Panel, 2000).

RTI involves analyses of prior and current instructional opportunities and the application of evidence-based instructional strategies related to positive child outcomes. Instructional variables that are assessed include alterable factors such as time allocated for instruction, academic learning time, pacing of instruction, number of opportunities to respond, and sequencing of examples and nonexamples of skills (Denton, Vaughn, & Fletcher, 2003; Carnine, Silbert, & Kame'enui, 1997; National Reading Panel, 2000; Witt, VanDerHeyden, & Gilbertson, 2004). An essential component of RTI involves the direct measurement of the treatment integrity of instructional or behavioral interventions in a general classroom setting.

## ALTERNATIVE ACTIONS FOR PREVENTION

### Screening for Academic and Behavior Problems

An essential step in preventing children's academic and behavior problems involves the systematic screening of a given school population to identify at-risk children. This screening process should begin as early as possible in the child's school career (e.g., kindergarten to first grade) because it is well known that academic and behavioral interventions are far more effective with younger children than with older children (Good, Gruba, & Kaminski, 2002; Juel, 1988; Kazdin, 1987; Severson & Walker, 2002; Walker, Severson, & Feil, 1995). The early signs of learning difficulties and behavior problems can be recognized during the preschool years (Hinshaw, Han, Erhardt, & Huber, 1992; Torgesen & Wagner, 1998). Walker et al. (1995) found that early signs of oppositional defiant disorder and conduct disorder can be identified as early as 3 years of age. In the absence of early detection, relatively mild difficulties early in life can escalate into more severe difficulties (e.g., severe reading problems and antisocial behavior) later on in a child's development (O'Shaughnessy, Lane, Gresham, & Beebe-Frankenberger, 2002).

It is unfortunate that schools do not use current knowledge about early identification and prevention strategies for children with learning and behavioral difficulties. Most schools adopt a "wait to fail" attitude in which they wait for teachers to refer children only *after* these children show persistent and severe academic and behavioral problems. In short, schools are reactive rather than proactive organizations and only intervene when children's problems become stressful and taxing to the school environment. Efficient and practical means are available for the early identification of children likely to develop learning and behavior problems. However, using them requires knowledge of decision rules used in the screening of children at risk for academic or behavioral difficulties.

### Decision Rules for Screening

Any use of screening procedures requires an understanding of various decision rules and associated statistics that allow for making correct decisions and avoiding incorrect decisions. The issue in screening is knowing whether the degree of predictive accuracy is high enough to justify the use of the selected screening measures (see Bennett et al., 1999). Table 1 shows key statistics that are useful in evaluating predictive accuracy. These are (a) sensitivity, (b) specificity, (c) positive predictive power, (d) negative predictive power, (e) prevalence, and (f) accuracy. *Sensitivity* refers to the percentage of individuals with an outcome (e.g., LD or ED) who have a risk indicator (e.g., poor reading fluency or noncompliance). *Specificity* refers to the percentage of individuals who do not have

**Table 1** *Calculating the Predictive Accuracy of Screening Measures*

| | Outcome Present | Outcome Absent |
|---|---|---|
| Risk indicator present | A<br>Accurate prediction | B<br>False positive |
| Risk indicator absent | C<br>False negative | D<br>Accurate prediction |

Sensitivity: A/A+C; specificity: D/B+D; positive predictive power: A/A+B; negative predictive power: D/C+D; prevalence: A/A+B+C+D; accuracy: A+D/A+B+C+D

the outcome and who also do not have the risk indicator. *Positive predictive power* is the proportion of people who have the risk indicator who eventually develop the outcome. *Negative predictive power* reflects the proportion of individuals without the risk indicator who do not develop the outcome. *Prevalence* (also called base rate) is the proportion of individuals in the population that have the outcome. The overall *accuracy* is the proportion of individuals correctly classified by the screening procedure.

Table 2 shows the classification of RTI outcomes using screening procedures. Obviously, the goal is to avoid false positive and false negative errors when using a screening procedure. A *false positive* represents an individual who responded adequately to an intervention but was classified with the outcome (e.g., LD and ED). A *false negative* is an individual who did not respond adequately to an intervention but was not classified with the outcome. The statistics described above can be useful in estimating classification accuracy in an RTI model and in avoiding diagnostic error. It should be clear from Table 2 that the goal is to identify children with a disability status (LD or ED) based on their inadequate response to intervention (*true positives*) and not to identify children with a disability status if they do show an adequate response to intervention (*true negatives*).

It should be noted that children should not be classified based on the presence or absence of a single risk factor. Most experts argue that using multiple measures of both risk factors and outcomes is highly recommended (Bennett et al., 1999; Loeber, Dishion, & Patterson, 1984). Severson and Walker (2002) argue for the use of a multiple gating procedure to increase the predictive accuracy for identifying children at risk for academic and behavior problems. Multiple gating uses a series of progressively more extensive and precise assessments, or gates, that

**Table 2** *Classification of RTI Outcomes in Eligibility Determination*

| Outcome Status | Responder | Inadequate Responder |
|---|---|---|
| Eligible | False positive<br>(adequate response) | True positive<br>(inadequate response) |
| Ineligible | True negative<br>(adequate response) | False negative<br>(inadequate response) |

provide for multimethod assessment of children's difficulties and that establish a decision-making structure collected from different information sources (Severson & Walker, 2002).

***Systematic Screening for Behavior Disorders (SSDB).*** SSBD is a multiple-gating screening procedure for the identification of children at risk for behavior disorders in Grades 1–6 (Walker & Severson, 1990). SSBD contains a series of linked, sequential assessments known as *gates*. The procedure uses a combination of teacher nomination (Gate 1), teacher rating scales and checklists (Gate 2), and direct observations of classroom and playground behavior (Gate 3) to accomplish early identification of children who are at risk for behavior disorders.

SSBD was nationally standardized on 4,500 cases for the Gate 2 measures and approximately 1,300 cases for the Gate 3 measures. Extensive empirical evidence supports the procedure's reliability and validity and is reported in the SSBD technical manual and in other sources (Severson & Walker, 2002; Walker, Severson, and Feil 1990, 1995). The major advantage of SSBD is its provision of behaviorally referenced criteria and a common set of standards for teachers to use in evaluating students' behavioral risk status. It identifies students with both externalizing and internalizing behavior problems and removes most of the idiosyncratic subjectivity characteristic of the current referral process. Proactive universal approaches to early identification, such as SSBD, provide opportunities for early intervention efforts that can prevent the escalation of problem behaviors into more virulent and resistant behaviors (Walker et al., 2004). A downward extension of SSBD known as the Early Screening Project is available for children ages 3–5 years. (Walker et al., 1995).

***Dynamic Indicators of Basic Early Literacy Skills (DIBELS).*** Measurement tools for assessing the growth and development of early literacy skills of children in kindergarten and first grade have been developed at the University of Oregon (Good et al., 2002; Kaminski & Good, 1998). These tools meet several relevant criteria in terms of content, practicality, technical characteristics, and individual decision making. In terms of content assessed, these tools measure three areas that are crucial to reading development: *phonological awareness*, *alphabetic principle*, and *accuracy* and *fluency* with reading connected text. DIBELS assesses this content in kindergarten using the following measures: initial sounds fluency, phonemic segmentation, nonsense word fluency, and letter naming fluency. In first grade, these measures include phonemic segmentation fluency, nonsense word fluency, oral reading fluency, and letter naming fluency. In second grade, one measure, oral reading fluency, is used to assess reading.

In terms of practicality, the above measures are efficient and economical and take only a minimum amount of time away from instructional activities. For example, the kindergarten battery consists of the following in terms of administration times: initial sounds fluency (3 minutes), phonemic segmentation (2 minutes), nonsense word fluency (2 minutes), and letter naming fluency (1 minute). Thus, the entire kindergarten battery takes only 8 minutes to administer. The first-grade battery involves the following administration times: phonemic segmentation fluency (2 minutes), nonsense word fluency (2 minutes), oral reading fluency (3 minutes). The first-grade battery also takes only 8 minutes to administer. Finally, the second-grade battery using oral reading fluency takes only 3 minutes to administer. Compared with traditional psychoeducational assessment, this represents a huge savings in time for school psychologists.

The above measures have demonstrated reliability and validity evidence that is based on a number of studies (see Good et al., 2002). All measures have multiple alternate forms and have excellent evidence for alternate form reliability. Test–retest reliabilities of the measures are in the 0.92–0.97 range. Concurrent validity evidence is based on relationships among the above measures and standardized tests of academic achievement (both individually and group administered). In addition to having strong psychometric characteristics, the above measures are highly sensitive to change and can be used as outcome measures in the RTI decision-making process (Good et al., 2002).

From the perspective of RTI, the DIBELS measures are accurate in identifying children who require additional instructional support to achievement reading goals for their respective grade levels. The measures also inform decisions about the effectiveness of instruction on a weekly, student-by-student basis. Decision making is aided by the use of benchmark assessments that are well established for each of the DIBELS measures. For example, in winter a kindergartener scoring less than 10 on initial sounds fluency may need intensive instructional support, whereas a child scoring 25–35 on this measure is considered to be meeting benchmark standards. A second-grade (spring) child reading less than 50 words correctly per minute would be at risk and in need of support, whereas a child reading 90 words correctly per minute would be meeting benchmark standards.

Good et al. (2002) suggest that individual decision making using DIBELS is based on a problem-solving model (Shinn, 2002; Tilly, 2002) called the outcome-driven model. This model consists of five steps: (a) identifying the need for support, (b) validating the need for support, (c) planning support, (d) evaluating and modifying support, and (e) reviewing outcomes. The level and intensity of instructional support is matched to the individual needs of a given student. Some students will require intensive support; others will need less intensive support. The entire logic behind this model is to prevent a pattern of reading failure by using early identification and intervention.

## ALTERNATIVE ACTIONS FOR INTERVENTION

Two basic types of approaches are used to deliver intervention services in an RTI approach: *problem-solving* approaches (Bergan & Kratochwill, 1990; Tilly, 2002) and *standard protocol* approaches (Fuchs, Mock, Morgan, & Young, 2003). Standard protocol approaches use evidence-based and empirically validated interventions for students who are struggling in a particular academic domain (e.g., reading). These approaches have been recommended by reading researchers and have a convincing body of empirical support (Foorman, Francis, Fletcher, Schatschneider, & Mehta, 1998; Torgesen et al., 2001; Vellutino et al., 1996). Because of space considerations, only the problem-solving approaches are presented in the following sections.

### Problem-Solving Approaches

Problem-solving approaches to intervention activities can be traced back to Bergan's (1977) original text on behavioral consultation and on Bergan's and Kratochwill's (1990) revised text. Behavioral consultation takes place in a sequence of four phases: (a) problem identification, (b) problem analysis, (c) plan implementation, and (d) plan evaluation. The goal in behavioral consultation is to define the referral problem in specific operational terms, to identify environmental conditions related to the referral problem, to design and implement an intervention plan with integrity, and to evaluate the effectiveness of the intervention (Bergan & Kratochwill, 1990).

***Problem identification.*** The most important task in any problem-solving model is to define the referral concern in specific behavioral terms. Teachers often describe behavior in vague or global terms that are not useful in the problem-solving process. Typically, behavioral consultants use teacher interviews as the initial means of defining behavior. Those behaviors subsequently defined in the interview are *directly* observed or measured in some way (e.g., classroom observations or administration of DIBELS measures).

However, an adequate definition of behavior does not necessarily establish its social significance. The social significance of behavior can be established in how consumers (teachers and parents) value certain behaviors. For example, reading at grade level or completing math worksheets with 90% or greater accuracy may be more socially significant than being on-task 100% of the time.

For social behaviors, it is more fruitful to define target behaviors for intervention in terms of positive social behaviors to be increased rather than negative social behaviors to be decreased or eliminated. Target social behaviors in problem identification must pass the "Dead Man's Test": If a dead man can perform the behavior, it is not a behavior. For example, staying in seat, being quiet, not talking out in class are all things a dead man can do. On the other hand, raising one's hand before speaking in class or asking permission to leave one's seat are all behaviors that a dead man cannot perform.

In selecting target behaviors for intervention, consultants should keep in mind that behaviors that allow for successful or adaptive functioning in school environments should be selected. That is, behaviors targeted in problem identification should have *habilitative validity* (Hawkins, 1991). Habilitative validity is the degree to which the goals, procedures, and outcomes of intervention maximize the overall benefits and minimize the overall costs to that individual and others. In terms of academic performance, behaviors that are highly predictive of subsequent reading skills should be targeted for intervention. For example, phoneme segmentation fluency that is well below benchmark levels (<10) represents a socially significant target behavior that has habilitative validity if it is increased to benchmark levels. In terms of social behavior, behaviors such as compliance, rule following, and cooperation have habilitative validity in general and special education classrooms (Gresham, 2002b).

***Problem analysis.*** The purpose of problem analysis is to identify those environmental events (both antecedent and consequent) that are related to the occurrence and nonoccurrence of behavior. Functional behavioral assessment is often used to identify the purposes or functions a behavior serves (see Gresham, Watson, & Skinner, 2001). Behavioral function has traditionally been classified into four categories: (a) social attention (positive reinforcement function), (b) escape or avoidance (negative reinforcement function), (c) access to preferred tangibles or activities (positive reinforcement function), and (d) automatic or sensory reinforcement. Many times children exhibit disruptive classroom behavior to escape aversive academic tasks. If disruptive behavior results in a removal of task demands, then that behavior will be negatively reinforced and will increase in frequency on future occasions. Other times or for other children, disruptive behavior might result in social attention from peers and teachers. In this case, if disruptive behavior results in social attention, it will be positively reinforced and increase in frequency in the future.

Witt and colleagues have provided the field with a useful approach for conducting functional behavioral assessments for children's academic problems (Witt, Daly, & Noell, 2000). They cite five reasons for children's academic difficulties: (a) The student does not want to do the work (lack of incentives), (b) the student has not spent enough time doing the work (few opportunities to respond), (c) the student has not had enough help to do the work (inadequate instructional support), (d) the activity is not teaching the student what the teacher wants the student to learn (low expectation or instructional mismatch), and (e) the work is too difficult for the student (skill deficit). These five reasons are useful in conceptualizing children's academic difficulties and lead directly to interventions to improve academic performance (Noell & Witt, 1998; Witt et al., 2000).

***Plan implementation.*** After successful problem identification and problem analysis, an intervention plan should be implemented. The consultee (the teacher) must have the skills to successfully implement the intervention plan. Often, a consultant may have to assist in the initial stages of plan implementation (Noell & Witt, 1998; Watson & Robinson, 1996). An essential component in plan implementation is ongoing *progress monitoring* of the child's behavior. Without monitoring the child's response to the plan, the effectiveness of the plan in changing behavior cannot be known. Progress monitoring is the crux of any RTI model; without it responsiveness to intervention cannot be evaluated.

Another key component of plan implementation is the systematic evaluation of *treatment integrity.* Treatment integrity refers to the degree to which an intervention is implemented as intended (Gresham, 1989). One can have the best intervention plan ever devised, but it may be useless in changing behavior if the teacher does not implement it or implements it poorly. Treatment integrity should be directly assessed in the classroom using well-established procedures (see Lane & Beebe-Frankenberger, 2004).

Noell et al. (2000, 2002, in press), borrowing from the performance management literature in business and industry (Balcazar, Hopkins, & Suarez, 1985) have shown that teachers can reliably implement a variety of academic and behavioral interventions. Specifically, these researchers have shown that follow-up contact by a consultant that includes a review of student progress and treatment implementation can lead to near perfect implementation of interventions (see Mortenson & Witt, 1998; Noell, Duhon, Gatti, & Connell, 2002; Noell et al., 2000; Noell et al., in press). The types of follow-up and support procedures in this research range from traditional performance management procedures, such as daily performance feedback or weekly performance feedback, to procedures derived from the school-based consultation literature, such as behavioral consultation or social influence (Noell et al., in press).

The above series of studies along with a huge literature in applied behavior analysis strongly suggest that behavioral and academic interventions developed in a behavioral consultation model can be implemented with integrity, but only with specific performance feedback from consultants. If they are implemented correctly, these interventions can produce substantial changes in students' academic and social behavior (Alberto & Troutman, 2003; Elliott, Witt, Kratochwill, & Stoiber, 2002; Gresham, 2002a; Greenwood, Maheady, & Delquadri, 2002).

***Plan evaluation.*** A critical aspect of the RTI approach is the determination of an adequate response to intervention. How does one know that the intervention has brought the target behavior into functional or adequate ranges? The answer to the question is easier for academic difficulties, particularly reading, than for social behavior. For example, benchmark assessments are widely available in the curriculum-based measurement (CBM) literature to determine whether the student's performance is in the normative range (see Good et al., 2002; Shinn, 2002). One could also adopt the criteria recommended by Fuchs and Fuchs (1997, 1998) in terms of expected growth over time as a standard for evaluating responsiveness to intervention.

In terms of social behavior, several methods have been suggested to evaluate treatment responsiveness. By far the most common means of evaluating treatment responsiveness for individuals is using visual inspection of graphed data. Unlike complex statistical analyses, visual inspection relies on the "interocular" test of significance. The problem with visual inspection, however, is that there is no universal standard to apply in determining adequate responsiveness to intervention. Barnett, Daly, Jones, and Lentz (2004) have provided useful guidelines for evaluating response to intervention using graphed data from single case designs.

As a supplement to visual inspection, one might quantify the magnitude of behavior change by calculating the percentage of change from baseline to intervention levels of performance. One calculates the percent change index by comparing the median data point in baseline with the median data point in the intervention phase. For example, if a child's median level of disruptive classroom behavior in baseline is eight occurrences and the median level of disruptive behavior in the intervention phase is two occurrences, then the percent reduction in disruptive behavior is 75%. This metric is not unlike the methods that physicians use to quantify degree of weight loss or reductions in blood cholesterol levels. The difference, however, is that there are well-established medical standards or benchmarks for ideal weights and cholesterol levels, but these don't exist for problem social behaviors (e.g., disruptive behavior) in classrooms.

Perhaps the best means of evaluating children's response to intervention is to determine the educational significance or *social validity* of behavior change. Kazdin (1977) first proposed socially validating intervention effects, and others extended those efforts (Fawcett, 1991; Hawkins, 1991; Wolf, 1978). Kazdin recommended three general approaches to social validation: social comparisons, subjective evaluation, and combined social validation procedures. *Social comparison* involves comparing an individual's behavior after intervention with the behavior of relevant peers. If the child's behavior subsequent to intervention is similar to nonreferred peers, then one might conclude that the intervention produced educationally significant changes in behavior. Walker and Hops (1976) and Nelson and Bowles (1975) presented examples of how social comparison could be used in classroom settings.

*Subjective evaluations* are another strategy in establishing the social importance of intervention effects (Kazdin, 1977; Wolf, 1978). These evaluations consist of having treatment consumers (teachers, parents, or team members) rate the qualitative aspects of the child's behavior after treatment. Subjective evaluations are used not only to assess the quality of behavior change but also to assess consumer satisfaction with treatment procedures.

*Combined social validation procedures* use both social comparisons and subjective evaluations in evaluating the social importance of intervention effects. The practical significance of any RTI could be bolstered if one demonstrates that child behavior moved into the same normative range (or higher) than nonreferred peers and if treatment consumers felt that the intervention had produced socially important changes in behavior. The combined approach captures not only how much a behavior changed (a quantitative criterion) but also how consumers perceive that change (a qualitative criterion).

## SUMMARY

Most applied psychologists working with children and youth do not use assessment tools that have a strong connection to intervention activities. There is often little connection between the referral concern, the assessments conducted, the interventions recommended, and the evaluation of intervention outcomes. In short, these assessments lack treatment validity. Treatment validity is defined as the extent to which assessment procedures lead to beneficial outcomes for individuals. For assessment procedures to have treatment validity, they must lead to identification of relevant areas of concern (academic or behavioral or both), inform treatment planning, and be useful in evaluating treatment outcomes.

The concept of RTI depends largely on the treatment validity of assessment procedures used to determine adequate or inadequate response to intervention. This chapter argues that the field of applied psychology should adopt RTI logic as a more beneficial way of addressing children's academic and behavioral needs. RTI can be defined as adequate or inadequate change in academic performance or behavior as a function of intervention. In an RTI approach, changes in programming, increased intensity of treatment, and special education eligibility determinations are based on how children respond to evidence-based interventions implemented with integrity.

Two basic approaches are available for delivering intervention services in an RTI approach: (a) problem-solving approaches and (b) standard protocol approaches. Only problem-solving approaches were described in this chapter because of space considerations. Problem solving typically takes place in four stages: problem identification, problem analysis, plan implementation, and plan evaluation. Several procedures were discussed for determining whether or not a child shows an adequate response to intervention. These included visual inspection of graphed data, percent change in behavior from baseline, and social validation procedures.

## RECOMMENDED RESOURCES

### Books and Other Printed Material

Bradley, R., Danielson, L., & Hallahan, D. P. (Eds.). (2002). *Identification of learning disabilities: Research to practice.* Mahwah, NJ: Erlbaum.

This edited volume contains the most up-to-date research knowledge that is basic to understanding learning disabilities. The volume contains comprehensive reviews of the research evidence underlying different aspects of the field of LD. The final chapter summarizes major findings and provides a consensus statement regarding what is known about the field of LD.

Reschly, D. J., Tilly, W. D., & Grimes, J. (Eds.). (1999). *Special education in transition: Functional assessment noncategorical programming.* Longmont, CO: Sopris West.

This edited volume argues for an outcomes-oriented system for providing special education and related services for children with high-incidence disabilities. It suggests a rethinking of the identification, assessment, and intervention services for students in special education. Throughout the volume, a noncategorical, function-based assessment and intervention approach is emphasized.

Shinn, M. R., Walker, H. M., & Stoner, G. (Eds.). (2002). *Interventions for academic and behavior problems II: Preventive and remedial approaches.* Bethesda, MD: National Association of School Psychologists.

This NASP-published volume contains comprehensive reviews of the most up-to-date knowledge in the field of academic and behavioral interventions. Chapters are based on the design of evidence-based behavioral, instructional, and parental interventions that emphasize environmental rather than within-child causes for most academic and behavior problems.

## Websites

*http://www.aimsweb.com*

AIMSweb is a formative assessment system that informs the teaching and learning process by providing continuous student performance data and reporting improvement to parents, teachers, and administrators to enable evidence-based evaluation and data-driven instruction. This website describes the AIMSweb system and provides psychometric and other research-based evaluation of the curriculum-based measurement (CBM) subtests contained in the system.

*http://www.dibels.uoregon.edu*

This website describes the Dynamic Indicators of Basic Early Literacy Skills (DIBELS), which are a set of standardized, individually administered measures of early literacy development. The measures are short (1 minute) CBM fluency measures used to regularly monitor the development of prereading and early reading skills. This website provides extensive information and links to the DIBELS data system, along with psychometric information and free download instructions.

*http://www.education.ucr.edu/reach*

This website was created to provide teachers with interventions that will help make their classrooms positive and productive environments for learning. Project REACH (Research Exploring Alternatives for Children) is a 5-year longitudinal investigation of the effects of interventions for children and youth with severe social, emotional, and behavioral difficulties. The website provides evidence-based interventions (e.g., self-management, social skills training, task interspersal, and choice) with step-by-step instructions for implementing the strategies, along with a troubleshooting section for each intervention.

## REFERENCES


Alberto, P., & Troutman, A. (2003). *Applied behavior analysis for teachers* (6th ed.). Upper Saddle River, NJ: Merrill/Prentice Hall.

American Psychiatric Association. (1994). *Diagnostic and statistical manual of mental disorders* (4th ed.). Washington, DC: Author.

Balcazar, F., Hopkins, B., & Suarez, Y. (1985). A critical, objective review of performance feedback. *Journal of Organizational Behavioral Management, 7,* 65–89.

Barnett, D., Daly, E., Jones, K., & Lentz, F. E. (2004). Response to intervention: Empirically based special service decisions for increasing and decreasing intensity using single case designs. *Journal of Special Education, 38,* 66–79.

Bennett, K., Lipman, E., Brown, S., Racine, Y., Boyle, M., & Offord, D. (1999). Predicting conduct problems: Can high-risk children be identified in kindergarten and grade 1? *Journal of Consulting and Clinical Psychology, 67,* 470–480.

Bergan, J. (1977). *Behavioral consultation.* Columbus, OH: Merrill.

Bergan, J., & Kratochwill, T. (1990). *Behavioral consultation and therapy.* New York: Plenum.

Bocian, K., Beebe, M., MacMillan, D. L., & Gresham, F. M. (1998). Competing paradigms in learning disabilities classification by schools and variations in the meaning of discrepant achievement. *Learning Disabilities Research and Practice, 14,* 1–14.

Bullis, M., & Walker, H. M. (1994). *Comprehensive school-based systems for troubled youth.* Eugene, OR: Center on Human Development, University of Oregon.

Carnine, D., Silbert, J., & Kame'enui, E. (1997). *Direct instruction in reading* (3rd ed.). New York: Merrill.

Clay, M. (1987). Learning to be learning disabled. *New Zealand Journal of Educational Studies, 22,* 155–173.

Cone, J. D. (1989). Psychometric considerations and multiple models of behavioral assessment. In A. Bellack & M. Hersen (Eds.), *Behavioral assessment: A practical handbook* (pp. 42–66). New York: Pergamon.

Cronbach, L. J. (1975). Beyond two disciplines of scientific psychology. *American Psychologist, 30,* 116–127.

Denton, C., Vaughn, S., & Fletcher, J. (2003). Bringing research-based practice in reading intervention to scale. *Learning Disabilities Research and Practice, 18,* 201–211.

Donovan, M., & Cross, C. (2002). *Minority students in special and gifted education.* Washington, DC: National Academy Press.

Elliott, S. N., Witt, J. C., Kratochwill, T., & Stoiber, K. (2002). Selecting and evaluating classroom interventions. In M. Shinn, H. Walker, & G. Stoner (Eds.), *Interventions for academic and behavior problems II: Preventive and remedial approaches* (pp. 243–294). Bethesda, MD: National Association of School Psychologists.

Fawcett, S. (1991). Social validity: A note on methodology. *Journal of Applied Behavior Analysis, 24,* 235–239.

Fletcher, J., Francis, D., Shaywitz, S., Lyon, G. R., Foorman, B., Stuebing, K., et al. (1998). Intelligent testing and the discrepancy model for children with learning disabilities. *Learning Disabilities Research and Practice, 13,* 186–203.

Fletcher, J., Lyon, G. R., Barnes, M., Steubing, K., Francis, D., Olson, R., et al. (2002). Classification of learning disabilities: An evidence-based evaluation. In R. Bradley, L. Danielson, & D. Hallahan (Eds.), *Learning disabilities: Research to practice* (pp. 185–261). Mahwah, NJ: Erlbaum.

Foorman, B., Francis, D., Fletcher, J., Schatschneider, C., & Mehta, P. (1998). The role of instruction in learning to read: Preventing reading failure in at-risk children. *Journal of Educational Psychology, 90,* 37–55.

Fuchs, D., Mock, D., Morgan, P., & Young, C. (2003). Responsiveness-to-intervention: Definitions, evidence, and implications for the learning disabilities construct. *Learning Disabilities Research and Practice, 18,* 157–171.

Fuchs, L. (1995). *Incorporating curriculum-based measurement into the eligibility decision-making process: A focus on treatment validity and student growth.* Paper presented at the National Academy of Sciences Workshop on Alternatives to IQ Testing, Washington, DC.

Fuchs, L. (2002). Three conceptualizations of "treatment" in a response-to-treatment framework for LD identification. In R. Bradley, L. Danielson, & D. Hallahan (Eds.), *Learning disabilities: Research to practice* (pp. 521–529). Mahwah, NJ: Erlbaum.

Fuchs, L., & Fuchs, D. (1997). Use of curriculum-based measurement in identifying students with disabilities. *Focus on Exceptional Children, 30,* 1–16.

Fuchs, L., & Fuchs, D. (1998). Treatment validity: A unifying concept for reconceptualizing the identification of learning disabilities. *Learning Disabilities: Research and Practice, 13,* 204–219.

Good, R., Gruba, J., & Kaminski, R. (2002). Best practices in using Dynamic Indicators of Basic Early Literacy Skills (DIBELS) in an outcomes-driven model. In A. Thomas & J. Grimes (Eds.), *Best practices in school psychology IV* (pp. 669–720). Bethesda, MD: National Association of School Psychologists.

Greenwood, C., Maheady, L., & Delquadri, J. (2002). Classwide peer tutoring programs. In M. Shinn, H. Walker, & G. Stoner (Eds.), *Interventions for academic and behavior problems II: Preventive and remedial approaches* (pp. 611–649). Bethesda, MD: National Association of School Psychologists.

Gresham, F. M. (1989). Assessment of treatment integrity in school consultation and prereferral intervention. *School Psychology Review, 18,* 37–50.

Gresham, F. M. (1991). Conceptualizing behavior disorders in terms of resistance to intervention. *School Psychology Review, 20,* 23–36.

Gresham, F. M., (2002a). Responsiveness to intervention: An alternative approach to the identification of learning disabilities. In R. Bradley, L. Danielson, & D. Hallahan (Eds.), *Learning disabilities: Research to practice* (pp. 467–519). Mahwah, NJ: Erlbaum.

Gresham, F. M. (2002b). Teaching social skills to high-risk children and youth: Preventive and remedial strategies. In M. Shinn, H. Walker, & G. Stoner

(Eds.), *Interventions for academic and behavior problems II: Preventive and remedial approaches* (pp. 403–432). Bethesda, MD: National Association of School Psychologists.

Gresham, F. M., & Gansle, K. A. (1992). Misguided assumptions of the DSM-III-R: Implications for school psychological practice. *School Psychology Quarterly, 7,* 79–95.

Gresham, F. M., Watson, T. S., & Skinner, C. H. (2001). Functional behavioral assessment: Principles, procedures, and future directions. *School Psychology Review, 30,* 156–172.

Grimes, J. (2002). Responsiveness to intervention: The next step in special education identification, service, and exiting decision making. In R. Bradley, L. Danielson, & D. Hallahan (Eds.), *Learning disabilities: Research to practice* (pp. 531–547). Mahwah, NJ: Erlbaum.

Hawkins, R. (1991). Is social validity what we are interested in? Argument for a functional approach. *Journal of Applied Behavior Analysis, 24,* 205–213.

Hayes, S., Nelson, R., & Jarrett, R. (1987). The treatment utility of assessment: A functional approach to evaluating assessment quality. *American Psychologist, 42,* 964–974.

Heller, K., Holtzman, W., & Messick, S. (1982). *National Research Council Special Task Force Report.* Washington, DC: National Academy Press.

Hinshaw, S., Han, S., Erhardt, D., & Huber, A. (1992). Internalizing and externalizing behavior problems in preschool children: Correspondence between parent and teacher ratings and behavioral observations. *Journal of Clinical Child Psychology, 21,* 143–150.

Juel, C. (1988). Learning to read and write: A longitudinal study of 54 children from first through fourth grades. *Journal of Educational Psychology, 80,* 437–447.

Kaminski, R., & Good, R. (1998). Assessing early literacy skills in a problem-solving model: Dynamic Indicators of Basic Early Literacy Skills. In M. Shinn (Ed.), *Advanced applications of curriculum-based measurement* (pp. 113–142). New York: Guilford Press.

Kauffman, J. M. (1999). How we prevent the prevention of emotional and behavioral disorders. *Exceptional Children, 65,* 448–468.

Kauffman, J. M. (2000). *Characteristics of emotional and behavioral disorders of children and youth* (7th ed.). Upper Saddle River, NJ: Merrill/Prentice Hall.

Kazdin, A. (1977). Assessing the clinical or applied significance of behavior change through social validation. *Behavior Modification, 1,* 427–452.

Kazdin, A. (1987). *Conduct disorders in childhood and adolescence.* London: Sage.

Lane, K. L., & Beebe-Frankenberger, M. (2004). *School-based interventions: The tools you need to succeed.* Boston: Allyn & Bacon.

Loeber, R., & Farrington, D. (Eds.). (1998). *Serious and violent juvenile offenders: Risk factors and successful interventions.* Thousand Oaks, CA: Sage.

Loeber, R., Dishion, T., & Patterson, G. (1984). Multiple-gating: A multistage assessment procedure for identifying youths at risk for delinquency. *Journal of Research in Crime and Delinquency, 21,* 7–32.

MacMillan, D. L., & Siperstein, G. N. (2002). Learning disabilities as operationally defined by schools. In R. Bradley, L. Danielson, & D. Hallahan (Eds.), *Learning disabilities: Research to practice* (pp. 287–333). Mahwah, NJ: Erlbaum.

Mann, L. (1979). *On the trail of process.* New York: Grune & Stratton.

Messick, S. (1995). Validity of psychological assessment: Validation of inferences from persons' responses and performances as scientific inquiry into score meaning. *American Psychologist, 50,* 741–749.

Mischel, W. (1968). *Personality and assessment.* New York: Wiley.

Mortenson, B., & Witt, J. C. (1998). The use of weekly performance feedback to increase teacher implementation of a prereferral intervention. *School Psychology Review, 27,* 613–627.

National Reading Panel. (2000). *Report of the National Reading Panel. Teaching children to read: An evidence-based assessment of the scientific research literature on reading and its implications for reading instruction.* (NIH Publication No. 00-4769). Washington, DC: U.S. Government Printing Office.

Nelson, R., & Bowles, P. (1975). The best of two worlds—observation with norms. *Journal of School Psychology, 13,* 3–9.

Noell, G. H., Duhon, G., Gatti, S., & Connell, J. (2002). Consultation, follow-up, and behavior management intervention implementation in general education. *School Psychology Review, 31,* 217–234.

Noell, G. H., & Witt, J. C. (1998). Toward a behavior analytic approach to consultation. In T. S. Watson & F. M. Gresham (Eds.), *Handbook of child behavior therapy* (pp. 41–57). New York: Plenum.

Noell, G. H., Witt, J. C., LaFleur, L., Mortenson, B., Ranier, D., & LeVelle, J. (2000). A comparison of two follow-up strategies to increase teacher intervention implementation in general education following consultation. *Journal of Applied Behavior Analysis, 33,* 271–284.

Noell, G. H., Witt, J. C., Slider, N., Connell, J., Gatti, S., Williams, K. et al. (in press). Treatment implementation following behavioral consultation in schools: A comparison of three follow-up strategies. *School Psychology Review.*

O'Shaughnessy, T., Lane, K., Gresham, F. M., & Beebe-Frankenberger, M. (2002). Students with or at risk for emotional-behavioral difficulties: An integrated system of prevention and intervention. In K. Lane, F. M. Gresham, & T. O'Shaughnessy (Eds.), *Interventions for children with or at risk for emotional and behavioral disorders* (pp. 3–17). Boston: Allyn & Bacon.

President's Commission on Excellence in Special Education. (2002). *A new era: Revitalizing special education for children and their families.* Washington, DC: United States Department of Education.

Reschly, D. J. (2002). Minority overrepresentation: The silent contributor to LD prevalence and diagnostic confusion. In R. Bradley, L. Danielson, & D. Hallahan (Eds.), *Learning disabilities: Research to practice* (pp. 361–368). Mahwah, NJ: Erlbaum.

Reschly, D. J., & Tilly, W. D. (1999). Reform trends and system design alternatives. In D. Reschly, W. D. Tilly, & J. Grimes (Eds.), *Special education in transition: Functional assessment and noncategorical programming* (pp. 19–48). Longmont, CO: Sopris West.

Reschly, D. J., & Ysseldyke, J. (2002). Paradigm shift: The past is not the future. In A. Thomas & J. Grimes (Eds.), *Best practices in school psychology IV* (pp. 3–20). Bethesda, MD: National Association of School Psychologists.

Sechrest, L. (1963). Incremental validity: A recommendation. *Educational and Psychological Measurement, 23,* 153–158.

Severson, H. H., & Walker, H. M. (2002). Proactive approaches for identifying children at risk for sociobehavioral problems. In K. Lane, F. M. Gresham, & T. O'Shaughnessy (Eds.), *Interventions for children with or at risk for emotional and behavioral disorders* (pp. 33–53). Boston: Allyn & Bacon.

Shaywitz, S., Shaywitz, B., Fletcher, J., & Escobar, M. (1990). Prevalence of reading disability in boys and girls: Results of the Connecticut Longitudinal Study. *Journal of the American Medical Association, 264,* 998–1002.

Shinn, M. (2002). Best practices in using curriculum-based measurement in a problem-solving model. In A. Thomas & J. Grimes (Eds.), *Best practices in school psychology* (4th ed., pp. 671–697). Bethesda, MD: National Association of School Psychologists.

Speece, D. (2002). Classification of learning disabilities: Convergence, expansion, and caution. In R. Bradley, L. Danielson, & D. Hallahan (Eds.), *Learning disabilities: Research to practice* (pp. 279–285). Mahwah, NJ: Erlbaum.

Speece, D., & Case, L. (2001). Classification in context: An alternative approach to identifying early reading disability. *Journal of Educational Psychology, 93,* 735–749.

Tilly, W. D. (2002). Best practices in school psychology as a problem-solving enterprise. In A. Thomas & J. Grimes (Eds.), *Best practices in school psychology IV* (pp. 21–36). Bethesda, MD: National Association of School Psychologists.

Tilly, W. D., Reschly, D. J., & Grimes, J. (1999). Disability determination in problem-solving systems: Conceptual foundations and critical components. In D. Reschly, W. D. Tilly, & J. Grimes (Eds.), *Special education in transition: Functional assessment and non-categorical programming* (pp. 285–301). Longmont, CO: Sopris West.

Torgesen, J., Alexander, A., Wagner, R., Rashotte, C., Voeller, K., & Conway, T. (2001). Intensive remedial reading instruction for children with severe reading disabilities: Immediate and long-term outcomes from two instructional approaches. *Journal of Learning Disabilities, 34,* 33–58.

Torgesen, J., & Wagner, R. (1998). Alternative diagnostic approaches for specific developmental reading disabilities. *Learning Disabilities Research and Practice, 13,* 220–232.

VanDerHeyden, A., Witt, J. C., & Naquin, G. (2003). Development and validation of a process for screening referrals to special education. *School Psychology Review, 32,* 204–227.

Vaughn, S. (2002). Using response to treatment for identifying students with learning disabilities. In R. Bradley, L. Danielson, & D. Hallahan (Eds.), *Learning disabilities: Research to practice* (pp. 549–554). Mahwah, NJ: Erlbaum.

Vaughn, S., & Fuchs, L. (2003). Redefining learning disabilities as inadequate response to instruction: The promise and potential problems. *Learning Disabilities Research and Practice, 18,* 137–146.

Vaughn, S., Linan-Thompson, S., & Hickman, P. (2003). Response to instruction as a means of identifying students with reading/learning disabilities. *Exceptional Children, 69,* 391–409.

Vellutino, F. (2002). On the role of intervention in identifying learning disabilities. In R. Bradley, L. Danielson, & D. Hallahan (Eds.), *Learning disabilities: Research to practice* (pp. 555–564). Mahwah, NJ: Erlbaum.

Vellutino, F., Scanlon, D., Sipay, E., Small, S., Pratt, A., Chen, R., & Denkla, M. (1996). Cognitive profiles of difficult-to-remediate and readily remediated poor readers: Early intervention as a vehicle for distinguishing between cognitive and experiential deficits as basic causes of specific reading disability. *Journal of Educational Psychology, 88,* 601–638.

Walker, H. M., & Hops, H. (1976). Use of normative peer data as a standard for evaluating classroom treatment effects. *Journal of Applied Behavior Analysis, 9,* 159–168.

Walker, H. M., Irvin, L., Noell, J., & Singer, G. (1992). A construct score approach to the assessment of social competence: Rationale, technological considerations, and anticipated outcomes. *Behavior Modification, 16,* 448–474.

Walker, H. M., Nishioka, V., Zeller, R., Severson, H., & Feil, E. (2000). Causal factors and potential solutions for the persistent under-identification of students having emotional or behavioral disorders in the context of schooling. *Assessment for Effective Intervention, 26,* 29–40.

Walker, H. M., Ramsey, E., & Gresham, F. M. (2004). *Antisocial behavior in school: Evidence-base practices.* Belmont, CA: Wadsworth/Thomson Learning.

Walker, H. M., & Severson, H. H. (1990). *Systematic Screening for Behavior Disorders: User's guide and administration manual.* Longmont, CO: Sopris West.

Walker, H. M., Severson, H. H., & Feil, E. (1995). *Early Screening Project: A proven child-find process.* Longmont, CO: Sopris West.

Watson, T. S., & Robinson, S. (1996). Direct behavioral consultation: An alternative to traditional behavioral consultation. *School Psychology Quarterly, 11,* 267–278.

Wiggins, J. (1973). *Personality and prediction: Principles of personality assessment.* Reading, MA: Addison-Wesley.

Witt, J. C., Daly, E., & Noell, G. H. (2000). *Functional assessments: A step-by-step guide to solving academic and behavior problems.* Longmont, CO: Sopris West.

Witt, J. C., VanDerHeyden, A., & Gilbertson, D. (2004). Troubleshooting behavioral interventions: A systematic process for finding and eliminating problems. *School Psychology Review, 33,* 363–383.

Wolf, M. M. (1978). Social validity: The case for subjective measurement or how applied behavior analysis is finding its heart. *Journal of Applied Behavior Analysis, 11,* 203–214.

Ysseldyke, J. (2001). Reflections on a research career: Generalizations from 25 years of research on assessment and instructional decision-making. *Exceptional Children, 67,* 295–309.

# 41

# School Readiness

**Ann Casey**

*Minneapolis Public Schools*

## BACKGROUND AND DEVELOPMENT

### School Readiness Defined

There is no universal understanding of what is meant by school readiness. Many believe it is a concept fraught with confusion. Do schools wait for children to be ready (Meisels, 1999)? Or do school professionals define important predictors of early school success and focus on ensuring that children have the opportunities to learn these skills in early childhood? Some would argue that schools need to be ready for the children, not the other way around. An even greater debate concerns how school readiness should be assessed and what the outcomes of the assessments should be. Finally, most professionals believe that early childhood education should be developmentally appropriate, but there is little agreement on how this concept should be defined.

Data from a recent study of state policies on readiness for kindergarten suggest that the main criterion for entry to kindergarten currently is age, with 5 years being the most common age criterion (Saluja, Scott-Little, & Clifford, 2000). The amount and kinds of skills 5-year-olds bring with them upon school entry vary considerably. This is especially true because the domains of early development are quite broad and can be categorized in a variety of ways. Generally, the child development literature addresses the different development domains: physical and health, social–emotional, language and literacy, self-care and independence, and cognitive. These domains are highly interrelated, interdependent, and difficult to tease apart, especially in early childhood. This interrelatedness, in addition to the wide range of maturation of individual skills, makes assessment of young children complex and often unreliable.

The first goal of Goals 2000 stated: "By the year 2000 all children will start school ready to learn" (National Educational Goals Panel, 1995). What was meant by "ready to learn" and how to measure it were quite unclear. The goals planning group concluded that five broad domains of development are important: physical well-being and motor development, social–emotional development, approaches to learning, language usage, and cognition and general knowledge. Although the term "ready for school" is a slight improvement over "school readiness," it still leaves much to debate. Regardless of definition, a focus on readiness suggests not only the need to assess development in the above five domains but also the need to consider factors that influence such development.

### Factors That Influence School Readiness

***Family and home factors.*** Family and home factors clearly have some bearing on children's readiness for school. Christenson (1999) highlighted four such factors: (a) an enriching environment, (b) management and discipline, (c) supportive relationships, and (d) language. To be sure, children from families who have greater resources tend to have more skills upon entry to kindergarten. Generally, they have had print-rich environments where they have observed family members reading and interacting with a variety of text formats (books, magazines, newspapers, checkbook, e-mail) and have had hundreds of hours of storybook reading with a parent. Hours of reading with a parent have also contributed to their language and cognitive development by introducing new vocabulary and new knowledge through reading and conversations about the books. Finally, children who have learned some self-regulation of their own behavior through consistent parental discipline are better prepared to follow teacher directions and attend during school instructional periods.

Socioeconomic status (SES) has long been a predictor of academic success. Despite this fact, Entwisle,

Alexander, and Olson (1997) found in their Beginning School Study that poor children make about the same amount of academic progress during the school year as their middle-class peers. This is gratifying news to many educators, yet the message is that a year's worth of growth is not enough progress to close the gap that exists in comparisons of poor children with their more advantaged peers. This achievement gap can be attributed to significant differences in skills upon entry to kindergarten and to what happens during the summer months for poor versus middle-class school-age children. Because the gap widens during elementary school, presumably because of middle-class children's summer enrichment experiences, the best opportunity to reduce the gap between low and middle SES children is in the years prior to kindergarten entry. A logical implication of these findings is to have well-developed preschool *and* summer programming for at-risk youngsters.

***Early language and literacy skills.*** A review of beginning reading research suggests quite conclusively that there is a set of early literacy skills that help children become competent readers (Adams, 1990). These skills include, but are not limited to, awareness of print and the functions print serves in our society, phonological awareness, letter recognition, letter–sound correspondence, language structure, and vocabulary knowledge. With the recent push for accountability, such as in the No Child Left Behind Act's dictate that "all children will be reading by the end of third grade," educators can begin to chart a sequence of skills children need to develop, beginning in early childhood. Juel (1988) found that oral reading fluency at the end of first grade predicts fourth-grade reading achievement. For children to be fluent in first grade, however, they should be able to understand letter–sound correspondence in kindergarten. Children who have had rich oral language experiences, exposure to a variety of print materials, and additional experiences interacting with books prior to school entry are most likely to have letter–sound correspondence in kindergarten.

Before children learn that letters represent sounds, they need to understand that the spoken words are made of individual sounds. This understanding is called *phonemic awareness*. Ideally, phonemic awareness develops in early childhood, ensuring that upon school entry children are ready to learn that sounds are represented by letters (Snow, Burns, & Griffin, 1998). If children do not have phonemic awareness in kindergarten, they will need explicit teaching to learn it. Phonemic awareness is a necessary skill but is not sufficient in learning to read in first grade.

In their longitudinal study of young children and their caregivers, Hart and Risley (1995) found that the amount and quality of verbal interaction between adults and their children predicted children's vocabulary development at age 3. The differences in vocabulary development were related to socioeconomic differences, with poor children receiving considerably less oral language stimulation. Age 3 vocabulary development further predicted early school achievement. Clearly, rich oral language experiences are foundational to the development of a child's vocabulary as well as to knowledge itself. Print exposure is also related to vocabulary and content knowledge (Neuman, 2001). One is much more likely to be exposed to unknown words and concepts through print than through daily conversation. This phenomenon is referred to as the Mathew Effect, taken from the biblical proverb of the rich getting richer and the poor getting poorer (Stanovich, 1986). Those who learn to read effectively read more, and those who struggle read less, leading to an increasing gap in reading achievement and, thus, content knowledge.

***School factors.*** In addition to discussion of the need to provide more quality early experiences and services for young children, some of the literature on school readiness has focused on "ready schools." This idea suggests that it is the responsibility of schools to educate children regardless of their early experiences. A one-size-fits-all approach to kindergarten is not acceptable when many children are identified as not being ready or as being immature because they do not have skills the teachers expect them to have. A more current concept is that child development is highly influenced by contextual variables. Of course, the community and family in which a child is raised are very important ingredients for a developing child. Interaction among child, family, community, and school variables is complex and creates learning environments for children that vary a great deal on an individual basis. Thus, educators have two choices: intervene before kindergarten or intervene during kindergarten. Rather than focus on child skills or the lack thereof, however, school staff should focus on the quality of early-grade experiences (Pianta & LaParo, 2003).

## PROBLEMS AND IMPLICATIONS

In a discussion about school readiness, educators need to consider a number of concerns and problems. Four of those are highlighted here: (a) the quality of preschool experiences, (b) screening, (c) curriculum and instruction, and (d) teacher quality.

## Quality of Preschool Experiences

Families that are most in need often have the least access to high-quality care and education for their young children. With the advent of the No Child Left Behind Act and the high-stakes accountability movement, examining the experiences children have prior to kindergarten entry has become increasingly important. The quality of both family and child care or preschool experiences has significant impact on children's development. If an educational goal is to have children enter kindergarten with skills that prepare them for more formal learning experiences, then the focus should be on improving the quality of experiences young children have with their families and early care providers. Nurturing relationships are a primary ingredient in the healthy development of young children (Shonkoff & Phillips, 2000). Because the differences in skills among children are highly correlated with socioeconomic circumstance, it is important that all children have access to high-quality early experiences.

## Issues of Screening

Screening serves a very useful purpose as long as high-stakes decisions are not made on the basis of the results. Most notably, screening measures can identify children whose skills and performance should be observed and assessed more carefully to determine if they could benefit from targeted interventions that will increase the likelihood of their being better prepared for success in school. Screening results may be used to determine that some children need more experience and practice in social interaction, whereas others might need additional practice in early literacy skills. Finally, screening also serves as a first step in finding young children who ultimately may have a disability.

Many districts conduct screening of all children entering kindergarten. The purpose of such screening is varied, although often it serves to determine readiness for kindergarten. In economically diverse school districts, screening may communicate to the public the need to address large gaps in skills between middle and low SES kindergarten students upon entry to the formal education system. Because achievement gaps are a persistent finding among school age students, it is important that the public understand that these gaps exist prior to school entry. Screening also serves as a baseline for accountability purposes to determine the amount of progress made in various kindergarten programs. In addition, kindergarten screening information can be useful to kindergarten teachers, so that they can differentiate instruction and foster the development of important skills for academic and social success. Although screening certainly has its advantages, it also has its problems. For example, although the results of screening should lead to differentiated instruction, this is not a common practice among many kindergarten teachers.

Another issue is that of the validity and reliability of screening instruments commonly used in the schools (Meisels, 1999). Given that development in early childhood is not linear, but instead tends to happen in spurts, it remains a difficult area to assess.

Perhaps of greatest concern is how screening results are used. Clearly, an undesirable consequence of screening is "red-shirting," or delaying kindergarten entry of children who score poorly on school readiness assessments. There is no empirical support for this practice, yet Wesley and Buysse (2003) found that the practice is still quite common when children do not score well on kindergarten screenings. Screening should be designed to identify those who may need more support in order to prevent negative outcomes later on, not to exclude them from support. Most children are not going to catch up by staying out of kindergarten; instead, they need to be in high-quality kindergarten programs where they have appropriate peer models and a chance for specialized instruction in skills necessary for school success.

Some parents delay kindergarten entry on their own, judging their child not ready. Research results challenge this practice. For example, the Early Childhood Longitudinal Study–Kindergarten Class of 1998–99 found that older kindergarteners—those who could have started school a year earlier but did not do so—tended to have higher frequencies of developmental problems in areas such as coordination and articulation than their 5-year-old peers (National Center for Education Statistics [NCES], 2001). Additional studies indicate that children who are overage for their grade tend to have higher dropout rates, greater behavior problems in adolescence, more substance abuse, and increased emotional distress (see chapter 8, "School Completion").

Another common practice that is problematic in many school districts is the retention of children judged not ready for first grade or assigned to a developmental kindergarten or transitional first-grade room. Neither of these approaches has empirical support (Gredler, 1997), and the result is the same as delaying kindergarten entry. The National Association for the Education of Young Children (NAEYC, 1995) recommends the following alternatives to retaining or delaying entry of kindergarten students: high-quality preschool, improved quality of child-care settings, full-time kindergarten, smaller class size, tutoring outside of class time, summer programs, after-school programs, and multi-age groupings.

To help address the above problems, public schools must be organized in such a way that they are adequately prepared to teach the wide range of children who enter kindergarten every year. Kindergarten programs should be designed to meet the particular needs of the children in the community they serve (Panter & Bracken, 2000). These early years are critical periods for learning foundational skills. It is not appropriate to deny targeted or more intensive interventions to children who need more experiences and practice than others. Children who are at risk will benefit from literacy-rich environments and opportunities to interact with more competent peers. When children are lagging in some of these skills, the best approach to avoid future school failure is to use a kind of inoculation approach or provide the practice the children need in order to develop the skills. Of course, the practice should be developmentally appropriate and connect children's background and culture to new knowledge.

## Curriculum and Instruction

With respect to curriculum and instruction, the concept of developmentally appropriate practice has divided the early childhood community. Many early childhood and kindergarten teachers have been taught that their programs should have a high degree of child-initiated activities and that the teacher's role is to guide the child's choices. They believe their programs should focus on the whole child with particular emphasis on social–emotional outcomes. On the face of it, there is nothing particularly wrong with this view, but it suggests a more passive role for the teacher. Somehow, a high degree of teacher direction has been viewed as developmentally inappropriate. As argued by Neuman (2001), too often early childhood programs have focused on process with little emphasis on content. Many programs claiming to be developmentally appropriate have focused on active learning, on *how* rather than *what* children learn, and have shown little concern for knowledge or skill acquisition. What is needed is a balanced approach between child- and teacher-directed activities.

The NAEYC position statement on school readiness (1995) suggests that isolated skills should not be taught to young children and that all skill development should occur in meaningful contexts. Again, on the face of it this is not controversial, but the interpretation of these statements plays out in a variety of ways. The NAEYC statement opposes drill as an instructional strategy. For the important early literacy skill of phonemic awareness, children need to learn to hear the sounds in words through frequent exposure to songs, rhymes, and word play. It is clear that some children will require more practice on this than others. Unfortunately, many teachers of young children would label this extra practice as drill, and therefore as developmentally inappropriate, essentially denying these children the practice they need to master this important skill. The more risk factors children have, the more likely they will need a teacher-directed approach to learning, which would ensure that they receive the right kinds and amounts of experiences that will contribute to strong developmental outcomes related to school success.

Children whose family's language is other than English face particular challenges in preschools where the language of instruction is English. The issues here are similar to those facing school-age English language learners (see chapter 49, "English Language Learners"). There is a paucity of research about what methods and in what language children are best instructed. Most Head Start programs have focused on English acquisition with the rationale that this will help prepare children for school, where English is also the language of instruction (Snow et al., 1998). Of concern is whether the emphasis on English acquisition is at the expense of developing other important skills, such as concept development and social interaction. A recent Head Start evaluation sheds some light on this question. It was determined that Spanish-speaking children gained in English vocabulary without losing their Spanish vocabulary (Administration for Children and Families, 2003). However, no gain in letter recognition skills was noted.

## Teacher Quality

A final problem related to school readiness, particularly with respect to preventing children's future problems and addressing current ones, is the quality of staff people who provide preschool services. Working as a child care or preschool provider is often a minimum-wage job. The low levels of pay attract staff people who have low levels of education, making it difficult to attract and retain qualified staff. For many, finding highly qualified staff people and keeping them in their jobs is one of the most serious issues facing the early childhood community ("Quality Counts," 2002).

## ALTERNATIVE ACTIONS FOR PREVENTION AND INTERVENTION

Success in school is determined largely by the type of early care and education children receive during the first 5 years of life. Given that factors related to poverty are significant predictors of poor academic and social outcomes, it is heartening to know that attention to contextual variables, particularly early care and education, can have significant lasting effects on changing this trajectory. As emphasized by the National Research Council (Bowman, Donovan, & Burns, 2000), "The course of development can be altered in early childhood by effective interventions that change the balance between risk and protection, thereby shifting the odds in favor of more adaptive outcomes" (p. 32). It should be no surprise, then, that national organizations such as the Committee for Economic Development (CED) advocate for making the early development of children a national priority (see *Preschool for All,* CED, 2002). Research supports such advocacy. Several well-designed longitudinal studies of children living in poverty have demonstrated the value of high-quality early care and education. For example, in the Perry Preschool Project, it was estimated that for every dollar that was invested, the public and participant reaped $8.74 of value in return (Schweinhart, Barnes, Weikart, Barnett, & Epstein, 1993).

### Characteristics of High-Quality Early Care and Education

In order to be ready for school success, children need highly stimulating environments that include rich oral language, print exposure, and knowledge development in the 5 years before they enter kindergarten. Quality preschool programs are one way to provide such an environment. All children could benefit from high-quality early care and education. Politics will likely influence whether investments are made in targeted preschool programs (e.g., Head Start and early childhood special education) or universal preschool programs (i.e., programs that are open to all young children). Some of the following facts have been compiled by the National Institute of Early Education Research to assist in informing policy discussions: (a) targeted programs are less expensive, (b) targeted programs can provide the level of intensity necessary for the neediest children, (c) universal programs are more likely to reach targeted children since all eligible children do not currently receive targeted preschool services, and (d) the public is more likely to support universal programs (Barnett, Brown, & Shore, 2004). Barnett et al. argue that the quality is likely to be higher in a universal program than a targeted one because many more stakeholders are invested in the outcomes. Currently, only three states are moving toward universal preschool for 4-year-olds: Georgia, New York, and Oklahoma. None is truly universal yet, although Georgia is closest and serves about 70% of the state's 4-year-olds in preschool. Unfortunately, because of the lack of full funding and other variables such as mobility of families, targeted programs do not reach many of the children who need them ("Quality Counts," 2002).

Despite a growing consensus about the importance of early education, the system of early care and education in the United States remains fragmented, with highly variable quality from one setting to another. Furthermore, this system has two separate traditions: child care and preschool. For years the major emphasis of many preschool programs was safety and social development. Responding to a growing body of evidence about what is important in early childhood, the National Research Council established the Committee on Early Childhood Pedagogy in 1997 to review the research in this area. The findings resulted in *Eager to Learn: Educating Our Preschoolers* (Bowman, Donovan, & Burns, 2000). This report provides a good synthesis of what is known about indicators of high-quality early care and education. The following are some of these indicators:

- Programs in which social–emotional and motor skills are mutually supportive in the development of cognitive skills.
- Quality relationships between teachers and children.
- Low adult:child ratios.
- Clear expectations about what children should learn.
- A curriculum that provides a broad base of experience in many knowledge domains and includes extensive language development.
- Variety in classroom structures, thought processes, and discourse patterns.
- Teachers who have access to high-quality professional development.
- A stable workforce that is adequately paid.

Of particular interest is the finding that no specific curriculum is best. What appears to be most important is that children be exposed to a breadth of curriculum domains (literacy, science, and math) and that there be a mix of direct instruction with more child-centered exploratory learning. In addition, social and other goals should be integrated with the cognitive aspects of the curriculum. Balance is key—balance in content and balance in the types of instructional techniques that are used. Currently, most preschool services are delivered to targeted groups and are educators' best hope for reducing gaps between children upon entry to kindergarten.

## Examples of Effective Preschool Programs and Interventions

The following examples of programs and interventions include many of the characteristics listed above. They also have been shown to be effective in promoting academic and social development.

***Abecedarian Project.*** The North Carolina Abecedarian Project is perhaps the best known study of high-quality early care and education involving a targeted group of poor children. (Other projects that provided as intensive an intervention as Abecedarian include the Milwaukee Project and the Syracuse Family Development Research Program; Campbell, Ramey, Pungello, Sparling, & Miller-Johnson, 2002). The Abecedarian interventions were labor intensive and supported families as well as the children, with children receiving full-day care and a curriculum that was appropriate given the developmental ages of the children. The original children in the Abecedarian Project were recruited as infants in the 1970s. The sample has been followed and data collected through age 21. Longitudinal studies (Campbell, et al., 2002) show that compared with children who received 5 years of treatment prior to school entry, children in the Abecedarian sample had a significantly higher number of years of total education and had stronger reading and math scores that persisted into adulthood. Those who received only 3 years of school-age support had weaker outcomes, but those who received both preschool and primary school services had the best reading skills.

***Head Start.*** Established in 1965, Head Start was the first nationally funded preschool program in the United States. Targeted to children from impoverished families (e.g., in 2003 that comprised families of four earning less than $18,400), Head Start has provided access to health care, developmental screenings, services to families, and preschool education to 3- to 5-year-olds. Head Start is a good example of a program that focuses on the whole child and also provides support services to families. More than a million children and their families received Head Start services in 2003 (Hart & Schumacher, 2004). Unfortunately, this is only about 60% of the children who are eligible for the program. Early research on Head Start found that it helps reduce gaps in children's skills as they enter kindergarten but also found that the effects tended to dissipate over time. The Follow-Through project from the 1970s was designed to determine which types of primary school programming could help maintain the gains made in Head Start.

More recently, Head Start developed the Family and Child Experiences Survey (FACES) to investigate both program quality and child outcomes. Using this instrument, the program reported that the gap between the 2000 cohort of children in Head Start programs and the general population of children the same age was reduced but that Head Start children continued to enter kindergarten with fewer skills than the national average (Administration for Children and Families, 2003). These findings, however, show improvement in children's skills from the 1997–98 cohort measured on the same skills.

Like many other organizations providing preschool services, Head Start has struggled with providing highly qualified teachers. The reauthorization of Head Start set a goal that 50% of its teachers would have associate degrees by 2003. FACES found that the 2000 cohort had an increase in the number of teachers with advanced degrees. Furthermore, the survey revealed a relationship between teacher credentials and gains in early writing skills, suggesting that teachers who are more qualified produce children with more readiness skills (Administration for Children and Families, 2003).

Expanding upon the success of Head Start, in 1995 the federal government created Early Head Start, which serves infants and toddlers birth to age 3 through both center-based and home-based programming (Irish, Schumacher, & Lombardi, 2003). In both Head Start and Early Head Start, the majority of children are from homes where parents have low levels of education; thus, the program aims to increase the quality of experience for these children. Unfortunately, Early Head Start teachers are not as well trained as Head Start teachers, with just 36% having their associate degree.

***Reading First and Early Reading First.*** More recently, the Bush administration has strongly supported the funding of two national early-intervention programs for improving reading: Reading First and Early Reading First. Reading First is a federal grant program to states for implementing evidence-based reading programs for kindergarten through third grade. Early Reading First is the preschool version, with grants going directly to existing early education programs and targeting those that serve low-income families. The goal is make these early education centers into high-quality programs so that children enter school with the oral language, phonological awareness, print awareness, and alphabetic knowledge they need for successful kindergarten entry.

***Storybook reading.*** There is considerable evidence that the practice of adults reading books to children contributes to their language development (Bus, van Ijzendoorn, & Pelligrini, 1995). When children become more active participants, their vocabulary is likely to grow even more. Hargrave and Senechal (2000) compared a storybook intervention with a dialogic reading intervention using the same books for two groups of preschool children who had poor expressive vocabularies. Although both groups of children increased their language on several measures, the children in the more active, dialogic intervention increased the most. This intervention can help many parents learn to use story time as a way to build oral language and to provide rich literacy and social interaction experiences. The strategy essentially requires children to take a more active role and for parents to provide feedback and gradually encourage their children to extend the dialogue (e.g., "Yes, the tree is green but what else do you notice about the tree?"). A goal is for the children to tell the story (Whitehurst, Arnold, Epstein, & Angell, 1994). A recent review of studies on dialogic reading found that it has a positive influence on language development in young children ages 2 and 3 who began with at least a 50-word vocabulary (Cutspec, 2004).

Teachers, school psychologists, and others often recommend reading at home when parents inquire about what they can do for their young children. This recommendation should be used cautiously, however, because parents who have not engaged in this activity before are likely to need more specific guidance and support. Parents may need help in locating and choosing appropriate reading materials for young children. They may also need information about the purpose of reading (e.g., not to finish the story without interruption but to have a conversation with their children about the story and its characters) and about how to engage their children. Clearly, an unwanted outcome would be that both the parent and child become frustrated with the activity and thus avoid it in the future. One way to help avoid this outcome is by connecting families of modest circumstances with their local public library. Children's librarians are a valuable community resource who not only provide families with assistance in choosing books for their children but also provide services such as "story hours" that foster print awareness and vocabulary development.

## Transition to Kindergarten Practices

Too often, the transition to kindergarten is not a well-planned process, resulting in a one-shot approach that does not meet the needs of families and children. The more the culture of the family diverges from the culture of the school, the more important transition activities become, but all children benefit from a well-planned transition from the preschool environment. Good transition practices are a long-term process that connects the K–12 school and staff, the family and child, and the early childhood care and education community (Pianta & Cox, 1999).

In a national survey of kindergarten teachers, Rimm-Kaufman, Pianta, and Cox (2000) found that teachers estimated that only about 50% of the children transition well. This suggests many children could benefit from significant transition planning to help them be better prepared for the expectations held by school personnel. The goal of such planning is not just to form better relationships. It is to form relationships that promote continuity that will help children be ready for the school culture and for the kinds of skills and behaviors expected of kindergarten children. Pianta and Kraft-Sayre (2003, p. 17) describe nine steps to effective kindergarten transition:

1. Establish collaborative teams.
2. Identify a transition coordinator.
3. Facilitate regular meetings and conduct a needs assessment.
4. Generate ideas for transition activities.
5. Create a transition time line.
6. Anticipate barriers.
7. Revise ideas and time lines.
8. Implement transition practices.
9. Assess, evaluate, and revise.

These authors found that when collaboration occurs early, kindergarten teachers learn about the preschool environments of the children they will be teaching, and the early childhood providers and families learn about the school environment. This type of transition planning produces good outcomes for children, making school entry successful.

## Kindergarten Screening and Interventions

Even with more effective preschool interventions and transition practices, kindergarten classrooms will continue to include children with large gaps in entry-level skills. Findings from the Early Childhood Longitudinal Study—Kindergarten Class of 1998–99 (ECLS-K) indicate that almost half of all children entering kindergarten in the United States come from families with one or more risk factors for school achievement (NCES, 2004). For these children, kindergarten needs to be a time of reducing the gap in skills between students. Beginning kindergarten assessments can help identify students' strengths and needs and provide school personnel with information to target specific interventions for particular groups of children.

In order for school to be ready for the children who enter kindergarten, school personnel need to shift from traditional kindergarten practices to those providing students with the skills they will need to profit from more formal academic instruction in first grade. In order to make the most of kindergarten, teachers need information to plan appropriate interventions for their students. Screening measures should be adopted or developed with the specific population of children to be screened in mind. Thus, a beginning kindergarten assessment might look different in an urban setting compared with one developed for a suburban school system. However, some items would be universal, because they are predictive of later school achievement. These would include letter naming, letter–sound identification, vocabulary, print concepts, listening comprehension, object counting, and number recognition. Good kindergarten assessments incorporate both direct and indirect measures of cognitive skills but also incorporate important social–emotional competencies such as self-regulation. These assessments would include not only individual screening instruments but also direct observations, record reviews, and parent and teacher interviews and rating scales (see Maxwell & Clifford, 2004, for more information on screening and assessment of young children).

One approach to ensuring that children receive appropriate interventions is to provide full-day kindergarten programs. Results from the ECLS-K indicate that children who attend full-day programs make greater gains in reading and math than those in half-day programs. Whereas child characteristics had some bearings on the findings (children in poverty made smaller gains), all groups of children in full-day programs had better outcomes (NCES, 2004).

In addition to the length of time in a program, the quality of kindergarten instruction also is a significant factor in determining program effectiveness. Without quality instruction, children become "instructional casualties" (Vaughn, Linan-Thompson, & Hickman, 2003). Avoiding instructional casualties is most critical for high-risk children. These children often need more intensive small group and direct academic instruction, as well as instruction in social skills, such as how to sit, wait, listen, and follow directions, whereas others will already have learned these skills prior to kindergarten. Small group instruction should not replace whole group instruction, such as when classroom teachers are introducing new concepts and vocabulary. Whenever possible, early-intervention small group instruction should not supplant the rich experiences provided to all students in the classroom.

# SUMMARY

School readiness has been an ill-defined concept, but nevertheless it is a much discussed goal for our nation's children as they enter kindergarten. Clearly, all children need access to high-quality preschool experiences. This access would include a well-balanced curriculum that provides children with a breadth of experiences and integrates the main skill domains of early childhood: social–emotional skills, physical well-being, cognition, independence, and language development. Among these domains, language development is perhaps of greatest importance in early childhood, especially the development of vocabulary and knowledge development. It also is important for children to understand the functions of print and to begin to use child writing (scribbling, drawing) to represent their ideas. A related skill that pervades all areas of child development is self-regulation. The development of language and of self-regulation exert a bidirectional influence; that is, each skill assists the other as well as the other domains of development. Finally, schools need to be ready for the children entering kindergarten. To achieve this, teachers, school psychologists, and other school staff need to adopt or develop valid and reliable screening measures and use the results wisely, coordinate transition to kindergarten practices, and work together with parents to ensure that children have an opportunity to develop the skills they will need for academic and social success.

## RECOMMENDED RESOURCES

### Books and Other Printed Material

Bowman, B. T., Donovan, M. S., & Burns, M. S. (Committee on Early Childhood Pedagogy, National Research Council). (2000). *Eager to learn: Educating our preschoolers.* Washington, DC: National Academy Press.

Developed by the National Research Council, this book will help readers fully understand what it will take to improve the quality of early care and education.

Pianta, R. C., & Kraft-Sayre, M. (2003). *Successful kindergarten transition: Your guide to connecting children, families, and schools.* Baltimore, MD: Brookes.

This is the how-to manual for putting effective practices for transition to kindergarten in place in schools and communities.

Shonkoff, J. P., & Phillips, D. A. (Committee on Integrating the Science of Early Childhood Development, National Research Council). (2000). *From neurons to neighborhoods: The science of early childhood development.* Washington, DC: National Academy Press.

This book is technically informative on the current science of early development. It offers both policy and practice recommendations.

### Websites

*www.ed.gov/programs/earlyreading/index.html*

This is the website for Early Reading First. The program is designed to transform existing early education programs into centers of excellence that provide high-quality early education to young children, especially those from low-income families.

*http://www.fpg.unc.edu/ncedl*

This is the website for the National Center for Early Development and Learning, which is a research project supported by the U.S. Department of Education's Institute for Educational Sciences. It has funded a multitude of early childhood research, including the work on transition to kindergarten.

*http://nieer.org/*

This is the website for the National Institute for Early Education Research. The institute supports early childhood education initiatives by providing objective, nonpartisan information based on research.

## REFERENCES


Adams, M. J. (1990). *Beginning to read: Thinking and learning about print.* Cambridge, MA: MIT Press.

Administration for Children and Families. (2003). *Head Start FACES 2000: A whole child perspective on program performance.* Washington, DC: U.S. Department of Health and Human Services.

Barnett, W. S., Brown, K., & Shore, R. (2004, April). The universal vs. targeted debate: Should the United States have preschool for all? *Preschool Policy Matters,* (6). New Brunswick, NJ: National Institute for Early Education Research.

Bowman, B. T., Donovan, M. S., & Burns, M. S. (Committee on Early Childhood Pedagogy, National Research Council). (2000). *Eager to learn: Educating our preschoolers.* Washington, DC: National Academy Press.

Bus, A. G., van Ijzendoorn, M. H., & Pelligrini, A. D. (1995). Joint book reading makes for success in learning to read: A meta-analysis on intergenerational transmission of literacy. *Review of Educational Research, 65,* 1–21.

Campbell, F. A., Ramey, C. T., Pungello, E. P., Sparling, J., & Miller-Johnson, S. (2002). Early childhood education: Young adult outcomes from the Abecedarian Project. *Applied Developmental Science, 6,* 42–57.

Christenson, S. (1999). Families and schools: Rights, responsibilities, resources, and relationships. In R. C. Pianta & M. J. Cox (Eds.), *The transition to kindergarten* (pp. 143–177). Baltimore, MD: Brookes.

Committee for Economic Development. (2002). *Preschool for all: Investing in a productive and just society.* Retrieved July 23, 2004, from http://www.ced.org/docs/report/report_preschool.pdf

Cutspec, P. A. (2004). Influences of dialogic reading on the language development of toddlers. *Bridges: Practice-Based Research Syntheses, 2*(2), 1–12.

Entwisle, D., Alexander, K. L., & Olson, L. (1997). *Children, schools, and inequality.* Boulder, CO: Westview.

Gredler, G. R. (1997). Issues in school readiness. In G. Bear, K. Minke, & A. Thomas (Eds.), *Children's needs II: Development, problems, and alternatives* (pp. 489–499). Bethesda, MD: National Association of School Psychologists.

Hargrave, A. C., & Senechal, M. (2000). A book reading intervention with preschool children who have limited vocabularies: The benefits of regular reading and dialogic reading. *Early Childhood Research Quarterly,* 75–90.

Hart, B., & Risley, T. (1995). *Meaningful differences in the everyday experience of young American children.* Baltimore, MD: Paul H. Brookes.

Hart, K., & Schumacher, R. (2004). Moving forward: Head Start children, families, and programs in 2003. *Center for Law and Social Policy, Head Start Policy Brief,* (5), 1–7.

Irish, K., Schumacher, R., & Lombardi, J. (2003). Serving America's youngest: A snapshot of early Head Start children, families, teachers, and programs in 2002. *Center for Law and Social Policy, Head Start Policy Brief,* (3), 1–7.

Juel, C. (1988). Learning to read and write: A longitudinal study of 54 children from first through fourth grades. *Journal of Educational Psychology, 80,* 437–447.

Maxwell, K. L., & Clifford, R. M. (2004, January). School readiness assessment. *Beyond the journal. Young children on the Web.* Retrieved April 17, 2005, from http://www.journal.naeyc.org/btj/200401

Meisels, S. J. (1999). Assessing readiness. In R. C. Pianta & M. J. Cox. (Eds.), *The transition to kindergarten.* Baltimore, MD: Paul H. Brookes.

National Association for the Education of Young Children. (1995). *School readiness: Position statement.* Retrieved on June 18, 2004, from http://www.naeyc.org/about/positions/pdf/PSready98.pdf

National Center for Education Statistics. (2001). *Entering kindergarten: A portrait of American children when they begin school.* (NCES 2001-035). Washington, DC: U.S. Government Printing Office.

National Center for Education Statistics, U.S. Department of Education. (2004). *Full-day and half-day kindergarten in the United States: Findings from the early childhood longitudinal study, kindergarten class of 1998-99.* (NCES 2004-078). Washington, DC: U.S. Government Printing Office.

National Education Goals Panel. (1995). *National educational goals report executive summary: Improving education through family-school community partnerships.* Washington, DC: U.S. Government Printing Office.

Neuman, S. (2001). The role of knowledge in early literacy. *Reading Research Quarterly, 36,* 468–475.

Panter, J. E., & Bracken, B. A. (2000). Promoting school readiness. In K. Minke & G. Bear (Eds.), *Preventing school problems—Promoting school success* (pp. 101–142). Bethesda, MD: National Association of School Psychologists.

Pianta, R. C., & Cox, M. J. (Eds.). (1999). *The transition to kindergarten.* Baltimore, MD: Paul H. Brookes.

Pianta, R. C., & Kraft-Sayre, M. (2003). *Successful kindergarten transition: Your guide to connecting children, families, and schools.* Baltimore, MD: Paul H. Brookes.

Pianta, R. C., & LaParo, K. (2003). Improving. *Educational Leadership* (April), 24–29.

Quality counts 2002: Building blocks for success. (2002, January). *Education Week, 21,* 1–170.

Rimm-Kaufman, S. E., Pianta, R. C., & Cox, M. J. (2000). Teachers' judgments of problems in the transition to kindergarten. *Early Childhood Research Quarterly, 15,* 147–166.

Saluja, G., Scott-Little, C., & Clifford, R. M. (2000). Readiness for school: A survey of state policies and definitions. *Early Childhood Research and Practice, 2,* 1–21.

Schweinhart, L., Barnes, H., Weikart, D., Barnett, W. S., & Epstein, A. S. (1993). Significant benefits: The high/scope Perry preschool study through age 27.

*Monographs of the High/Scope Educational Research Foundation, 10.* Ypsilanti, MI: High/Scope Press.

Shonkoff, J. P., & Phillips, D. A. (Committee on Integrating the Science of Early Childhood Development, National Research Council). (2000). *From neurons to neighborhoods: The science of early childhood development.* Washington, DC: National Academy Press.

Snow, C., Burns, S., & Griffin, P. (1998). *Preventing reading difficulties in young children.* Washington, DC: National Academy Press.

Stanovich, K. (1986). Matthew effects in reading: Some consequences of individual differences in the acquisition of literacy. *Reading Research Quarterly, 21,* 360–407.

Vaughn, S., Linan-Thompson, S., & Hickman, P. (2003). Response to instruction as a means of identifying students with reading/learning disabilities. *Exceptional Children, 69,* 391–409.

Wesley, P. W., & Buysse, V. (2003). Making meaning of school readiness in schools and communities. *Early Childhood Research Quarterly, 18,* 351–375.

Whitehurst, G. J., Arnold, D. S., Epstein, J. M., & Angell, A. L. (1994). A picture book reading intervention in day care and home for children from low-income families. *Developmental Psychology, 30,* 679–689.

42

# Gender Differences in Academic Development and Performance

**Linda M. Raffaele Mendez**
**Stephanie T. Mihalas**
**Robin Hardesty**
*University of South Florida*

## BACKGROUND AND DEVELOPMENT

The study of how a child's gender affects his or her education is a very broad area of inquiry. Current research in this area focuses on gender differences in numerous aspects of the educational process, including academic performance, social experiences in schools, perceptions of competence in different academic subjects (e.g., reading vs. math), special education placement rates, and frequency of school discipline (e.g., suspension or expulsion). Although a number of chapters in this volume include discussion of such gender differences, none includes much discussion of gender differences in academic development and performance. This is the focus of the present chapter.

A review of the literature on gender differences in academic development and performance among students in the United States over the past 25 to 30 years reveals some very interesting changes in the types of issues that are being discussed, researched, and debated. In the 1970s and 1980s, most of the research and writing focused on gender inequity in education for girls and women. Of primary concern was the academic development of girls in mathematics and the sciences. Researchers found that girls frequently stopped taking math and science coursework when it was no longer required (Sherman, 1983), performed more poorly on standardized math and science tests (see Campbell, Hombo, & Mazzeo, 2000), and perceived themselves to be less talented than boys in these subject areas (Eccles et al., 1983). Several explanations for these gender differences were offered in the literature, including biological differences in brain development (e.g., Benbow & Stanley, 1980), pervasive gender role stereotypes that girls are less competent in math and science than boys (e.g., Eccles & Jacobs, 1986), and differential expectations and treatment by parents and teachers (e.g., Eccles-Parsons, Adler, & Kaczala, 1982; Fennema, 1990). Concern about the underrepresentation of women in high-paying career fields led to the development of a number of initiatives to increase girls' awareness of and interest in mathematics and the sciences. Greater attention also was focused on instructional strategies that meet girls' gender-specific learning needs in these subject areas (Morrow & Morrow, 1992). These initiatives, over time, have resulted in a considerable narrowing of the mathematics achievement gap between boys and girls (see Freeman, 2005).

In the 1990s, as girls started to make gains on standardized tests in mathematics and their enrollment in male-dominated subjects in colleges and universities increased, the focus of the gender equity literature shifted away from a predominant concern about the performance of girls in mathematics and the sciences to a broader-based concern about their overall experiences in schools. Sadker and Sadker's (1994) seminal book on gender differences in classroom experiences reported that girls (a) received less attention from teachers in the classroom than boys, (b) were less likely than boys to be given active feedback by teachers after answering a question in class, and (c) were praised more often by teachers for their appearance than for the quality of their intellectual ideas. At about the same time, Gilligan and her colleagues (e.g., Brown & Gilligan, 1992) were publishing their qualitative research showing that many girls experience a decrease in self-esteem and personal agency as they move into adolescence, subverting their own needs and desires (i.e., their "true voice") in an attempt to maintain positive personal relationships with others. These authors hypothesized that such a trend had a negative impact on girls' educational development. Additionally, the American Association of University Women (AAUW) published several reports showing that girls' schooling experiences were negatively affected by sexual harassment by peers in schools (AAUW, 1993) as well as by gender bias in the curriculum (AAUW, 1992). The upshot of this research was a greater focus on a wider range of school-related variables related to girls' academic development and performance, including teacher–student relationships, peer relationships, and school climate and safety.

More recently, in the mid to late 1990s, the literature on gender equity in education has begun to include concerns about boys. In recent years, there has been considerable debate over which gender faces more educational challenges. For example, Hoff Sommers (2000) sharply criticized the conclusions reached by Gilligan and the AAUW, arguing that in the 1990s it was boys, not girls, who were performing poorly in the educational system. Similarly, Kleinfeld (1998) argued that the AAUW's mission to focus concern on girls' needs in schools drew attention away from the group most at risk for school failure: African American boys. Around the same time, several books on boys' development were published (i.e., Gurian, 1996; Kindlon & Thompson, 1999; Pollock, 1998). These books called attention to the effect of societal stereotyping on boys' development (similar to how this issue had been examined for girls in the 1970s and 1980s) and suggested that boys also had specific needs that were not being adequately addressed in schools. These publications resulted in greater awareness of the unique developmental challenges faced by boys and how gender role stereotyping limited their opportunities to communicate honestly and to actively pursue interests in female-dominated domains such as creative writing and art.

Recent research also has begun to pay closer attention to the interaction of gender and race in education. When one examines outcome data, it is clear that the group currently most at risk for school failure in our schools is African American boys. African American boys are far more likely than boys from other racial groups to be identified as having an educational disability (see Losen & Orfield, 2002) and to be suspended or expelled from school (Raffaele Mendez & Knoff, 2003). They also are much less likely than African American girls to graduate from high school (Roderick, 2003; Swanson, 2003). Roderick (2003) found that among the 98 African American boys and girls from inner-city Chicago in her study, there were few gender differences in school performance or teacher ratings in Grade 8. However, between Grades 8 and 9, boys experienced much more dramatic declines in their grades than girls. Boys also were viewed more negatively than girls by their ninth-grade teachers. Among these students, only 40% of boys graduated from high school compared with 80% of girls. Such findings suggest that the educational challenges faced by so many African American boys clearly merit attention and intervention from educators. Although further discussion of these challenges is beyond the scope of this chapter, interested readers are referred to the special issue of *Urban Education*, Vol. 38(5), which was dedicated to this topic.

Current research and writing on gender equity in education is continuing to explore differences between the genders with regard to both the educational process and outcomes. Recently, Meadows, Land, and Lamb (2005) reported the results of a large-scale national study examining gender differences across a variety of areas of well-being, including material well-being, social relationships, health, safety and behavioral concerns, productive activity (educational attainments), place in community, and emotional and spiritual well-being. These authors found few gender differences in their data, noting that any differences that did emerge were relatively small. Importantly, the only educational data they examined were scores on the National Assessment of Educational Performance (NAEP). Thus, Meadows et al.'s conclusions that boys and girls are similar across all domains of well-being are based on limited data and mask some important gender differences. When boys as a group are compared with girls as a group on other indicators of academic development and performance, it becomes clear that each gender reflects specific areas of concern. These differences are addressed in the next two sections of this chapter.

## PROBLEMS AND IMPLICATIONS

### Gender Differences in Academic Development and Performance

Multiple indicators are available to gauge gender differences in academic development and performance. In this section, school readiness, grades, standardized test scores, and gifted program placement are examined. These indicators of performance were chosen because they are commonly used to measure student progress and because state or national data are available for each indicator.

***School readiness.*** The issue of school readiness has received a considerable amount of attention in recent years (e.g., Coley, 2002; also see chapter 41, "School Readiness"). The growing interest in children's readiness for formal education is likely related to the fact that kindergarten is becoming increasingly academically focused (Shepard & Smith, 1988), with school systems expecting children to read, write, and perform mathematical operations earlier in their school careers than in years past. This increasing focus on academics in the early elementary years has particular implications for boys, who, on average, experience slower brain maturation than girls (Gogtay et al., 2004). This slower maturation results in girls as a group showing superior skills to boys as a group in a variety of areas related to school readiness, including early language development (particularly vocabulary development), fine motor skills, and self-control (Rawson & Rose, 2002). Research also shows that boys at age 5 have a higher activity level than girls (Martin, Wisenbaker, Baker, & Huttunen, 1997), a finding that has important implications for a child's capacity to engage in quiet seatwork (Sax, 2005). Because of these gender differences, when boys are compared with girls in the kindergarten setting, they often look less mature.

Research shows that fewer boys than girls meet kindergarten readiness expectations. For example, in Oregon in 2002 (McClanahan, 2002), 71.8% of male children met all dimensions of kindergarten readiness compared with 81.1% of female children. Similarly, a study of 19,000 children who began kindergarten in 1998 (Zill & West, 2001) found that girls as a group began kindergarten with significantly better reading skills than boys as a group. Significant gender differences were found in letter recognition (with 70% of girls vs. 61% of boys knowing their letters at school entry) and letter–sound association (with 32% of girls vs. 26% of boys able to identify the first letter of a word after hearing the word). Perhaps more important is the finding that girls were less likely than boys to have developmental difficulties and were more likely to demonstrate good social skills, positive classroom behavior, and a positive orientation toward learning activities.

***Grades.*** The literature is quite clear that girls have an advantage over boys in terms of grades earned (Halpern, 1997; Dwyer & Johnson, 1997). This is true across school subjects and across ages. In the United States in 2000, female high school graduates earned an overall grade point average (GPA) of 3.05 and male high school graduates earned an overall GPA of 2.83 (Perkins, Kleiner, Roey, & Brown, 2004). Of course, grade differences must be interpreted cautiously. As some authors have pointed out, the grade differences between boys and girls have been found to be small in some cases (Kleinfeld, 1998). Additionally, the fact that girls earn higher grades than boys does not mean that they necessarily perceive themselves as more competent than boys across subject areas. A recent study of 932 students in Grades 4–6 (Pomerantz, Altermatt, & Saxon, 2002) showed that girls earned significantly higher grades than boys in language arts, social studies, science, and math. However, when asked about their levels of competence in each subject, girls' ratings of their competence in math and science were significantly lower than boys' ratings.

It also is likely that classroom behavior has an influence on school grades. The literature is clear that boys demonstrate more behavior problems in the classroom than girls. For example, in 1995, the U.S. Department of Education reported that, among children in grades 1–3, parents of girls were less likely than parents of boys to be contacted by their child's school regarding problems with behavior or homework (Bae, Choy, Geddes, Sable, & Snyder, 2000). Boys also experience many more suspensions and expulsions than girls (Raffaele Mendez, Knoff, & Ferron, 2002). The complex interplay of factors that results in boys earning lower grades than girls clearly deserves further study.

***Standardized test scores.*** Although girls earn higher grades than boys across subject areas and grades, the latest information suggests that they do not necessarily earn higher scores than boys on standardized tests (Freeman, 2005). Two standardized tests are the basis on which gender comparisons are frequently made: the National Assessment of Educational Progress (NAEP) and the Scholastic Aptitude Test (SAT). The NAEP provides information on state and national student performance results in reading, mathematics, science, and writing, as well as national student performance results in various aspects of social science and foreign language. Gender comparisons in reading, mathematics, and science on the NAEP have been made for the past three decades. The SAT provides information on reading, writing, and math. Notably, because only students who plan to attend college typically take the SAT, a much narrower group of students is included in SAT scores than in NAEP scores.

The most recent information available from the NAEP (see Freeman, 2005), which is given in Grades 4, 8, and 12, shows that girls outperformed boys in reading and writing on the 2002 test. According to Freeman, gender differences in reading and writing have remained relatively stable over the past decade. However, these differences do not translate to higher scores for girls on advanced placement (AP) exams in English. Although more girls took AP exams in English in 2002, boys earned a higher average score.

With regard to scores on the NAEP in mathematics, the difference between the genders is negligible. Despite a common perception that males outperform females in mathematics, NAEP scores do not support this (Freeman, 2005). The differences between boys and girls in Grades 4, 8, and 12 remained similar from 1990 to 2003. Nonetheless, in 2002, more males than females took the AP exam in mathematics, and they also earned a higher average score than females. In science, 4th and 8th grade males scored higher than females on the NAEP, but the differences at 12th grade were not significant.

With regard to the SAT, the long-standing and frequently cited difference between boys and girls on the math portion of the exam continues to exist. In 2004, boys earned an average math score of 537 compared with 501 for girls. Boys and girls earned similar scores on the verbal section (512 vs. 501, respectively; College Board, 2004). Notably, although the gender difference on the math section is statistically significant, its practical significance is questionable. According to the College Board, there is about a 30 point margin of error in an individual SAT score, which is close to the mean difference between genders. Additionally, differences between racial groups on the SAT are much larger than between genders (College Board, 2004). The interaction between gender and race also is important to consider. Boys in every racial group score higher on the math section than their female counterparts, except for African American boys, who have scored lower on the SAT than African American girls in recent years (Coley, 2001).

***Gifted program placement.*** In addition to gender differences in grades and standardized test scores, differences in gifted program placement provide some indication of how girls and boys compare with regard to academic development and performance. Some of the most recent data on this issue are found in a report by Karnes and Shaunessy (2003), which included the composition of students enrolled in gifted programs in each state, by gender. Most states showed no appreciable differences in the percentages of boys and girls enrolled in gifted programs. However, a few states did have relatively large differences, with some having greater percentages of boys enrolled and others having greater percentages of girls enrolled.

## Gender Differences in Academic Problems

This section of the chapter examines gender differences in academic problems, including retention, special education placement, and school dropout. These indicators were chosen because national data are available on each, and each speaks in different ways to the issue of children's and youth's success or lack of success in school. In each of these areas the data are quite clear that more boys than girls are identified as having academic problems. Whether this means that boys actually have more academic problems than girls or that they are more likely than girls to be identified as having problems is unclear, because teachers may be more likely to recommend them for assessment or intervention as a result of concomitant behavioral issues.

***Retention.*** Retention in grade is a relatively common educational practice despite mixed evidence on the effectiveness of this practice in remediating academic deficits (e.g., McCoy & Reynolds, 1999; also see chapter 46, "Grade Retention and Promotion"). Recent national statistics on retention show that in 1999, 8% of boys ages 5 to 12 had repeated at least one grade compared with 5% of girls of the same age (Freeman, 2005). Boys from minority groups had the highest rates of retention, with 12% of African American boys and 11% of Hispanic boys having repeated a grade, compared with 7% of White boys (Freeman, 2005). The overrepresentation of boys in retention is not a new finding; similar percentages of boys and girls were retained in 1992 and 1995 (Bae et al., 2000).

***Special education placement.*** Similar to the findings for retention, placement in special education programs is more likely for boys than for girls in almost every disability category. Boys are particularly overrepresented in the categories of learning disabled and emotionally disturbed. For example, in 1999, 12.5% of boys versus 6.6% of girls were identified as having a learning disability, and 3.8% of boys versus 1.9% of girls were identified as having an emotional disability (Freeman, 2005). Boys also outnumbered girls by more than 2 to 1 among students with a speech impediment (5.1% of boys vs. 2.1% of girls).

***School dropout.*** The findings for school dropout are consistent with indicators of other academic problems. Although high school dropout rates have declined over the past 30 years (i.e., 1972 through 2002; ChildTrends DataBank, 2002), the gap between male and female rates of dropout has increased. In 2002, males' rate of dropout was about 12%, and females' was 9%. Differences were particularly marked for minority students, with Hispanic and Black females graduating at significantly higher rates than their male counterparts (Swanson, 2003).

## Gender Role Stereotyping and Academic Self-Concept

Although student outcome data (e.g., grades and school dropout rates) provide some important information about how boys and girls are faring in school, it is important to examine research that goes beyond these types of statistics to get a more complete picture of gender differences in academic development and performance. The issue of gender role stereotyping and its impact on children's perceptions of their skills, expectations for success, and valuing of varying academic subjects is an important part of the larger picture of how gender relates to academic development. As noted earlier in this chapter, although girls obtain higher grades in mathematics and science than boys, they rate their competence in these subjects lower than boys do (Pomerantz et al., 2002). Such a finding makes sense in light of the pervasive gender role stereotype in the United States that males are more talented in mathematics and females are more talented in reading and writing.

Eccles and her colleagues (e.g., Eccles et al., 1983) have written extensively about the effect of parents' socialization and gender role stereotypes on their children. Notably, these stereotypes shape the beliefs they hold about their children's abilities and aptitudes, which influence how they interact with their children. For example, a parent who believes that boys are good at math and girls are better at reading may encourage participation in activities designed to specifically develop these abilities, which further confirms the parent's gender stereotypes. Parents' gender role stereotypes also influence the value their children attach to activities such as math and science (termed subjective task values) and, consequently, their motivation to participate in such activities. Gender-specific messages received from parents help to shape children's perceived academic competence beliefs, or preconceived ideas the child possesses about his or her ability to complete a task successfully and correctly. Research shows that competence beliefs act as mediators of academic achievement, even after controlling for ability or prior achievement (Bleeker & Jacobs, 2004). In addition, children spend more time on activities in which they have higher competence beliefs. Therefore, a girl who does not believe she is good at math may spend less time engaged in math-related activities. Less time engaged in a task tends to lead to lower achievement, which further confirms competence beliefs and gender role stereotypes (Jacobs & Eccles, 2000).

Not surprisingly, research also shows that beginning in middle to late elementary school, children have competence beliefs that follow culturally stereotyped gender roles. Over a period of 10 years, Jacobs, Lanza, Osgood, Eccles, and Wigfield (2002) tracked domain-specific competence beliefs, task values, and levels of participation in reading and math among 761 elementary, middle, and high school students. Competence beliefs for both males and females were highest in early elementary school. By late elementary school, males' competence beliefs were higher than females' in math, and females' competence beliefs were higher than males' in reading. By high school, competence beliefs for males and females were significantly lower than in elementary school and fairly similar across genders for both math and reading. Thus, the gender differences in perceived academic competence beliefs that have been reported in the literature seem to vary by age, peaking in late elementary school and then declining as students move into high school. Gender differences were found in the subjective task value assigned to language arts, with females valuing such activities significantly more than males. No differences were found in the valuing of mathematics. Both genders were found to value math or language arts more when they rated themselves as highly competent in that domain.

In a similar study, Andre, Whigham, Hendrickson, and Chambers (1999) asked younger and older elementary school students (Grades K–3 and Grades 4–6) to rate their perceived competencies, subjective task values, and perceptions of gender differences in careers related to language arts and math. Additionally, their parents were asked to rate their perceptions of the child's competencies, their own subjective task value, and expectancies for their child's achievement. Overall, girls rated their abilities in reading higher than boys did, and boys rated their abilities in math higher than girls. Older (but not younger) elementary school boys also rated their competency beliefs for science higher than girls. In this study, no gender differences were found in parents' expected achievement for reading or math, but parents did expect that boys would perform better than girls in science.

Parents who hold stereotypic gender beliefs regarding math and science achievement, particularly mothers of girls, have been found to have negative perceptions of their child's ability to succeed in coursework, regardless of the child's ability and past performance (Jacobs & Eccles, 1992; Jacobs, 1991). Notably, Eccles and Jacobs (1986) found that parents who had been exposed to media coverage that espoused biologically based gender differences in math and science achievement believed that boys possessed innate mathematical abilities that girls did not have. Parents who had not been exposed to such messages believed that boys and girls were equally capable in math-related tasks. All parents, regardless of gender-biased media exposure, felt that advanced training in mathematics was of more value for males. Media reports that attribute differences in math achievement solely to innate factors may negatively affect parents' beliefs in their daughters' math abilities, which may have a greater influence on females' math self-efficacy beliefs than their actual performance in math.

Research also shows that parents' perceptions of their children's abilities (which are shaped by parents' gender role stereotypes) may affect students' academic self-efficacy beliefs and future career choices (Bleeker & Jacobs, 2004). In a longitudinal study of 354 students, their mothers, and their classroom teachers, some interesting gender differences emerged. In the sixth grade, teachers rated the mathematical abilities of female students as higher than males. However, a year later, when the children were in seventh grade, mothers of boys had higher expectations for their child's math achievement than mothers of girls. In 10th grade, boys rated their ability in math much higher than girls did, and boys were found to have higher self-efficacy beliefs for careers in math and science than girls. Also, mothers who held higher expectations for their child's success in mathematics in seventh grade had children who reported higher career self-efficacy beliefs in late adolescence (ages 19–20), and their children were more likely to select a career in physical science or computers than those whose mothers held lower expectations. These results suggest that parents' stereotypic beliefs about achievement may have a long-term effect on children's self-efficacy beliefs and performance in mathematics and the sciences.

In addition to messages received from parents (Eccles et al., 1983) and differential treatment by teachers in the classrooms (Sadker & Sadker, 1994), gender stereotypes also may be reinforced in curricular materials. Evans and Davies (2000) reviewed basal reading textbooks and found that male characters were typically depicted as aggressive, argumentative, competitive risk-takers, and female characters were typically affectionate and passive. Reading materials also may favor subjects girls enjoy. Gentry, Gable, and Rizza (2002) reported that girls in Grades 3–8 found their class activities and materials more interesting and enjoyable than boys. If boys are not interested in topics covered in the reading curriculum, they may be less motivated to read than girls.

Overall, educators need to be aware of the effects that gender role stereotypes have on students' self-perceptions. Students who are not performing well in particular academic subjects may be receiving messages at home that discourage their participation in or valuing of such subjects. Encouraging and providing opportunities for students to engage in activities that develop their academic self-efficacy beliefs in multiple domains have the potential to benefit both genders. Parents can also be provided with positive feedback regarding their children's strengths in all academic domains to minimize the effect of gender-stereotyped messages received through the media and the larger culture.

## ALTERNATIVE ACTIONS FOR PREVENTION AND INTERVENTION

### Single-Sex Classrooms

Since the 1970s gender segregation has been the focus of controversial debate in many nations, including Australia, Belgium, the United Kingdom, and the United States (Haag, 2000). In the United States, single-sex classrooms are most often espoused as benefiting girls; however, much of the research on single-sex schooling has been conducted in private and Catholic schools (Datnow, Hubbard, & Woody, 2001) or in other countries. Since Title IX was passed in 1972, which requires equal access to educational opportunity for boys and girls, single-sex schooling has been difficult to implement in public schools in the United States.

California was the first state to experiment with gender-segregated schooling in the public sector since the passage of Title IX. In 1997, six districts in California opened single-sex academies. The academies served students in middle school or high school (Grades 5–12, depending on the academy) and were relatively small in terms of overall number of students served (typically about 100 students each). Research on the academies (only one of which was still in existence in 2001, when the final report was written) showed that outcomes for students were mixed. Datnow et al. (2001) reported that the academies reinforced traditional gender role stereotypes, and gender segregation led to a dichotomous understanding of gender, where girls were seen as good and boys were seen as bad. More positive findings showed that gender segregation reduced classroom distractions from the opposite sex and also allowed for more opportunities for educators to impart important life messages to adolescents, because teachers were comfortable assuming a guidance role with students.

Another recent study, conducted by Younger and Warrington (2002) in England, examined the effectiveness of gender-specific classrooms on students' learning over a 12-year period. This study involved students in years 7–11 of schooling in one school. The students attended either mixed-gender or single-sex classes for English, math, and science. The primary aim of the study was to determine how teachers changed their behaviors when working only with girls, only with boys, or with both genders simultaneously. Three types of outcomes were addressed in this study: academic, classroom interaction, and affective. Academically, both male and female achievement improved over the 12-year period of the study, and achievement levels also were found to be above the national average. However, females' scores on the national exam were consistently higher than males'. Observations in the classroom found that teachers' tolerance of male behavior was higher in single-sex classrooms compared with mixed-sex classrooms. Boys in the single-sex classrooms were allowed to be more inattentive, fidgety, and active without receiving reprimands. Classroom interaction data also revealed that females participated more than males in both mixed-sex and single-sex classrooms. Affective reports from males indicated that they enjoyed being in single-sex classes because they did not experience pressure to impress girls or show off and thus were able to focus on their work. The same is true for females in this study, who reported that they felt safe and enjoyed developing their self-esteem around other females.

Parker and Rennie (2002) found similar results in their study of 10 high schools in Australia in which boys and girls were segregated for science and math in one or more years of the project. Results showed that both teachers and students tended to believe that single-sex classes were better working and learning environments than mixed-sex classes. Additionally, teachers noted that minority groups (in this case Aboriginal girls) had more opportunities to learn in single-sex classrooms because they did not experience a dual form of discrimination (i.e., gender and race). Also, the successful implementation of gender-sensitive strategies was directly linked to classroom management issues. Teachers noted that they were able to work more directly with students and modify their teaching styles when they did not have to focus on redirecting students in mixed-sex classrooms to stay on-task.

Although the focus of this chapter is on academic achievement, social development also must be considered in examining the efficacy of gender-segregated classrooms. Barton and Cohen (2004) researched the link between social development and gender classroom composition in 39 students across Grades 4–6. In this study, all students were in mixed-gender classrooms in Grade 4. In the second year of the study (i.e., in Grade 5), they were placed in single-gender classrooms. The initial assessment, in Grade 5, found that boys increased the number of same-sex friends from Grade 4 to Grade 5; however, females reported more aggression (e.g., overt, relational, and victimization) in Grade 5 than in Grade 4. At the 1-year follow-up, in Grade 6, boys continued to increase the number of same-sex friends but girls did not. However, the aggressive behaviors reported by girls in Grade 5 were not evident at the 1-year follow-up in Grade 6. Although classroom composition was not found to be related to measures of social competence, the findings did indicate that males and females differentially experienced changes in friendships and feelings of victimization. These findings have important implications for educators who are considering the implementation of gender-segregated classrooms. Specifically, program evaluation of such classrooms should not focus solely on academic outcomes but also take into account social and emotional outcomes for students.

Because of the mixed findings associated with gender-segregated classrooms and the controversy associated with educational segregation in general, further research clearly is needed in this area, particularly because gender-segregated schooling is increasingly being seen as a potential solution to address the needs of students at risk in public schools (see Datnow et al., 2001). In particular, more research is needed on outcomes for students in gender-segregated classrooms that are specifically designed to meet gender-specific needs (e.g., use of empirically supported strategies for teaching math to girls using cooperative learning). Additionally, when classrooms are segregated by gender, special attention must be paid to providing informal opportunities for students to socialize with the opposite sex, choosing teachers who are gender-aware themselves and can teach in a way that builds the confidence of students, and monitoring aggression and peer networks.

## Strategies and Initiatives for Boys

As has been discussed throughout this chapter, there are a number of concerns regarding boys in the current educational system. Although the complex interplay of factors that results in boys currently performing more poorly than girls in schools overall is not fully understood, some classroom-based techniques implemented by teachers have been shown to increase academic achievement in boys. The following is a list of practices that may be beneficial for teachers and educator support staff to abide by when working with boys (Connell & Gunzelmann, 2004):

- Use visually stimulating materials to tap into students' visual and spatial strengths such as blocks, Legos, and logs for math.
- Provide male role models, such as guest speakers, male mental health workers, and male teachers.
- Choose materials that appeal to males, such as books about sports and nature, hands-on materials, and use of technology.
- Allow opportunities for competition, such as spelling bees, brainteasers, and geography bees.
- Sustain a supportive environment in which students feel safe to express themselves, are encouraged to let feelings show, and are allowed to make mistakes.
- Provide alternative curricula, such as vocational and work-based learning (Ontario Ministry of Education, 2003).
- Set limits and high expectations.

Since writing is one of the areas in which boys are not performing as well as girls (e.g., on the NAEP), specific strategies have also been identified to promote improved writing performance for boys. Foremost is the way teachers approach and direct the writing process. Structured, explicit, and varied approaches and strategies have proved beneficial for males. Teachers are encouraged to clearly state goals and objectives and to work through the writing process by modeling and using visual diagrams such as grids and spider diagrams. Allowing boys to pick their own topics during narrative writing is effective because they feel empowered to be creative and independent. Active learning tasks, such as role-playing or drawing, also have been found to motivate boys to become more engaged with writing (Daly, n.d.)

Finally, educators must avoid comparing young boys with their female counterparts as the standard for behavior. Boys' greater activity levels and slower language development can make them look less mature than girls. Some authors (e.g., Rawson & Rose, 2002) have suggested that boys should be a full year older than girls when they start kindergarten. Others have suggested that boys should be at least 5½ years of age at kindergarten entry (e.g., Sax, 2005). Although delaying school entry may not be a practical strategy for most families, it is important for educators to recognize that boys as a group normally have slower development compared with girls as a group, and many of these boys will eventually catch up in the first few years of elementary school. As such, educators should recognize that boys and girls may have different needs in early elementary school, with boys often needing more opportunities for gross motor activity than girls. Recognizing these differences as normal would likely reduce the percentage of boys who are retained in kindergarten or referred to special education for behavioral problems, such as Attention Deficit Hyperactivity Disorder, which affect more boys than girls.

## Strategies and Initiatives for Girls

The progress that girls have made in academic achievement across stereotypically male-dominated domains (e.g., mathematics, science) over the past 10–20 years is notable. Such progress is likely attributable to initiatives designed to increase girls' interest and confidence in math and science, such as Operation SMART, Summer Math: EUREKA!, and Expanding Your Horizons. Within recent years, initiatives for girls have added engineering and technology to math and science, referred to as STEM. A recent report by the American Association of University Women (2004) synthesized 416 STEM gender equity projects that had been funded by the National Science Foundation (NSF) and the AAUW during the past decade. One of the key recommendations that came out of this report was that STEM gender equity activities should be infused into the general school curriculum. The authors noted that many of the projects included in the synthesis took place outside of school and provided girls with "important opportunities for hands-on learning and investigation that are often absent from the school curriculum" (AAUW, 2004, p. 28).

Another key recommendation that emerged from the AAUW synthesis was that data collection and project evaluation should be emphasized in future STEM efforts, as many of the projects did not report participant demographics or measurable outcomes. Although there are many STEM initiatives in the literature and on the Internet (see, in particular, *http://www.campbell-kibler.com*), few have been formally evaluated. Most programs also have been implemented solely with girls. An exception is Family Tools and Technology (FT2), which was developed at Rutgers University and implemented in 12 schools during the 1995–1996 school year (Campbell, Bachmann, & Steinbrueck, 1996). The goal of this program is to teach girls and their parents, within coeducational settings, how to use tools to solve problems in a manner that promotes comfort using tools and reduces gender role stereotyping. The program begins by training teachers, each of whom then recruits 10 elementary school students (70% of whom are girls) and their parents for a series of 12 hands-on family training sessions in which families engage in problem-solving activities using tools, such as programming a VCR, using a voltmeter, or fixing a bicycle chain. Results of a program evaluation using pre- and post-program surveys of students (Campbell et al., 1996) showed that student participants had significant decreases in gender role stereotypes. The positive results were associated with girls using tools and with students' significantly more positive attitudes toward tools and those who use them (particularly boys' attitudes toward girls who use tools).

Several other promising programs also are currently being evaluated. Researchers at the Wellesley Centers for Women (WCW) are evaluating two new programs that directly address STEM-focused activities. The first one, titled Hear Our Voices, is funded by the National Science Foundation. The program addresses the gender gaps in computer technology by developing and evaluating educational methods and learning modalities designed specifically for females ages 10 to 18. One of the driving elements of the program is its design to counteract avoidance patterns of females in the sciences. Some examples of what the program entails include writing and recording music in the studio; creating flash animation, 3-D, and robotics projects; and writing, filming, and editing original movies and video productions. The current evaluation intends to measure change in participants' attitudes toward computers and careers in computer-related fields (see Recommended Resources). The second project being evaluated is 4 Schools for Women in Engineering. This project is a consortium of four universities in Massachusetts: Northeastern University, Tufts University, Worcester Polytechnic Institute, and Boston University. Massachusetts recently became the first state to establish engineering as part of the mandated curriculum for K–12. These four institutions are working together to build a K–12 outreach program for girls and women to increase gender equity in the sciences, technology, engineering, and mathematics. The ultimate goal is to develop a middle school curriculum that encourages both sexes to stay on an educational path that could lead to an engineering degree. The program is expected to be available for national dissemination in the next 3 years. The intervention is highly replicable at low cost (i.e., hard copy manual, videotape, and web-based learning).

## SUMMARY

National statistics on indicators such as kindergarten readiness, grades, and standardized test scores in reading and writing show girls currently outperforming boys. Boys also have higher rates of academic problems than girls, including retention, special education placement, and school dropout. Nonetheless, boys continue to score significantly higher than girls on the mathematics portion of the SAT (although the difference between girls and boys on the mathematics section of the NAEP is negligible). Boys also continue to have more confidence in their skills in math and science than girls, even when girls are earning higher grades in these subjects.

The bottom line with regard to gender equity in academic development and performance is that specific areas of concern exist for boys and for girls. The promotion of gender equity in schools entails recognizing and addressing these areas of concern.

## RECOMMENDED RESOURCES

### Books and Other Printed Material

Campbell, P. B., Jolly, E. J., Hoey, L., & Perlman, E. K. (2002). *Upping the numbers: Using research-based decision-making to increase diversity in the quantitative disciplines.* Available from the

Campbell-Kibler Associates, Inc. website: *http://www.campbell-kibler.com*

This is one of many excellent reports authored by Patricia Campbell and her associates regarding how to increase female participation in male-dominated fields. This particular report, which was commissioned by the General Electric Foundation, examines achievement, course taking, and interest in mathematics at various grade levels and provides research-based implications to increase female representation in quantitative disciplines.

Freeman, C. E. (2005). *Trends in educational equity of girls and women: 2004* (NCES 2005–016).Washington DC: U.S. Government Printing Office.

This compilation of information from the National Center for Education Statistics provides comparisons of males and females in preprimary and elementary education, elementary and secondary education, postsecondary education, and educational outcomes. Available from the website of the U.S. Department of Education's National Center for Education Statistics: *http://www.nces.ed.gov/pubs2005/equity*

Sax, L. (2005). *Why gender matters: What parents and teachers need to know about the emerging science of sex differences.* New York: Doubleday.

This recently published book, written by a psychologist and family physician, provides a good overview of differences in development among boys and girls. Although this book is written for a lay audience, it includes numerous references to publications in refereed journals.

Swanson, D. P., Cunningham, M., & Spencer, M. B. (2003). Black males' structural conditions, achievement patterns, normative needs, and "opportunities." *Urban Education, 38,* 608–633.

This empirical investigation first appeared in a special issue of *Urban Education* devoted to the schooling experiences of African American boys. The study examined how structural conditions influenced school outcomes for 219 African American urban adolescents. This is an excellent article for those seeking an ecological understanding of the underachievement of African American boys.

### Websites

*http://www.wcwonline.org/o-rr26-1b.html*

Wellesley Centers for Women (WCW) is evaluating two new programs that directly address STEM-focused activities. Hear Our Voices, funded by the National Science Foundation, addresses the gender gaps in computer technology by developing and evaluating educational methods and learning modalities designed specifically for females ages 10 to 18. Readers can stay abreast of these findings and see how the program is implemented across various clubhouses (i.e., Sorenson Multi-Cultural Center-Salt Lake City, Lawrence Boys & Girls Club-Lawrence, and Break Away Technologies-Los Angeles).

*http://www.ithaca.edu/wise/topics/gender.htm*

The website Working to Improve Schools and Education (WISE), developed by Jeff Claus at Ithaca College, includes a variety of topics related to education and teaching. The Gender Issues page, which includes links to a wide array of topics related to gender and education, is highly recommended.

## REFERENCES

American Association of University Women. (1992). *How schools shortchange girls: A study of major findings on girls and education.* Washington, DC: AAUW Educational Foundation.

American Association of University Women. (1993). *Hostile hallways: The AAUW survey on sexual harassment in America's schools.* Washington, DC: AAUW Educational Foundation.

American Association of University Women (2004). *Under the microscope: A decade of gender equity projects in the science.* Washington, DC: American Association of University Educational Foundation.

Andre, T., Whigham, M., Hendrickson, A., & Chambers, S. (1999). Competency beliefs, positive affect, and gender stereotypes of elementary students and their parents about science versus other school subjects. *Journal of Research in Science Teaching, 36,* 719–747.

Bae, Y., Choy, S., Geddes, C., Sable, J., & Snyder, T. (2000). *Trends in educational equity of girls and women* (NCES 2000-030). Washington, DC: U.S. Department of Education.

Barton, B. K., & Cohen, R. (2004). Classroom gender composition and children's peer relations. *Child Study Journal, 34,* 29–46.

Benbow, C. P., & Stanley, J. C. (1980). Sex differences in mathematical ability: Fact or artifact? *Science, 210,* 1262–1264.

Bleeker, M. M., & Jacobs, J. E. (2004). Achievement in math and science: Do mothers' beliefs matter 12 years later? *Journal of Educational Psychology, 96,* 97–109.

Brown, L. M., & Gilligan, C. (1992). *Meeting at the crossroads: Women's psychology and girls' development.* Cambridge, MA: Harvard University Press.

Campbell, J. R., Hombo, C. M., & Mazzeo, J. (2000). *NAEP 1999 trends in academic progress: Three decades of student performance.* Washington, DC: U.S. Department of Education, Office of Educational Research and Improvement, National Center for Education Statistics.

Campbell, P. B., Bachmann, K. A., & Steinbrueck, K. (1996). *Tools are cool and so am I: The impact of family tools and technology on girls and boys: Executive summary.* Available: http://www.campbell-kibler.com/fttabs.htm

ChildTrends DataBank. (2002). *Dropout rates.* Available: http://www.childtrendsdatabank.org

Coley, R. J. (2001). *Differences in the gender gap: Comparisons across racial/ethnic groups in education and work.* Princeton, NJ: Educational Testing Service.

Coley, R. J. (2002). *An uneven start: Indicators of inequality in school readiness.* Princeton, NJ: Educational Testing Service.

College Board (2004). *2004 college bound seniors: A profile of SAT program test-takers.* Princeton, NJ: College Board.

Connell, D., & Gunzelmann, B. (2004). The new gender gap: Why are so many boys floundering while so many girls are soaring? *Instruction, 113*(6), 14–17.

Daly, C. (n.d.) *Literature search on improving boys' writing.* Office for Standards in Education. Retrieved May 10, 2005, from http://www.ofsted.gov.uk/publications/docs/3401.pdf

Datnow, A., Hubbard, L., & Woody, E. (2001). *Is single gender schooling viable in the public sector? Lessons from California's pilot program. Final report.* Toronto: Ontario Institute for Studies in Education.

Dwyer, C. A., & Johnson, L. M. (1997). Grades, accomplishments, and correlates. In W. Willingham & N. S. Cole (Eds.), *Gender and fair assessment* (pp. 127–156). Mahwah, NJ: Erlbaum.

Eccles, J. S., & Jacobs, J. E. (1986). Social forces shape math attitudes and performance. *Journal of Women in Culture and Society, 11,* 367–380.

Eccles (Parsons), J., Adler, T. F., Futterman, R., Goff, S. B., Kaczala, C. M., Meece, J. L., & Midgley, C. (1983). Expectancies, values, and academic behaviors. In J. T. Spence (Ed.), *Achievement and achievement motivation* (pp. 74–146). San Francisco: Freeman.

Eccles-Parsons, J. S., Adler, T. F., & Kaczala, C. M. (1982). Socialization of achievement attitudes and beliefs: Parental influences. *Child Development, 53,* 310–321.

Evans, L., & Davies, K. (2000). No sissy boys here: A content analysis of the representation of masculinity in elementary school reading textbooks. *Sex Roles, 42,* 255–270.

Fennema, E. (1990). Teachers' beliefs and gender differences in mathematics. In E. Fennema & G. Leder (Eds.), *Mathematics and gender* (pp. 10–26). New York: Teachers College Press.

Freeman, C. E. (2005). *Trends in educational equity of girls & women: 2004* (NCES 2005-016). Washington, DC: U.S. Department of Education, National Center for Education Statistics.

Gentry, M., Gable, R. K., & Rizza, M. G. (2002). Students' perceptions of classroom activities: Are there grade-level and gender differences? *Journal of Educational Psychology, 94,* 539–544.

Gogtay, N., Giedd, J. N., Lusk, L., Hayashi, K. M., Greenstein, D., Vaituzis, A. C., et al. (2004). Dynamic mapping of human cortical development during childhood through early adulthood. *Proceedings of the National Academy of Sciences 101,* 8174–8179.

Gurian, M. (1996). *The wonder of boys.* New York: Tarcher/Putnam.

Haag, O. (2000). Single sex education: What does the research say? *ERIC Digest:* ED444758.

Halpern, D. F. (1997). Sex differences in intelligence: Implications for education. *American Psychologist, 52,* 1091–1102.

Hoff Sommers, C. (2000). *The war against boys: How misguided feminism is harming our young men.* New York: Simon & Schuster.

Jacobs, J. E. (1991). Influence of gender stereotypes on parent and child mathematics attitudes. *Journal of Educational Psychology, 83,* 518–527.

Jacobs, J. E., & Eccles, J. S. (1992). The impact of mothers' gender-role stereotypic beliefs on mothers' and children's ability perceptions. *Journal of Personality and Social Psychology, 63,* 932–944.

Jacobs, J. E., & Eccles, J. S. (2000). Parents, task values, and real-life achievement-related choices. In C. Sansone & J. M. Harackiewicz (Eds.), *Intrinsic and extrinsic motivation: The search for optimal motivation and performance* (pp. 405–439). San Diego, CA: Academic Press.

Jacobs, J. E., Lanza, S., Osgood, D. W., Eccles, J. S., & Wigfield, A. (2002). Changes in children's self competence and values: Gender and domain differences across grades one through twelve. *Child Development, 73,* 509–527.

Karnes, F. A., & Shaunessy, E. (2003). *State of the states: Gifted and talented education report.* Washington, DC: National Association for Gifted Children.

Kindlon, D., & Thompson, M. (1999). *Raising Cain: Protecting the emotional life of boys.* New York: Ballantine Books.

Kleinfeld, J. S. (1998). *The myth that schools shortchange girls: Social science in the service of deception.* Washington, DC: The Women's Freedom Network.

Losen, D., & Orfield, G. (2002). *Racial inequity in special education.* Cambridge, MA: Harvard University Publishing Group.

Martin, R. P., Wisenbaker, J., Baker, J., & Huttunen, M. (1997). Gender differences in temperament at six months and five years. *Infant Behavior and Development, 20,* 339–347.

McClanahan, A. (2002). *2002 kindergarten survey report: Readiness to learn.* Salem, OR: Oregon Department of Education.

McCoy, A. R., & Reynolds, A. J. (1999). Grade retention and school performance: An extended investigation. *Journal of School Psychology, 37,* 273–298.

Meadows, S. O., Land, K. C., & Lamb, V. L. (2005). Assessing Gillian vs. Sommers: Gender-specific trends in child and youth well-being in the United States, 1985–2001. *Social Indicators Research, 70,* 1–52.

Morrow, C., & Morrow, J. (1992). Whose math is it anyway? Giving girls a chance to take charge of their math learning. *Initiatives, 55*(3), 49–59.

Ontario Ministry of Education (2003). *Me read? No way! A practical guide to improving boys' literacy skills.* Ontario: Author. Available: http://www.edu.gov.on.ca/eng/document/brochure/meread/meread.pdf

Parker, L. H., & Rennie, L. J. (2002). Teachers' implementation of gender-inclusive instructional strategies in single-sex and mixed-sex science classrooms. *Instructional Journal of Science of Education, 24,* 881–897.

Perkins, R., Kleiner, B., Roey, S., & Brown, J. (2004). *The high school transcript study: A decade of change in curricula and achievement, 1990–2000* (NCES 2004-455). Washington, DC: U.S. Department of Education, National Center for Education Statistics.

Pollock, W. (1998). *Real boys: Rescuing our boys from the myths of boyhood.* New York: Random House.

Pomerantz, E. M., Altermatt, E. R., & Saxon, J. L. (2002). Making the grade but feeling distressed: Gender differences in academic performance and internal distress. *Journal of Educational Psychology, 94,* 396–404.

Raffaele Mendez, L. M., & Knoff, H. M. (2003). Who gets suspended from school and why: A demographic analysis of school and disciplinary infractions in a large school district. *Education and Treatment of Children, 26,* 30–51.

Raffaele Mendez, L. M., Knoff, H. M., & Ferron, J. M. (2002). School demographic variables and out-of-school suspension rates: A quantitative and qualitative analysis of a large, ethnically diverse school district. *Psychology in the Schools, 39,* 259–277.

Rawson, M., & Rose, M. (2002). *Ready to learn: From birth to school readiness.* Stroud: Hawthorn Press.

Roderick, M. (2003). What's happening to the boys? Early high school experiences and school outcomes among African American male adolescents in Chicago. *Urban Education, 38,* 538–607.

Sadker, M., & Sadker, D. (1994). *Failing at fairness: How America's schools cheat girls.* New York: Simon & Schuster.

Sax, L. (2005). *Why gender matters: What parents and teachers need to know about the emerging science of sex differences.* New York: Doubleday.

Shepard, L. A., & Smith, M. L. (1988). Escalating academic demand in kindergarten: Counterproductive policies. *Elementary School Journal, 89,* 135–145.

Sherman, J. (1983). Girls talk about mathematics and their future: A partial replication. *Psychology of Women Quarterly, 7,* 338–342.

Swanson, C. B. (2003). *Who graduates? Who doesn't? A statistical portrait of public high school graduation, class of 2001.* Washington, DC: The Urban Institute.

Younger, M., & Warrington, M. (2002). Single sex teaching in a co-educational comprehensive school in England: An evaluation based upon students' performance and classroom interactions. *British Educational Research Journal, 28,* 353–374.

Zill, J., & West, N. (2001). *Entering kindergarten: A portrait of American children when they begin school: Findings from the condition of education 2000* (NCES 2001-035). U.S. Department of Education, NCES. Washington, DC: U.S. Government Printing Office.

# 43

# Ethnic and Racial Diversity

**Craig L. Frisby**
*University of Missouri*

In *Children's Needs II* (Bear, Minke, & Thomas, 1997), this chapter summarized critical issues related to the biological concept of race and the psychosocial concept of ethnicity. The chapter summarized universal problems that disproportionately affect groups (e.g., childbirth, family, health, and mortality statistics; and intelligence and academic achievement disparities) and problems unique to the psychology of race and ethnicity in the context of American schooling (self-esteem, acculturation, and ethnic identity issues). Intervention material focused on select school curriculum, testing, and assessment issues.

The current chapter updates relevant statistical information using the 2000 Census. In addition, this update describes popular ideas that have little or no empirical support for raising and sustaining the academic achievement of ethnically and racially diverse populations in schools to any significant degree. In the remaining sections, the chapter highlights empirically supported prevention and intervention practices for strengthening school learning for all children.

## BACKGROUND AND DEVELOPMENT

Racial and ethnic categories, as indicated in government census reports, are not anthropologically or scientifically based, but are sociopolitical constructs. Every 10 years or so, the U.S. Census Bureau collects detailed census data on ethnic and racial groups, primarily for the purpose of enforcing civil rights laws related, but not limited to, housing, education, and employment. The 1990 census categories for racial and ethnic groups have come under increasing criticism from advocates who believe that these categories do not reflect the increasing diversity in America, which has resulted primarily from growth in immigration and interracial marriages (Snipp, 2003). In response to the criticisms, the U.S. Office of Management and Budget (OMB) announced in July 1993 that it would undertake a comprehensive review of the current categories for data on race and ethnicity. Following the report of the Interagency Committee for the Review of the Racial and Ethnic Standards, in 1997 the OMB revised its Statistical Policy Directive No. 15 (Race and Ethnic Standards for Federal Statistics and Administrative Reporting).

As a result of these changes (for an extensive account, see Snipp, 2003), the 2000 Census survey asked each respondent to answer two questions regarding race and ethnicity. The first question asked the respondent to indicate whether or not they identify themselves as Spanish, Hispanic, or Latino (regardless of race). Approximately 12% of the American population indicated their ethnicity as "Hispanic or Latino," and 87% selected "Not Hispanic or Latino." The second question asked respondents to identify their racial group from six categories. These six categories, and their approximate percentages in the American population as indicated in the 2000 Census, are given below (Grieco & Cassidy, 2001):

- "White Only" (approximately 75%) refers to people having origins in any of the original peoples of Europe, the Middle East, or North Africa. It includes people who indicated their race or races as "White" or wrote in entries such as Irish, German, Italian, Lebanese, Near Easterner, Arab, or Polish.
- "Black or African American Only" (approximately 12%) refers to people having origins in any of the Black racial groups of Africa. It includes people who indicated their race or races as "Black, African American, or Negro," or wrote in entries such as a Nigerian or Haitian.

- "American Indian and Alaska Native Only" (approximately 0.9%) refers to people who have origins in any of the original peoples of North and South America (including Central America) and who maintain tribal affiliation or community attachment. It includes people who indicated their race or races by marking this category or writing in their principal or enrolled tribe, such as Rosebud Sioux, Chippewa, or Navajo.
- "Asian Only" (approximately 3%) refers to people having origins in any of the original peoples of the Far East, Southeast Asia, or the Indian subcontinent. It includes people who indicated their race or races as "Asian Indian," "Chinese," "Filipino," "Korean," "Japanese," "Vietnamese," or "Other Asian," or who wrote in entries such as Burmese, Hmong, Pakistani, or Thai.
- "Native Hawaiian and Other Pacific Islander Only" (approximately 0.1%) refers to people having origins in any of the original peoples of Hawaii, Guam, Samoa, or other Pacific Islands. It includes people who indicated their race or races as "Native Hawaiian," "Guamanian or Chamorro," "Samoan," or "Other Pacific Islander," or who wrote in entries such as Tahitian, Mariana Islander, or Chuukese.
- The category "Some Other Race Only" (approximately 5%) is included for respondents who were unable to identify with the five previous racial categories. This category also includes respondents who provided write-in entries (e.g., Moroccan, South African, Belizean, Mexican, or Cuban).

Race and ethnicity data from the 1990 Census is not directly comparable to 2000 Census data, since 2000 Census respondents were given the option of selecting "two or more races" to indicate their racial identities (approximately 2%).

Ethnicity is a much more psychologically and socially complex concept than what is indicated on the 2000 Census (for distinguishing features of ethnicity as a concept, see this chapter in *Children's Needs II*). According to the *Harvard Encyclopedia of Ethnic Groups* (Thernstrom, 1980), America hosts more than 100 distinct ethnic groups that constantly evolve, merge, and in some cases dissolve over time. Distinctions between ethnic groups are the result of a complex interplay between geographic origins, migratory status, race, language or dialect, religious faith, shared traditions, literature, folklore, music, food preferences, settlement and employment patterns, political interests, group maintenance institutions, perceptions of ethnic distinctiveness that are internal to a group, and perceptions of ethnic distinctiveness that are external to the group.

## PROBLEMS AND IMPLICATIONS

In the previous edition of this chapter, the point was made, and bears repeating here, that racial and ethnic diversity is not inherently a "problem" in itself. America has always been popularly described as a nation of immigrants. Although social and political tensions between groups can be found in all countries, the United States serves as an example to the world in efforts to accommodate diverse groups into the American mosaic. Civil rights and antidiscrimination laws are a common fixture of local, state, and federal governments. Although ethnic and racial prejudice exist to varying degrees in all societies, the open display of malice toward "outgroups" is socially unacceptable in American society and is aggressively ostracized and publicly condemned whenever it occurs in civic life. The contributions of a variety of cultural groups can be easily identified in American literature, gourmet cuisine, popular music, high fashion, sports, and the entertainment media.

Despite this encouraging picture, the issue that vexes educators involves seemingly intractable social problems (e.g., illegal immigration, poor English language proficiency, poverty and its correlates, chronic welfare dependency, out-of-wedlock births, fatherless households, prison and juvenile justice involvement, and drug or alcohol addiction) that are disproportionately represented across various ethnic and racial groups. Many of these problems are well beyond the school's control and require commonsense solutions that schools cannot provide. Stated bluntly, the optimal solution for a chronically absent father is a reliable and loving father in the home. Most school-based interventions designed to address the fallout from these problems must compensate by necessarily involving intentional efforts to promote positive interactions between teachers and students (see chapter 5, "Student–Teacher Relationships") and to raise students' and parents' sense of engagement with schools (see chapter 4, "School Engagement"). In addition, help, expertise, and resources outside of the educational system are crucial in addressing serious social problems. For example, the social services, mental health, and criminal justice systems often play important roles in helping at-risk ethnic and racial minority families (Gansle & Pogue, 2005).

## Indicators of Academic Achievement

Academic disparities across racial and ethnic groups are a constant source of hand-wringing and frustration among educators (Borman, Stringfield, & Rachuba, 2000; Thernstrom & Thernstrom, 2003). Arguably, no other country in the world has equaled the United States in its efforts to increase the academic achievement and to facilitate the school adjustment of low-performing and unsuccessful children and youth, many (but not all) of whom are ethnic and racial minorities.

It is not uncommon to encounter claims (from the research literature, lay public, or popular media) that a certain intervention has demonstrated "increased school achievement" among racial and ethnic minority students. For example, Gay (2000) favorably reviewed literacy programs for ethnic minority students, "culture-centered" schools, and research on ethnic minority students' involvement in cooperative learning studies. At the conclusion of this review, she wrote the following:

> When instructional processes are consistent with the cultural orientations, experiences, and learning styles of marginalized African, Latino, Native, and Asian American students, their school achievement improves significantly. (p. 181)

The proper evaluation of such claims require, among other things, a recognition that *school achievement* is an umbrella term that can refer to a wide variety of indicators. These indicators include, but are not limited to, student rates of participation in particular classroom activities, school truancy rates, frequency of school absences, school dropout and graduation rates, rates of homework completion, number of pages read in reading material, number of items completed in math worksheets, and school grades. For large-scale education research, however, the most objective method for determining an intervention's impact on academic achievement is by examining changes in scores on standardized academic achievement tests.

## Three Popular Myths About Raising Academic Achievement

The school psychology, educational psychology, and teacher education literatures are replete with opinions that purport to explain the reasons and remedies for disproportionately low achievement among cultural minority groups. Some of these opinions are formed from the empirical literature and are supported by a solid body of replicable and well-executed research studies. Unfortunately, too many of these explanations are little more than myths, and so-called remedies based on these myths inevitably reveal themselves as dead-ends, in the sense that they consistently fail to raise to a significant degree, and sustain, the academic achievement (as measured by standardized achievement tests) of cultural minority groups.

This is not to suggest that remedies that fail to raise academic achievement cannot lead to measurable benefits in other important domains (e.g., reduced truancy or increased graduation rates). Fundamentally, however, myths are ideas that have little to no evidence to support significant, long-lasting gains in standardized academic achievement test scores. Second, evidence that is presented in support of these ideas repeatedly withers when subjected to empirical scrutiny. Third, proponents of these ideas have no credible rebuttals to the evidence that contradicts claims of increased academic achievement. Nevertheless, for a variety of reasons these ideas resonate effortlessly with education audiences and the lay public, have an unusually long shelf life in scholarly journals, and may even be currently promulgated and celebrated as "best practice" in school psychology and teacher education training programs. Three popular myths for raising academic achievement that have a direct relevance to school psychology (or any profession interested in the psychological foundations of education) are briefly summarized below.

***Myth 1: Multicultural education increases academic achievement of pupils from ethnic or racial minority groups.*** Multicultural education is an ideological movement whose origins can be traced to the late 19th century. According to Marshall (2002), the term *multicultural education* was first introduced widely within American teacher education in the 1970s and experienced explosive growth during the 1990s. Multicultural education has been defined differently by different educators (e.g., Davidman & Davidman, 1994; Sleeter & Grant, 1994). According to one of its leading proponents (Banks, 1995), however, the broad goals of multicultural education are to (a) reform school curricula by redefining the content and organization of basic school subjects to include the contribution of various cultural groups; (b) design instruction that assists students in recognizing cultural assumptions, frames of reference, biases, and perspectives that inform knowledge encountered in the classroom; (c) eliminate and/or reduce attitudes, beliefs, and worldviews based in racism, sexism, and other forms of bigotry; (d) adapt teaching and instruction to the cultural characteristics of students when necessary; and (e) restructure the culture and organization of the school so that students from diverse racial, ethnic, and social-class groups will experience equality and empowerment.

Writers who are sympathetic to multiculturalism ideology typically blame the disproportionate educational problems of cultural minority groups on a "cultural discontinuity" between the home and the school (e.g., Allen & Boykin, 1992). The implicit (and sometimes explicit) assumption is that when multicultural education is consistently applied in schools in the manner intended by its advocates, improvements in self-esteem, ethnic identity, intergroup relations, and school achievement should naturally occur. Gay (2000) wrote:

> Culturally responsive practices unveil some solutions to the seemingly unsolvable mystery of the perpetual underachievement of marginalized students of color. They are not being taught in school as they learn in their cultural communities. This discontinuity interrupts their mental schemata and makes academic learning harder to achieve. (p.182)

The problem here is that there is no universal consensus as to how multicultural education can be operationalized in classroom or school settings. Multicultural education refers to anything from teaching an occasional unit on foods and customs from other lands, to altering textbooks to include contributions of ethnic groups, to incorporating classroom cooperative learning activities, to creating "cultural immersion" schools that marinate students in a particular cultural heritage, and everything in between. Articles in favor of multicultural education usually consist of conceptual pieces, advocacy articles, criticisms of educational practices, isolated program descriptions, or anecdotal stories (Sleeter & Grant, 1987; Stotsky, 1999). Critical reviews of multicultural education research reveal that rigorous evaluation studies of outcomes in actual K–12 classrooms are virtually nonexistent (Gay, 1994; Sleeter & Grant, 1987) or display meager positive effects (see Stotsky, 1999).

Virtually no rigorous and replicable experimental studies—with objectively defined variables and appropriate control groups—examine the effects of multicultural education on standardized academic achievement test scores. National Assessment of Educational Progress (NAEP) data showed no relationship between the infusion of multiculturalism in reading textbooks and improvement in minority children's NAEP test scores (Stotsky, 1999).

The important point to be made is not whether multicultural education is morally or philosophically preferable to other forms of education for cultural minority students, as this debate will ultimately be resolved (if it is at all) on ideological, not empirical, grounds. The essential point addressed here is whether multicultural education is a necessary or even sufficient ingredient for increasing and sustaining academic school achievement (evaluated through changes in scores on group-administered standardized achievement tests) of groups for whom it is designed. To date, there is little reliable research evidence that inspires confidence in this conclusion. Some evidence even suggests that multicultural education is an irrelevant factor for school success (e.g., Sowell, 1986, 2002).

***Myth 2: Adapting instruction to each student's culturally based learning style increases academic achievement.*** Teacher training programs typically encourage the individualization of learning and instruction in the classroom. The concept of a "learning style" is frequently touted as an important variable to which teachers must pay attention (Reiff, 2000). A *learning style* can be thought of as habitual patterns, consistent over long periods of time and across many areas of activity, in how a person learns or prefers to learn (Sternberg & Grigorenko, 2001). Most learning styles are identified through self-report paper-and-pencil survey instruments. According to Kane and Boan (2005), more than 3,000 manuscripts have been published on the topic of learning styles since the 1960s. According to received wisdom, teachers maximize students' potential for academic success if they adapt their teaching or instruction to a student's identified learning style.

A related idea, perpetuated among some learning style theorists, is the notion that reliable differences in learning style are associated with differences in learners' racial and ethnic background (for summaries of this research, see Kane & Boan, 2005). Disproportionate school failure among non-White students is often attributed to the failure of contemporary education to be sensitive to, and subsequently base instruction on, students' culturally based learning styles (Dunn & Griggs, 1995; Hale-Benson, 1986).

Despite its intuitive appeal, the use of culturally based learning styles as a means of discovering interventions that would raise academic achievement is both conceptually and empirically problematic (for extended discussion and relevant citations, see Frisby, 1993; Irvine & York, 1995; Kane & Boan, 2005; Kavale, Hirshoren, & Forness, 1998). Learning style theory ignores results from traditional research on the effects of general intelligence on learning and academic achievement (e.g., Jensen, 1989), and hence it fails to persuasively defend its added value in explaining learning problems. Distinguishing features that discriminate between different learning style models are based more on semantic descriptions, rather than on results from empirical investigations. Learning style models appear to be "instrument bound," which limits the generalizability of findings.

Independent empirical validation for many learning style instruments is poor, and evaluations that are done do not support the reliability, construct, or predictive validity of these instruments. Weaknesses of self-reported measures of learning style models include respondents' inability to accurately or objectively report behavior as well as social desirability effects. Given the sheer number of different learning style models and dimensions within models, adapting classroom instruction to students' identified learning styles in large classrooms is extremely unwieldy. The assumption that students can learn only through their identified learning styles, or that achievement is facilitated if classroom instruction is matched to students' identified learning styles, is unsupported by a consistent program of research and in some cases is contradicted by numerous case studies (e.g., Carter, 2000). Ethnic and racial groups are not homogeneous, and learning traits overlap across groups. Associating differences in learning style with racial, ethnic, and sex differences involves gross stereotyping that misleads educators.

***Myth 3: The use of alternative (as opposed to traditional) assessment for native-born English speakers will reveal previously hidden evidence of academic achievement.*** Performance on individually administered tests of cognitive ability and academic skills are in themselves forms of academic achievement. Long-standing ethnic and racial group differences in mean scores on these tests are well established (Jensen, 1998). Part of the controversy surrounding the use of tests in educational decision making concerns whether score differences merely reflect trait differences, or whether artifacts of the tests cause these differences in mean scores. Those who hold the latter view accuse traditional tests of various forms of bias (see Brown, Reynolds, & Whitaker, 1999). Presuming bias is the cause, test critics have responded to this challenge in four basic ways. First, some have attempted to design traditional tests with modified content to eliminate or reduce mean group differences in test scores (see Jensen, 1980, 1984). Second, some have designed nontraditional procedures that substantially alter the test content or modify the manner in which tests are administered or scored, which presumably provides a fairer assessment to culturally different test takers (e.g., see Armour-Thomas & Gopaul-McNicol, 1998). Third, some have used traditional tests but artificially manipulated the scoring or interpretation of scores to equalize results (e.g., System of Multicultural Pluralistic Assessment; "race norming"). Fourth, some have sought to drastically reduce or eliminate the use of standardized intelligence or academic achievement tests and to replace these with problem solving using curriculum-based, portfolio, or "authentic" assessment (Braden, 1999; Shinn, Collins, & Gallagher, 1998).

Although alternative methods have limited advantages in particular situations (see the discussion of curriculum-based assessment and curriculum-based measurement by VanDerHeyden & Burns, 2005), they have by and large failed to provide convincing evidence that bias or cultural insensitivity in traditional test design, administration, or interpretation is responsible for group differences in mean scores. A thorough analysis of these failures is well beyond the scope of this chapter. However, the following broad observations have been noted (see Braden, 1999; Brown, Reynolds, & Whitaker, 1999; Frisby, 1999, 2005; Gottfredson, 2000; Jensen, 1980; Kranzler, Miller, & Jordan, 1999):

- Alternative methods continue to display ethnic or racial group differences in scores, with some of these discrepancies being either larger or smaller compared with those found on traditional tests.
- Efforts to reduce group differences on traditional tests by modifying the content require a reduction in the $g$ loading of test content. When the $g$ loading of test content is reduced, predictive validity for important outcomes is also compromised.
- Assessment methods that stray too far from the design of traditional testing (either in their content, administration, or scoring) not only have been shown to be psychometrically weaker, but are viewed as too cumbersome and inefficient for widespread use in schools.
- Attempts to hide group differences may solve an immediate political problem, but these differences will nevertheless show up in other academic domains.

## The Perennial Paradox

These prescriptions for raising academic achievement are rooted in an implicit belief in, and subsequent search for, a "culture x treatment interaction" in American education. A *culture x treatment interaction* refers to the idea that culturally specific counseling, instructional, curricular, and assessment methods exist, that if matched to learners from targeted racial and ethnic backgrounds, would significantly and consistently lead to improved outcomes among such learners *over and above* what would be the case if such methods were not used. Many scholars express frustration that they cannot find a large body of literature that identifies "culturally specific" prescriptions for raising academic achievement for racially and ethnically diverse learners. The irony here is that this literature indeed exists, but much of it is not explicitly advertised as culturally specific (with the possible exception of situations involving English language learners; see chapter 49). For example, a research study may show significant positive effects for a school sample consisting of culturally different learners. However, because these learners did not constitute the majority of the sample, the study is not explicitly advertised as being effective with culturally different learners—which causes it to be overlooked by those looking for practices that help cultural minority children. Many factors that are most supportive of maximizing academic achievement have universal applications and can be discovered most readily in the literature on effective schools. Nevertheless, educators and psychological support personnel must also be aware of political, ideological, and cultural issues that are inevitably intertwined with this literature. This chapter addresses these issues in the following sections.

# ALTERNATIVE ACTIONS FOR PREVENTION AND INTERVENTION

Before discussing promising practices, a distinction first should be made between the concept of *maximizing* the achievement of traditionally low-performing groups versus *equalizing* achievement between all racial and ethnic groups (summarized in the popular catchphrase "closing the achievement gap"). These two are not to be confused. Differences in average levels of school achievement will continue to be a reality as long as there are mean subpopulation differences in cognitive ability (for a detailed discussion, see Gottfredson, 2005, and Jensen, 1998). The following review summarizes school- and classroom-level variables that most effectively neutralize negative influences on the academic achievement for racially and ethnically diverse children and youth.

## School-Level Effects

Schools that serve predominantly low-income ethnic minority children are disproportionately plagued with discipline problems, violence, poor attendance, low student achievement, failure to attain basic literacy skills, lower levels of parental support, and are less likely to attract and retain excellent teachers (see Truscott & Truscott, 2005). These problems are particularly salient for African American, Hispanic, and Native American groups. Furthermore, several studies have demonstrated that the socioeconomic (SES) backgrounds of all students attending a school can have an effect on student achievement *over* and *above* the effects associated with students' individual social class or ability (Teddlie & Reynolds, 2000). Fortunately, high-achieving, low-income minority (primarily Black) schools with higher-than-expected achievement have been studied extensively (e.g., see reviews by Brookover et al., 1982). The following characteristics exemplify these effective schools, particularly at the elementary level.

Effective schools for low-income urban minority students are characterized by themes in the general beliefs, norms, expectations, and feelings that pervade the school (i.e., the school's "ideology"). Among the school staff, there is "buy-in" to the belief that mastery of instruction objectives is the top priority, accompanied by the feeling that school-wide performance on achievement tests is an appropriate goal and measure of school success. The staff have a sense of high efficacy in their ability to instruct students in the school objectives, an expectation that all students will reach high standards of achievement commensurate with their capabilities, and that all students can learn school objectives (e.g., see Carter, 2000). Students in effective schools are aware of high performance expectations for all students, and they reinforce achievement norms among their peers. Students possess a belief in their ability to learn and have a low sense of "academic futility" (i.e., the perception that nothing one does will make a difference in school).

The organizational structure of effective schools defines role expectations for appropriate behavior primarily in terms of academic achievement; that is, the effective teacher instructs all students to high achievement, the "good student" is a high achiever, the effective principal is an instructional leader who promotes effective instruction, and good parent involvement facilitates the school's achievement goals. It follows, then, that the staff and student reward structure within the school is centered on achievement. In effective schools, differentiation of the instructional program is minimal—common instructional objectives, common expectations, and common instructional materials are used for all students. Flexible heterogeneous grouping is used rather than homogeneous segregation of students by ability, race, or socioeconomic status. Testing programs are used for diagnosis of learning rather than for sorting and selecting between levels of students. Compensatory and special education programs help students catch up to grade level and are conducted in and coordinated with the regular classroom.

Effective schools have orderly, relatively quiet, work-oriented environments. Each grade level has clearly stated standards for mastery, as well as procedures for certifying attainment of those standards. Academic competition is used to promote peer learning, and effective use of reinforcement principles promotes appropriate learning conduct. A high percentage of the total school day involves "academic engaged time" for all students. Assessment data are used effectively. Ongoing monitoring of student progress includes diagnosing problems and giving students regular feedback (for corrective instruction). Accurate record keeping of mastery of objectives by all students is required. School-wide data are used for evaluating and improving the school's instructional program.

Conclusions from the school effectiveness literature are not without critics of these principles. Stedman (1987) reviewed school effectiveness studies prior to the late 1980s and found that many schools serving low-income minority children that adopted the principles of effective schools still had a majority of students performing below grade level. Others have argued that this literature fails to appreciate the unique context variables associated with schools that are not situated in low SES urban settings.

With respect to this latter issue, Teddlie and Stringfield (1993) reviewed research that shifted the emphasis to the effects of context variables (e.g., SES; rural, suburban, or urban setting; or grade level) in influencing school effectiveness. Variables such as a clear academic mission and focus, an orderly environment, high levels of academic engaged time on-task, and frequent monitoring of student progress were found across all schools. However, the following characteristics distinguished effective low SES schools from effective middle SES schools:

- Low SES schools promoted high expectations for students' present academic behavior, whereas middle SES schools promoted high expectations for both present and future academic achievement (e.g., going to college).
- Low SES principals tended to take a directive role in the selection, development, and implementation of instructional and curricular programs, whereas middle SES principals exercised less direct control over classroom instruction.
- Low SES schools emphasized external reward structures for academic achievement for the purpose of helping high-achieving students to feel special. In contrast, middle SES schools de-emphasized external rewards for academic achievement, since achievement motivation is more frequently fostered in the home environment.
- Low SES schools tended to focus on basic skills first, with other curricular offerings offered after basic skills have been mastered. In contrast, middle SES schools offered expanded curricula beyond the basic skills.
- Low SES schools, situated within the context of toxic environments, tended to create boundaries to buffer the school against negative influences from the surrounding community. In contrast, middle SES schools tended to encourage contact and collaboration between the community and the schools.
- Low SES schools tended to have principals who exercised authority in hiring younger, more idealistic teachers, whereas middle SES schools tended to hire more experienced teachers.

## Classroom-Level Effects

Teachers in more effective schools have also demonstrated more effective teaching behaviors relative to teachers in less effective schools (see reviews by Teddlie & Reynolds, 2000). VanDerHeyden and Burns (2005) reviewed research applicable to effective instruction for at-risk minority populations. Consistent with the theme of this chapter, they do not conceptualize the topic as a search for "culturally specific" interventions. Rather, intervention is considered "multicultural" if research demonstrates its efficacy for all children from diverse backgrounds and in diverse settings. According to VanDerHeyden's and Burns' literature review, empirically supported effective classroom instruction for all students involves a triumvirate of task-centered, instruction-centered, and student-centered variables.

With respect to task variables, research consistently shows that children who are taught at their instructional level show gains in rates of task completion, task comprehension, and on-task behavior. Here, *instructional level* is enhanced when the match between the ratio of known to unknown units of a task and a student's prior skill levels allows for successful task completion and new learning (VanDerHeyden & Burns, 2005).

Instructional variables can be manipulated to maximize learning outcomes for all students. Teaching prerequisite skills, and selecting and sequencing appropriate examples (and, when necessary, nonexamples) during instruction, facilitates classroom learning. Reducing lectures into smaller units, and allowing student practice after each unit, improves acquisition and retention of lesson content. Increased retention and understanding of new material occurs when learners are taught using instructional units (called instructional sets) determined by their individual skill levels. The proportion of instructional time allocated to a content area during which students are actively and productively engaged in learning (called academic learning time, or ALT) has been shown to result in improved outcomes. Many techniques have been effective in increasing ALT. For example, high rates of student compliance to teacher directions can be facilitated by interspersing easier problems with more difficult problems, interspersing preferred tasks with nonpreferred tasks, giving students instructional choices, teaching and using transition routines to organize student behavior and reduce disruptive behavior during transitions, and effectively manipulating group and individual contingencies to increase on-task behavior (VanDerHeyden & Burns, 2005).

Finally, classroom teachers, particularly at the elementary levels, have considerable influence in managing student behaviors and developing social and emotional competence related to academic achievement (see chapters 1 and 3, "Social and Emotional Learning" and "Developing Self-Discipline"). An orderly, safe classroom environment is a necessary precondition for learning to occur. None of the prescriptions for good classroom instruction are likely to be present, let alone have any effect, if there is chaos and mayhem in the classroom. For starters, teachers can increase students' opportunities to practice skills and receive feedback on performance, which is necessary for retention of newly learned skills and fluent performance. The use of paired peer practice (either as a supplement to or substitution for independent seatwork) has been shown to be effective for improving reading and math performance of low SES, ADHD, learning disabled, and average-achieving children (see review by VanDerHeyden & Burns, 2005; also see chapter 48, "Peer-Assisted Learning Strategies"). Academic gains have been linked to cooperative learning activities that include structured activities, individual accountability, frequent interaction and feedback between pairs of students, and reciprocity of tutoring roles. Teachers can also teach children strategies for completing homework that have been shown to increase both the frequency and quality of homework (VanDerHeyden & Burns, 2005).

## The Role of Cultural Awareness in Meeting the Academic Needs of Culturally Diverse Students

Aside from occasional references to socioeconomic status, previous discussions in this chapter about prescriptions for effective practices make no reference to cultural variables. This is because the assumption of a "culture x treatment interaction" (when culture is defined as equivalent to race or ethnicity) rests primarily on philosophical rather than empirical grounds.

According to Rogers et al. (1999), "to respond to the psychological and educational needs of this diverse clientele, psychologists must attain *cross-cultural competence* and develop specialized skills" (p. 244; emphasis added). Unfortunately, studies that attempt to empirically validate the construct of cross-cultural competence are scarce. In one such study (Cunningham, Foster, & Henggeler, 2002), researchers examined the degree of agreement between a group of peer-nominated experts in cultural competence and a group of therapists who were highly experienced in working with African American clients. Participants examined items from three psychotherapy process measures and were asked to rate the degree to which each item was pertinent to the construct of cultural competence. The researchers found minimal chance agreement among all pairwise combinations of participants across the two groups. They concluded that the "therapist experts did not exceed chance agreement in the classification of specific therapist behaviors into categories of behavior that comprise cultural competence from the perspective of the peer-nominated experts" (p. 236). Despite these disappointing results, the literature continues to promote the assumption that "cultural competence" is a conceptually coherent construct (e.g., Rogers et al., 1999).

For better or worse, most writers consider ethnic and racial differences as a convenient proxy for "cultural" differences (see Frisby, 2005, for problems inherent in this perspective). Readers who attempt to make sense of the voluminous writing on the role of culture in influencing academic achievement will find a bewildering array of conflicting and contradictory messages (see Thernstrom & Thernstrom, 2003, for an extended discussion). For example, multiculturalists blame educational inequities between groups on the lack of "culturally sensitive" practices among teachers and a cultural discontinuity between the home and school (e.g., Allen & Boykin, 1992). In this view, educators are obligated to adapt to the child's culture in order for the child to succeed educationally. In contrast, other researchers will appeal to maladaptive cultural traits as an explanation of why some groups fail to take advantage of educational opportunities to the same degree as other higher performing groups. According to this view, it is the child's natural cultural characteristics that hold him or her back from succeeding academically, which places the onus of responsibility on the child and family to adapt to the broader culture (Richardson, 2003). In other words, "culture" functions as a Rorschach inkblot on which researchers can project their prescriptions for effective interventions, even when such prescriptions blatantly contradict each other.

These confusions underscore the highly politicized nature of cultural issues in education. Since these conflicts show no signs of reaching consensus anytime soon, the best that educators and school psychologists can do is to understand the political realities of dealing with cultural issues in educational settings. Two important concepts reflect these political realities: the concept of "cultural brokerage," and the ideology of "cultural maintenance."

*Culture brokers* are individuals, groups, or organizations who enjoy a self-styled or self-conferred status as mediators between a cultural group (for whom the mediator presumes to represent or speak) and a wider audience whose opinion the mediator seeks to influence. In the academic community, cultural brokerage enjoys wide representation among authors who write for ethnically oriented psychology journals and textbooks. In many school districts serving culturally diverse communities, individual schools and district offices have positions for "multicultural coordinators," "school-community liaisons," or others in administrative and teaching positions whose roles are to mediate school–community communications or to influence decision making about the content of multicultural education and curricula. Culture brokers may or may not be members of the specific cultural groups served by the school. However, culture brokers who are members of the targeted cultural group are given a certain amount of credibility as spokespersons or advocates for the best interests of the group in question.

Although culture brokers are the source of advocacy related to cultural issues in educational settings, the ideology of *cultural maintenance* provides its content. Educators who promote cultural maintenance believe that the "culture" of certain racial and ethnic minority and immigrant groups should be protected from the Americanization process (i.e., too much identification with the broader American culture) by proactively fostering and preserving a separate group identity. Thus, cultural maintenance becomes a top priority that influences who is hired to work with cultural minority children in schools, the content of curriculum materials, how schools interact with parents, and the school's overall educational mission.

In August 2001, for example, the Northwest Regional Educational Laboratory convened a panel of American Indian and Alaska Native (AIAN) principals, superintendents, curriculum specialists, school counselors, and tribal education officials to discuss and provide recommendations for effective school practices for AIAN students (Northwest Regional Educational Laboratory, 2001). The panel devised a "comprehensive inventory of indicators for the school community environment" (p. 5). The indicators serve as markers that schools can use to evaluate whether they are "serving [AIAN] students and supporting their needs" (p. 7). They include items categorized into nine domains. School improvement committees evaluate the extent to which indicators within domains are significantly developed, are in the process of being developed, or are not present in their respective schools.

Two common cultural themes pervade all aspects of the panel's recommendations: *self-determination*, defined as the right of AIAN communities to determine their own educational goals and the steps taken to meet those goals, and trust between AIAN and non-AIAN communities. Owing to the perceived past history of broken treaties and government policies that forced assimilation, AIAN communities often harbor a natural distrust of outsiders, and they are particularly sensitive to signs of disrespect or attitudes of "cultural superiority." Outsiders are expected to earn the trust of AIAN communities and respect community needs for cultural and political sovereignty (Northwest Regional Educational Laboratory, 2001).

These same issues are not unique to AIAN communities, but can be found in any racial and ethnic minority school in which cultural brokerage and the ideology of cultural maintenance is strong. The discussion here is not about whether there is consensus as to the meaning of concepts such as "culturally appropriate leadership" or "culturally appropriate instruction," as consensus may very well be unattainable. What is important is that many educators *believe* these concepts to be real. As long as there is a critical mass of like-minded educators and decision makers, then school psychologists and other support personnel must be able to effectively adapt to these political realities.

## SUMMARY

Since the 1990 Census, government classification of racial and ethnic groups has adapted to the increasing complexity of American life. Ethnic and racial diversity is not problematic in and of itself, however social problems often co-vary with this diversity. In the educational realm, efforts to improve the academic achievement levels of certain groups relative to others have met with varying degrees of success (when *academic achievement* is defined broadly). Interventions such as multicultural education, adapting classroom instruction to cultural learning styles, and using alternative assessment techniques may be popular in the education and school psychology literatures, but they have not been empirically supported as effective interventions for raising standardized academic achievement scores.

Academic achievement levels between American racial and ethnic groups to date have not been fully equalized; however, the educational experience of all children can be maximized by applying results from sound research on instructional interventions. The most conservative proposals for helping all learners succeed can be found in the literature on effective schools. However, in educational settings in which the dual concepts of *cultural brokerage* and *cultural maintenance* are strong, educators and school psychologists must be sensitive to these political realities.

## RECOMMENDED RESOURCES

Frisby, C. L., & Reynolds, C. R. (Eds.). (2005). *Comprehensive handbook of multicultural school psychology.* New York: John Wiley.

This handbook is patterned after the *Handbook of School Psychology* in providing scholarly literature reviews on a variety of topics relevant to multicultural issues in school psychology. The focus of this handbook is on research related to the intersection of race, ethnicity, language, social class, religion, and geographical location with school psychology research and practice. Chapters cover topics related to educational and psychological foundations, testing and intervention issues, cultural variation within American families, and international school psychology.

Snipp, C. M. (2003). Racial measurement in the American census: Past practices and implications for the future. *Annual Review of Sociology, 29,* 563–588.

This article provides a brief but interesting historical overview of how racial and ethnic data are collected by the federal government. The circumstances leading up to structural changes in the 2000 Census are discussed, followed by a discussion of how these revisions may affect social scientific research on the subject of race and ethnicity.

Thernstrom, A., & Thernstrom, S. (2003). *No excuses: Closing the racial gap in learning.* New York: Simon & Schuster.

This text, written by seasoned researchers and senior fellows at the Manhattan Institute, marshals a wealth of facts documenting the academic achievement gap among American racial and ethnic groups. The inadequacy of conventional explanations is explored, coupled with sober assessments of the limited impact of Title 1, Head Start, bilingual education, and other intervention programs. Case study examples are provided that describe pockets of effective schooling for low-performing minority groups.

## REFERENCES

Allen, B. A., & Boykin, A. W. (1992). African-American children and the educational process: Alleviating culture discontinuity through prescriptive pedagogy. *School Psychology Review, 21,* 586–596.

Armour-Thomas, E., & Gopaul-McNicol, S. (1998). *Assessing intelligence.* Thousand Oaks, CA: Sage.

Banks, J. A. (1995). Multicultural education: Historical development, dimensions, and practice. In J. A. Banks & C. A. McGee Banks (Eds.), *Handbook of research on multicultural education* (pp. 3–24). New York: Macmillan.

Bear, G., Minke, K., & Thomas, A. (Eds.). (1997). *Children's needs II: Development, problems, & alternatives.* Bethesda, MD: National Association of School Psychologists.

Borman, G. D., Stringfield, S., & Rachuba, L. (2000). *National trends and promising programs and practices: A report prepared for the national task force on minority high achievement.* New York: College Entrance Examination Board.

Braden, J. P. (1999). Performance assessment and diversity. *School Psychology Quarterly, 14,* 304–326.

Brookover, W., Beamer, L., Efthim, H., Hathaway, D., Lezotte, L., Miller, S., et al. (1982). *Creating effective schools: An inservice program for enhancing school learning climate and achievement.* Holmes Beach, FL: Learning Publications.

Brown, R. T., Reynolds, C. R., & Whitaker, J. S. (1999). Bias in mental testing. *School Psychology Quarterly, 14,* 208–238.

Carter, S. C. (2000). *No excuses: Lessons from 21 high performing high poverty schools.* Washington, DC: Heritage Foundation.

Cunningham, P. B., Foster, S. L., & Henggeler, S. W. (2002). The elusive concept of cultural competence. *Children's Services: Social Policy, Research, and Practice, 5,* 231–243.

Davidman, L. M., & Davidman, P. T. (1994). *Teaching with a multicultural perspective.* New York: Longman.

Dunn, R., & Griggs, S. A. (1995). *Multiculturalism and learning style: Teaching and counseling adolescents.* Westport, CT: Praeger.

Frisby, C. L. (1993). One giant step backwards: Myths of black cultural learning styles. *School Psychology Review, 22,* 535–557.

Frisby, C. L. (1999). Culture and test session behavior: Part II. *School Psychology Quarterly, 14,* 281–303.

Frisby, C. L. (2005). The politics of multiculturalism in school psychology: Part II. In C. L. Frisby & C. Reynolds (Eds.), *Comprehensive handbook of multicultural school psychology* (pp. 81–136). New York: John Wiley.

Gansle, K., & Pogue, R. (2005). Successful community programs for youth in multicultural environments. In C. Frisby & C. Reynolds (Eds.), *Comprehensive handbook of multicultural school psychology* (pp. 973–992). New York: John Wiley.

Gay, G. (1994). *Urban monograph series: A synthesis of scholarship in multicultural education.* Oakbrook, IL: North Central Regional Education Lab.

Gay, G. (2000). *Culturally responsive teaching: Theory, research, and practice.* New York: Teachers College Press.

Gottfredson, L. (2000). Skills gaps, not tests, make racial proportionality impossible. *Psychology, Public Policy, and Law, 6,* 129–143.

Gottfredson, L. (2005). Implications of cognitive differences for schooling within diverse societies. In C. Frisby & C. Reynolds (Eds.), *Comprehensive handbook of multicultural school psychology* (pp. 517–554). New York: John Wiley.

Grieco, E. M., & Cassidy, R. C. (2001). Overview of race and Hispanic origin: Census 2000 brief. Retrieved December 13, 2004, from http://www.census.gov/prod/2001pubs/c2kbr01-1.pdf

Hale-Benson, J. E. (1986). *Black children: Their roots, culture, and learning styles.* Baltimore: Johns Hopkins University Press.

Irvine, J., & York, D. E. (1995). Learning styles and culturally diverse students: A literature review. In J. Banks & C. Banks (Eds.), *Handbook of research on multicultural education* (pp. 484–497). New York: Macmillan.

Jensen, A. (1980). *Bias in mental testing.* New York: Free Press.

Jensen, A. (1984). The black-white difference on the K-ABC: Implications for future tests. *Journal of Special Education, 18,* 377–408.

Jensen, A. R. (1989). The relationship between learning and intelligence. *Learning and Individual Differences, 1,* 37–62.

Jensen, A. (1998). *The g factor: The science of mental ability.* Westport, CT: Praeger.

Kane, H., & Boan, C. (2005). A review and critique of multicultural learning styles. In C. Frisby & C. Reynolds (Eds.), *Comprehensive handbook of multicultural school psychology* (pp. 425–456). New York: John Wiley.

Kavale, K. A., Hirshoren, A., & Forness, S. R. (1998). Meta-analytic validation of the Dunn and Dunn model of learning-style preferences: A critique of what was Dunn. *Learning Disabilities Research and Practice, 13,* 75–80.

Kranzler, J. H., Miller, M. D., & Jordan, L. (1999). An examination of racial/ethnic and gender bias on curriculum-based measurement of reading. *School Psychology Quarterly, 14,* 327–342.

Marshall, P. L. (2002). *Cultural diversity in our schools.* Belmont, CA: Wadsworth/Thomson Learning.

Northwest Regional Educational Laboratory. (2001). *Learn-Ed Nations Inventory.* Portland, OR: Author. Retrieved December 20, 2004, from http://www.nwrel.org/indianed/LENI/Learn-Ed.pdf

Reiff, J. C. (2000). *Learning styles (What research says to the teacher).* Washington, DC: National Education Association.

Richarson, W. K. (2003, May 26). The sad truth of racial stereotypes in Memphis city schools. *FrontPage Magazine.* Retrieved June 6, 2003, from http://www.frontpagemag.com/Articles/ReadArticle.asp?ID=7996

Rogers, M. R., Ingraham, C. L., Bursztyn, A., Cajigas-Segredo, N., Esquivel, G., Hess, R., et al. (1999). Providing psychological services to racially, ethnically, culturally, and linguistically diverse individuals in the schools: Recommendations for practice. *School Psychology International, 20,* 243–264.

Shinn, M. R., Collins, V. L., & Gallagher, S. (1998). Curriculum-based measurement and its use in a problem-solving model with students from minority backgrounds. In M. R. Shinn (Ed.), *Advanced applications of curriculum-based measurement* (pp. 143–174). New York: Guilford Press.

Sleeter, C., & Grant, C. A. (1987). An analysis of multicultural education in the United States. *Harvard Educational Review, 57,* 421–444.

Sleeter, C. E., & Grant, C. A. (1994). *Making choices for multicultural education: Five approaches to race, class, and gender* (2nd ed.). New York: Macmillan.

Snipp, C. M. (2003). Racial measurement in the American census: Past practices and implications for the future. *Annual Review of Sociology, 29,* 563–588.

Sowell, T. (1986). *Education: Assumptions versus history.* Stanford, CA: Hoover Institution Press.

Sowell, T. (2002). The education of minority children. In E. P. Lazear (Ed.), *Education in the twenty-first century* (pp. 79–92). Stanford, CA: Hoover Institution Press.

Stedman, L. C. (1987). It's time we changed the effective schools formula. *Phi Delta Kappan, 69,* 215–224.

Sternberg, R. J., & Grigorenko, E. L. (2001). A capsule history of theory and research on styles. In R. J. Sternberg & L. Zhang (Eds.), *Perspectives on thinking, learning, and cognitive styles* (pp. 1–21). Mahwah, NJ: Lawrence Erlbaum.

Stotsky, S. (1999). *Losing our language: How multicultural classroom instruction is undermining our children's ability to read, write, and reason.* New York: Free Press.

Teddlie, C., & Reynolds, D. (2000). *The international handbook of school effectiveness research.* New York: Falmer Press.

Teddlie, C., & Stringfield, S. (1993). *Schools make a difference: Lessons learned from a 10-year study of school effects.* New York: Teachers College Press.

Thernstrom, S. (Ed.). (1980). *Harvard encyclopedia of American ethnic groups.* Cambridge, MA: Harvard University Press.

Thernstrom, A., & Thernstrom, S. (2003). *No excuses: Closing the racial gap in learning.* New York: Simon & Schuster.

Truscott, S. D., & Truscott, D. M. (2005). Challenges in urban and rural education. In C. Frisby & C. Reynolds (Eds.), *Comprehensive handbook of multicultural school psychology* (pp. 357–393). New York: John Wiley.

VanDerHeyden, A. M., & Burns, M. K. (2005). Effective instruction for at-risk minority populations. In C. Frisby & C. Reynolds (Eds.), *Comprehensive handbook of multicultural school psychology* (pp. 483–516). New York: John Wiley.

# 44

# Ability Grouping

**Carl M. Ross**

*Kyrene School District, Tempe, Arizona*

**Patti L. Harrison**

*The University of Alabama*

Ability grouping is the educational practice of placing students of similar ability into groups for instructional purposes. Grouping structures range from relatively restricted within-class ability grouping arrangements (e.g., reading groups) to extensive whole-class ability grouping structures (e.g., tracking). Although ability grouping has been a common practice in education for many years and is used at all grade levels (elementary, middle, and high school), its use has not been without controversy. Many educators and researchers argue that ability grouping, especially homogeneous grouping, has negative effects on academic achievement and social–emotional functioning and that the practice is discriminatory. Others, however, view ability grouping, including homogeneous grouping, as quite beneficial.

Research and issues concerning ability grouping are examined in this chapter. In addition to a review of relevant research investigating the effects of ability grouping, it also reviews special topics, such as ability grouping for gifted children and the importance of classroom practices when considering ability grouping. Although the special education practice of grouping students according to disability will not be directly addressed in this chapter, many of the issues discussed have relevance for special education practices and the current move toward greater inclusion of students with disabilities into the general education program. Finally, grouping practices that promote achievement and lessen inequity are considered as possible forms of effective intervention.

## BACKGROUND AND DEVELOPMENT

A number of different arrangements define the practice of ability grouping (Gamoran, 1992; Slavin, 1987; Tieso, 2003), as described below:

- *Homogeneous grouping.* Students are grouped according to some preset criteria, usually academic ability, with each resulting group containing students with similar ability levels.
- *Heterogeneous grouping.* Students are grouped systematically or randomly, with each resulting group containing students of all ability levels.
- *Within-class ability grouping.* Students from an otherwise heterogeneous class are grouped together within the class for instruction in one or more subjects.
- *Joplin and other cross-grade plans.* Students are primarily assigned to heterogeneous classes, but are regrouped according to ability across grade levels for instruction in specific subjects. The Joplin plan is a cross-grade plan specific to grouping across grade levels for reading instruction.
- *Comprehensive nongraded plans.* Students are not assigned to grades levels but are heterogeneously mixed by age and ability and served by teams of teachers who frequently regroup the students, depending upon the task, within the larger heterogeneous group.
- *Whole-class ability grouping* (also referred to as *tracking* and *XYZ grouping*). Students are separated into distinct classes by ability (generally low, average, and

high) and remain in those classes throughout most or all of the school day.

- *Enrichment classes.* Students, typically those identified as gifted, are grouped together for all or part of a day.
- *Accelerated classes.* Students, typically those identified as gifted, are allowed to advance to higher grades or educational levels than their same-age peers.
- *Cooperative learning groups.* Students work cooperatively on a task in small heterogeneous groups.

Research, particularly at the elementary school level, suggests that relatively restricted grouping practices such as within-class or cross-grade structures may effectively increase academic achievement without causing social–emotional harm (Elbaum, Vaughn, Hughes, Moody, & Schumm, 2000; Lou et al., 1996; Slavin, 1987). However, the effectiveness and appropriateness of extensive grouping practices, such as whole-class grouping and tracking, have been strongly criticized. Central among these criticisms of extensive grouping practices are the following four issues and concerns (National Association of School Psychologists, 1998; Oakes & Guiton, 1995; Slavin & Braddock, 1993).

1. *Is ability grouping as effective as other grouping arrangements in improving academic achievement?* Is ability grouping actually harmful to some students? Proponents of ability grouping believe that many students benefit, especially those of higher ability. Critics argue that students with lower ability are labeled and stigmatized and may even be harmed academically and socially or emotionally by participating in whole-class grouping or homogeneous classes.

2. *Is ability grouping inconsistent with the democratic ideal that all students should have an equal opportunity to learn?* Proponents of homogeneous ability grouping argue that heterogeneous grouping is unfair to students with higher ability because the instruction is "watered down" to focus on the needs of the students with lower ability. Critics, however, raise the concern that homogeneous grouping results in students in lower ability groups receiving inferior instruction.

3. *Does ability grouping promote a view that students' abilities are fixed and stable and that schooling has little effect on students' abilities?* Proponents of ability grouping argue that the practice accommodates students' inherent abilities and skills and that students should not be expected to accomplish any more than the limits of their fixed abilities. Critics of ability grouping, however, claim that homogeneous ability grouping results in a self-fulfilling prophecy, with students with lower ability performing poorly and students with higher ability performing well. Such critics believe that the abilities and skills of all students, even those with lower ability, can be altered through quality instruction and high expectations.

4. *Does ability grouping result in discrimination based on race, ethnicity, and socioeconomic status?* Proponents assert that ability grouping is not discriminatory but simply reflects the typical ability and motivational level associated with race, ethnicity, and socioeconomic status. Critics assert that ability grouping is a discriminatory practice that often coincides with poorer quality schooling and lower expectations for poor or minority students in lower ability groups. They suggest that specific race, ethnic, and socioeconomic status groups may be overrepresented in higher ability groups and underrepresented in lower ability groups.

## What Research Shows About Ability Grouping

Researchers have addressed issues such as those described above, and research results are not entirely consistent in conclusions about the appropriateness and effectiveness of ability grouping. It is easier to understand the conclusions drawn by various researchers when the different variables they consider are examined. These variables include (a) the type of grouping used (e.g., whole-class versus within-class grouping), (b) the curriculum used with the various groups (e.g., differentiated or undifferentiated), (c) the different instructional practices used in the various groups, (d) the outcomes being assessed (e.g., academic achievement or social–emotional factors), and (e) the ability level of the students in the groups (e.g., higher ability or lower ability).

Research has largely focused on the academic achievement of homogeneously and heterogeneously grouped students (e.g., Kulik & Kulik, 1982, 1984; Lou et al., 1996; Slavin, 1987, 1990, 1993). To a lesser extent, student social–emotional outcomes (e.g., Gamoran, 1992; Lou et al., 1996) and teacher and classroom factors related to ability grouping (e.g., Good & Brophy, 2003; Oakes, 1985) have also been investigated. Recent research has used meta-analytic techniques to analyze past research on the topic and provide comprehensive research syntheses (Elbaum et al., 2000; Kulik & Kulik, 1982, 1984; Lou, Abrami, & Spence, 2000; Lou et. al., 1996; Slavin, 1987, 1990, 1993). The results summarized below are based largely on these research syntheses.

## Effects of Ability Grouping on Academic Achievement

***Effects of whole-class ability grouping (tracking) on academic achievement.*** Research consistently shows that the homogeneous ability grouping practice of tracking, or whole-class ability grouping, is ineffective and does not improve student achievement for elementary school students at any ability group level (Kulik & Kulik, 1992; Slavin, 1987). Similar results are found for middle and high school students (Slavin, 1990, 1993). Some studies on tracking in secondary schools, in fact, have concluded that not only is tracking generally ineffective for students, it is detrimental to the achievement of students with low ability (Linchevski & Kutscher, 1998; Oakes, 1987). Tracking can take several forms at the secondary level, including placement in high, middle, or low tracks, advanced or basic tracks, and college preparatory or vocational and technical tracks. Although some forms of tracking used at the secondary level, such as a college preparatory track, may *appear* to show positive effects on the achievement of students with high ability, these effects may be related to factors such as the academic subjects taken, rather than the homogeneous grouping per se (Oakes, 1987).

***Effects of other forms of ability grouping on academic achievement.*** Although research consistently has shown that student achievement is not generally enhanced by tracking, research results for the effectiveness of other forms of ability grouping have not been consistent. For example, in the elementary grades, Slavin (1987) found inconclusive support for regrouping students into distinct classes for reading and mathematics but found greater support for the effectiveness of the Joplin Plan, within-class grouping, and similar nongraded homogeneous grouping. Though the Joplin/cross-grade plans showed inconsistent results (some studies found greater benefits for students with lower ability, some for students with higher ability, and some for all ability groups), none of the ability groups gained at the expense of another ability group. The greatest gains in within-class groups were for students with lower ability. Several studies (e.g., Lou et al., 1996; Lou et al., 2000) support within-class ability grouping, showing that, overall, students with similar ability who are placed together in within-class groups perform significantly better than students with different ability placed in within-class groups. However, the effects are different for students of different ability levels: Medium-ability students appear to benefit significantly from being placed with students of similar ability, while low-ability students benefit significantly from being placed with students of different ability.

Less research has investigated other forms of ability grouping with students older than elementary level. For example, Slavin (1993) identified only four studies that investigated within-class grouping and nongraded plans for middle school students. Unlike research with elementary students, these studies indicate no differences in the effectiveness of within-class or cross-grade plans for middle school students when compared with other grouping methods.

***Effects of ability grouping on the academic achievement of gifted students.*** Results are fairly consistent with respect to the effects of homogeneous ability grouping on gifted students. Research indicates that gifted students at all grade levels benefit academically from enriched or accelerated classes (Kulik & Kulik, 1992) as well as from homogeneous ability grouping in general (Rogers, 2002). However, research is inconclusive about the benefits for gifted students when placed in heterogeneous cooperative group settings (Robinson, 1990).

## Additional Factors Related to Ability Grouping

Other factors and their relationship to ability grouping have been examined. Factors include student social–emotional functioning, teachers' behaviors and practices, teachers' expectations, teacher tracking, placement procedures, and student segregation. Research on these factors has focused primarily on lower ability groups, particularly when the practice of tracking is used.

***Whole-class ability grouping (tracking) and students' social–emotional functioning.*** Research indicates that social–emotional factors such as self-esteem, self-concept, aspirations, and attitudes toward school are affected negatively by tracking, that is, by whole-class ability grouping (Marsh, 1989; Oakes, 1987; Slavin & Braddock, 1993). There also is evidence that student motivation and behavior are negatively affected by placement in a lower track classroom (Dawson, 1994; Eccles et al., 1993; Gamoran, 1992).

***Whole-class ability grouping (tracking) and teachers' behaviors and practices.*** Teachers' behaviors and practices also may vary significantly between higher and lower ability classes when whole-class ability grouping is used (Dawson, 1994; Good & Brophy, 2003; Oakes, 1985). Teachers in lower ability classes often communicate less effectively with their students, focus more on behavior management and less on academic skills, and use generally poorer instructional strategies. They treat low and high achievers differently and may interact with lower achievers differently—by paying less attention to them, calling on them less often, providing less helpful feedback, waiting less time for responses, requiring less effort, and positively reinforcing them less often for correct responses (Good & Brophy, 2003). Likewise, secondary teachers in low ability classes tend to spend more time on classroom management activities than those in high ability classes. For example, in high ability classes, secondary teachers maintain greater task orientation, deal more consistently with behavior, and present instructional objectives more clearly (Evertson, 1982). Teachers in lower ability classes tend to emphasize mainly behavioral requirements and expect students to conform, follow rules, and work quietly. In contrast, teachers in higher ability classes are more likely to expect active participation, critical thinking skills, creativity, and self-direction (Oakes, 1985). In general, instructional quality may be poorer in lower track classes.

***Whole-class ability grouping (tracking) and teachers' expectations and placement.*** Teachers' expectations of their students tend to vary across homogeneously grouped classes, with teachers in lower ability classes having lower expectations for their students (Good & Brophy, 2003). In addition to students in lower track classes receiving poorer quality instruction and being held to lower expectations, "teacher tracking" may also occur. That is, few teachers desire to teach the lower tracked classes, and higher tracked classes are often bestowed as an award to the best teachers (George, 1992).

***Whole-class ability grouping (tracking) and placement procedures.*** Many of the procedures used to place students in homogeneously grouped classes are questionable. Once placed, students may become locked into their track placement. These placements, which sometimes are made based on test score differences as small as one point, often make it virtually impossible for students to move to a higher track and can greatly affect a student's academic future (George, 1992).

***Whole-class ability grouping (tracking) and student segregation.*** Student segregation by race, ethnicity, and socioeconomic status appears to be an important factor in homogeneous ability grouping. Research indicates that low-income and minority students are placed in lower tracked classes in disproportionate numbers compared with the overall school population (George, 1992). Teachers' perceptions of students' suitability for various high school tracks and ability groups tend to be linked to the students' race, ethnicity, and socioeconomic status (Oakes & Guiton, 1995).

***Within-class grouping and students' social–emotional functioning.*** Although not as comprehensive as research relating to tracking, research relating to the effects of within-class grouping on student social–emotional outcomes (such as student attitudes and student self-concept) is more positive. Regarding overall effects of within-class grouping, students in small groups within classrooms, on average, have significantly more positive attitudes toward the subject matter they are grouped in and higher general self-concept than students in ungrouped classes (Lou et al., 1996).

***Within-class grouping and placement procedures.*** Although research investigating within-class grouping and its relationship to student achievement and social–emotional factors has suggested positive outcomes, there may be limitations in teaching practices in within-class groups (Kutnick, Blatchford, & Baines, 2002; Macintyre & Ireson, 2002). Some of the limitations are similar to those found for whole-class, tracked groups. Teachers may not appropriately consider the size and makeup of within-class groups. Improper group placement of students may be a significant phenomenon, and groups tend to be inflexible once they have been formed. After group placement has occurred, teachers may not teach group processes, provide students with training in group work skills, or allow students the opportunity to use group skills to promote learning.

## Implications

With the exception of the homogeneous grouping of gifted students, research suggests that extensive homogeneous, whole-class grouping structures such as tracking are not effective for the majority of students and generally have no significant impact on student achievement. Furthermore, research focusing on lower tracked classes suggests that tracking may have a negative impact on students' self-esteem, attitude, and class behavior. Teacher and instructional factors may also differ across whole-class ability grouped classes, with many students in lower tracked classes receiving poorer quality instruction and fewer academic advantages than students in higher tracked classes. Procedures to place students in groups may be flawed or biased, as well, with evidence showing that lower socioeconomic status students, African American students, and Hispanic students are overrepresented in lower tracked classes. Given these research findings, there is little support for the continuation of traditional whole-class tracking programs in elementary, middle, or high schools.

Other forms of ability grouping, however, have been shown to be effective academically and may have more positive social–emotional outcomes. Evidence for elementary school students indicates that two forms of homogeneous ability grouping, cross-grade/Joplin plans and within-class grouping, can increase student achievement. These two grouping plans can be of maximum benefit if they create homogeneous groups in the specific skills being taught, if the plans are flexible enough to allow for changes in groups after initial placement, if teachers modify their pace and instructional level to be consistent with the students' levels, and if teachers conduct frequent and careful assessments of student performance (Slavin, 1987). Positive effects of within-class grouping may be enhanced when teachers using small groups have more or different training than teachers who do not use small groups, when group placement is based on academic ability and on factors such as gender or group cohesion, and when teachers use cooperative learning strategies in instruction (Lou et al., 2000).

Although research on tracking at the middle and high school levels is extensive, there is less research on the use of within- or between-class grouping practices with older students. Perhaps whole-class tracking is so entrenched at the secondary level that no other grouping practices are attempted on a large-scale basis, despite the consistent research on the ineffectiveness of tracking. It is recommended that secondary schools systematically develop and implement other grouping strategies, such as the cross-grade and within-class plans used with elementary students, and evaluate the effectiveness of these alternative strategies.

Though students who occupy the upper end of the high ability spectrum seem to benefit substantially from enriched or accelerated classes (Kulik & Kulik, 1992; Rogers, 2002), ability grouping for gifted children is controversial in schools. Educators concede that accelerated programs may be effective for gifted students; however, equity concerns emerge when enrichment programs are limited to the upper 3% to 5% of students. Slavin and Braddock (1993) stated: "Even if there were evidence in favor of enrichment programs for the gifted, there would still be no evidence whatsoever to deny that such enrichment programs might be effective for all students, not just gifted ones" (p. 14). A continuing question appears to be whether both equity and excellence can be accomplished for gifted students and their nongifted peers.

A rationale for enrichment programs for gifted students has been that these students have special needs and require special attention (see chapter 34, "Giftedness"), as do students in special education programs for learning disabilities, mental retardation, and other disabilities. Students with disabilities have, in fact, been shown to benefit from alternative instructional groupings in reading (Elbaum et al., 2000). The question, then, is whether providing special services is as appropriate for gifted students as for students with disabilities related to learning and behavioral problems. Some critics of gifted programs have suggested that the achievement effects of enrichment and accelerated programs are due to differentiated instructional practices. Others have responded that all instruction is more effective when it is designed to meet the unique needs of different groups, and that all students, not only the gifted, benefit from effective differentiated instruction (e.g., Allan, 1991; Kulik and Kulik, 1992).

## ALTERNATIVE ACTIONS FOR PREVENTION AND INTERVENTION

One consistent theme is apparent in research concerning ability grouping: Actual classroom processes in the grouped classrooms may not be investigated adequately in research studies (Dawson, 1987; Gallagher, 1993; George, 1993; Lou et al., 1996; Slavin, 1987, 1990). However, some research has suggested possible mediating effects of instructional processes on group placement and achievement and has supported the idea that student achievement may be more consistently and positively affected if all groups are exposed to high-quality instruction. For example, one study found that controlling for instructional practices reduced the negative effects of track placement on reading achievement by 10%–20% overall (Carbonaro & Gamoran, 2002).

Research findings can be used to suggest a model of the complex relationship between instructional practices, within-class grouping, and student achievement (Lou et al., 2000). In the model, the most important predictors of student achievement in within-class groupings are teacher training, grouping specificity, type of small-group instruction, grade level, relative ability of students, and type of test used to measure student achievement outcomes. The model suggests that effects of within-class grouping are more positive when (a) teachers using small groups have more or different training than teachers who do not use small groups, (b) students' placement into groups is based on academic ability and other factors such as gender and group cohesion, and (c) cooperative learning is the instruction method used. When locally developed tests (as opposed to nationally standardized tests, for instance) are used to measure achievement outcomes, more positive gains in achievement may be demonstrated. When all these optimal conditions are in place, small-group instruction may have a large positive effect for elementary students at all ability levels. On the other hand, when none of these optimal conditions is in place, positive effects on student achievement may be minimal and can, in fact, be negative for postsecondary students.

Thus, to be successful, effective classroom practices are required for both heterogeneously and homogeneously grouped arrangements. Gallagher (1993) noted that "merely clustering students who have similarities does not guarantee that anything useful will occur. It is what *happens* to these students after they have been grouped that makes the difference" (p. 23). Gamoran and Weinstein (1998) added, "[De-tracking] brings no guarantee of high-quality instruction for all students. In some cases, detracking brought equality, but at a lower level for all" (p. 410). The challenge remains for schools to improve the performance of low-achieving students. Simply moving from homogeneous to heterogeneous structures is not, in itself, sufficient to achieve equity. If low achievers remain unsuccessful in heterogeneous groups, equity is still not achieved (Grossen, 1996). As such, the actual practices used by teachers in classrooms, such as behavioral management, instructional strategies, expectations for student achievement, provision of feedback, and teacher assignment to classes, should be carefully monitored. Grouping may, in fact, be of only secondary importance when actual classroom processes such as these are considered.

Regardless of whether grouping practices are of primary or secondary importance, some forms of ability grouping are generally associated with more favorable outcomes than others. As discussed earlier, research suggests that rigid tracking is detrimental to students in lower tracked classes and has no clear benefit for most other students, except for gifted students. Other forms of ability grouping, however, are likely to yield more favorable outcomes and may be beneficial in reducing inequity if appropriate instructional practices are used. In the following sections alternative grouping practices are described that are more likely to result in positive academic and social–emotional outcomes.

## Partial Untracking and More Flexible Tracking

If tracking cannot be eliminated altogether, the lowest tracks should be. If tracking is necessary, ways in which it could be implemented more effectively include (a) regularly reassessing students' capabilities, (b) regularly rotating high-quality teachers among the tracks, (c) using tutorials to allow students in lower tracked courses to make up work and advance to higher tracks, and (d) experimenting with new methods of placement and creating better tracking placement criteria (Braddock & McPartland, 1990; Gamoran, 1992).

## Other Forms of Homogeneous and Heterogeneous Ability Groups

Generally, the most effective grouping practices combine heterogeneous and homogeneous grouping strategies. Students should have a primary association with a heterogeneous group, but for specific activities, small homogeneous groups may be advantageous (Slavin, 1987). Alternative combinations of homogeneous and heterogeneous practices include the following (Dawson, 1994; Fuchs, Fuchs, & Burish, 2000; George, 1992; Slavin, 1987):

- *Flexible grouping and team teaching.* A very flexible grouping scheme in which grouping arrangements are changed based on the current instructional purpose. Team teaching is sometimes combined with this arrangement.
- *Mixed-ability grouping with additional support.* A grouping arrangement in which all students are placed in heterogeneous classes and extra support is provided to individual students as needed.
- *Cross-grade grouping.* Also known as the Joplin plan when used with reading; an arrangement in which students are primarily assigned to heterogeneous classes but are regrouped according to ability across grade levels for instruction in specific subjects.

- *Nongraded schools.* Arrangement in which students are not assigned to grades; rather students are heterogeneously mixed by age and ability and are served by teams of teachers who regroup the students frequently within the larger heterogeneous group, depending upon the task.
- *Teacher autonomy grouping.* Arrangement in which teachers are given the authority to group students in the way they feel is most effective for instruction.
- *Before- and after-school programs.* Arrangement in which lower or remedial tracks are eliminated during the regular school day and shifted to before school, after school, or on weekends.
- *Split-level grouping (Winchester plan).* Arrangement in which ability grouping is both maintained and minimized. Students are divided into ability groups and remain with those groups, but the groups are rotated during the day, and no one ability group remains with any other single ability group throughout the day.
- *Administrative or student choice grouping.* Arrangement in which both students and administrators have more choice in where the students are placed. Test scores, for example, may have less weight than student preferences or administrative decisions.
- *Peer tutoring.* Arrangement in which students work in pairs and one student provides tutoring to the other. The exact structure may take many forms, such as homogeneous pairs, heterogeneous pairs, within-grade, and cross-grade (see chapter 48, "Peer-Assisted Learning Strategies").

As the following two case studies illustrate, alternative ability grouping practices such as those described have been successfully implemented as part of comprehensive school restructuring. An elementary school (grades pre-K–8) near a large Midwestern city was selected to be "redesigned" during the 1997–1998 school year because it had persistently low achievement scores and was classified in the lowest category of its district's accountability system (Archibald & Odden, 2000). An integral part of the school's redesign was the comprehensive implementation of direct instruction, which included flexible ability grouping when the teachers believed it would be beneficial for students. Each grade level at the school was given the option of whether they would use ability grouping and for what subjects. For instance, a second grade might group students according to ability for reading, with each teacher teaching a different level; at the third grade, one teacher might teach reading to all students. As of the 1999–2000 school year, the investigators reported that the school had made gains toward the continued academic improvement of its students.

Another case study (Odden, Archibald, & Tychsen, 1999) describes the restructuring of an elementary school (grades K–5) near a major metropolitan area in the Northwest. The restructuring was a result of a reform agenda initiated by the school's district superintendent in 1995. As its restructuring model, the school community selected the Success for All program (Slavin, Madden, Dolan, & Wasik, 1996). An integral part of Success for All is the cross-grade grouping structure in which students are grouped according to reading levels rather than by age. For example, one reading group may have first, second, and third graders who are all reading at the same level. The students are evaluated every 8 weeks and reassigned to reading groups accordingly. The investigators reported that initial achievement results of the program's implementation have been promising.

Successfully moving from rigid tracking arrangements to alternative grouping practices, however, may be difficult (Gamoran & Weinstein, 1998). For example, de-tracking has been a goal that has been more idealized than actually achieved, particularly in secondary schools and in the area of mathematics. Other factors (such as intellectual rigor, commitment to equity, and use of differentiated instruction in a way that does not contradict equity) may be more fundamental in promoting academic excellence and equity than a school's grouping structure. Unless these factors are present and the technical difficulties of providing high-quality instruction to diverse students are solved, de-tracking brings no guarantee of success.

Perhaps because of mistaken assumptions, many parents and teachers may also resist changes to traditional tracked classrooms. Parents of bright students may feel that any move to de-track may be harmful to their children, whereas teachers accustomed to teaching tracked classes may be hesitant to teach heterogeneous classes. These fears and concerns must be addressed for successful de-tracking to occur, and a long-term plan must be implemented that begins by promoting viable ability grouping alternatives to both school personnel and the public (George, 1992).

## SUMMARY

Ability grouping is a broad term that encompasses a wide variety of grouping practices. These practices range from tracking to various forms of within-class and between-class ability groups. Tracking has not been shown to increase student achievement and may produce detrimental social–emotional and sociological outcomes, particularly for students in low ability classes. Given this record, there are few, if any, good reasons to continue tracking as currently employed. Influential educational organizations such as the National Education Association and the National Association of School Psychologists have called for an end to tracking.

Successfully moving away from traditional tracking, however, will require that practices be in place to ensure that high-quality instruction is provided to diverse groups of students. Furthermore, viable ability grouping alternatives to tracking must be promoted to both school personnel and the public.

Other forms of ability grouping have, in fact, been shown to be viable and to be associated with increased achievement and more positive social–emotional outcomes. Research based mostly on studies at the elementary school level supports the effectiveness of placing students primarily into heterogeneous groups but then organizing them into small homogeneous groups for specific activities, such as the organizations used in within-class or cross-grade grouping plans.

The appropriateness of targeting gifted students for homogeneous grouping arrangements continues to be debated. Although accelerated programs for gifted students may substantially increase achievement for those students, and enrichment programs may also be beneficial, equity concerns emerge when such programs are limited to the upper 3% to 5% of students.

An even more pressing and more practical question is the question of how important grouping practices are in education. Regardless of grouping arrangement, effective classroom practices are required for students to be successful, and classroom practices must be considered in any ability grouping discussion.

## RECOMMENDED RESOURCES

Gamoran, A. (1993). Alternative uses of ability grouping in secondary schools: Can we bring high-quality instruction to low ability classes? *American Journal of Education, 102,* 1–22.

This article offers a practical middle ground in the ability grouping debate. A description of high-quality instruction in low-ability classrooms is provided.

Grossen, B. (1996). How should we group to achieve excellence with equity? Available from http://darkwing.uoregon.edu/~adiep/grp.htm

This web article reviews the issues of excellence versus equity in the ability grouping debate and argues that, in itself, moving from homogeneous to heterogeneous groups is not sufficient to achieve equity. The author asserts that the challenge is for schools to improve the performance of low achieving students. If low achievers remain unsuccessful in heterogeneous groups, equity is still not achieved.

Lou, Y., Abrami, P. C., & Spence, J. C. (2000). Effects of within-class grouping on student achievement: An exploratory model. *Journal of Educational Research, 94,* 101–112.

Adding to meta-analytic results regarding the effects of within-class grouping on student achievement, this study also examines other factors (such as teacher training, grouping basis, and type of instruction) that help account for the significant variability found in the effects of within-class grouping on student achievement.

Rogers, K. B. (2002). Grouping the gifted and talented. *Roeper Review, 24,* 103–108.

This is a comprehensive review of issues and research regarding grouping and gifted students. It provides a compelling argument for those who assert that gifted students should be grouped with other gifted students.

## REFERENCES


Allan, S. D. (1991). Ability grouping research reviews: What do they say about grouping and the gifted? *Educational Leadership, 48,* 60–65.

Archibald, S., & Odden, A. (2000). *A case study of resource reallocation to implement a whole school reform model and boost student achievement: Parnell Elementary School.* Consortium for Policy Research in Education, University of Wisconsin–Madison.

Braddock, J. H., & McPartland, J. M. (1990). Alternatives to tracking. *Educational Leadership, 47,* 76–79.

Carbonaro, W. J., & Gamoran, A. (2002). The production of achievement inequality in high school English. *American Educational Research Journal, 39,* 801–827.

Dawson, M. M. (1987). Beyond ability grouping: A review of the effectiveness of ability grouping and its alternatives. *School Psychology Review, 16,* 348–369.

Dawson, M. M. (1994). Best practices in promoting alternatives to ability grouping. In A. Thomas & J. Grimes (Eds.), *Best practices in school psychology III* (pp. 347–357). Bethesda, MD: National Association of School Psychologists.

Eccles, J. S., Wigfield, A., Midgley, C., Reuman, D., Mac Iver, D., & Feldlaufer, H. (1993). Negative effects of traditional middle schools on students' motivation. *The Elementary School Journal, 93,* 553–574.

Elbaum, B., Vaughn, S., Hughes, M. T., Moody, S. W., & Schumm, J. S. (2000). How reading outcomes of students with disabilities are related to instructional grouping formats: A meta-analytic review. In R. Gersten, E. P. Schiller, & S. Vaughn (Eds.), *Contemporary special education research: Syntheses of the knowledge base on critical instructional issues* (pp. 105–135). Mahwah, NJ: Erlbaum.

Evertson, C. E. (1982). Differences in instructional activities in average- and low-achieving junior high English and mathematics classes. *Elementary School Journal, 82,* 329–350.

Fuchs, D., Fuchs, L. S., & Burish, P. (2000). Peer-assisted learning strategies: An evidence-based practice to promote reading achievement. *Learning Disabilities Research and Practice, 15,* 85–91.

Gallagher, J. J. (1993). Ability grouping: A tool for educational excellence. *College Board Review, 168,* 21–27.

Gamoran, A. (1992). Is ability grouping equitable? *Educational Leadership, 50,* 11–17.

Gamoran, A., & Weinstein, M. (1998). Differentiation and opportunity in restructured schools. *American Journal of Education, 106,* 385–415.

George, P. S. (1992). *How to untrack your school.* Alexandria, VA: Association for Supervision and Curriculum Development. (ERIC Document Reproduction Service No. ED348752).

George, P. S. (1993). Tracking and ability grouping in the middle school: Ten tentative truths. *Middle School Journal, 24,* 17–24.

Good, T. L., & Brophy, J. E. (2003). *Looking in classrooms* (3rd ed.). Boston: Allyn & Bacon.

Grossen, R. (1996). How should we group to achieve excellence with equity? Retrieved December 10, 2004, from http://darkwing.uoregon.edu/~adiep/grp.htm

Kulik, C. C., & Kulik, J. A. (1982). Effects of ability grouping on secondary school students: A meta analysis of evaluation findings. *American Educational Research Journal, 19,* 415–428.

Kulik, C. C., & Kulik, J. A. (1984). Effects of ability grouping on elementary school pupils: A meta analysis. Ann Arbor: University of Michigan. (ERIC Document Reproduction Service No. ED255329).

Kulik, J. A., & Kulik, C. C. (1992). Meta-analytic findings on grouping programs. *Gifted Child Quarterly, 36,* 73–77.

Kutnick, P., Blatchford, P., & Baines, E. (2002). Pupil groupings in primary school classrooms: Sites for learning and social pedagogy? *British Educational Research Journal, 28,* 187–206.

Linchevski, L., & Kutscher, B. (1998). Tell me with whom you're learning, and I'll tell you how much you've learned: Mixed-ability versus same-ability grouping in mathematics. *Journal for Research in Mathematics Education, 29,* 533–555.

Lou, Y., Abrami, P. C., & Spence, J. C. (2000). Effects of within-class grouping on student achievement: An exploratory model. *Journal of Educational Research, 94,* 101–112.

Lou, Y., Abrami, P. C., Spence, J. C., Poulsen, C., Chambers, B., & d'Appollonia, S. (1996). Within-class grouping: A meta-analysis. *Review of Educational Research, 66,* 423–458.

Macintyre, H., & Ireson, J. (2002). Within-class ability grouping: Placement of pupils in groups and self-concept. *British Educational Research Journal, 28,* 258–263.

Marsh, H. (1989). Age and sex differences in multiple dimensions of self-concept: Pre-adolescence to early adulthood. *Journal of Educational Psychology, 81,* 417–430.

National Association of School Psychologists. (1998). *Position statement on ability grouping.* Bethesda, MD: Author.

Oakes, J. (1985). *Keeping track: How schools structure inequality.* New Haven, CT: Yale University Press.

Oakes, J. (1987). Tracking in secondary schools: A contextual perspective. *Educational Psychologist, 22,* 129–153.

Oakes, J., & Guiton, G. (1995). Matchmaking: The dynamics of high school tracking decisions. *American Educational Research Journal, 32,* 3–33.

Odden, A., Archibald, S., & Tychsen, A. (1999). *Hollister Elementary School: A case study for resource reallocation.* Consortium for Policy Research in Education, University of Wisconsin–Madison.

Robinson, A. (1990). Point-counterpoint: Cooperation or exploitation? The argument against cooperative learning for talented students. *Journal for the Education of the Gifted, 14,* 9–27.

Rogers, K. B. (2002). Grouping the gifted and talented. *Roeper Review, 24,* 103–108.

Slavin, R. E. (1987). Ability grouping and student achievement in elementary schools: A best-evidence synthesis. *Review of Educational Research, 57,* 293–336.

Slavin, R. E. (1990). Ability grouping and student achievement in secondary schools: A best-evidence synthesis. *Review of Educational Research, 60,* 471–499.

Slavin, R. E. (1993). Ability grouping in the middle grades: Achievement effects and alternatives. *The Elementary School Journal, 94,* 535–552.

Slavin, R. E., & Braddock, J. H. (1993). Ability grouping: On the wrong track. *College Board Review, 168,* 11–18.

Slavin, R. E., Madden, N. A., Dolan, L. J., & Wasik, B. A. (1996). *Every child, every school: Success for All.* Thousand Oaks, CA: Corwin Press, Inc.

Tieso, C. L. (2003). Ability grouping is not just tracking anymore. *Roeper Review, 26,* 29–43.

# 45

# Grades and Grading Practices

**William Strein**
**Nicole Meshbesher**
*University of Maryland, College Park*

Grading and reporting of student achievement and progress are universal features of formal educational environments from kindergarten to graduate school. Many teachers believe that grades are overemphasized, but it is recognized that grades have important consequences for students' present lives (rankings, awards, failure), for postsecondary educational opportunities, and for employment (McMillan, Myran, & Workman, 2002). Grading issues are extremely controversial, with little consensus among stakeholder groups (e.g., parents, teachers, students, administrators, and community members), to the extent that efforts to make even moderate revisions in grading and reporting procedures are extraordinarily difficult (Guskey & Bailey, 2001). This chapter explores key issues in grading and reporting, and provides information from the literature that will assist educators, and those who consult with them, in improving grading and reporting practices for K–12 students in both general and special education programs.

## BACKGROUND AND DEVELOPMENT

### Functions and Purposes of Grading

Grading typically serves four basic purposes: (a) *certifying* that students have achieved a specific level of accomplishment or mastery (e.g., high school graduation), (b) *selecting* students for some educational or occupational path (e.g., college admission, or employment), (c) *informing* students and parents about the student's progress, and (d) *motivating* students (Natriello, 1992). Grading policies and practices that serve one purpose particularly well may actually hinder another purpose (Guskey & Bailey, 2001). For example, certification and selection are often well served by high standards and competitive grading practices, but when grading is used for these purposes, it tends to be most motivating to already high-achieving students, and may actually decrease motivation of lower achieving students (Natriello, 1987). As long as a teacher is using a single-indicator reporting system (e.g., one letter grade or percentage number for English), there seems to be no reasonable resolution to the problem of trying to ascertain clearly the meanings of the grade assigned.

Although assessment and grading are inextricably intertwined, it is helpful to distinguish between them. *Assessment* refers to the objective measurement of a student's learning. *Grading* refers to the teacher's evaluation of the adequacy of a student's learning.

### Typical Approaches to Grading

This section presents common approaches to grading (and discusses the advantages and disadvantages of each), research on what grading practices teachers actually use, and what factors affect teachers' grading practices. The majority of practices that are typically used are based on four broad approaches to grading: *letter grades, other categorical systems, percentage grades, and standards-based grades.*

Letter grades (ABCDF) remain the most commonly used system in secondary schools; they are less frequently used in elementary schools. Many experts (e.g., Stiggins, 2005) consider traditional grading to be inevitable, at least for the immediate future. One of the clearest advantages to traditional letter grading is that it is familiar to parents, teachers, and students alike. Letter grades also provide a succinct description of achievement and performance. Despite some reservations, teachers find letter grades to be generally helpful (Bursuck et al., 1996), at least for nondisabled students. Disadvantages of letter grades include (a) inappropriate collapsing of different information into one symbol, (b) arbitrary grade cutoffs that are difficult to make, and (c) lack of comprehensiveness of other methods, such as standards-based grading (Guskey & Bailey, 2001).

Other categorical systems of measurement are beginning to be used in place of letter grades. For example, the state of Kentucky (as reported in Guskey & Bailey, 2001) adopted a standards-based system that uses the categories of Distinguished, Proficient, Apprentice, and Novice. Advocates of such systems claim that they are more affirming of the student and are more descriptive than letter grades. Disadvantages are similar to those of letter grades. Also, there is little evidence as to whether such systems truly have fewer negative connotations (Guskey & Bailey, 2001). In addition, such systems may imply a carefully constructed standards-based system (see below), when in fact the categories are simply letter grades that are relabeled.

Percentage grades are second in popularity only to letter grades and have a long history of use in American schools. This system is typically more popular in middle and high schools. The strongest advantage of percentage grades is that they have the potential of providing large discrimination in evaluation of achievement. Again, a disadvantage includes collapsing of much information into a single indicator. For example, averaging scores on three quizzes and a major exam to produce an overall percentage may not give enough weight to the more comprehensive indicator of knowledge (Guskey & Bailey, 2001).

Standards-based grading (Guskey & Bailey, 2001) involves setting clear criterion-referenced standards in any given subject and then reporting levels of mastery in reference to each standard. A criterion-referenced approach bases grades on students' individual attainment of some previously defined levels of achievement, and it involves no comparison to other students. Most applications are currently geared to the elementary level. For example, a standards-based reporting system in elementary school math might include items such as "Subtracts single-digit numerals," "Subtracts two-digit numerals without regrouping," or "Subtracts two-digit numerals requiring regrouping." Each item might then be evaluated with a notational system such as "1 – Beginning Standard," "2 – Approaches Standard," "3 – Meets Standard," "4 – Exceptional: Exceeds Standard" (Guskey & Baley, 2001, p. 88). Such systems may summarize performance within an academic area with a notational system similar to an overall "grade" in math. Some systems dispense with summarized grades altogether.

Advantages of standards-based grading include providing important clear information about students' performance, and providing information that may be useful for both diagnostic and prescriptive purposes. Two disadvantages are that (a) such systems are labor-intensive, especially in terms of initially developing and implementing the system, and (b) reporting systems with large numbers of standards and corresponding indicators are often too complicated for parents to understand.

***Teachers' actual practices.*** Several recent large surveys (Bursuck et al., 1996; McMillan, 2001; McMillan et al., 2002) and a comprehensive review (Brookhart, 1994) of earlier research provide a clear picture of the extent to which teachers use the above practices of grading. Surveys of elementary and secondary school teachers produce generally consistent results. Additionally, the findings from six newer (1996–2002) studies are very consistent with Brookhart's conclusions arising from her review of 19 studies published from 1985 to 1993. Apparently, teachers' grading practices have been quite stable over at least two decades.

In principle, three general categories cover most criteria for grading. *Product* criteria are based on specific student achievement or levels of performance. *Process* criteria refer to how a student performs and not what the student has attained, for example, effort, work habits, and perhaps performance on daily assignments. *Progress* criteria emphasize student gains (or losses) over time and are highly individualized across students. One of the most enduring findings of research on teachers' grading practices is that at both the elementary and secondary school levels and across content areas, teachers nearly universally use hodgepodge grading, a practice that is supported widely by both students and teachers (Cross & Frary, 1999; McMillan et al., 2002). Hodgepodge grading refers to combining product, process, and progress criteria into a single grade. There is great variation as to how individual teachers weight such factors (Brookhart, 1994; McMillan, 2001).

Notwithstanding common perceptions, disruptive student behavior appears to contribute little to grading (McMillan et al., 2002). Although teachers routinely include nonachievement factors, sometimes referred to as *academic enablers*, such as effort, participation, and responsibility (Cross & Frary, 1999; McMillan et al., 2002), academic performance is consistently the most important factor in grading (McMillan, 2001; McMillan et al., 2002).

Parents and many educators stress the importance of considering academic enablers when grading low-achieving students, students who recently have made good progress relative to their own previous baseline, or students who are persisting despite some difficult personal obstacles. However, the increased focus on meeting standards has decreased the acceptability and use of nonachievement-based indicators in the grading process.

In elementary school, grading practices vary little across content areas (e.g. language arts and math), although increased importance is placed on homework and assessments in the upper elementary grades (McMillan, et al., 2002). Similar to their elementary school counterparts, secondary teachers use a variety of factors to guide their grading practices. Most notable among those are that (a) academic achievement is the most important factor, and (b) nonachievement factors are not always used in determining grades, whereas this practice is almost universal in elementary school (McMillan, 2001). Variation also occurs across content areas at the secondary level. For example, in surveying the grading practices of secondary teachers (Grades 6–12), McMillan found that social studies teachers used effort and participation and extra credit more often than math teachers. Similarly, high school science teachers used effort in only a minor way and rarely included other nonachievement factors (Feldman, Alibrandi, & Kropf, 1998).

At all grade levels, tests, quizzes, and in-class homework accounted for the majority of the basis for assigning grades, with tests and quizzes becoming increasingly emphasized at the secondary level (Bursuck et al., 1996). Out-of-class homework and class participation had moderate to strong effects on grades (Cross & Frary, 1999), with an increased importance placed on homework at later grades (McMillan et al., 2002). In terms of reference points for anchoring grades, Feldman et al. (1998) found that 50% of high school science teachers used criterion-referenced grading, 28% graded students relative to one another, 16% based grades on the student's individual ability, and 2% assigned grades based on the student's academic growth from some previous point.

Given the substantial variation in teachers' grading practices, it is useful to ask what factors influence teachers' decisions about grading practices. A substantial body of evidence indicates that teachers' philosophies and beliefs about education, learning, and instruction constitute the single greatest influence on teachers' grading practices. For example, in a large survey of the assessment and grading practices of teachers in Grades 3–5, McMillan et al. (2002) found no differences in grading practices across grade levels. Importantly, however, they found that variability in teachers' grading practices *within* schools was greater than the variability *between* schools. Using these results and other published research, which reported large and unpredictable between-teacher variability (e.g., Cizek, Fitzgerald, & Rachor, 1995), McMillan et al. concluded that, although school policies and other external factors have some effect, "individual teacher preferences are more important than are differences between schools in determining grading practices ... [and] school and student characteristics as a whole are less important than are individual beliefs" (p. 212). Similarly, in an interview study of 24 teachers of Grades 5–12, McMillan and Nash (2000) concluded that "[grading practices] were influenced most heavily by internal beliefs and values that were frequently idiosyncratic, reflecting teachers' philosophies of education" (p. 6).

Notwithstanding the overriding importance of teachers' beliefs, external influences such as school policies on grading (Christiansen & Vogel, 1998), subject areas and academic level being taught (e.g., regular vs. advanced placement classes; McMillan, 2001), and assessment systems being used (McMillan & Nash, 2000) influence teachers' grading practices. Easily available computer technology (e.g., special grade-book software) appears to have affected grading by fostering such practices as combining grades from various activities to form weighted composite grades (Feldman et al., 1998). Without question, the *standards movement* and the No Child Left Behind Act (NCLB) exert increasingly strong influence on teachers' grading practices (see later sections of this chapter).

## PROBLEMS AND IMPLICATIONS

### Relationship Between Assessment and Grading

Assessment and grading practices are interconnected but differentiable aspects of teaching. Greater attention and emphasis have been placed on classroom grading practices within the professional literature, whereas research pertaining to assessment has focused on standardized or large-scale testing as opposed to teacher–classroom assessment practices (McMillan & Workman, 1998). Classroom assessments are an integral part of instruction. The results often provide invaluable information about students' understanding of content that can guide teacher instruction. However, experts question teachers' competence in designing and evaluating classroom assessments that are consistent with recommended measurement principles. Teachers' limited assessment competencies can affect not only the quality and effectiveness of the assessment measure, but also have consequences for students' learning, their overall motivation, and their perceptions of their ability level (McMillan & Workman, 1998).

In an interview study of teacher classroom assessment and grading practices across Grades 5–12, McMillan and Nash (2000) found that teachers use a variety of assessments in order to balance external pressures and personal beliefs. For example, the majority of the teachers interviewed indicated that formative and more informal assessments (e.g., daily quizzes, observation, daily checks of student understanding), as well as constructed response assessments (e.g., open-ended essay and short-answer questions, and presentations) were very useful and provided the most valuable information regarding student performance. However, objective measures (e.g., selected response assessments) also were often used and incorporated into teachers' repertoire of assessments. The advantage of objective measures is that they do not possess the ambiguity and subjectivity inherent in evaluating constructed response assessments. Thus, using objective measures can alleviate conflicts with parents who may question or challenge the grade on constructed response assessments.

At the elementary school level, objective tests are used most often, but many teachers also use constructed response assessments. Also, elementary teachers distinguish between levels of assessment that require rote recall versus higher order thinking (McMillan et al., 2002). At the secondary level, English teachers use constructed response assessments more than math, social studies, and science teachers. Secondary teachers of above-average and advanced placement (AP) classes tend to assess higher order thinking skills, whereas teachers of average level or below-average classes tend to assess recall knowledge (McMillan, 2001).

## Alternative Assessments

Increased emphasis on alternative assessments that focus on higher order thinking and problem-solving skills has greatly influenced recommendations for classroom assessments. This emphasis represents a shift from traditional assessments, such as selected response and other objective measures. Generally, the advantage of using alternative assessments is that they "require the active construction of meaning rather than passive regurgitation of isolated facts" (McMillan & Workman, 1998, p. 2). The caveats, for schools that want teachers to implement alternative assessments, are that many teachers may need inservice training on using such assessments. Also, more frequent communication with parents may be needed in order to clarify the expectations for students' learning and how students will be evaluated using the alternative assessments (Carlson, 2003).

Alternative assessments include authentic assessments, portfolios, journals, grading rubrics, and individual and group projects (McMillan & Workman, 1998). Authentic assessments link the student evaluation to real-world situations. Portfolios include a collection of completed work, either electronic or hard copy. The benefits to using portfolios are that they offer a means of evaluating student performance over a period of time, as well as provide the opportunity for students to become actively engaged in the development, design, and content within the portfolio. Grading rubrics delineate the criteria by which student performance will be evaluated. The benefits of using grading rubrics are that they inform students of the teacher's expectations prior to beginning an assignment, which can help guide students as they complete the assignments, and rubrics provide a means to communicate clearly to parents how the student's grade on the assignment is derived (Jackson & Larkin, 2002). Individual or group projects are desirable because they foster active student participation. The primary advantages of using group projects are not only that they actively engage students, but that they also require cooperation among members of the group to jointly produce the project. One of the significant disadvantages associated with group projects is determining how to grade the participants so the grading is fair and so it accurately reflects the contributions of each student.

## Real-World Considerations Versus Expert Recommendations

A consistent finding in the research literature on grading practices is that teachers often do not follow established measurement principles, resulting in incongruence between the recommendations of experts in measurement and the actual practices of teachers (Brookhart, 1994). Measurement experts argue that basing grading on sound measurement principles would eliminate the subjectivity of grades that are based on the "hodgepodge of factors" and would also result in increased consistency of grading practices across teachers (McMillan et al., 2002). Experts recommend the following practices (e.g., Cross & Frary, 1999; Guskey & Bailey, 2001):

- Use product-oriented rather than process- or progress-oriented criteria. For example:
    - Base grading *exclusively* on measures of current achievement.
    - Eliminate "academic enablers" (grading for effort, participation, and responsibility) in grading.
- Base grading on the evidence that best depicts student achievement at the point at which the grade is assigned. For example:
    - Give greater weight for more recent evidence.
    - Give greater weight to the most comprehensive sources of information, e.g., comprehensive tests versus daily work.
    - Rank order evidence in terms of importance to learning.
    - Eliminate the assigning of zeros for missing work; use an Incomplete (I) instead.
- Eliminate the common practice of "hodgepodge grading," such as combining effort, achievement, ability, and so forth into a single grade.
- Inform students in advance about expectations and criteria used for grading (this being the only recommendation that teachers seem to adhere to).

Teachers' reluctance to follow the measurement experts' recommendation—to assign grades based solely on achievement—is likely related to teachers' understanding that grades serve other functions in addition to indicating students' level of achievement. It is also likely that the achievement-only approach to grading de-emphasizes the function of grades as a pedagogical tool, that is, "... [promoting] student success in general in many areas important to schooling, including both academic and [nonacademic] achievement [factors] such as responsibility, effort, improvement, participation, and cooperation" (McMillan et al., 2002, p. 212). Moreover, teacher grading practices are likely to be affected by taking into account individual student differences, wanting to encourage student involvement and motivate students, wanting students to succeed, and wanting to avoid too many failures (McMillan, 2001).

Many teachers lack training in recommended assessment and grading practices (Salend & Duhaney, 2002), but the literature is mixed as to whether such training actually increases teachers' use of recommended practices (Bursuck et al., 1996; Cross & Frary, 1999). Although teachers typically work in isolation, they do not work in a vacuum that is free of external pressures, demands, and challenges associated with teaching a class of diverse learners. Changes in existing grading practices are unlikely to occur unless measurement experts work collaboratively with educators to determine best practices for assessment and grading that both incorporate sound measurement principles and take into account daily classroom functioning (Brookhart, 1994).

## The Standards Movement and the No Child Left Behind Act: Implications for Grading Practices

At the beginning of the 21st century, there is probably nothing more influential or more controversial in American education than the increased emphasis on accountability standards. The history of and controversies surrounding the standards movement are far too extensive and complex to even summarize here (also see chapter 46, "Grade Retention and Promotion"). Although the details vary, the signature feature of the standards movement is the use of student evaluation procedures external to the classroom. That is, the standards and accompanying evaluation tools used are not designed by the classroom teacher. In addition, the standards movement promotes the use of statewide or even national criteria and evaluation methods for assessing the adequacy of student progress. This is in sharp contrast to traditional grading practices in which the evaluation standards are set, de facto, by the teacher, even when school district grading policies and guidelines are in place.

The No Child Left Behind Act of 2001 does not address the issue of grading per se. However, under NCLB all public school children must be tested annually on statewide tests in reading, math, and science (beginning in 2007) in certain grades, with reports of such testing sent to parents. State standards in each assessed area must define levels corresponding to "basic" (considered to be below-standard), "proficient," and "advanced." Accordingly, under NCLB parents receive regular reports indicating whether their child is performing adequately based on evaluations external to the child's classroom or school. (The NCLB Act and its accompanying federal regulations are very complex. The broad characterizations presented here have important nuances and exceptions that are too extensive to review in this chapter.)

An emphasis on external standards unequivocally is linked most closely with letter-grading practices that rely exclusively on evaluation of student products rather than process- or progress-oriented grading or the hodgepodge grading that is typically used (Cross & Frary, 1999). Descriptive standards-based grading, discussed earlier, is also consistent with the emphasis on external standards. Consider the disjuncture and confusion that would occur if a fifth-grade teacher awarded Bobby a B (signifying above average work) or even a C (average) in math based on his quiz scores, timely homework completion, and consistent good effort, only to have Bobby's parents receive a report from the end-of-year mandatory testing indicating only "basic" (i.e., less than adequate) achievement in mathematics. It's no surprise, then, that one large metropolitan area school district recently revised its grading policies for Grades 1–8 from a system previously based on attainment of "objectives assigned to the student" to one based on attainment of grade-level (Grades 1–5) or individual course (Grades 6–8) expectations, and based on achievement only (Montgomery County Public Schools, 2003).

Basing grades exclusively on attainment of uniform standards serves measurement functions well, but doing so may be seen as serving pedagogical functions (e.g., students' motivation, self-efficacy, etc.) less well (Bulterman-Bos, Verloop, Terwel, & Wardekker, 2003). However, Bulterman-Bos et al. found that secondary teachers in the Netherlands (where students must pass a national exam to graduate) employed "adjustment strategies," while still keeping an eye on eventual external-standards-based performance. Numerous adjustments in how students, parents, and teachers think about grades will need to occur as standards-based education moves ahead.

## Effects of Different Grading Practices

What is known about the effects of grading practices is mostly a matter either of speculation or of inferences from theory that are not empirically tested. Although there is a vast literature on grading (over 4,000 published articles), most of it consists of essays and surveys of teachers' practices (McMillan & Workman, 1998). The empirical research that does exist tends to investigate both grading and assessment practices, making it difficult to draw conclusions about the effects of grading alone. However, comprehensive reviews of research (Crooks, 1988; McMillan & Workman, 1998) and individual studies (e.g., Ring & Reetz, 2000) lead to several conclusions. First, types of evaluations conducted (e.g., evaluations accenting broad, connecting principles vs. those emphasizing rote memorization of facts) affect both student study strategies and what students learn. Although this conclusion refers more to evaluation methods than to grading practices, it is well supported by research and strengthens the inference that grading practices may also affect student learning and motivation.

A second conclusion is that higher, but attainable, standards tend to lead to greater student effort and greater performance on achievement tests (Bulterman-Bos et al., 2003; Crooks, 1988). The "but attainable" modifier is critical. Grades have some value as rewards, but no value as punishments: Low grades tend to cause students to withdraw from learning (Guskey & Bailey, 2001). Crooks (1988) summarizes this issue clearly, as follows: "In many teaching situations, [having high, but attainable standards] is not possible if all students are working simultaneously on the same tasks and trying to meet the same standards. Under such circumstances, some students will probably not be challenged, whereas others may find the standards unattainable" (p. 469).

By comparison to standards-based grading, which may have mixed effects, norm-referenced grading (i.e., grading systems that evaluate students relative to one another) is likely to be deleterious to far more students than it helps. Such evaluations decrease the learning and motivation of students who repeatedly score toward the bottom (Crooks, 1988) and are most motivating only for those toward the top of the distribution (Natriello, 1987).

A final conclusion is that some form of mastery grading, tied with a mastery learning approach to instruction, is well supported by the literature (Crooks, 1988; Guskey & Bailey, 2001). Mastery grading is a two-category (pass–fail) system, but mastery is typically defined at a very high level (corresponding to an A or B).

Mastery grading is inherently linked to the mastery learning approach. This approach to teaching uses both formative and summative evaluation, divides the curriculum into small units (e.g., about 2 weeks), and provides "corrective action" for students who did not reach mastery at the end of the unit. If unsuccessful on the first cycle of instruction and testing, students receive additional instruction and additional chances to demonstrate mastery. Mastery grading is the only grading method based specifically on a theory of student learning.

Mastery learning strategies have a strong record of improving both learning outcomes and students' attitudes at all educational levels (Guskey & Bailey, 2001), although the outcomes are much less clear in whole-school applications than in controlled studies (Haladyna, 1999). A disadvantage to the approach is that this integrated system requires extra time and work for teachers. This focus on integrated grading and instructional systems is consistent with the finding that although grading systems may affect students, instructional accommodations for low-achieving students likely have much greater impact than grading accommodations per se (Ring & Reetz, 2000).

## Grading for Students With Disabilities

Students with disabilities often have difficulty learning and demonstrating mastery of information through assignments and traditional means of evaluation, such as tests and quizzes. This does not suggest that such students are incapable of learning the required content. Instead, these students often need some type of differentiated instruction, modifications, or accommodations to tests and assignments (e.g., reducing the number of required problems or giving extended time), which are typically delineated in their Individualized Education Program (IEP). Consequently, under traditional grading procedures students with disabilities may receive a grade for completing an assignment or test that is not the same as one completed by their peers without disabilities (Bradley & Calvin, 1998). To explore this complex topic, the following sections address (a) the need for adaptations, (b) effective adaptations currently used, (c) teacher collaboration and grading, (d) issues of fairness, and (e) application to low-achieving, non–special education students.

***Need for adaptations.*** The increased focus on academic rigor and standards mandated by NCLB creates a sense of urgency to adhere stringently to the prescribed curriculum. As a result, it has rendered many teachers unwilling to differentiate their instruction or implement interventions that may compromise the integrity of the established standards. However, with the continuing increase in the number of students with disabilities who receive the majority of their instruction within general education environments, the individual needs of these students cannot be ignored. Those needs often require teachers to modify instruction as well as adapt their assessment and grading practices. Unfortunately, the demands associated with accountability for ensuring high student achievement, in conjunction with the requirement to meet the individual needs of students, pull teachers in different directions and force them to reconcile these requirements with their personal viewpoints about grading (McMillan & Nash, 2000).

Students with disabilities often are not successful in general education classes in which teachers do not adapt their grading practices. Students with disabilities in such classes either earn low grades or are at risk for failure (Munk & Bursuck, 2001). Moreover, students with disabilities in special education classes often receive higher grades than their peers with disabilities who are included in general education classes (Hendrickson & Gable, 1997). Because placing students with mild disabilities into self-contained special education classrooms is not consistent with the provisions and spirit of Individuals with Disabilities Education Act 2004, one possible method is for teachers to adapt their grading practices. Such adaptation is not a new concept: A survey of teachers revealed that half of general education teachers informally adapt their grading practices (Bursuck et al., 1996).

Munk and Bursuck (2001) contend that successful adaptation of grading practices depends in large part on the perceived purpose of grading, as discussed earlier in this chapter. Given the variety of perceived purposes, dissent among educators, parents, and students about adapted grading is not surprising. Additionally, the diverse purposes of grades are especially likely to cause conflict for students with disabilities. In the case of students with disabilities, hodgepodge grading may result in misleading grades and provide a false impression of the student's actual achievement level (McMillan et al., 2002).

***Effective adaptations.*** Research has identified grading adaptations that teachers most commonly use. Specifically, Bursuck et al.'s (1996) survey of teachers revealed that the most commonly used grading adaptations acceptable to teachers included using weighted grades; using multiple grades, such as separate grades for effort and achievement; grading based on student progress and improvement; and grading based on mastery of IEP objectives. Conversely, the teachers reported the following as unacceptable: using adapted grading that evaluated students on mastery of less content than for general education students, altering the grading scale (e.g., lowering the percentage score required to earn an A), and promoting students to the next grade in the absence of achievement.

One interesting solution to the challenge of grading students with disabilities is to devise a Personalized Grading Plan, or PGP (Munk & Bursuck, 2001). Developing a PGP, which consists of multiple steps, could be completed within the IEP development and revision process to avoid additional meetings. The first step is for the student, parent, and teacher to jointly identify what purposes they believe the grade should serve. Second, these participants review school policy on grading and develop a menu of possible adaptations. Third, participants agree to the perceived purposes for a grade in order to select an appropriate adaptation. Fourth, the participants implement the PGP. Finally, the effects of the PGP on the individual student's grades are evaluated, while soliciting the teacher's perceptions of accuracy of those grades and discussing the student's and parents' satisfaction with the PGP.

Munk and Bursuck (2001) conducted a study on the implementation of a PGP with four eighth-grade students with learning disabilities. The results indicated that the students' PGPs relied mostly on weighting the components differently (e.g., giving greater weight to homework versus tests) and slightly altering the criteria (percentage of points for a given grade), depending on the type of activity being evaluated. Additionally, the students' grades mostly improved with the PGP or were higher than they would have been for that marking period had traditional grading been used. Overall, the students, parents, and teachers were generally satisfied with the PGPs because they achieved the intended purposes delineated at the outset. The results from this small study suggest a promising alternative to grading students with disabilities. However, even if it is incorporated within the IEP review process, it may not be feasible to implement PGPs for all students with disabilities, given the time investment required for all parties. Conversely, investing the time needed to clearly identify grading expectations and to reach an agreement among all participants on grading adaptations may, in fact, prevent misunderstandings and avert future conflicts. Additional suggestions for grading adaptations are listed in Table 1.

**Table 1** *Suggested Grading Adaptations for Students With Disabilities*

- Incorporate improvement and progress on IEP objectives into students' grades.
- Modify the weight of assignments, homework, tests, and quizzes.
- Have students create portfolios that incorporate examples of their completed work over time.
- Schedule frequent parent, teacher, and student conferences to discuss student progress and to address difficulties.
- Award grades based on student improvement.
- Use a point system for grading by which the student earns a specified number of points for assignments, homework, or tests and quizzes, which can be calculated daily, weekly, and throughout a marking period (see Hendrickson and Gable, 1997, for a comprehensive list and description of various grading options).
- Use points and percentages to grade modified assignments so that students can then be graded on work completed (e.g., if an assignment was modified to reduce the number of problems from 30 to 15).
- Avoid using different grading scales for students with disabilities (e.g., lower grading scale to allow them to earn an A).
- Avoid posting grades by identification number because it increases competition, and since students with disabilities often have the lowest scores, it may reinforce the notion that they are unable to achieve.
- Develop and use grading rubrics.
- Use a variety of grading approaches and methods.
- Avoid grading solely on effort.

From "Grading Modified Assignments. Equity or Compromise?" by D. F. Bradley and M. B. Calvin, 1998, *TEACHING Exceptional Children, 31*(2), pp. 24–29; "Collaborative Assessment of Students With Diverse Needs: Equitable, Accountable, and Effective," by J. Hendrickson and R. A. Gable, 1997, *Preventing School Failure, 41*, pp. 159–164; and "Report Card Grading Adaptations for Students With Disabilities: Types and Acceptability," by D. D. Munk and W. D. Bursuck, 1998, *Intervention in School and Clinic, 33*, pp. 306–311.

***Teacher collaboration and grading.*** Opportunities for collaboration between teachers exist within elementary and secondary schools. The institution of grade-level teams at the elementary and middle school levels and the departmentalizing of high school teachers by content area give teachers the opportunity to discuss grading and instruction. Collaboration between teachers can lead to benefits for both teachers and students. It offers the potential to enhance camaraderie among teachers, and discussion regarding instruction and grading can increase the consistency of expectations across teachers, which helps students who have multiple teachers.

The use of coteachers—teachers who work together within one classroom—represents another form of collaboration that is used across all grade levels. Coteaching by a special educator and a general educator in order to instruct and maintain students with disabilities in the general education classroom now occurs frequently. Grading students with disabilities often presents a challenge for teachers, and it becomes even more complex with the involvement of more than one teacher, such as in a coteaching situation.

Grading traditionally is completed by individual teachers who employ their own philosophies. Most teachers have not been trained to grade collaboratively (Munk & Bursuck, 2001). As a result, many teachers have expressed confusion about their respective roles in terms of grading (Christiansen & Vogel, 1998). In an effort to address these difficulties, Christiansen and Vogel devised a decision model to be used by general and special educators who coteach and need to collaborate on grading for students with disabilities. This model is rooted in the problem-solving process and consists of four basic steps. First, the coteachers become aware of their school system grading policy, as well as state and federal policies. Second, each teacher identifies his or her basic philosophy of teaching and commonly used grading practices. Third, each teacher explicates his or her philosophy and grading practices to one another to become familiar with the other's approach to teaching and grading. And fourth, after completing the first three steps, the coteachers cooperatively determine the appropriate grading practice for individual students.

***Fairness.*** The issue of fairness has been noted throughout the research literature on grading practices, especially in reference to grading students with disabilities. Christiansen and Vogel (1998) delineated several reasons why many general education teachers are hesitant to alter their grading practices for students with disabilities. First, modifying grading for students with disabilities is seen as unfair to students without disabilities and potentially violates the school's established grading policy. Teachers view allowing the practice of adapting grades only for students with disabilities as being particularly unfair to students without disabilities (Bursuck et al., 1996). Additionally, many general education teachers believe that the integrity of standards and established curriculum will be compromised if assignments and grading are modified for students with disabilities. This raises the question as to whether it is fair for students with disabilities, who have not mastered the same objectives or the same number of objectives, to earn a grade comparable to their peers without disabilities (Bradley & Calvin, 1998). The issue of comparable mastery becomes especially salient at the high school level, because states have specified graduation requirements that students must complete in order to earn a diploma. High school students are not only earning grades, but also are earning credits to fulfill the diploma requirements. The question thus becomes, is it fair for students with disabilities to receive credit for a class required for graduation in which they did not complete the same objectives as their peers without disabilities?

Ring and Reetz (2000) identified additional teacher beliefs about grading students with disabilities. In their research with teachers of students with learning disabilities within inclusive middle schools they cited four basic teacher beliefs. First, it is the individual student's responsibility to achieve regardless of ability or disability. Second, accommodations are allowed based on student needs, but students should be held to grade level standards. Third, modifying assignments is acceptable. Fourth, grading can be based on effort and student functioning.

To obtain students' viewpoints, Bursuck (1999) conducted a survey of high school students with and without disabilities in Grades 9–12 to determine what these students believed to be fair and acceptable grading adaptations. The results indicated that the responses differed based on level of achievement (high or low) and with respect to the presence or absence of a disability. Specifically, the majority of students without disabilities did not rate any grading adaptation as fair. Giving students passing grades in the absence of effort or corresponding achievement, using a modified grading scale, and giving a higher grade based on improvement were identified as the most unfair. However, if grading adaptations were to be used, those considered to be most fair (or least unfair) by all students included giving multiple grades (one to reflect effort and one for achievement) and passing students that put forth the effort. The most significant difference between high- and low-achieving students was that high-achieving students viewed weighting grades and calculating grade point average (GPA) based on difficulty of the class as fair (e.g., giving higher weights to grades in AP classes), whereas their low-achieving peers did not. Students with disabilities were much more inclined to perceive grading adaptations as acceptable for some students.

***Application to low-achieving students.*** Much of the extant research, particularly that related to students with learning disabilities, has not identified educationally relevant differences between low-achieving students and school-identified students with learning disabilities (Stuebing et al., 2002). In fact, many low-achieving students have similar needs and experience similar educational difficulties as their peers identified with learning disabilities. Teachers of low-achieving students may find it beneficial to implement grading practices similar to those they employ with students with disabilities. However, a critical challenge will likely arise: Entitlements under IDEA 2004 do not extend to low-achieving students who are not formally identified as having an educational disability. Accordingly, issues of the appropriateness and fairness of using adapted grading with such students will loom large in the absence of mandated modifications and accommodations.

## RECOMMENDED GRADING PRACTICES

Given the functions of grading, both historically and currently, the real-world competing pressures on teachers, the mandates of NCLB, and advice from measurement experts, several recommendations can be made regarding grading.

***Articulate a clear policy on grading and disseminate it to parents and students.*** School systems should inform teachers, parents, and students about policies pertaining to grading so that consumers can correctly interpret the meaning of the grades. Articulate the bases allowed for grading. Say whether adaptations are allowed and, if so, for whom or under what circumstances. To the degree that teachers have some latitude in grading procedures, they should make clear their expectations and the basis on which grades will be assigned. Of course, this must be done in a developmentally appropriate fashion; information given to secondary school students will be much different than that given to those in early elementary school.

***Integrate assessment and grading practices.*** Although grades represent an *evaluation* of student achievement, they should be based solidly on valid *assessments* of that achievement and reflect clearly articulated instructional objectives. Grading and assessment practices need to be aligned. For example, a grading system that reports on specifics such as "student can write about material that he or she has read" must have some valid measure of assessment that links reading and writing beyond the teacher's mere global impression of student achievement.

***Ensure that grades that refer to academic content predominantly, or exclusively, reflect current achievement.*** If grades are to communicate clearly, a grade or other performance indicator in math should reflect the student's math achievement, not interest or effort or improvement, unless such intended nonachievement meanings are made explicit on the report card or on the student's work. Grades that indicate achievement should weight comprehensive sources of information (e.g., tests vs. quizzes) and the most recent evidence most heavily.

***Use multiple grades or indicators rather than large composite grades.*** Multiple indicators take two forms: (a) multiple indicators of achievement within an area, and (b) separate indicators for achievement and nonachievement outcomes. For example, rather than give a student one letter grade for math, a teacher might grade math calculation and math applications separately. This scheme increases the specificity of information provided to students and parents and decreases the inaccuracies that may result from averaging scores across disparate learning objectives. Similarly, report cards might include letter grades strictly for achievement and give a separate set of indicators for outcomes such as effort, study skills, attendance, and so forth.

***Use a criterion-referenced system at least through elementary school.*** Systems that evaluate student achievement against externally set standards will most clearly communicate information about student accomplishment. There is little evidence supporting the value or desirability of grading that focuses on normative evaluations such as superior, above average, or average (i.e., traditional interpretations of ABCDF grading), at least until there is a need for the school system to provide interindividual comparisons for competitive selection processes, such as college admissions.

***Develop a system for grading students with disabilities that is consistent with accommodations provided and/or with differential expectations.*** To the extent that the educational program for a student with disabilities is altered from the program for all other students, the grading system for that student should reflect such changes.

## SUMMARY

Grading and reporting is an essential feature of American education. How this function is performed has significant implications for the education and mental health of K–12 students. Educators, and the psychologists who work with them, need a better understanding of grading and reporting in order to improve this aspect of the educational process. Challenges abound and include (a) improving the alignment of assessment and grading practices with established measurement and evaluation principles; (b) developing reporting systems that, in the modern age of standards and high-stakes testing, accurately reflect the student's achievement status relative to mandated, external-to-the-classroom standards but do not drastically undermine the motivation of lower achieving students; and (c) grading students with disabilities fairly and accurately in the context of programs that specifically include accommodated instruction and individualized goals.

Grading and reporting almost certainly will continue to be one of the most controversial and passionately debated issues in education. Combining knowledge of the larger context in which grading and reporting is embedded with an understanding of stakeholders' views and sound measurement and evaluation principles should allow school psychologists and other educational consultants to navigate thoughtfully through this difficult terrain.

## RECOMMENDED RESOURCES

Guskey, T. R., & Bailey, J. M. (2001). *Developing grading and reporting systems for student learning.* Thousand Oaks, CA: Corwin Press.

This 200-page paperback is an excellent source for the professional who wants to understand issues and research in grading and reporting and to also obtain practical tips for improving these systems. Coauthored by one of the most prolific and most cited writers (Guskey) on this topic and including more than 240 references to the literature, this book should appeal to the scholar–practitioner. It is both substantive and practical.

Haladyna, T. M. (1999). *A complete guide to student grading.* Boston: Allyn & Bacon. (Available as a component of Allyn & Bacon's (2003) *Assessment of student achievement and assigning grades* (ISBN: 0205429408) package).

As the title implies, this 170-page paperback offers specific guidance to the teachers and teachers-in-training for whom it is designed. With separate chapters on nine different grading systems, plus one how-to chapter and five chapters addressing more general issues, this book is a handy, practical resource.

Stiggins, R. J. (2005). *Student-involved classroom assessment* (4th ed.). Upper Saddle River, NJ: Prentice Hall.

This textbook, as a whole, is a good reference on classroom assessment and associated topics. The extensive chapter on report cards presents a clear case for the measurement experts' position on achievement-only grading.

## REFERENCES

Bradley, D. F., & Calvin, M. B. (1998). Grading modified assignments. Equity or compromise? *TEACHING Exceptional Children, 31*(2), 24–29.

Brookhart, S. M. (1994). Teachers' grading: Practice and theory. *Applied Measurement in Education, 7,* 279–301.

Bulterman-Bos, J., Verloop, N., Terwel, J., & Wardekker, W. (2003). Reconciling the pedagogical goal and the measurement goal of evaluation: The perspectives of teachers in the context of national standards. *Teachers College Record, 105,* 344–374.

Bursuck, W. D. (1999). The fairness of report card grading adaptations: What do students with and without learning disabilities think? *Remedial and Special Education, 20,* 84–94.

Bursuck, W., Polloway, E. A., Plante, L., Epstein, M. H., Madhavi, J., & McConeghy, J. (1996). Report card grading and adaptations: A national survey of classroom practices. *Exceptional Children, 62,* 301–318.

Carlson, L. A. (2003). Beyond assessment to best grading practice: Practical guidelines. In J. E. Wall & G. R. Walz (Eds.), *Measuring up: Assessment issues for teachers, counselors, and administrators.* Greensboro, NC: ERIC Clearinghouse on Counseling and Student Services.

Christiansen, J., & Vogel, J. R. (1998). A decision model for grading students with disabilities. *TEACHING Exceptional Children, 31*(2), 30–35.

Cizek, G. J., Fitzgerald, S. M., & Rachor, R. E. (1995). Teachers' assessment practices: Preparation, isolation and the kitchen sink. *Educational Assessment, 3,* 159–179.

Crooks, T. J. (1988). The impact of evaluation practices on students. *Review of Educational Research, 58,* 438–481.

Cross, L. H., & Frary, R. B. (1999). Hodgepodge grading: Endorsed by students and teachers alike. *Applied Measurement in Education, 12,* 53–72.

Feldman, A., Alibrandi, M., & Kropf, A. (1998). Grading with points: The determination of report card grades by high school science teachers. *School Science and Mathematics, 98,* 140–148.

Guskey, T. R., & Bailey, J. M. (2001). *Developing grading and reporting systems for student learning.* Thousand Oaks, CA: Corwin Press.

Haladyna, T. M. (1999). *A complete guide to student grading.* Boston: Allyn & Bacon.

Hendrickson, J., & Gable, R. A. (1997). Collaborative assessment of students with diverse needs: Equitable, accountable, and effective. *Preventing School Failure, 41,* 159–164.

Jackson, C. W., & Larkin, M. J. (2002). Teaching students to use grading rubrics. *TEACHING Exceptional Children, 35*(1), 40–45.

McMillan, J. H. (2001). Secondary teachers' classroom assessment and grading practices. *Educational Measurement: Issues and Practice, 20,* 20–32.

McMillan, J. H., Myran, S., & Workman, D. (2002). Elementary teachers' classroom assessment and grading practices. *Journal of Educational Research, 95,* 203–214.

McMillan, J. H., & Nash, S. (2000, April). *Teacher classroom assessment and grading practices decision making.* Paper presented at the Annual Meeting of the National Council on Measurement in Education, New Orleans, LA. (ERIC Document Reproduction Service No. ED447195).

McMillan, J. H., & Workman, D. J. (1998). *Classroom assessment and grading practices: A review of the literature.* Richmond, VA: Metropolitan Educational Research Consortium. (ERIC Document Reproduction Service No. ED453263).

Montgomery County Public Schools. (2003). *Current status of grading and reporting.* Rockville, MD: Author.

Munk, D. D., & Bursuck, W. D. (1998). Report card grading adaptations for students with disabilities: Types and acceptability. *Intervention in School and Clinic, 33,* 306–308.

Munk, D. D., & Bursuck, W. D. (2001). Preliminary findings on personalized grading plans for middle school students with learning disabilities. *Exceptional Children, 67,* 211–234.

Natriello, G. (1987). The impact of evaluation processes on students. *Educational Psychologist, 22,* 155–175.

Natriello, G. (1992). Marking systems. In M. C. Alkin (Ed.), *Encyclopedia of educational research* (6th ed.). New York: Macmillan.

No Child Left Behind Act of 2001, Pub. L. No. 107-110, 115 Stat. 1425 (2002).

Ring, M. M., & Reetz, L. (2000). Modification effects on attributions of middle school students with learning disabilities. *Learning Disabilities Research and Practice, 15,* 34–42.

Salend, S. J., & Duhaney, L. M. (2002). Grading students in inclusive settings. *TEACHING Exceptional Children, 34*(3), 8–15.

Stiggins, R. J. (2005). *Student-involved classroom assessment* (4th ed.). Upper Saddle River, NJ: Prentice Hall.

Stuebing, K. K., Fletcher, J. M., LeDoux, J. M., Lyon, G. R., Shaywitz, S. E., & Shaywitz, B. A. (2002). Validity of IQ-discrepancy classifications of reading disabilities: A meta-analysis. *American Educational Research Journal, 39,* 469–518.

# 46

# Grade Retention and Promotion

**Shane R. Jimerson**
**Kelly Graydon**
**Sarah M. Pletcher**
*University of California, Santa Barbara*

**Britton Schnurr**
**Deb Kundert**
**Amanda Nickerson**
*University at Albany, State University of New York*

## BACKGROUND AND DEVELOPMENT

Grade retention is among the most controversial and fervently debated interventions in the field of education. Grade retention refers to the practice of requiring a student who has been in a given grade level for a full school year to remain at that same grade level in the subsequent school year. Estimates suggest that between 7% and 15% of students are retained annually in the United States, which translates to over 3 million children every year having to complete an extra year of school (Hauser, 1999). Retention rates vary according to geographic region, school type (e.g., suburban or metropolitan), and individual factors (e.g., ethnicity). Rates escalate rapidly as sociodemographic risk factors are combined. For example, using data from the Baltimore longitudinal study of urban children with multiple risk indicators, Alexander, Entwisle, & Kabbani (1999) reported that over half the students (41% of Whites and 56% of Blacks) repeated a grade over the first 9 years of their schooling. Furthermore, it is reported that by high school, the cumulative risk of grade retention in metropolitan school systems often exceeds 50% (Hauser, 1999).

### Sociopolitical Context

One reason for the increasing popularity of grade retention is the current sociopolitical climate that emphasizes high standards and accountability, as seen in the No Child Left Behind Act. Reading and writing standards have emerged as indicators of academic proficiency and students' readiness for promotion to the next grade level. For instance, in Florida 162,196 students were retained at the end of the 2001–2002 school year because of their failure to meet grade level standards in reading. Given that the annual cost of education per student is approximately $5,820, retaining these students essentially cost the state an extra $943,980,720 (nearly $1 billion; Florida Department of Education, 2003). The relative ratio of retained students by race was disproportionately Black (24%) and Hispanic (19%) compared to White (8%) and Asian and Pacific Islander (6%).

Ironically, given the current educational policies and practices, student statistics consistently indicate that a greater number of students are being *left behind* (experiencing grade retention) compared with previous decades, and at a great cost to taxpayers. Perhaps such educational costs would be less alarming if they were not largely being used to support a practice with undemonstrated effectiveness. As noted by the Educational Research Service (1998), "Perhaps no topic in public education suffers from a greater divide between the views of researchers and the views of practitioners and the public. The existing research overwhelmingly points to negative effects of retention" (p. 1).

### Characteristics of Retained Students

Retained students generally have lower achievement, particularly in reading and language arts, relative to most students in a classroom; however, those students often have peers who are equally low achieving but who are promoted (Jimerson, Carlson, Rotert, Egeland, & Sroufe, 1997). Thus, it is important to consider characteristics of retained students in addition to low achievement. Research reveals that compared with equally low-achieving and promoted peers, retained students do not typically have lower levels of intelligence (Jimerson et al., 1997). However, the characteristics of a student's parent have been associated with retention: Children who are retained are more likely to have mothers with lower IQ scores, lower parental involvement in school, and parents with poorer attitudes toward their child's education. In contrast, parents who are more involved in school and act as advocates for their child are less likely to have their child experience repeating a grade (Jimerson et al., 1997).

Although levels of intelligence and achievement do not necessarily distinguish retained from nonretained students, behavior often does. Research often highlights maladaptive behavior as a distinguishing characteristic of retained students (Jimerson et al., 1997). A prospective longitudinal study revealed that those students who were retained displayed more negative classroom behaviors. They were also perceived as being significantly less confident, less self-assured, less engaging, and less socially competent than their peers (Jimerson et al.).

Research has also delineated gender and ethnic characteristics of retained students. Males are about twice as likely to repeat a grade as females, and retention rates are higher for minority students (Black and Hispanic students in particular). Retained students are also likely to have missed a greater percentage of school days than nonretained students (Jimerson et al., 1997). These factors—gender, minority status, and attendance—may be related to other distinguishing variables, such as parental involvement and classroom behavior. Thus, research indicates that retained students are a heterogeneous group of children with an assortment of challenges influencing low achievement.

## PROBLEMS AND IMPLICATIONS

Educational professionals responsible for providing interventions to students who are struggling academically or emotionally must consider studies examining the effectiveness of grade retention. The following provides a brief review of research examining the effects of grade retention on academic achievement, socioemotional adjustment, and graduation rates.

### Effects on Academic Achievement

In general, research does not demonstrate academic advantages for retained students relative to comparison groups of low-achieving promoted peers. Holmes (1989) reported that 54 studies showed negative achievement effects when retained children went on to the next grade level. Of the nine studies that reported positive short-term achievement effects, benefits were shown to diminish over time and to disappear in later grades. A more recent meta-analysis (Jimerson, 2001) indicated that only 5% of 169 analyses of academic achievement outcomes resulted in significant statistical differences favoring the retained students. In contrast, 47% resulted in significant statistical differences favoring the comparison group of promoted low-achieving peers. Of the analyses favoring the retained students, two-thirds reflected differences during the repeated year (e.g., second year in kindergarten); however, initial gains were not maintained over time. Analyses examining the effects of retention on language arts and reading yielded moderate to strong *negative* effects, indicating that the group of low-achieving but promoted students outperformed the retained students in language arts and reading. Overall, the results of over 80 studies during the past 75 years fail to support the use of grade retention as an early intervention to enhance academic achievement.

### Effects on Socioemotional Adjustment

Fewer studies have addressed the social and behavioral adjustment outcomes, compared with academic achievement, of retained students. Those that have done so suggest that grade retention can have harmful effects. Holmes (1989) concluded that, on average, retained students display poorer social adjustment, more negative attitudes toward school, less frequent attendance, and more problem behaviors compared with promoted students (matched on achievement). Jimerson (2001) reported that of 16 studies of socioemotional adjustment outcomes of retained students relative to a matched comparison group of students, 8 resulted in statistically significant outcomes favoring the retained students and 13 favored the comparison group. Thus, of the 148 analyses conducted in these 16 studies, the majority (86%) indicated no significant differences in socioemotional outcomes between low-achieving students who were retained and those who were promoted. Other studies have shown that many retained students have difficulties with their peers (Shepard & Smith, 1990). Overall, the results of the meta-analyses of over 300 analyses of socioemotional and behavioral adjustment from over 50 studies during the past 75 years fail to support the use of grade retention as an early intervention to enhance socioemotional and behavioral adjustment.

Although the research clearly fails to support grade retention as an intervention and suggests that grade retention is associated with negative long-term outcomes, additional insight can be gained by exploring how children view retention. In one study, children were asked to rate 20 stressful life events, which included occurrences such as losing a parent, going to the dentist, getting a bad report card, and others (Yamamoto & Byrnes, 1987). The results indicated that by the time they were in sixth grade, children reported only the loss of a parent and going blind as more stressful than grade retention. This study was replicated in 2001, and it was found that sixth-grade students rated grade retention as the most stressful life event, similar to the loss of a parent and going blind (Anderson, Jimerson, & Whipple, in press). Both studies demonstrated a developmental trend, consistent with emerging social and cognitive skills, with the reported stress of grade retention increasing from first, to third, to sixth grade. Thus, research indicates that children perceive grade retention as an extremely stressful life event. Further research is needed, however, to examine the perceptions of students who have experienced grade retention.

## Effects on School Completion and Employment

Whereas few studies that examine the efficacy of early grade retention extend through high school, longitudinal studies consistently demonstrate that retained students are more likely to drop out than matched comparison groups of equally low-achieving but socially promoted peers (Jimerson, 1999; Jimerson, Ferguson, Whipple, Anderson, & Dalton, 2002). Likewise, there is considerable evidence indicating that grade retention is an early predictor of school dropout (Alexander, Entwistle, & Dauber, 2003; Hauser, Pager, & Simmons, 2000). Indeed, grade retention has been identified as the single most powerful predictor of dropout (Rumberger, 1995). A recent review of 17 studies, all of which examined factors associated with dropping out of high school prior to graduation, suggests that grade retention is one of the most robust predictors of school dropout (Jimerson, Anderson, & Whipple, 2002). All 17 studies found that grade retention was associated with subsequent school withdrawal. Several of the studies included statistical analyses that controlled for many individual and family level variables commonly associated with dropping out (e.g., socioemotional adjustment, socioeconomic status, ethnicity, achievement, gender, parental level of education, and parental involvement). The review provided by Jimerson et al. (2002) documented the consistent finding that students retained during elementary school are at increased risk for dropping out of high school. Retained students are between 2 and 11 times more likely to drop out during high school than nonretained students, and grade retention increases the risk of dropping out by 20%–50%. Thus, research consistently indicates that early failure (grade retention) is highly associated with the ultimate school failure (dropping out). Dropping out is associated with numerous deleterious outcomes, including fewer employment opportunities, substance abuse, and arrests (e.g., Cairns & Cairns, 1994; also see chapter 8, "School Completion"). Many students who are retained in elementary school join a cohort of younger children the following year and are considered to be "overage for grade" for the remainder of their education. Research reveals numerous negative effects associated with being overage for grade that are evident during adolescence, including an increased rate of school dropout, more behavior problems, higher levels of emotional distress, and more substance abuse and reckless behaviors (e.g., Byrd, Weitzman, & Auinger, 1997).

Few studies have examined the effects of grade retention on students after they have completed or dropped out of school. An exception was a study that followed children for 21 years and compared retained students with low-achieving promoted students and a control group (e.g., normal achievers; Jimerson, 1999). Results showed that retained students had a greater probability of poorer educational and employment outcomes during late adolescence. Retained students were less likely to receive a diploma by age 20 and less likely to be enrolled in a postsecondary education program. They also received lower education and employment status ratings, were paid less per hour, and received poorer employment competence ratings at age 20 compared with low-achieving students and the control group (whereas the low-achieving and control group students did not differ). The study also found that the low-achieving promoted group was comparable to the control group on all employment outcomes at age 20. Results from other longitudinal samples yield similar findings, suggesting poorer long-term outcomes for retained students relative to a comparison group of low-achieving but promoted students (Alexander et al., 2003; Temple, Reynolds, & Ou, 2000).

## ALTERNATIVE ACTIONS FOR PREVENTION AND INTERVENTION

Given that research has failed to support the efficacy of grade retention, it is essential to examine other prevention strategies and alternative interventions that *do* have research support for their utility. With the emphasis on standards and accountability in education, policy makers, administrators, and teachers are encouraged to implement evidence-based policies and programs. Thus, the remainder of this chapter addresses recommendations and strategies aimed at promoting the social and cognitive competence of students. Each is a possible evidence-based strategy that may be incorporated in a systematic plan to promote the academic and social success of students; however, school professionals must consider the individual strengths and needs of each child.

The professional literature is replete with calls for preventive strategies and alternatives to retention (e.g., National Association of School Psychologists, 2003). Specific programs are discussed later in the text and are presented in Tables 1 and 2. The following is a list of general suggestions for strategies aimed at reducing the number of children recommended for retention:

- Actively encourage parental involvement.
- Adopt age-appropriate and culturally sensitive instructional strategies.
- Establish multiage groupings in classrooms with teachers trained to work with students of mixed age and ability.
- Establish early intervention programs and preschool programs.
- Create the opportunity for students to have additional time to master material without becoming overage for grade through the use of high-quality summer school, intersession programs, and before and after school programs.
- Create personal intervention plans for students.
- Reduce class size.
- Increase the use of one-on-one tutoring.
- Identify specific learning or behavior problems and design interventions to address those problems.
- Provide appropriate special education services.
- Establish full-service schools to provide a community-based vehicle to meet the needs of at-risk students.

When preparing to implement any intervention, it is necessary to appropriately assess the individual needs of the student. This type of assessment can be done with norm-referenced tests, curriculum-based measurements, observations, and rating scales. Regardless of the specific assessment method that is implemented, it is important to obtain information from multiple sources in order to best understand the individual strengths, weaknesses, and needs of each child. When intervention and prevention strategies are implemented on a larger scale (e.g., school-wide or district-wide), it is essential that they be designed, implemented, and evaluated in a manner appropriate for the populations they serve. Effective interventions must consider and respect developmental, cultural, linguistic, and gender differences among students. Therefore, it is important to recognize that there is no "silver bullet," no single intervention that can meet the needs of all students; rather, the context and specific needs of the individual child receiving the prevention or intervention services need to be carefully considered.

In addition to understanding the needs of an individual student or the entire student population, educators must be familiar with specific evidence-based intervention strategies. A comprehensive review of preventive, remedial, and alternative approaches is beyond the scope of this chapter; however, it presents some evidence-based intervention strategies that may be implemented by educational professionals. Considering the diverse needs of retained students, educators can anticipate that systematic evidence-based interventions will aid in the academic and socioemotional development of students at risk of school failure.

Children are most often retained because of academic failure, behavioral difficulties, or a combination of the two. Alternatives designed to prevent academic failure, remediate academic deficits, and address behavioral problems can be grouped into preventive strategies

**Table 1** *Examples of Prevention Programs and Empirical Support*

| Description | Empirical Support/Relevance to Retention |
|---|---|
| *Preschool programs*[a] | |
| • Programs provide educational support and family services to children from economically disadvantaged families to increase school readiness.<br>• Components of Head Start include nutrition, physical, and mental health services, home visits, early-childhood education, parent involvement, and social services. | • Outcome studies of Head Start programs tend to use cognitive assessments and report that the positive effects taper off in the early elementary school years.<br>• Some have found improved cognitive abilities among Head Start participants.<br>• Chicago Child–Parent Centers (CPC) program participants experienced increased parental involvement, higher word recognition scores, lower rates of special education placement, school mobility, and grade retention.<br>• Each year of participation in the CPC program was associated with a reduction in grade retention, lower rate of special education placement, and less time spent receiving special education services. |
| *Creating positive school climate*[b] | |
| • Programs use a comprehensive systems approach to redesign schools and prevent academic and behavioral problems using proactive instruction, school-wide behavior support, and positive school climates. | • Student perceptions of caring and supportive classroom environments result in greater school satisfaction. |
| *Looping and multiage classrooms*[c] | |
| • Looping allows a core group of students and a single teacher to remain together for multiple years.<br>• Multiage classrooms consist of children of different ages and abilities. This allows children to advance at their own rate and creates the opportunity for children to learn from each other. | • With looping, parents are more involved and have more positive views of their children's school and teacher.<br>• Retention rates decreased 43% in one district that implemented looping.<br>• Multiage classrooms provide support for students who are at risk.<br>• Parents and students held positive feelings regarding placement in multiage classrooms. |
| *Parental involvement*[d] | |
| • Strategy enhances parents' attitude toward education, actions to create a home environment supportive of learning, and involvement in education at home and school. | • Parents' expectations and desire for their children's success have the strongest relationship with increased academic achievement.<br>• Parental involvement is associated with higher test scores and self-esteem, improved social skills, better attendance and work habits, and fewer behavioral difficulties. |

[a](e.g., Gilliam & Zigler, 2000; Reynolds, 2000; Ripple & Zigler, 2003)
[b](e.g., Sugai et al., 2002; Roeser, Midgley, & Urdan, 1996)
[c](e.g., Burke, 1997; Darling-Hammond, 1998; May et al., 1995; Rafoth & Carey, 1995; Reynolds et al., 1999; Yang, 1997)
[d](e.g., Epstein, 1990; Fan & Chen, 2001; Sheridan & Kratochwill, 1992)

and alternative interventions. In a discussion of the issues of grade retention, considering preventive strategies at both a primary and secondary level is helpful. At the primary level, preventive strategies include programs and educational techniques that are built on effective pedagogical methods and are culturally sensitive to the group being served. These include strategies that may reduce retention rates by meeting the diverse needs of many children through routine classroom structure and techniques. At the secondary prevention

**Table 2** *Examples of Alternative Interventions and Relevant Empirical Support*

| Description | Empirical Support/Relevance to Retention |
|---|---|
| *Early reading programs*[a] | |
| • In Success for All, small groups of students at the same reading level are placed together for 90 minutes of direct reading instruction. Reading tutors work individually with students to facilitate successful reading before the need for remediation.<br>• Reading Recovery is an individualized instruction program that provides one-on-one tutoring for 30 minutes each day for 12–20 weeks for first-grade students identified by their teachers as demonstrating poor performance in reading and writing. | • Results of programs designed for Spanish speaking students were positive, with third graders who were taught with Exito Para Todos performing better on English assessments than control students taught primarily in English.<br>• Positive outcomes for Reading Recovery include a decline in retention rates of first-grade students from 2.5% to 0.7% and a decrease in classification as learning disabled from 36% to 9% over 5 years. A high percentage of children continued to make progress for two or more years after treatment.<br>• Reading Recovery was found to be the most cost-effective among other programs used to address reading difficulties in children, including retention. |
| *Summer school and after school programs*[b] | |
| • Summer school focuses on providing instruction during the summer months of a traditional academic year.<br>• After school programs are academically oriented and focus on improving and enriching academic achievement by providing supplemental services after traditional school hours. | • Summer school programs that provide remedial intervention and focus on strengthening achievement enhance the development of knowledge and skills.<br>• Middle-class students may benefit more from summer school than same-age students from lower socioeconomic status backgrounds, although there was a significant benefit for all groups.<br>• Summer school programs that provided small-group or individualized instruction had larger positive effects.<br>• High-quality after school programs can increase the academic achievement of at-risk students, allow students additional "time on task" without being overage for grade, and allow students to reduce gaps in their knowledge base. |
| *School-based mental health programs*[c] | |
| • Mental health services based in school settings provide treatment to students who may not otherwise have access to services and coordinate services across settings and providers. | • Outcomes for students receiving school-based services and clinic- or community-based services are similar, but services provided in school-based settings were shorter in duration and more students were able to be served.<br>• School-based services are cost–effective, and the practitioner is better able to maintain contact with school personnel, observe the child in multiple settings, and design more generalizable treatments. |
| *Direct instruction*[d] | |
| • The instruction teaches strategies that enhance a student's academic engaged time (i.e., frequent student response, fast-paced instruction, teacher control of material). | • Research with children who have mild disabilities has consistently supported the use of this approach. Use of direct instruction increased academic engaged time by increasing opportunities for students to respond, thereby resulting in increased student achievement. |

*(Continued)*

**Table 2** *Continued*

| Description | Empirical Support/Relevance to Retention |
|---|---|
| *Mnemonic strategies*[e] | |
| • Memory-enhancing strategies have been found to improve students' organization (clustering) and higher order thinking (knowledge application involving inference) with learned information.<br>• Strategies are often used for learning vocabulary, processing tests, and studying science and history. | • Studies have found large effect sizes for mnemonic strategies.<br>• Students have increased confidence in their knowledge of information learned using mnemonics. |
| *Curriculum-based measurement*[f] | |
| • The process is used for designing, evaluating, and modifying instructional programs according to the results of regular assessment.<br>• The use of curriculum-based measurement in formative evaluation involves the development of appropriate probes and local norms. | • The process is associated with increased academic performance.<br>• A meta-analysis found that systematic formative evaluation (i.e., curriculum-based measurement) was effective regardless of student age, treatment duration, frequency of measurements, or disability status of the child. |
| *Cooperative learning*[g] | |
| • Instructional arrangement allows small groups or teams of students to work together to achieve team success (promoting the students' responsibility for their own learning as well as the learning of others). | • Achievement of students who were exposed to these techniques was higher than that of those who were not. Findings held across grade and subject areas. |

[a](e.g., Clay, 1987; Gredler, 1997; Slavin & Madden, 2001)
[b](e.g., Cooper et al., 2000; Darling-Hammond, 1998)
[c](e.g., Armbruster & Lichtman, 1999; Dwyer & Bernstein, 1998; Evans, 1999)
[d](e.g., Engelmann & Carnine, 1982; White, 1988)
[e](e.g., Dretzke & Levin, 1996; Mastropieri & Scruggs, 1998)
[f](e.g., Fuchs & Fuchs, 1986; Shapiro, 1996)
[g](e.g., Barnett, Clarizio, & Payette, 1996; Fuchs, Fuchs, Bahr, Fernstrom, & Stecker, 1990; May et al., 1995)

level are remedial practices that may be helpful for those children who exhibit academic difficulties or behavioral concerns that, if not addressed, could put them at risk for retention.

Alternative interventions are appropriate for consideration once a student has been identified for a potential retention. However, as emphasized above, there is currently no evidence from long-term studies that suggests that retention is beneficial for students or that interventions implemented concurrently with retention will ameliorate the risks associated with spending an extra year in the same grade. Until such long-term studies are conducted, the discussion needs to focus on alternative interventions that do not result in a student becoming overage for grade.

Although this chapter has divided the discussion of programs into the categories of prevention and intervention, in practice programs may simultaneously serve either function, depending on the timing of the strategy and the degree to which the student is exhibiting problems.

## Prevention

***Preschool.*** Preschool intervention programs are generally aimed at assisting at-risk students before they are detrimentally affected by the negative aspects of their environments. Head Start and the Chicago Child–Parent Centers are examples of two early childhood intervention programs that provide comprehensive educational and family support services to children from economically disadvantaged families in order to increase school readiness (see Table 1). In addition to literacy instruction, preschool programs may offer a range of individualized services in the areas of health, nutrition, and parental involvement that are designed to foster healthy development in children. For guidance on setting up preschool classrooms, including information on membership, relationships, and knowledge and skills that promote positive outcomes for children, see Schwartz, Garfinkle, and Davis (2002).

***Positive school cultures.*** Comprehensive school-wide efforts to prevent academic and behavioral problems should use a systems approach that entails proactive instruction, school-wide behavioral support, and promotion of positive school climates (Sugai, Horner, & Gresham, 2002). Students who perceive their classroom environments as caring and supportive and who report a higher quality of relationships with teachers and a greater affiliation with their class also report greater school satisfaction, which is important, because low levels of school satisfaction relate to problem behaviors, disengagement in academic work, and school drop out. Specific interventions may be implemented to strengthen children's social and academic skills and promote problem-solving and conflict resolution skills. Changing or enhancing overall school philosophies or implementing published school-wide programs requires a significant commitment by the school administration and faculty, including considerable training, personnel, and resources.

***Looping and multiage classrooms.*** Looping and multiage classrooms are two alternative grading structures that allow more flexibility in accommodating individual differences in learning and development. In looping classrooms, students spend two or more years with the same teacher. In multiage classrooms, students of different ages and abilities are educated in the same room, thus allowing students to move ahead at their own pace and to learn from one another (May, Kundert, & Brent, 1995). These strategies allow teachers to better understand and adapt to students' individual learning styles (e.g., Nichols & Nichols, 2002), and expectations are based on individual progress rather than on grade-based standards. Looping is often used in other countries, such as Japan and Germany, which have significantly lower retention rates than the U.S. schools (Reynolds, Barnhart, & Martin, 1999).

***Parental involvement.*** Studies have consistently demonstrated that parental involvement, defined as a combination of a parent's attitude toward education and willingness to assist in creating a home atmosphere that is conducive to doing homework, is associated with greater success among students (see chapter 6, "Parent–Teacher Relationships"). Parental involvement is often a key component of more broad-based interventions aimed at improving academic achievement, and adding a parent component may improve the outcomes of many interventions. Schools implementing such programs should consider cultural variations among parents and families and the ways in which cultural factors may interact with the school's outreach. For example, although positive effects of parental involvement are found when child IQ, socioeconomic status, and ethnicity are controlled for, low-income and ethnic minority parents generally are less involved in their student's schooling (Izzo, Weissberg, Kasprow, & Fendrich, 1999). Parents from diverse cultures may not know how to become involved, may not understand the educational system, or may not feel welcome at their child's school. However, Epstein (1990) found that school policies, teacher practices, and family practices were more important than demographic variables for understanding parental involvement. Policy changes that foster greater understanding among administrators and that welcome parents' involvement in all aspects of their children's education are strategies that may make parent involvement programs more feasible.

## Interventions

***Early reading programs.*** These programs focus on reading, an essential skill for subsequent knowledge acquisition, by attempting to facilitate children's reading success before they fall behind. Although individual children may require different types of instructional support (Gredler, 1997), the programs described in Table 2 are noteworthy in that they strive to prevent failure or provide intervention when children are experiencing difficulties.

***Summer school programs and after school programs.*** Summer school and after school programs are designed to provide students with extra instructional time to master the material without becoming overage for grade and thus being at a higher risk for negative outcomes, such as dropping out of school. In general, summer school programs focus on providing instruction during the summer months of a traditional academic year, and after school programs provide instruction and supplementary support outside of the normal school day. In addition, some districts offer support in the form of morning programs or Saturday school. Numerous studies have assessed the effects of summer school and after school programs; however, the quality and content of these programs vary greatly, making it difficult to make generalizations. Schools implementing summer school or after school programs as an intervention to improve student achievement should ensure that the programs contain key elements commonly found in effective programs (Cooper, Charlton, Valentine, & Muhlenbruck, 2000).

***School-based mental health programs.*** In addition to contributing to academic failure, behavioral difficulties are often associated with recommendations for retention. Children with significant mental health needs are often unavailable for learning and are likely to fall behind their classmates. In an effort to address the broad mental health needs of students in the most efficient manner possible, some schools have adopted school-based mental health programs. Although studies evaluating the effectiveness of these programs are scarce, preliminary evaluation results suggest that they are promising interventions for promoting social and emotional competence (Armbruster & Lichtman, 1999).

***Direct instruction, mnemonic strategies, curriculum-based assessment, and cooperative learning.*** Teaching techniques that increase student performance, such as direct instruction, mnemonic strategies, curriculum-based measurement, and cooperative learning, have been shown to improve academic performance (e.g., White, 1988; Forness, Kavale, Blum, & Lloyd, 1997). A natural outcome of improved academic performance is a reduction in the number of students who are recommended for retention. Therefore, if teachers implement effective, research-based teaching strategies, their students will be more successful and less likely to be recommended for retention. The school psychologist may support this process by sharing research findings regarding effective strategies or by conducting in-school research to document the effectiveness of methods for students at risk for being retained. Each of these techniques is described further in Table 2.

***Behavior modification and cognitive behavior modification strategies.*** Behavior modification and cognitive behavior modification strategies are aimed at reducing negative conduct and increasing positive classroom behaviors. Although these strategies are grouped together in this section, there are important differences between them. Many behavior modification strategies use token reinforcement systems and peer or adult monitors. Another behavior modification strategy involves the use of publicly posted positive group and individual behavior, which has been found to increase academic success.

Cognitive behavior modification addresses not only overt behaviors but also the underlying cognitions influencing external behaviors. This strategy involves combining behavioral approaches such as modeling, feedback, and reinforcement with cognitive approaches such as "cognitive think-alouds" to teach strategies such as anger control and self-coping. Both behavior modification and cognitive behavior modification strategies have consistently been found to increase on-task classroom behavior, reduce disruptive and inappropriate behavior, and increase academic skills and achievement.

## Discussion and Conclusion

Although an exhaustive list is beyond the scope of this chapter, the interventions just described illustrate a variety of successful strategies that can be used to help students achieve both academic and social competence. A natural by-product of the interventions is a reduction in the number of students who are recommended for retention.

Many teachers and schools are currently engaging in a number of positive educational practices to help their students, including prevention and intervention strategies. Those activities should be informed by theory and empirical research so that effective strategies can be supported and failed educational activities and interventions can be discarded. Educational professionals should select interventions that are effective, that have demonstrated integrity, and that will be accepted by teachers, parents, and other stakeholders. They also should consider the degree to which the interventions allow stakeholders to use existing skills and resources (Elliott, Witt, Kratochwill, & Stoiber, 2002).

The recommendation for retention is a dynamic process influenced by multiple variables. Simply adopting one empirically supported alternative will not, in itself, eliminate all of the problems being addressed by the intervention. Therefore, a comprehensive approach to preventing school failure, aimed at intervening on multiple levels, will likely result in the most productive school experience for children. From its inception, a well-designed intervention should begin by viewing students from diverse backgrounds as individuals who have specific needs, rather than as a group that is deficient or disadvantaged. Specifically, selected intervention strategies must consider and respect cultural, linguistic, and gender differences among students. Intervention programs should also use frameworks that are relevant to underrepresented populations within the cultural landscape of the schools and students they serve. Neglecting to develop positive relationships and failing to eradicate cultural, gender, and socioeconomic class bias may cause interventions to fail. Careful planning is needed to integrate promising prevention and intervention strategies into current school programs in a way that emphasizes both high academic standards and socioemotional development. Central to the goal of facilitating the overall development of children is the recognition that both cognitive and social competence are necessary for students to engage in a successful academic career (see chapter 1, "Social and Emotional Learning"). Planning of prevention and intervention strategies should involve careful consideration of the contextual environment, past history, and current events surrounding each student. It is crucial to have several proven and effective intervention strategies available to construct a program tailored to both the larger student body and the individual student.

Academic excellence remains a prominent national issue, and educators must accept the responsibility of facilitating the progress of students who do not meet school, district, or state standards. Children do not haphazardly fail to meet academic standards; rather, their lack of academic success often reflects the failure of adults to provide appropriate support and scaffolding for their early developmental and academic trajectories. To promote educational success, schools should move beyond the use of retention and social promotion and foster an understanding that students can be assisted through the implementation of empirically supported prevention and intervention programs. Educational professionals, policy makers, and families must collaborate in order to promote the social and cognitive competence of all children.

## SUMMARY

Advocates for the practice of grade retention often claim that students may do better during the following year. Opponents invoke research that consistently indicates that short-term gains are not maintained over time. The research shows that as retained students continue in the educational system, they are more likely to experience other negative outcomes and to ultimately drop out. In this chapter's exploration of the disparity between research and the increasing rates of grade retention, it can be suggested that many educational professionals are either unaware of the results of research or choose to disregard studies in favor of their own beliefs regarding the efficacy of grade retention. However, upon considering the literature examining grade retention that has been presented in this chapter, educators who are knowledgeable about this research are now challenged to transfer what has been found in the research to what is implemented in schools.

Promoting the social and cognitive competence of all students is fundamental to accomplishing our national educational goals. Given the failure of the practice of grade retention in achieving these goals, alternative strategies for the prevention and intervention of academic or social–emotional difficulties need to be implemented. Neither repeating a grade nor merely moving on to the next grade provides the necessary scaffolding for improving the academic and social skills of students at risk of academic failure. Alternative intervention strategies are needed. Incorporating effective, evidence-based interventions and instructional strategies into school policies and practices provides a foundation upon which educational professionals may facilitate the academic and social development of all students.

## RECOMMENDED RESOURCES

### Books and Other Printed Material

Alexander, K., Entwisle, D., & Dauber, S. (2003). *On the success of failure: A reassessment of the effects of retention in the primary grades* (2nd ed.). New York: Cambridge University Press.

This book provides information regarding analyses of a longitudinal study, a critique of the literature, and a discussion of implications for practice.

Jimerson, S. R. (2001). Meta-analysis of grade retention research: Implications for practice in the 21st century. *School Psychology Review, 30,* 420–437.

This article provides a systematic review of research published between 1990 and 1999 and also reviews previous meta-analyses.

Walberg, H. J., Reynolds, A. J., Wang, M. C., & Manning, J. B. (Eds.). (2004). *Can unlike students learn together?* Greenwich, CT: Information Age.

This book includes numerous chapters addressing grade retention, from longitudinal studies, to meta-analyses and reviews, and includes authors such as K. Alexander, S. Jimerson, A. Reynolds, and L. Shepard.

## Websites

*http://www.education.ucsb.edu/jimerson/retention/*

This website, titled *Beyond Grade Retention and Social Promotion,* is posted by Dr. Jimerson at the University of California, Santa Barbara. The website includes downloadable PDF files of research examining the effectiveness of grade retention.

*http://www.ncrel.org/sdrs/areas/issues/students/atrisk/at800.htm*

This website, titled *Beyond Social Promotion and Retention—Five Strategies to Help Students Succeed,* is posted by the North Central Regional Educational Laboratory. It posits that social promotion and grade retention are inadequate responses to low student achievement and suggests other alternatives.

## REFERENCES

Alexander, K., Entwisle, D., & Dauber, S. (2003). *On the success of failure: A reassessment of the effects of retention in the primary grades* (2nd ed.). New York: Cambridge University Press.

Alexander, K., Entwisle, D., & Kabbani, N. (1999, November). *Grade retention, social promotion, and "third way" alternatives.* Paper presented at the National Invitational Conference hosted by the Laboratory for Student Success at Temple University for Research in Human Development and Education, Alexandria, VA.

Anderson, G. E., Jimerson, S. R., & Whipple, A. D. (in press). Students' ratings of stressful experiences at home and school: Loss of a parent and grade retention as superlative stressors. *Applied Journal of School Psychology.*

Armbruster, P., & Lichtman, J. (1999). Are school-based mental health care services effective? Evidence from 36 inner city schools. *Community Mental Health Journal, 36,* 493–504.

Barnett, K. P., Clarizio, H. F., & Payette, K. A. (1996). Grade retention among students with learning disabilities. *Psychology in the Schools, 33,* 285–293.

Burke, D. L. (1997). Looping: Adding time, strengthening relationships. *ERIC Digest,* ED414098.

Byrd, R., Weitzman, M., & Auinger, P. (1997). Increased behavior problems associated with delayed school entry and delayed school progress. *Pediatrics, 100,* 654–661.

Cairns, R., & Cairns, B. (1994). *Lifelines and risks: Pathways of youth in our time.* Cambridge, UK: Cambridge University Press.

Clay, M. (1987). Implementing reading recovery: Systemic adaptations to educational innovation. *New Zealand Journal of Educational Studies, 22,* 35–58.

Cooper, H., Charlton, K., Valentine, J. C., & Muhlenbruck, L. (2000). Making the most of summer school: A meta-analytic and narrative review. *Monographs of the Society for Research in Child Development, 65*(1), 118. University of Chicago Press.

Darling-Hammond, L. (1998, August). Alternatives to grade retention. *School Administrator, 55*(7), 18–21.

Dretzke, B. J., & Levin, J. R. (1996). Assessing students' application and transfer of a mnemonic strategy: The struggle for independence. *Contemporary Educational Psychology, 21,* 83–93.

Dwyer, K. P., & Bernstein, R. (1998). Mental health in schools: Linking islands of hope in a sea of despair. *School Psychology Review, 27,* 277–286.

Educational Research Service. (1998). *Information for school leaders.* Prepared for Association of California School Administrators. Arlington, VA: Author.

Elliott, S. N., Witt, J. C., Kratochwill, T. R., & Stoiber, K. C. (2002). Selecting and evaluating classroom interventions. In M. R. Shinn, H. M. Walker, & G. Stoner (Eds.), *Interventions for academic and behavior problems II: Preventative and remedial approaches* (pp. 243–294). Bethesda, MD: National Association of School Psychologists.

Engelmann, S., & Carnine, D. (1982). *Theory of instruction: Principles and applications.* New York: Irvington.

Epstein, J. L. (1990). School and family connections: Theory, research, and implications for integrating sociologies of education and family. *Marriage and Family Review, 15,* 99–126.

Evans, S. W. (1999). Mental health services in schools: Utilization, effectiveness, and consent. *Clinical Psychology Review, 19,* 165–179.

Fan, X., & Chen, M. (2001). Parental involvement and students' academic achievement: A meta-analysis. *Educational Psychology Review, 13,* 1–22.

Florida Department of Education. (2003). *Student statistics and expenditures for the 2001–2002 academic year.* Available from the DOE Office of Funding and Financial Reporting website: http://www.firn.edu/doe/fefp

Forness, S. R., Kavale, K. A., Blum, I. M., & Lloyd, J. W. (1997). Mega-analysis of meta-analyses: What works in special education and related services. *Teaching Exceptional Children, 29,* 4–9.

Fuchs, D., Fuchs, L. S., Bahr, M. W., Fernstrom, P., & Stecker, P. M. (1990). Prereferral intervention: A prescriptive approach. *Exceptional Children, 56,* 493–513.

Fuchs, L. A., & Fuchs, D. (1986). Effects of systematic formative evaluation: A meta-analysis. *Exceptional Children, 53,* 199–208.

Gilliam, W. S., & Zigler, E. F. (2000). A critical meta-analysis of all evaluations of state-funded preschool from 1977 to 1998: Implications for policy, service delivery and program evaluation. *Early Childhood Research Quarterly, 15,* 441–473.

Gredler, G. R. (1997). Intervention programs. *Psychology in the Schools, 34,* 161–169.

Hauser, R. (1999). *How much social promotion is there in the United States?* Madison, WI: Center for Demography and Ecology, University of Wisconsin, Madison. (CDE Working Paper No. 99-06).

Hauser, R., Pager, D., & Simmons, S. (2000, October). *Dropout in relation to grade retention: An accounting from the beginning school study.* Paper presented at the National Invitational Conference hosted by the Laboratory for Student Success at Temple University for Research in Human Development and Education, Alexandria, VA.

Holmes, C. T. (1989). Grade-level retention effects: A meta-analysis of research studies. In L. A. Shepard & M. L. Smith (Eds.), *Flunking grades: Research and policies on retention* (pp. 16–33). London: Falmer Press.

Izzo, C. V., Weissberg, R. P., Kasprow, W. J., & Fendrich, M. (1999). A longitudinal assessment of teacher perceptions of parent involvement in children's education and school performance. *American Journal of Community Psychology, 27,* 817–839.

Jimerson, S. R. (1999). On the failure of failure: Examining the association between early grade retention and education and employment outcomes during late adolescence. *Journal of School Psychology, 37,* 243–272.

Jimerson, S. R. (2001). Meta-analysis of grade retention research: Implications for practice in the 21st century. *School Psychology Review, 30,* 420–437.

Jimerson, S. R., Anderson, G. E., & Whipple, A. D. (2002). Winning the battle and losing the war: Examining the relation between grade retention and dropping out of high school. *Psychology in the Schools, 39,* 441–457.

Jimerson, S. R., Carlson, E., Rotert, M., Egeland, B., & Sroufe, L. A. (1997). A prospective, longitudinal study of the correlates and consequences of early grade retention. *Journal of School Psychology, 35,* 3–25.

Jimerson, S. R., Ferguson, P., Whipple, A. D., Anderson, G. E., & Dalton, M. J. (2002). Exploring the association between grade retention and dropout: A longitudinal study examining socio-emotional, behavioral, and achievement characteristics of retained students. *California School Psychologist, 7,* 51–62.

Mastropieri, M. A., & Scruggs, T. E. (1998). Constructing more meaningful relationships in the classroom: Mnemonic research into practice. *Learning Disabilities Research and Practice, 13,* 138–145.

May, D. C., Kundert, D. K., & Brent, D. (1995). Does delayed entry reduce later grade retentions and use of special education services? *Remedial and Special Education, 16,* 288–294.

National Association of School Psychologists. (2003). *Position statement: Student grade retention and social promotion.* Bethesda, MD: Author.

Nichols, J. D., & Nichols, G. W. (2002). The impact of looping classroom environments on parental attitudes. *Preventing School Failure, 47,* 18–25.

Rafoth, M. A., & Carey, K. (1995). Best practices in assisting with promotion and retention decisions. In A. Thomas & J. Grimes (Eds.), *Best practice in school psychology III* (pp. 413–420). Bethesda, MD: National Association of School Psychologists.

Reynolds, A. J. (2000). *Success in early intervention: The Chicago Child-Parent Centers.* Lincoln: University of Nebraska Press.

Reynolds, J. C., Barnhart, B., & Martin, B. N. (1999). Looping: A solution to the retention vs. social promotion dilemma? *ERS Spectrum, 17*(2), 16–20.

Ripple, C. H., & Zigler, E. (2003). Research, policy, and the federal role in prevention initiatives for children. *American Psychologist, 58,* 482–490.

Roeser, R. W., Midgley, C., & Urdan, T. C. (1996). Perceptions of the school psychological environment and early adolescents' psychological and behavioral functioning in school: The mediating role of goals and belonging. *Journal of Educational Psychology, 88,* 408–422.

Rumberger, R. (1995). Dropping out of middle school: A multilevel analysis of students and schools. *American Educational Research Journal, 32,* 583–625.

Schwartz, I. S., Garfinkle, A. N., & Davis, C. (2002). Arranging preschool environments to facilitate valued social and educational outcomes. In M. R. Shinn, H. M. Walker, & G. Stoner (Eds.), *Interventions for academic and behavior problems II: Preventative and remedial approaches* (pp. 455–468). Bethesda, MD: National Association of School Psychologists.

Shapiro, E. S. (1996). Step 3: Instructional modification, general strategies. In S. N. Elliot & J. C. Witt (Eds.), *Academic skills problems* (pp. 138–164). New York: Guilford Press.

Shepard, L. S., & Smith, M. L. (1990). Synthesis of research on grade retention. *Educational Leadership, 47,* 84–88.

Sheridan, S. M., & Kratochwill, T. R. (1992). Behavioral parent-teacher consultation: Conceptual and research considerations. *Journal of School Psychology, 30,* 117–139.

Slavin, R. E., & Madden, N. A. (2001). *One million children: Success for All.* Thousand Oaks, CA: Corwin Press.

Sugai, G., Horner, R. H., & Gresham, F. M. (2002). Behaviorally effective school environments. In M. R. Shinn, H. M. Walker, & G. Stoner (Eds.), *Interventions for academic and behavior problems II: Preventative and remedial approaches* (pp. 315–350). Bethesda, MD: National Association of School Psychologists.

Temple, J., Reynolds, A., & Ou, S. (2000, October). *Grade retention and school dropout: Another look at the evidence.* Paper presented at the National Invitational Conference hosted by the Laboratory for Student Success at Temple University for Research in Human Development and Education, Alexandria, VA.

White, W. A. T. (1988). A meta-analysis of effects of direct instruction in special education. *Education and Treatment of Children, 11,* 364–374.

Yamamoto, K., & Byrnes, D. A. (1987). Primary children's ratings of the stressfulness of experiences. *Journal of Research in Childhood Education, 2*(2), 117–121.

Yang, X. (1997). Educational benefits in elementary school through looping and Friday in-services. *ERIC Digest,* ED425850.

# 47
# Homework

**Timothy Z. Keith**
*University of Texas at Austin*

**Patricia B. Keith**
*Keith Research & Evaluation*

## BACKGROUND AND DEVELOPMENT

Homework is a controversial topic. Despite its ubiquity, homework is no longer viewed by everyone as a way to help students achieve academically. For example, in a book titled *The End of Homework* (Kralovec & Buell, 2000) the authors argue that there is *no* valid reason for young children to do homework and that high school students should be given homework that they can do at school and not at home. The growing anti-homework movement argues that children need time to think, that homework disrupts family life while increasing stress, and that damage to the parent–child relationship can outweigh any educational improvement that homework can bring (Bantick, 2004). An Australian government report suggested "parents were concerned at the degree to which homework should be prescribed and the pressures it can place on the home environment when children are enjoying a range of social activities which parents see as vitally important" (Parents Victoria, 2000). Other reports in the popular press—with titles such as "Homework Doesn't Help" (Begley, 1998) and "The Homework Ate My Family" (Ratnesar, 1999)—likewise suggest a growing anti-homework trend. Yet, according to Cooper (2001), the outcries against homework may represent a small vocal group of individuals. One recent survey (Public Agenda, 2000) suggests that 64% of parents believe that their children are getting about the "right amount of homework," whereas only 10% of parents think their children are getting too much homework. In contrast, 25% of parents think their children are not getting enough homework.

Such debate is not new. The purposes, efficacy, and effects of homework have been debated since the early 1900s (Gill & Schlossman, 2000), and the debates continue in both the professional and popular press (Buell, 2004; Loveless, 2003). For example, a Phi Delta Kappa booklet designed to review homework research and draw practical implications for teachers concluded that little was known about the effects of homework (England & Flatley, 1985). On the other hand, the U.S. Department of Education's (1987) popular compilation of research concerning teaching and learning argued that both the quality and the quantity of homework affect student learning. Given such inconsistency, this chapter begins with a review of homework research, with the assumption that teachers, administrators, and support staff, including school psychologists, need to understand the effects of homework before they can develop coherent recommendations concerning homework.

Homework is defined here as work assigned for completion outside the normal class period. The work may be completed at home or at school, but it is assumed that most is completed at home. Furthermore, it is assumed that the primary purpose of homework is to supplement and improve academic learning.

### Effects of Homework on Learning

If homework does not substantially improve learning and achievement, the reasons for assigning it would be weak, at best. The research evidence provides some answers to the question of what effects homework has on learning; however, most homework research has focused on issues of *quantity* rather than *quality*. Perhaps this is because it is easy to measure how long it takes a student to complete homework, whereas it is difficult to categorize the quality of assignments. Thus, much of the research has focused on time spent doing homework, or homework versus no homework, and the effects of such conditions on learning.

***Quantity of homework.*** Much of the available homework research has been conducted at the high school level, with researchers often using large, representative data sets and nonexperimental research techniques for such analyses. For example, in a series of studies of the effects of homework and other variables on school learning, Keith and colleagues have consistently shown that the amount of time high school students spend working on homework has an important—although sometimes small—effect on their achievement (e.g., Keith, 1982; Keith & Benson, 1992; Keith & Cool, 1992; Keith, Diamond-Hallam, & Fine, 2004). In this research, homework had meaningful effects across different ages of students (sophomores and seniors), for cross-sectional as well as longitudinal analyses, and when a variety of other important influences were controlled (e.g., motivation, parental involvement, and quality and quantity of instruction). Time spent on homework was an important influence on learning, whether that influence was measured by grades or by test scores, and even after important background characteristics were controlled.

The importance of homework for high school students has been demonstrated in other research as well. For example, in a well-designed quasi-experiment using 10th graders and social studies assignments, students who were assigned homework achieved at a higher level than those who were assigned none (Foyle, 1985). Cooper and colleagues' analyses of survey data from triads of teachers, parents, and students suggested that the amount of homework assigned was not important but that the amount of homework completed was important for the grades of students in middle and high school (Cooper, Lindsay, Nye, & Greathouse, 1998). Of course, research does not consistently support the findings on the influence of homework on high school learning, but the majority of research indeed suggests positive effects for homework on high school students' learning and achievement (Cooper, 1989).

Similarly, homework seems an important influence on the learning of middle school youth (Cooper et al., 1998; Keith et al., 1993; Weiner, Sheridan, & Jenson, 1998), although some reviewers suggest that the effects of homework may be smaller for middle than for high school youth (Cooper, 1989). In one study, Keith et al. (1993) suggested that homework may help explain the positive effects of parental involvement. In that study, eighth graders with more involved parents completed more homework, and that homework, in turn, resulted in higher achievement test scores. Several intervention studies have shown success when parents are involved in planning and completing homework interventions for middle school youth (Cancio, West, & Young, 2004; Toney, Kelley, & Lanclos, 2003; Weiner et al., 1998). These interventions resulted in fewer homework problems and greater homework completion and accuracy. Student self-monitoring of homework was also beneficial (Cancio et al.; Toney et al.).

Less research has been done on the effects of homework for younger children. Mathematics homework has been a common focus of study, and a number of researchers have found significant positive effects for homework for elementary school students (Austin, 1979). Homework may have inconsistent positive effects for elementary students in other subject matter areas as well. Cooper and colleagues showed moderate effects for the amount of homework completed on the grades for students in Grades 2 to 4 (Cooper, Jackson, Nye, & Lindsay, 2001; Cooper et al., 1998). Parents' help with homework also had a positive effect (Cooper et al., 2001). But again, homework findings are less consistent for elementary-level than for older students (Muhlenbruck, Cooper, Nye, & Lindsay, 2000). Nevertheless, a comprehensive meta-analysis of homework research showed a significant but smaller positive effect for homework versus no homework for elementary students (Cooper, 1989, chapter 5).

***Quality of homework assignments.*** It seems logical that the quality of homework assignments should also be important. Although quality is more difficult to define than quantity, evidence supports this assumption. For example, there is evidence that homework that is graded or commented on has a stronger effect on achievement than does homework that is not (Paschal, Weinstein, & Walberg, 1984). Evidence from in-class assignments suggests that positive comments are particularly beneficial (Page, 1992). Furthermore, well-planned, systematic homework that is closely tied to the instruction in the classroom appears to be more effective than vague, less well planned assignments (Leonard, 1965).

Consequences for homework completion or noncompletion and parental checking of homework may add to its effectiveness (Rhoades & Kratochwill, 1998). On the other hand, in one of the few studies designed to compare the effectiveness of various types of homework, Foyle

(1985) found no difference in the effects of *practice* homework, designed to review and reinforce skills and materials covered in class, and *preparation* homework, designed to prepare students for an upcoming class topic. Such results do not necessarily mean that the two types of homework result in no meaningful differences. The lack of differences in the two experimental conditions may simply point to the need for the type of homework to be tied closely to the purpose of the assignment (Keith, 1986).

## Homework in Special Education

Relatively little research has been done on the effects of homework for students with special needs. There is evidence, however, that homework is equally effective for low-ability and high-ability youth (Keith, 1982) and that homework can help compensate for low ability (Polachek, Kniesner, & Harwood, 1978).

As might be expected, students who receive pullout or inclusive special education services often have difficulty with homework. In one study, 56% of children with learning disabilities had difficulty completing homework, compared with 28% of regular education students (Polloway, Foley, & Epstein, 1992). Students in special education had more difficulty completing homework assignments, spent less time doing homework assignments, and returned completed assignments that were of lower quality compared with those of students without disabilities (Epstein, Polloway, Foley, & Patton, 1993). Furthermore, students with learning disabilities and behavior problems were more likely to procrastinate, needed more reminding and monitoring, and were more easily distracted than average-achieving students (Epstein et al., 1993). Communication difficulties often occur as a result, with parents, general education teachers, and special education teachers blaming one another for homework problems (Buck et al., 1996; Epstein et al., 1997; Munk et al., 2001). In a study of school district homework practices, about one-third of districts had homework policies, and about two-thirds of those districts recommended that homework modifications be made for students with disabilities. Most such homework modifications were spelled out in Individual Education Plans (IEPs; Roderique, Polloway, Cumblad, Epstein, & Bursuck, 1994).

## Other Issues, Effects, and Purposes

The effects of homework may be greater for students of minority ethnicity and race. In particular, homework may have stronger effects on the achievement test scores of Black and Hispanic youth than of White youth (Keith, 1993) and stronger effects on the grades of students of Asian descent (Keith & Benson, 1992). Some researchers speculate that homework may further improve achievement by reducing leisure TV viewing (Paschal et al., 1984), although several studies have found little support for this hypothesis (Keith et al., 1993).

Some homework critics have argued that students should complete homework in school (Kralovec & Buell, 2000). Recent research suggests, however, that in-school homework has little or no effect on learning, whether measured by grades or by test scores (Keith et al., 2004). These analyses also showed an even stronger effect for homework done out of school than previous research, when separated from the effects of homework done in school. Homework has also shown stronger effects than supervised in-class study for middle school youth; however, supervised in-class study may be more beneficial for elementary school students (Cooper & Valentine, 2001).

Although the primary purpose of homework may be the improvement of immediate achievement and learning, homework can also provide students with long-term benefits (e.g., developing better study habits and study skills and developing lifelong learning interest) and some nonacademic benefits (e.g., better time management, greater self-direction and self-discipline, and more independent problem-solving abilities; Cooper, 2001).

Parents see homework as developing responsibility, providing independent study and preparation for future study, and strengthening the home–school bond (e.g., Warton, 1997). Olympia, Sheridan, and Jenson (1994) argued that homework is "a natural means of home–school collaboration" (p. 60). Other possible purposes of homework include the development of good work habits, the extension of the school day, the opportunity for practice and review, and the assessment of students' understanding of the lesson (for a more detailed discussion of these purposes, see Keith, 1986). Teachers also can individualize instruction by giving different assignments based on the students' instructional levels (Patton, Jayanthi, & Polloway, 2001). There is, in fact, some evidence that individualized homework assignments may produce higher achievement than "blanket" assignments (Bradley, 1967; Hong & Milgram, 2000). Nevertheless, such secondary purposes of homework need additional research support (Cooper, 1989).

A common complaint about homework is that it detracts from other worthwhile and family activities

**Table 1** *Recommendations for Normal Homework Guidelines, by Grade*

| Grade Level | Keith, 1986 | Cooper, 1989 |
|---|---|---|
| Grades 1–3 | 10–45 minutes per day, geared toward the "average" student | 1–3 assignments per week, 15 minutes or less each |
| Grades 4–6 | 45–90 minutes per day | 2–4 assignments, 15–45 minutes each |
| Grades 7–9 | 1–2 hours per day | 3–5 assignments, 45–75 minutes each |
| Grades 10–12 | 1½–2½ hours per day | 4–5 assignments, 75–120 minutes each |

(Bantick, 2004; Kralovec & Buell, 2000). However, recent findings suggest that students in the United States spend relatively little time on homework (Loveless, 2003). Indeed, many high school students appear to spend almost twice as much time during weekdays watching TV as doing homework (Keith et al., 2004).

## Developmental Issues

Education and school curricula are developmental processes; thus it follows that homework should change at different ages and grade levels. At the simplest level, the time students spend working on homework should vary depending on the child's age and grade level. Guidelines for the right amount of homework are difficult because that amount depends a great deal on the community, the school, and the teacher. Even more important, there is wide variability within a classroom for students' completion of the same assignment; the assignment that takes one student 10 minutes may take another an hour. Despite such caveats, several authors have made suggestions for general homework guidelines, which are summarized in Table 1 (e.g., Cooper, 1989; Keith, 1986).

Types of homework assignments should also vary by grade level and subject matter area. Lee and Pruitt (1979) classified homework as falling into one of four categories:

- *Practice homework*, the most frequent type, is designed to review materials and reinforce skills developed in the classroom.
- *Preparation assignments* are designed to prepare students for an upcoming class topic and often involve activities such as reading a text or doing library research.
- *Extension homework* is designed to extend or generalize concepts or skills learned from familiar to new situations, such as writing an essay on the similarities and differences in the causes of the American and the French Revolutions (Lee & Pruitt, 1979, p. 34).
- *Creative homework* assignments require the integration, extension, and creative application of a variety of skills (e.g., a TV production on some topic).

One type of assignment is not always better than another—each serves its own purpose and has its own strengths and weaknesses. Practice, for example, though a necessary component of learning, tends to be the most frequently used type of homework assignment, and it can degenerate into busy work if overused. Preparation assignments, on the other hand, require considerable initiative and thought but may not be helpful if the assignment is vague (e.g., read the next chapter in your social studies text).

Although one type of assignment is not always better than another, it seems likely that both the purposes and types of assignments should vary by grade level. If one of the purposes of homework is to increase students' initiative and responsibility as they grow older, then the mix of types of assignments should change accordingly as students enter higher grades. Thus, if the types of homework are placed on a continuum from practice to creative assignments, the proportion of higher order (extension and creative) assignments should increase as children enter higher grades. Similarly, some of the other purposes of homework change in importance as children mature. For example, the purpose of strengthening the home–school relation may be more important at younger grade levels than at older levels, whereas extending the school day may be more important at higher grade levels. Individualization as a purpose of homework is important for any student having learning difficulties.

# PROBLEMS AND IMPLICATIONS

Although homework may have benefits, homework problems are common and vexing for students, parents, and school personnel. Students may not understand homework or may not complete homework for a variety of reasons. Parents may be unable to provide the homework help students need. Teachers may not have the time or inclination to assign homework or to provide worthwhile feedback on homework that is assigned. Homework that is not completed will result in additional problems in learning. School personnel need to anticipate and be prepared to deal with these problems.

It seems obvious that homework should be closely tied to the curriculum and to a child's instructional level. Thus, the hallmarks of well-developed classroom instruction would seem to hold for homework as well. Homework assignments should have a clear purpose, with explicit, even foolproof directions. Similarly, the product of the assignment should be clear. Is the student expected to answer the questions at the end of the chapter or to complete an essay? Finally, homework generally should be evaluated in some way, either by grading assignments, quizzing the students on the assignment topic, or commenting on their assignments. Whatever system is chosen, work completed outside of school should be followed up in school, both to correct problems that arise and to reinforce the learning that has occurred. Many homework problems likely are the result of homework being poorly tied to the in-school curriculum.

Homework can be viewed from a variety of perspectives. On the one hand, homework can be seen as a means to an end, as a method of raising achievement or improving learning. Such a perspective leads to the notion of homework as an educational intervention, a technique used to improve the achievement of individuals or groups having learning problems (Olympia, Sheridan, Jenson, & Andrews, 1994). Alternatively, homework may be considered in its own right. This perspective is probably more useful when the presenting problem is compliance with homework assignments or difficulty with correct completion of the assigned homework (Miller & Kelley, 1991, 1994). Parents' and teachers' questions commonly come from this perspective: Homework is being assigned; why isn't the student completing it (Rhoades & Kratochwill, 1998)?

Homework concerns and questions can come from a group or an individual perspective. A child may be referred for a problem with homework or a problem for which homework might be a suitable intervention, such as low achievement. At a group level, schools and school districts often develop formal homework policies; informal policies are possible at the classroom and school level as well.

Thus, the *perspective* underlying the question may be among the first considerations addressed when school personnel are faced with questions concerning homework. Other information that may affect possible action toward the presenting question includes both school- and home-related concerns. At the school level, school personnel investigating homework problems will want to know if homework is being assigned and, if so, how much is being assigned. How long does it take the student to do the homework? What types of homework are being assigned? Are the types of assignments and the amount of homework appropriate for the child's grade and ability level? Is the purpose of the assigned homework clear? Does the student understand what he or she is to do and the expected product of the assignments? Is the homework being reviewed in some meaningful fashion in the classroom? Does the homework supplement classroom instruction?

Assigned homework will not fulfill any purpose if it is not completed. When homework problems arise, an assessment may begin with patterns of homework completion and noncompletion. Is assigned homework generally being completed? Are there clear contingencies for the completion or noncompletion of homework? How much homework is being completed? Are there differences in the types of homework the student is completing compared with homework that is not completed? Is completed homework done accurately? If the concern is with an individual student, are other students in the class completing homework correctly? If homework is being completed, but inaccurately, adjustments may be needed in directions for, types of, or difficulty level of homework assignments. Homework that is clearly defined, regularly assigned, of appropriate difficulty level, positively evaluated, and properly integrated into the curriculum will probably produce more learning, and will more likely be completed correctly, than homework that is not. Furthermore, students will likely complain less about homework that is expected, relevant, and appropriate.

Student attitudes toward homework are obviously important. What are student reactions to the homework they are assigned? Do they have valid reasons for not completing assignments? What changes would they suggest?

Homework is a shared school–home responsibility, and thus assessment of what happens in the home is needed when homework problems arise (Olympia, Sheridan, & Jenson, 1994; also see chapter 6, "Parent–Teacher Relationships"). What are parents' and other family members' attitudes toward homework? Do the parents convey a belief that homework completion, and learning in general, is important? There is evidence that such an orientation toward learning, called "the curriculum of the home," may be an important influence on learning (Walberg, 1984).

Table 2 lists many of the questions that are asked in this section, which may shed light on the locus or possible solution of homework problems. Beside each question is a continuum from positive to negative. After interviewing the teacher, student, or parent and after reviewing relevant records, one should simply mark his or her impressions of the answer to each question. The list is intended as an organizer for collected information, not as an interview or checklist. An alternative, more formal assessment is provided by the Homework Problem Checklist, a valuable tool for assessing the extent of homework problems (Anesko, Schoiock, Ramirez, & Levin, 1987). This short checklist provides parents' perspective on homework problems and may be useful in designing interventions.

## ALTERNATIVE ACTIONS FOR PREVENTION AND INTERVENTION

The action taken to address a homework question from a parent will depend on the nature of the problem. Questions about homework may focus on homework as a means to an end (homework as an intervention) or on issues of homework completion (homework itself as the focus). In addition, homework questions may be addressed at the group or individual level. Thus, this discussion of alternatives for prevention and intervention is divided into subsections, although the possible actions may overlap.

### Prevention of Problems at the Group Level

One of the best ways to avoid homework problems is to make sure students, parents, and school personnel know what the homework expectations are. School districts are increasingly interested in developing formal homework policies, and school psychologists can provide constructive input for the development of such policies. Informal policies at the district, school, or class level are also possible. There are advantages and disadvantages to both the formal and informal approach. For example, a district-wide policy creates consistent standards that let parents, children, teachers, and administrators know what is expected. On the other hand, informal policies or class-level policies may provide greater flexibility for individual classes and individual students. The general homework policy presented in Cooper (1989) may provide a good starting point for the development of district-wide policies.

Whatever the approach taken, the policy developed should be flexible. It should communicate different homework expectations for different grade levels. It also should allow flexibility within grade levels and subject matter areas and even within individual classes for students needing individualized study. An inflexible, unworkable homework policy is probably worse than none at all.

Any policy should be shared with students and parents to ensure that they are aware of expectations; the policy may also provide guidelines for parental involvement in homework. The policy should emphasize the need for variety in homework assignments and should encourage the assignment of homework on a consistent basis. Such regularly assigned homework will likely produce more learning than less consistently assigned homework, and students who expect homework on a regular basis will also be less likely to complain about assignments than students who do not expect homework. Homework policies should be developed with input from administrators, teachers, parents, and even students.

When developing district-wide homework policies the following should be considered: (a) design a homework hotline to help answer students' questions concerning homework, (b) encourage students to call or e-mail classmates with homework questions, and (c) create a homework policy website that answers frequently asked questions, provides homework resources, and lists class assignments (Salend, Duhaney, Anderson, & Gottschalk, 2004).

Any district, school, or class that institutes a homework policy or a homework program should be prepared to hear objections to those policies. Homework takes time for students to complete and for teachers to check over and grade. Some contend that students have too many other important out-of-school activities to spend time on homework, although several recent findings suggest the fallacy of this concern (Loveless, 2003). Student objections to homework can be minimized if homework is expected, its purpose is clear, time requirements are not excessive, and the scope and product of the assignment are explicit. High school teachers may be advised to let students know in advance what their assignments

**Table 2** *Homework Information That May Be Useful in Planning Homework Interventions*

| **Student Name:** ______________________________ | **Date:** ____________________ |
|---|---|
| **Information of Interest Concerning Homework** | Positive .................................... Negative |
| How many classes report homework problems? | 0 .................................... All |
| **Information From Teacher Interview and Observation** (Class: ______________) | |
| Is homework assigned regularly? | Always .................................... Rarely |
| Is the homework tied to the curriculum? | Closely .................................... Loosely |
| Is it appropriate for grade level? | Very appropriate .................... Not appropriate |
| Is it appropriate for ability level? | Very appropriate .................... Not appropriate |
| Is the purpose of the homework clear? | Very clear .................................... Vague |
| Are the directions explicit? | Very explicit .................................... Vague |
| Is the expected product of the homework clear? | Very clear .................................... Vague |
| Is the homework evaluated in some way? | Always .................................... Rarely |
| Is the student provided feedback about homework? | Always .................................... Rarely |
| Are there clear contingencies for failure to complete homework? | Always .................................... Rarely |
| Is reinforcement provided for completed homework? | Always .................................... Rarely |
| How much time is expected for homework? | Consistent with guidelines ..... None or excessive |
| Are other students completing homework accurately? | All .................................... Few |

*(Continued)*

**Table 2** *Continued*

| **Student Name:** ______________________ | **Date:** ______________ |
|---|---|
| Is individualization of homework possible? | Easy ........ Difficult |
| Are different types of assignments used? | Variety ........ No variety |
| **Information From Student and Review of Homework Products** | |
| How much time is spent on homework? | Consistent with guidelines ..... None or excessive |
| Are student reports of time consistent with teacher expectations? | Consistent ........ Inconsistent |
| Does the student write down the assignments? | Always ........ Rarely |
| Does the student understand the assignment? | Always ........ Rarely |
| Does the student bring home needed materials? | Always ........ Rarely |
| Normal rate of completion of homework | 100% ........ <60% |
| Normal rate of homework accuracy | 100% ........ <60% |
| Does the student have a quiet place to study? | Always ........ Rarely |
| Does the student study at a consistent time? | Always ........ Rarely |
| Student attitude toward homework | Positive ........ Negative |
| **Information From Parents** | |
| Does parent believe education is important? | Very important ........ Not important |
| Does parent believe homework is important? | Very important ........ Not important |

*(Continued)*

**Table 2** *Continued*

| **Student Name:** ______________________ | **Date:** ______________ |
|---|---|
| Does the student have a quiet place to study? | Always .................... Rarely |
| Does the student study at a consistent time? | Always .................... Rarely |
| Does parent check or supervise homework? | Always .................... Rarely |
| Does parent make sure all assignments are completed? | Always .................... Rarely |
| Is parent willing to check, supervise, reinforce, or help with homework? | Always .................... Rarely |

*Note.* This list of questions is intended as a means of organizing information collected concerning problems with homework. After discussing the problem with the teacher, student, and parent, the psychologist may use this form to check off areas that are problematic and those that represent no problems by placing an X in the appropriate place along each continuum. The list is *not* intended as an interview or checklist to be completed by parents, teachers, or students.

will be for the week to avoid having assignments from several classes get "bunched up" (Munk et al., 2001).

Homework also requires a time commitment from teachers. Good homework assignments are well planned and are an integral part of the curriculum. Most assignments should be graded, and practice homework may be followed profitably by a quiz. Teachers may want students to occasionally correct each other's assignments.

Most objections to homework revolve around the issue of time commitments on the part of students, teachers, and parents. Yet homework does seem to pay off in higher achievement: If it is decided that homework is important and that it produces desirable outcomes, then time will need to be budgeted for its assignment, completion, and correction.

## Group Interventions for Homework Problems

Many questions about homework center on methods of ensuring its completion; homework that is not completed will not fulfill any of its purposes. Homework should be assigned on a regular basis and every effort should be made to ensure that the assignments are consistent with in-class goals and activities. Teachers should strive to convey the purpose of each assignment and to make sure that the directions and expected products of assignments are so clear that they are virtually foolproof. It may be worthwhile to start assignments in class to clear up any questions or problems that arise, although the majority of the assignment should be completed at home. Parents should know that homework is being assigned.

Teachers should provide a mix of homework assignments, including practice, extension, preparation, and creative homework. Although practice homework is necessary it should not be overused. Other types of assignments will often fulfill the purpose better than practice assignments. Teachers should be encouraged to individualize assignments for students who are unlikely to benefit from the normal assignment; such individualization may benefit students' learning. For example, the majority of the class may be given extension homework in science, whereas several low-achieving children may be served better by an assignment that uses the class's new science vocabulary in writing sentences. Excessively long assignments will also reduce compliance: Teachers should be encouraged to think about how long a similar assignment would take in the classroom, and it may be worthwhile occasionally to ask a reliable student how long an assignment took to complete. Real-life assignments, homework planners, and the graphing of homework completion have been shown to improve homework completion for both regular and special education students (Bryan & Sullivan-Burstein, 1998). Such efforts to ensure the relevance and quality of homework assignments should also increase homework completion.

Finally, completed assignments should be assessed in some way; grades and positive comments on homework assignments will likely produce more learning and will also convey that the teacher thinks the assignments are important. Assignments may be followed by a short quiz on the assigned material. Contingencies can be added to increase motivation for homework completion.

A number of homework programs are available that may be appropriate for use in groups, such as classes, or with individual students. Such programs may focus on helping parents, teachers, or the students themselves intervene with homework problems. Olympia, Sheridan, and Jenson (1994) provide a valuable review of such programs. Parent training accompanied by teacher consultation is another way to increase the amount of homework students complete (Rhoades & Kratochwill, 1998).

## Individual Interventions for Homework Problems

Teachers and parents are often concerned about a child who does not complete or poorly completes assigned homework. The first step in such a referral should be the assessment of the homework that is being assigned using some of the interventions mentioned for groups. The homework assigned should be appropriate for the student's ability, achievement, and in-class performance. Individualization of homework assignments may be needed for students performing below the classroom average. The purpose of the assignment and the directions should be clear and the products well defined, and homework should be graded or evaluated. Given the adequacy of the assigned homework, individual cases of noncompletion of homework will often require working with the student and the student's parents to improve homework completion. The student may be questioned concerning reasons for not completing homework, and realistic objections and concerns should be addressed (see Table 2).

Behavior management techniques can be very useful for increasing homework compliance (Kahle & Kelley, 1994). Student-managed interventions have been shown to improve homework completion and accuracy (Olympia, Sheridan, Jenson, & Andrews, 1994). Goal setting and contingency contracting have also shown promise as methods for improving homework performance (Kahle & Kelley, 1994; Miller & Kelley, 1994).

Parental cooperation and support can be an important and effective aspect of homework interventions (Kahle & Kelley, 1994; Miller & Kelley, 1991; Olympia, Sheridan, & Jenson, 1994). Both monitoring by parents and self-monitoring have been shown to improve homework completion and accuracy (Cancio et al., 2004; Toney et al., 2003). If nothing else, parents should be informed of their child's failure to complete homework, and the extent to which they should expect the child to bring assignments home. If parents do not know how often homework is assigned, it is easy for their children to pretend they have no homework. Thus, regularly assigned homework will help ensure clear parental expectations as well.

Parents should be encouraged to provide a quiet, nondistracting place for their child to study, as well as a regularly scheduled time for study. Background music may be fine for studying, but television should be discouraged (Pool, Koolstra, & van der Voort, 2003a, 2003b). For some students, specifying regular times for homework may be necessary, while for others it may be better simply to specify a time by which homework must be completed. Parents should be encouraged to convey a belief in the importance of homework and the expectation that homework will be completed well. The extent of parental involvement in a child's homework, while negotiable, should also be discussed. Extensive involvement should probably be rare. Even when parents have the academic and teaching skills to help their children with homework, it is difficult to serve as teacher and parent at the same time. Parents should generally provide the structure and encouragement for homework completion and should be available to answer an occasional question, review completed assignments, and help review materials for a test, if they feel comfortable in this role.

Completion of homework is a first step; successful completion is obviously a more important goal. Students experiencing difficulty with homework may need to have adjustments made in the nature and type of assignments and may also need help in developing good study skills. The school psychologist may need to work with such students to teach them basic organizational and study strategies. For example, the SQ3R approach (survey, question, read, recite, review) is a valuable tool for ensuring understanding of material and is easy to apply to a variety of situations. The chapters on study skills and learning strategies in this book may be valuable resources for the development of learning interventions.

## Homework as an Individual Intervention

Homework can also be conceived of as an intervention for an individual student. A hypothetical case, such as the following, may best illustrate this possibility (see Olympia, Sheridan, Jenson, & Andrews, 1994, for a research example). The school psychologist receives a referral from a teacher concerning a sixth-grade boy achieving below the level of his peers; the teacher questions whether special class placement is needed. Screening and record review suggest low average abilities and achievement, and a consistent history of marginal classroom performance. Special education placement seems inappropriate, yet some sort of classroom intervention is obviously needed. Further checking reveals the presence of low homework demands (or alternatively, the regular assignment of homework that is too difficult and not completed).

A homework intervention may be appropriate for such a case, and the efficacy of such an intervention could be demonstrated using single-case design techniques. For example, the teacher may give weekly quizzes in math, and reading could be assessed weekly using curriculum-based methods. The quiz and curriculum-based assessment (CBA) scores for the first several weeks would serve as a baseline for the intervention. The school psychologist would then work with the teacher to develop nightly mathematics homework at an appropriate level and would work with the student and his parents to explain the mathematics intervention, to enlist their support, and to set up some guidelines at home for homework completion. Weekly assessment would be continued in both mathematics and reading, with the expectation being that the weekly math quizzes would improve while the reading assessments would remain relatively stable. After such a pattern emerged, reading homework assignments could similarly be started, with the expectation of subsequent improvement in the weekly reading CBA scores.

Such an intervention would help keep the student in the regular classroom; would enlist the aid of the teacher, parents, and student in improving his achievement; would clearly demonstrate whether the intervention was effective; and would require relatively little in-class individualization of homework. Of course, several assumptions are made in this hypothetical case. The first is that the homework assigned is appropriate for the student's age and achievement level and that it is closely tied to the in-class curriculum. Homework that does not meet these criteria will likely be ineffective. The second major assumption is that the student complies with the homework intervention. If not, reasons for noncompletion should be explored and adjustments to the intervention should be made. For example, the appropriateness of the level and time commitment of the assignments would need to be checked, as would the commitment of the parents and the student. It would also be relatively easy to build in some type of reinforcement for successful homework completion (e.g., Harvey, Lewis-Palmer, Horner, & Sugai, 2003; Madaus, Kehle, Madaus, & Bray, 2003).

## SUMMARY

Research evidence suggests that homework is an important influence on academic learning and may fulfill other worthwhile purposes as well. Yet to fulfill these purposes, homework needs to be a well-planned part of the curriculum and needs to be appropriate for the students who are to complete it.

Questions from teachers and parents concerning homework are likely to focus on groups or individuals and on homework as a means to an end (Is it improving student achievement?) or on homework itself (Is homework being completed?). As with other types of referrals, for educators to give meaningful answers to homework questions, they will need to understand the perspective and needs of the person asking the question and will need to gather additional information about the student, the student's classroom, and the nature of the homework. Homework provides an excellent opportunity for working collaboratively with the school, the student, and the home in an effort to improve a student's functioning.

Homework can be viewed as a cost-effective intervention for improving achievement or as a method of accomplishing other purposes. Yet homework requires a considerable time commitment from students, teachers, and often parents. For this reason, care must be taken to ensure that homework assignments fulfill their purposes and that they are clear, well-aligned with the curriculum, and appropriate for the students who are to complete them. Such a focus on quality of homework assignments should help ensure that assignments are treated as important rather than as busy work. Furthermore, with such a focus on quality, and with appropriate feedback, it is likely that homework's effect on learning will be even greater than that shown in research, where quality of assignments is rarely controlled.

## RECOMMENDED RESOURCES

### Books and Other Printed Material

#### *For Professionals*

Miller, D. L., & Kelley, M. L. (1991). Interventions for improving homework performance: A critical review. *School Psychology Quarterly, 6,* 174–185.

This review summarizes research findings on interventions designed to increase homework completion and accuracy. Miller and Kelley focus particularly on parental involvement and parent–child conflict and their relation to homework.

Olympia, D. E., Sheridan, S. M., & Jenson, W. (1994). Homework: A natural means of home-school collaboration. *School Psychology Quarterly, 9,* 60–80.

Olympia and colleagues provide a fine review of homework programs that can be used in the service of group or individual interventions. Programs may focus on parents, teachers, or students as the primary focus of the interventions.

Powers, T. J., Karustis, J. L., & Habboushe, D. F. (2001). *Homework success for children with ADHD: A family-school intervention program.* New York: Guilford.

This manual is an excellent resource for teachers, clinicians, or others who are interested in establishing a homework program with parents with elementary school-aged children with ADHD who are experiencing difficulties with homework completion. After providing an overview of homework and learning problems commonly experienced by children with ADHD, the book provides detailed chapters on how to set up and initiate the behavioral intervention with a group of parents or an individual parent. The intervention is organized into seven sessions with specific goals for each meeting; within the manual are numerous checklists, rating scales, and worksheets to be used during the program. Although this homework program was designed for students with ADHD, the program can be used for all students who are experiencing difficulties completing homework.

***For Parents, Students, and Teachers***

Dawson, P. (2004). Homework: A guide for parents. In A. S. Canter, L. Z. Paige, M. D. Roth, I. Romero, & S. A. Carroll (Eds.), *Helping children at home and school II: Handouts for families and educators* (S2: 41–46).

This handout provides a structured approach for parents interested in improving their children's homework completion by establishing daily routines, developing incentive systems, and involving siblings in the process.

Radencich, M. C., & Schumm, J. S. (1997). *How to help your child with homework: Every caring parent's guide to encouraging good study habits and ending the homework wars: For parents of children ages 6–13.* Minneapolis, MN: Free Spirit Publishing.

This book was written by two teachers. It provides parents with step-by-step techniques to use with children during the elementary school years. After a brief review of some issues related to homework (e.g., who should do homework), the book provides advice on setting up a homework schedule and a home study center; helping with reading, writing, spelling, mathematics, science, social science, and foreign language homework; using technology wisely; helping prepare for tests; and helping children develop study skills.

Zentall, S. (1998). Seven steps to homework success: A family guide for solving common homework problems. Plantation, FL: Speciality.

This book provides information that parents and teachers will find useful if their goal is to increase students' completion of homework assignments. Topics covered include understanding the importance of homework; the child's homework skills; homework alliances with the child; building a learning station; home–school communication; and basics about homework assignments. Of special note is chapter 4, which presents 11 common homework problems and provides some basic solutions for these problems.

## REFERENCES

Anesko, K. M., Schoiock, G., Ramirez, R., & Levin, F. M. (1987). The Homework Problems Checklist: Assessing children's homework difficulties. *Behavioral Assessment, 9,* 179–185.

Austin, J. D. (1979). Homework research in mathematics. *School Science and Mathematics, 79,* 115–121.

Bantick, C. (2004, May). Homework robs children of their childhood. *The Age.* (Australia) [Electronic version]. Retrieved May 21, 2004, from http://www.theage.com.au/articles/2004/05/20/1085028464584.html

Begley, S. (1998, March 30). Homework doesn't help. *Newsweek,* 50–51.

Bradley, R. M. (1967). An experimental study of individualized versus blanket-type homework assignments in elementary school mathematics. *Dissertation Abstracts International, 28,* 3874A.

Bryan, T., & Sullivan-Burstein, K. (1998). Teacher-selected strategies for improving homework completion. *Remedial and Special Education, 19,* 263–275.

Buck, G. H., Bursuck, W. D., Polloway, E. A., Nelson, J., Jayanthi, M. A., & Whitehouse, F. (1996). Homework-related communication problems: Perspectives of special education teachers. *Journal of Emotional and Behavioral Disorders, 4,* 105–113.

Buell, J. (2004). *Closing the book on homework.* Philadelphia: Temple University Press.

Cancio, E. J., West, R. P., & Young, K. R. (2004). Improving mathematics homework completion and accuracy of students with EBD through self-management and parent participation. *Journal of Emotional and Behavioral Disorders, 12,* 9–22.

Cooper, H. (1989). *Homework.* New York: Longman.

Cooper, H. (2001). Homework for all—in moderation. *Educational Leadership, 58*(7), 34–38.

Cooper, H., Jackson, K., Nye, B., & Lindsay, J. L. (2001). A model of homework's influence on the performance evaluations of elementary school students. *Journal of Experimental Education, 69,* 181–199.

Cooper, H., Lindsay, J. J., Nye, B., & Greathouse, S. (1998). Relationships between attitudes about homework, the amount of homework assigned and completed, and student achievement. *Journal of Educational Psychology, 90,* 70–83.

Cooper, H., & Valentine, J. C. (2001). Using research to answer practical questions about homework. *Education Psychologists, 36,* 143–153.

England, D. A., & Flatley, J. K. (1985). *Homework—And why.* Bloomington, IN: Phi Delta Kappa Educational Foundation.

Epstein, M. H., Polloway, E. A., Buck, G. H., Bursuch, W. D., Wissinger, L. M., Whitehouse, F., & Jayanthi, M. (1997). Homework-related communication problems: Problems of general education teachers. *Learning Disabilities Research and Practice, 12,* 221–227.

Epstein, M. H., Polloway, E. A., Foley, R. M., & Patton, J. R. (1993). Homework: A comparison of teachers' and parents' perceptions of the problems experienced by students identified as having behavioral disorders, learning disabilities, or no disabilities. *Remedial and Special Education, 14,* 40–50.

Foyle, H. C. (1985, November). *Homework variety: A way to educational excellence.* Paper presented at the annual meeting of the National Council for the Social Studies, Chicago, IL.

Gill, B., & Schlossman, S. (2000). The lost cause of homework reform. *American Journal of Education, 109,* 27–62.

Harvey, M. T., Lewis-Palmer, T., Horner, R. H., & Sugai, G. (2003). Trans-situational interventions: Generali-zation of behavioral support across school and home environments. *Behavior Disorders, 28,* 299–313.

Hong, E., & Milgram, R. M. (2000). *Homework: Motivation and learning preference.* Westport, CT: Bergin & Garvey.

Kahle, A. L., & Kelley, M. L. (1994). Children's homework problems: A comparison of goal setting and parent training. *Behavior Therapy, 25,* 275–290.

Keith, T. Z. (1982). Time spent on homework and high school grades: A large-sample path analysis. *Journal of Educational Psychology, 74,* 248–253.

Keith, T. Z. (1986). *Homework.* West Lafayette, IN: Kappa Delta Pi.

Keith, T. Z. (1993). Causal influences on school learning. In H. J. Walberg (Ed.), *Analytic methods for educational productivity* (pp. 21–47). Greenwich, CT: JAI Press.

Keith, T. Z., & Benson, M. J. (1992). Effects of manipulable influences on high school grades across five ethnic groups. *Journal of Educational Research, 86,* 85–93.

Keith, T. Z., & Cool, V. A. (1992). Testing models of school learning: Effects of quality of instruction, motivation, academic coursework, and homework on academic achievement. *School Psychology Quarterly, 7,* 207–226.

Keith, T. Z., Diamond-Hallam, C., & Fine, J. G. (2004). Longitudinal effects of in-school and out-of school homework on high school grades. *School Psychology Quarterly, 19,* 187–211.

Keith, T. Z., Keith, P. B., Troutman, G. C., Bickley, P. G., Trivette, P. S., & Singh, K. (1993). Does parental involvement affect eighth grade student achievement? Structural analysis of national data. *School Psychology Review, 22,* 474–496.

Kralovec, E., & Buell, J. (2000). *The end of homework: How homework disrupts families, overburdens children, and limits learning.* Boston: Beacon Press.

Lee, J. F., & Pruitt, K. W. (1979). Homework assignments: Classroom games or teaching tools? *The Clearing House, 53,* 31–35.

Leonard, M. H. (1965). An experimental study of homework at the intermediate-grade level. *Dissertation Abstracts International, 26,* 3782.

Loveless, T. (2003, October). *Brown Center report on American education 2003: How well are American students learning.* Washington, DC: Brookings Institute.

Madaus, M. M. R., Kehle, T. J., Madaus, J., & Bray, M. A. (2003). Mystery motivator as an intervention to promote homework completion and accuracy. *School Psychology International, 24,* 369–377.

Miller, D. L., & Kelley, M. L. (1991). Interventions for improving homework performance: A critical review. *School Psychology Quarterly, 6,* 174–185.

Miller, D. L., & Kelley, M. L. (1994). The use of goal setting and contingency contracting for improving children's homework performance. *Journal of Applied Behavior Analysis, 27,* 73–84.

Muhlenbruck, L., Cooper, H., Nye, B., & Lindsay, J. J. (2000). Homework and achievement: Explaining the different relations at the elementary and secondary school levels. *Social Psychology of Education, 4,* 295–317.

Munk, D., Bursuch, W. D., Epstein, M. H., Jayanthi, M., Nelson, K. J., & Polloway, E. A. (2001). Homework communication problems: Perspectives of special and general education parents. *Reading and Writing Quarterly: Overcoming Learning Disabilities, 17,* 189–203.

Olympia, D. E., Sheridan, S. M., & Jenson, W. (1994). Homework: A natural means of home-school collaboration. *School Psychology Quarterly, 9,* 60–80.

Olympia, D. E., Sheridan, S. M., Jenson, W., & Andrews, D. (1994). Using student-managed interventions to increase homework completion and accuracy. *Journal of Applied Behavior Analysis, 27,* 85–99.

Page, E. B. (1992). Is the world an orderly place? A review of teacher comments and student achievement. *Journal of Experimental Education, 60,* 161–181.

Parents Victoria. (2000). *Reporting and homework in Victorian government schools: Report to Department of Education.* Victoria, Australia: Department of Education, Employment, and Training.

Paschal, R. A., Weinstein, T., & Walberg, H. J. (1984). The effects of homework on learning: A quantitative synthesis. *Journal of Educational Research, 78,* 97–104.

Patton, J. R, Jayanthi, M., & Polloway, E. A. (2001). Home-school collaboration about homework: What do we know and what should we do. *Reading and Writing Quarterly: Overcoming Learning Difficulties, 17,* 227–242.

Polachek, S. W., Kniesner, T. J., & Harwood, H. J. (1978). Educational production functions. *Journal of Educational Statistics, 3,* 209–231.

Polloway, E. A., Foley, R. M., & Epstein, M. H. (1992). A comparison of the homework problems of students with learning disabilities and nonhandicapped students. *Learning Disabilities Research and Practice, 7,* 203–209.

Pool, M. M., Koolstra, C. M., & van der Voort, T. H. A. (2003a). The impact of background radio and television on high school students' homework performance. *Journal of Communication, 53,* 74–87.

Pool, M. M., Koolstra, C. M., & van der Voort, T. H. A. (2003b). Distraction effects of background soap operas on homework performance: An experimental study enriched with observational data. *Educational Psychology, 23,* 361–380.

Public Agenda. (2000). Survey finds little sign of backlash against academic standards or standardized tests. New York: Author. Retrieved October 13, 2005, from http://www.publicagenda.org/press/press_release_detail.cfm?list=29

Ratnesar, R. (1999, January 25). The homework ate my family. *Time, 153,* 55–56, 59–63.

Rhoades, M. M., & Kratochwill, T. R. (1998). Parent training and consultation: An analysis of a homework intervention program. *School Psychology Quarterly, 13,* 241–264.

Roderique, T. W., Polloway, E. A., Cumblad, C., Epstein, M. H., & Bursuck, W. D. (1994). Homework: A survey of policies in the United States. *Journal of Learning Disabilities, 22,* 314–322.

Salend, S. J., Duhaney, D., Anderson, D. J., & Gottschalk, C. (2004). Using the Internet to improve homework communication and completion. *Council for Exceptional Children, 36,* 64–73.

Toney, L. P., Kelley, M. L., & Lanclos, C. F. (2003). Self- and parental monitoring of homework in adolescents: Comparative effects on parents' perception of homework behavior problems. *Child and Family Behavior Therapy, 25,* 35–51.

U.S. Department of Education. (1987). *What works: Research about teaching and learning* (2nd ed.). Washington, DC: Author.

Walberg, H. J. (1984). Improving the productivity of America's schools. *Educational Leadership, 41*(8), 19–30.

Warton, P. M. (1997). Learning about responsibility: Lessons from homework. *British Journal of Educational Psychology, 67,* 213–221.

Weiner, R. K., Sheridan, S. M., & Jenson, W. R. (1998). The effects of conjoint behavioral consultation and a structured homework program on math completion and accuracy in junior high students. *School Psychology Quarterly, 13,* 281–309.

Zentall, S. (1998). *Seven steps to homework success: A family guide for solving common homework problems.* Plantation, FL: Speciality Press.

# 48

# Peer-Assisted Learning Strategies

**Marika Ginsburg-Block**
*University of Delaware*

**Cynthia Rohrbeck**
*George Washington University*

**John Fantuzzo**
*University of Pennsylvania*

**Nancy C. Lavigne**
*University of Delaware*

## BACKGROUND AND DEVELOPMENT

In contrast to teacher-led instructional strategies, peer-assisted learning (PAL) refers to dyadic and small group learning opportunities led by students, such as classwide peer tutoring (CWPT; Greenwood, Maheady, & Delquadri, 2002), reciprocal peer tutoring (RPT; Fantuzzo & Ginsburg-Block, 1998), and cooperative learning strategies (Johnson & Johnson, 1989). PAL strategies have been widely researched and used in schools for more than 30 years. In fact, a recent survey of classroom teachers showed that two-thirds of teachers offered opportunities for weekly student interaction, and nearly half of the teachers surveyed received professional development training on student–student interaction strategies within the past year (Henke, Chen, & Goldman, 1999). PAL strategies may be found in some school-wide curricula, such as the Success for All program (Slavin, Karweit, & Wasik, 1994). Even more commonly, PAL strategies are recommended for struggling students to bolster their academic and social skills. The research literature has documented the effectiveness of PAL in promoting significant academic, as well as social, self-concept, and behavioral effects for students (Ginsburg-Block, Rohrbeck, & Fantuzzo, 2004; Rohrbeck, Ginsburg-Block, Fantuzzo, & Miller, 2003). Familiarity with the use of PAL strategies in the schools is essential for any school-based practitioner.

### Definition and Purpose

Unfortunately, the research literature has no consistent, agreed-upon definition of PAL. For the purposes of this chapter, discussion of PAL strategies will be limited to peer-led strategies that focus on academic content, thereby excluding some peer-mediated strategies, such as peer counseling or peer mentoring, that are often included in discussions of PAL (Topping & Ehly, 1998). Structured, student-led cooperative learning strategies are also included in this chapter's definition of PAL. Others have excluded cooperative learning approaches from their definitions of PAL, since in their generic form, they may simply include small group instructional arrangements that lack peer-led interaction (Topping & Ehly, 1998).

### Benefits of PAL Strategies

The benefits of PAL are too numerous to fully document in this chapter, so only PAL's most compelling advantages are highlighted below.

***Superiority to traditional models.*** PAL's effectiveness above that of traditional independent or competitive learning has been demonstrated repeatedly in the research literature. Consensus among the available meta-analytic reviews of the PAL literature (Cohen, Kulik, & Kulik, 1982; Cook, Scruggs, Mastropieri, & Casto, 1985; Johnson, Johnson, & Stanne, 2000; Rohrbeck et.al., 2003) places PAL's effects on academic learning above the reported average for social, behavioral, and educational treatments (Lipsey & Wilson, 1993). The most recently published review reports an average overall unweighted effect size of .59 (.90 standard deviation [SD]) across 81 PAL studies comparing PAL strategies to traditional methods at the elementary level (Rohrbeck et al., 2003). This means that the average student receiving PAL performed more than half a standard deviation greater than the average peer in the control condition. Alternatively, the average child receiving PAL scored at the 72nd percentile of the students in the control condition. In terms of practical significance, this means that PAL could theoretically move a student from the very middle of the class to nearly the top quarter of the class.

***Effectiveness in promoting both academic and affective outcomes.*** PAL brings together strong academic learning strategies and strong affective learning strategies, addressing academic learning needs while simultaneously addressing social, self-concept, and behavioral learning needs. Parallel to those findings reported for PAL's academic effectiveness, the most recent meta-analysis examining PAL's affective effectiveness for elementary students reported effect sizes of .52 (.58 SD), .40 (.51 SD), and .65 (.42 SD) for PAL's social, self-concept, and behavioral conduct effects, respectively (Ginsburg-Block et al., 2004). Behavioral conduct involves positive classroom learning behaviors such as academic engagement, an often-cited advantage of PAL. The benefit of PAL for the promotion of social–emotional learning is that it is easily embedded in the daily curriculum and maintains a focus on academic learning while addressing the same needs as add-on curricula designed specifically to address social–emotional learning.

***Effectiveness with vulnerable student populations.*** One of the most concerning phenomena in American education today is the persistent achievement gap between majority and minority students. To address this issue, PAL researchers examined the effectiveness of PAL with urban, minority, and low-income elementary children across 36 studies in the research literature (Ginsburg-Block et al., 2004). On every outcome variable studied, urban students exposed to PAL demonstrated significantly greater outcomes than their suburban or rural counterparts who were also exposed to PAL, including the areas of academic, social, self-concept, and behavioral conduct. PAL resulted in significantly greater effects in the areas of academic achievement, social skills, and self-concept for predominantly minority students versus their predominantly majority peers. Finally, predominantly low-income students demonstrated greater self-concept effects as a result of their involvement in PAL, compared with their predominantly middle- or high-income peers. In some cases these reported gains were extremely dramatic. For instance, self-concept effects were six times greater for minority students than their majority counterparts. These findings, coupled with achievement gains greater than twice those of their majority counterparts (as demonstrated by Rohrbeck et al., 2003), suggest that PAL may be a promising strategy for reducing the troubling achievement gap between majority and minority students in our public schools.

***Versatility and cost-effectiveness.*** In terms of versatility, PAL strategies have been successfully implemented with a wide range of students, including students in Grades K–12, as well as adult learners, students in regular and special education classrooms, low-achieving students, high-achieving students, and students with limited English proficiency. PAL strategies have also been applied to a wide range of subject areas, including but not limited to mathematics, reading, science, and social studies. In addition, PAL strategies have been implemented for a variety of instructional purposes—to supplement or replace a particular curriculum, to reinforce previously learned material, or to teach new material. PAL strategies have been used with and without technology. They have also been used with intact classrooms or across grades, as push-in or pullout programs, by individual teachers, or in school- or district-wide efforts. In general, PAL strategies make use of resources that are readily accessible to all schools—that is, peers. One carefully conducted study of an urban school district in the western United States found that peer tutoring surpassed computer-assisted instruction, class size reduction, and instructional time as the most economical and effective method of raising reading and mathematics achievement (Levin, Glass, & Meister, 1987). This is merely one example; however, it illustrates the fact that PAL strategies require fewer resources than many other instructional interventions, and their results are consistently more impressive than those more costly strategies. Thus, PAL strategies may be considered cost-effective as well as versatile.

## Developmental Systems Framework

A developmental systems framework is useful for understanding the complex educational needs of diverse student populations and for informing the development and evaluation of intervention methods, such as PAL, to meet these needs (Rohrbeck et al., 2003). Fundamentally, this perspective explains the development of children's academic and social competencies by emphasizing the importance of the context in which development occurs (Bronfenbrenner, 1979). Developmental–ecological theory suggests that the way in which children interact with the salient influences in their environment (e.g., parents, peers, and teachers) determines their level of success in meeting developmental challenges, such as adaptation to school (Garcia Coll & Garrido, 2000). The application of a developmental systems framework to PAL is inherent, because PAL is a *classroom* strategy that employs *peers* in the learning process, both of which provide important contexts for child development.

Many ideas exist about the precise mechanisms underlying the effectiveness of PAL strategies. Based on a developmental systems framework, those ideas can be grouped into two broad conceptual categories: (a) student-centered classroom instruction, and (b) peer interactions.

***Student-centered classroom instruction.*** One hypothesis about the effectiveness of PAL strategies suggests that PAL's incorporation of student-centered instructional strategies supports learning by enhancing student motivation and self-concept. Contemporary achievement motivation theorists (e.g. Ryan & Deci, 2000) suggest that students are continually striving to establish self-regulation and mastery of newly learned concepts. Academic environments organized to achieve these goals have been linked to positive student achievement as well as affective outcomes, such as feelings of self-efficacy and motivation (Fantuzzo & Polite, 1990). Key elements of classroom structure associated with bolstering student affect include individualizing classroom tasks and evaluation techniques, structuring opportunities for learning, and providing opportunities for student self-management, many of which are used in PAL programs (Ames, 1992). Evidence linking each of these classroom structures to student outcomes exists (e.g., Daly, Martens, Kilmer, & Massie, 1996; Fantuzzo, King, & Heller, 1992).

The effectiveness of these classroom structures in the context of PAL was examined in two recent theory-driven meta-analyses (Rohrbeck et al., 2003; Ginsburg-Block et al., 2004). The authors found that academic and self-concept effect sizes were significantly higher for PAL interventions that provided students with more opportunities for autonomy. PAL programs employing individualized evaluation procedures that focus on individual progress produced greater academic, self-concept, and behavioral effects than normative evaluation procedures. Additionally, self-concept effects were significantly greater for structured as opposed to unstructured PAL programs. These findings support the hypothesis that, in part, PAL's effectiveness can be attributed to its successful support of the student as a learner through the use of student-centered instructional strategies.

***Peer interactions.*** Two major categories of peer influence explain the mechanisms by which peer interactions contribute to student learning: (a) peer influence on cognitive development and (b) peer influence on task engagement and achievement motivation. From a cognitive–developmental perspective (Piaget & Inhelder, 1972; Vygotsky, 1935), PAL provides students with formal peer learning opportunities in which peers help each other reexamine their own understanding and skills. This process leads to higher levels of thinking and learning and to the internalization of educational goals. Children are able to explain and successfully teach concepts to one another (Slavin, 1990), often more effectively than adults. Some research shows that peer tutors display more gains than the students they teach (Greenwood, Carta, & Hall, 1988), since providing explanations increases the explainer's retention of information. Studies of small group learning have linked mathematics achievement with the process of giving and receiving elaborated help and providing answers (e.g., Webb & Farivar, 1994). Overall, providing students with opportunities to engage in peer teaching and learning has been associated with cognitive gains.

Along with the cognitive benefits of PAL, peer relationships foster academic and social motivation for learning and, consequently, for academic success (Wentzel, 1999). When social influences provide students with consistent messages about the importance of academic success, students are more likely to internalize these values and pursue positive academic goals. In contrast, the often-incongruent values and demands placed on students across peer and school settings may contribute to school disengagement (Phelan, Davidson, Locke,

& Yu, 1998). Two conditions are necessary to provide students with incentives to help peers in their learning: group goals and individual accountability (Johnson, Maruyama, Johnson, Nelson, & Skon, 1981). In studies where rewards were used as incentives, Slavin (1990) found that interdependent reward contingencies, in which rewards were provided on the basis of group performance, were more effective than dependent or independent reward contingencies. Working toward a common goal, as in the case of group reward contingencies, promotes peer encouragement, reinforcement of effort, and the establishment of norms emphasizing academic achievement. Furthermore, researchers found that academic, social, and self-concept effect sizes were higher for PAL interventions that used interdependent reward contigencies rather than no reward contingencies (Rohrbeck et al., 2003; Ginsburg-Block et al., 2004). Given the consistently positive relationship between the use of interdependent group reward contingencies in PAL programs and favorable student outcomes, these practices serve to enhance the effectiveness of PAL programs and should be considered as complementary, if not essential, PAL components.

## PAL Models

Three widely researched and validated models of academic PAL strategies are highlighted in this section: (a) Classwide Peer Tutoring (CWPT), (b) Reciprocal Peer Tutoring (RPT), and (c) Cooperative Learning (CL). In addition, a brief overview of cross-age peer tutoring (CAPT), a popular arrangement for pairing students, will be discussed. CWPT, RPT, and CAPT employ peer dyads in the learning process, whereas CL makes use of small learning groups. Unlike the major PAL models, CAPT is simply an instructional arrangement and does not come with a set of validated procedures. Table 1 provides a summary of each of the major models, including their distinctive components, subapplications (i.e., many distinct PAL strategies have been modeled after CWPT and CL), populations, and subject areas for which the model has been tested.

## Classwide Peer Tutoring (CWPT)

CWPT was jointly developed in the early 1980s by researchers at the Juniper Gardens Children's Project of the University of Kansas and local classroom teachers who were interested in integrating students with mild disabilities into their regular education classrooms. CWPT incorporates components from the effective instruction literature, including the following: (a) reciprocal tutor and tutee roles, (b) frequent opportunities to practice and receive feedback on performance, (c) weekly performance evaluations, (d) self-management through performance monitoring, (e) individual and group reinforcement contingencies, and (f) public posting of performance outcomes (Greenwood et al., 2002).

CWPT engages entire classrooms in peer tutoring. Each student pair consists of a tutor and tutee. Student pairs rotate weekly and are assigned either randomly, matched by ability (i.e., same or adjacent levels), or by level of language proficiency. During the course of the tutoring session students switch roles, allowing each to participate in both the tutor and tutee roles. Pairs are assigned to one of two classroom teams to which their points are attributed. Tutors give their tutees points for correct and corrected responses, and tutors earn bonus points from the classroom teacher for following appropriate procedures. At the end of each session, the winning team for that day is applauded and may receive an optional certificate. The losing team is also applauded and encouraged to work harder next time (Arreaga-Mayer, Terry, & Greenwood, 1998).

The CWPT teacher's manual includes a description of 10 core procedures necessary to implement the intervention (see Table 1). At the elementary level, the purpose of CWPT is to supplement traditional content-area instruction by replacing seatwork, teacher lecture, and oral reading group activities. In secondary schools, the character of CWPT changes somewhat to include practice, skill building, application, and review. Study guides are used to structure student interactions, replacing those subject-matter procedures implemented at the elementary level (Greenwood et al., 2002).

CWPT has been used effectively with students in regular and special education classes, students with disabilities (including high-functioning students with autism, social competence deficits, Attention Deficit Hyperactivity Disorder, mild disabilities, and behavior disorders), low-achieving students, students with limited English proficiency, and students in Grades K–12 (Arreaga-Mayer et al., 1998). The most impressive research supporting the effectiveness of CWPT comes from a 12-year longitudinal experiment. In this study, CWPT participants showed (a) increased academic engagement in Grades 1–3; (b) increased achievement gains in Grades 2, 3, 4, and 6; (c) reduced special education enrollment by Grade 7; and (d) reduced

**Table 1** *PAL Models and Features*

| Model | Distinctive Components | Subapplications | Populations[a] | Content Areas[a] |
|---|---|---|---|---|
| *Classwide Peer Tutoring* (Greenwood et al., 1988) | 1. New material review<br>2. Content materials<br>3. New partners weekly<br>4. Partner pairing strategies<br>5. Reciprocal roles daily<br>6. Team competition<br>7. Individual points<br>8. Error correction<br>9. Public posting of scores<br>10. Team social rewards | 1. Peer-Assisted Learning Strategies (Fuchs et al., 1995)<br>2. Classwide Student Tutoring Teams (Maheady et al., 1988) | Elementary, secondary, students with disabilities, English language learners, low-achieving students | Reading, spelling, language, mathematics, social studies, science, history |
| *Cooperative Learning* | 1. Positive interdependence<br>2. Face-to-face interaction<br>3. Individual accountability and personal responsibility<br>4. Interpersonal and small group skills<br>5. Group processing | 1. Learning Together (Johnson & Johnson, 1999)<br>2. Teams–Games–Tournaments (DeVries & Edwards, 1974)<br>3. Group Investigation (Sharan & Sharan, 1992)<br>4. Creative Controversy (Johnson & Johnson, 1995)<br>5. Jigsaw (Aronson & Patnoe, 1997)<br>6. Students Teams Achievement Divisions (Slavin, 1990)<br>7. Complex Instruction[b] (Cohen, Lotan, Scarloss, & Arellano, 1999)<br>8. Team Accelerated Instruction (Slavin, 1990)<br>9. Cooperative Learning Structures[b] (Kagan, 1989)<br>10. Cooperative Integrated Reading and Composition (Stevens & Slavin, 1995) | Elementary, secondary, students with disabilities, English language learners, low-achieving students | Reading, language, writing, grammar, comprehension, mathematics, social studies, science |
| *Reciprocal Peer Tutoring* (Fantuzzo & Ginsburg-Block, 1998) | 1. Structured peerinteractions<br>2. Student-managed, interdependent group reward contingency<br>3. Reciprocal peer tutoring | | Elementary, low-achieving students | Mathematics (computation and problem solving) |

[a]These population and content areas are not exhaustive; they reflect the majority of the research conducted on these models.
[b]No evaluation studies are available comparing strategy to individualistic instruction.

school dropout by Grade 12 (see Greenwood et al., 2002).

***Peer-Assisted Learning Strategies (PALS).*** PALS is a form of CWPT developed in the early 1990s by researchers at the Peabody College of Vanderbilt University. Their purpose was similar to that of CWPT's developers, that is, to provide elementary school teachers with an effective and feasible classwide intervention that could be used in regular education classrooms accommodating mainstreamed special education students. PALS was developed on the basis of CWPT, although it includes some variations. The most prominent difference between CWPT and PALS is the inclusion of ongoing curriculum-based measurement (CBM) procedures, as well as links to computerized formative evaluation systems using CBM (Fuchs, Fuchs, Phillips, Hamlett, & Karns, 1995; Greenwood et al., 2002).

Consistent with CWPT, PALS follows a reciprocal tutoring format in each session. Students are paired according to ability level based on CBM pretest scores with higher performing students matched to lower performing students. Pairs work together on individually determined learning tasks that are selected to match the instructional level of the lower performing student. The higher performing student begins the session as the "coach," and the lower performing student begins as the "player." PAL coaches interact frequently with their players by modeling learning behaviors and providing feedback and error correction. Weekly CBM provides teachers with information about student performance. Twice-monthly student feedback sessions provide students with a graphic display of their progress and skills profiles that indicate areas of relative strength and weakness. PALS mathematics sessions include an acquisition instruction component in which students practice problem solving using a structured procedure. This is followed by a mixed problem–type drill. PALS reading sessions are organized to include partner reading, story retelling, paragraph shrinking (i.e., oral summarization), and prediction relay, that is, summarization and prediction of subsequent events in the story (Fuchs, Fuchs, Mathes, & Simmons, 1997; Fuchs et al., 1995; Greenwood et al., 2002).

Numerous studies support the effectiveness of PALS in the areas of reading and mathematics at the elementary level and reading and subject-matter instruction at the secondary level. Collateral effects of PALS include increased social skills for students and high levels of satisfaction among student and teacher participants. PALS has also been successfully implemented with students with learning disabilities and behavior disorders (Greenwood et al., 2002).

***Classwide Student Tutoring Teams (CSTT).*** CSTT is another application of CWPT developed specifically for content area instruction at the secondary level (Greenwood et al., 2002; Utley, Morweet, & Greenwood, 1997). It was developed during the late 1980s to enhance skill mastery of material previously introduced by the teacher. CSTT applies the peer teaching procedures of CWPT to small groups of four to five heterogeneous learning teams per classroom (i.e., at least one student at low, medium, and high levels of performance). These learning teams are modeled after teams–games–tournaments (TGT), a cooperative learning strategy involving competition among teams (see the section on cooperative learning). Another difference between CSTT and CWPT is the use of teacher-developed study guides.

CSTT sessions are recommended twice weekly for 30 minutes. Materials are distributed to each team, including a study guide for the week, paper and pencils, and a small deck of cards. All students take turns being the teacher. As "teacher," the student selects from the deck a card that contains a question and reads the question to the other students. Students write down their responses, which are checked by the student teacher against the answer key. Points are provided to students for correct or corrected answers, and the student teacher provides the correct answers. As in CWPT, the classroom teacher is responsible for monitoring teamwork and awarding bonus points for appropriate task-oriented behavior. Teams receive rewards for meeting a minimum standard or being most improved, and the most outstanding team members are also recognized. Winning point totals are posted publicly (Greenwood et al., 2002; Utley et al., 1997).

Research has demonstrated the superiority of CSTT compared with traditional methods in promoting mathematics achievement among 9th- and 10th-grade students at risk for school dropout (Maheady, Sacca, & Harper, 1988). In addition to its application for mathematics, CSTT has been applied to secondary social studies, science, and history classrooms with students in regular education and students with mild disabilities. The nonacademic effects of CSTT include increases in self-esteem and friendships (Greenwood et al., 2002; Utley et al., 1997).

## Reciprocal Peer Tutoring (RPT)

RPT was developed in the late 1980s for pairs of low-achieving urban elementary school children (Fantuzzo et al., 1992). Unlike strategies that rely on mixed-ability pairs or groups, RPT employs same-age student pairs of comparable ability, with the primary objective of keeping students engaged in constructive academic activity. RPT has been applied primarily to elementary mathematics instruction in the areas of computation and problem solving with children in Grades 3 through 6.

Although RPT provides numerous opportunities for student self-management, the role of the classroom teacher is critical. Implementation of RPT involves preparation, teamwork training, RPT training, and supervision of the RPT intervention, all of which involve the active participation of the classroom teacher (Fantuzzo & Ginsburg-Block, 1998). Preparation activities include the development of curricular materials, such as flash cards and drill sheets, and the assessment of student skill levels. Altogether, training involves approximately five 45-minute sessions during which students become familiar with teamwork, as well as with the specific procedures for RPT. Sessions are held twice weekly for 30–45 minutes and have been implemented for periods of 10 weeks to 5 months with positive results.

Each session of RPT includes a 20-minute problem-solving session in which students alternate between the roles of teacher and student. The student teacher presents his or her student with flash cards selected to match the skill areas in which the student needs strengthening (as determined through curriculum-based assessments). Each flash card has a problem on one side and the answer and solution steps on the reverse side. Students solve these problems on a structured worksheet divided into sections: Try 1, Try 2, Help, and Try 3. The student teacher provides the student with performance feedback and assistance after two unsuccessful attempts, and the student is encouraged to attempt the problem a total of three times. This problem-solving session is followed by the completion of individualized problem drill sheets (i.e., matched to student instructional levels), which are traded and scored within the student dyad. Dyads then compute a team score based on the scores of both team members. Team scores are compared with student-selected team goals to determine whether the team has met its goal and won for the day. Students select their own goals from a set of limited choices that reflect improvement from their baseline performance. After a predetermined number of wins, teams earn their rewards. A list of acceptable rewards is compiled by the classroom teacher and usually consists of special privileges rather than tangible items. Student dyads then select their desired reward from those available choices.

The core components of RPT include structured peer interactions, an interdependent group reward contingency, and reciprocal peer tutoring. Each component appears to provide a unique and significant contribution to the effectiveness of RPT. In component studies conducted by RPT's developers, the informational structure used by RPT was linked to higher levels of academic and behavioral competence in students, the group reward contingency was linked to higher conduct reports from classroom teachers, and active reciprocal peer tutoring was linked to achievement gains. In addition to these core components, a series of two studies explored the individual and additive benefits of a home-based parental involvement component in conjunction with RPT, demonstrating that the greatest benefits resulted from a combination of both RPT and parent involvement (Fantuzzo, Davis, & Ginsburg, 1995). Together, these studies linked parent involvement to higher teacher ratings of student readiness to learn in the classroom and to increases in students' academic and behavioral self-concept. The parental involvement intervention programmed regular opportunities for home–school communication about children's success in the RPT program, as well as opportunities for parents to reinforce student efforts through conversation and individualized celebrations.

RPT has been successfully implemented with low-achieving urban students as a pullout program, as well as with entire classrooms of students and with English language learners. Extensive experimental research supports RPT's effectiveness, yielding impressive results in the areas of achievement, self-concept, motivation, and behavior (Fantuzzo & Ginsburg-Block, 1998).

## Cooperative Learning (CL)

CL is defined as group work with the purpose of accomplishing mutual learning goals. This strategy is suitable when learning goals or mastery and retention of material are essential, a task is complex, problem solving or higher level reasoning strategies are required, creativity is desirable, or high-quality performance is expected (Johnson & Johnson, 1994). Although CL has been studied for well over a century, Roger T. and David W. Johnson of the University of Minnesota can be credited with popularizing the approach over the past 35 years through their extensive research and dissemination efforts both nationally and internationally. In CL the classroom teacher provides students with instruction followed by small group work. Students in each group work through the assignment until all group members successfully understand and complete it.

All CL models are based on five core components (see Table 1). However, the precise instructional format varies from model to model.

The first component, *positive interdependence*, refers to the two main responsibilities of students engaged in cooperative learning: to learn the material and to make certain that all group members learn the material. Positive interdependence is best achieved through a combination of goal interdependence, in which the group is working toward a common group goal, and reward interdependence, in which each group member receives a reward when the group achieves its goals.

In the second component, *face-to-face interaction*, group members encourage and help each other reach group goals by using feedback, challenging each other's ideas, and sharing materials and results from the positive interdependence component.

The third component, *individual accountability*, requires each group member to provide an individual contribution to the group. Structures such as keeping groups small, testing students individually, randomly calling upon individual group members to respond, closely monitoring groups, assigning roles to each member, and having each member teach a partner all serve to maintain individual accountability.

The fourth component, *interpersonal and small group skills*, may be a threatening or foreign notion to many students, particularly those with low skills or those who are more accustomed to a traditional independent or competitive learning model. Training and reinforcement of group skills is required to ensure that students acquire and use the skills necessary for working together in a group.

*Group processing*, the final CL component, is a technique to improve group effectiveness. Both small group and classroom processing are recommended. Small group processing involves group members discussing how well the group worked together, identifying what worked well and what did not, and making decisions about how to proceed. Classroom processing can be led by the teacher, who may share his or her observations of group work as well as encourage group members to contribute to the discussion (Johnson & Johnson, 1994).

The following sections briefly describe the eight most popular and well-researched CL strategies.

***Learning Together.*** LT, developed by the Johnsons at the University of Minnesota, engages heterogeneous groups of four to five students in a group assignment. Each group completes the assignment together and returns one product to the teacher. Students are tested individually and their scores are averaged. The group total is then compared with a predetermined criterion score to determine the group's grade. Praise and rewards are provided at the group level (Yager, Johnson, Johnson, & Snider, 1986).

***Academic Controversy.*** AC, another cooperative learning strategy developed by the Johnsons, uses intellectual conflict to promote learning (Johnson & Johnson, 1995). AC involves five distinct steps: (1) Students develop a set of arguments in favor of a position, (2) each student presents his or her argument, (3) the group discusses the positions, (4) students reverse their positions and present the case for the opposing position, and (5) students relinquish all positions and work to reach consensus.

***Student Team Learning.*** Student Team Learning consists of methods developed by Slavin and colleagues at Johns Hopkins University. All methods use team rewards, individual accountability, and equal opportunities for success, which involves the use of individualized performance expectations based on student improvement rather than normative achievement levels (Slavin, 1990). Student Teams–Achievement Divisions (STAD) uses heterogeneous groups of four members who work together over three to five class periods. The learning sequence consists of teacher presentation of a lesson, teamwork that encourages mastery of material for all members, and finally individual quizzes on the material. Points are assigned on the basis of individualized performance expectations, which enables all students to be successful, regardless of ability level. Teams earn rewards on the basis of the total points earned by all group members. Another method, Teams–Games–Tournaments (TGT), is similar to STAD; however, the quizzes are replaced with weekly tournaments, requiring students to compete with members of other teams to earn points. Students compete at "tournament tables" with three same-ability peers.

In contrast to STAD and TGT, which are considered universal methods appropriate for most grade levels and content areas, Team-Assisted Individualization (TAI) was designed specifically for mathematics instruction in Grades 3–6 (Slavin, 1990). TAI shares the teaming and reward features of the first two methods; however, it also incorporates an individualized instruction component and comes with instructional materials. Students are placed individually in an instructional sequence according to their skills, and they complete the units at their own pace. Team members check one another's practice problems and provide assistance. Final unit tests are taken individually and used to determine team point totals.

Like TAI, Cooperative Integrated Reading and Comprehension (CIRC) was designed for a specific content area—reading and writing at the upper elementary level (Slavin, 1990). Students follow a sequence of activities, including teacher-led reading group instruction, team practice, and team preassessments, followed by a final quiz. As with the other Student Team Learning methods, team rewards are provided on the basis of the average performance of all team members on final quizzes and written work. Teams are composed of heterogeneous pairs of students who read to one another, predict and summarize stories to one another, write responses to stories, and practice spelling, decoding, and vocabulary together. During writing instruction these pairs work together to write drafts, revise and edit each other's work, and create team books. CIRC has been incorporated into the Success For All (SFA) cooperative learning curriculum. SFA is a widely researched and disseminated school change program designed for low-achieving elementary schools.

***Task specialization methods.*** The final two models of CL are considered to be task specialization methods, in which students take on unique roles within the group in order to complete a joint task (Slavin, 1990). Group Investigation (GI) was developed by Shlomo and Yael Sharan and Rachel Hertz-Lazarowitz in Israel. GI requires training in group skills, cooperative planning, and teacher facilitation. It is implemented in six stages: students form heterogeneous groups on the basis of mutual interests, then they plan their approach and assign roles, carry out the investigation, prepare a final report, present the final report, and, finally, participate in an evaluation of student learning.

Jigsaw was developed by Aronson and colleagues in the late 1970s and later modified and renamed Jigsaw II by Slavin and colleagues. Jigsaw II follows the same principles as the original method; however, it is touted as being easier to implement and is therefore described here. Similar to how students perform other CL methods, Jigsaw II students work in heterogeneous teams and complete quizzes individually. The quiz scores are then combined to form team scores, and high-scoring teams are rewarded. Unique to Jigsaw II, however, is that although all students read the assigned material, each group member is responsible for mastering a different section or topic. Students from different teams who were assigned to the same section meet to discuss their section for 30 minutes in "expert groups." Then students return to their original teams, where they teach their section to the other team members.

CL has been applied across all academic content areas; across grade levels, including preschool and graduate school; with diverse populations of learners, including students with disabilities and at-risk, bilingual, and gifted students; and across educational settings, including regular and special education classrooms, after school programs, and nonschool educational programs (Johnson & Johnson, 1994). A recent review specifically examined the effectiveness of eight different cooperative learning strategies compared with individualistic or competitive strategies (Johnson et al., 2000). The average effect sizes of these strategies ranged from 0.13 to 1.04 across 164 studies. Overall, each of the strategies (see Table 1) produced positive effects on student achievement, with six of the eight strategies indicating moderate to high achievement effects when compared with traditional individualistic learning conditions (i.e., Cooperative Integrated Reading and Composition [CIRC] and Jigsaw yielded positive, but smaller effects). Cooperative learning environments also result in better social acceptance and social competence, mental health, and self-esteem compared with competitive and individualistic settings. In fact, CL experiences have been found to produce robust effect sizes ranging from 0.62 to 0.65 when students' opinion of the methods is measured (Johnson & Johnson, 1989).

## Cross-Age Peer Tutoring (CAPT)

CAPT is a generic approach to pairing students of different ages and grade levels for the purpose of reaching learning goals. Using this approach, the younger tutees enhance their skills by practicing with older peer tutors, while the peer tutors gain skills by teaching the material to their tutees. Similar to same-age homogeneous grouping arrangements, CAPT is quite useful for low-achieving students who may be reluctant to participate with peers because of low skill levels. In CAPT the tutee is usually more willing to work with the tutor, since it would be

**Table 2** *Developing PAL Programs in the Schools: A Partnership-Based Model*

| Stage | Description |
|---|---|
| 1. Developing partnerships | Partnership formation by consultant and teacher; program planning |
| 2. Field testing | Program implementation, evaluation, and sharing of results |
| 3. Expanding partnerships | Invitation to parents and community members to join partnership; roles established |
| 4. Refining procedures | Refinement and expansion to include more teachers, academic subjects, types of students |

expected that an older student would have more advanced skills. By the same token, an older low-achieving tutor may feel more comfortable working with a less-skilled younger peer. Several well-conducted research studies show promising student outcomes as a result of participation in CAPT, including substantial increases in mathematics and reading achievement and self-esteem for both tutors and tutees (e.g., Sharpley, Irvine, & Sharpley, 1983).

## Developing PAL Programs in the Schools: A Partnership-Based Model

This section describes a four-stage model for developing PAL programs in the schools. The model is based on a partnership approach to program development (see Table 2). There has been a growing recognition in the intervention literature that in order for programs to work they must be implemented using a partnership approach (Power, 2003). This approach acknowledges the long-standing gap between evidence-based practices described in the educational literature and those practices employed in schools, and it offers some promising solutions.

Partnership approaches differ from traditional approaches in that they recognize that educators' and stakeholders' acceptance of and investment in an educational program are equally as important as the demonstrated effectiveness of that program. Thus, the following model recognizes that partnership is essential to building the foundation for lasting and effective PAL programming, in particular, partnerships formed with those systems that are salient to child development—peers, teachers, parents, and community members. Finally, this partnership-based model recognizes the importance of either adopting programs whose effectiveness has been established in the literature or developing programs that employ evidence-based components.

Regardless of whether programs are adopted from an existing PAL model or developed for a particular setting, this implementation model calls for (a) the evaluation of program effectiveness based on the unique ecology of each classroom, school, or school district, and (b) the use of this information for program improvement, enhancement, and extension.

## Process of Developing PAL Interventions

The following description uses the terms *PAL consultant* and *PAL facilitator* to identify the initial collaborators in the implementation of a PAL program. The PAL consultant would typically be the school psychologist, teacher, educational specialist, or university-based educator providing technical assistance to the PAL facilitator, and the PAL facilitator would be the person implementing PAL. The facilitator may be a classroom teacher, educational specialist, special educator, librarian, or any educator who is interested in implementing PAL with a group of students. The model uses the classroom as the unit for initial implementation; however, this model may be applied to any number of settings, such as after school programs, nonschool tutorial programs, and entire grade levels.

The basis of this model relies on building a strong partnership among the PAL consultant, PAL facilitator, families, community members, and other stakeholders. The partnership principles underlying this model are taken from the work of Fantuzzo, McWayne, and Bulotsky (2003). First, the person or persons initiating the PAL program must refrain from entering the partnership with a predetermined agenda. This holds true for Stages 1 and 3 of the model. The initiators must work to understand the hesitation or concerns that exist among potential partners. For example, given all of the demands placed on classroom teachers, including meeting content standards and preparing their students for standardized testing, they may be justly reluctant to consider yet another new instructional approach. Families, who may feel either marginalized by the school or overwhelmed with other demands, also may be hesitant about becoming invested in such an effort.

These concerns must be shared and resolved as part of the partnership process. Next, this discussion should result in a mutual exchange of information and ideas. At this point the initiators should explain their rationale for wanting to proceed with a PAL program. Both initiators and new partners must then work to build a mutually agreeable agenda.

***Stage 1: Developing partnerships.*** This first stage is the foundation for developing a successful PAL program. Not only is a partnership developed between the PAL consultant and facilitator, but also the majority of initial program planning is accomplished during this stage. During this stage the principles of partnership are applied to identify mutual goals and roles for each of the partners. Although planning at this stage will most likely involve a single classroom or grade level, it is wise to conduct a larger-scale needs assessment. This information will be useful for initial as well as future PAL program planning. A needs assessment should identify faculty and other stakeholders who are interested in the PAL program, appropriate student groups, academic subjects and skill areas, and resources available for the program.

Key to the success of this first stage is the identification of strategies that are most likely to be both feasible and effective. With regard to feasibility, it is critical not only to identify and adopt elements that are acceptable to both the consultant and the facilitator (particularly the latter), but also to anticipate and plan for potential barriers to implementation. For example, planners should consider how parent and student consent will be obtained, how to accommodate potential increases in student noise levels as students work together, strategies to deal with student conflicts, and what to do about student absences, which will affect the composition of peer dyads and cooperative groups. With regard to program effectiveness, it is important to select or develop a program that contains the essential PAL components identified in this chapter: a program structure in which students are trained and assigned to clearly defined roles, individualized evaluation procedures that avoid social comparison and emphasize individual progress, interdependent group reward contingencies by which individual student performance contributes to group goals, and opportunities for student autonomy.

***Stage 2: Field testing.*** The major components of this stage include the initial implementation of the program, the evaluation, and the sharing of results. Aids to program implementation include clearly defined roles for both facilitators and participants, adequate training, tools such as implementation checklists, and opportunities for reflection and planning, particularly during the initial days of implementation.

Program evaluation should include both formative and summative evaluation components, allowing for the ongoing monitoring of student progress in addition to final achievement outcomes. Initial placement, progress monitoring, and program evaluation using curriculum-based measurement strategies are central to several PAL models (e.g., PALS). Depending on the goals of the program, measures of social–emotional development may also be warranted. In addition, treatment fidelity information, or the extent to which program procedures were carried out as planned, should be collected, as well as essential information about teacher and student satisfaction (also parent satisfaction, if parents were included).

Given the reality and constraints of school-based research, attempts should be made, if possible, to provide a rigorous evaluation of the program. Although experimental research designs may be unfeasible, quasi-experiments using an equivalent comparison group, or multiple baseline designs involving the collection of baseline and intervention data, should be seriously considered. More compelling evidence of program effectiveness may result in increased opportunities for garnering resources from the school district or outside agencies.

During this second stage, program evaluation results are shared among partners. Partners discuss their interpretations and the implications of these results and make decisions about the next steps. Partners may decide to return to Stage 1 to reconsider their selection of strategies, materials, or training procedures. Or partners may decide to proceed to Stage 3 and to expand the program. In this case, stakeholders such as other teachers and administrators may also be invited to share in the program evaluation findings. An important aspect of this model is that these stages are iterative and nonsequential, in that they may be repeated until a satisfactory product is obtained at each stage.

***Stage 3: Expanding partnerships.*** Parents and community members are invited to join the partnership at this stage, with the recognition that in order to reach high standards of achievement and social–emotional learning for all students, the collaboration of teachers, families, and community members is essential. A true commitment to partnering with families and community members must be made, including planning for potential barriers to participation such as language or cultural differences, transportation, and scheduling. Here, according to the partnership principles outlined previously, an exchange of information takes place between the initial and new members of the now expanding partnership. Parents and community members are encouraged to offer their opinions, expertise, and concerns. The consultant and classroom teacher share information about how the PAL program was implemented and what results were obtained. Together, partners work to establish a mutually acceptable plan of action and meaningful roles for each of the members. For the consultant and classroom teacher, this will involve redefining roles, whereas the parents and community members will be establishing new roles.

Research specific to the PAL literature clearly documents the benefits of including families in PAL programming (e.g., Fantuzzo et al., 1995). The use of community partners to facilitate school-based intervention programs has also been established as a beneficial strategy (e.g., Power, Dowrick, Ginsburg-Block, & Manz, 2004). The participation of family and community partners will likely improve the intervention's relevance, acceptability, and responsiveness to the needs of students and the community (Fantuzzo et al., 2003). Roles for families and community members might include assisting with the implementation of PAL training and tutorial sessions, developing program materials, raising funds, creating a program newsletter, or encouraging student participants by celebrating their successes.

Following inclusion of new parent and community member components in the PAL program, the newly improved program is again implemented and evaluated according to the guidelines established in Stage 2, and results are shared among all participants and stakeholders.

***Stage 4: Refining procedures.*** The last stage of this iterative process involves refining procedures based on the findings of the program evaluation and the initial needs assessment. Refinements may involve expanding the program to include more teachers, other academic subjects, students with special needs, or additional partners. To avoid creating a PAL program that will wind up being yet another short-lived initiative, PAL partners must work toward system-level integration and sustainability. One way of accomplishing this goal is to involve all major stakeholders mentioned above. A strong, vocal, and respected group of program supporters is essential to maintaining a program's momentum. Beyond initial planning, implementation, and evaluation, ongoing opportunities for sharing should be programmed. Schools tend to maintain isolation among educators, but continued cooperation is essential to effectively implement a program such as this (e.g., consider the merits of the fifth component of CL, that is, group processing). As students, families, and educators accept the principles of PAL and as its academic and social–emotional benefits become apparent, it will gradually become part of the school culture.

Topping (2001) suggests these additional ideas for sustaining and expanding PAL programs: (a) conduct a cost–benefit analysis that considers the costs and benefits for all stakeholders, (b) keep costs down by using readily available materials and resources, (c) consult with students to obtain and incorporate their ideas, and (d) evaluate long-term results by following student participants across years.

## SUMMARY

PAL strategies are promising classroom interventions for the promotion of not only academic, but also important social, self-concept, and behavioral outcomes in students. PAL strategies have been used successfully in Grades K–12, across varied subject areas, and with diverse groups of students. PAL is particularly effective in promoting positive outcomes for vulnerable groups of students, including low-income, minority, and urban students. PAL's effectiveness across an important array of student groups makes it an exciting, if not essential option for instruction. A developmental systems framework, including the examination of both classroom and peer applications used to structure PAL strategies, provides a lens for considering PAL strategies. Recent research has demystified the nuts and bolts of PAL by identifying its effective components, including opportunities for student autonomy, individualized evaluation procedures, structuring of student roles, and use of group reward contingencies. Although many versatile PAL models exist, a partnership-based process for program implementation is recommended in order to maximize program effectiveness and longevity.

## RECOMMENDED RESOURCES

### Books and Other Printed Material

Johnson, D. W., Johnson, R. T., & Holubec, E. J. (1998). *Cooperation in the classroom* (7th ed.). Edina, MN: Interaction Book Company.

The authors describe this as the foundational book for implementing cooperative learning. For additional practical resources, including training videos, see the description of their website (*http://www.co-operation.org*) below.

Topping, K. (2001). *Peer assisted learning: A practical guide for teachers.* Cambridge, MA: Brookline Books.

This practical guide for teachers provides a review of peer-assisted learning (PAL) techniques and instructions for getting started on implementing a PAL program in Grades K–12. It includes a reproducible planning format to guide readers through the process.

Topping, K. J., & Ehly, S. (Eds.). (1998). *Peer assisted learning.* Hillsdale, NJ: Erlbaum.

This edited volume provides an introduction to the PAL literature and various PAL models, such as classwide and reciprocal peer tutoring. It goes beyond the current chapter to describe nonacademic peer applications such as peer counseling.

### Websites

*http://www.co-operation.org*

The website for Roger and David Johnson's Cooperative Learning Center at the University of Minnesota provides an overview of cooperative learning and its various models, links to books and other resources, and a question and answer forum.

*http://www.jgcp.ku.edu/index.htm*

This is the website for the Juniper Gardens Children's Project at the University of Kansas, where classwide peer tutoring, or CWPT, was developed by Charles Greenwood and colleagues. The site has links to CWPT products that can be ordered, including materials for progress monitoring.

*http://www.kc.vanderbilt.edu/kennedy/pals*

The website for the Peer-Assisted Learning Strategies (PALS) program, developed by Fuchs and Fuchs, provides all the information needed to administer PALS in the classroom, along with demonstration videos, manuals, materials, and more.

*http://www.w-w-c.org*

The website for the What Works Clearinghouse, of the U.S. Department of Education, provides information on the effectiveness of educational interventions, programs, products, practices, and policies, including PAL.

## REFERENCES


Ames, C. (1992). Classrooms: Goals, structures, and student motivation. *Journal of Educational Psychology, 84,* 261–271.

Aronson, E., & Patnoe, S. (1997). *The jigsaw classroom* (2nd ed.). New York, NY: Longman.

Arreaga-Mayer, C., Terry, B. J., & Greenwood, C. R. (1998). Classwide peer tutoring. In K. J. Topping & S. Ehly (Eds.), *Peer Assisted Learning* (pp. 105–119). Hillsdale, NJ: Erlbaum.

Bronfenbrenner, U. (1979). Contexts of child rearing: Problems and prospects. *American Psychologist, 34,* 844–850.

Cohen, E. G., Lotan, R. A., Scarloss, B. A., & Arellano, A. R. (1999). Complex instruction: Equity in cooperative learning classrooms. *Theory into Practice, 38,* 80–86.

Cohen, P. A., Kulik, J. A., & Kulik, C. C. (1982). Education outcomes of tutoring: A meta-analysis of findings. *American Educational Research Journal, 19,* 237–248.

Cook, S. B., Scruggs, T. E., Mastropieri, M. A., & Casto, G. C. (1985). Handicapped students as tutors. *Journal of Special Education, 19,* 483–492.

Daly, E., Martens, B., Kilmer, A., & Massie, D. (1996). The effects of instructional match and content overlap on generalized reading performance. *Journal of Applied Behavior Analysis, 29,* 507–518.

DeVries, D., & Edwards, K. (1974). Student teams and learning games: Their effects on cross-race and cross-sex interaction. *Journal of Educational Psychology, 66,* 741–749.

Fantuzzo, J. W., Davis, G. Y., & Ginsburg, M. D. (1995). Effects of parent involvement in isolation or in combination with peer tutoring on student self-concept and mathematics achievement. *Journal of Educational Psychology, 87,* 272–281.

Fantuzzo, J., & Ginsburg-Block, M. (1998). Reciprocal peer tutoring: Developing and testing effective peer collaborations for elementary school students. In K. J. Topping & S. Ehly (Eds.), *Peer assisted learning* (pp. 121–144). Hillsdale, NJ: Erlbaum.

Fantuzzo, J. W., King, J. A., & Heller, L. R. (1992). Effects of reciprocal peer tutoring on mathematics and school adjustment: A component analysis. *Journal of Educational Psychology, 84,* 331–339.

Fantuzzo, J., McWayne, C., & Bulotsky, R. (2003). Forging strategic partnerships to advance mental health science and practice for vulnerable children. *School Psychology Review, 32,* 17–37.

Fantuzzo, J. W., & Polite, K. (1990). School-based self-management interventions with elementary school children: A component analysis. *School Psychology Quarterly, 5,* 180–198.

Fuchs, D., Fuchs, L. S., Mathes, P. G., & Simmons, D. C. (1997). Peer-assisted learning strategies: Making classrooms more responsive to diversity. *American Educational Research Journal, 34,* 174–206.

Fuchs, L. S., Fuchs, D., Phillips, N. B., Hamlett, C. L., & Karns, K. (1995). Acquisition and transfer effects of classwide peer-assisted learning strategies in mathematics for students with varying learning histories. *School Psychology Review, 24,* 604–620.

Garcia Coll, C., & Garrido, M. (2000). Minorities in the United States: Sociocultural context for mental health and developmental psychopathology. In A. J. Sameroff & M. Lewis (Eds.), *Handbook of developmental psychopathology* (2nd ed., pp. 177–195). New York: Kluwer Academic/Plenum.

Ginsburg-Block, M., Rohrbeck, C., & Fantuzzo, J. W. (2004). *A meta-analytic review of the social, emotional and behavioral outcomes of peer assisted learning.* Manuscript submitted for publication.

Greenwood, C. R., Carta, J. J., & Hall, R. V. (1988). The use of peer tutoring strategies in classroom management and educational instruction. *School Psychology Review, 17,* 258–275.

Greenwood, C. R., Maheady, L., & Delquadri, J. (2002). Classwide peer tutoring programs. In M. R. Shinn, H. M. Walker, & G. Stoner (Eds.), *Interventions for academic and behavior problems II: Preventive and remedial approaches* (pp. 611–649). Bethesda, MD: National Association of School Psychologists.

Henke, R. R., Chen, X., & Goldman, G. (1999). *What happens in classrooms? Instructional practices in elementary and secondary schools, 1994–1995.* Washington, DC: U.S. Department of Education, National Center for Education Statistics.

Johnson, D. W., & Johnson, R. T. (1989). *Cooperation and competition: Theory and research.* Edina, MN: Interaction Book Company.

Johnson, D. W., & Johnson, R. T. (1995). *Creative controversy: Intellectual challenge in the classroom* (3rd ed.). Edina, MN: Interaction Book Company.

Johnson, D. W., & Johnson, R. T. (1999). *Learning together and alone: Cooperative, competitive, and individualistic learning* (5th ed.). Needham Heights, MA: Allyn & Bacon, Inc.

Johnson, D. W., Johnson, R. T., & Stanne, M. B. (2000). *Cooperative learning methods: A meta-analysis.* Retrieved October 6, 2004, from http://www.co-operation.org/pages/cl-methods.html

Johnson, D. W., Maruyama, G., Johnson, R., Nelson, D., & Skon, L. (1981). Effects of cooperative, competitive, and individualistic goal structures on achievement: A meta-analysis. *Psychological Bulletin, 89,* 47–62.

Johnson, R. T. & Johnson, D. W. (1994). *An overview of cooperative learning.* Retrieved August 17, 2004, from http://www.co-operation.org/pages/overviewpaper.html

Kagan, S. (1989). The structural approach to cooperative learning. *Educational Leadership, 47,* 12–15.

Levin, H. M., Glass, G. V., & Meister, G. R. (1987). Cost-effectiveness of computer-assisted instruction. *Evaluation Review, 11,* 50–72.

Lipsey, M. W., & Wilson, D. B. (1993). The efficacy of psychological, educational, and behavioral treatment: Confirmation from meta-analysis. *American Psychologist, 48,* 1181–1209.

Maheady, L., Sacca, M. K., & Harper, G. F. (1988). Classwide peer tutoring with mildly handicapped high school students. *Exceptional Children, 55,* 52–59.

Phelan, P., Davidson, A., Locke, A., & Yu, H. C. (1998). *Adolescents' worlds: Negotiating family, peers, and school.* New York: Teacher's College Press.

Piaget, J., & Inhelder, B. (1972). *The psychology of the child* (pp. 152–159). New York: Basic Books.

Power, T. J. (2003). Promoting children's mental health: Reform through interdisciplinary and community partnerships. *School Psychology Review, 32,* 3–16.

Power, T., Dowrick, P., Ginsburg-Block, M., & Manz, P. (2004). Partnership-based, community-assisted early intervention for literacy: An application of the participatory intervention model. *Journal of Behavioral Education, 13,* 93–115.

Rohrbeck, C. A., Ginsburg-Block, M. D., Fantuzzo, J. W., & Miller, T. R. (2003). Peer-assisted learning interventions with elementary school students: A meta-analytic review. *Journal of Educational Psychology, 95*(2), 240–257.

Ryan, R. M., & Deci, E. L. (2000). Self-determination theory and the facilitation of intrinsic motivation, social development, and well-being. *American Psychologist, 55,* 68–78.

Sharan, S., & Sharan, Y. (1992). *Group investigation: Expanding cooperative learning.* New York: Teacher's College Press.

Sharpley, A. M., Irvine, J. W., & Sharpley, C. F. (1983). An examination of the effectiveness of a cross-age tutoring program in mathematics for elementary school children. *American Educational Research Journal, 20,* 103–111.

Slavin, R. E. (1990). *Cooperative learning: Theory, research, and practice.* Englewood Cliffs, NJ: Prentice Hall.

Slavin, R. E., Karweit, N. L., & Wasik, B. A. (Eds.). (1994). *Preventing early school failure: Research, policy, and practice.* Needham Heights, MA: Allyn & Bacon.

Stevens, R. J., & Slavin, R. E. (1995). Effects of a cooperative learning approach in reading and writing on academically handicapped and nonhandicapped students. *Elementary School Journal, 95,* 241–262.

Topping, K. (2001). *Peer assisted learning: A practical guide for teachers.* Cambridge, MA: Brookline Books.

Topping, K. J., & Ehly, S. (Eds.). (1998). *Peer assisted learning.* Hillsdale, NJ: Erlbaum.

Utley, C. A., Morweet, S. L., & Greenwood, C. R. (1997). Peer mediated instruction and interventions. *Focus on Exceptional Children, 29,* 1–23.

Vygotsky, L. S. (1978). Mental development of children and the process of learning (M. Lopez Morillas, Trans.). In M. Cole, V. John-Steiner, S. Scribner, & E. Souberman (Eds.), *L. S. Vygotsky: Mind in society* (pp. 7–8). Cambridge, MA: Harvard University Press. (Original work published 1935).

Webb, N., & Farivar, S. (1994). Promoting helping behavior in cooperative small groups in middle school mathematics. *American Educational Research Journal, 31,* 369–395.

Wentzel, K. R. (1999). Social-motivational processes and interpersonal relationships: Implications for understanding motivation at school. *Journal of Educational Psychology, 91,* 76–97.

Yager, S., Johnson, R. T., Johnson, D. W., & Snider, B. (1986). The impact of group processing on achievement in cooperative learning groups. *The Journal of Social Psychology, 126,* 389–397.

# 49

# English Language Learners

**Emilia C. Lopez**

*Queens College, City University of New York*

## BACKGROUND AND DEVELOPMENT

Over 4 million students with limited English language proficiency are enrolled in public schools in the United States (National Clearinghouse for English Language Acquisition and Language Instruction, 2001). They speak over 400 different languages and are from diverse cultural backgrounds. The majority speak Spanish (76%), Vietnamese (2.3%), Hmong (2.2%), Haitian Creole (1.08%), Cantonese (1.0%), and Korean (1.0%) as their first languages. States with the most significant numbers of these students are California, Texas, Florida, New York, Illinois, and Arizona. It is predicted that the number of English language learners will continue to increase; thus, there is a critical need for school professionals to understand and be able to address their needs.

Although students who demonstrate low levels of proficiency in speaking, comprehending, reading, and writing in English are typically referred to as *limited English proficient* (LEP), there is concern that the term emphasizes those students' language limitations. The term *English language learners* (ELL) recently emerged in the literature as a way to bring attention on the potential those students demonstrate as learners of English as a second language (Baca & Baca, 2004). Thus, in this chapter, ELL students will be used to refer to students who demonstrate limited English proficiency. *L1* and *L2* will also be used consistently to refer to ELL students' first and second languages, respectively.

ELL students exhibit a wide range of educational and mental health needs. For example, many enter schools with little or no prior educational experiences (Ovando, Collier, & Combs, 2003). They often exhibit school behaviors that are different from the students in the mainstream. Many also exhibit mental health needs associated with their immigration experiences (e.g., refugees escaping countries with political unrest). Irrespective of their behavior and needs, the fact that most of these students enter school with a broad range of language skills and instructional experiences is of significant concern to school professionals as they work to help these students achieve in school.

ELL students exhibit diverse developmental language patterns (Ovando et al., 2003). New immigrants, as well as many students born in the United States, enter schools with a diverse range of educational experiences and literacy skills in their native languages and in English. In addition to exhibiting varied levels of language proficiency in their primary and secondary languages, ELL students demonstrate a wide range of cultural language-related experiences including differences in writing systems, concepts of sound–symbol relationships, modes of discourse, story patterns, and nonverbal communication styles (Ovando et al.). Cultural differences imply that those students may not be familiar with patterns common to the English language and to communicating within the context of the American culture.

The wide range of language skills and experiences exhibited by ELL students is perhaps the most pressing rationale for focusing attention on these students' language skills. Language is one of the most important components for learning, achieving academically, and understanding classroom discourse. Thus, it is imperative that educators understand the processes of first and second language acquisition and that they develop skills to facilitate language learning for ELL students. This chapter explores a number of developmental and theoretical issues related to second language acquisition and discusses prevention and intervention strategies that are designed to target these students' language skills. (For additional information regarding ELL students and linguistically diverse students, see various chapters on the topic in *Best Practices in School Psychology IV*, Thomas & Grimes, 2002).

## Developmental and Theoretical Issues

A crucial aspect of working with ELL students is developing a knowledge base of the basic developmental and theoretical issues that inform instructional, assessment, and intervention practices. This section of the chapter explores that knowledge base by articulating a number of issues that will help school-based professionals understand the process of second language acquisition and apply such knowledge in their work. The information presented will be helpful to teachers instructing ELL students and to other professionals, such as school psychologists and other educational consultants, involved in planning and implementing interventions for ELL students.

## Developmental Processes That Underlie the Development of a Second Language

Three processes are key components of the development of a second language: (a) *automatic habit formation*, (b) *conscious rule learning*, and (c) *natural acquisition*. Automatic habit formation is evident when learners pick up "chunks" of language or prefabricated utterances that usually consist of common phrases in their everyday language (de Valenzuela & Niccolai, 2004). For example, a 6–year-old recently exposed to English might learn the sequence "Hello. How are you? I am fine, thank you!" and may use it automatically every time he or she meets a new person. These chunks of language are typically memorized and often, but not always initially, used within the appropriate social context. The strategy helps learners practice new knowledge within meaningful contexts and build on their understanding of syntax construction.

Conscious rule learning involves consciously learning the rules applicable to (a) producing and understanding the units of sounds (i.e., morphology), (b) understanding word meanings and word combinations (i.e., semantics), and (c) understanding grammatical functions and producing structurally correct sentences (i.e., syntax) (Krashen, 1982). Research suggests that there is a natural development to certain aspects of L2 acquisition (e.g., negation, interrogation, word order, and morpheme acquisition) and that formal instruction cannot speed up the process of learning particular rules because learners must go through certain developmental steps to master those rules (de Valenzuela and Niccolai, 2004). However, formal instruction can facilitate conscious rule learning as L2 learners' language skills mature.

In addition to conscious rule learning, Krashen (1982) argues that the natural acquisition of meaningful language is an important process in L2 development. The natural acquisition of language occurs within social contexts where learners are exposed to L2 in everyday situations and settings. In these scenarios language is learned within the natural patterns of communication and supported by models, feedback, and reinforcement.

## Primary Landmarks and Stages in L2 Development

Table 1 describes the general stages of L2 development (Krashen, 1982). At the initial stages, expressive and receptive skills grow continuously and steadily. During the preproduction stage, ELL students are particularly focused on developing receptive skills and may exhibit a silent period in which there is little or no production of language. The silent period usually lasts from 3 to 6 months, but cases have been documented of up to a year (Ovando, et al., 2003). Expressive and receptive language skills continue to grow steadily through the advanced fluency stage.

ELL students functioning within the preproduction to intermediate fluency stages typically exhibit interference, particularly during the early stages of L2 acquisition (McLaughlin, 1985). Interference occurs in speaking and writing modes when L2 learners apply the L1 rules to the morphology, semantics, and syntax rules of L2. For example, a Spanish speaker may transfer the Spanish rule applying to the possessive form to an English language structure (i.e., "the coat of the boy" instead of "the boy's coat").

Initially, ELL students may engage in code switching, or mixing languages over phrases or sentences (Timm, 1993). Learners in the earlier stages of L2 acquisition may use code switching because they lack access to vocabulary in L2 and they revert to L1 to convey meaning. As the language skills of ELL students become more proficient, code switching becomes part of their repertoire as a purposeful strategy to convey meaning (e.g., to make a joke or to put stress on a comment).

According to Krashen (1982), a key component leading to proficiency across all stages of L2 development is *comprehensible input*. Krashen defined comprehensible input as language input that is at the individual learner's level and slightly above that level. It is congruent to the concept of zone of proximal development and implies

**Table 1** *Stages of Second Language Acquisition*

Level 1: Preproduction
- Minimal comprehension
- Limited or no verbal production
- Silent period
- Learner focused on comprehension
- Learner dependent on modeling and contextual cues to obtain and convey meaning

Level 2: Early production
- Limited comprehension
- Production of isolated words in response to "comprehensible input"
- Learner beginning to respond to yes or no questions and to produce one- to two-word utterances

Level 3: Speech emergence
- Good comprehension
- Limited vocabulary
- Use of short phrases and simple sentences
- Ability to respond to literal questions that have been made comprehensible
- Errors in pronunciation and syntax

Level 4: Intermediate fluency
- Excellent comprehension
- Few errors in syntax
- Learner engagement in elaborate conversations and in production of full and complex sentences

Level 5: Advanced fluency
- Receptive and expressive language skills are well developed

*Note.* Adapted from *Principles and Practice in Second Language Acquisition*, by S. D. Krashen, 1982.

that language input that is beyond that zone of proximal development is too difficult or beyond an independent level of functioning (Vygotsky, 1962). Comprehensible input is important because if ELL students are exposed to difficult levels of language that are not comprehensible, they will likely become uninterested and even frustrated. Because L2 learners need language that is at the level of instruction and input that they can handle, teachers must monitor the comprehensible input they provide through instruction and must adjust their language output to each child's level of comprehensible input. Language that is more difficult to understand can be gradually introduced in increments and embedded within language that the student is already familiar with to provide contextual support and scaffolding.

## Development of L2 Skills and the Time Factor

Research generally indicates that basic interpersonal communicative skills (BICS) are the first L2 skills that develop. BICS are context-embedded skills negotiated by contextual cues such as face-to-face interactions, hands-on experiences, concrete manipulations, and authentic experiences. These skills tend to develop within 2 to 3 years at both the expressive and receptive levels (Cummins, 1984). However, development ranges of up to 5 years have been reported in the research literature (Ovando et al., 2003). In contrast, cognitive academic language proficiency skills (CALPS) tend to develop in 5 to 10 years (e.g., Collier, 1992; Cummins). CALPS are language skills that are more demanding and difficult to acquire because they are connected to academic experiences and situations that are more abstract and have fewer contextual cues (Cummins, 1999).

## Relationship Between L1 and L2

Research suggests that students who have well-developed CALPS in L1 are able to gain CALPS in L2 at a faster rate. Cummins (1986) argues that well-developed skills in L1 facilitate the transfer of knowledge to L2. For example, students who understand and can explain the process of metamorphosis in L1 will be able to understand and discuss the concept in L2 once they learn the vocabulary and syntax related to metamorphosis. Cummins explains that knowledge developed in L1 can be accessed in and transferred to L2 because of a common underlying proficiency facilitating the transfer of knowledge from one language to another. The empirical literature indicates that transference from L1 to L2 can lead to positive gains in L2 in reading and writing (Ellis, 1994; Ovando et al., 2003).

## Relationship of ELL Students' Difficulties to L2 Acquisition Process or Disability

In consultations, prereferrals, and special education referrals, school professionals often have difficulties differentiating between difficulties that are solely related to the expected L2 acquisition processes and those difficulties that are a function of both limited English skills and a disability. Thus, during both assessment and intervention, they should explore questions such as: Within what state of acquisition is the student functioning? How long is it taking the student to acquire BICS and CALPS? How proficient is the student in L1 and L2?

Difficulties in developing a second language can be attributed to factors both internal and external to the child and to the interaction of the two types of factors. Thus, both internal and external factors should be addressed during assessment and intervention. Table 2 provides a list of factors that directly influence language acquisition with ELL students. School professionals should examine each of those factors by observing; obtaining thorough background histories; interviewing parents, students, and school professionals; and examining school records. Various language proficiency tools are available (mostly in Spanish and English) and can be used to obtain a sense of the levels at which ELL students are functioning. In addition, observations, interviews, language rating scales, and other informal procedures (e.g., structured and unstructured language samples) are other useful tools to examine levels of L2 acquisition and rate of acquisition (Ovando et al., 2003).

***Problems inherent to English language learners.*** Cognitive deficits (e.g., mental retardation) and medical problems (e.g., hearing impairments) directly affect the speed and rate of acquisition of English as a second language (de Valenzuela & Niccolai, 2004). Deficits in the acquisition of a second language can also result from speech and language impairments. Speech and language impairments are evident in ELL students when the deficits exhibited interfere with communication and cause speech to be maladjusted. For an ELL student to be considered speech and language impaired in speech, language, or voice, the impairments must be evident in L1 or the most dominant language (de Valenzuela & Niccolai). Bilingual students must demonstrate deficits in both L1 and L2 to receive a classification of speech and language impaired.

De Valenzuela and Niccolai (2004) outline possible indicators of speech, language, or voice problems manifested as difficulties in both L1 and L2: (a) omission of the initial or final sounds of words, (b) sound substitutions, (c) hesitancy to participate orally in class in the dominant language, (d) malformation of the oral cavity, (e) chronic hoarseness, (f) consistently too loud or too soft speech, (g) raspy or gravelly sounding voice, (h) noticeably nasal tone or other difficulties with voice quality, and (i) stuttering or dysfluent communication.

**Table 2** *Factors That Influence the Process of Second Language Acquisition*

- Students' cognitive abilities and medical history.
- Students' motivation to learn the second language (i.e., intrinsic vs. extrinsic motivation).
- Affective variables such as anxiety and self-confidence.
- Personality characteristics (i.e., extroverted vs. introverted individuals).
- Attitudes about the adopted culture and the second language.
- Educational history in the first and second languages (e.g., access to prior educational experiences, types of programs exposed to, interrupted schooling, languages of instruction).
- Length of residence in United States.
- Access to literacy experiences in first and second language (L1 and L2).
- Frequency of contact with the native country (e.g., lengthy stays in native country).
- Level of proficiency in L1 facilitating transfer to L2.
- Access to, exposure to, and experiences with social and academic opportunities that promote the development of high proficiency in L1 and L2 and balanced bilingualism.
- Type of communities where students live and access to languages in those communities.
- Experiences with prejudice, discrimination, and bias that may negatively influence attitudes toward the second language.
- Educational policies that promote access to English as a second language services, taking into consideration the quantity and quality of support that is needed to acquire cognitive academic language skills in L2.

*Note.* For reviews of these factors, see de Valenzuela & Niccolai, 2004; Gersten & Baker, 2000; and Ovando et al., 2003.

Langdon (1992) urges school professionals to explore whether ELL students exhibit the following difficulties in their most dominant language: (a) delays in responding to verbal items, (b) difficulties following verbal directions, (c) gaps in labeling language, and (d) difficulties organizing verbal responses to open-ended questions.

Damico, Oller, and Storey (1983) focus on the need to examine the students' pragmatic skills or their ability to use effective language to communicate with others in social contexts. They note that deficits in pragmatic skills may include (a) linguistic nonfluencies such as repetitions, unusual patterns, and hesitations; (b) frequent revisions (i.e., the student continually revises what he or she is saying); (c) word-finding difficulties; (d) inappropriate responses when asked questions; (e) poor topic maintenance; and (f) the need for multiple repetitions.

Identifying ELL students with speech and language disorders and learning disabilities is a complex process that requires constant attention to the interplay between cultural and linguistic differences and a possible disability. Because ELL students' skills are dynamically growing and changing as they are exposed to L2 in social and academic situations, school professionals must remain mindful of the normal course of L2 development and its relationship to the development of L1 skills. As such, ELL students' skills should be carefully examined in both L1 and L2 while considering if those language deficits are the result of normal stages of L2 acquisition or to speech and language impairments. For example, problems in speech, language, and voice should be examined within the context of expected L2 developmental factors. Speech that is too loud or too soft may be related to appropriate cultural patterns of communication in specific cultural contexts. Delays in responding to verbal items, difficulties in following verbal instructions, difficulties organizing verbal responses to open-ended questions, and the pragmatic deficits described by Damico et al. (1983) are frequently exhibited by ELL students in English as they progress through the early stages of L2 acquisition. L1 loss as a result of a lack of exposure to L1 may also manifest itself in the form of delays in responses, poor vocabulary, hesitancies, and word-finding problems.

***External factors influencing English language learners' language acquisition.*** ELL students who enter schools in the United States with little or no prior educational experiences often encounter significant academic difficulties. A lack of literacy skills in their native language implies that those students are at a disadvantage in acquiring literacy skills in English because they lack much of the basic vocabulary knowledge and the concepts they need to catch up to their English-speaking peers. Immigrant students who exhibit disabilities may have lived in countries where access to special education programs was nonexistent or very limited. For many of those families, their arrival in the American school system is their first experience in obtaining comprehensive services for their children.

The quality of educational experiences to which students were exposed in their native countries must be considered, since many students may exhibit poor literacy in L1 as a result of exposure to poor-quality programs or the lack of services in their native countries. The question of quality services must also be explored for ELL students who have a history of obtaining educational services in American schools. Some literature suggests that U.S. school systems are not well equipped to educate ELL students (see August & Hakuta, 1997). School professionals involved in identifying ELL students who are at risk of developing learning difficulties must examine whether external factors are at the root of these students' difficulties.

## ACTIONS FOR PREVENTION AND INTERVENTION

Appropriate programs and effective strategies should be used to address language difficulties of ELL students. Little research has focused on the relationship between process and outcome variables directly linked to higher achievement and literacy for ELL students; however, a literature base exists that supports the use of a number of programs and interventions designed to promote language learning and high academic attainment for these students. This section of the chapter provides an overview of educational programs, instructional strategies, and collaborative frameworks designed to help school professionals facilitate the process of L2 acquisition.

### Educational Programs

ELL students may have access to a variety of educational programs focusing on advancing their L1 or L2 skills. These programs (described in Table 3) include bilingual education, two-way bilingual education, sheltered English, and pullout English as a second language (ESL) programs (Ovando et al., 2003). Bilingual education programs are transitional or maintenance. Students in transitional bilingual education programs tend to exit those programs within 2 or 3 years or once they have demonstrated sufficient proficiency to function in English-only classrooms. Maintenance bilingual education programs have the goal of maintaining students' bilingual skills by providing bilingual instruction for longer periods of time (e.g., 5 to 6 years). Well-designed bilingual education programs maintain a good balance, providing students with time, exposure, and access to English as they progressively acquire literacy skills in both languages. The effect is to not take time away from English and to capitalize on the common underlying proficiency that helps students transfer knowledge from one language to another and to access knowledge in both languages (Ovando et al., 2003).

**Table 3** *Educational Programs for English Language Learners*

| Educational Programs | Descriptions |
|---|---|
| Bilingual education | ELL students dominant in their native language are initially taught mostly in their native language. Students also receive instruction in English for part of the day. As the students' English language skills progress, the time spent on English language instruction increases progressively to provide more exposure to content in English. |
| Two-way bilingual education | Program includes a mix of students who are dominant in a language other than English (e.g., Spanish) and a group of students dominant in English. The goal is to work toward bilingual proficiency with both groups. |
| Sheltered English language | Instruction is delivered in English while adjusting the level of the language to the students' level of language proficiency. |
| Pullout English as a second language | Program is typically available to all students exhibiting limited proficiency in English, including those students who are taking part in the programs described above. Teachers trained in ESL methods instruct children in small groups. They focus on vocabulary, sentence construction, and concept formation. |

The empirical literature focusing on bilingual education is beset with methodological problems that render results difficult to interpret (Gersten & Jimenez, 1998). One of the major problems is inconsistently applied practices across bilingual education programs. For example, a bilingual program in one district may focus on delivering instruction mostly in the native language while providing inadequate opportunities for English language development. Another district may do the opposite and provide most of the instruction in English, with little instruction in the native language. It is difficult to ascertain the effectiveness of bilingual education programs when outcome studies fail to account for such inconsistent policies and practices. There is research to suggest that when ELL students are exposed to quality bilingual education programs for at least 5 to 6 years during the elementary grades, they are able to maintain grade level norms in L1 and reach grade level norms in L2 in about 4 to 7 years (see Collier, 1992).

At this time, there is a lack of well-designed research comparing outcomes across different instructional programs for ELL students. As such, placement decisions should take into consideration a variety of issues. For example, bilingual education and two-way bilingual education programs may not be readily accessible. Bilingual education legislation requires that a specific number of students must need bilingual services within any one grade in order for schools to obtain funds for bilingual programs (Ovando et al., 2003). Thus, bilingual education programs may not be feasible for many students who speak low-frequency languages such as Urdu or Tagalog. Bilingual programs may also not be feasible because of practical limitations of establishing programs in multiple languages (e.g., availability of bilingual staff, funding, or trained staff). Sheltered English language instruction and ESL programs are alternatives to bilingual education programs. Districts should develop clear criteria for identifying students for different programs.

A consistent recommendation in the ESL literature is to examine exiting criteria, since decisions are often made to exit students from available programs before they acquire the academic language skills they need in L2 (Gersten & Baker, 2000). One preventive action is to extend ELL students' enrollments in bilingual education programs to prepare them to acquire the language skills necessary to handle academic content in English.

ELL students are often provided with limited pullout ESL instruction and placed with general education teachers who are not trained in delivering effective strategies for this population (August & Hakuta, 1997). ESL programs are also typically provided for a predetermined amount of time (e.g., 2 to 3 years), and the discontinuation of services is determined on students' scores on language proficiency tests that fail to measure students' readiness to handle academic content in English (de Valenzuela & Niccolai, 2004). Once students are exited from those bilingual or ESL programs, district policies often deny them future ESL services, even when teachers and other school personnel have data to show that the students still need the services. Implementing prevention services would entail expanding ESL programs beyond a pullout format to either sheltered English programs or coteaching models in which ESL teachers and classroom teachers collaborate to develop and implement appropriate L2 learning strategies implemented throughout the curriculum.

Exiting decisions for these programs should also be based on the use of formal as well as informal procedures that carefully examine the curriculum and task demands, the students' skills to handle those demands, and their readiness to use their English language skills to learn the academic content (Rosenfield, 1987). Training teachers and support personnel in areas related to second language development, bilingualism, programs for ELL students, assessment of ELL students, and the implementation of effective instructional strategies is another strategy that has the potential to prevent the implementation of practices and policies that hinder ELL students' academic and language growth.

### Instructional Strategies in General Education Settings

Gersten and Baker (2000) suggest it is time to move away from the rhetoric about what language ELL students should be instructed in and to move forward by focusing on effective instructional strategies that promote ELL students' social and academic language skills in general education settings. The National Academy of Sciences (August & Hakuta, 1997) also recommended conducting research focusing on effective instructional strategies for ELL students.

Although little research is currently available examining effective instructional practices for ELL students, there is some research with the potential to guide practice within the context of evidence-based interventions. A discussion of evidence-based interventions is helpful to all school personnel involved in implementing instructional strategies for ELL students, including consultants such as school psychologists, speech and language specialists, and counselors working with teachers (i.e., consultees).

Table 4 provides a list of instructional strategies for ELL students that were compiled based on the review of literature on evidence-based interventions. For example, Gersten and Baker (2000) recently conducted an investigation to examine the knowledge base on using effective instructional practices with ELL students. They used a multivocal synthesis method to examine experimental and qualitative studies of instructional practices. They also used a third data source consisting of professional work groups that included practitioners and researchers. The work groups were used to identify relevant and irrelevant concepts, propositions, and practices "considered important by the most knowledgeable groups in the field" (p. 34).

## COLLABORATIVE INTERVENTIONS

The effective school literature has shown that one of the basic characteristics of effective schools is a collaborative environment in which teachers, administrators, other service providers, and parents work together to meet students' needs and solve problems (Levine & Lezotte, 2001). ELL students in general education programs are often instructed and supported by a number of school professionals across several programs in general education, including bilingual and ESL teachers and general education teachers (i.e., not part of a bilingual program). In addition, those students may receive support services from other personnel such as counselors, reading and math specialists, and school psychologists. Collaboration among those professionals should expand across several areas and include coordinating efforts for the following purposes:

- Identify ELL students' academic, social, and mental health needs.
- Develop programs with a unified philosophy for instruction, curriculum, and social skills within a multicultural framework.
- Provide a variety of services.
- Develop and implement interventions targeting specific needs for ELL students.
- Share instructional ideas and strategies.
- Gather and pool available resources.
- Monitor and evaluate the quality of interventions implemented.
- Evaluate the collaborative process.
- Plan and execute training experiences to help school professionals expand their knowledge and skills needed to work with ELL students.
- Work collaboratively with parents.
- Develop organizational structures supporting effective policies and services to meet the social and academic needs of ELL students.

Teacher assistance teams are one form of collaborative effort that can provide support to teachers while they

**Table 4** *Recommended Instructional Strategies for English Language Learners*

- Use traditional approaches that have been previously validated in the research literature, such as using classwide peer tutoring, increasing academic engagement, teaching decoding and word recognition in reading, preteaching critical vocabulary prior to student reading, and providing feedback.
- Implement language development programs that emphasize developing English proficiency and fluency in social and academic communication; teaching the formal, grammatical aspects of English; and teaching new academic content.
- Build vocabulary while restricting the number of new words presented to allow teachers to explore vocabulary at a deeper level of understanding (e.g., presenting about seven words instead of the typical 20 words in a third-grade class).
- Use visual aides such as concept and story maps, word banks, pictures, graphic organizers, and manipulatives to teach concepts and vocabulary.
- Use cooperative learning and peer tutoring strategies to teach complex and decontextualized academic concepts.
- Use the native language strategically to help students understand complex and challenging concepts that ELL students would not be able to understand in English. The constant dual translation method was identified as an ineffective strategy.
- Modulate the language and cognitive demands of instructional sequences by using simple language to introduce new and complex concepts and embedding difficult vocabulary within familiar language.
- Use both extended discussions and briefer question–response exchanges to explore academic content.
- Emphasize both a content-driven curriculum (i.e., focusing on teaching content in science or math) as well as English language instruction (i.e., teaching speaking, reading, and writing in English).
- Incorporate students' cultural and background experiences to enhance comprehension of content material and to make the learning experience more meaningful.
- Provide time for students to respond in English, since processing information in a second language is more demanding and the students may need additional time to compose their responses.
- Provide scaffolding experiences by reinforcing the students' language production and expanding on it to model higher vocabulary and sentence construction.
- Monitor comprehensible input so that students understand content.
- Incorporate speaking, listening, reading, and writing activities early in the L2 acquisition process.
- Create classroom environments that encourage self-confidence, high self-esteem, and low anxiety levels.
- Provide supports in the form of models, feedback, and hands-on activities to build background knowledge and familiarity with concepts.
- Use tasks that incorporate problem solving and stimulate the development of higher thinking skills.

*Note.* Adapted from de Valenzuela & Niccolai, 2004; Gersten & Baker, 2000; Gersten & Jimenez, 1998; Gersten & Woodward, 1994; and Reyes, 1992.

instruct ELL students (Harris, 2004). The purposes of the teams are to work toward developing, implementing, and monitoring interventions. Other collaborative efforts can include ESL and bilingual teachers who team teach with other-subject teachers or work together to coordinate and align the curriculum (Harris).

Consultation services provided by individual consultants (e.g., ESL teacher, bilingual teacher, school psychologist, social worker, counselor, or speech and language specialist) are another form of collaboration available to school staff instructing ELL students. Ingraham (2000) developed a multicultural consultation framework to guide consultants working with consultees through the stages of problem identification, problem analysis, intervention planning and implementation, and summative evaluation (i.e., a teacher in a general education classroom instructing ELL students). Multicultural consultation stresses the need to examine cultural issues throughout all stages of problem solving. The instructional consultation model developed by Rosenfield (1987) is appropriate for consultants addressing language instructional issues for ELL students. The instructional model provides instructional consultants with opportunities to examine questions such as the following: Is the curriculum appropriate for ELL students? Do the students have the prerequisite skills to succeed at the instructional tasks? What is the discrepancy between the students' skills and the expected levels of performance (Lopez & Truesdell, in press; Rosenfield, 1987)?

Collaboration between school professionals and parents is also important in the process of increasing students' English language skills. Research shows that parental involvement is correlated with increased academic performance in schools with significant numbers of culturally and linguistically diverse students (de Valenzuela, Baca, & Baca, 2004). De Valenzuela et al. encourage the development of ecologically based parent and community involvement models that invite parents to collaborate to obtain information about available resources and to formulate strategies for intervening in the schools. They argue that effective programs involve parents in identifying the unique needs of the community in which the programs function to create services to fulfill those needs. For example, a community with many recent immigrants may focus on developing a program for adolescent newcomers to provide information about the schools, community, and social services.

The involvement of ELL parents increases when school professionals use strategies such as providing interpreters during meetings or other events, and communicating in the parents' native languages when sending written materials such as letters home (Lott, 2003). School professionals who develop an awareness and a knowledge base of how culturally different families view educational issues are better equipped to work with those families because they have an understanding of how cultural differences influence parents' attitudes, perceptions, and patterns of collaboration with school professionals (Lynch & Hanson, 2004).

Culturally sensitive teachers, counselors, and school psychologists who develop a knowledge base of L2 acquisition issues can foster parental involvement by acknowledging the parents' contributions to the students' academic and linguistic functioning. For example, a common misconception among school professionals is that parents should stop talking and communicating with their children in their native language at home. The rationale is that using the native language at home will interfere with English language development. However, if the parents also have limited English proficiency, the decision to use the nondominant language can lead to a lack of interaction and poor communication in the home environment. Furthermore, many parents are uncomfortable using English at home because they feel that it will prevent their children from learning the family's native language and curtail their exposure to the native culture.

Several investigations have found that working with parents to develop L1 language and literacy skills at home has positive effects on L2 language and literacy skills (see de Valenzuela et al., 2004). Strategies that are effective in promoting parent involvement will lead to children's learning. Such strategies include encouraging parents to read to their children and discuss what they read in their native language, providing literacy workshops for parents, providing families access to libraries, and involving minority parents in curriculum planning and home–school collaboration activities (Lott, 2003).

## Special Education Evaluation and Placement

When preventive approaches are implemented within the general education setting and data from interventions or summative evaluations indicate that ELL students are not progressing adequately, school professionals should consider a special education referral. Bilingual evaluations performed by assessors who have the competencies to work with ELL students are strongly recommended. Trained interpreters should be used when bilingual evaluators are not available (Lopez, 2002). However, even for professionals with expertise in those areas, distinguishing between deficits caused by the L2 acquisition process and those caused by learning difficulties can be challenging. Many of the tools available to assess ELL students are inappropriate because they tend to exclude those students from norming samples and the content is culturally loaded (see Ortiz, 2002).

Best practices entail using an ecological assessment framework that takes into consideration internal as well as external factors influencing ELL students' academic functioning (Ortiz, 2002). Informal tools and procedures, such as the examination of school records and the use of observations, interviews, language samples, test–teach–test procedures, curriculum-based assessment, and portfolio assessment methods are recommended to assess students with limited English proficiency. Formal procedures can be implemented using approaches such as adaptations and testing of the limits, with results reported in descriptive and qualitative formats.

Special education settings that range from inclusion to resource room and self-contained classrooms should be considered, with priority given to the least restrictive environment that will meet the ELL student's needs (de Valenzuela & Niccolai, 2004). When special education services are needed, the question must be decided as to what language or languages students should receive instruction in and whether bilingual special education should be considered, if available. Some argue that bilingual special education is necessary in order to instruct ELL students in their native language using a rigorous curriculum instead of a "watered down" English curriculum (see Baca & Baca, 2004). According to de Valenzuela and Niccolai, research indicates that students with disabilities can become bilingual and that the common underlying proficiency principle also applies to this population because skills can be transferred from L1 to L2.

Other educators argue that imposing a bilingual instructional method makes the students' task of learning English difficult and even impossible because the demands of learning in two languages are excessive for students with disabilities (see Baca & Baca, 2004). In the absence of research guiding the decision-making process, educators are urged to consider a number of factors, such as the following, when they choose the language of instruction for ELL students with language and learning disabilities: (a) the family's language at home, (b) the extent to which the student's disability affects language and literacy development, (c) the student's current and future needs for both languages, (d) the strength of each language for instructional purposes, and (e) the student's and the family's language preferences (Cloud, 2002).

The concerns previously voiced in this chapter regarding the instruction of ELL students in general education settings also extend to special education settings (Baca, Baca, & de Valenzuela, 2004; Gersten & Woodward, 1994). Concerns have been voiced that special educators are not typically trained to work with ELL students and do not have an understanding of L2 instructional techniques. Special education services are sometimes inadequate for ELL students in that bilingual special education aids are used to provide native language instructional support, but those professionals do not have experience in teaching ELL students or knowledge about L2 acquisition issues. Limited access to ESL services for ELL students in special education settings may also hamper their language and academic growth.

According to Harris (2004), collaboration between special education teachers, general educators involved with ELL students (e.g., bilingual and ESL teachers), and other school professionals who provide support services to those students (e.g., school psychologists and speech and language specialists) is helpful in providing coordinated and integrated services to ELL students with disabilities. Special educators with expertise in bilingual issues are an important resource to address the needs of L2 learners in special education classrooms. Educators across the general, bilingual, and special education settings are able to share information about second language development and appropriate strategies for ELL students. In addition, as ELL students with disabilities are prepared for the transition to general education, collaboration between those professionals can help students succeed in the general education curriculum by identifying the demands of the general education setting and by developing strategies to help students meet those demands (Harris, 2004).

The match between special education strategies and strategies used to instruct ELL students has been another topic of discussion in the literature. Gersten and Woodward (1994) noted that special education instruction tends to adapt a "task-analytic, skill-building approach [that is] functionally and philosophically incompatible" with ELL instructional approaches that emphasize the acquisition of expressive and receptive skills in natural contexts (p. 317). They argue that the special education emphasis on teaching discrete aspects of language and reading, and the tendency to simplify language, results in deliberate and slow lessons that lack intellectual challenge and conceptual development. Such strategies are ineffective in teaching ELL students to use rich, academically based language and to acquire challenging concepts that will lead to higher order thinking skills and problem-solving abilities.

Gersten and Woodward (1994) note that it is important for L2 instruction in special education settings to be relevant rather than only a series of drills on grammar and usage. They recommend adapting methods of presentation and practice for ELL students' needs, using interesting reading materials, emphasizing language comprehension, monitoring and negotiating comprehensible output in instruction, focusing on a small number of vocabulary words at a time, offering multiple exposures to vocabulary and concepts, introducing vocabulary before content, exploring complex ideas and concepts by contextualizing instruction through visual and experiential means, and creating classroom environments driven by student involvement and discussion about the academic content.

In general, placing ELL students in special education settings is best accomplished when the evaluation process has integrated nonbiased methods to assess the students' language and academic functioning. Placement decisions should be made while considering the students' and families' needs. Collaboration between general education, bilingual education, and special education staff will be necessary to maximize students' learning in the areas of language development and academic functioning.

## SUMMARY

As the number of ELL students increases in our nation, school professionals will need to increase their knowledge base and skills to instruct, assess, and intervene with these students. Knowledge of developmental and theoretical issues such as the process of second language acquisition, the development of language proficiency skills, and the relationship between L1 and L2 acquisition are pivotal in efforts to understand how ELL students become proficient in speaking, understanding, reading, and writing in English. The process of distinguishing between L2 acquisition issues and learning difficulties is complex, and professionals must have the skills to explore the factors that influence learning a second language. Most importantly, practitioners and researchers must work collaboratively to identify effective instructional strategies that can be implemented within early intervention and prevention frameworks to help ELL students succeed and achieve in general education settings.

## RECOMMENDED RESOURCES

### Books and Other Printed Material

Baca, L. M., & Cervantes, H. T. (Eds.). (2004). *The bilingual special education interface* (4th ed.). Upper Saddle River, NJ: Pearson/Merrill/Prentice Hall.

This volume provides a comprehensive overview of issues relevant to special education and English language learners. A number of authors provide their perspectives on topics related to policies, assessment practices, and intervention design relevant to ELL students and bilingual students with disabilities.

Gersten, R., & Baker, S. (2000). The professional knowledge base on instructional practices that support cognitive growth for English-language learners. In R. Gersten, E. P. Schiller, & S. Vaughn (Eds.), *Contemporary special education research: Synthesis of the knowledge base on critical instructional issues* (pp. 31–79). Mahwah, NJ: Erlbaum.

The chapter is strongly recommended because it describes an investigation designed to identify effective instructional practices for English language learners. The researchers describe the methodology used and provide readers with a comprehensive discussion of instructional interventions that promote academic achievement for language minority students.

Ovando, C. J., Collier, V. P., & Combs, M. C. (2003). *Bilingual and ESL classrooms: Teaching in multicultural contexts* (3rd ed.). New York: McGraw-Hill.

Readers will find that this book provides a comprehensive discussion of instructional English language learners and bilingual children. It is a particularly useful resource for professionals who want to gain knowledge related to language development and instructional interventions for ELL students.

### Websites

*http://www.ncela.gwu.edu*

This website for National Clearinghouse for English Language Acquisition and Language Instruction Educational Programs (U.S. Department of Education) disseminates information about educational programs on language acquisition for ELL students.

*http://www.colorado.edu/education/BUENO/*

The Bueno Center for Multicultural Education implements research and training programs that focus on multicultural issues. The Center provides professional development opportunities and a variety of materials on bilingual and multicultural topics relevant to school professionals.

*http://www.crede.ucsc.edu*

The Center for Research on Education, Diversity and Excellence (CREDE) is a federally funded program that disseminates research findings, professional materials, multimedia products, and print publications. The CREDE website is helpful for practitioners, researchers, and parents.

*http://www.nasponline.org/culturalcompetence/index.html*

The National Association of School Psychologists (NASP) website offers a section on Culturally Competent Practice, which provides information related to consultation, intervention, and assessment. The resources are appropriate for school psychologists, other school professionals, and parents.

## REFERENCES

August, D., & Hakuta, K. (1997). *Improving schooling for language-minority children.* Washington, DC: National Academy Press.

Baca, L., & Baca, E. (2004). Bilingualism and bilingual education. In L. M. Baca & H. T. Cervantes (Eds.), *The bilingual special education interface* (4th ed., pp. 24–45). Upper Saddle River, NJ: Pearson/Merrill/Prentice Hall.

Baca, L., Baca, E., & de Valenzuela, J. S. (2004). Development of the bilingual special education interface. In L. M. Baca & H. T. Cervantes (Eds.), *The bilingual special education interface* (4th ed., pp. 100–123). Upper Saddle River, NJ: Pearson/Merrill/Prentice Hall.

Cloud, N. (2002). Culturally and linguistically responsive instructional planning. In A. Artiles & A. Ortiz (Eds.), *English language learners with special education needs: Identification, assessment and instruction* (pp. 107–132). McHenry, IL: Center for Applied Linguistics and Delta Systems.

Collier, V. P. (1992). A synthesis of studies examining long-term language minority student data on academic achievement. *Bilingual Research Journal, 16,* 187–212.

Cummins, J. (1984). *Bilingualism and special education: Issues in assessment and pedagogy.* Clevedon, England: Multilingual Matters.

Cummins, J. (1986). Language proficiency and academic achievement. In J. Cummins & M. Swain (Eds.), *Bilingualism in education* (pp. 138–161). New York: Longman.

Damico, J. S., Oller, J. W., Jr., & Storey, M. E. (1983). The diagnosis of language disorders in bilingual children: Surface-oriented and pragmatic criteria. *Journal of Speech and Hearing Disorders, 48,* 385–394.

de Valenzuela, J. S., Baca, L., & Baca, E. (2004). Family involvement in bilingual special education: Challenging the norm. In L. M. Baca & H. T. Cervantes (Eds.), *The bilingual special education interface* (4th ed., pp. 360–381). Upper Saddle River, NJ: Pearson/Merrill/Prentice Hall.

de Valenzuela, J. S., & Niccolai, S. (2004). Language development in culturally and linguistically diverse students with special needs. In L. M. Baca & H. T. Cervantes (Eds.), *The bilingual special education interface* (4th ed., pp. 124–161). Upper Saddle River, NJ: Pearson/Merrill/Prentice Hall.

Ellis, R. (1994). *The study of second-language acquisition.* Oxford, UK: Oxford University Press.

Gersten, R., & Baker, S. (2000). The professional knowledge base on instructional practices that support cognitive growth for English-language learners. In R. Gersten, E. P. Schiller, & S. Vaughn (Eds.), *Contemporary special education research: Synthesis of the knowledge base on critical instructional issues* (pp. 31–79). Mahwah, NJ: Erlbaum.

Gersten, R., & Jimenez, R. T. (1998). *Promoting learning for culturally and linguistically diverse students: Classroom applications from contemporary research.* Belmont, CA: Wadsworth Publishing.

Gersten, R., & Woodward, J. (1994). The language-minority student and special education: Issues, trends, and paradoxes. *Exceptional Children, 60,* 310–322.

Harris, K. C. (2004). The relationship between educational consultation and instruction for culturally and linguistically diverse exceptional (CLDE) students: Definitions, structures, and case studies. In L. M. Baca & H. T. Cervantes (Eds.), *The bilingual special education interface* (4th ed., pp. 336–359). Upper Saddle River, NJ: Pearson/Merrill/Prentice Hall.

Ingraham, C. L. (2000). Consultation through a multicultural lens: Multicultural and cross-cultural consultation in schools. *School Psychology Review, 29,* 320–343.

Krashen, S. D. (1982). *Principles and practice in second language acquisition.* New York: Pergamon.

Langdon, H. W. (1992). Speech and language assessment of LEP/bilingual Hispanic students. In H. W. Langdon & L. L. Cheng (Eds.), *Hispanic children and adults with communication disorders* (pp. 201–265). Gaithersburg, MD: Aspen Publishers.

Levine, D. U., & Lezotte, L. W. (2001). Effective schools research. In J. A. Banks & C. A. McGee Banks (Eds.), *Handbook of multicultural education* (pp. 525–547). San Francisco: Jossey-Bass.

Lopez, E. C. (2002). Best practices in working with school interpreters to deliver psychological services to children and families. In A. Thomas & J. Grimes (Eds.), *Best practices in school psychology IV* (pp. 1419–1432). Washington, DC: National Association of School Psychologists.

Lopez, E. C., & Truesdell, L. (in press). Conducting instructional consultation with English language learners. In G. Esquivel, E. C. Lopez, & S. Nahari (Eds.), *Handbook of multicultural school psychology.* Mahwah, NJ: Erlbaum.

Lott, B. (2003). Recognizing and welcoming the standpoint of low-income parents in the public schools. *Journal of Educational and Psychological Consultation, 14,* 91–104.

Lynch, E. W., & Hanson, M. J. (2004). *Developing cross-cultural competence: A guide for working with children and their families* (3rd ed.). Baltimore: Paul H. Brookes.

McLaughlin, B. (1985). *Second language acquisition in childhood: Vol. 2. School-age children* (2nd ed.). Hillsdale, NJ: Erlbaum.

National Clearinghouse for English Language Acquisition and Language Instruction. (2001). *Survey of the states' limited English proficient students and available educational programs and services, 1999–2001 Summary report.* Washington, DC: Author.

Ortiz, S. O. (2002). Best practices in nondiscriminatory assessment. In A. Thomas & G. Grimes (Eds.), *Best practices in school psychology IV* (pp. 1321–1336). Bethesda, MD: National Association of School Psychologists.

Ovando, C. J., Collier, V. P., & Combs, M. C. (2003). *Bilingual and ESL classrooms: Teaching in multicultural contexts* (3rd ed.). New York: McGraw Hill.

Reyes, M. de la L. (1992). Challenging venerable assumptions: Literacy instruction for linguistically different students. *Harvard Educational Review 62,* 427–446.

Rosenfield, S. (1987). *Instructional consultation.* Hillsdale, NJ: Lawrence Erlbaum.

Thomas, A., & Grimes, G. (Eds.). (2002). *Best practices in school psychology IV* (Vol. 1 & 2). Bethesda, MD: National Association of School Psychologists.

Timm, L. A. (1993). Bilingual code-switching: An overview of research. In B. J. Merino, H. T. Trueba, & F. A. Samaniego (Eds.), *Language and culture in learning: Teaching Spanish to native speakers of Spanish* (pp. 94–112). Bristol, PA: Falmer Press.

Vygotsky, L. S. (1962). *Thought and language.* Cambridge, MA: Harvard University Press.

# 50

# Healthy Family Systems

**Jenet Jacob**
**William J. Doherty**
*University of Minnesota*

Since its foundation, school psychology has been concerned with the home environment of the individual child. Yet, it was not until the late 1970s and 1980s that more direct methods for assessing and working with families were developed (Anderson, 1983; Fine & Holt, 1983). Extensive research has documented relationships between various demographic and status variables and child behavioral and academic outcomes (Armor, 2003; Amato, 2001). However, researchers have increasingly been led beyond socioeconomic variables to evaluate the significant role of family interaction patterns in the individual behaviors of children. Analyses of these interaction patterns have illuminated the ways in which individual development is affected by the interconnected, relational processes within the family. This understanding has increased the need for school practitioners to develop more systematic approaches to address these significant dimensions of family life.

Much of the understanding of family interaction processes has emerged from family systems theory. From a family systems perspective, the family is a dynamic, interdependent unit that interacts with other interdependent units in ways that affect the development of the individuals within it. Individual behavior is a product of complex interactions between persons and their environments, rather than the result of internal psychological processes or external forces. This view challenges traditional conceptions of cause and effect based on single identifiable causes and highlights the fluid process of mutual influence among individuals in relationships.

Family systems theory developed hand in glove with clinical interventions because the pioneers were all therapists or people interested in therapy (Bateson, 1972; Bowen, 1978; Minuchen, 1974; Haley, 1976). Using the ideas introduced by cybernetics and general systems theory, anthropologist Gregory Bateson and his team in Palo Alto, California, began by analyzing the interaction patterns in families of schizophrenic individuals. Their studies of family communication revealed the family as an interacting system with properties such as boundaries, subsystems, structures, and continuous inflow and outflow of energy (Bateson, Jackson, & Weakland, 1956). They concluded that the systemic patterns of the family are such that schizophrenia is a symptom of a family system pathology rather than isolated individual pathology. In the 1960s and 1970s, these ideas were expanded by family psychiatrists such as Murray Bowen (1978), Lyman Wynne et al. (1986), and Salvador Minuchin (1974), who pioneered the clinical application of family systems theory in the form of family therapy.

This new systemic perspective allowed the symptomatic behavior of individuals to be analyzed and treated within its context of habitual patterns of systemic interaction, the source of the behavior's purpose and meaning. By isolating these patterns in family therapy, systemic family processes could be altered to improve the well-being of the involved individuals. Family therapy thus provided the context for the development of family systems theory, which also explains much of its appeal to practitioners (Doherty & Baptiste, 1993).

Despite its potential, family systems theory has not been adequately applied in the school setting, largely because it has not been translated into terms educational practitioners find useful within their roles. Although families have always been recognized as a central influence on children's emotional well-being and school learning, school psychologists have not had an explicit conceptual framework for understanding family systems (Fine & Holt, 1983; Kramer, 1990). Professionals who do not have formal means of assessing families have had to rely on methods of evaluation that do not take complex family processes into account or lead to effective action (Doherty

& Peskay, 1992). This shortcoming suggests a significant need for more explicit models for assessing families of children in schools.

Furthermore, working with whole families around serious problems is generally thought to lie outside the role constraints, training, and interest of most school practitioners (French, 1990). This fact notwithstanding, when properly translated to the school context, family systems theory offers a way to transcend the current atheoretical approach of many school psychologists by giving them a framework for understanding the dynamics of family interactions and offering context-sensitive modes of intervention.

This chapter begins with an introduction to family systems theory through a systemic view of normal family functioning and problematic functioning. This is followed by a presentation of alternative actions for prevention and intervention of family problems from within the school context and a practical model of family involvement that practitioners may find useful. Our ultimate goal is to show how using insights from family systems theory within the unique role and position of school practitioners provides a powerful opportunity to promote positive changes in children and parents.

**Table 1** *Basic Principles of Family Systems Theory*

1. The family must be understood as a whole.
2. Family interaction patterns regulate the behavior of individuals and tend to repeat across generations.
3. Individual symptoms reflect family interaction patterns.
4. Key family interaction patterns occur in triangles.
5. Family health requires clear family boundaries.
6. Family health requires a balance between connection and individuation.
7. Flexibility is a key safeguard against serious family dysfunction.
8. Small perturbations can lead to major family change.
9. Professionals become part of the new family system.

## BACKGROUND AND DEVELOPMENT

### Basic Family Systems Theory

Contemporary family systems theory incorporates the following nine principles (see Table 1) to describe how the behavior of individual family members emerges through interactional structures and processes that then interface with other systems. We will briefly discuss the implications of each of the nine principles for understanding family functioning (much of this section is adapted from review chapters by Doherty and Peskay, 1992, and Vickers and Minke, 1997). This chapter does not include a separate Problems and Implications section because within the systems approach, both function and dysfunction are controlled by the same processes. An understanding of these principles will enable school practitioners to better identify and address the relationship between children's behavior at school and children's experience at home.

1. *The family must be understood as a whole.* The elements of the family system are the individual members, who are held together in an interdependent relationship in which each family member's behavior affects every other member. These patterns of mutual influence result in the creation of a system that is greater than the sum of individual parts and therefore cannot be comprehended by examining the individual elements in isolation (Whitchurch & Constantine, 1993). Within the family system are multiple subsystems of interaction, such as the parental relationship. Each subsystem may be analyzed separately in its exchanges with the larger family system and other subsystems. As with all systems, the family system and its subsystems are *goal seeking.* Each system seeks a *homeostatic equilibrium* (a balance of continuity and adaptation) through a process of feedback and control, much like a thermostat senses the ambient air temperature and adjusts the production of heat. In establishing this balance, the system must maintain and protect its boundaries, as well as build bridges between itself and other systems and subsystems. Individual behavior is better understood when seen as a reflection of the purposeful goal seeking of the whole system.

2. *Family interaction patterns regulate the behavior of individuals and tend to repeat across generations.* From the moment a couple meets, they establish behavioral sequences that form the repeated patterns of interaction that ultimately define how the family system functions. This idea of repeated behavioral sequences that form a coherent whole is the core of family systems approach. These interaction patterns are developed and perpetuated in everything, from mealtime activities and holiday rituals to the way the family deals with secrets and privacy.

When described metaphorically, this patterned interaction of human behavior has been characterized as a dance, in which the behaviors of an individual are moves in a complex family choreography. The total family dance takes on an identity of its own as the family members perform their complementary movements. These dancelike "vibrations" are characteristic of all living systems (Bateson, 1972). Individuals within a family vibrate to the oscillations of family patterns, which are in turn influenced by the oscillations of the individuals within the family. The patterned nature of these oscillations ensures that they are historical, reflecting the influence of past generations while already engaged in establishing those of future generations. The intergenerational transmission of these patterns or "rules" explains how families may sometimes become stuck in dysfunctional interactional styles for generations.

In their repetition, the patterns form a set of interactional rules and shared assumptions that define the appropriateness of behavior for individuals within the system. A few of these rules are clear and overt, such as finishing homework before playing with friends after school, or asking permission before taking the car. But the most powerful are those that are covert and unstated, those that are not consciously identified by individuals within the system. In setting out who may do what, where, when, how, and with whom, rules prescribe behaviors related to things such as expression of feelings, conflict resolution, sexuality, independence, and achievement (Barbarin, 1992). Once such a rule is established by its patterned redundancy, the homeostatic, goal-directed nature of the family system means that change to the system may be resisted, even if it is dysfunctional. Examples of such covert rules may include allowing mom to express anger but not dad, accepting poor school performance from a son but not a daughter, or allowing strong emotional reactions from one family member while the others must remain quiet (Ingoldsby, Smith, & Miller, 2004). When one family member begins to act in a manner that is outside the accepted limits of family behavior, the others will engage in negative or positive feedback loops to cause a return to the family's homeostatic equilibrium.

These rules organize themselves into belief systems about the internal dynamics of the family's system and define how a family sees itself. Some families, for example, have beliefs about the high achievement potential of all family members, or the importance of religious identity. This does not assume that all family members hold identical beliefs, but that there are identifying family belief patterns around which family members cohere or dissent. Major family crises occur when fundamental disagreements challenge these belief systems.

3. *Individual symptoms reflect family interaction patterns.* The complex choreography of family interaction patterns assumed by systems theory means that individuals who demonstrate dysfunctional behavior are expressing symptoms of family system pathology rather than individual pathology. From a family systems perspective, problems attributed to individual dysfunction are better conceptualized as disorders involving dysfunctional transactional patterns within the entire system (Whitchurch & Constantine, 1993). The eating disorders of bulimia and anorexia nervosa, for example, have been conceptualized as disorders involving the entire family system rather than the identified patient alone (Minuchin, Rossman, & Baker, 1978).

This link does not implicate family processes as the cause of the disorder but affirms the importance of concentrating on how the family organizes its processes around such problems (Doherty & Baptiste, 1993). Such problems may become entrenched in the family's relational system because they serve to maintain family homeostasis by stabilizing systemic function. For example, systemic family therapists might view a child's deteriorated functioning at home and school after the divorce of her parents as a way of prompting the divorced parents to cooperate. After the parents respond by cooperating, the child's improved functioning might indicate that the behavior served as a means of reconnecting the parents.

*Where* a symptom occurs in a relationship system is determined by the patterns of emotional functioning that predominate in that family system. Patterns that foster dysfunction in a particular member of the family will induce symptom development in that member during periods of high family stress. Symptoms may include a physical illness, emotional illness, or social illness defined as a conduct or criminal disorder (Kerr & Bowen, 1988).

In the case of an alcoholic father, roles may be established around the behavior that both maintain it and require it for homeostatic function. The mother may serve as the enabler by helping the father avoid the consequences of his behavior. The oldest child may become the caretaker by taking on the needs of the other children and being the ideal student, in contrast to a younger sibling who, as the delinquent, attempts to change dad by bringing attention to himself. Each of the individuals in the family fulfills a role in an attempt to absorb some of the family stress, which may cause any of them to exhibit symptoms of system dysfunction (Ingoldsby et al., 2004).

4. *Key family interaction patterns occur in triangles.* As the above example demonstrates, a systemic perspective assumes that it is never possible to adequately explain the emotional processes in one relationship if links to other relationships are not included. The process by which one relationship becomes intertwined with others is termed *triangling.* From a family systems perspective, triadic interactions are the smallest systemic units that can be analyzed to understand relationships, because dyadic relationships occur in a field with other people. Within the family, interlocking triangles form to equilibrate or stabilize relational transactions (Kerr & Bowen, 1988). Identifying these triadic relationships allows an analysis of the effect one relationship has on another relationship, such as how the marital relationship affects the father–child relationship (Doherty & Beaton, 2004). Sibling triangles, parent–child triangles, and intergenerational triangles are all important interlocking centers of interaction.

In understanding children's adjustment, a triangular perspective suggests that in addition to relating to the mother and father in separate dyads, the child also relates to the parents' relationship. The child lives in a "force field" of interactional pulls and pushes to and from each parent that is calibrated by the parents' own relationship. In its constructive role, this triangular interaction provides the collaborative parenting relationship needed to raise the child. When parents are conflicted or distant, however, the child will experience distress even when the dyadic relationships with each parent are not distressed. Dysfunctional triangling develops when, for example, a child is brought into a coalition with one parent against the other by telling secrets about the other in order to establish a stronger position (see Figure 1).

5. *Family health requires clear family boundaries.* A defining feature of all systems and of the interlocking triadic relationships that compose them is their boundaries. Boundaries define what is or is not included in the family system, and to the degree that the boundaries are closed or open, they enable or restrict the transfer of information and energy (Ingoldsby et al., 2004). Boundaries that allow appropriate exchanges of thoughts, feelings, and behaviors are considered optimal, whereas those that excessively inhibit access are less effective. Boundary permeability within the family system is often conceptualized by an assessment of the amount of exchange between the family and its environment and the amount of cohesion and emotional connectedness among the family members (Whitchurch & Constantine, 1993).

Subsystems within the family also have boundaries determined by the rules that define who participates and how. An interaction in which a mother tells her oldest child, "You aren't your brother's parent. If he is riding his bike in the street, tell me and I will stop him," lays out the rule defining the boundaries of their subsystem (Minuchin, 1974, p. 53). Such rules are essential because they protect the integrity of the system and provide for the development of interpersonal skills. Healthy boundaries are defined enough to allow subsystem members to carry out their functions without undue interference while also allowing contact between members of the subsystem and other subsystems. Inappropriate subsystem boundaries are present when, for example, parents share intimate details about their marital lives with their child or prevent a member of the family from participating appropriately in decision making.

Uncertainty about who is included in a system or how they are included is described as *boundary ambiguity* (Boss, 1988). Boundary ambiguity often occurs when there is psychological presence and physical absence, as in postdivorce families in which the children may regard the nonresidential father as a continuing member of the family, while the mother regards the family as a single-parent unit. In the case of families in which one or both parents have remarried, boundary ambiguity can be seen in situations where it is not clear whether the mother's new husband is in a father role or a friend role. Boundary ambiguity presents significant stress for families in these situations.

One of the most significant sources of stress on system boundaries in families results from changes inherent to the family life cycle. The birth of the first child, children's entrance into the school system, job-related spousal absence, adolescent children leaving home, loss of a spouse, loss of a parent, and remarriage all present unique stresses on the family that require system adjustment if the family is to survive. Some

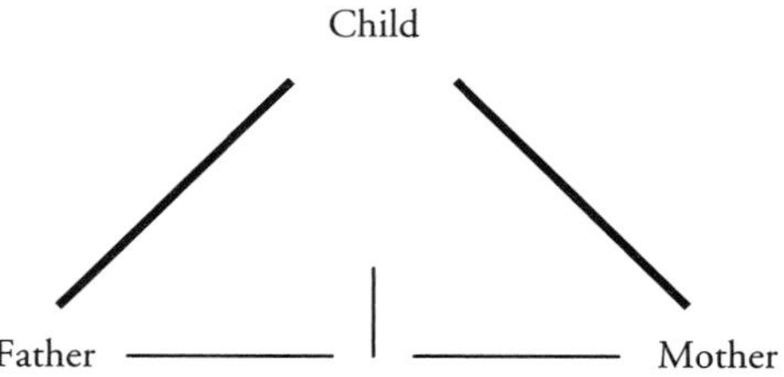


**Figure 1.** *Triangulated interaction between child and one parent, in coalition against the other parent.*

families are strengthened by adjusting to these developmental stresses, whereas others seem to enter a downward spiral toward dysfunction. The difference between these families seems to be the structural variability they allow as they accomplish the functions necessary for survival. For example, the survival of many African American families throughout history depended on their ability to adapt structural norms to allow people to enter and exit the family system as they needed (Boss, 1988).

6. *Family health requires a balance between connection and individuation.* An important corollary to appropriate boundary permeability is the necessity of systemic relationships that preserve individual autonomy while establishing solidarity. Family systems are defined by the degree of connection they expect and experience, which can range from too much (enmeshed) to too little (disengaged). A family system that supports both connection as well as autonomy provides a healthy systemic structure in which individual development can flourish. According to family systems theory, this structure requires both emotional closeness as well as emotional distance and differentiation.

A family system that requires excessive emotional connectedness is defined by intra-family boundaries that permit extreme and inappropriate exchanges of information, causing members to feel emotionally smothered and inhibited in their individual differentiation. At the same time, this family system also maintains boundaries that are strongly impermeable to exchanges with the outside environment, causing the system to close in on itself. In this family system, members become excessively dependent on one another for emotional cues about what to think, feel, or do (Rosenblatt, 1994). Individual autonomy is sacrificed for excessive emotional connection.

A family system that is disengaged is characterized by intra-family boundaries that are excessively impermeable to interpersonal engagement and the exchange of energy and information. Though these family members may function autonomously, they will have "a skewed sense of independence, and lack of feelings of loyalty and belonging" (Minuchin, 1974, p. 55). In disengaged families, nurturing and monitoring are sacrificed for individual autonomy. Identity differentiation is inhibited by a lack of interdependence. Inadequate bonding results, and individuals feel neglected, undervalued, and indifferent to the needs of others. In such systems only high levels of individual stress can activate the family's supportive system.

Families who experience symmetry between supportiveness and autonomy are defined by clear boundaries that allow appropriate exchanges of information and physical and emotional connectedness. From a systems perspective, such families have successfully walked the tightrope of solidarity and autonomy. Walking the tightrope is particularly important when considering the changing developmental needs for autonomy and connection as children grow. Younger children, for example, may need a qualitatively different level of involvement, structure, and autonomy than adolescents who are redefining family roles in preparation for departure from the family. Family systems that are able to appropriately adjust to these needs enable the healthy development of individual members.

The importance of appropriate family engagement is reflected in the school setting, where family disengagement is identified as an important distinguishing factor in adolescents who are at risk for academic failure and those who are not. Family rigidity, chaotic family functioning, and family enmeshment also negatively affect academic achievement (Chapin & Vito, 1988). Similar findings among Chinese adolescents demonstrate that more open communication between parents and adolescents also predicts better academic outcomes, indicating the importance of healthy systemic processes across cultures (Xia et al., 2001).

7. *Flexibility is a key safeguard against serious family dysfunction.* Adaptability is another cardinal principle related to the balance between unity and autonomy. Healthy systems are those that are flexible to the constant changes inherent in family life and development. Systems that are unable to appropriately respond to demands from inside the family or from the environment will experience stress that will undermine healthy functioning and even survival. Healthy adaptability requires appropriate responsiveness to the two opposing forces induced by pressure toward homeostasis and pressure toward adaptation or change. Families who are excessively rigid will maintain fixed patterns, restrict negotiation, and demonstrate an inability to address the needs of new members. Families defined as chaotic are characterized by continual change, unpredictability, confusion, arbitrary decision making, and constant negotiation. Appropriate flexibility in response to continual internal and external demands is defined by an ability to change rules, interaction patterns, beliefs, and roles in a way that promotes healthy functioning for all members.

From a systems perspective, adaptation occurs on two levels. The first order involves adjustments made according to day-to-day demands, and the second order involves more profound adjustments to greater interactional or organizational changes. First-order changes, for example, involve appropriate adjustments in rules and responsibilities according to the developmental age of children. Second-order changes are usually necessary when expected developmental changes take place, such as the birth of a baby, or when unexpected crises occur, such as death or divorce.

Effective family adaptation to the continual adjustments of parenting and to family crises such as illness or unemployment requires a constructive balance between support and autonomy as well as maintenance of clear family boundaries. Thus, all of the significant characteristics of healthy family systems identified previously come to bear in the appropriate flexibility of the family system. It is not the stressful events themselves that disable families. It is the family's flexibility that determines whether the outcome is positive, neutral, or negative (Minuchin, 1974; Olson et al., 1983).

8. *Small perturbations can lead to major family change.* The importance of the family's flexible responsiveness to both the small and large internal and external demands of family life is underscored by systems theory's notion that small alterations in a complex living system can lead to large-scale, unanticipated change. In science, the contemporary version of this is found in chaos theory (Glieck, 1987), which has shown how small perturbations—for example in air temperature—can be accelerated by other environmental conditions, leading to major changes that could not have been predicted. In families that are coping adequately in a stressful environment, a perturbation such as the birth of a new, sickly child, the broken leg of a family wage earner, or the death of a beloved grandparent can trigger changes that render the family disabled and send a child spiraling into trouble. Similarly, a family that has become dysfunctional may turn around after some event that initially is not so promising, such as a layoff resulting in the father acquiring a more satisfying or better paying job. Family systems theory emphasizes the power of small events for good or ill.

9. *Professionals become part of the new family system.* Family systems theory in the 1980s began to emphasize how professionals who work with families become incorporated into a "meta" system that can be examined with the same systems concepts as the family system (Keeney, 1983, as cited in Doherty & Peskay, 1992). Therefore, all of the family systems principles described above can be used to understand and assess the interactions between school professionals and families: repeated interaction patterns, beliefs, triangles, boundaries, flexibility, connectedness versus disengagement, the meaning of symptomatic behavior, and the role of small perturbations.

## ALTERNATIVE ACTIONS FOR PREVENTION AND INTERVENTION

Given the influence of the family system on children's well-being and behavior, and the fact that the school's relationship with the child includes a relationship with the child's family, one of the main avenues for problem prevention involves working with families in a collaborative, supportive way. A strong family–school relationship is perhaps the best preventive family support measure provided by the school. Establishing such relationships also makes it likely that when problems do occur, there will be effective, collaborative problem-solving between families, children, and schools (Epstein, 1996).

The goal of having a balanced relational collaboration between parents and school professionals for the welfare of the child is best established through respectful and caring relationships with parents. A healthy family–practitioner–child triangle requires boundaries that are permeable enough to allow school practitioners inside the family system and allow parents inside the school environment. Recognizing the important effect schools have on the level of parent involvement is fundamental to identifying and establishing programs that support and enhance collaborative family–school relationships (see chapter 6, "Parent-Teacher Relationships").

A growing focus in schools has been the development of school-based family intervention programs to address the needs of specific populations. Problems and populations of focus have included gifted students, students from divorced families, and those suffering parental abuse and neglect, among others (Gerrard, 1996; Montemayor, 1984; Berger, Fine, & Carlson, 1992). From recruitment to retention, the success of these programs requires that the functioning of the family systems of these at-risk populations be carefully considered. Such programs recognize that addressing family dynamics is essential for the intervention to be effective and sustainable. In a review of programs developed for families at risk for drug use, Glynn and Haenlein (1988) focused on the role of the family in the efficacy of such programs. Similar considerations have been important with intervention programs for pregnant and parenting school-age students. The fact that students who receive the most involvement and emotional support from their families are most likely to complete programs indicates the importance of specifically addressing family systems (Schnack, 1995).

## A Model of Family Involvement for School-Based Mental Health Service Providers

One of the most vexing problems for school practitioners is knowing how deeply to become involved with parents and other family members in the service of children's needs. Family problems can seem bottomless and outside of the competency and time constraints of education professionals. Indeed, some school psychologists resist developing much understanding of family systems because it is unclear how to apply knowledge that seems more suitable to the work of family therapists. The model presented here was originally developed for training family physicians in working with families experiencing illness and disability (Doherty & Baird, 1986). These professionals face a similar dilemma to that of school-based practitioners. They inevitably work with family members in emotional distress but are not equipped, by mission, training, and scheduling logistics, to engage in intensive family therapy.

The Levels of Family Involvement (LFI) model has provided a way to conceptualize a moderate degree of depth or intensity in physicians' work with families, that is, interaction that is more than just informational but not as intensive as therapy. The model has been widely adopted in family medicine training and has been put into operation in a series of research studies to document the degree of family-centered practice and skills used by academic family physicians and family practice residents (Marvel & Morphew, 1993; Marvel, Schilling, Doherty, & Baird, 1994). The model has also been applied to the work of parent and family educators (Doherty, 1995) and school psychologists (Doherty & Peskay, 1992). Following is an updated version of the LFI model, which has been adapted primarily from Doherty (1995). The model conceptualizes professional engagement with families along a continuum with five qualitatively different levels of intensity (see Table 2 for a list of the levels and skills). Each of the levels and corresponding interventions will be described in the following section.

***Level 1: Institution-Centered Interactions.*** Level 1 describes programs or activities in which parents and

**Table 2** *Levels of Family Involvement for Professionals*

**Level 1: Institution-Centered Interactions**

Interactions with families are institution centered, not family centered. Families are not regarded as an important area of focus but are dealt with for practical or legal reasons. One-way communication prevails.

**Level 2: Information and Collaboration**

*Knowledge Base:* Content information in the professional's specialty.

*Personal Development:* Openness to engage families in collaborative ways.

*Skills:*

1. Communicating information clearly.
2. Eliciting questions and areas of concern.
3. Conducting informative family conferences.
4. Making pertinent and practical recommendations.
5. Generating mutually agreed-upon action plans.
6. Respecting cultural concerns that families raise.
7. Providing information on community resources.

**Level 3: Feelings and Support**

*Knowledge Base:* Family development plus individual and family reactions to stress.

*Personal Development:* Awareness of one's own feelings in relation to family members, and ability to tolerate family members' feelings without fleeing or trying to fix them.

*Skills:*

1. Eliciting expressions of feelings and concerns.
2. Listening empathetically.
3. Normalizing feelings and reactions.
4. Creating an open and supportive climate.
5. In group settings, protecting a family member from too much self-disclosure.
6. Engaging families in collaborative problem-solving discussion that involves feelings and values as well as rational planning.
7. Tailoring recommendations to the unique needs and concerns of the family.
8. Sensitively exploring cultural issues.
9. Identifying family impairment and psychological dysfunction.
10. Tailoring a referral to the family's unique situation.

*(Continued)*

**Table 2** *Continued*

**Level 4: Brief Focused Intervention**

*Knowledge Base:* Family systems theory.

*Personal Development:* Awareness of one's own participation in systems, including one's own family, client family systems, and larger community systems.

*Skills:*

1. Asking a series of questions to elicit a detailed picture of the family dynamics.
2. Developing a hypothesis about the family dynamics involved in the problem.
3. Working with the family for a short period of time to change a stuck family interaction pattern.
4. Knowing when to end the intervention effort and either referring or returning to level 3.
5. Helping the family use its cultural resources to address a problem.
6. Orchestrating a referral by educating the family and the therapist about what to expect.
7. Working closely with therapists and community systems.

**Level 5: Family Therapy**

The following partial description is offered to show the boundary between Level 4 and Level 5 family therapy.

*Knowledge Base:* Family systems and patterns whereby distressed families interact with professionals and other community systems.

*Personal Development:* Ability to handle intense emotions in families and self and to maintain one's balance in the face of strong pressure from family members or other professionals.

*Skills:*

1. Interviewing families or family members who are quite difficult to engage.
2. Working intensively with families during crises.
3. Efficiently generating and testing hypotheses about the family's difficulties and strengths.
4. Escalating conflict in the family in order to break a family impasse.
5. Constructively dealing with a family's ambivalence about change.
6. Working on culturally related stress and conflicts that are impairing the family.
7. Negotiating collaborative relationships with other professionals and systems, even when these groups are at odds with one another.

*Note:* From "Developmental Levels of Family-Centered Medical Care," by W. J. Doherty and M. A. Baird, 1986, *Family Medicine, 18,* pp. 153–156; and from "Boundaries Between Parent and Family Education and Family Therapy," by W. J. Doherty, 1995, *Family Relations, 44,* pp. 353–358. Adapted with permission of the authors.

other family members are included only for practical or legal reasons. At this level of family involvement, the school practitioner does not see working with families as a professional skill to be developed. Professionals create educational and programmatic policies with little explicit attention to the needs of parents and family members, who are expected to support and cooperate with the professionals concerning their children's difficulties. Conferences concerning the children are conducted in a school-focused manner instead of a partnership manner, with parents having relatively little input. Fortunately, Level 1 programs are increasingly being seen as inadequate ways to work with families and, in the case of children with special educational needs, are contrary to federal law (Doherty & Peksay, 1992).

***Level 2: Information and Collaboration.*** Level 2 involves engaging family members in collaborative educational activities around the content knowledge of child development, parenting, and family life. At this level, both parents and school professionals have good skills in communicating information clearly, eliciting questions, engaging a group in the learning process, and making pertinent and practical recommendations. Examples of appropriate Level 2 activities include individualized education plan (IEP) meetings that engage parents in an informative and collaborative way. Although IEP meetings are often also conducted at Level 1, with a one-way flow of information from professional to parents, Level 2 requires more collaborative effort by professionals than standard practice. The principal limitation of Level 2, even when done well, is that it avoids the affective and experiential domains and does not lead to an understanding of the stresses, problems, concerns, and strengths of families.

***Level 3: Feelings and Support.*** Level 3 embraces the activities, knowledge, and skills of Level 2 but adds to them. This level includes eliciting the feelings and experiences of the parents and family members and using these personal disclosures as part of the educational process. The school practitioner uses the skills of listening empathetically, gently probing for feelings and personal stories, creating an open and supportive climate, engaging in collaborative problem-solving, and tailoring recommendations to the specific situation of the parent or family member. Unintrusively combining, as it does, the cognitive and affective domains, Level 3 is the optimal level of intensity for most ongoing educational activities with families. However, it is far less common than Level 2 and perhaps Level 1 because it involves a focus on family interaction patterns rather than school processes.

Level 3 interactions in educational settings generally deal with the normative stresses of family life rather than traumatic personal memories and experiences, although these may emerge, leading to referral to a therapist. A simple example of a Level 3 exchange would be when a parent nonverbally shows dismay at some new information and the professional reflects back the feeling, as in "This must be hard news to hear." Another example is when a parent changes the subject—from talking about the child to mentioning stresses going on at home or work that make it hard to focus on helping the child with school work—and the professional listens empathetically and responds. Skilled professionals with a Level 3 family orientation are able to let the parent feel heard as a person while not losing sight of making plans to help the child.

The most common mistakes at Level 3 are to move too quickly back to the cognitive level, either because of personal discomfort or the sense that other team members are not comfortable, or to give premature advice before the parent has had the chance to tell the story and express feelings. Another mistake is to probe too deeply into the sources of the parent's distress in an effort to help, thereby becoming too intrusive. When done well, however, the Level 3 balancing of depth and limits is the hallmark of skilled interaction with parents in an educational setting.

The principal limitation of Level 3 is that some parents' needs and problems are too intense to be worked with constructively in an educational setting or using a supportive group approach. In a group meeting, some parents may overdisclose and need gentle limit setting from the school practitioner. In a family educational group setting, these parents may overwhelm other parents with a need for air time. Or their problems may go far beyond parenting and child issues. In these situations, the school practitioner might meet with the parent alone to discuss a referral to a therapist.

***Level 4: Brief Focused Intervention.*** Level 4 subsumes Levels 2 and 3 and goes beyond by including an assessment of a family systems problem and a planned effort to help the parent change a troublesome parenting problem, broader family interaction pattern, or larger systems problem. Level 4 is primarily suited for work with families with special needs, that is, families who are in high-risk situations. These might include teen parents with family and peer problems, families involved in the mental health or child protective services systems, and parents facing the stress of having a severely ill or disabled child. Problems suitable for Level 4 interventions generally go beyond one-to-one parent–child issues to involve the parent's interactions with a co-parent, other family members, or professionals who are dealing with the child. Examples might include conflictual co-parenting with a divorced spouse, an interfering grandparent who is allied with one spouse, or struggles with a child protective services caseworker.

At Level 4, school practitioners have learned the skills of assessing family problems in their wider context and of developing basic interventions to ameliorate them. They have also done personal work to examine their feelings and relationships with their own family system and community systems in order to avoid becoming "triangled," that is, being set in opposition by one parent against the other people or groups in the parent's life.

In the LFI model, Level 4 is considered an elective competency level for school psychologists and other school-based mental health service providers (e.g., counselors or social workers), one that requires training beyond that normally provided in graduate programs and other training settings. It represents the upper boundary of education practiced by a minority of school professionals, who choose to work with special populations of parents and seek special training in family assessment and basic family intervention. Furthermore, Level 4 requires a clear contract with the parent or group of parents to engage in more intensive work than regular Level 3 information and support activities. In practice, Level 4 assessment generally involves asking a series of questions about the family dynamics in order to discover problematic interaction patterns such as triangulation and couple distress.

Experience suggests that the most common mistakes at Level 4 are (a) moving into this depth without realizing it, and then getting stuck or overwhelmed; (b) not having an agreement with the parents to engage in this kind of problem-solving discussion; (c) not spending sufficient time at Level 3 before moving into assessment and intervention; and (d) staying at Level 4 when it is not helping. On the latter point, a Level 4 intervention around a troublesome family interaction should be attempted only for a limited time, such as one discussion and a follow-up. If this degree of intervention is not being helpful, and if the problem is serious enough, the school practitioner should refer the family for therapy and return to Level 3 involvement. For example, if an adolescent is moving frequently between divorced parents' houses after arguments with each parent and is skipping school, the school professional might meet with the parents and the student a couple of times to see if they can work out an arrangement that will stick. If progress is not achieved within this time frame, the odds are that a therapy referral will be needed to sort out the conflicting agendas of the divorced parents.

Because Level 4 deals with the problems of parents, it is important to be clear what kinds of problems are suitable and not suitable for Level 4 work in schools. Level 4 deals only with issues of parenting, not marital functioning, psychological disorders, or personality problems of adults. Thus, co-parenting issues are appropriate to address, but marital issues are not. Anger management with a parent is appropriate, but anger management with the parent's mother-in-law or boss is not. A parent's self-defeating thoughts about herself as a parent or co-parent are appropriate for Level 4 work, but a parent's self-defeating thoughts about body image are not. Level 4 remains focused on the goals of the student's program of education.

Because the LFI model suggests that Level 3 should be the typical level of involvement for school practitioners, it is reasonable to ask why Level 4 is appropriate at all. Is it too intensive for school settings? The response is that as school-based professionals are increasingly asked to work with families with special needs and multiple stressors, the boundaries of the field are already being extended beyond informational and supportive services. In any case, the school practitioner working at Level 4 is likely to be involved in collaborative professional relationships with family therapists and other professionals who are usually working with the same families. Level 4 is inherently collaborative, both with families and with other professionals.

The most common misapprehension about Level 4 is that, because it is the most intensive level of involvement with families, it must be the preferred level. This is no truer than the assumption that surgery is generally preferable to less invasive treatment. Experience with the LFI model suggests that Level 4 should be the exception rather than the rule in educational settings for two reasons: the majority of families do not need this level of service, and few school practitioners are trained to provide it. The chief dangers of Level 4 are when the school practitioner is drawn unaware and unprepared into family interventions because of the family's serious problems and because of a frustration over the limits of informational and supportive efforts to help the family.

***Level 5: Family Therapy.*** Level 5 is outside of the boundaries of typical school settings unless the school has on-site family therapists. Family therapy generally involves an extended series of family sessions aimed at treating serious psychological and family problems by stimulating significant change in family interaction patterns. Whereas Level 4 is confined to parenting-related issues, Level 5 may move beyond parenting into couple relationship issues, family-of-origin problems, and mental disorders in individual family members. The skills specific to Level 5, some of which are mentioned in Table 2, involve dealing with the management of intense personal distress or interpersonal conflict, and ambivalence or resistance to change among family members. When families see a therapist, they know they are in mental health treatment and not in an educational program, although education is also likely to occur.

Each of the levels beyond Level 1 also has a set of skills used in relating to outside services and service providers. At Level 2 the school practitioner is knowledgeable about community resources, such as therapy services, and makes that information available in a form the family can understand. At Level 3 the school practitioner uses greater sensitivity to detect when a family might require a referral and also is able to tailor the referral to the unique situation of the family. At Level 4, the school practitioner has personal knowledge of family therapists and other family professionals and services and is able to orchestrate a referral by educating both the family and the professionals about what to expect from each other.

## Methods for Referring Families for Therapy

A referral to a therapist can be an option at any level of involvement. A referral can be appropriate when a parent or family problem is serious and interfering with the functioning of the family, the parents, or the child and when any of the following criteria are met: (a) it is outside of the scope of competence of the school practitioner to address, (b) there is insufficient time to devote to working with the family problem, (c) the problem extends well beyond the child's issues (for example, a parental depression or marital conflict), or (d) the school setting is not appropriate for the work needed to address the problem. The technique of making referrals to therapists is not well articulated in the literature and appears to depend on the idiosyncratic experiences of the referring professional. The following is an appropriate protocol for working with parents in the school setting.

1. Let the person describe the problem and show emotion.
2. Offer empathetic support.
3. Ask questions about the general problem, but avoid asking for a lot of specific details that could result in a Level 5 therapy conversation. Example: "How long has your husband had a drinking problem?" not "How many drinks a day does he have?" or "Are you afraid for your safety?" rather than "Does he hit you more when he is drinking?"
4. Reflect to the parent the deeper feelings involved, such as fear, frustration, and hopelessness—the kinds of feelings that are apt to propel someone to take action to get help. Example: "It sounds as if you are at the end of your rope with this problem," or "You're feeling pretty hopeless right now because nothing you have tried has lifted you out of the sadness you are living with all the time."
5. Ask a question or two that might generate hope. Example: "Have there been good times between you and your husband in the past?"
6. Ask the person if he or she has ever had counseling for this problem, or ever considered it.
7. Orient the person to what therapy is all about, for example, that it's a place for support, for clarity about problems and solutions, and for hard work to improve his or her life.
8. Ask directly if therapy is something the person is interested in pursuing. Come back to the question again if the answer is vague.
9. If the answer is yes, emphasize the importance of this first step toward addressing the problems. Encourage the person in his or her resolve to get help.
10. If the referral is for couples or family therapy, explore the person's perception of the willingness of a spouse or partner and other family members to participate. Coach the person on how to bring it up with the family: at a calm time, with a clear message (e.g., "I need help and the family needs help"), emphasizing others' participation. If the person seems ambivalent about asking others to participate, return to whether he or she wants to pursue the referral. Don't let the person express his or her own ambivalence by saying that someone else won't take part with them.
11. Link the person with a specific therapist or agency, if possible. Know what is involved in the referral and educate the person about the logistics and about what to expect. When appropriate, offer to call in advance to see if the therapist or agency can accept the referral. But make sure that the person being referred makes a personal call to set up the first appointment.
12. Offer to collaborate with the therapist and follow up, with permission, to see if the session took place and if you can be of assistance.

This can be considered a sophisticated Level 4 protocol for referring families to therapists. The referring professional allows enough depth to occur in the conversation for the problem and the feelings about it to be present in the moment, offers hope and encouragement, addresses ambivalence, and works to make the link between the family and the outside system actually happen. This level of engagement in the referral process may not be called for in all cases, such as when a parent simply requests referral information, but it is an option the school professional can put into practice when needed.

## SUMMARY

By illuminating the significant role of family processes, family systems theory contributes a unique perspective to an already rich repertoire of methods used by school practitioners. This chapter has attempted to show how the family systems framework might enhance the effectiveness of the methods currently used by school practitioners to promote understanding and positive changes in children and their families.

Basic family systems theory sees the family as a system in which repeated patterns of interaction regulate the behavior of individuals. A healthy family system must have internal and external boundaries that allow appropriate exchanges of thoughts, feelings, and behaviors that both preserve individual autonomy and support connection. The constant events and changes inherent in family life require the system to respond in ways that will preserve system functioning in facing pressure to change as well as pressure to maintain. When a system is not healthy, individuals within the system may become symptomatic and develop problems. If the symptomatic individual is a student of the school system, school professionals then become involved. Because the symptoms are really an expression of family system dysfunction, family dynamics must be considered to appropriately address the individual needs of the student.

The goal of school professionals is to establish a balanced relational collaboration between parents and the school for the benefit of the child. Successful school-based prevention and intervention programs are those that establish effective relationships for collaborative problem-solving between families, children, and schools. The Levels of Family Involvement model provides a way to conceptualize how school psychologists may work effectively with families at different levels of intensity.

This systemic approach invites a more complete view of the context from which the behaviors of children emerge and a more collaborative approach between school-based mental health service providers and families for the care and education of children. In this enhanced role, school professionals will be better able to address the needs of children along with the family, school, and community systems in which they develop.

## RECOMMENDED RESOURCES

### Books and Other Printed Material

Christenson, S. L., & Sheridan, S. M. (2001). *Schools and families: Creating essential connections for learning.* New York: Guilford Press.

This book presents specific processes for school professionals to collaborate with families to effectively support the students' learning. The text includes useful strategies for evaluating current school–home connections and for implementing more effective methods. School professionals will find this a useful resource for understanding home–school collaboration and how to facilitate it.

Mikesell, R. H., Lusterman, D., & McDaniel, S. H. (Eds.), (1995). *Integrating family therapy: Handbook of family psychology and systems theory.* Washington, DC: American Psychological Association.

This text provides useful information on the integration of traditional psychological approaches with systems theory. School professionals will find this a useful resource to identify how a systemic approach can be effectively implemented in the school setting.

### Websites

*http://www.wcer.wisc.edu/fast/*

The Families and Schools Together (FAST) website provides a description of the FAST program, a multifamily group intervention designed to build protective factors for children. FAST incorporates research on family systems theory, along with other theories, to achieve its four goals of enhancing family functioning, preventing school failure by the targeted child, preventing substance abuse by the child and other family members, and reducing stress from daily life situations for parents and children.

*http://www.soe.usfca.edu/institutes/ccfd/school_based_counseling.html*

School-Based Counseling: A New Paradigm is a website that describes the University of San Francisco's counseling program. It contains up-to-date rationales for and research on programs that incorporate a family systems perspective in school counseling.

## REFERENCES

Amato, P. (2001). Children of divorce in the 1990s: An update of the Amato and Keith (1991) Meta-analysis. *Journal of Family Psychology, 15,* 355–370.

Anderson, C. (1983). An ecological developmental model for a family orientation in school psychology. *Journal of School Psychology, 21,* 179–189.

Armor, D. (2003). *Maximizing intelligence.* New Brunswick, NJ: Transaction Publishers.

Barbarin, O. A. (1992). Family functioning and school adjustment: Family systems perspectives. In F. Medway & P. Cafferty (Eds.), *School psychology: A social psychological perspective* (pp. 131–163). Hillsdale, NJ: Erlbaum.

Bateson, G. (1972). *Steps to an ecology of mind.* San Francisco: Chandler.

Bateson, G., Jackson, D. D., & Weakland, J. H. (1956). Toward a theory of schizophrenia. *Behavioral Science, 1,* 251–264.

Berger, S. R., Fine, M. J., & Carlson, C. (1992). A school-based divorce intervention program. In M. J. Fine & C. Carlson (Eds.), *The handbook of family-school intervention: A systems perspective* (pp. 386–399). Boston: Allyn & Bacon.

Boss, P. G. (1988). *Family stress management.* Newbury Park, CA: Sage.

Bowen, M. (1978). *Family therapy in clinical practice.* New York: Aronson.

Chapin, S. L., & Vito, R. (1988, April). *Patterns of family interaction style, self-system processes, and engagement with school work: An investigation of adolescents rated at-risk or not-at-risk for academic failure.* Paper presented at the Annual Meeting of the American Educational Research Association, New Orleans, LA.

Doherty, W. J. (1995). Boundaries between parent and family education and family therapy. *Family Relations, 44,* 353–358.

Doherty, W. J., & Baird, M. A. (1986). Developmental levels of family-centered medical care. *Family Medicine, 18,* 153–156.

Doherty, W. J., & Baptiste, D. A., Jr. (1993). Theories emerging from therapy. In P. G. Boss, W. J. Doherty, R. LaRossa, W. R. Schumm, & S. K. Stenmetz (Eds.), *Sourcebook of family theories and methods: A contextual approach* (pp. 505–524). New York: Plenum Press.

Doherty, W. J., & Beaton, J. M. (2004). Mothers and fathers parenting together. In A. L. Vangelisti (Ed.), *Handbook of family communication* (pp. 269–286). Mahwah, NJ: Erlbaum.

Doherty, W. J., & Peskay, V. E. (1992). Family systems and the school. In S. L. Christenson & J. C. Conoley (Eds.), *Home-school collaboration: Enhancing children's academic and social competence* (pp. 1–18). Silver Spring, MD: National Association of School Psychologists.

Epstein, J. L. (1996). Perspectives and previews on research and policy for school, family, and community partnerships. In A. Booth & J. F. Dunn (Eds.), *Family-school links: How do they affect educational outcomes?* (pp. 209–246). Mahweh, NJ: Erlbaum.

Fine, M. J., & Holt, P. (1983). Intervening with school problems: A family systems perspective. *Psychology in the Schools, 20,* 59–66.

French, J. L. (1990). History of school psychology. In T. B. Gutkin & C. R. Reynolds (Eds.), *The handbook of school psychology.* (2nd ed., pp. 3–20). New York: Wiley.

Gerrard, B. (1996). School-based family counseling: A new paradigm: Review of the literature. Retrieved July 17, 2004, from the University of San Francisco Center for Child and Family Development website: http://soe.usfca/edu/institutes/ccfd/sbc_literature_review.html

Glieck, J. (1987). *Chaos: Making a new science.* New York: Penguin.

Glynn, T. J., & Haenlein, M. (1988). The family context of adolescent drug use: Family interventions. *Journal of Chemical Dependency Treatment, 1,* 255–243.

Haley, J. (1976). *Problem solving therapy.* San Francisco: Jossey-Bass.

Ingoldsby, B. B., Smith, S. R., & Miller, E. J. (2004). *Exploring family theories.* Los Angeles: Roxbury.

Kerr, M. E., & Bowen, M. (1988). *Family evaluation.* New York: Norton.

Kramer, J. J. (1990). Training parents as behavior change agent: Successes, failures, and suggestions for school psychologists. In T. B. Gutkin & C. R. Reynolds (Eds.), *The handbook of school psychology* (2nd ed., pp. 683–702). New York: Wiley.

Marvel, M. K., & Morphew, P. K. (1993). Levels of family involvement by resident and attending physicians. *Family Medicine, 25,* 26–30.

Marvel, M. K., Schilling, R., Doherty, W. J., & Baird, M. A. (1994). Levels of physician involvement with patients and their families: A model for teaching and research. *Journal of Family Practice, 39,* 535–544.

Minuchin, S. (1974). *Families and family therapy.* Cambridge, MA: Harvard University Press.

Minuchin, S., Rossman, B. L., & Baker, L. (1978). *Psychosomatic families: Anorexia in context.* Cambridge, MA: Harvard University Press.

Montemayor, R. (1984). Picking up the pieces: The effects of parental divorce on adolescents with some suggestions for school-based intervention programs. *Journal of Early Adolescence, 4,* 289–314.

Olson, D. H., McCubbin, H. I., Barnes, H. L., Larsen, A. S., Muxen, M. J., & Wilson, M. A. (1983). *Families: What makes them work?* Beverly Hills, CA: Sage Publications.

Rosenblatt, P. S. (1994). *Metaphors of family systems theory.* New York: Guilford Press.

Schnack, S. L. (1995). Factors related to pregnant and parenting high school students remaining in school. *UMI Dissertation Services, 1995*(3). (UMI No. 9616995).

Vickers, H. S., & Minke, K. M. (1997). Family systems and the family-school connection. In G. G. Bear & K. M. Minke (Eds.), *Children's needs II: Development, problems, and alternatives* (pp. 547–558). Bethesda, MD: National Association of School Psychologists.

Whitchurch, G. G., & Constantine, L. L. (1993). Systems theory. In P. G. Boss, W. J. Doherty, R. LaRossa, W. R. Schumm, & S. K. Stenmetz (Eds.), *Sourcebook of family theories and methods: A contextual approach* (pp. 325–352). New York: Plenum Press.

Wynne, L., McDaniel, S. H., & Weber, T. T. (1986). *Systems consultation: A new perspective for family therapy.* New York: Guilford Press.

Xia, Y. R., Xie, X., Zhou, G., Defrain, J., & Zhou, Z. (2001). *Chinese adolescents' involvement in family decision-making processes and its association with parent-adolescent communication and relationship.* Presentation given at the 63rd Annual Conference of the National Council on Family Relations, November 8–11, Rochester, NY.

# 51

# Adoption

**Gretchen Miller Wrobel**

*Bethel University*

**Zoe Hendrickson**
**Harold D. Grotevant**

*University of Minnesota*

Adoption is a dynamic process of family formation that is shaped by history and culture as well as by personal, social, and political attitudes. The U.S. population of adopted children and adolescents is becoming increasingly diverse and therefore increasingly difficult to characterize as a group. Infants and older children, sibling groups, and children with known disabilities are adopted by those who are married, unmarried in committed relationships, and single. Children who are adopted can be of a different race than their adoptive parents, be born in a different country, or have relationships with their birth family. Adoptive families and children face unique adoption-related normative tasks in addition to the typical developmental milestones experienced by all families and children. School professionals must be aware of the dynamics of adoption in order to effectively serve adopted children in U.S. schools.

American perceptions about adoption are generally positive. A national study of adoption attitudes (Evan B. Donaldson Adoption Institute, 2002) found that 94% of Americans surveyed have a favorable opinion of adoption, with 63% of that total holding very favorable opinions. Personal experience with adoption is also prevalent; 64% of respondents indicated that a family member or close friend either is adopted, has adopted, or has placed a child for adoption. This survey also found that Americans largely see no difference between adopted children's likelihood of problems compared with other children. In questions related to school, 47% of respondents indicated that adopted children were just as likely as other children to have problems at school. Yet a significant minority of Americans does not believe that adopted children are as emotionally healthy as nonadopted children. Of respondents, 22% believe adopted children are less likely to be happy, 32% think they are less well-adjusted, and 34% believe they are less self-confident. The goal of this chapter is to provide current research-based information that will help school professionals understand the dynamics of adoption and the experiences of adopted children.

## BACKGROUND AND DEVELOPMENT

Obtaining accurate adoption statistics in the United States is difficult, as there is no comprehensive reporting system for all public, private agency, and independent adoptions. The Adoption and Foster Care Analysis and Reporting System (AFCARS) tracks children adopted from foster care, and the U.S. State Department tracks international adoptions through the record of orphan visas issued each year (National Adoption Information Clearinghouse [NAIC], 2004). The U.S. Census included the category "adopted son/daughter" for the first time in 2000 and provides the most comprehensive figure for the total number of adoptions in the United States, placing the number of adopted children under the age of 18 at 2.5% of the population (Kreider, 2003). This percentage must be considered a broad estimate because it encompasses a wide range of adoptions, including adoption of step-children and biologically related children (e.g., grandparent adoption) in addition to biologically unrelated children and those adopted domestically, internationally, independently, and from informal adoptions.

## Adoption From Foster Care

The growing number of children in the foster care system has contributed to a shift in many adoption agencies' policies on foster parent adoptions. Several decades ago, professionals focused on reuniting the biological family and considered potential adoption by the foster parents in conflict with the child's best interests. But because the Adoption and Safe Families Act of 1997 emphasizes swift, permanent placements, the number of adoptions by foster parents has grown (McRoy, 1999). In a planned foster care–to-adoption arrangement, a child is placed in a foster family that has agreed to eventually pursue a legal adoption even though the parental rights of the child's birth parents have not yet been terminated. An unplanned foster adoption results when foster parents develop a close relationship with the child and later request to adopt if the birth parents relinquish their rights or if those rights are involuntarily terminated by the courts.

Most recent estimates for FY 2001 indicate that 18% of children who exited foster care were adopted, up from 14% in 1998 (NAIC, 2003). Financial subsidies are available to adoptive families to provide medical, maintenance, and special services to children adopted from foster care with physical, behavioral, or emotional disabilities (Grotevant & Kohler, 1999). Foster parent adoptions have proved to be successful and stable, especially when the foster care lasts for a year or more before the formal adoption. When the child is in the foster home for less than a year before adoption, the chances of disruption are about the same as for nonfoster adoptions (Barth & Berry, 1988; see also chapter 63, "Foster Homes").

## Kinship Care and Kinship Adoption

About 30% of the children in the formal foster care system are living with relatives in certified foster homes (NAIC, 2003), and an estimated 3% of all children in the United States may be living in households with relatives other than their mother or father (U.S. Dept. of Health and Human Services, 2003). These informal arrangements often result from substance abuse, HIV/AIDS, incarceration, or mental illness of one or both parents. Children of color, especially African Americans, are disproportionately represented in kinship care.

Kinship care is far less likely to culminate in formal adoption than other care arrangements. Relatives may be reluctant to contribute to the loss of a family member's parental rights, and caregivers already acknowledge a permanent bond of kinship, albeit not a parental one (Smith, Howard, & Monroe, 2000). Kinship care can provide continuity and familiarity, and children often have frequent contact with their parents. But because these arrangements are outside the service network, caregivers may not have access to community support services. In addition, kinship care can present a financial hardship for caregivers; in some states, subsidies for family members are much smaller than those provided to certified foster families (Boots & Geen, 1999).

## Adoption by Gay and Lesbian Parents

States vary widely in their laws on adoption by gays and lesbians. Although at the time this chapter was written only one state (Florida) specifically prohibited adoptions by gays or lesbians, few permit joint adoption by a couple. In most states, gays or lesbians are allowed to adopt as a single person; their partners may or may not be allowed to apply for guardian or second adoptive parent status. Adoption by gays or lesbians is still somewhat uncommon; most studies of homosexual parent couples involve children who were conceived in a heterosexual relationship (Perrin and the Committee on Psychosocial Aspects of Child and Family Health, 2002).

Questions have been raised about whether children with gay or lesbian parents experience more problems than those being raised by heterosexual couples. A recent research summary commissioned by the American Psychological Association concluded that "overall, results of research suggest that the development, adjustment, and well-being of children with lesbian and gay parents do not differ markedly from that of children with heterosexual parents" (American Psychological Association, 2004, p. 2).

## Single-Parent Adoptions

Single parents are more likely to be females who adopt a same-sex child. They tend to have a higher-than-average education level but their incomes are lower than for adoptive couples. For single adoptive parents, the support of family and community is a critical factor.

Because most adoption agencies give priority to placing children in homes with two parents, single parents are more likely to adopt special needs children for whom finding a permanent placement may be more difficult. In 1998, one-third of the children adopted from the public foster care system were adopted by single women. The majority of these women and children (about two-thirds) were African American. Most of the mothers (65%) had been the foster caregivers of the children they adopted (U.S. Dept. of Health and Human Resources, 2003).

In a study that tracked the adopted children of single parents over a 14-year period, Shireman (1996) found that single parents were skilled in handling crises and in accommodating the emotional needs of their children. The less complicated dynamics of the one-parent, one-child household may be especially beneficial for children with abusive backgrounds. Overall, the longitudinal data showed that the adjustment for adopted children of single parents is equivalent to that of adopted children in two-parent families.

## Openness in Adoption

The decision to adopt necessitates a decision regarding the amount or type of contact the adoptive family and child will have with the child's birth family, especially with his or her birth mother. Consideration of openness in adoption is driven by the desire of birth mothers to have some form of continued contact and by the increase in the number of children who know their birth parents, such as those in older child and sibling group placements. Agencies have adapted their practice to include consideration of openness (Henney, Onken, McRoy, & Grotevant, 1998), and it is now the norm for domestic infant adoption to involve some form of contact. Contact or openness in adoption can be described by a continuum that places confidential adoption at one end of the continuum and fully disclosed adoption at the other (Grotevant & McRoy, 1998). Confidential adoption is characterized by the absence of communication between adoptive and birth families, with only general and non-identifying information given to adoptive parents at placement. Fully disclosed adoption involves varying amounts of direct contact between birth and adoptive families, such as the sharing of letters, pictures, e-mails, phone calls, and visits. In the middle of the continuum is mediated adoption, which involves the exchange of non-identifying information through an intermediary, usually the adoption agency.

Beyond initial decisions made at placement, openness needs to be considered a dynamic process that is influenced across time by the desire for contact of adoptive parents, adopted children, and members of the birth family; by current amount and type of contact; and by family interactions. For those children who are adopted at an older age, openness includes the complexity of negotiating already established relationships with the birth family, especially if the child was removed from the family because of abuse or neglect. Families with children placed as infants work toward establishing a relationship with the birth family in the context of chosen contact. These relationships evolve as the adoptive kinship network of adoptive parents, adopted children, and birth family members work toward a level of contact that is comfortable for all (Grotevant & McRoy, 1998).

In families with children who were adopted as infants, some adolescents may want more contact with their birth family; others may be satisfied with their current situation (Berge, Mendenhall, Wrobel, Grotevant, & McRoy, in press). One group of adoptive parents reported that relationships with the birth family were maintained for the benefit of the adopted child, and if there was dissatisfaction with the amount of contact, the desire was for more contact rather than less (Grotevant, McRoy, Elde, & Fravel, 1994). Parents across all openness levels appear to feel secure in their role as parents, though differences do exist. Parents in fully disclosed adoptions are less fearful that the birth mother may reclaim their child; they have open communication with their children and demonstrate greater degrees of empathy about adoption than those parents in confidential adoptions (Grotevant et al., 1994). In families who have contact with the birth family, the greater collaboration in making decisions for the adopted child's well-being rather than for the needs of adults is associated with better emotional adjustment for the child (Grotevant, Ross, Marchel, & McRoy, 1999).

## Special Needs Adoption

For most education professionals, the term *special needs* typically refers to children with emotional, developmental, physical, or learning disabilities. In the realm of adoption however, the term has a much broader application. It incorporates not only the abilities or needs of the child, but also includes circumstances of the child's adoption. For example, children adopted after the age of 2, children adopted in sibling groups, children who have a different ethnic or racial heritage than their adoptive parents (even if adopted as healthy infants), and children with a known history of neglect or abuse may all be considered special needs adoptions. The legal definition of *special needs* varies from state to state and is linked to the provision of financial subsidies available to assist adoptive parents with the expenses associated with their child's physical or emotional needs. The North American Council on Adoptable Children (NACAC) maintains a compilation of specific state guidelines (NACAC, 2004).

Broad generalizations about special needs adoptions are problematic and unwise. Several decades of research have pinpointed only a few factors that consistently predict the success of the adoptive outcome: the age at placement and the development of problem behaviors (McRoy, 1999). These two factors are often interrelated. Children adopted at later ages are more likely to have encountered adverse experiences, such as abuse or neglect, and one or more temporary placements in foster homes or institutional settings, which can increase the probability of adjustment difficulties.

A growing number of children who experience abuse, neglect, or exposure to parental drug abuse are removed from their parents' homes by social services and placed in foster care (U.S. General Accounting Office, 1994). If attempts at family reunification are not successful, their parents' legal rights may be terminated by the courts and the children are then legally available for adoption. These children are typically included under the special needs umbrella, and their behavior often shows the emotional consequences of early neglect and abuse, as well as the physiological results of alcohol or drug use by the mother during pregnancy. Such children present enormous challenges for adoptive parents. However, because of the small number of healthy infants available for adoption as well as an increased governmental commitment to finding permanent placements for "hard to place" children in the foster care system (Adoption and Safe Families Act, 1997), more families are stretching their resources and their parenting skills to accommodate these special needs children. Of the estimated 500,000 children in foster care, about 25% are available for adoption; their parents' rights have been legally terminated and they are seeking permanent placement (U.S. Department of Health and Human Services, 2003.)

Special needs adoptions can be successful and satisfying when parents are given thorough background information on the child's disabilities and limitations, when they have reasonable expectations for the child's adjustment, and when they have strong support from their extended families, communities, and service organizations. However, children who have suffered severe trauma may develop behavior patterns and emotional disorders that appear years after the actual adoption and strain the parents' ability to cope. Although adoptive parents may be more accepting of a child's physical, mental, or developmental issues, studies show that parents have difficulty grappling with a child's problem behaviors, such as sexual acting out or chronic lying or stealing (Smith et al., 2000).

Because these behaviors may erupt in a school or public setting, parents must be given an opportunity to inform school professionals about their child's background in a way that preserves the integrity and privacy of the family. If school officials and staff do not have adequate information, adoptive parents can sometimes feel unfairly judged as negligent and inadequate. Helping the child alter the problem behaviors may require that the underlying psychological issues associated with the behavior (e.g., stresses of loss, anger, grief, and abandonment) be considered. If the child is receiving psychological services outside of school, it will be important to coordinate school strategies with such efforts. Although children with a history of abuse are somewhat more likely to develop later behavioral problems, in the clear majority of cases, a nurturing, supportive, and consistent environment can significantly reduce the damage of earlier trauma (Verhulst, 2000).

## International Adoptions

Over the past three decades, the reduced stigma of being an unwed parent and a downturn in the number of teenage pregnancies have resulted in a dramatic decrease in the number of healthy infants available for adoption. In 1995, less than 1% of pregnant, never-married women voluntarily relinquished their babies for adoption compared to almost 9% before 1973 (NAIC, 2003). Consequently, the number of infants brought to the United States from other countries (most notably China, Russia, Guatemala, and South Korea) has more than tripled, increasing from 7,093 in 1990 to 21,616 in 2003, as infertile, predominantly white couples have sought healthy children and babies to adopt (U.S. Department of State, 2004).

Research that compares internationally adopted children with domestically adopted children generally shows that both groups fare about equally well on a broad spectrum of measures, including self-esteem, social adjustment, and incidence of behavior and emotional problems. However, the complex array of adoption factors and outcome measures make it difficult to reach unequivocal conclusions. Adoption factors include country of origin, age at placement, circumstances of the birth, the child's environment and experiences prior to adoption, and characteristics of the receiving family. Outcome factors include the child's psychological and emotional adjustment, assimilation in the adoptive country's culture, and development of ethnic identity. Establishing a normative group for comparison raises the questions of whether internationally adopted children should be compared with transracial domestic adoptions or with children of the same ethnic background living with their families of origin. The interplay of racial identity with adoptive identity is intricate; both are major influences in the child's psychological and emotional stability and adjustment.

A number of studies have found that the child's age at the time of adoption, intersecting with the experience of early deprivation or abuse, is the greatest predictor of negative outcomes. For example, a British study of 111 adopted Romanian children who had been severely deprived in institutional settings prior to placement found that a large percentage demonstrated an unusual pattern of attachment disorder (O'Connor et al., 2003). These children were characterized as superficially exuberant and were likely to show the same attachment behavior toward strangers that they showed to their parents. Of the Romanian children placed at the ages of 6 to 24 months, 51% showed this atypical pattern, as did 39% of children placed at less than 6 months, compared with 16% of children from a nondeprived background. Despite these disheartening statistics, the study also found that a sizable number of children were able to establish positive relationships with their adoptive parents in spite of their early negligent care.

A key challenge for White parents who have adopted children internationally is that they must address issues of discrimination and the complexities of racial and ethnic identity, even though the parents may not themselves have personal experience in these arenas. Children whose parents acknowledge and celebrate cultural differences show better adjustment than those whose parents deny racial differences or overemphasize assimilating the child into the mainstream culture (Benson, Sharma, & Roehlkepartain, 1994). A child's desire to participate in his or her native culture may fluctuate. Children who eagerly attend culture camps during the elementary school years may suddenly lose interest when faced with adolescent peer pressure to conform. Also, searching for birth parents internationally is much more difficult than within the United States; however, should a child decide to do so, there is a growing movement favoring contact with the child's home country and potentially with his or her birth family.

## Transracial Adoption

International adoptions are often transracial and account for about 85% of all transracial adoptions (U.S. Department of State, 2004). Domestic transracial adoptions, though less common, are a subject of debate and controversy in many circles. For example, in 1972, the National Association of Black Social Workers (NABSW) passed a resolution declaring that adoption of African American children by White parents is a form of cultural genocide (1972). The NABSW (1994) urged that African American children removed from their biological families be placed only in same-race adoptive homes, arguing that Whites are ill-equipped to prepare Black children for the discrimination they will face and that they would be unable to socialize their children into African American culture. The Indian Children Welfare Act of 1978 mandated similar guidelines for placing Native American children.

Confounding these intentions is the current ethnic makeup of the foster care caseload: 60% of children awaiting adoption are African American, Hispanic, Asian American, or Native American. The Multiethnic Placement Act of 1994 and the subsequent clarifications of the 1996 Interethnic Adoption Provisions attempted to address this disparity by preventing the discrimination of adoption placement on the basis of race. Although future studies may help to clarify the specific elements that reliably predict successful transracial placements, the body of current research indicates that the majority of children in both domestic and international transracial adoptions show positive psychological, social, cultural, and racial identity adjustments (Lee, 2003).

## Sibling Groups

Research on the desirability of placing siblings in the same adoptive home has not drawn uniform conclusions.

In some cases, siblings have provided one another with an emotional buffer against the loss and grief of separation from their birth family. An older sibling may even act as a surrogate parent. But in other instances, a dysfunctional pattern of sibling interaction may interfere with the adoptive family's ability to incorporate the new members, especially when there are biological or other adopted children in the household (McRoy, 1999). In addition to considerations about the effects of siblings on each others' behavior, advocates have pointed to the desirability of keeping siblings together from a human rights standpoint. Though beneficial for the children, placing siblings together can be difficult; there are a limited number of adoptive families who have the inclination or resources to expand their household by several children all at once, and the age of the oldest child is often a deterrent when parents want to adopt only very young children. Consequently, sibling groups may stay in foster care longer than might be desirable while awaiting a permanent home (Schlonsky, Webster, & Needell, 2003).

## Attachment

Developing an affectional tie or attachment is a fundamental task for all parents and children; a warm, loving, and secure relationship with a parent is important for positive development. Attachment theory has important implications for adopted children, especially those adopted after the age of 6 months. For these children a first attachment may have been broken, developed without a full sense of security, or not developed at all due to neglect. Despite the equivocal nature of research evidence (Portello, 1993), attachments in adoptive families are often assumed to be less secure than in nonadoptive families because the child's first attachment may not have been with the adoptive mother. However, although early attachments are important, they do not solely determine future development (Thompson, 2001). Attachment is part of a developmental process that allows relationships to stabilize and change over time, and no one developmental period dominates the process (Johnson & Fein, 1991).

Children with difficult attachment histories can learn to develop multiple attachments beyond infancy (Watson, 1997). By considering attachment as a dynamic process, not one tied to critical periods of development with only good or bad outcomes, professionals are able to intervene in developmentally appropriate ways as necessary (Portello, 1993). This view of attachment development is especially helpful for families who are formed through the adoption of older children. By allowing time for attachments to develop between adopted children and their parents, realistic expectations about the effort and time it takes to become a family can provide room for the attachment process to take place (Portello).

Adoptive parents enter parenthood with many strengths and resources that facilitate the development of attachment with their children. They are generally older at the time they first become parents, are more financially secure, and have been married longer than first-time parents whose children are born to them (Brodzinsky & Pinderhughes, 2002). Adoptive parents have also been socialized to adoptive parenthood through the educational efforts of adoption agencies (Brodzinsky & Huffman, 1988). These resources allow adoptive parents to provide the warm, stable, and nurturing environment that aids in the development of attachment.

## Adoptive Family Communication

Positive and open communication about adoption-related issues is important for meeting the information needs of adopted children and adolescents. Such communication has been theorized as facilitating adopted children's maturation (Brodzinsky & Pinderhughes, 2002; Kirk, 1964), and begins when adoptive parents tell the adoption story to their children. How this story is told sets the atmosphere for future adoption-related communication.

Adoption-related communication is an ongoing process that should consider the unique communication needs of the child. Brodzinsky (1987) identified ways that adoptive families can facilitate communication at different developmental stages. Early childhood is described as a time for creating an atmosphere in which questions can be freely explored. Children at this stage are especially interested in the basic facts about their birth parents and reasons for placement. Maintaining this atmosphere of open communication is the task for middle childhood and adolescence. During this developmental period, adopted children come to understand all the social, biological, and legal meanings of adoption and begin to develop a sense of adoptive identity.

When children and adolescents ask their parents about their adoption, parents must decide how they will respond to and support their child's curiosity. Parents' response will be influenced by the amount of information they possess, the child's developmental level and intensity of curiosity, and what information the parents are willing to share or withhold. Four options are available: (a) share all available information, (b) share all available information while seeking more, (c) share some information and withhold other information, and (d) withhold all available information (Wrobel, Kohler, Grotevant, & McRoy, 2003). Parents report that often the decision to withhold information is based on age (Wrobel, Ayers-Lopez, Grotevant, McRoy, & Frederick, 1996); they believe that waiting until the child is older to share certain information will make it more likely that the child will be "ready" to hear it. Sometimes withholding reflects the challenge of dealing with difficult adoption stories (i.e., abuse or abandonment; Wrobel et al., 2003). Young adults whose adoptive parents decided to support their child's curiosity about adoption by being prepared to share information and answer questions throughout the adopted child's life described their family relationships as close (Sobol, Delaney, & Earn, 1994).

## Development of an Adoptive Identity

Adopted children and adolescents face the challenge of making meaning of their beginnings, which may be unknown or unclear. This meaning-making process presents different questions for children adopted under different circumstances. Children adopted as infants may wonder who their birth parents were and why they placed their child for adoption. Children placed at older ages may wonder if they have any more siblings, if their birth parents ever think about them, and if they will ever see their birth parents again. Children adopted from other countries may wonder why their parents abandoned them to an orphanage.

Exploration of these questions occurs in the process of identity development as the young person attempts to construct a narrative that will help him or her make sense of the past, understand the self in the present, and project himself or herself into the future (Grotevant, 1997). It is a lifelong process that is especially intense during adolescence because of young persons' emerging cognitive abilities that allow them to think beyond the present to what might have been in the past or might be in the future. Adoptive identity is the evolving answer to the question, "Who am I as an adopted person, and what does adoption mean in my life?" (Grotevant, 1997; Grotevant, Dunbar, Kohler, & Esau, 2000).

***Developmental subgroups of adopted adolescents.*** In a recent study of adoptive identity (Dunbar & Grotevant, 2004), researchers interviewed 145 adolescents (mean age 15.6 years) in depth about their adoption-related feelings, beliefs, and knowledge. All the adolescents in the study had been adopted as infants by same-race parents and had lived with those parents since placement. Four subgroups of adolescents were identified (see Dunbar & Grotevant, 2004, for details). The first group, those with *unexamined identity*, included adolescents who simply had not thought much about adoption issues and felt that, in general, such issues were not very central in their lives. The tone of their discussion about adoption was neither particularly positive nor negative. Adolescents in the second group, those with *limited identity*, had begun to explore ideas about adoption. Some talked with their friends about adoption or answered other peoples' questions about being adopted. But in general they did not view adoption as particularly important in their lives and did not think about it very much.

In contrast, those adolescents with *unsettled identity* had thought quite a bit about adoption, had explored its meaning in their lives, felt that it was very significant for them, but also had moderate to high levels of negative affect associated with adoption. Sometimes the negative affect involved anger or resentment toward their birth parents or adoptive parents; sometimes it bothered them that they did not know certain things about their past. Many of them felt "different" from their adoptive families. Those who had contact with birth parents tended to be dissatisfied with the contact, typically wanting more than they were able to bring about (Mendenhall, Berge, Wrobel, Grotevant, & McRoy, 2004). In general, adolescents in this group conveyed the feeling that they were trying to sort out their feelings about adoption, but that it was difficult.

Finally, adolescents with *integrated identity* had thought a great deal about adoption and felt clear and resolved about its meaning in their lives. Their discussion about adoption tended to be couched in positive terms. Although they felt that adoption was important to them, they were not preoccupied with it. They generally viewed themselves as fortunate and their family situation as positive. They thought about their birth parents with sympathy, compassion, and understanding.

This study of adoption narratives revealed that one identity pattern should not be concluded to be healthier than another, especially those occurring during adolescence. Adoption narratives should be thought of as snapshots in time rather than as identity endpoints, since identity development during adolescence is fluid. Different adolescents explore with different levels of intensity and with different internal timetables. By young adulthood, however, many of the teens in the study of identity narratives should have developed an integrated sense of adoptive identity.

In the ongoing process of identity development, changes may be triggered by experiences that challenge adolescents' current thinking about adoption. Such encounters may include teasing by other children, embarrassment at being asked to complete a family history assignment in school (when their family history is unknown), or resentment at being turned down for a date by a classmate who is of the same racial group as their adoptive family's but not their own. These situations can also lead adolescents to question fundamental aspects of themselves, how they fit in their adoptive family, or even how they fit into the world.

***Challenges in transracial adoptions.*** As noted earlier, the number of children being adopted internationally into the United States has grown steadily over the past two decades and continues to do so. Most of these children are adopted across racial lines and thus face multiple challenges (Lee, 2003). First, they must integrate their sense of membership in two families. If they have contact with birth family members, it may mean negotiating plans for contact among all the parties; if they do not have contact, it is still a significant cognitive and affective task. Second, they must integrate two cultures. What does it mean to be a Korean American or a Chinese American growing up in a White family in a small town, for example? Third, they must deal with the issue of difference in physical appearance: How can I really be a member of this family when I look so different? Finally, they must deal with societal attitudes, intrusive comments of strangers, and racism.

Parents play important roles in their adolescent's life, but identity exploration is a multifaceted process. The child's emerging cognitive abilities are engaged in an attempt to understand their adoption through the perspectives of time (past, present, and future), place (current living situation and origins), and relationships (peers, teachers, extended family, and other adults). Professionals who work with adolescents recognize that identity development occurs gradually over time, and they should understand that adopted teens, as others, navigate this process in diverse ways. In any group of adolescents, school personnel would likely find that adopted adolescents fall into each of the four identity categories described earlier in this section—the unexamined, limited, unsettled, and integrated identities. One of the most important things significant adults can do is to be good observers and receptive listeners, letting the adolescent set the pace whenever possible. Providing young people with access to information allows them to decide how and when to deal with that information.

### Searching

For adopted persons who do not have direct contact with their birth families, a desire for information about their adoption may lead them to search for members of their birth family, particularly their birth mothers (Müller, Gibbs, & Ariely, 2003). Searching can represent one way to gather information in an attempt to synthesize the dual identities offered by birth and adoptive families (Reitz & Watson, 1992), though not all adopted persons want to search for their birth families. Searching is typically thought of as a process for adopted adults of confidential adoptions, yet thinking about searching can begin in adolescence when approaching adulthood makes searching legally possible. Wrobel, Grotevant, and McRoy (2004) examined the search intentions of 93 adolescents with varied amounts of adoptive openness but no direct contact with their birth families. Wrobel et al. found that thinking about searching is normative in the adolescent experience, regardless of whether the adolescent decides to search. All adolescents, across all types of openness arrangements, were able to express their thoughts about searching and their particular desire for contact. However, not all adolescents were interested in searching. Those adolescents who were least satisfied with the amount of openness in their adoption were more likely to express an intention to search, and those with more information about their birth parents were more likely to search or had actually done so. In contrast to prior research that had been conducted primarily with adults, this work showed that search intentions and actions were not related to problematic relationships in the adoptive family or to adolescent maladjustment.

## PROBLEMS AND IMPLICATIONS

### Mental Health of Adopted Children

Mental health problems are the focus of a great deal of writing about adopted children and adolescents. Although the assertion that adoptees demonstrate higher rates of maladjustment than their nonadopted peers has been widely stated, recent work is acknowledging the significant degree of heterogeneity among adopted children and is attempting to pinpoint the particular mechanisms or risks that may be resulting in higher overall rates of problem behaviors.

Although numerous investigations of mental health problems have been done, most have focused on simple adoptee–nonadoptee differences in levels of problem behaviors or on differences in rates of clinical diagnoses. A meta-analysis of 66 published studies concluded that adopted children had higher levels of maladjustment, externalizing disorders, and academic problems than nonadopted children (Wierzbicki, 1993). However, developmental level appears to have had a moderating influence, in that relatively few differences were typically found between adopted and nonadopted children during infancy or preschool years, but by middle childhood and adolescence, differences began to emerge (Brodzinsky, 1993). Many studies assessing adoption outcomes have been based on convenience samples of adoptees and nonrepresentative samples of nonadoptees (Finley, 1999), raising some doubts about how firmly conclusions can be drawn.

Two studies, the first based on a nationally representative sample of U.S. adolescents, found that adoptive parents (in comparison to nonadoptive parents) are more likely to refer their children for mental health services (Miller et al., 2000; Warren, 1992). It is possible that adoptive parents are more comfortable working with social service providers because of their experience of adopting their child, or that they might feel their child is at risk for problem behaviors and want to investigate any potential problems early. This difference in referral rate may partly account for the perception that adoptees as a group experience more mental health problems.

Adopted children differ in terms of their prenatal histories (e.g., quality of prenatal care, or exposure to drugs or alcohol), their preplacement experiences (e.g., foster care, orphanage care, or variations in quality and length of preplacement care), and their adoption experiences (e.g., age of placement, cultural and ethnic match with characteristics of the adoptive family, and quality of care). Researchers studying mental health issues of adopted children are increasingly realizing that predicting and understanding such outcomes requires a better understanding of risk factors and mechanisms than of adoption status by itself. It is possible that differences in average levels of problem behaviors may be the result of a relatively small number of adoptees who have had extremely difficult preadoption experiences (e.g., Haugaard, 1999). In general, it seems safe to say that adoption status by itself is a less successful predictor of outcomes than are specific experiential and risk factors to which children may have been exposed. The more specific information available about an adopted child's history, the more effectively mental health services can be targeted, should they be needed.

### Educational Implications of Adoption

Compared with the large body of literature related to mental health issues of adopted children, little has been written regarding the educational implications of being adopted, such as special education rates or overall academic performance. One study reported a positive picture of school experience for adopted adolescents, with rates of school absenteeism and low desire to drop out of school similar to the general school population (Benson, et al., 1994). This group of adopted adolescents reported having a B or better grade average (62%), high achievement motivation (72%), and the desire to pursue postsecondary education (94%).

More recently, adopted adolescents in the National Longitudinal Study of Adolescent Health were compared to their nonadopted peers with regard to school grades, school connectedness, learning problems, and academic expectations (Burrow, Tubman, & Finley, 2004). Adopted adolescents reported significantly more academic learning problems and lower grades. Although statistically significant (in part because of the large sample size), the mean differences were small. No differences between the two groups of adolescents were observed for school connectedness or academic expectations, with all means in the positive range. These recent findings support a generally positive picture of the academic experience of adopted adolescents. For those adopted adolescents who do experience school adjustment and performance problems, these behaviors should be considered within the context of risk factors experienced by the adolescent, some of which may have been encountered prior to or in conjunction with adoption.

## ALTERNATIVE ACTIONS FOR SUPPORT

School professionals are in a position to educate others about adoption while serving the unique needs of adopted students. Through consultation with staff and students, adoption-related issues can be thoughtfully considered in the complex context of school-related adjustment. This section contains actions school professionals can take when working with the issues presented by adopted children, their families, and their teachers.

### Learn the Adoption Story

The complexities of adoption do not allow a single picture of the adoptive family to be formed. When considering adoption as part of a student's experience, school professionals must ask the student and family what type of adoption arrangement they have. The student's perspective is important to understanding the adoption arrangement. It is rare for a child not to know his or her adoption story, as adoption agencies help parents understand the importance and necessity of telling the adoption story to their child. By asking the child to relay his or her adoption story, school professionals can learn much about the context of that child's adoption. By listening to both the student and parents a more complete picture of the adoptive family will emerge.

## Determine if Counseling Is Needed

School professionals are well positioned to help families identify and evaluate counseling and other support resources, should they be needed. Counseling adopted children and adolescents is most likely to be successful when the counselor is knowledgeable about the special issues associated with adoption. Many resources are available to help, including general adoption support groups and adoption advocacy groups, as well as groups that are concerned with very specific situations (e.g., children adopted from specific countries with specific disabilities). Community counselors should be asked about their experiences working with adopted children and their families. Much information is available on the Internet, although it is important to critically evaluate the usefulness and validity of all such resources. Sponsorship by legitimate adoption agencies and professional groups is important. Research sites should include the name of the sponsoring institution to allow the legitimacy of the sites to be verified.

## Look Beyond the Child's Adopted Status

Although being adopted is not a predictor of future behavioral or academic difficulties, adopted children do face additional normative developmental tasks. Children's adoption-related experiences (e.g., early drug exposure or growing up in foster care) may contribute to such problems. Adoptive status is an important factor to consider when determining a course of action but should be considered in conjunction with other developmental and environmental factors.

School professionals may be unaware of a student's adoptive status and thus not have an important context for evaluating a student's behavior. It is appropriate when gathering demographic data to ask if a student is adopted. Some parents may be reluctant to share this information for fear that their child's adoptive status will become the primary explanation for the child's difficulties. School professionals should convey to parents their understanding that adoptive status is only one factor of influence within the wider developmental and environmental context.

## Support Student's Search for Context of Adoptive Identity

When identity is being developed during adolescence, an adoptive identity is also being formed. To support the development of an adoptive identity, school professionals can connect teens with peer and adult mentors who have a similar adoptive or ethnic background. Adoption agencies often have support groups for adopted teens, and some cultural communities in metropolitan areas have support networks available to the student. These supports may be helpful as the teen is exploring what it means to be an adopted person.

## Use Appropriate Language to Convey Awareness

The use of constructive adoption terminology is the mark of a well-informed professional. Birth mother and birth father refer to the adopted child's biological parents; mother and father refer to the child's adoptive parents. Children's and parents' adoptive status should be referred to only in the context of adoption-related discussion. It is inappropriate to ask parents who have had children join their family through adoption and birth which children are "their own." The adoption process is not one of "putting a child up for adoption" or "giving up" a child; rather, children are placed for adoption through the creation of an adoption plan.

## Become Familiar With Adoption-Related Issues

School professionals should familiarize themselves with adoption issues by reading a variety of adoption-related literature. The ideas presented by adoption professionals, first-person accounts, and ideas presented in the research literature together can provide a well-rounded view of adoption. Lists of local resources (e.g., support groups and knowledgeable therapists) can be compiled and given to families and teachers as needed, and workshops and inservice training using local professionals could be organized. These multiple sources of information will allow school professionals to combat any uninformed negative attitudes, stereotypes, expectations, and attributions school personnel may have about adoption and will enhance the healthy development of adopted children.

### Evaluate Curricula for Inclusiveness

Curricula should be evaluated to ensure that adoption is presented as one of the ways to build a family. Many children are nurtured and loved by adults who are not biologically related to them. Families may be formed through adoption, remarriage, temporary foster care, or relative care. Teachers should be aware that some routine class discussions or assignments may be a source of embarrassment or anxiety for adopted children. Asking the students in a class to create a family tree, write an autobiography, or bring in a baby picture or family photo can provoke strong feelings in adopted children and undermine their self-esteem. Holidays, with their emphasis on family togetherness and cultural history, can be particularly stressful for adopted children. Emphasizing the multiple ways families are formed, including adoption, can help children from all family types feel included.

### Inform Parents of Students' Discomfort

Children who are visibly different from their parents are especially vulnerable to teasing and unwanted comments such as "Why is your mom white?" Teachers and counselors should be sensitive to these potentially hurtful questions and help the adopted child to choose the method of response that feels most comfortable. Some children may want to have an adult help explain the situation. Others may prefer to simply ignore the comments. When situations arise at school, most adoptive parents would appreciate being informed so that they can address any emotional issues at home. What may seem like a harmless comment can be a catalyst for a complicated array of questions and feelings.

### Look for Ways to Share Information and Help Educate

Adoptive and foster parents and school personnel can be excellent resources for each other. Parents may be willing to speak to students or school staff about adoption myths and truths that can help sensitize teachers and students to the experiences of living in an adoptive family. At the same time, school professionals should be aware of postadoption support groups and services offered in their area. As developmental changes in children unfold, parents may need help from outside sources in knowing how to address questions and issues that emerge.

## SUMMARY

The complex nature of adoption requires that school professionals familiarize themselves with its many forms. Married couples, relatives, and single adults are adopting children from foster care, from foreign countries, and with special needs. Domestic adoption arrangements most often involve some form of contact between birth and adoptive families. Although Americans increasingly view adoption in a positive light, unfounded and negative ideas about the lives of adopted children and families persist and are sometimes given undue attention in the media. Adoption should not be viewed as a problem but as an important contextual influence on a person's development. Although adopted children and their families often require support from mental health and educational professionals, the vast majority of families and children function in a healthy manner. It is essential that school professionals view adoption as only one important factor among other developmental and environmental influences when considering a course of intervention for a student's school difficulties. School professionals, as informed and effective child advocates, can make an important difference in the lives of adopted children.

## RECOMMENDED RESOURCES

### Books and Other Printed Material

Brodzinsky, D. M., & Palacios, J. (2005). *Psychological issues in adoption: Theory, research and practice.* Westport, CT: Greenwood.

This book offers a comprehensive review of the adoptive experience, drawing from the research and clinical work of prominent experts in the field. It is a good source for gaining information concerning many adoption situations school personnel may encounter.

Grotevant, H. D., & McRoy, R. G. (1998). *Openness in adoption: Exploring family connections.* Thousand Oaks, CA: Sage.

This book summarizes the findings of a nationwide study of children adopted as infants into U.S. families through confidential, mediated, and open adoptions. It highlights the similarities and differences in children's experiences and family relationships.

In addition to the above, the journal *Adoption Quarterly: Innovations in Community and Clinical Practice, Theory and Research* presents empirical work that is of interest to both practitioners and researchers. Regular columns include book reviews and overviews of current legal issues related to adoption.

## Websites

*http://www.adoptioninstitute.org*

The website of the Evan B. Donaldson Adoption Institute highlights the work of the institute, a not-for-profit organization focused on improving adoption policy and practice. The organization's mission is to "improve the quality of information about adoption, to enhance the understanding and perception of adoption, and to advance adoption policy and practice." The website includes a fully searchable database of adoption research studies.

*http://naic.acf.hhs.gov*

The National Adoption Information Clearinghouse website is a service of the Children's Bureau, Administration for Children and Families, U.S. Department of Health and Human Services. "The mission of the Clearinghouse is to connect professionals and concerned citizens to timely and well-balanced information on programs, research, legislation, and statistics regarding the safety, permanency, and well-being of children and families."

*http://www.nacac.org*

The North American Council on Adoptable Children (NACAC) was founded in 1974 by adoptive parents to help meet the needs of waiting children and the families who adopt them and has grown into an internationally prominent advocacy and resource organization. The mission of the organization states, "Every child has the right to a permanent family. The council advocates the right of every child to a permanent, continuous, nurturing and culturally sensitive family."

*http://www.adoptivefamilies.com*

Published bimonthly, *Adoptive Families Magazine* has valuable information for adoptive parents and for those who work with adoptive families, paying special attention to developmental perspectives and giving attention to all types of adoptions.

## REFERENCES


Adoption and Safe Families Act of 1997, Pub. L. No. 105-89, 111 Stat. 2115. (1997).

American Psychological Association. (2004). *APA policy statement: Sexual orientation, parents, and children.* Retrieved September 1, 2004, from APA Online: Public Interest website: http://www.apa.org/pi/lgbc/policy/parents.html

Barth, R. P., & Berry, M. (1988). *Adoption and disruption: Rates, risks and responses.* New York: Aldine de Gruyter.

Benson, P. L., Sharma, A. R., & Roehlkepartain, E. C. (1994). *Growing up adopted: A portrait of adolescents and their families.* Minneapolis, MN: Search Institute.

Berge, J., Mendenhall, T., Wrobel, G. M., Grotevant, H., & McRoy, R. (in press). Adolescents' feelings about openness in adoption: Implications for adoption agencies. *Child Welfare.*

Boots, S. W., & Geen, R. (1999). *Family care or foster care? How state policies affect kinship caregivers.* Retrieved September 7, 2005, from http://www.urban.org/url.cfm?ID=309166

Brodzinsky, D. M. (1987). Adjustment to adoption: A psychosocial perspective. *Clinical Psychology Review, 7,* 25–47.

Brodzinsky, D. M. (1993). Long-term outcomes in adoption. *Future of Children, 3,* 153–166.

Brodzinsky, D. M., & Huffman, L. (1988). Transition to adoptive parenthood. *Marriage and Family Review, 12,* 267–286.

Brodzinsky, D., & Pinderhughes, E. (2002). Parenting and child development in adoptive families. In M. Bornstein (Ed.), *Handbook of parenting: Volume 1* (2nd ed., pp. 279–311). Hillsdale, NJ: Erlbaum.

Burrow, A. L., Tubman, J. G., & Finley, G. E. (2004). Adolescent adjustment in a nationally collected sample: Identifying group differences by adoption status, adoption subtype, developmental stage and gender. *Journal of Adolescence, 27,* 267–282.

Dunbar, N., & Grotevant, H. D. (2004). Adoption narratives: The construction of adoptive identity during adolescence. In M. W. Pratt & B. H. Fiese (Eds.), *Family stories and the life course: Across time and generations* (pp. 135–161). Mahwah, NJ: Erlbaum.

Evan B. Donaldson Adoption Institute. (2002). *2002 national adoption attitudes survey highlights.* Retrieved June 2, 2004, from http://www.adoptioninstitute.org/survey/survey_summary.html

Finley, G. E. (1999). Children of adoptive families. In W. K. Silverman & T. H. Ollendick (Eds.), *Developmental issues in the clinical treatment of children* (pp. 358–370). Boston: Allyn & Bacon.

Grotevant, H. D. (1997). Coming to terms with adoption: The construction of identity from adolescence into adulthood. *Adoption Quarterly, 1*(1), 3–27.

Grotevant, H. D., Dunbar, N., Kohler, J. K., & Esau, A. L. (2000). Adoptive identity: How contexts within and beyond the family shape developmental pathways. *Family Relations, 49,* 379–387.

Grotevant, H. D., & Kohler, J. (1999). Adoptive families. In M. E. Lamb (Ed.), *Parenting and child development in "nontraditional" families* (pp. 161–190). Mahwah, NJ: Erlbaum.

Grotevant, H. D., & McRoy, R. G. (1998). *Openness in adoption: Exploring family connections.* Thousand Oaks, CA: Sage.

Grotevant, H., McRoy, R., Elde, C., & Fravel, D. L. (1994). Adoptive family system dynamics: Variations by level of openness in the adoption. *Family Process, 33,* 125–146.

Grotevant, H., Ross, N., Marchel, M., & McRoy, R. (1999). Adaptive behavior in adopted children: Predictors from early risk, collaboration in relationships within the adoptive kinship network, and openness arrangements. *Journal of Adolescent Research, 14,* 231–247.

Haugaard, J. J. (1999). Is adoption a risk factor for the development of adjustment problems? *Clinical Psychology Review, 18,* 47–69.

Henney, S. M., Onken, S., McRoy, R. G., & Grotevant, H. D. (1998). Changing agency practices toward openness in adoption. *Adoption Quarterly, 1*(3), 45–76.

Johnson, D., & Fein, E. (1991). The concept of attachment: Applications to adoption. *Children and Youth Services Review, 13,* 397–412.

Kirk, H. D. (1964). *Shared fate: A theory of adoption and mental health.* New York: Free Press.

Kreider, R. (2003). *Adopted children and stepchildren: 2000 (Census 2000 Special Reports).* Retrieved May 12, 2004, from http://www.census.gov/prod/2003pubs/censr-6.pdf

Lee, R. M. (2003). The transracial adoption paradox: History, research, and counseling implications of cultural socialization. *The Counseling Psychologist, 31,* 711–744.

McRoy, R. G. (1999). *Special needs adoption: Practice issues.* New York: Garland.

Mendenhall, T., Berge, J., Wrobel, G., Grotevant, H., & McRoy, R. (2004). Adolescents' satisfaction with contact in adoption. *Child and Adolescent Social Work Journal, 21,* 175–190.

Miller, B. C., Fan, X., Christensen, M., Coyl, D., Grotevant, H. D., & van Dulmen, M. H. (2000). Adopted adolescents' over-representation in mental health counseling: Adoptees' problems or parents' lower threshold for referral? *Journal of the American Academy of Child and Adolescent Psychiatry, 39,* 1504–1511.

Müller, U., Gibbs, P., & Ariely, S. (2003). Adults who were adopted contacting their birthmothers: What are the outcomes, and what factors influence these outcomes? *Adoption Quarterly, 7*(1), 7–26.

National Adoption Information Clearinghouse. (2003). *Foster care national statistics.* Retrieved June 2, 2004, from http://naic.acf.hhs.gov/pubs

National Adoption Information Clearinghouse. (2004). *Adoption statistics.* Retrieved May 15, 2005, from the U.S. Department of Health and Human Services Administration for Children and Families website at http://naic.acf.hhs.gov/pubs/s_adopted/index.cfm

National Association of Black Social Workers. (1972, April). *Position statement on transracial adoptions.*

Paper presented at the National Association of Black Social Workers Conference, Nashville, TN.

National Association of Black Social Workers. (1994). *Position statement: Preserving African-American families.* Detroit, MI: Author.

North American Council on Adoptable Children, Adoption Subsidy Resource Center. Retrieved August 25, 2004, from http://www.nacac.org/adoptionsubsidy.html

O'Connor, T. G, Marvin, R. S., Rutter, M., Olrick, J., Britner, P., & The English and Romanian Adoptees Study Team (2003). Child-parent attachment following early institutional deprivation. *Development and Psychopathology, 15,* 19–38.

Perrin, E. C., and the Committee on Psychosocial Aspects of Child and Family Health. (2002). Technical report: Coparent or second-parent adoption by same-sex parents. *Pediatrics, 109,* 341–344.

Portello, J. (1993). The mother-infant attachment process in adoptive families. *Canadian Journal of Counseling, 27,* 177–190.

Reitz, M., & Watson, K. (1992). *Adoption and the family system.* New York: Guilford Press.

Schlonsky, A., Webster, D., & Needell, B. (2003). The ties that bind: A cross-sectional analysis of siblings in foster care. *Journal of Social Service Research, 29*(4), 27–52.

Shireman, J. (1996). Single parent adoptive homes. *Children and Youth Services Review, 18,* 23–36.

Smith, S. L., Howard, J. A., & Monroe, A. D. (2000). Issues underlying behavior problems in at-risk adopted children. *Children and Youth Services Review, 22,* 539–562.

Sobol, M., Delaney, S, & Earn, B. (1994). Adoptees' portrayal of the development of family structure. *Journal of Youth and Adolescence, 23,* 385–401.

Thompson, R. (2001). Sensitive periods in attachment? In D. Bail (Ed.), *Critical thinking about critical periods* (pp. 83–106). Baltimore: Brookes.

U.S. Department of Health and Human Services, Administration for Children and Families, Children's Bureau. (2003, March). Adoption and foster care analysis and reporting system. Retrieved August 25, 2004, from http://www.acf.hhs.gov/programs/cb/publications/afcars/report8.htm

U.S. Department of State. (2004). *Immigrant visas issued to orphans coming to the U.S.* Retrieved September 3, 2004, from http://travel.state.gov/family/adoption_resources_02.html

U.S. General Accounting Office. (1994). *Foster care: Parental drug abuse has alarming impact on young children. Report to the Chairman, Subcommittee on Human Resources, Committee on Ways and Means, House of Representatives.* (Publication No. HEHS-94-89). Washington, DC: U.S. General Accounting Office.

Verhulst, F. C. (2000). Internationally adopted children: The Dutch longitudinal adoption study. *Adoption Quarterly, 4*(1), 27–44.

Warren, S. B. (1992). Lower threshold for referral for psychiatric treatment for adopted adolescents. *Journal of the American Academy of Child and Adolescent Psychiatry, 31,* 512–517.

Watson, K. (1997). Bonding and attachment in adoption: Towards better understanding and useful definitions. *Marriage and Family Review, 24,* 159–173.

Wierzbicki, M. (1993). Psychological adjustment of adoptees: A meta-analysis. *Journal of Clinical Child Psychology, 22,* 447–454.

Wrobel, G. M., Ayers-Lopez, S., Grotevant, H. D., McRoy, R., & Frederick, M. (1996). Open adoption and the level of child participation. *Child Development, 67,* 2358–2374.

Wrobel, G., Grotevant, H. D., & McRoy, R. G. (2004). Adolescent search for birthparents: Who moves forward? *Journal of Adolescent Research, 19,* 132–151.

Wrobel, G. M., Kohler, J. K., Grotevant, H. D., & McRoy, R. G. (2003). The Family Adoption Communication (FAC) Model: Identifying pathways of adoption-related communication. *Adoption Quarterly, 7*(2), 53–84.

# 52

# Families of Children With Disabilities

**Kelly A. Powell-Smith**
**Bobbie J. Vaughn**
*University of South Florida*

## BACKGROUND AND DEVELOPMENT

During the 2000–2001 school year, about 8.2% of children in the United States ages 3 to 21 received special education services (U.S. Department of Education, 2002). When one adds in the numbers of children who participate in early intervention programs, these numbers increase substantially. Family participation in the special education process and the rights of parents and children are protected by law (e.g., Individuals with Disabilities Education Act [IDEA], 1997). Legislation acknowledges the important role that families play in their children's education by requiring schools to actively seek parents' participation in processes such as developing Individual Education Plans (IEPs) and Individual Family Service Plans (IFSPs). In fact, one of the explicit purposes of IDEA Part C was to "enhance the capacity of families to meet the special needs of their infants and toddlers with disabilities" (Section 631(a)(4)). Along with legislative changes, the trend in special education has continued to be that of serving more students with disabilities in inclusive settings.

All of these changes heighten the need for skilled school professionals to work with families of children with disabilities. To a large extent, the success of a child with a disability is related to the environment's ability to adapt to the child's needs both at school and at home. Thus, school professionals need to be well informed about the complex issues confronting families of children with disabilities. In this way, these professionals can bridge the home-to-school gap to create important partnerships with families, which can result in family empowerment.

School professionals must abandon the traditional focus on mothers and their children with disabilities and accept that families may be more broadly defined as "two or more people who regard themselves as a family and who perform some of the functions that families typically perform. These people may or may not be related by blood or marriage and may or may not usually live together" (Turnbull, Turnbull, Shank, & Leal, 1995, p. 24). Regardless of family composition, school professionals require a framework for understanding families' complexity. Family systems theory (e.g., Minuchin, 1974) provides such a framework. From this perspective, family structure is composed of four interrelated subsystems: marital, sibling, parental, and extrafamilial. Life events, such as the birth of a child with a disability, affect not only the parents, but also siblings, grandparents, and family friends. All systems influence one another both directly and indirectly, including school professionals in the extrafamilial subsystem (see also chapter 50, "Healthy Family Systems").

### Family Reactions Across the Life Span

Although researchers have attempted to document family responses to having a child with a disability (see Blacher, 1984, for a review), it is not possible to capture all potential family reactions, nor to predict a particular family's reaction based on child or family characteristics (Bailey, Blasco, & Simeonsson, 1992; Seligman & Darling, 1997). What is known is that families may experience and re-experience stress at various points in their lives as a result of their life circumstances and changing needs. Given the ongoing challenges facing families of children with disabilities, understanding family needs and concerns begins with acquiring knowledge about events and experiences across the child's life span.

## Anticipation of Birth

Differences in parents' initial reactions to the diagnosis of a disability may be related to factors and events that occur prior to the child's birth. Most parents expect the birth of a healthy child and dread the idea of having a child with a disability (Seligman & Darling, 1997). These expectations and anxieties are shaped by and shared with family, friends, and doctors, who often attempt to reassure the parents by discounting worries about the baby's health (Seligman & Darling). Alternatively, professionals may convey a negative attitude toward the diagnosis of a disability, and these attitudes also may shape the family's response to diagnosis (Turnbull & Turnbull, 2001). Even with a prenatal diagnosis of a disability, parents may still hope that there has been a mistake. Thus, most parents are not well prepared for the birth of a child with a disability (Seligman & Darling).

## Diagnosis

The birth of a child with a disability, or the diagnosis of a disability later in the child's life, may challenge the family's hopes, dreams, and expectations for the child. The realization that their child has a disability may produce a wide range of emotions from families, including depression, anger, shock, denial, fear, guilt, and confusion (Heiman, 2002). Negative reactions to a diagnosis are understandable given our culture's negative stereotypes about people with disabilities, parental expectations that may not be met, and the often secretive or negative reactions of delivery room doctors and nurses (Seligman & Darling, 1997). Of course, not all families react with the same degree of emotional response.

Parent–child attachment occurs through the process of parent–child interaction in all families, regardless of the nature of the disability. Though certain characteristics of children with disabilities (e.g., negative reactions to being held, or the child's appearance) may hinder attachment, most parents still form strong attachments with their child with a disability (Seligman & Darling, 1997). One fact to consider regarding the literature on family reactions is that much of it is written from a Euro-American perspective. Thus, Turnbull and Turnbull (2001) suggest that professionals consider the wide range of cultural variations in a family's response to the diagnosis.

The preschool years are another time when a child's disability may be first identified. The family may become concerned about their child when they notice that typical developmental milestones are not being achieved, especially in families where older siblings or other children are used as a reference point. Parents may observe other same-age children and notice that their child is not performing at the same level. Families' reactions to diagnoses at this later time may be very similar to those of families who receive a diagnosis at the time of birth or during infancy. Understanding that an intense response can occur at any time is especially important for school professionals, who may work with families in circumstances involving an accident or when identifying the need for special education.

## Postdiagnosis

Parents need to have accurate information so they can begin to adjust their expectations if necessary and to take an active role in interventions for their child. In fact, many families feel powerless until they start to do something to assist the child's development. A recent survey of parents of children with developmental disabilities validated this need for information. Parents ranked highest the need for information about teaching strategies, behavior management, child rights, and the availability of services, both present and future (Ellis et al., 2002).

Following a diagnosis, some families seek further evaluation and treatments. Professionals may interpret this behavior as a sign of denial or as a search for a cure, yet parents report that they are just trying to "do whatever they can to improve their children's quality of life" (Seligman & Darling, 1997, p. 49). Families also may seek additional evaluation to gain a particular diagnosis that gives them access to services. School professionals should attempt to determine the function of the family's "shopping" behavior before assuming they are denying the child's diagnosis.

As children grow, family concerns may shift. For example, all adolescents struggle with issues related to their physical development, independence, and preparation for adulthood. However, a disability may limit the level of independence a child can achieve without ongoing support. Although some families' concerns center on issues related to independence and adulthood, others worry about the stigma of disability (Hatter,

Williford, & Dickens, 2000). Some children may have less visible disabilities, and in such circumstances concerns may focus on the stigma that might occur if the disability is acknowledged to obtain services. Thus, families must consider the child's dependencies and issues related to the child's functioning beyond the immediate family support system. Depending on the nature of the disability, families may need to address the following issues during adolescence: (a) planning for the transition from school to work, (b) securing appropriate housing, (c) navigating social issues related to peers and dating, and (d) arranging for the child's support after the parents' death.

## PROBLEMS AND IMPLICATIONS

Approximately 10% to 25% of U.S. children have disabilities that range from learning disabilities to profound developmental disabilities. Many of these children are born to parents who live in poverty and abuse drugs and alcohol. These families are often single-parent families that relocate frequently, and children may suffer the effects of malnutrition and abuse as a result of family instability, parental stress, and maternal depression. They may experience further frustration in caring for their children as a result of the difficulty of accessing the necessary services. Given their very complex life circumstances, families of children with disabilities may develop a variety of needs across the life span of the child that affect both the family as a system as well as individual family members.

### Family System Needs

"Children with disabilities inevitably challenge families by making inordinate demands on their time, psychological well-being, relationships, economic resources, and freedom of movement" (Brantlinger, 1991, p. 250). The needs of these families vary greatly with the unique skills and attributes of each child, severity of the disability, environmental conditions, cultural and ethnic values, and demands placed upon the child. These individual characteristics may serve to either limit or strengthen the family as a whole (Turnbull & Turnbull, 2001). Thus, any discussion of needs must be tempered by respect for the individual variability that exists across families. Although having a child with a disability can prove challenging, the research literature has increasingly attended to the positive transformations families can experience as a result of having a child with a disability. This view goes beyond the notion of the family merely coping; rather, it includes a focus on significant changes for the better that might occur in families as a result of having a child with a disability (Scorgie & Sobsey, 2000). Within this context, however, some common needs still exist.

Empowerment is critical for meeting some of these common needs. For example, many families need to be empowered to address their basic needs, obtain appropriate respite care, and address any financial concerns. The daily care needs of the child with a disability may cause family members to overlook their own daily care or socialization needs. Resources (e.g., respite care) are needed to meet ongoing needs, especially at transition times, when families may experience several stressors at once (referred to as the pile-up factor; Minnes, 1988). Also, many children with disabilities have daily care needs, which include medical and health care concerns (e.g., dialysis, physical therapy, or medication). These children may encounter repeated visits to the emergency room, more frequent hospitalizations, and painful medical procedures (Stoneman, 1998). Thus, families may incur both direct costs (e.g., those related to child care, medical care, and special equipment) and indirect costs (e.g., those related to time off from work; Seligman & Darling, 1997). These costs may strain families' financial resources and create additional stress, which may be exacerbated by socioeconomic status or lack of access to adequate health insurance. Additional stress can also affect a family's resources for implementing interventions for the child with the disability.

Specific needs also may exist with families from various cultures. Limited English proficiency may result in a need to translate information into a different language (Turnbull & Turnbull, 2001). Reactions to having a child with a disability may differ from those of members of the majority culture. The family might experience "dual stigma—the stigma of being racially or ethnically different from the dominant culture and the stigma of having a child who is seen as 'different' because of a disability" (Rounds, Weil, & Bishop, 1994, p. 3). Finally, the family might receive different treatment of their child as a result of their ethnicity (Park, Turnbull, & Park, 2001).

### Needs of Specific Family Members

***The child with a disability.*** Children with disabilities often have daily care, educational or vocational, informational, and social–emotional needs beyond those of children without disabilities. Upon entering the educational system, they may experience wide-ranging needs in traditional academic skill areas (e.g., reading), independent living skills, communication, and specific vocational or career-related skills. They also may require extra assistance in learning how to interact appropriately with peers. These behavioral and social concerns may exist throughout childhood. Coupled with these concerns is the likelihood that these children and their families may experience stigma related to the disability, which could limit opportunities in the community.

Among the social–emotional needs children with disabilities experience is the need for self-determination. Self-determination for all ages is about choice making, decision making, and problem solving, all of which lead to autonomy, self-regulation, self-realization, and psychological empowerment (Wehmeyer, 1998). Historically, schools, providers, and policymakers often usurped choice and control in the case of children with disabilities, often with the best intentions. Children who have few freedoms may develop passive behaviors associated with learned helplessness or aggressive behavior problems as a result of a restrictive environment. A survey of 282 adolescents with disabilities showed that they lacked some of the characteristics necessary for self-determination (e.g., self-efficacy, internal locus of control). They believed less in themselves and tended to blame outcomes on the actions of others, failing to take responsibility for their own actions (Wehmeyer, 1994). Thus, without choice and control children may feel restricted and become disempowered, increasing the likelihood for further familial stress.

As adolescence and early adulthood approaches, needs may shift more toward finding appropriate housing and suitable job opportunities, plus planning for future financial needs (Turnbull & Turnbull, 2001). Needs related to transportation (e.g., knowing how to use public transportation because the person is unable to drive a car) and the need to find appropriately supportive housing (e.g., group home or assisted living center) also may become important. Once again, the family experiences challenges related to separation and uncertainty about the future.

***Siblings.*** The needs of siblings can be as wide ranging as those of children with disabilities themselves. However, much of the research on siblings has failed to account for differences in the nature of the disability experienced by the family (Stoneman, 1998). Characteristics such as family size, gender, and birth order may also affect sibling adjustment (Turnbull & Turnbull, 2001). Thus, some siblings have difficulty coping with the situation, others experience no ill effects, and still others describe the benefits of having a sibling with a disability. In essence, there is "no single definitive impact" (Turnbull & Turnbull, 2001, p. 119). Nonetheless, an empowerment perspective suggests that siblings, much like other members of the family, need information and skills to help them adjust to having a sibling with a disability, beginning at the time of diagnosis and continuing through the life span. This information helps siblings understand the nature of their brother's or sister's disability and alleviates worries and anxieties they may experience. For example, siblings may wonder if they carry a defective gene and worry that they may become parents of a child with a disability (Featherstone, 1980; Garland, 1993).

The social and emotional needs of children who have a sibling with a disability may be affected when they receive less attention from their parents who are focusing on the child with the disability (Stoneman, 1998). As a result, siblings may not have as much interaction with parents as they might need or want, and they may be asked to defer their needs (Siegal & Silverstein, 1994). Skills required to adjust to these circumstances are important because differential attention from parents has been associated with negative sibling outcomes (e.g., less prosocial behavior; Stoneman). Additional problems might include thinking that their assistance is taken for granted, resenting the differing behavioral expectations for the child with the disability, and feeling embarrassed by their brother or sister with the disability (Siegal & Silverstein). Finally, because of increased caregiving demands, siblings may spend less time in social activities with their peers or less time in activities outside the family, such as participating in scouting or organized clubs and sports. As adults, siblings may face increasing responsibility regarding the care of their brother or sister with a disability (Turnbull & Turnbull, 2001).

Regardless of the issues faced by siblings of children with disabilities, a number of positive outcomes also may result. Siblings have reported benefits of growing up with a brother or sister with a disability, such as being more altruistic, empathetic, and understanding of others with problems (Siegal & Silverstein, 1994). Also, siblings may learn skills such as tolerance and advocacy (Turnbull & Turnbull, 2001). Finally, relationships with siblings may serve as the model for future peer relationships (Siegal & Silverstein).

***Parents.*** The research on parent responses to having a child with a disability has resulted in varying conclusions. One problem is that much of the research on parents is focused on the negative impact of having a child with a disability and on having a child with severe disabilities (Seligman & Darling, 1997). Thus, little is known about the differing effects that various disabilities have on parents and families. For example, we know little about how children with mild disabilities affect their families in comparison to how children with severe disabilities affect their families. In addition, most of the available research has been focused on mothers (Schwartz & Rodriguez, 2001), leaving gaps in knowledge about the impact on fathers.

Despite conflicting research, some common needs exist. For example, parents need accurate diagnostic information about the disability and honesty in discussions regarding the impact across the life span. Parents also require information about their legal rights and provisions for their child under federal and state laws (e.g., IDEA). Some of the most useful information may come from other parents of children with similar needs and challenges, such as support groups and parent-to-parent groups.

Parents also may experience stress within the marital relationship, although conflicting research exists. One study of families of eighth-grade students with and without disabilities found a higher incidence of divorce and separation among the families of children with disabilities (Hodapp & Krasner, 1994–1995). Others, however (e.g., Scorgie, Wilgosh, & McDonald, 1998), have reported greater marital satisfaction as a result of having a child with a disability, and these higher levels of satisfaction appear to have a positive effect on family functioning. Establishing relationships with other parents through avenues such as support groups may buffer isolating or negative circumstances (e.g., increased marital stress or divorce).

***Extended family members.*** Despite an increasingly broad family focus, research on extended family members is even less plentiful than research on siblings (Turnbull & Turnbull, 2001). Extended families (including aunts, uncles, grandparents, friends, neighbors, and professionals) often provide a valuable support network to families of children with disabilities (Turnbull & Turnbull). Extended family members also have similar needs as parents for information and education (e.g., the nature of the disability and available programs and services), empowerment (e.g., training in strategies for being supportive of the child and family), and support and encouragement (e.g., from other grandparents who share similar experiences; Meyer, 1993). Yet extended family members may not know when or how to help, or they may want to help when the parents believe such help is not necessary. Thus, school professionals should encourage grandparents and other extended family members to participate in the child's education, such as IEP conferences (Turnbull & Turnbull). IEP conferences or other involvement may help extended family members gain a more complete picture of the child, gain access to information that otherwise may not be provided to them, and become a better support resource to the immediate family. Unfortunately, extended family members rarely have a peer group with whom to share common experiences regarding a family member's disability. Despite the growth of parent-to-parent support groups, a much smaller percentage of support programs exist for other family members.

## ALTERNATIVE ACTIONS FOR PREVENTION

The best preventive programs focus on intervening at the time the child is identified as eligible for IDEA Part B or Part C services. Preventive services for families and children include establishing partnerships and addressing risk factors through family empowerment and support.

### Empowering Families

School psychologists are often the first professionals that families of children with disabilities encounter after their child enters school or at the time of diagnosis, when families are most vulnerable. This time is most critical for creating supports that protect families against the cumulative effects of life circumstances and their child's disability as well as empower them to face the challenges ahead. This time is also when prevention efforts are most powerful.

One of the first preventive missions of school psychologists and other school professionals is to empower families to cope with their child's disability. *Empowerment* means to gain control or mastery over one's life (Jones, Garlow, Turnbull, & Barber, 1996). Exactly how this occurs for each family depends on their unique circumstances and available resources (e.g., community services). Families must have a clear idea of the available resources and then should be allowed to choose what services they need and when and how they will use those services (Jones et. al.). Finally, school professionals can empower families by supporting their decisions and minimizing the psychological cost of accepting help.

If school professionals realize they themselves lack the resources or knowledge to fully promote family empowerment, then they must band together with families to achieve a collective empowerment, rather than abandon this very important preventive process (Turnbull, Turbiville, & Turnbull, 2000). Power no longer falls within the professionals' purview but is shared and used to build capacity. Thus, competence is gained, partnerships are built, and families are provided the necessary opportunities to receive support and services.

***Developing rapport and effective communication.*** When establishing partnerships that empower families, one must first build a foundation of trust. This foundation is built upon effective communication and rapport. Rapport is best considered an ongoing process and not a one-time effort. Much like building a savings account, rapport requires continuous deposits and limits on withdrawals. Because rapport building requires good communication, difficulties often occur when families and schools fail to communicate effectively. Unfortunately, parents report that professionals seem to experience difficulty informing them of their child's disability. This difficulty may occur because these first interactions often take place at the time of the child's initial diagnosis (Upshur, 1991) when it is especially stressful to hear sensitive information from an unknown professional. School professionals must communicate with families in a manner that is respectful of their knowledge level and is sensitive to their comfort level with the professional. Thus, school professionals are cautioned to avoid speaking as the expert, but instead recognize families as the true experts on their children.

School professionals also must interact with families in their primary language, using simple, straightforward terms (i.e., jargon-free) and translators when necessary. School professionals must adopt practices that also take into consideration the method (e.g., telephone call or face-to-face) and frequency of contact. Contact needs may vary according to the family's life circumstances or the complexity of their child's disability.

***Attending to cultural and lifestyle differences.*** In partnering with families, school professionals must appreciate and respect family diversity. Diversity includes not only cultural and ethnic diversity, but also diversity in family values and beliefs. It is important for school professionals to accept that some families come with complex life circumstances and appreciate that these families approach their interactions with schools according to those circumstances. Every family brings strengths or positive attributes even in the most difficult family circumstances. When school professionals accept and understand family strengths and life circumstances, they take a very important step toward partnership. In doing so, they can tailor services with the family's lifestyle in mind. When school professionals create this "fit" between the family needs and the services or supports, they increase the likelihood of family participation and successful partnership (Albin, Lucyshyn, Horner, & Flannery, 1996).

***Involving families in school.*** Federal laws mandate the inclusion of families in the assessment process as well as in IEP and IFSP development. Including families in these activities also is critical for developing trust and a collaborative relationship with the family. Such an approach is consistent with a consultative service delivery model, NASP's Standards for the Provision of School Psychological Services (National Association of School Psychologists, 2002b), and both NASP and American Psychological Association ethical standards (National Association of School Psychologists, 2002a; American Psychological Association, 2002), along with recent calls for change within the field.

Families should be included from the beginning of the problem-solving process because they can provide information that might inform all aspects of the process, including their long- and short-term goals and their views about their child's strengths and needs (Hubbard & Adams, 2002). Families also provide valuable information about their child's activities and interests in home and community environments. Finally, legislation requires IFSPs to include a statement of present family strengths and needs (Bondurant-Utz & Luciano, 1994). Such information is best obtained directly from the family.

Family involvement also is ongoing. Parents have raised several concerns about the IEP/IFSP process. For example, they have voiced concern that their children's IEPs were repetitive from one year to the next, that meetings were routine, and that they had little influence in the process (Harry, Allen, & McLaughlin, 1995). The actions that were found to discourage parent participation primarily included (a) inflexibility in scheduling or notices being sent out late, (b) not enough time allowed for the meetings, (c) too much emphasis on signing the documents without supporting meaningful parent participation, (d) use of language or jargon unfamiliar to the parents, and (e) team dynamics that set up a power structure, or "us–them" posture, that made parents' advocacy efforts difficult (Harry et al., 1995).

Involving families also means communicating about things other than administrative tasks. Families often are called to the school to attend to their child's behavior or to participate in meetings but not to attend social events or events that might better prepare them to parent their child with disabilities. Unfortunately, if the family's only communication with school professionals involves business or problems, they may cease to respond to these invitations. Families, including those who have children with disabilities, want to feel a part of a school community and need multiple opportunities for participation (e.g., breakfasts, volunteer programs, and support groups). School staff must make every effort to create opportunities for these families to participate in important meetings and social gatherings, especially those that offer information, support, or a reprieve from business as usual. Thus, both mandated meetings and social activities need to occur at times that are convenient for the family.

## Preparing Parents to Work With Agencies

Families may require assistance in navigating the network of agencies that offer services to families with children with disabilities. The large number of agencies and the lack of coordination among them may present a challenge to the family. An important component of preparing families to work with agencies involves helping them interact with professionals outside the school system as well as inside (e.g., feeling empowered to ask questions or to challenge school placement). Useful information to provide to families includes (a) a glossary of the language and jargon used by educational, medical, and mental health professionals; (b) a detailed fact sheet on the rights given to parents and their children by federal and state legislation; and (c) a complete list of available service options.

## Helping Families Access Respite Care and Social Support

Respite care and social support services also may serve a preventive function. Respite care services provide assistance in caring for a child with a disability and allow family members to have a break from care demands and to take time for themselves (Westling & Fox, 2004). Although these services may not be needed by all families, school professionals should be prepared to help families obtain information about the variety of respite care services available in their community or to help the school's parent group organize such a service. Respite care services often are available through community service organizations or health and human services agencies (Westling & Fox). School professionals may want to develop a list (Ellis et al., 2002) of potential respite care providers that can be provided to families.

Support groups also can play an important role in providing assistance to families of children with disabilities. Support groups may help with social–emotional and informational needs and provide a way for family members to benefit from other families' experiences with and knowledge about the education system and community agencies. These groups also can provide parents and other family members with friendships that counter the social isolation they sometimes experience. For families with an adolescent child with disabilities, such groups can help the family cope with their child's emotional and physical changes, inform the family about leisure activities in their community, and identify skills needed for career or vocational settings (Turnbull & Turnbull, 2001).

Support groups for siblings can be especially helpful for children who must learn to cope with receiving less attention from their parents than they may want and with the emotional concerns created by having a brother or sister with a disability. Such groups, known as "sibshops," allow siblings to receive information about their brother or sister with disabilities as well as vent their feelings in a safe environment where they know others understand and empathize (Meyer & Vadasy, 1994). Forming local sibshops may improve children's relationships with their brother or sister with disabilities (Dyson, 1998).

Although support groups are designed to accomplish a variety of goals, the actual activities planned to achieve the goals will vary depending on the population for which the support group is intended (e.g., parents, siblings, grandparents, or extended family). Published curricula are available for those interested in beginning a support program for grandparents and siblings (e.g., Meyer & Vadasy, 1994).

## Assisting Families With Transition Planning

The goal of transition planning with families is to create a seamless change for their child regardless of age or reason for transition. Without proper planning, preparation, and family involvement, transitions to new systems of care (e.g., from early intervention service systems to the public school system) may prove stressful for families because of the subsequent loss of continuity across systems. Proactive, yet sensitive planning by school professionals may offset family stress in the face of transitions.

Transition planning may begin in the hospital (e.g., for children born with disabilities) or as soon as the child leaves the hospital, when families are faced with establishing Part C services. The next major transition, when a child exits Part C services, often poses many challenges for children as they enter a new setting, with unfamiliar adults and children and new expectations of the child with the disability that may differ from those under home-based services (Hanson et al., 2000).

Because services for children in Part B emphasize families less (Entwisle, 1995), it is vital for school professionals to look for creative ways to support family needs through the school and to reach out to community providers to create continuity of services. At this time, the school should create a team to assist with the transition to school-based care to prepare the child and the family for the separation and the possible loss of services, and to set a timeline of preparatory activities (Lillie & Vakil, 2002). By providing ample time for planning, the family can become more involved by visiting the school and classroom. During these visits, school professionals can seek family perspectives about strategies for promoting classroom success and about possible barriers to learning. Parents also could be given curricular activities that resemble classroom activities to implement within the home (Rosenkoetter, Hains, & Fowler, 1994).

Another major transition faced by families with a child with disabilities is the transition to independence and adulthood. By introducing this transition into the special education curriculum early in the child's school life, children and families become involved in preparatory activities that help them adjust to the notion of a life beyond graduation (West, Fetzer, Graham, & Keller, 2000). Early discussions of transitions provide professionals with knowledge about the family that can help them tailor supports and services to address family concerns. Families may approach this transition to adulthood and independence with trepidation and often with resistance (West et al.). A primary goal in helping families with this transition process is to alleviate the fear that often accompanies discussing their child's establishing independence as an adult. Often families' fears keep them too protective of their child and the child enters adulthood relatively unprepared. School professionals also can assist families and children by empowering them to weigh the benefits and costs of remaining in or abandoning adult service systems and make decisions that suit their unique needs (Hatter et al., 2000).

### Achieving Self-Determination

Families and school professionals must unite and become active in the self-determination process to prevent or curb children's overdependence and to provide children with more control over their lives. Families need to help their children participate in family decisions (e.g., what color to paint the house or where to go on vacation), decisions about everyday life (e.g., what to wear, what to eat, and what sports to play), and problem solving in difficult situations (e.g., resolving a disagreement with a friend or sibling or taking on a difficult chore). These activities help children feel in control and included in their family and community. School professionals can help by including all students when they address school-wide academic and discipline concerns, as well as by offering more choice in classroom materials and activities, accommodations and modifications for schoolwork, food at lunchtime, and school-wide events and activities. Finally, school professionals can encourage children with disabilities to become involved in planning and conducting their IEP meetings as well as planning for their future (see the discussion on Person-Centered Planning in the Interventions section).

In summary, as families become empowered, they develop the skills necessary to adapt, adjust, problem solve, and make decisions that minimize or arrest problems and issues as they arise. However, sometimes families reach an impasse that may result in the loss of an irreplaceable service or an important person, ill health, the need to make a major transition, or behavior problems that arise as a result of the disability. When these events occur, when prevention is not possible, or when preventive efforts fail to achieve the desired outcomes, it becomes necessary to pursue more formal efforts to intervene.

## ALTERNATIVE ACTIONS FOR INTERVENTION

Part of family empowerment includes families' ability to choose among an array of possible interventions.

Partnerships established with schools and agencies expose families to many different services, some of which prevent problems, others that function as interventions. Because families of children with disabilities have very complex needs, they may seek a variety of interventions at different times in their lives. Before school professionals approach a family about interventions, they must consider the family context and how it might help in determining the interventions best suited for the family. Family system variables to understand include the number of caregivers and siblings in the household, caregiver employment and socioeconomic status, cultural beliefs and values, childcare arrangements, the responsibilities of family members in operating the household, and the health of other family members. These variables, as well as myriad daily issues with which the family must contend, may affect their availability to participate in an intervention. Thus, school professionals must be well versed in widely used evidence-based practices to help the family determine what type of intervention best suits their needs at a given time.

The following sections describe three types of widely used evidence-based practices. These interventions should not be considered mutually exclusive or exhaustive. Families can participate in more than one of these interventions simultaneously, perform one at a time, or engage in a host of other interventions not described in this chapter. The interventions vary in the amount of time invested and comprehensiveness (Turnbull & Turnbull, 2001).

## Person-Centered Planning

Person-centered planning is a process that helps families and their child with disabilities develop a vision for the child's life with the necessary supports in place to accomplish that vision. Person-centered planning is grounded in the values, goals, and outcomes of the focus person (i.e., the individual with disabilities), but it also considers a variety of other perspectives, such as family culture and values, agency and school views, funding issues, and other community considerations (Lyle-O'Brien, O'Brien, & Mount, 1997). This process typically is carried out with a facilitator who helps the family articulate the desired life for the family and child and with a team of individuals important to the child and family (e.g., family, friends, teachers, counselors, school psychologists, or agency staff) who help identify and plan for ("problem-solve") the supports necessary to achieve their ultimate lifestyle goal (Kincaid & Fox, 2002). School psychologists who have been trained in a collaborative problem-solving model of service delivery are well positioned to facilitate or participate in the person-centered planning process.

Person-centered planning has evolved over the past decade to embody a number of different applications (described in Table 1). Though research is generally lacking on the efficacy of person-centered planning applications, a few studies document positive effects through caregiver accounts using a focus group format. Recently, one longitudinal comparison study of 38 individuals living in institutions, who also had challenging behavior, documented the success of person-centered planning (Holburn, Jacobson, Schwartz, Flory, & Vietze, 2004). Twenty of the 38 received person-centered planning, and the other 18 received individualized support plans as usual. Of the 20, only 2 returned to the institution and 18 moved to community living arrangements, whereas only 5 individuals in the contrast group moved to the community. Although this study focused primarily on adults with disabilities and challenging behaviors, it attests to the power of a team in making lifestyle change for persons with disabilities and challenging behaviors.

The process is relatively simple and includes casual meetings with food and drink. Team members begin by describing the child's strengths and reviewing their history, followed by identifying barriers that prevent the child and family from achieving a better lifestyle. Problem solving includes considering the child's preferences, strengths, and needs; brainstorming and evaluating options; developing a vision; and creating and implementing an action plan. Person-centered planning, regardless of method, creates a synergy among group members that focuses on the whole being greater than the sum of its parts. The synergy unites members around a common goal of supporting and problem-solving family and child concerns or issues.

## Parent Training

As a result of their child's disability and associated challenges, parents may need some specific strategies to address the child's needs. School professionals can convey helpful information to families in an effective and efficient manner through parent training groups (Webster-Stratton & Taylor, 2001). These groups are very successful in intervening with conduct and other behavior problems and also can be used to create parent support networks (Webster-Stratton & Taylor). Families often report that their children continue to experience

**Table 1** *Applications of Person-Centered Planning*

| Application | Description | Reference |
|---|---|---|
| Personal Profiling | • Uses group graphics to develop a series of frames that portray the child's identity and experiences.<br>• Includes important people and critical events in the child's life, and choices the child does or does not make in his or her life.<br>• Includes the child as an active participant. | O'Brien, Mount, & Lyle-O'Brien (1990) |
| Personal Futures Planning | • Helps the team focus on how to address issues in five areas (home, work or school, community, choices and preferences, and relationships).<br>• Helps team members when they do not know the child well, as it provides a comprehensive picture of the child's life. | Mount & Zwernik (1988) |
| Making Action Plans (MAPS) | • Helps the team achieve a roadmap for working toward their desired goals.<br>• Produces a framework for who the child is, his or her history, dreams, nightmares, strengths, and gifts, as well as the vision and a plan of action. | Pearpoint, Forest, & O'Brien (1996) |
| Planning Alternative Tomorrows With Hope (PATH) | • Works well with teams who know the individual well.<br>• Helps develop timelines for accomplishing the dreams and goals of the person. | Pearpoint, Forest, & O'Brien (1996) |
| Group Action Planning | • Provides a reciprocal and energetic problem-solving framework among committed individuals who come together to support the family and child with disabilities.<br>• Fosters an interdependent connection among participants in which suggestions by group members are viable and progress is "celebrated."<br>• Invites individuals who can support the family and child in important areas of their life (e.g., friendships, school, community, and home). | Turnbull & Turnbull (1996) |

behavior problems beyond the life of the parent training group, which can be attributed to the fact that only parents received intervention. Thus, research indicates that parent training is most promising when offered in concert with child training (Webster-Stratton & Hammond, 1997).

In parent training groups, the trainer must have the clinical background and expertise to administer the training in a collaborative atmosphere. Thus, school psychologists are well suited to be parent trainers. Parent trainers must listen to the stories of the family and the numerous issues and complex needs that accompany raising a child with disabilities, including challenging behavior. Parent trainers must also possess skills to respond to issues beyond the parent–child relationship.

Parent training programs typically last 3 to 4 months and incorporate a variety of strategies (Webster-Stratton & Taylor, 2001). Successful programs incorporate didactic presentations, role-playing, videotaped vignettes of parent–child interactions (e.g., including both effective and ineffective strategies), homework, and in-class discussions among participating families. Some of the researched parent training programs can be found in Webster-Stratton and Taylor (2001).

Although parent training has shown promising outcomes, it may prove inadequate for children with disabilities who demonstrate persistent or chronic behavior problems that have resulted in numerous disciplinary actions. In these cases, IDEA calls for the implementation of "strategies, including positive behavioral interventions, strategies and supports" when a child's behavior "impedes his or her learning or that of others" (34 C.F.R. §300.346 [a][2][i]).

## Positive Behavior Support

Positive Behavior Support (PBS) is a family-centered, assessment-based approach with a foundation in applied behavior analysis. It is designed to enhance quality of life while minimizing or eliminating children's challenging behavior. This approach was developed in response to the application of aversive consequences to students with extreme forms of behavior; efficacy has been demonstrated across environments, disabilities, and ages of individuals (Carr et al., 1999).

Individualized PBS is needed for the 1%–7% of students who do not benefit from a school-wide intervention (Sugai et al., 2000). PBS, for these students, begins with the formation of a team in which the family is central to the process. It then proceeds through a person-centered planning process, uses functional behavior assessment for creating hypotheses about the environmental triggers and responses as well as behavioral function, and culminates in a comprehensive behavior support plan that must be evaluated for its success.

***Developing a team and creating a vision.*** The team comprises the family and other school personnel such as the school psychologist and other individuals who interact with the child on regular basis (Vaughn, Dunlap, Fox, Clarke, & Bucy, 1997). One of the first activities of the team is to assist the family in creating a vision for their child using person-centered planning; or if time does not permit, the team may use an informal process by getting the family to describe what they want for their child's future.

***Conducting a functional behavior assessment.*** Central to positive behavior support is functional behavior assessment (FBA). FBA is the process of identifying, across settings, environmental variables that trigger or do not trigger the occurrence of the child's challenging behavior and contribute to its maintenance over time (O'Neill et al., 1997). Specifically, these variables include (a) setting events, which set the stage for challenging behavior (e.g., fatigue, illness, or social altercations; Horner, Vaughn, Day, & Ard, 1996); (b) antecedent events, which immediately precede the behavior (e.g., demands or attention to other students); (c) classes of challenging behavior by function (e.g., escape/avoidance, attention/tangible); and (d) events or responses that immediately follow or maintain the challenging behavior (e.g., positive or negative reinforcement). The FBA process occurs through a combination of record reviews, functional assessment interviews, and direct observations. The culmination of the FBA is the development of testable hypotheses and a contextually relevant behavior support plan.

***Developing hypotheses and behavioral support plans.*** Hypotheses are developed by the team from a summary of the FBA information and verified through observation (O'Neill et al., 1997). Hypothesis statements describe the antecedent conditions (e.g., setting events and immediate predictors), the challenging behavior, and the maintaining consequences or probable function of the behavior. These statements also guide the development of strategies within the behavior support plan.

The behavior support plan focuses on proactive intervention components that teach replacement behaviors, eliminate or minimize antecedent setting events or triggers, and engineer supportive environments (e.g., arranging the context of concern). Although behavior support plans emphasize preventive versus reactive procedures, they also must contain consequence strategies that involve adults and peers changing their responses to the child's challenging behaviors. These altered responses help render the challenging behavior ineffective and reinforce the desired behavior. The team creates these strategies by carefully considering the resources available in each context (e.g., home, school, and community) as well as the values, beliefs, and lifestyle of the family (Albin et al., 1996). The team then creates a script describing the who, where, and when of the implementation. Finally, for students with dangerous or destructive behaviors, the plan must contain crisis intervention procedures that ensure the safety of the child as well as other students in the setting.

## SUMMARY

Families of children with disabilities encounter a wide range of experiences and challenges throughout the family's lifecycle and the lifespan of their child. Individual differences are expected in terms of reaction to diagnosis and subsequent family needs. This variation necessitates an individualized approach to meeting the needs of families of children with disabilities. In addition, prevention and intervention services need to be coordinated across systems of care. School professionals are encouraged to take a proactive role when helping families to identify their needs and access services to meet those needs. Ongoing problem solving is used to create an environment of mutual respect in which family members and school professionals are empowered to be equal partners in team-based transdisciplinary decision making.

## RECOMMENDED RESOURCES

### Books and Other Printed Material

Meyer, D. J., & Vadasy, P. F. (1994). *Sibshops: Implementing workshops for siblings of children with special needs.* Baltimore: Brookes.

This guide serves as a helpful tool in organizing and conducting sibling support groups. The first half of the book focuses on concerns in approaching such a workshop and how to address specific needs of the children. The second half introduces program games and activities that could be used during a support group session. The authors include extensive appendices covering a sibshop model, information concerning specific disabilities, and an introduction to national organizations.

Turnbull, A. P., & Turnbull, H. R., III (2001). *Families, professionals, and exceptionality: Collaborating for empowerment* (4th ed.). Columbus, OH: Merrill/Prentice Hall.

The information in this text focuses on the central theme of empowerment for families, professionals, and students. The authors also focus on an applied family systems perspective and multicultural approach. This book includes the full range of exceptionalities and describes best practices for family–professional partnerships in both general and special education.

In addition, *The Exceptional Parent* (Boston: Psy-Ed Corporation) is an excellent magazine for parents of children and young adults with disabilities and special health care needs. The mission of the magazine is to provide a worldwide network of caring parents, encourage parents to become advocates for their children by joining local and national organizations, and assist parents as caregivers by providing information and support from other parents and professionals.

### Websites

*http://www.nichcy.org*

The National Dissemination Center for Children with Disabilities (NICHCY) serves as a source of information on IDEA, the No Child Left Behind Act (as it relates to children with disabilities), and research-based information on effective educational practices.

*http://www.beachcenter.org*

The Beach Center on Disability is affiliated with the University of Kansas's Schiefelbusch Institute for Life Span Studies and the Department of Special Education. The site provides both parents and professionals with a variety of information, which can be located by general topic area (e.g., disability policy or self-determination) or by disability category (e.g., Autism Spectrum Disorders or health impairments). Numerous research articles and other helpful documents are downloadable directly from the site.

## REFERENCES

Albin, R. W., Lucyshyn, J. M., Horner, R. H., & Flannery, K. B. (1996). Contextual fit for behavioral support plans: A model for "goodness of fit." In L. K. Koegel, R. L. Koegel, & G. Dunlap (Eds.), *Positive behavioral support: Including people with difficult behavior in the community* (pp. 81–98). Baltimore: Brookes.

American Psychological Association. (2002). Ethical principles of psychologists and code of conduct. *American Psychologist, 57,* 1060–1073.

Bailey, D. B., Blasco, P. M., & Simeonsson, R. J. (1992). Needs expressed by mothers and fathers of young children with disabilities. *American Journal on Mental Retardation, 97,* 1–10.

Blacher, J. (1984). A dynamic perspective on the impact of a severely handicapped child on the family. In J. Blacher (Ed.), *Severely handicapped young children and their families: Research in review* (pp. 3–50). Orlando, FL: Academic Press.

Bondurant-Utz, J. A., & Luciano, L. B. (1994). Family involvement. In J. A. Bondurant-Utz & L. B. Luciano (Eds.), *A practical guide to infant and preschool assessment in special education* (pp. 41–57). Boston: Allyn & Bacon.

Brantlinger, E. (1991). Home-school partnerships that benefit children with special needs. *The Elementary School Journal, 91,* 249–259.

Carr, E. G., Horner, R. H., Turnbull, A. P., Marquis, J. G., McLaughlin, D. M., McAtee, M. L., et al. (1999). *Positive behavior support as an approach for dealing with problem behavior in people with developmental disabilities: A research synthesis.* Washington, DC: American Association on Mental Retardation.

Dyson, L. L. (1998). A support program for siblings of children with disabilities: What siblings learn and what they like. *Psychology in the Schools, 35,* 57–63.

Ellis, J. T., Luiselli, J. K., Amirault, D, Byrne, S., O'Malley-Cannon, B., Taras, M., et al. (2002). Families of children with developmental disabilities: Assessment and comparison of self-reported needs in relation to situational variables. *Journal of Developmental and Physical Disabilities, 14,* 191–202.

Entwisle, D. R. (1995). The role of schools in sustaining early childhood program benefits. *The Future of Children, 5*(3), 133–144.

Featherstone, H. (1980). *A difference in the family.* New York: Basic Books.

Garland, C. W. (1993). Beyond chronic sorrow: A new understanding of family adaptation. In A. P. Turnbull, J. M. Patterson, S. K. Behr, D. L. Murphy, J. G. Marquis, & M. J. Blue-Banning (Eds.), *Cognitive coping, families, and disability* (pp. 67–80). Baltimore: Brookes.

Hanson, M. J., Beckman, P. J., Horn, E., Marquart, J., Sandall, S. R., Greig, D., et al. (2000). Entering preschool: Family and professional experiences in this transition process. *Journal of Early Intervention, 23,* 279–293.

Harry, B., Allen, N., & McLaughlin, M. (1995). Communication versus compliance: African-American parents' involvement in special education. *Exceptional Children, 61,* 364–377.

Hatter, R. A., Williford, M., & Dickens, K. (2000). Nurturing and working in partnership with parents during transition. In H. B. Clark & M. Davis (Eds.), *Transition to adulthood: A resource for assisting young people with emotional or behavioral difficulties.* Baltimore: Brookes.

Heiman, T. (2002). Parents of children with disabilities: Resilience, coping, and future expectations. *Journal of Developmental and Physical Disabilities, 14,* 159–171.

Hodapp, R. M., & Krasner, D. V. (1994–1995). Families of children with disabilities: Findings from a national sample of eighth-grade students. *Exceptionality, 5,* 72–81.

Holburn, S., Jacobson, J. W., Schwartz, A. A., Flory, M. J., & Vietze, P. M. (2004). The Willowbrook Futures project: A longitudinal analysis of person-centered planning. *American Journal on Mental Retardation, 109,* 63–76.

Horner, R. H., Vaughn, B. J., Day, H. M., & Ard, W. R., Jr. (1996). The relationship between setting events and problem behavior. In L. K. Koegel, R. L. Koegel, & G. Dunlap (Eds.), *Positive behavioral support: Including people with difficult behavior in the community* (pp. 81–98). Baltimore: Brookes.

Hubbard, D. D., & Adams, J. (2002). Best practices in facilitating meaningful family involvement in educational decision making. In A. Thomas & J. Grimes (Eds.), *Best practices in school psychology IV* (pp. 377–387). Bethesda, MD: National Association of School Psychologists.

Individuals with Disabilities Education Act (IDEA) (1997), 20 U.S.C. [subsections] 1400 et seq. (1999); 34 C.F.R. [subsections] 300.1 et seq. (1999); 64 Fed Reg. 12,406-12,672 (1999).

Jones, T. M., Garlow, J. A., Turnbull, H. R., III, & Barber, P. A. (1996). Family empowerment in a family support program. In G. H. S. Singer, L. E. Powers, & A. L. Olson (Eds.), *Redefining family support: Innovations in public-private partnerships* (pp. 87–112). Baltimore: Brookes.

Kincaid, D., & Fox, L. (2002). Person-centered planning and positive behavior support. In S. Holburn &

P. Vietze (Eds.), *Research and practice in person centered planning* (pp. 29–50). Baltimore: Brookes.

Lillie, T., & Vakil, S. (2002). Transitions in early childhood for students with disabilities: Law and best practice. *Early Childhood Education Journal, 30,* 53–58.

Lyle-O'Brien, C., O'Brien, J., & Mount, B. (1997). Person-centered planning has arrived ... or has it? *Mental Retardation, 35,* 480–484.

Meyer, D. J. (1993). Lessons learned: Cognitive coping of overlooked family members. In A. P. Turnbull, J. M. Patterson, S. K. Behr, D. L. Murphy, J. G. Marquis, & M. J. Blue-Banning (Eds.), *Cognitive coping, families, and disability* (pp. 81–92). Baltimore: Brookes.

Meyer, D. J., & Vadasy, P. F. (1994). *Sibshops: Implementing workshops for siblings of children with special needs.* Baltimore: Brookes.

Minnes, P. M. (1988). Family stress associated with a developmentally handicapped child. *International Review of Research in Mental Retardation, 15,* 195–226.

Minuchin, S. (1974). *Families and family therapy.* Cambridge, MA: Harvard University Press.

Mount, B., & Zwernik, K. (1988). *It's never too early; it's never too late* (Publication No. 421–88–109). St. Paul, MN: Metropolitan Council.

National Association of School Psychologists. (2002a). Principles for professional ethics. In A. Thomas & J. Grimes (Eds.), *Best practices in school psychology IV* (pp. 1615–1636). Bethesda, MD: National Association of School Psychologists.

National Association of School Psychologists. (2002b). Standards for the provision of school psychological services. In A. Thomas & J. Grimes (Eds.), *Best practices in school psychology IV* (pp. 1637–1646). Bethesda, MD: National Association of School Psychologists.

O'Brien, J., Mount, B., & Lyle-O'Brien, C. (1990). *The personal profile.* Lithonia, GA: Responsive Systems Associates.

O'Neill, R. E., Horner, R. H., Albin, R. W., Sprague, J. R., Storey, K., & Newton, J. S. (1997). *Functional assessment and program development for problem behavior: A practical handbook* (2nd ed.). Pacific Grove, CA: Brooks/Cole.

Park, J., Turnbull, A. P., & Park, H. (2001). Quality of partnerships in service provision for Korean American parents of children with disabilities: A qualitative inquiry. *Journal of the Association for Persons with Severe Handicaps, 26,* 158–170.

Pearpoint, J., Forest, M., & O'Brien, J. (1996). MAPS, Circles of Friends, and PATH: Powerful tools to help build caring communities. In S. Stainback & W. Stainback (Eds.), *Inclusion: A guide for educators* (pp. 67–86). Baltimore: Brookes.

Rosenkoetter, S. E., Hains, A. H., & Fowler, S. A. (1994). *Bridging early services for children with special needs and their families: A practical guide for transition planning.* Baltimore: Brookes.

Rounds, K. A., Weil, M., & Bishop, K. K. (1994). Practice with culturally diverse families of young children with disabilities. *Families in Society: The Journal of Contemporary Human Service, 75*(4), 3–15.

Schwartz, I. S., & Rodriguez, P. B. (2001). A few issues to consider: The who, what, and where of family support. *Journal of Early Intervention, 24,* 19–21.

Scorgie, K., & Sobsey, D. (2000). Transformational outcomes associated with parenting children who have disabilities. *Mental Retardation, 38,* 195–206.

Scorgie, K., Wilgosh, L., & McDonald, L. (1998). Stress and coping in families of children with disabilities: An examination of recent literature. *Developmental Disabilities Bulletin, 26,* 22–42.

Seligman, M., & Darling, R. B. (1997). *Ordinary families, special children: A systems approach to childhood disability* (2nd ed.). New York: Guilford Press.

Siegal, B., & Silverstein, S. (1994). *What about me? Growing up with a developmentally disabled sibling.* New York: Plenum.

Stoneman, Z. (1998). Research on siblings of children with mental retardation: Contributions of developmental theory and etiology. In J. A. Burack, R. M. Hodapp, & E. Zigler (Eds.), *Handbook of mental retardation and development* (pp. 669–692). Cambridge, UK: Cambridge University Press.

Sugai, G., Horner, R. H., Dunlap, G., Hieneman, M., Lewis, T. J., Nelson, C. M., et al. (2000). Applying positive behavior support and functional behavioral assessment in schools. *Journal of Positive Behavior Interventions, 2,* 131–143.

Turnbull, A. P., Turbiville, V., & Turnbull, H. R. (2000). Evolution of family-professional partnerships: Collective empowerment as the model for the early twenty-first century. In J. P. Shonkoff & S. J. Meisels (Eds.), *Handbook of early childhood intervention* (2nd ed., pp. 630–650). New York: Cambridge University Press.

Turnbull, A. P., & Turnbull, H. R., III (1996). Group action planning as a strategy for providing comprehensive family support. In L. K. Koegel, R. L. Koegel, & G. Dunlap (Eds.), *Positive behavioral support: Including people with difficult behavior in the community* (pp. 99–120). Baltimore: Brookes.

Turnbull, A. P., & Turnbull, H. R., III (2001). *Families, professionals, and exceptionality: Collaborating for empowerment* (4th ed.). Columbus, OH: Merrill/Prentice Hall.

Turnbull, A. P., Turnbull, H. R., Shank, M., & Leal, D. (1995). *Exceptional lives: Special education in today's schools.* Englewood Cliffs, NJ: Merrill.

Upshur, C. C. (1991). Families and the community service maze. In M. Seligman (Ed.), *The family with a handicapped child* (pp. 91–118). Needham Heights, MA: Allyn & Bacon.

U.S. Department of Education. (2002). *To assure the appropriate public education of all children with disabilities: Twenty-fourth annual report to Congress on the implementation of the Individuals with Disabilities Education Act.* Washington, DC: Author.

Vaughn, B. J., Dunlap, G., Fox, L., Clarke, S., & Bucy, M. (1997). Parent-professional partnership in behavioral support: A case study of community-based intervention. *Journal of the Association for Persons with Severe Handicaps, 22,* 185–197.

Webster-Stratton, C., & Hammond, M. (1997). Treating children with early onset conduct problems: A comparison of child and parent training interventions. *Journal of Consulting and Clinical Psychology, 65,* 93–109.

Webster-Stratton, C., & Taylor, T. (2001). Nipping early risk factors in the bud: Preventing substance abuse, delinquency, and violence in adolescence through interventions targeted at young children (0–8 years). *Prevention Science, 2,* 165–192.

Wehmeyer, M. L. (1994). Perceptions of self-determination and psychological empowerment of adolescents with mental retardation. *Education and Training in Mental Retardation and Developmental Disabilities, 29,* 9–21.

Wehmeyer, M. L. (1998). Self-determination and individuals with significant disabilities: Examining meanings and misinterpretations. *Journal of the Association for Persons with Severe Handicaps, 23,* 5–16.

West, T. E., Fetzer, P. M., Graham, C. M., & Keller, J. (2000). Driving the system through young adult involvement and leadership. In H. B. Clark & M. Davis (Eds.), *Transition to adulthood: A resource for assisting young people with emotional or behavioral difficulties.* Baltimore: Brookes.

Westling, D., & Fox, L. (2004). *Teaching students with severe disabilities* (3rd ed.). Columbus, OH: Merrill.

# 53

# Adolescent Pregnancy and Parenting

**Karen Callan Stoiber**
**Heather McIntyre**
*University of Wisconsin–Milwaukee*

## BACKGROUND AND DEVELOPMENT

At a national level, many important improvements have been achieved in the incidence of adolescent pregnancy and in the quality of prevention programs and resources since the last review of this topic in *Children's Needs II* (Stoiber, 1997). In general, adolescent pregnancy rates, birth rates, and abortion rates have been steadily declining over the past decade, and evaluation research in this field has advanced (Kirby, 2002a). Recent findings also indicate that fewer teens 15 to 17 years of age are sexually active; approximately 3 in 10 teens within this age group reported having sex in 2002, compared with 4 in 10 in 1995 (Alan Guttmacher Institute [AGI], 2004). Such trends are heartening for people who work with youth and who are dedicated to improving outcomes for students and their families.

Despite these positive indications, the United States continues to have the highest adolescent pregnancy rate among industrialized countries—twice as high as in England, Wales, or Canada and nine times as high as in the Netherlands or Japan. Approximately 860,000 adolescents become pregnant each year, and nearly half of those become adolescent mothers (AGI, 2004). Four out of 10 American adolescent women become pregnant before the age of 20 (Population Resource Center [PRC], 2004). Also, the number of adolescents initiating sexual activity at younger ages (15 years and under) has risen, and more youth report being sexually active by late adolescence than in previous decades (AGI).

Adolescent pregnancy and parenting thus continues to constitute one of the major challenges to American youth and society. Recent reports by the Centers for Disease Control and Prevention (CDC, 2002, 2003) and other agencies provide a compendium of staggering statistics documenting that too-early sexual activity and pregnancy remain an endemic public health and traumatic social health issue for the United States. For example, data provided by the Population Resource Center (PRC) show that the number of girls ages 15 to 19 in the United States is expected to increase by 2.2 million between 1995 and 2010. If the rate of adolescent pregnancy remains the same, the number of adolescent pregnancies and births will increase by 26%. Furthermore, although the adolescent pregnancy rate in the United States is the lowest since 1975, few changes have occurred in the types and extent of negative outcomes associated with this phenomenon (e.g., school dropout, impoverished living conditions, and poor quality of parenting).

An examination of adolescent sexual patterns and pregnancy rates indicates that younger and older adolescents differ in experiences and in the basis for their behavior. Twelfth-grade students (47.9%) are more likely to engage in sexual intercourse than ninth-grade students (29.7%; Grunbaum et al., 2001). Coercion is often involved for younger females who are sexually active. Approximately 75% of girls who engaged in intercourse before 14, and 60% of girls who had sex before 15, reported being forced to have sex against their will.

No single factor accounts for a youth's decision to engage in sexual activity; rather, layers of factors interact and build exponentially to create patterns of risk. An examination of adolescent pregnancy and parenting suggests two broad categories of contributing factors: dispositional characteristics and situational factors.

## Dispositional Characteristics

Dispositional factors include one's approach to thinking and behaving and are often conceptualized in the literature as personal risk factors (Jaffee, Caspi, Moffitt, Belsky, & Silva, 2001; Stoiber & Good, 1998). Adolescents, in general, are more prone to risk-taking behaviors when compared with adults, as they demonstrate less developed decision-making competence and reflective-thinking dispositions. Adolescents who become pregnant differ not only from adults in decision making, cognitions, and attitudes but also differ from their age peers (Coley & Chase-Linsdale, 1998). Furthermore, youth who partake in several risk-taking behaviors, including alcohol abuse, violence, and delinquency behavior, are more likely to follow a developmental pathway toward early sexual activity and adolescent pregnancy (Kirby, 2002a). Approximately 26% of sexually active teens reported alcohol or drug use, and 42% reported not using a condom during their last episode of sexual intercourse (Grunbaum et al., 2001). Unfortunately, risk-taking adolescents are prone to alcohol and drug use throughout pregnancy, as they often fail to recognize the potential detrimental outcomes for their unborn offspring.

Among the various dispositions associated with adolescent pregnancy, the cognitive profiles and attitudes of pregnant adolescents differ from those who do not engage in sex as teens (Jaffee et al., 2001). More specifically, youth who engage in early sexual activity frequently have unrealistic expectations regarding the outcomes and consequences of too-early pregnancy, an external locus of control, and lower self-efficacy (Young, Martin, Young, & Ting, 2001). These students also tend to show negative attitudes toward school and low achievement motivation. In contrast, adolescent girls who are least likely to become pregnant hold strong academic aspirations, realistic career goals, and sound decision-making competencies (Kirby, 2002a). Developing a positive school identity and having positive relationships with school staff also appear to serve as mediators, which in turn, motivate youth to avoid risky sexual behavior (Kirby).

## Situational Risk Factors

Situational risk factors are those related to educational, family, or economic conditions that may influence whether an adolescent will become sexually active, and ultimately, the likelihood of teen pregnancy. Situational factors are often conceptualized as ecologically based, with poverty and limited educational attainment considered as the two major underlying situational factors linked to adolescent childbearing (Santelli et al., 2004). Culture or ethnicity, family, and peers also are considered to influence adolescent pregnancy and parenting (Corcoran, Franklin, & Bennett, 2000). The role of poverty as one of the most powerful, if not most potent, factor associated with too-early pregnancy and birth is supported by the fact that nearly 85% of all teenage pregnancies occur among youth living in low-income families (PRC, 2004). Females who become pregnant during their teenage years often live in poor families and communities and are much more likely to remain poor throughout their adult lives (Jaffee et al., 2001). Unfortunately, the cycle of poverty is often perpetuated by intergenerational teenage childbearing.

Adolescent mothers, in general, tend to have lower cognitive and reading abilities as well as lower academic goals, levels of achievement, and formal schooling (Jaffee et al., 2001). The role of educational attainment is a pervasive factor in that adolescent pregnancy rates are disproportionately higher in schools having high dropout rates and in families having parents with lower educational levels. Students who become pregnant are at greater risk not only of school failure, but also of perpetuating a financially disadvantaged life because of the increased likelihood of being stuck in low-status and low-paying employment. An important advance, however, has been recent research that confirms the role of early intervention programs, and in particular early literacy support, in reducing adolescent pregnancy (Campbell, Ramey, Pungello, Sparling, & Miller-Johnson, 2002).

Race and ethnicity also emerge as important situational factors related to adolescent pregnancy rates. Recent statistics suggest that among youth 15 to 19 years of age, African American females are reported to have the highest pregnancy rate (153 per 1,000), followed by Hispanic (138 per 1,000) and White teenagers (71 per 1,000; AGI, 2004). Thus, despite recent declines in the overall number of teen pregnancies, particularly among African American youth, young women of color continue to be disproportionately affected by adolescent pregnancy. In interpreting these statistics, one should consider a probable link between race and socioeconomic status, as ethnic minorities are overrepresented at lower socioeconomic levels (Corcoran et al., 2000).

Several researchers have begun to use a sociocultural paradigm that emphasizes not only the role of race and ethnicity, but also the importance of family structure and family dynamics for understanding early motherhood among ethnic minorities (Stoiber, Ribar, & Waas, 2004). In particular, family dysfunction emerges as an important contextual risk factor for teenage pregnancy (PRC, 2004). Families with poor communication and relationship styles, physical or sexual abuse, lower levels of goal orientation, and coercive patterns of parent–child conflict are more likely to have teens who become pregnant (Jaffee et al., 2001). Although the constellation of family factors may differ somewhat among diverse cultures and family ethnicities, the parenting practices of relationship building, limit setting, parental monitoring, and conflict resolution are influential in reducing early sexual activity and pregnancy (Jaffee).

An adolescent's friends and peer group, in particular those of girls, strongly affect sexual behavior and dispositions for too-early pregnancy. Although the dynamics surrounding peer influence are complex, researchers are beginning to better understand the role of social norms, expectations, attitudes, and behaviors in an adolescent's sexual behavior. One longitudinal study of peer networks indicated that the behaviors of close friends influence whether or not female youth are sexually active. More specifically, girls who reported being virgins at the start of the study were more likely to engage in sexual intercourse if they had sexually experienced friends (see Wallander, Eggert, & Gilbert, 2004). Similarities in the sexual behaviors of peer groups have been documented, suggesting that risk-taking adolescents may connect with friends who reinforce their problem behavior; alternatively, positive peers seem to provide powerful motivation to resist engaging in sexual behavior.

### Sexual Behaviors of Males and Adolescent Fatherhood

Male students (49%) are more likely than female students (43%) to be sexually active (CDC, 2002) and to have used alcohol or drugs at last intercourse (30% vs. 18%). In addition, a significantly greater percentage of males than females reported engaging in early sexual activity before the age of 13 (9.3% vs. 4.5%) and to have had more than four sex partners (17.2% vs. 11.4%; Grunbaum et al., 2001). Sexual experience varies across races and ethnicities; of male high school students, 69% of African American, 53% of Hispanic, and 41% of non-Hispanic White reported having had sex. There is considerable fluctuation in 15- to 19-year-old males' reports of having sex during a 12-month period; for example, 10% said they did not have sex, and 23% reported having sex 50 or more times. In addition to adolescent males engaging in sex earlier and more frequently than females, their attitudes are of concern. Half of males 12–19 years of age agreed that teen boys often receive the message that teenage sex and pregnancy are not a big deal (CDC), and 40% reported the belief that "getting a girl pregnant will make you feel like a real man" (National Campaign to Prevent Teen Pregnancy [NCPTP], 2003, p. 4).

One interesting finding showed that adolescent males who father children with teenage girls tend to have similar problems as their female counterparts. Teen fathers are more likely to suffer from emotional, psychological, behavioral, and academic difficulties than their peers who delay childbearing, and they are twice as likely to be delinquent. They also are more likely to continue intergenerational teenage parenting (Coley & Chase-Lindale, 1998). These males tend to have limited educational attainment, be poor, and live in unsafe communities. Furthermore, low income and poor academic achievement appear to be predictive of teenage fatherhood (Fagot, Pears, Capaldi, Crosby, & Leve, 1998).

## PROBLEMS AND IMPLICATIONS

The deleterious effects of adolescent pregnancy are even more salient when one considers the increased likelihood of several serious, and often irreversible, developmental and health consequences. When compared with their same-age peers, pregnant teens are more likely to (a) drop out of high school; (b) live in poverty and rely on public welfare; (c) experience increased health and mental health problems, including depression, anxiety, and potentially fatal sexually transmitted diseases (STDs); (d) experience abortion or adoption; and (e) have offspring with cognitive and behavioral problems (Annie E. Casey Foundation, 1998).

### Economic Ramifications

Adolescent pregnancy has serious economic consequences because it places substantial financial burdens on both the young parent and society. Nearly 70% of adolescent mothers and their children live in poverty; only 2% of adolescent mothers eventually complete college (U.S. Census Bureau, 2000). Single adolescent mothers are more likely to live in unsafe neighborhoods and are less likely to have health insurance for themselves and their children. Adolescent fathers typically endure less economic adversity than single mothers. The cost of adolescent parenthood to taxpayers increases each year, with medical costs rising exponentially. Estimates suggest more than 50% of the federal budget for welfare aid goes to families begun by women who were adolescents when they first gave birth.

## Health and Mental Health Outcomes

One of the most serious consequences of early sexual activity is increased risk of exposure to sexually transmitted diseases (STDs). In 2000 approximately 19 million new cases of STDs were reported, of which 9 million (48%) occurred in persons 15 to 24 years of age (Weinstock, Berman, & Cates, 2004). Teen pregnancy also contributes to morbidity and overall health consequences for adolescents, with younger teens and those not receiving proper prenatal care, in particular, being at increased risk for premature delivery and childbirth complications (Kellogg, Hoffman, & Taylor, 1999).

Pregnant and parenting adolescents also are more likely to suffer from psychological and mental health problems than those who do not have children during their teenage years. For example, Stoiber, Anderson, and Schowalter (1998) found that more than 75% of pregnant or parenting teens harbored negative emotions during their pregnancy. Many resented the unexpected demands of parenting and reported difficulties meeting their child's developmental needs. Also, young mothers are more prone to depression and uncontrolled moods and provide less emotional support for their babies than older mothers (Coley & Chase-Lindale, 1998). More research is needed, however, to disentangle the relation between poverty and parental characteristics, as financial strain is linked to depressive symptoms and poor parenting quality.

## Children of Adolescent Mothers

Not surprisingly, grim child outcomes are associated with adolescent parenthood because these children often have low birth weight; experience health, coping, and developmental problems; and are more likely to be poor, abused, and/or neglected (Jaffee et al., 2001). Difficulties are most evident with adolescent mothers who experienced heightened levels of distress; these children showed less competent coping behaviors, such as poorer self-regulation, greater irritability, poorer social engagement and adaptation to situations, and sad or flat affect (Stoiber & Anderson, 1996). When compared with children born to older mothers, these offspring showed a variety of cognitive, language, and academic difficulties (e.g., Stoiber & Anderson), as well as behavioral difficulties, particularly low impulse control, and heightened aggression (Jaffee et al.). These children also are more likely to experience paternal abuse or have no contact with their biological father, live in poverty, experience deviant mother–child interactions, and have more siblings (Jaffee et al.). Children of adolescent mothers also are prone to risky behaviors such as substance abuse, sexual activity, criminal activity, and delinquency (Miller, Bayley, Christensen, Leavitt, & Coyl, 2003), with these problem behaviors often leading to increased rates of incarceration during adolescence (Jaffee et al.).

Not all children born to adolescent mothers display developmental problems. Responsive parenting appears to protect children from potential risks associated with too-early parenting (Stoiber & Anderson, 1996). The most successful children of adolescents have mothers who are employed, achieve higher education levels than the average teen mother, have fewer children, live in safer neighborhoods, and reside with a male partner. Rather than regarding all children of adolescent mothers as uniformly at risk for negative developmental outcomes, the ecological risk and resiliency model stresses individual differences in coping and adjustment. Adolescent parents who have support systems or access to parenting resources are more likely to engage in positive parenting practices.

# ALTERNATIVE ACTIONS FOR PREVENTION

In view of the potentially detrimental and often life-altering consequences of early sexual activity and adolescent pregnancy, the need for explicit prevention efforts is clear. Despite this obvious need, the complexities surrounding adolescent pregnancy have made it difficult to determine the most efficient and effective preventive solutions.

Adolescent pregnancy can best be conceptualized as a socially and psychologically complex problem that is influenced by an interrelated set of dispositional and situational factors (Santelli et al., 2004). Given this context, no single prevention strategy can or should be expected to resolve it. Thus, advocates of single-prong approaches are cautioned to be modest in their expectations of producing successful outcomes, as even those programs thought to be comprehensive have often actually achieved only modest results (Manlove, Franzetta, McKinney, Romano-Papillo, & Terry-Humen, 2004). Prevention of too-early pregnancy likely requires well-designed, specific, and directed activities (or a set of related strategies) implemented by a facilitator who relates in a positive and caring manner with those adolescents targeted in the prevention program.

Sexuality education is common in schools and is generally supported by the public. For example, survey results based on a nationally representative group of adolescents and adults highlight public support for prevention programs and for access to contraception for those students who are having sex (Albert, 2004). Specifically, the survey sponsored by National Campaign to Prevent Teen Pregnancy (NCPTP) found support for the following beliefs: (a) young people should receive more information about abstinence and contraception (endorsed by 81% of adolescents and 75% adults; only 1% of adults and 2% of teens believed adolescents are getting enough information about these two topics); (b) those students who are sexually active wish they had postponed having sex (endorsed by 66% of all sexually experienced teens); and (c) high school students should resist being sexually active (69% of surveyed teens stated that it's not okay for high school students to have sexual intercourse, including 59% of older teens 15–19 years of age).

As the most prominent public institution having the potential to reduce teen pregnancy rates, schools play a critical preventive role. However, schools face difficult choices in determining the best way to systematically address the issues surrounding adolescent sexual development and activity. Perhaps no area of prevention is more hotly debated than adolescent pregnancy prevention, especially when it is considered within the context of school-based approaches. The prevention approach implemented in a school should obviously reflect the values and priorities of the surrounding community and the needs of the adolescents.

Before reviewing the different types of adolescent pregnancy prevention programs, it is important to address the standards of evidence used to evaluate them. For a prevention program to have the desired characteristic of scientific soundness (i.e., demonstrates that it produces intended outcomes or works), it should have distinct process and outcome goals as well as corresponding procedures or steps for implementation (Stoiber & Kratochwill, 2002). Given the recent movement toward evidence-based interventions and practices (Stoiber & Kratochwill, 2000; Stoiber & Waas, 2002), decisions about program effectiveness should be based on specified criteria to establish the level of evidence needed to support a program. This is exactly what the NCPTP's Effective Programs and Research Task Force, as well as other empirical reviews of studies conducted by the NCPTP, have done (see, e.g., Solomon & Card, 2004).

Studies to evaluate whether a program or set of prevention strategies is effective should be evidence based and meet the following research criteria: (a) used experimental or quasi-experimental evaluation design; (b) collected follow-up data subsequent to program implementation; (c) employed appropriate statistical methods; (d) had a sufficient sample size to measure effects; and (e) showed significant positive effects on appropriate outcomes, such as actual sexual behaviors and refusal or negotiation skills (Kirby 2001, 2002b; Manlove, Romano-Papillo, & Ikramullah, 2004). However, it is often difficult for programs for preventing teen pregnancy to achieve statistically significant changes in health outcomes such as pregnancy, birth, or HIV/STD rates given the limited period of follow-up and small sample sizes that typically characterize prevention studies (Kirby, 2001). In addition, such health outcomes may be underreported or undetected. Nonetheless, considerable information on the features and components of the most effective prevention programs for altering early sexual behaviors has become available through recent systematic reviews of prevention programs.

Prevention programs can be categorized into three types: (a) abstinence-only and abstinence education approaches; (b) resistance-skills and abstinence-plus approaches; and (c) comprehensive, multicomponent programs.

## Abstinence-Only and Abstinence Education Programs

Not surprisingly, most teen pregnancy prevention programs focus on prevention of early sexual behavior. The main goal of abstinence programs is to deter or reduce early initiation of sexual intercourse and, subsequently, pregnancy among teenagers. These didactic or curricula-based programs often fall into two general types of programming: (1) abstinence-only (till marriage) and (2) abstinence education programs.

The primary intent of abstinence-only programs is straightforward—to delay the initiation of adolescent sexual activity. Virginity pledge programs (students take a pledge to be abstinent) and programs advocating postponing sexual involvement are two examples of abstinence-only approaches. These programs typically target values and provide alternative life options to deter teens from engaging in sexual behavior, essentially focusing on abstinence as the only healthy choice for teenagers (Kirby, 2001).

Most of the outcome data on abstinence-only programs have limited empirical significance because of poor research design characteristics (i.e., post-test only, nonrandom assignment of participants or no control group, poor measurement procedures, or faulty data analyses) and a focus on only short-term effects (Hoyt & Broom, 2002). As such, most abstinence-only programs fail to meet the evaluation criteria and thus are not considered evidence based or effective. Following his comprehensive review, Kirby (2002b) concluded that "there do not currently exist any abstinence-only programs with strong evidence that they either delay sex or reduce teen pregnancy" (p. 6). However, Kirby goes on to clarify that this conclusion does not mean that abstinence-only programs are ineffective or that they are effective. Rather, more well-designed research must occur to pinpoint whether abstinence-only programs delay the initiation of sex or reduce adolescent pregnancy.

Despite the lack of empirical support regarding the effectiveness of abstinence-only programs, they are among those prevention programs that receive the greatest level of federal funding (AGI, 2004). For example, U.S. budget funding for abstinence-only programs almost doubled, going from $140 million in 2004 to $270 million in 2005.

## Abstinence-Plus and Resistance Sex Education Programs

The conclusions for abstinence-only programs are in contrast to those found for abstinence-plus programs, which emphasize abstinence as the first and best choice for teens but also encourage teens to use contraceptives if they are sexually active. These programs attempt to increase adolescents' knowledge of sex, contraception, reproduction, and STDs, frequently by combining didactic and interactive components.

The need for incorporating contraceptive use in prevention programs is reflected in data compiled by CDC (2003): 42% of sexually active high school students did not use a condom the last time they had sex, and 14% of high school students have already had four or more sex partners. Providing access to contraceptives generally accompanies curricula-based sex education programs and is often cited as a key component of successful teen pregnancy prevention programs. Programs that provide knowledge about contraception, in addition to access, are among the most successful in reducing teen pregnancy (Manlove, Romano-Papillo et al., 2004). Providing access to contraceptives and reproductive health services for sexually active teenagers is viewed as beneficial, because once teens start having sex it becomes very difficult to stop or deter the behavior. Thus, providing access to condoms and contraceptives for sexually experienced adolescents will likely lead to more positive outcomes than providing information based solely on abstinence (Kirby, 2001). Also, successful prevention programs provide developmentally customized programs that target preteen and younger adolescents for abstinence-based programs before they become sexually active, and provide older, sexually active adolescents with access to contraceptives (Manlove, Franzetta et al., 2004).

Providing access to contraceptives, particularly in a school setting, often raises public concern; however, research indicates that distributing contraceptives to students does not increase the amount of sexual activity among students; rather, it leads to an increase in the degree to which sexually active students use contraception (AGI, 2004). In 2002 sexually active youth of all ages were more likely to be using contraceptives than in 1995. In addition, though 20% of the decline in teen pregnancy is the result of decreased sexual activity, 80% is the result of more effective contraceptive practices (AGI).

Some prevention programs attempt to simulate the experience of being a parent and provide role-playing experiences for teens. Baby Think it Over is one such program in which teen students must care for a 6 and ½-pound infant simulator over the course of several days. The simulator mimics specific care demands of an infant (i.e., feeding, diapering, and holding), which require response by the teen. Sensors within the simulator are sensitive to frequency, duration, and the physical nature of handling to determine whether the teen appropriately met the infant's needs (Hoyt & Broom, 2002). Results indicate that this program affects adolescents' perceptions of the responsibilities and demands required for parenting; however, no data are available on whether such simulation experiences reduce teen pregnancy and childbirth.

A recent empirical review of pregnancy reduction programs identified six sex and HIV education programs as meeting evidence-based evaluation criteria in reducing

**Table 1** *Common Characteristics of the Most Effective Sex Education Programs*

1. *Risky behavior focus:* Target reducing or stopping sexual behaviors that lead to unintended pregnancy or HIV/STD infection.
2. *Theoretical basis:* Incorporate components shown to influence other health-related behavior and that target specific sexual antecedents (e.g., social or peer influences).
3. *Clear message:* Communicate consistent messages about abstinence and contraceptive use. (This appears to be one of the most essential components distinguishing effective programs from ineffective ones.)
4. *Accurate information:* Provide factual information about the risks of early sexual activity as well as effective ways to avoid intercourse and to use contraception.
5. *Resistance activities:* Incorporate activities for resisting social pressures to have sex.
6. *Competency-based skills:* Introduce examples and practice through role-playing and other behavioral techniques to develop communication, negotiation, and refusal skills.
7. *Active participant involvement:* Use instructional methods designed to help participants personalize the information.
8. *Developmentally and culturally sensitive:* Employ behavioral goals, teaching strategies, and materials matched to students' age, sexual experience, and culture.
9. *Sufficient duration:* Implement over a sufficient period of time (i.e., more than one or two sessions occurring for a few hours).
10. *Effective instructors:* Select interventionists with appropriate training, who implement the program as intended, and who believe in the program's philosophy.

*Note:* adapted from Kirby, D. (2001). *Emerging answers: Research findings on programs to reduce teen pregnancy (Summary).* Washington, DC: National Campaign to Prevent Teen Pregnancy; and Kirby, D. (2002). Antecedents of adolescent initiation of sex, contraceptive use, and pregnancy. *American Journal of Health Behavior,* 26, 473–485.

risky sexual behaviors in adolescents (see Solomon & Card, 2004). The curricula of the most effective sex and HIV education programs incorporate 10 common characteristics (Kirby, 2001, 2002a), with the absence of any one of these components reducing the likelihood of producing successful outcomes (see Table 1).

## Comprehensive and Multicomponent Prevention Programs

The contributive factors leading to adolescent pregnancy tend to be broad and complex, so multimethod strategies are helpful for responding to diverse individual risk conditions. Because of the dynamic interplay of risk factors associated with early initiation of sexual activity and teen pregnancy, it is difficult, if not impossible, to target all known antecedents of teen pregnancy. Many prevention programs thus tend to focus solely on early risky sexual behavior in adolescents rather than address underlying and systemic problems (e.g., unrealistic goals, poor school motivation, or drug and alcohol use) associated with teen pregnancy (Kirby, 2001).

The most effective prevention programs appear to be comprehensive and incorporate multiple components that focus on increasing reproductive knowledge, improving social assertion and decision-making skills, promoting avoidance of risky behavior, and developing long-term goals and career options. Such prevention programs integrate a variety of services and target numerous antecedents of teen pregnancy. For example, Stoiber and Good (1999) reported significant outcomes on risk-taking attitudes, intentions, and behaviors for a comprehensive resiliency-centered program that targeted interrelated risk-taking behavior, including risky sex and drug and alcohol use, among students of culturally diverse urban middle schools. The resiliency-centered program focused explicitly on fostering adolescent responsible decision-making and future planning as well as on developing stronger connections between urban students and their school. The 20-week classroom-based curricula included having students (a) participate in classroom activities to help them develop realistic short-term plans for improving academic performance as well as attainable long-term career and other future plans; (b) make plans for spending time with other peers who support them in their goals; and (c) learn ways to evaluate their daily choices and to see the benefits of resisting drugs, alcohol, and sexual behavior through the use of media, interactive discussions, and mentoring.

In general, the most effective school-based prevention programs aimed at reducing sexually risky behavior include three main components (see Table 2): (a) group-based psychoeducational training; (b) decision-making and communication skills; and (c) behavioral skills training (Moore, McGlinchey, & Carr, 2002). Psychoeducational-type programs typically demonstrate gains with only females regarding knowledge about safe and risky sex (but with little effect shown on attitudes, intentions, or behaviors) and demonstrate limited or no effect for males. Programs incorporating communication and decision-making skills and behavioral resistance skills demonstrate gains in the domains of knowledge,

**Table 2** *Main Components of Prevention Programs for Reducing Sexually Risky Behavior*

| Component | Focus |
|---|---|
| Psychoeducational Training | Facts about teenage pregnancy and contraception. |
| | Class discussions and information sharing on safe sex and the effects of unwanted pregnancy. |
| | Facts about risk factors for teenage pregnancy, STD infection, and HIV infection. |
| Decision-Making and Communication | Assertiveness training and refusal skills training to manage peer pressure. |
| | Interpersonal skills for communicating (sharing opinions, listening, asserting beliefs) with parents and peers. |
| | Goal setting for a successful future, along with problem-solving plans to resist sexually risky situations. |
| Behavior Skills Training | Instruction and modeling of resistive behaviors with corrective feedback to rehearse, personalize, and refine skills for avoiding sexually risky situations. |
| | Anticipation and design of behavioral strategies for resisting peer pressure for sexual risk taking. |
| | Enactment of strategies to resist situations involving drug and alcohol use, as it increases likelihood of sexual risk taking. |
| | Purchase and use of condoms effectively. |

*Note:* adapted from Moore, N., McGlinchey, A., & Carr, A. (2002). Prevention of teenage pregnancy, STDs, and HIV infection. In A. Carr (Ed.), *Prevention: What works with children and adolescents* (pp. 287–313). New York: Taylor and Francis Inc.

attitudes, intentions, and behaviors (Moore et al.). Thus, prevention programs that integrate psychoeducational approaches with communication, decision-making, and behavioral components appear to be the most effective for reducing sexual practices or increasing safe sexual practices.

Two specific types of multicomponent programs have emerged as being evidence based: service learning approaches and sex education plus youth development approaches. The Teen Outreach Program (TOP; Allen & Philliber, 2001) is an example of a school-based service learning program for students in grades 9 through 12. The goals of TOP are to prevent high-risk behaviors such as school failure and adolescent pregnancy and to help students make educated decisions and develop social competence. The program uses structured, service-oriented activities in combination with didactic discussions related to aspects of the teen's future, such as life, career, and relationship choices. TOP incorporates three components: supervised volunteering, classroom-based discussions pertaining to volunteer experiences, and classroom activities connected to positive adolescent development.

During the intervention study, students met at least once a week across the academic year and volunteered for a minimum of 20 supervised hours, with the average student recording 35 hours. The overriding message to students who participated was that adolescents can and do make important contributions to society. When sex and related issues were discussed, abstinence was emphasized along with contraception.

Evaluations indicated that students randomly assigned to the TOP condition (342 students), when compared with the control group (352 students), were less likely to experience or cause a pregnancy, be suspended from school, or fail a course. Furthermore, adolescents in the control group experienced twice as many pregnancies (9.8% vs. 4.2%). An important finding of the evaluation was that data on TOP suggested similar positive outcomes for all racial and ethnic groups, socioeconomic status groups, household compositions, and grade levels (after controlling for demographic characteristics, grade level, and baseline problem behaviors). Better outcomes in altering behaviors occurred for female students compared with males. Non-experimental analyses found that the number of hours a student volunteered appeared to be negatively associated with the likelihood of having or causing a pregnancy and the likelihood of being suspended from school. Overall, TOP showed strong evidence of success (Solomon & Card, 2004), and similar programs are likely to be an important addition in preventing teen pregnancy.

The Children's Aid Society (CAS)–Carrera Program (Philliber, Kaye, Herrling, & West, 2002) is another example of a successful multicomponent program that served low-income, high-risk African American and Hispanic youth 13 to 15 years of age. It is based on a youth developmental approach and aims to reduce underlying risk and psychological factors associated with teen pregnancy (e.g., poverty, school failure, and inadequate health care). CAS–Carrera functions as an after-school and summer program, incorporating mentoring and ongoing counseling, health care, academic assistance, career counseling, crisis intervention, and access to performing arts and sports activities. This is an intensive program provided on a year-round basis, 5 to 6 days per week, until the student completes high school (at a cost of $4,000 per teen each year). The primary objective of the program is to assist youth in achieving productive goals by helping participants think about and plan carefully for their futures (including abstaining from sex or using contraception consistently as a key component of successful planning). CAS–Carrera aims to offer a parallel family structure for at-risk teens, and for many participants the program becomes their primary source of support.

Overall, the CAS–Carrera program was found to be effective in postponing first sex and to produce more positive outcomes for females than for males. At the end of the third year of program implementation, females in CAS–Carrera, compared with control group females, were significantly less likely to have sex (54% vs. 66%), less likely to become pregnant (10% vs. 22%), almost twice as likely to use a condom and a hormonal method of contraception (36% vs. 20%), and more likely to receive appropriate health care (74% vs. 61%). It should be noted that 26% of CAS–Carrera participants (15% of females and 38% of males) were already sexually experienced at baseline.

Table 3 presents a summary of several key understandings regarding what works to prevent and postpone teen sex. This information emerges from evaluations of successful programs (Kirby, 2001; Manlove, Franzetta et al., 2004; Manlove, Romano-Papillo et al., 2004).

## The Role of Parental Involvement

Most prevention and intervention programs fail to incorporate parental involvement, despite evidence that parents influence the sexual behavior of teens (Kirby, 2001), particularly risky sexual behavior. Data from a recent survey by the NCPTP (Albert, 2004) offered several critical understandings regarding parental influences, including the following:

- *Power of parental influence.* Teens reported that parents (37%) have a greater influence than friends (37% vs. 33%), the media (5%), or siblings (6%) on their decisions about sex. Parents, on the other hand, underestimate their influence (only 28% reported the belief that parents most influence their teen's decisions about sex) and overestimate the importance of other influences, including peers (47%) and the media (12%).
- *Parent–child dialogue about sex.* The majority of teens (87%) and adults (91%) agree that teens having more open, honest conversations with their parents would help delay sex and prevent adolescent pregnancy. However, nearly 4 in 10 teens (37%) indicated that they had not engaged in such conversations with their parents.
- *Support for parents.* Approximately 90% of parents of teens agreed that they should talk with their adolescents about sex but stated that they often don't know what to say, how to say it, or when to start the

**Table 3** *Summary of What Works in Preventing and Postponing Adolescent Sexual Behavior*

- Attempt to alter predispositions to risk-taking behaviors early and prior to the onset of adolescence and initiation of sexual intercourse. Once an adolescent has initiated sexual activity it becomes very difficult to deter or stop.
- Incorporate a combined focus on delaying sexual behavior and on consistent contraceptive use, as this seems to be among the most effective approaches in postponing the onset of sex, reducing the frequency of sex, and improving contraceptive use.
- Use longer-term programs, which show more lasting effects than those lasting shorter periods (e.g., less than 6 months). Booster sessions are an important addition to prevention programs.
- Combine education with active learning and behavioral skills training (e.g., social assertion, risk recognition, problem solving under peer pressure, practice purchasing condoms, and correct condom use).
- Promote practice of interpersonal and communication skills, including negotiation and refusal skills, through role-playing to effectively reduce risky sexual behavior.
- Employ outreach efforts through community-based programs to the most vulnerable of youth, such as homeless or runaway youth, juvenile offenders, and school dropouts.
- Address sexual activity within a comprehensive prevention model that recognizes the use of alcohol and drugs when many adolescents engage in sex.
- Encourage self-evaluation of potential dispositions, as adolescents usually make their decisions about sex in social situations, when decision making may be faulty, where time is limited, and when they are sexually aroused.

*Note:* Information adapted from Kirby, D. (2001). *Emerging answers: Research findings on programs to reduce teen pregnancy (Summary).* Washington, DC: National Campaign to Prevent Teen Pregnancy; Manlove, J., Franzetta, K., McKinney, K., Romano-Papillo, A., & Terry-Humen, E. (2004). *No time to waste: Programs to reduce teen pregnancy among middle school-aged youth.* Washington, DC: The National Campaign to Prevent Teen Pregnancy; and Manlove, J., Romano-Papillo, A. R., & Ikramullah, E. (2004). *Not yet: Programs to delay first sex among teens.* Washington, DC: The National Campaign to Prevent Teen Pregnancy.

conversations. Parents should initiate such conversations early (prior to or at the onset of adolescence) and do so on an ongoing basis so that both parent and child feel comfortable with the content and are not embarrassed to share their beliefs and experiences.

A recent review published by NCPTP (2004) further endorses the enormous importance of parents in influencing adolescent sexual activity, stating "the overall strength and closeness of parent/child relationships seems to be the best protection of all" (p. 1). More specifically, the NCPTP review concluded that parents who (a) communicate their values and expectations clearly, (b) express their concerns and love early and openly, and (c) exercise supervision raise children who are more likely to resist early sexual activity as well as other risky behaviors such as violence, substance and alcohol use, and school failure. Thus, although candid conversations about sex are essential, parents also should take active roles in supervising, monitoring, and engaging their adolescent children.

The effects of structured components for family involvement in prevention programs are less clear than the influential role parents play in mediating their teen's sexual decisions. In his review of effective programs, Kirby (2001) noted that including a parental component in sex and HIV prevention programs failed to produce significant changes in adolescents' reported sexual activity. Kirby's review, however, indicated that a parental component led to short-term increases in communication between teens and their parents. As prevention program developers and researchers better delineate appropriate methods and procedures for involving parents, benefits for a parental component will likely be documented.

## ALTERNATIVE ACTIONS FOR INTERVENTION

Prevention programs targeting teen pregnancy, as implemented to date, unfortunately have not achieved the desired effect of significantly reducing adolescent sexual activity and pregnancy rates. Hence, intervention programs are indicated, particularly for reducing repeat pregnancies among adolescent mothers and for improving parenting practices among adolescent parents (Coard, Nitz, & Felice, 2000).

### Intervention Programs for Reducing Repeat Pregnancies Among Teen Parents

Most prevention programs target first-time teen pregnancies (Kirby, 2001), despite data indicating the increased risk for repeat pregnancies among teenage parents. Adolescent parents have a 20% to 35% chance of becoming pregnant within 1 year of the birth of their first child (Coard et al., 2000; NCPTP, 2004). Several factors appear to contribute to subsequent births among adolescent mothers. First, younger teens and those who intentionally become pregnant are more likely to have a subsequent pregnancy during adolescence. Second, low levels of education attainment and of cognitive ability are associated with giving birth to a second child as a teen. Teens who experience second pregnancies further reduce their chances of marrying and of ever attaining economic self-sufficiency.

Intervention programs often focus on providing health and prenatal services for pregnant teens and their babies. Fewer intervention programs have targeted the psychological and social needs of parenting teens, despite the staggering number of adverse conditions and problems associated with adolescent parenting (Coard et al., 2000). Not only is there a paucity of intervention programs for adolescent parents, but most programs involved in rigorous evaluations have failed to produce significant results on intended outcomes (Klerman, 2004). For example, Klerman indicated in her review of 19 intervention programs that only 3 studies—two home visitation programs and one program in a medical setting—showed significant positive effects, based on randomized, controlled designs. No school-based programs showed documented, substantive, positive results.

The limited positive findings for intervention programs are due to, at least in part, the lack of school-based programs for adolescent parents and the difficulty in motivating, engaging, and securing adolescent mothers to regularly attend intervention programs. Unfortunately, adolescent mothers' high-stress circumstances often interfere with program involvement (Klerman, 2004). In addition, numerous interventions for pregnant or parenting teens have focused on less than optimal outcomes, such as helping the adolescent mother earn a GED when a high school diploma would lead to better employment opportunities and outcomes, or the interventions have not been carried out as intended. Table 4 summarizes components of successful programs for reducing or delaying repeat adolescent pregnancies.

**Table 4** *Summary of Features of Effective Interventions for Pregnant and Parenting Adolescents*

- Develop a positive, supportive, and sustained relationship with the pregnant or parenting adolescent. The strength of this relationship may be the most critical factor influencing positive outcomes.
- Start intervening early. Begin while the teenager is pregnant and continue the intervention until the child is at least 2 years old and the mother is 18 or older.
- Avoid relying on group forms of intervention, as adolescent mothers appear to require more intense, individualized treatment.
- Involve interventionists who have knowledge of and sensitivity toward family planning and domestic violence issues.
- Encourage adolescent mothers to live with their parents or other adults who can provide a stable and positive economic environment that allows them to stay in school. For new adolescent mothers who cannot live at home, assist them in finding a maternity group home that offers support and child care.
- Use approaches that are developmentally matched (treat 15-year-olds or those with cognitive disabilities differently than 19-year-olds) and culturally sensitive and that fit the characteristics of the targeted population.
- Provide ongoing, intensive support around issues of contraception and resistance toward repeat pregnancy.

*Note:* Information adapted from Kirby, D. (2001). *Emerging answers: Research findings on programs to reduce teen pregnancy (Summary).* Washington, DC: National Campaign to Prevent Teen Pregnancy; and Klerman, L. (2004). *Another chance: Preventing additional births to teen mothers.* Washington, DC: National Campaign to Prevent Teen Pregnancy.

## Parenting Programs for Teen Parents

School-based intervention programs for pregnant and parenting teens may include components such as individual counseling, parent education groups, social support groups, and groups that focus on the parent–child relationship (Stoiber et al., 2004). Whether the intervention is offered on an individual basis or through a therapeutic group for pregnant and parenting adolescents, the following topics should be addressed: (a) human development, reproduction, and body changes during pregnancy, including labor and delivery; (b) options related to pregnancy continuation and adoption; (c) nutrition; (d) negative effects of smoking, drinking, and drug use during pregnancy; and (e) family coping and relationship issues.

Schools should attempt to provide a range of services, including both school-based and school-linked intervention services, to accommodate the diverse needs and individual circumstances of pregnant and parenting adolescents. A common goal of interventions that focus on parenting practices is to ensure that teenagers learn and practice effective parenting strategies. In addition to providing support in handling the demands of parenting, these programs assist teens in achieving self-sufficiency. Teen parents require individualized support, guidance, and access to community and school-based resources.

They also benefit from job training for positions with higher wages, support to earn a high school diploma, financial aid for postsecondary education, and access to safe and affordable housing. Improving the teen mothers' environment and life options leads to better adjustment and outcomes both for them and their children (Jaffee et al., 2001).

Regardless of the form of interventions (e.g., individual vs. group, focus on career vs. focus on coping strategies), schools can be optimal sites for service delivery. School psychologists and other school personnel are especially well positioned for coordinating school-based and school-linked intervention programs for pregnant and parenting adolescents. For example, school professionals can function as an important resource for arranging and monitoring community services, such as medical follow-up, academic tutoring, and home visits from nursing staff specializing in adolescent parenthood. Collaboration between schools and community-based organizations as well as among school-based professionals will likely lead to better long-term pregnancy prevention and outcomes for parenting teens.

## SUMMARY

Despite declines in the rates of adolescent pregnancy and parenting, many adolescents remain at significant risk for early sex and parenting. In light of the serious consequences associated with having sex and being pregnant at a very young age, school-based prevention and intervention programs that successfully delay adolescent sex and pregnancy are critically needed. Although no program or component holds all the solutions, perhaps the most compelling indication stemming from the empirical literature is the powerful and often preventive role that relationships can play. First, strong parent–child relationships are influential in deterring an adolescent's engagement in early sexual activity. Second, an adolescent's peer relationships and friendships affect whether or not a teen becomes sexually active or uses contraceptives. Third, the quality of relationships that youth enjoy at school influences a student's decisions and aspirations, including decisions about abstinence and contraception use. Fourth, interventionists who establish caring student relationships produce more productive outcomes.

Although evaluation research has begun to provide some useful guidelines and strategies, further research is necessary to determine which types of programs work best for teens facing different types of life stressors and risk factors associated with early sexual activity, risky sexual behaviors, and teen pregnancy. Little is known regarding which strategies produce the best outcomes with different populations, such as different ethnicities or different family structures. As more information about what works in prevention and intervention programs becomes available, school professionals must use that knowledge to select and implement effective programs. Furthermore, they should engage in program evaluation procedures to examine the effects of the strategies and programs they use (Stoiber & Kratochwill, 2000, 2002). By incorporating evidence-based practices, school professionals will function as valuable resources in reducing adolescent pregnancy and in responding to the critical needs of at-risk adolescents.

## RECOMMENDED RESOURCES

### Books and Other Printed Material

Coley, R. L., & Chase-Lansdale, P. L. (1998). Adolescent pregnancy and parenthood: Recent evidence and future directions. *American Psychologist, 53,* 152–166.

This seminal article provides an overview of research on adolescent sexual activity, pregnancy, and parenting, with a primary focus on psychological antecedents and consequences. Parenting practices of adolescents, as well as the extent of involvement and impact of fathers and grandmothers, is discussed. Components of effective intervention and prevention programming are reviewed. Finally, policy implications with a focus on welfare reform of the social and financial burdens imposed by adolescent pregnancy and parenthood are discussed.

Kirby, D. (2002). Antecedents of adolescent initiation of sex, contraceptive use, and pregnancy. *American Journal of Health Behavior, 26,* 473–485.

This article was adapted from Kirby's (2001) *Emerging Answers: Research Findings on Programs to Reduce Teen Pregnancy,* published by the National Campaign to Prevent Teen Pregnancy. The primary focus of the article was to review antecedents associated with adolescent initiation of sex, contraceptive use, and pregnancy. Findings indicate the need to address multiple correlates of teen pregnancy, both sexual and nonsexual.

Solomon, J., & Card, J. J. (2004). *Making the list: Understanding, selecting, and replicating effective teen pregnancy prevention programs.* Washington, DC: National Campaign to Prevent Teen Pregnancy.

*Making the List* is a publication of the National Campaign's Putting What Works to Work (PWWTW) project, funded by the Centers for Disease Control and Prevention (CDC). The PWWTW project aims to publish and disseminate the latest research on teen pregnancy in an easy-to-understand language for parents, practitioners, and policy makers. This publication is an essential resource for understanding the use of evidence-based criteria in selecting effective teen pregnancy prevention programs and for examining components and outcomes of various programs for preventing teen pregnancy.

## Websites

*http://www.guttmacher.org*

Visit the website of the Alan Guttmacher Institute to retrieve updated information on teenage pregnancy and parenting statistics, trends, implications, and policies. It also contains links to other useful websites on adolescent childbearing and pregnancy prevention.

*http://www.teenpregnancy.org*

This website contains a variety of resources from the National Campaign to Prevent Teen Pregnancy, including fact sheets on the incidence of sexual activity, key answers to common questions about teen sexuality and pregnancy prevention, survey results and information on sexual attitudes among adults and youth, and empirical reports of effective teen pregnancy and STD/HIV prevention programs stemming from the Putting What Works to Work (PWWTW) project.

## REFERENCES


Alan Guttmacher Institute. (2004). *U.S. teenage pregnancy statistics: Overall trends, trends by race and ethnicity and state-by-state information.* New York: Author.

Albert, B. (2004). *With one voice 2004: America's adults and teens sound off about teen pregnancy.* Washington, DC: National Campaign to Prevent Teen Pregnancy.

Allen, J. P., & Philliber, S. (2001). Who benefits most from a broadly targeted prevention program? Differential efficacy across populations in the Teen Outreach Program. *Journal of Community Psychology, 29,* 637–655.

Annie, E. Casey Foundation. (1998). *When teens have sex: Issues and trends.* Baltimore: Author.

Campbell, F. A., Ramey, C. T., Pungello, E., Sparling, J., & Miller-Johnson, S. (2002). Early childhood education: Young adult outcomes from the Abecedarian Project. *Applied Developmental Science, 6,* 42–57.

Centers for Disease Control and Prevention (CDC). (2002). *Adolescent and school health programs that work.* Retrieved September 24, 2004, from http://www.cdc.gov/nccdphp/dash/rtc/index.htm

Centers for Disease Control and Prevention (CDC). (2003). *Health topics—Sexual behaviors.* Retrieved September 24, 2004, from http://www.cdc.gov/nccdphp/dash/rtc/index.htm

Coard, S. I., Nitz, K., & Felice, M. E. (2000). Repeat pregnancy among urban adolescents: Sociodemographic, family, and health factors. *Adolescence, 35,* 193–200.

Coley, R. L., & Chase-Lindale, P. L. (1998). Adolescent pregnancy and parenthood: Recent evidence and future directions. *American Psychologist, 53,* 152–166.

Corcoran, J., Franklin, C., & Bennett, P. (2000). Ecological factors associated with adolescent pregnancy and parenting. *Social Work Research, 24,* 29–39.

Fagot, B., Pears, K., Capaldi, M., Crosby, L., & Leve, C. (1998). Becoming an adolescent father: Precursors and parenting. *Developmental Psychology, 34,* 1209–1219.

Grunbaum, J. A., Kann, L., Kinchen, S. A., Williams, B., Ross, J. G., Lowry, R., et al. (2001). Youth risk behavior surveillance: United States, 2001. *Morbidity and Mortality Weekly Report, 51*(4), 1–64.

Hoyt, H. H., & Broom, B. L. (2002). School-based teen pregnancy prevention programs: A review of the literature. *The Journal of School Nursing, 18,* 11–17.

Jaffee, S., Caspi, A., Moffitt, T. E., Belsky, J., & Silva, P. (2001). Why are children born to teen mothers at risk for adverse outcomes in young adulthood? Results from a 20-year longitudinal study. *Development and Psychopathology, 13,* 377–397.

Kellogg, N. D., Hoffman, T. J., & Taylor, E. R. (1999). Early sexual experiences among pregnant and parenting adolescents. *Adolescence, 34,* 293–303.

Kirby, D. (2001). *Emerging answers: Research findings on programs to reduce teen pregnancy (Summary).* Washington, DC: National Campaign to Prevent Teen Pregnancy.

Kirby, D. (2002a). Antecedents of adolescent initiation of sex, contraceptive use, and pregnancy. *American Journal of Health Behavior, 26,* 473–485.

Kirby, D. (2002b). *Do abstinence-only programs delay the initiation of sex among young people and reduce teen pregnancy?* Washington, DC: National Campaign to Prevent Teen Pregnancy.

Klerman, L. (2004). *Another chance: Preventing additional births to teen mothers.* Washington, DC: National Campaign to Prevent Teen Pregnancy.

Manlove, J., Franzetta, K., McKinney, K., Romano-Papillo, A., & Terry-Humen, E. (2004). *No time to waste: Programs to reduce teen pregnancy among middle school-aged youth.* Washington, DC: National Campaign to Prevent Teen Pregnancy.

Manlove, J., Romano-Papillo, A. R., & Ikramullah, E. (2004). *Not yet: Programs to delay first sex among teens.* Washington, DC: National Campaign to Prevent Teen Pregnancy.

Miller, B. C., Bayley, B. K., Christensen, M., Leavitt, S. C., & Coyl, D. D. (2003). Adolescent pregnancy and childbearing. In G. Adams & M. Berzonsky (Vol. Eds.), *Blackwell handbooks of developmental psychology: Blackwell handbook of adolescence* (pp. 415–449). Malden, MA: Blackwell Publishing.

Moore, N., McGlinchey, A., & Carr, A. (2002). Prevention of teenage pregnancy, STDs, and HIV infection. In A. Carr (Ed.), *Prevention: What works with children and adolescents* (pp. 287–313). New York: Taylor and Francis Inc.

National Campaign to Prevent Teen Pregnancy. (2003). *The sexual attitudes and behavior of male teens.* Washington, DC: Author.

National Campaign to Prevent Teen Pregnancy. (2004). *Parental influence and teen pregnancy.* Washington, DC: Author.

Philliber, S., Kaye, J. W., Herrling, S., & West, E. (2002). Preventing pregnancy and improving health care access among teenagers: An evaluation of the Children's Aid Society–Carrera Program. *Perspectives on Sexual and Reproductive Health, 34,* 244–251.

Population Resource Center. (2004). *Adolescent pregnancy and childbearing in the U.S.* Retrieved September 1, 2004, from http://www.prcdec.org

Santelli, J. S., Kaiser, J., Hirsch, L., Radosch, A., Simkin, L., & Middlestadt, S. (2004). Initiation of sexual intercourse among middle school adolescents: The influence of psychosocial factors. *Journal of Adolescent Health, 34,* 200–208.

Solomon, J., & Card, J. J. (2004). *Making the list: Understanding, selecting, and replicating effective teen pregnancy prevention programs.* Washington, DC: National Campaign to Prevent Teen Pregnancy.

Stoiber, K. C. (1997). Adolescent pregnancy and parenting. In G. Bear, K. Minke, & A. Thomas (Eds.), *Children's Needs II* (pp. 567–579). Bethesda, MD: National Association of School Psychologists.

Stoiber, K. C., & Anderson, A. J. (1996). Behavioral assessment of coping strategies in young children at-risk, developmentally delayed, and typically developing. *Early Education and Development, 7,* 25–42.

Stoiber, K. C., Anderson, A. J., & Schowalter, D. S. (1998). Group prevention and intervention with pregnant and parenting adolescents. In K. C. Stoiber, & T. R. Kratochwill (Eds.), *Handbook of group intervention for children and families* (pp. 280–306). Needham Heights, MA: Allyn & Bacon.

Stoiber, K. C., & Good, B. (1998). Risk and resilience factors linked to problem behavior among urban, culturally diverse adolescents. *School Psychology Review, 27,* 380–397.

Stoiber, K. C., & Good, B. (1999, August). *Effects of a classroom-based intervention on reducing adolescent risk-taking and problem behavior.* Symposium presented at the Annual Meeting of the American Psychological Association, Boston, MA.

Stoiber, K. C., & Kratochwill, T. R. (2000). Empirically supported interventions and school psychology: Rationale and methodological issues: Part I. *School Psychology Quarterly, 15,* 75–105.

Stoiber, K. C., & Kratochwill, T. R. (2002). *Outcomes: Planning, monitoring, evaluating.* San Antonio, TX: PsychCorp.

Stoiber, K. C., Ribar, R., & Waas, G. A. (2004). Enhancing resilience through multiple family group interventions. In D. Catherall (Ed.), *Handbook of stress, trauma, and family* (pp. 433–451). New York: APA Press.

Stoiber, K. C., & Waas, G. A. (2002). A contextual and methodological perspective on the evidence-based intervention movement within school psychology in the United States. *Educational and Child Psychology, 19,* 7–21.

U.S. Census Bureau. (2000). *Current population survey.* Available from http://www.census.gov

Wallander, J. L., Eggert, K. M., & Gilbert, K. K. (2004). Adolescent health-related issues. In D. R. T. Brown (Ed.), *Handbook of pediatric psychology in school settings* (pp. 503–520). Mahwah, NJ: Erlbaum.

Weinstock, H., Berman, S., & Cates, W. Jr. (2004). Sexually transmitted diseases among American youth: Incidence and prevalence estimates, 2000. *Perspectives on Sexual and Reproductive Health, 36,* 6–10.

Young, T. M., Martin, S. S., Young, M. E., & Ting, L. (2001). Internal poverty and teen pregnancy. *Adolescence, 36,* 289–304.

# 54

# Child Care

**Kim M. Pierce**

**Deborah Lowe Vandell**

*University of Wisconsin–Madison*

## BACKGROUND AND DEVELOPMENT

Working parents' use of nonparental child care arrangements for children is common in the United States. In 1999, 58% of children ages 0–5 years and 64% of children ages 6–14 years had mothers who were employed (U.S. Census Bureau, 2003). Almost three-quarters (73%) of children younger than 5 years of age with employed mothers are reported to be cared for on a regular basis by someone other than their parents for an average 39.1 hours per week (Sonenstein, Gates, Schmidt, & Bolshun, 2002). Among school-age children in kindergarten through eighth grade, 31% of those whose mothers are employed full time participate in regularly scheduled nonparental care arrangements before school for an average 4.7 hours per week, and 68% are in care after school for an average 9.0 hours per week (Kleiner, Nolin, & Chapman, 2004). Participation in both early and school-age child care often is not restricted to a single arrangement; 28% of preschool children and 24% of school-age children of employed mothers have multiple care arrangements across a typical week (U.S. Census Bureau, 2003).

Common child care arrangements in the United States include center care, child care homes, in-home care, and relative care. Parents of school-age children also use before- and after-school programs. Each of these types of care is described below.

### Child Care Variations

***Child care centers.*** Child care centers provide care for children in school-like settings. National surveys (Sonenstein et al., 2002; U.S. Census Bureau, 2003) indicate that center care is used by 27%–28% of preschool children and 8% of school-age children (ages 6–14) of employed mothers. Features of care in child care centers vary widely. The National Institute of Child Health and Human Development (NICHD) Early Child Care Research Network (ECCRN; 1999) observed that child:staff ratios in centers range from 1:1 to 15:1 for infants, 1:1 to 11:1 for toddlers, and 1:1 to 15:1 for preschoolers; children are cared for in groups as large as 30 in infancy and 38 during the preschool years; and caregiver education varies from less than a high school diploma to an advanced academic degree. Child care centers typically have larger child:staff ratios and group sizes, and more educated caregivers, than other forms of child care.

***Child care homes.*** Child care homes (sometimes called family day care) represent another common child care arrangement in the United States. In this arrangement, the provider cares for a small group of children in the provider's home. Families often prefer child care homes for infants and toddlers because they see it as providing a home-like setting with one stable caregiver and relatively few other children. Of families with employed mothers, 21% use this kind of care for their children 5 years and younger, and 10% use it for their school-age children (U.S. Census Bureau, 2003). Some family day care providers have considerable education and training and others have very little. Group sizes as large as 14 (Clarke-Stewart, Vandell, Burchinal, O'Brien, & McCartney, 2002) and child:adult ratios as high as 12:1 (Burchinal, Howes, & Kontos, 2002) have been observed in child care homes catering to infants and preschoolers. Licensing requirements differ substantially by state and community; some states do not regulate child care homes, whereas other states have rules regarding group size, child:staff ratio, and caregiver training. Licensed homes typically provide higher quality care than unlicensed homes do (Burchinal et al.; Votruba-Drzal, Coley, & Chase-Lansdale, 2004). Child care homes in general feature smaller child:staff ratios and smaller group sizes than are seen in child care centers, and family day care providers have, on average, less education and training than caregivers in centers.

***In-home care.*** Another child care arrangement is for families to employ a person to care for the child in the child's own home. Because of the high financial cost, this type of care tends to be used by affluent families in which mothers are highly educated and have high-status occupations. Families also are more likely to use in-home care if they have several small children requiring child care. National surveys report that in-home care is used for 6% of preschool children and 4% of school-age children with employed mothers (U.S. Census Bureau, 2003). As is the case with other forms of child care, the training and education of in-home providers vary. Some are college-educated professional nannies with specialized child care training, whereas others have minimal education or training and may view child care as a temporary job.

***Relative care.*** Relatives, often grandmothers or aunts, are another source of child care. This arrangement is used for 41% of preschoolers and 26% of school-age children in families with an employed mother (U.S. Census Bureau, 2003). Relative care is more common when mothers are employed part time and when families have fewer financial resources. Parental beliefs also contribute to the use of this type of care. Families who have concerns about their children being cared for by non–family members are more likely to use relative care.

Wide variations have been observed in the quality of child care provided by grandmothers and other relatives. In one study that focused on relative care in low-income families (Kontos, Howes, Shinn, & Galinsky, 1995), 69% of the care was rated as insensitive to the needs of young children. However, research with more diverse samples has shown that grandmothers provide sensitive and stimulating care when they are caring for fewer children and when they have nonauthoritarian child-rearing beliefs. Grandmothers also have been observed to provide more positive caregiving than that observed in child care homes and centers, although this discrepancy was reduced by the time children were 3 years of age (NICHD ECCRN, 2000).

***Before- and after-school programs.*** The before- and after-school hours are challenging for families with employed mothers because children's school days typically are shorter than parents' workdays. Before- and after-school programs offer child care to families whose children need supervision outside of school hours. These programs consist of organized group activities that occur on a regular basis, typically 4 or 5 days each week, and are offered in a variety of settings, including schools, day care centers, community centers, and churches. In 1999, 6% of children ages 6–14 with employed mothers attended before- and after-school programs (U.S. Census Bureau, 2003). Child:staff ratios in these programs can range from 4:1 to 25:1, and staff education varies from less than a high school diploma to advanced degrees.

A primary goal of before- and after-school programs traditionally has been to provide supervision to children of working parents. However, the roles and functions of these programs are in some flux. Historically, the vast majority of families using programs paid fees for their children to attend. Recent initiatives such as the federally funded 21st Century Community Learning Centers, however, are free of charge and have substantially expanded the numbers of low-income children being served by programs. Changes also are occurring in the focus of the programs, with some programs continuing to offer an array of enrichment activities, whereas other programs, in response to increasing federal and state pressure on schools to improve academic achievement, have adopted an academic focus and emphasize preparation for standardized tests, tutoring and remediation, and academic skill development.

***Structural variations and process quality of child care settings.*** Researchers have devoted considerable attention to child care quality assessed by structural-regulable features such as child:staff ratio, group size, and caregiver training and education, and by process quality, which refers to the actual experiences that children have in child care, including interactions with caregivers and peers and opportunities to engage in stimulating activities—in other words, the social, cognitive, and physical environment of the care setting. Numerous studies have found that structural-regulable features predict process quality (Burchinal, Roberts, Nabors, & Bryant, 1996; Clarke-Stewart et al., 2002; NICHD ECCRN, 2000). For example, when child:staff ratios are lower, group sizes are smaller, and caregivers are more educated, the global process quality scores in early child care tend to be higher and caregiving is more socially and cognitively stimulating, responsive, warm, and emotionally supportive. In before- and after-school programs, these features are associated with fewer negative staff–child interactions and more positive psychosocial climates (Rosenthal & Vandell, 1996).

## Child Care and Children's Developmental Outcomes

A critical question asked by parents, educational and health professionals, and policy makers is how variations in the child care experience affect children's development. Researchers have worked to identify the conditions under which child care supports children's development as well as the conditions under which development is undermined in terms of child care quality, amount of child care, and type of child care.

***Child care quality.*** Studies have reported relationships between child care quality (measured by process quality and by structural-regulable features) and child developmental outcomes. For example, when quality is higher, as indicated by caregiving that is more positive and sensitive and by lower child:staff ratios, children appear more prosocial and positively engaged with peers in the child care setting (Howes, Phillips, & Whitebook, 1992). When caregivers have more formal education and more early childhood training, children are rated as more cognitively competent during free play (Kontos & Wilcox-Herzog, 1997).

Child care quality also is associated with children's concurrent functioning in other settings. For example, preschool children whose care is higher in process quality obtain better scores on cognitive and language tests and evidence better behavioral and social adjustment (Clarke-Stewart et al., 2002; NICHD ECCRN, 2000). Children in settings with smaller child:staff ratios, compared with children in settings with larger ratios, evidence better cognitive and language skills (Burchinal et al., 1996). The amount of caregivers' formal education is positively associated with cognitive development (Clarke-Stewart et al.), language skills (Burchinal et al., 1996), and task persistence and school readiness (Ruopp, Travers, Glantz, & Coelen, 1979). Smaller group sizes in child care centers have been shown in a large-scale experimental study to be associated with children's gains across a 9-month period on measures of receptive language, general knowledge, cooperative behavior, and verbal initiations, and with less hostility and conflict in their interactions with others (Ruopp et al.). The impact of structural-regulable features of child care settings on child developmental outcomes appears to be mediated by process quality; that is, better structural quality is associated with higher process quality, which in turn is associated with better child outcomes.

Child care quality also predicts longer term child developmental outcomes, particularly when quality is measured at several points in time rather than at a single point. These cumulative measures provide more reliable and robust indications of early child care experiences than a one-time assessment, because most children experience changes in settings and caregivers. In the NICHD Study of Early Child Care, a large national study of over 1,000 children (NICHD ECCRN, 2003a), measures of positive caregiving collected at regular intervals from infancy through age 4½ predicted children's school readiness and language scores at age 4½, controlling for amount and type of care and an extensive list of family covariates. Burchinal et al. (2000) similarly found that the quality of child care arrangements over time affects children's cognitive and language development. Higher quality child care from infancy to 3 years of age was associated with better cognitive development, better receptive and expressive language skills, and better functional communication skills over time.

Other longitudinal studies have examined associations between the process quality of early child care experiences and child developmental outcomes in the early grade school years. In the Cost, Quality, and Outcomes Study (Peisner-Feinberg et al., 2001), conducted in four states and involving over 500 children, children who had been enrolled in high-quality child care center classrooms displayed better receptive language skills prior to school entry and in kindergarten, and better math skills prior to school entry and during kindergarten and second grade. In further analyses that controlled for the quality of the elementary school classroom, the relations between child care quality and children's math skills were maintained.

Relations between structural features of child care settings and children's subsequent social and cognitive development in grade school also have been reported. Howes (1988), for example, examined structural-regulable factors at 3 years in relation to children's first-grade adjustment. Quality in the child care settings was defined in terms of meeting recommended guidelines for teacher training, child:adult ratio, group size, a planned curriculum, and space. During the intervening period, the children attended the same university lab school, meaning that they experienced classes with the same or similar structural-regulable characteristics. Howes determined that boys and girls who had attended higher quality child care programs (defined by structural-regulable composite scores) prior to enrollment in the university school were rated by their first-grade teachers as having fewer behavior problems and better work habits compared with children whose child care at 3 years was of lower quality. Additionally, boys whose child care was of higher quality prior to enrollment in the lab school received better first-grade teacher ratings of academic performance compared with other boys. In a different sample, Howes (1990) found that children were rated as more hostile by their kindergarten teachers when they had a history of poor-quality care, as measured by a composite score of child: adult ratio, caregiver training, and caregiver stability at 18, 24, 30, and 36 months.

A few studies have examined the impact of process quality in before- and after-school programs on children's developmental outcomes. For example, Pierce, Hamm, and Vandell (1999) found that variations in program quality were related to children's functioning at school in first grade. Boys who attended programs in which there was a more positive emotional climate were reported by their classroom teachers to exhibit fewer problem behaviors at school in comparison to boys who attended programs with less positive climates. A more negative emotional climate in the after-school programs, in contrast, predicted poorer academic performance at school. Additionally, boys who attended programs rated as fostering autonomy and providing activity choices had better social skills according to their first-grade teachers. In a follow-up study of these same children, observed program quality in Grades 2, 3, and 4 (defined as positive interactions with staff and with peers, opportunities for autonomy, and provision of developmentally appropriate activities) predicted better work habit ratings and higher academic grades in Grades 2–4, controlling for Grade 1 performance (Vandell & Pierce, 2001).

Relations between school-age program quality and child developmental outcomes have been reported in other samples as well. Vandell, Shumow, and Posner (2005) described pervasive differences in staff–child interaction, emotional climate, and provisions for child autonomy at two programs serving low-income elementary school children. Across the school year, students who attended the poorer quality program showed declines in their report card grades, work habits, and peer relations, whereas the performance of children in the more supportive program either improved or remained the same. In analyses of data from the NICHD Study of Early Child Care, less conflictual relationships with after-school program staff predicted higher reading and math achievement at the end of first grade and fewer problem behaviors according to both mothers and classroom teachers, controlling for child functioning at 4½ years, several child and family selection factors, and instructional and emotional quality of the first-grade classroom (Vandell, Pierce, & Lee, 2005).

Thus, the available evidence indicates that quality of early child care and after-school programs is related to child developmental outcomes during the early elementary school years. We do not know if these early relations are maintained after this period, if they disappear, or if they are magnified in the later elementary years and adolescence.

***Amount of child care.*** The amount of early child care experienced by children has been considered in relation to child developmental outcomes by the NICHD Study of Early Child Care (NICHD ECCRN, 1998, 2001, 2003b, 2003c). Amount of care was not associated with children's cognitive, language, or preacademic performance. There was evidence, however, that amount of care was associated with children's socioemotional adjustment. In particular, children who had spent more hours in child care were reported by their caregivers or teachers and mothers to have more behavior problems, to be less socially competent, and to have more conflicted relationships with caregivers and teachers at several ages (2 years, 4½ years, kindergarten, and first grade) than children who had spent fewer hours in child care. However, other studies have found that associations between high hours in care and externalizing behavior problems are evident only for those children whose child care is of poor quality (Votruba-Drzal et al., 2004).

Associations between amount of participation in before- and after-school programs and child outcomes also have been reported. Low-income children and adolescents who attend high-quality programs more often, compared with those who attend less often, have been shown to post greater gains in math achievement (Welsh, Russell, Williams, Reisner, & White, 2002) and to improve their academic grades and work habits at school (Vandell & Pierce, 1999). It is not clear if the same effects would be found with more advantaged samples or in lower quality programs.

***Type of child care.*** Other research has considered the effects of different types of child care arrangements. In general, preschool children who attend child care centers score higher on standardized cognitive, language, and school readiness assessments compared with children in less formal arrangements or exclusive maternal care (Loeb, Fuller, Kagan, & Carrol, 2004; NICHD ECCRN, 2004). On average, child care centers have more highly educated caregivers than other types of child care arrangements, and children in centers spend more time in lessons and structured activities than children in other forms of care, which may explain the cognitive benefits of participation in center care. The association between center care participation and cognitive outcomes holds for preschool children from a range of socioeconomic backgrounds, although center care may have a strong compensatory effect on low-income children's cognitive and language development since the child care center may offer a more stimulating and enriching environment than the home does.

A recent set of analyses of type and quantity of child care from infancy through 4½ years, controlling for child care quality (NICHD ECCRN, 2004), found that more time in center care during the toddler and preschool years was associated with better language development, whereas center care during infancy was associated with lower preacademic test scores. Additionally, more time in center care during infancy, toddler years, and preschool years was associated with more externalizing behavior problems (e.g., immature behavior, attention problems, and aggression) in the child care setting at 4½ years. Hours of participation in child care homes and in relative care was not associated with children's cognitive and social outcomes.

Participation in before- and after-school programs also has been linked to academic and socioemotional outcomes. For example, Posner and Vandell (1994) reported that low-income children who attended school- and community-based after-school programs during third grade had fewer antisocial behaviors and had better reading and math grades, work habits, emotional adjustment, and peer relationships at the end of third grade, compared with children who were in sitter care, parental care, or self-care after school. Benefits also have been reported for middle-class children: Kindergartners who participated in an extended day program had better relationships with peers than their classmates who did not participate in the program (Howes, Olenick, & Der-Kiureghian, 1987).

## Self-Care

Some families regularly use self-care arrangements, or time spent without adult supervision, for their children. Self-care can vary along several dimensions. Some children are at home, others are at the home of a friend, others are out in the neighborhood, and still others are in public places such as shopping malls or video arcades. Children may be alone or with siblings or peers. Some children in self-care are monitored by telephone or have parental rules to follow while caring for themselves, whereas other children do not experience adult supervision in any form. According to the U.S. Census Bureau (2003), 26% of school-age children and 4% of preschool children are in self-care, either alone or with a sibling, as a regular out-of-school care arrangement. For children of employed mothers, the figures are 32% and 4.5%, respectively. Use of self-care increases as children get older: Among children of employed mothers, 3% of 5- to 8-year-olds, 16% of 9- to 11-year-olds, and 43% of 12- to 14-year-olds are in self-care as a regular arrangement.

The available research evidence indicates that the different types of self-care are differentially associated with developmental outcomes. Steinberg's (1986) seminal study made clear the importance of the characteristics of the self-care situation for child and adolescent developmental outcomes. Steinberg determined the "usual" after-school situations of adolescents in Grades 5–9 and classified the unsupervised situations as unsupervised at home, unsupervised at a friend's home, and unsupervised "hanging out." Participation in each of these self-care contexts was analyzed in terms of self-reported susceptibility to peer pressure to engage in antisocial activity in response to hypothetical dilemmas. No differences in susceptibility to peer pressure were apparent between students who were supervised or unsupervised at home. However, girls and boys who hung out with peers in unsupervised settings reported greater susceptibility to peer pressure than students who were unsupervised at a friend's home, who in turn reported greater susceptibility than students who were home alone after school. The associations were strongest for adolescents whose parents did not know their whereabouts.

These results suggest that the more removed the adolescents were from adult supervision, the greater their potential to engage in antisocial behavior in response to peer pressure. Family factors buffered this effect: Adolescents in all the unsupervised care categories who perceived that their parents used an authoritative parenting style reported less susceptibility to peer pressure than adolescents who perceived their parents to be less authoritative. Similar results have been reported in an extension of Steinberg's work that examined actual antisocial behavior rather than responses to hypothetical dilemmas (Galambos & Maggs, 1991).

Other investigators have reported associations between unsupervised peer contact and a variety of poor adjustment outcomes, including poorer grades and academic achievement, more misconduct, more externalizing behavior, more substance use, and a greater likelihood of dropping out of school (Flannery, Williams, & Vazsonyi, 1999; Jordan & Nettles, 2000; McHale, Crouter, & Tucker, 2001). In addition to parenting quality, features of the neighborhood context and parental monitoring appear to moderate the relationship between unsupervised peer contact and developmental outcomes. Early adolescents who spend the most after-school time unsupervised with peers appear to be at the greatest risk for negative outcomes if they live in unsafe neighborhoods and parental monitoring is low.

The family and community contexts also appear to be important in moderating the effects of being home alone on children's developmental outcomes. Research that contrasts this type of self-care with supervised arrangements has identified few links between self-care at home and negative outcomes in rural and suburban samples. However, for low-income children in urban areas, self-care during the elementary school years has been associated with more externalizing and antisocial behavior problems compared to low-income children in supervised care (Marshall et al., 1997).

Other factors involved in associations between self-care at home and children's adjustment include the amount of time spent in self-care and the child's age. Children who spend 30 minutes after school without adult supervision experience the arrangement differently than children who spend 2 hours in self-care, and 1 day per week of self-care is a different experience for children than 5 days per week of self-care. Younger children may be more affected by these variations than older children. For example, Pettit, Laird, Bates, and Dodge (1997) reported that more time in self-care in Grades 1 and 3 was negatively associated with social and academic competence in Grade 6. The amount of time spent in self-care in Grade 5 was not associated with these outcomes, suggesting that self-care is more problematic for younger children than for adolescents. As children get older and desire greater autonomy, self-care may represent an opportunity to exhibit their ability to regulate their own behavior within the context of rules set by parents.

Some children spend the after-school hours in the care of older siblings. Despite the frequency of sibling care, this arrangement has received scant attention in the literature. The available evidence indicates that sibling care is associated with poor outcomes such as aggression, delinquency, susceptibility to peer pressure to engage in antisocial behavior, and substance use (Flannery et al., 1999), and lower social acceptance and global self-worth compared with children in self-care alone at home or supervised by adults (Berman, Winkleby, Chesterman, & Boyce, 1992). Berman et al. speculated that these effects may be due to limited nurturance and companionship provided by older siblings and older siblings' greater use of physical punishment compared with the punishment used by parents.

## PROBLEMS AND IMPLICATIONS

The quality of the child care that children receive prior to school entry has implications for their performance at school, both in the classroom and on the playground. High-quality child care experiences help to prepare children for school by supporting the development of cognitive and language skills, whereas poor-quality care can undermine school efforts by increasing the numbers of children with academic and social deficits. Negative effects of poor-quality care also are evident for school-age child care in terms of grades and social skills with peers.

Unfortunately, high-quality child care is in short supply. The available data from several large multisite studies indicate that much of the child care in the United States is of poor or barely adequate quality. In the Cost, Quality, and Outcomes Study (Peisner-Feinberg et al., 2001), conducted in California, Colorado, Connecticut, and North Carolina, only 14% of the classrooms were rated as providing developmentally appropriate, good-quality care, whereas 74% provided mediocre care and 12% provided poor-quality care. Center-based programs for infants appeared to be particularly problematic; 8% of the infant and toddler rooms were rated as being of good quality, and 40% were rated as poor quality. Quality of child care homes and relative care also appears problematic. In the Relative and Family Day Care Study (Kontos et al., 1995), 34% of the care was judged to be inadequate, 58% was adequate/custodial, and only 8% was of good quality. Similar proportions were reported in the NICHD Study of Early Child Care (NICHD ECCRN, 2000), in which quality of care was poor for 7% of the sample and fair for 53% of the sample. Only 10% of the sample received caregiving that was highly positive and sensitive.

The absence of consistently high-quality child care in the United States is believed to be the result of several factors. A major factor that contributes to the variable (but generally low) quality of child care is that there are no common standards that are enforced across the states. For example, only 10 states require providers in child care homes to have preservice training in early childhood education or child development, and only 14 states require preservice training of teachers in child care centers. Continuing education is required of teachers in child care centers in 48 states (range from 3 to 40 hours annually), but only 34 states require it for providers in child care homes (range from 4 to 20 hours annually). Table 1 shows the licensing thresholds for child care homes in terms of the number of children being cared for. As shown in the table, 41 states allow child care homes to serve anywhere from 2 to 13 children without licensure, and two states do not license child care homes at all.

**Table 1** *State Licensing Thresholds for Child Care Homes*

| Number of Children in Child Care Home | Number of States That Require Licensing at This Threshold[a] |
|---|---|
| 1 | 10 |
| 2 | 5 |
| 3 | 8 |
| 4 | 11 |
| 5 | 7 |
| 6 | 5 |
| 7 | 2 |
| 13 | 1 |

*Note.* Two states do not license child care homes.
[a]Includes the District of Columbia.

Very few states have regulations for child:staff ratios and group sizes in child care centers that are as strict as those recommended by professional organizations. Table 2 shows the ratios and group sizes recommended by the American Academy of Pediatrics and the American Public Health Association, and the number of states with regulations that meet these guidelines. As shown in the table, only three states require the recommended 3:1 ratio for infants. Thirteen states require the recommended 4:1 ratio for toddlers, but three or fewer states require the recommended ratios for older preschoolers and school-age children. In the NICHD Study of Early Child Care (NICHD ECCRN, 1999), only 36% of infant classrooms in child care centers met the recommended child:staff ratio; this figure was 20%, 26%, and 56% for classrooms when the study children were 15, 24, and 36 months old, respectively. Most states' requirements for maximum group sizes also do not meet the recommendations.

The importance of meeting recommended standards is reflected in research that shows that positive developmental outcomes accrue when children attend child care centers that are in compliance with the recommendations for structural and caregiver standards (Burchinal et al., 2000; NICHD ECCRN, 1999). Toddlers and preschool children whose centers adhere to the recommended child:adult ratios are reported by their mothers to exhibit fewer behavior problems, more positive social behaviors, and better language skills. When centers meet the recommended guidelines for group size, children score higher on tests of cognitive skills and academic achievement. When centers meet recommendations for staff education and training in early childhood education or child development, children exhibit fewer behavior problems and perform better on tests of school readiness, language comprehension, cognitive skills, and academic achievement. Furthermore, there appears to be a linear relationship between the number of standards that child care centers meet and children's behavioral adjustment, school readiness, and language comprehension.

A second problem is that child care expenses place considerable financial strain on many families because they require a substantial portion of family incomes. The Children's Defense Fund (Schulman, 2000) reported that statewide averages for annual center care costs ranged from $3,692 to $9,509 for infants, $3,380 to $7,389 for preschoolers, and $1,936 to $5,738 for school-age children. In child care homes, costs ranged from $2,600 to $7,410 for infants, $2,340 to $6,694 for preschoolers, and $1,404 to $4,528 for school-age children. Poor families report paying 33%–34% of their income for child care; working-class families spend 14%–15%, whereas middle-class families spend 5%–8% (U.S. Census Bureau, 2003). It is clear that child care costs can be an especially onerous burden for low-income families, making it so difficult for these families to use high-quality care that they often use relatives and other forms of low-cost care. Although there has been a substantial increase in federal child care assistance dollars in recent years, rules regarding eligibility for assistance are set at the state level, with income limits ranging from 123% to 325% of the federal poverty level and some states restricting subsidy receipt to families receiving Temporary Assistance to Needy Families.

The provision of developmentally appropriate afterschool arrangements is another challenge for families, schools, and communities. Older school-age children press for an opportunity to have some unstructured time

**Table 2** *Maximum Child:Staff Ratios and Group Sizes in Child Care Centers Recommended by the American Academy of Pediatrics and the American Public Health Association*

| Child Age | Recommended Child:Staff Ratio | Number of States Requiring Standard | Recommended Group Size | Number of States Requiring Standard |
|---|---|---|---|---|
| Infant | 3:1 | 3 | 6 | 1 |
| Toddler | 4:1 | 13 | 8 | 8 |
| 2 years | 4:1 | 3 | 8 | 2 |
| 3 years | 7:1 | 2 | 14 | 2 |
| 4 years | 8:1 | 1 | 16 | 0 |
| 5 years | 8:1 | 0 | 16 | 0 |
| 6–8 years | 10:1 | 2 | 20 | 4 |
| 9–12 years | 12:1 | 2 | 24 | 2 |

after school when they can relax, play with friends, and set their own agenda. This push is often juxtaposed against parents' and other adults' legitimate concerns about the dangers and risks associated with children being unsupervised by adults during the after-school hours. The challenge, then, is to develop after-school care arrangements in which children's needs to exercise greater autonomy and independence are met along with the children's continuing needs for contact and support from caring adults.

## ALTERNATIVE ACTIONS FOR PREVENTION AND INTERVENTION

Parents play a central role in selecting and monitoring their children's child care arrangements; however, they may have difficulty recognizing high-quality child care. In the Cost, Quality, and Outcomes study of 100 centers in four states (Peisner-Feinberg et al., 2001), 90% of parents rated their children's centers as good, whereas trained observers rated these same programs as poor or mediocre. An important step in improving the quality of care available to children is to educate parents on the dangers of poor-quality care for their children's development and to help parents identify high-quality care. School-based professionals (e.g., psychologists, counselors, social workers, and teachers) can play a key role in this educational effort.

The quality of children's experiences in child care also can be improved by instituting standards for structural-regulable features such as group size and child:staff ratio as well as caregiver qualifications. States that require more favorable group sizes, child:adult ratios, and caregiver training have centers with better quality care than states with less demanding licensing standards. Adopting standards such as those recommended by the American Academy of Pediatrics and the American Public Health Association will require concerted efforts by citizens as well as by professional organizations. These efforts should focus on changing the prevailing view of child care as serving a strictly custodial role that allows parents to work. Rather, child care should be viewed as one avenue for promoting child development by meeting children's needs for education, enrichment, and supportive relationships with caregivers.

Because establishing and enforcing higher child care standards will increase the costs of care, it will be necessary to develop ways to offset such costs, especially for families who cannot afford them. Public monies that support low-income families' use of high-quality care programs are particularly needed because this support helps low-income families in three ways. First, government support reduces the financial strain child care places on these families. Second, these programs serve as educational enrichment experiences that can contribute to the children's ability to succeed at school. Third, these programs act as a respite for parents, reducing the stress in their lives and improving the quality of their parenting. In 1999, only 15% of children who were eligible for federal child care assistance received funding. Both federal and state governments should expand support for low-income families' use of high-quality care.

Child care policy also should include modifications of existing parental leave policies as a way of meeting the need for high-quality infant care. Most industrialized countries offer parents an opportunity to stay home and care for an infant for at least part of the first year with wage replacement, as a means of supporting families and children's healthy development. For example, Canada offers 15 weeks of paid maternity leave and an additional 10 weeks of parental leave, both paid at 55% of prior earnings. The European Union has established a minimum of 14 weeks of paid parental leave, although most European nations are more generous, with paid leaves ranging from 18 weeks in the United Kingdom (at 90% of prior earnings for 6 weeks and a flat rate for the remaining 12 weeks) to 3 years in Norway (at 80% of prior earnings for 1 year and a flat rate for 2 years). The costs of these leave policies are paid through governmental social insurance programs and payroll taxes. The United States has much more limited parental leave provisions. Currently, parents employed by firms with more than 50 employees are allowed by federal law to take up to 3 months of *unpaid* leave. There is no federal policy of paid leave, although some employers allow employees to use sick leave or other benefits for a period following the birth of a baby. The National Research Council recommends that job-protected leave be mandated by the federal government for parents of infants less than 1 year of age.

Families of school-age children also have needs for child care. One way of meeting the need for high-quality before- and after-school care is to make more effective use of public schools. School professionals can serve as strong advocates within their districts for the development of age-appropriate programs and activities. Schools are an excellent location for before- and after-school child care programs because they have classrooms, gyms, equipment, and outdoor play areas. School-based programs make transportation to another setting unnecessary. For these programs to appeal to older school-age children and to middle schoolers, however, special attention needs to be paid to programming and activities. Inclusion of youth in program planning is particularly important. Done properly, these programs can provide rich contexts for positive development that encourage children's enrollment and participation, as opposed to serving a strictly custodial role. The National After School Association (*http://www.naaweb.org*) has identified 36 standards that are judged to promote quality in after-school programs. These standards, which can provide a useful guide to setting up and maintaining programs, are in the areas of human relationships (e.g., staff relate to children and youth in positive ways); indoor environment (e.g., indoor space allows children and youth to take initiative and explore their interests); outdoor environment (e.g., equipment allows children and youth to be independent and creative); activities (e.g., there are sufficient materials to support program activities); safety, health, and nutrition (e.g., children and youth are carefully supervised to maintain safety); and administration (e.g., staff are professionally qualified to work with children and youth).

School professionals also can assist children and families with self-care issues. Only two states legislate the age at which children can be alone at home. Maryland specifies that no child younger than 8 can be left alone, and Illinois law states that children younger than 14 cannot be left without supervision for an "unreasonable" period of time, with 15 factors considered in determining what is unreasonable. In lieu of guidance from the government, school professionals can implement self-care training programs within their schools and communities to assist families with deciding whether to use self-care arrangements. University cooperative extension offices have developed programs that could be adapted for use by school psychologists. National organizations also can be a source of information. For example, some local chapters of the American Red Cross offer Home Alone, a course to teach self-care skills to children. These programs can help children and families evaluate children's readiness for self-care and institute appropriate safety and monitoring features. The programs typically include information about personal, fire, and home safety; how to handle emergencies; first-aid; time management; and nutrition. Parents and children are encouraged to create family rules that the child should follow while home alone and to practice self-care skills together. Outcome evaluations of self-care training programs have documented that the programs effectively increase children's knowledge of safety and self-care practices. However, these programs must be implemented with considerable care, because they may be viewed as an endorsement of self-care for children who are not yet ready for it and they may provide children and families with a false sense of security.

Finally, school professionals may need to address both short-term and long-term failures in the child care system as they are manifested in individual children's school adjustment. Children who have experienced poor-quality and unstable child care are more likely than their classmates to appear uncooperative, aggressive, distractible, and withdrawn. Individual and small-group activities to address these behavior problems may be needed.

## SUMMARY

Millions of children in the United States participate in nonparental child care arrangements on a regular basis. These arrangements vary widely in their quality, amount, and type. Variations in child care are associated with child developmental outcomes. High-quality care can foster language and cognitive skills as well as greater social competencies, whereas poor-quality care is linked to increased behavior problems and poor social competence. Larger amounts of child care prior to school entry are associated with more behavior problems and less social competence. Preschoolers who attend child care centers display better cognitive and language skills, and greater readiness for school, than preschoolers who participate in other forms of child care. Children of low-income families appear to derive greater benefits from high-quality child care. The effects of self-care in elementary and middle school are dependent on multiple factors including the amount of time spent in self-care, the family and neighborhood contexts, and the presence of peers. The importance of child care experiences as both positive and negative contributors to children's development underscores the need for child care policies to ensure that children have access to care that does not compromise development.

## RECOMMENDED RESOURCES

### Books and Other Printed Material

Harvey, B., & Shortt, J. (2001). *Working together for children and families: A community's guide to making the most out of out-of-school time.* Wellesley, MA: Wellesley College. Wellesley Centers for Women, National Institute on Out-of-School Time. Available at *www.niost.org*

This publication provides an introductory guide to building high-quality school-age programs through collaboration with parents and the community at large.

National Institute of Child Health and Human Development (NICHD) Early Child Care Research Network. (Ed.). (2005). *Child care and child development: Results from the NICHD Study of Early Child Care and Youth Development.* New York: Guilford Press.

This compilation volume presents the findings of the NICHD Study of Early Child Care and Youth Development, a landmark study that has followed children since their birth in 1991. The latest findings on child care use and quality, and effects of child care on children's health, psychological development, and family relations are discussed.

Smolensky, E., & Gootman, J. A. (Eds.). (2003). *Working families and growing kids: Caring for children and adolescents.* Washington, DC: National Academies Press.

This book is the work of the Committee on Family and Work Policies that was convened for the National Research Council and the Institute of Medicine. It presents a review and evaluation of the effects of parental employment on child and adolescent development and describes policy applications that support working parents and their children.

### Websites

*http://www.afterschoolalliance.org*

The After-School Alliance works to raise awareness of the importance of high-quality, affordable after-school programs. This website provides news about after-school programs and links to research reports and publications.

*http://www.naeyc.org*

The National Association for the Education of Young Children promotes quality in educational and developmental services for children from birth to 8 years. This website includes the organization's accreditation standards for programs serving children, as well as policy statements and research reports.

*http://www.nccic.org*

The National Child Care Information Center is a service of the U.S. Department of Health and Human Services. The website serves as a clearinghouse for information about child care.

## REFERENCES

Berman, B. D., Winkleby, M., Chesterman, E., & Boyce, W. T. (1992). After-school child care and self-esteem in school-age children. *Pediatrics, 89,* 654–659.

Burchinal, M., Howes, C., & Kontos, S. (2002). Structural predictors of child care quality in child care homes. *Early Childhood Research Quarterly, 17,* 87–105.

Burchinal, M. R., Roberts, J. E., Nabors, L. A., & Bryant, D. M. (1996). Quality of center child care and infant cognitive and language development. *Child Development, 67,* 606–620.

Burchinal, M. R., Roberts, J. E., Riggins, R., Jr., Zeisel, S. A., Neebe, E., & Bryant, D. (2000). Relating quality of center-based child care to early cognitive and language development longitudinally. *Child Development, 71,* 339–357.

Clarke-Stewart, K. A., Vandell, D. L., Burchinal, M., O'Brien, M., & McCartney, K. (2002). Do regulable features of child-care homes affect children's development? *Early Childhood Research Quarterly, 17,* 52–86.

Flannery, D. J., Williams, L. L., & Vazsonyi, A. T. (1999). Who are they with and what are they doing? Delinquent behavior, substance use, and early adolescents' after-school time. *American Journal of Orthopsychiatry, 69,* 247–253.

Galambos, N. L., & Maggs, J. L. (1991). Out-of-school care of young adolescents and self-reported behavior. *Developmental Psychology, 27,* 644–655.

Howes, C. (1988). Relations between early child care and schooling. *Developmental Psychology, 24,* 53–57.

Howes, C. (1990). Can the age of entry into child care and the quality of child care predict adjustment in kindergarten? *Developmental Psychology, 26,* 292–303.

Howes, C., Olenick, M., & Der-Kiureghian, T. (1987). After-school child care in an elementary school: Social development and continuity and complementarity of programs. *Elementary School Journal, 88,* 93–103.

Howes, C., Phillips, D. A., & Whitebook, M. (1992). Thresholds of quality: Implications for the social development of children in center-based child care. *Child Development, 63,* 449–460.

Jordan, W. J., & Nettles, S. M. (2000). How students invest their time outside of school: Effects on school-related outcomes. *Social Psychology of Education, 3,* 217–243.

Kleiner, B., Nolin, M. J., & Chapman, C. (2004). *Before- and after-school care, programs, and activities of children in kindergarten through eighth grade: 2001* (NCES 2004–008). Washington, DC: U.S. Department of Education, National Center for Education Statistics.

Kontos, S., Howes, C., Shinn, M., & Galinsky, E. (1995). *Quality in family child care and relative care.* New York: Teachers College Press.

Kontos, S., & Wilcox-Herzog, A. (1997). Influences on children's competence in early childhood classrooms. *Early Childhood Research Quarterly, 12,* 247–262.

Loeb, S., Fuller, B., Kagan, S. L., & Carrol, B. (2004). Child care in poor communities: Early learning effects of type, quality, and stability. *Child Development, 75,* 47–65.

Marshall, N. L., Coll, C. G., Marx, F., McCartney, K., Keefe, N., & Ruh, J. (1997). After-school time and children's behavioral adjustment. *Merrill-Palmer Quarterly, 43,* 497–514.

McHale, S. M., Crouter, A. C., & Tucker, C. J. (2001). Free-time activities in middle childhood: Links with adjustment in early adolescence. *Child Development, 72,* 1764–1778.

National Institute of Child Health and Human Development (NICHD) Early Child Care Research Network. (1998). Early child care and self-control, compliance, and problem behavior at twenty-four and thirty-six months. *Child Development, 69,* 1145–1170.

NICHD Early Child Care Research Network. (1999). Child outcomes when child care center classes meet recommended standards for quality. *American Journal of Public Health, 89,* 1072–1077.

NICHD Early Child Care Research Network. (2000). Characteristics and quality of child care for toddlers and preschoolers. *Applied Developmental Science, 4,* 116–135.

NICHD Early Child Care Research Network. (2001). Child care and children's peer interaction at 24 and 36 months: The NICHD Study of Early Child Care. *Child Development, 72,* 1478–1500.

NICHD Early Child Care Research Network. (2003a). Does quality of child care affect child outcomes at age 4½? *Developmental Psychology, 39,* 451–469.

NICHD Early Child Care Research Network. (2003b). Does amount of time spent in child care predict socioemotional adjustment during the transition to kindergarten? *Child Development, 74,* 976–1005.

NICHD Early Child Care Research Network. (2003c). Social functioning in first grade: Associations with earlier home and child care predictors and with current classroom experience. *Child Development, 74,* 1639–1662.

NICHD Early Child Care Research Network. (2004). Type of child care and children's development at 54 months. *Early Childhood Research Quarterly, 19,* 203–230.

Peisner-Feinberg, E. S., Burchinal, M. R., Clifford, R. M., Culkin, M. L., Howes, C., Kagan, S. L., et al. (2001). The relation of preschool child-care quality to children's cognitive and social developmental trajectories through second grade. *Child Development, 72,* 1534–1553.

Pettit, G. S., Laird, R. D., Bates, J. E., & Dodge, K. A. (1997). Patterns of after-school care in middle childhood: Risk factors and developmental outcomes. *Merrill-Palmer Quarterly, 43,* 515–538.

Pierce, K. M., Hamm, J. V., & Vandell, D. L. (1999). Experiences in after-school programs and children's adjustment in first-grade classrooms. *Child Development, 70,* 756–767.

Posner, J. K., & Vandell, D. L. (1994). Low-income children's after-school care: Are there beneficial effects of after-school programs? *Child Development, 65,* 440–456.

Rosenthal, R., & Vandell, D. L. (1996). Quality of care at school-aged child care programs: Regulatable features, observed experiences, child perspectives, and parent perspectives. *Child Development, 67,* 2434–2445.

Ruopp, R., Travers, J., Glantz, F., & Coelen, C. (1979). *Children at the center: Final report of the National Day Care Study.* Cambridge, MA: Abt.

Schulman, K. (2000). *The high cost of child care puts quality care out of reach for many families.* Washington, DC: Children's Defense Fund.

Sonenstein, F. L., Gates, G. J., Schmidt, S., & Bolshun, N. (2002). *Primary child care arrangements of employed parents: Findings from the 1999 National Survey of America's Families* (Occasional Paper No. 59). Washington, DC: Urban Institute.

Steinberg, L. (1986). Latchkey children and susceptibility to peer pressure: An ecological analysis. *Developmental Psychology, 22,* 433–439.

U.S. Census Bureau. (2003). *Who's minding the kids? Child care arrangements: Spring 1999 detailed tables (PPL-168).* Retrieved July 13, 2004, from http://www.census.gov/population/www/socdemo/child/ppl-168.html

Vandell, D. L., & Pierce, K. M. (1999, April). Can after-school programs benefit children who live in high-crime neighborhoods? In N. Marshall (Chair), *Children's out-of-school time: The next generation of research.* Poster symposium conducted at the biennial meeting of the Society for Research in Child Development, Albuquerque, NM.

Vandell, D. L., & Pierce, K. M. (2001, April). Experiences in after-school programs and child well-being. In J. L. Mahoney (Chair), *Protective aspects of after-school activities: Processes and mechanisms.* Paper symposium conducted at the biennial meeting of the Society for Research in Child Development, Minneapolis, MN.

Vandell, D. L., Pierce, K. M., & Lee, D. (2005). Relationships with after-school program staff: Supporting (versus hindering) children's adjustment and achievement. In J. L. Mahoney & D. L. Vandell (Chairs), *Features of after-school programs that promote development: Type, quality, and content.* Symposium conducted at the biennial meeting of the Society for Research in Child Development, Atlanta, GA.

Vandell, D. L., Shumow, L., & Posner, J. (2005, April). After-school programs for low-income children: Differences in program quality. In J. L. Mahoney, R. W. Larson, & J. S. Eccles (Eds.), *Organized activities as contexts of development: Extracurricular activities, after school and community programs* (pp. 437–456). Mahwah, NJ: Erlbaum.

Votruba-Drzal, E., Coley, R. L., & Chase-Lansdale, P. L. (2004). Child care and low-income children's development: Direct and moderated effects. *Child Development, 75,* 296–312.

Welsh, M. E., Russell, C. A., Williams, I., Reisner, E., & White, R. N. (2002). *Promoting learning and school attendance through after-school programs: Student level changes in educational performance across TASC's first three years.* Washington, DC: Policy Studies Associates.

# 55

# Family Mobility and Schooling

**Karla Buerkle**
**Anastasia Hansen**
*University of Minnesota*

## BACKGROUND AND DEVELOPMENT

America has long been described as a nation on the move. Most children experience mobility sometime during their school years, either firsthand through a change of address or school, indirectly through a friend's leaving or coming, or peripherally through student turnover in their classrooms. Although the U.S. Census Bureau reports that moving rates show a downward trend, from 17% in 1994 to 14% in 2003, over 40 million Americans continue to move annually, with residence changes affecting 8½ million school-age children (Schachter, 2004). An estimated one in seven families moves during a given school year, with up to one of every two children experiencing a move during their elementary school years (Cohen, Johnson, Struening, & Brook, 1989). Children who transfer to a new school following a residence change face a double burden of adjustment to several new environments. In addition, school mobility has become a phenomenon on its own, with several recent studies describing nearly 40% of school change as happening separate from residential mobility or grade promotions. Instead, transfers may be tied to negative reasons, such as avoiding suspensions or expulsions, not feeling comfortable or welcomed in a particular school, or having logistics problems with transportation or start and end times (Rumberger & Larson, 1998).

The popular view of mobility focuses on the stress of moving, of having to leave friends and familiar places. Tasks of developing new friendships and establishing roots can be difficult and demanding. Beyond social adjustment issues, for school-age children there are significant academic implications. Children must adjust to a new academic system that may include differences in teaching style, novel materials, and a curricular mismatch with prior school experiences. If the move occurs during the school year, academic learning time may be lost. Teachers must deal with classroom turnover and academic accountability. School personnel incur additional paperwork and new student responsibilities. These experiences affect connections in school communities and investments in students.

Understanding the impact of family mobility may necessitate differentiating families who are "on the move" from those who experience a move as a discrete event. Families with limited economic resources may depend on others, moving from place to place to avoid placing too great a burden on or wearing out their welcome with one relative or friend. Mobility may occur regularly when money is used up on survival necessities such as food and none is left to pay the rent. Moving may be a temporary or chronic solution to get away from untenable housing or a dangerous situation. When a residence or school change co-occurs with these other family stressors, support networks may be unavailable or overtaxed. Families with sufficient economic and support resources, on the other hand, may be able to handle moves much differently, with more time to prepare and more choice about their new environments. Changing residences or schools may be positive for families and children when the move is to a better home or for a good job, when it is seen as a better environment fit, or when it is viewed simply as an exciting new start. Our understanding of mobility is challenged to encompass an ecological viewpoint on the multidimensional nature of residence or school moves and on the varied outcomes mobility has on the lives of mobile children and families.

## Ecological Approach

An ecological lens may help provide a better understanding of the influence of residential moves and school changes in children's lives. Bronfenbrenner (1979) provides a classic ecological analysis, viewing a child as part of a system, surrounded by personal, familial, school, community, and larger world influences. This network of systemic influences in a child's life can help to identify both risk and protective factors that influence adjustment to an event such as a move. For example, a child with a healthy social network of extended family members, multiple friends, involvement in extracurricular activities, and community–world ties such as religion, work, or volunteering may be protected from major upheaval in the wake of a move. Factors predicting risk include social isolation, family instability or additional stressful life events, and limited resources, including financial strain and unavailable connections with important others. An illustration of the ecological model applied to moving highlights interaction of risk and protective factors across personal, social, and environmental domains (see Figure 1). Personal factors include preparedness for and control over the move, social issues involve support networks, and environmental issues target satisfaction and fit with the new home or school (Carlisle-Frank, 1992).

The importance of connections to others cannot be overstated. Families need support, resources, and education to strengthen their ability to guide and foster competencies in children. This kind of social capital, defined as the support and relationships children need

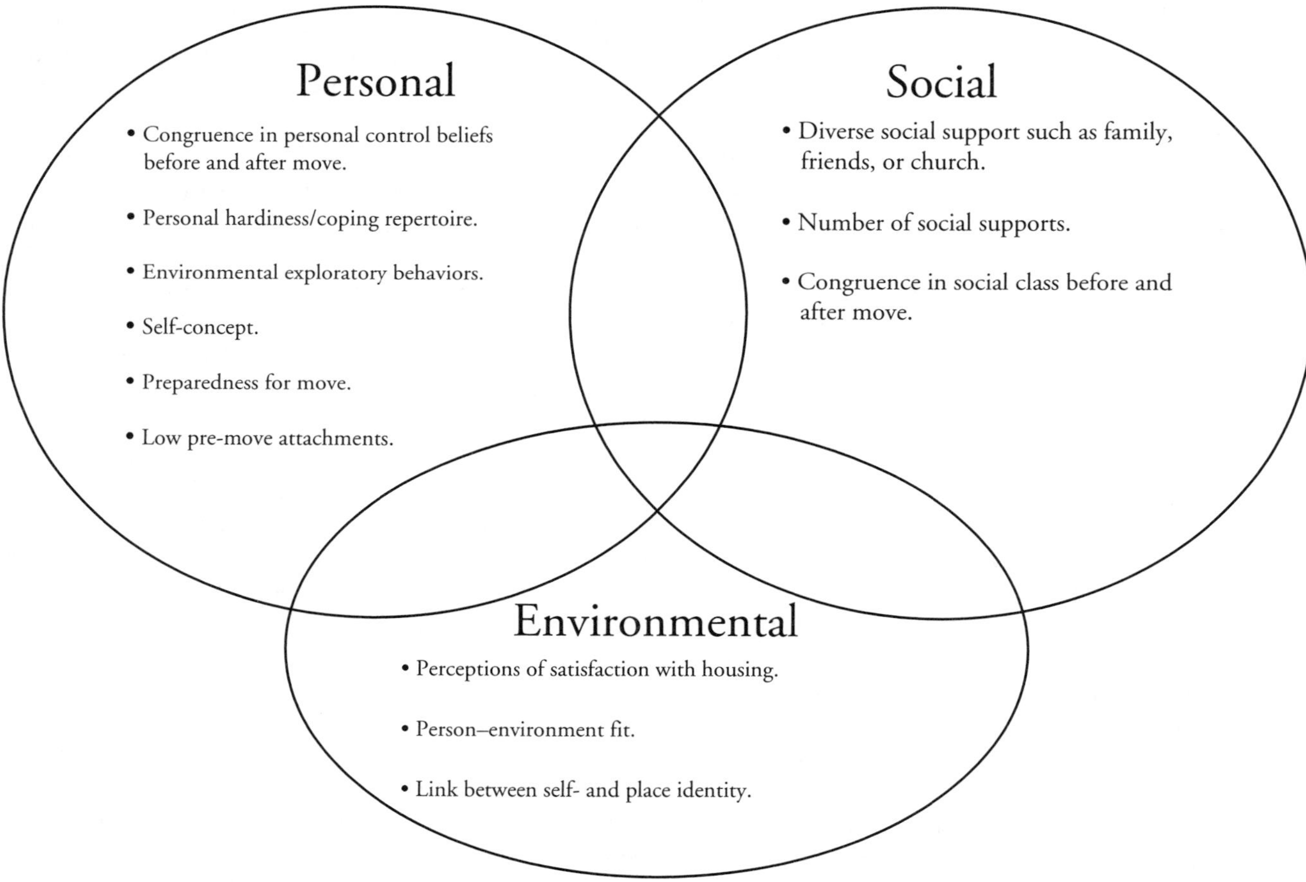


**Figure 1.** *Factors influencing adjustment to relocation.* Information adapted from *"The Relocation Experience: Analysis of Factors Thought to Influence Adjustment to Transition,"* by P. L. Carlisle-Frank, 1992, Psychological Reports, 70, pp. 835–838.

from adults in their lives (Coleman, 1987), is often eroded because of residential and school mobility. Moves often involve leaving behind important others, being unable or unwilling to make new connections, or simply not having the time or energy needed to establish relationships. Mobile families, on their own, may not be able to provide the social capital necessary for children's healthy development (Hagan, MacMillan, & Wheaton, 1996).

## Relationship to Educational Achievement and Social Development

Stability is important in children's lives, and mobility can shift the child's focus away from academic requirements and developmental challenges and require energy simply to adjust to new situations and surroundings. A largely negative relationship exists between frequent mobility and school adjustment and performance, but a causal connection has not been established and family characteristics are confounding influences (e.g., Wright, 1999). Adding to the equivocal nature of the mobility-achievement relationship is the co-occurrence of moves with other family stressors. In general, children from disadvantaged families have poorer school performance than their peers, with the added stress of frequent mobility resulting in even lower educational achievement (Temple & Reynolds, 1999). However, this appears to be an indirect relationship, perhaps mediated by a third variable such as school attendance. For example, children experiencing residential mobility miss more school, and poorer attendance has been shown to predict lower achievement (Kids Mobility Project, 1998). When viewed developmentally, there may be critical periods in children's lives during which residential or school change may be more problematic.

***Early childhood.*** Stability, continuity, and consistency in young children's lives are essential during the early childhood and preschool years. Adjustment to neighborhood and school environments outside the home taxes a child's competence, adding importance to experiencing stability at home. A focus of early childhood programs is to promote parent involvement and increase connections to the school community, thereby fostering school stability (Temple & Reynolds, 1999). Mobility, whether residential or school, adds stress and often brings about a sense of uncertainty as a change is happening. Continuity and consistency bolster a child's sense of security, safety, and attachment. If continuity (e.g., friends, extracurricular activities, and community-based activities) and consistency (e.g., same bedtime routines, weekend rhythms, home expectations, monitoring and discipline, and homework plans) across old and new environments can be accomplished, children's adjustment may be better (Buerkle, 1997).

***Elementary-age children.*** Early school years require children to adjust to the routines and demands of school away from their parents and home environment. School stability is associated with increased academic competence (Pianta & Early, 2001). Early mobility may be especially disruptive, as early elementary years are a critical period for developing a foundation in basic skills, and education is cumulative (Mantzicopoulos & Knutson, 2000). Young children have fewer coping skills and less developed personal competencies, so they may have more difficulty handling mobility-related changes than older children (Alexander, Entwisle, & Dauber, 1996). Residential stability and living with both biological parents have been identified as important protective factors and are considered social capital for young children (Tucker, Marx, & Long, 1998).

***Middle and high school students.*** Mobility affects peer relationships. This becomes more and more important as children get older, with junior high and high school presenting significant challenges to fitting in or breaking into established cliques. Adolescents' sense of identity may be threatened by a loss in their peer network and the resulting environment change (Brown & Orthner, 1990). A disruption in continuity and routine may be problematic in adolescence because of the need for a stable arena of comfort in the midst of teenage turbulence (Adam & Chase-Lansdale, 2002). One study found that school change in eighth to 10th grade was positive, often done using a plan, and accepted by peers, whereas later school mobility (10th to 12th grade) was detrimental to school achievement and completion (Swanson & Schneider, 1999). During the adolescent years, school changes may occur not because of family mobility but because of school choice options. Students may change schools for specific educational opportunities or for what they see as a better fit. Alternatively, school change resulting from behavioral or academic problems is viewed as a form of educational disengagement, a risk factor for dropout, and a predictor of poorer achievement (Rumberger & Larson, 1998).

# PROBLEMS AND IMPLICATIONS

## Costs of Moving

The costs of family and school mobility are high. Mobile children and families experience the financial strain of moving expenses, social vulnerability associated with the loss of established and familiar connections with friends and neighbors, and emotional uncertainty that accompanies a change in address and starting over. Families that move deal with residence or school change as a stressful life event; for those families chronically on the move, mobility is seen as a sign of underlying family instability. Families on the move are viewed as transient with their lack of stability affecting the makeup of their neighborhoods and schools, their ease of connecting within communities, and the willingness of others, including teachers and school personnel, to reach out to students considered short term. School personnel must help new students catch up on material already presented and adjust to new classrooms and peer groups, and they must deal with student turnover issues and academic accountability for students they did not teach.

## Mobility in Special Populations

Although mobility requires adjustment to new surroundings and environments for all children and families, certain groups, because of their increased rates of mobility, have even more significant obstacles to overcome (see Table 1).

**Table 1** *Special Populations Affected by High Rates of Family or School Mobility*

| Special Population | Specific Challenges |
|---|---|
| Homeless | • Unrecognized or unmet educational needs.<br>• Lack of stable social relationships. |
| Foster care | • High rates of school transfers with change in care. |
| Welfare-assisted families | • Housing instability due to economic strain, dangerous neighborhoods, and substandard housing. |
| Migrant | • Isolation, discrimination, and language barriers. |
| Immigrant | • High influx in target neighborhoods or schools, difficulty of meeting noneducational needs, and language barriers. |
| Special education | • Behavior that may lead to school-initiated mobility, program or school transfers that are required to meet needs, school changes leading to danger of disengagement and dropout. |
| Military | • High mobility that is the norm, building coping and adaptive skills. |

*Note:* Information adapted from (Special Issue) "Student Mobility: How Some Children Get Left Behind," C. Hartman & T. M. Franke (Eds.), 2003, *Journal of Negro Education, 72*(1).

***Families in poverty.*** Children and families living in poverty experience instability in many forms. Housing instability is one of the most insidious, and it often leads to greater school instability as well. Homelessness experienced by children has its own set of stressors, including the difficulty of handling residential change and instability. Rivlin (1990) described the importance of a stable home:

> Regardless of the quality of the housing, a person's home is the central organizing structure for the stream of activities that constitute a life. For children, this loss is most threatening since it occurs at a time when they are developing a sense of themselves, of their identity, of what they are capable of doing and of their own self-worth. The lack of consistency of setting threatens the acquisition of personal identity for children and challenges the identity and strength of adults. (p. 44)

Families are the fastest growing homeless group (Julianelle & Foscarinis, 2003). Poor school attendance, which often accompanies homelessness, leads to a lack of cognitive experiences, with a corresponding tie to poorer achievement (Kids Mobility Project, 1998). Similarly, children in foster care experience high rates of school transfer along with residence changes and oftentimes gaps in attendance due to systematic parameters (Conger & Finkelstein, 2003). Families receiving welfare assistance deal with reform measures that set limits on assistance with the aim of making families self-sufficient. For many, the loss of welfare benefits increases their mobility, leading to temporarily living with others or moving from home to home when unable to pay the rent (Nichols & Gault, 2003). A lack of affordable housing options increases mobility as families continue to move in a search for decent living quarters (Crowley, 2003).

***Immigrant and migrant families.*** Immigrant and migrant populations have specific cultural characteristics that often may be at odds with success in the American school system. Migrant families are mobile by virtue of following seasonal patterns of work, usually farm work or fishing, and are characterized by their nomadic qualities. They face obstacles including poverty, isolation, discrimination, and language barriers (Branz-Spall, Rosenthal, & Wright, 2003). Immigrant children often miss extended periods of the school year for trips back to the homeland to visit family or celebrate important cultural events, which interferes with educational continuity. Children in immigrant families may experience school changes while finding stable housing, a constant influx of new classmates, and a high turnover rate among teachers and administrators as their schools are stretched to capacity meeting noneducational needs (Hanna, 2003).

***Special education.*** Students with emotional, behavioral, and cognitive disabilities exhibit more behavioral problems than the general population of students (Mendez, Knoff, & Ferron, 2002). These behavioral incidences may lead to disciplinary actions, which in turn leave special education students more vulnerable to school-initiated mobility resulting from suspensions, expulsions, or involuntary transfers (Osher, Morrison, & Bailey, 2003). In addition, students receiving special education services may experience school change associated with finding a site or program that best meets their needs. To the extent that school change enhances a student's ability to benefit from an academic program or to establish positive relationships, mobility can be positive for the adjustment of children with learning and behavior challenges. Often, however, change has been shown to increase adjustment difficulties, which are related to school disengagement and dropping out (Osher et al.).

Considering risk and protective factors can be helpful when advocating for students with special needs. Examples of protective factors are good communication among team members, partnering with families, and increased mainstreaming experiences for students. Risk factors include isolating students within or out of the classroom (e.g., in a behavior room or principal's office) and high numbers of transitions (e.g., pullout services, teacher turnover). Protective factors can be seen as strengthening students' connections with schools, whereas risk factors tend to promote disengagement, mobility, and dropout potential.

***Military.*** The high mobility faced by military families is accepted as part of this lifestyle, rather than viewed as a problem, thus moves often are viewed as new and exciting opportunities. The Department of Defense Education Activity (DoDEA) schools provide specific information on their success (Joiner, 2003; Smrekar & Owens, 2003). Despite more than a third of their students moving each school year, DoDEA schools have developed a system of support and accountability that has led to impressive achievement results for a culturally and socioeconomically diverse student group. In fact, DoDEA schools have a noteworthy record of high achievement for largely minority, low-income students, compared with their civilian peers.

Highly qualified teachers, involved parents, individualized attention in small schools, and a transition support plan for mobile students appear to be key factors in these outcomes. Military families have networks, services, and opportunities in place to aid adjustment, and they know that everyone else is dealing with similar circumstances. Families and children are more likely to be open to making connections when they know others are looking for this as well. In addition, moving may positively affect school achievement through elevated social competence scores and high rates of participation in extracurricular activities (Marchant & Medway, 1987).

Despite overall positive findings of the adjustment of military children to frequent moves, families in the military are vulnerable, similar to their civilian counterparts, to co-occurring life stressors and poor adaptation or coping skills. In some military families, highly mobile teens perceive themselves as insecure, complaining, inconsistent, critical, and less intimate when compared with their less mobile peers (Shaw, 1979). Students with effective coping and problem-solving skills and positive attitudes find adjustment easier than students who are less adaptive.

# ALTERNATIVE ACTIONS FOR PREVENTION AND INTERVENTION

As the previous section indicated, the detrimental effects of frequent school changes for students are widespread. This section describes three categories of prevention and intervention actions. On a broad scale, national and state policies may have the power to reduce mobility of families who move frequently for reasons other than choice. At the school level, educators can reduce the likelihood of frequent moves by welcoming families and developing a strong school–community bond. Because some moves will occur, as a third level of action, schools must be prepared to provide services to make education accessible and effective for mobile students.

## Policy Implications

One of the United States' six educational goals is to increase high school completion and reduce the achievement gap between White and minority youth; it may well be that if this goal is to be fulfilled, school mobility must be reduced and its negative consequences alleviated (Rumberger & Larson, 1998). The primary public policy consideration in reducing the mobility of low-income families is to increase the availability of affordable housing. For example, in one U.S. metropolitan area, for 68,900 renter households with a yearly income below $10,000, only 31,200 housing units had rental prices that were affordable for this group (Kids Mobility Project, 1998). A single parent earning minimum wage from one full-time job cannot afford the fair market rate for a two-bedroom rental unit anywhere in the United States (Julianelle & Foscarinis, 2003). To protect the well-being of children, access to affordable, safe, and stable housing is critical, along with access to stable, quality school systems (Crowley, 2003; Kids Mobility Project, 1998; Nichols & Gault, 2003).

Next, district policies that do not require a direct relationship between residential address and school enrollment, along with flexible transportation options, reduce mobility by allowing residentially mobile students to maintain enrollment at their school of origin. Schools experiencing high rates of mobility as a result of homelessness or residential moves in general can team with district transportation systems through the efforts of a McKinney–Vento liaison or a school social worker who will track mobility and communicate with the transportation office (James & Lopez, 2003). The passage of the McKinney–Vento Act in 1987 gave homeless students the right to remain in their home school, with the aim of increasing educational stability, access, and success. Despite this effort, homeless children often suffer because of unrecognized or unmet educational needs and a lack of stable social relationships (Julianelle & Foscarinis, 2003). School transfers may be lessened if transportation is provided or, in the case of children in foster care, if placement focuses on extended families or neighborhood placements (Conger & Finkelstein, 2003). In addition, better coordination between welfare officials and school personnel could ease and reduce transitions (see chapters 62 and 63 on "Poverty" and "Foster Homes"). On a local level, schools can implement policies to reduce the level of mobility in their student bodies. General policies and practices that promote the overall effectiveness of the school can increase student engagement and therefore reduce voluntary turnover. Reducing grade retention and increasing teacher quality and salaries are specific policy areas that have been linked to reducing mobility (Rumberger, 2003). Schools should also examine their policies that dictate responses to problem behavior, including suspensions and referrals to the principal's office, in order to avoid pushing students out of school or further diminishing already limited instructional time for mobile students (Osher et al., 2003). Considering the important concepts of student engagement and school push-outs, it becomes clear that school policies have an impact on both voluntary and involuntary mobility (see chapter 8, "School Completion").

## Improvements in the Home–School Connection

Perhaps the most frequently cited intervention for improving the school experiences of students and families is forging a stronger bond between families and school (Nakagawa, Stafford, Fisher, & Matthews, 2002). Highly mobile families are likely to be experiencing several stressors; therefore, schools need to make a concentrated effort to reach out to these families and welcome them into the school community. Especially in urban areas, in which geographically concentrated, intra-district moves are the norm, schools that develop a positive relationship with families can increase parents' emotional investment in the school and their likelihood of taking steps to continue their child's enrollment even after a change in residence. Specific practices that schools have implemented in order to increase engagement of mobile families include hosting cultural events, providing parent and family resources in the style of full-service schools, offering adult education classes or family counseling services, and communicating directly with parents (see chapter 6, "Parent–Teacher Relationships").

Partnering with community resources and helping families to account for basic needs (food, clothing, and affordable housing) are ways to both decrease mobility and clearly communicate that the family is important to your school (Fisher, Matthews, Stafford, Nakagawa, & Durante, 2002; Franke, Isken, & Parra, 2003). This help is especially critical for families who are mobile because of forced moves. Providing resources for families to fulfill their basic needs helps to eliminate the likelihood that a parent will have to choose between buying food for their children and paying the rent with limited funds. Overall, it is important for schools to avoid the pitfall of treating highly mobile families as problems or clients; instead, schools should view these families as welcome partners and resources (Nakagawa et al., 2002).

Finally, simply sharing information with parents and families is critical. Details about the effects of mobility on students' school success may encourage parents to find a way to reduce or eliminate school mobility for their sons and daughters, either by waiting until the end of a school year to move, or by investigating ways to maintain enrollment after a move (Capps & Maxwell, 2002; Kerbow, Azcoitia, & Buell, 2003). Schools also can provide families with information regarding transportation options and advertise policies that may allow students to remain continuously enrolled in their original school despite a move (Kerbow, 1996).

Although studies have not specifically examined the link between strong family–school connections and benefits for mobile families, the literature on family–school connections in general as well as anecdotal and qualitative evidence from schools suggest that families are more likely to continue enrollment in one school and to support the academic development of their children at home when these bonds are created. In addition, developing a partnership with families promotes a common message across home and school that learning is important, and it improves support for student engagement and school completion. Only when families are invited and welcomed into schools can continuity and consistency exist, not only across home and school but also between changes in residence and enrollment.

## Accessible and Effective Education for Mobile Students

Much remains to be researched in the area of remediation of problems related to mobility in students. Still, several promising practices are being implemented in schools across the country that appear to improve school experiences for mobile students and families as well as for school personnel. These practices typically aim to (a) reduce the alienation of families by developing a stronger school–community connection, (b) alleviate the negative social and academic consequences for students, (c) ease the logistical struggles of school processes, and (d) smooth the transition process from one school to another. Each tactic helps to address one or more of the challenges associated with mobility.

***Social and academic success.*** Discontinuity in curriculum coupled with the challenge of adjusting to a new classroom make learning difficult for students who change schools frequently. Providing before- and after-school programs for academic and social development, along with tutoring during the school day, can help students fill in the gaps in skills developed during frequent moves (Fisher et al., 2002; Kerbow, 1996).

One critical influence on academic success for all students is attendance. Students who change schools frequently tend to have lower attendance rates than their more stable peers (Kids Mobility Project, 1998). Reducing the number of days these students are exposed to instruction further compounds the challenges they are already facing. A proactive school or district approach to improving attendance rates for all students can help mobile students maintain academic growth. One such district approach is a comprehensive attendance plan focusing on the characteristics outlined in Table 2.

Beyond ensuring attendance at school, schools must also ensure that a quality education is available and accessible. Rumberger (2003) presented several practical steps that teachers, families, and schools can take in order to prepare for transition and navigate it successfully:

- At the school level, prepare for new students by planning activities and materials (including extra sections of required courses) to accommodate large numbers of incoming students, preparing an orientation video about the school, training volunteer student coaches who have experience with mobility, and developing information packets about extracurricular activities.

**Table 2** *Comprehensive Attendance Plan Characteristics*

| Plan Component | Explanation |
|---|---|
| Clarity of policy | Policy should be clear enough to determine excused vs. unexcused tardies and absences and should include a clear statement on the number of absences allowed. |
| Equity from site to site | Equity in the enforcement of policy, rules, and procedures is facilitated by clarity of policy. |
| Communication to the public | Regular communication to staff, students, and families. |
| Use of data and technology to collect and use reliable attendance data | Data are used to analyze outcomes and solve problems by identifying students at risk, communicating with families in a timely manner, and avoiding mere calculation of buildings' average daily attendance. |
| Support between district and schools' staff | Support of district staff is critical, as is deployment of attendance support staff in *all* levels of school. Elementary schools are too often neglected, and that is where patterns of attendance are set. |
| Engagement of students in learning | Educators must address instruction, school climate, and diverse reasons for absences. |
| Engagement of families | This is best accomplished through early, frequent, and positive communication. |
| Development of a shared expectation about the district's responsibility to provide transportation | The district, school, and community must agree on the provision of transportation. |

*Note.* Information from "Student Attendance and Mobility in Minneapolis Public Schools," by E. Hinz, L. Kapp, & S. Snapp, 2003, *Journal of Negro Education, 72*(1), pp. 141–149.

- At the classroom level, prepare for new students by developing learning packets that cover background information on units, and by creating subject matter and reading and writing skills assessments.
- Provide late-enrolling students with opportunities to earn credits through independent study or to enroll in a class without credit to gain experience and then re-enroll the following semester.
- Encourage students to join extracurricular activities or counseling groups, if appropriate.
- Make an appointment with new students to meet on the telephone or in person 1 or 2 weeks after enrollment to check on students' progress.
- Provide ongoing activities for academic and social growth by forming a new students group at lunch, providing staff mentors, and monitoring student progress.

A qualitative study of one school's implementation of these tactics showed that over several years, faculty have cultivated a commitment to making every child feel welcome by actively reaching out to parents and creating an overall culture of caring to meet the needs of highly mobile students. Integrating a school-wide approach to easing transitions of incoming students enables the school staff to recognize and attend to individual student needs during the intake process (Beck, Kratzer, & Isken, 1997).

***School processes.*** Mobile students' learning problems may be exacerbated when information is not quickly exchanged between schools. Students may be reassessed for ability and achievement at every school entry in order to determine their instructional needs—assessments that may have already been conducted one or several times in previous schools—which detracts from instructional time for the student and delays transition into the new classroom. Expediting school processes for serving mobile students is an important step in providing appropriate educational services to this group.

Given that students in urban areas may be moving within clusters of schools, one viable option for easing the transmittal of records is to collaborate with other schools to expedite the process. Schools that tend to share a pool of mobile students within a district can work together to ensure prompt delivery of records, optimally through a portfolio assessment system that follows students wherever they go (Kerbow, 1996). A centralized data system may also be a way for schools to monitor attendance and enrollment and to access records for students on the move (Nakagawa et al., 2002). Solutions created by the Title 1 Migrant Education Program mirror this notion and include electronic records transfer systems and distance learning programs in an attempt to attenuate the barriers of isolation, discrimination, and language (Branz-Spall et al., 2003).

Another method for easing transitions for intradistrict moves is to establish one core curriculum across all schools (Kids Mobility Project, 1998). This option may help to reduce discrepancies between curricula for mobile students, but it also has drawbacks. For example, policy decisions may take a long time to trickle down to the classroom level, leaving different schools in different curricula for longer than intended. Also, mobile districts tend to be diverse districts—one curriculum may not be optimal for each school's population (Kerbow et al., 2003). A decision on this method would be best made after districts examine the relative pros and cons for their students.

***Smoothing transitions.*** Several tactics can be beneficial for helping mobile students become acclimated to their new schools more quickly and easily. One intervention commonly implemented to welcome students into a new school is a formal orientation process. This process may include a tour of the school, introduction to key adults, and a "welcome packet" of necessary supplies (Capps & Maxwell, 2002). In addition, an initial meeting and family history interview between a school staff member (principal, counselor, etc.) and the student and his or her family can help create a smooth transition. During this time, a brief academic assessment tailored to the school's curriculum can provide a preliminary picture of areas of strength or gaps in a student's academic preparation and can indicate what academic support or in-class help the student may need (Franke et al., 2003).

DoDEA schools may be a good model for easing transitions between schools for mobile children. These schools have integrated a transition support plan to provide children and parents with the tools to maintain continuity and consistency during moves (Joiner, 2003). Included in this support plan is an information packet for families that includes helpful websites, tips for moving during the school year, and even recommendations on what courses to enroll in based on age (Joiner). Other tactics include having counselors who are trained to do step-by-step orientations, setting up an interactive counseling center with videoconference capabilities for exchanging transcript information, pairing new and current students in a student buddies system, reserving spaces in advanced courses, and announcing arriving and departing students in a daily bulletin.

Many schools implement the practice of pairing a new student with a buddy in the classroom to help the student adjust to the new physical and social surroundings of the school (e.g., Franke et al., 2003). The buddy student may be a successful mobile student, or any other student the teacher deems appropriate. Encouraging new students to join school clubs or extracurricular activities can promote speedier social integration and bonding with the school (Franke et al.).

Overall, a comprehensive approach is needed to meet the needs of students and families on the move. A survey of school personnel in highly mobile schools suggests that the most effective programs for addressing the problems associated with mobility addressed all levels of mobility: antecedents, school processes, and student and family consequences (Fisher et al., 2002).

## SUMMARY

A majority of children and school personnel are affected by mobility, either directly through a residence or school change or indirectly through student turnover. Although preventing all mobility is not a realistic goal—since some moves may be positive in the lives of children and families—comprehensive interventions give schools and educators ways to address mobility-related issues for students. Addressing public policy and home–school connections may reduce mobility, and implementing practices to make education effective and accessible can improve school experiences of highly mobile students.

Actions for prevention and intervention should be far-reaching and inclusive. Preventing forced or unnecessary mobility can occur through partnerships with community agencies to provide families with resources to meet their basic needs, to encourage an increase in the availability of affordable housing, and to strengthen relationships between schools, families, and community. Such efforts should be combined for maximum effectiveness. Promoting consistency and continuity for mobile students means partnering with parents, addressing gaps in learning and identifying learning problems or strengths early, promoting high levels of attendance, and engaging students in learning. Furthermore, establishing public policies that support affordable housing and transportation; developing a strong home, school, and community bond to improve educational engagement, family involvement, and attendance; and improving services aimed at making education accessible and effective can support mobile children and increase student achievement. When children and families feel they are part of their school and the larger community, these stronger bonds may provide stability that helps to increase successful outcomes for all.

## RECOMMENDED RESOURCES

### Books and Other Printed Material

Hartman, C., & Franke, T. M. (Eds.). (2003). Student mobility: How some children get left behind [Special issue]. *Journal of Negro Education, 72*(1).

This special issue covers the antecedents, processes, and consequences of school mobility for students and families. The issue discusses the impact and shape of special populations such as migrant families, students with emotional and behavioral disorders, homeless youth, children in foster care, and others who transfer frequently. Also presented are educational considerations, along with several suggestions for prevention and intervention.

Kids Mobility Group (1996). *Kids Mobility Project Report.* Minneapolis, MN: City Planning Dept., Hennepin County Office of Planning & Development, Minneapolis School District, University of Minnesota Dept. of Educational Psychology and Center for Urban and Regional Affairs (CURA). Contact: Author.

This online report provides research results from two urban mobility studies. Research focused on the school achievement of mobile students and on the impact of moving on low-income families. Available online at *http://www.fhfund.org/_dnld/reports/kids.doc*, or as a PDF file at *http://www.fhfund.org/_dnld/reports/kids.pdf*

Rumberger, R. W., Larson, K. A., Ream, R. K., & Palardy, G. A. (1999). *The educational consequences of mobility for California students and schools.* Berkeley, CA: Policy Analysis for California Education.

This book reports the results of a study examining incidence, consequences, and causes of mobility. Data include surveys of eighth graders followed over 6 years as part of the National Education Longitudinal Study data set, interviews with mobile students and their parents, and interviews with educators. The book includes suggestions for reducing and coping with student mobility, plus a snapshot of a school in which suggested interventions have been implemented.

### Websites

The following websites belong to mobility-related special interest groups or programs. These contacts provide innovative ideas for collaboration with a variety of entities to address this multifaceted problem.

*http://www.mpls.k12.mn.us/printview/c1a6c1de-2064-4412-aec2-445946c28baa.html* or go to *http://www.mpls.k12.mn.us* and search Homeless and Highly Mobile Student Services.

This website provides links to documents intended to assist educators in serving homeless and highly mobile students.

*http://www.naehcy.org/index.html*

The National Association for the Education of Homeless Children and Youth website includes links to educational resources as well as legislation and policy concerning homeless youth.

*http://www.militarychild.org/MOA.asp*

The Military Child Education Coalition's Memorandum of Agreement outlines specific steps for schools to use to help transitioning students. Included are ideas to ease transitions between schools, transfer records expediently, expand access to extracurricular activities, provide professional development, and more. Much of the information pertains to military schools, but civilian schools are taken into account as well.

## REFERENCES

Adam, E. K., & Chase-Lansdale, P. L. (2002). Home sweet home(s): Parental separations, residential moves, and adjustment problems in low-income adolescent girls. *Developmental Psychology, 38,* 792–805.

Alexander, K. L., Entwisle, D. R., & Dauber, S. L. (1996). Children in motion: School transfers and elementary school performance. *Journal of Educational Research, 90,* 3–12.

Beck, L. G., Kratzer, C. C., & Isken, J. A. (1997). Caring for transient students in one urban elementary school. *Journal for a Just and Caring Education, 3,* 343–369.

Branz-Spall, A. M., Rosenthal, R., & Wright, A. (2003). Children of the road: Migrant students, our nation's most mobile population. *Journal of Negro Education, 72,* 55–62.

Bronfenbrenner, U. (1979). *The ecology of human development.* Cambridge, MA: Harvard University Press.

Brown, A. C., & Orthner, D. K. (1990). Relocation and personal well-being among early adolescents. *Journal of Early Adolescence, 10,* 366–381.

Buerkle, K. (1997). Mobile children and families: Qualitative and quantitative explorations of the meaning and impact of residential mobility and school changes (Doctoral dissertation, University of Minnesota, 1997). *Dissertation Abstracts International, 58*(6), 2067.

Capps, W. R., & Maxwell, M. E. (2002). Mobility. *American School Board Journal, 189*(5), 26–29.

Carlisle-Frank, P. L. (1992). The relocation experience: Analysis of factors thought to influence adjustment to transition. *Psychological Reports, 70,* 835–838.

Cohen, P., Johnson, J., Struening, E. L., & Brook, J. S. (1989). Family mobility as a risk for early childhood psychopathology. In B. Cooper & T. Helgason (Eds.), *Epidemiology and the prevention of mental disorders* (pp. 145–156). London: Routledge.

Coleman, J. S. (1987). Families and schools. *Educational Researcher, 16,* 32–38.

Conger, D., & Finkelstein, M. J. (2003). Foster care and school mobility. *Journal of Negro Education, 72,* 97–103.

Crowley, S. (2003). The affordable housing crisis: Residential mobility of poor families and school mobility of poor children. *Journal of Negro Education, 72,* 22–38.

Fisher, T. A., Matthews, L., Stafford, M. E., Nakagawa, K., & Durante, K. (2002). School personnel's perceptions of effective programs for working with mobile students and families. *Elementary School Journal, 102,* 317–333.

Franke, T. M., Isken, J. A., & Parra, M. T. (2003). A pervasive school culture for the betterment of student outcomes: One school's approach to student mobility. *Journal of Negro Education, 72,* 150–157.

Hagan, J., MacMillan, R., & Wheaton, B. (1996, June). New kid in town: Social capital and the life course effects of family migration on children. *American Sociological Review, 61,* 368–385.

Hanna, W. J. (2003). Mobility and the children of Langley Park's immigrant families. *Journal of Negro Education, 72,* 63–78.

Hinz, E., Kapp, L., & Snapp, S. (2003). Student attendance and mobility in Minneapolis Public Schools. *Journal of Negro Education, 72,* 141–149.

James, B. W., & Lopez, P. D. (2003). Transporting homeless students to increase stability: A case study of two Texas districts. *Journal of Negro Education, 72,* 126–140.

Joiner, L. L. (2003). A different kind of district. *American School Board Journal, 190*(7), 16–19.

Julianelle, P. F., & Foscarinis, M. (2003). Responding to the school mobility of children and youth experiencing homelessness: The McKinney-Vento Act and beyond. *Journal of Negro Education, 72,* 39–54.

Kerbow, D. (1996). Patterns of urban student mobility and local school reform. *Journal of Education for Students Placed at Risk (JESPAR), 1,* 147–169.

Kerbow, D., Azcoitia, C., & Buell, B. (2003). Student mobility and local school improvement in Chicago. *Journal of Negro Education, 72,* 158–164.

Kids Mobility Project. (1998). *Report from the Kids Mobility Project.* Minneapolis Public Schools, Hennepin County, University of Minnesota: CURA and CAREI, & the Family Housing Fund. Minneapolis, MN: Author.

Mantzicopoulos, P., & Knutson, D. J. (2000). Head Start children: School mobility and achievement in the early grades. *Journal of Educational Research, 93,* 305–311.

Marchant, K. H., & Medway, F. J. (1987). Adjustment and achievement associated with mobility in military families. *Psychology in the Schools, 24,* 289–294.

Mendez, L. M. R., Knoff, H. M., & Ferron, J. M. (2002). School demographic variables and out-of-school suspension rates: A quantitative and qualitative analysis of a large, ethnically diverse school district. *Psychology in the Schools, 39,* 259–277.

Nakagawa, K., Stafford, M. E., Fisher, T. A., & Matthews, L. (2002). The "city migrant" dilemma: Building community at high-mobility urban schools. *Urban Education, 37,* 96–125.

Nichols, L., & Gault, B. (2003). The implications of welfare reform for housing and school instability. *Journal of Negro Education, 72,* 106–116.

Osher, D., Morrison, G., & Bailey, W. (2003). Exploring the relationship between student mobility and dropout among students with emotional and behavioral disorders. *Journal of Negro Education, 72,* 79–96.

Pianta, R. C., & Early, D. (2001). Turnover in kindergarten classroom membership in a national sample. *Early Education and Development, 12,* 239–252.

Rivlin, L. G. (1990). The significance of home and homelessness. In D. G. Unger & M. B. Sussman (Eds.), *Families in community settings: Interdisciplinary perspectives* (pp. 39–56). New York: Haworth Press.

Rumberger, R. W. (2003). The causes and consequences of student mobility. *Journal of Negro Education, 72,* 6–21.

Rumberger, R. W., & Larson, K. A. (1998). Student mobility and the increased risk of high school dropout. *American Journal of Education, 107,* 1–35.

Schachter, J. P. (2004). *Geographical Mobility, 2002 to 2003* (Rep. No. P20-549).Washington, DC: U.S. Bureau of the Census.

Shaw, J. A. (1979). Adolescents in the mobile military community. *Adolescent Psychiatry, 7,* 191–198.

Smrekar, C. E., & Owens, D. E. (2003). "It's a way of life for us": High mobility and high achievement in Department of Defense schools. *Journal of Negro Education, 72,* 165–177.

Swanson, C. B., & Schneider, B. (1999). Students on the move: Residential and educational mobility in America's schools. *Sociology of Education, 72*(1), 54–67.

Temple, J. A., & Reynolds, A. J. (1999). School mobility and achievement: Longitudinal findings from an urban cohort. *Journal of School Psychology, 37,* 355–377.

Tucker, C. J., Marx, J., & Long, L. (1998). "Moving on": Residential mobility and children's school lives. *Sociology of Education, 71*(2), 111–129.

Wright, D. (1999). School mobility: A negligible and confounded influence on student achievement. *Journal of Educational Research, 92,* 347–353.

# 56

# Divorce

**Shannon M. Greene**
**Edward R. Anderson**
**Emily A. Doyle**
**Holly Riedelbach**

*Department of Human Ecology and Population Research Center*
*University of Texas–Austin*

Each year, more than 1 million American children experience their parents' divorce (U.S. Census Bureau, 2000). Cumulative projections indicate that by age 18, 40% of children will have experienced parental divorce. Thus, divorce and life in a single-parent household have become increasingly common for large numbers of families with children.

This chapter discusses children's adjustment to divorce and addresses some of the common misunderstandings that arise from research in this area. It then reviews the changes in family life children go through after a parental divorce, with a focus on key factors that may present challenges to adjustment. Finally, the chapter reviews alternative actions for prevention and intervention for children undergoing parental divorce.

## BACKGROUND AND DEVELOPMENT

### Risk Associated With Divorce

Divorce and its effects on child adjustment have been the focus of intensive study, although controversy exists over how best to integrate the findings. To illustrate, Table 1 presents seven statements that may be useful in assessing the relative risk associated with divorce on children's adjustment.

It may be surprising to learn that each statement is true in that it correctly summarizes a particular part of the empirical literature relating to children of divorce. The list of statements was derived from an earlier review of the literature (Greene, Anderson, Hetherington, Forgatch, & DeGarmo, 2003). This chapter examines empirical support for each in the sections that follow.

***1. Children of divorce are at serious risk for maladaptation.*** Parental divorce is associated with a doubling of the risk of children experiencing clinically significant behavior problems (e.g., Hetherington & Kelly, 2002). Estimates of children from divorced households show that 17% to 25% will experience elevated levels of behavior problems, as compared with approximately 10% to 15% for children from nondivorced households (see also Amato, 2001, and Amato & Keith, 1991, for meta-analyses of divorce research). Any event that is associated with a twofold elevation of risk certainly would warrant attention by researchers and clinicians.

***2. Most children display no serious difficulties after their parents' divorce.*** From the same data presented above, it also is clear that the overwhelming majority of children (i.e., the 75% to 83% without behavioral problems) show no serious difficulties in relation to their parents' divorce. Thus, although divorce is associated with an increased likelihood of risk, it is incorrect to conclude that most children will have substantial problems as a consequence. The data, in fact, support both statements 1 and 2, with the former emphasizing risk and the latter emphasizing resilience.

***3. Substantial numbers of children of divorce are better adjusted than those from nondivorced households.*** Because there is a sizable overlap in the distribution of adjustment between children from divorced

**Table 1** *A Quiz on Children and Divorce*

Consider whether each of the following statements is true or false:

1. Children of divorce are at serious risk for maladaptation.
2. Most children display no serious difficulties after their parents' divorce.
3. Substantial numbers of children of divorce are better adjusted than those from nondivorced households.
4. Many of the negative effects associated with divorce exist well before the marriage ends.
5. Adjustment in some children is enhanced by their parents' divorce.
6. Negative effects of divorce on children generally resolve soon afterward.
7. Children may be affected adversely by parental divorce even into adulthood.

versus nondivorced families, it also is correct to state that many children from divorced families (approximately 40% based on estimates from meta-analytic work of Amato, 2001) are functioning at levels above the mean for children from nondivorced families. Much of the empirical literature on children's adjustment after divorce provides evidence for the large variability in how children are affected by this transition. This research highlights that divorce does not inevitably lead to problems in all children (see Amato, 2003, for a detailed description of the extent of overlap between distributions).

***4. Many of the negative effects associated with divorce exist well before the marriage ends.*** In explaining why children from divorced families fare worse than children from nondivorced families, some researchers have argued that divorce is essentially a marker for other factors that create problematic adjustment in children. Thus, from this perspective, some of the problems exhibited by children stem not from the divorce itself but from earlier deteriorating conditions in the family. Block, Block, and Gjerde (1986), for example, found that behavioral problems, particularly in boys, predated the divorce by up to 11 years. The finding that children from divorced homes exhibit higher rates of difficulties prior to divorce has been confirmed in other studies (e.g., Peris & Emery, 2004; Sun, 2001).

***5. Adjustment in some children is enhanced by their parents' divorce.*** Recent evidence has indicated that children appear to be better off in cases where the divorce substantially reduces levels of conflict between parents (Booth & Amato, 2001). In related findings, children from the most conflicted homes are more likely to report feeling relief about the divorce (Amato & Booth, 1997). In contrast, children from less conflicted homes are more likely to report distress over the divorce, and dissolution of relatively low-conflict marriages is associated with greater negative effects for children (Booth & Amato, 2001). There is some evidence that divorces occurring today may contain a greater proportion of low-conflict marriages, and thus the proportion of children experiencing psychological distress may be increasing (Amato, 2001). Together with evidence in support of statement 4, these results show that the quality of the marital relationship prior to divorce is an important factor to consider in understanding children's adjustment.

***6. Negative effects of divorce on children generally resolve soon afterward.*** Longitudinal evidence has shown that much of children's postdivorce behavior improves after 1 to 2 years following a divorce, as families adjust to their new life situation (e.g., Hetherington & Kelly, 2002). Thus, some of the difficulties experienced by children may reflect short-term disadvantages; consequently, the relative time since divorce is critical to understanding the nature of children's risk. With the support and involvement of a caring, competent adult, such as a parent, teacher, or school counselor, children generally are able to adjust over time.

***7. Children may be affected adversely by parental divorce even into adulthood.*** A number of studies show that adults who experienced parental divorce in childhood continue to show decrements such as lower life satisfaction and more depression (e.g., Amato & Sobolewski, 2001; Cherlin, Chase-Lansdale, & McRae, 1998). In a meta-analysis of 37 studies linking parental divorce in childhood with eventual adjustment in adulthood, Amato and Keith (1991) found moderate-size negative effects for depression and diminished life satisfaction, along with lower marital quality, educational attainment, income, occupational prestige, and physical health. As married adults, children of divorce also are more likely than those from nondivorced families to display reciprocally negative and escalating exchanges with their spouses and to demonstrate less effective problem solving (Hetherington, 1999). Divorce rates are higher as well, at 70% for the first 5 years of marriage for those from divorced family backgrounds (Bumpass, Martin, & Sweet, 1991). Selection of a stable, supportive spouse from a nondivorced household, however, may substantially reduce the risk of marital instability associated with having divorced parents (Hetherington & Kelly, 2002).

### Toward a Comprehensive Picture of Children's Postdivorce Adjustment

Taken together, statements 1–7 demonstrate that there is a great deal of diversity in children's responses to divorce. Some adjustment problems may be transitory, some may persist, and some may be present long before the actual dissolution occurs. How children respond to divorce depends on factors within the family preceding the divorce and on stresses and supports available to children and families afterward. In addition, there is evidence that boys are at greater risk than girls for some types of behavior problems, namely, conduct problems, after divorce (Amato, 2001). Despite the difference in conduct problems, however, divorce is associated with a range of poor outcomes for both boys and girls.

Some have hypothesized that children's reactions to divorce vary by age. For example, qualitative information on a clinical population suggests that preschoolers regress behaviorally and older children react angrily (Wallerstein, Lewis, & Blakeske 2002). Meta-analytic work by Amato (2001) on broader populations shows divorce-related adjustment problems differing by age, with academic issues more prominent in primary school and psychological problems more prominent in secondary school. Amato points out, however, that interpretations of these data are hindered in that they reflect children's age at the time of data collection, not age at time of separation. Apparent age differences may reflect transitory difficulties associated with a recent divorce; thus, these data should be viewed with caution. Nevertheless, further attention to developmental changes is warranted, given that the resources available to children, such as cognitive coping skills and peer social support, change with age.

## PROBLEMS AND IMPLICATIONS

Divorce is not a single isolated event, but a complex chain of marital transitions and family reorganizations that alter roles and relationships, and affect individual and family adjustment (Hetherington, Bridges, & Insabella, 1998). Prior to divorce, there may be increases in conflict within the family, periods of physical separation between spouses, and attempts at reconciliation. Divorce itself may trigger further disruptions in daily routines, roles, activities, and social relationships, including additional shifts in living arrangements and visitation—physical separation for those who have not already done so, accompanied by changes in contact between the child and the nonresidential parent. Additionally, a series of transitions and reorganizations in family life may arise from parental efforts to establish new partnerships, including dating and nonmarital cohabitation. These changes present children and families with adaptive challenges, with the response to these challenges influenced by previous functioning and experiences and by subsequent stresses and resources (Amato, 2000; Hetherington et al.).

Many researchers adopt the view that parenting practices mediate many of the contextual changes that occur during and after divorce (e.g., Simons & Associates, 1996). Thus, divorce precipitates changes in family life that have the potential to disrupt effective parenting practices, such as monitoring children's whereabouts, providing consistent discipline, using constructive problem-solving strategies, and engaging in positive involvement. These changes, in turn, increase the likelihood of children exhibiting behavioral and emotional difficulties.

Available research suggests four key factors that have implications for how children and families adapt: economic hardship, interparental conflict, parental distress, and cumulative transitions and related life stress. Although these factors are related to one another (e.g., parents experience distress when conflict is high and economic resources are low), each has potential challenges and implications for child adjustment.

### Economic Hardship

Divorce often is associated with dramatic reductions in income, with per capita declines averaging between 13% and 35% in national samples (Peterson, 1996). Reduced income contributes to other stressful circumstances, such as changes in education, family living arrangements, and employment (e.g., a return to paid employment or increased hours) (Simons & Associates, 1996). Economic pressure faced by divorced families may involve being unable to meet material needs, falling behind in debt payments, and having to cut back on everyday expenses to live within available means (Conger, Ge, Elder,

Lorenz, & Simons, 1994). Economic hardship, when combined with high levels of life stress, is associated with increased psychological distress and decreased parenting skills. In these situations, some parents become distracted and either emotionally or physically unavailable to their children (Simons & Associates). These disruptions in parenting, in turn, lead to problematic behavior in children (Forgatch, Patterson, & Ray, 1996). Over time, levels of life stress usually dissipate, although families with lower incomes generally experience greater numbers of disruptive events. Thus, the increase in economic hardship following divorce is a potent factor in the emergence of problematic outcomes for children.

## Interparental Conflict

Accumulating research shows that the frequency and intensity of conflict, as well as more overt forms of conflict (e.g., verbal and physical aggression), are related to problematic adjustment in children, even independent of divorce (Amato, 1999). In fact, interparental conflict has been shown to be a better predictor of child maladjustment than changes in the parents' marital status (Davies, Harold, Goeke-Morey, & Cummings, 2002). Interparental conflict has been linked to increases in children's emotional distress, disruptions in peer relations and academic performance, and physical health difficulties. Children who have a family history of exposure to interparental conflict (particularly if the conflict remains unresolved) show increasing sensitivity or reactivity over time, with reactions that include fear, sadness, anger, and aggressiveness. They may be particularly affected by conflict that involves issues related to parenting, which has been shown to predict child behavior problems more strongly than factors such as the overall frequency of conflict. Moreover, when conflict concerns child-related issues such as child rearing or custody, children may feel a sense of shame, or blame themselves for the divorce, or fear becoming involved in the conflict (Grych, Harold, & Miles, 2003). Some have hypothesized that exposure to highly conflictual situations undermines children's sense of emotional security, as outwardly manifested by emotional and behavioral problems (Davies et al.). Others show that high levels of conflict disrupt parenting practices, with mothers demonstrating more negativity and inconsistent discipline, and fathers showing less overall involvement with their children, as opposed to those in low-conflict marriages (Gonzales, Pitts, Hill, & Roosa, 2000).

## Parental Distress

Divorce is one of the most stressful experiences adults may face. Not surprisingly, many individuals experience a variety of adjustment problems. Compared with the nondivorced, individuals who separate or divorce have increased risk of psychopathology, higher incidence of motor vehicle accidents, elevated drinking and drug use, alcoholism, suicide, and even death (see review by Amato, 2000). Individuals with a shorter separation time and greater emotional attachment to the former spouse have significantly poorer immune functioning, greater numbers of health problems, and depression (Kiecolt-Glaser, McGuire, Robles, & Glaser, 2002). However, there also may be positive effects, with some individuals reporting gains in autonomy, overall happiness, social involvement, and career development following a divorce (Hetherington & Kelly, 2002). Moreover, at 2 years, postdivorce women reported less depression, improved health, and better parenting than those who remained in unhappy, conflictual marriages.

Individuals who have difficulties in adapting to stressful postdivorce changes may have problematic relationships with their children (Tein, Sandler, & Zautra, 2000); problematic relationships, in turn, interfere with adjustment in children (e.g., Martinez & Forgatch, 2002). Within the context of the divorced family, parental adjustment assumes a critical role, given that child adjustment typically follows from how well adults in the household manage stress. Children's own adjustment difficulties also contribute to the custodial parent's level of stress and quality of parenting (Forgatch et al., 1996); thus, processes operating within the parent–child relationship contribute to the long-term adjustment of both family members.

## Cumulative Transitions and Related Life Stress

Several studies have shown that risk for adjustment problems also arises from additional transitions surrounding relationship dissolutions and consequent repartnering across formal and informal unions (e.g., Martinez & Forgatch, 2002). Most adults will enter into new relationships. One study shows, for example, that at the time of the divorce filing, half of the parents already had begun to date, and over one quarter were in a serious romantic relationship (Anderson et al., 2004). Within 10 years of separation, about two-thirds of families with two or more children have experienced a nonmarital cohabitation

(Bramlett & Mosher, 2002). Among remarriers, parents had dated an average of three to five partners prior to meeting the person they would eventually remarry (Montgomery, Anderson, Hetherington, & Clingempeel, 1992). Thus, a consideration of only formal changes in union formation is likely to underestimate substantially the number of transitions and reorganizations that children must adapt to as part of postdivorce family life (Raley & Wildsmith, 2004). Similar to risk factors discussed above, the effect of repartnering transitions on child adjustment is mediated by parenting practices. As transitions increase in number, there are corresponding decrements in parental problem-solving ability and increases in parent–child conflict (DeGarmo & Forgatch, 1997).

### Short-Term and Long-Term Adjustment to Divorce

How well children adapt to divorce depends on the particular combination of stresses and resources in their lives (Amato, 1993). As stresses abate and resources become more plentiful, children who had exhibited problematic adjustment will improve. Prolonged exposure to economic hardship, continuing conflict between former spouses, extended periods of parental distress and disrupted parenting, and experience with multiple life transitions are associated with long-term adjustment problems. Long-term effects of divorce also may persist because of disruptions in normal developmental trajectories during adolescence. Chase-Lansdale, Cherlin, and Kiernan (1995) found, for example, that effects in adulthood were mediated by problems arising in adolescence. The kinds of problems that children of divorce encounter as adolescents also are potentially more disruptive to their lives, such as school dropout, early parenthood, and elevated drug use (Sun, 2001).

Most families manage to avoid these more calamitous outcomes; however, parents may worry that their children, though not necessarily demonstrating clinically significant levels of problems, show some behavioral problems or emotional distress from the divorce (Emery, 1999). Many families seek help in addressing these concerns, with children of divorce being twice as likely as those from nondivorced homes to receive psychological treatment (Zill, Morrison, & Coiro, 1993). Some of the referral concerns relate to the child's achievement and behavior in the school setting. In fact, although results of meta-analysis show modest negative effects of divorce on academic achievement (Amato & Keith, 1991), the manifestation of related problems are wide ranging. Problems include lower grades and scores on standardized tests for reading and math; lower teacher ratings of motivation and academic achievement (e.g., Martinez & Forgatch, 2002); the presence of barriers to learning such as inattention, irrelevant talk, and lack of reflectiveness in the classroom (Emery, 1988); and low school attendance, poor homework completion, and less parental supervision of schoolwork (McLanahan, 1999). Thus, school-based prevention and intervention programs seek to prevent and ameliorate these kinds of problems.

## ALTERNATIVE ACTIONS FOR PREVENTION AND INTERVENTION

Prevention and intervention programs for children of divorce seek to strengthen supportive systems by enhancing children's coping strategies and understanding of divorce, promoting positive parenting practices, and identifying ways in which school personnel can foster children's postdivorce adjustment. At times, program efforts may address broader objectives, such as attempts to evoke change in the larger school population by minimizing any potential stigma associated with diverse family forms. Because many school-based programs for children of divorce do not implement a screening criterion to remove those displaying current adjustment problems, the same program may function as a preventive effort for those children in the group with no serious problems and as an intervention for those with problems. Because the same programs can comprise both prevention and intervention efforts, depending on the child's level of adjustment, this section combines the two topics. The following discussion describes programs that target children and those that target teachers and administrators.

### Programs That Target Children

There are a variety of school-based programs designed to assist children of divorce, with the relative popularity of these programs reflecting a number of advantages that schools offer over other settings (Grych & Fincham, 1992). With a clearly defined and reasonably accessible population, school-based programs have the potential to reach greater numbers of children than individual or community-based programs. Further, because schools are a normative part of children's daily lives, involvement in a school-based program may carry less stigma than those that occur in other settings (although some children may be sensitive to how their involvement in these programs is viewed by peers). School-based programs also offer greater ecological validity than individual or community-based programs because they are nested within a support network of teachers, counselors, and peers that is already known to the child. Finally, school-based programs may present the child with a more neutral set of circumstances than settings involving the parents or other family members, allowing the child a temporary reprieve from problematic processes occurring at home.

School-based programs often share overlapping goals, skills, and activities. With respect to goals, many programs seek to address children's specific divorce-related responses (e.g., fantasies of parental reconciliation or self-blame for the divorce), along with more broadly based efforts to increase academic achievement, improve self-esteem or self-concept, and foster appropriate emotional expression. Skill building typically concerns anger management and relaxation training, along with efforts to enhance communication and problem-solving abilities. Activities vary with the targeted age group but include role-playing, art projects, skits, bibliotherapy, discussions, and puppet play. Additionally, children may work toward creating a tangible product, such as collaborating on a divorce-related newspaper or developing a book of their personal experiences. These mementos serve as a reminder of program skills learned, and thus also may help to minimize termination issues.

School-based programs often have a similar structure. They typically follow a group format, which reflects time and cost constraints (Grych & Fincham, 1992; Emery, Kitzmann, & Waldron, 1999). Children themselves may prefer groups over individual sessions because the former allows them to meet others who have experienced divorce, which may normalize their experiences and lessen isolation (Lesowitz, Kalter, Pickar, Chethik, & Schaefer, 1987). Groups are typically organized around a specific age range (e.g., kindergarten and first grade), reflecting children's varying developmental capacities. Programs usually encompass 8 to 12 in-school sessions, with each session lasting about 45 minutes to an hour. As Lee, Picard, and Blain (1994) conclude in their review of divorce-related outcome studies, however, including more sessions does not necessarily lead to enhanced program effectiveness. Considerations of cost dictate that program selection be based on those with the fewest number of sessions but also with demonstrated efficacy.

With respect to efficacy, two school-based prevention programs are particularly noteworthy for having undergone the most empirical evaluation (Emery et al., 1999): the Children of Divorce Intervention Program (CODIP; Pedro-Carroll, Sutton, & Wyman, 1999), and the Divorce Adjustment Project (DAP; Stolberg & Mahler, 1994). Table 2 compares these two programs. Table 3 includes detailed reviews of other programs (Lee et al., 1994; Emery et al., 1999; Richardson & Rosen, 1999).

CODIP, which has program information and materials accessible on the Internet (see Recommended Resources), is noted for its programmatic efforts to carefully design, implement, and evaluate a group program to provide support and training in social competence. CODIP was originally designed for fourth to sixth graders, with subsequent adaptations for second and third graders in suburban and urban settings. The urban adaptation included program exercises with a revised format to include greater sensitivity to sociocultural factors (e.g., stronger emphasis on diverse family forms and program materials depicting ethnically diverse families). The urban adaptation also allowed for a broader definition of *divorcing* families, including children whose parents had ended a common-law or long-standing cohabitation arrangement. More recently, an adaptation of CODIP was tested on kindergarten and first-grade children (Pedro-Carroll & Alpert-Gillis, 1997). The authors also report an adaptation for seventh and eighth graders that has not yet been subjected to empirical testing.

CODIP is organized around three substantive sections. The first section (sessions 1–3) focuses on building group support and examining divorce-related feelings, misconceptions, anxieties, and family changes. Skits and role-playing are used to help children express their feelings, and a filmstrip further elucidates changes and attributions surrounding the experience of divorce. The second section (sessions 4–6) encourages skill building such as teaching strategies for handling interpersonal conflicts, with a key focus on helping children assess whether or not problems are within their control. The final section teaches skills for handling anger, including an examination of actual situations that were handled appropriately and inappropriately by the children. Role-playing allows students to practice alternative strategies.

In contrast to CODIP's exclusive work with children, DAP includes a child's group (ages 7–13) and a group for parents. In DAP, children receive peer support, along with efforts to address divorce-related misunderstandings and develop cognitive–behavioral skills to deal with

**Table 2** *School-Based Preventive Interventions With Follow-Up Evaluation*

| Intervention Program | Program Structure | Focus and Goals | Follow-Up Modifications |
|---|---|---|---|
| Children of Divorce Intervention Program (CODIP) (Pedro-Carroll et al., 1999) | • 12 weekly 1-hour sessions.<br>• Four units, three to five sessions each.<br>• Topics covered:<br>Feelings, families, and family changes.<br>Coping with feelings and problems.<br>Child–parent relationships<br>Perceptions of self and family. | • Provide supportive group environment.<br>• Help children identify and express appropriate feelings.<br>• Clarify divorce-related misconceptions.<br>• Enhance coping skills.<br>• Enhance children's perceptions of self and family. | Alpert-Gillis, Pedro-Carroll, & Cowen, 1989:<br>• Adaptation of existing program for urban children:<br>○ Broadened participation requirements to include termination of common-law marriages and long-term relationships.<br>○ Extended length of program to 16 sessions to solidify learned concepts.<br>○ Adjusted program content to reflect realities of urban life and ethnic differences.<br>• Inclusion of age-specific adaptations. |
| Divorce Adjustment Project (DAP) (Stolberg & Garrison, 1985) | • Children's Support Group (CSG), consisting of 12 1-hour, two-part sessions:<br>*Part I*: Discussion of specific topics, e.g., reconciliation fantasies, self-blame.<br>*Part II*: Development of coping and problem-solving skills, e.g., communication, relaxation, anger control.<br>• Single Parents' Support Group (SPSG). | • Regain lost support systems.<br>• Dispel damaging perceptions of marital hostility and environmental changes.<br>• Develop and practice coping and problem-solving skills.<br>• Improve social skills.<br>• Prevent school behavior problems, including acting out and poor academic performance.<br>• Improve self-esteem.<br>• Assist children in generalizing skills at home.<br>• Aid in personal development.<br>• Provide support for postdivorce adjustment. | Stolberg & Mahler, 1994:<br>• Home workbooks: *KidsBook* and *ParentsBook*.<br>○ Preparation for group meetings.<br>○ Practice exercises to facilitate the transfer of learned skills to real-world situations.<br>• Group structure:<br>○ Gamelike format to enhance child participation and interest. |

divorce-related stressors. Each session is divided into two sections. The first section consists of a discussion of a specific topic (e.g., Whose fault is it? What do I do on vacations? Do I worry about my dad? I wish my parents would get back together). The second section makes use of teaching, modeling, and rehearsing skills such as anger control, problem solving, communication, and relaxation training.

In contrast to the child group, which occurs at the school, the parent group takes place off-site at a mental health center. The parent group seeks to improve adult functioning and to reinforce children for their efforts to generalize program skills in the home. Topics include those with an individual focus (e.g., The Social Me, The Working Me, The Sexual Me, Controlling My Feelings)

**Table 3** *Other School-Based Interventions for Children of Divorce*

| Intervention | Program Structure | Focus and Goals |
|---|---|---|
| Developmental Facilitation Groups (Kalter, 1990) | • Eight 1-hour sessions for fifth and sixth graders.<br>• Five to nine children per group.<br>• One female and one male group leader.<br>• Postgroup parent meetings. | • Normalize and clarify divorce issues.<br>• Develop coping skills for feelings and family interactions.<br>• Provide parents with information on divorce-related concerns of fifth and sixth graders. |
| School Services Program of the Center for the Family in Transition (Goldman & King, 1985) | • 10 1-hour weekly meetings.<br>• Separate treatments for children experiencing recent family structural changes such as divorce versus those with long-standing school-related difficulties.<br>• Includes teacher participation (e.g. joint conferences with parent(s) and group leaders). | • Provide a protected environment in which children could develop effective coping skills in response to the family change.<br>• Lessen feelings of isolation and shame.<br>• Help emphasize the supportive aspects of the school environment. |
| Self-Confidence of 5th Grade Children of Divorce (Sanders & Riester, 1996) | • Classroom-size discussion led by group leader. | • Help children to understand divorce through topics such as:<br>○ Why people divorce.<br>○ Feelings children experience.<br>○ Ways to cope with feelings.<br>○ Changes since divorce, such as parents' dating and visitation.<br>○ Identification of positive aspects of divorce. |

and those with a parenting focus (e.g., Communicating with My Child, Communicating with My Former Spouse about Childrearing Matters).

Both DAP and CODIP have shown program effects, with CODIP yielding gains across a wider range of variables: decreased anxiety and improved competence (frustration tolerance, assertiveness, and peer sociability) as measured by teacher ratings, and increased ratings of overall adjustment at home as measured by parent ratings. Additionally, although not initially randomized, a 2-year follow-up of the kindergarten–first grade CODIP sample showed that teachers (unaware of condition) rated program children as having fewer classroom adjustment problems than controls. Health records for these children showed fewer visits to the school nurse over the same period, in contrast to those who declined participation in the program. These latter students had more visits for vague, general malaise (Pedro-Carroll et al., 1999). With respect to DAP, both adult and child groups have shown gains in functioning. The adult program did not yield gains in parenting, however, leading the authors to recommend that future parent programs be augmented with direct efforts to improve parenting skills (Stolberg & Mahler, 1994). This recommendation is underscored by positive results of two community-based preventive-intervention efforts that specifically target parenting skills for divorced parents (Forgatch & DeGarmo, 1999; Wolchik et al., 2002).

On an interesting note, DAP researchers credit CODIP's gamelike format for the program's success in changing a broader range of outcomes than DAP does. This format may have increased children's interest and active participation in CODIP (Stolberg & Mahler, 1994).

Neither CODIP nor DAP has yielded improvements in children's externalizing behavior as measured by teachers or parents; thus, practitioners should consider other alternatives for children whose problems are primarily externalizing. In fact, emerging evidence indicates that group-based support programs for heterogeneous student populations may be contraindicated in cases in which children, especially boys, are already experiencing elevated levels of conduct problems (Dishion, Poulin, & Burraston, 2001). Inclusion of children with high levels of externalizing behavior may create iatrogenic effects for other children. With respect to school-based programs for children of divorce, there is some evidence of possible deleterious effects, although they are neither large nor widespread (Stolberg & Mahler, 1994). Therefore, treatment modality should follow from the nature of the child's issues or concerns. School-based group programs may be more appropriate for problems such as anxiety, depression, or barriers to learning, or for children who would benefit from psychoeducational information on parental divorce. Externalizing problems may be more difficult to change through school-based programs, and they raise questions of potential iatrogenic effects for other children. Thus, externalizing problems may require alternate intervention approaches, such as individual and family-based therapy.

### Programs That Target Teachers and Administrators

A variety of recommendations have been made to help schools adequately meet the needs of children from divorced families, including inservice trainings for teachers to help them understand issues related to divorce. Goldman (1986) provides an outline for what a single session of staff development might look like, including background information on the prevalence of divorce, along with commonly observed classroom problems and proposed solutions. Inservice trainings also might make use of the quiz on children and divorce presented in Table 1 to increase interest in the topic and address common misunderstandings about children of divorce. Others have called for the use of vignettes—brief descriptions of typical scenarios involving students' problematic reactions to transitions related to divorce, along with questions for the leader and staff to discuss (Lamden, King, & Goldman, 2002). Montemayor (1984) recommended that trainings include strategies to help teachers effectively offer support and guidance, such as a seminar led by a school psychologist on problem recognition and interviewing techniques. He also suggested that teachers be given a list of local agencies and services to manage any requests for referrals that are received from parents or students.

Suggestions for administrators include encouraging the adoption of policies that are more inclusive of nonresidential parents (Lamden et al., 2002). Changes include redesigning registration forms to include both parents' information, issuing duplicate copies of report cards and school calendars, and scheduling parent–teacher conferences to make them more convenient for single-parent households and to include the nonresidential parent. Goldman (1986) also recommended creating curriculum around the general topic of "the changing family," to be incorporated into English, Social Science, or Family Life Education classes. Thus, school personnel have a number of ways in which to intervene in attempting to enhance the lives of children after divorce and to support them through this transition. Further work is needed in establishing the efficacy of these potentially promising approaches.

## SUMMARY

Parental divorce has the potential to create considerable risk for children, but there is large variation in how children respond to the experience. The research to date demonstrates the diversity—not the inevitable negativity—of children's responses to parental divorce. To understand children's adjustment to divorce, school personnel must be aware of the family environment both before and after the transition itself. Key risk factors for maladjustment after divorce include economic hardship, interparental conflict, parental distress, and cumulative transitions and related life stress. How children adjust to divorce will depend on the particular combination of stressors and available supports. Some children will experience internalizing or externalizing problems or will have problems with academic achievement and classroom behavior, such as lower grades and standardized test scores, greater inattention and irrelevant talk, and poorer school attendance and homework completion.

In response to known risks, researchers have developed a number of school-based prevention and intervention programs. Of these, CODIP is perhaps the most promising, with accumulating evidence showing positive effects for a variety of internalizing problems and classroom behaviors. Externalizing problems may be more difficult to change through school-based programs and thus may require alternate intervention approaches, such as individual and family-based therapy. Schools also should consider other ways to foster children's adjustment, such as by implementing administrative changes designed to increase the opportunity for the noncustodial parent to participate in the child's life at school.

## AUTHOR NOTE

Work on this chapter was supported by Grant #1 R01 HD41463-01A1 from the National Institute of Child Health and Human Development, awarded to the first and second authors.

## RECOMMENDED RESOURCES

### Books and Other Printed Material

Amato, P. R. (2000). The consequences of divorce for adults and children. *Journal of Marriage and the Family, 62,* 1269–1287.

This article reviews recent research in divorce and presents a general model of divorce, stress, and adjustment, covering risk and protective factors for adults and children.

Emery, R. E., Kitzmann, K. M., & Waldron, M. (1999). Psychological interventions for separated and divorced families. In E. M. Hetherington (Ed.), *Coping with divorce, single parenting, and remarriage: A risk and resiliency perspective* (pp. 332–344). Mahwah, NJ: Erlbaum.

This chapter provides an extensive review of both child-focused and parent-focused interventions for divorced families, along with divorce mediation programs. It also gives a critical analysis of program strengths and limitations.

Hetherington, E. M., Bridges, M., & Insabella, G. M. (1998). What matters? What does not? Five perspectives on the association between marital transitions and children's adjustment. *American Psychologist, 53,* 167–184.

This article reviews research on children's adjustment to divorce and remarriage and examines individual, family, and socioeconomic factors that contribute to children's adjustment in divorced and remarried families.

### Books for Children

Blackstone-Ford, J. (1998). *My parents are divorced, too: A book for kids by kids.* Washington, DC: Magination Press.

Jan Blackstone-Ford and her children, Melanie Annie, and Steven, provide a guidebook of their experiences and advice for dealing with divorce and remarriage. Awarded the American Bookseller Pick of the Lists. Ages: Preadolescence and older.

Brown, L. K., & Brown, M. (1986). *Dinosaur's divorce: A guide for changing families.* New York: The Atlantic Monthly.

Authors Laurene Krasny Brown and Marc Brown use a cartoon-style depiction of dinosaur characters to teach children about divorce, reasons for divorce, life in two households, how to tell friends, and stepfamily issues such as meeting parents' new friends and having stepsiblings. This book has received numerous awards and distinctions: American Bookseller Pick of the Lists, New York Times Notable Books, School Library Journal Best Books, and Publisher's Weekly Choice for the Year's Best Books. Ages 4–8.

Lansky, V. (1998). *It's not your fault, Koko Bear: A read-together book for parents and young children during divorce.* Minnetonka, MN: Book Peddlers.

Author Vicki Lansky has designed a picture book that depicts a young unisex bear whose parents are divorcing; the bear must go through adjustments and deal with emotions such as anger, guilt, and sadness. At the bottom of each page, bullet points outline comments and suggestions for adults to help them address issues raised by the story. Available in English and Spanish. Ages 3–7.

Ransom, J. F. (2000). *I don't want to talk about it.* Washington, DC: Magination Press.

Author Jeanie Franz Ransom presents the story of a young girl whose parents have told her they are divorcing. Her parents offer reassurances about feelings she may be experiencing, and she imagines herself to be various animals as a way to express feelings. The book concludes with advice to parents on how to deal with children's emotions. This book has been awarded Today's Librarian Best Children's Resource. Ages 4–8.

Rogers, F. (1996). *Divorce: Let's talk about it.* New York: G.P. Putman & Sons.

Author Fred Rogers describes three real families in this multicultural photo essay that presents divorce as an adult problem and makes children aware that reconciliation usually is not likely. He provides suggestions for dealing with normal feelings of sadness, anger, and crying that include talking, drawing, and playing with friends. This book was awarded the American Bookseller Pick of the Lists. Ages 4–8.

Stern, Z., Stern, E., & Stern, E. S. (1997). *Divorce is not the end of the world: Zoe's and Evan's coping guide for kids.* Berkeley, CA: Tricycle Press.

Ellen Sue Stern and her two children, Zoe (age 15) and Evan (age 13), take turns talking about various issues, such as why the divorce happened, fantasies for reconciliation, living across two households, and handling emotions. Ages: Preadolescence and older.

## Website

*http://www.childrensinstitute.net*

The website maintained by the Children's Institute of Rochester, New York, provides information on the CODIP program and how to establish this and other programs in schools.

## REFERENCES

Alpert-Gillis, L., Pedro-Carroll, J., & Cowen, E. (1989). The children of divorce intervention program: Development, implementation, and evaluation of a program for young urban children. *Journal of Consulting and Clinical Psychology, 57,* 583–589.

Amato, P. R. (1993). Children's adjustment to divorce: Theories, hypotheses, and empirical support. *Journal of Marriage and the Family, 55,* 23–38.

Amato, P. R. (1999). Children of divorced parents as young adults. In E. M. Hetherington (Ed.), *Coping with divorce, single parenting, and remarriage: A risk and resiliency perspective* (pp. 147–163). Mahwah, NJ: Erlbaum.

Amato, P. R. (2000). The consequences of divorce for adults and children. *Journal of Marriage and the Family, 62,* 1269–1287.

Amato, P. R. (2001). Children of divorce in the 1990s: An update of the Amato and Keith (1991) meta-analysis. *Journal of Family Psychology, 15,* 355–370.

Amato, P. R. (2003). Reconciling divergent perspectives: Judith Wallerstein, quantitative family research, and children of divorce. *Family Relations, 52,* 332–339.

Amato, P. R., & Booth, A. (1997). *A generation at risk: Growing up in an era of family upheaval.* Cambridge, MA: Harvard University Press.

Amato, P. R., & Keith, B. (1991). Parental divorce and the well-being of children: A meta-analysis. *Journal of Marriage and the Family, 110,* 26–46.

Amato, P. R., & Sobolewski, J. M. (2001). The effect of divorce and marital discord on adult children's psychological well-being. *American Sociological Review, 66,* 900–921.

Anderson, E. R., Greene, S. M., Walker, L., Malerba, C. A., Forgatch, M. S., & DeGarmo, D. S. (2004). Ready to take a chance again: Transitions into dating among divorcing parents. *Journal of Divorce and Remarriage, 40,* 61–75.

Block, J. H., Block, J., & Gjerde, P. F. (1986). The personality of children prior to divorce: A prospective study. *Child Development, 57,* 827–840.

Booth, A., & Amato, P. R. (2001). Parental divorce relations and offspring postdivorce well-being. *Journal of Marriage and the Family, 63,* 197–212.

Bramlett, M., & Mosher, W. (2002). *Cohabitation, marriage and divorce and remarriage in the United States.* (DHHS Pub. No. PHS 2002–1998). National Center for Health Statistics. *Vital Health Statistics, 23* (22).

Bumpass, L. L., Martin, T. C., & Sweet, J. A. (1991). The impact of family background and early marital factors on marital disruption. *Journal of Family Issues, 12,* 22–42.

Chase-Lansdale, P. L., Cherlin, A. J., & Kiernan, K. E. (1995). The long-term effects of parental divorce on the mental health of young adults: A developmental perspective. *Child Development, 66,* 1614–1634.

Cherlin, A. J., Chase-Lansdale, P. L., & McRae, C. (1998). Effects of parental divorce on mental health throughout the life course. *American Sociological Review, 63,* 239–249.

Conger, R. D., Ge, X., Elder, G. H., Lorenz, F. O., & Simons, R. L. (1994). Economic stress, coercive family process, and developmental problems of adolescents. *Child Development, 65,* 541–561.

Davies, P. T., Harold, G. T., Goeke-Morey, M. C., & Cummings, E. M. (2002). Child emotional security and interparental conflict. *Monographs of the Society for Research in Child Development, 67* (Serial No. 270).

DeGarmo, D. S., & Forgatch, M. S. (1997). Determinants of observed confidant support. *Journal of Personality and Social Psychology, 72,* 336–345.

Dishion, T. J., Poulin, F., & Burraston, B. (2001). Peer group dynamics associated with iatrogenic effects in group interventions with high-risk young adolescents. *New Directions for Child and Adolescent Development, 91,* 79–92.

Emery, R. E. (1988). *Marriage, divorce, and children's adjustment.* Thousand Oaks, CA: Sage.

Emery, R. E. (1999). Postdivorce family life for children: An overview of research and some implications for policy. In R. A. Thompson & P. R. Amato (Eds.), *The postdivorce family: Children, parenting, and society* (pp. 3–27). Thousand Oaks, CA: Sage.

Emery, R. E., Kitzmann, K. M., & Waldron, M. (1999). Psychological interventions for separated and divorced families. In E. M. Hetherington (Ed.), *Coping with divorce, single parenting, and remarriage: A risk and resiliency perspective* (pp. 332–344). Mahwah, NJ: Erlbaum.

Forgatch, M. S., & DeGarmo, D. S. (1999). Parenting through change: An effective prevention program for single mothers. *Journal of Consulting and Clinical Psychology, 67,* 711–724.

Forgatch, M. S., Patterson, G. R., & Ray, J. A. (1996). Divorce and boys' adjustment problems: Two paths with a single model. In E. M. Hetherington & E. A. Blechman (Eds.), *Stress, coping, and resiliency in children and the family* (pp. 67–105). Mahwah, NJ: Erlbaum.

Goldman, R. K., & King, M. J. (1985). Counseling children of divorce. *School Psychology Review, 14,* 280–290.

Goldman, R. K. (1986). Separation and divorce. In T. N. Fairchild (Ed.), *Crisis intervention strategies for school-based helpers* (pp. 22–69). Springfield, IL: Thomas.

Gonzales, N. A., Pitts, S. C., Hill, N. E., & Roosa, M. W. (2000). A mediational model of the impact of interparental conflict on child adjustment in a multi-ethnic, low-income sample. *Journal of Family Psychology, 14,* 365–379.

Greene, S. M., Anderson, E. R., Hetherington, E. M., Forgatch, M. S., & DeGarmo, D. S. (2003). Risk and resilience after divorce. In F. Walsh (Ed.), *Normal family processes: Growing diversity and complexity* (pp. 96–120). New York: Guilford Press.

Grych, J. H., & Fincham, F. D. (1992). Interventions for children of divorce: Towards greater integration of research and action. *Psychological Bulletin, 111,* 434–454.

Grych, J. H., Harold, G. T., & Miles, C. J. (2003). A prospective investigation of appraisals as mediators of the link between interparental conflict and child adjustment. *Child Development, 74,* 1176–1193.

Hetherington, E. M. (1999). Should we stay together for the sake of our children? In E. M. Hetherington (Ed.), *Coping with divorce, single parenting, and remarriage: A risk and resiliency perspective* (pp. 93–116). Mahwah, NJ: Erlbaum.

Hetherington, E. M., Bridges, M., & Insabella, G. M. (1998). What matters? What does not? Five perspectives on the association between marital transitions and children's adjustment. *American Psychologist, 53,* 167–184.

Hetherington, E. M., & Kelly, J. (2002). *For better or for worse: Divorce reconsidered.* New York: Norton.

Kalter, N. (1990). *Growing up with divorce: Helping your child avoid immediate and later emotional problems.* New York: Collier MacMillan.

Kiecolt-Glaser, J. K., McGuire, L., Robles, T. F., & Glaser, R. (2002). Psychoneuroimmunology: Psychological influences on immune functioning and health. *Journal of Consulting and Clinical Psychology, 70,* 537–547.

Lamden, A. M., King, M. J., & Goldman, R. K. (2002). Divorce: Crisis intervention and prevention with children of divorce and remarriage. In J. Sandoval (Ed.), *Handbook of crisis counseling, intervention, and prevention in the schools* (2nd ed., pp. 83–104). Mahwah, NJ: Erlbaum.

Lee, C. M., Picard, M., & Blain, M. D (1994). A methodological and substantive review of intervention outcome studies for families undergoing divorce. *Journal of Family Psychology, 8,* 11–13.

Lesowitz, M., Kalter, N., Pickar, J., Chethik, M., & Schaefer, M. (1987). School-based developmental facilitation groups for children of divorce: Issues of group process. *Psychotherapy: Theory, research, practice, training, 24,* 90–95.

Martinez, C. R., Jr., & Forgatch, M. S. (2002). Adjusting to change: Linking family structure transitions to parenting and boys' adjustment. *Journal of Family Psychology, 16,* 107–117.

McLanahan, S. (1999). Father absence and the welfare of children. In E. M. Hetherington (Ed.), *Coping with divorce, single parenting and remarriage: A risk and resiliency perspective* (pp. 117–146). Mahwah, NJ: Erlbaum.

Montemayor, R. (1984). Picking up the pieces: The effects of parental divorce on adolescents with some suggestions for school-based intervention programs. *Journal of Early Adolescence, 4,* 289–314.

Montgomery, M. J., Anderson, E. R., Hetherington, E. M., & Clingempeel, W. G. (1992). Patterns of courtship for remarriage: Implications for child adjustment and parent-child relationships. *Journal of Marriage and the Family, 54,* 686–698.

Pedro-Carroll, J. L., & Alpert-Gillis, L. (1997). Preventive interventions for children of divorce: A developmental model for 5- and 6-year-old children. *The Journal of Primary Prevention, 18,* 5–23.

Pedro-Carroll, J., Sutton, S., & Wyman, P. (1999). A two-year follow-up evaluation of a preventive intervention for young children of divorce. *School Psychology Review, 28,* 467–476.

Peris, T. S., & Emery, R. E. (2004). A prospective study of the consequences of marital disruption for adolescents: Predisruption family dynamics and postdisruption adolescent adjustment. *Journal of Clinical Child and Adolescent Psychology, 33,* 694–704.

Peterson, R. R. (1996). A re-evaluation of the economic consequences of divorce. *American Sociological Review, 61,* 528–536.

Raley, R. K., & Wildsmith, E. (2004). Cohabitation and children's family instability. *Journal of Marriage and Family, 66,* 210–219.

Richardson, C. D., & Rosen, L. A. (1999). School-based interventions for children of divorce. *Professional School Counseling, 3,* 21–27.

Sanders, D. R., & Riester, A. E. (1996). School-based counseling groups for children of divorce: Effects on the self-concepts of $5^{th}$ grade children. *Journal of Child and Adolescent Group Therapy, 6,* 27–43.

Simons, R. L. & Associates (Eds.). (1996). *Understanding differences between divorced and intact families: Stress, interaction, and child outcome.* Thousand Oaks, CA: Sage.

Stolberg, A. L., & Garrison, K. (1985). Evaluating a primary prevention program for children of divorce. *American Journal of Community Psychology, 13,* 111–124.

Stolberg, A. L., & Mahler, J. (1994). Enhancing treatment gains in a school-based intervention for children of divorce through skill training, parental involvement, and transfer procedures. *Journal of Consulting and Clinical Psychology, 62,* 147–156.

Sun, Y. (2001). Family environment and adolescents' well-being before and after parents' marital disruption: A longitudinal analysis. *Journal of Marriage and Family, 63,* 697–713.

Tein, J-Y., Sandler, I. N., & Zautra, A. J. (2000). Stressful life events, psychological distress, coping, and parenting of divorced mothers: A longitudinal study. *Journal of Family Psychology, 14,* 27–41.

U.S. Census Bureau. (2000). *Statistical abstract of the United States.* Washington, DC: U.S. Government Printing Office.

Wallerstein, J. S., Lewis, J., & Blakeslee, S. (2000). *The unexpected legacy of divorce: A 25 year landmark study.* New York: Hyperion.

Wolchik, S. A., Sandler, I. N., Milsap, R. E., Plummer, B. A., Greene, S. M., Anderson, E. R., et al. (2002). Six-year follow-up of prevention interventions for children of divorce. *Journal of the American Medical Association, 288,* 1874–1881.

Zill, N., Morrison, D. R., & Coiro, M. J. (1993). Long-term effects of parental divorce on parent-child relationships, adjustment, and achievement in young adulthood. *Journal of Family Psychology, 7,* 91–103.

# 57

# Custody Issues

**Christy M. Buchanan**
**Amber K. Williams**
*Wake Forest University*

This chapter focuses on issues parents and children face in different custody arrangements and with different amounts of contact following divorce or separation. When parents divorce, a legal arrangement (by parental agreement or by judge's decree when parents cannot agree) determines how children are supposed to split their time between parents. (The legal arrangement for physical custody of the child is different from legal custody, which specifies each parent's role in decision-making for the child. This chapter focuses on physical rather than legal custody.) The most common arrangements are sole mother custody (living most of the time with mother), sole father custody (living most of the time with father), or joint custody (living relatively equal amounts of time with each parent). No single accepted criterion is used by lawyers or researchers to distinguish between sole and joint physical custody. However, a commonly accepted minimum criterion for joint custody is that a child spend at least 25% of the time with each parent (Bauserman, 2002). Therefore, if one parent has the child more than 75% of the time, the arrangement is considered sole custody for that parent. In sole custody, the plan for physical placement specifies the degree of contact that the child is expected to have with the noncustodial parent.

The physical custody or visitation plan specified in the legal decree does not always match what parents do in practice (Maccoby & Mnookin, 1992). Unless indicated otherwise, *custody*, as discussed in this chapter, refers to a child's actual living arrangements, and *contact* refers to the actual amount of time a child spends with a noncustodial parent. We retain the generally accepted definitions of joint custody, mother custody, and father custody specified above.

Most research on custody and contact has been done with divorced heterosexual parents. Less information is available on custody and contact for children whose parents never married or are of the same gender. Recent research has examined custody and contact in ethnically and socioeconomically diverse samples, but we still know relatively little about the intricacies of visitation and custody for individuals from different backgrounds. The trends discussed in this chapter apply broadly, but school professionals will no doubt have experienced instances in which ethnicity, economic status, or other individual circumstances differ from the average trends researchers have studied.

## BACKGROUND AND DEVELOPMENT

When parents separate or divorce, children's lives change in fundamental ways. Such changes can affect the school-age child in ways that range from relatively minor disruptions, such as leaving homework at one parent's home when making a transition to the other parent's home, to more substantial difficulties, such as experiencing problems in mood or behavior that stem from relational or parenting problems in the family. This chapter focuses on the latter kinds of problems.

### Prevalence of Alternative Custody and Contact Arrangements

In the United States, most children (70%–80%) are in sole mother custody following divorce, but substantial numbers of children now live either in sole father custody or in joint custody (Emery, 1999). Father custody is more likely among adolescents than among younger children. Joint custody is more common for children in the late preschool and early elementary school years, for males, and for parents with more income (Cancian & Meyer, 1998; Maccoby & Mnookin, 1992).

For children in sole-custody arrangements, the amount of contact with the noncustodial parent varies. For most children, divorce leads to a reduction in contact with fathers, although complete loss of contact is atypical. In a national sample of families in the late 1980s, 11% of children under age 18 whose parents had been separated for 3–5 years had not seen their noncustodial father in the years since the separation, whereas 58% saw him once a month or more during that time (Seltzer, 1991). Contact does decrease with time; after 5 years, 25% to 33% of children lose contact with their fathers (Manning & Smock, 1999; Seltzer). More recent cohorts of fathers are maintaining a higher level of contact with their children after divorce (Hetherington & Kelly, 2002), but irregular and infrequent contact remains common, especially as time since parental separation increases (Emery, 1999).

Contact with noncustodial fathers varies by education, income, and ethnicity. Contact is more likely when fathers have higher income and education, and this is especially true of White fathers. Rates of contact for highly educated White fathers exceed rates for fathers from other ethnic groups, whereas White fathers with little education have especially low levels of contact with their children (King, Harris, & Heard, 2004). Compared with Black or Hispanic adolescents, White adolescents are more likely to have overnight visits with noncustodial fathers and are more likely to talk to their fathers by phone and to receive letters from fathers. Hispanic adolescents are more likely than White or Black youth to have no contact at all (King et al., 2004). The activities in which adolescents engage with their noncustodial fathers also differ by ethnic group. White adolescents are more likely to take part in sports or watch movies with their fathers, but Hispanic and Black adolescents and their fathers are more likely to work on school projects, and Black adolescents and their fathers are more likely to participate in religious activities (King et al.).

Father contact is higher when children were born within marriage rather than outside of marriage (e.g., Marsiglio, Amato, Day & Lamb, 2000), when fathers have multiple children living at the same residence, and when the distance between the father's and child's residence is lower (Cooksey & Craig, 1998). A distance of less than 75 miles is crucial to contact (Hetherington & Kelly, 2002). Father contact tends to decline when fathers enter new relationships, especially when they have new biological children (Cooksey & Craig; Manning & Smock, 1999). Rates of contact with noncustodial mothers are somewhat higher than with noncustodial fathers (Hetherington & Kelly; Seltzer, 1991).

### Reaching the Optimal Situation for Children of Divorce

Research that examines factors linked to adjustment among children of divorce is consistent in pointing to certain family factors that predict positive adjustment among those children (e.g., Buchanan, 2000; Hetherington & Kelly, 2002). In an optimal situation, divorced parents get along well with each other, or they at least handle conflict so that children are minimally exposed to, and are not used in, the conflict. Both parents encourage positive relationships between the child and the other parent, and children spend enough time with each parent to sustain a close relationship. Both parents have age-appropriate routines and rules in their home, and rules are tempered with warmth between parent and child. Parents of adolescent children allow increased choice and independence while still monitoring children's activities.

As we consider different custody and contact arrangements in this chapter, we examine how the aspects of optimal family functioning described above are enhanced or jeopardized by different custody or contact arrangements. For example, some arrangements might have more conflict between parents than others and some might be more conducive to consistency in routines and monitoring. Armed with such knowledge, school personnel can be alert to possible risk factors for particular students. Of course, a student and family might not fit the average description for their particular custody or contact arrangement, so this information should be used only to guide inquiry rather than to make absolute judgments.

## PROBLEMS AND IMPLICATIONS

Researchers have addressed questions about the living arrangements of children after divorce by studying custody arrangements (mother vs. father vs. joint) and the amount of contact children have with noncustodial parents in mother or father custody. Findings about relatively high levels of contact within sole custody (e.g., overnights every other weekend plus a mid-week visit with the noncustodial parent) are similar to those concerning joint custody (25%–50% of time with each parent). Yet some distinct issues concerning custody arrangements do not overlap entirely with issues involving amount of contact (e.g., the effects of living with father vs. mother as custodial parent, and issues of alternating homes when contact is as high as it is in joint custody). So in what follows, we first discuss research that examines *amount of contact* in sole-custody arrangements, followed by research that compares different *custody arrangements* (i.e., sole mother vs. sole father vs. joint).

## Contact With the Noncustodial Parent in Sole-Custody Arrangements

Most information about the effects of different levels of contact with a noncustodial parent on family functioning and children's adjustment comes from mother-custody families and refers to contact with the noncustodial father. Thus, the bulk of information in this section pertains to contact with noncustodial fathers, although information on noncustodial mothers is included where available.

In general, higher levels of contact with a noncustodial parent are associated with positive family functioning. Parents with low levels of conflict are more likely than those in high conflict to agree on and implement parenting plans that incorporate contact with both parents. Parents with high levels of conflict are more likely to have the court impose custody and contact plans (because they can't agree). They are also less likely to implement high levels of visitation (and joint custody) even when the legal decree calls for such, and they are less likely to sustain such arrangements over time (Pruett, Williams, Insabella, & Little, 2003; Whiteside & Becker, 2000). When families implement arrangements that permit high levels of access to both parents, conflict does not appear to be either exacerbated or reduced simply by virtue of the arrangement (Maccoby & Mnookin, 1992).

Most recent studies conclude that there is no consistent direct link between the amount of father–child contact and child adjustment (Hetherington & Kelly, 2002; Marsiglio et al., 2000; Whiteside & Becker, 2000). It is true that adult children of divorce often lament lack of father contact and believe that lack of contact affected their lives negatively, with the greatest feelings of loss reported by children who saw their fathers occasionally, rather than a lot or very little (Laumann-Billings & Emery, 2000). And clearly, fathers can provide important financial and social capital for children that ought to benefit their development (Amato & Gilbreth, 1999; King et al., 2004). Still, research that examines whether children's adjustment actually differs based on the amount of contact they have with father (controlling for factors related to both contact and adjustment, such as marital conflict) does not provide strong support for a direct link between father contact and children's adjustment. Rather, the research indicates two things: (a) that the quality of the relationship between the noncustodial parent and child is more important to the child's adjustment than is contact per se; and (b) that the effect of contact with noncustodial parents depends on other factors, including the amount of conflict that exists between the parents and the quality of noncustodial parenting. Children benefit from contact with fathers that promotes or maintains a good father–child relationship and from circumstances in which contact promotes the optimal family functioning described earlier.

***Quality of the noncustodial parent–child relationship.*** Higher levels of contact with a noncustodial parent are associated with greater reported closeness to that parent (e.g., Fabricius, 2003; Whiteside & Becker, 2000). Among adolescents, even arrangements with relatively small amounts of visitation (e.g., 2-week summer visits) have been found to maintain or promote emotional ties between adolescent children and their noncustodial parents (Buchanan, Maccoby, & Dornbusch, 1996). However, more substantial amounts of contact might be needed to maintain closeness with younger (i.e., preschool or early school-age) children.

The closeness maintained between children and noncustodial fathers is generally not as high as that between children and custodial mothers or between children and nondivorced fathers (Buchanan et al., 1996; Emery, 1999). Closeness to noncustodial mothers also appears to be somewhat higher than closeness to noncustodial fathers, especially for boys (Buchanan et al., 1996), but having contact with the noncustodial parent clearly enhances the child's chances for having a good relationship with that parent.

Maintaining a good relationship with the noncustodial parent (particularly if this means that the child has a close relationship with both parents) after divorce is clearly linked with positive outcomes for children (e.g., King, 2002; Pruett, Ebling, & Insabella, 2004). So although contact does not guarantee a good relationship between children and noncustodial parents—just as close relationships between custodial parents and children are not guaranteed—it enhances the chances for one. And a good relationship with the noncustodial parent is a positive factor in children's adjustment.

***Moderating factors.*** It would be naive to assume that contact with a noncustodial parent benefits all children in all circumstances equally. One factor that is likely to be important in affecting whether contact with a noncustodial parent leads to positive outcomes for the child is the level of conflict between the parents. Most evidence suggests that contact is less likely to be beneficial and can hold a greater potential for harm if interparental conflict is high (e.g., Hetherington & Kelly, 2002; Lamb, Sternberg, & Thompson, 1997). Similar findings emerge both for high levels of contact in sole-custody arrangements and for joint custody (although positive effects of joint custody might still exist despite conflict, as will be discussed later; Bauserman, 2002).

Contact with a noncustodial parent might not be as helpful to children in the face of high interparental conflict because negative effects of exposure to high conflict cancel any positive effects of a continued relationship with the noncustodial parent. Or perhaps high conflict between parents interferes with close relationships between children and their noncustodial parents, and such closeness is one of the proposed mechanisms by which contact has a positive effect. In support of this possibility, Buchanan et al. (1996) found that higher hostility toward the noncustodial parent on the part of the custodial parent was associated with less closeness between an adolescent and his or her noncustodial parent; closeness to the custodial parent was not associated with the level of interparental conflict. Any actual harm that results from a child's contact with the noncustodial parent in high-conflict situations might result from increased exposure to conflict or from an increased likelihood that children will become caught up in the conflict (Buchanan et al.; Kelly & Emery, 2003).

In contrast to the research cited thus far, some research suggests that contact with a noncustodial parent can be helpful in situations of high interparental conflict, presumably because maintenance of the relationship with the noncustodial parent buffers the negative effects of conflict. In one study of early adolescents whose parents were divorced, levels of social and academic competence were low only for children whose parents were in high conflict and who did not see their noncustodial fathers (Forehand et al., 1990). Adolescents whose parents were in high conflict but who also had contact with their noncustodial fathers functioned as well as adolescents whose parents experienced low levels of conflict. Thus, early adolescents might be better off in some respects having contact with a noncustodial parent (compared with not having such contact) even when there is high conflict between their parents.

Mixed findings—regarding whether contact with a noncustodial parent when parents are in high conflict is good, bad, or of no consequence—suggest that the effect of contact in high-conflict situations depends on other factors. One factor is how the conflict is handled. Although some parents might take advantage of a child's contact with the other parent to use the child in the conflict, not all parents will do so. If parents can avoid the temptation to involve children in the conflict, contact (or the continued positive relationship that contact enables) might in fact benefit the child despite the high levels of conflict. In general, when parents isolate personal conflicts from their parenting interactions—using cooperative or "parallel" parenting—children adjust more positively (e.g., Hetherington & Kelly, 2002), perhaps in part because children are then more likely to benefit from positive relationships with each parent.

Other important factors determining what the effects of contact will be include the adjustment and maturity of the noncustodial parent and the children's predivorce relationship with that parent. Contact with father is beneficial if the previous relationship was good and if the father was not "poorly adjusted or extremely immature" (Kelly, 1993, p. 38; see also Hetherington & Kelly, 2002). The quality of the ongoing parent–child relationship and what actually takes place during the time together are also important. In a meta-analysis of 63 studies published from 1970 to 1998, Amato and Gilbreth (1999) found that authoritative parenting by noncustodial fathers was a stronger predictor of children's well-being than either contact or children's feelings of closeness to their fathers. This was true across child age, race, and gender and despite the cause of the father's absence.

Longer time spent with fathers, more so than high frequency of contact, has been linked to better adjustment of elementary-school-age children (e.g., Pagani-Kurtz & Derevensky, 1997). Contact that is regular and predictable is better, especially for younger children (Leventhal, Kelman, Galatzer-Levy, & Kraus, 1999; Pruett et al., 2004), perhaps in part because a regular schedule reduces parental conflict over contact (Isaacs, 1988). Even young children (4–6 years of age) appear to derive some benefit from overnights with the noncustodial parent as long as they occur as part of a regular routine (Pruett et al.). Adolescents, in contrast to younger children, desire and appear to benefit more from flexibility in contact arrangements (Bray, 1991;

Buchanan et al., 1996). Although adolescents value and want time with their noncustodial parents, they can experience frustration and resentment when contact arrangements do not accommodate peer and extracurricular activities and when they have little say in when or how much contact occurs (Buchanan et al.). Some kind of predictable schedule is still warranted, because adolescents, like younger children, benefit from structure and regular supervision (Ravitz, 1999) and because contact that is irregular is more likely to fall by the wayside. But parents of adolescents need to be flexible about changes in the regular schedule to accommodate adolescents' increasing involvement outside the family.

The number of transitions the child has to make from one home to another in a given period of time is another important factor in the effect of contact. The time of transition, especially if children are younger and if parents are still in high conflict, can be stressful (Mayes & Molitor-Siegl, 1999; Wallerstein & Blakeslee, 1989). Thus, a contact plan that minimizes the number of transitions and makes transition times as low stress as possible will likely benefit children.

***Child-support compliance.*** Contact is related to more reliable payment of child support (Amato & Gilbreth, 1999; Emery, 1999), although it is not clear whether contact leads to better compliance, or whether more committed fathers both stay in contact with their children and pay child support. Some recent evidence suggests that more involved fathers are more likely to pay child support simply because they are more likely to have the money to do so (Seltzer, 1998). In any case, children who see their noncustodial fathers appear more likely to benefit from adequate financial and material resources. Child support compliance predicts better child adjustment, particularly with regard to cognitive development and academic achievement (Amato & Gilbreth, 1999; Lamb et al., 1997). In one study, adolescents were more likely to graduate from high school and to attend college if they had both contact with and financial support from their fathers, compared with adolescents who had only contact or financial support or neither (Menning, 2002). Thus, contact with fathers might enhance payment of child support and might also make the money given more beneficial.

## Custody Arrangement

Although mother custody of children after divorce is still the most common arrangement, father custody and joint custody became more prevalent in the 1980s and 1990s. Substantial numbers of today's children of divorce, especially school-age and adolescent children, experience these alternative forms of custody. Although progress has been made in studying these less frequent custody arrangements, it is still difficult to completely disentangle the effects of father or joint custody on children from the effects of other factors related to custody arrangements (e.g., conflict between parents, parental adjustment). In this section, we point to some of the potential risks or benefits of one form of custody over another, without drawing strong conclusions about causes.

***Mother custody versus father custody.*** Despite increases in father involvement in child care over recent years, women still perform the majority of child care and household management duties in most homes (e.g., Bianchi, 2000). Thus, when parents divorce, fathers typically have less experience in primary child care and household management. Coupled with the entrenched notion that mothers are the more natural and competent parent, especially for young children, most families as well as courts continue to assume that mother custody is a better option for children than father custody.

Research comparing mother custody and father custody suggests that the two arrangements are very similar. One of the most extensive comparisons of the two custody arrangements among families with adolescents found no differences in children's trust of parents, conflict between the child and parent, family decision-making practices, curfews, household organization and routines, the presence of a parent in the home after school, or assignment of chores (Buchanan et al., 1996). Yet adolescents did report feeling somewhat closer to custodial mothers than to custodial fathers, and custodial fathers were reported to be less effective monitors of their children's activities. Custodial mothers confided more in their children, and those children worried more about their mothers. Children in mother custody also felt a greater need to take care of their mothers than children in father custody felt with respect to their fathers.

This and other recent research on adolescents (e.g., Naevdal & Thuen, 2004) show elevated levels of emotional and behavioral problems among father-custody adolescents compared with mother-custody adolescents. In the Buchanan et al. (1996) study, the difference was partly accounted for by the differences in emotional closeness to and monitoring by custodial parents. Thus, father-custody children—at least adolescent children—might be at a somewhat elevated risk for behavioral problems compared with mother-custody children. That disadvantage is, in part, because fathers get custody of more difficult children and under more difficult family circumstances (Emery, 1999). In the Buchanan et al. study, father-custody adolescents were more likely to have moved into father custody after initially living with the mother or in joint custody (in contrast, more adolescents in mother custody had lived with their mothers all along). The reasons for a change into father custody, although sometimes positive, were more likely to be negative (e.g., conflict with mother, behavior problems that the mother couldn't handle) than were changes to other arrangements over time. Furthermore, father-custody arrangements were characterized by higher levels of hostility between the parents, and higher levels of overall life stress as reported by the adolescent. Thus, the average single father might face a more difficult parenting situation than the average single mother.

However, the poorer adjustment of the father-custody adolescents and the relationship among lower closeness, lower monitoring, and adjustment were not eliminated when background factors such as the stability of the residential arrangement and the hostility between parents were accounted for. Thus, the more difficult circumstances of some father-custody cases did not completely explain the original findings (Buchanan et al., 1996), and it is possible that fathers' lower levels of experience in parenting might also contribute to differences in parenting and in adolescent adjustment. However, regardless of the cause of the higher levels of problems in father-custody adolescents, these data illuminate some of the risk factors that children living in the sole custody of their fathers might face, as well as the kinds of information and support that custodial fathers might especially need (e.g., how to handle hostile relationships with an ex-spouse; the importance of monitoring adolescents).

Documented differences between mother and father custody are small in magnitude even when statistically significant. Family functioning varies considerably within both custody arrangements, and some research with preadolescent and early adolescent children has reported no differences in the adjustment of children in mother and father custody (e.g., Downey, Ainsworth-Darnell, & Dufur, 1998; Hilton, Descrochers, & Devall, 2001). Thus, several reviewers of the literature on custody rightly conclude that a child's custody arrangement is a less important factor in his or her adjustment than is the parenting and the nature of the relationships to which the child is exposed (Bray, 1991; Twaite & Luchow, 1996). In American society today, it is harder than ever to predict family functioning simply on the basis of which parent has primary custody.

***Joint versus sole custody.*** A meta-analysis by Bauserman (2002) of 33 studies conducted between 1982 and 1999 concluded that children in joint custody have consistently better outcomes on a wide array of psychological and behavioral indices than do children in sole custody. Just as high levels of contact are a benefit in sole-custody arrangements, a major potential benefit of joint custody appears to be that children can maintain close relationships with both parents (Buchanan et al., 1996; Luepnitz, 1986). Greater closeness to both parents appears to be one of the reasons that joint-custody adolescents have more successful adjustment compared with those in sole custody (particularly those in father custody; Buchanan et al.). Joint-custody adolescents are also the most satisfied with the division of time between their parents, compared with sole-custody adolescents (see also Warshak, 2003). Other concerns about joint custody, such as that it will exacerbate loyalty conflicts, increase conflict between parents, or make it difficult to monitor or supervise children, have not been substantiated (Buchanan et al.).

Interparental conflict is lower in families that have joint custody, but lower conflict does not completely account for benefits of joint custody (e.g., Bauserman, 2002). Furthermore, Bauserman found that positive outcomes in joint custody continued regardless of the level of conflict between parents. Nonetheless, some evidence shows that joint custody can have *less* favorable outcomes, and perhaps even negative outcomes, for children when parents are in especially high conflict (e.g., Buchanan et al., 1996; Johnston, Kline, & Tschann, 1989). Although court awards of joint legal custody are common now (Emery, 1999), and although joint legal custody is linked to higher levels of actual contact with both parents (Seltzer, 1998), a constellation of factors is often present in actual joint-custody arrangements that are sustained over time (Emery): the child has good relationships with both parents, and the parents are in less conflict, are older, and have more education and income. Researchers still don't know to what extent joint physical custody itself, apart from those factors, accounts for the positive adjustment of children (Bauserman). However, one study that looked at several of the factors jointly found that closer relationships with both parents was an important and direct predictor of better outcomes even after other factors were accounted for (Buchanan et al.).

As in the case of contact with a noncustodial parent, other factors might influence the success of a joint-custody arrangement, including the number and kind of transitions between homes, the distance between homes, and the temperament of the child. Not surprisingly, joint custody seems to work better for children who have more flexible, easygoing temperaments (Wallerstein & Blakeslee, 1989). Joint custody also appears to work better for preadolescent school-age children than for adolescents, perhaps for the same reasons that high and regular visitation becomes more problematic for adolescents. Yet some adolescents maintain a joint-custody arrangement without significant stress or problems managing and organizing their lives in two homes; as noted earlier, those adolescents are especially satisfied with their arrangements (Buchanan et al., 1996).

## ALTERNATIVE ACTIONS FOR PREVENTION

Helping parents make good initial decisions about custody and contact lies at the root of preventing problems. Most parents make parenting plans about custody and contact without going to court, but in making those decisions they might seek input and advice from professionals, including school personnel. The research reviewed in this chapter draws the following conclusions about what is in the best interests of children.

Children tend to benefit when both parents stay involved in their lives following divorce. Furthermore, most children want to maintain relationships with both parents (Lamb et al., 1997; Warshak, 2003). Fathers, who are at greatest risk of losing meaningful contact with their children after divorce, are more likely to maintain contact and good relationships with their children when they feel that they have an important parental role and that they have some control over their child's upbringing (Pruett & Pruett, 1998). Decisions (or court awards) for joint legal custody appear to be symbolically important in acknowledging the importance of fathers' involvement. Studies show that fathers awarded joint legal custody are more likely to stay in contact with children, even when those studies control for the quality of preseparation relationships (Seltzer, 1998). It is unknown whether a decree for joint legal custody has the same effect on involvement of noncustodial mothers. In most cases, school-based professionals should encourage children's contact with noncustodial parents, in the spirit of promoting a good relationship between the child and each parent. When conflict between parents is low or moderate, there is little reason to think that children will be harmed by visitation; rather, more evidence shows that children can benefit from the ongoing relationship such visitation provides. In situations of high conflict, there might be reason for concern about negative effects of contact with both parents. However, children can still benefit from contact in such contexts if parents can handle conflict between themselves in nondestructive ways. Even when parents cannot refrain from interpersonal conflict, contact plans that minimize the number of transitions and that use drop-offs by neutral parties can minimize the number of parental encounters and therefore the level of conflict to which children are exposed (Ellis, 2000).

Although school personnel typically should consider promoting contact and a good relationship between the child and the noncustodial parent, they clearly need to consider each situation individually. Factors to consider include whether parents are likely to use high levels of contact as an excuse to involve the child in conflict (such as by asking the child to carry messages or asking the child questions about the other parent or home), how well adjusted the parents are, and the strength of the existing relationship between the noncustodial parent and the child. In addition, the temperament of the child should be considered. For children with more adaptable, easygoing temperaments, frequent visitation or transitions between homes might pose little problem (Ellis, 2000). For less adaptable children, spending more time in one consistent home environment might be preferable, although as long as the routine of visitation is consistent, even those children might respond well to spending time in both homes on a regular basis.

Joint physical custody also can be encouraged if both parents are supportive of the arrangement and if parents are either amiable or able to handle their conflicts between themselves, with minimal exposure of the child to the conflict. Under those circumstances, joint custody would seem best able to promote (or allow maintenance of) good relationships between a child and both parents. Joint custody does not appear to interfere with effective supervision of children or with consistency of rules and management within or across homes, and in and of itself, does not promote conflict between parents (Buchanan et al., 1996). If parents are not in high conflict and can communicate with one another about parenting, this custody option might be most beneficial for children and can be recommended.

With regard to the logistics of joint custody or high levels of contact in sole custody, establishing schedules that minimize the number of transitions and are relatively predictable seems to work best, especially for younger children. Adolescents, as compared to younger children, need more flexibility within their routine to accommodate friends, jobs, and other extracurricular interests. Even so, using a predictable schedule that is viewed as flexible is more likely to promote continued visitation and positive outcomes than is allowing visitation to occur haphazardly or spontaneously.

With regard to father custody, each situation needs to be considered individually. Any single parent—whether mother or father—experiences challenges and difficulties in parenting alone (Emery, 1999; see also chapter 59, "Single Parenting and Stepparenting"), and in many ways the parenting of single fathers is similar to that of single mothers. However, fathers often have less experience in primary caregiving than do mothers and often get custody under unusual circumstances, so they might need extra support in creating a healthy, effective family environment. In particular, attention should be given to their efforts to develop close relationships with their children and to their monitoring of children's activities.

Another question to consider is to what extent children should have a voice in custody and visitation arrangements. Most experts believe that if children have opinions, those opinions should be considered (Kelly & Emery, 2003; Warshak, 2003). However, children—even adolescent children (Ravitz, 1999)—should not be forced to give an opinion or to make a decision about what custody will be or how much contact will occur. Even seemingly minor decisions about where to spend a weekend or a holiday can be stressful for children, because children feel as if they are choosing between their parents, and they worry about hurting their parents' feelings (Buchanan et al., 1996). Thus, parents and counselors must walk a fine line between, on the one hand, eliciting and considering children's wishes when they are offered and, on the other hand, not making children feel responsible for decisions concerning the amount of contact with each parent. The age of the child and the amount of conflict between parents will influence the child's willingness and ability to give honest input, and preadolescent children might say what they think their parents want to hear (Warshak, 2003). Yet Warshak recommends that parents feel free to treat children as collaborators in developing a parenting plan, or allow children's opinions to be elicited by mediators, custody evaluators, or family therapists. Ultimately, however, parents need to assume responsibility for decisions about custody and contact, even if their decisions are influenced by the child's wishes.

On a related point, it is normal for adolescents to express interest in changing custody or visitation arrangements, either to accommodate new activities and interests, or simply as a reflection of identity exploration. Changes that reflect an interest in trying something new, as opposed to those that reflect attempts to escape from or manipulate parents, are generally seen as reasonable and worth considering (Bray, 1991).

More important to children's adjustment than specific custody or visitation arrangements are the quality of children's relationships with each parent, the quality of parenting that children receive from each parent, and the level of conflict between parents after divorce. To enhance children's relationships with noncustodial parents who have legal custody rights, school personnel can send information about children's school activities and achievements to the noncustodial parent as well as to the custodial parent. Parent–teacher conferences can be conducted with both parents, either individually or together. Noncustodial parents can be invited to attend school events. Bray (1991) cites evidence that "attendance by the noncustodial parent at special events can facilitate the parent–child relationship" (p. 426). Noncustodial father involvement in school has been linked to better school outcomes for children (Nord, Brimhall, & West, 1997). Thus, unless a noncustodial parent's rights have been legally terminated, he or she can and should be permitted access to school information about his or her child (Jacob & Hartshorne, 2003).

Finally, when parents work together to make timely, clear, and mutually agreeable decisions about custody and contact, children benefit (Lamb et al., 1997; Leventhal et al., 1999). For parents having a hard time making such decisions, good decisions might be facilitated, and the chance of future problems and conflict reduced, by the use of divorce mediation. Although research is still limited (Emery, 1999, 2001b), mediation can help parents avoid the adversarial process of the court system, potentially reducing conflict between them and increasing their satisfaction with the custody or visitation outcome. Furthermore, evidence shows that fathers who use mediation maintain higher levels of contact with their children over time than do fathers who litigate (Emery, 2001b).

## ALTERNATIVE ACTIONS FOR INTERVENTION

Interventions for children who exhibit poor adjustment related to custody or contact arrangements would make use of the same information emphasized for prevention. Parents can be encouraged to alter difficult or unhealthy arrangements and move toward custody or contact plans that better fit their child's needs. For example, some children exhibit problems as a result of feeling (whether they are aware of it or not) that a noncustodial parent doesn't love or care for them. In such instances, parents could help by recognizing the importance of regular contact between a noncustodial parent and the child, as well as by learning about effective ways for a noncustodial parent to maintain a parental—rather than a visitor's—role (Pruett & Pruett, 1998). Noncustodial parents can be encouraged to communicate their love and concern for the child, both through the amount and quality of time they spend with the child and through symbolic expressions of love, such as remembering special days (Buchanan et al., 1996).

Individual counseling or group parenting education can help parents recognize the importance of the child's relationship with each parent along with other aspects of parenting. These interventions can address issues such as conflict resolution between parents and contact refusal by the child (for more specific information on these types of programs see, for example, Ellis, 2000; Emery, 1999, 2001a, 2001b; Whiteside & Becker, 2000). School-based professionals can provide resources and support to help parents address problems of custody or contact and to work together for the benefit of their children regardless of the custody arrangement.

Interventions regarding custody and contact often must address the issue of conflict between parents, and a word about handling conflict seems appropriate. Aside from generally educating parents about the negative effects of conflict on children, school psychologists and counselors might warn parents that young adults feel more anger and less closeness toward mothers who are perceived as interfering with or criticizing father involvement (Fabricius, 2003); although unstudied, the same is likely to be true of fathers who engage in such behaviors. School personnel also could help prevent negative outcomes for children by intervening to limit or stop parents from involving their children in the conflict. In some cases, it might be helpful simply to alert parents that certain behaviors, such as asking children to carry messages between homes, quizzing them about the other home, or denigrating the other parent in front of the child, are stressful for children. Counseling children about how to handle such situations would also be helpful. In cases of extreme conflict, including disputes over custody and contact, family therapies are available that can help families overcome high levels of conflict to reach workable, if not ideal, solutions (Lebow, 2003; Mannarino, 1997).

## SUMMARY

Children want and can benefit from contact with both parents after divorce. However, the benefits depend on a variety of factors, including the level of conflict between parents, characteristics of the child (e.g., age and temperament), and the logistics of the arrangement (e.g., distance between homes, regularity of contact, flexibility of the arrangement). Joint physical custody (or sole custody with a high level of contact with the noncustodial parent) can help families approximate the optimal post-divorce scenario described early in this chapter. Although arrangements involving a high level of contact with both parents can be risky under some circumstances (e.g., when conflict between parents is high or when the child, because of temperament, has trouble adapting to changes in routine), contact can be structured to minimize problems. Father custody might be associated with elevated risk for some, but it works well for many children.

The information provided in this chapter should help school personnel to understand processes and circumstances involved in a child's contact or custody arrangement; however, they should not be surprised to find situations that do not fit the average profile for that arrangement. Ultimately, school personnel will do the most to improve children's functioning after divorce by encouraging and supporting parents in their efforts to minimize conflict, develop and maintain positive relationships with their child, and provide consistent, authoritative parenting in each home in which the child resides.

## RECOMMENDED RESOURCES

### Books and Other Printed Material

Ellis, E. M. (2000). *Divorce wars: Interventions with families in conflict.* Washington, DC: American Psychological Association.

This book is written by a clinician for practitioners who work with divorced and divorcing families in legal or therapeutic settings. Drawing from the best research available, the author provides extensive information about potential problems of children in divorce contexts and details approaches to help families resolve problems that arise with divorce and conflict, including decisions about custody and contact.

Galatzer-Levy, R. M., & Kraus, L. (Eds.) (1999). *The scientific basis of child custody decisions.* New York: Wiley.

This volume covers a wide range of topics relevant to custody and visitation arrangements of children, including issues particular to children at different ages (infants, school-age children, and adolescents), children of same-gender parents, and adopted children. Clinical intervention and high-conflict divorces are also addressed.

Lebow, J. (2003). Integrative family therapy for disputes involving child custody and visitation. *Journal of Family Psychology, 17,* 181–192.

This article outlines negative outcomes associated with ongoing conflict over visitation and custody, and provides an integrative, multilevel family therapy model to help high-conflict families focus on behaviors that promote the best interests of the child.

Long, N., & Forehand, R. (2000). *Making divorce easier on your child: 50 effective ways to help children adjust.* Chicago: Contemporary Books.

This book gives helpful, clear, and research-grounded advice on a wide range of topics relevant to divorcing parents, including issues of visitation and custody.

## Website

*http://www.divorcesource.com/info/children/children.shtml*

This page is part of a larger support site for people experiencing divorce. Focused on child-related issues, the page has many links to sites with divorce tools, message centers, chat rooms, and legal and scientific information. A link for Custody, Visitation, and Child Support connects the reader to state-by-state legal information as well as to books on those topics.

# REFERENCES


Amato, P. R., & Gilbreth, J. G. (1999). Nonresident fathers and children's well-being: A meta-analysis. *Journal of Marriage and the Family, 61,* 557–573.

Bauserman, R. (2002). Child adjustment in joint-custody versus sole-custody arrangements: A meta-analytic review. *Journal of Family Psychology, 16,* 91–102.

Bianchi, S. M. (2000). Maternal employment and time with children: Dramatic change or surprising continuity? *Demography, 37,* 401–414.

Bray, J. H. (1991). Psychosocial factors affecting custodial and visitation arrangements. *Behavioral Sciences and the Law, 9,* 419–437.

Buchanan, C. M. (2000). The impact of divorce on adjustment during adolescence. In R. D. Taylor & M. Wang (Eds.), *Resilience across contexts: Family, work, culture, and community* (pp. 179–216). Mahwah, NJ: Lawrence Erlbaum Associates.

Buchanan, C. M., Maccoby, E. E., & Dornbusch, S. M. (1996). *Adolescents after divorce.* Cambridge, MA: Harvard University Press.

Cancian, M., & Meyer, D. R. (1998). Who gets custody? *Demography, 35,* 147–157.

Cooksey, E. C., & Craig, P. H. (1998). Parenting from a distance: The effects of paternal characteristic on contact between nonresidential fathers and their children. *Demography, 35,* 187–200.

Downey, D. B., Ainsworth-Darnell, J. W., & Dufur, M. J. (1998). Sex of parent and children's well-being in single-parent households. *Journal of Marriage and the Family, 60,* 878–893.

Ellis, E. M. (2000). *Divorce wars: Interventions with families in conflict.* Washington, DC: American Psychological Association.

Emery, R. E. (1999). *Marriage, divorce, and children's adjustment* (2nd ed.). Thousand Oaks, CA: Sage Publications.

Emery, R. E. (2001a). Behavioral family intervention: Less "behavior" and more "family." In A. Booth, A. C. Crouter, & M. Clements (Eds.), *Couples in conflict* (pp. 241–250). Mahwah, NJ: Lawrence Erlbaum Associates.

Emery, R. E. (2001b). Interparental conflict and social policy. In J. H. Grych & F. D. Fincham (Eds.), *Interparental conflict and child development: Theory, research, and application* (pp. 417–439). Cambridge, UK: Cambridge University Press.

Fabricius, W. V. (2003). Listening to children of divorce: New findings that diverge from Wallerstein, Lewis, and Blakeslee. *Family Relations, 52,* 385–396.

Forehand, R., Wierson, M., Thomas, A. M., Armistead, L., Kempton, T., & Fauber, R. (1990). Interparental conflict and paternal visitation following divorce: The interactive effect on adolescent competence. *Child Study Journal, 20,* 193–202.

Hetherington, E. M., & Kelly, J. (2002). *For better or for worse: Divorce reconsidered.* New York: W. W. Norton.

Hilton, J. M., Descrochers, S., & Devall, E. L. (2001). Comparison of role demands, relationships, and child functioning in single-mother, single-father, and intact families. *Journal of Divorce and Remarriage, 35,* 29–56.

Isaacs, M. B. (1988). The visitation schedule and child adjustment: A three year study. *Family Process, 27,* 251–256.

Jacob, S., & Hartshorne, T. S. (2003). *Ethics and law for school psychologists* (4th ed.). New York: Wiley.

Johnston, J. R., Kline, M., & Tschann, J. M. (1989). Ongoing post-divorce conflict in families contesting custody: Effects on children of joint custody and frequent access. *American Journal of Orthopsychiatry, 59,* 576–592.

Kelly, J. B. (1993). Current research on children's postdivorce adjustment: No simple answers. *Family and Conciliation Courts Review, 31,* 29–49.

Kelly, J. B., & Emery, R. E. (2003). Children's adjustment following divorce: Risk and resilience perspectives. *Family Relations, 52,* 352–362.

King, V. (2002). Parental divorce and interpersonal trust in adult offspring. *Journal of Marriage and the Family, 64,* 642–656.

King, V., Harris, K. M., & Heard, H. E. (2004). Racial and ethnic diversity in nonresident father involvement. *Journal of Marriage and the Family, 66,* 1–21.

Lamb, M. E., Sternberg, K. J., & Thompson, R. A. (1997). The effects of divorce and custody arrangements on children's behavior, development, and adjustment. *Family and Conciliation Courts Review, 35,* 393–404.

Laumann-Billings, L., & Emery, R. E. (2000). Distress among young adults from divorced families. *Journal of Family Psychology, 14,* 671–687.

Lebow, J. (2003). Integrative family therapy for disputes involving child custody and visitation. *Journal of Family Psychology, 17,* 181–192.

Leventhal, B., Kelman, J., Galatzer-Levy, R. M., & Kraus, L. (1999). Divorce, custody, and visitation in mid-childhood. In R. M. Galatzer-Levy & L. Kraus (Eds.), *The scientific basis of child custody decisions* (pp. 205–225). New York: Wiley.

Luepnitz, D. A. (1986). A comparison of maternal, paternal and joint custody: Understanding the varieties of post-divorce family life. *Journal of Divorce, 9,* 1–12.

Maccoby, E. E., & Mnookin, R. H. (1992). *Dividing the child: Social and legal dilemmas of custody.* Cambridge, MA: Harvard University Press.

Mannarino, A. P. (1997). Working with families with custody and visitation problems. In D. T. Marsh & R. D. Magee (Eds.), *Ethical and legal issues in professional practice with families* (pp. 127–139). New York: Wiley.

Manning, W. D., & Smock, P. J. (1999). New families and nonresident father-child visitation. *Social Forces, 78,* 87–116.

Marsiglio, W., Amato, P., Day, R. D., & Lamb, M. E. (2000). Scholarship on fatherhood in the 1990s and beyond. *Journal of Marriage and the Family, 62,* 1173–1191.

Mayes, L. C., & Molitor-Siegl, A. (1999). The scientific basis of child custody decisions. In R. M. Galatzer-Levy & L. Kraus (Eds.), *The impact of divorce on infants and very young children* (pp. 188–204). New York: Wiley.

Menning, C. L. (2002). Absent parents are more than money: The joint effect of activities and financial support on youths' educational attainment. *Journal of Family Issues, 23,* 648–671.

Naevdal, F., & Thuen, F. (2004). Residence arrangements and well-being: A study of Norwegian adolescents. *Scandinavian Journal of Psychology, 45,* 363–371.

Nord, C. W., Brimhall, D., & West, J. (1997). *Fathers' involvement in their children's schools* (NCES 98–091). Washington, DC: U.S. Department of Education, National Center for Education Statistics.

Pagani-Kurtz, L., & Derevensky, J. L. (1997). Access by noncustodial parents: Effects upon children's postdivorce coping resources. *Journal of Divorce and Remarriage, 27,* 43–55.

Pruett, M. K., Ebling, R., & Insabella, G. (2004). Critical aspects of parenting plans for young children: Interjecting data into the debate about overnights. *Family Court Review, 42,* 39–59.

Pruett, M. K., & Pruett, K. D. (1998). Fathers, divorce, and their children. *Child and Adolescent Psychiatric Clinics of North America, 7,* 389–407.

Pruett, M. K., Williams, T. Y., Insabella, G., & Little, T. D. (2003). Family and legal indicators of child adjustment to divorce among families with young children. *Journal of Family Psychology, 17,* 169–180.

Ravitz, A. (1999). Custody evaluations of adolescents. In R. M. Galatzer-Levy & L. Kraus (Eds.), *The scientific basis of child custody decisions* (pp. 226–235). Hoboken, NJ: John Wiley.

Seltzer, J. A. (1991). Relationships between fathers and children who live apart: The father's role after separation. *Journal of Marriage and the Family, 53,* 79–101.

Seltzer, J. A. (1998). Father by law: Effects of joint legal custody on nonresident fathers' involvement with children. *Demography, 35,* 135–146.

Twaite, J. A., & Luchow, A. K. (1996). Custodial arrangements and parental conflict following divorce: The impact on children's adjustment. *The Journal of Psychiatry and Law, 24,* 53–75.

Wallerstein, J. S., & Blakeslee, S. (1989). *Second chances: Men, women and children a decade after divorce.* New York: Ticknor & Fields.

Warshak, R. A. (2003). Payoffs and pitfalls of listening to children. *Family Relations, 52,* 373–384.

Whiteside, M. F., & Becker, B. J. (2000). Parental factors and the young child's postdivorce adjustment: A meta-analysis with implications for parenting arrangements. *Journal of Family Psychology, 14,* 5–26.

# 58

# Custodial Grandchildren

**Bert Hayslip, Jr.**
**Patricia L. Kaminski**
*University of North Texas*

## BACKGROUND AND DEVELOPMENT

This chapter explores the state of knowledge about grandchildren who are being raised by their grandparents, with particular attention paid to implications for school psychologists and other school-based practitioners. These children and their family structures also are referred to as *custodial grandchildren* and *grandfamilies*. Custodial grandchildren must be considered in the context of the family structure that makes them a unique subgroup. As such, the chapter also describes the various circumstances that place a grandparent in the role of primary caregiver, the challenges and needs of custodial grandparents, and factors bearing on the quality of the grandparent–grandchild relationship.

### The Increasing Prevalence of Grandfamilies

School psychologists, counselors, and social service agency personnel are more likely than ever to encounter children who are being reared by their grandparents. Indeed, custodial grandparents, defined here as adults who are caring for their grandchildren on a full-time basis, are becoming more prevalent. In 2000, 5.7 million grandparents lived with their grandchildren (U.S. Census Bureau, 2001), and approximately 2.4 million of those were raising their grandchildren. From 1990 to 2000, there was a 30% increase in the number of children (half of whom were under the age of 6) living in households maintained by grandparents (U.S. Census Bureau, 2000). This figure represents nearly 6 million children under the age of 18 or 8% of all children at that time. The reality for many *grandkin*, grandchildren being cared for by a family member (see Edwards, 1998), is that they may receive care not only from their grandparents, but also from aunts and uncles (who may or may not co-reside with them), friends, and neighbors.

### Diversity Among Grandfamilies

Understanding custodial grandchildren demands an appreciation for the diverse types of people who assume the role of parent to a grandchild. Although a majority of grandparent caregivers are under the age of 65 (72%), female (77%), and married (54%), (U.S. Census Bureau, 2000), significant numbers of grandchildren are being raised by grandfathers and single grandparents. Moreover, though most custodial grandparents are Caucasian (51%), significant numbers of African Americans (38%) and Hispanics (13%) also provide such care (American Association of Retired Persons [AARP], 2003). There is also more age diversity among custodial grandparents than there typically is among traditional parents. For example, it is not unusual for custodial grandparents of elementary school–age children to be in their 40s or their 70s.

Attending to subcultural differences among custodial grandparents is especially vital to understanding the context and needs of custodial grandchildren. For example, household composition is an important factor influencing childcare demands, needs for social support, and financial stress. Households in which grandparents are raising their grandchildren in the absence of the adult parent are referred to as *skipped-generation households*; those in which grandparents co-reside with the grandchild's parent but still assume primary parental responsibility are referred to as *co-parenting households*.

The likelihood of grandfamilies having a particular type of household composition varies according to ethnicity. For example, Pruchno (1999) found that Black (versus White) custodial grandmothers were more likely to have peers living with them, to have come from families with multiple generations living together, and to be receiving more formal social services. Hispanic American custodial grandparents are more likely to co-parent with an adult child other than the grandchild's parent (Burnette, 1999). However, Hispanics and African Americans are more likely than Caucasians to co-parent with one of their grandchild's parents, consistent with an emphasis on the family as an ongoing entity and with expectations of intergenerational assistance for the former two groups (Cox, Brooks, & Valcarcel, 2000). The effects of co-parenting versus skipped-generation caregiving on custodial grandparents' well-being also vary by ethnicity. For example, Latino grandmothers' well-being is positively related to co-parenting, whereas African American grandmothers fare better in custodial (skipped generation) families (Goodman & Silverstein, 2002).

Particularly relevant to understanding custodial grandchildren is an awareness of the diverse circumstances under which children arrive in the custody of their grandparents. Indeed, some circumstances are more socially stigmatizing than others and, therefore, raise different concerns relevant to their impact on the child's psychosocial adjustment. The permanency of the grandfamily arrangement, or whether its length can even be predicted, is also likely to influence a child's adjustment to it. Even under the best circumstances, however, simply being raised by one's grandparents at all affects children in that they are apt to feel different from their age peers.

Circumstances that lead to grandfamilies range from the practical (e.g., when a grandparent provides co-parenting help for a single parent who must work or go to school) to the tragic (e.g., when a child's parent dies) to the traumatic (e.g., when the court mandates that the grandparent care for the grandchild because of child abuse by the adult parent). Indeed, divorce, adult parent drug abuse, and child abuse most commonly lead to grandparent custody (see Hayslip & Kaminski, 2005). However, teen pregnancy, and the incarceration, disability, or death of an adult child, can also thrust grandparents into the custodial role.

Reflecting the difficulty in describing grandparent-headed families in general terms is the fact that grandparents choose to raise their grandchildren for differing reasons—they are the only relatives available, they believe they can provide better care than the parent, or they want to help their adult children in a time of crisis (Hayslip, Shore, Henderson, & Lambert, 1998). Among co-parenting grandmothers, the desire to help financially and the adult child's divorce are the most common reasons for role assumption, whereas among skipped-generation custodial grandmothers, parents' substance abuse, child neglect, mental or emotional distress, criminality, and child abuse are most common (Goodman & Silverstein, 2002).

## Strengths of Grandfamilies

The research and clinical literature overwhelmingly suggests that full-time custodial grandparents are at risk in terms of both their physical and mental health, relative to traditional, non-caregiving grandparents. Moreover, custodial grandchildren are more likely than their peers to have behavioral and emotional problems and to be in poorer physical health. Yet grandfamilies also have many strengths; indeed, it is these resources that allow them to function and even prosper despite the disruptions they have experienced in their personal and family lives.

First, grandparents have a wealth of life experience that can be useful in their newly assumed roles of parents to their grandchildren. They can draw upon a lifetime of having coped with life stresses, both within and outside the context of their marriages and relationships with their children and grandchildren. They can serve as role models, influence the values and life choices made by their grandchildren, and otherwise impart a sense of stability in the lives of children who typically have suffered the loss of their family of origin and a disrupted relationship with one or both parents.

Raising a grandchild can afford grandparents a second chance at parenting as well as numerous other benefits (see Reynolds, Wright, & Beale, 2003). Reflecting a strengths-based perspective, Ruiz (2004) described African American grandmothers raising their grandchildren as purveyors of moral, spiritual, and family values. Moreover, both the work of Cox (2000), which emphasizes the empowerment of custodial grandparents, and that of Whitley, White, and Kelley (1999), whose case management model stresses independence, self-confidence, and self-assurance among grandparent caregivers, rest on the assumption that grandparent-headed families are more appropriately thought of in terms of resources and strengths, rather than in terms of deficits or unmet needs.

## Developmental Considerations and Custodial Grandchildren

As members of a demographic group that has only recently come to the attention of researchers and professionals, custodial grandchildren have, with very few exceptions, yet to have their particular developmental needs addressed in the literature. The attention of researchers to date has been for the most part directed at describing and understanding the needs of grandparent caregivers, to the exclusion of the grandchildren they care for. To date, this relative lack of knowledge has not been remedied.

One assumption that can be made about custodial grandchildren is that the age of both a grandchild and a grandparent would affect their relationship and their adjustment to a custodial arrangement. It is also likely that their relative ages further affect the child's development. Further research is needed to determine whether such assumptions have merit.

## PROBLEMS AND IMPLICATIONS

Although the literature consistently suggests a relationship between the circumstances surrounding raising a grandchild and numerous physical and psychosocial outcomes among grandparent caregivers, less is known about such factors' *direct* effects on grandchildren. It is safe to assume that such effects on grandchildren are at least mediated by the negative effects of caregiving on their grandparents. In light of the dearth of work examining custodial grandchildren specifically, this section briefly reviews what is known about the difficulties faced by grandparent caregivers and discusses the implications for the grandchildren they are raising. Also, some tentative conclusions about the experiences and needs of custodial grandchildren can be extrapolated from the extant literature on populations of children with similar characteristics or life experiences. These populations include children from low-income families, children of guardians with high levels of stress or psychoemotional problems, children with emotional or behavioral difficulties, bereaved children, abused children, and youth who are making a transition to a new school.

### Custodial Grandparenting: Effects on Grandparents

Available data suggest that becoming a custodial grandparent is associated with a variety of negative consequences; chief among these are poorer physical and mental health (Hayslip et al., 1998). The incidence of illnesses such as depression, diabetes, hypertension, and insomnia is greater among grandparent caregivers, who often report more difficulty than their age peers in performing activities of daily living (Minkler & Fuller-Thomson, 1999). Of course, serious health problems can also affect the ability of custodial grandparents to provide consistent care to their grandchildren. For example, women's risk of coronary heart disease increases when they provide "high levels" of care (i.e., 9 hours per week) for grandchildren (Lee, Colditz, Berkman & Kawachi, 2003).

Grandparent caregivers often report experiencing loneliness, feeling different, and having a sense of invisibility (Wohl, Lahner, & Jooste, 2003). When either emotional (e.g., friendships or empathy) or instrumental (e.g., childcare or community services) support is lacking, custodial grandparents are at risk for depression and lowered self-esteem (Giarrusso, Silverstein, & Feng, 2000). Custodial grandparenting may also contribute to social isolation when custodial grandparents report feeling alone in their situation and suspect that their peers cannot relate to their experience (Kelley, Whitley, Sipe, & Yorker, 2000). Significantly, grandparent caregivers report that they have little in common with the parents of their grandchildren's friends (Erhle, 2001).

The percentage of grandparent caregivers living below the poverty line (19%) is greater than that for other types of families with children (14%; U.S. Census Bureau, 2000). Contributing to this dire situation, many grandmothers must reduce or give up paid work to raise a grandchild. In addition to a loss of income, the less tangible benefits of employment, such as better health and less parenting stress, may also be sacrificed (Musil, Schrader, & Matikani, 2000). Other factors also contribute to the financial burden of grandfamilies. For example, one-quarter of the custodial grandparents in one sample reported paying for their adult child's living expenses (Waldrop & Weber, 2001). Grandparents also commonly provide financial assistance for their adult child's psychiatric care, substance abuse treatment, and legal expenses. Although there are no published studies about the specific effects of poverty on grandfamilies, it is well documented that children from low-income households are at higher risk than other children for numerous academic, psychosocial, and health problems (see chapter 62, "Poverty").

### Custodial Grandparenting: Effects on Grandchildren

The prevalence of developmental, emotional, and behavioral difficulties among custodial grandchildren appears to be atypically high (e.g., hyperactivity, learning deficits, oppositionality, and depression; see Hayslip & Shore, 2000). Grandkin can also experience delays in the development of their socioemotional skills, self-concept, language, attention, and cognitive functioning, necessitating referrals to speech therapists or school counselors (Rogers & Henkin, 2000). In a sample of 170 inner-city grandchildren in kinship care (*M* age = 7.4), Grant and Kucera (1998) found the following symptoms (from most to least common) resulted in referral to school personnel: poor concentration, hyperactivity, depression, oppositional-defiant behavior, Attention Deficit Hyperactivity Disorder (ADHD), temper tantrums, mood swings, and social isolation. Numerous studies have reported high rates of grade retention (e.g., 23%–63%) and special education placement (e.g., 26%–28%) among custodial grandchildren (see Lawrence-Webb, Okundaye, & Hafner, 2003).

It is vital to mention that the adjustment reactions of some custodial grandchildren may be being misdiagnosed as more severe psychopathology. The one stressor these grandkin have in common—the temporary or permanent loss of their biological parents—is typically a severe stressor that would challenge the coping resources of most people. Given the frequency of additional stressful and traumatic experiences encountered (e.g., abuse or custody battles), it is not surprising that high numbers of custodial grandchildren exhibit symptoms of emotional, behavioral, and learning problems. To date, however, no longitudinal studies have been conducted to determine if such symptoms were preexisting (e.g., secondary to prenatal drug exposure or parental abuse), relatively normative temporary reactions to the immediate crisis, or psychopathology precipitated by the crisis. Additional research with rigorous assessment procedures is needed to investigate etiological factors and verify rates of various academic, emotional, and behavioral problems among custodial grandchildren.

In addition to the range of adjustment problems and psychiatric symptoms that have been associated with becoming a custodial grandchild, a host of feelings and psychological issues are expected responses to this event. Primary among these are grief, guilt, fear, embarrassment, and anger (see Smith, Dannison, & Vach-Hasse, 1998).

Grandchildren being raised by their grandparents, who have already experienced loss and rejection and are often angry about this, are likely to have more difficulty developing trusting relationships with grandparent caregivers, teachers, and peers (Rogers & Henkin, 2000). It is expected that a child who has been abandoned (either literally or figuratively) will fear abandonment in the future. Children's fears of abandonment are likely to be exacerbated when their custodial grandparents are in poor health or elderly. From the grandchild's perspective, wondering when an 80-year-old grandmother, who is either widowed or whose husband is also older, will die is a real concern. Such worries are not expected to be as intense for grandchildren whose grandparents are in their 50s, in good health, and still married.

Complications related to bereavement (i.e., complicated bereavement; see chapter 18, "Grief") are especially likely to occur when children feel stigmatized (as when a parent has died of AIDS or a drug overdose) and when they have not been given the opportunity to talk about their feelings related to the parent's dying. This latter factor often varies with the grandparent's own openness to doing so, especially if the deceased parent was a son or daughter. In cases in which the unwritten rule is to not discuss a parent's death, grandchildren are likely to harbor feelings ranging from sadness to anger, guilt, regret, or anxiety.

A grandparent's ability and willingness to attend to a grandchild's feelings over the loss of a parental relationship can be compromised by the fact that many custodial grandparents are also simultaneously grieving over the losses that placed them in that role, such as the death or incarceration of their adult child. Moreover, grandparents often express shame, guilt, and anxiety over an adult child's illness or death due to AIDS (Joslin, 2002). Thus, many grandparent caregivers must also cope with the secondary losses linked to a child's death or physical or emotional absence, as well as with their grandchild's grief related to parental loss. Recent evidence (Miltenberger, Hayslip, Harris, & Kaminski, 2003–2004) suggests that grandparent caregivers' grief may be disenfranchised (i.e., not publicly recognized or acknowledged by others), undermining their opportunities to express themselves, receive social support, and talk to their grandchildren about the latter's feelings. Thus, it is likely that grandchildren's grief is also disenfranchised.

In addition to custodial grandchildren likely feeling alone in their grief, many things related to their living situation—from the older appearance of their caregivers to the practical consequences of having caregivers who may not drive—tend to make them feel different from their peers. Feeling singled out is likely to be particularly stressful for children who also are required to change to a new school as a result of their new custody arrangement. Moreover, especially in cases in which the grandchild must relocate to a different city or state to live with a grandparent, friendship networks and other sources of stability are likely to be disrupted, leaving many children feeling lonely and displaced and adding to their sense of loss and abandonment.

Some custodial grandchildren are vulnerable to role-reversals with their grandparents, perhaps in an effort to earn love or because they never experienced appropriate caregiver–child boundaries. Thus, it is important to monitor custodial grandchildren for signs that they are having too many emotional or physical caregiving demands being placed on them (Kaminski & Hayslip, 2004). Such role-reversals can be detrimental to children, for the real "work" of childhood (i.e., intellectual, psychological, and spiritual development) cannot optimally occur when pseudo-adult behavior is required.

## ALTERNATIVE ACTIONS FOR PREVENTION

Grandparent-headed families have many strengths and resources, such as the wisdom and caring of a grandparent, on which a child can rely; therefore, it is inaccurate to assume that all children who are being raised by their grandparents are at risk for behavioral, emotional, and academic difficulties. Nevertheless, school personnel should be sensitive to the fact that custodial grandchildren face unique challenges and are more likely than most children to encounter certain difficulties; thus assessments of their needs should be performed more quickly so that some potential problems might be prevented. Moreover, by being proactive, school personnel can enhance the likelihood of a collaborative and mutually beneficial relationship with custodial grandparents.

### Building a Relationship Between Schools and Grandfamilies

The foundation of improved relationships between grandfamilies and schools rests on sensitivity to the needs of this population. First, educators, counselors, and school psychologists can model acceptance of and respect for diverse family constellations. For example, the term *guardian* can be easily substituted for *parent* so that custodial grandchildren are not continually reminded that their family is different. Routinely inviting the grandparents of any children to serve as classroom volunteers, participate as guest speakers, and attend school programs would help all older adults feel more included and less intimidated. As an added benefit, custodial grandparents would feel less out of the ordinary in the school environment.

Sensitivity also requires awareness of the fact that grandparents who are new to the custodial role may not have formally interacted with a school system in a decade or more. As such, the amount of information they need from school personnel may exceed that of other parents with children at the same grade level as their grandchild. For example, custodial grandparents may not be familiar with logistical requirements (e.g., required child immunizations, bus schedules), terminology (e.g., individualized education plans, zero tolerance policy), and the array of services and programs for which their grandchild may be eligible, such as school meals, special education, or counseling (Reynolds et al., 2003). In addition, older custodial grandparents are likely to feel rusty compared with most parents when it comes to academics. Many report anxiety about having to help their grandchild with homework (Glass & Huneycutt, 2002). By being aware of this potential problem, teachers may be able to intervene more quickly with a creative solution (e.g., arranging a peer tutor).

School officials should also be aware that custodial grandparents often have difficulty registering their grandchildren for school (Erhle, 2001). Such difficulties are greatest for grandparents who are caring for their grandchildren informally, without a legal basis for doing so, such as adoption, legal custody, or guardianship (Generations United, 2002). Some school districts have altered their policies to allow grandparents who do not have legal custody to nevertheless register their grandchildren (AARP, 1993).

After establishing an inclusive environment and reaching out to grandfamilies, schools may need to remove other barriers to increase the likelihood of custodial grandparents' involvement with the school. Specifically, childcare and transportation assistance may be a prerequisite for a grandfamily's participation in school-sponsored activities and programs. Even if providing transportation is not realistic for a particular school, educators should consider logistics such as public transportation schedules before planning events.

Whether or not custodial grandparents are able to attend school meetings and programs on a regular basis, school personnel must strive for consistent communication with grandparent caregivers. Not only are consistency and predictability critical ingredients to establishing trust, but a lack of such stability can unduly strain an already stressed family. Similarly, achieving consistency and predictability in a custodial grandchild's class schedule and routine can minimize unnecessary stress on the child (Smith et al., 1998).

## Advocating on Behalf of Grandfamilies

Another key to supporting the strengths of grandfamilies is ensuring that they are informed about or referred to the services to which they are entitled (see Grant, 2000, for a school-based advocacy program). Not only do a disproportionate number of grandfamilies live below poverty level, but only one in three custodial grandchildren is covered by health insurance (see Kirby & Kaneda, 2002). Furthermore, grandchildren who have recently been in the custody of an impaired parent may be undernourished and overdue for medical, dental, and eye checkups. Thus, particularly in school systems without social workers, school psychologists and other school-based professionals may need to play an active role in meeting the basic needs of these children (e.g., advocate for and facilitate access to federal and community programs for which grandparents and grandchildren may be eligible).

Advocates are vital because grandfamilies too often fall between the cracks of agency responsibility (McCallion, Janicki, Grant-Griffin, & Kolomer, 2000). The absence of advocacy for grandparent caregivers as well as other barriers to service use have contributed to the underutilization of resources from which grandfamilies could benefit (Butts, 2000). For example, 90% of grandparent caregivers do not receive social security benefits, and 85% do not receive any type of public assistance (Landry-Meyer, 2000). Furthermore, only a small number enjoy foster care status, which can provide child-care, monetary remuneration, and tutoring (Dellmann-Jenkins, Blankemeyer, & Olesh, 2002).

Fortunately, however, several organized, programmatic efforts are being implemented to address access problems. For example, the National Family Caregiver Support Program (NFCSP) was established in 2000 to enable states to make information available about, and improve access to, a variety of support services relating to physical health and well-being, financial and legal assistance, mental health counseling, and support group services (Beltran, 2003). Similarly, a number of public benefits programs can help grandparent caregivers by providing financial assistance and medical insurance. These programs include Supplemental Security Income (SSI), Social Security benefits for children age 17 and younger (Old-Age Survivors and Disability Insurance), Temporary Assistance to Needy Families (TANF), Medicaid, and the Children's Health Insurance Program (CHIPS; Biscarr, 2002). Information regarding the many state and federally funded programs for grandparent-headed families can be found on the websites of the AARP as well as Generations United (see Recommended Resources).

# ALTERNATIVE ACTIONS FOR INTERVENTION

This discussion on interventions with grandfamilies is based on clinical experiences and on the relevant literature on interventions with custodial grandparents because of the relative lack of published work specifically detailing interventions with custodial grandchildren. The majority of this literature is descriptive; very few controlled treatment outcome studies and no replication studies have been abstracted on any of the major databases (e.g., PsycInfo, ERIC).

After working to meet the basic needs of grandchildren, school personnel can turn their attention to higher-order needs, such as the child–primary caregiver relationship, social support, and psychoeducation. Custodial grandparents may also benefit from attending classes to refresh or enhance parenting skills. These activities aim to shore up anticipated vulnerabilities in the custodial grandparent–headed family. Further intervention may be needed to address any specific problems that persist, especially those related to family relationships and functioning, grief work, and child adjustment.

## Strengthening the Quality of the Grandparent–Grandchild Relationship

Fundamental to both prevention and intervention efforts is a focus on improving the quality of the relationship between a child and his or her primary caregiver. Indeed, the quality of this relationship can be viewed as the primary strength that characterizes grandparent-headed families, enabling both generations to cope with the many negative consequences that accompany their situation. In light of the adverse circumstances that often lead to grandchildren being raised by their grandparents, the quality of the grandparent–grandchild relationship is key to the grandchild's overall happiness and adjustment. Thus, efforts to foster a warm and mutually fulfilling relationship between grandparent and grandchild constitute a form of intervention. In some cases, impaired relationships with a parent may impede the formation of an emotional bond with a grandparent (e.g., 13% of adolescents reported nonoptimal relationships with both mothers and grandparents; Keller & Stricker, 2003). However, when possible, a secure relationship with a grandparent may nevertheless help compensate for earlier parental failures and may be a buffer against the child's experiencing depression, low self-esteem, and low social acceptance. The grandparent becomes a secondary attachment figure, one whose relationship with the child can be reparative, helping the child develop attachment security despite the initial insecure attachment with a primary caregiver. In the case of children who internalize their feelings, focusing on building the quality of the grandchild–grandparent relationship may be more effective than focusing on ameliorating behavior problems or impaired school performance (Keller & Stricker).

The mechanisms for facilitating a secure custodial grandparent–custodial grandchild attachment have yet to be empirically tested. However, Poehlmann (2003) proposed that factors that are likely to predict relationship quality in these dyads include the age of the child at placement, the sensitivity with which the grandparent responds to her or his grandchild, and the quality of the grandparents' marital relationship.

Though the quality of the grandchild–grandparent relationship is paramount to intervention, also important is ensuring that both the child and the grandparent have sources of social–emotional support and companionship outside of their relationship with each other. In particular, increasing social–emotional support may be especially helpful for those custodial grandparents who rely unduly on their grandchild to meet their needs, perhaps because of their isolation from age peers or friends.

## Coordinating Programs and Support Groups for Custodial Grandparents and Custodial Grandchildren

School professionals may be helpful in coordinating the formation of educational programs and support groups to assist custodial grandparents (see Smith, 2003). Model programs typically employ a professional facilitator and incorporate both didactic sessions and peer support for custodial grandparents (e.g., Glass & Huneycutt, 2002) and, occasionally, for grandchildren (e.g., Dannison & Smith, 2003; Rogers & Henkin, 2000).

One school-based intervention for school-aged custodial grandchildren, Grandma's Kids (Rogers & Henkin, 2000), aims to teach life skills (e.g., empathy training, anger management, and impulse control). The program includes information about drug abuse, provides academic tutoring, and engages custodial grandchildren in group counseling to help them build self-esteem, manage conflict, increase coping, and improve their relationships with others. Through this program, grandchildren can also interact with other children living with their grandparents and gain access to many activities (e.g., arts and crafts, summer camps and workshops, sports, tutoring, and mentoring). Preliminary findings suggest that the program's impact on grandchildren is positive (Temple University Center for Intergenerational Learning, 2005).

Support groups have been demonstrated to provide needed information and emotional support to grandparent caregivers, and such benefits seem to be especially important for minority grandparents (AARP, 2004) as well as for grandparents who are either isolated or live in rural areas. Although support groups likely mitigate some of the distress grandparent caregivers experience, groups sometimes merely allow participants to vent endless frustrations without moving to a more positive and constructive focus (Strom & Strom, 2000). However, support groups do provide the opportunity for expressing feelings and receiving empathy from others, especially important in light of the fact that grandparents report feeling invisible and judged by others as parental failures (Wohl et al., 2003). By disclosing how they became custodial grandparents, talking about their families, and comparing memories of raising their adult children with their current experiences, custodial grandparents can bring closure to unfinished business and work through feelings of guilt and regret (Smith, 2003; Wohl et al.).

In the context of the advantages of support groups in lessening the isolation felt by custodial grandparents and their grandchildren, KinNet, a project funded in 2000 through the Adoption and Safe Families Act (ASFA) and created through Generations United, established a national network of support groups for grandparent caregivers in the formal foster care system. These support groups, representing 16 states, consisted of grandparent caregivers residing in the community, many of whom were African American (61%). Recent evidence suggests that KinNet is effective in imparting information, providing needed social networking support to custodial grandparents, and improving the mental health of custodial grandparents (Generations United, 2004; Smith & Monahan, 2004). The Brookdale Foundation's Relatives as Parents Program (RAPP) funds demonstration projects that provide information, referral, and direct support to grandparent caregivers and their grandchildren. In addition, the American Association of Retired Persons (AARP) Grandparent Information Center (GIC) maintains a national database of grandparent support groups and an online source of information targeting the emotional, legal, and financial needs of grandparent caregivers (AARP, 2003). Information about such programs can be accessed on their websites listed in Recommended Resources.

## Improving Parenting Skills Among Custodial Grandparents

A crucial role that school professionals may play in the lives of grandchildren being raised by their grandparents is to assist custodial grandparents with their parenting. This is especially important for those grandparents who are raising children with emotional or behavioral difficulties that bring them into conflict with teachers, school officials, other parents, or age peers. Depression, ADHD, drug or alcohol abuse, or disruptive behavior disorders are likely to pose many challenges to the behavior management skills of teachers as well as to the parenting skills of grandparents. Grandparents may need to be educated about such difficulties as well as learn to know when problem behaviors in their grandchildren warrant a referral to a mental health professional.

Parenting skills training for custodial grandparents should encompass a variety of topics. Content might include (a) parenting skills, such as discipline styles (and their outcomes), limit setting, and consequences for actions; (b) communication skills on topics such as how to talk to a teenager or to a child's teacher; (c) advocacy issues that include legal and custody questions and knowledge about one's rights; (d) drug use and sexuality; and (e) grief and related issues of loss (Wohl et al., 2003). Training in this context can help address grandparents' lack of knowledge about mental health care for themselves or their grandchildren and their unfamiliarity with STDs, drug use, school violence, or peer influences on their grandchildren (Silverthorn & Durant, 2000).

It is important to point out that grandparent caregivers may resist parenting skills training, despite its potential benefits for grandparents and grandchildren, because it may imply they have not adequately parented their adult children (see Hayslip & Kaminski, 2005). Prefacing this training with a caveat that stresses how times have changed may help decrease grandparents' defensiveness about this issue.

Custodial grandparents report that a primary obstacle to participation in parenting programs is not having time to attend (Kaminski & Hayslip, 2004). Practitioners can develop creative solutions to these problems, such as providing either audiotaped or videotaped parent training materials for use at home.

Another innovative approach to improving parenting skills is based on an empowerment model (Cox, 2000). Custodial grandmothers were involved in designing a 12-class curriculum. In addition to modules on parenting and communication, the program covered topics such as developing advocacy skills and making presentations. Each participant also became expert on a topic of her choice and presented the material she learned to other grandparents in the community. Such presentations were quite beneficial to custodial grandparents, increasing their knowledge of community needs, enabling them to overcome cultural and language barriers with other grandparent caregivers, increasing community outreach, and allowing for the formation of ongoing and meaning support from other grandparents (Cox). In their efforts to educate one another and through the acquisition of knowledge and skills, they were empowered to change their relationships with their grandchildren and redefine their roles as grandparents.

## Considering Other Issues When Working With Custodial Grandchildren

For children who have already experienced numerous losses in their lives, fears about a grandparent's health or continued ability to care for them can be a significant source of distress. In cases in which the child has a poor relationship with a surviving parent, he or she may have a sense of divided loyalties, of being caught, emotionally, between a grandparent and a parent. The poorly defined nature of the child's relationship to both parent and grandparent can also inhibit the child's processing of his or her feelings of grief regarding the loss of the relationship with a parent who has either willingly given up parental rights or who has had such rights rescinded by the court. Continuing questions regarding legal custody, patterns of visitation by the child's parents, and the role a parent is likely to fill in the child's life (as communicated to the child by the grandparent) can either undermine or enhance the child's emotional well-being, social relationships, and school performance (Hayslip & Kaminski, 2005). It is entirely possible that the school professionals working with a custodial grandchild will interact not only with the grandparent raising him or her, but also with the biological parent who continues to play a significant role in that grandchild's life. This parent may or may not interact with the grandparent and thus may or may not help solve the grandchild's emotional, social, or academic difficulties.

In such cases, it may be beneficial for school professionals to play a role in helping a grandparent and grandchild forge a new relationship with the adult parent that permits some contact, yet does not interfere with the quality of the relationship that has been established between grandparent and grandchild (for discussions of family therapy approaches with custodial grandparents, parents, and children, see e.g., Brown-Standridge & Floyd, 2000). In many cases, there is a fine line to be walked wherein the grandchild's well-being is actually harmed by renewing a relationship with the adult parent, particularly when there is evidence that some physical, emotional, or sexual abuse has occurred.

Even parents who have not been abusive can cause harm when they unpredictably enter and exit the lives of their children (Dannison & Smith, 2003). Depending on the circumstances surrounding the custody arrangement; the relationships between the grandparent, parent, and child; the parent's emotional stability; and other factors, the sudden presence of a biological parent can cause significant distress. That distress will often appear as a change in mood or behavior at school. When this is the case, it is important for custodial grandparents and school personnel to be in communication. Clear communication from the school can help the child's grandparents understand the possible impact of parental visitation or absence, which may affect their decisions about parental contact in the future. Similarly, clear communication to the school can help the child's teachers anticipate and potentially minimize negative consequences of parental visitation or absence.

Attempts to understand the unique and often complex adjustments custodial grandparents and their grandchildren must make are just beginning. For example, little is known about the long-term consequences of either having been raised by a grandparent or about raising a grandchild later in life. As few longitudinal studies of custodial grandparents are available at present (see Hayslip & Kaminski, 2005), long-term longitudinal work, perhaps targeting vulnerable grandparents and their grandchildren, will be necessary to answer these questions; however, no such work is being done to target grandchildren who are being raised by their grandparents. Moreover, additional and more rigorous treatment outcome studies are needed, especially to address the particular lack of attention to the specific psychotherapeutic needs of custodial grandchildren. Future researchers would also do well to recruit participants about whom even less is known (e.g., rural grandparents, custodial grandparents and grandchildren of differing ethnicities, custodial grandfathers). By attending to these and other key variables (e.g., reasons for role assumption, the grandchild's adjustment, family system processes; see Goodman, 2003), researchers can improve the design and implementation of efforts to help grandparents and the grandchildren they are raising.

## SUMMARY

An increasingly prevalent family constellation is a home headed by grandparents who are raising their grandchildren. Understanding grandchildren who are being raised by their grandparents requires that they be considered in the context of their relationship to one another. This understanding should also reflect several key issues: (a) the costs and benefits of being raised by a grandparent, (b) the heterogeneity of grandparent–grandchild dyads, (c) the need for social support among custodial grandparents and their grandchildren, (d) the development of parenting skills among grandparents raising grandchildren, (e) school-based and social programs targeting the adjustments and problems experienced by such grandchildren, and (f) the importance of developing a trusting and secure relationship between grandparent and grandchild in light of the losses experienced by both.

## RECOMMENDED RESOURCES

### Books and Other Printed Material

Cox, C. (Ed.). (2000). *To grandmother's house we go and stay: Perspectives on custodial grandparents.* New York: Springer.

This edited text provides an excellent overview of custodial grandparenting. Throughout the text, the editor's perspective emphasizing the importance of empowering such grandparents is evident.

Hayslip, B., & Goldberg-Glen, R. (Eds.). (2000). *Grandparents raising grandchildren: Theoretical, empirical, and clinical perspectives.* New York: Springer.

This edited text explores the clinical, theoretical, and research-related bases for understanding grandparents and the grandchildren they are raising. The editors take a lifespan perspective in understanding custodial grandparents and their grandchildren, emphasizing the multiple antecedents of such roles.

Hayslip, B., & Patrick, J. (Eds.). (2003). *Working with custodial grandparents.* New York: Springer.

This edited text focuses on interventions with custodial grandparents, using case studies to emphasize the many levels and targets of intervention as well as quantitative research aimed at improving the psychosocial functioning of grandparent caregivers.

## Websites

*http://www.aarp.org/grandparents*

The American Association of Retired Persons Grandparent Information Center is an excellent resource both for grandparents raising their grandchildren and for professionals. It provides timely information on research and practice relevant to coping with the demands of raising a grandchild.

*http://www.brookdalefoundation.org*

The Brookdale Foundation established the Relatives as Parents Program in 1996, designed to expand services for grandparents raising grandchildren. It awards seed grants of $10,000 to state agencies for this purpose. The Brookdale Foundation is also an excellent source of information regarding state-specific resources of all types for custodial grandparents.

*http://www.gu.org*

Generations United provides fact sheets and other resources on grandparents and other relatives raising grandchildren. It is perhaps the premier source of information related to advocacy, programmatic support, and research on intergenerational relationships across the life span, with particular emphasis on grandparents raising their grandchildren.

## REFERENCES


American Association of Retired Persons. (1993). *Grandparents raising their grandchildren: What to consider and where to find help.* Washington, DC: Author.

American Association of Retired Persons. (2003). *Lean on me: Support and minority outreach for grandparents raising grandchildren.* Retrieved May 15, 2005, from http://www.aarp.org/research/family/grandparenting/aresearch-import-483.html

American Association of Retired Persons. (2004). *Raising grandchildren? Take care of yourself, too.* Retrieved May 15, 2005, from http://www.aarp.org/life/grandparents/helpraising/Articles/a2004-09-07-grandparents-raisinggrands.html

Beltran, A. (2003). *A guide to the National Family Caregiver Support Program and its inclusion of grandparents and other relatives raising children.* Washington, DC: Generations United. Retrieved May 15, 2005, from http://www.gu.org/publications.asp

Biscarr, M. (2002). *Grandparents and other relatives raising children: Support in the workplace.* Washington, DC: Generations United. Retrieved May 15, 2005, from http://www.gu.org/Files/Support-in-Workplace-Guide-final.pdf

Brown-Standridge, M. D., & Floyd, C. W. (2000). Healing bittersweet legacies: Revisiting contextual family therapy for grandparents raising grandchildren in crisis. *Journal of Marital and Family Therapy, 26,* 185–197.

Burnette, D. (1999). Physical and emotional well-being of custodial grandparents in Latino families. *American Journal of Orthopsychiatry, 69,* 305--317.

Butts, D. M. (2000). Organizational advocacy as a factor in public policy regarding custodial grandparenting. In B. Hayslip & R. Goldberg-Glen (Eds.), *Grandparents raising grandchildren: Theoretical, empirical and clinical perspectives* (pp. 341–350). New York: Springer.

Cox, C. (2000). Empowering grandparents raising grandchildren. In C. Cox (Ed.), *To grandmother's house we go and stay: Perspectives on custodial grandparents* (pp. 253–267). New York: Springer.

Cox, C., Brooks, L. R., & Valcarcel, C. (2000). Culture and caregiving: A study of Latino grandparents. In C. Cox (Ed.), *To grandmother's house we go and stay: Perspectives on custodial grandparents* (pp. 215–233). New York: Springer.

Dannison, L. L., & Smith, A. B. (2003). Custodial grandparents community support program: Lessons learned. *Children & Schools, 25,* 87–95.

Dellmann-Jenkins, M., Blankemeyer, M., & Olesh, M. (2002). Adults in expanded grandparent roles:

Considerations for practice, policy, and research. *Educational Gerontology, 28,* 219–235.

Edwards, O. W. (1998). Helping grandkin- Grandchildren raised by grandparents: Expanding psychology in the schools. *Psychology in the Schools, 35,* 173–181.

Erhle, G. M. (2001). Grandchildren as moderator variables in the family: Social, physiological, and intellectual development of grandparents who are raising them. *Family Development and Intellectual Functions, 12,* 223–241.

Generations United. (2002). *Grandparents and other relatives raising children: Caregiver support groups.* [Fact sheet]. Retrieved May 15, 2005, from http://www.gu.org

Generations United. (November, 2004). *Efficacy of support groups for grandparents raising grandchildren.* Paper presented at the Annual Scientific Meeting of the Gerontological Society of America, Washington, DC.

Giarrusso, R., Silverstein, M., & Feng, D. (2000). Psychological costs and benefits of raising grandchildren: Evidence from a national survey of grandparents. In C. Cox (Ed.), *To grandmother's house we go and stay: Perspectives on custodial grandparents* (pp. 71–90). New York: Springer.

Glass, J. C., & Huneycutt, T. L. (2002). Grandparents raising grandchildren: The courts, custody, and educational implications. *Educational Gerontology, 28,* 237–251.

Goodman, C. (2003). Intergenerational triads in grandparent-headed families. *Journal of Gerontology: Social Sciences, 58B,* S281–S289.

Goodman, C., & Silverstein, M. (2002). Grandparents raising grandchildren: Family structure and well being in culturally diverse families. *The Gerontologist, 42,* 676–689.

Grant, R. (2000). The special needs of children in kinship care. *Journal of Gerontological Social Work, 33,* 17–33.

Grant, R., & Kucera, E. (1998). *Social and environmental stressors affecting an inner city school population.* Washington, DC: National Academy on School Based Health Care.

Hayslip, B., & Kaminski, P. (2005). Grandparents raising their grandchildren: A review of the literature and suggestions for practice. *The Gerontologist, 45,* 262–269.

Hayslip, B., & Shore, R. J. (2000). Custodial grandparenting and mental health services. *Journal of Mental Health and Aging, 6,* 367–384.

Hayslip, B., Shore, R. J., Henderson, C., & Lambert, P. (1998). Custodial grandparenting and grandchildren with problems: Their impact on role satisfaction and role meaning. *Journal of Gerontology: Social Sciences, 52B,* S164–S174.

Joslin, D. (2002). *Invisible caregivers: Older adults raising children in the wake of HIV/AIDS.* Columbia, NY: Columbia University Press.

Kaminski, P. L., & Hayslip, B. (August, 2004). *Parenting attitudes of custodial grandparents.* Paper presented at the Annual Convention of the American Psychological Association, Honolulu, HI.

Keller, S., & Stricker, G. (2003). Links between custodial grandparents and the psychological adaptation of grandchildren. In B. Hayslip & J. Patrick (Eds.), *Working with custodial grandparents* (pp. 27–44). New York: Springer.

Kelley, S. J., Whitley, D. M., Sipe, T. A., & Yorker, B. C. (2000). Psychological distress in grandmother kinship care providers: The role of resources, social support and physical health. *Child Abuse & Neglect, 24,* 311–321.

Kirby, J., & Kaneda, T. (2002). Health insurance and family structure: The case of adolescents in skipped generation families. *Medical Care Research and Review, 59,* 146–165.

Landry-Meyer, L. (2000). Grandparents as parents: What they need to be successful. *Family Focus, 45,* F9–F10.

Lawrence-Webb, C., Okundaye, J. N., & Hafner, G. (2003). Education and kinship caregivers: Creating a new vision. *Families and Society, 84,* 135–142.

Lee, S., Colditz, G., Berkman, L., & Kawachi, I. (2003). Caregiving to children and grandchildren and risk of coronary heart disease in women. *American Journal of Public Health, 93,* 1939–1944.

McCallion, P., Janicki, M., Grant-Griffin, L., & Kolomer, S. (2000). Grandparent caregivers II: Service needs and service provision issues. *Journal of Gerontological Social Work, 33,* 57–84.

Miltenberger, P., Hayslip, B., Harris, B., & Kaminski, P. (2003–2004). Perceptions of the losses experienced by custodial grandmothers. *Omega: Journal of Death and Dying, 48,* 245–262.

Minkler, M., & Fuller-Thomson, E. (1999). The health of grandparents raising grandchildren: Results of a national study. *American Journal of Public Health, 93,* 1384–1389.

Musil, C., Schrader, S., & Matikani, J. (2000). Social support stress and the special coping tasks of grandmother caregivers. In C. Cox (Ed.), *To grandmother's house we go and stay: Perspectives on custodial grandparents* (pp. 56–70). New York: Springer.

Poehlmann, J. (2003). An attachment perspective on grandparents raising their very young grandchildren: Implications for intervention and research. *Infant Mental Health Journal, 24,* 149–173.

Pruchno, R. (1999). Raising grandchildren: The experiences of Black and White grandmothers. *The Gerontologist, 39,* 209–221.

Reynolds, G. P., Wright, J. V., & Beale, B. (2003). The roles of grandparents in educating today's children. *Journal of Instructional Psychology, 30,* 316–325.

Rogers, A., & Henkin, N. (2000). School-based interventions for children in kinship care. In B. Hayslip & R. Goldberg-Glen (Eds.), *Grandparents raising grandchildren: Theoretical, empirical and clinical perspectives* (pp. 221–238). New York: Springer.

Ruiz, D. S. (2004). *Amazing grace: African American grandmothers as caregivers and conveyors of traditional values.* Westport, CT: Praeger.

Silverthorn, P., & Durant, S. (2000). Custodial grandparenting and the difficult child: Learning from the parenting literature. In B. Hayslip & R. Goldberg-Glen (Eds.), *Grandparents raising grandchildren: Theoretical, empirical and clinical perspectives* (pp. 47–64). New York: Springer.

Smith, A. B., Dannison, L. L., & Vach-Hasse, T. (1998). When "Grandma is Mom." *Childhood Education, 75,* 12–16.

Smith, C. J., & Monahan, D. J. (2004, November). *Evaluating kinship care: Practice and policy implications.* Paper presented at the Annual Scientific Meeting of the Gerontological Society of America, Washington, DC.

Smith, G. (2003). How grandparents view support groups: An exploratory study. In B. Hayslip & J. Patrick (Eds.), *Working with custodial grandparents* (pp. 69–92). New York: Springer.

Strom, R., & Strom, S. (2000). Goals for grandparent caregivers and support groups. In B. Hayslip & R. Goldberg-Glen (Eds.), *Grandparents raising grandchildren: Theoretical, empirical and clinical perspectives* (pp. 171–218). New York: Springer.

Temple University Center for Intergenerational Learning. (2005). *Grandma's Kids: A kinship family support program. Research and valuation.* Retrieved May 15, 2005, from http://www.temple.edu/cil/ProgramsResearch.html

U.S. Census Bureau. (2000). *Current population survey.* Washington, DC: U.S. Government Printing Office.

U.S. Census Bureau. (2001). *Co-resident grandparents and grandchildren.* Retrieved May 15, 2005, from http://www.census.gov

Waldrop, D., & Weber, J. (2001). From grandparent to caregiver. *Families in Society: The Journal of Contemporary Human Services, 82,* 461–472.

Whitley, D. M., White, K. R., & Kelley, S. J. (1999). Strengths-based case management: The application to grandparents raising grandchildren. *Journal of Families in Society, 80,* 110–119.

Wohl, E., Lahner, J., & Jooste, J. (2003). Group processes among grandparents raising grandchildren. In B. Hayslip & J. Patrick (Eds.), *Working with custodial grandparents* (pp. 195–212). New York: Springer.

# 59

# Single Parenting and Stepparenting

**Cindy Carlson**
**Jennifer N. Trapani**
*University of Texas at Austin*

## BACKGROUND AND DEVELOPMENT

Fewer children today than 10 years ago can count on growing up in a household that includes both of their biological parents. The number of single-parent households rose from 22% in 1990 to 28% in 2000 (U.S. Census Bureau, 2002), and one-third of all children under 18 years of age reside in a stepfamily home (Bumpass, Raley, & Sweet, 1995). According to these statistics, 6 of 10 children in any school classroom are likely to live in some form of a single-parent or stepfamily home. Much of the knowledge of the effects of these family living arrangements on children is based on research that has focused on the non-Hispanic White, postdivorce single-mother home and subsequent remarriage that creates a stepfamily. Although remarriage rates following divorce continue to be high among the non-Hispanic White population, the recent census indicates a significant increase in living arrangements that are less often the focus of research: births to unmarried mothers, father-headed single-parent homes, grandparents raising children, and cohabitation as a precursor or substitute for marriage (U.S. Census Bureau, 2002, 2003). These demographic trends that affect the lives of children warrant closer examination.

Although the divorce rate is now declining in the United States, children remain unlikely to reside with two biological parents. The number of single-mother households has remained steady, and single-father households have increased, largely because of increased rates of nonmarital fertility (Casper & Bianchi, 2002). About one-third of the births in the United States are now to unmarried mothers, and the rate of nonmarital childbearing continues to increase for women of all races. As the rate of nonmarital births continues to rise, so too does the number of grandparents raising the children of their young unmarried daughters and sons. In 2002, 5.6 million children (8%) were living in a grandparent head-of-household home (U.S. Census Bureau, 2003). Cohabitation, another notable rising demographic trend, has become an antecedent or alternative to marriage and a normative mode of entry into remarriage. Across ethnic groups, cohabitation is likely for 1 in 10 children in the custody of mothers and 3 in 10 children in the custody of fathers (U.S. Census Bureau). Cohabitation blurs the boundaries between single-parent and step-parent living arrangements (Casper & Bianchi).

The 2000 Census highlights the diverse forms of families in which children are living. The census figures also point to several issues that must be considered in any discussion of the effects of different family composition on children's school-related behavior and learning. Among these are (a) the challenge of defining single-parent and stepfamily homes, (b) family stability versus transition for children, (c) ethnic diversity in the changing demographics, (d) the role of economic resources, and (e) negative stereotyping.

### Challenges of Identification

Despite recent census data, obtaining an accurate picture of the living arrangements of children is difficult. A single parent was defined by the 2000 Census as a parent who is not currently living with a spouse (U.S. Census Bureau, 2002). Using the census definition, single parents may be married but separated; they may be divorced, widowed, or never married; and the household may contain other related adults, such as grandparents, or it may contain unrelated adults, as in cohabitation. Each of these single-parent family compositions varies in stability, emotional processes, and economic and social resources that differentially affect children (for review see Carlson, 1987, 1992). Accurate numbers of children in stepfamilies are even more difficult to ascertain because the 2000 Census failed to include stepfamilies as a category of family type. Rather, the census merged biologically intact and stepfamily homes into the single category of two-parent households. This categorization is unfortunate because of the significant differences in both the family processes and child outcomes associated with stepfamilies compared with intact homes (for review see Carlson, 1995, 1996).

The literature broadly defines a stepfamily as a household containing a child who is biologically related to only one adult; however, this definition fails to account for children who live with a single parent and have contact with the remarried or partnered nonresidential parent (Visher, Visher, & Pasley, 2003). Thus, even studies of stepfamily processes may exclude variations in living arrangements that are relevant to the lives of children. Several of the population trends noted above have further compromised knowledge of single-parent and stepparent families. In sum, it is quite likely that statistical measures of the rate of occurrence of single-parent and stepparent homes are conservative and do not reflect the diversity of living arrangements that characterize the typical public school classroom.

## Stability Versus Transition

A focus on the number of single-parent and stepparent households implies a stability of living arrangement that is inconsistent with demographic trends. Children's lives today are more likely to be characterized by multiple family transitions than by long-term stability (Bumpass et al., 1995; Hetherington & Stanley-Hagan, 2000). The following is one possible scenario based on demographic data: One-third of all children are now born to unmarried mothers, who commonly live with a parent or parents for some period of time. Young unmarried mothers typically move out to marry or cohabitate; their children may subsequently reside with the new couple or remain in the custody of grandparents. Children in this scenario could reside in two forms of a single-parent home and one form of stepfamily; depending on the stability of the marital union of the mother, additional transitions may occur.

In a second scenario, also based on demographic statistics, a marital union that produced children has a 50% chance of ending in divorce. The number of mothers who return to live with parents following a divorce has doubled in recent years; 75% of men and 66% of women eventually remarry after divorce; one-half of all marriages are preceded by cohabitation; and 60% of remarriages end in divorce, especially when remarried couples have stepchildren. Children in this scenario may experience as many as 6 to 10 changes in living arrangements during their school-age years, and this estimate may be conservative given the possibility of a subsequent remarriage and divorce. Each family transition is marked by a period of disorganization, with restabilization requiring anywhere from 2 to 7 years (Hetherington & Stanley-Hagan, 2000).

The median duration for children to reside in some form of single-parent home prior to cohabitation by their parent is 3.7 years (Bumpass et al., 1995). Thus, any discussion of single-parent and stepparent homes must consider the impact of multiple family transitions on children's development, in particular if families have little opportunity for a period of stabilization between transitions.

## Ethnic Diversity

The pace and extent of family change has not been uniform across racial and ethnic groups in the United States. Dramatic racial differences exist in family living arrangements involving children. More than half of Black children (53%) live in a single-parent household, followed by Hispanic children (30%), non-Hispanic White children (20%), and Asian and Pacific Islander children (15%; U.S. Census Bureau, 2003). Black children are also more likely to live with grandparents (9%, compared with 6% for Hispanic and 4% for non-Hispanic White children) and more likely to reside with the grandmother only. Children more commonly reside with both grandparents in all other ethnic groups. Hispanic children are most likely among the race and ethnicity groups to reside in extended households that include parents and grandparents. Compared with non-Hispanic White and Hispanic women, Black women are more likely to have children out of wedlock, less likely to marry by age 30, less likely to make the transition from cohabitation to marriage, more likely to divorce after a first marriage, and more likely to have a failed remarriage, suggesting an overall higher rate of family instability (Teachman, 2000). Both Hispanic and Black parents are less likely to remarry than are non-Hispanic Whites, who represent 80% of the stepfamilies in the United States (Hetherington & Stanley-Hagan, 2000). Thus, the living arrangements of children vary significantly by race and ethnicity.

### Economic Resources

The role of economic resources is another theme that is relevant to consideration of single-parent and stepfamily homes. The economic well-being of children is clearly linked with family structure (Teachman, 2000). Sixty-five percent of children in single-mother families, 45% of children in single-father families, and 61% of children in households with neither parent present are below the poverty level (U.S. Census Bureau, 2003). Poverty is associated with greater probability of childhood injury and behavior problems, as well as lower cognitive and academic achievement (Teachman). Children in two-parent homes, including stepfamilies, are consistently more economically advantaged than children in single-parent living arrangements. The stress associated with economic disadvantage, therefore, is central to any discussion of the impact of single-parent homes on the development of children.

### Negative Stereotypes

Although it has become normative for children to be reared in some form of single-parent or stepfamily home, the view that these families are in some way deficient when compared with intact biological families continues to influence research as well as educational and social policy (Visher et al., 2003). Although undoubtedly both single-parent and stepfamilies face different challenges than biologically intact homes do, the majority of children in single-parent and stepfamily homes grow up to become well-adjusted adolescents and adults (Amato, 2000; Hetherington, 1999). Families, whatever the form, that are characterized by love, trust, mutual helping, respect, and commitment enhance the well-being of children (Amato, 2000; see also chapter 50, "Healthy Family Systems").

Diverse living arrangements, however, bring unique challenges to children and their parents that may influence behavior and learning in school. This chapter focuses on family processes that are characteristic of single-parent and stepfamily systems and highlights the diversity within these family structure categories. Particular attention is given to literature published since 1997 and to the family forms that have been documented by the 2000 Census to be increasing in numbers. The interested reader is referred to reviews of earlier research relevant to children and parents in single-parent and stepfamily living arrangements (see Carlson, 1987, 1992, 1995, 1996).

## PROBLEMS AND IMPLICATIONS

### Single-Parent Families

The 2000 Census defined the single-parent household as a parent who is not currently living with a spouse (U.S. Census Bureau, 2003). Non-Hispanic White single-parent homes are most likely to be organized as isolated, nuclear units in which parents have exclusive responsibility for rearing children; Black and Hispanic single parents are most likely to reside in or be supported by multigenerational family units or extended family networks (Baca-Zinn & Wells, 2000; U.S. Census Bureau).

Although children can and do thrive in single-parent families, a notable feature of this family form is the economic and role strain that is the byproduct of one parent assuming the primary responsibility for parenting and maintaining a household. Economic strain will affect the child both directly, in terms of access to a broad range of resources, and indirectly, through quality of parenting and parental mental health, which are related to financial strain. The many ways in which single parents cope with the challenge of resource strain are evident in the variety of family forms that are classified as single-parent homes.

***Never-married, multigenerational, single-parent homes.*** Although never-married single mothers may be older, 70% of nonmarried mothers are teenagers who have the lowest levels of education and least available economic resources compared with other parents (Entwisle & Alexander, 2000). Never-married single mothers are most common among the Black and Puerto Rican populations, and children in these homes tend to be among the most seriously economically disadvantaged in the nation (Casper & Bianchi, 2002). Black unmarried mothers commonly reside in multigenerational households composed of mothers, grandmothers, and children living either within a shared home or in close proximity to one another such that grandmothers can provide advice, emotional support, and practical assistance (Chase-Lansdale, Gordon, Coley, Wakschlag, & Brooks-Gunn, 1999). Puerto Rican single mothers are more likely to cohabitate with a partner; however, parenting assistance from a larger kinship network is common.

Poverty is the most overwhelming influence on unmarried single mothers and their children, including those residing in multigenerational homes (Anderson, 2003). Young, never-married mothers are commonly deficient in the school- and work-related skills they need to have to take advantage of educational and occupational opportunities that would allow them to achieve an adequate standard of living (Anderson, 2003; Amato, 2000). Employment rates for never-married mothers hover at 60%, and three of every five children who live with never-married mothers live in poverty (Casper & Bianchi, 2002). Compared with the effect of living in a single-parent home, the effects of poverty account for more of the variance in predicting both child outcomes and parental functioning (Brooks-Gunn & Duncan, 1997). Poverty is correlated with children's lower school achievement and higher incidence of behavior problems, even when factors such as mother's age at the child's birth, family structure, and community disadvantage are taken into account (Anderson). Children of never-married single parents are least likely to be enrolled in school-related gifted/talented programs, sports, clubs, and after-school lessons (Casper & Bianchi). Financial strain has also been associated with higher levels of depressive symptoms in parents, which directly and negatively influence the quality of their child rearing (Eamon & Zuehl, 2001). In contrast, parent's educational attainment has been shown to be negatively associated with depression and positively associated with physical health (Amato). Thus, poor, undereducated, frequently depressed and irritable single mothers face higher rates of child behavior problems as they cope with serious financial strain, itself a known stressor related to poorer parental psychological functioning, child functioning, and family relationships (Anderson).

Some researchers suggest that the multigenerational family structure reflects an adaptive response to harsh economic conditions, with impoverished families forming complex kin networks that pool resources and share childrearing across generational lines. Other scholars link multigenerational families more closely to high rates of young motherhood across generations, which, in turn, are associated with poverty (Chase-Lansdale et al., 1999; Anderson, 2003). The grandmother in multigenerational single-parent families has long been a hidden member, ignored by researchers, policy makers, demographers, and educators who view the single parent to be the person primarily responsible for his or her children. Many grandmothers play an important co-parenting or primary parenting role within multigenerational families. However, co-residence with a grandmother should not be considered a panacea for the problems associated with young motherhood (George & Dickerson, 1995). This living arrangement is complex, and its favorable impact depends on multiple variables, including the mother's age of first birth, the quality of the mother–grandmother relationship, the quality of parenting by the mother, and the quality of parenting by the grandmother (Chase-Lansdale et al.; see also chapter 58, "Custodial Grandchildren").

***The single-grandparent household.*** Four percent of children reside with neither parent, and 44% of these children live in their grandparent's household (U.S. Census Bureau, 2003). The single-grandmother home, in general, is at high risk for serious economic disadvantage and role strain. Grandparents are less likely to continue employment because of their age, so financial resources are severely limited. Census data found children living with grandparents were three times more likely to be welfare recipients, compared with multigenerational households, and children residing with a grandparent only were least likely of all family types to be insured (U.S. Census Bureau). In addition to economic strain, grandparents who serve as the sole caretaker of grandchildren are likely to experience considerable role strain associated with the resumption of parental duties when they are aging and in poorer health.

***The single-father family.*** Although only 5% of children in the United States are classified as living in father-headed single-parent homes (compared with 23% single-mother homes), the single-father family is the fastest growing family type for children of all races (Casper & Bianchi, 2002). In the past 20 years, the proportion of single-father households has tripled for non-Hispanic White and Hispanic men and increased by 42% for Black men (U.S. Census Bureau, 2002). One out of every seven children in a single-parent household lives with a father (Amato, 2000). As with single mothers, the rise in unmarried fertility and delay in marriage resulted in substantial increases in never-married single fathers (U.S. Census Bureau, 2003). For postdivorce fathers, both father-custody and joint-custody arrangements have become more common over the past few decades. Father-custody status may, on average, signal a higher risk situation in which special attention to the needs of adolescent children may be warranted (see chapter 57, "Custody Issues"). Although single fathers are two-thirds less economically secure than married fathers, when compared with single-mother households, children in single-father families have overall access to more resources as reflected in higher incomes, higher standards of living, and greater residential stability (Amato).

Single fathers, compared with single mothers, report more difficulty managing their households and greater role strain from the task of balancing work and parental roles (Buchanan, Maccoby, & Dornbusch, 1996). Single fathers report greater difficulty parenting their daughters than their sons, especially coping with their emotional needs and pubertal changes (Peterson, Bodman, Bush, & Madden-Derdich, 2000). Some of the strain on single fathers has been attributed to the fact that, unlike single mothers, they are more emotionally isolated (Anderson, 2003). Custodial fathers, however, more readily draw on extended family members or girlfriends to provide practical support and child care, and noncustodial mothers are more likely to stay involved in parenting responsibilities compared with noncustodial fathers in single-mother homes (Anderson).

Single fathers' performance of parenting roles differs from both single mothers' and married fathers' (Peterson et al., 2000). Compared with married fathers, single fathers use more flexible child-rearing approaches and gender-role socialization in their children (Weinraub & Gringlas, 1995). However, compared with single mothers, single fathers are less likely to talk with, praise, or hug their children; they are also less likely to monitor their children's television use, provide help on children's homework, or spend time with their children (Amato, 2000). Thus, single fathers are less likely to engage in an authoritative parenting style that combines warmth with monitoring, a combination generally associated with positive child outcomes. Fathers and children in father-custody homes report feeling somewhat less close to one another compared with children (both boys and girls) in single-mother homes (Amato; Buchanan et al., 1996).

Studies examining how children fare behaviorally and educationally in single-father households, based on parenting styles and the quality of the parent–child relationship, have yielded mixed results. Children's educational attainment, school performance, and standardized test performance did not differ between single-mother and single-father homes, especially when income was controlled (Buchanan et al., 1996; McLanahan, 1999). More behavioral problems, such as substance abuse, were associated with adolescents residing in single-father homes compared with single-mother homes (Buchanan et al.). High levels of adjustment and the absence of behavioral problems among adolescents residing in father-custody homes were found only for those father-custody adolescents who reported a close relationship with *both* their custodial father and noncustodial mother.

In summary, children in single-father homes benefit from greater economic resources and residential stability when compared with single-mother homes; however, they may experience lower levels of warmth, closeness, and parental monitoring. These parenting style differences do not appear to adversely affect children educationally, but they may be associated with higher frequency of behavior problems in adolescence, especially when relations between children and the noncustodial mother are strained.

***Postdivorce single-mother families.*** Forty percent of all children in the United States experience a parental divorce. Of those, nearly 90% are placed primarily in the physical custody of their biological mother (Greene, Anderson, Hetherington, Forgatch, & DeGarmo, 2003). On average, children in divorced families, in comparison with those in nondivorced families with high marital conflict, show more problems in adjustment as a result of the changes and stresses accompanying divorce and life in a single-parent, usually mother-headed, household (Hetherington, 1999). It is beyond the scope of this chapter to discuss the effects of divorce on children (see chapter 56, "Divorce"); however, characteristics of the mother-headed single-parent household that affect children's development are examined here.

One well-documented problem that arises for women and children in the aftermath of divorce is economic decline. Significant differences are consistently found between the income levels and standards of living for divorced mothers and divorced fathers (see chapter 56, "Divorce). Compared with unmarried single mothers, however, divorced mothers are in a much better position to financially support children and maintain a household. They are substantially better educated, and 80% of postdivorce single mothers are employed (Casper & Bianchi, 2002). Employed single mothers, even those who are highly educated, however, manage to attain only a per capita income level that is 53% of that in two-parent families (Casper & Bianchi). Racial differences further affect the economic challenges faced by single-mother families. Black and Hispanic employed single mothers earn incomes that are, on average, two-thirds of the income of non-Hispanic White single mothers. On a positive note, single mothers of all races, as a group, are increasingly more likely to be college graduates and employed in professional, managerial, and technical occupations (Casper & Bianchi).

Even in wealthy families the approximate loss of 50% of one's annual income following divorce exerts a powerful force on children's well-being (McLanahan, 1999). Adolescents who experience income loss associated with family disruption are more likely to drop out of high school and to give birth as teenagers (McLanahan). Financial strain may also require changes in residence and neighborhood, with lowered access to high-quality schools and extracurricular activities. Taken together, these changes lower the social capital that is available to support the development of children in single-parent homes. Economic instability has been found to account for roughly half of the disadvantage associated with growing up in a postdivorce single-parent home (McLanahan; Anderson, 2003). Bearing in mind that the majority of postdivorce single-mother families are non-Hispanic White persons who maintain a separate nuclear household, it is safe to assume that economic strain will be common and will be sustained throughout the duration of the single-parent home unless a remarriage occurs.

Such dramatic loss of income generally requires that single-parent mothers have full-time employment, which may reduce children's access to parental resources. Children need parents to read to them, discuss problems, help with homework, and give discipline and supervision; children in single-parent homes, for example, are not read to as frequently as in two-parent families (McLanahan, 1999). However, single mothers, despite employment, report spending as much, if not more, time with their children than did Baby Boom mothers, and single mothers do not substitute quality for quantity with children when they work long hours (Casper & Bianchi, 2002). Single mothers have also been found to monitor their children's behavior more capably compared with single fathers, although they report more difficulty than single fathers in disciplining and controlling children (Buchanan et al., 1996). In sum, single mothers appear to be more authoritative parents than single fathers.

In comparisons of parenting quality in single-mother and two-parent families, the bulk of the literature finds that, regardless of social class or ethnicity, single-parent homes, which are predominantly mother headed, tend to be less authoritative and authoritarian and more permissive and neglectful. Although differences in parenting style between mother-headed one-parent homes and two-parent homes are generally small, the single parent, whether mother or father, exhibits diminished parenting, especially in behavioral control and limit setting of children (Avenevoli, Sessa, & Steinberg, 1999). Parents who can maintain authoritative, supervisory parenting styles with their children are more likely than others to have children and adolescents that thrive in single-parent postdivorce homes. Numerous other factors affect the adjustment of children in postdivorce, mother-headed homes, including gender of children, custodial arrangements, quality of relationship, and level of involvement between the child and both parents.

***Cohabiting single-parent families.*** Most detrimental to children and adolescents' well-being following divorce is the cohabitation of his or her divorced parent (Buchanan el al., 1996). Despite the potential costs to children and adolescents, 11% of single mothers and 33% of single fathers who have primary custody of their children also have a cohabiting unmarried partner (U.S. Census Bureau, 2003). Cohabitation of the custodial mother with a new partner is associated with higher levels of behavior problems and lower levels of social competence in children when compared with children in remarried homes, and the effect of cohabitation is substantial (Buchanan et al.). Adolescent behavior problems associated with cohabitation of a parent were, in part, related to less acceptance of the parental authority of a cohabitating partner when compared with acceptance of the authority of a stepparent. Child outcomes associated with cohabitation by custodial fathers could not be examined because no published studies were located. Although unmarried fathers seldom co-reside with mothers in the Black community, father involvement with children is often extensive and should be considered in any assessment of intervention related to the child or family (Chase-Lansdale et al., 1999).

## Stepfamilies

A stepfamily is a household containing a child who is biologically related to only one of two adults who are partnered with one another (Visher et al., 2003). Because cohabiting single parents were discussed in the previous section, the term stepfamily refers here to those households that are reconstituted by marriage. Within the broad definition of a stepfamily, numerous variations of stepfamily structure exist that are linked with the diverse antecedents to the stepfamily household. Prior to becoming a stepfamily, for example, either or both adults may or may not have been previously married, they may or may not have given birth to or fathered children, and their former relationships may have ended with the death of their spouse, a breakdown in cohabitation, or divorce.

For children, the residential parents, nonresidential parents, or both may remarry.

Most stepfamily research concerns three types of remarriage families: (a) stepfather families in which the wife has custodial children in the household, (b) stepmother families in which the husband has custodial children in the household, and (c) complex stepfamilies (also termed blended or binuclear) in which both adults have custodial children in the household (Visher et al., 2003). Unfortunately, our knowledge of stepfamily life is biased toward non-Hispanic White populations who have the highest remarriage rates.

Whereas single-parent families are challenged to find ways to add economic and social resources to the system, stepfamilies are challenged to find ways to accommodate the complexity of relationships that result from remarried family systems. When two parents marry, each with children, the resultant complex stepfamily, for example, includes residential or nonresidential stepsiblings and biologically- and non–biologically related extended family members, such as aunts, uncles, cousins, grandparents and stepgrandparents (Hetherington & Stanley-Hagan, 2000). Slightly more than half of the remarried parents in a complex stepfamily go on to have children with their new spouses, bringing additional half-siblings into the family (Visher et al., 2003). The sheer complexity of the potential kin networks in stepfamilies represents not only a marked deviation from the composition of first-marriage families, but a need to regard each stepfamily as unique in its definition and, thus, its challenges (Cherlin & Furstenberg, 1994).

Changes in divorce and remarriage rates over the past three decades indicate that many children are negotiating developmental challenges associated with repeated family reorganization (Hetherington & Stanley-Hagan, 2000). Remarriage is a major family transition that involves multiple changes, stresses, and the need for a reorganization of family roles and rules. Major family transitions are generally accompanied by a period of disruption or disequilibrium in family relationships, gradually followed by the emergence of a new homeostasis that differs substantially from that found in nuclear families with biological children from first marriages. It may take between 2 and 7 years for adjustment to remarriage and stepfamily stabilization to occur (Hetherington & Stanley-Hagan). Adaptation trajectories are affected by multiple interacting factors, such as individual characteristics of children and parents and their relationships, support from extended family members, and the experience of concurrent changes in financial resources, employment or school, and residence (Hetherington & Stanley-Hagan). Although remarriage may add economic and social resources to the single-parent home, it can also lead to increased stress, problems in family relationships, and anger and acrimony that undermine the happiness, health, and adjustment of family members. The adjustment of children in stepfamilies appears to be more similar to that of children in divorced single-parent families than to that of children in first-marriage families.

Children's responses to marital transitions vary considerably. However, children from divorced and remarried homes are at greater risk for developmental, learning, or emotional problems compared with those from intact homes. In a longitudinal developmental study of children's response to remarriage, Bray (1999) found children to have greater externalizing problems in the first 6 months following a remarriage, a period of quiescence for several years, and then a reeruption of behavior problems in young adolescence after several years of seemingly healthy adjustment to stepfamily life. Longitudinal research on stepfamily processes by Hetherington and colleagues also found adolescents in stepfamilies to be at particular risk for externalizing disorders compared with counterparts in nondivorced families (Greene et al., 2003). A key factor in adolescent risk was the *cumulative* impact of transitions. Adolescents' externalizing behavior increased and social competence decreased when they had experienced all three of the following marital transitions—divorce, remarriage of the custodial parent, and remarriage of the noncustodial parent. Adolescents' conduct problems were associated, in general, with negative relationships within the family (including parent–child, stepparent–stepchild, new marital partners, former marital partners, and siblings), and remarried families with adolescents were more likely to display coercive, conflictual, and punitive exchanges. Stepfamily relationships were also characterized by more coalitions and triangles compared with nondivorced families (Bray, 1992, cited in Bray, 1999).

Compared with adolescents, preadolescent children appear to adapt more easily to remarriage, especially school-age boys' acceptance of stepfathers (Bray, 1999). Some researchers have suggested that living in stepfamilies can be more beneficial for Black youth, particularly males, compared with non-Hispanic White youth; however, remarriage among Blacks is more common among those with higher levels of education and economic resources, making such comparisons inconclusive (Hetherington & Stanley-Hagan, 2000). In summary, although many stepfamilies are able to establish warm, involved, and respectful relationships, the combination of entry to adolescence with remarriage appears to be a particularly challenging developmental transition for all members of the family.

Parenting in stepfamilies differs from parenting in nondivorced two-parent homes. Although authoritative parenting generally predicts positive outcomes for children and adolescents, stepchildren and adolescents rebuffed stepparents who assumed an active, authoritative parenting role early in remarriage, and these children displayed greater child behavior problems (Bray, 1999). Critical to the success of stepparenting is an initial focus on the formation of a friend relationship with stepchildren, with the custodial parent remaining the primary disciplinarian. After 2.5 years, stepparents played an important parental role in stepfamilies, and the use of an authoritative parenting style was then related to positive outcomes in children (Bray). Although an active parenting role by stepparents early in remarriage predicts conflict in family relationships, monitoring of the behavior of children and adolescents by both the parent and stepparent, early and later in remarriage, relates to better outcomes for children (Bray; Greene et al., 2003).

In sum, stepfamilies are notable not only for the advantage of additional economic and social resources but also for the stress associated with the formation of new roles and close relationships within the family. Just as numerous factors affect the transition to harmonious and stable stepfamily relations, variations in stepfamily structure also present unique benefits and challenges.

***Stepfather families.*** Stepfather families are one of the most common stepfamily structures. Research has shown that this type of stepfamily tends to experience less stress than other stepfamilies, especially when the stepchildren are younger at the time of the mother's remarriage and when the children are boys who are gaining a stepfather (Hetherington, 1993). Stepfathers who refrain from taking an active role in discipline and control behaviors report having not only better relations with their stepchildren but also higher marital satisfaction (Hetherington & Stanley-Hagan, 2000). Although research finds stepparents may safely increase their involvement in parenting over time, disengaged parenting remains the standard parenting style of stepfathers, with only a small percentage of stepfathers eventually establishing active, authoritative relationships with their stepchildren (Hetherington & Stanley-Hagan).

***Stepmother families.*** Stepmothers appear to have a much more difficult time integrating into stepfamilies than do stepfathers (Hetherington & Stanley-Hagan, 2000). Children, particularly girls, report greater stress when living with their father and stepmother than with their mother and stepfather (Visher et al., 2003). It has been suggested that unique dynamics are at work in stepmother families, creating special relationship problems (Hetherington & Stanley-Hagan). Stepmothers, like mothers in first marriages, are often expected by their new husbands to take on the primary caretaker role, including the role of disciplinarian. Children respond no more favorably to discipline from a stepmother early in remarriage than they do to discipline from a stepfather. Even when the amount of time stepmothers devote to childcare and parenting responsibilities is controlled, however, stepmothers experience more difficulties in their relationships with their stepchildren (MacDonald & DeMaris, 1996).

The greater tension in the stepmother–stepchild relationship may be a function of the greater emotional closeness that is characteristic between mothers and both sons and daughters. Since stepmother families are defined as father-custody homes, disturbances in the biological mother–child bonding patterns can be assumed to have occurred, and these may be more upsetting to children than disturbances in the father–child relationship during and after divorce (Visher et al., 2003). The uniqueness of the mother–child bond may also create competition and loyalty conflicts for children between their mother and stepmother. A final challenge to this family structure is the lack of parenting experience by resident stepmothers, who may not have had children themselves and may have unrealistic expectations for stepchildren and the stepparent role.

***Complex stepfamilies.*** Complex stepfamilies, families in which both adults have children from a previous marriage living in the household, account for 7% of stepfamilies (Visher et al., 2003). Successfully integrating the multiple relationship patterns within the complex stepfamily is a significant challenge that many couples fail to negotiate successfully. The likelihood of redivorce is highest in complex stepfamilies, and the greater the number of children involved, the more likely the couple will divorce (Hetherington, 1993).

Because the complexity of kinship relationships in this family form is staggering, children in the complex stepfamily home will be affected not only by the involvement of a stepparent in their lives, but also by co-residence with stepsiblings. Stepsibling relations can be particularly challenging among adolescents who are close in age. Also, approximately 50% of complex stepfamilies will have an additional child within the first 2 years of the remarriage. Research on the impact of the addition of a mutual child, although very limited, yielded mixed results (Visher et al., 2003). A child born prior to the successful integration of the remarried family increased stepfamily stress; however, a child born later contributed positively to the integration of the family and buffered the likelihood of divorce.

***Summary.*** Remarried parents or stepparents are different than parents in a first-marriage family, and growing up in a stepfamily can be much more complicated than growing up in a first-marriage family. The breach of emotional ties that occurs in postdivorce families, coupled with the time it takes to establish new emotional bonds in a remarried family and the ambivalence that many youth may experience with stepparent and stepsibling relationships, make the transition to stepfamily living a slow, and sometimes conflicted, process. Successful stepfamilies accept and understand the differences in roles and emotional closeness that are characteristic of new stepfamilies and allow the necessary time to accomplish the tasks that lead to successful integration (Visher et al., 2003). Though the addition of a stepparent may upset the equilibrium of a stabilized singleparent family, be met with resistance from children, and lead to disrupted family relations, it can also add significant economic and social resources for single parents and present an opportunity to form new, gratifying supportive relationships that can promote the well-being of children and adults. In healthy stepfamilies, children are better adjusted compared with children in conflict-ridden first-marriage families (Heatherington & Stanley-Hagan, 2000).

## ALTERNATIVE ACTIONS FOR PREVENTION AND INTERVENTION

Schools can do little to change children's living arrangements that may place them at greater risk for behavioral problems and lower achievement in school. Schools can, however, engage in preventive intervention to strengthen the resilience and coping of parents and children with regard to family processes and transitions. Schools can also provide a safe, structured, and authoritative community of care that may help buffer children's stressful living arrangements. Assessment domains and relevant questions to consider in evaluating the context of single-parent and stepparent families include family resources, parenting style and skill, interparental conflict, sibling relationships, child characteristics, and school environment characteristics (Carlson, 1996). A number of recommendations for intervention with single-parent and stepparent families were discussed in Carlson (1995) and are summarized in Table 1. Interventions are organized as a menu of multilevel prevention strategies from which parents might choose and are consistent with recommendations for school-based treatment (Dishion & Kavanagh, 2003).

Since the publication of these intervention strategies, the demand for evidence-based intervention programs has increased dramatically in both psychology and education. A review of the literature, however, revealed only evidence-based postdivorce interventions for parents and children and no published evidence-based interventions specifically directed to either single parents or stepfamilies. Given the lack of published evidence-based interventions specifically for single-parent and stepparent families, this section offers promising evidence-based preventive interventions for parents and families, in general, that are either school-based or demonstrate a change in school outcomes.

Although school-based mental health personnel may not be directly involved in the delivery of parent and family interventions, school professionals should be guided by evidence-based practice in their referrals and recommendations for treatment. Overall, family-based intervention demonstrates strong evidence of effectiveness with adolescent conduct disorders, whereas parent management training and parent consultation have a stronger evidence base for producing school-related behavioral change in younger school-age children (Sanders, 1998).

### Evidence-Based Parent Interventions

Parent interventions are those that deliver services to one or more parents with the goal of either preventing the emergence of a child problem, preventing the worsening of an emerging child problem, or treating an existing problem. Given that authoritative parenting is a significant mediator of children's adjustment in single-parent and stepfamily homes, and children residing in single-parent and stepfamily homes are, on average, at greater

**Table 1** *Menu of School-Based Services to Consider With Single Parent and Stepfamily Systems*

| **Child-Focused Interventions** | **Level** |
|---|---|
| Bibliotherapy | Universal |
| Structured support groups | Selected |
| Individual counseling or referral for more intensive services | Indicated |
| **Parent and Family-Focused Interventions** | |
| Parent/Family resource centers | Universal |
| Parent groups: educational/support | Universal |
| Parent consultation | Selected |
| Family check-up | Selected |
| Parent management training | Indicated |
| Brief family intervention | Indicated |
| Referral for more intensive services | Indicated |
| **Home–School Collaboration** | |
| Home–school notes | Selected |
| Parent tutoring in home | Indicated |
| Family–school meetings | Indicated |
| **Family-Focused School Policies** | Universal |
| Develop policies that include and inform all caregivers | |
| Maintain records consistent with the complexity of students' families | |
| Review curricula for bias, as well as education regarding family diversity | |
| Train school personnel in family-related issues | |
| Support working parents with after-school programs for children | |
| Support adolescent parents with child care on campus | |
| Consider working single parents in scheduling school activities | |

*Note.* Adapted from "Best Practices for working with Single-Parent and Stepparent Families," by C. Carlson, 1995, *Best Practices in School Psychology II* (pp. 1097–1110). Copyright 1995 by the National Association of School Psychologists.

risk for behavior problems and lower achievement, interventions to prevent or address these problems with improved parenting are appropriate. Parent-focused intervention methods include parent education and support, parent consultation, and parent training. *Parent education and support* is defined as group delivery of information about a particular topic; *parent consultation* involves the conjoint problem solving by a mental health professional and parent to solve a child problem; and *parent training* teaches specific parenting techniques, generally behavioral, to either a group of parents or an individual parent for use with a specific child problem.

Evidence-based reviews of effectiveness find parent consultation and parent training approaches that are rooted in behavioral theory to be effective in improving a variety of presenting child problems (Kazdin & Weisz, 2003; Sanders, 1998; Sheridan, Eagle, Cowan, & Mickelson, 2001). Two-parent training programs are considered to be well established in terms of evidence (Brestan & Eyberg, 1998): the Incredible Years: Parents, Teachers, and Children Training Series (e.g., Webster-Stratton & Reid, 2003) and parent management training programs based on *Living with Children: New methods for Parents and Teachers* (Patterson & Gullion, 1968). There is no evidence to support the effectiveness of commercial parent education programs, such as Parent Effectiveness Training, in changing the behavior of children, although such programs may positively affect parental attitudes (Sanders, 1998).

A limitation of the existing literature on the effectiveness of parent interventions, as pertains to this chapter, is that studies have not examined the differential effectiveness of these intervention methods with different groupings of parents. The majority of parent intervention effectiveness studies are conducted with biological mothers only and largely with middle-class, non-Hispanic White mothers. Thus, little is known about how the effectiveness of parent interventions might differ across racial and social class groups or differ when participation is expanded to include all the relevant caretakers of a child.

## Family-Based Interventions

Family-based interventions focus on the psychosocial relationships of the family (Sexton & Alexander, 2002). Given the well-established link between children's school-related behavior and learning and the quality of their relationships with family members in single-parent and stepfamily homes, family-based interventions appear particularly well-suited for coping with the relationship complexities of these living arrangements as they affect children in school. Reviews of the empirical support for family-based interventions (e.g., Sexton & Alexander, 2002; Liddle & Rowe, 2005) find the following models to be effective in reducing adolescent conduct disorders: Multidimensional Family Therapy (MDFT; Liddle, 2002); Functional Family Therapy (FFT; Sexton & Alexander, 2000); Multisystemic Therapy (MST; U.S. Department of Health and Human Services, n.d.); and Brief Strategic Family Therapy (BSFT; Szapocznik, Hervis, & Schwartz, 2003). Common to all approaches is a view of the adolescent's problem behavior as embedded not only within family relationships, but also within the larger social context of the neighborhood, peer group, and school. Both MST and MDFT have demonstrated changes in school achievement related to family treatment. The BSFT and MST models have demonstrated effectiveness with two ethnic minority populations, Cuban American and Black economically disadvantaged families, respectively.

Although MST is a home-based treatment, it is noteworthy because it specifically targets interventions to the school and peer group as well as the family. In MST, therapy teams work with four to six families, at times convenient to the family in their home, and are available to the family 24 hours a day. MST therapists focus on empowering parents and improving their effectiveness to enforce rules, decrease adolescents' involvement with deviant peers, improve academic performance, and cope with any criminal subculture that may exist in the neighborhood or school. At the school level, MST emphasizes the development of a collaborative relationship between the parents and school personnel to promote the academic efforts of the adolescent.

## School-Based Family-Focused Prevention and Intervention

One family-centered, multilevel prevention program deserves special recognition because it has demonstrated effectiveness in treating high-risk youth and because it is school based. The Adolescent Transitions Program (ATP) is a multilevel approach to family-based intervention within a middle school setting (Dishion & Kavanagh, 2003). Three tiers of intervention build on one another and represent universal (reaches all parents), selected (targets at-risk families), and indicated (treatment) family interventions. The universal intervention is the Family Resource Room, which permits the dissemination of information to parents, family–school collaboration, family health education, and voluntary parent self-assessment. Selected intervention consists of the Family Check-Up, which is designed to engage parents in an assessment process and motivate them toward change. The Family Check-Up is a three-session intervention that includes an initial interview, an ecological assessment, and a feedback interview. The initial interview uses motivational interviewing strategies to engage parents and adolescents to complete the next two sessions. The ecological assessment (session two) contains questionnaires for family members to complete, the parent daily record, and a family interaction task that is completed in either the home or school setting. The third session continues to use motivational interviewing techniques to provide feedback of the assessment to the family in four phases: self-assessment, support and clarification, feedback, and presentation of the menu of change options. Indicated treatment includes a menu of services, grounded in family management practices, from which families may select. The menu of change includes self-help, brief family interventions, school monitoring, parent networking, or family therapy and support.

ATP has been found to be effective in improving mothers' and adolescents' negative interactions, reducing teacher-reported externalizing behavior at school, and reducing substance use within a year following the intervention. Results have been independently replicated (Dishion & Kavanagh, 2003). This model of school-based mental health treatment appears to be the most promising evidence-based approach for assisting children, parents, and families with the challenges posed by the complex living arrangements characteristic of children's lives today.

## SUMMARY

Recent census data indicate that children in today's schools will be less likely to reside in a home with both biological parents and more likely to reside in some form of a single-parent or stepparent family living arrangement. The diversity of children's living arrangements is considerable, and what is normative varies significantly by race. Children today are also likely to experience multiple family transitions while attending school, with the effect of any transition being substantial. Although the majority of children in single–parent and stepparent families grow up to become well-adjusted adolescents and adults, the challenges associated with single-parent and stepparent families, for both parents and children, are considerable.

As a group, children and adolescents in single-parent and stepparent families continue to show higher risk for behavioral problems when compared with peers in low-conflict, biologically intact homes. Risk is intensified with economic stress, the cumulative effect of multiple family transitions, family relationships characterized by negativity and conflict, and the onset of adolescence. In addition, particular living arrangements may be especially stressful for children and adolescents, including cohabiting parents and grandparent-only households. There is a lack of evidence-based interventions to address the particular problems of single-parent and stepparent families. Parent training and parent consultation are recommended for treating children's behavior problems. Family-focused intervention is recommended for treating adolescent conduct problems. The model that is most strongly recommended for assisting children and their families is a multilevel, school-based prevention program with a range of service options that can help families deal with the complexity of single-parent family and stepfamily living arrangements discussed in this chapter.

## RECOMMENDED RESOURCES

### Books and Other Printed Material

Demo, D., Allen, K. R., & Fine, M. A. (Eds.). (2000). *Handbook of family diversity.* New York: Oxford Press.

This handbook is a comprehensive resource, primarily from a sociological perspective, that addresses the influence of diversity issues on the family. Included are chapters on diversity within the single-parent family and stepfamily systems, as well as useful chapters on diversity of family forms within particular ethnic and racial groups.

Hetherington, E. M. (Ed.). (1999). *Coping with divorce, single parenting, and remarriage: A risk and resiliency perspective.* Hillsdale, NJ: Erlbaum.

This compilation provides a resource and resiliency perspective on the various changes facing families today, including a wealth of empirical research on the outcomes of divorce, single parenting, and remarriage, as well as implications and interventions.

Walsh, F. (Ed.). (2003). *Normal family processes* (3rd ed.). New York: Guilford Press.

A comprehensive resource that contains up-to-date chapters on family processes within the single-parent family and stepfamily home. Chapters on ethnic socioeconomic variation in family processes are also relevant. The book emphasizes a family systems perspective and considers implications for treatment.

### Websites

*http://www.singleparentcentral.com*

This website offers a wealth of information on single parents and issues that face them and their families. A broad range of articles are represented in archives that cover topics such as single fathers, single mothers, child and adolescent development, divorce, and career and financial issues. Links to government resources can also be found, as well as recent statistics and facts relevant to single parents.

*http://www.saafamilies.org*

The official website of the organization Stepfamily Association of America, this website offers facts and statistics on stepfamilies as well as information about educational resources, including book reviews and articles. Information on a number of programs and services for stepfamilies is presented, as well as stepfamily law, policy, and advocacy.

## REFERENCES

Amato, P. R. (2000). Diversity within single-parent families. In D. Demo, K. R. Allen, & M. A. Fine (Eds.), *Handbook of family diversity* (pp. 149–172). New York: Oxford Press.

Anderson, C. (2003). The diversity, strength, and challenges of single-parent households. In F. Walsh (Ed.), *Normal family processes* (3rd ed., pp. 121–152). New York: Guilford Press.

Avenevoli, S., Sessa, F. M., & Steinberg, L. (1999). Family structure, parenting practices, and adolescent adjustment: An ecological examination. In E. M. Hetherington (Ed.), *Coping with divorce, single parenting, and remarriage: A risk and resiliency perspective* (pp. 65–92). Hillsdale, NJ: Erlbaum.

Baca-Zinn, M., & Wells, B. (2000). Diversity within Latino families: New lessons for family social science. In D. Demo, K. R. Allen, & M. A. Fine (Eds.), *Handbook of family diversity* (pp. 252–273). New York: Oxford Press.

Bray, J. H. (1999). From marriage to remarriage and beyond: Findings from the developmental issues in stepfamilies research project. In E. M. Hetherington (Ed.), *Coping with divorce, single parenting, and remarriage: A risk and resiliency perspective* (pp. 253–272). Hillsdale, NJ: Erlbaum.

Brestan, E. V., & Eyberg, S. M. (1998). Effective psychosocial treatments of conduct disordered children and adolescent: 29 years, 82 studies, and 5,272 kids. *Journal of Clinical Child Psychology, 27,* 180–189.

Brooks-Gunn, J., & Duncan, G. J. (1997). The effect of poverty on children. *Future of Children, 7*(2), 55–71.

Buchanan, C. M., Maccoby, E. E., & Dornbusch, S. M. (1996). *Adolescents after divorce.* Cambridge, MA: Harvard University Press.

Bumpass, L. L., Raley, R. K., & Sweet, J. A. (1995). Redefining single-parent families: Cohabitation and changing family reality. *Demography, 32,* 97–109.

Carlson, C. I. (1987). Children and single parent homes. In J. Grimes & A. Thomas (Eds.). *Children's needs: Psychological perspectives* (pp. 560–570). Washington, DC: National Association of School Psychologists.

Carlson, C. I. (1992). Single-parent families. In M. E. Procidano & C. B. Fisher (Eds.), *Families: A handbook for school professionals* (pp. 36–56). New York: Teachers College Press.

Carlson, C. I. (1995). Best practices for working with single-parent and stepparent families. In A. Thomas & J. Grimes (Eds.), *Best practices in school psychology II* (pp. 1097–1110). Washington, DC: National Association of School Psychologists.

Carlson, C. I. (1996). Single parenting and stepparenting. In G. Bear, K. Minke, & A. Thomas (Eds.), *Children's needs II* (pp. 937–953). Washington, DC: National Association of School Psychologists.

Casper, L. M., & Bianchi, S. M. (2002). *Continuity and change in the American family.* Thousand Oaks, CA: Sage.

Chase-Lansdale, P. L., Gordon, R. A., Coley, R. L., Wakschlag, L. S., & Brooks-Gunn, J. (1999). Young Black multigenerational families in poverty. In E. M. Hetherington (Ed.), *Coping with divorce, single parenting, and remarriage: A risk and resiliency perspective* (pp. 165–192). Hillsdale, NJ: Erlbaum.

Cherlin, A., & Furstenberg, F. F. (1994). Stepfamilies in the United States: A reconsideration. In J. Blake & J. Hagen (Eds.), *Annual review of sociology* (pp. 359–381). Palo Alto, CA: Annual Reviews.

Dishion, T. J., & Kavanagh, K. (2003). *Intervening in adolescent problem behavior: A family-centered approach.* New York: Guilford Press.

Eamon, M. K., & Zuehl, R. M. (2001). Maternal depression and physical punishment as mediators of the effect of poverty on socioemotional problems of children in single-mother families. *American Journal of Orthopsychiatry, 71,* 218–226.

Entwisle, D. R., & Alexander, K. L. (2000). Diversity in family structure: Effects on schooling. In D. Demo, K. R. Allen, & M. A. Fine (Eds.), *Handbook of family diversity* (pp. 316–337). New York: Oxford Press.

George, S. M., & Dickerson, B. J. (1995). The role of the grandmother in poor single-mother families and households. In B. J. Dickerson (Ed.), *Black single mothers: Understanding their lives and families* (Sage Series on Race and Ethnic Relations, Vol. 10, pp. 146–163). Thousand Oaks, CA: Sage.

Greene, S. M., Anderson, E., Hetherington, E. M., Forgatch, M. S., & DeGarmo, D. G. (2003). Risk and resilience after divorce. In F. Walsh (Ed.), *Normal family processes* (3rd ed., pp. 96–120). New York: Guilford Press.

Hetherington, E. M. (1993). An overview of the Virginia longitudinal study of divorce and remarriage with a focus on early adolescence. *Journal of Family Psychology, 7,* 1–18.

Hetherington, E. M. (1999). Should we stay together for the sake of the children? In E. M. Hetherington (Ed.), *Coping with divorce, single parenting, and remarriage: A risk and resiliency perspective* (pp. 93–116). Hillsdale, NJ: Erlbaum.

Hetherington, E. M., & Stanley-Hagan, M. (2000). Diversity among stepfamilies. In D. Demo, K. R. Allen, & M. A. Fine (Eds.), *Handbook of family diversity* (pp 173–196). New York: Oxford Press.

Kazdin, A. E., & Weisz, J. R. (2003). *Evidence-based psychotherapies for children and adolescents.* New York: Guilford Press.

Liddle, H. A. (2002). *Multidimensional family therapy for adolescent Cannabis users, Cannabis Youth Treatment Series.* (Vol. 5; DHHS Pub. No. 02-3660). Rockville, MD: Center for Substance Abuse Treatment, Substance Abuse and Mental Health Services Administration. Retrieved August 15, 2004, from http://kap.samhsa.gov/products/manuals/cyt/pdfs/cyt5.pdf

Liddle, H. A., & Rowe, C. L. (2005). Advances in family therapy research. In M. P. Nichols & R. C. Schwartz (Eds.), *The essentials of family therapy* (2nd ed., pp. 298–328). Boston: Allyn & Bacon.

MacDonald, W. L., & DeMaris, A. (1996). Parenting stepchildren and biological children: The effect of stepparents' gender and new biological children. *Journal of Family Issues, 17,* 5–25.

McLanahan, S. S. (1999). Father absence and the welfare of children. In E. M. Hetherington (Ed.), *Coping with divorce, single parenting, and remarriage: A risk and resiliency perspective* (pp. 117–146). Hillsdale, NJ: Erlbaum.

Patterson, G. R., & Gullion, M. E. (1968). *Living with children: New methods for parents and teachers.* Champaign, IL: Research Press.

Peterson, G., Bodman, D., Bush, K., & Madden-Derdich, D. (2000). Gender and parent-child relationships. In D. Demo, K. R. Allen, & M. A. Fine (Eds.), *Handbook of family diversity* (pp. 82–104). New York: Oxford Press.

Sanders, M. R. (1998). The empirical status of psychological interventions with families of children and adolescents. In L. L'Abate (Ed.), *Family psychopathology: The relational roots of dysfunctional behavior* (pp. 427–468). New York: Guilford Press.

Sexton, T. L., & Alexander, J. F. (2000). *Functional family therapy.* U.S. Department of Justice. Office of Juvenile Justice and Delinquency Prevention Bulletin (NCJ 184743). Retrieved August, 21, 2004, from http://www.ncjrs.org/pdffiles1.ojjdy/184743.pdf

Sexton, T. L., & Alexander, J. F. (2002). Family-based empirically supported interventions. *The Counseling Psychologist, 30,* 238–261.

Sheridan, S. M., Eagle, J. W., Cowan, R. J., & Mickelson, W. (2001). The effects of conjoint behavioral consultation: Results of a four-year investigation. *Journal of School Psychology, 39,* 361–385.

Szapocznik, J., Hervis, O., & Schwartz, S. (2003). *Therapy manuals for drug abuse. Manual Number 5: Brief strategic family therapy for adolescent drug abuse.* U.S. Department of Health and Human Services, National Institute on Drug Abuse. Retrieved August 21, 2004, from http://www.nida.nih.gov/TXManuals/bsft/bsftindex.html

Teachman, J. D. (2000). Diversity of family structure: Economic and social influences. In D. Demo, K. R. Allen, & M. A. Fine (Eds.), *Handbook of family diversity* (pp. 32–58). New York: Oxford Press.

U.S. Census Bureau. (2002). *Estimates of the population of the United States.* Washington, DC: U.S. Government Printing Office. Retrieved July 31, 2004, from http://www.census.gov/popest/estimates.php

U.S. Census Bureau. (2003, June). *Children's living arrangements and characteristics: March, 2002.* Retrieved July 8, 2004, from http://www.census.gov

U.S. Department of Health and Human Services. (n.d.) *Multisystemic therapy (MST).* Substance Abuse and Mental Health Services Administration, Center for Substance Abuse Prevention. Retrieved January 26, 2003, from http://www.modelprograms.samhsa.gov

Visher, E. B., Visher, J. S., & Pasley, K. (2003). Remarriage families and stepparenting. In F. Walsh (Ed.), *Normal family processes* (3rd ed., pp. 153–175). New York: Guilford Press.

Webster-Stratton, C., & Reid, M. J. (2003). The incredible years: Parents, teachers, and children training series: A multifaceted treatment approach for young children with conduct problems. In A. E. Kazdin & J. R. Weisz (Eds.), *Evidence-based psychotherapies for children and adolescents* (pp. 224–240). New York: Guilford Press.

Weinraub, M., & Gringlas, M. B. (1995). Single parenthood. In M. H. Bornstein (Ed.), *Handbook of parenting: Vol. D. Status and social conditions of parenting* (pp. 65–88). Mahwah, NJ: Erlbaum.

60

# Psychological and Physical Abuse

**Marla R. Brassard**
**Erin Rivelis**
*Teacher's College, Columbia*

The purpose of this chapter is to provide guidance for school psychologists and other school-based professionals confronted with cases of psychological and physical abuse. Following a review of definitions and indications for both types of abuse, this chapter describes the developmental consequences of abuse and the implications for school professionals. Alternative actions for prevention that can be incorporated as part of regular school practice are presented, including screening for abuse and managing difficult reporting issues. Finally, alternative actions for intervention with abused students of different ages are presented, including a list of important resources for school-based professionals.

## BACKGROUND AND DEVELOPMENT

Over 90% of physical abuse cases have co-occurring psychological abuse, whereas only about 20% of psychological abuse cases have co-occurring physical abuse (Binggeli, Hart, & Brassard, 2001). Thus, most of what is known about family dynamics comes from studies of children in families with both forms of abuse. Parental hostility, harshness, and lack of respect for a child's autonomy and feelings are common to both forms of abuse. Physically abused children are at much greater risk of cognitive problems than those psychologically abused alone because of shaken baby syndrome and head trauma, which are often unintentionally inflicted in frustration or during disciplinary efforts.

### Definitions and Indications of Psychological Abuse

Psychological abuse (a term used interchangeably with emotional abuse) is defined as caregiver acts of spurning, exploiting or corrupting, and terrorizing or threatening (American Professional Society on the Abuse of Children, 1995). *Spurning* is verbal and nonverbal caregiver behavior that belittles or degrades a child. Examples are shaming or ridiculing the child for showing normal emotions, such as affection, grief, or sorrow; consistently singling out one child to criticize and punish, to perform most of the household chores, or to receive fewer rewards; and publicly humiliating the child. *Exploiting and corrupting* are caregiver acts that encourage, model, or permit the child to develop inappropriate behaviors (e.g., self-destructive, antisocial, criminal, deviant, or other maladaptive behaviors). Examples include encouraging or permitting prostitution, performance in pornographic media, initiation of criminal activities, substance abuse, or violence toward or corruption of others; parentifying or infantilizing the child; and encouraging or coercing abandonment of developmentally appropriate autonomy through extreme over involvement, intrusiveness, or dominance (e.g., allowing little or no opportunity or support for the child's views, feelings, and wishes; micromanaging the child's life); and restricting or interfering with cognitive development. *Threatening* is caregiver behavior that threatens or is likely to hurt, kill, abandon, or place the child or child's loved ones or objects in recognizably dangerous situations. Examples include threatening to kill or hurt a loved one; causing the child to witness violence against a parent, sibling, or pet; and setting rigid or unrealistic expectations with threat of loss, harm, or danger if they are not met.

The most accurate and comprehensive source of information on the incidence of abuse in the United States comes from the third (and most recent) National Incidence Study of Child Abuse and Neglect (NIS-3; Sedlak & Broadhurst, 1996). The authors used a national sampling frame during a 3-month period to identify all cases known to Child Protective Services (CPS); to investigatory agencies such as police or sheriffs or child welfare agencies; and to professionals in schools, hospitals, and other major agencies, whether reported to CPS or not. Using NIS-3 data, psychological abuse occurs at a rate of 6.5 per 1,000 children if evidence of harm is required and 18.3 per 1,000 if the endangerment standard is used. Because the NIS-3 only samples cases known to CPS and mandated reporters, it underestimates the actual rate of abuse. The Family Research Laboratory at the University of New Hampshire conducts telephone surveys with a nationally representative sample of American parents on parent–child conflicts using a stratified probability design and random digit dialing (see Straus & Field, 2003, for the most recent report). This design yields much higher estimates.

According to these surveys, psychological abuse is the most frequent form of maltreatment, with 90% of American parents engaging in some form of psychological aggression with children age 2 and over during the past 12-month period. Fewer parents engage in severe psychological aggression or psychological abuse, with rates of 10%–20% for toddlers and up to 50% for teenagers. The difference in estimates has to do with comparison across cases that are identified by mandated reporters but not necessarily reported (NIS-3) versus cases that are known to parents but may not be identified or reported by someone outside the family and may not rise to a level of reportability.

Girls are as likely to be psychologically abused as boys. However, rates of psychological abuse differ greatly by income group. According to the NIS-3, children from families with low incomes were emotionally abused at a rate 13 times that of children in higher income families (those with incomes of $30,000 or more per year). Children in the middle-income group had a rate of emotional abuse five or more times that of children in the highest income group. Although lower income families may be more likely to be reported than higher income families, it is quite likely that these rates of abuse by income level findings are accurate due to the design of the NIS-3 (e.g., its inclusion of all suspected cases known to mandated reporters, regardless of whether a report was actually made; see Sedlak & Broadhurst, 1996, for a detailed rationale). The NIS-3 shows no difference in psychological abuse by family structure, but other studies have found less psychological abuse in two-parent households (Straus & Field, 2003).

## Definitions and Indications of Physical Abuse

Physical abuse is defined as acts of commission that are characterized by infliction of overt physical violence by adult caregivers or parents. "It includes hitting with the hand, stick, strap, or other object; punching; kicking; shaking; throwing; burning; stabbing; or choking a child" (Sedlak & Broadhurst, 1996, p. 10). In addition to physical injuries that result in death, abuse also may include skeletal injuries, neurological and ocular damage, loss of consciousness, interrupted breathing, broken bones, and burns. The most common types of abuse involve bruises, lacerations, and contusions.

Such acts of violence perpetrated by parents, guardians, custodians, or other individuals 18 years of age or older, including group home and day care center personnel, are reported to CPS agencies, whereas similar inflictions of injuries or abuse by other adults (e.g., neighbors, strangers) are reported to local law enforcement agencies if they rise to a level of assault and battery. Incidents involving school professionals are more complicated. They are usually left to the discretion of the principal and school board to resolve unless they are so serious that a complaint is filed with law enforcement and law enforcement agrees to accept the case (Childhelp USA National Child Abuse Hotline, 1-800-4-ACHILD, personal communication, April 21, 2005).

Physical abuse is usually identified through physical inspection by trained social workers or medical professionals. Typically, they use a combination of x-ray and diagnostic experience in determining that the injuries could not have occurred accidentally. If physical abuse is suspected, most states authorize schools to take color photographs of the child (although this is preferably done by CPS workers) and to hold a child at school until CPS arrives if there are concerns about a child's safety.

According to the NIS-3, boys were equally likely to be physically abused as girls. Children ages 12 to 14 were more likely to be physically abused then children ages birth to 2 years. However, most fatalities from physical abuse occur in children under the age of 2. Physical abuse was related to income in that the incidence rate for children in the lowest income families (less than $15,000 per year) was 2.25 times higher than that for children in the middle-income group ($15,000 to $29,999 per year) and 16 times the rate for children in the highest income group ($30,000 or more per year). Children living with both parents are much less likely to be physically abused than children living with either their mother or father or with neither parent.

Table 1 provides a description of parental behavior and circumstances that have been empirically and clinically tied to an increased likelihood of psychological and physical abuse.

**Table 1** *Parental Behavior and Circumstances That Might Indicate Abuse*

- Parents delay or fail to seek appropriate care for a child's illness, injury, learning or behavioral problems, or routine checkups and immunizations.
- Parents view child as bad or evil.
- Parents say that they were abused as children and it didn't hurt them, or they excuse or idealize the behavior of the adult who mistreated them. Parents who minimize their own abuse may think that their children won't be affected if they are abusing them, or they may think that their children deserve the maltreatment just like they did (McMillen, 2000).
- Parents display distorted belief regarding their children and their roles as parents.
- Parents make derogatory comments about a child, either to the professional or in front of the child.
- Parents have high, rigid, and unrealistic expectations for child behavior.
- Parents compare the child negatively to another child in the family.
- Domestic violence is occurring in the home.
- Parents lack friendships or long-term relationships. Parents seem isolated from friends, relatives, and neighbors, and are not involved with community groups or only involved in very short-term relationships, as interactions quickly become strained because of their abrasive personalities.
- Parents have family crises such as divorce, financial problems, unemployment, and housing problems.
- Parents have problems with alcohol or substance abuse.

*Note.* See Binggeli, Hart, & Brassard (2001) and Kolko & Swanson (2002) for comprehensive literature reviews on manifestations and risk factors for psychological and physical abuse, respectively.

# PROBLEMS AND IMPLICATIONS

## Developmental Consequences of Abuse

Psychological abuse and physical abuse are both manifestations of harsh, hostile parenting. Most maltreated children have anxious attachments to their parents (Erickson, Egeland, & Pianta, 1989). Because of their early experiences with caregivers, physically and psychologically abused children appear to see others as hostile and rejecting. This has implications for the quality of their relationships and their behavior in school. Across the developmental period, effects are seen in impaired interpersonal relationships and in resultant problems with emotional and behavioral regulation. For some children learning is affected, and many children end up in special education.

***Infants and toddlers.*** Psychological abuse is less frequent than other forms of maltreatment at this age (Straus & Field, 2003), but when it occurs in the form of harsh or verbally abusive parenting, it is related to attachment insecurity or disorganization at 12 and 18 months in infants (Erickson, Egeland, & Pianta, 1989). Psychological abuse is also related to significant internalizing and externalizing problems not seen in children physically neglected alone (Dubowitz, Papas, Black, & Starr, 2002). Psychological abuse and neglect together are related to externalizing behaviors, behavioral ratings of aggression, and lower ego resiliency (Manly, Kim, Rogosch, & Cicchetti, 2001). Toddlers who are rejected by their mothers, whether physically abused or not, respond to peer distress with fear, anger, and physical aggression and are more aggressive with teachers (Main & George, 1985). They are less likely than nonabused toddlers to approach their teachers and more likely to resist the advances (positive as well as neutral and negative) of both teachers and peers. This type of response makes it much more likely that abused children will be rejected by adults and peers, thereby confirming their wariness, distrust, and anger toward others. Physical abuse is particularly dangerous at this age because of the vulnerability of very young children. It can result in serious injuries, including neuropsychological impairments (shaken baby syndrome), even when the parent had no intent to harm.

***Preschool.*** By preschool, psychologically and physically abused children are significantly more noncompliant, avoidant, and negative in affect with their mothers, and they are less persistent and enthusiastic in learning (Erickson et al., 1989). A subset are compulsively compliant with adult requests (which protects against abuse) or compulsively noncompliant (e.g., oppositional defiant disorder; Crittenden, 1988). Psychologically abused and neglected children have higher rates of aggression and peer reports of fighting in preschool than nonabused children (Manly et al., 2001).

Physically abused children often have cognitive delays relative to nonmaltreated peers. This may be the result of either mild head injuries occurring in the course of physical abuse or just an additional result of environments that do not provide the emotional and intellectual nourishment needed for appropriate cognitive development. These cognitive delays appear early in life. Furthermore, as children begin attending school, they often have difficulty maintaining attention—they both receive less support and are less able to elicit adult support for learning. Most maltreated children in preschool master basic language but appear to have some specific deficits in the use of internal-state language (language about emotions and feelings). Additionally, they have a tendency to talk less about themselves than about their ongoing activities (Cicchetti, Toth, & Hennessey, 1989).

***Middle childhood.*** Erickson et al. (1989), in a longitudinal, prospective study of high-risk families, found that when maltreated children entered school, a variety of patterns emerged, depending on the caregiving they had experienced. Teacher reports indicated that physically abused children (who were also verbally abused) functioned more poorly on cognitive tasks than nonmaltreated peers. Half of these children were referred for special intervention and attention by the end of their first year at school because of the high rates of regressive, noncompliant, and acting-out behavior they exhibited.

The rejecting and aggressive behavior of psychologically and physically abused children predispose others to respond to them in ways that parallel the ways in which they are treated at home. It also leads to other patterns of behavior that negatively affect school performance. Cicchetti et al. (1989) found that physically abusive parents demonstrated a combination of high-achievement expectations for their children and a controlling, nonreasoning-based style of interaction with their children, which had a highly negative effect on their children's classroom performance. The authors noted that behavior problems exhibited by maltreated children in a classroom are likely to elicit overcontrolling teaching styles that tend to undermine an intrinsic motivation to learn and emphasize a learning style based on extrinsic rewards or punishment.

Studies using middle childhood or middle childhood and adolescent maltreatment samples (e.g., CPS agencies, battered women's shelters, and foster care), community samples, or both found that psychological abuse or psychological maltreatment (after controlling for the other forms of maltreatment and demographic factors) uniquely predicted a series of negative outcomes, including social–emotional problems (Herrenkohl, Herrenkohl, Egolf, & Wu, 1991), not having friends at school and other interpersonal problems (Vissing, Straus, Gelles, & Harrop, 1991), poor response to treatment in foster care (Dance, Rushton, & Quinton, 2002), poor behavioral adjustment (Moore & Pepler, 1998), and delinquency and aggression (Vissing et al., 1991).

***Adolescence.*** Adolescents are the victims of less physical and more psychological abuse than children, most likely because they can escape or fight back effectively, so parents stop the physical abuse and increase the verbal coercion. Children who are psychologically and physically abused in childhood are at great risk of conduct disorder in adolescence (Egeland, Yates, Appleyard, & van Dulman, 2002). Verbal abuse alone has been identified as a predictor of social phobia (Magee, 1999); increased risk of alcohol and tobacco use (Moran, Vuchinich, & Hall, 2004); and delinquency, aggression, interpersonal problems (Vissing et al., 1991), and dating violence (Lavoie et al., 2002).

# ALTERNATIVE ACTIONS FOR PREVENTION

## Reaching Out to Potential Victims

Most child abuse is not reported or substantiated by CPS. This can be seen in the clear discrepancy between substantiated cases (data collected by the U.S. Department of Health and Human Services Administration of Children and Families) and cases identified by mandated reporters, many of which are not reported (NIS-3), and cases known to families (Family Violence Survey). Thus, many children are silent victims of abuse. They often give evidence of distress in their problematic interpersonal relationships, problems in learning despite normal ability, social withdrawal, or acting-out behavior. However, abuse is only one of a number of potential causes of such behavior. Several methods can facilitate children's reporting so that a level of reasonable suspicion is reached. School-based professionals can (a) help teachers ask questions of children and adolescents they see as being possibly abused and (b) screen children for abuse either as part of routine special education evaluations or when children exhibit signs of distress that could be the result of a variety of factors, including abuse.

***Helping teachers with identification concerns.*** Teachers, with their frequent contact with children and adolescents, are the most likely to notice physical and behavioral indicators of abuse (Sedlak & Broadhurst, 1996), and they are the group of professionals to whom children are most likely to disclose abuse. Many teachers feel comfortable filing a report with the child abuse hotline when they see clear indications of burns, bruises, or welts. Some feel comfortable reporting clear verbal abuse or public humiliation. Most are less certain of what to do when they observe unusual behavioral changes or when they see troubling art projects or read troubling stories or journal entries in language arts and English classes. Another common scenario is a child who approaches the teacher in great distress but refuses to disclose what is upsetting them ("I can't talk about it!"). These situations often fall below the standard of "reasonable suspicion" but are indicative of some kind of problem. Teachers may then tell the school psychologist or other mental health professional that they are very concerned about a child or teen in their class and may seek advice on how to proceed or ask the mental health professional to speak to the child or adolescent.

Children often feel most comfortable talking about painful events in their lives with adults they know. A child is much more likely to reveal what's bothering him or her, including reporting parental abuse, to a teacher than to an unfamiliar school psychologist. A professional can give the teacher confidence to talk to the child by brainstorming or role-playing ways the teacher might approach the child or by providing similar training to all teachers. For example, a teacher might catch the child at a quiet moment and say:

"Laurie, I've noticed a real change in you in the last three weeks and I'm very concerned about it. You've gone from being happy and involved in class to seeming very sad and withdrawn. It's made me wonder if things are happening to you that are upsetting or hurting you. I really care about you and would like to help."

Even if the child or teen denies that there is a problem, the teacher has conveyed that the child's suffering has been noticed, that someone cares, and that an adult is available and willing to talk if the child wants to in the future.

***Identifying potential abuse victims during assessment and intervention activities.*** Many cases of abuse go undetected throughout a child's school years, but some of these cases might be revealed if school personnel were to routinely seek information about potential abuse. This could be done as part of any evaluation in which parental permission has been granted to assess a child's social–emotional and behavioral functioning. Children can be asked such questions as, "Have you ever been injured or hurt by someone older than you?" or "Tell me about events or situations that have happened to you that were upsetting, scary, or frightening" (Kolko, 2000, p. 77). Follow-up questions can be posed, such as, "Please tell me what happened." "Tell me what happened first." "Where did it happen?" "What happened afterwards?" If the child does report an event, he or she can be asked, "Was there an injury?" "How were you hurt? Or what happened that hurt you?" "How badly were you hurt?" "Has something like this happened before?"

School psychologists are ethically obligated to inform the child about limits to confidentiality as part of establishing a professional relationship for either assessment or intervention. If this is done and abuse is subsequently disclosed, the child expects the professional to report the abuse. Furthermore, once the threshold of reasonable suspicion is reached and the assessor knows that a report must be made, the assessor stops questioning the child for details, and the interview moves toward supporting the child through the reporting process.

If behavioral indicators or problematic parent–child interactions are observed that do not in and of themselves reach a level of reporting, school-based mental health service providers might want to interview the child in a nonthreatening way to obtain more information. Kolko (2000, p. 77) recommends open-ended, nonjudgmental questions about discipline, as many incidents of abuse occur in the context of discipline and punishment. Questions can be posed along the lines of, "Children can get punished (disciplined) for doing different things; how often do you get punished and in what ways?" Children can be asked follow-up questions such as:

- How often do you get punished—for example, get sent to your room, have privileges removed, and get lectured?
- How often does this involve screaming, name calling, and threats?
- How often does this involve any physical force or discipline such as spanking, slapping, or grabbing?
- What is the most extreme or serious kind of physical discipline or punishment that's used with you?
- How worried are you that someone living with you could lose control with you—that is, to the point that you could get hurt?

When reasonable suspicion of abuse emerges from these screening procedures, questioning for details ceases in order to avoid interfering with the subsequent investigation. Table 2 describes key considerations in reporting abuse, some of which are also discussed below.

## Managing Difficult Reporting Issues

According to Sedlak and Broadhurst (1996), schools identify over half of all cases known to mandated reporters, yet only 16% of the cases are investigated by CPS. In their review, the other 84% of cases were either not reported or not investigated if they were reported; the NIS-3 does not break these figures out (Sedlak & Broadhurst, 1996). Frustrating experiences with the system explain, in part, why so many school professionals do not report abuses they identify. Many school professionals are frustrated when cases they report are not "screened in" for investigation or, if screened in, are unsubstantiated (allegations of abuse are unfounded or there is insufficient evidence to determine if abuse occurred), or if they are substantiated, no services are offered to families that need them. The child abuse reporting system is set up to screen in all cases in which reporters show reasonable suspicion, a lower standard than that of substantiation or service provision. A case that meets a threshold of reasonable suspicion may not meet a higher standard of substantiation, which requires that the preponderance of evidence point to abuse. A higher standard yet is that for criminal prosecutions, such as child sexual abuse cases, in which the evidence must be beyond a reasonable doubt (Kalichman, 1999).

Reporting psychological abuse frustrates professionals because signs that a child is being abused are more likely to appear over time rather than be reportable as a single event or observation. The lack of clear-cut signs can make it difficult to decide that a reporting threshold has been reached, and it can make it harder to reach a threshold for screening in the report. To substantiate a case of psychological abuse, some states require evidence of harm (e.g., anxiety disorder, ulcers, or suicide attempt). Unless a mental health professional will testify to both the abusive caregiver behavior and an accompanying significant impairment in child functioning, a case will be considered unfounded. For example, the first author recently served as a consultant to one state's Department of Social Services on their policies regarding psychological abuse and neglect. In this state, no child under school age was screened in for psychological abuse or neglect because there was no school psychologist, social worker, or guidance counselor to serve in this expert role and the state had no money for independent mental health professionals.

**Table 2** *Key Considerations in Mandated Reporting*

- Get to know your state reporting laws by consulting the state Department of Social Services website.
- Inform all child and adult clients of the limits of confidentiality at the first meeting for assessment or intervention.
- Remember that your role is to report when you have a reasonable suspicion and not to investigate whether child abuse has occurred.
- The child's reported abuse does not need to be confirmed by a parent or other adult before reporting.
- Past abuse should be reported to protect future children from being abused, even if the child in question is not currently at risk.
- Secondhand reports describing abusive situations provide enough of a basis for a report.
- Verbal, emotional, and physical injuries should be reported regardless of the age of the perpetrator (e.g., an older sibling).
- Even if an abuse has been reported previously, whether screened in or not, a new report of suspected abuse should be filed. Child Protective Services takes into account the number and types of reports filed.
- Even if another professional (this includes the principal) says they are going to report, it does not excuse a mandated reporter from filing a report. Follow up to verify that a report was filed. Leave your name when you call.
- Keep a detailed record of all reports you file. Follow up reports with Child Protective Services workers to see how a case was resolved.
- Inform parents or guardians that you are reporting and why, unless doing so would endanger the child or the investigation.

Despite these frustrations and the limitations of the CPS system, school professionals are legally and ethically obligated to report all suspected abuse. If convicted of failure to report, school professionals are guilty of a misdemeanor, face sanction from professional associations and credentialing and licensing boards, and are liable for civil damages that may arise because they did not report. Furthermore, reporting makes a clear statement that every child has a right to psychological and physical safety. It also conveys to children subjected to abuse that what is happening to them is wrong and it is not because they are bad. In addition, reporting may prevent further abuse because caregivers are placed on notice that some parenting practices are unacceptable and will be sanctioned.

***What school professionals should do if they are not sure a report is required.*** Given the wide variety of ways children can be harmed by adult behavior, school professionals are often unsure about whether a particular incident constitutes abuse under state law or whether the threshold of reasonable suspicion has been reached. Several strategies should be considered in these cases.

School professionals should be thoroughly familiar with what constitutes abuse under their individual state law. State laws vary dramatically in the breadth and specificity of the reporting requirements. Some limit mandated reports to knowledge of abuse by direct observation, thus excluding self-disclosures of abuse by perpetrators, spousal reports, or any other source of information other than that from the suspected child victim (Davidson, 1988). In some states there is considerable ambiguity about whether events that are several years old need to be reported.

When unsure about whether or not to report, professionals should consult with colleagues experienced with child abuse cases. Professionals who discuss cases with colleagues are more likely to report suspected child abuse (Kalichman, 1999). However, talking with colleagues does not always clarify the issue. In such cases, it is helpful to call the child abuse hotline and discuss the situation with the worker without divulging the names of the suspected victim or perpetrator. This can be very helpful in clarifying whether a case does or does not fall under the reporting statute. Sometimes the hotline worker will give a definitive answer. In other instances the hotline worker may say that a case falls at a borderline level that may well be screened out; however, if certain other information were to become available, the case might be screened in. Unfortunately, not all states have child abuse reporting hotlines. Many of those that do not have their own hotline require reporters to contact a regional office. Child abuse reporting numbers can be found online or at the front of local telephone directories.

***What a school professional should do if the principal wants to preapprove all reports.*** The law is clear that all mandated reporters are obligated to report. Informing the school principal does not constitute a report unless the professional follows up to see that a report was made. Generally, the best approach is to make clear to a principal that having a preapproval policy is illegal and creates liability problems for the district and the professionals involved. This does not preclude a discussion with the principal about each case of suspected abuse prior to filing a report, if time permits. Administrators like to be informed and prepared for situations that force them to deal with outside agencies and potentially upset parents. They may also have information useful for filing the report.

***What to include in a report.*** Each state has its own requirements and forms. For making a telephone report, certain types of information are required in almost all states (Kalichman, 1999). The child's name, age, sex, race, address, and current location are always required. Agencies typically want the names and ages of siblings or other children in the home, as well as the names and addresses of parents or a legal guardian. The suspected perpetrator's name, address, and relationship with the child as well as his or her current location are typically required, if known. A description of the abusive incident also is required. This can include when the most recent incident occurred, the date and time that information was obtained, the type of abuse, the evidence that led the reporter to believe that the child was being abused, and some assessment of how severe the abuse was. Finally, many states require information on other people who may have knowledge of the abuse. Information about the child's current and future safety and risk for future abuse are also required. Actions the reporting source may have taken, such as taking color photographs or keeping a child at school, might also be requested.

Written reports, containing the same information as the telephone report, are generally due within 48 hours in those states that require them. Forms can be downloaded from the state's website if the school does not keep them on hand. Written reports typically are admissible in criminal proceedings, so care should be taken in making sure they are clear and accurate.

***What not to include in a report.*** Confidentiality is explicitly waived when school-based mental health professionals report suspected abuse. However, information beyond that required for reporting is still protected under privileged communication statutes for licensed psychologists and under NASP ethical guidelines. Reports should include only information for making determinations of abuse and for taking effective action on behalf of the child. This information includes the evidence that led the professional to believe that abuse was occurring, such as behavioral symptoms, verbal descriptions, self-reports or observations of abusive acts, or other verbal disclosures that clarify that abuse has occurred plus the facts of the family's location and family configuration. Care should be taken not to exceed what is needed when responding to follow-up inquiries by police or CPS workers (Kalichman, 1999).

***How to inform parents that a report has been made.*** When cases of suspected abuse are reported by the school, parents may respond with anger and shame. Parents of preschool children enrolled in special education programs have removed their child from nonmandated programs when the school reported them. Some parents will pull a child out of school for home schooling to reduce the likelihood that they will be reported for abuse again. Such responses can remove children from important developmental and educational experiences and permanently damage school–family relationships. An important objective for school professionals is to find a way to minimize such damage while still acting to protect children.

The first consideration is always to protect the child. The second is to enhance child well-being. If a telephone call to or meeting with the parents does not endanger the child or the CPS investigation, it may minimize the secrecy and shame around child abuse. It provides school professionals with an opportunity to communicate to the parent the concerns about the child's welfare, the school's commitment to child and family safety, and the sincere interest on the part of the professional in what happens to both the child and other family members. It is not the role of school professionals to determine if abuse occurred. Sometimes suspicions are unfounded. Sometimes it is easy to see how things escalated into verbal or physical violence. Often parents know that they have crossed the line from borderline to harmful parenting practices and they feel bad about it. Some parents are grateful that someone cared enough to intervene. Informing parents of a report and why it was made in a matter-of-fact, explanatory, and nondefensive way can be an effective response if the circumstances are right. It opens the door to a continuing and, perhaps, closer relationship between parents and the school, rather than closing the door, leaving shame and anger on one side and judgment and disgust on the other. A face-to-face meeting is ideal if it can be quickly arranged. With some families there may be enough of a relationship already established that a telephone call would suffice, as in the example below.

"Hello, Mrs. C. I am Ms. B, the school psychologist at H. Middle School. I wanted you to know that I filed a report with the child abuse hotline. Your daughter was very upset today at school. She said that last night you pulled a knife on your husband during an argument before dinner in the kitchen. She thought you were going to kill one another. When her brother tried to intervene, she said that your husband threw him against the wall and he dislocated his shoulder."

Stop and listen to what the parent has to say. Acknowledge feelings of distress, concern, and anger (e.g., "You and your husband are having a very hard time right now," "It sounds like his drinking is a major issue," "You are very upset that CPS has to get involved on top of everything else that is going on."). Ask the parent if there are things you or others can do to support their child or children at school and offer suggestions for services based on what the parent has shared about the family's circumstances (e.g., suggest a Children of Alcoholics support group). Encourage both parents to call if they want to talk with you. Give them the timeline for investigation that the hotline provided. Follow up with the child and the family later to see how things are going. In general, treat parents as you would like to be treated in a similar situation.

Although numerous risk factors may elevate the chances of a child experiencing physical or psychological abuse, the mere presence of risk factors does not necessarily imply actual child maltreatment. Certain protective factors in the child's family and in the child's environment—such as a positive self-concept, social skills, increased level of awareness, and a supportive social network—can minimize the impact of these risk factors as well as the adverse effects of maltreatment (Fortin & Chamberland, 1995). School and community services can provide families with support and model appropriate parenting techniques, which raise parents' self-esteem, decrease feelings of isolation, and diminish the impact of everyday stressors. Some efforts to educate and support families are reviewed below. These have proved to be effective preventive measures for minimizing the likelihood of abusive family dynamics and mitigating adverse circumstances.

## Educating Parents

***Educating parents on child development.*** Some parents lack knowledge of child development and skills for effective parenting, and thus have inappropriate expectations for their children (Wolfe, 1991). School-based parenting workshops can provide parents with valuable developmental information, as well as with stress management, anger management, and conflict resolution skills that may better equip parents to deal with everyday stressors and with their child's disobedient behavior.

***Teaching parents to play with and stimulate their children.*** Teaching parents techniques to play with their children can foster positive parent–child interactions while reducing problematic behaviors. Play can be used as a time to develop children's social competence and enhance positive self-concept (e.g., see the description of the Incredible Years Parent Training Series in the Alternative Actions for Intervention section).

***Teaching parents effective discipline techniques.*** Generally, positive discipline methods are associated with higher levels of child compliance (Hembree-Kigin & McNeil, 1995; McMahon & Forehand, 2003) as well as higher IQs and academic achievement (Herrenkohl et al., 1991). Programs aimed at teaching appropriate discipline and parenting skills emphasize how and when to attend, ignore, reward, issue commands, and implement time-outs (McMahon & Forehand; Webster-Stratton, 2001). These techniques have proved effective in reducing negative parent–child interactions and in decreasing conduct problems in preschool and elementary school–age children (Hartman, Stage, & Webster-Stratton, 2003; Hembree-Kigin & McNeil; McMahon & Forehand).

## Educating School Personnel

***Find an adult to take a special interest in a troubled child.*** Unfortunately, many children do not receive adequate attention in the home. Thus, it is extremely important that children receive this nurturance and attention from other responsible adults in their lives. One of the factors that separates children who cope well from those who do not is the presence of an adult who has taken an active interest in them and their lives (Sroufe, 1983). Schools can provide ample (and supplemental) opportunities for children to establish these bonds with a teacher, athletic coach, lunchroom aide, or counselor. Schools can also provide formal mentoring programs, which pair children up with older students or a caring adult.

***Provide a predictable, routine environment.*** A highly structured classroom environment is particularly beneficial for abused children who live in psychologically and physically unsafe environments (Binggeli et al., 2001). A structured classroom with a competent teacher provides a context in which children can gain experience in relating to peers and adults, competently reading social cues, and learning to clearly and competently signal their own needs and concerns (Davis & Fantuzzo, 1989). In addition to providing a highly structured environment, teachers who impose consistent demands on their students while treating them with sensitivity and respect experience fewer behavioral problems in the classroom (Rimm-Kaufman, La Para, Dowber, & Pianta, 2005).

***Do not tolerate abuse of children by school personnel or peers.*** Although it may be difficult for school personnel to ensure that children are treated properly outside of the school building, several steps can be taken to ensure the safety of students while they are in a school setting. Children must view school as a safe haven that provides relief and protection from unhealthy, home-based experiences. Hence, abuse by school personnel, whether physical or psychological, can have devastating effects on a child's academic, social, and emotional development. Staff training on conflict resolution, appropriate disciplinary techniques, behavior management, and stress and anger management will provide teachers, administrators, bus drivers, and others with the support and resources to overcome abusive inclinations.

If the situation is clearly abuse, administrators need to be contacted and reports made to CPS. If the behavior seems hurtful to a child or children but does not rise to a level of reportability, the observer should request a private meeting with the person and use "I" statements to convey their concerns. Allow the individual the opportunity to address any misinterpretations of their behavior. In some case, it may be important to involve the administration in the conversation. The goal is to prevent abuse by providing feedback, support, and resources for adults working within the school community (see chapter 10, "Bullying" for management of peer abuse).

## Educating Children

***Teach children to recognize and resist abuse.*** In addition to providing comprehensive support and educational services for parents, school-based preventive programs have shown promise in protecting children from the adverse effects of physical and psychological abuse. A national survey of 2,000 youth between the ages of 10 and 16 demonstrated that children receiving school-based prevention programs were more knowledgeable about abuse, more likely to confide in someone after an attempted victimization, and less likely to blame themselves (Finkelhor & Dzuiba-Leatherman, 1995). Dake, Price, and Murnan (2003) reported that third graders who attended two 1-hour sessions on the following topics demonstrated a significant increase in knowledge regarding child abuse: describing potential abuse problems; identifying support systems available to children, different types of touch, and personal safety rules; emphasizing that the child is a victim and should not be blamed; and stating that child abuse should never be kept a secret. Their study found that younger children gained significantly more knowledge than older children, demonstrating the importance of targeting children at an early age. However, knowledge does not necessarily equal ability to enact this knowledge in dangerous situations. As such, Dake et al. note that school-based abuse prevention programs "should not be 'one-shot' efforts but be part of a planned, sequential intervention of child abuse" (p. 81).

Teaching children to recognize and resist maltreatment assumes that they have both the confidence and language skills necessary to accurately identify and appropriately communicate their feelings and the ability to recognize appropriate and inappropriate acts. Many children find it difficult to recognize, accept, and express their feelings. Therefore, schools must teach children skills that lead to increased self-confidence, empowerment, self-protection, and development. Promoting personal safety and responsibility can be accomplished by ensuring that they understand concepts such as feelings and emotions, appropriate and inappropriate touch, trust, self-esteem, and assertiveness skills in various situations. However, effective programs must incorporate active practice alongside skills training.

***Teach and practice good communication and problem-solving skills.*** Abused children often inaccurately identify their own and others' emotional states and are inclined to attribute negative intent to neutral behavior of others (Crittenden, 1989). Therefore, providing such children with experience and skill in interpreting clear and consistent communications are essential. Using their personal experiences as a guide, abused children frequently expect adults and authority figures to act in coercive ways, and such predictions or expectations may actually provoke many of these coercive responses. Inservice training can help teachers and other school personnel learn how to step back from these provocations and thus reduce any explosive incidents as they model good communication skills (Colvin, 2004).

***Promote self-control and competence.*** Physically and psychologically abused children often suffer from poor self-control and low levels of self-esteem and self-confidence (Fantuzzo, 1990). Teaching children to control, regulate, and modulate their emotions and teaching them appropriate anger management techniques can significantly reduce aggressive and impulsive behavior, both in and out of the classroom (Larson & Lochman, 2002; see also chapter 3, "Developing Self-Discipline"). Cognitive deficits, inattention, low self-esteem, and low levels of motivation may all exacerbate behavioral problems. School professionals can help promote children's self-confidence by developing and emphasizing existing competencies, such as in academics, athletics, and social interactions, to buffer against adverse life circumstances.

School professionals can help abused children function competently by actively encouraging elementary school children and their parents to get and stay involved in sports and service activities. Participation in sports is inversely related to getting into trouble and positively related to increased self-esteem, good peer relationships, and increased likelihood of participation in adolescence, which confers additional protective benefits. Participating in sports helps mood and promotes an active lifestyle, leadership, and teamwork (Huston, 2003). Service activities, particularly religious groups, are also protective. They promote close relationships, prosocial behavior, and empathy. Increases in participation over time are related to increases in psychosocial competence (Huston).

## ALTERNATIVE ACTIONS FOR INTERVENTION

Several evidence-based interventions target emotional, behavioral, and adaptive problems experienced by abused children and youth and are appropriate for school-based interventions (see Table 3). As many psychologically and physically abused children display aggressive behaviors in addition to poor peer relations and problem-solving skills, many intervention programs have focused on reducing these aggressive impulses while emphasizing an interpersonal, problem-solving approach. The Incredible Years program (Webster-Stratton, 1991; Webster-Stratton, 2001), the Primary Mental Health Project (Cowen et al., 1996), and Functional Family Therapy (Alexander & Parsons, 1982) are all empirically supported intervention programs that have proved effective in treating the

**Table 3** *Comparison of Intervention Programs*

| Intervention Program | Purpose and Components | Number of Sessions | Empirical Findings | Training, Costs, and Contact |
|---|---|---|---|---|
| I Can Problem Solve (ICPS)(Shure, 1992) | An interpersonal problem-solving program aimed at reducing and preventing high-risk behaviors, including aggression, social withdrawal, poor peer relations, and low frustration tolerance.<br><br>Offers a companion program for parents.<br><br>*Primary Clients:* children 4–12 years.<br><br>*Practitioners:* teachers. | At least 1 20-minute class lesson daily for 4 months.<br><br>Can fit flexibly into the school day and can be incorporated into language arts curriculum. | In a 2-year study of preschool and kindergarten children, 70% of impulsive or inhibited children were rated as adjusted after the intervention, compared with only 6% of controls.<br><br>Fifth- and sixth-grade students involved in this program showed fewer negative behaviors, more prosocial behaviors, and improvement on standardized achievement test scores and reading grade book levels, compared with controls. | Manual ($39.95) + training costs ($1,000 per day usually ½ to 2 days).<br><br>Myrna B. Shure, PhD *mshure@drexel.edu*<br><br>*http://www.thinkingchild.com/icps.com* |
| The Incredible Years | Aimed at reducing and preventing conduct problems and drug abuse in children and promoting their social competence.<br><br>Offered as several components (described below). | | | Carolyn Webster-Stratton, PhD<br><br>*incredibleyears@seanet.com*<br><br>*http://www.incredibleyears.com* |

*(Continued)*

**Table 3** *Continued*

| Intervention Program | Purpose and Components | Number of Sessions | Empirical Findings | Training, Costs, and Contact |
|---|---|---|---|---|
| Parent Training Component (Webster-Stratton, 2001) | Teaches skills such as nonviolent discipline techniques, problem solving, and effective communication in a group setting.<br>Includes videotapes to improve parenting skills. | | Results of several studies indicate increases in parents' positive affective responses; decreases in the use of criticism, harsh discipline, and negative commands; increases in effective limit-setting; improvements in family communication and problem solving; increases in parental self-confidence; and reductions in conduct problems in children. | |
| | BASIC program<br>*Primary Clients:* parents of children 2–7 years. | 12 to 14 2-hour weekly sessions. | | 12 videotapes and leader manual ($1,300 + training costs which are additional, check with author). |
| | ADVANCED program<br>*Primary Clients:* parents of children 4–10 years. | 8 to 12 2-hour sessions as a supplement to the BASIC program. | | 6 videotapes and leader manual ($775) + training costs which are additional. |
| | *Practitioners (BASIC and ADVANCED):* many disciplines including nursing, psychology, social work, education, and psychiatry. | | | |
| Teacher Training Component (Webster-Stratton, 2001) | Teaches motivation through positive reinforcement, strengthened relationships with students, and increased problem-solving and social skills within the classroom.<br>*Primary Clients:* teachers.<br>*Practitioners:* many disciplines, including nursing, psychology, social work, education, and psychiatry. | 14 2-hour sessions or a 4-day intensive program. | Three randomized studies have demonstrated reductions in students' behavioral problems, increases in prosocial behaviors, improvements in teachers' and parents' interactions with children, and improvements in children's academic and social competence. | 7 videotapes and leader manual ($975) + training costs which are additional. |

| | | | | |
|---|---|---|---|---|
| Dina Dinosaur Social Skills and Problem-Solving Curriculum Component (Webster-Stratton, 1991) | Promotes social competence and positive peer interactions, develops conflict management skills, and reduces conduct problems.<br><br>*Primary Clients:* children 4–8 years.<br><br>*Practitioners:* teachers. | Groups of 5–6 children meet for 18 to 22 2-hour sessions.<br><br>For implementation in the classroom: 15- to 20-minute sessions several times a week. | Two randomized control group evaluations indicated clinically significant improvements in social competence and negative behaviors among high-risk Head Start children, as well as increases in problem-solving strategies. | 9 videotapes + lesson plan manual ($1,075 + training costs which are additional). |
| Aggression Replacement Training (Goldstein et al., 1998) | Designed to prevent and reduce aggression in adolescents.<br><br>3 components include: skill streaming, anger control training, and moral education training.<br><br>*Primary Clients:* adolescents.<br><br>*Practitioners*: teachers, counselors, school psychologists, child care workers, correctional officers. | Groups of 6–8 adolescents meet for 45- to 90-minute sessions three times per week (varying durations depending on nature and severity of the problem). | Compared with controls, individuals receiving the intervention acquired skills such as expressing a complaint, responding to anger, dealing with group pressure, and preparing for a stressful conversation. Other studies have shown improvements in moral reasoning, prosocial behaviors, self-control, and reductions in impulsivity. | Manual ($29.95), videotape training course, 10 copies of workshop supplements ($495), skill cards ($25).<br><br>*icart-usa@oasen.com*<br><br>*http://www.aggressionreplacementtraining.org* |

*(Continued)*

**Table 3** *Continued*

| Intervention Program | Purpose and Components | Number of Sessions | Empirical Findings | Training, Costs, and Contact |
|---|---|---|---|---|
| Anger Coping Program (Larson & Lochman, 2002) | To improve social cognitive skills of aggressive children by helping them recognize the physiological signs of anger, improve perspective taking, increase problem-solving skills, and expand their repertoire of appropriate behaviors. | 12 to 33 group sessions (mean = 18) of 5–7 children. | Treated aggressive elementary school boys had reductions in disruptive and aggressive off-task behavior as well as improvements in self-esteem. Follow-up studies have shown improved problem-solving skills, self-esteem, and lower levels of substance use than controls. | 3 full-day workshops, monthly follow-up workshops, telephone consultations, weekly planning meetings—check with authors for price.<br>John Lochman, PhD<br>*jlochman@gp.as.ua.edu* |
| | *Primary Clients:* children.<br>*Practitioners:* two cotherapists recommended. (All lead therapists should have a master's or doctorate degree in psychology, social work, counseling, or psychiatry. Teachers and school counselors are also encouraged to act as coleaders.) | 12 to 33 group sessions (mean = 18) of 5–7 children. | | |

| | | | | |
|---|---|---|---|---|
| Strengthening Families Program: For Parents and Youth 10–14 (SFP 10–14) (Molgaard et al., 1997) | Video-based program designed to increase appropriate interaction and communication between parents and adolescents, reduce risk and build protective factors, and improve parenting practices.<br><br>Offers individual and conjoint sessions for parents and their adolescents.<br><br>*Primary Clients:* adolescents ages 10–14 years and their parents.<br><br>*Practitioners:* requires 3 group leaders, 1 for parent sessions and 2 for youth; include teachers, school counselors, mental health staff, ministers, and skilled parents. | Seven sessions plus four booster sessions (3–12 months later).<br><br>Can be offered at schools, social service agencies, churches, community centers, etc. | Three controlled longitudinal studies have found positive effects on parenting behaviors (specifically setting limits and building positive relationships), reductions in teens' affiliations with antisocial peers, and lower rates of alcohol, tobacco, and cigarette use. Youth also demonstrated fewer conduct problems than the control group. | Manual ($175), 9 videotapes ($250), 2-day training ($2,500).<br><br>Virginia Molgaard, PhD, and Richard Spoth, PhD<br>*vmolgaar@iastate.edu* |
| Strengthening Families Program | Family skills training program designed to increase resilience and decrease risk factors for violence and aggression, delinquency, depression, and school failure.<br><br>Offers individual and conjoint sessions for parents and their children.<br><br>*Primary Clients:* 6- to 12-year-olds and their parents.<br><br>*Practitioners:* requires a part-time consultant, family recruiter, and 4 trainers (2 parents trainers and 2 child trainers). | 14 sessions | Controlled longitudinal studies illustrate improved parenting behaviors and child management. Children in the treatment condition displayed delayed initiation of alcohol, tobacco, and marijuana use, lower rates of alcohol and cigarette use, and lower levels of aggressive behaviors and hostility compared with controls. | Set of 6 manuals ($300), 2-day training ($2,700).<br><br>Karol L. Kumpfer, PhD<br>*karol.kumpfer@health.utah.edu* |

*(Continued)*

**Table 3** *Continued*

| Intervention Program | Purpose and Components | Number of Sessions | Empirical Findings | Training, Costs, and Contact |
|---|---|---|---|---|
| Parent-Child Interaction Therapy (Hembree-Kigin & McNeil, 1995) | Improve the quality of parent–child relationships, change parent–child interaction patterns, increase the child's prosocial behaviors, and decrease problematic behaviors.<br><br>*Primary Clients:* children ages 2–7 years and their parents.<br><br>*Practitioner:* licensed/certified mental health professionals. | 14 1-hour sessions. | Outcome studies have shown increases in parents' reflective listening, physical proximity to their children, and prosocial verbalization, and decreases in sarcasm and criticism of their children. Studies of preschool children with ODD, CD, and ADHD demonstrated improvement in overall behavior. | Sheila M. Eyberg, PhD<br>*seyberg@phhp.ufl.edu*<br><br>*http://www.PCIT.org* |
| Helping the Noncompliant Child (McMahon & Forehand, 2003) | Improves child behaviors and familial interactions by teaching parents appropriate child management and discipline techniques.<br><br>Serves as a preventive measure against serious conduct problems.<br><br>*Primary Clients:* children 3–8 years and their families.<br><br>*Practitioners:* professionals and para-professionals skilled in counseling parents of young children with bahaviour problems. | 8–10 75- to 90-minute sessions. | Research with noncompliant children has shown significant increases in compliance from pretreatment to posttreatment and improvements in behaviors such as tantrums, aggression, and crying. Studies with children with developmental and language disabilities have demonstrated greater changes in parental behaviors and attitudes compared with controls. | Manual ($38), recommended 2-day training ($3,000).<br><br>Robert J. McMahon, PhD<br>*mcmahon@u.washington.edu* |

| | | | | |
|---|---|---|---|---|
| Functional Family Therapy (FFT)(Alexander & Parsons, 1982) | Family-based intervention program for acting-out youth.<br>Improves family communication and interactions, problem-solving techniques, and parenting strategies.<br>*Primary Clients:* children 6–18 years.<br>*Practitioners*: family therapists. | 8–12 sessions for mild cases; up to 30 hours for severe cases. | Research supports the lower rates of adulthood recidivism of participants, improvements in family communication and problem-solving techniques, and reduced negative familial interactions. Results also indicate superiority of FFT over placement in a group home in the reduction of recidivism in juvenile delinquents. | $2,000 per family.<br>James F. Alexander, PhD *jfaffi@psych.utah.edu*<br>*http://www.fftinc.com* |
| Primary Mental Health Project (PMHP)(Cowen et al., 1996) | An early-detection and prevention program that addresses social, emotional, and behavioral problems in children through the use of play and relationship building.<br>*Primary Clients:* children in kindergarten–third grade.<br>*Practitioners*: child associates (e.g., college students, aides, and parents), supervised by mental health professionals. | Individual or small group sessions 1 to 2 times/week for 30–60 minutes. | Studies have shown improvements in self-efficacy and self-confidence, behavioral problems, social problem-solving, initiation and participation in activities, learning difficulties, and reductions in withdrawn behaviors. | Art/play materials ($200–300), screening instruments ($0.25/child), evaluation instruments ($1.00/child), workshop ($140).<br>Offers several options and combinations of training including program setup, consultation, & evaluation.<br>*http://www.pmhp.org* |

*(Continued)*

**Table 3** *Continued*

| Intervention Program | Purpose and Components | Number of Sessions | Empirical Findings | Training, Costs, and Contact |
|---|---|---|---|---|
| Adults & Children Together (ACT) Against Violence Training Program | Violence prevention program that teaches adults who raise, care for, or teach young children to be positive role models and promote nonviolent problem solving.<br><br>*Primary Clients:* children from birth to 8 years.<br><br>*Practitioners*: professionals in psychology, early education, social work, public health, and related disciplines. | Can be implemented in schools; number of sessions flexible. | | Kit includes manual, video, handbook, brochures ($100), 2½- to 3-day workshop (contact authors for cost).<br><br>*jsilva@apa.org*<br><br>*http://www.actagainstviolence.com* |
| Fourth R | Educates adolescents about forming healthy relationships by integrating topics of sexuality and substance abuse into the curriculum.<br><br>*Primary Clients:* adolescents 13–15 years.<br><br>*Practitioners*: teachers. | 21 lessons. | | David Wolfe, PhD<br>*dawolfe@uwo.ca* |

internalizing and externalizing problems of physically and psychologically abused youth.

Webster-Stratton's The Incredible Years program includes parent and teacher training components (Webster-Stratton, 2001) as well as a social skills and problem-solving curriculum for children (Webster-Stratton, 1991). The parent training component uses child-directed play and promotion of language skills through modeling to promote prosocial behaviors and reduce problem behaviors. A randomized, controlled trial illustrated that parents who received the program were significantly more involved with their children during free play than the control group (Hughes & Gottlieb, 2004). A trend was also noted for program mothers to provide more autonomy and support, including freedom of expression, meaningful feedback, flexibility, and encouragement than control mothers provided during free play.

The child component, the Dina Dinosaur Social Skills and Problem-Solving Curriculum (Webster-Stratton, 1991), addresses interpersonal difficulties in children 4 to 8 years of age by promoting social competence and positive peer interactions, teaching conflict management techniques, and increasing the child's ability to empathize with others. Webster-Stratton, Reid, and Hammond (2001) demonstrated decreases in externalizing problems at home, less aggression at school, more prosocial peer behaviors, and more positive conflict management techniques in children who completed the program. However, Webster-Stratton et al. noted that for children whose parents exhibit harsh and coercive parenting styles, it may be necessary to offer a parenting component in conjunction with the child intervention.

Finally, in addition to the child and parent components, The Incredible Years offers teacher training programs to strengthen teaching skills while preventing and treating behavioral problems in young children (Webster-Stratton, 2001). It consists of teaching appropriate discipline techniques, positive reinforcement, problem-solving strategies, and communication skills through group discussion, modeling, role-playing, and the use of videotapes. All three components have been shown to improve the behavior of both nonreferred and referred children, making the program components ideal for both prevention and intervention.

The Primary Mental Health Project's core component is the development of an ongoing relationship between children and a trained paraprofessional child associate (Cowen et al., 1996). The program targets several internalizing behaviors frequently encountered in physically and psychologically abused children. Children meet with their child associate alone or in small groups one to two times a week for 20 to 25 sessions over the school year. Meetings take place in a structured play room designed to foster expressive play and create learning experiences while placing limits on inappropriate behavior. An implementation of this program in an urban inner-city school district in New York City over 4 years showed improvements in self-efficacy and self-confidence ratings, social problem solving, and initiation and participation in activities, and reductions in shyness and behavioral problems (Meller, Laboy, Rothwax, Fritton, & Mangual, 1994).

Functional Family Therapy is a family-based prevention and intervention program that targets children 6 to 18 years of age and their families to improve family communication and interactions and reduce negativity within families. Other aspects of the therapy include developing appropriate problem-solving techniques, positive behavior change, and parenting strategies (Alexander & Parsons, 1982). Functional Family Therapy has significantly reduced arrest rates for at-risk youth at a 6- to 8-month follow-up as well as at a 2½- to 3½-year follow-up (Alexander & Parsons, 1973).

Overall, these programs focus on expanding children's and adolescents' repertoire of problem-solving techniques, helping them accurately attend to environmental stimuli, reducing hostile attributional biases, and improving social and communication skills. The parenting and teaching components focus on improving adult–child relationships by teaching adults to follow the child's lead and sensitively respond to the child's cues and developmental level while using positive and contingent discipline. Furthermore, many of these effective manual-based intervention programs are relatively flexible, as they can be easily modified and adapted based on the nature and extent of the presenting problem as well as on individual differences of the primary clients. In addition, they can be easily implemented by a broad range of school personnel. The interventions for parents and families require good group and family consultation and therapy skills, but training and supervision are available.

## SUMMARY

Schools identify more abuse than any other source, and yet relatively few cases are reported or investigated. Psychologically and physically abused children demonstrate relationship difficulties with parents, teachers, and peers. They have difficulty regulating emotions, particularly anger, aggression, and sadness. Some physical abuse victims demonstrate cognitive deficits, which may be related to mild head injuries as well as to a lack of appropriate stimulation and supervision in their home environment. Both groups have difficulty using language to identify and understand their own and others' emotions. School-based professionals should use efficient screening strategies to identify and clarify ambiguous cases. Although it can be difficult, school professionals can negotiate difficult reporting challenges to protect children and reach out to their families. A number of informal and formal school-based prevention and intervention strategies and programs have proved effective in improving parent–child relationships and moderating the emotional and behavioral problems associated with psychological and physical abuse.

## RECOMMENDED RESOURCES

### Books and Other Printed Material

Binggeli, N. J., Hart, S. N., & Brassard, M. R. (2001). *Psychological maltreatment of children.* Thousand Oaks, CA: Sage.

This book is part of the Sage series of study guides for professionals working in the area of child abuse and neglect. It provides a comprehensive review of research and clinical practice on the topic.

Kalichman, S. C. (1999). *Mandated reporting of suspected child abuse: Ethics, law, and policy.* Washington, DC: American Psychological Association.

This highly practical book is packed with research, legally relevant information, and, most importantly, detailed case studies with accompanying commentaries on a comprehensive set of reporting dilemmas facing psychologists.

Kolko, D. J., & Swanson, C. C. (2002). *Assessing and treating physically abused children and their families: A cognitive-behavioral approach.* Thousand Oaks, CA: Sage.

This clearly written treatment manual reviews and provides detailed descriptions of the use of empirically supported intervention techniques. Though focused on family treatment, a number of the child treatments described are similar to those used in schools to help children identify feelings, manage anger, improve social skills, and learn problem solving. The manual can help school professionals identify treatments that are likely to work, improve their ability to interact with families constructively, and help them develop school-based interventions for children whose families are unwilling to participate in or unable to find appropriate treatment.

### Websites

*http://www.childhelpusa.org*

The website of Childhelp USA has local reporting numbers (National Child Abuse Hotline, 1-800-4-ACHILD); descriptions of what to expect when making a report; help for parents, professionals, and children; symptoms; statistics; definitions; information in Spanish; and more.

*http://nccanch.acf.hhs.gov*

The website of the National Clearinghouse on Child Abuse and Neglect Information has information on types of abuse, signs of abuse, reporting information, statistics, prevention information, and more.

## REFERENCES

Alexander, J. F., & Parsons, B. V. (1973). Short-term behavioral intervention with delinquent families: Impact on family process and recidivism. *Journal of Abnormal Psychology, 81,* 219–225.

Alexander, J., & Parsons, B. V. (1982). *Functional family therapy.* Monterey, CA: Brooks/Cole Publishing Company.

American Professional Society on the Abuse of Children. (1995). *Practice guidelines on the psychosocial evaluation of suspected psychological maltreatment in children and adolescents.* Chicago: Author.

Binggeli, N. J., Hart, S. N., & Brassard, M. R. (2001). *Psychological maltreatment of children.* Thousand Oaks, CA: Sage.

Cicchetti, D., Toth, S. L., & Hennessey, K. (1989). Research on the consequences of child maltreatment and its application to educational settings. *Topics in Early Childhood Special Education, 9,* 33–55.

Colvin, G. (2004). *Managing the cycle of acting-out behavior.* Eugene, OR: Behavior Associates.

Cowen, E. L., Hightower, A. D., Pedro-Carroll, J. L., Work, W., Wyman, P. A., & Haffey, W. G. (1996).

*School-based prevention for children at risk: The Primary Mental Health Project.* Washington, DC: American Psychological Association.

Crittenden, P. M. (1988). Family and dyadic patterns of functioning in maltreating families. In K. Brown, C. Davies, & P. Stratton (Eds.), *Early prediction and prevention of child abuse* (pp. 161–189). New York: John Wiley.

Crittenden, P. M. (1989). Teaching maltreated children in the preschool. *Topics in Early Childhood Special Education, 9,* 16–32.

Dake, J. A., Price, J. H., & Murnan, J. (2003). Evaluation of a child abuse prevention curriculum for third-grade students: Assessment of knowledge and efficacy expectations. *Journal of School Health, 73,* 76–82.

Dance, C., Rushton, A., & Quinton, D. (2002). Emotional abuse in early childhood: Relationships with progress in subsequent family placement. *Journal of Child Psychology and Psychiatry, 43,* 395–407.

Davidson, H. (1988). Failure to report child abuse: Legal penalties and emerging issues. In S. J. Wells & A. Maney (Eds.), *Professional responsibilities in protecting children: A public health approach to child sexual abuse* (pp. 93–102). New York, England: Praeger.

Davis, S., & Fantuzzo, J. W. (1989). The effects of adult and peer social interactions on social behavior of withdrawn and aggressive maltreated preschool children. *Journal of Family Violence, 4,* 227–248.

Dubowitz, H., Papas, M. A., Black, M. M., & Starr, R. H. (2002). Child neglect: Outcomes in high-risk urban preschoolers. *Pediatrics, 109,* 1100–1107.

Egeland, B., Yates, T., Appleyard, K., & van Dulman, M. (2002). The long-term consequences of maltreatment in the early years: A developmental pathway model to antisocial behavior. *Children's Services: Social Policy, Research, & Practice, 5,* 249–260.

Erickson, M. F., Egeland, B., & Pianta, R. (1989). The effects of maltreatment on the development of young children. In D. Cicchetti & V. Carlson (Eds.), *Child maltreatment: Theory and research on the causes and consequences of child abuse and neglect* (pp. 647–684). New York: Cambridge University Press.

Fantuzzo, J. W. (1990). Behavioral treatment of the victims of child abuse and neglect. *Behavior Modification, 14,* 316–339.

Finkelhor, D., & Dzuiba-Leatherman, J. (1995). Victimization prevention programs: A national survey of children's exposure and reactions. *Child Abuse and Neglect, 19,* 129–139.

Fortin, A., & Chamberland, C. (1995). Preventing the psychological maltreatment of children. *Journal of Interpersonal Violence, 10,* 275–295.

Goldstein, A. P., Glick, B., & Gibbs, J. C. (1998). *Aggression replacement training: A comprehensive intervention for aggressive youth* (Rev. ed.). Champaign, IL: Research Press.

Hartman, R. R., Stage, S. A., & Webster-Stratton, C. (2003). A growth curve analysis of parent training outcomes: Examining the influence of child risk factors (inattention, impulsivity, and hyperactivity problems), parental and family risk factors. *Journal of Child Psychology and Psychiatry, 44,* 388–398.

Hembree-Kigin, T. L., & McNeil, C. B. (1995). *Parent-Child Interaction Therapy.* New York: Plenum Press.

Herrenkohl, R. C., Herrenkohl, E. C., Egolf, B. P., & Wu, P. (1991). The developmental consequences of child abuse: The Lehigh longitudinal study. In R. H. Starr & D. A. Wolf (Eds.), *The effects of child abuse and neglect: Issues and research* (pp. 57–81). New York: Guilford Press.

Hughes, J. R., & Gottlieb, L. N. (2004). The effects of the Webster-Stratton parenting program on maltreating families: Fostering strengths. *Child Abuse and Neglect, 28,* 1081–1097.

Huston, A. (2003, June). *Middle childhood development: What matters? Supports and opportunities.* Paper presented at the NIH-sponsored conference, Building Pathways to Success: Research, Policy, and Practice on Development in Middle Childhood, Washington, DC.

Kalichman, S. C. (1999). *Mandated reporting of suspected child abuse: Ethics, law, and policy.* Washington, DC: American Psychological Association.

Kolko, D. J. (2000). How do I interview a child about alleged physical abuse? In H. Dubowitz & D. DePanfilis (Eds.), *Handbook for child protection practice* (pp. 75–79). Thousand Oaks, CA: Sage.

Kolko, D. J., & Swanson, C. C. (2002). *Assessing and treating physically abused children and their families: A cognitive-behavioral approach.* Thousand Oaks, CA: Sage.

Larson, J., & Lochman, J. E. (2002). *Helping schoolchildren cope with anger: A cognitive behavioral intervention.* New York: Guilford Press.

Lavoie, F., Hebert, M., Tremblay, R., Vitaro, F., Vezina, L., & McDuff, P. (2002). History of family dysfunction and perpetration of dating violence by adolescent boys: A longitudinal study. *Journal of Adolescent Health, 30,* 375–383.

Magee, W. (1999). Effects of negative life experiences on phobia onset. *Social Psychiatry and Psychiatric Epidemiology, 34,* 343–351.

Main, M., & George, C. (1985). Responses of abused and disadvantaged toddlers to distress in agemates: A study in the daycare setting. *Developmental Psychology, 21,* 407–412.

Manly, J. T., Kim, J. E., Rogosch, F. A., & Cicchetti, D. (2001). Dimensions of child maltreatment and children's adjustment: Contributions of developmental timing and subtype. *Development and Psychopathology, 13,* 759–782.

McMahon, R. J., & Forehand, R. L. (2003). *Helping the noncompliant child: Family-based treatment for oppositional behavior* (2nd ed.). New York: Guilford Press.

McMillen, J. C. (2000). How do I assess a caregiver's personal history and its meaning for practice? In H. Dubowitz & D. DePanfilis (Eds.), *Handbook for child protection practice* (pp. 305–309). Thousand Oaks, CA: Sage.

Meller, P. J., Laboy, W., Rothwax, Y., Fritton, J., & Mangual, J. (1994). *Community School District Four: Primary Mental Health Project, 1990–1994.* New York: Community School District No. 4.

Molgaard, V. K., Kumpfer, K. L., & Fleming, E. (1997). *The strengthening families program: For parents and Iowa youth 10–14 leader guide* (Rev. ed.). Ames, IA: Iowa State University Extension.

Moore, T. E., & Pepler, D. J. (1998). Correlates of adjustment in children at risk. In G. W. Holden, R. Geffner, & E. N. Jouriles (Eds.), *Children exposed to marital violence: Theory, research, and applied issues* (pp. 157–184). Washington, DC: American Psychological Association.

Moran, P. B., Vuchinich, S., & Hall, N. K. (2004). Associations between types of maltreatment and substance use during adolescence. *Child Abuse and Neglect, 28,* 565–574.

Rimm-Kaufman, S. E., La Para, L. M., Dowber, J. T., & Pianta, R. C. (2005). The contribution of classroom setting and quality of instruction to children's behavior in kindergarten classrooms. *Elementary School Journal, 10,* 377–394.

Sedlak, A., & Broadhurst, D. (1996). *Executive summary of the Third National Incidence Study of Child Abuse and Neglect.* Washington, DC: U.S. Government Printing Office.

Shure, M. B. (1992). *I Can Problem Solve (ICPS): An interpersonal cognitive problem solving program.* Champaign, IL: Research Press.

Sroufe, L. A. (1983). Infant–caregiver attachment and patterns of adaptation in preschool: The roots of maladaptation and competence. *The Minnesota Symposium on Child Psychology, 16,* 41–83. Hillsdale, NJ: Erlbaum.

Straus, M. A., & Field, C. J. (2003). Psychological aggression by American parents: National data on prevalence, chronicity, and severity. *Journal of Marriage and Family, 65,* 795–808.

Vissing, Y. M., Straus, M. A., Gelles, R. J., & Harrop, J. W. (1991). Verbal aggression by parents and psychosocial problems of children. *Child Abuse and Neglect, 15,* 223–238.

Webster-Stratton, C. (1991). *Dinosaur social skills and problem-solving training manual.* Seattle, WA: Incredible Years.

Webster-Stratton, C. (2001). *The Incredible Years: Parents, teachers, and children training series.* Seattle, WA: Incredible Years.

Webster-Stratton, C., Reid, J., & Hammond, M. (2001). Social skills and problem-solving training for children with early-onset conduct problems: Who benefits? *Journal of Child Psychology and Psychiatry and Allied Disciplines, 42,* 943–952.

Wolfe, D. A. (1991). *Preventing physical and emotional abuse of children.* New York: Guilford Press.

# 61

# Sexual Abuse

**Connie B. Horton**

*Pepperdine University*

**Tracy K. Cruise**

*Western Illinois University*

## BACKGROUND AND DEVELOPMENT

Child sexual abuse (CSA), with few exceptions, was a virtually unrecognized phenomenon prior to the 1970s. It was not until the passage of the Child Abuse Prevention and Treatment Act (Public Law 93-247) in 1974 that federal mandates led all states to outlaw this behavior. The following two decades brought an explosion of research, clinical, and popular press literature on this form of maltreatment. Professional and public audiences found the alarming prevalence rates disturbing, and the effects could no longer be ignored. Schools were urged to be involved in the response.

Although to some extent, public interest in the topic has apparently waned, it is important for school professionals to realize that children continue to be sexually abused. The problem has not gone away. In fact, modern advances such as Internet technology have only expanded the ways in which offenders can obtain access to their victims (Finkelhor, Mitchell, & Wolak, 2000). Schools still have a critical role to play in the response.

CSA has no universal definition. Krugman and Jones (1987) defined sexual abuse as "the involvement of dependent, developmentally immature children in sexual activities that they do not fully comprehend and therefore to which they are unable to give informed consent and/or which violate the taboos of society" (p. 286). Sexual abuse may include acts of touching (e.g., fondling, oral sex, or intercourse) and noncontact (e.g., exposure to pornography, voyeurism, or watching the perpetrator masturbate). Sexual abuse may involve a combination of these acts and will often progress from less to more invasive forms in an attempt to desensitize the child to sexual content or contact (Kaufman et al., 1998).

Legal definitions of sexual abuse vary from state to state, but most describe a particular age difference between the adult and child. Typically, a 5-year age difference is necessary to constitute sexual abuse. However, a significant portion of offenders are under the age of 18, with a portion of their acts occurring with children less than 5 years younger. These victims may be less powerful in terms of physical size or intelligence and unable to refuse the act (e.g., Johnson, 1999).

The variation of definitions of sexual abuse leads to some discrepancy between incidence and prevalence rates. A recent national incidence study found that 12.3 children per 1,000 were abused or neglected in the United States in 2002, with 10% of those cases being sexual abuse (U.S. Department of Health and Human Services [DHHS], 2004). These figures include mostly children abused by adults, not by child or adolescent offenders. The figures do not include cases that were disclosed but never reported and cases that were never disclosed; therefore, they are likely to be underestimates of sexual abuse. Prevalence estimates of sexual abuse garnered mostly from retrospective research suggest ratios of 1:3–4 girls and 1:4–9 boys being sexually abused during childhood (Gorey & Leslie, 1997).

There is no typical profile of a child sexual abuse victim, as sexual abuse affects children of all ages, races, and socioeconomic levels. However, children are most vulnerable to sexual abuse between the ages of 3 and 15 years, with 9 being the median age (U.S. DHHS, 1999). The average duration of intrafamilial sexual abuse is 4 years, whereas duration of extrafamilial abuse is generally much shorter, probably because of more limited access to the child victim (Courtois, 1993). Children who are most vulnerable to sexual abuse are those who have lower self-esteem, are emotionally needy, or lack adequate supervision (Putnam, 2003). In the majority of cases (85%–90%) the perpetrator is male.

Early myths suggested that sex offenders were typically "creepy strangers" who attacked children. Later, as people began to understand that this was not true, fathers were thought to be the most common offenders. This too is incorrect. Although it is true that most children know their offenders, the offenders are not fathers in the majority of the cases. The latest incidence study found that 29% of sexual abuse offenders were classified as "other relative," meaning that they were not a parent, guardian, or parent partner (DHHS, 2004). Uncles, cousins, or grandparents are commonly reported in this category. Even more striking is the fact that 37% of sexual offenders were in other types of relationships with the child, such as camp counselor, school employee, clergy, or hospital staff (DHHS, 2004).

# PROBLEMS AND IMPLICATIONS

## Effects and Symptoms

There is no universal child sexual abuse syndrome, no single specific symptom profile for every child who has been sexually abused. Some victims do not display any initial or long-term damaging effects, whereas others have delayed, or *sleeper*, effects. Many children certainly experience immediate and/or long-term consequences (e.g., Rind, Tromovitch, & Bauserman, 1998), but there is significant heterogeneity in the extent and types of symptoms exhibited by sexually abused children. These potential symptoms occur in a variety of domains, including physical, emotional, behavioral and social, and cognitive and academic.

***Physical.*** In the majority of cases of CSA, victims demonstrate no physical effects; however, some are physically injured. Vaginal and rectal tears, lacerations, or bruising and bladder injuries have been observed as abuse effects (Johnson, 2004). Pregnancy, sexually transmitted diseases, and genital pain are other infrequent results of child sexual abuse. Somatic complaints (e.g., headaches, stomachaches, or irritable bowel syndrome) and problems with toileting, eating, or sleeping (e.g., insomnia or night terrors) can follow CSA (Kendall-Tackett, 2000). Additionally, chronic hyperarousal caused by maltreatment may be related to somatic symptoms, alterations in brain structures, hormone types and levels, growth patterns, and pain threshold level (e.g., Cohen, Perel, DeBellis, Friedman, & Putnam, 2002).

***Emotional.*** Children who have been sexually victimized are more likely than their peers to experience withdrawal, depression, anxiety, fear, hypervigilance, anger, low self-esteem, and blunted or restricted affect (e.g., see review by Horton & Cruise, 2001). Underlying these feelings may be a self-perception of being different, dirty, or "damaged goods" as a result of the abuse, or a misperception that their faults somehow caused the abuse. Many of these internalizing symptoms have also been noted as long-term consequences; adolescent and adult survivors often exhibit depression, anxiety, feelings of isolation and stigma, hyperarousal, and low self-esteem (Putnam, 2003). One additional affective response to maltreatment worthy of note is anger. Some children may be angry with their perpetrators, whereas others are also angry with the individuals who failed to prevent the CSA or who failed to believe the victim upon disclosure or discovery. This generalized anger toward others may lead to behavioral and interpersonal difficulties.

***Behavioral and social.*** Some victims of CSA, in response to their trauma, may develop angry, aggressive tendencies, initially demonstrated as a young child's instrumental aggression (e.g., see review by Horton & Cruise, 2001). This may lead to more serious conduct problems in adolescence, including fighting, property offenses, and other criminality. Less aggressive behavioral concerns include clingy and overly dependent behavior in young children or suicidal and other self-injurious behavior, alcohol and drug abuse, and cigarette smoking in adolescents (Paolucci, Genius, & Violato, 2001).

Some abused children may misinterpret the intent of peer behavior to be more hostile and will respond aggressively (e.g., Kaplan, Pelcovitz, & Labruna, 1999). For others, the symptoms of fear, mistrust, and negative self-perceptions interfere with the development and maintenance of friendships. As a result, some of these children may display more dependency on adults and demonstrate a need for an unusual degree of reassurance. Sexual behavior problems of abused children are most obviously related to sexual abuse. Children may have precocious sexual knowledge and language, be involved in extensive, age-inappropriate sexual play, masturbate excessively, or exhibit sexually aggressive behavior toward peers or adults (Johnson, 1999). Adolescent sexual difficulties include sexual dissatisfaction, indiscriminate sexual involvement, and an increased risk for revictimization (Paolucci et al., 2001). Sexual behavior problems occur on a continuum (Johnson). Some victims, though certainly not most, may begin to develop an offender mindset.

***Cognitive and academic.*** In addition to the behavioral and emotional consequences of child maltreatment, specific academic problems can occur in the aftermath of CSA. Sudden changes in school performance are common among victims of CSA, as are more chronic academic problems, including poor school achievement, failing grades, increased risk for retention, truancy, and dropping out (e.g., Leiter & Johnsen, 1997).

In sum, consequences of CSA vary in type and severity across children. Although negative outcomes are possible, they are not inevitable or invariable for children who are sexually abused. When victims of CSA do experience effects, symptoms may vary in type and severity. Factors that mediate the impact of CSA include child characteristics, preabuse family functioning, aspects of the abuse experience, cognitive interpretation, coping strategies used, and response and support from others (Whiffen & MacIntosh, 2005).

# ALTERNATIVE ACTIONS FOR PREVENTION

School personnel have been involved in the prevention of child sexual abuse through a variety of avenues for years and will undoubtedly continue to offer specific and ancillary prevention efforts. Therefore, school psychologists should continue to assist educators to be leaders in this cause. The five steps listed in the 2004 child abuse prevention campaign packet and described below are a simple reminder of ways in which educators can be involved in the prevention of child sexual abuse (National Clearinghouse on Child Abuse and Neglect [NCCAN], 2004).

## 1. Raise the Issue

School psychologists and counselors can encourage administrators and community members to provide programs for children and their families to reduce the likelihood of sexual abuse. Program review, consultation regarding program implementation, and program evaluation are just a few ways school professionals might raise the issue of child sexual abuse and begin prevention programming.

School mental health professionals also play a critical role in primary prevention as they stay abreast of the research and treatment of child sexual abuse and offer this information to staff and parents through inservice training sessions or at community group meetings. School psychologists and counselors can help educators and parents understand the rate of occurrence, risk and protective factors, and negative consequences of child sexual abuse.

## 2. Reach Out to Children and Parents in Your Community

The most commonly identified prevention effort undertaken by many schools (85%) occurs at this level. These are skill-based, personal safety, and victimization prevention programs that are presented to children during school hours (Daro, 1994). Some states even mandate such programs (see Recommended Resources).

Although the primary goal of these programs is to teach children that it is against the rules for adults to act in a sexual way with children, it is difficult to assess the level of success of such programs. One important observation regarding these prevention programs is that data demonstrating that they prevent anything are limited. One recent retrospective study did find that female college students who participated in a school prevention program were less likely to be sexually abused (Gibson & Leitenberg, 2000). Debate has even ensued over whether children should be expected to prevent their own abuse and whether these programs foster more guilt or blame by suggesting that the child should have stopped the abuse (Bolen, 2003).

Personal safety and victimization prevention programs are generally assessed on whether students are acquiring and retaining knowledge, obtaining and employing skills, and disclosing ongoing or previous abuse. Studies demonstrate that those programs employing multiple presentation styles (e.g., role-playing, discussions, films, and modeling) demonstrate significant changes in children's knowledge of both sexual abuse and prevention skills (Davis & Gidycz, 2000; Rispens, Aleman, & Goudena, 1997). Although initial findings regarding knowledge acquisition are promising, only a limited number of studies have assessed the retention of this knowledge. Again, programs offering multiple formats and more than three sessions appear to yield extended recall of the information (Davis & Gidycz). Because of ethical concerns surrounding a true assessment of children's acquisition of skills, few data are available to support an assumption that children will demonstrate the necessary prevention skills in a real-life situation. Most notably, programs that employ behavioral training (e.g., modeling, role-playing, and social reinforcement) report that students actively demonstrate the taught skills in that context significantly more than do students in programs without behavioral skills training (Rispens et al.). However, it is still unclear whether these skills generalize beyond the training environment.

School-based prevention programs consistently promote disclosures of both current and past abuse (Bolen, 2003). Although disclosure may not be a central goal for all programs, this secondary outcome is critically important. By allowing children to break their silence and receive support and intervention, these programs, when carefully implemented, may significantly reduce the amount of time a victim suffers in silence and thus reduce the likelihood of long-term trauma.

School psychologists, counselors, or social workers, who may be asked to select and implement such programs, should be aware of the many issues relevant to a successful program. Aspects to consider include the developmental sensitivity of the program and the empirical support for the specific program (see Horton & Cruise, 2001, for a complete review of program components and recommendations). More effective programs (a) are presented through multiple mediums and offer opportunities for skills practice, (b) offer repeat exposure, (c) address multiple forms of victimization (e.g., physical abuse, bullying), (d) include parent and public education components, (e) emphasize that most offenders are known to the victim and may even be another child, and (f) offer interventions for those already victimized (Davis & Gidycz, 2000; Rispens et al., 1997).

## 3. Remember the Risk Factors

Although school-based programs are the most easily recognizable abuse prevention efforts in schools, more recent reviews suggest that prevention should be aimed at promoting the overall well-being of children to offset some of the identified risk factors (Bolen, 2003). For example, providing children a chance for positive experiences through achievement and interpersonal relationships may bolster self-esteem and aid children in managing interpersonal interactions. Exposure to healthy role models who provide consistent care and support can help children learn how to express emotions and trust others. Prosocial behaviors need to be "interwoven throughout the curriculum" to help foster healthy relationships and promote healthy sexuality (Bolen, 2003, p. 182).

Some prevention efforts may be targeted specifically at children in the form of affective education and teaching of problem-solving skills. All children could benefit from such training, not just those who have experienced sexual abuse. In some cases the specific effects of abuse may be better handled in therapy sessions outside the school setting (e.g., because traumatic memories are too disturbing to address in short intervals, or school mental health professionals may lack competency in this area), but general coping skills and problem solving may be better addressed in the school environment, where relevant examples are present and where other children may assist in the development of such training efforts (see chapter 1, "Social and Emotional Learning").

Parent and teacher education programs can also offer participants an accurate explanation of normal sexual development in children. It is important for teachers and parents to understand what sexual behaviors are age-appropriate in children and when certain sexual behaviors may be problematic. Johnson's (1999) *Understanding Your Child's Sexual Behavior* provides useful descriptions and examples across developmental levels. Having this awareness will allow adults to determine when sexual behaviors are problematic and to raise the question of sexual abuse.

In an effort to assist children and families most at risk of harm, school professionals may offer parent support groups or community information sessions aimed at helping parents understand the relationship between their own physical and psychological well-being and the overall health of their children. Topics such as managing parental stress, awareness and treatment for mental health issues, and the importance of parental involvement for the physical and psychological safety of a child are often included in these parent education programs.

Finally, and probably most important, creating open communication among children, parents, and educators may allow individuals involved to develop closer interpersonal relationships that may reduce many of the risk factors for sexual abuse. Families that have open and direct dialogues foster more positive self-regard among children, remain aware of where children are and what activities they are engaged in, and allow for disclosures of feelings and experiences that might not otherwise be heard. Healthy families display effective communication patterns that result in healthier children. Open communication channels between home and school also allow parents and teachers to address the needs of children and to address any concerns early before problems are fully developed. Children who feel they can talk to their teachers and be heard and understood are more likely to experience acceptance and support. Moreover, school personnel are often the trusted adults with whom children first make disclosures of abuse (see chapters 5 and 6, "Student–Teacher Relationships" and "Parent–Teacher Relationships").

### 4. Recognize the Warning Signs

It is imperative that school psychologists develop a clear understanding of the potential physical, behavioral, and social–emotional indicators of sexual abuse (see Horton & Cruise, 2001, for a review). Although no single symptom confirms that a child has been sexually abused, the presence of a variety of indicators should raise the suspicion and compel school professionals to be open to the possibility (see Table 1).

### 5. Report Suspected Abuse or Neglect

School professionals must remember their role as mandated reporters and report any suspected cases of sexual abuse. Furthermore, they may also support other staff and parents through the reporting process and offer consultation to assist in open home–school communication (see Reporting CSA section below). As professionals trained in both the detection of and response to child sexual abuse, school psychologists and counselors may take a leadership role in coordinating the variety of services offered to children and their families following the detection of sexual abuse. These professionals can help ensure that a child's needs are being met and that all agencies involved are aware of everyone's goals to avoid duplication of services.

**Table 1** *Possible Warning Signs of Child Sexual Abuse*

*Physical*
- Difficulty walking, sitting, or standing.
- Pain during urination or urinary tract infections.
- Somatic complaints—stomachaches, headaches, general aches and pains.
- Sleep disturbances—difficulty sleeping, nightmares.
- Regressive behaviors—tantrums, baby talk, thumb sucking, enuresis or encopresis.
- Pregnancy, especially in early adolescence.
- Sexually transmitted diseases.
- Self-injurious behavior—cutting, burning oneself, suicide attempts.

*Cognitive Development and Academic Achievement*
- Age-inappropriate sexual knowledge.
- Sexually explicit drawings (not open to interpretation).
- Sudden changes in academic performance.
- Failing grades.
- Refusal to participate in certain activities (e.g., dressing out for PE).
- Difficulty concentrating.
- Truancy or absenteeism—maybe to avoid feeling stigmatized or in order to feel safe.

*Emotional, Psychosocial, and Behavioral Development*
- Sexualized play (i.e., frequent sexual themes with toys or other children).
- Frequent touching of genitals or masturbation.
- Inappropriate sexual expression with adults (e.g., frequent hugging of a female teacher that produces arousal).
- Aggressive sexual behavior with use of force or verbal threats.
- Social isolation or withdrawal.
- Extreme fear reactions—to people or situations.
- Dependent or clingy behavior.
- Social skill deficits—lack of prosocial behaviors, decreased empathy, inability to make friends.
- Substance abuse or delinquency, especially in adolescents.
- Difficulty trusting others.
- Fire setting.
- Cruelty to animals.
- Running away.

## ALTERNATIVE ACTIONS FOR INTERVENTION

To be prepared to respond to abuse in informed, sensitive ways, and to avoid the possible iatrogenic effects from the school's response, school professionals must avoid a number of problems or potential traps. A balanced perspective is often the key to avoiding the errors. School mental health service providers should ensure that their own response is balanced and that their consultation with teachers urges a balanced response as well. The following suggestions may help in achieving this goal.

## Recommendations for a Balanced Response

***1. Observations of symptoms should lead to hypotheses but not to conclusions.*** School professionals would do well to know the potential emotional, cognitive, and social consequences described above. This can be of assistance in two important ways. When working with a known victim of child sexual abuse, school professionals ought to make an extra effort to assess these domains and listen extra carefully for evidence of some of the thinking patterns, emotional symptoms, or social patterns that are frequently seen in victims (Horton & Cruise, 1997). Similarly, if a school professional learns of a child with symptoms, it is important to consider the *possibility* that this child may be a victim of abuse.

The risk, however, is that the school professional will go too quickly beyond generating hypotheses to drawing conclusions that are not yet warranted. For example, a practitioner is acting prematurely if he or she assumes that a child who has been victimized sexually must have certain symptoms and therefore needs a particular treatment. An assessment must be done first. Likewise, for a clinician to assume that because a child demonstrates particular symptoms, the child must be a victim of sexual abuse is erroneous. Although it is certainly appropriate to consider the possibility that a child has been abused, this should be one of many hypotheses that is explored. Jumping to conclusions in either of these scenarios is not helpful to anyone.

***2. Neither overreactions nor underreactions to child sexual behavior problems are helpful.*** Whether a symptom raises an abuse hypothesis should depend partly on the particular symptom. Some symptoms are generic signs of distress. For example, a child may show signs of anxiety for an infinite number of reasons. There may be a genetic tendency for individuals in this family to be anxious. Perhaps the child is not normally anxious but is exhibiting symptoms because of some family changes (e.g., a divorce, move, death, or financial problems). School factors such as being bullied, having difficulty with academic material, struggling with a learning disability, or having a harsh teacher could also be creating anxious feelings. The possibility that the anxiety is an outcome of abuse is real and so should be considered in some cases, but abuse is not the only, or even the most likely conclusion that can be reached.

Sexual behavior problems, on the other hand, are symptoms that are more likely to be correlated with a history of abuse. However, cause for concern depends on the nature of the sexual behavior problem. For example, if a child in kindergarten attempts to initiate oral sex with a peer on the playground, the hypothesis of sexual abuse should definitely be considered. This child has somehow received too much information too soon, but the details of that education are unknown. It is possible that the child has been victimized directly in this way. It is also possible that he observed others engaging in sexual behavior. It could be that he has been exposed to pornography. Compared with anxiety symptoms, this display of behavior, while not used to draw definitive conclusions, should raise more serious hypotheses. Neither a minimizing "boys will be boys" nor a harsh punitive response is helpful.

***3. School personnel should be open to potential disclosure but not lead children in that direction, nor feel the need to investigate reports.*** Although sexual behavior problems are a more reliable symptom than general distress symptoms, an even more reliable sign of abuse is a direct disclosure. School professionals can err by not trusting a child's report or by leading a child to make a report.

"Children will lie about anything." "You can't trust a child's abuse disclosure, especially during a divorce." "But that family seems so nice. I can't believe this would be true." These statements and attitudes, which may seem to be common sense, can cause school practitioners to fail to take seriously a child's disclosure or to avoid even beginning a conversation in which a disclosure might emerge.

Memory is a complex field, and much about it remains unknown. Suggestibility has been shown to vary depending on a child's age and the nature of the suggestions, questions, and props used (Reed, 1996). An important point for school practitioners to remember is that they are not investigators. If a child discloses that he or she has been sexually abused, the school professional has a responsibility to make a report but not to interrogate the child. At times, adults in the school may be concerned about a child, but there is not enough information to make a report to child protection services. In such circumstances, school professionals may ask *open-ended* questions (or invitations), which do not give the child direction or limit the child's response. "Tell me what has been going on" or "How's life?" are starter questions that allow a child to respond freely in any way he or she wishes. The positive side of this open-ended questioning approach is that the interviewer is clearly not leading. Thus, if a child discusses abuse in this conversation, it is clear that the suggestion came from the child, and that the school professional did not coerce the child to disclose. The potential downside of this type of questioning is that a child may choose to go in a very different direction and talk about what has been going on with soccer, school, or friends. According to Reed (1996), *focused* questions "introduce a new topic but do not combine the identity of an actor with a potentially abusive action" (p. 109). For example, a school psychologist might ask the child to "tell me about your weekend visits with your Dad." These types of prompts point the child in the direction of the question at hand, but do not lead.

*Direct* questions, though necessary as follow-up, connect actor and action (e.g., "Did your coach touch your penis?") and are to be used only by a child protection investigator, not by school personnel. *Leading* questions that "suggest new information and tempt, pressure, or coerce a child to agree to the suggested information" (Reed, 1996, p. 109) should not be used by anyone.

***4. School personnel should be compassionate toward children who have been victimized but should still hold them responsible for their behavior.*** Children who have been sexually abused will not be "cured" overnight. They will need the patience of school psychologists, teachers, and others involved in their care and education. At the same time, compassion and patience are not equal to excusing behavior or being overly lenient regarding disruptive behavior problems. School practitioners may need to find this balance in their own direct contact with victimized children and will have a critical role in helping teachers understand and employ the same balance.

It is unnecessary, unethical, and perhaps even illegal for school practitioners to share elaborate details of children's abuse histories with teachers. At times, however, teachers have some general sense that the child or adolescent has likely been abused in some way because he or she has been placed in a foster home or residential facility. Other times, children have shared their stories directly with the teachers. In both cases, many teachers, knowing that a child has been abused, may develop a compassionate stance and become so sad, worried, or sympathetic that they find it difficult to correct behavior or have high academic standards. A teacher may begin to understand a child's aggression as related to abuse, and therefore be reluctant to be too hard on the child, and may not use established classroom or school procedures in handling the matter. A teacher may be reluctant to give back tests or papers with weak grades so as not to further decrease an adolescent's postabuse low self-esteem.

Although these teachers are to be commended for their generosity and compassion, they need to understand the potential downside of an attitude that goes too far in that direction. For example, a child who is accidentally reinforced for his or her aggression may become more aggressive. Instead of helping the student recover from traumatic events, this approach may add further challenges. The student may have peer problems or get into serious trouble in other settings in which people are not interested in or aware of the abuse history. Over time, the student may internalize the identity as the tough guy or the bad girl, the abuser, not the victim. This potential trajectory, of course, is not at all what the compassionate teacher would want, but it is a risk. Regarding the second example, a teacher may need to be told that supporting the student's academic development—not "lowering the bar"—may be one of the greatest ways to help an abused child.

## Reporting of Suspected CSA

When child disclosures or professional observations of indicators have raised the question of CSA, the decision to make a report must be considered. In addition to the ethical and moral reasons for reporting suspected CSA, legislation has been passed by every state, requiring school personnel to report CSA (Horton & Cruise, 2001). State laws vary on certain specifics; therefore, it is critical for school professionals to be familiar with the laws in their state (see the Recommended Resources section).

Many important aspects of reporting laws are consistent across states. All states, for example, describe *mandated reporters*, that is, individuals who are required by law to report suspected child abuse and neglect, typically to child protection agencies and occasionally to the police. Mandated reporters who fail to report may be found guilty of a class B misdemeanor as a negligent party, and may be required to pay fines for the offense (Illinois Department of Child and Family Services [IDCFS], 1998). In every state laws clearly name school personnel as one of the professional groups of mandated reporters Additionally, states laws are consistent in establishing that mandated reporters are not required to have proof of abuse at the time of the report, but rather have only a "reason to suspect" before a report is mandated. School personnel, therefore, should not wait until they have irrefutable evidence. Finally, states generally have some type of "Good Samaritan" clause to protect mandated reporters who act in good faith. Therefore, school personnel who honestly suspect sexual abuse have immunity from civil liability or criminal penalty when they do make a report (IDCFS, 1998).

Schools frequently have policies in which all reports must go through the principal, response teams, or designated receivers. Teachers and other school personnel are asked to discuss suspected abuse with the designated person or team, which will then decide whether to make the report (Crenshaw, Crenshaw, & Lichtenberg, 1995). Though common, this practice is not ideal, and in some states it may be illegal, particularly if there is a gatekeeper or potential report suppression function. Such a procedure may delay a report or result in a less reliable second- or thirdhand report. Additionally, in many states (e.g., Illinois; see IDCFS, 1998) it is specifically illegal to suppress a report. Also, "mandated reporters remain liable for their suspicions even if they have reported to their designated receiver" (Crenshaw et al., p. 1110). Thus, if a teacher suspects that a child is being maltreated and reports this to his principal, who decides she disagrees and will not report it, the teacher is still mandated to report. Notifying a principal or other supervisor that a report has been made is a different, appropriate, and completely legal matter (IDCFS).

School personnel are responsible for the largest numbers of reports (DHHS, 1999); however, there is also reason to believe that schools are responsible for the largest numbers of failures to report (Crenshaw et al., 1995). School personnel who report abuse indicate that they do so for a variety of reasons. Most commonly, they cite that they hope the report will help stop the maltreatment and that they know it is their legal obligation to make the report (Crenshaw et al.). Although suspected sexual abuse is reported more commonly than suspected neglect or emotional abuse, it is less commonly reported than suspected physical abuse (Crenshaw et al.). Fear, lack of information or expertise, school-related obstacles, past problems with Child Protective Services (CPS), and concerns about the child are commonly cited reasons for failure to report (Horton & Cruise, 2001). School psychologists and other school-based mental health service providers may have an important role in helping counter these obstacles.

## Treatment Options

Once sexual abuse has been reported and CPS has completed its investigation, the child's treatment needs should be considered. The following factors should be considered in determining whether to suggest a community referral or school-based services: student factors (e.g., the severity of the abuse and the symptoms displayed, and whether the child wants counseling at school), family factors (e.g., residence of the child, parental attitudes, level of denial, and resources), community factors (e.g., other available options), institutional factors (e.g., administrative support and district philosophy regarding provision of this type of service), and school professional factors (e.g., expertise of school-based providers).

If, after considering the issues above, school professionals decide to recommend that the child receive primary services in the community, they should be thoughtful in making the referral. The Center for Mental Health in the Schools (1997) reports that follow-through rates regarding referrals made by school personnel are less than 50%. However, taking the time to make a good referral (i.e., knowing community providers, checking wait lists and sliding fee scales) can make a difference.

When it has been determined that the school will have a role in providing mental health interventions for a child or adolescent victim of CSA, a few options that should be considered include general mental health programming, CSA-focused groups, or individual abuse-focused counseling.

Students with CSA histories may benefit from a number of ancillary counseling programs already offered by a school. For example, groups focused on anxiety, depression, anger management, or social skills may be helpful to students in addressing the effects of their experience. In addition to matching group placements to the student's symptoms, school professionals may find it helpful to include students in programs that fit their current life situations. For example, students who are abused are much more likely to have moved, changed schools, or had other transitions, so it may be helpful to include them in a group for new students. In such groups, students may choose whether to disclose their abuse history, but even if they choose not to, the group may be helpful in developing increased self-understanding, enhancing coping strategies, and providing a positive, safe experience with peers.

Schools that provide abuse-specific group or individual interventions should use current best practices and empirically validated treatments. Unfortunately, information remains limited. Summarizing the status of the field, Saunders and Williams (1996) reported that although "treatment for abused children is viewed as appropriate, necessary, and even mandatory by most mental health professionals and child advocates ... scientific knowledge about the outcome of treatment for abused children lags far behind the clinical literature, the clinical practice, and the high volume of services being delivered" (p. 293). Although the field has room for improvement, valuable theoretical models have been described, key treatment goals and approaches have been discussed, and treatment manuals for model programs have been made available.

One important treatment model for school psychologists to consider is the Integrated Contextual Model proposed by Friedrich (e.g., 1996). This model, which is applicable to male and female students, is based on solid theoretical principles and empirical evidence. According to the model, attachment theory, behavioral and emotional regulation, and self-perception and development have made valuable contributions to understanding the effects of CSA and determining treatments that are likely to be effective. For example, an attachment perspective leads clinicians to work very intentionally to form a safe, therapeutic alliance with the child, and to work hard to encourage the attachment between the child and the primary caregiver. The dysregulation perspective suggests that sessions with these children should be structured and predictable. Teaching children self-soothing, tension-reduction skills also fits with this aspect of the model. Finally, self theory views the experience of acceptance and affirmation as important to the CSA victim, who may have adopted the offender identity and view himself or herself as bad. The model emphasizes that each of the three areas has applications for individual, group, and family work.

Cognitive–behavioral approaches also have been applied successfully in the treatment of CSA. Cognitive–behavioral therapists recognize the interactional nature of thoughts, feeling, and behavior (Feeny, Foa, Treadwell, & March, 2004). Commonly used cognitive–behavioral techniques, including affective education, cognitive restructuring techniques, and skills training, can be very helpful in addressing the needs of students with a CSA history (Kendall, 2000).

## Treatment Goals

Beyond the use of general models, case planning must be individualized. Abuse is a historical event, not a diagnosis, so treatment needs and therapeutic goals will vary significantly (Horton & Cruise, 2001). Multimethod and multi-informant assessments that include child, parent, and teacher interviews (see Horton & Cruise, 1997); general symptom instruments (e.g., the Children's Depression Inventory and the Child Behavior Checklist); and abuse-specific measures (e.g., the Trauma Symptom Checklist for Children and the Children's Sexual Behavior Inventory) may be important in helping to individualize treatment plans.

Although individualization is important, certain common goals and treatment considerations also apply when working with many clients with a history of abuse. The treatment of victims of CSA should recognize the importance of a therapeutic relationship and should address the affective, cognitive, behavioral, and social effects of the maltreatment experience. Additionally, school professionals working with victims of CSA may be confronted with abuse-specific symptomatology.

***Post-traumatic stress disorder (PTSD).*** Victims of CSA may need assistance in understanding a variety of PTSD symptoms (e.g., nightmares, flashbacks, or feeling numb or "on guard," worrying that they may be "going crazy" or that they are the only one with these feelings). Books that explain the symptoms and strategies to decrease symptoms may offer hope. For example the PTSD Workbook in Cunningham and MacFarlane's (1996) *When Children Abuse* includes a developmentally sensitive explanation (e.g., although the actual PTSD terminology is explained in child-oriented language, the authors also encourage child clients to think of it standing for "Pretty tough stuff, Dude"). Specific suggestions for coping are offered, and children are encouraged to draw and write about their experiences. In working with those children who do develop PTSD (fortunately, most child sexual abuse victims do not), this could be a useful resource.

***Dissociation.*** One specific symptom that may deserve focused attention is dissociation. Herman (1992) describes this phenomenon:

> The child victim prefers to believe that the abuse did not occur. In the service of this wish, she tries to keep the secret from herself. The means she has at her disposal are frank denial, voluntary suppression of thoughts, and a legion of dissociative reactions. The capacity for induced trance or dissociate states, normally high in school-age children, is developed to a fine art. (p. 102)

The following steps have been recommended for directly addressing dissociation (Gil, 1991): (1) Develop a terminology comfortable to the child; (2) determine dissociate sequencing (identifying the physiological, emotional, and cognitive responses that occur when the child is dissociating); (3) explain dissociation as adaptive; (4) understand precipitants; (5) address the troublesome emotion (e.g., anxiety); (6) learn alternatives to the "escape" of dissociation (e.g., relaxation, deep breathing when feeling anxious).

***Sexual behavior problems.*** Another abuse-specific behavior that school-based practitioners should have some familiarity with is improper sexual behavior, which can be quite difficult to extinguish (Finkelhor & Berliner, 1995). A thorough review of the treatment of these issues is beyond the scope of this chapter and, in fact, has been the sole subject of several books (e.g., Ryan & Lane, 1997). Few school practitioners need to develop expertise in this area because they are not typically the primary therapist for children with severe sexual behavior problems. However, school personnel may serve a supportive role and so it may be helpful for them to have some basic information and be aware of relevant resources.

***Cutting and other self-injurious behaviors.*** A phenomenon increasingly being observed among high school students is a pattern of intentional, self-injurious behavior, which is typically "cutting" (see chapter 72, "Self-Mutilation"). Victims of CSA typically have not learned to regulate affect well, and because they experience overwhelming emotion in response to the abuse, they are in a predicament; there is great desire to turn off the pain but no way to do it. Self-injurious behaviors are often the paradoxical result of a desperate effort to get relief. Linehan's (1993) *Skills Training Manual for Treating Borderline Personality Disorder*, which includes chapters on emotional regulation and distress tolerance, along with handouts and homework sheets, is very appropriate for high school students.

### Group Treatment

Group treatment has a number of advantages, including reducing isolation and the myth of being the only one, developing positive peer relationships and countering the "damaged goods" view of self, giving students opportunities for role-playing and active learning, and making efficient use of school-based clinicians' time (see Horton & Cruise, 2001).

### Treatment Curricula and Therapeutic Books

School professionals may find it helpful to have a collection of therapeutic curricula and therapeutic books available to inform their treatment of CSA victims. Sources such as Hindman's (1991) *When Mourning Breaks* and *Paper Dolls and Paper Airplanes: Therapeutic Exercises for Sexually Traumatized Children* (Crisci, Lay, & Lowenstein, 1998) may be helpful, as each of these sources has numerous treatment exercises to address victims of various ages (see Recommended Resources).

## SUMMARY

CSA is an insidious form of maltreatment that occurs in the lives of many students, in many cases resulting in deleterious physical, emotional, behavioral, and academic effects. Schools have long been identified as social institutions that could make a positive difference in preventing and intervening in these cases. School psychologists and other school-based mental health service providers who are well informed on child sexual abuse are in a good position to lead these efforts.

Prevention is certainly the ideal goal. Broad-based prevention programming, which raises the issue of child sexual abuse, includes parents and children, and addresses risk factors, has the potential to prevent significant numbers of children from being harmed. Schools are in a uniquely powerful position to implement such efforts.

When students have already been abused, school professionals with healthy, balanced attitudes will provide the most therapeutic response; they understand that it is important to be open to disclosure, avoid overreacting or underreacting to sexual behavior, and be compassionate while holding high standards for students' behavior. In addition, school professionals need to understand the legal and ethical issues in reporting and help the child work through fears, doubts, and other obstacles to end the child's victimization experience. Making sure that a student receives needed therapeutic services is an additional powerful intervention, regardless of whether the intervention is abuse specific or a more generalized treatment and whether the services are offered in the community or are school based.

## RECOMMENDED RESOURCES

### Books and Other Printed Material

Crisci, G., Lay, M., & Lowenstein, L. (1998). *Paper dolls and paper airplanes: Therapeutic exercises for sexually traumatized children.* Indianapolis, IN: Kidsrights.

Numerous exercises are presented for addressing the negative outcomes of child sexual abuse. Exercises are for various ages and may be used in individual or group therapy.

Horton, C. B., & Cruise, T. K. (2001). *Child abuse and neglect: The school's response.* New York: Guilford Press.

A part of the Guilford School Practitioner Series, this book is practically based and aimed at helping school professionals identify and respond to the issue of child maltreatment. The book integrates findings from recent research and applies them to school-based practice. Topics range from identification and reporting of child maltreatment to treatment and prevention. Case examples and concrete suggestions are offered to assist in understanding and addressing the complexities of child maltreatment.

Johnson, T. C. (1999). *Understanding your child's sexual behavior: What's natural and healthy.* Oakland, CA: New Harbinger Publications.

This book is a good resource for parents and professionals who want to understand normal sexual development in children. Specific examples help readers to distinguish between developmentally appropriate sexual behavior and those actions that may be problematic. The author offers tips on how to talk to children about sex and the possibility of sexual abuse.

### Websites

*http://nccanch.acf.hhs.gov*

The website of the National Clearinghouse on Child Abuse and Neglect provides the latest incidence data, articles and handouts on identifying and reporting child abuse and neglect (including state regulations), and links to numerous resources regarding the intervention and prevention of child maltreatment. The site also offers access to a series of resource manuals for school personnel and social service providers.

*http://usdemo.missingkids.com*

The website of the National Center for Missing and Exploited Children offers resources for parents and educators regarding risk factors for sexual abuse and safety tips. The recent report discussing online solicitation of children is presented, along with tips for Internet safety.

*http://www.prevent-abuse-now.com/register.htm*

The website of the State Registries of Sexual Offenders provides links to each of the state's sex offender registries. It also offers links to some cities' registries and state registry laws. Prevention and reporting information is also discussed.

*http://www.ucalgary.ca/resolve/violenceprevention/English/reviewprog/childsxintro.htm*

The website provides an extensive list of child sexual abuse prevention programs. Additionally, this resource includes important information on how to evaluate such efforts.

## REFERENCES

Bolen, R. M. (2003). Child sexual abuse: Prevention or promotion? *Social Work, 48,* 174–186.

Center for Mental Health in the Schools. (1997). *School-based client consultation, referral, and management of care.* Los Angeles: School Mental Health Project, Department of Psychology, University of California–Los Angeles.

Cohen, J. A., Perel, J. M., DeBellis, M. D., Friedman, M. J., & Putnam, F. W. (2002). Treating traumatized children: Clinical implications of the psychobiology of posttraumatic stress disorder. *Trauma, Violence, and Abuse, 3,* 91–108.

Courtois, C. A. (1993). *Adult survivors of child sexual abuse.* Milwaukee, WI: Families International.

Crenshaw, W. B., Crenshaw, L. M., & Lichtenberg, J. W. (1995). When educators confront child abuse: An analysis of the decision to report. *Child Abuse & Neglect, 19,* 1095–1113.

Crisci, G., Lay, M., & Lowenstein, L. (1998). *Paper dolls and paper airplanes: Therapeutic exercises for sexually traumatized children.* Indianapolis, IN: Kidsrights.

Cunningham, C., & MacFarlane, K. (1996). *When children abuse: Group treatment strategies for children with impulse control problems.* Brandon, VT: Safer Society Press.

Daro, D. A. (1994). Prevention of child sexual abuse. *Future of Children, 4,* 198–223.

Davis, K. M., & Gidycz, C. A. (2000). Child sexual abuse prevention programs: A meta-analysis. *Journal of Child Psychology, 29,* 257–265.

Feeny, N., Foa, E., Treadwell, K., & March, J. (2004). Posttraumatic stress disorder in youth: A critical review of the cognitive and behavioral treatment outcome literature. *Professional Psychology: Research and Practice, 35,* 466–476.

Finkelhor, D., & Berliner, L. (1995). Research on the treatment of sexually abused children: A review and recommendations. *Journal of the American Academy of Child and Adolescent Psychiatry, 34,* 1408–1423.

Finkelhor, D., Mitchell, K., & Wolak, J. (2000). Online victimization: A report on the nation's youth. Retrieved May 1, 2005, from http://www.missingkids.com

Friedrich, W. N. (1996). An integrated model of psychotherapy for abused children. In J. Briere, L. Berliner, J. A. Bulkley, C. Jenny, & T. Reid (Eds.), *The American Professional Society on the Abuse of Children (APSAC) handbook on child maltreatment.* Thousand Oaks, CA: Sage.

Gibson, L., & Leitenberg, H. (2000). Child sexual abuse prevention programs: Do they decrease the occurrence of child sexual abuse? *Child Abuse & Neglect, 24,* 1115–1125.

Gil, E. (1991). *The healing power of play: Working with abused children.* New York: Guilford Press.

Gorey, K. M., & Leslie, D. R. (1997). The prevalence of child sexual abuse: Integrative review adjustment for potential response and measurement biases. *Child Abuse & Neglect, 21,* 391–398.

Herman, J. (1992). *Trauma and recovery.* New York: Harper Collins.

Hindman, J. (1991). *When mourning breaks.* Ontario, OR: AlexAndria Associates.

Horton, C. B., & Cruise, T. K. (1997). Clinical assessment of child victims and adult survivors of child maltreatment. *Journal of Counseling and Development, 76,* 94–104.

Horton, C. B., & Cruise, T. K. (2001). *Child abuse and neglect: The school's response.* New York: Guilford Press.

Illinois Department of Child and Family Services. (1998). *A manual for mandated reporter.* Springfield, IL: Author.

Johnson, C. F. (2004). Child sexual abuse. *Lancet, 364,* 462–470.

Johnson, T. C. (1999). *Understanding your child's sexual behavior: What's natural and healthy.* Oakland, CA: New Harbinger Publications.

Kaplan, S. J., Pelcovitz, D., & Labruna, V. (1999). Child and adolescent abuse and neglect research: A review of the past 10 years. Part I: Physical and emotional abuse and neglect. *Journal of the American Academy of Child and Adolescent Psychiatry, 38,* 1214–1222.

Kaufman, K. L., Holmberg, J. K., Orts, K. A., McCrady, F. E., Rotzien, A. L., Daleiden, E. L., & Hilliker, D. R. (1998). Factors influencing sexual offenders' modus operandi: An examination of victim-offender relatedness and age. *Child Maltreatment, 3,* 349–361.

Kendall, P. C. (2000). *Child and adolescent therapy: Cognitive-behavioral procedures* (2nd ed.). New York: Guilford Press.

Kendall-Tackett, K. A. (2000). Physiological correlates of childhood abuse: Chronic hyperarousal in PTSD, depression, and irritable bowel syndrome. *Child Abuse & Neglect, 24,* 799–810.

Krugman, R., & Jones, D. P. H. (1987). Incest and other forms of sexual abuse. In R. E. Helfer & R. E. Kempe (Eds.), *The battered child.* Chicago: University of Chicago Press.

Leiter, J., & Johnsen, M. C. (1997). Child maltreatment and school performance declines: An event-history analysis. *American Educational Research Journal, 34,* 563–589.

Linehan, M. M. (1993). *Skills training manual for treating borderline personality disorder.* New York: Guilford Press.

National Clearinghouse on Child Abuse and Neglect. (2004). *2004 child abuse prevention community resource packet.* Washington, DC: Author.

Paolucci, E. O., Genius, M. L., & Violato, C. (2001). A meta-analysis of the published research on the effects of child sexual abuse. *Journal of Psychology, 135,* 17–37.

Putnam, F. (2003). Ten-year research update review: Child sexual abuse. *Journal of the Academy of Child and Adolescent Psychiatry, 42,* 269–278.

Reed, L. D. (1996). Findings from research on children's suggestibility and implications for conducting child interviews. *Child Maltreatment, 1,* 105–120.

Rind, B., Tromovitch, P., & Bauserman, R. (1998). A meta-analytic examination of assumed properties of child sexual abuse using college samples. *Psychological Bulletin, 124,* 22–53.

Rispens, J., Aleman, A., & Goudena, P. P. (1997). Prevention of child sexual abuse victimization: A meta-analysis of school programs. *Child Abuse & Neglect, 21,* 975–987.

Ryan, G., & Lane, S. (Eds.). (1997). *Juvenile sexual offending: Causes, consequences, and correction.* San Francisco: Jossey-Bass.

Saunders, B. E., & Williams, L. M. (1996). Introduction to special section regarding treatment outcome studies. *Child Maltreatment, 1,* 293.

U.S. Department of Health and Human Services, Administration on Children, Youth and Families. (1999). *Child maltreatment 1997: Reports from the states to the National Child Abuse and Neglect Data System.* Washington, DC: U.S. Government Printing Office.

U.S. Department of Health and Human Services, Children's Bureau. (2004). *Child maltreatment 2002.* Washington, DC: U.S. Government Printing Office.

Whiffen, V. E., & MacIntosh, H. B. (2005). Mediators of the link between child sexual abuse and emotional distress: A critical review. *Trauma, Violence, and Abuse, 16,* 24–39.

# 62

# Poverty

**Elizabeth M. Whitehouse**
*University of Minnesota*

## BACKGROUND AND DEVELOPMENT

Poverty has become a pressing issue that cannot be ignored in educational policy and practice. The current national poverty threshold is $19,157 annual income for a household of four with at least two minor children (U.S. Census Bureau, 2005). If the total family income, which includes unemployment compensation, social security, child support, and other sources, is less than this threshold, then the family is considered to be in poverty. This figure is updated annually to account for inflation. However, many government aid programs use a different poverty measure. For example, the poverty guideline of the U.S. Department of Health and Human Services is currently $19,350 for a household of four members (U.S. Census Bureau).

According to the most recent U.S. Census Population Survey, the poverty rate for children in 2004 was 17.8%, up from 16.7% in 2002 (DeNavas-Walt, Proctor, & Lee, 2005; Proctor & Dalaker, 2003). This rate represents 13 million children and is higher than the rate for adults ages 18 to 64 and for seniors age 65 and older. Both the number of people in poverty and the rate of poverty have increased for four consecutive years, from 31.6 million and 11.3% in 2000 to 37 million and 12.7% in 2004 (DeNavas-Walt et al.). Further in 2004, about 10.2% of all families lived in poverty, and 28.4% of families headed by single mothers were in poverty (DeNavas-Walt et al.). Thus, many children in schools are experiencing poverty, indicating a need to disseminate information to school professionals who work with these children in various capacities.

Aside from the income threshold set by the government, the concept of poverty can seem quite vague. Poverty has been defined as the "extent to which an individual does without resources" (Payne, 2001, p. 16), of which income is only one. Other resources that children in poverty often lack include emotional, mental, spiritual, and physical resources; support systems; relationships; and role models. Financial differences alone do not explain why some are able to leave poverty and others are not. Furthermore, the problems associated with poverty are complex, deeply rooted, and value laden. The intent of this chapter is to provide information for educators and suggest best practices for working with students in poverty, not to imply that solutions for every problem are known and are merely not carried out in schools.

School professionals should remember several key points when they work with students in poverty. The discussion of these points below is drawn from Payne (2001), except as otherwise noted. First, poverty is relative and exists only in terms of relationships and expectations. What seems normal to one student or educator might be quite different from what their peers experience. Not all poor students view their situation as atypical. Second, poverty occurs in all ethnic groups and in all countries, though it is more prevalent in some than others. For example, in 2003 Black and Hispanic fourth graders were more likely than White fourth graders to be in high-poverty schools and less likely to be in low-poverty schools (National Center for Education Statistics, 2004). Finally, the concept of social class is somewhat ambiguous, as families fall along a continuum of income levels. Although poverty is defined according to one point on this continuum, the idea of social class is often applied to all families on this continuous line. Families can move along this continuum, and just because a family earns a certain level of income does not mean the issues discussed in this chapter apply to each child in that family. Also, the study of children and families in poverty is based on patterns, and all patterns have exceptions. The following sections describe other terms and concepts that may be important to remember when thinking about how to intervene with students living in poverty.

### Generational Versus Situational Poverty

It is important to distinguish between generational and situational poverty, as these different circumstances may lead to disparate outcomes. Generational poverty exists when a family earns below the poverty level for two or more generations. Conversely, situational poverty is caused by specific circumstances (e.g., death or divorce) and occurs for a shorter period of time. Some differences are characteristic of people in generational versus situational poverty; for example, those who have experienced poverty for longer periods of time tend to adopt the cultural norms of that group, whereas those in poverty temporarily often bring many resources with them from middle-class culture. This chapter focuses primarily on those students who experience generational poverty. However, many of the preventive efforts and interventions discussed may be useful for educators working with children in situational poverty as well.

### Cultural Rules

The concept of culture can refer to any group of people with shared beliefs, practices, and values. Therefore, social classes can be considered cultures, as they generate norms that relate to patterns of thought, social interaction, and cognitive strategies. The culture of poverty produces rules that govern how people act and how they are perceived with respect to intelligence and capability. School systems and many other institutions operate under middle-class rules, which are not made explicit and thus may be hidden and confusing to students in poverty. Even when a student's family income increases, the patterns of thought and interaction strategies that were adaptive when the student was in poverty can remain. For example, students in poverty might be more accustomed to using action to solve problems, whereas middle-class students might be more likely to see words as an important negotiating tool.

Therefore, educators must strive to understand the norms associated with poverty, as well as teach some of the rules that will help all students succeed in school. These school rules should not be looked upon as "correct" but as alternatives that may be more effective in certain situations (e.g., school and work), whereas the current rules will be more useful under other circumstances (e.g., in the community). This is important to keep in mind when working with parents as well, since they will likely operate under the same cultural rules as their children.

### Language Differences

Variations in the form and use of language also differentiate social classes. The school system, through instruction and standardized tests, typically employs the formal register, or standard sentence syntax. However, many children experiencing poverty are raised using the casual register, or more general word choice supplemented by nonverbal messages. The use of formal register is one of the hidden rules of the middle-class culture and may have little meaning for students in poverty. The pattern of conversation differs across these registers. In the formal register stories focus on getting to the central theme quickly, whereas the pattern is more circular in the casual register. Middle-class teachers may encourage children and parents to get right to the point of a story, which can be confusing and interpreted as rude. This use of the formal rather than casual register affects story structure as well. Children may struggle academically when they are expected to conform to a standard organizational pattern, because they are more comfortable writing a story that winds around the point before getting there.

## PROBLEMS AND IMPLICATIONS

Growing up in poverty has far-reaching effects on children's developmental outcomes. The following discussion of these effects draws from reviews by Evans (2004) and McLoyd (1998), except where otherwise noted.

The negative effects linked to poverty are not due to one particular condition; rather, poor children experience multiple and cumulative stressors. These stressors are both more frequent and more intense than those experienced by children not living in poverty and can affect physical health, academic achievement, and social and emotional well-being. It is especially important for educators to be aware of potential problems, as students in poverty can become accustomed to their situation and fail to identify supports they need (Chapman, 2003). Also, many of these conditions are due to the family's struggle for survival and not the result of negative parenting practices or lack of ability and intelligence.

## Physical Environment

Neighborhoods stricken by poverty are subject to a number of conditions that have a negative effect on the children who live there. The majority of research looks at urban rather than rural poverty, as poverty has become more concentrated in inner-city neighborhoods, though some problems may be present in both areas. These neighborhoods are often located closer to toxic waste dumps, show a higher prevalence of unsafe lead levels, and have more air pollution than affluent neighborhoods. Lead-based paint is often found in older residences, which are common in poor communities, in addition to higher levels of poisonous gasses. Children living in these areas are more often exposed to pesticides and carcinogenic emissions from factories. These children have less access to safe drinking water and are exposed to more noise than their peers. There is more traffic in poor neighborhoods, and play areas are more dangerous.

The immediate physical environments of these children are often harmful as well. Children in poverty are more likely to live in crowded homes that have structural defects and rodent infestations. They are more likely to have inadequate heat in the winter and are less likely to have safety devices such as smoke detectors and fire extinguishers. These homes are also less likely to have amenities such as washers and dryers and air conditioning. Finally, children from low-income households have less access to nutritious food.

The physical condition of schools is also different for children in poverty. These schools are more likely to have leaky roofs, inadequate heating, and poor ventilation and are often overcrowded. This primarily results from the unequal per-pupil expenditure for schools, as large urban school districts receive less funding than their suburban counterparts.

Children who attend school in low-income areas are absent more often, are more likely to have unqualified teachers, and experience a higher rate of teacher turnover than middle- or upper-class neighborhoods (National Center for Education Statistics, 2004). Violence in low-income schools is more prevalent; weapons are more likely to be present and the number of physical assaults is greater. The same conditions are found in low-income daycare facilities. Schools in low-income areas are also less likely to have computers, and when they do, students use them in less advanced ways (Becker, 2000).

As a result of their harsh living conditions, children from low-income families are more likely to have chronic health conditions such as asthma. Less access to nutritionally adequate food leads to weight loss, tiredness, headaches, inability to concentrate, and irritability. Their mothers' undernutrition during pregnancy also puts children at risk for neurological and cognitive problems and increases the rate of premature births. All of these factors can lead to diminished performance in school.

The high prevalence of violence and dangerous traffic levels in low-income urban neighborhoods increases the rate of childhood injuries. Lack of access to healthy recreational activities can lead to unhealthy leisure options such as alcohol and other drug use. Living in these conditions is associated with higher rates of externalizing behaviors and less-effective coping skills (Park, Turnbull, & Turnbull, 2002).

## Academic Struggles

Children living in poverty may experience less cognitive enrichment in their home environment than children from higher income households. An extensive study related to speech patterns among various social classes (Hart & Risley, 1995) showed that professional parents use three to four times more verbalization with their children and are far more responsive to children's verbal and nonverbal behaviors. Parents from lower social classes also are more likely to talk to children for the purpose of directing behavior rather than sustaining conversation. Parents of poor children tend to use a simpler vocabulary as well. As a result of these differing speech patterns, children in poverty often come to school with less rich vocabularies, affecting their ability to acquire reading and other academic skills.

Parent behaviors can affect student achievement in other ways as well. Early skill deficits in reading are associated with a history of adverse caregiving and are especially important because they tend to become larger over time (Ackerman, Brown, & Izard, 2004). Parents from low-income households are less likely than those from middle-income households to participate in literacy activities with their children, such as going to the library or reading. Sometimes, families cannot afford necessary school supplies or cannot provide a quiet space for their children to complete their homework. Also, poor parents tend to monitor their children's education less closely, are less likely to know their child's teacher, volunteer less often, and do not keep up with their children's homework assignments. These patterns are often a consequence of strict working conditions and lack of job benefits (Heymann & Earle, 2000) and, as mentioned earlier, may relate to the structural language barriers between families in poverty and educators. Furthermore, poor parents may not feel competent to help with homework and may define their role in education differently from their children's teachers (see also chapter 6, "Parent–Teacher Relationships").

In order to address language differences, teachers must encourage students in poverty to use the formal register in school. However, this language must be acquired naturally to be effective, and there must be a significant relationship between teachers and students that encourages students to begin using that structure (Payne, 2001). Unfortunately, forming these relationships is difficult because most teachers spend only 1 year with a class. Therefore, students in poverty frequently continue to use the casual register, hindering their ability to perform well on classroom tasks and standardized tests. Several other useful skills that students in poverty may not obtain in their home environment include developing a systematic method of exploration, organizing and measuring objects in space and time, using precision and accuracy when gathering information, and learning how to compare and contrast.

## Social and Emotional Issues

Children from low-income households are more likely to be separated from their families, spend time in foster care, and experience greater levels of violence. Parents in low-income families tend to be less responsive and exhibit harsher, more punitive parenting styles, relying more frequently on corporal punishment. Children from impoverished backgrounds are also often forced to take on an adult role when they are young (Payne, 2001). As adults, they become caught between being dependent and independent, without reaching a level of interdependence. This unhealthy balance causes some to lose needed emotional resources (e.g., stable and positive relationships or role models).

Many educators of students in poverty complain about these students' negative and disrespectful behaviors. However, these behaviors often help low-income students survive outside of school and are an inherent part of the culture of poverty (Payne, 2001). For example, students may laugh when disciplined to save face, or argue loudly with the teacher because they are accustomed to participatory disputes and have distrust for authority. Inappropriate comments may be related to use of the casual register, and physical fights may be part of their language of survival.

Parent stress levels are often high in low-income families, leading to depression and other mental health problems. Mothers in low-income housing have higher lifetime and current rates of major depression and substance abuse than their peers, and many report childhood abuse by a caregiver as well as violence in adulthood by a male partner (Bassuk, Buckner, Perloff, & Bassuk, 1998). Children's stress levels in these environments are also high, leading to feelings of unhappiness and anxiety (Park et al., 2002). Economic hardship can have a negative influence on the self-esteem of both parents and children living in poverty.

Peer rejection is a common experience for children in poverty. Children often feel stigmatized by their living situation and may be teased by peers for not having the right clothes or good hygiene (Gray, 2004). This peer rejection contributes to the higher dropout rate and delinquency among this population. Recognition that their circumstances do not meet some arbitrary requirement set by society can lead to a focus on what they do not have, contributing to low self-esteem, depression, and isolation (Gray). In addition, frequent residence changes often lead to loss of friends and social connections (Ackerman et al., 2004).

All of the problems described above can have devastating effects on the lives of children in poverty. Children need a sense of stability and consistency in their lives in order to feel secure, and this basic need is frequently not met for children in poverty. The longer children remain in poverty, the more diminished their resources become and the less likely they are to succeed in school.

## Resiliency

An emerging body of literature now focuses on children who have faced adversity and persevered. Often referred to as resilient, these children are able to overcome the challenges they face and succeed in society. Masten (2001) suggests that these children are not rare, and their ability to rise above their problems comes from typical resources within themselves, their relationships, and their community. This idea gives a more hopeful outlook for working with students in poverty.

Also, children living in poverty develop many strengths that they may not have otherwise. These children often have a superior inner strength, persist when facing adversity, and form strong kin networks (Gray, 2004). They recognize the hard work and sacrifice made by their caregivers and have deep respect and admiration for their families. These strengths should be kept in mind when working with students from low-income backgrounds. These assets can be used effectively to overcome limitations and must be taken into account when planning prevention and intervention efforts.

However, Pianta and Walsh (1998) note that this literature should be viewed with caution, as the study of resilience is still new, and studies detailing success stories are lacking. Furthermore, much of the research is cross-sectional, and students identified as resilient one year may be considered problematic the next. These authors state that resiliency should not be seen as solely residing in the child, the family, or the school. Rather, resilience is distributed across systems, and all of these systems interact. Pianta and Walsh also highlight process over product, noting that competence is a process occurring in the interactions of the student and the context in which the competencies develop; therefore the focus must be on developing competencies over time rather than teaching isolated skills. In general, the validity of the construct of resilience has yet to be established.

## ALTERNATIVE ACTIONS FOR PREVENTION

Although it is beyond the ability of educators to prevent the occurrence of poverty, many efforts certainly can be made to help bring families out of poverty and to alleviate its effects. For the purposes of this chapter, prevention is conceptualized as efforts directed toward developing and implementing effective public policy and research that can help families escape poverty. Intervention efforts are conceptualized as those designed to ameliorate long-term effects of living in poverty.

### Policy

Policy initiatives should have the goal of getting children and families out of poverty permanently rather than providing a temporary fix (Gray, 2004). When families become self-sufficient with respect to income, many of the problems associated with poverty are alleviated. Policy should also focus on removing barriers to learning as well as offering supports to enhance learning for students in poverty (Adelman & Taylor, 2000). Educators can become involved in policy reform in order to promote programs that enhance the lives of students in poverty.

Park et al. (2002) provide several key suggestions for policy reform that should help improve the conditions of families living in poverty. Health care initiatives should be considered to increase access to nutritious meals through programs such as Women, Infants, and Children (WIC), food stamps, and free and low-cost meals at school. Eliminating barriers for health care providers to accept Medicaid recipients would increase access to affordable care for low-income families. Physical environment changes, such as improving access to good housing in safe neighborhoods, would certainly have a beneficial effect on children. Increasing the number of law enforcement officers on duty in poor neighborhoods may create a safer environment and reduce crime. Neighborhood watch programs could be funded as well, so that those living in low-income areas are invested in the safety of their communities (Chapman, 2003).

Mental health services are essential for families experiencing poverty. Increasing funding for community services would provide more convenient access and more qualified professionals. Public policy should also continue to address better early childhood education for children in poverty, as well as high-quality elementary, middle, and high school public education. Rather than supporting programs that encourage parents to find any job available, educators can support policy that advocates for postsecondary education and training for employment that will be long-lasting and provide enough earnings to support a family (Gray, 2004). Educators can encourage these policy decisions by serving on committees, supporting fundraising organizations, and writing letters to local political officials.

### Research

To develop and implement effective prevention and intervention programs, continued research is needed. Because educators often deliver these prevention and intervention efforts, it follows that they would be involved in the research behind them as well. First, researchers need to establish causal relationships between certain aspects of living in poverty and specific child outcomes in order to more accurately target variables that are amenable to change. Furthermore, the concentration on child- and family-level secondary interventions, such as education and support services, may be inadequate (McLoyd, 1998). Although these strategies can help alleviate some of the problems associated with poverty, research on more global, primary strategies is needed. These strategies include policies that directly reduce poverty by raising families' income level and providing universal insurance.

Because people living in poverty experience many negative outcomes, including depression, anxiety, stereotypes, and violence, it is essential to discover the mechanisms by which poverty contributes to these outcomes in order to prevent and combat them. Researchers in education should distribute this information broadly, effectively, and in a practical manner to those practitioners who are working with children in poverty (American Psychological Association, 2000).

### Individual Action

Park et al. (2002) also stress the importance of individual educators and practitioners acting as advocates for children in school districts. Educators should strive to learn more about children living in poverty and the effects of low income on their physical, social–emotional, and academic well-being. These individuals can also discover ways to use school resources in creative ways, find outlets to obtain more resources, and partner with other school staff as well as outside service providers to meet individual student and family needs. Having a list of resources available ensures that important supplies will be ready when they are needed.

Additionally, evidence shows that supplemental school programs for students in poverty are effective in keeping them from falling or remaining behind their peers academically (Alexander, Entwisle, & Olson, 2001).These include preschool and full-day kindergarten, which disadvantaged children are often the least likely to attend. Educators can also teach summer classes and provide supplemental support during the school year for these students. Reading is a central part of the curriculum in these programs, though supplemental physical activity and enrichment are also important. According to Alexander et al., these interventions are most effective when used in combination, so that each program can build on previous efforts.

## ALTERNATIVE ACTIONS FOR INTERVENTION

Though preventing problems before they start is the best way to eliminate them, the high poverty rate is a harsh reality. Therefore, it remains imperative that effective interventions be in place for students already experiencing the negative effects of poverty. Schools are essential to the provision of services for these youth, and school psychologists in particular have a responsibility to recognize their physical, academic, and social–emotional needs. Interventions should also take context into account, as well as be purposeful and targeted toward specific desired outcomes (Chapman, 2003). Providing effective intervention strategies will help ensure that students living in poverty receive the same educational opportunities as their peers. Several of the following interventions reflect school-based recommendations or are embedded within larger programs and therefore have not been evaluated as separate components.

### Practitioner Training

First and foremost, educators must have explicit knowledge of the culture and values of poverty, which will increase their ability to work effectively with these students. In general, practitioner training needs improvement in the area of working with high-poverty students. Coursework in graduate programs should provide training in cultural competence, as well as inform students of the causes and impacts of poverty and successful interventions.

At the school level, many staff members will need information regarding the special needs of students living in poverty and ways to work with parents of these students. Workshops are an efficient way to emphasize how these students should be treated and to make clear what interventions will be implemented. General information about developmental issues and resources should be discussed, as well as the terms, concepts, problems, and implications outlined earlier in this chapter. Of greatest importance is that information about students' living situations should be treated as confidential to protect students' privacy and emotional well-being (Mizerek & Hinz, 2004).

### Basic Needs

Students' physical needs must be met before they can be expected to perform academically or develop healthy relationships with staff and peers. Schools can provide breakfast for students that are not able to eat a nutritious meal at home before school, and school staff may keep a supply of snacks in their classrooms for students who do not arrive in time for breakfast. Schools may also consider providing laundry facilities, showers, extra clean clothes, toothbrushes, and hairbrushes for students who do not have these items available at home. Having a nap room for students who do not get enough sleep at night may be needed. Finally, providing school supplies to these students can also be helpful (Mizerek & Hinz, 2004).

## Academic Assistance

The high mobility of impoverished students requires that school staff make efforts to keep track of these students and make sure their records are transferred to their new schools. As attendance is critical for success in school, staff should attempt to determine where these students are if a pattern of absence develops as a result of mobility.

Students may need other forms of academic help as well, such as having a peer or adult volunteer tutor. Times should be provided for these students to receive one-on-one assistance in areas in which they may be falling behind. Skills that are developed naturally by some may not have been picked up by students in poverty and need to be taught explicitly when they are of school age (Payne, 2001). Peer tutoring, if implemented correctly, can provide this instruction, with extra benefits such as building confidence and forming peer networks. Students should be paired thoughtfully, so that each student is benefiting in some way (e.g., one student has strong social skills and the other excels academically). Tutors can provide help with homework as well as teach skills that may not have been learned at home, such as data gathering and comparing and contrasting.

One study that explored the effects of teaching on reading growth in high-poverty classrooms found that asking higher level questions increased engagement. Furthermore, reading achievement scores and use of comprehension strategies were related to writing growth (Taylor, Pearson, Peterson, & Rodriguez, 2003). Strategies such as continually engaging students in active reading and modeling also predicted writing growth. To be effective, these activities may require more time than a teacher alone can give, emphasizing the need for support staff or volunteers.

Payne (2001) suggests several strategies for breaking down the languages barriers that often exist between students and teachers. First, students can write in the casual register with which they are comfortable and practice translating this into formal register. Graphic organizers that detail patterns of discourse may help increase understanding among all students, and telling stories in both formal and informal registers may provoke discussions of how language patterns make stories different and how stories remain the same. Though students should be taught that the use of formal register may be necessary in many future employment opportunities, educators should recognize and respect that the casual register is the primary method of discourse for many students in poverty.

In addition, students from low-income families may need extra time and materials to complete their assignments. Educators should not assume that these students did not complete their work because they lack motivation or ability. Schools can help by providing a quiet area for students to finish their homework and by supplying necessary materials for everyone when handing out assignments, so as not to single out particular students.

A study of several schools in Illinois provides examples of effective program components that relate to academic supports for students in poverty (McGee, 2004). Some of the commonalities among the schools that were successful in bridging the achievement gap between high- and low-income students included visible leadership that promotes high academic standards, high expectations, the valuing of education, the attitude that all students can succeed, an emphasis on early literacy, and increases in effective academic learning time.

## Relationship Building

As a result of negative school experiences, children in poverty often feel a lack of connectedness with school, which is associated with lower attendance and higher dropout rates (Christenson, Sinclair, Lehr, & Hurley, 2000). Therefore, it is crucial that educators find ways to help these students become more engaged in their academic environments (see chapter 4, "School Engagement"). Positive, warm relationships are essential for children and can be particularly important in the lives of children living in poverty. Teachers and other school staff are more important as role models for children from low-income families than has previously been recognized (Payne, 2001). Relationships provide the context in which children form their self-perceptions (Gray, 2004), and children in poor families may have fewer opportunities to spend time with others, both adults and peers. Thus, educators must be purposeful in encouraging relationship building among students who may not have this opportunity naturally.

One of the interventions that will help children in poverty develop more positive relationships with others is that of teaching them self-regulation of their behavior, an expected skill in middle-class school systems (Payne, 2001). Effective discipline for these students must include clear expectations for behavior and clear, consistent consequences that are contingent upon their behavioral choices. Educators can remind students of several appropriate behaviors when they display inappropriate actions; they also can model respect and emphasize the negative consequences of aggression. It is essential to understand the reasons for behavior, negotiate when possible, and suggest alternatives to negative behaviors. To promote relationship development in the classroom, schools may consider a looping method of teaching, in which students have the same teacher for more than 1 year. This practice gives students the opportunity to spend more time with the same peers, which encourages the development of friendship networks. It may also promote a more positive attitude toward school for both students and parents (Nichols & Nichols, 2002).

Close contact with families is important in planning and implementing interventions. Reliable contact with families can help increase attendance and heighten academic achievement by making caregivers and students feel more connected to school (Christenson, 2004). Furthermore, a child's perception of the meaningfulness of school may be influenced by parental involvement (Chapman, 2003). Primary caregivers often know students best and can provide critical information to school psychologists and other educators regarding the child's life outside of school. To develop contacts with families, schools must find ways to accommodate complicated work schedules or provide transportation for families that do not have access to their own.

To foster relationship building, schools should consider establishing a mentor program with local high schools and universities. Some students experiencing poverty lack role models who are academically successful. Mentors can provide such models and can work with the child on academics, social skills, and problem solving. For older students, career workshops and job shadowing may be beneficial (Chapman, 2003). In addition to developing appropriate coping and problem-solving skills, these kinds of relationships can provide information and know-how, temporary relief from emotional and time constraints, and connections to new people and resources (Payne, 2001).

In general, several moderators of program effectiveness have been recognized that can help schools identify characteristics of mentoring programs that are most important (see DuBois, Holloway, Valentine, & Cooper, 2002). These include continuing training for mentors, setting expectations for participation, providing structured activities for students and mentors to complete, fostering parental involvement, and monitoring program implementation. Mentoring programs are potentially most effective for youth identified as experiencing environmental disadvantage, and the quality of the relationship between mentors and students is important.

A specific intervention that encompasses these characteristics and focuses on the development of relationships is Check & Connect, which promotes partnerships between students, teachers, parents, and a monitor (Anderson, Christenson, Sinclair, & Lehr, 2004; see also chapter 8, "School Completion"). As a central component of Check & Connect, the monitor encourages student engagement in school by meeting with students each week to problem solve, complete academic activities, and work on social skills. Monitors, who are typically graduate students, also meet with families and teachers to facilitate communication. Another key feature of the Check & Connect model is persistence; monitors commit to working with students for at least 2 years and follow the student to their new school if they move.

Both student and monitor ratings of the quality of their relationship are associated with increased engagement in school. Furthermore, monitor ratings of relationship quality predict teacher ratings of student engagement, and students who were at higher risk showed the same quality of relationships with monitors and the same level of engagement as their lower-risk peers (Anderson et al., 2004). Another study looked at high school students with emotional behavioral disorders who participated in Check & Connect (Sinclair, Christenson, & Thurlow, 2005). Over two-thirds of these students were eligible for free and reduced lunch, indicating a high rate of students in poverty. Results showed that students who participated in Check & Connect were significantly less likely to drop out of school than controls. They also attended school more consistently and were five times more likely to complete school within 5 years.

## Full-Service Schools

Perhaps the most comprehensive intervention for students and families experiencing poverty is to maintain a full-service school. These schools make a variety of services available to students and their families at one convenient location, and they have the potential to incorporate all of the prevention and intervention efforts described in the preceding sections. Through full-service schools, families have access to necessary resources and can become more connected to their child's educational environment, and students have access to resources that can improve their social, emotional, physical, and cognitive functioning. This approach provides a single point of entry into a system of services, coordinates service delivery, can offer innovative approaches to improving outcomes for students, and can link services to future employment opportunities for students and their families (Park et al., 2002).

Full-service schools typically rely on collaboration and cooperation among several different agencies. These schools provide a wide range of services for both students and families, including health care, recreation, community events, mental health services, family planning services, drug treatment, adult education, and job preparation (Dryfoos, 1996). Perhaps one of the most important features of full-service schools is the individualized attention that the students and families receive (Dryfoos). However, substantial resources are also needed. For example, space must be provided for physicians, psychologists, social workers, lawyers, and others to provide services, often necessitating a separate building on or near school grounds. Furthermore, for full-service schools to be effective, collaborative relationships between agencies must be developed, and legal and ethical concerns must be addressed (McMahon, Ward, Pruett, Davidson, & Griffith, 2000). Negotiating roles, identifying goals, maintaining open and consistent communication, recognizing potential threats and discussing how they will be addressed, and monitoring changes and progress will help foster the development of collaborative support teams. At the same time, those involved in full-service schools must seek legal consultation and develop a mechanism for addressing ethical questions to deal with issues of shared information and consent. Other potential barriers to forming successful full-service schools include local politics, fiscal issues, and poor school attendance (McMahon et al.). However, these barriers can be overcome with careful planning, support, and collaboration.

The implementation of full-service schools is still in its beginning stages and has not been evaluated fully. Preliminary results indicate improvements in attendance and graduation rates (Park et al., 2002). Studies of specific programs have shown great promise for urban, high-risk populations of various ages (e.g., Dryfoos, 1994; Garrison, Roy, & Azar, 1999; McMahon et al., 2000). One program in particular, the AMIGO program, seeks to enhance students' personal, social, and academic competence through the provision of a range of services (Garrison et al.). These services include therapy for families and individuals, consultation with schools, in-home intervention, crisis intervention, parent education, and case management. Teachers and parents fill out surveys to evaluate student progress, and changes in attendance, grades, and study skills are monitored. Results show that one-half to two-thirds of teachers and 90% of parents report significant improvement in students' academic, personal, and social adjustment; behavior; and sense of family well-being. At the end of the 1995–1996 school year, 70% of students attended school at least 90% of the time, and 90% of students attended school at least 80% of the time. Finally, two-thirds of students were at grade level in math and one-third were at grade level in reading by the end of the school year.

## SUMMARY

The high poverty rate in the United States has made the issue of children experiencing adversity a prominent one in schools. These students are at risk for physical, cognitive, and social–emotional problems that certainly affect their academic achievement and general competence. This chapter gave some background about the culture of poverty and discussed the adversity these students face as well as the consequences of these conditions. Educators must take the lead not only in understanding the culture of poverty and in working to intervene effectively with these students, but also in developing and advocating for relevant policy and research and the improvement of training programs for future educators. It is imperative that this topic become more widely addressed in order to ensure that students who experience poverty receive an enriching and engaging education.

## RECOMMENDED RESOURCES

### Books and Other Printed Material

Dryfoos, J. G., & Maguire, S. (2002). *Inside full-service community schools.* Thousand Oaks, CA: Corwin Press.

Written by a principal who has implemented a full-service school and a well-known researcher in this area, this book offers both theoretical and practical perspectives. Information regarding the formation of full-service schools is provided, as well as hints for overcoming barriers and sustaining such programs. The authors include models for urban, suburban, and rural settings.

Evans, G. W. (2004). The environment of child poverty. *American Psychologist, 59*(2), 77–92.

This article stresses the consequences of cumulative risk exposure on children in poverty. Evans comprehensively reviews the literature related to the physical, social–emotional, and cognitive risks associated with the environment of childhood poverty.

Payne, R. (2001). *A framework for understanding poverty.* Highlands, TX: aha! Processes.

Payne presents a practical approach for working with students in poverty. She discusses the environment of poverty as a culture that clashes with the middle-class norms in today's schools. Payne gives background on the issues associated with poverty, discusses characteristics of students, and presents realistic strategies for educators.

## Websites

*http://www.ssc.wisc.edu/irp*

This website of the Institute for Research on Poverty is based at the University of Wisconsin–Madison and offers detailed research reports related to various issues associated with poverty. It lists publications and conferences on the topic, and provides links to other related sources.

*http://www.nlchp.org*

The National Law Center on Homelessness and Poverty strives to end homelessness and poverty, and their website gives information about several key issues such as housing, income, and education. Statistics as well as a discussion of the causes of and solutions for poverty and homelessness are also available.

*http://www.census.gov/hhes/www/poverty.html*

The Census Bureau website provides current and past statistics on poverty rates, thresholds, and other data that are updated annually. The site also presents detailed definitions of the kinds of income used to compute poverty status and describes how the thresholds are calculated, as well as the history behind the poverty measure.

# REFERENCES

Ackerman, B. P., Brown, E. D., & Izard, C. E. (2004). The relations between persistent poverty and contextual risk and children's behavior in elementary school. *Developmental Psychopathology, 40,* 367–377.

Adelman, H. S., & Taylor, L. (2000). Looking at school health and school reform policy through the lens of addressing barriers to learning. *Children's Services: Social Policy, Research, and Practice, 3,* 117–132.

Alexander, K. L., Entwisle, D. R., & Olson, L. S. (2001). Schools, achievement, and inequality: A seasonal perspective. *Educational Evaluation and Policy Analysis, 23,* 171–191.

American Psychological Association. (2000). *Resolution on poverty and socioeconomic status.* Retrieved June 21, 2004, from http://www.apa.org/pi/urban/povres.html

Anderson, A. R., Christenson, S. L., Sinclair, M. F., & Lehr, C. A. (2004). Check & Connect: The importance of relationships for promoting engagement with school. *Journal of School Psychology, 42,* 95–113.

Bassuk, E. L., Buckner, J. C., Perloff, J. N., & Bassuk, S. S. (1998). Prevalence of mental health and substance use disorders among homeless and low-income housed mothers. *American Journal of Psychiatry, 155,* 1561–1564.

Becker, H. J. (2000). Who's wired and who's not: Children's access to and use of computer technology. *The Future of Children, 10,* 44–75.

Chapman, M. V. (2003). Poverty level and school performance: Using contextual and self-report measures to inform intervention. *Children & Schools, 25,* 5–17.

Christenson, S. L. (2004). The family-school partnership: An opportunity to promote the learning competence of all students. *School Psychology Review, 33,* 83–104.

Christenson, S. L., Sinclair, M. F., Lehr, C., & Hurley, C. (2000). Promoting successful school completion. In K. M. Minke & G. G. Bear (Eds.), *Preventing school problems – promoting school success: Strategies and programs that work.* Bethesda, MD: National Association of School Psychologists.

DeNavas-Walt, C., Proctor, B. D., & Lee, C. H. (2005). *Income, poverty, and health insurance coverage in the United States: 2004* (U.S. Census Bureau, Current Population Reports, P60-229). Washington, DC: U.S. Government Printing Office.

Dryfoos, J. G. (1994). *Full-service schools: A revolution in health and social services for children, youth, and families.* San Francisco: Jossey-Bass.

Dryfoos, J. G. (1996). Adolescents at risk: Shaping programs to fit the need. *Journal of Negro Education, 65,* 5–18.

DuBois, D. L., Holloway, B. E., Valentine, J. C., & Cooper, H. (2002). Effectiveness of mentoring programs for youth: A meta-analytic review. *American Journal of Community Psychology, 30,* 157–197.

Evans, G. W. (2004). The environment of child poverty. *American Psychologist, 5,* 77–92.

Garrison, E. G., Roy, I. S., & Azar, V. (1999). Responding to the mental health needs of Latino children and families through school-based services. *Clinical Psychology Review, 19,* 199–219.

Gray, K. (2004). Children's lives in and out of poverty. In P. B. Pufall & R. P. Unsworth (Eds.), *Rethinking childhood.* New Jersey: Rutgers University Press.

Hart, B., & Risley, T. R. (1995). *Meaningful differences in the everyday experiences of young American children.* Baltimore, MD: Brookes.

Heymann, S. J., & Earle, A. (2000). Low-income parents: How do working conditions affect their opportunity to help school-age children at risk? *American Educational Research Journal, 37,* 833–848.

Masten, A. S. (2001). Ordinary magic: Resilience processes in development. *American Psychologist, 56,* 227–238.

McGee, G. W. (2004). Closing the achievement gap: Lessons from Illinois' golden spike high-poverty high-performing schools. *Journal of Education for Students Placed At Risk, 9*(2), 97–125.

McLoyd, V. C. (1998). Socioeconomic disadvantage and child development. *American Psychologist, 53,* 185–204.

McMahon, T. J., Ward, N. L., Pruett, M. K., Davidson, L., & Griffith, E. E. (2000). Building full-service schools: Lessons learned in the development of interagency collaboratives. *Journal of Educational and Psychological Consultation, 11,* 65–92.

Mizerek, E. A., & Hinz, E. E. (2004, May). Helping homeless students. *Principal Leadership, 9*(4), 10–13.

National Center for Education Statistics. (2004). *The condition of education 2004* (NCES 2004–077). Washington, DC: U.S. Government Printing Office.

Nichols, J. D., & Nichols, G. W. (2002). The impact of looping classroom environments on parental attitudes. *Preventing School Failure, 47,* 18–25.

Park, J., Turnbull, A. P., & Turnbull, III, H. R. (2002). Impacts of poverty on quality of life in families of children with disabilities. *Exceptional Children, 68,* 151–170.

Payne, R. K. (2001). *A framework for understanding poverty.* Highlands, TX: aha! Processes.

Pianta, R. C., & Walsh, D. J. (1998). Applying the construct of resilience in schools: Cautions from a developmental systems perspective. *School Psychology Review, 27,* 407–417.

Proctor, B. D., & Dalaker, J. (2003). *Poverty in the United States: 2002* (U.S. Census Bureau, Current Population Reports, P60-222). U.S. Washington, DC: Government Printing Office.

Sinclair, M. F., Christenson, S. L., & Thurlow, M. L. (2005). Promoting school completion of urban secondary youth with emotional or behavioral disabilities. *Exceptional Children, 71,* 465–482.

Taylor, B. M., Pearson, P. D., Peterson, D. S., & Rodriguez, M. C. (2003). Reading growth in high-poverty classrooms: The influence of teacher practices that encourage cognitive engagement in literacy learning. *Elementary School Journal, 104,* 3–28.

U.S. Census Bureau. (2005). *How the Census Bureau measures poverty.* Retrieved September 29, 2005, from http://www.census.gov/hhes/www/poverty/povdef.html

# 63

# Foster Homes

**Nancy A. McKellar**
*Wichita State University*

Look at the faces in any elementary classroom. One or more of those children probably do go home to their parents and siblings. Instead, they live with a family that is not their own. In 2002 in the United States, 532,000 children were in foster care (U.S. Department of Health and Human Services, 2004). The government includes in this figure children who live in one of eight settings, including institutions and group homes. One-fourth of this total lived with relatives, a situation called *kinship care* (see Dubowitz & Sawyer, 1994, for a review of kinship care; also see chapter 51, "Adoption," and chapter 58, "Custodial Grandchildren"). Almost half, or over 240,000 children, lived in a family home with non-relatives. It is these children whose needs are discussed in this chapter.

## BACKGROUND AND DEVELOPMENT

### Demographics of Foster Children

Although the average age at which children entered foster care in 2002 was 8.5 years, 40% of children entering foster care were younger than 6 (U.S. Department of Health and Human Services, 2004). Black children and White children account for similar proportions of the foster children population (37% and 39%, respectively), indicating that Black children are overrepresented with respect to their numbers in the general population. Children remain in foster care for a median of 18 months and a mean of 32 months, although some remain much longer. In Shin's (2003) study of 16- and 17-year-olds about to exit foster care, the average time in out-of-home placement was 8 years.

In the past 20 years, beginning in the mid-1980s, there have been significant changes in the children in foster homes, in both their numbers and their needs. The number of children in foster care, how long they stay in foster care, and the probability that they will reenter foster care during their youth have all increased. In each year between 1998 and 2002, more children entered than exited foster care (U.S. Department of Health and Human Services, n.d.).

Originally, foster care was developed to assist poor children, but now it is also used to provide safety and protection to maltreated children (Cameron, 2002). Today most children enter foster care as a result of serious abuse and neglect (Kelly, 2000; see chapters 60 and 61, "Psychological and Physical Abuse" and "Sexual Abuse"). Parental substance abuse has affected children prenatally and after birth. Increasing numbers of foster children are infected with HIV/AIDS or are affected by their parents' illness.

In 2002, 54% of children who exited foster care returned to their biological parents (U.S. Department of Health and Human Services, 2004). Just over 19,500 youth, or 7% of those exiting foster care in 2002, were emancipated—commonly referred to as "aging out" of the system—because they turned 18 or finished high school. Many youth age out of foster care without jobs, adequate educational preparation, or support systems. Of homeless individuals, 30% are former foster children (Hunter College School of Social Work, 2004).

### Common Experiences of Foster Children

Some youth report how important and helpful their relationships with foster parents were to them (Gilligan, 2000a). Foster homes may provide more security and predictability than the home from which the child was removed. Foster parents may emphasize education and give the child support and resources to succeed. When former foster children are compared with members of their biological families, they often are doing better both financially and in maintaining consistent employment (Kelly, 2000).

From the perspective of the child, foster care means living with strangers (Cameron, 2002). Depending on the age at which children entered foster care and whether they have contact with their families of origin, children may know very little about their biological parents. They may not have contact with their brothers and sisters. They have very little control over their lives. Their preferences and aspirations may never be sought by those who make decisions about whom they will live with and for how long. They may even be hungry because the food in their new foster homes is different from what they are used to.

Children in foster care may always feel like guests and never really feel that they belong in their foster homes. The foster parents may be caring for more than one foster child (Bates & Dozier, 2002), and these other foster children may arrive and depart unexpectedly and without explanation, further threatening any sense of security that the child may have built (Palmer, 1995). Foster children may not dare to get excited about upcoming events or school trips that the teacher describes because they know that they can be moved to another foster home without warning or preparation. Children may be moved to a new foster home in the middle of the academic semester and lose high school credit for the work they have already completed (Evans, 1997). Children in foster care may yearn to be in a home where they look like everyone else and have the same last name that they do. They may have no ready answers to questions from other kids, such as "Where's your mother?" and "Why don't you live with your parents?"

When children in foster care turn 18 and are emancipated, or exited from foster care, most of their peers will be graduating from high school and starting out on their own. Youth who are former foster children do not have a family home where they can come and go as they try out their ability to live independently (Palmer, 1995). They may not receive the emotional and financial support they need during young adulthood.

In sum, when children enter foster care, they have left much more than their biological parents. Typically, they have left their siblings, extended family members, friends, and teachers. With each subsequent move within the foster care system, they are forced to leave friends, foster families, and teachers. Many express anger at having to leave friends and others with whom they have established relationships (Gilligan, 2000a).

## PROBLEMS AND IMPLICATIONS

Many of the young children who enter foster care have serious and complicated problems involving their development, mental health, and physical health (American Academy of Pediatrics, 2000). Children typically enter foster care when they have been neglected or abused. Not surprisingly, they may suffer post-traumatic stress, anxiety, dissociation, and depression (Urquiza, Wirtz, Peterson, & Singer, 1994). Many are at significant risk for cognitive, academic, and behavioral problems. Lack of stimulation associated with neglect, as well as the trauma of abuse, can impair the brain development of children up to 3 to 4 years of age. Such neglect has serious consequences for the development of young children (American Academy of Pediatrics). These children may fail to form healthy psychological attachments with caregivers or with any adult, putting their development of emotional security and social conscience in great jeopardy (see chapter 29, "Attachment"). The lack of stimulation associated with neglect can lead to poor physical development as well as impaired communication skills. Antisocial behavior may develop.

### Emotional Outcomes

Entering and living in the foster care system is stressful for children. The stress experienced by the foster child is expressed differently depending on the child's age (see chapter 19, "Stress"). Infants may exhibit failure to thrive, withdrawal, or temper tantrums. Without a trusted caregiver, the young child does not develop appropriate ways to regulate negative emotions (Dozier, Higley, Albus, & Nutter, 2002). Babies who are placed in foster care after their first birthday are more likely than those placed earlier to have spent longer in neglectful or abusive situations, to have experienced more change in caregivers, and to be less likely to go to their foster mothers for comfort (Bates & Dozier, 2002). All these factors tend to challenge foster mothers' nurturing efforts.

The separation associated with placement in foster care is most likely to result in emotional disturbance in children between 6 months and 3 years of age, particularly if they were exposed to family discord and disruption prior to placement (American Academy of Pediatrics, 2000). Children this age do not yet have sufficient language abilities to use to cope with change and loss. Also, they are naturally anxious around strangers, which their new foster parents are to them. Finally, young children have limited life experiences coupled with a sense of time that is focused on the present, without an understanding of the distinction between temporary and permanent, all of which exacerbate uncertainty and stress.

As foster children grow older, they may become detached and apathetic and may daydream excessively (American Academy of Pediatrics, 2000). They may become avoidant or resistant (Dozier et al., 2002). They are easily overwhelmed and disorganized by stress. When in a threatening situation, they may act as though they do not need their caregivers. Older children may react to environmental stress by immediately ceasing any motor movement; this response may be misinterpreted as defiance or oppositional behavior (American Academy of Pediatrics).

Long-term foster care is most likely to be emotionally beneficial if the child is able to spend most of that time in a single, stable placement, allowing the child to identify strongly with the foster family. However, many youth in foster care report feeling stigmatized (Gilligan, 2000a). They feel different from their peers and others may treat them as different.

## Health Outcomes

Many children enter foster care in poor health and remain at high risk for multiple health problems while they are in foster care (Risley-Curtiss & Kronenfeld, 2001). Many have chronic and complex illnesses. Young children who have come from environments in which sexual promiscuity and substance abuse were common are at high risk for becoming infected with sexually transmitted diseases, such as hepatitis and HIV (American Academy of Pediatrics, 2002). Although many problems surround the providing of routine medical care to foster children, they are even less likely to receive dental or mental health services than medical care. Furthermore, psychological and behavioral problems are even more likely than physical problems. Children in foster care are more likely to receive special education services, especially those for emotional disturbance, than are their age peers. In an Illinois study (Goerge, Van Voorhis, Grant, Casey, & Robinson, 1992), 30% of school-age foster children were in special education.

## Educational Outcomes

Foster children do not have a biological parent to monitor their education and advocate for them when necessary. A study of foster children's educational experiences in nine California counties identified several problems (Bay Area Social Services Consortium, 2001). There were delays in enrolling foster children because their cumulative records were not transferred promptly and their immunization records were difficult to obtain. As a result, children missed time in school, and in some cases foster parents were asked to get new immunizations for their children, a possible health risk. Foster parents and social workers were not always knowledgeable about special education services and how to obtain them for the children for whom they were responsible. In general, the educational and child welfare systems did not communicate well with each other, so there was little sharing of information.

Information from biological parents and former teachers is much more limited because the child's biological parents may be uncooperative or incapable of providing accurate information about the child, and the child may have been transferred to a new school upon entering foster care (Urquiza et al., 1994). As a rule, foster parents need about a month to get to know the child and to wait for any honeymoon period to pass before they can provide helpful information about the child (Urquiza et al.).

Schools have difficulty keeping track of children in foster care because such children are moved to new foster homes frequently. When foster children change schools, their current foster parents often do not have information about their prior educational performance and needs. Problems in locating and transferring educational records were reflected in the finding that for one-third of the school-age children entering foster care in Arkansas from 1995 to 1999, it was not known whether they were previously receiving special education services (Evans, Scott, & Schulz, 2004). Foster children also may not remain in a school district long enough to be assessed to determine their eligibility for special education services (Zetlin, Weinberg, & Luderer, 2004).

From the foster child's perspective, transferring to a new school means adjusting to new teachers and peers (Vera Institute of Justice, 2004). The curriculum may match poorly with that of the previous school. Special services may be disrupted. Foster children are often excluded from activities such as field trips, after-school tutoring, or sports teams because foster parents may believe that they do not have the authority to sign the required permission forms, and their caseworkers are too busy finding safe homes for children to attend to school permission slips.

Many foster children function at a lower educational level than their peers, below their own potential, or both (McDonald, Allen, Westerfelt, & Piliavin, 1996). Shin (2003) found that a third of youth who were aging out of foster care had reading levels below sixth grade. In their study of almost 3,500 school-age children entering foster care in Arkansas, Evans and his colleagues (2004) found alarming evidence of intellectual, achievement, and language problems: 10% had IQs below 70 and 88% had at least one academic or language score in the first (lowest) quartile. Achievement deficits were greatest in the skill areas of basic reading, math calculation, and written expression. Since learning these skills typically occurs through formal instruction, these deficits may reflect the harm of disruptions in regular school attendance related to foster care placement.

Being in foster care does not appear to be a direct cause of children's academic difficulties (McDonald et al., 1996). Instead, children enter foster care behind their peers academically and foster care does not compensate for the early deficiencies in their lives. They perform poorly in school even in comparison with other children in poverty (Vera Institute of Justice, 2004). Their academic difficulties are compounded when they miss school because they are moved among foster homes. Many are forced to miss classes for mandated medical and court appointments (Vera Institute of Justice). Those foster children with more emotional and behavioral problems, those with learning disabilities, and those who need or have an Individualized Education Plan are less likely to be succeeding in school (Bay Area Social Services Consortium, 2001). The high school graduation rate of youth in foster care is below that of the general population (McDonald et al.), and their educational attainment overall is lower (Shin, 2003).

## ALTERNATIVE ACTIONS FOR PREVENTION

Schooling is a key influence in the development of children. According to Sylva (1994), "Pre-school experiences put in motion a virtuous cycle of learning orientation at school entry, followed by teacher recognition and expectation, followed by pupil self concept, school commitment and finally success in adult life" (p. 162). School can be a stable force in foster children's lives and can provide the skills that they need to support themselves as adults (Vera Institute of Justice, 2004). In other words, providing foster children with high-quality educational experiences should be understood as primary prevention. The school has the potential to be a powerful force toward normalizing the lives of children in foster care (Gilligan, 1998). The first step is to get children into school and then to align the educational services with the skills and needs of the individual student.

In the Casey National Alumni Study (Casey Family Programs, 2003), nine characteristics predicted the level of success that former foster children achieved in adulthood. Five of these characteristics are ones that schools can positively affect: (a) life skills preparation, (b) completion of a high school diploma or the GED before exiting foster care, (c) scholarships for college or job training, (d) participation in organizations and clubs for youth while in foster care, and (e) use of tutoring services to minimize academic problems. Similarly, Shin (2003) found four variables that significantly predicted educational attainment, operationalized as reading achievement, in youth exiting foster care. Three of these variables can be the focus of prevention efforts by schools: (a) aspiration for higher education, (b) participation in extracurricular education, and (c) avoidance of illicit drugs.

Children who have experienced extreme adversity and lost much of the control that they had over their lives desperately need a sense of accomplishment and supportive relationships (Gilligan, 2000b). School is a setting in which the foster child may receive both. Supportive relationships may be formed with teachers, teacher aides, the school secretary, or the custodian (see chapter 5, "Student–Teacher Relationships"). Mentoring programs that provide students with adults who model problem solving, persistence, and achievement have the potential to enhance the foster youth's educational aspirations (Shin, 2003; see also chapter 33, "Achievement Motivation").

Accomplishment in academics is important but not the only possibility for achievement. Some children may gain their sense of accomplishment through extracurricular activities (e.g., school newspaper or choir), positions of responsibility (e.g., school crossing guard), or sports. Examples of hobbies and interests that can enhance resilience include music, swimming, football, skiing, art, dance, and care of animals (Gilligan, 2000b).

Professionals from social service agencies and education must collaborate in order to address the needs of foster children (Goerge et al., 1992). Periodic progress report meetings about the child's education can increase communication between the student, foster parents, caseworker, and teacher (Evans, 1997). Schools should take the initiative to schedule frequent, perhaps monthly, meetings of the teacher, foster parents, and caseworker to discuss the accomplishments and needs of the student in foster care. Written records of the information shared at these meetings can be added to the caseworker's file on the child. Then, if the student moves abruptly to another school, the caseworker will have educationally relevant information to share even if the child's school records are not transferred promptly.

## Foster Parents

Of the almost 50,000 children adopted from foster care in 2002, 61% were adopted by their foster parent or parents (U.S. Department of Health and Human Services, 2004), suggesting that these adults are more permanent in the lives of foster children than is sometimes assumed. Foster parents provide the day-to-day care of foster children. They are the adults who make sure the children are at school on time, have their homework completed, have had breakfast, and are appropriately dressed for the weather. Many young people report that their time in foster care was helpful because of positive relationships with foster parents or social workers involved in their daily lives (Gilligan, 2000a).

Foster parents report that they want to be involved in their children's schools to learn about their foster children's behavior at school and to help educators get to know the children (Bay Area Social Services Consortium, 2001). If foster parents are unsure what information to seek about their child, teachers can encourage and support their involvement by suggesting questions that they might want to ask (see Table 1). Teachers might structure the information shared at the conference around similar questions.

**Table 1** *Questions for Foster Parents to Ask at School Conferences*

1. How is my child doing? In what ways is my child doing well? What difficulties or challenges is my child having?
2. What is the best way for me to help my child with homework? How much help should I give?
3. Has my child completed all required work to date? What is he or she missing? Can the work be made up?
4. What are the academic standards for the grade? Is my child meeting them? If not, what can I do to help?
5. What standardized tests will my child take this year? How are students being prepared for these tests? What can I do at home to help?
6. What services are available in the school to help my child? What other resources are available?
7. If my child is not learning or behaving as well as expected, how will I be notified?

*Note.* From *Foster Children & Education: How You Can Create a Positive Educational Experience for the Foster Child*, by the Vera Institute of Justice, 2004, Appendix; retrieved August 27, 2004, from *http://www.vera.org/publication_pdf/241_452.pdf*

## School Professionals

The Committee on Early Childhood and Adoption and Dependent Care of the American Academy of Pediatrics (2000) has recommended that special attention be given to providing young children in foster care with basic stimulation coupled with stable, predictable, loving care from at least one adult. Multiple moves among foster homes as well as the premature return to the biological parents compound the child's emotional trauma. The implication for early childhood education of foster children is that teachers need to be sensitive and responsive to the children's need for stability and predictability (Dozier et al., 2002). A consistent, structured, warm classroom environment is recommended. Behavior problems, either internalized or externalized, can be the child's response to stress.

The teacher is the professional with whom foster children have the most contact (Gilligan, 1998). Teachers can help to counter instability in the life of a foster child by providing structure and predictability (Hunter College School of Social Work, 2004). Routines, opportunities for practicing skills, and prior discussion of schedule changes are important classroom practices. Foster children often feel stigmatized. Teachers and other educators should be careful to protect their right to privacy, no matter how tragic or sensational the circumstances that led to the child's placement in foster care. By using classroom materials and books that include foster and adopted children, teachers can help foster children to feel less different from their peers. Teachers need to be sensitive to the difficulties that foster children will have in completing certain assignments, such as bringing their baby picture to school or constructing a family tree, and to offer students alternative activities.

## School Policy

Schools must give special attention to maintaining the continuity of educational services and records when foster children change homes, whether to another foster home or to their biological parents' home. Multiple moves among foster homes and the resultant moves to new schools certainly contribute to the academic delays experienced by foster children. However, part of the problem is the lack of available services, such as tutoring, to help the child with school-related problems or the underutilization of available services (Curran & Pecora, 1999).

When secondary school students change schools in the middle of the semester, they typically lose credits for incomplete classes. If schools were to develop procedures for assigning credits in less than whole blocks, the academic progress of foster children would be less negatively affected by the abrupt moves to which these children are often subjected (Bay Area Social Services Consortium, 2001). Even when students move during the school year, they could receive credit for the work they have completed.

"Being in foster care affects both the way students behave in school and educators' reactions to them" (Alshuler, 2003, ¶ 17). Some children express their anger and frustration at school more readily than in their foster homes. On the other hand, educators may assume that every child in foster care will have problems, or they may attribute every behavior concern that the child has to the problems of the biological parents. The challenge to educators is to treat children in foster care like other children but with understanding and compassion for the challenges that they face. Educators need to provide consistent structure and clearly communicate expectations for both academic and behavioral performance.

## ALTERNATIVE ACTIONS FOR INTERVENTION

### Guidance and Emotional Support

Children and youth in foster care want to participate in the planning and decisions that affect their lives (Curran & Pecora, 1999). Though this is true of all children as they move into adolescence, foster children have had decisions about where they live, with whom they live, the contact they can have with their families and friends, and the school they attend made by persons who are not involved in their daily lives and with whom they may have only limited contact. Including foster youth in planning their educational programs responds to their need for control over their lives and can also be used to guide them in developing goals and self-advocacy skills.

Many foster children need a single adult who has the responsibility of monitoring the child's education and advocating for needed services (Vera Institute of Justice, 2004). If the child's caseworker or foster parents do not assume this role, then school personnel can choose to designate a teacher or related services staff to support the foster child in this way.

Experience has taught many foster youth to be hesitant about trusting adults (Hunter College School of Social Work, 2004). Their expectation may be that teachers will also fail them. Educators need to be patient and consistent as they work to develop trusting relationships with students in foster care.

### Information Sharing

If confidentiality rules are barriers to information sharing, child welfare agencies should seek ways to separate school information from the highly confidential information about the family and child in the case record so that the educationally relevant information can be shared more easily with the school (Bay Area Social Services Consortium, 2001). Two strategies to combat the current delays in transmitting records and sharing information are to create information databases that all schools statewide can access and to use Health and Education Passports (Bay Area Social Services Consortium). Eleven states use the health passport to record health care information and facilitate communication among those responsible for foster children (Risley-Curtiss & Kronenfeld, 2001). These documents contain information about the child's development, physical health, and immunizations (PEATC, n.d.). They can be expanded into health and education passports that also contain the schools the child has attended, attendance record, academic performance and grade level, and special needs. The passport stays with the child as he or she goes into new placements to facilitate the incumbent changes.

### Evaluation

Given the circumstances that lead to placement in foster care for most children, the American Academy of Pediatrics (2000) recommended that evaluations of young children include assessment of the following areas: gross and fine motor skills, cognition, speech and language, self-help skills, emotional well-being, coping skills, relationships to persons, behaviors, and adequacy of caregiver's parenting skills. Special attention needs to be given to the extent to which the child's instruction has been disrupted by multiple foster home placements.

Kirby and Hardesty (1998) recommend that a neuropsychological screening instrument be included in the assessment, because many foster children have been victims of physical abuse, have traumatic birth histories, and have physical abnormalities. Recommendations can be used to suggest to foster parents, as well as teachers, appropriate discipline approaches and ways to increase the child's sense of belonging and stability.

Psychoeducational evaluations of children in foster care present certain challenges. Foster parents may not have the long-term knowledge of the child that would enable them to provide accurate information for adaptive and other behavior rating scales (Urquiza et al., 1994). Curriculum-based assessment and observation will need to assume a prominent place in the evaluation.

Multidisciplinary teams face special challenges in determining whether children in foster care are eligible to receive special education services for learning disabilities or language disorders. Severe discrepancies between ability (as indicated by IQ) and achievement or language are found much more frequently in foster children than in the general population of children (Evans et al., 2004). Also, children in foster care have typically suffered environmental, economic, or cultural disadvantages. The multidisciplinary team must decide whether the severe discrepancy is primarily the result of these disadvantages. If the team automatically excludes foster children from special education services because of the presence of these disadvantages, then children in foster care are disenfranchised from potentially beneficial educational services simply because they are in foster care. However, with few or no records or access to biological parents or former teachers, distinguishing whether an exclusionary factor is the primary reason for the severe discrepancy can be extremely difficult.

**Table 2** *Serving the Needs of Students in Foster Care: Checklist for School Professionals*

Systems and procedures are in place to ensure that:

- New students in foster care are identified.
- Foster parents are welcomed into the school community and informed of the school's calendar, policies, and expectations.
- Records are transferred rapidly when a foster child changes schools.
- An individual or school team assumes the responsibilities of advocate for students in foster care.
- Teachers have been trained to assess the skills of new students to meet the educational expectations in their classrooms. Teachers submit their assessments within 2 weeks to the designated advocate.
- The school nurse assesses the vision, hearing, general health, and medical needs of new students within 2 weeks.
- Foster children are invited to participate in extracurricular activities and sports.
- Tutoring is available to minimize academic problems.
- Foster children participate in planning their educational programs.
- Periodic progress meetings are held with teachers, foster parents, and the caseworker. The caseworker is given written records of educationally relevant information discussed at the meeting for inclusion in the caseworker's file on the child.
- Secondary students receive proportional credit for partially completed courses.
- Guidance counselors help secondary school students obtain admission and financial support for college or postsecondary school training.

## Classroom Considerations

Effective classroom environments are exciting places to learn, where children are presented with new ideas to investigate. Children are encouraged to explore, take risks, and test limits in the acquisition of new knowledge and skills. However, the new and unknown in any sense is exciting only if one has a secure base. Foster children often lack that. For them, new activities and situations are more likely frightening. Educators need to explain new situations to foster children, clarifying expectations and limits. Teachers need to be aware that worry about biological parents and siblings may interfere with the foster child's focus on educational activities and assignments (Vera Institute of Justice, 2004).

Tutoring should be provided to foster children who have low academic skills as well as to those whose educational experiences have been disrupted by a move during the school year (Shin, 2003). These services need to be available to middle and high school students, not just elementary children (Avery, n.d.). Teens can be provided with volunteer mentors who advise them about course selection, volunteer and part-time job opportunities, college applications, and financial aid for higher education (see Table 2 for a checklist of school practices to meet the needs of students in foster care).

## SUMMARY

Children and youth in foster care face the challenges of growing up while living with families to whom they are not related. Most children enter foster care as a result of parental neglect, and these children have more physical, academic, and behavioral problems than their peers. They experience anxiety and stress in response to the separation from their biological parents and siblings and to the frequent, sudden changes that characterize life in foster care. Delays in transferring their educational records and in assessing their needs impede their progress in school.

Schooling can be a valuable preventive force in the lives of foster children by providing stability, belonging, skills, and successful experiences. Procedures for transferring medical and educational information and for increasing the involvement of foster parents in their children's schooling need to be implemented. Teachers should encourage and be supportive of foster children and also provide clear, consistent expectations and consequences. If no adult has assumed the responsibility of mentoring and advocating for the foster child, then the school should identify someone to support the child in this way.

## RECOMMENDED RESOURCES

### Books and Other Printed Material

Cameron, T. (2002). *Foster care odyssey: A black girl's story.* Jackson, MS: University Press of Mississippi.

The author was abandoned at birth and spent the first 19 years of her life in foster care because her mother did not legally free her to be adopted. Although she experienced the foster care system in the 1950s and 1960s, she gives a poignant description of the system from the child's perspective that is relevant today.

Kelly, G. & Gilligan, R. (Eds.). (2000). *Issues in foster care: Policy, practice and research.* London: Jessica Kingsley Publishers.

Research and practical suggestions are integrated well in chapters that address issues applicable to home and school, including managing children's behavior and promoting resilience.

### Websites

*http://www.casey.org*

The Casey Family Foundation's website contains publications and links to other resources related to foster care.

*http://www.fosterclub.com*

FosterClub, sponsored by the National Network for Youth in Foster Care, is a website for youth in foster care. There are companion websites for teens transitioning out of foster care (*http://www.fyi3.com*) and for adults (*http://www.fosterclub.com/grownups*). Youth can join the FosterClub, read letters from others in foster care and articles about foster care, and interact with other members on the message board.

*http://www.vera.org/publication_pdf/241_452.pdf*

The Vera Institute of Justice's *Foster Children & Education: How You Can Create a Positive Educational Experience for the Foster Child* contains practical information on minimizing the barriers that foster children face in getting an education. Appendices contain English and Spanish versions of handouts with questions for parents to ask at parent–teacher conferences and tips on helping with homework.

## REFERENCES

Alshuler, S. J. (2003). From barriers to successful collaboration: Public schools and child welfare working together [Electronic version]. *Social Work, 48,* 52–63.

American Academy of Pediatrics, Committee on Early Childhood, Adoption, and Dependent Care. (2000). Policy statement: Developmental issues for young children in foster care [Electronic version]. *Pediatrics, 106,* 1145–1150.

American Academy of Pediatrics, Committee on Early Childhood, Adoption, and Dependent Care. (2002). Policy statement: Health care of young children infoster care [Electronic version]. *Pediatrics, 109,* 536–541.

Avery, J. (n.d.). *Education and children in foster care: Future success or failure?* Seattle, WA: New Horizons for Learning. Retrieved August 27, 2004, from http://www.newhorizons.org/spneeds/inclusion/collaboration/avery.hym

Bates, B. C., & Dozier, M. (2002). The importance of maternal state of mind regarding attachment and infant age at placement to foster mothers' representations of their foster infants. *Infant Mental Health Journal, 23,* 417–431.

Bay Area Social Services Consortium, Center for Social Services Research, School of Social Welfare, University of California, Berkeley (2001). *Education for foster children: Removing barriers to academic success.* Retrieved July 22, 2004, from http://cssr.berkeley.edu/bassc

Cameron, T. (2002). *Foster care odyssey: A black girl's story.* Jackson, MS: University Press of Mississippi.

Casey Family Programs. (2003). *Assessing the effects of foster care: Early results from the Casey National Alumni Study.* Retrieved July 22, 2004, from http://www.casey.org/Resources/Publications/NationalAlumniStudy.htm

Curran, M. C., & Pecora, P. J. (1999). Incorporating the perspectives of youth placed in family foster care: Selected research findings and methodological challenges. In P. A. Curtis, G. Dale, Jr., & J. C. Kendall (Eds.), *The foster care crisis: Translating research into policy and practice* (pp. 99–125). Lincoln, NE: University of Nebraska Press.

Dozier, M., Higley, E., Albus, K. E., & Nutter, A. (2002). Intervening with foster infants' caregivers: Targeting three critical needs. *Infant Mental Health Journal, 23,* 541–554.

Dubowitz, H., & Sawyer, R. J. (1994). School behavior of children in kinship care. *Child Abuse & Neglect, 18,* 889–911.

Evans, B. (1997). *Youth in foster care: The shortcomings of child protection services.* New York: Garland Publishing, Inc.

Evans, L. D., Scott, S. S., & Schulz, E. G. (2004). The need for educational assessment of children entering foster care. *Child Welfare, 83,* 565–580.

Gilligan, R. (1998). The importance of schools and teachers in child welfare [Electronic version]. *Child and Family Social Work, 3,* 13–25.

Gilligan, R. (2000a). The importance of listening to the child in foster care. In G. Kelly & R. Gilligan (Eds.), *Issues in foster care: Policy practice and research* (pp. 40–58). London: Jessica Kingsley Publishers.

Gilligan, R. (2000b). Promoting resilience in children in foster care. In G. Kelly & R. Gilligan (Eds.), *Issues in foster care: Policy practice and research* (pp. 107–126). London: Jessica Kingsley Publishers.

Goerge, R., Van Voorhis, J., Grant, S., Casey, K., & Robinson, M. (1992). Special-education experiences of foster children: An empirical study. *Child Welfare, 71,* 419–437.

Hunter College School of Social Work. (2004). *Traditional toolkit.* Retrieved July 22, 2004, from http://www.hunter.cuny.edu/socwork/nrcfcpp/foster-care-month/trad-toolkit.html

Kelly, G. (2000). Outcomes studies of foster care. In G. Kelly & R. Gilligan (Eds.), *Issues in foster care: Policy practice and research* (pp. 59–84). London: Jessica Kingsley Publishers.

Kirby, K. M., & Hardesty, P. H. (1998). Evaluating older pre-adoptive foster children [Electronic version]. *Professional Psychology: Research and Practice, 29,* 428–436.

McDonald, T. P., Allen, R. I., Westerfelt, A., & Piliavin, I. (1996). *Assessing the long-term effects of foster care: A research synthesis.* Washington, DC: Child Welfare League of America.

Palmer, S. E. (1995). *Maintaining family ties: Inclusive practice in foster care.* Washington, DC: Child Welfare League of America.

PEATC. (n.d.). *Steps to overcoming barriers.* Retrieved August 27, 2004, from the Parent Educational Advocacy Training Center website: http://www.peatc.org/FosterCare/overcoming_barriers.htm

Risley-Curtiss, C., & Kronenfeld, J. J. (2001). Health care policies for children in out-of-home care. *Child Welfare, 80,* 325–350.

Shin, S. H. (2003). Building evidence to promote educational competence of youth in foster care. *Child Welfare, 82,* 615–632.

Sylva, K. (1994). School influences on children's development. *Journal of Child Psychology and Psychiatry and Allied Disciplines, 35,* 135–170.

Urquiza, A. J., Wirtz, S. J., Peterson, M. S., & Singer, V. A. (1994). Screening and evaluating abused and neglected children entering protective custody. *Child Welfare, 73,* 155–171.

U.S. Department of Health and Human Services, Administration for Children and Families, Children's Bureau. (2004). *The AFCARS report (9).* Retrieved April 19, 2005, from http://www.acf.hhs.gov/programs/cb/publications/afcars/report9.pdf

U.S. Department of Health and Human Services, Administration for Children and Families, Children's Bureau. (n.d). *Data and information systems: The AFCARS reports.* Retrieved July 22, 2004, from http://www.acf.hhs.gov/programs/cb/dis/afcars/publications/afcars.htm

Vera Institute of Justice. (2004). *Foster children & education: How you can create a positive educational experience for the foster child.* Retrieved August 27, 2004, from http://www.vera.org/publication_pdf/241_452.pdf

Zetlin, A., Weinberg, L., & Luderer, J. W. (2004). Problems and solutions to improving education services for children in foster care [Electronic version]. *Preventing School Failure, 48,* 31–36.

# 64

# Chronic Illness

**Kathy L. Bradley-Klug**
*University of South Florida*

**Elizabeth Chesno Grier**
*University of South Carolina School of Medicine*

**Erin E. Ax**
*University of South Florida*

## BACKGROUND AND DEVELOPMENT

More children than ever before in American schools are living with chronic illness. Chronic illnesses and disabilities consist of "congenital disorders involving the central nervous system (CNS; e.g., seizure disorders), acquired disorders of the CNS (e.g., traumatic brain injury), disorders not primarily involving the CNS (e.g., asthma, cancer), and biopsychosocial disorders (e.g., ADHD, substance abuse)" (Power, Heathfield, McGoey, & Blum, 1999, p. 251). For children with chronic illnesses, medication monitoring, special diets, invasive procedures, and frequent hospitalizations are a reality. These illnesses and their management can affect the child's cognitive, academic, educational, social, emotional, and behavioral functioning.

Recent medical advances have increased live birth rates and infant survival. Such advances have changed the way we characterize the conditions themselves, as many acute illnesses have become chronic conditions, and previously incurable illnesses are now often either curable or managed in such a way that individuals are able to function in everyday life activities (Eiser & Morse, 2001). This increased ability to manage diseases, coupled with recent health care reforms and increased access to treatment, has lengthened life expectancy and the functional capability of many children with chronic illness.

To address the increase in health and mental health services required by children, reforms in health care have shifted delivery of services from inpatient and outpatient clinics and hospitals to community organizations (Power, 2003). The school, as a community-based organization, is the place where most children are served. The academic, social, and emotional needs of children with chronic illness should be addressed through the use of a comprehensive assessment procedure followed by the implementation of interventions based on a decision-making process.

Within a comprehensive system of health care, school psychologists are seen as health care providers that supply services to children with chronic illness (Nastasi, 2000). They, along with other school-based professionals, are in a unique position to link school and other community organizations and, through these partnerships, to provide access to resources for children and families (Nastasi; Power, 2003). With this role, school professionals may need to develop new competencies to work with communities to better the quality of life for children with chronic illness. School personnel must familiarize themselves with available resources to assist in the development and maintenance of effective interventions. This involvement includes the initiation of collaborative relationships with medical personnel such as local pediatricians and hospital educators.

The purpose of this chapter is to provide an overview of the various problems children and adolescents with chronic illness may encounter. Primary, secondary, and tertiary approaches to prevention and intervention are discussed and examples are provided. A problem-solving model designed specifically to address the multiple challenges faced by children with chronic illness provides a decision-making framework for working with individual children. Finally, the chapter discusses future directions that may directly affect the training and daily practice of all educators.

# PROBLEMS AND IMPLICATIONS

Chronic illnesses and disabilities are common among children and youth, with estimates ranging from 10% to 15% of children age 18 years or under to 20% of the population of children in school (Brown & DuPaul, 1999). The prevalence rates of chronic illnesses in the pediatric population are surprising (see Table 1). Some of the more common chronic illnesses include asthma, cancer, diabetes, eating disorders, sleep disorders, and traumatic brain injury (TBI). Less common but just as critical conditions include cystic fibrosis, sickle cell disease, seizure disorders, and HIV/AIDS. Research indicates that although many children with chronic illness are able to successfully meet the expectations of the educational system, about 40% experience some type of school-related difficulties (Nabors & Lehmkuhl, 2004). This chapter will touch on issues relevant to all chronic diseases in children and adolescents; however, it will focus on life-threatening illnesses and their impact on the cognitive, academic, social, emotional, and behavioral outcomes of children and adolescents. The reader also is referred to specific chapters in this volume that cover the topics of asthma and allergies, HIV/AIDS, seizure disorders, TBI, overweight, and chronic headaches.

## General Cognitive Issues

Certain chronic illnesses and injuries may result in mild, moderate, or major cognitive impairments. The cognitive abilities of a child can be compromised as a direct result of the disease or injury itself, as a result of the medications used to treat the symptoms of the disease, or by the stress and anxiety associated with living with a chronic illness. For example, most research on children with cystic fibrosis (CF) suggests that this illness has a very mild impact on cognition. Although young children with CF may demonstrate some delays in intellectual functioning, these delays are typically resolved by 5 years of age and the intellectual functioning of older children is similar to that of their healthy peers (Batsche & Tunnicliffe, 1998). In comparison, 11% to 17% of children with sickle cell disease experience silent cerebral infarcts, which may be associated with moderate problems related to inattention and executive dysfunction (Kral & Brown, 2004). Children with acute lymphocytic leukemia (ALL) and brain tumors who survive are at risk for severe neurocognitive consequences as a result of CNS damage related to the disease itself and the indirect treatment effects (Moore, 2005). Only through consultation with medical professionals and comprehensive assessment can the specific impact of a chronic illness for an individual child be determined.

In many cases, medications used to treat the illness may result in disruption of cognitive abilities. Specifically, some research has shown that antipsychotic medications can have adverse effects on the cognitive performance of some individuals (Phelps, Brown, & Power, 2002). One must keep in mind that, to date, researchers have not been able to reliably predict the responses that individuals will have to various pharmacological treatments. Therefore, educators must work closely with prescribing medical personnel to continuously monitor the effects of medication on children's performance in school. In addition, educators should be notified when a change in pharmacological treatment occurs.

Given the stress and anxiety that may be experienced by an individual who has been diagnosed with a chronic illness or who is dealing with the daily effects of the symptoms of the disease, normal cognitive functioning may be disrupted. Often stress and anxiety in children and adolescents are manifested as inattentive and hyperactive behaviors. Thus, if educators are aware of the medical issues related to a particular child, positive preventive interventions may be implemented to help the child cope with the stress and anxiety and decrease the impact on educational performance.

## General Academic and Educational Implications

Children with chronic illness often are absent from school because of frequent medical appointments, illness-related complications, side effects of medications, and hospitalizations. As a result, these students miss valuable instructional time in the classroom and are often delayed in the acquisition of skills. Although some illnesses may have a direct effect on the child's ability to function well academically, many times the learning problems that are encountered by a child with a chronic illness are the result of missed opportunities to learn. In these cases, delays in learning can be prevented if individualized intervention is provided early (Armstrong, Blumberg, & Toledano, 1999). For example, without warning, children with

**Table 1** *Pediatric Prevalence Rates of Common Chronic Illnesses in the United States*

| Illness | Prevalence |
|---|---|
| Anorexia nervosa | 1 out of every 200 adolescents (typically girls) 12–18 years of age report behaviors of anorexia, as well as 3–10 out of every 200 children in early and middle adolescence. |
| Asthma | Asthma affects 4–5 million children under 18 years of age and is considered to be the most common chronic illness in children and adolescents. |
| Bulimia nervosa | 2%–19% of children and adolescents report behaviors of bulimia, including 12%–19% in high school and college-age adolescents. |
| Cancer | Approximately 8,500 children each year are diagnosed with some form of cancer before 15 years of age. |
| Cystic fibrosis | CF affects 25,000–30,000 primarily Caucasian individuals. More than 50% of individuals with CF are diagnosed by 6 months of age, and 70% are diagnosed by 1 year of age. |
| Diabetes | 1 in every 500–600 children under the age of 20 has Type 1 diabetes; Type 2 diabetes accounts for 10%–20% of new cases of diabetes in youth and disproportionately affects African American, Hispanic American, and Native American youth. |
| HIV/AIDS | 9,074 cases are reported in children below 13 years of age and 4,428 cases are reported in adolescents between 13 and 19 years of age. |
| Obesity | 11%–22% of children and adolescents are overweight. |
| Seizure disorders | 2.3 million Americans have a seizure disorder; 1%–2% of children experience a seizure disorder, and 10% of Americans will experience a seizure at some point in their life. |
| Sickle cell disease | 1 in every 400–500 African American newborns and 1 in every 1,000–1,400 Hispanic American newborns are diagnosed with sickle cell disease each year. |
| Sleep disorders | 10%–20% of children experience sleep difficulties throughout childhood, including 6%–22% in infancy and early childhood, 43% in later childhood, and 33% in adolescence. |
| Traumatic brain injury | 1 million children and adolescents sustain a brain injury every year. TBI is the most common cause of death of American children. |

*Note.* Information provided in this table was gathered from both the Centers for Disease Control and Prevention website (*http://www.cdc.gov*) and from "Prevention of Disease and Injury in Pediatric Psychology," by M. C. Roberts, K. J. Brown, R. E. Boles, J. O. Mashunkashey, and S. Mayes, 2003, in M. C. Roberts (Ed.), *Handbook of Pediatric Psychology* (3rd ed., pp. 84–98), New York: Guilford Press.

sickle cell disease may experience severe bouts of pain or pain crises that may result in hospitalization (Bonner, Gustafson, Schumacher, & Thompson, 1999). Coordination between school personnel, hospital educators, and homebound instructors is critical to limiting the amount of missed instruction these children may encounter.

Not all pediatric illnesses necessarily result in missed opportunities for learning or in learning difficulties. For example, children with asthma and other allergic disorders suffer minimal educational consequences if their conditions are well managed and if there is clear communication between caregivers and educators (Bender, 1999).

It appears that the severity of the disease is a critical variable in determining the impact on the child's cognitive and academic functioning. For instance, research in the area of Type 1 diabetes has shown that children at greatest risk are those with early onset and longer duration of the disease. Also, individuals who have difficulty maintaining metabolic control will likely have more problems in school (Holmes, Cant, Fox, Lampert, & Greer, 1999).

Educators, because of their lack of knowledge related to a chronic illness, may have difficulty setting appropriate expectations for a child who is ill. In some cases, expectations may be lowered when unnecessary. In other cases, particularly when the disease is less obvious (e.g., sickle cell disease), educators may be less willing to make accommodations or to reassess their expectations because of their lack of understanding of the impact of the disease on academic functioning. There also is a tendency to stereotype children based on the disease or illness type. For example, negative stereotypes often are associated with CF (e.g., delayed intellect). Knowledge of chronic illnesses can help to eliminate stereotypes and myths, allowing for individual problem solving around the specific needs of the child.

## General Family Issues

Families of children with chronic illness undergo a tremendous amount of stress and fatigue (also see chapter 52, "Families of Children With Disabilities"). Caregivers of children with pediatric health issues may even experience symptoms similar to post-traumatic stress disorder (Schwartz & Drotar, 2004). The financial impact on the family may be quite significant, particularly if one parent has to stop working in order to manage the day-to-day treatment of the illness or be available to attend regular medical visits. Depending on the family structure, some caregivers may be better able to cope with the experience of having a child with a chronic illness than others. Specifically, youth with chronic illness who come from families in which the father is absent tend to have more problems with treatment adherence and increased issues with psychological adjustment than those from families where the father is present (Wysocki & Gavin, 2004). Educators should be sensitive to the needs of the chronically ill child's siblings in the school system as well. For example, siblings of children with cancer may experience both behavioral and emotional distress (Labay & Walco, 2004).

Caregivers often are trying to cope with a significant amount of anxiety and stress that result from the long-term health, treatment adherence, and overall safety issues related to raising a child with a chronic illness (Mellin, Neumark-Sztainer, & Patterson, 2004). As a result, caregivers may either appear to be disconnected from issues related to education or very concerned about their child's level of functioning in school. In both cases, they may lack the physical and mental energy necessary to maintain ongoing relationships with school personnel. In addition, some parents may become overprotective of their child and may restrict their child's involvement in school and social activities because of their illness-related concerns (Anthony, Gil, & Schanberg, 2003).

An additional stressor for families may be lack of familiarity with school issues and uncertainty about how to communicate and collaborate with school personnel. In some cases, the family may equate a child's reentry to school with a return to normality and may not be prepared for the social and academic difficulties that lie ahead. Families may also be in need of guidance regarding services available at school.

In summary, if they are not acknowledged, family issues surrounding a child's experience with chronic illness can significantly affect the child's progress and development. Educators who are knowledgeable of family issues related to chronic illness and develop strategies to deal with these issues are important to the child's successful educational experience.

## General Social, Emotional, and Behavioral Issues

***Social issues.*** Children with chronic illness often struggle with issues related to peers in the school setting. In some cases, because of their lack of understanding, peers are concerned that they will "catch" the child's disease. Peers are reluctant to engage in contact with the child, particularly in circumstances in which the disease or treatment of the illness results in a change in the child's physical appearance (e.g., hair loss of child who has had chemotherapy or the short stature of children with CF). The child with the illness may also be embarrassed by his or her appearance and may choose not to interact with peers, instead withdrawing from social interactions. Educators need to be aware of these potential social implications of chronic illness and must be prepared to provide support for the child with the illness as well as education of the peers.

***Emotional and behavioral issues.*** Given the critical nature of the diagnosis and treatment of any type of pediatric chronic illness, especially life-threatening illnesses such as sickle cell disease, cystic fibrosis, or cancer, one would expect that the literature would be rife with studies showing significant differences in emotional and behavioral functioning in afflicted children compared with their healthy peers. However, this is not the case. Most of the research indicates that there are few differences between children with chronic illness and their normal peers. Studies that have shown differences are often criticized because of small sample size or weak methods. At best, the research is mixed in this area. The following paragraphs highlight some of the more recent research in the areas of sickle cell disease, cystic fibrosis, and cancer.

A growing body of literature suggests that "stress and mood play a role in the fluctuating course of symptoms in chronic illness" (Gil et al., 2003, p. 364). Episodes of pain experienced by individuals with sickle cell disease have been shown to lead to moodiness and stress in adolescents. It is also hypothesized that this increase in moodiness and stress may exacerbate pain (Gil et al.). Because pain associated with sickle cell disease can have an unpredictable onset, these individuals may experience stress throughout their daily activities because they do not know what may or may not precipitate an acute pain episode. Thus, this relationship between pain, stress, and mood appears to be cyclical.

Cystic fibrosis is a terminal illness, and the children and families affected by this disease must cope with the daily medical management of the disease along with the fact that CF inevitably leads to death. Despite the graveness of this disease, most research studies to date have not found significant differences in the emotional or behavioral functioning of children with CF when compared with their healthy peers. However, because of the delayed development of secondary sexual characteristics and because of short stature, some individuals with CF may express anxiety about being teased by peers and being less physically active than their peers (Stark, Mackner, Patton, & Acton, 2003).

Children with cancer who have been recently diagnosed may experience distress related to fear of the unknown, pain, disruption of routine, and discomfort caused by treatment. This emotional response does not appear to be pervasive, and children with cancer who return to school are not reported as behaving any differently than their peers (Vannatta & Gerhardt, 2003).

Clearly, individuals with chronic illness may suffer from time to time with a variety of emotional and behavioral outcomes. Although some of these emotional sequelae may be expressed in overt, observable behaviors, for other individuals these emotions are not as easily observed. What seems to be consistent across the literature on chronic illness is that each individual's level of functioning and adaptability are related to any number of factors, including the individual's understanding of the disease, family functioning, existence of supportive social relationships, and overall quality of life. Educators must be aware of the possible emotional and behavioral outcomes of chronic illness and consistently monitor the child in order to provide support when necessary.

### Quality of Life

Health-related quality of life (HRQoL) is a concept that considers an individual's ability to function in daily life when trying to cope with an illness (Quittner, Davis, & Modi, 2003). More specifically, HRQoL reflects the individual's perception of the impact of the illness and subsequent treatments on his or her overall well-being (Quittner et al.). Although the medical literature reflects an intensive focus on the assessment of HRQoL with regard to children and youth with chronic illnesses, there has been little focus on adapting these findings to the school setting. It is the role of school psychologists and other educators to develop appropriate, evidence-based interventions for academic, social, and emotional skill deficits that consider the whole child. When developing these interventions, educators need to take into account children's HRQoL, specifically addressing children's perceptions of how their disease and the interventions in place to assist them are affecting their daily functioning in the educational setting.

Educators are obligated to take into account children's perspectives of what is happening to them and for them, and must ask if children are truly benefiting from the current educational situation. As stated by Armstrong and colleagues (1999), "After saving the life of the child with cancer, salvaging their quality of life is the next most important priority" (p. 201).

## ALTERNATIVE ACTIONS FOR PREVENTION

School is becoming a more important setting for prevention efforts (e.g., Power & Blom-Hoffman, 2004), and school-based health centers are being developed to provide children and families easier access to a variety of services, including health-related needs (e.g., Fuemmeler, 2004; Meyers & Swerdlick, 2003; Shaw, 2003). School-based professionals can support children with chronic illnesses through a variety of primary, secondary, and tertiary interventions, including advocating for the child, providing direct services, consulting to support health promotion, coordinating services, developing programs, and engaging in research and evaluation to find efficient and successful methods to help these children (Power, DuPaul, Shapiro, & Parrish, 1998). The following subsections review in more detail the application of prevention efforts with the population of children with chronic illness.

## Primary Prevention

Chronic illnesses generally cannot be prevented. However, school professionals can be knowledgeable about health promotion in order to decrease the numbers of avoidable illnesses as well as those of preventable diseases and injuries that can affect a children's health. Primary prevention includes making changes to the environment, modifying human behavior, and influencing legislation (Roberts, Brown, Boles, Mashunkashey, & Mayes, 2003). Modifying the environment pertains to making structural changes to ensure safety and to promote health. For example, many schools unfortunately support unhealthy lifestyles by offering high-calorie and high-fat foods in school lunches and in snack machines, which can lead to poor nutrition and promote weight gain. Studies have shown a dramatic increase in the numbers of obese children, and these children have a high risk for developing Type 2 diabetes and cardiovascular disease (Jelalian & Mehlenbeck, 2003; see also chapter 74, "Childhood Overweight"). Changing menus and offering nutritional snacks can support health.

Changing behavior in children may include creating educational programs in the school setting to support healthy lifestyles (e.g., teaching the importance of nutrition, limited television time, strategies to reduce stress, and exercise) and to prevent problems affecting health (e.g., training to prevent smoking and substance abuse and educating students about sexually transmitted diseases; Meyers & Swerdlik, 2003). Also, injury risk can be reduced through awareness programs (Roberts et al., 2003). Finally, legislation can support health-related services in the school setting. For instance, major diseases (e.g., polio, measles, and rubella) can be avoided within the school setting by offering children immunizations to prevent health problems.

Another example of primary prevention related to health disorders is training in universal precautions to prevent the spread of disease. This training is required in most educational settings to promote the safety and wellness of all students and staff. Typically, training is facilitated through the school health coordinator or school risk management personnel. Training of school personnel in the potential transmission of blood-borne diseases such as HIV/AIDS has been shown to increase compliance with universal precautions, particularly in the use of disposable gloves (Grier & Hodges, 2001). Thus, it appears that primary prevention strategies can have an impact on the behavior of those in the educational setting.

## Secondary Prevention

Secondary prevention efforts are intended for populations of children who are at risk for chronic illnesses. For instance, children who have obese parents are at risk for being overweight, and research has been conducted to educate these parents about providing nutrition for their children with positive results (Jelalian & Mehlenbeck, 2003). Harrell and colleagues (1998) have designed a school-based intervention program to improve the heart health of children with such risk factors as obesity, physical inactivity, and smoking. The intervention was designed so that general education teachers, using kits provided by the American Heart Association, could teach children about the importance of getting regular exercise, making wise choices about heart-healthy foods, and choosing not to smoke. The program also involved an aerobic exercise component that can be adopted by physical education teachers in the school. The effectiveness of the program was demonstrated through reductions in cholesterol and higher health knowledge for students in the treatment group as compared with the control group.

Another population of individuals often targeted for secondary prevention efforts includes those at risk for HIV/AIDS (see chapter 65). In the area of HIV/AIDS, the risk groups to be targeted include children and adolescents suspected of alcohol or drug use, children and adolescents suspected or known to engage in sexual behavior, and pregnant teenage mothers. It is recommended that programs be developed and implemented that meet the specific and unique needs of each of these groups (Wodrich, Swerdlik, Chenneville, & Landau, 1999).

## Tertiary Prevention

Tertiary prevention is geared to the population of children who already have a diagnosed chronic illness and is intended to prevent associated problems. Prevention efforts can be aimed at several levels, including the individual child with the chronic illness, family members, educators, medical professionals, and community members. All of these levels involve several commonalities, including awareness, knowledge, and collaboration.

***Individual child.*** For the child with a chronic illness, interventions must be determined on an individual basis. One of the priorities with any illness is to educate the child about the symptoms, side effects of medications, importance of treatment adherence, and any limitations that they must accept in daily routines. Once children know about their illness, they can better serve as advocates for themselves within the educational setting. An example of a new program that has been developed to educate children and adolescents about CF is *Fitting Cystic Fibrosis into Your Life Everyday.* Developed by the STARBRIGHT Foundation, this 30-minute program on CD-ROM was designed to increase individuals' knowledge about their disease and to teach them coping skills. Children using the program increased their knowledge of CF and improved their ability to generate effective coping strategies (Davis, Quittner, Stack, & Yang, 2004). Consumer satisfaction reports from the participants recommend the program's use with parents, siblings, classmates, and teachers for providing basic information on CF in a way that is efficient and fun. Similar types of programs are available that focus on pediatric cancer, such as *Why? Charlie Brown, Why?*, a video published by the Leukemia and Lymphoma Foundation, and *The Sickle Cell Slime-O-Rama Game*, also offered through the STARBRIGHT Foundation.

***Family.*** Educating caregivers about their child's illness and its implications is crucial and should teach them specific ways to help their child be as successful as possible across settings. School personnel should encourage caregivers to become well versed in their child's illness and may assist caregivers in finding up-to-date, reliable, and valid information resources. Knowing the community resources that are available to families (e.g., Sickle Cell Disease Association, Children's Cancer Center, and Epilepsy Society) is invaluable. Educators are encouraged to contact their county or state health department for a list of resources available to children and families in their area.

Caregivers also need to be knowledgeable about the types of services available to their child. Children with chronic illnesses have several legal protections that also provide special services if needed. The Individuals with Disabilities Education Act (IDEA) includes an avenue through which children can receive services (the Other Health Impaired, or OHI category) if the illness *adversely affects* the child's learning (Jacob & Hartshorne, 2004; Grice, 2002). With OHI eligibility, children with chronic illnesses have access to special education support, depending on their individual needs. If the effects of the illness are not considered severe enough to reach the standard of adversely affecting the child's learning but still *substantially limit* one or more major life activities (which can include learning), then a Section 504 plan under the Rehabilitation Act of 1973 can be created to provide the child with accommodations within the general education classroom (Jacob & Hartshorne). Both legal options offer children interventions tailored to their individual needs to support their learning. However, the level and intensity of interventions, as well as the accountability, differ.

As a student eligible as OHI under IDEA, an Individual Education Plan (IEP) would be developed that allows the child access to special education services to help meet goals and objectives in areas such as academic, social, emotional, behavioral, language, development, and motor skills. In contrast, a Section 504 plan is created individually for the child to provide accommodation and intervention strategies. These would typically be implemented in the general education classroom setting or school environment to support the child's needs associated with his or her illness. Because both plans are intended to provide individualized interventions to the student with a chronic illness, both parents and educators often find it confusing to decide which route to take. Unfortunately, the literature offers school-based teams little guidance on how to decide which level of service is appropriate. The decision regarding whether a Section 504 plan or an OHI designation is warranted depends upon what options will best meet the child's individual needs ("Don't Confuse OHI's Definition," 2001).

Medical homebound is another placement option mandated by federal law (Madan-Swain, Katz, & LaGory, 2004) if a child cannot attend school as a result of health problems. A child is not required to have an IEP or Section 504 plan to have access to this intervention. It requires a doctor's statement detailing the reasons why a child is medically unable to attend school. For example, a child who is receiving chemotherapy may become very ill and weak for several weeks at a time. Or a child recovering from surgical treatment of a brain tumor may need substantial recuperation time. Medical homebound services can provide the child with learning opportunities at home so that absenteeism does not adversely affect educational progress. If a child who does not have a Section 504 plan or an IEP through OHI is being recommended for homebound services, a team of educators, parents, and health professionals should collaborate to determine what level of other services (i.e., OHI or Section 504 plan) the child may need in addition to homebound services. The commonality among all school options discussed is that a team meeting should be held to determine the appropriate level of services and interventions necessary to meet the needs of the individual child.

***Educators.*** Educators need to be informed about those children within their educational setting who have been diagnosed with a chronic illness. This information may be available in the child's cumulative school folder or through the school nurse if parents have disclosed the information to the school system. Not only must classroom teachers be knowledgeable of a particular student's illness and related issues, but all school personnel should be informed, including classroom aides, lunch room attendants, bus drivers, physical education teachers, administrators, and others. Because the chronic illness may affect the child in every activity he or she encounters during the course of the day, all personnel must be aware of the symptoms and must know what action to take if a crisis occurs. For example, if a child with sickle cell disease has a pain crisis on the bus, the bus driver should know how to respond in order to maintain the safety of the child with the illness as well as the safety of the other children. With the consent of parents or guardians, the school nurse, psychologist, counselor, and social worker can serve as excellent resources in the educational setting to ensure that appropriate knowledge and plans of action are distributed across all relevant school personnel.

The key to preventing further difficulties for a child with chronic illness is education and collaboration for all of those involved. There is a wealth of information and research about many childhood illnesses and their implications. Understanding these issues can lead to the prevention of problems associated with chronic illness. In order for interventions to be effective, educators need to be aware of the impact of chronic health issues on all aspects of the child and on that child's family.

## ALTERNATIVE ACTIONS FOR INTERVENTION

The impact of a chronic illness varies for each child, depending on the nature of the illness and the individual child's needs. Yet the implications on each area of a child's functioning can be significant if prevention efforts are not taken seriously. The literature is replete with the notion that collaboration is needed to support children in the school setting. It is necessary for school professionals to partner with medical professionals and families in order to proactively provide services to children with chronic illness and to implement intervention strategies for problems. Medical professionals and educators "have traditionally worked in parallel without regular communication or mutually identified objectives" (Farmer & Clippard, 1995, p. 49). It is suggested that without communication and collaboration, rehabilitation may not be as successful, and reentry into school after hospitalization may be compromised. Thus, the establishment of a strong link between medical professionals and educators is critical to the development of positive educational and functional outcomes for children with chronic health issues. Contacting local and state school health advisory councils is recommended to help facilitate this collaborative link.

### Collaborative Problem-Solving Approaches

The incorporation of a systematic and consultative problem-solving approach is another way to facilitate collaboration across professionals. It can help guide educators in understanding the problematic behavior of the child with a chronic illness as well as his or her ecology, resulting in the development and implementation of effective interventions. The research literature has not previously included an approach that is specifically aimed at addressing the unique needs of a child with a chronic medical condition in the educational setting. The Biopsychoeducational Model of Consultation for the assessment, intervention, and evaluation of children with pediatric health issues was recently introduced (Grier & Bradley-Klug, 2005). This model provides a structured guide to working with children with chronic illness in the school setting, addressing all areas of their functioning in the most efficient manner. The model also has a foundation of problem solving, an activity in which most school psychologists are well versed. As the team leader, the school psychologist or other school-based professional can guide the process while modeling collaboration to support each student. Table 2 gives an overview of the steps involved in the biopsychoeducational consultative model.

When applying the biopsychoeducational consultative model, key team collaborators need to be initially

**Table 2** *Steps Within the Biopsychoeducational Consultative Problem-Solving Model*

| | |
|---|---|
| Select key collaborators | Determine who can contribute to best help the child (teacher, school psychologist, medical personnel, school counselor, school nurse, parent, student, or administrator) and select team leader. |
| Problem identification | Define and describe behaviors in observational terms as a team. |
| Problem analysis | Develop and confirm or refute hypotheses for each factor to better understand the problem behavior as a team; prioritize problems. |
| Solution development and implementation | Develop and implement the plan of intervention as a team. |
| Evaluation | Monitor and evaluate results of intervention and collaboration as a team. |

identified and parents or caregivers should be involved. Also, educators in the school setting who have both direct contact (e.g., general education teacher, special education teacher, speech-language pathologist, and school nurse) and indirect involvement (e.g., assistant principal and school counselor) should be included. A school psychologist typically assumes the role of team leader, but others also may serve in that role, depending on the individual child's needs. For instance, some children with Type 1 diabetes require that their blood sugar levels be taken several times each day. A school nurse who helps monitor the child's blood sugar levels and who has direct daily contact with the child might serve as a team leader.

In addition to parents and educators, several medical professionals typically are involved in the care of children with chronic illness. These individuals should participate in the consultative problem-solving process to explain the medical implications of the illness and treatment and to assist in the development of interventions in the school setting to ensure that the child's needs are addressed appropriately. It should be noted that the involvement of medical professionals does not necessarily obligate them to attend all team meetings in the school setting. Just as educators are extremely busy, medical professionals also have strong demands on their time. So the team leader or another representative from the team can share the responsibility of making contacts, asking questions, sharing ideas, soliciting feedback, and seeking advice from medical professionals using other methods of communication, such as telephone or e-mail.

Next, problem identification is vital to understanding the nature of the concern or potential challenge. The best-case scenario is to meet with the team at school, including parents and educators, to identify and prioritize the problems or concerns related to the child with chronic illness. A thorough problem analysis, which involves a comprehensive assessment of the child's individual needs and factors within his or her ecology (see Table 3), will aid in explaining the child's presenting problems in order to develop an appropriate prevention and intervention plan. In this step, assessment may be warranted to better understand the medical diagnoses and their implications as well as to obtain data regarding the child's cognitive and neuropsychological profile; academic achievement levels; and social, emotional, and behavioral functioning. It is important to remember that assessment does not necessarily mean testing but is the gathering of data to understand all aspects of a child's needs. Ecological assessment also is very important. This includes investigating the school and classroom environment, teacher characteristics, family organization and preferences, and nature of the involvement of medical professionals (e.g., treatment issues) and other professionals (e.g., counseling and therapy).

Once the problem is understood fully, the third stage of the problem-solving approach, intervention development and implementation, is completed. School psychologists and other health service providers on the team engage in the following activities:

- Developing an awareness among team members of educational services available to students.
- Promoting awareness of health issues in schools—e.g., providing inservices to teachers.
- Serving as a liaison among those involved in the child's life—e.g., communicating and collaborating with medical professionals and family.
- Monitoring and supporting the student—e.g., providing counseling and social skills training to the student.
- Providing teacher or educator consultation and support—e.g., helping them design behavior management programs and classwide strategies.
- Offering peer education and support—e.g., teaching awareness and dispelling myths about chronic illness and providing social skills training.
- Providing family consultation and support—e.g., helping them understand the child's needs within both school and home settings.

The last stage involves evaluation of the intervention and prevention strategies. It is very important to frequently monitor, evaluate, and modify interventions as needed to continuously support the child with chronic illness. This ongoing monitoring and modification may occur during regular team meetings by assessing the child's medical needs, academic progress, social skills development, and emotional and behavioral progress.

Implementation of the biopsychoeducational consultative model may seem very time consuming; however, using the problem-solving process a few times teaches those involved about the many needs of the child with a chronic illness. The model, though based on this problem-solving process, has two additional key features that make it different from general problem solving. First, it requires the collaboration of key individuals. Second, and more importantly, it requires collaboration across the ecology of the child with a chronic illness.

Medical systems and educational systems have very different structures. Families of children who have chronic illnesses are sometimes floundering in the middle of these systems, listening to what the school says and what the doctor says and feeling caught between the two. Applying the biopsychoeducational consultative model helps to connect all of those involved with the child with chronic illness to better support their needs. In turn, successful intervention can occur early, which will lead to prevention of continuing problems and less stress for all involved. Ultimately, using this type of approach will save tremendous amounts of time. Research is currently under way about the outcomes of this model.

Use of a structured problem-solving model to guide the assessment-to-intervention link for children with chronic illness is essential to providing these children with positive educational experiences. Educators must collaborate with the child, caregivers, and professionals across a variety of settings in order to collect information, make reliable decisions, and monitor the effects of interventions.

**Table 3** *Factor Areas for Consideration Within the Biopsychoeducational Model*

| | |
|---|---|
| Child factors | • Individual strengths and weaknesses (cognitive abilities, learning style, emotional functioning, social skills, etc.) |
| | • Medical/psychiatric diagnoses |
| Family factors | • Family structure (single-parent family, blended family, etc.) |
| | • Family socioeconomic status |
| | • Family dynamics |
| | • Family acceptance/ability to cope |
| Educational factors | • School curriculum |
| | • Teacher characteristics and instructional style |
| | • Classroom environment |
| | • Peers issues |
| Medical factors | • Medical professional |
| | • Treatment & maintenance of pediatric illness |
| Other factors | • Other professional involvement |
| | • Community involvement |

## Future Directions

Most of the discussion thus far has involved the prevention and intervention efforts of school psychologists and educators within the school setting. A key aspect of helping children with chronic illnesses in the school setting, especially since their numbers and life capabilities are increasing as a result of advances in medical technology, is to begin training at a preservice level. Graduate training that offers knowledge of the impact of pediatric health issues in the schools can provide future teachers and school psychologists with a foundation for providing an educational program to best meet the needs of these students.

At the inservice level, practicing school psychologists and educators may search for workshops and presentations at regional, national, and state conventions where they can gain additional skills in the area of chronic illness in children and adolescents. Administrators can design inservices with a focus on medical issues and introduce faculty and staff to members in the community who are available as resources to educators and families.

# SUMMARY

It is critical that educators, and specifically school psychologists, redefine themselves as health care providers and, as such, broaden their scope of services and identity (Nastasi, 2000). This redefinition requires expanding the knowledge base of practitioners in the area of chronic illness in children and the impact on the educational experience (Nastasi; Power, Shapiro, & DuPaul, 2003). Chronic illness in children and adolescents can affect cognition, academic performance, and social, emotional, and behavioral outcomes. In addition, issues affecting the family can influence performance in school as well. Educators are obligated to become knowledgeable about the chronic illnesses affecting the children with whom they work. Using a structured problem-solving model to assess individual needs and develop effective interventions is critical. Training programs in education and school psychology need to integrate instruction in pediatric health issues into their curricula so that professionals gain this information at the preservice level. For those already in practice, opportunities must be provided at the local, regional, and national levels for dissemination of information on chronic illnesses. Optimal educational outcomes for children and adolescents with chronic illnesses can only be realized when knowledge of the impact of health issues is clearly understood and incorporated in the educational decision-making process.

## RECOMMENDED RESOURCES

### Books and Other Printed Material

Brown, R. T. (Ed.). (2004). *Handbook of pediatric psychology in school settings.* Mahwah, NJ: Lawrence Erlbaum.

This text is a good resource that was written specifically for school professionals about pediatric health issues and comprehensive school-based interventions that emphasize family, school, and healthcare collaboration.

Phelps, L. (Ed.). (1998). *Health related disorders in children and adolescents: A guidebook for understanding and education.* Washington, DC: American Psychological Association.

This comprehensive volume contains brief synopses of many chronic illnesses, their outcomes, and psychoeducational implications. Resources, websites, and organizations supporting each illness and disorder are useful for parents and school-based professionals.

Roberts, M. C. (Ed.). (2003). *Handbook of pediatric psychology* (3rd ed.). New York: Guilford Press.

This excellent resource for practitioners in the schools provides information about specific pediatric health issues, the health care system, and the need for collaboration across all professions and settings.

### Websites

*http://kidshealth.org*

KidsHealth, a website designed for kids, teens, and parents, includes descriptions and information about a variety of health concerns and medical problems. The site, which is produced by the Nemours Foundation, is noted for having physician-approved information.

*http://starbright.org*

Using innovative, technology-based programs, STARBRIGHT Foundation has a mission to empower seriously ill children. This is an excellent site for children, caregivers, and professionals in education.

## REFERENCES

Anthony, K. K., Gil, K. M., & Schanberg, L. E. (2003). Brief report: Parental perception of child vulnerability in children with chronic illness. *Journal of Pediatric Psychology, 28,* 185–190.

Armstrong, F. D., Blumberg, M. J., & Toledano, S. R. (1999). Neurobehavioral issues in childhood cancer. *School Psychology Review, 28,* 194–203.

Batsche, G., & Tunnicliffe, H. (1998). Cystic fibrosis. In L. Phelps (Ed.), *Health related disorders in children and adolescents: A guidebook for understanding and education* (pp. 204–212). Washington, DC: American Psychological Association.

Bender, B. G. (1999). Learning disorders associated with asthma and allergies. *School Psychology Review 28,* 204–214.

Bonner, M. J., Gustafson, K. E., Schumacher, E., & Thompson, R. J., Jr. (1999). The impact of sickle cell disease on cognitive functioning and learning. *School Psychology Review, 28,* 182–193.

Brown, R. T., & DuPaul, G. J. (1999). Introduction to the mini-series: Promoting school success in children with chronic medical conditions. *School Psychology Review, 28,* 175–181.

Davis, M. A., Quittner, A. L., Stack, C. M., & Yang, M. C. K. (2004). Controlled evaluation of the STARBRIGHT CD-ROM program for children and adolescents with cystic fibrosis. *Journal of Pediatric Psychology, 29,* 259–267.

Don't confuse OHI's definition; look at ADHD severity, limitations. (2001, December). *Section 504 Compliance Advisor, 5,* 3.

Eiser, C., & Morse, R. (2001). The measurement of quality of life in children: Past and future perspectives. *Developmental and Behavioral Pediatrics, 22,* 248–256.

Farmer, J. E., & Clippard, D. (1995). Educational outcomes in children with disabilities: Linking hospitals and schools. *NeuroRehabilitation, 5,* 49–56.

Fuemmeler, B. F. (2004). Promotion of health behaviors. In R. T. Brown (Ed.), *Handbook of pediatric psychology in school settings* (pp. 81–98). Mahwah, NJ: Lawrence Erlbaum.

Gil, K. M., Carson, J. W., Porter, L. S., Ready, J., Valrie, C., Redding-Lallinger, R., et al. (2003). Daily stress and mood and their association with pain, health-care use, and school activity in adolescents with sickle cell disease. *Journal of Pediatric Psychology, 28,* 363–373.

Grice, K. (2002, Summer). Eligibility under IDEA for other health impaired children. *School Law Bulletin, Institute of Government, University of North Carolina at Chapel Hill,* 7–12.

Grier, E. C., & Bradley-Klug, K. L. (2005). *A biopsychoeducational model of consultation for the assessment, intervention, and evaluation of children with pediatric health issues.* Manuscript submitted for publication.

Grier, E. C., & Hodges, H. F. (2001). HIV/AIDS: A challenge in the classroom. *Public Health Nursing, 15,* 257–262.

Harrell, J. S., Gansky, S. A., McMurray, R. G., Bangdiwala, S. I., Frauman, A. C., & Bradley, C. B. (1998). School-based interventions improve heart health in children with multiple cardiovascular disease risk factors. *Pediatrics, 102,* 371–380.

Holmes, C. S., Cant, M. C., Fox, M. A., Lampert, N. L., & Greer, T. (1999). Disease and demographic risk factors for disrupted cognitive functioning in children with insulin-dependent diabetes mellitus (IDDM). *School Psychology Review, 28,* 215–227.

Individuals with Disabilities Education Act—Amendments of 1997. (1997). U.S. Congress, Public Law 101-147; amended by Public Law 105-17.

Jacob, S., & Hartshorne, T. S. (2004). *Ethics and law for school psychologists* (4th ed.). New York: Wiley.

Jelalian, E., & Mehlenbeck, R. (2003). Pediatric obesity. In M. C. Roberts (Ed.), *Handbook of pediatric psychology* (3rd ed., pp. 529–543). New York: Guilford Press.

Kral, M. C., & Brown, R. T. (2004). Transcranial doppler ultrasonography and executive dysfunction in children with sickle cell disease. *Journal of Pediatric Psychology, 29,* 185–195.

Labay, L. E., & Walco, G. A. (2004). Brief report: Empathy and psychological adjustment in siblings of children with cancer. *Journal of Pediatric Psychology, 29,* 309–314.

Madan-Swain, A., Katz, E. R., & LaGory, J. (2004). School and social reintegration after a serious illness or injury. In R. T. Brown (Ed.), *Handbook of pediatric psychology in school settings* (pp. 637–655). Mahwah, NJ: Lawrence Erlbaum.

Mellin, A. E., Neumark-Sztainer, D., & Patterson, J. M. (2004). Parenting adolescent girls with Type 1 diabetes: Parents' perspectives. *Journal of Pediatric Psychology, 29,* 221–230.

Meyers, A. B., & Swerdlik, M. E. (2003). School-based health centers: Opportunities and challenges for school psychologists. *Psychology in the Schools, 40,* 253–264.

Moore, B. D. (2005). Neurocognitive outcomes in survivors of childhood cancer. *Journal of Pediatric Psychiatry, 30,* 51–63.

Nabors, L. A., & Lehmkuhl, H. D. (2004). Children with chronic medical conditions: Recommendations for school mental health clinicians. *Journal of Developmental and Physical Disabilities, 16,* 1–15.

Nastasi, B. K. (2000). School psychologists as health care providers in the 21st century: Conceptual framework, professional identity, and professional practice. *School Psychology Review, 29,* 540–554.

Phelps, L., Brown, R. T., & Power, T. J. (2002). *Pediatric psychopharmacology: Combining medical and psychosocial interventions.* Washington, DC: American Psychological Association.

Power, T. J. (2003). Promoting children's mental health: Reform through interdisciplinary and community partnerships. *School Psychology Review, 32,* 3–16.

Power, T. J., & Blom-Hoffman, J. (2004). The school as a venue for managing and preventing health problems: Opportunities and challenges. In R. T. Brown (Ed.), *Handbook of pediatric psychology in school settings* (pp. 37–48). Mahwah, NJ: Lawrence Erlbaum.

Power, T. J., DuPaul, G. J., Shapiro, E. S., & Parrish, J. M. (1998). Role of the school-based professional in health-related services. In L. Phelps (Ed.), *Health related disorders in children and adolescents: A guidebook for understanding and education* (pp. 15–26). Washington, DC: American Psychological Association.

Power, T. J., Heathfield, L. T., McGoey, K., & Blum, N. J. (1999). Managing and preventing chronic health problems: School psychology's role. *School Psychology Review, 28,* 251–263.

Power, T. J., Shapiro, E. S., & DuPaul, G. J. (2003). Preparing psychologists to link systems of care in managing and preventing children's health problems. *Journal of Pediatric Psychology, 28,* 147–155.

Quittner, A. L., Davis, M. A., & Modi, A. C. (2003). Health-related quality of life in pediatric populations. In M. C. Roberts (Ed.), *Handbook of pediatric psychology* (3rd ed., pp. 696–709). New York: Guilford Press.

Roberts, M. C., Brown, K. J., Boles, R. E., Mashunkashey, J. O., & Mayes, S. (2003). Prevention of disease and injury in pediatric psychology. In M. C. Roberts (Ed.), *Handbook of pediatric psychology* (3rd ed., pp. 84–98). New York: Guilford Press.

Schwartz, L., & Drotar, D. (2004). Effects of written emotional disclosure on caregivers of children and adolescents with chronic illness. *Journal of Pediatric Psychology, 29*(4), 309–314.

Shaw, S. R. (2003). Professional preparation of pediatric school psychologists for school-based health centers. *Psychology in the Schools, 40,* 321–330.

Stark, L. J., Mackner, L. M., Patton, S. R., & Acton, J. D. (2003). Cystic fibrosis. In M. C. Roberts (Ed.), *Handbook of pediatric psychology* (3rd ed., pp. 286–303). New York: Guilford Press.

Vannatta, K., & Gerhardt, C. A. (2003). Pediatric oncology: Psychosocial outcomes for children and families. In M. C. Roberts (Ed.), *Handbook of pediatric psychology* (3rd ed., pp. 342–357). New York: Guilford Press.

Wodrich, D. L., Swerdlik, M. E., Chenneville, T., & Landau, S. (1999). HIV/AIDS among children and adolescents: Implications for the changing role of school psychologists. *School Psychology Review, 28,* 228–241.

Wysocki, T., & Gavin, L. (2004). Psychometric properties of a new measure of fathers' involvement in the management of pediatric chronic disease. *Journal of Pediatric Psychology, 29,* 231–240.

# 65

# HIV/AIDS

**Steven Landau**
**Adena B. Meyers**
**John B. Pryor**
*Illinois State University*

## BACKGROUND AND DEVELOPMENT

With no known cure, Human Immunodeficiency Virus (HIV) has emerged as a significant threat to global health. In some developing countries, HIV has decimated entire communities, and is usually transmitted by individuals unaware of their infection. Internationally, it is spreading most rapidly among children and young women of childbearing age. Its effect has been dramatic: In developing countries (e.g., Uganda), life expectancy has dropped from 60 to 42 years of age.

As a result of advances in medical care, the course of HIV infection has changed dramatically in the United States. HIV is now considered a chronic illness with complex medical management required for long-term positive outcomes. Epidemiological data (Centers for Disease Control and Prevention [CDC], 2002) indicate that AIDS prevalence in the United States is approximately 380,000 patients, with a 14% decline in deaths attributable to AIDS since 1998. Among U.S. children, HIV infection is most likely the result of mother-to-child transmission. However, the rate of child infection has dropped so dramatically in recent years that the current prevalence rate reveals few cases per year, even in AIDS epicenters such as New York City. This marked decrease is largely the result of aggressive prenatal HIV counseling and testing and the subsequent treatment of HIV-infected pregnant women with Highly Active Anti-retroviral Therapy (HAART; see Wightman & Klebert, 2000).

In contrast, the rate of AIDS diagnosis for adult men increased 7% since 1999, and adult men represented 71% of all new cases of HIV/AIDS as of 2002 (CDC, 2002). In the United States, people of color are disproportionately infected with HIV: An African American woman is 25 times more likely than her European American counterpart to have AIDS (Logan, Cole, & Leukefeld, 2002), and 82% of current cases of pediatric AIDS involve African American or Hispanic children even though these ethnic groups represent less than 25% of the U.S. population (CDC, 2003).

HIV is a complex retrovirus that leaves the individual with a compromised immune system. Different terms are used to reflect the progression of illness through multiple stages of morbidity. *HIV infection* refers to infection with human immunodeficiency virus, regardless of the presence of overt illness or clinical manifestations. *HIV-related disease* refers to the presence of HIV infection and the presence of clinical manifestations that may or may not be life threatening. *Acquired immunodeficiency syndrome* (AIDS) represents the later stages of HIV disease. Persons with HIV/AIDS are vulnerable to a variety of opportunistic diseases that have less impact on people with functioning immune systems. The presence of such opportunistic illnesses in a weakened immune system can result in diminished health, decreased quality of life, and in some cases death. Clinical diagnosis of AIDS hinges, in part, upon the presence of these opportunistic infections. Progression through these stages is consistent across HIV-infected individuals, but with the advent of HAART, early death is no longer inevitable.

Despite encouraging epidemiological and longevity data in this country, HIV/AIDS remains a daunting challenge. Although the number of children infected with HIV has dropped precipitously in the United States, most children with HIV/AIDS live to reach school age. In fact, with current treatment success, many of these children are expected to reach adolescence and adulthood. As such, the educational needs of these children present a challenge for school personnel.

Even though school personnel may not know the identity of some students with HIV/AIDS (see Legal Issues, in this chapter), these children are likely to present with distinctive medical, neuropsychological, and psychosocial needs. School psychologists and other school-based professionals may be ill-prepared to address the multiple needs of these children. For example, HIV is unique among chronic illnesses in that the diagnosis may evoke a negative response bias in school personnel and parents in the community that is driven by social stigma. This stigma is often extended to the family members of HIV-infected students.

School professionals must take a leadership role in educating others to reduce prejudice against students with HIV/AIDS. Indeed, social stigma can lead to increased stress among caregivers of these children, which can then compromise the caregivers' adjustment to the catastrophic illness. Furthermore, the mental health of the caregiver may affect the child's adjustment to HIV (see Bachanas et al., 2001, for a review), and the psychosocial stressors experienced by the child with HIV can actually exacerbate the medical course of the disease (Bose, Moss, Brouwers, Pizzo, & Lorion, 1994). To meet the needs of these children, school professionals must become familiar with the relevant issues surrounding HIV and AIDS. These include numerous social, contextual, and cultural factors associated with HIV transmission, as well as the psychoeducational and psychosocial sequelae of the disease.

## Transmission of HIV

In the general population, the virus is transmitted through body fluids, primarily blood, sperm, and vaginal secretions. However, best estimates indicate that 93% of HIV-positive children acquired the virus from an infected mother through vertical or mother-to-child transmission (CDC, 2002). This transmission can occur during pregnancy (the virus has been isolated in amniotic fluid), during delivery (the time considered most likely), or post-partum through breast-feeding. Breast-feeding by an infected mother appears to double the infant's risk of HIV infection, especially if it occurs during the neonatal period.

Several known risk factors increase the fetus's vulnerability to HIV infection: decreased gestational age, low birth weight, and increased maternal viral load during pregnancy (Pulsifer & Aylward, 2000). From the perspective of prevention, mode of delivery, especially elective caesarian section, may reduce neonatal vulnerability to infection by 50%. In the United States, the use of antiretroviral medication during pregnancy for HIV-infected women has also significantly reduced the likelihood of vertical transmission. Unfortunately, the prophylactic use of these medications during pregnancy is not routine in developing countries where HIV is spreading rapidly.

In the absence of treatment, approximately 25% of infants born of HIV-infected women will be infected (Brown, Lourie, & Poa, 2000). All babies born of HIV-infected women have maternal antibodies to HIV. However, testing for the presence of these antibodies is often inaccurate. The current standard of care involves testing all infants born to HIV-infected women with HIV RNA testing (i.e., quantification of viral load, or the number of viral particles found in each millimeter of blood). The test allows health care providers to identify HIV-infected infants within the first weeks of life and to begin aggressive HAART treatment to prevent early disease progression.

Mandated systematic screening of the U.S. blood supply since 1985 has greatly reduced the number of children infected by blood transfusions or clotting agents. As such, it is unlikely that children in the United States will become infected through this blood-borne mode of transmission. In addition, the institution of universal precautions by the Centers for Disease Control and Prevention (CDC) since 1985 has greatly reduced the risk of exposure to infected blood and other bodily fluids.

HIV is not spread through casual contact. In studies of thousands of households where family members have lived with and cared for people living with HIV/AIDS (even when it was not known the person was infected with HIV), there is no known case of transmission through casual contact, including circumstances where kitchen and bathroom facilities, meals, or eating and drinking utensils were shared. Even so, sharing of razors or toothbrushes is discouraged. Theoretically, the virus could be transmitted in any body fluid. However, tears, urine, and stool have never been implicated. In addition, there are no known reports that HIV was casually transmitted in other social situations, such as schools and day care settings (National Association of State Boards of Education, 2001).

Among adolescents and adults, the primary means of transmission continues to be unprotected sex with an infected person. For males, infection likely results from same-sex contact with other boys or men; for females, heterosexual transmission is the most likely risk factor.

HIV may be present in either the semen or vaginal secretion of an infected person. Sexual activity in which a partner comes in contact with either of these fluids represents a risk for HIV transmission.

Almost all cases of HIV infection and AIDS in adults result from risky behaviors established during adolescence. For example, current national survey data (CDC, 2003) indicate approximately half of all 9th through 12th graders admit to being sexually active (with a steady decline in the age of sexual debut), and 14% have had four or more sexual partners. In addition, almost 20% of adolescent boys ages 13 to 18 report having at least one sexual experience with another male (Tinsley, Lees, & Sumartojo, 2004). Further increasing the risk of HIV infection, less than two thirds of teens admit to using a condom in their last sexual intercourse. This fact is disquieting, as approximately 90% of all high school students indicate they have been taught about HIV/AIDS prevention. Among teens, recent data suggest boys who have sex with both boys and girls represent the greatest behavioral risk profile of any group in the nation and are the most likely to drop out of school (Goodenow, Netherland, & Szalacha, 2002). As such, they are the least likely to be exposed to school-based safe-sex education.

There is also evidence that HIV can be transmitted in the context of child sexual abuse, although reliable estimates of this occurrence are difficult to establish. There are, however, reliable, troubling, and compelling data regarding the relation between individuals' sex abuse history in childhood and adolescent or adult risk-taking leading to HIV infection (see Repetti, Taylor, & Seeman, 2002, for details). For example, adolescents with a history of sexual abuse are known to use condoms significantly less often than peers, and they present with significantly higher rates of sexually transmitted diseases (STDs). In addition, a recent telephone survey revealed that women with a history of early and chronic sexual abuse are seven times more likely to engage in HIV risk-taking behaviors (see Logan et al., 2002, for an excellent review).

One hypothesis for the observed relation between victimization and sexual risk-taking is based on the notion that a painful history of physical or sexual victimization may lead to substance or alcohol abuse for the sake of self-medication (Logan et al., 2002). Evidence for this theory comes from repeated demonstrations that women with substance or alcohol abuse problems are much more likely to have physical abuse histories. In addition, young women who engage in binge drinking are five times more likely than non-heavy drinkers to have had 10 or more sexual partners in the past year. Among teens, one fourth of 9th through 12th graders acknowledged using alcohol or drugs during their last sexual intercourse (CDC, 2003).

The co-occurrence of alcohol or substance use and sexual risk taking is unequivocal: Alcohol has a deleterious effect on decision making, and risky behavior is more likely to occur when a person's judgment is impaired. Also, alcohol is known to reduce a woman's ability to resist physical aggression or unwanted sexual advances. Furthermore, data indicate that chronic exposure to alcohol or illicit substances may actually compromise the woman's immune system (Logan et al., 2002). As such, the presence of these toxins may increase *biological* vulnerability to STD infection of any type. If an STD is present, there is increased risk of HIV infection, and the presence of HIV increases the transmission risk of other STDs such as hepatitis. This association is troubling, as drug abuse also predicts the exchange of sexual favors for money and drugs, which in turn increases the risk of HIV infection. Finally, extant psychiatric difficulties, such as depression or post-traumatic stress disorder (PTSD), can lead to poor decision making, increased substance abuse for coping, and greater incidence of HIV.

## Epidemiology and the Culture of HIV/AIDS

It is widely acknowledged that pediatric HIV represents a family condition. Even so, it must also be considered in the context of culture and social class. Families serve as the principal medium in which health beliefs and healthy behaviors are taught to children. However, this socialization process is strongly influenced by the cultural identity of the family. Culture and ethnicity not only account for considerable variation in general attitudes about parenting, parenting behaviors, and child-rearing goals, they also affect the health socialization of youth (Tinsley et al., 2004).

***Cultural risk factors.*** Epidemiological data also make it clear that various conditions of poverty are robust correlates of HIV. The ethnic groups hardest hit by HIV also experience the greatest proportion of their members below the poverty line. Poverty is associated with increased stress, poor health status, reduced access to community (including health) services, greater incidence of psychiatric disorders, and higher rates of alcohol and drug abuse (see chapter 62, "Poverty"). In addition, low-income women are at elevated risk for partner violence, including sexual assaults (Repetti et al., 2002). Safe sex may not be an immediate concern if one needs to focus, instead, on insufficient funds for food or housing, inadequate medical care, and community violence. As such, it is no wonder HIV has become a compelling feature of the syndrome of hardship experienced by those living in impoverished urban environments.

The covert culture surrounding homeless and runaway teens must also be considered. These adolescents present a life history that places them at huge risk for STD infection and HIV. The risk profile of homeless and runaway adolescents is striking. Research by Booth and Zhang (1997) showed that, on average, these teens leave home at 13.1 years of age, having had 2.8 lifetime out-of-home placements. They have lived with their birth mothers an average of 8.3 years. Half of runaways report a history of sexual abuse, 55% report physical abuse, and most have been raised in a home where there was alcohol (52%) or drug (54%) abuse. Indeed, 95% of these teens admit to using drugs, and 60% meet diagnostic criteria for conduct disorders. Nearly one fourth report having used sex in exchange for drugs, with safe sex never a consideration (Booth & Zhang). Runaway teens live in a very dangerous world, a world made more threatening by the risk of HIV exposure. In addition, homeless or runaway adolescents are rarely in school, thereby precluding the preventative benefits of school-based safe-sex education.

***Culture and family communication.*** Cultural differences influence how families discuss sexual matters in general and HIV transmission in particular (except as otherwise noted, the following discussion is drawn from Tinsley et al., 2004). According to family systems theory, parents influence teens' risk of HIV infection by affecting adolescents' HIV knowledge, attitudes, and behavior. This can occur through two routes of influence. First, children's HIV knowledge and prevention behaviors are indirectly influenced by family dynamics. This process is represented by distal constructs pertaining to the general child-rearing environment and the emotional climate, or sense of connectedness, in parent–child relations. Parent monitoring is also represented by this process and can serve as a protective factor. For example, parental monitoring of adolescent behavior can delay the age of sexual debut among teens, especially in the African American community.

The second route of influence is a direct process that involves explicit communication between family members regarding sexual matters, especially safe-sex practices. Children's knowledge of HIV, attitudes toward persons with AIDS, and transmission myths are a product of this more proximal route in which culture accounts for some important cross-family differences. Consistent with family systems theory, there is strong evidence of the intergenerational transmission of HIV knowledge, with parent–child conversation being the means by which teens' HIV risk can be attenuated or exacerbated.

For example, Asian American high school students tend to engage in significantly fewer HIV prevention practices than European American students, a finding attributed to European American students' reportedly greater ability to communicate with parents about sex. European and African American teens report more sex-focused conversation with parents than is found among Hispanic teens. However, in both African American and Hispanic communities, especially when income and education are low, parents seem to have less accurate HIV knowledge, greater endorsement of HIV transmission myths, and less knowledge of condom use. Accordingly, their children tend to be the least informed, and present higher risk profiles. Unfortunately, parents who are most likely to disseminate incorrect information to their children represent segments of the population in which HIV is most prevalent.

Consistent with family systems theory, older siblings can serve as a deleterious model for their younger brothers and sisters. Specifically, pregnant teens or adolescent mothers of infants can have a negative influence on siblings' risk behaviors, especially younger sisters'. This is especially the case when younger sisters must assist in the care of these infants. Sisters of parenting adolescents use more drugs and alcohol and have a higher rate of teen pregnancy.

Culture also plays a role in the application of coping strategies when a family is confronted with catastrophic illness. For example, among African American and Hispanic parents, stressful parenting brought on by the presence of HIV can lead to increased frequency of unsafe sexual practices by the parents (Bachanas et al., 2001). Cultural differences also are evident when examining the impact of social stigma on coping. African American parents may be more comfortable than European Americans in disclosing their child's HIV status to immediate family members (see Brown et al., 2000). This can be an important coping strategy, as such disclosures tend to broaden the support network of stressed parents. In addition, research focusing on children's chronic illness has shown that greater family disclosure seems to reduce the child's sense of isolation, ultimately leading to enhanced adaptation by the child. In a related vein, among many Hispanic individuals, for whom death is a more culturally accepted event, one finds less denial (Brown et al.). Strong denial tends to compromise adaptive coping.

## PROBLEMS AND IMPLICATIONS

### Neurological Sequelae of HIV

In addition to affecting the immune system, HIV is known to directly attack the infected person's central nervous system (CNS). There is evidence that the virus enters the CNS shortly after infection, and it has been found in aborted fetuses as young as 15 weeks gestational age (Llorente et al., 2003). The consequences of this infection are more devastating in cases of pediatric HIV because the child's immune and neurological systems are still developing. In contrast to the progressive symptoms of AIDS in adults who experience neurological dysfunction late in the course of illness, HIV-infected children present neurological problems early in their illness. Between one third and two thirds of all pediatric HIV cases involve a compromised neurological system (Tepper et al., 1998).

The most common neurological indicator of infant HIV is progressive encephalopathy or neuro-AIDS (i.e., a decline in mental or motor status; Pulsifer & Aylward, 2000), which involves impaired brain growth, progressive motor dysfunction (the most salient indicator), developmental delays, and loss of developmental milestones. These effects can be chronic and pervasive, cutting across the child's cognitive, motor, and social–emotional development. In some cases, however, the neurological impairment is static (i.e., does not progress over time). Fortunately, early and aggressive use of HAART has been known to change the course of neurological impairments, and some evidence suggests loss of functioning may be reversed (Tepper et al., 1998).

***Cognitive development.*** Investigations into the cognitive development of HIV-infected children are fraught with methodological challenges, as many confounding variables must be addressed (Pulsifer & Aylward, 2000). For example, besides their *in utero* exposure to the virus, many of these children have also been exposed to drugs, alcohol, and nicotine during fetal development. In many cases, there was no prenatal care, and these children were born to mothers with limited education and low socioeconomic status. In addition, it is likely the family has been under considerable stress as a result of the mother's own HIV illness. Limited cognitive stimulation and out-of-home placements are common (Wachsler-Felder & Golden, 2002). Approximately one third of vertically infected infants will demonstrate significant cognitive delays, and the amount of viral load in the child predicts the degree of cognitive delay. Unfortunately, a low score on the Bayley MDI is also predictive of infant mortality, independent of other risk-related variables (see Llorente et al., 2003).

Among school-age children, the consequences of HIV show greater variability than indicated with infants and toddlers. Cognitive development of HIV-infected school-age children does not show the same pattern of impairment found in infants, as some studies indicate these children can function within normal limits or within the low-average range (see Pulsifer & Aylward, 2000, for a review). With disease progression, the infected child may show a decline in cognitive functioning. This deterioration may coincide with reduced interest in school, attentional difficulties, language problems, and psychomotor slowing (Llorente et al., 2003).

***Motor and language problems.*** HIV also affects the child's motor and language development. Indeed, motor delays serve as a hallmark characteristic of the encephalopathy presented by HIV-infected children. Toddlers may experience a change in gait, toe-walking or hyperreflexia, and increased muscle tone in the lower legs (Wachsler-Felder & Golden, 2002). In addition, clumsiness and fine-motor problems are observed. In rare cases, ambulation becomes compromised.

HIV has a deleterious effect on the child's language development, with expressive language more impaired than receptive language. These delays can appear during infancy and are most pronounced among children 12 to 24 months of age. Language acquisition problems are common, as are problems with the child's mean length of utterances (Pulsifer & Aylward, 2000). Among HIV-infected children, the severity of CT scan abnormalities predicts the degree of language impairment.

### Psychosocial Sequelae

In addition to cognitive, motor, and language dysfunction, children with HIV may also present with problems in social and emotional functioning. These effects tend to be most pronounced among those who contracted the illness through vertical infection. However, isolating the impact of this mode of transmission is difficult because many of these children also had prenatal drug exposure, impoverished child-rearing, death of a parent, and unstable living arrangements (see Pulsifer & Aylward, 2000, for a review). Among infected children, mental health difficulties can be exacerbated by frequent medical contacts and hospitalizations, social stigma surrounding HIV, and extensive school absence. It is very difficult to disentangle the causal role of disease from environmental stressors.

Even so, several large-scale studies indicate that many children with HIV show apathy, depressed or flat affect, social isolation, lethargy, anhedonia, attention difficulties, irritability or agitation, occasional impulsivity, and reduced goal-directed behavior. Nonsocial behavior is a prevalent complaint, as are anxiety and depression (see Pulsifer & Aylward, 2000, for a review of social–emotional effects). Historically, some HIV-infected children have been labeled autistic-like because they present severe withdrawal and non-purposeful behavior. However, it is not clear whether these behavioral outcomes are due to the disease itself or to the child's efforts at coping with the disease plus other environmental stressors. For example, maternal adaptation to a child's illness is known to affect the child's coping (Lwin & Melvin, 2001).

## HIV/AIDS Stigma and Disclosure

At times, children who have HIV also have a hidden stigma. Parents of school-age HIV-infected children often delay disclosing the diagnosis to their children (Waugh, 2003). One reason for this concealment is the fear that the infected child will divulge his or her HIV status to classmates and teachers, causing the child and family to be stigmatized (Lester et al., 2002). To complicate matters, almost all school-age children with HIV/AIDS have HIV-infected mothers. Thus, revealing a child's HIV status may directly implicate the mother's HIV status, as well as her possible use of illegal drugs or unprotected sexual activity.

The decision to tell a child he or she is infected is complicated. Knowing that they have HIV can help children seek social support (Battles & Weiner, 2002), and a child's disclosure to friends has led to improvement in immune functioning (Sherman, Bonanno, Weiner, & Battles, 2000). Children's knowledge that they are HIV-infected also increases the likelihood of medication adherence (Blasini et al., 2004). The solution for some parents is to identify "safe people" to whom children can disclose (Murphy, Roberts, & Hoffman, 2002). However, children who are asked to keep their HIV status a secret may suffer from stress (Kirshenbaum & Nevid, 2002). Issues regarding shame or guilt may also affect children who are not HIV-positive themselves but who have parents or other family members with the disease.

Blame is an important element of stigma. Generally, people are more likely to feel anger and less likely to show pity (or compassion) when they blame someone for their stigmatizing condition (Weiner, 1993). This effect applies to HIV/AIDS as well as to other stigmas (Crandall, 2000). With regard to pediatric HIV/AIDS, adults seem less likely to blame children who were infected perinatally rather than if they were infected through actions believed to be within their control, such as unprotected sex (Pryor, Reeder, & Landau, 1999). Even if the child does not have HIV, infection among other family members can lead to stigma, and blame becomes a very important issue. Speculations about family drug use may exacerbate children's fear of blame.

Recent research has begun to explore the psychology of people's reactions to perceived stigmas, including HIV/AIDS. These investigations suggest people have spontaneous emotional reactions followed by more reasoned, rule-based, or thoughtful responses (Pryor, Reeder, Yeadon, & Hesson-McInnis, 2004). Immediate emotional reactions to persons with HIV/AIDS can reflect the automatic associations people have between HIV/AIDS and stigmatized groups. For example, people who hold negative attitudes about homosexuality tend to have more negative immediate reactions to persons with HIV/AIDS. This is the case even when the person with HIV/AIDS is understood not to be homosexual. For example, anti-gay attitudes are associated with negative reactions to children with HIV/AIDS (Pryor et al., 1999).

# ALTERNATIVE ACTIONS FOR PREVENTION

Schools are an obvious place to reach the majority of young people to provide information and prevention strategies regarding HIV infection. Though some may question whether this type of program falls in the realm of school responsibility, others believe that, as a major social institution, schools cannot afford to ignore the devastating impact of the AIDS epidemic on children and adolescents (Starkman & Rajani, 2002). The vast majority of adults in the United States support the notion that schools should provide sexuality and HIV education, and most secondary schools do so. However, it is not clear whether schools routinely select effective sexuality and HIV education curricula, or if effective curricula, when selected, are implemented with fidelity (Kirby, 2002a).

In a survey of U.S. public school administrators, the majority (69%) reported that district-wide policies require their schools to offer sexuality education (Landry, Kaeser, & Richards, 1999). However, the definition and content of sexuality education vary considerably, particularly with respect to the relative emphasis placed on abstinence as opposed to condom use and other risk-reduction methods. Currently, three primary types of sexuality education policies are most common: (a) *comprehensive* policies that discuss abstinence as one option among many pathways to healthy sexual development; (b) *abstinence-plus* policies that promote abstinence as the best option for adolescents, but also address effective methods of contraception and disease prevention; (c) *abstinence-only* policies that present abstinence as the only acceptable option outside of marriage, and the discussion of contraception is either prohibited altogether or restricted to information about its failures and shortcomings. The relative merits and drawbacks of these very different approaches have been the subject of political as well as scholarly debate. Recent legislative mandates favor an abstinence-only approach, yet little evidence of its effectiveness has been documented (Starkman & Rajani, 2002; see also, chapter 53, "Adolescent Pregnancy and Parenting").

Clearly, it is important for schools to select prevention curricula that have been empirically supported. Kirby (2002b) recently reviewed research on numerous sexuality and HIV/STD education programs that promoted abstinence as the safest choice but also emphasized preventive benefits of condoms and other methods of contraception. Some of the studied programs led to delayed onset of intercourse, decreased numbers of sexual partners, and reduced frequency of intercourse. One study out of 28 reported earlier onset of intercourse and increased frequency of sexual behavior following the intervention, and approximately two thirds reported no impact on sexual behavior. More than half of the studies that assessed changes in condom use found significant increases; none of the studied programs resulted in decreased condom use. Programs that effectively reduced unprotected sex shared several key components (Kirby). Specifically, these programs:

- Focused on reducing specific risky behaviors.
- Provided clear, continually reinforced messages about sexual behavior.
- Provided accurate information about sex, its risks, and ways to avoid risks.
- Addressed social influences on sexual behavior.
- Taught skills through modeling and practice.
- Used teaching strategies that elicit active involvement and "personalize" the information.
- Were appropriate for the age, culture, and sexual experience level of the participants.
- Were of adequate length to complete important activities.
- Had leaders (teachers or peers) who were adequately trained and believed in the program.

For more details about specific prevention programs known to reduce sexual risk-taking among school-age youth, see Meyers and Landau (2000).

Currently, most HIV/AIDS education programs target adolescents in higher grade levels (Wodrich, Swerdlik, Chenneville, & Landau, 1998). However, it is possible to provide appropriate HIV/AIDS education at all grade levels while being sensitive to developmental differences across age groups. Clearly, implementing prevention programs in earlier grades can help to prevent high-risk behavior patterns before they become firmly established and more difficult to change.

Kirby's (2002b) model distinguishes between the sexual and nonsexual antecedents of sexual risk-taking. Sexual antecedents include knowledge, attitudes, and self-efficacy regarding sexual behavior. Nonsexual antecedents include such factors as beliefs about the future and connections with caring adults. Considering the social and economic contexts of young people at greatest risk for HIV infection, it is not surprising that messages to "just say no" or "use condoms" are often ineffective (Elders, 1994). Among teenagers raised in poverty, who lack adequate medical care and social support and who may feel helpless in their efforts to create change for the future, HIV infection is part of a network of difficult social and economic circumstances. Therefore, if HIV infection is to be prevented, larger social and economic issues must also be addressed. In this context, it is notable that a handful of well-designed studies (e.g., Allen, Philliber, Herrling, & Kuperminc, 1997) have demonstrated interventions that engage adolescents in meaningful career-related activities and connect them with supportive adults; these changes in turn lead to sustained reductions in sexual risk-taking among girls. Although more research on this approach is needed, studies suggest one promising route to HIV prevention, at least for girls, is to target nonsexual antecedents of sexual risk-taking.

## ALTERNATIVE ACTIONS FOR INTERVENTION

### Full-Service Schools

The multitude of physical, emotional, social, and cognitive concerns that emanate from HIV-related cases highlight the need for a holistic, multidisciplinary approach to service delivery. When a child with HIV infection attends school, the quality of his or her educational experience will be influenced by the availability and coordination of appropriate medical, social, and educational services. Full-service schools (Dryfoos & Maguire, 2002; Meyers & Swerdlik, 2004) represent a model of service delivery that could effectively address the complex needs of an HIV-infected child. This approach rests on two assumptions: that learning is enhanced when children's social, emotional, and physical needs are met, and that the institution of public education represents an appropriate and convenient center for the delivery and coordination of a wide range of services addressing children's developmental needs.

Some full-service schools provide on-site care in the form of school-based health centers that function as primary care facilities, providing examinations, acute treatment, health screenings, and in some cases preventive services (Meyers & Swerdlik, 2004). Other full-service schools link students and families with community resources using well-developed referral agreements. Both school-based and school-linked services of this type have the potential to help overcome the significant barriers to health care access that plague children from economically disadvantaged communities—often the same communities that are disproportionately affected by HIV/AIDS.

Worchel-Prevatt et al. (1998) described a model program aimed at facilitating school reentry for children with chronic illness. The program is consistent with the full-service school approach, in that it applies an ecological perspective by addressing the medical, social, and academic functioning of children with chronic illnesses. It is based on a model of coping with disability and illness that emphasizes risk factors, such as psychosocial stressors and disease-related variables, as well as resilience factors such as social supports. The program includes a school reentry team, whose members are responsible for meeting with the family and school to assess needs and develop a reentry plan, as well as a hospital liaison team, whose members are responsible for facilitating communication and collaboration between family, school, and hospital. The authors described a case study involving an 11-year-old girl with cancer. Following needs assessments with the family and school, an intervention plan was developed that involved educating staff and students about the child's medical condition and increasing communication between school and hospital personnel. Results indicated that the child experienced a reduction in depression and improved satisfaction and confidence with respect to social support and peer relationships. Although this example does not involve a child with HIV, the program was designed to be sufficiently flexible to be adapted for use with a variety of different chronic illnesses.

### Safety Precautions

Regardless of the disclosed presence of an HIV-infected student, training in the CDC's universal precautions (CDC, 1988) should be an important component in the training of school staff. Students and teachers should be made aware of modes of HIV transmission, and the myths surrounding this issue should be dispelled. Because commonly spread viruses, such as colds and influenza, can have a serious impact on the weakened immune system of an HIV-infected child, increased attention to good hygienic practices is necessary. All schools should adopt policies regarding the handling of blood and other body fluids, regardless of known attendance of an HIV-infected student.

If implemented properly, universal precautions not only will prevent the spread of HIV, they also will reduce the spread of hepatitis and other blood-borne contagions. Grosse (1999) outlines six recommended precautions that should be implemented and taught as part of children's contagion education:

- Use protective gear as a barrier when exposure to blood is possible. In schools, this usually involves vinyl or latex gloves, disposable cloth towels, and wads of gauze or paper towels.
- Remove protective gear by not touching the contaminated area, and dispose of materials in biohazard containers. Gloves should never be reused.
- Wash hands and any other body areas immediately with soap and water.

- Seek medical attention for any significant exposure to blood of another person.
- Clean all surfaces or objects that may have been contaminated. Household bleach can be used, but it must remain in contact with the contaminated area for at least 30 seconds.
- Use pickups (e.g., a broom and dust pan, or tweezers) to pick up sharp objects, such as broken glass. Dispose of sharp objects in containers reserved for biohazardous material. Do not use plastic or paper bags for the disposal of sharp objects.

## Psychoeducational Issues

The central nervous system is a direct and specific pathway by which HIV can affect a child's cognitive and psychomotor development (Knight, Mellins, Levenson, Arpadi, & Kairam, 2000). In the absence of treatment, pediatric HIV infection involves CNS dysfunction and progressive encephalopathy, which can result in deteriorating cognitive ability in extreme cases. This deterioration may involve global developmental degeneration over the course of the illness, with speech and motor performance worsening over time. However, most children with HIV do not present with this progressive pattern; instead, their development is permanently interrupted or slowed such that milestones are not acquired or are greatly delayed. However, by dramatically reducing the child's viral load, HAART combination therapies are known to ameliorate neurological degeneration and, in some cases, will reverse the child's neurodevelopmental dysfunctioning (Tepper et al., 1998).

Because HIV CNS disease can progress faster in children than in adults, repeated or serial assessment of the child's psychoeducational functioning is recommended. Such assessment should have a changes-over-time perspective, both to determine if the child's neurological functioning remains stable and to assess the effectiveness of academic and psychosocial interventions. For children under the age of 5, it is recommended that evaluations occur every 6 to 12 months, and once per year for those older than 5 years of age (see Armstrong et al., 1999, for a description of frequently used test batteries). The foci of serial assessment should be broad to capture all concomitants of HIV illness (i.e., cognitive, academic, speech and language, motor, and psychosocial functioning).

Psychoeducational dysfunction resulting from HIV infection is not different from impairment caused by other agents or factors. Therefore, regardless of the cause of impairment, children with HIV can benefit from early intervention and special education services that currently are in place for children with developmental disabilities, if needed. Many of these children will be eligible for special education and related services under IDEA or for accommodations under Section 504 because of their physical and cognitive impairment.

Children with HIV may have multifaceted needs that require interdisciplinary services. Interdisciplinary teams should focus on the multiple areas affected by HIV, including cognitive functioning, language, perceptual–motor abilities, memory, and adaptive behavior (Wachsler-Felder & Golden, 2002). A number of disciplines should be involved in these assessments, including school psychology, physical therapy, occupational therapy, speech pathology, special education, social work, and nursing. In addition, some psychological and neurodevelopmental evaluations may be done in a medical setting. With parental consent, results of evaluations should be shared across the medical and school settings. Assessments should be family centered and include a family and developmental history, especially given the prevalence of poverty and drug use among mothers of children with HIV. Interdisciplinary teams should assess for special family needs related to stress, financial hardships, respite care, and infection of other family members. The reader is encouraged to consult Armstrong et al. (1999) for further details regarding an excellent pediatric HIV psychoeducational assessment protocol.

## Legal Issues

Because of negative reactions and stigma associated with HIV/AIDS, a number of legal issues have surfaced, especially concerning confidentiality, right of privacy, and discrimination. At the federal level, civil rights laws protect school staff as well as students infected with HIV from discrimination. Under the 1990 Americans with Disabilities Act (ADA), it is illegal for employers to discriminate against employees with disabilities. Courts have interpreted disabilities to include HIV infection, whether or not symptoms are present. School staff members who are (or are perceived to be) infected with HIV cannot be penalized on the basis of their HIV status. All decisions concerning work assignments, hiring, promotion, training opportunities, and benefits must ignore the staff member's HIV status. An administrator or supervisor cannot require an HIV test, because the results are not relevant to one's job performance. However, ADA does not require any work-related preferences or special considerations due to HIV status in a performance evaluation.

The employment provisions of ADA apply to all sectors of the community, including the public schools. As a result, the school district can be liable for monetary damages if documentation indicates that school authorities were aware of harassment directed at a person with HIV and did not prevent its continuation. With regard to students, many states have adopted their own policies protecting the civil rights of people with HIV. Readers should consult *http://www.nasbe.org/HealthySchools/Safe_Healthy/sasha.html* for specific information regarding each state's policies and regulations.

All school professionals should have working familiarity with Section 504 of the Rehabilitation Act of 1973 and the Individuals with Disabilities Education Act (IDEA). Section 504 prohibits denial of services or discrimination as a result of any disabling condition. For example, a student with HIV cannot be denied participation in school athletics, transportation, extracurricular activities, or other school programs. In addition, school officials are proscribed from tolerating harassment of a student with HIV. In other words, Section 504 guarantees the public school student with HIV access to a "free, appropriate public education" to meet his or her educational needs. The child's HIV status per se is totally irrelevant to any decision made about that child in school. Instead, decisions must be based on the student's unique educational and health needs; circumstances must be considered on a case-by-base basis.

Often, state law determines whether educational personnel should or must be informed of a child's HIV status. In Illinois for example, if a school-age child tests positive for HIV, the state Department of Public Health is required to inform the child's principal (and in some cases the superintendent) of the test result, including the child's name. The principal, in turn, is legally authorized (although not required) to inform other school staff (e.g., school nurse, classroom teachers). These additional disclosures are considered necessary only when justified by public health or other legitimate reasons. Once school personnel have been informed, that information would be protected under the Education for All Handicapped Children Act (EHA) of 1975, as well as under IDEA and the Family Education Rights and Privacy Act (FERPA). These laws require that consent be given before the school can disclose a student's HIV condition. Because there is no evidence that HIV can be transmitted through casual contact, it may be appropriate for the principal or superintendent, exclusively, to know the status of an infected student.

The above represents a brief summary of the most noteworthy statutes that pertain to HIV and the schools. If more information regarding HIV and legal issues is sought, the reader should consult *http://www.megalaw.com/top/aids.php*. This website provides links to documents regarding relevant case law, government agencies that deal with HIV and the law, university AIDS and HIV programs, and numerous other websites relevant to HIV law.

### Bereavement Issues

Because of recent aggressive use of medications, it is no longer the case that most children with pediatric HIV will succumb to the illness. In this context, and according to current demographic and epidemiological data, the most likely AIDS-related bereavement scenario will involve a healthy child who loses a family member. In many ways this child's bereavement experience is no different than if a parent or older sibling was lost to any other terminal disease. Thus, the extant child-focused bereavement literature may provide guidance to educators trying to meet the needs of students affected by this loss (see chapter 18, "Grief"). However, some important attributes of AIDS-related bereavement may diminish the utility of this literature. First, there is some likelihood of losing multiple family members to AIDS. Second, children affected by AIDS may not be able to grieve openly in school because of the stigma associated with the disease; surviving family members may exert pressure to behave in a secretive manner. Finally, disintegration of the family is not uncommon. AIDS not only creates many orphans, it is the cause of other major stressors, including a move to the residence of extended family members, as well as legal battles regarding custody. School professionals must keep in mind that, prior to the AIDS-related loss of a parent, bereaved children not only witnessed the conspicuous deterioration of a loved one but, in many cases, also had to assume the role of caregiver to a dying parent.

## SUMMARY

Since the advent of HAART, most children with HIV in the United States are now living to reach adolescence and early adulthood. As such, the HIV-related challenges confronting school professionals will change over time. Although the developmental trajectory of children with HIV is looking more promising, the child with HIV is likely to have one or more parents with HIV, resulting in a highly stressful family context. Many of these students will live with extended family members while experiencing loss and bereavement. Finally, because HIV/AIDS disproportionately affects people living in poverty and people of color, numerous cultural factors must be considered when dealing with HIV children.

Almost all children with HIV were infected via mother-to-child (vertical) transmission of the virus. Prevention of vertical infection is dependent on sufficient prenatal care and aggressive drug regimens throughout the pregnancy of infected mothers. Adolescents with HIV, in contrast, were usually infected as a result of risky behaviors and tend to be unaware of their infected state during the teen years. Prevention of adolescent HIV depends heavily on early use of empirically validated health education curricula that focus on safe sexual practices. Unfortunately, teens at greatest risk of HIV infection are those most likely to prematurely drop out of school, making them inaccessible to school-based prevention efforts.

The HIV-infected child presents unique challenges in the arena of psychoeducational assessment. For severe cases, serial assessments are necessary to document any decline in functioning and to monitor the effectiveness of interventions. Existing early intervention and special education programs may be appropriate for HIV-infected children who present with psychoeducational dysfunction. Interdisciplinary services that address cognitive functioning, language, perceptual–motor abilities, memory, and adaptive behavior may be required. All individuals with HIV/AIDS are protected under the Americans with Disabilities Act and Section 504 of the Rehabilitation Act. Children with HIV may also qualify for special services under IDEA.

## RECOMMENDED RESOURCES

### Books and Other Printed Material

Meyers, A. B., & Landau, S. (2002). Best practices in school-based sexuality education and pregnancy prevention. In A. Thomas & J. Grimes (Eds.), *Best practices in school psychology IV* (pp. 1523–1536). Bethesda, MD: National Association of School Psychologists.

This chapter reviews recent research on school-based sexuality education and provides details about the characteristics of effective programs.

Richardson, J., & Schuster, M. A. (2003). *Everything you never wanted your kids to know about SEX (but were afraid they'd ask): The secrets to surviving your child's sexual development from birth to the teens.* New York: Crown Publishing.

This book, written by a psychiatrist and a pediatrician, presents accurate and up-to-date information about sexual development in a format parents will find useful and accessible.

### Websites

*http://www.nasbe.org/HealthySchools/Safe_Healthy/sasha.html*

The National Association of State Boards of Education has prepared an excellent handout for school personnel that addresses HIV in the schools. *Healthy Schools: Someone at School Has AIDS* can be downloaded as a PDF file from this site.

*http://www.aidslegal.com/media/pdfs/teens.pdf*

The AIDS Legal Council of Chicago has published an excellent resource for adolescents who suspect they may have HIV. The handout, *HIV: Issues for Teenagers, Your Legal Rights*, can be downloaded from this address and includes the following topics: getting an HIV test, disclosing HIV test results, HIV-positive teens in school, and planning for the future.

*http://www.siecus.org*

Professionals interested in school-based health education should consult the SIECUS website. This is a rich resource for information regarding coordinated school health programs, sexuality education, and HIV prevention education, as well as many other topics.

*http://psychology.ucdavis.edu/rainbow/index.html*

The work of Dr. Gregory Herek, an internationally recognized authority on sexual prejudice (also called *homophobia*), hate crimes, and AIDS stigma, can be found at this site. The interested reader will find current factual information to promote the use of scientific knowledge for education and enlightened public policy related to sexual orientation and HIV/AIDS.

*http://www.cdcnpin.org/scripts/index.asp*

The nation's largest collection of information and resources on HIV, STD, and TB prevention can be found at this site, which is maintained by the CDC's National Prevention Information Network.

# REFERENCES


Allen, J. P., Philliber, S., Herrling, S., & Kuperminc, G. P. (1997). Preventing teen pregnancy and academic failure: Experimental evaluation of a developmentally based approach. *Child Development, 68,* 729–742.

Armstrong, F. D., Harris, L. L., Thompson, W., Semrad, J. L., Jensen, M. M., Lee, D. Y., et al. (1999). The outpatient developmental services project: Integration of pediatric psychology with primary medical care for children infected with HIV. *Journal of Pediatric Psychology, 24,* 381–391.

Bachanas, P. J., Kullgren, K. A., Schwartz, K. S., McDaniel, J. S., Smith, J., & Nesheim, S. (2001). Psychological adjustment in caregivers of school-age children infected with HIV: Stress, coping, and family factors. *Journal of Pediatric Psychology, 26,* 331–342.

Battles, H. B., & Weiner, L. S. (2002). From adolescence through young adulthood: Psychosocial adjustment associated with long-term survival of HIV. *Journal of Adolescent Health, 30,* 161–168.

Blasini, I., Chantry, C., Cruz, C., Ortiz, L., Salabarria, I., Scalley, N., et al. (2004). Disclosure model for pediatric patients living with HIV in Puerto Rico: Design, implementation, and evaluation. *Journal of Developmental and Behavioral Pediatrics, 25,* 181–189.

Booth, R. E., & Zhang, Y. (1997). Conduct disorder and HIV risk behaviors among runaway and homeless adolescents. *Drug and Alcohol Dependence, 48,* 69–76.

Bose, S., Moss, H. A., Brouwers, P., Pizzo, P., & Lorion, R. (1994). Psychologic adjustment of human immunodeficiency virus-infected school-age children. *Journal of Developmental and Behavioral Pediatrics, 15,* S26–S33.

Brown, L. K., Lourie, K. J., & Poa, M. (2000). Children and adolescents living with HIV and AIDS: A review. *Journal of Child Psychology and Psychiatry and Allied Disciplines, 41,* 81–96.

Centers for Disease Control and Prevention (1988). Guidelines for effective school health education to prevent the spread of AIDS. *Journal of School Health, 58,* 142–146.

Centers for Disease Control and Prevention. (2002). *HIV/AIDS Surveillance Report (Vol. 14).* Atlanta, GA: Author.

Centers for Disease Control and Prevention. (2003). *Youth risk behavior surveillance system (YRBSS): 1991–2003.* Retrieved September 12, 2004, from http://www.cdc.gov/yrbss

Crandall, C. S. (2000). Ideology and lay theories of stigma: The justification of stigmatization. In T. Heatherton, R. Kleck, M. Hebl, & J. Hull (Eds.), *The social psychology of stigma* (pp. 126–150). New York: Guilford Press.

Dryfoos, J. G., & Maguire, S. (2002). *Inside full-service community schools.* Thousand Oaks, CA: Corwin Press.

Elders, M. J. (1994). Sexuality education for communities of color. *SIECUS Report, 22*(6), 1–3.

Goodenow, C., Netherland, J., & Szalacha, L. (2002). AIDS-related risk among adolescent males who have sex with males, females, or both: Evidence from a statewide survey. *American Journal of Public Health, 92,* 203–210.

Grosse, S. J. (1999). Educating children and youth to prevent contagious disease. *Eric Digest,* ED 437368. Retrieved March 15, 2004, from http://www.ericdigests.org/2000-3/disease.htm

Kirby, D. (2002a). The impact of schools and school programs upon adolescent sexual behavior. *Journal of Sex Research, 39,* 27–33.

Kirby, D. (2002b). Effective approaches to reducing adolescent unprotected sex, pregnancy, and childbearing. *Journal of Sex Research, 39,* 51–57.

Kirshenbaum, S. B., & Nevid, J. S. (2002). The specificity of maternal disclosure of HIV/AIDS in relation to children's adjustment. *AIDS Education and Prevention, 14,* 1–16.

Knight, W. G., Mellins, C. A., Levenson, R. L., Arpadi, S. M., & Kairam, R. (2000). Effects of pediatric HIV infection on mental and psychomotor development. *Journal of Pediatric Psychology, 25,* 583–587.

Landry, D. J., Kaeser, L., & Richards, C. L. (1999). Abstinence promotion and the provision of information about contraception in public school district sexuality education policies. *Family Planning Perspectives, 31,* 280–286.

Lester, P., Chesney, M., Cooke, M., Whalley, P., Perez, B., Petru, A., et al. (2002). Diagnostic disclosure to HIV-infected children: How parents decide when and what to tell. *Clinical Child Psychology and Psychiatry, 7,* 85–99.

Llorente, A., Brouwers, P., Charurat, M., Magder, L., Malee, K., Mellins, C., et al. (2003). Early neurodevelopmental markers predictive of mortality in infants infected with HIV-1. *Developmental Medicine and Child Neurology, 45,* 76–84.

Logan, T., Cole, J., & Leukefeld, C. (2002). Women, sex, and HIV: Social and contextual factors, meta-analysis of published interventions and implications for practice and research. *Psychological Bulletin, 128,* 851–885.

Lwin, R., & Melvin, D. (2001). Annotation: Paediatric HIV infection. *Journal of Child Psychology and Psychiatry and Allied Disciplines, 42,* 427–438.

Meyers, A. B., & Landau, S. (2000). Preventing early sexual behavior: Sociopolitical issues and the design of empirically supportable school-based interventions. In K. Minke & G. Bear (Eds.), *Preventing school problems – promoting school success: Strategies and programs that work* (pp. 229–336). Bethesda, MD: National Association of School Psychologists.

Meyers, A. B., & Swerdlik, M. E. (2004). Full service schools. In C. Spielberger (Ed.) *Encyclopedia of applied psychology* (*Vol. 1,* pp. 43–49). Oxford: Elsevier.

Murphy, D. A., Roberts, K. J., & Hoffman, D. (2002). Stigma and ostracism associated with HIV/AIDS: Children carrying the secret of their mothers' HIV+ serostatus. *Journal of Child and Family Studies, 11,* 191–202.

National Association of State Boards of Education. (2001). *Someone at school has AIDS: A complete guide to education policies concerning HIV infection.* Retrieved October 22, 2004, from http://www.nasbe.org/HealthySchools/Safe_Healthy/sasha.html

Pryor, J. B., Reeder, G. D., & Landau, S. (1999). A social psychological analysis of HIV-related stigma: A two-factor theory. *American Behavioral Scientist, 42,* 1193–1211.

Pryor, J. B., Reeder, G. D., Yeadon, C., & Hesson-McInnis, M. (2004). A dual-process model of reactions to perceived stigma. *Journal of Personality and Social Psychology, 87,* 436–452.

Pulsifer, M. B., & Aylward, E. H. (2000). Human immunodeficiency virus. In K. O. Yeates, M. D. Ris, & H. G. Taylor (Eds.), *Pediatric neuropsychology: Research, theory, and practice* (pp. 381–402). New York: Guilford Press.

Repetti, R. L., Taylor, S. E., & Seeman, T. E. (2002). Risky families: Family social environments and the mental and physical health of offspring. *Psychological Bulletin, 128,* 330–366.

Sherman, B. F., Bonanno, G. A., Weiner, L. S., & Battles, H. B. (2000). When children tell their friends they have AIDS: Possible consequences for psychological well-being and disease progression. *Psychosomatic Medicine, 62,* 238–247.

Starkman, N., & Rajani, N. (2002). The case for comprehensive sex education. *AIDS Patient Care and Standards, 16,* 313–318.

Tepper, V. J., Farley, J. J., Rothman, M. I., Houck, D. L., Davis, K. F., & Collins-Jones, T. L. (1998). Neurodevelopmental/neuroradiologic recovery of a child infected with HIV after treatment with combination antiretroviral therapy using the HIV-specific protease inhibitor Ritonavir. *Pediatrics, 101*(3), e7–e12.

Tinsley, B. J., Lees, N. B., & Sumartojo, E. (2004). Child and adolescent HIV risk: Familial and cultural perspectives. *Journal of Family Psychology, 18,* 208–224.

Wachsler-Felder, J. L., & Golden, C. J. (2002). Neuropsycho-logical consequences of HIV in children: A review of current literature. *Clinical Psychology Review, 22,* 441–462.

Waugh, S. (2003). Parental views on disclosure of diagnosis to their HIV-positive children. *AIDS Care, 15,* 169–176.

Weiner, B. (1993). AIDS from an attributional perspective. In J. B. Pryor & G. D. Reeder (Eds.), *The social psychology of HIV infection.* (pp. 287–302). Hillsdale, NJ: Erlbaum.

Wightman, S. I., & Klebert, M. K. (2000). The medical treatment of HIV disease. In J. Durham &

F. Lashley (Eds.), *The person with HIV/AIDS: Nursing perspectives* (pp. 314–350). New York: Springer.

Wodrich, D. L., Swerdlik, M. E., Chenneville, T., & Landau, S. (1998). HIV/AIDS among children and adolescents: Implications for the changing role of school psychologists. *School Psychology Review, 28,* 228–241.

Worchel-Prevatt, F. F, Heffer, R. W., Prevatt, B. C., Miner, J., Young-Saleme, T., Horgan, D., et al. (1998). A school reentry program for chronically ill children. *Journal of School Psychology, 36,* 261–279.

# 66

# Epilepsy

**David W. Dunn**

*Department of Psychiatry and Neurology, Indiana University School of Medicine*

**Joan K. Austin**

*Department of Environments for Health, Indiana University School of Nursing*

Seizures and epilepsy are among the most common neurological problems affecting children. As many as 10% of children will have a seizure at some time during the first 20 years of life, and approximately 1% of children and adolescents will develop chronic recurrent seizures (Hauser, 1994). These children are at an increased risk for both cognitive and behavioral problems.

## BACKGROUND AND DEVELOPMENT

The risk for seizures occurs when neurons begin to fire episodically and excessively. This abnormal firing is seen on the electroencephalogram (EEG) as spikes, sharp waves, or slow waves. This random firing may affect ongoing brain function (i.e., causing transient cognitive dysfunction) that is not evident to observers. When the firing spreads to adjacent areas of the brain, it can cause a seizure.

Certain children are at increased risk of developing seizures. Many seizure syndromes have been found to be familial, and gene loci have been identified. Thus, the child with a family history of seizures is at risk. In addition, brain damage may lead to seizures. The damage may be the result of a congenital malformation of the brain or may follow acquired damage, as seen with cerebral palsy, head injury, meningitis, or stroke. Damage to the frontal or temporal lobes is more likely to be associated with seizures than is damage to the occipital or parietal lobes.

### Seizure Types

A seizure is a single event, and epilepsy is defined as two or more unprovoked seizures. An unprovoked seizure is one in which there is no immediate cause of the seizure. Provoked seizures are caused by transient events such as low blood glucose, toxins, central nervous system infection, or a blow to the head. In describing seizures, parents and observers usually refer to changes before, during, and after the event. The seizure itself is called the *ictus* and the period after the seizure is the *postictal period*. A *prodromal period* may occur prior to the seizure, during which parents may notice changes in the child's behavior or thinking. An *aura* is a warning or change that occurs immediately prior to the seizure. The child is usually able to remember the aura, but may have limited or no recall of the seizure. Diagnosis of a seizure is based on the description of the event. Children usually have an EEG performed to help confirm that the episode was a seizure and to assist with classification of the seizure. Additional laboratory tests, including blood glucose, calcium, and electrolytes, and neuroimaging with computed tomography (CT) or magnetic resonance imaging (MRI) are performed to determine the etiology or reason for the seizure.

Seizures are first divided into *partial* and *generalized* seizures. Partial seizures begin in a single focal area in the brain; generalized seizures start with involvement of both hemispheres of the brain. The different types of seizures are listed in Table 1 (for a brief review of seizure types and syndromes see Browne & Holmes, 2004).

***Partial seizures.*** Partial seizures are also called *focal* or *localized* seizures. They are divided into simple partial seizures, which have no loss of consciousness, and complex partial seizures in which there is transient loss of contact with the environment. The simple partial seizure often consists of motor symptoms, such as an

**Table 1** *Seizure Types*

Partial Seizures
- Simple partial seizures: no loss of consciousness
- Complex partial seizures: loss of consciousness
- Partial with secondary generalization: seizures that evolve into tonic–clonic (grand mal) seizures

Generalized seizures
- Absence (petit mal) seizures
- Atonic seizures
- Myoclonic seizures
- Tonic seizures
- Clonic seizures
- Tonic–clonic (grand mal) seizures

Unclassified epileptic seizures

uncontrollable jerking of the hand and fingers with a spread to involve the face and arm. This type of seizure is also known as a Jacksonian march or Jacksonian seizure. Less often, simple partial seizures are sensory, such as an uncomfortable sensation that spreads over a portion of one side of the body. Rarely, they may have autonomic symptoms such as pallor or vomiting, or psychic symptoms such as brief emotions, hallucinations, or memories.

Complex partial seizures may start with a simple seizure or begin with loss of consciousness. The manifestations of the seizures will depend on the area of the brain involved in the spread of abnormal signals from the epileptogenic focus. The complex partial seizure may consist of automatisms such as lip smacking and picking or fumbling movements of the fingers and hands or may consist of various motor, sensory, psychic, or autonomic symptoms. Some complex partial seizures consist only of loss of consciousness. They are distinguished from *absence seizures* by a period of postictal confusion following the episode. Occasionally, partial seizures will be followed by a *generalized tonic–clonic seizure*. These are termed *partial seizures with secondary generalization*.

***Generalized seizures.*** Generalized seizures affect both cerebral hemispheres simultaneously. *Absence seizures* are brief staring spells. There is no warning or confusion, and no other physical or mental changes follow the episode. Most episodes are brief, lasting a matter of seconds. Although they occasionally are accompanied by a tremor of the hands or blinking of the eyes, they never result in a fall or injury to the child.

*Myoclonic seizures* cause a brief sudden contraction of muscle groups without apparent change in consciousness. Most are sudden episodes lasting less than a minute. *Tonic seizures* consist of a stiffening or contraction of muscle groups and involve both sides of the body symmetrically, with an associated fall and loss of consciousness. *Clonic seizures* are repetitive jerks that usually occur symmetrically and with an associated loss of consciousness, and a postictal period of confusion or lethargy follows. When tonic and clonic seizures occur together, the child has a classic *tonic–clonic* or *grand mal* seizure. It usually begins as a sudden stiffening and fall, followed by symmetrical jerking movements of the extremities and then a period of sleep, confusion, or lethargy. Children may be incontinent during these episodes and are at risk of injury from the fall. *Atonic seizures* cause a sudden loss of muscle tone that usually results in a fall.

## Epilepsies and Epilepsy Syndromes

Epilepsy is defined by the occurrence of two or more seizures not triggered by specific metabolic disruptions or other isolated events that cause a seizure. After seizure type is determined, the next step is the classification of epilepsies or epileptic syndromes (Table 2). Epilepsy syndromes are defined by a combination of seizure type, etiology, EEG findings, and natural history. The epilepsy syndrome classification is currently being revised because of changes in our knowledge of epilepsy. In both the old and new proposed classifications, the epilepsy syndromes are still divided into focal and generalized epilepsies.

Focal epilepsy syndromes may be called *localization-related, local,* or *partial* syndromes. The syndromes are then divided into idiopathic, symptomatic, or cryptogenic, depending on the assumed etiology. *Idiopathic* epilepsy syndromes are due either to familial seizures or to an unknown causation. *Symptomatic* epilepsies are associated with a known or suspected disorder or damage to the brain, and *cryptogenic* epilepsies are presumed to be due to central nervous system (CNS) damage, even though the etiology cannot be defined. In the more recent proposed change in classification, epilepsies may be divided into idiopathic, symptomatic, and familial disorders. The *idiopathic* seizures are of unknown origin, the *symptomatic* seizures are due to known underlying damage or dysfunction, and the *familial* seizures are due to a known genetic abnormality. Additional categories of epilepsies and syndromes are called *undetermined,* whether focal or generalized and *special syndromes.* Under special syndromes are *isolated* seizures, *febrile* seizures,

**Table 2** *Epilepsies and Epileptic Syndromes of Childhood*

- Localization-related (focal) epilepsies
  - Idiopathic epilepsies
    - Benign childhood epilepsy with centrotemporal spikes
    - Childhood epilepsy with occipital spikes
  - Symptomatic and cryptogenic epilepsies: frontal lobe, temporal lobe epilepsies
- Generalized epilepsies and epileptic syndromes
  - Idiopathic
    - Benign neonatal convulsions
    - Childhood absence epilepsy
    - Juvenile absence epilepsy
    - Juvenile myoclonic epilepsy
    - Isolated grand mal epilepsy
  - Symptomatic or cryptogenic epilepsies
    - Infantile spasms (West syndrome)
    - Lennox-Gastaut syndrome
- Epilepsies undetermined whether generalized or focal
  - Neonatal seizures
  - Acquired epileptic aphasia (Landau-Kleffner syndrome)
- Special syndromes
  - Febrile seizures
  - Provoked seizures due to metabolic, toxic, infectious, or traumatic events

and *provoked* seizures. This chapter describes only the most common epilepsy syndromes affecting school-age children. For the more unusual syndromes the reader might refer to one of the standard textbooks of epilepsy (e.g., Browne & Holmes, 2004).

The idiopathic, localization-related epilepsies are benign childhood epilepsy with centrotemporal spikes (or *rolandic* epilepsy) and childhood epilepsy with occipital paroxysms. Both begin in the preschool or elementary school years and usually resolve by the end of adolescence. Both disorders are probably familial and are not associated with underlying CNS damage. They have characteristic EEG changes with accentuation of spikes during sleep. During rolandic seizures, there is speech arrest, drooling, and clonic movements or abnormal sensations involving the face. Consciousness is preserved. These seizures are more common in the evenings and can become secondarily generalized. Most of these children have infrequent seizures and may require no antiepileptic drugs (AEDs). Occipital seizures are characterized by eye movements, visual hallucinations, and occasionally vomiting. As with rolandic seizures, they occur more often at night and can spread to become generalized seizures. They more often need to be treated with AEDs.

The symptomatic and cryptogenic localization-related epilepsies are defined by epileptiform disorders coming from a specific area of the brain and by a known or assumed focal area of brain damage or dysfunction. They most often arise in the temporal or frontal lobes. *Temporal lobe* seizures may begin with an aura. The most common manifestation of the seizure is a motionless stare. Other signs are mouth or facial movements, manual automatisms, and autonomic changes such as pallor, salivation, or flushing. As many as a fifth of the children with temporal lobe seizures may have generalized tonic–clonic seizures. During the postictal phase, the child may be sleepy or confused or complain of a headache. In contrast, *frontal lobe* seizures tend to occur during sleep. The seizure consists of tonic posturing movements and occasionally of more complex automatisms such as bicycling movements. These seizures are usually brief and are followed by little or no postictal confusion.

The idiopathic generalized epilepsies are childhood absence epilepsy, juvenile myoclonic epilepsy, and epilepsy with generalized tonic–clonic seizures. *Childhood absence* epilepsy begins during the preschool or elementary school ages and often remits by adolescence. These seizures consist of brief staring spells with no aura or postictal confusion. *Juvenile myoclonic* epilepsy starts during the adolescent years and, though easily controlled, tends to persist into adulthood. The usual manifestations are brief jerks of the shoulders and arms and occasional tonic–clonic seizures soon after awakening. Epilepsy with generalized tonic–clonic seizures may begin at any age but tends to start during adolescence. There is a sudden onset of stiffening followed by jerking of all the limbs. The episode is followed by postictal sleep or confusion and headache.

One group of uncommon but problematic epilepsies (affecting less than 1 child in 1,000) has a major impact on cognitive functioning. These include *infantile spasms* and the *Lennox-Gastaut syndrome*, which are cryptogenic or symptomatic generalized epilepsies that begin in the preschool ages. The children have a combination of seizure types, including myoclonic jerks and atonic seizures. The seizures can be difficult to control, and even with control they are often associated with mental handicap. The *Landau-Kleffner syndrome*, or *acquired epileptic aphasia*, begins in the preschool years and causes pronounced language disturbance with less obvious seizures.

*Febrile* seizures and *provoked* seizures are special syndromes. Both are very common. Approximately 5%–10% of children have one of these episodes at some time during their lives. Febrile seizures are generalized tonic–clonic seizures that occur at the initial rise in temperature, or onset of fever, associated with an infectious illness. They are seen in children 1 to 6 years of age and are not associated with any risk of cognitive or behavioral problems. Isolated seizures may occur with low blood sugar, hypocalcaemia, water intoxication, head injury, certain medications and drugs, and sleep deprivation. Treatment of the underlying problem should prevent subsequent epilepsy.

## PROBLEMS AND IMPLICATIONS

Children with epilepsy are at increased risk for mental handicap or learning disabilities. Infantile spasms, Lennox-Gastaut syndrome, and the other symptomatic generalized epilepsies are associated with significant mental handicap, with more than three fourths of these children having IQs in the mentally retarded range. Children with less severe epilepsies may have intelligence scores in the broad normal range but still experience more cognitive difficulties than siblings or control groups. On average, academic underachievement is found in about one third of children with epilepsy (Mitchell, Chavez, Lee, & Guzman, 1991). This does not seem to be solely an effect of chronic illness, as children with epilepsy have more academic difficulties than a comparison group of children with asthma (Austin, Huberty, Huster, & Dunn, 1998).

Children with epilepsy also are at increased risk for behavioral problems. In epidemiological studies, approximately one fourth of children with uncomplicated epilepsy and more than half of the children with epilepsy and other neurological problems have psychiatric problems. In comparison, behavioral problems are found in 10%–15% of children with chronic illnesses not involving the brain and 5%–10% of controls (Davies, Heyman, & Goodman, 2003). Studies have shown a higher rate of behavioral problems in children with epilepsy compared with children with cardiac disease, asthma, and other chronic illnesses not involving the central nervous system. Children with epilepsy also have consistently more behavioral problems than their siblings.

### Risk Factors for Cognitive and Behavioral Problems in Children With Epilepsy

Multiple risk factors for cognitive and behavioral problems are seen in children with epilepsy. These risk factors include gender, neurological dysfunction, seizure-related factors, use of antiepileptic drugs, and family variables (Dunn & Austin, 1999). Gender may have some predictive value. Boys with epilepsy seem to be at increased risk for academic difficulties. Gender has been a less consistent predictor of behavioral problems. The association between gender and behavioral problems varies by type of behavioral problem, the severity of epilepsy, and the age of the child. Thus, some studies suggest that boys have more difficulty, others suggest that girls do, and several studies show no difference.

Neurological dysfunction in addition to epilepsy consistently predicts both cognitive and behavioral problems. The child with both seizures and mental handicap is likely to have CNS damage as an explanation for both problems. Underlying neurological dysfunction also increases the risk of behavioral problems. More severe intractable seizures are a predictive factor for both behavioral problems and lower cognitive ability. Seizure type and seizure syndrome also may be important. Children with symptomatic or cryptogenic generalized epilepsies are at significantly increased risk for academic difficulty; other seizure types and epilepsy syndromes do not predict differences in frequency of cognitive or behavioral problems. Early age of seizure onset has been associated with cognitive problems but is less significant as a risk for behavioral difficulties (Schoenfeld et al., 1999).

Treatment of seizures with AEDs can result in academic and behavioral problems, though the effect is usually minimal. Nevertheless, certain AEDs may cause trouble for specific children. Phenobarbital, benzodiazepines, and topiramate are the agents most often associated with cognitive and behavioral difficulties. Phenobarbital has caused lowering of full-scale intelligence scores, hyperactivity, inattention, irritability, and depression, and benzodiazepines may cause sedation and cognitive impairment or disinhibition and worsening of behavior. Topiramate has had adverse effects on attention and verbal fluency and has been associated with both depression and psychosis (e.g., Loring & Meador, 2004). The incidence of behavioral and cognitive side effects from the newer AEDs seems to be low,

**Table 3** *Cognitive and Behavioral Side Effects of Antiepileptic Drugs*

| | |
|---|---|
| Barbiturates | Hyperactivity, irritability, depression. |
| Phenytoin | Poor concentration and slowing of motor speed (mild). |
| Carbamazepine | Lethargy, incoordination. |
| Valproic acid | Psychomotor slowing (minimal), dementia (very rare). |
| Lamotrigine | Lethargy, irritability and aggression (uncommon). |
| Gabapentin | Irritability and aggression (more frequently observed in children with mental handicaps). |
| Topiramate | Slow speech, depression, irritability, inattention. |
| Levetiracetam | Hyperactivity, aggression, lability. |
| Zonisamide | Psychosis. |

but side effects can occur in any individual child. School professionals can help monitor for adverse effects after introduction of a new AED or a change in dosage (see Table 3).

Family variables such as family relationships, parental education, parental participation in educational activities, and an organized and supportive family environment are important in predicting both cognitive and behavioral problems (Austin, Dunn, Johnson, & Perkins, 2004). In addition, child variables seem to be important in predicting behavior. A negative attitude toward illness has been associated with symptoms of depression and low self-esteem in children and adolescents with epilepsy (Dunn, Austin, & Huster, 1999).

Stigma continues to be a potential problem for children with epilepsy and their families. Individual perceptions of stigma can contribute to low self-esteem and depression in children and adolescents with epilepsy. In the school setting stigma also might result in lower expectations by teachers or parents for potential academic success of the child with epilepsy (Bishop & Slevin, 2004). Recent surveys have shown a lack of understanding about epilepsy and its effects on children's lives. A survey of adolescents in the general population found that adolescents thought that persons with epilepsy would be more likely to be bullied, and less likely to be popular than their healthy peers (Austin, Shafer, & Deering, 2002). More than half the respondents reported that they would not tell others if they had epilepsy. Surveys of both the general population and teachers have found that approximately one fourth to one third of individuals thought having a child with epilepsy in the classroom would negatively affect the school environment.

## Cognitive Difficulties in Children With Epilepsy

Children with mental retardation have a higher prevalence of epilepsy than children with normal intelligence. The prevalence of epilepsy in children with mental handicap is approximately 15%–20%, with higher rates of 35%–50% in the children with mental handicap plus additional brain injury such as cerebral palsy. Within the population of children with epilepsy, mental handicap is seldom due to just the effects of seizures and is far more often determined by the degree of underlying CNS damage.

Regression in cognitive function or academic abilities is uncommon in children with epilepsy. Studies that repeated neuropsychological testing over a course of years found no deterioration or change in scores on standard measures of intelligence and achievement (e.g., Bailet & Turk, 2000). Rarely, a loss of previously acquired skills or a persistent drop in IQ may be associated with intractable (difficult to control) seizures or may follow status epilepticus, a prolonged seizure lasting more than 30–60 minutes.

Children with epilepsy and normal intelligence are at risk for learning disability. As a group, children with epilepsy are more likely to have lower grades, to repeat a grade, or to score below average on achievement tests than siblings or children with other chronic illnesses. Multiple areas of underachievement have been documented. Evaluating children with epilepsy and a full-scale IQ of $\geq 70$, Seidenberg et al. (1986) found significant underachievement for word recognition in 10% of children, for spelling in 33% of boys and 16% of girls, for arithmetic in 28% of boys and 32% of girls, and for reading comprehension in 23% of boys and 13% of girls. Mitchell et al. (1991) described underachievement for general information in 50% of children with epilepsy, for spelling in 32%, for mathematics in 31%, and for reading comprehension in 38%.

Deficits in memory and attention are possible contributors to the academic underachievement seen in children with epilepsy, though memory impairment has not consistently been found. Some studies have found that children with epilepsy have lower scores on memory tests than population norms or sibling controls (e.g., Bailet &

Turk, 2000). Others found no memory deficits in a group of children with well-controlled epilepsy (e.g., Williams et al., 2001). In contrast, multiple studies have found impairment in sustained attention in children with epilepsy (e.g., Sánchez-Carpintero & Neville, 2003). Problems with attention have been found in children with chronic seizures and new-onset seizures, or the problems may precede the onset of seizures. In one study, parents of 10.7% of children with first-recognized seizures described attention problems in the 6 months prior to the beginning of seizures (Austin et al., 2001).

### Behavioral Problems in Children With Epilepsy

A variety of behavioral problems have been described in children with epilepsy. This increased prevalence of behavioral problems has been found in both epidemiological samples and clinical groups. In one large epidemiological study, Davies et al. (2003) reported behavioral problems in 37% of the children with epilepsy. They separated the children with epilepsy into two groups, those with additional neurological disabilities and those with uncomplicated epilepsy. In the sample of children with complicated epilepsy, 16% had a pervasive developmental disorder, 12% had Attention Deficit Hyperactivity Disorder (ADHD), 24% had oppositional defiant disorder (ODD) or conduct disorder, and 16% had unspecified emotional problems. None of the children with uncomplicated epilepsy had pervasive developmental disorder or ADHD. In the uncomplicated group, 17% had ODD or conduct disorder and 17% an emotional disorder. In comparison, in the control sample, the prevalence of emotional problems was 4%, ODD and conduct disorder was 5%, ADHD was 2%, and pervasive developmental disorder was 0.2%. In a sample of children with epilepsy recruited from an epilepsy clinic, Caplan et al. (1998) found disruptive behavior disorders (ADHD, ODD, and conduct disorder) in 25% and anxiety or mood disorders in 13%. They noted a schizophrenia-like psychosis in 10% of the children with complex partial seizures but not in the children with generalized seizures.

ADHD is the most common behavioral problem associated with childhood epilepsy and is a probable contributor to the academic underachievement seen in children with epilepsy. When formal diagnostic criteria are used, ADHD has been found in approximately 30%–40% of children with epilepsy. Symptoms of ADHD have been found in children with epilepsy regardless of seizure type. In contrast to children seen in a psychiatric clinic who present with ADHD but without epilepsy, children with ADHD and epilepsy seem to have an equal male:female ratio and more often have the inattentive type of ADHD. In one study of children with chronic seizures, symptoms of ADHD, combined type, were present in 11.4%; with ADHD, predominantly inattentive type, in 24%; and with ADHD, predominantly hyperactive–impulsive type, in 2.3% (Dunn, Austin, Harezlak, & Ambrosius, 2003).

Depression has been found in about one fourth of children and adolescents with epilepsy. Although depression has been associated with temporal lobe epilepsy in adults, there does not seem to be an association between seizure type and depression symptoms in children with epilepsy. Depression has been associated with higher seizure frequency and with a negative attitude toward illness, lower satisfaction with family relationships, and external or unknown locus of control (Dunn et al., 1999). Depression has often been overlooked and left untreated in children with epilepsy.

There are fewer studies of anxiety disorder in children with epilepsy. Symptoms of anxiety disorders are found in 15%–25% of children with seizures (Williams et al., 2003). Poor seizure control, polypharmacy, and comorbid learning and behavior problems are risk factors (Williams et al.). Anxiety also has been described as a withdrawal symptom occurring with the discontinuation of antiepileptic drugs.

The two most severe behavioral problems associated with epilepsy are psychosis and autistic disorder. True schizophreniform psychosis is more common in adults with complex partial seizures that began early in life. Psychosis is relatively uncommon in children with epilepsy, although illogical thought processing and hallucinations have been found in approximately 10% of children with complex partial epilepsy (Caplan et al., 1998). Autistic Disorder and Autism Spectrum Disorders are more common in children with both epilepsy and mental retardation. Approximately one third of children with autistic disorder will develop seizures during their lifetime.

## ALTERNATIVE ACTIONS FOR PREVENTION

Primary prevention of epilepsy is difficult. Attempts to prevent CNS damage include immunizing for meningitis and promoting use of car seats and bicycle helmets to reduce head injury, which could lead to a reduced incidence of symptomatic epilepsies. Currently, there is no way to prevent idiopathic or familial epilepsy. Thus, practitioners must focus on secondary or tertiary prevention of cognitive, behavioral, and psychosocial problems associated with epilepsy. Education and support are common components of interventions, and both should help ameliorate the problems experienced by children with epilepsy. Several published interventions have started with education of the child and family about epilepsy and then have tried to equip families and children with skills to master the medical and psychosocial challenges of seizures.

For example, Lewis, Hatton, Salas, Leake, and Chiofalo (1991) conducted a large group intervention designed to benefit children and families with epilepsy. They invited families to participate in four child-centered, family-focused sessions, each lasting 1.5 hours. Instruction was given separately to parents and children. Children were given information about seizures and seizure management and were taught coping skills and communication. Parents received support, education about seizures, and instruction on decision making, parenting, coping, and adaptation. Outcomes were compared to those of a control group that received three 2-hour lectures by a physician. Children in the treatment group had more knowledge of seizure management, an increased sense of social competence, and fewer behavioral problems. Parents in the experimental group were significantly less anxious by the end of the program. The major problem in the design of the intervention was the difficulty of scheduling four sessions for large groups of parents and children.

Tieffenberg et al. (2000) described a weekly 5-session group intervention to assist children and families with chronic illnesses, including epilepsy. The groups consisted of 8 to 10 families with either epilepsy or asthma. The sessions emphasized helping the child to develop autonomy, with the parents acting as facilitators. At the end of the intervention, both children and parents had increased knowledge of the illness. Parents reported decreased fears and less disruption in family life, and children had an increase in internal locus of control. In addition, the children with epilepsy made fewer emergency room visits and had fewer days absent from school.

Austin, McNelis, Shore, Dunn, and Musick (2002) developed an intervention that employed telephone conferences. Children and parents first were questioned about worries and concerns, knowledge of epilepsy, and information and support needs. After reviewing their responses, a nurse contacted the family by telephone and addressed questions and concerns. Next, families were offered the opportunity to participate in a telephone conference with other families to allow children to talk to other children with seizures and parents to talk to other parents dealing with epilepsy in a child. At the end of the intervention, both parents and children had improved knowledge and less need for information. Children had fewer concerns and parents had less need for support.

In a recent report, Snead et al. (2004) described a 6-week psychoeducational group intervention for adolescents and their parents. Topics included medical aspects of epilepsy, healthy behaviors and attitudes, stress management, social concerns, and relationships. Adolescents and parents were in separate groups. Assessments were completed at the first and last sessions. The adolescents reported better understanding of epilepsy and more comfort with disclosure of epilepsy. Parents found the information on managing seizures, dealing with schools, and coping with stress most helpful. No significant changes were seen in measures of quality of life, depression, or anxiety.

To combat the stigma associated with epilepsy, educational interventions should target peers and teachers as well as children with epilepsy and their families. Children and adolescents with epilepsy are reluctant to tell others about their seizures, and parents frequently do not disclose their child's condition to teachers, in part because of fears of stigma. Information and educational programs available from the Epilepsy Foundation can be used to improve understanding about epilepsy and its effects on children's lives (see Recommended Resources). Because fear of the unknown may be particularly challenging with seizures, instructions for teachers on managing a seizure in the classroom should result in a better sense of mastery and control. Improved communication between parents and teachers should follow if parents are less fearful of stigma within the classroom. Education about epilepsy could improve knowledge and attitudes and create a more realistic environment in the classroom that might promote optimal achievement by the child with epilepsy.

Some children and adolescents with epilepsy might benefit from more extensive interventions to reduce the risk of adverse outcomes. For example, Freeman, Jacobs, Vining, and Rabin (1984) described a comprehensive program for adolescents with seizures that included assessment, evaluation of classroom placement, and provision of counseling and vocational training. Participants in the program had fewer grade failures, were less likely to drop out of school, and were more likely to be employed than adolescents with epilepsy in regular school programs. The total cost of the intervention was approximately 10% higher than the cost of standard placement.

## ALTERNATIVE ACTIONS FOR INTERVENTIONS

### Responses to a Seizure at School

All school professionals should be aware of basic first aid for children with a seizure. Seizures may be very frightening to observers. This fear could be mitigated by having an appropriate plan. If a child has a generalized tonic–clonic or grand mal seizure, the observer should turn the child onto one side and place a soft object such as a pillow or folded coat under the head. Do not try to restrain the child or place anything in the mouth. Watch the time. Most seizures last less than 5 minutes. Stay with the child until the seizure ends and during the period of postictal lethargy. This postictal period may last several minutes. If the child has a nonconvulsive seizure, watch the child during the episode and gently guide him or her away from dangerous areas such as stairs or streets. Do not try to restrain the child. Most nonconvulsive seizures are brief, with a quick return of consciousness. Full descriptions of first aid for seizures are available on the Epilepsy Foundation website.

If the child has a known seizure disorder, call 911 only if (a) the seizure does not appear to be stopping within 5 minutes, (b) a seizure recurs after stopping, or (c) the child appears to have trouble breathing after the seizure. In the case of a child who has had no prior seizure or when the school is unaware of a previous seizure in a child, the parents should be notified immediately and the child should be seen by a physician that day. If the parents are not available, the child should go to an emergency room.

After the episode, the school professional should write a description of the event for the child's parents and physician that details what the child was doing when the seizure started, any warning signs that occurred just prior to the seizure, behavior during the episode, areas of the body involved, degree of contact with the environment, duration of the seizure, and the child's behavior immediately after the episode, including length of time until the child was back to normal. This information can be very helpful to the physician caring for the child. If the event occurs in front of other students, after the child with the seizure is safe, explain what happened to the other children in a calm, reassuring manner.

### Collaboration Between Physicians and School Professionals

The quality of care given to the child with epilepsy is in part dependent on the quality of information available to the physicians and nurses treating the child. At all follow-up clinic visits, the physician will need to know not only about adequacy of seizure control and possible side effects of medication, but also about behavioral or educational problems of the child with epilepsy. Teachers, school nurses, psychologists, counselors, or social workers should help provide this information to parents or directly to the physician once the parents have given permission for such communications to occur.

If parents or school personnel warn the physician about changes in behavior or academic performance, the physician will start by reviewing the history for recurrent seizure during the daytime or during sleep. Next, the physician will consider the possibility of psychiatric or cognitive side effects of medications. Physicians should repeat the EEG, as frequent epileptiform discharges might be associated with transient cognitive impairment that could contribute to cognitive or behavioral problems. Often, the physician may need a prolonged video EEG to sample the entire day and to capture events on both EEG and video that might not be clinically clear. For example, staring spells could be absence seizures, daydreaming, or a sign of ADHD. This distinction may be particularly important, as subtle seizures may have a significant effect on academic performance. A study of the effect of nonconvulsive seizures and epileptiform discharges on cognitive functioning showed that slowing of processing speed was associated with epileptiform discharges and with seizures occurring during psychological testing, whereas problems with attention and short-term memory deficits were associated only with seizures during testing (Aldenkamp & Arends, 2004). If there is a suggestion of nocturnal seizures resulting in next-day lethargy or inattention, the physician may request an overnight EEG recording to assess for nocturnal seizures and sleep disturbance.

In the school, the first step in providing adequate interventions for the child with epilepsy is recognizing that a problem exists and understanding that cognitive and behavioral problems are not an inevitable result of having epilepsy. Once a child with epilepsy is identified as having cognitive or behavioral problems, assessment should be broad enough to include biological and psychosocial factors that may be adversely affecting the child. First, teachers should watch for seizure control and should be aware of changes in medication. The child with cognitive problems will need psychological assessment and possibly modifications in the educational program. The child with behavioral problems may benefit from a combination of psychotherapy and psychopharmacological therapy.

In the classroom, cognitive or behavioral problems should prompt the teacher to watch for not only obvious seizures but also more subtle nonconvulsive seizures. During nonconvulsive seizures, the child may stare blankly and fail to respond to being called or touched. Sometimes there may be lip smacking or other subtle movements that will help distinguish nonconvulsive seizures from more common daydreaming or the inattention of ADHD. Good communication between teachers, parents, and physicians can clarify the nature of vague episodes and inform the teacher about the expected manifestations of the seizure type experienced by the child. Teachers should observe the child for daytime sleepiness, because unrecognized nocturnal seizures can cause sleep fragmentation, with subsequent reduction in daytime alertness. Furthermore, epilepsy in children and disrupted sleep has been associated with an increase in daytime behavioral problems.

Teachers should be aware of the introduction of a new AED, discontinuation of AEDs, or changes in AED dose. There are anecdotal reports of adverse cognitive or behavioral effects in most of the AEDs, suggesting that careful monitoring should follow introduction of or increase in a dose of any AED. It is essential that deterioration in academic performance or behavior following change in AEDs be reported to the treating physician.

## Academic and Behavioral Interventions

If adverse effects of seizure control or antiepileptic drugs are not the apparent cause of a change in cognitive function, psychological assessment should be obtained, with particular emphasis on memory, attention, and information processing (Fastenau, Dunn, & Austin, 2004). The results can be used to establish an individualized educational plan. Some children with epilepsy will need extra support and structure for attentional problems, and others will need educational interventions for learning disabilities. The programming needs of the child with epilepsy and ADHD or learning disability are no different from those of a child without epilepsy.

Children with epilepsy and behavioral problems may benefit from psychosocial interventions. Several studies have shown reduction in seizure number and improvement in self-esteem after participation in individual or group therapies that emphasized monitoring for emotional precipitants of seizures followed by instruction in relaxation techniques, self-control, and coping (e.g., Dahl, Melin, Brorson, & Schollin, 1985). Though not specific for children with epilepsy, individual cognitive–behavioral therapy and interpersonal therapy have been shown to be effective for children and adolescents with depression and anxiety (Lagges & Dunn, 2003).

Family therapy is another option. Prior studies by Austin et al. (2004) and Mitchell et al. (1991) have demonstrated an association between family stress and dysfunction and behavioral problems in children with epilepsy. Impaired communication between parents and children, excess maternal criticism, marital discord, and parental psychopathology are associated with behavioral problems. In a study of children with new-onset seizures, Austin et al. (2004) showed that parents' sense of mastery and control and their confidence in their ability to adequately discipline the child with seizures was associated with better behavior rating for children at baseline and 24 months after the first seizure. Though this was not an intervention study, it suggests that improvement in parenting abilities would result in improved child behavior.

When psychotherapeutic intervention is ineffective or only partially effective, psychopharmacology should be tried. Psychotropic drugs that lower the seizure threshold are best avoided, and attention should be paid to potential drug interaction between psychotropic medications and antiepileptic drugs (Alldredge, 1999). Children with ADHD and epilepsy have shown improvement in attention and no increase in seizure frequency after introduction of stimulant medication.

Depression and anxiety can be treated with serotonin reuptake inhibitors (SSRIs). Though there are no controlled studies demonstrating efficacy and safety of these medications in children with seizures, some double-blind placebo controlled trials of fluoxetine and sertraline for children and adolescents with depression and an open label study of sertraline for depression in adults with epilepsy have shown improvement in depressive symptoms without significant reduction in seizure control (Kanner & Dunn, 2004). Recent worries about activation and increase in suicidal ideation early in the course of treatment with SSRIs show that they demand careful monitoring of response and adverse events (see chapter 15, "Depressive Disorders"). In addition, the SSRIs may inhibit the metabolism of certain AEDs, leading to elevated serum drug levels (Alldredge, 1999).

Nevertheless, the SSRIs are better than the older tricyclic antidepressants, which lower seizure threshold and have not been shown to be more effective than placebos in controlled trials for depression in children and adolescents. The hyperactivity and aggression seen in some children with autistic disorder and the hallucinations and delusions that occur in childhood and adolescent onset psychosis may respond to antipsychotics. Both clozapine and chlorpromazine lower the seizure threshold and should be avoided; however, there does not seem to be a significant risk with haloperidol or risperidone (Alldredge, 1999).

## SUMMARY

Seizures and epilepsy are common and heterogeneous disorders of childhood. The childhood epilepsies vary from benign transient diseases to intractable disorders associated with significant impairments. Children with epilepsy are at risk for both cognitive and behavioral problems. The most consistent predictors of difficulty are additional neurological dysfunction and severe seizures. An early age of onset is more commonly associated with cognitive problems than with behavioral disturbance. Mental retardation is more commonly found in children with additional central nervous system damage. Learning disabilities may occur in all children with epilepsy and are often associated with memory and attentional problems. The most frequent behavioral disorders associated with epilepsy are ADHD, depression, and anxiety. Educational programs may be helpful in preventing behavioral problems. Treatment of cognitive difficulties is the same for children with and without epilepsy. Behavioral problems can be treated with psychosocial interventions or with medication, being careful to avoid drugs that lower the seizure threshold and to monitor for interactions between antiepileptic drugs and psychotropic agents.

## RECOMMENDED RESOURCES

### Books and Other Printed Material

***For parents or a general audience:***

Devinsky, O. (2002). *Epilepsy: Patient and family guide* (2nd ed.). Philadelphia: F. A. Davis.

This text is for both adults and children with epilepsy. It has a good section on legal rights and insurance.

Freeman, J. M., Vining, E. P. G., & Pillas, D. J. (2002). *Seizures and epilepsy in childhood: A guide* (3rd ed.). Baltimore, MD: Johns Hopkins University Press.

This book provides an up-to-date review of seizures and epilepsy. It covers medical aspects plus coping with epilepsy, school, sports, and driving.

***For mental health professionals:***

Ettinger, A. B., & Kanner, A. M. (2001). *Psychiatric issues in epilepsy: A practical guide to diagnosis and treatment.* Philadelphia: Lippincott Williams & Wilkins.

This book provides good coverage of a wide range of behavioral concerns and psychosocial issues, with less emphasis on cognitive problems.

Svoboda, W. B. (2004). *Childhood epilepsy: Language, learning, and behavioral complications.* New York: Cambridge University Press.

This is a new textbook that is divided into sections on speech and language problems, cognitive difficulties, and behavioral problems.

Trimble, M., & Schmitz, B. (2002). *The neuropsychiatry of epilepsy.* Cambridge, UK: Cambridge University Press.

Many of the chapters in this text are by European experts. The coverage is broad but focuses more on adults than children.

### Websites

*http://www.aesnet.org*

The website of the American Epilepsy Society is designed for professionals involved in research and treatment of people with epilepsy. It has some information for more general audiences.

*http://www.epilepsyfoundation.org*

The website of the Epilepsy Foundation provides information for all ages, a good section on first aid for seizures, and reviews of current medications and issues that are accessible to a general audience.

## REFERENCES

Aldenkamp, A., & Arends, J. (2004). The relative influence of epileptic discharges, short nonconvulsive seizures, and type of epilepsy on cognitive function. *Epilepsia, 45,* 54–63.

Alldredge, B. K. (1999). Seizure risk associated with psychotropic drugs: Clinical and pharmacokinetic considerations. *Neurology, 53*(Suppl. 2), S68–S75.

Austin, J. K., Dunn, D. W., Johnson, C. S., & Perkins, S. M. (2004). Behavioral issues involving children and adolescents with epilepsy and the impact on their families: Recent research data. *Epilepsy & Behavior, 5,* S33–S41.

Austin, J. K., Harezlak, J., Dunn, D. W., Huster, G. A., Rose, D. F., & Ambrosius, W. T. (2001). Behavior problems in children before first recognized seizures. *Pediatrics, 107,* 115–122.

Austin, J. K., Huberty, T. J., Huster, G. A., & Dunn, D. W. (1998). Academic achievement in children with epilepsy and asthma. *Developmental Medicine and Child Neurology, 40,* 248–255.

Austin, J. K., McNelis, A. M., Shore, C. P., Dunn, D. W., & Musick, B. (2002). A feasibility study of a family seizure management program: 'Be Seizure Smart.' *Journal of Neuroscience Nursing, 34,* 30–37.

Austin, J. K., Shafer, P. O., & Deering, J. B. (2002). Epilepsy familiarity, knowledge, and perceptions of stigma: Report from a survey of adolescents in the general population. *Epilepsy and Behavior, 3,* 368–375.

Bailet, L. L., & Turk, W. R. (2000). The impact of childhood epilepsy on neurocognitive and behavioral performance: A prospective longitudinal study. *Epilepsia, 41,* 426–431.

Bishop, M., & Slevin, B. (2004). Teachers' attitudes toward students with epilepsy: Results of a survey of elementary and middle school teachers. *Epilepsy and Behavior, 5,* 308–315.

Browne, T. R., & Holmes, G. L. (2004). *Handbook of epilepsy* (3rd ed.). Philadelphia: Lippincott Williams & Wilkins.

Caplan, R., Arbelle, S., Magharious, W., Guthrie, D., Komo, S., Shields, W. D., et al. (1998). Psychopathology in pediatric complex partial and primarily generalized epilepsy. *Developmental Medicine and Child Neurology, 40,* 805–811.

Dahl, J., Melin, L., Brorson, L. O., & Schollin, J. (1985). Effects of a broad-spectrum behavior modification treatment program on children with refractory epileptic seizures. *Epilepsia, 26,* 303–309.

Davies, S., Heyman, I., & Goodman, R. (2003). A population survey of mental health problems in children with epilepsy. *Developmental Medicine and Child Neurology, 45,* 292–295.

Dunn, D. W., & Austin, J. K. (1999). Behavioral issues in pediatric epilepsy. *Neurology, 53*(Suppl. 2), S96–S100.

Dunn, D. W., Austin, J. K., Harezlak, J., & Ambrosius, W. T. (2003). ADHD and epilepsy in childhood. *Developmental Medicine and Child Neurology, 45,* 50–54.

Dunn, D. W., Austin, J. K., & Huster, G. A. (1999). Symptoms of depression in adolescents with epilepsy. *Journal of the American Academy of Child and Adolescent Psychiatry, 38,* 1132–1138.

Fastenau, P. S., Dunn, D. W., & Austin, J. K. (2004). Pediatric epilepsy. In M. Rizzo & P. J. Eslinger (Eds.), *Principles and practice of behavioral neurology and neuropsychology* (pp. 965–982). Philadelphia: W.B. Saunders.

Freeman, J. M., Jacobs, H., Vining, E., & Rabin, C. E. (1984). Epilepsy and inner city schools: A school-based program that makes a difference. *Epilepsia, 25,* 438–442.

Hauser, W. A. (1994). The prevalence and incidence of convulsive disorders in children. *Epilepsia, 25*(Suppl. 2), S1–S6.

Kanner, A. M., & Dunn, D. W. (2004). Diagnosis and management of depression and psychosis in children and adolescents with epilepsy. *Journal of Child Neurology, 19*(Suppl. 1), S65–S72.

Lagges, A. M., & Dunn, D. W. (2003). Depression in children and adolescents. *Neurology Clinics of North America, 21,* 953–960.

Lewis, M. A., Hatton, C. L., Salas, I., Leake, B., & Chiofalo, N. (1991). Impact of the children's epilepsy program on parents. *Epilepsia, 32,* 365–374.

Loring, D. W., & Meador, K. J. (2004). Cognitive side effects of antiepileptic drugs in children. *Neurology, 62,* 872–877.

Mitchell, W. G., Chavez, J. M., Lee, H., & Guzman, B. L. (1991). Academic underachievement in children with epilepsy. *Journal of Child Neurology, 6,* 65–72.

Sánchez-Carpintero, R., & Neville, B. G. R. (2003). Attentional ability in children with epilepsy. *Epilepsia, 44,* 1340–1349.

Schoenfeld, J., Seidenberg, M., Woodward, A., Hecox, K., Inglese, C., Mack, K., et al. (1999). Neuropsychological and behavioral status of children with complex partial seizures. *Developmental Medicine and Child Neurology, 41,* 724–731.

Seidenberg, M., Beck, N., Geisser, M., Giordani, B., Sackellares, C., Berent, S., et al. (1986). Academic achievement of children with epilepsy. *Epilepsia, 27,* 753–759.

Snead, K., Ackerson, J., Bailey, K., Schmitt, M. M., Madan-Swain, A., & Martin, R. C. (2004). Taking charge of epilepsy: The development of a structured psychoeducational group intervention for adolescents with epilepsy and their parents. *Epilepsy and Behavior, 5,* 547–556.

Tieffenberg, J. A., Wood, E. I., Alonso, A., Tussutti, M. S., & Vicente, M. F. (2000). A randomized field trial of ACINDES: A child-centered training model for children with chronic illnesses (asthma and epilepsy). *Journal of Urban Health: Bulletin of the New York Academy of Medicine, 77,* 280–297.

Williams, J., Phillips, T., Griebel, M. L., Sharp, G. B., Lange, B., Edgar, T., et al. (2001). Factors associated with academic achievement in children with controlled epilepsy. *Epilepsy and Behavior, 2,* 217–223.

Williams, J., Steel, C., Sharp, G. B., DelosReyes, E., Phillips, T., Bates, S., et al. (2003). Anxiety in children with epilepsy. *Epilepsy and Behavior, 4,* 729–732.

# 67
# Traumatic Brain Injuries

**Elaine Clark**

*University of Utah*

## BACKGROUND AND DEVELOPMENT

According to the Centers for Disease Control and Prevention (CDC), each year between 1.2 and 1.5 million individuals in the United States sustain a traumatic brain injury (TBI) (Guerrero, Thurman, & Sniezek, 2000). For children below the age of 15, the rate is estimated to be 180 out of every 100,000 (Feeney & Ylvisaker, 2003). Falls are the most common cause of brain injury in children 5 years of age or younger, whereas motor vehicle accidents are to blame for TBIs among older children and adults (CDC, 1997; Lovasik, Kerr, & Alexander, 2001). High-velocity accidents are the most likely cause of serious brain injuries, in particular, those that result in death. Although epidemiological data over the past 20 years suggest that serious brain injuries are being prevented (e.g., a 50% decline in the number of hospitalizations for brain injuries; Thurman, Alverson, Dunn, Guerrero, & Sniezek, 1999), there is no clear indication that less serious injuries are being prevented. These less serious injuries represent the vast majority of TBIs. According to the CDC (1998), approximately 25% of individuals with TBIs have some type of negative consequence from their injuries, including problems such as poor learning and memory, language difficulty, physical impairment, and social–emotional and behavioral problems.

Although only 10%–15% of brain injuries are classified as severe (Thurman et al., 1999), some children with milder TBIs have sequelae that affect their functioning for several months. Although educators need to be aware of these children so that accommodations can be made when needed, the vast majority of these children recover from their injuries and do not have lasting impairment. This is not the case for the child with a severe brain injury. Educators can expect this child to have persistent, if not permanent, impairments in a number of functional areas (e.g., gait and coordination problems, problems learning and behaving at grade and age-appropriate levels, interacting socially with peers, and being well-adjusted from a psychological standpoint; Knights et al., 1991).

The inclusion of TBI in the 1990 amendments to the Individuals with Disabilities Education Act (IDEA) was intended for the student with significant impairment caused by a brain injury. According to data collected by the U.S. Department of Education (1999), students classified as TBI account for only 0.2% of the entire special education population. Although the number of students served (less than 12,000) under the designation TBI is small given the number of brain injuries that occur each year in school-age children (Thurman et al., 1999), having TBI be a part of IDEA has raised awareness about the effects of a brain injury and these students' educational and psychosocial needs. The purpose of this chapter is to help readers better understand the range of problems associated with a TBI and to educate them about ways to conduct assessments and design interventions.

### Nature and Severity of Brain Injuries

A closed head injury is caused by physical force to the head, often from receiving a blunt blow or from hitting a solid object, such as a windshield or pavement. A brain injury, however, can occur even if the head does not come in contact with an object, such as occurs in motor vehicle accidents where the brain is thrust against the skull and damaged from acceleration–deceleration forces. The brain can also be damaged by penetrating objects, such as knives and bullets. Although these injuries are often lethal (e.g., 90% death rate in the case of gunshot wounds; Lovasik et al., 2001), the damage is often more focal (i.e., impacts areas along the line of penetration).

A number of factors determine the likelihood that impairment will result from the injury; however, the most important factor is the actual damage (primary and secondary). Primary damage is caused by the rupturing of blood vessels (hemorrhage), bruising (contusions), fracture of the skull, and stretching or shearing of nerve pathways (axonal injury). Although these problems can play a significant role in determining effects of the injury, so can the secondary effects of damage, that is, swelling caused by accumulated blood and cerebrospinal fluid, increased intracranial pressure and blood volume, decreased cerebral blood flow, reduced oxygen, and tissue death.

Neuroimaging can help determine the effects of damage by discriminating brain structures that are affected. However, day-of-injury scans are notoriously unreliable (e.g., computer tomography, CT scans) and tend to underestimate the damage (e.g., mask tissue loss and changes in ventricle size; Bowen et al., 1997). Even the most sophisticated method, magnetic resonance imaging (MRI) cannot fully represent the damage immediately after injury and takes longer to conduct, making its use unfeasible. It may take weeks or months to fully appreciate the extent of the damage on scans; however, these data are nonetheless included in the initial assessment of injury severity. The other common measures of severity are those that assess consciousness and post-traumatic amnesia (PTA).

The Glasgow Coma Scale (GCS) is the most commonly administered measure of consciousness. The GCS assesses an individual's response to stimuli with eye opening, motor movement, and verbal response, with scores ranging from 3 to 15. A brain injury is considered mild when an individual has a GCS between 13 and 15, PTA less than 30 minutes, and no signs of neurological damage (i.e., no skull fracture or evidence of hemorrhage or edema). For a brain injury to be considered moderate in severity, the GCS needs to be between 9 and 13, PTA between 30 minutes and 24 hours, and clear evidence of neurological damage. Individuals who have a GCS of 8 or lower and a PTA greater than 24 hours (again with clear signs of brain damage) are considered to have a severe TBI.

## PROBLEMS AND IMPLICATIONS

### Common Sequelae of Brain Injury

Common problems associated with TBI include those directly associated with areas of the brain that are damaged and those that can be associated with the indirect effects of injury, including social and emotional problems. The following sections describe several associated physical, sensory-motor, language, cognitive, academic, behavioral, and social–emotional sequelae of a brain injury.

***Physical and sensory-motor problems.*** Children with TBIs often report problems with fatigue, change in appetite, headache, and dizziness immediately after injury, and in some cases continue to complain of problems for several months (e.g., headaches and dizziness 3 months out for 60% of children studied by Barry, Taylor, Klein & Yeates, 1996). For children with mild TBIs, the problems appear to remit earlier on, especially problems with fatigue, poor appetite, and sleep disturbance. However, Barry et al. also showed that for some children the problems get worse. For example, 26% had staring spells 6 months later, whereas only 22% had this problem shortly after injury. These researchers also showed that about the same number of children with sensory impairments soon after injury (i.e., children with moderate to severe TBIs) have problems 6 months later (e.g., 26% show immediate visual problems and 28% show persistent problems).

Typical sensory problems involving vision include poor acuity, double vision, and difficulty tracking. In more severe cases, however, children can have visual field defects and sometimes blindness. Hearing problems are also fairly common among children with severe brain injuries. However, the study by Barry et al. found that only 15% of the children reported reduced hearing acuity and tinnitus (ringing in the ears) after TBI. Hearing problems that are not permanent appear to remit sooner than visual ones.

Motor impairments, including abnormal gait, poor coordination, limb weakness, rigidity, tremor, and spasticity are also reported for children with severe brain injuries. Data from the Barry et al. study showed that nearly a third of the children had problems with clumsiness and coordination when tested 6 months after their injuries.

***Language, cognitive, and academic skill deficits.*** Expressive language problems are often related to motor impairments. The speech of children with severe brain injuries is often dysfluent immediately after injury. Although expressive language often improves soon after injury (along with other motor improvements), receptive language problems tend to persist (Anderson et al., 1997). In fact, some children's receptive language actually gets worse over the first 2 years following a severe brain injury (Ewing-Cobbs et al., 1997).

There is no evidence that cognitive functioning gets worse over time; however, severe TBIs slow the speed of information processing, interfere with attention and concentration, reduce memory capacity (storage and retrieval), and affect executive functions (e.g., the ability to set and prioritize goals, analyze tasks, plan and organize behaviors, and initiate and evaluate one's own actions (Battistone, 2003; Orme, 1997). Not surprisingly, brain injuries have been shown to interfere with acquisition of academic skills, even the most basic, such as mathematics and reading. Research on reading, for example, has shown that when a severe TBI occurs around 6½ years of age or younger, decoding skills are affected the most. On the other hand, when an injury takes place around age 9, it has a greater likelihood of affecting reading comprehension (Barnes, Dennis, & Wilkinson, 1999). The effect that a severe brain injury has on academic performance is of serious concern. Kinsella et al. (1997) found that 70% of children who sustained a severe TBI attended school only part time or were in special education. On the other hand, only 40% of children with moderate brain injuries were found to be in a similar situation, and none of those with a mild brain injury.

***Behavioral, emotional, and social problems.*** According to recent research, more than half of all children who sustain a serious brain injury are diagnosed with new-onset behavioral disturbance or psychiatric disorder, including personality disorder (Bloom et al., 2001; Max et al., 2000). These children are also three times more likely than noninjured peers to be placed in special education classrooms for severe emotional disturbance (Michaud, Rivara, Jaffe, Fay, & Dailey, 1993). Most often, the reason for placement in special education is for externalizing behaviors such as poor impulse control, anger outbursts, and aggressiveness (Taylor et al., 2002). Nearly a third of the children who have severe brain injuries have these types of problem behaviors (Schwartz et al., 2003). Verbal disinhibition and sexually inappropriate behaviors have been associated with damage to the brain, whereas noncompliance and aggressiveness (e.g., arguing, physical fights, and property destruction) have been associated with both physiological changes and reactions to impairment in functioning. Internalizing problems such as anxiety and depression can also be thought of as a result of both primary damage to the brain and psychological reactions to the injury (e.g., emotional response to suddenly being impaired and being uncertain about the prospects of recovering and leading a "normal" life).

Although some of the behavioral and emotional sequelae of a brain injury are temporary and mainly affect the child's participation in rehabilitation programming (Warschausky, Kewman, & Kay, 1999), these problems can persist and influence various aspects of a child's academic performance. These influences include having less exposure to instruction and being excluded at times from the classroom because of inappropriate acting-out behaviors. Depression can also result in reduced instructional time; however, it is less likely to result in the student spending more time with the principal than the teacher. Depression may lessen a child's motivation (and ability) to interact with peers. Children with TBIs report being more worried about losing friends than they are about other injury-related problems, such as physical well-being, performance in school, and participation in sports and recreation (Bohnert, Parker, & Warschausky, 1997).

Social rejection and isolation are some of the most common problems following a severe brain injury. This is not surprising considering the various ways that a brain injury can reduce opportunities for a child to interact with peers. These include reduced motor skills, affecting the child's participation in sports, and decreased confidence and motivation to initiate social contacts. These children also have difficulty maintaining social relationships, given their impaired problem-solving ability, poor impulse control, and immature behaviors (Russman, 1997). Children with severe TBIs have been described as having behaviors similar to those of children with an Attention Deficit Hyperactivity Disorder (ADHD); that is, they often make inappropriate comments, act without stopping to think, and fail to use rules of social engagement. Social problems for the child with a TBI also have a significant impact on the entire family, especially parents who are worried about their child's psychological well-being and who feel burdened by their child's lack of social contact (e.g., they try to serve as a friend substitute for their child). This adds more stress to the family, which in turn adds stress to the child and reduces the child's ability to function, both socially and cognitively (Taylor, Yeates, Wade, Drotar, & Klein, 1999; Wade, Taylor, Drotar, Stancin, & Yeates, 1998).

## Factors Affecting Outcomes

A number of factors determine the course of recovery and long-term outcomes. Severity of injury, however, has been found to be the most predictive (Stratton, 2000). This variable, plus the age of the child at the time of injury and the child's preinjury status, have been studied in relationship to the child's family environment. As a result, outcomes must be determined on a case-by-case basis. However, for convenience, the following sections describe these predictive factors separately.

***Severity of damage.*** Severity involves the degree to which the brain has been physiologically altered, including how diffuse the damage is (e.g., the extent to which various areas of the brain have been damaged) and what medical complications have contributed to the overall damage (e.g., other organ system damage that has further compromised brain function). Not surprisingly, children who have sustained a severe TBI have been shown to have the worst outcomes across cognitive, physical, social, and behavioral domains. Children with severe TBIs are the only ones who have been shown to have significantly lower scores on intelligence tests (Orme, 1997). This group has also been found to have the lowest scores on other neuropsychological tests and measures (Anderson et al., 1997). Deficits in the following areas have been found for children with severe TBIs: attention and concentration, memory, language (receptive and expressive), and executive functioning (e.g., ability to organize, plan, initiate, and follow through). These children also have greater psychological, behavioral, and social problems (Max et al., 2000).

Children with moderate brain injuries are often difficult to distinguish from those with mild brain injuries since neither group has been shown to have persistent brain injury sequelae (Ewing-Cobbs et al., 1997). Children with moderate TBIs, however, have not been studied as much as children with mild brain injuries, and often the two groups have been combined in studies (Stratton, 2000). What researchers have shown, however, is that the majority of children who sustain a mild TBI become symptom free within the first few months of their injury. Ponsford et al. (1999) demonstrated that at the end of 3 months, only 17% of children with mild TBIs had symptoms. Most of the children with mild brain injuries who had persistent difficulty also had prior problems or prior TBIs. This does not mean that the symptoms of a mild TBI should be ignored. Even the most transient symptoms can have negative consequences on the child, including headache, dizziness, fatigue, confusion, irritability, sleep disturbance, inattention and poor concentration, and memory problems.

***Age of the child at injury.*** Although infants and young children are less susceptible to brain contusions, lacerations, and axonal injuries (Spreen, Risser, & Edgwell, 1995), their injuries place them at greater risk for problems later on. This is especially true of young children who sustain a severe TBI. These children are at risk for intellectual impairment, memory problems, slowed information processing, poor attention and concentration, impaired spatial and perceptual–motor skills and sensory capacity, emotional and behavioral problems, and social difficulties (Max et al., 1999). Early TBIs disrupt normal development as a result of both damage to the brain (i.e., damage to certain areas that are critical for skill development) and the secondary effects of the damage. For example, when a toddler sustains a brain injury that affects the motor area of the brain, this may impair not only motor functioning but also learning that would typically take place from normal exploration of his or her physical space. Damage early in life can also affect skills that are not expected to emerge until later in life, for example, frontal lobe damage affecting a person's organization of thoughts, ability to plan and initiate behavior, and ability to think abstractly (Nybo & Koskiniemi, 1999).

***Child and family functioning.*** Not surprisingly, children who had problems before a brain injury—those with preinjury learning, behavior, and social–emotional problems—do worse afterward (Anderson et al., 1997). Children with families who had significant difficulties before the injury also do worse afterward (Taylor et al., 1999). The effect that a brain injury has on a family cannot be underestimated, because it influences nearly every facet of family life. The family's financial situation may deteriorate because parents have to quit jobs or dramatically reduce work hours. Families may incur increased health insurance costs as a result of loss of benefits following injury. Increased stressors often lead to divorce (Anderson et al., Wade et al., 1998). It is not surprising that as time goes on families have an increased number of psychological problems, despite adjusting to the physical burden of caring for a child with a TBI.

## ALTERNATIVE ACTIONS FOR PREVENTION AND INTERVENTION

Considerable effort has been made over the past several years to educate the public about ways to prevent brain injuries (Head Smart campaigns) and to enact laws that would require people to wear seatbelts and helmets when riding motorcycles (and for children, when riding bicycles). Although seatbelt laws are now common, only a handful of states have passed laws that require helmet use (laws that are credited with significant reductions in severe brain injuries). Since TBIs are not always preventable, interventions are needed to reduce the effects of a brain injury. Implementing effective interventions early in the course of recovery will improve a child's chances of being successful in the classroom as well as in the social environment. Since the majority of children with a TBI will be able to return to the regular classroom without visible signs of a brain injury (i.e., without mobility problems so often seen with a severe TBI), identifying students who have milder or moderately severe brain injuries but who need services is difficult. This identification is critical, however, given the fact that many children return to school near the start of the recovery process and are in school for the majority of their rehabilitation. Therefore, thorough assessments should begin before students return to school, preferably while they are still involved in rehabilitation.

## Educationally Relevant Assessments

One of the earliest steps in the assessment process is to contact medical-rehabilitation specialists who are familiar with the student's injury. If possible, this should be done before the child is discharged. In addition, the child and parents need to be seen and plans made for school reentry. This not only gives the child and the family a goal but gives the school time to prepare for the student's return. In some cases, the physical environment will have to be adapted for the student (e.g., improving access to facilities and materials in the classroom) and a number of services arranged (e.g., physical and occupational therapy, nursing, and speech and language services). Ongoing communication with the family will also ensure that school personnel are informed about the date of reentry and the amount of time the student will be able to be in school (i.e., partial versus full-day programming) and what adjustments need to be made to his or her schedule.

Not all children with brain injuries need special education services; in fact, those with mild to moderate TBIs may require only a few accommodations in the regular classroom (e.g., reduced workload and tutoring by a teacher or peer). To ensure that the educational needs of the students are understood, neuropsychological testing needs to be done. Children who are receiving rehabilitation services, however, often have been tested before discharge. School psychologists need to acquire this information and supplement the testing with whatever else needs to be done to ensure academic success. This includes administering more curriculum-based measures (CBM) and functional behavior assessments (FBA) in schools. Assessment data are needed to determine not only where the student stands (e.g., what percentile on standardized tests) but also what needs to be done to improve the student's chance of succeeding in the classroom. Practical assessments such as CBM and FBA not only help monitor student progress but also guide instruction and behavioral plans. Interviews are an important source of data for CBM and FBA. However, they are also important for understanding the course of recovery and the treatment needs of the student.

***Curriculum-based measures and functional behavior assessments.*** Use of CBM is especially important for assessing academic performance of children with TBIs, given its sensitivity to fluctuations in performance and its ease of use. CBM is brief and can be used frequently to monitor progress in the classroom (e.g., the student's response to instruction). Behavioral observations and routine probes are a critical component of the assessment; therefore, CBM can be used to adjust the curriculum as well as the instructional style if the student is not acquiring information as expected. Since the method is applicable to different subject areas, it can also help assess areas of weakness early on (i.e., before the student gets too far behind) and guide instructional decisions.

FBA is another assessment tool that is directly applicable to interventions in that it assesses environmental variables that are associated with a particular behavioral occurrence. Researchers have shown that FBA can be used to develop effective strategies for children with brain injuries (Feeney & Ylvisaker, 2003); however, the majority of support comes from studies of other children who have similar maladaptive behaviors, that is, problems with impulsivity, anger outbursts, and aggression. An FBA provides a description of the functions of a particular child's behavior (e.g., getting attention, avoiding certain tasks, or obtaining a tangible reward) with the use of direct observation, structured interviews (child, teacher, and parent), and manipulation of variables thought to be associated with the particular behavior (e.g., an antecedent). This method of assessment may provide critical information about what might have precipitated a problem behavior and will help in developing an intervention to prevent that behavior in the future. For example, it may be determined that a student smashes lockers after leaving second- and fourth-period classes. An FBA may show that the same peers are in the two classes and that these peers tend to ridicule the particular student. Knowing this helps educators alter the environment to prevent aggressive outbursts (e.g., put hall monitors near the lockers right after class and alert the classroom teachers that bullying may be going on in class and needs to be stopped). Understanding what triggers the aggression may allow the actual root of the problem to be addressed, so that the student with a TBI is not spending an inordinate amount of time in the principal's office for discipline.

***Standardized measures.*** Although the literature contains some practical suggestions about ways to use standardized test data for educational planning (see Heathfield, Pompa, & Clark, 2005), these measures tend to be less useful than CBM and FBA for structuring the classroom and planning curriculum changes. The advantage of standardized tests, however, is that they provide a measure of relative performance so that parents and teachers know how the student ranks among peers and what the student's strengths and weaknesses are (e.g., the student may have intact spatial abilities and math skills but impaired verbal memory). A number of tests and measures are available for use with school-age children who have sustained a brain injury. However, describing these is beyond the scope of this chapter. School psychologists are typically familiar with a wide range of measures; although in some cases they may need to consult with other professionals to ensure that all important functional domains are properly assessed (e.g., having a colleague administer unfamiliar neuropsychological tests). The range of these measures is likely to include tests of attention and concentration, memory, reasoning and problem solving, cognitive flexibility, organization, processing speed, motor speed and coordination, sensory–perceptual skills (visual, auditory, and tactile), language abilities (e.g., fluency and comprehension), executive function (e.g., planning, organization, and initiation), social skills, mood, and personality. Baron's (2004) text on neuropsychological evaluation of children is an excellent reference, as is Semrud-Clikeman's (2001) book on TBI assessments and interventions (see Recommended Resources).

## Educationally Relevant Interventions

***Behavioral interventions.*** Chronic behavior problems are some of the most devastating sequelae of a TBI. These problems not only affect a child's ability to learn but also interfere with positive family interactions and meaningful social relationships. It is, therefore, critical that interventions begin early (i.e., at the time of rehabilitation and reentry into school) and be implemented in a variety of settings (i.e., community, home, and school). Compared with studies of children with developmental disabilities, empirical studies with children who have acquired brain injuries are few. The data from other populations, however, have supported the use of behavioral interventions, in particular, applied behavior analysis (ABA). Although ABA has been shown to be useful in reducing negative behaviors, the procedure has been criticized for placing too much emphasis on contingency management and intrusive (aversive) methods. Research has shown that behavioral interventions that focus on antecedents hold the most promise for managing behaviors (e.g., classrooms with carefully planned routines and clear performance expectations), and if it is possible to use positive reinforcement only, then this is the preferred strategy.

Positive reinforcement of appropriate behaviors, using behavioral momentum techniques, can be an important intervention. Feeney and Ylvisaker (2003) showed that the chances of appropriate behavior occurring is increased by raising the rate of positive reinforcement for appropriate responding. For example, if one gives a series of commands with a high probability of compliance, then delivers a low-probability command (or one that is not likely to be followed), there is a greater chance of compliance. The high-probability event tends to increase the rate of reinforcement, which in turn creates the momentum that the student needs to respond positively to less desirable commands. Unfortunately, even when using this method, interventions do not generalize that well and are difficult to maintain after the treatment is withdrawn. The interventions that have shown maintenance with chronic behavior problems in children with TBIs tend to be those that are in place for extended periods of time (e.g., 3 or more years; Gardner, Bird, Maguire, Carreiro, & Abenaim, 2003).

In addition to methods that set the occasion for an appropriate behavior to occur, behavioral interventions that include consequences have been shown to be effective. Although considerable research has accumulated that shows that aversive consequences can be effective for managing severe conduct problems (Reavis, Jenson, Kukic, & Morgan, 1993), it is not the intervention of choice for children with brain injuries. Researchers in the field encourage use of more natural (and positive) consequences that are related to the behavior, for example, giving constructive feedback and assistance (Ylvisaker et al., 2001).

***Academic interventions.*** Individualizing academic interventions is critical for students with TBIs, although it is often difficult to know at first which intervention will work with what child. CBM can help determine the best academic interventions; however, interventions that address underlying problems are also important. These include slowed information processing, problems with mental tracking and cognitive flexibility, inattention and poor concentration, short- and long-term memory problems, deficits in receptive and expressive language, the inability to understand concepts, problems with organization, and the inability to solve problems in a coherent and logical way (Kinsella et al., 1997). Strategies that are often used to alleviate problems associated with poor academic performance include restructuring the classroom to reduce distractions, slowing the pace of instruction, reducing the difficulty level of the work, delaying new learning, teaching strategies to help with memory and organization, shortening assignments, reinforcing the student for completing work in class, assigning less homework, providing tutoring, giving students greater opportunity to receive positive reinforcements, precision commands, and direct instruction. Some of the methods, including direct instruction, have been shown to be effective specifically with students who have TBIs (Glang, Todis, & Cooley, 1997). This is not surprising, given that this method involves paced instruction for learning, frequent response opportunities, feedback, and reinforcement (essentially the principles of ABA).

Other interventions that are used to improve academics include teaching specific problem-solving skills (e.g., self-regulation, metacognition, and attribution) and helping students better manage (and organize) their time and accommodate for impairments (e.g., electronic spellers, computers with word processors, tape recorders, calculators, memory books, cueing tapes, and visual prompts). For a more detailed description of these and other teaching strategies, see Bowen (2005).

***Social interventions.*** Interventions that are often used to improve social relationships of children include cognitive behavioral methods (Suzman, Morris, & Morris, 1997), social skills training (Russman, 1997), and school-based friendship building and networking (Glang et al., 1997). Although researchers have suggested that the most effective interventions for children with TBIs are those that incorporate both a behavioral and a cognitive component (Feeney & Ylvisaker, 2003), for the most part, the benefits of these social skills interventions have been temporary. Russman, for example, found that improving cognitive problem-solving skills improved social interactions, but improvements were not maintained over time. Similarly, friendship-building programs that have shown dramatic increases in social interactions (i.e., students with TBIs interacting with noninjured peers) have also failed to show that the interactions were maintained after the intervention was terminated (Glang et al.).

Social relationships are extremely complex, and the development of friendships is difficult to prescribe. Although friendships often end because of inappropriate behaviors, they are formed based on proximity, similar abilities, and shared interests. Interventions that teach functionally equivalent skills or behaviors that replace inappropriate ones, including communication skills, may be helpful; however, research is needed to find ways to highlight shared interests and abilities so that natural friendships can be formed.

***Family interventions.*** Parents are often expected to be involved with the education of their child, including providing encouragement and assistance at home. Parents who are emotionally distressed following this type of injury, however, have been shown to be compromised in terms of their ability to parent and participate in home-based interventions (Warschausky et al., 1999). Although parents typically adjust to the physical demands of having a child with a brain injury within the first year, their ability to adjust psychologically is not as good. In fact, research has shown that when a brain injury is severe, the psychological burden gets worse over time, not better (Rivara et al., 1994). School professionals may be able to help parents by coordinating resources to help them cope better and to educate them about the ways a brain injury is likely to affect the child and the entire family (e.g., cause sibling resentments and negative behavioral reactions and create feelings of hopelessness in the family). Parents report that they do not feel they had enough time to discuss their child's brain injury with doctors and rehabilitation specialists (Resnick, 1993) and that they are frustrated by the lack of available resources after discharge. As a result, children are frequently brought back to school before they are physically and mentally ready and experience frustration themselves.

Providing effective treatments for families requires familiarity with parent intervention research. One important finding is that parents who participated in information-sharing support groups actually did worse after treatment, reporting more symptoms of depression and anxiety after therapy than before (Singer et al., 1994). Parents who participated in stress management interventions, on the other hand, showed improvement. The latter intervention provided specific instruction about ways to cope with grief using cognitive coping strategies and self-monitoring. These same strategies could be incorporated into parent training modules that teach parents effective parenting skills. Although parent management training has not been well studied using TBI populations, the literature involving parents of children with behavior disorders may be helpful (e.g., Maughan, Christiansen, Jenson, Olympia, & Clark, 2005). Identifying which families are in the greatest need of help, however, is critical, so that resources can be appropriately allocated and families can get appropriate help (Conoley & Sheridan, 1997). This initial identification can also help ensure that siblings of the child with a TBI get treatment if needed. Siblings are often frustrated by the fact that a family member's behavior has changed and a disproportionate amount of attention is being paid to that individual. Although resentment is natural, oftentimes siblings feel guilty about this and begin to have psychological problems of their own.

Given the range of problems that children and families face, school professionals may find themselves serving primarily as consultants. Connecting families with mental health services in the community and serving as a liaison may provide children with the best chances of success in school by informing teachers what services the child is (or is not) getting. All too often, the services for children with brain injuries are poorly coordinated, and professionals make assumptions about the services that are being rendered (i.e., thinking things are being done when they are not).

## SUMMARY

Given the degree to which a brain injury affects the life of a child and his or her family and friends, educators are faced with a formidable task in designing effective academic and behavioral interventions for this population. Although the inclusion of TBI as a category of special education classification under IDEA (1990) helped increase awareness and services to children with brain injuries, many children with TBIs are still not being identified and served. Part of the problem has to do with the lack of information among educators about the diverse ways in which a brain injury affects a student in the classroom. These effects include changes in learning, emotional and behavioral control, social interactions, and family life. Educators may not be able to provide all the services children with TBIs and their families need, but they can help by conducting thorough assessments and designing individualized interventions for children who sustain a traumatic injury.

As indicated in this chapter, the nature of brain injuries necessitates comprehensive, well-planned assessments of cognitive, academic, behavioral, and social functioning. Although standardized cognitive and intellectual measures may be helpful in the assessment of a child with a brain injury, it is critical that curriculum-based measures, classroom observations, and interviews be conducted. Records of performance and social–emotional functioning prior to the injury also must be reviewed in order to set appropriate expectations. Students receiving, or needing, services before a brain injury are likely to need these, and other, services afterward. Families are also likely to need support and help to find ways to cope so that the child is not affected further. School professionals will be best able to help children with TBIs when they are knowledgeable about brain injuries; have a neuropsychological testing background; are competent to conduct state-of-the-art academic and social, emotional, and behavioral assessments (e.g., CBM and functional behavior analysis); and can implement empirically based interventions. This knowledge base and skills are needed to design practical, effective strategies for classroom use (i.e., instructional and behavioral) and on the playground, at home, and in the community.

Much needs to be known about what interventions work best for children (and families) who suffer the effects of a brain injury. Research to date, however, suggests that interventions that manage antecedents and that are positive and context-sensitive have the best chance of working (Ylvisaker et al., 2001). In addition, many of the interventions that have been empirically supported for other students with learning and behavior problems can be used. The literature on empirically supported, school-based interventions for children with behavior problems, for example, is voluminous and would be worthwhile resources for educators and school professionals who work with children who have brain injuries (Bowen, Jenson, & Clark, 2004).

# RECOMMENDED RESOURCES

## Books and Other Printed Material

Appleton, R., & Baldwin, T. (Eds.). (1998). *Management of brain-injured children.* New York: Oxford University Press.

The chapters in this book highlight the importance of addressing TBI-associated problems from a multidisciplinary framework. The chapter authors describe various types of assessments and a wide range of interventions for children who are suffering the effects of a brain injury. Recommendations in the text are practical and can be used in different settings (e.g., at home and school, and in the community).

Baron, I. S. (2004). *Neuropsychological evaluation of the child.* New York: Oxford University Press.

The author has compiled published data on a number of neuropsychological tests that are applicable to children. Brief test descriptions and norms are included. In addition, the author has discussed important conceptual issues and neuropsychological assessment models.

Semrud-Clikeman, M. (2001). *Traumatic brain injury in children and adolescents: Assessment and intervention.* New York: Psychology Press.

The author provides a comprehensive overview of TBI, including a basic review of neuroanatomy and areas of functioning that are most likely to be affected by a brain injury (e.g., learning problems, emotional concerns, and family issues). Ideas for school-based assessments and interventions are included in the text, and case studies illustrate the various topics that are covered. Readers will appreciate the fact that Dr. Semrud-Clikeman has written the book in a manner that allows practitioners without an extensive neuropsychological background to benefit.

Tyler, J. S., & Mira, M. P. (1999). *Traumatic brain injury in children and adolescents: A sourcebook for teachers and other school personnel* (2nd ed.). Austin, TX: Pro-Ed.

This book is specifically designed for use by school personnel to address the problems that children with moderate to severe brain injuries face. The authors provide suggestions for a variety of interventions, including those intended to reintegrate children with TBIs into the classroom and strategies to use once they are there.

## Website

*http://www.biausa.org*

The website of the Brain Injury Association of America provides information and resources in both English and Spanish regarding prevention, assessment, and treatment of TBI. Readers are also encouraged to contact their state brain injury association.

# REFERENCES

Anderson, V., Morse, S. A., Klug, G., Catroppa, C., Haritou, F., Rosenfeld, J., & Pentland, L. (1997). Predicting recovery from head injury in your children: A prospective analysis. *Journal of the International Neuropsychological Society, 3,* 568–580.

Barnes, M. A., Dennis, M., & Wilkinson, M. (1999). Reading after closed head injury in childhood: Effects on accuracy, fluency, and comprehension. *Developmental Neuropsychology, 15,* 1–24.

Barry, C. T., Taylor, H. G., Klein, S., & Yeates, K. O. (1996). Validity of neurobehavioral symptoms reported in children with traumatic brain injury. *Child Neuropsychology, 2,* 213–226.

Battistone, M. (2003). *Drive & deficit: A study of motivational and cognitive aspects of processing speed deficiencies in traumatically brain injured individuals.* Unpublished doctoral dissertation, University of Utah, Salt Lake City, Utah.

Bloom, D. R., Levin, H. S., Ewing-Cobbs, L., Saunders, A., Song, J., & Fletcher, J. M. (2001). Lifetime and novel psychiatric problems after pediatric traumatic brain injury. *Journal of the American Academy of Child and Adolescent Psychiatry, 40,* 572–579.

Bohnert, A. M., Parker, J. G., & Warschausky, S. A. (1997). Friendship and social adjustment of children following a traumatic brain injury: An exploratory investigation. *Developmental Neuropsychology, 13,* 477–486.

Bowen, J. (2005). Classroom interventions for students with traumatic brain injuries. *Preventing School Failure, 49,* 34–41.

Bowen, J., Clark, E., Bigler, E. D., Gardner, M. K., Nilsson, D., Gooch, J., et al. (1997). Childhood traumatic brain injury: Neuropsychological status at the time of hospital discharge. *Developmental Medicine & Child Neurology, 39,* 17–25.

Bowen, J., Jenson, W. R., & Clark, E. (2004). *School-based interventions for students with behavior problems.* New York: Kluwer Academic/Plenum Publishers.

Centers for Disease Control and Prevention. (1997). Traumatic brain injury—Colorado, Missouri, Oklahoma and Utah, 1990–1993. *Morbidity & Mortality Report, 46,* 8–11.

Centers for Disease Control and Prevention. (1998). Traumatic brain injuries in the United States. Washington, DC: National Center for Injury Prevention and Control [Data file]. Available from CDC website, http://www.cdc.gov

Conoley, J. C., & Sheridan, S. M. (1997). Pediatric traumatic brain injury: Challenges and interventions for families. In E. D. Bigler, E. Clark, & J. Farmer (Eds.), *Childhood traumatic brain injury* (pp. 177–190). Austin, TX: Pro-Ed.

Ewing-Cobbs, L., Fletcher, J., Levin, H. S., Francis, D. J., Davidson, K., & Miner, M. E. (1997). Longitudinal neuropsychological outcome in infants and preschoolers with traumatic brain injury. *Journal of the International Neuropsychological Society, 3,* 581–591.

Feeney, T. J., & Ylvisaker, M. (2003). Context sensitive behavioral supports for young children with TBI. *Journal of Head Trauma Rehabilitation, 18,* 33–51.

Gardner, R., Bird, F., Maguire, H., Carreiro, R., & Abenaim, N. (2003). Intensive positive behavior supports for adolescents with acquired brain injury. *Journal of Head Trauma Rehabilitation, 18,* 52–74.

Glang, A., Todis, B., & Cooley, E. (1997). Building social networks for children and adolescents with traumatic brain injury: A school-based intervention. *Journal of Head Trauma Rehabilitation, 12,* 32–47.

Guerrero, J., Thurman, D. J., & Sniezek, J. E. (2000). Emergency department visits associated with traumatic brain injury: United States, 1995–1996. *Brain Injury, 14,* 181–186.

Heathfield, L. T., Pompa, J., & Clark, E. (2005). The translation of neuropsychological information into the IEP, school discipline plan, and functional assessments of behavior. In R. C. D'Amato, E. Fletcher-Janzen, & C. R. Reynolds (Eds.), *The handbook of school neuropsychology* (pp. 684–700). New York: Wiley.

Kinsella, G. J., Prior, M., Sawyer, M., Ong, B., Murtagh, D., Eisenmajer, R., et al. (1997). Predictors and indicators of academic outcome in children 2 years following traumatic brain injury. *Journal of the International Neuropsychological Society, 3,* 608–616.

Knights, R. M., Ivan, L. P., Ventureyra, E. C., Bentivoglio, C., Stoddart, C., Winogron, W., et al. (1991). The effects of head injury in children on neuropsychological and behavioral functioning. *Brain Injury, 5,* 339–351.

Lovasik, D., Kerr, M. E., & Alexander, S. (2001). Traumatic brain injury research: A review of clinical studies. *Critical Care Nursing Quarterly, 23,* 24–41.

Maughan, D. R., Christiansen, E., Jenson, W. R., Olympia, D., & Clark, E. (2005). Behavioral parent training as a treatment for externalizing behaviors and disruption behaviors: A meta-analysis. *School Psychology Review, 34,* 267–286.

Max, J. E., Koele, S. L., Castillo, C., Lindgren, S., Arndt, S., & Bokura, H. (2000). Personality change problems in children and adolescents following a traumatic brain injury. *Journal of the International Neuropsychological Society, 6,* 279–289.

Max, J. E., Roberts, M. A., Koele, S. L., Kindgren, S. D., Robin, D. A., & Arndt, S. (1999). Cognitive outcome in children and adolescents following severe traumatic brain injury: Influence of psychosocial, psychiatric, and injury-related variables. *Journal of the International Neuropsychological Society, 5,* 58–68.

Michaud, L. J., Rivara, F. P., Jaffe, K., Fay, G., & Dailey, J. L. (1993). Traumatic brain injury as a risk factor for behavioral disorders in children. *Archives of Physical Medicine and Rehabilitation, 74,* 368–375.

Nybo, T., & Koskiniemi, M. (1999). Cognitive indicators of vocational outcome after severe traumatic brain injury in childhood. *Brain Injury, 13,* 759–766.

Orme, S. F. (1997). *Methodological considerations in neuropsychological research: An empirical review of pediatric traumatic brain injury outcome studies.* Unpublished doctoral dissertation, University of Utah, Salt Lake City, Utah.

Ponsford, J., Willmott, C., Rothwell, A., Cameron, P., Ayton, G., Nelms, R., et al. (1999). Cognitive and behavioral outcome following mild traumatic head injury in children. *Journal of Head Trauma Rehabilitation, 14,* 360–372.

Reavis, H. K., Jenson, W. R., Kukic, S. J., & Morgan, D. P. (Eds.). (1993). Reprimands and precision requests. In Utah State Office of Education, *Utah's BEST project: Behavioral and educational strategies for teachers.* Salt Lake City: Author.

Resnick, C. (1993). The effect of head injury on family and marital stability. *Social Work in Health Care, 18*(2), 49–62.

Rivara, J., Jaffe, K., Polissar, N., Fay, G., Martin, K., Shurtleff, H., et al. (1994). Family functioning and children's academic performance and behavior problems one year following traumatic brain injury. *Archives of Physical Medicine and Rehabilitation, 75,* 369–379.

Russman, S. B. (1997). *Social skills training for children and adolescents with traumatic brain injury.* Unpublished doctoral dissertation, University of Utah, Salt Lake City, Utah.

Schwartz, L., Taylor, G., Drotar, D., Yeates, K. O., Wade, S. L., & Stancin, T. (2003). Long-term behavior problems following pediatric traumatic brain injury: Prevalence, predictors, and correlates. *Journal of Pediatric Psychology, 28,* 251–263.

Singer, G. H., Glang, A., Nixon, C., Cooley, E., Kerns, K., Williams, D., et al. (1994). A comparison of two psychosocial interventions for parents of children with acquired injury: An exploratory study. *Journal of Head Trauma Rehabilitation, 9,* 38–94.

Spreen, O., Risser, A. H., & Edgwell, D. (1995). *Developmental neuropsychology.* New York: Oxford University Press.

Stratton, T. A. (2000). *Meta-analyses of traumatic brain injury outcomes in children and adolescents.* Unpublished doctoral dissertation, University of Utah, Salt Lake City, Utah.

Suzman, K. B., Morris, R. D., & Morris, M. K. (1997). Cognitive-behavioral remediation of problem solving in children with acquired brain injuries. *Behavior Therapy and Experimental Psychiatry, 28,* 203–212.

Taylor, H. G., Yeates, K. O., Wade, S. L., Drotar, D., & Klein, S. K. (1999). Influences on first year recovery from traumatic brain injury in children. *Neuropsychology, 13,* 76–89.

Taylor, H. G., Yeates, K. O., Wade, S. L., Drotar, D., Stancin, T., & Minch, N. (2002). A prospective study of short and long-term outcomes after traumatic brain injury in children: Behavior and achievement. *Neuropsychology, 16,* 15–27.

Thurman, D. J., Alverson, C. A., Dunn, K. A., Guerrero, J., & Sniezek, J. E. (1999). Traumatic brain injury in the United States: A public health perspective. *Journal of Head Trauma Rehabilitation, 14,* 602–615.

U.S. Department of Education, Office of Special Education Programs. *Implementation of the Individuals with Disabilities Education Act: Twenty-First Annual Report to Congress.* Washington DC: Author.

Wade, S., Taylor, H. G., Drotar, D., Stancin, T., & Yeates, K. O. (1998). Family burden and adaptation during the initial year following traumatic brain injury in children. *Pediatrics, 102,* 110–116.

Warschausky, S., Kewman, D., & Kay, J. (1999). Empirically supported psychological and behavioral therapies in pediatric rehabilitation of TBI. *Journal of Head Trauma Rehabilitation, 14,* 373–383.

Ylvisaker, M., Todis, B., Glang, A., Urbanczyk, B., Franklin, C., DePompei, R., et al. (2001). Educating students with TBI: Themes and recommendations. *Journal of Head Trauma Rehabilitation, 16,* 76–93.

# 68

# Allergies and Asthma

**Elizabeth L. McQuaid**
**Daphne Koinis Mitchell**
**Cynthia A. Esteban**
*Brown Medical School*

Allergic diseases are very common among school-age children, and over the past several decades, the prevalence of many allergic diseases has grown (Academy of Allergy, Asthma and Immunology [AAAAI], 2000). These conditions exert a considerable impact on quality of life and health care costs. Allergic diseases generally require ongoing management through emphasis on (a) avoidance of allergens when possible, (b) administration of appropriate medications, and (c) measures to manage exacerbations or flare-ups of the symptoms. This chapter first provides an overview of the prevalence and etiology of allergic diseases, followed by a brief summary of clinical symptoms and existing guidelines for medical treatment for these disorders. It then assesses the developmental issues regarding allergic diseases, including expectations for appropriate self-care across childhood, and issues in self-management that are salient for children of different ages. Finally, the chapter reviews common problems that arise when attempting to implement medical treatments and provides a brief overview of educational and psychosocial treatment options. Throughout, the chapter offers examples of how school professionals can support children's self-management of allergic diseases.

## BACKGROUND AND DEVELOPMENT

Allergic diseases are caused by an overreaction of the immune system to substances in the environment. Allergic diseases include a range of chronic conditions, including asthma, hay fever (allergic rhinitis), skin allergies (e.g., atopic dermatitis), and food allergies. For the most part these conditions are chronic, although symptoms may wax and wane over time. However, some cases hold the potential for occasional, severe exacerbations, such as in severe asthma episodes or anaphylaxis. Anaphylaxis is a rapid, immune-mediated, systemic process that can be life-threatening. It occurs in response to an allergen to which an individual has been previously exposed and developed a sensitivity.

Some allergic diseases have increased in prevalence over the past few decades. As an example, the prevalence of allergic rhinitis has increased significantly over the past 15 years. It is now the most common allergic disease in the United States, affecting up to 40% of children (AAAAI, 2000). Asthma is also increasingly common and affects nearly 5 million children below the age of 18 in the United States (Centers for Disease Control and Prevention, 1996). Atopic dermatitis has also increased in prevalence and affects approximately 15% of children (Leung, 2003). Although food allergies are more difficult to diagnose and track, there is some evidence that peanut allergy has increased in prevalence as well (Grundy, Matthews, Bateman, Dean, & Hasan Arshad, 2002). No definitive explanation for these increases in allergic diseases exists; however, greater exposure to indoor allergens in recent decades may play a role. Possible causes, termed the "hygiene hypothesis," include frequent antibiotic use and decreased exposure to infection, which paradoxically may play a role in increasing the risk of allergic diseases and asthma (Strachan, 1989).

Allergic diseases may present at any age, and the expression of allergic disease is a dynamic process; that is, it can change dramatically over the course of childhood and into adulthood. For example, although food allergy is estimated to occur in approximately 8% of children below the age of 7, it is much less common in adults, affecting only 1%–2% of the population (Sampson, 1998). Later in childhood, respiratory allergies become more common. For some conditions, particularly asthma, significant disparities also exist across racial and ethnic groups. Ethnic minorities such as African Americans and Hispanics typically demonstrate higher rates of asthma, more frequent health care utilization, and more fatalities from asthma than their White counterparts (Lozano, Connell, & Koepsell, 1995).

A brief review of etiology, clinical symptoms, and current treatment approaches for various allergic disorders is described below. An overview of common prescription medications for allergic disorders and asthma is presented in Table 1.

## Etiology, Symptoms, and Treatment Approaches

***Allergic rhinitis.*** In the United States, allergic rhinitis is the most common of the allergic diseases. The typical onset is school age. Allergic rhinitis develops through allergic sensitization, over time, to a variety of mold spores and airborne pollens, such as from grasses, trees, and weeds. Symptoms tend to be seasonal, as children develop reactivity to specific allergens that are present at different times of year. Perennial allergic rhinitis can also occur, and may be linked to chronic exposure to indoor allergens such as animal dander, dust mites, cockroaches, or indoor mold. Rhinitis is frequently accompanied by sinusitis (inflammation of the sinuses with excess mucus secretion, loss of mucus clearance, and bacterial infection) or allergic conjunctivitis (inflammation of the conjunctiva, the thin mucus membrane that covers the inner eyelid).

Children with allergic rhinitis typically present with a variety of classic symptoms, including sneezing, profuse and watery nasal discharge (rhinorrhea), nasal stuffiness and congestion, and itching of various involved areas such as the nose, throat, or eyes. Treatment for allergic rhinitis consists of attempting to avoid the allergens that cause the symptoms, using medications, and, in some cases, receiving immunotherapy (allergy shots). The most common medications are antihistamines and nasal corticosteroids. As immunotherapy is expensive and time consuming, it is typically recommended when other conventional treatments have failed to provide adequate symptom relief.

***Skin allergies.*** There are a variety of skin allergies, but the most commonly seen are atopic dermatitis, contact dermatitis, urticaria, and angioedema. Atopic dermatitis, commonly referred to as eczema, is a chronic or recurrent skin inflammation. It has very early onset and often precedes the development of other allergic conditions (such as allergic rhinitis or asthma) in children. It presents as an itchy rash that typically occurs on the hands and flexural areas of the arms, legs, and neck, but it can cover the entire body. It can also present as very dry skin. Symptoms may wax and wane over the course of months or years. Contact dermatitis is a localized skin reaction (typically a red rash) that is caused by exposure to certain substances, such as rubber, cosmetics, or even certain plants (e.g., poison ivy). It may appear immediately in response to an irritant (irritant contact dermatitis), or may develop in 1–2 days if it is in response to an allergen (allergic contact dermatitis). Contact dermatitis typically resolves within a short time.

Urticaria, commonly known as hives, is an episodic condition that may or may not have an allergic component. It presents as red, itchy, and swollen areas on the skin. If allergic in origin, it may be caused by food, medication, or insect venom. Angioedema is caused by a similar pathogenic mechanism and often appears with urticaria. Angioedema involves swelling of tissue under the skin (most often in the face, tongue, extremities, or genitalia). As with contact dermatitis, most cases of urticaria/angioedema are acute, lasting from a few hours to a few days.

Treatment of these skin conditions typically involves identification and avoidance of the allergen or triggering substance, application of topical over-the-counter and prescription medications to relieve the rash and discomfort, and administration of antihistamines. A short course of oral corticosteroids may also be used to treat more severe symptoms. For urticaria, injection of epinephrine is recommended if anaphylaxis is suspected.

***Food allergies.*** A wide variety of medical and behavioral difficulties have been attributed to food allergies. Recently, researchers have increased efforts to distinguish true food allergies from what may be food reactions or intolerances. Food allergies are reactions caused by immunological responses to specific food proteins. Although many common childhood food allergies (e.g., cow's milk, wheat, eggs, and soy) abate over time, a few (e.g., tree nuts, peanuts, fish, and shellfish) can persist, and may present a risk for significant reactions, such as anaphylaxis.

An allergic reaction to food can present with a range of symptoms that are isolated to an organ system or

**Table 1** *Common Medications for Allergies and Asthma*

| Name | Indication | Administration |
|---|---|---|
| Antihistamines, anticholinergics, decongestants | | |
| *Antihistamines – Oral*<br>Acrivastine (Semprex-D)<br>Brompheniramine (Bromfenex, Bromfed)<br>Carbinoxamine (Rondec)<br>Chlorpheniramine (Chlor-Trimeton, Deconamine, Rynatan, Tanafed)<br>Clemastine (Tavist)<br>Cyproheptadine (Periactin)<br>Diphenhydramine (Benadryl)<br>Hydroxyzine (Atarax, Vistaril)<br>Promethazine (Phenergan)<br>Triprolidine (Actifed) | *Indication* (Note: Individual products may have only one or two and not all indications below): Allergic rhinitis, allergic conjunctivitis, urticaria, angioedema, allergic pruritis.<br>*Side effects*: Drowsiness, irritability.<br>*Less sedating*:<br>Cetirizine (Zyrtec),<br>Desloratadine (Clarinex),<br>Fexofenadine (Allegra),<br>Loratadine (Claritin, Alavert). | Administered in tablet or liquid form. |
| *Antihistamine – Intranasal*<br>Azelastin (Astelin) | *Indication*: Allergic rhinitis.<br>*Side effects*: Bitter taste, headache, somnolence. | Administered in nasal spray. |
| *Anticholinergic – Intranasal*<br>Ipratropium bromide (Atrovent nasal) | *Indication*: Rhinorrhea associated with allergic and nonallergic perennial rhinitis.<br>*Side effects*: Nosebleed, nasal dryness, dry mouth and throat. | Administered in nasal spray. |
| *Decongestants – Intranasal*<br>Oxymetazoline (Afrin)<br>Phenylephrine (Neo-Synephrine) | *Indication*: Rhinorrhea, nasal congestion.<br>*Side effect*: Rebound congestion. | Administered in nasal spray, nasal drops. Not to be used for more than 3 days. |
| *Decongestants – Oral*<br>Ephedrine<br>Pseudoephedrine | *Indication*: Nasal congestion.<br>*Side effects*: Agitation, insomnia, hallucinations, tremor. | Administered orally. |

*(Continued)*

**Table 1** *Continued*

| Name | Indication | Administration |
|---|---|---|
| *Antihistamine – Ophthalmic*<br>Azelastine (Optivar)<br>Emedastine (Emadine)<br>Levocabastine (Livostin) | *Indication*: Effective for itching in allergic conjunctivitis.<br>*Side effects*: Ocular burning or stinging, headache, bitter taste. | Administered in eyedrops. May be sensitizing. |
| *Vasoconstrictor/Antihistamine combination – Ophthalmic*<br>Antazoline, Naphazoline (Naphcon-A, Vasocon-A) | *Indication*: Combination relieves eye redness and itching.<br>*Side effects*: Pronounced dilation of pupil, increased intraocular pressure, local irritation. | Administered in eyedrops. Vasoconstrictors alone may result in rebound effect. |
| Anti-inflammatory medications | | |
| *Steroids – Intranasal*<br>Beclomethasone (Vancenase, Vancenase AQ, Beconase AQ)<br>Budesonide (Rhinocort, Rhinocort AQ)<br>Flunisolide (Nasalide, Nasarel)<br>Fluticasone (Flonase)<br>Mometasone (Nasonex)<br>Triamcinolone (Nasacort AQ, Nasacort HFA, Tri-Nasal) | *Indication*: Allergic rhinitis.<br>*Side effects*: Irritation, nosebleeds. | Administered in nasal spray. |
| *Mast cell stabilizer – Intranasal*<br>Cromolyn nasal (NasalCrom) | *Indication*: Prevention and relief of nasal allergy symptoms. Best when initiated before symptoms.<br>*Side effects*: Transient stinging, sneezing. | Administered in nasal spray. |
| *Mast cell stabilizer – Ophthalmic*<br>Lodoxadine (Alomide)<br>Cromolyn (Crolom, Opticrom)<br>Nedocromil (Alocril)<br>Pemirolast (Alamast)<br>*Combination antihistamine – Mast cell stabilizer (broad-based antiallergic effect)*<br>Olopatadine (Patanol)<br>Ketotifen (Zaditor) | *Indication*: Treatment of itching due to allergic conjunctivitis. Some mast cell stabilizers are used for vernal conjunctivitis, keratoconjunctivitis, vernal keratitis.<br>Best when initiated before symptoms.<br>*Side effects*: Headache, blurred vision, burning or stinging, dry eye. | Administered in eyedrops. |

*(Continued)*

**Table 1** *Continued*

| Name | Indication | Administration |
|---|---|---|
| *Nonsteroidal anti-inflammatory – Ophthalmic*<br>Ketorolac (Acular) | *Indication*: Ocular itch due to seasonal allergic conjunctivitis.<br>*Side effects*: Transient stinging, burning, irritation. | Administered in eyedrops.<br>Note: Ophthalmic corticosteroids are not discussed here because of side effects. They should be prescribed by an ophthalmologist. |
| *Steroids – Inhaled*<br>Beclomethasone (QVAR)<br>Budesonide (Pulmicort)<br>Flunisolide (AeroBid)<br>Fluticasone (Flovent, Advair combination)<br>Triamcinolone (Azmacort) | *Indication*: Asthma.<br>Long-term prevention of symptom exacerbations.<br>Reduce the need for quick-relief medications.<br>Reduce airway inflammation.<br>*Side effects*: Cough, dry mouth. | Administered through metered dose inhalers (MDIs), nebulizers, or dry power inhalers (DPIs).<br>Use of spacer is recommended for MDIs. Mouth should be rinsed after administration to prevent infection of the mouth. |
| *Mast cell stabilizer – Inhaled*<br>Cromolyn sodium (Intal)<br>Nedocromil (Tilade) | *Indication*: Asthma. Long-term prevention of symptoms; initiate prior to known trigger exposure.<br>*Side effect*: Throat irritation, cough. | Administered in inhaled or nebulized form. Less effective anti-inflammatory properties than corticosteroids. |
| *Leukotriene modifiers*<br>Montelukast (Singulair)<br>Zafirlukast (Accolate)<br>Zileuton (Zyflo) | *Indication*: Asthma, allergic rhinitis (Singulair only). Long-term prevention of symptom exacerbations.<br>*Side effect*: Headache, GI upset, flu/cold symptoms. Serious: Churg-Strauss syndrome (rare), Cholestatic hepatitis (rare). | Administered in tablet or granule form with once-daily dosing. Particularly beneficial for control of nocturnal symptoms. |
| *Steroids – Oral*<br>Dexamethasone (Decadron)<br>Methylprednisolone (Solu-Medrol)<br>Prednisolone (Prelone, Pediapred, Orapred)<br>Prednisone | *Indication*: Steroid-responsive disorders, allergic disorders, inflammatory conditions. Typically provided in short-term "burst" dosages to gain control over acute symptoms. May be used to control chronic symptoms through daily or every other day administration.<br>*Side effects*: Mild with short-term use. Many side effects, including mood and behavior changes, with long-term use. | Administered in tablet or liquid form. Administration of the lowest effective dose is recommended. Monitoring of side effects recommended when administered for sustained periods of time. |

*(Continued)*

**Table 1** *Continued*

| Name | Indication | Administration |
|---|---|---|
| *Steroids – Topical: Low, medium, high, very high potency*<br>Alclometasone Dipropionate (Aclovate)<br>Clocortolone pivalate (Cloderm)<br>Desonide (DesOwen, Tridesilon)<br>Hydrocortisone (Hytone)<br>Hydrocortisone acetate (Cortaid, Corticaine)<br>Betamethasone valerate (Valisone)<br>Desoximetasone (Topicort)<br>Flucinolone acetonide (Synalar)<br>Flurandrenolide (Cordran)<br>Fluticasone proprionate (Cutivate)<br>Hydrocortisone butyrate (Locoid)<br>Hydrocortisone valerate (Westcort)<br>Mometasone furoate (Elocon)<br>Triamcinolone (Aristocort Kenalog)<br>Amcinonide (Cyclocort)<br>Betamethasone dipropionate (Diprosone, Maxivate)<br>Desoximetasone (Topicort)<br>Diflorasone diacetate (Maxiflor)<br>Fluocinonide (Lidex)<br>Halcinonide (Halog)<br>Triamcinolone (Aristocort, Kenalog)<br>Betamethasone dipropionate (Diprolene, Diprolene AF)<br>Clobetasol (Temovate, Cormax)<br>Diflorasone diacetate (Psorcon)<br>Halobetasol propionate (Ultravate) | *Indication*: Steroid responsive dermatoses.<br><br>*Side effects*: Few side effects with low potency medications. Intermediate, high, and very high potency medications may cause many side effects if used for prolonged periods. | Administered in cream, ointment, lotion, solution, foam, tape, gel. Apply to affected areas on skin. |
| *Beta-adrenergic agonists*<br>Albuterol<br>Bitolterol (Tornalate)<br>Formoterol (Foradil)<br>Levalbuterol (Xopenex)<br>Metaproterenol (Alupent)<br>Pirbuterol (Maxair)<br>Salmeterol (Serevent)<br>Terbutaline (Brethine) | *Indication*: Bronchospasm.<br>Relief of acute symptoms through smooth muscle relaxation. Prevention of bronchoconstriction prior to exercise.<br><br>*Side effects*: Few side effects when inhaled. They are less effective and have more side effects when given orally. Side effects include increased heart rate, tremor, hyperactivity, insomnia. | May be administered in inhaled or nebulized form.<br><br>Overreliance on albuterol (e.g., more than one canister per month) indicates inadequate asthma control and need for additional preventive measures. |

*(Continued)*

**Table 1** *Continued*

| Name | Indication | Administration |
|---|---|---|
| *Bronchodilators-other*<br>Epinephrine<br>Ipratropium Bromide (Atrovent)<br>Theophylline (Uniphyl, Theo-24) | *Indication*: Bronchospasm in asthma, treatment of other chronic lung diseases, Anaphylaxis (Epi Pen).<br><br>*Side effects*: Palpitations, tachycardia, tremor, anxiety (Epinephrine). Increased heart rate, blurred vision, headache, dry mouth (Atrovent). Many, including hyperactivity and decreased attention span (Theophylline). | May be administered in injection, intravenous, or nebulized form (Epinephrine); administered in inhaled or nebulized form, not intended for use with exercise-induced symptoms, alternative medication for patients unable to take beta2 agonists (Atrovent); administered in oral form (Theophylline). |

occur in combination with other organ systems as part of an anaphylactic reaction. Symptoms of the skin are most common and range from an itchy rash to acute urticaria or angioedema. However, anaphylaxis should be suspected with feelings of a generalized warmth or flush, a sense of impending doom, and tingling and itching of hands, feet, and groin. This may progress to complaints of a lump or tightness in the throat, hoarseness, difficulty swallowing, wheezing, shortness of breath, chest tightness, or coughing. Gastrointestinal symptoms may include bloating, nausea, vomiting, or cramps. Food allergy symptoms, including anaphylaxis, typically appear within minutes to two hours after the person has eaten the food to which he or she is allergic, and may occur initially then subside for several hours before returning.

At this time, there is no treatment for food allergies. Strict avoidance of the allergy-causing food is the only way to avoid a reaction. In less acute cases, food allergy may contribute to chronic conditions such as atopic dermatitis, where avoidance of certain foods during school meals or snacks may help control exacerbations. If a food allergy progresses rapidly to anaphylaxis, epinephrine injections are necessary to control symptoms. Immediate injection of epinephrine, followed by a call to 911, can be critical to prevent the progression of anaphylaxis to death. Kits containing an antihistamine and syringe with epinephrine are available, as is the "Epipen," a prefilled epinephrine injection. Children with severe food allergies should have access to such tools at all times, and school personnel should be instructed in their use.

***Asthma.*** Asthma is a disorder of the airways that involves both chronic underlying inflammation and exacerbations characterized by reversible airway obstruction, or *bronchoconstriction* (National Institutes of Health, 1997). Symptoms occur as a result of airway hyperresponsivity to triggers. Triggers may be allergens that elicit symptoms among individuals with specific immunological sensitivities or sensitivity to airborne irritants (e.g., tobacco smoke or perfume). Physical activity, respiratory infections, and strong emotions can also trigger asthma exacerbations. Presentation of asthma symptoms varies from one individual to another, but the classic signs of an asthma episode can include wheezing, coughing, chest tightness, and shortness of breath. Some children become pale and listless. In more severe episodes, children may walk in a hunched-over position or may have difficulty speaking in full sentences. In life-threatening episodes, cyanosis (blue lips and extremities) can occur as a result of low oxygen saturation.

As with allergies, one of the key features of asthma prevention is avoiding triggers. Within the home, insects, pets, smoke, dust, cockroaches, mice, molds, and certain foods can contribute to ongoing symptomatology (AAAAI, 2000). Tools are available to enhance symptom identification and assess symptom severity. Most commonly, a peak flow meter, which measures the peak expiratory flow rate (PEFR), can be used to provide a simple objective measure of current airway obstruction. A PEFR value that is lower than a child's normal baseline indicates that an asthma episode is in progress or is about to begin.

Medications are used for symptom control and comprise two basic classes: quick-relief medications for immediate symptom control (i.e., bronchodilators), and long-term controller medications to reduce underlying inflammation and decrease bronchoreactivity (see Table 1). When an asthma exacerbation does not resolve easily through standard treatments, systemic corticosteroids can be used for more rapid anti-inflammatory action. As asthma management can be complex, education in the home and school is critical for effective disease control. National guidelines also recommend use of a written asthma management plan to help parents, teachers, and other caregivers coordinate their approach to care. Using these medical guidelines, school practitioners can recognize symptoms, identify their sources, and understand medication differences (e.g., medication taken daily versus only when there are problems) to better design and synchronize treatment plans for students.

### Developmental Issues

Because allergies and asthma are characterized by a complex and fluctuating clinical presentation, symptoms can vary considerably as children grow. This variability can be due to seasonal changes, changes in trigger exposure across settings, and gradual changes in the immune response over time. Although the underlying predisposition to allergy may remain constant, symptoms may be very episodic and, in the case of some conditions, may disappear completely or increase in severity. Children's symptoms and response to medications may also change throughout development. The amount and type of medications needed may change as children grow.

Throughout children's development, the family plays a crucial role in helping children learn to monitor and manage their symptoms, assist in trigger identification and control, administer medications, and monitor medication side effects. Regardless of the child's age, the effective management of asthma and allergies involves the successful integration of multiple systems of care, including the family system, the health care system, and the school setting.

Appropriate expectations for the self-care of allergic diseases and asthma change throughout development. For example, parents are centrally responsible for monitoring exposure to triggers and administering medications to toddlers and preschoolers. Younger children who are susceptible to anaphylaxis when exposed to specific triggers need to be monitored vigilantly, with appropriate treatment nearby should exposure occur. As children approach the early elementary years, they should learn to ask for assistance when having symptoms, begin to identify triggers, and understand the function of specific medications. School-age children have the capacity to notice symptoms and report to a responsible adult, and they may be more independent taking medications when in settings away from the family (e.g., playground or school). By the late elementary school years and early adolescence, children should know how to avoid allergens and other triggers, monitor their symptoms, and self-administer some medications.

Despite developmental advances, even older children still rely on the support of family to control the symptoms and manage allergic conditions and asthma. Adolescents vary in their ability to manage illness independently, and some may require ongoing assistance in order to address symptoms promptly and adhere to a treatment plan. Although adolescents' knowledge about asthma may improve during this age range, some take medication less regularly than they should (McQuaid, Kopel, Klein, & Fritz, 2003). At the same time, parental monitoring of illness management during adolescence decreases. Given that adolescents often need to negotiate their adherence to treatment in the context of social pressures, monitoring their level of motivation and self-management skills is an important part of coordinating treatment. School practitioners play an important role in understanding developmental milestones and recognizing opportunities to address potential developmental issues when planning school interventions.

## PROBLEMS AND IMPLICATIONS

Allergic diseases and asthma can pose several specific challenges to all children and families, even when the disease is managed effectively. Normal challenges related to the management of the allergic disease include dealing with the impact of allergic symptomatology and, in chronic conditions, adhering to treatment demands that can be complex. In some cases, illness management and the consequences of disease may present more significant challenges that may affect child functioning. A review of these issues is presented below.

### Academic Functioning

Allergic conditions can affect children's school functioning in a variety of ways. For example, the presence of symptoms as a result of being near unexpected triggers during the day can impair the student's concentration and the ability to attend to schoolwork. Nocturnal allergic symptoms can compromise children's quality of sleep and their ability to focus while in school (Diette, Markson, Skinner, Ngyuen, & Algatt-Bergstrom, 2000). Difficulty controlling symptoms can prevent children from attending school. Asthma, for example, is the leading cause of school absences in the United States (National Institutes of Health, 1997).

It is important for school personnel to be aware of factors that can intensify problems with illness management and affect students' learning in the school setting. For example, children with a history of significant food allergy, such as anaphylactic reactions to peanuts, clearly are at risk for experiencing disruptions in school and social functioning, particularly if dietary exposures are difficult to control. Children with the highest levels of asthma severity are at the most risk for experiencing morbidity related to asthma, such as more frequent nocturnal awakenings. It is important to be aware of the severity level of children's allergic disease, as it can be related to poor academic functioning and grade failure (e.g., Silverstein et al., 2001).

Medication side effects also have the potential to affect children's academic functioning. Although concern has been expressed regarding the potentially sedating properties of antihistamines, use of these drugs for allergic rhinitis does not affect children's memory and alertness (Bender & Milgrom, 2004). A direct relation between behavioral problems and use of allergy medication in children has not been found (McLoughlin et al., 1983). Furthermore, common quick-relief medicines for asthma, such as albuterol, do not appear to significantly increase the activity level of children with asthma (Hadjikoumi, Loader, Bracken, & Milner, 2002). Oral corticosteroids used in severe allergic conditions and severe asthma may impair school performance (Suess, Stump, Chai, & Kalisker, 1986) and can result in hyperactive symptoms (Hederos, 2004); however, this has not been demonstrated consistently (e.g., Bender, Lerner, & Poland, 1991). It is noteworthy that many children who use as-needed or preventive long-term medicines to treat allergic diseases have minimal side effects (Bender et al., 1991), and the benefits of using medication consistently to control symptoms likely outweigh the costs. Collaboration between the child's family, physician, and school system may ensure that proper monitoring of medication can identify potential side effects.

Although data are inconsistent, there does not appear to be a strong link between asthma, allergies, and learning disabilities. It has been argued that a common physiological pathway may lead to both immune problems and deviations with brain function (Speer, 1954). Findings linking food allergies with cognitive problems have been reported (Schnoll, Burshteyn, & Cea-Aravena, 2003), as have problems with learning in children with asthma (e.g., Halterman et al., 2001). However, consistent differences in intelligence and neurocognitive functioning between children with and without asthma have not been found (Annett, Aylward, Lapidus, Bender, & DuHamel, 2000). Taken together, these equivocal results suggest that several factors may explain the relation between allergies and learning problems, such as predisposing individual differences, illness severity, or treatment-related factors such as medication side effects. Proving that a causal link exists between allergies and learning problems is difficult, since studies have not followed children with allergies and assessed relations among these variables over time.

## Psychosocial Functioning

Consistent trigger avoidance may, by necessity, impose some social limitations on children with allergies and asthma. For example, some children cannot participate in sports, take field trips to the zoo, or eat certain items at parties, constraining their participation in normal, developmentally appropriate activities with peers and family. The stress of activity constraints can affect children's developing self-esteem. Children of school age have heightened concern for how others perceive them, which may influence their adherence to treatment. Physical changes due to skin allergies (e.g., eczema or hives), dietary restrictions due to food allergies, or the need to use an inhaler to manage asthma symptoms in public may increase self-consciousness (e.g., Velsor-Friedrich, Vlasses, Moberley, & Coover, 2004). Children who have had a severe allergic reaction or a significant asthma exacerbation may have to cope with the distressing symptoms, ongoing treatments, and even hospitalization. Those who have experienced anaphylaxis or a life-threatening asthma exacerbation may be very fearful of experiencing another attack.

Children with allergies and asthma are at some increased risk for exhibiting behavioral symptoms such as impulsivity, hyperactivity, poorly regulated arousal levels, and aggression (e.g., Marshall, 1989). Atopic dermatitis has been associated with increased behavioral symptoms in school-age children (Absolon, Cottrell, Eldridge, & Glover, 1997). Behavioral difficulties that are associated with asthma are found primarily in the anxiety and depression spectrum, and those with severe disease tend to have more risk of psychopathology (McQuaid, Kopel, & Nassau, 2001). However, not all children with allergic diseases will develop behavioral problems (e.g., McGee, Stantaon, & Sears, 1993).

Data regarding the link between allergic disorders and clinically diagnosed psychiatric disorders, such as Attention Deficit Hyperactive Disorder (ADHD), are more equivocal. It is difficult to draw firm conclusions, as studies tend to use different methods of measurement and focus on different conditions. Some evidence shows a small but consistent association between allergic rhinitis, specifically, and ADHD (e.g., Brawley et al., 2004).

There is less consistent evidence that food allergies or intolerances to food additives such as food coloring and preservatives are associated with significant behavioral symptoms or psychiatric disorders in children. Feingold (1975) first posed the theory that food additives were associated with hyperactivity. Despite widespread publicity, subsequent research has been mixed. Some recent work has linked food allergies with behavioral problems in children (e.g., Bateman et al., 2004). In contrast, a number of well-controlled studies of the Feingold hypothesis have led to the rejection of the idea that eliminating food additives through dietary changes has any benefit beyond the normal placebo effect (Krummel, Seligson, & Guthrie, 1996). Taken together, results suggest that food allergies or reactions to certain food additives are not likely to be a causal factor in hyperactivity, but they may have the potential to exacerbate symptoms in certain subgroups of children.

In general, children with asthma who have comorbid psychiatric problems may have more difficulty managing their asthma and, consequently, greater morbidity (Weil et al., 1999). A constellation of factors, such as severe asthma, psychiatric comorbidity, and increased functional limitations from these conditions, can have a significant effect on children's school functioning, including their ability to listen, pay attention, concentrate on schoolwork, and participate in mutually respectful social exchanges with peers and teachers (Fowler, Davenport, & Garg, 1992). School practitioners can play a critical role in enhancing child adaptation through collaboration with community mental health professionals and health care providers to coordinate effective treatment plans outside of the school setting.

### Familial and Cultural Factors

Children and families with significant allergic disease may be burdened by the stress of illness management tasks. Many children and families with chronic conditions find it challenging to remember to take their medications daily. Nonadherence is generally associated with subsequent morbidity (Bauman et al., 2002). Parents are also commonly concerned about medication side effects and their impact on children's functioning. Parents need to be educated about the distinction between common but harmless side effects and uncommon but dangerous side effects (see Table 1). Consistent communication with the child's physician can address any concerns that a parent may have about their child's medication use and the effect it may have on their functioning. School professionals can play an important role in helping parents and teachers identify behavioral patterns within the classroom that may be associated with medication use. They can also support children's efforts to take medication regularly, avoid triggers, and control symptoms.

Family stressors can also serve as risk factors for compromised illness management and, ultimately, morbidity. Family processes that affect family functioning and the emotional climate of the family, such as parental distress, conflict, stressful life events, lack of maternal social support, and parenting difficulties, can compromise illness management and contribute to the morbidity of children with allergic diseases and asthma (e.g., Bartlett et al., 2001).

Families' health beliefs also should be considered when schools attempt to support efforts to control allergic diseases or asthma (Flores, 2004). For example, for African American and Hispanic inner-city families, parents' beliefs or concerns about their child's medications (e.g., the dangers of dependence or long-term effects) can cause the underuse of daily preventive asthma medications (Riekert et al., 2003). In addition, there is a high rate of use of alternative practices (e.g., prayers, rubs, and herbal remedies) in African American (Braganza, Ozuah, & Sharif, 2003) and Hispanic (Bearison, Minian, & Granowetter, 2002) families with children who have asthma. School personnel need to consider families' cultural values and beliefs regarding disease, address misperceptions about medications, and help replace potentially harmful practices with medically acceptable alternatives that fit within families' belief systems.

## ALTERNATIVE ACTIONS FOR PREVENTION AND INTERVENTION

Treatment of allergic diseases comprises two basic strategies: *prevention* and *management*. Prevention strategies are based on different phases of the allergic process and include primary prevention (blocking initial sensitization), secondary prevention (blocking the expression of the disease post-sensitization), and tertiary prevention (avoidance of allergens known to increase symptoms; AAAAI, 2000). Primary prevention efforts to minimize initial sensitization include avoiding exposure to allergens and irritants for children who have a propensity to develop allergic diseases (e.g., waiting to introduce nuts into a child's diet until the preschool years). Secondary prevention efforts to block illness expression include consistent use of preventive medications, or medical interventions such as immunotherapy. Tertiary prevention efforts include avoidance of identified environmental allergens known to initiate symptoms. School personnel can help support prevention efforts by identifying potential triggers within the school environment that may pose risks to children with allergic sensitivity or immunologically sensitive airways, by supporting children's consistent use of prescribed medications, and by referring children directly to the school nurse when they present with allergy or asthma symptoms.

Once allergic disease is identified, a four-tiered strategy is often recommended for symptom management. This includes (1) having the child avoid or minimizing exposures to known allergens and irritants in the environment, (2) making sure the child uses medication as prescribed, (3) evaluating the child for immunotherapy, and (4) educating the child and family regarding the disease and its management (AAAAI, 2000). To effectively control allergic diseases and asthma, a number of different intervention approaches have been found to be useful. These include pharmacological management of the illness, control of environmental triggers, educational and psychosocial interventions to provide basic knowledge of the illness, strategies for optimal management, and support for the child and family's health-related behaviors (AAAAI).

Current standards of care in allergy and asthma management often propose integrating a variety of supplemental psychosocial, educational, and environmental interventions with pharmacological management of illness. The following sections outline commonly used supplemental interventions, including strategies for environmental control, educational interventions, psychosocial approaches, and treatment approaches that combine various elements of these approaches in a coordinated fashion.

## Environmental Control Strategies

Clinical recommendations for allergy control and asthma management commonly include measures for trigger reduction in the home setting. This approach can include counseling parents to quit smoking, to remove pets from the home, and to employ measures to reduce dust mites, such as washing bedclothes in hot water. Some specific measures to reduce individual triggers in the home, such as using mattress covers to minimize dust mite exposure, have been shown to reduce allergen levels (e.g., Marks et al., 1994). Impoverished households are more likely to be reservoirs for certain triggers (e.g., cockroaches and rodents), and some families may lack the resources to implement more expensive strategies for trigger control, such as carpet removal. Tailoring advice to the family based on their economic circumstances and the child's specific allergic profile can increase acceptance of recommendations. For example, offering low-cost alternatives (e.g., mattress covers that may be covered by insurance) or using an individualized approach, such as trigger reduction strategies based on the child's skin-testing profile, can help reduce allergen exposure and asthma symptoms (Morgan et al., 2004).

For triggers in the school environment, the U.S. Environmental Protection Agency (EPA) has developed a program called Tools for Schools. This novel program helps school staff identify potential problems in indoor air quality in the school environment. School staff members do a walk-through using a checklist to identify potential sources of problematic indoor air quality. Once potential sources are identified, such as inadequate ventilation, EPA recommends strategies to reduce indoor allergens and irritants and to improve the overall indoor air quality of the school. Although published data do not yet exist regarding the program's efficacy, it has been widely adopted and is available for public use.

## Educational Interventions

Patient education regarding the basics of disease etiology, symptom management, and trigger control are now thought to be central to effective care (AAAAI, 2000; National Institutes of Health, 1997, 2002). Patient education should begin at the physician's office with a written asthma action plan. The written plan should include early warning signs of an asthma episode, indicators for worsening symptoms (specific symptoms and peak expiratory flow measurements), the names and doses of medications in use (both long-term controller and quick-relief medication), how and when the medications are taken, and when to contact the clinician or emergency department. For the school setting, the plan also should include recommendations regarding self-administration of medication and plans to ensure access to medication,

medication pre-treatment to prevent exercise-induced symptoms, if applicable, and identification of triggers so that the school may help reduce exposure (National Institutes of Health, 1997).

Asthma education or self-management programs for asthma have been used for over two decades. Families typically have insufficient knowledge of asthma, including inaccuracies regarding medication usage, poor understanding of the etiology and course of asthma, and poor asthma management techniques (e.g., Zimmerman, Bonner, Evans, & Mellins, 1999). Numerous educational programs have been developed and implemented to address these problems. However, establishing the efficacy of programs is challenging, as the medical field of asthma is regularly transformed by the introduction of new medications, new delivery systems for medicine, and new methods of disease management.

## Psychosocial Interventions

Psychosocial interventions for asthma that are implemented in clinical practice include self-management training, problem-solving techniques, family-based interventions, and psychophysiologic modalities to reduce symptoms (i.e., relaxation training and biofeedback). More recently, some interventions have explicitly focused on increasing child adherence to medication use. For example, promising results from one study showed that targeting adherence to medication use during home visits helped increase appropriate use of daily medications in inner-city children (Bartlett, Lukk, Butz, Lampros-Klein, & Rand, 2002). Efforts to pilot test such an intervention included employing social–cognitive strategies (e.g., goal setting, monitoring, and feedback) and targeting known barriers to medication use. Psychosocial interventions such as these can play an important role in pinpointing difficulties in disease management, addressing poor treatment adherence, and facilitating cooperation between families and physicians (Lemanek, Kamps, & Chung, 2001).

Psychophysiological approaches such as relaxation training and biofeedback have also been implemented as adjunctive treatments, specifically for asthma symptoms. A review of different forms of biofeedback and relaxation techniques in pediatric asthma (McQuaid & Nassau, 1999) concluded that some forms of biofeedback to modify asthma symptoms have empirical support, yet more research is needed to determine if these strategies effect clinically significant changes in asthma symptoms.

## Combined Approaches

Although many interventions have focused on single behavioral or environmental targets (e.g., medication adherence and trigger abatement), it is increasingly acknowledged that approaches that combine several treatments in a coordinated fashion are likely to have the most significant and sustained results. As an example, one recent study evaluated a comprehensive school-based asthma program on indices of asthma morbidity and school functioning (Clark et al., 2004). This program included asthma education for the general school population through classroom sessions for children, asthma education for school personnel, and school fairs regarding asthma. Additionally, children with asthma participated in specific educational activities (an adaptation of "Open Airways for Schools"; Evans et al., 1987). School building walk-throughs to identify problems in indoor air quality were also implemented to work toward reduction of environmental asthma triggers. Finally, written communication regarding the child's participation in this school program was shared with the health care providers of children with asthma to encourage coordination of care. Results were impressive and indicated significant reductions in asthma symptoms, particularly for children with persistent asthma. Few differences in academic functioning were noted, with the exception of higher grades in science and fewer school absences related to asthma for the treatment group (Clark et al.). These results suggest that combined interventions, although costly and labor intensive, may be what is required for significant and sustained effects on disease control.

# SUMMARY

Allergic diseases, including asthma, are increasing in prevalence in school-age children. Allergic conditions are typically caused by an overreaction of the immune system to an otherwise harmless substance. Allergic diseases include allergic rhinitis (hay fever), skin allergies (atopic dermatitis, contact dermatitis, and urticaria and angioedema), food allergies, and asthma. Symptom presentation is varied; it can range from mild symptoms, such as a runny nose and itchy eyes, to life threatening, as in a severe asthma exacerbation or anaphylactic reaction to food. Treatment for allergic diseases and asthma comprises two basic strategies, (a) trigger control for symptom prevention and (b) medication use for symptom prevention and relief. The role of patient and family education in trigger avoidance, symptom monitoring, and appropriate use of medication has been increasingly emphasized in guidelines for effective medical care (AAAAI, 2000; National Institutes of Health, 2002).

School personnel should be made aware that children with allergic conditions face some ongoing challenges. These may include difficulties in concentration and attention as a result of medication side effects, self-consciousness regarding obvious symptoms or medication use, and the need to adhere to treatment regimens that may be complex. In addition, empirical work indicates that some allergic conditions are associated with increased behavioral difficulties, and individuals who have severe disease are most affected. Despite lay beliefs that food allergies cause hyperactivity, the majority of studies do not support this association.

A variety of psychosocial and behavioral interventions are available to supplement medical treatments for allergic conditions. The majority of programs address asthma; however, certain interventions, such as strategies for environmental control within the school, have the potential to benefit all students. A coordinated treatment plan that involves ongoing communication among the family, medical caregivers, and school personnel is necessary to best manage the disease for optimal outcome and to enable the child to achieve full academic potential.

# RECOMMENDED RESOURCES

## Books and Other Printed Material

American Academy of Allergy, Asthma, and Immunology. (2000). *The allergy report: Science-based findings on the diagnosis and treatment of allergic disorders.* Available through the AAAAI website: http://www.aaaai.org/ar/default.stm

This report provides a thorough description of current treatment approaches in allergic disorders.

National Asthma Education and Prevention Program, Expert Panel Report (1997, 2002). Available from the website of the National Heart, Lung, and Blood Institute of the National Institutes of Health: http://www.nhlbi.nih.gov/about/naepp/

This reference is a comprehensive overview of the current recommended guidelines for the diagnosis and management of the disease, including helpful handouts for patients. Slides regarding asthma are also available through the website.

Wood, R. A. (1995). *Taming asthma and allergies by controlling your environment.* Washington, DC: Asthma and Allergy Foundation of America.

This brief monograph, available from the website of the AAFA, provides recommendations regarding how children and parents can implement trigger control strategies in the home and at school.

## Websites

*http://www.epa.gov/iaq/schools/*

The U.S. Environmental Protection Agency (EPA), in this website for its Indoor Air Quality Tools for Schools Program, has put together specific resources for school personnel to help identify and target problems of indoor air quality in their schools. In addition, the website contains a link to EPA's Healthy School Environments web pages (*http://www.epa.gov/schools*), which provide direction to on-line resources to help school personnel and parents address environmental health issues in schools.

*http://www.aafa.org*

The Asthma and Allergy Foundation of America's website contains many books and resources, plus a hotline, an e-mail chat room, and more.

*http://www.starbright.org/projects/asthma/index.html*

STARBRIGHT Foundation (n.d.). *Quest for the code.* This interactive CD-ROM is a terrific resource for older children to learn about asthma. It is available through their website and also by calling (800) 315-2580.

# REFERENCES

Absolon, C. M., Cottrell, D., Eldridge, S. M., & Glover, M. T. (1997). Psychological disturbance in atopic eczema: The extent of the problem in school-aged children. *British Journal of Dermatology, 137,* 241–245.

Academy of Allergy, Asthma and Immunology (AAAAI). (2000). *The allergy report: Science-based findings on the diagnosis and treatment of allergic disorders.* Milwaukee, WI: Academy of Allergy, Asthma, and Immunology.

Annett, R. D., Aylward, E. H., Lapidus, J., Bender, B. G., & DuHamel, T. (2000). Neurocognitive functioning in children with mild and moderate asthma in the childhood asthma management program. *Journal of Allergy and Clinical Immunology, 105,* 717–724.

Bartlett, S. J., Kolodner, K., Butz, A. M., Eggleston, P., Malveaux, F., & Rand, C. (2001). Maternal depressive symptoms and emergency department use among inner-city children with asthma. *Archives of Pediatric Adolescent Medicine, 155,* 347–353.

Bartlett, S. J., Lukk, P., Butz, A., Lampros-Klein, F., & Rand, C. S. (2002). Enhancing medication adherence among inner-city children with asthma: Results from pilot studies. *Journal of Asthma, 39,* 47–54.

Bateman, B., Warner, J. O., Hutchinson, E., Dean, T., Rowlandson, P., Gant, C., et al. (2004). The effects of a double blind, placebo controlled, artificial food colourings and benzoate preservative challenge on hyperactivity in general population sample of preschool children. *Archives of Disease in Childhood, 6,* 506–511.

Bauman, L. J., Wright, E., Leickly, F. E., Crain, E., Kruszon-Moran, D., Wade, S. L., et al. (2002). Relationship of adherence to pediatric asthma morbidity among inner-city children. *Pediatrics, 110*(1 Pt 1), e6.

Bearison, D. J., Minian, N., & Granowetter, L. (2002). Medical management of asthma and folk medicine in a Hispanic community. *Journal of Pediatric Psychology, 27,* 385–392.

Bender, B., Lerner, J. A., & Poland, J. E. (1991). Association between corticosteroids and psychologic change in hospitalized asthmatic children. *Annals of Allergy, 66,* 414–419.

Bender, B., & Milgrom, H. (2004). Comparison of the effects of fluticasone propionate aqueous nasal spray and loratadine on daytime alertness and performance in children with seasonal allergic rhinitis. *Annals of Allergy and Asthma Immunology, 92,* 344–349.

Braganza, S., Ozuah, P. O., & Sharif, I. (2003). The use of complementary therapies in inner-city asthmatic children. *Journal of Asthma, 40,* 823–827.

Brawley, A., Silverman, B., Kearney, S., Guanzon, D., Owens, M., Bennett, H., et al. (2004). Allergic rhinitis in children with attention-deficit/hyperactivity disorder. *Annals of Allergy and Asthma Immunology, 92,* 663–667.

Centers for Disease Control and Prevention. (1996). Asthma morbidity and hospitalization among children and young adults—US 1980–1993. *Morbidity and Mortality Weekly Report, 45,* 350–353.

Clark, N. M., Brown, R., Joseph, C. L. M., Anderson, E. W., Liu, M., Valerio, M. A., et al. (2004). Effects of a comprehensive school-based asthma management program on symptoms, parent management, grades and absenteeism. *Chest, 1125,* 1674–1679.

Diette, G. B., Markson, L., Skinner, E. A., Ngyuen, T. T., & Algatt-Bergstrom, P. (2000). Nocturnal asthma in children affects school attendance, school performance and parents' work attendance. *Archives of Pediatric Adolescent Medicine, 154,* 923–928.

Evans, R., Mullally, D. I., Wilson, R. W., Gergen, P. J., Rosenberg, H. M., Grauman, J. S., et al. (1987). National trends in the morbidity and mortality of asthma in the U.S. Prevalence, hospitalization and death from asthma over two decades: 1965–1984. *Chest, 91*(Suppl. 6), S65–S74.

Feingold, B. (1975). Hyperkinesis and learning disability linked to artificial food flavors and colors. *American Journal of Nursing, 75,* 797–803.

Flores, G. (2004). Culture, ethnicity, and linguistic issues in pediatric care: Urgent priorities and unanswered questions. *Ambulatory Pediatrics, 4,* 276–282.

Fowler, M. G., Davenport, M. G., & Garg, R. (1992). School functioning of U.S. children with asthma. *Pediatrics, 90,* 939–944.

Grundy, J., Matthews, S., Bateman, B., Dean, T., & Hasan Arshad, S. (2002). Rising prevalence of allergy to peanut in children: Data from 2 sequential cohorts. *Journal of Allergy and Clinical Immunology, 110,* 784–789.

Hadjikoumi, I., Loader, P., Bracken, M., & Milner, A. D. (2002). Bronchodilator therapy and hyperactivity in preschool children. *Archives of Disease in Childhood, 86,* 202–203.

Halterman, J. S., Montes, G., Aligne, C. A., Kaczorowski, J. M., Hightower, A. D., Szilaygi, P. G., (2001). School readiness among urban children with asthma. *Ambulatory Pediatrics, 1,* 201–205.

Hederos, C. A. (2004). Neuropsychologic changes and inhaled corticosteroids. *Journal of Allergy and Clinical Immunology, 114,* 451–452.

Krummel, D., Seligson, F., & Guthrie, H. (1996). Hyperactivity: Is candy causal? *Critical Review of Food Science Nutrition, 36,* 31–47.

Lemanek, K. L., Kamps, J., & Chung, N. B. (2001). Empirically supported treatments in pediatric psychology: Regimen adherence. *Journal of Pediatric Psychology, 26,* 279–282.

Leung, D. Y. M. (2003). Atopic dermatitis (atopic eczema). In M. Hill (Ed.), *Fitzpatrick's dermatology in general medicine* (6th ed., pp. 1180–1194). New York: McGraw-Hill.

Lozano, P., Connell, F. A., & Koepsell, T. D. (1995). Use of health services by African American children with asthma on Medicaid. *Journal of the American Medical Association, 274,* 469–473.

Marks, G. B., Tovey, E. R, Green, W., Shearer, R., Salome, C. M., & Woolcock, A. J. (1994). House dust mite allergen avoidance: A randomized controlled trial of surface chemical treatment and encasement of bedding. *Clinical and Experimental Allergy, 24,* 1078–1083.

Marshall, P. (1989). Attention deficit disorder and allergy: A neurochemical model of the relation between the illnesses. *Psychological Bulletin, 106,* 434–446.

McGee, E., Stantaon, W. R., & Sears, M. R. (1993). Allergic disorders and attention deficit disorder in children. *Journal of Abnormal Child Psychology, 21,* 79–88.

McLoughlin, J., Nall, M., Isaacs, B., Petrosko, J., Karibo, J., & Lindsey, B. (1983). The relationship of allergies and allergy treatment to school performance and student behavior. *Annals of Allergy, 51,* 506–510.

McQuaid, E. L., Kopel, S. J., Klein, R. B., & Fritz, G. K. (2003). Medication adherence in pediatric asthma: Reasoning, responsibility, and behavior. *Journal of Pediatric Psychology, 28,* 323–333.

McQuaid, E. L., Kopel, S. J., & Nassau, J. H. (2001). Behavioral adjustment in children with asthma: A meta-analysis. *Journal of Developmental and Behavioral Pediatrics, 22,* 430–439.

McQuaid, E. L., & Nassau, J. H. (1999). Empirically supported treatments of disease-related symptoms in pediatric psychology: Asthma, diabetes, and cancer. *Journal of Pediatric Psychology, 24,* 306–328.

Morgan, W. J., Crain, E. F., Gruchalla, R. S., O'Connor, G. T., Kattan, M., Evans, R., et al. (2004). Results of a home-based environmental intervention among urban children with asthma. *New England Journal of Medicine, 351,* 1068–1080.

National Institutes of Health. (1997). *National Asthma Education and Prevention Program (National Heart, Lung, and Blood Institute), Second Expert Panel on the Management of Asthma. Expert panel report 2: Guidelines for the diagnosis and management of asthma.* Bethesda, MD: NIH.

National Institutes of Health. (2002). *National Asthma Education and Prevention Program, Expert Panel, Report. Guidelines for the Diagnosis and Management of Asthma-Update on selected topics 2002.* Bethesda, MD: Author.

Riekert, K. A., Butz, A. M., Eggleston, P. A., Huss, K., Winkelstein, M., & Rand, C. S. (2003). Caregiver-physician medication concordance and undertreatment in asthma among inner-city children. *Pediatrics, 111,* 214–220.

Sampson, H. A. (1998). Epidemiology of asthma and allergic diseases. In E. Middleton (Ed.), *Allergy, principles and practice* (5th ed., p. 1162). St. Louis, MO: Mosby.

Schnoll, R., Burshteyn, D., & Cea-Aravena, J. (2003). Nutrition in the treatment of attention-deficit hyperactivity disorder as a neglected but important aspect. *Applied Psychophysiology and Biofeedback, 28,* 63–75.

Silverstein, M., Mair, J., Katusic, S., Wollan, P., O'Connell, E., & Yungin, J. (2001). School attendance and school performance: A population-based study of children with asthma. *Journal of Pediatrics, 139,* 278–283.

Speer, F. (1954). Allergic-tension-fatigue in children. *Annals of Allergy, 12,* 168–171.

Strachan, D. P. (1989). Hayfever, hygiene, and household size. *British Medical Journal, 299,* 1259–1260.

Suess, W. M., Stump, N., Chai, H., & Kalisker, A. (1986). Mnemonic effects of asthma in children. *Journal of Asthma, 23,* 291–296.

Velsor-Friedrich, B., Vlasses, F., Moberley, J., & Coover, L. (2004). Talking with teens about asthma management. *Journal of School Nursing, 20,* 140–148.

Weil, C. M., Wade, S. L., Bauman, L. J., Lynn, H., Mitchell, H., & Lavigne, J. (1999). The relationship between psychosocial factors and asthma morbidity in inner-city children with asthma. *Pediatrics, 104,* 1274–1280.

Zimmerman, B. J., Bonner, S., Evans, D., & Mellins, R. B. (1999). Self-regulating childhood asthma: A developmental model of family change. *Health Education and Behavior, 26,* 55–71.

# 69

# Prematurity

**Gloria C. Maccow**

*Guilford County Schools*

**Anne M. Howard**
**Mark E. Swerdlik**

*Illinois State University*

## BACKGROUND AND DEVELOPMENT

The typical length of a pregnancy is 40 weeks. Babies are considered to be born full term (at-term gestation) if they are delivered between 37 and 42 weeks of pregnancy. They are considered preterm, also referred to as premature, if born before 37 weeks of pregnancy (i.e., less than 259 days from the first day of the mother's last menstrual period; World Health Organization, 1977). In the United States, approximately 12% of babies are born preterm. Of these preterm babies, approximately 84% are born between 32 and 36 weeks of gestation, approximately 10% are born between 28 and 31 weeks of gestation, and about 6% are born at less than 28 weeks of gestation (March of Dimes, 2004).

Although the international definition of prematurity focuses on gestational age, prematurity can also be defined in terms of birth weight (Amiel-Tison, Allen, Lebrun, & Rogowski, 2002). Low birth weight (LBW) refers to those infants weighing less than 2,500 grams, or 5 pounds 8 ounces; very low birth weight (VLBW) infants weigh less than 1,500 grams, or 3 pounds 5 ounces; extremely low birth weight (ELBW) refers to those infants weighing less than 1,000 grams, or 2 pounds 3 ounces. Low birth weight is associated with preterm birth, but it can also result when the infant is born at term (40 weeks gestation) but too small for gestational age (Alexander & Slay, 2002).

Advances in medical technology have reduced the rate of perinatal mortality related to premature birth. Between 1980 and 2000, the infant mortality rate, (i.e., the number of infants who died before their first birthday) was reduced from 12.6 to 6.9 per 1,000 live births (Centers for Disease Control and Prevention [CDC], 2002). However, premature births remain common. In fact, the rate of premature birth increased from 9.4% to 12.1% between 1981 and 2000 (March of Dimes, 2004). Specifically, LBW rates rose from 6.8% to 7.6% of live births, a 12% increase, and VLBW rates rose 24%, from 1.15% to 1.43% of live births. Correspondingly, preterm birth rates increased approximately 17% (Alexander & Slay, 2002).

Significant economic costs are associated with the intensive care that neonates require in order to survive. Compared with the average hospital charge of $1,300 for infants born without complications, the average cost is about $75,000 for infants diagnosed as premature (March of Dimes, 2004). The costs of prematurity continue after the infants leave the hospital, because a large percentage of the youngest and smallest babies live with long-term health problems (March of Dimes) and/or neurodevelopmental impairments (Msall & Tremont, 2002).

### Factors That Increase the Risk of Prematurity

Approximately 40% of women who deliver prematurely have no risk factors; however, certain variables place a woman at greater risk of preterm labor and birth. These include (a) previous preterm birth, (b) certain uterine or cervical abnormalities, and (c) pregnancies of twins, triplets, or more (March of Dimes, 2004). Certain lifestyle or environmental variables also increase the risk of premature birth. These include late or no prenatal care, smoking, consumption of alcohol or illicit drugs, and long working hours with long periods of standing (March of Dimes).

Other maternal risk factors include preeclampsia (toxemia or high blood pressure of pregnancy) and infections of the vagina, urinary tract, or fetal or placental tissues. A number of factors related to the pregnancy can place the mother and fetus at risk. Included are abnormal or decreased function of the placenta, placenta previa (low-lying position of the placenta), early detachment of the placenta from the uterus (placental abruption), premature rupture of membranes (amniotic sac), and too much amniotic fluid. Reproductive factors, including third-trimester bleeding and chorioamnionitis (inflammation of fetal membrane as a result of infection), pose a very high risk for premature labor (Heffner, Sherman, Speizer, & Weiss, 1993).

One reproductive risk factor, multiple gestation, is becoming more common because of assisted reproductive technology. Since 1983, when the first infant was conceived through in vitro fertilization (IVF) in the United States, there has been a substantial increase in the use of IVF and related procedures. Women who conceive using assisted reproductive technology are more likely to have multiple births than women who conceive without treatment. Associated with multiple births may be maternal complications of pregnancy (e.g., hemorrhage and hypertension), premature delivery, low birth weight infants, infant mortality, and long-term disability for infants who survive (CDC, 2003).

***Differential effects by ethnicity.*** Disparities by race in the rates of infant mortality, low birth weight, and preterm delivery are a persistent feature of U.S. pregnancy statistics. African Americans continue to have twice the risk of delivering a LBW infant and over 2.5 times the risk of a VLBW delivery, compared with Whites and other minority women (CDC, 2002). Considering that factors associated with ethnicity are also correlated with socioeconomic disadvantage, it is difficult to separate the contributions of each to prematurity. A number of studies using multivariate analysis techniques—adjusting for relevant variables, including maternal age, education, marital status, employment, and smoking and drug use—nevertheless have found that ethnicity itself strongly predicts the rate of premature birth (e.g., Shiono & Klebanoff, 1986). Higher prevalence of adverse social conditions during the mothers' gestations, infancies, or childhoods that compromised reproductive capability may explain at least some of the differences in rates of prematurity.

***Differential effects by age.*** Compared with older mothers, a teenager is more likely to deliver a baby that is preterm and low birth weight. Therefore, the babies are at greater risk for illnesses and developmental delays. As a group, teenage mothers are very likely to have dropped out of school, abuse drugs and alcohol, and live in poverty. When they become pregnant, they often delay seeking prenatal care. During pregnancy, they experience complications such as toxemia, hypertension, and urinary tract infections that may go untreated (Luster & Brophy-Herb, 2000). Premature delivery is often the result, and the infant tends to be small for gestational age.

## Effects of Prematurity

Premature infants are surviving at higher rates as a result of fetal monitoring to identify infants at high risk and delivery of high-risk infants in perinatal centers with sophisticated equipment and expertise in the management of high-risk newborns. Babies born near term may have few medical complications, but babies born before 32 to 34 weeks gestation can have complex medical needs. Resulting biomedical complications, such as brain damage, increase the risk of subsequent developmental disability (e.g., Allen, 2002). These medical needs and complications are the result of diseases experienced by premature infants because of the immaturity of their organ systems (see Table 1).

***Biomedical complications.*** Breathing problems are common among premature infants. Apnea, or interruptions in the infant's breathing, can occur and affect the heart rate. Respiratory distress syndrome (RDS) is especially common. Approximately 24,000 babies a year, most of whom were born before 34 weeks gestation, suffer from RDS. RDS is caused when the air sacs in the lungs of the newborn do not remain open because the lungs are too immature to produce the required protein, *surfactant*, in sufficient amounts. The fetus typically begins producing surfactant after about the 34th week of pregnancy. Therefore, many infants born before 34 weeks gestation are incapable of producing sufficient amounts to breathe on their own. When the physician diagnoses RDS, a surfactant preparation may be administered to the infant immediately after birth.

In addition to surfactant, increased oxygen concentration and respirators are used to treat RDS. The effect

**Table 1** *Common Diseases of Premature Infants and Possible Complications*

| Disease | Possible Complications |
|---|---|
| Hyperbilirubinemia (jaundice) | • Kernicterus (mental retardation, cerebral palsy).<br>• Inner ear damage. |
| Intraventricular hemorrhage (IVH) | • Neurological impairment.<br>• Hydrocephalus.<br>• Cerebral palsy.<br>• Mental retardation.<br>• Hearing impairment.<br>• Visual impairment. |
| Necrotizing enterocolitis (NEC) | • Damage to intestines. |
| Patent ductus arteriosus (PDA) | • Congestive heart failure.<br>• Necrotizing enterocolitis.<br>• Pulmonary edema.<br>• Oxygen or respirator dependency. |
| Respiratory distress syndrome (RDS) | • Bronchopulmonary dysplasia.<br>• Upper airway damage.<br>• Recurrent lower respiratory tract infections. |
| Retinopathy of prematurity (ROP) | • Impaired vision (myopia, partial loss of field of vision).<br>• Blindness. |

of using respirators for more than a month may be complications such as chronic lung disease (bronchopulmonary dysplasia), upper airway damage, and recurrent lower respiratory tract infections (e.g., Brown, 1993). Oxygen or respirator dependency may result when the blood vessel connecting the aorta and the pulmonary artery does not close as it should shortly after birth (patent ductus arteriosus; Manginello & DiGeronimo, 1998).

Because of its immaturity, the liver of some premature babies cannot remove from the blood a waste product called bilirubin. This leads to an overabundance of bilirubin (a yellowish-red pigment) in the infant's blood. Known as hyperbilirubinemia or jaundice, this condition can cause brain damage. Brain damage can also result from a condition known as intraventricular hemorrhage (IVH). IVH occurs in 20% to 30% of infants weighing less than 1,500 grams at birth (Moe & Paige, 1998), and the likelihood of its occurrence is inversely related to gestational age and birth weight (Linder et al., 2003). Some premature infants with IVH will die (Manginello & DiGeronimo, 1998), but the number is decreasing as a result of improvements in medical technology. Those who survive have a high risk of neurological or developmental disability (e.g., Ment, Schneider, Ainley, & Allan, 2000). The degree of risk is related to the severity of the bleeding. A grading system from 1 to 4 is used to describe the severity of the IVH. With Grade 1, the bleeding is present in just a small area of the ventricles. When the bleeding occurs inside the ventricles, the IVH is at Grade 2. Approximately three fourths of all IVH cases are Grades 1 or 2. Once the IVH is treated, there tend to be no further complications. The most serious IVH cases are Grade 3 (when the ventricles are enlarged by the blood) and Grade 4 (when the bleeding extends into the brain tissues around the ventricles). IVH at Grades 3 or 4 can result in long-term injury to the brain.

***Psychosocial complications.*** A facilitative environment can ameliorate some effects of biomedical complications (Horowitz, 1987). However, parents are sometimes unable to provide the care and stimulation required by an already vulnerable infant. Mothers may be preoccupied with their own feelings about the birth of the premature infant and may feel anxious about their ability to parent an infant with multiple needs. Even though most parents develop competence in caring for the premature infant, feelings of anxiety and inadequacy are likely to persist as the changing needs of the child demand different parenting skills. Some parents may not receive the education they need to develop effective parenting skills because their time is consumed by decisions regarding medical and daily care for the infant, as well as by the economic needs of the family (Minde, 1992).

Beyond the immediate impact of delivering a premature baby, families are faced with the challenges of caring for such an infant. Many preterm infants have difficulties communicating their needs because the caregiver is unable to understand their signals and cues. Add to this the unusual caregiving demands of some premature infants, and it is clear that child characteristics may produce parental stress, which in turn may affect the parent–child relationship. Medical and mental health professionals should be sensitive to the unique psychological needs of parents. It is important to recognize and define their loss and encourage parents to release themselves from guilt and focus on improving the life of their infant. Parental psychological health should also be monitored, as stress, anxiety, depression, low self-esteem, and marital discord can be associated with the birth of a premature infant.

## PROBLEMS AND IMPLICATIONS

Developmental difficulties in preterm infants can be severe, pervasive, and inversely related to gestational age. Approximately half of extremely premature infants who survive have mental or physical disabilities (Wood, Marlow, Costeloe, Gibson, & Wilkinson, 2000). Premature infants are at risk for a number of neurological abnormalities and developmental delays that could persist through adolescence and may not even manifest until school age. Developmental difficulties may range from mild conditions, such as muscular weakness, learning disabilities, and poor socialization, to more severe disabilities, such as cerebral palsy, blindness, deafness, or mental retardation. It is important to bear in mind that the majority of research in this area is conducted with VLBW, ELBW, and extremely premature infants and that most infants who are only a few weeks premature and of normal weight for gestational age usually do not have significant delays in their development. Nevertheless, some researchers are concerned that moderately preterm children are overlooked because of the belief that they experience no complications related to their premature birth (Amiel-Tison et al., 2002). In fact, children who are moderately premature experience more neurodevelopmental disabilities than infants of normal birth weight, although they experience fewer complications than VLBW infants.

### Developmental Outcomes

Although the sequence in which developmental milestones are achieved does not differ for most premature infants and full-term infants, premature infants initially acquire skills at a slower pace. If their development is compared with infants their own chronological age during their first 2 years of life, premature infants may appear to be significantly delayed in their attainment of developmental milestones. For this reason, professionals often adjust for prematurity in evaluating the development of preterm or LBW infants younger than 2 or 3 years. Appropriate progress of major developmental milestones is determined by "correcting" a premature child's age, that is, by subtracting the number of weeks premature from the chronological age. For example, a 6-month-old born 8 weeks prematurely would be expected to have reached motor development levels of a 4-month-old child. In general, there are low correlations between the performance of typically developing children on developmental tests in infancy and intelligence test scores obtained in later childhood (Sattler, 2001). For ELBW infants, this holds true even when adjusted ages are used. It is for this reason that a controversy exists about whether to use chronological age or corrected age in assessing cognitive development. However, there is agreement that corrected age should be used in assessing motor skills and other developmental milestones for the first 2 years of life.

Because of the interrelated nature of early development, specifically because motor skills affect performance on measures of mental ability (e.g., Bayley Scales of Infant Development; Bayley, 1993), it is difficult to justify the use of corrected age for motor ability and not for mental ability. Until further research is completed, caution should be used in deciding whether to adjust for degree of prematurity. When the goal of the assessment is to determine the child's relative strengths and weaknesses to identify appropriate intervention services, the uncorrected age should be used.

### Motor Development

Despite limited muscle mass, physical coordination, and strength, premature infants and full-term babies alike begin to explore their world from the moment of birth. They both also follow a universal sequence of motor skill development (e.g., holding head erect followed by sitting alone, which precedes crawling and standing alone). However, there may be noticeable differences in the rate of motor progress. For example, at the age of 4 months, typical children born at term gestation are able to hold their heads erect while being supported in a sitting position. A child born 8 weeks premature would be expected to reach this milestone at the age of 6 months.

Motor development begins with visual exploration, reaching, reflexes, and other sensorimotor behaviors. Because of damage to the central nervous system, infants who were born prematurely may be delayed in their development of the muscular strength required to navigate the environment. Specifically, premature infants may have muscle tone dysregulation and lack of postural control beyond that of full-term infants. This poor muscle control may interfere with the development of arm and hand function—reaching—and therefore limit social interaction and exploration. Early observations of weaknesses in muscle control may turn out to be symptoms of cerebral palsy. Cerebral palsy is the most common neurological abnormality of LBW children, affecting 5% to 37% of premature infants. In addition to minor developmental delays, some premature infants, especially those with ELBW and VLBW, experience lasting motor difficulties. For example, 7- and 8-year-old preterm children have been shown to present impairments of both fine and gross motor skills (Foulder-Hughes & Cooke, 2003). Furthermore, a relationship appears to exist between motor ability and cognitive performance; motor development at 1 year of age was predictive of cognitive performance at 4 years of age among ELBW infants (Burns, O'Callaghan, McDonell, & Rogers, 2004). Thus, it is important to conduct early assessments of motor abilities to inform intervention decisions.

## Touch, Vision, and Hearing

Given their delicate, vulnerable state at birth, premature infants are at a high risk for neurological impairments, which carry significant lifelong implications. Infants born prematurely are often sustained in isolettes in the neonatal intensive care unit (NICU). These small, closed beds filter air to prevent infection and regulate temperature because the babies cannot yet regulate their own body temperature effectively. However, these conditions make it difficult for parents to provide their infants with natural stimulation, warmth, and nurturing. When close interaction is possible, parents may find that their infant is unresponsive, irritable to touch or other stimuli, and stiff or withdrawn.

Preterm infants are more likely than full-term infants to have reduced vision as a result of significant abnormalities of all parts of the visual system. The most common problem is retinopathy of prematurity, which affects approximately one third of premature infants. ROP is an eye condition caused by the abnormal growth of blood vessels. It can result in vision loss and blindness. Consistent with other developmental outcomes, the frequency and severity of this disorder is inversely related to gestational age, with damage ranging from mild vision loss to blindness (Repka, 2002). Preterm infants are also at an increased risk of having amblyopia, strabismus (i.e., crossed eyes), refractive error, and cortical visual impairment. The occurrence of blindness in this population ranges from 7% to 11% (Hack & Fanaroff, 1999). Limited vision may preclude normal psychomotor and cognitive development, as the infant is unable to fully explore his or her environment. For example, an inability to observe the caregiver's smile inhibits the infant's ability to develop a smile.

Additionally, complications associated with prematurity including perinatal asphyxia and hyperbilirubinemia, and the use of ototoxic drugs may lead to hearing loss. Ototoxic drugs are used to treat neonatal sepsis, a bacterial infection to which premature infants are particularly vulnerable. However, the treatment can damage parts of the inner ear and lead to permanent hearing loss. The percentage of premature infants who are deaf ranges from less than 1% to 9% (Msall & Tremont, 2002). Hearing loss can hinder the infant's ability to discriminate voices, which affects language and communication.

## Language and Cognitive Development

In the first 2 years of life, infants become self-assertive, purposeful beings who make sense of their environment and begin to master the complexities of language. However, many premature infants have multiple sensory deficits and therefore often experience delays in language and cognitive development. Children with delayed sensorimotor development may have difficulty extracting and synthesizing visual, auditory, and tactile information from the environment. Language development, in particular, is dependent on vocal stimulation and visual input. Impaired sensory modalities may delay the development of a one-word vocabulary and lead to deficits in communication and language-based skills. Deficits in speech articulation and prereading skills are three to five times more frequent in very preterm children than in full-term children (Wolke & Meyer, 1999).

Infants with neurological impairments have difficulty paying attention. They tend to be irritable and have difficulty sleeping. As preschoolers, they have difficulty with fine motor tasks, such as cutting with scissors, coloring, buttoning, and tying shoes, and with gross motor activities, such as running. They have difficulty maintaining their balance and completing tasks requiring eye–hand coordination, such as throwing and catching a ball and copying. Because these skills are assessed by scales of infant development, children with neurological impairments are likely to score below the expected levels for their chronological ages on these instruments. Preterm children score significantly lower on all measures of cognitive and language abilities, including assessments of general intelligence, language comprehension, and expression. In fact, the effect of very preterm birth on cognitive abilities was found to be much larger than the effect of socioeconomic factors (Wolke & Meyer, 1999).

In general, the mean IQ of VLBW infants is in the low average range and is 3 to 9 points below that of typical birth weight peers. However, these scores may be less an estimation of true cognitive capacities and more an indication of deficits in the areas of visual–motor, visual–perceptual, language, academic, and attentional abilities (Aylward, 2002). Also, the verbal abilities of LBW children tend to be less impaired than their perceptual performance skills. Compared with full-term children in control groups, VLBW children display selective impairments in processing speed, mental arithmetic, visual–motor and fine motor skills, spatial abilities, expressive language, and memory.

## Social and Emotional Development

Attachment, the lasting affective bond between infants and their caregivers, has long been identified as a precursor to healthy emotional development. Child characteristics, such as temperament and behavior, may compromise the attachment between children with disabilities and their caregivers. Premature infants are significantly more distractible and less approaching than full-term infants at 6 weeks old, making parenting initially more challenging (Hughes, Shults, McGrath, & Medoff-Cooper, 2002). Also, preterm infants show high levels of stimulus overload and lower levels of alertness, expression, emotional self-regulation, and tolerance for tactile and sensory input.

Greater rates of behavioral problems are identified with decreasing birth weight. These problems are attributed, in part, to brain injury because they tend to occur in children with cognitive deficits and neuromotor dysfunction. A recent meta-analysis of behavioral outcomes revealed that preterm infants showed increases in externalizing and internalizing behaviors and had more than twice the risk for developing Attention Deficit Hyperactivity Disorder (Bhutta, Cleves, Casey, Cradock, & Anand, 2002). Premature children also exhibit higher levels of anxiety, depression, and aggression than full-term children, and they have lower self-concepts, resulting in more disturbances at home and school. Problem behaviors likely reflect a failure in self-regulatory functions.

## Effects on Education and Instruction

Although most children born prematurely are without major disabilities and attend mainstream schools, one third to one half of these children will experience learning and behavioral difficulties. Very premature infants are three to four times more likely to struggle in school than children born full term. Specifically, they are more likely to repeat one or more grades (33% versus 18%); receive special education (20% versus 5%); require additional teacher assistance in the areas of reading, spelling, math, and handwriting (16% versus 6%); and receive school-based therapies (47% versus 18%). Teachers report that children born preterm are more likely to exhibit behavior problems in the classroom and are overall less well adjusted to the school environment (Sykes et al., 1997). This risk could be compounded by inadequate environments. It is therefore important for professionals to identify biological and environmental factors that could compromise developmental outcome so that modifications can be made to improve the prognosis for the individual child.

## Predictors of Developmental Outcome

Once the infant has been delivered prematurely, developmental outcome can be predicted by a number of perinatal variables. Medical correlates associated with low birth weight and gestational age are the primary predictive sources for determining long-term prognosis. The risk of disability is higher in premature infants with respiratory distress syndrome (RDS), intraventricular hemorrhage (IVH) and bronchopulmonary dysplasia (BPD). Immediately following birth, medical professionals determine the infant's APGAR score based on appearance, pulse rate, grimace, activity, and respiration. This quick assessment is conducted on all live births and provides information about the infant's condition at 1 and 5 minutes following birth. A score between 7 and 10 indicates the infant is in good to excellent condition. Those with a score between 4 and 6 may need additional medical attention and careful monitoring. Scores below 4 indicate significant distress and likely require lifesaving measures. The APGAR score is used to inform decisions about the nature and extent of immediate treatment procedures and can help professionals communicate prognosis information.

In addition to biological risk, information on environmental and demographic variables allows professionals to identify whether an already vulnerable infant is at risk of further harm because of inadequate or nonfacilitative environments. Socioeconomic status, quality of attachment, maternal age, single parenthood, and parents' education level are also predictive of developmental status of preterm infants. In general, environmental factors, including caregiving interactions, play, and stimulation, are good predictors of intellectual outcomes. Thus, once perinatal risk factors have been identified, social workers should obtain information to describe the characteristics of the family and identify the family needs that should be met to foster the development of the child.

### Identification of Developmental Needs

The Individuals with Disabilities Education Act (IDEA) recognizes the importance of early intervention for children with special needs, and it supports efforts to provide services for children with disabilities from birth through age 5. In order to identify services likely to enhance the development of the child and family, professionals are required to describe the child's strengths and needs in five developmental areas: cognition; communication; social and emotional development; adaptive or self-help; and physical, including motor, vision, and hearing. Because of the interrelated nature of these aspects of early development, assessment of the child's strengths and needs typically is conducted by a team of professionals from different disciplines (i.e., multidisciplinary assessment).

Transdisciplinary play-based assessment (Linder, 1990) is a family-centered approach that involves collaboration among families and professionals. The professional team (e.g., physical and occupational therapist, speech and language pathologist, psychologist, and social worker) works with the child simultaneously rather than separately to identify the child's current functioning in several developmental areas. This method of assessment has received empirical support regarding validity and clinical utility, and it is more time efficient when compared with other traditional, standardized tests (Myers, McBride, & Peterson, 1996). Additionally, information gathered from play-based assessments is used to enhance the capacity of families to assist their children as outlined in the Individualized Family Service Plan (IFSP). Instruments that assess multiple domains can be used within the play-based assessment approach (see Table 2). Also, the Bayley Infant Neurodevelopmental Screener (BINS; Aylward, 1995) has been developed to identify infants who are developmentally delayed or have neurological impairments. This instrument, when used in conjunction with other known medical and social risk factors, is a satisfactory screening tool for LBW infants (Leonard, Piecuch, & Cooper, 2001).

## ALTERNATIVE ACTIONS FOR PREVENTION

Premature birth has many etiologies; therefore, reduction of its incidence requires effort at many levels (Fuchs, Fuchs, & Stubblefield, 1993). At the primary prevention level are approaches that can be used prior to or early in pregnancy. These include increased participation of females in family planning activities that focus on encouraging childbirth after age 17 and before age 40, and extending intervals between births. Other approaches seek to increase concern about nutrition and low weight gain of pregnant women, reflected in widespread use of supplemental nutritional programs. Prevention also emphasizes cessation of risk behaviors, such as smoking and the use of licit and illicit drugs, including alcohol. The need for universal prenatal care is stressed, as is the importance of resting in jobs with prolonged standing, treating specific illnesses early, and preventing genital infections. Many of these approaches have been emphasized through nationwide public information campaigns. In addition, primary prevention efforts have included the role of obstetrical medical technology, such as home monitoring of uterine activity, tocolytic drugs to suppress uterine contractions, corticosteroids to accelerate fetal lung maturity, and the use of bed rest to prevent preterm deliveries.

Although a number of expert panels have defined and recommended these primary or universal prevention programs (e.g., U.S. Public Health Services, 1989), there is a paucity of research supporting their effectiveness. Dryfoos (1994) provided some support for primary prevention programs with the finding that school-based health clinics reduced the rates of teen pregnancy. The in-school clinics, many in high schools, tend to be located in low-income areas. They integrate educational, medical, and social services to students and their families and focus on prevention of pregnancy and sexually transmitted diseases. Clinic staff may also educate teens about various birth control methods, and many dispense contraceptives.

Despite the lack of clear empirical support for primary or universal prevention efforts, there is a need for more and better-designed empirical studies investigating these programs. Research agendas for the future are

**Table 2** *Multidomain Instruments Suitable for the Developmental Assessment of High-Risk Premature Infants and Children*

| Instrument | Age Range | Description |
|---|---|---|
| Assessment, Evaluation, and Programming System (AEPS) for Infants and Children, Second Edition (Bricker, 2002) | Birth to 6 years | Evaluates the child's functioning in six domains: fine motor, gross motor, adaptive, cognitive, social–communication, and social. Also assesses family functioning. The AEPS links assessment, intervention, and evaluation. |
| Battelle Developmental Inventory, 2nd Edition (Newborg, Stock, Wnek, Guidubaldi, & Sviniski, 2004) | Birth through 8 years | Uses structured testing, parent interviews, and observations of the child to identify children with disabilities and to assess speech, social–emotional, cognitive, motor, hearing, and other health impairments. |
| Bayley Scales of Infant Development–II (Bayley, 1993) | 1 month to 42 months | Assesses current level of cognitive, language, personal–social, fine and gross motor development, and behavior during the testing situation. |
| Brigance Diagnostic Inventory of Early Development–II (Brigance, 2004) | Birth to 7 years | Uses comprehensive skill sequences to assess functioning in 12 developmental domains, including motor skills, prespeech behaviors, social and emotional functioning, and general knowledge. |
| Transdisciplinary Play-Based Assessment (Linder, 1990) | Infancy to 6 years | Uses play-based techniques to assess the child's cognitive, social, emotional, communication and language, and motor development. Participants include professionals from different disciplines, plus parents. |

proposed by a number of experts (e.g., Hernandez-Reif & Field, 2000) and include investigating more intense programs to help women discontinue smoking during pregnancy, in an attempt to identify mechanisms controlling the onset of labor and possible biological factors that contribute to Black women's increased vulnerability to having premature onset of labor. Another question for the research agenda is why racial differences persist in prevalence of preterm labor, low birth weight, and infant mortality, considering that socioeconomic or lifestyle variables do not adequately explain such differences.

Secondary prevention efforts focus on early identification of symptoms, such as increased uterine contractility or premature dilatation of the cervix, which may cause premature delivery. To assess the risk, and to eliminate specific risks for individual pregnant women, education is provided for pregnant women and health professionals. This training improves the ability of women to recognize symptoms of early preterm labor and to use home uterine monitoring, which is a safe and efficacious mode of health care delivery when compared with hospital care management (Goulet et al., 2001). At the same time, health professionals are educated to respond early, to provide special prenatal care for patients who are at high risk for prematurity, and to administer effective drugs to stop premature labor.

Preventive prenatal care is particularly important for teenage mothers. Intervention programs for economically disadvantaged pregnant adolescents, including programs in hospitals, clinics, or maternity shelters and home visitation by nurses, have improved birth outcomes by reducing infant mortality, morbidity, and pregnancy (e.g., Barnard, Morissett, & Spieker, 1993). Specific services provided as part of these intervention programs include on-site prenatal care to students and psychosocial support. Counseling services have focused on a family-management approach that helps pregnant teenagers plan for their immediate and long-term future. Increased numbers of educational programs are being established in segregated special schools or in regular school buildings because the law prevents girls from being excluded from schools because of pregnancy. Teenage mothers who continue to make progress toward their high school diploma during pregnancy maximize their ability to obtain gainful employment after their infants are born. Programs that allow pregnant teenagers to receive services in their home school increase their rate of graduation (see chapter 53, "Adolescent Pregnancy and Parenting"). A comprehensive review of outcome studies of secondary prevention programs is provided by Barnard et al. (1993).

## ALTERNATIVE ACTIONS FOR INTERVENTION

Interventions designed to reduce the negative effects of prematurity have focused on infant behavior, family organization and functioning, caregiving environments, and home discharge and community resources (Kleberg, Westrup, Stjernqvist, & Lagercrantz, 2002). Because biomedical risk interacts with environmental stressors to depress the development of many premature infants, children from families with fewest resources tend to profit the most from early intervention (Ramey & Ramey, 1998). The infant's attributes, which are affected by biomedical complications, operate continuously and reciprocally with environmental forces, such as schools and families, in determining the outcome for the infant. Thus, the developmental outcome of premature infants could be enhanced by reducing the biomedical risks, creating a facilitative environment, and providing early (education) intervention programs.

### Reducing Biomedical Risks

Tertiary preventive approaches seek to improve the outcome for the neonate when premature delivery is inevitable (Fuchs et al., 1993). These approaches include transportation of mothers to a perinatal center, treatment of the mother with specialized drugs and therapies after premature rupture of the membranes, and expert neonatal care. High-quality technological care of premature infants appears to significantly improve their immediate and long-term outcomes (Brooks-Gunn, McCarton, Casey, & McCormick, 1994). Supplemental stimulation has been used in NICUs to counteract neonatal sensory deprivation. This stimulation can be visual (e.g., pictures and mobiles), auditory (e.g., tape recordings of the mother's voice and of heartbeat sounds, music therapy), tactile–kinesthetic (e.g., skin-to-skin contact), olfactory (e.g., the odor of the mother's breast milk), or vestibular (e.g., the use of oscillating waterbeds, rocking cribs, cuddling, stroking, and flexing of limbs, and provision of physical and occupational therapy). One particular sensory stimulation program, known as Kangaroo Care, has been particularly effective with adolescent parents (Dombrowski et al., 2000).

Unfortunately, there is an ongoing bias in medical communities against extra stimulation or handling of premature infants during critical NICU hospital care. This bias persists despite findings of the positive impact of increased stimulation on the infant's development (Hernandez-Reif & Field, 2000). By age 3, developmental outcomes are related more to aspects of the early social environment than to early physiological factors, except for children with more severe brain injury (Nelson et al., 2001). Thus, it is important to provide interventions to facilitate the development of an effective early social environment.

### Creating a Facilitative Environment

Interventions have been developed to address parental feelings of loss and increased stress that typically occur after the birth of premature infants. In addition, interventions have focused on mother–child interactions and stressed the importance of frequent and consistent maternal and family visits to the neonatal intensive care unit (Brooks-Gunn, Klebanov, Liaw-Fong, & Spiker, 1993). Short-term self-help groups have specifically targeted facilitating the attachment process during identified critical periods and alleviating family stress. Programs that focus on supporting the family and facilitating the attachment process have reported many positive effects (Brisch, Bechinger, Betzler, & Heinemann, 2003), including improved cognitive and social–emotional functioning of the infant. Such programs have also reported enhanced satisfaction with and confidence in mothering, more favorable attitudes toward child rearing, a reduced degree of infant temperamental difficulty perceived by the mother, greater appreciation of the infant's motor capacity, and improved ability to recognize the infant's social and physiological cues and to engage the infant's attention and sustain social interaction. Although short-term increases in cognitive abilities have been reported for children as a result of these interventions, these increases tend to attenuate when many of the children enter inner-city schools with fewer educational resources.

Increases in parental feelings of competence and enhancement of their self-esteem are linked to early hands-on experiences with their infant. In addition, successful programs capitalize on the strengths of families and recognize that assessment of the needs of the family and infant must be ongoing and must respond to changes in factors that affect the family over time. The types of support likely to mediate the stress of families vary with the individual characteristics of the child and the family. Services must be tailored to meet these individualized needs at a given point in time and must assist families in developing and mobilizing support networks.

## Providing Early (Education) Intervention

Early education is available through IDEA for at least some children born prematurely. The most successful programs include a strong parent, educator, and physician partnership (e.g., Sparling et al., 1991) and integrate psychological, instructional, and therapeutic services. These services may be center based, home based, or a combination of the two (e.g., Hill, Brooks-Gunn, & Waldfogel, 2003). Centers sometimes appear to be more like hospital rooms than educational settings because they are heavily furnished with therapeutic equipment. However, recent research related to the quality of early intervention supported the use of more natural environments that promote the development of child-focused, age-appropriate target skills (e.g., Dunst & Bruder, 2002). These programs focus on children's intentional and incidental learning that occurs as part of daily living, family rituals, family and community celebrations, and special occasions and events, and stress the use of learning opportunities, such as eating during mealtime, splashing water during bath time, listening to adults sharing stories, learning greeting skills at family events, going for neighborhood walks, playing in the woods or in a neighborhood park, and going to children's festivals and fairs (e.g., Dunst & Bruder, 2002). Developmentally appropriate practices must provide a clear role for the teacher, a scope and sequence of content for the child to master, and opportunities to teach self-regulation. It is also important to (a) include the interplay among emotions, social understanding, and cognition within the child; (b) include classroom-specific factors such as the social–emotional climate and the teacher–child relationship; and (c) incorporate the larger context of the school, family, and community.

The positive parental feelings of competence referred to above are maintained by a problem-solving approach to education, which allows parents to develop their own skills for assessing the needs of their child and family and to design a program to address these identified individualized needs. Consistent with federal law and after a comprehensive assessment of the infant, an Individualized Family Service Plan (IFSP) is developed that stresses an integrated approach to service delivery.

A family-centered approach is vital in delivering the services documented on the IFSP. Parental involvement is a critical component of early-intervention programs because parents can play a significant role in the implementation of early-intervention services in the home (e.g., Bruder, 2000). In many early-intervention programs, parents are taught exercises and games to facilitate the infant's cognitive development, coordination, language, and socialization skills and are provided with information about infant development and caregiving skills, such as feeding. A central part of these early-intervention educational programs is parent education, which enhances the parents' ability to meet the special needs of their child. Provided by the school psychologist or school social worker, this component focuses on the normal development of the premature infant, atypical development, health-related problems that require immediate intervention, and effective parenting skills. As was true for other intervention programs, degree of impact is mediated by degree of temperamental difficulty, weight, and prematurity status (Blair, 2002).

Early education can improve developmental outcomes for at-risk children and their families (e.g., Blair, 2002). Participants in early intervention perform significantly better on measures of cognitive, language, and social–emotional development, and their parents are rated as more effective and knowledgeable on measures of parenting behavior and infant–toddler development (e.g., Schweinhart, 2003). Improvements are also observed in basic school readiness, such as recognition of colors and shapes. Larger effects are reported for public programs (i.e., public schools and Head Start) than for private child-care programs (e.g., National Institute for Early

Education Research). These differences are attributed to such factors as a stronger infrastructure, higher expectations for performance, higher standards, and a higher level of funding. Schweinhart (2003) uses data from the Perry Preschool Project to describe the possible long-term effects of high-quality early education.

## SUMMARY

Advances in neonatal care have made it possible for many premature infants to survive. However, these increased survival rates are not without cost. The medical costs of caring for extremely premature infants are enormous, and the most premature infants are likely to show long-term developmental difficulties. Because the environment can mediate the biological risks to the child, assessment of environmental variables will increase the accuracy of predictions about later development. A unified developmental approach to intervention that includes the infant, family, and community is necessary to maximize the positive outcomes for children born prematurely. The approach must include medical, psychological, developmental, and educational experiences and must target the whole child, including the infant's physiological and psychological needs and the needs of the family. Once the premature infant leaves the hospital, the family must be linked to a community-based support system, including the school and the services of the school psychologist. Intervention services must support families in their capacity to care for and facilitate the continued growth and development of their infants.

## RECOMMENDED RESOURCES

### Books and Other Printed Material

Allen, M. (Ed.). (2002). *Mental Retardation & Developmental Disabilities Research Review* [Special issue], *8*(4). John Wiley & Sons.

Professionals from a variety of medical and mental health fields contributed to this special issue that focuses on prematurity. Research is presented on epidemiology, cognitive and neuropsychological outcomes, motor disabilities, ophthalmological problems, macropremies, neurodevelopmental care in the NICU, and health-related issues of preterm children and their caregivers.

Tracey, N. (1999). *Parents of premature infants: Their emotional world.* Chichester, UK: Whurr.

This book recognizes the unique stress and emotions experienced by the parents of premature infants and the effect prematurity can have on the well-being of the infant and family as a whole. The author presents interviews with parents and explains related theoretical constructs to address the emotional needs of parents and their premature infants.

### Websites

*http://www.prematurity.org*

This website is an appropriate resource for parents of premature infants. Information regarding labor and delivery, the NICU, popular books for parents and practitioners, support options for parents, and the latest research on prematurity is provided.

*http://www.modimes.org*

The March of Dimes has the mission of improving the health of babies through prevention of prematurity, birth defects, and low birth weight. This website contains a link to a site on prematurity that educates and informs both parents and practitioners about preterm babies and their unique needs.

## ACKNOWLEDGMENTS

We gratefully acknowledge the contributions of Cynthia L. Elias, who was one of the authors of "Prematurity," in *Children's Needs II: Development, Problems, and Alternatives* (1997).

## REFERENCES

Alexander, G. R., & Slay, M. (2002). Prematurity at birth: Trends, racial disparities, and epidemiology. *Mental Retardation & Developmental Disabilities Research Reviews, 8,* 215–220.

Allen, M. (2002). Preterm outcomes research: A critical component of neonatal intensive care. *Mental Retardation & Developmental Disabilities Research Reviews, 8,* 221–233.

Amiel-Tison, C., Allen, M. C., Lebrun, F., & Rogowski, J. (2002). Macropremies: Underprivileged newborns. *Mental Retardation & Developmental Disabilities Research Reviews, 8,* 281–292.

Aylward, G. P. (1995). *Bayley Infant Neurodevelopmental Screener.* San Antonio, TX: Psychological Corporation.

Aylward, G. P. (2002). Cognitive and neuropsychological outcomes: More than IQ scores. *Mental Retardation & Developmental Disabilities Research Reviews, 8,* 234–240.

Barnard, K. E., Morissett, C. E., & Spieker, S. (1993). Preventive interventions: Enhancing parent-infant relationships. In C. H. Zeanah (Ed.), *Handbook of infant mental health* (pp. 386–401). New York: Guilford Press.

Bayley, N. (1993). *Bayley Scales of Infant Development–II.* San Antonio, TX: Psychological Corporation.

Bhutta, A. T., Cleves, M. A., Casey, P. H., Cradock, M. M., & Anand, K. J. S. (2002). Cognitive and behavioral outcomes of school-aged children who were born preterm: A meta-analysis. *Journal of the American Medical Association, 288,* 728–737.

Blair, C. (2002). Early intervention for low birth weight, preterm infants: The role of negative emotionality in the specification of effects. *Development and Psychopathology, 14,* 311–332.

Bricker, D. (Ed.). (2002). *Assessment, evaluation, and programming system (AEPS) for infants and children* (2nd ed.). Baltimore: Paul H. Brookes.

Brigance, A. H. (2004). *Brigance Diagnostic Inventory of Early Development–II.* North Billerica, MA: Curriculum Associates.

Brisch, K. H., Bechinger, D., Betzler, S., & Heinemann, H. (2003). Early preventive attachment-oriented psychotherapeutic intervention program with parents of a very low birth weight premature infant: Results of attachment and neurological development. *Attachment and Human Development, 5,* 120–135.

Brooks-Gunn, J., Klebanov, P. K., Liaw-Fong, R., & Spiker, D. (1993). Enhancing the development of low-birthweight, premature infants: Changes in cognition and behavior over the first three years. *Child Development, 64,* 736–753.

Brooks-Gunn, J., McCarton, C. M., Casey, P. H., & McCormick, M. C. (1994). Early intervention in low-birth-weight premature infants: Results through age 5 years from the Infant Health and Development Program. *Journal of the American Medical Association, 272,* 1257–1262.

Brown, E. R. (1993). Long-term sequelae of preterm birth. In A. R. Fuchs, F. Fuchs, & P. G. Stubblefield (Eds.), *Preterm birth: Causes, prevention, and management* (2nd ed., pp. 465–475). New York: McGraw-Hill.

Bruder, M. B. (2000). Family-centered early intervention: Clarifying our values for the new millennium. *Topics in Early Childhood Special Education, 20,* 105–115.

Burns, Y., O'Callaghan, M., McDonell, B., & Rogers, Y. (2004). Movement and motor development in ELBW infants at 1 year is related to cognitive and motor abilities at 4 years. *Early Human Development, 80,* 19–29.

Centers for Disease Control and Prevention. (2002). Infant mortality and low birth weight among black and white infants—United States, 1980–2000. *Morbidity and Mortality Weekly Report, 51,* 589–592.

Centers for Disease Control and Prevention. (2003, August 29). Assisted reproductive technology surveillance–United States, 2000. *Morbidity and Mortality Weekly Report, 52,* 1–16.

Dombrowski, M. A. S., Anderson, G. C., Santori, C., Roller, C. G., Pagliotti, F., & Dowling, D. A. (2000). Kangaroo skin-to-skin care for premature twins and their adolescent parents. *American Journal of Maternal Child Nursing, 25,* 92–94.

Dryfoos, J. F. (1994). *Full-service schools: A revolution in health and social services for children, youth and families.* San Francisco: Jossey-Bass.

Dunst, C. J., & Bruder, M. B. (2002). Valued outcomes of service coordination, early intervention, and natural environments. *Exceptional Children, 68,* 361–375.

Foulder-Hughes, L. A., & Cooke, R. W. I. (2003). Motor, cognitive, and behavioural disorders in children born very preterm. *Developmental Medicine and Child Neurology, 45,* 97–103.

Fuchs, A. R., Fuchs, F., & Stubblefield, P. G. (Eds.). (1993). *Preterm birth: Causes, prevention, and management* (2nd ed.). New York: McGraw-Hill.

Goulet, C., Gevry, H., Gauthier, R. J., Lepage, L., Fraser, W., & Aita, M. (2001). A controlled clinical trial of home care management versus hospital care management for preterm labour. *International Journal of Nursing Studies, 38,* 259–269.

Hack, M., & Fanaroff, A. A. (1999). Outcomes of children of extremely low birthweight and gestational age in the 1990s. *Early Human Development, 53,* 193–218.

Heffner, L. J., Sherman, C. B., Speizer, F. E., & Weiss, S. T. (1993). Clinical and environmental predictors of preterm labor. *Obstetrics and Gynecology, 81,* 750–757.

Hernandez-Reif, M., & Field, T. (World Association for Infant Mental Health). (2000). Preterm infants benefit from early stimulation. In J. D. Osofsky & H. E. Fitzgerald (Eds.), *Handbook of infant mental health.* (Vol. 4, pp. 295–318). New York: Wiley.

Hill, J. L., Brooks-Gunn, J., & Waldfogel, J. (2003). Sustained effects of high participation in an early intervention for low birth-weight premature infants. *Developmental Psychology, 39,* 730–744.

Horowitz, F. D. (1987). *Exploring developmental theories: Toward a structural/behavioral model of development.* Hillsdale, NJ: Erlbaum.

Hughes, M. B., Shults, J., McGrath, J., & Medoff-Cooper, B. (2002). Temperament characteristics of premature infants in the first year of life. *Journal of Developmental and Behavioral Pediatrics, 23,* 430–435.

Kleberg, A., Westrup, B., Stjernqvist, K., & Lagercrantz, H. (2002). Indications of improved cognitive development at one year of age among infants born very prematurely who received care based on the Newborn Individualized Developmental Care and Assessment Program (NIDCAP). *Early Human Development, 68,* 83–91.

Leonard, C. H., Piecuch, R. E., & Cooper, B. A. (2001). Use of the Bayley Infant Neurodevelopmental Screener with low birth weight infants. *Journal of Pediatric Psychology, 26,* 33–40.

Linder, N., Haskin, O., Levit, O., Klinger, G., Prince, T., Naor, N., et al. (2003, May). Risk factors for intraventricular hemorrhage in very low birth weight premature infants: A retrospective case-control study. *Pediatrics, 111,* 590–595.

Linder, T. W. (1990). *Transdisciplinary play-based assessment: A functional approach to working with young children.* Baltimore: Brookes.

Luster, T., & Brophy-Herb, H. (2000). Adolescent mothers and their children. In J. D. Osofsky & H. E. Fitzgerald (Eds.), *WAIMH handbook of infant mental health: Vol. 4. Infant mental health in groups at high risk.* New York: Wiley.

Manginello, F. P., & DiGeronimo, T. F. (1998). *Your premature infant.* New York: Wiley.

March of Dimes Birth Defects Foundation. (2004). Prematurity: Preterm birth. Retrieved July 25, 2004, from http://www.marchofdimes.com/prematurity/5196_5799.asp

Ment, L. R., Schneider, K. C., Ainley, M. A., & Allan, W. C. (2000). Adaptive mechanisms of the developing brain: The neurologic assessment of the preterm infant. In B. R. Vohr (Ed.), *Clinics in perinatology: Outcome of the very-low-birth weight infant* (pp. 303–323). Philadelphia: W. B. Saunders.

Minde, K. (1992). The social and emotional development of low-birthweight infants and their families up to age 4. In S. L. Friedman & M. D. Sigman (Eds.), *The psychological development of low birthweight children: Advances in applied developmental psychology* (pp. 157–185). Norwood, NJ: Ablex.

Moe, P., & Paige, P. L. (1998). Neurologic disorders. In G. B. Merenstein & S. L. Gardner, *Handbook of neonatal intensive care* (4th ed., pp. 571–603). St. Louis, MO: Mosby.

Msall, M. E., & Tremont, M. R. (2002). Measuring functional outcomes after prematurity: Developmental impact of very low birth weight and extremely low birth weight status on childhood disability. *Mental Retardation and Developmental Disabilities Research Reviews, 8,* 258–272.

Myers, C. L., McBride, S. L., & Peterson, C. A. (1996). Transdisciplinary, play-based assessment in early childhood special education: An examination of social validity. *Topics in Early Childhood Special Education, 16,* 102–126.

National Institute for Early Education Research. (n.d.). *What is known about the outcomes of programs operated under different auspices, including the public schools, Head Start, and private programs?* Retrieved

March 6, 2005, from http://nieer.org/faq/index.php?TAid=142

Nelson, M. N., White-Traut, R. C., Vasan, U., Silvestri, J., Comiskey, E., Meleedy-Rey, P., et al. (2001). One-year outcome of auditory-tactile-visual vestibular intervention in the neonatal intensive care unit: Effects of severe prematurity and central nervous system injury. *Journal of Child Neurology, 16,* 493–498.

Newborg, J., Stock, J. R., Wnek, L., Guidubaldi, J., & Sviniski, J. (2004). *Battelle developmental inventory screening test, second edition.* Allen, TX: DLM Teaching Resources.

Ramey, C. T., & Ramey, S. L. (1998). Prevention of intellectual disabilities: Early interventions to improve cognitive development. *Preventive Medicine, 27,* 224–232.

Repka, M. (2002). Ophthalmological problems of the premature infant. *Mental Retardation & Developmental Disabilities Research Reviews, 8,* 249–257.

Sattler, J. M. (2001). *Assessment of children: Cognitive applications* (4th ed.). San Diego, CA: Jerome M. Sattler.

Schweinhart, L. J. (2003). *The High/Scope Perry Preschool Study Through Age 40: Summary, conclusions, and frequently asked questions.* Retrieved March 6, 2005, from http://www.highscope.org/Research/PerryProject/perrymain.htm

Shiono, P. H., & Klebanoff, M. A. (1986). Ethnic differences in preterm and very preterm delivery. *American Journal of Public Health, 76,* 1317–1321.

Sparling, J., Lewis, I., Ramey, C. T., Wasik, B. H., Bryant, D. M., & LaVange, L. M. (1991). Partners: A curriculum to help premature, low birthweight infants get off to a good start. *Topics in Early Childhood Special Education, 11,* 36–55.

Sykes, D. H., Hoy, E. A., Bill, J. M., McClure, B. G., Halliday, H. L., & Reid, M. M. (1997). Behavioral adjustment in school of very low birthweight children. *Journal of Child Psychology and Psychiatry and Allied Disciplines, 38,* 315–325.

U.S. Public Health Services Expert Panel on the Content of Prenatal Health Care. (1989). *Caring for our future: The content of prenatal care.* Washington, DC: U.S. Government Printing Office.

Wolke, D., & Meyer, R. (1999). Cognitive status, language attainment, and prereading skills of 6-year-old very preterm children and their peers: The Bavarian longitudinal study. *Developmental Medicine and Child Neurology, 41,* 94–109.

Wood, N. S., Marlow, N., Costeloe, K., Gibson, A. T., & Wilkinson, A. R. (2000). Neurologic and developmental disability after extremely preterm birth. *New England Journal of Medicine, 343,* 378–384.

World Health Organization. (1977). Recommended definitions, terminology, and formulae for statistical tables related to the perinatal period and use of a new certificate for cause of perinatal death. *Acta Obstetricia et Gynecologica Scandinavica, 56,* 247–253.

# 70

# Communication Disorders

**Lea A. Theodore**
*Queens College, of the City University of New York*

**Melissa A. Bray**
**Thomas J. Kehle**
**Dana M. Bossio**
*University of Connecticut*

The ability to communicate with others is a fundamental and essential skill. When individuals are unable to interpret information they are receiving, or cannot express their thoughts or needs effectively, it is likely that they will be at risk for long-term problems in academic, social, and vocational functioning (Baker & Cantwell, 1987). Communication disorders are generally categorized into the broad areas of language, speech, and hearing, including central auditory processing disorders (CAPD). The American Speech-Language-Hearing Association (ASHA, 1993) defined a communication disorder as an "impairment in the ability to receive, send, process, and comprehend concepts or verbal, nonverbal and graphic symbols systems. A communication disorder may be evident in the processes of hearing, language, and/or speech" (p. 40).

Language disorders are further specified as *expressive* (i.e., deficits in speaking and/or written language), *receptive* (i.e., impairments in auditory and/or visual comprehension), or *global or mixed* (i.e., impairments in both expressive and receptive language skills). Language disorders affect approximately 7% of children in U.S. schools (Tomblin, 1997). Speech disorders, which affect approximately 5% of the school-age population, may be categorized as articulation, voice, and stuttering (Law, 2000). Finally, hearing disorders include sensorineural loss (nerve or inner ear damage), conductive loss (middle-ear damage), and CAPD. Sensorineural and conductive hearing losses occur in approximately 5% of school-age children (U.S. Department of Health and Human Services, 1991), whereas CAPD is estimated to occur in 3% of this same population (National Institute on Deafness, 2004).

The purpose of this chapter is to briefly summarize the types of communication disorders that are most relevant to school personnel, distinguish between language disorders and related disorders that involve language deficits as an influencing factor such as learning disabilities, and provide the reader with a number of intervention strategies that can be used to assist students with communication disorders in their varied academic and social endeavors. Additionally, it addresses collaboration among school-based practitioners in addressing the needs of students with communication disorders.

## BACKGROUND AND DEVELOPMENT

### Language Disorders

Children's acquisition and use of language are central to their lives, and when deficits are experienced in one or more areas of language, they have a greater risk of experiencing difficulties in social and academic pursuits (see chapter 38, "Language Development"). With regard to the categories of communication disorders, language disorders (also termed specific language impairments, or SLIs) are most germane to the role and function of school psychologists. SLIs are significant deficits in the production and/or comprehension of language that cannot be explained by general cognitive impairment, sensorimotor deficits, neurological damage, psychiatric diagnosis, or lack of exposure to language (Leonard, 1998). SLIs may involve any combination of the form of language (phonology, morphology, and syntax), the content of language (semantics), and the function of language in communication (pragmatics). Specifically, *phonology* refers to letter–sound correspondence and the grammatical rules for combining the two; *morphology* refers to the smallest part of a word that denotes meaning; *syntax* refers to grammar, *semantics* to word meaning, and finally, *pragmatics* to the social use of language.

Regarding etiology, language disorders may be developmental or acquired (e.g., through injury or disease), and at times there may not be an obvious or apparent cause (Owens, 2004). Although it has also been hypothesized that language disorders can be attributed to a simple delay in the development of language, which children will eventually outgrow, most evidence has indicated that this is not the case (Rice, 2000). Language disorders are likely contributors to other pervasive difficulties in functioning, such as learning disabilities and deficits in social competence.

***Expressive language disorder.*** Expressive language disorder is characterized by deficits in oral and/or written language relative to the form, content, and use of linguistic skills. Generally, school-based practitioners should pay particular attention to the extent that students express vocabulary and concepts and employ correct grammatical forms in their speech. They may be limited in the number of words spoken or the mean length of utterance, and may be able to express only very short and simple sentences. Furthermore, children with expressive language disorders often have difficulties with word retrieval and may misuse words, or they may substitute an incorrect word in spoken language. With regard to social language deficiencies, students with expressive language disorders may also have trouble initiating and maintaining conversations and responding to questions.

Preschoolers with expressive language disorders may exhibit difficulty with counting, naming colors, identifying shapes, and reciting days of the week. School-age children often struggle with reading and written language because of impairments with phonological processing skills such as rhyming, blending, segmenting, and sound deletion. Adolescents typically exhibit difficulty with higher-order language skills such as figurative language and expository writing (Mercer & Paige, 2005).

***Receptive language disorder.*** Impairments in auditory and visual comprehension of language characterize receptive language disorders. Problems with comprehension are often subtle and thus not always readily recognizable to school-based practitioners (Bishop, 2004). Students with receptive deficits may be limited in their lexical knowledge, concept understanding, and word-finding skills. These individuals may also experience difficulties in attending to, processing, retaining, or integrating spoken knowledge. Other common components of receptive language disorders are difficulty following directions, forgetfulness, and the misinterpretation of nonverbal cues or gestures. These individuals also often have difficulty responding appropriately to who, what, when, where, and why questions (Owens, 2004).

More specifically, preschool children with receptive language disorders have difficulty following one-, two-, and three-step directions, may exhibit poor play skills, and may be weak in their comprehension of basic stories. In elementary school children, deficits are mainly noted in the areas of comprehension of textbook material, synthesis of ideas, and understanding of oral class presentations (Mercer & Paige, 2005). During high school, students exhibit difficulty with note taking, organization, study habits, social skills, and understanding of lectures (Bray, Kehle, & Theodore, 2002).

***Mixed expressive–receptive disorder or global deficits.*** Students evidencing the characteristics of a mixed language disorder exhibit global impairments that include both expressive and receptive deficits. The specific constellation of deficits a child experiences is individual and unique. The majority of children with language disorders will exhibit difficulties with both receptive and expressive language. Rarely does one exist in isolation from the other (Owens, 2004).

***Pragmatics and the social use of language.*** Students with language disorders often experience a number of pragmatic difficulties that put them at risk for decreased peer interactions and friendships and an overall relative diminishment of social skills. Particularly troubling is the fact that deficits in the social use of language not only affect the child's current functioning, but also may persist into adulthood and influence future endeavors in academic, social, and vocational arenas (Owens, 2004). Children who exhibit difficulties with the pragmatics of language often have trouble answering questions and initiating or maintaining conversations. They exhibit limited flexibility in conversational language (relative to various listeners) and experience difficulty taking turns between speaking and listening. Additionally, individuals with pragmatic deficits often make off-topic or inappropriate comments relative to the conversation at hand (Owens, Metz, & Haas, 2000).

***Related disorders with language deficits as influencing factors.*** A variety of disorders that afflict children also have concomitant language deficits. More specifically, individuals with Attention Deficit Hyperactivity Disorder (ADHD), autism, mental retardation, emotional or behavioral disorders (e.g., anxiety and depression), physical or neurological damage, or learning disabilities often exhibit difficulties with regard to the form, content, and use of language (Botting & Conti-Ramsden, 2004). Many times the associated deficits are related to the ineffective use of pragmatic language and consequently lead to relatively poor social functioning. Most pertinent to the school-based practitioner, however, is the comorbidity of learning disabilities and language disorders.

It has been estimated that approximately half of all students with language disorders also evidence a comorbid learning disability (Mercer & Paige, 2005). Language-impaired, learning-disabled children often have receptive and expressive deficits with respect to the general organization of language. More specifically, a student with a learning disability may have difficulty defining words, retrieving words from his or her lexicon, understanding *wh-* questions, and comprehending and using pronouns and possessives (Seidenberg, 2002). Additionally, those who experience deficits in both learning and language may have trouble with abstract linguistic concepts relative to the expression of comparative, spatial, and temporal relationships.

Children with language-based learning disabilities purportedly have been shown to score lower on verbal IQ tests. This is not at all surprising in that their acquisition and comprehension of language is typically diminished. The salient point is that such children's IQs should not be based on verbal IQ tests. The more appropriate measure would be a nonverbal test.

The majority of students with a reading disability have difficulties with phonological processing (Mercer & Paige, 2005). Early childhood language indicators of subsequent literacy problems include difficulty with letter–sound correspondence; rapid naming of objects, letters, and words; phoneme segmentation; and identification of the first letter of words (Bray et al., 2002). Language disorders may also be evident in students with learning disabilities in written language and spelling. Furthermore, mathematical skills may be compromised as a result of the linguistic component often associated with mathematics. That is, acquiring some mathematical concepts, such as word problem solving, often necessitates lexical knowledge and complex written comprehension (Young et al., 2002).

Further, children with learning disabilities are likely to have pragmatic difficulties. In particular, these students may lack the social skills necessary for appropriately initiating, maintaining, and terminating interactions relative to greeting others, asking questions, responding, and using appropriate language and gestures (Mercer & Paige, 2005). Additionally, students with learning disabilities may have difficulty accepting criticism, receiving compliments, disagreeing, and giving positive feedback.

## Speech Disorders

***Articulation.*** An articulation disorder is defined as the mispronunciation of single or combinations of speech sounds (phonemes). Unintelligible speech can at times be related to phonological processing and often to subsequent academic functioning. Approximately 50% of children with learning disabilities, especially in reading, also have speech and language impairments (Mercer, 1997). Therefore, if the student who has articulation, language, or stuttering problems is also having reading trouble or other academic difficulties, it is recommended that a combined speech, language and psychoeducational evaluation be conducted.

***Stuttering.*** Stuttering, a fluency disorder, is typically characterized by sound, syllable, word, or phrase repetitions; prolongation of sounds; and blocking or immobility of the lips or larynx (Bray et al., 2002). Approximately 3% or more of emitted syllables or 5% of words must be stuttered upon in order to indicate a dysfluency disorder. Since language impairments have been related to stuttering, school personnel may want to consider assessing the language skills of individuals who stutter (Bray et al.).

## Central Auditory Processing Disorder

CAPDs are characterized by difficulty with information processing of verbally presented material in the presence of normal hearing. ASHA (1996) defined CAPD as "a deficiency in one or more of the following phenomena: sound localization and lateralization, auditory discrimination, auditory pattern recognition, recognition of temporal aspects of audition, auditory performance decrease with competing acoustic signals, and auditory performance decrease with degraded signals" (p. 43). Students with CAPDs present and struggle with a broad constellation of behaviors that are associated with language, learning, and attention difficulties, such as impulse control and distractibility issues, and poor language and academic performance (Friel-Patti, 1999; Keith, 1999).

## PROBLEMS AND IMPLICATIONS

### Language Disorders

Although language disorders may be effectively treated with early intervention, the majority of students will still experience problems as they progress through school (Leonard, 1998). For example, children previously identified as having deficits in language and who still experienced difficulties in kindergarten were also likely to experience long-term problems with language, literacy, and overall educational attainment (Stothard, Snowling, Bishop, Chipchase, & Kaplan, 1998). Essentially, children who are accurately diagnosed with poor language skills in kindergarten are not likely to "recover" from their impairments, nor will they "catch up" with their peers as they grow older (Tomblin, Zhang, Buckwalter, & O'Brien, 2003). The best outcomes are associated with those who have very specific deficits in expressive language only, and poorest for children with deficits in both expressive and receptive domains of language (Tomblin et al.).

### Language Disorders and Learning Disabilities

Substantial comorbidity exists between language impairments and learning disabilities. McArthur, Hogben, Edwards, Heath, and Mengler (2000) examined the relationship between students with specific reading disabilities (SRDs) and SLIs and found approximately 53% of the students were equally likely to be classified in either group. However, it is still possible to have pure language disorders devoid of any other influencing factors. To determine whether or not a child has only SLI or has both SLI and SRD, two independent evaluations should be conducted. One should be conducted by the speech pathologist to determine if an SLI exists; the other by the school psychologist to determine if an SRD exists. Problems with definitions, diagnoses, comorbidity, and the heterogeneity of deficits between individuals make it extremely difficult to diagnose SLIs (Bishop, 2004).

### Speech Disorders

The lack of intelligibility of speech has been related to difficulty with phonological processing skills and subsequent problems in reading, writing, spelling, and math. Auditory discrimination problems may also be evidenced. There are myriad causes for dysfluency, including oral motor, neurological, genetic predisposition, language, and learning factors.

Of interest to school practitioners would be the possibility that an individual who stutters may have concomitant language impairments and often a resulting learning disability. Additionally, individuals who stutter may also exhibit other motor repetitive problems, such as ADHD, Tourette's syndrome, and emotional disorders such as anxiety and depression (Mansson, 2000). Depending on the specific constellation of deficits, individuals who stutter may exhibit various academic and behavior problems. For instance, some individuals who stutter, especially those with language disabilities, will demonstrate reading problems.

### Central Auditory Processing Disorder

A controversy surrounds the notion of whether CAPD indeed exists as an independent entity. A well-established definition of central auditory processing disorders has not been clarified, which has resulted in diagnosis that is equivocal and open to speculation. In addition, the behavioral characteristics of CAPD are remarkably similar to those of other disorders, which further adds to the uncertainty and confusion of diagnosing CAPD. Consequently, there continues to be a great deal of debate regarding diagnosis and subsequent treatment. Individuals working with children with communication disorders have been trying to understand CAPD and its association with language and learning difficulties (Keith, 1999). Unfortunately, the critical issue of how CAPDs are distinct from other disorders has yet to be satisfactorily addressed (Cacace & McFarland, 1998).

At present, children diagnosed with CAPD exhibit a broad constellation of behaviors that include poor comprehension in the presence of background noise, distractibility, poor academic achievement despite normal hearing and cognitive ability, and poor auditory attention and concentration (Emerson, Crandall, Seikel, & Chermak, 1997). In addition, students with CAPD respond inconsistently to auditory information, exhibit deficits in auditory memory and discrimination, demonstrate poor sequencing skills, have difficulty attending to verbally presented information, exhibit poor comprehension, and frequently ask the teacher to repeat information (Friel-Patti, 1999; Keith, 1999). Academically, these students struggle with day-to-day achievement issues and failure to reach their expected potential. Further, they struggle with phonemic awareness, reading, spelling, handwriting, language, letter–sound and word recognition, articulation, and word recall (Keith, 1999). Again, these behaviors appear to coexist with other disorders, including speech and language, learning, and attention disabilities. Given that these characteristics overlap with other disorders, one should not necessarily assume that their presence is indicative of a diagnosis of CAPD. Further, the potential comorbidity with other disorders leads to the question of whether CAPD is the primary or secondary deficit in these children (Keith, 1999).

Problems also exist with regard to the use of performance measures designed to assess symptoms of CAPD (Friel-Patti, 1999). Implicit in CAPD diagnosis is the notion that auditory processing deficits underlie academic difficulties (Cacace & McFarland, 1998). Using this rationale, performance on tests that tap audition has been used as the sole vehicle to diagnose CAPDs. Deficits should be noted in tasks exclusively associated with the processing of auditory information. However, it is critical to understand that, given the similar symptomatology between central auditory processing disorders and other disorders, auditory processing deficits may be one of several areas of information-processing deficits. That is, if one solely evaluates auditory processing, and diagnosis rests on poor performance on one test in a battery, the likelihood of obtaining a false positive is greater (Cacace & McFarland; Friel-Patti).

To address this information processing issue, professionals also need to evaluate other modalities to increase certainty that auditory processing is the primary deficit. Further complicating diagnosis, instruments developed to assess CAPD may not focus exclusively on auditory processing skills, but rather focus on a constellation of information-processing factors (Friel-Patti, 1999). To date, no empirical evidence supports diagnosis in this manner, nor has any battery of tests yielded a unique profile of CAPD. Furthermore, the reliability and validity of the instruments used in diagnosing CAPD have been widely contested (Amos & Humes, 1998). Because individuals diagnosed with CAPD comprise a heterogeneous group, diagnostic decision-making appears to rest on clinical judgment rather than on scientific methodology.

## ALTERNATIVE ACTIONS FOR INTERVENTION

Prevention of communication disorders was not addressed in this chapter. Information on this topic can be found in chapter 38, "Language Development."

### Language Disorders

With respect to expressive language, school-based practitioners should model correct grammatical usage and encourage role-playing and storytelling activities (Mercer & Paige, 2005). An effective strategy is to use modeling, either in vivo or on videotapes, using peers to verbalize the target vocabulary that needs to be learned by language-impaired students. Imitation requires the child to not only view but also repeat the modeled speech directly after it is presented. When used together, modeling and subsequent imitation have had positive effects on children's syntax, vocabulary, and morphology (Owens, 2004).

Grammar consistently proves to be an area of difficulty for children with specific language impairments. Sentence recasting, in which an adult alters the child's incorrect grammar while retaining the child's original meaning, can improve children's use of grammar. Modifying or correcting the child's use of grammar in speech and writing gives the child immediate feedback and error correction in a natural environment (Fey & Proctor-Williams, 2000). This strategy alerts the child to the contrast between the specific grammatical characteristics of his or her own speech and that of the person responding. School-based practitioners can also teach strategies that will reinforce the student's use of his or her lexicon. Students with expressive language disorders often have trouble with word-retrieval. Semantic training (i.e., instruction in the definition of words), memory strategies, phonological awareness training (i.e., instruction in the letter sounds associated with common words that cannot be retrieved), and rehearsal of words that are problematic to recall can improve word-finding errors or retrieval of words in children with expressive language difficulties (German, 2002).

To maximize receptive language in children, educators should aim to minimize distractions in the classroom, cue important material, and allow students ample time to respond to prompts and questions. In addition, children may act out sentences and stories using creative dramatics to enhance comprehension (Mercer, 1997). Asking students to repeat or paraphrase instructions is an effective means to ensure the students' comprehension of presented information and allows the instructor time to provide immediate feedback (Donahue & Pidek, 1993). Students' listening comprehension can improve when they are taught strategies that help them clarify, summarize, and question verbal input (Aarnoutse, van den Bos, & Brand-Gruwel, 1998).

Mnemonic strategies (i.e., chunking of information, using acronyms to denote meaning, or linking new information to old for easy recall) are thought to promote comprehension and retention of information by enhancing the meaning of verbal input and linking it to previously acquired knowledge. Mnemonic devices have been found effective in helping students organize, categorize, and store new information for later retrieval. These strategies can enhance the recall and comprehension of abstract and concrete information (Mastropieri, Scruggs, & Fulk, 1990).

Metacognitive strategies (i.e., students are taught to silently pick out main ideas and information from verbal speech and ignore extraneous verbal information) have been found to be useful in enhancing the comprehension of auditory input. Schunk and Rice (1984) found that students were better able to comprehend orally presented material when they used explicit strategies such as self-verbalization prior to answering questions about the material. Additionally, using a multicomponent strategy for comprehension, including training for self-questioning during orally presented material, reciprocal peer questioning and discussion, enhanced students' comprehension of information presented in a lecture format (King, 1991).

In light of the concomitant pragmatic deficits experienced by children with language difficulties, programs are recommended that include multicomponent training in social skills and are designed to ameliorate and facilitate the social use of language. Overall, social skills training programs have been found to have moderate effects on the social competence of students with disabilities (Mercer & Paige, 2005). Training should specifically address initiating and maintaining conversation, appropriately terminating dialogue, understanding nonverbal body language, and taking turns. This may be accomplished using modeling or role-playing (Bray et al., 2002).

Most social skills interventions focus on three broad areas: social entry, maintenance of interactions, and problem solving. Some of the commonly addressed social skills that fit within one of these three areas are listening, learning pragmatics in conversations, asking questions, seeking help, sharing, and cooperating. Social skills training is most effective when a combination of modeling, coaching, and reinforcement are used to address specific, identified areas of strength and difficulty (Gresham, Sugai, & Horner, 2001).

## Related Disorders With Language Deficits as Influencing Factors—Learning Disabilities in Reading

Students with reading learning disabilities are likely to have difficulty with phonological processing, particularly if deficits in language are the influencing factor. One of several effective practices for these students would be to use the Dynamic Indicators of Basic Early Literacy Skills (DIBELS) system to identify and monitor students for reading problems based on measures of phonological awareness (PA), initial sound fluency (ISF), and phoneme segmentation fluency (PSF; Good & Kaminski, 1996). DIBELS allows practitioners to identify specific areas of deficit and target interventions to those skill areas. Typical PA curricula feature teacher-led games and activities aimed at promoting phonological analysis and manipulation through rhyming, identifying phonemes, blending, and segmenting (Justice & Pullen, 2003). PA training is particularly effective at improving the phonological processing and reading skills of students with learning disabilities or language impairments (Good & Kaminski).

Students with reading learning disabilities often have difficulty with reading fluency, a fundamental skill in the decoding and comprehension of written text. A number of instructional strategies are effective in improving the reading fluency of students, including *repeated readings* and *listening passage preview* (Eckert, Ardoin, Daly, & Martens, 2002; Mercer, Campbell, Miller, Mercer, & Lane, 2000). Interventions that use repeated readings as a strategy require a child to orally read a passage, while an accomplished reader provides immediate assistance to the child when he or she experiences difficulty or when errors are made. The child then must reread the passage until he or she reads it fluently. Listening passage preview requires an accomplished reader to read a passage aloud while the student reads along silently. After the passage preview, the student is given immediate feedback as he or she reads the passage aloud. The effectiveness of fluency interventions on students' reading problems may be enhanced with contingent reinforcement or performance feedback (Eckert et al., 2002).

## Speech Disorders

With regard to articulation disorders, strategies that may be used to ameliorate articulation problems include auditory discrimination training and promotion of phonemic awareness through activities such as word blending and segmentation (Owens, 2004). For example, students are exposed to audio tapes that model correct pronunciation of letter sounds, training them to discriminate between the sounds. Additionally, reinforcing correct speech and incorporating behavior modification techniques within the classroom (such as a combined token economy and response cost program) may be effective in addressing difficulties with articulation disorders (Owens).

Treatments for children who stutter are generally effective during the course of treatment; however, the long-term success of the treatments has been limited. Treatment for stuttering is typically directed by the speech pathologist. However, the school psychologist should work with the speech pathologist when the stuttering appears to have a learned component (i.e., the individual stutters in one setting and not in another). In such cases, behavioral (e.g., reinforcement strategies) and cognitive–behavioral (e.g., self-modeling) interventions may be helpful (Bray et al., 2002).

Behavioral interventions include successive approximations, systematic desensitization, positive reinforcement, and response cost. Self-modeling, which has also been used to improve stuttering, requires the repeated, spaced presentation of edited videotapes that depict the student engaging in the exemplary behavior of fluent speech in formerly problematic situations (Bray & Kehle, 1998). Finally, antidepressant medications such as fluoxetine (i.e., Prozac) or clomipramine have also been used successfully to diminish stuttering (Stager, Ludlow, Gordon, Cotelingam, & Rapoport, 1995).

For some students, stuttering is more likely to occur during times of excitement, stress, or anxiety. Stuttering may be significantly reduced in particularly relaxed social circumstances, such as conversing with friends. Therefore, within the classroom, teachers should disregard speech that is not fluent, allow the student plenty of time to respond to questions, avoid completing sentences for the student, model a slower rate of speech, and avoid interrupting the student when he or she stutters.

## Interventions for Central Auditory Processing Disorder

Unfortunately, there is little consensus in the literature regarding treatment of central auditory processing deficits, or CAPDs (Keith, 1999). This is primarily because children suspected of having a CAPD present with varied profiles, such as academic learning problems and language disorders (Friel-Patti, 1999). Thus, intervention strategies that are most frequently recommended are relatively generic in that they may be used to treat students with a wide variety of problems. These approaches include seating the student close to the teacher, managing and monitoring the classroom, enhancing the student's language skills, repeating instructions to ensure understanding, augmenting the student's listening skills, and gaining the child's full attention prior to speaking (Friel-Patti). In addition, collaboration among school psychologists, teachers, and speech–language pathologists is advisable in facilitating a supportive and effective academic environment.

## Collaboration Between School Psychologists and Speech Pathologists

There appears to be substantial opportunity for collaboration and much overlap in expertise between school psychologists and speech pathologists. Specifically, school psychologists are well trained with respect to behavioral and cognitive–behavioral interventions that may be applicable for students with communication disorders, and these interventions could complement the treatments implemented by the speech pathologist.

Most studies have indicated an urgent need for collaboration when assessing and addressing the difficulties of students with language disorders, yet empirical research that would document the effectiveness of such ventures is limited (Whitmire, 2002). The following example illustrates the potential for collaboration among school personnel to address the multiple needs of students with language and learning disabilities.

Jeanette, a 7-year-old second grader who reportedly had difficulty with following directions, grammatical usage, and reading instruction, was referred for assessment by her teacher. The speech–language pathologist concluded that Jeanette had a mixed expressive–receptive language disorder, with specific difficulties in word-retrieval, grammar, and comprehension of lengthy sentences. A comprehensive psychoeducational evaluation indicated that Jeanette was experiencing reading difficulties relative to decoding, fluency, and comprehension. The speech pathologist and school psychologist collaborated on a treatment plan. Specifically, they discussed implementing an intervention that would use phonological awareness training, cueing as a means to aid word retrieval and segmentation of phonemes, and a metacognitive strategy (i.e., self-instruction), which could be used while listening to orally presented material. The school psychologist further suggested implementing repeated readings and listening passage preview as means to address Jeanette's difficulties with fluency.

## SUMMARY

Communication disorders, or impairment in the ability to receive, send, process, and comprehend concepts or systems of verbal, nonverbal, and graphic symbols, may negatively influence academic, social, and vocational functioning. Communication disorders are categorized as speech (articulation and stuttering), language (expressive, receptive, and mixed), and hearing (conductive, sensorineural, and central auditory processing) deficits. Collaboration between speech pathologists and school psychologists may be beneficial in the early diagnosis and subsequent implementation of interventions designed to lessen the deleterious effects of these disorders.

## RECOMMENDED RESOURCES

Beitchman, J. H., Cantwell, D. P., Forness, S. R., Kavale, K. A., & Kauffman, J. M. (1998). Practice parameters for the assessment and treatment of children and adolescents with language and learning disorders. *Journal of the American Academy of Child and Adolescent Psychiatry, 37* (Suppl.), S46–62.

This extensive and thorough review of the literature provides the school-based practitioner with a wealth of information relative to language disorders and language-based learning disabilities.

Mercer, C. D., & Paige, C. P. (2005). *Students with learning disabilities* (6th ed.). Columbus, OH: Prentice Hall.

This text fully defines learning disabilities and their relationship with language and language disorders.

Telzrow, C. F. (1989). Guest editor's comments: Communication disorders in preschool and school-aged children. *School Psychology Review, 18,* 463–474.

This article reviews and comments on the implications for communication disorders relative to school psychology.

### Website

*http://www.asha.org*

The website of the American Speech-Language-Hearing Association (ASHA) is beneficial in understanding the relationship between communication disorders and social and academic functioning.

## REFERENCES

Aarnoutse, C. A. J., van den Bos, K. P., & Brand-Gruwel, S. (1998). Effects of listening comprehension training on listening and reading. *Journal of Special Education, 32,* 115–126.

American Speech-Language-Hearing Association (ASHA). (1993). Definitions of communication disorders and variations. *Asha, 35* (Suppl.), 40–41.

American Speech-Language-Hearing Association, Task Force on Central Auditory Processing Consensus Development (1996). Central auditory processing: Current status of research and implications for clinical practice. *American Journal of Audiology, 5,* 41–54.

Amos, N. E., & Humes, L. E. (1998). Scan test–retest reliability for first- and third-grade children. *Journal of Speech, Language, and Hearing Research, 41,* 834–845.

Baker, L., & Cantwell, D. P. (1987). Comparison of well, emotionally disordered and behaviorally disordered children with linguistic problems. *Journal of the American Academy of Child and Adolescent Psychiatry, 26,* 193–196.

Bishop, D. V. M. (2004). Specific language impairment: Diagnostic dilemmas. In L. Verhoeven & H. Van Balkom (Eds.), *Classification of developmental language disorders: Theoretical issues and clinical implications* (pp. 309–326). Mahwah, NJ: Lawrence Erlbaum Associates.

Botting, N., & Conti-Ramsden, G. (2004). Characteristics of children with specific impairment. In L. Verhoeven & H. Van Balkom (Eds.), *Classification of developmental language disorders: Theoretical issues and clinical implications* (pp. 21–38). Mahwah, NJ: Lawrence Erlbaum Associates.

Bray, M. A., & Kehle, T. J. (1998). Self-modeling as an intervention for stuttering. *School Psychology Review, 27,* 587–598.

Bray, M. A., Kehle, T. J., & Theodore, L. A. (2002). Best practices in the school psychologist's role in the assessment and treatment of students with communication disorders. In A. Thomas & J. Grimes (Eds.), *Best practices in school psychology IV* (pp. 1513–1522). Bethesda, MD: National Association of School Psychologists.

Cacace, A. T., & McFarland, D. J. (1998). Central auditory processing disorder in school-aged children: A critical review. *Journal of Speech, Language, and Hearing Research, 41,* 355–373.

Donahue, M. L., & Pidek, C. M. (1993). Listening comprehension and paraphrasing in content-area classrooms. *Journal of Childhood Communication Disorders, 15,* 35–42.

Eckert, T. L., Ardoin, S. P., Daly, E. J., III, & Martens, B. K. (2002). Improving oral reading fluency: A brief experimental analysis of combining an antecedent intervention with consequences. *Journal of Applied Behavior Analysis, 35,* 271–281.

Emerson, M. F., Crandall, K. K., Seikel, J. A., & Chermak, G. D. (1997). Observations on the use of SCAN to identify children at risk for central auditory processing disorder. *American Speech-Language-Hearing Association, 28,* 43–49.

Fey, M. E., & Proctor-Williams, K. (2000). Recasting, elicited imitation and modeling in grammar intervention for children with specific language impairments. In D. V. M. Bishop & L. B. Leonard (Eds.), *Speech and language impairments in children: Causes, characteristics, intervention and outcome* (pp. 177–194). Philadelphia: Taylor & Francis Group.

Friel-Patti, S. (1999). Clinical decision-making in the assessment and intervention of central auditory processing disorders. *Language, Speech, and Hearing Services in Schools, 30,* 345–352.

German, D. J. (2002). A phonologically-based strategy to improve word-finding abilities in children. *Communication Disorders Quarterly, 23,* 177–190.

Good, R. H., & Kaminski, R. A. (1996). Assessment for instructional decisions: Toward a proactive/prevention model of decision-making for early literacy skills. *School Psychology Quarterly, 11,* 326–336.

Gresham, F., Sugai, G., & Horner, R. H. (2001). Interpreting outcomes of social skills training for students with high-incidence disabilities. *Exceptional Children, 67,* 331–344.

Justice, L. M., & Pullen, P. C. (2003). Promising interventions for promoting emergent literacy skills: Three evidence-based approaches. *Topics in Early Childhood Special Education, 23,* 99–113.

Keith, R. W. (1999). Clinical issues in central auditory processing disorders. *Language, Speech, and Hearing Services in Schools, 30,* 339–344.

King, A. (1991). Improving lecture comprehension: Effects of a metacognitive strategy. *Applied Cognitive Psychology, 5,* 331–346.

Law, J. (2000). Prevalence in natural history of primary speech and language delay: Findings from a systematic review of the literature. *International Journal of Language and Communication Disorders, 35,* 165–188.

Leonard, L. B. (1998). *Children with specific language impairments.* Cambridge, MA: MIT Press.

Mansson, H. (2000). Childhood stuttering: Incidence and development. *Journal of Fluency Disorders, 25,* 47–57.

Mastropieri, M. A., Scruggs, T. E., & Fulk, B. M. (1990). Teaching abstract vocabulary with the keyword method: Effects on recall and comprehension. *Journal of Learning Disabilities, 23,* 92–96.

McArthur, G. M., Hogben, J. H., Edwards, V. T., Heath, S. M., & Mengler, E. D. (2000). On the 'specifics' of specific reading disability and specific language impairment. *Journal of Child Psychology and Psychiatry & Allied Disciplines, 41,* 869–874.

Mercer, C. D. (1997). *Students with learning disabilities* (5th ed.). Englewood Cliffs, NJ: Prentice Hall.

Mercer, C. D., Campbell, K. U., Miller, M. D., Mercer, K. D., & Lane, H. B. (2000). Effects of a reading fluency intervention for middle schoolers with specific learning disabilities. *Learning Disabilities Research & Practice, 15,* 179–189.

Mercer, C. D., & Paige, C. P. (2005). *Students with learning disabilities* (6th ed.). Columbus, OH: Prentice Hall.

National Institute on Deafness. (2004). *Auditory processing disorder in children.* NIH Publication No. 01-4949. Bethesda, MD: National Institutes of Health.

Owens, R. E. (2004). *Language disorders: A functional approach to assessment and intervention* (4th ed.). Boston: Allyn & Bacon.

Owens, R., Metz, D. E., & Haas, A. (2000). *Communication disorders: A life span perspective.* Boston: Allyn & Bacon.

Rice, M. L. (2000). Grammatical symptoms of specific language impairment. In D. V. M. Bishop & L. B. Leonard (Eds.), *Speech and language impairments in children: Causes, characteristics, intervention and outcome* (pp. 17–34). Philadelphia: Taylor & Francis, Inc.

Schunk, D. H., & Rice, J. M. (1984). Strategy self-verbalization during remedial listening comprehension instruction. *Journal of Experimental Education, 53,* 49–54.

Seidenberg, P. L. (2002). Understanding learning disabilities. In D. K. Bernstein & E. Tiegerman-Farber (Eds.), *Language and communication disorders in children* (5th ed., pp. 388–435). Boston: Allyn & Bacon.

Stager, S. V., Ludlow, C. L., Gordon, C. T., Cotelingam, M., & Rapoport, J. L. (1995). Fluency changes in persons who stutter following a double blind trial of clomipramine and desipramine. *Journal of Speech and Hearing Research, 38,* 516–525.

Stothard, S., Snowling, M., Bishop, D. V. M., Chipchase, B. B., & Kaplan, C. A. (1998). Language-impaired preschoolers: A follow-up into adolescence. *Journal of Speech, Language, and Hearing Research, 41,* 407–418.

Tomblin, J. B. (1997). Prevalence of SLI in kindergarten children. *Journal of Speech, Language, and Hearing Research, 40,* 1245–1260.

Tomblin, J. B., Zhang, X., Buckwalter, P., & O'Brien, M. (2003). The stability of primary language disorder: Four years after kindergarten diagnosis. *Journal of Speech, Language, and Hearing Research, 46,* 1283–1296.

U.S. Department of Health and Human Services. (1991). *Healthy people 2000: National health promotion and disease prevention objectives* (DHHS Publication Number 91-50121). Washington, DC: Author.

Whitmire, K. (2002). The evolution of school-based speech-language services: A half century of change and a new century of practice. *Communication Disorders Quarterly, 23,* 68–76.

Young, A. R., Beitchman, J. H., Johnson, C., Douglas, L., Atkinson, L., Escobar, M., & Wilson, B. (2002). Young adult academic outcomes in a longitudinal sample of early identified language impaired and control children. *Journal of Child Psychology and Psychiatry, 43,* 635–645.

71

# High-Functioning Autism and Asperger's Syndrome

**Frank J. Sansosti**

*District School Board of Pasco County, Florida*

**Kelly A. Powell-Smith**

*University of South Florida*

## BACKGROUND AND DEVELOPMENT

Autism is a neurobiological disorder of unknown etiology that is defined on the basis of observable behavioral and developmental features. Defined as a triad of impairments, autism is characterized by deficits in social development, communication, and repetitive behaviors or interests (American Psychiatric Association, 1994). Traditionally, autism was considered to have an almost uniformly poor prognosis that was associated with mental retardation and underdeveloped language. However, since the late 1970s, the categorization of children with autism and related disabilities has been recognized as a spectrum of disorders, which is used to describe the characteristics of the disability that may present themselves in various combinations, from very severe to very mild. At one end of the spectrum are children with classic autism. These children have more severe deficits, including significant cognitive and speech delays. At the other end of the spectrum are those children with similar characteristics of classic autism, but they display low average to above-average cognitive abilities and normal language abilities, at least superficially. Such children are commonly referred to as having high-functioning autism or Asperger's syndrome (HFA/AS).

No diagnostic guidelines for HFA currently exist; the term is most commonly used as a clinical descriptor. By convention, if a child meets the diagnostic characteristics for autism but displays cognitive ability in the low average to above-average range, he or she is said to have HFA. Although identified in the literature at about the same time as classic autism, AS is a relatively new classification of autism spectrum disorder (ASD) that was only recently recognized in the *Diagnostic and Statistical Manual of Mental Disorders, Fourth Edition* (DSM-IV; American Psychiatric Association, 1994). The current diagnostic criteria for AS include the presence of significant impairment in social interactions and displays of restricted behaviors and/or interests, but no significant delay in language or cognitive development.

At present, the *DSM-IV-Text Revision* (DSM-IV-TR; American Psychiatric Association, 2000) represents autism and AS as two distinct conditions with different sets of diagnostic criteria. However, recent research is unclear as to whether HFA and AS truly represent two distinct conditions or whether they differ only in symptom severity (Volkmar & Klin, 2000). In recent years, several studies have been devoted to examining the distinction, or lack thereof, between HFA and AS. Most of these studies examined the disparity in neurocognitive aspects and profiles between children with HFA and AS (e.g., Ozonoff, South, & Miller, 2000). A review of these studies presents mixed results and only promotes greater confusion over the differential diagnosis of HFA and AS. Although the advancements in neuropsychology are important, they are beyond the scope of this chapter. In this chapter, HFA and AS are combined because it is still undetermined whether their treatment requirements differ. Thus, for the purposes of prevention and intervention design, understanding the needs of these children is more important than attending to the specific diagnostic label (Kunce & Mesibov, 1998).

Overall, HFA/AS may involve the same fundamental symptomatology, differing only in degree or severity. HFA/AS is currently understood as a developmental disorder characterized by children who (a) have significant difficulties in social interactions and relationships despite a desire to engage socially; (b) display a lack of empathy that is usually milder than that seen in classic autism; and (c) engage in unusual patterns of interest, especially the tendency to focus too much on certain objects or topics (Gillberg & Ehlers, 1998; Howlin, 1998). Children with HFA/AS generally have average to above-average cognitive abilities (sometimes in the superior range), and language functioning is generally stronger than in classic autism, although it is often unusual in pragmatic ways (Landa, 2000; Twachtman-Cullen, 2000).

### Developmental Aspects

The developmental patterns of difficulties for children with HFA/AS vary among age groups. Key elements during the preschool years include difficulty with joint play skills, poor understanding of basic social stimuli (e.g., calling the child's name), and an appearance of being in one's own world (Mundy & Stella, 2000). As children with HFA/AS enter elementary school, concerns over behavior and lack of social skills become paramount. Elementary school–age children with HFA/AS often have difficulty changing routines and/or following directions, leading the child to be considered hyperactive, inattentive, and sometimes aggressive. In addition, elementary-age children with HFA/AS appear socially immature and display obsessive interests or strict adherence to routines. Difficulties in socialization and behavioral adjustment remain the most significant factors during middle and high school years. At this point, children with HFA/AS stand out from their peers, and obsessive interests may evolve into obsessive–compulsive behaviors. Their inability to make friends and fit in may result in further withdrawal and significant affective problems such as depression or anxiety (Volkmar & Klin, 2000).

### Prevalence

Over the past several years, the number of children and youth identified with ASD has increased substantially. Traditionally, the prevalence of autism has been reported to be 4 to 6 per 10,000 children (Lotter, 1967). However, recent statistics have suggested that the prevalence may be considerably higher. For example, Scott, Baron-Cohen, Bolton, and Brayne (2002) reported the overall prevalence of ASD to be 57 per 10,000 children. When considering just higher functioning individuals, Hyman, Rodier, and Davidson (2001) suggested prevalence rates of HFA/AS to be about 48 per 10,000 children. It has been argued that such increases are the result of the broader diagnostic schema of autism that now includes HFA/AS and PDD-NOS (Pervasive Developmental Disorder-Not Otherwise Specified) and may not indicate a change in the actual incidence of ASD. However, when separating the effects of a broadened spectrum of dysfunction, the prevalence rates across the autism spectrum remain remarkably high.

In addition to epidemiological increases, the U.S. Department of Education reports that the number of ASD-diagnosed children served under the Individuals with Disabilities Education Act (IDEA) has increased 1,354% between 1991 and 2001 (U.S. Department of Education, 2003). When services are examined at the state level, increases in services for children with ASD reportedly range from 10% to 48,600% (Massachusetts and Illinois, respectively). In round terms, for every two children with ASD registered through IDEA in 1991–1992, roughly 14 registered in 2000–2001. Unfortunately, no information was found regarding the percentage of students receiving services specifically for HFA/AS, suggesting that, given the higher prevalence of HFA/AS, there may be a large unserved student population. Given these data, it is likely that educators and other student support personnel increasingly will be called upon to restructure services to better serve children with HFA/AS.

## PROBLEMS AND IMPLICATIONS

### Social Interactions

As is the case with all ASD, HFA/AS shares a common characteristic of poor, or absent, social relatedness and erroneous use of social skills, which remains the most difficult life challenge for these children and their families (Volkmar & Klin, 2000). Children with HFA/AS may be anywhere from withdrawn to active on a continuum of social behavior. At times, they may prefer to spend time alone, or they appear to have little awareness of or interest in others. In some instances, children with HFA/AS may attempt to interact with others in abnormal, socially clumsy, or unacceptable ways (e.g., blurting out socially inappropriate comments and not understanding the effects of those comments on others). Despite individual variability, social behaviors of children with HFA/AS are characterized by a failure to (a) recognize and orient to social stimuli (e.g., name calling or clapping) and social cues (e.g., body language, gestures, facial expressions, or tone of voice); (b) understand the perspective of others; and (c) initiate and maintain conversations with others (Twachtman-Cullen, 2000).

Research on the social impairments of individuals with HFA/AS has led to a hypothesis involving a deficit in "theory of mind" (ToM). Theory of mind is the cognitive ability to infer the mental states of others (e.g., their perspectives and beliefs) and interpret another person's actions from observable external behavior. For example, if a child runs screaming away at the sight of a dog, one can infer that the child is scared. Likewise, if a child cheers at the sight of his or her mother or father walking into a room, one can infer that the child is happy to see the parent. Not only does ToM involve the ability to understand the perspective of another person, it also involves understanding that other individuals are able to form different perspectives about the events that exist within the environment (Happe & Frith, 1996). From this viewpoint, ToM is necessary for basic social understanding and, later, social communication because it involves the child's ability to respond to visual cues (e.g., facial expressions or gestures) for the purpose of sharing information regarding an object or event with another person (Mundy & Stella, 2000; Twachtman-Cullen, 2000). However, this ability is impaired in individuals with HFA/AS.

Baron-Cohen (1995) used the term *mindblindness* to describe the inability of individuals with ToM deficits to appreciate the feelings, knowledge, or beliefs in other people, or to fully recognize or interpret their own thought processes. Simply stated, a deficit in ToM interferes with the child's ability to distinguish his or her own thoughts or feelings from the thoughts and feelings of others. According to this view, a disturbance in ToM gives rise to the difficulties that children with HFA/AS have in social understanding and communication. Specifically, individuals with HFA/AS will exhibit deficits in identifying the communicative intents of others, understanding figures of speech (e.g., idioms), and following the conventions of topic maintenance when speaking (Landa, 2000; Mundy & Stella, 2000; Twachtman-Cullen, 2000). These difficulties have a major impact on the child's social reasoning skills and behavior. For example, a child with HFA/AS may have difficulty identifying whether being run into by another child in physical education class was intentional or accidental. Likewise, children with HFA/AS may have difficulty understanding how their own actions (e.g., engaging in specific routines during lunch or talking excessively about trains) may affect the thoughts of others.

The ability to read social situations and to adjust one's communicative behavior based on external behaviors is a task that is performed effortlessly in typically developing children (Twachtman-Cullen, 2000). Therefore, the capacity for ToM is governed largely by the indirect, socially mediated environmental cues, which can be particularly abstract. However, children with HFA/AS often are constrained by what is observable in a very concrete, physical world. Because children with HFA/AS have a specific difficulty in understanding and interpreting abstract social information, they are particularly compromised in their ability to engage in reciprocal social interactions.

## Functional Communication

Children with HFA/AS often develop good structural language skills. Thus, they may speak in syntactically and grammatically correct structures. In this sense, the *content* and *form* of language appear to be relatively intact. However, it is the *use* of language for communicative purposes (pragmatics) that is significantly impaired (Landa, 2000; Twachtman-Cullen 2000). The pragmatic use of language requires crucial knowledge and skill, not only to employ speech to express intentionality for a communicative purpose, but also to make judgments about the listener in order to regulate speech style and content. Despite their developed language skills, children with HFA/AS often have great difficulty communicating because of their inability to recognize the thoughts, feelings, and intentions of their listener. In this regard, pragmatic difficulties in children with HFA/AS appear to be directly linked to impairments in ToM skills (Landa; Twachtman-Cullen). That is, impaired social communication may be a reflection of the difficulty children with HFA/AS have with reading and understanding social cues.

The literature has identified several specific areas of difficulty children with HFA/AS have in the pragmatic use of language (see Landa, 2000, for review). Because of the variability of functioning and stages of development, not all children with HFA/AS will display each of these deficits. However, most children with HFA/AS will display limited use or severe impairments in areas such as eye contact, nonverbal behavior, affect, and prosody.

***Eye contact.*** It is not uncommon for a child with HFA/AS to display poor or inconsistent eye contact during social situations. As a result, others may limit or avoid interactions with the child with HFA/AS, because lack of eye contact is often perceived as unsociable behavior. It may be that children with HFA/AS avoid eye contact to escape from social interactions they perceive as aversive or difficult (Moore, 2002). Limited practice making eye contact may impair the communication of children with HFA/AS even further, because eye contact is necessary if they are to observe facial and social cues in the environment and to tailor subsequent communication to meet the needs of the listener. Without frequent eye contact, reciprocity in social communication is difficult for children with HFA/AS.

***Nonverbal behavior.*** Nonverbal aspects of communication, such as facial expression, body posture, and hand movements, exist in many areas of our daily lives. At times, the entire meaning of a message can be conveyed simply through body language rather than words (Twachtman-Cullen, 2000). However, children with HFA/AS often have difficulty using and understanding the messages that nonverbal mannerisms convey. For instance, children with HFA/AS may be less likely to pick up on typical nonverbal behaviors used in the classroom, such as a teacher putting one finger over her lips to call for quiet or shaking her head to indicate disapproval.

***Affect.*** Another common characteristic of children with HFA/AS is their absence or inappropriate use of affect. Most often, children with HFA/AS appear detached from their social environment because they display a placid expression without emotion (Myles & Simpson, 2003). However, there may be times when the child displays inappropriate affect, such as laughing when another person is hurt, failing to show excitement upon receiving a desired item such as a gift or toy, or displaying a fear response in nonthreatening situations.

***Prosody.*** Prosody refers to affective expression or intonation when speaking to indicate meaning. A disturbance in producing intonation during speech, or dysprosody, is a well-known feature of individuals with HFA/AS (Twachtman-Cullen, 2000). Very often, individuals with HFA/AS are described as having very flat, emotionless speech. However, speech characteristics of children with HFA/AS can range on a continuum at different points in development. For example, children with HFA/AS may display exaggerated inflections by talking with an excessively high pitch, at too high or too low a volume, or with a rapid, staccato delivery (Myles & Simpson, 2003).

When combined, these areas of pragmatic difficulty often lead to severe impairments in initiating and maintaining social interactions. Because they lack an understanding of appropriate social customs, many children with HFA/AS have difficulty initiating conversations. Initiation of conversations often centers on a favorite topic, which the child discusses with excessive detail, regardless of the cues provided by the conversation partner (Myles & Simpson, 2003). Favorite topics can range from popular childhood interests (e.g., Harry Potter or Yu-Gi-Oh!) to highly technical descriptions of places or objects (e.g., the Bermuda triangle, deep fry cookers). Perseveration on a favorite topic often leads to the inability to maintain a reciprocal conversation. Therefore, many children with HFA/AS are described as being verbose, carrying out a pedantic monologue while offering little or no opportunities for their listener to alternate roles (take turns) in conversational exchange (Landa, 2000; Twachtman-Cullen, 2000).

In addition, children with HFA/AS often take a literal interpretation of abstract language such as jokes, sarcasm, and idioms. For example, a child with HFA/AS might interpret a sarcastic expression such as, "Well, isn't that nice?" as meaning it really is nice. Likewise, it is unlikely that a child with HFA/AS would be able to identify the communicative purpose from the headline "Red Tape Holds Up New Bridge." Such descriptions provide some indication that children with HFA/AS organize the world of people and things into discrete labels according to more concrete, factual perceptions of their environment (Myles & Simpson, 2003; Twachtman-Cullen, 2000).

## Behavior

Problematic behaviors in children with HFA/AS span a wide range and tend to vary according to the child's development and intellectual ability. Although stereotyped, repetitive behaviors (e.g., body rocking or hand flapping) may occur in individuals with HFA/AS during highly stressful situations, they are most likely found in children with classic autism. More often, children with HFA/AS engage in restricted patterns of behaviors and insist on doing things in a certain way (Howlin, 1998). For instance, they may become distressed when not permitted to eat lunch in the same location each day. Likewise, they may insist that books and school supplies be arranged in a certain order. Any change in such routines is often perceived as difficult and may result in problematic or tantrum behaviors. Children with HFA/

AS may also display restricted patterns of behaviors through an all-absorbing preoccupation with a circumscribed topic (Howlin; Myles & Simpson, 2003). For example, they may be obsessed with learning extraordinary amounts of factual information about vacuum cleaners, dinosaurs, or freeway interchanges in Los Angeles. Over time, the topics of interest may change for a child with HFA/AS, but they tend to dominate every aspect of his or her life.

### Implications for Educational Practice

Several implications for educational practice exist in relation to the impairments that children with HFA/AS display. Perhaps the most common implication is the likelihood that children with HFA/AS will engage in poor or ill-mannered social behaviors. For instance, the child may tell the teacher what student was responsible for committing a disobedient act after the teacher asks, "Who did that?" Likewise, the child may stop someone in mid-conversation to comment on their bad breath. Aside from such social blunders, children with HFA/AS also are likely to demonstrate inattention and distractibility during structured and unstructured academic times. At any moment, the child may withdraw. For example, during a small group reading exercise, while one student was reading a passage on Spanish conquistadors, the child with HFA/AS commented on the materials used for constructing the fort depicted in a picture at the bottom of the page. Not surprisingly, educators frequently may have to redirect the child's attention or restate the directions for a given assignment or homework.

Children with HFA/AS also may have difficulty with organizational planning. Therefore, tasks that involve planning, prioritizing, and organizing are affected. Because of this, children with HFA/AS often have difficulty completing work on time or fail to turn in assignments. In addition, children with HFA/AS have difficulty extracting meaning and determining relevant from irrelevant information, leading to difficulties in comprehension (Myles & Simpson, 2003). Finally, children with HFA/AS are likely to demonstrate a poor appreciation of various problem-solving skills, using only one strategy for a variety of social and academic situations (Myles & Simpson, 2003). For this reason, abstract situations (e.g., tornado drills) or academic content (e.g., inferential reading comprehension questions, word problems, or algebra) are usually very difficult for children with HFA/AS to understand.

## ALTERNATIVE ACTIONS FOR PREVENTION

Despite the identified areas of difficulty, appropriate support and education can dramatically increase the independent functioning of children with HFA/AS. Because many of these difficulties stem from a lack of understanding or a misinterpretation of the world, preventive actions can substantially decrease the occurrence of inappropriate behaviors in children with HFA/AS. Carefully designed and individualized environmental supports help children with HFA/AS understand the world, help them accept change, and increase their independent functioning (Myles & Simpson, 2003). Strategies include using visual supports and incorporating choice and preference, as well as various academic accommodations. Unfortunately, the scientific support for some of these prevention strategies is limited (e.g., task presentation strategies and teacher communication strategies). Although the research on these strategies is increasing, it is necessary for practitioners to monitor progress through systematic data collection.

### General Strategies

***Visual supports.*** Visual supports consist of pictures, photographs, or lists that prompt or remind children with HFA/AS to engage in a particular behavior or prepare them for an upcoming activity or task. Because children with HFA/AS often have difficulty understanding the world in which they live, these visual supports provide the structure and predictability necessary for effective functioning in a variety of settings (e.g., classrooms and the community). Specifically, visual supports allow children with HFA/AS to anticipate upcoming events and any expectations regarding setting or task requirements, thereby creating a sense of security and reducing anxiety.

Visual supports can be used in a variety of forms such as schedules, rules, or other graphically represented cues to support the inclusion and education of children with HFA/AS. For example, Morrison, Sainato, BenChaaban, and Endo (2002) taught children with autism to use visual schedules representing activities in the classroom and documented improved independent transitions across activities. In addition, visual supports have been used to promote self-initiated social interactions and decrease problem behavior (Charlop-Christy, Carpenter, Le, LeBlanc, & Kellet, 2002). For a complete review of the variety of visual supports that have been used to increase flexibility and independence in children with HFA/AS, the interested reader is referred to Myles and Simpson (2003).

***Choice and preference.*** Historically, children with developmental disabilities have had very little choice regarding the events that affect their lives. More recently, there has been a push to allow children to exert greater control through choice making. *Choice making* refers to the process of allowing a child to select an activity among several available alternatives. For example, a child with HFA/AS may be given the choice of whether to complete math or reading work first during independent seatwork time. The expectation is that the student will complete tasks for both academic areas, but the choice regarding which one to do first is student directed. Related to choice making is the concept of preference. *Preference* refers to those objects, particular tasks, and activities that an individual finds most appealing and naturally rewarding. When choice making and preferences are incorporated, children with HFA/AS may exert more control over their lives and thus reduce some of the odd behaviors resulting from anxiety.

Over the past two decades, an increasing body of research has demonstrated the beneficial effects of allowing choice-making opportunities for children with various developmental disabilities, including children with HFA/AS. For example, incorporating choice making into daily tasks has resulted in increased task engagement, decreased disruptive behavior challenges (Moes, 1998; Peterson, Caniglia, & Royster, 2001), and increased homework completion (Moes). Likewise, incorporating individuals' preferences into activities has been shown to significantly decrease problematic behaviors and increase time engaged in academic and social contexts (e.g., Vaughn & Horner, 1997).

## Academic Strategies

A number of simple, cost-effective strategies work well in preventing the academic difficulties often experienced by students with HFA/AS. These strategies work to prevent inappropriate behaviors and promote the acquisition of appropriate academic and social behaviors by creating a structured and predictable environment. Primarily, these strategies are educator directed and can be grouped into those that focus on the environment, presentation of tasks, and teacher communication strategies.

***Environmental strategies.*** Students with HFA/AS function best in classrooms that are not only well organized and predictable (Attwood, 1998) but also minimally decorated and physically simply arranged. Thus, everything from the arrangement of desks to the layout of bulletin boards should be simple and uncluttered (Moore, 2002). Such efforts give the student with HFA/AS the kind of structure and predictability necessary to function effectively in the classroom, as well as increase the probability of maintaining the student's attention to academic tasks. According to Moore, if desks are grouped, groups should be kept to a maximum of four or five students. Also, under such circumstances it may be best to seat the student with HFA/AS toward the outside of the group. Similarly, if desks are put in rows, the student with HFA/AS should be seated near the end of the row. While facilitating social interactions, such desk arrangements allow the student with HFA/AS to have some distance from others when overstimulated, as well as allow the teacher to easily reach the student.

In addition to a simple classroom design, a variety of visual supports may be provided to help students with HFA/AS stay focused and on-task. For example, part of keeping the classroom structured and predictable is the establishment of a small number (e.g., three to five) of briefly stated classroom rules. Once established, rules should be posted where they are visible to all students (Paine, Radicchi, Rosellini, Deutchman, & Darch, 1983). In addition to clearly posting rules, providing the student with HFA/AS a visual schedule of activities for each day may be helpful (Moore, 2002; Kunce & Mesibov, 1998). Such visual schedules can be written or picture based, depending on the needs of the child. Regardless of the method, research on visual schedules suggests that they increase on-task behavior for students with HFA (Bryan & Gast, 2000). Schedules may be used for activities in a single classroom (i.e., at the elementary school level) or for activities across various classrooms (i.e., for middle school and high school). In a classroom setting, it is best to post the schedule in a clearly visible location (e.g., on the student's desk or on the chalkboard or whiteboard). Students may carry a printed copy of the schedule for use across classes. Schedules may also provide information on daily, weekly, or monthly activities for the student with HFA/AS (Kunce & Mesibov). The use of posted rules and schedules allows students with HFA/AS to anticipate what is expected of them academically and behaviorally.

***Task presentation strategies.*** Many of these strategies are consistent with the notion of eliminating distracting stimuli. For example, task directions should be briefly worded and provided in writing when possible. In a study by Kunce, Marcus, Bundy, and Sebolt (in press, as cited in Ozonoff, 2003), students with HFA performed significantly worse than control students when provided with oral instructions. However, when provided with written directions, the students with HFA in the study performed as well as control students. Wording can be simplified by using less complex vocabulary and shorter sentences (Kunce & Mesibov, 1998). In addition to providing written instructions, directions should be repeated as needed when they are complex or presented orally (Moore, 2002). Also, tasks that rely on inferential language skills, such as math word problems and some reading comprehension questions, may need to be reworded to make essential information obvious and to remove distracting information before presenting the questions to students with HFA/AS. For directions and word problems, teachers might also consider highlighting critical information for the student with HFA/AS.

In addition to strategies focused on keeping things uncomplicated, a number of visual task presentation strategies are available that can help children with HFA/AS organize their work. One strategy educators use is color-coding academic content areas. That is, all materials that pertain to a particular subject (e.g., worksheets, folders, and boxes used for handing in reading assignments) are kept the same color. Educators may also create task checklists or job cards that provide the student with a list of steps to be completed when engaging in a particular task that may be difficult to complete independently. Finally, strategies that use the physical layout of assignments can include using graph paper (or turning lined paper sideways) so students can use the lines as columns to complete math problems (Moore, 2002). In addition, organization of assignments can be improved by offering the child with HFA/AS advance organizers or study guides that help him or her differentiate relevant from irrelevant information. For a more detailed discussion of these strategies, the interested reader is referred to Moore (2002) and Kunce and Mesibov (1998).

Finally, it may be advantageous to incorporate the student's special interest into lessons when possible. These adjustments can cut across content areas (e.g., math, reading, science, and history) and likely will increase motivation. This strategy is consistent with the idea of incorporating preferences, as discussed earlier (Vaughn & Horner, 1997). For example, if a student has a strong interest in trains, the student might be required to complete a report on the history of trains in the United States for a history assignment, math problems might be constructed using travel distance from one train station to another, or the student could examine the various methods used to power trains for science.

***Teacher communication strategies.*** A large percentage of instruction is conducted through teacher communication (e.g., lecture and demonstration; Kunce & Mesibov, 1998). Given the social communication deficits often present with HFA/AS, a focus on teacher communication strategies is needed to prevent misunderstandings. Two primary strategies fall under this category: priming students and notifying students of changes in routine.

Priming consists of providing students with HFA/AS with lesson materials, schedules, descriptions of activities to occur, expectations for grading, and so forth prior to conducting the lesson (Wilde, Koegel & Koegel, 1992). Priming can be done either immediately before the lesson or test or done further in advance, such as the day or evening before (Moore, 2002). It is most useful to preview information or activities with which the student is likely to have the greatest difficulty. Priming may be conducted at home or at school and by various individuals (e.g., parents or teachers), but it is best done in a relaxed and encouraging environment with someone who will be patient with the student (Myles & Simpson, 2003).

In addition to priming, teachers should also consider how they communicate changes in routine to students with HFA/AS. Because surprises can lead to inappropriate behaviors or shutting down, educators would be wise to consider ways they can communicate such changes before they occur (Moore, 2002). For example, students can be notified in advance about an afternoon tornado drill. Students should be informed particularly of steps and behaviors expected of them during the upcoming event. Methods such as emergency cards and change in routine cards (Moore), checklists or advance organizers for alternative routines such as assemblies and field trips, and Social Stories (described in the following sections) may be useful for this purpose.

## ALTERNATIVE ACTIONS FOR INTERVENTION

Preventive actions in and of themselves are necessary, but sometimes not sufficient, for producing changes in the functioning and development of children with HFA/AS. Therefore, more specific interventions that are designed to increase the skill, frequency, or quality of behaviors emitted by children with HFA/AS may be necessary. In this chapter, interventions for social, behavioral, and academic skills are separated from preventive actions because they require direct teaching to the individual child with HFA/AS or require consultation or additional training for those staff who are working with the child. The following discussion of interventions recommended for children with HFA/AS is not exhaustive but represents those strategies that have the most empirical support for their use.

## Social Skills Interventions

***Group social skills training.*** In general, weekly group-based social skills training (SST) programs for children with HFA/AS are built around the components of structured learning. That is, regardless of the skills being taught, each lesson consists of breaking a particular social skill (e.g., initiating conversations) into its component parts (e.g., prepare ahead, ask yourself what you are going to say, make eye contact, say hello) and sequentially teaching toward a level of mastery. Mastery is achieved by first modeling appropriate use of the skills for students and then having the students engage in role-playing in situations closely related to real life. During role play, the child with HFA/AS could be required to initiate a conversation with another person as the other person is engaged in a separate task. The student with HFA/AS would have to ask to join in or ask the other person to join him or her in another activity. Following the role play, the student would receive feedback from other children in the group, as well as from the instructors.

Several important principles, or essential ingredients, that underlie the efficacy of SST were delineated by Krasny, Williams, Provencal, and Ozonoff (2003). First, SST for children with HFA/AS must be concrete. Children with HFA/AS are often very concrete and literal thinkers. Therefore, it is essential to specifically define behaviors for the child in terms of what the behavior looks or sounds like (e.g., personal space is defined as an arm's length away). Second, SST should be highly structured and predictable. Most lessons will change from week to week. However, maintaining certain elements within the group (e.g., starting each session with homework review; having game time halfway through each lesson) is essential to ensure predictability for the students. Visual schedules or activity lists can also be used. Third, in addition to being concrete and predictable, SST should foster group belonging. Allowing students to get to know one another and develop friendships outside of the group setting can be extremely important. Belonging to a group will not only decrease the level of stress children with HFA/AS may have, but also help them share interests and take the perspective of others. Finally, any SST group should be goal directed. Both group and individualized goals should be selected and practiced as part of the weekly lesson.

The research literature describes various methodologies and approaches in SST (e.g., role-playing, games) for children with HFA/AS. Much of this research has focused on improving conversational and perspective-taking skills (e.g., Bauminger, 2002). In most of these studies, positive trends were found (e.g., increases in initiation and maintenance of conversations, increased recognition of facial cues, increased social problem-solving ability). However, inability to generalize skills to other settings (e.g., home, school, community) was usually a major limitation. Despite the lack of evidence for skill generalization, group SST is an effective method for teaching the component skills necessary for effective social communication, and it should be considered a worthwhile intervention for children with HFA/AS.

***Social Stories™.*** Social Stories are individualized written stories that briefly explain challenging social situations through visual supports and text (Gray, 1998). The goal of any Social Story is twofold. First, a Social Story provides descriptive information regarding a target social situation, such as the people involved, the sequence of events, and the thoughts and feelings of others. Second, the story provides an appropriate way to respond to a given social cue or situation (e.g., how to remain calm and follow directions during a fire drill). In these ways, Social Stories offer information on how to understand and interpret social cues (i.e., theory of mind skills) and provide instruction in initiating, responding to, and maintaining appropriate social behavior (Sansosti, Powell-Smith, & Kincaid, 2004).

Social Stories can be developed by educators, parents, or others who work closely with the child with HFA/AS. Although Social Stories are relatively easy to create, considering the different types and correct ratio of sentences (e.g., descriptive, directive, and perspective sentences) is essential (see Gray, 1998, for review). Without adherence to the guidelines outlined by Gray, a Social Story is likely to become a list of directives for appropriate behavior. However, the goal of a Social Story is to teach understanding, with little emphasis on controlling inappropriate functioning.

Research examining the effectiveness of Social Story interventions for children with HFA/AS has grown in recent years (see Sansosti et al., 2004, for a detailed review). This research has investigated the effects of Social Story interventions for children with ASD on such things as increasing greeting and sharing behaviors (Swaggart et al., 1995), improving social interactions during lunch (Norris & Dattilo, 1999), and increasing social communication skills (Thiemann & Goldstein, 2001). From a review of the available literature, Social Stories appear to be an effective strategy when used in applied settings for children with HFA/AS.

***Video modeling.*** A recent strategy that has been shown to be effective for children with HFA/AS is the use of video modeling, in which the child with HFA/AS watches a videotape of a model engaging in the target behavior to be imitated. Compared with live modeling, video modeling has several advantages for teaching new skills and promoting maintenance and generalization of skills for children with HFA/AS. First, video modeling capitalizes on the visual strengths of children with autism. Second, videotape can be created for use in a variety of natural contexts (e.g., home, community), whereas live modeling is confined to the clinic or classroom. Third, it allows for repeated viewings of the same model, without the model having to be present. Fourth, video modeling allows for a standard model to be shared with a variety of individuals. Finally, children with HFA/AS often enjoy watching videos.

Research on video modeling has demonstrated its effectiveness for teaching behaviors such as conversational skills (Charlop & Milstein, 1989), functional living skills (Shipley-Benamou, Lutzker, & Taubman, 2002), perspective-taking skills (Charlop-Christy & Daneshvar, 2003), and play and daily living skills (Charlop-Christy, Le, & Freeman, 2000). In addition, video modeling has been shown to be more effective than live modeling (Charlop-Christy et al., 2000). Specifically, in a comparison with live modeling, video modeling led to both quicker acquisition and greater generalization of skills. Therefore, video modeling may be used to increase the generalization of skills for children with HFA/AS, a task that has been difficult to accomplish in previous research.

***Peer-mediated approaches.*** Access to peers who model appropriate social conventions is crucial to promoting the social–communicative development of children with HFA/AS (Howlin, 1998). However, mere access to peers does not constitute a successful intervention. Rather, a specific structure for using typically developing peers must be incorporated. In a peer-mediated approach (e.g., peer buddies and peer tutoring), typically developing peers take an instructional role by prompting and praising the social behaviors of children with HFA/AS. Specifically, peers are trained how to make social initiations and how to respond promptly and appropriately to the communicative attempts of children with HFA/AS. After such training, peers are placed in situations where they engage in social activities with children with HFA/AS free from adult interaction.

Despite the need for continued access to trained peers, peer-mediated approaches have the advantage of providing a natural means for promoting socialization in children with HFA/AS. That is, peer-mediated approaches are based on naturally occurring social behaviors rather than on artificial or simulated scenarios (Myles & Simpson, 2003). With a greater reliance on naturalistic training, peer-mediated approaches have the advantage of enhancing maintenance and generalization of skills.

Peer-mediated procedures represent a robust approach for teaching social interaction skills to children with HFA/AS. Investigators have employed a wide range of peer-mediated procedures to increase peer social initiations (e.g.,Odom & Strain, 1986) and social–communicative interactions (e.g., Laushey & Heflin, 2000). Peer-mediated interventions recently were expanded to teach peers how to effectively motivate children with HFA/AS to respond to multiple environmental cues within natural contexts. For example, peer-based Pivotal Response Training has demonstrated improved effects on incidental teaching approaches to increase social interaction, sociodramatic play, and communicative interactions of children with HFA/AS (e.g., Terpstra, Higgins, & Pierce, 2002).

## Behavioral Interventions

***Differential reinforcement.*** Differential reinforcement decreases problem behaviors through the use of rewards for an alternative or incompatible replacement behavior. By using differential reinforcement, undesirable or inappropriate behaviors are weakened, primarily through ignoring, while more desirable behaviors are reinforced. For instance, a child with HFA/AS who frequently takes objects from other students during recess is reinforced for asking for desired objects.

The effects of differential reinforcement on children with HFA/AS are well established in research literature. In fact, the use of differential reinforcement may be viewed as a tried and true approach because it is part of many of the traditional approaches to behavioral treatment for children with autism (e.g., discrete trial training). Currently, differential reinforcement strategies have been used to increase communicative intent and social interactions (e.g., Drasgow, Halle, & Ostrosky, 1998). In many of the studies in which differential reinforcement strategies have been used, a subsequent decrease in stereotypic or restricted behaviors also was observed.

***Self-management.*** Adherence to routines or preoccupied interests may be one of the few ways that children with HFA/AS cope successfully with stress (Howlin, 1998; Myles & Simpson, 2003). Simply trying to eliminate such behaviors may only increase levels of anxiety and result in an increased need for children with HFA/AS to engage in routines or in ritualistic or other inappropriate behaviors. Therefore, it is important to systematically teach children with HFA/AS how to manage their own behavior and, subsequently, develop self-control.

Self-management works by having children with HFA/AS actively record and evaluate whether their behavior was appropriate or inappropriate, then receive rewards. Depending on the frequency and type of reinforcement, behaviors are shaped to systematically increase levels of self-control. A major advantage of a self-management intervention is its capacity to teach independence. Because self-management strategies teach children with HFA/AS self-control, it is likely that their behavior will generalize to other settings where no intervention is in effect. That is, the emphasis of the self-management intervention changes from a short-term strategy to improve a single target behavior to a more global process of changing multiple behaviors across a number of environments and people (Koegel, Koegel, & Parks, 1995).

Self-management procedures have been used to increase productivity and accuracy of academic tasks, on-task behavior, and social skills across a wide variety of learners, including children with HFA/AS. When used specifically with children with HFA/AS, self-management procedures appear to be useful for decreasing stereotypic behaviors (Koegel et al., 1995), increasing the frequency and duration of on-task behaviors (Callahan & Rademacher, 1999), and enhancing maintenance and generalization of social skills (Shearer, Kohler, Buchan, & McCullough, 1996). Although the research base regarding the efficacy of self-management strategies for children with HFA/AS is emerging, this strategy should be considered effective because it is a logical extension of prior research among other populations.

## Academic Interventions

***Systematic and explicit instruction.*** Systematic instruction means that educators use, to the greatest degree possible, instructional methods that are validated, carefully planned, and evaluated to determine the efficacy of instruction (Iovannone, Dunlap, Huber, & Kincaid, 2003). In addition, strategies for promoting the generalization and maintenance of skills are incorporated into systematic instruction plans. Furthermore, systematic instruction employs strategies consistent with recommendations discussed in the prevention section of this chapter (e.g., advance organizers, simple concrete instructions, and discrete steps). These strategies will help the student with HFA/AS stay focused and engaged during teacher-directed instructional times. In addition to these efforts, teaching strategies derived from the field of Applied Behavior Analysis should be used. For example, the use of task analysis, shaping, and fading procedures can be very helpful when designing instructional interventions for students with HFA/AS, and these strategies have a long history validating their utility across a variety of learners. A final, but critical, component of systematic instruction is data collection to document progress in response to instruction. Frequent ongoing data collection is needed to make changes in response to student learning (or lack thereof) quickly before precious instructional time is lost.

***Comprehension strategy instruction.*** Students with HFA/AS are generally good readers. However, they often have difficulty with comprehension of written material. In fact, these students often can fluently decode material well above the level of material about which they can answer comprehension questions. Given this pattern, it is suggested that materials used for comprehension strategy instruction be at a level necessary for successful comprehension. In many cases, these materials may be at a lower level than these students are accustomed to reading (i.e., the level they are capable of decoding fluently; Moore, 2002). Using cloze tasks, in which the child must supply a missing word in a reading passage, may prove very helpful in teaching comprehension. While controlling the level of materials to ensure success with comprehension tasks, teachers will need to be careful to choose materials that are age appropriate to guard against motivational difficulties. Once again, incorporating special-interest content into comprehension instructional material may promote student motivation.

In addition to comprehension instructional materials, direct instruction in the use of visual supports such as story mapping (semantic maps), picture drawing, outlining, and charting may help build comprehension skills. These strategies help students with HFA/AS organize the information they encounter when reading content area material or fictional works and when completing math word problems, which typically rely heavily on reading comprehension skills. For example, story mapping involves the student answering a set of questions about important ideas conveyed in a story (e.g., who, what, where, why). These questions about story details provide the reader with a means to organize, remember, and integrate information from narrative text. Similarly, graphic displays (e.g., descriptive or thematic maps) provide a visual picture of the content in expository text as well as show important linkages across content (Baker, Gersten, & Grossen, 2002).

Similar to the visual strategies used for reading comprehension, strategies that have the student draw pictures and make charts for use with math word problems have been described by Moore (2002). Typically, drawing a picture is used much in the same way as manipulatives. Picture drawing would be used for a problem like the following, which involves making a comparison:

> Fifteen people board a fishing boat in Key West. Fourteen of the 15 people on the boat want to fish that day. The captain has 10 fishing poles on his boat. Before the boat can leave the dock, the captain needs to know how many more fishing poles he needs to get so all the passengers who want to fish that day can have their own pole. How many does the captain need to get?

Using the picture-drawing strategy the student would draw representations for both fishing poles and people and then use these drawings to help solve the problem (e.g., compare the number of people wanting to fish with the number of fishing poles available). In contrast, the charting strategy described by Moore (2002) is more useful for word problems involving multiple categories of items (e.g., types of furniture—desk, table, chair, bookshelf) and several items in each category (e.g., tables made out of different materials, different colors, etc.).

Because comprehension requires the student to use a complex set of skills simultaneously (e.g., knowing vocabulary, determining the purpose of the reading, and remembering only relevant information), it is important to explicitly teach the metacognitive strategies needed for eliciting the skills and knowledge necessary to adequately comprehend (Carnine, Silbert, & Kameenui, 1997). Therefore, in addition to teaching the use of the visual strategies described here, explicit instruction on the thinking processes involved in comprehension is needed. The implication is that students must understand, in a very concrete way, the processes required for adequate comprehension.

Students with HFA/AS have great difficulty with reading comprehension questions about sequencing, inferencing, making predictions, generalizing, drawing conclusions, and distinguishing between fact and fiction. Thus, explicit instruction should be provided regarding the strategies the student must employ to answer such questions. Similarly, for math problems requiring greater comprehension of language (e.g., for tasks beyond math computation), explicit direct instruction is needed. Explicit instruction makes the process of solving word problems or determining viable answers to comprehension questions very concrete.

One way to accomplish this is to use a "model—lead—test" teaching format (Kozloff & Rice, 2001). First, the educator models the steps one completes to determine a solution or answer. Once the process is modeled, the teacher carefully leads (responds with) the student through the process, prompting the student as needed. Next, students overtly demonstrate the process by themselves for the teacher so the teacher can see students go through each step. The teacher must provide corrective feedback and praise as part of this final step. The point of using an explicit instructional format is to not only make the process very concrete for the student, but also maintain student attention and prevent learning errors.

***Homework and study support.*** A homework support strategy that is helpful for students with HFA/AS is the use of assignment notebooks (Moore, 2002). Simple in design, these tools are used to track assignments and help teach responsibility to students with HFA/AS. Once a notebook has been established, each day after the student has recorded the assignment, the teacher checks the notebook before the child leaves school to ensure that assignments are recorded accurately. The child is then required to show the parent the notebook at home and the parent signs the notebook when the child has finished the designated homework. Finally, the student brings the notebook back to school the following day and shows it to the teacher. Typically, the teacher offers some sort of reinforcement for students' efforts to use the notebook and for completing homework.

In addition to homework support, students with HFA/AS benefit from assistance related to note taking. Students with HFA/AS often have difficulty listening and writing at the same time. They may experience problems separating main ideas from details. Also, these students may have motor difficulties that make writing more challenging. Each of these difficulties can lead to problems in taking accurate and useful notes. One intervention is to provide direct instruction in how to distinguish main ideas from detail information (Moore, 2002). Other interventions that may help include the teacher providing notes to the student, tape recording lectures, assigning a peer to take notes for or share notes with the student, or allowing the student to type his or her notes. Moore describes a number of assistive technology devices that may be useful for students with HFA/AS.

## SUMMARY

Children with high-functioning autism/Asperger's syndrome (HFA/AS) display a variety of social, behavioral, and communicative difficulties despite average to above-average cognitive functioning. Over the past several years, rates in the frequency of diagnoses and special education referrals for children with HFA/AS have increased at an alarming rate. With such an increase in the number of children identified with HFA/AS, it is increasingly important to understand how to effectively build supports and interventions to assist in the development of social competency, behavioral regulation, and academic learning.

To best support children with HFA/AS, it is necessary to develop an approach that integrates a number of prevention and intervention strategies. Preventative approaches are quick environmental change strategies that create structure and predictability for children with HFA/AS. Visuals (e.g., picture schedules) help the student understand when or where activities or tasks start, as well as what to do during and following those activities or tasks. Incorporating choice and preference motivates children with HFA/AS to engage in activities that may otherwise be less rewarding for the child. In addition to such prevention strategies, more direct interventions are often needed to increase the skill, frequency, or quality of behaviors displayed by children with HFA/AS. Often, these interventions involve teaching social skills and social understanding, reducing the frequency of inappropriate and/or rigid behaviors, and teaching academic content (e.g., comprehension) in a systematic and explicit manner. A combination of the prevention and intervention strategies discussed in this chapter, along with methods for collaboration, consultation, and evaluation of treatment effects, is necessary to ensure that the needs of children with HFA/AS are met.

## RECOMMENDED RESOURCES

### Books and Other Printed Material

Howlin, P. (1998). *Children with autism and Asperger Syndrome.* Chichester, England: John Wiley.

This book offers an excellent resource for understanding the characteristics of individuals at the higher end of the autism spectrum. Information is included on appropriate treatment approaches and educational practices. Full of practical treatment advice, this book is a good resource for both teachers and parents.

Iovannone, R., Dunlap, G., Huber, H., & Kincaid, D (2003). Effective educational practices for students with autism spectrum disorders. *Focus on Autism and Other Developmental Disabilities, 18,* 150–165.

This article provides an integration of years of research on autism spectrum disorders into a curricular model appropriate for implementation in many houses of education. Specifically, it offers descriptions of empirically supported core elements that should be part of any instructional program for students with autism spectrum disorders. Guidelines for developing, implementing, and evaluating instructional approaches are discussed in the framework of best instructional practice.

Moore, S. T. (2002). *Asperger syndrome and the elementary school experience: Practical solutions for academic and social difficulties.* Shawnee Mission, KS: Autism Asperger Publishing Company.

This text provides an accurate description of many of the social and academic difficulties experienced by elementary-age children with Asperger's syndrome. In addition, it describes practical preventive strategies that aim to increase organization and enhance academic productivity and accuracy for students with Asperger's.

## Websites

*http://www.maapservices.org*

The website of the Information and Support Network for More Advanced Persons with Autism and Asperger's Syndrome contains information regarding the characteristics of autism and related disabilities, relevant legal information, and teaching strategies. It also offers an international listing of persons, agencies, and organizations that support individuals and families afflicted with autism spectrum disorders.

*http://www.udel.edu/bkirby/asperger/*

This website, Online Asperger Syndrome Information and Support (O.A.S.I.S.), provides access to a host of links regarding the characteristics, assessment, education, research, and support of children with HFA/AS. In addition, it offers Web-based forums and private monitored message boards and chat rooms.

## REFERENCES


American Psychiatric Association. (1994). *Diagnostic and statistical manual of mental disorders* (4th ed.). Washington, DC: Author.

American Psychiatric Association. (2000). *Diagnostic and statistical manual of mental disorders* (4th ed., text rev.). Washington, DC: Author.

Attwood, T. (1998). *Asperger's syndrome: A guide for parents and professionals.* London: Jessica Kingsley Publishers.

Baker, S., Gersten, R., & Grossen, B. (2002). Interventions for students with reading comprehension problems. In M. R. Shinn, H. M. Walker, & G. Stoner (Eds.), *Interventions for academic and behavior problems II: Preventative and remedial solutions* (pp. 731–754). Bethesda, MD: National Association of School Psychologists.

Baron-Cohen, S. (1995). *Mindblindness: An essay on autism and theory of mind.* Cambridge, MA: MIT Press.

Bauminger, N. (2002). The facilitation of social-emotional understanding and social interaction in high-functioning children with autism: Intervention outcomes. *Journal of Autism and Developmental Disorders, 32,* 283–298.

Bryan, L. C., & Gast, D. L. (2000). Teaching on-task and on-schedule behaviors to high-functioning children with autism via picture activity schedules. *Journal of Autism and Developmental Disorders, 30,* 537–552.

Callahan, K., & Rademacher, J. A. (1999). Using self-management strategies to increase the on-task behavior of a student with autism. *Journal of Positive Behavior Interventions, 1,* 117–122.

Carnine, D. W., Silbert, J., & Kameenui, E. J. (1997). *Direct instruction reading* (3rd ed.). Upper Saddle River, NJ: Merrill.

Charlop, M. H., & Milstein, J. P. (1989). Teaching autistic children conversational speech using video modeling. *Journal of Applied Behavior Analysis, 22*(3), 275–285.

Charlop-Christy, M. H., Carpenter, M., Le, L., LeBlanc, L. A., & Kellet, K. (2002). Using the picture exchange communication system (PECS) with children with autism: Assessment of PECS acquisition, speech, social-communicative behavior, and problem behavior. *Journal of Applied Behavior Analysis, 35,* 213–231.

Charlop-Christy, M. H., & Daneshvar, S. (2003). Using video modeling to teach perspective taking to children with autism. *Journal of Positive Behavior Interventions, 5,* 12–21.

Charlop-Christy, M. H., Le, L., & Freeman, K. A. (2000). A comparison of video modeling with in vivo modeling for teaching children with autism. *Journal of Autism and Developmental Disorders, 30,* 537–552.

Drasgow, E., Halle, J. W., & Ostrosky, M. M. (1998). Effects of differential reinforcement on the generalization of a replacement mand in three children with severe language delays. *Journal of Applied Behavior Analysis, 31,* 357–374.

Gillberg, C., & Ehlers, S. (1998). High-functioning people with autism and Asperger syndrome: A literature review. In E. Schopler, G. B. Mesibov, & L. J. Kunce (Eds.), *Asperger syndrome or high-functioning autism?* (pp. 79–106). New York: Plenum.

Gray, C. A. (1998). Social stories and comic strip conversations with students with Asperger syndrome and high-functioning autism. In E. Schopler,

G. B. Mesibov, & L. J. Kunce (Eds.), *Asperger syndrome or high-functioning autism* (pp. 167–198). New York: Plenum.

Happe, F. G., & Frith, U. (1996). The neuropsychology of autism. *Brain, 119,* 1377–1400.

Howlin, P. (1998). *Children with autism and Asperger syndrome: A guide for practitioners and carers.* Chichester, England: Wiley.

Hyman, S. L., Rodier, P. M., & Davidson, P. (2001). Pervasive developmental disorders in young children. *Journal of the American Medical Association, 285,* 3093–3099.

Iovannone, R., Dunlap, G., Huber, H., & Kincaid, D. (2003). Effective educational practices for students with autism spectrum disorders. *Focus on Autism and Other Developmental Disabilities, 18*(3), 150–165.

Koegel, R. L., Koegel, L. K., & Parks, D. R. (1995). "Teach the individual" model of generalization: Autonomy through self-management. In R. L. Koegel & L. K. Koegel (Eds.), *Teaching children with autism: Strategies for initiating positive interactions and improving learning opportunities* (pp. 67–93). Baltimore: Brookes.

Kozloff, M. A., & Rice, J. S. (2001). *Direct approach to literacy instruction inventory of essential knowledge and skills.* Retrieved July 29, 2004, from http://people.uncw.edu/kozloffm/diinventoryrevised.html

Krasny, L., Williams, B. J., Provencal, S., & Ozonoff, S. (2003). Social skills interventions for the autism spectrum: Essential ingredients and a model curriculum. *Child and Adolescent Psychiatry Clinics in North America, 12,* 10–122.

Kunce, L. J., & Mesibov, G. B. (1998). Educational approaches to high-functioning Autism and Asperger's syndrome. In E. Schopler, G. B. Mesibov, & L. J. Kunce (Eds.), *Asperger syndrome or high functioning autism?* (pp. 227–261). New York: Plenum.

Landa, R. (2000). Social language use in Asperger syndrome. In A. Klin, F. R. Volkmar, & S. S. Sparrow (Eds.), *Asperger syndrome* (pp. 125–155). New York: Guilford Press.

Laushey, K. M., & Heflin, L. J. (2000). Enhancing social skills of kindergarten children with autism through training multiple peers as tutors. *Journal of Autism and Developmental Disorders, 30,* 183–193.

Lotter, V. (1967). Epidemiology of autistic conditions in young children: Prevalence. *Social Psychiatry, 1,* 134– 137.

Moes, D. R. (1998). Integrating choice-making opportunities within teacher-assigned academic tasks to facilitate the performance of children with autism. *Journal of the Association for Persons with Severe Handicaps, 23,* 319–328.

Moore, S. T. (2002). *Asperger syndrome and the elementary school experience: Practical solutions for academic and social difficulties.* Shawnee Mission, KS: Autism Asperger Publishing Company.

Morrison, R. S., Sainato, D. M., BenChaaban, D., & Endo, S. (2002). Increasing play skills of children with autism using activity schedules and correspondence training. *Journal of Early Intervention, 25,* 58–72.

Mundy, P., & Stella, J. (2000). Joint attention, orienting, and nonverbal communication in autism. In A. M. Wetherby & B. M. Prizant (Eds.), *Autism Spectrum Disorders: A transactional developmental perspective* (pp. 55–77). Baltimore: Brookes.

Myles, B. S., & Simpson, R. L. (2003). *Asperger syndrome: A guide for educators and parents.* Austin, TX: ProEd.

Norris, C., & Dattilo, J. (1999). Evaluating effects of a social story intervention on a young girl with autism. *Focus on Autism and Other Developmental Disabilities, 14,* 180–186.

Odom, S. L., & Strain, P. S. (1986). A comparison of peer-initiation and teacher-antecedent interventions for promoting reciprocal social interaction of autistic preschoolers. *Journal of Applied Behavior Analysis, 19,* 59–71.

Ozonoff, S. (2003, September). *Empirically supported interventions for school-age and more verbal children with autism spectrum disorders.* Paper presented at the Autism and Telehealth M.I.N.D. Bank Meeting. Sacramento, CA.

Ozonoff, S., South, M., & Miller, J. N. (2000). DSM-IV-defined Asperger syndrome: Cognitive, behavioral and early history differentiation from high-functioning autism. *Autism, 4*(1), 29–46.

Paine, S. C., Radicchi, J., Rosellini, L. C., Deutchman, L., & Darch, C. B. (1983). *Structuring your classroom for academic success.* Champaign, IL: Research Press.

Peterson, S. M., Caniglia, C., & Royster, A. J. (2001). Application of choice-making intervention for a student with multiply maintained problem behavior. *Focus on Autism and Other Developmental Disabilities, 16,* 240–246.

Sansosti, F. J., Powell-Smith, K. A., & Kincaid, D. (2004). A research synthesis on social story interventions for children with autism spectrum disorders. *Focus on Autism and Other Developmental Disabilities, 19,* 194–204.

Scott, F. J., Baron-Cohen, S., Bolton, P., & Brayne, C. (2002). Brief report: Prevalence of autism spectrum conditions in children aged 5–11 years in Cambridgeshire, UK. *Autism, 6,* 231–237.

Shearer, D. D., Kohler, F. W., Buchan, K. A., & McCullough, K. M. (1996). Promoting independent interactions between preschoolers with autism and their nondisabled peers: An analysis of self-monitoring. *Early Education and Development, 7,* 205–220.

Shipley-Benamou, R., Lutzker, J. R., & Taubman, M. (2002). Teaching daily living skills to children with autism through instructional video modeling. *Journal of Positive Behavior Interventions, 4,* 165–175.

Swaggart, B. L., Gagnon, E., Bock, S. J., Earles, T. L., Quinn, C., Myles, B. S., & Simpson, R. L. (1995). Using social stories to teach social and behavioral skills to children with autism. *Focus on Autistic Behavior, 10*(1), 1–16.

Terpstra, J. E., Higgins, K., & Pierce, T. (2002). Can I play? Classroom-based interventions for teaching play skills to children with autism. *Focus on Autism and Other Developmental Disabilities, 17,* 119–126.

Thiemann, K. S., & Goldstein, H. (2001). Social stories, written text cues, and video feedback: Effects on social communication of children with autism. *Journal of Applied Behavior Analysis, 34,* 425–446.

Twachtman-Cullen, D. (2000). More able children with autism spectrum disorders: Sociocommunicative challenges and guidelines for enhancing abilities. In A. M. Wetherby, & B. M. Prizant (Eds.), *Autism spectrum disorders: A transactional developmental perspective* (pp. 225–249). Baltimore: Brookes.

U.S. Department of Education. (2003). *24th Annual Report to Congress on the Implementation of the Individuals with Disabilities Education Act.* Washington, DC: Author.

Vaughn, B. J., & Horner, R. H. (1997). Identifying instructional tasks that occasion problem behaviors and assessing the effects of student versus teacher choice among these tasks. *Journal of Applied Behavior Analysis, 30,* 299–312.

Volkmar, F. R., & Klin, A. (2000). Diagnostic issues in Asperger syndrome. In A. Klin, F. R. Volkmar, & S. S. Sparrow (Eds.), *Asperger syndrome* (pp. 25–71). New York: Guilford Press.

Wilde, L. D., Koegel, L. K., & Koegel, R. L. (1992). *Increasing success in school through priming: A training manual.* Santa Barbara: University of California.

# 72

# Self-Mutilation

**Richard Lieberman**
*Los Angeles Unified School District*

**Scott Poland**
*NOVA Southeastern University*

School-based professionals are often called on to consult with school staff and parents when students exhibit self-injurious behaviors. The alarming numbers of adolescent students engaging in self-mutilation (SM) pose a challenge to all school mental health personnel. Complicating matters for the educator is that these behaviors can appear contagious, often running through schools, peer groups, or grade levels. SM behaviors such as cutting and burning have recently been the focus of the media, popularized by current movies and personalities who have publicly admitted to SM. The effect of such exposure on youth has not been adequately measured.

For some students, these harmful behaviors seem superficial, occurring in response to certain precipitating events that are typical in the life of the adolescent. For other students, these behaviors are clearly more habitual, repetitive, dangerous, and self-destructive. Most school psychologists and other school-based mental health service providers are skilled in assessing suicide risk, but they may have limited knowledge of intervening with students exhibiting SM, many of whom will assess at low risk of suicide. This chapter provides suggestions on ways school mental health professionals can respond to the unique individual and community needs that surround self-injurious students, but it is essential that the reader begin by gaining a better understanding of this puzzling, disturbing, and often misunderstood behavior.

## BACKGROUND AND DEVELOPMENT

### Classifications

SM has been referred to in the literature by a variety of terms, including self-harm, self-abuse, self-inflicted violence, and self-injurious behavior. It is important to distinguish SM behaviors from other culturally sanctioned behaviors such as ritualistic tattooing, piercing, and branding. Those behaviors, as traced by Favazza (1996), have been linked to such issues as salvation, social orderliness, spirituality, and healing and are distinct from the SM behaviors that are the focus of this chapter.

Favazza and Rosenthal (1993) proposed three classifications of pathological SM. *Major SM* is an infrequent act that occurs suddenly with a great deal of tissue damage. It is most commonly associated with individuals who are psychotic or acutely intoxicated. It rarely occurs at school. *Stereotypic SM* includes behaviors such as head banging, wrist and lip biting, and complex tics most associated with those who have developmental disabilities, autism, or Tourette's syndrome. *Moderate/superficial SM*, which is the focus of this chapter, includes cutting, burning, pinching, puncturing, scratching, nail-biting, and interference with wound healing. The arms, wrists, inner thighs, and abdomen are the areas most typically injured (Zila & Kiselica, 2001; Conterio & Lader, 1998). These areas are strategic in that they can be easily concealed by clothing. Cutting is one of the most common forms of self-injury found in the non-hospitalized population (Ross & Heath, 2002; Briere & Gil, 1998).

SM has been associated with a wide variety of disorders, including psychotic, antisocial, and borderline personality, mood, and anxiety disorders (Zila & Kiselica, 2001). To many clinicians SM is synonymous with borderline personality disorder, which is diagnosed more often in females and characterized by significant fears of abandonment (Favazza, 1996; Linehan, 1993). Although individuals with borderline personality disorder often engage in SM behaviors, this diagnosis is not appropriate for the majority of students engaging in SM. A history of physical and sexual abuse (Boudewyn & Liem, 1995; Turell & Armsworth, 2000), family violence (Conterio & Lader, 1998), and post-traumatic stress disorder (Favazza & Rosenthal, 1993; Kehrberg, 1997; Langbehn & Pfohl, 1993) have been identified as significant risk factors in SM. As a symptom of post-traumatic stress disorder, cutting may be seen as a reenactment of childhood trauma (Levenkron, 1998) in an effort to gain some control over what happened. All of these correlates can be useful in identifying at-risk adolescents for the purposes of intervention and prevention (Kress, Gibson, & Reynolds, 2004; Walsh & Rosen, 1988).

Clearly, SM is a complex behavior that may have compulsive or impulsive characteristics. Consequently, Favazza (1996) further broke down the classification of moderate/superficial SM into three types: compulsive, episodic, and repetitive. *Compulsive self-injury* includes such behaviors as hair pulling (trichotillomania), skin picking, and the binging and purging of eating disorders. These behaviors are responses to obsessive thoughts from which the child seeks relief. There is ample evidence of a relationship between SM and eating disorders, with as many as one half to two thirds of youth that exhibit SM experiencing concurrent or previous eating disorders (Favazza, 1996; Favazza & Conterio, 1988). Common to these disorders are the issues of regaining control and achieving a rapid respite from distressing, overwhelming emotions. *Episodic SM* and *repetitive SM* (RSM) are characteristic of impulse disorder and behaviors. They differ only in the degree and frequency of the act. Episodic impulse disorders include parasuicidal behaviors, alcohol and substance abuse, and shoplifting. All these behaviors have two factors in common: they are episodic and gratifying. *Episodic* implies the behaviors are occasional and in response to certain precipitating events. They are gratifying because of the complex endorphins, natural antidepressants released by the brain when an adolescent engages in SM (Favazza). This may be why so many teens do not report pain in response to SM but a sense of relief or release. This neurological, addictive component of impulse disorder may play a critical role in the behavior escalating from episodic SM to RSM (Pies & Popli, 1995).

We support Favazza's (1996) proposal of a new Axis 1 diagnostic category in the DSM, Repetitive Self-Mutilation Syndrome (RSM), which is defined as a "recurrent failure to resist impulses to harm one's body physically without suicidal intent" (p. 253). Because this category does not exist in the current DSM, Favazza urges clinicians to consider the diagnosis of Impulse Control Disorder, Not Otherwise Specified for individuals engaging in this kind of repetitive self-injury.

## Incidence

Approximately 3 million Americans engage in some form of self-injury, and 90% of them began in adolescence (Bowman & Randall, 2004). However, it is difficult to determine the actual incidence of SM in the adolescent population. Rough estimates range from 750 to 1,400 per 100,000 (Favazza, 1996). It has been estimated that 13% of adolescents and 12% of college-age youth have engaged in some form of SM (Ross & Heath, 2002; Favazza, DeRosear, & Conterio, 1989). The incidence increases significantly to 40% to 60% in adolescent inpatient settings (Darche, 1990).

## Developmental, Cultural, and Gender Issues

SM typically has an onset in late childhood to early adolescence and appears more common in females (e.g., Simeon & Hollander, 2001; Zila & Kiselica, 2001). A wider variety of self-injurious behaviors appear in the elementary school–age population, with a greater representation of males. Common harmful impulsive behaviors that school staff may observe can range from cutting, puncturing, poking, hair pulling, head banging, scratching, or burning with the use of erasers (Poland & Lieberman, 2002). SM is prevalent in all cultures and races and cuts across all socioeconomic boundaries.

## Suicidality

A common misconception is that adolescents who cut themselves do so with suicidal intent. SM is performed for different reasons than suicide, and it is distinguished from parasuicide (suicide attempts) in that "a person who truly attempts suicide seeks to end all feelings whereas a person who self-mutilates seeks to feel better" (Favazza, 1998, p. 262). Essentially, adolescents engaging in SM might harm themselves superficially in an effort to *not* attempt suicide.

Although most students exhibiting SM behaviors do not harm themselves with suicidal intention, many have extensive mental health histories that include parasuicidal behaviors. A well-intentioned adult may try to help by commanding the adolescent to stop these behaviors immediately. However, without identifying other coping skills and replacement behaviors to fall back on, the adolescent may, in desperation, attempt suicide (Favazza, 1989). Assessing a student for risk of suicide and obtaining a complete mental health history is always prudent and best practice when a student is referred for SM (see chapter 17, "Suicidal Ideation and Behaviors").

# PROBLEMS AND IMPLICATIONS

## Functions of SM

Evidence demonstrates that SM can fulfill a multitude of needs in the lives of troubled adolescents. Reasons that adolescents engage in self-harm include (a) feeling concrete pain when psychic pain is too overwhelming; (b) reducing numbness and promoting a sense of being real; (c) keeping traumatic memories from intruding; (d) modulating affect; (e) receiving support and caring for others; (f) discharging anger, anxiety, despair, or disappointment; (g) self-punishing; and (h) gaining a sense of control (Kress, Gibson, & Reynolds, 2004). In general, SM appears to function as a means to regulate and control emotions (Suyemoto & MacDonald, 1995).

## Precipitating Events

In today's complex society, situational crises challenge adolescents' coping capacities on a daily basis. However, a number of stressful, potentially traumatic life events have been identified as precipitants to episodes of SM. They include losing a parent, being sexually abused, having a sibling who engages in SM, and witnessing family violence (Walsh & Rosen, 1988). Some events more typically observed by school support personnel can include peer conflicts, intimacy problems, breakup of a romance, or rejection of human interconnection (Kehrberg, 1997; Zila & Kiselica, 2001). In addition, mood disorders and alcohol and substance abuse are substantial risk factors for both SM and suicide (Moscicki, 1995). The Centers for Disease Control and Prevention's Youth Risk Behavior Surveillance data (Grunbaum et al., 2003) revealed that almost 30% of youth reported feeling a prolonged sense of hopelessness during the previous year. These are youth who are at risk for SM and suicidal behavior.

## Isolation

Many adolescents choose to self-injure in isolation and attempt to avoid attention and embarrassment by wearing clothes that conceal their injuries very well (Alderman, 1997). Shrouded in shame and secrecy, they may go to great lengths to present themselves as uninjured and normal. Isolation from peers and the mental health community and feelings of being disconnected at school have been found to raise risk in youth to engage in SM. Girls were particularly vulnerable to SM if they abused alcohol and had friends who were not friends with each other (Bearman & Moody, 2004).

## Contagion

Contagion, or the imitation of behaviors by others in the environment, is a phenomenon associated with adolescent SM. Having a sibling, friend, or other acquaintance who engages in SM raises risk in youth to imitate the behavior (Walsh & Rosen, 1988). School administrators have observed self-injurious behaviors spread through peer groups, grade levels, and campus clubs. SM may serve as an occasional "rite of togetherness," used to cement certain friendships and romances (Froeschle & Moyer, 2004). Sometimes an adolescent will pick up the behavior from older siblings or peer group leaders and seek acceptance and inclusion through SM. Although every student referred for SM should be assessed for suicide risk and have parents contacted, mental health professionals should expect that many students will inevitably assess as low risk and not demonstrate any overt psychopathology or emotional disturbance. Studies have demonstrated repeatedly that with appropriate interventions, the majority of students develop better coping skills, and SM behaviors diminish (see Alternative Actions sections below).

As clinicians, we have observed that, within certain peer groups displaying similar SM behaviors (such as a group of fourth graders who were referred for having eraser burns on their arms), there is often one individual, "the alpha male/female," whose behaviors and emotional lability have set off other peers, who imitate the SM. That student, however, may in fact be in the early stages of a more serious borderline or antisocial personality disorder or be a victim of severe abuse or family violence. These students, once identified, require referral to appropriate community agencies that address such serious disorders. In the majority of cases, students who exhibit episodic SM need intensive monitoring and follow-up to ensure that better coping strategies have replaced poor ones and that episodic SM has not progressed to repetitive SM.

## ALTERNATIVE ACTIONS FOR PREVENTION

There is growing awareness of the importance of mental health services, especially primary prevention programs, in helping students succeed academically. The World Health Organization (2000) outlined a number of protective factors associated with children's mental health: good relationships with other youth, the ability to seek adult help when it is needed, access to mental health care, religiosity or a spiritual life, stable family environment, possession of coping and problem-solving skills, a connectedness to school, and involvement in extracurricular activities. The importance of supportive environments has also been demonstrated, specifically with respect to SM. Adolescents were less likely to harm themselves through SM or to engage in suicidal behavior if they attended schools where they felt safe, had a higher density of friendship ties, and had a more tightly knit school community (Bearman & Moody, 2004). Thus, prevention of SM is inextricably linked to the general promotion of children's mental health in schools and to districts' safety planning. Specifically, safety planning should include crisis preparation, training for staff, and implementation of primary prevention programs that reduce risk in youth (National Institute of Mental Health [NIMH], 2002).

### Crisis Preparation

Well-developed crisis preparation plans allow for sensitive and rapid response to a wide variety of problems, including SM. For example, the strong association between sexual and physical abuse and cutting behaviors makes it critical for schools to collaborate with child and family protective services in the community and to require all personnel to attend annual professional development events to learn the warning signs and procedures when referring students who are potential victims (see also chapter 60, "Psychological and Physical Abuse," and 61, "Sexual Abuse").

School crisis teams provide not only an opportunity for collaboration between the school's administration and school mental health and medical staff (e.g., psychologists, counselors, nurses, and social workers) but also a critical link to the mental health resources in their communities (Poland & McCormick, 1999; see Alternative Actions for Intervention, below). School mental health professionals play an important role in the referral of students to qualified professionals in their communities, and they are urged to update their lists of mental health resources annually. They need to be knowledgeable of the practitioners and treatment centers that have specific training in the management of self-injury, as well as those resources that provide culturally sensitive services (e.g., interpreters and therapists who reflect the ethnicities present in the school community). If possible, school-based professionals might use an inservice day to visit local treatment facilities and determine the steps a student would go through in seeking help and receiving treatment. When school professionals are aware of what the treatment process is like, they can better help students and their families make decisions and develop intervention plans (Kress, Gibson, & Reynolds, 2004). Brock, Lazarus, and Jimerson (2002) provide more detail on developing school-based crisis preparation teams.

### Training

The Surgeon General (U.S. Department of Health and Human Services, 2001) has identified two promising strategies for suicide prevention that have particular relevance in any discussion of SM prevention: gatekeeper training and screening programs (discussed in the following section). Gatekeeper training takes into account the fact that the self-mutilating, potentially suicidal student does not generally self-refer. The goals of this effective strategy are to raise awareness of the risk factors and warning signs of SM and suicide (see Table 1) and to provide clear, succinct intervention procedures to all adults, including school staff and parents. It also is helpful for all staff to be aware of the myths versus the facts regarding SM (see Table 2).

The National Association of Secondary School Principals provides these additional recommendations to administrators: incorporate SM training into your crisis team responsibilities, provide information to all adults on campus on how to recognize the risk factors and warning signs of SM and suicide, and train all staff to respond appropriately and refer students to crisis team personnel (Lieberman, 2004).

### Primary Prevention Programs

A myriad of evidence-based primary prevention programs exist that address and reduce health risks of adolescents, such as depression, alcohol and substance abuse, bullying, and suicide. Promoting appropriate, trusting

**Table 1** *Signs of Self-Injury*

- Frequent or unexplained bruises, scars, cuts, or burns.
- Consistent, inappropriate use of clothing designed to conceal wounds (often found on the arms, thighs, or abdomen).
- Secretive behaviors, such as spending unusual amounts of time in the student bathroom or isolated areas on campus.
- General signs of depression, social–emotional isolation, and disconnectedness.
- Substance abuse.
- Possession of sharp implements (razor blades, shards of glass, thumb tacks, or paper clips).
- Evidence of self-injury in work samples, journals, art projects.
- Risk-taking behaviors such as playing with guns, acting out sexually, jumping from high places, or running into traffic.

*Note.* From "Understanding and Responding to Students Who Self-Mutilate," by R. Lieberman, 2004, *National Association of Secondary School Principals: Principal Leadership, 4*(7), pp. 10–13. Adapted with permission.

adult–child relationships and creating caring environments where students feel welcomed, respected, and trusted are related benefits of any primary prevention program (Webster & Browning, 2002), and these programs should be beneficial in preventing SM as well.

For example, the SOS (Signs of Suicide) program has documented evidence of reducing adolescent suicide attempts (Aseltine & DeMartino, 2004). The goals of this program are to identify depressed youth at risk for self-injurious behaviors and increase their help-seeking skills. Presumably, improved help-seeking skills should also reduce students' risk for SM; however, the screening instruments used in the SOS program (and similar programs) do not specifically address SM.

## ALTERNATIVE ACTIONS FOR INTERVENTION

The following are just a few of the challenges that face school mental health professionals when they respond to referrals of students exhibiting SM behaviors:

> "Over the past few months I have had 12th, 7th, and now 2nd graders referred to my counselors for hurting themselves. Should I talk to my staff and parents about this, and if so, what should I say?"
> —*K–12 Principal*

> "I have eight hysterical seventh-grade girls in my office and they are all cutting themselves and talking about suicide. I need your help!"
> —*Middle School Assistant Principal*

> "I have a first-grade boy who keeps poking himself with thumb tacks in the classroom. I've assessed him and he is low risk for suicide. Now what do I do?"
> —*Elementary School Nurse*

> "I have identified six middle school students who are engaging in self-mutilation. I don't have a lot of time; can I work with them in a group?"
> —*Middle School Counselor*

> "I just discovered a bunch of cuts on my daughter's arm and she tells me all her friends are doing it. I have forbidden her to ever do this again and I've told her never to see those friends again. Was this OK?"
> —*Concerned Parent*

School personnel and parents are facing increasingly complex situations involving SM, and they often consult school-based practitioners for assistance. Responding to these requests requires knowledge and skills to educate the adults of the school community, provide guidance on treatments, and, in some cases, provide individual and group interventions in the school setting.

### Adult Education

School districts should take a proactive approach to educating faculty and school staff, particularly coaches, physical education instructors, health educators, resource officers, bus drivers, and nurses, on ways to recognize SM and to correct misunderstandings about the nature of this behavior. In addition, all staff members must know how to manage student self-disclosure of SM. All adults on the school campus should be aware of the referral procedures and should identify students who have injured themselves in any way. Such adult education could contribute to students feeling less shame, more optimism, greater trust of adults, and increased willingness to seek help.

### Response to Student Disclosures

School mental health professionals may lack the time, space, or diagnostic expertise to respond to the therapeutic needs of students referred for exhibiting SM behaviors. Their primary role, once the student has been

**Table 2** *Myths Versus Facts in Self-Mutilation*

*Myth 1*: Self-mutilators use this behavior to manipulate other people.

*Fact*: Physical pain is inflicted in an attempt to replace emotional rage. The victim's attempts to conform to expectations of normal behavior lead to silence about the event. Victims go to great lengths to present themselves as uninjured and normal and rarely seek to manipulate others through SM (McLane, 1996).

*Myth 2*: Self-mutilation is synonymous with suicide.

*Fact*: SM is a ritual performed for reasons other than suicide. The self-mutilator uses pain to mask emotional pain but does not intend to destroy the entire body (Zila & Kiselica, 2001; Levenkron, 1998).

*Myth 3*: Self-mutilators are dangerous and will probably harm others.

*Fact*: SM is generally secretive and most often performed in isolation. The behavior is not performed in an attempt to harm but rather to vanquish emotional pain. Violence is not directed toward others (McLane, 1996).

*Myth 4*: Self-mutilators just want attention.

*Fact*: Most self-mutilators perform their ritual and symbolic acts in private. They are often humiliated about their scars and keep them private (Levenkron, 1998).

*Note.* Information from "Just Cut It Out: Legal and Ethical Challenges in Counseling Students Who Self-Mutilate," by J. Froeschle and M. Moyer, 2004, *Professional School Counseling, 7*, pp. 231–236. Adapted with permission.

identified, is to assess the student for immediate risk, communicate with parents, and direct the family to the appropriate district and community mental health resources (see chapter 17, "Suicidal Ideation and Behaviors," for detailed information on assessment of suicide risk). Then, by obtaining the appropriate authorization for release of information, they can focus on "tightening the circle of care" around the student by facilitating communication among the adolescent, school, home, and community mental health agencies. School nurses are vital crisis team members who should be consulted on all cases of students referred for SM. The school nurse has medical expertise to address immediate wound treatment and the risk for possible secondary infections. The nurse also is familiar with medical and mental health resources in the community.

***Personal reactions.*** In general, students engaging in RSM are very difficult to work with, and it is not uncommon for practitioners to have strong emotional reactions to the self-injury. These feelings can include intense horror and repulsion, and reactions to the adolescent can range from helplessness, anger, guilt, and sadness to utter frustration (Kress, Gibson, & Reynolds, 2004). Mental health professionals must continually monitor and manage their personal reactions and recognize their limitations—the ratio of support staff to students and other work demands that are placed on them. Practitioners should work with only a few RSM students at one time, identify and refer to experts in the community, share regularly with colleagues, and routinely seek collaborative support and guidance from supervisors.

## Legal and Ethical Issues

Practitioners often must weigh legal and ethical responsibilities when responding to a student engaging in SM. Froeschle and Moyer (2004) provided succinct recommendations to assist in responding to these issues:

- Clarify the limits of confidentiality with both students and parents. When students are at risk for self-harm (as in the case of SM), counselors have a duty to warn parents and may be in legal jeopardy for nondisclosure if a student who reports SM behavior to the counselor is later seriously injured or dies.
- Practitioners should teach the student the importance of communication with parents and role-play such interactions.
- Practitioners should recognize the limits of their abilities; maintain accurate and objective records; familiarize themselves with state law, statutes, district policies, and procedures; collaborate and confer with colleagues regularly to make decisions in the best interests

of their students; and maintain liability insurance coverage.

Finally, child sexual abuse and family violence are distinct risk factors for RSM. If at any time the practitioner has a suspicion of abuse, neglect, or maltreatment or feels that parent notification would place a child in more danger, local child protective services should be notified immediately.

***Warning parents.*** Contacting parents about their child's depression and SM behaviors must be done with patience, tolerance, and cultural sensitivity. Inevitably, parents can provide critical information that will assist in assessing the appropriate level of risk of their child's behavior that will help guide interventions. Table 3 summarizes the information to be gleaned during parent notification interviews. Table 4 provides some suggestions for parents whose child is engaging in SM. Family counseling can be critical to resolving communication and attachment issues that often may be at the root of SM (Kehrberg, 1997).

***Using no-harm agreements.*** No-harm agreements, also known in the literature as no-suicide contracts or individual safety plans, may assist an adolescent in taking control over harmful impulses by identifying trusted adults, alternative behaviors, help-seeking and communication skills, grief resolution activities, and links with community and district resources. These agreements should be part of a comprehensive plan to control SM and never be used as a sole intervention. In cases in which no-harm agreements are used, students who refuse to sign and cannot guarantee their own safety should be considered high risk and should be supervised and released to a parent or emergency personnel only.

## School-Based Interventions

In addition to intervention steps already discussed, recent treatment approaches that have applications for school-based personnel and have been effective in decreasing self-injury include building communication skills and learning to use behavioral alternatives (Dallam, 1997). These approaches can easily be incorporated into a student's no-harm agreement.

***Communication skill building.*** SM may serve as a means for an adolescent to communicate intense feelings of anguish to the world (Levenkron, 1998).

**Table 3** *Information to Gather Through Parent Interview*

1. Is the parent available?
2. Is the parent cooperative?
3. What is the child's previous mental health history?
4. Has the child ever tried to harm himself or herself before?
5. Has the child suffered recent losses?
6. Has the child ever been traumatized or victimized?
7. Does the family possess mental health insurance?

*Note.* From "Suicide Intervention," by S. Poland and R. Lieberman, 2002, in A. Thomas & J. Grimes (Eds.), *Best Practices in School Psychology IV* (pp. 1151–1167). Copyright by National Association of School Psychologists. Reprinted with permission.

Communication skill building is essential in helping a teen learn and develop healthier coping strategies when the stresses of life seem overwhelming. Adolescents should be encouraged to identify and talk with trusted adults at home or at school about self-injurious impulses. However, when adults are unavailable, the school practitioner can help the teen vent his or her emotions using written journals or art projects. One example of journaling is a "trigger log," which can be included in the student's no-harm agreement. Students record each time they engage in SM and identify the precipitating events. They can also compare their experiences to days they did not self-injure. Use of age-appropriate techniques such as play and clay and art work also is recommended to aid communication, particularly when working with younger, elementary school–age children.

***Tension release and alternative behaviors.*** Stress management and tension release exercises and substitute behaviors empower adolescents with alternatives to self-injury. The stress response is just that, *a response*, and students can realize that they have some control over their responses. Techniques such as diaphragmatic breathing, meditation, and visualization can be effective exercises to reduce tension. One of the best prescriptions for the treatment of depression that also provides tension release is physical exercise. Exercise lends itself well to no-harm agreements because goals can be short term ("Let's exercise today") and then gradually extended. Adolescents who can manage to exercise every day or every other day for 3 weeks will not only feel better (physically and about themselves); they will also sleep and eat better. Other physical exercises include flattening recycling cans; hitting a punching bag or bean bag; playing tennis,

**Table 4** *Suggestions for Parents Whose Child Is Engaging in SM Behaviors*

**DO:**

- Accept your child even though you do not accept his or her behavior.
- Let your child know you love him or her.
- Understand that this is your child's way of coping.
- Make your home a safe place by removing anything that could be used as a tool for self-injury.
- Encourage participation in extracurricular activities and outreach in the community (e.g., volunteering to work with animals, in nursing homes, tutoring, or mentoring).
- Reach out to the school and tighten the circle of care.

**DON'T:**

- Discourage self-injury, threaten hospitalization, use punishment or negative consequences.
- Overreact or say or do anything to cause guilt or shame, and never publicly humiliate your child.
- Forbid your child to see friends, but monitor whom he or she does see. Contact other parents.
- Overprotect or blame yourself for your child's behavior.

*Note.* Information from *See My Pain! Creative Strategies for Helping Young People Who Self-Injure*, by S. Bowman and K. Randall, 2004, Chapin, SC: Youthlight, Inc.

handball, or karate; walking or running; or ripping phone books.

Substitute behaviors have been discussed in the media but have not yet been found to be effective treatments for SM in the literature. Clinicians have reported anecdotally some success with patients who have been encouraged to substitute ice for a cutting implement or to snap a rubber band around the wrist when the impulse to self-injure overwhelms them. Holding books at arm's length or standing on tip toes until exhausted are other common suggestions. School mental health personnel are urged to fully discuss alternatives with parents and obtain their permission before incorporating any of these substitute activities in a no-harm agreement.

***School interventions to limit contagion.*** Because contagion may play a role in SM, it is prudent to disseminate materials carefully when responding to an outbreak of SM in the school population. Educators must refrain from school-wide communications in the form of general assemblies or intercom announcements. Health educators should reconsider the classroom presentation of certain popular movies and music videos that glamorize such behaviors and instead seek appropriate messages in the music and movies of artists who are popular with students. When students within a particular peer group are referred together, it is appropriate to divide the group up among different support staff and respond to each adolescent individually. When numerous members of one peer group are referred, a leader, the alpha female or male, may be identified whose behavior may be setting others off. As a rule, school mental health professionals should refrain from running specific groups that focus on cutting; however, groups that focus on empowerment, exercise and tension release, or grief resolution are worthwhile alternatives.

## Community-Based Treatments

No single, correct therapeutic approach to SM has been identified in the literature. Although prevention appears to be the best form of treatment for SM, biological, psychosocial, and behavioral therapies have been used with some success (Favazza, 1996).

***Biological.*** Biological explanations for SM have focused on neurotransmitters in the brain and lowered functioning of serotonin. Prozac (fluoxetine), Paxil (paroxetine), and Zoloft (sertraline) are classified as SSRIs (selective serotonin reuptake inhibitors) and are the most frequently prescribed medications for adolescent depression and anxiety despite a growing concern of side reactions. Although published studies of the efficacy of SSRIs in the treatment of SM are few, they are consistently positive. SSRIs do not selectively treat SM but rather affect impulsivity and compulsivity. There are reports of their effectiveness in treating SM, nail biting, skin picking, scratching, and hair pulling (Hawton et al, 1998; Coccaro, Kavoussi, & Hauger, 1997).

***Psychosocial.*** Much has been published to outline the general principles of treatment of SM from a psychosocial perspective. Tantam and Whitaker (1992, cited in Favazza, 1996) reviewed the literature and suggested several treatment principles. First, the counselor should focus on forming and maintaining a working relationship with the client that includes clear limits. Second, the counselor should focus on helping the client stop the behavior, which is defined as a habit. Third, the counselor should assist the client in developing alternative, more effective means of expressing emotion and resolving conflicts.

***Behavioral.*** Cognitive–behavioral therapy (CBT) and dialectical behavioral therapy (DBT) have received empirical support in the treatment of SM. CBT seeks to connect thoughts, feelings, and behaviors in patients exhibiting SM. The process can be facilitated by redirecting the adolescents' attention away from environmental conflicts and toward their own controllable thoughts. Patients are guided to cope with overwhelming emotions by speaking about them, not acting on impulses to self-injure. They are trained to replace negative perceptions with a focus on their positive qualities and on aspects of their world in which they do have some control. CBT seeks to help the student make sense of self-injury.

Recent findings from the Treatment for Adolescents with Depression Study are consistent with work suggesting that CBT has a specific beneficial effect on self-injurious behaviors and, more importantly, that CBT combined with Prozac may confer a protective effect not only against suicidal ideation but also on SM and other harm-related behaviors (March et al., 2004).

Linehan (1993) pioneered DBT in her work with patients diagnosed with borderline personality disorder. DBT involves a structured combination of skills training and group and individual psychotherapy and addresses a hierarchical structure of treatment goals with clients. The focus is on first reducing high-risk behaviors, followed by learning to cope with post-traumatic stress responses, enhancing self-respect, and developing alternative coping skills. In weekly psychotherapy sessions, a particular problematic behavior or event from the past week is explored in detail, beginning with the chain of events leading up to it, going through alternative solutions that might have been used, and examining what kept the client from using more adaptive solutions to the problem. Both between and during sessions, the therapist actively teaches and reinforces adaptive behaviors, especially as they occur within the therapeutic relationship. The emphasis is on teaching clients how to manage emotional trauma rather than reducing or taking them out of crises. Telephone contact between the client and the therapist between sessions is part of DBT procedures. Linehan has documented success in reducing patients' parasuicidal, life-threatening, and self-injurious behaviors as well as reducing behaviors that interfere with the treatment process. School mental health personnel must become aware of the expertise that exists in their communities, especially for identifying therapists trained in CBT and DBT when responding to some of the most severe cases of students exhibiting RSM.

## SUMMARY

SM is a puzzling, disturbing, and poorly understood behavior. The overwhelming number of students engaging in some form of SM presents a significant challenge to school-based mental health personnel. With an onset in early adolescence, and with higher rates among females, SM has been associated with many disorders. SM is a complex behavior, with both compulsive and impulsive characteristics, that appears to fulfill a multitude of needs for the self-injurer. The family environments of SM students can be chaotic, abusive, and dysfunctional, and a history of being sexually abused and witnessing family violence have been identified as significant risk factors in SM. One widely accepted theory views these students as being unable to tolerate or express emotions, and as, at times, seeking a rapid respite from distressing thoughts, feelings, and tensions by engaging in repetitive SM. SM can have both organic and behavioral components that foster repetition. Cutting and burning are the most common forms of self-injury found in non-hospitalized populations. SM appears to be episodic, and is often performed ritualistically in isolation and culminates in pervasive feelings of shame and guilt. The typical SM adolescent female conceals her wounds well and takes great pains to appear normal and uninjured to others at school.

School mental health practitioners must be prepared to identify these students, effectively communicate with parents, and refer them to the appropriate, culturally responsive community mental health agency. In addition, school professionals can implement a myriad of school-based interventions that focus on teaching appropriate communication skills and tension release and coping skills. Professionals aim to "tighten the circle of care" that surrounds the student by educating school staff and parents and by facilitating communication among the adolescent, the school, the home, and the community mental health agency. In addition to identifying, advocating for, and referring the students, school professionals must be knowledgeable and skilled in developing and coordinating primary prevention programs, educating adults in the school community, assessing for suicidal tendencies, understanding the complex legal and ethical issues related to SM, establishing no-harm agreements, and providing guidance to school mental health staff on treatments and individual and group interventions. Finally, continued research is needed on interventions for adolescents with depression and impulse disorders, including SM, parasuicidal behaviors, and alcohol and substance abuse.

## RECOMMENDED RESOURCES

### Books and Other Printed Material

Alderman, T. (1997). *The scarred soul: Understanding and ending self-inflicted violence.* Oakland, CA: New Harbinger Press.

This book was one of the first written for victims of self-inflicted violence that sought to teach them what they could do to stop hurting themselves.

Favazza, A. (1996). *Bodies under siege* (2nd ed.). Baltimore, MD: Johns Hopkins University Press.

The American Medical Association has referred to this text as the most comprehensive historical, anthropological, ethnological, and clinical account of self-mutilation.

Levenkron, S. (1998). *Cutting: Understanding and overcoming self-mutilation.* New York: W.W. Norton.

With many examples from his practice, Levenkron provides clear and comprehensive information on the causes and effective treatments of self-mutilation.

### Websites and Other Contacts

*http://www.selfinjury.org*

ASHIC—the American Self-Harm Information Clearinghouse—strives to increase public awareness of the phenomenon of self-inflicted violence and the unique challenges faced by self-injurers and the people who care about them. This website provides assistance, outreach, and public education about self-harm.

*http://www.palace.net/llama/selfinjury/*

This page, maintained by Deb Martinson, provides comprehensive outreach, resources, and information on self-injury. Interactive pages include web boards, self-assessment questionnaires, and links to off- and online resources and downloads.

*Crisis Hotline Numbers: These numbers provide callers with immediate crisis response, information, and resources.*
(800)-SUICIDE and (800)-DONTCUT

## REFERENCES


Alderman, T. (1997). *The scarred soul: Understanding and ending self-inflicted violence.* Oakland, CA: New Harbinger Press.

Aseltine, T., & DeMartino, R. (2004). An outcome evaluation of the SOS Suicide Prevention Program. *American Journal of Public Health, 94,* 446–451.

Bearman, P., & Moody, J. (2004). Suicide and friendships among American adolescents. *American Journal of Public Health, 94,* 89–95.

Boudewyn, A., & Liem, J. (1995). Childhood sexual abuse as a precursor to depression and self-destructive behavior in adulthood. *Journal of Traumatic Stress, 8,* 445–459.

Bowman, S., & Randall, K. (2004). *See my pain! Creative strategies for helping young people who self-injure.* Chapin, SC: Youthlight, Inc.

Briere, J., & Gil, E. (1998). Self-mutilation in clinical and general population samples: Prevalence correlates and functions. *American Journal of Orthopsychiatry, 68,* 609–620.

Brock, S. E., Lazarus, P. J., & Jimerson, S. E. (2002). *Best practices in school crisis prevention and intervention.* Bethesda, MD: National Association of School Psychologists.

Coccaro, E. F., Kavoussi, R. J., & Hauger, R. L. (1997). Serotonin function and antiaggressive response to fluoxetine: A pilot study. *Biological Psychiatry, 42,* 546–552.

Conterio, K., & Lader, W. (1998). *Bodily harm.* New York: Hyperion Press.

Dallam, S. (1997). The identification and management of self-mutilating patients in primary care. *The Nurse Practitioner, 22,* 151–164.

Darche, M. A. (1990). Psychological factors differentiating self-mutilating and non-mutilating adolescent inpatient females. *Psychiatric Hospital, 2,* 31–35.

Favazza, A. R. (1989). Why patients mutilate themselves. *Hospital Community Psychiatry, 40,* 137–145.

Favazza, A. (1996). *Bodies under siege* (2nd ed.). Baltimore, MD: Johns Hopkins University Press.

Favazza, A. R. (1998). The coming of age of self-mutilation. *Journal of Nervous and Mental Disease, 186,* 259–268.

Favazza, A., & Conterio, K. (1988). The plight of chronic self-mutilators. *Community Mental Health, 24,* 22–30.

Favazza, A., DeRosear, L., & Conterio, K. (1989). Self-mutilation and eating disorders. *Suicide and Life-Threatening Behaviors, 19,* 352–361.

Favazza, A., & Rosenthal, R. (1993). Diagnostic issues in self-mutilation. *Hospital and Community Psychiatry, 44,* 134–140.

Froeschle, J., & Moyer, M. (2004). Just cut it out: Legal and ethical challenges in counseling students who self-mutilate. *Professional School Counseling, 7,* 231–236.

Grunbaum, J., Kann, L, Kinchen, S., Ross, J., Hawkins, J., Lowry, R., et al. (2003). *Youth risk behavior surveillance—United States, 2003.* Atlanta: Centers for Disease Control and Prevention, National Center for Injury Prevention and Control. *Surveillance summaries,* May 21, 2004. MMWR 2004;53(No. SS-2). Retrieved May 9, 2005, from http://www.cdc.gov/HealthyYouth/yrbs/

Hawton, K., Arensman, E., Townsend, E., Bremner, S., Feldman, E., Goldney, R., et al. (1998). Deliberate self-harm: Systematic review of efficacy of psychosocial and pharmacological treatments in preventing repetition. *British Medical Journal (Clinical Research Edition), 317* (7156), 441–447.

Kehrberg, C. (1997). Self-mutilating behavior. *Journal of Child and Adolescent Psychiatric Nursing, 10,* 35–40.

Kress, V., Gibson, D., & Reynolds, C. (2004). Adolescents who self-injure: Implications and strategies for school counselors. *Professional School Counseling, 7,* 195–202.

Langbehn, D., & Pfohl, B. (1993). Clinical correlates of self-mutilation among psychiatric patients. *Annals of Clinical Psychiatry, 5,* 45–51.

Levenkron, S. (1998). *Cutting: Understanding and overcoming self-mutilation.* New York: W.W. Norton.

Lieberman, R. (2004). Understanding and responding to students who self-mutilate. *National Association of Secondary School Principals: Principal Leadership, 4*(7), 10–13.

Linehan, M. M. (1993). *Cognitive–behavioral treatment of borderline personality disorder.* New York: Guilford Press.

March, J., Silva, S., Petrycki, S., Curry, J., Wells, K., Fairbank, J., et al. (2004). Fluoxetine, cognitive–behavioral therapy, and their combination for adolescents with depression: Treatment for Adolescents with Depression Study (TADS) randomized controlled trial. *Journal of the American Medical Association, 292,* 807–820.

McLane, J. (1996). The voice on the skin: Self-mutilation and Merleau-Ponty's theory of language. *Hypatia, 11,* 107–121.

Moscicki, E. K. (1995). Epidemiology of suicidal behavior. *Suicide and Life-Threatening Behavior, 25,* 22–35.

National Institute of Mental Health. (2002). *Mental health and mass violence: Evidence-based early psychological intervention for victims/survivors of mass violence. A workshop to reach consensus on best practices* (NIH Publication No. 02-5138). Washington, DC: U.S. Government Printing Office.

Pies, R., & Popli, A. (1995). Self-injurious behavior: Psychopathology and implication for treatment. *Journal of Clinical Psychiatry, 56,* 580–588.

Poland, S., & Lieberman, R. A. (2002). Suicide intervention. In A. Thomas & J. Grimes (Eds.), *Best practices in school psychology IV* (pp. 1151–1167). Bethesda, MD: National Association of School Psychologists.

Poland, S., & McCormick, J. (1999). *Coping with crisis: Lessons learned.* Longmont, CO: Sopris West.

Ross, S., & Heath, N. (2002). A study of the frequency of self-mutilation in a community sample of adolescents. *Journal of Youth and Adolescence, 3,* 67–77.

Simeon, D., & Hollander, E. (Eds.). (2001). *Self-injurious behaviors: Assessment and treatment.* Washington, DC: American Psychiatric Publishing.

Suyemoto, K. L., & Macdonald, M. (1995). Self-cutting in female adolescents. *Psychotherapy, 32,* 162–171.

Tantam, D., & Whitaker, J. (1992). Personality disorder and self-wounding. *British Journal of Psychiatry, 161,* 451–464.

Turell, S., & Armsworth, M. (2000). Differentiating incest survivors who self-mutilate. *Child Abuse & Neglect, 24,* 237–249.

U.S. Department of Health and Human Services. (2001). *National strategy for suicide prevention: Goals and objectives for action* (SMA01-3517). Rockville, MD: U.S. Department of Health and Human Services, Substance Abuse and Mental Health Services Administration, Center for Mental Health Services, National Institutes of Health, National Institute of Mental Health. Retrieved May 9, 2005, from http://www.mentalhealth.org/publications/allpubs/SMA01-3517

Walsh, B., & Rosen, P. (1988). *Self-mutilation: Theory, research and treatment.* New York: Guilford Press.

Webster, L., & Browning, J. (2002). Child maltreatment. In S. E. Brock, P. J. Lazarus, & S. R. Jimerson, *Best practices in school crisis prevention and intervention* (pp. 503–530). Bethesda, MD: National Association of School Psychologists.

World Health Organization (2000). *Preventing suicide: A resource for teachers.* Geneva: Author. Retrieved May 9, 2005, from http://www.who.int/mental_health/media/en/62.pdf

Zila, L., & Kiselica, M. (2001). Understanding and counseling self-mutilation in female adolescents and young adults. *Journal of Counseling and Development, 29,* 46–52.

# 73

# Adolescent Eating Disorders

**Catherine Cook-Cottone**

**LeAdelle Phelps**

*State University of New York at Buffalo*

## BACKGROUND AND DEVELOPMENT

Eating disordered behaviors continue to be significant medical and psychological concerns for today's practitioner (Neumark-Sztainer, Wall, Story, & Perry, 2003). For decades, the media-driven perpetuation of the ideal body as thin has created a deleterious cultural context in which body dissatisfaction is normative and eating disorder symptomatology epidemic (Cook-Cottone & Phelps, 2003). Specifically, adolescent eating disordered behavior is characterized by an intense preoccupation to be thin, accompanied by a pathological fear of gaining weight, that is manifest in severe disturbances in eating behavior (i.e., self-starvation, food restriction, purging of food, and/or cyclic binging and purging of food). *The Diagnostic and Statistical Manual of Mental Disorders, Fourth Edition, Text Revision* (DSM-IV-TR; American Psychiatric Association, 2000) currently lists two specific diagnoses: anorexia nervosa (AN) and bulimia nervosa (BN).

### Anorexia Nervosa

According to the DSM-IV-TR individuals diagnosed with AN refuse to maintain a minimally normal body weight (i.e., 85% of normal weight for a person's age and height), are intensely afraid of gaining weight, and demonstrate a significant perceptual disturbance regarding the size or shape of their body. Younger children may not experience loss of weight; rather, they fail to make expected weight gains as they increase in age and height. Primarily, individuals with AN pursue or maintain excessively low body weight through a reduction in food intake, or *food restriction.* However, other methods may include self-induced vomiting, misuse of laxatives or diuretics, and excessive exercise. Accordingly, the DSM-IV-TR provides for diagnostic specificity of two subtypes: restricting type (weight loss is accomplished primarily through restriction) and binge-eating/purging type (regular episodes of purging with or without binging). The statistics regarding prevalence are not encouraging, and many believe that the social stigma and secrecy associated with eating disordered behavior, especially in male populations, may contribute to an underestimation of true prevalence rates (Ray, 2004). The prevalence rate of AN in young females is approximately 3 to 5 per 1,000 (Hoek & van Hoeken, 2003), and the prevalence rate among young males is approximately 3 per 10,000 (American Psychiatric Association, 2000). Moreover, from 1953 to 1999, mortality rates for those diagnosed with AN averaged around 5%. Of the survivors, less than 50% recover, 33% improve but are not considered recovered, and 20% remain chronically ill (Steinhausen, 2002).

### Bulimia Nervosa

Individuals with BN manifest recurrent episodes of binge eating, use inappropriate compensatory behaviors to prevent weight gain (e.g., self-induced vomiting; misuse of laxatives, diuretics, or enemas; fasting; or obligatory exercise), and place an excessive emphasis on body shape and weight in their self-evaluation (American Psychiatric Association, 2000). Diagnostic criteria allow for the identification of two subtypes: purging type (regular engagement in the use of vomiting, laxatives, diuretics, or enemas) and nonpurging type (use of other compensatory behaviors such as fasting or exercise; American Psychiatric Association). The prevalence rate for BN is estimated at 1 in 100 for young women and 1 in 1,000 for young men (Hoek & van Hoeken, 2003). Outcomes have been relatively promising, with evidence of up to 75% of those diagnosed not meeting criteria at 5 years (Ben-Tovim, 2003).

### Developmental Considerations

The development of risk can be best conceptualized by a multifaceted developmental model in which individual factors (e.g., gender, emotional regulation, and specific physiological tendencies) and particular familial characteristics (e.g., lack of emotional validation and a focus on image or appearance) interact, creating a vulnerability that is expressed, in Westernized cultures, as eating disordered behavior. This pathogenic developmental trajectory involves a process in which individual vulnerabilities and familial experiences lead to difficulties with self-regulation and care, primarily involving behaviors linked to food intake and nutrition. Furthermore, these difficulties manifest within the context of a limited and disordered experience of the self, wherein physical appearance is disproportionably attended to and simultaneously assessed based on a gradually internalized set of unattainable and unhealthy standards. The result is a self-perpetuating disorder. Self-regulation and dissatisfaction become the central organizing features of the individual's life. In brief, the experience of the self is diminished almost solely to dissatisfaction with and control of the body (i.e., food restriction and binging and/or purging).

The trajectory toward risk can begin quite early in the child's development. However, initial diagnostic symptoms typically present in the early to mid-adolescent years, and childhood onset is rare (American Psychiatric Association, 2000). Though many predisposing factors may have been present for some time, manifestation of the clinical disorder requires, at least, later childhood cognitive and physiological development. That is, many of the diagnostic symptoms reflect more developmentally sophisticated cognitive processing. For example, in AN two of the four and in BN one of the five diagnostic criteria describe symptoms that involve evaluative and comparative thought (e.g., self-evaluation unduly influenced by weight and fear of becoming fat; American Psychiatric Association). Moreover, other criteria allude to cognitively mediated experiences or behaviors as well as the internal representation of an abstract ideal. Such cognitive processes are characteristic of later concrete operational or formal operative thought (e.g., a sense of lack of control and compensatory behaviors in BN, and refusal to maintain body weight in AN; American Psychiatric Association).

Physiological implications of these factors are twofold. First, as the young adolescent is becoming increasingly capable of comparative and evaluative thought, physical changes associated with puberty are emerging, creating a developmental period of unique vulnerability (Williams & Currie, 2000). Second, the final diagnostic criterion for AN depends entirely on later childhood physiological development: amenorrhea in postmenarchal females (American Psychiatric Association, 2000). The relative contributions of cognitive and physiological development change with age. That is, once an individual is capable of more advanced cognitive processes, the timing of clinical onset depends less on cognitive and physiological developmental issues and more on external influences. For example, this earlier period of vulnerability is followed by a later window of risk during the transition from adolescence to young adulthood (e.g., the transition to college; Cook-Cottone & Phelps, 2003).

Gender is a strong risk factor. Whereas a small proportion of clinical cases are male, 90% of individuals diagnosed with AN and BN are female (American Psychiatric Association, 2000). The cultural context appears to be involved in gender difference; the media-propagated thin ideal targets mainly women, with men presented at more normal weights. Also, subcultural effects may be apparent, as both females and males show increases in vulnerability and incidence in specific weight-sensitive athletic or social contexts (e.g, wrestling, boxing, ballet dancing, gymnastics, and possibly in the gay culture; e.g., Patel, Greydanus, Pratt, & Phillips, 2003). Though considerably less research has been done on males and eating disordered behavior, there is some evidence that risk factors for males include history of obesity, involvement in athletic activities, sexual identity conflict, comorbid mental disorders, familial history of eating disorders, and family chaos (American Psychiatric Association; Ray, 2004). The pathogenic developmental trajectory is thought to be similar for both genders (Ray); however, the research on eating disorders is based almost exclusively on female populations.

## PROBLEMS AND IMPLICATIONS

Programs designed for primary prevention (aimed at reducing the incidence of new cases) and secondary prevention (aimed at early identification and intervention prior to the onset of clinical disorder) must address each ecological dimension that contributes to the eating disordered developmental trajectory (Piran, 2001a), namely, cultural ideals and pressures, familial factors, and factors related to self.

## Contributing Cultural Characteristics

For years, researchers have cited the decreasing sizes of models and beauty pageant contestants in Westernized cultures and described the implicit message that to be beautiful, even acceptable, one must be thin (Cook-Cottone & Phelps, 2003). It is now well accepted that Westernized culture beholds thinness as ideal, and the media is accordingly abundant with extremely thin female representations (e.g., Tiggemann & Slater, 2004). Research documenting what appears to be a causal media influence continues to accumulate, including meta-analyses, experimental research, and cultural studies. To illustrate, a recent meta-analysis found that thin media images reliably led to increases in body image dissatisfaction (Groesz, Levine, & Murnen, 2002). In addition, using an experimental 2×2 factorial design, Tiggeman and Slater (2004) found that viewing music videos featuring thin women increased both social comparison and body dissatisfaction. Also, in an interesting study of the introduction of television into a culture, Becker, Burwell, Gilman, Herzog, and Hamburg (2002) measured the eating disordered behavior of two cohorts of Fijian adolescents: one cohort had been exposed to television for only a few weeks and the other cohort had been exposed for 3 years. Those who had been exposed to more television manifested higher levels of eating disordered behaviors (11%) than the group more recently exposed to television (none). Consequently, many believe that the media should be considered a causal factor in the development of body dissatisfaction and eating disordered behavior.

## Familial Factors

It has long been accepted that the family environment is a significant factor in the development of healthy psychological functioning (Davis, Shuster, Blackmore, & Fox, 2004). In findings specific to eating disorders, positive family relationships may protect, or insulate, children and adolescents from body dissatisfaction and eating disordered behavior (Byely, Archibald, Graber, & Brooks-Gunn, 2000) and foster the development of autonomous emotional regulation and healthy coping and problem-solving skills (Wisniewski & Kelly, 2003). Conversely, familial environment can also contribute to risk (Davis et al.). Eating disordered symptomatology has been associated with familial factors such as low levels of parental caring, low familial communication, and incidence of physical and sexual abuse (e.g., Wonderlich et al., 2001). These familial experiences are believed to be invalidating and incongruous with children's internal physiological and emotional experiences, and thus to perpetuate a tendency to overuse external stimuli (e.g., reactions, statements, and standards of others) and disregard internal stimuli (e.g., physiological states and emotions; Wisniewski & Kelly). Family members may also place children and adolescents at risk by modeling a preoccupation with physical appearance and eating disordered behavior (e.g., Davis et al.).

## Factors Related to Self

Risk factors related to individual vulnerability include problems associated with self-regulation, set point–related physiological disruptions, dieting, onset of puberty, and the disordered development of self-concept. For each child and adolescent at risk for manifesting eating disordered behavior, the respective contributions of the individual factors may vary proportionally. However, each is critical to prevention efforts focused on general and at-risk populations.

***Self-regulation.*** Functionally, eating disordered behavior may emerge, in part, from the subjective experience of dysregulation. In typical development, self-regulation evolves throughout the childhood and adolescent years. Though parenting and nurturing experiences are believed to play a role, the development of self-regulating behaviors may also be influenced by individual physiological differences (Wisniewski & Kelly, 2003). There is some evidence that these physiological differences may manifest as a heightened sensitivity to emotional and physiological stimuli and can place children and adolescents at increased risk for eating disordered behavior (Wisniewski & Kelly). Correlational as well as long-term prospective studies have found characteristics such as emotional sensitivity, reactivity, and impulsivity to be associated with body dissatisfaction as well as eating disordered behavior (e.g., Wonderlich et al., 2001).

Individuals with eating disorders may also experience a disruption in the hunger and satiety signaling systems (Wisniewski & Kelly, 2003). It may be that those at risk for eating disordered behavior do not experience, perceive, or interpret hunger and satiation signals accurately, causing disruption in, or dysregulation of, the self-nourishing process. It is not yet clear to what degree premorbid hunger and satiety difficulties play a role in placing individuals at risk or if the disruptions are more a result of familial invalidation or unresponsiveness, chronic dieting, eating disordered behaviors, or a combination of these factors.

***Set point theory.*** For some time, *set point* theory—the body's homeostatic tendency toward a genetically predetermined set point, or healthy weight range—has been implicated as playing a role in the risk for and onset of eating disordered behavior. According to the theory, the set point causes the body to metabolically adjust to variations in food intake, or fuel consumption (e.g., Goodman & Villapiano, 2002). For example, for individuals with a higher relative set point range (e.g., 125–140 pounds for a 5′1″ frame), losing weight to 115 pounds or lower might trigger metabolic adjustments (e.g., lowered metabolism or redistribution of body warming resources). Furthermore, at weights significantly below the set point range, symptoms can become more severe (e.g., hair loss, headaches, dizziness, sleep disturbance, weakness, edema or fluid retention, sensitivity to light and noise, and general gastrointestinal discomfort; Goodman & Villapiano). Because it is an individual process, someone with a lower set point, but the same height and weight, may not demonstrate any symptoms. Evidence suggests that individuals with a higher set point may be at greater risk, because lower weights, those closer to the thin ideal, are more difficult for them to maintain (e.g., Goodman & Villapiano). However, metabolic processes are difficult to study and involve many variables, thus the existence of a set point that homeostatically controls body weight is not yet considered a certainty (Macias, 2004).

***Drive for thinness and dieting.*** Previously considered a phenomenon that manifests in the later adolescent years, dieting behaviors have become apparent at increasingly younger ages. For example, half of an 8- to 10-year-old sample reported dieting at least some of the time (Thomas, Ricciardelli, & Williams, 2000). The function of early dieting has not been well explored; however, its presence appears to create significant risk for later eating disordered behavior (Thomas et al.). Notably, dieting behavior may be the earliest eating-related behavioral indicator of risk. Its manifestation may reflect the child's early eating and body-related attempts at self-control, critical self-analysis, and externalization of self-assessment.

Food restriction and dieting have also been implicated in exacerbating the experience of metabolic dysregulation. In *diet-induced thermogenesis*, it is believed that as food intake is decreased, metabolic processes such as temperature regulation (e.g., decreases in overall body temperature) and heat distribution vary accordingly in order to conserve energy (Goodman & Villapiano, 2002). Individuals often manifest lower body temperature and may feel cold. Because fuel consumption is targeted toward heating vital organs, they may complain of having cold hands and feet. Researchers also theorize that a period of caloric restriction may be followed by a rebound effect. That is, caloric restriction is followed by a persistent reduction in metabolic activity, accompanied by a tendency toward higher fuel consumption and a consequent increase in weight (Goodman & Villapiano). Collectively, these experiences may add to the sense of physiological dysregulation felt by those at risk for eating disordered behavior. However, metabolic responses to caloric intake are still not well understood and may depend on a variety of factors, including age, gender, stress, and hormonal cycles (Macias, 2004).

***Pubertal onset.*** At the onset of puberty, the associated hormonal cycles, physical changes, and shifts in social response can create, or further increase, subjective feelings of dysregulation and may be a trigger for body dissatisfaction. Specifically, hormonal and physical changes can occur quite quickly, creating a discontinuous experience of self (Piran, 2001b), and may be accompanied by many social implications (Piran; Williams & Currie, 2000). Generally, a child's physical growth and developmental experience, after the toddler years, is a relatively continuous process until puberty, when the body changes not only in size but in shape and function (e.g., increase in body fat, development of breasts and menstruation). Also, the emergence of secondary sexual characteristics is often accompanied by a more sexualized social response when others begin to see the individual as a young woman (including the sexual aspects of womanhood) rather than as a child. This change brings with it the cultural and social inequities suffered by women, especially in terms of the experience of body (Piran). The individual timing of pubertal onset may be particularly important regarding risk for body dissatisfaction and eating disordered behavior (Williams & Currie). Ohring, Graber, and Brooks-Gunn (2002) suggested that girls who experience early puberty have less time to develop cognitively and psychologically and also experience a more stressful social context because many male and female peers have not manifested pubertal changes.

For individuals developing disordered eating behaviors, the physical changes associated with pubertal onset may trigger body dissatisfaction and consequent dieting as changes in shape and increases in body fat and weight are evaluated in terms of the thin ideal (Littleton & Ollendick, 2003). Many researchers believe that increases in eating disordered behavior are related to the rapid accumulation of body fat, over which young girls have little or no control (e.g., Gowers & Shore, 2001). This combination of the adolescent's awareness of the thin ideal and the body's growing discrepancy from that ideal, with a seemingly uncontrollable increase in body fat, may create an overwhelming experience and set the stage for experimentation with eating disordered behavior.

***Self-concept.*** Variations in self-concept appear to be related to risk for body dissatisfaction, dieting, and eating disordered symptomatology (Geller, Zaitsoff, & Srikameswaran, 2002; Jacobi, Paul, deZwaan, Nutzinger, & Dahme, 2004). Specifically, risk appears to be related to the breadth, depth, and quality of schemata upon which a child or adolescent bases his or her individual assessment of self. For individuals with eating disorders, the shape and weight of the body become unduly important, and for some, the sole determinant of self-worth (American Psychiatric Association, 2000). In brief, the more the assessment of self converges on appearance and size, the more at risk the child. The developmental roots of this tendency are multifaceted and complex and may extend back to the early childhood years.

The reduction of self-concept to acceptability of the body occurs over time and within the context of many formative familial and cultural experiences. Invalidating familial or interpersonal experiences can create a tendency toward the use of external indictors of well-being (Wisniewski & Kelly, 2003). Children learn that the ability to assess situations, problems, even emotions does not lie within themselves. The many empirical findings associating risk and symptomatology to lack of competence and effectiveness (e.g., Jacobi et al., 2004) may be related to this developmental risk factor. Over time, repeated experiences emphasizing the importance of reliance on external signals combined with cultural (media images and messages) and even subcultural (encouragement to maintain a ballet figure or a low gymnastic weight) cues can result in a child's passionate and ego-syntonic assessment of self that is based disproportionately on appearance or size. Conversely, an environment that encourages autonomous assessment of internal states and validates children's needs allows the child to develop a sense of inner competence and to value his or her own inner experience as important when making choices and assessing self (Wisniewski & Kelly). Furthermore, children and adolescents who develop competency-based determinants of self-concept are at less risk as appearance and size take up a smaller proportion of the overall self-assessment (e.g., Geller et al., 2002).

## ALTERNATIVE ACTIONS FOR PREVENTION

Research on effective prevention of body dissatisfaction, dieting, and eating disordered behavior has evolved over the past 10 years. The growing base of empirical knowledge has informed the process of implementation and administration as well as the content of prevention programs. Specifically, the implementation process is gradually shifting from a primarily psychoeducational model toward an experiential and constructive model. Research also has explored effective administrative procedures, such as the best practices for mixed gender participation and integration of primary and secondary prevention efforts. In addition, the curricular content of prevention programs, once an inclusive list of the health risks associated with eating disorder behaviors, has undergone a paradigm shift as well. Much of the content is now shaped by positive psychology ideals and is geared toward the creation and fortification of resiliency.

### Changing Models of Prevention Program Format

In the current state of practice of eating disorder prevention, many practitioners implement a primarily psychoeducational model, use a mixed gender format, and see primary and secondary efforts as distinct. More recently, alternative models that emphasize active and constructive learning, single gender learning environments, and a pragmatic view of primary and secondary prevention efforts have emerged, and early results are promising.

***Psychoeducation.*** The most common prevention strategy for body dissatisfaction and disordered eating has been psychoeducation (Littleton & Ollendick, 2003). However, the efficacy of this strategy is questionable

(Ben-Tovim, 2003). For example, psychoeducational prevention programs have shown disappointing results, with the average effect size from pre- to posttest for eating disorders at a very small $d = .08$ (Littleton & Ollendick).

The primary shortcoming of the prevention programs we reviewed was the assumption that risk for body dissatisfaction and disordered eating was related to lack of knowledge about healthy eating and the negative consequences of engaging in eating disordered behaviors. Conversely, psychoeducational approaches that included critical analyses of media, the thin ideal, the representation of women in the media, and image editing have shown positive effects (Stice & Ragan, 2002). However, given the limited effectiveness of most psychoeducational approaches, the prevention community has moved toward cooperative, interactive, and participatory learning (e.g., Wade, Davidson, & O'Dea, 2003).

***Constructivism and learning by doing.*** In some cases, pure didactic delivery has been supplemented by interactive processes such as homework assignments, role-playing, and small group discussions (Littleton & Ollendick, 2003). Early findings suggest that these approaches have promise. For example, in a study of intervention groups that required a more active and constructive engagement of participants, researchers found decreases in thin-ideal internalization, negative affect, and bulimic symptoms at 1-, 3-, and 6-month follow-ups (Stice, Trost, & Chase, 2003).

***Gender diversity in participants.*** Currently, findings vary with regard to choosing single versus mixed gender format for prevention efforts. Although no empirically based conclusions have been presented at this time, early recommendations suggest mixed gender groups may be most suitable for younger children and when content is focused on new knowledge about nutrition and weight (Piran, 2001a). However, when discussions and activities are related specifically to the individual experience of body, a single gender group may provide a safer and more supportive context for learning (e.g., Phelps, Nathanson, Nelson, Sapia, & Dempsey, 2000). This may be especially true for middle school and high school students (Piran).

***Primary and secondary prevention efforts.*** Primary and secondary prevention efforts for eating disorders have been traditionally conceptualized as two separate processes. Primary prevention efforts focus on the promotion and maintenance of healthy development and the prevention of eating disordered attitudes and behaviors (i.e., before they begin). Secondary prevention efforts target the identification and correction of eating disordered attitudes and behaviors in the very early stages before full clinical disorders manifest. Primary and secondary levels of prevention may have unique developmental applications (see Piran, 2001a, from which the following discussion is drawn). Specifically, primary prevention programs that address acceptance of diversity in natural weights and healthy lifestyle choices may be most effective when completed in the lower elementary years before the individual's preoccupation with body shape and weight crystallize and become entrenched within the construct of self and social life. In later grades, prevention processes can be viewed more as helping students create a "stance of resistance toward adverse social prejudices and mores" (p. 261).

According to some clinical evidence, it may be efficacious, especially in the school setting, to combine primary and secondary prevention efforts. Because of the low prevalence rates of these disorders, secondary prevention programs may not be pragmatically feasible in other than exceptionally high-risk populations (Ben-Tovim, 2003). Also, combining prevention and early intervention efforts helps eliminate the stigma associated with attending a group as the focus is shifted to creating resiliency and wellness. Furthermore, as participants are identified as being preoccupied with body weight and shape or present with symptoms, they can be referred for individual treatment throughout the group process.

## Prevention Group Content Consistent with Positive Psychology Ideals

Recently, a paradigm shift has taken place in regard to the prevention of body dissatisfaction, dieting, and eating disordered behaviors (see Steck, Abrams, & Phelps, 2004, for a detailed discussion of the following). Historically, prevention programs have focused on the amelioration or attenuation of empirically identified risk factors and problematic behaviors. However, the risk and problem behavior approach has not proved to be a consistently effective prevention strategy. What was a well-meaning review of "warning signs" at times became a young girl's first exposure to eating disorder techniques and behaviors. That is, presentation of eating disorder information (e.g., on purging techniques and extreme dieting behaviors) may potentially contribute to onset of eating disorder symptomatology. Quite differently, a positive psychology approach to prevention focuses on enhancing empirically identified resiliency factors. Steck et al. believe that enhancing protective factors promotes wellness more effectively. In addition, by focusing on building wellness, the potential risks associated with participating in prevention groups are reduced as participants are no longer exposed to a list of dieting and purging "warning signs" (Cook-Cottone & Phelps, 2003).

***Media literacy.*** Media literacy, or the ability to critically evaluate media messages, has been a focus of many recent prevention efforts (e.g., Cook-Cottone, Kane, Scime, & Beck, 2004). Media literacy skills have been theorized to be the protective factor associated with attenuating the effects of media exposure (e.g., Wade et al., 2003). This approach deconstructs the media's presentation of the thin ideal, representative stereotyping of female societal roles, marketing motivations, image editing techniques, and consumer effects (Cook-Cottone et al.). For example, Stice et al. (2003), using an active problem-solving approach to media literacy, addressed the issue in a three-session dissonance intervention program in which the adolescent female participants (ages 13–20) were asked to help develop a body acceptance program for younger girls. In the first session, participants collectively defined the thin ideal, discussed its origin and effects, and identified beneficiaries of its dissemination. For a homework assignment, participants were asked to write a one-page statement about the "costs associated with the pursuit of the thin-ideal" (Stice et al., 2003, p. 13). In the second session, session leaders reviewed and expanded first-session content and conducted role–play exercises in which group members took turns trying to dissuade individuals playing various roles (e.g., a dieter or a person with anorexia nervosa) from pursuing the thin ideal. For homework, participants were asked to engage in a body acceptance mirror exercise. The last session allowed time for previous content review and provided participants with an opportunity to discuss potential difficulties they might encounter in resisting the thin ideal and to role-play solutions. They were asked to suggest ways to help younger girls accept their own bodies. This intervention showed reductions in thin-idealization, negative affect, and bulimic pathology (but, notably, not in body dissatisfaction or dieting), with many positive effects persisting at 1-, 3-, and 6-month follow-up.

Other prevention programs use a somewhat more standardized approach to media literacy, with specific objectives and accompanying curriculum. The Go Girls! Media Literacy, Activism, and Advocacy Project is one example (Piran, Levine, & Irving, 2000). Go Girls! (Giving Our Girls Inspiration and Resources for Lasting Self-Esteem) is a 12-week program of one 1-hour session each week, with a manualized curriculum designed for middle school and high school students. Beyond providing active learning of media literacy content, the Go Girls! program incorporates media activism in which the participants work to change media by protesting or praising particular media products. Participants also use the media to communicate messages in their own words to alter the media environment. Throughout their experience with Go Girls! participants practice critical analysis of media images, survey peers on body image and media, learn and practice activism and advocacy techniques such as letter writing and holding meetings with retail management. Initial outcomes (Piran et al.) as well as adapted implementations (Wade et al., 2003) show positive results. Positive outcomes included reduced internalization of the thin ideal, increased self-acceptance, and a greater sense of empowerment.

Given the current milieu of ubiquitous media messages and cultural pressures, Piran (2001a) and Neumark-Sztainer et al. (2003) have suggested that media literacy in children and adolescents may be enhanced by adding contextual supports and safeguards to prevention efforts. This would include parent- and teacher-focused prevention efforts that help to increase the media literacy and self-concept of important adults in the child's life. Also, additional support can be added by creating classroom and community rules of no tolerance for harassment or body teasing.

***Competence and assertiveness training.*** Fostering growth in the depth and complexity of an individual's self-concept reduces the risk for a developmental convergence of self-assessment on the appearance of the body and related eating behaviors. Such growth can be accomplished by providing opportunities for individuals to build the aspects of self that are associated with resiliency (e.g., competence, assertiveness, and physical self-concept). According to Piran (2001b) feeling competent is a critical protective factor. An important component of self-concept, competence evolves and matures with experience. In the healthy development of competence, children experience interpersonal interactions and respond to individual needs, accept failure as a necessary part of the problem-solving and learning processes, and ultimately learn to act autonomously and successfully. Accordingly, prevention efforts designed to enhance competence focus on the strategies involved in successful individual and interpersonal experiences (e.g., assertiveness training) as well as active problem solving (Cook-Cottone et al., 2004; McVey & Davis, 2002).

***Physical self-concept.*** Body dissatisfaction, specifically, appears to be negatively correlated with a positive physical self-concept. That is, children and adolescents who appreciate their bodies for their utility and function appear to present with less body dissatisfaction (a concept related more specifically to the appearance and size of the body and body parts; e.g., Phelps et al., 2000). Although research is just emerging related to the enhancement of physical self-esteem in eating disorder prevention, some promising practices are currently being studied, such as the teaching of yoga techniques (Cook-Cottone et al., 2004). Also, participation in other activities not specifically designed to prevent eating disorders (e.g., sports) may have a protective effect as children develop and attend to critical competencies (Tiggemann, 2001).

***Self-regulation and care.*** Risk for body dissatisfaction, dieting, and eating disordered behavior appears to be related to increased sensitivity, a sense of dysregulation, and metabolic regulatory difficulties (possibly diet-induced). Some researchers believe that eating disordered behavior is a misguided attempt to control dysregulated processes (Cook-Cottone et al., 2004). Accordingly, progressive program curricula often include the instruction and practice of specific self-regulation and care topics that are theorized to help individuals stabilize and regulate physiological and emotional experience. Curricula have included a variety of techniques such as developing healthy eating and exercise strategies to help maintain steady physiological status (e.g., hydration requirements, satiating and blood glucose, stabilizing food intake, daily nutritional needs, and the stabilizing effects of moderate exercise on the body). Curricula also include identifying physiological and psychological responses to stress, including recognizing somatic signs of fatigue, hunger, and emotions; being aware of and understanding emotional experiences associated with physiological experience; and identifying stressors and emotional challenges. Other elements include practice of coping and relaxation techniques, such as diaphragmatic breathing, imagery, progressive muscle relaxation, and yoga practice (Cook-Cottone et al.; Daubenmier, 2002; Littleton & Ollendick, 2003; McVey & Davis, 2002; Neumark-Sztainer et al., 2003; Stice et al., 2003).

# ALTERNATIVE ACTIONS FOR INTERVENTION

Once symptomatology reaches clinical levels, individuals with eating disorders require comprehensive and multifaceted care beyond what is appropriate in school treatment (American Academy of Pediatrics [AAP], 2003). However, school professionals should be knowledgeable about the most recent best practices treatment model. Recommended treatment for individuals with eating disorders typically involves a multidisciplinary treatment team that addresses health status and medication, nutritional rehabilitation and counseling, and psychosocial needs (American Dietetic Association [ADA], 2001; American Psychiatric Association Work Group on Eating Disorders [APAWGED], 2000).

## Health Status and Medication Issues

Medical treatment should be provided by a doctor trained to work with individuals with eating disorders. Outpatient medical treatment typically involves monitoring and treatment of physiological status (e.g., nutritional and refeeding issues, electrolyte levels, weight, vital signs, and physical symptoms). When needed, hospitalization is used to stabilize physiological processes and provide nourishment through a refeeding process (AAP, 2003).

Individuals with eating disorders present with a variety of health issues as a result of their symptomatology. Medical complications related to purging (i.e., self-induced vomiting and laxative use) include electrolyte imbalance and depletion of key nutrients, irreversible myocardial damage with use of ipecac (a product used to induce vomiting), esophageal damage, dental erosion, gastric rupture, metabolic acidosis, chronic dehydration, menstrual irregularities, and amenorrhea (AAP, 2003). Medical complications related to caloric restriction include moderate to severe cardiovascular complications, gastrointestinal problems (e.g., constipation, bloating, or liver malfunction), renal difficulties, anemia and iron deficiencies, endocrine problems, and neurological irregularities (e.g., cortical atrophy and seizures; AAP). Psychopharmacological medication may be provided by the treating physician or psychiatric consultation may be used. Psychopharmacological treatment has been found to be most efficacious in the treatment of bulimia nervosa (e.g., antidepressant agents), with little efficacy found in the inpatient treatment of anorexia nervosa (ADA, 2001; APAWGED, 2000; Roerig, Mitchell,

Myers, & Glass, 2002). There is some evidence that antidepressant medication may be helpful in relapse prevention in AN (Rosenblum & Forman, 2002). The efficacy of antipsychotics, lithium, and serotonin antagonists in the treatment of eating disorders is under investigation (Roerig et al.)

## Nutritional Rehabilitation and Counseling

The nutritional aspects of treatment are often provided by a registered dietitian or nutritionist. The American Dietetic Association (2001) offers clear guidelines for the role of the nutritionist. The guidelines include a therapeutic focus on food and nutrition issues and monitoring of physiological symptomatology. Specifically, the nutritionist works with the patient to determine individual caloric needs and develops a nutrition plan that allows the patient to meet those needs. Meal planning often consists of three meals a day plus snacks (one to three per day). All eating is prescribed in a structured fashion to prevent hunger and to address chaotic eating patterns that facilitate binging and purging cycles or restriction. Food records are often used to record food intake, behaviors, feelings, and associated thoughts. Nutritional guidance typically involves teaching about body weight regulation, the effects of starvation, energy balance, misconceptions about dieting and weight control, and the consequences of purging behaviors.

## Psychosocial Treatment

Psychosocial issues are typically addressed by a psychologist, psychiatrist, or other licensed mental heath professional with training in the treatment of eating disorders. Treatment may include individual as well as group therapy, support groups, or family therapy. Goals of psychosocial treatment include the following: (a) help patients understand and cooperate with treatment team members addressing the medical and nutritional aspects of their treatment, (b) facilitate patient understanding of the psychological function of eating disordered behaviors, (c) help patients decrease eating disordered behaviors and increase self-care and coping, (d) improve interpersonal and social functioning within the family and community contexts, and (e) address psychological issues that reinforce or maintain eating disorder symptomatology (APAWGED, 2000; Cook-Cottone et al., 2004). For the treatment of BN, research suggests efficacy in cognitive behavioral as well individual psychotherapy modalities (Rosenblum & Forman, 2002). For the treatment of AN, individual and family therapy are often recommended (APAWGED). To date, no specific type of individual therapy has been identified by research as most efficacious in the treatment of AN (APAWGED).

## School Supports and Transitions

Adequate support in the school setting can be an important part of the recovery process for individuals with eating disorders (Manley, Rickson, & Standeven, 2000). The support can be most readily provided within the context of a prevention-oriented school atmosphere that already promotes zero tolerance of in-school advertising, body teasing, harassment, and gender-biased discourse and that encourages healthy nutritional behaviors and opportunities for positive physical and expressive experiences (e.g., soccer, yoga classes, track, swimming, art, and music; Cook-Cottone et al., 2004). As with all programs for students in need, school supports should be provided in accordance with the level and type of student need (Cook-Cottone et al.). When necessary, a school support and transition team should be established that includes school personnel, medical and nutrition practitioners, and a licensed mental health professional (e.g., the treating psychologist or psychiatrist). Manley et al. offer some additional suggestions. A specific school liaison should be identified to communicate with the treatment team and to coordinate services and supports within the school setting. In some cases, identification as Other Health Impaired or enrollment in Section 504 services may be necessary in order to develop an individualized plan. Flexibility is important, as students in treatment for eating disorders frequently must miss school for medical and therapeutic appointments. Specific student needs may include supportive counseling, medical monitoring, release from physical education classes, meal monitoring or support, and ongoing communication with the treatment team and family. Special accommodations may be necessary to facilitate academic progress, such as reduced workload, extended time on assignments and tests, and access to quiet study locations. In cases of an extended inpatient hospitalization, academic consultation may be required.

# SUMMARY

Within the past decade, notable changes have taken place in the understanding of the prevention and treatment of eating disordered behaviors. The etiology of eating disordered behavior is now viewed as a pathogenic developmental trajectory influenced by individual, familial, and cultural variables that manifests as a restricted experience of the self, which is diminished to dissatisfaction with and control of the body (i.e., food restriction, binging and/or purging). The developmental model of eating disorder etiology guides strategic implementation of prevention efforts, in the elementary years, that address individual, familial, and cultural factors. Recognizing the ineffectiveness of didactic, psychoeducational prevention programs, prevention efforts have turned toward a more constructive learning model with program content that reflects positive psychology ideals. Prevention curricula include media literacy and activism, coping and self-regulating strategies, assertiveness and competence training, and the development of a positive physical self-concept. When a child or adolescent is clinically ill, school professionals provide support for all aspects of the treatment effort: health status and medication, nutritional rehabilitation and counseling, and psychosocial needs. Overall, by helping maintain a safe, positive, and healthy environment; by providing constructive prevention efforts that address areas known to promote resiliency; and by facilitating treatment and school transition efforts, school personnel can be a powerful component of efforts to prevent and heal eating disorders.

## RECOMMENDED RESOURCES

### Books and Other Printed Material

Piran, N., Levine, M. P., & Steiner-Adir, C. (1999). *Preventing eating disorders: A handbook of interventions and special challenges.* Philadelphia: Brunner/Mazel.

This text addresses cultural issues, age-specific primary prevention strategies, and population-specific secondary prevention strategies.

Goodman, J. L., & Villapiano, M. (2002). *Eating disorders: The journey to recovery workbook.* Philadelphia: Brunner/Mazel.

This workbook provides a step-by-step guide to the recovery process and addresses many key issues, including women's issues, the media, trauma and abuse, and comorbid disorders. Though written as a recovery workbook for the patient, it can also serve as a very readable guide and information source for the practitioner.

### Websites

*http://www.nationaleatingdisorders.org/p.asp?WebPage_ID=294*

The National Eating Disorders Association (NEDA) is the largest not-for-profit organization in the United States that is working to prevent eating disorders and provide treatment referrals to those suffering from anorexia, bulimia, and binge eating disorder and those concerned with body image and weight issues. The website offers program materials for practitioners (e.g., Go Girls! curriculum), information on eating disorders, and research grant opportunities.

*http://www.4girls.gov*

The mission of the 4 Girls Health website, developed by the Office on Women's Health in the Department of Health and Human Services, is to promote healthy, positive behaviors in girls between the ages of 10 and 16. The site gives girls reliable, useful information on the health issues they will face as they become young women and tips on handling relationships with family and friends at school and at home.

## REFERENCES

American Academy of Pediatrics (AAP). (2003). Identifying and treating eating disorders: Policy statement by the Committee on Adolescence. *Pediatrics, 111,* 204–211.

American Dietetic Association. (2001). Position of the American Dietetic Association: Nutrition intervention in the treatment of anorexia nervosa, bulimia nervosa, and eating disorders not otherwise specified. *Journal of the American Dietetic Association, 101,* 810–819.

American Psychiatric Association. (2000). *The diagnostic and statistical manual of mental disorders* (4th ed., text rev.). Washington, DC: American Psychiatric Association.

American Psychiatric Association Work Group on Eating Disorders (APAWGED). (2000). Practice guideline for the treatment of patients with eating disorders (revision). *American Journal of Psychiatry, 157,* 1–39.

Becker, A. E., Burwell, R. A., Gilman, S. E., Herzog, D. B., & Hamburg, P. (2002). Eating behaviors and attitudes following prolonged exposure to television among ethnic Fijian adolescent girls. *British Journal of Psychiatry, 180,* 509–514.

Ben-Tovim, D. I. (2003). Eating disorders: Outcome, prevention and treatment of eating disorders. *Current Opinion in Psychiatry, 16,* 65–69.

Byely, L., Archibald, A. B., Graber, J., & Brooks-Gunn, J. (2000). A prospective study of familial and social influences on girls' body image and dieting. *International Journal of Eating Disorders, 28,* 155–164.

Cook-Cottone, C. P., Kane, L., Scime, M., & Beck, M. (2004). *Group prevention and treatment of eating disorders: A constructivist integration of mind and body strategies.* Paper presented at the annual meeting of the New York Association for Specialists in Group Work, Buffalo, NY.

Cook-Cottone, C. P., & Phelps, L. (2003). Body dissatisfaction in college women: Identification of risk and protective factors to guide college counseling practices. *Journal of College Counseling, 6,* 80–89.

Daubenmier, J. J. (2002). A comparison of Hatha Yoga and aerobic exercise on women's body satisfaction. *Dissertation Abstracts International.* (UMI No. 9315947).

Davis, C., Shuster, B., Blackmore, E., & Fox, J. (2004). Looking good—Family focus on appearance and risk for eating disorders. *International Journal of Eating Disorders, 35,* 136–144.

Geller, J, Zaitsoff, S. L., & Srikameswaran, S. (2002). Beyond shape and weight: Exploring the relationship between nonbody determinants of self-esteem and eating disorder symptoms in adolescent females. *International Journal of Eating Disorders, 32,* 344–351.

Goodman, L. J., & Villapiano, M. (2002). *Eating disorders: The journey to recovery workbook.* Philadelphia: Brunner/Mazel.

Gowers, S. G., & Shore, A. (2001). Development of weight and shape concerns in the etiology of eating disorders. *British Journal of Psychiatry, 179,* 236–242.

Groesz, L. M., Levine, M. P., & Murnen, S. K. (2002). The effect of experimental presentation of the thin media images on body satisfaction: A meta-analytic review. *International Journal of Eating Disorders, 31,* 1–16.

Hoek, H. W., & van Hoeken, D. (2003). Review of the prevalence and incidence of eating disorders. *International Journal of Eating Disorders, 24,* 383–396.

Jacobi, C., Paul, T., deZwaan, M., Nutzinger, D. O., & Dahme, B. (2004). Specificity of self-concept disturbances in eating disorders. *International Journal of Eating Disorders, 35,* 204–210.

Littleton, H. L., & Ollendick, T. (2003). Negative body image and disordered eating behavior in children and adolescents: What places youth at risk and how can these problems be prevented? *Clinical and Child and Family Psychology Review, 6,* 51–66.

Macias, A. E. (2004). Experimental demonstration of human weight homeostasis: Implications for understanding obesity [commentary]. *British Journal of Nutrition, 3,* 329–330.

Manley, R. S., Rickson, H., & Standeven, B. (2000). Children and adolescents with eating disorders: Strategies for teachers and school counselors. *Intervention in School & Clinic, 35,* 228–231.

McVey, G. L., & Davis, R. (2002). A program to promote healthy body image: A 1-year follow-up evaluation. *Journal of Early Adolescence, 22,* 96–108.

Neumark-Sztainer, D., Wall, M., Story, M., & Perry, C. (2003). Correlates of unhealthy weight-control behaviors among adolescents: Implications for prevention programs. *Health Psychology, 22,* 88–98.

Ohring, R., Graber, J. A., & Brooks-Gunn, J. (2002). Girls' recurrent and concurrent body dissatisfaction: Correlates and consequences over 8 years. *International Journal of Eating Disorders, 31,* 401–415.

Patel, D. P., Greydanus, D. E., Pratt, H. D., & Phillips, E. L. (2003). Eating disorders in adolescent athletes. *Journal of Adolescent Research, 18,* 280–296.

Phelps, L., Nathanson, D. S., Nelson, L. D., Sapia, J. L., & Dempsey, M. (2000). An empirically supported eating disorder prevention program. *Psychology in the Schools, 37,* 443–452.

Piran, N. (2001a). The body logic program: Discussions and reflections. *Cognitive and Behavioral Practice, 8,* 259–264.

Piran, N. (2001b). Re-inhabiting the body from the inside out: Girls transform their school environment. In D. L. Tolman & M. Brydon-Miller (Eds.), *From subjects to subjectivities: A handbook of interpretive participatory methods* (pp. 218–238). New York: New York University Press.

Piran, N., Levine, M. P., & Irving, L. M. (2000). Go Girls! Media literacy, activism, and advocacy project. *Healthy Weight Journal, 14* (November/December), 89–90.

Ray, S. L. (2004). Eating disorders in adolescent males. *Professional School Counseling, 8,* 98–101.

Roerig, J. L., Mitchell, J. E., Myers, T. C., & Glass, J. B. (2002). Pharmacotherapy and medical complications of eating disorders in children and adolescents. *Child and Adolescent Psychiatric Clinics of North America, 11,* 365–383.

Rosenblum, J., & Forman, S. (2002). Evidence-based treatment of eating disorders. *Current Opinion in Pediatrics, 14,* 379–383.

Steck, E. L., Abrams, L. M., & Phelps, L. (2004). Positive psychology in the prevention of eating disorders. *Psychology in the Schools, 41,* 111–117.

Steinhausen, C. (2002). The outcome of Anorexia Nervosa in the 20th Century. *The American Journal of Psychiatry, 159,* 1284–1293.

Stice, E., & Ragan, J. (2002). A preliminary controlled evaluation of an eating disturbance psychoeducational intervention for college students. *International Journal of Eating Disorders, 31,* 159–171.

Stice, E., Trost, A., & Chase, A. (2003). Healthy weight control and dissonance-based eating disorder prevention programs: Results from a controlled trail. *International Journal of Eating Disorders, 33,* 10–21.

Thomas, K., Ricciardelli, L. A., & Williams, R. J. (2000). Gender traits and self-concept as indicators of problem eating and body dissatisfaction among children. *Sex Roles, 43,* 441–458.

Tiggemann, M. (2001). The impact of adolescent girls' life concerns and leisure activities on body dissatisfaction, disordered eating, and self-esteem. *Journal of Genetic Psychology, 162,* 133–142.

Tiggemann, M., & Slater, A. (2004). Thin ideals in music television: A source of social comparison and body dissatisfaction. *International Journal of Eating Disorders, 35,* 48–58.

Wade, T. D., Davidson, S., & O'Dea, J. A. (2003). A preliminary controlled evaluation of a school-based media literacy program and self-esteem program for reducing eating disorder risk factors. *International Journal of Eating Disorders, 33,* 371–383.

Williams, J. M., & Currie, C. (2000). Self-esteem and physical development in early adolescence: Pubertal timing and body image. *Journal of Early Adolescence, 20,* 129–149.

Wisniewski, L., & Kelly, E. (2003). The application of dialectic behavior therapy to the treatment of eating disorders. *Cognitive and Behavioral Practice, 10,* 131–138.

Wonderlich, S., Crosby, R., Mitchell, J., Thompson, K., Redlin, J., Demuth, G., et al. (2001). Pathways mediating sexual abuse and eating disturbance in children. *International Journal of Eating Disorders 29,* 270–279.

# 74

# Childhood Overweight

**Jessica Blom-Hoffman**
**Jessica B. Edwards George**
**Debra L. Franko**

*Northeastern University*

## BACKGROUND AND DEVELOPMENT

Overweight and obesity in the United States have reached epidemic proportions. Health experts caution that today's generation of children may be among the first to have a shorter life span than their parents as a result of obesity-related deaths. Among children and adolescents ages 6–19 years, the prevalence of overweight (defined as a body mass index [BMI]-for-age greater than or equal to the 95th percentile), has risen from 4%–5% in the late 1960s to 16% in 2002 (Centers for Disease Control and Prevention [CDC], 2004). In current terminology, *obesity* and obese are terms reserved for use with adults who have a BMI greater than or equal to 30 (CDC, 2003a). The terms *overweight* and *at risk for overweight* (defined as a BMI-for-age between the 85th and 94th percentile) are used for children and adolescents (CDC, 2003b).

Although the overweight and obesity epidemic affects all ethnic, racial, and socioeconomic groups, as well as both genders, some subgroups are disproportionately affected by this health condition. For example, American Indian (Caballero, Himes et al., 2003), African American, and Mexican American children and adolescents are more likely to be overweight than their White peers (e.g., CDC, 2002a). High rates of overweight in children and adolescents are particularly alarming because the probability of overweight and obesity persisting into adulthood among overweight adolescents is high (Guo & Chumlea, 1999).

It is estimated that between approximately 112,000 (Flegal, Graubard, Williamson, & Gail, 2005) and 400,000 (Mokdad, Marks, Stroup, & Gerberding, 2004) deaths in the United States are attributed to overweight and obesity each year. If this trajectory is not reversed, deaths related to poor diet and lack of physical activity will quickly become the leading cause of death in this country. Obesity is related to numerous serious medical conditions, including but not limited to cardiovascular problems (e.g., high cholesterol and blood pressure), endocrine disorders (e.g., type 2 diabetes), pulmonary complications (e.g., obstructive sleep apnea), and depression (U.S. Department of Health and Human Services, 2001).

Health experts have no doubt that overweight and obesity are the result of the interaction of multiple factors, including genetics, environment, and behavior. Despite the contributions of genetics to the expression of obesity, the human genome has not evolved so significantly in the past 40 years to explain sufficiently the current rates of this problem. What has evolved, however, is our 'obesogenic' or toxic environment, which provides ideal conditions for the development of overweight and obesity (Wadden, Brownell, & Foster, 2002). The overweight problem can be defined simply as an imbalance in the *energy in–energy out* equation (Dietz & Gortmaker, 2001). In other words, overweight results from a longstanding pattern of behavior that results in more energy (i.e., calories) being consumed than burned. Numerous environmental culprits contribute to the energy imbalance, including increased portion sizes, greater availability and consumption of soft drinks and fast foods, and time spent engaging in sedentary activities (e.g., computer use, television viewing, and video games; Ebbling, Pawlak, & Ludwig, 2002).

# PROBLEMS AND IMPLICATIONS

## Psychosocial Effects of Overweight

Children who are overweight tend to be stigmatized by others. In one study, elementary school–age children attributed negative characteristics (e.g., having fewer friends, being less liked by their parents, doing less well academically, being unhappy with the way they look, and wanting to be thinner) to pictures of overweight children (Hill & Silver, 1995). Relationships between bullying behaviors and overweight have been revealed as well. Among children ages 11–16 years, those who were overweight were more likely to be victims and perpetrators of verbal, physical, and relational aggression than children who were normal weight (Janssen, Craig, Boyce, & Pickett, 2004).

The social networks of children who are overweight were explored in a very large national sample of more than 17,000 adolescents (Strauss & Pollack, 2003). When compared to peers with BMIs in the normal range, adolescents who were overweight were more isolated. In general, these adolescents received fewer friendship and best friend nominations than their normal-weight counterparts. In addition, adolescents who were overweight were less likely to receive reciprocated nominations from their peers. Findings from this study highlighted ethnic and racial differences, indicating that not all adolescents' social networks are affected similarly by their overweight status. Specifically, the social networks of Non-Hispanic White boys and girls were affected most negatively by their overweight status. Hispanic boys and girls' and African American girls' friendship networks also were significantly affected by their overweight status, whereas among African American boys, friendship networks were not significantly affected by overweight status.

## Psychological Correlates of Overweight

Associations between overweight and depression in girls (Erickson, Robinson, Haydel, & Killen, 2000) and low self-esteem (Strauss, 2000) in adolescents have been documented. A large study of children ages 9–16 found that chronic overweight was associated with psychopathology in both girls and boys (e.g., oppositional defiant disorder and depression; Mustillo et al., 2003). In addition, negative self-image among overweight children as young as 5 years has been shown (Davison & Birch, 2001). There is evidence in a prospective study that both childhood overweight and parental obesity increase risk for the development of bulimia nervosa (Fairburn, Welch, Doll, Davies, & O'Connor, 1997).

Because children and adolescents who struggle with overweight are at risk for social stigmatization and marginalization, depression, and low self-esteem, it is critical that school professionals be aware of and sensitive to these issues. This can be addressed in part through school- and class-wide bullying prevention programs as well as through individual counseling and small group interventions.

# ALTERNATIVE ACTIONS FOR PREVENTION

Given the alarming rates of childhood overweight, the minimal effectiveness of treatments, and the associated life-threatening and costly health sequelae, considerable effort must be dedicated to the prevention of this condition. Because overweight in adolescence is a major predictor of obesity in adulthood, efforts to prevent the onset of overweight need to be targeted toward healthy, young children. A series of commonsense cures to prevent the development of overweight among children has been described by Ebbling and her colleagues (2002). Preventive behaviors at home include limiting television viewing and setting aside time for healthy meals and physical activity. Recommendations at school include (a) funding mandatory physical education, (b) establishing stricter standards for school lunch programs, and (c) replacing unhealthy foods with healthy alternatives in school vending machines. School professionals can be important advocates for changes in school policy and can disseminate information to parents, administrators, and school staff about the prevention of childhood overweight. To address this problem in a meaningful way, school communities must work together to change the obesogenic environment.

## School-Based Prevention Programs

***Child and Adolescent Trial for Cardiovascular Health (CATCH).*** The CATCH field trial represents one of the largest, most rigorously designed outcome evaluations in the area of school health. This 3-year, randomized intervention trial was funded by the National Heart, Lung, and Blood Institute from 1991 to 1994. The CATCH program was comprehensive in that it was implemented within the general education program, the food service program, the physical education program, and participants' homes. The CATCH intervention had three goals: (a) to reduce the total fat, saturated fat, and sodium content in food served in the school cafeteria, while maintaining the recommended levels of essential nutrients as well as student participation in school meals; (b) to increase the time students spent engaged in moderate to vigorous physical activity in physical education class; and (c) to reduce total cholesterol among students in the intervention group relative to students in the control group (Resnicow, Robinson, & Frank, 1996; Stone, 1996).

More than 5,000 students from 96 schools in four states (California, Louisiana, Minnesota, and Texas) participated in the CATCH intervention trial. The 96 schools were randomly assigned to one of three conditions (school intervention; school plus home intervention; control and usual programs; Stone, 1996). The classroom component of the program was based on social–cognitive theory and included behavior change strategies to improve self-efficacy, expectations, skills, and students' ability to set nutrition-related goals. The home component of the field trial consisted of 19 activity packets, which were completed by families during the 3-year intervention, and two family fun nights, offered once during third grade and once during fourth grade. Students from diverse ethnic and racial backgrounds (i.e., 68% White, 13% African American, 14% Latino) were included in the study, increasing the generalizability of the results (Stone). The outcome evaluation examined the program's effect on several variables: physiological (i.e., blood pressure, cholesterol, skinfold thickness, BMI), behavioral (i.e., nutrient intake), and psychosocial (i.e., dietary intention, usual food choice, dietary knowledge, and perceived social support for healthy food choices). At the end of the trial, no significant differences were reported between students in the experimental group and students in the control group on physiological variables (Webber et al., 1996). However, students did report a statistically significant decrease in the percentage of calories from fat they consumed relative to comparison students, as measured by 24-hour dietary recalls (Lytle et al., 1996). Students in the intervention group reported statistically significant improvements on all four psychosocial variables relative to comparison students. In addition, effect sizes indicated substantial and significant improvements with regard to diet (e.g., intentions, usual food choices, and self-efficacy for eating healthier foods) for students in the experimental group. The intervention also showed positive changes as a result of the school food service and physical education components. The mean percentage of total fat calories and saturated fat calories in school lunches decreased significantly in intervention schools relative to control schools (Resnicow et al., 1996). In addition, students in those schools demonstrated a significant increase in the percentage of time spent engaging in moderate to vigorous physical activity during gym classes, even though the average length of gym classes did not change (Luepker et al., 1996). In general, results indicated no greater benefit of the school plus home intervention over and above the school only intervention on behavioral and physiological variables. This was true even among students with high family participation (Resnicow et al.). CATCH planners concluded that because the planned dose of the family intervention (i.e., the number of family nights and home-based activities for families) was insufficient to affect behavioral and physiological variables, a more extensive and intensive intervention might be necessary to obtain the desired results. However, it is not clear how feasible that would be. Also, the results suggested that alternative strategies that involve families need to be examined.

***Pathways.*** The Pathways program was a multisite, randomized clinical research trial that investigated the effects of a school-based, primary prevention program targeted to American Indian children and their families. The outcome evaluation of the Pathways program was also funded by the National Heart, Lung, and Blood Institute. The full-scale trial, which was conducted from 1996 to 2000, incorporated a participatory action research framework consisting of a partnership between representatives of seven American Indian communities in the southwestern United States and a university-based research team (Davis & Reid, 1999). The program, developed for children in grades three through five, had four components: (a) classroom curriculum, (b) school food service modifications, (c) physical education modifications, and (d) a family involvement component. School staff implemented the program (i.e., teachers and food service personnel), and the research team was responsible for training and for the outcome evaluation (Davis et al.). The design and implementation of the Pathways program make it an outstanding example of school-based primary prevention efforts targeted toward elementary school children.

Unfortunately, the study showed no differences between children randomized to the intervention group and children in the control group with regard to the percentage of body fat (Caballero, Clay et al., 2003). This finding was consistent with those of other school-based overweight prevention programs (e.g., Webber et al., 1996), which demonstrates the difficulty of achieving change on this specific outcome variable. Despite this outcome, the study showed significant reductions in the amount of fat in school lunches at the intervention schools. Food service personnel incorporated more fresh fruit and vegetables and other low-fat foods in the school meals. In addition, at the end of the study, students in the intervention group reported significantly lower daily energy intake (i.e., calories/day) than students in the control group. Finally, significant improvements in students' health-related knowledge were associated with the program.

***Planet Health.*** Like the CATCH and Pathways randomized trials, Planet Health was a multiyear, school-based, universal overweight prevention program. The outcome evaluation of the Planet Health curriculum was conducted by the Harvard Prevention Research Center on Nutrition and Physical Activity and funded by the National Institute of Child Health and Human Development and the Centers for Disease Control and Prevention from 1995 to 1997. Planet Health targeted middle school students in sixth and seventh grades and had four behavioral goals, including (a) reducing television viewing to less than 2 hours per day, (b) increasing moderate and vigorous physical activity, (c) increasing fruit and vegetable consumption, and (d) decreasing consumption of foods high in fat (Gortmaker et al., 1999). The Planet Health curriculum, which was implemented by classroom and physical education teachers over 2 years, was based on behavioral–choice and social–cognitive theories. It involved 32 classroom lessons that were related to the general education curriculum and the state educational guidelines. In addition, the program included a 2-week campaign to reduce television viewing.

Nearly 1,300 students in 10 schools were randomized to experimental and control schools in the Boston metropolitan area. Primary outcome variables included BMI and triceps skinfolds. In addition, self-report measures of television viewing, activity level, and eating behaviors were administered.

The Planet Health study is among the few school-based prevention programs to demonstrate significant reductions in overweight. In the 2-year intervention period, overweight prevalence among girls increased from 21.5% to 23.7% in the control schools and decreased from 23.6% to 20.3% in the intervention schools (Gortmaker et al., 1999). A similar finding was not observed among boys. Significant reductions occurred in the number of hours both girls and boys watched television each day. At follow-up 2 years after the intervention ended, girls in the intervention group had increased fruit and vegetable consumption and consumed fewer calories (i.e., less total energy intake) compared with girls in the control group. Differences in intervention effects across racial and ethnic groups reported the largest effect of the program among African American girls. The authors concluded that the positive program effects were due only in part to reductions in television viewing, increased fruit and vegetable consumption, and decreased intake of total calories, indicating that other unmeasured variables also contributed to the program's effect. Information regarding purchase of the curricular materials for Planet Health, and Eat Well and Keep Moving (a similar curriculum for elementary-age children) can be found in the Recommended Resources section.

## Preventive Behavioral Interventions

***Reducing sugar-sweetened beverage consumption.*** In the past half century consumption of sugar-sweetened beverages, including soft drinks, has risen dramatically (nearly 500%; Ludwig, Peterson, & Gortmaker, 2001). A national survey of beverage consumption conducted among children and adolescents revealed that as children get older, their self-reported daily consumption of carbonated soft drinks increases steadily from approximately 6 ounces per day at age 8 to over 19 ounces per day at age 18 (Rampersaud, Bailey, & Kauwell, 2003). Concurrently, milk consumption decreases from approximately 10 ounces per day at age 8 to approximately 6 ounces per day at age 18. Excess consumption of sugar-sweetened soft drinks is particularly concerning because it is associated with increases in BMI (Ludwig et al.).

Children and adolescents have overwhelming access to sugar-sweetened beverages in their environments. Recently, the widespread availability of soft drinks in schools has come under intense scrutiny (see Wiehe, 2004). Historically, soft drink companies have looked to underfunded school districts as a way of promoting their products among impressionable young customers whose taste preferences are developing. In signing contracts with these companies, schools enable the unhealthy products to be marketed during or after school in exchange for needed funds to purchase physical education equipment, instructional materials, and computers. Products are marketed through students' purchases as well as through exposure to product logos on vending machines, banners, books and book covers, software, scoreboards, and T-shirts. Fortunately, many states and local school districts are becoming more aware of the association between the overconsumption of sugar-sweetened beverages and the development of childhood overweight. More school districts are reconsidering their contracts with soft drink companies, and state legislation is being introduced to prevent the sales of unhealthful foods in schools (Center for Science in the Public Interest, n.d.).

Recently, the American Academy of Pediatrics (Murray et al., 2004) published a policy statement recommending that pediatricians voice an opinion regarding the importance of eliminating sweetened drinks in schools, advocating for the establishment of school nutrition advisory councils, and having public discussions about vending machine contracts before school districts sign them. School professionals should be aware of the availability of sugar-sweetened beverages and high-fat foods with low nutrient density in their schools as well as of the district policies associated with the vending machines. School psychologists, in collaboration with parents, school nurses, and other school staff, can serve as important advocates to promote healthful vending machine policies in their districts. Specifically, they can encourage adding healthy options in the vending machines, such as water, milk, 100% fruit juice, and nutritious snacks.

Few studies have attempted to alter consumption of carbonated beverages in school-age children. Recently, however, a school-based study targeting reduced consumption of carbonated beverages in children 7–11 years of age demonstrated significant changes in self-reported consumption of soft drinks (James, Thomas, Cavan, & Kerr, 2004). The intervention involved four lessons taught by a diabetes nurse, which were delivered in the classroom environment with the teacher present. The study demonstrated significant differences between two randomly assigned groups in the development of overweight over a 12-month period. The prevalence of overweight among children in the experimental group remained the same, whereas the prevalence of overweight among children in the control group increased by over 7%.

***Reducing recreational screen time.*** Recreational screen time refers to leisure time spent watching television and videos, playing video games, and using the computer. Efforts to reduce recreational screen time are important in the fight against childhood overweight, as studies have demonstrated an association between those behaviors and BMI. In one study, children who watched less than 2 hours of television per day had significantly lower BMIs than children who watched 4 or more hours per day (Anderson, Crespo, Bartlett, Cheskin, & Pratt, 1998). The relationship between television viewing and childhood overweight is hypothesized to be the result of the following mechanisms of action: (a) reduced time spent engaged in physical activity, (b) increased caloric consumption resulting from eating and drinking while watching television, and (c) subsequent eating behaviors influenced by advertisements for high-calorie foods and beverages (Robinson, 2001). As a result, pediatricians recommend limiting recreational screen time to no more than 2 hours per day (Krebs & Jacobson, 2003).

Robinson (1999) developed, implemented, and evaluated an innovative, school-based approach to reduce television, video, and video game viewing at home. The intervention involved sending information home to families, instituting a 10-day TV turnoff, teaching children to self-monitor their television viewing, establishing a television budget of 7 hours per week, and teaching children to be intelligent viewers by being selective about what they chose to watch in their allotted 7 hours. Results indicated that an 18-lesson program, based on social learning theory and implemented by third- and fourth-grade teachers, was effective in reducing reported television time. Also, children randomly assigned to the intervention group had smaller increases in BMI and body fat measures at postintervention than did children in the control group. This study was the first to demonstrate experimentally the relationship between television viewing and increased body fat. It is important to note that this intervention was able to yield changes in body fat without encouraging changes in physical activity level.

***Health report cards.*** Providing families with personalized BMI information collected at school through a health report card is a somewhat controversial approach that was the basis of a recent study (Chomitz, Collins, Kim, Kramer, & McGowan, 2003). Chomitz et al. sent home personalized health report cards to nearly 1,400 kindergarten through eighth-grade children's parents. They demonstrated that the majority of parents who recalled receiving personalized BMI information about their child wanted this information on an annual basis. Caregivers of overweight children who received the health report card were more aware of their child's weight status than caregivers of overweight children who did not receive any health information. However, receiving personalized and general information about childhood overweight did not seem to affect caregivers' level of concern about their child's weight status. Despite efforts printed in the intervention materials to dissuade caregivers from initiating dieting activities, almost 20% of families indicated they were planning to begin dieting activities with their overweight children. Unfortunately (but not surprisingly), providing parents with specific health guidelines to prevent overweight (e.g., limiting television to 2 hours or less, increasing physical activity to at least 1 hour per day, and aiming to eat at least five servings of fruits and vegetables per day) was not effective in changing child health behaviors.

More research is clearly needed to understand how health report cards might be used more effectively. The collection of height and weight surveillance data in schools needs to be conducted in a sensitive manner and in a private environment by well-trained staff. If school districts decide to adopt a health report card approach, the report cards should be mailed to parents instead of sending them home with children. Also, parents of children who are overweight should receive contact information for community-based health care professionals who specialize in the treatment of childhood overweight. The effect of the report cards on children's self-esteem and unsupervised dieting behaviors needs study. School districts that adopt this approach need to recognize that the effects of providing sensitive information in this manner are not yet fully understood and should implement programs designed to monitor and evaluate outcome.

***School Health Index (SHI).*** The SHI is a structured assessment tool developed by the Centers for Disease Control and Prevention (2002b) for use by elementary and middle school teams to evaluate the school's health environment and to help schools plan. A team of school administrators, staff, parents, and students use the SHI to assess the school's health-related policies and programs and to determine targets for change that will promote physical activity, healthy eating, and tobacco use prevention. A site coordinator is required to facilitate the meetings and data collection. An entire module of the SHI is dedicated to the relationship between school counseling, psychological and social services, and the promotion of physical activity, healthy eating, and a tobacco-free lifestyle. All information needed to use the SHI can be obtained free of charge from the CDC (see Recommended Resources).

## ALTERNATIVE ACTIONS FOR INTERVENTION

Mental health professionals in the schools have an opportunity to identify children who are at risk for becoming overweight or are already overweight so that they can begin intervention activities as soon as possible. School professionals can be partners in students' weight reduction treatment plans by working as part of an interdisciplinary team, which may include the child's physicians, nurses, nutritionists, school psychologists, and social workers. Currently, diet and exercise goals are included too infrequently in the Individualized Education Programs of children struggling with health-related difficulties due to overweight. Although the main business of schools is not to promote nutrition and physical activity, but to provide children with a quality education, for maximum learning, children need to be as healthy as possible. Plainly stated, healthy children are better able to learn. Collaboration among school and medical professionals can help children and their families achieve healthier eating and activity behaviors that may persist throughout the child's development and into adulthood.

Changes in eating and activity behaviors of adolescents and adults have been found to be much more difficult to facilitate and maintain than changes achieved with children (Barlow & Dietz, 1998). Thus, intervening as soon as a child becomes overweight (or preferably at the earliest indication of the at-risk trajectory) is more effective in decreasing the likelihood of the physiologic and psychological sequelae of overweight. Mental health professionals in the schools can use screening instruments (e.g., the Overeating Questionnaire; O'Donnell & Warren, 2004) to assist in identifying children at risk.

A long-term, multidimensional approach that includes diet, activity, the use of behavior modification principles for habit changing, and the participation of the child's family and other caregivers, contributes to long-term weight maintenance in children (Epstein, Valoski, Wing, & McCurley, 1994). When facilitating this type of intervention approach, the primary goal is to regulate the child's body weight and body fat while sustaining sufficient nutrition for growth and development and at the same time developing healthy eating and activity patterns (Epstein, Myers, Raynor, & Saelens, 1998). Treatment of children who are overweight is typically a long-term process and requires ongoing support. The longer the treatment, the greater the weight reductions in children; in other words, as the duration of treatment increases, the percentage of overweight generally decreases (Goldfield, Raynor, & Epstein, 2002).

## Inclusion of the Family

Including the child's parents and other sources of support is essential in interventions designed to reduce childhood overweight by helping the child implement the necessary dietary and activity changes (Epstein et al., 1994). One study of a family-based behavioral treatment program demonstrated that support from family and friends is a predictor of change in percentage overweight across a 10-year period (Epstein et al.). The inclusion of the child's family was found to enhance the child's likelihood of short- and long-term weight control. Therefore, it is important to identify and involve caretakers and extended family who may be responsible for supervising the child's diet and activity (Barlow & Dietz, 1998). Caregivers who do not participate in interventions may accidentally or purposely undermine the treatment program. Also, assessing the family's readiness for change is important, as lack of readiness has been found to lead to treatment failure (Barlow & Dietz). Repeated failures may frustrate the family and child, thus averting future efforts at weight management. School psychologists and nurses can assist in educating families about the medical and psychological complications of overweight and about the implications of not intervening with their children and motivating them to pursue and remain in treatment.

## Communication Skills and Demeanor of Clinicians

The significance that society places on one's physical appearance and the widespread belief that overweight is a consequence of laziness or a lack of self-control can create feelings of humiliation and shame in overweight children and their families. The communication skills and demeanor of school-based mental health providers and others are critical in developing a positive therapeutic relationship with families who are trying to make positive changes in their eating and activity patterns (Barlow & Dietz, 1998). An impartial, empathic, and nonaccusatory manner of connecting with families will facilitate this relationship. At the same time, clinicians must compassionately remind families of the potential for significant physical and psychological problems if the child's weight issues are not treated. As in all therapeutic relationships, mental health professionals working with families struggling with weight problems should be optimistic concerning the child's and family's ability to produce change. If a family is not successful at first, clinicians should avoid criticizing and instead try to help the family determine why a failure has occurred and encourage them to renew their efforts. A clinician who understands all of the factors that contribute to the child's weight problems, such as living situation, schedule, and values, and who is able to individualize and refine treatment and recommendations will be an important asset to the family.

## Dietary Interventions

Dietary interventions are based on the premise that an overweight child's energy consumption surpasses his or her energy expenditure. Therefore, one way of obtaining the negative energy balance needed for weight loss is to reduce the child's daily caloric intake. A well-balanced, healthy diet that is reduced in calories (including liquid calories) and high-fat foods but does not make the child feel hungry or deprived can be accomplished by following a variety of dietary plans. Parents considering placing their child on a diet should consult with a registered dietitian or physician who specializes in the weight management of children to ensure an appropriate and safe course of action. It is critical that health professionals who suggest dietary changes to families understand the important roles various foods play in different cultures. Dietary modifications need to be respectful of these traditions by considering ways of altering food preparation methods (e.g., use and amount of fats) and reducing portion sizes while maintaining the presence of the foods in the diet.

Few studies have compared the effects of using different dietary approaches while holding other aspects of a treatment constant (Goldfield et al., 2002). Some diet plans that have been successful include individualized dietary interventions, the diabetic exchange system (Becque, Katch, Rocchini, Marks, & Moorehead, 1988), the 'traffic light' diet (Valoski & Epstein, 1990), the protein-sparing modified fast (PSMF) diet (Figueroa-Colon, von Almen, Franklin, Schuftan, & Suskind, 1993), the reduced calorie diet, and the reduced fat diet (Epstein et al., 1998). Children and adolescents who consume breakfast regularly have a lower BMI, suggesting an important target for intervention (Siega-Riz, Popkin, & Carson, 1998). School staff should communicate with treating physicians and other health care professionals, such as nutritionists, to obtain more information when children are prescribed special diets. In addition, trained professionals in educational settings can assist in obtaining a diet history with detailed information about eating habits and patterns, including eating during the school day that may cause the child to consume excessive amounts of calories and fat.

## Activity Interventions

Activity interventions are an essential component of a weight reduction plan. Gradual, targeted increases in the child's activity levels should be encouraged (Barlow & Dietz, 1998). A meta-analysis to determine whether adding exercise to diet during treatment leads to a greater reduction in adiposity than diet alone found that exercise combined with diet improved the treatment of childhood overweight by almost one half of a standard deviation beyond diet alone (Epstein & Goldfield, 1999). Incorporating general increases in activity in children's daily routine (e.g., increasing walking and taking the stairs instead of an elevator) appears to be more effective in reducing weight than higher-intensity aerobic exercise or calisthenics (Epstein, Wing, Koeske, & Valoski, 1985). School professionals should encourage and reinforce children's efforts to reduce sedentary activity and to increase physical activity (Epstein, Paluch, Gordy, & Dorn, 2000). Daily physical education and recess provide important opportunities during the school day for children to be physically active. School professionals should be aware of and work to address deterrents to physical activity, such as safety issues and the expense of participating in certain types of activity programs.

## Behavioral Interventions

To maximize the child and family's potential to succeed in treatment, intervention programs should include instruction in behavior modification principles to change established habits (Foreyt & Cousins, 1989). This approach will raise the family's awareness about current problem behaviors and provide them with the skills necessary to modify behaviors gradually and to maintain changes over time. Clinicians in the schools can help children and families become aware of existing eating routines, activity patterns, and parenting behaviors that may be linked to the child's weight difficulties. When developing behavioral interventions with families, school-based mental health professionals can guide families to create goals that are explicit, specific, and simple.

When developing goals, the clinician should target only a few (two or three) small, permanent changes in diet or activity at one time, rather than numerous, lofty changes (Barlow & Dietz, 1998). An example of a small, simple goal may be to replace eating potato chips with a healthy alternative snack, such as an apple or vegetable sticks. This type of goal is more attainable and typically more effective for families than is a large, general goal such as decreasing the child's overall fat intake. Children and their families should be reinforced frequently by their interdisciplinary team and by each other for meeting their goals. Only after they have mastered the changes should new goals be developed. School personnel can assist the family in recognizing and working through potential situations that jeopardize adherence to the child's dietary and activity goals.

Parenting skills training is also an important component in the treatment of childhood overweight (Barlow & Dietz, 1998). Parents should be taught the basic skills necessary to encourage their child's appropriate behaviors and to decrease inappropriate behaviors that are not aligned with weight management goals. Consistency and contingency are the hallmarks of effective behavior management. Children must be able to depend on reinforcement when they engage in behaviors that further positive change. Finding real reasons to praise the child, even in tough times, and rewarding the child for achieving and maintaining goals are essential for success. Food should never be used as a reward (including in the classroom). School professionals can help parents (and teachers) develop a list of appropriate alternative reinforcers to use with their child. Offering healthy food options and establishing daily family meals and snack times are a few ways to help the child make good food choices and reduce unsupervised eating time. In addition, parents and teachers need to recognize that their eating behaviors and activity patterns serve as models for the child's habits and that they may need to make changes in their own eating and exercise behaviors.

# SUMMARY

The problem of childhood overweight in the United States is widespread and rising. Children who are overweight suffer from serious psychosocial and medical difficulties. The current cultural and commercial environment in the United States provides the ideal opportunity for overweight to occur. Recognizing the context surrounding the obesity epidemic is important to understanding the full magnitude of the problem and realizing that no one group (e.g., families, medical providers, educators, or legislators) can make meaningful change by working in isolation. Environmental changes, in addition to individual efforts, are needed to reverse the obesity trajectory. Schools play important roles in the prevention and treatment of childhood overweight. School professionals, including school psychologists, must understand the multifaceted nature of this health issue and see a role for themselves with regard to prevention and intervention. School-based prevention programs, such as Child and Adolescent Trial for Cardiovascular Health (CATCH), Pathways, and Planet Health, provide illustrations of how schools can be active participants in the prevention of overweight. School staff can join with parents and administrators to advocate for school health policies that promote good nutrition and physical activity. To assist children who are already overweight, school psychologists and school nurses can collaborate with medical providers to help school staff understand children's specific medical regimens. Long-term multidimensional approaches that target diet, activity levels, and behavior modification principles for habit change have been found to be the most effective in reducing the weight of children who are overweight. School personnel can assist by including the child's family, caregivers, and extended family in the process and helping the child and family to choose small, explicit goals that facilitate gradual, long-term change. Childhood overweight is complex and will require the efforts of multiple stakeholder groups who can address the problem on numerous levels.

# RECOMMENDED RESOURCES

## Websites

*http://www.cdc.gov/nccdphp/dnpa/obesity/*

This website contains general information from the Centers for Disease Control and Prevention related to the obesity epidemic.

*http://www.cdc.gov/healthyyouth/SHI/index.htm*

This website provides access to the School Health Index, a self-assessment and planning tool to improve the effectiveness of schools' health and safety policies and programs. Information can also be obtained at (888) 231–6405.

*http://www.dole5aday.com*

This interactive website is designed to help children, parents, and teachers learn about the importance of eating fruits and vegetables. It provides free nutrition curricula information for teachers and helpful information for parents (from Dole Food Company, Inc.).

*http://www.hsph.harvard.edu/prc/projects.html*

Harvard University's Prevention Research Center on Nutrition and Physical Activity website has information about the Planet Health (middle school) and Eat Well and Keep Moving (upper elementary school) curricula. In addition, these programs can be ordered from Human Kinetics at (800) 747–4457.

# REFERENCES

Anderson, R. E., Crespo, C. J., Bartlett, S. J., Cheskin, L. J., & Pratt, M. (1998). Relationship of physical activity and television watching with body weight and level of fatness among children: Results from the Third National Health and Nutrition Examination Survey. *Journal of the American Medical Association, 279,* 938–942.

Barlow, S. E., & Dietz, W. H. (1998). Obesity evaluation and treatment: Expert committee recommendations. *Pediatrics, 102,* 29–37.

Becque, M., Katch, V., Rocchini, A., Marks, C., & Moorehead, C. (1988). Coronary risk incidence of obese adolescents: Reduction by exercise plus diet intervention. *Pediatrics, 81,* 16–23.

Caballero, B., Clay, T., Davis, S. M., Ethelbah, B., Holy Rock, B., Lohman, T., et al. (2003). Pathways: A school-based, randomized controlled trial for the prevention of obesity in American Indian schoolchildren. *American Journal of Clinical Nutrition, 78,* 1030–1038.

Caballero, B., Himes, J. H., Lohman, T., Davis, S. M., Stevens, J., Evans, M., et al. (2003). Body composition and overweight prevalence in 1704 schoolchildren from 7 American Indian communities. *American Journal of Clinical Nutrition, 78,* 301–312.

Centers for Disease Control and Prevention (CDC). (2002a). *Obesity still on the rise new data show.* Retrieved February 10, 2003, from http://www.cdc.gov/nchs/releases/02news/obesityonrise.htm

CDC. (2002b). *School Health Index: For physical activity, healthy eating, and a tobacco-free lifestyle.* [Elementary school version.] Atlanta, GA: Author.

CDC. (2003a). *BMI for adults: What is BMI?* Retrieved October 29, 2004, from http://www.cdc.gov/nccdphp/dnpa/bmi/bmi-adult.htm

CDC. (2003b). *BMI for children and teens.* Retrieved October 29, 2004, from http://www.cdc.gov/nccdphp/dnpa/bmi/bmi-for-age.htm

CDC. (2004). *Prevalence of overweight among children and adolescents: United States 1999–2002.* Retrieved October 29, 2004, from http://www.cdc.gov/nchs/products/pubs/pubd/hestats/overwght99.htm

Center for Science in the Public Interest (n.d.). Policy options: Public policy can make it easier for people to eat well, be physically active, and watch their weight. Retrieved October 21, 2004, from http://www.cspinet.org/nutritionpolicy/policy_options.html

Chomitz, V., Collins, J., Kim, J., Kramer, E., & McGowan, R. (2003). Promoting healthy weight among elementary school children via a health report card approach. *Archives of Pediatric and Adolescent Medicine, 157,* 765–772.

Davis, S. M., Clay, T., Smyth, M., Gittelsohn, J., Arviso, V., & Flint-Wagner, H., et al. (2003). Pathways curriculum and family interventions to promote healthful eating and physical activity in American Indian school children. *Preventive Medicine, 37,* 24–34.

Davis, S. M., & Reid, R. (1999). Practicing participatory research in American Indian communities. *American Journal of Clinical Nutrition, 69*(Suppl.), 755–759.

Davison, K. K., & Birch, L. L. (2001). Weight status, parent reaction, and self-concept in five-year-old girls. *Pediatrics, 107,* 46–53.

Dietz, W. H., & Gortmaker, S. L. (2001). Preventing obesity in children and adolescents. *Annual Review of Public Health, 22,* 337–353.

Ebbling, C. B., Pawlak, D. B., & Ludwig, D. S. (2002). Childhood obesity: Public health crisis, common sense cure. *Lancet, 360,* 473–482.

Epstein, L. H., & Goldfield, G. S. (1999). Physical activity in the treatment of childhood overweight and obesity: Current evidence and research issues. *Medicine and Science in Sports and Exercise, 31,* 553–559.

Epstein, L. H., Myers, M. D., Raynor, H. A., & Saelens, B. E. (1998). Treatment of childhood obesity. *Pediatrics, 101,* 554–564.

Epstein, L. H., Paluch, R. A., Gordy, C. C., & Dorn, J. (2000). Decreasing sedentary behaviors in treating pediatric obesity. *Archives of Pediatrics and Adolescent Medicine, 154,* 220–226.

Epstein, L. H., Valoski, A., Wing, R. R., & McCurley, J. (1994). Ten-year outcomes of behavioral family-based treatment for childhood obesity. *Health Psychology, 13,* 373–383.

Epstein, L. H., Wing, R. R., Koeske, R., & Valoski, A. (1985). A comparison of lifestyle exercise, aerobic exercise, and calisthenics on weight loss in obese children. *Journal of Pediatrics, 107,* 358–361.

Erickson, S. J., Robinson, T. N., Haydel, F., & Killen, J. D. (2000). Are overweight children unhappy? *Archives of Pediatric and Adolescent Medicine, 154,* 931–935.

Fairburn, C. G., Welch, S. L., Doll, H. A., Davies, B. A., & O'Connor, M. E. (1997). Risk factors for bulimia nervosa. A community-based case-control study. Archives of *General Psychiatry, 54,* 509–517.

Figueroa-Colon, R., von Almen, T., Franklin, F., Schuftan, C., & Suskind, R. (1993). Comparison of two hypocaloric diets in obese children. *American Journal of Diseases of Children, 147,* 160–166.

Flegal, K. M., Graubard, B. I., Williamson, D. F., & Gail, M. H. (2005). Excess deaths associated with underweight, overweight and obesity. *Journal of the American Medical Association, 293,* 1861–1867.

Foreyt, J. P., & Cousins, J. H. (1989). Obesity. In E. J. Marsh & R. A. Barkely (Eds.), *Treatment of childhood disorders* (pp. 405–422). New York: Guilford Press.

Goldfield, G. S., Raynor, H. A., & Epstein, L. H. (2002). Treatment of pediatric obesity. In T. A. Wadden and A. J. Stunkard (Eds.), *Handbook of obesity treatment* (pp. 532–555). New York: Guilford Press.

Gortmaker, S. L., Peterson, K., Wiecha, J., Sobol, A. M., Dixit, S., & Fox, M. K. (1999). Reducing obesity via a school-based interdisciplinary intervention among youth. *Archives of Pediatric and Adolescent Medicine, 153,* 409–418.

Guo, S. S., & Chumlea, W. C. (1999). Tracking of body mass index in children in relation to overweight in adulthood. *American Journal of Clinical Nutrition, 70*(Suppl.), S145–S148.

Hill, A. J., & Silver, E. K. (1995). Fat, friendliness and unhealthy: 9-year-old children's perception of body shape stereotypes. *International Journal of Obesity, 19,* 423–430.

James, J., Thomas, P., Cavan, D., & Kerr, D. (2004). Preventing childhood obesity by reducing consumption of carbonated drinks: Cluster randomized controlled trial. *British Medical Journal, doi:10.1136/bmj.38077.458438.EE.*

Janssen, I., Craig, W. M., Boyce, W. F., & Pickett, W. (2004). Associations between overweight and obesity with bullying behaviors in school-aged children. *Pediatrics, 113,* 1187–1194.

Krebs, N. F., & Jacobson, M. S. (2003). Policy statement: Prevention of pediatric overweight and obesity. *Pediatrics, 112,* 424–430.

Ludwig, D. S., Peterson, K. E., & Gortmaker, S. L. (2001). Relation between consumption of sugar-sweetened drinks and childhood obesity: A prospective, observational analysis. *Lancet, 357,* 505–508.

Luepker, R. V., Perry, C. L., McKinlay, S. M., Nader, P. R., Parcel, G. S., Stone, E. J., et al. (1996). Outcomes of a field trial to improve children's dietary patterns and physical activity: The child and adolescent trial for cardiovascular health (CATCH). *Journal of the American Medical Association, 275,* 768–776.

Lytle, L. A., Stone, E. J., Nichaman, M. Z., Perry, C. L., Montgomery, D. H., Nicklas, T. A., et al. (1996). Changes in nutrient intakes of elementary school children following a school-based intervention: Results from the CATCH study. *Preventative Medicine, 25,* 465–477.

Mokdad, A. H., Marks, J. S., Stroup, D. F., & Gerberding, J. L. (2004). Actual causes of death in the United States, 2000. *Journal of the American Medical Association, 291,* 1238–1245.

Murray, R. D., Taras, H. L., Frankowski, B. L., McGrath, J. W., Mears, C. J., Young, T. L., et al. (2004). Policy statement: Soft drinks in schools. *Pediatrics, 113,* 152–154.

Mustillo, S., Worthman, C., Erkanko, A., Keeler, G., Angold, A., & Costello, E. J. (2003). Obesity and psychiatric disorder: Developmental trajectories. *Pediatrics, 111,* 851–859.

O'Donnell, W. E., & Warren, W. L. (2004). *Overeating questionnaire (OQ).* Los Angeles: Western Psychological Services.

Rampersaud, G. C., Bailey, L. B., & Kauwell, G. P. A. (2003). National survey beverage consumption data for children and adolescents indicate the need to encourage a shift toward more nutritive beverages. *Journal of the American Dietetic Association, 103,* 97–100.

Resnicow, K., Robinson, T. N., & Frank, E. (1999). Advances and future directions for school-based health promotion research: Commentary on the CATCH intervention trial. *Preventative Medicine, 25,* 378–383.

Robinson, T. (1999). Reducing children's television viewing to prevent obesity. *Journal of the American Medical Association, 282,* 1561–1567.

Robinson, T. (2001). Television viewing and childhood obesity. *Pediatric Clinics of North America, 48,* 1017–1025.

Siega-Riz, A. M., Popkin, B. M., & Carson, T. (1998). Trends in breakfast consumption for children in the United States from 1965 to 1991. *American Journal of Clinical Nutrition, 67*(Suppl), 748–756.

Stone, E. J. (1996). Can school health education programs make a difference? *Preventive Medicine, 25,* 54–55.

Strauss, R. S., & Pollack, H. A. (2000). Childhood obesity and self-esteem. *Pediatrics, 105,* 15.

Strauss, R. S., & Pollack, H. A. (2003). Social marginalization of overweight children. *Archives of Pediatric and Adolescent Medicine, 157,* 746–752.

U.S. Department of Health and Human Services. (2001). *The Surgeon General's call to action to prevent and decrease overweight and obesity.* Rockville, MD: Author.

Valoski, A., & Epstein, L. (1990). Nutrient intake of obese children in a family-based behavioral weight control program. *International Journal of Obesity, 14,* 667–677.

Wadden, T. A., Brownell, K. D., & Foster, G. D. (2002). Obesity: Responding to the global epidemic. *Journal of Consulting and Clinical Psychology, 70,* 510–525.

Webber, L. S., Osganian, S. K., Feldman, H. J., Wu, M., McKenzie, T., & Nichaman, M. (1996). Cardiovascualr risk factors in children after 2 ½ years of intervention—The CATCH study. *Preventative Medicine, 25,* 432–441.

Wiehe, S. (2004). Sugar high: The marketing of soft drinks to America's school children. *Archives of Pediatric and Adolescent Medicine, 158,* 209–211.

# 75

# Recurrent Headaches

**Keith D. Allen**

*Division of Pediatric Psychology*
*Munroe-Meyer Institute for Genetics and Rehabilitation*
*and University of Nebraska Medical Center*

## BACKGROUND AND DEVELOPMENT

Recurrent headaches are characterized by repeated painful episodes that are experienced across several months and occur in the absence of a well-defined medical cause. The most common recurrent headaches in children are migraine headaches, which are characterized by sharp, throbbing, moderate to severe pain, and tension headaches, which are characterized by dull, mild to moderate diffuse pain. Migraine headaches usually involve pain that is on one side of the head, pulsates, is of moderate to severe intensity, is aggravated by routine physical activity, and is associated with nausea and sensitivity to light and noise. The pain usually lasts several hours. Tension headaches typically include pain lasting minutes to days that presses and tightens, is of mild or moderate intensity, is bilateral, and does not worsen with routine physical activity. Nausea is absent, but light or noise sensitivity may be present (International Headache Society, 1988).

Although the most common characteristics used to differentiate the two types of recurrent headaches involve intensity and frequency (i.e., migraine headaches are typically infrequent and intense; tension headaches are typically frequent and moderate), there is a good deal of overlap in characteristics across these two types of recurrent headaches. Headaches are increasingly being viewed as representing different points on a continuum of severity rather than distinct diagnostic categories (Ambulatory Sentinel Practice Network, 1987). This view is consistent with research suggesting that differentiating between migraine and tension headache may not be critical to treatment success (e.g., Arndorfer & Allen, 2001).

Recurrent headaches represent a clinically significant health problem for many children and youth. A recent international study of health behavior in school-age children found that over a third of all adolescents in the United States complain about headaches in general (U.S. Department of Health and Human Services, 2003). Furthermore, headaches have been ranked fourth on a list of the most common clinical problems encountered in primary schools (DiMario, 1992) and have been found to be the most common complaint presented to school nurses in high schools (Schneider, Friedman, & Fisher, 1995). Headaches are also reported to be the most common complaint to school nurses among adolescents in other countries (Larsson & Zaluha, 2003).

Although prevalence rates vary, actual recurrent headaches appear in about 10% of all preadolescent children and up to 15% of all adolescents (e.g., Newacheck & Taylor, 1992). By far, the majority of these recurrent headaches are diagnosed as migraines. In general, current evidence suggests that recurrent headaches (a) typically first appear around 6 to 7 years of age, (b) become more prevalent with age, (c) present more frequently in preteen boys than preteen girls, and (d) present more frequently in adolescent girls than adolescent boys (McGrath & Hillier, 2001). Although predicting who will develop recurrent headaches is difficult, those who have a family history of recurrent headaches, particularly in the maternal family, clearly have an increased risk (Waters, Silberstein, & Dalessio, 1993). No clear link exists between headaches and any psychological factors (McGrath & Hillier). The most significant problems associated with headaches in general involve the potential presence of organic pathology or disease. Therefore, repeated headache activity should always be evaluated initially by a physician to rule out the presence of disease processes. The most common causes include recent infections (e.g., sinus), increased intracranial pressure from excessive fluid or swelling, solid tumors, diseases such as hypertension, or dental problems (Dalessio & Silberstein, 1993). However, even if a child has been to a physician and disease has reportedly been ruled out, school professionals working with children with headaches should be aware of symptoms that might indicate a more serious condition and the need for a medical evaluation by a physician (see Table 1). Although these symptoms do not reliably predict more serious conditions, they are present in about 30% of children with infections or tumors and only in about 10% of children with migraine headaches (Silberstein & Marcelis, 1993). Once an organic cause has been ruled out, the diagnosis of recurrent headache is appropriate.

Although recurrent headaches do not involve significant pathology or disease, that does not mean that the pain is not real. This is an important point, because outdated disease models still persist in which pain in the absence of organic disease is considered to be evidence of psychological disease (i.e., psychopathology or malingering). It appears, however, that although individuals with recurrent headaches do not have organic disease, they do tend to have unstable or poorly regulated nervous systems that are easily activated or disturbed by stress (Rothner, 1995). That is, some children are more susceptible to developing headaches in response to stress. Indeed, half of all high school students who report headaches perceive that stress and emotional tension are important factors (Schneider et al., 1995).

Events that are commonly considered to be stressful might include tests at school, negative interactions with peers, public speaking, or physical fatigue (Singer, 1994). Conditions that create stress also include too little physical activity, sleep problems, and poor eating habits (e.g., Larsson & Zaluha, 2003). But stress might also include events more commonly considered to be positive, such as going to an amusement park, attending a birthday party, engaging in physical exercise, or even sleeping in on weekends. That is, susceptible children may have nervous systems that respond to these events as though they are stressful. Over time, repeated disturbance of the unstable nervous system, without recovery, can result in recurrent pain (Barlow, 1984). In this model, recurrent headaches are not evidence of psychopathology or malingering. They are not caused by stressful events (since not everyone gets headaches under these conditions), nor are the headaches caused by the child's reactivity (since not every stressful event leads directly to a headache). Instead, it appears to be a combination of physiological reactivity and stress over time that can eventually precipitate or trigger painful episodes.

**Table 1** *Red Flag Symptoms Indicative of Possible Tumor, Disease, or Infection*

| Symptom | Example |
|---|---|
| Progressive pain | Pain that continues to worsen over time. |
| First or worst pain | Rapid onset of severe, intense pain. |
| Intellectual decline | Difficulty reading, writing, or thinking. |
| Personality change | Changes in mood or motivation. |
| Pain in face or neck | Stiff neck or pain in cheeks, eyes, or jaw. |
| Waking at night with pain | Disruption of sleep by pain onset. |
| Motor or perceptual difficulties | Increased clumsiness even when pain free. |

In addition, learned responses to pain can play an important role in understanding recurrent pain (Fordyce, 1976). When children experience recurrent headaches, they may stay home from school, lie down, massage the temples, close the shades, take medication, demand quiet, or sleep. By doing so, they learn that these behaviors typically provide some pain relief. As a result, children are much more likely to engage in the behaviors again, precisely because the behaviors produce short-term pain reduction. This pattern makes sense, of course, but unfortunately almost none of these short-term pain relief strategies provide any long-term benefit. Furthermore, these strategies often interfere with adaptive functioning at school and at home. In addition, children may learn that some pain behaviors allow them to escape unpleasant demands (e.g., chores) or unpleasant experiences (e.g., tests) or allow them increased attention from parents, nurses, or peers. It is not difficult to see how these consequences could also encourage behaviors that interfere with adaptive functioning at home and at school. However, it is the pain relief children experience that is the primary factor in determining which behaviors they learn to use when they are in pain.

Not all pain behavior in children is determined by the consequences of that behavior. Still, the importance of learning as it pertains to recurrent headaches in children cannot be overemphasized (Allen & Mathews, 1998). Perhaps this fact more than any other—that children learn to respond to pain on the basis of consequences they experience—is what has led to the growing interest in behavioral methods of intervention.

## PROBLEMS AND IMPLICATIONS

The origins of recurrent headaches and their prevalence in school-age children have some important implications for day-to-day functioning. First, although clinical evidence suggests some spontaneous remission of recurrent headaches, there are no clear indicators of who may become pain free and who will continue to suffer. However, the longer children endure relatively unpredictable episodes of pain, the more likely they are to develop other emotional or behavioral difficulties, particularly if they do not have access to age-appropriate coping strategies (Allen & Mathews, 1998). For example, headaches are generally associated with increases in anxiety as pain intensity increases. Typically, the anxiety decreases as the source of the headaches is controlled. In recurrent headaches, however, the anxiety associated with painful episodes may persist and in some cases evolve into depression, particularly as the health care system fails in repeated attempts to identify and remediate organic pathology that does not exist. Children with recurrent headaches also are more likely than headache-free children to report somatic complaints (e.g., limb and abdominal pain), anxiety, and mild depression (Carlsson, Larsson, & Mark, 1995). Not surprisingly, headache sufferers are two to five times more likely to seek heath care, resulting in a significant impact on health care utilization and costs (Stang, Osterhaus, & Celentano, 1994). However, the differences in emotional adjustment between children who are headache sufferers and headache-free children are relatively small (Carlsson et al.), and attempts to associate significant psychiatric disorders with headaches have proven unsuccessful (Sillanpaa & Anttila, 1996). Although most children with recurrent headaches are unlikely to show clinically significant psychiatric impairments (Martin & Smith, 1995), school staff should be aware that there is an increased risk for emotional distress as a by-product of recurrent pain, and it may lead to social withdrawal, impaired school performance, and decreased ability to cope with demands in the classroom (e.g., Shaw, 1988).

The second important implication of recurrent pain is that it can result in prolonged absences from school (Stang & Osterhaus, 1992). Missing school, and the resulting inactivity, not only can be counterproductive to successful long-term management of headache pain (Allen & Mathews, 1998), it also can lead to deteriorating academic performance. Recent empirical studies have found significant morbidity in terms of lost time at school (Lee & Olness, 1996), with children who experience recurrent headaches missing 2.5 times more school days than headache-free children (Abu-Arefeh & Russell, 1994). In addition, in studies of the quality of life in children with recurrent headaches, specific areas of functional impairment have been noted in school and social functioning. Because of their pain or because of related efforts to relieve pain, children and youth with recurrent headaches may not complete homework assignments and may miss important social events with peers, extracurricular activities, or family weekend activities. In addition, even when children with recurrent pain force themselves to participate, pain can diminish performance and the satisfaction typically experienced in those types of activities. Children with migraines have been found to experience patterns of impairment in school and social functioning comparable to that of children with cancer and other chronic diseases, such as rheumatoid disease (Powers, Patton, Hommel, & Hershey, 2003).

In this context, school professionals, such as school psychologists and school nurses, are in a unique position to guide the integration of children with recurrent pain into the school ecology (Allen, Mathews & Shriver, 1999). Acting either as a consultant to teachers or counselors, or as a liaison between health and school professionals, school professionals who have already gained entry into the child's school or classroom will have information about relevant pain triggers and environmental stressors that health professionals do not have. This information may be useful in reducing headache activity. In addition, school professionals may be in a better position than either physicians or parents to implement some intervention strategies. Pain control (self-regulation) skills are likely to be easier to use within the school context if they are learned and practiced directly in the school. As consultants, these professionals are also in an ideal position to educate other school personnel about the validity of pain reports, the importance of teaching active pain management skills, and the importance of modifying the school environment (i.e., responses to pain) when necessary.

## ALTERNATIVE ACTIONS FOR PREVENTION AND INTERVENTION

### Stress Reduction

Decades of research have demonstrated that chronic exposure to stress without relief can result in physical symptoms. Given that stress is thought to be a contributing

**Table 2** *Common Pharmacologic Preparations for Treatment of Recurrent Headache*

| Common Abortive Medications | | |
|---|---|---|
| Simple Analgesics | Nonsteroidal Anti-inflammatories | Prescription Preparations* |
| Tylenol, Midrin | Advil, Motrin, Nuprin, Anaprox | Imitrex, Zomig, Maxalt, Amerge |

| Common Prophylactic Medications | | | | |
|---|---|---|---|---|
| Ergot Derivatives* | Antidepressants | Antihistamines | Beta-Blockers | Anticonvulsants |
| Cafergot | Elavil | Periactin | Inderal | Depakote, Tegretal, Topamax |

*higher incidence of side effects

factor to the etiology of recurrent headaches, generic stress reduction might be considered one type of universal headache prevention. Two approaches to generic stress reduction in children involve teaching general relaxation skills and improving family support (see also chapter 19, "Stress"). Relaxation therapies are well-established and efficacious treatments for reducing stress in children (Holden, Deichmann, & Levy, 1999). For example, typical children who were taught in a prevention program to concentrate on using short, repeated self-statements suggesting states of relaxation and calm reported significantly less stress and physical complaints (Goldbeck & Schmid, 2003). Likewise, strong family support and parent–child attachment have been shown to reduce stress in children (e.g., Greenberg, Siegel, & Leitch, 1983). However, there have been no specific attempts to link either relaxation therapies or family support interventions with universal headache prevention. So although universal headache prevention probably warrants further investigation, no empirically validated approaches can be recommended at this time.

## Medical Management

The most frequent point of intervention with recurrent headaches involves medical management. Most children will have been taken by their parents to a variety of physicians (e.g., pediatrician; ear, nose, and throat specialist; or neurologist) who will seek to identify and treat an obvious underlying pathological condition. Indeed, a physician is the most appropriate professional to initially assess and treat a child presenting with recurrent headaches. Physicians who treat headaches can include pediatricians, neurologists, and family practitioners. Common pharmacologic treatments fall into two categories: abortive agents (taken to reduce pain) and prophylactic agents (taken to prevent onset). Because most simple analgesics and nonsteroidal anti-inflammatories have few side effects (see Table 2), these abortive medications are the first line of treatment for children with recurrent headaches (Singer, 1994). Prophylactic medications have a higher likelihood of side effects such as nausea, sedation, fatigue, and lightheadedness, but no studies indicate the extent to which these might affect daily functioning or school performance in children. Furthermore, a recent review of pharmacologic treatment of childhood headache has shown that no abortive or prophylactic agents have been proved effective in controlled studies with children (Pakalnis, 2001). Because pharmacological management of headache activity is highly individualized, the effectiveness and possible side effects should be closely monitored by the child's physician. The general consensus is that the use of daily prophylactics or prescription abortives is not desirable for children, especially given the behavioral pain management strategies that are viable alternatives (Pakalnis).

## Removal of Headache Triggers

One alternative to medically managing recurrent headaches involves learning to remove or avoid stressors that produce the biological reactivity associated with headaches. Typically, the longer children experience recurrent headaches, the larger the number of headache triggers that are likely to be present (Zeltzer, Barr, McGrath, & Schechter, 1992). In the school setting, these may involve particularly stressful events such as taking tests, reading out loud in class, or having a negative interaction with a peer. Identifying these as triggers may suggest opportunities for intervention in terms of eliminating or avoiding some triggers. For example, a child whose headaches are triggered by test anxiety may need to be taught test-taking strategies. Headaches could also possibly be triggered by academic difficulties with a particular subject, and tutoring might help. Other common triggers include fatigue and diet. Numerous experimental studies have linked fatigue and headaches, and a recent treatment outcome study found that teaching children better sleep habits significantly reduced the frequency and duration of headaches (Bruni, Galli, & Guidetti, 1999). Parents might be prompted to help an adolescent develop a more consistent and predictable sleep routine (see also chapter 77, "Sleep and Sleep Problems"). Headaches can also be triggered by foods; most often those with caffeine (e.g., colas or chocolate), nitrates (e.g., processed meats), or MSG (e.g., Chinese foods). The removal of these substances from the diet at home and at school might offer some benefit. Finally, a child whose headaches are triggered by negative social interactions such as teasing may need to be taught relevant problem-solving skills, or the class may need a classwide management program to reduce teasing. Unfortunately, there is little research investigating trigger management as an intervention for recurrent headaches. This general lack of research on eliminating triggers as an intervention probably reflects the fact that there is little evidence that triggers alone account for a significant number of headaches.

## Self-Regulation Through Relaxation

Another alternative for treating the biological factors associated with recurrent headaches involves teaching the child to control the physiological reactivity that occurs in response to stress. This is one of the most well-researched and effective interventions for managing recurrent headache pain in children. Self-regulation training for children typically involves teaching simple relaxation procedures or biofeedback. Sufficient evidence now exists from treatment outcome studies to conclude that both approaches are well established as effective treatments for recurrent headaches in children (Holden et al., 1999). Moreover, researchers have extended clinic-based treatment into the home (Allen & Shriver, 1998), into primary care settings (Allen, Elliott, & Arndorfer, 2002), and into schools (Larsson, Melin, Lamminen, & Ullsted, 1987) and found equally significant improvements.

The actual self-regulation skills the child is taught can vary widely depending on how quickly the child learns the skills, the child's cognitive capabilities, and the resources available. Relaxation training might involve progressive muscle relaxation, guided imagery, diaphragmatic breathing, or some combination of these (see Cautela & Groden, 1978). In progressive muscle relaxation, children learn to identify the difference between a relaxed body and a tense body. Children are coached to progressively tighten and relax different body regions, usually starting with easy areas (e.g., fists) and gradually moving to other areas such as shoulders, neck, legs, arms, and face. The practice session is often recorded on audiotape so that the child can practice at home. Through practice, children learn to identify when the body is tense and how to relax it, even when in school. This type of approach has been successfully implemented by school nurses (e.g., Larsson & Carlsson, 1996), but it is labor intensive and may not be well received by all school nurses (Fichtel & Larsson, 2004) or by students (Schneider, et al., 1995) who go to the nurse's office to rest rather than to receive treatment.

In guided imagery, children are taught to imagine a previous experience, pleasant event, or fantasy that will help them relax and will distract them from the pain. Children are typically encouraged to use their senses to imagine the colors, feelings, sounds, tastes, and aromas that would accompany the image. For children, these images might be social events, sporting activities, tranquil situations, or even unusual fantasy scenes. Diaphragmatic breathing involves teaching children to take slow, deep breaths as they concentrate on breathing with the diaphragm.

## Self-Regulation Through Biofeedback

Biofeedback involves learning to relax and control muscle tension (electromyographic biofeedback) or learning to increase hand temperature (thermal biofeedback). Thermal biofeedback has received significant attention. Investigations have repeatedly demonstrated that thermal biofeedback is an effective, efficient treatment for pediatric headache, with more than two-thirds of the children experiencing a significant (50%) reduction in headache activity with biofeedback (e.g., Hermann & Blanchard, 2002). Thermal biofeedback can be efficiently and effectively applied in the home or in a primary care clinic, and can work for tension as well as migraine headache sufferers (e.g., Arndorfer & Allen, 2001).

The success of thermal biofeedback lies, in part, in the immediacy of the feedback, a feature known to be important when learning new behaviors. But biofeedback is also attractive because it holds particular appeal for children. Children sit in front of a computer screen with sensors taped to their skin, and they watch as the computer displays moment-to-moment changes in autonomic activity. In the case of thermal biofeedback, the information provided describes changes in hand temperature, an indirect measure of peripheral blood flow. In an era in which video and computer games are an established part of the culture, for many children biofeedback seems like a game in which the body serves as the joystick. Perhaps as a result, thermal biofeedback is extremely easy to learn and to teach. Some researchers have suggested that children are more enthusiastic and less skeptical than adults and that they learn more quickly than adults (e.g., Culbert, Kajander, & Reaney, 1996). Finally, the availability of inexpensive home temperature trainers makes thermal biofeedback portable and easy to use within a variety of settings, including the classroom.

Although biofeedback may not be viable or practical to teach in some school settings, muscle relaxation, imagery, and diaphragmatic breathing are self-regulation skills that a knowledgeable school psychologist could teach a child. However, both training and motivation are important components of effective delivery of these interventions in the school setting. In one study, training that relied on audiotaped instructions was insufficient to produce meaningful headache improvements when treatment was delivered by school nurses (Fichtel & Larsson, 2004). In addition, student motivation could be a significant factor, since home practice appears to be an important component of effective intervention with any of these self-regulation skills. There appears to be a relationship between the amount of home practice and improvement in pain (e.g., Allen & Shriver, 1997), so emphasis should be on regular practice of self-regulation skills.

## Management of Learned Responses to Pain

In addition to removing headache triggers or teaching self-regulation skills, selecting an intervention alternative that involves management of a child's learned responses to pain is important. The typical responses to headache pain—lying down in the nurse's office, shutting off lights and sound, staying home from school, or missing extracurricular activities—usually provide the child with some level of immediate pain relief. That is, most children respond as they do to pain, not because they are malingering or lazy, but because those responses reduce pain. Yet these same responses do not seem to produce significant reductions in long-term pain frequency, intensity, or duration (Allen & Mathews, 1998). Unfortunately, the immediate relief is a powerful consequence, so children are not easily persuaded to attempt alternative strategies such as biofeedback or relaxation. In addition, parents and teachers often encourage typical responses to headache pain precisely because it provides the child with some relief, if only for a short time.

Not surprisingly, creating an environment that supports alternative ways of responding to pain can be an important part of enhancing treatment outcome (e.g., Allen & Shriver, 1998). Table 3 presents an example of guidelines that may help caregivers discourage the child's typical pain responses and instead encourage adaptive responses that provide more long-term benefit. In particular, parents and teachers are asked to eliminate questions about the status of pain (e.g., how is the pain? where is it today?). In addition to being asked to provide prompts for children to use self-regulation strategies if needed, adults are encouraged to eliminate efforts to assist with pain management (i.e., no suggestions about how the pain should be handled). Finally, parents and teachers are asked to encourage active participation in normal activities by asking the child to try to remain in the classroom while managing pain, to participate in physical education, to complete after-school activities, and to complete chores. For example, children would be discouraged from lying quietly in a dark room with a compress on their head until the pain subsides, even though the inactivity may provide some degree of immediate relief. However, it provides no long-term solution for managing or eliminating pain. Parents who were given the guidelines presented in Table 3 were found to have children who exhibited more adaptive and independent coping with their headache pain (e.g., attending school, completing school work, and participating in daily activities), regardless of how much the children practiced self-regulation skills, while adults who did not follow through with or were not given the recommendations had children who exhibited less adaptive coping, regardless of how much they practiced self-regulation strategies.

Two cautions should be made with regard to the management of learned responses to pain. First, although adherence to these guidelines was found to improve treatment outcome, it was not found to be necessary for good treatment outcome (Allen & Shriver, 1998). Consistent with decades of research on the use of nondrug treatments such as biofeedback and relaxation therapies, good outcomes were also found without

**Table 3** *Pain Behavior Management Guidelines for Care Providers*

1. Eliminate status checks:

   Do not ask questions about pain intensity, frequency, duration, location.

2. Reduce response to pain behavior:

   Make no effort to assist the child in coping (other than to issue a single prompt to practice self-regulation skills). Do not offer assistance or suggestions for coping. Do not offer medication.

3. Reduce pharmacological dependence:

   Do not offer over-the-counter or abortive medication. If medication is requested, deliver only as prescribed and not as needed (i.e., follow directed timetable).

4. Encourage normal activity:

   Insist on attendance at school, maintenance of daily chores and responsibilities, and participation in regular activities (lessons, practices, or clubs).

5. Encourage independent management of pain:

   Praise and publicly acknowledge independent practice of self-regulation skills during pain-free episodes. If pain is reported, issue a single prompt to practice self-regulation skills. Praise and reward compliance with guideline 4 when report of pain has been made.

6. Recruit others to follow rules 1–5:

   School personnel should not send child home. Child should be encouraged and permitted to practice self-regulation skills in the classroom; workload should not be modified.

7. Treat pain that requires a reduction in activity as illness:

   If school, activities, chores, or responsibilities are missed, treat child as ill and send to bed for the remainder of the day, even if pain is resolved. Do not permit television viewing, games (video), or special treatment.

*Note.* Adapted from: "Role of Parent-Mediated Pain Behavior Management Strategies in Biofeedback Treatment of Childhood Migraine Headaches," by K. D. Allen and M. D. Shriver, 1998, *Behavior Therapy, 29,* pp. 477–490. Adapted with permission.

management of learned responses to pain. This is an important point, because parents or teachers may find adhering to these types of guidelines to be troublesome. Guidelines that dissuade adults from helping with pain management, that require children to stay active, or that ask that children practice pain management in the classroom rather than the nurse's office may seem harsh and dispassionate. In this regard, the recommendations are best viewed as guidelines, not rules. Research does not support slavish adherence to the guidelines regardless of individual circumstances, school policies, or personal level of comfort. Children will likely benefit if they are encouraged and supported in their use of alternative approaches to pain management, but flexibility and adaptation to particular circumstances may also be important.

## SUMMARY

Recurrent headaches represent a clinically significant health problem for many children and adolescents. If left untreated, headaches may have a significant impact on daily functioning in school. Recurrent headaches represent one type of childhood health problem that school psychologists can address through prevention and through a variety of evidence-based alternative intervention strategies. Intervention centers on the notion that recurrent headaches come from the interactive effects of biological reactivity, environmental stress, and learning. Intervention begins with a thorough medical evaluation by the child's physician and usually some attempt at medical management. Alternative behavioral interventions include modifying headache triggers, teaching simple self-regulation strategies such as relaxation or biofeedback, and developing a supportive environment that encourages adaptive coping. School staff should know that children can learn to control their body's reactivity, that the skills for controlling reactivity are easily learned, and that children who learn self-regulation can reduce the reactivity of the body and in many cases reduce the frequency of pain. At the same time, school staff should know that it is important to create an environment in which independent, adaptive coping is supported by encouraging the use of self-regulation skills along with active engagement in life. Improvements in pain management and adaptive functioning will likely occur if these recommendations are implemented both at home and at school, suggesting the importance of coordinating efforts through communication between family and school personnel.

## AUTHOR NOTES

Address correspondence to Keith D. Allen, Munroe-Meyer Institute, 985450 Nebraska Medical Center, Omaha, NE 68198-5450. This manuscript was supported in part by grant 5 T73 MC 00023-13 0 from the Maternal and Child Bureau, Health Resources Services Administration, Department of Health and Human Services, and by grant 90DD0533 from the Administration on Developmental Disabilities (ADD), Administration for Children and Families.

## RECOMMENDED RESOURCES

### Books and Other Printed Material

Abu-Arafeh, I. (Ed.). (2004). *Childhood headache.* New York: Mac Keith Press.

This is an edited book with an international team of medical experts who offer an up-to-date and excellent overview of possible genetic factors, various headache syndromes, common clinical features, and both medical and dietary management aspects of childhood headaches. It is intended more for clinicians than school practitioners, but it is a useful resource for anyone intending to regularly work with children with headaches.

Allen, K. D., Mathews, J. M., & Shriver, M. D. (1999). Children and recurrent headaches: Assessment and treatment implications for school psychologists. *School Psychology Review 28,* 266–279.

This article provides a more detailed problem-solving approach to school-based management of recurrent pain in children, and headaches in particular. It provides details regarding headache assessment procedures, includes examples of assessment instruments, offers specific suggestions for how to present information to children and parents, and presents strategies for evaluating outcomes and problem-solving treatment failures.

McGrath, P. A, & Hillier, L. M. (Eds.). (2001). *The child with headache: Diagnosis and treatment.* Seattle: IASP Press.

This book reviews the findings from extensive research and clinical practice that have occurred in the Pediatric Pain Program at the University of Western Ontario. The emphasis is on environmental stress as a primary causal factor of headaches. The authors provide excellent examples of how to sell the importance of stress management to children and families and how to develop and implement an array of management strategies. Included are numerous helpful tables and appendices that detail how to assess headaches and develop recommendations. From a practical standpoint, a clinician with very little background in pain management would find very specific help regarding how to assess, diagnose, plan, and deliver treatment.

### Websites

*http://www.headaches.org*

The website of the National Headache Foundation is an excellent, comprehensive, user-friendly site that offers information for both patients and professionals. The user can click on Headache Sufferer and then go to Educational Resources and review the modules on Children's Headaches and on Treatment. The website provides comprehensive reviews of behavioral interventions (e.g., relaxation, biofeedback, and stress management), as well as medical interventions, and it also covers preventive strategies.

*http://www.achenet.org/kids/children.php*

The website of the American Council for Headache Education: Headaches in Children focuses on the biological origins and medical management of childhood headaches. It provides a good overview of the clinical features of childhood headaches, the various triggers that affect children, some different prevention strategies that are available, and the basics of medical management of childhood headache.

*http://www.aafp.org/afp/20020215/625.html*

The website of the American Academy of Family Physicians: Headaches in Children and Adolescents is another article that provides primarily a medical orientation on the biological origins and management of headaches. It provides very nice tables on causes, prevalence, assessment, and medications and also provides patient information handouts and a PDF version for downloading and printing.

# REFERENCES


Abu-Arafeh, I. & Russell, G. (1994). Prevalence of headache and migraine in schoolchildren. *British Medical Journal 309,* 765–769.

Allen, K. D., Elliott, A. E., & Arndorfer, R. (2002). Behavioral pain management for pediatric headache in primary care. *Children's Health Care, 31,* 175–189.

Allen, K. D., & Mathews, J. R. (1998). Behavior management of recurrent pain in children. In T. S. Watson & F. Gresham (Eds.), *Handbook of child behavior therapy: Ecological considerations in assessment, treatment, and evaluation* (pp. 263–285). New York: Plenum Press.

Allen, K. D., Mathews, J. R., & Shriver, M. D. (1999). Children and recurrent headaches: Assessment and treatment implications for school psychologists. *School Psychology Review, 28,* 266–279.

Allen, K. D., & Shriver, M. (1997). Enhanced performance feedback to strengthen biofeedback treatment outcome with childhood migraine. *Headache, 37,* 169–173.

Allen, K. D., & Shriver, M. D. (1998). Role of parent-mediated pain behavior management strategies in biofeedback treatment of childhood migraine headaches. *Behavior Therapy, 29,* 477–490.

Ambulatory Sentinel Practice Network. (1987). A study of headache in North American primary care. *Journal of the Royal College of General Practitioners, 37,* 400–403.

Arndorfer, R. E., & Allen, K. D. (2001). Extending the efficacy of a thermal biofeedback treatment package to the management of tension headaches in children. *Headache, 41,* 183–192.

Barlow, C. F. (1984). *Headaches and migraine in childhood.* Philadelphia: J. B. Lippincott.

Bruni, O., Galli, F., & Guidetti, V. (1999). Sleep hygiene and migraine in children and adolescents. *Cephalalgia, 19* (Suppl. 25), 57–59.

Carlsson, J., Larsson, B., & Mark, A. (1995). Psychosocial functioning in schoolchildren with recurrent headaches. *Headache, 36,* 77–82.

Cautela, J. R., & Groden, J. (1978). *Relaxation: A comprehensive manual for adults, children, and children with special needs.* Champaign, IL: Research Press.

Culbert, T. P., Kajander, R. L., & Reaney, J. B. (1996). Biofeedback with children and adolescents: Clinical observations and patient perspectives. *Journal of Developmental and Behavioral Pediatrics, 17,* 342–350.

Dalessio, D. L., & Silberstein, S. D. (1993). Diagnosis and classification of headache. In D. J. Dalessio & S. D. Silberstein (Eds.), *Wolff's headache and other head pain* (6th ed., pp. 3–18). New York: Oxford Press.

DiMario, F. J. (1992). Childhood headaches: A school nurse perspective. *Clinical Pediatrics, 31,* 279–282.

Fichtel, A. F., & Larsson, B. (2004). Relaxation treatment administered by school nurses to adolescents with recurrent headache. *Headache, 44,* 545–554.

Fordyce, W. E. (1976). *Behavioral methods for chronic pain and illness.* St. Louis, MO: C. V. Mosby.

Goldbeck, L., & Schmid, K. (2003). Effectiveness of autogenic relaxation training on children and adolescents with behavioral and emotional problems. *Journal of the Academy of Child and Adolescent Psychiatry, 42,* 1046–1054.

Greenberg, M., Siegel, J., & Leitch, C. (1983). The nature and importance of attachment relationships to parents and peers during adolescence. *Journal of Youth and Adolescence, 12,* 373–386.

Hermann, C., & Blanchard, E. B. (2002). Biofeedback in the treatment of headache and other childhood pain. *Applied Psychophysiology and Biofeedback, 27,* 143–162.

Holden, W. E., Deichmann, M., & Levy, J. (1999). Empirically supported treatments in pediatric psychology. *Recurrent Pediatric Headache, 24,* 91–109.

International Headache Society. (1988). Classification and diagnostic criteria for headache disorders, cranial neuralgias and facial pain. *Cephalalgia, 8,* 19–28.

Larsson, B., & Carlsson, J. (1996). A school-based, nurse administered relaxation training for children with chronic tension-type headache. *Journal of Pediatric Psychology, 21,* 603–614.

Larsson, B., Melin, L., Lamminen, M., & Ullsted, F. (1987). A school-based treatment of chronic headaches in adolescent. *Journal of Pediatric Psychology, 12,* 553–556.

Larsson, B., & Zaluha, M. (2003). Swedish school nurses' view of school health care utilization, causes and management of recurrent headaches among school children. *Scandinavian Journal of Caring Sciences, 17,* 232–238.

Lee, L. H., & Olness, K. (1996). Clinical and demographic characteristics of migraine in urban children. *Headache, 37,* 269–276.

Martin, S. E., & Smith, M. S. (1995). Psychosocial factors in recurrent pediatric headache. *Pediatric Annals, 24,* 469–474.

McGrath, P. A., & Hillier, L. M. (Eds.). (2001). *The child with headache: Diagnosis and treatment.* Seattle: IASP Press.

Newacheck, P. W., & Taylor, W. (1992). Childhood chronic illness: Prevalence, severity, and impact. *American Journal of Public Health, 82,* 364–371.

Pakalnis, A. (2001). New avenues in treatment of pediatric migraine: A review of the literature. *Family Practice, 18,* 101–106.

Powers, S. W., Patton, S. R., Hommel, K. A., & Hershey, A. D. (2003). Quality of life in childhood migraines: Clinical impact and comparison to other chronic illnesses. *Pediatrics, 111,* 1–5.

Rothner, A. D. (1995). Pathophysiology of recurrent headaches in children and adolescents. *Pediatric Annals, 24,* 458–466.

Schneider, M. B., Friedman, S. B., & Fisher, M. (1995). Stated and unstated reasons for visiting a high school nurse's office. *Journal of Adolescent Health, 16,* 35–40.

Shaw, J. A. (1988). Childhood depression. *Medical Clinics of North America, 72,* 831–845.

Silberstein, S. D., & Marcelis, J. (1993). Headache associated with abnormalities in intracranial structure or pressure. In D. J. Dalessio & S. D. Silberstein (Eds.), *Wolff's headache and other head pain* (6th ed., pp. 438–461). New York: Oxford Press.

Sillanpaa, M., & Anttila, P. (1996). Increasing prevalence of headache in 7-year-old schoolchildren. *Headache, 36,* 466–470.

Singer, H. S. (1994). Migraine headaches in children. *Pediatrics in Review, 15,* 94–101.

Stang, P. E., & Osterhaus, J. T. (1992). Impact of migraine in the United States: Data from the National Health Interview Survey. *Headache, 33,* 29–35.

Stang, P. E., Osterhaus, J. T., & Celentano, D. D. (1994). Migraine: Patterns of healthcare use. *Neurology, 44* (Suppl. 4), s47–s55.

U.S. Department of Health and Human Services, Health Resources and Services Administration. (2003). *U.S. teens in our world.* Rockville, MD: U.S. Department of Health and Human Services.

Waters, W. E., Silberstein, S. D., & Dalessio, D. J. (1993). Diagnosis and classification of headache. In D. J. Dalessio & S. D. Silberstein (Eds.), *Wolff's headache and other head pain* (6th ed., pp. 3–18). New York: Oxford Press.

Zeltzer, L. K., Barr, R. G., McGrath, P. A., & Schechter, N. L. (1992). Pediatric pain: Interacting behavioral and physical factors. *Pediatrics, 90,* 816–821.

# 76

# Substance Abuse

**Susan G. Forman**
**Brenna H. Bry**
**Phuong-Anh Urga**

*Rutgers, The State University of New Jersey*

Substance abuse is typically defined as the use of alcohol or other drugs in ways that negatively affect life functions. These negative effects can be legal (e.g., arrests), physical (e.g., injuries), emotional (e.g., irritability), or behavioral (e.g., truancy, impaired academic performance, auto accidents, risky sex, violence, or delinquency). Most adolescents who use alcohol and drugs do not use them in ways that are considered abuse. Use that begins at an earlier than average age, however, increases the probability that use will escalate into abuse. Furthermore, use by children and adolescents at any age places them at greater risk for negative consequences than does abstinence.

Both substance use and abuse, of course, are hidden behaviors in that they are done out of sight of authority figures. Nevertheless, parents, school personnel, and others who care about children and adolescents will want to be as knowledgeable as possible in order to hold realistic expectations about this hidden behavior. Accordingly, they will find it helpful to know (a) the prevalence of use of different substances at different ages, (b) correlates of substance abuse, (c) how substance abuse works, (d) what schools and parents can do to prevent or discourage abuse, and (e) how best to intervene when substance abuse is discovered. This chapter reviews recent developments in these areas.

## BACKGROUND AND DEVELOPMENT

### Prevalence

The Monitoring the Future project has studied national prevalence of adolescent substance use since 1975 using yearly representative samples of public and private secondary school students (Johnston, O'Malley, Bachman, & Schulenberg, 2003). Results from the 2003 survey are summarized in Table 1. Although illicit drug use rates are down from their peak in the early 1980s, when roughly 66% of students surveyed had used an illicit substance in the past year, substance use is nevertheless still substantial. The 2003 survey estimated that 51% of the students had used a substance in the past year, meaning that more than half of secondary school students are placing themselves at risk for negative consequences.

Marijuana is by far the most widely used illicit drug. As early as the 8th grade, one out of every six students (17.5%) reported having tried marijuana. By the 12th grade, nearly half of all students (46%) reported some marijuana use in their lifetime. Furthermore, 6% of high school seniors had been daily marijuana smokers (for at least 1 month) at some time prior to the 2003 survey. Other classes of illicit drugs that are most widely used by adolescents are amphetamines, inhalants, hallucinogens (including LSD and ecstasy), tranquilizers, and barbiturates.

In addition to studying drug use among 8th, 10th, and 12th graders, the annual survey includes attitudinal indicators related to drug use. For the first time in several years, all three grade levels showed an increase in perceived risk for regular marijuana use and a decline in the perceived availability of marijuana. The reason for the decrease in illicit drug use since the 1980s is believed to be that more students now view use as risky.

Alcohol and cigarette use remains more widespread than use of any of the illicit drugs. Whereas the percentage of students using any illicit drug continued to decline, data from the 2003 survey suggest that alcohol use remains stable. Of 8th and 12th graders, 46% and 77%,

**Table 1** *Prevalence of Adolescent Substance Use*

| | Lifetime | 30-Day | Daily |
|---|---|---|---|
| **Cigarettes** | | | |
| Grade 8 | 28.4 | 10.2 | 4.5 |
| Grade 10 | 43.0 | 16.7 | 8.9 |
| Grade 12 | 53.7 | 24.4 | 15.8 |
| **Alcohol** | | | |
| Grade 10 | 66.0 | 35.4 | 1.5 |
| Grade 12 | 76.6 | 47.5 | 3.2 |
| **Marijuana** | | | |
| Grade 8 | 17.5 | 7.5 | 1.0 |
| Grade 10 | 36.4 | 17.0 | 3.6 |
| Grade 12 | 46.1 | 21.2 | 6.0 |
| **Any Illicit Drug Including Inhalants** | | | |
| Grade 8 | 30.3 | 12.1 | NA |
| Grade 10 | 44.9 | 20.5 | NA |
| Grade 12 | 52.8 | 24.6 | NA |

*Note.* Numbers represent percentages of the sample reporting use. Adapted from *Ecstasy Use Falls for Second Year in a Row, Overall Teen Drug Use Drops*, by L. D. Johnston, P. M. O'Malley, J. G. Bachman, and J. E. Schulenberg, 2003, Ann Arbor, MI: University of Michigan News and Information Services [Online]. Retrieved May 5, 2004, from *http://www.monitoringthefuture.org*

respectively, reported having at least tried alcohol. Of greater concern than just any use of alcohol is its use to the point of inebriation: 21% of the 8th graders, 44% of the 10th graders, and 62% of the 12th graders reported that they have been drunk at least once. Cigarette smoking showed a slight decrease from 2002; however, rates are still high: 28% of 8th graders and 54% of 12th graders reported having smoked a cigarette at least once; 24% of high school seniors identify themselves as current smokers who smoke less than daily, and 16% are current daily smokers.

The prevalence data in Table 1 are averaged across races and ethnicities; however, rates of use are consistently higher for White students than for Black or Hispanic students. For instance, whereas 56% of White seniors reported using alcohol in the past 30 days, only 34% of Black seniors did. In addition, White seniors were almost three times as likely as Black seniors (38% compared with 14%) to report having been drunk in the past 30 days (Johnston, O'Malley, & Bachman, 1998).

In addition to presenting prevalence rates, Johnston et al.'s (2003) survey provides estimates of age of initiation for various drug classes. By the end of sixth grade, between 15% and 20% of students have had their first cigarette, between 7% and 23% have had their first alcoholic beverage, and between 3% and 6% have tried marijuana. The age at which adolescents are introduced to substance use appears to be decreasing. This trend is of particular concern.

## Risk and Protective Factors

Not all adolescents who try alcohol or illicit drugs develop a pattern of abuse. To help explain the origins and pathways to abuse, researchers have developed a descriptive and predictive framework focused on factors that differentiate adolescents who may be more vulnerable to substance abuse from those who may be less vulnerable. A *risk factor* is defined as any characteristic or condition that, if present, increases the probability of substance abuse.

Empirical research supports a model that represents multiple risk factors. No single causal pathway appears to lead to drug abuse; rather, the more risk factors a child or adolescent is exposed to, the more vulnerable he or she is to developing substance abuse in adolescence or young adulthood. Additionally, an individual's vulnerability for developing substance abuse and related health and social problems decreases when the number of risk factors he or she is exposed to is reduced (Bry, 1996).

Exposure to even a significant number of risk factors does not necessarily result in the development of substance abuse and related behavioral problems. Many children are exposed to high-risk environments and do not experience significant problems or impairment. As noted above, the majority of children who initiate alcohol and substance use do not escalate to abuse. The presence of protective factors may account for this fact. Protective factors are influences that prevent, limit, or reduce substance abuse. In the presence of existing risk factors, a protective factor may interact with a risk factor to counter, buffer, or neutralize risk for substance abuse (Hawkins, Catalano, & Miller, 1992).

Risk and protective factors exist at every level at which a child or adolescent interacts with others and the surrounding environment. These factors are commonly organized into the following domains: individual (psychological, behavioral, and biological factors), family (function, management, and bonding), peer (norms and activities), school (bonding, climate, policy, and performance), and community and society (bonding, norms, resources, and policy/sanctions). Table 2 provides a framework for characterizing risk and protective factors in each of the five domains.

**Table 2** *Risk and Protective Factors Associated With Child and Adolescent Substance Use*

| Domain | Risk Factors | Protective Factors |
|---|---|---|
| *Individual* | • Certain physical, emotional, or personality traits:<br>○ Inherited genetic vulnerability<br>○ Low self-esteem<br>○ Violence and aggression<br>○ Impulsivity and risk-taking propensity<br>○ Maladaptive coping responses<br>○ Alienation<br>○ Rejection of prosocial values.<br>• Psychological disorders (e.g., conduct disorder, ADHD, depression).<br>• Early and persistent aggressive behavior.<br>• Early age of substance use initiation.<br>• Academic failure.<br>• No involvement in social or cultural activities.<br>• Lack of positive health behaviors. | • Positive relationships with adults.<br>• Knowledge regarding risks associated with substance use or abuse.<br>• Negative attitudes toward substances and substance use.<br>• Bonding to prosocial and conventional values.<br>• Social competence.<br>• Involvement in alternative activities.<br>• Sense of well-being and self-confidence.<br>• Positive future plans and goals.<br>• Academic achievement. |
| *Family* | • Lack of family bonding.<br>• Family conflict or domestic violence.<br>• Lack of clear expectations or consequences of behavior (including substance use).<br>• Lack of parental monitoring.<br>• Excessive or inconsistent punishment.<br>• Family history of substance abuse.<br>• Parental use of substances, toleration of use by children, or involvement of children in their own use ("Get me a beer"). | • Close family relationships.<br>• Members who share responsibilities, including decision making.<br>• Clear communication.<br>• Consistent parenting practices.<br>• Clear expectations and consequences of behavior.<br>• Parental monitoring.<br>• Parental support and involvement in school. |
| *Peer* | • Peers who reinforce negative norms and expectations regarding substance use.<br>• Peers who engage in substance use or delinquent behavior. | • Peers involved in substance-free activities.<br>• Friends who disapprove of substance use.<br>• Friends who encourage school involvement. |
| *School* | • Lack of clear expectations and consequences (academic and behavioral).<br>• Lack of sense of belonging to school.<br>• Lack of parental and community involvement. | • Promotes school bonding and attendance.<br>• Communicates high academic and behavioral expectations.<br>• Encourages goal setting, academic achievement, and social development.<br>• Sponsors substance-free events and activities. |

*(Continued)*

**Table 2** *Continued*

| Domain | Risk Factors | Protective Factors |
|---|---|---|
| *Community* | • Alcohol and substances readily available.<br>• Sale of alcohol and tobacco to minors.<br>• Unclear or inconsistent laws and ordinances (e.g., where alcohol use is permitted).<br>• Conflicting substance use messages ("beer gardens" at fairs versus "Just Say No").<br>• Lack of community bonding.<br>• Extreme economic deprivation.<br>• Lack of strong social institutions.<br>• Neighborhood disorganization. | • Opportunities for community involvement.<br>• Active religious organizations.<br>• Clear and consistent laws and ordinances.<br>• Policies and norms that encourage nonuse (higher taxation for alcohol and tobacco, strict regulations for licensing of establishments that sell alcohol).<br>• Available resources (e.g., housing, health care, child care, jobs, and recreation).<br>• Community prevention programs. |

*Note.* Developed from: "Psychological Approaches to Prevention", by B. H. Bry, 1996, in W. K. Bickel and R. J. DeGrandpre (Eds.), *Drug Policy and Human Nature: Psychological Perspectives on the Prevention, Management, and Treatment of Illicit Drug Use* (pp. 55–76), New York: Plenum Press. Also from "Risk and Protective Factors for Alcohol and Other Drug Problems in Adolescence and Early Adulthood: Implications for Substance Abuse Prevention," by J. D. Hawkins, R. F. Catalano, and J. Y. Miller, 1992, *Psychological Bulletin, 112*, pp. 64–105.

Risk and protective factors exert their influence within a developmental trajectory, or path. Children progress through different developmental stages, each of which is associated with unique social influences, demands, and challenges. Accordingly, the potential effects of specific risk factors and protective factors change with age. For example, risk factors within the family have greater impact on a younger child, whereas association with drug-abusing peers may be a more significant risk factor for an adolescent. Furthermore, critical or sensitive periods in development may heighten the importance of risk or protective factors.

The key risk periods for drug abuse occur during major transitions in children's lives (Schulenberg & Maggs, 2002). These transitions include significant changes in physical development (i.e., puberty) or social situations (e.g., transition from middle to high school). When children move from elementary to middle or junior high school, they often experience new academic and social situations, such as learning to interact with a wider group of peers and encountering greater expectations for academic performance. It is at this stage—early adolescence—that children are likely to encounter substances for the first time. The transition to high school presents additional social, psychological, and educational challenges. Exposure to substances, substance abusers, and social activities involving substances is also likely to increase. Negotiating these increasing demands may introduce new risk factors or exacerbate existing risk factors for an adolescent.

Two findings from research on protective factors have important implications for prevention efforts aimed at adolescent substance abuse. First, the transition from childhood to adolescence is an important developmental period during which protective factors may be especially influential (Scheier, Newcomb, & Skager, 1994). Second, protective factors may have a cumulative effect: the more protective factors a child has on his or her side, the greater the reduction in risk for developing problems related to substance use (Swadi, 1999). Current research encourages the use of preventive interventions that strengthen protection in the effort to reduce adolescent vulnerability.

The presence of psychological disorders has been identified as a risk factor for adolescent substance abuse. The three most commonly cited conditions are conduct disorder, Attention Deficit/Hyperactivity Disorder (ADHD), and depression (Swadi, 1999). Children with ADHD have an elevated risk of abusing alcohol and illicit substances (Wilens, Faraone, Biederman, & Gunawardene, 2003). When tracked to adulthood, those with ADHD show higher rates of transition to abuse compared with those without the disorder. Concern regarding this association includes the worry that ADHD treatment medications (i.e., prescription stimulants) increase the risk of substance abuse. However, treatment medications appear to actually help reduce the risk of substance abuse rather than elevate it. One study found that treating ADHD with medications appeared to reduce the risk of substance abuse or dependence by

84% (Biederman, Wilens, Mick, Spencer, & Faraone, 1999), and another study estimated that untreated children with ADHD have about twice the risk of substance abuse as children without the disorder (Wilens et al.). Researchers hypothesize that children with ADHD who are not being treated with medication are at elevated risk because they attempt to self-medicate their symptoms with alcohol and other substances. This hypothesis is important to keep in mind when considering other psychological disorders that co-occur with adolescent substance abuse.

Another risk factor that requires more discussion is an individual's genetic vulnerability. Knowledge regarding the genetic and biological determinants of substance abuse is primarily based on alcohol abuse and alcoholism research. The biological children of alcoholics are three to four times more likely to develop alcohol problems than children of nonalcoholic parents, regardless of who raised them (Schuckit, 1984). Although the evidence indicates that alcohol and substance abuse are in part genetically influenced, it is unlikely that a specific gene will be identified that can fully account for the vulnerability of some individuals. However, a genetic predisposition does not necessarily result in the development of alcohol or substance abuse.

Negative life events also appear important in risk for substance abuse. Higher prevalence rates for bereavement, unwanted and teenage pregnancy, and sexual victimization in childhood or adolescence have been found among adolescent substance users relative to nonusers (Swadi, 1999). The relationship between life events and substance abuse is likely bi-directional; therefore, the order of causality may not be clear. The coping theory of substance use, however, presupposes that increased negative affect following exposure to stressors increases the likelihood and intensity of substance use. For some adolescents, substance abuse may reflect a maladaptive coping response. Regardless of the order of causality, negative life events and substance abuse are risk factors for each other. For example, an adolescent who is sexually victimized is at greater risk for abusing substances; substance abuse, in turn, increases the risk for future victimization.

## PROBLEMS AND IMPLICATIONS

The above information regarding prevalence, risk and protective factors points to several problems and holds several implications for school personnel, parents, and others involved with children and youth. Adults generally are not likely to know whether particular individuals use substances, how much they use, or precisely when they initiate use. However, given that 50% of high school seniors will have tried an illicit substance and 77% will have used alcohol, it is important for parents and teachers to regularly include topics of drug and alcohol use in conversations with youth in a way that acknowledges that the adult does not know if the teen has decided to use or abstain. On the other hand, given that 50% of all high school seniors and more than 50% of all minority group members have *not* tried illicit drugs, it is equally important to avoid assuming that all teens have used. By communicating a willingness to talk about drug and alcohol use, though, adults retain the opportunity to influence youth's private decisions.

Some of the findings discussed earlier on risks and protective factors can guide adults' efforts to influence children and adolescents to abstain, or at least to delay initiating substance use for as long as possible. Youth are less likely to use substances when (a) they perceive the risks that are associated with use, (b) they are bonded to conventional institutions and values, and (c) they feel socially and academically competent. Thus, these protective factors can be targeted in conversations and in substance abuse prevention programming for all school-age children, from preschool through high school. All children can gain from these outcomes, and preventive programming with these goals can be applied universally.

Recent findings suggest that programming will be most effective if it is tailored to acknowledge students' racial and ethnic attributes. For example, African American youth are less likely to use substances if they feel a greater sense of racial identity and pride (Caldwell, Sellers, Bernat, & Zimmerman, 2004); Hispanic youth are less likely to use substances if they speak Spanish more often with family and friends (Epstein, Botvin, & Diaz, 2000), and Vietnamese American youth are less likely to use substances if they are more involved in their ethnic communities (Bankston, 1995). Perhaps the values that protect youth from substance abuse are actually the values that are considered conventional by their own specific cultural group.

There are youth, of course, for whom merely increasing protective factors is not enough to prevent substance abuse. The presence of some risk factors can make students quite vulnerable to the positive effects of substances. Once those students have discovered the positive effects firsthand, protective factors play a much smaller role. A useful way to think about why youth abuse substances, even though they experience negative consequences, is to remember that use always has immediate payoffs. Using a substance changes one's current experience in a positive direction. The changes are quick and easy to bring about. Thus, the reliable, short-term, reinforcing effects of each episode of alcohol or other drug use become far more powerful in determining future use than do the intermittent, long-term, negative consequences, such as detention for tardiness, lower grade point average, loss of abstinent friends, parental disapproval, or arrest. The strength of consistent, immediate reinforcement and the relative weakness of inconsistent, delayed punishment are two reasons that it is best to delay students' initiation of substance use developmentally as long as possible. One wants youth to be attached firmly to personally valued and attainable life goals (i.e., to have something to lose) and to have learned the ability to self-regulate and to delay gratification before they experience substances' positive effects.

Although earlier initiation of use definitely increases the probability of later abuse, there are also adolescents who initiate use later and escalate to abuse quickly. Compared with their classmates, these students tend to feel less competent academically, have more behavior problems, and feel less welcome or at home in schools; that is, they have less sense of belonging (Wills, McNamara, Vaccaro, & Hirky, 1996). Unlike some of the less obvious risk factors, students experiencing these three risk factors are easily identified. These students are certainly candidates for more intensive substance abuse prevention programming. Of course, identifying students who are at risk for substance abuse must be done carefully, in that many students with risk factors never develop substance abuse. Intensive preventive programming, however, can benefit even those high-risk students who will never abuse drugs. Reducing the above three risk factors not only reduces the probability of substance use but also reduces the probability of school dropout and juvenile delinquency.

## ALTERNATIVE ACTIONS FOR PREVENTION

To be effective, substance abuse prevention programs should target risk factors that can be modified and should strengthen protective factors. Professionals generally agree that early intervention with risk factors can have a greater impact than later intervention. Prevention programs that combine targeting of different levels of the social system for children and youth, such as family, school, and community, can be more effective than a program with a single social system target. Family-based prevention programs can strengthen protective factors for young children by teaching parents better family communication skills and appropriate discipline and family management skills. School-based programs have been the primary approach for reaching children and youth because they allow for universal access.

School-based programs focus on children's social and academic skills such as improving peer relationships, self-control, coping skills, social behaviors, and drug refusal skills. The programs also frequently include an education component about prevalence and the effects of drug use. Such prevention programs can be implemented as early as preschool to address risk factors such as aggressive behavior, poor social skills, and academic difficulties. Prevention programs for elementary school children can address self-control, emotional awareness, communication, social problem solving, and academic support. Prevention programs for middle and high school students can address study habits and academic support, communication, peer relationships, self-efficacy and assertiveness, drug resistance skills, reinforcement of antidrug attitudes, and strengthening of personal commitment against drug abuse.

Unfortunately, many schools use substance abuse prevention programs that are not evidence-based and that have not been shown to be effective in controlled outcome studies. A study of 1,656 public and 249 private schools found that the most prevalent curriculum (used by 53% of public and 54% of private schools) was Drug Abuse Resistance Education (DARE) (Ringwalt et al., 2002), a program that has shown little evidence of effectiveness even though it has been evaluated extensively (Lynam et al., 1999).

A meta-analysis of the effectiveness of school-based drug prevention programs indicated that effective programs were those that used interactive skills-training methods as opposed to didactic lecture methods, and that these programs sought to change behaviors by teaching skills and competencies rather than by changing knowledge and attitudes as a result of lectures (Tobler & Stratton, 1997). Effective programs have booster sessions, so they are long term; the effects of middle school programs diminish without high school follow-up programs (Scheier, Botvin, Diaz, & Griffin, 1999). Programs should address factors specific to the target population, with attention to age, gender, and ethnicity of the participants.

There are three levels or types of prevention programs, which are identified by the level for which they are designed. *Universal* programs are for the general population. *Selective* programs target groups at risk. *Indicated* programs are for those who already have abused drugs or engaged in other risky behaviors. The following sections describe a number of universal, selective, or indicated school-based substance abuse prevention programs that are evidence-based.

## Universal Prevention Programming

A variety of approaches have been used in universal prevention programs. These include cognitive and affective prevention education, social influence approaches, personal and social skills training, youth-led programs, school climate change, community partnerships, and parent involvement. Reviews of the literature on universal programs report that consistently positive effects have been found for programs that use social influence and life-skills approaches. Social influence approaches focus on social resistance skills training, psychological inoculation against advertising, and normative education. Life skills approaches focus on teaching generic self-management and social skills.

***Life Skills Training.*** This school-based, universal prevention program has repeatedly shown positive effects for middle school students (e.g., Botvin, Baker, Dusenbury, Botvin, & Diaz, 1995). Life Skills Training views substance use as a socially learned behavior that may serve a number of purposes, such as coping with anxiety or failure or reacting to the appeals of peers. The program teaches general personal and social coping skills as well as skills and information specifically related to substance use. The program extends over 3 years with 15 sessions of approximately 45 minutes each during the first year (sixth or seventh grade), 10 booster sessions in the second year, and 5 booster sessions in the third year. The sessions may be conducted consecutively every day, two to three times per week, or once a week.

Life Skills Training consists of three major components. The first, drug resistance skills, provides information about the prevalence and effects of tobacco, alcohol, and marijuana use and teaches resistance skills for dealing with peers and the media. The self-management skills component teaches how to improve self-image using a self-improvement plan and also teaches decision-making and problem-solving skills. In addition, sessions on coping with anxiety teach students how to use imagery, breathing, and muscle relaxation as coping strategies. The general social skills component addresses verbal and nonverbal communication skills, including guidelines for avoiding misunderstandings; skills to initiate, maintain, and end conversations; and skills needed to handle social requests. This component also teaches assertiveness skills that can be used to resist peer pressure to smoke, drink, or use drugs.

The program is designed to be carried out by classroom teachers, health professionals, or peer leaders. Implementation of the program requires a teacher's manual, a student guide, and a recording of guided relaxation exercises. Teacher training is highly recommended although not required.

Life Skills Training has been evaluated in a variety of studies over 25 years and has been found to reduce the prevalence of tobacco, alcohol, and illicit drug use relative to controls. In one study of over 4,400 students in 56 schools in New York State, significant prevention effects were found for cigarette smoking, marijuana use, immoderate alcohol use, normative expectations and knowledge concerning substance use, interpersonal skills, and communication skills (Botvin, Baker, Dusenbury, Tortu, & Botvin, 1990). A 6-year follow-up study with 3,600 students in 56 schools found that weekly polydrug use (use of multiple substances to enhance or counteract, such as tobacco, alcohol, and one or more illegal drugs) was 66% lower than in control schools and that any use of tobacco, alcohol, or marijuana was 44% lower than in control schools (Botvin et al., 1995).

Life Skills Training has been evaluated with Black and Hispanic youth, as well as with majority populations, and has been found to be effective. In a recent study, the effectiveness of Life Skills Training was tested with 3,600 predominantly minority, economically disadvantaged students in 29 New York City schools. Those who received the program reported less smoking, drinking, drunkenness, inhalant use, and polydrug use than controls. In addition, this program has been found to be effective in reducing binge drinking in minority, inner-city middle school students (Botvin, Griffin, Diaz, & Ifill-Williams, 2001).

Although Life Skills Training appears to be the universal school-based prevention program with the most evidence of effectiveness, a number of significant issues regarding its implementation require further examination. The program has many components and requires a significant time commitment over 3 years. The contributions and effectiveness of the individual components remain to be determined. In addition, studies have not examined the manner in which the program typically would be implemented in a school setting, without support from a university-based research team, and how program adaptations within a local setting might influence program effectiveness.

***Promoting Alternative Thinking Strategies (PATHS).*** Another universal prevention program, PATHS (Kusche & Greenberg, 1994), was designed specifically for elementary school students and has repeatedly shown positive results in controlled outcome studies. PATHS is based on the belief that behavioral and substance use problems can be prevented if children develop not only cognitive social problem-solving skills but also ways to accurately process and effectively regulate their emotions. The theory is that children, when faced with frustrating real-world situations, may use confrontational or unhealthy modes of coping, not because they do not know the cognitive steps of problem solving, but because they do not understand and regulate the emotional content of the situation. Accordingly, PATHS is designed to increase protective factors by enhancing social and emotional competence and to decrease risk factors by reducing conduct and emotional problems.

PATHS teaches kindergartners through sixth graders self-control, emotional awareness and understanding, and the steps of problem solving. The developers recommend that the program be provided for multiple school years, but positive short- and long-term effects have been shown even when it has been implemented for only 1 year.

The program materials include more than 100 interactive lesson plans that are designed to be continually integrated into classroom activities from kindergarten through sixth grade. The materials were developed to move children along a continuum of emotional and social competency during elementary school. Kindergartners are introduced to emotional literacy through the PATHS Turtle Kit. First through sixth graders learn how to identify emotions, change behaviors and attitudes that contribute to violence and substance use, express and control emotions effectively, and generate conflict-resolution strategies. Each grade level uses a different curriculum manual, which includes activities that can be adapted to suit individual classroom needs.

The effects of PATHS have been evaluated over the past 15 years in multiple controlled trials involving regular and special education students in rural, suburban, and urban schools. Some of the trials had 1- or 2-year follow-ups. Although elementary school children are too young to assess for substance use, one important risk factor—conduct problems—and one important protective factor—social–emotional competence—were each repeatedly affected in positive directions by PATHS. At the end of 1 year of programming and after a 2-year follow-up, teacher or peer reports of aggressive student behavior were reduced in students who had the programming versus students who did not. Effects of social–emotional competence were measured in several ways. When compared with students who did not have the program, students who had 1 year of PATHS repeatedly demonstrated increased fluency and vocabularies for discussing their feelings, ability to recognize others' feelings, and ability to solve social problems in nonconfrontational ways that show self-control (Greenberg, Kusche, Cook, & Quamma, 1995; Kam, Greenberg, & Kusche, 2004.)

## Selective Prevention Programs

Selective prevention programs are provided for at-risk children and youth, including children of alcoholics or drug abusers and students with behavior problems or academic failure. In general, less is known about the effectiveness of selective prevention programs because of the popularity of universal school-based prevention programs. Primary types of selective prevention programs include those that teach academic and behavior management skills, alternative activity programs that involve high-risk youth in activities that are free of substance use, tutoring or mentoring programs, and family strengthening approaches.

Project Toward No Drug Abuse is a selective prevention program that is based on a motivational skills decision-making model for high school students (Sussman, Dent, & Stacy, 2002). This highly interactive model views drug use as being related to three types of variables: motivation variables, including attitudes, beliefs, and desires regarding drug use; general social and self-control skills; and cognitive processing skills for making rational decisions. The program's goal is to correct deficits in these variables.

The program consists of 12 interactive sessions of 40 minutes each. The sessions address motivation, social skills, and decision-making skills regarding the use of cigarettes, alcohol, marijuana, hard drugs, and violent or aggressive behavior. Session topics include active listening, stereotyping, myths and denials associated with drug use, negative consequences of drug abuse, methods for coping with stress, the value of health, self-control methods, assertiveness, the links between positive and negative thinking and behavior, attitudes about substance use, and decision-making skills and commitment.

In three experimental field trials, more than 2,400 high school students from 42 schools in Southern California participated in the program. Two of the field trials involved students from alternative high schools that serve youth who are unable to be in a traditional public high school setting because of problems such as attendance, academic achievement, or drug use. Results indicated reductions in the use of cigarettes, alcohol, marijuana, hard drugs, weapon carrying, and victimization at 1-year follow-up. The program was effective in both regular and alternative high schools. The program was administered successfully by the project's health educators.

## Indicated Prevention Programs

Indicated prevention programs target youth who already have engaged in risky behaviors, such as aggression, substance abuse, and juvenile delinquency. These prevention programs are designed to prevent further episodes of the problem behaviors and to prevent the problems from becoming chronic. These programs frequently require more highly trained staff than do universal or selective programs.

***Reconnecting Youth.*** Reconnecting Youth (Eggert, Thompson, Herting, & Randell, 2001) is an indicated program for high school students who are at risk for dropping out of school as a result of poor grades or who have other problems such as history of substance abuse, aggression, depression, or suicidal risk behaviors. The goals of the program are to increase school academic performance, reduce drug use, and learn skills to manage emotions. The program consists of a semester of daily group sessions that focus on social skills training and positive peer bonding. The small group sessions are taught by a specially trained teacher or group leader and include self-esteem enhancement, decision-making, personal control, and interpersonal communication. Parental involvement is required for student participation. Studies have shown improved school performance; decreased school dropout; reduced hard drug use; decreased problems associated with drug use, such as adverse consequences and progression to heavier drug use; and decreased depression, perceived stress, and anger control problems.

## School-Based Program Implementation

Effective implementation of evidence-based programs for substance abuse prevention requires that schools consider a number of factors. Key stakeholders (administrators, teachers, parents, and students) should be involved in deciding which program fits the school's existing needs, its available resources, and its philosophy and practices. In the planning phase, school psychologists can use their knowledge and expertise to provide information about the content, structure, and potential effectiveness of programs being considered.

Once a decision is made about which program to implement, the school must provide adequate training to program implementers. A number of the programs described above have structured training and materials that can be accessed easily. After initial training, schools must then give program implementers ongoing support by making consultation and material resources available (space, equipment, and supplies). Other factors that have been identified as influencing the success of implementation include ease of program administration, implementers' attitudes toward and support for the program, implementers' sense of efficacy, and support for the program by other school staff and school administrators (Forman, Smallwood, & Nagle, 2005).

Substance abuse prevention is a long-term endeavor that requires a team of practitioners and other stakeholders to assess and consider indicators of success before deciding to continue or modify the program. As the team begins to implement the program, the quality of that implementation should be monitored. Practitioners also should recognize that the positive results obtained by researchers in trials are likely to be obtained in practice settings only when there is high fidelity of implementation. Fidelity of implementation is the degree to which the program is implemented as the program developers intended. Fidelity includes (a) adherence to theoretical guidelines and methods, (b) completeness and dosage (amount of program delivered), (c) quality of program delivery, (d) degree to which participants are engaged, and (e) degree to which significant elements are present that would differentiate the program from another type of program (Dusenbury, Brannigan, Falco, & Hansen, 2003).

Recently researchers have begun exploring how evidence-based programs may change students in the short term so that long-term outcomes (e.g., reduced substance use) can occur. These short-term signs of progress, or proximal markers of program effects, are termed *mediating variables or mechanisms of change*. For example, Greenberg et al. (1995) found that before they saw long-term effects of PATHS on conduct and emotional problems, they saw increases in children's "emotional literacy," or the ability to identify and name emotions. Before Botvin et al. (1995) found long-term effects of Life Skills Training on substance use, they found that students in their program were more likely than controls to report accurate (rather than inflated) estimates of prevalence of substance use by peers and to show antidrug attitudes, increased knowledge about substance effects, and greater refusal skills. Hansen (1996) compared students while they were in two different prevention programs and found that students in the program with greater documented effectiveness showed more positive changes in three other mediating variables: a greater intention not to use substances in the future, values and ideals that were more incongruent with use, and a greater sense of belonging to their school. All of these variables can be monitored during the implementation of substance abuse prevention programs, as potential proximal markers of long-term positive effects.

## ALTERNATIVE ACTIONS FOR INTERVENTION

When youth already are suffering from the negative effects of substance use, treatment must be considered. However, treatment outcome studies do not support referring substance-abusing youth to outpatient therapists or to clinics that do not have specific expertise in, and an evidence-based treatment protocol for, child or adolescent substance abuse. Adult treatment programs are not appropriate. On the other hand, referring adolescents to substance abuse treatment if they have been merely experimenting with substances in a way that is not affecting life functioning will introduce them to youth who are engaged in riskier behaviors. As Table 2 shows, spending time with other youth who abuse substances is a strong predictor of future abuse. Thus, careful assessment of the youth and collaboration with the family about treatment options are keys to successful interventions.

When parents are choosing substance abuse treatment settings, they should be advised that both residential and nonresidential settings can be effective, but that longer treatment produces more lasting improvement in substance use than does shorter treatment (Latimer, Newcomb, Winters, & Stinchfield, 2000). The range of treatment length in the Latimer et al. study was 3 to 98 days, with a mean of 39.19 days. Thus, parents should be prepared that treatment probably must be longer than the typical 14 to 21 days. If possible, they should find a treatment that is evidence-based.

Parents also should be told that most of the effective treatments target multiple areas in the youth's life, in addition to substance use, and that most of the effective treatments involve the family. Vaughn and Howard (2004) recently rated outpatient adolescent substance abuse treatments according to the strength of evidence that supports their effectiveness. Family therapy and cognitive–behavioral therapy interventions received high ratings. In another study, the Phoenix House residential treatment showed significantly better outcomes than the typical treatment settings used by probation officers (Morral, McCaffrey, & Ridgeway, 2004). Phoenix House is a highly structured 9- to 12-month treatment program in which residents progress through phases of increasing privileges and responsibilities.

Finally, parents and school personnel should know that substance abuse tends to be a chronic problem that is difficult for youth to overcome. Accordingly, one treatment episode may not be enough. It is generally accepted that the majority of participants relapse within 90 days of leaving treatment. Follow-up studies show that youth's participation in at least 6 months of aftercare programs can significantly reduce post-treatment problems for at least 1 year (Latimer et al., 2000). Having an abstinent friend or having a sense of connectedness to school also can reduce problems after treatment. Those studies' findings suggest that schools should take an active role in providing aftercare through programs such as Project Toward No Drug Abuse (Sussman et al., 2002) or Reconnecting Youth (Eggert et al., 2001).

## SUMMARY

Three decades of research on substance abuse prevention have yielded a number of school-based programs that appear to have a positive effect on the prevalence of substance abuse among youth. These programs, which focus on increasing protective factors and reducing risk factors, can be implemented as early as the preschool years. Effective substance abuse prevention programs use a behavioral skills training approach. These highly structured programs involve direct practice of skills and feedback. Some of the most widely used substance abuse prevention programs are not the most effective. With time and financial resources in short supply in our schools, and with the potential negative effects of failed intervention efforts, school professionals must advocate for and implement only evidence-based programs.

## RECOMMENDED RESOURCES

### Books and Other Printed Material

Hansen, W. B. (2002). Program evaluation strategies for substance abuse prevention. *Journal of Primary Prevention, 22,* 409–435.

This article comprehensively reviews state-of-the-art program evaluations. Issues such as data collection, informed consent, and fidelity measures are covered.

National Institute on Drug Abuse. (2003). *Preventing drug abuse among children and adolescents: A research-based guide* (NIH Publication No. 04-4212[A]). Bethesda, MD: National Institutes of Health

This publication summarizes recent research on risk and protective factors and evidence-based substance abuse prevention programs. Principles for effective prevention programming are provided.

Vaughn, M. G., & Howard, M. O. (2004). Adolescent substance abuse treatment: A synthesis of controlled evaluations. *Research on Social Work Practice, 14,* 325–335.

This article rates different types of outpatient adolescent substance abuse treatments according to the amount of evidence that exists regarding their effectiveness.

### Websites

*http://www.drugabuse.gov*

The website of the National Institute on Drug Abuse contains a range of current information on substance abuse and its prevention and treatment.

*http://www.modelprograms.samhsa.gov*

This website contains descriptions of programs that have been reviewed by the Substance Abuse and Mental Health Services Administration's National Registry of Effective Prevention Programs. Eighteen criteria were used to evaluate program effectiveness, and programs are categorized as promising programs, effective programs, or model programs.

*http://www.colorado.edu/cspv/blueprints*

This website of the Center for the Study and Prevention of Violence at the University of Colorado describes in detail 11 model and 18 promising evidence-based prevention programs to reduce crime and substance abuse. Programs are for infants through adolescents.

## REFERENCES


Bankston, C. (1995). Vietnamese ethnicity and adolescent substance abuse: Evidence for a community-level approach. *Deviant Behavior, 16,* 59–80.

Biederman, J., Wilens, T., Mick, E., Spencer, T., & Faraone, S. V. (1999). Pharmacotherapy of attention-deficit/hyperactivity disorder reduces risk for substance use disorder. *Pediatrics, 104,* 20.

Botvin, G. J., Baker, E., Dusenbury, L., Botvin, E. M., & Diaz, T. (1995). Long-term follow-up results of a randomized drug abuse prevention trial in a white middle-class population. *Journal of the American Medical Association, 273,* 1106–1112.

Botvin, G. J., Baker, E., Dusenbury, L., Tortu, S., & Botvin, E. M. (1990). Preventing adolescent drug abuse through a multimodal cognitive-behavioral approach: Results of a three-year study. *Journal of Consulting and Clinical Psychology, 58,* 437–446.

Botvin, G. J., Griffin, K. W., Diaz, T., & Ifill-Williams, M. (2001). Drug abuse prevention among minority adolescents: Posttest and one-year follow-up of a school-based preventive intervention. *Prevention Science, 2,* 1–13.

Bry, B. H. (1996). Psychological approaches to prevention. In W. K. Bickel & R. J. DeGrandpre (Eds.), *Drug policy and human nature: Psychological perspectives on the prevention, management, and treatment of illicit drug use* (pp. 55–76). New York: Plenum Press.

Caldwell, C. H., Sellers, R. M., Bernat, D. H., & Zimmerman, M. A. (2004). Racial identity, parental support, and alcohol use in a sample of academically at-risk African American high school students. *American Journal of Community Psychology, 34,* 71–82.

Dusenbury, L., Brannigan, R., Falco, M., & Hansen, W. B. (2003). A review of research on fidelity of implementation: Implications for drug abuse prevention in school settings. *Health Education Research: Theory & Practice, 18,* 237–256.

Eggert, L. L., Thompson, E. A., Herting, J. R., & Randell, B. P. (2001). Reconnecting youth to prevent drug abuse, school dropout, and suicidal behaviors among high-risk youth. In E. F. Wagner & F. B. Waldron (Eds.), *Innovations in adolescent substance abuse interventions* (pp. 51–84). Oxford, UK: Elsevier Science.

Epstein, J. A., Botvin, G. J., & Diaz, T. (2000). Alcohol use among Hispanic adolescents: Role of linguistic acculturation and gender. *Journal of Alcohol & Drug Education, 45*(3), 18–32.

Forman, S. G., Smallwood, D. L., & Nagle, R. J. (2005). Organizational and individual factors in bringing research to practice: What we know; where we need to go. *Psychology in the Schools, 42,* 569–576.

Greenberg, M. T., Kusche, C. A., Cook, E. T., & Quamma, J. P. (1995). Promoting emotional competence in school-aged children: The effects of the PATHS curriculum. *Development and Psychopathology, 7,* 117–136.

Hansen, W. B. (1996). Pilot test results comparing the All Star program with seventh grade D.A.R.E.: Program integrity and mediating variable analysis. *Substance Use & Misuse, 31,* 1359–1377.

Hawkins, J. D., Catalano, R. F., & Miller, J. Y. (1992). Risk and protective factors for alcohol and other drug problems in adolescence and early adulthood: Implications for substance abuse prevention. *Psychological Bulletin, 112,* 64–105.

Johnston, L. D., O'Malley, P. M., & Bachman, J. G. (1998). *National survey results on drug use from the Monitoring the Future study, 1975–1997: Vol.1. Secondary school students* (NIH Publication No. 98-4345). Washington, DC: U.S. Department of Health and Human Services.

Johnston, L. D., O'Malley, P. M., Bachman, J. G., & Schulenberg, J. E. (2003). *Ecstasy use falls for second year in a row, overall teen drug use drops.* Ann Arbor, MI: University of Michigan News and Information Services. Retrieved May 5, 2004, from http://www.monitoringthefuture.org

Kam, C., Greenberg, M. T., & Kusche, C. A. (2004). Sustained effects of the PATHS curriculum on the social and psychological adjustment of children in special education. *Journal of Emotional and Behavioral Disorders, 12,* 66–78.

Kusche, C. A., & Greenberg, M. T. (1994). *The PATHS curriculum.* Seattle: Developmental Research and Programs.

Latimer, W. W., Newcomb, M., Winters, K. C., & Stinchfield, R. D. (2000). Adolescent substance abuse treatment outcome: The role of substance abuse problem severity, psychological, and treatment factors. *Journal of Consulting and Clinical Psychology, 68,* 684–696.

Lynam, D. R., Milich, R., Zimmerman, R., Novak, S. P., Logan, T. K., & Martin, C., et al. (1999). Project DARE: No effects at 10-year follow-up. *Journal of Consulting and Clinical Psychology, 67,* 590–593.

Morral, A. R., McCaffrey, D. F., & Ridgeway, G. (2004). Effectiveness of community-based treatment for substance-abusing adolescents: 12-month outcomes of youths entering Phoenix Academy or alternative probation dispositions. *Psychology of Addictive Behaviors, 18,* 257–268.

Ringwalt, C. L., Ennett, S., Vincus, A., Thorne, J., Rohrbach, L. A., & Simons-Rudolph, A. (2002). The prevalence of effective substance use prevention curricula in U.S. middle schools. *Prevention Science, 3,* 257–265.

Scheier, L., Botvin, G., Diaz, T., & Griffin, K. (1999). Social skills, competence, and drug refusal efficacy as predictors of adolescent alcohol use. *Journal of Drug Education, 29,* 251–278.

Scheier, L., Newcomb, M. D., & Skager, R. (1994). Risk, protection, and vulnerability to adolescent drug use: Latent-variable models of three age groups. *Journal of Drug Education, 24,* 49–82.

Schuckit, M. (1984). Subjective responses to alcohol in sons of alcoholics and control subjects. *Archives of General Psychiatry, 41,* 879–884.

Schulenberg, J. E., & Maggs, J. L. (2002). A developmental perspective on alcohol use and heavy drinking during adolescence and the transition to young adulthood. *Journal of Studies on Alcohol, 6* (Suppl. 14), 54–70.

Sussman, S., Dent, C. W., & Stacy, A. W. (2002). Project Toward No Drug Abuse: A review of the findings and future directions. *American Journal of Health Behavior, 26,* 354–365.

Swadi, H. (1999). Individual risk factors for adolescent substance use. *Drug and Alcohol Dependence, 55,* 209–224.

Tobler, N. S., & Stratton, H. (1997). Effectiveness of school-based prevention programs: A meta-analysis of the research. *Journal of Primary Prevention, 18,* 71–128.

Vaughn, M. G., & Howard, M. O. (2004). Adolescent substance abuse treatment: A synthesis of controlled evaluations. *Research on Social Work Practice, 14,* 325–335.

Wilens, T. E., Faraone, S. V., Biederman, J., & Gunawardene, S. (2003). Does stimulant therapy of attention-deficit/hyperactivity disorder beget later substance abuse? A meta-analytic review of the literature. *Pediatrics, 111,* 179–185.

Wills, T. A., McNamara, G., Vaccaro, D., & Hirky, A. E. (1996). Escalated substance use: A longitudinal grouping analysis from early to middle adolescence. *Journal of Abnormal Psychology, 105,* 166–180.

# 77

# Sleep and Sleep Problems

**Deidre L. Donaldson**

*May Institute & Brown Medical School*

**Judith A. Owens**

*Brown Medical School*

## BACKGROUND AND DEVELOPMENT

Sleep problems are among the most common child-rearing problems reported by parents. Estimates suggest that as many as 25% of children between birth and 4 years of age experience difficulty sleeping through the night (Mindell, Carskadon, & Owens, 1999). For many of these children, sleep problems become chronic. Bedtime struggles and night awakenings are common among school-age as well as preschool children (Blader, Koplewicz, Abikoff, & Foley, 1997; Owens & Witmans, 2004). Estimates of sleep problems during adolescence, particularly insomnia, insufficient sleep, and daytime fatigue, range from 33% to 75% (Morrison, McGee, & Stanton, 1992; Ohayon, Roberts, Zulley, Smirne, & Priest, 2000). In addition to being pervasive, sleep problems may substantially affect daily functioning in many areas, including health, mood, behavior regulation, academic performance, and overall quality of life. Failure to properly identify the effects of sleep problems may lead to misdiagnoses and missed opportunities to successfully intervene to enhance student performance.

Sleep is one of the primary organizing activities of the brain in early development. It represents a complex interaction between physiology and environmental factors, which requires a biopsychosocial approach (Mindell & Owens, 2003). To properly assess and treat childhood sleep problems, professionals first need to understand how these factors present and interact during the course of typical sleep development.

### Sleep Development

The regulation of sleep is controlled by the circadian sleep–wake cycle and what has been termed the *homeostatic* process. Circadian rhythms, which also govern many other physiological processes in the body, are intrinsic, regular, and predictable rhythms of relative sleepiness and wakefulness that are responsive to environmental factors (light, daily schedule). The homeostatic sleep process, also known as sleep *pressure* or sleep *drive*, begins to build upon waking and continues throughout the day. It is largely determined by the amount and quality of prior sleep and the amount of time spent awake since the last sleep period. Chronic inadequate sleep may accumulate across days and weeks in what is known as a sleep debt, which must eventually be paid back with compensatory sleep.

Sleep *architecture* refers to the basic structure of sleep and consists of REM (rapid eye movement) and non-REM sleep. REM or dream sleep, known as active sleep in infants, refers to a sleep stage characterized by a desynchronized EEG pattern, rapid respirations, dream activity, and muscle paralysis that prevents us from acting out our dreams (Sheldon, Dahl, Kryger, & Ferber, 2005). Non-REM sleep, or quiet sleep in infants, is differentiated into four sleep stages by characteristic EEG patterns. Each stage represents a progressively deeper state of sleep. REM and non-REM sleep cycle in a regular way (every 60–90 minutes in children) throughout the night.

To better understand normative changes in sleep architecture across development, we summarize these changes across four specific developmental periods: infancy, early childhood, middle childhood, and adolescence. Common sleep problems for each period are presented and subsequently explained in the Problems and Implications section that follows. School professionals will not necessarily come into contact with all of these age groups or problems. Nevertheless, understanding how sleep architecture develops in children may make it easier to recognize deviations or symptoms indicative of sleep problems or disorders.

***Infancy: 0 to 1 year.*** During the first year of life, significant developmental changes in sleep architecture occur. These include increased duration of the ultradian REM/non-REM cycle, a shift from REM sleep onset to non-REM sleep onset, a significant decrease in the proportion of the sleep period spent in REM sleep, increasingly longer REM periods concentrated later in the sleep period (Sheldon et al., 2005), and a gradual decline in the percentage of *slow wave*, or the deepest stage of sleep. Sleep also becomes consolidated into one long, continuous nocturnal sleep period ("sleeping through the night") and one or two short naps in contrast to the short (3- to 4-hour) sleep bouts in newborns. About 70% of infants achieve this consolidation by 9 months. Infants also develop a greater reliance on external cues for the onset and cessation of sleep, for example, the light–dark cycle (Anders, Sadeh, & Appareddy, 1995), rather than relying on hunger–satiety cues alone. In addition, most infants develop the capacity for self-soothing (sleep regulation) by approximately 3 to 4 months of age.

Cosleeping, or sharing the sleeping space with a caregiver or sibling, is common during this period. This is especially true of certain groups in the United States (e.g., Hispanic and African American populations) as well as in other cultures (Asian, Southern European) (Owens, 2004). As a lifestyle practice, cosleeping seldom results in sleep problems or parental complaints. However, *reactive* cosleeping, or that initiated by parents in response to existing sleep problems (for example, difficulty self-soothing during night awakenings) can be more problematic and more difficult to eliminate (Owens & Witmans, 2004).

Irregular sleep patterns are also common during this period. Many parent-reported sleep problems are actually normal or transient variations and reflect a mismatch between normal sleep development and parental expectations. Such concerns include reversed day–night sleep patterns in the first 2 to 3 months of age, irregular sleep patterns prior to 4 months of age, and the perception that normal "active" sleep (characterized by movements, grimacing, smiling) is restless or disturbed (Mindell & Owens, 2003). An abrupt, persistent, and dramatic change in sleep patterns or behaviors is the best indicator of an actual sleep disorder in this age group. The most likely sleep disorder to be diagnosed during this period is sleep-onset association disorder, or dependence on certain sleep associations, such as parental presence, in order to fall asleep. Associated problems include prolonged night awakenings and rhythmic movement disorders, such as body rocking and head banging (Mindell & Owens, 2003).

***Early childhood: 2 to 5 years.*** By the end of the first year of life, most children sleep through the night. Transient awakenings are common, but disturbances resolve quickly when the child's physiological needs are met and parents remain neutral in response to such occurrences (Goodlin-Jones, Burnham, Gaylor, & Anders, 2001). Sleep changes during preschool or early childhood occur more gradually than during infancy. Most toddlers take only a single daytime nap by 18 months and by 2 years of age exhibit regular nighttime sleep architecture similar to that of adults (Sheldon et al., 2005). By the time children reach the age of 4 or 5 years, most give up daytime napping (Edwards & Christophersen, 1994). Bedtime routines develop around 2 years of age, last approximately 30 minutes, and typically involve toileting, drinking, reading a story, and separating from parents. Preschool children also exhibit increasingly longer sleep onset latency with age, ranging from approximately 15 minutes for younger children to 30 minutes for ages 5 and 6 years (Sheldon et al.). This may take the form of resistance to bedtime as they become more socially interactive. Preschool-age children often call out for parents after being put in bed ("curtain calls"), awaken frequently during the night, or experience nightmares and nighttime fears (Kuhn & Weidinger, 2000). Transitional objects become important at this age and serve to reduce separation anxiety. Bedtime routines and self-soothing behaviors enhance the initiation and maintenance of sleep, and set bedtimes are particularly important to enforce at this age.

School professionals may receive inquiries from parents regarding common sleep problems. These include naps, difficulties transitioning a child from crib to bed, maintaining a consistent bedtime routine, the child's ability to self-soothe during awakenings, and the possible development of bedtime resistance, which frequently occurs in conjunction with inconsistent sleep schedules

(Mindell & Owens, 2003). The most likely formal sleep disorders to emerge during this period are sleep-onset association disorder, limit-setting sleep disorder (bedtime resistance related to parental inability to set appropriate bedtime limits), rhythmic movement disorders, nightmares, obstructive sleep apnea, and partial arousal parasomnias, such as sleepwalking or sleep terrors (Mindell & Owens).

***Middle childhood: 6 to 12 years.*** Relatively few studies have examined sleep patterns during this age range. Existing information suggests that sleep–wake and REM/non-REM cycles continue to approach adult sleep patterns. Moreover, circadian preferences for phase-advanced or phase-delayed sleep ("morning person" versus "night owl") may emerge. Total sleep duration for school-age children averages between 9 and 11 hours per night, with older children exhibiting shorter sleep periods than younger children (Iglowstein, Jenni, Molinari, & Largo, 2003). Naps are rare for this age group in the absence of an underlying sleep disorder or insufficient sleep, and school-age children should be able to remain quite alert throughout the day (Sheldon et al., 2005).

Approximately 40% of parents report sleep problems during this developmental period, including bedtime resistance, sleep onset delays, nighttime fears, and daytime sleepiness (Mindell & Owens, 2003). Contributing issues include inconsistency between weeknight and weekend sleep patterns and disrupted sleep due to environmental factors, such as caffeine intake and the presence of video games, televisions, and computers in the bedroom. School professionals should be alerted to the potential for sleep problems in students when daytime drowsiness, inattention, disruptive behavior, moodiness, or impaired academic performance is present. Possible sleep disorders include sleepwalking, sleep terrors, bruxism (teeth grinding), obstructive sleep apnea, and insufficient sleep.

***Adolescence: 13 to 18 years.*** Adolescents experience dramatic physiological, sociological, and psychological changes that affect sleep. These include hormonal changes, growth, social demands and schedules, and increased independence. Average sleep need during adolescence decreases slightly from a prepubescent average of 10 hours per night to about 9 ¼ hours by age 16. However, a number of surveys have demonstrated that teenagers obtain approximately 7 ½ hours of sleep per night during the school week (e.g., Wolfson & Carskadon, 1998). Decreased sleep duration during school nights occurs largely as a function of a physiologically based phase delay (preference for later sleep onset in the evenings and awakenings in the mornings) due to pubertal hormonal influences. Thus, daytime sleepiness is a common adolescent complaint. This shortfall in total sleep time on school nights may result in a rebound effect on weekends to compensate (Carskadon, Wolfson, Acebo, Tzischinsky, & Seifer, 1998).

Potential sleep problems during this developmental period include difficulties falling asleep at night (delayed onset), variability between sleep schedules during the week compared with the weekend, insufficient sleep during the school week, daytime sleepiness, and the effect of insufficient sleep on daily functioning and performance. The most notable sleep disorders for this age group include insufficient sleep disorder, insomnia, delayed sleep phase syndrome, periodic limb movement disorder or restless legs syndrome, and narcolepsy. School professionals could be very helpful in educating adolescents and their parents about the high risk of insufficient sleep disorder as well as the significant effect of socioenvironmental factors on sleep quality and duration for this age group.

## PROBLEMS AND IMPLICATIONS

A *sleep problem* may be defined as a condition that interferes with the initiation and maintenance of normal sleep and "that is viewed as a problem by the child or caregiver, the significance of [which] may be characterized by its severity, chronicity, and frequency and associated impairment in daytime function in the child or family" (Owens et al., 2005, p. 49). Caregivers' expectations of sleep development and desired sleep behaviors should be considered in addition to the child's actual sleep behaviors. For example, a child who takes short naps may not allow a busy parent sufficient respite from childcare, resulting in parental complaints about the child's sleep patterns. The assessment of sleep problems should, therefore, include factors central to the reported problem as well as how those factors relate to adult expectations and desired child behaviors. Professionals working with children may not always have access to parental reports of child behavior. This is especially relevant for school personnel. Yet educators may be in a position to recognize daytime symptoms of and impairment associated with sleep problems before other adults in the child's life.

## Screening Methods for Common Sleep Problems in Children and Adolescents

Historically, sleep problems in both pediatric and adult populations have been classified using two primary diagnostic classification systems: *the International Classification of Sleep Disorders, Second Edition* (American Academy of Sleep Medicine [AASM], 2005) and the *Diagnostic and Statistical Manual of Mental Disorders* (i.e., DSM-IV-TR; American Psychiatric Association, 2000). However, sleep problems may also take the form of symptoms or clusters of symptoms and may not necessarily meet the criteria for a formal disorder. Screening tools can assist in recognizing such symptoms in various populations.

In this chapter we use the screening tool BEARS (Owens & Dalzell, 2005) to outline the most common childhood sleep problems professionals are likely to encounter (see Table 1). Each letter in the acronym represents a sleep domain important in children 2 to 18 years of age. BEARS provides a structured interview format to obtain information from both parent and child, with developmentally appropriate prompts for each domain. However, the tool was also designed to generate a comprehensive screening of sleep behaviors and symptoms, using limited information in a short period of time. Professionals can quickly and easily gather data across all five domains of assessment and determine possible mechanisms behind the symptoms. Overlap exists across the major domains, and many of the sleep problems may be related. For the purposes of this chapter, we have assigned each sleep problem to the most relevant domain.

## Bedtime Problems

The essential question associated with bedtime problems is, "Does the child have problems going to bed or falling asleep?" Bedtime problems frequently occur as a result of poor limit setting or ineffective routines. Poor sleep habits may also contribute. The most common types of bedtime problems include limit-setting sleep disorder, insomnia, and adjustment sleep disorder, all of which constitute behavioral insomnias of childhood (AASM, 2005).

***Limit-setting sleep disorder.*** Young children, especially those between the ages of 2 and 6 years, may refuse to go to bed despite being physiologically ready (Sheldon et al., 2005). In some cases, bedtime resistance represents a mismatch between the child's circadian preference for a later bedtime and parental expectations. As a result, bedtime struggles arise, and caregivers experience increasing difficulty separating from their child at night. Parents who wish to avoid bedtime conflicts with their child, who lack knowledge regarding appropriate limit-setting, or who are too tired to set firm limits may repeatedly allow a child to sleep in a place other than the child's bed. Caregivers may also try a variety of strategies to quiet the child during ensuing conflicts to minimize escalation, including sleeping in the child's bed or physical punishment. Unfortunately, those methods may only serve to exacerbate the problem.

Psychosocial stressors (e.g., substance abuse, depression, and marital conflict) may also minimize a caregiver's ability to effectively maintain limits around bedtime behavior (Sheldon et al., 2005). Busy family schedules contribute to inconsistent bedtimes that compromise sleep onset. This problem presents a serious difficulty for approximately 5% to 10% of the childhood population (AASM, 2005). Parents of children with this problem typically report conflicts around bedtime. Children may present with other complications as a result of inadequate sleep, including irritability, diminished attentional abilities, decreased academic performance, and family conflict.

***Insomnia.*** Children of all ages may experience difficulty falling or staying asleep (Sheldon et al., 2005). Insomnia is defined as significant difficulty initiating or maintaining sleep, resulting in a negative daytime effect for the child, the caregiver, or both. Insomnia has many potential causes, including primary sleep disorders, medication, chronic illness, and psychiatric disorders. A specific type of insomnia known as psychophysiological insomnia (AASM, 2005) is characterized by anxiety about sleep and awakenings that compromises the ability to fall asleep (Sheldon et al.) and results in daytime sleepiness. This type of insomnia is much more common in adolescents and adults than in younger children. As many as 30% of adolescents experience some form of insomnia, usually described as poor sleep (Mindell & Owens, 2003). Insomnia may exist in conjunction with other sleep problems or as a primary problem when all other possible etiologies have been ruled out.

***Adjustment sleep disorder and nighttime fears.*** Children may experience difficulty initiating sleep secondary to life stress that results in emotional arousal

**Table 1** *The BEARS Screening Algorithm of Pediatric Sleep Problems*

| Domain | Central Question | Examples |
|---|---|---|
| Bedtime problems | Are there problems going to bed or with sleep onset? | Limit-setting sleep disorder, insomnia, adjustment sleep disorder, nighttime fears |
| Excessive daytime sleepiness | Is there extreme fatigue, excessive napping, sleep onset problems? | Narcolepsy |
| Awakenings during the night | Can child maintain or reinitiate sleep after awakening? | Sleep-onset association disorder, nightmares, night terrors, sleepwalking, periodic limb movement disorder |
| Regularity and duration of sleep | Is sleep regular and sufficient? | Insufficient sleep, inadequate sleep hygiene, delayed sleep phase |
| Sleep-disordered breathing | Is there difficulty breathing during sleep? | Obstructive sleep apnea |

*Note.* See Mindell & Owens, 2003.

(Gallagher, Tobia, & Wolfson, 1995). Examples of life stressors that affect sleep include family conflict, traumatic events, and major life changes such as moving, parental separation, or the death of a family member. The essential features of this problem are sleep that differs from the child's typical pattern and an identifiable stressor preceding or associated with the disturbance. The symptoms and features of this disturbance remit in the absence of the stressor or with improved psychological adaptation to the stressor (AASM, 2005).

Children affected by this problem often present with insomnia, and daytime sleepiness may also be present. Additional symptoms, including irritability, lethargy, tearfulness, or anxiety, begin within approximately 3 months of the onset of the stressor (AASM, 2005). Impairment in social and educational functioning may result. The disorder tends to persist longer in response to chronic versus acute stressors. If the condition lasts longer than 6 months, or if more global symptoms of anxiety are present, the potential for a more pervasive anxiety disorder, such as generalized anxiety disorder or post-traumatic stress disorder, should be considered (AASM).

## Excessive Daytime Sleepiness

Excessive daytime sleepiness in childhood may present in a variety of ways, some of which may not be intuitively obvious to observers. A child may seem extremely overtired during the day, nap excessively, or have difficulty getting up in the morning. Alternatively, children may present with mood, behavior (hyperactivity, impulsivity, aggression), attention, or learning problems. Although we discuss only primary disorders of excessive daytime sleepiness, virtually any sleep problem resulting in inadequate sleep duration or interrupted sleep may cause daytime sleepiness.

Narcolepsy can be a cause of daytime sleepiness but this diagnosis is rarely made in childhood. Peak onset occurs during the second decade of life (Brooks & Mignot, 2002). However, many narcoleptic adults report the development of symptoms in later childhood and adolescence. The hallmarks of narcolepsy include (a) sudden, dramatic, and irresistible sleep attacks typically less than 1 hour in duration; (b) cataplexy, a sudden partial or complete loss of muscle tone triggered by emotions; (c) sleep paralysis, the perceived inability to move while falling asleep; and (d) visual and auditory hallucinations that occur at the beginning or end of the sleep period (Brooks & Mignot).

Narcolepsy is a rare condition, but secondary symptoms are relevant to the school setting, including poor school performance and behavioral problems as a result of excessive daytime sleepiness. The symptoms of narcolepsy may be over overlooked or misdiagnosed as psychiatric or behavioral disorders, such as Attention Deficit Hyperactivity Disorder (ADHD), depression, or psychosis (Mindell & Owens, 2003). An overnight sleep study is necessary for definitive diagnosis.

## Awakenings During the Night

Awakenings during the night refer to frequent awakenings during most nights, with an inability to self-regulate or reinitiate sleep once awakened. This category encompasses several sleep disorders, including sleep-onset association disorder, sleepwalking, night terrors, and periodic limb movement disorder. Nightmares are also associated with night awakenings.

***Sleep-onset association disorder.*** It is typical for children (and adults) to briefly arouse or awaken at the end of a sleep cycle (approximately every 60 to 90 minutes). Most individuals independently settle and fall back to sleep. In sleep-onset association disorder, children are unable to transition back to sleep once aroused because they have developed dependence on certain associations at bedtime, such as being fed or rocked to induce sleep (Mindell, 1999). The disorder occurs primarily between the ages of 6 months and 3 years (AASM, 2005). Parents of children with sleep-onset association disorder report that their children have difficulty sleeping through the night, in contrast to the bedtime struggles reported by parents of children with limit-setting sleep disorder.

***Sleepwalking.*** Approximately 40% of children exhibit sleepwalking at some time during childhood (Laberge, Trembly, Vitaro, & Montplaisir, 2000). Sleepwalking may occur any time after a child learns to walk, with peak incidence between 4 and 8 years of age (AASM, 2005). Sleepwalking behaviors range from calm to agitated. Children may perform complex tasks while sleepwalking, such as preparing and eating food or unlocking a door. They may also display inappropriate behavior such as urinating in a corner. Although activities appear purposeful, actions are often uncoordinated and clumsy. Vocalizations may occur but are typically senseless or unintelligible. The risk of self-injury is a central concern.

***Night terrors.*** Night or sleep terrors affect approximately 3% of older children, with peak incidence during school age or preadolescence (Mahowald, 2002). Night terrors and confusional arousals are both partial arousal parasomnias and present in similar ways. However, important differences distinguish the two. Whereas confusional arousals begin gradually, the onset of sleep terrors is sudden and intense. The child may sit up in bed, emit a piercing scream, and exhibit autonomic nervous system manifestations such as increased heart and respiratory rates, dilated pupils, and sweating. Some children also may get out of bed and run hysterically around the room yelling and crying. They often report the fear that something is going to get them. As with confusional arousals, attempts to console or waken the child will often exacerbate the incident. The episodes usually end as quickly as they began, lasting approximately 1 to 5 minutes.

***Restless legs syndrome and periodic limb movement disorder.*** Restless legs syndrome (RLS) is characterized by uncomfortable crawling sensations in the legs that are exacerbated by inactivity and alleviated by movement (Picchietti & Walters, 1996). The symptoms tend to peak at sleep onset and result in difficulty falling asleep. Since the disorder has only recently been found to occur in children as well as adults, the prevalence in childhood is largely unknown; however, RLS is known to affect about 10% of the adult population (AASM, 2005). Periodic limb movement disorder (PLMD) is a movement disorder characterized by leg twitching or kicking during sleep. These movements are repetitive, occur approximately every 20 to 40 seconds, tend to occur in lighter stages of sleep, are disruptive to sleep, and may persist for minutes to hours. Individuals with PLMD are not aware of these movements. The only recognized symptom may be daytime sleepiness secondary to disrupted sleep or arousals caused by the movement. Caregivers may report that the child is a restless sleeper, and daytime sleepiness may be observed. Secondary symptoms, such as behavior and academic problems are also possible, and ADHD symptoms in children have been found in association with both RLS and PLMD. The only way to definitively diagnose PLMD is by an overnight sleep study in conjunction with thorough medical and physical exams.

***Nightmares.*** Nightmares are long, frightening dreams that usually awaken the child from REM sleep. They may begin as early as 2 to 3 years of age, although children do not typically report them until 3 or 4 years of age (AASM, 2005). The content of nightmares often involves threats to the child or family members. If the child awakens screaming, nightmares can be difficult to distinguish from partial arousal parasomnias such as sleep terrors or sleepwalking. However, several defining characteristics can be used to differentiate them.

Nightmares usually occur during the longest REM period in the last third of the night, whereas partial arousal parasomnias occur during the first third of the night. Generally, when the child awakens from a nightmare, there is clear recall, and the child is alert and oriented. Furthermore, the child responds well to comforting. In partial arousal parasomnias, the child will appear confused and disoriented in response to awakenings, and adult intervention often exacerbates the symptoms (Sheldon et al., 2005). Unlike arousal disorders, nightmares rarely result in displacement from bed or self-injury. Partial arousal parasomnias are overall much less common than nightmares and often are exhibited by other family members.

## Regularity and Duration of Sleep

This domain encompasses problems in which children do not get regularly scheduled sleep of an age-appropriate duration. The most common are insufficient sleep resulting in a sleep debt, inadequate sleep hygiene, and delayed sleep phase syndrome.

***Insufficient sleep and cumulative sleep debt.*** Insufficient sleep refers to inadequate sleep relative to an individual's sleep need (Mindell & Owens, 2003). Chronic insufficiency results in a cumulative sleep debt, which eventually interferes with daily functioning. The most notable symptom is excessive daytime sleepiness. Secondary symptoms may include risk-taking behavior and symptoms associated with other sleep problems, such as behavior and mood problems, cognitive impairment, and compromised attention skills.

Average sleep duration across childhood and adolescence is 8 to 10 hours per night (Iglowstein et al., 2003). Failure to maintain an appropriate bedtime results in insufficiency. In childhood and adolescence, this is usually the result of lifestyle factors such as television viewing, part-time job hours, early school start times, late-night socializing, and homework.

***Inadequate sleep hygiene.*** Sleep hygiene refers to behaviors and habits that promote sleep. Inadequate sleep hygiene refers to practices that increase arousal or interfere with sleep organization (Mindell & Owens, 2003). Common factors that contribute to inadequate sleep hygiene in children and adolescents include failure to maintain consistent sleep–wake schedules, electronic media in the bedroom (TV, computer, video games), caffeine and nicotine intake, inadequate exercise or poor diet, absence of a bedtime routine, and drugs and medications.

Those suffering from inadequate sleep hygiene may present with insomnia, delayed sleep onset, nighttime awakenings, and early morning awakenings. As with other sleep problems, inadequate sleep hygiene can interfere with daily functioning, resulting in secondary mood and behavior changes, excessive daytime sleepiness, complaints of fatigue, cognitive impairment, difficulties with attention and concentration, and caffeine use to combat the fatigue.

***Delayed sleep phase syndrome (DSPS).*** Approximately 7% of all adolescents suffer from this disorder (AASM, 2005). The problem most commonly occurs as adolescents acquire responsibility for their own sleep schedule or experience changes in biological timing mechanisms, causing delayed sleep onset (Carskadon, Acebo, Richardson, & Tate, 1997). Also, staying up late, sleeping in, or taking late afternoon naps may contribute (Regestein & Pavlova, 1995; Dahl & Carskadon, 1995). Essentially, the circadian-determined sleep and wake times are discrepant with the desired bedtime and wake times required by daily schedules or school. Individuals with this problem report sleep onset insomnia as a result of the body's inability to shift sleep rhythms to earlier hours. Excessive morning sleepiness is also a problem. Phase delay may be distinguished from other causes of insomnia by the fact that when individuals with DSPS are allowed to sleep on their preferred schedule, they have no difficulty falling asleep.

## Sleep-Disordered Breathing

***Obstructive sleep apnea.*** Obstructive sleep apnea (OSA) is a medical condition in which brief, repeated episodes of obstructed airflow through the nose and mouth occur during sleep (Marcus, 2001). These periods of complete airflow cessation (apnea) or partial airflow obstruction (hypopnea) result in two problematic conditions (Gozal, 1998). First, chronic reduction in oxygen (hypoxia) and increases in carbon dioxide levels (hypercapnia) during the apneic periods may result in cognitive impairment. Empirical data are only now being collected in children, but clinical reports suggest subtle learning problems may result rather than generalized developmental delays. Second, partial awakenings frequently accompany the apneic episodes. Over the course of many nights, these awakenings result in poor sleep quality, chronic sleep deprivation, and daytime sleepiness.

The age range for this disorder is 2 to 15 years of age, with a peak incidence between 3 and 4 years (AASM, 2005). The prevalence is estimated to be 1% to 3% (Guilleminault, Palayo, Leger, Clerk, & Bician, 1996), with males and females equally affected. The most common underlying cause of OSA in children is enlarged tonsils and adenoids. In addition, certain populations show an increased incidence of OSA, including children with facial and oral anomalies, genetic syndromes such as Down syndrome, neuromuscular conditions, and morbid obesity.

Symptoms of OSA include sleep-related symptoms and daytime symptoms (American Academy of Pediatrics [AAP], 2002). The most common sleep-related symptom is loud snoring. This is usually accompanied by noticeable pauses in breathing sounds during the night, gasping, or choking. Children with OSA may also experience restless sleep, nocturnal sweating, and sleeping in abnormal positions to breathe more easily. There also may be an increased incidence of parasomnias, including bedwetting, nightmares, and night terrors. Daytime symptoms of OSA include chronic mouth breathing, a nasal vocal quality, and growth failure. Growth failure results from the child's relative difficulty in eating and breathing simultaneously, decreased taste sensation secondary to nasal obstruction, and interruption of the regular nocturnal secretion of growth hormone due to frequent partial awakenings. Other symptoms include morning headaches and difficult awakenings with morning irritability.

OSA may be associated with poor attention span, distractibility, low frustration tolerance, behavioral impulsivity, aggressive behavior, daytime sleepiness, social withdrawal, learning problems, and compromised academic performance (Chervin & Archibold, 2001). These symptoms result from chronic sleep deprivation, and they overlap considerably with symptoms of other problems, including ADHD (Corkum, Tannock, & Moldofsky, 1998). Differential diagnosis is made difficult by the fact that OSA and ADHD may coexist. If daytime behavioral symptoms are accompanied by nocturnal symptoms of OSA, referral for an evaluation and overnight sleep study should be made. When a child fits the criteria for ADHD, school personnel should question parents about the child's sleep to help rule out the possibility of OSA.

## Sleep Problems in Special Populations

Sleep problems occur at higher rates in children with special health care needs (Quine, 2001), which includes children with chronic medical problems, behavior and mood disorders, and developmental disabilities. Thus, it is important to screen for sleep problems in those populations. In general, the types of sleep problems afflicting children with special health care needs are not unique to them, but they tend to be the more frequent and severe forms of sleep problems that afflict the general population.

The relationship between sleep problems and chronic medical conditions has only recently begun to be investigated in children. The task is complicated because chronic medical conditions involve complex underlying disease processes, emotional and family responses, hospitalization and medications, and related secondary symptoms, such as pain, all of which can affect sleep. Nevertheless, studies have examined sleep in different chronic illness subgroups, including asthma, burns, cystic fibrosis, sickle cell anemia, and rheumatologic disorders (Owens, 2004). For example, children with asthma are more likely to have sleep problems related both to nocturnal circadian-mediated exacerbations of asthma symptoms (coughing, wheezing) and to some of the medications used to treat asthma, which affect sleep quality. Similarly, children with rheumatologic disorders, such as juvenile rheumatoid arthritis, may have sleep disturbances related to chronic pain or medication. Children with sickle cell disease and comorbid obstructive sleep apnea may have painful sickling crises exacerbated by the hypoxia (low oxygen) of OSA.

Sleep problems and behavior or mood disorders are also related. Specifically, behavior and mood difficulties often emerge as secondary functional impairments of sleep problems. In addition, preexisting behavior and mood disorders may be exacerbated in children who experience sleep problems, and vice versa. A good example of this is the relationship between sleep problems and ADHD (Mick, Biederman, Jetton, & Faragne, 2000). The central nervous system centers that regulate sleep and attention and arousal are indeed linked. A substantial proportion of children diagnosed with ADHD (up to 25%) actually have a primary sleep disorder (most notably OSA, restless legs syndrome, periodic limb movement disorder, or narcolepsy) that accounts for at least a portion of their behavioral dysregulation (Chervin et al., 2002). In addition, children diagnosed with ADHD may have sleep-onset delay or restless sleep related to comorbid psychiatric conditions (depression or oppositional defiant disorder), caused by concomitant psychotropic medications (e.g., stimulants), or intrinsic to the ADHD. Subjective parental measures of sleep in children with ADHD almost universally demonstrate significant sleep problems in comparison with controls, whereas more objective measures of sleep, such as sleep studies in general, do not show consistent differences (Corkum et al., 1998). The considerable night-to-night variability in sleep patterns found across a number of studies of children with ADHD may be at least a partial explanation for this discrepancy in the findings.

Sleep problems are also recorded with high frequency in children with developmental disabilities. For example, 30% to 80% of children with severe mental retardation, more than half of the children with severe cognitive impairment, and approximately 50% to 70% of children with pervasive developmental delay and autism experience significant sleep problems (Wiggs,

2001). This high prevalence may be related to a number of factors, including intrinsic abnormalities in sleep regulation and circadian rhythms, use of medications for treating associated symptoms, cognitive delays, sensory deficits, and increased parental stress.

## ALTERNATIVE ACTIONS FOR PREVENTION

Many of the sleep problems affecting children, especially those associated with lifestyle behaviors, are preventable. One practice in particular—parent education—has been identified as a well-established intervention in the primary prevention of sleep problems (Mindell, 1999). Specifically, pre- and perinatal education of parents around infant sleep minimizes sleep problems that result from inappropriate caregiver expectations. Consequently, primary care providers have been encouraged to implement sleep education at well-child visits. For example, educating parents of 2-month-olds to put their infants to bed when the children are drowsy but not asleep can prevent the development of sleep association disorders. Educating parents of 3-month-olds to introduce a consistent bedtime routine can prevent sleep onset problems. No studies of education efforts to prevent sleep problems in older children or adolescents have been reported.

Another avenue for prevention is sleep hygiene. Sleep hygiene refers to a variety of factors that promote sleep. Although sleep hygiene has not been investigated as a preventive intervention per se, educating parents about sleep hygiene practices with infants (in addition to sleep development) is known to be an effective prevention strategy (Kuhn & Elliott, 2003). Also, a variety of sleep hygiene factors are included in behavioral treatments for sleep problems (secondary and tertiary prevention), because poor sleep hygiene is the primary cause of sleep-onset and maintenance problems in older children and adolescents (Mindell & Owens, 2003).

We find it helpful to divide sleep hygiene factors into two categories: those that promote sleep organization and those that minimize physiologic arousal (see Table 2). Inconsistent sleep schedules (day-to-day as well as week-to-weekend) are particularly problematic for teenagers. Many adolescents suffer from insufficient sleep during the week and then attempt to recover by oversleeping on the weekend (Wolfson, 2002). This insufficiency is a significant problem and is associated with poor academic performance, school attendance, and engagement (Mindell & Owens, 2003). Adolescents should be encouraged to maintain a reasonable sleep schedule during the school week, which may require a decrease in extracurricular activities and part-time job hours. In addition, it is recommended that schools avoid early start times when possible because they are biologically inconsistent with maximal academic performance and contribute to sleep insufficiency (Wolfson).

Approximately 30% of children entering preschool still take naps (Mindell & Owens, 2003). The timing, rather than the duration, of naps is most likely to contribute to sleep problems when they occur too close to bedtime. An increasingly popular phenomenon is the presence of televisions, video games, and computers in children's bedrooms, all of which can disrupt sleep. A media-free zone in the bedroom is recommended for all children and adolescents.

The reduction of physiological and cognitive arousal is best achieved by controlling the sleep environment, food intake before bedtime, substance use, and exercise. Adolescents are more likely to consume large quantities of caffeine, smoke cigarettes, and use pharmacological sleep aids, all of which contribute to sleep problems. Daily exposure to outside light and exercise (although not within 3 hours of bedtime) is helpful in maintaining the circadian rhythm for all ages, but it is particularly recommended for adolescents because of sleep-phase delay.

School psychologists and other professionals can play an important role in prevention by educating students about both sleep development and sleep hygiene. Topics may include physiological changes in sleep that occur with the child's development, the typical sleep needs and common types of sleep problems at different points in development, and the implementation of sleep hygiene practices. Even more critical might be the education of caregivers and students at all ages about the contribution of good sleep to student academic performance and functioning.

School professionals also play an important role in the identification of sleep problems. Many sleep problems in children persist undiagnosed or untreated until secondary daytime symptoms such as excessive somnolence, learning problems, and behavioral difficulties are observed in the school setting (Stein, Mendelsohn, Obermeyer, Amromin, & Benca, 2001). School professionals can also be instrumental in referring students and their caregivers for behavioral treatment of suspected or known sleep problems.

**Table 2** *Principles of Sleep Hygiene, by Age Group*

| Principle | Children | Adolescents |
|---|---|---|
| *Promote Sleep Organization* | | |
| Sleep schedule | Have set times and follow daily (within 1 hour); consistent on school and nonschool nights. | Have set times and follow daily; avoid catch-up sleep on weekends. |
| Naps | Less than 1 hour. | Less than 1 hour, if any, in mid-afternoon. |
| Bedtime routine | Quiet time for 1 hour prior. | Quiet time 30–60 minutes prior; read, relax, calm music. |
| *Minimize Arousal* | | |
| Sleep environment | Sleep in the same location consistently; bedroom should be comfortable ($\leq$ 70 degrees), quiet, and dark—a media-free zone reserved for sleep only. | Same as for children. |
| Food intake | Avoid hunger; avoid large meals 2–3 hours prior (light snacks only). | Same as for children. |
| Substance use | Avoid caffeine after 12:00 noon. | Avoid caffeine after 3:00 p.m.; avoid smoking entirely or at least 1 hour before; avoid sleep medications. |
| Exercise | Fresh air daily; minimize heavy exercise 2 to 3 hours prior to bedtime. | Fresh air daily with exposure to sunlight; exercise regularly. |

## ALTERNATIVE ACTIONS FOR INTERVENTION

Sleep hygiene is important for the prevention of sleep problems, but it also is a necessary first step in combating existing sleep problems. Sleep hygiene principles are relatively easy to implement and thus are useful tools for school professionals to share with children and families. During the past decade, sleep researchers have made advances in identifying effective treatments for sleep problems and disorders. As in other areas of child intervention, researchers and practitioners borrow treatments for sleep problems from adult practice. Such treatments are more difficult to implement than interventions involving education and sleep hygiene; therefore, they may be of limited use in the school setting. However, making education professionals aware of the existence and effectiveness of these treatments will help them seek appropriate referrals or educate children and families about such interventions.

### Medical Interventions

Medical treatments often involve pharmacological interventions. Empirical studies of pharmacological interventions with child behavioral sleep problems suggest that their effectiveness is moderate at best, that treatment gains dissipate when medications are removed (Owens et al., 2005), and that behavioral interventions are likely to have the most long-lasting benefits. In addition, many pharmacological agents have paradoxical effects that exacerbate sleep problems. Although a number of different types of medications, such as antihistamines (Benadryl), tricyclic antidepressants, and clonidine, have been used for sleep problems in children, there are currently no FDA-approved medications for this use. Given the lack of information regarding the efficacy, tolerability, and safety of these medications in the pediatric population, pharmacological interventions should only be used to provide short-term amelioration of sleep problems. Moreover, they should be combined with behavioral interventions if used for long-term problem management.

Medications are, however, often indicated and appropriate in the treatment of some medically based sleep disorders, such as narcolepsy and PLMD (Mindell & Owens, 2003). And some medically based sleep problems require additional medical interventions. For example, children with OSA may have their tonsils and adenoids removed, use a breathing device called CPAP (continuous positive airway pressure) during sleep, or be required to lose weight if obesity is a contributing factor. Such interventions do not usually interfere with the child's daily functioning or routines.

### Behavioral Interventions

Recent reviews of the empirical literature in this area (Kuhn & Elliott, 2003; Mindell, 1999) point to three currently available, well-established treatments for bedtime problems and night awakenings in children: extinction, graduated extinction, and parent education. One additional treatment, scheduled awakenings, has been identified as probably efficacious. Parent education was discussed in the previous section and is not repeated here. The implementation of the other three interventions—extinction, graduated extinction, and scheduled awakenings—requires specialized knowledge and clinical judgment skills. These interventions also require regular contact with the child's caregivers and active support for monitoring the child's behaviors in the home. Improper application of behavioral interventions can render treatment ineffective and compromise the promise of their known effectiveness in the future. Referral to behaviorally trained professionals can be helpful in this regard.

***Extinction: Systematic ignoring.*** Systematic ignoring refers to intentionally refraining from contact with the child during the child's attempts to gain interaction (e.g., crying, screaming, calling out for a caregiver). Essentially, parents are instructed to put their child to bed at a designated bedtime and then ignore the child until a set time the next morning. Systematic ignoring continues regardless of the child's behaviors until the undesired behavior (in this case bedtime refusal) is extinguished. With good adherence, success is usually achieved quite quickly. However, many parents find it difficult to adhere to this treatment and report it to be a less than ideal treatment option.

***Graduated extinction.*** Graduated extinction, a modification popularized by Ferber (1985), allows a caregiver to respond to distress from the child on a progressively less frequent basis. The adult enters the child's room but limits the visit to a few minutes regardless of the child's responses. During the visit the adult provides brief, minimally stimulating contact and reassurance. On subsequent nights, the adult gradually increases the duration between return visits to the child's room until the child falls asleep without the adult present (Owens, France, & Wiggs, 1999).

It is often helpful to advise caregivers that initial attempts at setting limits around bedtime behavior may result in increased behavioral resistance before success is attained. Children may try hard to continue getting what they are accustomed to when limits are introduced. Setting limits will be effective only when caregivers are able to ignore the child's resistance and maintain the limit. Once a child learns that the caregiver is going to maintain the limit, the undesirable behavior will dissipate quickly. It is important to give caregivers permission to maintain bedtime limits despite the child's distressful displays and support them when they are successful in doing this.

***Scheduled awakenings.*** Scheduled awakenings are currently considered a probably efficacious treatment for partial arousals or nighttime awakenings (Kuhn & Elliott, 2003; Mindell, 1999). The treatment involves waking a child approximately 30 minutes before a partial-arousal incident is expected. First, a baseline of awakenings is established. Then, caregivers engage in preemptive awakenings with the same frequency, albeit different timing, as the baseline problem. The time between awakenings is then gradually increased until no longer needed. The duration of sleep increases as the problematic, spontaneous awakenings are eliminated. This treatment is hypothesized to work by disrupting slow-wave, deep sleep. Some studies examining scheduled awakenings have reported problems with treatment adherence, presumably secondary to having to get up in the middle of the night or waking a sleeping child (Mindell).

***Other behavioral interventions.*** Several other behavioral interventions are considered helpful in treating pediatric sleep problems despite the fact that their success has not been empirically documented. Examples include stimulus-control procedures for bedtime problems and insomnia and shifts in the sleep–wake schedule for sleep-phase delay.

Treatment of adjustment sleep disorder typically involves stimulus-control procedures to manage the symptoms of insomnia. The goals of stimulus-control procedures are to minimize behaviors incompatible with sleep and to regulate the circadian rhythm. For example, children are not allowed to play games or do homework in bed. In the event that sleep onset does not occur within 20 minutes of being in bed, the child is instructed to get up and engage in a monotonous, quiet activity until he or she feels sleepy (Owens, Palermo, & Rosen, 2002). This typically involves sitting in a straight-back chair and reading a nonstimulating book. These steps are repeated as often as necessary until sleep onset occurs.

For delayed sleep-phase disorder, the child's bedtime needs to be advanced to an earlier hour. Because falling asleep at an earlier time often proves difficult for many parents and children, interventions have been designed to first gradually advance (set earlier) the evening bedtime by small increments (15 minutes) over the course of many days while keeping the morning waking time constant, maximizing evening sleepiness. In severe cases, chronotherapy is recommended. This treatment requires the child's bedtime and waking time to be simultaneously and progressively delayed by 2 to 3 hours per 24-hour period around the clock over a period of days until the desired bedtime is attained (Sheldon et al., 2005). For example, if a child consistently falls asleep at midnight and awakens at 7:00 a.m., he or she would be kept awake until 2:00 or 3:00 a.m. the first night and allowed to sleep until approximately 10:00 the next morning. The intervention would continue with similar advancements until the earlier, desired bedtime is obtained.

Sleep-stage transition disorders, nightmares, and other parasomnias require minimal intervention. Unless disturbing to family members, sleep talking is not usually problematic, and no interventions are recommended. Children with nightmares usually respond well to comforting by caregivers and will often quickly return to sleep. Frightening stories and television programs should be eliminated. Rhythmic movement disorders rarely cause serious injury. Placing rhythmic objects in the child's room, such as a clock or a metronome, and moving the child's bed away from the walls are two strategies commonly recommended for younger children. Ensuring safety with an alarm system to alert caregivers to sleepwalking is paramount.

Further empirical study of treatment interventions is needed (Mindell, 1999). Some research is focusing on identifying effective treatments for specific types of individuals, such as those with special needs or different combinations of sleep problems, to enhance treatment efficacy. Similarly, a functional approach to pediatric sleep problems has been recommended to identify a greater variety and more effective treatments in the future (Brown & Piazza, 1999).

## SUMMARY

The development of sleep involves complex changes in the sleep–wake and REM/non-REM cycles. The most common types of sleep problems vary across development. Sleep disorders are rare in infancy; parent-reported problems most commonly result from a mismatch between infant sleep behaviors and parental expectations. During preschool or latency, bedtime struggles and frequent night awakenings with inability to self-soothe are most common. Adolescents tend to be most affected by insomnia, insufficient sleep, and delayed sleep phase. Sleep problems that persist over time may result in decreased academic performance and behavioral changes such as inattentiveness, problems concentrating, and increased irritability. Thus, school professionals play an important role in assisting children and their families to identify and address sleep problems. Professionals should routinely screen for sleep problems in children with special health care needs because increased rates of sleep problems have been documented in that population.

The best prevention for sleep problems at all levels of development is appropriate sleep hygiene. Good sleep hygiene includes factors such as the avoidance of caffeine, minimal exposure to electronic media at bedtime, and a consistent bedtime schedule and routine. Medical and behavioral strategies may improve children's sleep and consequently benefit others living in the home. Medications are only rarely indicated and may be limited by their potential side effects, short-acting effects, or minimal data supporting their use with children. Several behavioral interventions have been found to provide effective, long-term amelioration of pediatric sleep problems. Three strategies in particular are currently regarded as well-established treatments for child sleep problems: extinction, graduated extinction, and parent education. Scheduled awakenings are regarded as probably efficacious for partial arousals and awakenings. Ultimately, more research is needed to establish effective treatments for sleep problems.

## RECOMMENDED RESOURCES

### Books and Other Printed Material

Durand, V. M. (1997). *Sleep better: A guide to improving sleep for children with special needs.* Baltimore, MD: Brookes Publishing.

Parent-friendly descriptions of clinical and empirical strategies for sleep problems in children with a variety of special health care issues, especially developmental disabilities.

Ferber, R. (1985). *Solve your child's sleep problems.* New York: Simon & Schuster.

This is a helpful guide for professionals and parents alike. It includes how to recognize sleep problems across developmental levels, how to intervene in the home, and when to pursue a referral for professional intervention.

Mindell, J. A., & Owens, J. A. (2003). *A clinical guide to pediatric sleep: Diagnosis and management of sleep problems in children and adolescents.* Philadelphia: Lippincott, Williams, & Wilkins.

This guide for primary care practitioners presents information on normative sleep patterns across development and reviews commonly reported child sleep problems. It includes a chapter on sleep in special populations, a large appendix with intervention handouts, and a CD-ROM.

## Websites

*http://www.aap.org/healthtopics/Sleep.cfm*

The website of the American Academy of Pediatrics (AAP) presents an entire section of audio files with parent-friendly guidance on normative sleep patterns and sleep problems.

*http://www.aasmnet.org*

The website of the American Academy of Sleep Medicine (AASM) includes fact sheets and links to informative sites in its Patient Resources section.

*http://www.sleepfoundation.org*

The website of the National Sleep Foundation provides suggestions for solving sleep problems in a variety of populations, including children and adolescents. The site offers sleep journals, checklists of symptoms, a sleep dictionary, and more.

## REFERENCES

American Academy of Pediatrics. (2002). Clinical practice guideline: Diagnosis and management of childhood obstructive sleep apnea. *Pediatrics, 9,* 704–712.

American Academy of Sleep Medicine. (2005). *International classification of sleep disorders* (2nd ed.). Westchester, IL: Author.

American Psychiatric Association. (2000). *Diagnostic and statistical manual of mental disorders* (4th ed., text rev.). Washington, DC: Author.

Anders, T. F., Sadeh, A., & Appareddy, V. (1995). Normal sleep in neonates and children. In R. Ferber, & M. H. Kryger (Eds.), *Principles and practice of sleep medicine in the child* (pp. 7–18). Philadelphia: W. B. Saunders.

Blader, J. C., Koplewicz, H. S., Abikoff, H., & Foley, C. (1997). Sleep problems of elementary school children: A community study. *Archives of Pediatric Adolescent Medicine, 151,* 473–480.

Brooks, S. N., & Mignot, E. (2002). Narcolepsy and idiopathic hypersomnia. In T. Lee-Chiong, M. J. Sateia, & M. A. Carskadon (Eds.), *Sleep medicine* (pp. 193–202). Philadelphia: Hanley & Belfus.

Brown, K. A., & Piazza, C. C. (1999). Commentary: Enhancing the effectiveness of sleep treatments: Developing a functional approach. *Journal of Pediatric Psychology, 24,* 487–489.

Carskadon, M. A., Acebo, C., Richardson, G. S., & Tate, B. A. (1997). An approach to studying circadian rhythms of adolescent humans. *Journal of Biological Rhythms, 12,* 278–289.

Carskadon, M. A., Wolfson, A. R., Acebo, C., Tzischinsky, O., & Seifer, R. (1998). Adolescent sleep patterns, circadian timing, and sleepiness at a transition to early school days. *Sleep, 21,* 871–881.

Chervin, R. D., & Archibold, K. H. (2001). Hyperactivity and polysomnographic findings in children evaluated for sleep-disordered breathing. *Sleep, 24,* 313–320.

Chervin, R., Archibold, K., Dillon, J., Panahi, P., Pituch, K., Dahl, R., et al. (2002). Inattention, hyperactivity, and symptoms of sleep disordered breathing. *Pediatrics, 109,* 449–456.

Corkum, P., Tannock, R., & Moldofsky, H. (1998). Sleep disturbances in children with attention-deficit/hyperactivity disorder. *Journal of the American Academy of Child and Adolescent Psychiatry, 37,* 637–646.

Dahl, R. E., & Carskadon, M. A. (1995). Sleep and its disorders in adolescence. In R. Ferber & M. Kryger (Eds.), *Principles and practice of sleep medicine in the child* (pp. 19–27). Philadelphia: W. B. Saunders.

Edwards, K. J., & Christophersen, E. R. (1994). Treating common sleep problems of young children. *Developmental and Behavioral Pediatrics, 15,* 207–213.

Ferber, R. (1985). *Solve your child's sleep problems.* New York: Simon & Schuster.

Gallagher, K., Tobia, A., & Wolfson, A. (1995). Sleep and waking behaviors in kindergartens: Impact of stressful life events. *Sleep Research, 24,* 96–107.

Goodlin-Jones, B., Burnham, M., Gaylor, E., & Anders, T. (2001). Night-waking, sleep-wake organization, and self-soothing in the first year of life. *Journal of Developmental and Behavioral Pediatrics, 22,* 226–233.

Gozal, D. (1998). Sleep-disordered breathing and school performance in children. *Pediatrics, 102,* 616–620.

Guilleminault, C., Palayo, R., Leger, D., Clerk, A., & Bician, R. C. Z. (1996). Recognition of sleep disordered breathing in children. *Pediatrics, 98,* 871–882.

Iglowstein, I., Jenni, O., Molinari, L., & Largo, R. (2003). Sleep duration from infancy to adolescence: Reference values and generational trends. *Pediatrics, 111,* 302–307.

Kuhn, B. R., & Elliott, A. J. (2003). Treatment efficacy in behavioral pediatric sleep medicine. *Journal of Psychosomatic Research, 54,* 587–597.

Kuhn, B., & Weidinger, D. (2000). Interventions for infant and toddler sleep disturbance: A review. *Child and Family Behavior Therapy, 22,* 33–50.

Laberge, L, Trembly, R. E., Vitaro, F., & Montplaisir, J. (2000). Development of parasomnias from early childhood to early adolescence. *Pediatrics, 106,* 67–74.

Mahowald, M. W. (2002). Arousal and sleep-wake transition parasomnias. In T. Lee-Chiong, M. J. Sateia, & M. A. Carskadon (Eds.), *Sleep medicine* (pp. 207–214). Philadelphia: Hanley & Belfus.

Marcus, C. L. (2001). Sleep-disordered breathing in children. *American Journal of Respiratory & Critical Care Medicine, 164,* 16–30.

Mick, E., Biederman, J., Jetton, J., & Faragne, S. V. (2000). Sleep disturbances associated with attention deficit hyperactivity disorder: The impact of psychiatric comorbidity and pharmacotherapy. *Journal of Child & Adolescent Psychopharmacology, 10,* 223–231.

Mindell, J. A. (1999). Empirically supported treatments in pediatric psychology: Bedtime refusal and night wakings in young children. *Journal of Pediatric Psychology, 24,* 465–481.

Mindell, J., Carskadon, M., & Owens, J. (1999). Developmental features of sleep. *Child and Adolescent Psychiatric Clinics of North America, 8,* 695–725.

Mindell, J. A., & Owens, J. A. (2003). *A clinical guide to pediatric sleep: Diagnosis and management of sleep problems.* Philadelphia: Lippincott, Williams, & Wilkins.

Morrison, D. N., McGee, R., & Stanton, W. R. (1992). Sleep problems in adolescence. *Journal of the American Academy of Child and Adolescent Psychiatry, 31,* 94–99.

Ohayon, M. M., Roberts, F. E., Zulley, J., Smirne, S., & Priest, R. G. (2000). Prevalence and patterns of problematic sleep among older adolescents. *Journal of the American Academy of Child and Adolescent Psychiatry, 39,* 1549–1556.

Owens, J. (2004). Sleep in children: Cross-cultural perspectives. *Sleep and Biological Rhythms, 2,* 165–173.

Owens, J., Babcock, D., Blumer, J., Chervin, R., Ferber, R., Goetting, M., et al. (2005). The use of pharmacotherapy in the treatment of pediatric insomnia in primary care: Rational approaches (A consensus meeting summary). *Journal of Clinical Sleep Medicine, 1,* 49–59.

Owens, J., & Dalzell, V. (2005). Use of the "BEARS" sleep screening tool in a pediatric residents' continuity clinic: A pilot study. *Sleep Medicine, 6,* 63–69.

Owens, J. L., France, K. G., & Wiggs, L. (1999). Behavioural and cognitive interventions for sleep disorders in infants and children: A review. *Sleep Medicine Review, 2,* 281–302.

Owens, J. A., Palermo, T. M., & Rosen, C. L. (2002). Overview of current management of sleep disturbances in children: II. Behavioral interventions. *Current Therapeutic Research, 63,* (Suppl. B), B38–B52.

Owens, J., & Witmans, M. (2004). Sleep problems. *Current Problems in Pediatric and Adolescent Health Care, 34,* 154–179.

Picchietti, D., & Walters, A. (1996). Restless legs syndrome and period limb movement disorders in children and adolescents. *Child and Adolescent Psychiatric Clinics of North America, 5,* 729–740.

Quine, L. (2001). Sleep problems in primary school children: Comparison between mainstream and special school children. *Child Health and Development, 27,* 201–220.

Regestein, Q. R., & Pavlova, M. (1995). Treatment of delayed sleep phase syndrome. *General Hospital Psychiatry, 17,* 335–345.

Sheldon, S., Dahl, R., Kryger, M., & Ferber, R. (2005). *Principles and practices of pediatric sleep medicine.* Philadelphia: W. B. Saunders.

Stein, M., Mendelsohn, J., Obermeyer, W., Amromin, J., & Benca, R. (2001). Sleep and behavior problems in school-aged children. *Pediatrics, 107,* 60.

Wiggs, L. (2001). Sleep problems in children with developmental disorders. *Journal of the Royal Society of Medicine, 94,* 177–179.

Wolfson, A. R. (2002). Bridging the gap between research and practice: What will adolescents' sleep-wake pattern look like in the 21st century? In M. A. Carskadon (Ed.), *Adolescents' sleep patterns: Biological, sociological, and psychological influences* (pp. 198–219). Cambridge, UK: Cambridge University Press.

Wolfson, A. R., & Carskadon, M. A. (1998). Sleep schedules and daytime functioning in adolescents. *Child Development , 69,* 875–887.

# 78

# Enuresis and Encopresis

**Michael W. Mellon**

*Mayo Clinic Rochester, MN*

Enuresis and encopresis are fairly common developmental problems and may be encountered in schools, especially during the early elementary years. This chapter reviews how the problems of wetting or soiling of bedding or clothing present in the school setting and their coordinated management by medical providers. The chapter also discusses the important role of school psychologists and educators in implementing and overseeing effective interventions in the school setting.

## ENURESIS—BACKGROUND AND DEVELOPMENT

A distinction is drawn between diurnal enuresis (daytime wetting accidents occurring at least twice a week for at least 2 months with a child at least 5 years of age) and monosymptomatic nocturnal enuresis (wetting accidents that occur during sleep) that occurs, by definition, at night and at the child's home. Diurnal enuresis and nocturnal enuresis require different management and treatment strategies.

Nocturnal enuresis is the name given to a child's passing of urine into his or her clothing or bedding while asleep. The term applies when the child is over 5 years of age, frequency is at least twice per week for 3 consecutive months, and no organic cause can be found for the accidents (American Psychiatric Association, 1994). Bedwetting is estimated to affect as many as 8% to 10% of the school-age population (Jarvelin, Vikevainen-Tervonen, Moilanen, & Huttunen, 1988); and the symptoms of as many as 16% of those children spontaneously remit each year (Forsythe & Redmond, 1974). Daytime wetting (with or without nighttime wetting) is less common, with estimates ranging from 1% to 8% of school-age children (Bakker, van Sprundel, van der Auwera, van Gool, & Wyndaele, 2002). The incidence of nocturnal enuresis occurs twice as often in males as females up to about puberty (De Jonge, 1973). However, in a survey of over 4,000 Belgian school children, the single symptom of daytime wetting occurred twice as often in girls (Bakker et al.). Of the 343 children in the sample who exhibited both day and night wetting, 54% were girls. Primary nocturnal enuresis, which accounts for approximately 80% of all children who wet the bed, describes a child who has been wetting continuously since birth and evidencing less than 6 consecutive months of dryness (Rawashde, Hvistendahl, Kamperis, & Djurhuus, 2002). In the United States alone, it is estimated that as many as 4 to 6 million children wet their beds nearly every night.

What is most typical of the developmental aspects of both diurnal and nocturnal enuresis is that children's wetting symptoms may spontaneously remit. This is likely the reason that parents of enuretic children are often advised by healthcare providers to take a watchful waiting approach to the problem to see if the child will outgrow the wetting. However, diurnal enuresis is often associated with potentially serious medical problems that can actually lead to permanent damage to the urinary tract if not treated immediately. Although serious medical problems are rare for children with monosymptomatic nocturnal enuresis (Jarvelin et al., 1991), given the availability of effective treatments for nocturnal enuresis a watchful waiting approach is no longer justified. Therefore, parents should be advised to consult a healthcare provider for a medical examination and treatment.

Nocturnal enuresis is clearly influenced by genetic factors. The likelihood that a child will wet the bed is 40% if one of his or her parents wet the bed as a child. The likelihood increases to 70% if both parents wet the bed (Norgaard, Djurhuus, Watanabe, Stenberg, & Lettgen, 1997). Furthermore, the best predictor of when a child might remit their wetting symptoms is the age at which his or her parent spontaneously stopped wetting the bed (Fergusson, Horwood, & Shannon, 1986). In fact, Eiberg, Berendt, & Mohr (1995) demonstrated that the loci for nocturnal enuresis are on chromosomes 13q and 12q. Although genetic influences on nocturnal enuresis are apparent, this information has not contributed in a meaningful way to developing more effective treatment. Little is known about the genetic influences on diurnal enuresis.

## PROBLEMS AND IMPLICATIONS OF ENURESIS

Enuresis is best conceptualized as a biobehavioral problem (Mellon & McGrath, 2000). Emerging evidence demonstrates a complex interaction of genetics and physical maturation of the urological and neurological systems. These physical determinants of enuresis combine with both respondent and operant processes to account for the pathogenesis of bedwetting. Daytime wetting appears to have a greater influence of abnormal urinary tract functioning that directly affects the behavioral regulation of continence.

Urinary continence is maintained through a balance between the automatic processes of "spinal cord to brainstem mediated urination" and the cortical control of the pelvic floor muscles that act as an on–off switch for bladder emptying (Holstege & Sie, 2002). Automatic bladder contractions are perceived by the child and are thought to be the relevant signal for initiation of socially learned behaviors of continence (i.e., suspend current activities and visit the toilet). It is hypothesized that during sleep, the child does not perceive the signal of a full bladder, and the process of automatic bladder emptying occurs without inhibition. This may be because the upper centrum or cortical areas fail to perceive the signals governing urination, so the child doesn't act upon them by fully awakening to prevent wetting (Watanabe, Imada, Kawauchi, Koyama, & Shirakawa, 1997). Higher thresholds for arousal from sleep have been shown in enuretic children compared with normal controls (Wolfish, 2001). Collectively, these findings strongly suggest neurological explanations for the background noise that prevents the detection of the signal of a filling bladder. These maturational delays in the nervous system appear to occur within the context of a genetic predisposition for enuresis (Von Gontard, Schaumburg, Hollmann, Eiberg, & Rittig, 2001).

Others have speculated that reduced bladder capacity or polyuria (i.e., overproduction of urine) or both are primary etiological factors for enuresis (Djurhuus & Rittig, 2002). Simply put, children who wet the bed are thought to do so because their capacity to hold urine is less than the amount they produce during the sleeping period. These findings have not been consistently replicated but likely account for a subpopulation of children with nocturnal enuresis.

The role of the pelvic floor in the pathophysiology of and recovery from enuresis has yet to be fully investigated. The pelvic floor consists of a system of striated muscles supporting the organs in the lower abdomen and includes the external urinary and anal sphincters. With regard to bladder functioning and capacity, there is evidence that an extremely quiescent pelvic floor activates bladder instability, which leads to a diminished bladder capacity (Yeung, Chiu, & Sit, 1999). A model of enuresis proposed by Mellon & Houts (in press-a) has combined these disparate findings into an explanation that accounts for the etiology of nocturnal enuresis and the hypothesized mechanisms of action for the success of the urine alarm. The model describes the normal developmental process of achieving daytime and nighttime urinary continence, the failure to generalize urinary inhibition or the "guarding reflex" to the state of sleep as the mechanism accounting for nocturnal enuresis, and the respondent and operant mechanisms that reestablish the guarding reflex during sleep.

The problem of diurnal enuresis is considered to be the result of different kinds of physiological causes that create background noise that interferes with accurate bladder signal detection, or it may simply result from incomplete social learning of daytime continence. These influences include physical ones such as urinary tract infections, bladder instability with urgency and frequency, constipation and painful defecation, and inconsistent or passive permissiveness in toilet training (Bakker, van Gool, & Wyndaele, 2001). The physiological processes are thought to interfere with a child's ability to detect the signal and appropriately act on the need to exercise appropriate toileting behavior. In effect, the signal of a full bladder is either stifled by acute illnesses of the urinary tract or constipation. Furthermore, the signal may not have been appreciated in children whose parents exercised passive permissiveness and the child has yet to be completely and reliably toilet trained.

For children experiencing diurnal enuresis, it is important to inquire about the frequency of daytime wetting symptoms and their duration. The process should lead to a distinction between the typically younger child who has an occasional accident and who might have some reluctance or fear regarding the use of a public bathroom, and the child who might require a medical assessment of their wetting symptoms. If the child has more than one daytime wetting accident every two weeks and has persisted with this pattern for at least a month, a medical assessment is warranted. It is increasingly rare for an older child to have diurnal enuresis, given that 96% of 5-year-olds are continent during the day. Therefore, an older child should be suspected of having an organic cause for the wetting (Meadow, 1990).

When a child is experiencing nocturnal enuresis, it is important for healthcare providers to inquire about how long it has been happening and whether the child has had any chronic illnesses that could contribute to excessive urine production (i.e., diabetes, nephritis) in order to guide the family on how to obtain proper treatment. The distinction of primary vs. secondary enuresis has some utility in appreciating pathological influences versus the normal progression of the problem. Children who exhibit a sudden and persistent onset of their wetting symptoms (i.e., secondary enuresis), whether for diurnal or nocturnal enuresis, have a higher likelihood of physiological influences on their wetting problem, including painful urination, urgency and frequency, polyuria, urinary tract infections, or a history of chronic constipation and encopresis (Issenman, Filmer, & Gorski, 1999).

Day and night wetting has no reported adverse developmental implications; however, there are certainly social and emotional consequences. Incontinence in public can have long-lasting and detrimental social implications for the child and has been reported to be the third most stressful event mentioned by school-age children behind "losing a parent" and "going blind" (Ollendick, King, & Frary, 1989). If the daytime wetting symptoms are frequent enough, they may interfere with the child's educational progress simply because the child is out of the classroom with each accident to clean up.

Bedwetting is considered to be less stressful than day wetting, but it can prevent typical social opportunities such as sleepovers and summer camps because of the fear of wetting in those situations. There is also evidence that children with nocturnal enuresis have an improvement in self-esteem with successful treatment (e.g., Longstaffe, Moffatt, & Whalen, 2000). Enuretic children often seem to be very embarrassed by the wetting because they believe that they might be the only ones with the problem. Successful treatment may begin by demystifying the problem by informing the child about how common it is (Mellon & Houts, in press-b).

## ALTERNATIVE ACTIONS FOR ENURESIS PREVENTION

Prevention in the traditional sense is not really possible, given that nocturnal enuresis is best accounted for by maturational delays in the neuro-urological systems caused by a genetic predisposition. However, efforts can be made to support the development of toileting skills and minimize the physical, emotional, and social impact of enuresis after it manifests.

Children with bladder control problems tend to experience a later onset in toilet training and more punishment during toilet training compared with children who do not have bladder control problems (Bakker et al., 2001). Although medical literature regarding evidence-based toilet training procedures is sparse, parents welcome anticipatory guidance from their health care practitioners on the best ways to achieve a successful outcome with toilet training their children (Luxem & Christophersen, 1994). As part of the kindergarten screening that all children go through, schools could develop a health questionnaire that inquires about health problems and toileting difficulties. Parents with children with diurnal and nocturnal enuresis then could be provided with educational brochures or information packets about the problems and how to seek out help. These parents might also be referred to the school nurse, who might be able to provide short-term health counseling about enuresis and its treatment.

Primary medical care providers also could coordinate with school nurses and school psychologists to provide toilet training programs and teach good toileting hygiene in the schools. A special issue of the journal *Pediatrics* was dedicated to current knowledge regarding toilet training, with specific references to the role of day care providers and preschools (American Academy of Pediatrics, 1999). Tables 1 and 2 summarize the important and coordinated roles of health care providers and day care providers and educators in facilitating a pleasant and individualized approach for toilet training children. Many of the common problems that parents encounter in toilet training their children can be avoided by properly educating parents regarding the child's readiness for training and by using sensitive methods of instruction to make the experience positive and nonstressful.

Perhaps the most important role for school professionals is to provide early detection of enuresis problems and offer parents guidance on treatments. Schools could help health care providers implement a treatment plan in the school system to ensure that urinary incontinence will be effectively resolved early in its course, thus minimizing

**Table 1** *Toilet Training Guidelines for Clinicians: An Individualized Developmental Approach*

Determining the Child's Readiness (often between 2 and 3 years of age)

1. Child shows capacity to imitate.
2. Child follows simple verbal commands.
3. Child expresses interest in toilet training.
4. Child can communicate the need to use the toilet.
5. Child demonstrates the ability to pull clothes up and down.
6. Child's temperament can be described as cooperative and persistent.

Determining the Parent's Readiness (at child's 1- to 2-year-old well-child visits)

1. Instruct parent about child's signs of readiness.
2. Do the parents have time for toilet training?
3. Encourage parents to resist outside influence on when to start.
4. Do the parents have previous bad experiences with toilet training older siblings?
5. Are there other adults involved in the child's care that will be involved in training?

Addressing Specific Issues

1. Identify reasons for resistance in a child who is physically ready.
2. A nonstressful, patient, and positive approach avoids causing resistance in the child.
3. Is the problem of stool withholding or avoidance of toileting the result of emotional stressors, constipation, or both?
4. Introduce the process of toilet training with a potty chair and progress to the regular toilet when the child is physically large enough.
5. Become familiar with the culture of the child's family and its relationship to toilet training.
6. Child should be well and not involved in any significant transition (i.e., a move or the birth of a sibling) during toilet training.
7. Coordinate the toilet training plan with other day care providers and preschool staff.
8. Stress the importance of good nutrition and the role of dietary fiber for bowel regularity.
9. The use of diapers or disposable training pants is helpful in the process of training.

*Note.* From "Toilet Training Guidelines: Parents—The Role of the Parents in Toilet Training," by P. A. Gorski, 1999, *Pediatrics, 103*, pp. 1362–1363. Copyright by the American Academy of Pediatrics. Adapted with permission.

the potential social stigma. A plan that involves school professionals would necessarily maintain privacy to minimize the chance for detrimental social consequences for the child. The details of such a plan would be individualized for each child's specific circumstances.

## ALTERNATIVE ACTIONS FOR ENURESIS INTERVENTION

### Treatment for Diurnal Enuresis

The effective treatment of diurnal enuresis involves a multidisciplinary approach among physicians, mental health professionals, and educators. Parents and teachers also play an important role in the implementation of treatment. As many as 50% of 7- to 8-year-old girls with daytime wetting symptoms have active urinary tract infections; therefore, treating with antibiotics is a first step (Hansen, Hansen, & Dahm, 1997). For children with an unstable bladder, the use of anticholinergic medicines helps reduce spontaneous and spastic bladder contractions that are the precursors of urinary urgency, frequency, and ultimately wetting accidents. However, these medical treatments will not help all children with diurnal enuresis completely stop the wetting. Additional lifestyle and behavioral interventions will also be needed in many cases.

Behavioral interventions have the advantage of not producing side effects that often can occur with the use of

**Table 2** *Toilet Training Guidelines for Day Care Providers and Preschool Staff*

Developmental Signs of Readiness

1. Day care providers are often the first to recognize readiness.
2. Signs include child's ability to imitate adults, to put things where they belong, to show independence by saying "no," to express interest in toileting, to communicate the need to use the toilet, and to pull clothing up and down.
3. The temperament of the child who is ready for toileting includes adaptability, persistence, attentiveness to adult directives, and willingness to please the caregiver or educator. If the child has not yet toilet trained by 4 years of age, suggest an evaluation by a health care provider.

Training Practices in the Day Care/Preschool Setting

1. Toilet training can be incorporated into typical curriculum.
2. Day care providers and educators can establish a positive training environment.
3. Children have an opportunity to learn from peers through modeling and vicarious learning.
4. Day care providers and educators can stress the importance of proper nutrition to promote health and bowel regularity.
5. Day care providers and educators can promote good hygiene related to toileting through frequent handwashing and regular changing of diapers.

Partnership Between Day Care Providers or Educators and Parents

1. Day care providers and educators can inform parents about effective training practices and proper timing for optimal learning.
2. Day care providers and educators should be aware of cultural issues in training to develop individualized approaches to training.
3. Day care providers and educators should encourage open communication with parents to coordinate efforts at home and at day care or preschool. Record keeping of progress facilitates close monitoring of progress and communication.

Optimal Setting and Facilities

1. A clearly identified diaper-changing area that is separate from other activity areas will minimize health hazards and allow for easy disinfecting.
2. Small toilets and sinks facilitate training because they fit the size of the children. Potty chairs should be avoided, as they are difficult to keep clean.
3. Disposable diapers are preferred over cloth because they are easier to dispose of and reduce the risk of contamination.

*Note.* From "Toilet Training Guidelines: Parents—The Role of the Parents in Toilet Training," by P. A. Gorski, 1999, *Pediatrics, 103,* pp. 1362–1363. Copyright by the American Academy of Pediatrics. Adapted with permission.

medications. Behavioral approaches have included the use of positive reinforcement that targets appropriate use of the toilet and dry pants, the urine alarm used during the day, retention control training to increase bladder capacity, timed or scheduled voiding, and the use of pelvic floor strengthening exercises. Unfortunately, no randomized controlled trials have been conducted on these types of interventions, and they often include, at best, single case or single group designs with little or no follow-up.

Scheduled toileting has been investigated in the geriatric population and found to be as effective as medications (Edens & Surwit, 1995). It is often a standard practice among pediatric urologists for their patients with day wetting. Pelvic floor exercises (i.e., Kegel exercises) are often taught to children who exhibit pelvic floor contractions during bladder emptying. The training has been done with EMG biofeedback equipment to make the child aware of how a relaxed pelvic floor allows for more efficient and complete bladder emptying. Schneider, King, and Surwit (1994) demonstrated that 60% of day wetting children who received pelvic floor training were no longer wetting at follow-up. Furthermore, the 31% of the children who were also on pharmacological treatment for wetting did no better than the children who were not. Caution is warranted in drawing firm conclusions because this was not a randomized controlled trial.

Based on clinical experience, I have developed a behavioral approach to day wetting that incorporates many of the above-mentioned components. The intervention is designed to increase the appropriate use of the toilet and the child's bladder capacity by having the child self-monitor output into a urine hat placed in the toilet. Urinary output goals are set for each child to approximate the estimated bladder capacity for each urination episode and a total for the day. Rewards are given when these goals are met and also for dry days. All children thus far have found the procedure to be novel enough to maintain interest over the course of a few months of treatment. Educators can easily assist in implementing this method in the school environment by simply recording each appropriate use of the toilet or accidents and reporting this information to the parents.

## Treatment for Nocturnal Enuresis

Many decades of research regarding behavioral treatments for nocturnal enuresis have allowed confident conclusions to be drawn about effective treatments. Research consistently identifies the primary role of the urine alarm in empirically supported treatments. The urine alarm consists of a urine sensor attached by wire to an alarm module. It comes in numerous designs, but the common versions are a rubberized pad laid on the bed and a sensor worn by the sleeper. The alarm volume can range from 85 to 110 decibels and the tone varies (e.g., electronic tone, telephone bell, or fire-alarm bell). Other types of alarm feedback include vibrating devices. The prices also vary greatly, from around $50 to $120.

Urine alarm treatment has proved to be effective for approximately 60% to 80% of all monosymptomatic enuretic school-age children regardless of gender. This conclusion has been empirically supported in a meta-analytic review by Houts, Berman, and Abramson (1994) and was summarized in a review using criteria for defining empirically established treatments (Mellon & McGrath, 2000). Similar findings were reported in a recent systematic review (Glazener & Evans, 2003). The procedure for the urine alarm treatment requires the child to turn the sensor on or attach it at bedtime after voiding in the toilet. If the child has a wetting accident, the alarm is activated; the child then changes the wet bedding and clothing and finishes voiding in the toilet. The procedure is repeated for each accident during the night. The treatment continues until the child reaches a specified success criterion, typically 14 to 21 consecutive dry nights. The length of treatment required can vary greatly, with the usual length of time being 12 to 16 weeks.

Dry Bed Training, developed by Azrin, Sneed, and Foxx (1974), is another empirically supported treatment (Mellon & McGrath, 2000). This operant conditioning procedure, which includes the urine alarm, has an average overall cure rate of 75% in as few as 4 weeks. Dry bed training includes systematic waking of the child, overcorrection if wetting occurs (having the child repeatedly get out of bed to visit the toilet), and cleanliness training. Treatments that combine the urine alarm with other behavioral treatments such as retention control training (e.g., Full Spectrum Home Training by Houts and Liebert, 1984) or with medications such as desmopressin have cure rates of 79% and 75%, respectively (Mellon & McGrath).

The amount of supervision required for a given child varies greatly. Some families will be able to conduct treatment at home without any professional guidance, but most will require a minimal amount of support by mental health professionals or educators. Assistance includes a method of record keeping that tracks bedtimes, the number of times wetting occur and at what time, whether the child awakens on his own to avoid accidents or sleeps through the night dry, and ratings of the child's attitude during the treatment. If the child becomes discouraged during treatment, the mental health professional monitoring the treatment can offer support to the child and parents by helping them set realistic goals for treatment or implementing an incentive plan for the child to improve her adherence to the treatment regimen. This support is often needed, because the amount of time typically needed to complete treatment is 20 weeks.

# ENCOPRESIS—BACKGROUND AND DEVELOPMENT

Encopresis is the name given to a child's passing of fecal material into his or her clothing. The term applies when the child is over the age of 4 years, when frequency is at least once per month for at least 6 months, and when no organic cause can be found for the soiling (American Psychiatric Association, 1994). As many as 1.5% to 7.5% of school-age children meet the diagnostic criteria for encopresis (Bellman, 1966; Houts & Abramson, 1990). The symptoms of encopresis can unfold over a period of up to 5 years, including the constipation that leads to overflow soiling at the time the child presents for treatment (Partin, Hamill, Fischel, & Partin, 1992). As many as 68% to 86% of encopretic children experience years of pain with defecation, and the condition is often referred to as *retentive encopresis* (Loening-Baucke, 1993). Even after standard medical treatment for encopresis, as many as 36% to 42% of children will persist with constipation and soiling, attesting to the difficulty in effectively treating this childhood disorder (Procter & Loader, 2003; Rockney, McQuade, Days, Linn, & Alario, 1996).

Most children undergo a developmental process that culminates in fecal continence 85% of the time by the age of 4 years (Bellman, 1966). Fecal continence is maintained as a dynamic balance between the involuntary and voluntary nervous systems of the lower gastrointestinal tract and the consistency of fecal material. The anal canal has a rich network of sensory nerve cells that can differentially recognize and respond to various qualities of tactile stimulation. The sensitive tissue of the anal canal can thus discriminate between the physical states of rectal contents as solid, liquid, or gas, which enables the child to make socially appropriate decisions about how to respond in order to maintain continence (Bartolo & Macdonald, 2002).

If it is determined that a bowel movement is inappropriate, then the child voluntarily contracts the external anal sphincter, which pushes the contents back into the upper rectal area and reestablishes resting tone in the internal anal sphincter. When defecation is deemed appropriate, assuming a squatting position on the toilet allows for more efficient passage of stool. Simultaneously executing a Valsalva contraction and relaxing the external anal sphincter allows for formed and soft stool to pass without discomfort. Fecal continence is maintained by having greater muscle tone in the external anal sphincter compared to pressures in the sigmoid rectum, with the anus acting essentially as the valve that selectively allows feces or flatus to pass. Normal regularity ranges from a daily bowel movement to once every third day, with peristalsis being stimulated by meal ingestion or vigorous physical activity (Quigley, 2002).

This complex bodily function can be disrupted by a state of chronic constipation or severe fecal impaction in which the rectal area is stretched full, leading to fecal incontinence. Mental health professionals and educators will recognize the importance of achieving bowel regularity for normal functioning in the encopretic child and the need for a multidisciplinary approach to restore this functioning. Fecal incontinence in the absence of constipation and withholding behavior should be understood simply as failed toilet training and might suggest other psychosocial issues that could contribute to this failure, such as ineffective parenting or disruptions to normal family functioning (Taubman & Buzby, 1997).

## PROBLEMS AND IMPLICATIONS OF ENCOPRESIS

It is important to differentiate between the child who has an isolated soiling accident and the child who meets the criteria for retentive encopresis. Children may have an accident because they are embarrassed to ask for permission to go to the bathroom or may have social anxiety related to defecating in public and avoid using the toilet. Early recognition of retentive encopresis and intervention with effective treatments will prevent the soiling from becoming entrenched. Continued soiling will ultimately lead to its occurrence in the school setting and result in long-lasting emotional and social consequences, some of which can be severe (Young, Brennen, Baker, & Baker, 1995).

Constipation is considered the precursor to fecal soiling or encopresis in most cases, as it is associated with decreased rectal sensitivity (Loening-Baucke, 2002). The loss of sensation to rectal filling will lead to soiling when rectal pressures rise and exceed the weakened anal pressure before the child or adult is even aware of the need to defecate (Bartolo & Macdonald, 2002). Rectal sensitivity can be further compromised by stool consistency, with high volumes of liquid stool or small, hard pellets being difficult to discriminate (e.g., between flatus or liquid feces) or pass effectively (e.g., small and hard stool). Fecal incontinence results when the signal that indicates the need to defecate (i.e., rectal distention) is lost because of chronic constipation and impaction, which reduce rectal and anal sensitivity. Furthermore, intensely painful defecation that results from passing large-diameter stool and abdominal pain are thought to cause people to avoid defecation, which they can do by contracting the gluteal muscles and the pelvic floor while standing in a rigid posture until the urge to defecate subsides; however, this worsens constipation. Accidents occur when small amounts of stool in the distal end of the fecal mass break away or when liquid stool seeps around the impaction. The defecation avoidance response is also suspected of being overgeneralized by sufferers to more complex aspects of toileting: They may avoid visiting the bathroom to attempt defecation, not comply with treatment, or avoid the social consequences of soiling by ignoring accidents or hiding soiled underwear (Mellon & Houts, in press-a). In essence, all aspects of bowel functions become associated with aversive experiences because of the anticipation of pain and the frustration associated with losing control of toileting skills. It is at that point that a feeling of learned helplessness and indifference surrounding toileting begins.

The existing literature regarding the behavioral and emotional characteristics of children with encopresis is meager and somewhat inconsistent. However, several trends bear mentioning in preparing for effective management of the encopretic child in the school setting.

Psychological and behavioral factors are thought to have an effect not only on the evolution of fecal incontinence (e.g., coercive toilet training, birth of a sibling, start of school) but also on the maintenance of the problem (e.g., externalizing behavior and nonadherence, low self-esteem and hopelessness, family conflict, psychiatric problems in parents) (Cox et al., 2003). For example, children with soiling demonstrate significantly more symptoms of anxiety or depression, less expressiveness and organization in the family environment, greater attention and social problems, more disruptive behaviors, and poorer school performance than nonsymptomatic children (Cox, Morris, Borowitz, & Sutphen, 2002). Furthermore, 20% more of the encopretic sample exceeded clinical thresholds in their behavioral symptoms compared with nonencopretic children. Additional evidence suggests lower levels of social competency in encopretic children versus nonclinical children (e.g., Young et al., 1995). Thus, encopretic children appear to have demonstrable behavioral dysregulation. The question of whether these differences precede or are the result of the stress incurred by having encopresis has yet to be answered. However, the behavioral–emotional difficulties observed in encopretic children attest to the differences in the complexity of this problem compared with that of children who just wet the bed. This emotional–behavioral complexity, combined with the greater physiological complexity in the mastery of bowel continence, will likely have to be addressed in the design of effective treatments for childhood encopresis.

## ALTERNATIVE ACTIONS FOR PREVENTION OF ENCOPRESIS

Early identification of those children who might manifest encopresis could be achieved by administering simple questionnaires during the kindergarten screening that all children complete for public school education. Asking parents if there are any toileting concerns, whether any accidents are occurring, how regular the child's bowels are, and how long any symptoms have been present will provide essential information. Once identified, these children and their parents can be directed to effective, multidisciplinary treatment programs in order to prevent years of continued struggle with the problem of chronic constipation and fecal soiling. Parents may indicate that they have "seen all doctors" and have "tried everything" to treat their child's encopresis. In reality, most of these children manifested chronic constipation or difficult and painful defecation early in their development and have received treatment of inadequate intensity and consistency (Partin et al., 1992).

Schools should consider increasing dietary fiber in their school lunch menu. Given that encopresis treatment requires the reestablishment of bowel regularity to overcome the constipation that leads to soiling, the role of dietary fiber cannot be emphasized enough. The recommended amount of dietary fiber children should ingest each day is approximately their age plus 5 grams (American Academy of Pediatrics, 1999). Primary school–age children should approximate 15 to 20 grams of fiber each day, with adequate hydration, which promotes greater bowel regularity and softer stools.

The goal of preventing the social and emotional burden of encopresis can best be achieved through early detection and effective treatment. School psychologists can play the important role of coordinating the multidisciplinary treatment in the school with parents, teachers, school nurses, and the child. Specific actions that can be taken are discussed in the next section.

## ALTERNATIVE ACTIONS FOR ENCOPRESIS INTERVENTION

An optimal outcome requires the child to be in compliance with the treatment during all waking hours, many of which occur in school. Ensuring that treatment is properly delivered in the school setting will require substantial oversight, which can be achieved by reviewing the components of treatment to be sure they are occurring daily. The school psychologist can reduce emotionally and socially adverse consequences by providing supportive and short-term counseling as needed. School professionals can also help by providing for the practical needs, such as access to a private bathroom and changing area if an accident occurs. Having the child focus on those behaviors that will lead to recovery from soiling will help him remain positive in his attitude toward treatment rather than be discouraged when accidents occur.

Treatments for encopresis have included singular medical attempts to reduce the obvious problems of constipation using bowel cathartics and stool softeners, singular psychological treatments to reduce the obvious stool withholding and the avoidance of defecating by using reinforcement procedures for appropriate toileting, invasive biofeedback to eradicate the paradoxical contraction of the external anal sphincter, or combinations of all of the above. Because of methodological limitations in the published literature, only the most conservative conclusions can currently be drawn (see review by McGrath, Mellon, and Murphy, 2000). No empirically established treatments have emerged from the literature; however, treatments that combine medical interventions for constipation with behavioral procedures to increase appropriate toileting have an average cure rate of 55% to 63%. Combining biofeedback and medical management to treat abnormal defecation dynamics and constipation has an average estimated cure rate of 67%. However, recent reviews have cast doubt upon whether the inclusion of biofeedback in combined approaches contributes to a greater rate of recovery compared with standard medical management (Brazzelli, & Griffiths, 2001; Mellon & Houts, in press-a).

The work of a research team at the University of Virginia Health Sciences Center, led by Dr. Daniel Cox, is an excellent example of a biobehavioral model with demonstrated efficacy. The research team's unique biobehavioral treatment, known as "enhanced toilet training," includes the typical and intensive medical management of enemas and stool softeners with behavioral training of appropriate toileting. Patients are instructed about the pathophysiology of retentive encopresis and the reduced rectal sensitivity and paradoxical contraction of the anal sphincter resulting from chronic constipation. An incentive plan is developed to target independent toileting and clean underwear. The treatment is enhanced by the therapist instructing the patient in proper sitting technique and in recognizing the muscles involved in enacting a Valsalva contraction, with prompting to simultaneously relax the anal sphincter.

Once the sequence is understood by the child and parent, parents are instructed to prompt this practice at home while the child sits on the toilet after two meals during the day. The sitting practice lasts 12 minutes, the first 4 minutes of which the child is asked to repeatedly contract and relax the anal sphincter to localize control and to fatigue the sphincter. The second 4 minutes emphasizes nothing more than a fun activity, such as reading, to desensitize the child to toileting. The last 4 minutes involves the child actually trying to have a bowel movement while relaxing his or her feet, legs, and anal sphincter. This procedure is phased out 2 weeks after the final treatment session. The treatment also involves a unique monitoring method that uses an automated voicemail system to call the family at predetermined times and collect information about medicines used, bowel movements in the toilet, soiling accidents, and independent use of the toilet. The research team also developed an Internet tutorial website designed to inform families about the causes of encopresis and its treatment. The University of Virginia Health Sciences Center research team has reported acceptable success rates of 44% cured, 71% significantly improved, and a 109% increase in bowel movements in the toilet. These modest success rates may be explained by the fact that all of their patients had previously failed standard medical intervention alone (for more detail, see Borowitz, Cox, Sutphen, & Kovatchev, 2002; Ritterband et al., 2003).

An additional comprehensive behavioral treatment that also includes medical management is that of Stark, Owens-Stively, Spirito, Lewis, and Guevremont (1990) and Stark et al. (1997). This intervention is delivered in a group format with all children receiving an initial bowel cleanout, dietary fiber education with goals to increase the ingestion of fiber, a sitting schedule, reinforcement of appropriate toileting and fiber intake, and relaxation skills for enemas. Although their studies were not randomized controlled trials, the authors report impressive results, with 89% cured at the end of treatment and soiling decreased 84%. These studies are notable for the cost savings of delivering treatment in a group format and for the significant emphasis on dietary fiber intake.

In general, the most effective treatments begin with a thorough medical assessment that often will include a bowel cleanout with enemas, suppositories, or other oral cathartics. Bowel regularity is promoted with stool softeners, bowel lubricants, significant increases in dietary fiber, or a combination of these approaches. Successful treatment also requires healthy toileting habits through scheduled visits to the toilet (typically after a meal), instruction regarding proper sitting technique (i.e., knees level with hips and feet on firm surface), instruction regarding relaxation of the anal sphincter while pushing to initiate a bowel movement, and proper hygiene. Loening-Baucke (2002) provides a helpful summary article of the important components of treatment. As can be imagined, these treatments require effort and lifestyle changes. To motivate the child to adhere to treatment long enough to benefit, the use of reinforcement strategies is also required. Targets for positive reinforcement in the form of token economies include fiber intake goals, adherence with toileting schedule, parent-prompted and self-initiated bowel movements in the toilet, taking of prescribed medicines and stool softeners, and clean underwear. The combination of targets will vary from one child to the next. Interviewing the child and parents will provide insights into which types of rewards (i.e., tangible rewards, activity rewards) are most meaningful to the child in order to motivate his or her positive adherence to treatment.

With an appreciation of the biobehavioral conceptualization of encopresis, school professionals will be more effective in assisting in the multidisciplinary treatment of fecal soiling. Such assistance should include ensuring that the child is adhering to toileting visits, monitoring dietary fiber intake, establishing a routine for socially discreet cleaning up after accidents, implementing behavioral incentives, and keeping accurate records of treatment components. School professionals should help coordinate the treatment within the school environment and communicate progress to the health providers managing the treatment. Treatment progress is easily quantified in charts that provide frequency counts of target behaviors, times of day in which the behaviors occur, and ratings of attitude and beliefs that might be related to problems with adherence to treatment. Early detection and effective treatment of chronic constipation and encopresis will minimize the possibility of the devastating social and emotional consequences mentioned in the previous section.

## SUMMARY

School professionals can be well prepared to help families who have an enuretic child by becoming familiar with proper assessments and evidence-based treatments for both daytime and nocturnal wetting. Diurnal enuresis is more likely to present in the school setting. School professionals can be instrumental in early recognition and management of the wetting by directing the child and family to obtain a medical assessment and assisting in implementing the treatment in the school setting. The behavioral interventions often require close monitoring by an adult to ensure adherence, record keeping, and provision of earned rewards for the behavioral targets of treatment. Proper management of the problem will allow for appropriate amounts of privacy surrounding the treatment to minimize any stress and embarrassment if accidents do occur. Although treatment for bedwetting will occur in the child's home, routinely screening for nocturnal enuresis will allow school professionals to direct the child and parent to effective treatment resources. Providing reassurance to the child and family will also be helpful to reduce any stress related to their belief that the child with bedwetting is the only one in the school with that problem.

Successful treatment for encopresis begins with education of the child and parent regarding causes and treatment. That effort is followed by a combination of laxative therapy to address the constipation that typically leads to soiling and behavior modification to promote appropriate use of the toilet, reestablishment of regular toileting, increased intake of dietary fiber, and cleanliness training for accidents. Record keeping is essential to document progress and monitor important treatment variables, which provide information for effective communication between the child–family, physician, and mental health professional or school staff. This coordinated effort is consistent with the biobehavioral conceptualization of encopresis and will promote a positive outcome for the child.

## RECOMMENDED RESOURCES

### Websites on Enuresis

*http://www.bedwettingstore.com*

This and the following website provide trustworthy information regarding enuresis and how to manage the problem. The Bedwetting Store's website describes a variety of urine alarms, books, bedwetting treatment kits, and other accessories that are available for purchase. All of the kits include the urine alarm, which is consistent with the published literature. However, no studies directly compare therapist-supervised versus self-help treatments for bedwetting. Clinical experience strongly suggests that a minimum level of supervision and support from an experienced therapist is needed.

*http://www.healthsystem.virginia.edu/UVAHealth/peds_urology/enuresis.cfm*

The University of Virginia online Health System is a useful resource that describes the etiology, assessment, and treatment of both diurnal and nocturnal enuresis. The information provided is consistent with current medical and psychological science.

## Websites on Encopresis

*http://www.healthsystem.virginia.edu/internet/pediatrics/patients/Tutorials/Constipation/constipationhome.cfm*

*http://www.healthsystem.virginia.edu/UVAHealth/peds_digest/constipa.cfm*

*http://www.healthsystem.virginia.edu/UVAHealth/peds_digest/encopres.cfm*

The above websites are quite detailed, provide accurate information, and are visually appealing to the user. They provide a parent or health care professional with most of the information needed to understand the components of proper assessment, treatment, and long-term management of constipation. At the very least, parents will be well informed about what to look for in effective treatment. Mental health professionals and school staff will also find these websites helpful in understanding how they might assist the health care provider in effectively treating the encopretic child.

# REFERENCES


American Academy of Pediatrics. (1999). Physiological and clinical considerations regarding toilet training: An updated review. *Pediatrics, 103* (Suppl.), 1343–1368.

American Psychiatric Association. (1994). *Diagnostic and statistical manual of mental disorders* (4th ed.). Washington, DC: Author.

Azrin, N. H., Sneed, T. J., & Foxx, R. M. (1974). Dry-bed training: Rapid elimination of childhood enuresis. *Behaviour Research and Therapy, 12,* 147–156.

Bakker, E., van Gool, J., & Wyndaele, J. (2001). Results of a questionnaire evaluation of different aspects of personal and familial situation, and the methods of potty-training in two groups of children with a different outcome of bladder control. *Scandinavian Journal of Urology and Nephrology, 35,* 370–376.

Bakker, E., van Sprundel, M., van der Auwera, J., van Gool, J., & Wyndaele, J. (2002). Voiding habits and wetting in a population of 4332 Belgian schoolchildren aged between 10 and 14 years. *Scandinavian Journal of Urology and Nephrology, 36,* 354–362.

Bartolo, D., & Macdonald, A. (2002). Fecal continence and defecation. In J. Pemberton, M. Swash, & M. Henry (Eds.), *The pelvic floor—Its function and disorders* (pp. 77–93). New York: W. B. Saunders.

Bellman, M. (1966). Studies on encopresis. *Acta Paediatrica Scandinavica, 1* (Suppl. 170), 7–132.

Borowitz, S., Cox, D., Sutphen, J., & Kovatchev, B. (2002). Treatment of childhood encopresis: A randomized trial comparing three treatment protocols. *Journal of Pediatric Gastroenterology & Nutrition, 34,* 378–384.

Brazzelli, M., & Griffiths, P. (2001). Behavioural and cognitive interventions with or without other treatments for defaecation disorders in children. *Cochrane Database of Systematic Reviews, 4,* CD002240. Information retrieved February 25, 2004.

Cox, D., Morris, J., Borowitz, S., & Sutphen, J. (2002). Psychological differences between children with and without chronic encopresis. *Journal of Pediatric Psychology, 27,* 585–591.

Cox, D., Ritterband, L., Quillian, W., Kovatchev, B., Morris, J., Sutphen, J., & Borowitz, S. (2003). Assessment of behavioral mechanisms maintaining encopresis: Virginia Encopresis-Constipation Apperception Test. *Journal of Pediatric Psychology, 28,* 375–382.

De Jonge, G. (1973). Epidemiology of enuresis: A survey of the literature. In I. Kolvin, R. MacKeith, & S. Meadow (Eds.), *Bladder control and enuresis* (pp. 39–46). London: William Heinemann.

Djurhuus, J., & Rittig, S. (2002). Nocturnal enuresis. *Current Opinion in Urology, 12,* 317–320.

Edens, J., & Surwit, R. (1995). In support of behavioral treatment for day wetting in children. *Urology, 45,* 905–908.

Eiberg, H., Berendt, I., & Mohr, J. (1995). Assignment of dominant inherited nocturnal enuresis (ENUR1) to chromosome 13q. *Nature Genetics, 10,* 354–356.

Fergusson, D., Horwood, L., & Shannon, F. (1986). Factors related to the age of attainment of nocturnal bladder control: An 8-year longitudinal study. *Pediatrics, 78,* 884–890.

Forsythe, W., & Redmond, A. (1974). Enuresis and spontaneous cure rate: Study of 1129 enuretics. *Archives of Disease in Childhood, 49,* 259–263.

Glazener, C., & Evans, J. (2003). Simple behavioural and physical interventions for nocturnal enuresis in children. Cochrane Database of Systematic Reviews, 1, CD003637.

Hansen, A., Hansen, B., & Dahm, T. (1997). Urinary tract infection, day wetting and other voiding symptoms in seven- to eight-year-old Danish children. *Acta Paediatrica Scandinavica, 86,* 1345–1349.

Holstege, G., & Sie, J. (2002). The central control of the pelvic floor. In J. Pemberton, M. Swash, & M. Henry (Eds.), *The pelvic floor—Its function and disorders* (pp. 94–101). New York: W.B. Saunders.

Houts, A., & Abramson, H. (1990). Assessment and treatment for functional childhood enuresis and encopresis: Toward a partnership between health psychologists and physicians. In S. B. Morgan, & T. M. Okwumabua (Eds.), *Child and adolescent disorders: Developmental and health psychology perspectives* (pp. 47–103). Hillsdale, NJ: Erlbaum.

Houts, A., Berman, J., & Abramson, H. (1994). The effectiveness of psychological and pharmacological treatments for nocturnal enuresis. *Journal of Consulting and Clinical Psychology, 62,* 737–745.

Houts, A. C., & Liebert, R. M. (1984). *Bedwetting: A guide for parents and children.* Springfield, IL: Charles C. Thomas.

Issenman, R., Filmer, R., & Gorski, P. (1999). A review of bowel and bladder control development in children: How gastrointestinal and urologic conditions relate to problems in toilet training. *Pediatrics, 103,* 1346–1352.

Jarvelin, M., Moilanen, I., Kangas, P., Moring, K., Vikevainen-Tervonen, L., Huttunen, N., & Seppanen, J. (1991). Aetiological and precipitating factors for childhood enuresis. *Acta Pediatrica Scandinavia, 80,* 361–369.

Jarvelin, M., Vikevainen-Tervonen, L., Moilanen, I., & Huttunen, N. (1988). Enuresis in seven-year-old children. *Acta Pediatrica Scandinavia, 77,* 148–153.

Loening-Baucke, V. (1993). Constipation in early childhood: Patient characteristics, treatment, and long-term follow up. *Gut, 34,* 1400–1404.

Loening-Baucke, V. (2002). Encopresis. *Current Opinion in Pediatrics, 14,* 570–575.

Longstaffe, S., Moffatt, M., & Whalen, J. (2000). Behavioral and self-concept changes after six months of enuresis treatment: A randomized, controlled trial. *Pediatrics, 105,* 935–940.

Luxem, M., & Christophersen, E. (1994). Behavioral toilet training in early childhood: Research, practice and implications. *Developmental and Behavioral Pediatrics, 15,* 370–378.

McGrath, M., Mellon, M., & Murphy, L. (2000). Empirically supported treatments in pediatric psychology: Constipation and encopresis. *Journal of Pediatric Psychology, 25,* 225–254.

Meadow, S. (1990). Day wetting. *Pediatric Nephrology, 4,* 178–184.

Mellon, M. W., & Houts, A. C. (in press–a). Psychosocial treatments for enuresis and encopresis: Current knowledge and future directions. *Journal of Clinical Child and Adolescent Psychology.*

Mellon, M. W., & Houts, A. C. (in press). Nocturnal enuresis: Evidenced based perspectives in etiology, assessment and treatment. In W. O'Donohue & C. Fisher (Eds.), *Practitioner's guide to evidence based psychotherapy.* New York: Springer.

Mellon, M., & McGrath, M. (2000). Empirically supported treatments in pediatric psychology: Nocturnal enuresis. *Journal of Pediatric Psychology, 25,* 193–214.

Norgaard, J., Djurhuus, J., Watanabe, H., Stenberg, A., & Lettgen, B. (1997). Experience and current status of research into the pathophysiology of nocturnal enuresis. *British Journal of Urology, 79,* 825–835.

Ollendick, T., King, N., & Frary, R. (1989). Fears in children and adolescents: Reliability and generalizability across gender, age and nationality. *Behavior, Research and Therapy, 27,* 19–26.

Partin, J., Hamill, S., Fischel, J., & Partin, J. (1992). Painful defecation and fecal soiling in children. *Pediatrics, 89,* 1007–1009.

Procter, E., & Loader, P. (2003). A 6-year follow-up study of chronic constipation and soiling in a specialist paediatric service. *Child: Care, Health & Development, 29,* 103–109.

Quigley, E. (2002). Colonic motility and colonic function. In J. Pemberton, M. Swash, & M. Henry (Eds.), *The pelvic floor—Its function and disorders* (pp. 84–93). New York: W. B. Saunders.

Rawashde, Y., Hvistendahl, G., Kamperis, K., & Djurhuus, J. (2002). Demographics of enuresis patients attending a referral centre. *Scandinavian Journal of Urology & Nephrology, 36,* 348–353.

Ritterband, L., Cox, D., Walker, L., Kovatchev, B., McKnight, L., Patel, K., et al. (2003). An Internet intervention as adjunctive therapy for pediatric encopresis. *Journal of Consulting & Clinical Psychology, 71,* 910–917.

Rockney, R., McQuade, W., Days, A., Linn, H., & Alario, A. (1996). Encopresis treatment outcome: Long-term follow-up of 45 cases. *Journal of Developmental & Behavioral Pediatrics, 17,* 380–385.

Schneider, M., King, L., & Surwit, R. (1994). Kegel exercises and childhood incontinence: A new role for an old treatment. *Journal of Pediatrics, 124,* 91–92.

Stark, L., Opipari, L., Donaldson, D., Danovsky, M., Rasile, D., & Del Santo, A. (1997). Evaluation of a standard protocol for retentive encopresis: A replication. *Journal of Pediatric Psychology, 22,* 619–633.

Stark, L., Owens-Stively, J., Spirito, A., Lewis, A., & Guevremont, D. (1990). Group treatment of retentive encopresis. *Journal of Pediatric Psychology, 15,* 659–671.

Taubman, B., & Buzby, M. (1997). Overflow encopresis and stool toileting refusal during toilet training: A prospective study on the effect of therapeutic efficacy. *Journal of Pediatrics, 131,* 768–771.

Von Gontard, A., Schaumburg, H., Hollmann, E., Eiberg, H., & Rittig, S. (2001). The genetics of enuresis: A review. *Journal of Urology, 166,* 2438–2443.

Watanabe, H., Imada, N., Kawauchi, A., Koyama, Y., & Shirakawa, S. (1997). Physiological background of enuresis type I. A preliminary report. *Scandinavian Journal of Urology & Nephrology, 183*(Suppl.), 7–10.

Wolfish, N. (2001). Sleep/arousal and enuresis subtypes. *Journal of Urology, 166,* 2444–2447.

Yeung, C., Chiu, H., & Sit, F. (1999). Bladder dysfunction in children with refractory monosymptomatic primary nocturnal enuresis. *Journal of Urology, 162,* 1049–1054, 1055.

Young, M., Brennen, L., Baker, R., & Baker, S. (1995). Functional encopresis: Symptom reduction and behavioral improvement. *Developmental and Behavioral Pediatrics, 16,* 226–232.

# 79
# Tic Disorders

**Thomas J. Power**
**Marianne M. Glanzman**

*Children's Hospital of Philadelphia*
*University of Pennsylvania School of Medicine*

## BACKGROUND AND DEVELOPMENT

Tic disorders are movement disorders characterized by brief, repetitive, involuntary movements or vocalizations (or both) that tend to occur in clusters and typically fluctuate in type, frequency, and severity over time (Leckman, 2003). Tics may be difficult to distinguish from behaviors that are commonly considered nervous habits (also see chapter 80, "Habits"). An important difference is that habits, such as nail biting or hair twirling, generally have a continuous, effortful, "writhing" quality, whereas tics, such as eye blinking or throat clearing, typically have a brief, automatic, staccato quality. Complex tics may be more difficult to distinguish from habits or compulsions (see below) but usually occur along with more common simple tics. Tics are often misunderstood by laypersons and professionals and may be ascribed to visual disturbances, allergies, nerves, or purposeful disruptive behavior.

Tic disorders can have a significant effect on school functioning by interfering with attention to instruction or work production, causing physical discomfort, disrupting other students or classroom routines, and resulting in peer rejection. In addition, tic disorders are frequently associated with other conditions that interfere with school functioning, most notably Attention Deficit Hyperactivity Disorder (ADHD) and obsessive–compulsive disorder (OCD; Leckman, 2002). It is estimated that approximately 35% of students with Tourette's syndrome (TS), the most complex tic disorder, receive special education services (Spencer et al., 1998).

### Characteristics of Different Tic Disorders

Individual tics are described by their topology (motor or vocal) and their complexity (simple or complex). Simple motor tics involve only one or a few muscle groups, such as eye blinking. Complex tics involve several muscle groups acting in a series, such as punching or squatting. Simple vocal tics consist of single noises, such as throat clearing or sniffing, whereas complex tics include words or phrases. Table 1 gives common examples of each type of tic. Though characterized as involuntary, tics can be suppressed for short periods of time, such as while speaking in front of the class, but they tend to occur in a flurry after, or between, periods of suppression. Also, some tics, especially in older children, are triggered by a sensory urge such as a funny feeling or an itch, which builds in intensity and is relieved by performing the tic (Leckman, 2003). When asked by a parent or professional who is trying to assess whether or not a particular behavior is a tic, individuals who experience such sensory-triggered tics will often deny that their tics are involuntary, because they perceive that they are choosing to perform the tic (Lang, 1993). Less commonly, some individuals have dystonic tics, which involve unusual, twisted postures of a body part that get stuck in a certain position for a few seconds. Tics are most common in the face, neck, and shoulders.

Tics typically occur during transitions between activities and during times of particular stress, such as before a performance or competition, or during relaxation, such as when watching television. They tend to decrease or disappear during periods of concentration, and they do not occur during sleep. Many children with tic disorders also

**Table 1** *Examples of Common Tics*

| *Simple Motor Tics* | *Simple Vocal Tics* |
|---|---|
| Blinking | Throat clearing |
| Grimacing | Grunting |
| Rolling or darting eyes | Sniffing |
| Squinting | Snorting |
| Lip licking | Inspiratory or expiratory noises |
| Shoulder shrugging | Humming |
| *Complex Motor Tics* | *Complex Vocal Tics* |
| Manipulating clothing | Repeating |
| Dystonic posturing | Stuttering |
| Hopping/jumping | Animal noises |
| Touching rituals | Altered speech quality |
| Thrusting of body parts | Talking to oneself |
| Sequences of simple motor tics | Coprolalia |

**Table 2** *Diagnostic Criteria for Tic Disorders*

| Diagnostic Type | Criteria |
|---|---|
| Transient Tic Disorder | Single or multiple motor or vocal tics |
| | Almost daily occurrences |
| | Duration less than 12 months |
| | Onset before age 18 |
| | Not due to other medical condition |
| | One or more motor or vocal tics (not both) |
| | Almost daily occurrences |
| Chronic Motor or Vocal Tic Disorder | Duration more than 12 months |
| | Onset before age 18 |
| | Not due to other medical conditions |
| | Multiple motor and at least one vocal tic |
| | Almost daily occurrences |
| Tourette's Syndrome | No tic-free period greater than 3 months |
| | Onset before age 18 |
| | Location, frequency, severity fluctuate over time |
| | Not due to other medical conditions |

*Note.* For a further description of diagnostic criteria, see DSM-IV-TR (American Psychiatric Association, 2000).

have OCD symptoms. Obsessions are recurrent thoughts about a negative outcome that are briefly relieved by performing a compulsion (a physical routine), even though the individual is aware that the action does not make sense. For example, a child may fear contracting a disease that is relieved by hand washing, resulting in repetitive hand washing. The difference between a compulsion and a complex tic is that the former is triggered by an obsession, whereas the latter may be performed compulsively but not in relation to particular cognitive triggers.

Table 2 shows the characteristics of different types of tic disorders, as described in the *Diagnostic and Statistical Manual of Mental Disorders, Fourth Edition* (DSM-IV-TR; American Psychological Association [APA], 2000). The DSM-IV-TR criteria are similar to those developed by the Tourette Syndrome Classification Study Group (1993). Tic disorders are common in the general population. Transient tic disorder, the most common type, is estimated to occur in 5% to 24% of children. Chronic tic disorder (including TS) is estimated to occur in 1–2% of children (Leckman, 2002; Robertson, 2003). The majority of individuals with tic disorders, including TS, have relatively mild forms, and may be undiagnosed for many years.

## Course of Tic Development

Tics commonly emerge in children between 3 and 8 years of age. The majority of tics that occur in children between 3 and 6 years are simple motor tics that are transient, although there is no way to know if a tic will be transient or chronic when it initially occurs. Boys are 3 to 4 times more likely to be affected by tic disorders than are girls (Robertson, 2003).

Most of the research on tic disorders has focused on TS, so this discussion will summarize what is known about its developmental course. Given the substantial evidence that different tic disorders are genetically and functionally related, and that tic disorders lie on a continuum from least severe (transient) to most severe (TS; Kurlan, 1994), one can reasonably assume that conclusions drawn from studies of children with TS have implications for children with other tic disorders.

Children who will have TS frequently present to pediatricians for behavioral concerns (hyperactivity, attention problems, anxiety, ritualistic behavior, emotional intensity) in early childhood, well before the onset of tics. They may be diagnosed with ADHD, an autistic spectrum disorder, an anxiety disorder, or OCD before the onset of tics (although true OCD, as defined in the

DSM-IV-TR, does not typically occur until preadolescence or later). The first tic typically occurs between 6 and 8 years of age, and almost always has occurred by age 13. Usually simple motor tics occur first. Gradually, other tics begin, some replacing tics that disappear, others being added to the preexisting repertoire. One or more vocal tics typically begin later, as do sensory tics (approximately 8 to 10 years of age), and complex tics occur still later (Bruun & Budman, 1993; Robertson, 2003). Coprolalia, a complex vocal tic that consists of obscene or sexually explicit words or phrases, is a widely known though uncommon TS symptom that typically occurs in adolescence and adulthood. Individuals with TS may also display motor tics with sexual content, such as obscene gestures or pelvic thrusting. Disinhibition of pathways connecting limbic and motor brain regions is thought to underlie these highly troublesome symptoms (see below).

TS and other tic disorders tend to be chronic conditions, gradually worsening in severity from onset into early adolescence, then decreasing in severity from mid-adolescence into adulthood. Many adults no longer display tics but may continue to experience coexisting conditions (Bruun & Budman, 1993; Robertson, 2003).

## Etiology

The etiology of tic disorders is primarily genetic, though sometimes an individual with a tic disorder appears to be the first affected in a pedigree. Tic disorders probably have a common genetic etiology even though they vary in type and severity. It is not uncommon to have one individual in a family with a chronic single or multiple motor tic disorder and another with TS. In addition, ADHD and OCD are likely to be part of the genetic continuum (Comings, 1990). Not uncommonly, individuals in a pedigree have different combinations of ADHD, OCD, and tic disorders. Females inheriting the genetic predisposition for TS are more likely to have OCD, whereas males are more likely to have tics (Singer & Walkup, 1991).

The search for genes underlying TS has been an active area of investigation for over 20 years. Although it seems to behave as an autosomal dominant disorder with variable penetrance, this assumption has not resulted in the identification of related genes. Researchers have recently proposed that specific sites on multiple chromosomes contribute to vulnerability to TS. Thus far, association studies and genetic linkage studies have suggested that areas on chromosomes 2, 4, 5, 8, 11, and 19 may be related to TS, but specific genes in these areas remain to be identified (Pauls, 2003).

Nongenetic factors also play a role in the expression of TS. Monozygotic (identical) twins share the same genetic information but do not always share TS or have it to the same degree of severity. Clearly, being male affects the expression of tics, and it is theorized that testosterone or other male hormones may affect early brain development in ways that influence the expression of tic-related genes (Leckman, 2002). Twin studies also indicate that the smaller twin is likely to be more severely affected; thus, the quality of the intrauterine environment (placental blood flow and nutrition) also is hypothesized to affect genetic expression. In animal studies, maternal stress during pregnancy may result in tic-like abnormalities in offspring. Because stress causes the release of specific hormones and catecholamines, researchers think that these may also affect the expression of tic-related genes (Leckman, 2002).

A promising line of evidence indicates that immune factors, specifically an immune response to infection or other immune stimulation that cross-reacts with brain cell antigens, may induce or exacerbate tics and related symptoms in some individuals. In the 1990s, case reports appeared of children who developed tics and obsessive–compulsive symptoms following streptococcal infections (see Singer & Loiselle, 2003). Treatment strategies, including antibiotics, plasma exchange, and treatment with immunoglobulins, were reported to be effective. The condition was called PANDAS (pediatric autoimmune neuropsychiatric disorder associated with streptococcal infection) and has stimulated much research and much controversy in the field (Singer & Loiselle, 2003).

In spite of controversy about the conceptualization of PANDAS, evidence has gradually accumulated that shows altered immune function in children with tics and OCD. Viral infections also have been associated with tic exacerbations. Autoantibodies that react with the parts of the brain known to be involved in tic disorders have been identified at a higher rate in children with tic disorders compared with controls (Hoekstra et al., 2004). As more specific information becomes available about the nature of the association between tic disorders and immune function, new avenues of research will likely be pursued in the areas of genetics and treatment.

## Neurological Basis of Tic Disorders

A substantial body of evidence indicates that alterations in brain functioning underlie the motor and vocal manifestations of TS. The induction of repetitive movements in rodents and primates by destruction or stimulation of certain brain regions and by manipulations of certain neurotransmitter systems has been well described in the scientific literature for over 30 years (Comings, 1990). These animal experiments have helped to focus researchers on the brain regions most likely to be involved in humans. Multiple lines of evidence suggest that abnormalities in the basal ganglia underlie tic disorders. The basal ganglia consist of several nuclei that together regulate motor output to the thalamus and integrate it with cognitive and affective information. The striatum (consisting of the caudate and putamen) is the central nucleus of the basal ganglia. The basal ganglia receive information from all parts of the cortex and connect via looplike circuits to the thalamus and back to the prefrontal cortex for metacognitive processing. At least five anatomically and functionally distinct circuits connect different cortical regions through the striatum to the thalamus and back to the frontal cortex. These circuits interconnect sensorimotor, motor, oculomotor, cognitive, and limbic processes, respectively. A failure to inhibit recurrent transmission through one or more of these cortical–striatal–thalamic–cortical circuits is theorized to lead to tics, obsessions, and compulsions (Hoekstra et al., 2004; Singer & Minzer, 2003).

Though transmission through specific circuits cannot be detected visually in isolation, the use of advanced structural and functional neuroimaging techniques has provided supportive evidence for this theory. Carefully analyzed volumetric MRI (magnetic resonance imaging) scans of adults and children with TS indicate differences between subjects and controls in striatal, basal ganglia, and regional cortical volumes, though the specific findings are not necessarily consistent between studies. The most consistent findings include (a) reduced striatal volume in subjects compared with controls, (b) increases in certain regional volumes in children compared with adults (decreases in adults suggest that some of the findings in adult studies are the result of compensation, comorbidities, or the persistence of symptoms over time rather than primarily etiological), and (c) activation of the prefrontal cortex during attempts to suppress tics (Gerard & Peterson, 2003; Hoekstra et al., 2004).

## PROBLEMS AND IMPLICATIONS

Functional impairments related to tic disorders can arise in multiple domains, including academic performance, social competence, behavioral functioning, and family interaction. The level of impairment associated with tic disorders is related to several factors, in particular the severity of the tics and the presence and severity of comorbid conditions. In general, the child's functional impairment is likely to be more severe with greater severity of the tic disorder, including the presence of both verbal and motor tics, greater frequency of tics, and higher complexity of tics. Mild tic disorders, which are the most common variety, typically are associated with minimal functional impairment (Peterson & Cohen, 1998). More severe tic disorders are likely to have social consequences for the child, particularly during preadolescence and adolescence, and may be associated with diminished self-esteem. Also, the more severe the tic disorder, the more likely it is for the child to have comorbid conditions, which in turn are related to functional impairments. The most frequently occurring comorbid disorders are ADHD and OCD.

### Attention Deficit Hyperactivity Disorder (ADHD)

ADHD commonly occurs among children with tic disorders. The prevalence of ADHD among clinic-referred children with TS has been estimated to be in the 50% to 80% range (King & Scahill, 2001). The rate of co-occurring ADHD among clinic-referred children with less severe tic disorders is lower. However, the prevalence of ADHD among children with tic disorders in the general population appears to be below 20% (Peterson & Cohen, 1998), suggesting that the presence of ADHD among children with tic disorders may contribute to their referral to a clinic for treatment.

Children with tic disorders, in particular TS, who meet criteria for ADHD are much more likely to have impairments in social and family functioning than children with TS who do not have ADHD (Spencer et al., 1998; Sukhodolsky et al., 2003). A high frequency of aggressive behavior and mood lability has been reported among children with TS. Children with TS and ADHD are much more likely to demonstrate aggression and moodiness than those with TS without ADHD, although this hypothesis requires additional investigation (Sukhodolsky et al.). Although the presence of ADHD among children with tic disorders contributes strongly to the level of impairment, children with ADHD and comorbid TS appear to have a greater level of functional impairment than those with ADHD only (Spencer et al.).

Children with TS who have ADHD also appear to have more significant educational impairments than those who have TS without ADHD. For example, Spencer and colleagues reported that 41% of children with TS and ADHD had been placed into special education, whereas only 6% of children with TS but not ADHD were in special education (Spencer et al., 1998). At this point, it is not clear that there is a unique cognitive profile associated with TS.

## Obsessive–Compulsive Behavior

As indicated, there is considerable evidence that TS and obsessive–compulsive behavior are variable expressions of a common genetic risk factor. The prevalence of obsessive–compulsive behavior among children with TS is about 50%, although only an estimated 25% of children with TS meet diagnostic criteria for obsessive–compulsive disorder (Spencer et al., 1998). Obsessions are recurrent thoughts or images that are experienced by an individual as intrusive and unwanted and can lead to heightened levels of distress. Compulsions are stereotyped, repetitive behaviors that typically are performed to alleviate distress associated with obsessions (APA, 2000). For example, a student may worry obsessively about his shoes becoming untied and falling off while engaged in a competitive sports activity. The child may become increasingly bothered as more time passes since the last time he checked and retied his shoes. The discomfort may be alleviated temporarily by performing a compulsive ritual of stopping in the midst of the game and tying additional knots in his shoes.

Obsessions and tics are functionally related and can be difficult to distinguish. An urge to exhibit a tic, like an obsession, can become increasingly distressing to a person over time. The repeated performance of a tic or compulsion can temporarily alleviate that distress. In fact, some experts have speculated that compulsions are actually examples of highly complex tics, particularly for cases in which an obsession does not appear to be linked to a stereotyped behavior (e.g., the stereotyped behavior of squatting when going through a doorway, when this behavior is not associated with an obsession, could be considered a compulsion or complex tic).

The association between tic disorders and other anxiety disorders is much less clear. For example, Spencer et al. (1998) found that, in general, children with TS displayed similar levels of anxiety disorders to those without TS (controlling for the presence of comorbid ADHD). However, the researchers found an increased risk for specific phobias among children with TS as compared with those without the disorder.

## Factors That Contribute to Impairments

***Child factors.*** As described in the preceding sections, there is a high level of individual variability in the type, frequency, and severity of tics manifested by children. Children with more frequent and severe tics generally experience greater impairment than those with milder tics. The presence of comorbid conditions, particularly ADHD, can have a significant effect on level of impairment. Also, problems associated with tic disorders may vary greatly across the age span from the preschool years through adolescence. Unfortunately, a student's tics may be most severe during the preadolescent and early adolescent years when peer acceptance is a high priority and youth are particularly sensitive to feedback from peers. As they become increasingly self-conscious during preadolescence and adolescence, the presence of tics may be bothersome to them and result in diminished self-esteem.

***Family factors.*** Families vary substantially in their ability to cope with the mental health needs of children with tic disorders. Parenting stress or caregiver burden has been identified as a critical variable that strongly influences the ability of a family to cope with mental health problems. Higher levels of caregiver burden can be associated with greater willingness to seek help for mental health problems, but they also are associated with lower rates of participation in intervention and lower levels of adherence (Kazdin, Holland, & Crowley, 1997). Factors that may contribute to caregiver burden include parent–child conflict, sibling tension, school reports of academic or behavior problems, and family–school conflict (Janicke & Finney, 2001). Also, adult-related stressors, such as family health problems, financial problems, parental psychopathology, and parents' social isolation may contribute to caregiver burden.

Because tic disorders are genetically based, and the comorbidities most commonly associated with tics have a high level of heritability (i.e., ADHD and OCD), families of children with tics have a strong likelihood of having another family member with tics or related comorbidities, which may further complicate family interactions and lead to higher levels of parental strain. Furthermore, because stress may exacerbate tics, heightened levels of parental strain and family stress may aggravate children's tics, which in turn may increase the child's level of functional impairment at home and school.

***School factors.*** School can be a challenging environment for children with tic disorders, particularly if they are also coping with ADHD. Stressful school environments can aggravate tics, resulting in greater social and emotional impairment. The teacher–child relationship has been shown to be important in enabling children to function effectively in an educational environment (Pianta, 1999), and the quality of that relationship may be a critical factor in determining how a child with tics is able to cope in school. Teachers who are able to develop instructional and behavior strategies in response to the unique needs of these children, and who are able to maintain a positive teacher–student relationship despite the challenges, are likely to be successful in educating these children.

The quality of the family–school relationship has been demonstrated to have an effect on the teacher–child relationship and the child's ability to learn (Christenson & Sheridan, 2001). Therefore, fostering effective partnerships between family and school is essential to enabling a child with tic disorders to cope effectively in school. Furthermore, the quality of children's interactions with peers in school can affect their ability to learn and their overall adjustment to school (Pellegrini & Smith, 1993). Children with tics are vulnerable to peer rejection, particularly if they have ADHD. The ability of school professionals to monitor peer interactions and promote cooperative social behavior among children with tic disorders is important to promote school success.

**Table 3** *Strategies for Reducing Risk and Promoting Resilience for Children With Tics and Other Health Conditions*

1. Work to maintain strong, positive attachments between caregivers and the child.
2. Provide education to the family to develop effective parenting skills.
3. Assist caregivers in building strong social networks within the family and community.
4. Assist caregivers in managing stress and maintaining a healthy lifestyle.
5. Build strong partnerships between family and school.
6. Work to establish and maintain warm, caring attachments between teachers and the child.
7. Provide effective classroom instruction.
8. Monitor peer relationships and work to promote cooperative peer relationships across contexts, including classroom, playground, and neighborhood organizations.
9. Provide professional support to teachers.
10. Reduce barriers to accessing high-quality health care.
11. Establish and maintain collaborative partnerships between the health care and school systems.
12. Encourage children to become involved in enjoyable, enriching neighborhood activities.
13. Encourage families to become involved in advocacy efforts and to expand their social networks through participation in local and national support groups.

*Note.* For a further description of these strategies, see Power et al. (2003).

## ALTERNATIVE ACTIONS FOR PREVENTION

Prevention for children with tic disorders refers to minimizing the impairments associated with these disorders, reducing the risk that more serious impairments might arise in the future, and enhancing the child's resilience in coping with challenges in the home, school, and community. Prevention efforts ought to focus on addressing factors that have been demonstrated to reduce risk and promote resilience. A major focus of prevention programming should be on strengthening the key systems in which children develop, including the family, school, health, and neighborhood systems (see Power, DuPaul, Shapiro, & Kazak, 2003, for a description of these factors). Table 3 describes some actions that can be taken to reduce risk and improve resilience for these children. Many of these strategies are also useful in promoting health and resilience for children with a range of health and mental health conditions.

## ALTERNATIVE ACTIONS FOR INTERVENTION

### Assessment

The clinical assessment of tic disorders in the United States generally follows the guidelines outlined in the DSM-IV-TR (APA, 2000). The assessment typically is conducted by a physician (e.g., psychiatrist, neurologist, or developmental pediatrician), although it can be performed by a psychologist with physician input, and involves working in collaboration with educational and mental health professionals and the parents. The assessment entails the collection of behavioral information through parent reports, teacher reports, self-reports, and direct observations of the child in multiple contexts. It is also important to collect information about family and medical history to rule out the possibility of other neurological conditions and the potential that medication may be contributing to symptomatology.

Direct observation is useful in assessing tics, although the observation of children in clinical settings may have limited significance because children are often able to suppress tics in these settings for a limited time. Observations in naturalistic contexts, such as the classroom or playground, are much more useful clinically in assessing tics. The observation system developed by Kenneth Gadow and colleagues is particularly useful (see Gadow, Nolan, & Sverd, 1992). Because the frequency and severity of tics can vary greatly across contexts, observing children in multiple settings and at different times is important. Recording the time and place in which tics are most frequent and severe may be helpful in planning interventions.

Rating scales completed by parents and teachers are also useful in assessing tics. Two measures that are commonly used in research and practice are the Yale Global Tic Severity Scale (Leckman et al., 1989) and the Hopkins Motor/Vocal Tic Scale (Walkup, Rosenberg, Brown, & Singer, 1992).

Because tic disorders often occur in combination with other mental health conditions, assessment should also include a screening for attention, behavioral, social, emotional, and learning problems. Structured interviews, behavior rating scales, direct observation methods, family history questionnaire, and brief psychoeducational testing are highly useful in assessing possible comorbid conditions.

An assessment of tics and comorbid conditions requires evaluation of a child's functional impairment to determine the extent to which clinical symptoms are interfering with performance in major domains of functioning, including academic achievement, peer relationships, family relationships, and conduct in home and school settings. The Academic Competence Evaluation Scales (DiPerna & Elliott, 2000) and the Social Skills Rating System (Gresham & Elliott, 1990) are examples of measures that may be useful in assessing functional impairment and competence related to academic and social behavior.

## Pharmacological Intervention

Treatment of tic disorders with medication involves two separate considerations: treatment of tics and treatment of associated conditions or symptoms. The vast majority of children with tics have mild enough symptoms that the tics themselves are not usually treated pharmacologically. The medications that are effective in decreasing tic severity may have side effects that limit their use to situations in which educational and psychosocial treatments are insufficient to prevent functional impairment. However, even children with relatively mild tics may be helped by medication for ADHD, anxiety, OCD, or mood problems. Two factors complicate the medication management of children with tic disorders. First, the medication for one type of problem may exacerbate another problem. For example, stimulants for ADHD may increase tics; neuroleptics to decrease tics may impair concentration or increase anxiety. Second, the chronically fluctuating course of tic disorders complicates the assessment of medication effects. Some children, especially those with more severe disorders, will require multiple medications.

Table 4 provides information about medications used to treat tics. Fewer than 15 controlled studies have been performed for all of the medications listed. Neuroleptics are the most effective medications but may not be the safest. The newest neuroleptics have been designed to minimize the undesirable side effects of older ones, particularly tardive dyskinesia (rhythmic, repetitive, stereotypical movements). Most have been studied in adults with psychosis, and little is known about their longer term effects and side effects in children. Antihypertensives are often tried first, though they are typically less effective. Medications in other categories, including benzodiazepines, dopamine agonists, and others, may have a role based on anecdotal or preliminary evidence (Sandor, 2003).

Table 5 gives analogous information on medications used for the treatment of associated disorders. Stimulants may increase tic severity or frequency, but that does not occur often, and in fact, tics may improve when ADHD is treated (Tourette Syndrome Study Group, 2002). Exacerbation of the primary disorder may be temporary or may resolve with dose reductions. Some children will have tic exacerbation on one category of stimulant but not the other (e.g., methylphenidate versus amphetamine). For these reasons, and because ADHD is often more functionally impairing than tics, evidence-based treatment for ADHD should be pursued, and stimulants generally are not contraindicated when tics are present.

Atomoxetine (Strattera), a selective norepinephrine reuptake inhibitor indicated for the treatment of ADHD, is a promising option for children with ADHD and tic disorders. It has not been found to induce or exacerbate tics in general studies designed to evaluate its

**Table 4** *Medications Used to Treat Tics*

| Medication Type | Dose Range (mg/day) | Potential Side Effects |
|---|---|---|
| Antihypertensives | | |
| Clonidine (Catapres) | 0.05–0.50 | sedation, sleep disturbance, hypotension, depression |
| Guanfacine (Tenex) | 0.50–5.0 | sedation, sleep disturbance, anxiety, blurred vision |
| Neuroleptics | | |
| Fluphenazine (Prolixin) | 0.50–20.0 | sedation, irritability, akathisia, dysphoria, dystonia |
| Haloperidol (Haldol) | 0.25–6.0 | same as others in class, weight gain, anxiety, galactorhea |
| Pimozide (Orap) | 1.0–8.0 | same as others in class, EKG changes |
| Newer (atypical) neuroleptics | | |
| Olanzapine (Zyprexa) | 2.5–20.0 | weight gain, sedation, lipid and glucose abnormalities |
| Quetiapine (Seroquel) | 12.5–600.0 | sedation, weight loss or gain, dizziness, dysphoria |
| Risperidone (Risperdal) | 0.25–6.0 | same as others in class, primarily weight gain plus obsessive–compulsive symptoms |
| Ziprasidone (Geodon) | 5.0–40.0 | sedation, EKG changes |
| Aripiperazole (Abilify) | 1.25–15.0 | nausea, sedation, anxiety, insomnia, orthostatic hypotension |
| Benzodiazepines | | |
| Clonazepam (Klonopin) | 0.25–6.0 | sedation |

effectiveness in ADHD. Some physicians currently consider this a first-line treatment for children with both ADHD and tics; however, additional studies in children with tic disorders will be informative. Modafinil (Provigil) is a medication currently indicated for narcolepsy that works differently from either stimulants or atomoxetine. It has shown promising preliminary results for ADHD symptoms in both children and adults and does not appear to exacerbate tics. Modafinil is currently undergoing the additional studies necessary to receive FDA approval for its use in the treatment of ADHD. Thus, although the number of options available for treating ADHD in children with tic disorders is increasing, it may take trials of several medications and doses to find the best option for an individual child.

The serotonin reuptake inhibitors (SSRIs) generally are safe and effective medications for anxiety and OCD. Some individuals with tics will show greater improvement in anxiety and OCD with the addition of a neurolpetic to the SSRI antianxiety regimen (Miguel, Shavitt, Ferrao, Brotto, & Diniz, 2003). Additional treatment of depression or bipolar disorder is sometimes required using other antidepressants or mood stabilizers. At this time, no evidence suggests that medications in these other categories are particularly effective or problematic in individuals with tics, with the exception of the antidepressant bupropion. Bupropion has been found to be well tolerated in individuals with bipolar disorder and appears to have a lower incidence of inducing mania (Frances, Kahn, Carpenter, Docherty, & Donovan, 1998). It can also be somewhat effective for ADHD symptoms because of its dopaminergic (stimulant-like) effects. However, like stimulants, it may lead to an exacerbation of tics.

Recently, concerns have been raised about a potential increased risk of suicide in depressed children and adults who are prescribed antidepressants (also see chapter 15, "Depressive Disorders"). It is not clear whether this risk extends to children who are being treated with these medications for something other than or in addition to major depression. Antidepressants have long been known to increase disinhibition. Children with hyperactivity may become more active, impulsive, or agitated on them, and those with unstable moods may become manic or hypomanic. It is reasonable to consider the possibility that the increased suicidal ideation reported is an expression of disinhibition in depressed individuals. Some physicians have responded to the recent warnings by

**Table 5** *Medications Used to Treat Associated Disorders*

| Medication Type | Dose Range (mg/day) | Potential Side Effects |
|---|---|---|
| | Medications for ADHD | |
| *Stimulants* | | |
| Methylphenidate (Ritalin, Methylin, Metadate, Concerta) | 5–72 | appetite loss, insomnia, headache, stomachache, irritability, rebound, increased tics |
| Methylphenidate (Focalin) | 2.5–20 | same as others in class |
| Amphetamine (Adderall, Dexedrine, Dextrostat) | 2.5–60 | same as others in class |
| *Nonstimulant* | | |
| Atomoxetine (Strattera) | 10–100 | sedation, stomachache, appetite loss, irritability, constipation, rapid pulse, sexual dysfunction |
| *Tricyclic antidepressants* | | |
| Imipramine (Tofranil) | 10–300 | dry mouth, blurred vision, constipation, fatigue, appetite suppression, sleep changes, EKG changes |
| Nortriptyline (Pamelor) | 10–150 | same as others in class |
| Clomipramine (Anafranil) | 12.5–200 | same others in class |
| Desipramine (Norpramin) | 10–300 | same as others in class, arythmia |
| | Medications for OCD/Anxiety | |
| *Selective serotonin reuptake inhibitors (SSRIs)* | | |
| Fluoxetine (Prozac) | 10–80 | insomnia, nausea, diarrhea, headaches, agitation, mania |
| Sertraline (Zoloft) | 25–200 | same as others in class |
| Paroxetine (Paxil) | 10–60 | same as others in class |
| Fluvoxamine (Luvox) | 25–200 | same as others in class |
| Citalopram (Celexa/Lexapro) | 10–40 | same as others in class |
| *Other antidepressants* | | |
| Bupropion (Wellbutrin) | 75–300 | agtation, dry mouth, nausea, headache, insomnia, tremor, constipation, tics |
| Venlafaxine (Effexor) | 12.5–150 | insomnia, nervousness, nausea, sedation, dizziness |

discontinuing the use of these medications, whereas others have continued their use with increased monitoring for cases in which they have been helpful. It is important in such cases for school personnel to work with families and physicians to identify signs, not only of suicidal ideation, but also of its potential precursor, disinhibition, in students taking these medications. In children, this may take the form of increased impulsivity or agitation; cursing, talking back, other inappropriate verbalizations; mood swings; or physical risk taking that was not previously characteristic for the child.

Most medications are added one at a time and increased or decreased gradually. Some require monitoring of blood tests and EKGs. Feedback from teachers about effects and side effects when medication is added or eliminated or the dose is changed is critical to effective intervention. Standardized ratings of effects and side effects may be used. The occurrence of effects and side effects will depend on the half-life and other properties of the medication; thus, the timing of feedback is also important. Ideally, physicians and families will provide information to school professionals about the medications being used to treat children, which will help teachers monitor effects and side effects. Also, such information is typically available to the public through the customer service department and website of the pharmaceutical company that produces the brand-name product of a particular medication.

## Behavioral Intervention

Conducting a functional behavioral assessment (FBA) is a useful starting point for planning interventions for children with tics who require treatment. FBA may be helpful in identifying the conditions under which children have the most difficulty and in identifying certain factors that may exacerbate the severity of tics, such as avoidance of tasks or of teachers' or peers' attention. However, clinicians must keep in mind that tics are primarily a response to internal stimuli and are difficult for children to control.

Several behavioral interventions have been developed to reduce the frequency and severity of tics. The two most successful behavioral intervention strategies are habit reversal and massed negative practice. Habit reversal typically involves multiple components, including (a) awareness training that allows children to recognize antecedents and the occurrence of tics, (b) relaxation training to reduce the stress that may contribute to tics, (c) competing response training, whereby children are taught to perform a behavior that is incompatible with tics when there is an urge to emit these behaviors, and (d) positive reinforcement provided by adults when the child adheres to the intervention procedures (Azrin & Peterson, 1990; also see chapter 80, "Habits"). Massed negative practice entails having the child exert as much effort as possible to perform tic behaviors in rapid succession. Intervals of exertion are interspersed with periods of rest.

Habit reversal and massed negative practice are beneficial in that they reduce the frequency and severity of tics (Azrin & Peterson, 1990; Peterson & Azrin, 1993). However, the treatments may require up to 20 intervention sessions, and adults typically must be trained to prompt and reinforce the child's practice in naturalistic settings. As a result, these interventions may be challenging to implement and sustain over time.

Because a high percentage of children with tic disorders have ADHD, behavioral and pharmacological interventions for ADHD are often needed to enable children and families to successfully cope with this disorder (see DuPaul & Stoner, 2003, for a description of evidence-based interventions for treating ADHD in school settings). Behavioral interventions have also been highly successful in treating the obsessive–compulsive behaviors often associated with tic disorders. The most successful intervention for those behaviors is response prevention, which may involve the following components: (a) gradually exposing the child to the situations that provoke obsessive–compulsive behavior, (b) blocking the child from performing the compulsion associated with an obsession, (c) teaching relaxation techniques to reduce the distress induced when the child cannot perform compulsive acts, and (d) using positive reinforcement for adherence with intervention procedures (March, 1995). This procedure has been demonstrated to be a well-established intervention for OCD (Piacentini, 1999). The success of this intervention typically requires training and monitoring of adults at home and school to assist the child in blocking the compulsive behaviors related to obsessive thinking.

## Selection of the Most Appropriate Course of Intervention

Selecting an appropriate course of intervention for a child with tic disorders entails a consideration of several factors, including the following:

- The disorders or problems that account for the greatest impairment.
- The range of evidence-based behavioral and pharmacological interventions available to treat the primary intervention targets.
- The effects of prior attempts to treat the child's problems.
- The acceptability of potential treatment options available to the parents and child.

For most children with tic disorders, the tics themselves are not the most impairing conditions exhibited by the child. If the child has ADHD or OCD, difficulties related to those disorders are often the primary targets of intervention. If tics are contributing to a significant level of impairment and require treatment, behavioral and pharmacological options are available. The choice of a behavioral or pharmacological approach to treatment requires that clinicians consider potential beneficial and adverse effects of each type of treatment. Also, families vary markedly with regard to their preference for pharmacological rather than behavioral approaches. Medication may be helpful, although the approaches that are most beneficial often are associated with a risk of side effects, including exacerbating other existing problems. Behavioral interventions also can be beneficial, but the amount of effort required to initiate and maintain those approaches may be prohibitive for some families.

Ultimately, the best course of action is the approach that makes the most sense to families after they have consulted with health and mental health professionals and weighed the benefits and costs. Careful monitoring of intervention effects is then required to determine if the approach is helping or whether a change in the intervention plan is needed.

### Evaluation of Intervention Outcomes

The school psychologist is in an excellent position to assist with the monitoring of intervention outcomes for children with tic disorders and other mental health conditions. When evaluating outcomes, the following practices are recommended:

- Collaborate with members of the intervention team, including the child's physician, parents, and teachers, to identify the intended outcomes of intervention.
- Select measures, preferably multimethod measures (e.g., observations and rating scales), to assess change related to each intended outcome.
- Monitor potential adverse side effects.
- Monitor progress in areas of academic instruction.
- Employ single case designs, when feasible, to control for threats to internal validity.
- Assess intervention acceptability from the point of view of parents, teachers, and the child on an ongoing basis.
- Plan for periodic review with the intervention team.

## SUMMARY

Tic disorders are common in children and adolescents and represent a wide spectrum of problems. These disorders vary greatly in severity, from transient tic disorders, the most common and least severe type, to Tourette's syndrome, the least common and most severe form. The etiology of tic disorders is primarily genetic, although environmental factors can contribute to the manifestation of symptoms. More severe variants of these disorders, particularly TS, often occur in combination with ADHD and OCD. The assessment of tic disorders requires interdisciplinary team collaboration involving a medical professional, school professionals, and the child's parents. Multiple methods of assessment, including direct observations, ratings scales, and interviews of parents and teachers, are useful in assessing tic disorders and comorbid conditions. Because children with tic disorders are at risk for impairment academically and socially, it is important to monitor their functioning and to actively promote academic and social competence by building strong family–school partnerships, fostering caring teacher–child attachments, providing effective classroom instruction, and promoting cooperative peer relationships. Tic disorders usually are associated with minimal functional impairment, and therefore most children with these conditions do not require intervention. However, children who have more severe forms of the disorder, particularly those with TS who have comorbid conditions, typically require intervention. Pharmacological interventions are available for tic disorders, although the most effective treatments may result in side effects for some children. Behavioral treatments have also been developed and validated, although applying those approaches may be time consuming and labor intensive.

Determining the best course of treatment for children with tic disorders requires close collaboration between the child's physician, parents, and teachers. Also, monitoring intervention effects using multiple methods is important for determining if interventions are working and whether modifications in the treatment plan are needed.

## RECOMMENDED RESOURCES

### Books and Other Printed Material

Leckman, J. F. (2002). Tourette's syndrome. *Lancet, 360,* 1577–1586.

This article provides a brief overview of Tourette's syndrome. The article has a particular focus on the developmental trajectory, epidemiology, genetics, and neurobiology of this disorder. Also, it provides a brief discussion of issues related to assessment and pharmacological treatment.

Sandor, P. (2003). Pharmacological management of tics in patients with Tourette's syndrome. *Journal of Psychosomatic Research, 55,* 41–48.

This article discusses a range of pharmacological options for the treatment of Tourette's syndrome. In addition to presenting a broad spectrum of options, it provides a sensible sequence of steps in the pharmacological care of children with this disorder.

Sukhodolsky, D. G., Scahill, L., Zhang, H., Peterson, B. S., King, R. A., Lombroso, P. J., Katsovich, L., Findley, D., & Leckman, J. F. (2003). Disruptive behavior in children with Tourette's syndrome: Association with ADHD comorbidity, tic severity, and functional impairment. *Journal of the American Academy of Child and Adolescent Psychiatry, 42,* 98–105.

This article presents the results of a study comparing children with Tourette's syndrome (TS) with and without comorbid Attention Deficit Hyperactivity Disorder (ADHD). The findings indicated that children with comorbid TS and ADHD were more likely to demonstrate aggression and functional impairments than those with TS without ADHD.

## Websites

*http://www.tsa-usa.org*

This is the web address for the Tourette Syndrome Association. TSA develops and disseminates educational materials, including books, videos, and brochures, that are useful for families, adults, and educational and health professionals. The TSA funds and disseminates findings of innovative research into the genetics and neurophysiology of tic disorders, as well as the diagnosis and treatment of these conditions. Also, TSA has assembled a professional membership directory that is highly useful in identifying health and mental health providers in the local community. The association publishes a quarterly newsletter describing advances in research and clinical practice, as well as a newsletter written by children with Tourette's syndrome for children with Tourette's syndrome. TSA may also be contacted at 42-40 Bell Blvd., Bayside, New York 11361, (718) 224-2999.

## REFERENCES

American Psychiatric Association. (2000). *Diagnostic and statistical manual of mental disorders* (4th ed., text rev.). Washington, DC: Author.

Azrin, N. H., & Peterson, A. L. (1990). Treatment of Tourette syndrome by habit reversal: A waiting-list control group comparison. *Behavior Therapy, 21,* 305–318.

Bruun, R. D., & Budman, C. L. (1993). The natural history of Gilles de la Tourette syndrome. In R. Kurlan (Ed.), *Handbook of Tourette's syndrome and related tic and behavior disorders* (pp. 27–42). New York: Marcel Dekker.

Christenson, S. L., & Sheridan, S. M. (2001). *Schools and families: Creating essential connections for learning.* New York: Guilford Press.

Comings, D. E. (1990). *Tourette syndrome and human behavior.* Duarte, CA: Hope Press.

DiPerna, J. C., & Elliott, S. N. (2000). *Academic Competence Evaluation Scales.* San Antonio, TX: Psychological Corporation.

DuPaul, G. J., & Stoner, G. (2003). *ADHD in the schools: Assessment and intervention strategies.* New York: Guilford Press.

Frances, A. J., Kahn, D. A., Carpenter, D., Docherty, J. P., & Donovan, S. L. (1998). The expert consensus guidelines for treating depression in bipolar disorder. *Journal of Clinical Psychiatry, 59*(Suppl.), 73–79.

Gadow, K. D., Nolan, E. E., & Sverd, J. (1992). Methylphenidate in hyperactive boys with comorbid tic disorder: II. Short-term behavioral effects in school settings. *Journal of the American Academy of Child and Adolescent Psychiatry, 31,* 462–471.

Gerard, E., & Peterson, B. S. (2003). Developmental processes and brain imaging studies in Tourette syndrome. *Journal of Psychosomatic Research, 55,* 13–22.

Gresham, F. M., & Elliott, S. N. (1990). *Social Skills Rating System.* Circle Pines, MN: American Guidance Service.

Hoekstra, P. J., Anderson, G. M., Limburg, P. C., Korf, J., Kallenberg, C. G. M., & Minderaa, R. B. (2004). Neurobiology and neuroimmunology of Tourette's syndrome: An update. *CMLS, Cellular and Molecular Life Sciences, 61,* 886–898.

Janicke, D. M., & Finney, J. W. (2001). Children's primary health care services: A social cognitive model of sustained high use. *Clinical Psychology: Science and Practice, 8,* 228–241.

Kazdin, A. E., Holland, L., & Crowley, M. (1997). Family experience of barriers to treatment and premature termination from child therapy. *Journal of Consulting and Clinical Psychology, 65,* 453–463.

King, R. A., & Scahill, L. (2001). Emotional and behavioral difficulties associated with Tourette syndrome. In D. J. Cohen, C. G. Goetz, & J. Jankovic (Eds.), *Tourette syndrome* (pp. 79–88). Philadelphia: Lippincott, Williams, & Wilkins.

Kurlan, R. (1994). Hypothesis II: Tourette's syndrome is part of a clinical spectrum that includes normal brain development. *Archives of Neurology, 51,* 1145–1150.

Lang, A. E. (1993). The premonitory ("sensory") experiences. In R. Kurlan (Ed.), *Handbook of Tourette's syndrome and related tic and behavioral disorders* (pp. 17–26). New York: Marcel Dekker.

Leckman, J. F. (2002). Tourette's syndrome. *Lancet, 360,* 1577–1586.

Leckman, J. F. (2003). Phenomenology of tics and natural history of tic disorders. *Brain and Development, 25*(Suppl. 1), S24–S28.

Leckman, J. F., Riddle, M. A., Hardin, M. T., Ort, S. I., Swartz, K. L., Stevenson, J., & Cohen, D. J. (1989). The Yale Global Tic Severity Scale: Initial testing of a clinician-rated scale of tic severity. *Journal of the American Academy of Child and Adolescent Psychiatry, 28,* 566–573.

March, J. S. (1995). Cognitive-behavioral psychotherapy for children and adolescents with OCD: A review and recommendations for treatment. *Journal of the American Academy of Child and Adolescent Psychiatry, 34,* 7–18.

Miguel, E. C., Shavitt, R. G., Ferrao, Y. A., Brotto, S. A., & Diniz, J. B. (2003). How to treat OCD in patients with Tourette syndrome. *Journal of Psychosomatic Research, 55,* 49–57.

Pauls, D. L. (2003). An update on the genetics of Gilles de la Tourette syndrome. *Journal of Psychosomatic Research, 55,* 7–12.

Pellegrini, A. D., & Smith, P. K. (1993). School recess: Implications for education and development. *Review of Educational Research, 63,* 51–67.

Peterson, A. L., & Azrin, N. H. (1993). Behavioral and pharmacological treatments for Tourette syndrome: A review. *Applied and Preventive Psychology, 2,* 231–242.

Peterson, B. S., & Cohen, D. J. (1998). The treatment of Tourette's syndrome: Multimodal, developmental intervention. *Journal of Clinical Psychiatry, 59*(Suppl. 1), 62–72.

Piacentini, J. (1999). Cognitive behavioral therapy of childhood OCD. *Child and Adolescent Psychiatric Clinics of North America, 8,* 599–616.

Pianta, R. C. (1999). *Enhancing relationships between children and teachers.* Washington, DC: American Psychological Association.

Power, T. J., DuPaul, G. J., Shapiro, E. S., & Kazak, A. E. (2003). *Promoting children's health: Integrating school, family, and health.* New York: Guilford Press.

Robertson, M. (2003). Diagnosing Tourette syndrome: Is it a common disorder? *Journal of Psychosomatic Research, 55,* 3–6.

Sandor, P. (2003). Pharmacological management of tics in patients with Tourette's syndrome. *Journal of Psychosomatic Research, 55,* 41–48.

Singer, H. S., & Loiselle, C. (2003). PANDAS: A commentary. *Journal of Psychosomatic Research, 55,* 31–39.

Singer, H. S., & Minzer, K. (2003). Neurobiology of Tourette's syndrome: Concepts of neuroanatomic localization and neurochemical abnormalities. *Brain and Development, 25* (Suppl.), S70–S84.

Singer, H. S., & Walkup, J. T. (1991). Tourette syndrome and other tic disorders: Diagnosis, pathophysiology, and treatment. *Medicine, 70,* 15–32.

Spencer, T., Biederman, J., Harding, M., O'Donnell, D., Wilens, T., Faraone, S., et al. (1998). Disentangling the overlap between Tourette's disorder and ADHD. *Journal of Child Psychology and Psychiatry, 39,* 1037–1044.

Sukhodolsky, D. G., Scahill, L., Zhang, H., Peterson, B. S., King, R. A., Lombroso, P. J., et al. (2003). Disruptive behavior in children with Tourette's syndrome: Association with ADHD comorbidity, tic severity, and functional impairment. *Journal of the American Academy of Child and Adolescent Psychiatry, 42,* 98–105.

Tourette Syndrome Classification Study Group. (1993). Definitions and classifications of tic disorders. *Archives of Neurology, 50,* 1013–1016.

Tourette Syndrome Study Group. (2002). Treatment of ADHD in children with tics: A randomized, controlled trial. *Neurology, 58,* 527–536.

Walkup, J. T., Rosenberg, L. A., Brown, J., & Singer, H. S. (1992). The validity of instruments for measuring tic severity in Tourette's syndrome. *Journal of the American Academy of Child and Adolescent Psychiatry, 30,* 472–477.

# 80

# Habits

**T. Steuart Watson**

*Miami University*

## BACKGROUND AND DEVELOPMENT

Broadly defined, habits are repetitive patterns of behavior that appear to be independent of social contingencies. That is, most habits *appear* as though they are not related to any readily observable consequence. Some habits are relatively harmless to the individual performing the habit (e.g., hair twirling), but others may be more severe and can result in negative consequences for the individual (e.g., loss of gum tissue from teeth grinding or clenching, or teasing from peers about thumb sucking).

Repetitive patterns of behavior may appear very early in life. For instance, children in utero have often been observed sucking their thumbs. Habitual behaviors may also persist in some form throughout an individual's life. Some habits occur across many settings and situations, whereas others are fairly circumscribed and occur only under one or two conditions. Although habits are generally considered to be under the person's control, the person may be unaware that she or he is engaging in the habit. In addition, as children grow older, they may become more covert in their habit as they become more sensitive to the reactions of others (e.g., a teenager who still sucks her thumb but only does so in the privacy of her bedroom and not at school or around her parents).

### Key Concepts and Common Habits

A habit is a repetitive behavior that is considered to be voluntary because it is not caused by an underlying disease or biological process. A habit is differentiated from a tic, another type of repetitive behavior, in that tics are generally not considered to be under the control of the individual and they probably have a neurobiological component whereas habits do not (American Psychological Association [APA], 2000; see chapter 79, "Tic Disorders"). Habits, like tics, may involve motor behavior (e.g., arm waving), vocal behavior (e.g., coughing, throat clearing), or both. It is sometimes difficult to distinguish between complex tics or tics associated with Tourette's syndrome and habits that involve multiple behaviors. In addition, habits may be rather transient; they seemingly appear out of nowhere and then vanish quickly. Other habits may be more permanent and persist for long periods. Habits that do not spontaneously remit often change in appearance over time and may give rise to other habits. That is, children with one long-standing habit may be more likely to evidence additional habits (Woods & Miltenberger, 2001).

Common habits exhibited by children include trichotillomania (hair pulling), bruxism (teeth grinding or clenching), nail biting, thumb sucking, and a host of other associated behaviors (e.g., skin picking, lip biting). A diagnosis of trichotillomania requires a history of hair pulling with noticeable hair loss (alopecia), reported urges to pull hair, and a sense of relief once hair has been pulled. These last two criteria may be difficult to assess in older children with developmental disabilities or in younger children who are unaware of their urge to pull and lack the verbal skills to express a sense of relief. Bruxism, which can involve jaw clenching or teeth grinding, may result in irregular and premature wear on teeth, malocclusion, loss of gingival tissue, and damage to the temporomandibular joint. In addition, individuals who engage in either nocturnal or diurnal bruxism may experience muscle tenderness in the face and neck. Nail biting can result in cosmetic unattractiveness, scarring and infection of the nail bed or cuticles, and dental problems such as gingival damage and shortening of tooth roots as a result of excessive pressure. Thumb sucking in children is generally not considered socially or physically problematic until after the age of 6, when children begin to encounter negative social consequences such as teasing and physical consequences such as overbites, malocclusions, and narrowing of the dental arches, as well as deformities of the thumb or other fingers (Peterson, Campose, & Azrin, 1994).

## Prevalence of Habits

Prevalence data for more serious habits were presented by Peterson et al. (1994). Bruxism was estimated to occur in 7% to 88% of the population; rates varied because researchers used different definitions. The highest rates of bruxism were reported for 7- to 15-year-olds with mixed dentition (e.g., overbite, uneven bite, or underbite).

Estimates for the prevalence of trichotillomania are difficult to obtain because of the frequent denial of the disorder and the reluctance of many individuals to obtain treatment. Epidemiologic studies in the United States estimate that approximately 8 million people have trichotillomania, and more children than adults exhibit the disorder. Among children, equal numbers of males and females exhibit the disorder. Although the average age of onset of trichotillomania is 13, the peak period for childhood onset is between the ages of 5 and 8. Adults who still pull their hair report that they began pulling as children.

Nail biting occurs more commonly in females and peaks from preschool age to adolescence with rates as high as 45%, which then gradually spontaneously remit to about 4.5%. Thumb sucking occurs in about 30% to 40% of preschoolers with only 10% to 20% of children older than age 6 still sucking their thumbs or fingers. No data are available on rates of occurrence of habits among various racial or ethnic groups.

## Etiology

The precise etiology of a particular habit, and habits in general, is very difficult to ascertain. Although a number of possible explanations exist, six empirically based explanations apply to the occurrence of habits: arousal reduction, arousal induction, delay reduction, conditioned reinforcement, modeling, and direct reinforcement effects. Support for the arousal reduction hypothesis (i.e., automatic negative reinforcement) is seen in adults with habits, who often report the presence of an unpleasant sensation or urge just before engaging in the habit and say that performing the habit reduces or eliminates the unpleasant sensation or urge. Along the same lines, Azrin and Peterson (1990), two prominent habit researchers, suggested that habits may be behavioral reactions that reduce stress. There is promise in that premise, as Glaros and Melamed (1992) found that anticipated stress was a better predictor of bruxism than the actual amount of stress subjectively reported by the individual. In additional anecdotal support for the arousal reduction hypothesis, parents sometimes report that their child is more likely to exhibit a habit during a stressful situation, such as when being reprimanded, or in emotional situations.

In some instances, habits occur because they provide pleasant tactile or kinesthetic stimulation to the person performing the habit (arousal induction). For example, some children suck their thumbs across a variety of settings and situations because the thumb sucking provides tactile stimulation to both the soft palate of the mouth and the thumb (Watson & Allen, 1993). The performance of some habits is consistent with Fantino's (1969) delay reduction hypothesis, which states that behaviors that result in less delay to the onset of reinforcement acquire conditioned reinforcing properties. For instance, a child who sucks her thumb while going to sleep does so because thumb sucking results in her falling asleep faster than if she did not suck her thumb.

Another possible etiology of habits is that they become associated with other reinforcing activities and, over time, become conditioned reinforcers. For instance, children who engage in a repetitive activity (e.g., skin picking) while watching TV (a reinforcer) may associate the repetitive behavior with watching TV. Thus, the skin picking increases over time and may generalize to occur during other reinforcing activities (e.g., listening to music, eating, talking on the phone). Watson, Meeks, Dufrene, and Lindsay (2002) demonstrated a modeling effect for two siblings who both sucked their thumbs. When the older sibling stopped sucking, the younger sibling stopped as well. When the older sibling was prompted to suck his thumb with the reintroduction of a transitional object, the younger sibling began thumb sucking again. Still other children may engage in habits because they receive social attention for doing so. Consider the case of a child who normally receives little social attention from his parents. When he engages in skin picking, his parents reprimand him, which inadvertently reinforces the behavior with social attention (e.g., Watson & Sterling, 1998a).

In all likelihood, a combination of the above factors accounts for the emergence of habits. Consider the example of an 8-year-old male with trichotillomania (chronic hair pulling) who has likely been pulling for several years. The habit may have begun with hair twirling (because of arousal induction) that gradually progressed to hair pulling. During the transition from twirling to pulling, he may have learned that pulling resulted in both a pleasant sensation (arousal induction) or, during stressful events, a reduction in physiological arousal (arousal reduction). As the behavior increases in frequency, it may become associated with other reinforcing activities (such as watching TV) and may even be directly reinforced by negative social attention from parents or siblings.

It is generally acknowledged and empirically supported that habits in young children occur independently of more serious psychopathology. Although habits had been postulated to be reflections or behavioral manifestations of psychopathology (Freud, 1965; Shapiro & Shannon, 1966), current research has not found a link between habits and underlying psychopathology. Furthermore, when assessed on measures such as the Child Behavior Checklist or Eyberg Child Behavior Inventory, children with habits do not significantly differ from children who do not have habits (Friman, Larzelere, & Finney, 1994). Perhaps because habits are sometimes assumed to arise from anxiety or tension (Hadley, 1984), laypeople often refer to them as nervous habits. Thus, individuals with habits are seen as nervous, and the anxiety or tension that they feel causes them to exhibit these nervous habits. However, support has been mixed on the hypothesis that individuals who exhibit habits experience significantly more anxiety and tension than others (Glaros & Melamed, 1992; Woods & Miltenberger, 1996).

Although some researchers consider both habits and tics to be part of the obsessive–compulsive disorder (OCD) spectrum (Hollander, 1993), children with habits do not have high rates of comorbidity with other disorders such as OCD and Attention Deficit Hyperactivity Disorder, as is the case for children with Tourette's syndrome. In addition, individuals with developmental disorders and certain neurological conditions are more likely to engage in repetitive behaviors than their typically developing peers, but these behaviors are more commonly characterized as self-injurious (e.g., head banging) or stereotypic (e.g., body rocking) than as habits.

# PROBLEMS AND IMPLICATIONS

## Determining Which Habits Should Be Treated

Almost all people over the course of their lives engage in behaviors that may be called habits, such as foot tapping, jaw clenching, or hair twirling. Children at various ages and stages of development exhibit habits that are considered normal and do not warrant any type of intervention. For instance, thumb or finger sucking by young children below the age of 6 is considered normal. Because many habit behaviors exhibited by children (e.g., finger tapping, hair twirling, leg shaking) do not pose any potential negative physical or psychological consequences and are frequently transient, they do not require treatment. Some habits, like trichotillomania, bruxism, nail biting, thumb sucking (among older children), and their variants are considered more serious and may result in significant physical, social, academic, and psychological consequences for the individual and should be, at the very least, carefully observed and monitored, if not immediately treated.

One example of the potentially negative social implications of a common habit is the school-age child who sucks her thumb at school. Previous research has shown that school-age children who suck their thumbs may be teased by peers (Friman, McPherson, Warzak, & Evans, 1993) and reprimanded by teachers. In addition to the social implications, the child may also incur physical damage (e.g., malocclusions, an infected nail or skin). At home, parents may also be frustrated by the child's seeming unwillingness to give up the habit, which results in their scolding, punishing, and shaming the child in the hopes of eliminating the habit. Some habits, such as skin picking, are not only unsightly but can interfere with social opportunities because peers may not want to associate with the child with the habit (Woods, Friman, & Teng, 2001). When a habit results in substantial problems for the child (i.e., poses a health risk, interferes with academic performance, interferes with peer interactions, results in negative psychological consequences, or interferes with normal parent–child relations), the habit should be treated.

## Assessing and Monitoring Habits

The most efficient and effective protocol for identifying, assessing, and treating habits employs a multiple-method, multiple-informant approach (Haynes, 1998). This protocol includes interviews, direct observation, and measures of permanent products (e.g., length of nails, hair pulled out), when possible. For older children and adolescents, self-monitoring may also be used to measure habits.

***Interviews.*** Interviews should be conducted with parents, teachers, and the child to obtain a thorough history across several domains, including developmental, medical, social, and academic information—developmental, to help distinguish between a habit and stereotypic or self-injurious behavior; medical, to help distinguish between a tic and a habit; social, to help determine the effect on peer relationships and possibly any precipitating social stress or anxiety that may be related; and academic, to help determine if the habit is having a deleterious impact on academic performance. After gathering information, interviewers should direct questions specifically toward the habit behavior, in particular, when the behavior was first noticed, what the behavior looks like (by having the child or parent describe or demonstrate the behavior), and previous successful or unsuccessful treatment attempts. Other important factors include when the behavior is most frequently exhibited, events that precede the behavior (both physiological and environmental), and events that typically follow the behavior (e.g., social attention, removal of unpleasant physiological stimulation). This information can then be used to develop hypotheses about situations that seem to trigger the habit and the variables that may be maintaining the habit.

***Direct observation.*** Direct observation, which should follow the interviews, is especially useful for verifying information gathered during the interviews, obtaining additional information related to the habit, and detecting other factors in the environment that may be important. Ideally, direct observations occur across a number of occasions and settings and at times and places the habit is likely, or not likely, to occur. At the very least, frequency and duration data should be recorded to provide a baseline regarding the habit. Johnston and Pennypacker (1993) give a detailed discussion of various recording methods.

In addition to baseline data gathered by observation, the antecedents and consequences of the habit are especially useful for developing and verifying hypotheses regarding the potential environmental variables that are functionally related to the habit. Watson and Steege (2003) presented a number of reproducible forms that will assist in collecting antecedent and consequent data.

***Permanent products.*** Because some habits are difficult to detect and because some children do not engage in the habit in public, direct observation of a habit may not be possible. For instance, if the child pulls hair only when alone, direct observational data cannot be collected. In other situations, the awareness of being observed may result in reactivity, which may artificially suppress the habit during the observational period. In such circumstances, collecting permanent product data (if available) may be helpful. Permanent products refer to relatively enduring remnants of a behavior. In the case of trichotillomania, it may be possible to measure bald areas on the scalp or hair left on the pillow. In the case of nail biting, the length of the nails on each hand can be measured. Permanent product measures are especially valuable because they can be used to verify behaviors reported by parents, teachers, or the student. In addition, such measures may provide a baseline from which to evaluate treatment success.

***Self-monitoring.*** Self-monitoring is similar to direct observation, but the individual with the habit monitors and records his or her behavior as it occurs. With children, the most effective means for using self-monitoring involves several steps. The first step is to teach the child to become aware of the habit. The second step is to use a simple recording device, such as a golf-stroke counter or a note card that does not interfere with daily activities and is not conspicuous. The third step, for children who have little to no motivation to change their behavior, is to add a reinforcement component for accurately monitoring and recording behavior. An added benefit of self-monitoring is that reactivity to the self-monitoring actions and awareness may reduce the habit (Carr & Rapp, 2001).

## ALTERNATIVE ACTIONS FOR PREVENTION AND INTERVENTION

### Prevention Alternatives

No empirically documented strategies for preventing the emergence of habits, that is, primary prevention, are available. However, one might consider a general approach that includes both universal and indicated prevention strategies. Universal prevention strategies are those that strengthen the child's behavioral repertoire such that, at least theoretically, habits may be less likely to emerge. Examples of universal strategies may include those that promote social competence and positive peer interactions, improve academic competence, and teach positive discipline techniques to parents. Other examples might include strategies for children who seem to exhibit greater anxiety in certain situations or respond negatively to stressful situations. In such cases, the focus might be on teaching appropriate anxiety-reduction or coping skills that children could rely on to reduce anxiety and stress so they would not have to use a repetitive behavior (see chapter 21, "Performance and Test Anxiety"). Indicated prevention strategies are intended for children with habit disorders who are demonstrating potential risk for impairment in one or more domains of functioning (e.g., social or academic). Examples of these strategies might include academic skill building and social skill development.

## Treatment Alternatives

The most effective treatments for habits fall into one of two general categories: habit reversal and function-based treatments. Although pharmacological treatments are available, they are more commonly used for OCD and tics and are not considered to be the first choice when treating habits. The most common pharmacological agents used in the treatment of repetitive behaviors include fluoxetine (Prozac), fluvoxamine (Luvox), clomipramine (Anafranil), olanzapine (Zyprexa), and catapres (Clonidine). Scant data are available regarding the effectiveness of these drugs for treating habits that are not related to OCD or some type of tic disorder.

## Habit Reversal

Habit reversal is the most effective treatment procedure for habits. The original habit reversal procedure was developed by Azrin and Nunn (1973) and contained 13 steps. Follow-up research indicated that three of the original 13 components are sufficient for effective treatment: awareness training, competing response training, and social support (e.g., Rapp, Miltenberger, Galensky, Roberts, & Ellingson, 1999). This three-step approach has been labeled *simplified habit reversal* (SHR). The SHR protocol is implemented in a minimum three-session format, during which the individual is trained in each of the components. Woods and Miltenberger (2001) present a complete review of the SHR protocol. A synopsis of the session-by-session protocol and the components involved follows.

During the first session, the clinician conducts a functional assessment interview to operationally define the habit and identify, as much as possible, the covert antecedents and consequences (i.e., sensations) that are related to the habit. The clinician also should assess any comorbid problems and identify the social support person who will assist the child with later components. Homework is assigned that typically involves collecting baseline data on the habit or collecting a permanent product.

During session two, the data are reviewed and the child is taught to become aware of the habit by describing and demonstrating it. Awareness training may also involve the child watching the clinician demonstrate the habit or watching himself in a mirror as he slowly performs the motor movements of the habit. Competing response training, which follows awareness training, involves having the child select a competing response. Typically, the behavior chosen as the competing response is physically incompatible with the target response (e.g., hands in lap for trichotillomania, mouth slightly open for those who clench their jaws). The clinician then demonstrates the competing response, and the child practices it. The following are primary objectives in selecting a competing response: (a) It should be physically incompatible with the habit, (b) it should be a response that can be performed across settings without drawing undue attention to the child, (c) it should not interfere with the child's activity or performance in other areas, such as writing in school, and (d) it should be easily cued by adults in the environment who are providing support to the child. The child is instructed to engage in the competing response for 1 minute each time the habit occurs.

The third component of SHR is social support training. The purpose of social support training is to provide the child with a person who will help implement and monitor the procedures. The primary jobs of the social support person are to prompt the child to engage in the competing response and to reinforce successful exhibition of the competing response and decreases in the habit. In session three, and subsequent sessions if necessary, data are continuously reviewed to evaluate the effectiveness of treatment. In some instances, different competing responses need to be selected or the social support person needs to be encouraged to be more diligent in cueing the competing response and reinforcing the target responses. Studies have consistently shown that habit reversal, including simplified habit reversal, is the most effective treatment for a wide spectrum of habit behaviors (Woods & Miltenberger, 2001). Recent studies have also indicated the long-term maintenance of reductions in habits using habit reversal (Romaniuk, Miltenberger, & Deaver, 2003) and the effectiveness of habit reversal over a placebo (Twohig, Woods, Marcks, & Teng, 2003). In most cases, habits treated with SHR are either completely eliminated with several weeks to a couple of months of treatment, or SHR reduces the habits to levels that either are no longer dangerous to the individual or no longer interfere with some aspect of the individual's daily functioning. Sometimes, however, SHR may not result in elimination of the habit or reduction to more acceptable levels. In those cases, the recommended next step is to implement a function-based treatment, because the function of the habit may not have been directly addressed using the SHR protocol.

## Function-Based Treatments

Function-based treatments fall generally into one of two categories: antecedent interventions and consequent interventions. Antecedent interventions are possible when, during initial interviews and direct observations, specific antecedents are identified that reliably precede the habit. Antecedent interventions involve several steps, the first of which is to identify similar antecedents that do not trigger the habit. In the second step, the clinician arranges opportunities to present the similar antecedents and to reinforce all appropriate behaviors other than the habit. The third and final step is to gradually reintroduce the antecedent that preceded the habit along with the other antecedents and reinforce all appropriate behavior that does not involve the habit (e.g., Watson, Dufrene, Weaver, Butler, & Meeks, 2005; Watson, Meeks, Dufrene, & Lindsay, 2002). The studies by Watson, Dufrene et al. and Watson, Meeks et al. showed relatively rapid elimination of habits and, perhaps more importantly, improvements in social and academic functioning as the habits decreased.

The second category of function-based treatments, consequent interventions, is possible when clear maintaining consequences are identified for the habit. The intervention will depend on whether the maintaining variable is social attention, negative reinforcement, or arousal induction or reduction. If the assessment data indicated that social attention is maintaining the habit, the primary intervention would involve withholding attention when the habit is exhibited (extinction) and providing social attention when appropriate behaviors other than the habit are exhibited (differential reinforcement). For example, Watson and Sterling (1998b) found through functional assessment procedures that social attention was maintaining the coughing habit of a 4-year-old girl during mealtimes. Treatment consisted of withholding attention following coughing (extinction) and providing verbal statements (social attention) contingent upon the absence of coughing (differential reinforcement). Over the course of 6 days of treatment, coughing was reduced to zero on the 4th day and remained at zero at 6-month follow-up.

In some instances, a habit results in the escape from, or avoidance of, an unpleasant situation or task. In one case, a third-grade student engaged in excessive, and loud, pencil tapping primarily when he was given a multiplication worksheet. Observations indicated that tapping allowed him to escape his work, either because tapping interfered with using his pencil to complete the task or the teacher engaged in behaviors that allowed him to avoid his work (e.g., reprimanding him, sending him to another desk or work area). Because this particular habit was motivated by negative reinforcement, intervention consisted of two essential elements. First, the student was no longer allowed to escape or avoid the multiplication task by tapping his pencil (extinction). Second, he was allowed to take very brief breaks following completion of gradually increasing work requirements (differential reinforcement and shaping). After 1 week of intervention, his tapping had decreased by more than 75% and, more importantly, the percentage of work he accurately completed increased by about 400% (Watson, McCurdy, & Weaver, 2000).

For habits that result in arousal induction, several options for treatment are available. The first is to develop an intervention procedure that results in the habit no longer providing a reinforcing sensation. Watson and Allen (1993) demonstrated the use of this procedure. They prevented the sensory stimulation that resulted from thumb sucking by attaching a thermoplastic post to the child's thumb. The post prevented the tactile and kinesthetic stimulation provided by thumb sucking (extinction). Sometimes, however, it may not be possible to simply prevent access to sensory stimulation produced by the habit. In such cases, a second treatment alternative is to punish the habit. A very effective treatment for eliminating thumb sucking, for example, is to place an unpleasant tasting substance on the thumb (e.g., Stopzit, Thumbz). An integral part of the treatment, however, is a program that reinforces the absence of thumb sucking. Regardless of the habit or the punishment procedure, some type of reinforcement program is necessary to avoid many of the pitfalls associated with the use of punishment alone (Martin & Pear, 2003). For instance, using punishment as a solitary strategy does not teach a new or competing behavior, it often strains the relationship between the person delivering the punishment (i.e., the teacher or parent) and the child, it may result in aggressive or emotional behavior from the child, and it may actually worsen the habit.

## SUMMARY

Although many habits are considered a part of the normal developmental process and will remit without specific intervention, some are problematic at any age (e.g., trichotillomania, bruxism, skin picking). Others become problematic when they persist past the point of developmental appropriateness (e.g., thumb sucking), and still others are problematic because they annoy others in the environment (e.g., foot tapping, hair twirling, lip smacking). Also, a number of both medical and nonmedical sequelae often occur with habits and make treatment necessary. Regardless of the specific habit and why it is problematic, two treatment options have been shown to be highly effective. Simplified habit reversal has been shown to be effective for a variety of habits and is a relatively easy procedure to implement. Another viable option is to base treatment on the identified function. Although that research is still in its infancy, early studies have yielded promising results.

## RECOMMENDED RESOURCES

### Books and Other Printed Material

Miltenberger, R. G., & Woods, D. W. (2000). Assessment and treatment of habit disorders. In J. Austin, & J. E. Carr (Eds.), *Handbook of applied behavior analysis* (pp. 137–160). Reno, NV: Context Press.

This chapter provides an excellent overview of the assessment and treatment of habit disorders from an operant and behavioral perspective. A number of empirically based strategies are covered for a variety of common childhood habits.

Watson, T. S., & Sterling, H. E. (1998). Habits and tics. In T. S. Watson, & F. M. Gresham (Eds.), *Handbook of child behavior therapy* (pp. 431–450). New York: Plenum Press.

This chapter, though a bit dated, illustrates the use of a consultative and problem-solving model for assessing and treating common habit and tic disorders in children. It was perhaps one of the first chapters to address a model of habit treatment based on function.

Woods, D. W., & Miltenberger, R. G. (Eds.). (2001). *Tic disorders, trichotillomania, and other repetitive behavior disorders: Behavioral approaches to analysis and treatment.* Boston: Kluwer Academic Publishers.

This book is the most comprehensive treatment of repetitive behavior disorders available. Although edited, all of the authors are recognized experts in habits and/or tics and present cutting-edge information on assessment and intervention.

### Websites

*http://www.trich.org*

The official website of the Trichotillomania Learning Center gives lots of information on trichotillomania that is specifically for the professional, plus reproducible information for parents and teachers.

*http://www.emedicine.com*

E-Medicine Consumer Health is intended primarily for professionals. Much of the information is presented in a scientific format; however, the information on the site is quite up-to-date and scientifically sound.

## REFERENCES

American Psychiatric Association. (2000). *Diagnostic and statistical manual of mental disorders* (4th ed., text rev.). Washington DC: Author.

Azrin, N. H., & Nunn, R. G. (1973). Habit reversal: A method of eliminating nervous habits and tics. *Behavior Research and Therapy, 11,* 619–628.

Azrin, N. H., & Peterson, A. L. (1990). Treatment of Tourette syndrome by habit reversal: A waiting-list control group comparison. *Behavior Therapy, 21,* 305–318.

Carr, J. E., & Rapp, J. T. (2001). Assessment of repetitive behavior disorders. In D. W. Woods, & R. G. Miltenberger (Eds.), *Tic disorders, trichotillomania, and other repetitive behavior disorders: Behavioral approaches to analysis and treatment* (pp. 9–32). Boston: Kluwer Academic Publishers.

Fantino, E. (1969). Choice and rate of reinforcement. *Journal of the Experimental Analysis of Behavior, 12,* 723–730.

Freud, A. (1965). *Normality and pathology in childhood.* New York: International Universities Press.

Friman, P. C., Larzelere, R., & Finney, J. W. (1994). Exploring the relationship between thumb-sucking and finger sucking. *Journal of Pediatric Psychology, 19,* 431–441.

Friman, P. C., McPherson, K. M., Warzak, W. J., & Evans, J. (1993). Influence of thumb sucking on peer social acceptance in first-grade children. *Pediatrics, 91,* 784–786.

Glaros, A. G., & Melamed, G. G. (1992). Bruxism in children: Etiology and treatment. *Applied and Preventive Psychology, 1,* 191–199.

Hadley, N. H. (1984). *Nail biting.* New York: Spectrum.

Haynes, S. N. (1998). The changing nature of behavioral assessment. In A. S. Bellack & M. Hersen (Eds.), *Behavioral assessment: A practical handbook* (4th ed.). Needham Heights, MA: Allyn & Bacon.

Hollander, E. (1993). Obsessive-compulsive spectrum disorders: An overview. *Psychiatric Annals, 23,* 355–358.

Johnston, J. M., & Pennypacker, H. S. (1993). *Strategies and tactics of behavioral research* (2nd ed.). Hillsdale, NJ: Erlbaum.

Martin, G., & Pear, J. (2003). *Behavior modification: What it is and how to do it.* Englewood Cliffs, NJ: Prentice-Hall.

Peterson, A. L., Campose, R. L., & Azrin, N. H. (1994). Behavioral and pharmacological treatments for tic and habit disorders: A review. *Journal of Developmental and Behavioral Pediatrics, 15,* 430–441.

Rapp, J. T., Miltenberger, R. G., Galensky, T. L., Roberts, J., & Ellingson, S. A. (1999). Brief functional analysis and simplified habit reversal treatment of thumb sucking in fraternal twin brothers. *Child and Family Behavior Therapy, 21,* 1–17.

Romaniuk, C., Miltenberger, R. G., & Deaver, C. (2003). Long-term maintenance following habit reversal and adjunct treatment for trichotillomania. *Child and Family Behavior Therapy, 25,* 45–59.

Shapiro, S., & Shannon, J. (1966). Bruxism as an emotional reactive disturbance. *Psychosomatics, 6,* 427–430.

Twohig, M. P., Woods, D. W., Marcks, B. A., & Teng, E. J. (2003). Evaluating the efficacy of habit reversal: Comparison with a placebo control. *Journal of Clinical Psychiatry, 64,* 40–48.

Watson, T. S., & Allen, K. D. (1993). Elimination of thumb-sucking as a treatment for severe trichotillomania. *Journal of the American Academy of Child and Adolescent Psychiatry, 32,* 830–834.

Watson, T. S., Dufrene, B., Weaver, A., Butler, T., & Meeks, C. (2005). Brief antecedent assessment and treatment of tics in the general education classroom. *Behavior Modification, 29,* 839–857.

Watson, T. S., McCurdy, M., & Weaver, A. (2000, May). Investigating the relationship between habits and adjunctive behavior. In D. W. Woods (Chair) *Habit behaviors: A closer look at controlling variables.* Paper presented at the 26th annual meeting of the Association for Behavior Analysis, Washington, DC.

Watson, T. S., Meeks, C., Dufrene, B., & Lindsay, C. (2002). Sibling thumb sucking: Effects of treatment for targeted and untargeted siblings. *Behavior Modification, 26,* 412–423.

Watson, T. S., & Steege, M. W. (2003). *A practitioner's guide to school-based functional assessment.* New York: Guilford.

Watson, T. S., & Sterling, H. E. (1998a). Habits and tics. In T. S. Watson & F. M. Gresham (Eds.), *Handbook of child behavior therapy* (pp. 431–450). New York: Plenum.

Watson, T. S., & Sterling, H. E. (1998b). Brief functional analysis and treatment of a vocal tic. *Journal of Applied Behavior Analysis, 31,* 471–474.

Woods, D. W., Friman, P. C., & Teng, E. J. (2001). Physical and social impairment in persons with repetitive behavior disorders. In D. W. Woods, & R. G. Miltenberger (Eds.), *Tic disorders, trichotillomania, and other repetitive behavior disorders: Behavioral approaches to analysis and treatment* (pp. 9–32). Boston: Kluwer Academic Publishers.

Woods, D. W., & Miltenberger, R. G. (1996). A review of habit reversal with childhood habit disorders. *Education and Treatment of Children, 19,* 197–214.

Woods, D. W., & Miltenberger, R. G. (Eds.) (2001). *Tic disorders, trichotillomania, and other repetitive behavior disorders: Behavioral approaches to analysis and treatment.* Boston: Kluwer Academic Publishers.

# 81
# Pediatric Psychopharmacology

**Mary C. Kral**
**Angela LaRosa**
*Department of Pediatrics, Medical University of South Carolina, Charleston*

**Ronald T. Brown**
*College of Health Professions and Department of Public Health, Temple University,*

**Tom Kubiszyn**
*University of Houston*

## BACKGROUND AND DEVELOPMENT

Many school professionals have encountered a child who has been prescribed medication to manage a psychiatric disorder. For a number of reasons, the probability of this occurring is likely to rise. Almost every large-scale study or review of patterns of medication administration has reported an increase in the prescribing of psychotropic medications for children over time (Gadow, 1997; Jensen et al., 1999; Medco Health Solutions, 2004; Vitiello, 2001), including for preschoolers (e.g., Coyle, 2000; Delate, 2004; Zito et al., 2000).

Several factors that may account for this trend include greater public awareness of childhood psychiatric disorders and increased acceptance of a disease model of childhood psychopathology (Riddle, Kastelic, & Frosch, 2001). In addition, more precise identification of those children at risk, increased accuracy of diagnoses, and expansion of existing diagnostic criteria have led to the increased incidence of children diagnosed with childhood psychiatric disorders (Gadow, 1997). Advances in the ability to identify the biological bases of childhood psychopathology and the increasing availability of newer medications with more favorable side-effect profiles also have likely contributed to the increase in pharmacotherapy (Brown & Sawyer, 1998). Finally, a systematic effort to contain and drive down the costs of medical care has dramatically changed delivery of health care services in this country (Brown & Freeman, 2003). In this context, the accessibility of treatment has increased, with pediatricians and primary care providers prescribing the majority of psychotropic medications for children (Safer, Zito, & Fine, 1996).

School personnel also play a significant role in the evolving epidemiology of pediatric psychopharmacology. Teachers are fast becoming a primary referral source for further medical evaluation to assess the need for possible pharmacological interventions. One recent study estimated that school personnel initiate as many as 40% to 65% of all referrals for assessment and treatment of Attention Deficit Hyperactivity Disorder (ADHD; Snider, Frankenburger, & Aspenson, 2000). School personnel also are becoming increasingly responsible for the behavioral management and academic adjustment of children who are receiving psychotropic medications. For example, a recent survey (N = 258) revealed that school psychologists are highly involved in the referral, evaluation, and intervention of students diagnosed with ADHD (Frankenberger, Farmer, Parker, & Cermak, 2001). Specifically, 20% of the participating school psychologists' caseloads involved children diagnosed with ADHD. A similar survey (N = 571) reported that the majority of school psychologists provide services to students who are prescribed medications (e.g., stimulants, anticonvulsants, antidepressants, antipsychotics, and antianxiety agents; Kubiszyn & Carlson, 1995). In that survey, 77% of the school psychologists surveyed endorsed expanding the role of school psychologists to include evaluation of medication effectiveness.

Educational law can also have an effect on the relevance of pediatric psychopharmacology in the school setting. For example, efforts were made to insert language into the most recent revision of the Individuals with Disabilities Education Act (IDEA) to prohibit school personnel from discussing pharmacotherapy with parents, but these efforts were unsuccessful. The law explicitly prohibits states from requiring medication as a prerequisite for attending school or receiving services, but it also makes clear that there is no Federal prohibition against sharing information with parents regarding the need for evaluation, including assessment for possible pharmacological interventions (National Association of School Psychologists, 2004). This provision is important in that students would not be well served if school professionals were legally prevented from fulfilling what many would consider an ethical obligation to discuss potential treatment options, including pharmacotherapy, with families (De Leon & Wiggins, 1996). Given the increasing numbers of students taking psychotropic medications, school-based health and mental health service providers (e.g., school nurses, psychologists, counselors, and social workers) should have a working knowledge of pediatric psychopharmacology, including the influence of various pharmacotherapies on learning and behavior.

## Basics of Pediatric Psychopharmacology

*Psychopharmacology* is a subdiscipline of pharmacology that is concerned with the study of the effects of drugs on the central nervous system and specifically on psychological processes and behavior (Poling, Gadow, & Cleary, 1991). *Psychotropic medications*, which are administered by prescription only (e.g., antidepressants, antipsychotics, antianxiety agents, and stimulants), target attention, cognition, emotions, and behavior. In the applied field of psychopharmacology, medications typically are referred to either by the manufacturer's trade name or brand name (e.g., Ritalin) or by the generic name (e.g., methylphenidate). The generic name is derived from the chemical composition of the medication, and the brand name is patent protected by pharmaceutical corporations. In theory, the safety or efficacy of brand name and generic formulations should not differ. However, in clinical practice, some physicians may report anecdotal evidence that patients respond differently to either a generic or a brand name formulation. When a medication has demonstrated efficacy in the treatment of a particular disorder, it is said to be *indicated*, meaning it is considered appropriate for the treatment of a particular condition. A medication that is *contraindicated* is not recommended because of a patient's existing physical condition or potential interactions with other medications currently prescribed (Werry & Aman, 1999).

All pharmaceutical agents, regardless of their classification, are delivered through the circulatory system until they reach electrochemically complementary receptor sites on nerves or other cells. Psychotropic medications render a therapeutic effect by altering, either directly or indirectly, the functioning of the central nervous system. At the level of the nerve cell, the drug binds with a receptor until an electrochemical change releases it. This lock-and-key action affects a nerve cell's capacity to transmit or receive information from neighboring nerve cells by catalyzing intracellular and extracellular changes that lead to alterations in cellular membranes, receptors, neurotransmitters, and other molecules. The terms *affinity* and *specificity* describe the binding strength between the drug and the receptor's chemical structure and the magnitude of the electrochemical attraction. Affinity and specificity affect the amount of drug needed to achieve sufficient receptor binding (i.e., *saturation*) to elicit a therapeutic effect. In short, as specificity and affinity increase, the amount of a drug required to achieve a particular level of saturation is reduced. If less of a drug is needed, all other factors being equal, the lower the probability of adverse side effects, defined as any unintended or undesirable medical or behavioral abnormality. A more detailed review of pharmaceutical mechanisms of action can be found in Werry and Aman (1999).

The lock-and-key action of psychotropic medications has the potential for producing positive effects on behavior. All medications, including over-the-counter agents, also have the potential to produce adverse side effects or allergic reactions. Adverse side effects of psychotropic medications may include a few commonly experienced side effects and some relatively rare events and are typically categorized as mild, moderate, or severe. Mild adverse side effects may include temporary discomfort, such as headache or loss of appetite. Adverse side effects also are characterized as serious when significant, albeit rare, medical complications or life-threatening events occur, such as seizures, cardiac arrhythmias, or suicidal ideation. For example, in response to serious adverse events that have recently been reported in the clinical literature, the U.S. Food and Drug Administration (FDA) required a warning against the use of selective serotonin reuptake inhibitors (SSRIs), with the exception of Prozac (fluoxetine), for the treatment of depression in children and adolescents. The side-effect profile of a particular medication can vary depending on the class of medication, the unique responsiveness of the child (Riddle et al., 2001), and the subjective report of individuals reporting the side effects (Brown & Sawyer, 1998). Also, adverse side effects may result from an interaction with other prescribed medications and over-the-counter agents, vitamins, and supplements. Because children often do not report side effects of medications (Tosyali & Greenhill, 1998), it is incumbent upon the prescribing physicians to discuss the side-effect profile of medications with caregivers and to closely monitor, by obtaining reports from multiple informants, not only the effectiveness of the medication over time, but also any adverse effects that may develop.

### Psychotropic Medications Commonly Prescribed to Children and Adolescents

A thorough discussion of the various classes of psychotropic medications and research findings pertaining to each drug is beyond the scope of this chapter. Instead, Table 1 presents a summary of commonly prescribed psychotropic medications administered to children and adolescents, including indications for use, common as well as infrequent side effects, and the status of FDA approval (see Brown & Sawyer, 1998; Brown & Sammons, 2002; Phelps, Brown, & Power, 2002; and Werry & Aman, 1999).

## PROBLEMS AND IMPLICATIONS

### Adult Versus Pediatric Psychopharmacology

In contrast to adult populations, psychotropic medications prescribed for pediatric populations are typically used as an adjunct to more traditional psychotherapies. There have been tremendous advances in psychopharmacology and many pharmaceutical agents have been developed in recent years that show particular promise in enhancing cognitive functioning and improving behavior in children, including new classes of medications with fewer adverse side effects and greater efficacy. Nonetheless, the clinical use of most psychotropic medications for children far exceeds the data available regarding safety and efficacy (Brown & Sammons, 2002; Greenhill et al., 2003). Research pertaining to psychotropic medication for children is progressing at a much slower rate than investigations of the same medications prescribed for adult use (Werry & Aman, 1999). Before a new drug is made available for public use, it must be approved by the U.S. FDA. The FDA's approval of drugs is most often based on information gathered from research with adults. These drugs are then commonly prescribed by practitioners for children, with protocols extrapolated from adult studies. In a sense, these agents are prescribed "off-label," and are not necessarily sanctioned for use with pediatric populations. This poses a serious dilemma for prescribing physicians, given the ethical and legal considerations, physiological differences, psychological influences, and adherence-related issues that may differentiate pediatric from adult psychopharmacology.

### Ethical and Legal Considerations

Children and adolescents, unlike adults, rarely initiate their own referral for behavioral and learning problems, and children cannot legally consent to treatment. Younger children especially may have little influence on whether they receive treatment, including psychotropic medications. This situation places greater responsibility on physicians to accurately identify those children in need of pharmacotherapy and to expose them to the fewest adverse effects possible (Brown & Sammons, 2002). For example, Zito et al. (2000) reported a dramatic increase in the prescription of psychotropic medications for children ages 2 through 4 years between the years 1991 and 1995, in the absence of sufficient data regarding the safety and efficacy of medications for very young children. As a result, a White House Conference in 2000 reported that proper diagnoses by qualified professionals are essential; psychosocial interventions generally should be implemented prior to psychotropic treatment and these interventions should continue even if a medication trial is activated; and collaborative practice among medical, mental health, and school professionals is essential (cited in Phelps, Brown, & Power, 2002).

The ethical concerns regarding children's inability to provide true informed consent calls into question the generalization of adult data regarding safety and efficacy of psychotropic medication to children and adolescents. As noted above, many of the psychotropic medications prescribed for children and adolescents are done so *off-label,* meaning that although the drug is an FDA approved medication, it may not be specifically approved for use in children or for a specific disorder (Tosyali & Greenhill, 1998). However, physicians' decisions to

**Table 1** *Commonly Prescribed Psychotropic Medications Administered to Children and Adolescents*

| Medication | Indications for Use | FDA Approval | Side Effects |
|---|---|---|---|
| | **STIMULANTS** | | |
| **Methylphenidate Preparations** | Attention Deficit Hyperactivity Disorder (ADHD), narcolepsy | > 6 years | Decreased appetite, weight loss, insomnia, nausea, abdominal pain, headache, mood lability, weepiness, irritability, tachycardia, hallucination, increased blood pressure, rebound symptoms, exacerbation of tics. |
| *Short acting (3–4 hrs.)* | | | |
| Focalin | | | |
| Methylin | | | |
| Ritalin | | | |
| *Intermediate acting (6–8 hrs.)* | | | |
| Metadate ER | | | |
| Methylin ER | | | |
| Ritalin SR | | | |
| *Long acting (8–12 hrs.)* | | | |
| Concerta | | | |
| Metadate CD | | | |
| Ritalin LA | | | |
| **Dextroamphetamine Preparations** | ADHD, narcolepsy | > 3 years | |
| *Short acting (4–6 hrs.)* | | | |
| Adderall | | | |
| Dexedrine tablets | | | |
| Dextrostat | | | |
| *Intermediate acting (6 hrs.)* | | | |
| Dexedrine spansules | | | |
| *Long acting (10–12 hrs.)* | | | |
| Adderall XR | | > 6 years | |
| | **NONSTIMULANTS** | | |
| Atomoxetine (Straterra) | ADHD | > 6 years | Decreased appetite, nausea, vomiting, fatigue, somnolence, dizziness, irritability, tachycardia, increased blood pressure. |
| Pemoline (Cylert) | ADHD | > 6 years | Potentially fatal acute liver failure, nausea, anorexia, weight loss, insomnia, seizures. |
| | **ALPHA AGONISTS** | | |
| Clonidine (Catapres) | ADHD, aggression | Approved for treatment of hypertension | Sedation, hypotension, dizziness. |
| Guanfacine (Tenex) | Tourette's syndrome | | |

*(Continued)*

**Table 1** *Continued*

| Medication | Indications for Use | FDA Approval | Side Effects |
|---|---|---|---|
| | **ANTIDEPRESSANTS** | | |
| **Selective Serotonin Reuptake Inhibitors** | | | |
| Citalopram (Celexa) | Depression | > 18 years | Diarrhea, nervousness, headache, nausea, vomiting, sleep disturbances, decreased weight gain, activation of mania. |
| Escitalopram (Lexapro) | Depression | > 18 years | |
| Fluoxetine (Prozac) (4) | Depression | > 8 years | |
| | OCD | > 7 years | |
| | Bulimia nervosa, panic disorder | > 18 years | |
| Fluvoxamine (Luvox) | OCD | > 8 years | |
| Paroxetine (Paxil) | Depression, obsessive–compulsive disorder (OCD), panic disorder, social anxiety disorder | > 18 years | |
| Sertraline (Zoloft) | Depression, panic disorder, post-traumatic stress disorder, anxiety disorder, premenstrual dysphoric disorder | > 18 years | |
| | OCD | > 6 years | |
| **Tricyclic Antidepressants** | | | |
| Amitriptyline (Elavil) | Depression | > 12 years | Dry mouth, blurred vision, constipation, drowsiness, insomnia, blood dyscrasias, tachycardia, arrythmia, seizures, nightmares, delusions. |
| Clomipramine (Anafranil) | OCD | > 10 years | |
| Desipramine (Norpramin) | Depression | > 18 years | |
| Imipramine (Tofranil) | Depression | > 12 years | |
| | Enuresis | > 6 years | |
| Nortriptyline (Pamelor) | Depression | > 18 years | |
| **Other Antidepressants** | | | |
| Bupropion (Wellbutrin) | Depression | > 18 years | Agitation, dry mouth, insomnia, activation of mania, headache, seizures, nausea. |
| Mirtazapine (Remeron) | Depression | > 18 years | Increased appetite, weight gain, somnolence, dry mouth, dizziness, agranulocytosis. |
| Nefazodone (Serzone) | Depression | > 18 years | Constipation, dry mouth, dizziness, blurred vision, confusion. |
| Trazadone (Desyrel) | Depression, anxiety | > 18 years | Drowsiness, dizziness, dry mouth, nausea, vomiting. |
| Venlafaxine (Effexor) | Depression, anxiety | > 18 years | Anxiety, nervousness, somnolence, insomnia, nausea, anorexia, increased blood pressure, constipation, weight loss, dry mouth, dizziness, sexual dysfunction. |

*(Continued)*

**Table 1** *Continued*

| Medication | Indications for Use | FDA Approval | Side Effects |
|---|---|---|---|
| | **ATYPICAL ANTIPSYCHOTICS** | | |
| Aripiprazole (Abilify) | Psychotic Disorder | > 18 years | Weight gain, sedation, atherogenic lipid profile, tardive dyskinesia, diabetes, neuroleptic malignant syndrome, dysphagia, hepatotoxicity, dizziness, conduction abnormalities, hyperprolactinemia, potentially fatal agranulocytosis. |
| Clozapine (Clozaril) | | > 16 years | |
| Olanzapine (Zyprexa) | | > 18 years | |
| Quetiapine (Seroquel) | | | |
| Risperidone (Risperdol) | | > 16 years | |
| Ziprasidone (Geodon) | | > 18 years | |
| | **MOOD STABILIZERS** | | |
| Carbamazepine (Tegretol) | Seizure disorder | > 6 years | Dizziness, drowsiness, nausea, vomiting, induction of mania, aplastic anemia, agranulocytosis. |
| Lithium | Manic depression | > 12 years | Fine tremor, polyuria, polydipsia, fatigue, nausea, malaise, weight gain, headache, thyroid and renal abnormalities, acne, rash, leukocytosis. |
| Valproic acid (Depakote) | Mania<br>Migraine, seizure disorder | > 18 years<br>> 16 years | Nausea, vomiting, depression, hepatic failure, psychoses, aggression, thrombocytopenia. |
| Buspirone (Buspar) | Anxiety disorder | > 18 years | Dizziness, drowsiness, nausea, headache, insomnia. |

prescribe psychotropic medications to children and adolescents are informed by research, such as clinical trials. For example, clonidine, an FDA approved medication for use in adults with hypertension, often is used in children to treat symptoms of ADHD, and several investigations support the effectiveness of this medication for use in the management of this pediatric disorder (e.g., Hunt, Minderaa, & Cohen, 1985).

By 1990, as a result of the long-standing precedent to exclude children from drug trials, more than 80% of all medications prescribed to children and adolescents had not undergone investigation of safety and efficacy with this population (Riddle et al., 2001). In response, the last decade saw an increase in federally funded studies designed to investigate pharmacologic treatment of children and adolescents with psychiatric disorders. For example, the National Institute of Mental Health (NIMH) funded the Research Units of Pediatric Psychopharmacology (RUPP) in order to foster multisite, multimodal collaborative investigations of the safety and efficacy of psychotropic medications in children and adolescents (Greenhill et al., 2003). A number of federal regulations also have encouraged increased research interest in pediatric psychopharmacology. The FDA Modernization Act of 1997 offered marketing incentives to pharmaceutical companies conducting safety and efficacy studies among pediatric populations. An additional FDA regulation in 2000 mandated safety and efficacy data for any newly introduced medication prior to administration to children and adults (Riddle et al., 2001). These federal research initiatives and regulations provide an important step toward addressing the ethical and legal concerns of pediatric psychopharmacology, particularly for children with chronic psychiatric disorders who benefit from medication as part of their treatment over the long term (e.g., ADHD, bipolar disorder, obsessive–compulsive disorder, etc.).

Federally funded initiatives to monitor the long-term safety and efficacy of psychotropic medications administered to children and adolescents are currently underway (Greenhill et al., 2003; Vitiello et al., 2003). In addition, MedWatch is a government-sponsored forum that gathers, evaluates, and reports information about adverse events in pediatric psychopharmacology (Riddle, Kastelic, & Frosch, 2001). It should be noted that reports to MedWatch are voluntary, and thus several confounding variables may obscure the reported outcomes (e.g., level of drug exposure, polypharmacy) (Vitiello et al.). Clearly, the rigor of controlled clinical trials is of particular import when evaluating the safety and efficacy of pediatric psychopharmacology, especially concerning the long-term effects on the developing central nervous system. Although both short-term and long-term effects of exposing the developing brain to psychotropic medications are largely unknown, the possible risks of pharmacologic treatment must be weighed against the deleterious effects of an untreated psychiatric disorder (Vitiello, 2001).

## Physiological Factors

The rates at which medications are absorbed, distributed in the body, and metabolized by children differ markedly from adults (Werry & Aman, 1999). Therefore, prescribing physicians must act judiciously when deciding on particular medications or dosages for children, and changes in dosages require consultation with prescribing physicians who are familiar with physiological functioning in children. Many medications have shorter half-lives in children and adolescents as compared to adults, and therefore may require more frequent dosing (Tosyali & Greenhill, 1998). Age also plays a significant role in predicting the effect of a medication, with younger children typically having more unpredictable responses than older children. In addition, individual differences in medication responsiveness impact the efficacy of medication. Therefore, children need to be carefully monitored. Finally, when considering additional medications, prescribing physicians must take care to consider any adverse medication interactions that may occur from *polypharmacy* (the use of more than one psychotropic agent simultaneously), an increasingly common practice in pediatric psychopharmacology (Brown & Sammons, 2002).

## Psychological Factors

Because young children do not have the cognitive schema from which to describe accurately the physiological or psychological changes that may be associated with the use of psychotropic medications (for reviews, see Brown & Sammons, 2002; Brown & Sawyer, 1998; Zametkin & Yamada, 1999), obtaining data from other informants, such as parents and school professionals, is imperative. Parents and teachers can provide information about positive and adverse events that may be associated with pharmacologic interventions, along with information about the time course in which these changes are observed. Because the level of agreement among child, parent, and teacher reports of behavior is relatively poor (Achenbach, McConaughy & Howell, 1987), school professionals may assist prescribing physicians in obtaining and interpreting information obtained across sources regarding medication response or adverse effects.

## Adherence to Treatment Regimens

Adherence to pharmacologic regimens is a critical factor that influences the efficacy of treatment. Unlike adults, children do not arrange their own appointments for treatment, and because children may be reluctant to use psychotropic medication, prescribing medication for children is more complicated than for adults. Because caregivers typically take responsibility for administration of children's medication, parental attitudes invariably influence children's use of medication. Caregivers may be ambivalent about using psychotropic medication, particularly when school staff initiate the referral and when the child's behavior is not deemed to be a problem at home. Again, school professionals may serve as liaisons between home, school, and prescribing physicians in order to identify sources of treatment resistance and to facilitate treatment adherence (Power & Krain, 2003).

## Coordination With Other Treatment Programs

Psychotropic medication is only one component in the overall treatment program for children and adolescents. The decision to coordinate various treatments necessitates thorough and accurate assessment of targets for intervention, especially for children whose emotions and behavior naturally vary from day to day and week to week (Tosyali & Greenhill, 1998). In this regard, functional behavioral assessments performed by school-based teams may provide invaluable information in all phases of pharmacologic intervention–assessment of children who may benefit from pharmacologic interventions, monitoring of treatment effects and safety, and coordination of multiple interventions within the classroom.

## ALTERNATIVE ACTIONS

### Evaluation of the Efficacy of Medication

Many of the medications prescribed for the treatment of childhood psychopathology have effects on learning and behavior in the school setting. As such, school psychologists and other school-based mental health service providers are in a prime position to assess the clinical efficacy and ecological validity of medication in the classroom, where medications exert observable changes in behavior and cognition. Trained in assessment and measurement, school psychologists, in particular, have an arsenal of measures for careful monitoring of medication effects, including response to medication within the realm of behavior and learning, as well as quantifying adverse side effects. Moreover, these professionals can readily obtain behavioral observations in the classroom and academic performance data. Finally, school practitioners and prescribing physicians may collaborate productively in determining whether trials of psychotropic medication are appropriate, effective, and successful, and also whether one particular dose is more effective than another in unstructured versus structured activities (Brown & Sawyer, 1998).

Because children may respond in idiosyncratic ways to pharmacologic interventions, methods of behavioral analysis and single-subject design are well-suited to assess medication effectiveness and to determine optimal dosing. These procedures also can be used to assess the relative superiority of pharmacologic interventions versus psychosocial interventions, or a combination of both. The first step is to identify specific and objectively defined goals for treatment (e.g., reduction in a set of target symptoms). The second step involves the selection of outcome measures that are sensitive to changes in the target symptoms. Frequently employed outcome measures include behavior rating scales, laboratory-based psychometric measures of cognitive functioning, and structured behavioral observation systems. Table 2 provides a sampling of commonly used behavior rating scales for monitoring medication effectiveness.

Traditionally, parent- and teacher-completed behavior rating scales have been used to monitor medication effectiveness. These instruments have the advantage of providing psychometrically sound information and economy of administration, but often are insensitive to subtle changes in behavior. In addition, behavior rating scales often are subject to rater biases. Psychometric measures of cognitive functioning (e.g., alternate forms of learning and memory and continuous performance tasks) also have been employed to assess the cognitive enhancing effects of various psychotropic medications. Again, while these psychometric instruments provide reliable and objective information about specific cognitive functions, they have been criticized on the grounds of lacking ecological validity (Barkley, 1991) and yielding many false positives (DuPaul, Anastopoulos, Shelton, Guevremont, & Metevia, 1992). In contrast, behavioral observation systems provide systematic and objective assessments of specific and often subtle changes in behaviors that can offset some of the limitations of rating scales. Given the limitations associated with each of the aforementioned outcome measures, multiple measures of treatment effectiveness should be incorporated as the standard of assessment (Brown & Sawyer, 1998; Phelps, Brown, & Power, 2002).

Best practice in medication-monitoring protocols involves double-blind, placebo-controlled medication trials. To control for bias effects, medication is administered in a *blinded* fashion, such that the child and individuals involved in data collection are unaware of the intervention being used at a particular point in time. Also, pills are encapsulated so that the medication and a placebo are indistinguishable. Although double-blind, placebo-controlled trials are considered the gold standard for determining the effectiveness of pharmacologic intervention, this procedure may be challenging and time consuming in the real world setting (Phelps, Brown, & Power, 2002). A variety of more cost effective procedures has been proposed for the evaluation of stimulant medication effectiveness (Barkley, Fischer, Newby, & Breen, 1988; Gadow, Nolan, Paolicelli, & Sprafkin, 1991; Roberts, DuPaul, & Benjamin, 1999), which may be applied to the monitoring of other fast-acting medications (e.g., anxiolytics).

### Multimodal Treatment

The ideal intervention model is a multimodal one that includes empirically supported psychosocial and pharmacological interventions from multidisciplinary collaborators (Phelps, Brown, & Power, 2002). In the multimodal approach, psychotropic medications are used to reduce symptoms so that children are amenable to psychosocial and educational interventions in other settings, such as psychotherapy and special education accommodations. For example, while stimulant medication may enhance academic success in the short term for children with ADHD (Pelham et al., 1993), academic gains in the long term will require comprehensive educational and behavioral interventions that draw upon children's strengths

**Table 2** *Examples of Behavior Rating Scales Used to Assess Medication Effectiveness*

| Scale | Utility | Limitations |
|---|---|---|
| | **Broad-Band Measures** | |
| *Behavior Assessment System for Children* (Reynolds & Kamphaus, 1992)<br>*Revised Child Behavior Checklist and Teacher Report Form* (Achenbach & Rescorla, 2001) | Excellent psychometric properties; ability to assess the effects of medication across a broad range of behaviors; assessment of both internalizing and externalizing behaviors; multiple observer forms. | Time required to complete the rating scale, particularly if administered repeatedly. |
| | **Narrow-Band Measures** | |
| *Beck Youth Inventories* (Beck, Beck, & Jolly, 2001) | Child and adolescent self-report measures of both internalizing (anxiety and depression) and externalizing behavior problems; excellent psychometric properties; brevity in terms of administration time. | Lack of parallel parent- and teacher-completed forms; not a substitute for a diagnostic interview, should be used as a screener. |
| *Conners' Rating Scales,* Revised (Conners, 1997) | Large normative base; empirically supported factor structure; strong psychometric properties; multiple observer forms; brevity in terms of administration time. | Comorbidity subscales contain only a few items and may not improve diagnostic sensitivity. |
| *Home and School Situations Questionnaire* (Barkley, 1997) | Useful in assessing compliance with rules and quantifying effects of disruptive behaviors on daily living; sensitive to medication effects. | Not designed to assess particular disruptive behavior disorders; should be used as adjunct to diagnosis-based scales; normative data may be outdated. |
| *Vanderbilt ADHD Rating Scales* (Wolraich, 2003) | Academic performance and behavioral performance subscales address functional impairment; brevity in terms of administration time; available online at *http://www.nichq.org* | As a newer instrument, lacks sufficient validity evidence. |

and interests and accommodate their learning differences (Frankenberger et al., 2001). Yet another example of the effectiveness of a multimodal approach is the research support in favor of combined antidepressant medication and psychotherapy for the treatment of childhood depression, or for the treatment of ADHD when it co-occurs with other psychiatric disorders, such as anxiety (for a review of these studies, see Brown, Arnstein, & Simerly, 2005).

## Recent Developments

The trend toward increased prescribing of psychotropic medications for children and adolescents is likely to continue, especially as the biological bases of a number of childhood psychiatric conditions are more precisely defined and as newer classes of medications with greater effectiveness and more favorable side-effect profiles are introduced into the pharmaceuticals market (Riddle, Kastelic, & Frosch, 2001). Given the interest among both primary care providers and school professionals in evidence-based medicine and empirically validated treatments, a collaborative effort is anticipated between these two groups, which will significantly enhance treatment decisions as well as document the efficacy of particular psychotropic agents (Brown & Sammons, 2002). Specifically, school-based health and mental health service providers should expand their scope of practice to include: (a) disseminating accurate information to parents and professionals in the schools regarding pharmacological interventions; (b) advocating for evidence-based, efficacious treatments that will maximize the academic success of schoolage children; and (c) providing data to prescribing physicians regarding children's behavior, frequency of symptoms, and responses to medication so that the most effective treatment plan can be implemented for individual students.

## SUMMARY

Trends in the epidemiology of pediatric psychopharmacology include increased public acceptance of a disease model of child psychopathology, along with a steady rise in the practice of prescribing of psychotropic medications to children and adolescents. Although federally funded investigations of pediatric pharmacotherapy also are on the rise, the field of pediatric psychopharmacology is generally characterized by limited safety and efficacy data. Many psychotropic medications affect cognition, emotion, and behavior that may be readily apparent in the classroom context. Thus, school-based mental health service providers are particularly poised to identify those children at risk for psychopathology, and, more importantly, to identify those who might benefit from pharmacological interventions. In that context, the expanding role of these professionals is likely to include assessment of treatment effectiveness in the classroom, monitoring of adverse medication effects, and dissemination of accurate information regarding evidence-based treatment to parents and other school professionals.

## RECOMMENDED RESOURCES

### Books and Other Printed Material

Brown, R. T., & Sawyer, M. G. (1998). *Medications for school-age children: Effects on learning and behavior.* New York: Guilford Press.

This text provides information about current pharmacological interventions and their effects on children in school, at home, and among peers. Topics covered at length include short-term and long-term effects of specific medications for particular childhood disorders and the psychologist's role in assessing and monitoring medication effectiveness.

Phelps, L., Brown, R. T., & Power, T. (2002). *Pediatric psychopharmacology: Combining medical and psychosocial intervention.* Washington, DC: American Psychological Association.

This text describes medications demonstrated to be effective in the treatment of children and adolescents using double-blind studies, in addition to the various empirically supported nonpharmacological interventions. It also addresses the integration of psychosocial and pharmacological interventions, suggested solutions to the problem of nonadherence to treatment regimens, conduct of medication-monitoring protocols, and participation in multidisciplinary collaborative interventions.

Roberts, M., & DuPaul, G. (2000). Role for school psychologists: Evaluating medication effects for students with attention-deficit/hyperactivity disorder. *NASP Communiqué, 28*(6).

This *Communiqué* article describes a method for evaluating the effects of stimulant medication on the behavior and school performance of children with ADHD. The method achieves a balance between practicality (i.e., limiting time and resource requirements) and sensitivity to treatment effects. This practical procedure guides the school psychologist in the use of multiple outcome measures, including behavior rating scales, curriculum-based assessment, and direct behavioral observations.

### Websites

*http://www.fda.gov/medwatch*

This website is the homepage for MedWatch, a government-sponsored initiative for reporting safety and adverse event information about drugs and other medical products regulated by the U.S. Food and Drug Administration, including prescription and over-the-counter drugs, medical and radiation-emitting devices, and special nutritional products (e.g., dietary supplements and infant formulas). The website is used to disseminate product safety alerts, recalls and withdrawals, and important labeling changes that may affect public health.

## REFERENCES

Achenbach, T. M., McConaughy, S. H., & Howell, C. T. (1987). Child/adolescent behavioral and emotional problems: Implications of cross-informant correlations for situational specificity. *Psychological Bulletin, 101,* 213–232.

Achenbach, T. M., & Rescorla, L. A. (2001). *Manual for ASEBA school-age forms & profiles.* Burlington, VT:

University of Vermont, Research Center for Children, Youth, & Families.

Barkley, R. A. (1991). The ecological validity of laboratory and analogue assessment methods of ADHD symptoms. *Journal of Abnormal Child Psychology, 19,* 149–178.

Barkley, R. A., Fischer, M., Newby, R., & Breen, M. (1988). Development of a multimethod clinical protocol for assessing stimulant drug responses in ADHD children. *Journal of Clinical Child Psychology, 17,* 14–24.

Barkley, R. A., & Murphy, K. R. (1998). *Attention-deficit hyperactivity disorder: A clinical workbook, 3rd edition.* New York, NY: Guilford Press.

Beck, J., Beck, A., & Jolly, J. (2001). *Beck youth inventories of emotional & social impairment manual.* San Antonio, TX: Psychological Corporation.

Brown, R. T., Carpenter, L. A., & Simerly, E. (2005). *Mental health medications for children: A primer.* New York: Guilford Press.

Brown, R. T., & Freeman, W. S. (2003). Primary care. In D. Marsh, & M. Fristad (Eds.), *Handbook of serious emotional disturbance in children and adolescents.* (pp. 428–444). New York: Wiley.

Brown, R. T., & Sammons, M. T. (2002). Pediatric psychopharmacology: A review of new developments and recent research. *Professional Psychology: Research and Practice, 33,* 135–147.

Brown, R. T., & Sawyer, M. G. (1998). *Medications for school-age children: Effects on learning and behavior.* New York: Guilford Press.

Conners, C. (1997). *Conners' rating scales – revised.* North Tonawanda, NY: Multi-Health Systems, Inc.

Coyle, J. T. (2000). Psychotropic drug use in very young children. *Journal of the American Medical Association, 283,* 1059–1060.

Delate, T., Gelenberg, A. J., Simmons, V. A., & Motheral, B. R. (2004, April). Trends in the use of antidepressants in a national sample of commercially insured pediatric patients, 1998 to 2002. *Psychiatric Services, 55,* 387–391.

De Leon, P. H., & Wiggins, J. G. (1996). Prescription privileges for psychologists. *American Psychologist, 51,* 198–206.

DuPaul, G. J., Anastopoulos, A. D., Shelton, T. L., Guevremont, D., & Metevia, L. (1992). Multimethod assessment of attention-deficit hyperactivity disorder: The diagnostic utility of clinic-based tests. *Journal of Clinical Child Psychology, 21,* 394–402.

Frankenberger, W., Farmer, C., Parker, L., & Cermak, J. (2001). The use of stimulant medication for treatment of attention-deficit/hyperactivity disorder: A survey of school psychologists' knowledge, attitudes, and experience. *Developmental Disabilities Bulletin, 29,* 132–151.

Gadow, K. D. (1997). An overview of three decades of research in pediatric psychopharmacoepidemiology. *Journal of Child and Adolescent Psychopharmacology, 7,* 219–236.

Gadow, K. D., Nolan, E. E., Paolicelli, L. M., & Sprafkin, J. (1991). A procedure for assessing the effects of methylphenidate on hyperactive children in public school settings. *Journal of Clinical Child Psychology, 20,* 268–276.

Greenhill, L. L., Vitiello, B., Abikoff, H., Levine, J., March, J. S., Riddle, M. A., et al. (2003). Developing methodologies for monitoring long-term safety of psychotropic medication in children: Report on the NIMH Conference, September 25, 2000. *Journal of the American Academy of Child and Adolescent Psychiatry, 42,* 627–633.

Hunt, R. D., Minderaa, R. B., & Cohen, D. J. (1985). Clonidine benefits children with attention deficit disorder and hyperactivity: Report of a double-blind placebo-controlled crossover therapeutic trial. *Journal of the American Academy of Child and Adolescent Psychiatry, 24,* 617–629.

Jensen, P. S., Bhatara, V. S., Vitiello, B., Hoagwood, K., Fiel, M., & Burke, L. B. (1999). Psychoactive medication prescribing practices for U.S. children: Gaps between research and clinical practice. *Journal of the American Academy of Child and Adolescent Psychiatry, 38,* 557–565.

Kubiszyn, T., & Carlson, C. I. (1995). School psychologists' attitudes toward an expanded health care role: Psychopharmacology and prescription privileges. *School Psychology Quarterly, 10,* 247–270.

Medco Health Solutions. (2004). *Drug trends.* Retrieved May 1, 2005, from http://www.drugtrend.com

National Association of School Psychologists. (2004). *IDEA reauthorization timeline: Implications for ongoing advocacy.* Bethesda, MD: Author.

Pelham, W. E., Carlson, C., Sams, S. E., Vallano, G., Dixon, M. J., & Hoza, B. (1993). Separate and combined effects of methylphenidate and behavior modification on boys with attention deficit-hyperactivity disorder in the classroom. *Journal of Consulting and Clinical Psychology, 61,* 506–515.

Phelps, L., Brown, R. T., & Power, T. (2002). *Pediatric psychopharmacology: Combining medical and psychosocial intervention.* Washington, DC: American Psychological Association.

Poling, A., Gadow, K. D., & Cleary, J. (1991). *Drug therapy for behavior disorders: An introduction.* New York: Pergamon Press.

Reynolds, C. R., & Kamphaus, R. W. (1992). *Behavior assessment system for children.* Circle Pines, MN: AGS Publishing.

Riddle, M. A., Kastelic, E. A., & Frosch, E. (2001). Pediatric psychopharmacology. *Journal of Child Psychology and Psychiatry and Allied Disciplines, 42,* 73–90.

Roberts, M. L., DuPaul, G. J., & Benjamin, E. (1999). Comprehensive multimethod medication protocol: Using academic and behavioral performance to monitor treatment effects. *Proven Practice: Prevention & Remediation Solutions for Schools, 2,* 16–23.

Safer, D., Zito, J. M., & Fine, E. M. (1996). Increased methylphenidate usage for attention deficit disorder in the 1990s. *Pediatrics, 98,* 1084–1088.

Snider, V., Frankenburger, W., & Aspenson, M. (2000). The relationship between learning disabilities and attention deficit hyperactivity disorder: A national survey. *Developmental Disabilities Bulletin, 28,* 18–37.

Tosyali, M. C., & Greenhill, L. L. (1998). Child and adolescent psychopharmacology: Important developmental issues. *Pediatric Clinics of North America, 45,* 1021–1035.

Vitiello, B. (2001). Psychopharmacology for young children: Clinical needs and research opportunities. *Pediatrics, 108,* 983–989.

Vitiello, B., Riddle, M. A., Greenhill, L. L., March, J. S., Levine, J., Schachar, R. J., et al. (2003). How can we improve the assessment of safety in child and adolescent psychopharmacology?. *Journal of the American Academy of Child and Adolescent Psychiatry, 42,* 634–641.

Werry, J. S., & Aman, M. G. (Eds.). (1999). *Practitioner's guide to psychoactive drugs for children and adolescents* (2nd ed.). New York: Plenum Press.

Wolraich, M. L. (2003). *Vanderbilt ADHD teacher rating scale (VADTRS) and the Vanderbilt ADHD parent rating scale (VADPRS).* Available online at www.nichq.org or from the author, University of Oklahoma Health Sciences Center, Oklahoma City, OK.

Zametkin, A. J., & Yamada, E. M. (1999). Monitoring and measuring drug effects: 1. Physical effects. *Practitioner's guide to psychoactive drugs for children and adolescents* (2nd ed., pp. 69–97). New York: Plenum Press.

Zito, J. M., Safer, D. J., dosReis, S., Gardner, J. F., Boles, M., & Lynch, F. (2000). Trends in the prescribing of psychotropic medications to preschoolers. *Journal of the American Medical Association, 283,* 1025–1030.

# Index

**NOTE: Page numbers ending in *f* indicate figures; page numbers ending in *t* indicate tables.**

## B

## D

**H**